ENCYCLOPEDIA OF

RELIGION

SECOND EDITION

ENCYCLOPEDIA OF RELIGION

SECOND EDITION

14

TRANSCENDENTAL MEDITATION
•
ZWINGLI, HULDRYCH

LINDSAY JONES
EDITOR IN CHIEF

MACMILLAN REFERENCE USA
An imprint of Thomson Gale, a part of The Thomson Corporation

THOMSON
GALE™

Detroit • New York • San Francisco • San Diego • New Haven, Conn. • Waterville, Maine • London • Munich

THOMSON
GALE

Encyclopedia of Religion, Second Edition

Lindsay Jones, Editor in Chief

For more information, contact
Macmillan Reference USA
An imprint of Thomson Gale
27500 Drake Rd.
Farmington, Hills, MI 48331-3535
Or you can visit our Internet site at
http://www.gale.com

LIBRARY OF CONGRESS CATALOGING-IN-PUBLICATION DATA

Encyclopedia of religion / Lindsay Jones, editor in chief.— 2nd ed.
p. cm.
Includes bibliographical references and index.
ISBN 0-02-865733-0 (SET HARDCOVER : ALK. PAPER) — ISBN 0-02-865734-9 (V. 1) — ISBN 0-02-865735-7 (v. 2) — ISBN 0-02-865736-5 (v. 3) — ISBN 0-02-865737-3 (v. 4) — ISBN 0-02-865738-1 (v. 5) — ISBN 0-02-865739-X (v. 6) — ISBN 0-02-865740-3 (v. 7) — ISBN 0-02-865741-1 (v. 8) — ISBN 0-02-865742-X (v. 9) — ISBN 0-02-865743-8 (v. 10) — ISBN 0-02-865980-5 (v. 11) — ISBN 0-02-865981-3 (v. 12) — ISBN 0-02-865982-1 (v. 13) — ISBN 0-02-865983-X (v. 14) — ISBN 0-02-865984-8 (v. 15)
1. RELIGION—ENCYCLOPEDIAS. I. JONES, LINDSAY, 1954-

BL31.E46 2005
200'.3—dc22 2004017052

This title is also available as an e-book.
ISBN 0-02-865997-X
Contact your Thomson Gale representative for ordering information.

Printed in the United States of America
10 9 8 7 6 5 4 3 2 1

EDITORS AND CONSULTANTS

EDITOR IN CHIEF

LINDSAY JONES
Associate Professor, Department of Comparative Studies, Ohio State University

BOARD MEMBERS

DAVÍD CARRASCO
Neil Rudenstine Professor of Study of Latin America, Divinity School and Department of Anthropology, Harvard University

GIOVANNI CASADIO
Professor of History of Religions, Dipartimento di Scienze dell'Antichità, Università degli Studi di Salerno

WENDY DONIGER
Mircea Eliade Distinguished Service Professor of the History of Religions, University of Chicago

GARY L. EBERSOLE
Professor of History and Religious Studies, and Director, UMKC Center for Religious Studies, University of Missouri—Kansas City

JANET GYATSO
Hershey Professor of Buddhist Studies, The Divinity School, Harvard University

CHARLES HALLISEY
Associate Professor, Department of Languages and Cultures of Asia and Program in Religious Studies, University of Wisconsin—Madison

CHARLES H. LONG
Professor of History of Religions, Emeritus, and Former Director of Research Center for Black Studies, University of California, Santa Barbara

MARY N. MACDONALD
Professor, History of Religions, Le Moyne College (Syracuse, New York)

DALE B. MARTIN
Professor of Religious Studies, and Chair, Department of Religious Studies, Yale University

AZIM NANJI
Professor and Director, The Institute of Ismaili Studies, London

JACOB OLUPONA
Professor, African American and African Studies Program, University of California, Davis

MICHAEL SWARTZ
Professor of Hebrew and Religious Studies, Ohio State University

INÉS TALAMANTEZ
Associate Professor, Religious Studies Department, University of California, Santa Barbara

CONSULTANTS

GREGORY D. ALLES
Associate Professor of Religious Studies, McDaniel College
Study of Religion

SIGMA ANKRAVA
Professor, Department of Literary and Cultural Studies, Faculty of Modern Languages, University of Latvia
Baltic Religion and Slavic Religion

DIANE APOSTOLOS-CAPPADONA
Center for Muslim–Christian Understanding and Liberal Studies Program, Georgetown University
Art and Religion

DIANE BELL
Professor of Anthropology and Women's Studies, George Washington University
Australian Indigenous Religions

KEES W. BOLLE
Professor Emeritus of History, University of California, Los Angeles, and Fellow, Netherlands Institute for Advanced Studies in the Humanities and Social Sciences
History of Religions

MARK CSIKSZENTMIHALYI
Associate Professor in the Department of East Asian Languages and Literature and the Program in Religious Studies, University of Wisconsin—Madison
Chinese Religions

RICHARD A. GARDNER
Faculty of Comparative Culture, Sophia University
Humor and Religion

JOHN A. GRIM
Professor of Religion, Bucknell University and Co-Coordinator,

Harvard Forum on Religion and Ecology
Ecology and Religion

JOSEPH HARRIS
Francis Lee Higginson Professor of English Literature and Professor of Folklore, Harvard University
Germanic Religions

URSULA KING
Professor Emerita, Senior Research Fellow and Associate Member of the Institute for Advanced Studies, University of Bristol, England, and Professorial Research Associate, Centre for Gender and Religions Research, School of Oriental and African Studies, University of London
Gender and Religion

DAVID MORGAN
Duesenberg Professor of Christianity and the Arts, and Professor of Humanities and Art History, Valparaiso University
Color Inserts and Essays

JOSEPH F. NAGY
Professor, Department of English, University of California, Los Angeles
Celtic Religion

MATTHEW OJO
Obafemi Awolowo University
African Religions

JUHA PENTIKÄINEN
Professor of Comparative Religion, The University of Helsinki, Member of Academia Scientiarum Fennica, Finland
Arctic Religions and Uralic Religions

TED PETERS
Professor of Systematic Theology, Pacific Lutheran Theological Seminary and the Center for Theology and the Natural Sciences at the Graduate Theological Union, Berkeley, California
Science and Religion

FRANK E. REYNOLDS
Professor of the History of Religions and Buddhist Studies in the Divinity School and the Department of South Asian Languages and Civilizations, Emeritus, University of Chicago
History of Religions

GONZALO RUBIO
Assistant Professor, Department of Classics and Ancient Mediterranean Studies and Department of History and Religious Studies, Pennsylvania State University
Ancient Near Eastern Religions

SUSAN SERED
Director of Research, Religion, Health and Healing Initiative, Center for the Study of World Religions, Harvard University, and Senior Research Associate, Center for Women's Health and Human Rights, Suffolk University
Healing, Medicine, and Religion

LAWRENCE E. SULLIVAN
Professor, Department of Theology, University of Notre Dame
History of Religions

WINNIFRED FALLERS SULLIVAN
Dean of Students and Senior Lecturer in the Anthropology and Sociology of Religion, University of Chicago
Law and Religion

TOD SWANSON
Associate Professor of Religious Studies, and Director, Center for Latin American Studies, Arizona State University
South American Religions

MARY EVELYN TUCKER
Professor of Religion, Bucknell University, Founder and Coordinator, Harvard Forum on Religion and Ecology, Research Fellow, Harvard Yenching Institute, Research Associate, Harvard Reischauer Institute of Japanese Studies
Ecology and Religion

HUGH URBAN
Associate Professor, Department of Comparative Studies, Ohio State University
Politics and Religion

CATHERINE WESSINGER
Professor of the History of Religions and Women's Studies, Loyola University New Orleans
New Religious Movements

ROBERT A. YELLE
Mellon Postdoctoral Fellow, University of Toronto
Law and Religion

ERIC ZIOLKOWSKI
Charles A. Dana Professor of Religious Studies, Lafayette College
Literature and Religion

ABBREVIATIONS AND SYMBOLS USED IN THIS WORK

abbr. abbreviated; abbreviation
abr. abridged; abridgment
AD *anno Domini,* in the year of the (our) Lord
Afrik. Afrikaans
AH *anno Hegirae,* in the year of the Hijrah
Akk. Akkadian
Ala. Alabama
Alb. Albanian
Am. *Amos*
AM *ante meridiem,* before noon
amend. amended; amendment
annot. annotated; annotation
Ap. *Apocalypse*
Apn. *Apocryphon*
app. appendix
Arab. Arabic
ʿArakh. *ʿArakhin*
Aram. Aramaic
Ariz. Arizona
Ark. Arkansas
Arm. Armenian
art. article (pl., arts.)
AS Anglo-Saxon
Asm. Mos. *Assumption of Moses*
Assyr. Assyrian
A.S.S.R. Autonomous Soviet Socialist Republic
Av. Avestan
ʿA.Z. *ʿAvodah zarah*
b. born
Bab. Babylonian
Ban. Bantu
1 Bar. *1 Baruch*
2 Bar. *2 Baruch*
3 Bar. *3 Baruch*
4 Bar. *4 Baruch*
B.B. *Bavaʾ batraʾ*
BBC British Broadcasting Corporation
BC before Christ
BCE before the common era
B.D. Bachelor of Divinity
Beits. *Beitsah*
Bekh. *Bekhorot*
Beng. Bengali
Ber. *Berakhot*
Berb. Berber
Bik. *Bikkurim*
bk. book (pl., bks.)
B.M. *Bavaʾ metsiʿaʾ*
BP before the present
B.Q. *Bavaʾ qammaʾ*
Brāh. *Brāhmaṇa*
Bret. Breton
B.T. Babylonian Talmud
Bulg. Bulgarian
Burm. Burmese
c. *circa,* about, approximately
Calif. California
Can. Canaanite
Catal. Catalan
CE of the common era
Celt. Celtic
cf. *confer,* compare
Chald. Chaldean
chap. chapter (pl., chaps.)
Chin. Chinese
C.H.M. Community of the Holy Myrrhbearers
1 Chr. *1 Chronicles*
2 Chr. *2 Chronicles*
Ch. Slav. Church Slavic
cm centimeters
col. column (pl., cols.)
Col. *Colossians*
Colo. Colorado
comp. compiler (pl., comps.)
Conn. Connecticut
cont. continued
Copt. Coptic
1 Cor. *1 Corinthians*
2 Cor. *2 Corinthians*
corr. corrected
C.S.P. Congregatio Sancti Pauli, Congregation of Saint Paul (Paulists)
d. died
D Deuteronomic (source of the Pentateuch)
Dan. Danish
D.B. Divinitatis Baccalaureus, Bachelor of Divinity
D.C. District of Columbia
D.D. Divinitatis Doctor, Doctor of Divinity
Del. Delaware
Dem. *Demaʾi*
dim. diminutive
diss. dissertation
Dn. *Daniel*
D.Phil. Doctor of Philosophy
Dt. *Deuteronomy*
Du. Dutch
E Elohist (source of the Pentateuch)
Eccl. *Ecclesiastes*
ed. editor (pl., eds.); edition; edited by

'Eduy. *'Eduyyot*
e.g. *exempli gratia,* for example
Egyp. Egyptian
1 En. *1 Enoch*
2 En. *2 Enoch*
3 En. *3 Enoch*
Eng. English
enl. enlarged
Eph. *Ephesians*
'Eruv. *'Eruvin*
1 Esd. *1 Esdras*
2 Esd. *2 Esdras*
3 Esd. *3 Esdras*
4 Esd. *4 Esdras*
esp. especially
Est. Estonian
Est. *Esther*
et al. *et alii,* and others
etc. *et cetera,* and so forth
Eth. Ethiopic
EV English version
Ex. *Exodus*
exp. expanded
Ez. *Ezekiel*
Ezr. *Ezra*
2 Ezr. *2 Ezra*
4 Ezr. *4 Ezra*
f. feminine; and following (pl., ff.)
fasc. fascicle (pl., fascs.)
fig. figure (pl., figs.)
Finn. Finnish
fl. *floruit,* flourished
Fla. Florida
Fr. French
frag. fragment
ft. feet
Ga. Georgia
Gal. *Galatians*
Gaul. Gaulish
Ger. German
Giṭ. *Giṭṭin*
Gn. *Genesis*
Gr. Greek
Ḥag. *Ḥagigah*
Ḥal. *Ḥallah*
Hau. Hausa
Hb. *Habakkuk*
Heb. Hebrew
Heb. *Hebrews*
Hg. *Haggai*
Hitt. Hittite
Hor. *Horayot*
Hos. *Hosea*
Ḥul. *Ḥullin*
Hung. Hungarian
ibid. *ibidem,* in the same place (as the one immediately preceding)
Icel. Icelandic
i.e. *id est,* that is
IE Indo-European
Ill. Illinois
Ind. Indiana
intro. introduction
Ir. Gael. Irish Gaelic
Iran. Iranian
Is. *Isaiah*
Ital. Italian
J Yahvist (source of the Pentateuch)
Jas. *James*
Jav. Javanese
Jb. *Job*
Jdt. *Judith*
Jer. *Jeremiah*
Jgs. *Judges*
Jl. *Joel*
Jn. *John*
1 Jn. *1 John*
2 Jn. *2 John*
3 Jn. *3 John*
Jon. *Jonah*
Jos. *Joshua*
Jpn. Japanese
JPS Jewish Publication Society translation (1985) of the Hebrew Bible
J.T. Jerusalem Talmud
Jub. *Jubilees*
Kans. Kansas
Kel. *Kelim*
Ker. *Keritot*
Ket. *Ketubbot*
1 Kgs. *1 Kings*
2 Kgs. *2 Kings*
Khois. Khoisan
Kil. *Kil'ayim*
km kilometers
Kor. Korean
Ky. Kentucky
l. line (pl., ll.)
La. Louisiana
Lam. *Lamentations*
Lat. Latin
Latv. Latvian
L. en Th. Licencié en Théologie, Licentiate in Theology
L. ès L. Licencié ès Lettres, Licentiate in Literature
Let. Jer. *Letter of Jeremiah*
lit. literally
Lith. Lithuanian
Lk. *Luke*
LL Late Latin
LL.D. Legum Doctor, Doctor of Laws
Lv. *Leviticus*
m meters
m. masculine
M.A. Master of Arts
Ma 'as. *Ma'aserot*
Ma 'as. Sh. *Ma' aser sheni*
Mak. *Makkot*
Makh. *Makhshirin*
Mal. *Malachi*
Mar. Marathi
Mass. Massachusetts
1 Mc. *1 Maccabees*
2 Mc. *2 Maccabees*
3 Mc. *3 Maccabees*
4 Mc. *4 Maccabees*
Md. Maryland
M.D. Medicinae Doctor, Doctor of Medicine
ME Middle English
Meg. *Megillah*
Me 'il. *Me'ilah*
Men. *Menaḥot*
MHG Middle High German
mi. miles
Mi. *Micah*
Mich. Michigan
Mid. *Middot*
Minn. Minnesota
Miq. *Miqva'ot*
MIran. Middle Iranian
Miss. Mississippi
Mk. *Mark*
Mo. Missouri
Mo'ed Q. *Mo'ed qaṭan*
Mont. Montana
MPers. Middle Persian
MS. *manuscriptum,* manuscript (pl., MSS)
Mt. *Matthew*
MT Masoretic text
n. note
Na. *Nahum*
Nah. Nahuatl
Naz. *Nazir*
N.B. *nota bene,* take careful note
N.C. North Carolina
n.d. no date
N.Dak. North Dakota
NEB New English Bible
Nebr. Nebraska

Ned. *Nedarim*
Neg. *Nega'im*
Neh. *Nehemiah*
Nev. Nevada
N.H. New Hampshire
Nid. *Niddah*
N.J. New Jersey
Nm. *Numbers*
N.Mex. New Mexico
no. number (pl., nos.)
Nor. Norwegian
n.p. no place
n.s. new series
N.Y. New York
Ob. *Obadiah*
O.Cist. Ordo Cisterciencium, Order of Cîteaux (Cistercians)
OCS Old Church Slavonic
OE Old English
O.F.M. Ordo Fratrum Minorum, Order of Friars Minor (Franciscans)
OFr. Old French
Ohal. *Ohalot*
OHG Old High German
OIr. Old Irish
OIran. Old Iranian
Okla. Oklahoma
ON Old Norse
O.P. Ordo Praedicatorum, Order of Preachers (Dominicans)
OPers. Old Persian
op. cit. *opere citato,* in the work cited
OPrus. Old Prussian
Oreg. Oregon
'Orl. *'Orlah*
O.S.B. Ordo Sancti Benedicti, Order of Saint Benedict (Benedictines)
p. page (pl., pp.)
P Priestly (source of the Pentateuch)
Pa. Pennsylvania
Pahl. Pahlavi
Par. *Parah*
para. paragraph (pl., paras.)
Pers. Persian
Pes. *Pesahim*
Ph.D. Philosophiae Doctor, Doctor of Philosophy
Phil. *Philippians*
Phlm. *Philemon*
Phoen. Phoenician
pl. plural; plate (pl., pls.)
PM *post meridiem,* after noon
Pol. Polish
pop. population
Port. Portuguese
Prv. *Proverbs*
Ps. *Psalms*
Ps. 151 *Psalm 151*
Ps. Sol. *Psalms of Solomon*
pt. part (pl., pts.)
1Pt. *1 Peter*
2 Pt. *2 Peter*
Pth. Parthian
Q hypothetical source of the synoptic Gospels
Qid. *Qiddushin*
Qin. *Qinnim*
r. reigned; ruled
Rab. *Rabbah*
rev. revised
R. ha-Sh. *Ro'sh ha-shanah*
R.I. Rhode Island
Rom. Romanian
Rom. *Romans*
R.S.C.J. Societas Sacratissimi Cordis Jesu, Religious of the Sacred Heart
RSV Revised Standard Version of the Bible
Ru. *Ruth*
Rus. Russian
Rv. *Revelation*
Rv. Ezr. *Revelation of Ezra*
San. *Sanhedrin*
S.C. South Carolina
Scot. Gael. Scottish Gaelic
S.Dak. South Dakota
sec. section (pl., secs.)
Sem. Semitic
ser. series
sg. singular
Sg. *Song of Songs*
Sg. of 3 *Prayer of Azariah and the Song of the Three Young Men*
Shab. *Shabbat*
Shav. *Shavu'ot*
Sheq. *Sheqalim*
Sib. Or. *Sibylline Oracles*
Sind. Sindhi
Sinh. Sinhala
Sir. *Ben Sira*
S.J. Societas Jesu, Society of Jesus (Jesuits)
Skt. Sanskrit
1 Sm. *1 Samuel*
2 Sm. *2 Samuel*
Sogd. Sogdian
Soṭ. *Soṭah*
sp. species (pl., spp.)
Span. Spanish
sq. square
S.S.R. Soviet Socialist Republic
st. stanza (pl., ss.)
S.T.M. Sacrae Theologiae Magister, Master of Sacred Theology
Suk. *Sukkah*
Sum. Sumerian
supp. supplement; supplementary
Sus. *Susanna*
s.v. *sub verbo,* under the word (pl., s.v.v.)
Swed. Swedish
Syr. Syriac
Syr. Men. *Syriac Menander*
Ta' an. *Ta'anit*
Tam. Tamil
Tam. *Tamid*
Tb. *Tobit*
T.D. *Taishō shinshū daizōkyō,* edited by Takakusu Junjirō et al. (Tokyo,1922–1934)
Tem. *Temurah*
Tenn. Tennessee
Ter. Terumot
Ṭev. Y. *Ṭevul yom*
Tex. Texas
Th.D. Theologicae Doctor, Doctor of Theology
1 Thes. *1 Thessalonians*
2 Thes. *2 Thessalonians*
Thrac. Thracian
Ti. *Titus*
Tib. Tibetan
1 Tm. *1 Timothy*
2 Tm. *2 Timothy*
T. of 12 *Testaments of the Twelve Patriarchs*
Ṭoh. *ṭohorot*
Tong. Tongan
trans. translator, translators; translated by; translation
Turk. Turkish
Ukr. Ukrainian
Upan. *Upaniṣad*
U.S. United States
U.S.S.R. Union of Soviet Socialist Republics
Uqts. *Uqtsin*
v. verse (pl., vv.)
Va. Virginia
var. variant; variation
Viet. Vietnamese

viz. *videlicet,* namely
vol. volume (pl., vols.)
Vt. Vermont
Wash. Washington
Wel. Welsh
Wis. Wisconsin
Wis. *Wisdom of Solomon*
W.Va. West Virginia
Wyo. Wyoming
Yad. *Yadayim*
Yev. *Yevamot*
Yi. Yiddish
Yor. Yoruba
Zav. *Zavim*
Zec. *Zechariah*
Zep. *Zephaniah*
Zev. *Zevaḥim*

* hypothetical
? uncertain; possibly; perhaps
° degrees
+ plus
– minus
= equals; is equivalent to
× by; multiplied by
→ yields

T
CONTINUED

TRANSCENDENTAL MEDITATION. Beginning as a method discovered by Maharishi Mahesh Yogi (b. 1911), Transcendental Meditation (TM) became an international movement in 1958, when it was presented as a scientific response and practical remedy to the various problems of modern life. This thrust was stressed even more when its founder and teachers denied that the movement was a religion, or that it had been founded as such. Instead, they argued that it was an easy technique that could be mastered by anyone. By using this method, a person could overcome ordinary problems such as mental and emotional stress and high blood pressure while obtaining greater relaxation, gaining greater physical energy and mental clarity, and achieving more advanced stages of consciousness. In spite of its many modern benefits, this new method of yoga claimed to be part of an ancient Hindu spiritual lineage.

Maharishi Mahesh Yogi, who was born Mahesh Prasad Varma on October 18, 1911 in Uttar Kashi, India, traced his spiritual heritage to the great Advaita Vedānta thinker Sankara (c. 788–820), and beyond him to ancient Vedic literature. Maharishi studied for fourteen years with Swami Brahmananda Saraswati (1869–1953) at the Jyotimath, a monastic community located high in the Himalayan mountain range of India, although he was never appointed successor to his own teacher. Before his student apprenticeship, Maharishi earned a college-level degree in physics and mathematics at Allahabad University in India. His educational background partially explains his tendency to wrap his message in scientific jargon and to stress the scientific advantages of his method. The Science of Creative Intelligence (SCI) is, for instance, the official name of his belief system, which is conceived as dynamic due to its ever expanding and increasing nature.

The use of scientific language to convey a religious message accomplishes at least two objectives: (1) it gives the belief system legitimacy, and (2) it forms a cognitive connection to the contemporary Western worldview that is dominated by science. TM operates from the basic presupposition that there is a compatibility between Advaita Vedānta, the Vedas, and Western science. Since 1988 TM has, for instance, worked intensively to demonstrate the parallels between quantum physics and its method.

Clockwise from top left corner. The Golden Pavilion, or Kinkakuji, in Kyoto, Japan. *[©Dallas and John Heaton/Corbis]*; Thor's hammer amulet, tenth century. National Museum of Iceland, Reykjavik. *[©Werner Forman/Art Resource, N.Y.]*; Tenth- to twelfth-century stone carving of Chacmool near the Temple of the Warriors at Chichen Itza in Mexico. *[©Kevin Schafer/Corbis]*; Temple of Hatshepsut in Luxor, Egypt. *[©Dallas and John Heaton/Corbis]*; Nepalese Tārā. *[©Christie's Images/Corbis]*.

MISSION TO THE WEST. Before making his mission to the West, Maharishi began his spiritual mission beyond India in April 1958 with a trip to Rangoon, Burma. He then traveled to Bangkok, Thailand; the island of Penang; Kuala Lumpur, Malaysia; Singapore; Hong Kong; Hawai'i; and finally the U.S. mainland. On a subsequent journey in 1960 to Germany he opened nine yoga centers, and later that year he traveled to the Scandinavian countries, beginning with Norway, before going to Italy, Greece, and Nairobi, Kenya. Later trips were made to South America, which made his movement a truly global enterprise.

Maharishi's introduction of his spiritual discovery to the West was preceded by the efforts of Swami Vivekananda (1863–1902) and Yogananda (1893–1952). Vivekananada traveled to America to attend the World Parliament of Religions in 1893 and launched the Vedanta Societies, whereas Yogananda traveled to America to attend the International Congress of Religious Liberals, organized by the Unitarian Church in Boston in 1920, and established the Self-Realization Fellowship with more than 150 centers throughout the world. Following in their footsteps, Maharishi arrived in America in 1959 and lectured on yoga in San Francisco, with additional trips to Los Angeles, New York, London, and Germany. His movement was initially called the Spiritual Regeneration Movement, which later became the name of the adult branch of the movement. The other wing of the movement was named the Students International Meditation Society (SIMS), established in 1964 in Germany. An early emphasis of the movement was its mission to college campuses, which was given a huge impetus in the mid-1960s when the British rock group the Beatles studied with the Maharishi in India. This event generated worldwide publicity for his movement. After his estrangement from the Beatles, the Maharishi initiated, instructed, and toured with the Beach Boys. Maharishi used his celebrity status with icons of popular culture to endear himself with the youth culture. By the 1970s, student centers could be found at over one thousand campuses. By the beginning of the 1980s the movement estimated that 1.5 million people had practiced Transcendental Meditation with a teacher. The college-campus focus of the movement culminated with the establishment of Maharishi International University in Fairfield, Iowa, in 1974 on the campus of the bankrupted Parsons College.

Pushing the margins of science, Maharishi established the Maharishi European Research University in 1975 at two lakeside hotels on Lake Lucerne in Switzerland. The purpose of the university was to research the effects of Transcendental Meditation and to determine the existence of higher states of consciousness. During the following year Maharishi envisioned his own world government with the ancient Indian Vedas as the basis of its constitution. He appointed ministers to various positions with titles like the Development of Consciousness, Prosperity, and Fulfillment and Health and Immortality. During the 1980s Maharishi began a program called TM-Sidhi with the purpose of teaching students to achieve yogic powers, such as the ability to fly or levitate. There was a public demonstration before 120 journalists in Washington, D.C., on July 9, 1986 that did not correspond with the media hype for the event and resulted in media ridicule of the movement. The members of the media were amused at the sham performance of students jumping on mats imitating acts of levitation.

MEDITATIVE TECHNIQUE AND MESSAGE. The meditative technique of Maharishi is grounded in a Neo-Vedānta metaphysical philosophy in which an unchanging reality is opposed to an ever-changing phenomenal world. Maharishi's book *Science of Being and Art of Living: Transcendental Meditation* (1963) expresses his basic philosophical position. The unchanging reality is equated with Being, which represents a state of pure existence that is omnipresent, unmanifested, and transcendental. Not only is Being beyond time, space, causation, and ever-changing phenomena, it remains unrecognized by human beings because their minds do not realize their essential identity with Being, since minds are captive to the outward-projecting senses. The essential nature of Being is further identified with absolute blissful consciousness, which radiates from Being. Maharishi compares Being to the ocean, upon which there are many waves. These waves are like the field of continually changing phenomena. What is really important for Maharishi is for human beings to realize Being, because without this realization a person's life is without foundation, meaningless, and fruitless. This realization is within the capabilities of everyone by means of TM.

This form of meditation is intimately connected to a person's breath (Prāṇa), which is an expression of Being in the sense that it represents a tendency of the unmanifested to reveal itself. The breath represents the latent power of Being within a person. As the nature of Being, breath plays a role as the motivating force of creation and evolution. The breath can be harnessed and used to help the mind of a person realize Being directly. This is accomplished by Transcendental Meditation, which enables a person to extricate oneself from a state of relative experience, transcend ordinary thinking, and gain the permanent state of Being. This means that a particular mind loses its individuality. It becomes instead a cosmic mind that is omnipresent, pure, and eternal.

Before achieving this cosmic state of mind, the human mind is like a seed that produces a tree. What this analogy attempts to show is the interdependent nature of the mind and karma (action). It is impossible for action to occur without a mind. In turn, it is karma that produces the mind, which in turn creates more karma. This suggests that karma owes its existence to the mind, and in turn creates the mind. By means of karma, the original, pure consciousness of Being is transformed into conscious mind. If karma represents what is temporary and perishable, Being is its exact opposite because it represents eternal unity. Karma creates diversity within the unity of Being.

Within the context of this metaphysical edifice, the technique of Transcendental Meditation involves saturating the mind with Being by harnessing one's breath and making it harmonious with the rhythm of nature and cosmic life. Maharishi emphasizes the naturalness of his technique. Moreover, the technique is a simple, easy, and direct way to development one's mental capabilities and latent potentialities. In contrast to ancient ascetic traditions of India, in TM it is not necessary to renounce the world or withdraw from one's family. That is an ascetic practice which can be performed within the context of the ordinary activities of the world.

Instruction in the technique of meditation stresses that it is an easy and natural process. Students are instructed to devote twenty minutes each day to practice, ideally in the morning and early evening. At the beginning stage, a student does not have to be convinced that the method will work. What is important is the correct practice. If a student performs the technique properly, positive results will follow automatically. The proper technique involves seven steps. The initial step involves attending a introductory lecture that is intended to prepare a person for what is to follow. In the second step, the theory of Transcendental Meditation is presented through a preparatory talk. The third step involves an interview with the teacher, at which time a student is given a sacred mantra (repetitive formula) that is personally fitted to a person, who is not to reveal it to others. By focusing on the mantra, persons are able to concentrate their attention on it. The final steps involve periodic verification and validation of a person's experiences by returning to and checking with a teacher.

Maharishi identifies seven levels of consciousness, with the final one culminating in a state of unity. The fifth state represents a cosmic consciousness that represents an awareness of Being even after the cessation of meditation, whereas the fourth stage stands for the transcendental state, which is a state of pure consciousness described as beyond the previous state of waking, dream, and deep-sleep consciousness. The fifth stage is an expansion of the pure consciousness achieved on the fourth level from an individual to a wider cosmic dimension. The sixth state is called God consciousness. Traditional yogic postures are unnecessary—in TM a person can simply sit upright and comfortably on a chair with eyes closed. The movement tends to stress that anyone can learn this simple, effortless, and easy mental technique.

From the perspective of Maharishi, this yogic technique and Neo-Vedānta metaphysical edifice are not a form of Hinduism. In fact, Transcendental Meditation is not a religion at all. By de-emphasizing its Hindu roots, stressing its nonreligious nature, and focusing on the scientifically demonstrable value of the technique, TM created a successful message that was embraced by many spiritual seekers and a scientifically minded audience. The movement used scientific means to demonstrate how the technique calmed the mind, increased awareness, relaxed the body, and lowered metabolism.

MILLENNIAL EXPECTATIONS. When Maharishi initially arrived in the United States, he stated at a press conference his rationale for coming to America. He confessed that he had learned a secret, swift, deep form of meditation that he was now motivated to share with the world for the spiritual regeneration of its inhabitants. A few years later, he established the Spiritual Regeneration Movement of Great Britain, located in northern London. In 1975 Maharishi announced the Dawn of the Age of Enlightenment. His bold and optimistic pronouncement suggested the commencement of a period during which humans can reach their fullest potential and that will be characterized by boundless happiness, harmony, peace, and personal fulfillment. This new dawn will also represent a period when science will verify and validate the teachings of the Maharishi. Moreover, even those who did not meditate would enjoy the benefits of this new age. The Maharishi took this message on tour to various countries. The impetus for such millennial hope continued in December 1983–January 1984, when he created the Taste of Utopia Assembly, which was staged at Maharishi International University. The purpose of this gathering was to unite Vedic wisdom and the practice of the TM-Sidhi program. Their fusion would usher into existence a utopian age of peace and prosperity. This vision represented a fuller expression of a utopian hope embodied within the movement from its earliest moments.

As Transcendental Meditation grew in the awareness of ordinary citizens, many tended to associate it with New Age religion. During the 1960s and 1970s, people were experimenting with drugs like LSD to induce altered states of consciousness and bliss. Within the context of the drug culture and New Age religion, TM appeared to ordinary people to be offering similar results. Thus, numerous practitioners of various forms of New Age religion and former drug experimenters were attracted to the TM movement because of its apparent kinship with these other forms of spiritual experimentation. Besides such perceived forms of kinship among TM, drug culture, and New Age spirituality, Transcendental Meditation shared with New Age spirituality a holistic view of life. This was a form of thinking and living that attempted to extricate itself from all forms of dualism, such as the dichotomy between body and mind. The Transcendental Meditation movement also intersected with New Age spiritualities with respect to organic and vegetarian dietary practices and alternative forms of medicine. In 1985, for instance, Maharishi launched the World Plan for Perfect Health along with a medical institution, the World Center for Ayurveda, in India.

The Transcendental Meditation movement promised a transformation of both the individual and society by means of an expansion of consciousness to unimagined states. In short, TM aimed to create a perfect society inhabited by perfect individuals. The movement offered a realized eschatology for a transformed mode of living in the present moment that promised a horizon of economic well-being, psychological and somatic healing, peace, and mental comfort.

The Transcendental Meditation movement has attracted disenfranchised, disaffected, and disenchanted seekers looking for spiritual experience, healing, community, a general sense of well-being, and happiness because of the decline of community, the rise of impersonal organizations, alienation, fragmentation of life, secularism, competing multicultural messages, and religious pluralism. With the promise of a perfect society, TM offered a personal and private form of spirituality for many disenchanted seekers.

See Also Millenarianism; New Age Movement; New Religious Movements; Vedānta; Vivekananda; Yogananda.

Bibliography

Eck, Diana L. *A New Religious America: How a "Christian Country" Has Now Become the World's Most Religiously Diverse Nation.* New York, 2001. A look at the impact of Eastern religions on America based on research for the Pluralism Project at Harvard University.

Ellwood, Robert S., Jr. *Religious and Spiritual Groups in Modern America.* Englewood Cliffs, N.J., 1973. A useful reference work on new religions and New Age cults that is dated in some places.

Mahesh Yogi, Maharishi. *Science of Being and Art of Living: Transcendental Meditation.* New York, 1963; reprint, New York, 2001. This book sets forth his basic philosophy, yogic method, and its connection to science.

Mahesh Yogi, Maharishi. *Maharishi Mahesh Yogi on the Bhagavad-Gita: A New Translation and Commentary: Chapters 1–6.* London, 1967. Maharishi's incomplete commentary on this important text from his own perspective.

Rothstein, Mikael. *Belief Transformations: Some Aspects of the Relation between Science and Religion in Transcendental Meditation (TM) and the International Society for Krishna Consciousness (ISKCON).* Aarhus, Denmark, Aarhus University Press, 1996. A comparative study of TM and the International Society for Krishna Consciousness (ISKCON). The author explores the former movements embrace of the scientific world-view and the latter movements reject of it.

Russell, Peter. *The TM Technique.* London, 1976. A study of the method and levels of consciousness by a member of the movement who studied with Maharishi.

Carl Olson (2005)

TRANSCULTURATION AND RELIGION

This entry consists of the following articles:

AN OVERVIEW
RELIGION IN THE FORMATION OF MODERN CANADA
RELIGION IN THE FORMATION OF THE MODERN CARIBBEAN
RELIGION IN THE FORMATION OF MODERN JAPAN
RELIGION IN THE FORMATION OF MODERN INDIA
RELIGION IN THE FORMATION OF MODERN OCEANIA

TRANSCULTURATION AND RELIGION: AN OVERVIEW

The term *transculturation* was first used by the Cuban sociologist Fernando Ortiz to describe the formation of Cuban culture from the coming together of indigenous, Spanish, and African populations. (Ortiz gave prominence to the term in two chapters of his book *Tobacco and Sugar,* 1947: chapter two is entitled "The Social Phenomenon of Transculturation and Its Importance," and chapter seven has the title, "The Transculturation of Tobacco.") In his studies, Ortiz shows how these groups interrelated, adopted, and adapted themselves in modes of language, music, art, and agricultural production. The contemporary usage of the term owes its academic parlance to the work of Mary Louise Pratt, who, in her book *Imperial Eyes: Travel Writing and Transculturation* (1992), following Ortiz, tells us that processes of this kind occur within "contact zones," "zones where cultures meet, clash, and grapple." These zones, according to Pratt, express the improvisational dimensions of colonial encounters in the modern period. The contact zones show that the encounters between colonizers and colonized, while characterized by the domination of the colonizers, did not simply define separateness but many complex interlocking relations. Within this overall context of domination, Pratt foregrounds the copresence, interaction, and improvisational dimensions of the contact zones (p. 7).

Pratt and others who make use of the term use it primarily to describe the contact of Western culture with other cultures over the last five hundred years. These contacts have taken on several overlapping forms—conquest, domination, reciprocity, adaptation, amalgamation, and so on. The phenomenon of the contact of cultures is not peculiar to the modern period, however. Given the human capacity for locomotion, different and diverse groups of people have been "in contact" since human beings have been on earth; cultural contacts have taken place throughout the history of humankind. Prior to the Neolithic period, when humans domesticated animals and began to practice agriculture, small transhumance bands of humans were in constant movement over designated parts of their regions. With the beginnings of early citied existence in China, Mesopotamia, and then in regions all over the world, the sedentary and centered human mode of being gained prestige. Though cities represented the human mode as sedentary and centered, movement, travel, and meetings and encounters with human groups outside the city centers increased rather than diminished.

Mary Helms's *Ulysses' Sail* (1988) examines the meaning of geographical distance and foreign places in premodern periods in several cultures of the world. Just as the vertical distance between the heavens and the earth expressed the spaces and loci for cosmological and theological speculation, the horizontal traversal of space revealed structures of power and knowledge. Long-distance spaces were traversed by long-distance travelers who were either themselves elite or represented the elite orders of society. Helms does not deny that trade went on through this travel but her emphasis is upon the creation of the symbolic spaces made through geographical travel.

Various kinds of knowledge, including literacy, navigation, the forging of metals, and astronomy, attended those who made these journeys, thus enhancing their power and prestige. The symbolic power also accrued from the knowledge of "outside phenomena." Thus, in Helms's study, boundaries are equal or even more important than zones. Long-distance travel involved going outside boundaries and thus the knowledge gained was understood to have the power of transformation. Helms's study "rest[s] upon the assumption that the significance of interchanges of people and material goods across geographical distances can better be understood if we know something of the qualities attributed to space and distance in various situations" (p. 10).

PILGRIMAGES. One aspect of the kind of long-distance travel discussed by Mary Helms has taken the form of pilgrimages in various cultures throughout the world. While Helms has pointed to long-distance travelers as people who went beyond, even transgressed, boundaries in their search for knowledge and power, the pilgrimage, though still emphasizing travel, specifies a definite destination and purpose for the traveler. It is this form of long-distance travel that is the precursor of the long-distance travels of Western peoples beginning in the fifteenth century of the Common Era.

The contact of Western cultures from the fifteenth century with the cultures of the world should be seen against the practice, rhetoric, and literature of pilgrimage. Pilgrimage has a long tradition in European cultures. By the fourteenth century one can discern two major meanings arising out of the pilgrimage: pilgrimage as a soteriological act or pilgrimage as an act of grace. The archetypal pilgrimage was the Christian pilgrimage to Jerusalem. Jerusalem for the Christian defined the symbolic and geographical center of the world; this space was saturated with the life and meaning of the Christian savior and thus was the most powerful and prestigious place in all Christendom. The pilgrimage to Jerusalem defined a penitential journey, where believers undertook a kind of ascesis en route that prepared them for the receptive beneficence of being in the Holy Land.

Following Helms, the pilgrimage to Jerusalem, and in like manner all other Christian pilgrimages, was based upon the vertical meaning of space, with the heaven above, the human as sinner in the middle, and the earth below. In the pilgrimage to Jerusalem, the penitent was congruent with the fundamental orders of divine power. At this center, the penitent could experience the most potent meanings of grace and redemption. The pilgrim nevertheless had to travel through space to arrive at Jerusalem, and in so doing, the old specter described by Helms in the horizontal traversal of the earth came back into play. The change of places and spaces through the journey of the pilgrimage piqued the curiosity of the traveler. Christian Zacher in *Curiosity and Pilgrimage* (1976) describes the tension between the soteriological and liturgical meaning of pilgrimage and the meaning of the pilgrimage as a journey of curiosity. The growing emphasis with curiosity as a major aspect of pilgrimage came to constitute another and often separate motivation for undertaking a pilgrimage.

Obviously, theological formulations were given for the liturgical meaning of pilgrimage; equal theological attention was paid to curiosity. It was pointed out that curiosity—wanting to know on one's own—was the original source of human sin. It was human curiosity in the Garden of Eden that led to the first disobedience to God. Curiosity represented the human will to know apart from God's command, and thus in this independent mode of knowing, humans transgressed the meaning and roles of proper knowledge. These summary statements by Zacher show the marked difference between the two modes: "the temptation to *curiositas* referred to any morally excessive and suspect interest in observing the world, seeking novel experience, or acquiring knowledge for its own sake" (p. 4). Regarding the liturgical meaning of pilgrimage, Zacher states the contrast: "As a form of religious worship, pilgrimage allowed men to journey through this present world visiting sacral landscapes as long as they kept their gaze permanently fixed on the invisible world beyond" (p. 4). Pilgrimage as a movement through space expressed an inner and outer process of spiritual meanings.

Two major changes took place that began to transform the pilgrimage from a liturgical ritual of travel into a more purposeful and pragmatic endeavor. The first occurred when Pope Urban II in 1095 called for a pilgrimage from the armed knights of Christendom to free the Holy Land from the Muslims and by so doing reconstitute the meaning of the sacred center of Christendom. This action allowed armed knights to undertake a ritual act while still part of a military order (Elsner and Rubiés, 1999, p. 24). The other change took place when monks and priests from the eleventh century on began to undertake missionary movements to other lands to convert nonbelievers to the true faith of Christianity. Missions took on a more rationalistic ideological bent that led to rationalistic narratives. Missions and crusades were allied during the late medieval period and this pattern was adopted by explorers of Africa and the Atlantic in the fifteenth century.

Though liturgical ritual pilgrimages were undertaken for soteriological purposes, it is clear that a great deal of curiosity was expressed through them. This curiosity had to do with the empirical observations of other lands and habits. Victor Turner in his anthropological analysis of pilgrimage suggests that a kind of tacit curiosity is part of the very structure of pilgrimage itself.

The language and style of the pilgrimage structure pervaded the travel narratives and discourses of Europeans commencing with the voyages of Columbus in the fifteenth century. The pilgrimage model from this time on entered into the travel stylistics and rhetoric of all long-distance travels of Europeans. Thus, from the earliest pilgrimage traditions of the church to the pilgrimage voyages of the Reformation Puritans to the New World, the pilgrimage model served as both umbrella and reservoir for the meanings of travel, discovery, conquest, and even scientific curiosity.

Henri Baudet has noted that the languages of travel and discovery embodied a duality that found expression in two relations of Europeans to the non-Europeans they "discovered."

> One is in the realm of political life—in the concrete relations with concrete non-European countries, peoples and worlds. . .The other relationship is an expression of the domain of the imagination, of all sorts of images of non-western people not derived from observation, experience or perceptible reality, but from a psychological urge—an urge that creates its own reality which may be different from the realities of the first category. (Baudet, 1988, p. 6)

Long-distance travel, the salvation of souls, and military missions coalesced into an amalgam of ideology and practice that became the basic structure of Western explorations, discoveries, and conquests over the last five hundred years. This ideological orientation led Daniel Defert to make the following remark concerning Western expansion:

> The early Europeans were pilgrims, *prudentia peregrandi.* They were taught languages as *languae pereginae,* that is not languages of a given territory but language necessary for the activity of traveling. . .This vast universe, known only to a few people, absent from the sacred texts and of which Antiquity knew nothing could have provided a field of endless invention and exaggeration. But the writer's obligation to the truth was the result of a hierarchal network of competition and confrontation. No doubt the voyage of discovery should be situated historically between medieval crusades which it miniaturizes and the organization of a laboratory. (1982, p. 12)

NORMATIVE MODES OF WESTERN TIME. From the time of Constantine through the medieval period the West was dominated by a Christian conception of the temporal process. Following the missionary commandment from the Gospels to preach and baptize all humanity, notions of time and space were made to conform to this injunction. Geographical space and the temporal process were believed to aid and abet this dictum. While other temporal modes among other peoples and cultures were acknowledged, they were understood as stages of preparation for the reception of the true time of Christian faith and practice. It was this conception and understanding of time based on a biblical paradigm that accompanied both the Roman Catholic missionary orders and Protestants in their explorations, discoveries, and conquests in various parts of the globe at least until the sixteenth century.

Following certain developments stemming from the Protestant Reformation and various technologies in the West, new notions regarding the temporal process emerged from the Western Enlightenment. Both had to do with the secularization of time. One conception offered a critique and alternative to the biblical structure of time from creation, to the passion and resurrection of Christ, to the last days; the other, while accepting the basic Christian ordering of time as formative and necessary for the West, nevertheless exorcised all the mystical and theological meanings from this temporal process, thus equating and identifying the time of Western culture with the meaning, structure, and order for a normative understanding of all human time.

It is a generally accepted notion in the Western social sciences that the history of humankind can be divided into four stages of development: the hunting-gathering, the pastoral, the agricultural, and the commercial. These stages did not arise from empirical observation but as a result of a kind of conjectural history. Ronald L. Meek in *Social Science and the Ignoble Savage* (1976) traces this conjectural history as it emerges from several thinkers during the eighteenth century. One prominent element in the development of the theory grew from various theories put forth to account for America, the lands across the Atlantic. America was seen as the first stage of some kind of development of human culture. Meek tells us that the decisive influence in the general adoption of the four-stage theory of cultural evolution and development was the Scottish moral philosophers, the most influential being Adam Smith. In his lectures on jurisprudence in 1762 and 1763, Smith used the four-stage theory as the underpinning for explaining the nature and meaning of property within several types of societies. With the growing acceptance of the theory, several scholars and literary authors undertook research and wrote texts that presupposed these stages as the "natural" evolution of human cultures. For the popular cultures of Europe, the four-stage theory could be turned into the binary of primitive/civilized. This theory and its shorthand became a convenient taxonomy for the classification of the cultures that Europeans encountered in various parts of the world.

While several events, technologies, and ideas contributed to the notion of a purely secular temporal process, the sustained treatment of this conception can be found in eighteenth- and nineteenth-century German philosophy, most especially in G. W. F. Hegel and those influenced by him. Karl Löwith's *From Hegel to Nietzsche: The Revolution in Nineteenth-Century Thought* (1964) traces the way in which these thinkers undertook a critical analysis of the meaning of time within Western culture. Their philosophies were not a simple rejection of a religious or Christian notion of time. While Christian notions of time and history were subjected to critique, they also attempted to show that for a certain period of Western history, Christianity was the bearer of what was objectively real in human time. This objective reality of history has in the modern period moved from the framework of the Christian faith and is now embodied within the secular structures of Western culture. While Hegel was the progenitor of these notions, Löwith points to Johann Friedrich Overbeck as the seminal thinker in the Hegelian school who summarized the theory of the ultimate reality of modern historical temporality.

When Europeans made contact with non-European cultures in various parts of the world, they were armed with ideological cultural notions not simply regarding what was normative for them but, in addition, their norms were understood to be normative for all humankind. While they were more often than not bearers of superior military, navigational, and other forms of technology, it was their normative understandings of time and space that they desired to enforce upon those whom they met. The encounter with others must perforce create a "contact zone," a zone of time/space that must be adjudicated regardless of the dominating power. Conquerors had to learn from the conquered if they were to maintain their authority and the conquered had to adjust, adapt, and respond to those who came from afar. It is clear that since the fifteenth century, the entire globe has become the site of hundreds of contact zones. These zones were the loci of new forms of language and knowledge, new understandings of the nature of human relations, and the creation and production of new forms of human community. These meanings have for the most part been ignored due to the manner in which the West, in an uncritical manner, absolutized its meaning of itself as the norm for all humankind.

EXCHANGES: LANGUAGES, RATIONALITIES, AND MATERIALITIES. The model of pilgrimage was always caught within a tension between curiosity, on the one hand, and the liturgical ritual meaning of a soteriology, on the other. It is equally the case that much travel was motivated by desire for the form of knowledge that came from visits to distant places. The narratives, discourses, and practices hardly revealed the kind of contingency and descriptions that would open these journeys to a full portrayal of the wide variety of exchange relations that were attendant to these travels.

Kathleen Biddick in *The Typological Imaginary* (2003) traces the origins of the stylization of the kind of "absoluteness" that became the favored narrative structure. In her research she shows that this stylization of the absoluteness of time and space can be traced back to what she calls the "Christian typological imagination." This form of historical thinking grows out of the way in which Christianity worked out its relationship to the history of Judaism and the Jews. The history of the Jews was subsumed into the Christian canon through their creation of the Christian Old Testament. From this perspective, the history of the Jews ended or should have ended with the coming of Jesus Christ. Though the history of Judaism continued and continues to this day, because of the canonization of the Christian Bible and the ensuing cultural power of Christianity, the Jews and Judaism were destined to always be seen as a people and tradition who were relegated to a temporal past, Christian time becoming the normative meaning of temporality as history. As Biddick put it, "They believed that the Christian new time—as 'this is now'—*superseded* a 'that was then' of Israel" (p. 1). She makes it clear that Western secular time took over this meaning of supercession from the Christians. Now given the fact that Western historical time in either its mundane or philosophical modes carries this sense, modes of time in transcultural contact zones are often seen as "unhistorical." Biddick refers to this kind of time as temporalities—ones not about divisions between then and now, but about passages, gaps, intervals, in betweeness. "These unhistorical temporalities that do not use time as a utilitarian resource to ground identity are temporalities that can never be one" (p. 2).

Temporalities within contact zones are very complex. The time of the pre-Western contact is no longer normative, though dimensions of it may inhere within the language; inhabitants are forced to accept the official historical time of their conquerors, and those oppressed within these spaces must express a temporality of their own "lived time," which is neither the precontact time of their traditional cultures nor the official time of the conquest.

From the fifteenth century to the present several different Western empires have dominated various cultural areas of the world. While dominance and conquest were common traits, all empires did not undertake these modes of control in the same manner. Neither did all the cultures within the dominated areas respond or adapt in the same manner. The processes and dynamics of these interactions define the varying meanings from within the contact zones.

These contact zones had an effect upon the literary productions of Europeans, indicating how the Europeans were responding and the impact of these non-European cultures upon European sensibilities. Peter Hulme in his *Colonial Encounters: Europe and the Native Caribbean, 1492–1797* (1986) shows how Europeans styled the encounters in literary form. For example, the encounters of Columbus and other Europeans in the New World are expressed in the dramas of Prospero and Caliban, John Smith and Pocahontas, Robinson Crusoe and Friday, and Inkle and Yarico; these dramas are attempts to express these encounters in ways that would fit within the orders of European cultures (p. xiii). Hulme makes it clear that there is much more going on than simply literary production. These literary forms, he says, should be seen as colonial discourses. By this he means,

> an ensemble of linguistically based practices unified by their common deployment in the management of colonial relationship, an ensemble that could combine the most formulaic and bureaucratic of official documents. . .underlying colonial discourse, in other words, is the presumption that large parts of the non-European world were *produced* for Europe through a discourse that imbricated sets of questions and assumptions, methods, of procedure and analysis, and kinds of writing and imagery. (1986, p. 2)

These literary productions taken on face value enabled Europeans to create stereotypical images of the non-Europeans encountered in colonial and imperial projects. These images enhanced the images of the exotic, the oriental, and the noble savage as products of the distances from the center of European metropolises. They fed into the stadial theories of the historical development of humankind, congealing this difference into cultural categories of the West.

The conjectural theory of history that formed the base upon which the stadial theory was erected was correlated with a cultural theory of human intelligence. Thus, various stages were expressions of forms of intelligence. This led to notions of "how natives think," or "prelogical mentality," and the like. Such theoretical postulations were based upon the normative structure and meanings of Western thought. Seldom were these issues of thought asked from within the contact zones, where oppressive administrative colonial structures, Europeans, and non-Europeans carried on their lives.

Thus, cultural, literary, philosophical, and scientific languages and discourses employing this supercessionary and absolute language of temporality normalized a Western understanding of the nature of the encounters with non-Western peoples. Interwoven and concealed within these linguistic productions were the actual and authentic relationships that were taking place in the contact zones. Two instances of the meaning of contact as it relates to the exchange of material products can be seen in the events and discourses surrounding the meaning of *fetish* and *fetishism* and the phenomena referred to as *cargo cults.*

The fetish and fetishism became popular in European discourses of the eighteenth century as a definition of the earliest form of religion. This definition and its usage was part and parcel of a stadial evolutionary variation of supercessionary history. The etymological origin of the word *fetish* is the Portuguese *feitico,* which means "manufactured" or "fabricated." William Pietz, who has recently undertaken the most extensive research into the history of this term and its various usages in modern times, traces its beginning with the Portuguese to its usage by the Dutchmen Pieter de Marees and Bosman through a succession of other European writers, finally appearing in the work of the first historian of religions, Friedrich Max Müller. It later becomes an important term in the writings on political economy of Karl Marx and in the theories of sexuality of Sigmund Freud. Given such a wide range of significations and connotations, Pietz notes that,

> fetish has never been a component in a discursive formation. Fetish rather describes not societies, institutions, or cultures but cross-cultural spaces. From this standpoint, the fetish must be viewed as proper to no historical field other than that of the history of the word itself, and to no discrete society or culture, but to a cross-cultural situation formed by the on-going encounter of value codes of radically different social orders. (1985, p. 11)

At one level the fetish is about a new conception of matter and materiality as these notions undergo transformations within the Atlantic world of exchanges and discourses. While the religious world of Christianity was predicated upon the creation of all matter by God, a form of matter was necessary in the Atlantic that carried only an exchange and not an inherent value. The notion of the fetish, as originating in the Atlantic encounters with radically different cultural notions of the value of matter, developed into the language of the fetish, which performed the dual roles of hiding the true and authentic exchanges that took place in the Atlantic encounters, and creating a form of matter that would not bear the weight of any human meaning of tradition or origination. The fetish in Pietz's description fits perfectly the kind of significations that arise from transcultural contact zones.

Another phenomenon of such spaces is the cargo cult. The term *cargo cult* was coined in 1923 in *The Vailala Madness and the Destruction of Native Ceremonies in the Gulf Division,* a report by government anthropologist F. E. Williams, to describe what he considered to be strange ritual phenomena among the population in Papua New Guinea. These rituals involved an interpretation of matter from within the contact zone. Although Westerners brought a wide variety of material products to Melanesia during the colonial period, their notion of matter was under the sign of inanimate products whose value lay only in their potential for exchange. The natives of Papua New Guinea understood matter and exchange in very different ways. In addition, Westerners were accompanied by Christian missionaries, who preached a gospel of the inherent value of each human soul as the basis for salvation. The natives of this area quickly perceived that though Christians preached a message of the salvation of human souls, they acted in terms of a soteriology based upon the accumulation and distribution of material goods. From this perspective they were able to understand the strange and almost magical characteristics between money as a mode of exchange, the inanimate nature of material products, and the hidden relationship obtaining between these items. Their response to this conundrum was in the form of rituals involving Western made products, the cargo, and millenarian hopes.

All forms of human expression, including language, took on different forms within the contact zones. There were several languages: the language of the official colonizing culture, the original or indigenous languages, and languages that were mixtures of the official and indigenous languages. These mixed, creole, or pidgin languages were not simply derivatives from the mixture but equally a system of communication that was uniquely suited to render adequately the experiences of those who lived outside and underneath the official legitimated orders of officialdom.

Exchanges were not limited to languages, products, and services; there were exchanges of sexualities as well. Exchanges of sexualities produced offspring of the mixtures in the contact zones. Every situation of contact included classes of persons resulting from the union of Westerners and non-Westerners. These "illegitimate" offspring became in turn complex aspects of the communication systems of the other exchanges between dimensions of work, products, and sexualities. For example, Magali Carrera (2003) has demonstrated how the complex mixtures of Spaniards, Indians, and Africans in Mexico led to taxonomies of cultural valuation that were expressed and normalized in a genre of *casta* paintings. Exchanges were not limited to human expressions; in the United States human beings as enslaved persons were legally defined as chattel and exchanged as property. This mode of exchange created almost imponderable issues regarding definitions and meanings of human freedom in a democratic society. One can see how various forms of fetishism enter into and serve to hide the true situation, often making it impossible for the official linguistic traditions to deal with the meanings and expressions that lie hidden within their legal and civil pronouncements.

Karen Fields's *Revival and Rebellion in Colonial Central Africa* (1985) shows in a precise manner "how natives think." The "natives" were very capable of not only "living in," but also "thinking about" and reflecting upon their situation. As over against an anthropological wisdom that Africans had no objective knowledge of the forces determining their behavior, she shows that they not only possessed such knowledge but were capable of making creative, critical, and intelligent use of it. Her book also enables us to see that within the contact zone the cultural categories of the West are taken up and reinterpreted in ways that give them a freshness and novelty. In the search and desire for another source of power that is no longer derivative of traditional resources, nor simply acquiescent to colonial authorities, the native in question, Shadrack, saw the God of the Watch Tower Society as the foundation for a critical and revolutionary meaning within the contact zone.

Another example of reason and intelligence from the contact zone can be seen in Margaret J. Wiener's *Visible and Invisible Realms: Power, Magic, and Colonial Conquest in Bali* (1995), which demonstrates the persistence of the meaning of the "other" and the invisible world of value and orientation in the midst of contemporary life. She also makes clear that Klungkung, the Balinese kingdom, did not anticipate the entrance into Western civilization as a heralded event.

John D. Kelly (1991) studied the meaning of virtue as a value within the structures of imported indentured workers from India on the island of Fiji in the early part of the twentieth century. His discussion raises issues regarding the nature of virtue when one wishes to be modern and at the same time appreciates the authentic limits placed upon one by tradition. These issues bear upon the nature of work, sexuality, kinship systems, and anti-colonialist organization and agitation. This study from within a contact zone adds much to the range of the meaning of virtue. Michael Taussig's *The Devil and Commodity Fetishism in South America* (1980), following a neo-Marxist methodology, is able to show a new valorization of the meaning of the devil from within the contexts of several contact zones in South America. Fernando Cervantes's *The Devil in the New World: The Impact of Diabolism in New Spain* (1994) shows how this same figure of the devil brought by the Spanish missionaries developed in opposition, on the one hand, and in parallel, on the other hand, to the understandings of the Aztecs. Cervantes's thorough study lays the grounds for a mature notion of evil emerging from the realities of the contact zone.

One might identify transculturation and contact zones as corollaries of a creole or a creolization process. The term *creole*, from the Spanish *criollo*, was initially used to identify persons born in the Americas but who claimed white European ancestry. From this point of view, all of the "Founding Fathers" of the United States could be called creoles. The term took on other connotations from within the situations of transculturation and the many "contact zones" throughout the world. More often than not, it now refers to the processes and dynamics of the fluid improvisational meanings of cultures that express the survival, critique, and creativity of those who occupy these situations and sites.

The Martinican intellectual Edouard Glissant has proposed the term *creolization* to describe a more general philosophical stance of transculturation and contact zones. Such a stance undertakes a critique of the official histories and the implicit notions of time and space embedded within them. Glissant calls for a "creolization process" of relationship and relativity. In the introduction to Glissant's *Caribbean Discourses*, J. Michael Dash characterizes one of his positions: "But the world can no longer be shaped into a system. Too many Others and Elsewheres disturb the placid surface. . .Glissant is a natural deconstructionist who celebrates latency, opacity, infinite metamorphosis" (Glissant, 1989, p. xii).

These works and several others of this genre are the result of serious questions asked from within contact zones rather than from the ideologically normative positions of Western categories. While the term *globalization* is used to refer to the various aspects of a worldwide capitalistic market-consumer system, the term might equally specify the myriad contact zones throughout the world where Western cultures and non-Western cultures have encountered each other. In these in-between spaces inhabited by both, exchanges, violent and reciprocal, have taken place. From places such as these a more authentic sense of humankind's place in the world might be forged.

BIBLIOGRAPHY

In *On the Social Phenomenon of "Transculturation" and its Importance in Cuba*, Fernando Ortiz opened the door to the significance of cultural contact through his studies of the formation of the Afro-Cuban dimensions of Cuban culture. His publication, *Tobacco and Sugar*, translated from the Spanish by Harriet de Onis (New York, 1947) marks the first scholarly usage of the term "transculturation." The contemporary study of cultural contact within an orientation of transculturation as both a description and critique of colonialism and imperialism was initiated by Mary Louise Pratt's *Imperial Eyes: Travel Writing and Transculturation* (London, 1992). Pratt's work served as a catalyst for other works published before and subsequent to her work, including Fredi Chiapelli, ed., *First Images of America: The Impact of the New World on the Old*, 2 vols. (Berkeley, 1976). Henri Baudet's *Paradise on Earth: Some Thoughts on European Images of Non-European Man*, translated by Elizabeth Wentholt (New Haven, 1965; reprints, Westport, Conn., 1976, and Middletown, Conn.,

1988), shows how travel leads to images of non-European peoples, even though these images are not based upon observation or perceptions. See also Nicholas Thomas's *Entangled Objects: Exchange, Material Culture, and Colonialism in the Pacific* (Cambridge, Mass., 1991). Charles H. Long devoted a section of his *Significations: Signs, Symbols, and Images in the Interpretation of Religion*, 2d ed. (Aurora, Colo., 1995), to an understanding of cultural contact and religion. Arjun Appadurai, ed., *The Social Life of Things: Commodities in Cultural Perspective* (Cambridge, U.K., 1986), extends the meaning of *transculturation* to the nature and meaning of objects. The display and meaning that objects take in this process were enhanced by the "world fairs" that became international exhibits for exotic and esoteric objects. Two important works discuss this aspect, Paul Greenhalgh's *Ephemeral Vistas: The Expositions Universelles, Great Exhibitions, and World Fairs, 1851–1939* (Manchester, U.K., 1988), and John Burris's *Exhibiting Religion: Colonialism and Spectacle at International Expositions, 1851–1893* (Charlottesville, Va., 2001). The impact of studies of cultural contact on the discipline of anthropology can be seen in Johannes Fabian's *Time and the Other: How Anthropology Makes Its Object* (New York, 1983) and Nicholas B. Dirks, ed., *Colonialism and Culture* (Ann Arbor, Mich., 1992).

The literature on travel as pilgrimage is extensive. Mary Helms's study of travel in *Ulysses' Sail: An Ethnographic Odyssey of Power, Knowledge, and Geographical Distance* (Princeton, 1988) adds a new dimension to the meaning of travel and the nature and quality of knowledge. Victor Turner's analysis of Christian pilgrimage in *Image and Pilgrimage in Christian Culture: Anthropological Perspectives* (New York, 1978) specifies the ritual elements and processes within the structure of Christian pilgrimages. For discussion of medieval European pilgrimages see, Christian Zacher, *Curiosity and Pilgrimage: The Literature of Discovery in Fourteenth-Century England* (Baltimore and London, 1976); Lionel Rothkrug's several studies include "Popular Religion and Holy Shrines: Their Influence on the Origins of the German Reformation and Their Role in German Cultural Development," in *Religion and the People, 800–1700*, edited by Jim Obelkevich (Chapel Hill, 1979); and *Religious Practices and Collective Perceptions: Hidden Homologies in the Renaissance and Reformation* (Waterloo, Ont., 1980).

Two edited works on pilgrimage contain excellent articles with extensive bibliographies: *Implicit Understandings: Observing, Reporting, and Reflecting on the Encounters Between Europeans and Other Peoples in the Early Modern Era* (Cambridge, U.K., 1994), edited by Stuart B. Schwartz; and *Voyages and Visions: Towards a Cultural History of Travel*, edited by Jaś Elsner and Joan-Pau Rubiés (London, 1999)—see in particular Elsner and Rubiés's introduction: "Travel and the Problem of Modernity." Daniel Defert's "The Collection of the World: Accounts of Voyages from the Sixteenth to the Eighteenth Centuries," *Dialectical Anthropology* 7 (1982): 11–20, presages the world fairs mentioned above in the works of Greenhalgh and Burris. For a discussion of the tension in liturgical time that ensued in medieval societies under the impact of technology and trade, see Harald Kleinschmidt, *Understanding the Middle Ages: The Transformations of Ideas and Attitudes in the Medieval World* (Woodbridge, U.K., 2000). Norbert Elias's *Time: An Essay*, translated by Edmund Jephcott (Oxford, 1967), is a good discussion of social time; it should be read along with Fabian's work, cited above. Kathleen Biddick's *The Typological Imaginary: Circumcision, Technology, History* (Philadelphia, 2003) demonstrates how medieval Christian time, later inherited by secular time, was based upon the placement of Jews and Judaism in time and space; this work should be seen as a counter to the kind of conjectural history that produced a stadial theory of cultural development as discussed in Ronald L. Meek's *Social Science and the Ignoble Savage* (Cambridge, U.K., 1976). The relationship of time, travel, and literary images is explored in Peter Hulme's *Colonial Encounters: Europe and the Native Caribbean, 1492–1797* (London and New York, 1986; reprint, 1992). The philosophical justification and amalgam of Christian time with secular time is the task of Karl Löwith's *From Hegel to Nietzsche: The Revolution in Nineteenth Century Thought*, translated by David E. Green (New York, 1964; reprint, 1991).

One of the earliest reports of a contact site in a transcultural situation is F. E. William's classic statement in *The Vailala Madness and the Destruction of Native Ceremonies in the Gulf Division* (Port Moresby, Papua New Guinea, 1923). This report, which led to the notion of "cargo cults," was followed by several works, the most notable being Peter Lawrence's *Road Belong Cargo: A Study of the Cargo Movement in the Southern Madang District, New Guinea* (Manchester, U.K., 1964) and the following works by Kenelm O. Burridge: *Mambu: A Melanesian Millennium* (London, 1960; reprint, Princeton, 1995) and *Tangu Traditions: A Study of the Way of Life, Mythology, and Developing Experience of a New Guinea People* (Oxford, 1969). A comprehensive study of this area is found in G. W. Trompf, *Payback: The Logic of Retribution in Melanesian Religions* (Cambridge, U.K., 1994).

Examples of historical empirical studies of contact zones include: for Africa, Karen E. Fields, *Revival and Rebellion in Colonial Central Africa* (Princeton, 1985); for Fiji, John D. Kelly, *A Politics of Virtue: Hinduism, Sexuality, and Countercolonial Discourse in Fiji* (Chicago and London, 1991); and for Bali, Margaret J. Wiener, *Visible and Invisible Realms: Power, Magic, and Colonial Conquest in Bali* (Chicago and London, 1995), which shows in stark relief how religious powers and resources of an "invisible world" emerge and come to play decisive roles in the Dutch conquest of Bali. Magali Carrera's *Imagining Identity in New Spain: Race, Lineage, and the Colonial Body in Portraiture and Casta Paintings* (Austin, Tex., 2003) demonstrates not only how the complex issue of race, class, and gender were managed but equally how they were normalized in domestic portraiture in the Mexican colonial family. John Cowley's *Carnival, Canboulay, and Calypso: Traditions in the Making* (Cambridge, U.K., 1996) describes how the carnival tradition becomes the container, expression, and critique of an ongoing tradition in the Caribbean. Finally, Fernando Cervantes's *The Devil in the New World: The Impact of Diabolism in New Spain* (New Haven, 1994) and Michael Taussig's, *The Devil and Commodity Fetishism in South America* (Chapel Hill, N.C., 1980) present, on the one hand, theological ramifications of this Christian symbol in a contact zone, and, on the other, the popular manifestations of this meaning as related to work and the economic system.

No discussion of transculturation or contacts zones can proceed very far without dealing with the issue of the fetish or what is implied in the modern discourse about fetishism. The most profound researches on the fetish are those of William Pietz, whose essays have been published in several issues of the journal *RES: Anthropology and Aesthetics.* These include: "The Problem of the Fetish I," *RES* 9 (1985): 5–18; "The Problem of the Fetish II: The Origin of the Fetish," *RES* 13 (1987): 23–41; and "The Problem of the Fetish, IIIa: Bosman's Guinea and the Enlightenment Theory of Fetishism," *RES* 16 (1988): 105–124. The importance of Pietz's research is shown by the fact that it is made use of by Biddick (cited above) and constitutes a significant part of the discussion of another important text dealing with issues related to contact zones, Anne McClintock's *Imperial Leather: Race, Gender, and Sexuality in the Colonial Context* (New York and London, 1995).

Almost all of the above works state explicitly or imply theoretical or methodological positions. However, a few texts directly set forth theoretical and methodological positions based upon transculturation and the contact zones. These include Ashis Nandy's *The Intimate Enemy: Loss and Recovery of Self Under Colonialism* (Delhi, 1983). Another text containing an unique interpretation and extension of thought is Vinay Lal's *Dissenting Knowledges, Open Futures: The Multiple Selves and Strange Destinations of Ashis Nandy* (New Delhi, 2000). Edouard Glissant's *Caribbean Discourse: Selected Essays,* translated by J. Michael Dash (Charlottesville, Va., 1989), comes from a completely different experience of the contact zone, and expresses many of the same meanings and styles as does Nandy.

CHARLES H. LONG (2005)

TRANSCULTURATION AND RELIGION: RELIGION IN THE FORMATION OF MODERN CANADA

The history of modern Canada has been characterized by a concurrence of dichotomies typified by the ongoing discord between French and English Canadians. This dichotomy, however, has been only one of a number of defining antitheses involving ethnicity, religion, and regionalism. Historians have long recognized the preeminent role of religion in the formation of the nation, and the relationship of religion—particularly the churches—to the growth of the specific dichotomies that define the Canadian Confederation. The churches, and religion more broadly, have been thoroughly bound to the political, social, and cultural development of this nation whose designation of "dominion," and motto, "from sea to sea," are both taken from the seventy-second Psalm.

THE CHURCHES. The relationship between churches and state in Canada was inaugurated in 1534, when Jacques Cartier erected a cross at the Gaspé Peninsula around which he and his companions knelt to pray. Cartier had sailed from Saint Malo, a French seaport connected with the transatlantic fishery that had emerged in the wake of the discovery of cod stocks off the coast of Newfoundland by Giovanni Caboto (John Cabot) and his son Sebastian, who had been commissioned by Henry VII in the late fifteenth century to seek out spices. By the end of the sixteenth century French fishers and aboriginal peoples had established a lucrative trade in furs, laying the foundation for a staple trade that would continue to bring the French to the northern part of the continent. The first permanent French settlements were established in Acadia in 1604 and Quebec in 1608. At the time of their founding, France was undergoing a period of religious revitalization. The counter-reformation had engendered a firm association between an increasingly missionary Catholic Church and the state, and all colonial ventures were consequently required to carry Catholicism with them and to missionize among native peoples. Aside from a few itinerant priests among the Mi'kmaq of Acadia from 1604 to 1613, active evangelization in North America was undertaken by religious orders, beginning with the Récollets who arrived at Quebec in 1615, and then the Society of Jesus (Jesuits) in 1625. French/aboriginal relations were relatively amicable during this period, due to the fact that French settlements were tied primarily to the trade in furs, an enterprise that did not give rise to large-scale colonization and required a level of cordiality among interested parties. Additionally, the French fostered alliances through the extension of trading privileges to baptized aboriginals.

In 1627, the French crown transferred control of the colony to the Company of New France, whose charter required the importation of four thousand French settlers with the services of priests, who would also evangelize among the native population. Baptized aboriginals were to be afforded the same rights as French citizens. Over the next quarter century the Jesuits established missions among the Algonquin, Montagnais, Abenaki, and to a lesser degree, Mohawk. The order assumed a prominent role in New France, due primarily to the fact that it was the principle purveyor of education, health care, and social assistance. Over time, much of this work would be undertaken by French and Canadian religious orders of women, such as the Ursulines, who arrived at Quebec in 1639 and established a boarding school for French and native girls.

By 1700, France controlled most of North America, aside from some parts of Newfoundland and the thirteen colonies. New France, however, was not isolated from the English colonies; indeed, conflict between them began in 1613, when Samuel Argall sailed from Virginia and destroyed the French trading post on Mount Desert Island (in present-day Maine). In 1627, the Kirk brothers took Quebec, and maintained control of the colony until 1633; and in 1690, William Phips unsuccessfully attacked Quebec. French control began to wane with the conquest of Acadia by seven hundred New England soldiers in 1710. By the Treaty of Utrecht (ending the War of the Spanish Succession in 1713), France surrendered Hudson Bay, Newfoundland, and Acadia (Nova Scotia); while maintaining control of the Saint Lawrence colonies, Ile Saint-Jean (Prince Edward Island), and Ile Royale (Cape Breton). The Treaty established two separate legal structures for the French Acadians and the Mi'kmaq population in the region, and guaranteed freedom of religion to the Acadians in return for oaths of allegiance, which they refused to take. The legal separation of ethnic groups was unstable, given that trade, intermarriage, and missionization had created an Acadian community that lacked such distinctions. The situation was epitomized by the request by the Acadians for a ruling on whether a 1744 order placing bounties on Mi'kmaq scalps applied to mixed-blood peoples. Frustrated with resistance from an allied Acadian and Mi'kmaq population, the English began forcibly deporting the Acadians in 1755.

The Seven Years' War (1756–1763) marked the end of French control in North America, but colonial animosities had reached a pitch before the end of the war. On September 13, 1759, the Canadians surrendered Quebec, following a confrontation with the New Englanders on the Plains of Abraham. A year later, Montreal followed suit. Until the end of the Seven Years' War, the two cities were occupied by the British. The treaty ending the war was signed in 1763; within a year, the colony was renamed the Province of Quebec and the Royal Proclamation of 1763 established the administration of the country. England had no clear policy toward the colony in the decade following the fall of Quebec. The Proclamation was vague, apparently presuming that English immigration would define the colony's political, economic, and religious temperament; but a consistent policy was not articulated during the 1760s due to the fact that England was politically unstable, with six administrations in the span of a decade. This haphazard mode of control was ended by the need to counter revolutionary rumblings in the thirteen colonies, and the result was the Quebec Act of 1774, the first constitution created by a parliamentary statute for a British colony. The Act inaugurated England's "second empire," a period during which parliament became chiefly responsible for imperial affairs. The Quebec Act guaranteed freedom of religion to French Catholics in return for an oath of allegiance that was modified to exclude potentially offensive references to religion. The Coutume de Paris remained the civil law of Quebec, while English law applied in criminal cases. There was no habeas corpus. The Act made no provision for an elected legislature, and left the Canadians comparatively free of taxation. Many in the thirteen colonies regarded the Act as an assault, objecting to the creation of nonrepresentative government, the "establishment" of Roman Catholicism in the colony, and the prerogative assumed by the British Parliament in its enactment. It is consequently cited as one of the causes of the American Revolution. More critically for Canada, it was the first British statute that conceded the presence of multiple ethnic groups in a colony.

At the time of the conquest of Quebec, French Catholics represented 95 percent of the province's non-aboriginal population. Although a few thousand European immigrants arrived after 1750, the influx of American loyalists instigated by the Revolutionary War dramatically altered the population balance. Between 1750 and 1800, English immigrants attempted to establish the Church of England, an effort that failed in Quebec, but succeeded to varying degrees in Nova Scotia, Prince Edward Island, Newfoundland, and what would become Ontario. In 1758, for instance, the Nova Scotia legislature instituted the Church of England, allowed freedom to Protestant dissenters, and prohibited Catholic priests from ministering in the province. In 1769, Prince Edward Island limited the rights of Roman Catholics, and by the turn of the century established the Church of England.

Following the American Revolution, seven thousand loyalists claimed land in Quebec, where there were ninety thousand French Catholics. Loyalist demand for constitutional amendments resulted in the Constitutional Act of 1791, which divided Quebec into two provinces: Upper and Lower Canada. The Act implemented elected assemblies, set aside one-seventh of the land as clergy reserves for the support of the Anglican Church, and stipulated that only Anglican ministers could perform marriages. Ultimately, however, it effectively gave power in each of the Canadas to a leadership that could override legislation passed by their assemblies. Upper Canada's political elite, the Family Compact, was firmly allied with the Anglican Church, despite the fact that Anglicans constituted a minority of Protestants in the province (by 1800 there were, among others, Presbyterians, Methodists, Quakers, Congregationalists, Lutherans, and Mennonites); and the Compact's counterpart in Lower Canada, the Chateau Clique, was controlled by the English and their French supporters. Popular rebellions were crushed in both provinces in 1837 and 1838, and Lord Durham was dispatched from England to report on the causes of the unrest. His recommendations, which included the granting of responsible government, the union of the two provinces, and the systematic assimilation of the French, resulted in the Act of Union of 1841. The Union created an inevitable tension between French Catholics demanding protection for their national distinctiveness, and English Protestants who began to lobby for denominational equality in a definitively Protestant society (the secularization of clergy reserves in 1854, for instance, was an offshoot of these efforts). Evangelicalism within both groups became prominent after 1840, as each sought to influence the fabric of Canadian institutions and laws. Catholic energies were focused on French Canada, while Protestants concentrated on the nation as a whole.

By the British North America Act of 1867, Ontario, Quebec, New Brunswick, and Nova Scotia were united into a Confederation: the Dominion of Canada. Newfoundland, Prince Edward Island, and British Columbia were identified as "colonies or provinces" that could join the Confederation by means of a joint action of their legislatures and the federal parliament. A year later, the Imperial Parliament enacted the Rupert's Land Act, providing for the surrender of Hudson's Bay Company land to England (Charles II had granted the entire territory surrounding Hudson Bay to his cousin Prince Rupert and seventeen associates in 1670), and the subsequent transfer of the territory to the Canadian government. No provision was made for the territory's admittance into the Confederation; it was regarded as a colony of a colony, a foundation that would perpetually cause western resentment toward central Canada.

In one respect, the Dominion was the project of politicians and advocates for a transcontinental railroad; and in this sense, the nation had a secular foundation. Still, Confederation provided for substantial provincial autonomy in matters of religion, language, and education, provisions that acknowledged the failure of the attempt, by means of the Union of 1840, to submerge French Catholic nationalism within a dominant English political structure. The British North America Act addressed more fully the constitutional rights of religious minorities, than those of ethnic groups; yet, although the Act confirmed the rights of French Canadians, the Confederation itself did not mitigate their fear of cultural eclipse within a prevailing English national culture. As early as 1871, for instance, the New Brunswick legislature prohibited the teaching of religion and the use of the French language in state-supported schools. During the same period, rival Protestant factions were creating coalitions that expressed a desire for the newly formed nation to assume an Anglo-Protestant character. The move toward Protestant unification was widespread in Anglo-Saxon nations during the nineteenth century; but Canadian churches generally accomplished the move earlier than others. Nineteenth-century intradenominational unions established a model that was expanded following Confederation, and that ultimately resulted in the creation of the United Church of Canada in 1925 (bringing together Methodists, Congregationalists, and many Presbyterians).

The acquisition of the west aroused in many evangelical Protestant churches a millennial desire to extend "His" dominion from one ocean to another, by assimilating immigrants into a dominant Protestant national culture. Competition among denominations quickly became economically unfeasible, and the need for a united response to the task lent urgency to the movement for union. Interest in a national church was fueled also, in part, by the desire to influence legislation, and by Anglo concern over increasing Roman Catholic influence in politics, especially in Quebec. By 1902, a number of anti-Catholic associations were already in existence whose aim it was to curb the expansion of Catholic influence. Unionists believed that a single Protestant church would foster an Anglo-Protestant form of national unity, a sentiment that was expressed in the preamble to the United Church's 1908 Basis of Union, which described "a national church with a national mission."

Although no formal agreement was reached until 1925, local Protestant churches in Ontario, the Maritime Provinces, and the west began to initiate their own unions in 1908. The unions coincided with a general wave of social action in Canada within which churches were deeply implicated. Among Protestants generally, the Social Gospel had become prominent by the late nineteenth century, a movement motivated by the belief that social reforms would establish God's kingdom, and that capitalism must be tempered by cooperation between business, workers, and consumers. The United Church of Canada institutionalized the vision of the Social Gospellers, and is acknowledged as having contributed significantly to the development of the Canadian welfare state.

While Protestants generally pressed for the development of an English-Protestant nation, the Catholic Church was engendering its own forms of social action. Catholic social action emerged in Nova Scotia in the 1930s in cooperative organizations like the Antigonish Movement that involved fishers and farmers. In the late 1920s, Action Catholique became prominent in Quebec, contributing to a general growth of social and political awareness in the province. Many of its young members eventually assumed prominent roles in academia and the media in Quebec during what was called the Quiet Revolution. Quebec underwent a dramatic transformation during the 1960s, whereby a social order that had functioned relatively uninterrupted since the Union of 1841 was overturned. The Quiet Revolution profoundly altered the province's social structure, where an Anglophone elite had for over a century controlled the economy, and the Catholic Church had assumed responsibility for protecting Francophone culture through education and social welfare. In 1960, the Quebec government began nationalizing major industries, providing for the rise of trade unions, and assuming control of health, social welfare, and education. As the Catholic Church lost control of these institutions, church attendance plummeted.

Declining church attendance ultimately affected not only the Catholic Church in Quebec. Prior to 1950, two-thirds of Canadians attended a church on a regular basis; by 1980, only one-third did so. Scholars have noted that evangelical Protestantism and Catholicism, which had been assertive forces for more than a century, had ceased to inspire Canadians. In addition to the Quiet Revolution, an obvious reason for this decline was the fact that Canada's ethnic composition no longer lent itself to the traditional cultural duality of English/French: by the early 1960s, over one third of the nation's population did not identity with either group. For Protestants in particular, any aspiration for a monolithic Protestant nation was simply anachronistic. Additionally, a transformation of higher education during the period may have contributed to the decline. Until the 1960s, most Canadian universities and colleges were owned and managed by churches, but increased costs forced the churches to turn to government for subsidization, and provincial legislatures refused to support church-controlled institutions. Some closed, while others secularized. The trend toward secularization has continued, with the result that churches no longer exercise direct influence over the public sphere. Many believe, consequently, that religion has become a private phenomenon for Canadians, involving such things as belief in the supernatural, the questioning of life's meaning, and institutional memory that draws them back to the churches for selective events (Bibby, 2002). The public role of religion, as typified by the churches, has been all but eliminated.

BETWEEN THE DICHOTOMIES. The churches have indelibly marked the development of modern Canada. In this respect, religion has played a key role in the creation of the nation but, since the 1960s, has ceased to pervasively define the public sphere, nor to influence Canadians' collective sense of national identity. This aspect of religion in Canada has essentially revolved around a series of dichotomies: English/French, Catholic/Protestant, native/white, east/west (metropolis/hinterland). Within this framework of dichotomies, another modality of religion has expressed itself from the margins of the dominant culture and its various national visions. The impact of this religious mode upon the formation of modern Canada is not immediately discernable in traditional narratives of the nation's religious history, but it has been, in many instances, profound. Although examples of this form of religion are numerous (Grant, 1980), one of the most significant instances is the religiously inspired leadership of Louis Riel in the North-West Rebellion of 1885. Riel provides a vantage point from which to explore another relationship between religion and the formation of Canada, one that may well continue to have an effect on the nation during its so-called secular period.

This relationship is imbedded in an abiding historical pattern foreshadowed by events in Acadia at the turn of the seventeenth century. In 1610 a secular priest in Acadia, Jessé Fléché, baptized the Mi'kmaq chief Membertou and twenty members of his family. Given that Fléché could speak no Mi'kmaq (and Membertou appears to have been under the impression that he was entering into a trading alliance), the legitimacy of these baptisms was called into question by the Church and by Jesuits who arrived in Acadia a year later. To redress the problem, the Jesuit Enemond Massé availed himself of the hospitality of the Mi'kmaq, choosing to live within the community and learn their language, a move made possible by a half century of previous goodwill between aboriginals and French fishers in Acadia, and that would define the nature of Jesuit/native relations in North America. His residence among the Mi'kmaq was short-lived. In 1613, the New Englander, Samuel Argall captured Acadia. During the battle for control of the region, Gilbert Du Thet was shot fatally, making him the first Jesuit to die in New France. Du Thet was killed while manning a canon. The events of 1610 to 1613 to a great degree established a pattern within which much of Canada's subsequent history can be situated. The pattern involves at least three distinct aspects: (1) a French/aboriginal foundation based on trade and Catholicism; (2) a violent English overlay that results in a French/English dichotomy that takes precedence over the aboriginal foundation; and (3) the implication of religion in this dichotomy.

This Acadian configuration is an especially apt model in respect to Louis Riel and the North-West Rebellion of 1885. Riel was born at Red River (in what would become the province of Manitoba) in 1844. He was Métis—a member of a community created by the Canadian fur trade, the descendants predominantly of French Catholic men and aboriginal women. The Métis, and in particular, the Métis buffalo hunt, were integral components of the society of the nineteenth century north-West until the transfer of the territory from the Hudson's Bay Company to the Dominion. The transfer was badly managed, with the Canadian government initiating land surveys before the territory had been formally transferred to the Dominion. Residents of the area around Red River (a large number of whom were Métis) were led to believe that existing land titles would not be acknowledged, and under the leadership of Riel formed a provisional government to oppose the transfer without legitimate attention to their grievances. Central to the negotiations between Canada and Riel's provisional government was the assurance of representative government and recognition of land claims. The result was the Manitoba Act, which created the province of Manitoba in 1870. Among other assurances, the Act guaranteed that land grants would be made to all mixed-blood residents of the territory. In the immediate wake of the creation of the province, Riel, the Métis, and the region's aboriginal population found themselves very much enmeshed in the Acadian pattern outlined above. Riel had expected to be a central figure in the transition of the territory to a province, but instead, a warrant for his arrest was issued (pertaining to an execution that had occurred in the course of the Métis resistance), and the Ontario legislature subsequently placed a $5000 bounty on him. He was a fugitive until 1875, when the federal government imposed a five year banishment. The Métis and aboriginals fared little better. The Métis land base did not materialize, and they were forced to migrate north and west as immigrants from central Canada inundated the province. Meanwhile, Canadian and American hunters were decimating the buffalo, which had been the foundation of both Métis and aboriginal life. The disappearance of the buffalo, in addition to epidemic disease, and insufficient assistance to native peoples who had signed treaties extinguishing land rights in return for reserves, led to starvation. Cree leaders petitioned the Canadian government and Prime Minister John A. Macdonald, but received no replies.

During his exile Riel began receiving visions, beginning at Washington Cathedral in Washington, D.C., in 1875, where the Holy Spirit anointed him "Prophet of the New World." His visions would ultimately map out a different kind of Canada. From his position between the dichotomy of ethnicity, Riel perceived a creative space within which a new orientation emerged with the potential for a different kind of unified national body. This nation was defined between the various Canadian dichotomies of ethnicity (English/French, native/white), religion (Catholic/Protestant), and metropolis/hinterland. In respect to ethnicity, he envisioned massive immigration of Italians, Poles, Belgians, Scandinavians, converted Jews, and Germans who together with the aboriginal population, the French, the Métis, and the "great Anglo-Saxon race" would each inhabit equal shares of the nation's territory, creating hybrid ethnicities. The Germans would, for instance, "make a new German-Indian world" (Morton, 1974, pp. 355, 366). Religion, too, was to undergo a radical transformation through which the dichotomy of Catholic/Protestant would be subsumed by a new universal Catholicism. "I wish to leave Rome aside," he said,

> Inasmuch as it is the cause of division between Catholics and Protestants. . . . If I have any influence in the new world it is to help in that way and even if it takes 200 years to become practical. . .then my children's children will shake hands with the Protestants of the new world in a friendly manner. I do not wish these evils that exist in Europe to be. . .repeated in America. (Morton, 1974, p. 319)

Finally, the dichotomy of metropolis/hinterland was recast with Canada as the center of a new world. It was obvious to Riel that the territories, the hinterland of central Canada, would be the fulcrum of this new order: "although the Province of Ontario is great it is not as great as the North-West" (Morton, 1974, p. 321). The north-West was also to be the seat of a new Roman Catholic church, with Saint Boniface (present-day Winnipeg) as the new Rome, the Métis as the new "sacerdotal people," and A. A. Taché, archbishop of Saint Boniface, the new pontiff. The removal of the papacy from Rome was warranted by the simple fact that "Rome did not pay attention to us" (Morton, 1974, p. 322). Ultimately it was clear to Riel that with all these transformations, Canada was to "become one of the most prosperous centres of the world, thanks to God" (Flanagan, 1974, p. 26).

Driven by this vision of a new Canada in which existing dichotomies would be rendered meaningless, Riel led a second Métis rebellion against the Dominion in present-day Saskatchewan in 1885. It coincided with similar uprisings from the region's aboriginal population, and both resistances were crushed by Dominion forces. Riel was tried and found guilty of high treason, and was hanged on November 16, 1885. Riel's religiously inspired resistance to central Canada seemed to have little effect on the formation of the nation, beyond apparently intensifying an existing historical pattern of an English Protestant/French Catholic dichotomy and an increasingly marginalized aboriginal and Métis community. The hanging of Riel fueled the French press and leadership, who found common cause with Riel's French ancestry, and accused the English of ethnic prejudice and religious fanaticism. Reaction among English Canadians quickly turned to an anti-Quebec sentiment, and amplified calls for national unity based on Anglo-Protestant patriotism. The execution has been linked to subsequent attacks on French Catholic education, resistance to the creation of French divisions in the world wars, and opposition to the institution of official bilingualism after 1960.

In 1885 aboriginal grievances were not the same as those of the Métis, and although at least two native actions may have been prompted by news of successful Métis action, this resistance was in no way executed under the leadership of Riel. Nonetheless, contemporary authorities melded the resistances, going so far as to accuse Riel at his trial of "arousing the Indians" and letting "loose the flood-gates of rapine and bloodshed" (Morton, 1974, p. 371). In the year following the events of 1885, aboriginal peoples were increasingly marginalized from mainstream society. The Department of Indian Affairs began to assume greater control over their lives, a trend that continued for almost a century, and resulted in wide-ranging regulation from education to the writing of wills. An aboriginal pass system was introduced, effectively restricting native peoples to their reserves. This was justified by the contention that participation in the rebellion constituted a violation of treaty agreements. Later "pass laws" adopted by the South African apartheid regime were patterned on this Canadian model.

As for the Métis generally (who were not afforded status by the Canadian government until 1982), the community became virtually invisible to the dominant culture. Many changed their names, others immigrated to the United States, some moved onto native reserves, while others moved northward. It seems that Riel's religiously-inspired rebellion did not immediately inform the creation of modern Canada, except insofar as it solidified a basic Canadian pattern that would inform the nation's next century.

The Twenty-First Century. Turning to Canada a century after the hanging of Riel, a number of dramatic alterations in this pattern have occurred. First, as church historians have noted, the nation has become secularized, and increasingly Canadians no longer associate themselves with the churches that informed so much of the nation's development. Additionally, the delicate antagonism between English and French entered into a new phase in the final decades of the century, through which their ongoing dichotomous relationship could well be dissolved. On October 16, 1970, the federal government declared the War Measures Act (a presumption of virtually unlimited power) in response to the kidnapping of British senior trade commissioner, James Cross, and Pierre Laporte, a Quebec cabinet minister. The kidnappings and subsequent murder of Laporte were attributed to the Front de Liberation du Québec. Although the events of October 1970 did not initiate further efforts to secure an independent Quebec through violence, the question of separation remained a serious political issue, culminating in the election in Quebec of the separatist Parti Québecois in 1976, and two narrowly rejected referendums on sovereignty in 1980 and 1995. Additionally, constitutional changes have created a context for the assertion of aboriginal and Métis land claims, which are only beginning to be felt. The Constitutional Act of 1982 (through which Canada gained its own constitution) vaguely recognized "existing" aboriginal and treaty rights, and recognized the Métis as aboriginal peoples. Land claims recognition has been slow but profound. In the mid-1990s, for instance, Donald Marshall was found guilty in the Nova Scotia Court of Appeal of fishing eels illegally. A team of lawyers (four of whom were Mi'kmaq) took the case to the Supreme Court of Canada, and in 1999 the Court upheld Marshall's right to catch and sell fish in accordance with treaties ratified in 1760 and 1761. The same year that the constitution was patriated, the Constitutional Alliance of the Northwest Territories was formed to press for the division of the Northwest Territories into two distinct territories. The subject had been discussed for a number of decades, and on April 1, 1999, the central and eastern part of the territories (a region constituting nearly one-fifth of Canada's land mass) was established as the territory of Nunavut, marking the largest aboriginal land claim settlement in Canadian history. The creation of Nunavut effectively gave the population (85% Inuit) control over education, health and social services, and the management of natural resources. In September 2003, the Supreme Court overturned an earlier conviction of Métis Steve Powley for hunting illegally. In the landmark ruling, the court declared that Powley could exercise the right to hunt without a license on the basis of the definition of the Métis as "aboriginal" in the Constitution of 1982 (council for Powley included lawyer Jean Teillet, great-great-grandniece of Louis Riel).

As Canada entered the twenty-first century many aspects of the national pattern of English overlay on an aboriginal/French foundation were disintegrating, while longstanding dichotomies were reshaping the national landscape. What might now be said of Louis Riel, who was religiously inspired to conceive of the nation in a radically different way, but whose life seemed to have accomplished little beyond the reification of the established order? This man was situated in the space between the dichotomies of ethnicity, was called by God to break with Rome and refashion a new universal Catholicism, envisioned the geographical center of Canada as the defining center of the nation, and was tried and executed as a Canadian traitor. Yet, a statue of Riel now graces the grounds of the Manitoba Legislature, and an accompanying plaque reads: "In 1992, the Parliament of Canada and the Legislative Assembly of Manitoba formally recognized Riel's contribution to the development of the Canadian Confederation and his role, and that of the Métis, as founders of Manitoba." Riel is the hero of over twenty plays, an opera, radio and television dramas, novels, poetry, music, cartoons, and a comic book. He is the only Canadian public figure whose writings have been published in their entirety (Riel, 1985), a project undertaken jointly by the federal government and a number of universities to mark the one hundredth anniversary of Riel's execution; in recent years, he has emerged as a national hero, especially, among English-speaking writers. Riel has been called a mythic figure, a mad messiah, a prophet, a savior, a mystic, a visionary, a Canadian Joan of Arc, a saint, and a martyr. Such frankly religious language is not accidental. As scholars announced the triumph of secularization and the privatization of religion in Canada at the end of the twentieth century, Riel was simultaneously emerging as a religious figure implicated in the meaning of a changing nation. As such, he may well constitute a resource for the continued role of religion in the formation of a twenty-first century Confederation.

BIBLIOGRAPHY

Bibby, Reginald W. *Restless Gods: The Renaissance of Religion in Canada.* Toronto, 2002.

Campeau, Lucien. *La mission des jésuites chez les Hurons 1634–1650.* Montreal, 1987.

Choquette, Robert. *Canada's Religions.* Ottawa, 2003.

Dickason, Olive Patricia. *Canada's First Nations: A History of Founding Peoples from Earliest Times.* Toronto, 1992.

Flanagan, Thomas. "Louis Riel's Religious Beliefs: A Letter to Bishop Taché." *Saskatchewan History* 27, no. 1 (1974): 15–28.

Flanagan, Thomas. *Louis "David" Riel: Prophet of the New World.* Rev. ed. Toronto, 1996.

Grant, John Webster. "Missionaries and Messiahs in the Northwest." *Sciences Religieuse/Studies in Religion* 9, no. 2 (1980): 125–136.

Grant, John Webster. *Moon of Wintertime: Missionaries and the Indians of Canada in Encounter since 1534.* Toronto, 1984.

Miller, J. R. *Skyscrapers Hide the Heavens: A History of Indian-White Relations in Canada.* Rev. ed. Toronto, 1991.

Moir, John S. *Church and State in Canada, 1627–1867.* Toronto, 1967.

Moir, John S. *The Church in the British Era.* Toronto, 1972.

Mol, Hans. *Faith and Fragility: Religion and Identity in Canada.* Burlington, Ont., 1985.

Morton, Desmond. *The Queen v Louis Riel.* Toronto, 1974; reprint, New York, 1992.

Murphy, Terrence, and Roberto Perin. *A Concise History of Christianity in Canada.* Toronto, 1996.

Rawlyk, George A. *The Canadian Protestant Experience, 1760 to 1990.* Burlington, Ont., 1990.

Reeves, Ted. *Claiming the Social Passion: The Role of the United Church of Canada in Creating a Culture of Social Well-Being in Canadian Society.* Etobicoke, Ont., 1999.

Riel, Louis. *The Collected Writings of Louis Riel/Les écrits complets de Louis Riel.* 5 vols. Edited by George F. G. Stanley. Edmonton, Alberta, 1985.

Voisine, Nive, ed. *Histoire du catholicisme québécois.* Vol. 2: *Les XVIIIe et XIXe siècles*; and Vol. 3: *Le XXe siècle.* Montreal, 1984–1991.

Westfall, William. *Two Worlds: The Protestant Culture of Nineteenth-Century Ontario.* Kingston, Ont., and Montreal, 1989.

JENNIFER I. M. REID (2005)

TRANSCULTURATION AND RELIGION: RELIGION IN THE FORMATION OF THE MODERN CARIBBEAN

Ciboney, Arawak-speaking Taíno, and Carib Amerindians crisscrossed the islands of the Caribbean archipelago for a millennium prior to the arrival of Europeans. Columbus learned from the Lucaya, a subgroup of the Taíno, that the island in the Bahamas where he first alighted was named Guanahani. He nevertheless christened (and Christianized) it as San Salvador before taking six Lucaya back to Spain as exotica to present at court in 1492—the first transculturation between Europe and the Caribbean. In 1493 the second voyage carried sugar cane from Europe to Hispaniola (Isla Española), and the Taíno gave Europe tobacco in return—a further and consequential moment of transculturation. By 1501 Nicolás de Ovando, governor of Hispaniola, ordered the delivery of the first Africans (Spanish-speaking Ladinos already enslaved in Iberia) to the New World. The Africans replaced dying Amerindians in the gold mines in a third moment of transculturation, in which the powers guiding all future exchange became transparent.

Thus began the recurrent economic and social pattern that created the Caribbean, built from its florid exploitation and from the regular resistance to it. Already in 1511 the Taíno had rebelled against the new order on Puerto Rico, and Africans on Hispaniola revolted not long after in 1521.

Three centuries later, following the abolition of slavery in the British holdings of Jamaica and Trindidad in 1834, East Indians and Chinese were imported en masse as indentured workers to labor next to or as overseers of Africans. Here was yet another moment of transculturation, bringing new rites and new gods: Kālī, Hanumān, Lakṣmī, and Rāma. Indian deities were now ritualized in the same zones as African *orishas,* and the signs and symbols of European Masonic secret societies shared the same space as those of Afro-Cuban *cabildos.*

During the intervening centuries, a solid social template emerged from between the same grinding continental plates that had thrust up Caribbean volcanoes. Europeans ruled over slaves whose labor produced sugar, the source of wealth that built the palaces of Antwerp and Versailles and fomented the Industrial Revolution of England. Yet if the lands of the Caribbean took on a shared economic form in the first global economy, they also developed unique religious patterns in accord with the particular objects, ideas, migrants, and languages that arrived at each place. Even when those objects, ideas, and peoples were similar, they were adopted by different means and with varying effects as they were received and made to signify in relation to specific landscapes, needs, histories, and contexts of implementation.

This essay proceeds by first examining the term *transculturation* as itself a product of the Caribbean. It then considers four cases of religious transculturation: Cuba, Jamaica, Saint Vincent, and Brazil. For each case, a different issue of transculturation is interpreted: in Cuba, the material and temporal niches in which old religions were received, remade, or lost; in Jamaica (and Rastafarians), the problem of indigenizing English, the colonial idiom, to make it able to "speak" religiously; in Saint Vincent, the phenomenon of physical emigration and the shifts in Garifuna religion that occur through the modern exodus to globalized cities such as New York; and in Brazil, the forging of a new religion in the contact zone out of the cross-fertilization of religious ideas from Africa and Europe. All four cases address the issue of reception and change—how ideas, objects, and people produced in one place take on new meaning when displaced, circulated, and rerooted in new soil in new ground.

The entry does not give an exhaustive account of the region but rather illuminates key processes through select examples. As the inclusion of Brazil indicates, this essay is on the "big Caribbean," defined not only by territorial contiguity but also by shared social history.

TRANSCULTURATION AS A CARIBBEAN PRODUCT. The term *transculturation* is itself an intellectual product of the Caribbean, appearing in Fernando Ortiz's *Contrapunteo cubano del tabaco y el azúcar* (Cuban counterpoint: Tobacco and sugar), first published in 1940. Ortiz proposed that the new word was superior to *acculturation* (a term especially associated with Melville Herskovits) because it did not imply a unilineal process of adopting a new culture—the idea that the former slate is completely erased before the new one is written. Rather, it suggested the nuances of culture loss or *deracination*; as such, losses and the responses to them continue to inform the experience of the new situation. It also connoted the only partial and fragmentary assimilation of a new culture as well as the completely novel creations that were bound to arise in what Ortiz called "neo-culturation."

More important than this semantic dexterity was the way Ortiz wrote about culture in the history of Cuba, as the process of human interaction with and thinking through the material resources at hand. Tobacco and sugar in Ortiz's hands became nothing less than a total semiotic system of contrasts through which the world was humanly experienced. For example, whereas tobacco recalls magic and is immutably dark, sugar connotes the commodification of a product born brown, then standardized to become white. In Ortiz's view, the material products of the island provided the lens through which issues of race and religion were perceived, contemplated, worked, and transformed.

If tobacco and sugar could be detached from their status as mere agricultural products to be recirculated as a symbolic system of meanings applied to every domain of experience, no less are the deracinated people of the Caribbean transcultured through their interactions with each other and with the products through which they know and make themselves.

CUBA: MATERIAL NICHES OF REMEMBRANCE IN THE CONTACT ZONE. Most prominent among distinctively Cuban religions is Santería. The name of Santería, implying the devotion to saints by *santeros,* was an innovation of the 1930s initiated by the Afro-Cuban scholar Romulo Lachatañeré. The new moniker was intended to counter state witch hunts levied against what was popularly called witchcraft (*brujería*) by granting the religion a more legitimate, Catholic resonance. Hence the very naming of the religion, which has real effects on religious practice, stands as testimony to the interaction between religion and political power.

Whether called Santería or La Regla de Ocha (The Rule of the *Orisha*), the religion derived from the quest of African slaves to reconstruct a shared religion out of disparate African traditions, which had been lumped together in the new territory. The great majority of African slaves disembarked in Cuba were set to work on giant sugar plantations, especially after the Haitian revolutions that began in 1791 and left Cuba the dominant world supplier of sugar. In the cities, however, especially Havana and Matanzas, a thriving free black society grew up in the niches of the slave economy. Out of these came black Catholic *cabildos* and *cofradías*, the councils and brotherhoods that, under the mantle of their devotion of Catholic saints, offered sites of mutual aid. By 1800 there were *cabildos* of fourteen different African "nations," each with its own king and queen, flag, and house. These were veritable rebuilt African monarchies, albeit with few temporal powers, in which the devotion to African gods could be remembered and recreated. Preeminent among the nations were the Yoruba, who were brought in great numbers after 1790 and carried with them a mythically rich, colorful, compelling pantheon of gods called *orisha* (Yoruba *ori-se*, literally "head-source"). Also prominent were the Kongo peoples, who comprised by far the largest group of slaves brought during the trade's first three centuries. These created another distinct Afro-Cuban religious lineage, Palo Monte. Palo invoked spirits of central West Africa, called *minkisi,* and contracted them to the living ritualizer through "binding" and "enclosing" their symbols in cauldrons, bottles, or bundles.

In every case, the religion had to be reconstructed out of the available materials and within the limited available spatial and temporal niches presented by colonial Cuba. West African religious were based above all in ritual practices choreographed out of a vast and complex set of iconic, culinary, musical, sartorial, and spatial cues. The gods were present only insofar as they could be rendered present through ritual work correctly executed to produce spirit possession. This meant that the gods that did not fit the niches presented were eventually lost, forgotten, or rendered superfluous. For example, the African gods related to agriculture remained important in Haiti because the religion of vodou emerged in a peasant farming society of small landholders after the revolution. Yet the analogous deities became largely inconsequential in Cuba and Brazil, because Santería and Candomblé took shape in and around cities where agriculture was not a pressing concern of everyday experience.

A progressive condensation and canonization of a relatively fixed set of *orishas* took shape. The Afro-Cuban Catholic *confradías* celebrated these *orishas* in the temporal and material niches available under slave law. For example, Changó, the *orisha* of kingship, lightning, and male seductive power was (and is) celebrated on December 4, the day of the Catholic calendar devoted to Santa Barbara. Her red and white banners and chromolithographs depicting a lightning strike (in Catholic hagiography Barbara's father was struck by lightning) provided a semiotic set into which Changó, a deity of lighting whose colors are red and white, could visually be integrated. Therefore devotees of Changó were able to ceremonialize and cognitively retain his memory. Many of the gods found no such fit, no material or calendrical niches of remembrance, and these gods died with those who last carried and incorporated them.

Condensation was one process, and aesthetic innovation was another. The aesthetics of African royal power had to be transferred to the idiom of European finery adopted from the Spanish colonial court. Santería initiates undergoing the day of enthronement and public display were (and are) dressed in long gowns of fine silk brocades and lace that emulated Spanish royalty but also served as memory bridges to recall African royalism. Likewise, the containers (*sopera*) of sacred stones that served as indexes of the sacred union between initiated persons and the *orisha,* were in many cases of fine porcelain, another European import applied to ritually sustaining the memory of Africa.

The importance of such transcultured ritual objects is revealed by the periodic persecutions that were suffered by practitioners of Santería, in which invasions of cult houses focused on the confiscation of objects such as drums, clothing, scepters, and the vases and porcelain bowls that held the iconic seats of the saints. Similarly transcultured material niches were also created in the Kongo legacy of Palo Monte. The *palos* (sticks) assembled in a cauldron signify a contract of power between a practitioner and an ancestral spirit, but they also contain a specific Cuban history within them. They recall the palisades (defenses built of sharpened sticks) runaway slave communities erected for their protection from slave hunters. Those palisades have now been transcultured to serve the purpose of protecting their users in contemporary urban centers.

JAMAICA: TRANSCULTURING SPEECH IN THE CONTACT ZONE. Named from the Arawak word *Xayaca* (Land of Wood and Water), Jamaica has loaned its soil to manifold ethnic groups. Arawak and then Carib Amerindian societies were followed by Spaniards, Africans, the British, and then Asians. Africans were brought and set to labor by 1513, and during the late 1600s Jamaica's sugar production was the most advanced in the Caribbean. Following emancipation in 1834, Great Britain tapped another of its colonies for thirty thousand East Indians who were imported as laborers. Hence diverse religious expressions converged and combined: Myal and Obeah (the latter derived from the West African Ashanti word *obeye,* meaning sorcerer); central African-derived Pukumina; the indigenized Christianity of Zion Revivalism; and during the twentieth century, Rastafarianism.

In its simplest form, Rastafarianism viewed the crowning of the new Ethiopian emperor, Haile Selassie (1892–1975), as the arrival of a new messiah, a Black Christ who would lead black Jamaicans back to Africa. Indeed, this projected return was to be the salvation of the people. Rastafarianism presented a fusion of diverse factors: revival millenarianism; Marcus Garvey's (1887–1940) back-to-Africa movement; Jamaican urbanization, industrialization, and the creation of an urban underclass; an Ethiopianism inspired by Garvey applied to a selective reading of the Hebrew Bible; the timely ascent of Haile Selassie—or Ras (Prince) Tafari—as emperor of Ethiopia in 1930; and the inversion of key markers like dreadlocks and ganja (marijuana) use from outcast symbols to expressions of defiant power.

Any of these elements moreover can be further divided into more complex transculturations. Garvey's message was a product not only of his Jamaican birth but also of his trajectory passing through Central America, Europe, Africa, and most important, the Pan-African centers of Harlem and Paris. The adoption of dreadlocks in the late 1940s may have imitated one or all of several influences: Kenya's anticolonial Mau Mau revolt against the British in the 1950s, the emulation of the styles of East Indian ascetics, or the Youth Black Faith movement of the 1940s that was indigenous to Jamaica. Similarly, ganja arrived with East Indian laborers before being adopted by revival millenarianism and later Rastafarianism as a key component of its "reasoning" rituals, in which it was used to inspire impassioned exchanges of religiopolitical speech.

It is such idiosyncratic speech that is the key transcultured marker of Rastafarianism. Because standard English is regarded as a colonial and compromised tongue and yet is the sole language of most Jamaicans, Rastafarian practitioners developed a means of at once distancing themselves from that language even as they worked through it by communicating in the dialect of "dread-talk." This occurs through multiple linguistic innovations. In the first, terms of standard English are varied or endowed with new meanings (e.g., *reason,* for ritually inspired discourses; *chalice,* for the pipe used to inhale the smoke of the herb; and *bald-tail,* for shorn, unenlightened non-Rastas). A second innovation is playing with standard words, which are altered in relation to phonological implications, such as *politricks* (politics), *live-icate* (as opposed to dedicate), or *jollification* (enjoyment). The most important revision of standard English occurs in the creation of *I*-words: *Ital* (natural), *Irie* (truth), *I-ration* (creation), *I-thiopia* (Ethiopia), plus the reference to oneself and others as "I and I." Explanations for the invocation of "I and I" in dread-talk include: (1) the refusal to make a subject of another person, hence the use of only first person address; (2) the verbal expression of the idea that one is never utterly separate from God (Jah) or from other persons, hence always "I and I"; and (3) the rejection of the term *me,* which connotes slave speech and subservience compared with *I,* a term of agency and choice.

Whereas English was the language given to members of the urban underclass in Kingston, the Rastafarian community transcultured it to signify distinction from rather than inclusion in the British linguistic legacy. Yet the fact that Rastafarianism is practiced in a variant of English is precisely that which aided and abetted its global dissemination as a Pan-African symbol. This was accomplished above all through reggae, disseminated during the 1970s by Bob Marley, Peter Tosh, Jimmy Cliff, and others as well as through the aesthetic codes rendered fashionable through the popularity of that music. At the beginning of the twenty-first century African identity is commonly expressed in Bahia, Brazil, Bronx, New York, and Port of Spain, Trinidad, through the colors, flags, clothes, music, and hairstyles of Rastafarianism. In this sense, the English language as a transcultured linguistic object cuts in two ways: dissented from, it also allows for that dissent to travel and be heard.

THE GARIFUNA: TRANSMIGRATION AND THE MULTIPLYING OF CONTACT ZONES. The Garifuna stand as the finest exemplars of the simplest cause of transculturation: human migration. An ethnic group born on the island of Saint Vincent in the seventeenth and eighteenth centuries through the exchange between African and Carib groups, they were initially known as the Black Carib. They were deported en masse by the British in 1797 to the coast of Central America. In addition to their own Arawak-derived language, many also spoke French and English, a repertoire to which they rapidly added Spanish. Garifuna religion reflected these transmigrations, including elements of African, Amerindian, and Roman Catholic Christian belief and practice. During the nineteenth century, the Garifuna emigrated up and down the Central American coast of the Caribbean by canoe as dedicated traders and travelers and in the process settled in some forty villages from Nicaragua to Belize.

That relative territorial stability changed dramatically in the twentieth century, during which time a third of Garifuna emigrated abroad, especially to the United States. The phenomenon of frequent migration and returns, related to contemporary labor patterns, had two dramatic effects on the religious life of the Garifuna and by extension of the Caribbean region in general. One effect is the burgeoning Protestant neo-Pentecostal affiliations. Employing high-tech sound systems, formal dress codes, and dramatic preaching styles, these neo-Pentecostal groups emulate—and are often funded by—U.S. denominational patrons. The second effect is the revivalist acceleration of discourses and practices of traditional ritual events, whose meanings are transformed in the process of being revived. For the Garifuna, traditional ancestor rituals that were once simply considered indigenous to themselves are increasingly understood as African in origin. As Garifuna migrants to U.S. cities have been exposed to the religions of their neighbors, such as Cuban Santería, Haitian vodou, Trinidadian *orisha,* and Puerto Rican Santerismo, they begun to view their religion in relation to that set and to perceive themselves as members of the religious African diaspora.

The two new directions of Garifuna religious change—toward Pentecostal modernity and reformed tradition—are not socially bifurcated but rather work in tandem, because they signify over and against and in rivalry with each other. Both proffer membership in global networks rather than local, village-based ones, and both are reliant on modern technologies of semiotic reproduction (e.g., videos, compact discs, books, and magazines) as they compete for adherents in the marketplace of identities and for recognition from state and international authorities. The Garífuna, like practitioners of other religions in the Caribbean region, are in the process of mastering and transculturing new objects of modernity to make them their own: communication systems, recording devices, legal documents, and other devices of "making history" in rationalized forms that can be used for pedagogy and legal defense. For the Garifuna, as elsewhere in the Caribbean, there exists a growing sense that local religion must be given global range—witnessed to, recorded, publicized, discursively defended, and disseminated—to acquire exchange value in the marketplace of religions. Otherwise, they risk losing their place.

Through migrations of the last generation, some Caribbean religions of the region like Santería have already become sophisticated transnational religions with a solid footing in legal and academic settings. Others, like practitioners of the ancestor religion of the Garifuna, remain ambivalent in relation to such processes of deliberate transculturation and what hidden risks they may hold.

BRAZIL: MAKING NEW RELIGIONS IN THE CONTACT ZONE. Like Cuban Santería, the Afro-Brazilian religion of Candomblé traces its origins to one of the city-states of the Yoruba, Dahomean, or Kongolese peoples of West and West Central Africa. It was forcibly brought to Brazil during the Portuguese slave trade over four centuries. As in Santería, Candomblé reconstructs a link to Africa through the reverence of deities (*orixás*) to generate power, or *axé,* for human use in its most worldly forms—luck, fertility, wealth, prestige, and health.

Axé can imply transformative capacity, charisma, fecundity, success, or physical force like electricity. As a quality of a house or a drum, however, it connotes tradition, lineage, and legitimate foundations. Producing *axé* entails a series of material practices that contain, enclose, and bind the elusive *axé* into loci (e.g., altars, vases, heads) from which its force can be received and redistributed. The techniques and tools of condensing and containing *axé* are known as the foundational secrets (*fundamentos*) of the religion. One gains access to this secret knowledge or, more properly, to the places and practice of secrecy by performing progressive initiations into increasingly important functions in the house (*terreiro*). The import of religious secrecy was augmented, however, by the new terrain from which Candomblé grew during the 1800s. Secrecy was transcultured and began to signify doubly: first in relation to West African ideals of contained, "cool" power and second as resistance to the police forces of the national context in which the rituals were practiced. Yoruba ideals of religious secrecy were overlapped with the Afro-Brazilian notion of *fundamentos,* deep knowledge based in practices hidden from the gaze of potential noninitiate encroachers.

In the contact zone, religious identities take on force through boundary work, that is, the marking and parsing of differences and similarities between a given religion and its neighbors. So Candomblé also began to be defined by its relation to, resistance against, and adaptation from other popular Brazilian religious expressions, such as French-descended spiritism.

Spiritism arrived in Brazil in the late nineteenth century via the teachings of Allan Kardec, also known as Hippolyte Léon Denizard Rivail. Its popularity derived from its healing techniques, enacted through mediums in ways as emotionally compelling as they seemed scientific. For spiritists, mediums became effective healers when possessed by more ancient, enlightened souls. In the twenty-first century the mediums dress in white or blue medical clothing to offer *passos* (passes) over the bodies of their subjects, moving their hands over the skin to attract negative vibrations to their own hands and cast them into the air. The healing spirits come from members of civilizations considered to be evolved—doctors or healers from Europe, ancient Egypt, or the Aztec Empire. Sickness is regarded as obsession, and the ritual intervention is a disobsession wherein one medium incorporates the obsessing spirit, while other mediums use their evolved entities to advocate for their client's release. Meetings reflect a high degree of rational bureaucratic organization.

The Afro-Brazilian religion of Candomblé and French-derived Spiritism transcultured each other. Spiritist groups were inspired by the African deities of Candomblé, and Candomblé groups were rationalized in similar ways to spiritism. Adopting elements of both, Umbanda is the result of the convergence of these two groups into a new, national religion. Umbanda was born in the industrializing south of Brazil in the 1920s. It shared aspects with Candomblé (such as possession, specific drumming patterns that call the spirits and *orixás* as heads of spirit divisions) and with spiritism (such as the manifestation of spirits of the dead for the purpose of consultation and healing and a rigid hierarchy of more and less evolved spirits).

Umbanda spirits are organized hierarchically in a complex system of seven lineages, called phalanxes, each headed by an *orixá* or saint. One kind of spirit of light is the *caboclo,* the spirit of the indigenous Brazilian Indian. Another is the *preto-velho,* the spirit of the old African slave, who manifests humility, kindliness, comfort, and sympathy. The *erês* or *crianças* are spirits of children who are playful and innocent. Finally, the *exús,* derived from the Yoruba trickster-messenger Eshu, are considered evil and must be rigorously controlled.

Although these are the most characteristic, traditional spirit roles in Umbanda, there is enormous flexibility for new spiritual entities to emerge, such as manifestations of homeless street children or the folkloric, hard-drinking bandits (*cangaçeiros*) of the arid northeast. Embedded in the spirits of Umbanda and the material processes through which they are incorporated is the ongoing transculturation of Brazilian history as it continually reworks the national mythology of the "three races"—Amerindian, African, white European—for a new time.

SEE ALSO Caribbean Religions, article on Afro-Caribbean Religions; Garvey, Marcus; Rastafarianism; Santería.

BIBLIOGRAPHY

Bastide, Roger. *The African Religions of Brazil: Towards a Sociology of the Interpenetration of Civilizations.* Translated by Helen Sebba. Baltimore, 1978.

Benítez-Rojo, Antonio. *The Repeating Island: The Caribbean and the Postmodern Perspective.* Translated by James E. Maraniss. 2d ed. Durham, N.C., 1996.

Blier, Suzanne. *African Vodun: Art, Psychology, and Power.* Chicago, 1994.

Brandon, George. *Santeria from Africa to the New World: The Dead Sell Memories.* Bloomington, Ind., 1993.

Brown, David. *Santería Enthroned: Art, Ritual, and Innovation in an Afro-Cuban Religion.* Chicago, 2003.

Brown, Diane D. *Umbanda and Politics in Urban Brazil.* Ann Arbor, Mich., 1986.

Brown, Karen McCarthy. *Mama Lola: A Vodou Priestess in Brooklyn.* Berkeley, Calif., 1991.

Cabrera, Lydia. *Reglas de Congo. Palo Monte. Mayombe.* Miami, 1979.

Chevannes, Barry. *Rastafari: Roots and Ideology.* Syracuse, N.Y., 1994.

Coronil, Fernando. "Introduction to the Duke University Press Edition: Transculturation and the Politics of Theory: Countering the Center, Cuban Counterpoint." In *Cuban Counterpoint: Tobacco and Sugar,* by Fernando Ortiz, pp. ix–lvi. Durham, N.C., 1995.

Cosentino, Donald J., ed. *Sacred Arts of Haitian Vodou.* Los Angeles, 1995.

Edmonds, Ennis Barrington. *Rastafari: From Outcasts to Culture Bearers.* New York, 2003.

Gonzalez, Nancie L. *Sojourners of the Caribbean: Ethnogenesis and Ethnohistory of the Garifuna.* Urbana, Ill., 1988.

Harding, Rachel. *A Refuge in Thunder: Candomblé and Alternative Spaces of Blackness.* Bloomington, Ind., 2000.

Herskovits, Melville. *Acculuration: The Study of Culture Contact.* Locust Valley, N.Y., 1938.

Hess, David J. *Spirits and Scientists: Ideology, Spiritism, and Brazilian Culture.* University Park, Pa., 1991.

Houk, James T. *Spirits, Blood, and Drums: The Orisha Religion in Trinidad.* Philadelphia, 1995.

Johnson, Paul Christopher. "Migrating Bodies, Circulating Signs: Brazilian Candomblé, the Garífuna of the Caribbean, and the Category of 'Indigenous Religions.'" *History of Religions* 41, no. 4 (2002): 301–328.

Johnson, Paul Christopher. *Secrets, Gossip, and Gods: The Transformation of Brazilian Candomblé.* New York, 2003.

Kerns, Virginia. *Women and the Ancestors: Black Carib Kinship and Ritual.* 2d ed. Urbana, Ill., 1997.

McAlister, Elizabeth. *Rara! Vodou, Power, and Performance in Haiti and Its Diaspora.* Berkeley, Calif., 2002.

Mintz, Sidney W. *Sweetness and Power: The Place of Sugar in Modern History.* New York, 1985.

Mintz, Sidney W., and Richard Price. *The Birth of African American Culture.* Boston, 1992.

Murphy, Joseph M. *Santería: An African Religion in America.* Boston, 1988.

Murphy, Joseph M. *Working the Spirit: Ceremonies of the African Diaspora.* Boston, 1993.

Murrell, Nathaniel Samuel, William David Spencer, and Adrian Anthony McFarlane, eds. *Chanting Down Babylon: The Rastafari Reader.* Philadelphia, 1998.

Olmos, Margarite Fernández, and Lizabeth Paravisini-Gebert. *Creole Religions of the Caribbean: An Introduction from Vodou and Santería to Obeah and Espiritismo.* New York, 2003.

Ortiz, Fernando. *Cuban Counterpoint: Tobacco and Sugar.* Translated by Harriet de Onís. Durham, N.C., 1995.

Palmié, Stephan. *Wizards and Scientists: Explorations in Afro-Cuban Modernity and Tradition.* Durham, N.C., 2002.

Pollard, Velma. *Dread Talk: The Language of Rastafari.* Kingston, West Indies, 1994.

Pratt, Mary Louise. *Imperial Eyes: Travel Writing and Transculturation.* London, 1992.

Thompson, Robert Farris. *Flash of the Spirit: African and Afro-American Art and Philosophy.* New York, 1983.

Voeks, Robert A. *Sacred Leaves of Candomblé: African Magic, Medicine, and Religion in Brazil.* Austin, Tex., 1997.

Wafer, Jim. *The Taste of Blood: Spirit Possession in Brazilian Candomblé.* Philadelphia, 1991.

PAUL CHRISTOPHER JOHNSON (2005)

TRANSCULTURATION AND RELIGION: RELIGION IN THE FORMATION OF MODERN JAPAN

Japan began forming a modern culture when it came into contact with the West. Then the Portuguese brought matchlocks to Japan, and Francis Xavier brought Christianity. In the nineteenth century, Japan underwent crucial development as a result of exchanges with the West, and this development has continued to the present with ongoing cultural contacts.

This was not the first time that Japan borrowed from other cultures. Yet Japanese borrowing in the modern period was much different from Japanese contacts with Chinese and Korean civilizations between the fifth and thirteenth centuries. In the case of these earlier contacts, because seafaring voyages were full of danger, the oceans surrounding the Japanese archipelago provided a buffer zone. Moreover, the cultures and civilizations of China and Korea, imbued with Confucian, Taoist, and Buddhist philosophies, were not as aggressive as modern Western powers, armed with steam ships, modern military forces, modern capitalism, and imperialist tendencies. As a result, Japanese assimilation of Chinese and Korean civilization was more gradual, gentler, and more deeply penetrating.

GUNS AND CHRISTIANITY. As mentioned, Japan's contact with the West began around the time when Portuguese merchants drifted ashore a southern island of the Japanese archipelago in 1543. The matchlocks they brought with them were mastered quickly, reproduced in large quantities by native craftsmen, and spread quickly and widely throughout the country. These guns not only changed military tactics but also transformed the structure of castles and other fortifications. Eventually, Oda Nobunaga (1534–1582), Toyotomi Hideyoshi (1538–1598), and Tokugawa Ieyasu (1542–1616), successive unifiers of the country, used such guns quite successfully in battles to unify the country.

The Catholic Church began missionary activities in Japan when Francis Xavier and other Jesuit priests arrived in 1549 on Kagoshima to evangelize in western Japan. In the beginning, Christianity was well received by warlords and later the Tokugawa shogunate. Portuguese merchants began international trade with Japan, followed by the Spanish in 1580, the Dutch in 1609, and the British in 1613. Japanese mercantile ships, which had trading abroad since the middle of fourteenth century, continued trade with China, Korea, Formosa, the Philippines, Java, Vietnam, Malaysia, and Thailand. Japanese leaders were interested in new information about Europe and the outside world, and in new scientific and technical knowledge, including knowledge about imported European firearms. Since Catholic missionary activities and the merchant trade were intimately connected, many warlords interested in the profits of trade readily converted to Christianity.

In 1587 Hideyoshi banished the missionaries and prohibited the Christian faith among the warlords. But only a few missionaries left Japan, and those who remained successfully propagated Christianity among the masses, gaining as many as 700,000 devotees by the early seventeenth century, more than two times the population of the capital city of Kyoto at that time. Later the Tokugawa shogunate, perceiving the colonialist interests of foreign powers and fearing uprisings among the masses, started to ban the Christian faith by issuing successive ordinances in 1614, 1616, and 1623. During this time the government destroyed churches, deported missionaries, and tortured and executed defiant Christians. All the Christian warlords but a few famous converts renounced their faith.

Some Christians went underground and maintained their faith for generations until the reopening of the country in the nineteenth century. Underground Christianity, separated from the Catholic orders, became indigenized and syncretized with folk Buddhism for outward appearances. The virgin Mary was amalgamated with Kannon (Avalokiteś-vara), Buddhist goddess of mercy, and called "Maria Kannon."

After the Shimabara uprising of Christians, in which forty thousand people fought on the Christian side, the Tokugawa government, in 1639, took the extreme measure of closing Japan to all foreign trade. The only exception was trade with the Dutch, who did not engage in any missionary activity, at the port of Nagasaki, from then on the only port officially open for international trade and exchanges. The Tokugawa feudal regime thus started the policy of seclusion, which was to last for 260 years.

PROSPERITY AMIDST SECLUSION. Several external factors made possible the long, peaceful seclusion of Japan. Vast oceans lay between Europe and Japan. At the time the center of political and economic power in Europe was shifting from Spain and Portugal to England and Holland, and this affected the ability of these counties to develop colonial empires. Also, the industrial revolution had not yet taken hold in Europe. Later, in the eighteenth and nineteenth centuries, when steam ships and the accelerating industrial revolution enabled Western countries to project power all over the world, Japan was revisited, this time by the fleets of various Western nations to force open its doors. The vast oceans were no longer a barrier to Western civilization. The oceanic space was becoming domesticated more and more by the power of capitalism, colonialism and imperialism as well as the science and technology of the West.

Domestically, the Tokugawa regime carried out an apt set of policies to order society and stabilize the country. It established a rigid social hierarchy consisting of four main social classes—warriors, farmers, artisans, and merchants—and prohibited upward mobility. In another important policy it confiscated weapons, allowing only hunters to use firearms and only warriors to use swords. And it rigidly regulated Buddhist temples and Shintō shrines. On Buddhist temples it imposed the temple parish system (*jidan seido*). This policy required individuals to be certified by their local Buddhist temples not to be a member of the "evil religion" Christianity.

Neo-Confucian philosophy provided the Tokugawa regime with a powerful political ideology, with distinctions of rank and status, for ruling feudal society. As a result, Confucian studies prospered under the patronage of the shogunate and many daimyo. The regime used neo-Confucian philosophy to regulate all Buddhist temples and Shintō shrines and suppress underground Christians. The Bureau of Buddhist Temples and Shintō Shrines organized Buddhist temples, in sectarian divisions, into a hierarchy of a central temple on top and more local temples further down. Temples thus functioned as a bureaucracy to control the spiritual life of the people. The government also banned new doctrines and interpretations in Buddhist and Shintō communities. Though the Tokugawa government recognized Buddhist sects as official religions, Buddhist priests thus lost their religious freedom and spontaneity. Young novices trained as priests at head temples, upon completing their training, went back to local temples to teach children Confucian ethics and the *Analects*. The official schools of the clans (*hankō*) and the many private temple schools (*terakoya*) greatly contributed to the prevalence of literacy among the populace in Tokugawa period (1603–1867). With its power to proscribe sects, the regime controlled the scope of activities of the temples.

The Tokugawa government, by establishing the peace and making life secure, encouraged the growth of industry and commerce, as well as the development of a transportation system centered around the waterways of sea, rivers, and canals. Within the feudal social-class system there developed a mercantile economy with currency and credit, and this encouraged the production of various agricultural and industrial commodities within the country. People were already consuming such commercial products as cotton, sugar, silk, and tea, all of which had a foreign origin. These commodities became important trade goods when Japan resumed trading with Western nations: Japanese imported cotton products and sugar and exported silk and tea.

JAPANESE THOUGHT. The neo-Confucian school not only synthesized the concept of *li* (reason, principle) with the Great Ultimate, material forces *(qi)*, human nature, and the mind; in Japan it also later equated *li* with the Way of the Gods (the literal meaning of "Shintō"). Joseph Kitagawa points out that since warrior-administrators translated philosophical ideas into practical measures for governing the country, the Tokugawa regime tended to be free from Chinese models. Since neo-Confucianism provided the ideological foundation of the regime, this school produced many famous scholars.

Equally important was the Wang Yangming school, which interpreted *li* as identical with the mind and viewed each individual mind as the manifestation of the Universal Mind. Though the regime did not support the Wang Yangming school, the idea of moral cultivation based on the Universal Mind appealed to many Japanese and gave rise to many important social reformers. Mind Learning (Shingaku), a popular version of Confucianism with Shintō and Buddhist elements, taught commoners the importance of disciplining the mind with simple, easy-to-understand language.

Besides these three schools of Confucianism, a variety of other schools of learning thrived during the Tokugawa period. Ancient Learning (Kogaku) advocated directly studying the texts of Confucius and Mencius. This gesture of returning to origins by reading the classical texts was a radical criticism of the neo-Confucian and Wang Yangming schools as later departures from the original Way.

National Learning (Kokugaku) was born as the antithesis of Chinese Learning, specifically the school of Ancient Learning, which advocated returning to classical Chinese texts. The school of National Learning created a tradition of textual criticism for the interpretation of Japanese classical texts that did away with all Chinese influences on the interpretation of Japanese texts. The most outstanding scholar of National Learning was Motoori Norinaga (1730–1801), who studied the *Kojiki* (Records of ancient matters), which is written in *manyōgana* (Chinese characters used phonetically). As is often pointed out, he tried to return to the world of meaning revealed by the ancient text itself, to grasp the meaning of the text by directly participating in it without any intervening Chinese influences and by living it as the Way of the Gods. Motoori deciphered and interpreted the *Kojiki* as sacred. Motoori's scholarship came to be accepted by Shintō theologians as the foundation of Shintō theology and, together with the scholarship of Hirata Atsutane, one of Motoori's posthumous disciples, laid the foundation for later nationalist Shintō movements during the Meiji period (1868–1912).

Dutch Learning (Rangaku) was primarily the learning of Dutch medicine. Dutch Learning produced such positivistic spirits as Yamawaki Tōyō, who studied the internal organs of the dissected body, and Maeno Ryōtaku and Sugita Genpaku, who not only examined the anatomized body but also translated a Dutch book on anatomy as *Kaitai shinsho* (New anatomy).

A positivist attitude can also be observed in the social reformer Andō Shōeki (d. 1762), who criticized traditional Confucian and Buddhist thinking as artificial and asserted the importance of learning directly from nature. For Andō, everyone must return to the Way of Nature (or the Life of Nature) by partaking in production, that is, agriculture. Nature is not an object of observation or contemplation, but what life partakes in. "By human participation, the True Way of Life reveals itself as the Truly Wondrous Way of Life." "Farmers cultivate land, weave cloths, eat simple food, wear simple cloths, selflessly and self-containedly. They are the direct children of Nature" (*Shizen Shin-ei-do,* vol. 4, pp. 57-69). Andō repudiated the feudalistic social hierarchy of Tokugawa society as artificial and to be avoided.

These schools of learning sought to return to the old, that is, to go back to origins in classical texts or back to original paradigms, and realize them here and now, or they sought to prove texts in a positivist spirit. These traditions later became the basis for responses to Western civilization, whether the response be to introduce a new approach, to appropriate critically, or to oppose.

The Tokugawa period also witnessed the development of popular arts, such as painting, woodblock prints, poetry, Kabuki theater, and puppet theater (Ningyō Jōruri). Each of these genres responded to the imaginary needs of the people in highly creative ways. These arts were sustained by wealthy merchants living in urban centers and later spread to local villages.

THE RISE OF RELIGIOUS MOVEMENTS. The Tokugawa regime rigidly controlled and manipulated the Buddhist sects and Shintō shrines as official religions. Institutional forms of religion, when they emerged, were suppressed and went underground during the Tokugawa period. Having lost freedom and mobility within the feudal parish system, Buddhism and Shintō, as institutions, lost their religiosity and degenerated into funeral services and administrators of ancestor veneration, respectively.

But various important folk religious movements emerged spontaneously from the lower strata of society. One such movement was large scale pilgrimages, which often undercut feudal space boundaries. There were mass pilgrimages to the Grand Shrine of Ise, repeated every sixty years, which developed into the Anything-Goes Dance (Eejanaika Odori), in which the masses, dancing and singing, went toward Ise. Other pilgrimages were the Pilgrimage to the Eighty-Eight Sacred Places of Shikoku (Shikoku Henro) and the Pilgrimage to the Thirty-Three Sacred Places of Kannon in Western Japan (Saigoku Junrei). All of these pilgrimages expressed a yearning for a worldly paradise apart from the realities of the contemporary world.

Three religions—Kurozumikyō, Tenrikyō, and Konkōkyō—emerged from the villages toward the end of the Tokugawa period. These popular religions became the prototypes of new religions in modern Japan. Each of these religions was based upon the religious experience of its founder and sustained people with simple but universal teachings.

Responses to Foreign Civilizations. In Japanese contacts with the Chinese and Korean civilizations in the fifth to ninth centuries, Kitagawa finds a threefold response: a welcome introduction, integration and assimilation, and rejection or transformation. This threefold process greatly enriched indigenous culture and tradition through the assimilation and integration of Buddhism, Confucianism, and Daoism. These contacts even stimulated the native religious tradition to develop Shintō and gave birth to many new religions, including indigenous forms of Buddhism. By this contact, Japanese culture and society was greatly enriched.

Prior to direct contact with modern Western powers, various aspects of Tokugawa feudal society were becoming modern. But the need to modernize took on a whole new meaning and urgency after Japanese contact with the West. When Portuguese traders and Jesuit Catholicism arrived in Japan, in the initial phases they were welcome. Later on in the historical process, however, Western culture could not be assimilated or integrated well because the Catholic Church demanded wholehearted allegiance and the Western powers had aggressive colonial interests. Thus, in a natural response, the Tokugawa regime rejected Western culture and Christianity except for Dutch trade, although many fragmental influences from Western culture remained.

The second cycle of contact with Western civilizations began in the late eighteenth century. Since 1792 Russians repeatedly sent diplomatic missions and battleships to Japan asking for the opening of trade. In 1808 England sent a battleship to Nagasaki to take over the Dutch trading base there. And when a team of administrators representing various clans visited Shanghai at the time of the Opium War (1840–1842) to investigate, they observed China succumbing to British military power and discovered that most of the East Asian coastal regions except Manchuria, Korea, and Japan had been colonized. Fearing Western colonialism, they felt the need to build up power to protect Japan. Many Dutch schools of medicine and schools of the feudal clans were soon transformed into naval strategy research institutes and naval academies. Then, in 1853, the four "black ships" led by Commodore Matthew Perry, with their powerful cannons, appeared off the shore of Japan and asked for the opening of Japanese ports.

The regime was forced to make treaties with the United States, Holland, England, France, and Russia on unequal terms, granting extraterritorial rights and giving up the right to levy tariffs. To avoid colonization and attain equilibrium with the Western powers, leaders felt the need to plan for enriching the nation and building up defenses. The whole country was divided into two factions: one for the shogunate and the other for the emperor, one for opening the country to foreigners and the other for excluding foreigners. The peaceful country, suddenly surrounded by the powerful military powers of the West, was thrown into an unprecedented crisis. Thus began a new cycle of contact with the West. It was the beginning of the perpetual fast changes in life and society that have continued into the twenty-first century.

Out of the crisis, people searched for a new unity and new order for the nation and ultimately chose to reinvigorate the country by reverting to the ancient ideal of an emperor-centered religious, political, and national polity. The design of the Meiji imperial regime was to construct a modern nation-state by negating the recent past (the feudal Tokugawa tradition) and restoring the monarchical rule of the eighth century, centered on the traditional Japanese notion of a sacred emperor at the top of all hierarchies. This was another phase of traditional Japanese "immanent theocracy," to use Kitagawa's term. Meiji leaders followed the ancient model of unity of religion and state *(saisei itchi)*. In this new regime, the former social hierarchy of warrior, farmer, artisan, and merchant was eliminated, and all the people were now treated equally as the subjects of the semidivine emperor.

Westernization. The modernization of Japan was not imposed on the Japanese people from the outside by colonialism. Rather, it was what the Japanese were determined to accomplish to overcome the disequilibrium of Western and Japanese power. A basic strategy of the regime was to use the Japanese spirit and Western knowledge *(wakon-yōsai)*. Learning the knowledge of the West was the secret to equalization and rectification of the power imbalance.

Recognizing that the Western powers would not revise the unequal treaties, Japanese leaders adopted various elements of European jurisprudence in the French, German, and English codes. This produced contradictions, since French codes were progressive and the German codes were conservative. Etō Shinpei (1834–1874), one of the chief designers of the modern state in the early stage of its formation, highly appreciated the French civil code, especially on the rights of the people, and incorporated aspects of the French code into the Meiji civil code. The Meiji code also had to embrace incoherences due to differences of culture and society.

Japan started modernizing not only in jurisprudence but also in many other areas of culture and society. Japan adopted many Western institutions, such as government offices, a solar calendar, police, an army, a navy, railways, gaslight, a postal system, electricity, compulsory education, banks, a parliament, and a constitution.

These measures for Westernizing Japan were accompanied by a policy of enlightenment and civilization (*bunmei kaika*), which promoted Western culture and civilization in all aspects of life and society, from modern Western sciences and rationalism to people's hairstyles and Western-style clothes. Japanese intellectuals translated many works of Western philosophers and scientists, starting with Darwin, Mill, Huxley, and Spencer and following with Voltaire, Rousseau, Descartes, Kant, Shopenhauer, Hegel, Spinoza, Locke, Hume, Nietzsche, W. James, Dewey, Bergson, Sartre, and Heidegger. They also translated many novelists and poets, such as Shakespeare, Goethe, Maupassant, Tolstoy, Ibsen, Dostoevskii, Hemmingway, Kafka, Zola, Heine, and Baudelaire. Many of these works were accepted as new paradigms in their genres.

As for policies toward religion, the Meiji government, like the Tokugawa regime, required religious registration. However, in place of Buddhist temples, the Meiji government required every Japanese subject to register at the local Shintō shrine. The architects of the Meiji government took the Western model of Christianity as the unifying force of the nation-state and modified it so that the Shintō pantheon of spirits *(kami)* served as the religious foundation of Japan, and they attempted to make Shintō the state religion in Japan. After encountering criticism and resistance from various sectors, other religious groups in Japan, and international societies, the government relaxed this religious policy.

During the formation of modern Japan, Japanese intellectuals absorbed Western ideals, rationalism, technology, and economic systems. Many young students and bureaucrats were dispatched to Western countries to study Western laws, institutions, sciences, and technologies. The Japanese government invited and employed many foreign advisors, professors, technocrats, and specialists to establish and develop a modern nation-state with industrial capacity and military strength.

Cultural Values and Criticism. To say the least, Western notions of science, which were based on the diversification of knowledge into various branches, had a strong impact on the minds of Japanese scholars, who had been accustomed to a holistic approach to learning. Within the Western sciences, for instance, religion was separated from all other branches of knowledge, such as politics, economy, culture, society, philosophy, mathematics, and physics. In the holistic orientation of the Japanese tradition, in contrast, Chinese Learning, National Learning, and Dutch Learning did not have clear divisions of knowledge. Therefore, for Japanese, being educated in the new tradition of Western sciences often meant exposure to an entirely new cultural and epistemological orientation based on a different set of values. This orientation required Japanese to evaluate Japanese and Western values against each other before accepting Western orientations and integrating them into Japanese culture. Japanese culture had to adjust itself to these new concepts and ideas. How to adapt Japanese culture was always open to criticism.

One such critic was Okakura Tenshin (1862–1913), an art critic and leader in modern Japanese art circles. Before the Russo-Japanese War, Okakura criticized Western colonialism and imperialism, saying that Asia is one. In the year after the war (1906), he also criticized "moderns" who judged the Japanese victory in bloody battles over Russia as "civilized" and who regarded such peaceful pastimes as the tea ceremony and other aesthetic activities as "barbarian." Okakura's critiques were published in English in London; the former was written in India, and the latter in Boston. He knew the problems of the East and the West, of Japanese culture and Western culture, because he lived in and knew both worlds.

Another critic was Minakata Kumakusu (1867–1941), a folklorist and natural historian. Minakata protested against the government's policy of consolidating Shintō shrines throughout the country to clear virgin forests belonging to the shrines. The government undertook this measure to create land for increased farm production and further industrialization. This measure, begun in 1906, met vehement criticism from Minakata, who had returned to Japan after a long sojourn of research in the United States and England. The policy was abandoned in 1915.

Though individuals raised severe criticisms of the direction of modernization at critical junctures in modern Japanese history, Japanese commoners often meekly accepted policies for Westernizing the nation. The Japanese tended to embrace recklessly the ideals of modern Western civilizations—rationalism, industrialization, capitalism, progress, and development—even when such ideals were incompatible with traditional Japanese values.

The Impact of Modernization on Religion. During the past 150 years, Japanese society has undergone many radical cultural and social changes involving all aspects of life. Included here are such great transformations as the overthrow of the feudal Tokugawa regime; the establishment of the modern Meiji imperial state; the rapid introduction of policies to modernize in the fields of government, law, education, technology, and culture; the development of capitalism; colonialist and militaristic involvement in Asia; the Sino-Japanese War (1894–1895); the Russo-Japanese War (1904–1905); the further development of industry and capitalism; greater economic and military involvement in Asia; the Second World War (which ended in Japan's defeat); the U.S. occupation; postwar modernization and democratization; and phenomenal economic growth. These rapid changes in society brought forth serious existential crises, including the disintegration of traditional communities and values, along with new types of human alienation and identity crises.

Modern Western concepts and views of religion were introduced in the early Meiji period into Japanese universities, which in themselves were modeled after Western universities. The Japanese word *shūkyō* was coined to translate the Western notion of religion, and when the word was applied to Japanese religionlike institutions, it often created problems. Buddhists, for instance, were uncomfortable with the theistic connotations of the word. Followers of other Japanese religions found their own problems. Because of its amorphous conception of the sacred, the Japanese indigenous religion Shintō does not fit well into the category of religion. Moreover, many studies of Japanese religion completely ignore the whole folk-religious tradition, a strong undercurrent of Japanese religious culture, because none of these folk religions had coherent, systematically articulated doctrines comparable to the Western ideal, Protestant Christianity.

Japanese religions responded to the changed intellectual climate. Shintō was now a state religion and took on all the trappings of state ideology. The elite Buddhist sects busily readjusted themselves to Western influences and the new political and social situations surrounding them. The True Pure-Land Sect was foremost in these attempts. It sent young students to study at Oxford University (where Max Müller was) and at other European institutions even before the Meiji Restoration in 1868. This sect drafted a constitution and experimented with a parliament even before the governmental did. It appropriated ideas of Western philosophy to develop its doctrines. The Zen Sect also actively developed its scholarship. In the process, elite Buddhist sects rediscovered the importance of the doctrines of their founders in the Kamakura period (1185–1333). Yet these sects were still bound to the powerful remnants of their hereditary parishes, inherited from the Tokugawa period. Thus these established religions, Shintō and Buddhism, developed doctrinally but remained aloof from the religious needs of the people. Christian sects, which were treated as an "evil religion" during the Tokugawa period, became tolerated and resumed their activities, but never became as potent a force as before.

New Religions. Western civilization thrust itself upon Japan in an age of imperialism. To survive, Japan absorbed Western ideals, rationality, technology, and economic systems. Thus did the Japanese elite seek to emulate and overcome the West. And yet they also sought to distinguish Japan from the West. This is important to note, because Japan, despite all the evidence to the contrary, is still presented as a homogeneous culture with little or no individuality. This notion of a homogeneous culture owes much to sudden contact with the West and to the Meiji effort to create a modern state to rival Western powers by forming a new political center consisting of a people united under an emperor.

The political myths created by the Japanese elite notwithstanding, Japanese commoners displayed their individuality in new religions. While the established religions and their leaders were busily trying to adjust to ongoing changes and remained aloof from the religious needs of the common people, new religious movements emerged spontaneously from the lower strata of society. The established religions tended to accept government policies, but there were signs of resistance among many of the new religions. But as soon as these new religions were more or less established within society, other new religions would emerge from lower strata of society or from the fringes of established new religions. The emergence of new religions has followed this general historical pattern up until the explosion of new religions in the 1990s, including Aum Shinrikyō, which in 1995 released Sarin gas in Tokyo subways during the morning rush hour.

Under the religious policy of the Meiji government, Shintō shrines were elevated to the status of the official state religion. After Buddhist, Christian, and liberal scholars resisted and criticized this move, the government eventually designated Shintō as a national cult rather than as a religion. By this move, all Shintō shrines were transformed from places of veneration to nonreligious places of national rituals. Buddhism lost its status as the state religion, which it had enjoyed during the Tokugawa period, but it remained an established religion supported by hereditary parishioners. During the Meiji period, three newly formed religions and some syncretic folk-religious associations were officially recognized as Shintō sects. Within the framework of Meiji imperial Shintō, all religious groups were officially recognized and tolerated.

By the policy of enlightenment, various age-old folk-religious practices, including yin-yang divination calendars, magico-religious practices, and symbolism, were suppressed as superstition, evil religion, and even licentious worship. All religions—Buddhism, Christianity, and the new religions—compromised with the ideology of a sacred emperor to survive in the framework of Meiji policy toward religion.

One of the most far-reaching influences of the enlightenment policy of the Meiji was that religion disappeared from the public domain. Religion became a private matter within a secular, modern state, although a sacred and inviolable emperor ruled over it. Politicians did not confess their faith, and schools and universities did not teach religion as a core subject.

Many students and scholars went abroad to study Western sciences and philosophy. After returning to Japan, many became leading intellectuals, civil servants, and political leaders. As Uchimura Kanzō states, the Japanese accepted Christian civilization but not Christianity itself (*Questions and Answers on Christianity*). Soon intellectuals found themselves in an intellectual climate in which they could not be persuasive unless they could skillfully manipulate modern Western scientific concepts. Even Buddhist scholars (figures such as Kiyosawa Manshi, Kimura Taiken, and Nishida Kitarō) had to use Western philosophical and scientific concepts to articulate their doctrines and ideas. For this reason, various sciences, including folklore and the study of religion, have had to follow modern Western models devoutly until into the twenty-first century. Despite this tendency, some thinkers also developed profound and articulate critiques of the West, as can be seen in the work of Okakura Tenshin, D. T. Suzuki, Nishida Kitarō, Nishitani Keiji, and Yanagita Kunio. Except for Nishida, all of these men were directly exposed to modern Western civilization, and all were aware of the need to straddle the two worlds.

The intellectual climate for novelists was similar to that for philosophers. Both Natsume Sōseki (1867–1916) and Mori Ōgai (1862–1922) were well versed not only in Chinese and Japanese literature, but also in Western languages and literatures. Sōseki expressed concern about the impossible task of synthesizing the enlightenment spirit of the externally imposed (the Western) and the spontaneous spirit of the indigenous. For him, "An enlightenment that was triggered from the outside was unknown until recent times. We must catch up with the West. But by incorporating the external, we become anxious and fret over it." Mori wrote, "The new Japan is in the midst of a whirlpool in which Eastern culture and Western culture are coming together. There are some scholars who stand in the Eastern, and others who stand in the Western; both stand on a single leg. This age calls for scholars who stand firmly on two legs."

The Taishō Intellectual Climate. The internal conflicts and agonies observed in novelists and philosophers of the Meiji period became weaker among intellectuals in the post-Meiji period, that is, after the Russo-Japanese War. In that war Japan struggled to defend itself against Russia's powerful military expansion with colonial intent. Japanese victory meant that it succeeded at building a strong nation by Westernizing, and that Japan was now a player in the power game among the world powers over East Asia. Although Japan had succeeded in its struggle for treaties ending extraterritoriality and allowing it to impose tariffs, it now had to contest with the world powers in a struggle for survival. After the Russian revolution in 1917, the First World War ended.

Intellectually, instead of agonies over how to maintain Japanese identity in the face of the Western onslaught, Japanese now faced the influences of Marxism, nihilism, and vitalist philosophy. This new intellectual climate, stemming from the thought of Karl Marx, Friedrich Nietzsche, and Henri Bergson, reflected contemporary Western social and political crises. Also swirling about in the atmosphere of the Taishō period (1912–1926) were liberalism and democratic thought, which helped give rise to movements for people's rights and socialism.

Soon, social, political, and economic crises visited Japan, and the newspapers frequently carried news about socialist movements. The novels of Akutagawa Ryūnosuke, who committed suicide by taking poison, represented a contemporary Japanese world reflecting the apocalyptic vision of the Western world. Nishitani Keiji, a leading philosopher of religion in twentieth-century Japan, stated that when Japanese intellectuals became aware of the crises of the West from Western philosophers and novelists, they attempted to go back to their own tradition, but when they tried to rediscover it, they also became aware that their own tradition had already partially broken down. To overcome this crisis, Nishitani thinks, "the Japanese have to overcome a double nihilism, for one aspect of the problem is a Western crisis, and the other aspect is a Japanese crisis."

The Postwar Period. Japan's defeat in the Second World War and the atomic bombing of Hiroshima and Nagasaki terminated Japan's colonialist and imperialist ambitions. During its occupation of Japan, the United States imposed on Japan a new constitution instituting democratic reforms, disarming the nation, separating church and state, radically revising the civil codes, giving the emperor the status of symbol of the nation.

Thus began another phase of the radical transformation of Japan due to contact with the West. Japan started to rebuild its country as a modern democratic, secular state by further Westernizing and rationalizing its institutions, but since the new structure of the state was imposed by an external force, many problems arose. In postwar Japan, many new religions again spontaneously emerged. Almost all of these new religions emphasized the veneration of ancestors by focusing on the form of the family altar, the proper way to hold services, the meaning of ancestor spirits, and so on. The United States sponsored a reform of the civil code along liberal Western lines that ensured the rights of every individual in the family at the risk of the continuity of the family. In reaction to this drastic change in the structure of the family, these new religions attempted to ensure the continuity of the family and family ties.

Mishima Yukio. An outstanding postwar critique of Japan's Westernization is found in the life and work of the novelist Mishima Yukio (1925–1970). Mishima wrote many creative novels in the literary style of twentieth-century Western literature. He also wrote many important essays before he committed suicide in the traditional samurai style of slitting his bowels. He wrote, "A characteristic of contemporary culture is probably that many different illusions—including ideals, norms, and ideologies—that had inspired people toward life have broken down. The idea of the absolute was lost, and people are forced to face naked life as materialistic and naturalistic, deprived of all designs. This is the cause of the irredeemable nihilism of today." When any community is eroded by other culture, its rules and customs break down, and the community gradually falls apart morally and spiritually. In such circumstances, life destroys itself, whatever efforts may be tried to fulfill life.

Mishima was desperately warning against the tendency of life to destroy itself in Japan's headlong effort to Westernize and modernize. When he criticized the Japanese emperor for proclaiming that he was a human being, not a living *kami*, he also pointed out the contradiction of modern constitutional emperorship. For Mishima, it is impossible to

Westernize the sacred; the sacred cannot be embodied within the framework of a Western secular nation-state.

See Also Buddhism, article on Buddhism in Japan; Buddhism, Schools of, article on Japanese Buddhism; Domestic Observances, article on Japanese Practices; Fiction, article on Japanese Fiction and Religion; Folk Religion, article on Folk Buddhism; Japanese Religions, article on Popular Religion and article on The Study of Myths; New Religious Movements, article on New Religious Movements in Japan; Politics and Religion, article on Politics and Japanese Religions; Shintō.

Bibliography

Ando Shoeki. *Ando Shoeki Zenshu.* 21 vols. Tokyo, 1983.

Anesaki Masaharu. *Nihon shukyo shi.* Tokyo, 1998.

Kawakatsu Heita. *Nihon Bunmei to Kindaiseiyo.* (Japanese civilization and the modern West). Tokyo, 1991.

Kitagawa, Joseph M. *Religion in Japanese History.* New York, 1966.

Kitagawa, Joseph M. *On Understanding Japanese Religion.* Princeton, 1987.

Murakami Shigeyoshi. *Japanese Religion in the Modern Century.* New York, 1980.

Natsume Soseki, "Gendai Nihon no Kaika" (Enlightenment of today's Japan). In *Natsume Soseki Bumnmei-ronshu.* Tokyo, 1986.

Thomas, Nicholas. *Entangled Objects: Exchange, Material Culture, and Colonialism in the Pacific.* Bambridge, 1991.

Uchimura Kanzo. *Kirisuto-kyo Mondo* (Questions and answers on Christianity). Tokyo, 1981.

Michio Araki (2005)

TRANSCULTURATION AND RELIGION: RELIGION IN THE FORMATION OF MODERN INDIA

To put into historical perspective the multifaceted pattern of Hindu socioreligious modernism, scholars have chronicled the origins of British Orientalism and the Bengal Renaissance. Similar to the European Renaissance, which occurred prior to the Reformation, nineteenth-century India also underwent a period of cultural renaissance followed by an era of religious reformation.

British Orientalism and the Bengal Renaissance. The Bengal Renaissance occurred in eastern Gangetic India—specifically, in the colonial metropolis of Calcutta—from the year 1773, when Warren Hastings designated the city as the future capital of British India, until 1828, when Governor-General Lord Bentinck challenged Orientalist cultural policy. During this period, Calcutta operated schools using European textbooks and teaching methods. In addition, the newly created Hindu middle class had founded Hindu College, the only Western-style institution of higher learning in South Asia. The government supported newspapers, journals, and books printed in English and the vernacular languages of India. Calcutta boasted a modern public library. Perhaps most significantly, the metropolis contained native intelligentsia, whose members were familiar with happenings in contemporary Europe, fully cognizant of their country's own historical legacy, and, as a renaissance elite, hopeful about its future as a culture in the modern world.

The agents of Western colonial rule who sympathetically supported these endeavors were "acculturated" civil, military, and judicial officials of the British East India Company (as well as some missionaries) referred to as Orientalists, largely because of the cultural policy that was followed by the government. Most of these so-called Orientalists did not harbor nationalistic or imperialistic ambitions, nor did they support the increasingly bureaucratic mentality that developed after 1870. On the contrary, the Orientalists had been shaped by the eighteenth-century world of the Enlightenment, with its open-minded curiosity about other civilizations. Orientalists were encouraged by official policy to master at least one Indian language and to use that language fruitfully for scholarly research. It was no accident that the Asiatic Society of Bengal, established in Calcutta in 1784 as the first modern organization of its type to study Asian civilizations in all their aspects, was a direct result of a British East India Company cultural policy. Orientalists such as William Jones, William Carey, James Prinsep, H. T. Colebrooke, and H. H. Wilson made important discoveries in such fields as pre-Muslim Indian history, religion, and archaeology. Research into the kinship of Indo-European languages and the rediscoveries of the historic Buddha, Aśoka, and the Mauryan Empire were some of the lasting achievements of this coterie of devoted civil servants. There is no evidence that they ensconced themselves in clubs, as did the later bureaucrats, nor did they construct a barrier of racial privilege between themselves and their "subject races." Instead, the Orientalists reached out to the Bengali intelligentsia, forming relationships with them, serving as sources of knowledge about contemporary Britain and, above all, working together on projects designed to promote social and cultural change in Calcutta.

The Bengal Renaissance arose from interaction between the Bengali intelligentsia and the British Orientalists. Between 1800 and 1830, in Calcutta, the Bengali intelligentsia consisted of uncertain but hopeful people who were adopting alien values and ideas to reform indigenous traditions. They established relationships with the British, both for material gain and to use them as windows to the West. Fortunately for them, the distance between London and Calcutta was vast, and the Orientalists with whom they associated had already become sufficiently "Indianized." The Bengali's favorable view of the West during this sympathetic Orientalist period helped to maintain good rapport and goodwill between the representatives of the two civilizations.

Rammohun Roy, Father of Modern India. Of all the Bengalis in the Orientalist period, none was more influential in creating a legacy of Hindu socioreligious reform than Rammohun Roy (1772–1833). Long before Vivekananda laid the foundation of his Ramakrishna Mission, before Nehru wrote his monumental *Discovery of India* in a British prison, and before Gandhi built his nationalist ideology on the bedrock of Hindu and Buddhist morality, Rammohun had already utilized the Orientalist rediscovery of the ancient tradition, which the progressive intelligentsia readily accepted in their quest for a new identity in the modern world.

Rammohun had studied Asian religions from primary sources and met countless Europeans in Calcutta who imparted to him their thoughts on Western civilization in the nineteenth century. Missionaries at the Danish enclave of Serampore had tried unsuccessfully to convert Rammohun to their Baptist form of Protestant Christianity. Some other members of the intelligentsia who were xenophiles did become Christians, deciding that their salvation lay in copying the West or in accepting that modernization equated to Westernization. But Rammohun, supported by the scholarly evidence of Orientalist research into Hindu antiquity, contrasted the age he lived in—with its *kulin* polygamy, sati practices, caste rigidity, idolatry, and the abuse of women—to the classical age, which was free of dark-age excrescences. For Rammohun, he and his fellow Indians did not need to surrender themselves to an alien way of life in order to accept modernistic values. Ancient Hindus were mathematical and scientific sophisticates; Brahma of the Upaniṣads was as superior a notion of the godhead as anything produced in the Middle East; ancient India overflowed with philosophic diversity; and ancient art, literature, and medicine flourished among Indians in classical times. Moreover, evidence existed that women were considered equal to men.

From 1815, when Rammohun settled in Calcutta, until 1833, when he traveled to England to meet with Unitarians (he died there later that same year), he labored intensely, keeping up with Orientalist scholarship, translating ancient scriptures, organizing meetings of the Calcutta Unitarian Society and Brāhmo Sabhā (society of God), and becoming involved in journalistic ventures and debates. As he sought to recreate the Vedantic tradition, he was often attacked by missionaries and other Christians, who ridiculed his efforts. In 1823, for example, he defended the Vedānta as containing a rational exposition on the unity of God without the superstitious verbiage that he claimed was so common in many Christian sources. Unlike the Bible, Rammohun argued, the Vedanta did not attempt to categorize the attributes of the Almighty, a gesture he found anthropomorphic and futile. He also contended that, whereas Christianity required a blood sacrifice to expatiate the sins of humanity, the Vedānta taught that the only means necessary to overcome sin is sincere repentance and solemn meditation. He asked whether popular Christianity was any better than popular Hinduism. How could the crucifixes, the saints, miracles, trinity, and holy water be justified?

Ultimately, Rammohun chose to reform Hinduism against the backdrop of a liberal faith emanating from former Christians in America and Britain who were highly dissatisfied with the same dubious beliefs and practices that troubled Rammohun and many of his cohorts in Calcutta. It is no coincidence that Rammohun established a Calcutta Unitarian Society in Calcutta in 1823, or that he died while visiting the home of the Reverend Lant Carpenter, a prominent Unitarian in Bristol, and that, had he lived, Rammohun would have traveled across the ocean to Boston and met with William Ellery Channing, the leading spokesman of liberal Unitarianism in the United States. Though Unitarianism was never a mass movement, like-minded sentiments regarding religion and society brought East and West together, with important consequences for socioreligious reform in India. Three simple but highly controversial ideas for the time (1815–1835) provided the link between the renaissance intelligentsia in Calcutta and the enlightened, liberal-minded elite in England and the United States.

First, a national faith would replace the predominant religions of the world, believed to be restricting the freedom of human beings by enslaving them to performing mechanical rites and rituals, listening to irresponsible anecdotes that served no moral purpose, and holding meaningless superstitions and otherworldly beliefs that served no useful purpose in improving the lot of the human race. Second, social reform would emancipate the exploited classes such as workers, peasants, and women through education and the extension of civil rights, allowing all to benefit equally from modern civilization. Finally, universal theistic progress would occur; human perfectibility could not be confined to a particular race or ethnicity but could happen worldwide.

Mindful of these three objectives, Rammoh̩un Roy helped establish the Brāhmo Sabhā, precursor of the Brahmo Samaj, on January 23, 1830. He then left for Europe to meet with persons who shared his beliefs. Though he never returned to India, he did leave behind the outline of a program for Hindu reformation.

The Brāhmo Samāj and the Hindu Reformation. The work of developing the Brāhmo Samāj after Rammohun's death was taken up by Debendranath Tagore (1817–1903), son of Rammohun's close friend, Dwarkanath Tagore. Like Rammohun, Debendranath identified true Hinduism with the Vedantic tradition; he also fought Christian missionaries' attempts at converting members of the new educated Bengali elite. In this endeavor, Debendranath received assistance, often against his better judgment, from an American Unitarian missionary, Charles Dall, who came to Calcutta in 1855 hoping (but failing) to find Rammohun's philosophical convictions in Debendranath's leadership. Unlike his father and Rammohun, who both voluntarily traveled to England, Debendranath remained suspicious of Westerners most of his life. Dall had to wait until 1866, when a more radical Brahmo named Keshub Chandra Sen rebelled against Tagore's conservatism and founded his own Brāhmo Samāj. Dall considered Keshub to be Rammohun's true successor.

Debendranath's significant contribution to the Hindu Reformation was his intellectual preoccupation with formulating the principles of a new middle-class ethic for Brahmos and their counterparts throughout India. Debendranath had begun a process that was similar to Christian reformers of earlier centuries, transforming the religion to become more puritanical so as to serve the needs of the new European Protestant middle class. Brāhmo missionaries translated his book, published in 1855 as *Brahmo Dharma* (Brāhmo ethic), into the languages of other Indian peoples as they traveled throughout South Asia spreading the gospel of Hindu reform. Debendranath redefined *dharma,* which in ancient times had meant caste duty, as a modernized set of precepts for the true Hindu. Debendranath offered the emancipated Hindu guidance and edification in everything from family responsibilities to behavior in the workplace to being a devotee of the one true God.

Debendranath never claimed to be creating something new, however. He began by stressing the duties that each member of the household owed to one another. He emphasized the social good from which a family can profit if its members practice sincerity, devotion, purity, forgiveness, and gentleness. In the workplace, Debendranath advocated the good Hindu to rely on one's self, persevere always, and work hard continually. He believed that poverty could be overcome by laboring in the path of righteousness. He advised doing one's own work rather than being dependent on others, and against choosing to beg.

In 1866 one of Debendranath's followers, Keshub Chandra Sen (1839–1884), led the militant wing of the movement to form a separate Brāhmo organization, dedicated to what they believed to be Rammohun Roy's ideological path. Keshub accused Debendranath of doing nothing as a social reformer, especially with regard to female emancipation. Furthermore, the activists saw Debendranath as a hypocrite because he attacked caste privilege but continued to wear the sacred thread as a Brahman. They also criticized Debendranath's suspicion of foreigners, such as Charles Dall, whom Keshub and his militant supporters viewed as a spokesman for liberal religion throughout the Western world. Keshub also felt that the Brāhmo mission to reach out to like-minded Hindus in Maharashtra, Gujarat, the Punjab, Tamilnadu, and elsewhere needed a more radical approach to a wide variety of issues, many of which Debendranath avoided.

Keshub's greatest influence on the course of Hindu reformation, outside of promoting female education, was probably his remarkable eclecticism. In this sense, he was very much like Rammohun, who had studied all the world's major religions, including Islam. But Keshub went much further than his predecessor, both in his quest for knowledge of comparative religion and in his attempts to understand the patterns of change and continuity in the history of South Asian religions.

In 1880 Keshub started conducting his pilgrimages to the saints. These were elaborate devotional seminars designed to trace the history of human crises and the role of ethical and religious reformers as saviors seeking to arrest the chaos. One of the saints was Socrates, who offered a practical morality and an exemplary life, in contrast to the corruption of his age. Before staging the seminar on Buddha, Keshub went to Bodh Gaya and meditated under the bodhi tree. His seminar on Jesus taught Keshub that Christ equated the love of man with the will of God. And as for Muḥammad, Keshub learned that the way to achieve the brotherhood of man was through practicing a rigid monotheistic faith.

Keshub's eclecticism—especially when studying Indian reformers throughout history—gave him a very different perspective on Hindu classical and postclassical developments. Unlike Rammohun and most other Brahmos up to his time, Keshub did not identify with one classical tradition, such as the Vedantic. Rather, Keshub viewed the Hindu faith as a pluralistic phenomenon in which various traditions emerged in their authentically pristine forms at different times to meet a pressing spiritual need, but they became distorted later through internal institutional decay or by the effects of disruptive foreign influences.

One illustration was Keshub's positive influence on Swami Dayananda Saraswati (1824–1883), who proved to be the earliest modern reformer of the Vedic tradition. Most nineteenth-century Hindu reformers were ambivalent about the Vedic tradition because they associated it with caste rigidity, the subjection of women, idolatry, and worse. Dayananda repudiated these charges and spent his mature life denouncing what he called the evils of post-Vedic Hinduism. Because he argued that the true Vedas rejected idol worship, untouchability, child marriage, and the rest of the evils attributed to them, Dayananda's followers called him the "Luther of India."

Keshub also encouraged other Brahmos to research the roots of Indian sectarian faiths. Bijoy Krishna Goswami (b. 1841), a radical modernist, translated early Vaisnava songs which declared equal rights for men and women and the repudiation of caste privilege. Aghore Nath Gupta (d. 1881) conducted Keshub's seminar on the Buddha, in which he declared that the great reformer was not an atheist but a compassionate humanist who taught us how to live in a world that was false and full of illusion. Keshub also influenced Dharmapala, a neo-Buddhist from Sri Lanka, to start the Maha Bodhi Society.

Narendra Nath Dutt, better known as Vivekananda (1863–1902), joined Keshub's coterie in 1880. Scholars have difficulty assessing Vivekananda's contribution to the Hindu Reformation because, though he owed much to Keshub's teaching, and though his view of the Vedantic tradition came largely from Brahmo sources, he chose as the name of his own organization or mission that of a Kamakrishna, a contemporary mystic saint from Calcutta. Vivekananda was the earliest non-Brahmo to be accepted by religious liberals in the West. In fact, his talk at the Parliament of Religion in 1893, which was organized by American Unitarians, was considered to be among the best of the conference.

Vivekananda has erroneously been considered a Hindu nationalist because scholars believe he defended such things as caste and icons. However, a close study of his ideological development reveals that he neither defended the negative aspects of caste nor promotes the external worship of images. For Vivekananda, there was nothing wrong with hierarchical structures, since every society on earth had one. What was wrong—as happened in India—was the corruption of the system, which then would become oppressive. Rather than abolish caste, he wanted to democratize it. As Vivekananda would argue, if you teach the fisherman the Vedanta, he will say "I am as good a man as you are." As for images in the service of religion, Vivekananda refused to assume a rigidly iconoclastic position, such as those of Islam or Protestantism. He did not understand why worshipping a God without form was necessarily more spiritually uplifting than creating an image by which to convey the same message.

The Hindu Renaissance and Reformation Challenged. In the final decades of British Indian rule, the renaissance and reformation movements were very much challenged by forces in every direction. Orientalism, with its profound interest in all facets of civilization in India, had long since disappeared by the turn of the twentieth century. It had ceased to be the cultural policy of the British East India Company in 1835, when it was replaced by the liberal Anglicized cultural policy advocated by Thomas Babington Macaulay during the famous Anglicist-Orientalist controversy. Macaulay, who never learned an Indian language while he served in Calcutta, challenged the Orientalist belief that modernism among South Asians could be achieved by cultivating their languages and by identifying with a classical tradition. Macaulay argued that if Indians wanted a progressive future for themselves, they ought to anglicize their lives, becoming proficient in the English language and choosing Western careers and professional ethics. But the successful expansion of the British Empire after 1870 led to another shift in cultural policy. Both liberal-minded Orientalism and Anglicism gave way to cultural imperialism, or the excesses of ethnocentric self-glorification. This policy held that, except for military prowess, East was East and West was West, and never the two shall meet. The grandeur of the British Empire seemed to testify to the superiority of the British race, while the subjected state of India at that time appeared to confrm the inferiority of the Indian race.

On the Indian side, renaissance and reformation were challenged by a more radical generation of freedom fighters, who surrendered their moderate politics for an extremist form of nationalist agitation. When the British imperialists denied human equality between citizens of India and the West, a xenophobia swept over the English-educated Indian intelligentsia, which led to increased cultural apologetics about everything Indian, including popular religion. Bal Gangadhar Tilak (1856–1920), the Maharashtran ultranationalist, totally rejected what he called the Pax Britannica. He believed that the establishment of English schools and British administrative and legal institutions were an imperialist deception secretly designed to exploit the country. Though Tilak did not urge violent methods to win freedom, others did, and several British officials were assassinated as a result. Some scholars assert that had Mahatma Gandhi (1869–1948) not assumed the leadership of the Congress Party after World War I, with his message of nonviolence, the Indian nationalist struggle would have become a movement drenched in blood. Gandhi admired Vivekananda's approach to Hindu reform.

The Orientalist legacy of the Bengal Renaissance and the Brāhmo legacy of Hindu Reformation were kept vividly alive throughout the first half of the twentieth century by India's greatest writer, Rabindranath Tagore (1861–1941), who in 1914 became the first Asian to win the Nobel Prize in Literature. As the grandson of Dwarkanath Tagore, who had started the Calcutta Unitarian Committee and Brahmo Sabha with Rammohun Roy in the 1820s, and as the son of Debendranath Tagore, who revitalized the Brahmo Samaj in the 1840s following Rammohun's death, Rabindranath struggled for decades to protect renaissance and reformation against the inroads of imperialism and nationalism.

In a manuscript compiled during World War I entitled *Nationalism*, Rabindranath saw the conflict as a crucial stage in the breakdown of all that was hopeful and positive in the progress of civilization. To him, the war's genocide in the trenches represented the butchery of nations feeding upon other nations. The Russian ideologue Karl Marx is reputed to have said that religion was the opiate of the people; for Tagore, nationalism had become the opiate of the people.

His opposition to nationalism did not mean that Tagore supported British imperialism. On the contrary, he attacked it vigorously, perhaps with more candor and understanding than any other thinker before him. Tagore dramatically surrendered his knighthood following the Jallianwala Bagh massacre on May 30, 1919.

In July 1921, Rabindranath inaugurated Visva Bharati University in Santineketan, hoping the institution would embody the ideals of Brahmo universalism. Three years earlier, on December 22, 1918, he had declared that Visva Bharati would carry on the efforts of scholars such as Keshub Chandra Sen, who had sought to understand the religions of India and the world by studying primary sources.

See Also Brāhmo Samāj; Vedānta; Vivekananda.

Bibliography

Basham, A.L. *The Wonder That Was India.* New York, 1963.

Bose, Nirmal Kumar. *Studies in Gandhism.* Calcutta, 1962.

Cannon, Garland. *Oriental Jones.* London, 1964.

Cannon, Garland, and Kevin Brine, eds. *Objects of Enquiry: The Life, Contributions and Influences of Sir William Jones.* New York, 1995.

Erickson, Eric. *Gandhi's Truth.* New York, 1969.

Gordon, Leonard. *Bengal: The Nationalist Movement, 1876–1940.* New York, 1973.

Isherwood, Christopher. *Ramakrishna and His Disciples.* New York, 1965.

Joader, Safruddin, and David Kopf, eds. *Reflections on the Bengal Renaissance.* Rajshahi, Bangladesh, 1977.

Joshi, V. C., ed. *Rammohun Roy and the Process of Modernization in India.* New Delhi, India, 1975.

Kejariwal, O. P. *The Asiatic Society of Bengal and the Discovery of India's Past, 1784–1830.* Calcutta, 1988.

Kopf, David. *British Orientalism and the Bengal Renaissance: The Dynamics of Indian Modernization, 1773–1835.* Berkeley, Calif., 1969.

Kopf, David. *The Brahmo Samaj and the Shaping of the Modern Indian Mind.* Princeton, N.J., 1979.

Kopf, David. "The Bengali Prophet of Mass Genocide: Rabindranath Tagore and the Menace of Twentieth-Century Nationalism." In *Rabindranath Tagore: Perspectives in Time,* edited by Mary Lago and Ronald Warwick, pp. 50–66. London, 1989.

Kopf, David. "European Enlightenment, Hindu Renaissance and the Enrichment of the Human Spirit: A History of Historical Writings on British Orientalism." In *Orientalism, Evangelicalism and the Military Cantonment in Early Nineteenth-Century India,* edited by Nancy G. Cassels, pp. 19–53. New York, 1991.

Lago, Mary, and Ronald Warwick, eds. *Rabindranath Tagore: Perspectives in Time.* London,1989.

Nehru, Jawaharlal. *The Discovery of India.* London, 1956.

Thomas, Nicholas. *Entangled Objects: Exchange, Material Culture, and Colonialism in the Pacific.* Cambridge, Mass., 1991.

DAVID KOPF (2005)

TRANSCULTURATION AND RELIGION: RELIGION IN THE FORMATION OF MODERN OCEANIA

In 1601, after a Spanish historian published a map showing the islands of the Carolines and the Marianas, north New Guinea, and most of the Solomon Islands, Pacific Island peoples became part of the general history of humankind. Even before geographers accepted French *savant* Dumont d'Urville's 1832 classification of Polynesia, Melanesia, and Micronesia, the islands entered the European imagination. Polynesia, largely through voyagers' experiences at Tahiti, evoked a new kind of paradise, one including sexual freedom as well as escape from social restrictions in the Old World; to a large extent, the region remains a "legend that sells" for pleasure-seeking holiday-makers. Melanesia, in contrast, has always presented ambiguity—home of untold treasures accompanied by frightful, perhaps monstrous dangers. For example, the world's largest gold and copper mine at Freeport, on the south coast of Irian Jaya, coexists with tourists' common anxiety about law-and-order issues, especially in nearby Papua New Guinea and the Solomons. Significantly, the European explorers who discovered Micronesian and Polynesian (sometimes referred to as "Austronesian") peoples viewed their lighter skins, more "welcoming" approach, and "recognizable" social structures (even kingship) as corresponding to the Enlightenment's (1780s–1840s) popular notions of "the noble savage." Conversely, the Europeans placed the "black islanders" of the southwest Pacific near the bottom of the evolutionary scale and often saw them as ignoble, miserable, and treacherous. These biased images affected transcultural outcomes.

For their part, the indigenous islanders had to make sense of these highly mysterious newcomers, whose dress and accouterments were utterly alien and whose vessels were significantly larger than and different from their own. Each island culture had its own postures of response and interaction, and in this vast region, which contains twenty-five percent of the known discrete languages and religions, this complexity is daunting. In general, however, each society had periods of initial contact, longer periods of adjustment to serious intrusions into its local ways of life, and the increasingly more common, yet nonetheless creative, absorption of modernity.

In terms of religious change, the Pacific Islands are noted for a massive shift towards Christianity (with over 90% nominal adherence for the whole region). This general change has entailed varying consequences for the myriad of isolated, small-scale, and survivalist cultures, some of which have been so accommodating to the new faith that their traditions have become highly muted, and others which have been highly resistant to conversion. Typically, Christianity has provided a window of opportunity for very localized peoples to participate in modernity, with all its accompanying bewilderments that in turn have occasionally subverted the religious life.

Pacific "contact scenarios" with outsiders can be plotted from the sixteenth century to the early twenty-first, since some mountain cultures in easternmost Irian Jaya have yet to interact with the outside world. When their content can be (re)constructed, most indigenous responses to external contacts appear "religious," in that newcomers are taken to be deities, strange and powerful spirits, or returning ancestors. On Hawai'i Island, in 1779, the "natives" thought Captain James Cook was the long-awaited, returning fertility god Lono, and he was feted by Chief Koah at much cost to the locals. After Cook's departure, however, when a storm forced him to return to the island, the natives killed him because of what they saw as his deception. Over half a century earlier, Rapanui, or Easter Islanders, apparently reacted to the enigma of passing vessels (before Jacob Roggeveen's landfall of 1722) by feverishly erecting many of their great statues to face the sea at Rano Raruku—a most untraditional act, considering that the effigies of chiefs were meant to gaze over their ancestral lands. In Polynesia, with its more vertically oriented cosmologies (sky/earth/underworld), the newcomers were often thought to have arrived from above: the Samoan term *papala[n]gi* (sky people), for instance, is used to describe the white visitors. Later on, as in Papua New Guinea, where a horizontal view of the cosmos prevailed, the first appearances of outsiders mostly suggested the return of the dead. In 1877, for example, the Papuan Koitabu thought Ruatoka, a Rarotongan co-worker of missionary James Chalmer, was an ancestral spirit because of his ghostly white suit; in 1946, isolated Ke'efu highlanders who stumbled upon thirteen dead white people in a strange shelter—a crashed plane—buried their bodies and offered sacrifices to them as "new beings" who could die like themselves.

Once interaction with outsiders continued, however sporadic, islanders had to decide whether to resist them or trade with them. Epidemic diseases caused by contact often stalled the progress of possible relationships, but the islanders also found the newcomers themselves to be vulnerable to trouble, sickness, and death. Once their weaknesses were known, the outsiders were classified as strangers, and thus became worth attacking. Spirit power would be needed to hold back the intruder; for example, patrol officer Jack Hides remembers a day in 1935 on the Papuan Plateau when a swaying Etoro medium, playing a drum while perched on another's shoulders, sang a repelling clan into action.

Although the islanders killed various newcomers, many of whom were unarmed missionaries, the superior weapons of whites and their parties eventually subdued any reprisals. In any case, trade offered a popular and profitable way of dealing with the new uncertainty. Seafarers usually bore attractive items for exchange, and they were soon considered as possible prizes of (group) possession. Sometimes exchange activity was not satisfying, however; Tongans, as a result, would pirate visiting vessels, such as the *Port-au-Prince* in 1806. The more hierarchical (mostly Polynesian) societies, though, were in the best position to negotiate a high-level, stable *rapprochement* with European officialdom. Tonga, after all, had held together a far-flung island empire, from as far west as the Isle of Pines (in southern New Caledonia) to Samoa. Other, smaller societies had to capitalize on their limited opportunities. Theft often occurred, explaining how so many steel axes filtered into the Papuan Highlands years before European miners did. Sometimes individuals got lucky without having to resort to stealing. The earliest Catholic missionaries to the New Guinea highland Chimbu, for instance, gave tools to the local people to help them establish an outpost in 1936. When the fortunate recipients arrived back in their hamlets, however, news of their prizes had preceded them; the missionaries then found queues of people, with gifts to trade in order to acquire the new instruments.

Outsiders often selected relatively safe locations to begin trading or mission work, and as a consequence, some groups earned privilege over others. Since inter-tribal hostilities had long been endemic to the region, recipients of new weapons could use them to create havoc among their enemies. For example, Maori tribes procured muskets from the 1810s, convincing even missionaries to trade them for hunting purposes. In Fiji, the European Charles Savage, remaining out of the range of traditional weaponry, was "employed" by Naulivou, chief of Mbau, to shoot down his foes at the forefront of inter-tribal battles (1808–1809).

Even during peacetime, however, the new religion could be manipulated to secure special advantages and keep up old enmities. Christianity came in more than one guise, and if one tribe was benefiting from the presence of a mission station, another might be tempted to invite in the representative of a different denomination. Before the 1950s, Catholic/Protestant missionary competition made possible the local politics of playing one against the other. Sectarian Protestant elements also competed for loyalties. In Papua after 1908, for example, dissident families or clans often achieved social separation as a means of satisfying their local grievances by becoming Seventh-day Adventists. In Polynesia, Mormonism grew rapidly at the expense of more mainstream churches, partly because of the material benefits it offered such as superior housing and medical services. In fact, the Mormons had established their small "kingdom" in the Tuamotos as early as 1844—even before the founding of Salt Lake City.

With the establishment of towns, missions, trading posts, and plantations, there arose the possibility of access to increased power and new goods. Traditionally, wealth was not only a mark of social status (of nobility in Polynesia, and often of successful management in Melanesia), but it was also a sign of blessing from the spirit order. In smaller societies, moreover, prosperity was cherished by the group; the common people looked to their chiefs for magnanimity, and a Melanesian big-man achieved his leadership through generous relinquishment—giving gifts so that many were put in his debt. Now, however, since the longest-staying possessors of the new goods were missionaries, the indigenous people deduced that special material blessings would flow through practicing the new religion. Ships' cargo was already mysterious in origin, and the connection of the strange goods with the availability of new spiritual power heightened expectations of collective well-being. This notion, called "cargoism," led people to try worshiping in the churches. Especially in Melanesia, though, where traditional rituals focused on the tangible fecundity of plants and animals, group agitations occurred, sparked by local prophesiers filled with hope that "cargo" (European-style trade goods invested with a religious aura) would arrive in abundance. The bearers of cargo were often thought to be returning ancestors, but also possibly the "Jesus" spoken of by the evangelists. Makeshift wharves, even airstrips, were erected to receive the marvels. What had been almost exclusively directed to the expatriate strangers would now come to the local peoples. Such "cargo cults," as they have been dubbed, expressed frustration that indigenes had only limited access to these wonderful items, an inequity that seemed to contradict values of reciprocity and sharing.

Acculturative activity surrounding the introduced, internationally marketed commodities has a complex history of its own. It has often involved mimicry, yet with suggestions of ritual. Closer to contact, for instance, isolated villagers began setting their own imitation tables with wooden copies of knives and forks. In later colonial times, with new jobs available and liquor restrictions removed, islander office workers could put on the airs of sophisticated white drinkers in hotels, uncharacteristically sitting with crossed legs and drooping cigarettes. Experimentalism abounded. Setting up a store to become wealthy enticed many, yet businesses commonly failed because the owners expected magical results, and their relatives quickly absorbed the earnings. Islanders often combined the new technology with traditional causal beliefs. For instance, Melpa highlanders have been known to sacrifice chickens when their trucks break down, and some bureaucrats have become convinced they have been bewitched through their computers.

The remarkable effect of Christian missions in Oceania influenced the transculturative processes involved in the massive shift to a universal religion. A number of transformations deserve special recognition. One is epistemic—traditionalist islanders and incoming Christians shared a general worldview in terms of retributive (or "payback") logic, but each supposed their grasp of its operations was correct. Indigenes supposed, for example, that trespassing into spirits' sacred groves and lairs would mean certain death; when missionaries, without this fear, did trespass without dire consequence, they were taken to possess a superior understanding of how the world worked, even while they had their own assumptions about sacrilege. Again, islanders explained most sicknesses and deaths in terms of spiritual causes and damaged relationships with deities that provoked ancestral punishments. Results of the missions' modern health services, however, often defied such expectations, even while Christians taught that bodily blessings derived from relying on "the true God." Consequently, knowledge passed on at initiations could not compete with a mission education.

In some earlier civilizations in Polynesia with kings as rulers, the long-term establishment of Christianity followed the *dénouements* of major wars. In Tahiti in 1815, Pomare II, who had lost power because of the emergent cult of the war god Oro, regained it in a holy war with the backing of the London Missionary Society (LMS) from the Leeward Islands. In Tonga, the powerful, pro-Christian secular chief Taufa'ahau, who dominated the Ha'apai, subdued his enemies by 1837. He unified the conquered peoples by first assuming the role of the supreme sacral kingship of Tu'i Tonga (1852), and then by attempting to place the Wesleyan Mission under his divine rule (although he had only partially succeeded by 1875).

Conversion to the new religion mandated by high-level, local decision-makers also occurred in other places: in Hawai'i under Kaahumanu in 1822, for example, and in Fiji under Cakabao in 1854). Legitimatization of local rule by missionaries prior to colonization was often marked by the acceptance of royal insignia (e.g., whales' teeth on Fiji), signs of authority which became very important when royal courts and councils of chiefs had to negotiate European annexations. Although missionaries disdained beliefs and rites that appeared to contradict their faith, they sometimes worked to save the culture by solidifying a weakened traditional government, as did Benjamin and Lydia Snow in the Marshall Islands in the 1860s.

More generally, religious change occurred through evangelically charged, politically disengaged individuals. Many pioneer "European" missionaries have stolen the historical limelight, but an immense unknown number of islanders also chose to participate in the evangelizing process. Important centers sprang up for the training of islander evangelists; with the eastern Pacific being evangelized first, the emissaries have generally moved westward. Thus, Takamoa and Malua Theological Colleges, established by the LMS on Rarotonga (Cook Islands) in 1839 and Apia (Western Samoa) in 1844, respectively, have produced both preachers and teachers that exposed Melanesia to the new faith. Many of these evangelists—103 out of 203 of the pioneer Polynesian LMS personnel—died in dangerous and malaria-ridden places, unfortunate deaths that were taken as signs of spiritual vulnerability in Melanesian cultures. Methodist Fijians were prominent among the earliest Melanesians to work among their fellow black islanders to the west (notably in New Britain and Bougainville).

These islander missionaries on Melanesia created a three-tiered chain of "pastoral power," which was comparable to colonial military structures. The religious hierarchy, however, set an example for ways that people other than the "white masters" could lead congregations. In western Melanesia, Indonesians filled these mediating roles; the Dutch Reformed missionaries typically deployed Ambonese, and the Catholics sent Flores Islanders. Melanesia did experience a time lag, however, before the highly populous and volatile highlands received missionaries in 1920; various coastal Melanesians were entrusted with this "frontier" activity. Devout Lutheran converts from the Huon Peninsula became the first native evangelists to the eastern highlands of Papua New Guinea, and rather aggressive Gogodala preachers were sent by the Unevangelized Fields Mission into the southern highlands. Throughout Catholic mission history in Melanesia, many catechists were trained to perform non-clerical religious duties in dispersed villages that were visited infrequently by expatriate missionaries. As celibacy was required of its religious, though, the Catholic Church always dawdled in the creation of indigenous clergy—in a world of island societies that expected everyone to marry. Nevertheless, new orders have been created in the region, such as the 1935 founding of a sisterhood called The Handmaids of our Lord in Papua. And in 1925, the Anglicans founded the Melanesian Brotherhood in the eastern Solomon Islands.

Overall, the European and American overseas missions have established mainstream Christian denominations throughout the Pacific Islands. Historical circumstances usually caused different church traditions to predominate in different areas. Once a given mission gained a foothold in a particular region, not even colonial shifts could readily change it. France, for example, which generally favored Catholic mission activity, did not deter LMS-originated Protestantism in Tahiti (with its famous "Temple," famous for choral competitions, in Papeete) or in the Loyalty Islands (part of France's Oceanic province of New Caledonia). Germany's takeover of New Guinea in 1885 resulted in strong Lutheran and Catholic missions, especially on the mainland, but did not prevent the growth of Methodism (after the pioneering work of Australian George Brown) on the islands of New Britain and New Ireland. How these missions established themselves sometimes depended on formal agreements. At a time of comity between missions in the British Empire, for example, the Governor of British New Guinea (or Papua) Sir William McGregor negotiated spheres of influence for missions within his jurisdiction in 1890. As a result, the LMS work expanded along the southern coast where Catholic missions were not already established, while the Anglicans consolidated in the northeast and the Methodists further east again, in the Trobriand Islands. Not being party to this agreement, and with a lot of non-British personnel, the Catholics managed to evade this arrangement to their advantage, however, as did the Adventists.

Each mission's presence in a given region generated group loyalties, which are often reflected in the provincial organizations of the newly independent Pacific nations; the groundwork of new social strata was laid through mission schooling and indigenous ministries; and distinctive expressions of Christianity arose that often reflected the primacy of the first cultures affected in a given region. In the Papua, for instance, annual ceremonies of LMS-originated churches along the coast are largely modeled on the Motu traditional exchange ceremony—called *bobo*—because the Motu were the first converts. In Catholic areas, the short, less schooled, and more aggressive Papuan Highlanders, called "bush kanakas," have often suffered in comparison to the tall, educated, coastal Mekeo, who have had a longer experience with the outside world and who dominate the betel-nut market in the capital city of Port Moresby.

All throughout the Pacific, distinctive regional expressions of mainstream Christianity abound. What would a Samoan or Tongan Christian funeral be without the proverbial exchange of woven mats? How would agreements between secular and ecclesiastical leadership be achieved in central Polynesia and much of eastern Melanesia without sharing the common cup of pressed *kava* root? Dramatic reenactments of tensions upon the arrival of the first missionaries—of Methodist minister Dr. Bromilow on Dobu Island in east Papua in 1891, or of Anglican bishop George Selwyn on Santa Ysabel in the central Solomons in 1862—become annual celebrations in particular places.

Moreover, local rituals have become complicated due to varying limitations placed on the interaction between gospel and culture. In the central New Guinea Highlands, for instance, at the Wahgi people's great pig-killing festivals, in which a host tribe gives with astounding generosity to nonhostile tribes around it, a wooden cross will often be planted on the dance ground and a Catholic priest will open proceedings with a blessing. Members of the Swiss Brethren's mission, on the other hand, would prohibit their adherents from attending these ceremonies. Across the Pacific Islands, pork and crab have been familiar dietary components, yet the Seventh-day Adventist Church, which has proportionately its largest following in the Pacific, proscribes such food in accordance with the Levitical code. Consequently, the first outward sign of any Adventist village is the presence of foreign livestock—especially goats and cattle.

As the churches grew, the model of the Christian village usually prevailed. Both the government and the mission discouraged dispersed hamlets and encouraged larger communities, often nestling around well-kept places of worship. This proximity did not prevent various frictions, however. Sorcerers, especially in Melanesia, had once been accepted as useful agents to retaliate against enemies in other tribes; now, however, the new peace was disturbed by the unnerving possibility that the remaining sorcerers could be paid to perpetuate evil acts for jealous and disgruntled families within the same village. Similarly, denominational or sectarian differences and tensions often disrupted rural peace, occasionally dividing villages. Group reactions also arose from dissatisfaction with the outcomes of introduced religion. In Polynesia and Micronesia, where both hierarchical social structures and cosmologies pertained, unsatisfied groups often responded to dissident prophets who accentuated the lack of spirit power in ordinary church life. Thus, in these regions, missionaries could gain new followers on the pretext that a prophet has an extraordinary access to heaven's blessings. For example, between 1930 and 1932 on Onotoa (now part of Kiribati), the prophet Ten Naewa tried to outwit the LMS missionaries by announcing that God would descend in person, and he himself "fathered" the Father's arrival, as he led his waiting "Sheep." In Melanesia, however, where cargo cults were more prevalent, the common complaint was the churches did not bear material results (pidgin: *kaikai,* or food). In the Solomons before World War II, local prophets such as Sanop, on Bougainville, announced the arrival of rifles, motor cars, and aircraft that were delivered by ancestors, thus rendering the colonial authorities unnecessary.

Eventually, independent churches emerged—many with indigenous leaders who rejected the mainline forms of Christianity as foreign. In Melanesia, where over twenty such churches have emerged, a third of them originated in cargo movements. Others stress concrete experiences of faith, such as dreams, visions, or collective ecstasies; the latter are notable among members of the Christian Fellowship Church, in New Georgia, the Solomons. This church was once led by the white-robed "Holy Mama." In Polynesia, independent church leaders are commonly believed to have direct access to heaven or to have come down from the heavens. The Maori church, founded by Ratana in 1928, accepted him as God's "mouthpiece"; prominent in this church's iconography is a ladder linking an airplane (representing heaven) with a car (representing Earth). In 1985, the LMS Cook Islands Christian Church began to attempt to heal a long-standing internal rift, caused by a remarkable female healer named Apii Piho and her followers, who believed her claim that she was Jesus.

The resilience of traditions in certain pockets of the Pacific has sometimes kept Christian influences at bay. Virtually all the strong neo-traditionalist movements are in Melanesia, and some of these are cargo cults. Latter-day followers of the large movement in Madang (north-coastal New Guinea) during the 1950s and 1960s maintained that the indigenes should be left to develop their own salvation stories, in which the ancestors and cult founder Yali are the heroes, rather than the Biblical prophets and Jesus. In the Solomons, on the western and southern parts of Guadalcanal, one Moro sect has created a movement—complete with its own schools—that is deliberately designed to preserve tribal culture and keep out Western influences. Not far to the north, the mountainous center of Malaita is home to the Kwaio, who reject any "Christian interference."

All these expressions of independence, as well as the many different varieties of indigenously generated new religious movements in the Pacific, have shown that islanders believe in expressing religiosity in their own cultural terms. Tensions and altercations at the village level have inevitably served to instruct churches in the Oceanic region, preparing them for their own self-determination. In intercultural relations, the balance of forces until the end of the twentieth century favored preserving sound beliefs and practices borne by the West. Religious leaders wanted to ensure that the different peoples receiving the Christian message were properly acculturated and did not lapse into the curious misunderstandings that had produced "cargo cults." They made some concessions, however, in terms of sculpture (of crucifixes, for instance) and architecture (Port Moresby's handsome Catholic cathedral, designed in the shape of a Sepik *haus tambaran* [spirit house] in 1967). A few missionaries, such as Maurice Leenhardt—Protestant pastor to the Houailou on eastern New Caledonian mainland in the 1930s—asked themselves whether they had learned more from "the natives" than they taught them. Others, such as Percy Chatterton, submitted to the spirit of independence arising from local congregations; he quietly facilitated the post-LMS *Papua Ekalesia* (Church of Papua), the first independent church of mainstream background in Melanesia formed between 1963 and 1968. The local people's confidence in their own leadership eventually caused a decisive shift away from church communities operating under mission control toward regionally autonomous ecclesiastical structures, or separate Catholic episcopies, under islander supervision. By the early twenty-first century, the prevailing missiological discourse stressed inculturation, or the advisability of imbedding the gospel into the local culture, both honoring the latter's pre-existing values while also transforming and redeeming its weaknesses from within.

The general movement towards national ecclesial emancipation—or, rarely, transnational status, as with the United Church in Papua New Guinea and the Solomon Islands after 1968—proceeded with the emergence of new political independencies in the region. Excluding New Zealand (1947), the newly decolonized nations—Western Samoa (1962), Nauru (1968), Fiji (1970), Papua New Guinea (1975), Solomons, (1978), Kiribati (1979), and Vanuatu (1980)—have been governed by indigenous leaders. Even where independence has not been achieved (with France and the United States as the two notable powers prolonging their possession of Pacific islands), national churches have been created, such as the *l'Église évangelique* in France's New Caledonia or the United Church in the Marshall Island in American Micronesia. Whether politically autonomous or not, the whole region has increasingly become affected by monetarization, foreign investment, and transnational companies' pursuit of opportunities in the metal, oil, gas, and timber industries. For example, one of the world's richest copper deposits is on Bougainville; natural gas is now piped out of the Lake Kutubu area in Papua New Guinea's Southern Highlands; while New Caledonia has become well known for its extensive nickel deposits.

Pacific islanders have embraced modernity in highly varying ways. Money has become the medium of exchange in towns and cities, but is still used in tandem with traditional valuable items (such as mats, shells, feathers) in villages and in rites (especially marriages and funerals). In rural areas, money can therefore be incorporated into ritual life and suggest new ritual forms. Old coins seem to circulate forever within single villages through ritualized gambling games. Money can now be pinned on a branch by New Guinea highlanders and paraded as a "money tree" to apologize for a killing or a road accident in a specific tribal area—quite an innovation, since compensation payments in kind were traditionally exchanged between allies, not adversaries. Some late-twentieth-century cargo cults were actually money cults; the followers were persuaded that the money that was already in the red boxes held by the leaders would multiply through weekly rituals. Overall, the islanders' quest to make money has been strong, however. Sepik craftsmen have sold traditional effigies of the dead for money and have carved spirit figures for the tourist market. *Hula* dancing to entertain tourists in Hawai'i exemplifies adaptation of local dance forms in order to earn money from visitors. Even in rural areas, today's leading dance performers in traditional ceremonies would compete for prizes at town shows or the privilege to represent their nation at Pacific arts festivals.

Success in business and in the modern economy, although reserved for the few, has had religious consequences.

Protestant Tongans employed in Honolulu or Sydney, for example, or Cook Islanders in Auckland, have started important diaspora congregations, importing their pastors from their home regions. In Melanesia, capitalist success may sometimes cause a business leader to develop political aspirations, yet those ambitions inevitably lead him or her to the traditional cultivation of dependents through the practice of generous gift-giving as a neo-traditional "big-man." Wealthy people may build large new houses in their home villages, only to find themselves the objects of jealousy and thus of paid sorcery attacks. In this context, the persistence of sorcery can be defended ideologically as a social equalizer to counter the inequities that threaten old reciprocities and village values.

Religious factors also influence modern Pacific politics. National constitutions typically invoke the supreme God, sometimes along with a worthy customary inheritance. Clergy have also achieved political prominence, such as Anglican Fr. Walter Lini, first Prime Minister of Vanuatu, or Catholic Fr. John Momis, the foundation Minister for Decentralization in Papua, New Guinea. Furthermore, internal military conflicts have sought religious inspiration. The Papuan Liberation Army (OPM) partly legitimates itself as a defense of Christianity against what is perceived as Indonesia's neo-colonial promotion of Islam, and its members look to the collective martyrdom of followers of the prophetess Angganita under the Japanese in 1943 as an inspiring precedent for their actions. In the Solomon Islands, civil strife in the late twentieth century, as well as religious differences between largely Anglican Malaitans and mostly Catholic Guadalcanalese, exacerbated the clash. In such post-colonial conflicts, political slogans have carried neo-traditional religious import. From 1990 to 2003, ideologues for the Bougainville Liberation Army, for example, fought for the independence of Bougainville as *Mekamui* (the Sacred Island). More generally, throughout what is a predominantly peaceful region, thinly disguised appeals to Christian principles often lurk behind the apparently secular political agendas of new national parliaments promoting better health, education, and social security.

Despite frustrating realities sometimes experienced by many outsider investigators, especially anthropologists, the Pacific Islands are remarkable for their strengthening indigenous Christianity. As a result, traditional cultures are being transformed, and, rather than being devastated, showing their resilience in change. Contrary to some historians, outsiders did not destroy Pacific cultures. While terrible epidemics did make many island communities very vulnerable, by and large, the missionaries did not impose religious change by force, and the islanders can no longer be preconceived as credulous, lacking any ability to make sensible decisions of their own. In fact, cultural relinquishments sometimes occurred spontaneously. LMS personnel, for instance, encouraged the preservation of the Motu people's harvest festival, during which worshipers wore extraordinary fifteen-foot high masks. When the Japanese unexpectedly bombed Port Moresby in 1942, however, the Motu never celebrated the festival again—not because they were forced to give it up, but because it had somehow lost relevance in a changing world.

Oceania's religious scene in the early twenty-first century should be assessed for what it has become. Anthropologists can now begin evaluating specific congregations; observing sociological differences in the region, such as the sedate, hierarchical Polynesian churches compared to the dynamic congregations of Melanesia, with their spiritistic and charismatic worship; and studying indigenous theological endeavors and liturgical innovations, appreciating them as important new developments within the wider world of religious affairs.

See Also Christianity, article on Christianity in the Pacific Islands; Politics and Religion, article on Politics and Oceanic Religions.

Bibliography

Barker, John, ed. "Christianity in Oceania: Ethnographic Perspectives." In *ASAO Monographs* 12. Lanham, Md., 1990.

Garrett, John. *To Live among the Stars: Christian Origins in Oceania.* Geneva, 1982.

Siikala, Jukka. *Cult and Conflict in Tropical Polynesia.* Academia Scientarum Fennica, FF Communications 99/2. Helsinki, 1982.

Smith, Bernard. *European Vision and the South Pacific: 1768–1850.* Oxford, 1960.

Swain, Tony, and Garry Trompf. *The Religions of Oceania.* New York, 1995.

Trompf, Garry. *Payback: The Logic of Retribution in Melanesian Religions.* Cambridge, U.K., 1994.

Garry W. Trompf (2005)

TRANSMIGRATION

TRANSMIGRATION denotes the process by which, after death, either a spiritual or an ethereal, subtle, and thinly material part of the personality, leaves the body that it previously inhabited; it then "migrates" to enter (i.e., is reborn in) another body, either human or animal, or another form of being, such as a plant or even an inanimate object. Other terms often used in this context are rebirth, especially in connection with Indian religions, *palingenesis* (from Greek *palin,* "again," and *genesis,* "birth,"), metempsychosis (from Greek *meta,* "again," and *psychê,* "soul") and, increasingly in modern popular parlance, reincarnation (from Latin *re* "back" and *caro,* "flesh"). Manichaean texts in Syriac use the expression *tašpikha* or *tašpikha denafshata,* corresponding to Greek *metangismos* (from Greek *metangizesthai,* "pour from one vessel into another one, decant"; similarly, Latin *transfundi*) and conveying the underlying notion of a transfusion or change of vessel whereby the soul is "poured" from one body into another. The Latin church father Augustine of Hippo (354–430) in his anti-Manichaean writings also uses the noun *revolutiones* and the verb *revolvi,* which happen to be identical with the later qabbalistic technical term *gilgul:* the soul "revolves" (i.e. rotates) through successive bodies. Earlier qabbalistic terms were *sod-ha-ʿibbur* ("the mystery of transition") and *haʿtaqah* ("displacing, changing place"), the latter equivalent to the Arabic *tanasukh.*

It is obvious that the notion of a non-physical entity (soul) existing separately from the physical body is assumed by most beliefs that posit an afterlife. The detailed elaboration of other cultures' views of afterlife and transmigration depends on the psychology and anthropology of those cultures, explicitly or implicitly. Thus the word soul may mean the whole human minus the body or a special substance or collection of substances non-physical in nature. In the former case, it is the whole albeit disincarnate person that survives (and goes on, for example, to the underworld, the land of the dead); in the latter case it is a specific soul-substance that persists and returns to its ancestral or heavenly home or haunts the living or is reborn. Many belief systems, especially among non-literate societies, know of multiple souls, but the idea is also not uncommon in literate societies: examples include the *ba* and *ka* of the ancient Egyptians, the oldest Greek *psychê* and *thymos,* and the fivefold division among contemporary Jewish qabbalists (*nefesh, ruah, neshamah, hayyah, yehidah*).

Unfortunately, contemporary knowledge of most small-scale indigenous cultures is often based on the information of single informants and passing travelers, but rarely on the sustained investigation of an anthropologist remaining in a culture for many years. The once-predominant idea among anthropologists that a single informant could be sufficient to "decode" a culture has proved to be a profound mistake, and it should be noted while using such sources that much of the information is incomplete. Even the material from older literate civilizations is not always that easy to analyze. The fragmentary character of the texts and the modern, often Christian and philosophically influenced ideas about the soul and the body tend to color interpretations and should preclude facile conclusions. Last but not least, scholarly approaches often tend to present a uniform picture (the Christians believe, the Buddhists believe, etc.), whereas especially in eschatological matters people often have their own private ideas. One final point is the appropriateness of the terminology of reincarnation or rebirth. Although it is used here in order not to complicate an understanding, it must be stressed that the terms regularly, especially in Africa, do not presuppose that the ancestors now leave the area of the dead, or how the afterlife is imagined. On the contrary: ancestors may reincarnate but they often do stay present in the world of the dead as well. In other words, among many communities there is a belief that the ancestors have a multiple presence, in this world and the world hereafter.

ORIGIN OF CONCEPT. Edward Tylor (1832–1917), one of the fathers of social anthropology, was perhaps the first modern scholar of transmigration, but he still interpreted his material in an evolutionary key, starting with the birth of the concept of the soul. Yet that stage in human history is unrecoverable and speculations in that direction are rarely fruitful. A modern approach should look at the geographical spread, the nature, and the functions of transmigration in society. This survey will examine first non-literate societies and progress to the major literate cultures and modern Western society.

CROSS-CULTURAL OVERVIEW OF NON-LITERATE SOCIETIES. The acceptance of the belief in some form of transmigration or return of the dead person to terrestrial life is a widely occurring concept that is evident in many cultures. Whereas older studies often claim that there is little evidence of belief in transmigration in most non-literate societies to the extent that they have been reliably and systematically studied by ethnologists, contemporary studies have uncovered a wealth of evidence to the contrary. This new research has been especially successful in America, where evidence suggests that such beliefs once were present among all North American Indian tribes. The first notices go back to the earliest stages of contact with European arrivals to the continent. For example, it was recorded in 1636 that the Hurons believed a human soul can return into the body of a child, as evidenced by the child's strong resemblance to a deceased person. The prevalence of this belief among the Northwest Coast Indians and the Inuit strongly suggests that here was the development of an ancient cultural complex, which may have been introduced by the first American immigrants who came via the Bering Strait. There is less evidence of this in Middle and Latin America, and the evidence becomes even scarcer in investigations into the cultures of the southernmost region of Latin America.

About Africa, there are mentions of reincarnation ranging from quite extensive reports to mere scattered observations. Not surprisingly they seem to be limited to the south of North Africa where the adoption of Christianity and Islam likely prevented the survival of older beliefs in this direction. It seems that in West Africa, especially, the belief in reincarnation was prevalent. The beliefs can assume various forms. In many instances, there is the belief that a recently and honorably deceased ancestor—a warrior, for example—is reborn in a baby, although the connection with the ancestor becomes weaker as the child grows. There also seems to be a gender aspect to the belief, for some tribes, like the Konkomba, stress that women reincarnate, too. The Nigerian Yoruba believe that every living person is a reincarnation. Apparently, the encroachment by Europeans even incited some Akan to formulate a belief in a return as white people, as the Dutch traveller Willem Bosman (b. c. 1672) noted.

The existence of a belief in reincarnation among the Australian Aranda (Arunta) was the subject of a vigorous debate in the early 1900s between Baldwin Spencer and Frank Gillen, on one side, and German missionary Carl Strehlow, on the other, who disputed the findings of the former. Yet the outcome seems to be that here, too, reincarnation existed, even though rather by mythical ancestors than by "real" people. The fact that several neighboring tribes mention a reincarnation of ancestors supports the interpretations of Spencer and Gillen.

In the area of Melanesia, Micronesia and Polynesia, many tribes tell about reincarnation, but the best information comes from the Trobriand Islands, where Bronislaw Malinowski (1884–1942) carried out detailed investigations in the framework of his interest in the islanders' sexual lives. As he noted, the inhabitants explained pregnancies as the reincarnation of ancestors.

There is more information regarding Siberia, the Arctic and the subarctic circle, where the belief in reincarnation was virtually ubiquitous. Here shamanistic "theology" even stressed that shamans could remember their former lives and some were able to show scars of their former lives. Among the Jakuts it was rather exceptionally believed that one could be reborn even outside one's own tribe. In general, it is the ancestors who were believed to return.

From this survey, it follows that the belief in reincarnation is evidently very old. It is less easy to understand, though, why it was originally absent from Egypt and the ancient Near East, from ancient Japan and China as well as from the Indo-European peoples. Unfortunately, contemporary knowledge of the roads by which beliefs have traveled in prehistory are so obscure that explanations of this geographical spread can only be speculative.

There is more certainty about the nature and function of this belief in reincarnation, however. Firstly, there is a distinction between the transmigration of a deceased person into an animal and the reincarnation into a person. The former is much less current than the latter, but it is well attested. Among some Alaskan Inuits, for example, it was believed that the souls of the dead migrated into their dogs. On the other hand, the most frequent belief is that the birth of a new child signifies the rebirth of an ancestor. From the ancestors, it is nearly universal that it is usually a deceased grandparent who is the favorite incarnated person, as is also indicated by the identity of the name; in West Africa the identity between ancestor and reincarnated child seems particularly marked. Through the reincarnation the young child becomes incorporated, so to say, in the ancestral line, which reinforces or creates new kinship relationships; reincarnation is very much a social process. This identity between ancestor and young child often is so strongly linked in some cultures that corporal punishment of children was prohibited out of respect for the ancestors. At the same time, the ancestor functions as a kind of guardian spirit for the youngster.

In addition to being evidence of an older ancestor, a newly born baby is sometimes perceived as the reincarnation of a previously deceased young child. It is plausible that this belief has originated in an attempt to comfort parents regarding the loss of an earlier child.

India. The notion of transmigration and reincarnation is a pivotal aspect of the general socio-religious belief system in India. In the Hindu religious tradition, the concept of transmigration is a vital aspect of the cultural milieu and has played a dominant role in shaping the actions, ethics, and ideologies of the people. Thus, the Indian subcontinent and the cultures influenced by it are dominated by the notion of *saṃsāra*, "what turns around forever," the wheel of birth and death. Whereas in the West the idea of reincarnation was always felt to be something exotic, strange, and at any rate required special justification, in India it came to be an accepted presupposition of life.

The history and development of this notion are not yet quite clear. However, there is consensus that the weary round of *saṃsāra* is not yet part of Vedic religion. The *locus classicus* of Indian reincarnation can be found in two parallel passages of the oldest Upaniṣads (*Brhad Aranyaka Upaniṣad* 6.2 and *Chandogya Upaniṣad* 5.3–10), which mention reincarnation and salvation. The fact that the notion was taken for granted—and indeed even made the basis of their respective doctrines of salvation—by Jainism and Buddhism suggests that by the sixth century BCE it was already widespread in India. Among the presuppositions of this doctrine is the notion that space and time are endless. The identity of the self depends on (moral) karmic determinants. Life is an unending, eternal, weary round of suffering, governed by an automatic causality of reward and punishment (*kamma*) that takes the soul from one existence to another through all six spheres of being, from that of the gods to that of "hungry spirits" and demons.

In Indian religious sensibility the emphasis is not so much on the duality of life/death as on birth/dying. The problem about rebirth is that of necessity it also implies "redying," that is, death recurring ad infinitum, unless a person succeeds in escaping from the vicious circle of *saṃsāra* (also depicted iconically as the monstrous wheel of unending existences, the *bhavacakra*, and described graphically in the Buddhist Avadana and Nidana literature) into ultimate liberation (Hindu *mokṣa*, Buddhist *nirvāṇa*). It should be emphasized that the ultimate goal (*artha*) is release and escape; the heavens (*svarga*) are still part of the samsaric world. Doctrinal differences of opinion relate to the method of liberation (yoga, mortifications, the "middle path") as well as to the precise definition of the liberated state.

The descriptions in the *Brhad Aranyaka Upaniṣad* 6.12.15f. (cf. also *Kausitaki Upaniṣad* and *Mundaka Upaniṣad*) still exhibit a somewhat mythological character. Those who have achieved perfection and have realized their true self go, after death, the "way of the sun," namely, the path of the gods (*devayana*): they enter the abode of *brahman* (*brahmaloka*) never to return again. Those who have not achieved ultimate self-realization but have lived a life of sinless piety and devotion, through sacrifices, penance, and charity, go along the path of the ancestors (*pitryana*) to the world of the moon, where they become rain and subsequently food: "Gods feed on them, and when that passes away from them, they start on their return journey to the reborn as human beings. . .Thus do they rotate." Evildoers are reborn as insects and vermin. According to the *Chandogya Upaniṣad* 5.10.7, they are reborn as dogs and pigs. As has been noted above, heaven too is part of the samsaric cycle, and hence gods too are reborn, even as human beings can be reborn as *devas,* to be subsequently reborn once again.

What or who exactly is it that is reborn? Unorthodox sramanic teachings as well as Upanisadic speculation provide a varied technical vocabulary (*atman, jiva, purusa*) to deal with the questions of empirical ego, real self, and so forth. Some systems of thought conceive also of spiritual entities in terms of a subtle, ethereal matter; one such example in Western history would be the Stoics.

Jainism. In the Jain system, the living entity is called *jiva* (the eternal "soul" or "life"), and it is doomed to unending rebirths as long as it is covered and encumbered (as if by a thinner or thicker film) by *kamma,* which is conceived as a kind of fine matter. The generation of new *kamma* must be stopped, and the accumulated *kamma* already present must be removed if liberation is to be achieved. That such liberation can be achieved is demonstrated by the line of *jinas* (lit., "conquerors").

Buddhism. The Buddha left no writings himself. Because Buddhist teachings were written down much later, the oldest stage of Buddhist teaching about transmigration is unknown. The fascinating problem of Buddhist doctrine concerning karmic rebirth arises from the fact that Buddhism denies the existence of an *atman*—that is, self, or ego-substance beyond the empirical ego, which is a transitory combination of "heaps" of "elements" (*skandhas*). Regardless of whether the anti-Brahmanic doctrine of *anatman* ("no-self") was already explicitly taught by the Buddha himself or was developed later, it is a central concept of historical Buddhism. It is clear, though, that reincarnation did not yet occupy a position of prime importance in the teachings of the Buddha himself, but was elaborated in minute detail only by his later pupils, as in the *Abhidharma Pitaka* of the Pali canon.

Tibet. The application of the doctrine of rebirth in Tibet, a culture decisively shaped by one particular form of Buddhism, deserves special mention because of its relevance to the social system and its political institutions. Buddhism was established late in Tibet, not before the seventh century CE. However, it would last to the fifteenth century before the characteristic connection between the worldly and spiritual powers started to receive its well-known contemporary form. Whereas initially it was only the leader of one of the many monk communities whose rule was determined by reincarnation, in the seventeenth century Mongolian support stabilized the rule of the Dalai Lama, which endured until the Chinese conquered Tibet in 1951 and eliminated the theocracy. The influence of the exile of the renowned fourteenth Dalai Lama on the Tibetan ideas of reincarnation still remains to be properly assessed.

GREEK RELIGION. Reincarnation in ancient Greece was "invented" by Pythagoras, an aristocrat from Samos, who came as an exile to Croton in southern Italy around 530 BCE. Here he developed his teachings about reincarnation that are only vaguely known, due to the fact that no writings of Pythagoras himself have been preserved and his community was almost completely massacred in the middle of the fifth century BCE. Yet his contemporary Xenophanes of Colophon (sixth century BCE) (fragment B 7, ed. Diels/Kranz) already told the following, uncomplimentary anecdote: "And once, they say, when he passed by a dog which was being maltreated, he pitied the animal and said these words: 'Stop! Don't beat him! For he is the soul of a friend whom I recognized straightaway when I heard his voice.'" Regrettably, it is not known how often Pythagoras thought of a reincarnation, but both Pindar (fragment 133, ed. Maehler) and Plato (*Phaedrus* 249a) speak of three times, of which the first reincarnation has been occasioned by a mistake in the underworld. Aristotle (384–322 BCE) notes: "as though it were possible, as in the tales of the Pythagoreans, for just any soul to clothe itself in just any body." Apparently, Aristotle thought that Pythagorean reincarnation went from body to body, but the mid-fifth-century philosopher Empedocles clearly taught differently, as he wrote: "already I have been a boy and a maiden, a bush and a bird and a fish jumping up from the sea" (fragment B 117, ed. Diels/Kranz). This process could last an extremely long time, as Empedocles speaks elsewhere of wandering "thrice ten thousand seasons" (fragment B 115, ed. Diels/Kranz). The origins of Pythagoras's views are unknown. Earlier generations of scholars liked to connect him with Buddhist views as he was nearly a contemporary of Buddha, but the down dating of the Buddha (above) has made this improbable. It seems possible, however, to isolate a few factors that may have played a role to a smaller or larger degree.

First, reincarnation could only come about when the Greek concept of *psychê* had developed into humankind's immortal self. It seems indeed that Pythagoras was also the first Greek to develop this particular idea of the soul. Second, the aristocratic Greeks were historically more interested in group survival than in personal survival. Yet at the end of the archaic period, there seem to be signs of an increasing interest in a more personal form of survival. Reincarnation can be seen as a more radical answer to this general development. Pythagoras's loss of political power around 500 BCE may have been an extra stimulus for developing the doctrine of reincarnation, since the survival of the soul singled out those reincarnated from those who were not. In other words, the doctrine may have been a kind of comfort to those of his pupils and friends that followed him into his exile. It might echo in the thesis of Max Weber (1864–1920), which posits that the rise of religions of salvation, such as Christianity, was also the consequence of the depoliticization of the educated classes.

It was probably only a short while after Pythagoras that somebody in southern Italy developed a new set of doctrines and practices which were promulgated not under their own name but that of the most famous singer of the Archaic Age, Orpheus. The so-called Orphics introduced vegetarianism, and modified existing Bacchic mysteries. At the same time they also produced new teachings (1) on the coming into being of the cosmos, gods and humankind; (2) on eschatology; and (3) reincarnation. Pindar (fragment 133 Maehler) already declares that the best roles in future reincarnations will be for those "from whom Persephone accepts compensation for ancient grief (viz. because the Titans had killed her son Dionysos)" and this "ancient grief" is also alluded to on recently found Orphic Gold Leaves. On an Orphic bone tablet that was found in Crimean Olbia c. 400 BCE, the terms "life-death-life: truth; Dio(nysos)-Orphik(?oi)" are legible, and in his *Meno* (81a) Plato (c. 428–348 or 347 BCE) attributes the doctrine of reincarnation to "priests and priestesses who try to give an account for the functions of their activities," that is, to wandering Orphics. It is part of this doctrine that the body is looked at rather negatively and considered to be the "prison of the soul."

As with Pythagoras, there are few particulars about Orphic reincarnation, but it is certain that Plato used Pythagoras and the Orphics. His views on reincarnation have to be deduced from his dialogues, whose temporal order still is debated. It seems that in his oldest dialogues Plato still is not completely convinced of the reality of reincarnation, but in the middle ones (*Phaedo*, *Phaedrus* and the *Republic*) the doctrine has become an important part of his eschatological views, even though the content varies depending on the dialogue. It is important to note that Plato's *Phaedo* gives evidence of the important process of ethicization, to use the term employed by Gananath Obeyesekere (2002), in which the bad receive a bad reincarnation (into animals) and the philosophers go to the gods.

Plato's ideas were rejected by some of his pupils and Aristotle, but the Pythagoreans carried them into later antiquity. The doctrine is found with philosophers like Plutarch (before 50–after 120 CE), the *Corpus Hermeticum,* and the so-called Chaldaean Oracles, but it became far more influential among the Neoplatonists like Plotinus (205–270 CE) and Porphyry. Unlike Plato, the former even considers a reincarnation into plants a possibility. Moreover, Plotinus clearly had precise thoughts about the different stages of reincarnation. Whereas the first rebirth is seen as an entry, the subsequent ones he calls *metensōmatōsis*, or "re-enbodyment"; people can remember their previous lives, and there is no liberation from the cycle of rebirths. Later philosophers had much difficulty with the thought of a transmigration into animals and it is striking that in the second half of the sixth century, Olympiodorus, one of the last Neoplatonists, rejected the doctrine of reincarnation.

CELTS. According to Caesar in his *Gallic Wars* (6.14) the Druids believed that souls did not perish but wander after death; for this reason Clement of Alexandria (*Stromateis* 1.15) already compared them with the Brahmans. As reincarnation was clearly not part of Indo-European traditions and there is little reliable evidence about such views in medieval Celtic literature, the Druids may well have taken over Greek views, perhaps via Massilia (Marseilles). Unfortunately, there are no further detailed sources, and this intriguing possibility remains an unsubstantiated one.

EARLY CHRISTIANITY. The early Christians firmly believed in the resurrection of the body and therefore opposed the doctrine of reincarnation. Although there were a few exceptions that were prepared to consider its validity, such as Origen, even he came to a negative conclusion. In the second and third centuries CE, especially, church leaders tried to refute the belief, but around 400 CE reincarnation no longer played a role in the internal and external Christian debates. Apparently, this decline in polemics went hand in hand with the loss of pagan interest in reincarnation.

It was different with the Gnostics. They opposed the idea of resurrection, and thus it is hardly surprising that some of them—in particular the Carpocratians—were more sympathetic to reincarnation, even though they limited its numbers. It seems possible that the Gnostics had reinterpreted the older Greek beliefs in a more optimistic way, but the fact that the Gnostics are viewed in this respect only through the prism of Christian theology makes every interpretation a somewhat dubious affair.

MANICHAEISM. Manichaeism is the only world religion that has disappeared. It was founded by Mani, who was probably born on April 24, 216. He was may have been descended from Persian aristocracy but certainly grew up in a Jewish-Christian group, the Elcasaites, and died in 277 in a Persian prison. His followers carried his beliefs to the West, where they found in Augustine a temporary convert, and to the East, where they were more successful. Via the Silk Road, Manichaean faith traveled to China, where the last Manichaeans probably died in the sixteenth century. Mani worked in a geographical area that was influenced by Zoroastrian, Jewish, Christian and Buddhist views and this plurality makes it difficult to isolate the precise origin of many of his ideas. The difficulty is compounded by the need to reconstruct the Manichaean doctrines from a whole series of languages, ranging over many centuries from Latin and Coptic until Sogdian and Chinese.

The Elcasaite community in which Mani grew up practiced vegetarianism, which in antiquity often went concomitant with a belief in reincarnation. Indeed, a Christian source reports that one of the Elcasaites, Alcibiades, taught that Christ had experienced already many a rebirth before being born from the Virgin Mary. This information points to a Greek origin rather than an Indian one, as later Arab historians suspected.

The Manichaeans taught that the soul could be reborn in humans, plants and animals. The aim was to be reborn in an elite Manichaean, a so-called *electus*, and in this way to become liberated from the cycle of rebirths. It is clear that the Manichaeans dreaded their rebirths, as they could become birds, mice, or even grass.

ISLAM. From the eighth century CE onward, Islam received a clear impetus regarding the doctrine of reincarnation from the Manichaeans and Neoplatonists. Yet whereas conventional Islam strictly rejected reincarnation, "heretical" currents embraced the doctrine, in particular the Syrian Alawites, the Lebanese Druze, and the Anatolian Alevites. Their heretical position explains why they kept their teachings highly secret. It was only in the nineteenth century that apostate Alawites started to publish some of their texts. These show that reincarnation is meant to enable the light souls to ascend to heaven through their reincarnations. The believers can reach this goal in seven times, but the non-believers have to die and be born again a thousand times. Particularly bad is the transmigration into an animal or plant. It seems that the doctrine also helps to explain human misfortune as a penalty for misdemeanors in previous lives.

JUDAISM. Like normative Christianity and Islam, normative Judaism also rejected reincarnation, and it is not mentioned in the texts of biblical and rabbinical Judaism. The first exposition of reincarnation in a primary Jewish source occurs around 1200 CE in the book *Bahir*, which was probably written in southern France. It is a typically Jewish touch that the cycle of rebirths ends with the Messiah, who himself stands outside the cycle. Allusions to and discussions of reincarnation can be found before *Bahir* and go back at least to the eighth century CE. This suggests a possible influence from Islam, but a Neoplatonist and/or Manichaean background cannot be excluded either, given that some Manichaeans were still present in Mesopotamia around that time.

Since the thirteenth century the notion of *gilgul* has been a central qabbalistic tenet, which also found a place in the most influential qabbalistic text of that era, the *Zohar* by Moses de Léon (d. 1305). After the expulsion of the Jews from Spain, the doctrine of reincarnation went with them to other areas where Jews were living. This meant that via Galilee Safed in sixteenth-century Galilea it eventually reached eastern Europe, where Hasidic leaders regularly tried to legitimize their position by claiming to be a reincarnation of previous great rabbis and scholars. This tradition largely ended after the upheavals of World War II and the Holocaust.

WESTERN CHRISTIANITY. Around the same time as *Bahir*, if not already a few decades earlier, reincarnation can be found among the Cathars of southern France. The best information comes from the protocol of interrogations in the Pyrenees by Bishop Jacques Fournier (1285–1342). Cathar belief was strongly dualistic: people had a good soul in a bad body. Souls traveled from body to body until they finally, if they had become a Cathar, could return to heaven. It is in this final body also that the resurrection will take place. The Cathars clearly admitted to a transmigration into animals and, as a rule, seemed to have limited the number of reincarnations to about seven. Although all kinds of solutions have been offered to the question from where the Cathars derived their doctrine—from Jewish, Islamic or "heretical" Christian traditions—it is only fair to say that none has been demonstrated in a satisfactory manner.

The Romans had not been overly interested in reincarnation, but it was Publius Ovidius Naso (43–17) who, through Book XV of his *Metamorphoses*, kept the memory of Pythagoras and his teachings alive through the Middle Ages. This meant that the doctrine was regularly discussed and always rejected. Even during the Renaissance and the immediate successive centuries, followers of the doctrine are extremely hard to find. Giordano Bruno (1548–1600) was a rare exception to this. Yet it is only in the later seventeenth and eighteenth centuries that evidence arrives of a renewed interest in the doctrine, undoubtedly favored by the growing questioning of normative Christianity by leading intellectuals amongst whom Gotthold Ephraim Lessing (1729–1781) played a leading role.

THEOSOPHY, ANTHROPOSOPHY, NEW AGE. Despite a growing interest in reincarnation among European intellectuals in the nineteenth century, the continuing rejection by normative Christianity meant that it was only in alternative circles that the doctrine of reincarnation could gain a permanent position. The source of all modern views is the Theosophical Society, which was founded by Helena Petrovna Blavatsky (1831–1891) in 1875. This imaginative dilettante found traces of reincarnation even in Egyptian sources and the Bible, where previous scholars had not. It was her encounter with India that led her to develop her views on reincarnation—which, however, were filled with typically European ideas, in particular the evolutionary development of the personality. Blavatsky was still trying to come to terms with the combination of Asian and European concepts, but Rudolf Steiner (1861–1925) attempted especially in the last years of his life, to make reincarnation one of the central tenets of his anthroposophy. Steiner was much impressed by the scientific progress of the nineteenth century and tried to make his views on reincarnation acceptable to a public that admired the latest insights of science. His views, however, must be gleaned from his voluminous writings, because he never succeeded in delivering a systematic exposition. The reincarnation, according to Steiner, starts in prehistory where the soul arises from a kind of sea "of the spiritual (German: *des Geistigen*)" and where it also ends. In the time between the reincarnations, which may last on average between 1,000 to 1,300 years, the souls wait on one of the planets. During this period the soul keeps its memory and before reentering a body it looks for an appropriate pair of parents. Steiner himself usually concentrated on male reincarnations and was not averse to speculations about his own historical "ancestors."

Over the course of the twentieth century, the idea of reincarnation gained increasing popularity, in particular among adherents of what is loosely called New Age religion, and is even accepted by some Christian theologians. It is also not unusual to find acceptance of the belief that people choose their own incarnation. Yet contemporary believers are less interested in the physical rebirth than in the progressive spiritual evolution through successive "realities." They often no longer think of a surviving mortal "I" but rather prefer to believe in a True Individuality or Higher Self, which constitutes the link between this life and the previous or coming ones. Some New Age sources even claim that reincarnation transcends space and time and that past and future lives coexist with the present lives. But such views occur especially in authors who tend to theoretical speculations and often have a science-fiction background.

Recovery of the past lives can now also be used for therapeutic purposes. In a twist that is not altogether surprising, a belief that once was typically religious is used to achieve psychological improvement.

See Also Orpheus; Pythagoras; Reincarnation.

Bibliography

All previous general expositions have now been supplanted by the brilliant, erudite and balanced survey by Helmut Zander, *Geschichte der Seelenwanderung in Europa* (Darmstadt, Germany, 1999); note also Gananath Obeyesekere, *Imagining Karma. Ethical Transformation in Amerindian, Buddhist and Greek Rebirth* (London, 2002). For the non-literate cultures see Michael Bergunder, *Wiedergeburt der Ahnen* (Münster, Germany, 1994). For the earliest Indian stages see H. Bodewitz, "The Hindu Doctrine of Transmigration. Its Origin and Background," *Indologica Taurinensia* 23–24 (1997–98): 583–605. For Greece and the Cathars see Jan N. Bremmer, *The Rise and Fall of the Afterlife* (New York, 2002). For the Celts see Helmut Birkhan, "Druiden und keltischer Seelenwanderungsglaube," in Johann Figl and Hans-Dieter Klein (eds.), *Der Begriff der Seele in der Religionswissenschaft* (Würzburg, Germany, 2002) 143–158. For New Age see Wouter J. Hanegraaf, *New Age Religion and Western Culture* (Albany, N.Y., 1998). A Rosicrucian approach can be found in Édouard Bertholet, *La réincarnation* (Lausanne, Switzerland, 1970). Other works of merit are *La Réincarnation: Théories, Raisonnements et Appréciations,* ed. Carl-A. Keller (Berne, Switzerland, 1986); *Karma and Rebirth in Classical Indian Traditions,* ed. Wendy Doniger O'Flaherty, (Berkeley, Calif., 1980); Hans-Peter Hasenfratz, *Die Seele* (Zürich, Switzerland, 1986), and Hasenfratz, "Seelenwanderung," in Gerhard Krause, Gerhard Müller, et al. (eds.), *Theologische Realenzyklopädie,* vol. 31 (New York, 2000), pp. 1–4.

R. J. Zwi Werblowsky (1987)
Jan N. Bremmer (2005)

TRANSSEXUALITY See GENDER ROLES

TREASURE TRADITION.

The Treasure (*gter ma*) tradition has some precedents in Indian Buddhism. One striking example is a prophecy by the Buddha in the *Pratyutpannasamādhi Sūtra* that predicts the sūtra would come to be hidden in the ground for future times when it could be propagated again. The Treasures also draw widely on a range of notions about revelation and visionary inspiration from both Indian and Chinese religions. However, as a well-defined movement with far-reaching political and cultural significance, Treasure is a distinctively Tibetan phenomenon.

Treasure-like claims can be found in the colophons of some of the early Tibetan Snying thig (Nyingthig, "Heart Sphere") scriptures, but the Treasure tradition in its full form only emerges gradually. It is common both to certain branches of Tibetan Buddhism and to the adherents of Bon, another religious tradition that has ancient roots in Tibet but that comes together as a school at around the same time as the appearance of Buddhist Treasure adherents. An early Bonpo "treasure discoverer" (*gter ston*) is said to be Gshen chen Klu dga' (Shenchen Luga) of the eleventh century. A formative moment for the Buddhist Treasure tradition is to be identified in the work of Nyang ral Nyi ma 'Od zer (Nyangral Nyima Ozer, 1136–c. 1204), a visionary and scholar of the Rnying ma (Nyingma) school of Tibetan Buddhism. This Treasure discoverer codified a full-length hagiography of Padmasambhava, the Indian Tantric master who is said to have been invited to the royal court in the eighth century to teach Buddhism to the Tibetans. This story included seminal passages about Padmasambhava's concealment of Treasure as part of his mission in Tibet.

Nyang ral Nyi ma 'Od zer and his hagiography of Padmasambhava are concerned primarily with the triumph of Buddhism over Tibet's older religions, especially the traditions called Bon, but the Bon tradition produced many Treasures of its own and flourished throughout the same time period that the Buddhist treasure tradition did. These Bon Treasure scriptures contain much of the same range of types of meditative and ritual practices as the Buddhist Treasures, but their narratives of the period of the royal court are told from a different perspective, focusing upon Bonpo struggles with the Buddhist faction and the persecution of Bon by the Buddhist kings. They trace the ultimate origins of Treasure teachings to the founder of the Bon religion, Gshen rab Mi bo (Shenrab Miwo), and to early Bon masters in Tibet.

In the Buddhist version of the Treasure story, the rationale for hiding Treasures is said to have been formulated when Padmasambhava discerned the future, a time when Tibetans would need special teachings to get them through certain difficult periods. He therefore designed special Buddhist practices and scriptures just for those times and proceeded to set up the circumstances for those special teachings to be revealed at just the right moment. This involved designating some of his own disciples to reveal those teachings in a future lifetime. Padmasambhava then uttered an empowering prophecy about that future revelation and proceeded to hide the teachings in a way that they would not be available until the proper prophesied moment in the future.

As the Treasure tradition develops, the manner in which Padmasambhava and other treasure concealers—both Buddhist and Bon—hide these teachings comes to be distinguished into several types. The basic form of the story is that the Treasures are buried in the physical world—in, for example, the ground or a stone or a pillar. But another mode soon appears by which the concealer buries a Treasure in the memory of the future discoverer. This alternate means relying on mental processes and visionary experiences and is often said to be set into motion when the concealer transmits ritually to the future discoverer an especially impressive communication. This makes it memorable enough to be held in mind over the course of several lifetimes. In either case—of the "earth Treasures" or the "mental Treasures"—the buried teaching is usually encoded in some way, often said to be a special abbreviated language or script distinctive to the *ḍākinīs*, a class of female enlightened spirits. Padmasambhava's consort and disciple Ye shes mtsho rgyal (Yeshe Tsogyal), a former Tibetan queen, is herself cast as a *ḍākinī* and served as Padmasambhava's principal helper in the effort to conceal treasure. Ye shes mtsho rgyal often is said to have been both the scribe for the Buddhist treasure teachings and their encoder.

Concealing the Treasure in code helps protect it against discovery by the wrong person at the wrong time. The other element that ensures that the Treasure reaches its correct destination in the future is the prophecy uttered at the time of the treasure's concealment. In the case of the Buddhist Treasures, these prophecies are uttered by Padmasambhava and serve to name the future discoverer and some of his (and sometimes her) circumstances, also often in coded or abbreviated form. When a discoverer in later times comes to present a teaching that is claimed to have been originally hidden as Treasure, one of the things that adds to the credibility of that claim is if the Treasure does indeed contain this prophetic utterance, with specific reference to the discoverer's name and other characteristics.

Most Treasure texts do include such prophecies as part of the narrative sections that advance the legitimacy of the Treasure itself. When one considers what Treasures are from the perspective of the discoverer, one can understand why legitimacy is such a key issue. Treasure teachings usually come in the form of texts although they can also come in the form of objects, such as ritual instruments or symbolic images. To claim that such things, be they textual or otherwise, were indeed concealed in the past for a particular purpose to be fulfilled in the present and additionally that the discoverer is a reincarnation of a person in the past specifically appointed to uncover that Treasure now requires support and evidence in order to be believed.

In fact the Treasures were regularly subject to criticism by skeptical members of most schools of Tibetan Buddhism. Partially such skepticism had to do with institutional and sectarian competition. In large part the Treasure tradition served as a vehicle for religious figures to distinguish themselves outside of the conventional monastic and academic avenues for self-advancement. But that was precisely what made them subject to doubt. This doubt is also represented in psychological and personal terms in accounts of the experiences of the discoverers themselves. In fact it is for this reason that the Treasure tradition spawned prodigious autobiographical writing throughout its history, often focused on narratives, sometimes idiosyncratic and poetic, of dreams, visions, and meditative experiences. In these experiences the visionary would make contact with the teachers of the past who had originally concealed the Treasure, such as Padmasambhava or an exalted Bon po master. The discoverers were often preoccupied with "reading the signs" of their lives, their bodies (which often included special marks and patterns on the skin), and their surroundings in order to pick up signals and evidence that would connect them with their prophecy texts and elements of a past life as a disciple of the original concealer. Once the discovers did access the actual Treasure itself—which often came in abbreviated form either in a dream, in a vision, or in "reality" in the form of a small scroll of paper with just a few cryptic linguistic indications—they would struggle with "decoding" the initial Treasure signs, a struggle that itself would have to draw on a whole range of esoteric yogic practices and skills. In short, a key part of what made the Treasures credible was just such genuine doubts and heroic struggles on the part of the visionary introducing them.

The successful effort to access Treasure material and then decode and unpack it to serve as a teaching tradition served to bolster the reputation of the discoverer himself or herself, and indeed the success of a Treasure often rode on the discoverer's charisma and personal power. But other kinds of evidence were also marshaled. In many ways it was frequently the virtues of the teachings themselves—their ritual or soteriological efficacy, their aesthetic qualities, and their compelling narratives—that made them believable and worthy of veneration as representations of truth and reality, that is, as teachings of an enlightened figure like Gshen rab Mi bo or Padmasambhava who served as an intermediary for primordial enlightenment itself.

In the Buddhist case, the Treasure promoters argued that their teachings should actually be considered to be originally and most basically the actual words of a buddha, on a par with other canonical Buddhist scriptures translated from Indic languages into Tibetan. Evidence of the success of these Treasure scriptures may be seen in the careers of the discoverers and the kinds of following they attracted and the communities and institutions they built. It can also be assessed in the longer term legacy: how often a given Treasure cycle was published, how often it was ritually performed. In fact there have been hundreds of Treasure discoverers introducing treasure texts and objects from the twelfth century CE to the twenty-first century. Many achieved great fame, and their works had lasting influence upon Tibetan literature, religious practices, and especially narratives about Tibet's royal past and its present religious identity. Some of the discoverers, like Klong chen pa (Longchenpa), were also scholars of the highest order. Others, such as 'Jigs med gling pa (Jigme Lingpa), introduced Treasure ritual cycles that had far-reaching popularity and influence.

It should also be noted that Treasure activity was sometimes the site of collaboration between Buddhists and Bon pos. In the nineteenth century the principal Buddhist Treasure cycles were collected by the polymath Kong sprul blo gros mtha' yas (Kongtrul Lodro Taye), himself originally a practitioner of Bon. Kong sprul worked in association with the visionary 'Jam dbyangs mkhyen brtse' i dbang po (Jamyang Khyentse Wangpo) and other colleagues and codified a corpus of Buddhist Treasures in a single collection, the *Rin chen gter mdzod*, of over one hundred volumes. A product of the nonsectarian Ris med (Rime) movement, this collection is organized by literary genre and ritual purpose. It contains a wealth of meditation techniques, ritual actions, and descriptions of deities. It also includes key narratives about Tibet's royal dynasties, the glories of its kings, the defeat of (in this version) anti-Buddhist demons and ministers, and the process by which the Buddhism that Padmasambhava taught to the court was taken in to become Tibet's national religion. The Bon po Treasure literature was also collected, codified, and divided into two main sections that are similar to those of the more mainstream Tibetan Buddhist canon, the Kanjur and Tanjur. But unlike the Buddhist Kanjur and Tanjur, this massive Bon po collection of several hundred volumes consists almost entirely of Treasure texts. Its date of compilation is not entirely clear, but it almost certainly predated the Buddhist *Rin chen gter mdzod* (Repository of the precious Treasures), possibly by a few hundred years.

For both the Bonpos and Buddhists, Treasure text production constituted a way to formulate new teachings suited to particular situations and audiences while giving them an aura of authenticity, antique pedigree, and religious power. Their specifically Tibetan character is evident in both Treasure traditions. The Bon po Treasures are replete with detailed rituals and deity lore that have no analogue in India and are clearly of ancient Tibetan origin. In the Buddhist Treasures Tibetanness becomes salient in debates about canonicity, authorship, and origins. Tibetan Buddhist orthodoxy had it that all genuinely original and canon-worthy Buddhist teachings had to come from India. By tracing a Treasure's origins back to a primordial Indic buddha or buddha principle, the treasure theorists managed to have it both ways: to give the Treasure an aura of authenticity even while allowing historical Tibetan teachers to formulate new materials under the Treasure tradition's aegis. In both cases it is thus no accident that the Treasure narratives display so much concern with Tibetan history, its leaders, its invasions, its glories, and its disputes. Treasure became a venue for Tibetan religious production qua Tibetan. It eventually became a popular means to acquire spiritual charisma not just by the unconventional yogis of the Bon po and Rnying ma schools who predominated in treasure production but also among some of the more monastic communities and other schools of Tibetan Buddhism. One particularly notable example is that the powerful fifth Dalai Lama had Treasure discoveries, and other Dalai Lamas had important connections with Treasure figures.

It is not coincidental that Treasure discovery continues to be a popular means for lamas to produce teachings and gain followers inside Tibetan areas in China in the early twenty-first century. The potentially nationalist implications of the tradition have not been lost on the governmental authorities, who for the most part have enforced a ban on Treasure discovery and have imposed tight restrictions on flourishing communities that continue to grow up around such visionaries.

SEE ALSO Bon; Dzogchen; Klong chen rab 'byams pa (Longchenpa); Kong sprul Blo gros mtha' yas (Kongtrul Lodro Taye); Padmasambhava; Ye shes Mtsho rgyal (Yeshe Tsogyal).

BIBLIOGRAPHY

Germano, David F. "Re-membering the Dismembered Body of Tibet: The Contemporary Ter Movement in the PRC." In *Buddhism in Contemporary Tibet*, edited by Melvyn Goldstein and Matthew Kapstein. Berkeley, Calif., 1998.

Gyatso, Janet. "The Logic of Legitimation in the Tibetan Treasure Tradition." *History of Religions* 33, no. 1 (1993): 97–134.

Gyatso, Janet. "Guru Chos-dbang's *gTer 'byung chen mo*: An Early Survey of the Treasure Tradition and Its Strategies in Discussing Bon Treasure." In *Tibetan Studies: Proceedings of the Sixth Seminar of the International Association of Tibetan Studies*, edited by Per Kvaerne, vol. 1, pp. 275–287. Oslo, 1994.

Gyatso, Janet. *Apparitions of the Self: The Secret Autobiographies of a Tibetan Visionary.* Princeton, N.J., 1998.

Hanna, Span. "Vast as the Sky: The Terma Tradition in Modern Tibet." In *Tantra and Popular Religion in Tibet*, edited by Geoffrey Samuel, Hamish Gregor, and Elisabeth Stutchbbury, pp. 1–13. Delhi, 1994.

Karmay, Samten G. *The Treasury of Good Sayings: A Tibetan History of Bon.* London, 1972.

Kvaerne, Per. "The Literature of Bon." In *Tibetan Literature: Studies in Genre*, edited by José Ignacio Cabezón and Roger R. Jackson, pp. 138–146. Ithaca, N.Y., 1996.

Thondup, Tulku. *Hidden Teachings of Tibet: An Explanation of the Terma Tradition of the Nyingma School of Buddhism.* London, 1986; reprint, Boston, 1997.

JANET GYATSO (2005)

TREES are a form of nature that represent life and the sacred continuity of the spiritual, cosmic, and physical worlds. A tree is often used to symbolize a deity or other sacred being, or it may stand for what is sacred in general. The religious beliefs that surround a tree may include as sacred any one or all of the physical parts of the tree: its trunk, branches, leaves, blossoms, sap, or roots. Sacred objects constructed from the wood of special trees are also used for religious purposes.

The physical properties of trees are combined with supernatural or sacred ideas, the beliefs that surround a tree's connection with what constitutes religion in different cultures. Trees are not only sacred in the major religions of the East and West, but also in other traditions where belief in the sacred is combined with beliefs in the power of ancestors, in the creation of life in birth, about death and the afterworld, and about health and illness. Trees that represent certain deities or ancestors, serve as mediators or links to the religious realm, and are associated with cultural beliefs in heaven or the afterlife. Trees may be valued as spiritual and physical contributors of life because they furnish liquids valued as sacred beverages used in ritual or as medicines for curing a variety of illnesses.

Through association with a particular religious or historical event, an individual tree or species of tree acquires the symbolic significance of the event as part of its meaning. The oak, date palm, and willow were used in the building of Solomon's temple and in constructing booths at Sukkot (*Lv.* 23:40). Deodar wood is used in the construction of Hindu temples. The oak is commonly taken to be the tree under which Joshua set up a pillar at Shechem to commemorate the nation's covenant with God (*Jos.* 24:26). The Jewish captives in Babylon in 597 BCE hung harps on weeping willows along the banks of the Euphrates (*Ps.* 137). The religious significance of this act established the willow as a symbol of mourning, death, and rebirth. The branches of the palm tree stand for Christ's triumphal entry into Jerusalem on Palm Sunday as well as for his rebirth. These associations are still prevalent in Christian tradition.

A society's religious beliefs about what kinds of trees are sacred generally depends on the nature and number of trees found in its territory. If trees are plentiful, the forest as a whole will also be an important part of the religion's spiritual beliefs and rituals. The Kwakiutl Indians of Pacific North America, like many other societies living in a tree-filled environment, believe that their heavily forested inland region is the home of supernatural beings.

THE INNATE POWER OF TREES. Religious or spiritual power may be inherent in a tree or in the elements that make up the tree. For example, in Taoist thought, trees and all forms of nature contain *yin* and *yang* energies, that is, the opposing forces of the universe. Each tree has spiritual power as it contains and balances these inequalities: the light and dark colors of the leaves and bark, and the opposition between light and shadow. In southwest China *fengshui* stands for the interaction of *yin* and *yang* and represents a power that affects the world and everything in it. *Fengshui* may be found especially in strange and awe-inspiring trees and stones. The contemplation of these powers or the active cultivation of trees to enhance their spiritual force, as in the Japanese art of *bonsai,* builds gentleness of character, religious spirit, and respect for humankind.

The Andaman Islanders use the intrinsic qualities of hibiscus trees to aid them in their struggles to catch large turtles and fish. It is through the spiritual qualities of these trees that the Islanders are able to succeed in overcoming their prey and to protect themselves from harm. The particular qualities of the tree represent essential elements of physical and spiritual life and ward off dangers associated with turtles and the sea.

The Haida Indians of North America used a power inherent in hemlock branches to scrub themselves in ritual baths. The tree had the power to purify and protect the Indians and to enable them to attain the degree of cleanliness required during their rituals and thus remain on good terms with their supernatural beings.

Power to avert illness and evil. Trees offer protection from both physical and spiritual illness through their associations with the divine. For the Ainu of Japan, *ramat* (literally "heart," translated as "spirit" or "soul") is a power that resides in all things in varying degrees. Wood is especially rich in *ramat,* which is provided by the spirit of Shiramba Kamuy, the upholder of the world and male god of vegetation. The Ainu believe that nothing is more effective for protection against evil and spiritual problems than *inaw* (carved wood offerings). The wood of over fifteen kinds of trees including oak, willow, lilac, dogwood, and magnolia may be used in the carving of *inaw,* which are then offered to good *kamuy* (spirits). Similarly three trees—the thorn, elder, and alder—are predominantly used to carve *inaw* for bad *kamuy. Inaw* are also hung in houses to provide general protection for the home and its occupants.

In the Konkan district of western India it is believed that barrenness can be cured by planting a tree for the uneasy spirits that wander about and inhabit women, preventing conception. Under favorable circumstances the evil spirit will leave a woman suffering from barrenness to take up residence in the newly planted tree, allowing the woman to conceive. The Indian mimosa tree is believed to provide spiritual protection against wicked spells and the evil eye. The illness caused by Sītalā-Māyā, the Indian goddess of smallpox, may be averted by setting up a branch of the neem tree just as Buddhists invoke certain sacred trees for health.

Trees may represent a spiritual healing for and protection from evil. The oil of the olive was traditionally used to soothe pain and so the olive tree or a sprig of the tree has become a symbol of the grace of Jesus Christ through which the sorrowful sinner finds eternal peace.

The cosmic tree. In many religions the universe is portrayed as multilayered, the layers kept distinct and in place by a world tree running through the exact center of the cosmos. Salish Indians of North America hold that their deity made three worlds, one above the other: the sky world, the earth, and the underworld. All are connected by a single tree that passes through the middle of each. The Babylonians believed that their cosmic tree, Kiskanu, was the home of the god of fertility and Ea's mother, Bau, the goddess of plenty. Heaven, or the home of Bai Ülgen, is believed by the Altai people to be on the top of a giant fir tree that grows at the earth's navel. The Vasyugan Ostiak (Khanty) believed that the cosmic tree's branches touched the sky and its roots extended to the underworld. A copy of the celestial tree of the Siberian Tatars stands before the palace of Erlik Khan, the lord of the dead.

Similarly, in Scandinavian mythology the cosmos is connected by a sacred ash, Yggdrasill. Its roots reach to Niflheimr, the lowest region of Hel; its trunk, enwrapped by the snake of the ocean, is in Midgarðr, the realm of humans; and its branches reach to Ásgarðr, the home of the gods. Other versions of the myth depict the great ash with three roots: Niflheimr or Hel under one, Utgarðr, the realm of giants and demons, under the second, and Midgarðr under the third. On top of Yggdrasill sits the eagle of Óðinn (Odin), chief of the gods; nearby is the Spring of Urðr ("fate"), where the gods dispense justice and determine the fate of the world. At Ragnarok, the doomsday of the gods, Yggdrasill will shake its roots, freeing the monsters of the lower regions.

Indian tradition offers many variations of the cosmic tree. In the Upanisads the tree is inverted with its roots in the sky while its branches cover the earth. The eternal *asvattha* ("fig tree"; *Ficus religiosus*) is a manifestation of Brahmā in the universe. This forest tree is also described as rising from the navel of Varuṇa or of Nārāyaṇa as he floats in the waters of the universe.

The ancient Egyptians believed that the sky was a huge tree that overarched the earth. The stars were fruits or leaves on the tree and the gods perched on its boughs. This tree separated the ocean from the sky, the upper from the lower worlds. Osiris, lord of the dead, was identified with this celestial tree. The sun was born from the tree every day while the celestial tree disappeared each morning, thus marking the periods of night and day. The year was also symbolized by 365 trees representing the days of their calendar year.

Cosmic space is also defined horizontally by trees. In addition to the center of the earth and the sacred tree, with its roots deep in the underworld and its trunks and branches defining the world of humans and the gods, many American Indian religions add sacred trees, and their associated colors, birds or other animals, and gods, to each of the four cardinal directions. The Maya, the Aztec, and the Indian cultures that later took part in their cultural heritage believed that five sacred trees (the four corners of the world and the center) were responsible for the organization of the universe; they allotted particular times of the year, or entire years in some cases, to serve under the dominion of each direction.

The tree of life. Many religions believe that the cosmic tree stands for the sacrality of the world, its creation, continuation, and fertility. Thus in many cases the world tree is also a tree of life and immortality as well. The patronesses of the cosmic tree for the Warao of South America are the Grandmothers, deities who are also associated with seasonal change and the winter solstice. The trees of the cardinal points and the Warao deities take on an especially interesting form. The southeast represents the soul of the Mother of the Forest, a deity of the world of light, while the southwest is the body of the Mother of the Forest. For the Warao, deities of the northeast and northwest represent the Tree of Life, the moriche palm, and so symbolize sustenance and fertility. Hebraic teaching and Islamic tradition describe the Tree of Life with its roots in heaven and its branches overarching the earth. Zoroastrianism teaches that the Tree of All Seeds, or the Tree of All Healing, which grows in the cosmic sea, Vourukasha, is responsible for life on earth.

In ancient Egypt, the celestial tree was also a tree of life. Its fruit kept the gods and the souls of the dead in eternal youth and wisdom. Out of this tree of life emerge divine arms some of which bear gifts while others pour out the water of life from an urn. In the Vedas, Varuna lifted up the celestial tree of life and by squeezing its fruit between two stones obtained *soma,* or *amrta,* the drink of immortality. Ancient Egyptian religion also associated this tree with fate. Sekhait, the goddess of writings or fate, sits at the foot of the cosmic tree where she records on the tree itself, or in its leaves, all future events as well as the important events of the present for the benefit of future generations.

The tree of knowledge. For Buddhists, the bodhi tree, or bo tree, is both the source of life for all beings and the tree of enlightenment. Śākyamuni Buddha made a special resolution at the foot of this tree of wisdom to remain under its branches until he attained supreme enlightenment. It was under this tree that he attained enlightenment after he was tempted and threatened by Māra and his three daughters Tanhā, Rati, and Rāga, who were like swaying branches of a young leafy tree singing songs of the season of spring.

The Babylonians believed that two trees guarded the eastern entry to heaven: the tree of truth and the tree of life. Similarly, in the Garden of Eden described in *Genesis* stood the Tree of Life and the Tree of the Knowledge of Good and Evil. After Adam ate of the fruit of the Tree of Knowledge of Good and Evil offered by Eve, God said, "Behold, the man is become as one of us, to know good and evil: and now, lest he put forth his hand, and take also of the tree of life, and eat, and live forever" (*Gn.* 3:22). Adam and Eve were driven from the garden, marking the beginning of humankind's troubles on earth.

Trees as food. In many religions trees are believed to be responsible for spiritual nurturance and sacred food. The Polynesians of Futuna believe that in Polotu, the abode of the gods, grows a sacred tree, the Puka-tala. The leaves of this tree will change into a wide variety of foods when they are cooked and so may supply all needs. For the tribes of South America's Gran Chaco, the god Cotaa created a wondrous tree that would provide food and drink for hungry people.

The bark of the alder tree is credited by the Karok Indians on the Klamath River in northwestern North America with providing salmon, an important food source. The creator of the world, Kareya, built a dam at the entrance of the Klamath River that prevented salmon from coming upstream to the Karok. The bark of the alder tree looks like salmon when it is broken off the tree and wetted. A Karok myth relates how this bark was used by Coyote to trick the women who guarded the dam into allowing the salmon to come up from the ocean, forever supplying food for the Karok. Salmon play both a life-sustaining and a religious role among these Indians, as does the wood of the alder tree.

Creation of humankind. In many religions the myth of a people's origin relates how a cosmic tree played an important role in either the actual creation of people or the emergence of humankind in this world from some other world. These beliefs are intimately tied to what is believed to be sacred. For example, among the Ainu the human backbone is regarded as the seat of life, and was originally made from a willow branch. But more frequently the cosmic tree or tree of life is responsible for the creation of the people of a society. Kiowa religion features a girl child, Pekeahaidei, carried by a growing tree into the sky where she marries and has a boy child. Carrying her child with her, she falls through a hole in her world. The child survives the fall to this world and is raised by Spider Old Woman, a very sacred being. Later the child creates Kiowa culture.

The Uyurucares of Bolivia believe that their god Tiri split a tree and from the opening came all the people of the earth. The Zuni, in their story of creation, are brought up from the lowest world level, where all is darkness, with the aid of the two sons of the sun. Branches from the pine tree to the north, the spruce to the west, the silver spruce to the south, and the aspen tree to the east had to be gathered before they could leave the Darkness World. The Zuni climbed the long prayer stick made from the pine of the north to the third world; scaled the crook from the spruce of the west to the second world; used the prayer stick from the spruce of the south to rise to the world below this one, and finally emerged into the Daylight World (this world) by climbing the prayer stick made from the aspen tree. This emergence story blends the cosmic tree, the trees of the four corners, and the tree of life as sacred elements that bring the Zuni to their present world and that serve as important parts of their religious beliefs.

The Seneca Indians of northeastern North America also give an account of the discovery of the world originating with the sacred people of the sky. In the middle of their village stood a tree covered with white blossoms, which gave light to the people when the tree was in bloom. When the blossoms fell, there was darkness. A woman of the Seneca dreamed three times that the tree must be pulled up by the roots. After the third dream, her people uprooted the tree. Upon discovering their actions, the chief became angry and ordered the woman who had had the dream to be pushed into the hole where the tree had been. The falling woman then discovered this world, an event that marks the beginning of the Seneca culture.

Trees as ancestors. A common extension of the notion of the cosmic tree as the source of all life is the belief in a tree as an ancestor and creator. This belief can take many forms. The Warramunga of northern Australia, for example, believe that the new life present in the womb of a mother receives its spirit or soul from certain trees, entering the womb through the navel. The Lakota on the upper Missouri River say that the first man and woman were two trees and that a snake chewed their roots off in order to allow the couple to walk away.

The Sauras of India honor the banyan tree, for they believe that "it is our mother." The banyan tree succored two fatherless children whose mother had abandoned them under its branches. The children would have perished but for the milk of the banyan that dripped into their mouths and fed them.

For the Ndembu, the "milk tree" *(mudyi)* is a dominant symbol of their culture and religious beliefs. The white latex sap of the tree is believed to represent breast milk and semen, suggesting the creation and nurturance of life. This tree stands for what is good in Ndembu society and is used in rituals to counter evil forces. The tree also stands for the spirits of the ancestors of the matriline, the important lineage of descent, and so represents social custom and structure.

In another vein, trees can be associated with a shrine dedicated to a deceased relative, who, in time, becomes an ancestor. Among the Nuer a *colwic* is the spirit of those people struck by lightning. These people are believed to have been chosen to enter into close kinship with the god Kwoth. A person killed by lightning is said to become a Child of Kwoth, a spirit of the air. The blood relatives of the deceased, his patriline, erect a *riek* or shrine over his funeral mound and plant a sapling of the nyuot tree at its side. The nyuot tree is associated with the *colwic* spirit and with the rain and the sky to which the soul of the dead person has been taken. When this sapling is planted during the rains (when most lightning occurs), the tree takes root. If it were to die another would be planted in its place. This tree becomes a shrine for the deceased's lineage. It is through this shrine that the deceased's spirit may become active in the everyday affairs of his relatives.

This idea of a sacred tree representing the lineage or clan is an old one. For many cultures, the ancestors are the deities and are responsible for life, death, and spiritual happines. The wooden totem pole used particularly by cultures of the Pacific Northwest coast of North America is not merely a name or emblem of different family groupings. The totem is a collective label, but it also has a religious character: the totem's origins related to the special relationship to the ancestors and the sacred world. The *inaw* of the Ainu, mentioned above, were originally the receptacles of ancestral *ramat*; later, the winged *inaw* (*shutu inaw*) came to represent ancestors. Some of these winged *inaw* became minor *kamuy* owing to their concentrated *ramat*, and were effective in warding off injurious magic.

Trees and Divine Powers. Trees may be viewed as having souls or spirits themselves or they may be a part of some divine being. Thus trees may symbolize a deity either by serving as the visible embodiment of a sacred presence or by marking a sacred spot that a deity frequents. Sacred trees may be the abode of deities or may be the divine beings themselves. For instance, the sacred heath worshiped in the time of Plutarch grew around the sarcophagus of Osiris and was known as the "soul of Osiris."

Trees with souls or spirits. Many religions include beliefs that trees have souls or are sentient sacred beings. The Australian Aborigines believe that the spirit of humanity resides in the land and that a tree, a bush, or a rock is the present incarnation of this spirit and has great religious value. A group of relatives thus includes humans and the spirits of these natural features of the landscape. If an Aboriginal leaves the area, he would leave a vital part of himself behind.

The pre-Islamic *jinn* are associated with certain kinds of trees. These trees are conceived as animate and rational, for a supernatural life and power resides in the trees. In Greece the dryads were oak nymphs, and the *tengu* of Japan are forest spirits.

The Trobriand Islanders of the western Pacific depend both spiritually and physically on the spirit of their canoe and the tree from which it is made. Once a tree is selected, the owner, builder, and helpers must perform a short ceremony before the tree can be cut down. A small cut is made in the trunk, and a bit of food is placed in the incision. This is an offering to the tree's *tokway*, or wood sprite, to induce the spirit to leave the tree so that the workers may begin the process of converting the tree into a canoe.

The Japanese have a story about the spirit of a very large and old willow tree that grows near a temple. The village decides to build a bridge and use the willow's wood for part of its construction. A young man, who like his ancestors before him loves and respects the old tree, saves it by offering to substitute wood from his own land in place of the willow tree. The village accepts and the tree is saved. Returning from work one day the young man meets a beautiful young woman under the willow. They marry with the understanding that the young man never ask his wife where she came from or who her parents were. He agrees. The emperor declares that a temple is to be built nearby. The village is eager to have the willow included in the building materials for the good fortune it will bring. One morning when the willow is being cut down the wife wakes up and tells her husband that she is the spirit of the willow, that she married him to make him happy in return for saving her (and the willow) so many years ago, but that now she must return to the willow to die with it because she is a part of it.

The spirit of a Buddhist nun of the eighth century CE is believed to be embodied in a giant ginkgo tree in Japan. This tree is called the Nurse Goddess Tree of Miyagi Field because of hanging formations that resemble human breasts, from which moisture drips in wet weather. This tree's "moisture" is believed to have the power of restoring milk to a woman who is unable to nurse. The tree itself is worshiped as a sacred mortal who has become a god and is filled with divine power.

Deities as trees. Trees may give birth to deities, or sacred beings may be made from trees. Among the Ainu of Japan, A-e-oina Kamuy, a sky god, is born to the elm tree spirit as is Kamuy Fuchi, supreme ancestress and ruler of all departed spirits. She was born from the elm tree impregnated by Kando-loro Kamuy, the possessor of the heavens. Her spirit is manifested in the sacred fire of the hearth and in vegetation.

In Asia Minor the almond tree and the river Sangarius were believed to have given birth to the god Attis, and consequently maturing almond trees became his symbol. The Tupari of the Mato Grosso region of Brazil believe that two of their male gods were born from a large rock. Since they had no wives, they cut down two trees, and each carved himself a woman and so populated the world.

Trees may also represent the essence of the deity. For example, the Buddha's fig tree, *asvattha*, is the chosen symbol of his essence, synonymous with all existence and all life. Among the Mandan Indians along the Missouri River in North Dakota, the world had two creators: First Creator and Lone Man. Lone Man leaves the cedar with the Mandan as a protection from all harm. The cedar is the body of Lone Man and contains his essence. Among the Arikara the cedar trees grown in front of their lodges are the body and spirit of Mother Corn, an important deity.

Deities symbolized by trees. Wreaths and crowns of foliage, usually laurel, olive, myrtle, ivy, or oak were sacred to Apollo and so symbolized some particular personification of him. The myrtle was also a symbol of both Venus and Neptune, the male and female deities of the productive and fertile powers of the waters. Several species of oak were symbols of Zeus.

Frequently a tree is held to be sacred because a deity resides in its branches. The *aśvattha* is said by some to be the abode of Brahma as well as embodying his essence and serving as the tree of wisdom and life. Other sources say that in this sacred tree abide Brahmā, Viṣṇu, and Śiva, as well as Viṣṇu in his incarnation as Kṛṣṇa. Among the ancient Semites, the goddess Al-Ozza had her abode in a sacred acacia at Nakhla.

Some trees are taken as symbols of a sacred person because of particular religious qualities the tree possesses. The myrtle is believed to be the symbol of pure maidenhood in Christianity and so is ascribed to the Virgin because of her pure life and sacred character. The palm, cypress, and olive are also symbols of the Virgin during her annunciation. They denote peace, heaven, and hope.

Greek beliefs frequently describe the actions of the gods in transforming human or divine beings into trees. The virginal Daphne, fleeing Apollo's embrace, is turned into a laurel tree by her mother, Gaia, the earth. Apollo breaks off a branch and crowns himself with it. In another myth, Aphrodite takes pity on Smyrna, mother of the slain Adonis, and tranforms her into a myrrh tree.

TREES AS VEHICLES OF COMMUNICATION WITH DEITIES. Trees serve as a means of communicating with the divine in three ways: through their use in shrines, the meeting place on earth of a sacred being and humankind; through the relationship between sacred trees and shamans, the religious mediators of the divine; and through the use of sacred drinks or drugs made from trees that allow a mystical contact with the sacred.

Trees and religious shrines. Sacred trees may be found along with bushes, shrubs, rocks, or even with a temple to make a shrine. In ancient Egypt, by order of Pepi II, a new center of worship was officially recognized by planting a Syrian fir in the town. Among the Pare of Africa, religious shrines were sacred groves of trees and depended in size upon the size of the comunity who would worship in them. Many Shintō shrines are built under the branches of an ancient tree as an alternate abode for the deity of the tree. The usual sacred tree of Shintō is the evergreen sakaki. It is usually on the grounds of the shrine, protected by sacred ropes. One of the most powerful shrines in Java lies in the center of Modjokerto, where at the foot of a huge banyan tree lies a small stone statue of Gaṇeśa, the Hindu elephant god of wisdom, surrounded by a white fence.

A shrine in the town of Kagami in Japan is dedicated to Musubi no Kami, the god of love, and built in honor of a cherry tree, Kanzakura. A myth tells of the spirit of a sacred cherry tree. A young girl falls in love with a handsome young man and will not accept the marriage arranged for her by her father. When the girl discovers she has fallen in love with the spirit of the cherry tree, she chooses to become a caretaker of the shrine devoted to the tree. There she stayed for the remainder of her life, representing religious perfection and dedication.

Sacred trees pass on communications from deities by speaking directly to humans, or indirectly through their whispering leaves whose sounds must then be interpreted by priests. At Dodona in Epirus, the talking Oak of Zeus delivered divine messages to humans through priests. Wood from this oak was also used to build the *Argo* and spoke to the heroes with a human voice. At Delphi, the laurel tree served as the voice of Apollo. The famous sacred tree near Shechem called the "tree of the revealer" in *Genesis* 12:6, was originally a Canaanite tree oracle.

Trees and shamans. Shamans or priests are frequently associated with sacred trees as oracles or interpreters of divine will. The shaman may be spiritually connected to the cosmic tree. Most frequently the shaman uses the cosmic tree as a vehicle to ascend to the sky or to the deities of the universe to gain sacred information.

In addition to the ability to transverse the universe and communicate with the deities by means of the sacred tree, shamans can communicate with the spiritual realm through divination, frequently using parts of sacred trees for ritual communication. According to the religion of the Sisal, an ethnic group in the Tumu district of northern Ghana, the first diviner or shaman descended from God shortly after humans descended to earth using the baobab tree. Shamans also frequently have spirit helpers to aid them in their ceremonials. Among the Coast Salish of North America, one of the most powerful spirit helpers is known as Biggest Tree and aids the shaman in acquiring gifts made from cedar. These gifts are "alive" for those who possess the power to perceive and use them.

Religious objects made of wood may also act as messengers. The wooden *inaw* of the Ainu are messengers (*shongokoro guru*) or intermediaries between the Ainu and the *kamuy* or between the *kamuy* themselves.

Trees and divine intoxicants. Many religions include the use of a divine potion, made from sacred plants, as necessary vehicles to the divine. Shamans frequently incorporate the use of such potions into their practices. Varuṇa obtains *soma,* or *amṛta,* the fruit of immortality, by squeezing the fruit of the celestial tree of life between two stones. The palmyra palm is a symbol of Śiva, yielding an intoxicating and powerful juice. In Chan Kom, descendants of the Maya use a favorite Mayan intoxicant and purge that has strong religious associations. They make a ceremonial mead of fermented honey and add the bark of the balche tree during the process for its narcotic effect. This drink, *balche,* enables communication with the deities and is necessary for all religious rituals, especially those for fertility, abundance of crops, rain, health, and family.

THE RITUAL USE OF TREES. Sacred trees have a ritual significance. The trees and their meanings may be incorporated into rituals of curing, initiation, marriage, and death. Trees used in any of these contexts stand for the divine and represent the sacred beliefs being honored through the ritual.

Trees appear in rituals in various forms as symbols for the divine. Sacred beverages are made from tree bark. Incense made from the sap and bark of sacred trees calls deities down to this world and then "feeds" them while they are here. *Copal,* an incense made from a tree sap and used by many cultures in Latin America, not only aids communication with the deities but protects the ritual participants from harm by driving away evil and purifying the area. Most frequently, wood is used to construct powerful religious paraphernalia, such as the sacred poles erected to symbolize the presence of the ancestral spirits or the cosmic tree during the ritual. The symbol of the cross is used in different religions to symbolize specific divine beings or the sacred in general.

The Zinacantecos, descendants of the Maya in Chiapas, erect cross shrines for every kind of ceremony. Three small pine trees are fastened to crosses and pine needles are strewn on the ground around the crosses to set off the area as sacred and ritually pure. There must be three crosses for a ceremony, and one is generally a permanent wooden construction, supplemented by two crosses made entirely from fresh pine boughs. The triadic symbol displays the Catholic religious use of three crosses as well as the traditional Native American beliefs. Crosses are "doorways" to the houses of the ancestral deities. They mark the boundaries between the sacred and the profane realms.

In Christian belief, the cross may be referred to as a symbol of the Tree of Life that stands in the Garden of Eden. The wood from the True Cross was believed to have the power to restore the dead to life. A variety of different trees are credited with being the wood chosen for Christ's cross: cedar of Lebanon, dogwood, mesquite, ash, and oak.

Trees in rituals of initiation and marriage. Many African cultures mark the transition from youth to adulthood through rituals of initiation, and some of the most powerful symbolism of this change is represented through the use of trees. Among the Ndembu, the milk tree, the mudyi, a symbol of life and the ancestors, is used in both male and female initiation ceremonies to transform boys and girls into fertile, productive adults. Traditionally, a girl's initiation ceremony and the use of the milk tree served as her marriage ceremony as well.

Every young girl among the Newari of Nepal is married to a small tree *(bel)* from early childhood. In India, the "marriage of trees" may be performed when a woman has been married for many years and has not yet borne children. One tree representing her husband and one tree symbolizing her fertility are planted side by side so that their combined growth may symbolically and spiritually increase her fertility and the growth of life within her womb.

The "marriage tree" is common in South India as a representation of a male or female ancestor. This tree is necessary for all weddings and is adorned as a part of the ceremony. In Java large "plants," are assembled from banana stems and scalloped tree leaves of various types, and wrapped with green coconut branches. These "flowers" made from trees are essential ritual elements for the wedding ceremony, representing the virginity of the bride and the groom.

Trees associated with death and rebirth. A variety of trees are specifically associated with religious beliefs about the fate of the dead and the rebirth or passage of their souls to the afterlife. Christian death symbolism involves the use of willows and cedar trees. These trees symbolically stand for the death of the body as well as heralding a rebirth of the soul. These trees are almost always present in cemeteries in America and may be accompanied by conifers or other kinds of evergreens: a promise of everlasting life. Wood is the most common material from which coffins are made for burial in Christian practice in the United States. The leaves of the baine palm used by the Coorgs of South India are associated with death and are used in funeral rituals.

Many religions practice tree burial as the appropriate spiritual resting place for the deceased. The Khasiyas of eastern India leave the deceased in the hollow trunk of a tree. Many North American Indian groups placed their dead in trees or on wooden structures grouped together to form a sacred burial ground. The Nootka and Southern Kwakiutl used another form of tree burial. They folded the body up and put it in a large box, which was then placed high in a tree. A wooden mortuary column was erected to display the family crest of the deceased.

In many religions, without proper religious burial the soul of the departed would be in danger and could harm the deceased's living friends and relatives. For the funeral pyre, the Coorgs of South India cut down a mango or pavili tree that grows in the burial ground. The entire tree must be used for cremating the corpse; improper use of the tree's parts may result in another death in the community in the near future.

SEE ALSO Axis Mundi; Beverages; Incense; Rites of Passage; Vegetation.

BIBLIOGRAPHY

Mircea Eliade provides a thorough discussion of the many different beliefs and practices that involve sacred trees in *Patterns in Comparative Religion* (New York, 1958). Eliade places religious belief associated with trees into seven categories. Clifford Geertz's *The Religion of Java* (New York, 1960) describes the syncretism of Hindu, Muslim, and folk beliefs that constitutes Javanese religion. Geertz's book is noteworthy for its discussion of ritual objects made from trees. Victor Turner's seminal treatment of the African milk tree in *The Forest of Symbols: Aspects of Ndembu Ritual* (Ithaca, N.Y., 1967) is an insightful and extensive consideration of a dominant symbol in Ndembu culture, the mudyi, or sacred tree. Turner explores the ritual use of trees in life-cycle rites of passage.

M. N. Srinivas has provided an important contribution to the understanding of Hindu beliefs about sacred trees, especially their role in rituals of the life cycle, in *Religion and Society among the Coorgs of South India* (London, 1952). A. R. Radcliffe-Brown provides an account of the religious beliefs in the powers of trees and the rituals associated with them as found among the people who live on a chain of islands extending from Burma to Sumatra in *The Andaman Islanders* (1922; 3d ed., Glencoe, Ill., 1948). In *Argonauts of the Western Pacific* (1922; New York, 1953) Bronisllaw Malinowski provides a fascinating account of the beliefs and rituals that surround the use of trees among the Trobriand Islanders.

The use of trees as discussed in Buddhist scriptures is presented by Ananda K. Coomaraswamy in *Elements of Buddhist Iconography* (1935; New Delhi, 1972). The mixture of Roman Catholic and Mayan beliefs is explored in Evon Z. Vogt's *Zinacantan: A Maya Community in the Highlands of Chiapas* (Cambridge, Mass., 1969). This is an extensive study of the Tzotzil-speaking Indians of Guatemala and includes a full account of their religious beliefs and the importance of sacred trees. Douglas Sharon's *Wizard of the Four Winds: A Shaman's Story* (New York, 1978) contains some encapsulations of North American and Mesoamerican cosmologies, including beliefs about sacred trees. Sharon's treatment of Mesoamerican shamans' use of trees as a source of power is noteworthy. Mircea Eliade's *Shamanism: Archaic Techniques of Ecstasy,* rev. & enl. ed. (New York, 1964), also provides an insightful discussion on the relationships between shamans and the cosmic tree.

One of the best discussions of the interrelationship between spirit, soul, God, and elements of nature is found in E. E. Evans-Pritchard's *Nuer Religion* (New York, 1977). Neil G. Munro's *Ainu Creed and Cult* (London, 1962) neatly describes the Ainu belief in ramat (spirit or soul), which inhabits trees, and the sacred and magical qualities ramat passed on to the ritual objects made from trees.

New Sources

Aburrow, Yvonne. *The Enchanted Forest: The Magic Lore of Trees.* Milverton, U.K., 1993.

Altman, Nathaniel. *Sacred Trees.* San Francisco, 1994.

Brosse, Jacques. *Mythologie des Arbres.* Paris, 1989.

Caldecott, Moyra. *Myths of the Sacred Tree: Including Myths from Africa, Native America, China, Sumeria, Russia, Greece, India, Scandinavia, Europe, Egypt, South America, Arabia.* Rochester, Vt., 1993.

Gifford, Jane. *The Wisdom of Trees: Mystery, Magic, and Medicine.* New York, 2000.

Goelitz, Jeffret. *Secrets from the Lives of Trees.* Boulder Creek, Calif., 1991.

Karas, Sheryl Ann. *The Solstice Evergreen: History, Folklore, and Origins of the Christmas Tree.* 1990; reprint, Fairfield, Conn., 1998.

Martin, Laura C. *The Folklore of Trees and Shrubs.* Guilford, Conn., 1992.

Pamela R. Frese (1987)
S. J. M. Gray (1987)
Revised Bibliography

TRENT, COUNCIL OF.

TRENT, COUNCIL OF. Also known as the nineteenth general council of the Roman Catholic Church, this council opened on December 13, 1545, and closed on December 4, 1563, after twenty-five formal sessions. The road to Trent, long and tortuous, passed through Constance, Basel, and Pisa. The cry for a sweeping reform of the church from top to bottom—"reformatio capitis et membrorum"—had been raised one hundred years before Luther posted his theses. It continued to ring out through the fifteenth century, accompanied more often than not by the insistence that serious reform could be achieved only within the framework of a general council. Basic to this coupling of reform and council was the widespread conviction that the papacy was incapable of or unwilling to put right the tangle of abuses that threatened to smother the ecclesiastical life of Christendom. Indeed, it was argued by many that the popes' chronic misuse of their dispensing powers, particularly with regard to the appointment to benefices, was the root cause of those abuses.

The demand for a council became the standard rhetoric not only of churchmen but also of princes and statesmen. Conciliar preeminence assumed doctrinal status in many of the best universities in Europe and found its way into a thousand pamphlets, treatises, and broadsides. Preachers thundered the message from their pulpits, and echoes were heard in busy chancelleries no less than in silent Carthusian charterhouses. No pope could be elected until he had assured the cardinals in conclave that he would summon a council within a year or two of his coronation.

Such were the shock waves loosed at the Council of Constance (1414–1418). The questions addressed there were at once constitutional, procedural, and moral. With whom or what lies ultimate authority within the church? The monarchical concept of the papal primacy had taken its classical form in the days of Gregory VII (d. 1085), had pressed its brief even further under the great lawyer popes of the thirteenth century (e.g., Innocent III, d. 1216, and Clement IV, d. 1268) and, scarcely checked by the extravagances of Boniface VIII (d. 1303), had reached a kind of practical hegemony, at least in fiscal affairs, at Avignon (1305–1376). But the protracted scandal of the Western Schism (1378–1417), when two and then three rival "popes" competed for the allegiance of Christendom, brought the notion of papal monarchy into severe disrepute, just as the solution of the crisis by a general council convened at Constance under the aegis of the German emperor enhanced the idea of conciliar superiority. The council's deposition of the three squabbling claimants, its election of a successor (Martin V, 1417–1431), and its solemn decree, *Sacrosancta,* all combined to stake out a constitutional position: a general council, representative of the emperor and other Christian princes, the learned elite of the universities, the experts in canon law, and the college of bishops, acted for the whole church, of which the pope was a functionary, albeit an exalted functionary.

The decree *Frequens,* which called for such a council to be held every ten years, concerned itself with the procedural problem. *Frequens* presumed the doctrine of *Sacrosancta.* Since final and decisive authority belonged to the council, the pope's position was that of chief executive or prime minister responsible to the council, which therefore had to meet frequently. The conciliar movement of the fifteenth century based itself on these grounds. Due partly to the temper of the time, that movement did not succeed. The secular counterparts of the aristocratic ecclesiastical assemblage the conciliarists had in mind were in retreat everywhere in Europe and, in most places, on the eve of dissolution. Ambitious dynasts were in the process of bringing the powers to tax, to maintain military establishments, and to appoint government personnel under their own bureaucratic control, and thus reducing and even eliminating the prerogatives of the great medieval parliaments. It was unlikely that the church, the first great Western institution to adopt this centralizing model, would have reversed direction in favor of a polity that was demonstrably anachronistic.

But there were other, more proximate causes for the collapse of the movement, not least the tendency of the conciliarists to quarrel among themselves. The popes, for their part, ignored the doctrine of *Sacrosancta* and evaded the provisions of *Frequens.* A council was indeed convoked at Basel in 1431, but it soon fell out with the pope, who withdrew from it and convened a more tame assembly under his own presidency at Florence. The rump council continued to meet at Basel until 1449, when it broke up into bitterly contending factions. After that, conciliar rhetoric sounded increasingly hollow, especially when engaged in by secular rulers who routinely invoked the threat of a council as a device to influence papal policy in Italy. So the conciliar movement died a lingering death, its last gasp coming at Pisa in 1511, when the king of France, in league with a dissident minority of the college of cardinals, summoned a council whose declared purpose was to strip the pope, the king's bitterest political enemy, of his office. This *conciliabulum* did not survive the French military reverses of the following year.

The effective end of the movement, however, did not put a quietus to the theory. The teaching of *Sacrosancta* continued to flourish in university circles, notably at the Sorbonne. Nor did those who rejected *Sacrosancta* necessarily repudiate *Frequens* as well. The two decrees had doubtlessly been wedded in the minds of the fathers of Constance, but as the century wore on a distinction between them was often drawn by those who, while not prepared to admit the constitutional superiority of the council, nevertheless believed that only a council could bring about meaningful reform.

The moral issue raised at Constance went unresolved for a hundred years. There had occurred a kind of spontaneous reform of the members in some places—the Devotio Moderna in the Netherlands, a florescence of mysticism in England and Germany, an evangelical revival in northern Italy, a dedication among the educated classes everywhere to the scholarly endeavors of Christian humanism. But these were hardly more than specks upon a dark sea of clerical illiteracy, popular superstition, jobbery, and pastoral neglect. The belief was almost universal that such abuses perdured because the Curia Romana, the pope's own administration, permitted and even encouraged them. Curial fees, taxes, and charges proliferated, most of them designed to allow what traditional law and common sense declared to be perilous to the life of the church. The members would never be properly reformed, it was said, unless the head were reformed too.

The Renaissance popes, whose lifestyles and political ambitions were hardly calculated to inspire confidence, stubbornly refused to put their houses in order or to permit any other organ of the church to do so. They tried to keep to the high ground of constitutional theory. The papal primacy, they argued, was a datum of divine revelation that they were pledged to defend as they had received it. They also declined to have any outside agency oversee and most likely interfere with the workings of their own court, the central bureaucracy of the church. Reform of the Curia, they proclaimed, was the business solely of the supreme pontiff.

Whatever the theoretical value of this argument, the trouble with it was that the supreme pontiffs, themselves products of the curial system, were clearly not prepared to go beyond platitudes and gestures in correcting the colossal financial chicanery that corrupted the various papal departments and that reached a stunning climax in the election and pontificate of Alexander VI (r. 1492–1503). Since Constance, the conviction that everything was for sale in Rome—offices, judgments, indulgences, dispensations from the law—had grown, not lessened, and the poison of simony seeped down through the whole body of the church. Julius II did indeed summon a council in 1512, largely as a counter to the French-sponsored gathering at Pisa, but the meanderings of the Fifth Lateran Council (1512–1517) produced reform decrees that were no better than scraps of paper and that served merely to confirm the cynical mistrust of the papacy's moral resolution.

The popes' highest card in this game of stalemate was the reluctance of even fervent conciliarists—aside from a handful of academics—to challenge the doctrine of the Petrine office. But the year that saw the conclusion of the futile Fifth Lateran Council was also the year of the ninety-five theses. By 1520, Luther declared himself ready to jettison the papacy if that institution obstructed the full flowering of the gospel as he understood it. And Luther soon proved he was no effete intellectual but the leader of a potentially vast popular movement. Over the next decade the character of the debate about a council was drastically altered. As early as 1523, the German estates, gathered in the Diet of Nuremberg, called for "a free Christian council in German lands." Here was conciliarism with a new twist. Now, besides the old clamor for a council to reform ecclesiastical abuses, there came the demand from a growing constituency in northern Europe for a reform of dogma as well.

The Council of Paul III. The pope who had to contend with this new situation, Clement VII (r. 1523–1534), avoided it as best he could, and though he paid lip service to the conciliar idea, he was as obstructive as his predecessors had been. His successor was cut from a different cloth. Alessandro Farnese, who upon his election assumed the name Paul III (r. 1534–1549), had long been a champion within the Curia of a reform council, and he had carefully distanced himself from Clement VII's duplicitous policy in this regard. Not that Farnese had the credentials of a reformer. His youthful career—Alexander VI had made him a cardinal when he was twenty-six—had revealed many of the more seamy features of the Renaissance papal court. In his middle years he had undergone something of a religious conversion, which, though it did not eradicate all the bad habits of his past, led him at least to a greater earnestness and gravity of purpose. Never a moral zealot himself, he signaled his good intentions by promoting men of genuine probity and even holiness to high ranks and, most of all, by immediately moving to fulfill his pledge to summon a general council.

From the beginning of Paul III's initiative, everything seemed to work at cross-purposes. For a council to succeed, both great Catholic sovereigns—the German emperor and the king of France—had to support it, but they were bitterly at odds with each other. The emperor, Charles V, pressed for a council of reconciliation to bring peace to Germany, which meant a council to correct abuses, to satisfy the *gravamina* of the German estates against the Curia, with as little attention as possible paid to divisive doctrinal issues. Francis I wanted no council at all, because religious unrest in Germany, which discomfited his Habsburg rival, was much to his liking. Had Paul III had his way, he would have preferred a council over which he could keep careful watch, a kind of "Sixth Lateran," which would emphasize doctrine and, with a preponderance of bishops from the Papal States in attendance, protect the prerogatives of the Curia. But he knew he had no chance for that, and so he proposed what appeared to be the next best scenario. Mantua was a petty Italian city-state whose duke was vassal to the emperor; on June 2, 1536, the pope, ignoring the unanimous advice of his cardinals, summoned a general council to convene at Mantua the following May and ordered all the bishops, abbots, and other prelates of the whole world to appear there.

Immediately obstacles sprang up all around him. The duke of Mantua demanded a large papal army to garrison the town. The Protestants promptly declined to attend because of the presence of this hostile force, and then, when security arrangements were altered to meet their objections, they refused anyway. The king of France also refused to participate or to allow any French prelates to do so. The emperor, pointing out how Francis I had connived with the Lutheran princes and even with the Turks, urged Paul III to join him in an assault upon the French and thus guarantee a successful council. The war duly broke out in 1536, but without the pope, who shrank from a step that might have provoked Francis into following the schismatic example of Henry VIII and that at the same time might have contributed to eliminating the only check upon Habsburg power, which he feared as much as the French king did. Instead, the pope postponed the Mantuan council twice, then translated it to Vicenza, postponed it again, and finally, in 1539, suspended it altogether.

The failure was more than a disappointment. It tended to sustain the view—not only among Protestants—that this pope was no more serious about reform than his predecessors had been. Paul III did not help his cause much by the simultaneous campaign he was carrying on—in the best Renaissance style of his first mentor, Alexander VI—to make a ruling dynasty of his children and grandchildren. The Farnese did indeed become dukes of Parma, but only at the cost of diminishing further the pope's limited fund of goodwill. Even so, whatever Paul III's flaws of character, lack of persistence was not one of them. The intricate diplomacy involved in the conciliar enterprise never really ceased, even when the distrustful emperor turned to another tack and urged a conference of leading theologians, Protestant and Catholic, who could discuss all the religious discontents and find solutions to them. The pope cooperated in this venture, but the distinguished participants in the Colloquy of Ratisbon, which occupied most of the summer of 1541, failed to reach a meeting of minds. Any hope of religious reunion was fast slipping away.

The pope responded by returning to his conciliar project. With the assent of the somewhat chastened emperor, he formally announced the opening of a general council for November 1, 1542. The site this time was Trent, a small italianized town northwest of Venice that was nevertheless an imperial free city and thus juridically "in German lands." But the earlier pattern of delay, postponement, and obstructiveness by Francis I and outright rejection by the Protestants, quarrels between pope and emperor, and intermittent warfare between France and the empire was bitterly repeated. Not until December 13, 1545, did Paul III's council finally begin in the Cathedral of Saint Vigilius in Trent. The process had consumed eleven years and had produced only thirty-four voting participants. It was no wonder the mood was somber throughout the Mass of the Holy Ghost and the formal reading of the bull of convocation, which reminded the fathers that their solemn task was to heal the confessional split, to reform those abuses that sullied Christ's body, and to promote amity among Christian princes.

Those princes, though their influence over the council was enormous, did not participate directly in its decision making, nor did anyone else outside the higher clergy. In its procedure Trent was more akin to the papal councils of the high Middle Ages than to Constance or Basel. Franchise belonged only to the "fathers" of the council, that is, to the bishops present—not their proctors—and to the generals of the mendicant orders. The presiding officers were the legates appointed by the pope. They were empowered to set the agenda, although each bishop was free to request inclusion of any proposal he pleased. This arrangement met with few serious difficulties once the basic compromise between the pope's and the emperor's positions was accepted: that matters of dogma and matters of reform would be treated simultaneously.

The work schedule followed a consistent pattern. It began with a "particular congregation," at which theologians and canonists would discuss the draft of a particular decree. The fathers formed the audience for these technical expositions. Then, meeting alone in a "general congregation," they debated the matter themselves until they reached agreement upon a final text. A "session" was a public meeting at which that text was read out, formally voted upon, and promulgated at the council's decree. Since it was thought to have a liturgical as well as a juridical significance, a session was always convened in the cathedral or some other church. Between

1545 and 1563 the Council of Trent held twenty-five sessions, of which seventeen were substantive in the sense that they were occasions for the proclamation of doctrinal definitions and reform legislation, while the rest were ceremonial affairs.

The first particular congregation met on February 20, 1546, to examine Luther's assertion of *sola scriptura.* On April 8, at the fourth session, the council declared that apostolic traditions, "which have come from the mouth of Christ or by the direction of the Holy Spirit and have been passed down to our own times," deserve to be accepted by believers "with as much reverence *[pari pietatis ac reverentia]"* as scripture itself. The fifth session, on June 17, renewed earlier conciliar legislation setting up structures for the theological training of the parochial clergy and placed upon bishops and pastors a stern obligation to preach to their flocks every Sunday and holy day. On the dogmatic side this session issued six "canons," terse condemnatory statements on the Pelagian as well as the Lutheran view of original sin.

Then began the most protracted debate of the council, devoted to the central Lutheran doctrine of justification. The first draft of a decree on this controversial subject was submitted to the fathers on July 28 and promptly rejected. For the next seven months the arguments raged through forty-four particular and sixty-one general congregations, until finally an acceptable text was hammered out and promulgated at the sixth session, on January 13, 1547. There was nearly unanimous assent to the sixteen chapters of the decree and the thirty-three canons, which repudiated Luther's view of justification by faith alone. But there was no such unanimity when the next great issue of reform was introduced. The fathers and their theologians wrangled through the succeeding months over the requirement that bishops reside in their dioceses. When the proposed decree was presented the first time, only twenty-eight fathers out of a total grown by early 1547 to sixty indicated their agreement by voting *placet.* The divisions over the matter were so deep that it had to be set aside for later consideration. The seventh session, on March 3, 1547, therefore contented itself with asserting a bishop's right to supervise parishes in his diocese administered by members of religious orders. The dogmatic decrees of the same session defined the nature of the sacraments, fixed their number at seven, and asserted their effective spiritual power *(ex opere operato).* The doctrine of baptism and confirmation was also treated in detail.

Meanwhile, in the midst of all this intellectual labor, various discontents revealed themselves. Trent was a small town with limited accommodations. Its location made it a difficult place to supply with provisions, and its climate was harsher than the southerners in attendance were accustomed to. Many of the fathers complained of the discomfort in which they were forced to live. During the summer of 1546, fighting between the emperor and the Smalcald League surged close enough to the city that dissolution of the council was seriously contemplated. This danger passed away, only to be replaced by a typhus epidemic that broke out in the vicinity early in 1547 and that caused the council to translate its deliberations to Bologna (eighth session, March 11, 1547). The emperor was furious at what he considered the pope's maneuver to bring the council under his direct control by removing it to a city in the Papal States. Fourteen imperialist bishops remained in Trent, but the majority of the fathers went dutifully off to Bologna, where they labored through intense debate in both particular and general congregations on the rest of the sacraments, the sacrificial character of the Mass, purgatory, veneration of the saints, and monastic vows—all doctrinal issues raised by the Protestant reformers. But Paul III allowed no formal sessions or decrees, lest he push the angry emperor too far. The significance of the Bologna phase of the council, until its suspension on February 16, 1548, proved to be the use to which its work was put when the council assembled again at Trent three years later.

The Council of Julius III. Giovanni Maria del Monte, who had been senior legate during the first phase of the council, was elected pope in February 1550 and took the name Julius III. Immediately he came under pressure from the emperor to reconvene the council and, specifically, to get on with the business of reform. The new pope faced many of the same political problems as his predecessor, and it was in the teeth of strong resistance from the German Protestant princes and the new king of France, Henry II, that the council reopened at Trent on May 1, 1551. The fifty or so fathers did little serious work before the end of the summer, but thanks to the deliberations at Bologna they were ready at the thirteenth session, on October 11, to issue a decree on the Eucharist that in eight expository chapters and eleven canons reasserted the traditional dogma of the real presence as well as the mechanism of transubstantiation. Six weeks later, at the fourteenth session, the sacraments of penance and extreme unction received doctrinal definition. The landmark character of these dogmatic decisions, however, was not matched by the reform legislation passed in the thirteenth and fourteenth sessions. Directives about rights and duties of bishops with regard to their clergy, and regulations governing procedures in ecclesiastical courts, did not, as the council's critics were quick to point out, strike at the roots of the accumulated abuses.

At the beginning of 1552 a faint flicker of hope for reunion flared up and then quickly died out. On January 15, ambassadors and theologians from several Protestant states, having come to Trent under a safe-conduct, appeared at the council's fifteenth session. But their brief presence only served to demonstrate that the confessional divisions could no longer be healed or that at any rate a council managed by the pope and already committed to *traditio* no less than to *scriptura* as a font of revelation could never be an instrument of reconciliation.

So the fathers returned wearily to their own debates, now treating of the sacrament of orders and the sacrifice of the Mass. The congregations dragged on inconclusively into the spring, as the emperor went to war yet again with the German princes allied with France. This time he was badly defeated, and when he fled to nearby Innsbruck the fathers at Trent decided it was too risky to remain there. They used the sixteenth session, April 28, 1552, to adjourn the council *sine die.* Julius III, at heart an indolent and self-indulgent man, made no effort through the rest of his pontificate to revive it. His successor, Paul IV (1555–1559), was fiercely determined to effect reform, but he had no patience for conciliar ways and preferred instead to impose doctrinal and moral purity by liberal use of the inquisition, of which he had once been head. This policy was an utter failure, as indeed was Paul IV's whole reign, and when the cardinals entered the conclave of 1559 the scandal of an unfinished council cast a long shadow over it.

THE COUNCIL OF PIUS IV. The conclave of 1559 lasted more than three months, and the pope who emerged from it, Pius IV (Giovanni Angelo de' Medici), was committed to bringing the Council of Trent to a satisfactory conclusion. The obstacles he encountered in persuading the Catholic powers to take up the conciliar enterprise once again were different but hardly less daunting than those Paul III and Julius III had had to face. The Peace of Augsburg (1555) and the Treaty of Cateau-Cambresis (1559) had indeed removed for the time being the threat of war that had so plagued the earlier stages of the council. But the Catholic monarchs—three of them, now that Charles V had departed the scene and had divided the Habsburg territories between his brother, Ferdinand I, and his son, Philip II of Spain—were deeply at odds over the crucial problem of whether the council Pius IV formally convoked (November 29, 1560) was to be a continuation of the former one or an entirely new undertaking. France, now troubled as Germany had been for a generation by a growing and aggressive Protestant faction, joined the imperialists in demanding a new council unencumbered by any decisions arrived at earlier. The king of Spain conversely insisted that the work begun before be allowed to run its course. The pope agreed with this view, though he dared not say so publicly. Instead he adopted a policy of studied ambiguity, confident that once an assembly had been lured back to its original site the problem would solve itself. After months of the most convoluted diplomacy, this tactic succeeded. On January 18, 1562, some 113 fathers gathered at Trent—their number would ultimately swell to 277—and implicitly accepted continuation by deciding to resume deliberations at the point at which they had been suspended ten years before.

By March the council had returned to the discussion of episcopal residence and found itself mired once again in argument. Everyone agreed that bishops should reside in their dioceses and that their widespread failure to do so was a fundamental cause of corruption in the church. But was the requirement one of divine law or ecclesiastical law? This seemingly abstract question had vast implications, because if residence were an obligation *jure divino,* it could mean that bishops exercised their office independently of the pope. A vote on April 20, revealed that the fathers were divided almost evenly on the subject. Tempers ran so high that the legates managed to calm the situation only by postponing discussion of the question until a later date. Dogmatic deliberations meanwhile continued, and at the twenty-first session (July 16, 1562) the council defined the sacrificial character of the Mass and the whole presence of Christ in each of the eucharistic species of bread and wine. The disciplinary decision as to whether the laity should be allowed to share the chalice—something taken seriously by the emperor and by Germans generally—was referred to the pope for implementation after the council.

Next on the agenda came discussion of the sacrament of orders, which involved once more the thorny issue of episcopal residence. By autumn the council had reached an impasse. No formulation, however ingenious, could budge the determination of either side. The winter of 1563 arrived, and then the spring, and still no resolution was in sight. The conciliar machinery ground to a halt, and after ten months of wrangling, the breakup of the council appeared imminent. Then, in early March, the senior legate suddenly died, and Pius IV replaced him with Giovanni Cardinal Morone. This proved to be the decisive intervention.

Morone, the ablest papal diplomat of the century, recognized that behind the arguments advanced by the proponents of *jus divinum* lurked the conviction that the papacy intended no real reform. He moved swiftly to defuse this radical mistrust, especially in the minds of the emperor and the king of Spain, by guaranteeing that a sweeping reform schema, blessed in advance by the pope, would be proposed to the council in short order. Employing a variety of formal and informal commissions, and playing skillfully upon the vanity of the heretofore unpredictable French delegation, Morone put the council back to work again. When the emperor expressed misgivings, Morone went off to Innsbruck to reassure him; when the pope hesitated to support his program, Morone threatened to resign. At the twenty-third session, on July 15, 1563, the council approved his first package of reform legislation. Perhaps its most important provision was the directive to establish a system of seminaries to provide intellectual and moral training for the parochial clergy. As for the conciliar crisis at hand, Morone evaded the insoluble problem by ignoring it. "It is a divine precept that the pastor know his flock," the decree began, but, though strictly obliging bishops to reside, it did not try to define the basis of that obligation. Moreover, cardinals were explicitly included in the requirement, and thus was struck down one of the worst and most resented of the abuses, the accumulation of benefices by officers of the Curia.

The logjam broken, there followed a hectic summer and autumn of congregations dealing with a flood of reform ideas. The whole clerical estate was refashioned during these months. Morone moved easily through all the factions, the pope's man indeed but the council's man too, always urging accommodation, compromise, the practical attainment of the goal of restoring spiritual primacy to the workings of the church. Special emphasis was placed upon eliminating the chaos in ecclesiastical administration which had opened the door to so many abuses. Morone spared little time for theoretical discussion; the question of indulgences, for example, which had occasioned the Lutheran reformation, was settled not in a dogmatic decree but in a reform decree. This also was the case with the veneration of the saints and relics. The council indeed defined the sacramentality and the indissolubility of matrimony, but it was even more intent on suppression of clandestine marriages. Statistically the achievement was prodigious: three times as much reform legislation was passed by the council during Morone's brief legateship than in all the sessions before him combined.

By the twenty-fourth session, on November 11, 1563, the end was finally in sight. The last session, at which all the conciliar decrees since 1545 were to be formally promulgated, was scheduled for December 9. However, news from Rome that Pius IV was severely ill led Morone to move the date forward. Therefore, the twenty-fifth session was held on December 3 and 4, 1563, when each of the 229 fathers gave his *placet* to all the work the council had done over its eighteen years of life. A *Te Deum* was sung, and tearful fathers embraced one another, in many cases embracing those with whom they had often violently disagreed.

SEE ALSO Boniface VIII; Gregory VII; Innocent III; Luther, Martin; Papacy; Reformation.

BIBLIOGRAPHY

The official collection of Tridentine decrees is *Canones et decreta, Concilii Tridentini* (Rome, 1564), many times reprinted, now to be found most conveniently in the volume edited by Giuseppe Alberigo and others, *Conciliorum oecumenicorum decreta* (Bologna, 1972). Relevant documents can be found in *Concilium Tridentinum: Diariorum, actorum, epistularum, tractatuum; Nova collectio,* 13 vols. (Freiburg, 1901–1967), an immense deposit and an indispensable tool of research.

The two classic studies are Paolo Sarpi's *L'istoria del Concilio Tridentino* (1619), 3 vols., edited by Giovanni Gambarin (Bari, 1935); and Sforza Pallavicino's *Storia del Concilio de Trento* (1656–1657), 3 vols., edited by Mario Scotti (Turin, 1968). The polemical camps trace themselves back to either Pallavicino, a defender of the council, or to Sarpi, an attacker of it.

The definitive history of the council has now been written: Hubert Jedin's *Geschichte des Konzils von Trient,* 4 vols. in 5 (Freiburg, 1949–1975), the first two volumes of which have been translated into English by Ernest Graf as *A History of the Council of Trent* (London, 1957–1960). Jedin also published many monographs on Trent, including *Girolamo Seripando,* 2 vols. (Würzburg, 1937), translated into English (but without the full scholarly apparatus) as *Papal Legate at the Council of Trent, Cardinal Seripando* (Saint Louis, 1947); and *Krisis und Abschluss des Trienter Konzils, 1562–63* (Freiburg, 1964), badly translated as *Crisis and Closure of the Council of Trent: A Retrospective View from the Second Vatican Council* (London, 1967).

A useful survey of ecclesiastical history during the time the council was sitting is Leon Cristiani's *L'église à l'époque du Concile de Trente,* "Histoire de l'église," no. 17 (Paris, 1948). Special studies of note include *Il Concilio di Trento e la Riforma Tridentina,* 2 vols. (Rome, 1965), a collection of distinguished essays by a panel of international scholars; Dermot Fenlon's *Heresy and Obedience in Tridentine Italy* (Cambridge, U.K., 1972), on Italian humanism and its import upon reform; James A. O'Donohoe's *Tridentine Seminary Legislation: Its Sources and Its Formation* (Louvain, 1957); and Wolfgang P. Fischer's *Frankreich und die Wiedereröffnung des Konzils von Trient,* 1559–1562 (Münster, 1973), on the resumption of the council after the death of Paul IV. On the diplomacy during those crucial few years, H. Outram Evennett's *The Cardinal of Lorraine and the Council of Trent* (Cambridge, U.K., 1930) is still useful, as is Gustave Constant's *La légation du Cardinal Morone prés l'empereur et le concile de Trente, avril–décembre, 1563* (Paris, 1922), a collection of documents and commentary. The best analysis of the council of Pius IV is Robert Trisco's "Reforming the Roman Curia: Emperor Ferdinand I and the Council of Trent," in *Reform and Authority in the Medieval and Reformation Church,* edited by Guy F. Lytle (Washington, D.C., 1981).

MARVIN R. O'CONNELL (1987)

TRIADS, groups or sets of three persons, things, or attributes, are found in many concepts of the divine. Because triads involve an uneven number they have been considered to be perfect expressions of unity and proportion, corresponding to a threefold division in nature or to images of the nuclear family.

In Indian mythology, the *Ṛgveda* suggests a threefold classification of its many divinities into gods of heaven, air, and earth. In its prayers three chief gods represent the powers of these natural elements: "May Sūrya [sun] protect us from the sky, Vāta [wind] from the air, Agni [fire] from the earthly regions" (10.158.1). Agni, god of fire and messenger to the gods during fire sacrifice, took three forms, as the sun in the sky, lightning in the aerial waters, and fire on earth. Commentators on the Vedas considered that the number of gods could be reduced to three, Agni, Vāyu, and Sūrya being considered as sons of the lord of creatures, Prajāpati.

A famous dialogue in the Brāhmaṇas and Upaniṣads asks how many gods there are. In reply, a traditional invocatory formula in a hymn to all the gods is quoted as indicating three hundred and three and three thousand and three. Further questioning reduces these figures to thirty-three, six, three, two, one and a half, and finally one, and that one is *brahman* (*Bṛhadāraṇyaka Upaniṣad* 3.9).

In the same Upaniṣad, Prajāpati is said to have had three kinds of offspring—gods, humans, and demons—who lived with their father as students of sacred knowledge. Each class of beings asked for a divine word, and to all Prajāpati gave the same reply: *dā.* This word was like the rolling thunder, *dā, dā, dā.* Each interpreted the word according to its own needs, and three definitions resulted: self restraint, giving, and compassion (*Bṛhadāraṇyaka Upaniṣad* 5.2). This concept was used by T. S. Eliot in the closing lines of *The Waste Land:* "then spoke the thunder. . . ." Eliot ended with another threefold borrowing from the Upaniṣads: "Shantih Shantih Shantih" ("Peace, peace, peace").

The Upaniṣads refer to three *guṇas*, strands or qualities that characterize all existing beings. These qualities are goodness or purity (*sattva*), passion or force (*rajas*), and darkness or dullness (*tamas*). The *Maitri Upaniṣad* affirms that in the beginning the three qualities were differentiated within the supreme self: "That One become threefold." This supreme self (*brahman*) is indicated by the sacred syllable *oṃ,* with which every recitation of the Veda begins. The sacred syllable divides itself threefold, for *oṃ* consists of three units: /a/, /u/, and /m/. *Aum* is the sound form of this being, and "one should worship it with *aum* continually" (*Maitri Upaniṣad* 6.3–4). A later description of *Brahman* was *satcit-ānanda,* or *saccidānanda:* being, intelligence or consciousness, and bliss.

In the *Bhagavadgītā,* goodness, passion, and darkness are declared to be the strands or qualities that spring from nature, binding the embodied self although it is changeless. But the world was deluded by these three strands and did not recognize that they come from God alone, that they are in him but he is not in them. God is higher and eternal. Because nature is the uncanny power of God, all elements must ultimately derive from him (*Bhagavadgītā* 7.12–13).

TRIMŪRTI. In Hindu mythology and popular theology many gods appeared, though Viṣṇu and Śiva (Rudra) became dominant. Early in the common era a *trimūrti* ("having three forms") was proposed that created a triad of these two and a creator, Brahmā. These three were regarded as forms of the neuter absolute *brahman,* or corresponding to the three *guṇas* of the Absolute. The epic *Mahābhārata* tells of these gods separately and not as a unity, and when the Trimūrti concept appeared its exposition varied according to the preferences of the writers for one or another deity.

A story in the *Bhāgavata Purāṇa* says that there was once a dispute among the gods as to which member of the triad was greatest. The sage Bhṛgu went to each of them in turn to decide the matter by tests. First he saw Brahmā but omitted to bow to him, whereupon the god blazed out in anger. Next he visited Śiva and did not return the god's salutation, so that Śiva raised his trident (*triśūla*) to destroy him; the sage was spared only by the intercession of Śiva's wife. Lastly Bhṛgu called on Viṣṇu, found him asleep, and woke him with a kick on the chest. Instead of becoming angry, Viṣṇu begged the sage's pardon for not having greeted him and said that he was highly honored by the kick, which had left an indelible mark on his breast, and that he hoped the sage's foot had not been hurt. Bhṛgu decided that Viṣṇu was the mightiest god because he overcame his enemies with weapons of gentleness and generosity. This Vaiṣṇava story indicates the diversity and rivalry of different sects and the problems of a triad.

It was debated whether the three gods were equal or had interchangeable functions. Each in turn might be the Supreme Lord, Parameśvara, and take the place of the others. The poet Kālidāsa, in his *Kumārāsambhava* (2.4ff.), expressed his adoration for the Trimūrti unified before creation but afterward divided in three qualities, proclaiming its threefold glory as "knower and known, priest and oblation, worshiper and prayer." These verses inspired Emerson's poem *Brahma* and its line "I am the doubter and the doubt, I am the song the Brahmin sings." But rather than teaching the equality of three persons in one God, Kālidāsa seems to have been addressing the personal Brahmā as the supreme god, despite his use of the term *Trimūrti.*

For the Vaiṣṇava believer Brahmā was an emanation of Viṣṇu, a demiurge or secondary creator; he is described in the vision of the *Bhagavadgītā* (11.15) as sitting on a lotus throne emerging from the body of Viṣṇu, the god of gods, a scene illustrated in many paintings. Whatever his former status, Brahmā has long since declined in popular esteem. His temple at Pushkar in Rajasthan is said to be one of only two in India, though this is difficult to verify in such a vast land with innumerable shrines. At Pushkar the temple of Brahmā has four black faces, supposedly directed at the four cardinal points though three of them face the worshiper. A *lingam* of Śiva nearby also has four human faces carved on it, no doubt to show affinity with Brahmā. But in popular religion in most of India today Brahmā has virtually disappeared, while Viṣṇu and Śiva have vast followings. (The two groups are considered almost as distinct religions.) The third most popular cult today follows the great goddess Mahādevī, the all-pervading power *śakti,* known under many names and notably today as Kālī.

A famous sculpture of the Trimūrti dating from the fifth to eighth centuries CE is in the Great Cave on Elephanta Island near Bombay. It is a massive stone bust nineteen feet high, with three faces each four or five feet long. This figure represents Śiva, who is the dominant deity among the sculptures in these caves. The eastern face is Rudra the destroyer, the front is Brahmā the creator, and the western face is Viṣṇu the preserver. All three are regarded as aspects of the character of Śiva, and all show the impressive serenity that marks representations of divine activity.

Early students of Hinduism in the West often considered that parallels exist between the Trimūrti and the Christian doctrine of the Trinity, and attempts were made to apportion common functions to the three persons in one God. There are still writers who call Brahmā, Viṣṇu, and Śiva "the Trinity," but the parallel with Christianity is not close, and the Trimurti concept never became popular or embodied an orthodox and catholic creed. Hindu writers and artists tended to favor one god of the three, and Viṣṇu and Śiva came to dominate in their own schools.

TRIKĀYA. In Indian Buddhism there were triadic concepts from an early date, and some that developed in Mahāyāna Buddhism and outside India showed parallels to Chinese triads. The Three Refuges (*triśaraṇa*), or Three Jewels (*triratna*), appeared in Buddhism at an early date. In the Tripiṭaka, or "Three Baskets" of scripture, the invocation of these refuges is attributed to the first lay believer in the Buddha. Recited every day in Theravāda Buddhism by the laity as well as by monks, the Triple Refuge is a simple affirmation of trust in the central objects of religion: the Buddha, the Dhamma or doctrine, and the Sangha or monastic order. The formula reads thus: "I go to the Buddha for refuge, I go to the Dhamma for refuge, I go to the Sangha for refuge." The Buddha is credited with saying that whoever trusts firmly in the virtues of the Three Jewels has "entered the stream," has set out on the way to enlightenment.

In the development of Buddhism the term *yāna* ("vehicle, means of progress") was used to indicate a way of attaining enlightenment. The Mahāyāna claimed to be the "one vehicle" (*ekayāna*), and its followers called their opponents Hīnayāna, followers of a "lesser vehicle." But, occasionally, more tolerant texts spoke of the major ways as *triyāna,* "threefold means."

Mahāyāna Buddhist philosophy wrestled with the problems of the absolute and the relative and of one or many Buddhas. A solution was found for philosophy in the doctrine of the *trikāya* ("three bodies"). This was expressed in essence in the *Laṅkāvatāra Sūtra* and developed by the Yogācāra school. According to this theory the body of the Buddha is threefold. The *dharmakāya* ("doctrine body or essential body") is self-existent and absolute, the same for all Buddhas. It supports the other two bodies, for ultimately only it exists. The *sambhogakāya* ("bliss body or communal body") is the channel through which the Buddhas communicate with *bodhisattvas* in the heavens. This notion was used to interpret texts that describe many Buddhas preaching to assemblies of *bodhisattvas* and gods in all the universes, while at the same time they had passed away to *nirvāṇa.* The *nirmāṇakaya* ("transformation body") is that by which the Buddha works for the good of all creatures, including the historical Buddha, who appeared on earth, and in other existences, and then passed away into *nirvāṇa.*

The *trikāya* doctrine sought to reconcile different expressions of the nature of the Buddha. In early texts the *dharmakāya* was simply the body of doctrine; once the Buddha had died, he existed thereafter in the doctrine. In popular beliefs the Buddhas were many, and they continued to exist in a state of bliss to hear the prayers of worshipers. Buddhist art from Gandhara to Japan often grouped three Buddhas or *bodhisattvas* together, the individual personages differing according to the environment. Parallels that have been drawn between the *trikāya* doctrine and the Christian teaching of the Trinity are strained and unproved. The Chinese triads appear to have been separate developments, although in popular religion triads of gods may be confused with several Buddhas.

THREE PURE ONES. Chinese speculations on a divine Triad and its representation in worship may have developed from Daoist philosophical notions of an original unity that produced diversity. In the Dao de jing 42 (fourth to third century BCE?) it is declared that "Dao produced the one, the one produced the two, the two produced the three, and the three produced the ten thousand things." This is not unlike an idea in the *Chāndogya Upaniṣad* (6.2) of one neuter being that entered into three divinities to produce the many. However, Arthur Waley in his translation of this verse rendered it thus: "Dao gave birth to the One, the One gave birth successively to two things, three things, up to ten thousand" (Waley, 1934, p. 195).

The concept of an inseparable triad of Heaven, earth, and man became popular in Chinese thought. Philosophers aimed at formulating systems that would deal with all questions concerning the divine, natural, and human worlds, so that all human activity might be in harmony with divine and natural orders. Such a system of knowledge and behavior was set out in the *Lüshi Chunqiu* (Spring and Autumn Annals of Mr. Lü), a work by various hands early in the common era. The book is in three sections, representing the triad of Heaven, earth, and humanity. The first section is in twelve chapters, the number associated with Heaven. The second is in eight chapters, the number associated with earth. The third is in six chapters, the number associated with man. Each chapter indicates actions appropriate for each season, stating that if humans fail to perform them properly they will cause disturbances in nature and bring calamity from Heaven.

Perhaps early in the common era, popular Daoist religion developed the worship of a triad, the Three Ones, Sanyi. It has been suggested that the concept of three celestial persons derived from Christian influence, although it is rather early for that to have happened unless some Christian ideas had filtered through via gnostic speculations. It is more likely that the idea of a religious triad developed from philosophical notions of diversity arising from unity, or that philosophical and religious concepts developed independently and were merged by priests who claimed authority for three deities worshiped as one.

An ancient Daoist divinity was Daiyi, the Grand Unity, introduced into official worship during the Han dynasty as the greatest of all gods, above the five legendary emperors. The Grand Unity became the personification of the Dao, as the Dao emanated itself into creation, a triad developed that controlled the whole universe. To the Grand Unity were added Dianyi, the Heavenly Unity, and Diyi, the Earthly Unity. It is strange that Diayi, the original all-embracing unity, was egarded as one of three. It seems more natural for Diayi to have been conceived as three in one, but there was great complexity in the multiplication of Daoist deities. From the second century of the common era Daoist liturgies spoke of the Great Mysterious Three in One, Taixuan Sanyi comprised the Sagely Father, the Lord and Master of the Human Spirit, and the Pivot of All Transformations. The Daoist imagination peopled the universe with a great variety of gods, natural forces, and deified heroes, forming a heavenly hierarchy, under the presiding supreme triad that controlled the universe like a state bureaucracy.

In the Daoist triad the three gods were said severally to control time past, present, and to come. By the Sung dynasty the triad of Three Pure Ones had become associated with chronological functions. The Precious Heavenly Lord, the First Original Heavenly Venerable One, controlled time past; some have compared him to the Father in the Christian Trinity. The Precious Spiritual Lord, the Great Jade Imperial Heavenly Venerable One, controlled time present; scholars have compared him to the Son. The Precious Divine Lord, the Pure Dawn Heavenly Venerable One appearing from the Golden Palace, controlled time to come; scholars have compared him to the Holy Spirit. Joseph Needham wrote that "there can be little doubt that the Taoists [Daoists] had intimate contact with Nestorian Christians at the capital during the T'ang dynasty. The really interesting question is where their trinity came from eight centuries previously" (*Science and Civilization in China,* Cambridge, 1956, vol. 2, pp. 158–160).

Whether there was a Christian influence or not (Nestorian missions did not arrive in China until the seventh century at the earliest), there was abundant contact between Daoism and Buddhism, which from the first century established itself as one of the three great ways of Chinese religion. Buddhist triadic concepts could be found in the *trikāya* doctrine, or in the concept of the Dhyāni Buddhas, which were regarded as personifications of creative aspects or manifestations of a primordial Ādi-Buddha. In popular Buddhist religion there were triads of Buddhas, such as Śākyamuni (Gautama), Amitābha of the Pure Land, and Maitreya, the Buddha to come. Another triad comprised the mythical Avalokiteśvara, Mañjuśri, and Samantabhadra, who have been worshiped in temples and pagodas in China and neighboring lands down to modern times, often alongside Daoist gods.

Laozi, the great saint of Daoism and the supposed author of the *Dao de jing,* was often assimilated to the Three Pure Ones. Influenced by Buddhist teachings on multiple Buddhas and *bodhisattvas* and the various incarnations of the Buddha, the Daoists came to espouse similar beliefs. Laozi was said to have been born before heaven and earth appeared and to have experienced numerous later births. Like the Buddha, he became an object of worship.

In Japanese Shintō the first verse of the *Kojiki* names three gods who all came into existence at the time of the beginning of heaven and earth. Later gods of storm, sea, and fire were grouped in threes, notably the storm god Susano-o no Mikoto, who was considered under three aspects ("three-treasure-rough-god"). The supreme sun goddess, Amaterasu, when asked for permission to erect a great Buddhist statue at Nara, is said to have identified herself with Vairocana, a member of a Buddhist triad, the personification of truth and purity.

The Shintō *kami* were regarded either as *avatāras* of the Buddhas (from the Buddhist point of view) or as their originals (from the Shintō point of view). Chinese triadic influences appeared in Japanese symbolism, as in paintings with three parallel curves and three or more flamelike signs, which were taken as symbols of the soul. A characteristic Shintō symbol is the *tomoe,* which is chiefly found in groups of three in the crest of many shrines. The *tomoe,* three pear-shaped sections of a circle, is often associated with the Chinese *yin* and *yang,* the two pear-shaped halves of a circle indicating complementary opposites, such as heaven and earth, male and female. The threefold *tomoe* is found even in the great Shintō shrine center at Ise, though this site is said to have been kept free from foreign influences.

HYPOSTASES AND FAMILIES. Triadic concepts can be traced in the ancient Mediterranean world, though not as clearly, with the exception of Egypt, as in India and China. Plato in the *Republic* (book 4) distinguished two elements in human nature, the rational and the irrational or lustful, not unlike the Indian *sattva* and *tamas.* But he found himself obliged to distinguish a third element, the spirited or passionate, similar to the Indian *rajas.* When there is a division between rational and irrational, the spirited should array itself on the side of the rational. The three elements in man, according to Plato, correspond to the social classes of guardians, auxiliaries, and producers. These were not unlike Indian classes or priests, warriors, and merchant farmers, although Plato's classes served different functions. Individuals and societies are wise when the rational element prevails, as when *sattva* prevails in Indian thought. They are courageous because of the spirited element, and they are temperate when the rational element governs with the consent of the other two, producing balance and harmony.

The Greeks wrestled with the problems of the divine nature and action in ways different from those of the Indians or Egyptians. In the *Timaeus* Plato proposed an account of the universe. The world came into being as a living creature endowed with soul and intelligence by the providence of God; the world is an image of what is eternal and true, a reflection of the changeless; the ultimate truth is God the creator. This was a unitary view, though Christian theologians later found a foreshadowing of the Trinity in the *Timaeus,* even from its first verse, which simply said, "One, two, three, but where is the fourth of my guests?"

There was more triadism in Neoplatonic teachings of three primal hypostases, a favorite theme of Christian theologians. Plotinus claimed that earlier Greek philosophers had established three degrees of reality, the primary realities or hypostases. These were represented triadically as the Good or the One, the Intelligence or the One-many, and the World Soul. These three are in the very nature of things, and they are also in human nature, so that our individual soul is something divine, possessing intelligence, and perfect.

In popular Greek religion various gods were grouped together, as, for example, Demeter, Kore, and Dionysos. Demeter, the corn goddess (Lat., Ceres), had an early double, Kore, who in time was regarded as her daughter, Kore or Persephone (Lat., Proserpina). Demeter's search for Persephone in the underworld was a vegetation myth represented in the Eleusinian mysteries under the symbol of the growing seed that assures a happy future life. Dionysos was also a fertility god; his mystery flourished in the Hellenistic age when Christianity was expanding.

The Etruscans had a triad of gods—Tinia, Uni, and Menerva—who presided over the destinies of towns and were identified by the Romans with their Capitoline triad of Jupiter, Juno, and Minerva. In Rome the flamens (priests or sacrificers) were led by three major and twelve minor priests. The three major priests were the *flamen Dialis* (of Jupiter), the *flamen Martialis* (of Mars), and the *flamen Quirinalis* (of Quirinus). These gods of the triad were invoked in formulas of devotion recited before battle, on receiving spoils, and when sanctifying treaties. Jupiter represented the sky-universe, like the celestial gods of Greece and India, and his priest was preeminent. Mars was the god of war, and months and festivals were named after him. Quirinus was a god of Sabine origin, but little is known of him except that his functions resembled those of Mars and his flamen formed the third of the threesome with those of Jupiter and Mars. The triad of Jupiter, Mars, and Quirinus was later overshadowed by the triad of Jupiter, Juno, and Minerva. A great new temple was dedicated to the latter three on the Capitoline hill in Rome in 509 BCE, the first year of the republic; inside was a statue of Jupiter.

Among the many gods of the ancient Western world, the clear examples of triads are found in Egypt and Mesopotamia. One reason for the concept of triads in Egypt, and no doubt in other lands, was the fusion of the cults of different places. When a victorious ruler brought several towns under his dominion, they would be subject to both political and religious control. New gods encountered local deities whose worship could hardly be suppressed. A simple solution for the conqueror and his priests was to admit the gods of the vanquished into general worship, without giving them too much independence. Neighboring gods joined the principal deity, the patron of the city. Thus at Heliopolis the local god Atum was joined with the lion pair Shu and Tefnut from the nearby town of Leontopolis. At Memphis there was a triad of Ptah, Sekhmet, and Nefertum. At Elephantine was a triad of Khnum, Sati, and Anukis.

However different the gods might have been originally, the ancients regarded them as members of a divine family, taking the roles of father, mother, and son. But the coincidence of different family relationships in the mythologies of the merging cults could cause confusion, as when the father became the son of his wife, or the mother the wife of her son.

The most famous triadic divine family of ancient Egypt was that of Osiris, Isis, and their son Horus. Osiris was a very popular god, whose cult flourished throughout Egypt from prehistoric times. In the texts Osiris was said to have been killed by his brother Seth, though according to one tradition he was drowned. The body of Osiris was divided into several parts and was sought and embalmed by his wife Isis, who became pregnant by the dead god. Isis gave birth to Horus, who avenged his father by killing Seth and reigning as successor to Osiris. This complicated mythology was recorded most clearly by Plutarch in the beginning century of the common era. Fundamental to the myths of this divine triad were the death and resurrection of Osiris, his place as a nature god, and his role as a model for earthly rulers. These myths provided links with both gnostic and Christian teachings.

Egyptian priests refined their ideas of the divine triads from early anthropomorphic myths to more abstract conceptions. Thus the god Ptah had two of his faculties, heart and tongue (spirit and word), personified under the visible forms of the gods Horus and Thoth. Or the family associations became the union of three spiritual aspects of the same god: his supreme intelligence, active spirit, and creative word. Or God was conceived of as three persons animated by the same will, like the founders of the towns of Thebes, Heliopolis, and Memphis. Re was the thinking head of this triad, Ptah its body, and Amun its invisible intelligence. This was not far from the Neoplatonic doctrines of a God who comprised intelligence, mind, and reason.

In Mesopotamia there were triads of deities organized according to the elements of heaven and earth. The high god Anu ruled in the sky, Enlil inspired the wind or storm and was god of the land, and Enki or Ea ruled the waters or abyss on which the world rested. The positioning of the deities varied over time. For instance, Enlil was once regarded as the first of the triad, though from the beginning of the second millennium BCE he was regarded as second. Another triad of Babylonian deities was composed of the moon god Sin, the sun god Shamash, and the storm god Adad. The popular goddess Ishtar was associated with both this and the previous triads, ousting colorless figures with whom they had earlier been associated. She was connected also with the ancient Sumerian god Tammuz, a vegetation deity like Osiris who descended into the underworld where Ishtar went to seek him. The return of Osiris and Ishtar in the spring brought joy and fertility.

Of the surviving religions of Semitic origin, Judaism and Islam rejected triadic notions of the godhead, while Christianity developed them. The Hebrew Bible was strongly monotheistic, although traces of female elements in the deity can be discovered, as when Jeremiah revealed that incense had been offered to the queen of heaven in Jerusalem and the cities of Judah (*Jer.* 44:17). Scholars have noted that there was goddess worship among Hebrew emigrants at Elephantine in Egypt. In a more abstract way *Proverbs* 8 and 9 referred to wisdom personified as the female companion of God before and during creation, a notion akin to the Logos doctrine of the Fourth Gospel. In the Qabbalah sexual imagery was used to describe the love of God for the Shekhinah, a sacred union of king and queen. But in general, Jewish teaching was alien to dualities or triads.

Islam was even more adamant, attacking the Christian doctrine of the Trinity, or what it considered that to be. Thus the Qurʾān exhorts, "Do not say, Three. Refrain, it will be better for you. God is only one God" (4:169). And again, "Surely they have disbelieved who say: 'God is one of three.' There is no god but one God" (5:77). Orthodox Christian doctrine did not say God was one of three, though no doubt the doctrine could be perverted in that way in popular use. Any suggestion of a divine family, of God begetting or procreating, or having a partner associated with him, was repugnant to Islam. Thus in the Qurʾān Jesus was credited with denying that he said, "Take me and my mother as two gods apart from God" (5:116). This was quite proper, and belief in the unity and absoluteness of God was fundamental to Islam. Some writers have pointed out that Islamic theology alludes to diversity in the divine nature through "the most beautiful names of God" (*al-asmāʾ al-ḥusnā*); these many attributes and titles are recited on prayer beads in popular devotion. And theologians have discussed the eternity of the Qur'an, which was held to be uncreated, almost like a divine hypostasis. In Islamic art the name of God, *Allāh,* may be seen written three times in the prayer niche in mosques, but the main current of Islam has been against both triad and trinity.

Christian doctrine developed, against an Old Testament background, from devotion to Christ, but as it developed it came into contact with triadic concepts of the divine from Egypt and the Near East. Belief in a divine family emerged, for the concepts of Father and Son were in Christianity from the beginning. The Holy Spirit was regarded as the third hypostasis in the Trinity, but it was often a vague or neglected notion. With the growth of the cult of the Virgin and Mother the female side of a triad seemed guaranteed. If Mary had been called God the Mother, like Isis, she would have completed a divine family. In popular religion that might have happened, but trinitarian theology was anchored in the Bible, and Christian teachings developed from those scriptures that gave a threefold baptismal formula and a triadic blessing. As with other religions, the threefold doctrine is best understood in its historical context, however attractive seeming cultural parallels may be.

See Also Numbers; Trinity.

Bibliography

Useful general introductions to Indian and Chinese thought, with selections from texts, are available in *Sources of Indian Tradition* (New York, 1958) and *Sources of Chinese Tradition* (New York, 1960), compiled by Wm. Theodore de Bary and others. A. L. Basham's *The Wonder That Was India,* rev. ed. (New York, 1963), ranges over Indian history and society but devotes its longest chapter to religion, and Robert C. Zaehner's *Concordant Discord* (Oxford, 1970) speculates about Chinese triads and other doctrines of the divine nature. Joseph Needham's great series on China has been usefully abridged in *The Shorter Science and Civilisation in China* (Cambridge, 1978) with chapters on Daoism and Confucianism. Of the many books by Edward Conze on Buddhism perhaps the best introduction is *Buddhism: Its Essence and Development* (Oxford, 1951), although *Indian Buddhism,* by Anthony K. Warder (Delhi, 1970), has fuller accounts of both Theravada and Mahayana primary sources. Arthur Waley's *The Way and Its Power* (London, 1934) is a classic that has been reprinted many times, although other translations need to be compared with it, and Holmes Welch's *The Parting of the Way: Laozi and the Daoist Movement* (London, 1957) gives more information on Daoism in general. Short, useful introductions to the major religions of ancient Greece, Rome, Egypt, Mesopotamia, and indeed of Asia as well, are provided in my *Man and His Gods* (London, 1971), reprinted with slight changes as *An Illustrated History of the World's Religions* (London, 1983).

Geoffrey Parrinder (1987)

TRICKSTERS

This entry consists of the following articles:

AN OVERVIEW
AFRICAN TRICKSTERS
NORTH AMERICAN TRICKSTERS [FIRST EDITION]
NORTH AMERICAN TRICKSTERS [FURTHER CONSIDERATIONS]
MESOAMERICAN AND SOUTH AMERICAN TRICKSTERS

TRICKSTERS: AN OVERVIEW

Trickster is the name given to a type of mythic figure distinguished by his skill at trickery and deceit as well as by his prodigious biological drives and exaggerated bodily parts. The myths of many cultures portray such a comic and amoral character, who is sometimes human but is more often animal in shape, typically an animal noted for agility and cunning: the wily coyote, the sly fox, the elusive rabbit, or the crafty spider. Sometimes the trickster is the agent who introduces fire, agriculture, tools, or even death to the human world. As such, he plays the part of another mythic archetype, the transformer, or culture hero, who in a mythic age at the beginning of the world helps shape human culture into its familiar form. However, the trickster's distinction lies not so much in his particular feats as in the peculiar quality of his exploits—a combination of guile and stupidity—and in the ludicrous dimensions of his bodily parts and biological drives. In those cultures where he stands independent of other mythic figures, his adventures are recounted in a separate cycle of myths and lore.

The trickster represents a complicated combination of three modes of sacrality: the divine, the animal, and the human. Myth relates that the trickster existed in the early times when the world was still taking shape and was inhabited by supernatural beings. As one of these important supernaturals, the trickster possesses extraordinary powers more divine than human. He frequently thwarts the supreme being's creative intentions. In one North American Indian myth, for example, the Winnebago trickster Wakdjunkaga scatters all living creatures across the face of the earth with an enormous fart, which leaves them laughing, yelling, and barking. This is an ungracious parallel to the Winnebago's solemn account wherein Earthmaker creates a quiet and static world order in which each species remains in a separate lodge. The trickster may assume an even more active role on the mythic stage in the absence or weakness of a supreme being. However, there is no need to pair the trickster in a dualism with the supreme being in order to understand his unique character.

The trickster is remarkable for the carnality that he shares with humans and animals. In his case, however, bodily functions and features are extreme: voracious appetite, insatiable lust, stupendous excretions, cosmic flatulence. He reorders (or has reordered for him) his bodily parts: His head may be fastened to his bottom, or his penis to his back. The trickster is usually male, but he often assumes female form in order to conceive and give birth. His (or her) most conspicuous bodily parts are passages (mouth, nostrils, anus, ears, vagina) and members that bridge or penetrate those passages (e.g., head, penis, or, in the case of the spider figure, the filament with which he spins his web). The trickster's appetites cannot be exhaustively explained in terms of the biology of sex or the physiology of hunger. He craves modes of being other than his own: animal, plant, and so on.

On a grand scale, the trickster mimics human needs, drives, and foibles, especially the imperfections of an ambitious but flawed intelligence. He often fumbles his tricks, and his mishaps lead to a comic apotheosis of wit into wisdom. The nature of his deception is especially complicated: a pretended ignorance and a pretended cunning. The irony of his maladroit trickery is so pervasive that one cannot decide whether the trickster is really ignorant or whether he is so clever that he successfully exculpates himself by pretending to be stupid. Reflections on his nature call into question the deeper nature of reality in an imperfect and changing world of the senses. By his duplicity, the trickster would have one believe that he intends his elaborate schemes to fail so that benefits might arise from catastrophe.

Ironically, it is just in his animal-like biological constraints and imperfections of intelligence—the human frame of meaning—that the trickster affirms a sacrality different from that of divine immortals. This sensate sacrality of foibles stumbles into other sacred realms with penetrating burlesque. For these reasons, trickster stories have been called a mythology of incarnation, and he a symbol of the human condition. The religious dimension of comic figures in folk literatures and dramas is often illumined by comparison with the strictly mythic personality of the trickster found in sacred texts relating the beginnings of the world.

The trickster parodies all pretensions to perfection. He mocks the gods, institutional religious figures, the techniques of humans, and himself. By poking fun at anything that parades as permanent, important, or impermeable, he exposes a penetrable (i.e., accessible, comprehensible) reality. In the process of penetrating it, he reveals the sacrality both of passage and of mundane flaw. He images the process of the religious imagination itself, which sees to it that human beings experiment with the sacred and which sometimes leads not to the serenity of faith in a static, eternal paradise but to an exciting, unpredictable turmoil of the senses in sacred music, dance, and sexuality. The trickster represents not a mystical contemplation of the singular but a sensuous appreciation of multiplicities and contraries.

As the trickster flounders toward a sacred life rooted more in carnate being than in divine being, ambiguity, irony, change, and humor fill the emptiness caused by the *kenōsis* of immortality. The trickster unites things by passing them through the senses and the imperfect reflections of his intelligence. His bodily parts and "all too human" intelligence admit no firm distinction between corporeal and spiritual existence. His exorbitant and active penis offers him access to realms of reality in which he ought properly to have no business. His (or her) bodily passages become the loci where worlds meet, come together, and even pass through and interpenetrate one another. Wherever he appears, the trickster enacts the human comedy as a sacred drama, displaying the ironic condition of a limited mind served by limited senses but with an unlimited desire to relate to the realms of meaning around it.

BIBLIOGRAPHY

The best overview of general interpretations of the trickster is chapter 1 of Robert D. Pelton's *The Trickster in West Africa: A Study of Mythic Irony and Sacred Delight* (Berkeley, Calif., 1980). For psychological interpretations that now appear overdependent on developmental models without consideration of religious depth, see three essays in Paul Radin's *The Trickster: A Study in American Indian Mythology* (1956; reprint, New York, 1969): C. G. Jung's "On the Psychology of the Trickster Figure," Karl Kerényi's "The Trickster in Relation to Greek Mythology," and Radin's title piece. For an overview that makes healthier use of the social context of the trickster in interpreting its meaning, see Laura akarius's "Le mythe du 'Trickster,'" *Revue de l'histoire des religions* 175 (1969): 17–46. For an attempt to place the figure within the history of ideas, see Ugo Bianchi's "Pour l'histoire du dualisme: Un Coyote africain, le renard pâle," in *Liber Amicorum: Studies in Honor of Professor Dr. C. J. Bleeker* (Leiden, 1969), pp. 27–43. Angelo Brelich has done admirably by examining the uniqueness of the trickster vis-à-vis other mythical figures in "Il Trickster," *Studi e materiali di storia delle religioni* 29 (1958): 129–137. I have pointed to the kind of close reading of trickster texts necessary to disclose their full religious value in "Multiple Levels of Religious Meaning in Culture: A New Look at Winnebago Sacred Texts," *Canadian Journal of Native Studies* 2 (December 1982): 221–247. I have also drawn out the comic aspects of incarnate saviors and loutish literary figures in "The Irony of Incarnation: The Comedy of Kenosis," *Journal of Religion* 62 (October 1982): 412–417.

New Sources

Hynes, William J., and William G. Doty, eds. *Mythical Trickster Figures: Contours, Contexts, and Criticisms.* Tuscaloosa, Ala., 1993.

Kun, Mchog Dge Legs, Ldan Bkra Shis Dpal, and Kevin Stuart. "Tibetan Tricksters." *Asian Folklore Studies* 58/1 (1999): 5–30.

McNeely, Deldon Anne. *Mercury Rising: Women, Evil, and the Trickster Gods.* Woodstock, Conn., 1996.

Mills, Margaret. "The Gender of the Trick: Female Tricksters and Male Narrators." *Asian Folklore Studies* 60, no. 2 (2001): 237–258.

LAWRENCE E. SULLIVAN (1987)
Revised Bibliography

TRICKSTERS: AFRICAN TRICKSTERS

African tricksters speak and embody a vivid, subtle language of sacred transformation. Through it they strike up absurd conversations between laundresses and goddesses, sex and death, flatulence and spiritual power, breaking the univocal by the anomalous and so opening human life—bodily, daily, defined—to its sacramental immensity. Like their counterparts in Amerindian myth and folklore, African tricksters inject bawdiness, rebellion, and wild lying (one might aptly call it polymorphous perversity) into the mythic history and the common experience of divine-human relations wherever they appear. Unlike many tricksters elsewhere, however, these multiform world-shatterers and pathfinders in Africa are woven not only into the fabric of myth but also into the stuff of everyday life, playing a part in economics, rites of passage, and ordinary conversation. This observation may tell more about the history of Western colonialism and ethnography than it does about the tricksters of non-Westerners, but it does suggest that anyone who wants to know the trickster in Africa must study the particular ways and speech of many different African peoples.

Such study is only now passing into its second phase. Travelers, ethnographers, and, more recently, Africans themselves have studied hundreds of African societies. Trickster-like myths and stories have emerged from many of their reports, but only a few collections of trickster tales have been gathered and examined within the context of their social and religious settings. Rarely do we have the tales in their original languages, or in more than a single version, together with the indigenous commentary that would make deep translation and comparison more reliable. Nevertheless, these barest beginnings have already demonstrated that the transforming power of the trickster—what the Yoruba refer to when they say that "Ẹṣu turns feces into treasure"—works in the present as well as in the primordial past.

In the first place, Africans have delighted in using animal tricksters to shape their children's "moral imagination," as T. O. Beidelman (1980) has put it. He has analyzed the complex ways that the Kaguru use Hare, Hyena, and other animals as metaphors, partly for the surface rules and patterns of their life, but much more for the deeper intuitions and meanings that make them, the Kaguru, who they are. The Kaguru, like the Ashanti in their *anansesem* ("spider stories") and the Azande in their tales of Tore, the spider, understand that the intricate lies and outrages of their tricksters reveal the social order as sacred in its supple particularity. Too bawdy to be taken as cautionary fables, too confident of the unity between specific and ultimate aims to be reduced to sets of binary opposition, too attuned to animals' lives to use them univocally, these stories provide an education in wit. They insist that the core of human existence, a meeting place of every sort of force, is displayed by—not prior to, withdrawn from, or obliterated by—the twists of disease, the denial of hospitality, the crazed lens of sexual rivalry. Ananse is "wonderful" because he makes all multiplicity a symbol of the Ashanti oneness that exists here and now. Telling the trickster's stories, then, is an anamnesis. In displaying his power to dismember everything, a people celebrates its capacity for remembering its own way of being.

African trickster figures are images of an ironic imagination that yokes together bodiliness and transcendence, society and individuality. Ananse of the Ashanti, Mantis of the San, Ogo-Yurugu of the Dogon, and others contend with animals and gods, spirits and humans; they exploit every liminal space to claim all speech for human language. Thus the differences among these figures are as significant as their similarities. Indeed, the trickster in Africa shows by his witty juggling with meaning and absurdity that he is more accurately understood as a spectrum of commentaries on mythic commentary than as a "category." This epistemological playfulness seems to represent a sophisticated African form of religious thought. It is perhaps a commonplace to insist that in every system the order of the center and the wildness of the periphery are linked. It is a bold piece of spiritual logic to make this insistence a joke—or even more, a joking relationship.

Legba, the trickster god of the Fon, personifies such logic clearly. The youngest of the seven children of the female-male high god, Mawu-Lisa, Legba is her linguist. All who approach her, even the other gods, must first address him. His trickery provoked Mawu into distancing herself from the newly formed earth, and his unpredictable mediation reminds both gods and humans that autonomy requires the perils of relationship. Legba's phallic image stands before all Fon dwellings as a symbol that every passage reshapes the world; like Ananse, he reveals that each transaction releases a sort of anti-entropic energy that turns muteness into conversation, randomness into meaning.

Legba is the master of the Fon dialectic. Fon mythology has kept alive the memory of their historical adaptiveness, which enabled them to borrow liberally from the institutions of their neighbors (especially from the Yoruba, whose Ẹṣu-Ẹlẹgba inspired Legba). By grasping their history in mythic terms as well as in secular terms, the Fon have insisted that their assimilation of others' creations is both revelation and ingenuity, and their traditional order has delighted in elaborating the movement from dark, female inside to bright, male outside—and back again. The patterns of kingship and clan, the stages of inner growth, the interweavings of gods and nature, and even the structures of juridical process became images of the dual being of the high god, the bipolar principle of all life. In the intercourse between visible and invisible universes, Legba is the living copula. The Fon say that Legba, or Aflakete (a name meaning "I have tricked you"), "dances everywhere like a man copulating." He infuses cosmic dialectic into social order as the laughter he provokes becomes the sacramental sign that the male-female processes of Fon life are both human and transcendent.

The link between divination and the trickster represents a still deeper level of meaning that West Africans especially have found in him. The Yoruba, like the Fon (who have adopted much of the Yoruba system of divination, known as Ifa) and the Dogon, see their trickster god as the chief possessor of divination's language. Ẹṣu is a disruptive mediator, "the anger of the gods," who stirs up trouble to increase sacrifice, yet his quickness of eye and hand symbolizes a metaphysical slipperiness that makes him both sociotherapist and iconographer. At moments of conflict the meetings that create a world become collisions. Lines of connection break down, intersections turn into dead ends, and, as the myths say, all becomes as fluid as water, as destructive as fire. Divination seeks to transform these dead ends into thresholds of larger meaning; Yoruba divination particularly knows that to give answers to knotted social and spiritual questions is, finally, to redraw an *imago mundi*, to restore the shattered icon of the Yoruba cosmos. Ẹṣu is not the source of most divinatory responses, but he enables divination to run its course. Some depiction of him is carved into every divining tray, and that portion of the tray is always turned to the east, from which both light and darkness come. Ẹṣu brings confusion so that order may encompass the unencompassable. In their art and cities the Yoruba image the world that the relationship between sky and earth, Ọlọrun and Onile, with all their attendants and rituals, has brought into being. Lord of exchange in the market beginning and ending each Yoruba week, Ẹṣu reveals that the meeting of these beings creates human business, truly Yoruba ground. At every kind of crossroads Ẹṣu's mastery of interchange ensures that the design of this ground includes all movement—even explosion and decay.

The central figure of the vast spiral of correspondences that is Dogon life and myth is the tricksterlike Ogo-Yurugu. Created by Amma, the high god, to become one of the androgynous semidivine founders and overseers of life on earth, Ogo rebelled against his "father's" plan because he feared he would be deprived of his female twin. He seized part of his primordial matrix and sought to shape the world with its help. After a long struggle, Amma rendered him mute and put him to wander alone on the fringes of human society as Yuru-gu, the "pale fox," but his concupiscent itch, his desire to possess the source of fecundity, led his obedient male twin (Nommo) to offer himself to Amma as a sacrifice that brought the world as it is into being. The Dogon believe that Yurugu still speaks a revelatory, if twisted, word in divination and that his story is embedded in the human personality, especially in males. The navel bears witness to his premature separation from the divine womb; children resemble him in their play; the joking relationship between an adolescent boy and his maternal uncle's wife repeats the pattern of Ogo's quest for twinness; and funeral dances bear the traces of his mistaken celebration of victory over Amma. Ogo-Yurugu is a paradigm of Dogon irony, for his "going and coming" discloses that wholeness is an "achieved gift," one both won and bestowed: as man thrusts outward, he discovers the inner unity of personal individuation, social integration, and cosmic intelligibility.

The Dogon find Ogo-Yurugu within the soul and on the peripheries of life, in the present and in the farthest past, in solitary rebellion and in every relationship. Like Ananse, whose lies defeat Kyiriakyinnyee ("hate to be contradicted") and bring contradiction into Ashanti life, Ogo symbolizes the human imagination reaching everywhere to create worlds as filled with both order and meaning as language itself. The African trickster, then, teaches both dexterity and insight. His dance does not signify abandonment of either worship or intelligence; it signifies delight that the unsayable is quite precisely said in the never-final failures of this world's words. If, then, the realm of the sacred is shaped by human play as well as by divine work, so that the least fragment of life can become an icon of boundlessness, what could be more practical than learning how to imagine? And how could one better celebrate the meeting of transcendence and human wit than with sacred laughter?

See Also African Religions, article on Mythic Themes.

Bibliography

T. O. Beidelman has made an intensive study of trickster figures and their social meanings in the oral literature of the Kaguru. His important interpretive essay, which argues for a moral rather than an epistemological interpretation of the trickster, is "The Moral Imagination of the Kaguru: Some Thoughts on Tricksters, Translation and Comparative Analysis," *American Ethnologist* 7 (1980): 27–42. It includes a bibliography of his more than twenty-five articles on the Kaguru: collections and translations of tales, analyses of their significance, and other commentaries on Kaguru society. See also Beidelman's "Ambiguous Animals: Two Theriomorphic Metaphors in Kaguru Folklore," *Africa* 45 (1975): 183–200.

Other major collections of trickster stories are E. E. Evans-Pritchard's *The Zande Trickster* (Oxford, 1967), R. S. Rattray's *Akan-Ashanti Folk-Tales* (Oxford, 1930), Charles van Dyck's "An Analytic Study of the Folktales of Selected Peoples of West Africa" (Ph.D. diss., University of Oxford, 1967), and Melville J. Herskovits and Frances S. Herskovits's *Dahomean Narrative: A Cross-Cultural Analysis* (Evanston, 1958). Tales, divination verses, and analyses of Ẹṣu-Ẹlẹgba can be found in 'Wande Abimbola's *Ifa Divination Poetry* (New York, 1977); William Bascom's *Ifa Divination: Communication between Gods and Men in West Africa* (Bloomington, Ind., 1969); John Pemberton's "Eshu-Elegba: The Yoruba Trickster God," *African Arts* 9 (1975): 20–27, 66–70, 90–91, and "A Cluster of Sacred Symbols: Orisa Worship among the Igbomina Yoruba of Ila-Orangun," *History of Religions* 17 (1977): 1–28; and Joan Wescott's "The Sculpture and Myths of Eshu-Elegba, the Yoruba Trickster," *Africa* 32 (1962): 336–354. The major work on Dogon myth and life is that of Marcel Griaule and Germaine Dieterlen: *Le renard pâle*, vol. 1, *Le mythe cosmogonique*, pt. 1, "La création du monde" (Paris, 1965).

For a study of four West African trickster figures in their social and mythic settings, see my book *The Trickster in West Africa: A Study of Mythic Irony and Sacred Delight* (Berkeley, 1980), which concludes with a discussion of the theory of the trickster. For a comparative study of African and North American tricksters and an analysis of the trickster's role among the Azande, see Brian V. Street's "The Trickster Theme: Winnebago and Azande," in *Zande Themes*, edited by Andre Singer and Brian V. Street (Oxford, 1972), pp. 82–104. In addition to Beidelman's bibliography and the one in my book, see also that of Martha Warren Beckwith in her *Jamaica Anansi Stories* (1924; reprint, New York, 1969).

New Sources

Bennett, Martin. *West African Trickster Tales Retold by Martin Bennett.* New York, 1994.

Hyde, Lewis. *Trickster Makes this World: Mischief, Myth, and Art.* New York, 1998.

Hynes, William J., and William G. Doby, eds. *Mythical Trickster Figures: Contours, Contexts, and Criticisms.* Tuscaloosa, 1993.

Owomoyela, Oyekan. *Yoruba Trickster Tales.* Lincoln, 1997.

Schmidt, Sigrid. *Tricksters, Monsters and Clever Girls: African Folktales—Texts and Discussions.* Cologne, 2001.

ROBERT D. PELTON (1987)
Revised Bibliography

TRICKSTERS: NORTH AMERICAN TRICKSTERS [FIRST EDITION]

The most prominent and popular personage, generally speaking, in the varied oral traditions of the numerous Amerindian peoples living north of the Rio Grande is the figure known as the trickster. Although the trickster may be spoken of in the singular as a type, there are in fact many tricksters, of whom a great variety of stories is told across the North American continent. Some are purely tricksters, but the most significant and central mythic figure in many tribes is a trickster who is also the tribe's culture hero and the creator (usually by transformation) of the present world order. Sometimes he is the maker of the earth and its beings, or alternately the co-creator, often antagonistic to the principal creator.

With rare exceptions, North American tricksters are beings of the mythic age only; they are not believed to be living gods or spirits, and they have no cult (other than the semiritualistic narration of their stories). Their relationship to shamanism, the definitive religious form in most of the region, is debated. Tricksters' activities in myths often resemble shamans' journeys to the spirit world, but tricksters ordinarily employ no "helpers," and shamans do not seek help from "trickster spirits." Although a history of oral traditions can be only a matter of speculation, it appears that the trickster figure belongs to a very ancient stratum of Indian mythology, since certain universally disseminated motifs, such as the theft of fire and the origin of death, are regularly attributed to him.

The concept of the trickster as a type is based upon his most essential trait: his trickiness. Tricksters everywhere are deceitful, cunning, amoral, sexually hyperactive, taboo-breaking, voracious, thieving, adventurous, vainglorious—yet not truly evil or malicious—and always amusing and undaunted. Even though his activities are usually motivated by ungoverned desire, the trickster is capable of performing deeds that benefit others: releasing imprisoned game, the sun, the tides, and such; vanquishing and/or transforming evil monsters; and, like the shaman, journeying to the land of the spirits or the dead to rescue a lost loved one. The significant element in all these deeds is trickery. But the trickster's tricks are not considered evil: as a weak "animal-person" or mere human in a world of strange animals and spirit beings, the trickster must use strategy to survive. Moreover, as a being of insatiable appetites (for food and sex), he cannot afford the luxury of scruples. Thus he breaks incest taboos (rapes or marries in disguise his daughter or mother-in-law) and hoodwinks small animals into dancing with eyes closed so he can kill them. His overweening pride prevents him from asking for help, or from acknowledging it when he receives it, and leads him into countless misadventures. Often behaving like a fool and coming to grief, he reacts invariably with buoyant good humor, refusing to accept defeat. Nothing is sacred in his eyes: all holy institutions may be mocked or mimicked with impunity by the trickster. Shamanism, especially, seems parodied in such continent-wide stories as those of a trickster's flight with geese or on the back of a buzzard, ending in his crashing to earth, often being fragmented, and his laughing it all off as a big joke.

In addition to humorous trickster folk tales, which are remarkably similar all over North America, each region has its own set of traditions about the mythic age, and in a majority of instances the leading personage of that time was a trickster.

Raven is the dominant mythic figure all along the Alaskan and Canadian Pacific coast. Some tribes attribute to him the creation of the land (e.g., by dropping pebbles on the water), probably following a world flood. The central myth of the Raven cycle is about his theft of the sun, which was being kept in a box by a "powerful chief." Making himself a tiny particle in the drinking water of the chief's daughter, Raven contrives to be reborn as a baby in the chief's house.

He cries for the box and is given it, whereupon he resumes his raven form and flies away, bringing light to the world. (Theft of the sun is a mythic theme found over much of North America, attributed almost always to the principal trickster or to a group of animals headed by him.)

In the Plateau region of the northwestern United States, Coyote is usually regarded as the maker or procreator of the people, sometimes using the body of a river monster he kills, sometimes by cohabitation with trees after a flood. His principal cycle concerns his release of the salmon and his subsequent journey up the Columbia River, leading the salmon. He demands a "wife" at each village, and if his request is granted, he makes that place a good fishing spot. The cycle is prefaced with a tale of jealousy, lust, and deceit. Coyote, desiring his son's two wives, treacherously and magically causes his son to be taken into the sky world. Coyote pretends to be his son while the son in the sky is gaining supernatural powers, unbeknownst to Coyote. Later the son returns, reclaims his wives, and takes revenge by causing his father to fall into the river and be carried away. Thus Coyote arrives at the mouth of the river where the salmon are kept; by turning himself into a baby, he tricks the women who keep them and releases them to swim upstream.

In California and the Great Basin region, Coyote usually is involved in a dualistic relationship with a wise, benevolent creator (Eagle, Fox, Wolf, or an anthropomorphic figure). Set against the backdrop of a world flood (or fire), the earth is remade and repopulated by the two, with Coyote ordaining the "bad" things such as mountains, storms, and fruit growing out of reach. Coyote decrees death—and then his son is the first to die. So Coyote establishes mourning rites for people to "enjoy." He also decrees conception by sex and painful childbirth. Here and in the Plateau, where "spirit helpers" were commonplace in everyday life, Coyote too has his "helpers": two chunks of excrement that he voids when in need of advice, but to which he always replies, "Just what I was going to do anyway!"

The Paiute and Shoshoni of the Great Basin consider Coyote the progenitor of the people (through intercourse with a mysterious woman following the flood). But among the Pueblo, whose mythology centers on an emergence from the underground, Coyote plays a rather minor role in most tribes. The Navajo assign him a larger part than the others: he causes the flood that necessitates the emergence; then he scatters the stars in the sky haphazardly, ordains death, and establishes sex. On the Great Plains, Coyote is known primarily as a trickster only. Some northern tribes credit him with the recreation of the earth after the deluge, and the Kiowa consider themselves the people of Sendah, a Coyote-like figure, who led them out of a hollow log in the beginning. Inktomi ("spider") of the Lakota is very similar to Coyote, except in the unique esoteric traditions reported from the Oglala Lakota. Here he is a veritable "fallen angel," who caused the first human family to be banished from their subterranean paradise and who subsequently induced the whole human race to emerge onto the earth by making them think life here would be better. The Oglala are one of the few groups in North America who consider the trickster genuinely evil, and almost the only tribe that believes the trickster to be a living spirit.

Hare, the chief trickster in the poorly preserved traditions of the Indians of the Southeast, seems not to be implicated in the emergence-origin traditions of these tribes. Rather, he is a culture hero (stealing the sun, fire, and such; transforming monsters), and he is the bungling rival of the youthful "blood-clot boy," a pure hero type. Siouan-speaking peoples seem to have brought a tradition of Rabbit stories to the Great Plains when they migrated there from the Southeast. Their Rabbit or Hare is a precocious boy, living with his grandmother, who by his foolish and/or heroic deeds makes the world habitable, as it is today. He is not, however, credited with any demiurgic activities.

The Algonquins, inhabiting a large part of eastern and midwestern Canada, New England, and the area around the three western Great Lakes, have mythologies centered on anthropomorphic culture heroes who were also tricksters, though seldom foolish, plus several minor theriomorphic tricksters. The leading figures are Gluskabe in Maine, Tcikapis in northern Quebec, and Manabush and Wisakejak (various spellings) in the most westerly tribes. The few Tcikapis tales recorded show him a monster-killing dwarf, whose greatest exploit was the snaring of the sun. Gluskabe, Manabush, and Wisakejak have much in common: they live with their grandmother and younger brother, Wolf—who is abducted and killed by water monsters and must be rescued and revived by the hero. (A remarkably similar tale is told of Coyote and Wolf far to the west, in the Great Basin.) The myth has been elaborated in the esoteric traditions of the Midewiwin, a secret curing society of the western Algonquins. Some investigators report a vague belief that the hero of this myth lives now somewhere in the north. The neighboring Iroquois make no place for their trickster, S'hodieonskon, in their dualistic creation myth.

In some tribes humorous trickster tales are relegated to a category apart from the more serious "myths," but because all these narratives are set in "myth times," they are never confused with quasi-historical legends or accounts of shamanic experiences. Thus, to some degree, a quality of sacredness adheres to the person of the trickster everywhere, despite the seemingly profane nature of many of the narratives.

The oral traditions of North America present a variety of combinations of trickster traits with others (culture hero, demiurge, etc.); but all are reducible to the idea of a being who lives by his wits and his wit, who represents a mythical perception of man making his cosmos and finding a place within it.

SEE ALSO North American Indian Religions, article on Mythic Themes.

BIBLIOGRAPHY

The term *trickster* was coined by Daniel G. Brinton in his *Myths of the New World* (Philadelphia, 1868). The only serious study of the American trickster to have been published in book form remains Paul Radin's *The Trickster* (1956; reprint, New York, 1969), which contains important essays by C. G. Jung and Karl Kerényi. It is not, however, a general study of tricksters in North America, but is mainly about those of the Winnebago tribe. My article "The North American Indian Trickster," *History of Religions* 5 (Winter, 1966): 327–350, is based on an earlier work, "The Structure and Religious Significance of the Trickster-Transformer-Culture Hero in the Mythology of the North American Indians" (Ph. D. diss., University of Chicago, 1965), which is a study of the entire continent north of the Rio Grande. Edward H. Piper sees the trickster as basically a child figure in his psychological analysis, "A Dialogical Study of the North American Trickster Figure and the Phenomenon of Play" (Ph. D. diss., University of Chicago, 1975). Laura Makarius has written several articles on tricksters from various parts of the world, viewing the trickster as a taboo-breaking magician; on the North American trickster, see her study "The Crime of Manabozo," *American Anthropologist* 75 (1973): 663–675. Barbara Babcock-Abrahams has published an interesting anthropological study, "'A Tolerated Margin of Mess': The Trickster and His Tales Reconsidered," *Journal of the American Folklore Institute* 2 (1975): 147–186. A recent popular collection of trickster stories, without significant interpretation, is by Barry Holstun Lopez: *Giving Birth to Thunder, Sleeping with His Daughter: Coyote Builds North America* (Kansas City, 1977). See also the February 1979 issue of *Parabola* (4, no. 1), which is devoted to the trickster. For the texts of the stories, one must resort to the hundreds of volumes of reports of pioneer American anthropologists published by the Bureau of American Ethnology, the American Folklore Society, and other organizations.

MAC LINSCOTT RICKETTS (1987)

TRICKSTERS: NORTH AMERICAN TRICKSTERS [FURTHER CONSIDERATIONS]

These are exciting times for the trickster. As suggested above, the term *trickster* is used to describe a character that has "trickiness" as his main attribute and is adept at surviving by his "wits." Yet, absent from this description is any critical appraisal of the trickster concept. The comparative analyses of trickster types in varied American Indian cultural traditions often ignore the bias of the analysts. Indeed, some critics suggest that the trickster that we encounter when reading cross-cultural accounts is not the indigenous trickster, but the trickster through the eyes of the analyst. But even as scholarly accounts of tricksters were being debated, the trickster became, in the 1980s and 1990s, a paradigm for overturning accepted practices in the academic world. During the height of the postmodern movement in the humanities and sciences critics of the status quo invoked the name of Trickster to undermine and question accepted practices. Marginalized groups fighting to have their voices heard over the dominant discourse also adopted the trickster as a model. Ironically, contemporary American Indians witnessed the cooptation of their tricksters by everyone else and so began to employ trickster tactics themselves. True to the trickster's nature, the practice of trickster tactics of destabilization, irony, foolishness, and deceit became a contest of one-upmanship. The happy result is evident in current American Indian manifestations of the trickster, a figure that cannot be analyzed as a phenomenon rooted in a mythic past anymore. Trickster stories are still told with the same awe and laughter, but the trickster has become a model for action as well.

The kinds of actions engaged in by contemporary tricksters can in many ways be analyzed like the actions of the mythic trickster. On the one hand, there are actions that are foolish and lead to embarrassing consequences. On the other hand, there are actions that are creative and heroic and lead to community leadership and personal accomplishment. Examples of the foolishness of tricksters most often impart lessons relevant to day-to-day life situations. The conflict between personal wants and needs and the order and limitations of an impersonal social order leads to constant evaluations of what actions to take in relation to the costs the actions will exact. Will the trickster engaged in quotidian situations prompt foolish acts? Will the embarrassment of failure (or success) be acceptable or will it prevent action? Do the trickster stories compel one to act or prevent one from acting? It is in these debates over trickster actions and responses to the everyday that the importance of trickster stories for self-identity can be explored. By recognizing that contemporary peoples do not just enjoy trickster stories as a humorous tale set in the mythic past, but see in them a parable of actions and consequences that affect daily decisions, we begin to see that tricksters continue to have a high degree of salience for contemporary American Indians.

Can the trickster figure be said to have any religious or spiritual significance or efficacy in today's world? As stated above, tricksters' roles in religion and spiritually are continually debated. However, in acknowledging the creative influence that trickster figures have had in forming the landscape to make it suitable for human habitation we come closer to the spiritual nature of tricksters. Many examples in the earlier part of this article illustrate how tricksters of many cultural traditions have been responsible for preparing the world for humans. Tricksters have done so both consciously and unconsciously. In the end (of mythic time), the landscape has become the physical manifestation of all of trickster's activities. Be it the freeing of game, the leveling of mountains, the creation of waterfalls, the destruction of monsters, or the changing of proportions and countenances of animals, all these actions are embedded in the landscape and the cultural traditions of the native North Americans. For many American Indians the Native landscape is a sacred landscape, full of stories that reinforce their connections to this world as well as to the mythic world that existed before humans. These worlds are not separate, just as the trickster of the mythic time and world is not separate from today's world.

Trickster is not an object for analysis held at an objective distance, but tather serves as a model for survival. Many American Indian artists, writers, leaders, and community members use trickster tactics—and thereby embody the trickster—to negotiate social injustices, preservation of traditional values, and repatriation of self-identity and self-determination. Trickster, then, is alive and well in Native North America.

See Also Anishinaabe Religious Traditions; Cosmology, article on Indigenous North and Mesoamerican Cosmologies; North American Indian Religions, article on Mythic Themes.

Bibliography

The analysis of the trickster from non-Native perspectives and to serve non-Native purposes has been a part of the translation processes since trickster tales were recorded. Paul Radin's classic *The Trickster; a Study in American Indian Mythology. With Commentaries by Karl Kerényi and C. G. Jung* (New York, c1956; reprint, 1972) is an example from the perspective of psychoanalysis. Lewis Hyde would later follow with his cross-cultural perspective in *Trickster Makes This World: Mischief, Myth, and Art* (New York, 1998). The postmodern incarnation of tricksters as a mode of critique is clearly articulated in Donna Harray's "Situated Knowledges:The Science Question in Feminism and the Priviledge of Partial Perspective" in her *Simians, Cyborgs, and Women: The Reinvention of Nature,* (New York, 1991). A trickster mode of analysis for semiotics is also explicitly stated in C. W. Spinks's *Semiosis, Marginal Signs and Trickster: A Dagger of the Mind* (Houndmills, Basingstoke, U.K., 1991), and most recently in his edited volume *Trickster and Ambivalence: The Dance of Differentiation* (Madison, Wis., 2001). For discussions on trickster and marginal literature see Jeanne Campbell Reesman's *Trickster Lives: Culture and Myth in American Fiction* (Athens, Ga., 2001) and Jeanne Rosier Smith's *Writing Tricksters: Mythic Gambols in American Ethnic Literature* (Berkeley, 1997). In this same period, Native American writers and artists began to re-appropriate trickster discourses in their creative works. Gerald Vizenor's *Dead Voices: Natural Agonies in the New World* (Norman, Okla., 1992) is a novel that grapples with the trickster role in contemporary Native American oral traditions and his *Narrative Chance: Postmodern Discourse on Native American Indian Literatures* (Albuquerque, N. Mex., 1989) uses the postmodern appropriations of trickster discourse to re-present a native analysis of Native American literature. Native American artists were also exploring the possibilities of a revitalized trickster discourse in their creative works as discussed and presented in Allan J. Ryan's *The Trickster Shift: Humour and Irony in Contemporary Native Art* (Vancouver, 1999). More locally inspired trickster projects are embedded in larger cultural reinscription projects such as the Tlinkit project *Will the Time Ever Come?: A Tlingit Source Book,* edited by Andrew Hope III and Thomas F. Thornton (Fairbanks, 2000) and the Western Apache project described by Keith Basso in his *Wisdom Sits in Places: Landscape and Language Among the Western Apache* (Albuquerque, 1996).

Bernard C. Perley (2005)

TRICKSTERS: MESOAMERICAN AND SOUTH AMERICAN TRICKSTERS

The peoples of Mesoamerica and South America maintain lively traditions concerning a cunning and deceitful mythic figure, the trickster. Although tricksters are ludicrous rather than solemn beings, they cannot be discounted as trivial because their activities and transformations touch on religious issues. For instance, they steal fire, which is deemed the center of social and physical life, and their clever bungling frequently introduces death. They stir up such a riot of the senses with their playful conduct, that sex, food, and song become sacred emblems of incarnate life. The trickster's scheming prefigures human intelligence, which is based, ironically, on the realm of the senses.

Tricksters are usually animals that have bodies riddled with passages, or they may have excessively large orifices, any of which may be cut open or penetrated. The contemporary Huichol, who live in the Sierra Madre Occidental, in north-central Mexico, consider Káuyúumaari ("one who does not know himself" or "one who makes others crazy") one of their principal deities (Myerhoff, 1974). Káuyumarie is the animal sidekick of the supreme Huichol deity, Tatewari ("our grandfather fire"). Irreverent, clever, and amusing, Káuyumarie brought about the first sexual intercourse between man and woman. He guides pilgrims to Wirikúta, where the Huichol believe the beginning of time and the center of space are located, and where, as the Sacred Deer, he was dismembered. Pilgrims learn at Wirikúta that all paradoxes and contradictions—even the distinctions between deer, maize, and peyote—arise from the division of Káuyumarie's body (Myerhoff, 1974). The four directions are colored by his body parts, and these colors can be seen in flowers or in the visions induced by eating his flesh—the sacred peyote plant. The horns on Káuyumarie's head enable humans to penetrate the contradictions that make up human experience (Furst, 1976).

Tricksters distort sight and sound purely to create illusion and noise. The Aztec divinity, Tezcatlipoca ("smoking mirror"), uses an obsidian mirror to distort images. He was able to trick Quetzalcoatl, for example, into looking into the mirror in which Quetzalcoatl saw a repulsive and misshapen being. Tezcatlipoca in one of his assumed shapes is Huehuecoyotl ("drum coyote"), the puckish patron of song and dance, who was an ancient Chichimec divinity known for being a sly contriver (Brundage, 1979).

Extraordinary body designs or cross-sex dress, which the trickster sometimes manifests, is a way in which the contrary conditions of existence are mediated. In her study of Zinacantecan myth from the Chiapas Highlands of Mexico, Eva Hunt links contemporary female tricksters to the sixteenth-century goddess Cihuacoatl, a female deity with a tail, a fake baby, and a snake, which emerges from under her skirt and from between her legs. In the contemporary Cuicatec region and the Puebla-Nahuatl area of Mexico, she is embodied as Matlacihuatl, and she is also known as Mujer Enredadora ("entangling woman"). Her name derives from *maxtli,* a loincloth. Matlacihuatl is adulterous and promiscuous, and she specializes in seducing homosexual men. She is sexually anomalous, having a vagina at the back of her neck that opens like a mouth. If a man does seduce her, he will become pregnant and give birth to a child that looks like excrement (Hunt, 1977).

A female turtle is the trickster of the Desána people in southern Colombia. She constantly outsmarts primordial monkeys, jaguars (the dominant supernatural beings of the primordial age), foxes, deer, and tapir, using their body parts to her advantage; for example, she uses the leg bone of the jaguar as a flute.

Tricksters often opposed the dominant supernatural beings of their day and embarrassed or humiliated the divine patrons of priests, shamans, and other privileged religious specialists. For example, the Maquiritaré, Carib-speakers of Venezuela, tell of divine twins; Iureke revives his twin brother, Shikiemona, who has been fixed in the form of a fish by the Master of Iron. In an effort to save his brother, Iureke assumes the form of a kingfisher and covers his brother with excrement. When the Master of Iron washes Shikiemona clean, the water removes the excrement and revives the dying twin, and he swims away (Civrieux, 1980). Later, the twins destroy the supernatural jaguar by exploiting his will for power. "I want some wind. I need some power," the jaguar exclaims. So the twins trick him into swinging on a vine after eating a smelly agouti (a kind of rodent). The jaguar breaks wind, filling the air with a foul smell on a cosmic scale, and ultimately the jaguar is propelled to the end of the earth, where he lands with a bang and breaks all his bones.

In other myths tricksters steal various forms of life from the underworld. For example, the Sanumá (Yanoama) of the Venezuela-Brazil border region, tell of Hasimo, a mythic bird-man, who steals fire from a primordial alligator, which stores fire in its mouth, by shooting excrement into its face, forcing the alligator to laugh (Taylor, 1979).

Manipulation of flesh and of bodily openings and closings is a key stratagem of tricksters. Among the Waiwai of Venezuela, an old man, who is a known liar and master of disguise, rescues his child from buzzards by making himself smell like putrid flesh (Fock, 1963). Yaperikuli, the transformer and trickster of the Baníwa of the upper Rio Negro region of northwestern Brazil, killed the chief of the Eenunai ("sky people") by opening his body and leaving it in a hammock like a "dummy." The trickster's role in general consists of his becoming enmeshed in a predicament and then rescuing himself through the use of his incarnate intelligence and the physical transformation of his body. Tricksters are sometimes wedged in the dangerous passages between two states of being, and through their efforts to rescue themselves—using perhaps a hole, or vine, as a passage—these states of being become altered forever.

The Yukūna people of the northwest Amazon region tell the story of two heroic brothers. The younger brother, Maotchi, is extracted from a hole in a tree by a female agouti with whom he has promised to have sex in exchange for being rescued. Once night falls, he fears making love with her, and so they sleep foot-to-foot. However, she begins to devour him through her anus, and by midnight she has "swallowed" him up to his anus, which then begins to swallow her. On another occasion, Maotchi tricks his elder brother, Kawarimi, into jumping with him into an enormous hole that leads to another world at the center of the earth. Maotchi saves himself by grabbing a vine as he falls, uprooting the vine in the process. As his brother falls into the hole, Maotchi shouts "Stone, stone!" to make his brother fall faster and, eventually, break all his bones (Jacopin, 1981).

Cross-dressing constitutes another tactic of the trickster. In eastern Ecuador, the Shipibo trickster is an ant eater who manages to trade "clothes" with a jaguar. The result is the human world, in which appearances and body forms can be deceiving: that is, where an ant eater is really a jaguar, a jaguar really an anteater, and so on (Roe, 1982). Because death is the ultimate transformation, tricksters have been linked with it; they also mock death and extract benefit from its appearances. For example, in Brazil, the Tapirapé culture hero, Petura, is able to steal fire from the primordial king vulture by pretending to be a cadaver: When the king vulture comes to devour the maggots infesting the corpse, Petura steals his "red fire." He also gives the anteater its shape by thrusting a club up its anus and a wooden stick into its nostrils (Wagley, 1977).

In the Gran Chaco area of southern South America, the Mataco trickster Tokhwáh—also known as Tawkx-wax, Takwaj, Takjuaj, Tokhuah—is both good and bad, and, although he advances human capabilities, every step forward brings comic disaster (Simoneau and Wilbert, 1982). Tokhwáh acts bisexually, chasing women and often seduced by men. His exploits require an entire cycle of myths, and he is at once divine and earthly, creative and destructive. In order to retain nourishing foods, Tokhwáh uses mud to close up his anus, which had been torn open through intercourse with an iguana. In another episode, he is blinded with excrement that comes flying through the air when Tokhwáh strikes a pile of dung that has answered his questions by making inarticulate dropping noises, "pa pa pa pa." On another occasion, as punishment for eating a child, all of Tokhwáh's orifices are plugged with clay or wax. When a woodpecker reopens his orifices, various bird-beings are spattered with blood and waste, giving the various species their distinguishing marks (Simoneau and Wilbert, 1982).

The actions of Mesoamerican and South American tricksters reveal the contradictions at the heart of human experience: carnal and spiritual, living but mortal, ambitious but finite. With a blend of humor and tragedy, trickster myths describe the calamities that occur when contrary conditions of being collide and overlap in a single experience.

See Also Jaguars; Tezcatlipoca.

BIBLIOGRAPHY

For a consideration of trickster figures as general mythical types among American Indian people, see Åke Hultkrantz's *The Religions of the American Indians* (Berkeley, Calif., 1967). For a treatment of trickster figures in Mesoamerica, see Barbara G. Myerhoff's *Peyote Hunt: The Sacred Journey of the Huichol Indians* (Ithaca, N.Y., 1974); Burr C. Brundage's *The Fifth Sun: Aztec Gods, Aztec World* (Austin, 1979); and Eva Hunt's *The Transformation of the Hummingbird: Cultural Roots of a Zinacantecan Mythical Poem* (Ithaca, N.Y., 1977).

For tricksters in various parts of South America consult the excellent series of volumes on folk literature of South American peoples edited by Johannes Wilbert and Karin Simoneau and published by the UCLA Latin American Center at the University of California, Los Angeles. Each volume contains extensive indices directing the reader to specific trickster motifs. For example, this article refers to Johannes Wilbert and Karin Simoneau's *Folk Literature of the Mataco Indians* (Los Angeles, 1982). Gerardo Reichel-Dolmatoff, *Amazonian Cosmos: The Sexual and Religious Symbolism of the Tukano Indians* (Chicago, 1971) presents the mythic figures of southern Colombia. For references to tricksters in the northwest Amazon region, see the excellent collections of myths in Robin M. Wright's "History and Religion of the Baníwa Peoples of the Upper Rio Negro Valley," 2 vols. (Ph.D. diss., Stanford University, 1981), and in Pierre-Ives Jacopin's "La parole generative: De la mythologie des indiens yukuna" (Ph.D. diss., Université de Neuchâtel, 1981). Trickster mythologies from Venezuela may be found in Marc de Civrieux's *Watunna: An Orinoco Creation Cycle* (San Francisco, 1980); Niels Fock's *Waiwai: Religion and Society of an Amazonian Tribe* (Copenhagen, 1963); and Kenneth I. Taylor's "Body and Spirit among the Sanumá (Yanoama) of North Brazil," in David L. Browman and Ronald A. Schwarz's *Spirits, Shamans, and Stars: Perspectives from South America* (The Hague, 1979), pp. 201–221, which discusses people living on the Brazil-Venezuela border. Mention may also be made of Charles Wagley's *Welcome of Tears: The Tapirapé Indians of Central Brazil* (Oxford, 1977); the special study made by Mario Califano, "El ciclo de Tokjwaj: Analisis fenomenológico de una narración mítica de los Mataco Costaneros," *Scripta ethnológica* (Buenos Aires) 1 (1973): 156–186; and Peter G. Roe's *The Cosmic Zygote: Cosmology in the Amazon Basin* (New Brunswick, N.J., 1982).

New Sources

Basso, Ellen B. *In Favor of Deceit: A Study of Tricksters in an Amazonian Society.* Tucson, 1987.

Bierhorst, J. *Myths and Tales of the American Indians.* New York, 1992.

Erdoes, Richard, and Alfonso Ortiz, eds. *American Indian Trickster Tales.* New York, 1998.

Vizenor, Gerald. "Trickster Discourse." *American Indian Quarterly.* 14 (1990): 277–287.

LAWRENCE E. SULLIVAN (1987)
Revised Bibliography

TRIGLAV, a three-headed deity of the heathen Slavs, was literally named: from *tri,* "*three,*" and *glava,* "*head.*" Worship of him in the temple at Szczecin (Stettin), Pomerania, is attested by Herbord, Ebbo, and Monachus Prieflingensis, the three biographers of Otto, a twelfth-century bishop of Bamberg. According to Herbord, the image of Triglav at Szczecin had three heads joined to one another. Ebbo states that the image was of gold; Monachus Prieflingensis asserts that all three heads were silver-plated. Another idol of Triglav stood in the town of Wolin. Both images were destroyed by Otto.

No detailed description of the image of Triglav exists. One of the interesting features of this god is that he was connected with the number three. His idol stood on the largest of the three hills of Szczecin, and the black horse consecrated to him and used in divination was led thrice across nine (thrice three) lances that were placed in front of the temple, about a yard apart.

In the words of the high priest of the temple at Szczecin, Triglav had three heads in order to make it known that he ruled over three realms: heaven, earth, and the underworld. Ebbo refers to him as the "summus deus" ("highest god"). Hence, Triglav may have been either a manifestation of three major gods or three aspects of one god. The black horse and the mention of the underworld suggest Triglav's ties with Veles-Volos, the god of death and the underworld, a deity standing in opposition to Sventovit, the god of heavenly light, who was associated with a white horse. Triglav may also have been related to Chernoglav, the "black god," who had a silver mustache and who was worshiped at Rügen, as mentioned in the *Knytlingasaga* (1265).

Tricephalous sculptures, mostly undated, have been found in South and East Slavic areas (Yugoslavia, Bulgaria, Russia); in France, Gallo-Roman sculptures of three-headed gods date from the second to the fourth century CE. A tricephalous figure called the Thracian Rider was known in the ancient Balkan world, particularly in Bulgaria, and his image is preserved on hundreds of stelae of the second and third centuries CE. The name of Triglav has been retained in the toponymy of all Slavic areas, proving its common Slavic origin.

BIBLIOGRAPHY

Machál, Jan. "Slavic Mythology." In *The Mythology of All Races,* vol. 3, edited by Louis H. Gray and George Foot Moore, pp. 217–220. Boston, 1918.

Palm, Thede. *Wendische Kultstätten: Quellenkritische Untersuchungen zu den letzten Jahrhunderten slavischen Heidentums.* Lund, 1937.

Pettazzoni, Raffaele. "The Pagan Origins of the Three-Headed Representation of the Christian Trinity." *Journal of Warburg and Courtauld Institutes* 9 (1946): 135–151.

Pettazzoni, Raffaele. "West Slav Paganism." In his *Essays on the History of Religions,* pp. 151–163. Leiden, 1967.

New Sources

Kapica, F. S. *Slavyanskije tradicionnije verovanija, prazdniki i rituali* [Slavic traditional beliefs, festivities and rituals]. Moscow, 2001.

Petruhin, A. Y., T. A. Arapkina, L. N. Vinogradova, and S. M. Tolstaya. *Slavyanskaja mifologija* [Slavic mythology]. Moscow, 1995.

Shaparova, N. S. *Kratkaya enciklopedija slavyanskoj mifologii* [A short dictionary of Slavic mythology]. Moscow, 2001.

Tokarev, S. A. "Mifi narodov mira [World myths]." *Bolshaya Rossijskaya Enciklopedija*, vol.1–2. Moscow, 1998.

MARIJA GIMBUTAS (1987)
Revised Bibliography

TRINITY. Trinitarian doctrine touches on virtually every aspect of Christian faith, theology, and piety, including Christology and pneumatology, theological epistemology (faith, revelation, theological methodology), spirituality and mystical theology, and ecclesial life (sacraments, community, ethics). This article summarizes the main lines of trinitarian doctrine without presenting detailed explanations of important ideas, persons, or terms.

The doctrine of the Trinity is the summary of Christian faith in God, who out of love creates humanity for union with God, who through Jesus Christ redeems the world, and in the power of the Holy Spirit transforms and divinizes (*2 Cor.* 3:18). The heart of trinitarian theology is the conviction that the God revealed in Jesus Christ is involved faithfully and unalterably in covenanted relationship with the world. Christianity is not unique in believing God is "someone" rather than "something," but it is unique in its belief that Christ is the personal Word of God, and that through Christ's death and resurrection into new life, "God was in Christ reconciling all things to God" (*2 Cor.* 5:19). Christ is not looked upon as an intermediary between God and world but as an essential agent of salvation. The Spirit poured out at Pentecost, by whom we live in Christ and are returned to God (Father), is also not a "lesser God" but one and the same God who creates and redeems us. The doctrine of the Trinity is the product of reflection on the events of redemptive history, especially the Incarnation and the sending of the Spirit.

DEVELOPMENT OF TRINITARIAN DOCTRINE. Exegetes and theologians today are in agreement that the Hebrew Bible does not contain a doctrine of the Trinity, even though it was customary in past dogmatic tracts on the Trinity to cite texts like *Genesis* 1:26, "Let us make humanity in our image, after our likeness" (see also *Gn.* 3:22, 11:7; *Is.* 6:2–3) as proof of plurality in God. Although the Hebrew Bible depicts God as the father of Israel and employs personifications of God such as Word *(davar)*, Spirit *(ruaḥ)*, Wisdom *(ḥokhmah)*, and Presence *(shekhinah)*, it would go beyond the intention and spirit of the Old Testament to correlate these notions with later trinitarian doctrine.

Further, exegetes and theologians agree that the New Testament also does not contain an explicit doctrine of the Trinity. God the Father is source of all that is (Pantokrator) and also the father of Jesus Christ; "Father" is not a title for the first person of the Trinity but a synonym for God. Early liturgical and creedal formulas speak of God as "Father of our Lord Jesus Christ"; praise is to be rendered to God through Christ (see opening greetings in Paul and deutero-Paul). There are other binitarian texts (e.g., *Rom.* 4:24, 8:11; 2 *Cor.* 4:14; *Col.* 2:12; *1 Tm.* 2:5–6, 6:13; *2 Tm.* 4:1), and a few triadic texts (the strongest are *2 Cor.* 13:14 and *Mt.* 28:19; others are *1 Cor.* 6:11, 12:4–6; *2 Cor.* 1:21–22; 1 *Thes.* 5:18–19; *Gal.* 3:11–14). Christ is sent by God and the Spirit is sent by Christ so that all may be returned to God.

The language of the Bible, of early Christian creeds, and of Greek and Latin theology prior to the fourth century is "economic" (*oikonomia,* divine management of earthly affairs). It is oriented to the concrete history of creation and redemption: God initiates a covenant with Israel, God speaks through the prophets, God takes on flesh in Christ, God dwells within as Spirit. In the New Testament there is no reflective consciousness of the metaphysical nature of God ("immanent trinity"), nor does the New Testament contain the technical language of later doctrine *(hupostasis, ousia, substantia, subsistentia, prosōpon, persona)*. Some theologians have concluded that all postbiblical trinitarian doctrine is therefore arbitrary. While it is incontestable that the doctrine cannot be established on scriptural evidence alone, its origins may legitimately be sought in the Bible, not in the sense of "proof-texting" or of finding metaphysical principles, but because the Bible is the authoritative record of God's redemptive relationship with humanity. What the scriptures narrate as the activity of God among us, which is confessed in creeds and celebrated in liturgy, is the wellspring of later trinitarian doctrine.

Dogmatic development took place gradually, against the background of the emanationist philosophy of Stoicism and Neoplatonism (including the mystical theology of the latter), and within the context of strict Jewish monotheism. In the immediate post–New Testament period of the Apostolic Fathers no attempt was made to work out the God-Christ (Father-Son) relationship in ontological terms. By the end of the fourth century, and owing mainly to the challenge posed by various heresies, theologians went beyond the immediate testimony of the Bible and also beyond liturgical and creedal expressions of trinitarian faith to the ontological trinity of coequal persons "within" God. The shift is from function to ontology, from the "economic trinity" (Father, Son, and Spirit in relation to us) to the "immanent" or "essential Trinity" (Father, Son, and Spirit in relation to each other). It was prompted chiefly by belief in the divinity of Christ and later in the divinity of the Holy Spirit, but even earlier by the consistent worship of God in a trinitarian pattern and the practice of baptism into the threefold name of God. By the close of the fourth century the orthodox teaching was in place: God is one nature, three persons *(mia ousia, treis hupostaseis)*.

Questions of Christology and soteriology (salvation) occupied theologians of the early patristic period. What was

Christ's relationship to God? What is Christ's role in our salvation? The Logos Christology of the apologists identified the preexistent Christ of Johannine and Pauline theology with the Logos ("word") of Greek philosophy. The Stoic distinction between the immanent word *(logos endiathetos)* and the expressed word *(logos prophorikos)* provided a way for Justin Martyr (d. 163/165) and others to explain how Christ had preexisted as the immanent word in the Father's mind and then became incarnate in time. Third-century monarchianism arose as a backlash against Logos theology, which was feared to jeopardize the unity of God; the modalism of Sabellius admitted the distinctions in history but denied their reality in God's being. Origen (died c. 254) contributed the idea of the eternal generation of the Son within the being of God; although other aspects of Origen's theology later were judged to be subordinationist, his teaching that the Son is a distinct hypostasis brought about subtle changes in conceptions of divine paternity and trinity. In the West, Tertullian (d. 225?) formulated an economic trinitarian theology that presents the three persons as a plurality in God. Largely because of the theology of Arius, who about 320 denied that Christ was fully divine, the Council of Nicaea (325) taught that Christ is *homoousios* (of the same substance) with God. The primary concern of Athanasius (d. 373), the great defender of Nicene orthodoxy, was salvation through Christ; if Christ is not divine, he cannot save. Like the bishops at Nicaea, Athanasius had a limited trinitarian vocabulary; *hupostasis* (person) and *ousia* (substance) could still be used interchangeably.

The fourth-century Cappadocian theologians (Basil of Caesarea, Gregory of Nyssa, and Gregory of Nazianzus) formulated orthodox trinitarian doctrine and made it possible for the Council of Constantinople (381) to affirm the divinity of the Holy Spirit. The speculatively gifted Cappadocians made a clear distinction between *hupostasis* and *ousia* (roughly equivalent to particular and universal), thereby establishing orthodox trinitarian vocabulary. At the close of the patristic period John of Damascus (d. 749) summarized Greek trinitarian doctrine with the doctrine of *perichōresis* (Lat., *circumincessio),* or the mutual indwelling of the divine persons.

Western trinitarian theology took a different course because of Augustine (d. 430). Instead of regarding the Father as source of divinity, Augustine's starting point was the one divine substance, which the three persons share. He sought the image of the Trinity within the rational soul and formulated psychological analogies (memory, intellect, will; lover, beloved, love) that conveyed unity more than plurality. The Augustinian approach served to effectively refute Arianism, but it also moved the doctrine of the Trinity to a transcendent realm, away from salvation history, from other areas of theology, and from liturgy. In the Latin West Boethius (died c. 525) formulated the classic definition of person, namely, "individual substance of a rational nature." Augustinian theology was given further elaboration in medieval theology, especially by Anselm (d. 1109) and in the Scholastic synthesis of Thomas Aquinas (d. 1274). Still Augustinian but focusing on person rather than nature, Richard of Saint-Victor (d. 1173) and Bonaventure (d. 1274) developed a psychology of love; charity is the essence of Trinity.

Although there are important exceptions to any typology, in general, Greek theology emphasizes the hypostases, the "trinity in unity," whereas Latin theology emphasizes the divine nature, or "unity in trinity." The Greek approach can be represented by a line: Godhood originates with the Father, emanates toward the Son, and passes into the Holy Spirit who is the bridge to the world. Greek theology (following the New Testament and early Christian creeds) retains the "monarchy" of the Father who as sole principle of divinity imparts Godhood to Son and Spirit. The Greek approach tends toward subordinationism (though hardly of an ontological kind) or, in some versions, to tritheism since in Greek theology each divine person fully possesses the divine substance. The Latin approach can be represented by a circle or triangle. Because the emphasis is placed on what the divine persons share, Latin theology tends toward modalism (which obscures the distinctiveness of each person). Also the Trinity is presented as self-enclosed and not intrinsically open to the world.

PRINCIPLES OF TRINITARIAN DOCTRINE. Trinitarian theology is *par excellence* the theology of relationship. Its fundamental principle is that God, who is self-communicating and self-giving love for us, is from all eternity love perfectly given and received. The traditional formula "God is three persons in one nature" compactly expresses that there are permanent features of God's eternal being (the three persons) that are the ontological precondition for the three distinct manners of God's tripersonal activity in the world (as Father, Son, Spirit).

Technical terms, theological theories, and official (conciliar) statements function together as a "set of controls" over the correct way to conceive both of God's self-relatedness as Father, Son, and Spirit, and God's relatedness to creation as Father, Son, and Spirit. Although one must guard against reducing the mystery of God to a set of formal statements, precise distinctions are useful insofar as they refine theological vocabulary or protect against distortions ("heresy"). Still, doctrinal statements are inherently limited; they address specific points of controversy, leaving other questions unsettled and sometimes creating new problems. Conciliar statements and theological principles guard against egregious errors (for example, "the Holy Spirit is a creature") and serve as boundaries within which trinitarian discourse may take place.

First, God is ineffable and Absolute Mystery, whose reality cannot adequately be comprehended or expressed by means of human concepts. Trinitarian doctrine necessarily falls short of expressing the full "breadth and length and height and depth" of God's glory and wisdom and love. Even though God who "dwells in light inaccessible" is impenetrable mystery, the doctrine of the Trinity is not itself a mystery, nor is the doctrine revealed by God, nor is the doctrine a substitute for the knowledge of God gained in the union of love that surpasses all concepts (see *Eph.* 3:18–19). Trinitarian doctrine is a partial and fragmentary exegesis of what has been revealed, namely, that God is self-communicating love. Further, because God is a partner in love and not an object to be scrutinized or controlled by the intellect, speculative theology must be firmly rooted in spirituality, doxology, and a concrete community of faith so that trinitarian doctrine does not become "heavenly metaphysics" unrelated to the practice of faith.

Second, the revelation and self-communication of the incomprehensible God, attested in the concrete images and symbols of the Bible and celebrated in Christian liturgy, is the proper starting point of trinitarian theology. Theological thinking proceeds from "God with us" ("economic" Trinity) to the nature of God ("immanent" Trinity). The starting point "within" God led to an overly abstract doctrine in the West and to a virtual divorce of the "immanent" Trinity from the Trinity of history and experience. Friedrich Schleiermacher (d. 1834) reacted against the cleavage between "God" and "God for us" by relegating the idea of the essential Trinity to an appendix to his summary of Christian theology. Karl Rahner's (d. 1984) widely accepted axiom is pertinent: "the 'economic' Trinity *is* the 'immanent' Trinity and vice versa." God is who God reveals God to be. Concepts that describe the ontological intrarelatedness of God must be drawn from and are subject to control by the "facts" of redemptive history.

Third, because the three persons together and inseparably (though without mingling or confusion) bring about salvation and deification, and because the one God is worshiped as Father, Son, and Spirit, no divine person is inferior to any other person. Although undivided, God exists as the pure relationality of love given and received. The decree of the Council of Florence (1442) that "everything in God is one except where there is opposition of relation" was regarded as a final answer to tritheism (belief in three gods), Arian subordinationism (ontological hierarchy of persons), Sabellian modalism (no real distinctions "in" God), and Macedonianism (denial of the divinity of the Holy Spirit).

There are two divine processions: begetting and spiration ("breathing"). Each divine person exists by relation to the other two persons (Gr., "relation of origin"; Lat., "relation of oppositon"), and each fully possesses the divine substance. In Greek theology the three hypostases have the distinguishing characteristics (sg., *idiotes*) of "being unbegotten" *(agennēsia),* "being begotten" *(gennēsia),* and "proceeding" *(ekporeusis).* The Father is the fountainhead of Godhood *(fons divinitatis),* who imparts divinity to Son and Spirit. According to Latin theology there are four relations (begetting, being begotten, spirating, being spirated) but only three "subsistent" relations: paternity, filiation, spiration. Latin theology (following Augustine) understands divine unity to reside in the divine nature that is held in common by Father, Son, and Spirit; Greek theology (following the Cappadocians) understands the unity to reside in the "perichoretic" relatedness of the three persons.

A corollary of the inseparability of the three coequal divine persons is the axiom that "all works of the triune God *ad extra* are indivisibly one" ("opera trinitatis ad extra indivisa sunt"). According to Latin theology it is the three-personed substance of God that acts in history; according to Greek theology every action of God toward creation originates with the Father, passes through the Son, and is perfected in the Spirit (Gregory of Nyssa). In any case, the axiom must not be understood to obscure what is distinctive to each divine person.

Fourth, a false distinction must not be set up between what God is and what God does, between essence and existence, between unity and threefoldness, between nature and person (relation). There are no "accidents" in God; the statement of the Fourth Lateran Council (1215) that each divine person is the divine substance countered the claim of some theologians (Joachim of Fiore) that God is a quaternity (three persons + essence = four persons).

Fifth, since the nature of God is to love, and love naturally seeks an object, it might appear that God "needs" the world as a partner in love. This would make the world coeternal with God. Many Scholastic theologians speculated on this question. Thomas Aquinas admitted that while he saw no philosophical reason to deny the eternity of the world, the testimony of the *Book of Genesis* and his Christian faith constrained him to do so. In 1329 Meister Eckhart was condemned for asserting the eternity of the world. With respect to trinitarian theology, even though Rahner's axiom (see above) suggests that God's relations to us, including creation, are constitutive of God and vice versa, theologians traditionally speak of a perfect and reciprocal exchange of love "within" God, that is, among Father, Son, and Spirit independent of their relationship to creation, in order to preserve the absolute character of God's freedom.

CURRENT DIRECTIONS AND REMAINING PROBLEMS. After centuries of disinterest in trinitarian doctrine in the West, the riches of this vast tradition are once again being explored. Three basic directions may be observed. First, some theologians have revised analogies of the "immanent" Trinity according to contemporary philosophy (for example, process metaphysics), linguistics, or interpersonal psychology. While this approach overcomes some of the aporia of classical expositions, it perpetuates the metaphysical starting point "within" God apart from salvation history. A second approach focuses on soteriology and Christology and is circumspect about the "immanent" Trinity, though without denying that historical distinctions are grounded ontologically in God. A third approach uses trinitarian symbolism to describe God's deeds in redemptive history but resists positing real distinctions in God. Despite basic differences in method, these three approaches all move in a more personalist (relational) direction and, in the case of the latter two, a more "economic" direction.

Theologians who specialize in trinitarian doctrine suggest that several areas warrant further attention. First, most trinitarian doctrine is so abstract it is difficult to see its connection with praxis. The "summary of Christian faith" and the living out of that faith should be brought to bear more directly on each other. Creeds, doxologies, and liturgy are important loci of the trinitarian faith recapitulated in trinitarian doctrine.

Second, unlike the "mystical theology" of the Orthodox tradition, theology in the West has been separated from spirituality since the thirteenth century. Reintegrating theology and spirituality would help to overcome the rationalist tendencies of Western theology, to provide the field of spirituality with theological foundation, and also to strengthen the weakest component of Western theology, namely, pneumatology.

Third, the *filioque* ("and from the Son") clause, inserted into the Western creed in the sixth century but denounced by the Orthodox church, remains a serious obstacle to reunion between East and West. Theologians should work assiduously for ecumenical agreement.

Fourth, to speak of God as "three persons" always has been problematic and remains the same today. In the modern framework "person" means "individual center of consciousness." To avoid the tritheistic implications of positing three "persons" in God, the relational, or "toward-the-other" character of "person" should be reemphasized.

Fifth, the exclusively masculine imagery of trinitarian doctrine hinders full recovery of the trinitarian insight into the essential relatedness of God. The fatherhood of God should be rethought in light of the critique of feminist theologies and also in view of the nonpatriarchal understanding of divine paternity to be found in some biblical and early theological writings.

Sixth, revising trinitarian theology along soteriological lines raises the question of its place in the dogmatic schema, that is, whether it ought to be treated as a separate "tract," as prolegomenous to theology, as its apex and summary, or as an undergird that is presupposed throughout but never alluded to explicitly.

Seventh, trinitarian theology must be pursued within the context of the "God question" of every age, whether this question takes the form of existentialist atheism, secular humanism, or some other.

Eighth, the Christian doctrine of God must be developed also within the wider purview of other world religions. Trinitarian doctrine cannot be Christomonistic, excluding persons of other faiths from salvation, nor can it surrender its conviction that God is fully present in Christ.

For trinitarian doctrine to be recovered as a vital expression of God's nearness in Christ, theologians must translate into a contemporary idiom the mystery of God's triune love in a way that does justice not only to the testimony of our predecessors but also to the ongoing and ever-new features of God's relationship with a people.

BIBLIOGRAPHY

Biblical and Historical Sources

For the New Testament origins of trinitarian doctrine, see the article and bibliography by Franz Josef Schierse, "Die neutestamentliche Trinitätsoffenbarung," in *Mysterium Salutis,* edited by Johannes Feiner and Magnus Löhrer, vol. 2 (Einsiedeln, 1967), and Arthur W. Wainwright's *The Trinity in the New Testament* (London, 1962). A standard and nearly complete exposition of patristic and medieval, Greek and Latin trinitarian doctrine is Théodore de Régnon's four-volume *Études de théologie positive sur la Sainte Trinité* (Paris, 1892–1898). Organized chronologically and full of helpful textual references is "Trinité," by G. Bardy and A. Michel, in *Dictionnaire de théologie catholique* (Paris, 1950), vol. 15.2, cols. 1545–1855. Standard English-language works include George L. Prestige's study of shifting terminology and concepts in early Greek trinitarian theology in *God in Patristic Thought,* 2d ed. (1952; reprint, London, 1964), J. N. D. Kelly's historical study, *Early Christian Doctrines,* 5th rev. ed. (New York, 1977), and Edmund J. Fortman's *The Triune God* (Philadelphia, 1972). Yves Congar's three-volume *I Believe in the Holy Spirit* (New York, 1983) is more impressionistic but contains many historical gems and a seasoned approach to this vast field.

Theological Works

In Protestant theology, Karl Barth placed the doctrine of the Trinity as a prolegomenon to dogmatic theology in *Church Dogmatics,* vol. 1, pt. 1 (Edinburgh, 1936). See also Claude Welch's summary of recent Protestant theology in *In This Name: The Doctrine of the Trinity in Contemporary Theology* (New York, 1952). Trinitarian theology that centers on the cross is represented in Eberhard Jüngel's *God as the Mystery of the World* (Grand Rapids, Mich., 1983) and Jürgen Moltmann's *The Crucified God* (New York, 1974). In Catholic theology, Karl Rahner's monograph *The Trinity* (New York, 1970) summarizes but also seeks to go beyond standard Western trinitarian dogma. Heribert Mühlen's *Der heilige Geist als Person,* 2d ed. (Münster, 1966) and *Una Mystica Persona* (Paderborn, 1964) develop a pneumatological and interpersonal analogy of the "immanent" Trinity. Walter Kasper's *The God of Jesus Christ* (New York, 1984) is a magisterial summary of classical and contemporary trinitarian theology, developed against the backdrop of modern atheism and in light of current studies in Christology. On Orthodox theology, see Vladimir Lossky's *The Mystical Theology of the Eastern Church,* 2d ed. (Crestwood, N.Y., 1976).

New Sources

Bobrinsky, Boris. *The Mystery of the Trinity.* Translated by Anthony P. Gythiel. Crestwood, N.Y., 1999.

Boff, Leonard. *Holy Trinity, Perfect Community.* Translated by Phillip Berryman. Maryknoll, N.Y., 2000.

Butin, Philip Walker. *Reformed Ecclesiology: Trinitarian Grace According to Calvin.* Princeton, N.J., 1994.

Collins, Paul M. *Trinitarian Theology, West and East: Karl Barth, the Cappadocian Fathers, and John Zizioulas.* Oxford and New York, 2001.

Davis, Stephen T., Daniel Kendall, and Gerald O'Collins, eds. *The Trinity.* Oxford and New York, 1999.

Schwöbel, Christoph, and Colin E. Gunton, eds. *Persons Divine and Human.* Edinburgh, 1991.

Thompson, John. *Modern Trinitarian Perspectives.* New York, 1994.

Torrance, Thomas Forsyth. *The Christian Doctrine of God.* Edinburgh, 1996.

CATHERINE MOWRY LACUGNA (1987)
Revised Bibliography

TROELTSCH, ERNST (1865–1923), German Protestant theologian and cultural philosopher. Ernst Peter Wilhelm Troeltsch is considered "the most eminent sociologically oriented historian of Western Christianity" (Talcott Parsons, quoted by James Luther Adams, "Why the Troeltsch Revival? Reasons for the Renewed Interest in the Thought of the Great German Theologian Ernst Troeltsch," in *The Unitarian Universalist Christian* 29, 1974, pp. 4–15). With regard to the impact of his work, Troeltsch was the most significant evangelical theologian since Friedrich Schleiermacher (1768–1834). As the central figure in German Protestant theology in the early twentieth century, he was able to exercise an enduring influence on philosophy, religion, sociology, and the study of history.

Troeltsch was born in Haunstetten, a small town near the old southern German imperial city of Augsburg. He spent his childhood and youth in Augsburg. Through the efforts of his father, a well-to-do physician, Troeltsch became acquainted at an early age with the modern natural sciences, and the famous preparatory school at Sankt Anna gave him the sense of a cosmopolitan Christian humanism.

In 1883, Troeltsch began the study of philosophy for two semesters at the Roman Catholic preparatory school in Augsburg and then, in the fall of 1884, of Protestant theology in Erlangen. He was particularly interested in the reconciliation of faith with knowledge and, therefore, attended lectures in art history, political science, national economics, history, psychology, and philosophy. Since the theological faculty at Erlangen was dominated by a neoorthodox Lutheranism, Troeltsch transferred, in 1885, to Berlin for a year and, in the fall of 1886, finally to Göttingen. Here the systematic theologian Albrecht Ritschl (1822–1889), the most prominent contemporary representative of a liberal, Lutheran, cultural Protestantism, exercised a primary and profound influence upon him.

As early as 1891, however, Troeltsch formulated a sharp criticism of Ritschl's ethicizing modernization of Luther's theology. He emphasized the far-reaching cultural differences between the "Old Protestantism" of the sixteenth and early seventeenth centuries and the modern world, which had emerged only with the Enlightenment of the eighteenth century. Insofar as Luther had remained committed to the ideal of a religiously dominated, homogeneous culture and had represented a pacifist ethic that sanctioned submission to the status quo, he was, for Troeltsch, still part of the Middle Ages. Thus for Troeltsch's own theological development, Enlightenment traditions were more important than the theology of the reformers. He believed that theology must be changed from the old dogmatic paradigm to a "historical method" and must be based upon a general, rational theory of religion.

Already in the *Disputationsthesen,* published on the occasion of his doctoral degree in 1891 (text in *Troeltsch-Studien I,* 2d. ed., Gutersloh, 1985, pp. 299–300), Troeltsch designated such a theology, which he believed compatible with modern consciousness, a "religious-historical discipline." It is not yet clear to what extent this statement was influenced by the Göttingen religious historian and Septuagint scholar Paul Anton de Lagarde (1827–1891). Troeltsch was part of a very close and friendly exchange in Göttingen with the church historian Albert Eichhorn (1856–1926), as well as the exegetes Hermann Gunkel (1862–1932), Alfred Rahlfs (1865–1935), Wilhelm Wrede (1859–1906), Heinrich Hackmann (1864–1935), and especially Wilhelm Bousset (1865–1920). These "young Göttingers" wanted to transform traditional biblical scholarship into an undogmatic, sociologically informed religious history of Judaism and early Christianity. They therefore attempted to understand the origins of Christianity from the perspective of the ancient religions, especially of late Judaism. Since they were not interested in historically secondary theological dogmatics, but rather in the original productivity of religious consciousness, they, along with Johannes Weiss (1863–1914), emphasized very strongly the eschatological character of Jesus' preaching of the kingdom of God, and also the autonomy of religion within culture. Troeltsch was considered the "systematician" of this "little Göttingen faculty," which as a so-called religious-historical school exercised a significant influence on the theology of the early twentieth century.

In a well-known essay, *Über historische und dogmatische Methode in der Theologie* (On Historical and Dogmatic Method in Theology; 1900, included in his *Gesammelte Schriften,* vol. 2, Tübingen, 1913, pp. 729–753), using the historiographic principles of critique, analogy, and correlation, Troeltsch drew the radical conclusion of definitively separating a supranaturalistic view of Christianity as the only true religion from the old dogmatic understanding of Jesus Christ as the extraordinary and exclusive revelation of God. The breaking down of the traditional isolation of Christianity from other religions should not, however, imply any skeptical relativism, but rather should serve as a foundation for the specific validity that Christianity claims. The program for a general theory of religion, which Troeltsch first outlined in 1895 in *Die Selbständigkeit der Religion* (The Independence of Religion), should, therefore, produce a metacritique of modern religious criticism. It should demonstrate, moreover, in dialogue with Ludwig Feuerbach's "suspicion of illusion," the real meaning of religious consciousness, in order to prove thereby the special validity of the Christian tradition. Thus the connection of historical-empirical analyses of the history of Christianity with a variety of attempts at a systematic philosophy of religion is characteristic of Troeltsch's lifework. The difficulties of making such a connection, however, demanded extensive epistemological, historical, and philosophical analyses of the relationship between historical contingency and the absolute. This Troeltsch was not able to bring to completion. To that extent, his massive literary work is, for the most part, fragmentary.

After a short lectureship in Bonn, and at the age of only twenty-nine, Troeltsch was called to Heidelberg in 1894 as professor of systematic theology. After the turn of the century, he became known far beyond the narrow borders of academic theology. This was a result of his intensive engagement in ecclesiastical politics on behalf of different organizations in liberal Protestantism, and also his prominent position within the University of Heidelberg. From 1909 to 1914, Troeltsch represented the university in the lower chamber of the parliament of the grand duchy of Baden. He was especially known for his numerous publications. On the basis of religious-historical comparison in his famous lecture *Die Absolutheit des Christentums und die Religionsgeschichte* (The Absoluteness of Christianity and the History of Religion, Tübingen, 1902), he denied to Christianity its traditional claim of absoluteness and relative superiority as the religion of personality. In *Psychologie und Erkenntnistheorie in der Religionswissenschaft* (Psychology and Epistemology in the Study of Religion, Tübingen, 1905), an essay presented to the International Congress of Arts and Sciences in Saint Louis in 1904, he connected William James's psychological pragmatism with the Neo-Kantian assumption of empirically independent structures of consciousness to form a theory of the "religious *a priori*." In accordance with this, the production of religious ideas is seen as a constitutive accomplishment of human subjectivity. In *Wesen der Religion und der Religionswissenschaft* (Writings on Theology and Religion, 1977, pp. 82–123), Troeltsch sought to explicate the independence of religion on four levels: First, empirically given religion should be analyzed according to a psychology of religion as an autonomous phenomenon of life that is constitutive for all culture. Second, in the epistemology of religion, the level of reality proper to religious consciousness must be rationally justified. Third, within a special historical philosophy of religions, the general concept of religion should be realized specifically and concretely in terms of the plurality of real existing religions for comparative religious-historical studies. Fourth, a metaphysics of religion bases the religious understanding of worldly reality upon the self-revelation of God. In this way, the universal history of religion should be proven to be the progressive revelation of God, and the presence of the absolute would be demonstrated in finite consciousness.

Troeltsch was not, however, able to carry out this great program. The concept of the religious *a priori* remained especially unclear. For Troeltsch only partially appropriated Kant's understanding of *a priori* structures of consciousness. He could do justice to the statement that the pious subject knows itself—or all finite reality—to be grounded in a divine substance only insofar as he understood the *a priori* as a product not proper to the intellect. To presuppose objects of cognition as directly given, however, contradicted the Kantian point of departure of his argumentation. The more Troeltsch sought to explain, in numerous small monographs on the philosophy of religion, the relationship of the religious consciousness to reality, the less he could still do justice to Kant's criticism. Although in close personal contact with the leading German representatives of Neo-Kantianism, Troeltsch did not share their basic assumptions.

After the turn of the century, in addition to his studies in the philosophy of religion, Troeltsch published in relatively quick succession several cultural-historical investigations into the profound transformation of the Christian consciousness during the transition to the modern period. These include the large treatise, *Protestantisches Christentum und Kirche in der Neuzeit* (Protestant Christianity and the Church in the Modern Age, in Paul Hinneberg, ed., *Die Kultur der Gegenwart,* Part 1, Section 4.1, Berlin and Leipzig, 1906; 1922, 3d ed.), on the basis of which the University of Greifswald conferred on him an honorary doctorate in philosophy, and a famous lecture, *Die Bedeutung des Protestantismus für die Entstehung der modernen Welt* (Munich, 1906; 1911, 2d ed.; abridged English version, *Protestantism and Progress: A Historical Study of the Relation of Protestantism to the Modern World,* London and New York, 1912). Both show the strong influence of Max Weber's investigations of 1904–1905 into the genetic connections between Protestant ethics and the spirit of capitalism. And Weber, in turn, was strongly influenced by Troeltsch's understanding of Lutheranism as a politically as well as economically premodern, patriarchal religion. Moreover, indications of the significance of the ascetic work-ethic of Calvinism for the development of capitalism can already be found in Troeltsch's work before the appearance of his friend's famous essays on Protestantism. The very close, seventeen-year friendship meant a substantial scholarly enrichment for both Troeltsch and Weber.

It is true that Troeltsch had established a sociological foundation for his understanding of the church even before the meeting with Weber. However, it was only under the influence of his friend that he distinguished precisely between church and sect as different types of religious community-building. *Die Soziallehren der christlichen Kirchen und Gruppen* (The Social Doctrines of Christian Churches and Groups), which, already partially published in 1908–1910, appeared in 1912 as the first volume of Troeltsch's collected works, also shows, however, significant sociological differences between the friends. Troeltsch wanted to present the social and ethical consequences of the Christian conceptual world and its interaction with cultural phenomena. The eschatological ideal of the kingdom of God of the Gospels stands in a relationship of unresolvable tension to the facticities of culture. Nevertheless, in that the church institutionalizes the grace of redemption sacramentally, it can become the place of salvation for the masses and fit the Christian concepts to the political-social order and its needs for legitimation. In contrast to this, the sects, small groups on the margin of society with demands for high achievement on their members, radicalize the tensions of religion and society to the point of absolute opposition between the norms of culture and the *lex Christi,* the Sermon on the Mount.

From the types of church and sect, Troeltsch further distinguished mysticism as the third particular social form of Christianity. Here the opposites of religion and society are reconciled within the pious subject himself, to the extent that he knows himself to be a participant in the divine spirit and he glimpses the true reality of the kingdom of God in a purely spiritual and universal brotherhood of those gifted by God. Troeltsch especially ascribed to his third type significant historical effects for modern Christianity. Weber, however, did not consider mysticism to be a separate social form of religion. This difference is the expression of contradicting evaluations of the real meaning of religion for modern societies. Unlike Weber, Troeltsch was convinced that, even under the conditions of Western rationalism, religion was an extremely important factor in societal formation. He understood the Christian tradition primarily as a force for the strengthening of individual autonomy over against the depersonalizing developmental tendencies of modern capitalism. Moreover, the church's tradition had to be provided with a new cultural credibility; that is, "religious individualism," inspired by the mystical tradition, which had been forced out of the evangelical church, had to be again given a right to exist within a "flexible church of the people" (*Gesammelte Schriften,* vol. 2, Tübingen, 1913, p. 105). In connection with Schleiermacher's program of a practically oriented theology of consciousness, Troeltsch interpreted dogmatic statements as self-communications of the genuine Protestant consciousness, as is shown especially in *Die Bedeutung der Geschichtlichkeit Jesu für den Glauben* (1911; translated as *The Significance of the Historical Existence of Jesus for Faith,* in *Writings on Theology and Religion,* 1967, pp. 182–207) and in his posthumously edited lectures on *Die Glaubenslehre* (Munich and Leipzig, 1925).

In the spring of 1915 Troeltsch was transferred to Berlin by the minister for cultural affairs. The chair he occupied there was renamed specifically for him, as a professorship in "religious, social, and historical philosophy and the history of Christian religion" and was transferred from the theological to the philosophical faculty.

With his moving to the capital of the empire, Troeltsch's intensive political activity quickly gained in public significance. Troeltsch interpreted World War I as an imperialistic power struggle, at the root of which lay not only economic antagonisms, but also deep-seated political and cultural contradictions between the German spirit and Western rationality. In spite of this connection with his earlier analyses of the social and ethical differences between Lutheranism and Calvinism, Troeltsch was not a theoretician of a separate political way for Germany. Since 1916 he had been fighting for a thorough democratization of the imperial constitution, the political integration of the parties of the workers' movement, and economic reforms aimed at breaking down class differences. This was reflected in manifold activities for the limitation of war and for peace negotiations. Troeltsch was a delegate of the leftist-liberal German Democratic party in the Prussian state assembly and undersecretary in the Prussian ministry for cultural affairs. After defeat and revolution, he was one of the leading representatives of that small minority in German Protestantism that interceded for the acceptance of the constitutional compromise of Weimar and for its concrete actualization as a social democracy.

In close connection with his political and practical activity, Troeltsch turned his attention in Berlin primarily to this question: to what extent could normative approaches to the solution of the present cultural crisis be found in the European cultural tradition? Because of his sudden death on 1 February 1923, Troeltsch was not able to realize concretely his program for a "European cultural synthesis." However, the basic theological structure of Troeltsch's philosophy of history can be recognized in the lectures *Christian Thought: Its History and Application* (London, 1923), edited by his friend Friedrich von Hügel (1852–1925), the so-called lay bishop of Roman Catholic modernism, and also the concluding part of *Das logische Problem der Geschichtsphilosophie* (The Logical Problem of the Philosophy of History), the first book of *Der Historismus und seine Probleme* (Historicism and its Problems), which appeared in 1922 as the third volume of the *Gesammelte Schriften.* Troeltsch now expressly restricted to the European-American cultural arena the old claim of Christianity to a position of relative superiority among the world religions. To pretend to understand foreign cultures was cultural imperialism. Against monistic worldviews, which presuppose that a universal history of humanity can be recognized, Troeltsch argued for a pluralistic understanding of reality. In that he was guided by the theological insight that an overview of history is possible only for God, but not for finite persons.

In the antiliberal, mostly antidemocratic, German Protestant theology of the 1920s, Troeltsch's cultural relativism encountered intensive criticism. Since the 1960s, however, one can see—on the international level as well as on an interdisciplinary level—a notable renaissance of interest in Troeltsch's thought. Indeed his theology of cultural modesty is important, in that it permits central problems of contemporary theological and philosophical discussion—for instance, the pluralism of religious traditions, the dependency of theology upon contexts, the relationship of Christianity to cultural modernity—to be grasped outside of all claims of dogmatic absolutism.

BIBLIOGRAPHY

A comprehensive listing of published works by Troeltsch is now offered by *Ernst Troeltsch Bibliographie,* edited and with an introduction and commentary by Friedrich Wilhelm Graf and Hartmut Ruddies (Tübingen, 1982). This inclusive bibliography indicates numerous previously unknown publications of Troeltsch and various of Troeltsch's own editions of the same texts. Summaries of texts that have been published in English can be found in Jacob Klapwijk's "English Translations of Troeltsch's Works," in *Ernst Troeltsch and the Future of Theology,* edited by John Powell Clayton (Cambridge, 1976); see also the appendix, "Troeltsch in English Translation," in Troeltsch's *Writings on Theology and Religion,* translated and edited by Robert Morgan and Michel Pye (London, 1977).

Several introductions to Troeltsch's work have been published: Trutz Rendtorff's "Ernst Troeltsch, 1865–1923," in *Theologen des Protestantismus im 19. und 20. Jahrhundert,* vol. 2, edited by Martin Greschat (Stuttgart, 1978); Karl-Ernst Apfelbacher's *Frömmigkeit und Wissenschaft: Ernst Troeltsch und sein theologisches Programm* (Munich, 1978); Giuseppe Cantillo's *Ernst Troeltsch* (Naples, 1979); Robert J. Rubanowice's *Crisis in Consciousness: The Thought of Ernst Troeltsch,* with a foreword by James Luther Adams (Tallahassee, 1982); Trutz Rendtorff's and my discussion of Troeltsch in *Nineteenth Century Religious Thought of the West,* vol. 3, edited by Ninian Smart et al. (Cambridge and New York, 1985); and my and Hartmut Ruddies' "Ernst Troeltsch: Geschichtsphilosophie in praktischer Absicht," in *Grundprobleme der grossen Philosophen,* vol. 8, edited by Joseph Speck (Göttingen, 1986). A critical biography of Troeltsch does not yet exist. However, there are detailed studies for a biography of the young Troeltsch in *Troeltsch-Studien,* vol. 1, *Untersuchungen zur Biographie und Werkgeschichte: Mit den unveröffentlichten Promotionsthesen der "Kleinen Göttinger Fakultät" 1888–1893,* edited by Horst Renz and Friedrich Wilhelm Graf (Gutersloh, 1982).

Jean Séguy's *Christianisme et société: Introduction à la sociologie de Ernst Troeltsch* (Paris, 1980) offers an instructive introduction to Troeltsch's sociology of religion. Intensive work has also been done on Troeltsch's dogmatics and theory of religion. See *Ernst Troeltsch and the Future of Theology,* edited by John Powell Clayton (Cambridge, 1975); B. A. Gerrish's *The Old Protestantism and the New: Essays on the Reformation Heritage* (Edinburgh, 1982); Walter E. Wyman, Jr.'s *The Concept of Glaubenslehre: Ernst Troeltsch and the Theological Heritage of Schleiermacher* (Chico, Calif., 1983); Sarah Coakley's *Christ without Absolutes: A Study of the Christology of Ernst Troeltsch* (Oxford, 1986); and *Troeltsch-Studien,* vol. 3, *Protestantismus und Neuzeit,* edited by Horst Renz and Friedrich Wilhelm Graf, (Gutersloh, 1984). In addition to studies in the reception of Troeltsch's thought in the Anglo-American world, in Italy, and in the Netherlands, this last volume contains detailed examinations of Troeltsch's political activity. Moreover, an instructive introduction is offered by Arrigo Rapp in *Il problema della Germania negli scritti politici di E. Troeltsch, 1914–1922* (Rome, 1978).

Friedrich Wilhelm Graf (1987)
Translated from German by Charlotte Prather

TRUBETSKOI, EVGENII (1863–1920), Russian Orthodox philosopher. Evgenii Nikolaevich Trubetskoi, a brother of Sergei, was professor of philosophy at the University of Moscow from 1905 to 1918. He developed his philosophical views within the same general context as did Vladimir Solov'ev and was the author of a major study on him, *Mirosozertsanie Solov'eva* (Solov'ev's Worldview, 2 vols., Moscow, 1913). A theoretical disagreement with Solov'ev, which did not stand in the way of their friendship, led Trubetskoi to study Western theocratic ideas. In his two-volume *Religiozno-obshchestvennyi ideal zapadnogo khristianstva* (The Religio-Social Ideal of Western Christianity, Moscow, 1892; Kiev, 1897), which focused on Augustine and the medieval papacy, he concluded that a religious institution's primary responsibilities were incompatible with that institution's exercise of political power.

In his philosophy, Trubetskoi blended philosophical idealism, traditional Orthodoxy, and a voluntaristic-exhortative creed that shaded off into political activism. His posthumously published *Smysl zhizni* (Meaning of Life) was popular among the Russian émigrés whom it provided with the much-needed assertion that there was meaning in existence.

Trubetskoi was instrumental in stimulating increased interest in religious philosophy. He was active in the Moscow Psychological Society, in the Religio-Philosophical Society of Vladimir Solov'ev (named after the philosopher), and in the publishing house Put' (The Way). All three, on different levels, popularized metaphysics, religion, and, tangentially, liberalism. Trubetskoi worked for reform of the Russian Orthodox church and for a greater involvement of the laity in the church. He was appointed to the pre-Sobor meeting in 1906 that prepared for institutionalizing self-government in the church and was elected to the church council that pronounced the reestablishment of the patriarchate in 1917.

Evgenii Trubetskoi in his writing focused both on the individual, as the carrier of value, and on the state, which establishes conditions that can make moral value effective. He published a number of important works in law, and led between 1906 and 1910 a small moderate political party, the Party of Peaceful Regeneration. At the same time he edited the *Moskovskii ezhenedel'nik* (Moscow Weekly), a journal in which he expounded upon public issues. In 1910 he joined the Constitutional Democratic Party. During World War I his patriotic brochures, especially one containing an analysis of icons titled *Umozrenie v kraskakh* (Speculation in Colors), were quite popular.

Trubetskoi based his liberalism not on the will of the majority but on the rights inherent in each individual. He saw the state as a necessary buffer between the majority, which could, on occasion, be illiberal, and the individual. Equally outspoken about the dangers of violence from the left as from the right, he condemned the terrorist actions of radicals that the Russian progressives tended to condone.

Trubetskoi was an early and uncompromising foe of the Bolsheviks. In the last years of his life he placed great hopes on the innate religiosity and conservatism of the Russian peasants to overthrow the oppressive Bolshevik regime. He died in Novorossisk, fleeing the Bolsheviks and predicting their early demise.

Bibliography

There is no comprehensive study of Evgenii Trubetskoi. His philosophical views are discussed in the standard works on Russian philosophy. I have written an introduction to a new edition of his memoirs, *Iz proshlago* (Newtonville, Mass., 1976), in which can also be found a bibliography of his major works.

Martha Bohachevsky-Chomiak (1987)

TRUBETSKOI, SERGEI (1862–1905), scion of an old noble family in Russia, was professor of philosophy at the University of Moscow. Weeks before his death Sergei Nikolaevich Trubetskoi became the university's first elected rector. He was instrumental in popularizing philosophical idealism. His philosophical and religious convictions led him to take public stands on the major issues of the day, positions which brought him national prominence. At an audience with the tsar in June 1905 Prince Trubetskoi was the spokesman of the moderate liberals. A close confidant of Vladimir Solov'ev, Trubetskoi worked within the philosophical tradition of idealism that encompassed Plato, Kant, the Russian Slavophiles, especially Ivan Kireevskii, and the Western mystics, particularly Jakob Boehme. Trubetskoi's interest in the history of philosophy led him to the history of religion. He wrote an introduction to the Russian edition of Karl Barth's *Religions of India* and prepared a bibliography on the history of religion for the Russian edition of P. D. Chantepie de la Saussaye's *Illustrated History of Religions.*

Trubetskoi's work was based on philological as well as historical study and demonstrates an amalgamation of philosophical and religious concerns. He maintained that while no strictly philosophical system can solve all the problems raised by philosophy, Christianity does hold solutions to these problems. For Trubetskoi, *sophia* (wisdom) is an intermediary between the absolute and humanity. He argued that the Logos, which he traced not to the philosophy of the Greeks but to Jewish gnosticism, refers to the concrete person of Christ rather than to a rational concept that might be linked to *sophia.* He rejected the notion of God as the absolute actualizing itself in history since, in his view, the absolute, by its very nature, could not be in the process of becoming. Trubetskoi held that Christianity, with its absolute and autonomous system of morality, is the vehicle through which the potential for the kingdom of God can be realized.

The source of true knowledge, according to Trubetskoi, lay in reason, sensibility, innate ideas, mystical experience, and faith, all of which reflect what he refers to as the "concrete consciousness" of each individual. Knowledge is possible because the human being is conscious of an external reality and is also part of that reality. Consciousness is not solely the function of the individual but of the species collectively. Hence, Trubetskoi considered the consciousness of causality to be both innate and based upon external reality. In his statement, "Whenever I make any decision I hold within myself a conference about all with all," Trubetskoi encapsulated a theory he characterized as "metaphysical socialism."

Because human beings have the capacity to reason, Trubetskoi argued, it follows that humankind can rise above natural causes and act morally. Eventually, humanity or society can develop the capacity to become a real organism, an eternal person. Although Trubetskoi posited the collectivity of consciousness, he maintained that value lay with the individual, since it is the individual who can reason and know. He defended the immortality of the individual soul and the freedom of the individual from external constraints. His conscious attempts to popularize philosophy drew him into the public arena. The reactionary wing of the Russian Orthodox clergy, which resented lay interference and the intrusion of philosophy into religion, accused Trubetskoi of undermining religion, while in actuality he sought to make it meaningful to the educated.

Bibliography

Among Trubetskoi's major works are *Metafizika v drevnei Gretsii* (Metaphysics in Ancient Greece; 1890), *Uchenie o logose v istorii* (A Study of the Logos in History; 1900), "Psikhologicheskii determinizm i nravstvennaia svoboda" (Psychological Determinism and Moral Freedom; 1894), "Etika i dogmatika" (Ethics and Dogmatics; 1895), "Osnovaniia idealizma" (Foundations of Idealism; 1896), and "Vera v bezsmertie" (Belief in Immortality; 1902). The articles were published in *Voprosy filosofii i psikhologii* (Issues in Philosophy and Psychology), a journal Trubetskoi was instrumental in founding. His collected works are available as *Sobranie sochinenii kn. Sergeia Nikolaevicha Trubetskogo,* 6 vols. in 5, edited by L. M. Lopatin (Moscow, 1907–1912). For further discussion of Trubetskoi, see my book *S. N. Trubetskoi: An Intellectual among the Intelligentsia in Pre-Revolutionary Russia,* with an introduction by Georges Florovsky (Belmont, Mass., 1976).

Martha Bohachevsky-Chomiak (1987)

TRUTH. The concept of religious truth expresses various aspects of human experience: reality that is permanent, immeasurable, unconcealed, effective, powerful; personal character that is sincere, good, genuine, valuable; and knowledge that is certain, accurate, pure, clear, and convincing. Truth emerges out of the basic human experience of valuation (both as assessment and appreciation) as a necessity for human survival and well-being. Human life is characterized by the need to distinguish between what is real and unreal, powerful and powerless, genuine and deceptive, pure and contaminated, clear and confused, as well as relative degrees of one extreme or the other. In an attempt to understand the character and variation of the existential engagement with truth in different religious traditions, we can recognize three aspects of truth: (1) the character of accurate knowing, (2) the nature of the reality known, and (3) the formation of value as the power to actualize this reality in authentic living. As a general concept, religious truth can be defined as the knowledge and expression of what-is for the purpose of achieving the greatest well-being possible (i.e., salvation, absolute freedom, or total harmony).

Inherent in religious truth is the recognition that a person who knows, manifests, or orients his or her life to ultimate reality is achieving ultimate transformation—for example, being saved or attaining complete liberation. In knowing the truth a person becomes authentic because he or she places his or her self-consciousness in a comprehensive context of what-is. The object of religious knowing is not simply information about another thing or person; it is recognition of the deepest reality or resource for fulfillment of life. Such an object, called God, the Dharma, the Dao, *tathatā* ("thusness"), or *nirvāṇa,* is not a conventional object in a subject-object relationship, but the original source, the nature, or quality of all conventional objects as they really are. This understanding of truth cannot be limited to a conception of truth as a relationship between words or between ideas and things (though words, ideas, and mental images may evoke the quality of truth whereby self-consciousness responds appropriately to what-is). Religious truth entails the continuing development of a valid relationship between self-consciousness and one's most extended and most profound environment (reality).

When people express religious truth, they are aware of different levels, kinds, or functions of truth. At the extremes are absolute and relative truth, or transcendent and conventional truth. The former expresses the deepest reality, the sacred, God, or "what-is"; the latter indicates accurate information about life the importance of which is limited to specific situations and short-term goals. The assumption of all religious truth is that personal estimations of what-is or decisions of momentary value must be affirmed only insofar as they are an aspect of the transcendent or absolute truth. Such absolute truth transcends and incorporates the concerns defined by information dependent on time-space conditions; it establishes an overarching value in relation to which the information has significance and meaning. This value is not external to the reality experienced, as an idea about something or a momentary feeling would be. Rather, it is experienced as a total orienting impetus providing coherence for the ideas and feelings that prompt a person to act in a certain way. Thus, truth is the valuation achieved by self-consciousness as it becomes a particular organizing center of self-awareness, meaning, feeling, and action—an individual participating in, and responding to, reality.

To respond appropriately or accurately to what-is can be understood as a release of ultimate power enabling a person to avoid self-deception and dissipating entanglement with unimportant activities and destructive forces. Religious truth is a transforming orientation leading to superlative well-being, known in traditional religious terms as the conversion from sin to salvation, illusion to insight, bondage to freedom, and chaos to order. It expresses not only what is apparent or of relative worth but also what-is at the deepest level. From the standpoint of sin, bondage, or chaos, this ultimate reality is experienced as what *ought* to be. By affirming the highest truth, a person declares a strategy for both knowing the ultimate reality and actualizing it in his or her daily experience, because such truth is of highest value for achieving superlative well-being. It expresses a comprehensive purpose as part of a person's perception of reality.

In world religions, truth is advocated as a corrective to three general sorts of deception: (1) intentional deception between people, or lying; (2) error due to lack of information; and (3) an inclination toward self-deception. These are interrelated because, in the last analysis, the expression of truth between people and the correction of ignorance find their capacity in the awareness developed through a continuing effort to avoid self-deception about "the way things really are." People often lie to each other in the sense that they deceive themselves about their own deepest resource; they lack information about ultimate values and reality because they are too easily satisfied by short-term pleasures.

At the same time, there is a wide range of solutions to self-deception in the different world religions. This is due to the fact that there are different orientations having different structures of valuation for determining which way of being authentic is really the best and which is derivative or secondary. Since truth is a solution to a process of self-deception, the correcting process that communicates and actualizes what-is at the deepest level, and thus what ought to be, is a comprehensive transformation of one's life-orientation. To examine different expressions of truth in world religions, we must not only look at different ideas about truth as a conceptual formulation but describe the processes in which the truth as description or information about reality is also a re-evaluation of what is significant in life. We will look at five different approaches or ways of knowing the truth so that it might actualize the deepest well-being possible, sometimes specified as the good, heaven, salvation, liberation, or total harmony. These approaches to truth are (1) intimate experience of spiritual presence(s), (2) symbolic duplication of sacred reality through myth and ritual, (3) cultivation of appropriate relationships, (4) awakening transcendent consciousness, and (5) cognition of necessary and eternal realities. Then we will consider some of the problems of formulating and reformulating the deepest truth in relation to other, general claims to truth in changing historical and social contexts.

Intimate Experience of Spiritual Presence(s). One way of knowing the ultimate truth is the awareness of what-is through the extraordinary experience of spiritual presence(s). These are most often unseen but powerful, controlling forces in life. This type of truth does not appeal for its validity to universal ideas or the coherence and meaning of culturally accepted symbols, even though the social-mythic system communicates the reality of these powerful presences in symbolic and mythic language. For this type of truth the adequacy and meaning of reality is encountered by direct personal acquaintance with usually unseen spiritual presences as they provide healing, regenerative resources, wholeness, and joy. The validity of this truth depends on the intimate and direct experience of such a presence. I shall describe two kinds of intimate knowledge of sacred presence. The first is found in many archaic cultures in North and South America, Africa, Siberia, and the South Pacific islands; it is expressed in the ecstatic experiences of diviners and shamans. The second is found in the ecstatic devotion to, and often prophetic utterance for, God in Judaism, Christianity, Islam, and the theistic forms of Hinduism.

An essential element of this religious knowledge is the rupture of conventional, everyday experience, a personal, heightened sensitivity to the usually hidden, but ultimately real, presence of power(s). While the wisdom of the shaman is often described as "supernatural," it is probably better to regard this—from the standpoint of the advocates—as a deeper or clearer knowledge of the natural forces that make all life possible. For example, the *kilumba* or *nganga* (one who possesses a healing vision) among the Bantu-speaking Luba in Africa is a man who is "seized" by a spirit or disembodied ancestor in order to reveal why some person or a society has inappropriately interfered with the powers of life and therefore has manifested disease, social disharmony, or natural catastrophe. Or, among the Huichol of north-central Mexico, the shaman (*mara'akáme*) is a person who is more deeply aware of the hidden forces contending with each other; he has transcended the apparent conditions of conventional existence and becomes the medium or mouthpiece of these forces in life. The unusual character of his knowledge is described as coming from the spirits (divine powers), who know and determine everyday happenings.

The shamanic communication requires crossing over from the biosphere to a hidden (spiritual) plane and then returning to the mundane world. The mundane sphere is a state of separation, pollution, and mortality, as evidenced by illness and social conflict. The hidden, but more powerful (spirit) realm is also one of contending forces who (which) can be benevolent or beneficent toward the members of the biosphere. The shaman needs to have the capacity and skill to maintain a balance between the contending forces; he engages the spirit forces as they "possess" him while deftly remaining balanced between two worlds. According to the Tucano of the Amazon forests, the soul of the shaman (*payé*) is said to be luminous, penetrating the darkness, and generative of life and health—like the sun. His skill and purity of soul allow him to ascend to the sky or descend into the netherworld, described as "death" or "dismemberment," and then return to the everyday world.

When the shaman becomes "possessed" by a spirit, his ecstatic experience is interpreted by the audience within a cosmology that affirms hidden vital forces, and his "seizure" is seen as a sign that they will soon hear the voices or sounds of these spirits that will aid them in dealing with vital problems. The truth of the shaman's utterances, then, is part of a total orientation to life in which the members of the community respond emotionally, socially, and physically to the perceived forces affecting them day in and day out. Shamanic utterances are distinguished in these societies from psychotic experiences among the people by their predictive force and concrete results in solving problems. At the same time, when the utterances of a recognized shaman are not effective by empirical examination, some extenuating circumstance, such as impurity or inadequate following of a prescription, can be given to account for the failure.

The second kind of religious truth that requires an intimate knowledge of a sacred presence is the overwhelming experience of a devotee to God. This, too, requires a sense of a usually hidden force that directs one's life as well as all existence. Direct personal experiences of God in Judaism, Christianity, and Hinduism are described as awesome, uncanny; they can provoke fear and terror. At the same time, they can provide deep comfort, evoke a sense of wonder and joy of life, and transform one's self-consciousness from a feeling of weakness, corruption, and worthlessness to strength, purity of heart, and profound value. In the theistic traditions of all cultures are found examples of pious devotees whose personal experiences of God are described as spontaneous eruptions of a divine force that, on the one hand, compels them to lead a new kind of existence and, on the other, provides a serene strength to meet life's traumas of personal loss, illness, and death. The devotee who lives his or her life in the presence of divine love and judgment feels reconnected with the source of life, so that even when mundane life is seen as full of evil and impotency, there is confidence in the divine power's ability to overcome the apparent meaninglessness and self-destructiveness.

The validity of the truth known from personal experience depends directly on an evaluation of one's self-consciousness within the context of a transcendent presence of the powers of life or the Holy One. The awareness is perceived as an overwhelming disclosure that transcends other norms of validity, such as empirical verification or rational analysis. Such divine disclosure provides a direction for living and a principle for knowledge not available in other norms of validity. The response to this disclosure is faith or trust in the final control of a powerful, loving, and caring divine presence. In the last analysis, such a divine presence remains a mystery, one that cannot be controlled by personal wants or verified by the mundane experience of health or prosperity. The response of faith is one of service in (and servitude to) the divine will. The truth known in such response is validated by the devotee in the experience of being known by the Holy One.

SYMBOLIC DUPLICATION OF SACRED REALITY THROUGH MYTH AND RITUAL. Symbolic expressions of truth in the form of divine words, sacred myths, and sacramental rites and initiations are found throughout the world. They reflect the power of symbolic gestures and language to construct a realm of meaning. While often combined with the experience of powerful forces and the sense of social obligation and order, the communicative power of religious symbolic forms is found in their capacity to express several levels of meaning simultaneously, so that such activities as dancing, eating together, body marking, telling stories, and the use of special words or sounds can have more than a single signification. Verbal language, especially, has the mental-emotional force to construct multiple levels of meaning whereby self-consciousness attends to, and structures, experienced reality. The formation of ideas woven together by syntax (i.e., language) identifies and orders (often overlapping) conceptual units of consciousness into meaningful awareness. Thinking or imagining is more than a presentation of external sensations to the mind; the formation of ideas is a projection of self-consciousness toward, and into, the sensations of the experienced world. To speak about the world creates a relationship of symbolic meaning between self-consciousness and the world. The use of language demands a choice whereby a person separates one "thing" from another, classifies similar appearances into concepts, and makes evaluations between more or less significant features of one's experience.

The power of language to construct a symbolic realm of meaning relates self-consciousness to the world by creating a "center" in the individual and, at the same time, placing the individual in a universe "as it is"—that is, as it appears directly to self-consciousness. Thus, symbols that express truth are those consistent with the deepest (often presumed) valuation inherent in one's experience. Religious symbols are those mental-emotional lenses that provide images of oneself (a psychology) and the universe (a cosmology); they teach human beings not only what to see, but how to see. As scholars of mythology have pointed out, religious myths are those symbolic expressions that are recognized as true simply by being expressed.

A religious symbol, such as a divine name, sacred myth, ritual action, or visual image of a deity, is seen by religious advocates as the manifestation of a pure, original, mysterious, and powerful reality in a particular concrete form. The symbolic bodily gesture, sound, or physical image is a paradigm of reality—divine reality. Myths and rituals are repetitions of original life-creating actions by the gods, primal ancestors, and cultural heroes and, therefore, must be carefully preserved and meticulously duplicated. They disclose the divine resource that makes any life at all possible. It is the sacred that is eternal, genuine, whole, and pure—the opposite of the profane, corrupt, and fragmented mundane human experience—yet, paradoxically, it is expressed in and through the mundane form, where it usually remains hidden. The religious power of the symbols derives precisely from the fact that they claim to repeat the primal action of creation, the divine rescue of the world from devouring demons, or to describe the joys of paradise in the eternal realm. In providing the paradigmatic truth regarding reality, myth and ritual also provide a model for successful human living. The appeal to divine action is a basic principle of justification for social relations, morality, and, in many cases, all human activities.

Sacred words (divine names, sacred actions and laws, blessings, curses) and sounds (*mantras*, chants) are perceived by religious devotees to have a special capacity to release power. According to the perspective of Mīmāṃsā, a school of Hindu philosophical thought, the sacredness of *mantras* (sacred sounds, phrases, or verses) derives from the eternity of the word. The use of the *mantra* in prayer, meditation, or worship reveals the deity or divine energy because the sound is intrinsically related to the divine energy; it is an eternal causal principle. The sound (*śabda*) of words is not arbitrary; it represents an eternal principle or force that is manifested in many forms of changing existence. The *mantras*, thus, express the essence of divine powers in their very repetition; the sacred utterance in the hymns of the *Ṛgveda* is a direct testimony to the primal energies of the universe. This view is basic for several subsequent Hindu theistic schools that appealed to the validity of verbal testimony on the basis of the intrinsic power of sound (speech) to express the eternal principles so long as the revealer, the source of knowledge, is adequate.

In Zoroastrianism, a sacred utterance, the Ashem Vohu, is used in most devotions to concentrate a person's mind on *asha* ("truth"). *Asha* is the name of an abstract principle of truth or righteousness in the cosmos, but also the name of a divinity often invoked in the *Gāthās*, one of the Amesha Spentas ("bounteous immortals"). As one of the immanent powers who maintain the universe, Asha is also symbolically identified with fire, a focus of much Zoroastrian ritual. In this religious tradition, truth is symbolically expressed in a divine name, a concrete ritual image, and evoked through a sacred prayer. In Islam, "truth," as identical to reality (*al-ḥaqq*), is an attribute of God, the creator of the world and maintainer of righteousness. *Al-ḥaqq* is that which is steadfast and permanent; it is genuine and authentic. God, as the reality, is the source of truth for humanity, especially as found in the sacred recitation (Qurʾān) given to Muḥammad.

The validity for truth in religious symbolic expression, then, is found in the recognition that its source is eternal, of the realm of the sacred. The activity of God, of bounteous spiritual beings, or of primal ancestors is the real and significant activity. The duplication of the sacred realm in symbolic gestures, physical objects, names, stories, and sounds provides the paradigm for meaning, regeneration in life cycles, and the norm for righteousness. True human knowledge and behavior imitates that of the gods or God. In religious initiations, sacrifices, and sacraments, people release eternal power that purifies as it discloses the foundation for human well-being. The deepest problems in life arise from forgetting one's sacred source, neglecting to repeat the sacred action symbolically, or rejecting the sacred word (such as the Jewish Torah, Jesus Christ as the divine word made flesh, or the Muslim Qurʾān) as the basis for all well-being. When the effects expected from following the sacred rituals and words are not attained, the devotee usually recognizes some failure in perfectly duplicating the sacred paradigm. When there are conflicting myths competing for the loyalty of believers, the sacred reality of one myth is often judged to be demonic power by those holding another myth (an exclusive position), or it is seen as a lesser but related aspect of the true sacred reality according to advocates of another myth (an inclusive position).

Cultivation of Appropriate Relationships. Another approach to truth that expresses self-consciousness of what-is is through practical moral wisdom characterized by honesty, trustworthiness, and sincerity. Here the emphasis is on moral action that is consistent with personal integrity. This approach holds that a person cannot truly know the nature of reality without demonstrating what it means to "be" in everyday activities. The means for attaining wisdom combines intuition with observation and learning drawn from ancient tradition. We will discuss first the expression of this truth from Chinese and Indian sources, which appeal to a natural cosmic order (law), and then briefly note several theistic expressions whose ultimate source is divine but that emphasize the moral character of truth.

In the classical Chinese expression of truth there is no sharp distinction between the knowledge of what-is and a person's moral action. Authentic awareness of reality is expressed more in daily practice than formulated in arguments about the nature of the good. The law of life is known not through a personal experience of a divine presence, duplication of a sacred word, or rational reflection; rather it is known through living out a sensitivity to the inherent cosmic harmony within the self and the world. Moral wisdom is found typified in the ancient Sage Kings by the phrase "sageliness within and kingliness without." The goal is to develop a moral attitude that is tested in social relationships, one that is based on the general notion that there is an intrinsic order in all things that must be actualized in concrete relationships with nature and society.

Truth in both verbal expression and behavior is defined as *chang* ("constant"). A statement or behavior is "constant" when it promotes appropriate relationships within an organic order. Thus, truth is not an idea or abstraction but a human expression that shapes practical behavior. It has a practical function in communication that attempts to promote good behavior. In the Confucian classic *Zhong yong* (Doctrine of the Mean) the insight into the way (*dao*) of life focuses on "sincerity" (*zheng*). Sincerity is the demonstration that one perceives the reality of all life; it is a manifestation of the ultimate coherence between self-consciousness and the objective world. The capacity to cultivate such sincerity or integrity is inherent in human beings, but its actualization is not inevitable, so the potential must be fulfilled by constant personal effort.

In classical Hinduism, also, there is the recognition that truth about what-is is most profoundly expressed in everyday activity. From the beginning of the common era, when the Brahmanic tradition that grew out of Vedic rituals was synthesized with a concern for social order, down to the present a prominent notion has been that of *dharma* ("law, reality, truth"). The cosmic order that pervaded all things is expressed also in appropriate social relationships. The *dharma,* what people should do, is the correct arrangement of everything in life. Knowledge of oneself is found in following one's *dharma,* one's way of being in relation to the organic whole. Everything and everybody has a place in the universe. The moral duties of farmer and ruler, husband and wife, or child and parent were defined by their appropriateness to each person's station. To act contrary to one's obligations and responsibilities destroys one's own character and creates chaos in society and nature.

According to the Brahmanic text *Manusmṛti* (The laws of Manu) the sources for knowing one's *dharma* were first the Veda, then the tradition, then the virtuous conduct of the religious leaders and holy men, and, finally, self-satisfaction. Most of the society did not study the Vedas, so they learned appropriate conduct from the tradition as expressed in popular stories, festivals, and social rules as they were reinforced by interaction with others. The truth of one's existence was defined by participation in the fabric of society, and the cultivation of personal character was found in the virtues of sincerity, self-restraint, and honesty.

In the theistic traditions of Zoroastrianism, Judaism, and Islam there has also been a deep sense of expressing truth through moral behavior. Truth is expressed in the qualities of veracity, integrity, and trustworthiness. In Zoroastrianism, truth (*asha*) is the order that governs human conduct. Those who are honest, keep their oaths and covenants, and are loyal to Ahura Mazdā are the righteous ones (*ashavan*), those who uphold *asha.* They look for the final victory over the wicked (*drugvant*), those who follow falsehood. In Judaism, truth (*ʿemeth*) is expressed in righteousness, justice, and peace. In such actions Jews worship "the God of truth." God keeps his word, and those who speak the truth come near him. Thus, those who avoid deceit and hypocrisy in all their dealings practice the truth. In Islam, the word *ṣadaqa* means integrity, honesty, and trustworthiness. It is the quality of expression when one tells the truth; it requires that a person be honest with himself or herself and with others, as well as recognize the actual situation with which one is dealing. To express the truth is to follow the will of God, since he is the source of everything. A statement that corresponds to reality is an action that is trustworthy.

Awakening Transcendent Consciousness. A fourth religious way that truth is viewed as the accurate self-consciousness of what-is focuses on the quality of consciousness. Rather than centering the nature of truth on the intimate experience of a spiritual presence, on the symbolic structuring of a sacred realm of meaning, or on cultivating appropriate relationships within a cosmic network, the power by which one can attain comprehensive well-being is the liberating insight that purifies inner dispositions, attitudes, and the thinking-feeling processes—all aspects of consciousness.

The truth of oneself and the world is perhaps partially expressed in symbolic imagery, ideas, and behavior, but the key condition for attaining true (or transcendent) knowledge, say the practitioners of this way, is the avoidance of attachment to these conventional habits of knowing. Here the concern to transform the manner or mode of knowing from a self-limiting, fabricating, and distorting process to a freeing, direct-intuitive insight is crucial because it is assumed that there is an intrinsic and reciprocal relation between the knowing process and the reality known. It is also assumed that there are different qualities of knowing, each of which leads to one or another kind of "becoming real." For anything to exist, it has to come into existence, or "become something," within the context of some manner of perception, process of knowing, and mode of consciousness. The concept of realization includes the two elements of knowing and becoming, as when we say that someone realizes certain possibilities. To realize transcendent consciousness requires a shift away from the conventional habits of consciousness aimed at perceiving (understanding) what-is. In this shift to another process of knowing, a person also comes to exist, "becomes," in a new way.

The highest truth, then, in this approach requires insight into the nature of the process of becoming; it stresses how a person contributes positively or negatively to this process by the manner or quality of his or her awareness. This means that the expression of truth must "fit" the level or quality of the hearer. Truth is not a single idea or proposition that stands eternally and to which all particular forms partially correspond. Ideas and concepts are useful as pointers to truth, or catalysts for freeing a person from habitual mental-emotional entanglements, but a statement that would "fit" a lower spiritual condition, and thus be "true," might be denied as an appropriate expression for someone at a higher level of spirituality. Because thought, emotions, and inner dispositions are interrelated, say the teachers of this way, a true statement is not a universal abstraction, an idea known by the intellect, but a catalyst for insight. Also, the hearer of truth must be prepared to receive it; for a religious idea to bear spiritual fruit, it must be received with a pure heart, or liberated mind. Such an apprehension requires more than intellectual skills or socially conditioned reflex responses; it is cultivated through serenity, courage, diligence, and love (compassion). To know the highest truth, then, is an illumination of "becoming" as an aspect of what-is, which is experienced as unconditional freedom.

The methods for attaining insight, which liberate one from self-imposed bondage according to several spiritual disciplines in India, include quieting the mind through meditation, separating oneself from conventional perceptual and emotional stimuli, sustained and detailed awareness of the factors in one's self-conscious "becoming," concentration (*samādhi*) on the unmoving or unifying center of consciousness, and various levels of mental absorption (*dhyāna*). These are techniques through which a person is reeducated to "see" himself or herself in relation to the world so that he or she is not constructing mental-emotional chains that cause suffering. For example, in Theravada Buddhist practice, the meditation procedures are intended to help one to withdraw from external conditioning forces and to concentrate one's consciousness, so that one can avoid the habitual confusion of one's pure consciousness with the shifting appearances of things, people, ideas—all aspects of the "objective" world. Once a person is not attached to conventional perceptive and ideational imagery, he or she can expand consciousness through trance or mental absorption and eventually, in a freed state of mind, be intuitively aware of "the immeasurable" or "emptiness." In such a state of awareness, say the Buddhist *suttas*, the Buddha perceived the nature of "becoming" as dependent coarising and also understood the root cause of suffering and the possibility of its elimination. Similarly, classical Hindu Yoga advocated the use of certain body positions, controlled breathing, detachment of the senses from external objects, and concentrated mental states to quiet—that is, to avoid producing—conventional procedures of knowing, such as habitual perceptions, inference, memory, or authoritative (sacred) words. These conventional means of knowing are useful as practical vehicles for business, getting physical pleasure, or establishing social relationships, but they are not useful in knowing the deepest reality, pure consciousness (*puruṣa*). Yoga intends to free one from the small, limiting consciousness, or the image of one's ego, so that one may become directly aware of universal consciousness.

A common metaphor in both theistic and nontheistic religious traditions for the transcendent consciousness is the identity or union of the self with ultimate reality (God). Well-known examples of this are found in Advaita Vedānta Hinduism, in Muslim Ṣūfī recollection of God, and in Christian mysticism. Śaṅkara (eighth century CE), as an exponent of "nondual highest knowledge" (*advaita vedānta*), asserted that a genuine and deep investigation into *dharma* led to the inquiry into *brahman*, the single undifferentiated reality that pervades all differentiated existence. The eternal *brahman* is pure being-consciousness-bliss (*sat-cit-ānanda*), and the most profound spiritual truth is to realize that self-consciousness (*atman*) is identical to *brahman*. The Ṣūfī master Ibn al-ʿArabī expresses a comparable insight in his assertion that true submission to God is an all-pervading sense that the self vanishes in the only true reality, God. He says in his *Fuṣuṣ al-ḥikam*: "When you know yourself, your 'I'-ness vanishes and you know that you and God are one and the same."

The Spanish Christian mystic John of the Cross (1542–1591) makes a similar claim in his manual on spiritual discipline, *Ascent of Mount Carmel*, when he writes: "This union comes to pass when God grants the soul this supernatural favor, that all the things of God and the soul are one in participant transformation; and the soul seems to be God rather than a soul, and is indeed God by participation." The soul, then, is like an unstained window that allows the divine rays to illumine it and "transform it into its own light." These examples indicate a common concern to know the highest truth through emptying the self of its conventional consciousness so that the ultimate reality itself is manifest; however, because mystics each use a distinctive method interwoven with their own psychological and cosmological concepts, their statements about the nature of consciousness and ultimate reality remain significantly different.

COGNITION OF NECESSARY AND ETERNAL REALITIES. A fifth approach to the expression of truth is that found in classical Greek reflection on the nature of reality. While Greek philosophy is not a religious tradition in the conventional contemporary sense, Greek philosophers such as Socrates, Plato, and Aristotle wrestled at a profound level with the relation between self-consciousness, the perceived world, and eternal reality (or realities). Their reflection had a significant influence on patristic and medieval Christian theology and on Islamic theology, as well as on the post-Renaissance European philosophical discussion of truth. Despite important differences in the understanding of truth found in the philosophies of Plato and Aristotle, they shared several assumptions in their approach that have been carried forward in the way Western philosophers, and some Christian and Muslim theologians, have addressed the issue of truth.

One of the basic assumptions is that reality (the being of things) is universal, necessary, and, consequently, prior to any knowledge of it. Truth (Gr., *alētheia*, from *alētheuein*, "to disclose") is a disclosure of what-is. Whether the eternal being is defined in terms of eternal ideas, as in Plato, or in terms of substances, as in Aristotle, the object of true knowledge is a necessary reality that is effective (even active) in the experienced world. The being of things is objective, presenting itself to the mind. Another important assumption is that whatever is real is intelligible; reality is that which can be known by the intellect. It has a signifying character, or a meaning of its own, which is known by cognition and, for Plato, intellectually contemplated by the mind. The "being" of things is the subject of any true judgment, which is basically a response to the disclosure of being. Whatever is real has a universal potential—it is potent and is a possibility—and is disclosed in particular forms and events. Plato asserted that being is itself a unity expressed by many particular forms, and such being is known by an integration of self-consistent judgments. By means of the intellect, human beings can know the universal potentials (reality), that is, can identify their meanings as they disclose themselves. By knowing the eternal ideas, especially the Good, human beings respond appropriately to life and achieve their own well-being.

In this context true knowledge is the mind's inner appropriation of the universal potentials that are disclosed by cognitive judgments pertaining to the continually changing appearances of the outer world. The mind has both a passive and an active role in becoming aware of the meaning that is exposed in the changing appearances. The passive aspect receives the impressions through observation, while the active aspect constructs the meaning mentally, by thinking or judgment. In this act the self-consciousness appropriates to some degree the meaning inherent in the being of things. The truth cognized is the valuable quality of the meaning appropriated, and it is evident to the degree that the mind signifies to itself what is disclosed by what-is. In this approach to truth, then, the primary effort is to respond with the intellect to a meaning found in an impersonal but active reality outside the mind. Truth is universal and has an inherent signification that must be reflected by the intellectual grasp of that objective meaning. The basic conceptual signification of reality should be the same in the mental experience of all human beings, regardless of their particular languages or symbolic systems.

Unlike the approach to truth through myth and symbol (which establishes the true meaning in symbolic duplication of a sacred realm), the meaning in this approach is assumed to be in an external reality that is only reflected in corresponding concepts. When mental images or concepts that intend to signify the meaning inherent in nonsymbolic facts conflict with each other, it is an indication that one or more of the symbolic significations do not correspond to the meaning, or self-signification, of reality. Such meanings are simply "beliefs," which may have emotional force but are not regarded by people taking this approach as signifying what-is. In the Western religious traditions, this approach has led to both dogmatism and scientific theorizing: the former identifies eternal, universal, and objective signification with divine revelation and its explication in theological dogmas; the latter identifies eternal, universal, and objective signification with scientific theories based on empirical verification and general inferences that are presumed to function alike in the experience of all people.

INTERPRETATION, COMMUNICATION, AND VERIFICATION. All religious truth, as an existential expression of what-is, is tested and verified by ever-changing human experience. Regardless of the nature of ultimate reality and its relation to the process of its becoming actualized in self-consciousness, as discussed in the approaches to truth given above, the quality of one's awareness, symbolic expression, or social relationship is tested in the changing circumstances of personal maturation and cultural-historical development. There is a basic question arising in each religious and cultural tradition: how is knowledge of the transcendent reality related to a general human means of knowing, for example, perception and inference? Another question arises: how is the original, eternal truth—which itself became manifest in a specific historical-cultural-linguistic situation—to be known in changing and sometimes quite different cultures? We will look at various answers to these questions by first considering the issues of continuity, meaning, and interpretation of symbolic and moral truth. We shall then examine levels of meaning, practical techniques, and the use of language to communicate the special awareness found in the experience of spiritual presence(s) and transcendent consciousness.

In the claims of truth that are based on a sacred word (divine revelation) and/or found in a tradition of trained scholars (such as priests, lawyers, or Confucian literati) who conserve and interpret the eternal moral law, there is a profound concern to understand or make intelligible the meaning of the sacred word and the eternal moral law. Great effort is made to learn, preserve, and interpret the normative teaching so that it is relevant to a community of believers in a specific lived experience. The difficulty in exposing the genuine intention of the original symbolic expression in light of new situations and personal differences of interpretation has resulted in the development of various schools or denominations within all religious traditions. For example, the center of Jewish life is the study and interpretation of the Torah. In this tradition there are different interpretations regarding the relation between the written Torah and the oral Torah. All faithful Jews try to live in the basic myth of the Exodus and according to God's commandments, but there are different interpretations of the purpose of God relative to the historical experience of the Jewish community, the nature of the promised salvation (in this life and the next), and the degree to which certain customs and ritual laws are to be observed in different cultural situations, as well as the centrality and character of study, prayer, moral action, and observance of sacred days. For the past two millennia the leadership of the Jewish community has centered on the rabbi, who not only was trained to interpret the Torah in a creative fashion but also served in many communities as judge and administrator of the law. Especially since medieval times, the rabbis and philosophically inclined thinkers have had to relate the expressions of the Torah to reason and, in the last two centuries, to scientific analysis of the human condition. Such questions as the nature of free will, divine providence, and the psychological conditions for faith are important considerations for contemporary efforts to worship God in truth and to fulfill divine moral obligations of justice and love.

Similarly, Christian faith is based on the divine revelation in Jesus Christ, and study of the Bible, especially of the New Testament, has been central to the life of the Christian community. Already in the first centuries of the Christian church, as the New Testament canon was taking shape and the creeds (the "symbols" of the church) were formulated to define the normative understanding of faith, the impact of the Classical Greek philosophical language helped to shape the doctrines of the Trinity, the person of Christ, and the nature of humanity. A continuing issue in the proper interpretation of scripture, devotional life, and worship was the authority of one or another bishop to declare the official understanding of Christian faith, which was settled by the convening of councils in the fourth and fifth centuries.

The concern to formulate statements of belief that would gain intellectual assent by believers has pervaded the history of the Christian church. During the thirteenth century a watershed formulation was made by Thomas Aquinas that eventually was recognized as authoritative and has remained the supreme theological statement for the Roman Catholic Christian community. In his *Summa theologiae* and *De veritates* he synthesized an understanding of Christian faith with Greek philosophical thought, especially from Aristotle, affirming that truth is a transcendental property of being that, in turn, is dependent on God, the ultimate intellectual cause. According to him, faith is human understanding, but the truth of faith rests on the truth of God, and belief—which includes church dogma—is a result of divine grace. In the sixteenth and seventeenth centuries, however, Christian reformers, such as Martin Luther and John Calvin, rejected the medieval understanding of a single ministerial (papal) office and, thus, many Roman Catholic dogmas; they emphasized the need to base Christian faith on the primal sacred word, the Bible. During the past three centuries, Christians in western Europe and America have engaged in theological reflection in a cultural context dominated by rationalism, scientific analysis, and industrial socioeconomic structures. These intellectual influences condition the formulation of Christian faith on issues such as the nature of human life, the meaning of revelation, and the role of men and women in the political and social order.

Some basic problems encountered by advocates of truth derived from an intimate experience of spiritual presence(s) and from transcendent awareness are (1) communicating an inconceivable reality through the use of words or appeals to conventional human experience, (2) relating unusual inner experience to general criteria of verification in common-knowledge perception or inference, (3) justifying the claims for a superior inner spiritual quality within the person who claims unusual and authoritative states of consciousness, and (4) avoiding the apparent circularity entailed in the claim that those who do not affirm the validity of supraconscious truth are not qualified to understand or judge the validity of this truth. The manifestation of the ultimate source of truth in an experience of spiritual presence(s) or an unconditional transcendent awareness is seen by its advocates to be a source of knowledge beyond logic, symbolic imagery, and conventional perception.

Nevertheless, advocates use words, symbols, and inference to argue by analogy or by logical analysis. For example, the vision of Lord Viṣṇu in the Hindu classic *Bhagavadgītā* (Song to the Lord) includes such imagery as "many mouths and eyes," and "the light of a thousand suns springing forth simultaneously in the sky" to portray the Lord. The Muslim devotional mystic Jalāl al-Dīn Rūmī (d. 1273) describes the true devotee as a person with "a burning heart." With regard to the use of inference to communicate transcendent awareness, a prime example is the second-century CE Indian Buddhist philosopher-monk Nāgārjuna, who used a rigorous logical dialectic to reject the claim of unchanging essences as the reality of existence. Or, in the Zen Buddhist tradition, logical riddles (*kōan*) are used to break the habits of language and conceptual imagery that cause attachment to things or ideas. Logic and symbolic imagery, then, are never wholly descriptive of the transcendent reality—only suggestive, or preparatory to moving to a new level of awareness.

Critics, on the other hand, argue that since the religious reality that its advocates claim to know is so different from any communicable description of it, religious experiences indicate more about the simply subjective (perhaps only psychological) conditions of the knower than about any universal reality. Or, since the nature of religious truth requires a change in the quality of apprehension through special techniques or through transcendent power (e.g., God's grace), any special appeal to unusual states of consciousness cannot provide the norm of validity for a general theory of truth that also relies on conventional inference or perception.

Truth in world religions, then, is a concept that not only has different meanings and uses in religious language but also indicates different approaches to the religious concern for the becoming self-conscious of what-is that makes possible the attainment of the highest well-being. Each of the approaches described here provides an evaluative process that structures the conditions, goals, and nature of truth. The different approaches each have their own development, principles of validation, and impact on people's lives. While different religious and cultural traditions emphasize one or two approaches to truth, the major world religions and civilizations have included several of them as sometimes permissible options.

In the contemporary world, where people of different, and sometimes conflicting, religions and ideologies are in a network of political, economic, and ecological relationships, there is a heightened sense of urgency to develop strategies for at least existing safely within a plurality of ultimate commitments, if not for integrating or discovering the principle of unity in that truth that declares the source of well-being for all humanity. One of the most difficult issues in attempting to integrate the various approaches is that each holds that a distinction must be made between lesser, conventional truth and the highest, or divine, truth. Each approach is itself a system of evaluations about the nature of ignorance, the ultimate reality, and the mechanism of knowing the truth that rejects alternate systems of evaluation.

Especially in those communities that identify their survival and highest fulfillment with a single *form* of truth, through orthodoxy (normative or prescribed teaching) or orthopraxis (normative or prescribed behavior), the tolerance of alternative approaches to truth is difficult to maintain. Paradoxically, a society often holds rigidly to a form of truth when there is change in, or confusion about, the underlying system(s) of evaluation (as, for example, the conflict between the epistemological assumptions of the scientific method and those of the symbolic self-consciousness attained in myth and sacrament), and often an openness to explore alternative forms (contents) of truth emerges when there is stability in the basic system of evaluation.

The contemporary world is characterized by rapid changes in technology and the development of a worldwide communication network. This situation requires new concepts of the self and the universe and an exchange of cultural and religious approaches to truth. The challenge for contemporary people is how to live within some system of comprehensive evaluation (as found in a religion or ideology) and how to respond in a mutually life-enhancing way with people committed to another system of evaluation. The survival and well-being of people in all cultures necessitates a creative reexamination and critical assessment of varied truth claims that implicitly give weight to different ways of valuation.

SEE ALSO Epistemology; Knowledge and Ignorance; Philosophy; Religious Experience.

BIBLIOGRAPHY

Introductory discussions of the concept of truth in world religions can be found in the following works: William A. Christian, Jr.'s *Meaning and Truth in Religion* (Princeton, 1964) and his *Oppositions of Religious Doctrines* (New York, 1972); *Truth and Dialogue in World Religions: Conflicting Truth-Claims*, edited by John Hick (Philadelphia, 1974); Wilfred Cantwell Smith's *Questions of Religious Truth* (New York, 1967); and my *Understanding Religious Life*, 3d ed. (Belmont, Calif., 1985).

For introductions to the nature of truth in shamanism and the symbolism of archaic cultures, see Joseph Campbell's *The Masks of God*, 4 vols. (New York, 1959–1968); Mircea Eliade's *The Sacred and the Profane* (New York, 1959) and his *Shamanism* (New York, 1964); S. F. Nadel's *Nupe Religion* (London, 1954); and Gerardo Reichel-Dolmatoff's *Amazonian Cosmos* (Chicago, 1971).

The religious significance of truth in Western traditions is discussed in Mary Boyce's *A History of Zoroastrianism*, 2 vols. (Leiden, 1975–1982); Jacob Neusner's *The Way of Torah* (Belmont, Calif., 1979); *Understanding Jewish Theology*, edited by Neusner (New York, 1973); Stephen Reynolds's *The Christian Religious Tradition* (Belmont, Calif., 1977); Leslie Dewart's *Religion, Language and Truth* (New York, 1970); W. Montgomery Watt's *Islamic Philosophy and Theology*, 2d enl. ed. (Edinburgh, 1984); and *Islam from Within*, edited by Kenneth Cragg and R. Marston Speight (Belmont, Calif., 1980).

The nature and cultivation of truth in Eastern traditions is described in Hajime Nakamura's *Ways of Thinking of Eastern Peoples* (Honolulu, 1964); *Revelation in Indian Thought*, edited by Harold Coward and Krishna Sivaraman (Emeryville, Calif., 1977); K. Kunjunni Raja's *Indian Theories of Meaning* (Madras, 1963); Padmanabh S. Jaini's *The Jaina Path of Purification* (Berkeley, 1979); Kulitassa Nanda Jayatilleka's *Early Buddhist Theory of Knowledge* (New York, 1963); Francis Dojun Cook's *Hua-Yen Buddhism* (University Park, Pa., 1977); *Tantra in Tibet*, translated and edited by Jeffrey Hopkins (London, 1977); Toshihiko Izutsu's *Toward a Philosophy of Zen Buddhism* (Tehran, 1977); *A Source Book in Chinese Philosophy*, translated and edited by Wing-tsit Chan

(Princeton, 1963); Fung Yu-lan's *The Spirit of Chinese Philosophy* (Boston, 1962); *Invitation to Chinese Philosophy*, edited by Arne Naess and Alastair Hanney (Oslo, 1972); and Tu Wei-ming's *Centrality and Commonality: An Essay on Chung-yung* (Honolulu, 1976).

A critical assessment of various principles of validity emerging from different cultures is found in Eliot Deutsch's *On Truth: An Ontological Theory* (Honolulu, 1979); *Modes of Thought: Essays on Thinking in Western and Non-Western Societies*, edited by Robin Horton and Ruth Finnegan (London, 1973); and *Knowing Religiously*, edited by Leroy S. Rouner (Notre Dame, 1985). For an examination of the relation of language, meaning, and truth in the mystical experiences of different religious traditions, see *Mysticism and Philosophical Analysis*, edited by Steven T. Katz (Oxford, 1978).

New Sources

Allen, Barry. *Truth in Philosophy.* Cambridge, Mass., 1993.

Blackburn, Simon, and Keith Simmons, eds. *Truth.* New York, 1999.

Field, Hartry H. *Truth and the Absence of Fact.* New York, 2001.

Gupta, Anil, and Nuel Belnap. *The Revision Theory of Truth.* Cambridge, Mass, 1993.

Hill, Christopher S. *Thought and World: An Austere Portrayal of Truth, Reference, and Semantic Correspondence.* New York, 2002.

Kölbel, Max. *Truth without Objectivity.* New York, 2002.

Luntley, Michael. *Reason, Truth and Self: The Postmodern Reconditioned.* New York, 1995.

Lynch, Michael P., ed. *The Nature of Truth: Classic and Contemporary Perspectives.* Cambridge, Mass., 2001.

Soames, Scott. *Understanding Truth.* New York, 1999.

Williams, Bernard Arthur Owen. *Truth and Truthfulness: An Essay in Genealogy.* Princeton, N.J., 2002.

FREDERICK J. STRENG (1987)
Revised Bibliography

TSADDIQ.

TSADDIQ. The Hasidic *tsaddiq* (righteous one), also called *rebbe* (teacher) or *admor* (acronym for "master, teacher, and guide"), is the spiritual leader of a Jewish community, to whom members look for guidance in both spiritual and mundane matters. Throughout history, with a few exceptions, the overwhelming majority of Hasidic *tsaddiqim* (plural for *tsaddiq*) have been male. The *tsaddiq* is the officially designated intercessor to God (*shaliah tsibur*) whose prayers on behalf of the community or the individual, while not absolving them of their religious responsibility to address only God in prayer, are considered to be more efficacious than their own, due to his perceived close intimacy with—and influence on—divine providence. He prays with his community and often presides over sacred meals with them, where his followers observe his holy comportment and participate in his charisma, expressed in both communal song and verbal teaching. The source of his charisma is said to be his having transformed his material being into spiritual form and sacred presence. His teachings often take on two forms: (1) exoteric explanations of biblical or rabbinic lore, said with his eyes open; and (2) esoteric teachings on the soul or on other mystical matters, which he says with his eyes closed, often in trance.

BIBLICAL AND RABBINIC DOCTRINES. The Hasidic use of the term *tsaddiq*—the righteous one—has deep roots in biblical and classic rabbinic literature, and was further informed by qabbalistic and late-medieval ethical treatises. Some of these sources shall be illustrated here.

In biblical writings, the term *tsaddiq* was used to designate both the divine nature—righteousness—and the one who carries out God's will. Given the biblical mythos that regards the human being as created in the divine image, the term represents the human ideal. The *tsaddiq* is one who has chosen to be an instrument of the divine nature and will. Attaining charisma thereby, he or she employs it for sacred purposes.

The persona of the *tsaddiq*, as reflected in the teachings of the rabbinic period (second century BCE—fifth century CE) often suggests the functions of one who in biblical times was described by the word *navi* (prophet). The rabbis state that a *tsaddiq* transforms divine wrath into divine compassion: God issues a heavenly decree, and the *tsaddiq* may annul it (Midrash Genesis Rabba 33:3). The divine presence (*shekhinah*) is said to be the *tsaddiq*'s constant companion.

The rabbis appraised the deeds of the *tsaddiqim* as being even more valuable than the creation of heaven and earth; for the latter are the product of divine justice, whereas the *tsaddiqim* add kindness to the creation (Babylonian Talmud Ketubot fol. 5a). The *tsaddiq* is sometimes also called a *Hasid*—one who acts with kindness towards God and creation, beyond the obligations of the law; upon acquiring both wisdom and humility. The rabbis detested the ignorant *Hasid*, whom they regarded as a public nuisance. (The term *Hasid*, meaning "follower of a particular Hasidic *rebbe*," has no textual witness before the 1880s.) In classical Midrash, the biblical Joseph was given the appellation *tsaddiq*, and refraining from sexual impropriety was regarded as the *tsaddiq*'s hallmark.

In Babylonian Talmud Yoma there are esoteric statements such as: "the entire world was created for the sake of one *tsaddiq*"(fol. 38b)—where either or both God and the righteous individual are indicated; or "The *tsaddiq* is a foundation upon whom the entire world stands"(fol. 38b)—a source for the idea of the Hasidic *tsaddiq* as *axis mundi* (Green, 1977). The rabbis state that prior to creation, God's "first thought" was the creation of *tsaddiqim*, and that their primordial presence was "consulted" in the creation of the human being (Midrash Genesis Rabbah 8:7). The *tsaddiq* functions as the conduit through whom divinity pours blessings and liberation into creation; and it is stated that due to the merit of *tsidqaniyot* (female *tsaddiqim*), Israel was delivered from the bondage of Egypt (Babylonian Torah Sotah fol. 11b). In the Qabbalah of the *sefirot*, which hypostasized the divine attributes, Joseph represents the archetype of the *tsaddiq*—the procreative power.

The sages declare that male and female *tsaddiqim* are exempted from the curses of Adam and Eve—meaningless toil and the pain of childbirth (Babylonian Torah Sotah fol. 12a). In this Edenic vein another rabbinic teaching that plays an especially important role in qabbalistic and *Hasidic* thought pronounces that: "By the light that was created on the first day, one could simultaneously gaze from one end of the world to the other. God, having observed that it could be abused by the wicked, hid this light and vouchsafed it for the *tsaddiqim* in 'the future time'"(Babylonian Torah Hagiga fol. 12a).

It is within the potential of every human being, regardless of national affiliation, to be a *tsaddiq*. As for the minimal qualification of the title *tsaddiq*, the rabbis state that a *tsaddiq* is one who has chosen, more often than not, to function as a divine instrument: doing more good than evil, and attempting to establish a conscience-driven rapport with the divine presence (Babylonian Torah Qidushin fol. 40b).

Yet, even the greatest *tsaddiqim*—even the angels—are not perfectly free of fault. King David was accorded the role of the repentant *tsaddiq* who defeated his evil inclination by practicing austerities although the ascetic ideal was not universally embraced by the rabbis. According to some rabbis, human beings—endowed with freedom of choice—are more precious to God than the angels, who were expressly created to suit their particular functions (Babylonian Torah Sanhedrin fol. 93a). The principal inner voice of the human *tsaddiq* is the inclination to the good, construed as an angel nurtured by the *tsaddiq's* good deeds, and the impetus that sustains the *tsaddiq* is faith in divine righteousness. All of these form the ideal of the Hasidic *tsaddiq*.

QABBALAH AND HASIDISM. Regarding the "light of the first day" in qabbalistic literature, we find a difference of opinion as to the meaning of "the future time" when it is stored away for the *tsaddiqim*. According to the *Sefer haBahir*, one of the earliest works of the Qabbalah (anon., twelfth century CE?), members of the Provence and Gerona schools of Qabbalah (1180–1230), the authoritative *Sefer haZohar* (anon., late thirteenth century), and the *Sefer haTemunah* (anon., early fourteenth century); this light is available to *tsaddiqim* during their earthly lifetime, by means of Torah study and contemplative prayer. Through uniting with the light, the *tsaddiq* theurgically and devotionally draws blessings to the entire creation. But according to the more conservative *Ma'arekhet haElohut* and the introductory qabbalistic treatise *Gates of Light* by R. Joseph Gikatilla (both are late thirteenth century), as well as the *Sefer haPeliah* (early fourteenth century?) "the future time" refers to the after-death state. In the sixteenth century, R. Moshe Cordovero (1522–1570) and R. Isaac Luria (1534–1572), both of whom greatly influenced Hasidic thought, accepted the view of the Zohar. In early Hasidic teaching, this light was said to inhere in the sacredness of the letters of the Torah—through which the world itself was created. These holy letters are themselves a central object of contemplation. The famous *Epistle of the Besht* indicates that the Messiah revealed to R. Israel Baal Shem Tov (henceforth, Besht, an acronym for Baal Shem Tov; 1700?–1760), the founder of the Hasidic movement, that each letter contains aspects of the outer world the realm of the soul, and the divine realm, which all unite within divinity. Practice in this form of contemplative-union was said to have afforded the *Besht* ("Master of the Good Name") clairvoyant vision.

This qabbalistic difference of opinion is similar to one found in medieval Jewish philosophy that deals with the possibility of conjunction—or *devequt*—during one's lifetime with the active (or agent) intellect, which is regarded as divinely emanated. This *devequt* union results from human awareness transcending the physical body, focusing on the divine presence within the human mind. Formulae to this effect are found in the explanations to the *yihudim* (unifications)—practices promulgated by the sixteenth-century Qabbalah of R. Isaac Luria, whereby the *tsaddiqim* unify their own conscious presence with the divine attributes, and raise them to higher levels, thereby drawing bounty from more sublime levels within the divine source for the sake of *tiqun*—the repair of the divine-human interface. Lurianic Qabbalah stipulates eight basic levels of theurgic union that provide sustenance, increase, renewal, or innovation, on the spiritual and/or material planes. During the millenia of the exile, nearly all unifications that occur are, in effect, the *tsaddiqim* uniting with the *shekhinah*—as it were, embodying the place of God—by uniting the divine primordial union with the temporal state. During the Temple period (first Temple, c. ninth century BCE to late fifth century BCE ; second Temple, fourth century BCE to 70 CE) and in the Messianic era (yet to occur), we read that it is God who directly enacts this union.

LEVELS OF *TSADDIQIM*. Hasidism, following the Zohar and Lurianic Qabbalah, divided the soul into five levels: (1) *nefesh*, the animating soul of the material plane; (2) *ruah*, the emotive spirit; (3) *neshamah*, the consciousness soul; (4) *hayah*, the emanated wisdom-soul of divine Imminence; and (5) *yehida*, transcendent unity.

These soul levels correlate with four worlds and their defining *sefirot* (divine attributes) as follows:

1. *nefesh* = action-sovereignty;
2. *ruah* = formation-harmony;
3. *neshamah* = creation-understanding;
4. *hayah* = emanation-wisdom; and
5. *yehida* = crown of emanation = primordial Adam = unity within the absolute infinite. Each level contains all five, within its own context.

Whereas emanation is understood and experienced as a seamless divine dialectical unity, creation represents the unfolding of the individual's participation in this dialectic process. Formation represents the emotional contours of this participation, and action, righteous effectuation. Given that all souls were originally within Adam, this schema was understood as forming a collective, living, human-form organism.

The potential of the human being as such, whether male or female, is likened to all five levels, as explicated in the Lurianic corpus. One who purifies all five levels of the *nefesh* attains to periodic transcendent unification with the aspect of sovereignty-in-emanation. This level constantly descends into the world of creation and needs to be raised to emanation by the *tsaddiq*, who has also descended. This is also the case with one who is in the process of purifying the fourth level of the*nefesh.* These two constitute the levels of most *tsaddiqim.* If one succeeds in purifying all five levels of the *ruah*, one would be in constant communion with the *Ruah haQodesh,* the Holy Spirit, and would abide—as active or passive—in the world of emanation, even when in descent to the "lower worlds," and would no longer be subject to jealousy and competitiveness. This is perhaps the qabbalistic analog to the conceptions of the *tsaddiq* developed by R. Nahman of Bratslav (1772–1810), a great-grandson of the *Besht,* and by the founder of Habad Hasidism, R. Shneur Zalman of Lyadi (1745?–1814). The archetypal image of *tsaddiqim* mentioned in the Bible has them working on the five aspects of the *neshamah.* The biblical forefathers, for example, were regarded as the "Divine Chariot"—the instruments of the emanated divine attributes: kindness, judgment, and harmonizing compassion—uniting the second and the third levels of the cosmic *neshamah.* Moses was said to have attained the union of its third and fourth levels and received, as a gift from God, the emanated light of the fifth level. According to the Zoharic-Lurianic Qabbalah, Moses incarnates in every generation, and is potentially present in all Israelite and convert-souls. Upon completion of the *tiqun* of the fifth level of the *neshamah,* he will be in constant union with the unchanging compassion of the *yehidah,* and will manifest as the Messiah.

Luria states that *tsaddiqim* who during the course of their lifetime have always striven to "unite the part with the whole" are constant companions of the divine presence (*shekhinah*) and are themselves present in spirit whenever anyone enacts a *yihud.* Furthermore, these *tsaddiqim* may "impregnate" with their own souls the soul of one who contemplates in this way (striving to unify the part with the whole), thereby aiding the person's spiritual development. According to the Lurianic explanation of the Zohar, higher-level *tsaddiqim* are able to voluntarily reincarnate, and they do so for the sake of furthering the cosmic *tiqun.* With this background it is easier to understand the insistence of R. Yaakov Yosef of Polnoya (died c. 1782), the chief spokesman of the doctrine of the *tsaddiq* as expounded by the *Besht,* that for the untutored laity as well as for the lesser *tsaddiq* to experience *devequt* with God, he or she must be aligned with the *tsaddiqim.*

In every generation a soul-spark of the Messiah is sent to incarnate, to redeem the generation that shows itself worthy; or, if there are worthy *tsaddiqim* in the generation, to illuminate them. By means of messianic consciousness, all the holy potential in human beings will be realized, and numerous texts of early Hasidic teaching (1750–1825) suggest that even the wicked will be transformed and released from hell. This transformative work, according to the Zohar and Lurianism, is performed by *tsaddiqim* in the present (both in this life and in the hereafter), rescuing the souls of those people who are associated with their own Adamic roots.

This work is the source of the Hasidic doctrine of "the descent of the *tsaddiq,*" who must periodically leave exalted states of divine union in order to raise up those for whom they are responsible. Lower-level *tsaddiqim* leave involuntarily, and may even temporarily fall. For higher-level *tsaddiqim* who have cultivated equanimity (as taught by the *Besht* and his disciples), in the words of Rabbi Elimelech of Lizansk (1716?–1787), "*oyven-hinten, hinten-oyven*" ("below [integrated with] above, and above [with] below") (*Or Elimelekh,* p. 98, number 148). And as said by Rabbi Pinchas of Koretz (1726–1791), a companion of the *Besht*: "great *tsaddiqim* love the exceedingly wicked, and lesser *tsaddiqim* love the less wicked" (*Imrei Pinchas haShalem* vol. 1, p. 474, number 72). Elimelech and his disciples also stressed the practice of union with all the *tsaddiqim.* Since the appearance of the pioneering work of Mendel Piekarz (1978), scholars no longer believe that these aspects of Hasidic spirituality were influenced by the Sabbatean false-messiah movement (c. 1666). The anti-Hasidic *mitnagdic* (opponent [to Hasidism]) theology of Rabbi Elijah of Vilna (1720–1797) concurs with the conception of the *tsaddiq* in all of the above, and differs from the early Hasidic model on the public aspect of the intercessory role of the *tsaddiq* and on the breakdown of elitist stratification in the community. Indeed, the Hasidic "social revolution" and its displacement of previous rabbinic and communal forms became possible only as a result of the complete breakdown of centralized Jewish authority (and its well-established universal educational system) in Poland and Lithuania due to the continuing upheavals in the kingdom of Poland between the years 1648 and 1772 which resulted in a smaller and weakened state. In addition, the aforementioned failed popular messianic movement resulted in the near-interdiction of qabbalistic literature, which became the preserve of the elite, who were perceived as having coldly distanced themselves from the greater, largely uneducated, community. These two events seemed to have engendered a novel construal of social solidarity and a replacement of authority.

MODELS OF HASIDIC LEADERSHIP: A BRIEF HISTORY OF THE *TSADDIQ* IN HASIDISM. Defining the archetype of Moses as leader of his people was central to the formulation of the ideal *tsaddiq* in the teachings of the Besht, who described such a *tsaddiq* as encompassing all and uniting with all, from the pharoah to the sage. The *tsaddiq*'s sense of responsibility is mirror-like; all facets of the world, both wicked and holy, become located in *tsaddiqim,* through recognition of their subtle forms within themselves. This causes them to repent, and opens the way for the wicked to repent as well. When they discern that heavenly inspiration is offered, they give honest and loving rebuke, being present within the dialectic of humility and innate worth, and realizing that the rebuke applies to themselves as well. Deriving from the qabbalistic procreative metaphor of the *tsaddiq*, Rabbi Yaakov Yosef of Polnoya regarded the desire, enthusiasm, and pleasure that a person has in performing the good as the expression of the attribute of the *tsaddiq* within the individual.

In early Hasidic applications of these teachings to petitionary prayer, the Besht and his successor, the *magid* (preacher) of Mezritch (1710?–1772) had always stressed the importance of the needs of the *shekhinah* as being the foremost of the *tsaddiq's* concerns; the Besht, making allowance for personal petition when one's sincerity would be compromised by pretense. They counseled the *tsaddiqim* to observe their needs, and by applying qabbalistic tools of symbolic analogy, to discern the spiritual needs of the *shekhinah*. The *magid*, being of an ascetic bent, and having accepted the leadership of what was fast becoming a religious movement that was attracting the cream of the young spiritually and intellectually gifted, placed his entire stress on the needs of the divine presence. This emphasis was passed on to Rabbi Shneur Zalman of Lyadi, who asked his followers not to trouble him with personal petitions.

The *magid*, acting as the Hasidic movement's advocate, distinguished between two types of *tsaddiqim*, based on *Psalm* 92:12: "The *tsaddiq* shall blossom like a palm; like a cedar of Lebanon shall he rise high." The solitary *tsaddiq*, who may rise high as "a perfect *tsaddiq*," produces no fruit. But the one who causes others to flourish, raising the lower elements outside himself, although he may not rise "as high" as the cedar, will blossom with new fruit. It is interesting to note that this distinction is not found in the teachings of the *Besht* as recorded by Rabbi Yaakov Yosef and other disciples. This fact seems to conform to the view of scholars as of the 1980s that Hasidism cannot be construed as a movement prior to the succession of the *magid*.

Indeed, the recruitment efforts of the *magid's* disciples enabled them to become the next generation's elite rabbinic authorities in most of the Ukraine and part of Poland (1772–1800), no doubt facilitated by the final division of Poland in 1772 and the vacuum in Jewish centralized authority. The socioreligious change that Hasidic ideology advocated in the teachings of the Besht, as recorded by Rabbi Yaakov Yosef, called for "men of form" to spiritually transform the "people of matter." This is in keeping with a narrative in the aforementioned *Epistle of the Besht*, which contains an exchange between the Besht and the Messiah. The Besht asked: "when will the Master (Messiah) come?" The Messiah answered: "when your teachings will be so well-publicized and revealed in the world . . . that they too will be able to enact unifications (*yihudim*) and soul-ascents as you do. Then the cosmic obscurations will come to an end and the time of divine favor and salvation will be upon us." Whereas the Besht was distressed by this answer, his numerous teachings instructing the would-be *tsaddiq* in the ways of humility and the acceptance of mutual social responsibility reflect acceptance of the messianic challenge, albeit with the understanding that it is a slow process. Indeed, this messianic ideal is in keeping with Moses' aspiration (*Num.* 11:29) that "the entire People of God be prophets."

It is this ambivalence that led to differences of opinion among scholars as to whether early Hasidism was messianic, or represented a neutralization of acute messianism. In addition, we find statements from the Besht regarding the messianic spark inherent in all who serve God, and the proviso that one must pray for personal redemption before one can pray for cosmic redemption. We also find anecdotal testimony regarding at least two Hasidic masters who realized this spark within themselves, while renouncing pretensions of public messianic identity: Rabbi Menachem Mendel of Vitebsk (1730–1788), a senior disciple of the *magid* who guided Rabbi Shneur Zalman after the *magid's* demise, before emigrating to the Holy Land in 1777; and Rabbi Menachem Mendel of Rymanov (d. 1815).

THE THIRD GENERATION AND THE NINETEENTH CENTURY. Rabbi Elimelech of Lyzansk was an elder disciple of the *magid* who came to him after having already developed into a fairly accomplished *tsaddiq*. He is credited with the formulation of a new Hasidic model—"Practical *Tsaddiqism*." His understanding of the exigencies of the time empowered the Hasidic *tsaddiq* to directly intercede on behalf of the material needs of the Jews. This was acknowledged by Rabbi Ephraim of Sudlykov (1740–1800), a grandson and respected disciple of the Besht, as legitimate, even as he stated that it represents a change from previously accepted emphasis on the needs of the *shekhinah*.

The chief disciple of Rabbi Elimelech was Rabbi Jacob Isaac Hurwitz (1745–1815), the "Seer of Lublin," whose disciples (1795–1870) became the rabbinic leaders of Poland and Galicia and even penetrated into the Austro-Hungarian Empire. Hurwitz was allowed to function as a public *tsaddiq* during the lifetime of Elimelech. The Seer's school produced great practitioners of Lurianic theurgy, and further applied its practices to petitionary prayer. The rationale given for this was the conviction that with fewer material concerns, the laity would better apply themselves to spiritual pursuits. This gave rise to anti-acute-messianism and informed a proto-anti-Zionist ideology. Rabbi Tsvi Elimelech of Dynov (1783–1841), a disciple of the Seer, asserted in the name of the Besht that it is easier to attain the level of *Ruakh ha-Qodesh* (inspiration of the Holy Spirit) in exile than in the Holy Land, where the standards are more demanding. His descendants, the *rebbes* of Munkacs, were among the foremost anti-Zionist Hasidic leaders in the pre–World War II period.

Returning to the theme of the Lurianic "cosmic organism" with its levels and shortcuts, the early Hasidim claimed that the *tsaddiq* can raise up some people only by eating or engaging in other mundane matters in a mode of holy intention, whereas others had to be elevated through the *tsaddiq*'s direct engagement in sacred matters. One of the contemplative innovations of the Besht involves the "raising up" of improper, distracted thought by recognizing the holy essence-nature of the thought: physical desire is rooted in kindness, anger and its effects are rooted in judgement, and pride is rooted in harmonious beauty. By subduing the evil impulse in these negative manifestations and recognizing their specific nature in holiness, the *tsaddiq* "sweetens them at their roots." Rabbi Yaakov Yosef quotes the Besht as saying that one who doesn't believe that divinity inheres in everything, and who doesn't believe that an untoward thought during prayer contains a holy spark sent to the person by divine providence so as to find redemption, shows a lack of faith. Some of the disciples of the *magid* held that thought-transformation practices were reserved only for the elite, whereas some *tsaddiqim* from the school of the Seer of Lublin—notably, the great Hasidic qabbalist Rabbi Isaac of Komarno (1806–1876)—advocated them for anyone who can maintain honesty in the course of these practices.

There is an early Habad tradition (which traces its provenance to the Besht) that states that whereas in earlier times, souls were incarnated within a stratified rubric (peasants possessing souls from the world of action, business people possessing souls from the world of formation, and scholars possessing souls from the world of creation), as of the advent of the Besht, which constitutes the "footsteps of the Messiah," the souls that enter the world contain sparks from all worlds. Thus, at one moment, one can be engaged in a sublime religious experience, and at the next, one can find oneself in totally different inner circumstances. For this reason the Besht counseled against self-satisfaction—the surest way to forsake the sacred path. Yet, Habad reserved thought-transformation practices for *tsaddiqim.* On the other hand, there is an oral tradition from the fifth Lubavitcher *rebbe,* Rabbi Shalom Dov-Ber (1860–1920), who recommended that each of his followers spend at least fifteen minutes a day cultivating the persona of the *tsaddiq,* observing all things as rooted in primordial Adam.

INTERNAL DISSENT; EXCEPTIONAL WOMEN; EXTERNAL OPPOSITION; DECLINE AND ACCOMMODATION. The Hasidism of Preshischa, formulated at the beginning of the nineteenth century by disciples of the Seer of Lublin as a breakaway reform of Hasidism, attempted to purify Hasidism from an ethos of the vain petitionary seeking of the miraculous. Instead. it stressed the values of inner truth and the study of the law, and demurred from the study of Qabbalah. This movement conquered Poland for the Hasidism of Kotzk, Gur, Aleksander, Biala, Amshinov-Worka, and Izbica-Radzin. During the first three generations, it upheld its antipetitionary position. There was mutual criticism between the schools of Lublin and Preshischa. The great *magid* of Kozienice, Rabbi Israel Hopstein (1733–1815), a prolific writer of qabbalistic works and close friend of both the Seer and Rabbi Simha Bunim of Preshischa (1765–1827), attempted to act as a bridge between them.

His daughter, Perele (d. 1849?) observed many of the biblical commandments ordained specifically for men, and was recognized as a *tsadeqet* by Rabbi Elimelech of Lyzansk, who, together with her father, urged his followers to visit her with their prayer petitions. *The Rebbe's Daughter: Memoir of a Hasidic Childhood* (2002), a memoir by Malka Shapira, a descendent of the *magid* of Kozienice, sheds light on the elevated status of women in this branch of Hasidism. Harry M. Rabinowicz, a scholar of the Hasidim in the late twentieth century, profiled more than ten women who made their mark in the nineteenth-century Hasidic world, including one who was not born into a family of Hasidic *rebbes.* Rabbi Hannah Rachel Werbmacher (1805–1892), an exceptional self-taught *tsadeqet* known as the "Maid of Ludmir," acted as a full-fledged Hasidic *rebbe,* receiving prayer petitions and delivering Torah sermons in public from a cordoned-off room. Since the late 1980s there has developed a controversy among scholars of Hasidism as to the correct assessment of these phenomena. Certainly, there is much research yet to be done in this field.

As of the 1870s, the elite of Preshischa renewed their interest in Qabbalah, including the works of Rabbi Isaac of Komarno, an opponent to the Preshischa path. Particularly good examples of such integration can be found in numerous works of Rabbi Tsaddoq haKohen of Lublin (1823–1900), a disciple of Rabbi Mordehai Joseph of Izbica (1788?–1854) who often placed his teacher's and his own deep psychological insights in a qabbalistic context, and also emphasized the aspect of the *tsaddiq* potential in all his followers; and Rabbi Yehudah Leib of Gur (1847–1905), whose voluminous *Sefat Emet* integrated many of the insights of the early Hasidim.

Throughout this period, Hasidism faced staunch opposition from the *maskilim* (enlighteners), who advocated antitraditional modernization and often attempted to accomplish it through government lobbying. Recriminations of unscrupulous manipulation were rife on both sides. The historiography of this period needs to be reevaluated, as its scholarship has been colored by modernist agendas that misvalue the efforts of the traditionalist Hasidim to preserve their culture. Although most Hasidic groups held secular education, and even job-training, as anathema, many Preshischa-influenced Hasidic courst (including Gur) were among the first to allow their communities access to Jewish trade schools, and to permit the formation of political parties that were more accommodating to the Zionist movement.

Piekarz has gathered evidence to produce a profile of the deteriorated state of East European *tsaddiqism* based on certain early twentieth-century Hasidic texts (c. 1920). This decadent tendency sustains an insular conformist mentality that fears and attacks all change. It views the stratification of souls as innate and unchanging—everyone has his station, and must place their faith in an unerring *tsaddiq* who is described as "the root of all worlds, transcending and filling and giving life to them all." These *tsaddiqim* and their families and close kin would often spend their time at Western European resorts, financed by their less-than-wealthy Hasidic followers (in accord with Hasidic perspective: in exile, the *tsaddiq* replaces the *Cohen*-priest, whose upkeep is incumbent on the laity), whom they encouraged to oppose other Hasidic "dynasties." However, there is not enough data to ascertain the extent of this trend. Indeed, traditional Hasidism allowed for pluralism of opinion and indeed, by stressing the uniqueness of the individual, encouraged it. One of the reasons for this deterioration over time is surely the nepotism of Hasidic "dynastic succession"—appointing successors regardless of merit. This emerged from the process of institutionalization that took place during the nineteenth century.

During the interwar period (1918–1939), some of the conservative Hasidic elite began reluctantly opening up to the modern world. Overcoming opposition, but not precipitating a break, gifted members of various leading Hasidic families, such as Rabbi Dr. A. J. Heschel (1907–1972) and R. Menachem Mendel Schneerson (1902–1994), the seventh Lubavitcher *rebbe*, were among the significant few who studied in some of Western Europe's major universities. In addition, Rabbi Abraham Isaac Kook (1865–1935), the first chief rabbi of modern Palestine (but not, strictly speaking, not a Hasidic *tsaddiq*), emphasized the role of the contemporary *tsaddiq* as one who also embraces the openness of modernity and forges new paths of creative spiritual speculation out of humanistic and scientific developments.

As for the period of the war itself, two works composed during that period are notable. *Esh Qodesh* (1960; Sacred Fire) was written by Rabbi Kalonymus Kalmish of Piasetzna (1889–1943), who was descended from some of the chief disciples of the Seer, and before the war was a renowned educator. This work contains his sermons delivered in the Warsaw Ghetto until 1943, and its heartrending theodicy of faith is a testament to this *tsaddiq* and his internalization of some of the central messages of the Besht. The second book was written in occupied Hungary by Rabbi Yissachar Shelomoh Teichtal (1885–1945), a leading disciple of the brilliant scholar Rabbi Haim Elazar, the *rebbe* of Munkacs (1868–1937) and an irascible compassionate and extremely opinionated Hasidic leader of the Hungarian anti-Zionist movement. Rabbi Teichtal's book, *Em haBanim Smeha* (A joyful mother of children), was an unpretentious repudiation of his teacher's theological arguments for opposing Zionism. Rabbi Teichtal also left behind a wartime diary that was published in 1995.

POST-HOLOCAUST HASIDISM. Despite their population being decimated by the Holocaust, in the post-Holocaust world Hasidism made a remarkable recovery in the United States and in Israel, rebuilding their institutions and replenishing their numbers. Many of the eligible "future *rebbes*" who resurrected old dynasties were trained in the postwar period by the few surviving elders. Most notable of those who trained these future *rebbes* was Rabbi Joel Teitelbaum (1887–1987), the Satmar *rebbe*, whose lineage goes back to Rabbi Moshe of Ujhely (1759–1841), a leading disciple of the Seer of Lublin. An ultra-conservative and brilliant scholar-charismatic, the Satmar *rebbe* saw his mission as rebuilding Hungarian and Galician Hasidism in the United Sates so that it would be as similar as possible to prewar times. A complex elitist, he discouraged the public teaching of Qabbalah and Hasidism, while apparently also training serious cadres of Hasidic-qabbalistic scholars. Following his death there was a flurry of publications of classic Hasidic works with extensive commentaries, originating both from his own community and from those aligned to it. Also, since the mid-1990s, several large anthologies of the teachings of the disciples of the Besht, such as Rabbi Pinchas of Koretz (1726–1791) and Rabbi Michael of Zlotchov (1734–1786) have appeared; these include manuscript material previously withheld by Hasidic dynastic leaders. In addition, some rare works written and published during the first four decades of the twentieth century which attest to the continuing creativity of Hasidic Qabbalah have been reissued. After the death of the Satmar *rebbe* in 1987, his surviving wife, Alte Feiga, held the primary charismatic attention of a significant portion of his followers until her own death in 2001. The Lubavitcher *rebbe*, another brilliant charismatic *tsaddiq*, built a worldwide network of Hasidic institutions and outreach programs. A look at the messianic pretensions of this movement is beyond the scope of this article, but while the deep contemplative traditions of this movement are being cultivated by small numbers of his followers, the recent voluminous publications (many for the first time) of the teachings of the seven *rebbes* of this dynasty (1777–1992) has led to a renaissance in the learning and teaching of this tradition.

In Israel Rabbi Shalom Noah Barazofsky (1918?–2000) the late *rebbe* of Slonim, had his discourses published in modern vernacular Hebrew. Like Rabbi Tsaddoq haKohen of Lublin, the *Slonimer rebbe*'s teachings addressed the *tsaddiq* potential in all who came to hear him or read his sermons. The *Amshinover rebbe*, Rabbi Yaakov David Milikofsky (b. 1947), is a premier type of charismatic *tsaddiq* in the Preshischa mode. His manner of prayer exemplifies genuine piety, and he is known as an extremely compassionate and astute listener in the private audiences that he freely grants. During the final decades of the twentieth century the charismatic authoritative and intercessory model of the Hasidic *tsaddiq* was widely adopted in the ultra-Orthodox Jewish world at large, both by the anti-Hasidic Lithuanian *mitnagdim* and by the renascent Orthodox communities of Jews originating from Moslem-dominated lands. Due to the unquestioned authority obliged by their homogeneous communities, which in each group results in stable voting patterns, these leaders have been increasingly sought after by politicians, and at times have been instrumental in shaping the balance of power in the larger political arena.

Finally, the twentieth century has also witnessed a surging of secular interest in the Hasidic ethos, thanks to both the person and the writings of Martin Buber (1878–1965), whose collections of Hasidic tales introduced the world at large to the spiritual relevance of this otherwise Jewish sectarian spirituality. In addition, numerous aphorisms as well as whole tracts of Hasidic teachings have been translated into English and other Western languages as of the second half of the twentieth century. The universal and ecumenical potential within Hasidic spirituality was further developed by Rabbi Dr. A. J. Heschel, who produced various academic studies on Hasidic history, the phenomenology of Hasidic piety, and wonder, and who also provided a living example of the religious activist-humanist *tsaddiq*. In the next generation, postmodern New Age spirituality found a Hasidic expression in Rabbi Zalman Schachter Shalomi (b. 1924), a Habad-educated spiritual master whose academic work on the *rebbe*-Hasid personal interview gave rise to a form of counseling that stresses the inner *tsaddiq*. He has continued the ecumenical trend by his intensive interactions with traditional spiritual teachers of non-Western religious traditions, and he champions a cross-cultural creative-Jewish paradigm in collaboration with traditional Hasidic texts. During the last decade of the twentieth century, he and Rabbi Arthur Green (b. 1941) established numerous retreat centers of Jewish contemplation that incorporate elements of Eastern (i.e., Sufi-Hindu-Buddhist) meditative traditions. Together in the late 1960s they began the Hasidic-influenced "conscious community" *havurah* movement in the Unites States. Rabbi Shlomo Carlebach (1925–1994), a charismatic Hasidic teacher and prolific composer and musician educated in the great traditional academies of Europe and the United States, was Rabbi Schachter-Shalomi's lifelong partner in ecumenical activity, often providing its ecstatic element. As a teacher, he was largely responsible for the popular renewal of interest in Izbica, Bratslav, and Piasetzna thought, and touched countless lives with his unconditional personal expressions of universal love.

See Also Hasidism, overview article; Judaism, article on Judaism in Northern and Eastern Europe since 1500; Luria, Isaac; Qabbalah.

Bibliography

There is as yet no scholarly history of Hasidic usage of the terms *tsaddiq*, *rebbe*, and *admor*. With regard to teaching with open or closed eyes, see Rabbi Hayim Elazar Shapira's *Divrei Torah* (Munkacz, 1930; Israel reprint, n.d.), series 3, number 36.

The biblical and rabbinic theology of the *tsaddiq* was analyzed in the classic study by Rudolf Mach, *Der Zaddik in Talmud und Midrasch* (Leiden, 1957), which together with Ephraim E. Urbach's *The Sages: Their Concepts and Beliefs* (Jerusalem, 1975), pp. 483–511 and elsewhere, formed the basis for the discussion of the classical period in Gershom Scholem's "*Tsaddik*: The Righteous One" in his *On the Mystical Shape of the Godhead: Basic Concepts in the Kabbalah* (New York, 1991), see pp. 88–140 and 283–293. Scholem's essay goes on to discuss the early and classical Qabbalah, but then ignores Lurianic Qabbalah and discusses Hasidism. Additional sources come from the excellent collection *Otsar haAgadah*, edited by Moshe David Gross (3 vols., Tel Aviv, 1954; 13th ed., Jerusalem, 1993), see vol. 3, pp. 1032–1057, which adduces over 500 rabbinic quotes regarding the *tsaddiq*; and from the works of Abraham J. Heschel, including *The Prophets* (New York, 1962), see pp. 200–205. *Theology of Ancient Judaism* (New York, 1965, Hebrew), see pp. 200–205. Also see Arthur Green's "The Zaddiq as *Axis Mundi* in Later Judaism" in *Journal of the American Academy of Religion* 45 (1977): 327–347. Regarding the colloquial use of the term *Hasid* meaning "follower of a particular Hasidic *rebbe*," the earliest citation found is in a text of Preshischa provenance, *Ramatayim Tsofim* by Shmuel of Shinyava (Warsaw, 1881), see pp. 200–205, based on the teachings of Rabbi Menachem Mendel of Kotzk (1787–1959) recalling events that took place in the 1820s that involved the Kotzker's teacher, Rabbi Simha Bunim of Preshischa (1765–1827). The history of this usage requires further investigation.

The qabbalistic aspect of the "hidden light" was briefly discussed in Scholem, pp. 113–115, where he adduces the Zohar II, 166b–167a. See Isaiah Tishby's *The Wisdom of the Zohar: An Anthology of Texts* (Oxford, 1989, vol. 1),, p. 442. See also Zohar II 147b and Daniel Abrams's *The Book Bahir: An Edition Based on the Earliest Manuscripts* (Los Angeles, 1994), numbers 97–100, 106, and related references in Scholem. And see, by Rabbi Azriel of Gerona, *Perush haAgadot*, edited by Isaiah Tishby (Jerusalem, 1945–1983), p. 111, and regarding the theurgic application, see "Principles Concerning the Secrets of Prayer" (Hebrew), included in Scholem's "Newly Discovered Writings of Rabbi Azriel of Gerona" (Hebrew) in *Festschrift for A. Gulak and Sh. Klein* (Jerusalem, 1942), pp. 214–216, and see Moshe Idel's "Some Remarks on Ritual and Mysticism in Geronese Kabbalah" in *Journal of Jewish Thought and Philosophy* 3 (1993): pp. 111–130. See also *Sefer haTemunah* (vol. 3 of *Torat haQaneh*, Jerusalem, 1997), pp. 176a–177b. This is to be contrasted with *Ma'arekhet haElohut* (Mantoba, Italy, 1558; reprint, Jerusalem, n.d.), folio 101b–102b; *Gates of Light*, by Rabbi Joseph Gikatilla (translated by Avi Weinstein, New York, 1994), pp. 76 and 327, and *Sefer haPeliah* in volume 1 of *Torat haQaneh*, p. 230a–b. Regarding Rabbi Moshe Cordovero, see Bracha Sack's *The Kabbalah of R. Moshe Cordovero* (Jerusalem, 1995, Hebrew), p. 323 and sources there; and on his influence on Hasidism, see Moshe Idel's *Hasidism: Between Ecstasy and Magic* (Albany, N.Y., 1995). With regard to Lurianic Qabbalah, see Menachem Kallus's *The Theurgy of Prayer in Lurianic Kabbalah* (Ph.D. dissertation, Hebrew University, 2002), chapter 4, sections 12–14, and pp. 281–282; and for his influence on Hasidism, the same source at pp. 280–281, and chapter 3. See also Menachen Kallus's "The Relation of the Baal Shem Tov to the Practice of Lurianic Kavvanot," *Kabbalah: Journal for the Study of Jewish Mystical Texts*, vol. 2 (Los Angeles and Jerusalem, 1997), pp. 151–167. As for the *Besht* and the "hidden light," see *Sefer Baal Shem Tov al haTorah* (ed. Rabbi Nathan Nata of Kalbiel and Shimeon Menachem Mendel of Gowarchov, Lodz, Poland, 1938; reprint, Jerusalem, 1993), vol. 1, "Noah," p. 107, col. 1 of note number 13, and also p. 14, number 27 and notes. This is the most complete anthology of the teachings of the Besht, and will be referenced here several times (cited as *Sefer Besht,* followed by volume number, Torah Portion and the number of teaching). A translation of it is due to appear in 2006–2007. Regarding the opinions of medieval philosophers, see Dov Schwartz's *The Philosophy of a Fourteenth Century Jewish NeoPlatonic Circle* (Jerusalem, 1996, Hebrew), pp. 153–208. See also the fascinating monograph by A. J. Heschel, *Prophetic Inspiration After the Prophets: Maimonides and Other Medieval Authorities;* translated and edited by Morris M. Faierstein (Hoboken, N.J., 1996). Returning to Lurianic Qabbalah, see *Sha'ar haYihudim* (Lvov, Ukraine, 1855; reprint, Jerusalem, n.d.), chapters 4 and 5, and see Kallus's dissertation, chapter 4 towards the end of note 357, and section 6 of note 383.

Regarding the levels of the soul and the implications of their perfections, see Menachem Kallus's "Pneumatic Mystical Possession and the Eschatology of the Soul in Lurianic Kabbalah" in *Spirit Possession in Judaism: Cases and Contexts from the Middle Ages to the Present,* edited by Matt Goldish, foreword by Joseph Dan (Detroit, Mich., 2003), pp. 159–184. See also, Gershom Scholem's "*Gilgul*: The Transmigration of Souls" in his *On the Mystical Shape of the Godhead: Basic Concepts in the Kabbalah* (New York, 1991), pp. 140–197, 300–312. And regarding *tsaddiqim* who have always striven to "unite the part with the whole" and are present in spirit whenever anyone enacts a *yihud,* see the Lurianic *Sha'ar Ruah haQodesh* (Jerusalem, 1912; reprinted 1983), folios 13a and 28a; and *Sha'ar Maamarei Rashby* (Jerusalem, 1898; reprint, 1978), folio 12b–c, and compare *Sefer Besht* vol. 2, Behukotai number 3. On the alignment of the laity to *tsaddiqim,* see *Sefer Besht,* vol. 2, VaEthanan number 66, and Eqev numbers 12–15, 30, and 66–70. And see Samuel Dresner's *The Zaddik: The Doctrine of the Zaddik According to the Writings of Rabbi Yaakov Yosef of Polnoy* (New York, 1960), pp. 75–142. Regarding the "descent of the *tsadyq*" and release from hell, see *Zohar* II, 128b–129a and elsewhere, and *Sefer Besht* vol. 1, Bereshit numbers 70–75, Lekh Likha number 19; vol. 2, Eqev number 68 and elsewhere. And see from Rabbi Pinhas of Koretz, *Imrei Pinchas haShalem,* edited by Yehezkiel Shraga Finkel (Bnei Beraq, Israel, 2003), pp. 370, numbers 31–32 and 474, number 72; and see from Rabbi Elimelekh of Lizansk, *Or Elimelekh,* edited by Alter Elisha haKohen Paksher (Jerusalem, 1984), pp. 65–66, number 84, p. 89, number 129, p. 91, number 131, and p. 98, number 148; and from Rabbi Menachem Mendel of Rymanov, *Menachem Tsion,* edited by Tsvi Elimelekh Pannet (Jerusalem, 2004), p. 11, col. b. Regarding previous scholarship on the "descent of the *tsadyq,*" see Dresner's *The Zaddik,* chapters 7 and 8; and regarding earlier sources of this doctrine, including Lurianic Qabbalah, and the refutation of Sabbatean influence, see Mendel Piekarz's *The Beginning of Hasidism: Ideological Trends in Derush and Mussar Literature* (Jerusalem, 1978, Hebrew), pp. 280–395. On *Mitnagdic* opposition to Hasidic conceptions of the *tsaddiq,* see Allan Nadler's *The Faith of the Mithnagdim: Rabbinic Responses to Hasidic Rapture* (Baltimore, Md., 1999), chapter 2.

For the sources of the teachings on Moses and the *tsaddiq,* see *Sefer Besht,* vol. 1, Bereshit numbers 121, 127, Noah, numbers 61, 62, 80, 81, 156–158; vaYishlakh, numbers 6–7; vol. 2, Shemot number 19; Ki Tisa number 9; Metzorah numbers 9, 10, 24; Qedoshim numbers 2–18; Qorah numbers 1–5; Eqev number 72, and elsewhere. Regarding the attribute of the *tsaddiq* within the individual, see *Sefer Besht,* vol. 1, Noah, number 2. With regard to the teachings of the Besht on petitionary prayer, see *Sefer Besht,* vol. 1, Noah, numbers 128–129 and 153–155, and on not compromising one's integrity in this, see especially ibid. numbers 124 and 152. For the teachings of the *magid* see ibid. numbers 80, 84, 87, 89–94, and especially, 130–131. For Rabbi Shneur Zalman's views on prayer, see Roman A. Foxbrunner's *Habad: The Hasidism of R. Shneur Zalman of Lyady* (Montogmery, Ala., 1992), pp. 19–22, 38, and 186–194. Regarding the two types of *tsaddiq* in the works of the *magid,* see *Liqutim Yeqarim* (Jerusalem, 1974), numbers 256 and 273, and for the version quoted here from the teachings of Rabbi Elimelekh, where the dialectic between the two types is more pronounced, see *Torat Shimeon* by Rabbi Shimeon of Yaroslav, a disciple of Rabbi Elimelekh (Jerusalem, 1974) (beginning of Parshat Emor). On Hasidism during the generation of the *Besht,* see Immanuel Etkes's "Hasidism as a Movement: The First Phase" in *Hasidism: Continuity or Innovation,* edited by Bezalel Safran (Cambridge, Mass., 1988), pp. 1–26. On the teachings of the Besht regarding the role of the "men of form," see Gedalya Nigal's *Manhig vaEdah* (Jerusalem, 1962) and Dresner's *The Zaddik: The Doctrine of the Zaddik According to the Writings of Rabbi Yaakov Yosef of Polnoy* (New York, 1960). The *Epistle of the Besht* was translated into English several times, most recently in the monumental work of translation and commentary by Norman Lamm, *The Religious Thought of the Hasidim: Text and Commentary* (New York, 1999); see there pp. 541–555, and for our text, p. 550. For the textual problems of this epistle, the history of scholarship, and possible resolutions, see I. Etkes's *Ba'al Shem: The Besht—Magic, Mysticism, Leadership* (Jerusalem, 2000), pp. 292–310. On the scholarly controversy concerning early Hasidism and messianism, see Gershom Scholem's "The Neutralization of the Messianic Element in Early Hasidism" in his *The Messianic Idea in Judaism and other Essays on Jewish Spirituality* (New York, 1971), pp. 176–203, and see Ben Zion Dinur's "The Beginnings of Hasidism and its Social and Messianic Foundations" (translated, originally in Hebrew, 1945) in *Essential Papers on Hasidism,* edited by Gershon Hundert, pp. 86–209 (New York, 1991), whose insightful readings regarding the early Hasidic social "program," although attacked ad homonym have not been effectively countered. See also Isaiah Tishby's "The Messianic Idea and Messianic Trends in the Growth of Hasidism" (Hebrew) *Zion* 32, no. 1 (1967): 1–45. Regarding the messianic spark-potential and the emphasis on personal redemption, see *Sefer Besht,* vol. 1, Bereshit number 166 and Shemot number 5; and vol. 2, Nitzavim number 8. As regards Rabbi Menachem Mendel of Vitebsk, see Mordechai Hayim Perlow's *Liqutei Sipurim* (Brooklyn, N.Y., 1992), p. 284, number 8. And regarding Rabbi Menachem Mendel of Rymanov, see *Torat haMagid meZlotchov,* edited by Eliezer Eliyahu Horowitz (Jerusalem, 1999), p. 176, number 6.

On Rabbi Elimelekh of Lizansk, see Nigal's *Mehqarim beHasidut* (Jerusalem, 1999; originally, 1978), pp. 116–233, and the more recent work by Piekatz, "R. Elimelekh miLizensk uMamshichei Darko," *Gil'ad* 15–16 (1998): 42–80, where he also discusses Rabbi Ephrayim of Sydlakov, and the later development of the school of the Seer. On the Seer of Lublin see Rachel Elior's "Between Yesh and Ayin: The Doctrine of the Zaddik in the Works of Jacob Isaac, the Seer of Lublin" in *Jewish History: Essays in Honour of Chimen Abramsky,* edited by Ada Rapaport-Albert and S. J. Zipperstein (London, 1988), 393–455. Regarding the easier availability of access to *Ruah haQodesh* in the exile, see *Sefer Besht,* vol. 1, VaYeshev number 4 and note 5. On Munkasz Hasidism, see Efraim Gottleib's *Studies in the Kabbalah Literature,* edited by Joseph Hacker (Tel Aviv, 1976), pp. 584–586. For the techniques of and variety of Hasidic opinion on the "raising-up of distracted thought," see *Sefer Besht,* vol. 1, Noah numbers 97–124, and especially note 94 (pp. 152–155) for the range of third- to fifth-generation Hasidic opinion. This matter seems to be a litmus test with regard to the contrast between social realism and antielitist idealism in the development of Hasidic thought and its relation to the original democratizing impulse (see Scholem's "*Devekut,* or Communion with God" in his *The Messianic Idea in Judaism and other Essays on Jewish Spirituality,* pp. 208–226). Regarding the *Habad- Besht* tradition concerning the nature of the soul in later generations, see Rabbi Aaron of Staroselye's *Shaarei haYichud vihaEmunah* (Jerusalem, 1966), folio 3b, marginal note. On this important mystical thinker see Louis Jacobs, translator, *Tract on Ecstasy* (London, 1963) and Rachel Elior's *Paradoxical Ascent to God* (Albany, N.Y., 1993).

Regarding the Hasidic "revolt" of Preshischa, see A. J. Heschel's *Kotzk: The Struggle for Integrity,* 2 volumes (Tel Aviv, 1963), see vol. 1, pp. 285–320 and 388–370; Morris Faierstein's *All Is in the Hands of Heaven: The Teachings of R. Mordechai Joseph of Izbica* (Hoboken, N.J., 1989); Shaul Magid's *Hasidism on the Margin: Reconciliation, Antinomianism, and Mysticism in Izbica/Radzin Hasidism* (Madison, Wis., 2003); and for later developments, see Arthur Green's *The Language of Truth: The Torah Commentary of the Sefat Emet* (Philadelphia, 1998), especially his introduction, and Alan Brill's *Thinking God: The Mysticism of Rabbi Zaddok of Lublin* (New York, 2002). On women and Hasidism, see Harry M. Rabinowicz's *Hasidism: The Movement and its Masters* (Northvale, N.J., and London, 1988), 341–351; Nehemia Polen's *The Rebbe's Daughter: Memoir of a Hasidic Childhood/Malka Shapiro* (Philadelphia, 2002) and Nathaniel Deutsch's *The Maiden of Ludmir: A Holy Jewish Woman and Her World* (Berkeley, Calif., 2003); and for a contrary view, see Ada Rapoport-Albert's "On Women and Hasidism: S.A. Horodecky and the Maid of Ludmir" in *Jewish History: Essays in Honour of Chimen Abramsky,* edited by Ada Rapaport-Albert and S. J. Zipperstein (London, 1988), pp. 45–525. On the early anti-Hasidic slander (Vienna, 1819) by the *Maskilim,* see Dov Taylor (ed. and tr.), *Joseph Perl's "Revealer of Secrets": The First Hebrew Novel* (Boulder, Colo., 1997), and see Heinrich Graetz's *A History of the Jews* (Philadelphia, 1967), volumes 4 and 5 regarding his bias against Qabbalah and Hasidism. For a more recent treatment, see Raphael Mahler's *Hasidism and the Jewish Enlightenment: Their Confrontation in Galicia and Poland in the First Half of the Nineteenth Century,* translated from the Yiddish by Eugene Orenstein (Philadelphia, 1985), and see Israel Bartal's "The Imprint of Haskalah Literature on the Historiography" in *Hasidism Reappraised,* edited by Ada Rapoport-Albert (London, 1996). On the development of Polish-Hasidic political parties, see Alan L. Mittleman's *The Politics of Torah: The Jewish Political Tradition and the Founding of Agudat Israel* (Albany, N.Y., 1996). On decadent forms of Hasidism, see Mendel Piekarz's "Religious Spiritualism against Zionism and Determinist Elitism: Lessons from the Discourses of the *Admor* of Partzava (1866–1930)" in *Hasidism in Poland,* edited by I. Bartal, Rabbi Elior, and C. Shmeruk (Jerusalem, 1994), and his earlier book, *Ideological Trends of Hasidism in Poland during the Interwar Period and the Holocaust* (Jerusalem, 1990). On the early life of Rabbi Dr. A. J. Heschel, see *Abraham Joshua Heschel: Prophetic Witness* by Edward K. Kaplan and Samuel H. Dresner (New Haven, Conn., 1998), and on the seventh Lubavitcher *rebbe,* see *Larger Than Life: The Life and Times of the Lubavitcher Rebbe, Rabbi Menachem Mendel Schneerson* by Shaul Shimeon Deutsch (New York, vol. 1 1995, vol. 2 1997). Although written by a follower of the late Lubavitcher *rebbe,* this work is an honest attempt at critical biography. For other examples of this trend, see Hillel Goldberg's *Between Berlin and Slobodka: Jewish Transition Figures from Eastern Europe* (Hoboken, N.J., 1989). Much has been written on Rabbi A. I. Kook. For some translations of his writings, see *The Essential Writings of Rabbi Abraham Isaac Kook,* translated with introduction by Ben Zion Bokser (Amity, N.Y., 1988), and *When God Becomes History: Historical Essays by Rabbi Abraham Isaac Hakohen Kook,* edited and translated with introduction and notes by Bezalel Naor (New York, 2003); and see *Rabbi Abraham Isaac Kook and Jewish Spirituality* by Lawrence Kaplan and David Shatz (New York, 1995). On Hasidic thought during the Holocaust, and on Rabbi Kalonymus of Piasetzna, see Nehemia Polen's, *The Holy Fire: The Teachings of Rabbi Kalonymus Kalman Shapira, the Rebbe of the Warsaw Ghetto* (Northvale, N.J., 1994). Three of his works on educational philosophy were translated: *A Student's Obligation: Advice from the rebbe of the Warsaw Ghetto* (tr. Micha Odenheimer; Northvale, N.J., 1991); *To Heal the Soul: The Spiritual Journal of a Chassidic rebbe* (tr. Yehoshua Starrett; Northvale, N.J., 1995) and *Conscious Community: A Guide to Inner Work* (tr. Andrea Cohen-Keiner; J. Aronson, N.J., 1996). See also regarding him, and on Rabbi E. Teichtal: Mendel Piekarz op. cit. (Jerusalem, 1990), and Eliezer Schweid: *Wrestling Until Day-Break: Searching for Meaning in the Thinking on the Holocaust* (Lanham, Md., 1994); idem. *From Ruin to Salvation* (Hebrew) (Hakibbutz Hameuchad, Israel, 1994).

Regarding Satmar, see Israel J. Rubin: *Satmar: Two Generations of an Urban Island* (New York, 1997) The Hasidic classic, *Toldot Yaakov Yosef* by Rabbi Y.Y. of Polnoye (originally published in Koretz, 1780) was published by Rabbi Shimeon Weiss, a *Hasid* of Satmar in a five volume edition with extensive commentary (Monroe, N.Y., 1998). The anthologized teachings of Rabbi Pinchas of Koretz and Rabbi Michael of Zlochov are referenced above, in sections 3 and 4. And see A.J. Heschel: *The Circle of the Baal Shem Tov* (ed. S. Dresner; University of Chicago Press, 1985) for monographs on these and other members of this circle. There have not yet been any studies on the *rebbes* of Slonim and Amshinov. For a perspective on the political life of Post-Holocaust ultra-Orthodox society, see: "Religious Fundamentalism and Religious Jews: The Case of the Haredim" by Samuel C. Heilman and Menachem Friedman, in *Fundamentalisms*

Observed (ed. Martin E. Marty and Rabbi Scott Appleby; Chicago, 1991; pp. 197–264). Some of Martin Buber's voluminous writings bear directly on Hasidism, such as his classic: *Tales of the Hasidim* (translated by Olga Marx; Schocken, N.Y., 1947 and 1991) and his novel based on the dramas of the circle of the Seer of Lublin: *For the Sake of Heaven* (Schocken, N.Y., 1945). Regarding Heschel, see also *The Earth is the Lord's* (London, 1945; reprint, Jewish Lights, Woodstock, N.Y., 1995); *God in Search of Man* (New York, 1955); and a posthumous collection of his essays: *Moral Grandeur and Spiritual Audacity* (edited by Susannah Heschel, New York, 1996). Some of Rabbi Zalman Meshulam Schachter-Shalomi's books include: *Spiritual Intimacy: A Study of Counseling in Hasidism* (Northvale, N.J., 1991); *Paradigm Shift: From the Jewish Renewal Teachings of Reb Zalman Schachter-Shalomi* (Northvale, N.J., 1993) and *Wrapped in a Holy Flame: Teachings and Tales of the Hasidic Masters,* edited by Nataniel M. Miles-Yepes (San Francisco, 2003). Also see Jacob Yuroh Teshima's *Zen Buddhism and Hasidism: A Comparative Study* (Lanham, Md., 1995). On Rabbi Shlomo Carlebach, see, by Meshulam Brandwein, *Reb Shlomele: The Life and Work of Shlomo Carlebach,* translated by Gavriel A. Sivan (Jerusalem, 1997), and Yitta Halberstam-Mandelbaum's *Holy Brother: Inspiring Stories and Enchanted Tales about R. Shlomo Carlebach* (Northvale, N.J., 1997).

MENACHEM KALLUS (2005)

TS'AO TAI SEE CAO DAI

TSEVI, SHABBETAI SEE SHABBETAI TSEVI

TSONG KHA PA

TSONG KHA PA (1357–1419) is the founder of the Dga' ldan pa (Gandenba) or Dge lugs pa (Gelukba) school of Tibetan Buddhism. His official, monastic name was Blo bzang grags pa, but he is more typically known in the Dge lugs pa tradition under the honorific titles of Rje rin po che (Precious Lord) and Jam dgon bla ma (Lama who is the Protector Mañjuśrī). Tsong kha pa lived during a period of Tibetan history in which large portions of the country had been unified under a central authority. It was a time of great religious efflorescence, brought about in large part by the high level of political stability that the country enjoyed.

TSONG KHA PA'S LIFE. Tsong kha pa was born in the Tsong kha region of A mdo in Eastern Tibet. Hagiographical accounts tell us that Tsong kha pa's birth was prophesied by the twelfth abbot of Snar thang monastery, Blo bzang grags pa (1299–1375), who told his student Chos rje don grub rin chen (1309–1375) to find the boy and give him his own name. His birth was augured by all of the traditional auspicious signs. Chos rje Don grub rin chen traveled back from Central Tibet to his home region of A mdo, recognized the young boy, and took him under his tutelage. Tsong kha pa took lay vows at the age of three from the Karma pa Rol pa'i rdo rje (1340–1383), and novice *(dge tshul)* ordination from Don drup rin chen at the age of seven. He spent the next decade or so receiving tantric initiations and teachings, and learning Buddhist doctrine. When he was sixteen or seventeen, following the advice of his teacher, he traveled to Central Tibet.

Central/Western (Dbus Gtsang) Tibet was the intellectual center of the country at this time. Tsong kha pa studied at many of the great monastic academies of the day, gaining expertise in all of the major texts and subjects of the Indian Buddhist scholastic tradition. In 1381 Tsong kha pa took full monastic *(dge slong)* ordination. He then began to focus more intentionally on the esoteric teachings of Tantra. It was during this period that he also met one of his major teachers, Bla ma Dbu ma pa (fourteenth century), a mystic and visionary, and a specialist on the practices of the deity Mañjuśrī, who, it was said, spoke to Tsong kha pa through Bla ma Dbu ma pa, answering his questions about the doctrine of emptiness.

Although Tsong kha pa studied with many teachers from all of the major schools of Tibetan Buddhism, it was the great Sa skya pa scholar Red mda' ba Zhon nu blo gros (1349–1412) whom Tsong kha pa would come to regard as his chief spiritual master. He studied with Red mda' ba extensively during this period, but eventually Red mda' ba and Tsong kha pa would become each other's teacher, spending a great deal of time together both teaching and in retreat.

By the early 1390s Tsong kha pa had completed his philosophical studies, and he had established his abilities and reputation as a scholar by engaging in the so-called monastic rounds (*grwa skor*), the practice of submitting to public examinations at various institutions. He continued to take teachings and initiations from various masters during this next phase of his life, receiving many lineages that would be important to the later Dge lugs order. But what really characterized this phase of Tsong kha pa's life was an emphasis on practice, teaching, and writing. For the next decade, he would alternate periods of teaching and learning with periods of retreat, all the while dedicating himself to "composition."

Tsong kha pa was also gathering disciples. One close group of students, the so-called eightfold pure retinue, accompanied him into a four-year intensive retreat at 'Ol kha, during which Tsong kha pa and his students had many visions of various deities. Visionary experiences, both in waking life and in dreams, had been a part of Tsong kha pa's life from his youth, but they became more frequent during this time, and would continue for the rest of his life. Especially important are a series of visions he had of Indian and Tibetan saints that were seen by Tsong kha pa (and by the later Dge lugs tradition) as legitimating his unique interpretation of the doctrine of emptiness.

Tsong kha pa had already begun to write before this period, but it was really during and after his time in intensive retreat that he wrote some of his most important philosophical and tantric works. In 1408 the Ming emperor invited Tsong kha pa to the Chinese court, but he declined, sending a close disciple in his stead. Clearly, Tsong kha pa thought that he still had much to accomplish in his native land.

In 1408, with the help of two patrons, Tsong kha pa founded the tradition of the Great Prayer Festival (Smon lam chen mo) in Lhasa, a New Year festival where the focus was on making offerings, both to the assembled clergy and to the image of the Jo bo rin po che (Tibet's most famous Buddha statue). This tradition would become one of Tibet's most important festivals, observed until the final Chinese takeover of Tibet in 1959. It also marks a turning point in Tsong kha pa's life, initiating a period of more public engagement, and one of greater concern with the institutionalization of his tradition.

The spectacle of the Great Prayer Festival brought even greater prominence to Tsong kha pa. With the help of patrons, he founded in 1409 the monastery of Dga' ldan, an institution that would become his principal seat (and that of his successors). He remained chiefly at Dga' ldan, giving extensive teachings and composing principally tantric works from 1410 until 1416. The monasteries of 'Bras spungs and Sera, the other two "seats" (*gdan sa*) of the Dge lugs pa school, were founded by two of Tsong kha pa's disciples in 1416 and 1419, respectively. In 1419 Tsong kha pa took ill. He passed away at Dga' ldan on the twenty-fifth day of the tenth Tibetan month. His body was preserved there in a golden reliquary, where it remained for over five hundred years until the monastery was bombed (and his tomb sacked) by Chinese troops.

TSONG KHA PA'S THOUGHT. Tsong kha pa believed himself to be following an intellectual and spiritual trajectory that extended from the Buddha, through the great scholar-adepts of India and Tibet, up to his own time. Whether or not he saw himself as actually reviving the Bka' gdams pa tradition, founded almost half a millennium earlier by the Indian scholar-saint Atiśa, Tsong kha pa's early followers came to refer to themselves as the "New Bka' gdams pa."

Conservative in his approach, Tsong kha pa believed that the great texts of Indian Buddhism were the standard by comparison to which the authenticity of doctrines and practices was to be judged. Bemoaning the fact that in his day "those who strive at yogic practice have studied little, while the learned are uninformed about the details of practice," Tsong kha pa sought to steer the tradition back to its Indian roots, grounding yogic practice in textual learning and philosophical analysis. He believed that the essence of Buddhism was not preserved in secret, oral lineages (*man ngag*), but that it was instead publicly accessible in the writings of the Indian Buddhist masters. His written work, therefore, can be seen as an attempt to critically reappropriate the Indian classics, and to show their relevance to practice.

His writings are holistic and synthetic, characterized by the impulse to harmonize all of the Buddha's teachings into a consistent whole. He especially sought to do this in his summa. His *Great Exposition of the Stages of the Path* (*Lam rim chen mo*) and his *Great Exposition of the Stages of Tantra* (*Sngags rim chen mo*) are erudite, grand syntheses of exoteric and esoteric Buddhism that offer the reader complete maps of these traditions. His *Essence of Eloquence* (*Legs bshad snying po*) attempts to reconcile the apparent contradictions in the Mahāyāna philosophical corpus through the hermeneutical distinction between the provisional *(drang ba'i)* and definitive *(nges pa'i)* meaning of texts. Tsong kha pa devoted many of his works to the interpretation of emptiness. Candrakīrti's (seventh century) interpretation of emptiness—called the Consequentialist, or Prāsaṅgika (*thal 'gyur pa*), interpretation—was for Tsong kha pa the highest expression of the Buddha's philosophical view (*lta ba*). Tsong kha pa saw emptiness as a corollary of the Buddhist doctrine of dependent arising *(rten 'brel)*, and this became a hallmark of his analysis of "Middle Way" (Madhyamaka) philosophy. All told, Tsong kha pa's collected works comprise about seventeen volumes.

As is obvious from Tsong kha pa's own life, study, learning, and theory was only part of the equation. Equally important was practice. As he states in a letter:

> Over many years I strove to understand the meaning of the [texts]. Based on that [understanding], and taking as the basis [for practice] the safeguarding of the moral discipline to which I had committed myself, I practiced many forms of accumulating [merit] and purifying [sin] [*bsag sbyang*], and devoted myself to the cultivation of the various meditational objects that constitute the path in its entirety. With this as the cause, I was able to achieve insight into at least the rough features of the path of Sūtra and Tantra.

Following in the footsteps of the Bka' gdams pa masters, Tsong kha pa believed that moral discipline (*tshul khrims*), epitomized by the monk's life, was the basis for the practice of both the sūtra and the tantric paths. The later tradition maintains that so crucial was the practice of monasticism to him that he eschewed taking a consort—and thereby postponed his own enlightenment until the after-death, intermediate stage—so as to teach to his followers the importance of celibacy.

THE CULT OF TSONG KHA PA. Like many Tibetan masters of his day, Tsong kha pa came to be considered an emanation (*sprul pa*) of a specific deity: in his case, Mañjuśrī, the deity of wisdom. Iconographically, Tsong kha pa is most often represented as a monk wearing a pandit's hat, with a text emanating from his left shoulder and a blazing sword (the symbol of Mañjuśrī) from his right shoulder. Tsong kha pa's apotheosis is celebrated in a variety of rites, arguably the most famous of which is a visualization/recitation practice called "The Hundred Deities of Dga' ldan" *(Dga ldan lha rgya ma)*, that concludes with the recitation of a verse of homage to Tsong kha pa called "The Object[less] Compassion [Verse]" (*dmigs rtse ma*). The mantra-like "accumulation" (or repetition) of the verse is a common practice, and is touted as efficacious in everything from curing illness to achieving enlightenment.

The cult of Tsong kha pa has taken more popular forms as well. Pilgrimage to Dga' ldan monastery (and to his tomb) has always been a favorite practice among the laity and clergy alike. Devotees circumambulate the monastery, prostrate before his tomb, and collect small pieces of dough that have been molded (and thereby blessed) by coming into contact with a relic of Tsong kha pa's tooth. Finally, Tsong kha pa's death date is celebrated throughout Tibet in the religious festival called the "Dga' ldan Offering of the [Twenty] Fifth" *(Dga' ldan lnga mchod)*, which culminates in offerings of butter lamps after nightfall. On this occasion, during a midwinter's night, entire monasteries become filled with the flickering of butter lamps, making it one of the most beautiful events in the Tibetan liturgical calendar.

SEE ALSO Buddhism, Schools of, article on Tibetan and Mongolian Buddhism; Mañjuśrī; Worship and Devotional Life, article on Buddhist Devotional Life in Tibet.

BIBLIOGRAPHY

Various Tibetan-language editions of Tsong kha pa's collected works (*gSungs 'bum*) have been preserved and published in India, China, and Japan. These remain the standard references for his life and thought. In European languages, on Tsong kha pa's life, see Rudolf Kaschewsky, *Das Leben des lamaistischen heilegen Tsongkhapa bLo-bzaṅ-grags-pa (1357–1419), Dargestellt und erläuert anhand seiner Vita: "Quellort allen Glückes"* (Wiesbaden, 1971), 2 vols; and Robert A. F. Thurman, ed., *The Life and Teachings of Tsong khapa* (Dharamasala, India, 1982). The latter work also contains translations of some of Tsong kha pa's minor works. The last two decades have seen the translation of some of Tsong kha pa's major works. The *Lam rim chen mo*, arguably his most important work, has now been translated as *The Great Treatise on the Stages of the Path to Enlightenment: Lam rim chen mo* by Joshua Cutler, Guy Newland, et al. (Ithaca, N.Y., 2000–2003), 3 vols. *Tsong Khapa's Speech of Gold in the Essence of True Eloquence*, translated by Robert A. F. Thurman (Princeton, 1984), is a translation of Tsong kha pa's *Legs bshad snying po*; this work has also partially been translated in Jeffrey Hopkins's *Emptiness in the Mind-Only School of Buddhism* (Berkeley, 1999). *Tantra in Tibet* and *Deity Yoga* (both Ithaca, N.Y., 1987) are translations by Jeffrey Hopkins of portions of the *Sngags rim chen mo*, with the commentary of the Dalai Lama. *Tsong kha pa's Six Yogas of Naropa* (Ithaca, N.Y., 1997) is Glenn Mullins's translation of the *Yid byes gsum ldan*, Tsong kha pa's main work on this subject. Tsong kha pa's *Dbu ma dgongs pa rab gsal*, his commentary to Candrakīrti's *Madhyamakāvatāra*, has been partially translated by Jeffrey Hopkins in *Compassion in Tibetan Buddhism* (Ithaca, N.Y., 1980), and by Jeffrey Hopkins and Anne Klein in *Path to the Middle* (Albany, N.Y., 1994).

JOSÉ IGNACIO CABEZÓN (2005)

TSUNG-MI SEE ZONGMI

TSWANA RELIGION.

Traditional religion among the Tswana of the high veld of southern Africa centered upon the supreme being, Modimo, and ancestor spirits known as *badimo.* The fact that *badimo* is the plural form of *modimo,* an honorific term used to express awe and reverence toward elders as well as toward the supreme being, indicates that the difference between Modimo, the ancestors, and human beings is one of degree rather than kind. While they occupy different positions in a complex hierarchy of spiritual power, all beings—whether spiritual or human—are intimately connected with each other. As the Tswana Christian theologian Gabriel Setiloane indicates, it is a basic premise of Tswana thought that a representative is identical with the person being represented or that a symbol is that which it symbolizes. Hence, the Tswana say, "Motho ke modimo" ("Man is *modimo*"), something that implies a far greater degree of interaction than the English "There is something of the divine in every man" (Setiloane, 1976, p. 21).

Modimo is believed to be the source and root of all existence. Intangible and all-pervasive, irreparably part of human experience but not directly sensed, he is a source of appeal in times of affliction and the guardian of the moral order. The complexity of the Tswana concept of the supreme being is best indicated by the wide range of praise names that are used to characterize him. Modimo is *mme* ("mother") and *lesedi* ("light"), but he is also known as *selo* ("monster") insofar as he possesses dangerous powers that go far beyond those of normal humanity.

Because a person cannot come into direct contact with Modimo and remain unchanged, the Tswana have recourse to the *badimo,* ancestors who act as intermediaries between humanity and the supreme being. Closely involved in everyday life, the *badimo* function to preserve harmony in social relations and to ensure the fertility of humans, animals, and crops. Their attitude toward humans is basically parental—looking to the welfare of the community as a whole, they seek to correct faults and protect their descendants from harm. In return, they expect *tirelo* ("service"). The essence of *tirelo* is the sharing of benefits with others. The *badimo* are said to love company and are especially gladdened by feasts. Whenever food or beer is prepared, a portion is set aside or poured on the ground for the *badimo.* This is done to maintain their good favor, for without it, life cannot be kept in proper balance and lived to the full. When an individual has neglected to honor the *badimo,* the Tswana say that he suffers from *bolwetse,* a term that covers both physical illness and a range of other maladies. Principally, it indicates that an individual is in disharmony with the spiritual forces (including Modimo) that engender and sustain his existence.

The concern for the community as a whole that is a central part of Tswana religion is expressed in the Tswana theory of human personality, or *seriti* (pl., *diriti*). Each person is born with a "heavy" or "light" *seriti* that can act for evil or for good. If a child is born with a light *seriti,* it must be strengthened and imbued with good intentions. Healthy *seri-*

ti brings dignity, respect, and properity; bad *seriti* causes ill will and discord in the social realm. A father of a household or a chief with good *seriti* strengthens the *diriti* of those who live in the house or chiefdom and vice versa. Because a man's *seriti* pervades much of his world, if he does wrong, his children, crops, or animals may suffer. Also, insofar as *seriti* originates from the *badimo* and is upheld by them, it functions as a spiritual force that knits together social and spiritual relations.

In times of suffering, people have access to religious specialists, or "doctors," known as *dingaka* (sg., *ngaka*). Both men and women can become doctors. There are six kinds of doctors in Tswana society, each classified according to the various divinatory and medicinal skills that he or she possesses. The best known, however, are the "horned" and the "hornless" doctors. The horned doctors divine by interpreting the pattern created by the throwing of four tablets, which represent an older and younger male and an older and younger female, or of pairs of astragalus bones, which represent the male and female of every common animal species. The hornless doctors divine by examining the patient. There are few doctors today and their practices, though still common, are officially illegal.

Human suffering is largely caused by incurring the displeasure of the *badimo* or by the actions of sorcerers. The complex Tswana term *boloi,* often translated as "sorcery" or as "magic," refers to both of these occurrences. There are two kinds of *boloi* that are socially constructive: *boloi* of the heart and of the mouth. Both involve offenses against a senior member of the kin group. If the senior member is slighted in some way, it is believed that he "puts the *badimo*" on the offender. The senior member need not be conscious of ill will toward the offender. In response to the offense, the *badimo* withdraw their support from the offender's *seriti* in order to call attention to his fault, and he is then susceptible to disease and other malign influences. Because of the encompassing nature of his *seriti,* much of his world is similarly threatened. In order to restore proper relations within the community (which includes the *badimo*), the offender provides an animal for slaughter; after it has been killed, the senior member uses a mixture of chyme and aloe to "wash" the offender and strengthen his *seriti.*

Two other types of *boloi* exist that are unquestionably evil. *Boloi ba bosigo* ("night sorcery"), which seems to be a form of witchcraft rather than sorcery, refers to the belief that certain witches (usually elderly women working in covens) cavort at night and cause mischief. Essentially tricksters, such witches gather naked, enter houses through closed doors and windows, upset pots, suck milk from nursing mothers or cows so that their yield is insufficient, exhume new corpses, and use owls as sentinels and hyenas as steeds. Day sorcery (*boloi ba motshegare*) is much more serious. It involves the purposeful manipulation of material substances for evil ends—usually to inflict disease or death upon a particular individual. Sorcerer and victim are often close relatives, such as husband and wife, parent and child, or brother and brother, who are overcome by feelings of greed, envy, or vengeance. *Bongaka,* therapy performed by the various *dingaka,* is essential to the prevention of sorcery.

Contemporary Tswana religion can only be explained in light of the tragic history of the people since the beginning of the nineteenth century. The impact of Western civilization coincided with the beginning of the nineteenth century, and chaos reigned in Tswanaland from 1810 until 1840. The first Christian mission was established in 1816 and four others were set up in the next thirty years; by 1870, missions had spread throughout Tswanaland. The dispersal of Tswana groups—both by the onslaught of marauding refugees resulting from the Zulu expansion known as the Mfecane and by the Boers, who took Tswana lands and subjected the people to forced labor—greatly weakened orthodox religious practices. The Boers drove the Tswana into reserve pockets of land in the Transvaal, the northern Cape of Good Hope, the Orange Free State, and the territory that became the Botswana state. Here, the remnants of once cohesive groups recombined into artificial units.

The Tswana have therefore been subjected to a great deal of pressure and turmoil inimical and destructive to their own religion. The official religion of most Tswana groups is now Christianity. Although the public rituals of the indigenous religion are seldom encountered, the more private and individualized practices of witchcraft, sorcery, and traditional healing persist strongly, even among Christians. The relationship between old and new beliefs is complex; much more of the former may remain than meets the eye. As Setiloane points out, many zealous and longstanding Christians have never given up the old worldview but have instead fitted Christianity into it. A number of traditional religious skills and rituals, including *pha badimo,* a thanksgiving ritual that is performed to show gratitude to the *badimo,* continue to play an important role in Tswana Christianity. The new social, political, and economic order brought about by the colonial system had more impact in christianizing the Tswana than the missionaries' religious teaching, which was too blatantly contradicted by the harsh oppression and racism of southern Africa to carry conviction.

The fundamental belief in the supreme being and the *badimo* continues to inform convictions about the earth and home as sacred and holy as well as attitudes toward cattle, which still have strong emotional, religious, and practical value, for they form the basis of important transactions between Tswana. Such exchanges continue to provide a binding conception of marriage, paternity, kinship, and family bonds that Christianity cannot replace. Initiation ceremonies, with their acutely emotional and religious accompaniments, also retain central and unassailable roles, as they induct the young into the profound continuities and solidarities of community life, earth, kin, and cattle. These values can still give a fundamental sense of psychological security, personal adequacy, and proper place in the cosmic scheme of things, and they function as an anchor in the stormy upheavals that afflict the Tswana in southern Africa in the early twenty-first century.

BIBLIOGRAPHY

Brown, J. T. *Among the Bantu Nomads: A Record of Forty Years Spent among the Bechuana.* London, 1926.

Mackenzie, John. *Ten Years North of the Orange River: A Story of Everyday Life and Work among the South African Tribes from 1859–1869.* Edinburgh, 1871.

Pauw, B. A. *Religion in a Tswana Chiefdom.* London, 1980.

Schapera, Isaac. *The Tswana.* London, 1953.

Setiloane, Gabriel M. "How the Traditional World View Persists in the Christianity of the Sotho-Tswana." In *Christianity in Independent Africa,* edited by Edward Fashole-Luke et al., pp. 402–413. Bloomington, Ind., 1978.

Willoughby, W. C. *The Soul of the Bantu.* London, 1928.

New Sources

Setiloane, Gabriel M. *The Image of God among the Sotho-Tswana.* Rotterdam, 1976.

AIDAN SOUTHALL (1987)
Revised Bibliography

TUATHA DÉ DANANN.

The Tuatha Dé Danann are the gods of pagan Ireland whose social order reflects the structure and values of early Irish society and includes poets and storytellers, kings and warriors, and practitioners of other professions and crafts. The name Tuatha Dé Danann (The Tribes or Peoples of the Goddess Danu) may originally have been simply Tuatha Dé—meaning simply the Tribes or Peoples of the Gods or of the Goddess—with Danann a later addition. Both Danu (genitive, Danann) and Anu are identified as personal names of the goddess of warfare and destruction known as the Morríghan (Great Queen or Phantom Queen), wife to Eochaidh Ollathair (Great Father), also called the Daghdha (Good God). Danu may, however, once have been a separate figure, parallel to the Welsh Dôn and Indic Danu, mother of the gods. The Tuatha Dé Danann war against and intermarry with the Fomhoire, a supernatural people associated with the sea, much as the Indic Devas and Asuras are both foes and kin.

Sources for information about the Tuatha Dé Danann include *Leabhar Gabhála Éireann* (The book of the taking of Ireland), a compendium of medieval prose and poetry associating legendary settlements of pre-Christian Ireland with classical and biblical chronology and presenting the gods as mortals descended from Noah. Additional sources, in which the Tuatha Dé are often explicitly called gods and goddesses, include texts whose language often reflects many chronological layers, some as early as the eighth century. These sources, including mythic and epic narratives, glossaries, and place-name lore, show elaboration and reshaping in response to cultural and political changes including those arising through Viking and Norman influences.

THE BATTLES OF MAGH TUIREDH. In the pseudo-historical framework of *Leabhar Gabhála Éireann* the Tuatha Dé are the fifth group to invade Ireland, conquering the previous settlers in the First Battle of Magh Tuiredh. After losing an arm in that combat, the Tuatha Dé king Nuadhu (subsequently called "Silverhand" for his artificial silver arm) resigns the kingship. The Tuatha Dé form an alliance with the Fomhoire, and Nuadhu's successor is the half-Fomorian, Bres, whose rule proves oppressive. After Bres flees to his Fomhorian kinsmen for reinforcements, Nuadhu (his natural arm miraculously reattached) is reinstated and invites Lugh, who is skilled in every art, to prepare the Tuatha Dé for war. Lugh's strategies are successful, and against great odds the Fomhoire are defeated in the Second Battle of Magh Tuiredh.

The subsequent treaty brings the Tuatha Dé specialized knowledge about agriculture, offered by Bres in exchange for his life and the end of Fomhorian aggression. After a long and peaceful rule, the Tuatha Dé are defeated by the Sons of Míl, legendary ancestors of Ireland's present inhabitants. The Tuatha Dé Danann retreat into Ireland's lakes and hills and into pre-Celtic sacred mounds, such as Newgrange, and their association with magical underground dwellings (*sídhe*) survives in beliefs about the fairies of later folk tradition. The Sons of Míl receive sovereignty over the surface of the land after promising that Ireland will continue to bear the names of three territorial goddesses, including Ériu (hence the name Erin).

FUNDAMENTAL CHARACTERISTICS. The Second Battle of Magh Tuiredh reveals fundamental characteristics of leading members of the Tuatha Dé when Lugh, practitioner of all the arts, asks how each will help defeat the Fomhoire. As a royal surrogate, whose many arts give him a rank equal to that of a king, Lugh both coordinates the preparation for battle and leads the Tuatha Dé to victory after Nuadhu is slain. Oghma, the strongman and champion, brings prowess as a warrior. Dian Cécht, grandfather of Lugh, serves as physician to the wounded. Goibhniu ("Smith") manufactures swords and spears. Eochaidh Ollathair, the "god of druidry," is a figure of extreme sexual potency (symbolized by his three testicles) and is known for his great strength, skill with a club as well as a sword, and mastery of magical arts. Morríghan, the goddess of battle who can take the form of a crow, determines the outcome of battles and can ensure victory through verbal magic. Other Tuatha Dé women appear as experts in magical practice, in the arts of warfare, in healing, and as artisans. Lugh's muster includes many other major and minor deities, some with highly specialized skills, facilitating comparisons with other Indo-European divine societies.

Tales about the gods illustrate early Irish social institutions and beliefs and were sometimes used as leading cases in native Irish law. Members of the Tuatha Dé Danann are cited as sources of specialized professional knowledge and are recognized as initiators of cultural practices. The Daghdha's daughter Brígh (Brighid), for example, is identified as the first to keen (lament the dead) in Ireland when she mourns her son who was slain in battle. This goddess, whose name is linked to healing and smith craft as well as to poetry, is also associated with domestic animals, and the folk practices connected to the cult of Saint Brighid may reflect early beliefs about Brígh's influence over crops and herds. Her husband, Bres, is associated with agricultural and pastoral prosperity. Laws addressing legal liabilities for illness and injury are attributed to Dian Cécht, who is invoked in early healing charms; his daughter, Airmedh, was reportedly the first to recognize all healing properties of herbs. Lost laws associated with smith work and other crafts are attributed to Goibhniu and other craftsperson deities.

KINGS AND GODDESSES. Sovereignty, a key theme in mythic and epic tales involving the Tuatha Dé, is often represented by the relationship between the king (divine or human) and the goddess of the land he rules. Many women of the Tuatha Dé serve as goddesses of territorial sovereignty and are associated with sacred wells and rivers and with the land of Ireland itself. Tales surrounding Édaín, who becomes the wife of Midhir of Brí Léith, explore aspects of kingship and the necessary presence of the queen—whether she is seen as divine or as a symbol of the sovereignty of the land. Midhir woos Édaín through several reincarnations and finally reclaims her from her mortal spouse Eochaidh Airemh, king of Ireland. Interaction between the gods and human society often occurs when sovereignty is in jeopardy. For example, in the tragic destruction of Conaire Mór, a king descended from Édaín, the people of the *sídhe* surround him at the time of his death.

SEE ALSO Celtic Religion, overview article; Fomhoire; Lugh.

BIBLIOGRAPHY

Gray, Elizabeth A. *Cath Maige Tuired: The Second Battle of Mag Tuired.* Irish Texts Society, vol. 52. Leinster, Ireland, 1982. Provides text and translation, contains extensive indices of references to the Tuatha Dé Danann and Fomhoire in early and later medieval Irish literature.

Mac Cana, Proinsias. *Celtic Mythology.* New York, 1970; reprint, 1973. Succinct, authoritative and comprehensive survey, extensively illustrated with photographs of significant items of Celtic material culture, includes chapters on the Tuatha Dé Danann and on the Irish heroic tradition.

Mac Neill, Máire. *The Festival of Lughnasa.* 2 vols., 2d. ed. Dublin, 1982. Provides an extensive discussion of both learned and popular literary sources related to Lugh and details folk customs associated with the celebration of Lughnasa.

Rees, Alwyn, and Brinley Rees. *Celtic Heritage: Ancient Tradition in Ireland and Wales.* London, 1961. Far-reaching and ahead of its time, this work explores the range of Celtic mythic tradition in the Indo-European context, including references to the work of Georges Dumézil, with exhaustive notes that provide access to both specialist studies and more general works.

ELIZABETH A. GRAY (2005)

TUCCI, GIUSEPPE

TUCCI, GIUSEPPE (1894–1984), Italian scholar of Asian religions. Giuseppe Tucci was born in Macerata in the Marche region of Italy on June 5, 1894, and died on April 5, 1984, in his house in San Polo dei Cavalieri, near Tivoli, in the province of Rome. Tucci fought during World War I, and after the war he graduated from the University of Rome (1919). From 1925 to 1930 he resided in India, teaching Chinese and Italian at the universities of Santiniketan and Calcutta. In 1929 Tucci was elected to the Accademia d'Italia, and in 1930 he accepted the chair of the department of Chinese language and literature at the Istituto Universitario Orientale of Naples. He then accepted the chair of the department of religion and philosophy of India and the Far East at the University of Rome (1932), where he remained until his retirement in 1969.

In 1933 he was instrumental in the founding of the Istituto Italiano per il Medio ed Estremo Oriente (IsMEO), the first president of which was Tucci's colleague and friend Giovanni Gentile. Tucci himself was president of the institute from 1947 to 1978; from 1979 he was its honorary president.

He was the editor of several periodicals, including *Alle fonti delle religioni* from 1921 to 1924, *Bollettino del'IsMEO* (which became *Asiatica* in 1935) from 1933 to 1943, *Le scienze del mistero e il mistero delle scienze* in 1946, and *East and West* from 1950 to 1984. He founded many series of scholarly publications of the IsMEO, such as the "Serie Orientale Roma" (the first fifty-two volumes of which he edited) in 1950, "Reports and Memoirs" (documenting research) in 1962, and "Restoration" in 1969. From 1950 to 1973 he directed the series "Il nuovo Ramusio," published by the Libreria dello Stato. He edited many other works meant to diffuse and popularize knowledge about Asian civilizations.

Tucci's scholarly research was complemented by his field explorations—he was, perhaps, the last of the great explorers—as well as by his impassioned interest in the contemporary Asian world. The six years he spent in India were fundamental in his life, as were his eight expeditions to Tibet (1929–1948), his six expeditions to Nepal (1950–1954), and his missions of exploration to Pakistan (starting in 1955), Afghanistan (1957), and Iran (from 1959); Tucci continued to conduct archaeological research on field explorations such as these until 1976.

The highest honors of the countries of Afghanistan, Japan, India, Indonesia, Iran, Nepal, Pakistan, and Thailand were conferred upon Tucci. He received honorary doctorates from many European and Asian universities, including those of Delhi, Kathmandu, and Tehran; he was given various academic and scientific titles in Italy (from the Accademia d'Italia, the Accademia delle Scienze of Turin, the Accademia of San Luca, and the Società Geografica Italiana), in Austria (from the Österreichische Akademie der Wissenschaften), in France (from the Société Asiatique), in Germany (from the Deutsches Archäologisches Institut), in Japan (from the Imperial Academy and the Tōyō Bunko), in India (from the Asiatic Society of Calcutta and Vishvabharati University of Santiniketan), and in England (from the British Academy and the Royal Asiatic Society).

Tucci received many international prizes, including the gold medal of the Calcutta Art Society (1965), the Sir Percy Sykes Memorial Medal (1971), the medal for archaeology of the Academy of Architecture of Paris (1972), the Jawaharlal Nehru Award for International Understanding (1976), and the Balzan Prize for History (1979). The Jawaharlal Nehru Award was always especially dear to Tucci because of his friendship with Nehru and his ties with great figures of modern India such as Rabindranath Tagore, Sarvepalli Radhakrishnan, and Mohandas K. Gandhi.

The entire Indian subcontinent and Tibet were the main areas of Tucci's interest as a scholar and explorer. A complete bibliography of his works contains 360 titles, including many dozens of books, about two hundred articles, numerous encyclopedia entries, reviews, and so on. His research actively touched on many fields other than Indian and Tibetan studies, however, and he focused especially on the study of religious and philosophical thought and on historical investigation. His interest in the latter field led him to study the archaeology of Hindukush and Iran; this study was also inspired by his perennial interest in the various points of encounter of the great Asian civilizations of the Himalayan regions, Northwest India, Pakistan, and Afghanistan.

He undertook his studies of China primarily during the first stage of his scholary activity in works such as *Scritti di Mencio* (1921), *Storia della filosofia cinese antica* (1922), and *Saggezza cinese* (1926). At any rate, the most important object of his studies was Buddhism in the various forms it had taken as it expanded from India toward Tibet, Central Asia, China, and the Far East. Tucci interpreted Buddhism as the highest form of Asian humanism. Always in search of universal values in a humanistic perspective, Tucci felt that the history of Asia was closely interconnected with that of Europe, and he thus always considered Eurasia to be a single continent in cultural as well as geographical terms.

His most important scholarly works are *Linee di una storia del materialismo indiano,* 2 vols. (1923–1929); *Indo-Tibetica,* 6 vols. (1932–1941); *Tibetan Painted Scrolls,* 2 vols. (1949); *Teoria e pratica del Mandala* (1949); *The Tombs of the Tibetan Kings* (1950); *Minor Buddhist Texts,* 2 vols. (1956–1958); *The Religions of Tibet* (1970); *The Ancient Civilization of Transhimalaya* (1973); and *On Swāt: The Dards and Connected Problems* (1977).

Endowed with vast humanistic knowledge and intensely interested in religious and philosophical thought, Tucci possessed great erudition, extraordinary knowledge of languages, and philological skill. He knew Sanskrit and Tibetan in depth, and also had significant knowledge of Chinese and Pali (and other Indian languages). Nevertheless, he did not disdain the public at large, to whom he addressed many works, among which are *Santi e briganti nel Tibet ignoto* (1937), *Forme dello spirito asiatico* (1940), *Asia religiosa* (1946), *Tra giungle e pagode* (1953), *To Lhasa and Beyond* (1956), *The Discovery of the Mallas* (1962), *La via dello Swat* (1963), *Il trono di diamante* (1967), *Tibet, Land of Snows* (1967), and *Rati-Līlā* (1969).

Many of Tucci's minor writings are collected (partially revised by him) in his *Opera Minora* (1971) published by the Oriental School of the University of Rome. The Istituto Universitario Orientale of Naples dedicated two volumes of Asian studies to him titled *Gururājamañjarikā: Studi in onore di Giuseppe Tucci* (1974), and the IsMEO published an international collection of Asian studies in three volumes dedicated to Tucci's memory, titled *Orientalia Iosephi Tucci Memoriae Dicata* (1985–1988).

BIBLIOGRAPHY

On May 7, 1984, the Istituto Italiano per il Medio ed Estremo Oriente solemnly commemorated its founder with the publication of my *Giuseppe Tucci* (Rome, 1984); an English version of this work, accompanied by an updated bibliography of Tucci's writings, appeared under the title "Giuseppe Tucci" in *East and West,* n.s. 3 (1984): 11–12 and 23–42. A year after Tucci's death, the institute published *Ricordo di Giuseppe Tucci* (Rome, 1985) by Raniero Gnoli with contributions from Luciano Petech, F. Scialpi, and G. Galluppi Vallauri; this work includes a biographical note, a discussion of Tucci's *cursus honorum* and his scholarly concerns, and a bibliography.

Short commemorative notices have been published in various scientific reviews, including S. Cleuziou's in *Universalia 1984* (the annual supplement of the *Encyclopaedia Universalis*), pp. 614–615; P. Corradini's in *Mondo cinese* 45 (1984): 101–105; Mircea Eliade's in *History of Religions* 24 (1984): 157–159; K. Enoki's in *Tohogaku* 68 (1984): 127–154; Luciano Petech's in the *Journal of the International Association of Buddhist Studies* 7 (1984): 137–142; B. J. Staviskij's in *Narody Azii i Afriki* 1 (1985): 213–214; M. Taddei's in *AIUON* 44 (1984): 699–704; and R. Tamburello's in *Il Giappone* 24 (1984): 211–213.

A special commemorative issue (no. 2) of *India Past and Present: A Biannual Journal of Historical Research* (Bombay, 1985), is dedicated to Tucci and contains (pp. 3–11) an editorial on his life and work. Corrado Pensa's study "L'occidente e le religioni orientali nella prospettiva di Giuseppe Tucci," in *Paramita: Quaderni di Buddhismo* 16 (1985): 19–25, deals with the West in relation to Eastern religions following the perspective of Giuseppe Tucci.

New Sources

Melasecchi, Beniamino, ed. *Giuseppe Tucci nel centenario della nascita.* Rome, 1995.

Tucci, Giuseppe. *On Swat: Historical and Archaeological Notes.* Rome, 1997.

GHERARDO GNOLI (1987)
Translated from Italian by Rodica Blumenfeld-Diaconescu
Revised Bibliography

TU KUANG-T'ING SEE DU GUANGTING

TULSĪDĀS, late medieval Indian poet whose plays and other works have had great influence on Hindu devotionalism, especially in communities that make Rāma the focus of worship. Despite his great popularity, or perhaps because of it, very little accurate information is available about the life of Tulsīdās. There is abundant material about him in the form of hagiographies and oral legends, but these legitimize his saintly life and the holy nature of his literary works rather than record the actual events of the biography.

While there is disagreement as to the date of Tulsī's birth, his death is generally agreed to have occurred in 1623. The traditionally accepted date of his birth is 1503, which would mean that he lived for 120 years. This is logical from the point of view of his hagiographers, because the full life span of a sinless human being is believed to be 120 years. Modern scholars consider that he was born probably in 1532 to a brahman family in an eastern Hindi-speaking area. In his *Kavitāvali,* Tulsī writes that he was born to a very poor family and that his father and mother did not welcome his birth. It is believed that he was born under an unfortunate conjunction of planets, which meant that for astrological reasons his parents had to abandon him.

Tulsī says that in his childhood his mind was always on Rāma, but that he later fell into the ways of the world. Sometime during his life Tulsī went to Banaras, where he lived until his death.

In 1574 Tulsī began the composition of his most renowned work, the *Rāmcaritmānas,* or *The Holy Lake of the Deeds of Rāma.* Tulsī became famous through this work, and he himself remarks in his *Kavitāvali* that "the world even likens me to the great sage Vālmīki." In addition to the *Rāmcaritmānas* and the *Kavitāvali,* at least ten other works can be ascribed to Tulsī with certainty. Chief among them are *Vinay-patrika, Dohāvali,* and *Gītāvali.*

As a poet, Tulsīdas combines the grandeur and the majesty of Sanskrit with the lyrical grace and power of Vraj (or Braj) Bhāṣā, a dialect of Hindi. A master of alliteration and rhythm, Tulsī also shows great restraint in his use of words, blending the epic and the lyric styles. His choice of dialect and style was not in conformity with the scholarly standards of his time. Tulsī describes himself as *prākrit kavi* ("uncultivated poet"), and from a scholarly viewpoint his language was *grāmya*—of the village, uncultured. Yet because of its poetic excellence, *Rāmcaritmānas* was the most revered of all Hindi texts both by scholars and by ordinary people.

The greatest achievement of Tulsī lies in making the popular devotional style acceptable to the orthodox Hindu community and the philosophical interpretations of the high culture accessible to ordinary people. His reinterpretation of the *Rāmāyaṇa,* based on the Sanskrit *Adhyātma-Rāmāyaṇa* and *Bhusundi-Rāmāyaṇa,* revolutionized the nature of the epic and transformed it into a popular devotional poem.

SEE ALSO Bhakti; Hindi Religious Traditions; Poetry, article on Indian Religious Poetry; Rāmāyaṇa.

BIBLIOGRAPHY

Hill, W. Douglas P., trans. *The Holy Lake of the Acts of Rāma* (1952). Reprint, Oxford, 1971.

McGregor, Ronald S. *Hindi Literature from Its Beginnings to the Nineteenth Century.* Wiesbaden, 1984.

Tulsī Das. *Kavitāvali.* Translated and with a critical introduction by Raymond Allchin. London, 1964.

New Sources

Lutgendorf, Philip. *The Life of a Text: Performing the Ramcaritmanas of Tulsidas.* Berkeley, 1991.

VELCHERU NARAYANA RAO (1987)
Revised Bibliography

TUNG CHUNG-SHU SEE DONG ZHONGSHU

TUNGUZ RELIGION. The peoples of Siberia speaking Tunguz languages numbered 65,900 persons, according to the 1989 census of the U.S.S.R. The most numerous of them are the Evenki (30,000) and Eveny (17,000), who are collectively called Tunguz in the older literature. Sometimes the ethnonym Lamut ("sea person") is employed, applying only to certain groups of Eveny. The close racial and cultural relationship of these two peoples makes it possible to examine their beliefs in the framework of a single system, which may be designated "Tunguz religion." Other peoples speaking Tunguz languages are the Nanay (Goldi; 12,000), Ulchi (3,200), Udege (1,900), Oroki and Orochi (1,200), and Negidal'tsy (600). They represent a special cultural area, extending as far as the basin of the lower Amur River and Sakhalin Island, that includes the ancient cultural legacies of the Ainu and Nivkhi (Giliaks) and the inhabitants of northeastern China. A common religion has long been the primary factor uniting the atomized society of Tunguz hunters who, in small groups, mastered the vast space of taiga and tundra between the Yenisei River on the west and the Sea of Okhotsk on the east and between the Arctic Ocean on the north and Lake Baikal on the south.

The periodic religious ceremonies of the Tunguz are closely tied to their mythology, and in several instances they directly reproduce myths of creation and of the heroic deeds of their first ancestors, beginning with the words *tarnīmngākāndu bičen* ("this was in *nimngākān*"). The term *nimngākān* means "myth, tale, legend; warm fairyland; bear ritual; shamanic séance." Each group of Tunguz has a myth on the creation of *bugha*—its own inhabited territory. *Bugha* has a variety of meanings: "locality, world, native land; cosmos, sky, earth; spirit master of the upper world/lower world/hunt, God, devil; paradise, hell; icon." The Tunguz also use this term to designate the entrance into a bear den or a small hut made of young larches with small figures of beasts and birds placed therein in preparation for shamanic performances. The basic meanings of the term *bugha* embrace, in this way, notions of the creator, creation of the world, and of a model of the world. For designating the deity of the upper world the Tunguz also use the names Mayin, Ekseri, Seweki, and Amaka. The first of these names is tied to the concept of "success" or "hunting luck," whereas the last is a kinship term referring to representatives of the older age groups: "grandfather, father, uncle," and, in general, "ancestor." The word *amaka* also has other meanings: "bear; God; sky."

According to the perceptions of the Tunguz, the upper world (*ughu bugha*) is connected to the middle world (*dulu bugha*) through the North Star, termed *bugha sangarin,* "sky hole." In turn the middle world is also connected to the lower world (*hergu bugha*) through an opening within it. In the *nimngākān* the first ancestors were able to move between all three levels of the world. Thereafter this became the privilege of the shamans, who use for this purpose Tuuruu, the Tunguz variant of the World Tree, or its equivalent. Engžekit, the mythical river called "the place that no one sees." It flows from the place termed Timanitki ("toward morning; east"), transects the middle world, and enters into the place called Dolbonitki ("toward night; north"), beyond which stretches the realm of the dead, Bunikit or Buni. Into Engžekit flow the many branch rivers of individual shamans. Somewhere at the confluence of these tributaries with the mythical river are the Omiruk, territories inhabited by souls *(ōmī);* these lands comprise the sacred wealth of each clan.

One of the myths associated with Engžekit tells of the origin of the first people, of reindeer, and of cultural objects from the various parts of the mythic bear's body. He voluntarily sacrificed himself to the heavenly maiden, who was carried off on an ice floe in the current between the upper and middle worlds. In other myths the bear, representing the ancestor of one or another Tunguz tribe, is similarly depicted as a culture hero, the creator of reindeer breeding, bequeathing after his inevitable death the ritual of the Bear Festival. This festival, which is essentially the same among all the Tunguz, is associated with the seasonal hunt of the animal in its den, which takes place in early spring or late autumn. The most important detail of the Tunguz bear ceremony, which has an explanation in their religio-mythological perception of the world, is the way in which they handle the bear's eyes. Hunters, having cut off the head of the slain beast, take out its eyes with great care, seeking to touch them neither with a knife nor with their fingernails. Then they wrap the eyes in grass or birch bark and carry them away into the forest, where they place them high in a tree. The Udege did this in the hope that the bear's eyes might be illuminated by the first rays of the rising sun. In the tabooed language of Tunguz hunters the bear's eyes are called *ōsīkta* ("stars"). The connection of the bear with heavenly luminaries is well illustrated in a Tunguz myth in which the bear, named Mangi, follows the reindeer or moose who had stolen the sun. Having caught up with his prey, the bear returns the sun to its place. Both protagonists in this myth form the constellation of Ursa Major, the Big Dipper, in Tunguz cosmology (Chichlo, 1981, pp. 39–44).

This myth of the heavenly (or cosmic) hunt was reenacted by the Tunguz during the greatest festival of the year, Ikenipke (a name derived from the word *ike,* "to sing"), which took place in a specially constructed cone-shaped dwelling *(žumi),* whose name designates not only "house, household, or family" but also "bear den" and *uterus animalis.* In the center of this dwelling is placed a pole called Tuuruu, along which Ekseri, the spirit of the upper world, and Hargi, the spirit of the lower world, travel in order to hold conversations with the shaman. The festival, which may be called the Tunguz New Year, consists of eight days of dancing, singing, and pantomine. The people, led by the shaman, would move inside the *žumi* in a circle in the direction of the sun's movement as they traveled up the river Engžekit behind an imaginary reindeer. In his song, the shaman would describe all the details of the travel, which lasted a year—all the animals, spirits, and obstacles encountered. At the end of the festival the men would shoot from a shamanic bow at wooden reindeer figures, shattering them into pieces that each man kept until the next festival.

Other important shamanistic rituals of the Tunguz took place in specially constructed dwellings in the taiga. With complex auxiliary structures, these represented a model of the supernatural world. The first, *nimngāndek,* signifies "the place where *nimngākān* is fulfilled." The second, *sevenčedek,* is "the place where a ceremony with *seven* is performed." Among all Tunguz peoples, *seven* means "shaman's spirit helper," but this word is connected to one of the names of the high God, Sevek or Seveki, and to the taboo reindeer of light coloring, *sevek,* which is also called *bughadi oron,* "heavenly reindeer." The ritual of dedicating the chosen reindeer as *sevek* is either independent or part of the ritual cycle in the Ikenipke festival. From the moment of this dedication, the *sevek* serves only for the transport of sacred objects. After its death, this reindeer is laid out on a platform set up in a tree.

The word *seven* also signifies the ritual dish at the Bear Festival, which is prepared from rendered bear fat mixed with finely chopped bear meat. Scooping the *seven* with a spoon, the hunter must swallow it without its touching his teeth. This method of partaking of the body of the beast deity is identical to the rules of handling bear eyes. The boldest hunters may swallow them but only without touching them with their teeth; otherwise the hunter will become blind. The meaning of these rules becomes more understandable in light of the strong prohibitions associated with the domestic hearth. The firewood and coals must not be stirred with a sharp object, nor may broken needles be thrown into the fire. Even to place a knife with its point toward the fire may put out the eyes of the spirit of the fire. This spirit, according to an Orochi myth, is a pair of bear cubs born from the mating of a bear and a woman. According to the Evenki, the bear is a culture hero who gave people fire. Reconstructing the Tunguz spirit of the domestic fire discloses his bisexual nature, corresponding to an androgynous deity like the bear. It is therefore understandable why hunters do not risk swallowing *ōsīkta* ("bear's eyes"), preferring to return them to the taiga. The luster of these "stars" on top of the World Tree assured hunting success, and the projections of the luster are the light and warmth of domestic hearths.

When considered as a system, the myths, concepts, rituals, and customs of the Tunguz show what a large, if not central, role the bear occupies. The most powerful shamans have him as a guardian spirit. At the time of the séance they don his skin, thus receiving power over all zoomorphic spirits, which they gather in the darkness of the sacred dwelling that represents, in essence, the cosmic bear den. The moose as well plays a significant role in the religious life of hunters and shamans, but its significance cannot be explained, as it is by most scholars, by economic functions alone. It must be noted that, according to myth, the moose emerges from the bear's fur and is, in consequence, part of him. And if Ursa Major is termed Heglen ("moose") by the Tunguz, this denotes a shift of stress in the direction of one member of a binary opposition composing the structure of the myth (and constellation), in which prey and hunter can change places. In their ritual practice Tunguz shamans preferred to place this stress on the figure of the hunter, inasmuch as they considered Mangi, who tracked the cosmic moose, to be their forefather.

Traces of the myth of the cosmic hunt in the religious life of Tunguz peoples still remain, as attested by ancient wooden disks of the Nanay that represent the sun (*siū*). On the upper part of one of them is a drawing of a bear, and on the lower is the representation of a moose turned upside down. The Nanay hung such disks on the door of a dwelling or on a child's cradle; to the shamans they were an indispensable accessory of their costume. Possessing healing and protective functions, these disks are concise and expressive signs of the fundamental myth of the beginnings of human history. In the Nanay culture area, the myth of the bear Mangi, who freed the sun from captivity, and the myth of the hunter Khado, who killed the excess suns, which were burning all living things, came into contact with each other. Both myths are similar insofar as the Orochi, neighbors of the Nanay, consider Khado the father of the shamanistic spirit Mangi, the representation of which is on the shamans' staffs.

The Tunguz, whose livelihood depends upon success in hunting, conducted simple ceremonies that gave the hunter confidence in his own powers and in the benevolence of fate. He could do without a shaman, having enlisted the support of the master spirit of a locality and having gained a personal spirit helper. One of these rites is Singkelevun, "obtaining *singken* (success)." This ritual appears to be the simplest imitation of the concluding ceremony of the Ikenipke rite: the hunter makes an image of a reindeer or a moose, takes it with him into the taiga, and then shoots at it with a small bow. If the image is hit immediately, it becomes a *singken.* The dried parts of previously killed animals (hearts, jaws, noses), which the hunter saves, are also guarantors of success. Certain groups of Tunguz began to call the spirit master of the taiga Singken. The Evenki and Orochi conducted a Singkelevun ceremony in October, before the beginning of the winter hunting season. It was performed among them as a complex shamanistic ceremony consisting of several cycles.

For the preservation of human life, the Tunguz prepared special repositories of souls, which were "earthly" miniature copies of *ōmīruk* found in the basin of the Engzekit River in the upper world. The domestic *ōmīruk* are small boxes with little figurines placed in them. Each figurine holds the soul of a person placed there by a shaman. Certain shamans placed tufts of hair from persons needing protection in the *ōmīruk.* Such little boxes were strapped to the saddle of the heavenly reindeer. The *ōmī* was evidently a reincarnated substance circulating within the limits of a determined social group. Among the Nanay, for example, the *ōmī* lived in the form of small birds on the clan tree, from which they descended into women's bodies. Depictions of these trees are still found on the robes of Nanay women today.

In the case of frequent deaths of children, the shaman had to set out for the upper world, where he snared one of the soul birds and swiftly descended to earth. Evidence of his successful trip was a fistful of wool strands pressed together, which he threw into a white handkerchief held up for him by an assistant during the séance.

The traditional method of disposing of the dead among the Tunguz was aerial: the body, washed in the blood of a sacrificial reindeer and clothed and wrapped in a hide, tent cover, or birch bark, was laid on a scaffold set up in the branches of a tree. Coffins, when used, were made of hollowed-out tree trunks and set upon tree trunks or on posts dug into the ground. The belongings of the deceased were left with him, and his reindeer was strangled and left at the place of burial. After christianization in the eighteenth century, the Tunguz began to practice underground burial. However, the traditional ritual persists in the Siberian taiga even today.

The Tunguz considered the cause of death to be the departure or theft by evil spirits of the *beye* soul, the name of which translates as "body." In conducting the mourning ceremony for the dead a year later, the Tunguz sometimes prepared a temporary "body" from a section of a tree trunk, which they clothed in part with the deceased person's clothing, provided with food, and bade farewell to forever. The shaman, completing the conveyance of the deceased into Buni, asked him not to return again nor to disturb the living. Among the Nanay, the initial conveyance of the deceased, termed Nimngan, took place on the seventh day. Here, the deceased was represented by a bundle of his clothing, in which the shaman placed the *han'an,* the "shadow" soul of the deceased, which he had caught. This bundle of clothes was treated like the living for a period of three years, until the final farewell with him at the large *kasa* memorial festival, lasting several days. But even here, under the unquestionable influence of Manchurian Chinese customs, the Nanay and other Tunguz peoples of the lower Amur region observed traditional division between the living and the dead. An ancestor cult did not unfold here nor, more forcibly, was it characteristic of the Evenki and Eveny, the nomads of the Siberian taiga.

Shamanism and the traditional religion of the Tunguz have not totally disappeared, as is commonly believed, notwithstanding atheist propaganda and prohibitions. As recently as 1958, four nomadic Even communities, living in isolation for more than thirty years in the mountainous forest-tundra of Magadan oblast, were headed by eight authoritative shamans, one of whom was called by the honorific Amanža (Amaka). But, in spite of their forced settlement, these Evens (Berezovka village, north-east of Yakutia) preserved their religious beliefs and behavior. Thus at the beginning of October 2000, to cause a fall of snow waited so much by the reindeers herders and the hunters of the village, a woman left her house with a bear skin, shook it vigorously, then suspended it outside. People of the village while arriving in the taiga after the snowfall, achieved the following ritual: Men sacrificed a reindeer and a woman copiously coated three selected larches with the blood of the animal. Then they threw in fire some drops of vodka and pieces of meat. Thus they wanted to thank the spirits of the forest and to be ensured of their benevolence.

SEE ALSO Bears; Shamanism.

BIBLIOGRAPHY

Anisimov, A. F. *Religiia evenkov.* Moscow and Leningrad, 1958.

Chichlo, Boris, "Ours—chamane." *Études mongoles et sibé-riennes,* 12 (1981): 35–112.

Delaby, Laurence. "Chamanes toungouses." *Études mongoles et sibériennes,* 7 (1976).

Diószegi, Vilmos. "The Origin of the Evenki 'Shaman Mask' of Transbaikalia." *Acta orientalia Academiae Scientiarum Hungaricae* 20 (1967): 171–200.

Diószegi, Vilmos. "The Origin of the Evenki Shamanistic Instruments (Stick, Knout) of Transbaikalia." *Acta Ethnographica Academiae Scientiarum Hungaricae* 17 (1968): 265–311.

Diószegi, Vilmos, ed. *Popular Beliefs and Folklore Tradition in Siberia.* Translated and revised by Stephen P. Dunn. Budapest, 1968. See especially the essays by V. A. Avrorin (pp. 373–386) and G. M. Vasilevich (pp. 339–372).

Diószegi, Vilmos, and Mihály Hoppál, eds. *Shamanism in Siberia.* Budapest, 1978. See especially the essays by A. V. Smoliak (pp. 439–448) and V. A. Tugolukov (pp. 419–428).

Lopatin, I. A. *The Cult of the Dead among the Natives of the Amur Basin.* The Hague, 1960.

Mazin, A. I. *Traditsionnye verovaniia i obriady evenkov-orochonov.* Novosibirsk, 1984.

Michael, H. N., ed. *Studies in Siberian Shamanism.* Toronto, 1963. See the essays by A. F. Anisimov (pp. 84–124) and G. M. Vasilevich (pp. 46–84).

Paproth, Hans-Joachim. *Studien über das Bärenzeremoniell: I. Bärenjagdriten und Bärenfeste bei den tungusichen Völkern.* Uppsala, 1976.

Priroda i chelovek v religioznykh predstavleniiakh narodov Sibiri i Severa. Leningrad, 1976. See especially the essays by S. V. Ivanov (pp. 161–188), N. B. Kile (pp. 189–202), and A. V. Smoliak (pp. 129–160).

Shirokogoroff, S. M. *Psychomental Complex of the Tungus.* Beijing and London, 1935.

Smoliak, A. V. Shaman: lichnost', funktsii, mirovozzrenie. Moscow, 1991.

Vasilevich, G. M. "Preshamanistic and Shamanistic Beliefs of the Evenki." *Soviet Anthropology and Archeology* 11 (1972).

BORIS CHICHLO (1987 AND 2005)
Translated from Russian by Demitri B. Shimkim

TUONELA, which means "the abode," is the mythical place of sojourn for the deceased in the religious traditions among Finns, Karelians, Ingrians and speakers of many other Finnish-related languages. The word concerns a sacred place in the otherworld, and is often used as a synonym of the words for the netherworld (*Manala, maanalainen*: "underworld") or for the mythical kingdom of the extreme north (Pohjola: "Northern Land"). In oral epics, laments, and lullabies it refers to "the home of the Tuoni," where Tuoni refers to the ruler of the world of the dead. The term *tuonilmainen* refers to "the other air," which is another term for the otherworld. A parallel Mansi word, *tammaa* (the otherworld) refers to the final destination of the journey of the breathing spirit *(lil)* of the deceased one in the northernmost edge of the universe. The spirit flies to *tammaa* across the Arctic Ocean in the shape of a migrating goose. In addition to its meaning as the mythical geographical destination of the spiritual voyage of a soul, *tuonela* also refers to the filled grave of an individual dead person, as well as the entire village graveyard.

Karelian, Ingrian, and Veps cemeteries at the Finnish-Russian border provide a good example of the long-lasting encounter between traditional folk belief and the deep influence of Russian Orthodox Christianity. Small log huts were erected above the graves, with a window set at one end, towards the direction of home, to let in light, and also to enable the dead to look out and guard the life and behavior of relatives at home for the benefit of family fortune and social control. A hole is made at another end through which the *löyly* (breathing soul) can leave the grave to visit its former home or to make its final journey to the home of the Tuoni in the shape of a bird.

Similar huts have been found in the cemeteries of other Finno-Ugric peoples (e.g., the Mordvins, Komi, and Mansi) in Russia. The custom of erecting huts in cemeteries was borrowed from the Russians, who erected similar house-shaped, pitched-roof structures over their graves. (These structures were forbidden by the tsarist government in the nineteenth century.) The cutting of trees and the breaking of twigs was forbidden in such places.

Scholars of Finnish folk beliefs, epics, and rituals (Martti Haavio, Uno [Holmberg-]Harva, Lauri Honko, Aili Nenola-Kallio, Juha Pentikäinen, and Anna-Leena Siikala) have emphasized the importance of death as the essential element of Finnish culture. Within that culture the extended family unit extended beyond those members still living on this earth and those who have died and passed on to the "other air": the realm of Tuoni. The deceased ones had strong power to enforce the values and norms of the society, and could punish the living for violating taboos. The dead were believed to have the same needs as the living—clothing, food, and work tools, so it was the duty of the living to provide these necessities. Of special importance was the provision of Tuoni footwear, in which the dead were dressed with woolen socks. Women who died unmarried were given the kerchiefs that married women wore, so that they could marry in the otherworld. Care for the dead continued beyond the funeral, for they continued to share in the family's proceeds. On personal and annual commemoration days, plenty of food was taken to the graves. It was believed that the dead ones came to the graves in the form of birds, and ate the food that was left there as a sacrifice.

The topography of Tuonela varies in Finnish folklore and mythology. Beliefs and practices which are clearly based on neighboring cultures and missionary religions have also been adapted to Finnish-Karelian cosmography, and are elaborated in funeral laments, for example. According to these beliefs, the realm of the dead may be situated in heaven or at the northern end of the world, separated from the world of the living by a deep precipice. At the base of the precipice flows the black river of Tuonela, unilluminated by the sun or moon. The river contains a whirling, wild cataract and a stream of fire in which spears, swords, and needles stand upright and the dead can be seen swimming in bloody clothes. The crossing of the river was associated with great danger. The dead could wade through it, or they could cross a bridge made of thin thread. More frequently, the dead were transported across the river in a boat steered by the daughter of Tuoni. If a person heard a ringing in his or her ears, it meant that relatives in Tuonela were calling for the boat.

Fingernails and locks of hair were especially significant in the Karelian and Ingrian beliefs about Tuonela. The nails of the deceased were clipped on Saturday night, cut in two, and slipped into the neck-hole of the deceased person's shirt. The clippings were thought to help the dead ascend Tuonela mountain, which was smooth as an eggshell. However, the nails had to be cut in pieces; otherwise, the Evil One would make a boat from the whole nails and use it to ferry the deceased to Hell. The picturesque nature of these beliefs about Tuonela stems partly from Baltic-Slavic, Byzantine, and Old Egyptian traditions, and partly from medieval Christian visionary literature and hagiography. In Finnish epics, these traditions have been merged with the older tradition of shamanic visions and journeys to the Land of the Dead. Lemminkäinen, who appears in folklore as both a god and a shaman is an example of how traditional shamanic epics have been combined to include elements of Egyptian Osiris mythology.

See Also Finnish Religions; Finno-Ugric Religions.

Bibliography

Haavio, Martti. "Suomalaisten tuonela-kuvitelmia." *Kotiseutu*, 1939, pp. 65–67. A discussion of Finnish images of Tuonela, based on folk songs.

Haavio, Martti. "Väinämöinen's Journey to Tuonela." In his *Väinämöinen, Eternal Sage*, translated by Helen Goldthwait-Väänänen, pp. 83–105. Helsinki, 1952. The journey of Väinämöinen, the chief protagonist of the *Kalefala*, to Tuonela.

Holmberg, Uno. *The Mythology of All Races*, vol. 4: *Finno-Ugric, Siberian.* Boston, 1927.

Honko, Lauri. "Jenseitsvorstellungen." In *Wörterbuch der Mythologie*, vol. 2, edited by H. W. Haussig. Stuttgart, West Germany, 1973. A section from Honko's longer article "Finnische Mythologie", this offers a fine general account of Tuonela.

Järvinen, Irma-Tiitta. "Communication between the Living and the Dead through Rituals and Dreams in Aunus Karelia." In *Folklore and the Encounters of Traditions: Finnish-Hungarian Symposium on Folklore and the Encounters of Tradition, 18–20 March 1996, Jyväskylä.* Jyväskylä, Finland, 1996.

Mansikka, V. J. "Itkujen Tuonela." In *Kieli-ja Kansatieteellisiä*, edited by E. N. Setälä, pp. 160–180. Helsinki, 1924. On Finnish ideas about the journey to Tuonela, as reflected in funeral laments.

Nenola-Kallio, Aili. *Studies in Ingrian Laments* (Folklore Fellows Communications 234). Helsinki, 1982.

Pentikäinen, Juha. *The Nordic Dead-Child Tradition.* Helsinki, 1968.

Pentikäinen, Juha. *Kalevala Mythology.* Translated and edited by Ritva Poom. Bloomington and Indianapolis, Ind., 1989. Originally published in Finnish as *Kalavalan mytologia.* Helsinki, 1987.

Siikala, Anna-Leena. *Suomalainen šamanismi. Mielikuvien historiaa.* (Suomalaisen Kirjallisuuden Seuran Toimituksia 565). Helsinki, 1992. Discusses shamanistic survivals in Finnish Charms and in the practices of Finnish wise men, including ideas about the abode.

Felix J. Oinas (1987)
Juha Pentikäinen (2005)

TURKIC RELIGIONS.

TURKIC RELIGIONS. Throughout the course of their long history, the Turkic peoples have simultaneously or successively practiced all the universal religions (Christianity, especially Nestorian Christianity; Judaism; Manichaeism; Buddhism; and Mazdaism) before the majority of them were won over to Islam. However, before yielding to these religions, they held their own system of beliefs, their own personal representations. These are generally identified as "animism" or "shamanism," even though the last term cannot even begin to cover the whole of the religious phenomena. Their "national" religion, largely shared by the Mongols and certainly the Tunguz, is still practiced today. It has been kept alive among certain Siberian and Altaic groups and, to a much greater extent than is realized, within the very institution of Islam, to which it has more or less adapted without abandoning or altering many of its original characteristics.

This is not to say that the indigenous Turkic religion is free of every foreign element. It developed in contact with other ideas, notably those from China and Iran. It has continually evolved and grown richer over the course of centuries, either through internal development or the influence of great civilizations. It is, in fact, quite flexible and is based on tolerance and religious coexistence. Certainly, it is essentially a mystic religion. Its beliefs have never been solidly unified, and, as we are beginning to better understand, they are like two diverging branches of a common trunk: the popular one is centered on shamanism, totemism, and a vigorous polytheism; the imperial one is antishamanist, antitotemist, and has monotheistic tendencies in its advocacy of the supremacy of Tengri, the sky god.

Although they are separate, these two branches have not escaped interpenetration. One branch developed under the tribal regime, the other during the formation of the great empires of the steppes, such as those of the Hsiung-nu, the T'u-chüeh or Türk (sixth to eighth century), the Uighurs (eighth to ninth century), or the Mongols (thirteenth to fourteenth century). It must be remembered that the Turkic peoples played a major role in the Mongol empire. This is reflected in the use of the name *Tartar* (Turkic, *Tatar*), which was used to refer to the armies of Chinggis Khan and is none other than the name of a very ancient vassalized Turkic tribe. This expressive name also evoked an infernal river of antiquity, the Tartarus, and had the connotation of "barbarian" as well.

Whether tribal or imperial, however, the prevailing political and social regime allowed a memory of the former to remain, and when the prevailing order was temporarily abolished, along with it was abolished a part of what it had imposed. Nevertheless, it is important to consider the beliefs common to both the popular religion and the imperial religion apart from the beliefs that pertain more particularly to one or the other.

Until recently, it had been considered impossible to understand the religion of the Turkic people in its ancient form. Studies, especially ethnographic ones, have been written on groups of people who continued to practice the religion in modern times (nineteenth to twentieth century). Only recently has it been observed that the inscribed Turkic stelae of the sixth to the tenth century, certain manuscripts (including the dictionary of Maḥmūd al-Kāshgharī, eleventh century), and foreign sources (especially Chinese but also Byzantine, Arabic, Latin, Armenian, and Syrian) present a considerable wealth of information. This information takes on full meaning when compared with ethnographic notes, medieval Mongolian sources, and pre-Islamic remnants in Turkic-Muslim plastic and literary works. Thus we begin to have, if not a complete knowledge of the ancient Turkic religion, at least a satisfactory view of the overall picture.

Of course, we have acquired more information on some periods and peoples than on others. We have a fair understanding of the religious situation under the empires but know little of the religious situation of the tribes, at least before the modern era. We know something of certain ethnic groups but nothing at all of others. In general, we have sufficient documentation on the period between the foundation of the Türk empire (sixth century) and the conversion of the Oghuz to Islam (eleventh to thirteenth century), as well as on the present era.

THE COMMON HERITAGE. With a few small exceptions, the Turkic religion has offered structures to all peoples of all social classes in all regions of the Turkic world throughout history. Admittedly, there was a less influential period during which the religion was developing, but it appears to have been firmly established as early as the first century CE. It would be incorrect to believe, for example, that at the beginning of the Türk empire, the western Türk borrowed a cult of fire that was unknown to the eastern Türk from Iran (where it is known to have flourished), for the cult was already pan-Turkic. Because Sogdian, the language of an Iranian people, was used as a written language as far north as Mongolia in the early sixth century, the fact that literary evidence for the fire cult exists in an Iranian language cannot be used to prove that the cult was of Iranian origin. Far less important practices seem to be known in the east but not in the west, such as the wearing of plumes, which did not spread to the west until the Mongolian invasions.

Although the religion was fairly well established early on, certain innovations appeared over the course of time. Without doubt, the dualism already apparent in the Turkic religion has been accentuated through the influence of Manichaeism. From Buddhism has come a conception of hell as a cosmic zone situated under the earth in symmetry with the sky (a deity), as well as the transformation of one of the great mythological characters, Erlik or Erklik ("the virile one, the valiant one") from a warrior who killed the stars at daybreak to the god of the underworld, a king of innumerable demons who not only live on the earth but haunt the entire universe. Equivalent to the Indo-Iranian Yama, he is attested to in Turkic sources as early as the 1200s. The idea of paradise seems to have taken shape in a similar way; the Sogdian word for it, *utchmaq,* has been confused with the Old Turkic infinitive *utchmaq,* which means "to fly away" and which was traditionally used, at least in speaking of great individuals, to signify "to die." An innovation that seems to be more important was observed by the Chinese in about 628: "In the past, the Türk had the custom of burning the dead; now they bury them." However, one must consider that the Turkic peoples have always fluctuated between incinerating and burying the dead. Of the pre-Slavic Bulgarians and, in a general way, of the western Türk, it is said, "One phratry burns its dead, the other buries them." The Kirghiz continued to use incineration until they came into contact with Islam.

Ideas that have remained unchanged are those relative to death, the afterlife, and funerary rites (apart from the issue of burial versus incineration). Death, which one hopes will be violent and unnatural (in spite of the respect that is occasionally shown the elderly) is considered the Necessity, Kergek (perhaps a deity). However, it is deeply dreaded and has given rise to bitter regrets, supposedly issued from the mouths of the deceased. Death is eminently contagious and requires a sober approach toward the dying one (generally abandoned) or the deceased. The type of afterlife to be attained depends primarily on the treatment accorded the skeleton. It must be cleaned perfectly: the flesh must be scraped off and the cadaver set on a platform in a tree and exposed. When the bones are clean, they are either buried in the ground (if the deceased is to retain his earthly ties) or burned (if he is to lose them and gain access to the kingdom of the dead). The funerary ceremonies have also survived the centuries without having been changed: they include lamentations and ritual mutilations, declamations *(agit)* of the virtues of the deceased, a sacrifice, and a communal meal. The meal has been especially important, so much so that the word *yog,* originally designating the funeral as a whole, would eventually connote only the meal.

The varying forms of the obsequies clearly demonstrate the margin of liberty or of uncertainty that remained within a well-defined context. This latitude occurs again and again primarily in the view of the world. The universe is generally represented as composed of two parallel plains, the sky and the earth (ultimately extended to three with the addition of the underworld). At the same time, it is also seen as a square plateau (earth), covered by a circumscribed dome (sky), with the four corners of the earth being allowed to exist outside the shelter of the sky. The cosmic axis that links the sky, the earth, and the underworld can be a mountain or a tree with seven branches, each branch representing a level of the sky. The levels of the sky are in turn derived from the seven planets still known to have been popularly believed in during modern times but also attested to by prehistoric engravings and by every construction with symbolic value, for example, the pillar of the tent, the ensemble formed by the central hearth of the yurt, and its upper opening, through which the smoke escapes. This axis is at once the support for the sky and the path that permits access to it. Among the numerous microcosms consonant with this view, the yurt, a circular tent in the form of a bell, is the most characteristic. It is protected from exterior influences by the powerful deity of the threshold, which one must kiss upon entering. Although circular in shape, the yurt was oriented first toward the rising sun and then toward the south.

It is possible that the sky and the earth originally may have been placed side by side, but there is more speculation than truth to this. The Orkhon inscriptions (eighth century) speak about origins in two lines: "When the sky above was blue and the earth below was dark, the son of man appeared between them." The Turkic peoples were little interested in the cosmogonical problem or in eschatology. Of the more recent cosmogonies (after the tenth century), the well-known one reported by Wilhelm Radloff (1884, vol. 2, p. 3) and all allusions to the creative power of the sky god were influenced by foreign religions.

The observation of stars is an important occupation. The phases of the moon are considered lucky or unlucky. No projects are to be undertaken when the moon is in its last quarter, although a good time to launch a military campaign is when the moon is waxing or is full. The last days of the lunar month are favorable for obsequies because they mark an end and announce a rebirth. Similarly, human life closely parallels plant life. Trees are born each spring and die each autumn; thus the cadaver is saved for the biannual obsequies, which take place either when the leaves begin to fall or as they grow green again, a fact that explains the aforementioned techniques used to preserve the skeleton. When great personages are taken to their place of final rest, an attempt is made to be in harmony with the vegetative season, the phases of the moon, and the beneficial moments of the solstices and the equinoxes.

The four classic elements make up the universe. Water and fire are of exceptional value. Moreover, they are antagonists and complementary components: fire comes from wood, which is born from water. The last has a fertilizing capacity but above all is pure. It is forbidden to dirty water, even though water does not purify. A "mass of water" is a symbol of knowledge and intelligence, qualities of the sovereign. Fire, which eventually would become a god, is an alter ego of the shaman because of its hypnotic, elevating, and healing powers. It is the great purifier. All defiled objects or those suspected of being defiled, notably anything that enters the camp, must pass between two fires, jump over the fire, or go around it. However, this ancient belief became obsolete in the nineteenth century, while fumigation, also a purifier, remained popular. The hearth, considered the reflection of the family, is protected by numerous taboos. To extinguish it and disperse the ashes would amount to destroying the race. Since ancient times, the great priest of this fire has been the "prince of fire," the *ottchigin* (derived from *ot tegin*), the youngest son to inherit the paternal residence—the heart of the empire—after the older sons had been provided for or endowed with a distant appanage. Today, this office is held by various members of the family, occasionally women. Like thunder, lightning—fire from the sky—arouses terror and is seen as a divine punishment against the one it strikes.

Every existing thing is inhabited by a force of varying intensity that we could call, although not quite accurately, "spirit," "soul," or "master-possessor." Each force can be broken down into a multitude of forces or can be combined with others to constitute a more vast, collective force. The tree is powerful, but the grove or forest is more powerful. The "eternal" stone is fully effective only when combined with others to form cairns *(obo)*, piles generally located in dangerous passages or passages recognized as such by a sacred mystery. Anything complex like a man or woman, has several souls; human souls reside particularly in the blood (the shedding of which is forbidden), breath, hair, skull, sexual organs, and elsewhere. Thus nothing is simple or stable; everything has variable dimensions, a sort of ubiquity. But everything makes reference to the animal, zoomorphism being the form par excellence—the form of all spirits and of human spirits before their birth, during their life, and after their death. Consequently, everything that exists can appear as it is or in animal form.

In one way or another, all animals have had a numinous role, but certain animals are different from others: the bird of prey, the eagle or falcon, is a divine messenger that flies near Tengri and sits enthroned on the summit of the cosmic tree; the stag is often considered a saint, but is hunted nevertheless; the hare's position is as ambiguous as that of the camel, which is totemized or tabooed as impure; the bear is the quintessential lunar animal, whose hibernation stirs the imagination; geese or swans, which appear in the widespread legend of the swan maiden, may symbolize the celestial virgin; all birds are souls; and the horse, a member of the clan, is the epitome of the sacrificial animal and also often a solar or aquatic symbol.

With the exception of the act of killing another human, combat between an animal and an adolescent, or another animal designated to represent him, constitutes the principal rite of passage. This rite allows a male youth to become part of adult society and gives him rights to women or, rather, constitutes marriage in itself. In effect, the match is an enactment of the sexual act: to conquer the animal is to become both its spouse and its son. It renews and reenacts the primordial ancestral struggle: murder, copulation, and birth. This rite is an ancient legacy clearly attested by the animal art plaques of the steppes, medieval manuscripts, and modern commentary.

Despite a strong family structure, accounts of adoption by animals or humans are numerous, and fraternity is not dependent upon birth alone. Fraternity can be pledged between two strangers through the exchange of significant gifts (osselets, arrows, horses) and particularly through the mixing of blood. The rite that establishes fraternity consists of the two postulants' joining their slashed wrists or drinking mixed drops of their blood from a cup that is often made from the dried skull top of a murdered enemy chief. This giving of one's blood to another man is actually only one variant of the oath. The other form is the giving of blood to the earth, realized through the pouring of one's blood or the blood of a sacrificed animal; this act is performed before the sky, which deeply involves those making the pledge.

The Popular Religion. Despite the pretensions of certain shamans to positions of tribal leadership, shamanism is essentially a religious phenomenon, a dominant one in the religious life of contemporary non-Muslim Turkic peoples and one that is at the heart of the popular religion. It speaks to the people of things that interest them most—the preservation of their life (magical healings), their future (divination), and their relations with the familiar gods and spirits (the shaman's sacerdotal role, his cosmic voyage). The institution of shamanism is surely quite ancient. Although poorly discernible in antiquity, it was in full bloom by the time of the Middle Ages, despite the total silence of the Türk inscriptions on the subject. This silence does not prove the nonexistence of shamanism but, rather, reflects the care taken to exclude it from imperial records. The oldest descriptions of shamanic séances date back almost to the era when the Old Turkic word for shaman, *qam*, clearly appears, and when magical healings and divinations were attested to among the Oghuz. Descriptions of such rites among the nomadic Turkic tribes come to us from Ibn Sīnā (Avicenna), while similar accounts regarding the Kirghiz come from Marvazī.

Shortly after this period, numerous traces of shamanism appeared among the tribes converted to Islam who became part of the Seljuk hordes. From then on, the information continues to increase and become more precise. In the thirteenth century, van Ruusbroec provided a remarkable description of the séance. From all this medieval information, it appears that the shaman had the ear of the people, communicated with the sky god, was visited by demons, and went into trances to accomplish his cosmic voyages, during which he met many spirits and their auxiliary, or adversary, spirits. His objectives were to cure the sick by expelling the spirits that had entered them or by finding the spirits that had left their bodies, to predict the future, and to exercise certain sacerdotal and political powers. In other respects, the shaman seems to have been a sort of blacksmith, a manipulator of two numinous objects, fire and metal. In any case, he already had rivals: for healing, the first official doctors; for divination, the astrologers (seers who were closer to the princes than to the people) and all kinds of sorcerers, diviners, and prophesiers who waved their wands or arrows and used osselets and dice, who used haruspicy, scapulimancy, and, especially, oneiromancy, and who interpreted divinatory texts. One type of sorcerer who became the shaman's most threatening rival was the "rainmaker," the *yadadji*, who, with the help of a bezoar, produced thunderstorms on demand. These sorcerers, like the astrologers, worked more freely under the imperial religion than did the shamans, because the sorcerers had no pretensions to power or claims of intimacy with the sky.

The totemic system, which can exist only in tribal societies that employ it to determine basic structures (families, clans), plays a role in the popular religion that is almost as important as that of shamanism. For a long time, totemism was unknown among the Altaic peoples in general; however, in the mid-twentieth century pioneering research by P. J. Strahlenberg, Cho-dzidlo, A. Billings, N. Shchukin, and others revealed a totemic system among both contemporary and extinct Turkic societies, such as the Bashkirs, the Oghuz, and the western Türk. Since the eighth century, the Arabs (as confirmed by certain medieval Turkic texts) have observed a tie between clans of certain tribes and certain animals. The study of these observations reveals, beyond all possible doubt, a totemism, naturally misunderstood in the Arab and medieval Turkic accounts.

It is clear that the people, organized under the tribal system, worshiped numerous gods of human dimension and that they cared little about great deities, notably the Sky. We have seen that they were surrounded by innumerable forces that they had to use or protect: natural forces and even fabricated objects (the "master" of the weapon, its "soul," could render the weapon ineffective). The "masters" of the herd, of game, fish, hunting and fishing territories, and doubtless others all had to be conciliated. The masters that the Old Turkic texts call *iduq yer sub,* "sacred lands and waters," concerned them most. These also could be the ensemble of indivisible lands inhabited by the tribe, or better, their "master-possessors" (those of other tribes and of foreigners such as the Chinese were recognized). It could also refer to certain privileged parts of this ensemble, often cited by name. The latter lands were "left free," as conveyed by the word *iduq.* In these areas it was forbidden to carry out any secular activity: hunting, fishing, or felling trees. The idea that the parts of a whole should always be respected was extended to everything. There were also *iduq* animals within the herd that could not be milked, sheared, or mounted. It was important for the hunters to allow some animals to escape from the game they encircled. At least the first fruits of the harvests had to be set aside unused. At each milking and at each meal, it was customary to set apart a portion of milk or meat to be offered to the gods.

Out of a desire to maintain control over the earth's products, the people made "soul supports"; these represented the spirit protectors of animals and harvests. They were among the numerous idols placed in the yurts and were also transported in carts, which became veritable traveling altars. Constructed of felt, wood, and metal, these zoomorphic or anthropomorphic idols could also represent and contain the soul of ancestors and of all imaginable powers. One took care of them, fed them, and painted them with blood. Ethnographers eventually began to call these idols by the Mongol word *ongon* (Turkic equivalents: *töz, tyn, kürmes*), although *ongon* actually refers to totems. Some of the highest deities were affected by this idolization, either through a spontaneous irruption of the practice as applied to the lower spirit protectors or through absorption of elements from the imperial religion. In a general way, the cave, the waters, the trees, and the stars were venerated. Every elevation of ground became a place of cult worship: it established the image of an ascent toward the sky, a distant and vague god.

Whereas the tribal and familial deities of ancient periods are poorly understood, it is almost impossible to define the possible ties of the people to the great gods as revealed to us by the imperial texts alone, at least for the period during which the people were not under the empire.

The Imperial Religion. It is difficult to comprehend the significance and the success of the imperial religion without taking into account the tribal organization of society, with its attendant instability, internecine wars, anarchy, and misery. Divided, the inhabitants of the steppes were powerless. United, they became invincible. Therefore, their strength assured free commerce and made possible raids and conquests of the rich lands of sedentary peoples. Despite the tribes' pronounced taste for independence and their attachment to tradition, the empire presented certain advantages that the tribes were prepared to accept, even if it meant losing part of their patrimony along with their autonomy. Certainly the sovereign, promoted through his own genius or through circumstances, was descended from the tribal regime and practiced the popular religion. This fact, together with his need to secure mass support, inclined him to tolerate the tribal religion; but he reorientated it, promoting elements that had been secondary, diluting or eliminating elements that were in essence antimonarchist. The two great victims were shamanism and totemism.

From the imperial viewpoint, shamanism had no alternative but to adapt. During the long medieval periods, shamans had not only attained positions of tribal leadership (without necessarily having the gifts or the means for leadership) but had also pretended to maintain privileged relationships with the invisible, to climb to the sky. As tribal chiefs, they had to accept a superior authority, something that was more difficult for them than for others. As religious leaders, they had to acknowledge that the *kaghan,* the emperor, had relationships with the invisible world and the sky, relationships much closer than their own. Thus, there was an inevitable conflict between the shaman and the sovereign. However, the contest being unequal, it often ended abruptly or resulted in the inevitable elimination of the shaman. Chinggis Khan's suppression of the influence of the great shaman at his court can be seen as an epitome of this conflict. Even though we have no information, we can assume that the process was the same in other political structures with pan-Turkic tendencies. It is characteristic that the Old Turkic texts do not contain a single word about shamanism: we have already seen why. Nevertheless, it took real courage on the part of the sovereign to disregard the fear inspired in the Turkic peoples by all those who held religious or magical powers, including priests of the religions with which they came in contact.

Totemism was an equally formidable obstacle erected by the tribal regime against the empire. Classificatory and divisive by definition, it was diametrically opposed to the imperial ideal. The duty to which the sovereign was thus called to devote himself consisted of renouncing the various totems of the clan cults and insistently promoting the totem or totems of the ruling dynasty. The ruling dynasty, like every family, like every tribe, was descended either from two united animals or from an animal that had had sexual relations with a human. The sex of the animal or human was not as important in this matter as was the complementarity of the different species. The latter was indicated more clearly and can be seen in the animal art of the steppes: a wildcat and a herbivore, a bird of prey and a rodent, an animal and a human. The myth of origin that was the most widely believed (because it simultaneously served the Türk, the Mongols, and other, smaller, groups) first presented a she-wolf who fed a young boy, married him, and gave him children, thus becoming his mother and wife at the same time. Later this was changed: a wolf was believed to have united with a doe. The content of this myth is particularly rich, especially among the Türk, because it involves the intervention of fertilizing water (the marsh where the she-wolf finds the child), the cave (where she gives birth), and even the bird of prey, which flies above the couple.

However, widespread as it is, this myth is only one among many. One could say that there are as many myths as there are Turkic peoples. Hence, the ancestor of the Kirghiz was a bull or a dog married to forty virgins; the ancestors of the Karakhanids, a lion and a camel. The Oghuz have demonstrated how a theme was able to change owing to unknown influences. Oghuz Kaghan, the eponymic ancestor of the confederation (whose name was etymologically *ogush,* "tribe") was first named "colostrum" *(agiz),* then "young bull" *(oghuz)* after his ancestor, while the wolf remained his guide and protector. Later, the Oghuz had six birds of prey as "totems" when they were divided into six clans and twenty-two or twenty-four when the number of their tribes increased. The exaltation of one's ancestors was emphasized in the Türk empire. Each year the sovereign either went in person or sent a high dignitary to the birthplace (cave) of his family. Türk flagpoles were topped with golden wolves' heads; thus the wolf continued to lead his descendants into battle and also to march ahead of them in migrations.

The imperial ancestor was clearly a divine animal who came from the sky. He was "blue" like the sky and, as described in a relatively recent (post-Chinggisid) text, he could be associated with luminous rays that emanated from the sun and moon. Thus, two different traditions concerning the origins of great men seem to have existed—one involving the sexual union of animals, one involving light that came and impregnated a woman or that, itself a radiant daughter, seduced heroes like Oghuz Kaghan. Some attempt was made to combine the two traditions, but never with much success, not even in the case of the Mongols, whose *Secret History* reveals the efforts made in this respect, or in the Turkic *Oghuz name,* which owes much to the former.

The popular gods suffered less from the imperial religion. Any major force that contributed to the power of the empire was welcomed, and the Turkic peoples, with their fundamental beliefs in the diffused divine, opposed the disappearance of these gods. (Popular sentiment also had to be respected.) Nevertheless, their fate was not always the same. Some were more or less forgotten, while others were promoted. Still others were obviously approached from a new perspective. The various *iduq yer sub,* the "forbidden places," the "master-possessors of the earth and waters," were apparently reduced to those originally belonging to the imperial family. The mountains saw their strength become concentrated in two or three summits, such as the Ötükän, where the prince was seated. On the other hand, everything that appeared to be universal, common to all humankind, grew disproportionately. The earth goddess was often associated with the sky god and partook of his indivisibility. The sky himself, principally Tengri, became the sky god and was "blue," "elevated," and "endowed with strength"; he clearly became, at least eventually, "eternal," the supreme god above all others because he was the god of the emperor and was as exceptional as the latter was. The sovereign was "born from the sky," "resembled the sky," and was some times the sky's son, acting in his name as if he were his great priest; but he was also more, something like the sky's projection, his "shadow," as the Muslims would say. He directed the sky's cult, the collective prayers and ceremonial sacrifices in which he had all his people participate. From then on, Tengri concerned all people, all animals, all vegetables. He gave them life, made them grow, and protected them through two specific gifts, *kut,* a viaticum and celestial "soul," and *ülüg,* "luck."

The national god of the Turkic peoples, Tengri, was also the god of all men and demanded that all recognize him, that is, that they submit to the Turkic *kaghan*—a demand that caused him to take on the characteristics of a god of war. The worst transgression was to revolt against the prince, that is, against Tengri, and the god knew no other punishment for this than death. Before sending death, Tengri "applied pressure," sent messengers, and intervened in a purely psychological manner. In serious cases, he intervened simultaneously with the more popular gods. In medieval times, at least, there does not seem to have been any notion of retribution or postmortem punishment.

If the popular religion has been passed over in silence by imperial Turkic texts, and often by others, there are nonetheless numerous deities that appear around the sky god without our knowing their connections to him: the earth goddess, the *iduq yer sub* and other master-possessors, the sacred springs and rivers, the trees, fire, and the mountain. Whether this last represented the "god of the earth," as with Boz Tengri, or whether it constituted the earth's axis, the center of the empire, like the famous Ötükän (in the Greater Khingan Range), its role eventually became so great and imposing that it was generally designated in Central Asia, as the god of the earth. (For example, the sacred mountain of the Mongolians is the Burkhan Qaldun.) The most powerful and stable of these deities that appear around the sky god is Umai (often still called this today but also known by other names, for example, Aĭyysyt among the Siberian Yakuts), a placental goddess of whom al-Kāshgharī says, "If one worships her, a child will be born." She protects newborns and mares and safeguards against puerperal fever. Certain attempts seem to have been made to bring her closer to Tengri; she has been called "close to the khatun," that is, to the empress.

Finally, in addition to grandiose ceremonies (in terms of the empire), the imperial religion apparently promoted cults and new rites. The banner cult supported a particular soul, either of an ancestral animal (often evoked through a statuette or horse or yak tails atop a pole) or of one of the sovereign's ancestors. This gave rise to the feast of the unfurling of standards and to solemn sacrifices. The imperial family adopted the ancient practice of bloodless animal slaughter: they were strangled, suffocated, or stoned. Funerary temples, erected structures that are the only Turkic temples outside of natural sanctuaries (caves, groves, springs, mountains) or domestic sanctuaries (tents, carts carrying idols), have unfortunately come down to us in a deplorable condition. What remains of them, the *balbal* and the *baba,* may also be an imperial innovation. The *balbal* are shapeless stones (eventually wood was used, for instance among the Cumans and Kipchaks) erected to represent enemies slain in combat or immolated during obsequies. The slain enemies represented by the *balbal* are supposedly at the service of their murderers. For great personages, these monoliths number in the hundreds.

The *baba* are the funerary statues of deceased princes and, occasionally, princesses. They were not viewed as images of the departed but as images of the living, who, after their death, remained among the people. Not of great aesthetic value, these huge, crude statues, of which a good number of specimens are known, represent the individual standing or seated, always holding a cup in the right hand, which is drawn back over the stomach. These works were the original image of the "prince in majesty" of classical Islam.

It is impossible to know whether belief in an afterlife in the sky was of imperial or popular origin, although there is no lack of presumptions that favor imperial origins: having come from the sky and belonging to it, the prince can only return there. In so asserting, one says that he "flies away," later that he "becomes a gyrfalcon" or that he "climbs up to the sky" where he is "as among the living." But there are also attestations of a celestial beyond for those who did not attain sovereignty—a place for those close to the prince, his servants, horses, concubines, and all those who could serve him or be useful to him. However, even if the sky was easily accessible to all—something we do not know—there was nothing to prevent the various souls of the same man, even those of a *kaghan,* from finding other places to inhabit (the tomb, the banner, the *balbal,* the *baba*), from being reincarnated in a new body, or from roaming the universe as an unsatisfied phantom.

See Also Chuvash Religion; Erlik; Islam, article on Islam in Central Asia; Ongon; Tengri; Umai.

Bibliography

Much research has been done on the formation of religious concepts among the people of the steppes and of Siberia. Mario Bussagli's *Culture e civiltà dell'Asia Centrale* (Turin, 1970) is a good historical presentation of nomadic cultures. For earlier periods, see Karl Jettmar's *Die frühen Steppenvölker* (Baden-Baden, 1964), translated by Ann E. Keep as *The Art of the Steppes* (New York, 1967). For the Huns, see Otto J. Mänchen-Helfen's *The World of the Huns: Studies in Their History and Culture* (Berkeley, 1973), which has a complete bibliography. Wilhelm Barthold gives the historical context of medieval Central Asia in *Turkestan down to the Mongol Invasion* (1900), 2d ed., translated from the Russian (London, 1958). For a comprehensive overview of Turkic religion, see my *La religion des Turcs et des Mongols* (Paris, 1984), which has a vast but nonexhaustive bibliography. For contemporary religious practice, Uno Harva's *Die religiösen Vorstellungen der altaischen Völker,* "Folklore Fellows Communications," no. 125 (Helsinki, 1938), is a useful reference work, although quite biased. It has been translated as *Les représentations religieuses des peuples altaïques* (Paris, 1959). Wilhelm Radloff has devoted himself to a vast study, most of which can be found in *Aus Sibirien,* 2 vols. in 1 (Leipzig, 1884). Wilhelm Schmidt collected considerable documentation in volume 9 of his *Der Ursprung der Gottesidee* (Münster, 1949), see also volumes 10–12 (Münster, 1955). On the subject of funeral rites and the beyond, see my *La mort chez les peuples altaïques anciens et médiévaux* (Paris, 1963). On the position of animals and vegetables, see my *Faune et flore sacrées dans les sociétés altaïques* (Paris, 1966). For a study of the phenomenon of shamanism, see Mircea Eliade's *Shamanism: Archaic Techniques of Ecstasy,* rev. & enl. ed. (New York, 1964). For examples of pre-Islamic relics in Turkic Islam, see John K. Birge's *The Bektashi Order of Dervishes,* "Luzac's Oriental Religious Series," no. 7 (1937; reprint, New York, 1982), and my *Les traditions des nomades de la Turquie méridionale* (Paris, 1970). Much work on Turkic religion has been widely published in journals, notably in *Central Asiatic Journal* (The Hague, 1957–). Noteworthy articles in English include those by John Andrew Boyle in *Folklore:* "A Eurasian Hunting Ritual," *Folklore* 80 (Spring 1969): 12–16; "Turkish and Mongol Shamanism in the Middle Ages," *Folklore* 83 (Autumn 1972): 177–193; and "The Hare in Myth and Reality: A Review Article," *Folklore* 84 (Winter 1973): 313–326. See also *Glaubenswelt und Folklore der sibirischen Völker,* edited by Vilmos Diószegi (Budapest, 1963).

New Sources

Bainbridge, Margaret, ed. *The Turkic Peoples of the World.* London, 1993.

Baldick, Julian. *Animal and Shaman: Ancient Religions of Central Asia.* New York, 2000.

Elverskog, Johan. *Uygur Buddhist Literature.* Turnhout, Belgium 1997.

Garrone, Patrick. *Chamanisme et islam en Asie centrale: la baksylyk hier et aujourd'hui.* Paris, 2000.

Jettmar, Karl. "Die Religion der Alttürken." In *Die vorislamischen Religionen Mittelasiens,* edited by Karl Jettmar and Ellen Kattner, pp. 219–228. Stuttgart, 2003.

Lieu, Samuel. *Manichaeism in Central Asia and China.* Leiden, 1998.

Roux, Jean-Paul. *L'Asie centrale: histoire et civilisations.* Paris, 1997.

Van Deusen, Kira. *Singing Story, Healing Drum: Shamans and Storytellers of Turkic Siberia.* Montreal, 2003.

JEAN-PAUL ROUX (1987)
Translated from French by Sherri L. Granka
Revised Bibliography

TURNER, HENRY MCNEAL. Henry McNeal Turner (1834–1915) was the twelfth bishop of the African Methodist Episcopal (AME) Church and the U. S. Army's first African American chaplain. He studied history, theology, law, Latin, Greek, Hebrew, and German and received an LL.D from the University of Pennsylvania in 1872. Turner also served as vice president of the African Colonization Society (1877) and was a major spokesperson for the Back-to-Africa movement. The movement was an African American led effort that advocated their emigration to Africa. Most black leaders had been opposed to such schemes since the option was first pursued in 1816 with the formation of the American Colonization Society by whites. However, emigration became a viable option for some blacks in the 1880s, when many black leaders were becoming increasingly disillusioned about the prospects of achieving equal rights in America. Matters became especially bleak in 1883 when the United States Supreme Court outlawed the Civil Rights Act of 1875. This action by the Supreme Court paved the way for state legislatures to enact laws that segregated all aspects of southern society. In 1896 segregation was upheld in the Plessy v. Ferguson Supreme Court decision that set forth the "separate but equal" doctrine. Turner's career was profoundly shaped by these events. Elected to the Georgia legislature during the Reconstruction era following the Civil War, Turner became known as the "Apostle of Foreign Missions" because of his travels to West Africa to found two churches, one in Sierra Leone and the other in Liberia. Turner was also famous for frequently asserting that "God is a Negro."

Turner was converted to Christianity at the age of thirteen while attending a Methodist revival. At the age of fifteen he took a job as a janitor with a law firm in Abbeville, South Carolina. Turner's intelligence so impressed his employers that they provided him with his basic education in law and history. He received his preacher's license in 1853 and traveled as an itinerant evangelist throughout the South as far west as New Orleans. He also traveled to Missouri and then to Baltimore, where he furthered his study of grammar, Latin, Greek, Hebrew, and German while overseeing a small mission congregation. Turner was ordained a Methodist deacon in 1860 and an elder in 1862.

Turner married Eliza Peacher, the daughter of a wealthy African American house builder in Columbia, South Carolina, in 1856. The threat of slavery that hung over free blacks in the South before the Civil War caused Turner to move with his family to St. Louis, Missouri. Over the course of the next five years he filled pastorates in Baltimore, Maryland, and Washington, D.C.

Turner became a friend of Charles Sumner, Thaddeus Stevens, and other influential Republicans in the years before the Civil War. When war broke out in 1861, Turner was commissioned as the first black chaplain in the U.S. Army. After the war Turner helped to establish AME congregations throughout Georgia, but he was frustrated by the lack of trained clergy to continue his work.

With Congress's passage of the Reconstruction Acts in 1867, Turner involved himself more directly in politics by helping to organize Georgia's Republican Party. He was elected to Georgia's House of Representatives from the city of Macon. The white-controlled legislative body, however, ousted the African American representatives in 1868. After Turner protested this injustice, he received threats from the Ku Klux Klan. In 1869 he was appointed postmaster of Macon by President Ulysses S. Grant, but he was forced to resign from this position a week later. He finished his term in the Georgia legislature in 1870, after which he moved to Savannah, Georgia, where he served in local churches (including the prestigious St Philip's AME Church) and served as an inspector for the U.S. Customs Service.

In 1876 Turner assumed the management of the AME Book Concern in Philadelphia and the editorship of the *Christian Recorder.* In 1880 he became the bishop of the denomination in a hotly contested election.

Turner was extremely effective as bishop. After the Supreme Court circumscribed the civil rights of African Americans in 1883, Turner's critique of mainstream American society became scathing. Equally scathing were Turner's criticisms of black meekness in the face of white oppression. He urged blacks to defend themselves against mob violence and saw his educational and missionary initiatives as vehicles for enhancing black self-worth and freedom. He published a catechism, a hymnal, and such books as *The Genius and Theory of Methodist Polity* (1885) and *The Black Man's Doom* (1896). He founded the *Southern Christian Recorder* in 1889 and the *Voice of Missions* in 1892, as well as encouraging the organization of the Women's Home and Foreign Missionary Society (1896) and the formation of the *Women's Christian Recorder.* Turner was also the first AME bishop to ordain a woman to the office of deacon, which he did in 1885. Turner served as the editor of the *Theological Institute* and as the denomination's historiographer from 1908 to 1912. He died in 1915 while traveling on church business. Turner is numbered with Richard Allen (1760–1831) and Daniel Payne (1811–1893) as one of the greatest bishops in the history of the African Episcopal Methodist Church.

SEE ALSO African American Religions, overview article; Allen, Richard; Methodist Churches.

BIBLIOGRAPHY

Angell, Stephen Ward. *Bishop Henry McNeal Turner and African American Religion in the South.* Knoxville, Tenn., 1992.

Ponton, M. M. *Life and Times of Henry M. Turner.* Atlanta, Ga., 1917.

Redkey, Edwin S. *Black Exodus: Black Exodus and Back to Africa Movements, 1890–1910.* New Haven, Conn., 1969.

Redkey, Edwin S., ed. *Respect Black: The Writings and Speeches of Henry McNeal Turner.* New York, 1971.

JAMES ANTHONY NOEL (2005)

TURNER, VICTOR

TURNER, VICTOR (1920–1983). Scottish-born American anthropologist and comparative religionist. On the basis of fieldwork in central Africa, Victor Witter Turner produced the richest ethnographic achievement of the period after World War II, and he explained the nature of religious ritual and symbolism in an African society in more detail than anyone had before.

Turner was born in Glasgow, Scotland. In 1943, in the midst of his five years of military service, he married Edith Davis, who was to collaborate with him in field research and writing throughout his career. He received his B.A. degree with honors in anthropology in 1949 from the University of London, where he studied with some of the leading figures of structural-functionalism: A. R. Radcliffe-Brown, Meyer Fortes, Raymond Firth, and Edmund Leach. He went on to graduate study at the University of Manchester under Max Gluckman and was introduced to conflict theory and political anthropology. During 1950–1954 he was a research officer at the Rhodes-Livingstone Institute in Lusaka, Zambia (then Northern Rhodesia), where he undertook, with his wife, a two-and-a-half-year study of the Ndembu people. In 1954 he returned to the University of Manchester and was appointed to the positions of lecturer and senior lecturer in social anthropology. From 1963 to 1968 he was professor of anthropology at Cornell University, and from 1968 to 1977 he was professor of anthropology and social thought at the University of Chicago. From 1977 until his death he was the William R. Kenan Professor of Anthropology at the University of Virginia. He held numerous fellowships, visiting appointments, and distinguished lectureships at universities in the United States and around the world. He organized major international conferences and was editor of the important series "Symbol, Myth and Ritual" published by Cornell University Press.

Like other leading anthropologists, Turner's ideas were shaped by his field experience. In the course of fieldwork he decided to abandon the social structural emphasis of his teachers and their bias against religion and to pursue a microsociological investigation of the actual processes of Ndembu village life that, he found, were articulated and resolved in ritual performances. Since Ndembu society is prone to conflict because of its inherent inconsistencies, he also rejected the static and mechanistic models of functionalism together with its goal of constructing universal social laws. Instead, he treated Ndembu society as a dynamic social process whose events were analyzable as "social dramas," consisting of phases of breach, crisis, redressive action, and reintegration (or schism), in which ritual played a central role. He also set aside the analytical perspective and alien categories of the outside observer and oriented his studies around the experiential context and cultural criteria of the Ndembu world, an approach that he later called the "anthropology of experience."

Although his initial study, *Schism and Continuity in an African Society* (1957), was labeled "difficult" and "experimental," Turner continued to refine his ideas about social drama and ritual process. He wrote one of the most detailed and perceptive studies of African divination, *Ndembu Divination: Its Symbolism and Techniques* (1961), viewing the subject in the context of social process and analyzing its use of social and ethical symbolism. He also wrote a short but brilliant clarification of methodological issues in African witchcraft studies, "Witchcraft and Sorcery: Taxonomy versus Dynamics" (1964), in which he treats a subject that had become bogged down in functionalist theorizing and confused definitions. He argues that witchcraft has to be viewed as a complex matter involving social process, cosmology, ecology, and biological factors. In addition he wrote a pioneering study of an Ndembu cult of affliction, *Chihamba, the White Spirit* (1962). In this work he attempted to go beyond the examination of social process and symbolic action and to formulate the implicit content of Ndembu thought by means of Thomistic concepts, long before the subjects of ethnophilosophy and ethnotheology had gained currency in anthropology. It was a venturesome effort and did not receive an entirely positive response. In subsequent and more detailed studies he examined Ndembu ethnomedical and ethnobiological concepts in the context of cults of affliction. One of these studies, *The Drums of Affliction* (1968), became the *locus classicus* of later scholarship in the field of African medical anthropology.

In the course of these ritual studies, Turner began to develop a theory of religious symbols. He noted in the field that certain symbols were dominant in ritual contexts and that they exhibited properties of condensation, unification of disparate significata, and polarization of meaning. Because of such semantic complexity, contextual variation, and attachment to ritual sequence, Turner rejected as overly simplistic the structuralist method of interpreting symbols in terms of synchronic, binary relationships. Instead, he proposed a threefold hermeneutic, based upon "exegetical," "operational," and "positional" levels of meaning. Moreover, he suggeted that in the context of intense ritual experience, the ideological, or "normative," and the sensory, or "orectic," poles of meaning came together and reinforced one another in such a way as to produce powerful emotional effects and real transformations of character and social relationships. Herein, Turner felt, lay the power and efficacy of ritual.

Although he wrote two detailed accounts of Ndembu boys' and girls' initiation rites (the first appearing in *The Forest of Symbols,* 1967, the second in *The Drums of Affliction,* 1968), it was in the context of a brief comparative study of rites of passage, "Betwixt and Between: The Liminal Period in *Rites de Passage*" (1964), that he began to focus upon the work of the Belgian anthropologist Arnold van Gennep. He found van Gennep's analysis of rites of passage into the phases of separation, threshold or *limen,* and reaggregation to be not only a useful cross-cultural model but also the source of a fundamental insight: the regenerative and transformational possibilities of ritual liminality. Whereas van Gennep emphasizes only the outward change of social status accomplished by these rites, Turner emphasizes the inward, moral, and cognitive changes that occurred, and where van Gennep examines only the social aspects of the liminal state, Turner examines its deconstructive and reconstructive processes. Thus Turner concentrated upon the heretofore neglected, strange, and amorphous properties of symbols and actions of the liminal phase. He regarded such symbols and actions both as channels for communicating basic social and cultural values and as channels for discovering new moral and metaphysical insights that tend to subvert as well as support established religious and social orders.

Turner developed his theory of liminality further in the seminal work *The Ritual Process* (1969). Here he defines the social form of liminality as *communitas,* the direct, egalitarian encounter and fellowship between people as people, which characterized both temporary ritual states and certain more enduring social groups. In this context he defined three forms of *communitas,* the "spontaneous," the "ideological," and the "normative," and he elaborated a host of contrasting liminal and status system forms. In addition to illuminating past religious and political movements as well as popular currents in American society of the 1960s, Turner brought his theory of liminality to bear upon the phenomenon of religious pilgrimage, a generally ignored subject in the history of religions. His contribution, presented in another important essay, "The Center Out There: Pilgrims' Goal" (1973), was to see pilgrimage as a rite of passage whose goals include both the experience of *communitas* and the liminal encounter with the sacred at the pilgrimage center. There followed a series of lectures and articles on this theme, and they inspired other scholars to take up the subject. Together with Edith Turner, he explored the subject further in relation to Mexican, Spanish, and Irish pilgrimage sites in a fieldwork study, *Image and Pilgrimage in Christian Culture* (1978). His subsequent search for liminality in the modern secular world led to his use of the word *liminoid* to represent the nonreligious genres of art, sport, and performance.

Although Turner often emphasized his departure from social functionalism, his vision of religion and society remained partly indebted to it. Like Émile Durkheim, he saw social order to be dependent upon ritual and ceremonial performances, and like Max Gluckman, he emphasized the cathartic effects of ritual reversal that helped to restore and legitimate established social structures. But he went beyond both Durkheim and Gluckman by examining the processes of social change and the ways in which ritual helped to create new social realities. His work, along with that of anthropologists Claude Lévi-Strauss, Clifford Geertz, and Mary Douglas, also helped to revive comparative studies in religious anthropology, which had been abandoned by British and American functionalists. But, although he agreed with Douglas and Geertz on the cognitive importance of ritual symbols, he refused to tie them closely to social structure as in Douglas's theory or to construe them as "texts" according to Geertz's formulation.

Following the American anthropologist Edward Sapir, Turner held that culture is not a completely or consistently articulated system, a set of dogmas or logically arrayed or Lévi-Straussian symbolic codes, but rather a changing entity, influenced by "root paradigms," that is, by axiomatic frames, or deep myths, that propel and transform people and groups at critical moments. In this respect Turner came to see that the Ndembu are not exceptional but typical, and thus that social order is fundamentally "processual" in form and "dramatic" in character.

Turner called his analytical method "dramatistic," because, like Freud, he believed that examination of disturbances of the normal and the regular often gives greater insight into the normal than does direct study. Because of the episodic character of social systems, Turner preferred the sociologist Kurt Lewin's image of society as "social fields." He also saw affinities with the phenomenological sociology of Alfred Schutz and his followers, who regarded culture as a constantly negotiated set of meanings, and he found useful Wilhelm Dilthey's theory that the meanings and values of life are to be found in the "structures of experience" and not in the formal categories of thought. This approach led him to welcome a shift in anthropology away from such concepts as structure, equilibrium, function, and system to such concepts as process, indeterminacy, and reflexivity, and he envisioned a new anthropology based upon a synthesis of disciplines instead of the usual disciplinary specialization. Turner himself was not, however, given to sustained theoretical exposition, and he often let unclarities remain in his writings, for which he was sometimes taken to task by his colleagues. He preferred to forge his concepts as he went along. His approach was regarded as highly original, and he put forward his ideas with a strong personal conviction that gave his analyses great force.

His final studies led him into the field of performance theory. In theater, especially experimental theater in the United States in the late 1960s and early 1970s, Turner saw the same kind of liminal reflexivity, the public cognizance of social situations, that he encountered in rituals associated with the redressive phase of Ndembu social dramas. Together with the drama theorist and director Richard Schechner, Turner understood theater to be an important means of communicating a society's self-reflections and a means of cross-cultural understanding. Thus he encouraged anthropologists to study theatrical performances as well as ordinary social life. In the course of his teaching he also guided students in the performance of ethnographic rituals as a means of learning about ritual and about the societies from which the students came.

At this juncture, he became interested in the subject of the neurobiology of ritual. It appeared that the contrasting functions of the cerebral hemispheres, the right and left brain, might correspond to the two aspects of society Turner had been looking at, structure and liminality. In a major essay, "Body, Brain and Culture" (1983), Turner speculated that the right hemisphere might also be the source of universal symbolic patterns, such as C. G. Jung's archetypes or his own root paradigms and deep myths, which seemed to exist at the subliminal level until activated and brought into the articulate realm of the left brain. The existence of different brain levels, especially the neocortex and the midbrain, also seemed to resemble the ideological and orectic poles of dominant symbols. Perhaps at the height of ritual, Turner speculated, it was the interaction between these two levels with the right and left hemispheres of the brain that produced the transformational effect that was essential to successful ritual performance. Although these were but speculations about the possible biological mechanisms of the ritual process, they were consistent with Turner's fundamental conviction that it was in the dynamics and dramatics of social, ritual, and theatrical events that one came to understand the lives of others and oneself.

BIBLIOGRAPHY

From 1980 until his death in 1983, Turner was an editor of this encyclopedia, to which he contributed two articles: "Bodily Marks" and "Rites of Passage: A Few Definitions." His previously published works include the following.

Schism and Continuity in an African Society: A Study of Ndembu Village Life. Manchester, 1957.

Ndembu Divination: Its Symbolism and Techniques. Manchester, 1961. Reprinted in *Revelation and Divination in Ndembu Ritual.*

Chihamba, the White Spirit: A Ritual Drama of the Ndembu. Manchester, 1962. Reprinted in *Revelation and Divination in Ndembu Ritual.*

"Betwixt and Between: The Liminal Period in *Rites de Passage.*" In *Symposium on New Approaches to the Study of Religion,* edited by June Helm, pp. 4–20. Seattle, 1964. Reprinted in *The Forest of Symbols.*

"Witchcraft and Sorcery: Taxonomy versus Dynamics." *Africa* 34 (1964): 314–325. Reprinted in *The Forest of Symbols.*

The Forest of Symbols: Aspects of Ndembu Ritual. Ithaca, N. Y., 1967.

The Drums of Affliction: A Study of Religious Processes among the Ndembu of Zambia. Oxford, 1968.

The Ritual Process: Structure and Anti-Structure. Chicago, 1969.

Dramas, Fields, and Metaphors: Symbolic Action in Human Society. Ithaca, N.Y., 1974.

Revelation and Divination in Ndembu Ritual. Ithaca, N.Y., 1975.

Image and Pilgrimage in Christian Culture: Anthropological Perspectives. Written with Edith Turner. New York, 1978.

From Ritual to Theatre: The Human Seriousness of Play. New York, 1982.

"Body, Brain, and Culture." *Zygon* 18 (September 1983): 221–245.

On the Edge of the Bush. Edited by Edith Turner. Tucson, 1985.

New Sources

Ashley, Kathleen M., ed. *Victor Turner and the Construction of Cultural Criticism: Between Literature and Anthropology.* Bloomington, Ind., 1990.

Barnard, H. G. "Victor Witter Turner: A Bibliography (1952–1975)." *Anthropologica* 27 (1987): 207–233.

Haviland, William A. *Anthropology.* 6th edition. Fort Worth, 1991.

Lett, James. *The Human Enterprise: A Critical Introduction to Anthropological Theory.* Boulder, Colo., 1987.

McLaren, P. L. "A Tribute to Victor Turner." *Anthropologica* 27 (1987): 17–22.

BENJAMIN C. RAY (1987)
Revised Bibliography

TURTLES AND TORTOISES. There is a widespread belief that the earth rests on the back of a turtle or tortoise. This archaic idea is found not only among North American Indians but also in South Asia and Inner Asia. The turtle now appears even as a symbol of the entire universe (e.g., in China). Moreover, according to creation myths involving an earth diver, the turtle, sometimes as an incarnation of the divine being, plays a prominent part in the cosmogony of various cultures.

According to the Maidu in California, a turtle dived to the bottom of the primeval ocean and procured a little soil under its nails. When it surfaced, God scraped its nails carefully and made a ball like a small pebble. The ball of soil then grew miraculously until it became as large as the universe itself. The Yokut narrate how at the time of beginning the eagle and the coyote sent a turtle into the waters. The motif of the turtle's successful dive is known also among the Algonquin. According to the Onondaga and the Mohawk (i.e., the Iroquois), it was a turtle that directed several different animals into the ocean; a beaver tried in vain, an otter also failed, but a muskrat returned successfully with soil in his claws and mouth. This soil was placed on the back of the turtle, and then the miraculous growth of earth began.

Inner Asia has preserved similar stories. According to the Buriats, in the beginning there was nothing but water and a turtle. God turned the turtle on its back and built the world on its stomach. In other versions, Mandishire (the *bodhisattva* Mañjuśrī) transforms himself into a great turtle and supports the earth he has made on the surface of the waters.

The great tortoise is often represented in India as the sustainer of the four elephants upon whose backs the world rests. In the *Mahābhārata* the tortoise, as an avatar of Visnu, supports the earth when the gods and demons churn the primeval ocean to obtain ambrosia.

In China, the turtle symbolizes the universe; its dome-shaped back represents the sky, while its belly, square in shape, stands for the earth. It also appears as the god of the waters, presiding over the north, one of the four cardinal points of the universe. Black in color, it is symbolically associated with winter and other aspects of the *yin,* or female principle; as in ancient Egypt and Greece, the tortoise in China is a symbol of erotic power and fecundity. Moreover, the great age to which the tortoise supposedly lives has made it a symbol of longevity and immortality; in the mythico-iconographical tradition the tortoise often forms a complex together with immortality, the moon, and paradise. There are "stone" turtles in South Korea and southern Japan (Kyushu), at its seashore facing the Korean Peninsula. Dating from prehistoric times, these monuments indicate that people believed in the turtle bestowing new life or immortality on the dead and escorting them to the otherworld far across the sea or to paradise under the waters.

BIBLIOGRAPHY

On the turtle in cosmogonic myths, much useful information has been collected by Charles H. Long in his *Alpha: The Myths of Creation* (New York, 1963), pp. 192ff. On turtle symbolism in China, see Marcel Granet's brilliant discussion in his *La pensée chinoise* (1934; reprint, Paris, 1968), pp. 173ff. Johannes Maringer has studied "stone" turtles in East Asia in his article "Vorgeschichtliche Grabbauten Ostasiens in Schildkrötenform und ihr mythischer Prototyp," *Antaios* 5 (1963): 368–374.

New Sources

Süss, Rudolph. *Vom Mythos der Schildkröte: das Urtier als Glücksringer.* Dortmund, 1991.

MANABU WAIDA (1987)
Revised Bibliography

TU-SHUN SEE DUSHUN

ṬŪSĪ, NAṢĪR AL-DĪN.

Naṣīr al-Dīn Ṭūsī (Muḥammad ibn Muḥammad ibn Ḥasan, AH 597–672/1201–1274 CE), addressed in general Islamic literature as *khawājah* (master) and the *muḥaqqiq* (scholar) of Ṭūs, was a Persian Shīʿī philosopher, theologian, mathematician, astronomer, and statesman. He is by far the most celebrated scholar of the thirteenth century in eastern Islamic lands. Very little is known about his childhood and early education, apart from what he reveals in his autobiography, the *Sayr wa sulūk.* He was born in Ṭūs, in northeastern Iran into an Ithnā ʿasharī (Twelver) Shīʿī family and died in Baghdad. He lost his father at a young age. Fulfilling the wish of his father, Ṭūsī took learning and scholarship very seriously and traveled far and wide to attend the lectures of the renowned scholars of the time. In a relatively short period, Ṭūsī mastered a number of disciplines. At a time when religious education was a priority, especially in his own family, which was associated with Twelver Shīʿī scholars, Ṭūsī seems to have shown great interest in mathematics, astronomy, and intellectual sciences.

In the *Sayr wa sulūk,* Ṭūsī gives a brief account of his theological and philosophical education, but he does not go into details about the scholars with whom he became acquainted, nor of his studies in mathematics and astronomy, which latter became important areas of investigation for him. But we know from other sources that Ṭūsī was a precocious learner and by the time he was seventeen he had studied the philosophy of Ibn Sīnā (d. 1037) with Farīd al-Dīn Dāmād (d. c. 1246) and attended the lectures of Quṭb al-Dīn Sarakhsī (d. 1221) in Nīshāpūr, where he is said to have met the famous poet and mystic Farīd al-Dīn ʿAṭṭār (d. 1220). At around this time, it is also certain that he studied jurisprudence.

At the age of twenty-two, Ṭūsī joined the court of Nāṣir al-Dīn Muḥtashim (d. 1257), the Ismāʿīlī governor of Quhistān, in northeast Iran, where in his own words he was accepted into the Ismāʿīlī community. It is probable that in Nīshāpūr, which at the time was an active center of Ismāʿīlī preaching, he had become acquainted with its teachings. Later, in a journey from Iraq to Khurāsān, he met Shihāb al-Dīn Muḥtashim (d. c. 1245), a highly renowned Ismāʿīlī scholar, and gradually he became more acquainted with Ismāʿīlī teachings through the religious writings of the Nizārī Ismāʿīlī Imām Ḥasan ʿAlāʾ Dhikrihī al-Salām (d. 1166).

In Quhistān, Ṭūsī developed a close personal relationship with the governor and dedicated to him and his family a number of scholarly works, such as the *Akhlāq-i Nāṣirī, Akhlāq-i Muḥtashimī,* and *Risāla-yi muʿīniyya,* which ultimately paved the way for his move to Alamūṭ, the seat of Ismāʿīlī political power in Iran.

Apart from editing, translating, and composing a variety of philosophical and scientific works, Ṭūsī produced a number of Ismāʿīlī texts, adding his scholarly background and talents to the unique collection of literature and archival materials in Alamūṭ. An example of this genre is his strong philosophical and esoteric interpretation of Ismāʿīlī thought, as represented in the *Rawda-yi taslīm* in particular.

The Mongol invasions of western Asia led to the collapse of Ismāʿīlī political power and the massacre of Ismāʿīlīs, who were perceived by the Mongols as a serious threat. Under these circumstances, Ṭūsī sought alternative patronage and was able to obtain employment in the emerging court of the Mongol conquerors, who wished to show support for learning and science. He also embarked on writing a series of Twelver Shīʿī works.

In the Mongol court, Ṭūsī witnessed the fall of the Abbasid caliphate, and after securing the trust of Hūlegū (d. 1265), he was given the full authority of administering the *awqāf* (religious foundations). His primary concern during this period was to protect the life of scholars and their freedom to pursue learning. He also established probably the most important observatory and center of scientific learning of his time in Marāghah, in the northwest of Iran. Under these circumstances Ṭūsī acted as a senior advisor to Hülegü and continued his scholarly activities and writing on various aspects of Shīʿī thought.

The corpus of Ṭūsī's writings comprise approximately 135 titles on a wide variety of subjects, including astronomy, ethics, logic, mathematics, philosophy, theology, Sufism, poetry and popular sciences. Some of these works—for example, his commentary on Ibn Sīnā's *al-Ishārāt wa-al-tanbīhāt* on philosophy and the *Akhlāq-i Nāṣirī* on theoretical and practical ethics—are still used as textbooks in many centers of learning in the Muslim world.

Ṭūsī's interest in ethical writings begun in Quhistān when, in answer to the request of Nāṣir al-Dīn Muḥtashim, he produced a number of ethical works, namely the Persian translations of Ibn Muqaffah's (d. 759) *al-Adab al-wajīz lil-walad al-ṣaqīr, Akhlāq-i Muḥtashimī*, and *Akhlāq-i Nāṣirī*, as well as the twenty-second chapter of the *Rawda-yi taslīm*, which, in line with the content of *Akhlāq-i Nāṣirī*, could be classified as a text on philosophical ethics.

A proper scholarly investigation into Ṭūsī's contribution to philosophy, astronomy, trigonometry, and mathematics has only recently begun. His importance in religion lies partly in his being one of the subtlest and most learned of the Shīʿī theologians, and partly in his application of philosophical ideas and methods to Islamic contexts and problems, as well as his active involvement in the politico-religious debates of his time. Within the overall domain of Islamic philosophical thinking, by defending Ibn Sīnā's philosophy, Ṭūsī should be considered as representing a revival of philosophical thinking in the eastern Islamic lands. For him, differences between Muslim sects and persuasions were merely theological debates, allowing the partisans to move freely from one stand to another without necessarily having to take parochial positions. It is from such a perspective that his ideas contributed to the development of *ḥikmah mutaʿāliyah* (higher wisdom), later developed by Mullā Ṣadrā (d. 1641) and the school of Isfahan.

BIBLIOGRAPHY

There are still no comprehensive studies on Ṭūsī in European languages. See H. Daiber and F. G. Ragep, "al-Ṭūsī, Naṣīr al-Dīn," in *Encyclopaedia of Islam*, new edition (Leiden, 1999), vol. X, pp. 747–757; as well as Wilferd Madelung, "Naṣīr al-Dīn Ṭūsī's Ethics between Philosophy: Shiʿism and Sufism," in *Ethics in Islam* (Ninth Giorgio Levi Della Vida Conference, May 6–8, 1983; Malibu, Calif., 1985), edited by Richard G. Hovannisian, pp. 85–101; Hamid Dabashi, "Khwāja Naṣīr al-Dīn al-Ṭūsī: The Philosopher/Vizier and the Intellectual Climate of His Times," in *History of Islamic Philosophy*, edited by Seyyed Hossein Nasr and Oliver Leaman (London, 1996), pp. 527–584; Herman Landolt, "Khwāja Naṣīr al-Dīn Ṭūsī, Ismāʿīlīsm and Ishrāqī Philosophy," and Farhad Daftary, "Naṣīr al-Dīn al-Ṭūsī and the Ismailis of the Alamut Period," in *Naṣīr al-Dīn Ṭūsī*, ed. N. Pourjavady and ž. Vesel (Tehran, 2000), pp. 13–30 and 59–67, respectively. Translations of some of Ṭūsī's works include: *Taṣawwurāt*, edited and translated into English by Vladimir A. Ivanow as *Rawāatu't-Taslīm, Commonly Called Taṣawwurāt* (Leiden, 1950), and into French by Christian Jambet as *La convocation d'Alamūt: Somme de philosophie ismaélienne* (Lagrasse, France, 1996); *Akhlāq-i Nāṣirī*, translated in English as *The Nasirean Ethics* by G. M. Wickens (London, 1964); *al-Tadhkirah fī ʿilm al-hay'a*, edited and translated into English by F. G. Ragep in *Naṣīr al-Dīn Ṭūsī's Memoir on Astronomy* (New York, 1993), and the *Sayr wa sulūk*, edited and translated into English by S. J. Badakhchani as *Contemplation and Action: The Spiritual Autobiography of a Muslim Scholar* (London, 1998).

S. J. BADAKHCHANI (2005)

TWELVERS SEE SHIISM, *ARTICLE ON* ITHNĀ ʿASHARĪYAH

TWELVE TRIBES. The Twelve Tribes (previously known as the Northeast Kingdom Community Church because of its location in the northeast corner of Vermont, and later as the Messianic Communities) is a communal, millenarian Bible-based movement that emerged from the Jesus Movement in the 1970s counterculture of the United States. Many of the Christian sects that emerged from this movement, such as the Children of God (the Family), Shiloh, and Jesus People USA, developed communal patterns of living. The Twelve Tribes is one of the few Jesus groups that survived from this period without disbanding or being absorbed into the U.S. religious mainstream.

Elbert Eugene Spriggs (b. 1937) had worked as a personnel manager and former schoolteacher when he joined a charismatic church in Glendale, California, in 1971. When the church disbanded, he moved back to his hometown, Chattanooga, Tennessee, with his new wife, Marsha Ann Duval. There the couple set up a small coffee shop in 1972 called the Light Brigade, where they held Bible study groups in the evenings. Attracting both young conservative Christians and hippies from the "lost generation," these Bible study sessions extended long into the night, so people brought their sleeping bags and gradually moved in with the Spriggses, who shared their resources with their flock. The coffee-house ministry expanded to include five Victorian houses that were renovated by Spriggs and his followers. They also opened as a "court of the gentiles" a small health-food café called the Yellow Deli. The Spriggses attended the First Presbyterian Church with their flock, and worked closely with the New Covenant Apostolic Order, a short-lived Christian group.

The group's break with the mainstream Christian church occurred in 1975, when the Spriggses and their friends arrived for the Sunday morning service at the local Presbyterian church and discovered that the service had been canceled on account of the Super Bowl. The Spriggses and their friends began to hold Sunday services in their communal homes, and called themselves the Vine Community Church. Spriggs began to baptize members in the local pond, an act that alienated the Chattanooga Christian community, because he was not ordained in any denomination. They also began observing the Saturday Sabbath, following Jewish custom. In 1980 the group relocated to Island Pond, Vermont, where they were called the Church in Island Pond, and as they spread through New England, they adopted a new name, the Northeast Kingdom Community Church.

"Gene" Spriggs is recognized by his followers as an "Apostle" (authoritative teacher). Although all community members believe that they are inspired by God and have the gift of prophecy, they believe that he exhibits these gifts on a higher level, and they call him *Yoneq* (Hebrew for "sapling"). This millenarian movement has grown to around 2,500 members (half of them are second and third generation) living in communities in nine countries on four continents as far-flung as New Zealand, Brazil, England, France, Germany, Spain, and Canada. Their early communities were established in New England—Vermont, Rhode Island, and Massachusetts, where the largest concentration of members can be found. Each community names itself after its local town or area.

Over their thirty-year history, the Twelve Tribes have come to believe that they are the restoration of the messianic Hebrew New Testament community of the first century CE. This belief evolved through members' study of the Bible and personal experiences. They reject the "white-bread" Christianity of mainstream churches that worship a remote impersonal God and does not sustain the soul, and they replace it, both literally and symbolically, with the "wholegrain, home-baked bread" of their living communal "church" that seeks to bring about the return and loving union with Yahshua (Jesus). The community attempts to restore the New Testament church by developing a physical and artistic culture that interprets first-century messianic Judaism in twenty-first-century terms. They are divided into "tribes" that correspond to their geographical regions. Men grow full beards and women cover their heads with scarves, following the Jewish custom.

In the "church" (community), members follow a strict code of ethics, dress, and diet, and must surrender to the hierarchical authority that descends from God through Yoneq, the Elders, the Teachers, the fathers, and the mothers, to the children. The Twelve Tribes is dedicated to ushering in the millennium by "raising up a people" who are truly loving and free of sin and selfishness. The church defines itself as the "pure and spotless bride" of *Revelation* who is preparing for the return of her king, Yahshua—the second coming. The path of the Tribes is the restoration of the primitive Jewish/Christian church, as described in *Acts* 2:37–47 and 4:32–35. This restoration is both theological and practical, and has led to a whole new way of life based on renouncing possessions, worldly habits, and attachments, and sharing all goods in common.

Members give each other Hebrew names, accessed through inspired moments of prophecy. They consider themselves to be part of the Commonwealth of Israel forming in the last days, bound by the New Covenant in the blood of the Messiah (*Eph.* 2:12). The Tribes are strongly evangelistic, but instead of sending out missionaries to spread their doctrines, they seek to win converts by inviting outsiders into their communal houses in order to demonstrate the reality of a loving, sharing, orderly communal and family life. Visitors are invited to share their meals, and to witness their happy family life and joyful revival meetings, which combine circle dancing, singing, sermons, and prayer. Once there, visitors encounter a unique, spiritual culture that resembles the historic Shaker villages in its "hands to work, hearts to God" ethic. Twelve Tribes women are skilled in the crafts of baking, painting with watercolors, sewing and macramé, and making soaps and body lotions. The men are skilled in leatherwork, cabinet-making, candle-making, and making stained-glass windows. Their renovated Victorian houses preserve the historic style, and they repair antique furniture, expressing their doctrine of restoration. Their children sing and compose an impressive repertoire of original devotional songs. Boys work alongside their fathers in the candle factories and farms, and daughters assist their mothers in the kitchen and sewing rooms. All members spend at least two hours a day in devotional dancing and singing, and many play and even build their own musical instruments.

Another missionary strategy employs the community's famous double-decker buses, which appear at Grateful Dead festivals, the Billy Graham Crusade, the Rainbow Gathering, and other mass events. Men, women, and children make friends by offering hospitality that includes free distribution of wholegrain baked goods, apple cider tea, and first-aid services, and members invite the crowd to join in their circle dancing and musical jams. They distribute the *Freepaper*, their missionary tract which portrays a utopian vision of perfect, loving families and service to one's brothers and sisters preparing for the return of Yahshua.

Considering that this new religious movement is relatively small and lacks the controversial features of some other Christian millennial groups—such as the use of firearms or illegal drugs, and polygamy or "free love"—level of conflict between the group and the larger society has been extraordinarily high. The trouble began in Chattanooga in the mid-1970s with a series of eight kidnappings and "deprogrammings" of Spriggs's youthful followers by Ted Patrick, the cofounder of FREECOG, the first anticult organization that formed in opposition to the Children of God (COG). FREECOG and was superseded by the nationally based Citizen's Freedom Foundation, which networked with the media, labeling the Tribes a cult and attributing their success in winning converts to brainwashing. The conflict escalated in 1982 when a series of custody battles launched by parents who had left the community drew attention to the group's sectarian methods of child rearing and their strict, Bible-based practice of corporal punishment of children. Stigmatizing news reports proliferated, portraying the Island Pond Community Church as a scary, gothic, puritanical "neo-Salem," where children were routinely neglected and abused.

The Twelve Tribes guidelines stipulate that children who do not obey upon first command must be punished, and the millenarian rationale is that they must be alert and ready to respond to Yahshua's call when he returns. Chastisements usually consist of a few blows to the palm with a flexible stick, and they must not be given in anger. Through this discipline, parents believe that their children will achieve eternal life; otherwise, they are in danger of "dying" into sin.

On June 22, 1984, the Island Pond Community was the target of a massive raid to seize their children. Ninety Vermont state troopers and fifty social rehabilitation services workers arrived in the predawn hours with a court order; they searched the households and took 112 children into protective custody. Parents accompanied their children to the hearing in Newport, Vermont, where District Judge Frank Mahady held forty individual hearings in one day. At the end of the day, he ruled that the search warrant issued by the state was unconstitutional, and he noted that the children involved had been detained solely in order to provide evidence for charges of abuse, and that no concrete evidence other than hearsay had been produced by the state. The church-state confrontation thus ended abruptly, and the children were returned to their parents. Ten years after the raid, the Twelve Tribes held a festival (which has become an annual event) to commemorate their "deliverance" from the raid. Some of the children of the raid, many of whom are married with their own children, speak out in defense of their parents and their community.

The Tribes have also become a target for Christian countercult groups who are combating Christian heresy. Reverend Robert Pardon founded the New England Institute of Religious Research, and through his website he disseminates discrediting accounts of the Twelve Tribes's Apostle, their "heretical" doctrines, and what he perceives to be excessive control by the group over the lives of individuals.

The two executive leaders of the Tribes are a married couple, Eddie Wiseman ("Hakam") and Jean Swantko, a lawyer who experienced a religious conversion while working on Wiseman's legal defense. They have responded to anticult pressure and social-control efforts by secular authorities by opening up dialogues with scholars at conferences, holding press conferences, and making persistent efforts to correct misinformation and reach out to their critics. The Twelve Tribes, who have adopted the colonialist hero Roger Williams as a sort of patron saint, have managed to realize their own "separation of church and state" by preserving strict boundaries between their community and the "sinful" society that surrounds them, while softening some of their sectarian attitudes. Their millenarian drama has evolved from an uncompromising and imminent catastrophic scenario in which all outsiders will fall into a lake of fire, to a more gradual process in which, before the return of Yahshua, the Tribes must raise up a people of seven generations before the Yo-bell, the last trumpet of revelations, will be blown. A new revelation laid out in the *Stone Kingdom Freepaper*, a special edition of the *Freepaper*, adds a middle ground between the saved and the damned, where "just men," or people who have never encountered the Tribes, will live.

See Also Family, The; Jesus Movement; Millenarianism, overview article.

BIBLIOGRAPHY

Bozeman, John, and Susan Palmer. "The Northeast Kingdom Community Church of Island Pond, Vermont: Raising Up a People for Yahshua's Return." *Journal of Contemporary Religion* 12, no. 2 (May 1997): 181–190.

Palmer, Susan J. "Helpmeets in the Messianic Communities." In *Moon Sisters, Krishna Mothers, Rajneesh Lovers: Women's Role in New Religions*, edited by Susan J. Palmer. Syracuse, N.Y., 1994.

Palmer, Susan J. "Apostates and Their Role in the Construction of Grievance Claims against the Northeast Kingdom/Messianic Communities." In *The Politics of Religious Apostasy: The Role of Apostates in the Transformation of Religious Movements*, edited by David G. Bromley, pp. 191–208. Westport, Conn., 1998.

Palmer, Susan J. "Frontiers and Families: The Children of Island Pond." In *Children in New Religions*, edited by Susan J. Palmer and Charlotte E. Hardmann, pp. 153–171. New Brunswick, N.J., 1999.

Palmer, Susan J. "The Messianic Communities' Stone Kingdom." In *Christian Millennialism from the Early Church to Waco*, edited by Stephen Hunt. London, 2001.

Swantko, Jean A. "A 25 Year Retrospective on the Impact of the Anti-Cult Movement on Children of the Twelve Tribes Community." Paper presented at the Thirteenth International Conference of CESNUR. Bryn Athlyn, Penn., 1999.

Swantko, Jean A. "An Issue of Control: Conflict between the Church in Island Pond and State Government." Available from http://religiousmovements.lib.Virginia.edu/nrms/tribes.html.

Susan J. Palmer (2005)

TWINS

This entry consists of the following articles:

AN OVERVIEW
BALTIC TWIN DEITIES

TWINS: AN OVERVIEW

The notion of duality, which must be distinguished from dualism, is common to every human culture. It finds a particular expression in the concept of the couple, an idea understood as a generating agency not only in the field of animal physiology but also in numerical and metaphysical symbology (as, for example, in Pythagorean speculation). According to this, the One and the Two, as generating principles, are perceived as masculine and feminine. The kind of duality expressed by the generating couple need not be viewed as dualistic in itself, but the shift from duality to dualism is obvious when the constituent elements (the One and the Two, male and female) are understood as principles that are, in effect, principal: that is, when their mutual relationship is responsible for the first origins of the world and of human beings and, at the same time, is one characterized by a strong disparity of value (or even a total opposition) between them.

Another privileged expression of duality, in both physiology and symbology, is the notion of twinship. The concept of twinship is not reducible to the projection of a physiological experience on a symbological plane. In fact, physiology requires the possibility of more than two twins, a possibility that is normally excluded in the symbological use of the notion. Thus, the duality of twins, an essential constituent of the notion in symbology, is given a peculiar function in the field of ontology, different from that of the couple. First, the couple is understood as a generating agency from the dynamic perspective of a sonship, which, on the symbological plane, can be unitary (as in the triadic pattern of father, mother, and son) or indefinitely plural. The notion of twins, however, is oriented toward stasis, whether there is a perfect symmetry between the two constituent elements, or, inversely, disparity between them. In fact, twinship is founded on the physiological experience of the diachrony of twins' conception in or emergence from the maternal womb. (This diachrony is the motivation behind seniorship, the notion that the twin born second was conceived first.)

Historical Examples. Diachrony is a decisive element in a famous mythical story about twins, the myth of the birth of Ōhrmazd and Ahriman, the God and the Antigod of Zoroastrian religion; this narrative is not explicitly accounted for in Zoroastrian literature but only in Christian and Islamic sources arguing against Zoroastrianism. It was not intended to resolve the radical dualism of Zoroastrianism but to provide an explanation of the origins of evil. Zurwān, the personification of time, performed a sacrifice in order to generate Ōhrmazd, the potential creator of all good things. But Zurwān doubted the efficacy of his sacrifice, and as a result he gave birth to twin sons, Ōhrmazd and Ahriman. The former was a result of his sacrifice, and the latter the consequence of his doubt. Since Zurwān had pledged to concede the royal privilege to the first son who appeared before him, the perverse Ahriman broke out of the maternal womb prematurely and demanded the fulfillment of his father's promise. Zurwān did not acknowledge him as a true son but was obliged to honor his promise; he declared that Ahriman would be king for nine thousand years, but that Ōhrmazd would be king forever.

Despite Zurwān's probable existence in the mythology of older times (in the cuneiform tablets of Nuzi and, according to some scholars, in a silver relief coming from Luristan), a similar myth of twinship appears in later religious contexts. More significant and much older is a text belonging to the very old *Gāthās* in the Zoroastrian Avesta (*Yasna* 30.3). This poem mentions two spirits (Spenta Mainyu and Angra Mainyu) who "were seen in sleep as twins"; they are respectively good and bad in thought, word, and action and the foundations of life and its opposite. According to a recent translation of this text by Helmut Humbach, their aspects as the foundations of life and its opposite are not to be interpreted specifically in a chronological sense (that is, in the sense of a cosmogony); but one may still consider the two spirits as opposite principles that exist prior to any manifestation of their existence in this world and hold them accountable for the existence of good and bad, life and death. Thus, they express a radical formulation of dualism, not only moral but ontological.

It is not clear, however, whether the two spirits are literally twins. According to most scholars, they are sons of one and the same father, Ahura Mazdā (the former spelling of the name *Ōhrmazd*), because other texts in the *Gāthās* state that Ahura Mazdā is the father of the beneficent Spenta Mainyu. Moreover, the same scholars, noting that the text quoted above mentions a "choice" made by the two twins (a good choice by the first and a bad choice by the second), think that these choices were made freely, in keeping with the then-current Zoroastrian notion of the free choice between good and bad that can be made by any human being in this world. This interpretation appears highly improbable. Good and bad seem natural choices for the first and second spirit respectively (otherwise, why should there be precisely two?), in the sense that the spirits prefigure the radical character of the choice. Or, rather, they embody it, but as principles and preformate referents of the choice itself and its consequences for people and *daēvas*, that is, life and its opposite. This is the only interpretation that can account for the pregnancy and the profound intermixture of ontology and ethics (as well as cosmogony and moral struggle) that is characteristic of Zoroastrianism in every period of its history. Moreover, it would be impossible to conceive the great god Ahura Mazdā as the father of the evil spirit, for the simple reason that their respective essences have nothing in common. In conclusion, the term *twins,* as applied to the two spirits, should be understood in that Gathic text not as designating brothers, sons of one and the same father, but as a strong expression of their symmetrical and perfectly contrary essences. In order to compare this notion of the twin spirits with the myth of Zurwān and his two sons (who are also good and bad already in their respective natures and not as a consequence of a contrary choice made by them), one must take into account the precisely different natures of Ahura Mazdā and Zurwān. The former is a supreme being completely endowed with personality and ethics; the latter—as time or destiny personified—is not so endowed; he is an entity apt to have materially with himself and to generate from himself such contrary personal agents as the twin characters, God and Antigod, that is, Ōhrmazd (the old Ahura Mazdā) and

Ahriman (the old Destructive Spirit) and their mutually opposing activities.

These two examples show the mythical theme of twinship in the context of the dualistic conceptions of Zoroastrian religion. As has been seen, the opposition between the two twins in the *Gāthās* and in the myth of Zurwān is, in a sense, horizontal. A different use of the theme of twins is present in Manichaeism. Mani was said to have a counterpart in the celestial realm, a twin, (Syr., *at-Taum*) a pneumatic-divine entity who was both his protecting agency and his alter ego. In the Manichaean Codex of Cologne, a Greek biographical text, the term *suzugos* ("he who is bound in marriage") is substituted for *twin.* This is reminiscent of the fact that in Valentinian Gnosticism the soul of the Gnostic was conceived of as feminine, destined to marry her divine counterpart, her angel. In Mani's case, the terms *twin* and *husband* both point to a relationship that implies the Gnostic notion of the perfect consubstantiality of the celestial element and its counterpart active in the terrestial realm. The terrestrial element waits to be reunited with the celestial element, the pneumatic self. At the same time, the heavenly twin and the angelic husband are an expression of transcendence in relation to whatever lives in the terrestial realm: "The mysteries and [vi]sions and the excellence of my Father, and concerning me, who I am, and my *suzugos* . . . who he is" (*Manichaean Codex of Cologne* 23.1–5). It is clear that this ambivalence concerning the perfect consubstantiality (or even identification) between Mani and his twin and at the same time the difference between them (i. e., their respective, actual identities) before the final return of Mani's soul to its original abode implies a vertical structure, well adapted to the general Gnostic notion of a devolution of some pneumatic essence or of its mission in this mixed world. This notion is antithetical to the radical, horizontal opposition of essences expressed in Zoroastrianism in the notion of twin spirits.

Among the nonliterate cultures in which dualistic and (needless to say) dual myths and conceptions exist, explicit radical dualisms are rare. The notion of two symmetrically opposed twins is found in the Iroquois myth of Iouskeha ("sprout") and Tawiskaron ("flint"). More primitive tribes that profess a dualistic mythology do not share the idea of a symmetry between two opposed, superhuman beings (as, for example in the myth of Coyote, who has nothing in common—as far as his origin and ontological meaning are concerned—with the creator). The Iroquois are agriculturalists with matriarchal institutions. This may imply that the dualistic structure expressed in their myth, both in terms of the symmetry of opposing twins and their common origin from a maternal entity, derives from a lunar mythology. On the other hand, this symmetry must be distinguished from that found in Zoroastrianism between the opposed "twin" spirits, or between Ahriman and Ōhrmazd. The Zoroastrian notion of the ontological opposition between the two spirits or between God and Antigod is radicalized to such an extreme that it denies any dialectical or complementary function for Ahriman (with the exception of some brief, very heterodox tales in which he is given some positive capacities that render him rather akin to the figure of a trickster: For example, it is he who knows what Ōhrmazd must do in order to create the great luminaries). However, some comparisons may be drawn between the Iroquois myth and the myth of the birth of Ōhrmazd and Ahriman from Zurwān. Some of the characteristics of the bad Tawiskaron may remind one of the deeds of Ahriman. The bad Iroquois twin breaks out of the maternal womb, emerging from his mother's side. Iouskeha's demiurgical activity, like that of Ōhrmazd, calls the good creatures of the world into existence; the creations of his twin are monstrous and maleficent. Tawiskaron calls into existence a gigantic frog who absorbs all the water in the world, causing aridity—a mythical motif that also exists in the Zurwān mythology. All in all, differences predominate. Even though Iouskeha (or Oterongtongnia) triumphs, he does not transcend his identity as a twin and grandson—not even the privileged one—of the female, primordial character, Ataentsic. Therefore, he has very little in common with the high god of Zoroastrianism, who does transcend his earthly role.

There are numerous problems connected with the myths of twins found among American Indians because of certain sociological elements common to many tribes; the tendency toward a dual organization, for instance, is shared by many populations of North and South America. It appears that the two moieties of a tribe are frequently connected with two mythical twins. According to Werner Müller (1956), this prevents one from interpreting the opposition between such twins as a crude opposition between good and evil. According to Mircea Eliade, the Iroquois myth "is a dualist myth, the only North American myth susceptible to comparison with the Iranian dualism of zurvanite type. . . . Nevertheless, as shall presently be seen, such an irreducible antagonism does not reach the Iranian paroxysm, and this for the simple reason that the Iroquois refuse to identify in the 'bad' twin the essence of 'evil,' the *ontological evil* that obsessed Iranian religious thought" (Eliade, 1969, p. 147f.). Moreover, the ontological basis of the Iroquois dual and (because connected with cosmogony) dualistic mythology is intertwined with sociological and cultural motivations; it implies a question not only of essence but also of function. Tawiskaron's activity, though essentially negative in its value, is considered to have an effect on Iroquois institutions (their cult and calendar) and way of life. As Eliade observes (on the basis of Werner Müller's argumentation), it was a prophet of the Seneca tribe, Handsome Lake, who, at the beginning of the nineteenth century "substituted for the couple of the mythical Twins that of the Great God, Haweniyo (the 'Great Voice') and the Devil, Haninseono ('Who Dwells in the Earth')" (ibid., p. 148). This substitution could be a result of the prophet's monotheistic tendency, but as Müller and Eliade point out, it could also be a response to the accusation made by the Europeans that the Iroquois "adored the Devil." This accusation has been leveled several times in response to dualistic theologies and mythologies; it implies that there is a cult around the second element of the couple. This element may be a demiurge-trickster, a culture hero, or a twin, in no way an exclusively bad character because it is also connected with an important, complementary aspect of reality. Such a notion is a reminder of the Egyptian myth (as expounded by Plutarch) that Seth, the opposing and destroying agency complementary to Osiris, was defeated but not annihilated in order that the equilibrium of the universe remain unchanged.

According to Åke Hultkrantz, the theme of twins in American Indian culture is connected with the figure of the culture hero. This hero may be the father of the twins; in some instances, at least one of the twins has some of the hero's characteristics. One even gets the impression that the twins incorporate respectively the two essences or tendencies present in the culture hero: "the vocation to produce and the vocation to destroy" (Hultkrantz, 1963, p. 41). Hultkrantz maintains that there is also a kind of parallelism between the relationship linking the supreme being and the culture hero on the one hand and the relationship between the two twins on the other. "It seems verisimilar that the myth of the twins be a variation of the mythological theme expressed in the relationship between the Supreme Being and the cultural hero, and that it influenced the latter only secondarily, possibly emphasizing dualism present in this" (ibid., p. 41f.).

In other cases, the twins have nothing in common with the culture hero, but they may accomplish—individually or together—some of the deeds traditionally attributed to him. According to Paul Radin (1949), three types are to be distinguished at the core of American Indian myths of twinship. First, the mother of the twins dies as a result of outside aggression or the unnatural birth of the bad twin (as among the Iroquois). In both myths, the second twin is negative and violent, but the first—at least in the first type of myth—is scarcely more commendable in his *modus operandi.* Second, the twins are children of the Sun. They are different in character, but they cooperate. The third type of myth is a combination of the first two. The first type seems to be common among the northern regions of North America; the second is concentrated in the southwestern regions of the same continent; the third belongs exclusively to South America.

Particularly interesting is the respective quality of the achievements of the twins in the context of their demiurgical activity, an issue that adds new particulars to the generic statement that the second twin, as Eliade points out, "does not incarnate the idea of, 'evil' but only the negative, dark aspect of the world" (Eliade, 1969, p. 149). Thus, among the Tuscarora, an Iroquois tribe, the bad twin, "animated by a bad spirit," came violently to light, so killing his mother. The good twin tried to create plants and animals, but the other, trying to imitate him, succeeded only in bringing desert lands and reptiles into existence. The bad twin also created the bodies of human beings; his brother gave them souls. In the end, the bad twin was vanquished but not annihilated; he became the king of the dead (Hultkrantz, 1963). One cannot but concur with Eliade that the twins in these mythologies form a complementary couple ruling "the two modes or two 'times,' which together constitute the living and fertile universe" (ibid., p. 149).

Another character from these Iroquois myths, the Grande Bosse, a double of Tawiskaron, who fought against the creator and introduced sickness and other evils, was finally defeated but was given the task of curing and helping people. This double lives on the cliffs at the borders of the world, in the land where diseases are born, accompanied by the False Faces, the abortive creations of Tawiskaron, who had tried in vain to imitate the human beings created by his brother. But, as Müller points out, as known from ritual, these creatures "in spring and autumn, drive away the maladies from the villages" (Müller, 1946, p. 272). This is a notion widespread both in North America and in Australia, namely, that bad entities or spirits that are guilty of homicide are endowed with the capacity to heal: They know the "medicine." In the Menomini cult of Manabozo, for example, the evil spirits responsible for the death of the brother of the hero are obliged to impart the medicine to those initiated in the cult, that is, to act against their previous homicidal activity. The same applies to the dreadful character of Crow in some Australian myths and also to the Egyptian myth already mentioned, in which the evil Seth is defeated but not annihilated. A providential decision by Isis allows him to continue his struggle against Apophis, the serpent, who day after day attacks the cosmic boat of the sun crossing the heaven. Eliade's discussion applies to the Egyptian situation as well as to the Indian:

> In other words, though the adversary has been defeated by the Great God, his works, the "evil," persist in the world. The Creator does not seek to, or perhaps he cannot, annihilate the "evil," but neither does he permit it to corrupt his creation. He accepts it as an inevitable negative aspect of life, but at the same time he compels his adversary to combat the results of his own work. (1969, p. 149)

Eliade points out, too, that the Iroquois worldview displays a clearly dualistic view of evil. Considered a "disastrous innovation" brought about by some bad superhuman personage, evil is nonetheless

> accepted as a henceforth inevitable modality of life and of human existence. . . . The universe is imagined to have a central portion, i. e., the village and the cultivated fields, inhabited by men; this central portion is surrounded by an exterior desert full of stones, swamps, and "False faces." (ibid., pp. 149–150)

The same situation is found in old Egypt, where the Nile and the land that is periodically flooded by it belong to Osiris; the desert and the barren sea (with the foreign, Asiatic) countries belong to the "red" Seth (red being the color of the desert), who is characterized by loneliness, infertility, and aggressiveness. A similar notion is found among the Dogon of West Africa. Nommo, the god of water (that of the Niger), may resemble the high god of numerous mythologies in his creative activity. The infelicitous attempts of his evil brother, Yurugu, or Ogo (who is not properly a twin), at creation result in misshapen, monstrous creatures. Compelled by his experience of failure, he introduces pain into the existence of the good creatures. In doing so, Yurugu joins the ranks of the demiurge-tricksters at least in terms of his inability to imitate the efficacy of the creator. But a difference remains. The demiurge-trickster is more interested in particular occurrences in purposedly worsening the quality of life than is the bad twin or brother; he introduces painful conditions of life, creates cliffs and mountains that are difficult to cross, and causes people to become mortal (as does Coyote among some Californian tribes and the bad demiurge of some Asiatic mythologies). But he also justifies his actions by claiming that he challenges human cultural creativity by providing obstacles to survival.

Another important feature of American Indian mythologies of twins is that in South America and in the southwestern regions of North America twins are conceived as sons of the sun. Their birth is characterized by the violent death of their mother. The twins are not necessarily portrayed as rivals. The difference between them is sometimes attested to by the difference of their respective destinies; one of them experiences death but is resurrected by the other (a motif found in the classical myth of the Dioscuri). These twins represent universal duality at the cosmological and sociological levels, which fact, however, does not prevent a consideration of them as disparate in terms of their ontological consistency and their axiological evaluation. Similar interpretations apply when the mythical referents of the twins are respectively Sun and Moon, such as among the Apinagé (or Apinayé; see Nimuendajú, 1939). Among the Caribbean population of the Kaliña, the first twin, Tanusi, is a kind of high god and ancestor, the creator of all good things, living in the "land without evening." Yolokantamulu, his twin brother, is connected with obscurity and the pains of humanity and lives in the "land without morning." By the standard tendency implicit in this kind of duality, the inborn disparity of the twins is not to be explained only as an expression of mere opposition between good and evil but also (or even preeminently) as an expression of ontological and cosmological (and sometimes sociological and psychological) complementarity (but see also the discussion by Josef Haekel, 1958, concerning Tanusi's feature as high god). At the same time, a notion of the disparity of value between the twins in the American Indian mythologies and religions can find a counterpart, as Eliade (1969, pp. 137f.) has observed, in the conception of the two souls in humans, one of heavenly origin and the other of "animal" nature (as among the Apapocúva of Brazil). As for the Caribbean Kaliñas, they characteristically claim that things existing on earth have their spiritual counterpart in heaven. On the sociological plane, the twins may sometimes represent respectively the two moieties of a tribe, as among the already quoted Apinagé.

The principle of twinship is fundamental to the ideology of the Dogon of Mali. For them, twinship means perfection. One of the main characters of their cosmology and cosmogony is Nommo. He is perfect and beneficent. His personality is equivalent to a pair of twins, masculine and feminine, who represent the ideal couple. This couple is not to be imitated on this earth because the marriage between twins is prohibited as a result of the troubles caused by Yurugu, or Ogo, the first son of Amma and the Earth. Nommo as a spiritual entity is a married couple, which is, because married, completely perfect. Yurugu alone is single, imperfect, and unhappy. He personifies deficiency, ontological and ethical. Not directly linked to a twin (Nommo is his younger brother), Yurugu is only understandable as Nommo's misshapen opposite. But it is exactly this opposition (and not the twinship inherent in the entity that is Nommo) that introduces a crucial dialectic between completeness and deficiency in the Dogon ideology. In this ideology, there is a kind of articulated totality in which deficiency—as represented by Yurugu—is an indispensable component. All in all, it may be concluded that in the Dogon ideology, twinship attains a higher status than in American Indian mythologies, because in those mythologies the principle of twinship is directly engaged in a dialectic of completeness and incompleteness as an element constituting a totality (so that even the "dark" element of a pair of twins is considered positive from a functional point of view).

According to the Dogon conception, twinship as such transcends evil but is pledged to coexist with it (i.e., with the single Yurugu). This kind of triadic ontology is very similar to that expressed in the Egyptian myth of Osiris and Seth told by Plutarch. The good Osiris and the bad Seth are not twins but brothers. Osiris' counterpart is his wife, Isis; Seth is infecund and alone—which does not prevent him from being an element of a universal totality. Yurugu's status as the older son of Amma is a feature not uncommon in dualistic conceptions. For instance, the birth of Ahriman precedes (though as a consequence of a trick and a violent act) that of Ōhrmazd in the Zurvanite myth, while Satan is the younger (or older) brother of Christ in the dualistic and sectarian doctrine of the Bogomils. The violence that characterizes the birth or coming to light of a bad twin or brother is typical of such twinship mythologies; this feature probably expresses a kind of recrimination against the bad twin, which is intended to diminish but not to abolish his "legitimacy."

Finally, as far as the "incompleteness" of Yurugu is concerned (i.e., his deprivation of the benefits of both twinship and marriage, or of the marriage implied in twinship), one can conclude that for the first entities of some cosmogonies the duality of twinship and the duality of the married couple are the same. (An example can be found in the Zoroastrian myth of the first human couple, Mashya and Mashyane, who were twins due to the fact that they were brought into existence as the result of a split within a rhubarb plant.) On the contrary, this identification between the two main forms of duality on the anthropological level—between marriage and twinship—is prohibited in the actual life of the Dogon as a lasting consequence of the rupture of harmony caused by the "previous guilt" committed by Yurugu, a guilt that is both a cause and a consequence of his deficiency. According to a version recorded by Montserrat Palau Marti (1957), Yurugu's deficiency was due to the fact that he was born irregularly to Amma and the Earth, a couple whose feminine component had not yet been excised and was therefore not yet ready for marriage and generation.

Another version ascribes the guilt to Yuguru himself, who could not believe that Amma would give him a wife for his twin. This ambivalence concerning the ontological level to which the first origin of deficiency is attributed reminds one of the sin of Sophia according to Valentinus and his followers. Sophia failed to obey the law that regulated the order and fecundity of the aeons, those spiritual couples (or syzygies) that exist in the divine Pleroma ("fullness"). Yurugu did not find his "twin soul" (literally, the feminine part of his soul) because of his lack of belief or, alternatively, because of his inborn deficiency, and therefore he cohabited incestuously with his mother, the Earth; this resulted in the birth of certain malevolent entities who live in the woods, outside of the culturalized and purified (i. e., ritually cultivated) land. On the other hand, the impurity and sterility of Yurugu does not prevent him from being an important element in the cosmological process; he is an essential part of the ordinary life of the Dogon. His "words" are essential to the development of life. Nommo, that is to say, one of the twins that compose his double personality, was sacrificed, and some cosmic entities were derived from him; he was later resurrected. Once the world is put in motion, the androgynous condition of existence (which was also peculiar to Nommo, whose two souls, masculine and feminine, were twins) is abolished, and sexual differentiation obtains—a differentiation, of course, that is different from the loneliness and incompleteness of Yurugu, the inhabitant of the woods. All in all, Yurugu remains a representation of limitation, but, for the same reason, also a referent of the growing cosmos of culture and agriculture. This corresponds to the will of Amma, that all be found and all be functional in nature, the perfect and the imperfect. Dogon dualism has its roots higher in the vertical series of the ontological levels; it affects the divine to some degree particularly if the first origin of deficiency is seen as deriving from the irregular maternity of Earth, whose feminine part was not yet excised.

One can conclude that the motif of twins in the ideologies of nonliterate cultures takes two main expressions: (1) symmetry, which being partial and not specular as in the Zoroastrian (Gathic) notion of the two spirits, is an adequate expression of the complementarity of twins; and (2) disparity in value, which also includes in itself a dynamism motivating some peculiarities related in the myth (e.g., when the second twin undergoes a crisis and is rehabilitated by the first). This complementarity, which is capable of integrating within itself the "bad" aspect, or simply the inferior quality, of the second twin, is not unqualified and static but articulated and dynamic; a distant equivalent is to be found in Platonic, Middle Platonic, and Neoplatonic speculation, where the existence of the lower, imperfect world, made after the image of the ideal one, is a requisite for the completeness of the All.

It is clear that this notion of an imperfection, which is a necessary component of a perfect totality, is extraneous to biblical creationism. It is dualistic in itself (when the two members of the couple are seen as disparate "principles" in the context of a cosmogony), and it in turn expresses a dialectical form of dualism. It must be distinguished from two other forms of dualism, where the "harmony" of the dialectical position is broken. The first is the Zoroastrian conception of the twins, one beneficent and the other maleficent; their relationship is one of radical opposition and mutual exclusion (a condition also present in the myth of Zurwān, despite the fact that the idea of Time as father of both Ōhrmazd and Ahriman is not to be confused with the Zoroastrian conception of the twin spirits, who cannot have God as their common father). The second form is found in Gnostic speculation, particularly Manichaeism, where matter, the substance of this visible world, is condemned, and Mani, the inspired founder, has a spiritual twin who is a heavenly counterpart of himself (i.e., his true self), to which he is to be "reduced" after his corporeal death.

INDO-EUROPEAN CULTURES. This article comes finally to some myths of twins in the Indo-European cultures. In India, Yama, whose name means "twin," is accompanied by a female counterpart, Yamī, the feminine form of his name. But he underwent some essential modifications and became the king of the dead, a function well suited to his original quality as first man. In Iran, Yima (the equivalent of Yama), with his female twin, Yimak, remained a prototype of humanity. (Other prototypes were Gaya-maretan, a total figure with no female counterpart or twin, and Mashya and Mashyane, the primordial twins and human progenitors.) Yima later became the inhabitant of Var, a subterranean world in which different categories of living beings wait for the final rehabilitation. Yima's connection with the principle of twinship is an important confirmation of the principle of duality in the field of cosmogony, no less important than another principle in the same field, androgyny.

The mention of a pair of Indian twin deities, the Nasatyas (or Aśvins), connected with the realm of health and fecundity (the third function of Indo-European tripartite ideology according to Georges Dumézil) provides an introduction to Castor and Pollux, the Dioscuri of Greek mythology. These can be seen as a privileged expression of ontological disparity, which is not necessarily ethical, contained within a set of twins. According to the characteristic and prevailing (but not necessarily older) formulation of the myth (first mentioned in the old epic poem *Kypria*, fragment 5k), Pollux was immortal, the son of Zeus—the supreme god—and of Leda; Castor was mortal, son of Tyndareus, the human husband of Leda. A very particular mythical element mediated their relationship so that they were neither wholly disparate nor wholly equal: The immortal Pollux renounced half of his immortality in favor of his mortal brother when the latter was fatally wounded by some common enemies. As a consequence of this, Castor and Pollux live alternatively in the heavens and in the netherworld (or they sojourn in their tomb in Laconia, at Therapnae near Sparta). This particular aspect of the myth represents a very peculiar expression of the twinship motif. The twins' symmetrical affinity is emphasized by their common attribute of the *pilos*, a piece of headgear later interpreted as representing half of Leda's egg; on the other hand, their radical, original disparity is emphasized by the opposite natures of their respective fathers (Zeus and a human hero). However, this dialectical situation—of partial affinity and radical disparity—is transcended by the attribution to the mortal twin of one-half of the immortality of the other; this leads to the situation of an artificially produced, balanced equality. In this sense, twinship is both an ontological presupposition and a final acquisition for them: a pattern different from, or opposed to, that of other myths concerning twins or brothers who, on the basis of an ontological or merely ethical or behavioral disparity, come to represent opposing elements (sun or moon, life or death, etc.).

Unfortunately, there are versions of the myth of the Dioscuri that modify this basic pattern. In some texts, Castor and Pollux are sons of the same father, Tyndareus, whose name can also designate Zeus ("he who strikes"). According to other sources, they are sons of Zeus (hence the name *hoi Dioskouroi*, "the young sons of Zeus"). Moreover, there are different interpretations concerning the modalities of their alternating destinies apart from the fact that in old sources (Homer) they live as typical heroes in their tomb at Therapnae. The more widespread interpretation (Lucian) is that one lives in heaven and the other in his tomb or in the netherworld, and vice versa. There are also good reasons for understanding that they experience life and death together in alternation. In a famous song of victory (*Nemean Odes* 10), Pindar immortalizes this episode, making brotherly love the motivation behind the generous deed of Pollux, who renounces one-half of his (still to be experienced) immortality to show that life (even immortal life) is hard without friends. This throws a different light on the whole myth, more in accordance with the old Homeric statement that the two are together in their Laconian tomb, or *hērōion*.

Thus, the myth of the Dioscuri may be distinguished from such myths as that of the Sumerian Dumuzi, who alternates his stay in the netherworld with that of Geshtinanna, his sister. In other words, the Dioscuri do not belong fundamentally to the typology of the dying god (even a dying god split into two figures who take turns dwelling in the netherworld); they represent instead a special (duplicate) version of the hero, who lives in his tomb, from which emanates his protecting influence on the town and the territory. More precisely, the Dioscuri (*theoi hērōes*, "divine heroes") belong to a typology in between that of the chthonic hero and the heavenly god. Their shared immortality, based on their geminate personality, allows them to act together as heavenly gods; as such, they manifest themselves on the summit of a ship's mast during a tempest, or they appear at the decisive moment during a battle. Their stay in a tomb links them to the classical heroes. All in all, this is a polytheistic interpretation of the motif of twins, different from those that are familiar in nonliterate cultures.

The most famous set of twins in myth and legend is Romulus and Remus, the founders of the Eternal City. Although the Dioscuri were worshiped in old Latium, as demonstrated by an archaic Latin inscription from Lavinium (fifth century BCE) dedicated to them, these twins were unrelated to the Roman twins. In contrast to the Dioscuri, who tended to be equated in their destiny and function (although Castor has special relations with the cavalry, and the temple on the forum was originally dedicated to—or at least named after—him, and only later after the Castores, the Roman name of the Dioscuri), Romulus and Remus tended to be differentiated, to the extent that the former kills the latter immediately after the marking of the sacred pomerium, which was intended to separate the domestic soil of the city from all external territory. The killing of the offender, Remus, because he had violated the pomerium, may be interpreted as prototypical of the drastic measures associated with this boundary for the protection of the city.

The legendary killing of Remus, however, did not prevent the Romans from continuing a ritual celebration, the Lupercalia, at which time two groups of Luperci, those allegedly instituted by Romulus (the Fabiani) and those said to be instituted by Remus (the Quinctiales), acted as rivals running around the old city acting out a rite intended to promote health and fertility and to reaffirm the ominous destiny of Rome. The rite was modified in 44 BCE, when a third group of Luperci was instituted (the Julii), the tradition behind the festivity being somewhat misunderstood. The owner of the third flock of Luperci, Caesar, who in those months was striving after kingship, could automatically be compared to the first founders of Rome as a candidate for kingship. All in all, the celebration of the Lupercalia—strictly ritualized and thus made inoffensive—could perpetuate in Rome's historical memory a significant notion, that of an endogenous source of rivalry and destruction, a duality threatening to become a dualism and, as such, dangerous; for this reason it was allowed to survive only within a strictly controlled ritual.

TWINS AND THE MYTHS OF ORIGINS. One must note some considerations concerning the cultural-historical setting in life of at least some of these traditions of twinship within the context of myths of origins. Such traditions are dualistic in character, whether they emphasize a horizontal or a frontal, mutually exclusive opposition between the twins (as in the case of Zoroastrianism), or, alternatively, a dialectical relationship between them. It would seem that this dialectic, as it is manifested among the American Indians, has something in common with an ideology of agriculturists, based on matriarchal and lunar aspects (e.g., the Kaliña situated the twins respectively on the bright and on the dark side of the moon). In the same way may be interpreted the extreme specialization and absoluteness of the dualism of the Iroquois twins, deriving probably from a lunar, female entity, as well as the type of culture present in the South American and Caribbean tribes. This means, as Hultkrantz (1963) has observed, that dualism in America (at least this kind of dualism) is a southern phenomenon (as opposed to that of the Arctic hunters). To be sure, one cannot forget, as Müller (1956) points out, that some mythologies of hunters, both in Canada and in California, are also dualistic. But this dualism (e.g., the well-known myth concerning the demiurge-trickster, Coyote, who opposes the high being in his creating activity and thus introduces death and the "heavy" physiology of human beings) is structurally very different from the dialectical symmetry of twins. The high being and the demiurge-trickster are of very different extraction; they cannot be reduced to a symmetrical, bipartite form of totality. On the other hand, dialecticism is not absent in the Californian myths of the supreme being and Coyote. The supreme being is a giver of life, but death is introduced by Coyote on the basis of an argument that tends to emphasize the cultural utility rather than the negative aspect of death.

Another issue concerning the twins motif in mythology concerns the direct impact of the physiological experience of twinship on the psychology of the relevant populations. According to Hultkrantz (1963, p. 45) the "superstitious" attention paid to the phenomenon of twinship could have been inspired by its appearance in the symbological language of myth. On the other hand, what is exceptional on earth could also be seen as primordial, so that the inauguration of the terrestrial (imperfect) status of humanity would have meant also the transition from (perfect) twinship to (imperfect) singleness. Twinship, as it is experienced in this world, comes to mean something extraordinary. In addition, the rather extraordinary phenomenon of twinship has been differently evaluated in different cultures. In Africa, for instance, one moves from a feeling of dread before twins (in some cases, one or both of them may be killed) among the San and Damara in southern Africa to a feeling of happiness and expectation of good fortune in their presence, as in Sudan. One could also venture that the typical ambivalence found in the disparities between twins (the second twin as bad, or simply as terrestrial, or, as a part of a totality, destined for a sacrifice from which he is ultimately rescued, as among the Dogon) is not unrelated to the problematical nature of physiological twinship, in which the different values of duality (completeness, but also distinction or even disparity) can put in motion a plurality of interpretations, both at the mythological and the ritual-sociological level. The reverse possibility, namely that the motif of twinship, which originally developed on the mythological level, could have motivated with its different expressions the contradictory nature of twinship on the ritual-sociological level, is perhaps too far-fetched.

See Also Androgynes; Clitoridectomy; Culture Heroes; Dualism; Tricksters.

Bibliography

Baumann, Hermann, and Diedrich Westermann. *Les peuples et les civilisations de l'Afrique.* Paris, 1948.

Bianchi, Ugo. *Zaman i Ōhrmazd: Lo zoroastrismo nelle sue origini e nella sua essenza.* Turin, 1958.

Bianchi, Ugo. *Selected Essays on Gnosticism, Dualism and Mysteriosophy.* Leiden, 1978. Compares Egyptian and Dogon mythology (see especially pages 86–102) and discusses the Egyptian myth of Seth (pages 103–125) and the Zoroastrian doctrine of the twin spirits and the myth of Zurwān (pages 361–416).

Bianchi, Ugo. *Il dualismo religioso: Saggio storico ed etnologico.* 2d ed. Rome, 1983.

Boyce, Mary. *A History of Zoroastrianism,* vol. 1. Leiden, 1975.

Chapouthier, Fernand. *Les Dioscures au service d'une déesse.* Paris, 1935.

Cirillo, Luigi, ed. *Atti del primo Simposio internazionale sul Codex Manichaicus Coloniensis.* Cosenza, 1986.

Count, Earl W. "The Earth-Diver and the Rival Twins: A Clue to Time Correlation in North-Eurasiatic and North American Mythology." In *Indian Tribes of Aboriginal America,* edited by Sol Tax, pp. 55–62. Chicago, 1952.

Dumézil, Georges. *Les dieux des Indo-Européens.* Paris, 1952.

Eliade, Mircea. *The Quest: History and Meaning in Religion.* Chicago, 1969. See especially pages 127–175.

Farnell, Lewis R. *Greek Hero Cults and Ideas of Immortality* (1921). Oxford, 1970.

Griaule, Marcel, and Germaine Dieterlen. *Le renard pâle,* vol. 1, *Le mythe cosmogonique.* Paris, 1965.

Gusinde, Martin. "Das Brüderpaar in der südamerikanischen Mythologie." In *Proceedings of the Twenty-third International Congress of Americanists, 1928,* pp. 687–698. New York, 1930.

Haekel, Josef. "Purá und Hochgott." *Archiv für Völkerkunde* 13 (1958): 25–50.

Harris, John R. *The Cult of the Heavenly Twins.* Cambridge, 1906.

Hewitt, J. N. B., ed. *Iroquoian Cosmology,* 2 pts. Washington, D.C., 1903, 1928.

Hultkrantz, Åke. *Les religions des indiens primitifs de l'Amérique: Essai d'une synthèse typologique et historique.* Stockholm, 1963.

Humbach, Helmut, ed. and trans. *Die Gāthās des Zarathustra.* Heidelberg, 1959.

Insler, Stanley. *The Gāthās of Zarathustra.* Tehran and Leiden, 1975.

Krickeberg, Walter, ed. *Die Religionen des alten Amerika.* Stuttgart, 1961. Translated as *Les religions amérindiennes* (Paris, 1962).

Métraux, Alfred. "Twin Heroes in South American Mythology." *Journal of American Folklore* 59 (April–June 1946): 114–123.

Müller, Werner. *Die Religionen der Waldlandindianer Nordamerikas.* Berlin, 1956.

Nimuendajú, Curt. *The Apinayé.* Washington D.C., 1939.

Palau Martí, Montserrat. *Les Dogon.* Paris, 1957.

Radin, Paul. "The Basic Myth of the North American Indians." In *Eranos–Jahrbuch* (Zurich) 17 (1949): 359–419.

Wide, Sam. *Lakonische Kulte* (1893). Stuttgart, 1973.

Zaehner, Robert C. *Zurvan: A Zoroastrian Dilemma.* Oxford, 1955.

New Sources

Schwartz, Hillel. *The Culture of the Copy: Striking Likenesses, Unreasonable Facsimiles.* New York, 1996.

Ward, Donald. *The Divine Twins; An Indo-European Myth in Germanic Tradition.* Berkeley, Calif., 1968.

UGO BIANCHI (1987)
Revised Bibliography

TWINS: BALTIC TWIN DEITIES

The twin myth and various folk beliefs associated with the idea of twins and the concept of duality have an important place in Baltic religion. The divine or deified twins usually are demiurges, with various associated cosmogonic and anthropogonic functions. Thus, for Latvians, Dievs, the personification of light, is the twin of Velns. The world was created, according to ancient folk legend, as a result of their fight on a stone in the middle of the sea (*vidū jūras uz akmeņa*) or on an island in the middle of the sea (*vidū jūras saliņā*), a place that at a later date became the central axis of the cosmos.

The Baltic divine twins have often been associated with the cycle of death and rebirth. Thus in Latvian mythological folk songs the theme of the sons of Dievs marrying their twin sisters, the daughters of Saule (the sun), is widespread. Before the wedding a ritual wooing of Saule's daughters takes place, which Dievs's sons accomplish by looking through the petals of poppies (*Caur magoņu lapiņām*), flowers that at weddings symbolize death, rebirth, and also puberty. On the wedding night, while waiting for the appearance of Saule's daughters at the vault of heaven, the sons light two candles at sea. These heavenly weddings end unsuccessfully because of an implied but never quite articulated suggestion of a serious violation—incest.

In antiquity it is probable that sacral incest was differentiated from profane incest, the first being committed by a primeval human or demiurge, the second by a trickster. Incest demonstrably pointed to two diverse forms of sexual behavior: the cultured versus the natural (as exhibited in nature), or, in other words, the civilized versus the savage. Sacral incest likely occurred only in illo tempore (the beginning of time) when there was no other coupling possible except between brother and sister. Angered by the violation of incest being committed, Pērkons, the god of thunder, struck the cosmic tree, or tree of life. For three years Saule collected the scattered branches of the damaged tree, the oak. It was only in the fourth year that she found the tip of the tree and, by piecing together all of the branches, made rebirth of the cosmos possible.

Another variation of this theme has it that during the heavenly wedding a daughter of the sun drowned. Her body was carried down the river into the sea, from the sea it was washed ashore, and in this spot grew a linden tree with nine branches. In Latvian mythology the number nine is an indicator of time and space in the cosmos. While carving from this linden tree a *kokles* (psaltery), a Latvian musical instrument considered to be the embodiment of a female deity or, in a broader sense, the soul and life of a woman, the son of Dievs recognized his twin sister, the daughter of Saule. Death and rebirth of the gods and of the seasons is the basis of this myth; it is analogous to the ancient Greek myth about Persephone. Latvian mythology scholars have tried to interpret the daughters of Saule as the sunlight at dawn or dusk (in autumn and winter, but also in the evening, the sun and its beams seem to die, while in the spring and at dawn they appear to be reborn), while the sons of Dievs are interpreted as Venus, which the Baltic people believed to be embodied in the two stars Rīta and Vakara (morning and evening). The divine twin sons of Dievs, in both Latvian and Lithuanian folklore, sources are associated with horses. In mythological folk songs the twins travel by boat or by horse, often transforming into or fusing with the horse. They appear also as water-loving beasts, otters, or beavers, dancing in either otter or beaver skins. They are also associated with the cosmic tree, the oak.

The sons of Dievs, usually two in number, are typically both called by the same name, but in some instances, each has a different name. Thus, in the spring season, the son of Dievs, as the embodiment of rebirth, is named Ūsiņš (from the verb *aust,* literally, "the rising of the sun," or "the emergence of light"). In autumn, the son of Dievs is the embodiment of death called Mārtiņš, possibly linked to the word *mirt* (to die). Both twins mirror the mythological idea of sequential change and continuity of the cycle of life and death. The sons of Dievs are perceived as the protectors of humans, primarily of men and specifically during war, at sea, when fishing, and when caring for horses. In Latvian mythological folk songs they reveal themselves as two candles in the sea to fishermen and sailors, thus lighting their way:

Div svecītes jūrā dega Sudrabiņa lukturos;
Tās dedzina
Dieva dēli, *Zvejnieciņus gaidīdami.*
Two candles burn at sea
In silver lanterns;
They're lit by the sons of *Dievs,*
Awaiting fishermen.

The divine twins are also associated with fertility cults and productivity. For Latvians this is revealed in a particularly striking fashion in the cult of Jumis and his twin sister Jumala, at one time either his betrothed or his wife. *Jumis* and

Jumala are words for which parallels can be found in several Indo-European traditions: in ancient Gaelic, *e(a)main*; in Avesta, *yima*; in Indo-Iranian, *yama*—as found, for example, in the hymn in *Ṛgveda* about Yama and his twin sister Yamī, wherein Yamī tries to entice her brother to take part in incestuous relations. The Iranian twins Yima and Yimāk, by getting married, become the predecessors of humanity. This theme is also found in Latvian mythological folk songs, where there is a direct allusion to incestuous relations between the brother and sister Jumis and Jumala (Jumīts and Jumaliņa are diminutive forms):

Jumīts meklēj Jumaliņu
Pa tīrumu staigādams;
Brālīts meklēj līgaviņas
No māsiņas vaicādams.
Jumīts looks for
Jumaliņa
Walking in the field;
The brother is seeking a bride
Asking his sister.

Latvians and Lithuanians also give the name *jumis* to any two fruits or nuts that have grown together, or to two sheaves of grain on one stalk. In ancient times (and still today), having harvested the rye, barley, and wheat, people tried to find and save two sheaves of grain intertwined, or they tied two bundles of the harvested grain together, saving this *jumis* over winter to ensure fertility and productivity for the coming year. On the subject of birth and fertility, according to Latvian folk beliefs, if a young woman wanted to have twins, she had to find and eat a *jumis*, such as two nuts or berries or some other fruit that have grown together. The Latvian Jumis and Jumala are associated with the idea of the death and rebirth of nature. Another testimony to the Jumis myth can be seen in the *jumis* nut found buried in a young girl's grave during an archeological dig of an eighth- to eleventh-century burial ground in Latvia called Kaugaru Beites.

Another son of Dievs who is mentioned in Latvian folklore, particularly in summer solstice songs called *Jāņu dziesmas* (Jānis's songs), is Jānis (*'Ai Jānīti, Dieva dēls;* Oh Jānītis [dim. of Jānis], son of Dievs). Jānis is typologically similar to Baldr in the Scandinavian indigenous religions; that is, he is a seasonal deity embodying the ideas of fertility and productivity associated with summer. We can assume that Jānis, like the Roman Janus, is two-faced—the two sons of Dievs united in one person, one linked to the spring and summer seasons, the other linked to autumn and winter. When one of them appears in the sky as a heavenly body (a star), the other, being underground, is not visible. The idea of promoting fertility predominates in the summer solstice songs. Folksong texts indicate that during this time the mythical heavenly wedding takes place between the divine twins—the sons of Dievs and the daughters of Saule.

Twins also figure as the founders of ancient social organizations, such as tribes, nations, states, and cities. For the Prussians, the twin brothers Widewuttis and Brūtens are the founders of a tribe. Widewuttis is the founder of secular power and the first king of the Prussian tribe, while Brūtens is the founder of its spiritual power and the *romow* sanctuary, being its first *Krive krivaitis* (high priest). In later times the Prussians worshiped Widewuttis and Brūtens in the form of two posts, one called Worskaito (the elder), the other called Iszwambrato (i.e., *Svais brāti,* "his brother").

Even as late as the end of the nineteenth century (and into the twentieth), twins appear in Lithuanian and Latvian historical legends. A Latvian legend recorded in the nineteenth century tells of the twin brothers Turo and Tusko, who both loved the same girl. They were so similar that the girl could not tell them apart, and for this reason gave one a gold ring and the other a silver ring to wear. Turo finally succeeded in winning the girl's love, but Tusko, in a dreadful act of betrayal, posed as his twin brother and stole his betrothed. When the betrothed of Turo, on recognizing the ring, learned that she had been deceived, she killed herself with a sword, while the twin brothers killed each other. The graves of all three are located in Zilais kalns (Blue Hill), an important and legendary sanctuary in Latvia, located near the city of Valmiera. This legend about the twins, along with other legends that abound regarding Zilais kalns, reflects the concepts of death and rebirth associated with the twin myths.

There is another interesting element in the Turo/Tusko legend. The names Turo and Tusko start with the same letter. This also occurs in the Roman Romulus and Remus, the Germanic Hengist and Horst, and in another Latvian myth about twins, Auseklis and Ūsiņš (both of which are derived from the Indo-European root-form **aus/*us*, with the ancient form of the latter being Ausiņš).

The divine twins as special patrons of the fertility and productivity cult are also revealed in traditional wood architecture in Latvia. Even today, one can find fastened to the ends of gables on houses or buildings two identical, symmetrically placed wooden horses, goats, or figurative carvings of other animals and birds. This tradition was practiced by all Baltic peoples, as can be seen from ethnographic drawings and written records of the eighteenth and nineteenth centuries, as well as from photographs taken during the first half of the twentieth century in Latvia, Lithuania, and East Prussia. Paradoxically, one of the places where zoomorphic and ornithomorphic images of twin deities have been preserved is East Prussia, which was most devastated during World War II and which now forms part of the Russian Federation as the Kaliningrad region and part of northeastern Poland. In districts where prewar buildings have been preserved, one can still see carved twin horse heads at roof gables and in the wooden trim above windows. This tradition has also been retained in the Curonian Spit in the Baltics. One part of the Curonian Spit territory is located in Lithuania, while the second part belongs to Russia; in Lithuania this twin-horse tradition at gable ends is being preserved, with the horse heads being restored, whereas in Russia such carvings are going to ruin, along with the buildings themselves. It is significant that in Latvian Jumis and *jumts* (roof), as well as the verb *jumt* (to roof, to thatch) and the term *debesu jums* (vault of heaven), are derived from the same root-form, based on the Indo-European root **ieu* (to tie together). Not only does the twin deity Jumis consist of two tied into one, but also a house roof having two sides joined into one whole.

The significance to the Baltic peoples of the twin myth, particularly as it relates to the birth of twins, was noted in the nineteenth century by such scholars as the German-born ethnographer and folklorist August Bielenstein. However, the Baltic twin myth has merited special attention and comparative analysis only since the 1960s, when it was included in an overview of various Indo-European twins written by Donald Ward (1968), and later by Vjačeslav Ivanov (1972 and 1983) and the Latvian-born folklorist Liene Neuland (1977). Evidently scholars have noted the similarities between the Baltic divine twins and the broader Indo-European twin concept, as in, for example, the Greek Dioscuri, Castor and Pollux (Polydeuces), and the ancient Indian twin, Aśvin.

BIBLIOGRAPHY

Beresnevičius, Gintaras. "Brutenio ir Videvučio religinė reforma." In *Baltų religinės reformos*, pp. 77–125. Vilnius, 1995.

Bielenstein, August. "Die Dieva dēli des lettischen Volksliedes." *Magasin*, Vol. 19, 4th ed., pp. 240–282. Mitau, Russia, 1896.

Biezais, Haralds. "Dievi un dievu dēli." In *Smaidošie dievi un cilvēka asara*, pp. 54–81. Senatne, 1991.

Bučas, Jurgis. *Kuršių nerijos nacionalinis parkas.* Vilnius, 2001.

Ivanov, Vjačeslav. "Otraženie indoevropejskoj terminologii bliznečnogo kul'ta v baltijskih jazykah." In *Balto-slavjanskij sbornik*, pp. 193–205. Moscow, 1972.

Ivanov, Vjačeslav. "K probleme latyšskogo Jumis i baltijskogo bliznečnogo kul'ta." In *Balto-slavjanskie issledovanija.* Moscow, 1983.

Neuland, Lena. *Jumis die fruchtbarheitsgottheit der alten Letten.* Uppsala, Sweden, 1977.

Rūsiņš, Valdis. *Divdaļīgums sakrālā veseluma struktūrā latviešu reliģiskajos priekšstatos.* Platforma, pp. 67–72. Riga, Latvia, 2003.

Ward, Donald. *The Divine Twins: An Indo-European Myth in Germanic Tradition.* Los Angeles, 1968.

JANĪNA KURSĪTE (2005)
Translated by Margita Gailītis and Vija Kostoff

TWO BOOKS, THE. The relationship between religion and science in the Christian West has often found expression in metaphors and models. Since the nineteenth century the strident "warfare model" has dominated interpretations of these different realms of human knowledge. However, a renaissance is occurring of a far more ancient metaphor, that of God's self-revelation through a pair of complementary books, the book of nature and the book of Scripture. Pope John Paul II proclaimed, "From the greatness and beauty of created things comes a corresponding perception of their Creator (*Wisdom* 13:5). This is to recognize as a first stage of divine Revelation the marvelous book of nature, which, when read with the proper tools of human reason, can lead to knowledge of the Creator" (John Paul II, 1998, p. 19).

ORIGINS OF THE METAPHOR. The origins of the "two books" metaphor are embedded in the conviction of the Abrahamic faiths that God is knowable through revelation. The Hebrew Scriptures and the New Testament were understood to be transmitting the very word of God, and thus the "book" became of paramount importance in their respective traditions. *Psalms* 19:1 majestically articulates the idea that "the heavens declare the glory of God, and the firmament proclaims his handiwork." The theme in the *Book of Wisdom* that God is known through the divine works even by Gentiles is echoed in the New Testament locus classicus for the natural knowledge of God, the Pauline declaration in *Romans*: "For what can be known about God is plain to them, because God has shown it to them. Ever since the creation of the world his invisible nature, namely, his eternal power and deity, has been clearly perceived in the things that have been made" (*Rom.* 1:19–20). Paul elsewhere describes the visible worlds as "images of the invisible" (*Heb.* 11:3).

In patristic literature one finds the first full expression of the metaphor. Elements may be found as early as the second century in Justin Martyr's adoption of the Stoic idea of the *logos spermatikos* (*Second Apology*, chap. 8) and in Irenaeus of Lyons (130–202 CE) the idea of the works and the word of God (*Adversus haereses* IV.20). Tertullian prefigured it in his antiheretical argument that, because Marcion has eviscerated Scripture, he cannot provide a counterpart in revelation to the knowledge of God derived from nature (*Adversus Marcionem*, V.5). Athanasius (c. 296–373 CE) offered a protostatement of the theme in his claim that nature and Scripture are the sole sources of knowledge of God (*Vita S. Antoni*, 78).

The clearest patristic statements of the metaphor of "the book of nature" were offered by John Chrysostom (c. 354–407 CE) and Augustine of Hippo (c. 354–407 CE). Chrysostom declared:

> If God had given instruction by means of books, and of letters, he who knew letters would have learnt what was written, but the illiterate man would have gone away without receiving any benefit. . . . This however cannot be said with respect to the heavens. . . . Upon this volume the unlearned, as well as the wise man, shall be able to look, and wherever any one may chance to come, there looking upwards towards the heavens, he will receive a sufficient lesson from the view of them. (*Homilies to the People of Antioch*, IX.5, 162–163).

Augustine proclaimed:

> There is a great book: the very appearance of created things. Look above you! Look below you! Note it. Read it. God, whom you want to discover, never wrote that

> book with ink. Instead He set before your eyes the things that He had made. Can you ask for a louder voice than that? Why, heaven and earth shout to you: "God made me!" (City of God, 11:22).

But although these passages establish the complementarity of natural and revealed theology among the fathers, the metaphor only reached full articulation with the progressive rediscovery of Aristotelian natural philosophy, when the "two books" became a primary model for expressing a mature binary epistemology of revelation.

ESTABLISHMENT OF THE "TWO BOOKS" METAPHOR. Medieval thinkers employed the model of a twofold revelation with great plasticity. Alain of Lille wrote, "*Omnis mundi creatura / Quasi liber et pictura / Nobis est et speculum*" (Every creature is to us like a book and a picture and a mirror). Hugh of Saint Victor regarded both the creation and the incarnation as "books" of God and compared Christ as primary revelation to a book. Saint Bonaventure's (1217–1274) model of revelation included three volumes: sensible creatures are "a book with writing front and back," spiritual creatures are "a scroll written from within," and Scripture is "a scroll written within and without" (*Collations on the Hexaemeron,* 12.14–17). Thomas Aquinas in his *Summa Contra Gentiles* likewise speaks about a threefold knowledge that humanity may have of divine things: ascent through creation by the natural light of reason, descent of divine truth by revelation, and elevation of the human mind to a perfect insight into things revealed. For Dante, for whom the book in which everything is contained is the Godhead, perfect insight is eschatological in paradise, where everything that has been scattered throughout the entire universe like loose pages is now "bound in one volume" (*Paradiso* XXXIII, 82).

Raymond of Sabunde offered the fullest late-medieval articulation of the metaphor in *Theologia Naturalis* (1436):

> Hence there are two books given to us by God, the one being the book of the whole collection of creatures or the book of nature, and the other being the book of sacred scripture. The first book was given to human beings in the beginning, when the universe of creatures was created, since no creature exists that is not a certain letter, written by the finger of God, and from many creatures as from many letters is composed one book, which is called the book of the creatures. Within this book is included humanity itself, and human beings are the first letters of this book. But the second book, Scripture, was given to human beings secondarily to correct the deficiencies of the first book, which humanity could not read because it is blind. The first book is common everyone, but the second book is not common to all, because only clerics are able to read what is written in it. (*Theologia Naturalis sive Liber Creaturarum,* 35–36)

Sabunde's incautious exaltation of the book of nature and his insistence that the book of Scripture is less accurate led to the condemnation of the work as heretical in 1595.

EARLY MODERN VARIATIONS ON THE THEME. The "book of nature" enjoyed its greatest currency in the early modern period. The Reformers' emphasis on the literal sense of Scripture cut through the profusion of "meanings" and "signatures" found by medieval scholars in nature and reinforced the idea of two books. However, the book of nature was clearly subordinate to biblical revelation in the theology of John Calvin, who held Scripture to be a necessary corrective to the deficiencies of nature (*Institutes,* I.6.1). The Reformed tradition retained this Calvinist interpretation of the two books in the *Belgic Confession* adopted by the Dutch Reformed Church. In contrast, Paracelsus suggested an empirical approach: whereas Scripture was to be explored through its letters, the book of nature had to be read by going from land to land because every country was a different page.

The metaphor was affected in the seventeenth century by both the elaboration of natural theology and the development of the sciences in novel empirical and theoretical directions. Pierre Gassendi (1592–1655) saw purpose in all of nature and suggested that if René Descartes wanted to prove the existence of God he ought to abandon reason and look around him and that the two books were not to be kept on separate shelves. Although Francis Bacon seems in practice to have kept the two books distinct, he articulated their essential complementarity:

> The scriptures reveal to us the will of God; and the book of the creatures expresses the divine power; whereof the latter is a key unto the former: not only opening our understanding to conceive the true sense of the scriptures, by the general notions of reason and rules of speech; but chiefly opening our belief, in drawing us into a due meditation of the omnipotency of God, which is chiefly signed and engraven upon his works. (*The Advancement of Learning,* VI, 16)

Bacon set the tone for the seventeenth-century scientific enterprise in his redirection of the "two books" metaphor toward the improvement of the human estate.

Galileo Galilei argued that the book of nature is written in the language of mathematics, not only implying that mathematics is the sublimest expression of the divine word but de facto restricting its full comprehension to those who are appropriately educated:

> And to prohibit the whole science [of astronomy] would be but to censure a hundred passages of holy Scripture which teach us that the glory and greatness of Almighty God are marvelously discerned in all his works and divinely read in the open book of heaven. . . . Within its pages are couched mysteries so profound and concepts so sublime that the vigils, labors, and studies of hundreds upon hundreds of the most acute minds have still not pierced them, even after continual investigations for thousands of years. (*Letter to Grand Duchess Christina*)

Galileo's famous dictum that Scripture teaches "how the heavens go and not how to go to heaven" should be interpreted in light of his conviction of the complementarity of the two books.

The metaphor flourished in the natural theological climate of seventeenth-century England, particularly in the "physico-theology" of the Boyle Lectures, where the idea was used by many divines as shorthand for the assumed validity of the design argument. But its two terms were not always held in comfortable balance. The dissenting theologian Richard Baxter, for example, argued that "nature was a 'hard book'; which few could understand, and that it was therefore safer to rely more heavily on Scripture" (*The Reasons for the Christian Religion,* 1667). In contrast, Sir Isaac Newton saw nature as perhaps more truly the source of divine revelation than the Bible, although he spent decades of his life investigating the prophetic books. It has been argued that in virtually abolishing the distinction between the two books, which he revered as separate expressions of the same divine meaning, Newton was attempting to keep science sacred and to reveal scientific rationality in what was once a purely sacral realm, namely biblical prophecy (Manuel, 1974, p. 49). By the early eighteenth century there was a significant faction within the Royal Society opposed to any mention of Scripture in a scientific context.

Decline and Survival of the "Two Books." Although the metaphor of the book of nature persisted vigorously into the nineteenth century, various movements began to weaken its cogency. The Enlightenment critiques of David Hume and Immanuel Kant undermined the project of natural theology in broad strokes, and the deist movement challenged the uniqueness of the Christian revelation. Thomas Paine asked defiantly: "Do we want to know what God is? Search not the book called the Scripture, which any human hand might make, but the Scripture, called the creation" (*The Age of Reason,* 1794).

The revolutions in geology and biology eroded longstanding traditions of a young earth and an immutable creation and wore away the bedrock beneath a coherent "book of nature" temporally coextensive with the "book of Scripture." Whereas John Mason Good argued that the Bible must be the word of God, "for it has the direct stamp and testimony of his works" (*The Book of Nature,* 1833), Charles Babbage advanced a view that seemed almost to verge on asserting the superfluity of scriptural revelation in light of the book of nature (*Ninth Bridgewater Treatise,* 1838). Parallel to the "historicization" of geology and biology, the development of a historical critical approach to study of the Scripture challenged the profoundly rooted tradition about the Bible as an integral and timeless record of the word of God.

Despite the developments outlined above, the "two books" metaphor continued to thrive during the nineteenth century among both conservative anti-Darwinians and more liberal thinkers who enthusiastically adopted the principles and discoveries of contemporary science. For the Scottish Freechurchman Hugh Miller, the "two books" became the "two theologies" (*Testimony of the Rocks,* 1857). A decade after Charles Darwin's *On the Origin of Species* (1859), Herbert Morris argued that Scripture and nature represent respectively the verbal and the pictorial representations of divine wisdom, correlating the "inspired record of creation" with contemporary science (*Science and the Bible,* 1871). Paul Chadbourne regarded nature as an unchangeable record, written in the language of the sciences of which geology comprised the most clearly comprehended volume (*Nature and the Bible from the Same Author,* 1870). The geologist Joseph Le Conte declared that "the whole object of science is to construct the theology or the divine revelation in nature." Although quite clear about the limits of science as a commentary on the book of Scripture, he held that "of these two books, nature is the elder born, and in some sense, at least, may be considered the more comprehensive and perfect" (*Religion and Science,* 1902).

The innovations in hermeneutics and science pushed the more religiously conservative wings of society in a precritical direction of maintaining verbal inerrancy and defending the ancient understanding of earth history. The metaphor of the "book of nature" gained weight as one of the cornerstones of their position, thriving in evangelical and fundamentalist-creationist circles right through the end of the twentieth century.

However, in both liberal and neo-orthodox theology the metaphor of "God's two books" entered into steady decline after 1900. Parallel to the development of historical geology and biblical criticism was the erosion of confidence that one can easily interpret natural processes teleologically, as William Paley had once argued. The discovery of extinction in the fossil record disproved the ancient assumption of the immutability of species, rendering it increasingly difficult to read the "book of nature" as self-evidently revealing the divine plan or at least as a plan worthy of admiration. Additionally the metamorphosis of "natural philosophy" or "natural history" into the variety of sciences as understood in the early twenty-first century undercut both terms in the metaphor of "God's two books." As each new scientific discipline developed its own sphere of study, the "nature" underlying the "book of nature" lost its metaphorical coherence, and the replacement of science as commentary on authoritative texts by the empirical investigation of the natural world essentially removed the "book" from the "book of nature." Finally, the gradual recognition over the nineteenth and twentieth centuries that the human community embraces a plurality of religious faiths has had the effect of relativizing the Bible as a source of revelation. The "two books" metaphor truly functions only if the claim can be defended that the Bible is the book of Scripture.

The complex metaphor of the "two books" has enjoyed a long and convoluted life cycle. For nearly two millennia the idea variously framed, constituted, negated, or otherwise reflected the relationship between the two human institutions now referred to as science and religion. It is an open question whether as a rhetorical device it can be rehabilitated in a world of historical critical interpretation of all sacred Scriptures and in which evolutionary or developmental models hold sway in scientific disciplines ranging from cosmology and geology to biology and neuroscience. But the changing fashions of metaphor cannot mask the conviction of believers that God does speak to God's creatures in pluriform ways: through religious traditions, through immediate intuition, through personal relationships, and through the revelations found in sacred writing and in nature.

BIBLIOGRAPHY

Blumenberg, Hans. *Die Lesbarkeit der Welt.* Frankfurt am Main, Germany, 1981.

Bono, James J. *The Word of God and the Languages of Man: Interpreting Nature in Early Modern Science and Medicine.* Madison, Wis., 1995.

Curtius, Ernst Robert. *European Literature and the Latin Middle Ages.* Translated by Willard R. Trask. New York, 1953.

Harrison, Peter. *The Bible, Protestantism, and the Rise of Natural Science.* Cambridge, U.K., 1998.

Howell, Kenneth J. *God's Two Books: Copernican Cosmology and Biblical Interpretation in Early Modern Science.* Notre Dame, Ind., 2002.

John Paul II, Pope. *Fides et Ratio.* Casale Monferrato, Italy, 1998.

Manuel, Frank E. *The Religion of Isaac Newton.* Oxford, 1974.

Pedersen, Olaf. *The Book of Nature.* Vatican City State, 1992.

Raymond of Sabunde. *Theologia Naturalis Seu Liber Creaturarum.* Stuttgart, Germany, 1966.

PETER M. J. HESS (2005)

TYLOR, E. B. (1832–1917) was an English anthropologist, often called "the father of British anthropology." Edward Burnett Tylor was born in London on October 2, 1832, the son of a brass-founder. Both his parents were members of the Society of Friends, and it was within the Quaker community that Tylor grew up. He entered his father's brass foundry at the age of sixteen, but a breakdown in health followed, and in 1855 he was sent to America in search of a cure. In Cuba in 1856 he met the noted archaeologist Henry Christy, who was also a Quaker, and they traveled together for some time. Out of this visit came Tylor's first book, *Anahuac, or Mexico and the Mexicans, Ancient and Modern* (1861), written and published before he was thirty. He had no university education of any kind, but he was a gifted writer and a tireless researcher in the emergent anthropological field. The two books for which he is chiefly remembered were written in his thirties: *Researches into the Early History of Mankind* (1865) and the even better known work *Primitive Culture* (2 vols., 1871). Although he wrote many more articles and reviews, he was to publish only one more book, the popular handbook *Anthropology* (1881). Gradually he gained academic recognition. He received an honorary doctorate from the University of Oxford in 1875. In 1883 he became keeper of the Oxford University Museum, and in 1884 reader in anthropology. From 1896 to his retirement in 1909 he was professor of anthropology, the first in Britain. He was knighted in 1912 and died on January 3, 1917.

During the years of Tylor's greatest activity, the question of the origin and evolution of religion was high on the agenda of social scientists, the dominant theorists being F. Max Müller on one level and Herbert Spencer on the other; Müller worked exclusively with language, while Spencer proceeded by way of vast generalizations learned in large measure from Auguste Comte. Tylor was no less interested than Müller in language, but he began at an earlier point in its evolution, far beyond "Aryan" roots and their meanings. To reach this point it was necessary for Tylor to formulate a comprehensive theory to bridge the gap between the present and the remote past. This was the theory of "survivals"—elements of culture or society that evolution has left behind. Gesture probably preceded language, though Tylor was too cautious to claim gesture to have been a separate stage in human communication. In matters concerning religion, he believed himself to be on firmer ground.

It was in 1866, in an article in the *Fortnightly Review* titled "The Religion of Savages," that he first introduced his idea of "animism," "the belief in Spiritual Beings," as the earliest form of known religion—and of course accessible only through the study of survivals and by placing a particular interpretation on the difficult matter of "savage" mental processes. His theory was given a definitive statement in *Primitive Culture,* and the word *animism* is still widely used today, though more in a descriptive than in an evolutionary sense.

Otherwise, Tylor's approach to early forms of human religion has often been criticized as being too intellectual and too moral. According to one of his disciples, R. R. Marett, he was "a little blind to the spontaneity of the process whereby Man becomes at once religious and moral, without taking conscious thought to it, until he is fairly involved in an incoherent striving that is neither because it is both together" (Marett, 1936, p. 168). Looking into the past for a certain type of moralized religion, and failing to find it beyond a certain point, Tylor missed much of importance. He had no feeling for the ecstatic side of religion, perhaps partly because of his intense dislike of nineteenth-century spiritualism. Also he cannot be exonerated from having overlooked or deliberately ignored all the evidence later produced by Andrew Lang in support of "high gods of low races," gods who were neither ghosts nor spirits. "Spirit" was perhaps the only category open to a pioneer such as Tylor, but when linked with "belief" (as it was in his celebrated "minimum definition" of religion), it had the effect of relegating much else to a subordinate place in the structure of religion and culture.

In the running debate between evolutionism and diffusionism it is generally supposed that Tylor was wholeheartedly on the side of the unilinear evolutionists. But he was prepared to consider diffusionism on its merits, and to stop only when the evidence would carry his argument no further. In his early years he was indeed something of a diffusionist, even to the extent of speculating that the Aztec god Quetzalcoatl was not only a man but may even have been an Irishman! Later his habitual caution prevented any further such flights of fancy, and on the whole he sided with the evolutionists, while stopping short of absolute dogmatism.

It was characteristic of Tylor's immediate disciples that sooner or later they were forced to part company with his findings in the form in which he stated them. The ubiquitous and enigmatic Andrew Lang broke away on the issue of "high gods," the urbane R. R. Marett on the matter of "preanimism" and later on questions concerning performative ritual. But these scholars and others retained a deep affection for their mentor. Marett wrote that throughout his career Tylor appears as "the most ingenuous of men, open-minded because he is simple-minded, the friend of all mankind because he would be incapable of feeling otherwise; and withal hardheaded, of business antecedents, not easily fooled, pedestrian enough to prefer solid ground under his feet" (ibid., p. 214). In short, though often unacknowledged, he laid foundations on which the study of primal religion has built for more than a century.

See Also Animism and Animatism; Manism.

Bibliography

For discussions of Tylor's contribution to the science of religion, see R. R. Marett's *Tylor* (London, 1936); Richard M. Dorson's *The British Folklorists: A History* (Chicago, 1968), pp. 187–197; J. W. Burrow's *Evolution and Society: A Study in Victorian Social Theory* (Cambridge, 1970), pp. 228–259; and Eric J. Sharpe's *Comparative Religion: A History* (London, 1975), pp. 53–58.

New Sources

Segal, Robert A. "Tylor's Anthropomorphic Theory of Religion." *Religion* 25 (January 1995): 23–30.

Tylor, Edward Burnett. *The Collected Works of Edward Burnett Tylor.* London, 1994.

Eric J. Sharpe (1987)
Revised Bibliography

TYNDALE, WILLIAM (1494?–1536), Bible translator and Reformation scholar. William Tyndale came from a well-established family in Gloucestershire in the west of England. After an excellent education at a local Grammar School, he was for ten years at the University of Oxford. In 1516 Tyndale's life took a decisive turn when the New Testament was for the first time printed in Greek, its original language, in an edition made by Desiderius Erasmus in Basle, Switzerland. Along with scholars throughout Europe, and particularly Martin Luther in Germany, Tyndale recognized the importance of a readily available Greek New Testament, and the need for a printed translation which could reach English readers and hearers at any level.

After spending perhaps a year in Cambridge (where Erasmus had been teaching Greek), Tyndale returned to Gloucestershire to begin work on an English New Testament. Such an enterprise was forbidden by the Church, for whom any vernacular deviation from the Latin translation (made in the fourth century) was heresy. This censorship was at its most severe in England, where it was rigidly applied: in the 1380s, alarmed by the spread of handwritten Bible translations made from the Latin into English under the influence of John Wyclif, the English Church had punished many "Lollards," as Wyclif's followers were nicknamed, often by burning them alive. Tyndale needed the permission of a Bishop, and sought it from Erasmus's friend Cuthbert Tunstall, Bishop of London. He was snubbed.

With money from courageous London merchants, Tyndale went to Germany, and in Cologne began printing his English translation. He had reached Matthew's Gospel chapter 22 when the print shop was raided. Tyndale and his helper fled up the Rhine to the safe Lutheran city of Worms. There in 1526 he produced 6,000 copies of his first English New Testament, pocket-size like all his works. Smuggled down the Rhine and eagerly received in England and Scotland, copies were ruthlessly hunted and destroyed: Tunstall supervised their burning at St Paul's. Only three copies now survive, one on permanent display in the British Library.

In Germany, Tyndale learned Hebrew (unknown in England) and in 1530 printed in Antwerp his translation of the "First Five Books of Moses"—the first time that Hebrew had been translated into English. Finding that knowledge of Hebrew deepened his understanding of the Greek biblical text, Tyndale produced a revision of his New Testament, printed in Antwerp in 1534. He worked in Antwerp also on the second quarter of the Old Testament, the Historical books Joshua to 2 Chronicles.

Tyndale's 1534 New Testament, and half of the Old Testament, were reproduced largely unchanged in successive English Bibles throughout the rest of the century, culminating in the influential version made in the name of King James in 1611: five-sixths of that New Testament, and only slightly less of the Old Testament, were there taken over directly from Tyndale, without acknowledgement.

Tyndale's greatness lay in his accurate translation of the original Greek and Hebrew; his clarity of expression; and in his choice of a linguistic register just a little above ordinary speech. He gave English speakers very many phrases still in use, such as "Let there be light." His Plain Style, a Saxon vocabulary in a neutral word order, through his wide Bible readership established English as a good written language that anybody could use. Much of the remarkable development of literature in the hundred years after him came out of his work: it is not fanciful to remark "Without Tyndale, no Shakespeare."

His New Testament affected the nation. A neat definition of the Reformation is "people reading Paul." The Epistle to the Romans in particular, the bedrock of New Testament theology, and read or heard—as Tyndale famously intended—even by "the ploughboy," showed the believer's direct access to God through faith. Moreover, in the newly available Bible a large number of the Church's practices and dogmas were not found: confession to the ear, the celibacy of the priesthood, Purgatory, and so on.

Tyndale wrote other important books. *The Parable of the Wicked Mammon* (1528) demonstrates the New Testament emphasis on faith rather than works. His *The Obedience of a Christian Man* (1528) countered the lie put about by his enemies that the reformers preached sedition.

Tyndale had a price on his head as a heretic. Commissioned to do so, Thomas More attacked him at length. In Antwerp, Tyndale was tricked into arrest; he was imprisoned near Brussels for sixteen months, and in October 1536 taken out, strangled, and burned. His heresy was the making of the English Bible: his influence, long ignored, was very large.

SEE ALSO Wyclif, John.

BIBLIOGRAPHY

Daniell, David. *William Tyndale: A Biography.* New Haven, Conn., and London, 1994.

Tyndale's New Testament. Introduction by David Daniell. New Haven, Conn., and London, 1989. A modern-spelling edition.

Tyndale's Old Testament. Introduction by David Daniell. New Haven, Conn., and London, 1992. A modern-spelling edition.

DAVID DANIELL (2005)

TÝR ("God") is a Scandinavian deity associated with law and war. Although his name reflects the Indo-European words for "god" and "day" (IE, **deywos* >; PGmc., **Tíwaz;* cf. Sansk. *dyaus*, Gk. *Zeus*, and Lat. *deus*), Týr no longer represents the transcendence and majestic glory of the luminous sky. He must have played a more important role at some stage, for his name can simply mean "god," both originally and in Viking times. His sovereign powers also meant that Norse court poets could substitute his name for that of Óðinn when it was combined with an object or characteristic associated with Óðinn: Victory-Týr, Týr of the Hanged, and Týr of Ships' Cargoes all designate Óðinn. More mysterious is the occurrence of *Týr* as the name of a young boy in the Eddic poem *Hymiskviða*; this figure may not have any relationship to the god.

By the time of the first written sources, Týr was not a supreme being, a creator of the world, or a heavenly father, but he still had an honorable position among the leading Æsir, the primary group of Norse gods. According to Snorri Sturluson, Týr is the boldest and most courageous of the gods and is invoked by warriors because he can grant victory. He possesses extensive knowledge, whence the Old Norse expression *týspákr* (as wise as Týr). Yet few other details are given: the identity of his father is uncertain, he does not appear to be married, and the only myth in which he plays a significant role is the story of the fettering of the wolf Fenrir.

The gods had been warned that the monstrous offspring of Loki and the giantess Angrboða—Fenrir, the witch Hel, and the serpent Miðgarðsormr—would cause them great harm. Óðinn cast Hel into the cold, dark world of Niflheimr and dispatched the Miðgarðsormr to the rim of the cosmic ocean, but the wolf was still in the custody of the Æsir. As the whelp grew up, only Týr dared to feed him, and the gods thought it time to chain him. They tried twice, but the wolf easily broke loose. The Æsir got the dark elves to manufacture an unbreakable fetter. From the rustle of a moving cat, the beard of a woman, the roots of a cliff, the breath of a fish, the sinews of a bear, and the spittle of a bird, the elves made a band as soft as silk yet able to withstand any force. The gods took Fenrir to a remote island, where they challenged him to free himself again. Having prided himself on snapping the other bonds, he did not deign to pit himself against something so fragile-looking. When the gods insisted, he became suspicious and only consented to be bound with the ribbon if one of them placed a hand in his mouth as a pledge of good faith. All were reluctant to do this except Týr, who lost his hand when the wolf found himself bound fast. The gods chained Fenrir to a huge boulder and gagged him with a sword, where he remained until the Æsir's final battle against the giants and monsters at Ragnarǫk. Each god had his own special opponent in that conflict, and Týr was killed by Garmr, the monstrous dog that guarded the entrance to Hel's realm.

Týr's action is an example of heroic abnegation, and Georges Dumézil (1974; 1985, pp. 268–274) has noted the parallel between Týr and Mucius Scaevola, who sacrificed his right hand to convince Lars Porsena, the Etruscan leader threatening Rome, that he and three hundred young men were ready to give up their lives to kill him. Porsena then signed a peace treaty that saved Rome from destruction. There are also parallels with non-Germanic gods: the Irish god Nuadu and the Indian god Súrya are one-armed as well. Týr the one-handed seems to be juxtaposed with the spell-working, one-eyed Óðinn, just as Nuadu with his one hand stood beside Lug with his magic and his closed eye.

Týr's sacrifice has been correlated with his function as god of law (De Vries, 1967, pp. 13–14, 22–24; Dumézil, 1973, p. 45), mainly on the basis of his association with the Germanic *thing* (the assembly of the warriors), where priests, perhaps of Tíwaz, kept the peace (cf. Tacitus, *Germania* 11), and the Germanic concept of war as a *vápnadómr* (judgment by arms) with set rules. The *interpretatio Romana* of Germanic Tíwaz as Mars (cf. the translation of Lat. *dies Martis* as OE. *Tiwesdæg*, Eng. *Tuesday*) can thus be correlated with Dumézil's view of Týr as the Germanic representative of the juridical aspect of sovereignty (Dumézil, 1977, pp. 196–200; Dumézil, 1985, pp. 265–272; Polomé, 1984, pp. 402–405). Dumézil, however, sees Týr's action not as heroic but as the embodiment of fraudulence, because it involves deliberate perjury—the gods had promised Fenrir that they would release him if he could not break the band. Most scholars view the deceit as ethically acceptable because it neutralizes an uncontrollable danger threatening the community of the Æsir. Clunies Ross (1994, p. 221) points out that both the wolf and Týr show courage, and both suffer. She interprets this myth as illustrating the interrelatedness of the worlds of gods and giants: giant nature does not lie in a world different from that of the gods, but instead lies inside it.

Evidence for the worship of Týr is scanty outside of Denmark, where place-names such as Tislund (Týr's grove) attest to his widespread veneration. Týr is commemorated in only two place-names in Norway (Tysnes, "Týr's peninsula"; Tysnesø, "Tysnes island" or "The island near Tyr's peninsula"); here the cult appears to have been adopted from Denmark. Týr's name has also been seen in some of the place-names of southern England, and Old English writers occasionally glossed the Latin *Mars* by *Tiw* or *Tig*. There are no Swedish place-names associated with Týr. Most likely, the importance of his cult elsewhere in the Germanic region diminished over time. He is also associated with the t-rune, which was called the "victory rune." Warriors engraved it on their sword hilts and guards, thereby invoking Týr twice.

SEE ALSO Dumézil, Georges; Eddas; Germanic Religion, overview article; Óðinn; Runes.

BIBLIOGRAPHY

Clunies Ross, Margaret. *Prolonged Echoes: Old Norse Myths in Medieval Northern Society*, vol. 1: *The Myths*. Odense, Denmark, 1994.

De Vries, Jan. *Altgermanische Religionsgeschichte*, vol. 2. 2d rev. ed. Berlin, 1967.

Dumézil, Georges. *Gods of the Ancient Northmen*. Berkeley, Calif., 1973.

Dumézil, Georges. "'Le Borgne' and 'Le Manchot.'" In *Myth in Indo-European Antiquity*, edited by Gerald James Larson, pp. 18–20. Berkeley, Calif., 1974.

Dumézil, Georges. *Les dieux souverains des Indo-Européens*. Paris, 1977.

Dumézil, Georges. *L'oubli de l'homme et l'honneur des dieux*. Paris, 1985.

Polomé, Edgar C. "The Indo-European Component in Germanic Religion." In *Myth and Law Among the Indo-Europeans*, edited by Jaan Puhvel, pp. 55–82. Berkeley, Calif., 1970.

Polomé, Edgar C. "The Indo-European Heritage in Germanic Religon: The Sovereign Gods." In *Athlon: Satura Grammatica in honorem Francisci R. Adrados*, edited by Alberto Bernabé et al., vol. 1, pp. 401–411. Madrid, 1984.

ELIZABETH ASHMAN ROWE (2005)

TYRRELL, GEORGE (1861–1909), leading Roman Catholic theologian of the so-called modernist movement. Adversity and agitation marked Tyrrell's life from the beginning. Born in Dublin on February 6, 1861, two months after his father had died, Tyrrell was raised in penury and vagabondage by his devoted mother and schooled in gospel kindness by Charles W. Benson of Rathmines School, but was swayed oppositely by the acerbity and agnosticism of his elder brother William.

William's untimely death sent Tyrrell on a search for stable footing in the externals of religion. Experimentation with Anglicanism and Roman Catholicism led to friendship with Robert Dolling, the later famous "Father Dolling," who served briefly as Tyrrell's mentor and spiritual director, first securing his matriculation at Trinity College (1878), then inviting him to London to see sane Anglo-Catholicism at work, hoping thereby to prevent his anticipated conversion to Roman Catholicism. Dolling's strategy failed. On May 18, 1879, Tyrrell was received into the Catholic church and a year later into the Jesuit order as well.

Although Tyrrell felt confirmed in those momentous decisions, he was unprepared to conform to the rigid ultramontanism and rationalist neoscholasticism of the post–Vatican I church and to the mechanistic spirituality of the "restored" Society of Jesus. Two of Tyrrell's seminary professors suggested more congenial paths. Thomas Rigby encouraged him to bypass the scholastics and to read Thomas Aquinas for himself, while Joseph Rickaby was no doubt the one who gave him John Henry Newman's *Grammar of Assent* in 1885 and thus occasioned "a profound revolution in my way of thinking." From Thomas, Tyrrell learned the principle of modernization, or *aggiornamento;* from Newman, he derived an experience-based psychology of religion and an inductive, historical method, as opposed to the *a priori*, deductive method of scholasticism.

In 1894 Tyrrell was appointed to the chair of ethics at the Jesuit school of philosophy at Stonyhurst, but two years later, no longer tolerable to the established faculty, he was removed to London and the staff of the Jesuit religious periodical, the *Month*. Thus began a writing career that would propel him into ever-widening circles of liberals, modernists, and modernist sympathizers (among them Wilfrid Ward, Friedrich von Hügel, Maude Petre, and Henri Bremond) and lead him to the thought of a host of nonscholastic scholars (Bergson, Blondel, Dilthey, Harnack, Loisy, Sabatier, Schweitzer, Troeltsch, and Weiss).

Tyrrell's work anticipated Vatican II's effort to bring church polity and doctrine into constructive dialogue with the best and most enduring elements of post-Enlightenment thought. Initially Tyrrell allied himself with Ward's mediating tactic of palliating ascendant policies with liberal doses of Newmanism, but as he encountered historical and biblical criticism, he concluded that Newmanism could not be made to answer questions it had never asked. In *Christianity at the Cross-Roads* (1909) Tyrrell sought to establish Newman's assumed identity between the "idea" of Christ and Christianity and the "idea" of Roman Catholicism by showing that the categories of apocalyptic and eschatology had carried the "idea" of Christianity unadulterated from epoch to epoch.

He also went beyond Newman in criticizing not only the doctrinal expression of faith but the act of faith itself.

On February 19, 1906, Tyrrell was dismissed from the Society of Jesus for refusing to retract a published excerpt from his *Letter to a University Professor* (1903). The following year, on October 22, 1907, he was excommunicated for publicly criticizing Pius X's encyclical *Pascendi dominici gregis,* which condemned modernism. Tyrrell died on July 15, 1909, a victim of Bright's disease, and was buried in the Anglican churchyard in Storrington, Sussex.

BIBLIOGRAPHY

Tyrrell's early apologetic essays are collected in *The Faith of the Millions,* 2 vols. (New York, 1901), while his later essays on the revelation-dogma-history issue are given in *Through Scylla and Charybdis* (London, 1907). His most substantive monographs are *Lex Orandi, or Prayer and Creed* (New York, 1903), on psychology of religion; *The Church and the Future* (1903; reprint, London, 1910), originally published under the pseudonym Hilaire Bourdon, an apologetic for Roman Catholicism; and *Christianity at the Cross-Roads* (London, 1910), an attempt to incorporate the implications of eschatology and apocalypticism. M. D. Petre's *Autobiography and Life of George Tyrrell,* 2 vols. (London, 1912), of which Tyrrell wrote volume 1, is an indispensable, if biased, account. My own book, *George Tyrrell: In Search of Catholicism* (Shepherdstown, W.Va., 1981), with extensive notes and bibliography, provides the fullest introduction to Tyrrell's thought.

DAVID G. SCHULTENOVER (1987)

TZU CHI SEE CIJI

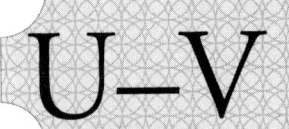

U–V

UCHIMURA KANZŌ (1861–1930), Japanese essayist, scholar of the Bible, and Christian leader. Uchimura's unique place in modern Japanese thought results from his insistence on human independence before the biblical Christian God. Four prophetic acts by Uchimura dramatize and represent themes in his writing. In two of these acts Uchimura questioned the growing authoritarianism of the government. His scrupulous hesitation in 1891 to bow before the signature of the emperor and his outspoken avowal of pacifism in 1903, immediately before the onset of the Russo-Japanese War, raised the issue of Christian loyalty to the state. He also proclaimed the imminent return of Christ in 1918 and appeared to renounce in a posthumously published document the Christian movement associated with his name.

These acts resulted from a heightened sense of individual worth and responsibility apparent in Uchimura's personal history. His father, a capable samurai civil servant, lost his status, position, and self-respect with the political changes that followed the revolution of 1867–1868. He turned the leadership of the family over to his sixteen-year-old son after the boy received a government scholarship large enough to support the whole family. Uchimura studied at a government agricultural college, where, under the influence of evangelical American Calvinist teachers, he became a Christian.

After graduation in 1881, dissatisfaction with government service as a fisheries scientist and a disastrous marriage drove him to the United States. There he found sympathetic mentors at Amherst College and obtained a second bachelor's degree in 1887. Back in Japan, Uchimura administered a school manned largely by American missionaries. Disagreement over evangelical methods—he wanted to cite Japanese examples of the upright life before he taught Christianity—led Uchimura to resign and forsake cooperation with missionaries. His hesitation before the imperial signature while a teacher in a government school cost him the possibility of further official employment. As a result, he determined to live by writing. After several lean years, he became the editor of a newspaper that he was to make into Japan's largest daily, but his declaration of pacifism cost him that posi-

---

Clockwise from top left corner. A deceased man sails through the underworld in a painting on papyrus from the ancient Egyptian *Book of the Dead.* Kunsthistorisches Museum, Vienna. *[©Erich Lessing/Art Resource, N.Y.]*; Venus of Milo, c. 130–120 BCE. Louvre, Paris. *[©Erich Lessing/Art Resource, N.Y.]*; Sixth-century Guatemalan funerary mask. Museo Nacional de Arqueologia, Guatemala City. *[©Erich Lessing/Art Resource, N.Y.]*; Cham Temple in My Son, Vietnam. *[©Luca I. Tettoni/Corbis]*; Detail from a fourth-century BCE Etruscan vase depicting Athena with her owl in flight and Poseidon holding the trident. Louvre, Paris. *[©Réunion des Musées Nationaux/Art Resource, N.Y.]* .

tion. He had already started in 1900 a monthly called *Seisho no kenkyū* (Biblical Studies). This publication fulfilled a long-standing ambition to write popular Bible commentaries and provided him with a livelihood until his death. Through his magazine, numerous individuals came to look upon Uchimura as their spiritual mentor. His many large lecture meetings after he joined the Second-Coming Movement in 1917 returned him to the center of national attention. The meetings developed into two-hour commentaries on the Bible for weekly audiences of five to seven hundred. He continued his magazine and lectures until death stilled his voice.

All of Uchimura's writings reflect a concern for a Japan suddenly introduced into the modern world. At the time, "the modern world" signified the European and North American nations, whose people believed in a hierarchy of states with those of the Christian culture ranked highest. Uchimura, through his English-language works, interpreted Japanese concerns to Westerners, emphasizing the rectitude of traditional Japanese virtues. His early Japanese-language works commented on contemporary Japanese society. His later writings introduced the Bible and the fruits of Christian culture to Japan. These essays were frequently based upon the notes he had written for his weekly lectures. The commentaries on the Bible form a major part of these writings and constitute the largest corpus of biblical studies by one author in the Japanese language.

The concept associated with Uchimura's name is *mukyōkai* or *mukyōkai shugi,* usually translated as "no church," "nonchurch," or, in Uchimura's translation, "Christianity of no-church principle." It proclaims a faith linking humans to God through prayerful use of the Bible alone. The church as it existed in the Christian nations seemed to Uchimura so burdened with the associations of Western history and tradition as to lack meaning for Japanese. On the other hand, Japanese, through faithful reading of the Bible, could develop a Christianity true to their needs and consistent with their traditions. Uchimura's denial in an article published after his death of "what is today commonly called *mukyōkai*" did not reflect any change in his belief. Instead, it expressed his dismay at the incipient development among his followers of a church based on their interpretation of *mukyōkai shugi.*

Uchimura's followers, most concerned that they must not start a church, continue in small Bible-study groups known collectively as *mukyōkai.* They have no other organizational ties than their respect for the Bible and the works of Uchimura. Adherents include a number of figures important in the shaping of Japanese institutions after 1945: Tanaka Kōtarō, Yanaihara Tadao, Nambara Shigeru, Takagi Yasaka, and Matsumoto Shigeharu.

BIBLIOGRAPHY

The definitive *Uchimura Kanzō zenshū,* 20 vols. (1932–1933; reprint, Tokyo, 1961–1966) has been replaced by another work of the same name in 38 vols. (Tokyo, 1981–1984). The latter version will include some more articles and many more letters. The best biography is by Masaike Megumu, *Uchimura Kanzō den* (1950; Tokyo, 1977). In English, *Culture and Religion in Japanese-American Relations: Essays on Uchimura Kanzō, 1861–1930,* edited by Raymond A. Moore, Michigan Papers in Japanese Studies, no. 5 (Ann Arbor, 1981); and my article "Uchimura Kanzō," in *Pacifism in Japan: The Christian and Socialist Tradition,* edited by Nobuya Bamba and me (Kyoto, 1978), discuss aspects of Uchimura's legacy. I have written a complete critical biography, which is ready for publication.

JOHN F. HOWES (1987)

UFO RELIGIONS. The rise of interest in unidentified flying objects (UFOs) has been amply demonstrated over the last few decades. It is not surprising that in an age of scientific discoveries, especially in the field of astronomy, the search for extraterrestrial life is a legitimate and respectable enterprise. But the quest for alien life on planets both within and outside our galaxy appears to have gone beyond the usual pursuit of scientific data supported by empirical evidence. It has also surpassed the quest for adventure beyond the confines of planet Earth. Many people do not just speculate about the possibility of alien life elsewhere but claim to have actually encountered or been visited by aliens. The search for UFOs has become the center of a belief system with most, if not all, of the features that are usually linked with religion. The phrase *UFO Religions* can thus be applied to those organizations that exhibit many of the various dimensions that have been routinely applied to other, more established, religious organizations.

While the precise definition of *religion* is still a matter of debate among scholars, there seems to be some agreement about those key features or characteristics that are central to any religious system. Among these are a communally shared belief system or worldview in which a sacred or transcendent reality figures prominently; a belief that the human race needs some kind of salvation or redemption from its present condition; an ethical system; experiences such as devotion, ecstasy, rebirth, and inner peace; central myths or stories, especially those dealing with the creation and future of humankind; and rituals. Many of these features are also found in UFO religious groups, though not all have been accorded the central place given them in most of the world's religions. Several UFO groups are noted for forming well-knit communities with a mission to propagate the teachings of their faith. Others stress individual spiritual development and/or healing. Still others, while having some of the main features of religion, are mail-order organizations and thus lack the communal and ritual aspects typical of some UFO religions.

HISTORY. The rise of the modern UFO religions can be traced to Kenneth Arnold who, in the mid-1940s, reported to have seen several flying saucers. Sightings by other individuals followed, and soon people were relating their experiences of meeting and communicating with aliens from other planets.

George Adamski (1891–1965) was the first contactee of the modern era. Believing that he had been visited by a being from the planet Venus on November 20, 1952, Adamski saw himself as the chosen person with the mission of communicating important messages from the aliens to human beings. Adamski never founded a religious organization as such, but he attracted a following interested in the wisdom and knowledge that the aliens had to offer to the human race. This led to the foundation of the International Get Acquainted Club. Several organizations to disseminate his teachings were later founded by his followers. The largest is the George Adamski Foundation, which has since 1965 continued to circulate his works and to promote his view that contacts with aliens have been made throughout the ages and that advancement in various sciences has been achieved through such contacts.

The George Adamski Foundation became the spearhead of the religiously oriented UFO groups that have emerged since the 1950s. The leaders of these groups reported contact with aliens, mainly from various planets in our solar system, and at times maintained that they had traveled to other planets, where they were shown advanced civilizations that made human cultures look rather primitive. Some of these leaders were charismatic and/or prophetic and succeeded in gathering a clientele around them, eventually forming cult movements, "which are full-fledged organizations that attempt to satisfy all the religious needs of the converts" (Stark and Bainbridge, 1985, p. 29). They became an elite group of individuals who were accepted as contactees with extraterrestrial intelligences who delivered their messages and teachings through their chosen mediums or prophets.

Some UFO groups, such as the Aetherius Society, Unarius Academy of Life, and the Association for Sananda and Sanat Kumara, with the passing away of their leaders in the 1990s, are now becoming institutionalized and have continued to survive and carry on their agenda without the presence of a contactee.

Some scholars have pointed out that there is a connection between UFO beliefs and the Theosophical Society and the I AM Religious Activity, though these latter groups cannot, strictly speaking, be called UFO religions if for no other reason than that the existence of, and communication with, aliens is not one of their central characteristics. Yet many of the aliens are similar and at times identical to the masters of the Theosophical Movement. The teachings of quite a few UFO religions have incorporated Eastern religious notions, such as karma and reincarnation, that were already made popular by theosophy. The Association of Sananda and Sanat Kumara is an excellent example of the link between theosophy and extraterrestrials. The late Sister Thedra, the founder of this organization, channeled for years the ascended masters, while later on she also communicated with the angel Moroni (prominent in Mormonism), with beings from other planets, and with Sananda (Christ). In the same way, George King, the founder of the Aetherius Society, maintained contact with aliens, many of which are identical to the ascended masters, which include founders of world religions such as Jesus and the Buddha.

General Worldview and Aims. The worldview adopted by UFO groups is much broader than that proposed by traditional religions. It indirectly includes modern astronomical discoveries and takes for granted the existence of intelligent creatures on other planets in the vast cosmos. These beings are superior to the human race intellectually, scientifically, and spiritually. In spite of this expansive view of the universe, the main concern is still planet Earth, which is conceived as a somewhat backward planet where men and women need outside help to advance in the course of evolution.

While UFO religions offer little, if any, speculation about the origin of the universe, they often have elaborate theories of the origins of the human race and its condition here on Earth. Raëlians, for instance, hold that human life on Earth was created by beings from another planet through their knowledge of DNA and its use. A similar view had already been popularized in Erich von Daniken's book *Chariots of the Gods* (1969) and has become part of UFO mythology.

Central to any UFO religion is the belief that contact with aliens is the way to salvation and improvement. The teachings of Adamski describe the aliens as "beings of amity, intelligence, understanding and compassion," while the Semjase Silver Star Center in California points out that they come with a mission to assist the human race out of its present ignorance. Some groups, especially those that originated in the 1950s such as the Aetherius Society, White Star, the Ashtar Command, and Cosmic Star Fellowship, stress the need to be saved from the dangers of the atomic (or nuclear) age that can lead humans to self-destruction. Others, such as the Solar Light Retreat, expect aliens to help solve the energy and environmental crisis. Spiritual development, a higher consciousness, healing from spiritual, psychological, and physical maladies, emancipation from the fear and chaos that beset human beings, and evolution to higher spiritual and self-awareness levels are among the benefits that many UFO groups hope to accrue with the advent of intelligent and advanced beings from other planets. In some UFO groups, such as the Aetherius Society and Unarius, healing is one of the main ritual practices. In others, such as the Extraterrestrial Earth Mission and Mark-Age, the stress is on achieving a higher consciousness or a more advanced evolutionary stage.

The belief system of UFO religions is often considered as part of the New Age movement and tends to be syncretistic. Thus, Chen Tao (God's Salvation Church), which in 1997 migrated from Taiwan to North America, is a prime example of such amalgamation, with Buddhist, Daoist, and folk beliefs intertwined and later combined with a Christian apocalyptic and millenarian worldview.

One of the common features of UFO religions is that their founders are convinced that they have been contacted by aliens. Adamski related how he had been visited by a humanlike being from Venus who imparted certain knowledge that he was instructed to pass on to humankind. He also could communicate with the aliens by telepathy. Other contactees who followed him made the same claim. George Hunt Williamson of the now defunct Brotherhood of the Seven Rays had contact with Martians via automatic writing. William Ferguson of the Cosmic Circle of Fellowship was transported to both Mars and Venus, where he was given messages to bring back to Earth. George King, of the Aetherius Society, received messages from aliens either while in a trance or by telepathy. The founders of Unarius, Ernest and Ruth Norman (known as Archangels Raphael and Uriel respectively), authored books containing teaching received from advanced intelligent beings living in other worlds. Nada-Yolanda (Pauline Share) of Mark-Age, Inc., uses both automatic writing and telepathy to convey messages from beings in spacecrafts. In like manner Valerie Donner of the Ground Crew uses channeling as a means of communication with extraterrestrial beings. Claude Vorilhon (now known as Raël) of the Raëlian Movement met several times with an alien who entrusted him with the good news of the true origins of human beings and of the return of the Elohim. The two leaders of the Extraterrestrial Earth Mission (known since 1993 as Drakar and Zrendar) go a step further and proclaim that different aliens have periodically taken possession of their bodies, presumably enabling them to communicate more freely and regularly to human beings.

As in the classical monotheistic religions, where God takes the initiative to call prophets, it is the aliens who approach specially selected individuals and commission them to act as messengers to the human race. The aliens, though not elevated to the status of gods or goddesses, are obviously transcendent and suprahuman beings even in those UFO religions like the Raëlian movement in which belief in God or supernatural beings is not found or does not occupy an important place.

Besides an elaborate soteriology, UFO groups also teach an eschatology, the chief element of which is the actual arrival of the aliens, an advent that, as Solar Light Retreat teaches, will initiate a new heaven and a new earth. The Ground Crew maintains that at least one angel will accompany each spaceship and that Earth will be transformed into a paradise.

The advent of aliens can be apocalyptic and/or millenarian. In most instances the time of the extraterrestrials' arrival is not specified but is expected to be relatively soon. Probably the most recent attempt to pinpoint the time of arrival was made by Chen Tao in Garland, Texas. In typical prophetic fashion, its leader, Hon-Ming Chen, said that God would announce his descent by taking control of the television networks on March 25, 1998. In similar fashion Unarius Academy of Science has foretold the advent of the aliens in their flying saucers. As in many prophetic instances, the failure of the prophecy to materialize has not led to the demise of the group.

Another UFO religion, Mark-Age, believed that the arrival of the aliens would be around the year 2000 and stated that its mission was to externalize on Earth the Hierarchical Board, namely, the spiritual government of our solar system, in preparation for the advent of the aliens. Borrowing the concept of the second coming from Christianity, it teaches that this Christian belief has a dual meaning, namely (1) the second coming of each one's I Am Self, expressed through the mortal personality; and (2) the second coming of Sananda/Jesus the Christ, Prince of Earth, in his resurrected, light body.

Other groups are more cautious. The Aetherius Society expects a new master, presumably to precede the advent of the aliens, but does not give a specific date. While many members believe that it will be soon, the society states that he will come when human beings are ready for his arrival. Raëlians think the extraterrestrials will arrive around the year 2020. But before they arrive, human beings must first have established world peace and built an embassy for them in or near Jerusalem.

SIGNIFICANT FIGURES AND ORGANIZATIONS. While many people believe in UFOs, the number of UFO religious organizations and of those who have joined their ranks is rather small. J. Gordon Melton (2003) lists twenty-three flying saucer groups, while Mikael Rothstein (2002) estimates that they are twenty-five different groups active today, but he does not list them. Melton's list, only slightly updated from the previous edition of his encyclopedia, omits such groups as Heaven's Gate, Chen Tao, the Nuwaubians, and the Ground Crew and its splinter group the Planetary Action Organization (PAO). It still remains, however, the most complete and provides short descriptions of the origins and belief systems of each group.

Melton's list also indirectly points to the some of the difficulties involved in studying these groups. Thus, Melton states that two of the groups he lists are defunct. He could not trace the addresses of eight groups and found that six provide only a post office box address. Nine of the groups mentioned have a web page, as have the more recent ones. The vast majority do not report the number of members of the organization. The membership of most groups may be somewhat fluid and probably consists of a few hundreds or thousands at most. At least two, the Ground Crew and ZetaTalk (the latter led by Nancy Lieder), exist only on the internet. By far the largest UFO group is probably the Raëlian movement, which boasts sixty thousand members in almost a hundred countries. Unarius Academy of Science states that tens of thousands of individuals have participated in its programs. It is not clear how each organization counts its membership. The Aetherius Society lists three levels of membership, full, associate, and friends, the last including interested individuals and scholars, but it provides no figures.

Not all UFO groups prefer to be called a religion. The Aetherius Society's web page states explicitly: "This is not a religion. . . . It's a spiritual path to enlightenment and the cosmic evolution of mankind." Unarius Academy of Science tends to view itself as a philosophy of life, while the Nuwaubians prefer to call themselves a fraternal organization. One group in particular, the Raëlian movement, is highly critical of established religion, particularly Christianity. It describes itself as an "atheist, spiritual organization" and states that one of its goals is to lead human beings to understand true religion. Its founder, Raël, starts by reinterpreting the biblical concept of Elohim, which, he asserts, refers not to God but to beings from another planet who created life on Earth.

CONTROVERSIES. Until recently, UFO religions have not been controversial. They rather left the impression of being innocuous, eccentric groups. In 1997, however, the members of Heaven's Gate took the initiative to transport themselves to a spacecraft by committing suicide in order to move into a higher state of being. This was perceived by many as a warning sign that UFO religions might be dangerous. Chen Tao's claim that God would speak over the television networks and then come down in flying saucers to save people created quite a stir and raised the fear that its members might follow in the path of those of Heaven's Gate. Such fear proved unfounded, and when the prophecy failed, many members abandoned the group, though some have remained loyal to Hon-Ming Chen's teachings and prophetic utterances.

The view that UFO religious are dangerous has been buttressed by the fact that several UFO groups, including the Raëlian movement, the Ground Crew, Unarius, and the Nuwaubians, share the apocalyptic view that the arrival of extraterrestrials is imminent. In fact, however, most UFO religions are benign and pose no threat to their members or to the public. Their predictions, no matter how far-fetched they might appear to be, are not of doom and disaster but of the betterment of the human race on Earth.

In late 2002 and in early 2003 the Raëlian movement made headlines by announcing that its scientists had succeeded in cloning human beings. Cloning is considered by Raëlians as the first step in the human quest for eternal life, and although the scientific reactions to their claim have been negative, it still remains part of their agenda.

During the last few years the Nuwaubians, who moved from New York to the Georgia countryside in 1993, have become one of the most controversial UFO groups. They have been accused repeatedly of child abuse and of encouraging Black Nationalism. Their leader, Malachi York, has spent three years in jail for assault, resisting arrest, and possession of weapons. In January 2004 he was convicted of sexual abuse of children and sentenced to a long jail term. Other, much less serious charges have been leveled at leaders of several UFO groups. George Adamski and Eduard Meier of the Semjase Silver Star Center were both accused of faking photographs and plagiarism, while William Ferguson of the Cosmic Circle of Fellowship was convicted of fraud and sentenced to a year in prison.

CONCLUSIONS. The presence of UFO religions has elicited the attention of many scholars from different academic fields. Both sociologists and psychologists have offered different interpretations of why they might come into being and of the psychological and mental state of their members.

The rise of belief in UFO religions is interesting from the point of view of both religious studies and theology. UFO religions seem to be making an attempt to relate religion with science more positively. The adherents of UFO religions see their beliefs confirmed by scientific data regarding the nature of the universe and the possibility of intelligent extraterrestrial life. Ryan Cook (2002) has called them "Technospiritualities."

From a theological standpoint, UFO religions attempt to incorporate a scientific view of the universe in their ideology. Traditional theology is Earthbound. In terms of myths of creation, beliefs regarding the origin of the human race, its current problems and destiny, and spirituality, theology has been confined to the planet Earth. Although theological speculations about the possibility of other worlds have been going on long before modern astronomy and its discoveries (O'Meara, 1999), Earth still remained the theological center of the universe. Speculations about the spiritual nature of beings in other worlds, their need for salvation, and the possibility of divine intervention were never considered in the context of contact with extraterrestrials who visit Earth in flying saucers. UFO religions offer a new worldview and propose a novel vision of the future. Whether these will captivate the human imagination further or not remains to be seen.

SEE ALSO Heaven's Gate; I AM; New Age Movement; New Religious Movements, article on New Religious Movements and Millennialism; Nuwabians; Raëlians; Theosophical Society; Unarius Academy of Science.

BIBLIOGRAPHY

"The Aetherius Society." Available from http://www.aetherius.org/index.htm.

Cook, Ryan J. "Nuwaubians" (2002). Available from http://home.uchicago.edu.

Lewis, James R., ed. *The Gods Have Landed: New Religions from Other Worlds.* Albany, N.Y., 1995.

Lewis, James R. *UFOs and Popular Culture: An Encyclopedia of Contemporary Myth.* Santa Barbara, Calif., 2002.

Lewis, James R., ed. *Encyclopedic Sourcebook of UFO Religions.* Amherst, N.Y., 2003.

Melton, J. Gordon. *Encyclopedia of American Religions,* 7th ed., pp. 798–805. Farmington Hills, Mich., 2003.

O'Meara, Thomas F. "Christian Theology and Extraterrestrial Intelligent Life." *Theological Studies* 60 (1999): 3–30.

Partridge, Christopher, ed. *UFO Religions.* New York, 2003.

Rothstein, Mikael. "UFO Religions." In *Religions of the World: A Comprehensive Encyclopedia of Beliefs and Practices,* vol. 4, edited by J. Gordon Melton and Martin Baumann, p. 1325. Santa Barbara, Calif., 2002.

Stark, Rodney, and William Sims Bainbridge. *The Future of Religion: Secularization, Revival, and Cult Formation.* Berkeley, Calif., 1985.

Von Daniken, Erich. *Chariots of the Gods?: Unsolved Mysteries of the Past.* New York, 1969.

JOHN A. SALIBA (2005)

UGARITIC RELIGION SEE CANAANITE RELIGION

ŬICH'ŎN (1055–1101), also known as National Master Taegak; Buddhist cataloger and founder of the Ch'ŏnt'ae (Chin., Tiantai) school of Korean Buddhism. Ŭich'ŏn was the fourth son of the Koryŏ king Munjong (r. 1046–1083), and one of the premier scholiasts of the Koryŏ (937–1392) Buddhist church. Early in his life, he is said to have mastered all of the main currents of Buddhist philosophy as well as much of Chinese classical literature. Korean Buddhism during his time was bifurcated between two increasingly hostile traditions: the scholastic schools (*kyo;* Chin., *jiao*), dominated by Hwaŏm (Chin., Huayan) philosophy, and the Nine Mountains schools of Sŏn (Chin., Chan), which were chiefly concerned with meditative practices. Ŭich'ŏn deplored the sectarianism that had infected the order and criticized adepts of both the Sŏn and scholastic schools for their intransigence.

To resolve this conflict, Ŭich'ŏn proposed an approach to Buddhist religious training that placed equal stress on both scriptural study and meditation practice. Ŭich'ŏn developed a curriculum based on such seminal texts as the *Abhidharmakośa, Vijñaptimātratāsiddhi Śāstra, Dasheng qixin lun,* and *Avataṃsaka Sūtra,* in order to engender a comprehensive understanding of the Buddhist teachings in his students. While acknowledging the value of scriptural study in conceptualizing the goal of practice and the course to be followed in reaching that goal, Ŭich'ŏn recognized its limitations. Formal meditative training was also essential if the adept were to achieve any personal experience of what was learned in Buddhist doctrinal writings. Hence, a viable Buddhist vocation would maintain a careful balance between both learning and meditation.

Ŭich'ŏn seems to have anticipated drawing upon his royal prerogative as a means of reconciling the rift between the Sŏn and *kyo* schools. In order to effect his vision of a unified Buddhist tradition in which equal stress was placed upon both study and practice, Ŭich'ŏn traveled surreptitiously to China in 1085, where he received transmission in the Tiantai lineage, one of the more ecumenical of the Chinese Buddhist schools. After returning to Korea the following year Ŭich'ŏn then attempted to merge the Sŏn and Kyo branches of the Korean church into a new Ch'ŏnt'ae school, which he felt provided a banner under which both branches could unite. While Ch'ŏnt'ae was known in Korea before his time, it was Ŭich'ŏn who was first able to establish the school as a fully viable, autonomous school; it is for this reason that he is regarded as the founder of the Korean Ch'ŏnt'ae school. Whatever his chances for success might have been, Ŭich'ŏn's death at the young age of forty-seven brought his efforts to a premature end, and Korean Buddhism remained divided until the similar endeavors of Chinul (1158–1210), some three generations later.

Along with his efforts to unify the Korean church, Ŭich'ŏn was also an avid bibliophile and one of the first Buddhist catalogers to recognize the importance to the tradition of native East Asian treatises and commentarial writings. In 1073 Ŭich'ŏn made a vow to compile a complete collection of such indigenous Buddhist literature, and dispatched agents to all areas of East Asia to obtain copies of texts not then available in Korea. Many of these books were obtained by exchange, as, for example, in the Khitan Liao region of northern China, where Wŏnhyo's works were traded for twenty-nine books by Liao authors. On his own trip to Southern Song-dynasty China, Ŭich'ŏn reintroduced a number of seminal works by noted Chinese exegetes that were no longer extant in China, including treatises by the Huayan patriarchs Zhiyan (602–668), Fazang (643–712), and Chengguan (738–840); these were exchanged for over three thousand fascicles (*kwŏn*) of Chinese materials. Finally, in 1090 he published his renowned catalog of this collection, the *Sinp'yŏn chejong kyojang ch'ongnok* (New compilation of a comprehensive catalog of the repository of the teachings of all the schools; T.D. no. 2184), with listings of 1,010 titles in a total of 4,740 *kwŏn.* Xylographs were carved for each of these texts, forming what was termed *Sokchanggyŏng* (Supplement to the canon). Unfortunately, the woodblocks of the supplement were burned by the Mongols during their invasion of the Korean peninsula in 1232, and many of the texts so painstakingly collected by Ŭich'ŏn were lost to history. Nevertheless, his catalog does survive, and remains one of the most valuable sources of information on the scholastic literature of medieval East Asian Buddhism.

SEE ALSO Buddhism, article on Buddhism in Korea; Chinul; Tiantai.

BIBLIOGRAPHY

Buswell, Robert E., Jr. trans. "Preface to a New Catalog of the Teachings of All the Schools." In *Sourcebook of Korean Civilization,* volume 1: *From Early Times to the Sixteenth Century.* edited by Peter H. Lee, pp. 424–425. New York, 1993.

Cho Myŏng-gi. *Koryŏ Taegak kuksa wa Ch'ŏnt'ae sasang.* Seoul, 1962; reprint 1982. The only comprehensive treatment in any language of Ŭich'ŏn's life and thought.

Munjip P'yŏnch'an Wiwŏnhoe, ed. *Taegak kuksa munjip.* Seoul, 1997.

Ōya, Tokujō. *Korai zokuzō chōzō ko,* 2 vols. Kyoto, 1937; reprinted *as Ōya Tokujō chosaku senshū,* vol. 7. Tokyo, 1988. The definitive study of Ŭich'ŏn's supplement to the Buddhist canon.

ROBERT EVANS BUSWELL, JR. (1987 AND 2005)

UIGHUR RELIGION SEE INNER ASIAN RELIGIONS

ŬISANG

ŬISANG (625–702), also known as the National Master Taesŏng Wŏn'gyo; founder of the Hwaŏm (Chin., Huayan) school of Korean Buddhism. Ŭisang, one of the most important scholiasts of the Unified Silla period (688–935), helped to forge the doctrinal perspectives that would become characteristic of the mature Korean Buddhist tradition.

Ordained as a monk at the age of twenty-nine at Hwangbok monastery in the Silla capital of Kyŏngju, he soon afterward decided to travel to Tang China together with his friend Wŏnhyo (617–686) to study under Chinese masters. As Ŭisang's biography relates, on their first trip in 650 (during the unification wars that were then raging between the three kingdoms of early Korea) the two pilgrims were arrested for espionage in the Liaodong area by Koguryŏ border guards and were only repatriated after several weeks of incarceration. In 661 they tried again, this time traveling to a seaport in the Paekche region of southwestern Korea, which had been conquered by Silla the preceding year, where they hoped to board a ship bound for Tang China. Prior to their embarkation, however, Wŏnhyo is said to have gained enlightenment and returned home to Silla, leaving Ŭisang to continue on alone.

Arriving in Yangzhou on the lower Yangtze River, Ŭisang made his way to Zhixiang monastery on Mount Zhongnan, where he studied under Zhiyan (602–668), the putative second patriarch of the Chinese Huayan school. Ŭisang's arrival at Zhixiang monastery is said to have been anticipated by Zhiyan, and he quickly became one of his chief disciples along with Fazang (643–712), who would eventually be recognized as the third patriarch of the school.

After Zhiyan's death in 668, Ŭisang became one of the leaders of the developing Chinese Huayan tradition. In 670, Ŭisang learned from two Korean envoys detained in the Tang capital that a Chinese invasion of Silla was imminent. Ŭisang returned to Korea to warn King Munmu (r. 661–680), and, thanks to his monition, Silla was able to forestall the attack. Partially out of gratitude, the king sponsored the construction of Pusŏk monastery on Mount T'aebaek and installed Ŭisang as its abbot. This monastery became the center of the Hwaŏm school, from where the new teachings that he had brought from China were propagated throughout the peninsula. His fame was so widespread in Korea that more than three thousand students are said to have congregated there to hear his lectures. Due in large part to Ŭisang's efforts, Hwaŏm philosophy came to dominate Korean Buddhist scholasticism.

Ŭisang's Hwaŏm thought is epitomized in his *Hwaŏm ilsŭng pŏpkyedo* (Diagram of the *Avataṃsaka* one-vehicle realm-of-reality), a short poem of 210 logographs in a total of 30 stanzas written in 668 while he was still a member of Zhiyan's congregation. The poem is arranged in a wavelike form, the "ocean seal diagram" (*Sāgaramudrā Maṇḍala*), which symbolizes the Hwaŏm teaching of the "six marks" (*yuksang*)—that is, of universality and particularity, identity and difference, and integration and disintegration. The entire structure of the diagram represents the marks of universality, identity, and integration, while its curves designate the particularity, difference, and disintegration marks. The chart is woven into one continuous line to show that all phenomena are interconnected and unified in the *dharma*-nature; the fact that this line ends at the same place where it began illustrates the cardinal Hwaŏm doctrine of interpenetration. The diagram is divided into four equal blocks, indicating that the *dharma*-nature is perfected through such salutary practices as the four means of conversion: giving, kind words, helpfulness, and cooperation. Finally, the fifty-four corners found along the meanderings of the line of verse indicate the fifty-four teachers visited by the pilgrim Sudhana in his quest for knowledge as narrated in the *Gaṇḍavyūha* chapter of the *Avataṃsaka Sūtra.* Hence, the diagram serves as a comprehensive summary of all the teachings found in the sixty-fascicle recension of the *Avataṃsaka Sūtra.* Besides Ŭisang's autocommentary to this poem, his only other extant work is the short *Paekhwa toryang parwŏn mun* (Vow made at the White Lotus enlightenment site), which combines Avalokiteśvara piety with Hwaŏm philosophy.

Although Ŭisang may not have been a prolific writer, his mastery of Huayan thought was highly regarded throughout East Asia. Fazang, for example, continued to correspond with Ŭisang even after the latter's return to Korea and, in one of his letters to Ŭisang in 692, he asks for corrections and suggestions on one of his manuscripts. Indeed, an examination of Fazang's writings reveals that the Korean exegetes Ŭisang and Wŏnhyo exerted strong influence on the development of his own thought, and, by extension, on the evolution of Chinese Huayan philosophy.

SEE ALSO Buddhism, article on Buddhism in Korea; Fazang; Huayan; Wŏnhyo.

BIBLIOGRAPHY

Chŏng, Pyŏng-sam. *Ŭisang Hwaŏm sasang yŏn'gu.* Seoul, 1998.

Forte, Antonino. *A Jewel in Indra's Net: The Letter Sent by Fazang in China to Ŭisang in Korea.* Italian School of East Asian Studies Occasional Papers 8. Kyoto, 2000.

Odin, Steve. *Process Metaphysics and Hua-yen Buddhism: A Critical Study of Cumulative Penetration vs. Interpenetration.* Albany, 1982.

"Ŭisang and the Flower Garland School." In *Sourcebook of Korean Civilization,* volume 1: *From Early Times to the Sixteenth Century,* edited by Peter H. Lee, pp. 159–166. New York, 1993.

ROBERT EVANS BUSWELL, JR. (1987 AND 2005)

UKKO

UKKO. Finnish incantations dating from the Middle Ages call upon Ukko, the supreme god or the god in heaven. Typical is the following such invocation: "O Ukko, god supreme, old man in heaven, god of the skies." His name, which means "old man," and other of his epithets, Isä ("father") or Vaari ("old man, grandfather"), reveal the dominant character of this deity. On the other hand, *ukko* and its diminutive form, *ukkonen,* also mean "thunder." Ukko is in fact most often connected with thunder; like Jupiter, he was thought to drive a chariot that caused the sound of thunder during storms. Above all, Ukko is described in incantations as ruler of the weather and giver of rain. His protection was also sought in healing and at births, on behalf of cattle or humans against evil spirits, and in hunting. It seems that Ukko, originally the god of thunder and rain, gradually emerged under the influence of the Christian concept of God to become the supreme god, helping humans in all their worldly needs.

Ukko's attributes are widely known symbols of lightning: a golden club, hammer, ax, sword, and arrow. "Ukko's wedges," ax-shaped stones found in the ground, have often been ascribed to the god of thunder as the implements with which he smote a tree or carved off shavings. Stones thought to belong to Ukko were used to protect their owners from fire or from evil spirits. Ukko's characteristics are reminiscent of the Scandinavian god of thunder, Þórr (Thor); Viking pendants depicting Þórr have also been found in Finland. In eastern and northern Finland thunderstones are called "Ukko's claws," suggesting that in the oldest Finnish beliefs thunder was represented as a giant bird with stone claws, as in northern Asia and America.

The list of Finnish deities given by the Finnish prelate Michael Agricola in the preface to his psalter (1551) notes that a toast was drunk to Ukko when seeds were sown in spring. Various later sources also describe village beer festivals, Ukon Vakat, held in Ukko's honor in spring or summer whenever there was threat of drought. In Karelia these rites merged with the worship of Saint Ilja, or Elias. The rites in question were performed to bring rain and to ensure a successful crop. Agricola mentions that women drank during the festival, following which "many shameful deeds took place." Ukon Vakat has in fact been connected with the rites reenacting the holy alliance of the god of fertility and his wife, the god of the earth, known, for example, to the farming cultures of eastern Europe. Agricola further mentions Rauni as Ukko's wife. The Saami (Lapps) also knew of Ukko's wife Ravdna, a childless deity to whom rowan berries are dedicated. The names *Rauni* and *Ravdna* are derived from the Scandinavian word meaning "rowan" (Swedish, *rönn;* Old Icelandic, *reynir*). The rowan is mentioned in Scandinavian mythology as being Þórr's "castle," his savior in times of danger. No mention is made of Ukko's wife in later descriptions of rites, but the Earth Mother is sometimes mentioned alongside Ukko in eastern Finnish incantations in which he appears as the Sky Father.

According to accounts written between the seventeenth and nineteenth centuries, the beer for the festivals held in honor of Ukko was sometimes made from malt germinated on the roof in a birchbark container. Food was also served. The site of the festival was often the organizer's farm, a lake shore, or, in inland areas, on "Ukko's hill" (*Ukon vuori*), a hill to which Ukko's share of the beer and sacrifices was brought. A ritual poem performed at festivals in Ukko's honor and asking him to increase the crop has been preserved in Ingria and Karelia.

SEE ALSO Finnish Religions.

BIBLIOGRAPHY

Haavio, Martti. *Heilige Heine in Ingermanland.* Folklore Fellows Communication, no. 144. Helsinki, 1963.

Harva, Uno. *Suomalaisten muinaisusko.* Porvoo, Finland, 1948.

Honko, Lauri. "Finnische Mythologie." In *Wörterbuch der Mythologie,* edited by H. W. Haussig, vol. 2, pp. 261–371. Stuttgart, 1973.

New Sources

Jauhiainen, Marjatta. *The Type and Motif Index of Finnish Belief Legend and Memorates.* Translated by Laura Stark-Arola. Helsinki, 1998.

Siikala, Anna-Leena. *Myth and Mentality: Studies in Folklore and Popular Thought.* Helsinki, 2002.

Virtanen, Leea, and Thomas DuBois. *Finnish Folklore.* Seattle, 2000.

ANNA-LEENA SIIKALA (1987)
Translated from Finnish by Susan Sinisalo
Revised Bibliography

ʿULAMĀʾ ("the learned"), the religious scholars of Islam, are the guardians, transmitters, and interpreters of its sciences, doctrines, and laws and the chief guarantors of continuity in the spiritual and intellectual history of the Islamic community. The term is a generic one and embraces all who have cultivated the religious disciplines or fulfilled certain practical functions such as judgeship. [*See figure 1 for individual titles given to ʿulamāʾ.*]

It is an axiom that the scholars are the heirs of the prophets; the emergence of the *ʿulamāʾ* as a distinct group had, therefore, to await the passing of the prophet Muḥammad and the completion of revelation. However, the Qurʾān itself indicates the necessity and excellence of a learned class, quite apart from extolling, in numerous verses, the virtue of knowledge (*ʿilm*). The word *ʿulamāʾ* appears in *sūrah* 35:28, although obviously not in the precise sense later usage conferred on it, and the expressions "those well rooted in knowledge" (3:7), "the people of remembrance" (16:43), and "those who have been given knowledge" (58:11) have also been interpreted as referring to the *ʿulamāʾ*. Numerous utterances attributed to the Prophet define the purpose and status of the *ʿulamāʾ:* in addition to being "the heirs of the prophets," they are described as "the best of my community," "the trustees of the prophets" (in the sense of being repositories of the laws promulgated by the prophets), "the trustees of God over his creation," "the lamps of the earth" (in that through their knowledge they dissipate the darkness of ignorance), and "equivalent to the prophets of the children of Israel" (in stature and authority). The authenticity of some of these utterances has been questioned, but their content has shaped the self-image of the *ʿulamāʾ* and their role in Muslim society.

The antecedents of the learned class of Islam may perhaps be sought in the *ahl al-ṣuffah* ("the people of the bench"), a group that customarily gathered outside the mosque in Medina for the cultivation of religious knowledge and from whom lines of transmission went forth to the great early authorities in Qur'anic exegesis, prophetic tradition, and law. Antecedents may be found also in certain individuals who excelled in a particular branch of learning (such as Ibn ʿAbbās, described by the Prophet as "the foremost of the exegetes"). It was not until the ninth century that a distinct class of learned men crystalized, bearing the title of *ʿulamāʾ*. This development went together with the elaboration and differentiation of the various branches of religious knowledge, with the vast expansion of the Islamic realm beyond the Arabian Peninsula, and with the accelerating conversion of non-Arab peoples to Islam (the high proportion of Iranians among the *ʿulamāʾ* of what has been called the formative period of Islamic thought cannot be overlooked). But the most important single impetus to the emergence of the *ʿulamāʾ* class was the desire of the Islamic community to codify the provisions of Islamic law, for the *ʿulamāʾ* were primarily concerned with law, of which other subjects were the virtual adjunct. Jurisprudence has remained the core of the *ʿulamāʾ* curriculum down to the present.

Various explanations have been offered for the emergence of the *madrasah*, the institution for the training and formation of the *ʿulamāʾ*, but once the *madrasah* appeared and spread throughout the Islamic world, it remained remarkably stable, and its resistance to change became one of the most important elements in the ability of the *ʿulamāʾ* to function as guarantors of continuity. The *madrasah* had a hierarchy of posts ranging from the *mubtadiʾ*, or beginning student, to the *mudarris*, or fully qualified professor of law; intermediate stages were the *mutawassiṭ* ("intermediate"), the *muntahī* ("terminal"), the *mufīd* ("docent"), the *muʿīd* ("repetitor"), and the *nāʾib mudarris* ("deputy professor").

Two elements lay at the heart of the *madrasah* education: the study of texts and the personal relationship between student and teacher. Particularly from the eleventh century onward, when all major developments in the field of jurisprudence had been completed, it was texts rather than the subjects they treated that defined the *madrasah* syllabus. The text was made the object of assimilation, discussion, elaboration, commentary, and criticism, so that an important part of *ʿulamāʾ* writing came to consist of glosses and commentaries on curricular texts.

The relationship between teacher and student consisted of far more than the transmission of a fixed body of knowledge. An entire worldview and distinct method of thought, as well as a sense of corporate identity, were also passed on. Accordingly, dealings between teachers and students were regulated by ethical and behavioral norms that were codified in a number of handbooks. These twin elements, the text and the teacher, were recorded in a document known variously as the *sanad* and the *ijāzah*, in which the competence of the student to teach various books was attested and the entire chain of authorities, to which his name was added as the most recent link, was enumerated.

Ākhūnd: Originally a title given to scholars of unusual merit, primarily in Iran, it was subsequently devalued and became a pejorative term for the lowest stratum of *ʿulamāʾ*. From it is derived the Chinese *ahung*, meaning any Muslim religious functionary.

Āyatullāh (anglicized Ayatollah; "sign of God"): A title of recent origin given to the highest ranking Shīʿ scholars in Iran.

Faqīh: Originally one who had a broad and complete understanding of religion as a whole; it occurs in this sense in several of the traditions of the Prophet that delineate the general rank of the *ʿulamāʾ*. It later came to designate a specialist in Islamic jurisprudence *(fiqh)*.

Ḥujjat al-Islām ("proof of Islam"): Originally a title reserved for scholars of quite exceptional status, it is now applied in Iran to scholars beneath the rank of *mujtahid*.

Imām Jumʿah: Leader of the congregational prayers performed at midday on Friday.

Khaṭīb: The scholar who delivers the Friday sermon *(khuṭbah)*.

Marjaʿ-i taqlīd ("source of imitation"): A *mujtahid* whom the ordinary Shīʿī believer is obliged to follow in the details of religious law.

Mawlānā ("our master"): A title of respect for a senior scholar.

Mawlawī: A variant form of the preceding, used in South Asia and Afghanistan to designate any religious functionary.

Muftī: A jurisconsult; one who delivers binding opinions on a matter of religious law.

Mujtahid: One who exercises *ijtihād*, that is, the search for a correct opinion in deducing the specific provisions of the law from its principles.

Mullā (anglicized Mullah): In origin probably a corrupt form of the Arabic *mawlā* ("master"), it has had the same semantic history as *ākhūnd*.

Qāḍī: Judge of the religious law.

Shaykh ("elder"): A title of respect used particularly in the Arabic-speaking lands and not implying the exercise of any particular function.

Shaykh al-Islām: The main religious dignitary of a Muslim city in Iran and Central Asia; in Ottoman usage, the head of the entire scholarly hierarchy.

Wāʿiẓ: Preacher.

FIGURE 1. Glossary of titles given to *ʿulamāʾ*.

Although the *ʿulamāʾ* were defined as a social unit by their cultivation and transmission of religious learning (together with the application of that learning in their own lives: *ʿilm* had always to be complemented by *ʿamal*, "practice"), they also exercised a variety of practical functions that made them indispensable to traditional society. Apart from preaching and leading congregational prayers in the mosque (a task that, outside the largest and most prestigious mosques, was often delegated to junior members of the class), they acted as judges, notarized and witnessed all important civil and commercial transactions, served as trustees for the estates of minors, and arbitrated popular disputes. All of these activities created a closeness between them and the rest of society (particularly the mercantile and artisan classes of the cities) that was singularly lacking in the relations of the state with its subjects.

Early *'ulamā'* (like early Ṣūfīs) appear not to have drawn salaries or charged fees for the functions they fulfilled, and down to the present some *'ulamā'*, particularly in the countryside, have continued to earn their livelihood from the practice of a trade. But despite initial misgivings, it soon became normal for the *'ulamā'* to charge fees for exercising notarial functions and issuing legal opinions (*fatwās*) and to accept stipends from the endowments that were settled on the learned institutions. Because the stipends were not always generous, it was often necessary to supplement them with income from other sources; *'ulamā'* biographies are replete with stories of material hardship. But certain *'ulamā'* are recorded to have accumulated great wealth, particularly when religious learning and prestige became hereditary in some families.

Islamic political theory, especially as elaborated by the Sunnī segment of the community, quickly came to an accommodation with the dynasties (often of military origin) that seized rule over the Islamic lands from the tenth century on; rebellion was generally equated with irreligion. Despite this, the *'ulamā'* sometimes acted as the spokesmen for popular grievances. In addition, there was the lasting conviction that the *'ulamā'* should shun close association with the state and its officers in order to maintain the superior degree of piety that was meant to undergird their learning. A frequently quoted tradition made the successorship of the *'ulamā'* to the prophets conditional on their "not associating with the sultan." Those who did associate were designated by the celebrated al-Ghazālī (d. 1111) as "scholars with worldly motivation" (*'ulamā' al-dunyā*) or "scholars of evil" *'ulamā' al-sū'*) by contrast with "scholars of otherworldly motivation" (*'ulamā' al-ākhirah*), that is, those who shunned such association. Tangential association with the state was, however, inevitable in the case of posts—above all, judgeships—that were at its disposal, and in Ottoman times the entire corps of *'ulamā'* became in effect part of the state bureaucracy and thus lost its autonomy.

It is often supposed that a fundamental and consistent opposition existed between the *'ulamā'* and the Ṣūfīs, the other great class of religious specialists in Muslim society, and certainly cases of mutual hostility are to be encountered. The overall historical record suggests, however, that a symbiotic relationship existed between the *'ulamā'* and the Ṣūfīs: while the *'ulamā'* cultivated *'ilm*, formal knowledge acquired through mental exertion, the Ṣūfīs pursued *ma'rifah*, inward knowledge resulting from the purification of the heart. The *'ulamā'* were designated as "scholars of the exoteric" (*'ulamā' al-ẓāhir*) and the Ṣūfīs as "scholars of the esoteric" (*'ulamā' al-bāṭin*); the purview of religion was seen to include harmoniously the concerns of both groups. Theoretical Ṣūfīsm was often taught in the *madrasahs*, and the Ṣūfīs recognized the authority of the *'ulamā'* in matters of law. From the fifteenth century onward, it was even common for many of the *'ulamā'*, especially in India and the Ottoman empire, to be affiliated with one of the Ṣūfī orders, often the Naqshbandiyah. One who combined formal scholarship with Sufism in this way would be designated as "the possessor of two wings" (*dhū al-janāḥayn*).

In modern times, the authority of the *'ulamā'* in Muslim society has generally declined. The increasing secularization of law and education has deprived them of many of their most important functions, so that in some cases they have become little more than state-supported dignitaries with purely cultic and ceremonial responsibilities; vigorous and ambitious minds have found little stimulus to join the ranks of the *'ulamā'*. In addition, the emergence of Islamic movements that bypass the *'ulamā'* and even criticize them for alleged failings, such as intellectual stagnation and political passivity, has undercut their standing with the believing masses. In some cases, however, the *'ulamā'* have collaborated with these movements, as in late twentieth-century Syria, where prominent *'ulamā'* were involved in the Muslim Brotherhood. Independent *'ulamā'* ventures in politics with parties such as the Nahdatul Ulama in Indonesia and the Jamī'at al-'Ulamā' in Pakistan have not been notably successful. The case of Iran, where the *'ulamā'* not only defied the secularizing bent of the state but led a revolution to victory and founded an Islamic republic, is an exception to the prevailing trend of diminishing influence, owing to a number of special factors such as the organizational autonomy of the Iranian *'ulamā'* in the prerevolutionary period and the charismatic appeal of Imām Khomeini. It is nonetheless possible that the present current of Islamic renewal may ultimately enhance the prestige and position of the *'ulamā'* in other countries.

SEE ALSO Ijtihād; Madrasah; Mosque, article on History and Tradition; Qāḍī; Shaykh al-Islām.

BIBLIOGRAPHY

There is no single work describing the origins, development, functions, and present status of the *'ulamā'*. The formation of the *madrasah* and the salient features of the pedagogical tradition have, however, been expertly discussed in George Makdisi's *The Rise of Colleges: Institutions of Learning in Islam and the West* (Edinburgh, 1981). Developments in the *madrasah* system under the Ottomans are the subject of Hüseyin Atay's *Osmanlilarda yüksek din eğitimi* (Istanbul, 1983). Among the many works delineating the ethical norms that surrounded the cultivation of learning mention may be made of Ibn Jamā'ah's *Tadhkirat al-sāmi' wa-al-mutakallim fī adab al-'ālim wa-al-muta'allim* (Beirut, 1974). Relations between the *'ulamā'* and the state, with particular reference to *'ulamā'* defiance of injustice, have been surveyed by 'Abd al-'Azīz Badrī in *Al-Islām bayn al-'ulamā' wa-al-ḥukkām* (Medina, 1966). The organization and functions of the Ottoman learned hierarchy are described by Ismail Hakkı

Uzunçarşili in *Osmanlı devletinin ilmiye teşkilâti*, 2d ed. (Ankara, 1984). Two collective works that contain essays on the *ʿulamāʾ* in different periods and lands are *The ʿUlamāʾ in Modern History*, edited by Gabriel Baer (Jerusalem, 1971), and *Scholars, Saints and Sufis*, edited by Nikki R. Keddie (Berkeley, 1972). See also my study *Religion and State in Iran, 1785–1906: The Role of the Ulama in the Qajar Period* (Berkeley, 1969).

HAMID ALGAR (1987)

ÜLGEN, sometimes called Bai Ülgen ("rich Ülgen"), is a deity venerated by the Turkic peoples living in the Altai and Sayan mountains in southern Siberia. Ülgen is also known to the east, among the Mongol Buriats.

In Altai-Sayan Turkic mythology Ülgen figures as the highest deity. He created earth and heaven and all living beings. He is the master of the good spirits, the lord of the upper world, the realm of light; he is the protector of humankind. After him stands Erlik Khan, the lord of the lower world, the realm of darkness; Erlik is the master of the evil spirits. Both Ülgen and Erlik Khan determine the fate of human beings, who live in the middle world.

In the Buriat pantheon Ülgen plays a secondary but revealing role: the deity is regarded as female, a goddess of earth. The Buriats call her Ülgen Ekhe ("mother Ülgen") and consider her the female counterpart of Ünder Tengeri ("high heaven"). Ülgen becomes directly equated with earth in the expression *ülgen delkhei,* which connotes both "wide earth" and "mother earth."

The Buriat Ülgen seems to be a relic of an ancient Turco-Mongol cult dedicated to Ülgen as a terrestrial deity. Her character, however, has undergone an essential transformation in the religion of the Altai-Sayan Turkic people. Ülgen has gradually usurped functions of the male deity Tengere Kaira Khan ("heaven, the gracious khan"), the highest god of heaven, thus changing herself into a male deity. But Ülgen has not been able to supplant Tengere Kaira Khan completely. Thus Ülgen sometimes figures as the first of Tengere Kaira Khan's sons, not residing, as he does, on the seventeenth level of heaven, but on the sixteenth.

Nevertheless, in some of the myths, as well as in popular belief, Ülgen has succeeded in attaining the rank of highest deity. His name has been placed beside those of other deities used by Turkic and Mongol peoples to designate their highest being: Tengri ("heaven"; Türk); Köke Möngke Tengri ("blue eternal heaven"; Mongols, Buriats); Esege ("father") and Malan Tengeri (Buriats); Khormusta (Mongols, Buriats, Tuvin, and Altaic Turkic peoples); Iuriung Aĭyy Toĭon ("white good lord"; Yakuts); Burkhan Bagši ("teacher Buddha"; Tuvin); and Kudai ("god"; Altaic Turkic peoples).

The various sources do not give a uniform description of Ülgen's character. Several indigenous conceptions of different historical and regional origin became mixed with foreign ideas, owing to Russian Orthodox missionary work and contact with Buddhist neighbors. Nevertheless, Ülgen's form and functions are sufficiently clear, in spite of discrepancies and contradictions in detail.

Hovering over the primeval ocean, Ülgen and the first man, in the form of two ducks, create the earth from mud taken from the bottom of the sea. In other traditions Ülgen uses mud to create the first human. Both motifs are indigenous conceptions. Christian influence may be evident in two other motifs: Ülgen makes the first woman from two ribs of one of the first seven men, who then becomes her husband; the woman, seduced by a snake, eats forbidden food from the first tree and then gives it to her husband.

Having attempted to become like Ülgen, the first man is expelled to the lower world by the deity, who names him Erlik—a figure also well known in Buddhist mythology. The second man, Mangdyshirä, the Buddhist *bodhisattva* Mañjuśrī, directs the three fish that support the earth, using a leash that is fastened to heaven. Thereby he controls heaven and earth. Having created the first parents of humankind, Ülgen retreats into his castle on the top of the cosmic mountain. He entrusts the supervision of humans to the third man, Maitärä, the Buddha Maitreya.

Ülgen is described as an old man with a long beard. Thus he becomes identical with White Old Man, a fertility god who is also known among other peoples. Ülgen also preserves distinct characteristics of a tribal deity. He has a wife, sons, daughters, and servants; many of his sons are spirits of Altaic clans.

The fact that Maitärä, the third man, is Ülgen's representative on earth does not exclude people from direct contact with Ülgen and does not prohibit them from asking him, for instance, for abundant cattle, for good crops, or for protection against all kinds of evil. The means that can be used for this purpose are prayer and sacrifice, which are also offered to other good gods and spirits, including Erlik Khan. The animals used for sacrifice seem primarily to be horses and sheep. Sacrifices can (but need not) be made with the help of a shaman, as in the famous horse offering described by Wilhelm Radloff. The shaman kills a horse and, accompanying its soul, penetrates through all the layers of heaven until he reaches Ülgen. The deity informs the shaman whether or not the offering has been accepted favorably, and the shaman learns of impending dangers, such as bad harvests. It is uncertain if the cult of Ülgen has survived to the present day.

SEE ALSO Buriat Religion; Erlik; Tengri.

BIBLIOGRAPHY

Ülgen's character, cult, and position in the religion of the Turkic peoples of southern Siberia have been discussed in great detail by Wilhelm Schmidt in volume 9 of his classic *Der Ursprung der Gottesidee* (Münster, 1949). Schmidt gives ample quotations from the works of Russian scholars, particularly from Wilhelm Radloff's *Proben der Volksliteratur der türkischen Stämme,* vol. 1 (Saint Petersburg, 1866), and *Aus Sibirien* (Leipzig, 1893), and from A. N. Anokhin's *Materialy po shamanstvu u altaitsev* (Leningrad, 1924). Ülgen and the horse sacrifice dedicated to him have also been dealt with by Mircea Eliade in his *Shamanism: Archaic Techniques of Ecstasy,* rev. & enl. ed. (New York, 1964). Brief but valuable elucidations of Ülgen's role in Turkic and Buriat religions have been given in recent Soviet publications by such authors as V. P. D'iakonova, T. M. Mikhailov, and S. Iu. Nekliudov.

New Sources

Rinchen. *Les matériaux pour l'etude du chamanisme mongol.* Wiesbaden, 1959.

Roux, Jean P. "Les Religions dans les Societes Turco-Mongoles." *Revue de l'Histoire des Religions* 201 (1984): 393–420.

Urbanaeva, I. S., and Institut mongolovedeniia buddologii i tibetologii. *Shamanskaia filosofiia buriat-mongolov: tsentral'noaziatskoe tengrianstvo v svete dukhovnykh uchenii: v 2-kh chastiakh.* Ulan-Ude, 2000.

KLAUS SAGASTER (1987)
Revised Bibliography

ULTRAMONTANISM is the tendency of Roman Catholicism that emphasizes the authority of the papacy in the government and teaching of the church. Originally articulated in opposition to Gallicanism, ultramontanism stressed the unity of the church centralized in Rome ("over the mountains") and its independence from nations and states. Ultramontane principles can be traced to the struggles of popes and councils in the fifteenth century. The papalist position received a full exposition by the Jesuit Roberto Bellarmino at the end of the sixteenth century. However, ultramontanism acquired its definitive meaning in the conflict over the Gallicanism of Louis XIV in the seventeenth and eighteenth centuries. The term *ultramontanism* seems to date from the 1730s, although *ultramontane* was used with various meanings in the Middle Ages. During the eighteenth century, exponents of ultramontanism waged a generally losing struggle against Gallicanism and similar statist movements in other countries, such as Febronianism and Josephism.

The French Revolution dealt a fatal blow to Gallicanism by destroying the monarchy on which it had rested. In the ensuing age of uncertainty, the attractiveness of the papacy as the only stable source of authority stimulated a Roman Catholic revival, of which ultramontanism was the essence. Count Joseph de Maistre forcefully expressed this position in *Du pape* (1819), proposing absolutism in state and church under the ultimate supremacy of the pope. The traditionalism of Viscount Louis de Bonald disparaged individual reason, for which Félicité de Lamennais (*Essay on Indifference,* 1817) substituted the "universal consent" of humanity, as embodied in the pope, as the ultimate test of truth. But Lamennais, developing the democratic implications of "universal consent," appealed not only to the pope but also to the people, seeking the freedom of the church in the freedom of society. Thus he commenced the liberal Catholic movement in the context of ultramontanism. The appeal made to Pope Gregory XVI by Lamennais and his associates on the journal *Avenir* was rejected (*Mirari vos,* 1832) by a papacy still seeking safety in alliance with authoritarian monarchies. Lamennais left the church. Nonetheless, his more moderate colleagues, notably Count Charles de Montalembert and Henri Lacordaire, were able to build a party, at once ultramontane and liberal, that supplanted Gallicanism as the political expression of French Catholicism. This party seemed to triumph during the revolution of 1848, securing its chief goal, freedom of Catholic education, with the passage of the Falloux law in 1850.

The Falloux law brought to the surface a latent division in the Catholic party, many of whose members had followed Montalembert's quest for liberty only as a means toward the end of the ultimate dominance of the church in French life. Louis Veuillot, editor of *L'univers,* led an intransigent group that rejected the compromises inherent in the Falloux law and advanced the most extreme claims on behalf of the church and, within it, of the authority of the pope. This new ultramontanism thus rejected liberal Catholicism, a product of the older ultramontanism, and set itself against all forms of liberalism in church, state, and intellectual life.

The attitude of the papacy was decisive. Although Pope Pius IX (1846–1878) had flirted mildly with liberalism early in his reign, he reacted sharply after the revolution of 1848, which had driven him out of his temporal dominions. After 1850, the church under his leadership regarded itself as besieged and embattled, hostile to all liberalism in political and intellectual life, and concentrating in the pope himself both the devotion of the faithful and the plenitude of authority. This was the final meaning of ultramontanism. Having already overcome Gallicanism, it now fought and defeated liberal Catholicism. Veuillot in France, the Jesuits associated with the periodical *Civiltà Cattolica* in Italy, William George Ward and Henry Edward Manning in England, Paul Cullen in Ireland, and, more moderately, the Mainz school led by Wilhelm von Ketteler in Germany were the leading exponents of a movement that rapidly triumphed among committed Catholics. The *Syllabus of Errors* (1864), a set of theses condemned by Pius IX, marked the height of ultramontane militancy. The definition of papal infallibility by the First Vatican Council in 1870 set the seal on its victory. However qualified the wording of this definition, it was manifest that the ultramontane program of a centralized and authoritarian church under an irresistible pope had been achieved.

From the First to the Second Vatican Council, ultramontanism was effectively synonymous with orthodox Roman Catholicism. The movement in its final form had won so complete a triumph that the term itself fell out of use.

SEE ALSO Gallicanism; Modernism, article on Christian Modernism; Papacy; Pius IX; Vatican Councils.

BIBLIOGRAPHY

Encyclopedic or reference entries on ultramontanism tend to be either partisan or unhelpful, but F. F. Urquhart's essay "Ultramontanism," in the *Encyclopaedia of Religion and Ethics,* edited by James Hastings, vol. 12 (Edinburgh, 1926), is a solid brief sketch. Good extended treatments of nineteenth-century ultramontanism can be found in Wilfrid Ward's *William George Ward and the Catholic Revival,* 2d ed. (London, 1912); Adrien Dansette's *Religious History of Modern France,* vol. 1, translated by John Dingle (New York, 1961); and especially Roger Aubert's *Le pontificat de Pie IX, 1846–1878,* "Histoire de l'Église," vol. 21 (Paris, 1952).

JOSEF L. ALTHOLZ (1987)

UMAI. The name *Umai* (*Umay*) first appears in the Old Turkic inscriptions of Mongolia (mid-eighth century CE), where it is borne by a feminine deity of unspecified but benevolent functions. There is a gap of more than a thousand years in the relevant documentation, but belief in Umai has remained alive among some of the Turkic peoples of the Altai region, and also among the Tunguz of northeastern Siberia. Here Umai may be male or female, or even androgynous. In one set of beliefs, where Umai is personified, the role of the spirit resembles that of a guardian angel of small children. Illness may signal Umai's abandonment of her ward, and a shaman's intervention may be sought to effect her return. Often Umai is thought of as the keeper of the soul of unborn children.

Among the Turkic Sagays, Shors, and Beltirs, *umai* is the term applied to the soul of a child from the moment of his birth until about the time when he walks freely and speaks with some fluency. On occasion, the help of a shaman may be requested for the sinister purpose of transferring the *umai* of a healthy infant either into the body of one seriously ill, or into the womb of a woman thought to be sterile. As a result of such an abduction, referred to as Umay (or Imay) *tutargha,* the donor will die. The term *umai* is applied also to the umbilical cord, which, after being cut, is placed in a small leather pouch and attached to the child's cradle.

The inconsistencies and contradictions shown by nineteenth- and twentieth-century beliefs and practices suggest that these are but surviving fragments of an ancient cult no longer definable. Since *umai* is the standard Mongol word for "womb" or "placenta," it can safely be assumed that, although the name *Umai* first appears in a Turkic text and the cult of Umai is strongest among Turkic peoples, originally the deity was part of a Mongol religious system.

SEE ALSO Turkic Religions.

BIBLIOGRAPHY

Most works dealing with Siberian mythology in general, or with the spiritual civilization of the peoples of the Altai in particular, devote some space to Umai. By far the best and most up-to-date study is that of L. P. Potapov, "Umai: Bozhestvo drevnikh tiurkov v svete etnograficheskikh dannykh," *Tiurkologicheskii sbornik* (1972): 265–286, which contains many references to earlier, mostly inaccessible studies. Important observations are made on pp. 234–235 of S. V. Ivanov's *Materialy po izobrazitel'nomu iskusstvu narodov Sibiri XIX-nachala XX v.,* "Trudy Instituta etnografii im. N. N. Miklukho-Maklaia," vol. 22 (Moscow, 1954). S. M. Shirokogoroff's *Psychomental Complex of the Tungus* (London, 1935) gives valuable Tunguz data. My article "'Umay,' a Mongol Spirit Honored by the Türks," in *Proceedings of the International Conference on China Border Area Studies, National Chengchi University* (Taipei, 1984), shows the Mongol origin of the cult.

DENIS SINOR (1987)

UMĀPATI ŚIVĀCĀRYA (fourteenth century CE) was a Tamil Śaiva Siddhānta teacher, author, and theologian. Umāpati Śivācārya, who flourished in the South Indian temple city of Chidambaram during the early fourteenth century, was the last of the four *santāna ācāryas* ("hereditary teachers," a term here referring to four theologians in teacher-disciple succession) of the Tamil Śaiva Siddhānta school of philosophy-theology. (The other three *ācāryas* were Meykaṇṭār, Aruṇanti, and Maṟaiñāṉa Campantar, all of whom lived in the thirteenth and fourteenth centuries.) According to tradition, Umāpati was a Vaiṣṇava brahman from Koṟṟavaṉkuṭi, near Chidambaram. One day, coming from the temple, he encountered the Śaiva *ācārya* Maṟaiñāṉa Campantar. This meeting resulted in Umāpati's conversion to Śaivism. Under the tutelage of Maṟaiñāṉa Campantar, who became Umāpati's guru, Umāpati studied Śaiva religious texts and himself became a prolific contributor to the Tamil Śaiva Siddhānta literature.

Fourteen theological texts are considered canonical in the Tamil Śaiva Siddhānta school and are collectively referred to as the Meykaṇṭaśāstra. Umāpati wrote eight of these treatises, the most important of which is the *Civapirakācam* (The Light of Śiva). The *Civapirakācam* is a hundred-stanza "supplementary treatise" (*cārpunūl*) related both to Meykaṇṭar's "root treatise" (*mutaṉūl*) the *Civañāṉapōtam,* the basic sutra of the Tamil Śaiva Siddhānta, and to Aruṇanti's secondary treatise-commentary (*vaḻinūl*) on the *Civañāṉapōtam,* the *Civañāṉacittiyār.* This clearly situates Umāpati's work and thought within a typical medieval Hindu sectarian lineage, scholastic in style and substance. Umāpati shares with the other Tamil Siddhāntins a threefold ontology—*pati* ("the lord," i.e., Śiva), *pacu* ("the creature," i.e., souls), and *pācam/malam* ("bondage"/"dirt," i.e., phenomenal reality and consciousness). In the *Civapirakācam* he displays considerable psychological acumen in delineating the various levels of knowledge-experience that the soul passes through on its journey from an original benighted state of intimate connection with malam to an ultimate illumination with the light of Śiva.

Other works by Umāpati in the *Meykaṇṭaśāstra* are briefly described as follows. The *Tiruvaruṭpayaṉ* contains ten sets of ten couplets in the style of the renowned Tamil ethical work known as the *Tirukkuṟaḷ.* Since the *Tirukkuṟaḷ 's* maxims treat only right conduct (*dharma*), wealth and power (*artha*), and eros (*kāma*), Umāpati offers the *Tiruvaruṭpayaṉ* to supply a section on *mokṣa,* the fourth Hindu "aim of life" (*puruṣārtha*). The thirteen-quatrain *Viṉāvenpa* records a dialogue between the author and his guru concerning details of Siddhānta ontology and epistemology. The *Poṟṟippakṟoṭai,* a ninety-five-stanza composition in the form of a hymn of praise, describes the soul's transformation thanks to Śiva's grace. The *Koṭikkavi,* a mere four quatrains, plays upon an analogy between the ascent of the soul to Śiva and the raising of a flag at a temple festival. The 125-stanza *Neñcuviṭutūtu* casts the author's heart as a messenger to her beloved (Śiva), who is described as a king, and expounds the soul's transformation by him. The *Uṉmaineṟiviḷakkam* contains six quatrains treating the soul's development and enlightenment. The *Caṅkarpanirākaraṇam* consists of twenty stanzas refuting other sectarian views, especially those of Advaita Vedānta.

Besides the works in the *Meykaṇṭaśāstra,* Umāpati is also the traditionally ascribed author of a number of Tamil Puranic works: a condensation of Cēkkiḻār's great hagiography on the lives of the Tamil Śaiva devotional saints; a sacred biography of Cēkkiḻār himself; the *sthalapurāṇa* ("sacred history of a place") of Chidambaram; and a *purāṇa* on the origins of the Tamil Śaiva collection of sacred hymns the *Tirumuṟai.* Umāpati also wrote a Sanskrit commentary on the *Pauṣkarāgama* and compiled an anthology of the ŚaivĀgamas, the Śataratnasaṃgraha.

SEE ALSO Meykaṇṭār; Śaivism, article on Śaiva Siddhānta; Tamil Religions.

BIBLIOGRAPHY

Two of Umāpati's Tamil works have been more or less adequately translated into English: the *Civapirakācam* in Henry R. Hoisington's *Tattuva-kaṭṭaḷei, Siva-gnāna-pōtham, and Siva-pirakāsam* (New Haven, Conn., 1854); and the *Tiruvaruṭpayaṉ* translated by G. U. Pope in the introductory "appendix" of Pope's *The Tiruvāçagam* (1900; reprint, Madras, 1970), pp. xxxix–lxxxvii. There is a translation with commentary on the anthology of the Āgamas: Periyaperumal Thirugnanasambandhan's *Śataratnasaṅgraha of Śrī Umāpati Śivācārya* (Madras, 1973). For an extended summary and discussion of Umāpati's contributions to the *Meykaṇṭaśastra,* see Mariasusai Dhavamony's *Love of God according to Śaiva Siddhānta* (Oxford, 1971), pp. 260–324. On Umāpati's Puranic works, see Kamil V. Zvelebil's *Tamil Literature* (Leiden, 1975), pp. 200–201, 221.

GLENN E. YOCUM (1987)

ʿUMAR IBN AL-KHAṬṬĀB (assassinated AH 23/644 CE), second caliph and founder of the Muslim Arab empire. Born in pagan Mecca, he accepted the mission of Muḥammad as God's prophet before the emigration (*hijrah*) of that city's nascent Muslim community to Medina. Muḥammad later married his daughter Ḥafṣah, whose name is linked with the collation of the Qurʾān. ʿUmar's fame as caliph (634–644) justly rests on his energetic leadership and shrewd counsel during the expansion of the Medinan commonwealth, which was ultimately transformed into an imperial structure displacing both Byzantine and Persian power in the Middle East.

While traditional accounts attribute a great number of "firsts" to ʿUmar, modern scholars have not always been able to distinguish ʿUmar's achievements from those of a later period. His adoption of the title Amīr al-Muʾminīn ("counselor of the believers") rather than Khalīfat Rasūl Allāh ("successor of the Messenger of God"), as his predecessor Abū Bakr was called, indicates at least the emergence of a selfconscious, permanent community, if not that of a well-defined political office. It seems clear that he set the precedent for religious endowments *(awqāf,* plural of *waqf*), first on his own land and then on the conquered land of the Sawād in Iraq, the revenue from which was to be used for the benefit of future generations of Muslims. He probably also instituted the prayers (*al-tarāwīḥ*) during the fasting month of Ramaḍān, the obligatory pilgrimage (*ḥajj*), and the Hijrah as the commencement of the Muslim era (622 CE). Of more doubtful origin are the specific punishments for drunkenness, adultery, and lampooning, and most controversial of all is the so-called Covenant of ʿUmar, promulgating fiscal, religious, and civil regulations with regard to the non-Muslim population. The document is almost certainly a conflation, with only the fiscal and religious provisions properly belonging to ʿUmar's time.

BIBLIOGRAPHY

A fifteenth-century account of ʿUmar's life is available in H. S. Jarrett's English translation of al-Suyūṭī's *History of the Caliphs* (1881; reprint, Karachi, 1977). A modern account, useful albeit brief, is the biographical entry by Giorgio Levi della Vida in the *Shorter Encyclopaedia of Islam* (1953; reprint, Leiden, 1974). Daniel C. Dennett's *Conversion and the Poll Tax in Early Islam* (Cambridge, Mass., 1950) summarizes various views on and details of the Covenant of ʿUmar. Also of interest is Hava Lazarus-Yafeh's "ʿUmar b. Al-Khaṭṭāb—Paul of Islam?" in *Some Religious Aspects of Islam: A Collection of Articles.* (Leiden, 1981), published as a supplement to *Numen,* vol. 42.

DAVID WAINES (1987)

ʿUMAR TĀL (1794/7–1864), known in Fūta as al-Ḥājj ʿUmar ibn Saʿīd ibn ʿUthmān of Gede, was an intellectual and military leader in the central and western Sudanic region. Born in Fūta Tōro, a Fulbe state in the middle valley of the Senegal River, ʿUmar first achieved prominence during the pilgrimage to Mecca and Medina, which he completed three times in the years 1828–1830. At the same time he obtained an appointment as the chief representative (*khalīfah*) in West Africa for the Islamic order called the Tijānīyah, which had been founded in North Africa in the eighteenth century. With these credentials 'Umar returned to West Africa, visited the capitals of the principal Islamic states, attracted a following of disciples, wives, and slaves, and established a reputation as a brilliant scholar, miracle worker, and military strategist. Much of his reputation emerged during a stay of seven years in Sokoto, the capital of the Islamic confederation of northern Nigeria. In 1839 'Umar traveled through the inland delta of the Niger River, where another Fulbe-dominated Islamic state called the caliphate of Hamdullāhi held sway. In 1840 he settled in Fūta Jalon, yet another Fulbe polity in the mountains of Guinea. In the small town of Jegunko he taught, formed his growing community, and completed his major work, *Rimāḥ,* which serves an an important guide for Tijānīyah clerics today.

Beginning in 1846 'Umar moved in the direction of a military *jihād,* or war against unbelievers. He recruited in his original homeland of Fūta Tōro. He moved his rapidly expanding community to Dingiray, a settlement east of Fūta Jalon under the control of the Mandinka king of Tamba. In Dingiray the Umarian forces collected arms, built fortifications, and created the conditions of conflict with the Mandinka. Their victories over Tamba in 1852–1853 launched the *jihād,* established 'Umar's reputation as a military leader, and attracted thousands of new recruits.

'Umar subsequently directed his forces to the north, to the upper valley of the Senegal River. With an army of about 15,000 he defeated the Bambara kingdom of Kārta, which had dominated the upper valley for decades. In 1857 'Umar laid siege to Medine, a new post established by the expanding French, but he suffered heavy casualties when Governor Louis Faidherbe arrived with new troops from the coast. 'Umar then led his survivors to the east to regroup, then back to the west in 1858–1859 in a bold recruiting campaign along the river valley. With his predominantly new army he defeated the renowned Bambara kingdom of the Middle Niger, Segu, and made the city of the same name the capital of his far-flung but poorly organized state.

In 1862 'Umar led most of his troops against the caliphate of Hamdullāhi in retaliation for Hamdullāhi's assistance to Segu against the *jihād.* He achieved an initial victory, but the Hamdullāhi Fulbe, aided by the Kunta clerics of Timbuktu, revolted in 1863, destroyed the Umarian forces, and killed 'Umar in 1864. The Umarian *jihād* ended at this point, but the fragile polity it created endured until the French conquest some thirty years later. The principal leader of the state was 'Umar's oldest son, Aḥmad, commonly called Amadu Sheku, and its principal capital was Segu.

The basic structure of the Umarian *jihād* consisted of recruitment of men and weapons in the west, in the regions of Senegal and Fūta Jalon, to wage war in the east, against the Mandinka and Bambara. 'Umar relied particularly on the Muslims of the west who, like himself, were dissatisfied citizens of the Fulbe states of Fūta Jalon, Bundu, and Fūta Tōro. He fought against people who could be generally classified as non-Muslims and who blocked the emergence of Islam in the western Sudan. The Segu Bambara were regarded as particularly notorious "pagans." The campaign against Hamdullāhi was not part of the original design of the *jihād.* When 'Umar decided to undertake it he wrote a long apologia to justify his actions, and the dissension produced by the conflict of Muslim against Muslim, and Fulbe against Fulbe, helped produce the revolt of 1863–1864.

The basic structure of the Umarian *jihād* contrasts with the experience of earlier Fulbe-led *jihād*s and the states (Sokoto, Hamdullāhi, and the two Fūtas) that resulted from them. The earlier pattern consisted of internal revolutions against "pagan" or nominal Muslim ruling classes, followed by expansion to the exterior. This pattern was codified in the writings of the Sokoto leadership and adopted by 'Umar himself in his own writings. 'Umar could not, however, lead a second internal revolution in his native land, and he decided to recruit in the west and fight to the east. He was highly successful militarily, but he laid little basis for an Islamic administration or for the incorporation or conversion of his new subjects. His twelve years of war have left decidedly different impressions in today's Senegal and Mali: In the first he is the crusading Islamic hero; in the second he is the invader who used Islam as a pretext.

'Umar left one lasting precedent to Muslims of all persuasions in West Africa: the example of emigration (*hijrah* in Arabic, *fergo* in Fulfulde) away from European expansion. In his desperate recruiting drive of 1858–1859, he called on Senegalese Muslims to leave a land that had become "polluted" by French expansion. His son Amadu followed his example in the 1890s at the time of French conquest of the interior, and other Muslim leaders, such as the caliph of Sokoto in 1903, did the same thing. They journeyed to the east, along the old pilgrimage routes, in search of places where the faithful could preserve Islamic state and society.

BIBLIOGRAPHY

The most complete work on the holy war of 'Umar Tal is my own book *The Holy War of Umar Tal: The Western Sudan in the Mid-Nineteenth Century* (Oxford, 1985). The most complete account of the state after 'Umar is B. O. Oloruntimehin's *The Segu Tukulor Empire* (London, 1972). Sidi Mohamed Mahibou and Jean-Louis Triaud have produced an excellent annotated translation of 'Umar's apologia for his campaign against Hamdullahi in *Voilà ce qui est arrivé: Bayān mā waqa'a d'al-Ḥāgg 'Umar al-Fūtī* (Paris, 1983), while John Ralph Willis has studied 'Umar's earlier works in "*Jihād fī sabīl-Allāh:* Its Doctrinal Basis in Islam and Some Aspects of Its Evolution in Nineteenth Century West Africa," *Journal of African History* 8 (1967): 395–415.

New Sources

Hanson, John M. *Migration, Jihad and Muslim Authority in West Africa: The Futanke Colonies in Karta.* Bloomington, Ind., 1996.

Oumarou Watta. *Rosary, Mat and Molo: A Study in the Spiritual Epic of Omar Seku Tal.* New York, 1993.

Robinson, David. *The Holy War of Umar Tal: The Western Sudan in the Nineteenth Century.* Oxford and New York, 1985.

Willis, John Ralph. *In the Path of Allah: the Passion of al-Hajj Umar: An Essay into the Nature of Charisma in Islam.* London, 1989.

DAVID ROBINSON (1987)
Revised Bibliography

UMBANDA SEE AFRO-BRAZILIAN RELIGIONS

UMMAH is an Arabic term denoting a grouping of individuals constituting a larger community with a single identity. The term is often translated as "community" or "people," and the plural (*umam*) is commonly used in Arabic with the meaning "nations." Other Semitic languages also employ this root *(ʾMM)* to designate social groups that share a common language, ethnicity, or set of laws and customs.

QURʾĀN AND ISLAMIC EXEGESIS. The term *ummah* and its plural occur numerous times in the Qurʾān, referring to groups of animals (Qurʾān 6:38) and people. According to Qurʾān 7:34 and 15:5, each *ummah* has an appointed time, which is fixed and cannot be delayed. To every *ummah* is sent a messenger (Qurʾān 10:47) or warner (35:24), calling each *ummah* back to the worship of God. Muslim exegetes relate that on the Day of Judgment the prophet Muḥammad will intercede on behalf of all the *ummahs* to whom prophets had been sent.

Perhaps this is reflected in Qurʾān 16:120, where Abraham is said to be an *ummah* obedient to God, being *ḥanīf,* and not one of those who associate things with God. In Qurʾān 2:124, God tells Abraham that he is making him an example (*imām*) for people. The terms *imām* and *ummah* are derived from the same root, and are sometimes understood as being a necessary pair. The *imām* shows by example and the *ummah* follows that example. Muslim exegesis on Qurʾān 3:94 equates the religion (*millah*) of Abraham with the *ummah* of the prophet Muḥammad, and Qurʾān 4:125 refers to the *millah* of Abraham, being *ḥanīf,* whom God took as a friend *(khalīl).* Qurʾān 43:22–23 also uses the term *ummah,* as *millah,* to refer to a religion or a community following a particular religion.

Qurʾān 10:19 states that all people are a single *ummah* (*ummah wāḥidah*), but the people disagreed. According to several early exegetes, this refers to the primordial existence of all humanity as a single *ummah* with a single religion, a state that was ruined by sin as exemplified by the murder of Abel by Cain. In Qurʾān 2:128, Abraham and Ishmael ask God to make their offspring an *ummah* submitting (*ummah muslimah*) to God. In Qurʾān 3:103, God says that there will be an *ummah* that commands right and forbids wrong. Exegetes interpret this to be a reference to the faithful remnant of the original single *ummah* that, on the Day of Resurrection, will demonstrate the righteousness of those who submitted to God.

ISLAMIC LAW AND PRACTICE. Islamic law does not define the *ummah* in a direct sense, but it does outline in detail the structure of Muslim society. Human actions are divided into two types: rituals (*ʿibadāt*) and social acts (*muʿamalāt*). In general, rituals define a relationship between God and individuals, or between God and the *ummah,* as a whole. Laws relating to social acts govern relations among individuals within a society, and between different societies or nations, and vary according to different Muslim schools of law in certain respects.

Laws defining purity do not make social distinctions outside of allowing for certain variations in practice based upon natural differences. For example, menstruation requires women to perform certain purification rituals, but men are also required to purify themselves from blood flowing from their own bodies, such as from the nose or a wound. The causes of impurity include both substances (urine, feces, semen, vomit, blood, pus) and activities (sleep and unconsciousness, sex, menstruation, parturition, touching of certain body parts). Those substances and activities that require ablution (*wuḍūʾ*) are natural occurrences necessary to human life. Activities and substances that require washing *(ghusl)* are all related to sexual reproduction and are thus necessary to the continued existence of human society.

Other rituals, such as prayer, offering, fasting, and pilgrimage, do make social distinctions. For example, in certain legal texts women are not to attend the group prayer (*jumʿah*) on Fridays and are not allowed to pray in mixed groups with men, nor are virgins allowed to perform any prayers or fasting during the month of Ramaḍān. The qualifications of the prayer leader are based upon social standing according to age, piety, and learning. Thus, the free person is better suited than the slave, the city dweller than the nomad, the healthy than the handicapped, the heir than the bastard. Similarly, the standing order for the group prayer places the pure before the impure, the literate before the illiterate, and the clothed before the naked. Other rituals are restricted to certain segments of society. *Zakāt* is only required of relatively wealthy people with extra income over and above that required for their regular upkeep, just as the *ḥājj* and *jihād* is not required for a person who does not have the means to both perform the duty and provide for his family during that time.

Certain rituals are made responsible upon the *ummah* as a whole. Islamic law distinguishes between individual ritual requirements (*farḍ ʿayn*) and communal requirements (*farḍ kifāyah*). Individual daily prayers, for example, are incumbent upon each individual. Those rituals that are incumbent upon the community as a whole, such as the group prayer (*jumʿah*) on Fridays and defense of the *ummah (jihād)* are not obligatory on each individual. The *ummah* is required to provide a group prayer on Fridays, which would necessitate a certain number of individuals to attend, but not all eligible members of the *ummah* must attend.

Spatial and temporal distinctions are also demarcated through ritual. For example, when traveling outside of a civilizational center (*miṣr*), people are not allowed to perform the congregational prayer. Nor is purification without water (*tayammum*) allowed within the confines of a civilizational center. People traveling more than three days distance from their home are only required to pray three daily prayers. These rituals parallel commercial and criminal laws, such as the prohibition against a city dweller selling goods for a desert dweller, or a bailed defendant being deposited in a market (*sūq*) but not in open country.

Laws regulating social acts differentiate a number of social spheres within the *ummah*. The most localized are individuals and their interactions with other individuals. In commercial law, exchanges are regulated between specific individuals. Jurists hold that the basic principle underlying commercial law is establishing equity between the two individual parties. Criminal law also regulates activity between individuals. Punishment for murder, for example, takes the form of an exchange between the murderer and the individuals affected by the murder. The payment of wergild is a compensation for the loss of the life. In adjudicating such exchanges or punishments, the role of the state is to facilitate the establishment of this "balance" (*ʿadl*) between individuals.

The second major social sphere within the *ummah* is that of the family. According to jurists, personal law regulates the balance among family members. Laws of marriage, divorce, maintenance, and inheritance are designed to maintain the fundamental structures of the *ummah*. Fornication, which is defined as specific types of sexual activity outside of marriage, is punishable by death because it threatens the balance of the family and the relation of the family to the larger society. The laws of slavery, and particularly those concerning concubines, found in classical Islamic law are also based upon the principle of social balance.

The third major social sphere is that of the society as a whole. This includes laws relating to land reclamation, which would affect productivity and ownership rights of large areas pertinent to the *ummah* as a whole. It also includes the laws of *jihād* or *siyār*, which require certain segments of the *ummah* (capable adult men) to defend the *ummah* in case of attack. Jurists conceptualize two realms: the "Place of Islam" (*Dār al-Islām*) and the "Place of War" (*Dār al-Ḥarb*). The *Dār al-Islām* designates civilized area in which Islamic law is practiced, whereas the *Dar al-Ḥarb* is the place of barbarism, lacking law and order.

POLITICAL THEORY AND PRACTICE. Medieval Muslim political theorists defined the *ummah* vis-à-vis the relation of the *ummah* to its ruler and the relation of both to God through the law as formulated by jurists on the basis of revelation. According to the political theorist al-Māwardī (974–1058), the *ummah* is constituted by its allegiance to the *imām* in a sort of contractual relationship. The responsibility of the *imām* is twofold: to enforce laws pertaining to social relations (*muʿamalāt*), and to ensure that the *ummah* can fulfill its ritual obligations (*ʿibadāt*). Māwardī maintained that the office of the *imām* is required by revelation and necessary to the proper functioning of the *ummah*, but the legitimacy of any individual *imām* is based on his adherence to the well-being of the *ummah*. Ibn Khaldūn (1332–1406) similarly argued that God created human beings so that they would be required to work together as a society and develop civilization in order to survive on the earth after the fall from Eden. This requires a state that provides individuals with food, shelter, and the opportunity to abide by God's commandments.

Some contemporary Muslim theorists contend that the *ummah* can still only be constituted with an *imām* or caliph, and must be inclusive of all Muslims regardless of ethnic or national origin. Some older theorists, such as Ibn Jamāʿa (1241–1333) argued that any effective leader could be considered an *imām*. Others, such as Ibn Taymīyah (1263–1328) and the ayatollah Khomeini (1902–1989), maintained that jurists could take the place of an *imām* even when the *ummah* already had an otherwise de facto ruler. The Iranian-born Jamāl al-Dīn al-Afghānī (1839–1897) proposed a pan-Islamic *ummah* to replace the fragmentation of modern states. The Ottoman sultan Abulhamid II (r. 1876–1909) attempted to reestablish the caliphate and the notion of a pan-Islamic *ummah*.

Modern reformist movements, such as the Ḥizb al-Taḥrīr, have called for the return to a caliphal state as a means to reconstitute the *ummah* and defend Islam against colonialist and imperialist incursions. Reformist political theorists include Sayyid Quṭb (1906–1966) from the Muslim Brotherhood in Egypt, Mawdūdī (1903–1979), founder of the Jamāʿat-i-Islāmī in Pakistan, and ʿAlī Shariʿatī (1933–1977), a leader in the Iranian revolution. According to these theorists, Islam is in the midst of a new age of ignorance (*jahilīyah*), which requires the reformation of the *ummah* under the aegis of an Islamic state upholding the principles of Islamic law.

Other groups define the *ummah* in more restrictive terms. ʿAlid or Shīʿī political theorists define the *ummah* more restrictively, based on its allegiance to an *imām* who is chosen because he possesses special attributes. Non-Shīʿī groups, such as the so-called Five Percenters, also restrict the *ummah* to an elect and narrowly construed group of believers, possessed of secret knowledge or other special characteristics. Early Kharijī leaders denied membership in the *ummah* to any Muslim who refused to follow the strict interpretation of the Qurʾān laid down by acknowledged Kharijī authorities. The Nation of Islam under Elijah Muhammad (1897–1975) delineated the *ummah* in exclusivist historical ties and racial terms.

In the modern period, nationalists have tied the definition of the *ummah* to ethnic and national identities. The Egyptian writer Rifāʿah al-Ṭahṭāwī (1801–1873) argued for a national *ummah* based on patriotism for a homeland (*waṭan*). Muḥammad ʿAbduh (1849–1905) broadened this national *ummah* to include all Arabs in a capacity that would allow Arabs to purify and establish a more international Islamic *ummah.* Muslim thinkers in East and Southeast Asia have called for a recognition of the Arab roots of the *ummah* while championing their own cultural and regional identities as the flowering of a true international *ummah.*

In 1924 Mustafa Kemal Atatürk (1881–1938) abolished the caliphate and founded the secular state of Turkey. Political movements in Arab states, such as the Ummah Anṣār or Sudanese Ummah Party founded in 1945 by supporters of the son of the founder of the Mahdist movement, sought to rally support for political causes with an ideology of the *ummah.* Many Arab states, especially in the 1960s, have legislated separate religious and national identities in an attempt to create a secular society distinct from and overriding religious allegiances. Some contemporary states with large Muslim populations sanction an official Islamic identity as a means to gain legitimacy and protect against threats from nonsanctioned religious groups. Certain forms of Islamic expression are considered subversive to the state and are outlawed as expressions of allegiance with an *ummah* that represents a different political order.

BIBLIOGRAPHY

For a historical overview of the concept of *ummah,* see Riḍwān al-Sayyid, *Al-Ummah wa al-jamāʿa wa al-sulflah: Dirāsāt fī al-fikr al-siyāsī al-ʿarabī al-Islāmī* (Beirut, 1984). This can be supplemented with Naśīf Naṣṣār, *Mafhām al-ummah bayna al-dīn wa al-taʾrīkh* (Beirut, 1978), and his *Taṣawwurāt al-ummah al-maʿāṣirah* (Kuwait, 1986). On *ummah* in the Qurʾān and exegesis, see Fred Denny, "The Meaning of Ummah in the Qurʾān," *History of Religions* 15 (1975): 34–70, and his "Ummah in the Constitution of Medina," *Journal of Near Eastern Studies* 36 (1977): 26–59. For studies on Islamic practice within the *ummah,* see Louis Gardet, *La cité musulmane: Vie sociale et politique* (Paris, 1954; 4th ed., 1976). An introduction to Islamic political thought with an emphasis on the *ummah* can be found in Erwin Rosenthal, *Political Thought in Medieval Islam: An Introductory Outline* (Cambridge, U.K., 1958). On the contractual relationship of the leader and the *ummah,* see Fazlur Rahman, "The Principle of *Shura* and the Role of *Umma* in Islam," *American Journal of Islamic Studies* 1 (1984): 1–9. Specific issues are treated in Louis Massignon, "L'Umma et ses synonymes: Notion de communauté sociale en Islam," *Revista des études Islamiques* (1947): 152; Elias Giannakis, "The Concept of Ummah," *Graeco-Arabica* 2 (1983): 99–111; and H. A. R. Gibb, "The Community in Islamic History," *Proceedings of the American Philosophical Society* 107 (1963): 173–176. On modern and contemporary thought, see Albert Hourani, *Arabic Thought in the Liberal Age,* 1798–1939 (London, 1962; reprint, Cambridge, U.K. 1983), and Leonard Binder, *Islamic Liberalism: A Critique of Development Ideologies* (Chicago, 1988). For studies of nationalism and the *ummah,* see Abdullah al-Aḥsan, *Ummah or Nation? Identity Crisis in Contemporary Muslim Society* (Leicester, UK, 1992), and Hans Kruse, "The Development of the Concept of Nationality in Islam," *Studies in Islam* 2, no. 1 (1965): 7–16.

BRANNON WHEELER (2005)

UNARIUS ACADEMY OF SCIENCE. Ernest Norman (1904–1971) and Ruth Norman (1900–1993) founded in 1954 the Unarius Science of Life, which began with a small circle of students and clients who requested psychic readings. Members refer to their practice as the "Science" and to themselves as "students." Ernest Norman purportedly possessed clairvoyant abilities that he used to read the past lives of people who requested the service and to contact ascended masters living in other realms of existence. Believing himself to be the reincarnation of Jesus Christ and other cosmic dignitaries, Ernest Norman channeled messages about his trips to Mars and Venus (Norman, 1956). He also channeled extended lessons in "highly advanced" Unarian Science that is sometimes called *interdimensional physics.* These basic lessons of Unarian Science are delineated in Ernest Norman's early work, *The Infinite Concept of Cosmic Creation* (1970). Ruth served as Ernest's helpmate as they built the small organization out of their series of homes in different locations throughout southern California. In 1971, Ernest Norman died, leaving Ruth in charge. Mrs. Norman carried on the "mission" with the help of two early followers, Thomas Miller and Charles Spaegal. Together they channeled messages from the cosmos, which they compiled into a book series called Tesla Speaks.

Ruth Norman and her followers opened a storefront center in 1975 in El Cajon, California. This center includes its own classrooms, library, offices, and print shop, and continues to serve as the spiritual hub of Unarian Science. Although Mrs. Norman claimed many distinguished incarnations, she is best known for her persona of Uriel the Archangel, or her higher self—the Goddess of Love and the Healing Archangel from what Unarians believe is the planet Aries. In order to display her divine nature as Uriel, Mrs. Norman would pose in an elaborate costume, complete with a glittering tiara, as she waved some type of a scepter. Frequently photographed and interviewed by news organizations, she promoted her prophecy of the coming of thirty-three spaceships that would save the earth in 2001.

According to Unarian millenarian prophecy, the Space Brothers, as the extraterrestrials are called, would usher in a new age of logic, reason, love, and peace for all the beings in the universe. They would solve all social and ecological problems by ending privation and want with their spiritual science. The large spaceships (usually depicted in Unarian art as flying saucers) would land on top of one another in order to form a towering university that would serve humankind. Using the construction materials brought by the ships, the Space Brothers would build a "Power Tower" that could supply every earthly energy need from a nonpolluting cosmic source. The planets of the Interplanetary Confederation that would supposedly send spaceships are called: El, Rey, Basis, Yessu, Luminus (once called Severus), Valneza, Osnus, Idonus, Vixall, Earth II, Vidus, Anzea, Po, Deva, Endinite, Dollium, Ballium, Dal, Shunan, Brundage, Kallium, Delna, Farris, Serena, Vulna, Emil, Sixtus, Eneshia, Glenus, Din,

Zeton, Jena, and Myton. Each ship would contain one thousand Space Brother scientists, who could teach the people of earth how to use their advanced technology.

In anticipation of this prophesied landing, Unarius purchased acreage for the ships in nearby Jamul, California, during the 1970s. Despite the fact that no ships landed in 2001 as predicted, Unarians believe that the landing will take place "when earth people are ready." Unarians frequently receive clairvoyant channeled messages from the spaceships and their deceased leaders, which are published in their literature. An annual celebration that honors the prophecy and features a parade of the banners of the planets occurs every October.

CURRENT ORGANIZATION. Ruth Norman headed the Unarius Academy of Science until her death in 1993. Charles Spaegal, whose spiritual name was Antares, succeeded her by running the center until he passed away in 1999. Thereafter Unarius was guided by a board of directors composed of long-term committed students of the Science. All jobs that entail the daily running of the Unarian center are unpaid volunteer positions. Current local members attend classes at the center, where they study Unarian literature and give testimonial accounts of the benefits of their spiritual science. Although some followers expressed a deep prior interest in UFOs, adherents more frequently report a familiarity with beliefs in the paranormal before joining Unarius. The local core membership ranges from forty to sixty dedicated students, while considerably more people are in contact with the organization through various types of correspondence, such as phone, email, and letters. Unarius has translated some of their works into Spanish in an attempt to reach out to American Latinos and those in Central and South America. Thousands of people remain on the Unarian mailing list after having either seriously or casually contacted the group. Through mail-order supply, those interested in Unarian Science can take correspondence lessons, read books, and watch video lessons.

Unarians insist that their pursuit is a science not a religion. Unarius offers classes in past-life therapy, interdimensional physics, and art therapy. Trusted students who are considered advanced in the science facilitate the classes. When a person regularly attends classes and participates in the volunteer activities that keep the group operational, he or she is considered a good student, or good member, of the group. More responsibility falls to those students who are able to channel messages from the Space Brothers. In addition, Unarian channelers contact Ernest and Ruth Norman as part of the "Spiritual Hierarchy" that communicates with the group.

Although there is no tendency toward androgynous clothing or expression, gender roles tend toward an egalitarian model partly because of the strong belief in reincarnation. Members believe they have lived as both sexes in their past incarnations. They share tasks and cooperate without making reference to any gender specificity, except in the case of lifting heavy objects, when men are usually called upon to do the job.

HEALING. Unarian philosophy focuses strongly upon healing through past-life therapy. Healing comes from the recognition of past-life imbalances and indiscretions that surface through feelings, visions, or dreams. Unarians welcome these so-called memories of past lives, a phenomenon called *recovered memory* in modern psychology. As a recommended healing process, members act out "memories" of past lives in psychodramas, which are often videotaped. Historically and contemporaneously, Unarian films have recorded many stories of past lives that are available to the general public when they play on local cable access stations in many American cities.

The Unarius Academy of Science remains significant because it is one of the oldest and most enduring UFO religions. The history of Unarius exemplifies a typical feature of such religions inasmuch as it initially functioned around charismatic leaders who telepathically communicated with supernatural extraterrestrials. Despite the eventual loss of both Ernest and Ruth Norman, Unarius continued to operate, and it even withstood a failed prophecy in 2001 without any appreciable loss of membership. Like other such groups, it considers the advent of extraterrestrials as a millenarian act of spiritual salvation, and this belief persistently gains adherents in the postmodern age.

SEE ALSO UFO Religions.

BIBLIOGRAPHY

Norman, Ernest. *The Voice of Venus.* El Cajon, Calif., 1956. Norman narrates his astral trip to Venus by describing life on the planet. See also *The Truth about Mars* (1956) by the same author, published by Unarius.

Norman, Ernest. *The Infinite Concept of Cosmic Creation: Home Study Lesson Course.* Glendale, Calif., 1970. This is the original, hard-to-find, large volume that explains Unarian Science. Individual lessons can be ordered through Unarius.

Norman, Ruth E. *Tesla Speaks,* Vol. 7: *Countdown!!! To Space Fleet Landing, or George Adamski Speaks Again from Planet Venus.* El Cajon, Calif., 1974. In this volume of the Tesla Speaks series, Mrs. Norman published one of the first predictions of a millenarian nature.

Norman, Ruth E. *Interdimensional Physics: The Mind of the Universe.* El Cajon, Calif., 1989. Channeled messages from outer space explain the physics of the universe.

Spiegel, Louis (Antares). *I, Bonaparte: An Autobiography.* El Cajon, Calif., 1985. Charles Spaegel, or Antares, explains his past lives, including one as Napoleon.

Tumminia, Diana. "How Prophecy Never Fails: Interpretive Reason in a Flying-Saucer Group." *Sociology of Religion* 59 (1998): 157–170. This theoretical and historical examination of the Unarian unfulfilled prophecies is supplemented by ethnographic information about the ways members rationalize away the evidence that does not support their beliefs.

Tumminia, Diana G. "In the Dreamtime of the Saucer People." *Journal of Contemporary Ethnography* 31 (2002): 675–705.

This ethnographic work describes how knowledge in Unarius is constructed through dreams, visions, and psychic readings.

Tumminia, Diana G., and R. George Kirkpatrick. "Unarius: Emergent Aspects of a Flying Saucer Group." In *The Gods Have Landed: New Religions from Other Worlds*, edited by James R. Lewis, pp. 85–104. Albany, N.Y., 1995. This chapter in a popular anthology about UFO religions details some of the many beliefs held by Unarians; it also contains demographic information from an earlier study of Unarius students.

Uriel and Unarius students. *The Proof of the Truth of Past Life Therapy.* El Cajon, Calif., 1988. Unarius students give testimonials about their healings that resulted from the use of Unarian Science, and they explain how memories of their past lives surfaced.

DIANA G. TUMMINIA (2005)

UNCTION

SEE SACRAMENT, *ARTICLE ON* CHRISTIAN SACRAMENTS

UNDERHILL, EVELYN

UNDERHILL, EVELYN (1875–1941) was an English poet, novelist, and writer on mysticism. Born in Wolverhampton, England, the daughter of barrister Arthur Underhill, Evelyn Underhill supplemented her secondary education by studies at King's College, London, and by travel abroad. Underhill's early letters show some precocity for self-study and her personal and literary career may be regarded in light of this capacity. Her marriage in 1907 allowed Underhill the kind of financial support and unencumbered way of life necessary for her both to seek personal guidance essential to her spiritual growth and to undertake the voluminous research that her work would demand.

Underhill was both beneficiary and catalyst in the revival of the metaphysical discussion current in the early years of her career. She was influenced by Arthur Waite, a figure of manifold interests in the occult, magic, and religion, associating herself for some time with the Hermetic Order of the Golden Dawn. Later, and in another vein, Underhill shared in the enthusiasm aroused by the ideas of contemporaries Henri Bergson and Rudolf Eucken and fell briefly under the influence of Hindu poet Rabindranath Tagore. More significant influences, however, were William Ralph Inge, the eminent dean of Saint Paul's Cathedral in London, and the Roman Catholic scholar Friedrich von Hügel, whose erudition and sensitivity had the most profound and lasting effect on her.

Underhill's work reveals her deep personal commitment to spiritual development. It reflects, for the most part, her conviction that Christianity provides an exceptionally vital medium for mystical communion. Although the focus of her work does not exclude the pagan experience, her insights are developed primarily within the Christian tradition.

Underhill's book *Mysticism* (1911) is her most important work. It is a decidedly nonacademic study of mystical experience. In part historical and primarily comparative, its lasting significance lies, however, in the psychological insight of Underhill's commentary. The experiences of mystics from a wide range of disciplines and cultures are presented. Underhill, emphasizing their similarity of expression, asserted the essential kinship of mystical experience wherever it is found. Early editions of *Mysticism* depict Christianity as exceptional only in its greater facility for fostering this experience. The appearance in 1930 of the revised twelfth edition revealed a significantly greater awareness of the differences between the Christian and non-Christian experience. The clarity and depth of understanding with which *Mysticism* was written have given it an unsurpassed value and accessibility as a guide to the mystical tradition.

Subsequent work was taken up in the midst of a growing preoccupation with the contemplative life. Prayer, public service, and guidance from devout and intelligent people such as von Hügel served to deepen Underhill's already substantial appreciation for the uniqueness of the Christian way. This is borne out in her revision of *Mysticism.* In general such changes in Underhill's perspective tended to move her work toward the center of the Anglican faith to which she had returned. This tendency is manifest in her last major work, *Worship* (1936). This book deals with more orthodox forms of Christian practice. It stresses the practical virtues of prayer and the great importance and centrality of the Eucharist in Christian life.

BIBLIOGRAPHY

In addition to the works cited above, see *The Mystic Way: A Psychological Study in Christian Origins* (London, 1913) in which Underhill describes the unique character of Christian mysticism, distinguishing it from its Greek predecessors. *Practical Mysticism* (1914; reprint, New York, 1948) is a shorter introductory companion to *Mysticism* (1911; 12th rev. ed., New York, 1961). Underhill's novels produced between 1903 and 1909 are best represented by *The Column of Dust* (London, 1909). For selections of verse as well as representative prose excerpts see *An Anthology of the Love of God,* edited by Lumsden Barkway and Lucy Menzies (1953; reprint, Wilton, Conn., 1976). A very balanced and lucid introduction is Christopher J. R. Armstrong's *Evelyn Underhill (1875–1941): An Introduction to Her Life and Writings* (Grand Rapids, Mich., 1976).

New Sources

Griffin, Emilie, ed. *Evelyn Underhiil: Essential Writings.* Maryknoll, N.Y., 2003.

Hogan, Kevin. "The Experience of Reality: Evelyn Underhill and Religious Pluralism." *Anglican Theological Review* 74 (Summer 1992): 334–347.

Jantzen, Grace M. "The Legacy of Evelyn Underhill." *Feminist Theology* no. 4 (September 1993): 79–100.

Miles, Margaret R. "Fragments from an Inner Life: The Notebooks of Evelyn Underhill." *Anglican and Episcopal History* 64 (June 1995): 246–247.

Underhill, Evelyn *Radiance: A Spiritual Memoir of Evelyn Underhill.* Edited by Bernard Bangley. Brewster, Mass., 2004.

GREGORY F. PORTER (1987)
Revised Bibliography

UNDERWORLD. The term *underworld* refers to the subterranean region inhabited by the dead. It is often the place of punishment of the wicked, the unrighteous, the unredeemed, the unbelieving, or the lost. The concept of an underworld is an ingredient in most belief systems in the history of religions, but there is no definite evidence indicating that the idea was present in the earliest stages of human culture. In the oldest strata of Egyptian and pre-Vedic Indian cultures, however, there exists a rich store of archaeological material suggesting that the aristocratic segments of society, at least, believed in some kind of an afterlife. But even in these early records of postmortem existence, there does not seem to have been a distinction between heaven, the realm of the blessed, and hell, the realm of the damned.

Later, when the two realms came to be differentiated, each religion appealed to its own set of criteria when determining the fate of an individual after death, whether blessed or damned. These criteria could be defined by birth, by ritual initiation into the community, by the performance of prescribed sacramental rites, by belief in a deity or in a set of teachings, and so on. Such standards were commensurate with the way the religion defined the proper relationship to the sacred.

PRIMITIVE AND ARCHAIC RELIGIONS. Tales of heroic journeys to the underworld, often undertaken on behalf of the entire community, are extremely widespread among tribal peoples throughout the world. Particularly notable for such lore are the Maori of New Zealand; the Algonquin, the Ojibwa, and various Plains tribes of North America; the Zulu, the Ashanti, and the Dogon of Africa; and numerous other societies in North Asia (especially Siberia and Mongolia), Central America, and South America.

If one disregards for the moment the detailed differences among the various accounts of the postmortem journey to the underworld, one can observe a common theme among many such stories. A heroic figure undertakes a descent into the belly of a chthonic or marine monster, a creature often identified as Mother Earth, the Mother of Death, or the Queen of the Night. He pursues a strenuous journey through her body, during which he encounters numerous obstacles and dangers. He finally reemerges into the world of the living, either through a natural orifice in the monster's body or through an opening that he himself creates. As numerous scholars have convincingly demonstrated, the ordeal of being ingested by a theriomorphic creature and of passing through the various channels of its body is symbolic of an initiatory ordeal whereby the hero conquers death or the fear of death and, in some cases, wins the prize of immortality.

The hero is submitted to a test or an ordeal in which he must either prove himself capable of overcoming the obstacles that lie in his path or prove himself capable of defeating the enemy that blocks his passage. The descent into the underworld is also a quest for special, esoteric knowledge or wisdom that is denied all other living beings who have not undertaken such a journey. As the possessor of this secret knowledge, the hero often serves as a mediator between the living and the dead or as a psychopomp who personally conducts the souls of the deceased to the underworld.

The typical shamanistic story of the descent into the underworld is exemplified in a tale of the Goldi peoples of Siberia. A shaman traps the soul of the deceased in a sacred pillow by beating his sacred drum. After mounting a notched tree in order to get a preview of the journey to follow, he summons two tutelary spirits to assist along the way and then, with the deceased and his ghostly companions, sets off on a specially prepared dogsled, furnished with a basket of food for nourishment. After encountering numerous obstacles along the way, the travelers arrive in the underworld. Using a fictitious name to protect his identity, the shaman deposits the deceased with his relatives in the underworld. He then returns immediately, armed with warm greetings and small gifts for the living from their subterranean kinsmen.

A prototypical example of the story in which the descent into the underworld is symbolically identified with the return to the mother's womb is found in the religious lore of the Maori of New Zealand. Maui, the heroic representative of the Maori, returned at the end of his life to the hut of his ancestress, Hine-nui-te-po, the Great Mistress (of the Night). He leapt into her body as she slept, made his way without difficulty through the various channels within her body, and had just emerged halfway from her open mouth when the birds that had accompanied him burst into laughter. Aroused by the screech of the birds' laughter, the ancestress abruptly clamped her mouth shut and cut the hero in two with her sharp teeth. Because of this misfortune, humans ever since have been mortal; had Maui successfully escaped his ancestress's body, they would have become immortal.

Many tribal peoples situate the land of the dead in the west, on the western side of the world, or simply at some distance west of the village. Many scholars (most notably E. B. Tylor and F. Max Müller) have argued that this practice is confirmation that most myths and rituals pertaining to the journey to the underworld are elaborations of a core solar myth.

While there no doubt is a kernel of truth in this view, there are other equally significant layers of meaning invested in these stories and practices. One important theme concerns the descent of a hero into the belly of a ferocious marine creature and his reemergence through the mouth or anus of the beast in an effort to conquer death and gain immortality. A second theme is of an arduous journey through wild and monster-infested areas in search of a precious object (magical ring, sacred fruit, golden vessel, elixir of immortality, etc.)

that will benefit the hero or his people. In a third theme, a tribesman submits himself to a deadly ordeal in order to pass from a lower to a higher stage of existence and thereby achieves a superhuman or heroic state of being. In yet another theme, a hero shoulders the onerous task of traveling to the subterranean regions where the Mother of Death or the Queen of the Night reigns supreme, thereby gaining knowledge of the route to the shadowy realm and of the fate of those who reside there.

ANCIENT EGYPT. The afterlife of the Egyptian nobility is described in the Pyramid Texts. Royalty were believed to ascend at death to the Blessed Lands, or Fields of the Blessed, in the heavens. According to the Pyramid Texts, members of the aristocracy traveled to the celestial spheres to dwell there like gods, often traveling on the ship belonging to Re, the sun god. Highly elaborate and expensive mortuary rites, charms, and incantations were offered for the nobility to guarantee that the soul of the deceased would enjoy a blissful existence in the world beyond. The life in that world is largely similar to this one but is free of the difficulties and misfortunes that plague the lives of even the powerful and wealthy. The afterlife of the common people is outlined in the Coffin Texts. Commoners were believed either to remain near the tomb after death or to travel to the netherworld.

The dead traveled to many different realms, some to the east but most to the west. It is now believed that the dead went in different directions because the disembodied spirits were thought to move about with the sun and the stars. The west was the primary destination of the souls (*ka*) of the dead. Darkness and night were identified symbolically with death and postmortem existence. The realm of the dead was located sometimes in the sky and sometimes beneath the earth. This region was ruled by Osiris, the king of the dead. While still a mortal, Osiris was murdered by his brother Seth and then resurrected by his sister-wife Isis. He subsequently became the chief ruler of the nether realm.

ASSYRIA AND BABYLONIA. In the views of the ancient Akkadians and Babylonians, the underworld is a dreadful place. To get there one has to pass through seven gates and remove a piece of clothing at each. The realm is organized on the order of a political state under the tyrannical rule of a king and a queen, Nergal and Ereshkigal. In the text entitled "Descent of Ishtar to the Nether World" (Pritchard, 1969, p. 107), this realm of the dead is described as

> the Land of no Return . . . the dark house . . . which none leave who have entered it . . . the road from which there is no way back, the house wherein the entrants are bereft of light, where dust is their fare and clay their food. Where they see no light, residing in darkness, where they are clothed like birds, with wings for garments, and where over the door and bolt is spread dust.

Once in the underworld, the fate of the deceased is improved or worsened depending on whether the body is buried according to the prescribed funeral rites and is provided by the living with food, clothing, and other accoutrements required for the journey to the other realm.

One name for the netherworld is Kigal ("the great subterranean realm"). *Kigal* is an element in the name of Ereshkigal, the "queen of the underworld" and sister of Ishtar. This domain was also known as Kutu, the sacred city of Nergal, a chthonic deity who was lord of the netherworld. The gateway through which each soul is required to pass is situated in the west, where the Babylonians watched the descent of the sun. All graves provide entrance to this shadowy realm. Having entered the main gate, the dead are then ferried across the river Hubur by a four-handed, fierce-faced ferryman to "the Great City." This city is a gigantic metropolis, encircled by seven walls, each wall surmounted by a gate and each gate guarded by a demon. At the very center of the complex is the lapis lazuli of Ereshkigal. Befitting her position as queen of the realm, she is surrounded by numerous attendants: a plague god who executes her orders, a scribe who announces the names of the new arrivals, and seven fierce, iron-willed judges called the Anunnaki. There are a host of demons who spread pestilence and suffering throughout humanity and keep the queen plentifully supplied with new residents.

GREECE AND ROME. In ancient Greece the belief in the postmortem survival of the soul stretches back to earliest times, as is suggested by evidence of food, drink, clothing, and entertainment provided in the grave. Already in Homer a clear distinction between the corpse and the ghost was made. The *Iliad* (3.278-279, 19.259) contains the belief that the gods punished or rewarded souls at death. It was thought that the souls of the living are supplied from the stock of souls in Hades.

Despite the rich stock of ideas native to the Greek islands regarding the dead and the underworld, from the time of Homer Greek writers showed no hesitation in drawing freely from other religious traditions and in synthesizing these foreign elements with indigenous material. Most of the borrowed elements were derived from Egypt (particularly the Osiris cult and the *Book of Going Forth by Day*) and from Mycenae. From Crete they adopted the idea of *elusion* ("paradise") and the figure of Rhadamanthys (one of the three infernal judges). From Mycenae they received the idea of weighing the soul in the balance.

The earliest Greek accounts of the postmortem journey of the soul to the underworld are to be found in the *Iliad* (1.595, 3.279, 5.395–396, 15.187–188) and in the *Odyssey* (11). At the moment of death, the soul (*psuche*) is separated from the body, transformed into a ghostly double of the person (*eidōlon*), and transported down to Hades, an enormous cavern below the surface of the earth (*Odyssey* 11.204–222). Here the souls of the dead are capable only of "flitting around as shadows while exuding shrill chirping sounds." This dismal domain is the very antithesis of the realm of the "blazing sun"; it is a place where one sees only "the cold dead" and is an altogether "joyless region." The shades of the dead are unconscious and incommunicative until they have imbibed a quantity of blood, the essence of life. So morally neutral is the life of the dead that all distinctions pertaining to social station, political position, and religious latitude are obliterated, thus rendering even a mean and destitute existence in the world highly preferable (*Odyssey* 11.487–491) to the office of rulership over Hades.

In ancient Greek cosmology, Hades lies within the ocean, perpetually shrouded in clouds and mist. Here there is no sunlight, only eternal darkness. The shades are depicted as being weak and extremely melancholy, always in search of escape from their sufferings and finding none. Especially painful are the sufferings of those who were either not properly buried on earth or not suitably nourished with sacrificial food offerings. The dire nature of the torments suffered by the inmates is graphically depicted in the story of Tantalos. Standing in water up to his chin, he found to his chagrin that the water mysteriously evaporated each time he sought to quench his thirst; surrounded by flowering fruit trees, he found that the wind blew the fruit away as he reached out to grasp it (*Odyssey* 11.582–592). Hades is separated from the realm of the living by a treacherous body of water, made up of five rivers (Lethe, Styx, Phlegethon, Acheron, and Cocytus). The entrance is guarded by Kerberos, a ferocious dog with three (earlier poets said fifty or one hundred) heads whose necks are encircled by venomous serpents. Here Minos judges the deeds of the deceased and provides the laws that govern them in the underworld. But the evidence seems to indicate that none of the laws meted out justice in the form of rewards for the righteous and punishment for the wicked.

According to Vergil, Rhadamanthys presides over a court of justice in which a variety of corporeal, mental, and spiritual retributions are distributed according to the nature of sins committed in the upper world. Nowhere in all of world literature is the drastic distinction between the two destinies after death presented in more painfully dramatic terms than in his *Aeneid:*

> This is the place where the road divides and leads in two directions: one way is to the right and extends under the ramparts of Dis [i.e., Pluto] to Elysium [i.e., Paradise], but the left path leads to the evil realms of Tartarus, where the penalties for sin are exacted. To his left Aeneas spots a deep cave enclosed by a triple fortification around which flows Phlegethon, seething with flames and tossing rocks about in its tumultous torrents. (6.540–579)

Aeneas encounters a gargantuan door that even the gods are powerless to penetrate, guarded by the ever-wakeful Tisiphone (one of the Furies). From inside, he hears horrifying groans and wailings from victims being lashed with whips and chains. Within this dismal kingdom of darkness and death reside a host of personifications of abstract entities: Grief and Cares, Diseases, Senility, Fear, Hunger, Toil, War, Discord, and countless other forces that afflict the life of every creature with misfortune and distress.

Not until the time of Plato does one encounter the notion that the righteous will be feted with sumptuous banquets "with garlands on their heads," or that the wicked will be plunged into a pit filled with mud, "where they will be forced to carry water in a sieve" (*Republic* 2.373c–d). Plato may have believed that the earthly experience of the fear of Hades is equivalent to being there already and that the suffering inflicted by a guilty conscience is sufficient punishment for the wicked act committed. This view coincides with the theory that Plato adopted many primitive beliefs about the fate of the soul and gave moral and psychological interpretations to allegorical tales (see *Gorgias* 493a–c). Similarly, for the poet and philosopher Empedocles the *psuche* ("soul") is the bearer of guilt, and the world of the senses is the Hades where the individual suffers for that guilt (frags. 118, 121). Also, Plato, who perhaps more than any other ancient thinker shows a genuine concern for the immortality of the soul and the judgment it undergoes after death, presents divine rewards and punishments in terms of reincarnation into a better or worse earthly life, rather than in terms of heaven and hell. In the *Laws* (904d) he suggests that Hades is not a place but a state of mind and adds that popular beliefs regarding Hades should be invested with symbolic value only.

JUDAISM. References to the underworld in the Hebrew scriptures are vague and derive largely from beliefs common throughout the ancient Near East (especially Egypt and Babylonia). Numerous terms are used to designate this shadowy realm, the two most popular names being *She'ol* (a word that seems peculiar to Hebrew) and *Gei' Hinnom* (Gr., *Geenna;* Eng., *Gehenna*). Some euphemistic substitutes for the latter are *erets* ("earth" or "underworld," *1 Sm.* 28:13, *Jb.* 10:21–22), *qever* ("grave," *Ps.* 88:12), *'afar* ("dust," *Is.* 26:5), *bor* ("pit," *Is.* 14:15), and *shaḥat* ("pit," *Ps.* 7:16; "the land of darkness," *Jb.* 10:21).

The historical Gehenna, or Gei' Hinnom—"Valley of ben Hinnom," or "Valley [of the son(s) of] Hinnom"— was located near the city of Jerusalem at the site of a cult in which children were sacrificed (*2 Kgs.* 23:10, *Jer.* 7:31); it was known popularly as the "Valley of Slaughter" (*Jer.* 19:5–6). Even before this time, the valley was used as a site for human sacrifices to the god Moloch (*2 Chr.* 33:8), and afterward, as a place where the city's rubbish was burned. In mythology, Gehenna was located beneath the earth or at the base of a mountain range (*Jon.* 2:7) or beneath the waters of the cosmic ocean (*Jb.* 26:5). This realm is sometimes pictured as a horrifying monster with mouth agape (*Is.* 5:14), a realm where persons of all classes are treated as equals (*Ez.* 32:18–32).

She'ol is another term used to designate the realm of the dead or the subterranean spirit world, where the destinies of the righteous and the wicked are the same. Heaven and She'ol are thought to be the two farthest extremities of the universe (*Am.* 9:2). She'ol is positioned at the nadir of a dark pit at the very base of the universe, into which the blasphemer who aspires to be equal with God will fall. But the term also refers simply to the state of death or to the grave (see *Prv.* 23:13–14, *Ps.* 89:49). The viability of this interpretation of the term is further confirmed by the fact that the Septaugint frequently translates *she'ol* as *thanatos* ("death").

The Hebrew scriptures place the domain of the dead at the center of the earth, below the floor of the sea (*Is.* 14:13–15, *Jb.* 26:5). Some passages locate the gates that mark the boundary of She'ol in the west. This realm has been depicted as a place pervaded by dust and darkness (*Jb.* 10:21–22), as it was in Mesopotamian thought. In contrast to the Babylonian netherworld, which boasted a large company of demonic creatures, both the Hebraic underworld and heaven are ruled over by one and the same God whose sovereignty extends throughout the universe (*Ps.* 139:7–8, *Prv.* 15:11, *Am.* 9:2). There is a strong suggestion in Psalm 73 that God will manifest his grace to the righteous by taking them to heaven, where they will exist eternally with him. The people of God will, therefore, be saved from She'ol to live with God forever, but the unrighteous will face a deprived existence in the chambers of the subterranean regions (*Ps.* 49).

According to the Ethiopic *Apocalypse of Enoch* (22:9–13), She'ol is not an abode of all the dead, where the souls merely exist as vague shadowy figures devoid of individual characteristics, but is a spacious realm with three subdivisions: One realm is allotted to the righteous who have been vindicated in life, one to sinners who were not submitted to divine judgment before death, and one to those whose deeds were judged during life and found wanting. in time, She'ol came to be identified with Gehenna, the pit of torment, an idea that, in turn, informed the Christian concept of Hell (*Hb.* 2:5).

In the postbiblical Jewish apocalyptic tradition, among the seven heavens that extend above the earth, sinners are confined to the second heaven to await final judgment. North of Eden lies Gehenna, where dark fires perpetually smolder and a river of flames flows through a land of biting cold and ice. Here the wicked suffer numerous tortures (*2 En.* 3–9).

Elsewhere within the same book, the Angel of Death inquires of Jehoshua whether there are any gentiles (or "descendants of Esau") in Paradise or any Children of Israel in Hell. Included in the reply is the observation that those descendants of Esau who performed righteous deeds on earth are rewarded here but sent to Hell after death; Israelites on the other hand receive punishment while living and inherit the joys of Paradise after death. According to Josephus Flavius (37–100 CE), historian of the Jewish War of 66–70, the Essenes of the Dead Sea area believed that the righteous retire to the western region, where their lives are undisturbed by rain, cold, or heat and where they enjoy cooling breezes continuously. The wicked, however, are condemned to a dark, chilly hell where they suffer eternal torments.

CHRISTIANITY. New Testament writers drew upon the postexilic Hebraic picture of Gehenna in formulating their understanding of the destination of the damned. Gehenna was imagined to be an enormous, deep pit that perpetually ejects clouds of putrid-smelling smoke from burning garbage, a pit where bodies of criminals and lepers are disposed of. Two significant alterations in the Hebraic concept of hell deserve mention: (1) there is a much sharper distinction between the realm of the blessed and the realm of the damned, and (2) the standard applied at the Last Judgment is defined by a person's attitude toward the person of Jesus and his teachings. In the Gospels the prevailing concept of the underworld is epitomized in the story of the rich man and Lazarus (*Lk.* 16:19–31). It would appear that the rich man is sent to Hell merely on account of his great wealth in this realm, whereas Lazarus is transported to "the bosom of Abraham" (Heaven, Paradise) in recompense for his sufferings and poverty. Hell is imagined as an invisible world, situated beneath the realm of the living, a blazing inferno of such intensity that even a drop of water applied to the tip of the tongue could bring welcome relief. It is also a distant land beyond a great gulf across which no movement is possible in either direction.

Whereas Hades remains at a great remove from the realm of the living, Paradise is situated in the immediate presence of God. The wicked in Hades and the righteous dead "at home with the Lord" await the final resurrection.

According to the eschatology of the *Book of Revelation,* a millennial reign is followed by the resurrection of the saints, and then by a period of universal conflict at the end of which Satan will be cast into a lake of fire and brimstone, preparatory to the resurrection of the remaining dead and the Last Judgment. Both Death and Hades are hypostatized as subterranean vaults that surrender the dead to be judged, after which Death and Hades themselves are thrown into the lake of fire, thus actualizing "the second death," that is, condemnation to the eternal fires of Hell (*Rv.* 20:11–15, 21:8). The remarkable feature of this account of "final events" is that Hell is homologized with the lake of fire to which the wicked are condemned, and it is itself punished by being cast into the same lake of torment. Supposedly the cosmic cataclysm that signals the termination of the current world order, the final defeat of Death and Satan and the Last Judgment, is a preview of the fate of the wicked in Hell. The nature of Hades can be inferred from the depiction of the realm of the blessed as a perpetually sunlit land in which the righteous are never discomfited by the blazing sun. There they are faithfully fed by the divine shepherd, refreshed by ever-flowing fountains, and relieved of their tears of grief.

Augustine (354–430 CE), the father of early medieval theology, perpetuated the concept of Hell as a bottomless pit containing a lake of fire and brimstone where both the bodies and the souls of humans and the ethereal bodies of devils are tormented (*City of God* 21.10). Thomas Aquinas (1225–1274) laid much of the foundation for the philosophical concept of Hell that shaped and informed the idea of Hell in the minds of poets, painters, sculptors, and novelists for centuries to come. For him, Hell never lacks space to accommodate the damned. it is a place where unhappiness infinitely exceeds all unhappiness of this world, a place of eternal damnation and torment where the suffering of the damned is intensified by recalling the glory of the blessed while no longer able to perceive the glory firsthand.

Dante (1265–1321) derived the theological framework for his notion of the underworld from the Old and New Testaments and Thomas. In the third chapter of the *Inferno* he describes the descent into Hell. Accompanied by his guide Vergil, Dante approaches the Inferno and sees the gate of Hell, the entrance to the city whose inhabitants live in suffering and eternal pain. Dante is conducted along a circular pathway leading from the gateway to the bottommost zone of Hell. He passes in succession through nine separate circular zones, each of which contains smaller cells where individuals or groups of the damned live. Charon waits on the near bank of the river Styx, ready to ferry his miserable passengers across the waters. As Dante and his guide move from circle to circle they encounter a variety of types of sinners sorted into groups according to their chief vices. On reaching the fourth ring of the ninth circle, the two travelers are confronted by Dis (Lucifer), who with his three mouths devours Judas, Brutus, and Cassius. The arduous journey of Dante and Vergil through the Inferno is completed with a horrifying descent into the interior of the body of Lucifer. Finally they arrive at a spot situated directly beneath the place of Christ's crucifixion on Mount Golgotha from where they once more see the stars.

The history of Christianity is dotted with periodic expressions of heretical dissent concerning the existence of Hell, notably by Origen, Erigena, Voltaire, and Nietzsche. But it was not until the seventeenth and eighteenth centuries, when rationalism began to find its voice, that a widespread decline of belief in Hell developed in Western culture. The concept of Hell as an actual spatial domain has virtually disappeared or been reduced to the level of allegorical interpretation. This transformation of the idea is exemplified in *The Fall* in Camus's warning "Don't wait for the Final Judgment. It takes place every day" and in Sartre's declaration in his play *No Exit* that "hell is other people."

ISLAM. Cosmology appears to have been a matter of interest in early Islam not for its own sake but "only as a doctrinal framework for understanding the cosmic field of divine providence and human accountability" (Smith, 1981, p. 9). Muhammad himself does not seem to have held to a clearly defined and detailed picture of a realm of the dead.

According to the Qur'ān, there are seven layers of heaven extending above the earth toward the celestial abode of God. Corresponding to the layers of heaven are seven descending depths of a vast funnel-shaped fire (*alnār*). The topmost level of the netherworlds is Gehenna. This realm of death and torment is connected to the world of the living by a bridge that all the souls of the dead must traverse on the day of judgment. The varieties of punishment meted out to the damned become more painful and severe with each level of descent.

At the partition between Paradise and the Fire stands Zaqqum, a tree that exudes a stifling odor and has blossoms composed of demons' heads. Eating the fruit of Zaqqum burns the stomach like molten metal (surah 7:46–50). The tree separates the two worlds, yet provides a point from which a person can see both realms simultaneously. Beside it is a wall or barrier that divides humanity into separate classes according to the moral quality of their deeds in the temporal world.

Each of the seven fiery realms is assigned a specific name. An inventory of these names reflects the Muslim attitude toward nonbelievers: *hāwiyah* (abyss for hypocrites), *jaḥīm* (fierce fire for idolators), *sa'īr* (blazing fire for Sabaeans), *jahannam* (purgatorial fire for Muslims), *lazā* (flaming fire for Christians), *saqar* (scorching fire for the Magi), and *ḥuṭamah* (raging fire for Jews).

The Qur'ān depicts Gehenna in highly pictorial and terrifying terms. It is referred to as the "Fire of Hell" (89:23) and is depicted as a kind of four-legged beast. Each leg is composed of seventy thousand demons; each demon has thirty thousand mouths. Each of the seven layers of the Fire is punctuated by a gate manned by a guardian who torments the damned. The term *Gehenna* refers both to the topmost sphere and to the entire realm of seven spheres. Whenever this beast of hell is transported to the place of final judgment, it sends forth a buzzing, groaning, and rattling noise, along with sparks and smoke that shrouds the entire horizon in total darkness (15:43–44, 39:71).

The realms of the blessed and the damned are separated by a towering wall. Those who inhabit the heights of this partition can view the inhabitants of both worlds and recognize each group by their distinguishing marks. The blessed are recognizable by their smiling countenances; the damned, by their black faces and blue eyes (57:13). There is also a hint of the existence of a purgatory or limbo for beings whose deeds are neither extremely good nor extremely bad.

Both the Qur'ān and the *ḥadīth* present a wide variety of reasons why a person may be condemned to a life of torment. The fundamental cause is lack of belief in God and in the message of his prophet, Muḥammad. Other reasons include the following: lying, corruption, lack of faith, blasphemy, denial of the advent of the judgment day and of the reality of the Fire, and lack of charity. Leading a life of luxury and believing that wealth brings immortality also lead to condemnation.

The postmortem journey of the soul of the redeemed or the blessed through the various layers of Heaven in the company of the archangel Gabriel is contrasted with the difficult and painful journey of the souls of the damned downward through the many spheres of Fire. The victims of the torments of Gehenna are represented as sighing and wailing in their wretched condition (11:106). Their skins are alternately scorched to a black crisp and then renewed so that they can suffer the torments of Fire over and over again. They are compelled to wear garments made of fire or scalding pitch, and boiling water is poured onto their heads, melting their insides and skins. Iron hooks are used to retrieve them every time they try to escape (22:19–22).

In time, Muslim theologians began to emphasize God's grace and mercy and to downplay his anger and wrath. The belief arose that after a certain period of purgation the angel Gabriel would intercede on the sinner's behalf and release him from the Fire. It was later believed that in time the Fire would be extinguished and all sinners pardoned.

HINDUISM. Vedic references to an underworld are so few in number and so vaguely conceived that many scholars have argued that Vedic religion lacked a concept of hell. More recent studies (see Brown, 1941) have demonstrated that references to a realm of postmortem suffering do signal a genuine, if relatively undeveloped, conception of hell in the Vedic literature.

According to *Ṛgveda* 7.104 and *Atharvaveda* 8.4, the Vedic Hell is situated beneath the three earths, below the created order. It is characterized as a gigantic, bottomless chasm or abyss, a place of no return. In this infinitely deep pit, there is no light, only deep darkness (cf. *Ṛgveda* 2.29.6). In the very deepest realm lies the cosmic serpent, the archdemon Vrtra (*Ṛgveda* 1.32.10), who fell there after Indra slew him.

Some texts describe the Vedic Hell as insufferably hot or unbearably cold. It is a realm of absolute silence (*Ṛgveda* 7.104.5) and of total annihilation, a state that is depicted semi-anthropomorphically as lying in the lap of Nirṛti, the destroyer. This region of eternal torment is populated not by those who committed wrongs inadvertently but by those who consciously and intentionally pursued unrighteous ends: Vṛtra, antidivine forces (*asuras* and *dasyus*), demonic powers (*rākṣasas*), and sorceresses (*yoginīs*) dwell here. The inhabitants of Hell are those who live at cross-purposes with the universal law (*ṛta*).

Hell stands in an antithetical relation to the ordered universe, based not on *ṛta* but *anṛta*. Here there is no order, no gods, no sun, no warmth, no fecundating waters, nor any of the elements vital to the creation and maintenance of creaturely existence. Here in the lap of destruction (*nirṛti*), there is only death and nonexistence (*asat*). It is the opposite of the created, ordered, and illuminated realm.

Later, in the Vedānta, hell came to be conceived in more strictly philosophical terms as the realm of pure nonbeing. Contrasted with this was the realm of being (*sat*), the realm of living beings and of life itself that came to be referred to as *brahman,* the limitless and indefinable fulcrum of being.

In the Upaniṣads, the paths leading to the realms of the blessed and the wretched are envisioned as the way of the ancestors and the way of the gods, respectively. Little importance is accorded to the idea of hell as the destiny of the unrighteous. The emphasis is rather on rebirth as the consequence of an unrighteous past life. In the Yama-Naciketas episode in the *Kaṭha Upaniṣad,* the young man Naciketas receives instruction on the postmortem state from Yama, the lord of the dead. Rather than directly addressing a matter so subtle that not even the gods understand it, Yama informs Naciketas of two paths leading to different ends: the way of pleasure and the way of goodness. Yama recommends that Naciketas choose the latter, thereby avoiding rebirth.

But in the Purāṇas (collections of classical Hindu mythologies), hells are depicted in terrifyingly graphic terms as places of extreme suffering and deprivation. In the *Rāmāyaṇa* (7.21.10–20), Rāvaṇa, the ten-headed demon, witnesses a scene of indescribable wretchedness on entering Yama's abode. He hears the agonizing cries of the wicked being gnawed by dogs and devoured by worms. Pitiful screams shoot across the Vaitarani River from parched people on hot sand who are being sawed in half. The thirsty cry out for water; the hungry, for food. Pale, emaciated specters run to and fro. The righteous, on the other hand, inhabit grand palaces and dine on sumptuous meals, surrounded by beautiful, sweet-smelling maidens dressed in exquisite garments. In the *Mahābhārata* (12.2.25) Yudhiṣṭhira is ushered into an enormous dark chamber that is cluttered with foul-smelling hair, heaps of raw flesh, and countless pools of blood, corpses, worms, deformed animals, hideous monsters of incomparable ugliness, and ghosts of terrifying presence. As will become standard in the later Purāṇas, a specific form of punishment is assigned to each of the subterranean chambers. In the underworld called Kumbhīpāka ("cooked victuals") the wicked are boiled alive in giant vats of boiling oil; in Śalmali, thorns from a silk-cotton tree are used to torture the wicked.

The *Agni Purāṇa* (chaps. 340 and 342), one of the eighteen major collections of classical mythology, perpetuate a theme that blossomed in the Upaniṣads. This is the idea that the course of a person's life in this world is governed by the ritual and moral quality of his deeds. One's experience in the next world is governed by the fruits of those deeds. Yama determines the infernal region to which each wicked soul repairs or the womb into which it is to be born, according to the deeds of the previous existence. The terrifying members of Yama's retinue usher the soul to a place where they prepare an account of its good and evil deeds. The soul initially reaps the benefits of its good deeds in the form of physical and spiritual delights, after which it is returned to hell for a period of suffering in order to purge the residual effects of its evil deeds. If the number of merits outweighs the demerits, the person is reborn into a pure and prosperous family; if the obverse is the case, he may be committed to a lengthy life of suffering in one of the hells or be reborn as an animal, insect, or other base form of life.

The pathways connecting this world with the various hells are dreadful to behold and extend for a total of 164,000 human miles. According to most classical cosmologies, there are a total of 28 major infernal regions situated below the lowest stratum of another 7 netherworlds. Each region lies along a vertical line of descent and is subdivided into 144 smaller chambers, to each of which is assigned an appellation describing its definitive characteristics, for example: Ghora ("horrifying"), Taralatara ("trembling"), Bhayanaka ("terrifying"), Kālarātri ("dark night of devouring time"), and Dīpta ("the blazing realm").

Each chamber is presided over by five guards with the terrifying faces of carnivorous animals and birds, who administer the form of punishment appropriate to the place. The guards cast their condemned wards into dreadful places of punishment. Some souls are cast into gigantic frying skillets or into caldrons filled with boiling oil, molten copper, or iron, while others are tossed onto the upturned tips of sharp pointed lances. Others are submitted to severe lashings with leather straps or heavy bastinados or are forced to drink beverages of boiling metals or noxious solutions of animal urine and human excreta. Still others are broken physically on the rack, dismembered, and then parceled out to vultures, hyenas, and other avaricious creatures of the infernal regions. Each of these dreadful realms is filled with the sounds of screaming, wailing, and moaning.

SECULAR VISIONS. Among a growing number of religious intelligentsia the world over, both heaven and hell are gradually being sublimated or transmuted into psychological entities or realms, with the personal and collective unconscious serving as the source of both positive and negative feelings, images, and attitudes. Even the general mass of people in industrialized countries who claim to retain a belief in an underworld of some description have, in practice, largely transposed many of the ideas and themes previously associated with the underworld (e.g., divine judgment, suffering, torment, disease, death, and mental and physical anguish) into the arena of contemporary human affairs.

SEE ALSO Afterlife; Hades; Heaven and Hell.

BIBLIOGRAPHY

General Works

Brandon, S. G. F. *The Judgment of the Dead.* London, 1967.

Mew, James. *Traditional Aspects of Hell (Ancient and Modern)* (1903). Ann Arbor, 1971.

Ancient Near Eastern Religions

Heidel, Alexander. *The Gilgamesh Epic and Old Testament Parallels.* 2d ed. Chicago, 1963.

Frankfort, Henri. *Kingship and the Gods.* Chicago, 1948.

Pritchard, James B., ed. *Ancient Near Eastern Texts Relating to the Old Testament.* 3d ed. Princeton, N.J., 1969.

Greek and Roman Religions

Dietrich, B. C. *Death, Fate and the Gods.* London, 1965.

Farnell, Lewis R. *Greek Hero Cults and Ideas of Immortality* (1921). Oxford, 1970.

Nilsson, Martin P. *A History of Greek Religion.* 2d ed. Translated by F. J. Fielden. Oxford, 1949.

Judaism

Charles, R. H. *A Critical History of the Doctrine of a Future Life.* 2d ed., rev. & enl. London, 1913.

Ginzberg, Louis. *The Legends of the Jews* (1909–1928). 7 vols. Translated by Henrietta Szold et al. Philadelphia, 1946–1955.

Graves, Robert, and Raphael Patai. *Hebrew Myths.* New York, 1966.

Christianity

Dante Alighieri. *Inferno.* Translated by Allen Mandelbaum. Berkeley, 1980.

Jeremias, Joachim. "Hades." In *Theological Dictionary of the New Testament,* vol. 1, edited by Gerhard Kittel. Grand Rapids, Mich., 1968.

Mew, James. "Christian Hell." In his *Traditional Aspects of Hell (Ancient and Modern)* (1903). Ann Arbor, 1971.

Walker, Daniel P. *The Decline of Hell: Seventeenth Century Discussions of Eternal Torment.* Chicago, 1964.

Islam

Asín Palacios, Miguel. *Islam and the Divine Comedy.* Translated by Harold Sunderland. London, 1926.

Smith, Jane I., and Yvonne Y. Haddad. *The Islamic Understanding of Death and Resurrection.* Albany, N.Y., 1981.

Morris, James W. *The Wisdom of the Throne: An Introduction to the Philosophy of Mulla Sadra.* Princeton, 1981.

Hinduism

Brown, W. Norman. "'The Rigvedic Equivalent for Hell." *Journal of the American Oriental Society* 61 (June 1941): 76–80.

Gombrich, Richard F. "Ancient Indian Cosmology." In *Ancient Cosmologies,* edited by Carmen Blacker and Michael Loewe, pp. 110–142. London, 1975.

Jacobi, Hermann. "Cosmogony and Cosmology (Indian)." In *Encyclopaedia of Religion and Ethics,* vol. 4, edited by James Hastings. Edinburgh, 1914.

Hopkins, E. Washburn. *Epic Mythology* (1915). New York, 1969.

Macdonell, A. A. *Vedic Mythology.* Strassburg, 1897.

New Sources

Albinus, Lars. *The House of Hades.* Aarhus, 2000.

Ariès, Philippe. *L'homme devant la mort.* Paris, 1977.

Ariès, Philippe. *The Hour of Our Death.* New York, 1981.

Armstrong, John. *The Paradise Myth.* London, 1981.

Badham, Paul. *Christian Beliefs about Life after Death.* New York, 1976.

Bernstein, Alan. *The Formation of Hell: Death and Retribution in the Ancient and Early Christian World.* Ithaca, 1993.

Betz, Hans Dieter. "Fragments from a Catabasis Ritual in a Greek Magical Papyrus." In *Gesammelte Aufsätze,* vol. 1, *Hellenismus und Urchristentum,* pp. 147–155. Tübingen, 1990.

Bonfante Warren, Larissa, ed. *Etruscans and Afterlife. A Handbook of Etruscan Studies.* Detroit, 1986.

Borman, William A. *The Other Side of Death: Upanisadic Eschatology.* Dehli, 1990.

Bosworth, Clifford Edmund. *The Banū Sāsān in Arabic Society and Literature. The Medieval Islamic Underworld.* Leiden, 1976.

Brandon, S.G.F. *The Judgement of the Dead.* London, 1967.

Brandon, S.G.F. *Man and His Destiny in the Great Religions.* Manchester, 1963.

Bremmer, Jan N. *The Rise and Fall of the Afterlife.* London, 2002.

Cantilena, Renata, ed. *Caronte: un obolo per l'aldilà.* Napoli, 1995. (Special issue of the journal *La Parola del Passato*).

Carey, John. "The Irish Other-World: Hiberno-Latin Perspectives." *Éigse. A Journal of Irish Studies* 25 (1991): 154–159.

Cavendish, Richard. *Visions of Heaven and Hell.* New York, 1977.

Chiavacci,Leonardi, and Anna Maria, ed. Dante Alighieri. *La Divina Commedia.* Milano, 1997.

Chirassi Colombo, Ileana. "La salvezza nell'aldilà nella cultura greca arcaica." *Studi Classici* 15 (1973): 23–39.

Clark, R. J. *Catabasis. Vergil and the Wisdom Tradition.* Amsterdam, 1978.

Coley, Alison E. *Indo-European Views of Death and the Afterlife as Determined from Archaeological, Mythological and Linguistic Sources.* Los Angeles, 1990.

Colvin, Howard. *Architecture and Afterlife.* New Haven, 1991.

Cumont, Franz. *Lux Perpetua.* Paris, 1949.

Eilen, Gardiner, ed. *Visions of Heaven and Hell before Dante.* New York, 1989.

Eliade, Mircea. *Death, Afterlife, and Eschatology: A Thematic Sourcebook.* New York, 1974.

Formanek, Susanne, and William R. La Fleur, eds. *Practicing the Afterlife: Perspectives from Japan.* Vienna, 2004.

Gowan, Donald E. *Eschatology in the Old Testament.* Philadelphia, 1986.

Griffiths, John Gwyn. *The Divine Verdict: A Study of Divine Judgement in the Ancient Religions.* Leiden, 1991.

Hillman, James. *The Dream and the Underworld.* New York, 1979.

Himmelfarb, Martha. *Tours of Hell: An Apocalyptic Form in Jewish and Christian Literature.* Philadelphia, 1983.

Hinard, Françoise, ed. *La mort, les morts et l'au-delà dans le monde romain. Actes du Colloque de Caen 20–22 novembre 1985.* Caen, 1987.

Hughes, Robert. *Heaven and Hell in Western Art.* New York, 1968.

Iverson, Kenneth W. *Death to Dust: What happens to Dead Bodies.* Tucson, 1994.

Klostermaier, Klaus. *Mythologies and Philosophies of Salvation in the Theistic Traditions of India.* Waterloo, 1984.

Lang, Bernhard. "Afterlife: Ancient Israel's Changing Vision of the World Beyond." *Bible Review* 4 (1988): 12–23.

Le Goff, Jacques. *La naissance du Purgatoire.* Paris, 1981 (English ed. *The Birth of Purgatory*, transl. by Arthur Goldhammer. London, 1984).

Moraldi, Luigi. *L'aldilà dell'uomo, nelle civiltà babilonese, egizia, greca, latina, ebraica, cristiana e musulmana, con il testo dell'Apocalissi di Paolo.* Milano, 1985.

Murray, [Sister] Charles. *Rebirth and Afterlife. A Study of the transmutation of some pagan imagery in early Christian funerary art.* Oxford, 1981.

Park, Joseph S. *Conceptions of Afterlife in Jewish Inscriptions.* Tübingen, 2000.

Rohde, Erwin. *Psyche. Seelenkult und Unsterblichkeitsglaube der Griechen.* Tübingen 1898².

Russell, Jeffrey Burton. *A History of Heaven: The Singing Silence.* Princeton, 1997.

Spronk, Klaas. *Beatific Afterlife in Ancient Israel and in the Ancient Near East.* Kevelaer, 1986.

Toon, Peter. *Heaven and Hell: A Biblical and Theological Overview.* Nashville, 1986.

Whaley, Joachim, ed. *Mirrors of mortality. Studies in the Social History of Death.* London, 1981.

Xella, Paolo, ed. *Archeologia dell'inferno: l'aldilà nel mondo antico vicino-orientale e classico.* Verona, 1987.

J. BRUCE LONG (1987)
Revised Bibliography

UNGARINYIN RELIGION. Members of the Ngarinyin (Ngarinjin) language group, along with their regional neighbors the Worrorra (Worrora/Worora), Wunambal (Unambal), and Gambre (Gamberre), whose combined, adjacent territories cover the northern Kimberley region of Western Australia, share a religious tradition primarily focused on the figures known as *wandjina* and *wunggurr* and an associated set of beliefs and practices. While variants of *wunggurr*, the Rainbow Serpent motif, are evident in Aboriginal cosmologies across Australia (Radcliffe-Brown, 1926), in the northern Kimberley region the Rainbow Serpent beliefs take on a distinctive cast through their interaction with the *wandjina* complex (cf. Elkin, 1930, "Rock Paintings of North-West Australia," p. 279).

***WANDJINA* AND *WUNGGURR*.** Whereas *wandjina* and *wunggurr* are in some respects distinguishable from each other, in local beliefs and practice they are not entirely separate entities. *Wandjina* are named and localized "spirits of place" believed to reside in specific tracts of country associated with a particular patrifilial clan and appear in narratives that describe their travels and adventures in the *Larlan* (the originary creative epoch). *Wunggurr* is a more diffuse life force animating and underlying the particular manifestations of its power that find expression in all species of things, including the *wandjina*. Some local expressions use the terms *wandjina* and *wunggurr* interchangeably in contexts where powerful forces emanating from the land are discussed in general. A further set of terms, *gulingi* (properly translated as "rain," but also a personage or group of personages indistinguishable from *wandjina*) and Galaru (a sky-snake personage particularly associated with the more dangerous aspects of cyclonic rain and lightning) are also at times used to refer to both *wandjina* and *wunggurr*. One further term, Wanjad, is used to refer to an aspect of *wunggurr* that becomes incarnate in the Rock Python. Representations of *wandjina* and *wunggurr* often occur together, alongside depictions of various natural species, in the painted cave galleries of this region. It is believed that *Wandjina* came to dwell eternally in the caves, in which they painted themselves. An oneiric mirroring between *wandjina* and *wunggurr* was noted by Andreas Lommel, who reported on the neighboring Wunambal's belief that "Ungud [*wunggurr*] finds the soul of a Wondschina [*wandjina*] in a dream in the water" (Lommel, 1997, p. 16).

D. Mowaljarlai explained the relationship between *wandjina* and *wunggurr* in this way:

> Every man or girl they come out from each *wunggurr* water. *Wandjina* gives us back. Then we know where that child come from. Everybody know. And that is where the land is because all the power connected. We find children from water. That's why we're water people. We spirits hide in the water come out in the open. We all belong water because *wandjina* belong water. He not a dry *wandjina*. He belong rain. (Doring, 2000, p. 238)

Wandjina are usually depicted as mouthless, anthropomorphic figures representing the body of an apical clan ancestor (or rarely an ancestress). They occur as polychromatic paintings in sandstone caves and in stone arrangements throughout the region. *Wandjina* are also identified in other features of the landscape, in various animal and plant (especially aquatic) species, in pools of freshwater and sometimes saltwater, and most importantly in the cumulonimbus rain-bearing clouds (*gulingi* or *angguban*) that move across the Kimberley landscape in the cyclone season, *Winjin* (December through to April). The actions of moving and then laying down performed by the *wandjina* in their travels in the creative epoch, *Larlan*, by the rain clouds (also known as "the travelers") each wet season, and by the flowing rivers gradually contracting to isolated pools are all perceived as processual moments in the continual reanimation of Dreaming forces that works toward everything in the country becoming *yayi-yurru* (also transcribed as *yorro yorro*), "standing up together in a bunch" (Redmond, 2001, p. 227; also Mowaljarlai and Malnic, 1993).

Wandjina are most often represented only with head and shoulders, though occasionally an entire anthropomorph (usually with no gender marking) is depicted. In such cases the torso, arms, and legs are often filled in with a series of parallel red ochre lines representing falling rain. The head is generally encircled with radiating lines said to be both feathered head decorations and lightning. The head commonly shows a horseshoe-shaped red-ochre band said to be the encircling body of *wunggurr*, the Rock Python.

Wandjina cave paintings are regarded by the Ngarinyin people as the imprint or "shadow," *anguma*, left by the *wandjina* after their creative travels across the landscape in the *Larlan*. The word *anguma* also denotes a person's "spirit" or "soul," linking *wandjina* closely to beliefs about conception (see below). *Wandjina* are said to be visible in the present because they pressed their bodies into the rock faces of this landscape during the earth's formative period, while its surface was still soft. The apparent absence of a mouth has been explained by some senior Ngarinyin men as resulting from the fact that the mouth is located on the inner side of the visible image, facing in toward the rock upon which the image appears. *Wandjina* sometimes left behind other sorts of markings, such as the footprints said to be visible in the rock at Aynggulura. Paddy Neowarra, a senior Ngarinyin man, tells how "*wandjina* walked through that flat ground, through the opening and made his print behind him for us to see" (Redmond, 1998, p. 24). At the painting site known as *Yalgi andi*, on the central Kimberley Plateau, the qualities of this primordially soft world are still said to be clearly evident. Here an extensive series of cup-shaped markings appear in both vertical and horizontal rock faces. These small hollows, *dagula* or *bindingarri*, are said to have been created by the action of the "sweat of *wandjina*" falling onto the soft rock in the *Larlan* (Redmond, 1996, p. 35).

The painted *wandjina* images, then, are regarded not as the artistic work of the ancestors of present-day people but rather as actual ancestors, autochthonous creations whose images have merely been maintained by human agency: "kept bright" by ritual repainting. This periodic repainting is believed to have profound consequences as far as maintaining the natural and social balances of the cosmos (Mowaljarlai and Malnic, 1993; Rumsey and Mowaljarlai, 1994; Crawford, 1968; Blundell and Layton, 1978). Persons of both genders feel a ritual obligation to countries where they have a strong connection deriving from one of a number of potential links (i.e., patrilocality, mother's country, conception site). It seems that socially mature persons other than patriclan members could be invited to repaint an image in another person's clan country. Such persons would then be given gifts (*ngurli*), such as kangaroo meat or wild honey. Paddy Neowarra explained, "In *Winjin* [Cyclone Season] time when that *wilmi* [mist] come out from the stone in early morning, *jurri* we call it, the 'smoke' goes into the paint and renews it and it's just like it paint up again so we can go always go back and renew it" (Redmond, 1995, p. 98).

In this sense even the act of retouching is not seen as being initiated by humans but by the saturated air emanating from the sun-warmed rocks that gives a new life to the painted images. There is indeed a noticeable glow in the paintings at this time of year because the kinds of ochre used in the paintings (the white huntite, particularly) absorb moisture readily, enriching the colors, restoring to them something of the vividness these paints display when wet (cf. Crawford, 1968).

Ngarinyin use the term *we awani* for the "laying down" of the *wandjina* as they pressed themselves into the soft jelly-like surface of the earth in the *Larlan*. They speak of the rock caves (tight niches into which painters often had to squeeze themselves) as actually being cloud formations, stating unequivocally "that stone is a cloud" (cf. Mowaljarlai and Vinnicombe, 1995: 236; see also Crawford, 1968).

The annual wet-season deluge finds its earliest mythic archetype in the focal story of Wanalirri. This story and its associated painting site and songs tell of a primordial flood of cataclysmic proportions that submerged the world and all within it. In this saga a boab tree (*Adansonia gregorii*), actually a disguised *wandjina*, "opened its legs" and swallowed up two juvenile miscreants who had originally provoked the wrath of the *wandjina* by plucking the feathers from Dumbi the Owl, an animal highly favored by *wandjina* (Redmond, 1995, p. 89). The boys were then trapped inside the boab body forever despite the efforts of their relatives (who then appeared to be saved from the flood) on the outside of the boab tree. These two boys who were trapped in the boab were said to be the only survivors of the great flood, but having grabbed a kangaroo by the tail to escape the floodwater, they were tricked into a premature burial. As in the various Arnhem Land versions of the swallowing myths and rites given by L. R. Hiatt "as a substitute for the natural model of female generation," the two boys of the Wanalirri story were imprisoned, but the other people of the world were regurgitated after the flood (Hiatt, 1975, p. 157).

This cosmogonic event is replicated in the floods of the wet season and in the radical contraction of the river systems as the dry season moves in. Thus there is an annual recurrence of the "breaking up" of the visible body of *wunggurr* into distinct pools. The long ribbons of the river courses, which are visible from the elevated rock ledges in which many of the *wandjina* caves are located, slowly break up into large, relatively isolated rock pools, the *ngawan* or "living water" that never disappears, no matter how dry the season.

The night sky is also said to be replete with pools of freshwater that are made most visible in the body of the originary *wandjina*, Walanganda, the Milky Way. This galaxy is said to be the body of Walanganda lying across the heavens, with his head in the north and feet in the south. Within this body of swirling white mists are pools of "dark, sweet water" that are pointed out in one dark hole in particular just to the east of the Southern Cross constellation (Redmond, 1996, p. 18). All freshwater on the earth is said to have come from water that originally "fell down" from these dark pools of freshwater in the body of Walanganda.

The whiteness of the body of Walanganda is said to come from the smoke from the cooking fires of the two moiety heroes: Jun.gun (Owlet Nightjar), who was cooking *yali* (female kangaroo), and Wodoy (Spotted Nightjar), who was cooking *jebarra* (emu) in the *Larlan.* These two totemic figures are central to the foundational myths of Ngarinyin sociality. They are said, for example, to have come to blows over the issue of primordial incestuous desire, leading to the introduction of the all-important law of moiety exogamy through daughter exchange. At the Walanganda *wandjina* painting in Jibilingarri clan country, the *wandjina* and a smaller second figure, identified as his son, are represented on the roof of a cave. In the burnished rock floor immediately below them is a dark, well-polished depression said to be the *wunggurr* pool visible in the Milky Way itself. Here the *wandjina* and his son are perpetually "mirrored" in the "water" that forms part of Walanganda's own body. Parallel red lines emanating from the *wandjina* body are said to be the swirling mists making up the galaxy. Importantly, these lines of celestial mist also formed an *angga* (or *coolamon*), traditionally used by women for carrying vegetable foodstuffs, babies, and the bones of the dead (cf. Love, 1936, p. 158). The curved outside surface of *angga* are usually decorated with the same kind of striated red lines carved into the wood. J. R. B. Love noted that at Kunmunya "the mother will often paint her child with stripes of red ochre" (Love, 1936, p. 118).

DEATH AND FUNERARY PRACTICES. The relationship of continuity between living persons and the *wandjina* of their clan was traditionally underscored by the practice of interring the skulls and femur bones of deceased men in the main *wandjina* cave of their patriclan. Most modern burials take place in township or community graveyards following a Christian service accompanied by country gospel singing interspersed with the intense keening of the women in a maternal kinship relationship to the deceased. These funerals are marked by strict observance of avoidance relationships that prescribe that the widow of a deceased man (but not vice versa) enters a lengthy period of seclusion from other members of the community. The occasional performance of precolonial burial practices, in conjunction with the narratives of senior Ngarinyin people about these practices when they were more widespread, permits considerable insight into Ngarinyin beliefs about death.

Once the bones of the deceased were regarded as sufficiently "clean and dry," after perhaps a year or more exposed to the elements in a stone cairn, they were gathered and given a final scrub in water by people in a maternal kinship category to the deceased (Redmond, 1997, p. 34). The skull and long-limb bones were anointed with a mixture of fat and red ochre before being wrapped in sheets of *wulun* (paperbark). The paperbark wrapping, particularly associated with femininity, symbolically "restores" to the bones their fleshy envelope. In this regard it is important to note that babies were also usually rubbed with fat by the maternal kin in the early days of their lives (cf. Love, 1936, p. 113).

Grieving relatives thus participate in ceremonies that "return" the individual subject to the ancestral realm, reunifying the deceased person with the enduring *wandjina* ancestor and ancestral clan country. This *wandjina* identity endures through various reincarnations of the ancestral being (through the *abi* relationship). A deceased person's *anguma* (shadow or spirit) is believed to rejoin with the body of *wunggurr* when his or her bones are lodged in the cave. The person's spirit travels to Dulugun, an island in the western sea (Numenbu, Champagny Island) and, after some indefinite interval, resurfaces through a water hole and attaches itself to the person it has chosen as its new father, thus enacting the *abi* identity of a person with his or her father's father's brother or sister. Each of these reciprocal relationship categories are glossed in English simply as "brother" and "sister." Afterward, one part of the *anguma* is said to remain in the rock cave where the bones are deposited. In Dulugun, spirit children are said to be mired in *jalad-gu,* a green water grass in the water holes where the *anguma* reside. It is said that this water grass acts as a kind of sponge that absorbs the *anguma* in Dulugun until they are ready to be reborn.

The identification of the sandstone caves in which the bones of the dead are placed with *an.guban* (rain clouds) is a crucial element in the understanding of the cosmography of this region—it is in these "watery" recesses that the *wandjina,* as the living part of a person's patri-identity, continues to dwell (Mowaljarlai and Vinnicombe, 1995; Mowaljarlai and Malnic, 1993; cf. Lommel, 1997; Crawford, 1968). The symbolic equivalence of cloud and stone highlights the series of transformations that link living persons, their *wandjina,* and the more universalizing aspect of the creative forces believed to be immanent in the figure of *wunggurr.*

CONCEPTION BELIEFS. *Wunggurr* also embodies *yarri,* dreaming activity in a general sense. This is most evident in the reciprocity of "dreaming" child spirits between the father-son dyad in the Ngarinyin social world, in which a person is identified as a reincarnation of an *abi* (father's father's brother or sister, depending on the gender of the child) from whom one's name is taken. *Wandjina* are thus personified in contemporary living persons, who identify with a particular *wandjina* by referring to him as "I" or "me," or as the speaker's *abi* when narrating stories of that personage in the *Larlan.* The association of *wandjina* and *wunggurr* with fertility is clearly apparent in the affectionate calling of newborn babies *"wandjina,"* and in the practice of divining where a fetus's *wunggurr* (conception place) is by family discussions about where the mother first knew herself to be pregnant, what happened on that day, where the husband was, and what he might have caught hunting or fishing that day, thus conferring the name of that place upon the child.

The senior Wunambal man W. Goonack stated, "We born from water, from *wulu*" (Redmond, 1995, p. 28). *Wulu* is a polysemous Ngarinyin term that Paddy Neowarra glosses as the "colour seen in water when a man finds dream for baby" or simply "dreams in the water" (Redmond, 1997, p. 72). This color, the spectral dispersion of light in water, is regarded as having "strong *wunggurr*" just as the rainbow is regarded as a powerful embodiment of *wunggurr.* In the latter case the shimmering spectral light is as important to the image of *wunggurr* as the snakelike shape it forms arching across the sky from one point on the earth to another.

***WUNGGURR* AND *BARNMARN*.** Beneath the *wunggurr* pools it is said that there are entire "worlds—big dry ground" in which *wandjina* dwell, worlds that are mirrors of the airy world above the rock pools but are contained in world-sized caves complete with kin, game, and vegetation. These worlds, also identified with Dulugun, the realm of the dead (see below), are believed to have something like "trap-doors with lid" or "windows" that allow entry and exit for those with the knowledge to do so, such as the *barnmarn,* a traditional healer and composer. A human being can enter and exit this realm through these "windows" or "trapdoors" as though in a "lift" (i.e., an elevator). The sensation of vertiginous descent was said to be similar (Redmond, 1996, pp. 56–59). According to D. Mowaljarlai, "A man who had healing powers came to that *wunggurr* place, snake place, punched a hole there with his heel, with foot, and he made a window . . . hollow ground, it just went down in a door" (Lommel and Mowaljarlai, 1994, p. 285).

The process of "dreaming" songs requires a composer to travel in a dream on the back of *wunggurr* through the air or deep beneath the water to Dulugun, the land of the dead. The composer's mortal body meanwhile remains on the ground, where it is cared for by the composer's assistants. The sleeping body remains connected to the *wunggurr* self by *buyu,* a long, thin, invisible thread connected to the body, now colloquially known as "radar" or "fishing line."

Miriru (or *mururu*) is a name for the *wunggurr* power possessed by the *barnmarn.* D. Mowaljarlai has explained that *mururu* is the "clear vision, no longer blind" imparted from *wunggurr.* Others have described it as "strong *wunggurr* dreams" and also as the "blood, juice of kangaroo" (Redmond, 1995, p. 25). There are a number of senses in which the *wunggurr* power of the composer-healer is comparable to that which comes from a person's dreaming of a spirit child. Both are referred to by the same term in Kimberley Aboriginal English: "finding" a song or "finding" a spirit child, respectively. Both require a penetration of the screen that normally shields humans from the spirit realm. Composers take the journey through the bottom of the water hole to Dulugun, where bundles of green leaves are held in front of their eyes so they will not be too frightened to look at the emerging dancing spirits. In the case of a man finding a child, the *anguma* itself takes the journey out of the water hole and lands on the body of the prospective father.

Beliefs about *wandjina* and *wunggurr* continue to have a powerful salience in contemporary Kimberley Aboriginal communities, despite great changes in economic and social circumstances. The people of this cultural domain continue to place these images and beliefs at the very heart of their social and cultural identity vis à vis other Aboriginal groups of the region and the encompassing non-Aboriginal world. In everyday discourse and the interpretation of events, *wandjina* and *wunggurr* figure prominently for all age groups, even though the differences in levels of knowledge and specificity are marked. One of the ways in which all participate in this shared body of beliefs is in the attribution of "uncanny" and troubling events to the actions of *wandjina, wunggurr,* and the host of other supernatural beings in this cosmology. The practice of depicting *wandjina* and *wunggurr* on canvases for sale in the contemporary art world is another means by which the salience of these images is transmitted across generations.

ADOLESCENT MALE INITIATION. Another continuing aspect of Ngarinyin religious life is the annual performance of ceremonies at which boys who have reached adolescence are circumcised. This may take the form either of the local tradition of *walungarri* (a circle dance performed over three nights accompanied by a long and intricate song cycle and clapping sticks) or *wangga* (imported to the Kimberley in the 1930s from the Daly River area of Northern Territory in which the *didjeridu* is employed as an accompaniment to singing in a Murin-patha language).

The practices of *walungarri* are said to have come from the ancestral bird personages, Gwion Gwion (Doring, 2000; cf. Lommel, 1997, and Crawford, 1968, where their role is understated). The local origins of circumcision are also given in myths such as the Worrorra story of Ngayanggananyi (Mount Trafalgar) and the Wunbangguwa people, told by Elkin Umbagai as "the Mountain of Initiation" (McKenzie, 1980, p. 76). Here the Ancestral Beings first dug a trench around a mountain so it was cut off from its surrounding stone matrix. To celebrate their achievement they instituted "the first initiation ceremony for young men" (McKenzie, 1980, p. 76). Here the *walungarri* circle dance is an emulation of digging around the base of the mountain. Flying Fox and several other ancestral animals, including Ring-Tail Possum, Crab, and Shovel-Nose Shark, "change their shapes"—that is, attained their present animal morphology through the process of digging out the trench around the mountain (McKenzie, 1980, p. 76). Flying Foxes, the first initiates (said to show circumcision marks on their penises), play a particularly prominent role in this story. The whirling flight of flocks of flying foxes when roused from sleep is said to be a re-enactment of the *walungarri* circle dance. The *walungarri,* says Umbagai, "goes on all night. When the first streak of daylight shows, the lads are taken away from the families—from the women and children" (McKenzie, 1980, p. 76). The women then "wail and sometimes beat their heads with stones" (in the manner of widows at the deaths of their husbands), and the initiate is entrusted to the care of a classificatory brother-in-law (a potential wife's brother), who will nurse him through the circumcision and its aftermath. This relationship remains significant to both parties throughout their lives.

Extensive travels to gather initiation performers are an important part of the ceremonial process and foster close ties of reciprocity between individuals and groups in far-flung settlements across the Kimberley. Other forms of exchange (*wurnan*) of both a ceremonial and mundane nature, the arrangements for which which tend to be all-consuming for the participants, are instituted and perpetuated through these visits, which in turn impart vitality and complexity to Kimberley social and religious life.

See Also Rainbow Snake; Wandjina.

Bibliography

Blundell, Valda. "Symbolic Systems and Cultural Continuity in Northwest Australia: A Consideration of Aboriginal Cave Art." *Culture* 2, no. 1 (1982): 3–20.

Blundell, Valda, and Robert Layton. "Marriage, Myth, and Models of Exchange in the West Kimberleys." *Mankind* 11 (1978): 231–245.

Capell, Arthur. *Cave Painting Myths: Northern Kimberley.* Sydney, Australia, 1972.

Crawford, Ian M. *The Art of the Wandjina.* Melbourne, 1968.

Doring, Jeff, ed. *Gwion Gwion.* Cologne, Germany, 2000.

Elkin, Adolphus P. "Rock Paintings of North-West Australia." *Oceania* 1 (1930): 257–279.

Elkin, Adolphus P. "The Rainbow-Serpent Myth in North-West Australia." *Oceania* 1 (1930): 349–352.

Hiatt, Lester R. "Swallowing and Regurgitation in Australian Myth and Rite." In *Australian Aboriginal Mythology: Essays in Honour of W. E. H. Stanner,* edited by L. R. Hiatt, pp. 143–162. Canberra, Australia, 1975.

Lommel, Andreas. *The Unambal: A Tribe in Northwest Australia* (1952). Translated by Ian Campbell. Carnavon Gorge, Australia, 1997.

Lommel, Andreas, and D. Mowaljarlai. "Shamanism in Northwest Australia." *Oceania* 6, no. 4 (1994): 277–287.

Love, J. R. B. "Rock Paintings of the Worrora and Their Mythological Interpretation." *Journal of the Royal Society of Western Australia* 16 (1930): 1–24.

Love, J. R. B. *Stone-Age Bushmen of To-day: Life and Adventure among a Tribe of Savages in North-Western Australia.* London and Glasgow, 1936.

McKenzie, Maisie, ed. *Visions of Mowanjum.* Adelaide, Australia, 1980.

Mowaljarlai, D. and Jutta Malnic. *Yorro Yorro: Everything Standing up Alive: Spirit of the Kimberleys.* Broome, Australia, 1993.

Mowaljarlai, D., and Patricia Vinnicombe. "That Rock Is a Cloud: Concepts Associated with Rock Images in the Kimberley Region of Australia." In *Perceiving Rock Art: Social and Political Perspectives,* edited by Knut Helskog and Bjørnar Olsen, pp. 228–246. Oslo, 1995.

Petri, Helmut. *Sterbende Welt in Nordwest-Australien.* Brunswick, Germany, 1954.

Radcliffe-Brown, A. R. "The Rainbow-Serpent Myth of Australia." *Journal of the Royal Anthropological Institute* 56 (1926): 19–25.

Redmond, Anthony. "Places That Move." In *Emplaced Myth: Space, Narrative, and Knowledge in Australian Aboriginal and Papua New Guinea Societies,* edited by Alan Rumsey and James Weiner, pp. 120–138. Honolulu, 2001.

Redmond, Anthony. "Rulug Wayirri: Moving Kin and Country in the Northern Kimberley." Ph.D. diss., University of Sydney, 2001.

Rumsey, Alan, and D. Mowaljarlai. *Report on Survey of Painting Sites in the Roe and Moran River Areas of Western Australia.* Canberra, Australia, 1994.

Anthony Redmond (2005)

UNIATE CHURCHES.

UNIATE CHURCHES. *Uniate* is the name given to former Eastern Christian or Orthodox churches that have been received under the jurisdiction of the Church of Rome and retain their own ritual, practice, and canon law. The term carries a strong negative connotation and is seldom used by these churches to describe themselves.

The term was first used by opponents to the Union of Brest-Litovsk (1595) to indicate a betrayal of Orthodoxy and a yielding to political pressure enforced by alleged violence. The problem of this terminology emerged again in the new alignment of eastern Europe after communism. Many Orthodox view these churches as an obstacle in the way of reconciliation between the Catholic and Orthodox churches. They feel that their very existence constitutes a denial by Catholics of the ecclesial reality of the Orthodox Church and that these unions grew from efforts to split local Orthodox communities.

Attempts at the reunion of the Christian churches of the East and the West usually ended in failure, especially in the centuries immediately after the mutual excommunications of 1054. Later political necessity forced Emperor Michael VIII Palaeologus (1234–1282) to seek the help of the Western powers for the support of Byzantium at the Council of Lyons (1274). Subsequently, this agreement was revoked by the new pope in Rome, Martin V (r. 1281–1285). In the East its acceptance was forced, and it was soon repudiated by Michael's son, Andronicus II (1260–1332). The Council of Florence, after long negotiations, issued a bull of reunion, *Laetentur coeli,* on July 6, 1439, but the Greek signatories began to deny the reunion as soon as they arrived in their home environment. Yet all these attempts at union were not futile because they kept the idea of union alive in Christian consciousness. After the initial optimism of the post–World War II ecumenical movement and the World Council of Churches in the Protestant dialogue with the Orthodox and in the Catholic International Dialogue with Orthodoxy after the Second Vatican Council, a period of retrenchment set in.

MELKITE CATHOLICS. The term *Melkite* refers to a Christian of the Byzantine rite—Catholic or Orthodox—from the patriarchates of Alexandria, Antioch, or Jerusalem. (The word derives from the Syriac word *malka* and the Arabic word *melek,* which mean "king" or "emperor." These Christians were given this name by the anti-Chalcedonian party because they adhered to the Christological position of the Byzantine emperor after the Council of Chalcedon in 451 CE.) Until the 1300s the Melkites used the Antiochene rite. In the countryside the liturgy was celebrated in West Syriac or Aramaic and in the cities in Greek. With the advent of Islam, Arabic gradually replaced Syriac. Over the course of the fourteenth century the Byzantine rite replaced the Antiochene rite.

The Melkite faithful tried to preserve allegiance to both Rome and Constantinople. By 1724, renewed communication with Rome had resulted in the creation of a Catholic Melkite Church alongside the Orthodox Melkite Church, although no formal written agreement of union was ever drawn up. In the intervening history the Melkite Catholic patriarch of Antioch, Maximos Mazloum (1833–1855), added the sees of Alexandria and Jerusalem to his title. Patriarch Maximos IV Sayegh (1947–1967) defended the traditions of the East in his patriarchate and at the Second Vatican Council. The Melkite bishops, including Patriarch Maximos IV, have supported the idea that, in the event of a reconciliation between the Orthodox and Catholic churches, their church should be reintegrated into the Orthodox Patriarchate of Antioch. A bilateral commission for dialogue between the Melkites and Antiochene Orthodox was established in 1995, and both sides expressed the firm intention to heal the schism of 1724. The Melkites have achieved the closest union with their former counterparts in practice if not yet in name. Many Melkite Catholics immigrated to North and South America at the beginning of the twentieth century and formed two eparchies (dioceses) in Newton, Massachusetts, and in São Paulo, Brazil.

MARONITE CHURCH. The Maronite Church traces its origins to the fourth century CE and the monk Maron (d. c. 423), who received a Greek and Syrian literary education and went to Antioch to complete his studies. In Antioch he met and befriended John Chrysostom (c. 347–407 CE), who soon became the bishop of Constantinople. Centuries later a community of Maronites grew up around the monastery of Saint Maron on the banks of the Orontes River in northern Syria. Seeking to escape from the persecutions of the caliphates of Damascus and Baghdad, Maronites began to seek refuge in the mountains of Lebanon. Although the Maronite Church never rejected the primacy of the Roman See, communication between the two churches was interrupted for centuries, and only after 1182 and the advent of the Crusaders was Roman recognition of the Maronite rite restored. During the time of the Crusades, Maronite priests and faithful were the only Eastern Christians allowed to worship in Latin churches. Maronites had the same rights as Latins, and their own magistrates judged them according to their own customs and laws. The head of the Maronite Church began to use the title "patriarch" during the fifteenth century. The title became definitive in a bull of Pope Paul V (ruled 1605–1621) in 1608.

The Maronite Church is one of two Uniate churches that do not have a parallel Orthodox hierarchy. The other is the Italo-Albanian Catholic Church. The Maronite Church has undergone many influences tending to conform it to the Latin rite. The rite of the Maronite Church belongs to a group of Antiochene rites, and its liturgical language is West Syriac or Aramaic. The Maronites adopted more and more the use of Arabic as that language became the vernacular. The words of institution in the canon of the liturgy are usually sung in Syriac; the rest of the liturgy is usually recited in the vernacular language of the place. Political and economic turmoil in the Middle East has caused the immigration of a large number of Maronites to the United States, where they have established two dioceses.

RUTHENIANS. The term *Ruthenian* designates former Orthodox who come from the region that is bounded on the north by the Vistula and Neman Rivers and on the south by the Danube and Dnieper, and that includes territories of present-day Poland, the former Soviet Union, Czechoslovakia, Hungary, and Romania. *Ruthenian* is derived from the Latin *Rutheni,* meaning "Russian," and is used by Western historians to designate Catholic Slavs of the Polish-Lithuanian state or of the Austro-Hungarian Empire. The Russian authorities preferred the term *Little Russian* to distinguish those people from the Russians to the north. The Ruthenians divided into two branches. To the north of the Carpathian Mountains under Polish or Russian control were the Galicians. The Subcarpathians lived on the southern side of the mountains and were influenced by Austro-Hungarian political and social conditions. The Galicians rapidly formed a church as a result of the Union of Brest-Litovsk (1595), which was signed by several bishops. The Union of Uzhgorod (1646) initiated a series of unions through the course of the next 125 years before Subcarpathian union was actually achieved and a see established at Mukacheve in 1771.

The subsequent political division of Galician territory subjected Byzantine Catholics there to persecution by their Orthodox brethren, who thought they had changed their traditions by allowing Latin rite deviations. The Catholics belonged to the peasant classes and lived in the villages, whereas the Orthodox for the most part belonged to the lesser landed nobility. Catholics were obliged to pass over to Orthodoxy under threat of violence, despite the assurances of Russian officials. In 1805 the See of Kiev was abolished. The Ruthenians were placed under the protection of the Austro-Hungarian Empire and the jurisdiction of the archbishop of L'viv (Lemberg), who was recognized as the primate of the Ruthenians of Galicia, Subcarpathia, Hungary, and Slovakia.

Nascent nationalism began to divide the Galician Church. After 1848 the term *Ukrainian* designated the people and nation to the north of the Carpathian Mountains. The term *White (Byelo) Russian* meant those inhabiting the northern regions around the Pripet Marshes. The remaining Ruthenians slowly developed a national consciousness in the Subcarpathian region and continued to refer to themselves as *Greek Catholics*, an ethnic as well as a religious term. Those Ruthenians who assumed Hungarian culture called themselves Hungarians. The creation of the Czechoslovak state and the advent of the Soviet Union reinforced these divisions. Ruthenian immigration to Yugoslavia in the sixteenth century created a substantial community there that survived persecution after World War II.

After World War II the Soviet government actively persecuted Ruthenian Catholics to force them into the Russian Orthodox Church. The major hierarchs of the Ukrainian Catholic Church were arrested in 1945 and 1946 and exiled to Siberia or killed. In a council of reunion held at L'viv, the remaining faithful, whose families had been threatened with deportation, voted in March 1946 to abolish the union with Rome. The metropolitan see of Galicia was placed under the jurisdiction of the Patriarchate of Moscow. In the case of the Subcarpathian Ruthenians, the territory of the diocese of Uzhgorod was ceded to the Soviet Union by Czechoslovakia after its occupation by the Soviet army. The Orthodox began to occupy Catholic churches under the protection of the civil administration. The Ruthenian bishop, Theodore Romzha (b. 1911), died mysteriously in 1947. The abrogation of the union with Rome was signed in August 1949 in the Monastery of Saint Nicholas in Mukacheve. The underground Ukrainian Catholic Church began to reemerge even before the fall of the Soviet regime.

The liturgy and ritual of the Ruthenian Catholics remained conservative for centuries and followed the main lines of the Orthodox tradition. Ancient Greek melodies were preserved in the Ruthenian *prostopenie* (plainchant) at the time that the Russian Orthodox Church introduced polyphony and Renaissance melodies into their church music. The Synod of Zamość (1720) introduced a number of innovations as a result of pressure from the Polish government to conform the Ruthenian usage to the Latin. These included the addition of the phrase "and the Son" (*filioque*) into the text of the creed; the commemoration of the pope; the teaching that the sacred moment of the liturgy, when the transformation of the elements occurs, was at the words of institution ("This is my body"), and not at the *epiklesis* (the calling down of the Holy Spirit) as had been taught in the East; the prohibition of communion to infants; the prohibition against using sponges to clean the *diskos* (paten); the prohibition against pouring hot water into consecrated wine; and the use of only one priest as well as a shortened formula in the administration of the anointing of the sick. Western types of Marian devotion and devotion to the Sacred Heart were introduced under the influence of the Polish Jesuits. Popular hymnody was often Western-inspired or based on folk melodies.

Austro-Hungarian emigration in large numbers began in the 1870s as a result of poor distribution of agricultural land, rising expectations from industrialization, and political and social pressures. A second wave of immigrants, consisting mostly of Ukrainian professionals and intellectuals, reached the United States after World War II, but large numbers of this group settled in Europe and other countries.

ROMANIANS. The Jesuits began to work as missionaries among the Transylvanian Romanians in 1693. Their efforts, combined with the denial of full civil rights to the Orthodox and the spread of Protestantism in the area, which caused growing concern among the Orthodox clergy, contributed to the acceptance of a union with Rome by the Orthodox metropolitan Atanasie of Transylvania (Atanasie Anghel [1697–1713]) in 1698. He later convoked a synod that formally concluded the agreement on September 4, 1700. At first this union included most of the Romanian Orthodox in the province. But in 1744 the Orthodox monk Visarion Sarai led a popular uprising that sparked a widespread movement back to Orthodoxy. In spite of government efforts to enforce the union with Rome, even by military means, resistance was so strong that Empress Maria Theresa (1717–1780) reluctantly allowed the appointment of a bishop for the Romanian Orthodox in Transylvania in 1759. In the end, about half of the Transylvanian Romanians returned to Orthodoxy. It proved difficult for the new Greek Catholic community, known popularly as the United Greek Catholic Church, to obtain in practice the religious and civil rights that had been guaranteed it when the union was concluded. Bishop Ion Inochentie Micu-Klein (1692–1768), head of the church from 1729 to 1751, struggled with great vigor for the rights of his church and of all Romanians within the empire. He died in exile in Rome.

COPTIC CHURCH. Despite attempts at union in the twelfth, thirteenth, fifteenth, sixteenth, and eighteenth centuries, the numbers of Uniate Copts remained small. Pope Leo XIII (r. 1878–1903) created a Coptic Patriarchate of Alexandria, Egypt, in 1895, and a Catholic Coptic synod elected Cyril Makarios (1867–1909) as patriarch in 1898. The see remained vacant from 1908 to 1947, when Mark II Khouzam (1888–1958) was elected patriarch. Four dioceses were erected, and the number of faithful began to increase dramatically. Upon the death of Mark II in 1958, Stephanos I Sidarouss (1904–1987) was elected patriarch and subsequently was made the first Coptic cardinal. After that, great progress was made on the resolution of understanding of Christological differences between the Catholic and Oriental Orthodox churches. In no other ecumenical relationship has a dogmatic disagreement of this type been overcome so unequivocally and with such official approbation. This was achieved without any official bilateral dialogue. The interplay of unofficial theological consultations and official pronouncements made by church leaders proved to be an effective means of resolving a centuries-old problem. The solution of the ecclesiological and ministerial differences remained much more elusive.

MALABAR CHURCH OF INDIA. The Malabar Church, according to tradition, was founded by the apostle Thomas. Hence the Malabarians refer to themselves as "Thomas Christians." From remote times Malabar fostered relations with the churches of Persia and Seleucia. From the ninth century to the sixteenth century the Syro-Chaldean patriarchs alone usually sent bishops to Malabar. Little is known about the Malabar Church before the sixteenth century. Portuguese missionaries arrived in India in 1498. The Malabarians, who did not consider themselves separated from Rome, welcomed the Portuguese as brothers in the faith, but they refused to allow Latin practices into their church. After 1552, two lines of Syro-Chaldean patriarchs sent bishops to Malabar, but only the bishops of the line of Sulaqa were confirmed in office by the pope of Rome.

When Mar Abraham, the last Chaldean bishop, died in 1597, the Portuguese archbishop of Goa, Alexis de Menezes (1559–1617), acted against what he thought were Nestorian errors in the Malabar Church. He convoked and presided at the synod of Diamper in 1599. At the synod the Malabar liturgy was changed. The anaphoras of Theodore of Mopsuestia (c. 350–428 CE) and of Nestorius (d. c. 451 CE) were suppressed; the formula "mother of God" was introduced wherever "mother of Christ" was discovered; the calendar of saints was rejected; and many Latin practices were introduced into the eucharistic liturgy and other sacramental rites.

Membership of Uniate Churches

Rites And Churches	Members	Bishops
Alexandrian		
Coptic	197,000	7
Ethiopian	203,000	5
Antiochene		
Malankar	327,000	4
Maronite	3,220,000	42
Syrian	138,000	15
Byzantine		
Byelorussian	5,000	1
Bulgarian	15,000	1
Greek	2,345	2
Hungarian	282,000	1
Italo-Albanian	64,000	3
Melkite	1,284,000	28
Romanian	1,119,000	6
Ruthenian	533,000	7
Slovak	222,000	1
Ukrainian	5,160,000	27
Yugoslav	49,000	3
Chaldean		
Chaldean	304,000	22
Malabar	3,886,000	25
Armenian	363,000	18

TABLE 1.

Further the creed was inserted immediately after the reading of the gospel; unleavened bread and communion of the faithful under one species only was introduced; and a consecration prayer, translated from the Latin, was inserted at the fraction rite instead of before the anamnesis and epiclesis.

Rome appointed Bishop Francis Roz (1557–1624), a Jesuit, as Abraham's successor in November 1599. His policy of Latinization met with great opposition. Archdeacon George, who had earlier been given the right of succession to Abraham by Rome, died in 1637. George's nephew Thomas assumed the leadership of the opposition. In 1653, when the Portuguese sent Ahattallah, a Syro-Chaldean claiming authority from Rome, to Goa, the opposition swore that they would never be under the control of the Jesuits. This was called the Coonan Cross Oath. Four months later twelve priests ordained Thomas as their bishop. Rome made efforts to heal this breach. Over the course of the next decade, eighty-four opposition congregations returned to Rome, and thirty-two remained with Thomas. This party, now called the "new party," accepted Jacobitism and the Syro-Antiochean rite, and from them descend the Malankara Catholics. Attempts at reunion made by Mar Thomas IV and Mar Thomas V in the early eighteenth century were fruitless. On September 20, 1930, Mar Ivanios George Thomas Panickerveetil (1882–1930), metropolitan of the Bethany congregation of Jacobite monks, Mar Theophilos

James Abraham Kalapurakal (1891–1956), bishop of Tiruvarur, and their whole community signed a union agreement with Rome. These Malankar Catholics retain the West Syrian liturgy but use the native dialect of Malayalam as their liturgical language.

See Also Schism, article on Christian Schism.

Bibliography

For an honest assessment of contemporary difficulties with Uniatism see Robert Taft's "The Problem of 'Uniatism' and the 'Healing of Memories': Anamnesis, Not Amnesia," *Logos: A Journal of Eastern Christian Studies* 41–42 (2000–2001): 155–196. A good historical survey is Robert Roberson's *The Eastern Christian Churches: A Brief Survey* (Rome, 1999). An in-depth study of the Slavic unions is Oscar Halecki's *From Florence to Brest, 1439–1596* (Rome, 1958), in which the Polish historian works almost exclusively with primary sources to debunk some established positions about the motives of those who sought union. A good case study of an individual union is Michael Lacko's *The Union of Užhorod* (Cleveland, Ohio, 1966). For a good treatment of Subcarpathian nationalism, politics, and intellectual life see Paul Robert Magocsi's *The Shaping of a National Identity: Subcarpathian Rus', 1848–1948* (Cambridge, Mass., 1978). A modern treatment of the complexities of Ukrainian nationalism and religion is Serhii Plokhy and Frank E. Sysyn's *Religion and Nation in Modern Ukraine* (Edmonton and Toronto, Canada, 2003).

Thomas F. Sable (1987 and 2005)

UNIFICATION CHURCH.

The Unification Church is a messianic, millenarian religion, dedicated to the goal of restoring the kingdom of heaven on earth. It was founded in Korea in 1954 by the Reverend Sun Myung Moon (b. 1920) as the Holy Spirit Association for the Unification of World Christianity (HSA-UWC). Within a quarter of a century it had become one of the best known and controversial of the contemporary wave of new religious movements. In Korea it is known as the Tong Il movement; in the West it has been referred to by various names such as the Unified Family, or the Moon Organization; then, during the 1990s, it was reconceived as the Family Federation for World Peace and Unification (FFWPU), with the Unification Church being merely the religious arm of the movement. However, despite their attempts to be rid of the label, the movement's members continue to be widely known as "Moonies."

History. Moon was born in what is now North Korea in 1920. He claims that on Easter Day 1936 Jesus appeared and asked him to assume responsibility for the mission of establishing God's kingdom on earth. During the next two decades Moon is said to have communicated with various other religious leaders (such as Moses and the Buddha) and with God himself. This resulted in a body of teachings eventually published in English as the *Divine Principle* (1973).

During the movement's early days in Korea it met with considerable opposition from both the established churches and government officials. Moon was imprisoned several times, and at one point spent two and a half years in a Communist labor camp. In the late 1950s Unification missionaries went to Japan and the West, but it was not until the early 1970s, when Moon himself moved to the United States, that the movement became known to more than a handful of Westerners. Over the next ten years, however, Moon's name became a household word as he spoke on lecture tours and at large rallies, and hosted leading academics at international conferences and local and national dignitaries at lavish dinners. The movement also received considerable attention by supporting U.S. president Richard Nixon during the Watergate crisis.

Several valuable properties (including the New Yorker Hotel and the Tiffany building in Manhattan) were acquired by the organization. Businesses affiliated with the movement (including fishing concerns and ginseng production companies) appeared to prosper. Cultural activities (including the Little Angels dance troupe, the Go World Brass Band, and the New Hope Singers) flourished. The Unification Theological Seminary was established in Barrytown, New York, in 1975, Sun Moon University appeared in Korea (1993), and the University of Bridgeport, Connecticut, which had been founded in 1927 as the Junior College of Connecticut, was rescued from financial disaster by the Professors' World Peace Academy, an organization created and supported by Moon, in 1992. Newspapers and other publications, including the *Washington Times* (in 1982), were launched in Tokyo, New York, Latin America, and elsewhere.

Clean-shaven, well-groomed Unificationists became a familiar sight on the streets of North America and Europe, selling candles, candy, cut flowers, potted plants, Unification literature—and the Unification Church itself. Those who joined as full-time members in the 1970s and 1980s were disproportionately white, middle-class people in their early twenties. As in Japan, they lived in communal centers, but by the early 1990s most grass-roots members had been sent to their hometowns, where (like the Korean members) they tended to live as nuclear families, no longer working full-time for Unification-related businesses.

Partly because of a high drop-out rate, the number of fully committed members has always been considerably lower than the media (or the movement itself) have suggested; indeed, there have never been, at any one time, many more than 10,000 full-time members in the West, where the movement has not grown substantially since the 1970s, but has come to rely on second-generation members to sustain its membership (although, following the fall of the Berlin Wall in 1989, a modest number of new converts were recruited in Eastern Europe and the former Soviet Union). In Asia, full-time membership is unlikely to have exceeded two or three times that number. There is, however, a considerably larger category of people who express support for Unification beliefs and/or other aspects of the movement while, perhaps, maintaining allegiance to another religious tradition. Indeed, with the passage of years, it has become increasingly difficult to distinguish between core Unificationists (rather like priests or monks) and those who are more or less loosely associated members of the wider Unification congregation. As with many new religions, the aging of converts and the arrival of second and subsequent generations has been accompanied by a tendency towards "denominationalization," or general accommodation to the wider society with a lessening of sharp dichotomies between "them" and "us."

BELIEFS. Unification theology is one of the most comprehensive among the contemporary new religions. The *Divine Principle* offers an interpretation of the Bible that, it is claimed, can unite all religions. God is portrayed as a personal being who created the world according to a few universal principles. All creation consists of positive and negative (male and female) elements; these unite into larger units, which in turn unite to form still larger wholes. Adam and Eve were created so God could have a loving "give-and-take" relationship with them. The original plan was that they should mature to a stage of perfection when they would be blessed in marriage; their children and their children's children would populate a sinless world in complete harmony with God. This, however, was not to be. The fall is interpreted not as the result of eating an apple, but as the consequence of a disobedience that involved the misuse of the most powerful of all forces: love. The archangel Lucifer, whom God had entrusted to look after Adam and Eve, became jealous of God's love for Adam and had a (spiritual) sexual relationship with Eve. Eve then persuaded Adam to have a (physical) sexual relationship with her. As a result of this premature union, which was Lucifer-centered rather than God-centered, the fallen nature, or original sin, of Adam and Eve has been transmitted to subsequent generations, and the whole of history can be seen as an attempt by God and man, especially key figures in the Bible, to restore the world to the state originally intended by God.

Ultimately, restoration is possible only through the person of a messiah, who with his wife will perform the roles in which Adam and Eve failed—that is, those of True Parents. They (and those whom they bless in marriage) will have children born without original sin. But for this to happen, humankind has to create a foundation ready to receive the messiah. In practical terms this involves the concept of "indemnity," whereby a good, sacrificial deed can cancel "bad debts" accumulated by a person or his ancestors. The role of the messiah is seen as an office filled by a man born of human parents, but free of original sin. Jesus was such a man, but, largely through the fault of John the Baptist, he was murdered before he had a chance to marry. Thus, he was able to offer the world spiritual but not physical salvation through his death. Numerous parallels between the period before the time of Jesus and the past two millennia are believed to indicate that the present is the time of the second coming. In 1992 Moon publicly declared what his followers had long believed—that he was that messiah, he and his wife being the True Parents of all humanity.

Unification teachings now extend well beyond the *Divine Principle.* In particular, there has been the development of what might be termed *Moonology,* which elaborates on the achievements of Moon and his immediate family, both on earth and in the spirit world. In 1993 Moon announced that the first True Family had been established (by him and his wife, children, and grandchildren) and that the world had entered the Completed Testament Age (CTA). In 1997 Moon instituted a new tradition, *Hoon Dok Hae,* meaning to meet for reading and disccusion, enjoining members to read, from 6:00 to 7:00 every morning, passages from his speeches, which now constituted the basic scriptures for the CTA. On the first day of each week, month, and year, and on the movement's holy days, members take the Pledge, a short statement in which they vow allegiance to God and "True Parents" (Moon and his wife), but on May 5, 2004, Moon announced the change from the "era before heaven" to the "era after the coming of heaven," and, henceforth, the pledge services would be observed every eighth day. The most important Unification rites are the mass weddings, known as Blessings. In the movement's early days, members were "matched" with a partner suggested by Moon, and were expected to practice celibacy before and for some time after the Blessing. By the mid-1990s, however, Blessings were extended to include millions of couples, many of whom did not attend the ceremony and had little awareness of their being associated with a Unification practice, let alone the practice's spiritual significance.

Moon has always spoken of a close relationship between activities in this world and the spirit world, but the connection became increasingly pronounced with two revivalist movements. First, several members claimed to have received messages from Moon's son, Heung Jin Nim, following his death in 1984; then, in the late 1980s, Moon's family recognized his embodiment in a young Zimbabwean member. For several months "Black Heung Jin Nim" enjoyed a privileged position, traveling the world and meting out punishments to members who confessed to having strayed. Eventually, however, he was denounced and returned to Africa, where he started his own movement. Another Unificationist revival, associated with Chung Pyung Lake in Korea, dates from the mid-1990s and involves the channeling of messages from Mrs. Moon's mother (and others in the spirit world). Members are expected to attend forty-day workshops for healing, contact with the spirit world, and participation in ceremonies to liberate their ancestors. According to the Unification Church, billions of couples have been Blessed in the spirit world, and in 2003 advertisements appeared in major newspapers containing testimonies from religious and political leaders (including Moses, Jesus, Muḥammad, Karl Marx, Pol Pot, and John F. Kennedy) declaring Moon to be the True Parent of humanity.

CONTROVERSIES. Throughout the world, the Unification Church has attracted considerable hostility from the media, cult-awareness movements, several government bodies, and, indeed, the general public. Among the many accusations are that it uses brainwashing or mind-control techniques to recruit and keep its members; that it breaks up families; that its leaders live in luxury while the rank and file are exploited and oppressed; that it manufactures armaments; that it is politically right-wing and has had connections with the South Korean intelligence agency (KCIA); that it is merely a front for a seditious organization that is attempting to take over the world and establish a theocracy with Moon at its head; and that it violates tax and immigration laws. (In 1982 a federal-court jury convicted Moon of conspiracy to evade taxes and sentenced him to eighteen months' imprisonment.) Other controversies have surrounded the financial situation of Unification-related businesses and the church's attempt to establish a large community, New Hope East Garden, in South America.

Attacks on Moon's personal behavior have come from a variety of sources. In 1993 an early member, Chung Hwa Pak, published *The Tragedy of the Six Marys,* claiming that Moon had frequently indulged in the sexual "restoration" of the world by having sex with women who would then be expected to have "restoring" sex with six men. In 1995, however, Pak publicly retracted his account. Another book, published in 1998 by Nansook Hong, the estranged wife of Moon's eldest son, described how her husband was addicted to hard drugs, committed adultery, and beat her while she was pregnant. The book also mentioned Moon's illegitimate son and suggested that, far from presenting the ideal example of a God-centered family, the Moons seem to constitute an uncommonly dysfunctional unit, with several of their children deserting the movement. The movement has vehemently denied the criticisms leveled against it, expressing particular concern where such accusations have been used to justify kidnapping members to make them renounce their faith (although, apart from Japan, few countries continue this practice of "forcible deprogramming"). Except for the occasional, short-lived exposé, the media and cult-watching organizations for the most part have lost interest in the movement as it has matured and become less high profile than it was in the 1970s and 1980s.

Bibliography

Unification theology exists in various versions. *Exposition of the Divine Principle* (New York, 1996). There have been many versions of this text, and this is the most recent version. Basically the theology is the same, though stresses and presentation vary. The first full translation into English from the Korean is *Divine Principle,* New York: Holy Spirit Association for the Unification of World Christianity, 1973. Moon has not actually penned any of the versions; they were taken down by his disciples from his talks/sermons and later plished/translated/interpreted by other Unificationists. English version is is accessible at http://www.unification.net/dp96. Numerous books, mostly partisan, have been written by members and close associates of the movement, ex-Unifications, and conservative Christians; Nansook Hong's *In the Shadow of the Moons: My Life in the Reverend Sun Myung Moon's Family* (Boston, 1998) is one of the most critical exposés, and the 600-page volume *40 Years in America: An Intimate History of the Unification Movement 1959–1999* (New York, 2000), by Michael Inglis and Michael L. Mickler, provides an extremely useful overview of public and internal developments from the church's own perspective. Sebastian Matczak's *Unificationism: A New Philosophy and World View* (New York, 1982) provides a theological critique and comparison with other thought systems. For sociological approaches, see John Lofland's *Doomsday Cult: A Study of Conversion, Proselytization, and Maintenance of Faith,* enl. ed. (New York, 1977); David G. Bromley and Anson D. Shupe Jr.'s *"Moonies" in America: Cult, Church and Crusade* (Beverly Hills, Calif., 1979); and Eileen Barker's *The Making of a Moonie: Choice or Brainwashing?* (Oxford, 1984). Massimo Introvigne's slim volume *The Unification Church* (Turin, Italy and Salt Lake City, Utah, 2000) follows events up to the end of the twentieth century.

Eileen Barker (1987 and 2005)

UNION, MYSTICAL See MYSTICAL UNION IN JUDAISM, CHRISTIANITY, AND ISLAM

UNITARIAN UNIVERSALIST ASSOCIATION.

The Unitarian Universalist Association is a religious denomination that is the result of the 1961 merger of the American Unitarian Association and the Universalist Church of America. Those two denominations derived from different backgrounds.

Unitarianism. Unitarianism is a religious view that was organized in institutional form in Poland, Transylvania, England, and the United States. Its emergence is primarily the result of indigenous factors in each country. The separate movements had common characteristics: affirmations of the unity of God, the humanity of Jesus, and human religious responsibility, and rejections of the doctrines of the Trinity, the divinity of Jesus, and human corruption or total depravity. Formulations of these views differed in each country.

In Poland, disputes in the Polish Reformed Church in 1555 led to a schism and the formation of the Minor Reformed Church of Poland in 1565. The physician and theologian Giorgio Biandrata (1515–1588) encouraged Gregory Paul, Martin Czechowic, Georg Schomann, and other leaders of the new movement in their views. A central community was founded at Racow in 1579. Fausto Sozzini (1539–1604), who came to Poland in that year, became the recognized leader of the Polish Brethren, who adopted his name by calling themselves Socinians. Sozzini's theology emphasized prayer to Christ, as the man whom God resurrected and to whom God gave all power in heaven and earth over the church. The Lithuanian Brethren, a sister group led by Simon Budny, were nonadorantist in theology, which meant they rejected prayer to Christ. The Polish and Lithuanian movements flourished primarily from 1580 to 1620. Roman Catholic opposition resulted in the destruction of the Socinians' famed school and printing press in Racow in 1632 and finally in a legislative decree in 1658 that required the Socinians to become Roman Catholics or go into exile or be executed. A few Socinian exiles found refuge with the Transylvanian Unitarians in Kolozsvár (present-day Cluj-Napoca).

Ferenc Dávid (1510–1579) was the outstanding leader of Transylvanian Unitarianism. Dávid converted from Roman Catholicism to Lutheranism after studying in Wittenberg and then became a leader, with Biandrata's encouragement, of the Reformed Church in Transylvania after debates with Peter Mélius. Together, Dávid and Biandrata published *Two Books on the False and True Knowledge of the One God the Father, of the Son, and of the Holy Spirit* in 1568, an antitrinitarian book that contained Lelio Sozzini's interpretation of the prologue to John's gospel. Sozzini, an uncle of Fausto Sozzini, denied that Christ's person was that of the cosmological Logos.

In 1568 John Sigismund, the Unitarian king of Transylvania, granted religious freedom to Catholics, Lutherans, members of the Reformed church, and Unitarians. (The name Unitarian gradually came into use after debates at Gyulafehérvár in 1568 and at Nagyvárad in 1569.) The Transylvanian diet (legislature) gave these four Received Religions constitutional recognition in 1571, shortly before Sigismund's death. The next king, Stephen Báthory, forbade innovations, that is, religious beliefs that were different from those that had prevailed under Sigismund. Dávid became increasingly insistent about his nonadorantist Christology, but his view was an innovation, which could endanger legal protection of the Unitarian church. Therefore Biandrata cooperated in the arrest, trial, and imprisonment of Dávid in 1579, and Dávid died that year in prison. His nonadorantist theology eventually prevailed. The Transylvanian Unitarians still survive in Romania and Hungary.

In England, John Biddle (1615–1662) published *Twelve Arguments Drawn Out of the Scripture* (1647) and other works that based Unitarian beliefs on New Testament texts. Thomas Firmin and others spread Biddle's views. Unitarians were excluded from the protection of the Act of Toleration (1689), but their views lived on both in the Church of England and among Dissenting churches in the form of an Arian Christology, which was named after the theologian Arius (c. 256–336), who maintained the Son was inferior to the Father, placing the Son among created things. When Dissenting ministers met at the Salters' Hall in London in 1719, they split into two groups. One group insisted on agreement with confessional statements, the other group required only the use of biblical terms and conformity with biblical views. Members of the latter group and their congregations gradually moved toward Unitarian views.

Theophilus Lindsey (1723–1808) opposed the Anglican church's creedal restrictions, left that church's ministry, and founded Essex Street Chapel in London in 1774, the first English Unitarian congregation. Joseph Priestley (1733–1804) was an outstanding Unitarian leader whose scriptural rationalism, materialist determinism, and humanitarian Christology influenced many Unitarians. Richard Price (1723–1791) emphasized free will in opposition to Priestley's determinism. Priestley and Thomas Belsham, Lindsey's successor at Essex Street Chapel, made a humanitarian Christology the dominant view, driving out Arian views.

The British and Foreign Unitarian Association, founded in 1825, was aided by the repeal of laws against nonconformity and by parliamentary approval of the Dissenters' Chapels Act (1844), which assured Unitarians of their churches.

James Martineau (1805–1900), who exercised great influence among English Unitarians, challenged Priestley's theology with his emphases on ethics and intuition. Martineau, who desired comprehension in a national liberal church, preferred the name *Free Christian* to *Unitarian.* In 1928, English Unitarian denominationalists and those who were influenced by Martineau's Free Christian views united to form the General Assembly of Unitarian and Free Christian Churches. The Non-Subscribing Presbyterian Church of Ireland, which derives from the influence of Thomas Emlyn (1633–1741), and some Welsh and Scottish churches, are different expressions of English Unitarianism.

American Unitarianism gradually emerged during the eighteenth century within Congregationalism, largely because of the influence of Arminian theology, which stressed the human capacity to respond to grace, and Arminian Christology. This gradual development resulted in conflicts that culminated in the appointment of a liberal, Henry Ware, as Hollis Professor of Divinity at Harvard College in 1805. The liberals were accused of covertly agreeing with Belsham's humanitarian Christology. Boston minister William Ellery Channing (1780–1842) replied that, instead, most of the liberal ministers were Arians, for they believed that Christ's character included ethical, intellectual, and emotional perfection, and that he was subordinate to God.

Channing's famous Baltimore sermon "Unitarian Christianity" (1819) gave the liberals a coherent theological view that embraced assertions of the unity and moral perfection of God; of the unity of Jesus Christ, his inferiority to God, and his mediatorial mission; and of human moral responsibility. The American Unitarian Association (AUA), an association of individuals, not of churches, was organized in 1825. Ralph Waldo Emerson, in his Cambridge Divinity School address (1838), and Theodore Parker in his sermon "The Transient and Permanent in Christianity" (1841), challenged the prevailing Unitarian emphasis on the authority of rationally interpreted scripture. These addresses initiated a controversy over Transcendentalism within Unitarianism. Parker has influenced many Unitarians as an exemplar of public ministry, for he expressed his theology in outspoken sermons on social and economic issues, ceaseless efforts for social reform, and a willingness to disobey the Fugitive

Slave Act of 1850, which he regarded as immoral, in obedience to a higher moral law.

Henry Whitney Bellows led the effort to organize the National Conference of Unitarian Churches (an association of churches) in 1865. The preamble to the constitution was almost a Christian creed, so Francis Ellingwood Abbot and others withdrew in protest and formed the Free Religious Association in 1867. In 1886 in the Western Unitarian Conference, a regional organization founded in 1852, a similar controversy emerged over whether the conference should be limited to those who accepted a Christian, theistic religious belief. William Channing Gannett wrote a nonbinding statement, "Things Commonly Believed among Us," which was adopted in the Western Conference in 1887. In 1894 the National Conference revised its constitution in a manner that enabled many members of the Free Religious Association to rejoin the conference. In 1925 the National Conference, which had been renamed the General Conference, was merged with the AUA.

In the early twentieth century, religious humanism appeared within Unitarianism under the leadership of John Dietrich and Curtis Reese, who were among those who signed the Humanist Manifesto (1933). A serious decline among the Unitarian churches during the depression led to the creation of a denominational Commission on Appraisal (1934–1936), whose chair, Frederick May Eliot, reluctantly agreed to become president of the AUA. Eliot's leadership revived the movement.

UNIVERSALISM. Universalism is a religious view that affirms the ultimate salvation of all humans. In some formulations, that has meant the ultimate reconciliation of all, even Satan, with God. *Acts* 3:21 is one of the scriptural bases for the belief that some Universalists have in a universal restoration (Gr., *apokatastasis*). Modern Universalism derives from radical Pietism and from dissenters from the Baptist and Congregational traditions.

In 1681, Jane Leade (1624–1704) became the recognized leader of a Philadelphian Society of Pietists in London. The group's name came from the sixth church mentioned in *Revelation* 3:7–13. In Germany, Johann Wilhelm Petersen, a follower of the founder of Pietism, Philipp Jakob Spener, became a convinced chiliast, anticipating the reign of Christ after his second coming. Petersen led a group of German Philadelphian pietists. He reinterpreted Leade's views, gave them scriptural foundations, and published his reinterpretation in *The Mystery of the Restoration of All Things* (2 vols., 1700–1710). Volume 1 contains a small treatise by one of Petersen's disciples, Georg Klein-Nicolai, under the pseudonym Paul Siegvolck. This effective treatise was reprinted frequently, for both in the original German, *Das von Jesu Christo . . . Evangelium . . .*, and in English translation, *The Everlasting Gospel. . . .*, it converted many people to Universalism. The title was taken from *Revelation* 14:6. Groups of German Philadelphian Pietists and people from other groups took copies of the treatise with them when they migrated to Pennsylvania in the eighteenth century. George de Benneville (1703–1793), who moved to Pennsylvania in 1741, maintained contacts with different groups in colonial Pennsylvania whose members affirmed Universalism and thus prepared the way for Universalism's later growth in America.

James Relly (1720–1778) left George Whitefield's movement in England in 1750. He wrote *Union, or A Treatise of the Consanguinity and Affinity between Christ and His Church* (1759), in which he argued that a result of the indissoluble union of Christ with his people is that there is no guilt and punishment for sins because Christ bore both the guilt and the punishment. All humans are among the elect, for whom Christ suffered. John Murray (1741–1815) brought Relly's universalized variation of Calvinist theology to New England in 1770. He became minister of the first Universalist congregation in America at Gloucester, Massachusetts, in 1780.

Elhanan Winchester (1751–1797), a Baptist minister, was converted to Universalism by *The Everlasting Gospel* and by his friend de Benneville. Winchester argued in *The Universal Restoration. . .* (1794) that future punishment is both finite and remedial in nature, to be followed by the ultimate reconciliation of all, even of the devil and his angels, with God.

Individuals in several European countries affirmed Universalism, but they founded no effective organizations. In England, however, Universalism survived within Unitarianism after Winchester converted William Vidler (1758–1816), a General Baptist minister, to Universalism. Vidler succeeded Winchester as minister of Parliament Court Chapel, London, and then became, also, a Unitarian, together with some members of his congregation. This congregation and other English Unitarian congregations soon contained as members former General Baptists and other persons who held universalist views.

The institutional growth of Universalism was to be in America, where Hosea Ballou (1771–1852) wrote *A Treatise on Atonement. . .* (1805), which made him the movement's preeminent authority in the nineteenth century. Ballou argued that sin is finite in nature, that its effects are completely experienced in this life, and that therefore all will be saved. He rejected the doctrine of the Trinity and affirmed an Arian view of Christ. These views were soon widely accepted by American Universalists.

In 1803 at Winchester, New Hampshire, the General Convention of Universalists in the New England States adopted a statement of agreement that is referred to as the Winchester Profession. The wording of the document embraced the varied Universalist views of the time. Between 1831 and 1841, a temporary schism occurred when believers in finite, future punishment founded the Massachusetts Association of Universal Restorationists in opposition to Ballou's view. By the end of the nineteenth century, restorationism was the predominant view, at the time characterized by movements attempting to transcend the divisions of denominationalism and to restore Christianity. In 1870 the Universalist General Convention approved a resolution that required the Winchester Profession to be interpreted so as to affirm the authority of scripture and the lordship of Jesus Christ. This creedal period ended in 1899, when the restrictions were rescinded and a noncreedal statement was adopted in Boston. A revised noncreedal Bond of Fellowship, known as the Washington Profession, was adopted in 1935 and revised in 1953.

Clarence Skinner (1881–1949), dean of Crane Theological School, was the leading spokesperson for Universalists in the twentieth century. His influence and that of others led to a reinterpretation of Universalism as focused on the unities and universals of human life rather than on an endless life after death. Thus many Universalists no longer hold a supernatural worldview.

THE UNITARIAN UNIVERSALISTS. Sporadic contacts between the Unitarians and the Universalists in the nineteenth and early twentieth centuries were followed in 1953 by organization of the Council of Liberal Churches (Universalist-Unitarian). Cooperation in this council's departmental programs prepared the way for the churches' merger in 1961 into the Unitarian Universalist Association (UUA), of which Dana McLean Greeley became the first president.

The churches and fellowships of the UUA are primarily located in the United States and Canada. (There are a small number of fellowships in other countries in Central and South America, Europe, Africa, and Asia.) Ministers and ministers of religious education who are granted associate or full professional fellowship are required to have completed training at a theological school or through a supervised program of independent study. The UUA follows the practice of congregational ordination.

Unitarian Universalists hold a wide variety of religious views, including liberal Christianity, naturalistic theism, mysticism, religious humanism, scientific theology, and aspirations toward a universal religion. They emphasize such values as human dignity, freedom of religious belief, the use of reason in formulating religious beliefs, and the expression of such beliefs in movements for social reform.

The theological diversity that characterizes Unitarian Universalists is expressed in worship that varies greatly from congregation to congregation, ranging from structured liturgy to thematic or sermon-centered emphases. Von Ogden Vogt (1879–1964), minister of the First Unitarian Society of Chicago, contributed the view that worship, as the celebration of life, is the central discipline of religion. His books *Art and Religion* (1921), *Modern Worship* (1927), and *The Primacy of Worship* (1958) led many religious liberals to modify thematic or sermon-centered emphases in the direction of patterns of worship that express basic communal religious experiences: attention or vision, humility, exaltation, illumination, and dedication. The hymns and worship materials contained in *Hymns of the Spirit* (1937), jointly produced by Unitarian and Universalist commissions on hymns and services, were predominantly liberal Christian in character, with some expressions of religious humanism. *Hymns for the Celebration of Life* (1964), which was prepared by a new commission after the merger of the two denominations, contained an increased proportion of materials expressive of religious humanism, particularly through the hymns and readings of Kenneth L. Patton, who portrayed humanist worship in *A Religion for One World: Art and Symbols for a Universal Religion* (1964) and *Services and Songs for the Celebration of Life* (1967). In 1980 the UUA's Commission on Common Worship continued the task of the preceding commissions, that of providing materials that will enable people holding widely differing theological views to worship together.

The UUA is one of forty-nine member groups of the International Association for Religious Freedom. In 2002, adult membership in the UUA, including those in the affiliated Canadian Unitarian Council, totaled about 220,000 in 1,051 churches and fellowships.

SEE ALSO Emerson, Ralph Waldo; Sozzini, Fausto Pavolo.

BIBLIOGRAPHY

The basic history of Unitarianism can be found in Earl Morse Wilbur's *A History of Unitarianism: Socinianism and Its Antecedents* (Cambridge, Mass., 1945) and *A History of Unitarianism in Transylvania, England, and America* (Boston, 1952). An important companion volume for the seventeenth-century period is *The Polish Brethren: Documentation of the History and Thought of Unitarianism in the Polish-Lithuanian Commonwealth and in the Diaspora, 1601–1685,* 2 vols., translated and edited by George H. Williams (Missoula, Mont., 1980). *The English Presbyterians: From Elizabethan Puritanism to Modern Unitarianism,* by C. Gordan Bolam, Jeremy Goring, H. L. Short, and Roger Thomas (London, 1968), is an illuminating description of English Unitarianism. *The Beginnings of Unitarianism in America* by Conrad Wright (Boston, 1955) gives a precise analysis of theological issues in the eighteenth century. Wilbur's few chapters on American Unitarianism have been supplemented by *A Stream of Light: A Sesquicentennial History of American Unitarianism,* edited by Conrad Wright (Boston, 1975).

Universalism in America, 2 vols. (Boston, 1884–1886), by Richard Eddy, had been the basic history for nearly a century, until publication of the two-volume work by Russell E. Miller, *The Larger Hope,* vol. 1, *The First Century of the Universalist Church in America, 1770–1870* (Boston, 1979) and vol. 2, *The Second Century of the Universalist Church in America, 1870–1970* (Boston, 1986). Ernest Cassara edited a selection of basic source documents, *Universalism in America: A Documentary History* (Boston, 1971). Charlotte Irwin provided a useful description of the European background of American Universalism in "Pietist Origins of American Universalism" (M.A. thesis, Tufts University, 1966). The original theological interpretation by George H. Williams in *American Universalism: A Bicentennial Historical Essay* (Boston, 1971) is an important contribution. Another study of the merged denominations is David Robinson's *The Unitarians and the Universalists* (Westport, Conn., 1985).

New Sources

Ross, Warren. *The Premise and the Promise: The Story of the Unitarian Universalist Association.* Boston, 2001.

JOHN C. GODBEY (1987)
Revised Bibliography

UNITY is the largest movement in the New Thought tradition and shares New Thought's formative influences and general worldview. Founded in Kansas City, Missouri, by Myrtle Fillmore (1845–1931) and Charles Fillmore (1854–1948), a married couple, Unity is the second oldest and most distinctly Christian community within New Thought. The impetus to the formation of Unity was Myrtle Fillmore's recovery from tuberculosis through the use of mental healing rituals.

The founding of the movement occurred in 1889, one year after Myrtle Fillmore pronounced herself healed. The first venture for Unity, the periodical *Modern Thought*, began publication in 1889, and in 1890 the movement's original prayer ministry was established—The Society of Silent Help. In 1891 the name Unity was given to the Fillmores' enterprise, and the couple began publishing a new periodical, *Unity*, whose masthead bore what would become the traditional symbol for the movement, a winged globe. Concurrent with the initiation of the movement, the Fillmores studied with New Thought founder, Emma Curtis Hopkins (1849–1925), who had established a Christian Science ministry and seminary in Chicago, which was independent of the Boston-based religion of Mary Baker Eddy (1821–1910). Of the various influences on the Fillmores' religious development (e.g., Spiritualism, Vedānta, New England Transcendentalism), Hopkins's teachings were the most significant.

The movement's first formal institutional expression was the Unity Society of Practical Christianity (1903), and in 1906 Unity ordained its first ministers—including Myrtle and Charles Fillmore. In harmony with the practice initiated by Hopkins and consistent with all other New Thought groups, from this time onward Unity has ordained women along with men and maintained a thoroughgoing egalitarianism with regard to all ecclesiastical roles and functions. It is notable that the majority of Unity ministers are women, making it perhaps the largest Christian community in which this is the case.

When incorporated as the Unity School of Christianity in 1914, Unity was a fully developed religious organization with an international outreach. Unity School's withdrawal in 1922 from the International New Thought Alliance and its initiation of its own annual convention the following year accelerated Unity's growth and development, soon making it the largest and most recognized movement within New Thought. It remains so to the present, with nearly one thousand ministries in more than sixty countries worldwide.

Unity is represented by two major corporate bodies, Unity School of Christianity, located at Unity Village, Missouri (just outside Kansas City), and the Association of Unity Churches in nearby Lee's Summit. The two groups are independent but work in harmony with one another. Unity School, which was originally founded by the Fillmores, publishes religious books and periodicals, serves as a retreat and education center, and operates the movement's prayer and healing ministry (Silent Unity, the successor of the Society for Silent Help). Governance of the school is vested in a board of directors, with a president and chief executive officer holding senior executive authority. From its inception to the early twentieth century, members of the Fillmore family have served as president of Unity School, with Connie Fillmore Bazzy, the founders' great-granddaughter, being the last member of the Fillmore family to hold the office.

The Association of Unity Churches, a successor to the earlier Unity Ministers' Association, was established as an independent corporation in 1966. The association is responsible for management and direction of the vast majority of the movement's congregations, supervising ministerial education, granting ordinations, sanctioning churches, and assisting in the placement of ministers. The association is governed by a board of trustees that is elected by representatives from member churches, regional organizations, and the board itself. Senior executive authority is vested in a president and chief executive officer.

In the 1990s, two Unity organizations emerged, independent of and in some tension with Unity School and the association—the Unity-Progressive Council and the Federation of Independent Unity Churches. A related organization, the Universal Foundation for Better Living, bases its teachings on the works of the Fillmores, although it affirms no formal linkage with the Unity movement.

Important to Unity has been its publishing enterprise. Although all of Charles Fillmore's books have remained in print, during the latter part of the twentieth century, Unity School began to reduce its list of titles, eliminating some of the movement's classic texts. Its periodical list has also shrunk, so that Unity now publishes only two magazines, *Unity* and *Daily Word*. By far the more popular is *Daily Word*, a prayer manual for each day of the month, initiated in 1924. Another important periodical, *Wee Wisdom*, Unity's children's magazine, was discontinued in 1991. First published in 1893, it holds the record as the longest continuously published children's periodical in American history.

In addition to the books by Myrtle and Charles Fillmore, Unity School has remained committed to the publication of *Lessons in Truth*, by H. Emilie Cady (1848–1941), a homeopathic physician and student of Hopkins. First appearing in serial form in *Unity* magazine in 1894, *Lessons in Truth* is Unity's all-time best-seller and the most widely circulated book in all of New Thought. Together with the works of Charles Fillmore (most notably *Christian Healing*

[1909] and *Metaphysical Bible Dictionary* [1931]), Cady's book is the primary source of Unity's theological system.

The system itself is largely consistent with the general principles of popular religious idealism found in New Thought as a whole and, like other New Thought groups, Unity allows individuals and affiliated churches significant freedom in matters of belief and practice. Although decidedly Christian in its terminology and self-affirmation, Unity has no formal creed or doctrine. This has led to considerable variation in teachings and practices within the movement, with some congregations de-emphasizing ideals and practices deemed significant to the founders. This phenomena has become especially noticeable since the 1980s, largely due to the appeal of various New Age teachings to Unity teachers and ministers. Despite the evident diversity in the movement and the appearance of nontraditional teachings in individual churches, a number of beliefs can be specified as foundational and generally accepted throughout the movement. Derived from the works of Cady, Charles Fillmore, and other representative thinkers, the more important beliefs are:

1. The ultimate basis of existence is mental (God as Mind), and all material/physical conditions are secondary to and products of mental states and conditions.
2. God (Divine Mind) is understood as supremely good (the Good) and the ground of perfection.
3. God (the Good) is omnipresent and, as a consequence, evil (typically referred to as "error") is unreality.
4. As spiritual beings, humans are innately divine and one with God. This innate divinity is referred to variously as the Christ within, the superconsciousness, and the Christ Mind.
5. Through realization of their innate divinity and appropriation of ideas in Divine Mind, humans are able to transform their lives, replacing negative states and conditions with positive ones.
6. Individuals have full freedom in matters of personal belief.
7. Christian doctrine, idealistically interpreted, is normative.

As with New Thought as a whole and individual movements within the tradition, Unity has received little scholarly attention, although it has received more attention than other New Thought groups, such as Religious Science, Divine Science, and the Universal Foundation for Better Living. In this regard, encyclopedias and general texts on new religious movements and religion in the United States often have brief sections on Unity. There are no critical histories of the movement and no significant scholarly treatments of its theology. Unity has published a biography of Myrtle Fillmore and two nonscholarly histories, all of which are generally reliable in terms of facts and data. In addition, a book by Hugh D'Andrade and two by Neal Vahle, although written for a Unity audience and largely informed by perceptions and understandings of Unity insiders, supply helpful information not found elsewhere. The chapters on Unity in Charles Braden's *Spirits in Rebellion* (1963) and J. Stillson Judah's *The History and Philosophy of the Metaphysical Movements in America* (1967) remain the best critical sources on the movement.

See Also Fillmore, Charles and Myrtle; Hopkins, Emma Curtis; New Thought Movement.

Bibliography

Bach, Marcus. *The Unity Way.* Unity Village, Mo., 1982. Sympathetic but reliable sketch of Unity's history and teachings.

Braden, Charles S. *Spirits in Rebellion: The Rise and Development of New Thought.* Dallas, 1963. See chapter on Unity. Now dated, but highly detailed academic history of the movement from founding until the early 1960s.

D'Andrade, Hugh. *Charles Fillmore: Herald of the New Age.* New York, 1974. Sympathetic but reliable biography of Unity's cofounder. Contains historical information not found elsewhere.

deChant, Dell. "Myrtle Fillmore and Her Daughters: An Observation and Analysis of the Role of Women in Unity." In *Women's Leadership in Marginal Religions: Explorations outside the Mainstream,* edited by Catherine Wessinger, pp. 325–350. Urbana, Ill., 1993. Study of Unity's theological supports for female leadership and the institutional structures of the Unity School and Assocaition of Unity Churches.

Freeman, James Dillet. *The Story of Unity.* Unity Village, Mo., 1954. Sympathetic but reliable history of Unity by major leader of the movement.

Harley, Gail M. "Unity in the Harmonial Family." In *America's Alternative Religions,* edited by Timothy Miller. Albany, N.Y., 1995.

Judah, J. Stillson. *The History and Philosophy of the Metaphysical Movements in America.* Philadelphia, 1967. See chapter on Unity. Now dated, but well-documented academic study of the history and teachings of the movement from its founding until the early 1960s. The most sustained critical analysis of Unity's teachings yet published.

Simmons, John K. "The Forgotten Contributions of Annie Rix Militz to the Unity School of Christianity." *Nova Religio: Journal of Alternative and Emergent Religions* 2, no. 1 (1998): 76–92. Study of the impact of a major theorist from the movement's formative period.

Teener, James W. "Unity School of Christianity." Ph.D. diss., University of Chicago, 1942. Hostile critique of the movement, but rich in historical data unavailable elsewhere.

Vahle, Neal. *Torch-Bearer to Light the Way: The Life of Myrtle Fillmore.* Mill Valley, Calif., 1996. Although written for a Unity audience and largely informed by perceptions and understandings of Unity insiders, supplies helpful information on the cofounder that is not found elsewhere.

Vahle, Neal. *The Unity Movement: Its Evolution and Spiritual Teachings.* Philadelphia, 2002. Although written for a Unity audience and largely informed by perceptions and understandings of Unity insiders, offers a reliable study of the movement's history.

Witherspoon, Thomas E. *Myrtle Fillmore: Mother of Unity.* Unity Village, Mo., 1977. Sympathetic but reliable biography of Unity's cofounder. Contains historical information not found elsewhere.

GAIL M. HARLEY (2005)
DELL DECHANT (2005)

UNKULUNKULU is a mythic figure among the Zulu people, a large ethnic group in South Africa. Properly speaking, uNkulunkulu, a name meaning "the old, old one," is not a deity (the Zulu had a weakly developed pantheon) but is rather the "first man." One oral tradition identifies uNkulunkulu as a man and a woman (often identified as uThlanga), but the common myth holds that uNkulunkulu is the first man. He appeared, or was created, by the "breaking off" of reeds—it is said of him that he "came out of, or broke off from, a bed of reeds." Thus, he is also called uMvelinqangi ("the first outcomer," i. e., "the ancestor of all"). All humans are derived from him and from his design and plan. It is also thought by some that uNkulunkulu was merely an early ancestral figure, understood as the ancestor of the Zulu, who was later believed—perhaps under the influence of Christianity—to have been the creator. There is a possibility, from the early sources, that uNkulunkulu was originally thought of purely as an ancestor and human being.

Because uNkulunkulu has no identifiable children there are no ancestral rites or specific families that can claim to be descended from him. Nonetheless, he created humanity and even gave humans their social institutions, such as marriage and chieftainship. In addition, he gave them spirits (of the dead), diviners to discover the past and the future, and doctors to treat various diseases.

BIBLIOGRAPHY

Berglund, Axel-Ivar. *Zulu Thought-Patterns and Symbolism.* London, 1976; Bloomington, Ind., 1989. A thoughtful and careful work.

Callaway, Henry. *The Religious System of the Amazulu* (1870). Reprint, Cape Town, 1970. One of the earliest, and best, introductions to Zulu religion.

Hexham, Irving, ed. *Texts on Zulu Religion: Traditional Zulu Ideas About God.* (Lewiston, N.Y., 1987).

New Sources

Berglund, Axel-Iver. *Zulu Thought-Patterns and Symbolism.* Bloomington, Ind.,1989.

Hexham, Irving, ed. *Texts on Zulu Religion: Traditional Zulu Ideas about God.* Lewiston, N. Y., 1987.

JAMES S. THAYER (1987)
Revised Bibliography

UNTOUCHABLES, RELIGIONS OF. At the beginning of the twenty-first century there are well over 160 million untouchables on the Indian subcontinent. They belong to numerous *jātīs* at the bottom of the caste order, their low position deriving from the belief that they embody extreme impurity. Throughout the twentieth century, constitutional categories such as "depressed classes" and "scheduled castes" and the term *harijan* ("people of god"), coined by the nationalist leader Mohandas Gandhi, have all been widely used to refer to untouchable communities in nonprejudicial ways. The practice of untouchablity was legally abolished in 1948, but the disabilities suffered and discrimination faced by untouchable individuals and groups have been only partially mitigated and have at the same time acquired new shapes in independent India. Strong links between their religious and social subordination and their widespread poverty and economic exploitation make untouchables some of the most disadvantaged groups in South Asia. Furthermore, the lowly position of the untouchables under Hinduism also extends to those sections of Christian, Muslim, Buddhist, and Sikh populations that belonged to untouchable castes before their conversion. It is thus entirely meaningful to speak of the religions of untouchables, especially if the term untouchable is aligned with the word *dalit* ("broken" or "oppressed"), an untouchable self-description that challenges subordination and reveals the limitations of ready separations between religious-ritual patterns and social-political processes in any discussion of untouchable castes.

DEBATES. Discussions of untouchable religions turn on charged questions. Does the extreme impurity of the untouchables place them outside the caste order? Do they have entirely separate religions? Or, does the very ritual lowness of the untouchables hierarchically yet vitally link them to other castes through an encompassing, consensual caste ideology of purity and pollution? Is their religion, then, primarily a lower form of the one practiced by those higher up in the caste order?

When scholars such as Louis Dumont and Michael Moffatt present the untouchables as primarily reproducing the homogeneous scheme of the ritual hierarchy of purity and pollution, they ignore the other matrices—for example, of ritual kingship, colonial governance, non-Brahmanic religions, and the modern state—that shape caste. By focusing singularly on concepts of purity and pollution as cementing the caste structure, they also externalize the terms of power that inhere in caste, especially as these bear on untouchables. Finally, such emphases underplay the creation within untouchable religions of novel meanings and distinctive practices. Conversely, various scholarly and commonplace positions stressing the radical disjunction between untouchable norms and practices and the caste order tend to overlook the manner in which the ideologies and relationships of caste not only exclude untouchable peoples from several processes but also hierarchically include them in other arrangements. Furthermore, they underplay the structures of hierarchy and authority in the religions of untouchables themselves, reflected in practices of endogamy and commensality, within various occupations, and in interactions between untouchable castes.

Questions of untouchable religions do not admit singular solutions. Shaped as part of wider hierarchies and relationships of caste, which differ from one region to another, these religions show marked regional variations. Even within a particular region, untouchable religions can display distinct expressions in different locales depending on the distribution of land ownership and on arrangements of authority among castes that diverge across villages. Further, far from being static and timeless, untouchable religions have undergone profound changes as a part of historical processes such as state formation, agrarian and urban mutation, and political transformation. The salience of these religions is found precisely within such variety and change.

Exclusion and Inclusion. The extreme impurity attributed to untouchables has denied them entry into Hindu temples and the services of the Brāhmaṇ *purohit* (priest), has spatially segregated their living quarters at the margins of rural and urban settlements, and has excluded them from the several sets of ranked relationships, ritual exchanges, and social interactions among discrete castes that are at the core of quotidian life. Highly codified prescriptions, such as those requiring deferential bodily movements and speech patterns in the presence of members of the upper castes, have governed the appropriate conduct of untouchables in public spaces, and have frequently forbidden them the use of various markers of honor and status, from modes of transport such as elephants, horses, and palanquins to apparel and accessories such as upper-body garments, turbans, and shoes. On the other hand, the very impurity of the untouchables has included them in the practices and processes of caste. They have exclusively performed the most defiling activities, entailing contact with severely polluting substances, in rural and urban arenas: from the scavenging of waste to work with leather and labor on cremation grounds, and from cleaning toilets and clearing human excrement to rearing unclean animals such as pigs and removing the impure carcasses of sacred cattle. Some of these tasks constitute the primary occupations of discrete untouchable castes; others are undertaken by untouchables who are more generally employed as agricultural or manual laborers. This situation simultaneously defines the subordination of the untouchables and places them at the core of caste, because only they can perform such pollution-ridden yet essential activities. Unsurprisingly, the untouchable presence in the social order has been variously acknowledged: they have received customary dues, especially on ritual occasions, for their caste-sanctioned duties and their agricultural labor; their participation has been critical in ceremonies celebrating the unity of the village; and their deities—like those of "tribal" or indigenous groups that bear an ambiguous relationship with the caste order—have been feared as violent yet venerated as guardians of villages. Thus, untouchable religions have been integrally related both to *dalit* exclusion from and *dalit* inclusion in caste hierarchies and ritual processes.

Hierarchy, Power, and Distinction. Untouchables have not accepted and experienced such processes passively. Rather, precisely while participating in hierarchical relationships, untouchable actions and understandings have imbued their religions and caste formations with specific distinctions. The untouchable religions in all their staggering heterogeneity have emerged bound to the historical constitution of Hinduism itself. They have been shaped through the wider interplay between Brahmanic hierarchical conventions that emphasize purity and pollution within a schema positing partial continuity between the human and the divine, and non-Brahmanic Hindu traditions that manifest rather different, even contending, orientations toward hierarchy, impurity, divinity, and worship.

Specific untouchable castes have been intimately associated with particular divine beings—such as the village goddess of smallpox (called Mariammaṉ in South India) and Mātā Māī—who are figures that are also feared and venerated by other castes as part of non-Brahmanic Hindu traditions. The worship and festivals of the lower castes, including untouchables, emphasize the use of blood sacrifice, liquor, possession, and different degrees and various forms of bodily chastisements and self-inflicted tortures. All over India the untouchables have also venerated major Hindu gods such as Viṣṇu and Śiva as well as the formless divine, through diverse means—including mystic-ecstatic cults, esoteric adoration, and ascetic piety—that engage and extend various modes of *bhakti* (devotional) practice, often preestablished by non-Brahmanic traditions. In each of these cases, untouchable religions have displaced and interrogated—as well as negotiated and negated—concepts of purity and impurity and established Hindu hierarchies, through ecstatic worship and possession, sensuous devotion, and pilgrimage. Sometimes this even entails religious, social, and gender inversions in which men acquire female attributes and Brāhmaṇs become impure.

Conversely, the origin myths of untouchables all over India have subverted and rejected upper-caste representations of their ritual lowness, yet they have done so by retaining notions of their own collective impurity. Throughout the nineteenth and twentieth centuries, untouchable communities such as the Satnāmīs of central India have elaborated new mythic traditions and distinctive caste/sect practices centered on their *gurūs* and on a formless God, and have also constructed novel depictions of deities such as Śiva and Draupadī. These innovative religious formations have questioned and contested but also reworked and reiterated the forms of power encoded in caste schemes of purity and pollution and kingly authority. Still other untouchable groups have participated in spirit cults, and while propitiating ancestors and ghosts have both articulated and reproduced labor bondage and caste hierarchy. The worship among untouchable castes of demonic figures and personal deities has negotiated yet accepted caste and ritual inequalities. This tension can also been seen in the way untouchable religions have distinctively absorbed the attributes of Hindu worship *(pūjā)* and sacrifice *(bali)* as well as the patterns of village festivals.

Furthermore, untouchable membership of sects such as the Kabīrpanthīs, Dādūpanthīs, Ravidāsīs, and Rāmnāmīs has led to an elaboration of relatively egalitarian devotional practices developed precisely through a broader acceptance of caste divisions. While the untouchable religions have widely expressed the distinctions of their own actions and understandings, these have generally been articulated in relation to the ritual authority encoded within Hindu hierarchies.

Taken together, distinct yet overlapping tendencies have characterized the untouchable religions. In each case, these religions have created their own forms of faith and practice, which have variously negotiated and subverted caste hierarchies. On the one hand, discrete dispositions of the untouchable religions have far exceeded an exclusive preoccupation with Brahmanic conventions of ritual hierarchy. On the other hand, within the untouchable religions the unequal relationships and ritual power at the core of caste have also been differently reproduced, reworked, and reconfigured. These contradictory tendencies have defined the identities, resistance, and solidarities of untouchables, as well as their submission, vulnerability, and subordination. The distinct dispositions of untouchable religions have, however, far exceeded an exclusive preoccupation with ritual hierarchy. These faiths have been more concerned with the *dalit* struggle to achieve political and social power than with efforts to improve the untouchable's position within the ritual caste system. At the same time, within the untouchable religions the unequal relationships and ritual power at the core of caste have been reproduced and reconfigured. Taken together, these contradictory tendencies have defined the identities, resistance, and solidarities of untouchables, as well as their submission, vulnerability, and subordination.

RITES AND GENDER. Among untouchable castes, rites of passage associated with every life stage from birth to death suggest varying degrees of concern with ritual purity. Karin Kapadia argues in *Śiva and Her Sisters* that among the untouchable Paraiyar caste in southern India the puberty rituals occasioned by a girl's first menstruation show marked differences from the Brahmanic concern with the pollution and purification of the menstruating woman: instead such rites involve quintessentially non-Brahmanic attempts to safeguard "the precious, distinctively female ability to create children" (1998, p. 93) and to symbolically construct fertility as sacred female power. The implication here is that pollution motifs are less important for the untouchables. In contrast, another account, focused on a specific Paraiyar woman (see Viramma, Racine, and Racine), reveals more ambivalent and earthy orientations to purity and pollution and female sexuality. It is not only that the untouchables' elaborations of purity/impurity and auspiciousness/inauspiciousness entail varied negotiations of shifting arrangements of caste and power, but also that even when certain untouchable groups closely follow the rules governing purity and pollution—during rites of birth and death, for example—they do so by conjoining such observances with the distinctive symbols and practices of their own castes and sects.

Marriage and gender among the untouchables have been characterized by practices common to most lower-status and varied middle-ranked castes, such as secondary marriages for men and women, widow remarriage, the payment of a bride price (rather than dowry), and women's freedom from the requirements of physical seclusion. Yet such arrangements have been themselves embedded in wider patterns of patrilineal kinship in their regional manifestations. This has meant that even though untouchable women have often possessed a degree of autonomy to negotiate hierarchical relationships of kin and community and marriage(s) and motherhood, and even though their physical labor has been positively valued, practically and symbolically, they have nonetheless not escaped the asymmetries of gender and caste and the inequalities of ritual and class. This is reflected in a multitude of ways, from widespread depictions of women as inherently engendering yet equally subverting the religious and social order to representations of the deviant sexuality of untouchable women, and from the sexual and economic exploitation of untouchable women by upper-caste and socially superior men to attempts at controlling their bodies and labor within their communities. Within these overlapping and constraining contexts, the actions and desires of untouchable women have left their mark on untouchable religions and life-cycle rituals, as well as on wider gender arrangements and caste hierarchies.

BEYOND HINDUISM. Much of what has been said above concerning untouchable religions within Hinduism also holds for the other untouchables faiths. In principle, Christianity, Islam, and Sikhism should have no place for caste, but in practice caste divisions in South Asia have found particular configurations within these religions. Indian Islam refers not so much to the *varṇa* distinctions of caste Hinduism, with their constitutive concerns with purity and pollution, as to the social separation between *ashraf* (well-born) and *ajlaf* (low-born) Muslims. High and low Muslims might worship together in the mosque, but in relations of marriage, commensality, and occupation they remain separate. Further, low-born Muslims who were converts from untouchable and other lower castes have distinctively understood and practiced Islam, especially by vigorously participating in popular religious traditions such as the cults of various saints whose veneration cuts across religions. The untouchables who became Sikh have created specific faiths that combine their understandings of the official doctrines and purity norms of Sikhism with popular practices of Hinduism and Islam.

In the case of Indian Christianity, the Roman Catholic Church, with an extensive membership in southern India, has historically accepted caste divisions, including their expressions in endogamy and commensality, on the grounds that these are "social" rather than "religious" mores and institutions, and has traditionally provided entirely separate or spatially segregated services for their higher and lower caste constituents. Even though Protestant churches all over South Asia have opposed caste, the taint of impurity and its attendant discrimination have clung to their untouchable members. Untouchable Christians have retained yet reworked prior practices and wider principles of caste and worship and ritual and kinship, creating distinct forms of untouchable identity and indigenous Christianity—including novel representations of Hindu and Christian divinities in which the former can complement but also oppose the latter.

HISTORY AND POLITICS. Historical transformations during the colonial and postcolonial periods have profoundly shaped untouchable religions. The coalescing of forms of British administration and indigenous authority from the late eighteenth century and the emergence by the mid-nineteenth century of an agrarian order clearly characterized by discrete agricultural castes together served to distinctly delineate untouchable groupings, and also led to their creation of and conversion to new faiths. Such processes among the untouchables were further heightened from the 1860s through the 1940s by the colonial state's emphasis on caste categories and religious communities in census enumeration and representative politics, by diverse non-Brahmanic movements in western and southern India, and by an increase in Christian missionary activity that challenged upper-caste authority. In this wider context, the untouchables formed caste associations and joined movements that undertook internal social reform. As they did so, they claimed a higher ritual status or contested their low position and pressed the state for concessions in high school education, government jobs, and political office. Untouchables also converted to Christianity, created distinctive forms of devotional worship, participated in the nationalist struggle, and initiated and endorsed movements to allow them entry into Hindu temples. Here the untouchables' questioning of upper-caste domination and the powerful affirmation of their identities were expressed as part of changing yet still relevant hierarchies of caste, religion, and politics.

Since the 1920s, political processes in which untouchables have participated have crucially influenced their religious and caste practices. The politics and legacy of B. R. Ambedkar have played a key role here. Belonging to the large untouchable Mahar caste of western and central India, Ambedkar received a Ph.D. from Columbia University and entrance to the bar from Grey's Inn, London, and served as chairman of the drafting committee of the Indian constitution in the 1940s. Drawing on earlier devotional and non-Brahmanic traditions of religious dissent as well as on constitutional law and rationalist individualism, Ambedkar's formulations on caste, Hinduism, and untouchable action were directly opposed to the Gandhian perspective within Indian nationalism, which condemned untouchability without renouncing the *varṇa* concept of caste. The political parties founded by Ambedkar were only partially successful and his demand that untouchables be recognized as a separate electorate drew wide criticism as a proposal that would divide both Hindus and the nation, but he nonetheless exerted significant political influence through arguing the position that discrimination against untouchables constituted the very core of caste—a position leading to his rejection of Hinduism in 1935. When Ambedkar converted to Buddhism in 1956, he was followed by a significant section of his own Mahar caste as well as by members of the Jātav caste of northern India, resulting in a *dalit* Buddhism that has combined distinctive caste practices with the egalitarian emphases of the new faith. Increased *dalit* resistance to upper-caste authority has also been seen in southern India, where it has been strengthened by regional, non-Brahmanic political initiatives present since the early twentieth century. Political developments emphasizing the role of the lower-castes after the late 1970s have further extended such processes to North India. *Dalits* in rural and urban areas have seized upon these advances not only to participate in electoral politics but also to express their identities and articulate power relationships in local and national arenas, and in so doing have defined the changing contours of untouchable religions and caste practices in contemporary India. At the same time, precisely such *dalit* expressions have repeatedly led to violent higher-caste reprisals and have engendered a political reaction centered on ideologies of a homogeneous Hindu nation. The gradual emergence in late colonial and independent India of a *dalit* middle-class through policies of affirmative action in public education, government employment, and political office has been accompanied, especially since the 1970s, by the growth of a vigorous *dalit* consciousness and by creativity in literature and art drawing on experiences of widespread discrimination and religious exclusion. This assertiveness continues to be reflected in, for example, the claims of *dalit* women, the terms of *dalit* Christian theology, and campaigns for *dalit* human rights that draw parallels between the injustices of caste and the wounds of race, not only in South Asia but also in the *dalit* diaspora. Today, as in the past, the religions of untouchables play a central part in these varied negotiations of, interactions with, and challenges to ritual authority, caste hierarchy, and political power.

SEE ALSO Varṇa and Jātī.

BIBLIOGRAPHY

Bandyopadhyay, Sekhar. *Caste, Protest, and Identity in Colonial India: The Namasudras of Bengal, 1872–1947.* London, 1997. A case study of a lower-caste movement in undivided Bengal.

Clarke, Sathianathan. *Dalits and Christianity: Subaltern Religion and Liberation Theology in India.* New Delhi, 1998. An important work on *dalit* Christianity in contemporary India.

Dangle, Arjun, ed. *Poisoned Bread: Translations from Modern Marathi Dalit Literature.* Bombay, 1992.

Deliege, Robert. *The World of the "Untouchables": Paraiyars of Tamil Nadu.* Delhi, 1997. An anthropological study of both Christian and Hindu members of an untouchable caste in southern India.

Dr. Babasaheb Ambedkar and His People. Dalit Website, available from http://www.ambedkar.org.

Dube, Saurabh. *Untouchable Pasts: Religion, Identity, and Power among a Central Indian Community, 1780–1950.* Albany, N.Y., 1998. An ethnographic history of the Satnāmīs, a numerically and politically significant untouchable caste/sect. The work discusses wider theoretical questions of Hinduism, caste, gender, and power.

Dube, Saurabh. *Stitches on Time: Colonial Textures and Postcolonial Tangles.* Durham, N.C., 2004. Examines faith and practice among untouchable converts to Christianity and gender and law among untouchable communities in central India.

Dumont, Louis. *Homo Hierarchicus: The Caste System and Its Implications.* Translated by Mark Sainsbury. London, 1970. An anthropological classic projecting untouchables as participants in a consensual ideology of purity and pollution.

Freeman, James M. *Untouchable: An Indian Life History.* Stanford, Calif., 1979. A rich life-historical account of a colorful *dalit* man from Orissa, eastern India.

Ilaiah, Kancha. *Why I Am Not a Hindu: A Sudra Critique of Hindutva Philosophy, Cuture, and Political Economy.* Calcutta, 1996. A provocative polemic against Hinduism and caste.

Jaffrelot, Christophe. *India's Silent Revolution: The Rise of the Low Castes in North Indian Politics.* New York, 2002. A wide-ranging survey of lower-caste, including *dalit,* participation in electoral politics.

Juergensmeyer, Mark. *Religion as Social Vision: The Movement against Untouchability in Twentieth-Century Punjab.* Berkeley, Calif., 1982. Discusses the untouchable Ad Dharm movement in North India.

Kapadia, Karin. *Śiva and Her Sisters: Gender, Caste, and Class in Rural South India.* Boulder, Colo., 1998. A feminist ethnography that explores the interplay between gender and power — including considerations of marriage, ritual, kinship, possession, and reproduction — in a village in southern India by examining the perspectives of both women and men of five castes, while especially focusing on the experiences of untouchable Pallar women.

Khare, R. S. *The Untouchable as Himself: Ideology, Identity, and Pragmatism among the Lucknow Chamars.* New York, 1984. Discusses empirical and analytical issues relating to untouchable ascetics and asceticism in North India.

Lamb, Ramdas. *Rapt in the Name: The Ramnamis, Ramnam, and Untouchable Religion in Central India.* Albany, N.Y., 2002.

Lorenzen, David, ed. *Bhakti Religion in North India: Community Identity and Political Action.* Albany, N.Y., 1995. Contains several essays on different dimensions of lower-caste devotional traditions.

Lynch, Owen M. *The Politics of Untouchability: Social Mobility and Social Change in a City of India.* New York, 1969. An early and important study of religious, social, economic, and political transformation among the *dalit* Jātav caste in post-Independence urban North India.

Mendelsohn, Oliver, and Marika Vicziany. *The Untouchables: Subordination, Poverty, and the State in Modern India.* Cambridge, U.K., 1998. An overview of the situation of the untouchables in contemporary India.

Moffatt, Michael. *An Untouchable Community in South India: Structure and Consensus.* Princeton, N.J., 1979. An important ethnography that draws on Louis Dumont's emphasis on the ideological consensus of purity and pollution to examine social relations and religious structure among an untouchable caste in a southern Indian village. The work contains a valuable discussion of the debate on the relation of untouchable castes to Hindu hierarchy.

Moon, Vasant. *Growing Up Untouchable in India: A Dalit Autobiography.* Translated by Gail Omvedt. Introduction by Eleanor Zelliot. Lanham, Md., 2001. An account by a close associate of B. R. Ambedkar.

Omvedt, Gail. *Dalits and the Democratic Revolution: Dr. Ambedkar and the Dalit Movement in Colonial India.* New Delhi, 1994. A historical study of *dalit* politics in twentieth century western and southern India.

Prashad, Vijay. *Untouchable Freedom: A Social History of a Dalit Community.* New Delhi, 2000. Primarily discusses the urban Balmikis of North India in the late nineteenth and twentieth centuries.

Ram, Kalpana. *Mukkuvar Women: Gender, Hegemony, and Capitalist Transformation in a South Indian Fishing Community.* Sydney, 1991. A feminist ethnography set among a marginal, low status, Catholic fishing community of Kerala in southern India. The work carries critical discussions of femininity and divinity and ritual and worship in both popular Catholic and non-Brahmanic traditions.

Valmiki, Omprakash. *Joothan: A Dalit's Life.* Translated by Arun Prabha Mukherjee. New York, 2003. An autobiography of a *dalit* writer from North India.

Viramma, Josiane Racine, and Jean-Luc Racine. *Viramma: Life of a Dalit.* Translated by Will Hobson. London, 1997. A richly textured life-history of a remarkable *dalit* woman from rural southern India.

Zelliot, Eleanor. "Learning the Use of Political Means: The Mahars of Maharashtra." In *Caste in Indian Politics,* edited by Rajni Kothari, pp. 29–69. New Delhi, 1970.

SAURABH DUBE (2005)

U NU.

U NU. U Nu's life (1905–1995) extends over decades of profound political and social change in Burma (Myanmar). He was a prominent member of the Thirty Comrades during the struggle for independence and played a historic role in the country's transformation from a British colony to an independent nation-state. He served as Prime Minister of democratic Burma between 1948–1956, 1957–1958, and 1960–1962. U Nu was a gifted politician, a deeply religious man, and a remarkable writer.

LIFE. U Nu's politics and worldview reflected the values of the early nationalist era in which he grew up. His father was a merchant in Wakema, a town in the delta region of Lower Burma where he was active in the local chapters of the Young Men's Buddhist Association (YMBA) and later in the General Council of Buddhist Associations (GCBA). These anticolonial organizations equated national identity with Burmese language, culture, and Buddhism, and Nu's father would consent only to enrolling his son at a local Anglo-vernacular government school. Unlike many of his political contemporaries, U Nu never studied abroad. He finished high school in Rangoon and graduated from Rangoon University in 1929. For a number of years he taught English, English history, and Burmese in the national school system.

By 1934, U Nu, now married to Daw Mya Yee, returned to the capital to join the civil service, but soon decided to seek a law degree at Rangoon University. U Nu emerged as a leader in the student strike of 1936, together with Aung San and others in the anti-colonial elite who later also gained prominent positions in the post-independence era. Like many of his peers, Nu adopted the anti-colonial title *Thakin* (Master). He rose to leadership positions in the pre-war nationalist Dobama Asiayone and the post-war Anti-Fascist People's Freedom League (AFPFL). In the aftermath of Aung San's murder, U Nu became the first Prime Minister of independent Burma in 1948. On several occasions, he withdrew from public life strategically to meditate and thus force a favorable resolution of political struggles.

Ethnic insurgencies, factionalism over the state's role in religious education, and the constitutional amendment to establish Buddhism as Burma's state religion led to Ne Win's final military takeover in 1962. Like the British in 1942, Ne Win imprisoned Nu from 1962–1966. In 1973 U Nu traveled to Thailand and then to exile in India. He was pardoned and returned to Burma in 1980 to oversee the new Pali text editions commissioned by the Mahasangha Nayaka Council. Following the popular uprising and the collapse of Ne Win's regime in 1988, U Nu established an interim government in a futile effort to regain political office. Ne Win's successor regime, the State Law and Order Restoration Council (SLORC) placed U Nu under house arrest from 1989 until 1992. He passed away on February 14, 1995.

POLITICAL VIEWS. A pragmatist about political ideologies and a skilled negotiator, U Nu advocated democracy or the Burmese Way to Socialism as exigencies dictated. His politics indicated a greater nexus to his Buddhist beliefs as he became increasingly religious in his adult life. As early as his twenties, he took vows to affirm his disciplined actions: to abstain from liquor; to be faithful to his wife; to observe temporary celibacy to effect political outcomes; and in 1948, to remain sexually abstinent. He meditated daily for hours, observed a vegetarian diet, and removed himself from his family's affairs. U Nu's ascetic practices and charisma were significant facets of his public persona.

The inception of parliamentary governance in post-independent Burma coincided with millennial expectations of an imminent, powerful Buddhist ruler (*cakkavatti)* in the Theravāda world where many believed that the second half of the Buddha's dispensation had begun. In popular Burmese culture, U Nu was often seen as that future king or future Buddha. On the advice of Nehru, he promoted a programmatic Buddhist revival (1947–1958) to further nationalism. The revival was intended to secure world peace and progress, ensure the expansion of the state into tribal areas, bring stability, and institute Buddhism as Burma's state religion. It culminated in the construction of a religious complex, Kaba Aye Pagoda, to house the Buddhist canon (*tipitaka*) and the convocation of the Sixth Theravāda Buddhist Synod, *Buddha Sasana Sanghayana* (1954–1956) that was modeled after earlier Buddhist councils, especially King Mindon's Fifth Buddhist Council (1871). Kaba Aye was the site of important state rituals, including the veneration of the Buddha's Tooth relic that had been temporarily conveyed from Sri Lanka to Burma. Such diplomatic exchanges celebrated Buddhist identity among some new Asian nations.

U Nu's political career eclipsed when his policies failed to integrate ethnic minorities into the national community. His government further deteriorated under economic pressures despite, or as his critics assert, because of, U Nu's practice of and the state's support for Buddhism. The political crisis escalated when he could not restrain demands by monks to require Buddhist instruction in public schools and to prohibit ethnic minorities from offering equivalent religious instruction. Ne Win's coup d'etat in 1962 ended parliamentary democracy and limited the role of Buddhism in the modern state until the 1980s.

LITERATURE. Writing and translating literature into Burmese (e.g. Dale Carnegie's *How to Win Friends and Influence People*) was U Nu's first passion in college. He soon gained a reputation as a gifted speech writer and orator, both talents that fostered his rise in politics. He authored plays, novels, translations, political speeches, and essays on Buddhism. Although his written work is extensive, some of it has been termed polemic, underscoring an intended message rather than an art form. His novel, *Man, the Wolf of Man*, emphasized personal themes, while his best known play, *The People Win Through*, focused on a communist insurrection and political rule by force as unmoral. He authored other plays like *Converting the Elder Brother*, a drama about political and personal betrayal, and *Thurya*, an allegorical fable about political corruption under colonialism. In *Saturday's Son*, an autobiographical novel, he recounted the turbulent events of his life until 1962. His religious writings primarily followed traditionalist forms. In *Buddhism: Theory and Practice* he detailed the moral and mental stages of meditation.

Throughout his life, U Nu's religiosity encompassed both modernist meditation and cosmological beliefs. In his 1987 inaugural speech for the Center for Burma Studies at Northern Illinois University, he affirmed the power local spirit lords (*nat*) exert over worldly matters. U Nu was deeply committed to Buddhist practice as moral legitimation for public office and employed religion to promote national culture and nation building. He achieved a prominent place among charismatic statesmen in twentieth century Asia.

BIBLIOGRAPHY

Butwell, R. *U Nu of Burma*. Stanford, Calif., 1963; reprint 1969.

Mendelson, M. E. *Sangha and State in Burma, A Study of Monastic Sectarianism and Leadership*. Edited by J. P. Ferguson. Ithaca, N.Y., 1975.

Nu, U. "Burma Looks Ahead." Translation of selected speeches by the Honorable U Nu, Prime Minister of the Union of Burma, delivered on various occasions from 1951 to August 4, 1952. Ministry of Information, Government of the Union of Burma, 1953.

Nu, U. *Saturday's Son*. Translated by U Law Yone. New Haven, Conn., 1975.

Nu, U. *Buddhism: Theory and Practice.* Bangkok, 1983.

Nu, U. "Nats." In *Crossroads: Journal of Southeast Asian Studies,* Vol. 4:1, Special Burma Studies Issue. Singapore, 1988. This speech was delivered on the occasion of the dedication of the Center for Burma Studies, Northern Illinois University, July 30, 1987.

Sarkisyanz, E. *Buddhist Backgrounds of the Burmese Revolution.* The Hague, 1965.

Smith, D. E. *Religion and Politics in Burma.* Princeton, 1965.

JULIANE SCHOBER (2005)

UPANIṢADS. The Upaniṣads are codified Sanskrit philosophical speculations of varying lengths in both prose and verse form, composed orally and set to memory mostly by anonymous South Asian sages, primarily in the classical and medieval periods. While the most important and influential Vedic Upaniṣads date from the eighth to the fourth centuries BCE, some lesser-known sectarian Upaniṣads appear as late as the sixteenth century CE. Individually and as a whole, the Upaniṣads present insights and doctrines that serve as the foundation for much of India's philosophical thought.

Traditional South Asian teachings based on the Upaniṣads have been called the Vedānta, the "end of the Veda," for the Upaniṣads chronologically and formally set the closure of the Vedic canon. Perhaps more to the point, Upaniṣadic lessons are said to be the end of the Veda in that they purport to present the "hidden meaning" or the "real message" of religious practice and thought.

The central teaching presented by the Upaniṣads as a whole centers on the notion that behind all of the spatial swirl and temporal flux of the world as it is experienced by the senses is a subtle, pervasive, timeless, and unchanging reality that is identical to the undying essence of the human being as well. The early Vedic Upaniṣads call this unified and imperishable world soul *brahman* or *ātman,* the former applying more typically to the godhead and the latter signifying the correlative divine "self" residing at the deepest level of one's person. The theistic Upaniṣads teach that this *brahman* or *ātman* is a single deity known generically as Īśv Īśa (Lord) living deep within one's being and identified particularly as Śiva, Viṣṇu, or the Goddess by particular sectarian communities.

While they explicitly or implicitly admit the difficulties of comprehending a hidden reality that either transcends or simply cannot be known through the structures of time, space, and causation, the Upaniṣads hold that through disciplined practices of meditation and the cultivation of extraordinary knowledge, it can in fact be discerned. Such discernment releases one from the apparent cycles of life and death caused by one's ignorance of the fact that the essential self does not die. Thus, Upaniṣadic religious anthropologies, theologies, and soteriologies all revolve around a key lesson that appears ubiquitously but that might well be characterized by the *Adhyātma Upaniṣad's* assertion that "he is a free person who through insight sees no distinction between his own self and *brahman,* and between *brahman* and the universe" and the *Kaṭha Upaniṣad's* proclamation that, having comprehended this identity, "one is released from the jaws of death" (3.5).

The Upaniṣads were first put into written form in 1656 CE, when Sultan Dara Shakoh sponsored the translation of fifty Upaniṣads from Sanskrit into Persian. In 1801–1802, these Persian works were then translated into Latin by Antequil du Perron, becoming the first, although poor, European version. Since that time, all of the Upaniṣads have been rendered into various Indian scripts, and the more important or influential ones have been translated into virtually all of the world's major languages. The Upaniṣads stand as works of monumental significance in the history of India and of the world.

CONNOTATIONS OF THE TERM *UPANIṢAD.* Built from the Sanskrit verbal root *sad* ("sit") and the prefixes *upa-* and *ni-* ("nearby"), the word *upaniṣad* represents the act of sitting at the feet of someone. The pedagogical tradition in which a student in search of sacred knowledge sat on the ground in front of a *guru* typifies, in part, the practices of the Vedic *vānaprastha*s ("forest dwellers") and *saṃnyāsin*s ("renunciants") who had retired to forest retreats to meditate and study. The practice also appears in various Agamic and Tantric traditions, many of whose followers lived beyond the boundaries of settled civilization, where they practiced yogic meditation under the guidance of a guru. Through combinations of dialogues, monologues, questions and answers, riddles, and speculative discourses, the student privately heard from the teacher secret lessons that had been passed down through the generations of the sacred lineage. Such a "secret lesson" was an *upaniṣad.* Isolated as a textual genre, the collections of such secret teachings are known as the Upaniṣads.

The term *upaniṣad* thus connotes an element of esotericism. In fact, the Upaniṣads state explicitly that such lessons are not intended for the general population: "Let none who has not maintained the vow think on this," demands *Muṇḍaka Upaniṣad* (3.12.11), and the *Rāmapūrvatāpanīya Upaniṣad* warns the teacher to "give not [his lessons] to common people" (84). That the teachings were to be heard by only select ears is demonstrated by the texts themselves, for synonyms and appositions of the word *upaniṣad* include not only such terms as *satyasya satyam* ("the truth of truth," *Bṛhad. Up.* 2.1.20), but also *rahasyam* ("that which is hidden," *Nṛsimhottaratāpanīya Up.* 8) and *paramam guhyam* ("that which is a supreme secret," *Kaṭh. Up.* 3.17).

The esoteric tone of the Upaniṣadic teachings derives in part from the place they hold in the larger Vedic literary corpus. The earliest Vedic literatures are the inspired hymns, chants, and incantations of the *Ṛgveda, Sāmaveda, Yajurveda,* and *Atharvaveda,* which were composed by the visionaries and priests of the various Vedic traditions and codified around 1200 BCE (although some are earlier and some later). To these Saṃhitās ("collections") of poems and songs are attached ritual instructions known as the Brāhmaṇas, which date to roughly 1000 to 800 BCE. As early as the ninth century BCE, individuals and small groups of people, most often of the *kṣatriya* (warrior) rather than the *brāhmaṇa* (priestly) class of society (see *Bṛhad. Up.* 1.4.11), began to leave the villages to live and meditate in the forest. There, unable or unwilling to perform the sometimes elaborate and expensive Vedic religious ceremonies, they contemplated the allegorical rather than literal significance of the hymns and rituals. These allegorical interpretations formed the basis of texts known as the Āraṇyakas, or "forest books." Toward the early part of the eighth century BCE these contemplative sages began to formulate more abstract philosophical interpretations of the metaphors and homologies used in the Brāhmaṇas and Āraṇyakas as they sought to gain knowledge of the deeper ontological status of the world and of the place the human being holds in that world. Out of this context came the Upaniṣads, the non-sacerdotal philosophical musings on the nature of reality itself.

The composers of the Upaniṣads diverged from the religious tradition of their time in that, unlike earlier Vedic poets and visionaries, they found little interest in proclaiming the wonder of the objective world or in praising the gods said to have enlivened that world. The forest sages understood the outer world to be less significant than the inner, and the gods to be nothing more than reflections or expressions of subjective processes within one's own being. "All of the gods are within me," asserts an early forest work, the *Jaiminīya Upaniṣad Brāhmaṇa* (1.14.2). The *Kaivalya Upaniṣad,* a later text, teaches that "the highest *brahman,* which is all forms, which is the supreme reality of the universe, which is the most subtle of the subtle and which is eternal, is nothing but yourself." The Upaniṣadic stress on the inner world rather than on external religious practices similarly distinguished the forest sages from the composers of such ritual texts as the Brāhmaṇas and, later, the Kalpasūtras; for the forest sage had no need for "ritual baths, nor periodic rites, nor deity, nor location, nor sacred space, nor worship" (*Tejobindu Up.* 4).

The lines separating the Brāhmaṇas and the Āraṇyakas, and the Āraṇyakas and Upaniṣads, as textual genres are not distinct; the early Āraṇyakas resemble in form the later Brāhmaṇas, and the later Āraṇyakas are nearly indistinguishable from the early Upaniṣads. Some traditions hold that the first true Upaniṣad is the *Ṛgveda's Aitareya Āraṇyaka* (ninth century BCE), while most others mark that line with the emergence of the *Śukla* ("White") *Yajurveda*'s *Bṛhadāraṇyaka Upaniṣad* and the *Sāmaveda*'s *Chāndogya Upaniṣad,* both of which date to the eighth century BCE.

UPANIṢADIC TEACHINGS. Symbolic representations in the Upaniṣads of ultimate reality are consistent with the notion that such reality is unmanifest yet vital. *Brahman* (*ātman,* Īśvara, etc.) is described as life-giving breath (*prāṇa*), wind (*vāyu*), or empty space (*ākāśa*); as pure consciousness (*cit*), bliss (*ānanda*), or eternity (*ananta*); and as the infinite subject by whom all objects are known, the "inner guide" (*antaryāmin*) of all that is.

Given its acknowledged immanent yet transcendent nature, ontological discourses in the early Vedic Upaniṣads depict *brahman* both cosmically (*saguṇa,* "with characteristics") and acosmically (*nirguṇa,* "without characteristics"). *Saguṇa brahman* is understood to be the finest essence (*aṇimā, rasa,* etc.) of all things in the world, as honey is the essence of beeswax and oil is the essence of sesame seeds (see *Ch. Up.* 6.9ff.). Understood cosmically, therefore, *brahman* is the substance of the universe. This does not mean that *brahman* is the material stuff of the world that can be perceived sensually. Rather, it is the hidden and subtle reality that allows all things to exist in the first place. Thus, when the sages of the *Muṇḍaka Upaniṣad* note that "this whole world is *brahman*" and that *brahman* is the "hidden mover . . . within all that moves, breathes, and winks" (2.2.1–2), they imply the cosmic ontological notion that *brahman* is the very "beingness" of all beings, including the human being. Transformative insight allows one to understand that this cosmic substratum is unified and indivisible, or—as the *Chāndogya Upaniṣad*'s Uddālaka Āruṇi teaches his son, Śvetaketu—"Thou art That!" (6.9.1–6.16.3).

Understood acosmically, *brahman* cannot be described through definitive or positive statements, because *brahman* transcends the limitations of language. Thus, *nirguṇa brahman* is not subject to categorization, and therefore, can neither be perceived nor conceived. *Brahman* "cannot be heard, nor touched. It has no form [and] is imperishable. Similarly, it has no flavor, nor odor. It is eternal, without beginning [and] without end" (*Kaṭh. Up.* 3.5), and it "cannot be known through language, nor by the mind, nor by sight" (6.12). That the content of ultimate reality cannot be depicted is summarized most succinctly in the *Bṛhadāraṇyaka Upaniṣad*'s recurring assertion that "the self [*ātman*] is not this, not that" (4.4.22ff.).

Thus, while the Upaniṣadic student seeking knowledge of *suguṇa brahman* was to comprehend the unity of all things in a world constructed on the essence of *brahman,* the student who looked for an understanding of *nirguṇa brahman* was to "deconstruct" the phenomenal world, as it were, in order to comprehend the imperishable self that lies behind the world of life and death.

Whether they considered *brahman* to be cosmic or acosmic, Upaniṣadic teachers generally distrusted empirical knowledge gained through sensual experiences. According to these thinkers, the physical world is a "measured" or "constructed" world, the world of *māyā,* a term that in the Upaniṣads denotes those aspects of the world that are empirically perceived but not ultimately real. *Māyā,* in other words, characterizes the world of time, space, and causation. According to Upaniṣadic teachings, then, that world which the ignorant call the "real world" is not, in truth, real.

Upaniṣadic ontologies are thus closely linked with epistemology. They are similarly related to physiology and psychology. Drawing on Sāṃkhya metaphysics, the Upaniṣads generally recognize a dualism of matter (*prakṛti*) and spirit (*puruṣa*). The former constitutes the objective and phenomenal world. The latter comprises the knowing subject that has no temporal or spatial limitations, and at times is used as a synonym for *ātman.* Within the world of *prakṛti,* the human body and mind may be divided into the gross body (*sthūla-śarīra*) and the subtle body (*sukṣma-* or *liṅga-śarīra*). Everyday consciousness revolves around the gross body made up of the senses and the objects of those senses (known collectively as the *indriyas*). Sensations gained from the gross body are then categorized by the subtle body, which consists of the mind (*manas*), the mechanism of personal identity or "ego" (*ahaṃkāra*), and the "awareness" (*buddhi* or *antaḥkāraṇa*), the basis of one's ability to live and act in the world.

Upaniṣadic physiology declares that both the gross and subtle bodies, however, are phenomenal (and therefore unreal) constructions relative to the spirit, the true self (see *Kaṭh. Up.* 3.10–11). Thus, the farther one's awareness is removed from its attachment to the external world experienced by the gross and subtle bodies, the closer one comes to a full yet nonempirical experience of the true self. Accordingly, the Upaniṣads emphasize the importance of dream states in the comprehension of deeper realities (see, e.g., *Bṛhad. Up.* 4.3.9). In sleep one loses awareness of the outside world, a world that is in effect a bad dream to begin with. The deeper one sleeps, the closer to eternal reality one gets.

The Upaniṣads recognize four states of waking and dreaming awareness, each successively purer and closer to the direct comprehension of *ātman.* The grossest psychological level is that of waking consciousness, a level in which apparent objects are mistakenly understood to be distinct entities and in which the subject does not recognize itself. The second, more refined, level of awareness is that of active dreaming, a state in which objects lose their solidity and appear more as they really are—as changing and unreal events. The dreaming subject is a "creator" (*kartṛ*) of the world, which exists only because he "projects" (*srjate*) it (see *Brhd. Up.* 4.3.10). The third level is that of dreamless sleep (*samprasāda, suṣupti*), in which one loses all awareness of oneself as an object in relation to other objects and no longer experiences the constrictions of time and space. In dreamless sleep one is said to have gained complete tranquillity. Here, one momentarily enjoys complete reunion with *brahman* and experiences, albeit nonempirically, the highest bliss (*paramānanda;* see *Bṛhad. Up.* 4.3.32).

Later Upaniṣads, especially those influenced by the practices and ideologies of Yoga, add to these states another level to one's psychological being, known simply as *turīya* or *turya,* "the fourth." *Maṇḍukya Upaniṣad* 7 describes this state: "It is not cognitive, nor is it noncognitive. It is unseen, unable to be spoken of, ungraspable, without any distinguishing characteristics, unthinkable, unnameable. It is the essence of the knowledge of the One Self [*ekātma-pratyaya-sāram*], that into which the world resolves. It is peaceful and benign. It is indivisible." Such a state sounds like the Upaniṣadic notion of ultimate reality. Indeed, the passage continues: "It [*turīya*] is *ātman.* It is to be known."

The waking somatic body, therefore, is unreal relative to ultimate reality, a point that carries ethical and eschatological implications. The "self" of one's being leaves the body at death, as the mango fruit at maturity separates from its stalk (see *Bṛhad. Up.* 4.3.36). If one has not renounced one's attachment to the world of the senses, then one will be reborn in another physical body, the existential situations of which are determined by the ethical laws of *karman;* and sooner or later one will suffer and die again. This continually turning wheel of death and rebirth (*saṃsāra*) is understood to be a painful trap from which one is released only when one understands that the physical body is not the real self, and that the world which the senses perceive is an insubstantial and effervescent illusion.

Most of the Upaniṣads agree that the best way one would cultivate such a freeing insight would be through the rigors of yogic meditation. While the Vedic Upaniṣads as a whole reflect the influence of yogic practice and ideology (see, for example, *Maitri Up.* 6.19–30 or *Śvet. Up.* 2.8–10), it is in the Yoga Upaniṣads that such teachings are most fully presented. For example, the *Amṛtabindhu, Śāṇḍilya,* and *Yogatattva* Upaniṣads, among others, contain long passages on the eight "branches" (*aṣṭānga*) of yogic practice (discipline, self-restraint, correct body posture, breath control, suppression of sensory awareness, mental concentration, intuitive meditation, and final union with the Absolute), the proper means to master each, and the characteristics of the successive levels of yogic "powers" (*siddhis*) one gains as one becomes more adept at the particular practices.

While continuing to uphold the efficacy of yogic practice, some of the Upaniṣads also present the more theistic teaching that one cannot truly know one's soul without what might be termed the "grace" of the soul. Such appears to be the position of *Kaṭha Upaniṣad* 2.23, which maintains that "this soul [*ātman*] cannot be attained through instruction, nor through rational thinking, nor by great learning. He is to be attained only by the one whom [the supreme self] chooses. The soul [*ātman*] reveals his own nature to such a one." The soteriological dimensions of this theistic teaching are much more explicit in the *Śvetāśvatara Upaniṣad*'s statement that "more subtle than the subtle, greater than the great, is the soul [*ātman*] that is set within the heart of the creature. One beholds it to be actionless and becomes free of sorrow, when through the grace of the Creator [*dhātuḥ prasadāt*] he sees the Lord [*Īś*] and his greatness" (3.20).

CLASSIFICATION OF THE UPANIṢADS. It is somewhat problematic to arrive at a precise number of Upaniṣads, because if all Sanskrit works claiming to present secret teachings were to be classified as Upaniṣads the number would be indefinite. Nearly 250 texts call themselves Upaniṣads—including the *Allopaniṣad* ("secret teachings about Allāh," composed at the time of Akbar) and the *Christopaniṣad,* dated well after the rise of Christian communities on the subcontinent—but it appears that most of these do so merely as a way to align themselves with a respected literary genre or religious tradition.

The *Muktika Upaniṣad* and other medieval South Indian works mention 108 separate Upaniṣads in an enumeration that has become somewhat of a stock list. Using the methods of historical, thematic, and textual criticism, twentieth-century scholars have isolated 123 genuine Upaniṣads. These works may be classified into two general categories, the Vedic Upaniṣads and the later Upaniṣads.

The Vedic Upaniṣads. Virtually all Vedic and most sectarian traditions recognize ten to eighteen Upaniṣads as revealed authoritative scripture *(śrūti).* Furthermore, all of the more important traditional theologians and philosophers throughout classical and medieval India recognized the central importance of these ancient works, and have written extensive commentaries on them. For these reasons, the Vedic Upaniṣads have also been called the Major, or Principal, Upaniṣads. They may be divided into three historical and textual groups.

1. The earliest Upaniṣads (the *Bṛhadāraṇyaka, Chāndogya, Taittīriya, Aitareya,* and *Kauṣītaki* Upaniṣads and the prose parts of the *Kena Upaniṣad*) predate the rise of Buddhism in the sixth century BCE, the *Bṛhadāraṇyaka* and the *Chāndogya* being the earliest and the *Kena* being the latest. All are explicitly aligned with one or another of the various *sakhās*, or "schools" of Vedic interpretation, and are composed in a prose that closely resembles Vedic Sanskrit. These texts make frequent use of allegorical modes of interpretation and are often almost indistinguishable in style from the Āraṇyakas. In many ways these six works serve as the philosophical foundation for all of the later Upaniṣads.

2. A second group of Upaniṣads (the *Kaṭha* [or *Kaṭhakā*], *Īśa, Śvetāśvatara, Muṇḍaka,* and *Mahānārāyaṇa* Upaniṣads and the metrical parts of the *Kena Upaniṣad*) reflects a growing sectarian orientation and dates to the sixth and fifth centuries BCE. These works, which are composed primarily in verse, are only loosely attached to the Vedic *sakhās*, and make less use of metaphorical, allegorical, or other tropic means of expression.

3. The Upaniṣads of a third group (the *Praśna, Maitri* [or *Maitrāyaṇīya*], *Jābāla, Paiṅgala,* and *Māṇḍūkya* Upaniṣads) return to prose form, but in a language that resembles classical Sanskrit much more than Vedic Sanskrit. They probably emerged in the late fifth and early fourth centuries BCE although the dates for a few of them are uncertain.

All of these works are attached to the textual collections of specific priestly Vedic traditions. The *Aitareya* and *Kauṣītaki* Upaniṣads belong to the *Ṛgveda.* The *Kaṭha, Maitri, Taittrīya,* and *Śvetāśvatara* Upaniṣads are attached to the *Kṛṣṇa* ("Black") *Yajurveda,* while the *Bṛhadāraṇyaka Īśa,* and *Paiṅgala* Upaniṣads are aligned with the *Śukla* ("White") *Yajurveda.* The *Chāndogya* and *Kena* Upaniṣads belong to the *Sāmaveda,* and, finally, the *Muṇḍaka, Māṇḍūkya, Praśna,* and *Jābāla* Upaniṣads form a part of the conclusion of the *Atharvaveda.*

The later Upaniṣads. To this list of principal Vedic Upaniṣads most authorities would add a large number of less known and, for the most part, medieval works that may be classified as the later Upaniṣads. These works are not universally accepted as *śrūti,* and they have not received the extensive attention from traditional South Asian philosophical commentators as have the Vedic Upaniṣads. This does not mean that they are less important than others. Indeed, these texts may well be more influential in their respective communities than the principal Vedic Upaniṣads. Such works reflect the increasing influence of Sāṃkhya philosophy, Yoga practice and ideology, and sectarian theistic traditions through the classical and medieval periods. While many align themselves with the *Ṛgveda, Yajurveda,* or *Sāmaveda,* most of these Upaniṣads are attached, at least nominally, to the *Atharvaveda.* Most are in prose form and are composed almost entirely in classical Sanskrit.

The number of the later Upaniṣads is too large to list all of them here. Only the most important or representative ones will be mentioned; readers seeking a more complete list are directed to the bibliography.

1. Vedānta Upaniṣads. These works, which include the *Muktika, Piṇḍa, Garba, Ātman, Prāṇāgnihotra, Adhyatman,* and *Brahmā* as well as perhaps two dozen other Upaniṣads, fairly consistently maintain the general doctrines presented by the Vedic Upaniṣads, and show relatively little sectarian influence. They differ from the Vedic Upaniṣads only in that they are not cited in traditional commentaries.

2. Yoga Upaniṣads. These texts arose out of a more specifically ascetic context than did many of the Vedic and Vedānta Upaniṣads, and reflect the influence of Yoga ideologies and practices within Upaniṣadic circles. This group includes the *Yogakuṇḍalī, Nādabindhu, Śāndilya, Yogatattva, Tejobindhu, Haṃsa, Amṛtabindhu, Dhyānabindhu,* and *Varāha* Upaniṣads. These works center on the direct experience of the eternal self (*ātman*) through specific techniques of Yoga and through the meditation on the sacred syllable *oṃ.*

3. Saṃnyāsa Upaniṣads. These works tend to extol the life of the wandering ascetic's search for release from the cycle of rebirth (*saṃsāra*) and teach ways in which such release may be obtained. They include the *Nāradaparivrājaka, Bhikṣuka, Paramahaṃsa, Āśrama,* and *Saṃnyāsa* Upaniṣads.

4. Mantra Upaniṣads. These teachings center on esoteric interpretations of specific sounds and syllables and place those interpretations into Yogic as well as Śaiva, Vaiṣṇava, and Durgā theistic contexts. Typical of such works would be the *Tārasāra, Kalisantāraṇa,* and *Nārāyaṇa* Upaniṣads.

5. Śaiva Upaniṣads. The earliest Śaiva Upaniṣad might well be said to be the Vedic *Śvetāśvatara Upaniṣad,* which praised the role of Rudra (a Vedic precursor to the god Śiva) in the religious quest. The more well-known of the medieval Śaiva Upaniṣads would include the *Nīlarudra, Kālāgnirudra, Kaivalya,* and *Atharvaśiras* Upaniṣads, all of which understand the person of Śiva (also known as Maheśvara, Bhairava, Īśana, and other names) to be an embodiment of the deepest self, *ātman.*

6. Vaiṣṇava Upaniṣads. These texts tend to interpret the various incarnations of the god Viṣṇu as representative forms of the *ātman.* Some Vaiṣṇava traditions look to the *Īśa Upaniṣad* as the Vedic antecedent to, or oldest sectarian representative of, this particular genre. Works associated with this group include the *Nṛsimha-pūrvatāpanīya, Nṛsimhottaratāpanīya, Mahā, Rāmapur-vatāpanīya,* and *Ramottaratāpanīya* Upaniṣads.

SEE ALSO Brahman; Māyā; Samādhi; Saṃnyāsa; Soul, article on Indian Concepts; Vedānta; Yoga.

BIBLIOGRAPHY

Readers seeking a stock list of what have been termed Vedic and later Upaniṣads should turn to the opening lines of the *Muktika Upaniṣad,* which lists 108 such works. J. N. Farquhar, a historian of Indian religious literatures, has distinguished 123 distinct Upaniṣads, which he lists in his *An Outline of the Religious Literature of India* (1920; reprint, Delhi, 1967), p. 364.

The last hundred years have seen the publication of a large number of Upaniṣads in modern languages, many of which suffer from a lack of perspicuity due to the somewhat esoteric nature of the original works. The most objective English translation of most of the Vedic Upaniṣads remains Robert Ernest Hume's somewhat stilted *The Thirteen Principal Upanishads,* 2d rev. ed. (Oxford, 1949). A more fluid translation is Sarvepalli Radhakrishnan's *The Principal Upaniṣads* (New York, 1953). Radhakrishnan's work is better than Hume's in that it includes the Sanskrit and it translates sixteen rather than thirteen works. Some students will find Radhakrishnan's commentaries on the works to be of some help, although many of them reflect his neo-Vedantic bias. Another good translation, and one that openly admits an Advaitic point of view, is Swāmī Nikhilānanda's *The Upanishads,* 4 vols. (New York, 1949–1959). Readers interested in the later Upaniṣads would be advised to look to Paul Deussen's *Sechzig Upanishads des Veda* (Leipzig, 1897), to K. Nārāyanasvāmi Aiyar's *Thirty Minor Upanishads* (Madras, 1914), and to Jean Varenne's *Upanishads du yoga* (Paris, 1974). Readers seeking only selections from the Vedic Upaniṣads might turn to Sarvepalli Radhakrishnan and Charles Moore's edited volume, *A Source Book in Indian Philosophy* (Princeton, N.J., 1957), pp. 37–96, or to Juan Mascaró's *The Upanishads* (Baltimore, 1965), although the latter is somewhat colored by a theistic understanding of the texts.

Those readers interested in short introductions to Upaniṣadic thought are advised to consult Paul Deussen's *The Philosophy of the Upanishads* (1906), 2d ed., translated by A. S. Geden (New York, 1966); Arthur Berriedale Keith's *The Religion and Philosophy of the Veda and Upanishads,* 2 vols. (1925), 2d ed. (Westport, Conn., 1971), pp. 551–570; or to Surendranath Dasgupta's *A History of Indian Philosophy,* vol. 1 (1922; reprint, Cambridge, 1951), pp. 28–61.

WILLIAM K. MAHONY (1987)

UPĀYA is a Sanskrit and Pali term meaning "device, strategem," or "means." The term has a technical function in Buddhism, especially in the Mahāyāna, where it is frequently used in the compound *upāyakauśalya* ("skill in means"). In Buddhist usage, it refers to certain manners of teaching or forms of practice that may be employed along the path to final release, and in which a buddha or *bodhisattva* is especially skilled. Often, these involve the skillful evaluation of the spiritual capacities of beings on the part of a buddha or *bodhisattva,* and a concomitant revelation of just that degree of truth that is most beneficial to the specific religious needs of the devotee. The usual Chinese equivalent is *fangbian* (Jpn., *hōben*). Although *fangbian* is an ordinary Chinese word with its own distinct meaning, owing to various terminological conflations its meaning in East Asian Buddhist texts is "(skillfully applied) means." The usage has given rise to the convenient English expression "skillful means." The concept of *upāya* also figures prominently in other Mahāyāna Buddhist cultures, notably that of Tibet.

PALI USAGE. The terms *upāya* or *upāyakusala* occur in the Theravāda canon, but only incidentally or in late texts. The *Dīgha Nikāya* and the *Anguttara Nikāya* speak of three kinds of skill: skill in entering *(aya),* skill in leaving *(apāya),* and skill in approach or means *(upāya).* Leaving etymological speculation aside, it is clear that this terminology refers to the spiritual attitude of a monk who is supposed to be expert in the management of his practice on the road to Buddhahood. In the *Suttanipāta,* it is the expert boatman taking others across a swift stream who is described as a "skillful knower of the means."

In spite of the paucity of references in Pali writings, it is remarkable that *upāya* here assumes a double aspect, referring to the activities both of aspiring monk and good teacher, skilled in the ways of helping others across the spiritual threshold. Variously emphasized, this double usage is frequently found in early Mahāyāna, although not direct textual lineage should be assumed. Other Pali usage is either nontechnical or late and incidental. This relative inattention to the term in Pali texts does not mean, however, that the way of thinking assumed in this terminology is foreign either to Theravāda Buddhism in its fully developed form or to the earliest Buddhists in general. Admittedly, there is no direct evidence that the Buddha himself made use of this specific term to explain the way his teaching was to be understood. Nevertheless, there are many indications that his message was presented with conscious, pragmatic skill. In support of this, one need only think of such well known scriptural similes as the raft, the poisoned arrow, the pith, and the water snake, in which the provisional and practical nature of the Buddha's teachings is made clear.

Upāya in the Lotus Sūtra. The opening chapters of the *Lotus Sūtra (Saddharmapuṇḍarīka Sūtra)* are an extended reflection on the nature of the Buddha's teaching. This reflection is advanced partly by means of a series of parables and partly by a retelling of the story of the Buddha's decision to teach others the religious path he had perfected (chaps. 2 and 7). The concept of skill in means plays an important role throughout, occurring over eighty times in the first eight chapters.

Traditionally, the story of the Buddha's decision to teach following his enlightenment had portrayed him as hesitant to do so because of the depth and subtlety of the Dharma and the sensuality and ignorance of humankind. In this account, only the urging of the god Brahmā led to the Buddha's decision to teach the four noble truths and the Middle Way. To this hesitancy was linked the Buddha's perception of the diversity of human faculties and dispositions, a diversity that is likened to a pond full of lotuses, only some of which rise undefiled above the water. In the retelling of this story in the *Lotus Sūtra,* the discrepancy between the Buddha's knowledge and the ignorance of living beings provokes an explanation that the teaching of the Buddha is an *upāya,* that is, a provisional expedient able to draw people into the Buddha's Dharma. In other words, although the Buddha realizes that the true, ultimate, and indeed originally nirvanic quality of things cannot be precisely stated in words, he nevertheless teaches the doctrine of *nirvāṇa* as a "means" to lead people toward detachment.

A parable in the third chapter of the *Lotus Sūtra* tells how a father lures his children from a burning house by the expedient of offering them three fine chariots for their enjoyment. Only on emerging from the fire do they realize that they have been tricked, as it were, into safety by the attractive inducements offered by their father: their real reward, their lives, far outweighs their original expectations. So too, according to the parable, does the Buddha lure sentient beings from the "burning house" that is *saṃsāra* (the round of birth and death) by proposing a variety of apparently distinct religious careers, all of which are in fact reducible to one: the path leading to Buddhahood. Thus understood, the otherwise polemically differentiated "vehicles" *(yāna)*—*śrāvaka* ("hearer of the Dharma"), *pratyekabuddha* (self-enlightened Buddha), and *bodhisattva*—are only provisional constructs designed to appeal to persons of different religious capacities. Ultimately, it is only the path of the Buddhas *(buddhayāna)* that is real.

While the means used to ensure deliverance may thus seem to involve an element of deception, or at least, of withholding the full truth, the discrepancy between the form in which the message is couched and its ultimate meaning is understood to arise owing to the relative ignorance of the living beings who receive it. The sincerity and the consistency of the Dharma regarded from the point of view of the Buddha is considered to be unimpeached. In chapter 5, the simile of a rain cloud, which bestows on diverse plants moisture equal to their needs, explicitly treats this point. Other parables stress that the religious path eventually brings rewards out of all comprehension to those just beginning their practice. In chapter 4, the process of winning enlightenment is compared to that of a son who abandons his father's estate. When the prodigal returns years later, in dire poverty and ignorant even of the fact that he has come to the place of his birth, his father only gradually reveals his patrimony to him, fearing that a premature revelation of the truth would frighten his son away once again.

Finally, not only is the teaching of the Buddha declared by this text to comprise a series of skillfully devised expedients, but the very appearance of the Buddha in this world is declared (chap. 15; chap. 16 in the Chinese) to be a mere strategem to draw beings to the Dharma. The actual Enlightenment is an event that took place, if it occurred in history at all, aeons ago. The Buddha's apparent *pārinirvāṇa* at age eighty is a mere simulacrum, comparable to that of a physician who feigns death in order to induce his willful sons to take an essential medicine. Chapter 7 tells of a guide who leads his charges to a magic city he has conjured up as a resting place for the weary. Only when they have rested do the travelers learn that the city is a mirage, not the ultimate goal of their journey after all.

Thus, in the *Lotus Sūtra* it is not merely a question of particular teachings being regarded as secondary formulations. The very appearance of the Buddha, his setting the wheel of the Dharma in motion, and his winning of *nirvāṇa,* have a provisional, dialectical nature related to the needs of living beings in their diversity.

Upāya in the Perfection of Wisdom Literature. In the early Mahāyāna sūtras, known as the Prajñāpāramitā ("perfection of wisdom") literature, the notion of skill in means is closely linked to that of *prajñā,* that is, to wisdom or insight into the true character of things. Such insight implies a recognition of the metaphysical voidness or insubstantiality of all phenomena and all factors of experience (*dharmas*). Insight and skill in means are two of the perfections in which a *bodhisattva* has to school himself. Hence, this usage (especially in the *Aṣṭasāhasrikā-prajñāpāramitā Sūtra*) complements that of the *Lotus.* As an adept in training, the *bodhisattva* must manage the various features of practical religion that articulate his path, but without becoming attached to them in any way. He must, for example, practice *dhyāna* ("meditation, trance") without being subject to its karmic consequences, that is, without rebirth in the various *deva* heavens that such meditation entails. These heavens, the teaching holds, are pleasant but religiously irrelevant existences; attachment to them is an impediment to the religious life: "But what is the skill in means of a Bodhisattva? It is just this perfection of wisdom. And he applies himself to this skill in means in such a way that, endowed with it, the Bodhisattva enters into the trances without being reborn through the influence of the trances" (Conze, 1973, p. 250).

Upāya, however, is not only a matter of individual spiritual welfare. The *bodhisattva* would lose his own way if he abandoned living beings.

> If the mind of a Bodhisattva forms the aspiration not to abandon all beings but to set them free, and if in addition, he aspires for the concentration on emptiness, the Signless, the Wishless, i.e., for the three doors to deliverance, then that Bodhisattva should be known as one who is endowed with skill in means, and he will not realise the reality-limit midway, before his Buddhadharmas have become complete. For it is this skill in means which protects him. (Conze, 1973, p. 225)

Thus the *bodhisattva* is both the adept and the benefactor. In Mahāyāna thinking it is not possible to be the one without also being the other.

A closely related early Mahāyāna text, the *Vimalakīrtinirdeśa Sūtra* (Teaching of Vimalakīrti) dramatizes this principle with a narrative centered on an illness feigned by the *prajñā*-adept Vimalakīrti. In conversation with Mañjuśrī he declares that his illness is without characteristics but arises only through compassion as a skillful means. It will be healed only insofar as all beings depart from belief in self and from dualistic thought. The close connection between *upāya* and *prajñā* ("insight") is evident in statements such as: "Again, insight without (skillful) means is bondage, but insight with (skillful) means is release; (skillful) means without insight is bondage, but (skillful) means with insight is release" (T.D. no. 14.545). Applied to the body, that fundamental object of Buddhist meditation, the implications of this are as follows:

> Yet again, seeing the body in terms of impermanence, suffering, emptiness and non-self, this is called insight. To stay in birth-and-death even though the body is sick, bringing benefits to all and not getting disgusted or tired, this is called (skillful) means . . . To see that the body is never without sickness . . . and that there is no renovation and no passing away, this is called insight. To recognize that the body is sick and yet not to enter eternal cessation, this is called (skillful) means. (T.D. no. 14.545)

IMPLICATIONS. The concept of *upāya* plays an incidental role in many other Mahāyāna texts, especially in connection with *bodhisattvas* as savior figures. Its implications are also clearly present, however, in the more philosophical Madhyamika distinction between two levels of truth. Both provisional truth *(lokasaṃvṛtisatya)* and supreme truth *(paramārthasatya)* are essential, according to the *Mādhyamakakārika* (Middle stanzas) of Nāgārjuna, for the proclamation of Buddhist Dharma.

Skill in means, or skillful means, is an idea known to every experienced monk in Mahāyāna Buddhism and has often been used to interpret the function of various aspects of Buddhist teaching or practice. Its role as a regulative principle in situations of accommodation or syncretism should never be overlooked. At the same time, many implications of its use as a principle of interpretation both in Buddhism and in a wider religious sense remain to be explored.

SEE ALSO Bodhisattva Path.

BIBLIOGRAPHY

A general discussion of *upāya* can be found in Sawada Kenshō's "Bukkyō ni okeru hōben no shisō ni tsuite," *Bukkyō bunka kenkyū* 12 (1963): 97ff. Masuda Hideo's "*Hannyakyō* ni okeru 'hōben' no imi ni tsuite," *Indogaku Bukkyōgaku kenkyū* 23 (1964): 112–117, discusses *upāya* in the Prajñāpāramitā literature. Kumoi Shōzen's "Hōben to shinjitsu," in *Hoke shisō*, edited by Ōchō Enichi (Kyoto, 1969), pp. 321–351, concentrates on the use of the term in the *Lotus Sūtra.* Leon Hurvitz's *Scripture of the Lotus Blossom of the Fine Dharma* (New York, 1976) and Edward Conze's *The Perfection of Wisdom in Eight Thousand Lines and Its Verse Summary* (Berkeley, 1973) are reliable translations of these two seminal texts. Eugène Burnouf's translation of the *Lotus,* rendered from Sanskrit, contains a discussion of *upāya* in the appendix: *Le lotus de la bonne loi,* vol. 2, Appendice, 2d ed. (Paris, 1925), pp. 594ff.

Other secondary sources include Alicia Matsunaga's *The Buddhist Philosophy of Assimilation: The Historical Development of the Honji-Suijaku Theory* (Tokyo and Rutland, Vt., 1969), which discusses issues closely related to the notion of *upāya;* "The Concept of Upāya in Mahāyāna Buddhist Philosophy," *Japanese Journal of Religious Studies* 1 (March 1974): 51–72, by the same author; my "Assimilation and Skilful Means," *Religion* 1 (Autumn 1971): 152–158; and my *Skilful Means: A Concept in Mahāyāna Buddhism* (London, 1978), a full-length study with further bibliography. For Pali usage, see the editions of the Pali Text Society, especially *Dīgha Nikāya,* edited by J. E. Carpenter (London, 1910), vol. 3, p. 220, and *Anguttara Nikāya,* edited by E. Hardy (London, 1958), vol. 3, pp. 431ff.

New Sources

Franck, Frederick. "Upaya: Stratagems of the Great Compassion." *Eastern Buddhist* 30, no. 2 (1997): 287–293.

Hamlin, Edward. "Magical Upaya in the Vimalakirtinirdesa Sutra." *Journal of the International Association of Buddhist Studies* 11, no. 1 (1988): 89–121.

Miller, Alan L. "Spiritual Accomplishment by Misdirection: Some Upaya Folktales from East Asia." *History of Religions* 40, no. 1 (2000): 82–108.

Pye, Michael. *Skillful Means: A Concept in Mahāyāna Buddhism.* 2d ed. New York, 2003.

Schroeder, J. W. *Skillful Means: The Heart of Buddhist Compassion.* Honolulu, 2001.

MICHAEL PYE (1987)
Revised Bibliography

URMONOTHEISMUS SEE SCHMIDT, WILHELM; SUPREME BEINGS

USENER, HERMANN

USENER, HERMANN (1833–1905), was a German classical philologist and historian of religion. From 1866 to

1902 Usener was professor at Bonn. His major writings include *Das Weihnachtsfest* (1889); *Religionsgeschichtliche Untersuchungen* (2 vols., 1889); *Götternamen: Versuch einer Lehre von der religiösen Begriffsbildung* (1896); and *Die Sintfluthsagen* (1899).

In *Götternamen,* Usener presented a once-influential theory. Taking his method from philology and his data mainly from demons (the *indigitamenta*) invoked by name in ancient Roman rites, Usener claimed to show that the history of the idea of deity had three phases. First, the concept of deity emerges as that of momentary gods (*Augenblicksgötter*) whose power is manifested during some fleeting experience, such as plowing and harrowing, but then vanishes. Next, as activities are repeated, these deities gain a certain continuity; they come to stand as functional powers over an entire class of phenomena or activity. Usener calls these "special gods" (*Söndergotter*). In a later phase still, when the name of the god is no longer connected with his function, the god is seen as an autonomous being or personality. Such gods often have many divine names, but this means only that several special gods with different names have become fused into one. Usener also cited data on Lithuanian religions in support of his views.

Usener's heavy reliance on philology and his claim that the history of the concept of deity could be adequately clarified through the history of the names of the gods was attacked by Jan de Vries, who pointed out that there is no instance of a specialized functional god having evolved into a principal deity. According to de Vries, the momentary gods likely represent a late phase of priestly speculation or juridical elaboration (de Vries, 1967, pp. 134–138). Georges Dumézil has argued similarly that a comprehensive historical approach shows that the *indigitamenta* are relatively unimportant phenomena (Dumézil, 1970, vol. 1, pp. 32–38).

Usener's other major effort was to show how Christianity took over pagan rites and feasts. He traced the Christmas festival to the birthday of the pagan sun god celebrated on the winter solstice (December 25, according to the Julian calendar), and he argued that certain saints derived from pagan prototypes (e.g., Pelagius from Aphrodite).

Bibliography

For brief and telling criciticms of Usener's theory of momentary gods, see Jan de Vries's *The Study of Religion* (New York, 1967) and Georges Dumézil's *Archaic Roman Religion,* 2 vols. (Chicago, 1970). Ernst Cassirer, the German philosopher of "symbolic forms," sympathetically discusses Usener in *Language and Myth* (New York, 1946), pp. 15–36, 72–83.

New Sources

Bremmer, Jan N. "Hermann Usener." In *Classical Scholarship: A Biographical Encyclopedia,* edited by W. Ward Briggs and William M. Calder III, pp. 462–478. New York-London, 1990.

Calder, William M., ed. *Usener und Wilamowitz: ein Briefwechsel (1870–1905)* Stuttgart, 1994.

Calder, William M. III, Hellmut Flashar, and Theodor Lindken, eds. *Wilamowitz nach 50 Jahre.* Darmstadt, 1985.

Clemen, Carl. "Hermann Usener als Religionshistoriker." *Studi e materiali di storia delle religioni* 11 (1935): 110–124.

Dieterich, Albert. "Hermann Usener." *Archiv für Religionswissenschaft* 8 (1905): i–ix. Reprited in *Kleine Schriften,* pp. 354–362. Leipzig and Berlin, 1911.

Jaeger, Werner. "Classical Philology at the University of Berlin: 1870–1945." In *Five Essays,* translated by Adele M. Fiske, pp. 45–74. Montreal, 1982.

Kany, Roland. *Mnemosyne als Programm. Geschichte, Erinnerung und Andacht zum Unbedeutenden im Werk von Usener, Warburg und Benjamin.* Tübingen, 1987.

Mette, Hans Joachim. "Nekrolog einer Epoche. Hermann Usener und seine Schule. Ein wirkungsgeschichtlicher Rückblick auf die Jahre 1856–1979." *Lustrum* 22 (1979–1980): 5–106.

Scardigli, Barbara. "Lettere inedite di Hermann Usener." In *Munus amicitiae. Scritti in memoria di Alessandro Ronconi,* pp. 263–298. Firenze, 1986.

Schlesier, Renate. "'Arbeiter in Useners Weinberg.' Anthropologie und antike Religionsgeschichte in Deutschland nach dem Ersten Weltkrieg." In *Altertumswissenschaft in den 20er Jahrhundert. Neue Fragen und Impulse,* ed. by Hellmut Flashar, pp. 329–380. Stuttgart, 1995.

Schröder, Wilt Aden. *Der Altertumswissenschaftler Eduard Norden (1868–1941): das Schicksal eines deutschen Gelehrten jüdischer Abkunft. Mit den Briefen Eduard Nordens an seinen Lehrer Hermann Usener aus den Jahren 1891 bis 1902.* Hildesheim, 1999.

Wessels, Antje. *Ursprungszauber. Zur Rezeption von Hermann Useners Lehre von der religiösen Begriffsbildung.* Berlin-New York, 2003.

Burton Feldman (1987)
Revised Bibliography

UṢŪL AL-FIQH.

The Arabic phrase *uṣūl al-fiqh,* which means literally "the roots of understanding," takes on a specialized sense in the classical literature of Islam; it may be rendered either as "sources of law" or as "principles of jurisprudence." The former rendering may be regarded as best expressing the primary sense of the phrase and the latter as conveying a broader, extended sense. It must be kept in mind that "law" in Islam is much more comprehensive than Western law: It includes not only civil and criminal law but also regulations pertaining to worship, hygiene, and other aspects of the private lives of individuals. It furthermore recommends and disapproves actions as much as it requires and forbids them, and while it specifies temporal penalties for certain offenses, its ultimate sanctions are otherworldly.

There are two Arabic terms that may be translated as "law"—*sharīʿah* and *fiqh.* The *sharīʿah* is the law of God, immutable, all-encompassing, and transcendent. Strictly speaking, *fiqh* is the understanding of the law of God that jurists acquire through pious scholarship. However, because it is this understanding of the law of God, as expressed in concrete rules formulated by the jurists themselves, which governs the daily lives of Muslims, it may be considered law in its own right. It is, in fact, the nearest thing to a positive law that the Islamic tradition affords. *uṣūl al-fiqh* thus designates, in its primary sense, the sources of this positive law, that is, the sources of a human *prudentia juris* conceived as a norm of human conduct. A source *(aṣl)* is that from which something else is derived. The law of God cannot, in its essence, be a derivative of anything; only human constructions of law can have that status.

The necessity for the distinction between the law of God and the positive law as the expression of the human understanding of that law becomes evident when reflecting on cases where the jurists differ among themselves in their construction of rules. Although some Muslim jurists subscribed to a kind of relativism, according to which any rules that emerged from the deliberations of a particular jurist constituted the law of God for him, the majority of Sunnī jurists insisted upon the absolute uniformity and prevenience of that law such that, where jurists propounded conflicting rules, they could not all be right and the possibility of error had necessarily to be admitted. But as the Sunnī jurists acknowledged no higher authority that might resolve differences among them, they were constrained to regard all rules propounded by duly qualified jurists on the basis of a diligent investigation of the sources of law as equally valid and normative, even if contradictory. What was required for a rule to be normative, therefore, was not that it be an infallible statement of the divine law but simply that it express a qualified jurist's genuine understanding of that law. It is the fallibility of that understanding that compels one to draw a clear line between it and the law of God, its object.

The derivation of positive law from its proper sources is governed by carefully formulated methodological principles so as to leave as little as possible to human ingenuity. These principles, which are partly hermeneutical, partly text-critical, and partly theological, are included in the extended meaning of *uṣūl al-fiqh*. They, together with the sources of law, constitute the "principles of jurisprudence."

The Theory of the Four Sources and Its Origin. Classical Sunnī Muslim legal thought enumerates four primary sources of positive law: the Qurʾān; the *sunnah,* or custom, of the prophet Muḥammad; consensus (*ijmāʿ*); and analogical deduction (*qiyās*). The first three of these sources consist of, or are embodied in, texts and as such may be described as the material sources of positive law. The Qurʾān and the *sunnah* of the Prophet (as recorded in the special literature called *ḥadīth*) have, by virtue of their inspired character, a special status not accorded the consensus: They alone have been compiled into discrete textual corpora classified as *nuṣūṣ*. The consensus, though not ranked among the *nuṣūṣ*, is nevertheless necessarily expressed in relatively fixed verbal formulations that may be regarded as essentially textual, or at least quasi-textual, in character. These are preserved *within* the larger literature of Islamic jurisprudence. The fourth source of positive law, on the other hand, is, in contrast to the other three, a *method* of deriving from texts rules of law that are not contained within the meaning of the texts. It may accordingly be described as a formal source of law. To the extent that the principle of analogy is strictly applied, the exclusive authority of the texts as material sources of law is maintained, for although the derived rule may not be said to be contained within the meaning of the texts, it may quite definitely be said to have its ultimate basis in the texts, that basis being an analogous rule contained within the texts' meaning. To these four sources of law most theorists add further "supplementary" sources, to be considered shortly.

Joseph Schacht's monumental study of the early development of Islamic jurisprudence (*Origins of Muhammadan Jurisprudence,* Oxford, 1959) singled out the famous jurist Muḥammad ibn Idrīs al-Shāfiʿī (d. 820) as the real architect of the "four source" theory. As Schacht showed, Shāfiʿī formulated this theory in response to the interaction of two movements that had been contending for supremacy in the shaping of Islamic law before his time. The earliest of these was represented by what Schacht called the "ancient schools of law." These schools, which were located in the principal Muslim urban settlements of the Umayyad period (661–750), especially Kufa and Medina, despite certain differences shared a common acceptance of the consensus of legal scholars as constituting the ultimate criterion of correct legal doctrine. While in no way minimizing the preeminence of the prophet Muḥammad, which the passing of generations only enhanced, the representatives of these schools came to view the *sunnah* of the Prophet as most faithfully represented in the unanimously agreed-upon doctrine. Thus the ancient schools in effect identified the *sunnah* of the Prophet with the consensus of legal scholars. In reaction to this view, the second movement, namely that of the traditionists (*ahl al-ḥadīth*), took the position that the consensus of the legists, far from adequately representing the *sunnah* of the Prophet, was in reality the product of human reasoning and was therefore of no value whatsoever and that the *sunnah* of the Prophet was properly represented only by formal traditions (*aḥadīth*; literally, "narratives") reporting actual sayings or deeds of the Prophet and accompanied by lists (*isnāds*) of accredited transmitters. The *sunnah* of the Prophet was thus, in their view, categorically distinct from the consensus of the legists. Both the ancient schools and the traditionists recognized, as any Muslim must, the authority of the Qurʾān, but as the Qurʾān supplies relatively little material of a specifically legal nature, the question of whether the consensus of legists or formal traditions from the Prophet was to be the primary norm after the Qurʾān was of crucial importance for the development of Muslim legal thinking.

Shāfiʿī himself leaned decidedly toward the traditionist point of view. At the same time, being a lawyer by disposition, like the representatives of the ancient schools in whose circles he had studied (and unlike the traditionists, who though much preoccupied with piety had little instinct for legal matters), Shāfiʿī realized that some principle of legal construction beyond that of sheer adherence to texts was necessary if law was to develop in accordance with the ongoing needs of the community. He therefore affirmed the validity of analogical deduction, a technique of legal construction that had been developed to near perfection by the ancient schools. However, he distinguished analogical deduction sharply from the purely private judgments of the legists, which the ancient schools had permitted in certain cases. The latter he ruled out entirely, as he did likewise the consensus of the legists, which, like the traditionists, he believed to be the product of private judgment. In its place he did, however, accept the general consensus of the entire Muslim community on essentials. Thus did Shāfiʿī assemble as complementary principles of legal construction four items: the Qurʾān, the *sunnah* of the Prophet as represented by formal traditions, the consensus of the community as a whole, and analogical deduction from any of the foregoing. By insisting on adherence to formal traditions, which in Shāfiʿī's time were fast being fashioned into a textual corpus, Shāfiʿī secured for Islamic law a strong literary base, thus introducing into juristic activity a larger measure of stability and predictability than had previously existed.

The Classical Theory of the Four Sunnī Madhhabs. During the third century of the Islamic era (roughly the ninth century CE), the ancient schools of law gave way to a new type of school called the *madhhab*. Whereas the ancient schools had been essentially regional in character, encompassing all legists in a particular locality such as Kufa or Medina, the *madhhabs* derived their identity (and their names) from particular authoritative teachers of law, whom they claimed as their founders and whose essential doctrine they claimed to uphold. Two such "personal schools" (Schacht's term)—the Ḥanafī and the Mālikī schools—emerged out of the ancient schools of Kufa and Medina, within which they had originated as circles of followers of two teachers of great prominence, Abū Ḥanīfah in Kufa and Mālik ibn Anas in Medina. The emergence, after Shāfiʿī's death, of another school claiming to uphold his doctrine gave added impetus to the development of the new type of school. By the early tenth century at least seven such schools were in existence within Sunnī Islam, although only four of these survived beyond the thirteenth century: the Ḥanafī, Mālikī, Shāfiʿī, and Ḥanbalī schools.

Despite certain differences that persisted between them and despite the diversity of their origins, the four *madhhabs* came eventually to agree upon a version of the theory of the four sources that is often described as the classical theory. This theory differed in one important respect from Shāfiʿī's version: It accepted the consensus of legal scholars as equal in weight to the consensus of the entire Muslim community, and because the latter was scarcely if at all ascertainable after the Muslim community had spread beyond its place of origin in Medina, it was the former alone that became the effective principle of legal construction (despite many difficulties in its application). Thus in effect the classical theory allowed the cardinal principle of the ancient schools, which Shāfiʿī had rejected, to creep back into Muslim legal thinking. Within the classical theory, it had, however, a position far less exalted than the one it had enjoyed in the thinking of the ancient schools, for it was now subordinated, not only to the Qurʾān, but also to the vast body of traditions. The classical theory, which inherited from Shāfiʿī the notion that the authority of the *sunnah* of the Prophet was grounded in the Qurʾān, went on to make the authority of the consensus dependent on both of these.

The differences between the four *madhhabs* in the realm of legal theory have to do with the so-called supplementary principles of legal construction alluded to above. Of these, two are predominant, namely those referred to by means of the terms *istiḥsān* ("preference") and *istiṣlāḥ* ("consideration of public utility"). The first, which is acknowledged by the Ḥanafī school, allows a jurist to set aside a rule deduced analogically from a text in favor of another rule, whose basis in the text is less obvious but that in the jurist's personal judgment provides a more equitable solution to the case at hand. The second, which originated within the Mālikī school but was also later accepted by some legists of the Shāfiʿī and Hanbali schools, allowed a jurist to formulate a rule on the basis of a perceived contribution to the common good (*maṣlaḥah*). Discussions of what was entailed in the notion of the common good proceeded from the conviction that the essential guidelines were to be found in the texts and culminated in some very profound probings into the "ultimate purposes" (*maqāṣid*) of the law of God. Because *istiḥsān* and *istiṣlāḥ* are kindred principles, and because neither in its classical formulation entailed a conscious turning away from the texts in favor of a totally independent use of human reason but looked to the texts for ultimate guidance, the differences between the *madhhabs* in regard to these principles may be assessed as relatively minor.

The large measure of agreement that the four *madhhabs* eventually arrived at in the theoretical realm helped to foster toleration of the differences between them in the realm of positive legal doctrine. The formulation of rules of law on the basis of the recognized sources was understood to be an arduous scholarly task, leading frequently to results of a quite tentative nature. A jurist who was qualified for this task was, in fact, called a *mujtahid* ("one who strives"), and the work of the *mujtahid* is accordingly called *ijtihād* ("striving"). The result of this work was classified as "opinion" (*ẓann*). Thus the rules formulated by the *mujtahids* represented at best their considered opinion, reached after much "striving," as to what the sources dictated with respect to specific cases presented to them. This recognition of the tentativeness of at least part of the positive law constructed by the jurists militated against a dogmatic attachment to any one *madhhab* as the sole valid expression of the law of God.

Alternatives to the Classical Theory. Although the espousal of the classical theory by the four Sunnī *madhhabs* assured it a position of undisputed predominance within the larger world of Islam, this theory by no means monopolized Muslim thinking completely.

The Ẓāhirī theory. Among the earlier Sunnī *madhhab* s that eventually disappeared, one—the Ẓāhirī *madhhab*—propounded a literalist theory of legal construction that, through the writings of the *madhhab*'s greatest representative, Ibn Ḥazm of Cordova (d. 1064), was to remain after the demise of the *madhhab* as a permanent challenge to the classical theory, to be considered whenever the works of Ibn Ḥazm were studied. The most distinctive feature of the Ẓāhirī theory was its decisive rejection of analogical deduction. Its literalism was of a radical sort requiring exclusive adherence to legal rules contained within the text's meaning as determined solely through the tools of the Arabic linguistic sciences. Analogical deduction was considered too speculative, as it seemed, in the Ẓāhirī view, to entail a purely human determination of a legal rule, even if the presumed basis (*ʿillah*) were said to be inferred from the texts; and rules, according to the Ẓāhirīyah, were not for humans to determine in any degree. The presence of the Ẓāhirī legacy within the Islamic legal tradition promoted intensive reflection among the legists upon the fundamental question of what constitutes the meaning of a text. The Ẓāhirīyah, in the interests of legal development, tended to stretch the concept of meaning to include much of what the four principal *madhhabs* considered to be established by analogy, so that the dispute was, partly at least, over methodological

The Shīʿī theory. Even more potent than the Ẓāhirī theory as a challenge to the thinking of the four *madhhabs* were the theories developed within Shīʿī Islam and especially within that branch known as Imāmī, or Twelver, Shiism. Twelver theory, like the Ẓāhirī, rejects analogical deduction, but the prevailing school of thought among the Twelvers, that of the Ūṣūlīyah, posits in its place "reason" (*ʿaql*) as the fourth source of law. Included under this rubric are a number of "rational" operations. Some of these are essentially interpretative activities and as such are considered to be "dependent" upon the texts, in the sense that they do not lead to any conclusion apart from the texts; others are completely autonomous. Of the latter operations, the most significant is the rational perception of good and evil, a notion derived from an early Muslim school of thought known as the Muʿtazilah but denied universally by later Sunnī thinkers. The three remaining sources posited by the Sunnī *madhhabs* are accepted in Twelver theory but with important modifications. The *sunnah* of the Prophet is expanded into the *sunnah* of the "infallible authority" (*al-maʿṣūm*) so as to include also the sayings of the imams, or spiritual heads of the community, who are deemed no less infallible than the Prophet. As for the consensus, which Twelver theorists take to be the general consensus of the community as a whole, it is reduced to the role of disseminator of the doctrine of the infallible authority, and the notion of an infallible consensus coequal as a material source of law with the Qurʾān and the *sunnah* of the Prophet is regarded as a Sunnī aberration stemming from the treasonous election of Abū Bakr as the first caliph. During the long period intervening between the entry of the twelfth imam into a state of "occultation" (believed to have occurred in 876) and his anticipated return, the community depends on the spiritual guidance of *mujtahids*, who, though not infallible—even when in agreement—are qualified by virtue of their superior knowledge of the Qurʾān and the *sunnah* of the "infallible authority" (as enshrined in Shīʿī *ḥadīth* collections) to carry on the task of developing the positive law in response to communal needs. Unlike the Sunnī legists, however, these *mujtahids* are not divided into a plurality of *madhhabs*—a most reprehensible situation, to the Shīʿī way of thinking—but constitute one unified and exclusively valid *madhhab*, that of the imams and the Prophet themselves.

ʿIlm Uṣūl al-fiqh. Interest in the methods and principles governing the derivation of positive rules from the sources of law gave rise to a special Islamic science called *ʿilm uṣūl al-fiqh*, whose business it was to spell out these methods and principles in detail and to deal with every conceivable issue that might arise in connection with them. This science was distinguished from *ʿilm al-fiqh*, the science of positive law as such. Together, these two sciences constitute the two main branches of what may be called, in the broadest sense of the term, Islamic jurisprudence.

Although Shāfiʿī, described already as the architect of the theory of the four sources, may also be regarded as the founder of ʿilm *uṣūl al-fiqh*, especially by virtue of his treatise known generally as the *Risālah*, the primary agents in the development of this science in the century or so after Shāfiʿī were a number of prominent members of the Muʿtazilī school, mentioned above. There is, in fact, a close connection between the development of ʿilm *uṣūl al-fiqh* and that of speculative theology (*ʿilm al-kalām*), in which the Muʿtazilah played a prominent role; and as the agents in the one were also the agents in the other, it is not surprising that the method of investigation that prevailed in speculative theology, namely that of dialectic, prevailed also in ʿilm *uṣūl al-fiqh*. After the eclipse of the Muʿtazilī school of theology by the "orthodox" Ashʿari and Māturidi schools, the further development of *ʿilm uṣūl al-fiqh* was carried on by theorists of all four *madhhabs*, many of whom adhered to these two later schools.

It should be noted, finally, that despite its great thoroughness and finesse *ʿilm uṣūl al-fiqh* was seldom put to practice for the purpose either of producing new law or of reforming existing law. The greater part of the legal doctrine of the four *madhhabs* was formulated long before *ʿilm uṣūl al-fiqh* reached maturity and is, in fact, in large measure a legacy of the ancient schools of law, as Schacht has shown. The methods and principles elaborated in *ʿilm uṣūl al-fiqh* were consequently viewed as identical with those presumed to have been employed by the great masters of an earlier period, especially the eponyms of the four *madhhabs*. *ʿIlm uṣūl al-fiqh*—at least in its later mature form—sought simply to articulate what was supposed to have been implicit in the work of the masters. At the same time it always stood as a potential resource for any daring mind that might wish to take a fresh and independent look at the inherited doctrine and embark on a new *ijtihād* in emulation of the masters themselves.

See Also Islamic Law.

Bibliography

Coulson, Noel J. *A History of Islamic Law.* Islamic Surveys, vol. 2. Edinburgh, 1971.

Goldziher, Ignácz. *The Ẓāhirīs: Their Doctrine and Their History.* Translated and edited by Wolfgang Behn. Leiden, 1971.

Löschner, Harald. *Die dogmatischen Grundlagen des šī'itischen Rechts.* Cologne, 1971.

Schacht, Joseph. *An Introduction to Islamic Law.* Oxford, 1964.

Weiss, Bernard. "Interpretation in Islamic Law: The Theory of Ijtihād." *American Journal of Comparative Law* 26 (1978): 199–212.

Bernard G. Weiss (1987)

UTOPIA.

UTOPIA. The term *utopia* (from the Greek *ou-topos,* "no place," or *eutopos,* "good place," and evidently coined as a pun by Thomas More for the title of his book published in 1516) has very diverse, often confusing connotations. Sometimes it is used to mean any idealization of the distant or primordial past, when humans lived closer to the gods (or God), as found in Sumero-Akkadian cuneiform accounts of Dilman; in the Hebrew story of Eden of *Genesis;* in portrayals of the Golden Age by Hesiod, Vergil, Symmachus, and other Greek and Roman writers; in myths of the "perfect great period" (*kṛtayuga, suśamā,* etc.) in later Vedic, earlier Jain, and Buddhist traditions; or in accounts of the early age of the four (mythic) emperors of popular Chinese thought. In some ancient cultures, the original inhabitants of certain foreign regions were imagined to live in an innocent, trouble-free state (the Greeks, for instance, wrote of the Ethiopians, Scythians, and others in this fashion), while not a few students of prehistory in modern times have visualized the earliest humans as herbivores, free from war (as held by Richard Leakey), or as without the sexual constraints and inequalities of later ages (as held by Friedrich Engels).

In contrast, the term *utopia* at other times refers to the future realization of some perfect place and time. It can take on futurist instead of primitivist associations, thus becoming a lost paradise regained, the projection of the hopes and dreams of a millenarianism (the kingdom of God or its equivalent on earth), or the establishment of an ideal society divinely or otherwise sanctioned to replace the glaring ills of the day. Occasionally notions of heavenly worlds—such as the mythic Isles of the Blessed in Greco-Roman belief, the Chinese Māhāyana Buddhist Pure Land of the West, or the Qur'anic vision of heaven as fertile gardens with maidservants—have been described as utopian, as also have visions of an eternal city set above the known order, such as Augustine's City of God, which nevertheless partakes of earthly affairs.

A more traditional understanding of utopia (as in More) is that of a distant, wondrous land allegedly discovered and described by a traveler returning home. Hints of this are found in Homer's *Odyssey* (the account of the Phaeacians), and the earliest extant written description of utopia is that of Euhemerus, who not only argued that the gods were originally deified mortals but also described an idyllic social order outside the bounds and difficulties of ordinary human life. Interestingly, priests are the effective rulers of the Sacred Isle, although they have no official political status.

Pertinent comparisons here include the Greek romancer (and perhaps Cynic) Iambulus writing on the island City of the Sun (early first century BCE), the church historian Socrates on the location of Eden (440 century CE), More's *Utopia* (1516), the Spanish explorer Garcilaso de la Vega's impressions of the Inca empire (1617), the Rosicrucian Johann Valentia Andreae's *Christianopolis* (1619), the Dominican Tommaso Campanella's *City of the Sun* (1623), empiricist Francis Bacon's *New Atlantis* (1627), and *philosophe* Denis Diderot's *Tahiti* (1772), all Western in origin. More's crescent-shaped, two-hundred-mile-long, substantially urbanized island utopia is the most famous, remarkable for its religious tolerance and its endearing priests, who do not persecute but instead constrain those few who happen to hold to the three destructive, forbidden views: that the soul is mortal, that the world is the outcome of mere chance, and that there is no reward or punishment after death.

Possible Eastern analogues to these strangely removed lands are found in Chinese and particularly Daoist beliefs from the fourth century CE onward. Accordingly, select individuals could secure, by some potion or other means, virtual immortality, and "not somewhere else out of this world," as Joseph Needham puts it, "nor in the underworld of the Yellow Springs, but among the mountains and forests here and forever." Looking further afield, from the pre-Christian Americans one learns of South American Indian migrations (the Guariní, in particular) in quest of the "land without evil" to the east. In transitional Melanesia, individuals who have managed to journey well beyond their own cultural bounds during colonial times (such as police, recruited laborers, and others) have often spun together novel mythic histories about where the whites came from—Britain, Germany, Jerusalem, Sydney, and so on—and how they acquired "cargo" (European goods). From such far-off utopias, where God, the ancestors, and culture heroes are present, cargo came as transformation and blessing to the islanders.

In the present day, the idea of utopia has become inseparable from utopianism, the systematic attempt to engineer a preferable, even perfect society. The origins of utopia in this sense might be said to go back to the construction of the first cities (according to Lewis Mumford) or at least to the schemes of Plato (and the lesser-known Greek thinkers Hippodamus and Phaleas). But many scholars do not consider this exercise in model building for revolutionary social transformation much older than the eighteenth century (the moderately aristocratic *Oceana* scheme by the Englishman James Harrington in 1656 being only faintly precursory), and they have pointed out the central role of the Western ideal of universal progression toward utopianism's realization. They also recognize the secondary importance of practical experimentation in the Americas, where, especially in North America, European colonists attempted to establish new kinds of community or sought a new paradise in the wilderness away from the evils of the Old World.

Utopianist designs for social reconstruction have not always been distinctly religious, except insofar as their ethical stances reflect spiritual values. As the chief protagonist in Plato's *Republic,* Socrates was an atheist when it came to the old gods, yet the guardians of his new polity were to be fully enlightened by the supreme idea of the good (the equivalent of God). In modern times, utopianists have voiced radically anticlerical, if not anti-Christian sentiments, yet they have been dominated by a vision of what is ethically right regarding human relationships. The first utopia as a projected, future program rather than a millennial fiat was that of the French progressivist Sebastian Mercier. In his tract on the year 2440 (written in 1770) he expressed his wish that the church as he knew it would not survive, but nonetheless he imagined an initiation ceremony using telescopes and microscopes, in which young people would discover God, the author of nature (which, in turn, would serve as the basis of justice). Disillusioned with ecclesiastical orthodoxy, in 1825, one of his successors, Saint-Simon, wrote *New Christianity,* and the renowned Charles Fourier described a New Earth in the dawning of the Third Age, like Joachim di Fiore's Age of the Spirit (1847). If François-Noël Babeuf and Pierre-Joseph Proudhon, two other French utopianists, were secular communists in their approach, each nevertheless preached with a religious intensity against injustice. There were other European utopian thinkers in the nineteenth century, both English and continental, from Scottish industrial reformer Robert Owen, a man touched by Christian millennial hopes in his *New Vision of Society* (1813), to vehemently antireligious anarchists, including Petr Kropotkin, a Russian litterateur active at the end of the century.

Marxism has been characterized as a species of secular utopianism, even millenarianism, for presaging a future, supranational society free of classes following a series of proletarian revolutions. Both Karl Marx himself and his collaborator Engels, however, detached themselves from the utopians (especially Proudhon) by arguing that the historical process rather than artificial reorganization would produce a radically better order. However, the fact that the programs of Lenin and Stalin in Russia, Mao Zedong in China, Kim Il Sung in North Korea, and others reveal massive political manipulation and forced mobilizations to support communist state policies suggests that where Marxism has been dominant in certain societies, politics have typically drifted toward the utopian, social-engineering model that Marx himself disdained. The end product of these maneuvers was meant to be a society free not only from classes but from religion.

Communism and socialism take a number of forms, although many less obviously political expressions are often referred to as communalisms, commutarianisms, or communes. Many and varied small-scale utopian communities have been established in the modern-day West, with the greatest number in North America. One discovers parallel and prototypic communities in earlier religious history: the Chinese Daoist and Neo-Confucian retreats of sagehood (Zhang Daoling at Dragon Tiger Mountain, Kiangsi, during the first century CE, or Zhou Dunyi at Lu Shan, c. 1050); in the early monasticisms (both the Jain and Buddhist traditions in India, the Jewish Qumranites and Therapeutae, the Christian Pachomians, Benedictines and their medieval successors, etc.); in the elitist, and for all appearances sectarian, spiritual fraternities (Indian *āśramas*, the ancient gnostic and hermetic schools of Egypt, the medieval Brethren of the Free Spirit in Germany and the Low Countries, the Rosicrucian Order, and other esoteric groups in seventeenth-century England and Germany); and in the communities of the radical Reformation (Anabaptists, Hutterites, etc.) with this tradition generating Mennonite, Amish, and other experiments in North America, including the Quaker City of Brotherly Love, Philadelphia.

By the nineteenth century the United States was sprinkled with many religious communities, at that time often dubbed "socialisms" (John Humphrey Noyes documented at least forty-eight in his *History of American Socialisms,* 1870) but today more likely called utopias or (somewhat pejoratively) "cults." The most famous, distinctly religious examples were Amana in Iowa, New Harmony in Indiana (inspired by Owen), the Shaker and Oneida communities (in New York and elsewhere), as well as the Mormon settlements in Utah. During the first half of this century such communities were spawned in the northwestern states, and since World War II the popularity of life in communes or special retreats has grown, especially in California because of the impact of Eastern meditative traditions and the rejection of highly mechanized and plutocratic North American society (in favor of, for example, a drug culture, anarchy, or a more highly disciplined, ascetic way of life). Some have been inspired by Thoreau's *Walden* and other American celebrations of seclusion in the wild, others by ravaged Amerindian traditions. Comparable postwar communes were established in northern Europe and Australia.

In view of these developments and the growth of state communism, Christian theologians have debated whether Christianity is a utopian faith. Reinhold Niebuhr characterized the Christian position as anti-utopian because evil can never be eradicated from society, while Paul Tillich argued that utopian dreaming has positive value in setting ideal goals but must be transcended when only enslavement or force can secure its long-lasting actualization. Modern Eastern philosophers, particularly Indian gurus who have encouraged or founded new communes, characteristically teach that such communities are but transitory supports before liberation from the realm of physical contingency and karmic law.

Utopia is a subject for both the sociology and psychology of religion. When attempts are made to realize a utopian scheme, it is important to ask questions about social dynamics, the role of a charismatic leader or elders, its degree of durability, and the rate of attrition. A stringently prestructured scheme usually results in a more legalistic orientation and a greater resort to authoritarianism, while in looser efforts at cooperation unity is maintained more by common hope of labors rewarded or a coming transformation. A shared sense of purpose, however, especially by the genuinely faithful, is crucial for the survival of either kind of movement. Apropos to religious categorization, utopianism tends to characterize sectarian, spiritualistic, and mystical persuasions, just as most utopists in the political arena tend to reject the current order of realpolitik, feeling it reflects the morally bankrupt established system.

Utopianism in practice is as attractive psychologically as millenarianism is for idealists, or for those in quest of some certainty and an anxiety-free existence in a sea of cultural, religious, and ethical pluralism. Utopia can also provide, as can the millennial transformation to come, satisfaction for feelings of resentment toward the world's ills or the society from which utopists secede. A need for the certainty a utopia can provide often coincides with extensive rule making and authoritarianism, while recriminatory tendencies can lead to isolationism and relative xenophobia.

Utopianism, when viewed as an oneiric tendency to project a vision of a better life or as exercises of the imagination that lead to social questioning, is more a product of the mind and religious intellectual activity than social organization. The contemplation of happiness and what it entails is a perennial feature of philosophical reflection in religious or quasi-religious traditions, and utopianism is one of its clearer manifestations. Students of the unconscious will note that the displacement of reality for imagined visualization can compel archetypally vivid dreams and rich symbols. Psychoanalytically interesting, moreover, is the aspect of utopias that touches on sexual mores. Thomas More imagined an ideal marriage state, with children being brought up by the community as a whole. An actual attempt at reconstructing Eden-like conditions of the male-female union came with the Adamites, one pre-Reformation group of which was isolated on an island in the river Elbe in Germany from the fifteenth century onward. Members went naked (a reminder that nudist colonies are essentially utopian), and the "naturalness" in the sexual relations of later groups are portrayed in the indelible symbols of Hieronymous Bosch's *Garden of Worldly Delights* (1506?). A modern utopia of particular interest regarding the relationship of religion and sexuality is the Oneida community which was governed by Noyes's complex books of instruction.

Whether as a product of thought or action, or analyzed in a sociological or psychological sense, utopianism characteristically betrays assumptions about the limited relevance of historical change. Utopias are often conceived, sometimes unwillingly, "as good patterns of life in an ahistorical cosmos" (Olson, 1982). Little thought is given to what may lie beyond or develop out of these Utopias in the future, since, like the millennium, they constitute an end or proper fulfillment of the known order. Unlike the millennium, however, utopia can be discovered, and although it may also be the product of dreaming and imagination, it can be devised rationally and is not constructed only from the elusiveness and ambiguities of apocalyptic literary authorities. Admittedly some forms of millennialism, particularly those of American theologians who preached that the kingdom of God had to be worked for on earth (as documented best by Ernest Lee Tuveson), compare better with utopian visions. On the other hand, such visions are not intrinsically incompatible with noneschatological or more decidedly secular approaches to social reform. Marx, Freud, and other atheist commentators, however, suggest that all religion is inherently utopian in reflecting the presumptions or hypothesizing about a given realm—especially the afterlife—that escapes the ordinary contingencies of material existence and selfhood. And if this is at least arguable, so too it can be proposed that utopia is fundamentally a given of religious consciousness.

See Also Cargo Cults; Community; Golden Age; Millenarianism; Noyes, John Humphrey.

Bibliography

Ferguson, John. *Utopias of the Classical World.* Ithaca, N.Y., 1975.

Holloway, Mark. *Heavens on Earth: Utopian Communities in America, 1680–1880.* 2d ed., rev. New York, 1966.

Kanter, Rosabeth Moss. *Commitment and Community: Communes and Utopias in Sociological Perspective.* Cambridge, Mass., 1972.

Lasky, Melvin J. *Utopia and Revolution: On the Origins of a Metaphor.* Chicago, 1978.

Lovejoy, Arthur O., and George Boas. *Primitivism and Related Ideas in Antiquity.* Baltimore, 1935.

Manuel, Frank E., ed. *Utopias and Utopian Thought.* Boston, 1967. Includes important articles by Lewis Mumford and Paul Tillich.

Needham, Joseph. *Science and Civilisation in China.* 5 vols. Princeton, N.J., 1954–1983.

Noyes, John Humphrey. *History of American Socialisms.* Philadelphia, 1870. Reissued as *Strange Cults and Utopias of Nineteenth-Century America.* (New York, 1966).

Olsen, Theodore. *Millennialism, Utopianism, and Progress.* Toronto, 1982.

Pöhlmann, Robert von. *Geschichte der Sozialen Frage und des Sozialismus in der antiken Welt.* 2 vols. Munich, 1925.

Richter, Peyton E., ed. *Utopias: Social Ideas and Communal Experiments.* Boston, 1971.

Thrupp, Sylvia L., ed. *Millennial Dreams in Action.* New York, 1970.

Tuveson, Ernest Lee. *Millennium and Utopia.* Berkeley, Calif., 1949.

Venturi, Franco. *Utopia and Reform in the Enlightenment.* Cambridge, 1971.

Yates, Frances A. *The Rosicrucian Enlightenment.* London, 1972.

New Sources

Collins, Steven. *Nirvana and Other Buddhist Felicities.* Cambridge, 1998.

Dawson, Doyne. *Cities of the Gods: Communist Utopias in Greek Thought.* New York, 1992.

Eaton, Ruth. *Ideal Cities: Utopianism and the (Un)built Environment.* Antwerp, 2001.

Eliav Feldon, Miriam. *Realistic Utopias: The Ideal Imaginary Societies of the Renaissance, 1516–1630.* Oxford, 1982.

Hardy, Dennis. *Utopian England: Community Experiments, 1900–1945.* London, 2000.

Levitas, Ruth. *The Concept of Utopia.* New York, 1990.

Neville-Sington, Pamela, and David Sington. *Paradise Dreamed: How Utopian Thinkers Have Changed the Modern World.* London, 1993.

GARRY W. TROMPF (1987)
Revised Bibliography

UTU. Utu was the Sumerian god of the sun (he is identified with the Akkadian Shamash) and the city god of both Sippar and Larsa, where he had temples bearing the same name "shining house." Utu was the son of the moon god, Nanna, and therefore brother of Inanna and Ishkur. Hence he belongs to the fourth generation of gods after the supreme god An, and he represents the third cycle, coming after that of the *annus sideralis*—related to the sky vault of An—and that of the lunation of the moon god Nanna—who is the first divinity of light, a bridge between the "invisible" (New Moon) superior divinities, namely Enlil, Enki, and Ninhursaga, and the "illuminator" divinities, namely the sun, Venus, and lighting. The cycle attributed to Utu is the diurnal one, not the annual one, and it is this aspect that determines his functions. As god of the sun, Utu was believed to ride the heavens from sunrise to sunset in a chariot pulled by four storm-beasts and then to descend to the netherworld at sunset to continue his circuit until the morning. A frequent scene in cylinder-seal iconography shows Utu rising in the eastern mountains holding a "saw" (the sun's rays).

Utu held an important position in the pantheon, although he does not figure prominently in mythological tales. According to the myth of Enki and the world order, Enki entrusted Utu with the borders of the universe; all of Utu's other functions derived from this role. Foremost was the administration of justice by defining the borders of rights and wrongs; in this task his attendants were Justice and Righteousness, two deities of his suite which included—among others—his wife Aja and his main assistant Bunene. Judgment actually took place in the morning, when the gods assembled; without Utu's rising, there could be no justice. Hence kingship—regulating society according to the divine laws and defending or enlarging the borders of the cosmos (i. e., the kingdom,) against the chaos—is placed under Utu's jurisdiction. The evil actions of ghosts and the harm brought about by demons or sorcerers—all affecting the outlines of the cosmic order—are battled by the god, who, for this reason, is invocated in the incantations. Yet an Utu hymn, which also concerns ghosts, may be imploring Utu to allow a dead man into the netherworld (Cohen, 1977).

UTU AS HELPER AND RESCUER. In the same cultural frame Utu plays a crucial role in purification ceremonies such as the *bit rimki,* an ablution ritual against evil caused by eclipses. Of capital importance too is his role in the counter-witch *maqlû* ("burning") ritual. After the night trial that convicted the witch and absolved her victim (originally judgement took place by day) and the witch's consequent destruction in the morning under the sun's beams, the purifications were carried out, thus freeing the victim from evil and restoring his or her previous relationship with his or her personal god (Abusch, 2002). Sunlight also provides the means of detection, and consequently Utu is the one who knows the most hidden aspects of the universe. Because of this skill he (together with Ishkur/Adad) is the "lord of the *omina,*" for the truth the oracle manifests reveals the ways of the cosmic order known to the god. The omen is signifier of other realities; hence in the poem "Enmerkar and the Lord of Aratta" the god plays a determining role in the invention of writing. Being all-knowing of hidden connections, he can also indicate the right direction to anyone who is lost or does not know the way (see the myths of Gilgamesh and Huwawa and of Lugalbanda). In addition he is merciful. Misfortune is a consequence of the actions of evil entities, and the god repels them into the darkness. Utu was considered to be the helper and advocate of the oppressed, safeguarding the orphan, the widow, and the poor (a task entrusted to the sovereigns), a role that was also attributed to the goddess Nanshe. It was Utu's function to right injustice, and the oppressed turned to him with their cry "I-Utu" ("O Utu!"), a phrase that came to mean oppression itself, and even (complaining) malcontents. As master of the borders, of the signs, and of the laws that govern them all, he is also master of all physical features, that is, of people's borders. In fact Utu transforms Dumuzi, pursued by the demons, into different animal forms in order to rescue him.

COROLLARIES. Utu has control over access to and egress from the netherworld, a power possibly related to his own ability to enter the netherworld every evening and emerge at sunrise as lord of the border between day and night. Thus in the myth of Gilgamesh, Enkidu, and the netherworld, Enkidu is trapped in the netherworld until Enki has Utu open a "window" so that Enkidu may ascend. Utu also served as judge of the netherworld, a function shared somewhat with the deified dead Gilgamesh and Dumuzi. This judgment of the dead and of the other denizens of the netherworld does not seem to have involved a concept of eternal reward and punishment, and it probably consisted of settling disputes and keeping the peace between the souls there. The character of Utu/Shamash, as mentioned above, is an element wedged between two related systems: binary (invisible versus visible divinities) and trinary (year, month, day). This could be the reason for his limited diffusion outside Mesopotamia (although his qualities of omniscience, justice, and mercifulness made him popular where Mesopotamian culture penetrated). A solar divinity is mentioned in the Eblaite texts (twenty-fifth century BCE) with the Sumerian cuneiform ideogram *Utu.* Although a Semitic reading *Sipish* for that ideogram is supported by a geographic name, it is not clear whether only a masculine sun god was meant, as in Mesopotamia, or a solar goddess, in accordance with the Western Semite tradition of the eastern Mediterranean coast in later times. The most realible hypothesis is that two sun divinities were present in Ebla, a masculine one occurring in royal rituals (which were cerainly Eblaite in origin) and a feminine one found in an exorcism. From Hittite Anatolia comes an important hymn—with evident and very strong Babylonian influences—to the sun god Iltanu, notwithstanding the importance of the sun goddess of Arinna.

In later times the "sophisticated polytheism" led the major divinities to be considered aspects of Marduk (Lambert, 1975). Shamash was Marduk when exercising justice. It was perhaps with this configuration that Shamash was emancipated from his original double frame, and his importance was felt even outside the bounds of Mesopotamia. Thus in Hellenistic times he was ready to meet—possibly through the mediation of the ancient Iltanu of Hittite times—the character of Apollo, who was in many aspects similar and who had been formerly present on the Anatolian coasts from the end of eighteenth century BCE. For more on the diffusion in late antiquity Hellenistic culture of the god Shamash in Hatra, in the Nabatean site of Khirbet Tannur, and in the Syrian region, in towns such as Harran, Edessa, Dura Europos̀, Palmyra, and Heliopolis (Baalbek in the Beqaa Valley), see Tubach 1986 and Fauth 1995.

SEE ALSO Dumuzi; Kingship; Mesopotamian Religions; Sun.

BIBLIOGRAPHY

For a general treatment of Utu, see Pietro Mander, "La difesa del Debole e la Giustizia nella Civiltà Sumerica: Dal Piano Divino e della Speculazione Teologica al Piano Sociale," in *Non Violenza e Giustizia nei Testi Sacri delle Religioni Orientali,* edited by C. Conio and D. Dolcini (Pisa, Italy, 1999), pp. 13–28. For peculiar aspects of the god, see Mark E. Cohen's "Another Utu Hymn," *Zeitschrift für Assyriologie* 67 (July 1977): 1–19; W. Heimpel, "The Sun at Night and the Doors of Heaven in Babylonian Texts," *Journal of Cuneiform Studies* 38 (1986): 127–151; B. Alster, "Incantation to Utu," *Acta Sumerologica* (Japan) 13 (1991): 27–69; Mark J. Geller's "Very Different Utu Incantations," *Acta Sumerologica* (Japan) 17 (1995): 101–126; and W. G. Lambert, "The Historical Development of the Mesopotamian Pantheon: A Study in Sophisitcated 'Polytheism,'" in *Unity and Diversity,* edited by H. Goedicke and J. J. M. Roberts (Baltimore and London, 1975), pp. 191–200. For discussion of Shamash as judge, see the Shamash hymn in W. G. Lambert's *Babylonian Wisdom Literature* (Oxford, 1960), pp. 121–138; and T. Abusch, *Mesopotamian Witchcraft* (Leiden, 2002).

For Ebla, see A. Archi, "Substrate: Some Remarks on the Foundation of the West Hurrian Pantheon," in *Hittite and Other Anatolian and Near Eastern Studies in the Honor of Sedat Alp,* edited by H. Otten, E. Akurgal, and A. Süel (Ankara, Turkey, 1992), pp. 7–14. For Syria in late antiquity, see Jürgen Tubach, *Im Schatten de Sonnen Gottes: Der Sonnenkult in Edessa, Harran und Hatra am Vorabend der christlichen Mission* (Wiesbaden, Germany, 1986); and Wolfgang Fauth, *Helios Megistos: Zur synkretistischen Theologie der Spätantike* (Leiden, 1995).

TIKVA FRYMER-KENSKY (1987)
PIETRO MANDER (2005)

VAIKHĀNASAS. The chief "priests" (*arcakas*) in more than half the Viṣṇu temples in the South Indian states of Tamil Nadu, Andhra Pradesh, and parts of Karnataka—including the renowned Hindu pilgrimage center, Tirupati in Andhra Pradesh—Vaikhānasas are a tiny, widely dispersed brahman community of about 3,000 families. Claiming to be a surviving school of Vedic ritual performance, the Taittiriya *śākhā* of the *Kṛṣṇa Yajurveda,* Vaikhānasas have their own complete Vedic Kalpasūtra in addition to prescriptive manuals on temple performances exemplifying the so-called Āgama literature. Beyond the intrinsic interest of their literature and the evidence it provides for further inquiry into questions of continuity and change in India's religious traditions, Vaikhānasas command special interest and attention because of their contemporary temple activities and efforts to maintain community integrity despite accelerating social and technical change.

Manū's discussion of *vanaprastha* ("forest-dweller," the third of the four classical *āśramas* mentions a "Vaikhānasa rule" (*Mānava Dharmaśāstra* 6.21). As other ancient authorities seem to support this reference, it appears quite likely that there existed a distinct Vaikhānasa reclusive community some time before the beginning of the common era, though the extant Vaikhānasa *sūtras* seem to be no older than the fourth century CE. The Vaikhānasa Gṛhyasūtras prescribe a daily worship of Viṣṇu that involves the fabrication of an image and is said to be "equal to the worship of all the gods" (*Vaikhānasa Gṛhyasūtra* 4.10–12). In essential details, this devotional service "prefigures" the *arcana* (service to images) detailed in the Vaikhānasa Saṃhitās; and it is plausible that Vaikhānasa literature documents the community's transition from a Vedic "school" of ritual observance to a "school" of the religious performances characteristic of Hindu devotional cults.

Louis Renou proposed (*L'Inde classique,* vol. 1) that the Vaikhānasa is a *bhāgavata* tradition that, while emphasizing Viṣṇu-Nārāyaṇa *bhakti,* did not exhibit the sectlike exclusivity apparently characteristic of early Pāñcarātra *ekāntins* ("monotheists"). Certainly, the Vaikhānasas's own insistence that they are *vaidikas* and not *tāntrikas* clearly evidences their concern with distinguishing themselves from *pāñcarātrikas.* This concern is further illustrated in their refusal (at least since the mid- to late nineteenth century) to undergo *Vaiṣṇavadīkṣā* ("initiation" as a Vaiṣṇava) on the grounds that they are "Vaiṣṇavas at/from birth" because their mothers underwent a particular life-cycle rite (*saṃskāra*) during their first pregnancies. Still, the exact historical relationship between Vaikhānasas and *pāñcarātrikas* remains unclear.

Inscriptions from perhaps the eighth century CE identify Vaikhānasas as temple functionaries. According to Vaikhānasa tradition, the sage Vikhanas (a manifestation of Brahmā or Viṣṇu) composed the *Vaikhānasa Kalpasūtra* and taught four disciples—Atri, Bhṛgu, Kāśyapa, and Marīci—the procedures of *samūrtārcana* ("devotional service [to Viṣṇu] with images"). Saṃhitās ("collections") of versions of these instructions, said to have been authored by these four disciples, constitute the core of Vaikhānasa literature.

More so than their Pāñcarātra counterparts, the Vaikhānasa Saṃhitās are the literature of ritual prescription, providing detailed instructions from priest to priest for constructing and dedicating temples and images and for conducting religious ceremonies involving them. While not negligible (as some scholars have asserted), the explicit *jñāna* sections of these texts are brief, and thus certain important features must be inferred from their discussions of ritual. These texts emphasize the distinction between Viṣṇu as the pervasive, unfigured (*niṣkala*) presence in the universe and his figured (*sakala*) presence occasioned in his graceful response to intent devotional meditation. Initially, this is the meditation of the *arcaka* who conducts the proceedings through which the deity comes to dwell in prepared images; subsequently, it is the essence of the behavior of devotees toward images so enlivened. Discussion of cosmogony in the Vaikhānasa texts principally traces the backgrounds of the human predicament: being caught in *saṃsāra.* According to Vaikhānasa teaching, *mokṣa* is "release" into Viṣṇu's heaven, and the nature of one's *mokṣa* depends on a devotee's service: attentive repetition of prayer (*japa*), sacrifice (*huta*), service to images (*arcana*), or meditation conforming to yogic regimen (*dhyāna*). Among these four, the *Marīci Saṃhitā* declares that *arcana* is the realization (*sādhana*) of all aims.

SEE ALSO Tamil Religions; Vaiṣṇavism.

BIBLIOGRAPHY

Those who read French will profitably consult Gérard Colas's *Viṣṇu, ses images et ses feux: Les métamorphoses du dieu chez les vaikhānasa* (Paris, 1996), a comprehensive study of Vaikhānasa teachings and ritual. Colas's earlier *Le temple selon Marīci* (Institut Français d'Indologie, Pondichéry, 1986) provides annotated translation of passages in the *Marīcisaṃhitā* dealing with the construction of temples and icons. In English, Jan Gonda's summary overview of Vaikhānasa literature in his *Medieval Religious Literature in Sanskrit* (Wiesbaden, 1977), pp. 140–152, remains useful as does Willem Caland's landmark essay *On the Sacred Books of the Vaikhanasas* (Amsterdam, 1928).

Caland's translation of the *Vaikhānasasmārtasūtram* (Calcutta, 1929) gives reliable access to a crucial text and is complemented by Wilhelm Eggers's *Das Dharmasūtra der Vaikhānasas* (Göttingen, 1927). Of the Vaikhānasa ritual handbooks, or Saṃhitās, the *Kāśyapajñānakāṇḍa* is ably translated into English by Teun Goudriaan as *Kāśyapa's Book of Wisdom* (The Hague, 1965). Also, Teun Goudriaan's "Vaikhānasa Daily Worship According to the Handbooks of Atri, Bhṛgu, Kāśyapa, and Marīci," *Indo-Iranian Journal* 12 (1970): 161–215, is an invaluable reference. Supplemented by the appropriate sections of Carl Gustav Diehl's *Instrument and Purpose* (Lund, 1956) that outline daily performances in South Indian Śiva temples, Goudriaan's essay affords an excellent idea of the essential structure and details of Agamic temple performances. And my "Mahāsaṃprokṣaṇa, 1981: Agama and Actuality in a Contemporary Temple Renovation," *Agama and Silpa* (Bombay, 1984), pp. 69–102, and "Tradition, Text, Person," *History of Religions* (May 1986) shed some light on the Vaikhānasas' contemporary circumstances.

G. R. WELBON (1987 AND 2005)

VÄINÄMÖINEN is the protagonist of the Finnish national epic, the *Kalevala,* and an important figure in ten ancient Finnish poems in *Kalevala* meter. He is the inventor of the *kantele* (the ancient psaltery used to accompany the chanting of the *Kalevala* epics), an expert singer, and a master musician. Väinämöinen has taken part in the primeval acts of creation; were he to be killed, joy and song would depart this earth.

Väinämöinen's name is derived from the word *väinä,* meaning a strait or a wide, slowly flowing river. The derivation seems to indicate that Väinämöinen was originally associated with water, but scholars are not in agreement about this or any other explanation of the hero's original character. He often goes by the epithet "the old one," and he is repeatedly characterized as "the everlasting wise man."

The images of Väinämöinen that occur in folk poetry can be grouped into four basic types: (1) creator of the primeval sea, (2) culture hero, (3) shaman hero, and (4) sea hero and suitor.

1. As creator of the primeval sea, Väinämöinen shapes the seabed by creating holes and shoals in it. Once his work is done, a bird—an eagle, a scaup duck, or a goose—makes a nest on his knee and lays an egg (in some versions, eggs). When Väinämöinen shifts his knee the egg breaks, and the pieces become the various elements of the world:

What was the egg's upper shell
became the heavens above

what was the egg's lower shell
became mother earth below

what was the white of the egg
became the moon in the sky

what was the yolk of the egg
the sun in the sky

what on the egg was mottled

became the stars in heaven

what on the egg was blackish
became the clouds in the sky.

(Bosley trans., in Kuusi et al., 1977)

Väinämöinen then joins his brother Ilmarinen in the upper aerial regions to strike a spark that falls through the nine heavens to Lake Alue. Väinämöinen's association with celestial bodies is reflected in the old Finnish names for Orion and the Pleiades, which mean "Väinämöinen's scythe" and "Väinämöinen's birchbark shoes," respectively.

2. As culture hero, Väinämöinen builds the primeval boat, which one day strikes a great pike from whose bones he makes the first *kantele,* which he uses to enchant the world. In Ingria (the region between Estland and Lake Ladoga) various goods are made from the great oak felled at Väinämöinen's command. In some regions Väinämöinen was believed to be the first cultivator of flax and hemp as well as the inventor of the fishnet. He is also credited with concocting various ointments and curing diseases and with the ability to stop the flow of his own blood. Like most culture heroes, Väinämöinen departed from the world, in his case in an iron-bottomed boat, once humanity had reached a certain level of development, and is prophesied to return in the future.

3. As shaman hero, Väinämöinen uses his singing to charm the young Saami (Lapp) Joukahainen, a rival shaman, into a swamp, where he abandons him by revoking his magical song. Other shamanistic motifs include Väinämöinen's crossing a river to visit Tuonela (the land of the dead) and returning as a snake, and his obtaining knowledge from Antero Vipunen, a dead wise man. Väinämöinen also resorts to shamanistic power in his quest for the *sampo,* a support of the world. A belt worn by Finnish shamans up to the nineteenth century, from which magic objects were hung and which was used as an aid in incantation, was known as "the belt of old Väinämöinen."

4. As sea hero and suitor, Väinämöinen appears in those parts of the extensive *Sampo* epic cycle concerning his theft of the *sampo* and the contest among heroes for the mistress of Pohjola ("homestead of the north"). In one episode a Saami shoots Väinämöinen, who falls into the sea and drifts until he is rescued by the mistress of Pohjola. At other times he engages in a dispute with Ilmarinen's sister Anni or makes an unsuccessful attempt to capture a mermaid. Finally, he orders the killing of a fatherless half-month-old boy in a marsh. When the baby suddenly begins to speak, deprecating the old man, Väinämöinen is compelled to rescind his order. In Elias Lönnrot's redaction, this final scene of the *Kalevala* is intended to be an allegory for the retreat of paganism and the rise of Christianity.

The tradition of poem-cycles and miniature epics with Väinämöinen as chief protagonist began in the distant past. The oldest stratum of this tradition represents Väinämöinen as an epic or cosmological figure. The newer stratum depreciates his role, or even satirizes him. The two strata tended to mix during the eighteenth or nineteenth centuries; Lönnrot brought this process to its logical conclusion when he compiled and edited the *Kalevala.* At the same time, he strengthened Väinämöinen's central position by casting him in roles originally occupied by other characters. He also divested him of mythological features and endowed him with human, though manifestly heroic, traits.

SEE ALSO Finnish Religions; Ilmarinen; Lemminkäinen; Tuonela.

BIBLIOGRAPHY

Haavio, Martti. *Väinämöinen, Eternal Sage.* Translated by Helen Goldthwaite-Väänänen. Folklore Fellows Communications, no. 144. Helsinki, 1952. An essay in which the shamanistic traits in the poems on Väinämöinen are emphasized.

Krohn, Kaarle. *Kalevalastudien,* vol. 5, *Väinämöinen.* Folklore Fellows Communications, no. 75. Helsinki, 1928.

Kuusi, Matti, Keith Bosley, and Michael Branch, eds. and trans. *Finnish Folk Poetry: Epic; An Anthology in Finnish and English.* Helsinki, 1977.

MATTI KUUSI (1987)

VAIŚEṢIKA. The Vaiśeṣika school of Indian philosophy, founded by Kaṇāda (sixth century BCE?), has concentrated mostly on issues and themes of ontology and has closely cooperated with the Nyāya, its sister philosophical school, on matters of epistemology. Like many other schools of Indian philosophy, it upholds that all living beings, human or nonhuman, have souls that are different from the body, eternal, and ubiquitous; that the supreme goal of life is liberation from the bondage of *karman* and the cycle of birth and rebirth; and that the attainment of liberation is the only means of ensuring freedom from all suffering.

According to Vaiśeṣika teaching, the soul is a kind of substance that is conceived as the substratum of quality particulars *(guṇas)* and motion. Both quality particulars and motion are related to the substance by way of inherence *(samavāya). Samavāya* is a special kind of relation as well as an independent ontic category that binds only those two kinds of relata, one of which must be destroyed with the severance of the relationship. Substances, quality particulars, and motions share common properties, or universals, that are eternal and independent of their substrates and yet related to them by way of inherence. Physical substances are produced from combinations of atoms, which are eternal, indivisible, and imperceptible. Each eternal substance is characterized by an ultimate differentiator *(viśeṣa),* which serves as a basis of distinction under circumstances where no ordinary means of distinction is available. Besides the above six kinds of positive ontological categories—substance, quality particular, motion, universal, inherence, and ultimate individuator—there is a negative ontic category, including such entities as absence (as of a book on the table), difference (as of one thing from another), and so on.

The Vaiśeṣika school seeks to prove the existence of the soul by arguing that desire, cognition, and other attributes are quality particulars and must be supported by a substance that is nonphysical because they are radically different in many ways from the quality particulars of physical substances. Such a substance must also be permanent and endure through time; otherwise no satisfactory account can be given of such phenomena as memory. It must further be eternal and in particular, preexistent before birth, or else one cannot account for the fact that a newborn child reaches out for its mother's milk, given that the infant's action is claimed to be purposive and involve memory (which can only have been acquired in a previous life).

One of the souls, called Īśvara (God), is said to be endowed with superhuman qualities such as omniscience. Īśvara's existence is inferred from the premise that a conscious agent is required not only for the creation of artifacts such as a pot, but indeed for all effects, and that the conscious agent responsible for bringing about a conjunction of atoms leading to the production of macrocosmic objects can only be Īśvara. He is also inferred as the author of revealed scriptures and further as the original bestower of significance on linguistic symbols, an act making all communication possible.

SEE ALSO Nyāya.

BIBLIOGRAPHY

The best book on Nyāya-Vaiśeṣika philosophy is Gopinath Bhattacharya's edition and translation of the *Tarkasaṃgraha-dīpikā* (Calcutta, 1976). For readers who are less technically minded, but still want a comprehensive and precise account, the best book is *Indian Metaphysics and Epistemology: The Tradition of the Nyāya-Vaiśeṣika up to Gaṅgeśa*, edited by Karl H. Potter (Princeton, 1977), volume 2 of *The Encyclopedia of Indian Philosophies.* The general reader may profitably consult Mysore Hiriyanna's *Essentials of Indian Philosophy* (London, 1949).

KISOR K. CHAKRABARTI (1987)

VAIṢṆAVISM

This entry consists of the following articles:

VAIṢṆAVISM: AN OVERVIEW

The origin of Vaiṣṇavism as a theistic sect can by no means be traced back to the Ṛgvedic god Viṣṇu. In fact, Vaiṣṇavism is in no sense Vedic in origin. Indology has now outgrown its older tendency to derive all the religious ideologies and practices of classical India—indeed, all aspects of classical Indian thought and culture—from the Veda. It must be remembered that when the Vedic Aryans migrated into India, they did not step into a religious vacuum. On the strength of newly available evidence, it is possible to identify at least two pre-Vedic non-Aryan cults. One was the *muni-yati* cult, which must be distinguished from the exotic Vedic Aryan ṛṣi cult. The *muni-yati* cult, with its characteristic features such as yoga, *tapas*, and *saṃnyāsa*, was an intrinsic component of both the Śiva religion, which had been deeply rooted and widely spread in pre-Vedic India, and the ancient Magadhan religiophilosophical complex, which later served as the fountainhead of such heterodox religions as Jainism and Buddhism. The second cult, that of *bhakti*, is more pertinent to our present purpose. The autochthonous character of *bhakti* in the sense of exclusive devotion to a personal divinity, as evidenced by several aboriginal Indian religions, is now generally accepted. These two cults can be seen to have influenced the hieratic Vedic cult to a certain extent both positively and negatively. Positively, the Vedic religion adopted into its pantheon the pre-Vedic non-Aryan Śiva in the form of Rudra. Similarly, there is every reason to assume that some of Vasiṣṭha's hymns to Varuna in the seventh book of the *Ṛgveda* reflect certain essential traits of *bhakti.* Negatively, the hieratic Vedic religion clearly betrays its aversion to such adjuncts of the Śiva religion as *yatis*, *śiśnadevas*, and *mūradevas.*

Once established, the Vedic religion succeeded in keeping the indigenous religious cults of India suppressed for a fairly long time. When, however, about the end of the period of the major Upaniṣads (eighth to sixth centuries BCE), the authority of Vedism began to decline, the non-Vedic religious cults again came into their own. Whereas some of them, like the ones that later developed into Jainism and Buddhism, refused to accept Vedic authority, the theistic cults sought its blessing and sanction.

VĀSUDEVISM. The theistic cult centered on *bhakti* for the deified Vṛṣṇi hero Vāsudeva, who is not mentioned in any early text. With the decline of Vedism, the cult emerged as a significant force. Strangely, the available evidence shows that the worship of Vāsudeva, and not that of Viṣṇu, marks the beginning of what we today understand by Vaiṣṇavism. This Vāsudevism, which represents the earliest known phase of Vaiṣṇavism, must already have become stabilized in the days of Pāṇini (sixth to fifth centuries BCE), for Pāṇini was required in his *Aṣṭadhyāyī* to enunciate a special rule (4.3.98) to explain the formation of the word *vāsudevaka* in the sense of a "*bhakta* or devotee of the preeminently venerable god Vāsudeva."

The tradition of the Vāsudeva religion continued almost uninterrupted since that time. Megasthenes (fourth century BCE) must be referring to this religion when he speaks of the Sourasenoi (people of the Śūrasena or Mathura region) and their veneration of Herakles. A passage in the Buddhist *Niddesa* also points to the prevalence of Vāsudeva worship in the fourth century BCE. The *Bhagavadgītā* (third century BCE) eulogizes the man of knowledge, who, at the end of many births, betakes himself unto the god in the conviction that "Vāsudeva is All" (7.19). According to the Besnagar inscription (last quarter of the second century BCE), the Garuḍa column of Vāsudeva, the "god of gods," was erected by Heliodoros, the Bhāgavata, of Takṣaśilā. The historical tradition that Vāsudeva originally belonged to the tribe of the Vṛṣṇis is also well attested. In the *Bhagavadgītā* (10.37) Lord Kṛṣṇa declares that of the Vṛṣṇis he is Vāsudeva. The *Mahābhāṣya* of Patañjali (150 BCE) also clearly speaks of Vāsudeva as belonging to the Vṛṣṇi tribe (*vārttika* 7 of 4.1.114). The inscriptions of Ghosundi and Nanaghat (both of the first century BCE) and the grammatical work *Kāśāika,* all of which associate Vāsudeva with Saṃkarṣaṇa (another deified Vṛṣṇi hero), further confirm the Vṛṣṇi lineage of Vāsudeva.

It may be noted that the Pāṇinian *sūtra* which establishes the Vāsudeva religion also suggests the existence of an independent religious sect, with Arjuna as its chief god. It would seem, however, that even in the initial stages of its development the Arjuna religion was subsumed by the Vāsudeva religion and thus disappeared completely from literature and history. The religion of Saṃkarṣaṇa also seems to have arisen independently of the Vāsudeva religion. In the *Mahābhārata,* Saṃkarṣaṇa (or Balarāma) is represented as the elder brother of Vāsudeva, but there is no indication in the epic of any religious sect having developed around him. However, the *Arthaśāstra* of Kauṭilya (fourth century BCE) refers to spies disguised as the ascetic worshipers of Saṃkarṣaṇa (13.3.67). The Mathura sculpture (second century BCE) which depicts Saṃkarṣaṇa by himself is also highly suggestive in this context. The evidence of the *Niddesa,* the *Mahābhāṣya* of Patañjali, and the Ghosundi and Nanaghat inscriptions, on the other hand, shows that, presumably on account of their original Vṛṣṇi affiliations, the Saṃkarṣaṇa and Vāsudeva religions had come to be closely allied. With the development of the doctrine of the *vyūhas,* whereby Saṃkarṣaṇa came to be regarded as one of the *vyūhas* (standing for the individual self) subordinate to Vāsudeva (standing for the Highest Self), the Saṃkarṣaṇa religion lost its independent existence.

KṚṢṆAISM. Another theistic cult which gathered strength with the decline of Vedism centered on Kṛṣṇa, the deified tribal hero and religious leader of the Yādavas. There is sufficient evidence to show that Vāsudeva and Kṛṣṇa were originally two distinct personalities. The Yādava Kṛṣṇa may as well have been the same as Devakīputra Kṛṣṇa, who is represented in the *Chāndogya Upaniṣad* (3.17.1) as a pupil of Ghora Āṅgirasa and who is said to have learned from his teacher the doctrine that human life is a kind of sacrifice. Kṛṣṇa seems to have developed this doctrine in his own teaching, which was later incorporated in the *Bhagavadgītā.* In time, the Vṛṣṇis and the Yādavas, who were already related to each other, came closer together, presumably under political pressure. This resulted in the merging of the divine personalities of Vāsudeva and Kṛṣṇa to form a new supreme god, Bhagavān Vāsudeva-Kṛṣṇa. Evidence in Megasthenes and in Kauṭilya's *Arthaśāstra* indicates that this new divinity was established as early as the fourth century BCE. Indeed, the names *Vāsudeva* and *Kṛṣṇa* began thereafter to be used indiscriminately to denote the same divine personality.

A third current was soon added to this swelling religious stream, in the form of the cult of Gopāla-Kṛṣṇa, which had originated among the nomadic cowherd community of the Ābhīras. Suggestions that the Gopāla-Kṛṣṇa cult shows traces of Christian influence or that it developed from Vedic sources are unacceptable. On the contrary, the religion of Gopāla-Kṛṣṇa seems to have spurned the Indra-dominated Vedic religion (as is evidenced by the Govardhana episode) and to have promoted religious sublimation of sensuous love (as represented by Kṛṣṇa's relationship with the *gopīs*). The amalgamation of the Vāsudeva cult of the Vṛṣṇis, the Kṛṣṇa cult of the Yādavas, and the Gopāla cult of the Ābhīras gave rise to what may be called Greater Kṛṣṇaism. New legends came to be invented whereby Vāsudeva, Kṛṣṇa, and Gopāla were integrated into a single homogeneous mythological pattern. If Vāsudevism represented the first phase of Vaiṣṇavism, Greater Kṛṣṇaism represented its second (and perhaps most outstanding) phase.

VAIṢṆAVISM. The seventh to fourth centuries BCE were a period of great philosophical ferment in India. Vedism was on the decline, and non-Vedic religions such as Jainism and Buddhism were gradually gaining ascendancy. That period also saw vigorous attempts by the vanguards of Vedism to resuscitate the Vedic way of life and thought through the Sūtra-Vedāṅga movement. Kṛṣṇaism followed an eminently practical course with a view to consolidating its position in the face of the expanding heterodoxy on the one hand, and the resurgence of Vedism on the other. The amalgamation of the three theistic cults was an important step in the direction of such consolidation.

The other line of action adopted by Kṛṣṇaism was of a more vital character. Non-Vedic in origin and development, Kṛṣṇaism now sought affiliation with Vedism so that it could become acceptable to the still not inconsiderable orthodox elements among the people. That is how Viṣṇu of the *Ṛgveda* came to be assimilated—more or less superficially—into Kṛṣṇaism. Viṣṇu had already been elevated from the subordinate position that he had occupied in Rgvedic mythology to the position of supreme godhead (*Aitareya Brāhmaṇa* 1.1). Further, the belief had already become well established that whenever *dharma* (righteousness) languishes and *adharma* (nonrighteousness) thrives, Viṣṇu, the supreme God, incarnates in order to save the world. Kṛṣṇa accordingly came to be regarded as an incarnation (*avatāra*) of Viṣṇu. Kṛṣṇaism thus grew in its mythological and practical scope so that in some ways it became a form of Vaiṣṇavism. One of the classic works of Kṛṣṇaism, the *Bhagavadgītā,* reflects the syncretic use of Vedic as well as Vāsudeva traditions in such a way that Kṛṣṇa himself is said to be the supreme Lord.

PĀÑCARĀTRA; BHĀGAVATA. The inclusion of the Nārāyaṇa cult into Kṛṣṇaism is generally regarded as the second major factor in the process of the so-called brahmanization of Kṛṣṇaism. However, the Nara-Nārāyaṇa cult itself seems to have originated in Badari (the northern ridge of the great Hindu Kush arch) independently of the Veda. Indeed, tradition assigns great antiquity to that cult (*Mahābhārata* 7.172.51). It is not unlikely that the ancient non-Vedic concept of Nara-Nārāyaṇa was absorbed into the Vedic ideology in the form of Puruṣa Nārāyaṇa of the *Śatapatha Brāhmaṇa* (12.3.4). The latter, in its turn, was perhaps later transformed into the pair Arjuna (Nara-Puruṣa) and Kṛṣṇa (Nārāyaṇa) of Kṛṣṇaism. Nārāyaṇa is represented as the founder of one of the two early sects of Vaiṣṇavism, namely, Pāñcarātra, as distinguished from the other early sect, namely, Bhāgavata. The distinction between these two sects is emphasized if we consider that the Pāñcarātrins were the worshipers of Nārāyaṇa, whereas the Bhāgavatas were the worshipers of Vāsudeva-Kṛṣṇa; that the Pāñcarātrins were the followers of Tantric Vaiṣṇavism, whereas the Bhāgavatas were the followers of brahmanic Vaiṣṇavism; an Vaiṣṇavism d that the Pāñcarātrins accepted the doctrine of *vyūhas* (according to which Vāsudeva, Saṃkarṣaṇa, Pradyumna, and Aniruddha were the four "emanations" [*vyūhas*] of God, standing respectively for the Highest Self, the individual self, mind, and egoism), whereas the Bhāgavatas accepted the doctrine of *avatāras* (ten incarnations of Viṣṇu).

Vaiṣṇavism in History. Vaiṣṇavism has generally enjoyed the patronage of various ruling dynasties, although foreign tribes like those of the Śakas and the Kushans (first centuries before and after the beginning of the common era) do not seem to have been favorably inclined toward that religion. Similar was the attitude of the early Vākāṭakas and the Bhāraśivas (second and third centuries CE). On the other hand, epigraphic and numismatic evidence shows that most of the Gupta sovereigns (who reigned from the fourth to the seventh century CE) were devout Vaiṣṇavas or Bhāgavatas, although their overall religious policy was remarkably liberal and tolerant. It was also during the age of the Guptas that most of the Vaiṣṇava Purāṇas and the Saṃhitās of Tantric Vaiṣṇavism took final shape. In the course of the post-Gupta millennium (700–1700 CE), Vaiṣṇavism, like Hinduism in general, came to be fragmented into further sects and subsects. The emergence of these sects and subsects usually followed a certain set pattern: some particular religious leader would start a movement either to reform the existing vulgarized religious practices of the parent sect or to widen the appeal of that sect by abjuring social inequalities. The main purpose of these new sects and subsects was not so much to sponsor any specific philosophical or theistic tenets as to establish and popularize certain distinct kinds of *bhakti*. This renewal of *bhakti* is known to have received its main impulse from South India. It is, indeed, striking that Nakkirār (late first century CE) should mention in one of his poems "the blue one with the eagle flag" (i. e., Kṛṣṇa) and "the white one of the plowshare and the palmyra flag" (i. e., Baladeva). But it was the Āḻvārs (sixth to ninth centuries CE) who denounced all social distinctions and expressed in their Tamil songs a deeply emotional and intensely personal devotion for Viṣṇu. The *bhakti* tradition of the Āḻvārs was given a Vedantic foundation by the *ācāryas* of the Śrī Vaiṣṇava school, such as Nāthamuni, Yāmunācārya, and Rāmānuja. Two subschools evolved out of the Vaiṣṇava theology of Rāmānuja: the southern school (the Teṅkalai) insisted that *prapatti*, or complete surrender to God, was the only way to obtain God's grace, whereas the northern school (the Vaṯakalai) required the devotee to resort also to other ways of salvation prescribed by the scriptures.

Vaiṣṇava Bhakti Cult. It is in northern and central India that one sees a truly exuberant ramification of the Vaiṣṇava *bhakti* cult (thirteenth to seventeenth centuries CE). Two main currents of devotional worship can be distinguished in this connection, one relating to Rāma and the other to Kṛṣṇa. In the case of the latter, again, there are two distinct lines of development, one centering on Kṛṣṇa and his spouse Rukmiṇī (as generally sponsored by the saints of Maharashtra) and the other centering on Kṛṣṇa and Rādhā (as popularized by, among others, Nimbārka, Caitanya, and Jayadeva). One of the most remarkable Vaiṣṇava saints of India, Kabīr (fifteenth century), was born to the family of a Muslim weaver of Banaras. Early in life he became influenced by the Hindu ascetic Rāmānanda (the fifth in descent from Rāmānuja), who symbolized for the young aspirant the spirit of revolt against religious exclusivism and abstruse philosophizing. Kabīr taught Sahaja-Yoga, which aimed at an emotional integration of the soul with God. The Kabīr sect extended to Kathiawar and Gujarat but in the process split up into twelve different Kabīrpanthas. Dādū (sixteenth century CE, Gujarat-Rajasthan), for instance, was a follower of Kabīr, but he founded his own Brahma-Saṃpradāya with a view to uniting the divergent faiths of India into a single religious system. Another outstanding Vaiṣṇava saint, Caitanya (or Gaurāṅga, 1486–1533), though not the founder of Bengal Vaiṣṇavism, left the indelible mark of his personality on that religious movement. He initiated a new mode of congregational worship, called *kīrtana*, which consisted of choral singing of the name and deeds of God, accompanied by drums and cymbals and synchronized with rhythmic bodily movements, all this culminating in ecstasy. Among other typical teachers and saints who fostered Vaiṣṇava *bhakti*—each in his or her own way—may be mentioned Jñāneśvara (thirteenth century, Maharashtra), Narsī Mehtā (fifteenth century, Gujarat), Śrīpādarāja and Purandaradāsa (both fifteenth century, Karnataka), Śaṃkaradeva (c. fifteenth-sixteenth century, Assam), Mīrā Bāī (sixteenth century, Rajasthan), Tulsīdās (sixteenth century, Uttar Pradesh), and Tukārām (seventeenth century, Maharashtra).

Literature. In the literature of Vaiṣṇavism, the first place—in time as in importance—has to be conceded to the *Mahābhārata*. Notwithstanding its ultimate encyclopedic character, there is no doubt that the *Mahābhārata* was, at an earlier stage, redacted in favor of Kṛṣṇaism, Kṛṣṇa having been represented almost as its prime mover. The inclusion in the Great Epic of such Vaiṣṇava religious tracts as the *Bhagavadgītā* and the *Nārāyaṇīya* and of the *Harivaṃśa* (as an appendix) confirms its basic Vaiṣṇava orientation. The Rāmāyaṇa, on the other hand, can hardly be called sectarian.

Among the eighteen Purāṇas, six—the *Viṣṇu, Nārada, Bhāgavata, Garuḍa, Padma,* and *Vārāha*—are traditionally regarded as Vaiṣṇava or *sāttvika.* Out of these, the *Bhāgavata Purāṇa* has all along been looked upon as an authoritative scripture of Vaiṣṇavism. From among the sectarian Upaniṣads, which, incidentally, are fairly late (second to fifteenth centuries CE), seventeen are said to be Vaiṣṇava. Several of them are of the nature of Tantras. However, the principal Tantric Vaiṣṇava sect is the Pāñcarātra. Traditionally, 108 Saṃhitās of the Pāñcarātra are mentioned, although their number is sometimes given as 215 or even 290. Among the Pāñcarātra Saṃhitās, which are variously referred to as *Ekāyanaveda, Mūlaveda,* or *Mahopaniṣad,* the *Sāttvata,* the *Pauṣkara,* and the *Jayākhya* are said to constitute the "jewel triad" (*ratnatrayī*). The more commonly known *Ahirbudhnya Saṃhitā* is believed to have been produced in Kashmir in the early fifth century. The four main Tantric topics dealt with in the Saṃhitās are *jñāna* (soteriological theology), *yoga* (psychophysical discipline), *kriyā* (cultic practices), and *caryā* (personal and social behavior). Side by side with the Pāñcarātra, there also developed a Tantric Vaiṣṇava cult known as Vaikhānasa. It may be noted that specific Saṃhitās govern the religious practices at specific Vaiṣṇava temples. Profuse philosophical literature has originated in the four major schools of Vaiṣṇava Vedanta. Reference may also be made to the various manuals dealing with *bhakti,* such as the *Bhaktisūtras* of Śāṇḍilya and Nārada (tenth century).

There are also quite a large number of prayers and hymns of praise (*stotras*), known for their great literary and religious appeal, which are addressed to Viṣṇu in his various forms. All this literature is in Sanskrit. However, many of the newly arisen sects and subsects of Vaiṣṇavism adopted as their gospels the sayings and sermons of their promoters (or of the immediate disciples of those promoters), which were usually delivered not in Sanskrit but in the vernaculars of the people for whom they were meant, and these were preserved in oral or written form.

BIBLIOGRAPHY

Bhandarkar, R. G. *Vaiṣṇavism, Śaivism and Minor Religious Systems* (1913). Reprint, Poona, 1982.

Bhattacharyya, Haridas, ed. *The Religions,* vol. 4, *The Cultural Heritage of India.* Calcutta, 1956.

Dandekar, R. N. *Some Aspects of the History of Hinduism.* Poona, 1967.

Dandekar, R. N. *Insights into Hinduism.* Delhi, 1979.

Gonda, Jan. *Aspects of Early Viṣṇuism.* Utrecht, 1954.

Gonda, Jan. *Viṣṇuism and Śivaism, a Comparison.* London, 1970.

Jaiswal, Suvira. *The Origin and Development of Vaiṣṇavism.* Delhi, 1967.

Schrader, F. Otto. *Introduction to the Pāñcarātra and the Ahirbudhnya Saṃhitā.* Madras, 1916.

R. N. DANDEKAR (1987)

VAIṢṆAVISM: BHĀGAVATAS

Quite probably Hinduism's most famous and widely encountered epithet for divinity conceived as ceaselessly and actively solicitous of human welfare is *Bhagavat* ("having shares"). *Bhagavān* (the more commonly cited nominative singular form of the word) occurs as early as the *Ṛgveda.* It expressly refers to Rudra-Śiva in the *Śvetāśvatara Upaniṣad* (5.4), and it is the common honorific of the Buddha in the Pali texts. But *Bhagavān* doubtless is most familiar in reference to Viṣṇu-Nārāyana/Vasudeva-Kṛṣṇa. Indeed, *bhāgavata* ("related to/devoted to Bhagavān") may be the most common, even earliest, general designation of a devotee of Viṣṇu.

If it is readily agreed that history's most prominent *bhāgavatas* are Viṣnu *bhaktas*, there is disagreement and not a little confusion concerning what—if anything—distinguishes them from *pāñcarātrikas* and other Vaiṣṇavas. In fact, *bhāgavata* frequently has meant simply a Vaiṣṇava (or proto-Vaiṣṇava) as such without further characterization. Until perhaps the eleventh century, this nonsectarian sense generally prevailed, and *bhāgavatas* were part of a growing but diffuse movement that emphasized a personal, active devotional relationship between the human and the Absolute but did not have a single, fixed set of specific beliefs and rituals. The variety of attitudes is readily seen by comparing Bhagavatism's most famous texts, the *Bhagavadgītā* and the *Bhāgavata Purāṇa.* The *Bhagavadgītā* is formal and intellectualized, and offers *bhakti* as a refined yoga, a way of release. Thus, its tenor contrasts distinctively with the vibrant emotionalism of the *Bhāgavata Purāṇa's bhakti.* Further, the religion of the *Bhagavadgītā* harkens expressly to Vedic sacrificial models, whereas the religious inspiration of the *Bhāgavata Purāṇa* is more varied.

Some have claimed that Bhagavatism and, indeed, the "*bhakti* idea" are rooted outside of Vedic ceremonialism altogether—that they originated from "indigenous" or "tribal" sources or perhaps are linked to extra-Indian (Iranian) prototypes. Suggestions that they are ultimately alien impositions or incursions, however, ought to be treated cautiously. For one thing, the available evidence will allow only the most hedged, vague, and inadequate historical account. For another, no aspect of Bhagavatism is encountered apart from the embracing set of characteristics of Hindu religious civilization that interpenetrate and link it with Vedic/Brahmanic values. Extant texts and current practices are embedded in this larger context, and this enables a reference without discomfort to "Hinduism" and to mean by it more than a mere collocation of discrete sects. As the *śāstris* and *paṇḍits*—the erudite commentators whose explications are the dynamics and the definition of Hindu tradition—have consistently attempted to show, often with considerable ingenuity, it is diversity rather than simple pluralism that ultimately characterizes Hinduism.

Linguistically, *bhaga, Bhagavat/Bhagavān,* and *bhakti* are derived from the Sanskrit root *bhaj,* meaning "apportion, distribute" as well as "partake, participate, choose." Already in the *Ṛgveda Saṃhitā, bhaga* means "portion, share," *inter alia,* and it occurs also as the name of one of the divine *Ādityas*. *Bhagavān* thus denotes "having a share(s), lucky, fortunate, blessed." But the Bhagavān is more than simply fortunate. He is someone (human or divine) who both "takes a share in" and bestows shares. Being lucky encompasses beneficence.

Crucially, the Bhagavān known to the historical Bhāgavata movement is no other than the Absolute itself. Bhāgavatas identify themselves as beneficiaries of the Bhagavān's essential nature: "choosing, loyal to, devoted to" the Bhagavān. While "sectarian" Bhāgavatas answer variously when asked the precise nature of their relation with the Bhagavān and how they, as *bhaktas,* can achieve some kind of union with Him, they often refer to a "perfect embrace."

EARLIEST BHĀGAVATAS AND THE PĀÑCARĀTRIKAS. Perhaps the earliest inscriptional evidence of Vaiṣṇava *bhāgavatas* dates from about 115 BCE, at a temple site at Beshnagar (Bhilsa District, Madhya Pradesh). Here, Heliodoros, native of Takṣasilā and ambassador of the Greco-Bactrian king Amtalikita (Gr., Antialkides), declares himself a *bhāgavata* in the dedication of a Garuḍadhvaja (a column with Garuḍa, the bird that is Viṣṇu's distinctive vehicle, as its capital) to Vāsudeva, *devadeva,* "lord of lords." The inscription attests to Vāsudeva-Viṣṇu worship in North India in the late second century BCE among "foreigners" as well as native Indians (Heliodoros's mission was to king Bhāgabhadra, apparently another *bhāgavata*). Despite his name, of course, it is not known how "foreign" this Heliodoros was; and the suggestion that the Vasudeva "sect's" popularity among foreigners indicates its distance from Brahmanic convention, or even its particular success among the *kṣatriyas* (nobles), is only conjecture.

Somewhat later—in the first century BCE—a cave inscription at Nanaghat (Western Maharastra) includes reference to Vāsudeva and Saṃkarṣaṇa (the latter known from the *Mahābhārata* as Vāsudeva-Kṛṣṇa's brother); at Ghosundi (Rajasthan), Vāsudeva and Saṃkarṣaṇa are also invoked in a fragmentary inscription at what is presumed to be a temple enclosure. Similar evidence is found near Mathurā (Uttar Pradesh), a celebrated center of Kṛṣṇa devotion.

These lithic records, in addition to references in the Pali Buddhist *Niddesa,* Pāṇini's *Aṣṭādhyāyī* (4.3.92–95), and Patañjali's *Mahābhāṣya* seem to confirm the existence of a *bhāgavata* movement in north-central and northwest India in the centuries immediately preceding the common era. Still, none of this evidence clears up Vāsudeva's background or the way he became identified with Viṣṇu. There is unmistakable evidence of identifications but no clear pattern of the process(es) whereby they emerged. Even in the face of the most familiar evidence there is controversy. Witness, for example, J. A. B. van Buitenen's insistence that Viṣṇu "does not figure at all in the *Gītā* as author of the Kṛṣṇa *avatara*" (*The Bhagavadgītā in the Mahābhārata,* Chicago, 1981, p. 167; cf. pp. 27–28), and Alf Hiltebeitel's counterargument that such claims (that Kṛṣṇa in the *Bhagavadgītā* "is not yet identified with Viṣṇu") are made "despite the clear evidence of the text" ("Toward a Coherent Study of Hinduism," *Religious Studies Review,* 1983, vol. 9, p. 207).

Beyond the psychological likelihood that certain aspects of Vedic belief and ceremony engendered at least some "proto-*bhakti*" sentiments, there are more substantial hints of *bhakti*-like attitudes discernible in a few hymns of the *Ṛgveda Saṃhitā.* Surely the *Śvetāśvatara Upaniṣad* shows that the basic elements of a Bhāgavatism are essentially in place, even though the Bhagavān in this text is Rudra-Śiva. However, it is in three works—the *Mahābhārata* (Book Twelve), the *Harivaṃsa* and the *Bhagavadgīta*—that a quite elaborate "Vaiṣṇava" Bhāgavatism first emerges in literature. Ironically, though, the *Mahābhārata*'s *Nārāyaṇīya* section (12.326–352) is almost too rich a source. It refers to "Sāttvatas," "Bhāgavatas," "Ekanti-bhāgavatas," and the "Pāñcarātra;" and, again, it is difficult to tell if these designate essentially one and the same movement or discrete sectarian groups.

Commonly, Bhāgavata and Pāñcarātra are held to be distinct movements. It also has been proposed that the Pāñcarātrikas are historically the first Bhāgavata sect or school. In both views, the majority of Bhāgavatas are considered to be both "eclectic" and conservative, concerned with reconciling and integrating *bhakti* with Vedic social and ritual order. Pāñcarātrikas, on the other hand, are characterized as coming from the fringes of the Aryan cultural and religious universe. This view tries to persuade one to see Bhāgavatas in a strict sense as *smārtas* ("orthodox" brahmans) of sorts and, by extension, *gṛhasthas* ("householders"). By contrast, the original Pāñcarātrikas would be socially marginal renunciant-ascetics—even "proto-*tāntrikas.*" Some scholars also point out that the absence of the distinctive Pāñcarātra notion of *vyūhas* ("manifestations" of the divine) or, indeed, of any direct reference to the Pāñcarātra in either the *Bhagavadgītā* or the *Bhāgavata Purana* signals discrete historical traditions. Similarly, some have argued that the cosmogony and cosmology depicted in the Pāñcarātra Saṃhitās (the earliest of which date perhaps from the sixth century CE) emphasize distinctively the world-creating and world-maintaining instrumentality of Viṣṇu-Nārāyaṇa's *śakti,* whereas the *Bhagavadgītā,* in making roughly the same point, draws rather on other imagery: the Bhagavān is fully and freely at work in the world without being limited by it in any way.

But early Bhāgavatas and Pāñcarātrikas seem rather to represent different tendencies of conceptualization and ritual orientation than formally distinct sects. Early Pāñcarātrikas, then, may well have been certain among the Bhāgavatas who were closely associated both with renunciant and with formal ritualist traditions. Their developing ideas and ritual practices possibly yielded, in their Saṃhitās, the first sectlike tradition among the Bhāgavatas. As Adalbert Gail put it succinctly, all Pāñcarātrikas were Bhāgavatas but not all

Bhāgavatas were Pāñcarātrikas. (Adalbert Gail, *Bhakti im Bhāgavatapurāṇa,* Wiesbaden, 1969, p. 7.)

BHĀGAVATAS, SMĀRTAS, AND VAIKHĀNASAS. Although it would be entirely wide of the mark to think of the earliest Bhāgavatas principally as brahmans accommodating ideas newly discovered by renunciant adventurers or encroaching from tribal or other extra-Vedic populations, the manifest processes whereby Bhagavatism becomes an idiom of Hinduism center among brahmans. Of them, those who carefully uphold and observe the precepts set forth in Vedic Smārtasūtras are known as Smārta brahmans. Historically, this appellation has come to designate in particular those brahmans who adhere to principles and teachings usually attributed to Śankara (or, occasionally, to Kumārilabhaṭṭa). These Smārtas are often mistakenly identified simply as Śaivas, but in fact, Smārta ritual centers expressly on observances enjoined by the *sūtras* and performance of *pañcāyatanapūjā* to five divinities: Śiva, Viṣṇu, Durgā, Sūrya, and Gaṇeśa.

Even taking into account Śaṅkara's (or Kumārila's) traditional reforming role, most scholars see in the Smārtas not a sect but rather a formalization and renewal of persisting Vedic values better thought of as constituting a Hindu "orthodoxy" or "orthopraxy." And, too, reaffirming obligations to Smārtasūtra injunctions was to some extent a reaction to the emerging strength and popularity of the general *bhakti/bhāgavata* movement. In a sense, then, the Smartas are an "antisect."

Some have claimed that it is precisely among groups or "schools" of careful adherents to one or another Smārtasūtra that there is found a Bhagavatism that is consciously concerned with linking itself to Vedic and Brahmanic proprieties. Hence it has been suggested that the Vaikhānasas represent either a Vedic ritual school accommodating Bhāgavata elements or a group of Bhāgavatas attempting Brahmanic legitimation by adopting the trappings of Smārtahood. Which hypothesis is closer to the historical truth cannot be determined now, but certainly Vaikhānasas are Bhāgavatas; and Vaikhānasas differ from Pāñcarātrikas in important part by identifying themselves as strict *vaidikas* (i.e., conforming to the Vedas) who carefully maintain Smarta standards.

EARLY BHĀGAVATAS OF TAMIL NADU: THE ĀḺVĀRS. Although assumed to be rooted in North India, both Pāñcarātra and Vaikhānasa traditions are historically more prominent in south India than in the north, particularly in Tamil Nadu and Andhra Pradesh. The spread of such movements as the Pāñcarātra, however, most likely was not the first introduction of Viṣṇu *bhakti* to the South, for Tamil literature of the first and second centuries already attests to the existence of a Viṣṇu cultus. Together with the Śaiva Nāyaṉārs, the most famous early South Indian *bhaktas* are the Āḻvārs, Tamil Vaiṣṇava poet-ecstatics who apparently lived and sang praise to Viṣṇu from the seventh to the ninth centuries.

In fact, what is especially noteworthy about these Tamil Bhāgavatas—a fitting designation although the word *Bhagavān* does not appear in their poetry—is the strongly emotional nature of their *bhakti.* In an important sense, it is in and through the Āḻvārs that bhakti and Bhagavatism acquire a voice independent of Vedic or Vedantic formalism. With the Āḻvārs, bhakti is neither the crowning achievement of yoga nor, as Śaṅkara especially would have it, the foremost among preliminary practices prior to final realization; rather, it is a self-validating expression of sentiment and a definition of the human-divine relationship. In the Āḻvārs' Tamil poetry, *bhakti* is first heard in its independent maturity—as song.

THE BHĀGAVATA PURĀṆA AND ITS INFLUENCE. Certainly written in South India and receiving more or less final form by the tenth century, the *Bhāgavata Purāṇa* was strongly influenced by the Tamil Alvars to such a degree that some portions of the text are little more than paraphrases or outright Sanskrit translations of Alvaric originals. It is in *Bhāgavata Purāṇa* that an intellectually and emotionally rich Bhāgavata perspective first appears in Sanskrit literature.

Only subsequent to the appearance of the *Bhāgavata Purāṇa* does a vigorous, specifically sectarian Bhagavatism emerge; the most famous Vaiṣṇava devotional sects trace their origins or crucial reforms to a period from the twelfth and (particularly) the thirteenth centuries to the sixteenth and seventeenth centuries. Especially prominent among these are the four so-called classical *sampradāyas* ("traditions, sects"), all linked in one way or another to South India: Rāmānuja's Śrīsampradāya, Madhva's Brahmasampradāya, Nimbārka's Sanakādisampradāya, and Viṣṇusvāmin's Rudrasampradāya, this last-named absorbed by Vallabhācārya's Vāllabhāsampradāya. Connecting these sects are commentaries in which their founders elaborate not only Bhāgavata devotional attitudes but also alternative interpretations of the Vedantic *pramāṇatraya* ("three authorities"): the *Bhagavadgītā,* the Upaniṣads, and the *Brahma Sūtra.* Through these commentaries Vaiṣṇava Bhagavatism becomes a full, articulate participant in Vedantic Brahmanism. No doubt the adherents of Hinduism's various sects have tended to be relatively few. Most Hindus are not sectarians in any rigorous sense, identifying rather with individual *sampradāyas* without becoming initiates or being strictly bound to their teachings and practices. But if it could be written at all, a "history" of Bhagavatism would trace the rise of individual Bhāgavata sects, and, cumulatively, the particularities of each would highlight the concrete actualities of Bhagavatism.

THE BHĀGAVATAS OF KARNATAKA AND THE MĀDHVAS. The movement founded by Madhva (also known as Ānandatīrtha; 1199–1278) is commonly held to be the first founded solely on the *Bhāgavata Purāṇa.* (Although the preexistent Śrisampradāya of Rāmānuja is usually considered a Pāñcarātra-based sectarian development, its principal indebtedness may be rather to the Āḻvārs.) Earlier than Madhva and even the *Bhāgavata Purāṇa,* a formal Bhāgavatasampradāya had emerged in the Kannara/Tulu country of western Karnataka. Probably influential in the development of Madhva's thought and still active today, this group descends from certain Smārta brahmans who became increasingly attached to Viṣṇu (possibly due to the growing general popularity of an informal Bhagavatism flowing in particular from the Maharashtra region).

Madhva's fame in the history of Vedantic thought rests on his unconditionally "dualist" position. According to him, the ineradicable distinction between the Absolute and humans must be understood. Madhva's goal is neither to become one with the Absolute nor to realize essential unity with it but rather to participate in it. Knowledge and its concomitant joy in eternal individuality are the heart of Madhva's teaching, which represents the most eloquent articulation in traditional Vedantic idiom of devotees' heartfelt sentiments. And it is perhaps in Madhva's traditions and practices that the complexities of earliest Bhagavatism most authentically survive.

VĀRAKARĪS AND OTHERS: BHAKTAS OF MAHARASHTRA. Bhāgavatas are known to have existed in Maharashtra from before the beginning of the Common Era. A particularly vigorous and complex vernacular Maratha *bhakti* tradition began to emerge in the thirteenth century, however, partly in consequence of the coming together of several traditions both within and beyond Maharashtra. Most significant of these appear to have been the Mādhvas, the Nāthas, the Sants, and the resurgent Vārakarī tradition.

The so-called Haridasas or Vaiṣṇavadāsas, vernacular hymnists to Viṣṇu, seem to have been inspired directly or indirectly by Madhva's teachings. Their influence quickly spread beyond the Kannada-speaking area, partly because of increasing attention they paid to Viṭhobā/Viṭṭhal, the regional divinity whose cult center was and remains Pandharpur in Maharashtra. Viṭhobā may originally have been (partly) the focus of a Śaiva cult, but the identification "Viṭhoba-Kṛṣṇa-Rāma" quickly established Pandharpur as the principal pilgrimage center for Maharashtrian Bhāgavatas—a very significant factor in the spread of this popular, vernacular Bhagavatism in Maharashtra and also farther south and east.

In the mid-1200s the "radical" and secretive Mahānubhāva (Manbhau) sect arose in Maharashtra, founded by Cakradhāra, who was a Gujarati. This Kṛṣṇa-centered movement evidences influences as various as Pāñcarātra and Vīraśaiva. But toward the end of the century, Jñāneśvar (or Jñāneśvara; also known as Jñāndev or Jñānadeva) founded or "reformed" the Vārakarī order, which was to become the most celebrated of Maharashtra's bhakta traditions. The *Jñāneśvari,* a Marathi commentary on the *Bhagavadgītā,* is Jñāneśvar's best-known work. His *abhaṅgas* (lyrical devotional hymns), however, may well have been more influential in the development of Maharashtrian bhakti, remaining a favored devotional vehicle of his successors. Tradition has it that Jñāneśvar's father had been a Nātha, which suggests that there were some Śaiva influences on the development of Jñāneśvar's own thought.

Possibly more important even than Jñāneśvar for the growth of the Vārakarīsampradāya was Nāmdev (or Nāmadeva; 1270–1350?), a native of Pandharpur. Maharashtrian Bhagavatism owes to Nāmdev a strong tradition of depreciating the externalities of devotional service. Giving up *pūjā* and pilgrimages and rejecting monkish asceticism, Nāmdev celebrated an inner quest for purity of spirit and direct communion with the Bhagavān through reciting his holy names. This rejection of the image cult has suggested an Islamic influence, but although Muslims were a significant minority in Maharashtra in Nāmdev's time, no clear evidence supports this suggestion. In addition, Nāmdev's influence has remained strong, even though subsequent important Maharashtrian Bhāgavatas such as Eknāth (or Ekanātha; 1548–1598?) and Tukrām (or Tukārāma; 1608–1649) did not advocate abandoning *pūjā* and the image cult. However, they stressed that cult images are more significant as "symbolic" aids to worship than as the literal, living presence of divinity.

Another noteworthy feature of Kṛṣṇa Bhagavatism in Maharashtra is the emphasis on Kṛṣṇa as the faithful husband of Rukmiṇī, herself viewed as embodying the Bhagavān's dynamic and creative nature. This contrasts markedly with the focus of many Kṇa-Bhāgavatas farther north and east—especially in Bengal and Orissa—for whom the central female is rather Rādhā, Kṛṣṇa's "mistress" and the personification of the Bhāgavata's longing for the Lord.

RĀDHĀKṚṢṆA BHĀGAVATAS. Young Kṛṣṇa's amorous play with the *gopīs* epitomizes the many ways that *bhakti* is "new" in the *Bhāgavata Purāṇa. Kāma* ("desire"), traditional enemy of the spiritual quest, is transformed through erotic imagery and becomes a symbol for the Bhāgavata's devotion to the Bhagavān. Selfless maternal affection for the child Kṛṣṇa influences the *gopīs*' love for the mature Kṛṣṇa. Their passion becomes *prema, kāma* transcendent: a love transcending the worldly, selfish love in the structured dharmic realm of spouse and family. The *Bhāgavata Purāṇa* hints that one *gopī* may be special to Kṛṣṇa, but does not name her. By the twelfth century, however, Rādhā is known in North India as Kṛṣṇa's favorite, eventually taken as an *avatāra* of Śri-Lakṣmī. Rādhā is first celebrated in Sanskrit in Jayadeva's *Gītagovinda* (early thirteenth century?). Subsequently, Rādhā and Kṛṣṇa together are central to Bhāgavata sects founded by Viṣṇusvāmin, Nimbārka, Vallabha, and Caitanya.

NIMBĀRKA. Possibly a friend of Jayadeva and a contemporary of Madhva (though doctrinally linked rather to Rāmānuja), Nimbārka (thirteenth century?) was a Telugu brahman who settled early and permanently at Vṛndāvana. As was characteristic of Bhāgavatas, Nimbārka was captivated by the problem of the relation of the Absolute to the world. As a Vedantin, he proposed an alternative to the positions of Śaṅkara, Rāmānuja, and Madhva through a realistic *dvaitādvaita* doctrine of *bhedābheda,* "distinct yet not different [from the phenomenal world]."

Unfolding in Nimbārka's writings (all in Sanskrit) is the notion of *prapatti* ("surrender"); the idea was derived from Rāmānuja and was especially elaborated by certain of Rāmānuja's successors. According to Nimbārka, this is the necessary first of two stages of the Bhāgavata's right relationship to the Bhagavān. The roles of human and divine in the drama of salvation are at issue; *prapatti* proposes that the initiative for this process is exclusively the Bhagavān's. The Bhāgavata can only surrender utterly to the Bhagavān's grace, abandoning all sense of personal capacity for efficacious action. To the sincere *prapanna* ("suppliant") the Bhagavān gracefully bestows direct perception of himself.

Although Nimbārka's Sanakasampradāya, extensively reformed in the fifteenth century, is itself generally restricted to an area around Mathurā and to some centers in Agra and in Bengal, Nimbārka's influence seems apparent in the teachings of Caitanya. Strongly influenced by Ramanujist tradition, Nimbārka distanced himself from an early, rather eclectic *smārta* Bhagavatism, emerging as among the most adventuresome of those Bhāgavatas who explored bhakti's more radical implications.

VIṢṆUSVĀMIN AND VALLABHA. Viṣṇusvāmin was the reputed founder of the Rudrasampradāya, which was regarded, along with those of Rāmānuja, Madhva, and Nimbārka, as one of the four great Bhāgavata schools or sects. Viṣṇusvāmin lived perhaps in the thirteenth century and, according to one account, was the *mantrī* ("minister") of a South Indian prince. Some traditions hold that Viṣṇusvāmin was a teacher both of Maharashtra's Jñāneśvar and of Madhva, but the evidence is meager and conflicting. And, although Viṣṇusvāmin apparently was a Vedantin, his commentaries on the *Bhagavadgītā* and the *Brahma Sūtra* have not survived. Tradition holds that he was a "dualist" who taught that "creation" was inspired by Brahmā's primordial loneliness and that individuals and the world itself proceeded from the Absolute as sparks leap from a flame.

Apparently, it is in Vallabhācarya's teachings that Viṣṇusvāmin's thought survives. Vallabha (1479–1531), son of a Telugu brahman and *Yajurveda* schoolman, was born in what is now Madhya Pradesh and spent his childhood mostly in Banaras. His Vedantic teachings are known as *śuddhādvaita* ("pure, or purified, nondualism"). In his view, Vallabha "corrected" or "purified" Śaṅkara's *advaita* by demonstrating that *māyā* ("appearance, illusion") is entirely a power of the Absolute (that is, Kṛṣṇa), and thus is in no sense independent of it. Real fragments of that Absolute, individuals are lost in forgetfulness and egotism until Kṛṣṇa manifests himself. That crucial act of grace inaugurates the *puṣṭimārga* ("way of sustenance [of the soul]"), leading to eternal, joyous (re-)union with Kṛṣṇa.

Vallabha's personal example was no less consequential than his theology. Tireless pilgrim, dedicated attendant on images, he became for his followers the preeminent, paradigmatic *sevaka* ("servant") of Kṛṣṇa. Decrying external acts empty of sincere emotion, Vallabha the ritualist urged that all acts be performed fully in a spirit of sweet and playful joy, a spirit captured most impressively in the *raslīlā* celebrations associated with the Vallabhācārīs.

In literature, the emotional fervor engendered amongst the Vallabhācārīs is particularly evident in the poetry of Sūrdās (1483–1563). Occasionally, the emotional abandon urged by Vallabha's example and nurtured by his successors led to "excesses" that, in the nineteenth century, even summoned restrictions from civil authorities. The teachings of Vallabhācārya are part of the inspiration for the "radical" Rādhāvallabhī and Sakhībhava movements in which Rādhā rather than Kṛṣṇa becomes central, Sakhībhava adherents going so far as to wear women's clothing and to attempt to lead the life of Rādhā. Overall, Vallabhācārya's *puṣṭimārga*—prominent and influential across North India—is a particularly impressive and vital expression of Bhagavatism and its pervasive influence on learned tradition and popular piety.

CAITANYA. Bengal's Sena dynasty (fl. twelfth through thirteenth centuries) championed the *Bhāgavata Purāṇa,* and its spirit is witnessed early in the Bengal/Orissa region in the Sanskrit *Gītagovinda* as well as in the devotional Bengali lyrics of such poets as Ḍimboka, Candidāsa, and Vidyāpati, who flourished from the twelfth through the sixteenth century. Doubtless the most famous Bhāgavata of this complex cultural region is Viśvambara Miśra, known best by the name he assumed as a *saṃnyāsin:* Kṛṣṇacaitanya. Born in Nadiya, probably in 1486, Caitanya is reported first to have been influenced by an itinerant Madhva teacher, though it is reasonable to assume that vibrant local devotional traditions were very significant as well. A definitive "conversion" to Kṛṣṇa Bhagavatism seems to have occurred in his early manhood. Henceforth, Caitanya was a phenomenon rarely observed even in Bengal's diverse culture. He became an extreme example of "god-intoxication"; and, swept at one moment by the ecstasy of experiencing Kṛṣṇa directly, and at the next moment by the agony of separation (*viraha*), he is reported to have staggered, fallen, danced, sung, roared, wept, laughed, and ranted in ways that attracted, challenged, and even threatened many of his contemporaries.

Only a few lines traditionally attributed to Caitanya survive. But his personal example and direct teachings drew about him disciples whose biographical, ritual, and theological writings—especially in the course of the sixteenth century—quickly and securely established an enduring religious movement that is the basis of the Gauḍīyasampradāya and the Hare Krishna group of the present time.

From the writings of his principal immediate disciples, the Gosvāmins, it is learned that Caitanya's "religious Vedanta" is most aptly characterized as *acintyabhedābheda:* Kṛṣṇa, the Absolute, and the individual *jīvas* ("souls") are "inconceivably discrete (yet) not different." But it is less for this variant on a familiar theme of Vaiṣṇava Vedānta than for the living example of his person that Caitanya is most significant historically. From "intentional" enactment of Kṛṣṇa's sports Caitanya drifted almost insensibly to a personal sense of reactualizing them, or, at least, so he was experienced by many of his followers. Devotees and object of devotion lost clear-cut boundaries in such "performances," which became nearly a "Tantric" *sādhana* ("actualization"). As such, these witness also the potent influence of Bengal's (ultimately Buddhist?) Sahajiya tradition. However, the latter's monistic thrust properly differentiates it from the fundamentally dualistic vision evident in Caitanya's alternating joy and despair in his separateness from Kṛṣṇa. Caitanya, as other Bhāgavatas, remained a *bhakta,* a devotee whose enduring problematic was also his raison d'être.

See Also Āḻvārs; Bengali Religions; Bhagavadgītā; Bhakti; Caitanya; Hindi Religious Traditions; Jayadeva; Līla; Madhva; Marathi Religions; Nimbārka; Rādhā; Rāmānuja; Vaikhānasas; Vallabha.

Bibliography

Jan Gonda's *Die Religionen Indiens,* vol. 2, *Der jüngere Hinduismus* (Stuttgart, 1963) continues to be the single most valuable general account of Bhāgavata backgrounds and individual sectarian developments; the notes contain numerous important bibliographical references. Anne-Marie Esnoul's "Le courant affectif à l'interieur du Brahmanisme ancien," *Bulletin de l'École Française d'Extrême Orient* (1956): 141–207, is a stimulating and beautifully nuanced comprehensive account. Although dated, R. G. Bhandarkar's classic *Vaiṣṇavism, Saivism, and Minor Religious Systems* (1913; reprint, Varanasi, 1965) and J. N. Farquhar's *An Outline of the Religious Literature of India* (Oxford, 1920) remain obligatory reading.

Among the most significant and appealing of relevant primary sources in English translation are A. K. Ramanujan's translation of selected hymns of Nammāḻvār, *Hymns for the Drowning* (Princeton, 1981); Barbara Stoler Miller's rendering of Jayadeva's *Gītagovinda, Love Song of the Dark Lord* (New York, 1977); and Edward C. Dimock, Jr. and Denise Levertov's translation of representative Bengali lyrics, *In Praise of Krishna* (1967; reprint, Chicago, 1981).

G. R. Welbon (1987 and 2005)

VAIṢṆAVISM: PĀÑCARĀTRAS

A movement or sect called Pāñcarātra figures significantly in some of the earliest textual evidence used by scholars to trace the historical emergence of Hindu, specifically Vaiṣṇava, devotional (*bhakti*) cults. Pāñcarātra is known to have influenced the development of Vaiṣṇava sectarian thought in several parts of India, and it remains a vigorous presence in South India today as an essential constituent of Śrī Vaiṣṇava religion and one of two Vaiṣṇava *āgamas* (traditions) that inform South India's Hindu temple culture.

The beginnings of the historical Pāñcarātra—and even the original sense of the word *pañcarātra*—remain matters of uncertainty and considerable scholarly dispute. Initially, the movement may not have been associated with any single doctrinal position. And when it first became associated with one, that position seems only secondarily to have been Vaiṣṇava. "The origin of Pañcarātra is obscure," J. A. B. van Buitenen observed, "because it has no[t] one origin" (van Buitenen, 1971, p. 6).

The problems begin with the word itself. Deprived of context, the compound *pañca-rātra* yields no clue beyond its literal sense: as a noun, it means "five nights" or "night of (the) five"; as an adjective, "five-night (ed)." Explanations given in the Pāñcarātra Saṃhitās (classical school manuals, none of which may be earlier than the sixth century CE) seem clearly ex post facto rationalizations embedded in apologetic and polemic. However faithfully such explanations record what certain Pāñcarātrikas (members of the Pāñcarātra tradition) came to mean by the word, they offer no secure insight into what it meant originally.

Śatapatha Brāhmaṇa 13.6.1.1 asserts that the primordial Puruṣa Nārāyaṇa, "wishing to become all things," performed Puruṣamedha ("human sacrifice"), a *pañcarātra sattra* ("five-day sacrifice"). In light of this occurrence (apparently the earliest) of the word in Vedic-Brahmanic literature, some scholars have found irresistible the temptation to seek the original meaning of the name *Pāñcarātra* in the Vedic sacrificial milieu. Thus, as F. Otto Schrader concluded, "it appears . . . that the sect took its name from its central dogma which was the Pāñcarātra Sattra of Nārāyaṇa interpreted philosophically as the fivefold self-manifestation of God by means of his Para, Vyuha, Vibhava, Antaryāmin, and Arcā forms" (Schrader, 1916, p. 25). Quite possibly this passage from the *Śatapatha Brāhmaṇa* evidences Nārāyaṇa's integration and legitimization into the Vedic ritual and intellectual world; but it may as well be an accommodation of certain Pañcarātric associations as the source of them. In any case, except for Nārāyaṇa's centrality, the details of the *Śatapatha Brāhmaṇa* ritual neither confirm nor reinforce the preoccupations and central features of historical Pāñcarātra literature and practice.

Moreover, van Buitenen has argued persuasively that particular literary, doctrinal, and ritual associations such as those mentioned above are only secondary or subsequent specifications of an older, more wide-ranging acceptation of the word. In his view, *pañcarātra* initially referred to a characteristic of the way of life of itinerant recluses: their living apart from "towns" (that is, major settlements) except during the two-month rainy season. A *pāñcarātrika* in such early texts as the *Bṛhatkathāślokasaṃgraha,* then, "is not distinguished by any particular faith or creed, but by a more or less ascetic life-rule," one prescribing five nights in the forest for every night spent in a town (van Buitenen, 1971, pp. 14–15). If van Buitenen is correct, it would not be the first time in India that practice has crucially preceded systematic theory. And his thesis would support a plausible solution to the longstanding puzzle concerning the relationship between Pāñcarātrikas and Bhāgavatas: the former may simply have been Bhāgavatas who led generally reclusive and ascetic lives.

EPIC PĀÑCARĀTRA. While certain texts (e.g., Ānandagiri's *Śaṅkaravijaya*) distinguish between Pāñcarātras and Bhāgavatas—and, indeed, consider Vaiṣṇavas distinct from both—it is not clear that the two necessarily were discrete in any sectlike way. The essence of "epic" Pāñcarātra is *bhakti:* unconditional devotion to the Lord (Bhagavat). The earliest unambiguous evidence of this "historical" Pāñcarātra seems to be that found in *Mahābhārata* 12.321ff, the *Nārāyaṇīya,* or *Nāradīya,* section, which introduces a religious attitude and a cosmology that agree in essential details with the teachings of the later Saṃhitās. Responding to a query concerning what god to worship, this "secret" teaching tells of a "hidden" god, invisible to all but his *ekānta-bhaktas* ("exclusive devotees"), to whom he graciously reveals himself. Such an *ekāntin* ("exclusivist") was King Uparicara, who worshiped Nārāyaṇa according to Sātvata rites and, believing kingdom, wives, and wealth to be his by Nārāyaṇa's boon, offered all these possessions to the Lord (*Mahābhārata* 12.322.17ff). Other *ekāntins* inhabited Śvetadvīpa ("white, or pure, island"), located to the north in the Milk Ocean. Knowing Pāñcarātra teachings, they saw Brahman-Nārāyaṇa while others were blinded by his radiance (*Mahābhārata* 2.323.26ff).

Sātvata is another name for the Vṛṣṇi, who are part of a larger population of Yādavas, commonly thought to have been the society in which Kṛṣṇa-Vāsudeva *bhakti* rose. Epic Sātvatas are Nārāyaṇa *bhaktas* ("devotees"); but the *Nārāyaṇīya* explains that Nārāyaṇa, "formerly single-imaged," caused himself to be born as the "fourfold" son of Dharma: Nara, Nārāyaṇa, Kṛṣṇa, and Hari (*Mahābhārata* 12.321.15–16).

The unitary god's multiple births or manifestations are familiar in Vaiṣṇava religious thought in general; and the historical Pāñcarātra seems to have contributed significantly to developing and enriching this notion. Doubtless, the epic Nārāyaṇa's four *vyūhas* ("appearances, modes of being") elaborate upon longstanding habits of identifying (or confusing) one divinity with another (or a divinity with a devotee), habits reinforced by factors such as the multiplication of divine epithets and the intensifying interaction between socio-religious groups, their ideologies and practices. Practically, this scheme facilitated the organization and "rationalization" of historically discrete devotional cults under a single, overarching principle, here Nārāyaṇa-Vāsudeva. In the *Nārāyaṇīya,* in fact, is found not one but two sets of multiple births that possibly developed independently. In addition to the more or less abstract Nara-Nārāyaṇa-Kṛṣṇa-Hari tetrad, there is the genealogical series Kṛṣṇa-Saṃkarṣaṇa (=Balakṛṣṇa)-Pradyumna-Aniruddha; that is, Kṛṣṇa, his brother, his elder son, and his grandson. Which set is the prior cannot be determined, although the latter is ultimately the more significant.

But something even more important is at work here: Pāñcarātrikas wanted to show how their supreme god could pervade the world and yet not be limited by it. To account for this, they drew upon several explanatory aids. And *vyūhas* were not the least important among them; for, as Jan Gonda observes, "already in Vedic ritualism the idea of *vyūha* implied an effective arrangement of the parts of a coherent whole" (Gonda, 1970, p. 50).

Epic *pāñcarātrikas,* then, are first and foremost *bhāgavatas* and *ekāntabhaktas*; and it is reasonable to conclude that the roots of their devotionalism are extra-Vedic. The Pāñcarātrikas are distinguished from similar groups of devotees by their particular efforts to show that their Lord is the underlying reality of all gods and that he is everywhere in the world without being subject to its manifest limitations. Crucial in this enterprise is their thoroughgoing exploitation of a theistic Sāṃkhya to explain the relation between this world and the supreme reality, as will be elaborated upon in the next section. Further, there is an equally insistent attempt to link the Nārāyaṇa-Vāsudeva-Kṛṣṇa of religious experience to prestigious Vedic explanations, which, by allusion, include even the fourfold Puruṣa of the *Puruṣasūkta* (*Ṛgveda* 10.90).

PĀÑCARĀTRA THOUGHT IN THE SAṂHITĀS. The principal texts of historical Pāñcarātra are the Saṃhitās ("collections"), of which there are 108 works according to tradition, and more than double that number reckoning all titles cited in lists. Far fewer texts are readily available for study, and among them the most significant seem to be *Pauṣkara, Jayākhya, Sāttvata* (constituting the "three gems" and presumably among the oldest), *Ahirbudhnya, Pārameśvara, Sanātkumāra* (quoted more than once by Yāmuna), *Parama, Padma, Īsvara,* and *Lakṣmī.* It is uncertain exactly when any of these was composed. Some may be as early as the sixth or seventh century CE although confirming citations date no earlier than the tenth century, and several are referred to only in the thirteenth or fourteenth century and later.

Formally, these texts closely resemble the Śaivāgamas (indeed, in this context, the terms *saṃhitā, āgama, tantra,* and *śāstra* are essentially interchangeable). Traditionally, they purported to deal with four topics: *jñāna* ("knowledge"), *yoga* ("disciplined concentration"), *kriyā* ("action"), and *caryā* ("conduct"). In fact, only one or two actually approximate this paradigm. The majority concentrate almost exclusively on *kriyā* and *caryā:* prescriptions for constructing and consecrating temples and "images" (of various materials) in which Bhagavān Nārāyaṇa is pleased to dwell, and for conducting the appropriate daily and festival services. Essentially, this is the literature of temple priests, and the bulk of it deals with practical details. The explicit *jñāna* sections (*pādas*) are usually brief and bound up with stories about the creation of the world.

The Pāñcarātra's cosmogony is complex and many-tiered; and it incorporates influences and otherwise distinct ideas from many sources, Vedic and extra-vedic. But, while they differ on certain details and in the elaborateness of their presentations, the extant Saṃhitās share an understanding about the principal features of the three-stage "order of creation" (*sṛṣṭikrāma*); and this core account may be sketched here in simplified outline. At the beginning (of every world age), the *śakti* ("energy, force, power") of *parabrahman* Nārāyaṇa-Viṣṇu awakens, opening her eyes as "action" (*kriyā*) and "becoming" (*bhūti*). She is Lakṣmī, distinct from Viṣṇu yet at the same time as inseparable from him as sunlight from sun. Although she acts independently, each act merely implements a wish of Nārāyaṇa-Viṣṇu's. As *kriyāśakti,* Lakṣmī is the "instrumental cause of the universe" and identical with Viṣṇu's great discus, Sudarśana. As *bhūtiśakti,* she is the "material cause," governed by *kriyāśakti* "as the thread governs pearls in a necklace."

In this *śuddhasṛṣṭi* ("pure creation"), the first *guṇas* (qualities) appear. Non-prakritic (because they are "pre-prakritic"), these qualities of the supreme Lord number six: knowledge (*jñāna*), lordship (*aiśvarya*), power (*śakti*), strength (*bala*), virility (*vīrya*), and splendor (*tejas*). The *guṇas* then pair together as knowledge/strength, lordship/virility, and power/splendor; and these three pairs respectively constitute the *vyūhas* Saṃkarṣaṇa, Pradyumna, and Aniruddha. The Lord is entirely present (with all his six qualities) in every *vyūha,* but only one pair of qualities is openly manifest in each.

These *vyūhas* appear successively, then act together—again sequentially—in the second, intermediate or "mixed" (*śuddhāśuddha*) creation. There, "impure" creation initially is carried embryo-like as an undifferentiated potentiality in Saṃkarṣaṇa's body. Pradyumna differentiates it as *puruṣa* and *prakṛti* ("spirit" and "material potential") and transfers it to Aniruddha, who in turn organizes it by means of his *śakti.* He is the *brahman* and *māyā* (apparent reality) of the material world, presiding over the cosmic eggs whence life as humans know it—the "prakritic" *guṅas* (*sattva, rajas, tamas*), *karman,* and time—devolves in the third, impure (*aśuddha*) creation, itself consisting first of a subtle and then a gross stage. Here the account links to familiar Sāṃkhya categories: Vāsudeva appears as the supreme *puruṣa.* Through his contact with the (material) body arises the *jīva,* otherwise called Saṃkarṣaṇa, who in turn produces *manas,* that is, Pradyumna. And from Pradyumna issues the creative agent, the *ahaṃkāra* who is Aniruddha.

In addition to their cosmogonic roles and cosmological significance, the *vyūhas* have important moral, theological, and pedagogical functions: Saṃkarṣaṇa teaches the true monotheism; Pradyumna translates that teaching into practice; and Aniruddha instructs about Pāñcarātra doctrine and the attainment of release.

Vibhavas ("manifestations") or *avatāras* ("descents") of the Lord are subordinate to and dependent upon the *vyūhas.* They are of two kinds: those belonging to *śuddhasṛṣṭi* are *mukhya* ("primary"), and the major Saṃhitās agree that they number thirty-nine. "Secondary" (*gauṇa*) *avatāras* usually are said to descend from Aniruddha. Primary and secondary *avatāras* differ importantly in their natures and in the benefits to be derived by devotedly concentrating on them. Those who seek mokṣa should worship primary *avatāras,* which spring directly from the Lord's body "like flame from flame." Secondary *avatāras* are "ordinary" beings pervaded by a fraction of the Lord's *śakti* to accomplish particular purpose for world maintenance. Worshiping them yields worldly rewards such as wealth or sovereignty.

With this theory of secondary *avatāras* one reaches the central preoccupations of the compilers of the Saṃhitās. It is not only "ordinary beings" who are fit receptacles for the Lord's descent: properly consecrated through Pāñcarātra ritual, a representation in stone, metal, wood, or clay also can become an *avatāra.* Descending into the material form with a part of his inexhaustible *śakti* when the appropriate consecration rituals are performed, the Lord thereby becomes fully present in the object, which is then known as *arcā avatāra,* or "worthy of worship."

PĀÑCARĀTRA IN PRACTICE. At the heart of epic and later Pāñcarātra is the driving insistence that salvation comes only through knowledge of ultimate truth, a knowledge that is the grace of the Lord revealed by single-minded devotion. This knowledge, open to members of all four *varṇas* (classes), depends on an understanding of the Pāñcarātra teachings. Such understanding requires the assistance of a qualified teacher (*guru*), who guides the aspirant until he determines that the student is fit to be initiated. Initiation (*dīkṣā*) consists of five rituals (*pañcasaṃskāra*): branding the initiate's shoulders with the discus and conch emblems (Tāpa), instruction in the application of the cosmetic sectarian mark on the forehead (Puṇḍra), assigning a new name to the initiate (Nāman), confiding a secret *mantra* and explaining its sense (Mantra), and teaching the details of external ritual (Yāga). In addition, the adept learns a yoga for internal worship, that performed in the heart.

Services to the Lord combine with a life of purity and harmlessness (*ahiṃsā*) to the end of realizing "devotional union" with the Lord. The Pāñcarātrika is assured that there will be moments when "absolute union" with the Lord will be experienced. But this is not a realization of primordial unity in any metaphysical sense. Rather, it is an active experience of rapt devotion to the Lord, whereby individuals never lose their individuality. Indeed, as "parts" of Lakṣmī or Śrī, they too are eternally distinct from the Lord. Even during the intervals between world ages, they remain separate from if latent in him.

Pāñcarātrikas have made a considerable point of stressing that they are *vaidikas,* hence that Pāñcarātra not merely ranks alongside the Veda but is in fact part of it. Nārāyaṇa-Vāsudeva, according to them, is the god of the Upaniṣads, author of the Veda and the world. They assert, in effect, that the known world is incomprehensible in terms of *karman* alone. Underlying it, grounding everything, must be the supreme person.

The mildest rejoinders to such Pāñcarātra apologetics suggested that, at the very least, there was no way to prove their Vedic claims. Most responses were more severe. *Manusmṛti* 10.23 declares, for example, that Sātvatas and *ācāryas* are offspring of despised unions. And commentators identified both as temple functionaries. Denying the propriety of the lifestyles of temple priests, Smārta brahmans consider all their claims suspect. Association with a presumably extra-Vedic (i.e., tribal or nomadic) society—the Sātvata-Yādavas—combined with the importance assigned to the dynamic, creative, female principle, Lakṣmī, doubtless contributed strongly to the (negative) assessment that Pāñcarātrikas were *tantrikas* (practitioners of Tantra). In an important sense, the assessment is correct; indeed, even the Pāñcarātrikas themselves called their system a *tantra.*

Pāñcarātra in History. It is generally accepted that the historical Pāñcarātra first emerged in northern, probably northwestern, India—it being clear, however, that Pāñcarātra itself was more an increasingly detailed set of cosmological speculations and devotional attitudes and procedures than it was a sect proper. This Pāñcarātra "system of thought" became the rationale of increasing numbers of Vaiṣṇava Bhāgavatas who were involved in temple and domestic devotional ritual. Its influence seems especially strong among the Mahānubhāvas of Maharashtra (from the mid-thirteenth century) and among the Narasiṃhas.

Even more apparent than its northern heritage is the fact that Pāñcarātra has prospered more obviously in South India than in the north for at least the past millennium. Pāñcarātra's destiny in the south is closely related to the rise of the Śrī Vaiṣṇava tradition, in which Pāñcarātra cosmological and ritual theory and practice combine with the unique vernacular devotional poetry of the Āḻvārs. The early Śrī Vaiṣṇava "doctors" Nāthamuni, Yāmuna, and Rāmānuja become the most noteworthy personalities associated with the propagation and defense of Pāñcarātra ideas. Later developments in Śrī Vaiṣṇava theology and the emergence of two distinct traditions—Vaṭakalai and Teṉkalai—realize and expand upon more of what was present in Pāñcarātra thinking from the start than is often recognized. Through the Śrī Vaiṣṇavas, Pāñcarātra thought informed Rāmānanda (fl. mid-fifteenth century?) and his following of Rāma *bhaktas*, thus reentering North India. Again through Śrī Vaiṣṇavism, Pāñcarātra teachings strongly influenced the non-brahman Sātānis in Karnataka.

The circumstances of Pāñcarātra's introduction into South Indian temples are not entirely clear. Perhaps temple procedures had earlier been only customary and generally informal. In that case, the Pāñcarātra systematically introduced order and regularity. It is also possible, however, that (at least some of) the earlier Viṣṇu temple ritual was conducted according to Vaikhānasa prescriptions. More self-consciously linked to Vedic ceremonial, Vaikhānasas tended to a certain conservatism, resisting the incorporation of devotional material from the Āḻvārs (to which the Pāñcarātra were quite receptive). At the same time, Vaikhānasas are closer to earlier Pāñcarātra than to its later form in their conception of such deities as Rudra-Śiva as manifestations of Viṣṇu, and thus both groups appropriately included ritual proceedings that the evolving Śrī Vaiṣṇavas often found offensive. On the other hand, however, modern-day Vaikhānasas have argued that both Pāñcarātra "*tāntrikas*" and the Śrī Vaiṣṇavas offend the Lord precisely because they allow "saints" and teachers of Śrī Vaiṣṇava tradition to intrude into temple devotional ritual in ways that improperly detract from the worship of Lord Viṣṇu.

See Also Āḻvārs; Avatara; Bhakti; Hindu Tantric Literature; Kṛṣṇaism; Marathi Religions; Śrī Vaiṣṇavas.

Bibliography

Jan Gonda's *Medieval Religious Literature in Sanskrit* (Wiesbaden, 1977) is the most helpful comprehensive account of Pāñcarātra (and other major Agamic) literature and ideas. His two-volume *Die Religionen Indiens* (Stuttgart, 1960–1963) contains the best overview of the Pāñcarātra in the context of India's religious history, and chapter 3 of his *Viṣṇuism and Śivaism* (London, 1970) significantly augments discussions of early Vaiṣṇava "theology." Of assistance in sorting out *tantra* and *āgama* is *Hindu Tantrism* by Teun Goudriaan, Dirk Jan Hoens, and Sanjukta Gupta (Leiden, 1979), especially Goudriaan's survey (pp. 3–67). J. A. B. van Buitenen's crucial thesis concerning the original sense of the term *pañcarātra* is included in the introduction to his translation of Yāmuna's *Āgamaprāmāṇyam* (Madras, 1971), itself a primary source of great importance, and his "On the Archaism of the *Bhāgavata Purāṇa*," in *Krishna: Myths, Rites, and Attitudes*, edited by Milton Singer (Honolulu, 1966), pp. 23–40, remains important. Walter Neevel's *Yāmuna's Vedānta and Pāñcarātra*, "Harvard Dissertations in Religion," no. 10 (Missoula, Mont., 1977), gives valuable information especially on Yāmuna's "Vedantic gentrification" of Pāñcarātra. Suvira Jaiswal's *The Origin and Development of Vaiṣṇavism* (Delhi, 1967) is useful so long as its historical reconstructions are read with caution.

Of course, one wants to encounter Pāñcarātra through primary sources. For this, F. Otto Schrader's classic *Introduction to the Pāñcarātra and the Ahirbudhnya Saṃhitā* (Madras, 1916) remains the best point of departure. H. Daniel *Smith's A Descriptive Bibliography of the Printed Texts of the Pāñcarātrāgama*, vol. 1 (Baroda, 1975), and vol. 2, *An Annotated Index to Selected Topics* (Baroda, 1980) are indispensable guides. Sanjukta Gupta's translation of the *Lakṣmī Tantra* (Leiden, 1972) is excellent, and S. Krishnaswami Aiyangar's reading of the *Paramasaṃhitā* (Baroda, 1940) is adequate. Finally, a precious record of actual practices is Kadambi Rangachariyar's *The Sri Vaishnava Brahmans* (Madras, 1931).

G. R. Welbon (1987 and 2005)

VAJRABODHI (671–741) was an Indian Buddhist monk and Zhenyan teacher in China. Vajrabodhi (Chin., Jingangzhi) was the second of three Vajrayana missionaries to eighth-century China. He was born of a South Indian brahman family, and his father was a priest for the royal house. Vajrabodhi probably converted to Buddhism at the age of sixteen, although some accounts place him at the Buddhist university of Nālandā at the age of ten. He studied all varieties of Buddhism and was said to have studied for a time under the famous Buddhist logician Dharmakīrti. Under Śāntijñāna, Vajrabodhi studied Vajrayāna teachings and was duly initiated into yoga, the "Three Mysteries," and *dhāraṇi.* Leaving India, Vajrabodhi traveled to Sri Lanka and Śrīvijaya (present-day Sumatra), where he apparently was taught a Vajrayāna tradition distinct from that taught at Nālandā. From Śrīvijaya he sailed to China and by 720 was ensconced in the Jianfu Temple at the Chinese capital, Changan. Accompanying him was his soon-to-be-famous disciple, Amoghavajra.

Like Śubhākarasiṃha, who preceded him by four years, Vajrabodhi spent most of his time in ritual activity, in translating texts, and in the production of Esoteric art. Particularly important was his partial translation of the *Sarvatathāgatatattvasaṃgraha* (T. D. no. 865) between the years 723 and 724. This Yoga Tantra— along with the *Mahāvairocana Sūtra* (T. D. no. 848), translated by Subhakarasimha the same year—provides the foundation of the Zhenyan school in China and the Shingon and Esoteric branch of the Tendai school (Taimitsu) in Japan. Like Śubhākarasiṃha, Vajrabodhi had ties to high court circles and enjoyed the patronage of imperial princesses; he also worked with the Chinese monk Yi Xing. Vajrabodhi died in 732 and was buried south of the Longmen caves. He was posthumously awarded the title Guoshi, "Teacher of the Realm."

Vajrabodhi's importance was twofold. Although the doctrines of the Yoga Tantras were known to Śubhākarasiṃha, Vajrabodhi was the first translator and systematic teacher in China of the *Sarvatathagatatattvasamgraha* and of Vajrayāna as practiced in South India and in Srivijaya. Second, Vajrabodhi reinforced the presence and visibility of the Vajrayana at the Chinese court, a presence that, under his disciple Amoghavajra, would become the dominant force in the court during the second half of the eighth century.

See Also Mahāsiddhas; Zhenyan.

Bibliography

Zhou Yi Liang provides a copiously annotated translation of the standard biographies of Vajrabodhi, Subhakarasimha, and Amoghavajra in his "Tantrism in China," *Harvard Journal of Asiatic Studies* 8 (March 1945): 241–332.

Charles D. Orzech (1987)

VAJRADHARA

VAJRADHARA (Tib., Rdo rje chang [Dorje chang]; Mongolian, Ochirdana) is, in the last stages of Indian Tantric Buddhism and in the continuing Tibetan traditions, the distinct embodiment of the highest state of being, the primordial Ādibuddha, and the revealer of all the Tantras. But he was not always thus, for in the beginning in India *Vajradhara* was simply another name for Vajrapāṇi (Tib., Phyag na rdo rje [Chagna dorje]), both *bodhisattva* and deity. One can explain this development as the logical expansion of the tiny terminological difference between the less concrete "bearer (*-dhara*) of the *vajra*" and the unambiguous "*vajra* in hand." Vajrasattva (Tib., Rdo rje sems dpa' [Dorje sempa]; Chin., Wo tzu lo sa tsui; Jap., Kongosatta) further complicates the historical picture. "*Vajra* being" was at first another early synonym for Vajrapāṇi, then both a synonym for Vajradhara and a distinct deity in his own right. Nor had Vajrapāṇi played a single unitary role in the history of Buddhism in India and beyond.

The Real Vajradhara. Given the logic of terminological abstraction, one might expect Vajrasattva to be loftier than Vajradhara (when they are distinguished). But it is Vajradhara alone who represents one of just two possible representations of the *dharmakāya,* the highest, in Tibetan Buddhism. The other is Samantabhadra ("All Good"; Tib., Kun tu bzang po [Kuntu zangpo]), depicted completely naked to illustrate his distance from conventions. In the Mahāyāna and Tantric Buddhist analysis of the nature of enlightenment, the *dharmakāya* is the least compromised form of the Buddha or a buddha, out of space and time. Thus its representation should not be taken literally, however anthropomorphic in appearance.

Vajradhara is indeed depicted seated cross-legged in a *vajraparyaṅka* pose, on a moon disk and lotus, two-armed, hands crossed over his heart in the *vajrahūṃkara* or union gesture. His left, female hand is inside (signifying his inner wisdom and emptiness) and bearing the bell; his right, male hand holding the *vajra* is above the left to symbolize the method and compassion directed outwards. He is blue, like his historical "forefather," Vajrapāṇi. If in union, Vajradhara's consort is red Vajrayoginī (Vajravārāhī), embodiment of *prajñāpāramitā* (the "perfection of wisdom"), skull in left hand and flaying knife in right. Emptiness expanded, like the personification of *prajñāpāramitā,* he should not be mistaken for an individual buddha-being. Although *dharmakāya,* and therefore not individual, he wears the regal finery of a *saṃbhogakāya*—eight jewel ornaments and five silks. In paintings he is frequently surrounded by the eighty-four *mahāsiddhas,* Tantric Buddhist saints.

In Rdzogs chen (Dzogchen), the "Great Perfection," or Atiyoga traditions of the Rnying ma (Nyingma, "old") school of Tibetan Buddhism, and in Bon, the so-called pre-Buddhist religion of Tibet, Samantabhadra, not Vajradhara, is the *dharmakāya,* albeit also known as Mahāvajradhara Samantabhadra (Kun bzang rdo rje chang chen [Kunzang dorje chang chen]). Vajradhara instead manifests as the *saṃbhogakāya,* while the Rdzogs chen Samantabhadra is utterly separate from the Mahāyāna *bodhisattva* of that name.

At these rarefied elevations of the *dharmadhātu*, the pure *dharma* realm, Vajradhara is real, definitive (Skt., *niścitārtha*; Tib., *nges pa don gi*), sheer concept, and the nature of everything. Such pantheism requires that nothing is not Vajradhara, if one could but realize this truth. Vajrasattva, meanwhile, is simply the *saṃbhogakāya* of the intangible Samantabhadra.

RELATIVE/CONVENTIONAL VAJRADHARA. To teach *bodhisattvas* and humans, the ultimate essence takes a form, a provisional symbolic (Skt., *neyārtha*; Tib., *drang don rtags*) one. This side of the dichotomy further subdivides into *saṃbhogakāya* and *nirmāṇakāya*, bodies of so-called "enjoyment" and "emanation." The first is supramundane, visible only to enlightened audiences such as dwell in paradisiacal buddha-realms, Akaniṣṭha, and so forth. The *nirmāṇakāya* is a buddha's manifestation in the world, as Śākyamuni or *bodhisattva*.

Vajradhara revealed the *mahāmudrā* teachings in India to Tilopa (c. 988–1069), thereby founding the Bka' brgyud (Kagyu) lineage. Bka' brgyud subsects agree that Tilopa instructed the Bengali Nāropa (1016–1100), who taught the Tibetan seeker Mar pa (Marpa, 1002/12–1097), who then carried the lineage back to Tibet and passed it on to Mi la ras pa (Milarepa, 1028/40–1111/23). In the Bka' brgyud traditions, Vajradhara receives special worship as both the revealer of mysteries and the mystery itself.

Vajradhara's ultimate position is as Khyab bdag rigs drug pa, all-pervasive lord of the sixth family (Khyab dag, Samantabhadra in Rdzogs chen traditions). The six families are the typical Indian upward extension of the earlier *maṇḍala* of five, in turn the expansion of the earlier three (via an occasional intermediate four). These structures belong to different historical phases of Tantric Buddhism, chronologically successive, but carried along and incorporated into succeeding classification systems. Kriyā Tantras have three families; Yoga Tantras, five; and the highest, Yoganiruttara Tantras, six. The sixth is overlord of the five as the zenith above four cardinal directions around a unifying center. Sometimes Vajrasattva, a further essentialization of Vajradhara's immanent nature, is conceptually located symmetrically opposite him at the nadir.

More than a millennium earlier, Vajrapāṇi had been a mere *yakṣa* sprite, albeit the "master of the mysterious [*yakṣas*]" (*guhyakādhipati*). The epithet stayed with him and grew ever more meaningful until he was the "master of the mysterious" truth at the heart of the secret esoteric tradition, and, as Vajradhara, the ultimate source of all its unfolding scriptures.

VAJRAPĀṆI UNARMED. Vajradhara was once but a synonym of Vajrapāṇi, originally the Buddha's humble attendant who happened to wield a mighty weapon. In early Indian Buddhist art his weapon is personified, in the form of Vajrapuruṣa. But by the time Vajradhara is clearly distinct from his namesake, the attribute has been further depersonified into its essence, with the *vajra* no longer a weapon but the underlying principle of phenomenal reality.

SEE ALSO Vajrapāṇi.

BIBLIOGRAPHY

Beer, Robert. *The Encyclopedia of Tibetan Symbols and Motifs.* London, 1999.

Davidson, Ronald M. *Indian Esoteric Buddhism: A Social History of the Tantric Movement.* New York, 2002.

Himalayan Art. "Buddhist Deity: Vajradhara." Shelley and Donald Rubin Foundation. Available from: www.himalayanart.org. A collection of Tibetan paintings, bronzes, and prints of Vajradhara, thirteenth to twentieth centuries CE.

Lamotte, Étienne. "Vajrapå-i en Inde." In *Mélanges de Sinologie offerts à Monsieur Paul Demiéville*, pp. 113–159. Paris, 1966. Translated as "Vajrapå-I in India." In *Buddhist Studies Review* 20, 1 (2003): 1–30, and 20, 2 (2003): 119–144.

Snellgrove, David L. *Indo-Tibetan Buddhism: Indian Buddhists and Their Tibetan Successors.* 2 vols. Boston, 1987.

ISABELLE ONIANS (2005)

VAJRAPĀṆI. "As for Vajrapāṇi . . . I confess to finding him by far the most interesting divine being throughout the whole history of Buddhism, for he has a personal history and considerable personal character." David Snellgrove's words were published in his magnum opus, *Indo-Tibetan Buddhism* (p. 134) in 1987, the year of this encyclopedia's first edition. Only now has Vajrapāṇi (Tib., Phyag na rdo rje [Chagna dorje]) gained his own independent entry. His promotion in the secondary literature echoes his unparalleled rise within the history of Indian and Tibetan Buddhism (with successes also in Central Asian, Chinese, Southeast Asian, and Japanese Buddhisms). From a half-tamed spirit who became the Buddha's constant companion, this protean shape-shifter graduates first into a *bodhisattva* and then into a deity before transcending everything as the primordial Ādibuddha, Vajradhara. However, Vajrapāṇi's progress extends backwards too, before Buddhism, to the beginnings of Sanskrit literature, the Vedas.

INDO-EUROPEAN ETYMOLOGY AND DIVINITY. In Sanskrit, *vajrapāṇi* means "he who has a *vajra* in hand." The word *vajra* refers to a thunderbolt, thunder crash, or lightning flash, and to its embodiment in unbreakable diamond (cf. the Tibetan neologistic translation *Rdo rje* [*dor je*], "Lord of Stones") and the invincible weapon made thereof. *Vajra* is linguistically related to its Indo-European cousin, the Zoroastrian Zend *vazra*, Mithra's "club" (cf. Vedic Mitra), and the English cognates *vigor*, *wacker*, and *wake*.

In pre-Buddhist Indian literature, the *vajra* is wielded by powerful gods, above all Indra, lord of the gods, sky, and rains. From the *Ṛgveda* onward, Indra's attribute is the *vajra*. Nevertheless, while the *Ṛgveda* often refers to *vajrabāhu*: (*vajra* in arm) and *vajrahasta* (*vajra* in hand), their synonym, *vajrapāṇi*, is not found before the *Ṣaḍviṃśabrāhmaṇa*.

The *vajra's* bearer has close correspondents in Greek, Roman, and northern European mythology. Zeus and Jupiter, kings of the gods and sky gods, hold the thunderbolt, while the Norse Þórr (Thor) brandishes a meteoric hammer that flashes lightning. Greco-Roman depictions of the bundle of thunder and lightning are barely distinguishable from the double-ended trident *vajra* used today across the northern Buddhist world. A Buddhist legend explains the adapted form, since the Buddha had grasped Indra's weapon and blunted it, forcing the aggressive open prongs together to create a peaceful regal scepter.

Following his Ṛgvedic supremacy, Indra, whose avatar Vajrapāṇi originally is, comes down in the world. A second-rank divinity, his supremacy is usurped by his storm-god colleague Rudra (Śiva), an opponent Vajrapāṇi will meet again many centuries later. In the *Mahābhārata,* for example, Indra is defeated, kidnapped, and humiliated, whether with the epithet *vajrapāṇi* or *vajradhara.* By this point, Vajrapāṇi had begun an alternative career that would lead him to the innermost heart of the Buddhist fold.

Separated from his godly prototype, Vajrapāṇi is an ambivalent *yakṣa,* neither divine nor human, albeit the general of the *yakṣa* army (*yakṣasenādhipati*) and master of the whole *guhyaka* (secret) class of *yakṣas* (*guhyakādhipati*). His mastery over secrets was reinterpreted to apply to the mysteries of esoteric Buddhism. With him, military metaphors are always explicit and sustained, and his *vajra* was conceptually assimilated to the legal staff (*danda*) of a law enforcer.

VAJRAPĀṆI AND THE BUDDHA. Although Vajrapāṇi's initial Buddhist incarnation may have been as the Buddha's associate, he was not a pushover. In a rare appearance in the Pali canon, Vajrapāṇi extracts a response from Ambaṭṭha to the Buddha's twice-unanswered question about his ancestry. To illustrate the threat that a third refusal will result in his head being shattered, Vajrapāṇi appears in the sky, visible to only the two interlocutors, wielding a blazing iron thunderbolt. The terrified Ambaṭṭha's tongue is loosened, and he keeps his head.

In the fifth century CE Buddhaghosa, the preeminent Pali commentator, glosses Vajrapāṇi as Indra, possibly reflecting the contemporary Brahmanization of Buddhism during and after the Gupta period. But the memory of their earlier identity is re-remembered everywhere in Indian Buddhist history. Vajrapāṇi and Indra are certainly depicted together enough times to have autonomous existences.

Numerous postcanonical narratives depict Vajrapāṇi's feet on the ground. Many Gandharan Buddhist bas reliefs from northern Pakistan from the first centuries of the Common Era show a Herculean strongman, under obvious Hellenistic influence, holding a *vajra.* Like a bodyguard, Vajrapāṇi is ever-present (*nityānubaddha*), mostly silent, at the Buddha's side. His desolation at the Buddha's deathbed even inspired an entire sūtra, transmitted in Chinese: *On Guhyaka Vajrapāṇi's Grief and Love When the Buddha Entered into Nirvāṇa.*

However close to the Buddha, Vajrapāṇi remained a menial. Smashing a boulder dropped by Devadatta, Vajrapāṇi's ill-judged blow sent a shard into his Lord's foot. Later, to spare the Buddha's nonviolent reputation, he defeated the *nāga* dragon Apalāla. Varying accounts of the episode, detailed in Étienne Lamotte's authoritative *Vajrapā-i en Inde* (2003), eventually credit him with single-handed conquest, in the *Mūlasarvāstivāda Vinaya,* localizing the event in northwest India.

When with the Mahāyāna, the historical Buddha and his human entourage lost their preeminence, while Vajrapāṇi, still judiciously aggressive, became venerable.

THREE *BODHISATTVAS.* Around the beginning of the Common Era, the young Mahāyāna Buddhism enthusiastically adopted Vajrapāṇi, if at first as a glorified protecting assistant, in such early classics as *Aṣṭasāhasrikāprajñāpāramitā Sūtra* (The perfection of wisdom in eight thousand verses sūtra).

With the Mahāyāna multiplication of *bodhisattvas,* Vajrapāṇi also becomes one, and he too is multiplied in the new tradition's proliferating style. The *bodhisattva* equivalent of the Buddha's intimate attendant, he mirrors Ānanda's function, with added Mahāyāna expansiveness: just as Ānanda guards and transmits the Śrāvakayāna sūtras, Vajrapāṇi protects and compiles fresh Mahāyāna sūtras. He is by the side of countless buddhas in multiple buddha realms, and constantly attends any *bodhisattva* who has attained the eighth to tenth of the ten *bodhisattva* stages.

Of the myriad Mahāyāna *bodhisattvas,* few merited dedicated religious cultivation. Apart from Maitreya, in particular, three stand out. Early Buddhist protectors, the Brahmanical gods Indra and Brahmā, are consequently recast as Vajrapāṇi and Padmapāṇi, bearers of the *vajra* and lotus respectively. Padmapāṇi became identified with the great *bodhisattva* of compassion, Avalokiteśvara, a Mahāyāna discovery, prompting Vajrapāṇi's subsequent parallel upgrade. With Mañjuśrī as the *bodhisattva* manifestation of Śākyamuni Buddha, the triad is complete.

In *Mañjuśrīmūlakalpa* (Mañjuśrī's fundamental instructions) in the earliest Kriyā Tantra phase of Tantric Buddhism, the trio lead three families (Skt., *trikula*), symbolized by the wheel, lotus, and *vajra,* specializing in wisdom, compassion, and power or energy (positive transmutations of the immemorial Buddhist root poisons: ignorance, greed, and hatred). Spiritual sons and heirs of the three crowning buddhas (Vairocana, Amitābha, and Akṣobhya (Tib., Mi bskyod pa [Mi kyö pa]), immoveable as the adamantine *vajra*), the three are ranked vertically, or at least on a slope. On the less auspicious left, Vajrapāṇi, with his entourage of fierce goddesses, remains inferior to the two embodiments of more primary Buddhist qualities. Their inequality means that one consecrated in the *vajra* family is entitled to perform fierce activities (coercing, destroying, and slaying), but not the beneficent ones, while those initiated into the gentler families are also entitled to perform the fierce activities in an emergency.

Bodhisattvas, not buddhas, the lords of the three families (Tib., *Rigs gsum mgon po* [Riksum gönpo]) are commemorated throughout the Himalayas wherever there is Buddhism, in wayside shrines, images, or a row of three stupas—white for compassionate Avalokiteśvara, orange for wise Mañjuśrī, and black or blue-grey for powerful Vajrapāṇi. Most common are *maṇi* walls of piled-up flat stones carved with the *mantras* of the three *bodhisattvas*: *oṃ maṇi padme hūṃ; oṃ vāgīśvarī hūṃ; and oṃ vajrapāṇi hūṃ.* Later Tibetan historians retrospectively identified their incarnations in the three kings who promoted Buddhism in Tibet: Srong brtsan sgam po (Songtsen gampo, r. 627–649/650); Khri Srong lde btsan (Trisong detsen, r. 755–c. 797); and Ral pa can (Rälpachen, r. 815–838), respectively Avalokiteśvara, Mañjuśrī, and finally the fierce Vajrapāṇi. Many people have been, and continue to be, recognized as incarnations of Vajrapāṇi, and of the others. While Mañjuśrī and Avalokiteśvara inspired philosophers and enduring Mahāyāna cults, Vajrapāṇi was going right to the top.

FIVE BUDDHAS. Tantric Buddhism is the Vajrayāna, the "Vajra Way." Naturally, the *vajra* holder will be most powerful in such an eponymous religion. In earlier Kriyā and Caryā Tantras, the *vajra* family had been inferior, but in the Yoga Tantras, the family system operates with theoretical equality, graphically expressed in the *maṇḍala*'s horizontal layout.

In the Yoga Tantra *Sarvatathāgatatattvasaṃgraha* (Congregation of the truth of all the buddhas, seventh century CE at the latest), Vajrapāṇi comes to the fore. With the main Vajradhātu *Maṇḍala*, his family is paramount, pervading all others. The buddha family's Vajradhātu *Maṇḍala* is scarcely distinguished from the *vajra* family's Trailokyavijaya *Maṇḍala*, where the expertise remains slaying and destroying. Here are located the non-Buddhist deities that Vajrapāṇi has forcibly converted, the achievement that gave him everlasting fame in Indian and Tibetan Tantric Buddhist institutional literature.

Without a single Tantric Buddhist origin myth, alternative stories compete. The literary winner is the account of Vajrapāṇi's defeat of Maheśvara Śiva. Many texts narrate Śiva's slaying and subjugation by Vajrapāṇi. Key is the *Sarvatathāgatatattvasaṃgraha's* telling, translated in Snellgrove (1987, pp. 136–140). Enlightened, Vairocana generates Vajradhara, from whom arises Vajrapāṇi to order Maheśvara into the *maṇḍala.* Śiva objects to obeying a mere *yakṣa*, but Vajrapāṇi threatens to destroy the whole threefold world (*trailokya*). Even when reduced to a prostrate corpse and then resurrected, the proud god refuses to submit. Finally, Vajrapāṇi triumphs and stands with his right foot on Maheśvara, and his left on that god's consort, Umā. Thus is mythologized the assimilation of non-Buddhist traditions, mediated by Vajrapāṇi, who acquires a new title, Trailokyavijaya, "Conqueror of the three worlds."

In the *Sarvatathāgatatattvasaṃgraha,* Vairocana had been in the center of the *maṇḍala,* but in the transitional Yoga/Yogottara *Guhyasamāja Tantra* (Secret union Tantra), the *vajra* family's buddha, Akṣobhya, takes the central position as the direct Sambhogakāya incarnation of Vajradhara. Vajrapāṇi's erstwhile synonym is now the sum of everything, and will be of supreme importance in the Tibetan tradition. In Yoganiruttara cycles the chief deities are all *vajra* family. Akṣobhya's emanations—Heruka, Hevajra, Saṃvara, Yamāri, Vajrakīla, Buddhakapāla, and Mahāmāya are buddhas in the style of Vajrapāṇi, with Akṣobhya on their crown, blue, fierce, and personifications of *vajra* power.

MULTIPLE VAJRAPĀṆIS. Already before the plethora of Yoganiruttara wild buddhas, VajrapāṇI—the *bodhisattva* himself—had multiple wrathful aliases in addition to Trailokyavijaya, conqueror of Śiva: these included Mahābala (great strength), subjugator of Māra and subject of the *Mahābala Sūtra* (dateable to between the *Mañjuśrīmūlakalpa* and the *Sarvatathāgatatattvasaṃgraha*); Ucchuṣma (the "incinerator" of impurities); Kuṇḍali; "fierce" Caṇḍavajrapāṇi (Tib., Phyag rdor gtum po [Chagdor tumpo]); and four-armed Bhūtaḍāmara (Tib., 'Byung po'i dul byed [Chungpö dulched]), his spirit-subduing form. Many of these independent deities are still cultivated today in the Tibetan tradition. The triple practice of Hayagrīva, Vajrapāṇi, and Garuḍa for the removal of obstacles, particularly *nāga* afflictions, reflects Vajrapāṇi's association with Garuḍa, natural enemy to snakes and *nāgas.*

ICONOGRAPHY. Given the wealth of identity-shifts Vajrapāṇi has enjoyed over the last 2,500 years, his iconography is manifold. From his late Mahāyāna phase on he is crowned with the *vajra* family buddha, Akṣobhya. Like Akṣobhya, he is blue, the color of space or the night sky, or black like thunderclouds or kohl. Vajrapāṇi wears the tiger skin that represents hatred harnessed (elephant skin signifies ignorance, and a flayed human skin, desire). The tiger skin's phallic stripes make it male, while the consort wears a female leopard skin. Yet, Vajrapāṇi is rarely depicted in union. The emphasis on wrath seems to have precluded passion, however explicitly phallic the *vajra* is in Tantric Buddhism (where it is regularly united with the female "lotus"). Usually Vajrapāṇi wields only a *vajra* (five- or nine-pronged) in his raised right hand, while his left is held at the heart in the threatening (*tarjanī*) gesture. His left hand can hold the noose to bind enemies, actual or metaphorical, or a bell. In more wrathful manifestations, the big-bellied dwarf has three eyes, a skull crown, and a snake necklace, and he steps towards the right to show his energy, standing on a sun disk on an open lotus, orange hair flaring upwards as if on fire. His *bodhisattva* form is peaceful, holding a lotus with *vajra* atop in his right hand, and making the gesture of generosity with his left.

VAJRAPĀṆI'S COMMENTARY. In addition to all his ahistorical history, Vajrapāṇi was also the name of one of the three "*bodhisattva*" authors who interpreted Tantric Buddhism in the light of the *Kālacakra Tantra* (Wheel of time Tantra) in the late tenth century CE. His *Laghutantraṭīkā* (Commentary on the shorter Tantra) analyses the first ten and a half stanzas of the *Cakrasaṃvara Tantra* (Wheel of bliss Tantra).

SEE ALSO Vajradhara.

BIBLIOGRAPHY

Beer, Robert. *The Encyclopedia of Tibetan Symbols and Motifs.* London, 1999.

Bischoff, Frédéric A. *Contribution à l'étude des divinités mineures du bouddhisme tantrique: Arya Mahabalanama-Mahayanasutra, tibétain (mss. de Touen-Houang) et chinois.* Paris, 1956.

Cicuzza, Claudio. *The Laghutantraṭīkā by Vajrapāṇi: A Critical Edition of the Sanskrit Text.* Rome, 2001.

Davidson, Ronald M. "Reflections on the Maheshvara Subjugation Myth: Indic Materials, Sa-skya-pa Apologetics, and the Birth of Heruka." *The Journal of the International Association of Buddhist Studies* 14, no. 2 (1991): 197–235.

Davidson, Ronald M. *Indian Esoteric Buddhism: A Social History of the Tantric Movement.* New York, 2002.

Himalayan Art. "Buddhist Deity: Vajrapani." Shelley and Donald Rubin Foundation. Available from: www.himalayanart.org. A collection of paintings, bronzes, and prints of Vajrapāṇi, from across the northern Buddhist world, ninth to twentieth centuries CE.

Lalou, Marcelle. "Four Notes on Vajrapani." *Adyar Library Bulletin* 20 (1956): 287–293.

Lalou, Marcelle. "A Fifth Note on Vajrapani." *Adyar Library Bulletin* 25 (1961): 242–249.

Lamotte, Étienne. "Vajrapå-i en Inde." In *Mélanges de Sinologie offerts à Monsieur Paul Demiéville,* pp. 113–159. Paris, 1966. Translated as "Vajrapå-I in India." In *Buddhist Studies Review* 20, 1 (2003): 1–30, and 20, 2 (2003): 119–144.

Linrothe, Rob. *Ruthless Compassion: Wrathful Deities in Early Indo-Tibetan Esoteric Buddhist Art.* London, 1999.

Mayer, Robert. "The Figure of Maheshvara/Rudra in the rNying ma pa Tantric Tradition." *Journal of the International Association of Buddhist Studies* 21 (1998): 271–310.

Snellgrove, David L. *Indo-Tibetan Buddhism: Indian Buddhists and their Tibetan Successors.* 2 vols. Boston, 1987.

Stein, Rolf A. "La Soumission de Rudra et autres contes tantriques." *Journal Asiatique* 283 (1995): 121–160.

ISABELLE ONIANS (2005)

VAJRASATTVA (Tibetan, Rdo rje sems dpa' [Dorjé Sempa]; Chinese, Jingang sadou; Japanese, Kongōsatta), the "Adamantine Being," is a *bodhisattva* affiliated primarily with the Buddha Akṣobhya (Unshakeable) but in many contexts is identified conceptually with Vajradhara (Vajra Holder). Vajrasattva is traditionally depicted iconographically as white in color with one face and two hands. In his right hand he holds close to his heart a *vajra* (thunderbolt), representing the active means toward enlightenment, and in his left hand beside his left hip an upturned bell (*ghaṇṭā*), a symbol of emptiness (*śūnyatā*) and the perfection of wisdom (*prajñāpāramitā*). Lavishly attired in the colorful garments of a princely *bodhisattva,* he sits with legs crossed in the *vajra* posture (*vajrāsana*) on a moon disk above a white lotus blossom. In some cases he is shown sitting with his right leg outstretched, and in others he is standing. He wears a crown often inscribed with an image of Akṣobhya. From his richly adorned body, rays of light (often dark blue) radiate outward to form a golden halo adorned with wish-fulfilling jewels and an outer rainbow. In this way he represents the embodied essence of all the peaceful buddhas.

Iconic images of Vajrasattava are found in statuary form and more frequently in paintings, especially of the *maṇḍala.* As a central deity of esoteric Buddhism or Vajrayāna (Adamantine or Thunderbolt Vehicle), Vajrasattva first rose to prominence in the Yoga class of Tantras. The ritual practices centered on him, including visualization of the *maṇḍala* and recitation of his hundred-syllable *mantra,* are popular among all followers of Tantric Buddhism, particularly in Tibet and in Japan. Vajrasattava's significance in the development of the Buddhist Vajrayāna tradition in India and in neighboring regions and beyond is well confirmed, although the precise details of his role in that historical process are complicated and require understanding of his divine adamantine allies, the closely related deities Vajrapāṇi (Vajra-in-Hand), Vairocana (Resplendent), and Vajradhara.

VAJRASATTVA IN INDIA. Vajrasattva first emerges as a central deity in the Yoga Tantras. The foundational text of this literary category is the *Sarvatathāgatatattvasaṁgraha* (Symposium of Truth of All the Tathagathas), also known simply as the *Tattvasaṁgraha.* Other significant Yoga Tantras include the *Sarvadurgatipariśodhana Tantra* (Tantra on the Elimination of All Evil Rebirths), the *Vajraśekhara Tantra* (Vajra Pinnacle Tantra), and the *Mañjuśrīnāmasaṃgīti* (The Litany of Names of Mañjusrī). Evidence suggests that the *Tattvasaṁgraha* and associated Tantric works date to the beginning of the eighth century, although some scholars now argue that the *Tattvasaṁgraha* itself may have been completed slightly earlier at the end of the seventh century.

Vajrapāṇi, a closely affiliated divine precursor to Vajrasattva, first takes center stage, along with the famous *bodhisattvas* Avalokiteśvara (Lord Who Looks Down) and Mañjuśrī (Gentle Glory), in the proto-Tantric *Mañjuśrīmūlakalpa* (Fundamental Ordinance of Mañjuśrī). In this text, the three deities are described as taking up honorable positions around the Buddha Śākyamuni: Avalokiteśvara, identified here as Padmapāṇi (Lotus-in-Hand), to his right; Vajrapāṇi to his left; and Mañjuśrī (Gentle Glory) appearing below Śākyamuni at the center. This formal arrangement of Buddhist deities seems to represent an early and simplified prototype of the more elaborate fivefold arrangement of buddhas that would later become fully systematized in the Yoga Tantras. In the *Mañjuśrīmūlakalpa,* Avalokiteśvara is associated with the symbol of the lotus, the divine emblem of purity and compassion. The central figure of Mañjuśrī is symbolically identified as *tathāgata* (Thus Gone), a term synonymous with the Buddha and enlightenment. For Vajrapāṇi and his retinue, the preeminent symbol is the *vajra,* signifying divine and magical power—the power to pacify, augment, control, and destroy. It is largely for this reason, owing to the power associated with the *vajra,* that Vajrapāṇi is the one given the daunting task of subjugating and converting to Buddhism the Hindu god Śiva (Maheśvara) in a dramatic and influential tale first recounted in the *Tattvasaṁgraha.*

It is in this work, also, that Vairocana first appears as a manifestation of the unity of all buddhas. The *maṇḍala* of Vairocana, introduced in the *Tattvasaṁgraha* with the name Vajradhātu (Adamantine World), places Vairocana in the center surrounded by the Buddhas Akṣobhya in the eastern quarter, Ratnasambhava (Jewel Born) in the south, Amitābha (Boundless Light) in the west, and Amoghasiddhi (All Accomplishing) in the north. In time this symmetrical arrangement of five principal buddhas became standard, though with the identity of the central deity frequently changing to reflect the affiliated lineage of a particular Tantric ritual tradition. Nevertheless, the Yoga Tantras continue to maintain that in whatever form the central deity manifests, whether as Vairocana, Vajradhara, Vajrasattva, or some other buddha figure, he is always to be understood as the same in essence, that is, as the unity of all buddhas.

With the development in the Yoga Tantras of this fivefold buddha *maṇḍala* coincided the expansion of various buddha families (*kula*). It was in the proto-Tantric *Mañjuśrīmūlakalpa* that this concept of families first emerged, with the introduction of three divine groups, Tathāgata/Buddha (Mañjuśrī), Lotus (Avalokiteśvara), and Vajra (Vajrapāṇi). The *Tattvasaṁgraha* added to this list a Gem (*ratna*) family, and a fifth, Action (*karma*) family, seems first to have been introduced in the *Vajraśekhara Tantra.* The Yoga Tantras, moreover, refer also to a transcendent sixth family represented by a supreme primordial buddha (Ādibuddha), understood as the source of the five principal buddhas. This supreme buddha is known variously as Mahāvairocana (Great Resplendent), Samantabhadra (Universal Goodness), Vajradhara, or more commonly, Vajrasattva.

Given the overall emphasis on power in Tantric Buddhism, it is the Vajra family that reigns supreme in the Tantras. Thus, it is the buddhas and *bodhisattvas* who embody the symbolism of the *vajra*—identified as such in the very names themselves—that stand at the center of the Tantric universe represented graphically in the form of the *maṇḍala.* Although originally Vairocana held the central position in the *maṇḍala* outlined in the *Tattvasaṁgraha,* it is Vajradhara, the transcendent sixth buddha, who, linked by name and power to the older Vajrapāṇi, comes eventually to replace Vairocana as the quintessential Tantric deity. Vajradhara is also identified with Vajrasattva, the *bodhisattva* associated most closely with the fierce Buddha Akṣobhya. In some of the later Tantras, therefore, Akṣobhya is placed in the center of the *maṇḍala* and Vairocana is shifted to the east in Akṣobhya's former position. Vajradhara and Vajrasattva, both symbolically identical, and thus interchangeable, remain the transcendent embodiments of adamantine power, the source and unity of all buddhas.

VAJRASATTVA IN TIBET. In Tibetan Buddhism, the iconography and ritual traditions of Vajrasattva are derived largely from the class of Indian Buddhist Yoga Tantras referred to above, though additionally in Tibet there are other primary Tantras associated with this deity. The most significant is the eighth-century *Gsang ba'i snying po* (Sanskrit, **Guhyagarbha,* "Secret Nucleus"), a work belonging to a distinctively Tibetan cycle of *mahāyoga* scriptures collectively titled *Sgyu 'phrul drwa ba* (Sanskrit, *Māyājāla,* "Web of Magical Emanation"). In the *Gsang ba'i snying po,* Vajrasattva appears at the center of the *maṇḍala* of the peaceful deities (Tibetan, *zhi ba'i lha*). This *maṇḍala* is the tranquil counterreflection of an elaborate arrangement of fierce divinities (Tibetan, *khro bo'i lha*). Together, both *maṇḍalas* constitute the Tantric system of the peaceful and wrathful deities most famously represented in the *Tibetan Book of the Dead* literature.

In Tibet there are numerous ritual programs (Tibetan, *sgrub thabs;* Sanskrit, *sādhana*) dedicated to Vajrasattva, and their practice is widely popular among all the main orders of Tibetan Buddhism. These Vajrasattva rituals serve as purificatory practices and constitute a key component of the preliminaries (*sngon 'gro*) to Tantric initiation and empowerment. In this context, Vajrasattva's hundred-syllable *mantra,* recited during the preliminary rites, is held to be a particularly potent method for purifying past sins and unwholesome *karma.*

For the Rnying ma pa (Ancient Ones) school of Tibetan Buddhism, Vajrasattva is also celebrated as a key lineage holder of the Rdzogs chen (Great Perfection) teachings, and is credited with the transmission of this esoteric system into the human realm in a vision revealed to the Indian mystic Dga' rab rdo rje (Sanskrit, Prahevajra).

VAJRASATTVA IN JAPAN. The identification of Vajrasattva as a divine lineage holder of the Tantric Buddhist teachings is found also in Japan, specifically in the esoteric (*mikkyō*) sūtras of the Japanese Shingon tradition. Here, Vajrasattva, known as Kongōsatta in Japanese, is recognized as the direct recipient of the esoteric teachings of the supreme Buddha Mahāvairocana (Japanese, Dainichi), the teacher of the *Mahāvairocana* and the *Vajraśekhara Sūtras.* Vajrasattva thus appears as second patriarch after the Great Vairocana in all established Shingon transmission lineages. From Vajrasattva the teachings were then transmitted in the human world to Nāgārjuna, and, through a succession of further Indian masters, eventually extended to the Japanese Buddhist priest Kūkai (774–835).

As in the Indian and Tibetan traditions, Vajrasattva in Japanese Shingon represents the adamantine enlightenment of all buddhas. Recognized as the active and manifest power of Mahāvairocana, he holds leadership positions within the two exclusive *maṇḍalas* of the Shingon tradition, the *taizō* (Sanskrit, *Garbhadhātu,* "Womb/Matrix World") and *kongōkai* (Sanskrit, *Vajradhātu,* "Diamond World"). In the ritual arena, during the esoteric initiation ceremonies and construction of the *maṇḍala,* Vajrasattva is invoked by practitioners to help them attain buddhahood in this lifetime.

BIBLIOGRAPHY

Abé, Ryuichi. *The Weaving of Mantra: Kūkai and the Construction of Esoteric Buddhist Discourse.* New York, 1999.

Beyer, Stephan. *The Cult of Tārā: Magic and Ritual in Tibet.* Berkeley, Calif., 1978.

Davidson, Ronald M. *Indian Esoteric Buddhism: A Social History of the Tantric Movement.* New York, 2002.

Snellgrove, David L. *Indo-Tibetan Buddhism: Indian Buddhists and Their Tibetan Successors.* 2 vols. Boston, 1987.

ten Grotenhuis, Elizabeth. *Japanese Mandalas: Representations of Sacred Geography.* Honolulu, 1999.

Thupten Yeshe. *Becoming Vajrasattva: The Tantric Path of Purification.* Edited by Nicholas Ribush. Boston, 2004.

Tucci, Giuseppe. *Tibetan Painted Scrolls.* 3 vols. Rome, 1949.

Yamasaki, Taiko. *Shingon: Japanese Esoteric Buddhism.* Translated and adapted by Richard and Cynthia Peterson. Edited by Yasuyoshi Morimoto and David Kidd. Boston, 1988.

BRYAN J. CUEVAS (2005)

VAJRAYĀNA SEE BUDDHISM, SCHOOLS OF, *ARTICLE ON* TANTRIC RITUAL SCHOOLS OF BUDDHISM

VALHǪLL is the hall of Óðinn (Odin) in Norse mythology. The fullest descriptions of it are found in the *Prose Edda* (c. 1220–1230) of the Icelandic mythographer Snorri Sturluson and in the Eddic poem *Grímnismál* (Lay of Grímnir), one of Snorri's main sources; tenth-century skaldic poems also make particular use of the conception. These and other texts describe Valhǫll as a stately palace, with a roof of shields and spears. A wolf hangs by the west portal and an eagle droops above; both these animals are associated with Óðinn, the god of the spear, and their actions recall his self-sacrifice. Valhǫll had 540 doors, through each of which 800 warriors could pass at once. (These numbers probably employ the Germanic long hundred and should be read as 640 and 960, respectively.)

Valhǫll served specifically as a hall for the *einherjar,* the dead warriors of Óðinn. These chosen heroes were fetched from the battlefield by valkyries, who also served them mead in Valhǫll, a scene probably reflected on such picture stones as the eighth-century Ardre VIII from Gotland, Sweden. Legendary heroes, human kings, and even the god of poetry, Bragi, are numbered among the *einherjar* in Valhǫll. The god Baldr's arrival is mentioned once, although the mythology usually associates him with Hel. The *einherjar* spend their days in endless combat, but in the evenings they join in reconciliation for feasting and drinking. The boar Sæhrímnir is boiled each day for their food but is restored again each night. Mead runs from the udders of the goat Heiðrún. She stands above Valhǫll, feeding on the foliage of Læráðr (Yggdrasill), the World Tree. The stag Eikþyrnir also chews on the tree; from his horns fluid runs into Hvergelmir, the Well of Wisdom, and thence into mighty rivers. The proximity of the tree and well suggests that Valhǫll is located at or near the center of the world.

The *einherjar* (those belonging to one army, or splendid warriors) share a special relationship with Óðinn. Called his *óskasynir* (adopted sons, or beloved sons), they are his retainers, destined to fight with him in the final battle at Ragnarǫk. This relationship may be the key to the religious background of Valhǫll. Some scholars have sought this background in ecstatic cults of Óðinn, characterized by initiation into warrior bands (perhaps secret cult groups that used animal masks). Valhǫll would then represent a mythic projection of the Germanic chieftain's hall, and the activities within would be a similar projection of the warrior life. Certainly other sources emphasize the ritual importance of feasting and drinking.

Many scholars believe that the Norse sources express a late development of conceptions of Valhǫll, appropriate particularly to the warrior elite of the Viking age. At an earlier period, Valhǫll may have simply indicated a grave mound. Supporting this notion is the Icelandic conception of a local mountain inhabited by dead family members; the sagas report that feasting was occasionally glimpsed within. Furthermore, in Sweden, certain rocks associated with the dead are called *valhall.* If this explanation is correct, *valhǫll* (carrion hall) may actually be derived from *valhallr* (carrion rock, or carrion hill,). Since *val-* may also mean "foreign," *valhǫll* might also denote "foreign hall," and the term is used of kings' halls in the Eddic poem *Atlakviða.*

SEE ALSO Baldr; Eddas; Óðinn; Snorri Sturluson.

BIBLIOGRAPHY

The standard treatment of Valhǫll remains that of Gustav Neckel, *Walhall: Studien über germanischen Jenseitsglauben* (Dortmund, Germany, 1913). Franz Rolf Schröder's *Germanentum und Hellenismus* (Heidelberg, Germany, 1924) discusses the development of the concept of Valhǫll under Middle Eastern influence; for instance, he points out that the sacred number 432,000 is the product of the 540 doors multiplied by the 800 warriors. In an important article, "Valhall med de mange dørrer," originally published in 1931 and reprinted in his *Norrøne studier* (Oslo, 1938), Magnus Olsen argues for Roman influence in the form of amphitheaters, perhaps even the Colosseum; there, crowds surged through many doors, warriors fought regularly, and the emperor presided, not unlike a god. On ecstatic cults of Óðinn, see Otto Höfler's *Kultische Geheimbünde der Germanen* (Frankfurt am Main, Germany, 1934); this volume is all that appeared of a projected two-volume work. In her *Prolonged Echoes,* vol. 1, *The Myths* (Odense, Denmark, 1992), pp. 253 ff, Margaret Clunies Ross discusses the picture of what she calls the "Valhǫll complex" in Snorri Sturluson's *Edda* as an attempt to portray Óðinn as warrior chieftain in charge of a warrior elite. Ann-Lili Nielsen, "Hedniska kult—och offerhandlingar i Borg," in *Religion från stenålder till medeltid,* edited by Kerstin Engdahl and Anders Kaliff (Linköping, Sweden, 1996), discusses cult activities in the chieftain's farm found in Lofoten, Norway, some of which may be relevant to notions of Valhǫll.

JOHN LINDOW (1987 AND 2005)

VALKYRIES, supernatural female figures of Norse myth and literature, share many features with the *dísir, fylgjur, hamingjur,* Norns, and *landvættir* in the extant texts, and there is little terminological consistency. A primary function of the valkyries is indicated by the etymology of the word *valkyrja,* a compound of *valr* (carrion) and a *nomen agentis* based on the verb *kyrja* (to choose). Regarded as the maidens of Óðinn, the valkyries chose who was to die in battle and brought the chosen ones to him in Valhǫll, where they joined the *einherjar,* Óðinn's warriors. Valkyries rode through the air, bore weapons, and could be fierce in appearance, although they may have been shape-changers. Their personal names ordinarily make reference to battle. In Valhǫll, valkyries served mead to the *einherjar,* a scene perhaps portrayed on the Ardre VIII picture stone (Gotland, Sweden; eighth century) and elsewhere. Sometimes, however, valkyries protected heroes in battle, a characteristic shared with the *fylgjur.* The valkyrie Sigrdrífa of the Eddic poem *Sigrdrífumál* may be associated with healing, which suggests the *matronae* of early Germanic religion. Like the Norns, valkyries weave fate in the poem *Darraarljóð.* There is also confusion with human or semidivine heroines, and in one heroic cycle a valkyrie is twice reborn in different identities.

Given the existence of the *matronae* in ancient Germanic times, the general prominence of male gods and the relative importance of the Æsir over the Vanir in Norse mythology, it seems apparent that female figures were of greater importance in Germanic religion than Norse mythology would indicate. Scholars have regarded the valkyries as derived from earlier goddesses of death or perhaps a fertility cult, but their association with Óðinn may be ancient and primary. If so, believers may once have attributed to valkyries shape-changing powers and the ecstatic "sending" of their spirits.

SEE ALSO Eddas; Óðinn.

BIBLIOGRAPHY

Nils Lid discusses the various female figures of Scandinavian religion in the section "Valkyrjer og diser" of his "Gudar og gudedyrking," in *Religionshistoria,* edited by Nils Lid (Oslo, 1954). Folke Ström's *Diser, norner, valkyrjor* (Stockholm, 1954) treats three of these groups and argues for association with a fertility cult and sacral kingship. Useful studies of the literary valkyrie are those of Lise Præstgaard Andersen, *Skjøldmøer—en kvindemyte* (Copenhagen, 1982) and Helen Damico, *Beowulf's Wealhtheow and the Valkyrie Tradition* (Madison, Wis., 1984).

JOHN LINDOW (1987 AND 2005)

VALLABHA (1479–1531), also called Vallabhācārya, was a Vaiṣṇava Hindu philosopher and religious leader. Vallabha was born in central India at Campāraṇya (Raipur District, Madhya Pradesh) into a family of Vaiṣṇava brahmans originally from the Telugu country. During his childhood, which was spent in Vārāṇasi (Banaras), Vallabha displayed unusual precocity in mastering the scriptures of orthodox Hinduism. In the course of his life he visited most of the holy places of India, publicly expounding his own interpretation of the events of Kṛṣṇa's life as presented in the *Bhāgavata Purāṇa.* In a series of debates with adherents of the nondualism (*advaita*) promulgated by the eighth-century philosopher Śankarācārya, Vallabha defended the doctrines of devotional worship (*bhakti*). On one of these occasions he was offered and accepted the position of leader (*ācārya*) of the Vaiṣṇava school established earlier by Viṣṇusvami.

Vallabha's own sect, the Vallabh Sampradāy, originated from two events that occurred in the Braj region around the city of Mathura. In the first of these, Kṛṣṇa appeared to Vallabha in a vision and revealed to him the *brahmasambandha mantra* by which human souls could be brought into direct relationship (*sambandha*) with the Supreme Being (*brahman*). In the second, Vallabha discovered on Govardhan Hill the stone image called Śrī Govardhananāthajī ("the auspicious lord of Govardhan"), usually abbreviated as Śrī Nāthjī; the statue is a representation of Kṛṣṇa holding up Govardhan Hill as a shelter for his devotees. The *brahmasambandha mantra* remains to this day the primary component of the rite of initiation into the Vallabh Sampradāy, and Śrī Nāthjī, now at Nathdwara (Udaipur District, Rajasthan), is the sect's chief divine image. Vallabha was married and had two sons, Gopīnātha (1512–1543) and Viṭṭalanātha (1516–1586).

After Vallabha's death, first Gopīnātha and then Viṭṭalanātha took charge of the sect. Each of Viṭṭalanātha's eight sons formed his own branch of the sect and the leadership within these branches passes down by inheritance through Vallabha's male line. With most of its membership drawn from the mercantile section of Hindu society, the Vallabh Sampradāy is found in all important Indian cities but is strongest in the states of Rajasthan and Gujarat and in the city of Bombay. Vallabha's sect was in decline during most of the nineteenth century, but in recent years it has regained its position of eminence among devotional varieties of Hinduism.

According to Vallabha the chief philosophical flaw in Śankarācārya's concept of *advaita* is that it accepts illusion (*māyā*) as a force independent of *brahman.* Vallabha rectified this defect by presenting *māyā* as one of the powers of the Supreme Being. In this way he made pure (*śuddha*) the nondualism of his philosophical system, which is, in consequence, called *śuddhādvaita.* The fundamental principles of *śuddhādvaita* are as follows: Kṛṣṇa is the Supreme Being and sole existent entity. Both human souls and the material universe are real but limited manifestations that Kṛṣṇa projects out of himself. The souls on earth have, however, forgotten their true nature as fragments of the divine and have become centered on themselves. This egoism is the primary sin that dooms human beings to separation from Kṛṣṇa and to an endless succession of births and deaths. In his mercy Kṛṣṇa himself came in human form to earth in the Braj area and showed through his own actions the way to salvation through *bhakti.* The divine grace, which cannot be earned through mere piety or ritual, is available to anyone, regardless of sex or caste, who will forget the ego and center himself or herself on Kṛṣṇa. Since Kṛṣṇa's grace is said to be the way (*mārga*) for the nourishment (*puṣṭi*) of the soul, followers of Vallabha call their religion the Puṣṭmārg. Salvation, the goal of the Puṣṭmārg, consists of eternal association with Kṛṣṇa in his paradise beyond ordinary time and space.

See Also Bhakti; Kṛṣṇa; Vaiṣṇavism, article on Bhāgavatas.

Bibliography

The most important of Vallabha's writings, all of which are in Sanskrit, is his *Subodhinī* commentary on the *Bhāgavata Purāṇa.* There is no satisfactory English translation, but the text has been well edited by Nandkishor Sharma (Nathdwara, 1928). Vallabha outlined his basic philosophical ideas in the *Tattvārtha-dīpa-nibandha,* which has been edited in two volumes by Harishankar Onkarji Shastri, with introduction and notes in English by J. G. Shah (Bombay, 1943). This edition includes both English and Gujarati translations of the text together with expository material. In sixteen short works collected together as the *Ṣoḍaśagranthāḥ,* Vallabha explained his approach to *bhakti.* An excellent three-volume edition of the *Ṣoḍaśagranthāḥ* with commentaries has been published under the title *Mahāprabhu Śrīmadvallabhācārya Viracitāḥ Ṣoḍaśagranthāḥ* (Nathdwara, 1980–1981), and an English translation of all but two of the sixteen works is included in Manilal Chhotalal Parekh's *Sri Vallabhacharya: Life, Teachings and Movement,* 2d ed. (Rajkot, 1943). A general introduction to Vallabha's teachings and sect is provided by my study *The Bhakti Sect of Vallabhācārya* (Faridabad, 1976), and a survey of his philosophical thought is given by Mrudula I. Marfatia in *The Philosophy of Vallabhācārya* (Delhi, 1967).

New Sources

Tagare, Ganesh Vasudeo. *Brahma-Vada: Doctrine of Sri Vallabhacarya.* New Delhi, 1998.

R. K. Barz (1987)
Revised Bibliography

VALLÉE POUSSIN, LOUIS DE LA See LA VALLÉE POUSSIN, LOUIS DE

VĀLMĪKI. Legendary sage and author of the Hindu epic *Rāmāyaṇa,* Vālmīki also plays a role in the epic itself. The first book of his *Rāmāyaṇa* tells the story of the invention of poetry by Vālmīki: One day Vālmīki saw a hunter kill the male of a pair of birds making love. Filled with compassion for the birds, the sage spontaneously uttered a curse at the hunter for his cruelty. Vālmīki's words came forth as well-formed, beautiful verse. The sage himself was surprised by his utterance, which was immediately memorized and recited on the spot by his disciple Bharadvāja, who had accompanied him. Later, after Vālmīki returned home, Brahmā, the creator, visited him and asked him to compose the story of the virtuous hero Rāma as outlined by the *ṛṣi* Narada, using the new meter that Vālmīki had created. Indian literary tradition therefore considers Vālmīki as the first poet (*adikavi*) and his *Rāmāyaṇa* the first poem (*adikavya*).

In the seventh book of the epic, Vālmīki is spoken of as a friend of King Daśaratha. Rāma's brother Lakṣmaṇa leaves the pregnant Sītā (Rāma's wife) in Vālmīki's hermitage. Finally, it is Vālmīki who shelters Sītā, raises her twin sons, and plays the role of reconciler between Rāma and Sītā by testifying publicly to Sītā's purity. In this context, Vālmīki describes himself as a son of Pracetas, which makes him a member of the family of Bhṛgus, an influential lineage of brahmans in ancient India.

A folk legend records that the sage was born out of an "anthill" (Sanskrit, *valmīka*) and therefore was called Vālmīki. This legend also records that he was originally a bandit, but some sages, pitying him, taught him the *mantra* "marā, marā, marā." As he repeated the syllables, they produced the name *Rāma,* and while he was deeply immersed in meditating on the name of Rāma, ants built anthills around him. This story appears with minor variations in the *Skāndapūrāṇa* and also in the *Adhyātma Rāmāyaṇa* and *Ānanda Rāmāyaṇa.* Many popular *bhakti* Rāmāyaṇas, including the *Krittivāsa Rāmāyaṇa* of Bengal, adopt this story.

Thus, there are two kinds of biographies for Vālmīki. One type describes Vālmīki as a sage-poet born of a high-caste brahman family and endowed with supreme wisdom and the divine sensibilities that made him the creator of poetry, while the other type describes him as a sinner transformed into a saint. The first type of biography is in conformity with the status of the *Rāmāyaṇa* as the great epic that it is in the Brahmanic tradition. The second type of biography relates to the status of the *Rāmāyaṇa* as a *bhakti* poem that transforms its readers from sinners into devotees of the god Rāma. The two types of biographies thus reflect the two major orientations and interpretations of the *Rāmāyaṇa* in Hindu culture.

Scholars have suggested a historical Vālmīki, who probably was a resident of Kosala (a region of the modern state of Uttar Pradesh) and traveled extensively in North India, though he did not know much of the South. This opinion is based on the textual evidence from the *Rāmāyaṇa* that gives detailed and geographically correct descriptions of

North India, whereas its descriptions of South India are purely fanciful. It is also suggested that Vālmīki was one of the *kuśīlavas* ("singers, bards") who sang the epic. No firm evidence is available, however, in support of a historical Vālmīki. Tradition holds, however, that Vālmīki is also the author of the medieval work *Mahārāmayaṇa,* or *Jñānavāśiṣṭa,* a philosophical text in the form of a dialogue between the sage Vaśiṣṭa and Rāma.

See Also Rāmāyaṇa.

Bibliography

Bulcke, Camille. "The Rāmāyaṇa: Its History and Character." *Poona Orientalist* 25 (January–October 1960): 36–60.

Goldman, Robert P., trans. *The Rāmāyaṇa of Vālmīki,* vol. 1, *Bālakaṇḍa.* Princeton, N.J., 1984. See especially the introduction (pp. 3–59).

Velcheru Narayana Rao (1987)

VAN DER LEEUW, GERARDUS See LEEUW, GERARDUS VAN DER

VAN GENNEP, ARNOLD See GENNEP, ARNOLD VAN

VAN RUUSBROEC, JAN See RUUSBROEC, JAN VAN

VANUATU RELIGIONS.

Formerly known as the New Hebrides, Vanuatu is a Y-shaped archipelago of mostly volcanic islands located about sixteen hundred kilometers northeast of the Queensland coast of Australia. The physical, linguistic, and cultural diversity of the 100,000 or so indigenous inhabitants of the sixty-three occupied islands is extreme even for the western Pacific, a diversity that is fully reflected in religious belief and practice. While the dominant traits in all contexts may be described as Melanesian, Polynesian influences, including those pertaining to religion, are sufficiently widespread and important to set this area apart from the rest of Melanesia. This article will ignore the profound impact of Christianity on contemporary religion, but it should be stressed, however, that much of what is described here as traditional continues today to be a major part of belief and practice, even among those who have been converted to Christianity for some generations.

Supernatural Powers and Spirit Beings. The traditional religions of Vanuatu, like religions universally, have as their identifying theme the cultural and social elaboration of people's ideas and emotions concerning the nature and locus of supernatural powers. Throughout the archipelago such powers, though mostly associated with various classes of spirit beings, are also commonly attributed to a wide range of "natural" phenomena, including humans, animals, birds, fish, plants, and stones. It is this diffuseness of supernatural power, together with its transferability, by means of ritual, from its various sources to human agents, that gives Vanuatu religions their distinctive character. The primary aim of Vanuatu religious practitioners is, through ritual, to gain direct control of extraordinary powers, rather than to supplicate spirit beings to act on their behalf. The ni-Vanuatu ("people of Vanuatu"), though deeply concerned with establishing and maintaining positive relations with the relevant power sources, cannot be said to worship such sources. Their religions, though replete with the powerful, the sacred, and the tabooed, are almost wholly devoid of deities, priests, and acts of worship.

As R. H. Codrington (1891, p. 123) long ago noted, the ni-Vanuatu recognize two classes of spirits, those who were once living people and those who were not. Though the former, which include both the ghosts of the dead and ancestral spirits, are everywhere the prime focus of ritual attention, it is the latter who figure most prominently in an elaborate body of mythological tales.

Mythology. A widespread feature of Vanuatu mythology is the representation of the leading figures as of two distinct kinds—on the one hand, the exclusively male beings whose personal names are often local variants of such well-known Polynesian gods as Tangaroa or Māui, and on the other, the sexually variable, though frequently female, beings whose personal names are of a purely indigenous kind. The Polynesian-type beings—such as Qat and his eleven Tangaro brothers in the Banks Islands; Takaro and his brothers or supporters on Maewo, north Raga, and Ambae; Tahar in the Small Islands; Takaru and Tokotaitai in Malo; Barkulkul (or variant) in south Raga and north Ambrim; Ambat, Hambat, Kabat, and so forth on Malekula; and a variety of local variants of Māui from Efate southward—are commonly associated with the sky, mountain peaks, treetops, volcanic fires, the sun and the moon, acts of a creative or originating kind, and the attainment of a satisfactory life after death. By contrast, the non-Polynesian-type beings—such as Sukwe or Marawa in the Banks; Gaviga in Maewo; Mwerambuto or Nggelevu in Ambae; Lehevhev (or variant) in Malekula and surrounding islands; Marrelul in south Raga; Bugliam in north Ambrim—are commonly associated with the underground, caves, mazes, snakes, spiders, rats, acts of a devouring or destructive kind, and the failure to attain a satisfactory afterlife.

Pig Sacrifices. Though both classes of mythological beings are often depicted as having transformative powers that are greatly in excess of those normally possessed by humans, they are only rarely the subject of ritual attention and are generally deemed to be of small consequence in human affairs. There is, however, one major exception: Throughout the northern and central islands there existed in the past, and still exists today in modified form in some of the northern islands, an elaborate institution that centers on the ceremonial slaughter of pigs, most especially tusked boars and hermaphrodites. Though this institution has important secular functions throughout the area, most notably in providing an elaborate social and political hierarchy, the key symbolic act, that of pig sacrifice, is nevertheless of deep religious significance. This is evident in two contexts, one of which relates the institution to the mythological beings and the other to the ancestral spirits. In mythology there is a widespread belief that there are two alternative fates that await the spirits of the recently dead: All those who have sacrificed at least one high-grade tusked boar are admitted to a pleasant abode presided over by the principal benign spirit; all others are excluded from this abode, usually through being devoured by the principal malignant spirit.

These mythic themes are, however, of relatively minor significance in accounting for the religious importance of the institution compared with the belief that the sacrificial act results in the transfer of ancestral power from the slaughtered animal to its human executioner. Through a complex cognitive and emotional process the killing of the pig has as its end result a further advancement in the spiritual progress of the sacrificer toward the attainment of full ancestral status. Men who have advanced to high rank through the slaughter of numerous tusked boars are regarded as having attained a spiritual condition not very far removed from that of the ancestors. Such men must eat and sleep alone because of the danger that their high spiritual condition poses for others, especially women and children.

Ancestral Spirits. Further evidence for the importance of the ancestral spirits, especially in the context of the sacrificial rites, can be found in the Ambrim practice of setting up carved tree-fern effigies of the dead. Also on Ambrim, as on Malekula, Epi, and as far south as Efate, the slit-gongs, which are used both at pig sacrifices and at funerary rites, stand upright on the ceremonial ground and are carved and painted so as to represent human forms. On the Small Islands, and most probably elsewhere also, the sounds that issue from the gongs are said to be the voices of the ancestral spirits. In the southern districts of Malekula, life-size effigies of the dead are made in which the head is formed from the deceased's skull. These effigies are kept for some generations in the men's clubhouse and, though not the focus of specific rituals, are nevertheless treated as being in some degree sacred.

On Ambae Island, where one finds none of the above iconographic representations of ancestral spirits, they are nevertheless regularly made small offerings of food in the hope that they will not cause their descendants any problems. Such offerings are usually made in a generalized way to any potentially troublesome spirits that may be lurking in the vicinity of the living. Occasionally, ghosts, as well as other varieties of spirit beings, are believed to befriend individual humans and to assist them by imparting magical knowledge.

Secret-Society Rites. In the period immediately prior to the spread of Christianity, there existed on many of the northern and central islands, though especially in such matrilineal areas as the Banks, Maewo, north Raga, and Ambae, a variety of more secret and voluntary cults that centered around the acquisition of highly dangerous powers of a predominantly destructive kind. Whereas the kinds of powers invoked through pig sacrifices derive from the benign ancestors and impart to practitioners a positive and highly esteemed form of sanctity, those invoked in the secret society rites derive either from malignant ghosts of the dead or from what may be described as the "dark" side of human spirituality. Prominent symbolic themes include representations of ghosts and sharks, usually in the form of masks and headdresses worn by members, and of such normally abhorrent and dangerous activities as incest, genital exposure, contact with menstrual blood, and sodomy. The powers generated in the context of these rites were primarily utilized by participants to create fear in others, and were hence closely associated both with warfare and sorcery. It is therefore no surprise that such rites mostly ceased to be practiced at about the same time that warfare was prohibited and sorcery came under increasing Christian and governmental attack.

Male Initiations. Though similar cultural themes figure in the ritual corpus of the more patrilineal areas of north Vanuatu (notably in Malekula, the Small Islands and Ambrim), in these communities they occur in the context of compulsory initiations into manhood rather than voluntary initiations into discreet secret societies. That the two institutions are closely related is evident in the common occurrence of shark symbolism, representations of threatening ghosts, long periods of seclusion, the importance of the phallus as a locus of power, and either real or symbolic ritual male homosexuality. But whereas the secret rites were deemed both dangerous and antisocial, the compulsory versions were, and in most communities still are, positively valued as generating a form of sanctity similar to that attained by pig sacrifices. Everywhere the key symbolic act is the removal of either part or all of the novice's foreskin and the subsequent wearing of a penis wrapper. Through such an act a boy takes his first step toward achieving spiritual maturity, a goal only fully attained when, after the slaughter of numerous additional tusked boars throughout his life, he finally succeeds, at death, in breaking his dependence on and identification with women. Needless to say, many men do not progress very far in their efforts to attain such a goal.

Women's Rites. The ritual life of women, though everywhere less elaborate than that of men, is nevertheless of importance in those relatively few areas about which there exists adequate knowledge. In some of the districts of Malekula there is a ritual association known as Lapas whose membership is restricted to women and which in many respects parallels the principal male ritual association, Nimangki. As in the latter, the women kill pigs, purchase sacred insignia, erect effigies of the dead, and are secluded for some days in a ceremonial house that may not be entered by nonmembers of the association, especially men. Furthermore, just as the men are believed to generate through their ritual actions a specifically male form of sanctity or holiness, so too are the women deemed to generate a specifically female sanctity. These two forms of sanctity, though both ultimately derived from the ancestral spirits, are nevertheless so entirely antipathetic to one another that they must be rigorously kept apart. Hence the pervasive importance of the sex dichotomy in the religious life of the people of Malekula, the Small Islands, and Ambrim.

Elsewhere (though most notably in the northern matrilineal islands of Maewo, north Raga, and east Ambae, where the sex dichotomy is a great deal less pervasive and important) the women, though the principal participants in and organizers of rites that are of primary concern to themselves, such as first menstruation or body tattooing, do not exclude the men from such activities. Likewise, the men, though again the key actors in the sacrificial rites of the graded society, encourage their womenfolk to kill an occasional pig and take supplementary titles. In west Ambae the women even participate as novices in the local versions of what are elsewhere exclusively male secret-society rituals.

SORCERY AND MAGIC. Various kinds of sorcery and magic are practiced throughout Vanuatu, though the former was, at least until recently, of special importance in Ambrim, while magic, rather than religion, seems to be the dominant ritual theme in some of the southern islands, notably Tanna. Indeed, in Tanna there are no major communal rites of the clearly religious kind that have been described for the northern islands. Even the male initiation rites, which, as in the north, focus on circumcision, seclusion, and the donning of penis wrappers, are seemingly of a more secular and ceremonial, rather than religious and ritual, character; the emphasis is primarily on individual status transition rather than on joint initiation into a secret male cult. However, ethnographic information concerning the traditional cultures of all the southern and central islands, including Tanna, is either fragmentary and unreliable or nonexistent. Since this applies most especially to their traditional magico-religious systems, the intention here is to not be too emphatic in thus relegating the religious component to a secondary position.

MOON WORSHIP. Such caution seems especially relevant in the case of Aneityum, where, in addition to the widespread practice of making offerings, usually of food, though sometimes also human sacrifices, to a variety of unnamed spirit beings (*natmas*), a more elaborate ritual of worship, including prayer, song, dance, and offerings of food and kava placed on wooden altars, was periodically performed in sacred groves dedicated to the moon. As on the neighboring islands of Aniwa and Futuna, the moon, who is known by the Polynesian name *Sina,* is represented in mythology as the wife of the sun. Unfortunately, little has been recorded of this mythology and even less of what seems to have been an important religious practice.

BIBLIOGRAPHY

Allen, Michael. *Male Cults and Secret Initiations in Melanesia.* Melbourne, 1967. Chapter 5 provides a summary of previously published ethnographic data on male initiations in the northern islands.

Allen, Michael, ed. *Vanuatu: Politics, Economics and Ritual in Island Melanesia.* Sydney, 1981. Fifteen articles written by professional anthropologists, twelve of them based on fieldwork carried out on eight islands during the 1960s and 1970s, with the remaining three providing comparative and theoretical overviews. Most articles contain data on both traditional and contemporary religions.

Capell, Arthur. "The Stratification of Afterworld Beliefs in the New Hebrides." *Folk-lore* 49 (1938): 51–85. A useful compendium of early accounts, mostly from missionary sources (some unpublished), of beliefs and myths concerning the afterworld and sky-dwelling spirit beings with Polynesian-type names. See also a later article by the same author on the same theme: "The Maui Myths in the New Hebrides," *Folklore* 71 (1960): 19–36.

Codrington, R. H. *The Melanesians: Studies in Their Anthropology and Folklore* (1891). Reprint, New Haven, Conn., 1957. An early classic written by an exceptionally knowledgeable and sympathetic missionary. This book still remains the primary source of information on the traditional religious beliefs and myths of the northern islands, especially the Banks.

Deacon, A. Bernard. *Malekula: A Vanishing People in the New Hebrides.* Edited by Camilla H. Wedgewood. London, 1934. An excellent early ethnography that still contains by far the most detailed and reliable information on the elaborate rituals and mythology of Malekula, especially in the Seniang district.

Guiart, Jean. *Société, rituels et mythes du nord Ambrym (Nouvelles Hébrides).* Paris, 1951. A useful ethnographic account, which should be read in conjunction with Patterson in Allen (1981).

Guiart, Jean. *Un siècle et demi de contacts culturels à Tanna, Nouvelles-Hébrides.* Paris, 1956. Still the only ethnographic monograph on the important island of Tanna, it should be read in conjunction with Brunton, Lindstrom, and Bastin in Allen (1981).

Lane, R. B. "The Melanesians of South Pentecost, New Hebrides." In *Gods, Ghosts and Men in Melanesia,* edited by Peter Lawrence and M. J. Meggitt, pp. 250–279. Melbourne, 1965. An excellent overview of the traditional religion of an isolated community on Raga (formerly south Pentecost) that was still predominantly pagan when Lane carried out his fieldwork.

Layard, John. *Stone Men of Malekula.* London, 1942. By far the best and most detailed extant account of a Vanuatu religion, based on fieldwork carried out in 1914 on Vao Island, off the northeast coast of Malekula.

Layard, John. "Identification with the Sacred Animal." *Eranos-Jahrbuch* 24 (1955): 341–406. A highly perceptive psychological analysis, from a Jungian perspective, of boar sacrifice on Malekula.

Rivers, W. H. R. *The History of Melanesian Society* (1914). 2 vols. Reprint, Oosterhout, 1968. A remarkable early attempt to carry out a comparative and historical analysis of the then extant body of ethnographic data on island Melanesia. Though the attempted historical reconstruction, which is mostly contained in volume 2, has been subjected to strong and generally well-merited criticism, the detailed ethnographic sections include valuable data on the magico-religious systems of the Banks and other more northerly Vanuatu islands.

New Sources

Hume, Lynne. "Church and Custom on Maewo, Vanuatu." *Oceania* 56, no. 4 (1986): 304–313.

Jolly, Margaret. "Sacred Spaces: Churches, Men's Houses and Households in South Pentecost, Vanuatu." In *Family and Gender in the Pacific: Domestic Contradictions and the Colonial Impact*, edited by Margaret Jolly and Martha Macintyre. Cambridge, Mass., 1989.

Lindstrom, Lamont. "Knowledge of Cargo, Knowledge of Cult: Truth and Power on Tanna, Vanuatu." In *Cargo Cults and Millenarian Movements: Transoceanic Comparisons of New Religious Movements*, edited by G. W. Trompf. Berlin, 1990.

Young, Michael W. "Kava and Christianity in Central Vanuatu: with an Appendix on the Ethnography of Kava Drinking in Nikaura, Epi." *Canberra Anthropology* 18, nos. 1–2 (1995): 62–96.

MICHAEL ALLEN (1987)
Revised Bibliography

VĀRĀNASĪ SEE BANARAS

VARDHAMĀNA MAHĀVĪRA SEE MAHĀVĪRA

VARṆA AND JĀTI.

The two separable but intertwined concepts of *varṇa* and *jāti* may be regarded as different levels of analysis of the Indian system of social structure called *caste.* While some scholars regard *varṇa* and *jāti* as reflecting quite separate dimensions of Indian social and religious thought, others insist, following the native traditions of Hinduism, that the two are inextricably linked. In any event, whereas the term *caste* is sometimes applied to social formations in places other than India, the terms *varṇa* and *jāti* are invariably applied exclusively to the Indian social (and religious) contexts.

The caste system has occasionally been regarded as so intrinsic, so enduring, and so distinctive to India and its long history that it is thought to be both the kernel of Indian culture and virtually identical to the definitional essence of Hinduism. While there are many different beliefs and practices associated with the Hindu religion, and while sectarian, regional, linguistic, and other variables make it difficult indeed to see any unifying features in that religion, it has been argued that the caste system and its attribution of hierarchical superiority to the *brahman* caste is one (and perhaps the only one) feature all (or at least the vast preponderance) Hindu traditions share. Although there are many problems in defining *Hinduism* as "the religion of caste" (not the least of which being that in India caste cuts across religious boundaries; there are Muslim, Sikh, Parsi, and Christian—as well as Hindu—castes), the fact that the two are sometimes equated indicates the importance, ubiquity, and deep roots of caste in Indian society and history.

The word *varṇa* means "color"—not, as was previously thought, to refer to "race" but rather in the sense of "characteristic" or "attribute." The best translation is probably "class." As applied to the realm of society, it refers to four social classes that epitomized Vedic (and Aryan) India: the *brahmans* or priests, the *kṣatriyas* (warriors and rulers), the *vaiśyas* (commoners; merchants and agriculturalists), and the *śūdras* (servants). These four classes, while separate in terms of function and given hierarchically different values, are also quite obviously interdependent. Taken together, they constitute a complete and well-ordered society according to a religiously and ideologically imbued indigenous social vision.

Evidence of such a division of society into four classes (ideologically, at least, if not in actuality) first appears in a cosmogonic hymn found in the earliest text of Indian history, the *Ṛgveda.* In that hymn, the entire universe is produced from the primordial sacrifice and dismemberment of a Cosmic Man, including the four classes of the social order: "When they divided the Cosmic Man, into how many parts did they apportion him? What do they call his mouth, his two arms, his thighs and feet? His mouth became the *brahman*; his arms were made into the *kṣatriya*; his thighs the *vaiśya*; and from his feet the *śūdras* were born" (*Ṛgveda* 10.90.11–12).

Here, then, is the much repeated and cited charter myth of an ideal Indian society. Each class is produced from the body part of the Cosmic Man that most resembles the supposed traits and assigned function of that class. From the mouth comes the *brahman* class, the priests charged with ritual functions and the oral preservation of sacred texts. From the arms, the source of physical strength and power, derive the *kṣatriya* warriors and rulers, and from the "thighs" (perhaps a euphemism for the genitals) arise the *vaiśya* commoners, who are charged with material wealth and fecundity. And from the feet, the lowest and most impure of the body parts but also the foundation upon which everything rests, come the *śūdras,* or servants.

In this system (as it was represented in the religious texts composed and preserved by the *brahmans*), the *brahmans* are invariably portrayed as hierarchically superior. They are created prior to others and therefore take precedence over others; they are created from the uppermost portion of the creator god and therefore are at the top of the social order; they are charged with (and indeed have a monopoly on) religious functions and are therefore the most pure, the most sacred, of the four classes. The *brahmans,* it is said, are also the most "complete," or the perfected instance of the human being. Indeed, some texts go much further and claim that members of this class are "human gods" (*manushya devas*): "There are two kinds of gods, for the gods are gods, and those *brahmans* who have studied and teach the Veda are human gods. . . .With oblations into the fire one pleases the gods, and with sacrificial fees one please the human gods" (*Śatapatha Brāhmaṇa* 2.2.2.6).

As such, the *brahmans* are sometimes said to represent the principle of "purity" in Indian social thinking. The supposed inherent characteristics and distinctive activities (the sacerdotal duties, but also practices such as nonviolence and vegetarianism) are thought to be the standard against which others are gauged. The other classes (and castes) are thus ranked into a hierarchical order of relative purity—to the extent they resemble the *brahman*, their status increases, while to the degree that they diverge from the *brahman* and the principle of purity their place in the system is diminished.

This elegant and orderly vision is complicated and compromised, however, by the high place of the second of the four *varṇas*, the *kṣatriyas*. Even in the religious texts, they are ranked only below the *brahman* priests, and it is possible, if not likely, that in actuality throughout Indian history (at least up until the time of the British Raj, when traditional political power was dispossessed) they took the highest places in the social order. The characteristics and duties of the *kṣatriyas*, however, are quite different from those of the *brahmans* (and the "purity" they supposedly embody). They control the worlds of politics and power, coercion and physicality. The functions of both rulership and the military are, ideally, monopolized by the class most suited to them, the *kṣatriyas*.

The high place of the *kṣatriya* in a hierarchy supposedly governed by relative resemblance to the *brahman* has sometimes been explained as the pragmatic insertion of a secular principle of "power" into a system otherwise organized according to religious "purity." Be that as it may, together, the two highest *varṇas* clearly constitute the "ruling classes" of the caste system. In the religious texts, the cooperation of the two is constantly emphasized for the proper ordering and operation of society (and, indeed, the cosmos as a whole). And in practical ways, bonds between the two highest *varṇas* are both symbolized and actualized in the important traditional (and symbiotic) relationship between the king and his court priest (the *purohita*).

The *vaiśya* class comprises all those engaged in the many professions other than, on the one hand, those of the priests and rulers and, on the other, those of the lowly servants. Farmers, traders, proprietors, bankers, herders—all these, and others involved in professions entailing wealth, increase, and productivity of all kinds, were classified as *vaiśyas*. Finally, at the base are the *śūdras* who, it is said, have but one duty to perform: to serve the others. While the *brahman, kṣatriya*, and *vaiśya varṇas* are designated the "twice-born" classes (because of the ritual "second birth" that boys from these classes undergo, which makes them eligible to study the sacred Veda), the *śūdras* are labeled "once-born" and are prohibited from studying (or even hearing) the Veda and from other religious prerogatives.

The relationship between the "classes" or *varṇas* and the "castes" or *jātis* (the latter term is related to the word for "birth," indicating that one is "born into" his or her caste) is a subject of scholarly debate among anthropologists and Indologists. For some, the terms are virtually interchangeable, and indeed the texts of the indigenous tradition often use the terms synonymously. Other scholars, also following the native traditions, see the *jātis* as historically deriving from intermixtures between members of an original four classes. Still others see the two as fundamentally different but nevertheless intellectually related, noting that the *varṇa* system forms the superstructure for the more complex system of *jātis*. The *varṇas*, under this conceptualization, are the "base categories" of social analysis, which can then generate any number of new, ranked social groupings, which may be termed *jātis*. Many anthropologists observe that while there are but four *varṇas* there are thousands of discrete *jātis* found "on the ground" in Indian society. For some of these observers, the *varṇas* are at best "theoretical," while it is the *jātis* that form the real social units of actual Indian society.

For many in Indian society, however, the *jāti* to which they belong is conceived of in terms of one or another of the classical *varṇas*. All *brahmans*, regardless of their identification as members of a wide variety of locally various, distinct, and endogamous *jātis*, claim membership in a pan-Indian and ancient *varṇa*, and the same is true with members of various *jātis* identifying themselves as *kṣatriyas, vaiśyas*, and *śūdras*. There are also large numbers of people assigned to *jātis* regarded by those of higher rank to be outside of or below the *varṇa* system altogether. These are what were once termed *untouchables* or, to use the preferred term of self-identification, the *dalit* castes.

In anthropological discourse, it is usually the *jātis* that are the referent of the term *caste*. Each *jāti* typically preserves a mythical account of its origins and a distinctive set of life-cycle rites observed by its members. Each is overseen by a local council that oversees and enforces a set of rules governing, among other things, acceptable occupation. It is, indeed, occupation that usually lends its name to the *jāti* (e.g., Barber, Potter, Leatherworker), although, especially outside the traditional rural areas, these caste labels no longer necessarily apply to the actual economic pursuits of individuals. While the indigenous tradition insists on ancient roots for these occupational assignments, some modern scholars have suggested that the castes of present-day India need not ever have been derived from ancient occupational associations that over time became hereditary and endogamous marriage groups.

Another definitive characteristic of the *jātis* is the set of rules governing marriage. A member of a particular caste is not to marry outside of that caste, and to disobey the rules of endogamy usually results in expulsion from the group. Those who are so punished become, literally, "outcastes." This practice reinforces the widely held belief that the multitude of *jātis* came into existence from the four original *varṇas* through an intricate series of mixed unions and subsequent expulsions.

Commensality, food exchange, and other transactions between castes are also highly regulated. Acceptance or nonacceptance of food (cooked in different ways or uncooked), grain, water, and leftovers play a large role in the relative placement of castes at the local level.

The *jātis*, like the *varṇas*, are organized hierarchically, although with many local variations. Often enough, these hierarchical placements are disputed and subject to constant renegotiation and jockeying for position. Research on the caste system has focused on the following areas: criteria for ranking, regional differences in ranking, ranking and social distance, local conflicts over rank order, strategies and circumstances of change in rank order, and the significance of hierarchy in Indian thought and society.

Essential to the traditional underpinnings of both the *varṇas* and the *jātis* is the belief in *karma* and rebirth. Birth into a particular class or caste was traditionally understood to be the result of *karma* created in the past, and thus any attempt or even inclination toward changing one's social situation in this life was severely discouraged. Caste was religiously ordained and legitimated in the concept of one's "own duty" or *svadharma.* And, as it is put in one of the sacred texts of the Hindu tradition, the *Bhagavadgītā,* "it is better to do one's own duty poorly than to do another person's duty well." If one performs his inborn caste duty well in this life, the promise is of a higher birth in the future.

The religious basis of the caste system is perhaps the principal reason for its endurance and pervasiveness in Indian history and society. The caste system can provide a modicum of stability, especially in times of political chaos or change. In the past there have, however, also been religious movements that have challenged, but never successfully undermined, the caste system. These include some of the cults within Hinduism itself, as well as certain elements within Buddhism, Sikhism, and some of the groups associated with the Neo-Hindu movement of the nineteenth and early twentieth centuries. And while the caste system endures in modern India, many forces are challenging its traditional pillars and especially the abuses that often have accompanied the system. The political rise of the *dalits,* the breakdown of traditional caste boundaries due to urbanization and modernization, reformational movements, and the general influx of democratic, secular and, to some extent, Western values into contemporary India have shaken, but not destroyed, this millennia-old institution.

SEE ALSO Priesthood, article on Hindu Priesthood; Rites of Passage, article on Hindu Rites; Untouchables, Religions of.

BIBLIOGRAPHY

For a comprehensive overview of the *varṇas* in ancient Indian texts, consult Brian K. Smith, *Classifying the Universe: The Ancient Indian Varna System and the Origins of Caste* (New York, 1994). For important and influential works on the caste system and its theoretical underpinnings, see A. M. Hocart, *Caste: A Comparative Study* (London, 1950); J. H. Hutton, *Caste in India* (London, 1963); Louis Dumont, *Homo Hierarchicus: An Essay on the Caste System,* translated by Mark Sainsbury (Chicago, 1970); Celestin Bougle, *Essays on the Caste System,* translated by David Pocock (Cambridge, UK, 1971); McKim Marriot, "Hindu Transactions: Diversity without Dualism," in *Transaction and Meaning: Directions in the Anthropology of Exchange and Symbolic Behavior,* edited by B. Kapferer, pp. 109–142 (Philadelphia, 1976); Gloria Raheja, *The Poison in the Gift: Ritual, Prestation, and the Dominant Caste in a North Indian Village* (Chicago, 1988); and Steven Parish, *Hierarchy and Its Discontents: Culture and the Politics of Consciousness in Caste Society* (Philadelphia, 1996).

BRIAN K. SMITH (2005)

VARUṆA replaced the earlier god Dyaus as the sky god in the Vedic pantheon, but early in his mythological career he became the god of the night sky; the myriad stars were his eyes and, still later, his spies. The importance of such a sky god seems to belong to the pastoral history of the nomadic Aryans. The Bogazköy inscription of the fourteenth century BCE mentions a Mitanni god, Uru-van-nas-sil, Varuṇa's prototype. Ouranos, Varuṇa's Greek parallel, was also a sky god.

With his thousand eyes, Varuṇa watched over human conduct, judging good and evil deeds and punishing evildoers. Varuṇa is the only god in the Vedic pantheon with such strong ethical bearings. The word used in the Vedas to refer to his eyes, *spaśa,* derived originally from the verbal root *spac* ("see"), later came to mean "spy." Still later, in the epics and the Purāṇas, the word underwent further linguistic evolution and became *pāśa* ("noose"); Varuṇa then ensnared the wicked in his noose.

Scholars have traced Varuṇa's name to various Indo-European roots such as *uer* ("bind"), *ver* ("speak"), *vṛ* ("cover"), *vār* ("shower"), as well as to noun stems like Lithuanian *weru* ("thread"). It is possible that these all contributed to the many layers of his mythological attributes.

Ahura Mazdā, the supreme god of the Avesta, is another parallel of the Vedic Varuṇa. In Vedic the Avestan name would be rendered *Asura Medhya* ("holy spirit"), and indeed the Vedas frequently refer to Varuṇa as an *asura.* In the Avesta, Mithra is closely related to Ahura Mazdā, just as the Vedic Mitra is related to Varuṇa. Mitra is the god of the daytime sky whose eye is the sun. Together Mitra and Varuṇa constitute the sky god and replace the earlier Dyaus. In the *Ṛgveda,* Varuṇa enjoyed sovereignty and supremacy for a brief period; he was frequently called *samrāj* ("emperor"), an epithet used only occasionally for Indra. The Rājasūya sacrifice, offered for attaining imperial grandeur, belongs to Varuṇa and Mitra; in the *Ṛgveda* Varuṇa is said to have performed this sacrifice, presumably with the intention of becoming the supreme god in the pantheon.

Because of his innumerable star-eyes, Varuṇa was regarded as omniscient. His knowledge and his function as a moral judge were the chief sources of his power, as he had no remarkable achievements to his credit. He watched over human beings: When two persons conversed, he was the invisible third; when anyone sinned, Varuṇa afflicted the transgressor with disease, and until the god relented, the victim would not be restored to health. In the solemn Varuṇapraghāsa rite, a seasonal sacrifice, the sacrificer's wife was required to confess her sin (i.e., conjugal infidelity) before the officiating priest. This is a unique instance of confession of sin in the early Vedic literature, and Varuṇa was the god associated with this sacrifice. The punishment he meted out in such cases was called a "seizure," hence the elaborate prayers to Varuṇa for forgiveness of sins.

In later literature Varuṇa's ethical role diminishes, but early texts frequently associate his majesty or supremacy with his function as upholder of the moral order referred to in the *Ṛgveda* as *ṛta* or, sometimes, *dharma* (i.e., "that which upholds") or *satya* ("truth"). In the Avesta this all-pervasive moral order that controls and regularly maintains the cosmic forces is *arata, aša, urta,* or *arta;* a cardinal concept in Zoroastrianism, it is first mentioned in the Tel-el-Amarna Tablet (c. fourteenth century BCE). *Ṛta* is Varuṇa's special domain, and it is often mentioned in connection with him.

Another concept associated with Varuṇa is the magical power known as *māyā;* for example, Asura's (i.e., Varuṇa's) *māyā.* In the Vedic context *māyā* meant both wisdom and power. With his *māyā* Varuṇa envelops the night and creates the dawn. *Māyā* predominantly links him with demons, for in later literature *asura* meant "demon," and demons wielded *māyā.*

Varuṇa's dark associations bring him close to the primarily chthonic gods such as Yama, Nirṛti, Soma, and Rudra. As a chthonic god, Varuṇa is associated with snakes (indeed, in Buddhist literature he is sometimes called the "king of snakes"), with barren black cows, or with deformed and ugly creatures. His ritual symbols are dark, depraved, and deformed things or creatures. His son Bhṛgu is said to have descended into hell. His connection with Vasistha, however, goes back to Indo-Iranian times: In the Avesta, Asha Vahishta (Vedic, Ṛta Vaśiṣṭha) is one of the Amesha Spentas who were Ahura Mazdā's active assistants. Varuṇa is Soma's brother. Of his wife, Varuṇani, nothing more than her name is known.

The dynamic character of Varuṇa's mythological career subsided in the later Vedic literature, where he is associated with the celestial waters. In the epics and Puranas, however, his domain shifted from the firmament toward the earth, and he became the overlord of the terrestrial waters, rivers, streams, and lakes, but primarily of the ocean. He dwelt in royal splendor in an underwater palace. Like Poseidon, Greek god of the ocean, he is often associated with horses. Finally, he is relegated to the position of "lord of the West," another dark and chthonic association. Here the circle of his mythological career closes, because as a *dikpāla* ("lord of a quarter [of the sky]") he is no more than a wholly passive god.

BIBLIOGRAPHY

Apte, V. M. "Varuṇa in the *Ṛgveda*." *New Indian Antiquary* (Bombay) 8 (1946):136–156. Deals with Varuṇa's Vedic background.

Bhattacharji, Sukumari. *Indian Theogony: A Comparative Study of Indian Mythology from the Vedas to the Puranas.* Cambridge and New York, 1970. See especially pages 22–47.

Dandekar, R. N. "Varuṇa, Vaśiṣṭha and Bhakti." In *Añjali: Papers on Indology and Buddhism, a Felicitation Volume Presented to Oliver Hector de Alwis Wijesekera on His Sixtieth Birthday,* edited by J. Tilakasiri, pp. 77–82. Peradeniya, Ceylon, 1970.

Dumézil, Georges. *Ouranos-Varuna.* Paris, 1934. A comprehensive treatise on Varuṇa and his Greek counterpart, Ouranos, and the traits they share.

Hiersche, Rolf, "Zur Etymologie des Götternamens Varuṇa." *Mitteilungen des Instituts für Orientforschung* (Berlin) 4 (1956): 359–363. Explores Varuṇa's identity from the various derivations of his name.

Kuiper, F. B. J. "The Bliss of Asa." *Indo-Iranian Journal* 8, no. 2 (1964): 96–129.

Lüders, Heinrich. *Varuṇa.* 2 vols: Vol. 1, *Varuṇa und die Wasser.* Vol. 2, *Varuṇa und das Rta.* Göttingen, 1951–1959.

Renou, Louis. "Varuna dans l'Atharvaveda." *Paideuma* 7 (1960): 300–306 (*Festgabe für Herman Lommel*).

Thieme, Paul. "Patañjali über Varuṇa und die sieben Ströme." In *Mélanges présentés à Georg Morgenstierne à l'occasion de son soixante-dixième anniversaire,* pp. 168–173. Wiesbaden, 1964.

Thieme, Paul. "Varuṇa in the Mahābhārata." In *Proceedings of the Twenty-Sixth Congress of Orientalists,* edited by R. N. Dandekar, vol. 3, p. 329. Poona, 1969.

SUKUMARI BHATTACHARJI (1987)

VASUBANDHU (fifth or fourth century CE) was an eminent Indian Buddhist teacher. Said to be a younger brother of the great Māhāyana teacher Asaṅga, Vasubandhu was first ordained in the Hīnayāna Sarvāstivada school but later converted to the Mahāyāna. Like his brother Asaṅga, Vasubandhu became a great exponent of the Yogācāra-Vijñānavāda teachings. He is believed to be the author of the *Abhidharmakośa* and many Māhāyana treatises.

Various problems continue to vex historians concerning the biography of Vasubandhu. The *Bosoupandou fashi zhuan* (Biography of Master Vasubandhu, T.D. no. 2049), translated—or rather, compiled—by Paramārtha (499–569), one of the main exponents of Yogācāra doctrine in China, is preserved in the Chinese Tripiṭaka and is the only complete biography. Apart from this, fragmentary information is found in various Chinese sources, the most important of which are the writings of the great Chinese translator Xuanzang (600–

664). Various histories of Buddhism written by Tibetan historians also give accounts of Vasubandhu's life. But Chinese and Tibetan sources alike disagree with the *Biography of Master Vasubandhu* (hereafter *Biography*) in many places. Moreover, two or three persons in Buddhist history bear the name *Vasubandhu:* According to some texts, a *Vasubandhu* is the twenty-first patriarch in the transmission of the Buddha's Dharma; elsewhere, Puguang (one of the direct disciples of Xuanzang) refers to an "ancient Vasubandhu" who belonged to the Sarvastivada school; and both Puguang and Yaśomitra, a commentator on the *Abhidharmakośa,* refer to a third, known as Sthavira-Vasubandhu. The identification of and relationship between these three persons is still unclear.

BIOGRAPHY. Vasubandhu's *Biography* can be divided into three sections. The first section is introductory. It begins with a legend of Puruṣapura (modern Peshawar), the native city of Vasubandhu, and then introduces his family: his father, the brahman Kauśika, and the latter's three sons, Asaṅga, Vasubandhu, and Viriñcivatsa. After a brief reference to Viriñcivatsa's life, an account is given of Asaṅga's life, including the famous story of his meeting with the *bodhisattva* Maitreya in the Tusita Heaven.

Vasubandhu's life comprises the second section. It begins by sketching the history of the Sarvāstivāda school in Kashmir and tells of the composition of the Abhidharma treatises and the great commentary on them, the *Mahāvibhāṣā,* there. Knowledge of the *Mahāvibhāṣā*'s contents was jealously kept secret from outsiders, the account alleges, but somehow it became known in Ayodhyā (near modern Faizābād), a city far removed from Kashmir. At the time, Vasubandhu was residing in Ayodhyā, then the capital of the Gupta dynasty. Vindhyavāsin, a Sāṃkhya teacher and a disciple of Vārṣaganya, came to Ayodhyā to challenge the Buddhists there to a debate while Vasubandhu and his colleague Manoratha were absent. Their fellow teacher Buddha-mitra thus had to meet the challenge alone, but because of his age he was defeated. This defeat deeply mortified Vasubandhu, who wrote a treatise, *Paramārthasaptatikā,* in order to confute Vindhyavāsin. It was after this that Vasubandhu composed his *magnum opus,* the *Abhidharmakośa* (hereafter *Kośa*), in six hundred verses (*kārikās*). The *Kośa* was an eloquent summary of the purport of the *Mahāvibhāṣā,* and it is reported that the Kashmiri Sarvāstivādins rejoiced to see in it all their doctrines so well propounded. Accordingly, they requested a prose commentary (*bhāṣya*), which Vasubandhu wrote. But the Kashmiris soon realized, to their great disappointment, that the work in fact *refuted* many Sarvāstivāda theories and upheld the doctrines of the Sautrāntika school. With the composition of the *Kośa,* however, Vasubandhu came to enjoy the patronage and favor of two Gupta rulers, Vikramāditya and his heir Bālāditya, who can be identified, respectively, as Skandagupta (r. about 455–467) and Narasiṃhagupta (r. about 467–473). Vasurāta, a grammarian and the husband of the younger sister of Bālāditya, challenged him to a debate but was defeated. Then Saṃghabhadra, a Sarvāstivada scholar from Kashmir, appeared to dispute the *Kośa.* He composed two treatises, one consisting of 10,000 verses and another of 120,000 verses. (According to Xuanzang's report, it took twelve years for Saṃghabhadra to finish the two works.) He challenged Vasubandhu to a debate, but Vasubandhu refused, saying, "I am already old, so I will let you say what you wish. Long ago, this work of mine destroyed the Vaibhāṣika (i.e., the Sarvāstivāda) doctrines. There is no need now of confronting you. . . . Wise men will know which of us is right and which is wrong."

The third section of the biography describes Vasubandhu's conversion to Mahāyāna Buddhism. According to this account, Vasubandhu, now proud of the fame he had acquired, clung faithfully to the Hīnayāna doctrine in which he was well versed and, having no faith in the Mahāyāna, denied that it was the teaching of the Buddha. His elder brother, Asaṅga, a Mahāyānist, feared that Vasubandhu would use his great intellectual gifts to undermine the Mahāyāna. By feigning illness he was able to summon his younger brother to Puruṣapura, where he lived. There Vasubandhu asked Asaṅga to explain the Mahāyāna teaching to him, whereupon he immediately realized the supremacy of Mahāyāna thought. After further study the depth of his realization came to equal that of his brother. Deeply ashamed of his former abuse of the Mahāyāna, Vasubandhu wished to cut out his tongue, but refrained from doing so when Asaṅga told him to use it for the cause of Mahāyāna. After Asaṅga's death, Vasubandhu composed commentaries on various Mahāyāna *sūtras,* including the *Avataṃsaka, Nirvāṇa, Saddharmapuṇḍarīka, Prajñāparamitā, Vimalakīrti,* and *Śrīmālādevī.* He himself composed a treatise (or treatises) on the "representation only" *(vijñaptimātra)* theory and commented on the *Mahāyānasaṃgraha, *Triratna-gotra, *Amṛta-mukha,* and other Mahāyāna treatises. He died in Ayodhyā at the age of eighty.

The *Biography* contains legendary or even mythical elements; the time sequence of events is ambiguous and differs greatly in places from the accounts in Xuanzang's *Xiyu ji.* For example, the *Biography* has Vasubandhu composing the *Kośa* at Ayodhyā and states that his conversion takes place at Puruṣapura; the *Xiyu ji* places the composition of the *Kośa* in the suburbs of Puruṣapura, and the conversion at Ayodhyā. According to the *Biography,* Vasubandhu's teacher was called Buddhamitra, who, it relates, was defeated in a debate by Vindhyavāsin. The *Xiyu ji,* however, never mentions Buddhamitra and names Manoratha as the teacher of Vasubandhu. In the *Biography,* Vasubandhu engages in his literary activity on behalf of the Mahāyāna after Asaṅga's death. Xuanzang, however, tells a strange story that suggests that Vasubandhu died before Asaṅga. Paramārtha and Xuanzang are the two most credible authorities for Vasubandhu's life, but serious discrepancies still exist between their accounts.

THE DATE OF VASUBANDHU. Vasubandhu's life has been variously dated at 900, 1,000, and 1,100 years after the Buddha's *nirvāṇa.* The figure 900 appears in the *Biography,* but elsewhere Paramartha is also said to have given another figure, 1,100. The figure 1,000 is found in Xuanzang's report, but the figure 900 seems also to have been adopted by his disciples. Various theories concerning the date have been offered by scholars. Noël Péri and Shiio Benkyō give as Vasubandhu's dates the years 270 to 350 CE. Ui Hakuju places him in the fourth century (320–400). Takakusu Junjirō and Kimura Taiken give 420 to 500, Wogihara Unrai gives 390 to 470, and Hikata Ryūshō gives 400 to 480, placing him in the fifth century.

In order to resolve these issues, Erich Frauwallner (1951) proposed a new theory whereby two Vasubandhus, Vasubandhu the elder and Vasubandhu the younger, are distinguished. The elder would be the younger brother of Asaṅga. It is his activity that, according to this theory, is described in the first and third sections of the *Biography* and may be dated at around 320 to 380. The younger would be the author of the *Kośa.* His activity constitutes the second section of the *Biography.* Since he was associated with the two Gupta rulers, he may be dated around 400 to 480. Frauwallner supposes that Paramārtha confused the two Vasubandhus and conflated them into a single person. This mistake, he maintains, was inherited by later historians, including Xuanzang.

Frauwallner's lucid and revolutionary theory has been endorsed by many scholars. But it does not seem to convince all. Especially doubtful is his treatment of early Chinese documents, many of which have been claimed by scholars to be spurious. Japanese scholars, who opposed the theory of dating in the fourth century by negating the evidence employed in its support, would reject Vasubandhu the elder for almost the same reasons. At any rate, Frauwallner's theory and the issues it raises remain a hypothesis.

LITERARY ACTIVITY. Vasubandhu is renowned as the author of one thousand works, five hundred in the Hīnayāna tradition and five hundred Mahāyāna treatises. However, only some forty-seven are extant, nine of which survive in the Sanskrit original, twenty-seven in Chinese translation, and thirty-three in Tibetan translation.

Among the independent expositions of Vasubandhu's own philosophy and doctrines, the *Abhidharmakośa* is the most voluminous. In the countries of "northern" Buddhism, including Tibet, it came to be regarded as a fundamental text to be studied by all students of the tradition. The *Karmasiddhi* (Demonstration of Karma) is a short, quasi-Hīnayāna treatise colored, as is the *Abhidharmakośa,* by Sautrāntika leanings. From the Yogācāra point of view the most important of Vasubandhu's works are the *Viṃśatikā* (Twenty verses), *Triṃśikā* (Thirty verses), and *Trisvabhāvanirdeśa* (Exposition on the three natures). Although these three texts are all very brief (and the last was totally unknown in China), they form a sort of trinity and represent Vasubandhu's final accomplishment as a Yogācāra-Vijñānavāda teacher. The *Triṃśikā* is especially important in that it became the basic text of the Faxiang (Jpn., Hossō) school. The *Foxing lun* (Treatise on Buddha nature), although thought to be apocryphal by not a few scholars, exerted great influence on Sino-Japanese Buddhism by advocating the concept of *tathāgata-garbha,* or Buddha nature. Vasubandhu's works also include books on logic, polemics, and other sciences.

Vasubandhu's commentaries on sūtras and *śāstras* are by no means less important than the above-mentioned independent treatises. He wrote commentaries on three treatises: the *Madhyāntavibhāga* (Discrimination between the middle and the extremes), *Mahāyānasūtrālaṃkāra* (Ornament of the Mahāyāna Sutras), and *Dharmadharmatāvibhāga* (also, *-vibhaṅga;* Discrimination between existence and essence). These three treatises are all ascribed to Asaṅga's teacher Maitreya and are therefore fundamental texts for the Yogācāra school. Vasabandhu also composed a commentary on Asaṅga's *Mahāyānasaṃgraha* (Compendium of Mahāyāna), the first systematic presentation of the Yogācāra-Vijñānavāda doctrines. His commentary (*upadeśa*) on the *Sukhāvatīvyūha Sūtra* is important in that it became a basic treatise of the Pure Land faith in China and Japan. The Indian Yogācāra-Vijñānavāda is represented in China by three schools, all of which developed around Vasubandhu's works. The first to appear, the Dilun school (established in the first half of the sixth century), took his commentary on the *Daśabhūmika Sūtra* as its central text. The second, the Shelun school, emerged in the second half of the same century organized around a Paramārtha's translation of the *Mahāyāna-saṃgraha.* The last to appear, the Faxiang school, founded by Xuanzang and his disciple Kuiji in the seventh century, took the *Triṃśikā* as its basic text.

With these works, Vasubandhu proved to be a highly influential Mahāyāna teacher. He is reverently called a *bodhisattva,* or even "the second Buddha," in various traditions from India to China. Vasubandhu brought to fruition doctrinal developments in the Mahāyāna, especially in the Yogācāra-Vijñānavāda tradition, that had been begun by Maitreya and Asaṅga and advanced by other unknown teachers. He thus marks a culmination in Buddhist history. Before him, his school concerned itself chiefly with Buddhist practice (hence the name *Yogācāra*); after him, it emphasized theoretical problems such as the analysis of consciousness (hence the name *Vijñānavāda*), so that various ontological, epistemological, and logical investigations became more and more conspicuous. Compared with Asaṅga, who was gifted as a religious leader, Vasubandhu seems more scholarly, abhidharmic, and theoretical.

SEE ALSO Asaṅga; Buddhism, article on Buddhism in India; Buddhism, Schools of, articles on Chinese Buddhism, Mahāyāna Buddhism; Maitreya; Yogācāra.

BIBLIOGRAPHY

A bibliography appended to Erich Frauwallner's *On the Date of the Buddhist Master of the Law, Vasubandhu* (Rome, 1951) is highly helpful in that it exhausts almost all discussions, hence almost all evidences, relevant to Vasubandhu's date.

After Frauwallner, there is no independent biographical study on Vasubandhu, except a paper by Hikata Ryūshō, "A Reconsideration on the Date of Vasubandhu," *Bulletin of the Faculty of the Kyushu University* 4 (1956): 53–74, which does not refer to Frauwallner and a criticism of Frauwallner's theory by Padmanabh S. Jaini, "On the Theory of Two Vasubandhus," *Bulletin of the School of Oriental and African Studies* 21 (1958): 48–53.

Vasubandhu's thought is the subject of numerous studies. Among the most useful are Louis de La Vallée Poussin's *Vijñaptimātratāsiddhi, la siddhi de Hiuan-tsang,* 2 vols. (Paris, 1928–1929); Sylvain Lévi's *Un système de philosophie bouddhique: Materiaux pour l'étude du système Vijñaptimātra* (Paris, 1932); and Yuki Reimon's *Seshin Yuishiki no kenkyū* (Tokyo, 1955–1956).

There have been several publications of English translations of the French translations of Vasubandhu's work. Among these are *Abhidharmakośabhasyam,* by Louis De La Vallée Poussin, English translation by Leo Pruden (Berkeley, Calif., 1988–1990), and *Karmasiddhiprakarana: The Treatise on Action.,* by E. Lamotte, English translation by Leo Pruden (Berkeley, Calif., 1988). Stefan Anacker's *Seven Works of Vasubandhu* (Delhi, 1984) includes translations of Vasubandhu's *Vādavidhī, Pañcaskandha-prakaraṇā, Karmasiddhi-prakaraṇa, Viṃśatika, Triṃśikā, Madhyāntavibhāgabhāṣya,* and *Trisvabhāvanirdeśa;* another important translation is Hermann Jacobi's *Triṃśikāvijñapti des Vasubandhu, mit bhāṣya des ācārya Sthiramati* (Stuttgart, 1932). Louis de La Vallée Poussin translated the most influential work of Abhidharma as *L'Abhidharmakośa de Vasubandhu,* 6 vols. (1923–1931; reprint, Brussels, 1971). My *Chūkan to yuishiki* (Tokyo, 1978) contains articles discussing some philosophical ideas of the Vijñānavāda; see also *Seshin ronshū* (Tokyo, 1976) by Kajiyama Yūichi, Aramaki Noritoshi, and me.

NAGAO GADJIN (1987 AND 2005)

VATICAN COUNCILS

This entry consists of the following articles:

VATICAN I
VATICAN II [FIRST EDITION]
VATICAN II [FURTHER CONSIDERATIONS]

VATICAN COUNCILS: VATICAN I

When Pius IX decided to convoke an ecumenical council, his purpose, clarified by advice solicited from various bishops whom he regarded as trustworthy, was to complete the work of reacting against naturalism and rationalism. He had been pursuing this goal since the beginning of his pontificate by endeavoring to establish Catholic life and thought once again on the solid foundation of divine revelation. As a result of suggestions from the bishops he had consulted, he added to this purpose, first, defining the true nature of the relation between church and state while taking into account the new situation produced by the French Revolution and its consequences and, second, adapting church law in ways made necessary by the profound changes that had taken place during the three centuries since the last ecumenical council.

PRELIMINARY DISCUSSIONS. Despite the reservations of some in the Curia Romana, which caused him to delay for two years, Pius IX was encouraged by prominent members of the episcopate to announce his intention of convoking a council; on July 29, 1868, he officially summoned all the bishops of Christendom to come to Rome by December 8, 1869, along with others who had the right to attend (especially the superiors general of the major religious orders). During the preliminary consultations a number of bishops had suggested taking advantage of the council to try to renew contacts with separated Christians. Two apostolic letters, dated September 8 and 13, 1868, invited the Eastern prelates not in communion with Rome, the Protestants, and the Anglicans in order that they might be able to take part in the council. But this clumsy approach was considered very insulting by those addressed and may be regarded, from an ecumenical viewpoint, as one of the most distressing examples of a lost opportunity.

In the Catholic world the announcement of the council almost immediately intensified the opposition between currents of thought that had been in confrontation for several years: Neo-Gallicans and liberal Catholics, on the one hand, and ultramontanes and opponents of modern freedoms, on the other. The choice of the consultors who were to prepare the drafts of the conciliar decrees—the group included sixty Romans and thirty-six from abroad, almost all of them known for their ultramontane and antiliberal views—disturbed those who had been hoping that the council would provide an opportunity for bishops from the outer reaches of the church to open up the church somewhat to modern aspirations and who thought they could discern a strategy at work: namely, to prepare for the council in secret, with no challenges raised by debate and with the curial viewpoint alone represented, and then to have the fathers accept without discussion a series of ready-made propositions.

The unfortunate "Correspondence from France" that was published on February 6, 1869, in *La civiltà cattolica,* the organ of the Jesuits in Rome, seemed to confirm this expectation by predicting a definition of papal infallibility by proclamation and thus without any possibility of restatement or discussion by the fathers. The reaction was especially intense in the Germanic countries. In particular, Ignaz von Döllinger, the well-known professor at the University of Munich, whose hostility toward the Curia had been on the increase for a number of years, published under the pen name *Janus* a violent and one-sided polemic against the overemphasis on papal primacy and Roman centralization. Polemical articles, though more moderate in tone, were also published in the newspapers of France, where liberal Catholics regarded as inopportune the definition of papal infallibility for which the ultramontanes were calling. The question of papal infallibility, which had not come up in the initial program for the council, suddenly became a major issue during the months preceding the opening of the council. A number of prominent bishops, such as Victor Deschamps, archbishop of Malines, and Henry Edward Manning, archbishop of Westminster, asked insistently that advantage be taken of the council for a solemn definition of this truth, since it was now being publicly challenged. On the other side, at their annual meeting in Fulda (September 1869), the majority of the German bishops discreetly expressed clear-cut reservations with regard to such a definition.

Though unmoved by such theological discussions, a number of European governments did become apprehensive about possible conciliar decrees on civil marriage, the place of religion in public education, and the legitimacy of freedom of worship and the press. Such apprehensions could only be intensified by the desire that many bishops and some Catholic newspapers expressed, namely that the *Syllabus of Errors* (1864) be made the basis for the council's deliberations, a desire that seems to have been welcome in Rome. All those in the church who feared the triumph of the ultramontane party at the council did what they could to intensify this governmental mistrust in the hope of procuring diplomatic warnings and cautions. At one point, France considered appointing a special ambassador to the council, as it had at the time of the Council of Trent, while Prince von Hohenlohe, chancellor of Bavaria, attempted to have the European governments take joint steps. In the end, these governments chose to limit themselves to an attitude of distrustful expectation.

Conciliar Debates. The council opened on December 8, 1869, in the presence of about 700 bishops, about two-thirds of those with the right to attend. Among them were 70 prelates of the Eastern rite who were in union with Rome, most of these being from the Middle East, and almost 200 fathers from non-European countries: 121 from the Americas (49 from the United States), 41 from Southern Asia and the Far East, 11 from Oceania, and 9 from the African missions, which were then in their infancy. One must remember that while the prelates from other parts of the world made up a third of the gathering, many of them were actually from Europe (the missionaries in particular) and that there was as yet no native bishop in Asia or Africa. This predominantly European gathering was also predominantly Latin. There was indeed a sizable English-speaking group (in which those of Irish origin were predominant) and about 75 Germans and Austrians. Spaniards and Latin Americans numbered barely one hundred; the French made up 17 percent of the gathering (the majority of the missionaries of that time were from France), and the Italians over 35 percent. In addition, two-thirds of the consultors, or experts, and all of the secretaries of the commissions were Italians, as were the five presidents of the council; of the primary leadership offices, only that of secretary general was not occupied by an Italian, namely, the Austrian Joseph Fessler.

The first three sessions of the council were spent on the election of the commissions. The most important of these was the doctrinal commission (*Deputatio fidei*), from which all bishops suspected of being opposed to a definition of papal infallibility were excluded by the maneuvering of a pressure group of which Archbishop Manning was one of the main leaders. This maneuver, which many wrongly believed was ordered by the Curia, was a serious mistake for two reasons: first, it gave the impression that the elections were only a front, with the result that fathers in various groups now began to have doubts about the freedom of the council; and, second, it prevented a possible dialogue that might have reconciled the two opposing viewpoints.

On December 28 the council began at last to examine the first drafted constitution, which was directed "against the numerous errors deriving from modern rationalism." This draft, which was the work of the Jesuits Johannes Baptist Franzelin and Clemens Schrader, drew strong criticism because of its substance, which some found to be out of touch with contemporary forms of rationalism and too apodictic on points freely discussed among theologians, and especially because of its form, which was judged to be overly polemical and insufficiently inspired by pastoral concerns. After six meetings for discussion, which had the advantage of showing that the council would be freer than some had feared, the presidents announced on January 10 that the draft would be sent back to the commission for recasting and that meanwhile the council would tackle the drafts on church discipline. In this area twenty-eight drafts had been prepared that were rather tame and showed hardly any pastoral openness to the future; to these were added eighteen others, much superior in character, on the adaptation of canon law to the new circumstances of the religious orders and congregations. The discussion of the first four drafts that were distributed quickly got bogged down in details, especially since the time available to the speakers was unlimited. As a result, in order to speed up the pace of the work (as the great majority of the fathers wanted), the pope, on February 20, 1870, amended the regulations that had been distributed at the opening of the council. By and large, the modifications were to the good, but some fathers, who had already resented having a set of regulations imposed on them from above, saw in these modifications a new threat to full freedom of discussion.

While the examination of texts that had little chance of proving explosive was advancing with prudent caution in the council hall, the attention of both the fathers and the public was increasingly focused on the question of infallibility. Raised again by a clumsy statement of Bishop Felix Dupanloup in November 1869, the question soon led the fathers, who had initially tended to group together along national and linguistic lines, to form new groups that were inspired by ideological considerations.

On the one side, many fathers who were very hostile to their contemporaries' infatuation with liberalism were not at all reluctant to have the council restate the principles according to which, in classical teaching, the relations between church and state should be ruled in an ideal Christian society. Many—often the same— wanted a solemn definition of the personal infallibility of the pope. Even though they did not approve of all the centralizing steps taken by the Curia, they were convinced that the Gallican and Febronian theses, which tended to diminish the primacy of the pope in favor of the episcopate, were simply a departure from the ancient tradition to which, as they saw it, witness was given by certain scriptural texts (esp. *Mt.* 16:18), certain patristic formulas (e.g., the maxim "Rome has spoken, the question is closed"), and the whole body of great scholastic doctors from Thomas Aquinas to Roberto Bellarmino and Alphonsus Liguori. Those fathers met the historical difficulties of their adversaries with an appeal to the living faith of the church and were especially impressed by the almost universal acceptance, in the church of their time, of the thesis of the pope's personal infallibility, a thesis repeated on a number of occasions during the preceding twenty years by many provincial or regional councils. Reasons of a nontheological kind strengthened many of these prelates in their conviction: their veneration of Pius IX; their belief that an increased emphasis on the monolithic character of the Roman church could only draw to this church various non-Catholics who were distressed by the hesitancies and lack of resoluteness of the churches separated from Rome or by the contradictions of philosophical systems (Manning, a convert, laid great stress on this point); their concern to lend as much weight as possible to the principle of authority in a world weakened by aspirations toward democracy, a type of government they regarded as a mitigated form of revolutionary anarchy; and their desire, in the face of the religious crisis they saw growing before their eyes, to give an increasingly centralized form to the defensive and offensive strategy of the church.

A comparable mixture of doctrinal considerations and nontheological motives inspired other prelates to think that such projects would overthrow the traditional constitution of the church and might well threaten the most legitimate aspirations of civil society. Some bishops remained very attached to a conception of the ecclesiastical magisterium according to which the pope can never decide a point of doctrine independently from ratification by the body of bishops. More widespread seems to have been the concern to safeguard the second element in the divinely appointed structure of the hierarchy; to many of the fathers the proposed definition of papal infallibility seemed part of a program aimed at practically destroying the episcopate. In addition, the way in which the question of infallibility was presented in the most prominent ultramontane newspapers could only confirm in their views those who were convinced that "the intention was to declare the pope infallible in matters of faith in order thereby to make people think him infallible in other matters as well" (Leroy-Beaulieu), that is, in matters more or less related to the political order. But surely it was to be expected that the governments would not permit a development along these lines without reacting to it, to the great detriment of the local churches.

Over and above immediate tactical considerations there was a question of principle that greatly disturbed all those who believed that the future in the political realm belonged to liberal institutions and that the church had everything to lose by standing forth as the champion of autocratic authoritarianism. There were also concerns of an ecumenical kind: the proposed definition would render even more difficult any rapprochement with Eastern Christians; it would intensify the militant hostility of some Protestant groups; it might even lead to a new schism in German intellectual circles, which had been deeply impressed by Döllinger's campaign. Those who declared their opposition to the definition were less numerous than those in favor of it—thus the designation of them as the "minority"—but the most prominent among them enjoyed great authority by reason either of their theological competence or of the important sees they occupied: the entire Austro-Hungarian episcopate under the leadership of Cardinal Othmar Rauscher, a renowned patrologist and strong defender of the rights of the Holy See against Josephist, or liberal, claims; all the major sees of Germany; a sizable number of French prelates, including the archbishops of Paris and Lyons; several archbishops of North America; the archbishop of Milan, the most populous of the Italian dioceses; and three Eastern patriarchs.

The two groups had an opportunity to count heads as early as January. The infallibilist pressure group, again acting independently (but in close contact with the Jesuits of *La civiltà cattolica*), circulated a petition asking the pope to put on the assembly's agenda a draft definition of papal infallibility, which the preparatory commission had preferred not to offer on its own initiative. The petition finally collected 450 signatures, and, despite a counterpetition signed by 140 bishops, Pius IX decided on March 1 to include the desired passage in the draft of the constitution on the church that had been distributed to the fathers some weeks earlier on January 21.

The minority, now deeply disturbed, busied itself organizing the resistance that had until then been scattered and unfocused. The real center of this opposition was a young layman, John Acton, who as a historian shared the prejudices of his master, Döllinger, against the dogma and who feared even more the indirect effects of the definition on the future chances of Catholicism in a society increasingly based on the idea of freedom. Conzemius's publication of the Acton-Döllinger correspondence (3 vols., Munich, 1963–1971) has made fully clear the important role, unsuspected until now, that Acton played in organizing the conciliar minority.

The leaders of the minority did not limit themselves to making personal appeals to fathers they hoped they could win to their side. Convinced as they were of the deadly effects on the church of the definition now being readied and of the legitimacy of taking all effective means to stop it, a number of them thought it necessary to rouse public opinion and so bring outside pressure to bear on the authorities of the council. Several of these fathers even tried to win governmental support, especially at Paris, because they knew how influential any mediation by Napoleon III would be, since his military and diplomatic support was indispensable in preserving what was left of the pope's temporal power.

CONCILIAR CONSTITUTIONS. Amid the growing restlessness outside the council in the salons, newspapers, and chancelleries, the assembly itself was going ahead with its work. The draft of the constitution against rationalism, which had been recast by bishops Martin, Deschamps, and Pie with the help of the Jesuit Joseph Kleutgen, came before the council again on March 18. The new version was favorably received by the fathers, and any discussion was now concerned only with individual points or improvements of details. On April 24 the council unanimously gave its solemn approval to its first dogmatic document, the constitution *Dei filius*, which responded to pantheism, materialism, and modern rationalism with a substantial exposition of Catholic teaching on God, revelation, and faith; this exposition was to be for almost a century the basis of the treatises which made up fundamental theology.

Chapter 1 condemns pantheist views and briefly sets forth Catholic teaching on providence. Chapter 2 defines, against atheism and traditionalism, the possibility of knowing the existence of God with certainty by the natural light of reason and, against deism, the absolute necessity of revelation if man is to have knowledge of the supernatural order. Chapter 3 defines the reasonableness of the act of faith as against the illuminism of some Protestants and against those who deny the value of the external motives of credibility, such as miracles. It states that faith is both a free assent and a gift of grace and reaffirms the obligation of believing all the truths the ordinary ecclesiastical magisterium proclaims to have been revealed. It asserts that the church, which proposes the truths to be believed, at the same time carries within itself the guarantee of its own divine origin and that with his grace God confirms believers in their faith. Chapter 4 explains the relations that should exist between faith and reason, science and revelation: there are mysteries that cannot be demonstrated by reason, but reason can legitimately reflect on supernatural truths. While claiming a proper freedom for science, the council warns against abuses of this freedom. Finally, it explains what true dogmatic development is and condemns systems according to which philosophy may give new and more perfect meanings to revealed dogmas.

It quickly became clear that, given the pace at which work was proceeding, the constitution on the church, the text of which had been distributed to the fathers on January 21, would not come up for discussion for several months; this was even more true of its eleventh chapter, which dealt with the special prerogatives of the pope. Consequently, as early as March, new petitions requested that this chapter, which made the council restive, be discussed out of its proper order as soon as the examination of the constitution against rationalism was concluded. Despite the reservations of three of the five presidents of the council, Pius IX, who was increasingly displeased at the opposition of the minority group, decided to alter the schedule. In order to avoid the anomaly of treating this chapter before the others, it was expanded into a short, independent constitution devoted entirely to the pope.

The general debate on the text as a whole began on May 13 but was reduced from the outset to a discussion of the opportuneness of the definition; at times the discussion was impassioned. After some fifteen meetings, the fathers went on to examine the details of the texts; this discussion focused essentially on the chapter devoted to the definition of papal infallibility. The proposed text, although the commission had already improved it by comparison with the original draft, did not yet take sufficient account of the legitimate role that belonged to the episcopate, alongside and in collaboration with the pope, in the supreme teaching office of the church. Fifty-seven speakers took the floor, emphasizing theological arguments or historical difficulties, as well as the practical advantages or drawbacks of a definition in the circumstances of that time. These debates, though often tedious, at least gave an opportunity to qualify certain expressions and led to the elimination of some opposition.

Meanwhile, the behind-the-scenes lobbying intensified. For, apart from the zealots of the majority and the partisans of unyielding resistance, the great majority of the fathers were men of moderation who were deeply grieved and troubled by all the agitation. Far from desiring to see their opponents crushed, they wanted only to find a compromise formula that would keep the divisions within the assembly from becoming public. This was especially true of the Italians, as Michele Maccarrone has clearly shown. By reason of their numbers these men, who had played no part in the initial steps taken to introduce the famous question, were a decisive bulwark of the informal "third party" that had been taking shape since the beginning and was finally able to win the day against the neo-ultramontane and anticurialist extremists.

There is reason for thinking that a much larger section of the minority would have finally accepted the nuanced solution that was gradually worked out if Pius IX had not been so intransigent. For recent research has also shown, with the help of previously unstudied documents, that the pope several times directly intervened on the side of the majority extremists as the discussion became protracted. Whatever the personal responsibility of Pius IX may have been, it is a fact that last-minute efforts to rally the opponents through small concessions proved fruitless, despite the good impression made by the recapitulatory explanation given by Bishop Gasser in the name of the theological commission (this authoritative commentary is of key importance for a grasp of the nuances of the conciliar text). When a final appeal of the minority to Pius IX had no result, some sixty bishops decided to leave Rome before the final vote in order not to have to cast a negative vote in the presence of the pope on a question that directly concerned him. The other members of the minority judged that the successive improvements of the text as well as Bishop Gasser's commentary had removed the principal substantive objections and they decided therefore to approve the final text. This text was solemnly accepted on July 18 by nearly everyone present.

Officially entitled First Constitution on the Church of Christ, the constitution *Pastor aeternus* expounds Catholic teaching on the privileges of the pope. After a lengthy introduction on the institution of the church by Christ and on the place therein of papal primacy as the foundation of the church's unity, chapter 1 asserts, against some Gallicans and Febronians, that Peter received directly from Christ, and not through the church, a primacy of jurisdiction over the entire church. Chapter 2 states that by Christ's will this primacy is to be continued perpetually in the successors of Peter, the bishops of Rome. Chapter 3 solemnly defines the nature of the pope's primacy: the pope has an ordinary, immediate, "episcopal" jurisdiction not only in questions of faith but also in matters of church discipline, and this authority, which does not depend on approval by an ecumenical council, is to be exercised over pastors as well as the faithful. The concern to provide explicit safeguards for the authority of the bishops is at the root of the third paragraph, the main point of which is that bishops govern their flocks as "true pastors" and are therefore not mere delegates of the pope.

The fourth chapter declares that authority as supreme teacher is included in the primacy and then recalls how over the course of time the popes had always exercised this function by drawing upon the faith of the universal church as expressed in particular by the teaching of the bishops. The chapter then goes on to define solemnly that this supreme teaching office has attached to it the prerogative of infallibility, provided the pope is speaking *ex cathedra*, that is, provided that "in exercising his office as teacher and shepherd of all Christians he defines, in virtue of his supreme apostolic authority" (that is, with the intention of unequivocally putting an end to all discussion) "that a doctrine concerning faith or morals must be held by the universal Church; such definitions are irreformable of themselves and do not require ratification by the episcopate (*ex sese non autem ex consensu Ecclesiae*)." This final formula is a bit ambiguous, for, according to the commentary given by Bishop Gasser in the name of the doctrinal commission, while the words reject the *consensus Ecclesiae* as the source of papal infallibility, they do not mean to deny that the pope, as spokesman for tradition, must remain in constant close contact with the "mind of the Church" (*sensus Ecclesiae*) in the exercise of his ministry.

After the vote taken on July 18 the council continued its work for two more months, but at a slower pace, since the majority of the fathers had left Rome for the summer. The occupation of Rome by the Italians on September 20 brought the work to a definitive end, and on October 20 the pope announced that the council was adjourned indefinitely.

The termination of the debates did not immediately bring a calm to all hearts. The agitation continued for some time, and there were sad apostasies, especially in the Germanic countries where the Old Catholic schism developed around some university professors who appealed to Döllinger's writings. Among the bishops of the minority a few, Hefele and Strossmayer among them, wavered for several months, but in the end none of them refused to accept the new dogma.

When the immediate results of the council were compared with its ambitious program (fifty-one drafts had still to be voted on) and especially with the great hopes the convocation of the council had raised, the First Vatican Council seemed to many to have been a failure, its principal outcome having been to aggravate the disunity among Christians. With the passage of time, however, people became aware of important results flowing from the intense intellectual ferment the convocation of the council had produced. The work done by the commissions which dealt with the improvement of church law was not wasted, nor were the many suggestions sent in writing by those at a distance. Extensive use was to be made of these materials in the encyclicals of Leo XIII and especially in the revision of the Code of Canon Law under Pius X. The first dogmatic constitution that had been passed in April 1870 exercised a clarifying influence on subsequent theological teaching, especially in the burning question of the relations between reason and faith. On the other hand, it also strengthened the tendency to enlarge the role of authoritative doctrinal interventions in the development of Catholic thought; this tendency was strengthened even more by the definition of papal infallibility.

While the solemn approbation given to the ultramontane movement, which continued to develop for another half century, did not bring about the revolution in church government that some opponents had anticipated, it did nonetheless lead to more numerous direct interventions of the Holy See in the dioceses and to an emphasis on Roman centralization. At the same time, however, it must be recognized that by defining very strictly the rare cases in which the privilege of papal infallibility comes into play, the council ruled out the exaggerated ideas that were beginning to spread abroad before 1870 under the influence of bishops like Manning and journalists like Veuillot. In the final analysis, the nuanced character of the definition, which was the result of impassioned discussion and satisfied the legitimate demands of many minority bishops, was the best safeguard against the excesses of what has been called "neo-ultramontanism," a fashion of excessive devotion, more sentimental than theological, to the pope.

SEE ALSO Döllinger, Johann; Gallicanism; Modernism, article on Christian Modernism; Pius IX; Ultramontanism.

BIBLIOGRAPHY

The main documents that inform us of the preparation and course of the council have been published in volumes 49–53 of the *S. Conciliorum nova et amplissima collectio* (Arnhem, 1923–1927). The two most detailed histories of the council are tendentious: Johann Friedrich's *Geschichte des vatikanischen Konzils*, 3 vols. (Bonn, 1877–1887), is excessively critical from an Old Catholic point of view; Theodor Granderath's

Geschichte des vatikanischen Konzils, 3 vols. (Freiburg, 1903–1906), is a systematic defense by a Jesuit who refuses to allow any legitimacy to the reservations of the minority. Good presentations are Edward Cuthbert Butler's *The Vatican Council*, 2d ed., 2 vols. (London, 1965), and Michele Maccarrone's *Il Concilio Vaticano I*, "Italia Sacra," vols. 7 and 8 (Padua, 1966). A shorter presentation is my *Vatican I* (Paris, 1964).

Worthy of special mention among the studies of the national episcopates are James Hennesey's *The First Council of the Vatican: The American Experience* (New York, 1963); Frederick J. Cwiekowski's *The English Bishops and the First Vatican Council* (Louvain, 1971); Klaus Schatz's *Kirchenbild und päpstliche Unfehlbarkeit bei den deutschsprachigen Minoritätsbischöfen auf dem I. Vatikanum* (Rome, 1975); and Constantin Patelos's *Vatican I et les évêques uniates* (Brussels, 1982). Doctrinal commentaries on the constitution *Dei filius* include Alfred Vacant's *Études théologiques sur les constitutions du Concile du Vatican d'après les actes du concile*, 2 vols. (Paris, 1895), and on the constitution *Pastor aeternus*, Gustave Thils's *La primauté pontificale* (Gembloux, France, 1972), and the same author's *L'in-faillibilité pontificale* (Gembloux, France, 1969). August B. Hasler's *Pius IX (1846–1878), päpstliche Unfehlbarkeit und 1. vatika-nisches Konzil*, 2 vols. (Stuttgart, 1977), raises real questions but is spoiled by a lack of historical criticism. See also Giacomo Martina's "Pio IX e il Vaticano I, di A. B. Hasler, rilievi critici," in *Archivum historiae pontificiae* 16 (1978): 341–369, and Joseph Hoffmann's "Histoire et dogme: la definition de l'infaillibilité pontificale à Vatican I," in *Revue des sciences philosophiques et théologiques* 62 (1978): 543–557 and 63 (1979): 61–82. A very complete analytical and critical bibliography is J. Goñi Gastambide's "Estudios sobre el Vaticano I," *Salman-ticensia* 19 (1972): 145–203, 381–449.

New Sources

Bermejo, Luis M. *Infallibility on Trial: Church, Conciliarity and Communion.* Westminster, Md., 1992.

Costigan, Richard F. "The Consensus of the Church: Differing Classic Views." *Theological Studies* 51 (March 1990): 25–49.

O'Gara, Margaret. *Triumph in Defeat: Infallibility, Vatican I, and the French Minority Bishops.* Washington, D.C., 1988.

Pottmeyer, Hermann Josef. *Toward a Papacy in Communion: Perspectives from Vatican Councils I and II.* Translated by Matthew J. O'Connell. New York, 1998.

Thils, Gustave. *Primaute et Infallibilite du Pontife Romain a Vatican I et Autre Etudes d'Ecclesiologie.* Leuven, 1989.

Thompson, Daniel Speed. *The Language of Dissent: Edward Schillebeeckx on the Crisis of Authority in the Catholic Church.* Notre Dame, Ill., 2003.

ROGER AUBERT (1987)
Translated from French by Matthew J. O'Connell
Revised Bibliography

VATICAN COUNCILS: VATICAN II [FIRST EDITION]

The idea of holding a church council, which can be attributed to Pius XI and Pius XII, four hundred years after the Council of Trent and one hundred years after the First Vatican Council, as well as the realization of this idea, must be seen in historical perspective. The principal formative influence on the life of the Roman Catholic church until the Second Vatican Council, besides the impact of the institutional and doctrinal differentiation of Christian churches resulting from the Reformation, was the Council of Trent (1545–1563), especially through its decisions on faith and morals. Although the First Vatican Council, through its definition of the universal jurisdictional primacy and infallibility of the pope, had expanded to some extent the decisions made at Trent, it did so without addressing the question of the relationship of primacy and episcopacy. The problem of conformity between proclamation of the faith and pastoral care was not considered, nor were the altered circumstances resulting from industrialization. On the one hand, the French Revolution and secularization had shaken the foundations of radical episcopalism evidenced in such national movements as Gallicanism, Josephism, and Fabronianism, but on the other hand, an extreme papalism (or rather curialism) was no longer possible after the dissolution of the Papal States.

The way was clear, however, for new forms of thinking about and actualizing the church and its relationship to the world. Before discussing the conduct of the Second Vatican Council itself, we shall examine these tendencies briefly.

THE CHURCH BEFORE THE COUNCIL. The liturgical movement, whose roots go back to the time of the Reformation, reached a peak of activity in the twentieth century. The movement sought to revive liturgical forms in order to create the church anew by means of daily participation in the objective events of liturgy and the mysteries of the church. Connected with this was a new valuation of sacramentality and of the proclamation of the word (for example, in kerygmatic theology, that is, pastoral theology, culminating in the development of a new practical theology). The liturgical movement found magisterial support in the encyclical *Mediator Dei* (1947) of Pius XII.

Paralleling the liturgical movement was the biblical movement, which rediscovered the immediate religious meaning of holy scripture by means of new translations into vernacular languages and the formation of Catholic Bible associations. The Bible was studied according to the norms of modern scholarship and the canons of scientific exegesis. The epoch-making encyclical *Divino afflante Spiritu* (1943) of Pius XII removed the prevailing ecclesiastical obstacles to a truly critical study of the Bible.

The involvement of the laity in the ministry of the church also changed. Catholic Action was founded in 1923. Laypeople were becoming conscious of their responsibilities and rights in the church. Manuals on doctrine and moral theology written especially for lay-people appeared, culminating in Yves Congar's *Lay People in the Church* (rev. ed.; Westminister, Md., 1965).

The church's consciousness of itself changed. This was primarily a matter of the dissolution of the one-sided canonical understanding of the church as juridical, an understanding that had been set forth in the late Middle Ages and was firmly established once and for all by the Code of Canon Law (1917). The change was signaled in 1922 by Romano Guardini, who declared the "awakening of the church in souls," and was confirmed in 1943 by the understanding of the church as the mystical body of Christ set forth in Pius XII's encyclical *Mystici corporis,* which, however, still identified the church with the official hierarchical Roman church. The change culminated in ecclesiological projects during and after World War II that engendered an understanding of the church as people of faith subject to the Word.

The ecumenical movements, which since the beginning of the twentieth century had brought together and united the non-Catholic Christian church communities through world church conferences and the founding of the World Council of Churches, stood distanced for a long time from the Roman Catholic church. The opening of the Roman offices for ecumenism by John XXIII was made possible by contacts and conversations between Protestant and Catholic theologians and church leaders that took place for mutual defense against antiecclesiastical totalitarianism. These contacts were expanded after the founding of a Catholic ecumenical board in Fribourg, Switzerland, in 1951. The question of the reunification of all Christians appealed to parts of Catholic Christendom and exercised a great influence on theological reflection about the church's unity in diversity and its understanding of ministry, eucharist, and primacy.

Another important tendency in the Roman Catholic church before the calling of the council involved changes in theology itself. Certain theological efforts and approaches went beyond basic or scholastic theology and carried on a dialogue with the consciousness of the times and with the theologians of the separated Christian churches. The most important stages were attempts to overcome through kerygmatic theology the objectivistic and unhistorical or superhistorical point of view of neoscholasticism; "nouvelle théologie," which emphasized open thinking and opposed scholasticism; transcendental theology, which reflected on the conditions of the possibilities of man; the acquisition of a genuinely theological understanding of history in hermeneutical theology; and finally the inclusion of the societal dimension in political theology. These positions gained more and more significance with regard to the church's self-understanding and its relationship to the world. It became a church that no longer defined itself in the triumphalist terms of the Counter-Reformation but understood itself as a pilgrim church waiting for its eschatological completion.

The inner transformation of the church corresponded to a new orientation in the relationship of the church to the world. Integralism, the world viewed simply as material for the activity and self-preservation of the church, and esotericism, the world as irrelevant for salvation, prompting flight from it, needed new alternatives. Here especially the theology of earthly realities (Gustave Thils), the theology of the world, and the various projects in moral theology or ethics were preparatory for a new outlook. The true relationship of the Christian and of the church to the world lies between integralism and esotericism. And this middle ground must not be understood as a cheap compromise necessitated by circumstances, a compromise possible only because, unfortunately, the world cannot ever be integrated totally into the ecclesial-religious sphere or because the pious cannot avoid serving the profane reality of life. This is a middle that stands above the extremes as an original unity. Of itself, it actually constitutes the unity and difference between the explicitly Christian and churchly, on the one hand, and the world and worldly activity, on the other. And here there must be a clear distinction between the relationship of the official church to the world and that of the Christian to the world.

History and Themes of the Council. The Second Vatican Council was the twenty-first ecumenical council (according to the official count of the Roman Catholic church), held from 1962 to 1965 at Saint Peter's Basilica in Rome. On May 17, 1959, after the first official announcement on January 25, 1959, John XXIII designated a commission that was to make preparations for the council under the direction of the cardinal secretary. All bishops, the Curia Romana, and the theological and canonical faculties voted on topics for discussion. On June 5, 1960 the pope ordered ten specialized commissions to work on the schemata (protocols). There were also two permanent secretariats (one for the mass media, another for Christian unity). A central preparatory committee was responsible for organizing the work of the council. The formal summoning of the council to Rome occurred on December 25, 1961. On January 2, 1962 the opening was set for October 11, 1962. According to the rules of procedure, ten cardinals were to head the ten council commissions assigned to work into the protocols the suggestions introduced in the general assembly. Two-thirds of the members of these commissions were to be chosen by the assembly; one-third were to be named by the pope. The council decisions required a two-thirds majority.

As so-called *periti* (expert advisers), about two hundred theologians (generally professors of theology) were called to Rome. Of the 2,908 legitimate delegates, 2,540 participated in the opening. Of the invited non-Catholic Christian churches and communities, seventeen were present through thirty-five representatives. In the end, twenty-eight non-Roman churches, including the Russian Orthodox church, were represented by ninety-three observers. There were eighty-six governments and international bodies represented at the opening.

The council met in four sessions: October 11 to December 8, 1962; September 29 to December 2, 1963; September 14 to November 21, 1964; and September 4 to December 8, 1965. Ten public sessions and 168 general assembly meetings were held.

From the time of its proclamation, the council was intended to have a double goal: reform within the church and preparation for Christian and world unity. But already in the opening address this goal was expanded and deepened. The council was given the task of proclaiming the entire Christian truth "through a new effort" whereby it was of great consequence to distinguish between the truths and the "way in which they are proclaimed." *Aggiornamento* (Ital., "coming together") was to demonstrate the credibility of the church, and the church's relationship to non-Christians was to be improved.

In the first session, which included the first thirty-six general assemblies, the commission members were not chosen according to the prepared list but rather, at the suggestion of Cardinal Achille Liénart (Lille), according to recommendations of the different groups of bishops. John XXIII died on June 3, 1963. His successor, Paul VI, continued the council. At the reopening of the second session (general assemblies 37–89) on September 29, 1963, Paul VI emphasized the pastoral orientation of the council. It was to deal with the nature of the church and the function of the bishops, to make efforts toward the unity of Christians, and to set in motion a dialogue with the contemporary world. From the presidency, which had been expanded to twelve members, four moderates were named (Cardinals G. P. Agagianian, Julius Döpfner, Jacobus Lercaro, and L. J. Suenens), who were alternately to direct the general assembly. The protocols were contracted to seventeen, and a press bureau was set up. In the third session (general assemblies 90–127), the pope, by way of the theological commission, had the so-called *nota explicativa praevia* ("previous explanatory note") included in the Constitution on the Church as an authoritative explanation of the chapter on the collegiality of pope and bishops in their responsibility for the whole church. The decisions of the First Vatican Council were thereby once again maintained. At the opening of the fourth session (general assemblies 128–168), Paul VI announced the establishment of a synod of bishops to be convened regularly. This was to emphasize the idea of collegiality between the pope, the bishop of Rome, and the other bishops. All the decisions of the council were confirmed and proclaimed in public session. Paul VI solemnly closed the council on December 8, 1965. The task of carrying out the decisions of the council was assigned to the appropriate commissions. The Secretariat for Christian Unity continued in existence, and two new bodies were set up: a secretariat for relations with non-Christian religions and one for relations with unbelievers.

The Second Vatican Council was a council of the church about the church. In order to protect its freedom, John XXIII specifically avoided formulating a systematic plan of discussion. The council was to be pastorally oriented so that the church could ask itself all the questions about the contemporary situation that were being asked within it and in the world. Beyond that, however, nothing was really prescribed. That fact is demonstrated by the seventy preconciliar proposals for future council decrees, which had to do with almost everything with which the church could at all concern itself. Although the selected topics, reflected in the sixteen documents accepted by the council, may appear to be haphazard, these four constitutions, nine decrees, and three declarations do form a unified network that makes the council a council about the church.

The subjects treated in the documents produced by the council can be summarized briefly. The basic self-understanding of the church is addressed in the Dogmatic Constitution on the Church. The inner life of the church is discussed in various documents: the work of salvation through liturgy (the Constitution on the Sacred Liturgy); the church's function of oversight (the Decree on the Bishops' Pastoral Office in the Church and the Decree on Eastern Catholic Churches); the teaching office (the Dogmatic Constitution on Divine Revelation, including discussions of scripture, tradition, and teaching office, and the Declaration on Christian Education); and vocations (the Decree on the Ministry and Life of Priests, the Decree on Priestly Formation, the Decree on the Appropriate Renewal of the Religious Life, and the Decree on the Apostolate of the Laity). The mission of the church to the world is likewise elaborated on in several documents: the church's relationship to non-Catholic Christianity (the Decree on Ecumenism and the Decree on Eastern Catholic Churches); its relationship to non-Christians (the Declaration on the Relationship of the Church to non-Christian Religions, which makes special reference to the Jews, and the Decree on the Church's Missionary Activity); its relationship to the contemporary secular situation of the world in general (the Pastoral Constitution on the Church in the Modern World and the Decree on the Instruments of Social Communications); and its relationship to the philosophical pluralism of the present age (especially in the Declaration on Religious Freedom).

The council's understanding of the church. The church is the subject not only of the Dogmatic Constitution on the Church *(Lumen gentium)* but also of all the other documents. The Second Vatican Council, in contrast to Trent and to Vatican I, was oriented neither toward dogma nor toward theological controversy; rather it was pastorally oriented in that it set forth the meaning of the church, its message, and its missions for the world and for humanity. The church, it declared, wishes to encounter humanity through acceptance and solidarity, through dialogue and cooperation.

In *Lumen gentium* the council set aside juridical and controversial questions and defined the church first as a mystery, as a sacrament of unity between God and human beings and among human beings themselves. It presented the mystery of the church in the perspective of salvation history as people of God, body of Christ, and temple of the Spirit, and it articulated the mission of the church for faith and for service in word and sacrament. It made the designation of the church as people of God its central statement and thereby set aside a one-sided hierarchical understanding of the church. It emphasized the pilgrim character and historicity of the church as well as its instrumental quality and its non-identity with the kingdom of God. The ministry of the church was characterized as gift and service. The council, in full support of Vatican I, dealt extensively with the college of bishops. It accentuated the principles of collegiality and synod as structural elements of the church and the meaning of the local church as representative of the whole church. With reference to the priesthood of all believers, the council stressed the dignity, role, and responsibility of the laity as well as the presence of the church in the world, which is often possible only through the laity.

Concerning the question of the identification of the Roman Catholic church with the church of Jesus Christ, the exclusive *est* ("is") was replaced by the more open *subsistit* ("subsists," *Lumen gentium* 8). The council characterized the church's relationship to the other churches and Christian confessions not through the instrumental definition of union with Rome but through the living realities in these communities that are constitutive of church. These realities make it legitimate, and also necessary, to address and recognize other churches as means of salvation. The relationship of these churches to the Roman church is defined by the formula *"coniunctum esse"* ("to be joined together"). This union is rooted in baptism, faith in God and Christ, and in other sacramental and spiritual realities. The call to Christian unity is understood not merely as a summons to the others but as an appeal to the church itself, a call for its own constant conversion. According to Vatican II, therefore, the unity of the church is not to be sought by imposing uniformity, that is, by an all-defining centralization, but in a legitimate plurality that strengthens unity and does not endanger it.

A council of the world church. The council seemed to be the first act in which the Catholic church began to realize itself as a truly worldwide community, but this does not dispute the importance of preceding events. In the nineteenth and twentieth centuries, the church slowly and tentatively developed from a potential world church to an actual world church, from a European, Western church with European settlements around the world, to a universal church present in the whole world, even if in very differing degrees of intensity, and no longer seen in terms of European-North American affiliates. Throughout the world the church was developing a native clergy that was conscious of its independence and responsibility for itself. This world church acted for the first time at the council with historical clarity concerning faith and morals. In spite of the undeniably powerful presence and influence of the European and North American regional churches, the members of this council, in contrast to all previous councils, were bishops from the whole world and not simply, as at Vatican I, European missionary bishops sent out to the whole world.

The council was also the cause of the abolition of Latin as the common cultic language. There will always be an ultimate liturgical unity among the regional liturgies because of the unity of the church and the sameness in theological essence of the Christian cult, but from the diversity of cultic languages there will develop, in a necessary and irreversible process, a diversity of liturgies. The relationship between sameness and diversity of the regional liturgies cannot be certainly and precisely predicted. In the long run, the liturgy of the universal church will not be a mere translation of the liturgy of the Roman church but rather a liturgy formed from the unity in diversity of regional liturgies in which each has its own unique form that does not result from its language only but also from other cultural factors such as gesture and dance. If the essence of the church, and thereby the essence and character of a local church, derives essentially from the liturgy, which is one of its highest actualizations, then a truly independent local church is formed. Such a church is more than an administrative district of a uniform, centrally organized state.

Relationship to the world. In several decrees, to which belong primarily the Pastoral Constitution on the Church in the World *(Gaudium et spes)* and the Decree on Religious Freedom, the council attempted to describe its fundamental relationship to the secular world on the basis of its nature and not simply by the force of external circumstances. The council spoke about the renunciation of external means of force in matters of religion, the dignity even of an errant conscience, and the building of a legitimate secular world that was not to be judged by ecclesial standards alone. These may seem like statements forced upon the church against its most inner sensibilities by a secularized world rather than as objective expressions of the reality of Christianity itself. One must consider, however, that the church, even where it has or could have greater power in the secular realm, must support the renunciation of that power, as the council stated, because this is required of the church by virtue of its own nature (although in its history it has all too often disregarded this requirement). The temptation for the church to reassert a false superiority over the world continues to exist, but since the decisions of Vatican II the church in principle can no longer yield to this temptation, because the council formulated an irrevocable norm. No longer, since the decrees of the council, can the limitation of freedom in the name of goodness and justice be so easily rationalized by the church. For the sake of the common good, as the council says, there will always be force and power in the world. But with Vatican II the church renounced a share of that power, which it had previously claimed without inhibitions whenever it could. A border over which it was no longer possible to return, not even in small matters, had thus been crossed.

Theology of the council. The theological situation in which the council found itself was transitional and difficult to define. On the one hand, neoscholastic theology was self-evident; it was the dominant theological position represented in the proposals that had been prepared for the council by Roman commissions. Linked inextricably with the Latin language, this neoscholastic theology used the New Testament in the old style as a collection of proofs *(dicta probantia)*. On the other hand, the theology of the council was more critically related to scripture than was neoscholasticism. It had opened itself to subject matter that did not originate in the repertory of neoscholasticism. It exercised a certain braking effect against theological excess (for example, in Mariology). It made an effort to be considerate of ecumenical needs. It also held that one could say something theologically important even if one did not proclaim it solemnly as dogma. The theology of the council was, then, a theology of transition. The question still remains whether, how, and how quickly this theology will be further developed now that it has received a certain official legitimation by the council. Although impulses from the conciliar theology can be felt in the work of the Sacred Congregation of the Doctrine of the Faith since the close of the council, that office remains too neoscholastic in its anxious defense against certain modern theological efforts and too fearful and not creative enough about the questions that engage contemporary theology.

Roman theology will not be able to lead the theology of the whole church back over the border crossed at the council. On the contrary, theology will almost of necessity become a world theology, in accord with the council. That is, it will no longer exist in the non-European and non-North American countries simply as a Western expression. Latin America and sub-Saharan Africa have already announced a claim to a theology of their own. Liberation theology does not have to remain the only watchword for such an independent Latin American theology. Perhaps East Asia will also soon develop a theology of its own in a creative dialogue with its own culture and history. These theologies will have to concern themselves with the questions that are foremost in the respective cultural arenas and are not the same everywhere. The undeniable diversity that emerges from this process will help shape and determine the character of the whole of theology. European and North American theology can actually contribute to the development of non-Western theologies, in spite of the hoped-for independence of the rest of the world, because the West, with its Enlightenment and technological rationality, is becoming in increasing measure a partner in the fate of the rest of the world practically and theologically.

Change in ecumenical attitude. The council signified a break in the history of the relationship of the Catholic church both with other Christian churches and communities and with the non-Christian religions of the world. Naturally there were always contained in the faith consciousness of the church convictions that in principle legitimized the newly emerging relationship of the Catholic church with other Christian churches and communities and the non-Christian religions. But in the past these convictions had no effective impact. The theological grounds that legitimized this new breakthrough were already present in the past: the conviction of God's will for universal salvation in Christ and the doctrines of the possibility of justification without sacraments, of the implicit desire to belong to the church, and of the validity of baptism even outside the Catholic church, among others. This legacy, which is theologically self-evident and was always present, can give the impression that nothing has actually changed in the relationship between the church and the rest of humanity. But the Catholic theologian, in contrast to an all too naive nontheologian, cannot understand the new closeness and the positive relationship of the Christian confessions among themselves and the relationship of Christianity with the non-Christian religions as if serious differences, divisions, or tasks for unification do not exist. The Catholic theologian does not understand the Catholic church to be only a particular form of historical coincidence, which religious history or church history has produced among many other equally valid forms.

Christianity has always been convinced that there is a true history of revelation and faith in which the same thing does not just happen again and again but in which new and radical changes occur. Naturally, with the event of Jesus Christ there occurred an unsurpassable summit and irreversible stage of revelation history that should not be hidden or trivialized. Nonetheless, the council initiated a point of view that it ratified as truly Christian, namely, that Catholic Christianity had assumed a different and new position relative to other Christians and their churches and relative to the non-Christian religions of the world.

The crucial point in this ecumenical change of attitude, in the broadest sense, is that the extent and radicality of this change is hidden and rendered innocuous in our ordinary consciousness by a modern liberal and relativistic mentality that assumes *a priori* that such a new ecumenical openness and readiness to learn is banal and self-evident. It should not be denied that this modern liberal mentality was part of the climate in which the new ecumenical consciousness could grow for the first time. But this consciousness also and especially grew out of a genuinely Christian root; it is in itself Christian. It definitively leaves behind an older mentality that had been operative for a millennium and a half; moreover, it remains obligatory for the history of the church, like other great decisive moments of faith history.

Without denying the seeds of the future in the past, it is necessary to maintain that before the council the Catholic church considered the non-Roman Catholic churches and communities to be organizations and societies of people who differed with the old church only through errors and deficiencies and who ought to return to it in order to find in it the full truth and fullness of Christianity. From the point of view of the old attitude, the non-Christian religions were all forms of paganism, that is, religion that human beings, sinfully and without grace, produced on their own. (This was also the opinion of Martin Luther and Karl Barth.) It was not at all explicit in the actual consciousness of the church that the non-Catholic churches could bring with them in an ecumenical accord a positive legacy of Christian history into the one church of the future, or that the non-Christian religions could exercise in their institutionality a positive salvific function for non-Christian humanity. Those views were changed by Vatican II, and since then a position of acceptance can no longer be excluded, because it is understood not as an aspect of the liberal modern mentality but rather as an integral element of Christian conviction.

Universal optimism about salvation. Given the multifaceted nature of Augustine's theology, the following characterization may not do him justice in every respect. One may also not ignore the fact that the history of the church's faith consciousness has progressed by many small steps from Augustine to the present. But if one considers these limitations and that many historical causes have functioned as catalysts in the above-mentioned change of faith consciousness of the church, one can still say that Augustine inaugurated and gave to Christianity a consideration of world history in which, because of the incomprehensibility of God's providence, world history remained the history of the damned, of whom in the end only a few were saved through a rarely given grace of election. The world was dark for Augustine and only dimly illumined by the light of God's grace, the gratuitousness of which was manifested in its rarity. Even if Augustine knew that there were many in the church who seemed to be outside it, and vice versa, the circle of those who are to be saved was nearly the same as the group of those who believed explicitly in a Christian and ecclesiastical way. The rest, because of an incomprehensibly just judgment of God, were among the damned of humanity. On the whole, hell was the future of world history.

Augustine's pessimism about salvation was slowly reconstructed and transformed in the theoretical and existential consciousness of the church by an extremely painstaking process. The emerging optimism about salvation, consisting of insights acquired one by one, was viewed as limited only by the bad will of the individual, and even then it was hoped that the power of grace would once again transform this malice into free love for God. Until the council, however, the church had not yet actually ratified and taught these insights with dogmatic finality. It did teach, however, that even those who are convinced atheists are connected with the Easter mystery of Christ as long as they follow their consciences; moreover, all human beings who know God in some way are in touch with God's revelation and can, in the theological sense of a saving act, believe. The church through Vatican II declared that even those who search in shadows and images for the unknown God are not far from the true God who wills that all human beings be saved if only they make an effort to lead a righteous life. It was emphasized by the council that the church is not so much a society for those who are saved but the primary sacramental symbol and germination cell of salvation for the whole world.

One could say that the council's optimism about universal salvation remained hypothetical, that salvation could fail for individuals through unrepented guilt, and that, hypothetically, such optimism was the normal teaching of the church even before the council. It is true that the church, even after the council, does not proclaim universal reconciliation. It is likewise true that before the council the church already taught belief in a universal salvific will. But this preconciliar teaching was thought of very abstractly and was equipped with not a few "ifs" and "buts" that could no longer be maintained after the council. The council courageously postulated a real revelation and therefore a real possibility of faith where the Christian proclamation does not yet reach. It did not even consider a profession of atheism to be unequivocal proof of the hopelessness of salvation, which certainly did not agree with the traditional doctrine previous to the council. With its rejection of a *theoretical* doctrine of universal salvation, the church, in the council and in its practical attitude, proceeded from the principle that the grace of God is offered to a person's free choice and that in this freedom it is also universally effective. This attitude has naturally had a long developmental history. In Vatican II, however, it became clear and irreversible because such a hope can certainly grow, but it cannot actually any longer diminish.

The world church made its appearance as such in the council, and it says to the world, at once incomprehensibly and self-evidently, that in all the abysses of its history and all the darkness of its future this world is surrounded by God and God's will. In boundless love this God is self-communicated to the world as its ground, power, and goal. Out of such love, God assures the effectiveness of this offer to the freedom of history. In the council the church became new because it became a world church. As such, it proclaims to the world a message that, although it certainly has always been the heart of the message of Jesus, is proclaimed today more unconditionally and more courageously than before—and thus it is new. In both respects, in the proclaimer and in the message, something new has happened that is irreversible.

SEE ALSO Roman Catholicism; Trent, Council of.

BIBLIOGRAPHY

The best complete presentations of the course of the council are given by Hanno Helbling in *Das Zweite Vatikanische Konzil* (Basel, 1966), Hubert Jedin in *Kleine Konziliengeschichte* (Freiburg, 1978), and René Laurentin in *Bilan du Concile: Histoire, textes, commentaires* (Paris, 1966). The best introduction to the topical problems is given in Joseph Ratzinger's *Die erste Sitzungsperiode des Zweiten Vatikanischen Konzils: Ein Rückblick* (Cologne, 1963), *Das Konzil auf dem Weg: Rückblick auf die zweite Sitzungsperiode* (Cologne, 1964), *Ergebnisse und Probleme der dritten Konzilsperiode* (Cologne, 1965), and *Die letzte Sitzungs-periode des Konzils* (Cologne, 1966). A comprehensive chronicle of the council is provided in *Il Concilio Vaticano II,* 5 vols. (Rome, 1966–1969). An English-language chronicle can be found in *Council Daybook,* 3 vols., edited by Floyd Anderson (Washington, D. C., 1965–1966).

Texts, minutes, and concordances concerning the proceedings can be found in *Acta et documenta Concilio oecumenico Vaticano II apparando,* "Series Antepraeparatoria," 5 vols. (Vatican City, 1960–1961), and "Series Praeparatoria," 3 vols. (Vatican City, 1964–1969); *The Documents of Vatican II in a New and Definitive Translation,* edited by Walter M. Abbott (New York, 1966); *Commentary on the Documents of Vatican II,* 3 vols., edited by Herbert Vorgrimler (New York, 1967–1969); and *Acta synodalia Concilii oecumenici Vaticani II* (Vatican City, 1970–1978). Concordances of the council texts can be found in *Indices verborum et locutionum decretorum Concilii Vaticanii II* (Florence, 1968–). An outstanding council bibliography can be found in the *Archivum Historiae Pontificiae* (Rome, 1963–).

KARL RAHNER (1987)
ADOLF DARLAP (1987)
Translated from German by Charlotte Prather

VATICAN COUNCILS: VATICAN II [FURTHER CONSIDERATIONS]

Until Vatican II (1962–1965) pronouncements of the Catholic Church were deduced from objective truths expressed in essentialist, ahistorical language. In contrast, the sixteen documents of the Twentieth Ecumenical Council are marked by a sense of historicity. Analogously, before Vatican II, authority in the church was exercised in a monarchical manner. In the documents of Vatican II, collegiality and subsidiarity became hallmarks of authentic authority.

THE METHODOLOGICAL SHIFT. Neither the implications of historicity for morality and doctrine nor a more inclusive understanding of the exercise of authority have run a smooth course since the close of the council. Nothing, however, that has transpired during that time remains unaffected by these two characteristics that permeated the council's deliberations. Indeed one's attitude toward the work of the council is most frequently dictated by one's acceptance or nonacceptance of the paradigm shift in ecclesial self-understanding occasioned by the twin concepts of historicity and shared authority. Further, developments in liturgical practice, more than in any other area, illustrate the interplay of historicity and authority.

HISTORICITY. Common to modern philosophers of history and cultural anthropologists is the understanding that humans are shaped by the empirical, particular circumstances of their lives. Within these circumstances a set of meanings and values emerges that develops into particular cultures, which, because of their particularity, cannot claim absolute universality for their values. Cultures generate horizons in which participants of that culture live, think, ask questions and receive answers, seek meaning, perceive value, and create symbol systems. However, these cultures are not static. Due to various influences, they change and develop. Some would say cultures are open-ended and that the ever-receding horizon is God—a horizon, however, never reached. The Jesuit theologians Karl Rahner (1904–1984) and Bernard Lonergan (1904–1984) worked with this notion of horizon. If one adopts this position, one can speak of absolute truth only within a certain horizon. Human beings can know truth but never completely possess it. Indeed within this understanding truth is more a lure, urging individuals and communities to a fuller self-appropriation, than it is an object to be possessed.

This understanding of human history and culture profoundly influenced the documents of Vatican II and the theology developed from these documents. Pius XII's landmark encyclical *Divine Afflante Spiritu* (1943) marked the beginning of a new era in Catholic biblical studies, one marked by an acknowledgement of the historicity of sacred texts. However, not until after Vatican II and the promulgation of *Dei Verbum* (1965) were nonscholars introduced to new ways of appropriating the Scriptures and modern biblical scholarship found its way into seminaries. Consequently whole areas of doctrine, such as original sin, which had been based on a literal understanding of Scripture, had to be rethought.

Besides applying the concept of historicity to Scripture, theologians applied it to theology. Whereas most theologians would agree that truth may be unchanging, they would also stipulate that it is expressed in historically conditioned categories and that, as history and culture change and develop, so do doctrines. This profoundly affected the study of Christology. As Elizabeth Johnson has pointed out, the emphasis on the historicity of Jesus, coupled with the fifteenth centenary anniversary of the Council of Chalcedon (451 CE), opened a whole new corpus of reflections on the humanity of Jesus and its relation to divinity. If Jesus was historically conditioned, so were his life choices and teachings and so was the founding of the church.

Once historicity has been accepted as a category or lens through which one looks at the dogmas of faith, the entire symbol system is open to reinterpretation. The hierarchy—those entrusted with the authentic passing on of the faith—often equates historicity with the danger of relativism. As philosophers and theologians have pointed out, historicity is not antithetical to truth, nor does it necessarily result in relativism. The relation between historicity and relativism remains, however, a principal focus of magisterial concern.

Of special concern to the hierarchy is the preservation of the teachings that Jesus is the universal savior of humankind and that Christianity is not simply one great religion among others. The Vatican II document on the church, *Lumen Gentium* (1964), spoke to both issues. Concerning the latter, it invited a renewed discussion of interfaith dialogue with its striking but somewhat ambiguous statement that truth subsisted (*subsistit*) in the Catholic Church while inviting the faithful to discover the truth in other religions. Pontiff John Paul II, following in the footsteps of John XXIII, has been particularly open to Christian-Jewish relations. He has, however, at the same time been extremely cautious in accepting any account of the salvific quality of religions, which would, in his opinion, relativize the absolute role of Christ. Various of his writings have addressed this issue. Notable among them are *Redemptor Homines* (1979) and *Ecclesia Asia* (1999), which was a response to the Synod of Asian Bishops and their attempt to enter into dialogue with indigenous and world religions in their respective areas.

AUTHORITY. It is perhaps in the area of authority that the church reveals its deepest frustration. This is not unexpected and perhaps unavoidable. Although the council enunciated the principals of collegiality and subsidiarity, it retained as fundamental its hierarchical structure. For example, *Lumen Gentium* (21–23) specified that bishops receive their authority from Christ, not from the pope, and that the universal church results from the union of local churches. It further stated that the pope and bishops form a college of discourse. Yet bishops may not exercise their authority without the approbation of the pope, but there is no imperative that the pope consult the bishops. This situation represents a clash of concepts regarding the exercise of authority. What was intended as a complement to Vatican I's promulgation of papal infallibility remains a source of frustration because of its conceptual ambiguity.

Subsidiarity, the principal that decisions and actions should occur at the lowest possible level of authority and competence, is vexed by the same concern. The fathers of the council clearly had in mind a new model of leadership, but their trust that the ambiguities resulting from the document's conflicting models of authority would be resolved in the life of the church was overly optimistic.

Symbolic of this and bringing together the various issues relative to authority is the 1968 encyclical of Paul VI, *Humanae Vitae.* In this encyclical Paul VI restated the traditional prohibition of artificial birth control although the majority of members of a panel of experts constituted by him, consisting of scientists and theologians, clergy and laity, advised him to do otherwise. This event marked a crisis of papal authority because many laity and moral theologians dissented from this teaching, something nearly unthinkable before Vatican II. To stem the increasing occurrences of dissent on this and other issues, the Vatican commissioned *The Catechism of the Catholic Church,* which was published in 1994. This publication offers the official teaching of the Catholic Church in all areas of faith and morals.

Christus Dominus (1965), *The Decree on the Pastoral Office in the Church,* provided for regional synods of bishops to address particular questions of their cultures and jurisdictions. In 1968 the bishops of Latin America met in Medellín, Colombia, and from this meeting liberation theology was born. This must be ranked among the most far-reaching effects of the council. Liberation theology is based on the premise that the appropriation of the gospel's message of the Kingdom of God implies the responsibility of the church, actualized in local communities, to seek not only the spiritual but also the material welfare of its members.

Liberation theology recognized too the systemic nature of sin and advocated a more just distribution of the world's goods. Often a Marxist economical analysis (although not a Marxist ideology) was applied to an oppressive situation. This use of Marxist economic categories raised the suspicions of ecclesial authorities. Although warnings were issued, liberation theology was never condemned by John Paul II. Born on Latin soil and addressing issues of the materially oppressed, liberation theology also gave impetus to the liberation movements of women, African Americans, and other marginalized groups. The fundamental option for the poor voiced by these liberation theologians has remained the motif of those movements throughout the world that strive for social justice.

LITURGY. Modifications in liturgical rites, especially the Eucharist, are the most notable results of the council and have affected the laity more than most other outcomes of the council. The changes in the liturgy also illustrate the ancient maxim, *Lex orandi, lex credendi* (as the church prays, so the church believes). Most conspicuous of these transformations are the celebration of Mass in the vernacular, the change from the celebrant facing the altar to facing the people, receiving the sacred host in one's hand rather than on the tongue, receiving the consecrated wine, and the incorporation of the laity into the ritual, including the introduction of lay lectors and lay ministers of the Eucharist into the celebration.

These changes bespeak a new ecclesiology that stresses the communion that exists among the members of the church and the fact that the priest leads the congregation rather than acts as a mediator between God and the assembly. These modifications also lessen the mystique that previously surrounded the celebrant as well as the emphasis on the distinction between the ordained and the laity. The architecture that characterized most churches constructed in the first few years after the council also emphasized these ecclesiological changes. Many of these were churches in the round, with the pews surrounding the altar. Except for statues of Mary and Joseph and perhaps the patron saint of the community, there was an absence of statues. This was to emphasize the centrality of Christ and direct the congregation's attention to the celebration of his mysteries in the Eucharistic observance. Consequent on this new emphasis, there was a great reduction in the number of private devotions such as novenas and the public recitation of the rosary.

It is in regard to the liturgy that the magisterium exercises the most caution and control. As lay persons become more involved in ministry, at times out of necessity, the Vatican has found it necessary to institute regulations that emphasize the difference in kind between clergy and laity. Any modifications initiated by the local church, including the use of inclusive language, must be approved by Rome, and that approval is difficult to obtain. Rahner had great hope that the Roman Church would finally become a world church. This, he said, would involve not only the celebration of the liturgy in the vernacular but the liturgy's being celebrated in the cultural idiom of a particular people. The Roman Church insists on the translation of the Roman liturgy into the vernacular. In the spirit of Rahner, one must ask if one must put on the mind-set of a white European male to embrace Catholicism.

Lumen Gentium declared that all persons were called to the perfection of love. For the first time in centuries the vocations of married couples and single men and women were regarded as having the same potential for holiness as those called to priesthood and religious life. A perhaps unforeseen consequence partially accounted for by this teaching was a vast exodus of men and women from consecrated life. Coupled with a great decrease in the numbers of those embracing such a life, the church is facing a dilemma in how to provide the Eucharist for the faithful. Paul VI in his declaration *Inter Insigniores* (1976) declared that women could not be admitted to ministerial priesthood. This position has been even more forcefully stated by John Paul II. Both Paul VI and John Paul II have restated the dedication of the Roman Church to the discipline of mandatory celibacy. This issue of who may preside at the Eucharist remains a central point of contention among the magisterium, theologians, and laity, especially as the number of priests continues to decline. The same may be said for the issue of optional celibacy. Perhaps the questions of ordination and celibacy, more than many others, illustrate the crisis resulting from the clash of cognitive viewpoints and the tension that sometimes characterizes the relationships among the pope, theologians, and laity since Vatican Council II.

SEE ALSO Liberation Theology; Lonergan, Bernard; Priesthood, overview article; Rahner, Karl; Roman Catholicism.

BIBLIOGRAPHY

Baum, Gregory. *Man Becoming: God in Secular Language.* New York, 1970. Based largely on the philosophy of Maurice Blondel (1861–1949), the book shifts Christian doctrine from a propositional method to a method incorporating historical consciousness.

Brown, Raymond E. *The Critical Meaning of the Bible.* New York, 1981. One of the foremost Catholic biblical scholars interprets the Bible using modern biblical scholarship.

Brown, Raymond E., Joseph S. Fitzmyer, and Roland E. Murphy, eds. *The New Jerome Biblical Commentary.* Collegeville, Minn., 1992. Using modern biblical scholarship, this book includes commentaries on every book in the Bible. Included also are scholarly articles on various areas of biblical studies, such as the various forms of criticism.

Burns, Robert A., O.P. *Roman Catholicism after Vatican II.* Washington, D.C., 2001. The author gives a balanced view of the thinking about various questions, such as women's issues, ordination, Christology, and Catholicism and world religions.

Catechism of the Catholic Church. *A Translation of Catechismus Ecclesiae Catholicae.* New Jersey, 1994. This is the officially sanctioned catechism of the Catholic Church. It includes short essays on doctrine and morality. The method is uneven, at times employing contemporary categories of scholarship and at other times using premodern categories.

Cernera, Anthony J., ed. *Vatican II: The Continuing Agenda.* Fairfield, Conn., 1997. Various experts outline the work they believe remains to be done in the church's reception of Vatican II.

Dupuis, Jacques. *Jesus Christ at the Encounter of World Religions.* Translated by Robert R. Barr. New York, 1991. The author explores the position of Jesus Christ in view of the claims of other world religions.

Dupuis, Jacques. *Toward a Christian Theology of Religious Pluralism.* Maryknoll, N.Y., 1997. A groundbreaking work that considers other world religions in their own right without comparison to Christianity.

Fiorenza, Elisabeth Schüssler. *In Memory of Her: A Feminist Theological Reconstruction of Christian Origins.* New York, 1983. This is a masterful study of New Testament scholarship based on principles of feminist interpretation.

Flannery, Austin, O.P., ed. *Vatican Council II.* Rev. ed. New York, 1992. An authorized translation of the sixteen documents of Vatican II and selected postconciliar writings. Each entry has a summary introduction.

Gutierrez, Gustavo. *A Theology of Liberation: History, Politics, and Salvation.* Translated and edited by Sister Caridad Inda and John Eagleson. New York, 1973. Gutierrez is considered the father of liberation theology. This book is an exposition of the basic premises of that theology.

Guzie, Tad. *Jesus and the Eucharist.* New York, 1974. The book is a careful study of the Catholic doctrine of the real presence using nonscholastic philosophical and theological principles.

Guzie, Tad. *The Book of Sacramental Basics.* New York, 1981. A clear and accessible account of the symbolic nature of sacramentality as well as an exposition of individual sacraments.

Johnson, Elizabeth. *Consider Jesus.* New York, 1990. The book constitutes a series of essays that emphasize the humanity of Jesus and Jesus as liberator.

Johnson, Elizabeth. *She Who Is: The Mystery of God in Feminist Theological Discourse.* New York, 1992. Based on significant research and firmly rooted in the tradition of Christianity, Johnson's work recasts the mystery of the Trinity in feminist concepts.

Lonergan, Bernard J. F. *Method in Theology.* New York, 1972. A systematic work that bases theological method on an empirical cognitive theory of intentionality analysis.

Lonergan, Bernard J. F. *A Second Collection.* Philadelphia, 1975. A collection of essays that treats various questions from the viewpoint of historical consciousness.

Rahner, Karl. *Foundations of Christian Faith: An Introduction to the Idea of Christianity.* Translated by William V. Dych. New York, 1978. This is a comprehensive and systematic overview of Christian faith.

Rahner, Karl. *Concern for the Church,* vol. 20 of *Theological Investigations.* Translated by Edward Quinn. New York, 1981. This work is among the more accessible of Rahner's works. Rahner's vision of the post–Vatican II church is drawn out in a series of essays.

Schillebeeckx, Edward. *Christ: The Sacrament of the Encounter with God.* Translated by Paul Barret. New York, 1963. A landmark work on the sacramentality of the humanity of Christ.

Schillebeeckx, Edward. *Ministry: Leadership in the Community of Jesus Christ.* Translated by Paul Bowden. New York, 1981.

A study of ministry in the early church from a historical-critical perspective.

Segovia, Fernando. *Decolonizing Biblical Studies.* New York, 2001.

Theobald, Christoph, and Dietmar Mieth, eds. *Unanswered Questions.* Maryknoll, N.Y., 1999. This volume of concilium discusses areas opened by Vatican II, such as sexuality, interfaith dialogue, and images of God, that remain in the state of development.

NANCY C. RING (2005)

VEDĀṄGAS. Vedāṅgas (Sanskrit, "limbs of the Veda") are subjects supplementary and subsidiary to the Vedas, the sacred texts of the pre-Hindu religion of ancient India. While the earliest sections of the Vedas date back to at least 1000 BCE, and probably earlier, the first works classified as Vedāṅga were composed not before the sixth or seventh centuries BCE, and the initial appearance of much of the classic literature of this genre is usually dated to no earlier than the fifth and fourth centuries BCE.

The Vedāṅgas are those subjects that were to be studied in order to correctly understand the Vedas and perform the rituals those texts enjoin. The texts categorized as Vedāṅgas are in the form of technical treatises written in the extremely condensed, aphoristic, and mnemonic style known as *sūtra* (literally "thread," referring to the idea that each aphorism is woven together with the others into a whole rather than tied sequentially into a linear chain). Because of the brevity and concision of their prose style, these works require further explication on the part of a teacher or through written commentary.

Although clearly appendages to the sacred Vedas, the Vedāṅgas were among the earliest texts to be categorized as *smṛti,* that is, "remembered" or traditional texts passed on from teacher to pupil and ultimately traceable back to a human author. While thus differentiated from the absolutely authoritative Vedas (which were classified as "revealed" or *śruti,* and regarded as not being the product of human beings), the Vedāṅgas are nevertheless often treated as approximating, if not fully equaling, the status of the Vedas themselves. The Vedāṅgas are, as one scholar has said, "at the same time without and within the Veda."

The Vedas and Vedāṅgas depict a religion entirely concerned with the performance, meaning, and implications of ritual and fire sacrifice. But as opposed to the often loosely structured hymns, myths, and speculative prose characteristic of the Vedas per se, the Vedāṅgas are precise, rationally and systematically organized, and highly technical.

The subjects covered in the six primary Vedāṅgas—ritual action *(kalpa),* grammar *(vyākaraṇa),* phonology or phonetics *(śikṣā),* prosody *(chandas),* etymology *(nirukta),* and astrology and astronomy *(jyotiṣa)*—all emerged out of necessities related to correct ritual performance. In this sense it can be said that all the earliest sciences of ancient India spring from ritual (and not, as in ancient Greece, for example, from mathematics). The Kalpasūtras are directly concerned with the rules for the correct performance of the ritual acts. Grammar, phonology, prosody, and etymology originated in order to ensure the proper and exact preservation and recitation of the Vedic *mantras* (inherently powerful verbal spells) that were an essential part of the performance of the ritual. And the science of *jyotiṣa* came into being to guarantee precision in the calculations for accurately timing the occurrences of the various rituals.

The Vedāṅgas, then, are "limbs" of the Vedas in that they help one correctly preserve, understand, and apply the material in those sacred texts. It is said in later texts that grammar is the mouth of the Vedas, etymology is its ears, ritual procedure is its hands, phonetics is its nose, prosody its feet, and astronomy/astrology its eyes.

Of the six primary Vedāṅgas, phonetics or Śikṣā (literally meaning "the study" or "teaching") is usually listed first and is regarded as the most important. Because the Vedas were preserved and transmitted orally, rules for precise pronunciation were crucial for maintaining the accuracy and integrity of the texts. Phonetics emerged as the first branch of linguistics, and its categories—*sound, accent, quantity, articulation, recital,* and *connection*—were fundamental for the subsequent development of linguistic studies. Important works on phonetics were composed by Pāṇini, Nārada, Vyāsa, and others.

Vyākaraṇa ("distinction," "separation") is so termed because grammar distinguishes roots, suffixes, and prefixes: it is the science that analyzes the parts and structure of a word and the method for such divisions. It also explains how correct words and sentences are formed from basic elements so that the intended meaning is clearly expressed, and is therefore also a crucial science for both the preservation and the understanding of the Vedas. Pāṇini's *Aṣṭādhyāyī* (Eight chapters) is the foundational text on grammar, along with important commentaries by Kātyāyanīputra (Kātyāyana) and Patañjali.

Chandas, or prosody, is the Vedāṅga that gives rules for the various meters in which the Vedas are recited, and lays out their classification and characteristics. The meters are divided into fourteen types ranging from those with twenty-four letters (the *gāyatrī*) to those with seventy-six. The word *chandas* is sometimes used a synonym for Vedic speech itself, as opposed to common language *(bhāṣā).*

According to tradition, there were originally some fourteen works of etymology included in the Vedāṅga designated *Nirukta.* Only one of these survives. The sole extant representative of the Vedāṅga dealing with etymology is the *Nirukta* by Yāska (dated ca. 500 BCE), which is a commentary on an older work (called the *Nighantu*) consisting of lists, groupings, and synonyms of words from the *Ṛgveda.* Yāska provides etymologies for these words and explanations of the stanzas from the *Ṛgveda* in which they occur. In the *Nirukta,* Yāska says he composed his text to insure that the correct meaning of the Veda is preserved even as people's abilities decline the further removed they are from the time of the original seers, who "heard" the Veda with direct intuitive insight. Without the aid of etymology, Yāska claims, the meaning of the Veda cannot be properly determined.

Vedic rituals were performed regularly at the various "junctures" of time: sunrise and sunset, the advent of new and full moons, the turn of the seasons, and the beginning of the new year. The ancient Indian science of astronomy developed out of the need for exact computations of the proper times for performing those rituals. Additionally, works on this subject also address what we would label astrology: the casting of horoscopes and predictions made on the basis of the location of the planets and stars, which helped the specialist adduce the most auspicious times for important events.

Finally, the Vedāṅga called *Kalpa* (from the Sanskrit root meaning "to prepare, design, arrange, or accomplish") consists of the rules and procedures for the actual performance of rituals. Kalpasūtras were produced by different ritual schools attached to one or another of the Vedas and are named after their mythical or semi-mythical founders (e.g., Baudhāyana, Āpastamba, etc.). A full Kalpasūtra consists of four principal components. First, there is the Śrautasūtra, which deals with the rules for performing the most complex rituals of the Vedic repertoire. Next comes the Gṛhyasūtra, which lays out the injunctions governing performance of the simpler "domestic" or household rituals. Third is the Dharmasūtra, which extends the reach of ruled, ritualized behavior to ethics and purity as they pertain to nearly every sector of daily life. Finally, a complete Kalpasūtra will also contain a Śulbasūtra that gives the rules of measurement for the construction of ritual altars. From this last component developed the Indian sciences of geometry, trigonometry, and algebra.

In addition to these six primary Vedāṅgas, four secondary "limbs" *(upāṅgas)* to Vedic literature are also sometimes listed: history *(purāṇa),* logic *(nyāya),* ritual exegesis *(mimamsa),* and teachings on religious duty *(dharmaśāstra).* To this list of four Vedas, six Vedāṅgas, and four Upāṅgas are added four so-called "secondary Vedas" *(upavedas)*—medicine *(āyurveda),* the science of archery *(dhanurveda),* musicology *(gandharvaveda),* and political science *(arthaśāstra)*—to complete the list of eighteen divisions of the literature of the "orthodox" tradition stemming from the Vedas.

SEE ALSO Nyāya; Purāṇas; Śāstra Literature; Sūtra Literature.

BIBLIOGRAPHY

For a summary of the Vedāṅgas, see Kanchi Kamkoti Peethadheeshwar, *The Vedas and Vedangas,* rev. ed. (Kumbakonam, India, 1988); Maurice [Moriz] Winternitz, *History of Indian Literature,* vol. 1 (1907; reprint, Delhi, 1981), esp. pp. 249–270; Arthur A. Macdonnell, *A History of Sanskrit Literature* (London, 1913); and Arthur Berriedale Keith, *The Religion and Philosophy of the Veda and Upanishads* (Cambridge, Mass., 1925). For particular Vedāṅgas, consult (for the Kalpasūtras) Jan Gonda, *The Ritual Sūtras* (Wiesbaden, Germany, 1977); (for grammar, phonetics, and etymology), Hartmut Scharfe, *Grammatical Literature* (Wiesbaden, Germany, 1977); and (for astronomy/astrology), David Pingree's *Jyotihśāstra: Astral and Mathematical Literature* (Wiesbaden, Germany, 1981).

BRIAN K. SMITH (2005)

VEDĀNTA.

The word *vedānta* literally means "end [*anta*] of the Veda," that is to say, the concluding part of the *apauruṣeya,* or revealed Vedic literature, which is traditionally believed to comprise the Saṃhitās, the Brāhmaṇas, the Āraṇyakas, and the Upaniṣads. Vedānta thus primarily denotes the Upaniṣads and their teachings. Metaphorically, Vedānta is also understood to represent the consummation or culmination (*anta*) of the entire Vedic speculation, or indeed of all knowledge (*veda*). The Hindu philosophical tradition, however, generally recognizes three foundations (*prasthānas,* literally, "points of departure") of Vedānta, namely, the Upaniṣads, the *Bhagavadgītā,* and the *Brahma Sūtra.* Of these three, the *Bhagavadgītā,* which primarily deals with the problems of social ethics, and which attempts a kind of religio-philosophical synthesis, can hardly be characterized as a strictly Vedantic treatise. Historically, one may speak of three periods of Vedānta—the creative period represented by the Upaniṣads, the period of systematization and harmonization of the Upaniṣadic teachings represented by the *Brahma Sūtra,* and the period of exposition, elaboration, and diversification represented by the commentaries on the *Brahma Sūtra,* the commentaries on those commentaries, and many independent treatises. The traditional grounding of Vedānta is thus consistently emphasized, it being implied that Vedānta is largely an exercise in scriptural exegesis rather than an independent philosophical formulation.

UPANIṢADS. More than two hundred texts call themselves Upaniṣads, but they include even such recent works as the *Christopaniṣad* and the *Allopaniṣad.* The *Muktikopaniṣad* gives a traditional list of 108 *Upaniṣads,* but, even out of these, many texts seem to have been called Upaniṣads only by courtesy. Usually 13 Upaniṣads, namely, *Īśa, Kena, Kaṭha, Praśna, Muṇḍada, Māṇḍūkya, Taittirīya, Aitareya, Chāndogya, Bṛhadāraṇyaka, Svetāśvatara, Kauṣītaki,* and *Maitrāyaṇī,* are regarded as the principal Upaniṣads (eighth to fourth century BCE). They are traditionally connected with one Vedic school (*śākhā*) or another, and several of them actually form part of a larger literary complex.

The Upaniṣads do not, by any means, constitute a systematic philosophical treatise. They rather represent the fearless quest for truth by essentially uninhibited minds. They seek, among other things, to investigate the ultimate reality "from which, verily, these beings are born, by which, when born, they live, and into which, when departing, they enter" (*Taittirīya Upaniṣad* 3.1.1), to delve into the mystery of the *ātman* "by whom one knows all this" but whom one cannot know by the usual means of knowledge (*Bṛhadāraṇyaka Upaniṣad* 4.5.15), and generally to promote "that instruction by which the unheard becomes heard, the unperceived becomes perceived, and the unknown becomes known" (*Chāndogya Upaniṣad* 6.1.3). It is true that the Upaniṣads arose out of a kind of intellectual and social revolt against the closed mechanical sacerdotalism sponsored by the Brāhmaṇas. But the Upaniṣadic teachers soon realized that the ultimate reality could not be comprehended through mere logical reasoning, for "words return [from it] along with the mind, not attaining it" (*Taittirīya Upaniṣad* 2.9.1). "Not by reasoning is this apprehension attainable," they declared (*Kaṭha Upaniṣad* 1.2.4). It is accordingly seen that the Upaniṣads present only the results of their speculation without making much ado about the logical processes, if any, which lead to those results. For the Upaniṣads the true consummation of all knowledge lies in the direct experience of the ultimate reality.

The Upaniṣads, however, presuppose a certain development of thought. The origin of some of their doctrines can be traced back to the *Ṛgveda,* or in certain cases, even to the pre-Vedic non-Aryan thought complex. It will also be seen that, from the methodological as well as from the conceptual point of view, the Upaniṣads owe not a little to the Brāhmaṇas, as a reaction against which they were largely brought into existence. The word *upaniṣad* is usually understood in the sense of esoteric teachings imparted by the teacher to his pupils who sit (*sad*) near (*upa*) him in a closed exclusive group (*ni*). But literally the word would rather seem to denote "placing side by side; equivalence, correlation," and then, secondarily, doctrines taught through equivalences or correlations. In a sense, the Upaniṣads represent an extension of the tendency of the Brāhmaṇas toward *bandhutā,* that is, toward perpetually establishing equivalences between entities and powers apparently belonging to different levels and to different spheres. It is, of course, inevitable that there should be no uniformity of method and teaching in such composite and heterogeneous texts as the Upaniṣads, but there certainly is a definite uniformity of purpose and outlook in them.

The Upaniṣads clearly betray a trend toward inwardization and spiritualization, which presumably has its origin in their general aversion for the physical body and sensual experience (*Maitrī Upaniṣad* 1.3). The Upaniṣadic teachers have consistently emphasized the view that the essential or real self (*ātman*) has to be differentiated from the empirical or embodied self (*jīva*). Indeed, true philosophical knowledge consists in not confusing the one for the other. This teaching is very well brought out in the famous parable from the *Chāndogya Upaniṣad* (8.7–12), in which Prajāpati is seen leading Indra progressively on the path of true knowledge and ending with the final instruction that the essential Self is different from and transcends the embodied self in its conditions of wakefulness, dream, and deep sleep. The essential Self is of the nature of pure self-consciousness. It is neither the knower nor the known nor the act of knowing, though this last necessarily presupposes the existence and direct awareness of the essential Self. The essential Self does exist—it is *sat* (existence)—but not in any particular form; it is pure *sat,* that is to say, it is of the nature of existence *as such.* It is also conscious, but not of any particular object, internal or external; it is pure *cit* (consciousness), that is to say, it is of the nature of consciousness *as such.*

In another significant analysis of the human personality (*Taittirīya Upaniṣad* 2.2.5), the Upaniṣadic teacher proceeds from the grosser to the subtler forms of the Self, it being implied that each succeeding subtler and more internal form is more real and essential than the preceding one. He there speaks of the physical form (*annamāyā*), the vital form (*prāṇamāyā*) which inheres within the physical form, the mental form (*manomāyā*) which inheres within the vital form, the form of consciousness (*vijñānamāyā*) which inheres within the mental form, and finally concludes by affirming that within the form of consciousness inheres the subtlest and the most internal, and, therefore, the most real and the most essential form, namely, the form of bliss (*ānandamāyā*). The essential Self is thus pure existence (*sat*), pure consciousness (*cit*), and pure bliss (*ānanda*).

Side by side with the analysis of the human personality, the Upaniṣadic thinker has attempted an analysis of the external world as well. The thinker has thereby arrived at the conclusion that at the basis of this gross, manifold, changing phenomenal world—which ultimately is a conglomeration of mere names and forms—there lies one single, uniform, eternal, immutable, sentient reality (see, e.g., *Chāndogya Upaniṣad* 6.1). The natural and logical next step is to identify the deepest level of the subjective person, namely, the essential Self (*ātman*), with the ultimate basis of the objective universe, namely, the cosmic reality (*brahman,* also called *sat*). The world appearance or the relation of the world to *brahman* are not major concerns in the Upaniṣads.

The Upaniṣads have not developed any epistemology. Nor have they enunciated any ethical system as such. They are more or less exclusively concerned with the ideal of *mokṣa,* or humanity's release from its involvement in the phenomenal world and its realization of the identity of its essential self with the cosmic reality. Even the doctrine of *karman* has not been systematically elaborated in the early Upaniṣads. It is regarded as something not to be spoken of openly (*Bṛhadāraṇyaka Upaniṣad* 3.2.13). As for the doctrine of rebirth, its first clear indications are seen in a passage of the *Bṛhadāraṇyaka Upaniṣad* (6.2.15–16), where it is mentioned as one of three eschatological alternatives.

BRAHMASŪTRAS. For various reasons, the period immediately following the major Upaniṣads marked a kind of break in the continuity of Brahmanic thought and tradition. But it proved to be only an interregnum. Soon a vigorous and comprehensive cultural movement was set in motion that sought to resuscitate the Brahmanic way of life and thought by reorganizing, systematizing, simplifying, and popularizing it. The literary monuments of this movement were generally clothed in a practical literary form, namely, the *sūtras*, or aphorisms, that were defined as being at once brief but unambiguous and to the point. By their very nature, the Upaniṣadic teachings, which were often sheer flashes of spiritual radiance rather than coherent philosophical formulations, were characterized by inherent ambiguities, inconsistencies, and contradictions. In order that they should prove reasonably meaningful, it was necessary to systematize and, more particularly, to harmonize them. This is exactly what the *Brahma Sūtra* (also called *Vedānta Sūtra* or *Uttara-mīmāṃ Sūtra*) of Bādarāyaṇa (third to second century BCE) attempted to do.

Apparently, the *Brahma Sūtra* was not the only work of this kind, for Bādarāyaṇa mentions several predecessors, as, for example, Ātreya, Āśmarathya, Kāśakṛtsna, and Jaimini. Little is known about the writings of these teachers except for Jaimini, who is believed to have been the author of the *Pūrva-mimāṃsa Sūtra.* The literary form of the *Brahma Sūtra* no doubt eminently suited its original purpose; in the course of time, however, it inevitably rendered the *sūtras* multivocal. By themselves they could hardly be made to yield any cogent philosophical teaching. Yet it seems that the *Brahma Sūtra* favors a kind of *bhedābheda,* or doctrine of distinction-*cum*-nondistinction. The world is represented as a transformation of the potency of God, God himself remaining unaffected and transcendent in the process. Hardly any of Bādarāyaṇa's *sūtras* can be shown to be unequivocally nondualistic in purport. It also seems that the *Brahma Sūtra* is specifically disposed against Sāṃkhya dualism and Mīmāṃsā ritualism. But after all, the Vedānta of the *Brahma Sūtra* is what the different commentators have chosen to derive from them. Indeed, each commentator exploits Bādarāyaṇa's work to develop his own peculiar thesis with a relentless vertical consistency regardless of the consequences such a procedure may have on collateral issues.

GAUḌAPĀDA. The earliest complete extant commentary on the *Brahma Sūtra* is that of Śaṅkara (788–820 CE). But in his thinking Śaṅkara is more vitally influenced by Gauḍapāda (fifth to sixth century) than by Bādarāyaṇa. It is true that the doctrine of *bhedābheda* and, to a certain extent, the Yoga of Patañjali provide the technical framework for Śaṅkara's philosophy, but it is the uncompromising nondualism reclaimed by Gauḍapāda from the Upaniṣads that Śaṅkara strongly vindicates, though he never goes so far in the direction of phenomenalism as does Gauḍapāda.

Gauḍapāda is traditionally believed to have been the teacher of Śaṅkara's teacher Govinda, although there is clear evidence that he must have lived at least three centuries before Śaṅkara. True to the usual practice of Hindu thinkers, Gauḍapāda has set forth his philosophy in his commentary, in the form of *kārikās* or memorial verses. The *Gauḍapādakārikā* constitutes the earliest treatise on absolute nondualism (*kevala advaita*). The very names of the four books that make up the work—namely, *Āgama* (Scripture), *Vaitathya* (Unreality of the World Experience), *Advaita* (Nondualism), and *Alātaśānti* (Extinction of the Revolving Firebrand)—bring out the entire teaching of Gauḍapāda in a nutshell. The first book the *Gauḍapādakārikā,* which alone is directly related to the *Māṇḍūkya Upaniṣad,* deals with the self in its four states: wakefulness, dream, deep sleep, and the "fourth" state (*turīya*), identified with *mokṣa.* In the second book, Gauḍapāda for the first time asserts that the world does not exist in reality, but that "the Self (*ātman*) apparently creates the self by the self" through its own *māyā* and cognizes various things (*Gauḍapādakārikā* 2.12). In other words, the world subsists in *ātman* through *māyā.* The third book teaches that duality does not exist in reality. Just as space (*ākāśa*), which is without duality, is manifested as portions of space, such as the space enclosed in a pot (*ghaṭākāśa*), so too is the Self manifested as *jīvas*. Similarly, just as when the pot is destroyed the space that it had enclosed merges into *ākāśa,* so too do *jīvas* merge into the Self. In reality no *jīva* is ever born. The fourth book speaks of the two standpoints—*saṃvṛti,* or the practical standpoint, and *paramārtha,* or the highest standpoint—and of the three stages in understanding, namely, *laukika* ("ordinary"), in which both objects and a subject are cognized as real; *śuddha laukika* ("purified ordinary"), in which perceiving itself, but not the objects of perception, is cognized as real; and *lokottara* ("supramundane") in which neither objects nor perceiving is cognized. This section emphasizes that consciousness (*vijñāna*) alone is real, though it may appear in various guises as objects with beginnings and ends, movements, and so on. It is analogous to a revolving firebrand that appears as a fiery hoop; in the same way *vijñāna,* when it flickers, appears as both perceiver and perceived.

There can be hardly any doubt about the strong Buddhist influence on Gauḍapāda's thought. The Buddhist terminology used in books two to four is quite unmistakable. One may leave aside such questions as whether Gauḍapāda himself was a Buddhist, or whether the authorship of all four books belongs to him, yet the *Gauḍapādakārikā* creates an irresistible impression that the Buddhist Śūnyavāda and the Vijñānavāda schools present philosophical positions that are in no small measure consistent with those presented by the major classical Upaniṣads.

ŚAṄKARA. Śaṅkara is by far the most outstanding and the most widely known exponent of Vedānta, particularly of the doctrine of absolute nonduality (Kevala Advaita). Many works pass as having been written by him, but among the philosophical works that can be ascribed to him with reasonable certainty are the commentaries on nine Upaniṣads; the commentaries on the *Brahma Sūtra,* the *Bhagavadgītā,* the *Gauḍapādakārikā,* the *Yogasūtra-bhāṣya,* and the *Adhyātmapaṭala* of the *Āpastamba Dharmasūtra;* and the *Upadeśasahāśrī* (with its nineteen verse tracts and three prose tracts). Some scholars have suggested that Śaṅkara was originally an adherent of Pātañjala Yoga and only later became an Advaitin. His background of theism and a kind of doctrine of distinction-*cum*-nondistinction, though not directly discernible, may also be validly assumed. But it is clearly Gauḍapāda who influenced Śaṅkara's teachings the most. Many of Śaṅkara's doctrines, illustrations, and arguments are clearly anticipated by Gauḍapāda, though in rather extreme forms. Indeed, in his teachings Śaṅkara may be said to have represented Guadapada's philosophy without its overtones of Buddhist Vijñānavāda and Śūnyavāda.

Śaṅkara's philosophy, like most Indian philosophy, is oriented toward the one practical aim of *mokṣa,* which implies liberation from suffering and regaining of the original state of bliss. It is based on *śruti* (scripture), especially the Upaniṣads, rather than on *tarka* (logical reasoning), which according to Śaṅkara belongs to the realm of *avidyā.* Śaṅkara takes for granted the validity of the Upaniṣads as an embodiment of the highest truth, and uses logic either to support his interpretation of the Upaniṣads or to refute other systems of thought. In his commentary on the *Brahma Sūtra* he seeks to harmonize the apparently contradictory teachings of the Upaniṣads through the assumption of two points of view, the ultimate (*pāramārthika*) and the contingent (*vyāvahārika*). He has obviously inherited this device of argumentation from Gauḍapāda. Indeed, it is in the many portions of his commentary that do not relate directly to the text of the *Sūtra* (that is, in the *utsūtra* discussions) that one gets glimpses of Śaṅkara's original philosophical contribution.

The main plank of Śaṅkara's philosophy is the belief in the unity of all being and the denial of the reality of the many particular entities in the universe. Reality is that which is one without a second, which is not determined by anything else, which is not sublated at any point of time, which transcends all distinctions, to which the familiar categories of thought are inapplicable, and which can be only intuitively realized. Such is *brahman* of Śaṅkara's Advaita. Śaṅkara's most distinctive contribution is the philosophical and dialectical development of the concept of *brahman* as without qualities (*nirguṇa*). *Nirguṇa brahman* is not to be understood as "void" or "blank"; it only signifies that nothing that the mind can think of can be attributed to it. *Sat* (pure, unqualified being), *cit* (pure consciousness), and *ānanda* (pure bliss), which are often affirmed of *brahman,* are not qualifying attributes of *brahman* but rather together constitute the essential nature of *brahman.*

Śaṅkara's main problem is how to reconcile the Upaniṣadic accounts of creation and the Upaniṣadic denial of plurality. He resolves it by pointing out that the world belongs to a level of being that is different from that of reality, namely, the level of appearance. The world (*jagat*) may be regarded as the imaginary translation of *brahman*—which is the only reality in the ultimate sense—to the space-time plane. The world is grounded in *brahman* as the illusory appearance of a serpent is grounded in a rope. The causal relationship between *brahman* and *jagat* is of the nature of *vivarta* ("manifestation, appearance"), which is to be clearly distinguished from *pariṇāma* ("evolution, transformation"). The ultimate reality that is one does not *become* many; it can only *appear* as many. *Jagat* is thus not absolutely real, for the experience of the world with its diversity of particular phenomena is sublated by realization of the one ultimate reality; but it is also not absolutely unreal, for until the world appearance is sublated by true knowledge it does possess empirical viability. Śaṅkara propounds a kind of phenomenalism without any suggestion of either nihilism or subjective idealism.

The world appearance, according to Śaṅkara's absolute nondualism, is the result of *avidyā* ("nescience"), which is a radical constitutive adjunct of the embodied self (*jīva*). *Avidyā* not only conceals (*avaraṇa*) the true nature of *brahman* but it also distorts (*vikṣepa*) it, so that *brahman,* for the time being, appears as the phenomenal world. The oneness of *brahman* experience is made to give way to the multiple experience of the world of names and forms. Viewed from yet another angle, the world is described as the result of *māyā.* If *avidyā* represents the weakness of *jīva, māyā* represents the potency imagined of *brahman* for cosmological purpose. It is by means of *māyā* that *brahman,* or rather the empirically posited creative aspect of *brahman* that is referred to as *saguṇa brahman* (God), produces the illusion of the world. It is emphasized, however, that *māyā* does not constitute a duality with *brahman,* that it does not affect *brahman,* and that it is not a permanent character of *brahman,* for when, as the result of true knowledge, the world appearance vanishes, *māyā* also vanishes and only pure *nirguṇa brahman* remains as the ultimate reality. In a sense, *māyā* and *avidyā* may be regarded as the two sides of the same coin.

The "why" of *avidyā* is, however, beyond comprehension. One, indeed, finds oneself in *avidyā.* For *jīva* is the Self (*ātman*), who, under the influence of *avidyā,* which is beginningless, has forgotten his essential identity with the one ultimate reality, namely, *brahman.* Like the world, *jīva* also is empirically real albeit transcendentally unreal; but whereas with the dawn of true knowledge the world completely vanishes, *jīva* sheds its body and other appurtenances occasioned by *avidyā* and regains its essential nature, namely, identity with *brahman.*

Śaṅkara has not developed any significant epistemology. Nor has he specifically discussed any ethical issues. He seems to take the observance of *dharma* in the phenomenal world for granted. For him the four prerequisites for *brahman* realization are discrimination between the eternal and the temporal, renunciation of nonspiritual desires, moral equipment, consisting of tranquility, self-control, and so forth, and an intense longing for *mokṣa.* Śaṅkara's personality is, in many respects, paradoxical. While strongly advocating the doctrine of Kevala Advaita, he is believed to have composed some very beautiful and moving hymns; while sponsoring a life of complete renunciation, he is himself known to have traveled almost the whole length and breadth of India as an active religious missionary with a view to founding *maṭhas* (monasteries) for the propagation of his teachings.

POST-ŚAṄKARA TEACHERS OF KEVALA ADVAITA. The school of Śaṅkara's Kevala Advaita can boast of a long line of teachers and pupils who through their writings have brought tremendous popularity to that school. Some of them have reinforced Śaṅkara's teachings with keen dialectic, some others have elaborated certain specific aspects of those teachings, while still others have presented those teachings in the form of more practical compendia. Again, some of Śaṅkara's followers have given a significant twist to the original doctrines of the great master and are, therefore, credited with having founded more or less independent subschools of Advaita.

Maṇḍana Miśra was a contemporary, perhaps a senior contemporary, of Śaṅkara. He was originally a Mīmāṃsaka and had written several treatises on Mīmāṃsā. But later he became an Advaitin. His *Brahmasiddhi* shows that he is directly influenced by Śaṅkara's philosophy. Indeed, there is a strong tradition—which is, however, equally strongly contested—that identifies Maṇḍana Miśra with Śaṅkara's pupil Sureśvara. Maṇḍana Miśra emphasizes that it is the *jīvas* who by their own individual *avidyā* create for themselves the world appearance on the changeless *brahman;* he discountenances the theory that the world originates from the *māyā* of *brahman.* Tradition is unanimous in holding that Sureśvara was a direct pupil of Śaṅkara. Sureśvara's *vārttika* on Śaṅkara's commentary on the *Bṛhadāraṇyaka Upaniṣad* is one of the longest philosophical treatises extant in Sanskrit. Its introductory part, called *Saṃbandha-vārttika,* deals with the relationship between the two sections of the Veda, the ritualistic and the spiritualistic. Sureśvara is also the author of the *vārttika* on Śaṅkara's commentary on the *Taittirīya Upaniṣad* and of an independent Vedantic treatise called *Naiṣkarmyasiddhi.* Some of the important points made by Sureśvara are that ritual action is in no way helpful to attainment of *mokṣa;* that *māyā* is only an aperture (*dvāra*) through which the one *brahman* appears as many; that *avidyā* is based not upon *jīvas* but upon pure *cit* itself; and that there is no reason to characterize the world as unreal before realization of the oneness of *ātman.*

Padmapāda is believed to have been the first pupil of Śaṅkara, and was, according to a tradition, nominated by the master as the first pontiff of the *maṭha* at Puri. His only available work, though called *Pañcapādikā* ("gloss [or *ṭīkā*] on five quarters"), actually consists only of the *ṭīkā* on Śaṅkara's commentary on the first four *sūtras* of the *Brahmasūtras.* Padmapāda invests *māyā* with a sort of substantiality and also assigns to it cognitive as well as vibratory activity. *Brahman* in association with *māyā* as characterized by this twofold activity is, according to Padmapāda, the root cause of *jagat,* while *avidyā* manifests itself in *jīva.*

It is, however, Vācaspati (fl. 841), author of the *Bhāmatī,* a commentary on Śaṅkara's commentary on the *Brahmasūtras,* who may be said to have founded an independent subschool of Śaṅkara's Vedānta. Vācaspati has sought to merge the teachings of Śaṅkara and Maṇḍana Miśra into one system. He propounds the view that *avidyā* has *brahman* as its object (*viṣaya*) and *jīva* as its support (*āśraya*). The *Saṅkṣepaśārīraka* of Sarvajñātmamuni (tenth century), a pupil of Sureśvara, is a popular treatise in verse on the main teachings of Śaṅkara. Sarvajñātman asserts that *brahman* is the ultimate cause of everything through the instrumentality of *avidyā.* Like the Bhāmatī subschool of Advaita, Prākaśātman (fl. 1200) inaugurated another independent subschool—the Vivaraṇa subschool—through his *Vivaraṇa* (exposition) of Padmapāda's *Pañcapādikā.* Prākaśātman endorses the view of Sarvajñātman that *brahman* is both the support and the object of *avidyā.* While in respect of *jīva* the Bhāmatī subschool puts forth the doctrine of limitation (*avaccheda*), the Vivaraṇa subschool puts forth the doctrine of reflection (*pratibimba*). The *Khaṇḍanakhaṇḍakhādya* of Śrīharṣa (fl. 1190) is a Vedantic dialectic against Nyāya, while the *Vedāntaparibhāṣā* of Dharmarājādhvarīinda (sixteenth century) deals with, among other things, the epistemology of Vedānta. Among other writers belonging to the school of Śaṅkara are Vidyāranya (fourteenth century), author of the famous *Pañcadaśī;* Prakāśānananda (sixteenth century), who wrote the *Vedāntasiddhantamuktāvalī;* Madhusūdana Sarasvatī (sixteenth century), author of the *Advaitasiddhi* and the *Siddhāntabindu;* Appayya Dīkṣita (sixteenth century), who wrote the *Siddhantalesamgraha* and the *Parimala,* a commentary on the *Kalpataru* of Amalānanda (thirteenth century); and Sadānanda Vyāsa (seventeenth century), who commented on the *Advaitasiddhi* of Madhusūdana Sarasvatī and also wrote a handy compendium called *Vedāntasāra.*

ŚABDĀDVAITA. Although there is generally evident a tendency to equate Vedānta with Śaṅkara's Kevala Advaita, one cannot afford to ignore the other schools of Vedānta that have been substantially influential. The doctrine of *śabdādvaita,* a monistic ontology presenting language as the basis of reality, was propounded by Bhartṛhari (d. 651) in his *Vākyapadīya;* this doctrine cannot be said to belong to Vedānta proper, since it is not derived from any of the three *prasthānas.* Still, according to Bhartṛhari the ideas that the ultimate reality, *brahman,* which is without beginning and end, is of the nature of the "word" and that the world proceeds from it can be traced back to the revelation of the Word *par excellence,* the Veda itself. This ultimate reality is one, but because of its many powers it manifests itself as many in the form of experiencer, the object of experience, and experience itself (the purpose of experience also being sometimes mentioned). This view of Bhartṛhari may be regarded as a precursor of Śaṅkara's theory of *vivarta.* The most important of the powers of *brahman,* according to Bhartṛhari, is time (*kāla*). The different kinds of actions and changes that bring about multiplicity in being all depend upon *kāla.* Bhartṛhari, however, adds that time itself is the first result of *avidyā.* In the state of true knowledge, there is no place for time.

BHĀSKARA. The proper post-Śaṅkara Vedānta begins with Bhāskara (fl. 850). Unlike the other post-Śaṅkara schools of Vedānta, Bhāskara's Vedānta does not seem to have gained wide currency, presumably because it was not linked up with any theistic sect. From his commentary on the *Brahma Sūtra* it becomes clear that Bhāskara knew Śaṅkara's commentary, for he follows Śaṅkara's arguments for refutation point by point. It further becomes clear that, for much of their interpretation, both Śaṅkara and Bhāskara must have drawn on a common traditional source. According to Bhāskara, *brahman* has a dual form: *brahman* as pure being and intelligence, formless, the causal principle, which is the object of one's highest knowledge; and *brahman* as the manifested effect or the world. Thus *brahman* represents unity (*abheda*) as well as distinction (*bheda*), both of which are real. *Jīva* is *brahman* characterized by the limitations of the mind substance. Thus, unlike the material world, *jīva* is not the effect of *brahman.* Bhāskara is at one with most of the post-Śaṅkara schools of Vedānta in rejecting outright Śaṅkara's view of the world appearance. Indeed, such rejection was the main obsession of those schools.

VIŚIṢṬĀDVAITA. To Rāmānuja (1017–1137) belongs the credit for successfully attempting to coordinate personal theism with absolutistic philosophy. Indeed, Rāmānuja may be said to have secured for Vaiṣṇavism the sanction of the Upaniṣads. In this, of course, he was heir to a fairly distinguished tradition of teachers such as Nāthamuni (fl. 950) and Yāmunācārya (fl. 1000), who is believed to have been Rāmānuja's teacher's teacher. Among the followers of Rāmānuja are Sudarśana Sūri (fl. 1300), Veṅkatanātha, more popularly known as Vedāntadeśika (fl. 1350), and Śrīnivāsācārya (fl. 1700). Rāmānuja's commentaries on two of the three *prasthānas*, namely, the *Brahma Sūtra* (called *Śrībhāṣya*) and the *Bhagavadgītā,* have been preserved. Rāmānuja is also the author of an independent philosophical treatise called *Vedārthasaṃgraha.* According to Rāmānuja, God, who possesses supremely good qualities, is the only absolute reality and therefore the only object worthy of love and devotion. Matter (*acit*) and souls (*cit*), which are equally ultimate and real, are the qualities (*viśeṣaṇas*) of God, but, as qualities, they are entirely dependent on God in the same way as the body is dependent on the soul. They are directed and sustained by God and exist entirely for and within him. Rāmānuja's doctrine is therefore known as Viśiṣṭa Advaita or the doctrine of one God qualified by *cit* (souls) and *acit* (matter). These three factors (*tattva-traya*) form a complex (*viśiṣṭa*) organic unity (*advaita*). The omnipotent God creates the world of material objects out of himself, that is, out of *acit* (which is eternal in him), by an act of will. Rāmānuja emphasizes that creation is a fact, a real act of God. What the Upaniṣads deny is the independent existence of material objects and not their existence as such. *Jīva* is made up of the human body (which is related to *acit*) and the soul (which is related to *cit*), which become associated with each other on account of *karman.* Souls are eternal and atomic and are conscious and self-luminous by their very nature. The liberated soul, which is completely dissociated from the body, becomes similar to, but not identical with, God.

In Rāmānuja's theory, God can be known only through scripture; besides the Veda, Rāmānuja recognizes the *Pañcarātra Āgama* also as revealed. For him, religious acts comprehend both Vedic ritual and the practices (*kriyāyoga*) prescribed by the Āgama. Rāmānuja recommends to all persons, irrespective of caste, rank, or sex, complete self-surrender to God (*prapatti* or *śaraṇāgati*) as the most efficacious means of attaining the *summum bonum.*

DVAITĀDVAITA. The philosophy of Nimbārka (fl. mid-fourteenth century?) is generally known as Svābhāvika Bhedābheda or Dvaitādvaita. It is set forth briefly, precisely, and without much polemic or digression in his commentary on the *Brahma Sūtra,* called *Vedāntapārijātasaurabha,* and which is elaborated in such works as the *Vedāntakaustaubha* of Śrīnivāsa (who is believed to have been a direct pupil of Nimbārka), the *Vedāntaratnamañjūṣa* of Puruṣottama (a pupil of Śrīnivāsa), and the *Vedāntakaustubhaprabhā* of Keśava Kāśmīrin (fourteenth century). Presumably influenced by Rāmānuja, Nimbārka assumes the ultimate reality of the three entities, namely, Paramātman or Puruṣottama (God), Jīva, and Jagat. He does not accept *avidyā* as a cosmic principle producing the world appearance. Rather, according to him, God actually transforms himself into the world of material objects and individual souls, but does not lose himself in these. He is simultaneously one with (*abheda*) and distinct from (*bheda*) the world of *jīvas* and matter. This is so, not because of any imposition or supposition (*upādhi*), but because of the specific peculiarity of God's spiritual nature (*svabhāva*). God alone has independent existence, while individual souls and matter, which are but derivative parts of God, are entirely dependent on and controlled by him. Liberation in Nimbārka's theory implies realization of and participation in the true nature of Lord Śrī Kṛṣṇa (who is the ultimate *brahman*) and is possible only through Kṛṣṇa's grace.

ŚUDDHĀDVAITA. Tradition speaks of four main schools of what may be called Vaiṣṇava Vedānta, namely, the Śrī school of Rāmānuja, the Sanaka school of Nimbārka, the Brahma school of Madhva, and the Rudra school of Viṣṇusvāmin, which last is more commonly associated with its later exponent Vallabha (1479–1531). Many works, large and small, are ascribed to Vallabha, the most important among them being the *Aṇubhāṣya,* a commentary on the *Brahma Sūtra* (up to 3.2.34); the *Tattvārthadīpanibandha,* an independent philosophical treatise; and the *Subodhini,* a commentary on a major part of the *Bhāgavata.* Vallabha's son Viṭṭhalanātha (1516–1584) completed the unfinished *Aṇubhāṣya* and also composed independent works such as the *Vidvanmaṇḍana* and the *Śṛṅgārarasamaṇḍana.* The *Śuddhādvaitamartaṇḍa* by Giridhara (1541–1621) and the *Prameyaranārṇava* by Bālakṛṣṇa Dīkṣita (seventeenth century) are other notable works of the Rudra school. *Śuddha advaita* ("pure nondualism") and *puṣṭimārga* are the two fundamental tenets of Vallabha's Vedānta. *Śuddha advaita* implies that the one *brahman,* free from and untouched by *māyā,* is the cause of the individual souls and the world of material objects. *Jīvas* and the material world are, in reality, *brahman,* for they represent but partial manifestations of the essential attributes of *brahman. Brahman* (God) pervades the whole world. Vallabha's doctrine is therefore also known as *brahmavāda.* While explaining the relation between *brahman* and the world, Vallabha propounds *avikṛtapariṇamavāda,* the theory that the world is a transformation of *brahman,* which latter itself, however, remains unchanged. It is like gold, which always remains itself no matter how it is formed into various ornaments or objects. God manifests his qualities of *sat* and *cit* in the form of *jīvas*, but the quality of bliss (*ānanda*) remains unmanifested. Vallabha teaches that it is through *puṣṭi* (literally, "nourishment, spiritual nourishment"), or the special grace of God, that *jīvas* attain *goloka* ("the world of cows"), the world of bliss, and participate in the eternal sport presided over by Lord Śrī Kṛṣṇa.

MADHVA. Among the Vedāntins, Madhva (1238–1317) is reputed to be a confirmed dualist (*dvaitin*). One wonders, however, whether the doctrine that Madhva advocates in his commentaries on the three *prasthānas* and in his other works—a doctrine endorsed by other teachers of his school, such as Jayatīrtha (fourteenth century) and Vyāsarāya (1478–1539)—can be designated strictly speaking as dualism in the sense in which the Sāṃkhya doctrine is designated as dualism. Madhva no doubt speaks of two mutually irreducible principles as constituting reality, but he regards only one of them, namely, God, as the one infinite independent principle, whereas the finite reality comprising matter, individual souls, and other entities is regarded as dependent. He emphasizes that Lord Śrī Hari, who is omnipresent, omniscient, omnipotent, and without beginning and end, is the highest independent reality. The ungodly traits that are sometimes imputed to his character in descriptions of his various incarnations are not native to him but are intended to delude the demons and similar evil beings. The material world is essentially real, for whatever is created by God by veridical volition cannot be unreal. Furthermore, on the strength of the evidence of direct perception, inference, and scripture (which Madhva considers to be the only valid sources of knowledge) it can be established that the distinction between God and *jīva* is real and beginningless. Indeed, Madhva asserts the verity of the fivefold distinction, namely, the distinction between God and *jīvas*, the distinction between God and insentient objects, the mutual distinction among *jīvas*, the distinction between *jīvas* and insentient objects, and the mutual distinction among insentient objects. *Jīvas*, which are infinite in number, are subject and subservient to God. There is a gradation of high and low among them in accordance with their *karman,* and this gradation persists even in the state of emancipation. *Mokṣa,* according to Madhva, implies the unblemished blissful experience of one's pure intrinsic nature as a servant of Lord Śrī Kṛṣṇa, and devotion to him is the chief means of attaining *mokṣa.*

SEE ALSO Avidyā; Bādarāyaṇa; Brahman; Gauḍapāda; Madhva; Māyā; Mīmāṃsā; Mokṣa; Nimbārka; Rāmānuja; Śaṅkara; Sūtra Literature; Upaniṣads.

BIBLIOGRAPHY

Agrawal, Madan Mohan. *The Philosophy of Nimbārka.* Agra, 1977.

Dasgupta, Surendranath. *A History of Indian Philosophy.* 3 vols. London, 1922–1940.

Deutsch, Eliot. *Advaita Vedānta: A Philosophical Reconstruction.* Honolulu, 1969.

Hacker, Paul. *Untersuchungen über Texte des frühen Advaitavāda,* vol. 1, *Die Schüler Śaṅkaras.* Wiesbaden, 1953.

Hacker, Paul. "Śaṅkara der Yogin and Śaṅkara der Advaitin. Einige Beobachtungen." In *Festschrift für Erich Fraunallner,* special issue of *Wiener Zeitschrift für die Kunde Süd- und Ostasiens* 12/13 (1968–1969): 119–148.

Hacker, Paul. "Śaṅkārācarya and Śaṅkarabhagavatpāda: Preliminary Remarks Concerning the Authorship Problem." In *Kleine Schriften,* edited by Lambert Schmithausen, pp. 41–58. Wiesbaden, 1978.

Hiriyanna, Mysore. *Outlines of Indian Philosophy.* New York, 1932.

Sharma, B. N. K. *A History of the Dvaita School of Vedānta and Its Literature.* 2 vols. 2d rev. ed. Bombay, 1981.

New Sources

Comans, Michael. *The Method of Early Advaita Vedanta: A Study of Gaudapada, Sankara, Suresvara, and Padmapada.* Delhi, 2000.

Sharma, Arvind. *The Rope and the Snake: A Metaphorical Exploration of Advaita Vedanta.* New Delhi, 1997.

Tagare, Ganesh Vasudeo. *The Veda and Vedanta.* Delhi, 1996.

R. N. DANDEKAR (1987)
Revised Bibliography

VEDAS. Specifically, the Vedas are often understood to comprise four collections of hymns and sacrificial formulas. In a more general sense, however, the term *Veda* does not denote only these four books, or any single book, but a whole literary complex, including the Saṃhitās, the Brāhmaṇas, the Āraṇyakas, the Upaniṣads, the Sūtras, and the Vedāṅgas. The many texts, varied in form and content, that make up the Veda were composed over several centuries, in different localities, and by many generations of poets, priests, and philosophers. Tradition, however, will not admit the use of the word *compose* in this context, for the Veda is believed to be *apauruṣeya,* "not produced by human agency." It is eternal. Its so-called authors have merely "seen" or discovered it, and they are thus appropriately called *ṛṣis*, or seers.

Vedic tradition notes that the *apauruṣeya* character of the Veda accords it ultimate validity in every respect. Moreover, the Veda is said to comprehend all knowledge (*veda*). Indeed, most of the later Brahmanic disciplines claim the Veda as their fountainhead. The Veda has been passed from generation to generation by oral transmission. This fact explains the name *śruti* ("what is heard") by which the Veda is known. In order to preserve this extensive literature intact without the aid of writing, and to facilitate its precise memorizing, the Vedists devised various ways of reciting the Veda (*pāṭhas* or *vikṛtis*) that involve permutations and combinations of the words in *mantras* (versus) and prose formulas. The emergence of various schools (*śākhās*) and subschools (*caraṇas*) of Vedic study has also substantially helped the preservation of this large corpus of literature. At the same time, oral transmission may have resulted in the loss of a considerable portion of Vedic literature in the course of time.

Early History of the Veda. The literary history of the Veda is usually divided into four periods: the Saṃhitā period (c. 2000–1100 BCE), the Brāhmaṇa-Āraṇyaka period (c. 1100–800 BCE), the Upaniṣadic period (c. 800–500 BCE), and the Sūtra-Vedāṅga period (c. 500 BCE onward). Broadly speaking, these four periods represent a chronological sequence, and a thread of logical development running through them invests them with a kind of unity. Yet only the literature of the first three periods is traditionally regarded as *apauruṣeya.* In particular, four collections of texts from the Saṃhitā period are commonly referred to as the four Vedas. These are the *Ṛgveda Saṃhitā* (the oldest collection), the *Atharvaveda Saṃhitā,* the *Sāmaveda Saṃhitā,* and the *Yajurveda Saṃhitā.*

Before the Vedic Aryans migrated into the northwestern region of India, then called Saptasindhu ("land of seven rivers"), their ancestors had lived together with the ancestors of the Iranian Aryans, presumably in Balkh and its environs, for a fairly long time (2200–2000 BCE). It was there that the Proto-Aryan language and religion acquired their specific characteristics. The religion of the Proto-Aryans consisted mainly of the concepts of cosmic law (Vedic, *ṛta;* Avestan, *aša*) and its administrator (Vedic, Asura Varuṇa; Avestan, Ahura Mazdā), a simple fire worship, and a cult centering on the sacred drink (Vedic, *soma;* Avestan, *haoma*). *Mantras* (magically potent verses) or hymns (groups of *mantras* usually involving a single theme) relating to this religion were composed by the ancestors of the Vedic Aryans in an earlier form of Vedic Sanskrit. In the course of time, the ancestors of the Vedic Aryans left their home in Balkh and proceeded toward the alluring "land of seven rivers," while the ancestors of the Iranian Aryans migrated toward Iran. During their expedition to Saptasindhu and because of subsequent conflicts and colonization in that region, a significant strain was imposed on the old Vedic religion in the form of a hero cult with Indra as its chief divinity. The activity of composing *mantras* and hymns relating to the old (Proto-Aryan) as well as the new Vedic (Indra) religion continued unabated throughout this time. Side by side with this religion of the "classes" among the Vedic Aryans developed the religion of the "masses," which was largely constituted of magic, sorcery, and witchcraft, and relating to which *mantras* were also being composed. When, soon after, the Vedic Aryans had settled down in their new home to a life of comparative peace, leisure, and prosperity, poet-priests collected all the scattered mantras, old and new and relating to both the Proto-Aryan and Vedic religions. They revised and edited them, grouped them together into suitable hymns (where they were not already so grouped), and arranged those hymns according to a certain plan. As a result, two primary "collections" (*saṃhitās*) were brought into existence: the *Ṛgveda Saṃhitā* and the *Atharvaveda Saṃhitā* (2000–1700 BCE).

Ṛgveda Saṃhitā. The *Ṛgveda Saṃhitā* has come down to the present according to the recension of the Sakala school. It consists of 1,028 *sūktas* (hymns) made up of varying numbers of metrical verses (*mantras*, more commonly called *ṛks*, which accounts for the name *Ṛgveda*). The hymns are assembled in ten different books or *maṇḍalas* whose formation is governed mainly by the criterion of authorship. Among the classes of the Vedic Aryans, a few families had already acquired some measure of socioreligious prestige. The *mantras* or hymns, which were traditionally believed to have been "seen" by the progenitor and other members of a particular family, were collected together to form the book of that family. The nucleus of the *Ṛgveda* is formed of six such family books, which are numbered from two to seven and which are ascribed respectively to the families of Gṛtsamada, Viśvāmitra, Vāmadeva, Atri, Bharadvāja, and Vasiṣṭha. Within a family book, the hymns are grouped according to the divinities to whom they are related. These divinity groups are then arranged in a certain fixed order, the group of hymns relating to Agni being placed first. Within each divinity group, the hymns are arranged in descending order according to the number of stanzas. The majority of hymns in the eighth book belong to the Kaṇva family. The first book is a collection of miniature *maṇḍalas*. Book nine is ritualistically oriented, all the hymns included in it, irrespective of authorship, being related to *soma.* The tenth book, which contains the same number of hymns as the first book (191), is a collection of residual hymns. There is another, later mechanical arrangement of the *Ṛgveda* that is obviously directed to the purpose of memorizing the *Saṃhitā.* According to this system, the entire *Ṛgveda Saṃhitā* is divided into eight divisions (*aṣṭakas*), each division into eight chapters (*adhyayas*), and each chapter into about thirty-three sections (*vargas*) of about five stanzas each.

The bulk of the *Ṛgveda* consists of mythology and the panegyrics and prayers that are either dependent on or independent of that mythology. The exclusively naturalistic, or ritualistic, or mystic interpretation of Vedic mythology is now generally discountenanced, and an evolutionary approach is increasingly favored. One may speak of three main phases of the evolution of the Rgvedic mythology: the phase represented by Ṛta-Varuṇa, Agni, and Soma; the phase represented by Indra and other heroic gods; and the phase represented by the admission into the Vedic pantheon of popular Aryan divinities (e.g., Viṣṇu) and pre-Vedic non-Aryan divinities (e.g., Rudra). Apart from mythology, the *Ṛgveda* also contains a few hymns of sociohistorical and philosophical purport.

ATHARVAVEDA SAṂHITĀ. The *Atharvaveda,* which is aptly described as the Veda of the masses, is more heterogeneous and less inhibited than the *Ṛgveda.* The name *Atharvāṅgirasaḥ,* often used in reference to this Veda, indicates the twofold character of its contents—the wholesome, auspicious "white" magic of Atharvan, and the terrible, sorcerous "black" magic of Aṅgirgas. Another name of this Veda is *Brahmaveda.* The name has been explained by the fact that the *Atharvaveda* consists of *brahmans* (magically potent formulas), or by the fact that this Veda is the special concern of the brahman priest in the Vedic ritual. There is another explanation of the name. Because of the peculiar character of the contents of this Veda, it was for a long time not recognized as being as authoritative as the other three Vedas (*trayī*). In reaction against this exclusivism, the Atharvavedins went to the other extreme and stated that the *Ṛgveda,* the *Sāmaveda,* and the *Yajurveda* were essentially "limited," for *brahman* alone was infinite, and this *brahman* was truly reflected only in the *Atharvaveda.* Thus, the *Atharvaveda* was called *Brahmaveda.* The *Atharvaveda* is also known by several other names, each of which emphasizes a specific trait of its character: It proves particularly efficacious in the performance of the duties of the *purohita* (royal priest), and is thus known as the *Purohitaveda;* it contains many hymns pertaining to the *kṣatriyas* (ruling or warrior class), and is thus called the *Kṣatraveda;* and it is the guide for the performers of the practices described in the five (*pañca*) main ancillary texts (*kalpas*) of this Veda, and thus is known as the *Veda of the Pañcakalpins.*

The *Atharvaveda* is available in two recensions, the *Śaunaka* and the *Paippalāda* (which is only partially available). The *Śaunaka* recension consists of 730 hymns grouped into twenty books (*kāṇḍas*). About five-sixths of these hymns are metrical (*arthasūktas*), whereas the remaining ones (*paryāya-sūktas*) are made up of prose units (*avasānas*). The *Atharvaveda* is less sophisticated in its meter, accent, and grammar than the *Ṛgveda.* The contents of the *Atharvaveda* may be broadly classified under the following headings: charms to counteract diseases and possession by evil spirits; prayers for health and longevity and for happiness and prosperity; spells pertaining to various kinds of relationships with women; hymns concerning the affairs of the king, as well as those intended to secure harmony in domestic, social, and political fields; and formulas for sorcery and imprecation and for exorcism and counterexorcism. Finally, the *Atharvaveda* contains quite a few hymns embodying highly theosophic and philosophical speculations.

SĀMAVEDA AND YAJURVEDA SAṂHITĀS. The *Sāmaveda* and the *Yajurveda* are essentially liturgical collections and conceptually mark the transition from the Saṃhitā period to the Brāhmaṇa period. The *Sāmaveda Saṃhitā* is a collection of *mantras* to be chanted at the various soma sacrifices by the *udgātṛ* priest and/or his assistants. The name *Sāmaveda* is, however, a misnomer; it is not a collection of *sāmans,* or chants, but rather a collection of verses, mostly derived from the *Ṛgveda,* which are intended to form the basis of proper *sāmans* (*sāmayoni mantras*). Out of the traditionally mentioned thirteen *śākhās* of the *Sāmaveda,* only three are known today: the *Kauthuma,* the *Rāṇāyanīya,* and the *Jaiminīya,* or *Talavakāra.* The *Kauthuma Saṃhitā* of the *Sāmaveda* is made up of two parts, the *Pūrvārcika* and the *Uttarārcika.* The *Pūrvārcika* consists of 585 *mantras* and the *Uttarārcika* of 1,225 *mantras.* However, the total number of *mantras* in the *Sāmaveda,* not counting those that are repeated, is 1,549—all but 78 of them having been taken from the *Ṛgveda,* mostly its eighth and ninth *maṇḍalas.* For their use in the *soma* ritual, the *sāmayoni mantras* are transformed into chants or ritual melodies, called *gānas,* by means of such devices as the modification, prolongation, and repetition of the syllables in the *mantras* and the occasional insertion of additional syllables (*stobhas*). Such *gānas* are gathered in four books: the *Grāmageyagāna,* the *Araṇyagāna,* the *Ūhagāna,* and the *Ūhyagāna.* Of course, these *gāna* collections are quite distinct from the *Sāmaveda.* Since one *sāmayoni mantra* can be chanted in a variety of ways, it gives rise to several *gānas.* Consequently, the number of *gānas* is much larger than the number of *sāmayoni mantras.* For instance, the number of *gānas* belonging to the Kauthuma school is 2,722.

Whereas the *Sāmaveda* concerns itself exclusively with just one feature of the *soma* sacrifice, the *Yajurveda* treats the entire sacrificial system. Indeed, the *Yajurveda* may be regarded as the first regular textbook on the Vedic ritual as a whole. It deals mainly with the duties of the *adhvaryu,* the priest responsible for the actual performance of the various sacrificial rites. There are two major recensions of the *Yajurveda,* the *Kṛṣṇa* ("black") *Yajurveda* and the *Śukla* ("white") *Yajurveda.* The difference between them lies not so much in their contents as in their arrangement. In the *Kṛṣṇa Yajurveda,* the *mantras* and the *yajus* (sacrificial formulas in prose) and their ritualistic explanation and discussion (called *brāhmaṇa*) are mixed together. Thus, in its form and content the Saṃhitā of the *Kṛṣṇa Yajurveda* is not particularly distinguishable from the Brāhmaṇa or the Āraṇyaka of that Veda. In contrast, the *Śukla Yajurveda* contains only the *mantras* and the *yajus,* the corresponding ritualistic explanation and discussion being reserved for the *Śatapatha Brāhmaṇa* that belongs to that Veda.

The Saṃhitās of four schools of the *Kṛṣṇa Yajurveda*—namely, the Taittirīya, the Kaṭha (or Kāṭhaka), the Maitrāyaṇī, and the Kapiṣṭhala Kaṭha—are available today either whole or in fragments. Incidentally, it may be noted that the Taittirīya school has preserved its literature perhaps most fully of all the Vedic schools, maintaining the continuity from the Saṃhitā period, through the Brāhmaṇa-Āraṇyaka-Upaniṣad periods, up to the Sūtra period. The *Taittirīya Saṃhitā* is divided into seven *kāṇḍas,* and, together with the *Taittirīya Brāhmaṇa* and the *Taittirīya Āraṇyaka,* it covers almost the whole gamut of Vedic ritual. However, in these texts, the different sacrifices are not dealt with in any rational order.

A significant feature of the *Śukla Yajurveda* is that its entire literary corpus has come down in two distinct versions, the *Mādhyandina* and the *Kāṇva.* However, there is little essential difference between them in content and arrangement. The *Śukla Yajurveda Saṃhitā,* which is also known as the *Vājasaneyi Saṃhitā* in the *Mādhyandina* version, consists of forty chapters (*adhyāyas*). The first twenty-five *adhyāyas* contain *mantras* and formulas relating to the principal sacrifices; the next four *adhyāyas* include additions to these basic *mantras* and formulas; *adhyāyas* 30–39 deal with such sacrifices as the Puruṣamedha, the Sarvamedha, the Pitṛmedha, and the Pravargya; and the last *adhyāya* constitutes the well-known *Īśa Upaniṣad.*

See Also Brāhmaṇas and Āraṇyakas; Pristhood, article on Hindu Priesthood; Sūtra Literature; Upaniṣads; Vedāṅgas; Vedism and Brahmanism.

Bibliography

Translations of the *Ṛgveda* can be found in *Hymns from the Rigveda,* translated by A. A. Macdonnell (Calcutta, 1922); *The Hymns of the Rigveda,* 2 vols., translated by T. H. Griffith (Varanasi, 1920–1936; reprint, 1967); *Ṛgveda Maṇḍala VII,* translated by Hari Damodar Velankar (Bombay, 1963); and *The Soma-hymns of the Ṛgveda,* 3 vols., translated by Shrikrishna Sākhāram Bhawe (Baroda, India, 1957–1962).

Translations of other Vedas include three works translated by T. H. Griffith: *The Hymns of the Samaveda* (Varanasi, 1893; reprint, 1963), *The Texts of the White Yajurveda* (Varanasi, 1899), and *The Hymns of the Atharvaveda,* 2 vols. (Varanasi, 1895–1896; reprint, 1968); *The Veda of the Black Yajus School Entitled the Taittiriya Sanhita,* translated by Arthur Berriedale Keith (Cambridge, Mass., 1914); and *Atharvaveda Samhitā,* edited by C. R. Lanman and translated by William Dwight Whitney (Cambridge, Mass., 1905).

The few English translations of the Brāhmaṇas include *Rigveda Brāhmaṇas,* translated by Arthur Berriedale Keith (Cambridge, Mass., 1920); *Pañcavimśa-brāhmaṇa,* translated by W. Caland (Calcutta, 1931); and *The Śatapatha-Brāhmaṇa,* translated by Julius Eggeling (Oxford, 1882–1900; reprint, Delhi, 1966).

The Āraṇyaka literature is represented in English by *The Aitareya Āraṇyaka,* edited and translated by Arthur Berriedale Keith (Oxford, 1909; reprint, 1969).

Secondary sources on Vedic religion include Maurice Bloomfield's *The Religion of the Veda* (New York, 1908; reprint, Varanasi, 1972); Arthur Berriedale Keith's *The Religion and Philosophy of the Veda and Upanishads* (Cambridge, Mass., 1925); Hermann Oldenberg's *Die Religion des Veda,* 2d ed. (Stuttgart and Berlin, 1917); Louis Renou's *L'Inde classique* (Paris, 1947); and my *Exercises in Indology* (Delhi, 1981), especially the chapter entitled "The Cultural Background of the Veda," pp. 68–93.

The religion of the Brāhmaṇas is discussed in *Religion and Mythology of the Brahmanas,* "Govind Vinayak Devasthali Series" (Poona, 1965); Jogiraj Basu's *India of the Age of the Brāhmaṇas* (Calcutta, 1969); and Sylvain Lévi's *La doctrine du sacrifice dans les brāhmaṇas* (Paris, 1898).

Secondary sources on Vedic literature include my *Vedic Mythological Tracts* (Delhi, 1979) and *Insights into Hinduism* (Delhi, 1979), especially the chapter entitled "Literature of Brahmanism in Sanskrit," pp. 320–372, and Jan Gonda's *Vedic Literature* (Wiesbaden, 1975).

New Sources

Choudhary, B. K. *From Kinship to Social Hierarchy: The Vedic Experience.* Patna, 1999.

Elizarenkova, Tatyana J. *Language and Style of the Vedic Rsis.* Albany, 1995.

Facets of Vedic Studies. Edited by Bidyut Lata Ray. New Delhi, 2000.

Inside the Texts, Beyond the Texts: New Approaches to the Study of the Vedas: Proceedings of the International Vedic Workshop. Harvard University, June 1989. Cambridge, Mass., and Columbia, Mo., 1997.

Jamison, Stephanie W. *The Ravenous Hyenas and the Wounded Sun: Myth and Ritual in Ancient India.* (*Myth and Poetics.*) Ithaca, N.Y., 1991.

Jamison, Stephanie W. *Sacrificed Wife/Sacrificer's Wife: Women, Ritual, and Hospitality in Ancient India.* New York, 1996.

Mahony, William K. *The Artful Universe: An Introduction to the Vedic Religious Imagination.* Albany, 1998.

Malamoud, Charles. *Cooking the World: Ritual and Thought in Ancient India.* Translated from the French by David White. Delhi; New York, 1996.

R. N. Dandekar (1987)
Revised Bibliography

VEDISM AND BRAHMANISM.

VEDISM AND BRAHMANISM. The somewhat imprecise terms *Vedism* and *Brahmanism* refer to those forms of Hinduism that revolve primarily around the mythic vision and ritual ideologies presented by the Vedas. These terms are classifications that have been used by historians to categorize in a typological manner a variety of religious beliefs and practices in ancient and contemporary South Asia. Vedic and Brahmanic religious sensibilities are thereby distinguished from Agamic, Tantric, and sectarian forms of Hinduism, which look to a variey of non-Vedic texts as the source of religious authority. Vedism is older than Brahmanism, which developed from and remains true to the Vedic worldview but accommodated and remolded the religious ideas and practices of non-Vedic South Asian traditions.

Vedism applies more specifically to the religious ideas and expressions of the Indian branch of the Indo-Europeans who gradually entered the valley of the Indus River in successive waves in the second millennium BCE. These communities regard as sacred and authoritative texts only those orally transmitted collections of poetic hymns (*mantras*), ritual instructions (Brāhmaṇas), and some of the early philosophical speculations (Āraṇyakas and Upaniṣads) of the Vedic literary corpus. Together, these works are said to constitute sacred "knowledge" (*veda,* hence *Vedism*) and are known as *śruti,* "revealed truth."

Brahmanism developed as the Vedic Indians moved further into the subcontinent to settle in the regions drained by the Ganges River and then southward to the tip of India. It is loosely known as Brahmanism because of the religious and legal importance it places on the *brāhmaṇa* (priestly) class of society. Brahmanism takes as sacred truth, in addition to the Veda, various law books (the Dharmaśāstras and Dharmasūtras), mythic epics (the *Mahābhārata* and *Rāmāyaṇa*), and a wide range of non-Vedic myths recounted in the Purāṇas. These texts, the earliest of which may date to the second part of the first millennium BCE and the lattermost of which to the medieval period, are known as *smṛti,* "remembered truth."

Both Vedism and Brahmanism, then, accept the Veda as sacred. The difference between the two is that Brahmanism also includes doctrines and mythic themes that do not specifically derive from the Vedas and therefore is ideologically more inclusive than Vedism. Some of these ideas find expression in various ritual practices such as temple worship and the domestic ceremony known as *pūjā,* in the notion of a society arranged according to vocational function (*varṇa*) and stage of life (*āśrama*), in meditation and renunciatory practices, in vegetarianism and reverence for the cow, in the importance of the teacher (*guru*) for transmitting the tradition, and in other non-Vedic themes that play important parts in Hindu religious life and thought.

TEXTUAL CORPUS. The collection of metric and prose texts that form the Veda (or, taken individually, Vedas) is by far the largest single documentary source of archaic Indo-European religious thought. At the same time, however, this collection amply documents a particular line of intellectual development that went far beyond its archaic beginnings and gave the Veda its pivotal but never undisputed place in Indian religion and philosophy.

Though no definite dates can be assigned to the Veda or any of its parts, some of its materials, especially in the metrical texts, may be dated back to the twelfth century BCE, or even earlier, when the later Indo-Aryans were still in direct contact with the Iranian branch of the Indo-European peoples. This common Indo-Iranian period is attested by linguistic, lexical, formulaic, and cultic similarities between the Veda and the Avesta (e.g., the sacred beverage, *soma* in the Veda and *haoma* in the Avesta, and the use of these beverages in the cult; the Vedic *hotṛ* priest and his Avestan counterpart, *zaotar*). The formation of the Veda as currently known extended over the first half of the last millennium BCE, bearing witness to a gradual move from the northwest of the subcontinent, the upper Indus area, where the *Ṛgveda* had its original home, to the watershed between the Indus and Ganges basins and into the Ganges plain. This movement is epitomized in the story of the sacrificial fire, which was forced by means of a ritual formula to come out of the mouth of the legendary sacrificer Videgha Māthava (whose name recalls Videha, present-day Bihar); the fire then relentlessly rolled eastward from the Sarasvatī River in the west to the Sadanira, the boundary river of Videha, in the east, and finally was established even beyond that boundary (*Śatapatha Brāhmaṇa* 1.4.1.10–19). Bengal (Vanga), however, remained, as far as the Veda is concerned, a "barbarian" country.

Apart from its antiquity, the most striking features of the Veda are its rigid codification and internal organization as well as its faithful oral transmission among specialized brahmans up to the present day. Although no decisive arguments can be adduced, the codification of the Veda may date from the middle of the first millennium BCE. (This is to be distinguished from partial compilations, which are generally assumed to have already been in existence at the rise of Buddhism in the sixth century BCE.) During the second half of that millennium further ancillary texts were added to the corpus.

Organization of the Veda. The primary principle of the internal organization of the Vedic corpus is strictly ritualistic, the texts being arranged according to their function with regard to the sacrificial ritual. The initial textual layer consists of formulas (*mantras*)—both metrical and in prose—to accompany the ritual acts (*karman*) and descriptions of the ritual (Brāhmaṇas). The latter are thus differentiated in rules regulating the ritual (*karmavidhāna*) and in explanation or discussion (*arthavāda; Āpastamba Śrautasūtra* 24.1.31–34). Though this primary division gives no special place to the Upaniṣads, the speculative extension of the Brāhmaṇa texts, it clearly illustrates the ritualistic divide between *karman,* or act, and *mantra,* or formula.

The repositories of the *mantras* are known as the Saṃhitās (named after the continuous mode of recitation involving *saṃdhi,* or changes taking place at the juncture of words succeeding each other), first collected in the *Ṛgveda* or "Veda of the Stanzas." Though the time of its final compilation may not greatly differ from the period of the Brāhmaṇas, the *Ṛgveda* contains, generally speaking, the oldest materials. The exposition of the ritual (including the explanation of the *mantras* and their use) in the Brāhmaṇas provides the second layer. The third layer is formed by the Āraṇyakas ("forest books") and the Upaniṣads. They are attached to the Brāhmaṇas and are composed in the same style. The Āraṇyakas, which derive their name from their having to be studied outdoors, in the wilderness (*araṇya*) because of their supposedly dangerous or secret nature, deal with particular parts of the ritual. The Upaniṣads start from and often refer to the ritual but their meta-ritualistic content goes beyond and even supersedes it.

To these three layers of texts, which form the *śruti* (lit., "hearing"), the "revealed" tradition in the strict sense, the Kalpasūtras (*kalpa,* "arrangement"; *sūtra,* "guideline"), concisely worded manuals, must be added. These comprise the Śrautasūtras—manuals for the *śrauta* (derived from the *śruti*), or "solemn" ritual based on the Brāhmaṇas—and the Smārtasūtras, summarizing the *smṛti* ("remembrance"), the secular tradition. The latter are again divided into the Gṛhyasūtras, manuals for the domestic ritual (*gṛha,* "house"), which exhibit a ritual close to the *śrauta* pattern, and the Dharmasūtras, on religious law and custom, which are at a greater distance from the *śruti,* though they are supposedly authorized by it.

The Kalpasūtras belong to the six Vedāṅgas ("members of the Veda"), ancillary branches of knowledge meant to explain the Veda and to sustain its preservation. In addition to the Kalpa, the system of ritual rules, these branches of knowledge are Śikṣā ("phonetics"), Chandas ("meter"), Vyākaraṇa ("grammar"), Nirukta ("etymology"), and Jyotiṣa ("astronomy"). While the systematic elaboration and standardization of Kalpa has the rationalistic trappings that qualify it as a "prescientific" science, astronomy and especially grammar developed into full-fledged sciences independent of the Veda.

The partly chronological division in Saṃhitās, Brāhmaṇas, Āraṇyakas, Upaniṣads, and Kalpasūtras is joined by a second, equally ritualistic, principle of organization running vertically through the successive layers. This division corresponds to the four priestly functions in the performance of the *soma* sacrifice, that is, the functions of the *hotṛ* ("reciter"); the *udgātṛ* or *chandoga* ("cantor" or "chanter"); the *adhvaryu* (officiating priest), who is in charge of the ritual acts and so of the overall proceedings; and the *brahman,* who acts as a mainly silent overseer and corrects possible mistakes in the performance of the ritual. To each of these four functions a separate Veda is assigned, consisting of its own Saṃhitā, Brāhmaṇa, and Kalpasūtra. Thus the *hotṛ*'s Veda is the *Ṛgveda,* from which the invitatory and offering stanzas as well as the longer recitations (*śastra*) are taken. The Śāmaveda cites the texts of the *Ṛgveda* and their "melodies" (*sāman*) that are to be chanted by the *udgātṛ.* The *adhvaryu* operates with the *Yajurveda* or "Veda of the Formulas" (*yajus*). These "formulas" are defined as non-*ṛc* (that is, non-Ṛgvedic), although the Saṃhitā contains many Ṛgvedic *mantras* as well. Finally, the *brahman* relies, at least in theory, on the *Atharvaveda,* but because of his overseeing function he should also be conversant with the other three Vedas.

There are, then, four Vedas. Tradition, however, emphasizes the "Triple Veda" (*trayī vidyā,* "threefold sacred knowledge"), that is, *Ṛgveda, Yajurveda,* and *Śāmaveda.* The *Atharvaveda* was added as a fourth according to a well-known pattern based on the numbers three and four: the three "twice-born" *varṇas* (social classes) of *brāhmaṇas* (Eng., brahmans), *kṣatriyas,* and *vaiśyas*—their second birth being their initiation to the Veda—joined by the fourth *varṇa* of the *śudras.* The pattern also represents the three aims or duties of life: *dharma* (religious law), *artha* (wealth), and *kāma* (sexuality)—to which *mokṣa* (liberation from mundane existence) is added as a fourth.

The position of the *Atharvaveda* as regards the other three Vedas is somewhat puzzling. The name of a legendary priest and his descendants, *Atharvan* is related to the Old Iranian *āthravan,* or fire priest, but does not refer to a specific priestly function in Vedic ritual. The relationship of the *Atharvaveda* with the *śrauta* ritual is a slight one. The connection with the *brahman's* function is made no earlier than in the comparatively late Brāhmaṇa of the *Atharvaveda* (*Gopatha Brāhmaṇa* 1.2.9). The contents of its Saṃhitā appear to be related to special rites for promoting well-being, for averting or undoing evil, for curing illness, and for harming enemies, which belong to the sphere of activity of the *purohita* (domestic priest or royal chaplain) rather than to the *brahman*'s function in the *śrauta* ritual. This seems also to be underlined by the fact that the *Atharvaveda*'s Gṛhyasūtra has priority over its Śrautasūtra in both age and importance. Although the *Atharvaveda*'s codification patterned after the "Triple Veda" is comparatively late, this does not mean that its contents are equally late in origin. Thus the so-called rice-dish sacrifice (Savayajña), though recast to parallel the *soma* sacrifice, may well have ancient roots. The Savayajña gives prominence to the sacrificial meal, which in the *śrauta* ritual is reduced to a minimum. Generally speaking, it would seem that the *Atharvaveda* became a repository of rites and incantations for which the fully developed *śrauta* system of ritual had no place anymore—such as, for instance, the exaltation of the *vrātya,* the warrior-sacrificer to whom the fifteenth book of the Saṃhitā is devoted.

Finally, there is still a third principle subdividing the Vedic texts, namely by "schools," each having its own recension of one of the four Vedas. If such a "school" has its own version of the Saṃhitā it is known either as a *śākhā* ("branch") or as a *caraṇa* (liturgical observance). The most subdivided of the four Vedas is the *Yajurveda.* First, there is the division between the so-called *Kṛṣṇa* ("black") *Yajurveda* and *Śukla* ("white") *Yajurveda* schools. The older *Black Yajurveda* is characterized by alternating *mantra* and Brāhmaṇa portions in its Saṃhitās, while the younger *White Yajurveda* neatly separates the *mantras* from the Brāhmaṇa, the celebrated *Śatapatha Brāhmaṇa.* Whereas the *White Yajurveda* has two closely related *śākhās* (*Mādhyandina* and *Kanva*), the *Black Yajurveda* shows marked differentiation between *śākhās* and their subdivisions, or *caraṇas* (the *Maitrāyaṇī Saṃhitā* with the *Mānava* and *Vārāha Sūtras*; the closely related *Kāṭhaka,* whose *sūtra* has been lost; and the *Taittirīya Saṃhitā,* with the *Āpastamba, Hiraṇyakeśin, Bhāradvāja, Baudhāyana, Vaikhānasa,* and *Vādhūla Sūtras*).

The Saṃhitā of the *Ṛgveda* is known in only one recension but has two subdivisions, Āsvalāyana (with the *Aitareya Brāhmaṇa* and the *Āsvalāyana Sūtra*) and Śānkhāyana (with the *Śānkhāyana Brāhmaṇa*—also known as the *Kauṣītaki Brāhmaṇa*—and the *Śānkhāyana Sūtra*). The *Śāmaveda* boasts two *śākhās* that in fact differ only minimally, the Kauthuma-Rānāyanīya and the Jaiminīya; the Brāhmaṇa of the latter is called *Jaiminīya Brahmaṇa,* and it is known for the richness of its mythical and legendary data. Finally, the *Atharvaveda* knows two *śākhās,* the Saunaka and the Paippalāda.

Though scholarly attention has mostly been directed toward the *Ṛgveda* and the problems raised by its language, stylistics, and mythological conceptions, from the strictly Indian point of view the main interest of Vedism is in the structure and development of ritual. This is evident in the internal organization of the Vedic corpus of texts, which, as has been seen, are arranged according to the needs of the *śrauta* system of ritual. The elaboration and standardization of this system are, however, a late Vedic development. The division of *mantra* and Brāhmaṇa is more than a technical-ritualistic one. It represents a caesura between, on the one hand, the older state of cult and belief that forms the background of the *Ṛgveda's* stanzas, and on the other the standardized system of ritual that developed in the Brāhmaṇas and was perfected in the Sūtras. It is also to be observed that, although the standardized ritual draws liberally on the *Ṛgveda* as a source of metrical *mantras*, only part of it is actually used in the ritual. Only the ninth of the ten books (*maṇḍalas*) of the *Ṛgveda,* which contains the hymns (*sūkta*) addressed to the god Soma (in the form of the *soma* beverage), is directly related to the ritual, namely to the decanting and filtering of the *soma* (*soma pavamāna*). These hymns were assembled for the purpose of the ritual in a separate collection that was added at a later date to the *Ṛgveda* as the ninth of its ten *maṇḍalas*. Otherwise, the arrangement of the *Ṛgveda* is not related to the later ritual. In general, this text provides few, if any, clear indications about its cultic context or about the occasions at which or for which the hymns were composed.

The *Ṛgveda,* then, for all its size and suggestive contents, does not allow a clear view of Vedic religion, its cult, or its beliefs, nor do the Brāhmaṇas, with their single-minded concentration on ritual. Non-Vedic testimonies, such as the early Buddhist scriptures, may be put to use—regarding, for instance, the cult of spirits (*yakṣas*)—but they will not suffice for a well-rounded picture. Nor does archaeology offer any reliable clues. It has not even been possible to find indubitable evidence linking the Vedic data with the preceding Indus civilization. The only source for Vedic religion is the Vedic corpus, but it can only give part of the spectrum. Moreover, one must take into account the sharp divide between the *Ṛgveda* and the Brāhmaṇas.

MYTHOLOGY. As regards mythology the *Ṛgveda* is a vast storehouse of mythic motifs that are partly taken up again and recast by the Brāhmaṇas in their explanation of the ritual. It would be a mistake, however, to expect a consistent mythology or a clearly structured pantheon. Individual outlines tend to be blurred and areas of activity indeterminate, whereas attributes and positions are to some extent interchangeable among the gods. The reason for the apparent indeterminateness of Ṛgvedic mythology is not to be found in the fluidity of archaic thought. In fact, the *Ṛgveda* bears witness to a highly developed state of verbal art. Though conventional and even formulaic, the mode of expression is characterized by great sophistication and flexibility, geared to interchangeability and conflation of images and formulations. The aim is not to arrive at a precise delineation of the deity invoked and his power, but, on the contrary, to compress several associations and layers of meaning within the bounded, metrical compass of a stanza. In this respect Ṛgvedic mythology is essentially different from the mythological statements of the Brāhmaṇas. The *Ṛgveda* works by multi-interpretable suggestion and allusion rather than by explicit statement, leaving unexpressed the inner connection of the images and meanings that are suggested or alluded to. In this way a vast or even unbounded field of symbolic relationships is evoked to enhance (and exploit) the power of the deity. Hence the indeterminacy of Ṛgvedic mythology, which is a matter of principle rather than of pristine fluidity.

This feature has given rise to F. Max Müller's well-known but misleading term *henotheism,* or *kathenotheism,* to characterize Vedic religion. Insofar as it describes the apparent tendency to provide the invoked deity with a maximum of divine associations to enhance its power, the term may still be useful. It should, however, not be taken as an intermediary stage on the way to some form of strict monotheism, nor can it serve to define Ṛgvedic religious thought. It does no more than indicate a marked feature of Vedic hymnology.

The mythological statements of the Brāhmaṇas, by contrast, are directly and unequivocally linked to the ritual and its details, which they are meant to explain and justify. The tersely and concisely recounted mythical and legendary episodes lack the sophisticated associativeness and multi-interpretability that characterize the *Ṛgveda.* Their only—and explicit—association is with the ritual. The many layers of meaning are reduced and systematized in three tiers referring respectively to the ritual (*adhiyajña*), to the godhead (*adhidaiva*), and to the person of the sacrificer (*adhyātma*). Given the structure of the ritual as a collection of separate sacrifices and of each sacrifice as a lineal concatenation of clearly distinguishable acts and accompanying *mantras*, the mythological statements that refer to the separate sacrifices or to the successive acts of each of them cannot, by their nature, present a consistently structured mythology and cosmology. Moreover, there are clear traces of non-Aryan themes—often revealed by non-Aryan names—that raise the question of their whole or only partial integration. The search for an underlying unified pattern of mythic and cosmic conception will therefore to a large extent remain a matter of speculation.

Keeping in mind this caveat as well as the indeterminacy of the *Ṛgveda* and the ritualism of the Brāhmaṇas, one may now proceed to a brief survey of Vedic mythology. In accordance with the not specifically Vedic or Indian custom of expressing the idea of totality by a number, the *Ṛgveda* often speaks of thirty-three gods. The Brāhmaṇas break down this number as eight Vasus, eleven Rudras, and twelve Ādityas, leaving two open slots. Essentially such numbers are, however, not meant to be filled out by a complete list.

Ādityas. In the same way, the most important group among the gods, the Ādityas, is equally marked by a number, namely seven or eight (although only six are named) and later, in the Brāhmaṇas, twelve. They are defined as the sons of the goddess Aditi, whose name means "boundlessness." Her name has given rise to an opposite counterpart, the goddess Diti (dropping the privative *a*), who later is considered the mother of the gods' enemies, the demonic *daityas*, better known as *asuras*. The notion of a mother goddess or Magna Mater is, however, not very prominent in the Veda. The Ādityas are connected with light and with celestial phenomena. Āditya also occurs as the name of the sun (otherwise Sūrya), and it has been proposed that the seven Ādityas be equated with the sun, the moon, and the five planets. On the other hand they are thought to represent various aspects of rulership or sovereignty; the first three, Varuṇa, Mitra, and Aryaman, especially represent this capacity, whereas Bhaga ("dispenser"), Aṃśa ("share"), and Dakṣa ("capability") are associated with social concepts. Some of these names, such as *Mitra, Aryaman,* and *Bhaga,* have direct correspondences in Old Iranian, but the functions associated with them differ considerably. Apart from that, the Ādityas as a group have been equated with the (somewhat different) Amesha Spentas in the Avesta.

The foremost among the Ādityas—and at the same time the most problematic—is Varuṇa. His name is, not without doubts, connected with the Greek Ouranos. He is a sovereign god, often characterized as *samrāj,* establishing and maintaining universal order, punishing transgressions, and binding the sinner with his ties. In this perspective one can also place his connection with *ṛta* (cosmic truth) and guardianship of the oath as well as with the waters, which are the abode of *ṛta.* At the same time Varuṇa exhibits a sinister and dark side, especially in his opposition to the warrior god Indra, who appears to have robbed Varuṇa of his virility and dethroned him (*Ṛgveda* 4.42; 10.124). In this connection Varuṇa's qualification as an *asura* should be mentioned. Being preeminently an *asura,* a lordly being, he can be considered as the Vedic counterpart to the Avestan Ahura Mazda, with whom he shares the connection with *ṛta* (OIran., *asha*). Varuṇa's *asura* quality would seem to oppose him to the *devas*, or heavenly gods, even though the *deva/asura* opposition is less pronounced in the *Ṛgveda* than it is in the Brāhmaṇas. The problem Varuṇa presents is his two-sidedness. As the first among the Ādityas he is a *deva,* while at the same time he is prominent as an *asura.*

Varuṇa often occurs coupled with another Āditya, Mitra, who (in accordance with his name) represents contract and alliance. In the Veda he remains somewhat in the background. In the Avesta, however, he is more prominent and receives a fuller treatment; he is also a warrior and is associated with heaven and the sun. In contradistinction to the *Ṛgveda,* the Brāhmaṇas emphasize an opposition between Mitra and Varuṇa, the former being equated with the daylight, the latter with the night. The third Āditya, Aryaman, is concerned with marriage and hospitality.

Indra. The god most often encountered is the warrior god Indra, who receives the most elaborate mythological treatment of all the Vedic gods. Although he does not belong to the Ādityas he is mentioned at least once as the fourth Āditya (*Ṛgveda* 8.52.7), so as to connect him with the three first, and sovereign, deities among the Ādityas. A few times in the *Ṛgveda* he is called an *asura,* as is Varuṇa. His appearance, strength, and liberality, and his prowess in battle, in drinking *soma* (sometimes obtained forcibly), and, later, in amorous ventures—as well as his chariot, his horses, and his weapon, the *vajra* (the thunderbolt)—receive ample attention. He is, however, not only a warrior and divine prototype of the *kṣatriya* or *rājanya:* He also exhibits priestly or Brahmanic traits and as such is related to Bṛhaspati, or Brāhmaṇaspati (lord of the greatness or of the *brahman*), who is credited with some of the heroic deeds usually ascribed to Indra. (Hanns-Peter Schmidt has even argued that *Bṛhaspati* may originally have been an epithet of Indra. Incidentally, this should warn against setting too early a date for the separation of the four *varṇas* as closed, mutually exclusive status groupings.)

Indra's most vaunted deeds are the liberation of the waters by killing the monster Vṛtra ("obstruction")—hence his epithet *Vṛtrahan,* which equates him with the Avestan Verethraghna—and the freeing of the cows (metaphorically, the heavenly lights) from the Vala cave or from the cave where the Paṇis hid their cattle. In the Vala episode he is associated with the priestly Angirases, who assist him by their chanting in opening the cave or enclosure. Here, Indra's relationship, or rather overlap, with Bṛhaspati/Brāhmaṇaspati is most clear.

Maruts and Vāyu. Indra's usual companions and warband are the Maruts, the sons of Pṛśni, the spotted cow. They are depicted as chariot fighters and support Indra in the Vṛtra battle, but they also have a priestly quality as bardic chanters. In a naturalistic perspective the Maruts are the violent storm gods, just as Indra's weapon, the *vajra,* is the thunderbolt. As such, the Maruts are akin to Vāyu ("wind"). Equally a charioteer and associated with Indra, Vāyu is linked with the Maruts. His pneumatic character seems to connect him with ancient initiation rites as well as with the later, Upaniṣadic speculations on the life breath, or *prāṇa.*

Trita. As a dragon slayer Indra has a minor double in Trita ("the third") Aptya ("the aquatic one" [?]), who is equally credited with slaying Vṛtra and Vala. These exploits, however, burden him, like Indra, with the guilt of manslaughter, which makes Trita into a kind of scapegoat. In the Brāhmaṇas he is identified with Agni, the fire, who hides from his cruel duty as the sacrificial fire. Trita is also known to the Avesta in a double form, as Thraetaona (Pers., Farīdūn) Āthwya, the slayer of the dragon Azhi Dahāka, and as Thrita, the father of Kereśāspa, equally a dragon slayer. Trita, and not Indra, may have been the original hero of the dragon fight.

Aśvins. The twin Aśvins ("possessing horses"), or, by their original name, the Nāsatyas, are chariot warriors—the chariot being typically manned by a pair, the driver and the fighter—conveying Sūrya, the bride of the sun. Equally, they are associated with the goddess Uṣas, or Dawn. They obtain the secret of the cultic *surā* beverage (distilled from grain) from the demon Namuci and honey mead (*madhu*) from the horse-headed Dadhyañc. In this connection they are also known for their qualities as healers and miracle workers.

Rudra. A different type of warrior is the terrible archer Rudra ("the red one," or "the howler"), who inhabits the mountains and the wilderness. He is identified with the destructive, uncontrolled aspect of Agni, the fire. Generally, Rudra is surrounded by fear and taboo. In the ritual he typically receives the remainder of the oblation, thus being set apart from the gods and "bought off." The group of Rudras—their later standard number is eleven—are identified with the Maruts, Rudra being said to be their father. In post-Vedic religion Rudra developed into the transcendent god Śiva.

Viṣṇu. Another Vedic god who was destined for post-Vedic prominence is Viṣṇu, who in many ways became a counterpart to Śiva. In the Vedic hymns Viṣṇu is a minor figure, associated with Indra in the Vṛtra battle. In the Brāhmaṇas he is identified with the institution of sacrifice. His characteristic deed, however, is the feat of crossing, measuring out, or conquering the universe by his three steps. This feat may be linked with his solar (and, possibly, also phallic) character as also with his later association with the *axis mundi.* As against the fearsome Rudra-Śiva, who resides outside human society, the consistently benevolent Viṣṇu takes up his position in the center of the universe and in the middle of the settled world, encompassing and organizing the universe with his three steps.

Pūṣan. The pastoral Pūṣan is the guardian of the roads, a trait that should probably be viewed against the background of the movement of cattle. The furthering of prosperity to which his name (from *puṣ,* "prosper") refers is primarily concerned with cattle (especially cows), the epitome of wealth. His guardianship of the roads easily connects Pūṣan with the path of the sun, which leads from heaven to earth. In this respect he may be viewed as a solar deity.

Agni. From the ritualistic point of view the most important deities are Agni, the fire, and Soma, the deified cultic beverage and draft of immortality (*amṛta*). In cosmic perspective they represent the fiery and watery elements. As the sacrificial fire, Agni is produced with the help of two special pieces of wood known as the "two *araṇis*" that are manipulated in a way explicitly imitating the sexual act. The domestic fire, on the other hand, is the fire used in the marriage ritual and so is derived from the bride's paternal home. This notion should be a warning to any misunderstandings regarding the "ancestral fire"; insofar as it is ancestral it is transmitted in the female line. Moreover, the upkeep of the actual domestic fire ends with the death of the householder, when it is used for the last time at his cremation. The fire—both domestic and sacrificial—is discontinuous, its transmission broken and its possession uncertain. The mythology of Agni is replete with his fleeing and hiding in plants or trees but especially in the waters, illustrating the basic though paradoxical interrelationship between the watery and fiery elements. This paradox is further indicated by one of the names for Agni, Apāṃ Napāt ("son of the waters").

Time and again Agni has to be retrieved from his hiding places, that is, the fire must be obtained from elsewhere, from other people. Even though the "two *araṇis*" would, in principle, ensure the undisturbed possession of the fire, which then can be produced at will after a period of inactivity or hiding when it has been symbolically taken up in the sacrificer's person, these drilling sticks are not an ancestral heirloom, but are obtained from the *adhvaryu* priest (fittingly, he is rewarded with a gift when fire is produced). Less ritualistically, the fire appears to be obtained by force or theft, as occasionally shown in the ritual texts. Conversely, the *śrauta* ritual for setting up the sacrificial fires (*agnyādhāna*)—obviously meant to have only one performance, whose effects were permanent—can be repeated after some, not clearly specified, mishap. This seems to point in the same direction: The fire may have been robbed or lost as the result of a hostile encounter. Although the Vedic myth of Mātariśvan ("swelling in the mother"[?], probably a name of Agni), who brings the fire to the human world, does not mention agonistic proceedings, the ritual seems to recall the well-known Indo-European myth of the theft of the heavenly fire.

On the other hand the fire is identified with the person of its possessor in a way that suggests the notion of an "external soul." It defines the household and its master; in the sacrificial ritual it leads the triumphant procession to the sacrificial hearth (*āhavanīya*), where it is to be installed. In this latter triumphal aspect Agni is a victorious warrior moving about on his chariot and bringing the gods to the sacrifice or conveying the offerings to them as well as receiving offerings himself. In short, he is the linchpin of the universe viewed as sacrificial process. Although the *śrauta* ritual identifies Agni with the *hotṛ* priest, it would seem that originally this functionary is no other than the sacrificer striving to prevail over other sacrificers and their fires, as is still noticeable in the rite of the Pravara, the "election" of the *hotṛ,* immediately preceding the burnt offerings.

Both mythologically and ritually, then, the relationship of humans with Agni, dispersed throughout many separate (and competing) fires as well as regularly disappearing, is critical and insecure. In his "terrible" (*ghora*) form, as Rudra, he may even endanger the sacrificer's life.

Soma. *Soma* (Avestan, *haoma*) is predominantly the plant from which the cultic beverage is prepared as well as the beverage itself. Like the fire, Agni, it has to be won or obtained from elsewhere. "The one [Agni] Matarisvan brought from heaven, the other [Soma] the eagle [*śyena*] took by force from the mountain" (*Ṛgveda* 1.93.6). In the Brāhmaṇas this bird is identified with the *gāyatrī,* which, having three eight-syllable feet, is the shortest of the Sanskrit meters and is emblematic of chant and recitation. The mountain where the *soma* plant grows is named Mūjavat. The main distinguishing feature of *soma* is that it is to be won or brought from the wilderness, far away from the settled world. In the ritual the stalks of the *soma* plant are bought from an outsider in exchange for a cow, after which the *soma* seller is beaten and chased. This latter feature, as well as other less explicit details, suggests that behind the trading lies a contest in which the seller represents the guardians of the *soma,* the heavenly Gandharvas.

Another way of winning the *soma*—or rather the *soma* draft—is by forcibly obtaining access to another's *soma* sacrifice. Though the ritual does not account for this it is a well-known mythical theme. Thus Indra robs Tvaṣṭṛ and drinks the *soma* from his ritual vessels. In another myth Indra slays Tvaṣṭṛ's son, the three-headed monster Viśvarūpa, at the sacrifice in order to obtain the *soma* draft. Or again, Indra obtains the *soma*—as well as Agni—by slaying Vṛtra, who is holding them within himself.

As a god, Soma rules over the waters and their cosmic circulation. As such he takes up a central position in the universe, parallel to that of Agni, with whom Soma is often coupled as a dual divinity in the ritual texts. Significantly the *Ṛgveda* associates him with the sun, illustrating once more the solIḍārity of the fiery and the watery elements.

As in the case of Agni, Soma's relationship with man (i. e., winning him or losing him) is of crucial importance. However, unlike Agni, he is not identified with the sacrificer, but remains external to him. He is "the king" *par excellence,* ceremonially received as such on the place of sacrifice and often referred to by this title alone in the ritual manuals. This may perhaps explain why, whereas the fire is simply brought from heaven and the evidence for force or stealth is reduced to scattered and fragmentary indications, conflict and violence are involved in winning the *soma.* If the fire, as the sacrificer's "external soul," were to be the subject of an equally open direct conflict, the consequences would be disastrous: Just how disastrous can be seen upon considering the position of Soma, "the king." After his reception, he is pressed—that is, "killed." Having been prepared, sacrificed, and consumed, Soma is, in short, immolated. Obviously, this rules out the direct identification with the sacrificer. Such an identification is, however, still discernible, but shrouded in mystery as a dark, undeclared truth. Thus, when the royal sacrificer of the Rājasūya is proclaimed king, the priests inaudibly add "Soma is our king."

The original mystery of the sacrificer's immolation has been preserved in a different and innocuous form in the ritualistic mythology of the Brāhmaṇas, where the sacrificer is stereotypically identified with Prajāpati, the "lord" (*pati*) of "beings" (*prajā*). One of the many *pati* gods, he makes a fleeting appearance in the late tenth book of the *Ṛgveda* but reaches overall preeminence in the Brāhmaṇas. This Prajāpati, then, is the epitome of sacrifice, being at once the sacrificer and sacrificial victim. By that time, however, the ritual had developed into a closed, autonomous system that is ideally parallel to but not directly linked with the reality of the sacrificer's actual life and death.

A particularly knotty problem is the original identity of the *soma* plant. From the texts it appears that it must be a plant, often thought to be a creeper, with juicy stalks delivering the *soma* juice when crushed. R. Gordon Wasson's seductively argued theory of *soma* as the "divine mushroom of immortality," specifically fly agaric, is not generally accepted. The main difficulty is that fly agaric is not indigenous to the geographical area of the *Ṛgveda.* But if Wasson is right, this would mean that the elaborate imagery of the *soma* hymns would revolve around a substance no longer used or even known. Given the conventional nature of Vedic hymnology, this is certainly not impossible. The stalks actually used in the ritual appear anyway to be a substitute for the lost original.

As to the god Soma's celestial nature and abode the question of whether he represents the sun or the moon was at one time hotly debated. Though regularly associated with the sun in the *Ṛgveda,* Soma is usually identified with the moon in the Brāhmaṇas. The waxing and waning of the moon easily lend themselves to serve as an expression of the cosmic processes of growth, death, and renewal over which Soma presides. This led Alf Hillebrandt to postulate a lunar origin and character for Soma, which he expanded into a mythology involving other gods as well. This interpretation has, however, not been generally accepted, nor has Hermann Lommel's suggestion that Soma's identification with the moon would have come about by a restructuring under external, non-Aryan influences found favor. When the naturalistic and celestial interpretation of Vedic mythology receded in favor of more sociologically, cosmogonically, or ritually oriented views, the question of the lunar as opposed to the solar interpretation slipped into the background. The naturalistic viewpoint has once again gained favor, and the debate may in some form or other be reopened. At any rate the central point of Soma's mythology is the circulation of the cosmic waters holding the ambrosia (*amṛta*) and linked with the alternation of life and death.

Female deities. As mothers, sisters, wives, and lovers of the gods, female deities receive frequent mention, but, with the exception of Uṣas (Dawn), they remain diffuse, lacking in profile and to a high degree interchangeable with one another.

First there are are the deified (primordial) waters, Āpaḥ (plural of *ap,* water), which hold the germ of life and are the abode or hiding place of Agni (Fire), the "son of the waters" (Apāṃ Napāt). As has been seen, they are also associated with Soma. Their most direct manifestation is formed by the rivers, especially those of the Punjab, such as the Sindhu (grammatically both masculine and feminine), also called Indus, and its tributaries. Mythologically the most important of them is the Sarasvatī, in the Brāhmaṇas identified with the goddess Vāc (Speech), especially in connection with the hymnic or ritual utterance. Aditi, the mother of the Ādityas, has already been mentioned. The Brāhmaṇas explain the latter's birth as the result of Aditi's eating the remainder of the rice mess (*odana*) prepared and offered by her to the gods. Other female deities are Śrī (Luster), Puraṃdhi (Bounty), and Iḍā, or Iḷā (Food, both as offering and as sacrificial meal).

The most individualized of the goddesses is Uṣas (Dawn). She is depicted as a nubile, eternally young woman, wife or lover of the sun and companion of the Aśvins. Her most important feature is her bounty and her association with the gift, especially the *dakṣiṇā,* the gift to the priests at the sacrifice. The Brāhmaṇas transfer the incest motif of the otherwise featureless sky god, Dyaus, and his daughter to Prajāpati, father of all and epitome of sacrifice, and Uṣas. Prajāpati is then chastised by the archer Rudra who shoots an arrow at him; the wound is represented by a small piece from the offering cake, "Rudra's portion," which is, because of its potency, given to the *brahman* priest to eat. It is striking that Uṣas, notwithstanding her clear delineation and the hymns addressed to her, does not have a part in the sacrificial cult.

Ancestors. Finally, mention must be made of a separate class of divine beings, the Ancestors (*pitaraḥ,* "the fathers"). To them belong the *ṛṣis,* the seers to whom the Ṛgvedic hymns are ascribed. Stereotypically the ancestors form a group of seven (lsuch as the Ādityas) to which an eighth, Agastya, is added. They are the eponyms of the *gotras* (brahman lineages) systematically listed in the Pravara ("election") rite in the *śrauta* sacrifice where the names of the *ṛṣis* defining the sacrificer's *gotra* are mentioned.

Otherwise, the householder's lineage is defined by the last three ancestors—father, grandfather, great-grandfather—who receive offerings of water and rice balls (*piṇḍas*) in both the domestic (*gṛhya*) and the solemn (*śrauta*) ritual. The feature distinguishing the cult of the ancestors from that of the gods is the use of the left hand; the right hand is used in the cult of the gods. Thus, though regularly associated with the gods and their deeds, the *pitaraḥ* are sharply differentiated from them. Similarly, the "way of the fathers" (*pitṛyāna*) is distinguished from the "way of the gods" (*devayāna*), the first "way" being associated with the moon and the second with the sun.

Yama. Another set of ideas regarding the world of the dead focuses on Yama and his twin sister Yamī (*yama,* "twin"). Also known in Old Iranian mythology, they form the primordial pair. The *Ṛgveda* knows, but apparently rejects, their incest: In a dialogue hymn (*Ṛgveda* 10.10) Yama refuses to respond to Yamī's entreaties. Yama is the first mortal and, in ancient Iran, the first king. In India his kingship is reserved for his righteous rule over the world of the dead, which he is the first to enter. In the *Ṛgveda* he is the son of Vivasvat, a solar figure ("the wide-shining") whom the Brāhmaṇas make into an Āditya. Although it is only in later Hinduism that Yama is equated with Dharmaraja, the king of the universal order, the idea underlying this notion does not seem to be alien to the Veda.

Interpretations of Vedic mythology. The interpretation of the Vedic mythological data has, in the last hundred years or so, variously emphasized naturalistic, ritualistic, and sociological approaches. Abel Henri Joseph Bergaigne's *La religion védique d'après les hymnes du Ṛgveda* was the first and, thus far, unequaled attempt at a unitary synthesis combining both the naturalistic and ritualistic viewpoints. The mythical motifs are classified on two levels: on the one hand the celestial processes of light and darkness, on the other the atmospheric phenomena (clouds, rain, lightning) parallel to the celestial level. Both levels are further characterized by the opposition and interaction of male and female elements. The natural processes structured in this way are then seen as reflected in the cult. Bergaigne has been criticized for his allegorical schematism and his tendency to view the *Ṛgveda* exclusively in terms of its rhetorics. But his lasting achievement is in his systematic textual approach, involving a rigorous attention to the phraseology and its formulaic aspects. On this basis, modified by Hermann Oldenberg, it has also been possible to obtain a clearer view of the formation of the *Ṛgveda.* In general, Bergaigne can be considered the founder of Vedic philology, which then is brought to full growth by Hermann Oldenberg.

The sociological approach has been forcefully represented by Georges Dumézil, who stresses the three functions of sovereignty, both spiritual and worldly (Varuṇa as against Mitra), physical force (exemplified by Indra), and fecundity or productivity (represented by the Aśvins and other groups of gods, such as the Vasus, in association with female divinities). The three functions or principles are at the same time seen as the (Indo-European) ideology governing a tripartite social organization exemplified by the three "Aryan" or "twiceborn" *varṇas* (classes): *brāhmaṇas*, *kṣatriyas*, and *vaiśyas*. The problem with the social and ideological tripartition is that the number three, which is indeed strikingly frequent, is usually associated with either the number two—the third forming a link or intermediary—or four, when the fourth is an indeterminate or opposite element rounding out the whole (thus the three *varṇas* are supplemented by a fourth, the *śudra varṇa;* compare also such configurations as seven or eight Ādityas). The theory of the three functions is, however, not primarily directed at the interpretation of Vedic (and later, epic) mythology as such, but at comparative Indo-European mythology—a field of study revived and stimulated by Dumézil's numerous and erudite publications.

Another approach, which is reminiscent of Bergaigne's cosmological comprehensiveness but is not dependent on naturalistic or ritualistic viewpoints, singles out cosmogony as the key to "the basic concept of Vedic religion." The cosmogonic approach, propounded by F. B. J. Kuiper, has been influenced by earlier work (in the 1930s) of Dutch structuralist scholars on Indonesian religion and society; it is an approach in which psychoanalytic insights also are heuristically brought to bear on cosmogonic thought. In this perspective, the central feature of Vedic cosmogony and of the world it brought about is the sudden breakup of the undifferentiated primeval unity of the waters into a dualistic cosmos. The cause of this dramatic change was Indra's heroic deed. The *asuras*, who were associated with the primeval state of affairs, are defeated and replaced by the "younger" *devas*. Henceforth, the dualistic cosmos of upper and nether world—rent apart by Indra—is determined by the conflict of *devas* and *asuras*, which periodically breaks out again at the joints of the time cycle (as at the New Year) and is reenacted in verbal and other contests, particularly chariot races. In this scheme, the primordial unity is guaranteed by Viṣṇu, who, far from being a minor figure in the *Ṛgveda* as is usually assumed, transcends the conflict by his third step. The cosmogonic exegesis entails complex problems of textual analysis. Thus the opposition between *devas* and *asuras*, though clear and systematic in the Brāhmaṇas, is far from unambiguous in the *Ṛgveda*. The main problem is the nature of Varuṇa, an *asura* who belongs equally to the *devas*. In Kuiper's view Varuṇa went over to the victorious *devas* (keeping a hidden allegiance to the *asuras*), much as Agni and Soma left Vṛtra for Indra.

Whether cosmogony can deliver a basic or unitary concept underlying Vedic religion, or at least the Veda as known to the modern scholar, is of course debatable. One may even doubt whether such a concept did indeed exist. At any rate the metaphorical language of the hymns, with its tendency to pack various meanings and images in a single suggestive stanza while leaving the connecting idea or concept unexpressed, makes it particularly hard to isolate and define such a basic concept.

There can, however, be no doubt about the importance attached to Indra's cosmogonic battle, if the number of references both in the hymns and in the prose texts is taken as a criterion. More generally, competition, conflict, and combat appear to permeate the Vedic world. If the gods are bountiful or the human patrons munificent, the point is more often than not that the bounty and munificence should not go to the opponent. In the Brāhmaṇas conflict is stereotyped as the perennial struggle between *devas* and *asuras*, but conflict does not stop there. The *devas* are also competing (often by running chariot races) or fighting among themselves. The hostile tension between Indra and his followers, the Maruts, that is noticeable in some hymnic passages is crudely expressed in the Brāhmaṇas as Indra plundering the Maruts. In the ritual texts the *bhātṛvya* (rival kinsman), or the *dviṣat* (the foe), is all but ubiquitous. There clearly is the idea of a stable unalterable order—often associated with the unforgiving rule of Varuṇa—but this order is destabilized from within by the dualism of conflict for the goods of life. These goods, known under various, mostly indeterminate, all-encompassing terms, are mythologically luminous and celestial in nature and are associated with the waters. Thus, for instance, Indra's freeing Agni and Soma, the fire and the waters, from Vṛtra.

The "real life" substratum of the goods of life is cattle, especially cows, which then are transformed into theriomorph divinities (as, for instance, Pṛśni, the mother of the Maruts). In this connection the complex of female deities seems to be particularly important. Thus Uṣas is directly associated with the cow given as *dakṣiṇā* (gift to the priests), and the *soma* cow (the price for which the *soma* is traded) is addressed (among other names) as Dakṣiṇā (the deified gift cow), Aditi "facing both ways" (*ubhatakṣ́īrṣṇī*), Rudrā (feminine form of Rudra), and Ādityā (belonging to Aditi); her footprint is that of Iḍā. Especially suggestive is the double-headed Aditi: She is reminiscent of the Brāhmaṇa motif of the rejected and therefore angered personification of the *dakṣiṇā* threateningly standing between the two parties of the Ādityas and the Aṅgirasas (a clan of ancient fire priests, especially associated with the *Atharvaveda* but here identified with the *asuras*); the two parties soothingly try to lure her, now identified with the goddess Vāc (Speech), each to his own side (*Śatapatha Brāhmaṇa* 3.5.1.18–22). The complex of female deities, then, are intimately connected with the cows (i. e., the goods of life) for which the conflicting parties contend.

This may explain the rather indeterminate nature of the female deities. They are the movable stakes in the ever-repeated contest. As such they have no fixed place or allegiance but keep shifting between the contending parties, dividing and connecting them. In this way it can perhaps also be understood that Uṣas (Dawn), though profusely eulogized, does not receive a sacrificial cult: Standing for the bounty spent, contended for, distributed, and consumed, she is—like Iḍā, the sacrificial meal—not a recipient but the gift itself.

As party to the conflict the *asuras* are originally not so much demoniacal opponents and spoilers but rather settled rulers and holders of the goods of life. They are being despoiled by the aggressive wandering *deva* warriors led by Indra, who aspire to the status of settled lords. As the *Śatapatha Brāhmaṇa* has it in a lapidary but probably ancient phrase: "The *devas* drove about on wheels, the *asuras* sat in their halls" (*Śatapatha Brāhmaṇa* 6.1.1.1). But eventually the *devas* prevail over the *asuras*, and that is why the "moving-about warrior" (*yāyāvara*) holds sway over the settled people (*kṣemya*), as a parallel passage explains (*Taittirīya Saṃhitā* 5.2.1.7). Similarly, an isolated but telling rule recommends the would-be sacrificer who is going to set up his *śrauta* fires to take his cooking fire (*dakṣiṇāgni*, lit., "southern fire") from the house of a man of substance (*puṣṭa*) who is "like an *asura*" (*asura iva*; *Kāṭhaka Saṃhitā* 8.12; cf. *Āpastamba Śrautasūtra* 5.14.1).

This does not mean that the world of the gods is modeled after human society, but rather that there is no sharp dividing line separating them. The worlds of gods and humans smoothly blend into each other, forming a universe permeated by the divine and the sacral. If Indra's heroic warrior deed established the cosmic order, it is an order of perennial conflict over the possession and the redistribution of the goods of life—a conflict in which gods and men equally take part—and the outcome is open to reversal at the next turn. This may explain the fact, usually considered a secondary extension, that Indra is in a few Ṛgvedic passages called *asura.*

The arena where the conflict was fought out was the microcosm of the place of sacrifice. The central institution that regulated and contained conflict was sacrifice (*yajña*). Though the *śrauta* ritual has no place for the enemy it does contain many mock contests, prominent among them verbal contests (*brahmodya*) and chariot races. The Brāhmaṇas do not tire of referring to enemies, and the explanatory passages continually link the sacrificial ritual and its details with the fights of *devas* and *asuras*, while the place of sacrifice is made the battleground.

Though researchers are ill-informed about the cultic background of the hymns, which may have known a great variety of concepts and forms, sacrifice, especially the *soma* sacrifice, clearly must have been of overwhelming importance. As the *Ṛgveda Saṃhitā* (1.164.50 and 10.90.16) says in an enigmatically involute statement: "With sacrifice the gods sacrificed sacrifice, these were the 'first ordinances' (*dharmāṇi prathamāni*)." The second passage concludes the hymn celebrating the sacrifice of the *puruṣa,* the cosmic man, out of whose immolated body the ordered universe, including the four *varṇas,* was created. Although this cosmogonic sacrifice recalls Indra's Vṛtra-slaying, there is no reference to a fight or contest. Rather, it suggests the "monistic" form of the *śrauta* sacrifice propounded by the Brāhmaṇas, mythologically represented by Prajāpati, who creates the world by sacrificing himself. However, judging by the explanations in the Brāhmaṇas as well as by many features of the *śrauta* ritual itself, the form of the sacrifice preceding the one taught by them appears to have been characterized by a dualistic and agonistic structure.

The dualistic character is already implied in Paul Thieme's fundamental observation that the *śrauta* sacrifice is in all its details characterized as a guest reception, the sacrificer being the host. The guests at the sacrificial feast are not only the gods but equally the priestly participants who drink the *soma* and partake of the sacrificial food and who are identified with gods. The dualism of hosts and guests is clearly marked by tension and competition. Thus the Ādityas and the Aṅgirases—who have been seen already in their (verbal) contest over the *dakṣiṇā* bounty—competed over the honor of inviting the other party to their own sacrifice. First the Aṅgirases invite the Ādityas, but the latter manage to be "one up." Devising an equally important sacrificial ritual that can be performed on short term before the time set by the Aṅgirases, the Ādityas invite the latter and win out (*Aitareya Brāhmaṇa* 6.34).

Apparently, being invited to a sacrifice is a challenge that one cannot honorably refuse. On the other hand, not being invited is a dishonor. And so uninvited guests force their way in to obtain or rather to contend for their share, as did the Śyāparṇas at the sacrifice performed by Viśvantara Sauṣademana (*Aitareya Brāhmaṇa* 7.27), or as did Indra at Tvaṣṭṛ's, where Indra even killed Viśvarūpa, Tvaṣṭṛ's son. It is this dualistic and agonistic form of sacrifice that the ritualists of the Brāhmaṇas and the Sūtras reformed and turned into the rigidly "monistic" system of ritual that is the apogee of Vedism.

RITUAL. The most striking feature of Vedic ritual is the thoroughly systematic nature of its structure and textual presentation. Whereas the Brāhmaṇas still show in many ways, but especially in the *arthavāda* discussions, traces of the formative process and sometimes explicitly mention former practices as against the new rules, the Sūtras, or "guidelines," are fully systematized to the extent of stating a set of "metarules" (*paribhāṣā*) for the proper interpretation and handling of the ritual prescripts. This systematic character, definitively clarified by Willem Caland, caused Oldenberg to speak of "prescientific science" and Sylvan Lévi of "doctrine." Frits Staal has again called attention to what he considers to be the ancient Indian "science of ritual" as a system of "rule-governed activity" per se.

The ritual system. In the first place, there is the principle of the unity of act and formula. Unless stated otherwise each act is accompanied by a formula. The system is then built up in the way of nesting units, simpler acts being integrated to form ever more intricate complexes. The basic sacrificial unit is the pouring of a small portion of the oblational substance—milk, ghee (clarified butter), cake, gruel, meat, or *soma*—into the offering fire. This smallest unit, indicated by the verb *juhoti* ("he pours"), occurs as a separate act in all *yajñas*, but it is also an integral part of a more complex sacrificial act. The simple pouring is performed by only one person, usually the *adhvaryu,* but the more complicated form requires the cooperation of several priests. While standing at the offering fire the *adhvaryu* calls out to the *āgnīdhra, "oṃśrāvaya"* ("let there be hearing"), and the latter answers with *"Astu śrauṣaṭ"* ("be it, one should hear"); then it is again the turn of the *adhvaryu,* who now calls on the *hotṛ* to recite the offering verse (*yājyā*). The verse begins with the name of the god to whom the oblation is addressed and is followed by the instruction to "worship" (*yaja*), that is, to recite the appropriate verse; the *hotṛ* complies, prefixing the words *ye yajāmahe* ("we who worship," also known from Old Iranian) and ending with the word *vauṣaṭ,* at which the *adhvaryu* pours the oblation in the fire and the sacrificial patron (*yajamāna*) pronounces the *tyāga* ("abandonment"): "for [name of the god addressed], not for me."

This scheme, indicated by the verb *yajati* ("he [i. e., the *hotṛ*] worships"), is the one used in the standard ghee libations preceding and following the main offering (*pradhāna*) in the vegetal sacrifices. In the case of the main offering the scheme is enlarged by a preceding invitatory verse (*anuvākyā* or *puronuvākyā*) to be recited by the *hotṛ,* who is called upon by the *adhvaryu* to do so. The same scheme is then further elaborated in the animal sacrifice by the participation of one of the *hotṛ*'s assistants, the *maitrāvaruṇa,* who relays to the *hotṛ* the *adhvaryu's* call for the *anuvākyā* and *yājyā* verse. In the *soma* sacrifice this complex is further enlarged by the chanting of the *stotra* ("laud," from the verb *stu,* "to praise"), which is the task of the *udgātṛ* and his assistants, and the *śastra* (recitation) of the *hotṛ,* which follows the libation and the drinking of the *soma* by the participants. In all this the basic sacrificial act remains the libation in the offering fire.

This summary description of the basic sacrificial act and its enlargement cannot do justice to the intricate detail of the rules that, apart from the sacrificial act itself, also cover the no less complicated preparatory acts—taking the vow, choosing the priests, collecting the ingredients and implements (*saṃbhāra*), arranging the place of sacrifice, readying the fires, preparing the oblational substance (*havis*), its consumption and disposal, the *dakṣiṇās*—as well as the concluding phase. But the brief summary adequately illustrates the systematic buildup of the ritual. Each sacrifice consists of a lineal succession of such standardized units of act and formula, primarily the basic sacrificial act with or without its extensions. The alignment of acts again shows the nesting principle by boxing in a unit on both sides by two other mutually connected or similar units, as for instance is the case of the main offering (*pradhāna*), which is preceded by the "fore-offerings" (*prayāja*), and followed by the "after-offerings" (*anuyāja*). In this way a complicated concatenation is achieved spanning the whole of the sacrifice, its beginning and conclusion, mirroring each other so as to enclose the whole.

The same nesting principle governs the hierarchical taxonomy of types of sacrifices, the simpler types being incorporated in the more complicated ones. The simplest type of sacrifice is the Agnihotṛa, the evening and morning offering of boiled milk. It is essentially the basic sacrificial act of the *juhoti* type, requiring only the service of the *adhvaryu.* More complicated is the *iṣṭi* (from the verb *yaj,* "to worship"), a vegetal sacrifice of one or more cakes (*puroḍāsa*), cereal boiled with butter and milk (*caru*), or a dish of coagulated milk (*sāṃnāyya*). It involves the taking out, husking, and grinding of the grain, preparing the dough, baking the cake (on a specified number of potsherds heated on the embers), and dividing it into portions to be distributed to the deity and among the sacrificer and his priests. Moreover, before the main offerings are made, the sacrificial fire is fueled with pieces of wood (*samidh*). The *hotṛ* recites a verse (*sāmidhenī*) as the *adhvaryu* places each *samidh* as an offering into the fire.

This series of sacrificial acts is then followed by the *pravara* ("election") of *hotṛ* and *adhvaryu,* in which the sacrificer's ancestral names are mentioned, and finally the main offerings are made according to the *yajāti* scheme. Of course, separate *juhoti* offerings are equally part of the *iṣṭi* ritual. A more complicated version of this type of sacrifice requires four priests: apart from the *adhvaryu,* the *hotṛ,* the *āgnīdhra* (counted with the *adhvaryu,* but as to his function associated with the *hotṛ*), and the *brahman.*

The next type, the *paśubandha* ("binding the animal victim"), or animal sacrifice, incorporates the *iṣṭi.* The acts concerned with the cake offering (*paśu-puroḍāśa*) are neatly intertwined with those of the animal sacrifice proper. Two more priests are added: the *maitravaruṇa,* who is associated with the *hotṛ,* and the *pratiprasthatr,* who assists the *adhvaryu.*

The most complicated type is the *soma* sacrifice, which incorporates both *iṣṭis* and *paśubandhas.* Its distinctive liturgical feature is the extensive use of the *Śāmaveda,* practically absent in the other sacrifices, for the chanted "lauds" (*stotra*), while the *soma* ritual proper is intertwined with an animal sacrifice. This involves the services of four specialized chanters (*chandoga*) led by the *udgātṛ.* Altogether the *soma* sacrifice needs sixteen or, according to some *sūtras,* seventeen priests, including the previously mentioned ones, divided into four groups according to the four Vedas: four *adhvaryu* priests (*Yajurveda*), four *hotrakas* (*Ṛgveda*), four *chandogas* (*Śāmaveda*), and four in the *brahman's* group (*Atharvaveda*); the seventeenth, the *sadasya,* is assigned to the *brahman.* At the same time, however, seven, instead of only four, of these priests are counted as *hotrakas,* six of whom are actually charged with *śastra* recitations from the *Ṛgveda.*

In the *śrauta* system of ritual the *iṣṭi* in the form of the fortnightly New and Full Moon sacrifices (*Darśapūrṇamāsa*), the *paśubandha* and the one-day *soma* sacrifice known as Agniṣṭoma ("liturgy of Agni") form the basic paradigms, or *prakṛti.* These *prakṛtis* can then be modified mainly as to the sacrificial substance and the deity or deities addressed (such a modification is known as *vikṛti*). The modified part therefore is primarily the *pradhāna* offering(s) involving (apart from differences in the sacrificial substances used) different invitations and offering verses. The rest of the ritual, the *aṅgas* (members) or *tantra* ("the warp," the sacrifice regularly being said to be woven), remains, but for a few minor adaptations, essentially unchanged. Thus a particular sacrifice is said to be characterized by three criteria: *dravya* (sacrificial substance), *devatā* (deity, or deities, first addressed at the beginning when the sacrificial substance is taken out), and *tyāga* (the sacrificer's "abandonment" formula, again specifying the deity after the offering; cf. *Kātyāyana Śrautasūtra* 1.2.2).

Furthermore, sacrifices can be strung together either in a continuous series (*ayana,* "course") or in periodical clusters. The latter is the case, for instance, with the fortnightly New and Full Moon sacrifice (comprising two main offerings within the same *tantra*) or with the seasonal Four Month sacrifices, which are essentially clusters of *iṣṭi*-type offerings at the beginning of a four-month period. The *soma* sacrifice in particular has lent itself to such strings, which may stretch over a number of years (theoretically even a hundred years). Although a *prakṛti* form, the Agniṣṭoma lasts only one day (apart from the preparatory days) and as such is an *ekāha;* there are strings of up to twelve days known as *ahīna.* A twelve-day series can be performed either as *anahīna* or a *sat-*

tra ("session"). The difference is that at a *sattra* there is not a sacrificer with his sixteen (or seventeen) priests but all the participants are homogenized into a single band of sacrificers who have put together their sacrificial fires, while at the same time each performs the task of a particular priest. Their leader is then called the *gṛhapati* ("master of the house"). The modifications that are needed make the twelve-day *sattra* into the *prakṛti* for all other, longer *sattras,* while the yearlong *sattra* or *gavām ayana* ("course of the cows") is again the model for all other *sattras* within the duration of a year or longer.

The feature by which the *soma* sacrifices are usually distinguished, however, concerns the arrangements of the *stotras* and *śastras*. The *stotras* involve intricate rules regarding the formation of the different standardized numbers of chanted units (*stotriyā*), composed of a group of two or three Ṛgvedic stanzas. These numerical arrangements are known as *stoma* ("liturgy"), which, like *stotra,* derives from the root *stu.*

Soma sacrifice. The *soma* sacrifice is the most important as well as the most intricate of the *śrauta* rituals. Its basic paradigm, the Agniṣṭoma, consists of an elaborate concatenation of sacrifices spanning five days and involving a whole pantheon. The first day is marked by the consecratory bath (*dīkṣā*) of the sacrificer, who remains a *dīkṣita* (initiate) and as such subject to restrictions of diet and behavior until the concluding bath (*ava-bhṛtha,* "the carrying away," i. e., of ritual matter by means of the waters). Special libations and an *iṣṭi* are connected with the *dīkṣā.* The next three days feature, in the morning and at midday, the ritual known as Pravargya and a ghee offering in the form of an *iṣṭi* called *upasad* ("sitting near" or "besieging"), after which these three days are called *upasad* days. The Pravargya ("to be removed," referring to the implements after the last performance) centers on a special clay pot (called *mahāvīra,* "great hero," or *gharma,* "heat"). Fresh milk is poured into this pot, which has been heated in the fire; of the milk boiled in this way a libation is made.

On the first *upasad* day the introductory (*prāyaṇīyā*) *iṣṭi* is performed. The *soma* stalks are bartered for the *soma* cow, and "King Soma" (in the form of the *soma* stalks) is given a ceremonial reception that takes the form of another *iṣṭi.* On the second *upasad* day the outline of the place of sacrifice (the *mahāvedī*) is traced and the earthen elevation for the offering fire is made. The third *upasad* day sees the construction of the other fire-places and of the various sheds on the *mahāvedi;* fire and *soma* stalks are brought forward in an elaborate procession and a *paśubandha* is performed. The *soma* sacrifice proper, entwined with another animal sacrifice, falls on the next, the fifth day, known as the *sutya,* or pressing day.

The *soma* stalks are pressed three times, in the morning, at midday, and in the afternoon, providing for three "services" or *savanas* ("pressings"). The pressing is done by four of the priests, who crush the stalks, spread on a bull's hide, with the pressing stones (*grāvan*). The *soma* juice is mixed with water and poured through a woolen filter into the wooden *soma* tub (*droṇakalaśa*). It is to this latter operation that the *pavamana* hymns of the *Ṛgveda* refer. Apart from the *soma* pressing, the distinctive feature of the *sutyā* day is formed by the twelve rounds—five each during the morning and midday *savanas*, and two in the afternoon—of pouring the *soma* libation, drinking the *soma,* and conducting the liturgy of the variously arranged *stotra* chants and *śastra* recitations. The afternoon service is followed by the final bath (*avabhṛtha,* "carrying away" of ritual matter to the waters), which forms the counterpart of the *dīkṣā* bath. Next is performed the concluding (*udayaniyā*) *iṣṭi,* which corresponds to the introductory (*prāyaṇīyā*) *iṣṭi.* But this is not yet the end, for a last *paśubandha*—a cow for Mitra and Varuṇa—must still be conducted. Only then is the "breaking up" (*adavasānīyā*) *iṣṭi* performed, after which the sacrificer and the other participants return home (the *śrauta* sacrifice, and especially the *soma* sacrifice, take place outside the settled community, in the wilds).

This basic scheme allows for an unlimited but mostly unspectacular variation. Such variation concerns in the first place the numerical arrangement of the *stotras* and the melodies (*sāman*) to which they are sung. Second, as already mentioned, the number of *sutyā* days can be multiplied so as to form *ahīnas* and *sattras*. Third, special rites can be inserted, both regular sacrificial acts and rites that are, strictly speaking, external to the *śrauta* system. Prominent among the latter are consecratory baths (*abhiṣeka,* comparable to an elaborate *dīkṣā*), which have given rise to a special class of sacrifices called *sava* ("instigation"), as well as agonistic rites: chariot races, dice games, and verbal and other contests. Storytelling, singing (as different from the Śāmavedic chanting), and dancing are occasionally prescribed. Such rites are mostly inserted in the middle of the *sutyā* day, during the midday service. A well-known case is provided by the *mahāvrata* ("great vow"). Technically a *sutyā* day at the end of the yearlong *gavāmayana,* it offers an interesting array of popular, apparently ancient rites, including a chariot race, arrow shooting, and a tug-of-war between an *ārya* and a *śudra* for a hide (believed to represent the sun), as well as the copulation of a "man from Magadha" (possibly meaning a musician) and a courtesan, and, of course, singing and dancing.

Similarly, the royal sacrifices, Vājapeya, Rājasūya, and Aśvamedha (horse sacrifice), are marked by such insertions. The Vājapeya ("booty" or "victory draft") follows the scheme of a one-day *soma* sacrifice which, however, combines the *soma* rites with those of the (popular) *surā* (grain liquor). Moreover, it features a race of seventeen chariots and a curious pole-climbing rite in which the sacrificer and his wife "ascend to heaven." The Rājasūya ("royal consecration") is essentially a series of five periodical *soma* sacrifices interconnected by *iṣṭi*-type sacrifices that stretch over two or three years. The important insertions are an elaborate *abhiṣeka* (water consecration), the enthronement, a game of dice, a chariot drive or race, and the recitation of the interesting legend of Śunaḥśepa (a brahman boy bought by King Hariścandra as a substitute for his own son, whom he was bound to sacrifice to Varuṇa, the point of the story being how Śunaḥśepa liberated himself by "seeing" and reciting stanzas in praise of Varuṇa). These rites are inserted in the second *soma* sacrifice, the Abhiṣecanīya (connected with the *abhiṣeka*).

The prestigious horse sacrifice (Aśvamedha) is a three-day *soma* sacrifice. The horse, accompanied by warriors, is left to roam about for a year on a tour of "world conquest" and is immolated, together with other animals, on the second *sutyā* day (thus providing the animal sacrifice of the basic *soma* paradigm). The insertions concern first of all the treatment of the horse; the chief consort of the sacrificer has to go through a sham copulation with the immolated horse while exchanging prescribed obscene and enigmatic phrases with the other consorts. Further there is again a chariot race and a full-scale verbal contest (Brahmodya).

The Puruṣamedha, or human sacrifice, is modeled on the Aśvamedha. In this form it would seem to be no more than a theoretical possibility reflecting the Ṛgvedic *Puruṣa* hymn (*Ṛgveda* 10.90). It does, however, raise the question of human sacrifice in general, outside the strictly bounded realm of the *śrauta* ritual. Although the idea of such sacrifices appears to have been known to the ritualists, as witnessed by the Śunaḥśepa legend, the actual practice would go against the grain of the *śrauta* ritual. The Brāhmaṇas repeatedly indicate that the sacrificer offers himself in sacrifice—like his mythical prototype Prajāpati or the Ṛgvedic Puruṣa—but the ritualistic solution is to "buy oneself free" (*niṣkrīṅīte*) by substitution. Or rather, the sacrificial ritual effectively cancels the ultimate violence of self-sacrifice. In a comparable way the royal sacrificer is mysteriously identified with the sacrificed "King Soma," a mystery that as such is not meant to be concretely realized but can only be hinted at. Nor is there a need for a *human* substitute. The Puruṣamedha, then, appears to be a theoretical construct that may reflect non-*śrauta* practices translated into the terms of the *śrauta* systems.

Separate mention should be made of the Sautrāmanī, named after Indra Sutrāman ("savior"). It is the sacrifice of *surā*, the grain liquor. In terms of the *śrauta* system it is an animal sacrifice in which three male animals are immolated for the Aśvins (who mythologically obtained the *surā* by force from Namuci), Sarasvatī, and Indra. The special feature is, however, the preparation, offering, and drinking of the *sura*. The way the animal sacrifice and the *surā* beverage are intertwined is patterned after the *soma* ritual (though without the *stotra-śastra* liturgy). The Sautrāmanī, though also given as an independent sacrifice, is to follow a *soma* sacrifice in which an *abhiṣeka* has been inserted (a *sava*, as in the Rājasūya). Apparently it is meant to remedy any unspecified bad effect of such sacrifices, as it is also said to cure the sacrificer from excessive *soma* drinking. In this connection, the function of the Aśvins as healers is relevant. It should be observed, however, that the *sura* beverage is not favored by the ritualists, who concentrate on *soma* instead, and later, in the *dharma* texts, *surā* is even prohibited.

Place of sacrifice and fires. In contradistinction to the domestic (*gṛhya*) ritual, the *śrauta* ritual requires a place of sacrifice separate from the home. Of the *soma* sacrifice it is even said, "One undergoes the *dīkṣā* at home; in the wilderness one performs the sacrifice." Although the *śrauta* ritual requires the presence of the sacrificer's wife, it appears originally to have been linked with life outside the settled community. Accordingly, the place of sacrifice is a temporary structure that is left when the sacrifice has been complete.

Just as the *śrauta* sacrifices are ordered by degrees of complexity, so also the place of sacrifice goes from simpler to more complex, enlarged forms. The basic form is that used for Agnihotra and *iṣṭi*. An oblong shed, oriented to the east, with openings to the four directions, shelters the three fire hearths. The round *gārhapatya* ("householder's") hearth, where the vegetal or dairy oblations are prepared, is on the west side, the square *āhavanīya* (offering hearth) is on the east side, and the half-moon-shaped *dakṣiṇāgni* ("southern fire"), where the food given to the priestly guests is cooked, is to the southeast of the *gārhapatya*. Between the *gārhapatya* and the *āhavanīya*, the *vedi*, the altar on which the oblations are placed, is arranged in the form of a trapezium. The upper layer of earth is taken off and the dug-out space is covered with grass. With its base to the west, its upper side to the east, and its sides bent inward, it is meant to suggest the form of a woman, broad-hipped and narrow-shouldered, holding the bounty of sacrifice (that is, the oblations placed on the *vedi*). To add to the *vedi*'s symbolism, the two shoulder points encompass the sides of the *āhavanīya*. Furthermore, there is a small mound (*utkara*) formed by the earth taken from the place of the *vedi* and used for rubbish disposal on the northern side. North of the *āhavanīya* a vessel with water is put down. The sacrificer has his seat south of the *āhavanīya*, as does the *brahman*, whose place is to the east of the *yajamāna*'s seat; the *hotṛ* is seated at the northwestern "hip" of the *vedi* and the *āgnīdhra*, north of the *vedi*; the *adhvaryu*, who mostly moves around on the place of sacrifice, has no fixed place.

For the *paśubandha* (animal sacrifice) the place of sacrifice is enlarged by adding an open space, the "great *vedi*" (*mahāvedi*), equally traced out in the form of a trapezium and covered with grass, immediately east of the fire shed. On the east side of the *mahāvedi* the new *āhavanīya* hearth (*uttaravedi*, "further *vedi*") is arranged, and east of it the sacrificial pole (*yūpa*) is erected. The center of the action is shifted to the east: The fire is brought from the old *āhavanīya* hearth in the fire shed and the latter serves henceforth as the *gārhapatya*. Outside the *mahāvedi*, to the north of it, sits the *śamitra*, the shed where the *śamitṛ* ("appeaser") kills the victim (by suffocation) after it has been taken from the *yūpa*. The same special arrangement with fire shed and trapezoid *mahāvedi* is used for the *soma* sacrifice. The *mahāvedi* is considerably larger, as various sheds are built on it. West of the new *āhavanīya* is the *havirdhāna* shed, where the two *soma* carts (one of which was used to bring up the store of *soma* stalks) are kept, as well as the *soma* tub (*droṇakalaśa*) and the other implements. On the western side, the north-south oriented *sadas* (seating hall) is erected. In the *sadas* six small fire hearths (*dhiṣṇiya*) are made, one for each of the six reciting *hotrakas*; further on are the seats of the four chanters who perform the *stotra*. The drinking of the *soma*, after the libation in the fire, takes place in the southern part of the *sadas*. The entrances of the *sadas* are on the east and the west sides. When the participants enter the *sadas* in procession, they do so in a peculiar way "as if stalking a deer" (*prasarpaṇa*, "creeping," possibly the remnant of a hunting dance). Finally there are two more sheds, each with a small fire hearth, the *āgnīdhrīya* (the *āgnīdhra's* place) and the *mārjalīya* ("cleansing"), respectively on the north and south sides of the *mahāvedi*. Outside the *mahāvedi* is placed the *utkara*, as is the *cātvāla* (cesspit), from which the earth has been taken for the fire hearths.

Normally the hearths are made of earth mixed with other materials, such as gravel, earth from an anthill, mud from a dried-up pool, and so forth. In the case of the *soma* sacrifice it is also possible to enhance the prestige of the ceremony by using brick fire hearths. For the horse sacrifice this is obligatory. The focus of attention is the *āhavanīya*, which rests on the *mahāvedi*. The *āhavanīya* consists of a five-layered brick construction. This requires a full thousand bricks of various shapes and sizes so as to fit into the prescribed pattern—the form of a bird with spread-out wings representing Agni (the bricks, being fired, are intimately connected with Agni). At the same time the brick-built *āhavanīya* is equated with the immolated and reconstructed body of Prajāpati or of the cosmic man (Puruṣa). Various objects are buried in the ground beneath the brick construction, including the skulls of a man and of four animals (horse, bull, ram, he-goat) and a gold image of a man. This rather suggests a funerary tumulus (not unrelated to the Buddhist *stūpa*). The construction of the brick hearths (Agnicayana, "piling the fire") is a complicated ritual of fetching the clay in a ceremonial procession (which can be shown to derive from a razzia or war expedition), firing the bricks, and finally building the hearths, especially the bird-shaped *āhavanīya*. The Agnicayana takes place during the *upasad* days, so as to be ready for the animal sacrifice on the last *upasad* day. After the sacrifice the brick-built fireplaces, like the place of sacrifice itself, are abandoned, not to be used again.

In this connection, mention should be made of the special ritual for the first installation of the *śrauta* fires, which forms the starting point of the *śrauta* sacrificer's career. This ritual, called Agnyādhāna or Agnyādheya, concerns the transition of the domestic householder-sacrificer to the status of an *āhitāgni*, one who has set up the *śrauta* fires. Hence the first part of the ritual is still domestic in nature, namely the cooking of a rice dish (*odana*) on a fire taken from the domestic hearth. This rice dish is offered to four brahmans (the number four characterizing the smallest possible community, as it does in the case of the Buddhist monks' community). Over the dying embers the drilling sticks (the two *araṇis*) are held and then given by the *adhvaryu* to the sacrificer. In the early morning of the next day the fire is drilled and put on the *gārhapatya* hearth. From the *gārhapatya* a burning piece of wood is taken and brought to the *āhavanīya* hearth, accompanied by a horse and a chariot wheel that is rolled in the same direction. This procedure for bringing over and setting up the *āhavanīya* fire, though easily interpreted as a solar charm, rather suggests a warlike expedition, especially when the accompanying *mantras* (referring to unnamed enemies) are taken into consideration. The *dakṣiṇāgni* is either drilled separately, is taken from elsewhere, or is taken from the remainder of the *odana's* cooking fire.

The ritual involves the installation of two more fires: the *sabhya* ("of the assembly," *sabhā*) and the *āvasathya* ("of the residence," *āvasatha*, i. e., of the guests). Their installation involves a dice game for the portions of a cow, which may, however, be replaced by an *odana*. The total number of fires, then, is five, a number that is in later speculations connected with the five *prāṇas* (vital breaths). In the *śrauta* sacrifices these two additional fires are not used, but they may well represent an ancient tradition of communal sacrificial festivals—a tradition that may live on in the *Mahābhārata's* description of the royal *sabhā* where the Rājasūya of the Pāṇḍava protagonists took place, as well as the fatal game of dice that set off the all-consuming war between the Pāṇḍavas and the Kauravas.

The Agnyādhāna is then rounded off by the first Agnihotra and *iṣṭi*. The main point of the Agnyādhāna is, however, the bridging of the gap between the *gṛhya* (domestic) and the *śrauta* spheres. The two sorts of fire, domestic (called *aupāsada* or *āmātya*) and *śrauta*, are discontinuous. They are to be linked to each other by the person of the sacrificer, who after the completion of the sacrifice symbolically takes the fires into himself to reproduce them for the next sacrifice with the help of his *araṇis*.

Domestic ritual. The domestic (*gṛhya*) ritual requires only the domestic fire (*aupāsada* or *āmātya*). It is, in principle, performed by the master of the house with the help of a house priest (*purohita*, lit., "put forward," apparently to ward off evil). The domestic sacrifices, including a domestic Agnihotra, cake and gruel offerings (*pākayajña*), and animal sacrifices, have undergone the influence of the *śrauta* system but are not directly derived from them. In many respects they may be nearer to the common source of both types of ritual, the material of this common source having been "recycled" and rigidly systematized in the *śrauta* ritual.

A prominent occasion for the animal sacrifice is the reception (*arghya*) of a prestigious guest to whom a cow is offered. The guest must then either order to kill and prepare the cow for a meal or release it. The burden for the killing falls on the guest, not on the host. This point is not without importance in connection with later notions about *ahiṃsā* (nonviolence) and the prohibition of cow slaughter. It may also explain the Buddha's refusal to have meat prepared for him.

The main part of the domestic ritual concerns the life cycle rituals. The first of these is marriage, at which time the domestic fire, derived from the fire lit for the occasion in the bride's home, is established in the new home. Further rituals are the furthering of the birth of male progeny (Puṃsavana), the birth rites (Janmakarma), first taking of solid food (Annaprāśana), first haircutting (Cūḍākaraṇa, "making the hairtuft," *cūḍā*).

Then follows the important initiation to the Veda (Upanayana, "leading up to" and acceptance of the boy by the teacher). This is said to be the "second birth" of the "twice born" *varṇas* of *brāhmaṇas*, *kṣatriyas*, and *vaiśyas*, which qualifies them for the use of Vedic *mantras* and for becoming, if they so wish, *śrauta* sacrificers. The period of pupilage or fosterage (*brahmacārin,* "walking in *brahman*" lasts, in theory at least, a varying number of years according to the *varṇa* of the pupil and is concluded by the Samāvartana, the "turning around" or return from the teacher. The former *brahmacārin* is now a *snātaka,* "one who has taken the bath" that ends his duties and restrictions as a pupil; the restrictions of the *brahmacārin* include chastity and are generally similar to those of the *dīkṣita.* Originally, the *brahmacārin* would seem to have been a young warrior who commends himself as a vassal to a magnate or warlord rather than a pupil peacefully devoted to learning by heart the Veda. His "return" as a *snātaka* is preferably by chariot and thereby recalls the *dīkṣita,* who, according to the older Śrautasūtras, also sets out on a chariot to the place of sacrifice. The term *samāvartana* seems, moreover, more appropriate to the warrior's art of turning around the horse-drawn chariot at high speed than to returning home. The long period of initiation to Vedic lore, then, appears to be largely a theoretical construct preserving the memory of an older situation rather than a generally applied rule. Accordingly, the Upanayana is the decisive rite that gives access to the Veda, whether or not there is an extended period of pupilage and a *samāvartana* rite.

To the domestic ritual also belong the funerary rites. These concern the cremation of the body, the Pitṛmedha ("ancestor sacrifice"), which, as the name indicates, is viewed as a (holocaust) sacrifice. The cremation fire is the household fire or, in the case of a *śrauta* sacrificer, his three sacrificial fires, which are placed around the pyre. The wife of the deceased lies down with the body of her husband on the pyre but is then ordered with a *mantra* to stand up again before the pyre is lit (the Veda apparently knows but rejects the burning of the widow). Then the parts of an immolated cow (or other female animal) are placed on corresponding parts of the body and burned with him. If the deceased was a *śrauta* sacrificer his sacrificial implements are also placed on his body. Afterward the ashes are gathered and at a later date interred under a tumulus (*loṣṭaciti,* "earth piling").

The period of mourning and impurity (*āśarca*) of the relatives at the death of a full-grown family member lasts for twelve days and is completed by a purificatory rite including a bath. The next stage is the incorporation of the deceased (who as a *preta,* or "one gone forth," is thought to roam about) into the ranks of the ancestors (*pitṛ*) to receive his part of the cult. The cult consists in the festive Śrāddha (from *śrāddha,* "faith"), a meal offered to brahmans. On this occasion three rice balls (*piṇḍas*) are put on the ground for the three immediate ancestors, represented by three brahmans who silently wait till the rice balls are cooled and they emit no steam. The ancestors are supposed to be fed by the steam of the hot rice balls, which are set on the ground and left there. Apart from the Śrāddha, which is very much a social occasion and is performed periodically as well as at particular auspicious occasions (such as the birth of a son), there are also daily offerings of water and food to the ancestors.

The *piṇḍa* offering to the ancestors has also found a place in the *śrauta* ritual, most notably on the preparatory day of the *iṣṭi.* Rice is cooked on the southern fire, offerings are made from it into the same fire, and three *piṇḍas* are placed on a special *vedi* near the fire. An enlarged version of this *piṇḍa-pitṛ-yajña* is incorporated as the "great ancestor sacrifice" (Mahāpitṛyajña) in the Sākamedha, the third of the seasonal four-month sacrifices.

As already mentioned, the cult of the ancestors is characterized by the use of the left side and the left hand as well as by uneven numbers.

Interpretations of Vedic ritual. Vedic ritual is usually interpreted in the sense of magic, the Veda being the means to bring about well-being and to avoid pain, as is stated by the fourteenth-century commentator Sāyaṇa. This interpretation is supported by the fact that the ritual texts dutifully declare which desire will be fulfilled by the performance of a particular sacrifice: health, wealth (especially in cattle), progeny, headmanship, or, less materialistically, (access to) heaven. More important, the ritual system as such is given in the Brāhmaṇas as a perfectly ordered mechanism to dominate and regulate the cosmic processes, both as regards the individual's life and the universe at large. In this context the gods are not free agents but, being themselves cosmic forces, they are compelled to do the sacrificer's bidding. The place of sacrifice is a microcosmos encompassing heaven and earth, and the ritual is identical with the cosmic order. When set in motion and correctly executed the ritual automatically controls the universe. Thus, for instance, it is said that the sun would not rise if the morning libation of the Agnihotra were not offered in the fire (*Śatapatha Brāhmaṇa* 2.3.1.5).

The Brāhmaṇas relate the ritual microcosmos to the macrocosmos and to the individual's life through the identification of ritual acts, objects, and implements with the elements of the macrocosmos and with parts of the sacrificer's body, the sacrificer being identified with Prajāpati, the mythical embodiment of sacrifice. Although these identifications, which form the central feature of the Brāhmaṇas, suggest a rich and multilayered network of symbolic relations, they are not so much multi-interpretable symbolic statements as one-to-one equations of ritual items with human and macrocosmic ones. They are, each one separately, isolated identificatory statements. As they occur in the Brāhmaṇas they make a singularly atomized impression. Taken together they are no more than a collection lacking consistency. Whereas Vedic hymnology capitalizes on the associative ramification of symbolic connections, such connections (*nidāna, bandhu*) are, in the Brāhmaṇas, reduced to single, unmistakable identifications. The connection on which the identification is based is often a number characterizing both items, which are then said to "coincide" *(saṃpad)* or to exhibit the same count (*saṃkhyāna*): for instance, three fires, three worlds; 360 *stotriyās*, 360 days in the year. Such equivalences are, of course, known to the Vedic hymns, but they are not directly made explicit as they are in the Brāhmaṇas. The explicit use of equivalence appears to have been viewed by the ritualists as an innovative technique—indeed their premier intellectual tool—to identify the ritual with the universe and so to reduce the universe to a strict, ritually controlled order.

The significance of identification and of the ritual system it underwrites is clearly set out in a ritualistic myth given in explanation of the *mahāvrata soma* sacrifice. Its theme is the sacrificial contest of Prajāpati and his antagonist Mṛtyu (Death). In this contest Prajāpati's "weapons" are the *stotra,* the *śastra,* and the ritual act. The arsenal of Death consists of lute playing, singing, dancing, and improper acts. For many years the contest remains undecided. But the breakthrough comes when Prajāpati finally discovers ("sees") the (numerical) equivalence, namely, of his own "weapons" with those of Death. Once the equivalence is established, Prajāpati effortlessly subjugates Death's panoply to his own, cancels the rival sacrifice, and so defeats Mṛtyu (*Jaiminīya Brāhmaṇa* 2.69–70). It is to be noted that Prajāpati's "weapons" are elements of the *śrauta* system of ritual, such as *stotra, śastra,* and regular sacrificial acts. It is through their equivalences that Prajāpati overcomes and integrates the countervailing power of Death. The latter's rival sacrifice, incorporating singing, dancing, and improper acts, is clearly non-*śrauta.*

Such acts are indeed part of the *mahāvrata,* which features a number of contest rites and even copulation. What the ritualistic myth relates, however, is that these rites are made harmless and are in fact superseded by Prajāpati's victory. Indeed, the term *mahāvrata* generally means no more than a *sutyā* day characterized by a particular arrangement of its *stotras* and forming part of a *sattra* made up of similarly differentiated *soma*-pressing days. In the same way other non-*śrauta* rituals and sacrifices were remodeled and fitted into the *śrauta* system. For instance, the guest reception offered to King Soma is made into a vegetal *iṣṭi,* not essentially different from any other *iṣṭi.* A more complicated example is provided by the so-called *vrātyastomas*, which are related to the *mahāvrata.* The *vrātya* (from *vrāta,* "gang, band," possibly derived from *vrata,* "vow") is a consecrated warrior in many ways related to the *dīkṣita.* The *Atharvaveda* in a long hymn celebrates the *vrātya* as a sacral cosmic figure. However, his disturbingly aggressive habits, which still shine clearly through the Brāhmaṇas, ill suit the perfect order of the ritual. The ritualists solved the problem they presented by remodeling the sacrifice of the *vrātyas* into the regular *soma* sacrifices of the *ahīna* type.

The Brāhmaṇa myth of Prajāpati's and Mṛtyu's sacrificial contest brings out the extent and depth of the reflection that went into the formulation of the ritual system. It also shows the aim of the ritualists' work. This is made clear by the story's conclusion: "Now there is no sacrificial contest (*saṃsava*) anymore; what was the other (rival) sacrifice, that came to nought; the sacrifice is only one; Prajāpati is the sacrifice." That is: Conflict is canceled; the enemy, Death, has been subjected to the rule of ritual. Henceforth, the single sacrificer stands uncontested on his place of sacrifice where he establishes his own perfectly ordered universe governed by the ritual. The mythological battle of *devas* and *asuras* has been decided by the ritual system. Enemies, like the *asuras*, are still profusely mentioned in the Brāhmaṇas, but only as disembodied entities defeated in advance by the unfailing means of the ritual. The only remaining uncertainty is the ritual mistake, which, however, can be repaired by ritual means (*prāyaścitta,* "removal of concern").

The ritual system is an absolute, universal, and nonconflicting order: It is, in other words, transcendent. While the hymn's world of the gods imperceptibly shaded over the world of men, the suprahuman (*apauruṣeya*) *śruti* and its ritual is now separated by a gap from the mundane world of conflict. The *śrauta* sacrifice has been individualized and desocialized. It is the exclusive affair of the single sacrificer. He and his priests should form one single body; otherwise, they are separate individuals within a group of priests, all of whom are at once sacrificers in the *sattra.* The situation in which more than one sacrificer would exist in addition to the priests on the place of sacrifice is explicitly ruled out. This may explain the striking lack of public religious ceremonies. Although the royal *śrauta* sacrifices such as the Rājasūya (consecration of the king) contain ample indications of a former public festival, the royal sacrificer is a single sacrificer, no different from any other *soma* sacrificer. The public rites have been remodeled in accordance with the standard paradigms of the individualized ritual, or else they are dismembered as separate acts inserted into the standard *soma* paradigm. The Rājasūya, formally speaking, does not make a sacrificer a king, for it is stated that "a king who wants to attain heaven should perform the Rājasūya" (*Āpastamba Śrautasūtra* 18.8.1). That is: He is already a king who for his own reasons performs the sacrifice. This is recognized in the later *dharma* texts, which do not prescribe it as the required consecration. Similarly, the Aśvamedha sacrificer should already have the status of a world ruler (*Āpastamba Śrautasūtra* 10.1.1).

The *śrauta* ritual, as many details of its rules and the Brāhmaṇa explanations make clear, has its origin in the heroic and essentially tragic world of the warrior who like the gods must "move about on wheels" and contend for the goods of life with the *asura*-like settled magnate who "sits in his hall." He can only hope that he may survive and eventually quit the life of the warrior (*kṣattravṛtti*) so as to become a settled householder and magnate himself. The warrior lives in the wilds (*araṇya*); hence the sacrificer's setting out from home. The settled community (*grāma*) on the other hand is the sphere of the magnate. The two spheres, *grāma* and *araṇya,* are clearly hostile to each other but equally complementary. The point of contact that held both together was their conflict contained by the sacrificial contest that lived on in the hypertrophical imagination of the epic "sacrifice of battle" (*raṇayajña*). Both epics, the *Mahābhārata* as well as the *Rāmāyaṇa,* still show the alternation between the wandering warrior's life in the wilds and the sphere of settled rulership.

The *śrauta* ritual indicated a clear break with the cyclical alternation of *grāma* and *araṇya* and with the sacrificial contest as the joint holding the two together. By the elimination of conflict from the desocialized and individualized sacrifice the two spheres were definitively broken apart. This is illustrated by the *agnyādheya,* which physically separates the domestic fire from the *śrauta* fires. The resulting gap must then be bridged by the single sacrificer who alternates between his life in the world and the transcendent rule of the *śruti.* Put differently, he must fuse the two opposite rules of a substantial householder and a wandering warrior. Hence, only a householder can be an *āhitāgni,* that is, one who has set up the *śrauta* fires permanently and thereby submits himself to the absolute order of the *śruti.* This gives him access to transcendence, but by the same token this does not change his social position. Whether king or commoner, under the rule of ritual all sacrificers are equal. Sacrifice can only impoverish the *āhitāgni,* since he has to go on spending his wealth in sacrifices and *dakṣiṇās* without a chance to recoup through reciprocity at the sacrifices of others. Accordingly, there is no obligation for the qualified householder to set up the fires and to submit to the strict discipline of *śrauta* sacrifice. If he does, he must be sure of himself and his fortune, or, as the texts put it, he must have absolute faith (*śraddhā*). It is true that the *śrauta* sacrifice promises him the fulfillment of his wishes. In the sacrificial contest the possibility of fulfilling one's wishes was clear. The goods of life were concretely set out as the stakes and prizes of the contest. The *śrauta* ritual by contrast does not and cannot make clear how the desired results are to be brought about. It is *adṛṣṭārtha* (without visible object), that is, transcendent.

It is clear, then, that the *śrauta* ritual hinges on a paradox. It offers itself as an effective magical means for the gratification of the sacrificer's worldly desires. On the other hand it withdraws from all worldly concerns from which desocialization and individualization have cut it free. It is a closed system of rationalistically devised rules, complete in itself and regardless of the uses and abuses to which it may be put. In the last resort it rejects its own potential for magical and sacral meaning. Beyond magic and sacrality it stands by itself in sovereign transcendence.

BRAHMANISM. Though admittedly a vague term, *Brahmanism* is best defined in relation to Vedism. It does not primarily concern religious cults or institutions but rather propounds particular views, laid down in texts, about humanity and the universe. These views are, however, equally fundamental to Hinduism in general. Their specificity resides in the claim to be related to or directly derived from the Veda. Brahmanism is, therefore, usually considered to be the Veda-oriented form of Hinduism, immediately following Vedism. However, since the textual tenets of Brahmanism are generally authoritative also in later Hinduism, a three-tiered succession of Vedism, Brahmanism, and Hinduism tends to be misleading. Moreover, like Vedism, Brahmanism is not likely to cover the whole of early Hindu religious belief and practice. Brahmanism is characterized by its acknowledgment of the Veda as the ultimate source of transcendent authority. Thereby it is clearly marked off from the "heterodox" sects or movements such as Buddhism, Jainism, Ajīvakas, and the materialist schools (Lokāyata, Cārvāka), which reject the authority of the Veda.

In Indian terms, the relationship between Vedism and Brahmanism is that of *śruti* ("hearing"), the transcendent "revelation" as against the worldly or human tradition, called *smṛti* ("remembrance"). The word *śruti* does not refer to the mode of receiving the revelations: The standard term is "seeing," not "hearing." *Śruti* thus refers to the transmission of the fixed and systematized texts. In this sense it is not essentially different from the *smṛti,* except for the unique care and efforts spent on its preservation and transmission. But the differentiation marked by the two terms is significant. Although the *smṛti* equally tends to give itself as revelation, namely by the godhead, the transcendent authority of the *śruti* does not derive from any godhead. It stands by itself without the intermediary of a divine agency. Its authority being ultimate, it can have no other, higher source. It therefore functions as the unassailable basis of the fluid and adaptive worldly *smṛti.* Another word for *smṛti* is *dharma,* universal law, which then is said to be derived from or to be already contained in the *śruti.* At any rate the *dharma* should not go counter to the *śruti.* In fact, however, the relationship is more complex and indeed problematic.

Texts. In addition to the Vedas and Brāhmaṇas, the texts to which Brahmanism, or, to use the Indian term, the *smṛti,* refers are the Upaniṣads, the Dharmasūtras and Dharmaśāstras, the epics (*Mahābhārata* and *Rāmāyaṇa*), and the Purāṇas. The Upaniṣads can be chronologically distinguished by their form: The older prose Upaniṣads are extensions of the ritualist Brāhmaṇas. Most of the younger ones, often of sectarian origin and with a wide variety of contents, are metrical. The latter genre has been productive over a long period reaching far beyond the late Vedic texts, until at least the sixteenth century CE. The Upaniṣads belong to the *śruti,* and this title is a claim to ultimate authority. In the same way, the set of 108 Upaniṣads (listed in the *Muktikā Upaniṣad*) are ascribed to the Vedic *śākhās* (schools), but it is significant that a large proportion is ascribed to the *Atharvaveda,* in which have been collected many other materials that do not fit into the *śrauta* system.

The Dharmasūtras are in the same condensed style as the Vedic *sūtras* and are equally affiliated with Vedic "schools" (*caraṇa*). This affiliation becomes looser with the metrical Dharmaśāstras. No less important as a storehouse of mythology, religious notions, and *dharma* are the wide-ranging *Mahābhārata* (especially its twelfth book, the *Śāntiparvan,* and its sixth book, which contains the celebrated *Bhagavadgītā*) and the *Rāmāyaṇa,* which has known a great number of reworkings. The encyclopedic Purāṇas ("ancient stories") deal, in principle, with five topics (*pañcalakṣaṇa,* "five characteristics"): creation, periodical recreation, genealogy (of gods and holy men), the world periods (*yugas*), and the dynasties. But many other materials have been added at various unspecified times: *dharma* precepts, pilgrimage, hymns, and sectarian treatises. They have functioned over a long period as a storehouse receiving all manner of materials. The Purāṇas (the term occurs already in the *Atharvaveda*) continued the tradition of legends (*itihāsa*) that occasionally make an appearance in the *śrauta* ritual (e.g., the Śunahśepa story in the Rājasūya). *Chandogya-Upaniṣad* 3.4.1. mentions *itihāsa-purāṇa* as the "fifth Veda," which is later taken to comprise the epics as well.

Brahmanism, though primarily textual, does not have a fixed corpus of texts. Its tenets are recorded in a variety of texts stretching over a long and, in fact, indefinite period of time. Its impact has made itself felt in Hinduism, increasing and decreasing in various regions at different times. It would seem that rising regional dynasties have been instrumental in creating waves of "brahmanization." This will also have been responsible for the incorporation in the texts of materials of regional and sectarian origin. But such brahmanization equally carried the *śruti* with it, which as the source of ultimate authority was of singular importance for the ruler's legitimation.

Interiorization of the ritual. The crucial issue here is the relationship of Brahmanism with the Veda, that is, between *śruti* and *smṛti.* The *śruti* has exhausted itself in creating a closed system of ritual order. But the price that had to be paid for this achievement was the alienation from the worldly concerns of the mundane order. The *śruti* was—purposely—desocialized and individualized. This created the problem of reconnecting it again with the mundane order. Propounding an absolute and seamless order, the *śruti* rejects conflict and places the rival beyond the pale. It therefore cannot speak to man's worldly concerns. Notwithstanding the proclaimed dependence of the *dharma* on the *śruti,* the latter's contents do not provide specific guidelines for the tensions and conflicts of social life.

Once it was desocialized and individualized there was only one way open to the *śruti:* interiorization. What then takes priority is no longer the faithful execution of the ritual but knowledge of the ritual and of the identifications on which it rests. This is already prefigured in the recurrent Brāhmaṇa phrase that a particular ritual act is effective only for him "who knows thus," that is, for him who knows the relevant identification. It is thus possible to perform the ritual in thought alone (*manasā*). The transcendent order of the ritual is realized internally in the way of discipline meditation.

An illustrative example is provided by the Agnihotra, offered in five breaths that are equated with the five sacrificial fires (*prāṇāgnihotra*). In mundane terms it is simply eating one's meal embellished with mouth rinsings and simple *mantras*. But the same pattern enables the brahman to participate in a festive meal to which he is invited (a Śrāddha, for instance). He is thus not just a guest obliged to his munificent host but an individual sacrificer who performs the sacrificial ritual independent of his host and the surrounding society. In other words, it enables the brahman to square the circle of living in society and of transcending it at the same time.

World renunciation. From the individualized sacrificer and his internalized sacrifice there runs a straight line leading to the extramundane world renouncer (*saṃnyāsin*), who gives up the three aims of mundane life—the socioreligious duties of the householder (*dharma*), the acquisition and management of wealth (*artha*), and sensual gratification (*kāma*)—to devote himself single-mindedly to a strict inner discipline that results in his liberation from earthly life (*mokṣa*). Though there is a wide variety of such inner disciplines they all share the ritualistic strictness of an internalized transcendent order. The renouncer's discipline obviously goes beyond, and in many if not most cases even rejects, Vedic ritualism. But it is the desocialization and individualization of Vedic ritual that has prepared the ground for the institution of *saṃnyāsa,* or renunciation.

In this connection two sets of ideas, both deriving from ritualistic thought, are fundamental. The first such notion is the Upaniṣadic identification of *ātman,* the individual "soul," with *brahman.* In the Vedic hymns *brahman* is the multilayered and multi-interpretable, often paradoxical or enigmatic formulation. The unexpressed inner connection is the essence of the *brahman.* The Brāhmaṇa ritualists reduce the *brahman* to the explicit identification. In both cases, however, it is this fundamental force that makes the poetic statement as well as the rite effective. In this way the *brahman* came to be seen as the transcendent principle of universal order. The *saṃnyāsin's* discipline, as already announced in the Upaniṣads, means the internal realization of the *brahman* as the principle of transcendent order through its identification with the *ātman.* It is the ultimate identification tying together and thereby canceling the dispersed identifications of the Brāhmaṇas in the single person of the renouncer, as was in fact already the case with the individualized *śrauta* sacrificer who was identified with Prajāpati or the *puruṣa.*

The other set of ideas, equally ritualistic in origin, is the concept of *karman,* or work. In the Brāhmaṇas *karman* is the sacrifice. Originally this sacrificial "work" had a social context. It rested on the competitive reciprocity of hosts and guests, the latter having to redeem themselves by acting in their turn as hosts. The individualization of the *śrauta* sacrifice, however, put an abrupt stop to all exchange and reciprocity. This meant that now the sacrificer had to exchange his *karman* with himself alone, one's *karman* inexorably bringing the next *karman* in its wake. This, combined with the not exclusively Indian notion of an unending alternation of birth, death, and rebirth (*saṃsāra*), created the urge to terminate the endless chain of ever-renewed *karman* that could no longer be transferred to the rival. The only way open was then to renounce all *karman,* all activity, by realizing internally the stasis of absolute order. Obviously, this signifies rejection of the external sacrifice as well. Even though it cancels Vedic ritualism, the ideal of terminating all *karman* can be seen as the consequence of ritualistic thought.

The crucial importance of the institution of world renunciation in Brahmanism and in Hinduism in general is that it created two opposite and incompatible spheres: the transcendent sphere of the renouncer's individualistic rejection of society as against the social world and its requirements. At the same time, however, the renouncer paradoxically needs society, which must provide for his upkeep so as to enable him to preserve his discipline. On the other hand society wants to draw him into its web again as the holder of transcendent authority. That is: The *saṃnyāsin* will gather a following. He is therefore especially known as the founder of a sect. The Indian sect typically has a *saṃnyāsin* as founder, who will be succeeded by one of his pupils to lead the worldly lay followers.

Varṇa and āśrama. The *dharma* or world order, being universal, must regulate both worldly and renunciatory life. This is the subject of *varṇāśramadharma,* the order of caste (*varṇa*) and life stages (*āśrama,* "place of exertion," hence also dwelling place of ascetics). While caste orders worldly society, the life stages give a place to its opposite, renunciation. As regards caste, it is to be noted that the *smṛti* knows two terms, *jāti* (genus) and *varṇa* (shape, color). The two terms are to some extent interchangeable, but there is a marked difference. Although there are only four *varṇas*—*brāhmaṇas* (Eng., brahmans), *kṣatriyas* (warriors), *vaiśyas* (producers), and *śūdras*, who serve the three "twice-born" *varṇas* (that is, those who have been initiated to the Vedic *mantras*)—the number of *jātis* is unlimited. The latter are said to have arisen in the first instance from mixed unions of the four *varṇas*. However, the scriptural order of the *varṇas* is based on their strict separation, that is, neither intermarriage nor commensality is allowed. As no society can exist on the basis of the single principle of separation, the *jātis* make society function. But this equally means that *jāti* society is based on a serious transgression, namely *varṇasaṃkara,* or "mixing of the *varṇas*."

The principle of separation can be seen as deriving from the individualization of the Vedic sacrificer that resulted from the exclusion of conflict and competition. In fact, individualization did not stop at the boundary of the *varṇa.* The scriptural rules forbid marriages among even distant relatives, and so are directed against the formation of extended marriage networks. As in the case of the sacrificer's individualization, the separation of the *varṇa* aims at a static, conflictless order through the exclusion of social relations. The scriptural order of the separate *varṇas* is in the last resort incompatible with the reality of the associative and conflictive jātis.

Although it is not stressed in the texts, the religious principle of the *jāti* order appears to be the asymmetric interdependence of pure and impure, the impure being the "fallout" of life processes, including death and decay. Their hierarchy as well as their obvious complementarity led the French sociologist Louis Dumont to his impressive analysis of the Indian caste order as based on and encompassed by the religious principle of the pure-impure hierarchy. Although this analysis holds for the *jāti* order, it is undermined by the scriptural *varṇa,* which rejects relations of complementarity and interdependence in favor of separation and independence.

This problem is particularly clear in the case of the brahman. As the ideal repository and upholder of the transcendent *śruti* the brahman should be immaculately pure. But this requirement threatens to make him dependent on the impure—such as the sweeper or the washerman—and such relations of dependence would fatally impair his purity. Purity, then, is the absence of relations. Strictly speaking he should not be a priest, because this would involve him in social relations of a particularly dangerous—because sacral—nature. Ideally, the brahman should stand outside of society, the highest brahman being the one who has no power or wealth or even provisions for the next day, and who performs the ritual in and for himself alone. Thus he bears the brunt of the incompatibility between *jāti* interdependence and *varṇa* separation. In other words, the ideal brahman should be a renouncer. The tension between *jāti* and *varṇa* is akin to the one between society and renunciation, and derives from the same source.

The scriptural theory of the four stages of life (*āśrama*) brings social and renunciatory life together in a single scheme. These four stages are those of the pupil memorizing the Veda (*brahmacārin*); the married householder (*gṛhastha*); the cenobitic forest dweller (*vānaprastha*), who still keeps up his domestic fire; and the individualized renouncer (*saṃnyāsin*), who has interiorized the fire and consequently the ritual. Of these four it is only the *gṛhastha* who is fully a member of society and as such must perform the scriptural duties toward the Vedic seers by upholding the *śruti,* toward the ancestors by progeny, and toward the gods by sacrifice. Only after these duties, especially the continuation of the lineage, have been fulfilled, is the householder free to withdraw from the world and strive for final liberation (*mokṣa*). It would seem that the basic principle is again the opposition of social and renunciatory life. Originally, the two opposites were given their due in a pattern of the cyclical alternation of life in the established community, setting out into the wilderness and returning again. When this alternating cycle was broken, the opposite and now-incompatible phases were given their due by placing them in the linear succession of the four *āśramas*, spanning the individual's life.

Ahiṃsā, vegetarianism, and the cow. *Ahiṃsā* (nonviolence) brings out the problematic character of the relationship between *śruti* and *smṛti.* It categorically forbids the killing of animals. Yet the *śruti* prescribes animal sacrifice and the consumption of the victim's meat, albeit only an insignificant part of it (the *iḍā*). Ludwig Alsdorf has distinguished three stages. First, there is no question of a general rule against meat consumption, but only against particular kinds of animals. Next, meat-eating is forbidden, except in the isolated context of the animal sacrifice. The third and last stage brings the absolute prohibition of meat (together with intoxicating drinks, such as *surā*). This does not, however, explain the reason for the rise of *ahiṃsā.* Non-Hindu influences, such as Buddhism and Jainism, have often been assumed to be important factors. Alsdorf suggests the pre-Aryan Indian civilization as the source of the prohibition. Hanns-Peter Schmidt, however, has pointed out that the Vedic ritual itself evinces a strong aversion to the violence of immolation. Part of the ritual is concerned with undoing the harm of the sacrificial killing. In Schmidt's view it was the internalization of the ritual that brought about *ahiṃsā.* Internalization canceled the external acts needed to undo the evil of killing, which is still involved, even in the internal food sacrifice (of the *prāṇāgnihotra* type). From then on the only way open was the absolute prohibition of meat.

The problem is further complicated by the sacrosanctity of the cow and the consequent prohibition—equally alien to the *śruti*—of cow's meat. Nevertheless, both *ahiṃsā* and the prohibition of cow's meat can be seen as deriving from the *śrauta* ritual, though in a different way from the one proposed by Schmidt. Originally it may have been a matter of alternating phases, namely the phase of the trekking consecrated warrior (the *dīkṣita*), who should preserve and, if possible, increase his cow herd (and consequently should not eat meat) as against the homecoming celebrated by a sacrificial festival that lifts the prohibition of meat-eating. The trekking phase of the warrior was decidedly violent, but vegetarian; the settled phase reversed the situation: Meat-eating is allowed, even prescribed, but social relations should be marked by nonviolence. In this way vegetarianism and the cow taboo can be seen as different in origin and even opposite to each other, deriving from opposite phases. With the collapse of their cyclical alternation, both the trekking warrior and the peaceful householder had to be homogenized into the single householder-sacrificer. As such he was required not only to be both nonviolent and to abstain from the cow, but at the same time to perform the sacrifice, which, even if vegetal, still involved the killing (grinding and pressing being explicitly considered as "killing") of the sacrificial substances.

Although this may explain the origin of vegetarianism based on *ahiṃsā* and of the sacrosanctity of the cow, the fact remains that there is an unresolved conflict between the *śruti* and the *smṛti.* This conflict is formulated in terms of the two opposite spheres of social life and renunciation. Eating meat is the ongoing way of the world (*pravṛtti*), but abstention (*nivṛtti,* the term for the cessation of worldly processes) brings ultimate spiritual rewards (*Mānava Dharmaśāstra* 5.56).

Cultic institutions. Separate from—but not wholly dissociated from—the impersonal cosmic principle there lies in the texts a profuse mythology. The Vedic ritual itself came to overshadow the gods as the central cosmic force and reduced them to mere names whose only place was in the *mantras*. Accordingly, the Veda is fundamentally aniconic. Brahmanism by contrast gives way to a rich stream of theistic beliefs and practices (which may never have been absent but were simply ignored by the Vedic scriptures). The *Śvetāśvatara Upaniṣad,* considered as the gate to theistic Hinduism, places the "Lord" (*īśa* or *īśvara*) in the center. Being intimately connected with the impersonal *brahman* he is both transcendent and, in his relation to humans, immanent. Such transcendent and immanent gods, who as such are to be distinguished from the great many divinities, are Śiva (Rudra), to whom the title *īśa* or *īśvara* primarily refers, and Viṣṇu. Together with the personified Brahma (who hardly receives a cult) they are often represented iconographically as the *trimurti,* the "triple body" or trinity.

Theism opened the way to cultic institutions, the first of which may be considered the temple, which developed from a simple open-air sanctuary to ever more elaborate complexes with a central cella and deity (*mūrti*) in an awe-inspiring towerlike and massive structure surrounded by smaller sanctuaries and niches for other gods, the whole of which was marked off by an outer wall. Second is the *pūjā* as the fundamental cult form, both in the household and more elaborately in the temple. Though the *pūjā* had existed before, its textual canonization by Brahmanism was a new development. Its basic pattern is the hospitable reception of an honored guest who is offered a bath, clothes, food, and a resting place. In the great temples of Śiva and Viṣṇu the *pūjā* is elaborated into a full and regal ceremony involving also the god's consorts and divine retainers. In the sense of a hospitable reception offered to the guest the *pūjā* is closely related to the Vedic ritual, which, as Thieme has shown (see above), derives from the same pattern. This does not mean that the *pūjā* evolved out of the Vedic ritual. Rather, the two are different realizations of the same basic pattern.

The individualization achieved by Vedic ritualism is also a characteristic of Brahmanism. This is clearly noticeable in the *pūjā.* The domestic *pūjā,* like the Vedic *gṛhya* ritual, is strictly a family affair. The individualistic tendency is displayed most clearly in the temple. Although great crowds are usually present at the temple during particular festivals, they do not participate in the actual *pūjā.* To pay their obeisance and to obtain a view (*darśana*) of the deity, the devotees pass, one by one, before the opening of the cella. Like Vedism, Brahmanism is devoid of regular *sacra publica.* Public and royal festivals, such as the raising of the "Indra pole" (*Indradhvaja,* a sort of Maypole), are described in the epics and Purāṇas but are not in any way prescribed. In this respect it is significant that although the Śrāddha in honor of the ancestors can be celebrated as a social gathering with a large number of guests, the *dharma* texts explicitly prefer the patron to invite no more than three brahmans, or even only one (*Mānava Dharmaśāstra* 3.125, 126, 129). Whereas Hinduism involves large public festivals, Brahmanism holds on to the individualism of Vedism.

The most important cultic notion to pervade Indian religiosity as a whole is *bhakti* ("participation"), the single-minded loving devotion to the godhead (in this context usually known as the *bhagavat,* the "felicitous one"), in whose being the devotee (*bhakta*) strives to share. Though at the opposite end from Vedic ritualism and Upaniṣadic thought, *bhakti* appears to be ancient. Its attitude of loving devotion is already commended in relatively early Upaniṣads (especially the *Katha Upaniṣad*). The term makes its first entry in the *Śvetāśvatara Upaniṣad,* which is generally known for its theistic stance. It is, however, in the *Bhagavadgītā* (*Mahābhārata* 6.25–42) that *bhakti* is canonized as the third "way" (*mārga*), next to (Upaniṣadic) knowledge (*jñāna,* that is, "knowledge" of *brahman*) and ritualism (*karman*). There *bhakti* is connected with the concept of disinterested worldly action (*karmayoga,* "harnessing oneself to action"). This means that the devotee should perform all actions that his station in life requires of him (even if this means that the warrior Arjuna must kill his relatives), but without any self-interest. It is a renunciatory attitude: The devotee renounces the result, the "fruit" (*phala*) of his actions. This attitude is the answer to the gap that divides life in the world from world renunciation. But the fusion of worldly and renunciatory life can only be achieved at the price of a paradox: The devotee fully engages in worldly activity, including violent conflict, but does not engage himself.

The Bhagavat (or Bhagavan), the god of the *bhakta,* is most commonly a form of Viṣṇu. His connection with the cosmic pillar and his *avataras* or "descents" in the world to restore the *dharma* and save humankind made him the ideal mediator between humans and transcendence. The devotee's *bhakti* is especially directed toward two of his forms of *avataras*, namely Kṛṣṇa and Rāma. Kṛṣṇa is worshiped as the divine child or as the cowherd (*gopāla*), the beloved of the *gopīs*, the cowherd girls. As a charioteer and bard (*sūta:* the combination of the two functions is a standard one) he proclaims the *Bhagavadgītā* to the warrior Arjuna. His story is told in the tenth book of the *Bhāgavata Purāṇa,* a fundamental text for the *bhakti* cult and for religious art, especially miniatures. King Rāma is the protagonist of the epic *Rāmāyaṇa.* The basic text of Rāma devotionalism is the Old Hindi *Rāmacaritamānasa* of Tulsīdās (fifteenth century), one of the many reworkings of the classical epic.

Concentrating on the inner life and attitude of the devotee, *bhakti* as a cult form does not need specific installations or institutions. It does know, however, a "congregational," though informal, form of worship: the singing of devotional hymns (*bhajan*). Both in its individual interiorized and in its "congregational" forms *bhakti* easily associates itself with temples and with organized sects. In fact, *bhakti* imbues all Hindu religiosity. As such it translates the Western concept of religion better than the word *dharma,* which has come into use in this sense only in the last century, and misleadingly stresses religious law and doctrine.

In the marked absence of a well-defined clergy, the most important figure in Brahmanism, as well as in Hinduism in general, is the *guru,* the spiritual teacher and guide. Ideally, he is a world renouncer or at least is known for his lack of self-interest. Although not a priest in the sense of an officiant or dispenser of sacraments, he holds an all but absolute authority—even in matters not necessarily of a spiritual nature—in the personal affairs of his devotees. Even in the context of *bhakti,* which emphasizes the direct personal relationship of the devotee to his god, the *guru* is the indispensable mediator. He can be seen as the actual recipient of the cult. Indian religiosity would be able to dispense with its gods on the condition that there is a *guru.*

Itself not a cult or a sect, Brahmanism is receptive to a great variety of beliefs, practices, and institutions. Its characteristic as well as its specific contribution to Hinduism is the faithful acknowledgement of the authority of the *śruti.* More importantly, Brahmanism carries on the individualistic tradition of interiorization that resulted from Vedic thought.

Smārtas. Brahmanism is still represented to the present day by the Smārtas (adherents of the *smṛti*). Characteristically, they are not a sect in an institutional or doctrinal sense but a loose category of (South Indian) brahmans who uphold nonsectarian orthodoxy. Their cultic practices are primarily private in character and reserve an important place for the Vedic *gṛhya* ritual. Smārtas will frequent particular temples, especially Śaiva ones, but they have no specific temples of their own. Worship takes place in the house, where a special room is kept for the *pūjā.* Smārta worship is especially concerned with the five gods Śiva, Viṣṇu, Durgā (consort of Śiva), Sūrya, and the elephant-headed Ganeśa, who are placed in the corners of a square with the preferred deity in the middle.

The Smārtas derive their tradition from Śānkara, the eighth-century founder of Advaita (monistic) Vedānta. Accordingly, they recognize the head of the monastic establishment (*maṭha*) and center of the Śānkara tradition at Śṛngeri (in present-day Karnataka) as their spiritual leader. Another tradition connects the Smārtas with Kumārila, the eighth-century teacher of Mimāṃśa (the interpretation of the Vedic ritual rules and so of the *dharma*). In this way the Smarta tradition claims to derive from both aspects of the *śruti,* the ritualistic and the Upaniṣadic (and thus the knowledge of *karman* and that of *brahman,* respectively), represented by the Vedanta tradition of Sankara and the Mimāṃśa tradition of ritualism.

The Brahmanic Smārta tradition lacks the colorful drama and institutions often and not without justification associated with Hinduism. It does not propound an enchanted world of magic and numinous power. Instead, it focuses on the central problem of *karman* and *brahman* already prefigured in later Vedism. It therefore holds on to the *śruti* as the ultimate truth and source of *dharma.* Tolerant of sectarian doctrines and practices, which it tends to harmonize, the Smarta tradition is not a sharply outlined orthodoxy. But it does represent the central concerns of Hinduism, past and present.

SEE ALSO Agni; Ahiṃsā; Bhagavadgītā; Bhakti; Brahman; Brāhmaṇas and Āraṇyakas; Dharma, article on Hindu Dharma; Domestic Observances, article on Hindu Practices; Goddess Worship, article on The Hindu Goddess; Hinduism; Indian Religions, article on Mythic Themes; Indra; Karman, article on Hindu and Jain Concepts; Kṛṣṇa; Mahābhārata; Maṇḍalas, article on Hindu Maṇḍalas; Mantra; Mimāṃśa; Mokṣa; Prajāpati; Prāṇa; Priesthood, article on Hindu Priesthood; Pūjā, article on Hindu Pūjā; Purāṇas; Rama; Rāmāyaṇa; Rites of Passage, article on Hindu Rites; Rudra; Saṃnyāsa; Śānkara; Sarasvatī; Śastra Literature; Soma; Sūtra Literature; Temple, article on Hindu Temples; Tulsīdās; Upaniṣads; Vaiṣṇavism, article on Bhāgavatas; Varṇa and Jāti; Varuṇa; Vedāṅgas; Vedānta; Vedas; Viṣṇu; Vṛtra; Yama; Zoroastrianism.

BIBLIOGRAPHY

General

The classic work is still Hermann Oldenberg's *Die Religion des Veda* (1894; 2d ed., Stuttgart, 1917). Arthur Berriedale Keith's *The Religion and Philosophy of the Veda and Upaniṣhads,* 2 vols. (1925; 2d ed., Westport, Conn., 1971), is a useful and detailed survey. Arthur Berriedale Keith and A. A. Macdonell's *Vedic Index of Names and Subjects,* 2 vols. (Varanasi, 1958), is outdated but still useful, especially for its text references. An up-to-date survey is provided in Jan Gonda's *Die Religionen Indiens,* vol. 1, *Veda und alterer Hinduismus* (1960; 2d rev. ed., Stuttgart, 1978). The nature, style, and composition of the text corpus are extensively dealt with in Jan Gonda's *A History of Indian Literature,* vol. 1, *Vedic Literature* (Wiesbaden, 1975).

Mythology

A. A. Macdonell's *Vedic Mythology* (1897; reprint, New York, 1974) gives a comprehensive survey. Full-scale studies are Abel Henri Joseph Bergaigne's *La Religion védique d'après les hymnes du Rig-veda,* 4 vols. (1878–1897; reprint, Paris, 1963), known for its systematic cosmological approach, and Alfred Hillebrandt's *Vedische Mythologie,* 2 vols. (1927–1929; reprint, Hildesheim, 1965), which also brings in the ritual prose texts. Important specialized, although wide-ranging, studies are Heinrich Lüders's *Varuṇa,* 2 vols., edited by Ludwig Alsdorf (Göttingen, 1951–1952), Hanns-Peter Schmidt's *Bṛhaspati und Indra: Untersuchungen zur vedischen Mythologie und Kulturgeschichte* (Wiesbaden, 1968), and F. B. J. Kuiper's *Ancient Indian Cosmogony,* essays selected and introduced by John Irwin (New Delhi, 1983). Georges Dumézil has argued his sociological and comparative Indo-Europeanist view in many publications; a useful analysis is given by C. Scott Littleton in *The New Comparative Mythology: An Anthropological Assessment of the Theories of Georges Dumézil,* 3d ed. (Berkeley, Calif., 1980). Leading scholars in the field are Louis Renou, some of whose significant contributions have been reprinted in *L'Inde fondomentale,* edited by Charles Malamoud (Paris, 1978), and Paul Thieme, whose work is among other things concerned with the Ādityas: see, for example, his *Mitra and Āryaman* (New Haven, Conn., 1957) and *Kleine Schriften,* 2 vols. (1971). In his fine ethnomycological study, *Soma: Divine Mushroom of Immortality* (New York, 1968), R. Gordon Wasson has forcefully argued that the *soma* plant originally was fly agaric; his thesis is, however, not generally accepted.

Ritual

Alfred Hillebrandt's *Ritual-Litterature: Vedische Opfer und Zauber,* "Grundriss der Indo-Arischen Philologie und Altertumskunde," no. 3.2 (Strassburg, 1897), still offers the best comprehensive survey. The foremost authority on Vedic ritual was—and still is—Willem Caland, whose translations definitely clarified the intricacies of the Vedic system of ritual. Special mention should be made of his *Das Śrautasūtra des Āpastamba,* 3 vols. (Göttingen and Amsterdam, 1921–1928). For the role of the *Śamaveda* in the ritual, his translation of the *Pañcaviṃ śa Brāhmaṇa* (Calcutta, 1931) should be consulted. Caland also initiated the study of the Jaiminīya School of the *Śāmaveda:* see his *Das Jaminīya-Brāhmaṇa im Auswahl* (Amsterdam, 1919). Julius Eggeling's five-volume translation of the *Śatapatha Brāhmaṇa* in "Sacred Books of the East," vols. 12, 26, 41, 43, and 44 (1882–1900; reprint, Delhi, 1963) still stands as a masterly achievement. *The Veda of the Black Yajus School Entitled Taittirīya-Sanhitā,* 2 vols., has been translated by Arthur Berriedale Keith (1914; reprint, Delhi, 1967); it should be checked with Caland's translation of the *Āpastamba Śrautasūtra.* Keith also translated the Ṛgveda Brāhmaṇas: *The Aitareya and Kauṣitaki Brāhmaṇas* (1920; reprint, Delhi, 1971). For the domestic ritual *The Gṛhya-sūtras,* translated by Hermann Oldenberg, "Sacred Books of the East," vols. 29 and 30 (1886–1892; reprint, Delhi, 1964), should be mentioned. For the "solemn" (*śrauta*) ritual there is now the compendium of texts and English translation edited by C. G. Kashikar, *Śrautakosa* (Poona, 1958–1982).

The basic paradigms of the vegetal, the animal, and the *soma* sacrifices have been described in Alfred Hillebrandt's *Das altindische Neu- und Vollmondsopfer in seiner einfachsten Form* (Jena, 1879); Julius Schwab's *Das altindische Thieropfer* (Erlangen, 1886); and Willem Caland and Victor Henry's *L'Agniṣtoma: Description complète de la forme normale du sacrifice de Soma dans le culte vedique,* 2 vols. (Paris, 1906–1907). The *sūtras* for the Agnihotṛa have been translated by Paul-Émile Dumont as *L'Agnihotṛa* (Baltimore, 1939) and the relevant Brāhmaṇa passages in H. W. Bodewitz's *The Daily Evening and Morning Offering according to the Brāhmaṇas* (Leiden,

1976). The Agnyādheya has been extensively studied by Herta Krick and Gerhard Oberhammer in *Das Ritual der Feuergründung* (*Agnyādheya*) (Vienna, 1982), giving full translations of the Brāhmaṇa portions. While Krick's interpretation is oriented toward Indo-European comparison, Timothy Moody's treatment in "The Agnyādheya" (Ph.D diss., McMaster University, 1980) is more factual. The royal rituals of the horse sacrifice and the Rājasūya have been analyzed by Paul-Émile Dumont in *L'Aśvamedha* (Paris, 1927) and by me in *The Ancient Indian Royal Consecration* (The Hague, 1957). The Agnicayana has been described from the texts and from Frits Staal's 1975 observations of the ritual as executed by Nambudiri brahmans in *Agni: The Vedic Ritual of the Fire Altar,* 2 vols., edited by Staal, with cassette recordings of chants and recitation (Berkeley, Calif., 1983).

The worldview of the Brāhmaṇas and especially their identification by modern scholars as the "prescientific" intellectual tool for ritual control of the universe have been dealt with by Sylvain Lévi in his *La doctrine du sacrifice dans les Brāhmaṇas* (1898), 2d ed., with a preface by Louis Renou (Paris, 1966), and by Hermann Oldenberg in *Die Weltanschauung der Brāhmaṇa-Texte* (Göttingen, 1919). Frits Staal has argued against the magico-cosmic meaning of ritual in general and, in particular, of Vedic ritual in "The Meaninglessness of Ritual," *Numen* 26 (June 1979): 2–23; Hans H. Penner's "Language, Ritual and Meaning," *Numen* 32 (July 1985): 1–16, emphasizes structure per se as against meaning. The continuity of the Vedic concept of sacrifice in Hinduism is the subject of Madeleine Biardeau and Charles Malamoud's *Le sacrifice dans l'Inde ancienne* (Paris, 1976). For the view of Vedic sacrificial ritual as originating in the conscious reform of a previous agonistic sacrifice, see my *The Inner Conflict of Tradition: Essays in Indian Ritual, Kingship, and Society* (Chicago, 1985). A detailed bibliography is provided by Louis Renou's *Bibliographie védique* (Paris, 1931). It has been continued by R. N. Dandekar's *Vedic Bibliography,* vol. 1 (Bombay, 1946) and vols. 2–4 (Poona, 1961–1985).

Brahmanism

As a singular topic, Brahmanism has not been the subject of special monographs. Its definition fluctuates between a particular period of post-Vedic religious development (older Hinduism) and mainstream orthodoxy. Louis Renou and Jean Filliozat's *L'Inde classique: Manuel des études indiennes,* 2 vols. (Paris, 1947–1953), brings together the whole of the written records of Hinduism, including those in the regional languages, under the heading "Brahmanism" (vol. 1, chap. 6). Among older works may be mentioned Auguste Barth's *The Religions of India,* translated by J. Wood, 6th ed. (Delhi, 1969), chap. 2.

Central to Brahmanism is *dharma.* The best introduction is provided by Robert Lingat's *The Classical Law of India,* translated with additions by J. D. M. Derrett (Berkeley, Calif., 1973). P. V. Kane's *History of Dharmaśāstra,* 5 vols. in 7 (1930–1962; 2d ed., rev. & enl., Poona, 1968–1975) is an exhaustive survey of the topics that traditionally come under the heading of *dharma.* The institution of world renunciation has been analyzed from a sociological point of view by Louis Dumont in "World Renunciation in Indian Religions," *Contributions to Indian Sociology* 4 (April 1960): 53–62. The same author has dealt with caste and *varṇa* in his influential *Homo Hierarchicus: An Essay on the Caste System,* rev. ed., translated by Mark Sainsbury (Chicago, 1980). He argues that Indian caste society (and even Indian civilization as a whole) is encompassed and held together by the religious principle of hierarchy. This view, however, is debatable because of the textual concept of *varṇa,* which refers not so much to hierarchic encompassment as to strict separation, while the religious institution of renunciation tends to break up society.

The vexing matter of *ahiṃsā* is discussed in Ludwig Alsdorf's *Beiträge zur Geschichte von Vegetarismus und Rinderverehrung in Indien* (Wiesbaden, 1962) and in Hanns-Peter Schmidt's "The Origin of *Ahiṃsā*," in *Mélanges d'indianisme à la mémoire de Louis Renou,* edited by Jacques Robert (Paris, 1968), pp. 625–655. Like Schmidt, I argue for the ritualistic origin of *ahiṃsā* in "Nonviolence and Sacrifice," in *Indologica Taurinensia* (forthcoming).

As regards mythology, E. Washburn Hopkins's *Epic Mythology,* "Grundriss der indo-arischen Philologie und Altertumskunde," no. 3.1.13 (Strassburg, 1915), gives a useful survey. *Classical Hindu Mythology: A Reader in the Sanskrit Purāṇas* (Philadelphia, 1978), edited and translated by Cornelia Dimmitt and J. A. B. van Buitenen, offers an illustrative selection. Wendy Doniger O'Flaherty's discussions of Puranic mythology, such as *The Origin of Evil in Hindu Mythology* (Berkeley, Calif., 1978), are of considerable interest.

New Sources

Choudhary, B. K. *From Kinship to Social Hierarchy: The Vedic Experience.* Patna, 1999.

Elizarenkova, Tatyana J. *Language and Style of the Vedic Rsis.* Albany, 1995.

Facets of Vedic Studies. Edited by Bidyut Lata Ray. New Delhi, 2000.

Inside the Texts, Beyond the Texts: New Approaches to the Study of the Vedas: Proceedings of the International Vedic Workshop. Harvard University, June 1989. Harvard oriental series. Opera minora; v. 2. Cambridge, Mass., and Columbia, Mo., 1997.

Jamison, Stephanie W. *The Ravenous Hyenas and the Wounded Sun: Myth and Ritual in Ancient India.* (*Myth and Poetics.*) Ithaca, N.Y., 1991.

Jamison, Stephanie W. *Sacrificed Wife/Sacrificer's Wife: Women, Ritual, and Hospitality in Ancient India.* New York, 1996.

Mahony, William K. *The Artful Universe: An Introduction to the Vedic Religious Imagination.* Albany, 1998.

Malamoud, Charles. *Cooking the World: Ritual and Thought in Ancient India.* Translated from the French by David White. Delhi; New York, 1996.

JAN C. HEESTERMAN (1987)
Revised Bibliography

VEGETARIANISM SEE AHIṂSĀ; GREEK RELIGION; VEGETATION

VEGETATION. The world's mythology and folklore offer one example after another of sacred plants, both wild and cultivated, as well as stories about the divine origins of plants, their magic or medicinal properties, and heroic quests to obtain them. These stories reflect a dual tendency, shared by humanity's forebears in history and by its contemporaries in the so-called nonliterate societies: On the one hand there has been the tendency to "humanize" nature with sacred narratives whose purpose is to explain how the world and humankind came to be the way they are; on the other hand analogies have been consistently drawn from the physical world—in this case, plants or perhaps the tools and techniques for cultivating them—to express those things about human living that can never be fully expressed, especially the perennial anxieties, fervent hopes, and nostalgias that expose immediately the limits of one's situation in the world.

For example, the Warao Indians of the Orinoco Delta in South America have endowed basket making with a quite explicit religious meaning derived ultimately from their experience with a certain plant. Besides calabashes and makeshift containers put together by folding leaves or palm stipules, the Warao have only baskets for storage and carrying. The raw material used in the manufacture of baskets is the cortex of the stem of the *itiriti* plant, which grows in most parts of the delta. The Warao say that they owe the existence of the plant to the selfless sacrifice of an ancestor in primordial times who, seeing that his people were in need of baskets to survive, transformed himself into the first *itiriti* plant and enjoined his descendants to employ his body in the manufacture of many useful things.

The plant itself has a number of magico-religious properties, the most important being its effect on the craftsman's hands. A Warao basket maker observes that over the course of his career his palms whiten as the pithy interior of the *itiriti* passes through his hands. He believes that eventually a small hole that only he can see will appear in each palm. Often, when the craftsman splits open an *itiriti* stem to get at the pith, he can see that a small snake has tunneled up from the roots of the plant, and he understands then by analogy what the Itiriti Spirit, conceived of as a snake, is accomplishing in his body. The spirit, he believes, is boring a tunnel from his chest, where the tutelary spirits reside, through both arms to the openings in his palms. When the craftsman finally observes the exit holes in his palms, he knows he has undergone a transformation from an ordinary human to a shamanic craftsman with the same healing powers and social status as the other religious specialists in his tribe.

At least two points deserve mention. First, when the Warao craftsman produces baskets, he complies with his divine ancestor's original intention that many useful things be made of his serpentine body. He validates the Spirit's sacrificial deed through the knowledge and practice of his craft, and by having the body of the god pass continually through his hands, he effectively reconstitutes the sacrality of the primordium. In other words, he "humanizes" nature, here not so much by narrating what took place in the beginning as by acting it out.

Second, thanks to the analogies he draws from the plant, the snake, and the physical effect of his contact with the sacred fiber, the basket maker possesses a language suitable for expressing—as well as a technique suitable for achieving—the transformation from ordinary status to that of shamanic craftsman, by means of which he gains a place for himself after death in the presence of the Creator Bird of Dawn. Such is the spiritual achievement to which he dedicates the better part of his life. Just as he masters his craft by understanding the nature of the material he employs and the secret of the manufacturing process, so, by analogy, does he achieve spiritual mastery over himself and the world. The Warao example thus illustrates an important function of religious symbols generally: By making it possible for the human situation to be translated into cosmological terms and vice versa, religious symbols reveal a fundamental oneness between human life and the structure of the world, drawing human beings out of their isolation in subjectivity and allowing them to take a stance vis à vis their own lives and the world that one could easily describe as a kind of transcendence.

Warao basket making describes only one of the ways that plants have entered and shaped religious life. The effectiveness of medicinal plants is often ascribed to the spirit or power they embody. For example, the Apinagé of South America believe that for each species of edible animal there is a corresponding wild plant that can be used should a person undergo the harm of ingesting the animal's soul.

Poisons have played extremely important roles in human affairs, especially in the hands of sorcerers and priest-physicians charged with knowing how to treat their toxic effects and who are themselves capable of using the poison against an enemy. The Canelos Quichua and the Jivaroan people in Ecuador say that forest demons reside in plants from which the poisonous curare is prepared, and it is they who kill the victim when a poisoned arrow penetrates the body.

The beer that the Chaco Indians brew from algaroba or other fruits is said to derive its intoxicating powers from the spirit present in the tree and especially in its fruits. As the beverage ferments, the indwelling spirit approaches the height of its powers. The mysterious process of fermentation can be hurried along by various ceremonies, the beating of drums, or the shaking of rattles.

Any plant that somehow bears or manifests the vital forces at work in the world, spontaneous growth and renewal, may host divine or magic powers; contact with such a plant will commonly transfer those powers for the benefit of one who understands its secret. An endless variety of agricultural rites and beliefs entail the recognition of a force manifested in the harvest. The Indochinese have a rice spirit that makes their crops grow and bear fruit. They treat the rice in flower as they would a pregnant woman, taking care to capture the spirit in a basket and store it carefully in the granary where rice is kept. When barley starts to germinate, the Ewe of West Africa ensure the fertility of the fields by consecrating a number of young girls to the python god. As the god's representatives, priests consummate a sacred marriage, and the girls or women thus consecrated engage in ritual prostitution for a period of time in the enclosure of the sanctuary. Elsewhere the presence of the sacred tree at wedding celebrations underscores the link between vegetation and human sexuality. In Java, when rice blossomed it was customary for the husband and wife to mate in the field.

These examples all express not only a certain solidarity between plants and human beings but also an ambiguous vulnerability or susceptibility to the spirits of plant life that causes humans to wish to coordinate their activities with the mysterious rhythms and circulating energies of vegetation.

It should also be clear that the sacrality of vegetation differs in marked ways from, for example, the sacred as it is revealed through the sky and its symbols. Whereas the latter communicates distance, overarching sovereignty, and "spirituality" in the sense of being elevated, not physical, and timeless, human relations with the plant world are characteristically close, physical, and time-bound (owing especially to the cyclic nature of plant life).

It is exceedingly difficult to account for the distance between ours and a properly religious world in which the spiritual powers of vegetation are a self-evident truth, at least not without demeaning the intelligence of religious people by repeating arguments akin to the Greek polemics against Egyptian religion or the Israelite polemics against the worship of idols. The Greek writer Plutarch, for example, insisted that the Egyptians worshiped plants, and they did so, he said, because of a verbal misapprehension. According to Plutarch, primitive peoples had once believed that the food plants they consumed were gifts from the gods, but later the habit of associating the gods' names with various plants caused their descendants to forget, that is, people of later times began to confuse the plant with the divinity who made it. Scarcely more helpful were writers in the twentieth century who, influenced by Darwin, simply reversed the order of Plutarch's hypothetical "devolution" of religion into superstition. Their claim was that theism came late not early in human history and that the known nonliterate peoples, like the earliest peoples on record, are as yet incapable of consistent, complex religious thought and self-understanding.

By contrast, a historian of religions would choose to say that even an expression such as "plant worship" is something of a misnomer, for it is usually not the plant itself that is worshiped but the sacred power present or embodied in the plant or symbolized by the plant; and that wherever the sacred is revealed, whether in vegetation, animal life, stones, or sky, it engages the whole human person—meaning his or her emotional, imaginative, and intellectual faculties taken together—in a vital relationship. There is no reason to assume that the earliest human forebears were any less intelligent than than those of the present. In fact, if one compares the mythopoeic thought of nonliterate or "primitive" peoples with modern scientific thought, the differences—and in this most scholars would now agree—turn out to be due to emotional attitude and intention rather than to any disparity of intellect.

In what follows this article has tried to simplify things as much as possible by reducing the topic of vegetation to its two most important and revealing elements: the symbolism of the tree and the ideas and practices made possible by the discovery of agriculture. These two are in any case the models without which further discussion of vegetation as a religious phenomenon would prove difficult.

TREE SYMBOLISM. In myth and ritual, trees serve as symbols of orientation, knowledge, and life.

The cosmic tree. One of the most widely disseminated motifs in mythology and religious iconography is that of the sacred tree as both *imago mundi* and *axis mundi.* There seems no way to reconstruct with certainty the process whereby the tree came to represent both the cosmos as a whole and its cardinal axis, joining the three domains (heaven, earth, and underworld) together and making communication among them possible.

It is known that the earliest sacred places were small-scale reproductions of the world in toto achieved by forming a landscape of stones, water, and trees. Australian totem centers were often located in a sacred group of trees and stones, and the tree-altar-stone pattern characterized sacred places throughout India and East Asia. Often a vertical post or pillar was added, presumably as a stylized tree meant to enhance the sacred power already present in this microcosmic landscape. Finally, it would seem that over the course of time the elements of such a landscape were reduced to the single most important element: the tree or sacred pillar.

One does not have to go far in the history of religions to find examples of the cosmic tree as an image of the world. The ancient Babylonians knew the black Kiskanu Tree that grows at Eridu, the center of the world. It shines like lapis lazuli—meaning that it shines like the night sky—and spreads its branches out toward the cosmic ocean that surrounds and supports the world. The Upaniṣads speak of the universe as an inverted tree that buries its roots in the sky and spreads its branches over the whole earth. A Scandinavian creation story in the *Vǫluspa* tells of a cosmic tree called Yggdrasill with branches that reach to heaven and cover the whole world and roots that run under the earth and support it. At the base of the tree lies the cosmic serpent Niðhǫggr, gnawing at its roots, and at the top is an eagle who battles daily with the serpent. Yggdrasill thus mirrors the precarious fate of the cosmos; though it may be bruised and shaken, the tree's ultimate renewal will mark the beginning of a new age and a new earth.

Furthermore, the cosmic tree also expresses one of the most profound nostalgias of religious people, namely, the desire to orient themselves to the center of the world. Like other symbols for the center, the tree image calls attention to the vertical plane of the universe, and that means to the underworld as well. Chinese mythology tells of a miraculous tree that grows at the center of the universe and that unites the Nine Springs and the Nine Heavens. In other words, it marks the point at which the various cosmic levels intersect. The Abakan Tatars describe an iron mountain on which grows a birch tree with seven branches symbolizing the seven levels of heaven. A shaman is said to climb this tree in his ecstatic ascent. The Qurʾān refers in several places to the tree Zaqqūm, which has its roots in the lowest reaches of Hell. Its leaves are small, and its fruits bitter. It reverses the image of the heavenly Tuba Tree that is situated at the celestial Kaʿbah directly above the earthly Kaʿbah and linking the two.

The Tree of Knowledge. Perhaps partly because of its role in the cosmos as the cardinal axis and partly because of its connections with certain deities, the sacred tree sometimes has oracular functions, making it a tree of knowledge. Two of the roots of Yggdrasill reached to the sources of divine wisdom: one to the Spring of Mímir ("meditation" or "memory"), the other to the Fountain of Urðr ("fate"). Similarly, the Oak of Zeus at Dodona was said to have oracular powers on account of the extreme depth to which its roots extended. Whether in the creation story of the *Book of Genesis* the Tree of Life and the Tree of Knowledge are in fact one tree or two has been open to dispute, but some have argued persuasively that only by eating first of the Tree of the Knowledge of Good and Evil could the hidden tree that conferred immortality be found.

The Tree of Life. When historians speak of the cosmic tree, they have in mind those meanings conveyed through the symbolism of the tree that refer specifically to the structure and organization of the cosmos. But the tree, quite simply because of its other vegetative qualities—those related to its growth cycle and regenerative capacities—also conveys to religious people another set of ideas, expressive of the world's inexhaustible fertility. Most scholars, when they consider tree symbols with an eye to this latter array of meanings, refer to the tree of life as opposed to the cosmic tree; and it is true that in specific instances one or the other tends to be more fully expressed. Still, in some myths they are the same tree or at least are located near one another at the center of the world. For example, the second chapter of *Genesis* states that immediately after the Lord God breathed into Adam's nostrils, he

> planted a garden in Eden, in the east; and there he put the man whom he had formed. And out of the ground the Lord God made to grow every tree that is pleasant to the sight and good for food, and the tree of life also in the midst of the garden, and the tree of the knowledge of good and evil. (*Gn.* 2:8–10)

The garden stands, then, at the center of the world, and the tree at its center.

Numerous myths and iconographic motifs connect the tree of life (or its equivalent) with the Great Goddess and water and so confirm the basic meaning conveyed through the symbol: that is, a common concern for, and perhaps a deep anxiety over, life's changing cycles of fruitfulness and decay, youth and old age, poverty and abundance, sickness and health.

One of the most common themes associated with the tree of life describes how the cosmos itself and the various deities came into being. According to the Egyptian Pyramid Texts, Atum first emerged from a lotus drifting over the primordial watery abyss, but the rest of the gods originated from trees, including Hathor, the Great Mother, from the sycamore.

Excavations in the Indus Valley have unearthed artifacts picturing goddesses of the *yakṣinī* type beside a *Ficus religiosa* or plants emerging from a goddess's genital organs. In a pictorial theme found over a wide expanse of Africa and Asia, the goddess rises between two branches of a tree in the center of a circle.

The lotus, while not a tree, shares the same connection with the Great Goddess and cosmic fertility. The lotus is already a sacred flower in the Brāhmaṇas, where it represents the female generative organ, and that is its root meaning whether it becomes the female goddess, the cosmic lotus of Viṣṇu's navel and hence the womb of all creation, or the seat of divinity and spiritual power. It tells the story of being issuing forth pure and bright from the dark possibilities of watery chaos.

The legendary soma plant also has a connection with water, for the *Ṛgveda* describes it both as a spring or stream and as a paradisiacal plant that promises life, fertility, and regeneration. The *Book of Revelation* makes even clearer the cosmological and redemptive significance of water and the tree together:

> Then he showed me the river of the water of life, bright as a crystal, flowing from the throne of God and of the lamb through the middle of the streets of the city; also, on either side of the river, the tree of life with its twelve kinds of fruit, yielding its fruit each month; and the leaves of the trees were for the healing of the nations. (*Rv.* 12:1–2)

One last theme deserves mention. Often a hero goes off in search of the tree of life (or some other divine plant for which the tree is a model) and the immortality it will bring. The quest usually entails great dangers and trials, for the tree of life is hidden (as the Tree of Life in the Garden of Eden may have been) or guarded by monsters, like the golden apples in the Garden of Hesperides, and therefore difficult if not impossible to reach. For example, in the Babylonian variant of the theme, Gilgamesh seeks a thorny herb of life that the sage Utanapishtim tells him is at the bottom of the sea. A serpent thwarts his attempt and gains immortality for itself instead.

Similarly, Iranian tradition has an earthly tree of life with a heavenly counterpart. Like soma, earthly *haoma* is sometimes thought of as a plant and sometimes as a spring.

The heavenly variety gives immortality to all who eat of it and grows where Ahura Mazdā first planted it, among the thousands of other medicinal herbs at the source of the waters of Ardvisura, on an island in the great sea Vourukasha. Angra Mainyu counters Ahura Mazdā's creation with a creation of his own in the shape of a lizard that swims through the waters to attack the miraculous *haoma* tree.

The Discovery of Agriculture. The term *Neolithic Revolution,* its second component notwithstanding, denotes a period of gradual technological, economic, and religious innovation that took place roughly between 9000 and 7000 BCE, during which time many societies drifted away from their hunting and gathering economies toward an economy based on the domestication of animals and plants. Domestication resulted in the appearance of agriculture as a special form of animal and plant production and put human beings in the position of being, in a sense, creators of their food.

This new food-producing role brought with it many changes. For one thing, agriculture altered the division of labor, as women began to assume the better part of the responsibility for subsistence. It meant that early cultivators had to develop more accurate techniques for reckoning time, inasmuch as the complex activities in which they were now engaged had to be planned months in advance and coordinated both with the yearly cycles and with the different cycles of plant life.

Agriculture also enriched the meaning of work. To be sure, farming is a profane skill, but for religious people it has always been first and foremost a ritual. It deals, for example, with the mysterious forces of growth somehow at work in the seed and furrow. It is carried out on the body of Mother Earth herself. It requires the planter to integrate his movements with beneficent and dangerous periods of time; and it forces him to contend with the spirits of vegetation, particularly those, like the tree and forest spirits, who grow angry when the land is cleared. It requires ceremonial action to assist the growth of crops and renew the earth's life-giving energies, and it draws the farmer into contact with the dead, for the earth is their abode.

Above all, agriculture provided for a vast store of analogies that made it possible for human beings to see the necessary links that joined plant life, women and sexuality, earth, moon, water, death, initiation, and resurrection in a single, integrated view of life. In effect it allowed the whole world to be apprehended as a living organism, governed by rhythmic cycles in which death and life belong necessarily to one another, and in which rebirth is all the more miraculous for the astonishing increase of new life that accompanies it. Long and intimate dealings with the soil and its seasons fostered the great hope that, like the seed hidden in the earth, the dead can hope to return to life in a new form: that is, death might be no more than a provisional change in the human mode of being. On the other hand, it also pointed to life's essential transitoriness and fragility.

Simply put, the discovery of agriculture created an opportunity for the human mind to grasp certain truths that had been much harder to grasp before. A primitive hunter, for example, would have understood the rhythm of the seasons perfectly well, but for agriculturalists that rhythm was the basis for a theoretical construction that gave meaning to life, and they experienced this rhythmic quality of life amplified many times over in patterns of activity and rest or of scarcity and plenty; in rituals meant to drive out the old season; in rites of sowing and harvest; and even in orgies, whose aim was to reproduce on the human level what was taking place in the ground and what did take place in the beginning—like seeds that lose their shape, disintegrate, and become something different, human beings lose their identities and try to enter a state of chaotic formlessness analogous to the formless state prior to the creation of the world.

Agriculture had certain tragic implications as well. As producers of their food, early humans learned to take responsibility for the vegetable kingdom, for its perenniality, even if that meant, as in the case of human sacrifice or cannibalism, the killing of their own kind so that life could be renewed. For example, an important Aztec festival dedicated to the maize goddess Chicomecoatl began every year just as the maize plant attained its full growth. A young female slave or captive, painted red and yellow to represent the colors of the plant, performed a ritual dance nightly for the duration of the festival. On the last night all the women in the community danced with her and chanted the deeds of Chicomecoatl. At daybreak, the men joined them in a solemn dance of death that brought the exhausted victim to the top of the pyramid of sacrifice. There the woman was finally offered up in a gruesome rite to the goddess. In this way the maize goddess, herself exhausted by her season's labors, was thought to be restored. For precisely the same reasons, the Khonds, a Dravidian tribe of Bengal, practiced human sacrifice at least until the middle of the nineteenth century, consecrating their victims to the earth goddess, Tari Pennu or Bera Pennu.

These examples give some hint of the essential, underlying ambivalence toward farming and vegetable life that has found expression in almost every known myth concerning the origins of agriculture and the introduction of food plants. The German scholar Adolf E. Jensen divides these myths into two categories. One group of myths he attributes to cultivators of tuberous plants. Perhaps the most famous story comes from the Ceramese Islanders in Indonesia and tells how a young maiden, Hainuwele, was killed and buried on the ninth night of the Maro festival. Her father dug up the corpse, cut it in pieces, and buried the pieces around the sacred dancing ground. Then from the various parts of her body food plants sprang forth. This primordial murder radically changed the human condition. On the one hand, it was a creative death that permits the goddess to be continually present in the lives of her descendants, for every time one of them consumes a plant that sprang from her divine body, he or she partakes of the actual substance of the goddess. On the other hand, the story reveals how death and sexuality first entered the world and attributes all the religious and social institutions that are still in place to a criminal act at the beginning of time.

Myths belonging to Jensen's second category he attributes to cereal growers, and they recall a primordial theft of the food plant in question from heaven. The Dogon, for example, tell of a primordial blacksmith who stole cereal grains from the sky god and brought them back to earth hidden in his hammer. The Gula and Kulfa of the central Sudan say that a female spirit pressed beeswax to the soles of her feet so that the grain that the sky god had spread out would adhere. The Chané in the western Gran Chaco believe that the fox god hid the small seeds of the algaroba fruit in a hollow tooth.

While there are differences between the two types of myths, a rigid distinction between them would be difficult to defend, partly because the origin of cereals is often attributed to a primordial murder as well; but it would also distract attention from the variety of origin myths and the different themes they choose to emphasize. For example, one could construct another category of myths that tell of a benevolent woman who secretly provides food for human beings until she is discovered in the act of producing plants asexually from her body. According to one variant of the story, food plants (tubers and cereals both) came originally from the sweat or excreta of the goddess. Members of the tribe learn about the revolting source of their food and kill her; but following the advice she gives just before her death, they also bury the pieces of her dismembered body, whereupon food plants and other elements of culture (agricultural implements, for example) spring from the corpse.

All of the foregoing myths have one thing in common: They present the introduction of agriculture as an ambiguous event caused by a crime or mistake that took place during primordial times and fraught with difficult consequences. It would seem, in fact, that myths that account for the origins of agriculture also have things to say about the highly ambiguous achievement of civilization itself, and to the degree that *civilized* is the equivalent of *human,* they address those ambiguities that define humanity's common lot.

Many of those ambiguities can be seen played out in the myth of Prometheus and in that story's profound effects on the religious life of the ancient Greeks. It is a story that recounts much more than just the origins of agriculture. In the myth from Hesiod, gods and humans lived together and shared food in the primordial Golden Age. On the day he distributed the share from the first sacrificial animal, Prometheus established the diet that differentiates humans and the gods. Through Prometheus's deceit, humans received the edible portions, leaving the gods with only the bones and fat. Zeus took his revenge by hiding fire so that it was impossible for humans to cook their meat. Prometheus then stole the seed of fire, hiding it in the hollow stalk of a fennel plant, and presented it as a gift to humankind. Feeling cheated, Zeus hid the seed of wheat, burying it in the earth, with the result that henceforth men would have to labor in the fields for food. At the same time, he created the first woman, whom Hephaistos modeled out of clay, and thus sexuality entered the world too.

The myth of Prometheus was commemorated in ancient Greece as the passing of the Golden Age and the beginning of human time. For the Greeks, Prometheus had fulfilled the will of Zeus, who condemned human beings to the experience of hunger and death, but he had also provided the food needed to survive. Moreover, in leaving nothing for the gods except, significantly enough, the smells rising from the sacrifice, he validated the gods' supremacy, for in a sense the need to consume food is inversely proportional to the vital energy that makes gods different from humans in the first place.

The state sacrifice, though it was the cornerstone of Greek religion in the cities, reflected the ambivalence of the myth that served as its model or charter: On the one hand it brought gods and humans together to commemorate the start of human life, but it also underscored the distance separating people from the gods they worshiped. Various religious groups opposed the sacrifice out of a desire for a religious experience that was unlike that offered by official religion and that promised the devotee closer contact with the divine. Among the most important of these groups were the followers of Pythagoras, who embraced vegetarianism as a way of rejecting wholesale the type of communion with the gods that animal sacrifice had established as the norm. The foods they valued were cereals such as wheat and barley and plants such as mallow and asphodel, for in the Golden Age those plants—even though the first two are cultivated grains—were said to have sprung spontaneously from the earth and were the foods that men and gods had once eaten together. In other words, through rediscovering this lost commensality, the Pythagoreans hoped to achieve a return to the Golden Age. Like other forms of vegetarianism, the Pythagorean type is an example of ascetic practice that aims to purify and transform human life and, in a way, to undo the effects of civilization. Recalling the equivalence of the terms *civilized* and *human,* one might interpret Pythagorean vegetarianism as an example of one of the many different ways that people living in a world shaped by the ideas and values of agriculture have expressed their lives and imagined ways of transcending their all-too-human circumstances.

See Also Agriculture; Center of the World; Greek Religion; Haoma; Human Sacrifice; Lotus; Quests; Soma; Trees.

Bibliography

The single most important source on vegetation and the religious significance of agriculture is Mircea Eliade's *Patterns in Comparative Religion* (New York, 1958), chap. 8, "Vegetation: Rites and Symbols of Regeneration," and chap. 9, "Agriculture and Fertility Cults." Both chapters include extensive bibliographies. In addition, James G. Frazer's *The Golden*

Bough: A Study in Magic and Religion, 3d ed., rev. & enl., 12 vols. (London, 1911–1915), remains a valuable sourcebook.

On the sacred tree, a useful study is E. O. James's *The Tree of Life: An Archaeological Study* (Leiden, 1966), but see also the illuminating insights of Gerardus van der Leeuw in his *Religion in Essence and Manifestation,* translated by J. E. Turner (London, 1938), pp. 55ff.

On the origins of agriculture in the Neolithic period, see Mircea Eliade's *A History of Religious Ideas,* vol. 1, *From the Stone Age to the Eleusinian Mysteries* (Chicago, 1978), esp. chap. 2, "The Longest Revolution: The Discovery of Agriculture—Mesolithic and Neolithic." For the prehistoric worship of vegetation goddesses, see Marija Gimbutas's *The Goddesses and Gods of Old Europe, 6500 to 3500 B.C.: Myths and Cult Images* (Berkeley, Calif., 1982). Another important study of the religious life of the early cultivators is Vittorio Lanternari's *La Grande Festa: Storia del Capodanno nelle civiltà primitive* (Milan, 1959).

Adolf E. Jensen has written extensively about myths of the Hainuwele type and other myths of the origins of agriculture. See his *Myth and Cult among Primitive Peoples,* translated by Marianna Tax Choldin and Wolfgang Weissleder (Chicago, 1963). Note that Ileana Chirassi has identified themes of the Hainuwele type in Greek mythology. An excellent bibliography is appended to her *Elementi di Culture Precereali nei miti e riti Greci* (Rome, 1968).

New Sources

Heinrich, Michael. "Herbal and Symbolic Medicines of the Lowland Mixe (Oaxaca, Mexico): Disease Concepts, Healer's Roles, and Plant Use." *Anthropos* 89, nos. 1–3 (1994): 73–83.

Swain, Brajakishore. "Plant Ecology and the Law of the Relationship between Action and Result." *Journal of Dharma* 16 (1991): 218–228.

PETER C. CHEMERY (1987)
Revised Bibliography

VELES-VOLOS. The alternative names *Veles* and *Volos* denote different aspects of a deity of the pre-Christian Slavs, the god of death and of cattle. The bifurcation in meaning must have taken place in the East Slavic area, since *Volos* is confined to East Slavic; in South and West Slavic, the only known form is *Veles. Volos* very likely derives from the older **Velsu.* Some scholars (e.g., Michael Shapiro) consider Veles-Volos not as a composite figure but as distinct twin gods. It is true that the names *Veles* and *Volos* never occur together; however, both are associated with death and evil and with pastureland and cattle, as linguistic analysis suggests. Furthermore, the two aspects of Veles-Volos have close parallels in individual gods of other Indo-European pantheons, such as the Baltic Vels and Velinas, the Germanic Odin, the Indic Varuna, and the Iranian Ahura Mazdā.

Downgraded to a demon in the Christian era, Veles is known in Czech demonology of the fourteenth to sixteenth century as well as in the toponymy of the South Slavic area. The medieval Czech phrase *k Velesu za more,* used to denote "beyond the sea (or water)," literally means "to Veles in the otherworld."

The character and function of Veles-Volos can, to some degree, be reconstructed by linguistic analysis, especially of names of parallel deities in other Indo-European pantheons. The Lithuanian name **Velinas* (now *Velnias,* "*devil*") and the Latvian name *Vels* or *Velis,* for example, identify a Baltic god of death and the underworld (recorded as a god at the end of the eighteenth century and later described as a devil, an adversary of Perkūnas, the Lithuanian god of thunder. The Lithuanian term *vėlė* or *velė* means "shade of the dead." Other related terms include the Latvian *Velu laiks* and Lithuanian *vėlinės* ("days of the dead"), the Tocharian *wäl* ("to die") and *walu* ("dead"), and a host of Germanic relatives: Old Icelandic *valr* ("dead on the field of battle") and *Valhǫll* (abode of warriors fallen on the field of battle), Old English *wæl* ("corpse left on the battlefield"), and Old Norse *vollr* ("meadow," i.e., "the pastureland of the departed"), a term paralleled in meaning by the Hittite *wellu-* (**wel-nu*).

The Indo-European root **wel-* ("sight, insight, foresight") underlies the name of the Baltic deity Velinas or Velis, whose clairvoyance (by means of a single eye) is one of his chief attributes. The Old Russian "*Velesov vnuk*" ("grandson of Veles") is an epithet for the musician and prophetic poet Boian of the epic *Slovo o polku Igoreve,* and the Old Russian word *v'lkhv* means "sorcerer, magician, poet."

Another name for Veles is *Chernobog,* signifying the "black god" known to all Slavs. This name is still preserved in Slavic toponymy, and a curse invoking Chernobog is still used in the Ukraine: "May the black god kill you."

Volos is first mentioned in the Russian *Primary Chronicle* (c. 1111 CE), and in two tenth-century treaties with the Greeks, as *skot'i' bog* ("god of cattle"). The etymology of the phrase reveals connections with theriomorphism, disease, and evil spirits. The Russian word *volos* ("hair, fur") also refers to a parasite that lodges under the skin of human beings and animals; the disease it causes is variously called *volos, volost',* or *vo-losti.* The carrier of the disease, a worm, is also called *volosets* or *zmeevik,* from *zmei* ("serpent"). The related Russian words *volosen* and *volosatik* mean "evil spirit" or "devil." *Medved'* ("fierce beast"), a term meaning "bear" in Russian dialect, is known from literary texts of the eighteenth and nineteenth centuries and is used as an epithet to describe the adversary of the prophet Elijah, the Christian successor of the Slavic thunder god, Perun.

The importance of Volos is indicated in various references to his idols. The eighteenth-century Russian collection *Skazanii o postroenii grada Iaroslavlia* (Legends about the Founding of Yaroslavl), first published in 1876, mentions a place where a statue of Volos once stood: "The sounds of heavy breathing, of the psaltery, and of singing could often be heard from there, and dancing could be seen." Another text in the *Skazanii* mentions that cattle were driven around the idol of Volos. Of great interest also is a description of how a priest, Volkhv, first offered by fire a sacrificial victim, prophesied in the name of Volos, and was then himself sacrificed to the god, a parallel of the Germanic deity Odin's sacrifice to himself.

Etymologies, historical records, and comparative studies of Indo-European mythologies allow us to reconstruct the ancient Veles-Volos as a multifaceted god who was, on the one hand, a frightening god of death and, on the other, a divine seer: a god who ruled over the magic art and over cattle, who was a steadfast protector of peaceful settlements and a stern chastiser of their violation, and who was an adversary of the thunder god.

In the Christian era, Volos became identified with the saints Blasius (Vlasii) and Nicholas (Nikola), the patrons of flocks and crops. The connection between Volos and Blasius may be based on actual and functional similarity, considering that Blasius was "the guardian of the flocks" to the Byzantines. Northern Russian icons portray Vlasii seated on a horse or on a stone, surrounded by cows, sheep, and horses. In central and northern Russia, particularly in the Yaroslavl and Novgorod districts, the cult of Vlasii was popular up to the end of the nineteenth century. On February 11, his name day, peasants did not work, thereby appealing to the god to preserve their village against epidemics of plague or cholera. Icons depicting Vlasii were placed in stables, and there was a custom of carrying the icon around each sheep, horse, and cow. In springtime, when the animals were driven out to pasture, special prayers were said: "Let the smooth lambs, the fat oxen go out playing, and let them come back hopping." The saying "Those who celebrate Saint Vlasii will always be in plenty" points to his ancient role as god of wealth.

BIBLIOGRAPHY

Gimbutas, Marija. "The Lithuanian God *Velnias.*" In *Myth in Indo-European Antiquity,* edited by Gerald J. Larson, pp. 87–92. Berkeley, 1974.

Ivanov, Viacheslav, and V. N. Toporov. "A Comparative Study of the Group of Baltic Mythological Terms from the Root **vel-*." *Baltistica* (Vilnius) 9 (1973).

Ivanov, Viacheslav, and V. N. Toporov. "K probleme dostovernosti pozdnikh vtorichnykh istochnikov v sviazi s issledovaniiami v oblasti mifologii: Dannye o Velese v traditsiiakh severnoi Rusi i voprosy kritiki pis'mennykh tekstov." *Trudy po znakovym sistemam* 6 (1973): 46–82.

Jakobson, Roman. "The Slavic God *Veles* and His Indo-European Cognates." In *Studi linguistici in onore di Vittore Pisani,* edited by Giancarlo Bolognesi et al., pp. 579–599. Brescia, 1969.

MARIJA GIMBUTAS (1987)

VENERABLE BEDE SEE BEDE

VENERATION SEE ANCESTORS; CULT OF SAINTS; ICONS; IMAGES, *ARTICLE ON* VENERATION OF IMAGES; RELICS; SAINTHOOD; WORSHIP AND DEVOTIONAL LIFE

VENIAMINOV, INNOKENTII SEE INNOKENTII VENIAMINOV

VENUS is perhaps the most singular example from among the divinized abstractions that make up the Roman pantheon. The word *venus,* in its origin, is a neuter noun of the same kind as *genus* or *opus.* It is discernible in the derived verb *venerari* (**venes-ari*), which is confined to religious usage by all the authors of the republican period, especially Plautus. The Plautinian construction (not maintained by classic use) is of particular interest: *veneror . . . ut,* which can be translated, "I work a charm [upon such-and-such a divinity] in order to [obtain a result]." This notion of charm or seduction that defines the word *venus* is represented in Hittite (*wenzi*) and in the language of the Veneti (*wontar*). Yet the root *ven-* did not produce a divinity anywhere except in Latin. It is significant that, in the Oscan region (where is recorded a form that is probably borrowed from Latin), the homologue of the Latin *Venus* is *Herentas,* formed from another root: *her-,* "to will."

The neuter *venus* is part of a remarkable semantic series of the same kind as *genus/Genius/generare,* except that here the first term and not the second was divinized, passing from the neuter to the feminine: *Venus/venia/venerari* (sometimes *venerare* in Plautus). To the persuasive charm that the goddess embodies and that the *venerans* ("he who venerates") practices upon the gods, there corresponds the symmetric notion of *venia* in the sense of "grace" or "favor"—a notion that belongs to the technical vocabulary of the pontiffs (Servius, *Ad Aeneidem* 1.519).

This metamorphosis of a neuter noun into a goddess (in contrast, it is the shift from feminine to masculine that marks the divinization of Cupido) was very likely furthered by the encounter of this divinity with the Trojan legend. This legend must have facilitated the relation drawn between a Venus embodying charm in its religious meaning and an Aphrodite personifying seduction in the profane sense. The notion of Aphrodite as mother of the Trojan hero Aeneas, the legendary founder of the Roman race, allowed for the application of a Greek legend to Roman benefit. The myth illustrated the rite. It made explicit in plain language the ritual employed by a Roman *venerans* when soliciting the *venia deum,* the favor of the gods. Set forth as their ancestor, the "pious" Aeneas conferred upon the Romans a privileged status in the eyes of the gods. Was it not therefore their lot as his descendants, the Aeneads, to be assured of obtaining the *pax veniaque deum* (the peace and grace of God), as frequently expressed by Livy, thanks to the mediation of Venus, the preferred daughter of Jupiter? This, to be sure, was on the condition that they fulfill the duties of *pietas* ("piety"). This explains the famous declarations whereby the Romans claimed the title of "the most religious people in the world" (Cicero, *De natura deorum* 2.3.8, *De haruspicum responsis* 9.19).

The divinization of the notion of *venus* had to take place in a syncretic environment, Lavinium, which lent to Venus the smile of Aphrodite. According to tradition, Aeneas established at Lavinium, in Latium, a cult of Venus Frutis (the appellation *Frutis* is very likely connected etymologically to *Aphrodite*), and in the same place a federal temple of Venus, common to all Latins, was set up. Archaeology has uncovered at that site a *hērōiov*, the shrine of a hero, which the discoverer identifies as the mausoleum of Aeneas mentioned by Dionysius of Halicarnassus (1.64.1–5).

The Trojan interpretation of Venus explains the development of her cult. Thanks to the enlightenment afforded by the association with the Trojan legend, the Romans were able to recognize their national Venus in the Aphrodite of Mount Eryx in Sicily at the time of the First Punic War and so erected a temple to her later on the Capitoline. On the basis of this same enlightenment, the goddess was associated with Jupiter in the cult of the Vinalia, the wine festival thought to have been instituted by Aeneas. The first temple erected in the goddess's honor had been dedicated to Venus Obsequens ("propitious Venus"). It had been vowed in 295 BCE by Q. Fabius Gurges while battle raged against the Samnites. Its dedication day, August 19, coincided with the Vinalia Rustica. The Trojan interpretation was imposed in definitive and official fashion in the first century BCE: Julius Caesar offered a temple in the middle of the forum to Venus Genetrix as the grandmother of the Julian gens and the mother of the Aeneades. Lucretius's literary expression *Aeneadum genetrix* thus was awarded liturgical consecration.

BIBLIOGRAPHY

Dumézil, Georges. *Idées romaines.* Paris, 1969. See pages 245–252.

Dumézil, Georges. *La religion romaine archaïque.* 2d ed. Paris, 1974. Translated from the first edition by Philip Krapp as *Archaic Roman Religion,* 2 vols. (Chicago, 1970).

Schilling, Robert. "Le Culte de l'Indiges' à Lavinium." *Revue des études latines* 57 (1979): 49–68.

Schilling, Robert. *Rites, cultes, dieux de Rome.* Paris, 1979. See pages 290–333.

Schilling, Robert. *La religion romaine de Venus depuis les origines jusqu'au temps d'Auguste.* 2d ed. Paris, 1982.

New Sources

Freyburger, Gérard. "Vénus et Fides." In *Hommages à Robert Schilling,* pp. 101–108. Paris, 1983.

Johnson, Patricia J. "Construction of Venus in Ovid's Metamorphoses V." *Arethusa* 29 (1996): 125–149.

Lloyd-Morgan, Glenys. "Roman Venus: Public Worship and Private Rites." In *Pagan Gods and Shrines of the Roman Empire,* edited by Martin Henig and Anthony King, pp. 179–188. Oxford, 1986.

Magini, Leonardo. *Le feste di Venere. Fertilità femminile e configurazioni astrali nel calendario di Roma antica.* Rome, 1996.

Speidel, Michael. "Venus Victrix. Roman and Oriental." In *Aufstieg und Niedergang der Römischen Welt* 2.17.4, pp. 2225–2238. Berlin and New York, 1984.

Wlosok, Antonie. *Die Göttin Venus in Vergils Aeneis.* Heidelberg, 1967.

ROBERT SCHILLING (1987)
Translated from French by Paul C. Duggan
Revised Bibliography

VERGIL (also spelled Virgil; Publius Vergilius Maro; 70–19 BCE) was born in Andes, near Mantua, and educated in Cremona and Milan before coming to Rome. His youthful poems include *Catalepton* 5 and 8. After publication of the *Eclogues* in about 39 to 38 BCE, he joined the literary circle of Maecenas, the close friend and ally of Octavian (the future Augustus).

Vergil's early poems reflect his Epicurean orientation, and evidence of his participation in the Epicurean community at Naples is found in a papyrus from Herculaneum, where he is mentioned by name (Gigante, 1983). The *Eclogues* reflect the turbulence during the civil wars following the death of Julius Caesar, the defeat of the tyrannicides, and the narrow avoidance of war between Octavian and Antony by the signing of the Treaty of Brundisium. In *Eclogue* 4, Vergil celebrates this treaty, proclaiming that an unnamed child is about to be born, and his birth will usher in a new Golden Age. Vergil's Golden Age in the fourth *Eclogue* resembles that of Hesiod, where little human effort is required, but Hesiod's negative connotation of decline is reversed by Vergil's proclamation that the Golden Age is about to return. The idea that it can recur is linked with a Sibylline prophecy of the "final age" before a new cycle of ages begins again. The role of Dikē (Justice) and agriculture derives from Aratus's version (*Phaenomena* 96–136); that Apollo will rule this age is consistent with Augustus's coming religious renewal. The theme of the Golden Age appears again in the *Georgics,* where Vergil says that Jupiter deliberately brought an end to the inertia characteristic of the Hesiodic Golden Age and imposed *labor* (toil) on mortals so that they could develop skills and intelligence. Vergil here develops the idea that a new Golden Age will be based on agriculture rather than leisure. In the *Aeneid* he says that Saturnus brought a Golden Age to Italy, where it was enjoyed by the Latin people but was lost through war. Jupiter prophesies it will recur under the rule of Augustus (Johnston, 1980).

Scholars have tried in vain to identify the child with whose birth the new Golden Age will begin. Candidates have included a child of Mark Antony, of Augustus, or of Pollio (for identifications, see Coleman, 1977; and Clausen, 1994). Christians associated it with *Isaiah* 7:14 and 9:6–7, a theme supported by the Jewish associations of Pollio, the poem's dedicatee. References to Sibylline oracles, the return of Virgo

(Justice), and other references in the poem were given biblical interpretations. Lactantius interpreted the poem as a prophecy of the birth of the Christ child, and Vergil was thus viewed as a "pre-Christian" and "a vehicle of divine inspiration" (Tarrant, 1997). The emperor Constantine, who had been associated earlier with the reference to Apollo in *Ecclesiastes* 4:10, accepted this reading, although saints Jerome and Augustine rejected it (Clausen, 1994, pp. 119–129). The messianic or Christian interpretation reigned through the nineteenth century despite scholars such as Christian Gottlob Heyne, who rejected it (1767). Eduard Norden (1924) connected the poem with Egyptian and Middle Eastern theology and rituals of Helios (December 25; which H. J. Rose associated with Apollo) and of Aion (January 6, formerly the winter solstice). Günther Jachmann (1952) argued that the child was meant to be a symbol of the new age.

At the end of the Republic, a prevailing attitude of neglect toward the gods caused great concern among intellectuals and leaders. Julius Caesar, and then Augustus, engaged in a series of religious reforms. Augustus was concerned with maintaining the traditional values of an agricultural society in the new Rome; he did not return to such republican practices as auguries and prodigies, which had been abused, but focused on reforms in Roman private religion, such as developing the priesthood of the *Fratres Arvales* (Arval brothers), and restoring neglected rites as well as the temples of the gods. Particularly important is the cult of Apollo, who, before the time of Augustus, was worshiped outside the *pomerium* with other foreign gods; under Augustus his temple was placed in the heart of the city on the Palatine Hill. Vergil's *Georgics* (completed in 29 BCE and read by Vergil to Augustus), a poem on the art of agriculture, invokes the gods of the countryside as well as the deities whom Augustus elevates.

VERGIL'S *AENEID*. The *Aeneid* (published by Varius after Vergil's death in 19 BCE) tells of the fall of Troy and the search by the surviving Trojans, led by Aeneas, to found a new homeland. The poem embodies the religious motifs of Vergil's earlier works: the struggles (*labores*) necessary to build a new society, embodied in the suffering of Aeneas, who was later depicted on the Ara Pacis as a heroic founder figure, like Romulus. In the poem Aeneas, whose regular epithet is *pius* (pious), is the embodiment of *pietas* (piety, which many medieval readers interpreted as "pity" and hence interpreted his killing of Turnus as a lack of *pietas*). Aeneas's piety is reflected in his religious attitude, in his patriotic mission, and in his relations with his father, son, and companions as he labors selflessly to fulfill the commands of the gods and to found a new home for his people and his family. The motifs of the loss and promised return of a Golden Age are prominent, particularly in the second half of the poem, in the prophecies of the gods that such an age will recur under Augustus, and in the revelation that the Latin race, which once enjoyed such an age, lost it through the madness of war.

In the *Aeneid* fate and the gods provide divine machinery that advances the plot: Aeneas is driven by his destiny or fate to found a new civilization, and the anthropomorphized gods aid him in his pursuit of that destiny. Although his destiny is fixed, Aeneas's mortal failings threaten to undermine his pursuit of that goal, as when he is motivated to die in battle in Book 2 or when he is tempted to remain at Carthage with Dido in Book 4. Jupiter, who to some degree is the personification of fate, serves throughout the poem as the final power who resolves conflicts between other gods who oppose what fate has ordained. Venus, mother of Aeneas, supports his quest, and Juno, for a variety of reasons, opposes it. The deities participating in the action include Greco-Roman gods, particularly Apollo (who is closely associated with Augustus and Actium) and Herakles (who serves as a model for Aeneas and for Augustus), as well as Eastern deities (Cybele) and indigenous deities (Faunus, Tiber-god, and Portunus). For Aeneas, as representative of the Trojans, prayer and ritual are constant concerns. This is reflected throughout the poem, as when the Trojans arrive at or depart from Thrace, Delos, Actium, and Castrum Minervae; after visions of the Penates, Anchises's ghost, and the Tiber-god; at signs from Venus; when Aeneas's ships are converted into nymphs; and in the honors he pays to the dead.

The underworld in Book 6 of the *Aeneid*. Aeneas enters the underworld at Lake Avernus in Cumae, guided by the Cumaean Sibyl, after performing funeral rites for Misenus and obtaining the Golden Bough, required for passage into the underworld. His descent to the underworld to consult with his deceased father, Anchises, is the main theme of Book 6. Vergil's underworld is more complex than previous accounts. Whereas Homer's Odysseus goes only to the entrance, Aeneas descends through each level until the road diverges, one leading to Tartaros, the lowest level, which he is not permitted to enter (the sinners and their punishments are described by the Sibyl), and one leading to Elysium, a *locus amoenus* (a pleasant place), thus providing the first distinction in destinies according to the manner in which one has lived one's life.

Vergil describes the levels of the underworld, beginning with the evil shapes and spirits at the entrance, which are harmless. On one side of the River Acheron huddle the dead who have not been properly buried. After crossing the river, they confront the dog Kerberos, then those who have died prematurely, including Dido. Next he sees Trojans and Greeks who died at Troy, and finally he comes to the parting of the ways, which leads him to Elysium, where he meets with Anchises and beholds the future heroes of Rome. His departure from the underworld, through the gates of ivory, is mysterious because Vergil says that *falsa insomnia* (false dreams) pass through these gates (6.896), as opposed to the "true dreams," which pass through the alternate gates of horn.

VERGIL AS A SUITABLE MODEL FOR CHRISTIAN SPECULATIONS UNTIL DANTE. By the fourth century CE Vergil had become the common property of pagans and Christians. Not only were his works central to literary education, but the themes of his works—the miraculous child of the fourth *Eclogue* as a prophecy of the birth of Christ, the reading of the first half of the *Aeneid* as an allegory for the progress of the soul to maturity, and Vergil's description of the underworld in Book 6—were seen as suitable models for Christians. Like the Cumaean Sibyl guiding Aeneas through the underworld, Vergil guides Dante Alighieri to the brink of *Paradiso,* which he is not permitted to enter because, having lived before the time of Christ, he cannot be a Christian. Vergil leads the way to a Christian era and represents the imperial values that a Christian must leave behind.

SEE ALSO Afterlife; Descent into the Underworld; Fate; Golden Age; Roman Religion; Sibylline Oracles.

BIBLIOGRAPHY

Armstrong, David, Jeffrey Fish, Patricia A. Johnston, and Marilyn B. Skinner, eds. *Vergil, Philodemus, and the Augustans.* Austin, Tex., 2004.

Barnes, W. R. "Virgil: The Literary Impact." In *A Companion to the Study of Virgil,* edited by Nicholas Horsfall, pp. 257–291. Leiden, Netherlands, 2000.

Büchner, Karl. *P. Vergilius Maro: Der Dichter der Römer.* Stuttgart, Germany, 1959.

Burrow, Colin. "Virgils, from Dante to Milton." In *The Cambridge Companion to Virgil,* edited by Charles Martindale, pp. 79–90. Cambridge, U.K., 1997.

Carcopino, Jérôme. *Virgile et le mystère de la IVe éclogue.* Paris, 1930. Discusses neo-Pythagorean coloring.

Clausen, Wendell, ed. *Virgil: "Eclogues," with an Introduction and Commentary.* Oxford, U.K., 1994.

Coleman, Robert, ed. *"Eclogues" of Vergil.* Cambridge, U.K., 1977.

Comparetti, Domenico. *Virgilio nel medio evo.* 2 vol. Florence, 1872; Translated as *Vergil in the Middle Ages* by E. F. M. Benecke (Princeton, N.J., 1997).

Courcelle, Pierre. *Lecteurs païens et lecteurs chrétiens de l'Enéide.* Rome, 1984.

Enciclopedia virgiliana. Rome, 1984–1991. Includes several articles pertaining to religion, including articles on deities, festivals, heroes, and forms of piety.

Galinsky, Karl. *Augustan Culture: An Interpretive Introduction.* Princeton, N.J., 1996.

Gigante, Marcello. "Virgilio fra Ercolano e Pompei." *Atene e Roma* 28 (1983): 31–50.

Hagendahl, Harald. *The Latin Fathers and the Classics: A Study on the Apologists, Jerome, and Other Christian Writers.* Göteborg, Sweden, 1958.

Jachmann, Günther. "Die vierte Eklge Vergils." *Annali della Scuola Normale Superiore di Pisa,* 2d ser., 21 (1952): 13–62.

Johnston, Patricia A. *Vergil's Agricultural Golden Age: A Study of the "Georgics."* Leiden, Netherlands, 1980.

Johnston, Patricia A. "Juno and the Sibyl of Cumae." *Vergilius* 44 (1998): 13–23.

Johnston, Patricia A. "Piety in Vergil and Philodemus." In *Vergil, Philodemus, and the Augustans,* edited by David Armstrong, Jeffrey Fish, Patricia A. Johnston, and Marilyn B. Skinner. Austin, Tex., 2004.

Mayer, Joseph B., W. Warde Fowler, and R. S. Conway. *Virgil's Messianic "Eclogue," Its Meaning, Occasion, and Sources: Three Studies.* London, 1907.

Mynors, R. A. B., ed. *"Georgics" by Vergil, with a Commentary.* Oxford, U.K., 1990.

Nisbet, R. G. M. "Virgil's Fourth *Eclogue*: Easterners and Westerners." *Bulletin of the Institute of Classical Studies* 25 (1978): 59–78.

Norden, Eduard. *Die Geburt des Kindes: Geschichte einer religiösen Idee.* Leipzig, Germany, 1924. Connects the fourth *Eclogue* with Egyptian theosophy.

Norden, Eduard, ed. *P. Vergilius Maro Aeneis buch VI.* 4th ed. Stuttgart, Germany, 1957.

Rand, Edward Kennard. *The Magical Art of Virgil.* Cambridge, Mass., 1931.

Rose, H. J. *The "Eclogues" of Vergil.* Berkeley, Calif., and Los Angeles, 1942.

Royds, Thomas Fletcher. *Virgil and Isaiah: A Study of the Pollio.* Oxford, U.K., 1918. Discusses Vergil as a prophet of Christ.

Solmsen, Friedrich. "Greek Ideas of the Hereafter in Virgil's Roman Epic." *Proceedings of the American Philosophical Society* 112 (1968): 8–14.

Tarrant, R. J. "Aspects of Virgil's Reception in Antiquity." In *The Cambridge Companion to Virgil,* edited by Charles Martindale, pp. 56–72. Cambridge, U.K., 1997.

Wagenwoort, H. *Pietas: Selected Studies in Roman Religion.* Leiden, Netherlands, 1980.Westendorp Boerma, R. E. H. *P. Vergili Maronis libellum qui inscribitur Catalepton.* Assen, Netherlands, 1949.Wilkinson, L. P. *The "Georgics" of Virgil: A Critical Survey.* Cambridge, U.K., 1969.

Williams, G. "A Version of Pastoral: Vergil, *Eclogue* 4." In *Quality and Pleasure in Latin Poetry,* edited by Tony Woodman and David West, pp. 31–46. Cambridge, U.K., 1974.

PATRICIA A. JOHNSTON (2005)

VERIFICATION SEE LOGICAL POSITIVISM

VESTA. The name *Vesta,* with the archaic suffix *-ta,* is derived from the root **a*1eu, "to burn." It encompasses two stems: stem 1, **a*1eu-s, is found in the Greek *heuo* and the Latin *uro,* "I burn"; stem 2, **a*1u-es, lies at the base of the Latin *Vesta* and most probably also of the Greek *Hestia.* The intrinsic bond between the goddess and fire, *ignis Vestae* ("fire of Vesta"; Paulus-Festus, ed. W. M. Lindsay, 1913, p. 94 L.), was understood perfectly by the ancients, even though they were sometimes tempted to propose fanciful etymologies; Festus, for example, in order to explain Vesta's round sanctuary identifies her with the round earth (Paulus-Festus, ed. W. M. Lindsay, 1913, p. 320 L.). The semantic connection between the Latin goddess and the Greek goddess was conceded by Cicero (*De natura deorum* 2.67), who also believed that Vesta had been borrowed from the Greeks.

Although the cult of Vesta was known throughout the Italic regions, evidence of it comes above all from Latium.

The cult of Vesta was established at Lavinium, so that it is possible that her worship with colleges of virgins in attendance was at one time more widespread throughout Latium. The goddess is clearly listed in the famous catalogue of Sabin divinities introduced in Rome in archaic times (Varro, *De lingua Latina,* 5.74). The tradition that the *virgines Vestae,* like most other Roman religious institutions, were instituted by king Numa is given by Livy (1. 20.3), Gellius (1.12.10) and Ovid (*Fasti* 6.259) but may be no more than a reconstruction from the established connexion between Numa and the nymph Egeria who inspired him: the Vestals drew water from the well of the Camenae, where Numa and Egeria met (Plutarch, *Numa* 13). Another origin, Romulean or Alban, may be infered: according to Livy (1.3.11), Ovid (*Fasti* 3.11–52), and Plutarch (*Romulus* 3), Rhea Silvia, daughter of Numitor and mother of the twins Romulus and Remus, was consecrated to the cult of Vesta by King Amulius, who wanted to deprive her of descendants. Tarpeia, who betrayed the Romans during the war between Romulus and Titus Tatius, was also perhaps a Vestal Virgin (Livy 1.3.11).

Since the cult of Vesta goes back to the origins of the Latin city, it escaped the anthropomorphism of the Etruscan and Greek environments, as evidenced by Ovid, who writes that even in his time the *ignis Vestae* was sufficient by itself and had no cultic statue (*Fasti* 6.295–298). When Cicero (*De natura deorum* 3.80) tells of the episode in which the *pontifex maximus* Q. Mucius Scaevola was slain in 82 BCE in front of "the statue of Vesta" he must be referring to an honorific statue located in the vestibule or outside the sanctuary.

Situated near the *via Sacra* in the Forum, in front of the *Regia* and linked with the *Atrium Vestae* ("house" of the Vestals), the goddess's round sanctuary (*rotunda aedes;* Paulus-Festus, ed. Lindsay, 1913, p. 321 L.; Ovid, *Fasti* 6.267) was differentiated from a four-sided temple oriented to the four cardinal points. This contrast, which the ancients attempted to explain by gratuitously comparing the goddess with the earth, becomes clear in the light of comparative studies. Vedic religion distinguished "the fire of the master of the house," which is "this world and, as such, is round," from "the fire of offerings," the smoke of which "carries men's gifts to the gods: this is oriented to the four cardinal points and is thus four-sided" (Dumézil, 1974, p. 320).

Vesta's influence was upon the altars and hearths (Cicero, *De natura deorum* 2.67). The recommendation that Cato (*De agricultura* 143) made to the farmwife *(vilica),* who held the same place in the country as did the mistress of the house *(domina)* in the city, was appropriate for anyone responsible for the hearth: "Let the hearth be maintained by being swept each day before bedtime."

Since the goddess also watched, "as it were, over the hearth of the city" (Cicero, *De legibus* 2.29), she was designated *Vesta publica populi Romani Quiritium* in the official religion. At her service there were the six Vestal Virgins, whose principal task was to maintain the fire (Cicero, *De legibus* 2.29). This fire was renewed once a year on March 1, the beginning of the ancient year (Ovid, *Fasti* 3.135–144). "If by chance this fire were extinguished, the virgins would be flogged by the pontiff. Custom then obliged them to rub on a piece of 'fertile' wood [*felix materia*] until the fire thus produced could be carried by a Vestal in a bronze sieve to the sanctuary" (Paulus-Festus, ed. W. M. Lindsay, 1913, p. 94 L.). Although the Vestals were directed by a superior, the *virgo Vestalis maxima,* they were placed under the authority of the *pontifex maximus,* who was to flog them in case of carelessness. They had to maintain absolute chastity for the entire duration of their service (Ovid, *Fasti* 6.283ff.). The loss of virginity meant capital punishment: the guilty Vestal was buried alive in the Campus Sceleratus ("field of crime") near the Porta Collina. Cicero (*De legibus* 2.8.20) gives two reasons for the virginity of the priestesses. The first is a practical one: married women have others duties. The second is inspired by Roman morality, and Cicero imagines the Vestals as setting a public example for all women. The preparation of the various items needed for sacrifices was also entrusted to the Vestals. The *muries,* a brine produced by adding water to oven-cooked coarse salt (Festus, p. 152 L.), and the *mola salsa,* baked wheat flour sprinkled with salt (p. 124 L.), which was spread over the heads of the victims *(immolare)* before they were slain *(mactare),* were both prepared by the Vestals (Paulus-Festus, ed. W. M. Lindsay, 1913, p. 97 L.). Scholars have defined the duties of the Vestals as a kind of housekeeping at the state hearth, and there is a debate as to whether they represent, in the cult, the king's daughters or the king's wife.

The girls chosen to be "priestesses" of Vesta were said to be "seized" (*capere*) by the *pontifex maximus,* and this "capture" had important juridical consequences: from that moment, the girl was no longer subordinate to the *patria potestas* (Gellius, *Noctes Atticae*1.12.9; Gaius, *Institutiones* 1.130), nor to a tutor (Gaius, *Institutiones* 1.145); she may, of her free will, dispose of her fortune, and she also may appear in court as a witness (Gellius 7.7.2). So the Vestals Virgins enjoyed a number of civil rights that originally a Roman woman did not possess. From the beginning, this female priesthood was endowed with outstanding rights (civil rights and not only cultic honors), which led some scholars to regard the Vestal Virgins as forerunners of the "emancipation" of Roman women (Guizzi, 1968, p. 200). Some scholars pretend that there was cooperation and solidarity between Vestal Virgins and Roman women (Gagé, 1963). But only "presence" is attested and there is no proof for an act of solidarity (Cancik-Lindemaier, 1990, 1996).

The goddess's feast, the Vestalia, was held on June 9. From June 7 to 15, her sanctuary was open exclusively to women, who were allowed to enter only with bare feet. On the last day it was cleaned. The end of this operation was noted in the calendars by the letters *Q(uando) ST(ercus) D(-elatum) F(as)* (literally, "Once the dung is removed, the day is profane"). This archaic notion, which marks the specific moment at which the day changes from being a *dies nefastus* ("forbidden or holy day," a day on which no public business could be transacted) to being *fastus* ("profane"), recalls the time "when a pastoral society in camp had to clean away the *stercus* [dung] of its flocks from the site of its sacred fire" (Dumézil, 1974, p. 320).

The sanctuary also contained some talismans that served as pledges of Rome's perpetuity. Among these was the Palladium, the statue of Pallas Athena, reputedly of Trojan origin (Servius, *Ad Aeneiden* 7.188; Livy, 27.27.14; Cicero, *Pro Scauro* 48). In contrast to the sacrificial ingredients preserved in the anterior part of the sanctuary *(penus exterior),* these "pledges of destiny" (*pignora fatalia;* Ovid, *Fasti* 6.445) were kept in the "holy of holies" *(penus interior)* that was closed off by a tapestry (Festus, p. 296 L.) and accessible only to the Vestals. This gave rise to the anecdote about the *pontifex maximus* L. Caecilius Metellus, who in 241 BCE, after having saved the Palladium from a fire, penetrated to the forbidden place and was struck blind (Pliny, *Natural History* 7.141) Thus, the symbolism of the "eternal fires" of Vesta (Ovid, *Fasti* 3.421) was reinforced by the presence of these "pledges of destiny."

The importance of Vesta is evident in the liturgy. The goddess was invoked at the end of every prayer and sacrifice (Cicero, *De natura deorum* 2.67), paralleling the opening invocation of Janus, who led the sequence of divinities. (This liturgical rule was the opposite of the Greek practice, which prescribed "beginning with Hestia."). Esteem for the Vestals followed naturally. Once a year they appeared before the *rex sacrorum* ("king of sacrifices") and said to him, "Vigilasne rex? Vigila!" ("Are you watchful, king? Be watchful!"; Servius, *Ad Aeneidem* 10.228). In a solemn ceremony at the Capitol, the *pontifex maximus* officiated along with the chief Vestal (Horace, *Odes* 3.30.8). One can thus understand Cicero's statement *(Pro Fonteio* 48): "If the gods were to scorn the Vestal's prayers, it would be the end of our power."

In the third century BCE Vesta did not entirely escape a syncretism that made her the homologue of Hestia: during the *lectisternium* of 217 BCE she was coupled with Vulcan/Hephaistos. Thus the beneficial fire, kept inside the city, was uncustomarily associated with the harmful fire, relegated to outside the *pomerium,* the religious and ritual boundary of the city (Vitruvius, 1.7.1). Another innovation started with Augustus, who upon becoming *pontifex maximus* in 12 BCE, even while respecting the old sanctuary of the Forum, had a chapel of Vesta (Aedicula Vestae) built on the Palatine near his palace and adorned it with a cultic statue (*Corpus inscriptionum Latinarum,* Berlin, 1863, vol. 1, no. 317).

BIBLIOGRAPHY

Brelich, Angelo. "Vesta." *Albae Vigiliae* 7. Zurich, 1949.

Dumézil, Georges. *La religion romaine archaïque.* 2d ed. Paris, 1974. This work has been translated from the first edition by Philip Krapp as *Archaic Roman Religion,* 2 vols., Chicago, 1970.

Cancik-Lindemaier, Hildegard. "Kultische Priviligierung und gesellschäftliche Realität." *Saeculum* 41, no. 1 (1990): 1–16.

Cancik-Lindemaier, Hildegard. "Priestly and Female Role in Roman Religion.The *uirgines Vestae.*" *Hyperboreus* 2, no. 2 (1996) 138–150.

Cornell, Tim, "Some Observations on the *crimen incesti.*" In *Le délit religieux dans la cité antique* (Collection de l'Ecole française de Rome, 48), Rome, 1981, pp. 27–37.

Fraschetti, Augusto. "La sepoltura delle Vestali e la città," in *Du châtiment dans la cité. Supplices corporels et peine de mort dans le monde antique* (Collection de l'Ecole française de Rome, 79), Rome, 1984, pp. 97–129.

Gagé, Jean. *Matronalia. Essai sur les dévotions et les organisations cultuelles des femmes dans l'ancienne Rome* (coll. Latomus LX). Brussels, 1963.

Giannelli, Giulio. *Il sacerdozio delle Vestali Romane.* Florence, 1913.

Guizzi, F. *Aspetti giuridici del sacerdozio Romano. Il sacerdozio di Vesta* (Pubblicazioni della Facoltà Giuridica dell'Università di Napoli). Naples, 1968.

Hommel, Hildebrecht. "Vesta und die frührömische Religion." *Aufstieg und Niedergang der römischen Welt* 1, no. 2 (1972): 397–420.

Latte, Kurt. *Römische Religionsgeschichte,* Munich, 1960 (2d ed., 1967), pp. 108–110.

Paulus-Festus. *Sexti Pompei Festi de uerborum significatu quae supersunt cum Pauli epitome.* Edited by W. M. Lindsay. Leipzig, 1913.

Radke, Gerhard. *Die Götter Altitaliens.* Münster, 1965, pp. 320–335.

Radke, Gerhard. " Die 'dei Penates' und Vesta in Rome." *Aufstieg und Niedergang der Römischen Welt,* II, 17, no. 1 (1981): 343–373.

Wissowa, Georg. *Religion und Kultus der Römer.* 2d ed., Munich, 1912, pp. 153–161.

ROBERT SCHILLING (1987)
CHARLES GUITTARD (2005)
Translated from French by Paul C. Duggan

VESTMENTS SEE CLOTHING

VIA NEGATIVA is a technical term for the negative way of theology, which refuses to identify God with any human concept or knowledge, for God transcends all that can be known of him. Yet the term points to the possibility of union with God and the experience of his presence.

Via negativa was described by Dionysius the Areopagite (c. 500 CE) in his treatises *Divine Names* and *Mystical Theology.* He developed further the ideas of the fourth-century Cappadocian fathers, particularly that of Gregory of Nyssa, but the term derives originally from the writings of the Neoplatonic philosopher Proclus (411–485). The writings of Dionysius were translated by John Scottus Eriugena (c. 810–880), who made *via negativa* the basis of his theology, arguing that it was more effective than the affirmative path. Since

Eriugena the term *via negativa* has been used by other theologians of mystical contemplation, particularly by Meister Eckhart (1260–1327) and Nicholas of Cusa (1401–1464).

The affirmative way of theology, *theologia kataphatika,* uses terms from one's own experience to describe God and his qualities. According to the affirmative theology, every term that refers to the good and the beautiful in this world can be applied analogously to God: "God is good," "God is love," "God is light," "God is truth." Yet the seeker after God becomes aware that God transcends all qualities or attributes that are applied to the creator by his creatures. God is good, but he is beyond and above any concept of goodness that one may imagine. What humans affirm about God does not express his reality. Whatever one may say of God one can also deny. People call him "Person," but, at the same time, they know that he transcends personal categories and empirical existence. God dwells in light that none can approach (*1 Tm.* 6:16), or he dwells in darkness, in which all names disappear. He transcends any concept that may be applied to him. This *via negativa* is the basis of "negative theology" (*theologia apophatika*), which presents God as ineffable and a mystery.

Via negativa is both a way to the knowledge of God and a way of union with him. God is known by *via negativa* when upon removal from the names, definitions, and statements used about God all that he is not. God cannot be named or defined. Any name or definition imposes limits, and God is above (*huper*) them. Incommensurable and incomprehensible, he cannot be reached by discursive reasoning; he is not an object of knowledge, for he is above knowledge. *Via negativa* means radical denial of all definitions, transcending reason while not abandoning it. The person following *via negativa* in order to know God engages in a paradoxical search. On the one hand, he or she denies that God can be identified with anything or that God can be expressed in words or concepts; on the other hand, the seeker must follow the road of *via negativa* to be united with the ultimate reality. The life of those who seek union with God is one of purification of soul and overcoming of passion as an approach to that union. God is nearer to people than they are to themselves, yet he is inconceivable. Hence, those who experience union with God speak in negative rather than positive terms; God is even more incomprehensible than he is at the beginning of the religious quest. Worship, expressed in prayers and hymns, reflects *via negativa.* God, who transcends reason and thought, is honored in silence as well. Negative theology conveys the purest form of devotion and the experience of God's ineffable presence.

Dionysus the Areopagite thought of God as a being beyond any conception or name, who "transcends all affirmation by being the perfect and unique cause of all things, and all negation by plenitude of his simple and absolute nature." Any concept that can be applied to the world cannot be used regarding God. He is present in the world by providence, but not in his essence. Yet one can know God in the silence of unknowing. "Unknowing" (*agnosia*), a key word in the mystical theology of Dionysius, means much more than absence of knowledge. To know God by unknowing is to surrender one's mind to him. God is not an object of knowledge. As the soul is saved by losing itself, so the mind knows God by unknowing. The mind is abandoned to be found and saved, for it is the mind itself that sees God at the last stage of union and contemplation. Knowledge of God is not simply knowledge but union with him. Still, God is incomprehensible even when this union is realized. To attain "superessential darkness" is the goal of *via negativa.*

The Christian experience of God must be distinguished from that of Neoplatonic mysticism. Although Dionysius the Areopagite was a devoted disciple of Proclus, the last great Neoplatonist, his description of the experience of God is not Neoplatonic. The Neoplatonists would say that God is incomprehensible to the human soul, but that this is because of the soul's union with the body. The "unbodying" of humans leads to liberation: When the soul, free from the body or from finitude, returns to the One, it attains perfect unity with it. The One is no longer incomprehensible. The apophatic, negative way is transformed into a cataphatic, positive one. This Neoplatonic outlook is far from the views of Dionysius.

Via negativa was important in later Christian theology as well, as in the work of the fifteenth-century German Catholic cardinal Nicholas of Cusa, who built upon and developed some ideas of Dionysius and Eriugena. With his conception of "learned ignorance," Nicholas teaches that God is ineffable, infinitely greater than anything that words or concepts can express, and that by the process of elimination and the use of negative propositions one comes nearer to the truth about Him. Negative propositions are true, whereas affirmative ones are inadequate, Nicholas asserts. He emphasizes that negative theology "is so indispensable to affirmative theology that without it God would be adored, not as the Infinite but rather as a creature, which is idolatry."

Via negativa is present in the Eastern religious traditions as well. The Hindu seeker's goal is union with *brahman,* the ineffable, the nonconceptual. The Upaniṣads contain innumerable statements expressing or reflecting the unknowability and intangibility of ultimate reality. *Brahman* is "without beginning, without end, eternal, immutable, beyond nature, is the Self" *(Kaṭha Upaniṣad).* The Self is to be described as *neti, neti* ("not this, not this"). The ignorant do not know *brahman,* for *brahman* remains hidden behind names and forms. To know *brahman* is to know what is beyond knowledge, and one who knows *brahman* becomes one with *brahman (Muṇḍaka Upaniṣad).* Having attained the ultimate reality, the sage declares: "I am life" *(Taittirīya Upaniṣad).* Meditation as practiced in Eastern religions reflects *via negativa* more strongly than is the case in modern Western religions.

The Dao of Daoism, like *brahman* of Hinduism, is ineffable, indescribable, indefinable, ungraspable. The Dao is actionless, yet active. The Dao, the way of all life, is "beyond the power of words to define." The terms applied to the Dao are all relative, "none of them absolute" (Bynner, 1944, p. 25). The Dao gives life to everything, yet it is humble and lowly: "Existence, by nothing bred, breeds everything" (Bynner, p. 27).

Via negativa also permeates the Buddhist view of *nirvāṇa.* According to the Theravāda teaching, *nirvāṇa* is a state into which one enters by achieving victory over craving through the extinction of desire. The nature of *nirvāṇa* is beyond ordinary human existence; no images or concepts derived from the world of human experience are adequate for describing or analyzing it. By using only negative terms, such as "unborn, not become, not made, uncompounded," the Buddha pointed to the nature of *nirvāṇa.* Something very positive is conveyed in this negative way, for these negative terms overcome limitations that are implicit in positive terms.

The Mahāyāna conception of *nirvāṇa* dispenses with the image of entering *nirvāṇa* and emphasizes the state of ultimate perfection. The *arahant,* the saint of the Theravāda, is interested in "entering" *nirvāṇa;* but the *bodhisattva,* the saint of the Mahāyāna, when he reaches the state of perfection, does not "stay" in *nirvāṇa* but brings perfection back into *saṃsāra,* the flux of events in this world. How is this state of perfection of the *bodhisattva* described? Again, only a negative approach is found to be adequate. The experience of the *bodhisattva* does not fit ordinary experience. The perfection of the *bodhisattva* is experienced as "compassionate oneness with others," when any thought of the self as separate is transcended, when *nirvāṇa* and *samsara* are known to be not two different realms of existence but one. To refuse to "enter" *nirvāṇa,* to remain in the world for the sake of others, is in fact to be in *nirvāṇa.* This state of perfection can be adequately expressed only in negative terms: "*nirvāṇa* is the annihilation of ego conception," or, "*nirvāṇa* is bliss unspeakable," that is, perfect, timeless bliss. A notion common to these and similar statements is that human language is inadequate for the expression of *nirvāṇa,* which is "the recognition of the oneness of existence." The Buddha said, "I will teach you the truth and the path of the truth." The truth is *nirvāṇa,* but *nirvāṇa,* the experienced eternal in Buddhism, is ineffable. *Brahman* is ineffable. Dao is ineffable. God is ineffable.

What positive theology affirms about God is not false, but it is inadequate. Negative theology affirms that God excels in everything. Yet the apophatic way alone, without the cataphatic, may lead anywhere. Cataphatic theology, without an apophatic dimension, may build a system of concepts without an underlying experience of God. The absolute terms of negation that are common to the mystical traditions (*emptiness, void, darkness, nothingness*) are paradoxically positive in content. They are the product of the experience of the divine, the numinous. They are symbols that point to God, who is the "Wholly Other," with whom nothing in this world can be compared. *Via negativa* indicates and expresses his unconditional existence.

BIBLIOGRAPHY

Burtt, Edwin A., ed. *The Teaching of the Compassionate Buddha.* New York, 1955. A valuable collection of excerpts from early and later Buddhist texts.

Bynner, Witter. *The Way of Life According to Laotzu.* New York, 1944. An attempt to produce a simple, free, and suggestive translation of the *Daode jing.*

Dionysius the Areopagite. *On the Divine Names and the Mystical Theology.* Translated, edited, and with an introduction by C. E. Rolt. New York, 1940. A good introduction and clear translation of this Christian classic.

Meyendorff, John. *Byzantine Theology.* 2d ed. New York, 1979. A very readable and informative account of trends in Byzantine theology.

Nicholas of Cusa. *On Learned Ignorance.* Translated by Jasper Hopkins. Minneapolis, 1981. Indispensable for the thought of this great mystic.

Otto, Rudolf. *The Idea of the Holy.* 2d ed. Translated by John W. Harvey. New York, 1950. Still the best book on the subject: a modern classic on the basic experience of the holy.

Prabhavananda, Swami, and Frederick Manchester, trans. *The Upanishads: Breath of the Eternal.* Hollywood, Calif., 1948. An easily followed translation of some of the most important parts of the Hindu scriptures.

Sigmund, Paul E. *Nicholas of Cusa and Medieval Political Thought.* Cambridge, Mass., 1963. A good, reliable source of information about the period.

New Sources

Bulhof, Ilse Nina, and Laurens Ten Kate, eds. *Flight of the Gods: Philosophical Perspectives on Negative Theology.* New York, 2000.

Carlson, Thomas. *Indiscretion and the Naming of God.* Chicago, 1999.

Coward, Harold, and Toby Foshay, eds. *Derrida and Negative Theology.* Albany, N.Y., 1992.

Davies, Oliver, and Denys Turner, eds. *Silence and the Word: Negative Theology and Incarnation.* New York, 2002.

Milem, Bruce. *The Unspoken Word: Negative Theology in Meister Eckhart's German Sermons.* Washington, D.C., 2002.

VESELIN KESICH (1987)
Revised Bibliography

VICO, GIOVANNI BATTISTA (1668–1744), Neapolitan philosopher of history and culture. Vico was born and lived his life in Naples except for nine years (1686–1695) spent as tutor to the Rocca family at Vatolla. He received a degree in law from the University of Naples (Salerno) in 1694. Vico was professor of Latin Eloquence, that is, rhetoric, at the University of Naples from 1699 to his retirement in 1741. Because of the low salary of his position, Vico provided for his family by working as a private tutor and by writing on commission.

As part of the duties of his professorship, Vico presented a series of inaugural orations marking the beginning of each university year. The last of these, *De nostri temporis studiorum ratione* (On the Study Methods of Our Time), published in 1709, contains the first statement of Vico's original philosophical position. This was followed by an attack on Descartes, *De antiquissima Italorum sapientia* (On the Ancient Wisdom of the Italians) in 1710, in which Vico states his famous principle of *verum et factum convertuntur*—the convertibility of the true and the made. Between 1720 and 1722 Vico wrote two works and a series of annotations that comprise a large study known as *Il diritto universale* (Universal Law), in one chapter of which Vico gives a first sketch of his concept of a new science of nations. The first version of his major work, now known as the *Scienza nuova prima* (First New Science), was published in 1725. The two parts of his autobiography were completed between 1725 and 1728. The definitive version of his major work, entitled *Principi di scienza nuova di Giambattista Vico d'intorno alla comune natura delle nazioni* (Principles of New Science of Giambattista Vico Concerning the Common Nature of Nations), was published in 1730 and revised in the year of his death. This version has come to be known as Vico's *Scienza nuova seconda* or simply as Vico's *New Science.* Vico's work was very little known in his time. It was revived in the nineteenth century by Jules Michelet and early in the twentieth century by Benedetto Croce and Fausto Nicolini. More recently Vico's thought has been given a further revival in works by a number of European and Anglo-American scholars.

In the *New Science* Vico claims that religion, marriage, and burial are the three "principles" *(principi)* at the basis of all human society. Vico intends to emphasize the genetic and etymological meaning of the word *principi* as "beginnings." The institutions of religion, marriage, and burial are the necessary and sufficient conditions required for a minimal human society, one that can generate and transmit culture. Vico's emphasis is on religion, the first term in this list of principles or institutions; through its beginning, marriage and burial begin.

In Vico's view, religion arises from a primordial fear of the actions of a divine being and from the attempt to establish a relationship to this being through auspices. The primordial phenomenon through which the divine appears is thunder and humankind's fear of it. In Vico's account, the first humans, who have grown to gigantic size and who are living in the great forests of the earth since the biblical flood, produce the first act of human speech by calling the thunderous sky Jove. Every people, or nation, has its Jove. Human speech and the culture of any nation begin at the sudden transformation of the physical states of the thunderous sky and humankind's fear of it into a spiritual meaning, the presence of a god. Jove is the first name forged in human consciousness. This is done not through an act of reasoning but through an act of imagination, or what Vico calls *fantasia. Fantasia* is not the passive formation of images from sensation, but an active power to form or make something true in human experience. Vico calls Jove an "imaginative universal" *(universale fantastico),* which is the term he uses for the form of thought that characterizes the primordial religious-mythic or poetic mind.

In Vico's view, the nations of humanity begin at various times and places independent of each other, but all share a common nature. They all have structurally similar beginnings in the Jove experience and they all undergo the same course *(corso)* of historical development that passes through three ages, that of gods, heroes, and men. Within a *corso* various organized religions evolve from the impetus of the original religious mentality and life. The world of nations is a panorama of *corsi* and *ricorsi.* That all nations have a common nature—that they begin in an act of naming the divine and develop according to the pattern of three ages—is in Vico's view evidence of providence in history.

Providence, for Vico, is evident in this three-stage life of any nation. In the age of gods men see all of nature and social institutions in terms of the presence of gods. Social order exists through fathers who found cities and take auspices of the divine. In the age of heroes *fantasia* is directed to form not gods but certain human figures, such as Achilles, as imaginative universals. In the age of men all life and thought becomes secularized: abstract thought rather than *fantasia* dominates; natural piety fades; the forms of social life become dissolute. When this occurs a given *corso* comes to an end and a civilization falls. At this point God reestablishes the providential structure of history by a *ricorso* in which a new beginning is made by a return of the survivors to the original severe conditions of life and primordial religious experience.

BIBLIOGRAPHY

Works by Vico

The standard edition of Vico's writings is by Fausto Nicolini, *Opere di G. B. Vico,* 8 vols. in 11 (Bari, 1911–1941). The standard English translation of Vico's major work is *The New Science of Giambattista Vico* (Ithaca, N. Y., 1961; rev. trans. 1968). Complementary to this is *The Autobiography of Giambattista Vico* (Ithaca, N. Y., 1944). Both of these works are translated by Thomas G. Bergin and Max H. Fisch and are admirable in their style and accuracy. Both contain prefaces and notes that are indispensable. Vico's *De nostri temporis studiorum ratione* (1709) has been translated by Elio Gianturco as *On the Study Methods of Our Time* (Indianapolis, 1965). Partial translations of Vico's works, including *De antiquissima Italorum sapientia* and *La scienza nuova prima,* are available in *Vico: Selected Writings,* edited and translated by Leon Pompa (Cambridge, 1982). For a comprehensive description of the Italian and English editions of Vico's works, see Michael J. Mooney's "Vico's Writings" in *Giambattista Vico's Science of Humanity,* edited by Giorgio Tagliacozzo and me (Baltimore, 1976).

Works about Vico

The classic bibliography is Benedetto Croce's *Bibliografia vichiana,* revised and enlarged by Fausto Nicolini (Naples, 1947–1948). Also useful is *A Bibliography of Vico in English, 1884–1984,* edited by Giorgio Tagliacozzo et al. (Bowling Green,

Ohio, 1986), and its supplements published by the Institute for Vico Studies in New York. For a full, paragraph-by-paragraph commentary on Vico's *Scienza nuova,* see Fausto Nicolini's *Commento storico alla seconda Scienza nuova,* 2 vols. (Rome, 1949–1950). For the classic interpretation of Vico's thought from the standpoint of Hegelian idealism, see Croce's *The Philosophy of Giambattista Vico,* translated by R. G. Collingwood (London, 1913). Three recent interpretations of Vico in English are Leon Pompa's *Vico: A Study of the 'New Science'* (Cambridge, 1975), which examines Vico's ideas as they constitute a science of society and history; Isaiah Berlin's *Vico and Herder* (New York, 1976), which considers Vico from the perspective of the history of ideas; and my own *Vico's Science of Imagination* (Ithaca, N.Y., 1981), which examines Vico's conception of "imaginative universals" as the basis of his thought. Several volumes of essays by European and American scholars have been edited by Giorgio Tagliacozzo, director of the Institute for Vico Studies, and others. Many of these essays show the connection of Vico with other thinkers; one of the most recent volumes is *Vico: Past and Present* (Atlantic Highlands, N.J., 1981). See also the yearbook, *New Vico Studies* (1983–), edited by Tagliacozzo and me.

DONALD PHILLIP VERENE (1987)

VICTORINES SEE HUGH OF SAINT-VICTOR

VIERKANDT, ALFRED

VIERKANDT, ALFRED (1867–1953), was a German sociologist. His early work focused on anthropology and social psychology. Born in Hamburg, Vierkandt studied at the University of Leipzig, where he was awarded the Ph.D. degree in 1892. He began teaching at the University of Berlin in 1900. In 1921 he was given the newly founded chair in sociology at Berlin, and he was awarded an honorary doctorate in 1932 by the University of Würzburg. Forbidden by the Nazis to lecture and give examinations, he was forced into retirement in 1934. After 1945 he took over the leadership of the Kant Society, and in 1946 he resumed teaching at the University of Berlin. He died in Berlin in 1953.

The influence of his teacher at Leipzig, Wilhelm Wundt, can be seen in Vierkandt's first major anthropological work, *Naturvölker und Kulturvölker* (1896), in which his differentiation between "primitive" and "civilized" peoples reflects Wundt's distinction between association and apperception. In his lectures Vierkandt dealt with the psychology, religion, art, and social conditions of "primitive people" with special attention to ethics and the philosophy of religion. Vierkandt focused upon the impact of a culture upon the individual through language, myth, and custom in his idea of the determining influence of the group on the individual's character development. In *Die Stetigkeit im Kulturwandel* (1908) Vierkandt not only presented a theory of cultural continuity and cultural change but also attacked the mechanical theories of diffusionism then prevalent.

After World War I Vierkandt shifted his focus and sought to outline the contents and methodology for the discipline of sociology. In *Gesellschaftslehre: Hauptprobleme der philosophischen Soziologie* (1923; 2d ed., 1928), he described sociology as the study of the "ultimate facts" of society, which, for him, were manifested in the specific properties of the group and in the characteristics of group life, the group being the carrier of interaction between its members. He further proposed a phenomenological method for this study. Vierkandt also acted as editor for a comprehensive dictionary, the *Handwörterbuch der Soziologie* (1931; reprint, 1959), to which most of the leading German sociologists of his day contributed. His study *Familie, Volk, und Staat in ihren gesellschaftlichen Lebensvorgängen* (1936) received little attention during the Nazi period but was republished in 1949 under the title *Kleine Gesellschaftslehre.*

Vierkandt's focus on the group as having an identity in itself instead of just being the sum of its individual members suggested a new approach to understanding the phenomena of religious life. Although his attempt to introduce phenomenology as a methodology for sociology has been rejected as not acceptable if sociology is to be a science, his view of religion as a distinctive phenomenon to be studied has been taken up and developed by historians of religions. Vierkandt understood culture as a historical phenomenon, something that gradually develops with its own inherent dynamism, and thus he advocated a nonreductive approach that does not seek to explain the phenomenon by some outside "key" but rather looks at the inner essence of the thing itself. This has been the basis for most approaches to the study of religions.

BIBLIOGRAPHY

The most recent appraisal of Vierkandt's work in English is Paul Hochstim's *Alfred Vierkandt: A Sociological Critique* (New York, 1966). Hochstim's work focuses primarily on a critical evaluation of Vierkandt's significance in the history and development of sociological thought, but it is more comprehensive and moves beyond the negative criticism of Vierkandt's phenomenological methodology found in Theodore Abel's *Systematic Sociology in Germany* (1929; reprint, New York, 1965). A brief treatment of Vierkandt's contributions to cultural sociology is found in *Social Thought from Lore to Science,* 3d ed., vol. 3, by Howard S. Becker and Harry Elmer Barnes (New York, 1961). A more philosophical appraisal of Vierkandt's contributions is Dora Peyser's "The Sociological Outlook of Vierkandt," *Australasian Journal of Psychology and Philosophy* 15 (1937): 118–136. Finally, more biographical details on Vierkandt's life and work can be found in the *Handwörterbuch der Sozialwissenschaften,* edited by Erwin von Beckerath et al., vol. 11 (Stuttgart, 1961).

WALLACE B. CLIFT (1987)

VIETNAMESE RELIGION.

VIETNAMESE RELIGION. Like the whole complex of Vietnamese culture, Vietnamese religion has long been presented as a pure copy of the Chinese model. Trained for the most part in the discipline of Chinese studies and associating mostly with the literati class and the townspeople, scholars have been constantly confronted by their interlocutors with the Chinese ideal, notably in the domains of moral and aesthetic norms, and they have gauged the value of a rite or particular behavior according to its degree of conformity with the rules laid down by the Han Chinese texts.

Historically, the Red River Delta, cradle of Vietnamese civilization, was occupied by the Han for more than a thousand years. Moreover, the Middle Kingdom, as highly centralizing as the Roman Empire, had an especially effective organization wherein each parcel of conquered territory was put under absolute control and strict surveillance militarily, administratively, and ideologically. Chinese writing served as a unifying and assimilating instrument of the first order. Nonetheless, Dongsonian civilization, which flourished in this region before its destruction by the Han invasions, must have possessed a certain vigor, for despite the very long coercive occupation that followed it, the Vietnamese preserved their language and a part of their culture, finally succeeding in the tenth century of the common era after numerous revolts in liberating themselves from their deeply implanted Chinese occupants. Paradoxically, the consolidation for independence reinforced the prestige of the Chinese model among the literati. Their influence in this regard even resulted in the promulgation in 1812 by Emperor Gialong, who had recently reunified the country, of a new code that was nothing more than a translation of a Manchu dynasty treaty, despite the fact that for more than three centuries, the Vietnamese had a set of original laws known as the Lê Code.

Yet, in a population that was more than 90 percent rural, ideology directly concerned only a relatively small number of people, those who wielded power and prestige. The ideals and beliefs they held touched but superficially the great masses, who remained bound to a set of rules transmitted orally and put to the test through daily observance. That the Vietnamese spoke a language belonging to a different family (Austroasiatic rather than Sino-Tibetan) was a considerable asset for the preservation of these rules. In addition, the development in the tenth century of the *chu nôm*, a demotic system of writing based on Chinese graphs, allowed for a closer contact between this popular culture and the literati class. This open attitude toward national beliefs and practices was reinforced with the extension of the *quôc ngu*, the romanized system of writing introduced in the seventeenth century by Alexandre de Rhodes. This system acquired its full acceptance, however, only in the nineteenth century and did not become universal until the twentieth century.

In the religious sphere, this situation created a coexistence, on the one hand, of a Chinese model followed strictly by the most erudite or those instructed in the faith, and on the other, of popular cults observed by the great mass of people. Between the two there evolved a phenomenon of osmosis leading to a syncretism with multiple nuances.

The expansion southward along the entire length of the Vietnamese territory added further to this diversification of the religion by the absorption, on the small coastal plains, of the Chams, whose religious affiliation was divided between Brahmanism and Islam, and on the Mekong Delta, of the Khmer adherents to Theravāda Buddhism. These three religions, with that of the Proto-Indo-Chinese on which they were grafted, effected a syncretism probably more intimately overlapping than was the Triple Religion (Buddhism, Confucianism, and Daoism) of the Vietnamese with these same Proto-Indo-Chinese foundations. Even at its source, at the edge of the Red River Delta, mention must be made, albeit in passing, of the Tai influence on the beliefs and practices not only of the Muong, who speak archaic Vietnamese, but also on those of the Vietnamese, properly speaking, who inhabit the villages of the foothills.

The twenty-year separation between the northern and southern halves of the country introduced further variations in the religions. A great number of Catholics from the North took refuge in the South in 1954, where their political weight allowed them to extend their influence. It should not be forgotten that outside of the Philippines, where the majority of the population is Catholic, Vietnam has the strongest Christian minority in Asia.

Whatever the case may be, this article examines Vietnamese religion before the entry of the country into its Marxist period, focusing not on the Chinese model, already treated elsewhere, but rather on those aspects that touch directly on Vietnamese religion.

On the level of the individual, a fundamental concept is that of souls or vital principles. This concept governs as many aspects of daily conduct as it does basic rituals such as funeral rites or ancestor worship. In this domain, Chinese influence predominates. One encounters the scholarly Han tradition of the three souls and the seven corporeal souls. They too carry Sino-Vietnamese names: *hôn* (Chin., *hun*) and *phach* (Chin., *po*). However, if one follows Leopold Cadière, to whom we owe the most profound study on the subject, notable variations appear between the system of the literati and the vocabulary and conceptions of the common people. For example, with regard to *phach*, the inferior vital principles, its Vietnamese equivalent, *voc*, remained confined to the physical aspect of the body (especially the external appearance of the body). Moreover, the most current term used is in fact Vietnamese: *via*, which is in the same semantic range as *phach* (from form of the body to animal soul). Qualities of these *via* vary according to individuals as well as within the same individual. A person endowed with heavy *via* exercises a harmful influence on others, while light *via* brings beneficial influence.

Appropriate funeral rites are absolutely essential for the benefit of the departed. There is fear of two categories of malevolent spirits, the *ma* (Chin., *ma*) and the *gui* (Chin., *gui*), souls of the dead without sepulchers. In contrast, one can benefit from the aid of the *thân* (Chin., *shen*), souls of ancestors, understood in a noble sense. These three entities, expressed in Sino-Vietnamese words, testify to the survival of the *hon.*

From words of the same family comes the Vietnamese *hoi,* with its Sino-Vietnamese doublet *khi* (Chin., *qi),* whose meaning ranges from breath, inhalation, emanations from living or dead bodies, to supernatural influence over a person's life and destiny. This influence can emanate not only from a human but also from an animal, the ground, stones, plants, and so forth. The concept provides the essential basis of popular cults as well.

The Chinese model reposes on the complex called *tam giao* (Chin., *sanjiao,* triple teaching or triple religion), that is, Buddhism (Phât giao; Chin., Fojiao), Confucianism (Không giao; Chin., Kongjiao), and Daoism (Lao giao; Chin., Daojiao), or the teachings of the Buddha, Confucius, and Laozi, respectively. Prior to 1975, when asked his religion, an educated Vietnamese generally would have answered that he was a Buddhist. On the civic or family level, however, he followed Confucian precepts; on the affective level or in the face of destiny, he turned to Daoist conceptions. Even if Mahāyāna Buddhism had an effect on his relationship with the otherworld, his personal behavior would have remained impregnated with Daoism. This fact was evident in his concern to conform with cosmic harmony, to pay careful attention to sources and currents of energy traversing the universe, and to parallel equivalents between these and the human body. These concerns were manifested in his desire to withdraw into nature as well as in his recourse to geomancy and diverse divinatory procedures, even to magic. It was primarily Confucianism and Buddhism, however, that affected his moral conduct.

It goes without saying that, as in China, each of the elements composing the Triple Religion in no way presented itself as impervious to the other two. Mutual borrowings throughout the course of centuries increased to the point that it was sometimes difficult to know with certainty which rite or belief to attribute to which element. During the twelfth and thirteenth centuries, disputes, sometimes very intense, pitted Buddhists against Daoists and caused them to accuse each other of plagiarism on a number of points. Recourse to divination in its multiple forms was not a monopoly of Daoists; Confucians also employed this means of decoding destiny.

This mixture was more deeply rooted among the common people, where features of each of the Three Ways were known only very superficially. Nevertheless, their respective dosages seem to have been in inverse proportion to that predominating among the literati. There was among the common people much less preoccupation with correct rules of government and with mandates from Heaven than with recourse to aid of supernatural beings to resolve the grievous problems of the here and now or to assure for oneself a decent future, both here and in the otherworld. It is true that the observance of ancestor worship attested to the ascendancy of Confucianism, but the different Buddhas and *bodhisattvas* tended to join the ranks of the multiple divinities and deities of the Daoist pantheon. Daoism itself was immeasurably enriched with popular autochthonous beliefs and practices, to which it lent a certain respectability by a tint of sinicization; furthermore, magic played a proportionally more important role in activities of a religious type.

The geographical situation of Chinese-occupied Vietnam placed it in a privileged position on the route of Indian merchants and missionaries traveling from India to China and of Han and Vietnamese pilgrims taking the reverse route. From the first centuries CE, Indian monks were personally active in spreading Buddhist doctrine throughout the Middle Kingdom, including South China. It is thus that some Vietnamese participated in the first translations of canonical texts. From the sixth century, and especially the seventh century, Theravāda Buddhism in Vietnam gave way to Mahāyāna, which was also prevalent in China. And in the pagodas, the three Buddhas (*tam thê phât*; Chin., *sanshi fo*) of the present, the past, and the future occupied the principal altar, other altars being invaded by statues of numerous *bodhisattvas*. Distinctly autochthonous *dhyāna* (*thiên*; Chin., *chan*) sects sprang up in the course of the centuries, and Vietnamese, in ever-increasing numbers, went on pilgrimage to India. The assistance given by eminent Buddhist monks to those who liberated the country from the Chinese accorded to Buddhism a considerable hold over the first dynasties. One was even to see kings abdicating to end their days in monasteries.

Confucianism, which regulated the examinations for the recruitment of the literati (in other words, the mandarin cadres), was from the time of the Ly (1009–1225) the dominant official ideology. Moreover, beginning with the reigns of the Lê, Confucianism provided the state and family moral code and rituals of a once-again independent Vietnam that subsequently was to behave as a southern replica of the Celestial Empire. Before the image of the Son of Heaven, its suzerain, the emperor of Dai-Viet, was responsible for his acts before the all-powerful God. If he did not observe the rules correctly, the mandate to govern that he received from Heaven would be withdrawn from him by different means: war, revolution, lack of a male heir, and so forth.

In matters of cult ministry, the eminent positions occupied by Heaven and earth found expression through the sacrifices offered to them by the sovereign, who officiated in person. These ceremonies, said to belong to the *nam giao* (Chin., *nanjiao,* sacrificial mound), appanage of imperial power, had always been vested with exceptional majesty and pomp. The *lê tich điên* (Chin., *jitian,* opening ceremony of the rice fields) also belonged to this cult complex. Here, too, the sovereign himself officiated—although he soon came to delegate the performance of this ceremony to a high-ranking mandarin. By tracing nine furrows on the royal field, the sovereign or his representative would open the plowing season.

Ancestor worship occupied a central place in the family cult. It represented the ritual expression of a cardinal virtue, filial piety (*hiêu;* Chin., *xiao*), the pivot of interpersonal relationships. The Vietnamese followed with devotion the precept of Mengzi, "duty toward parents is the foundation of all others," that permeated all rules of conduct. The necessity of perfecting oneself morally and intellectually, loyalty to one's friends, respect for one's superiors, fidelity to the sovereign—all these were believed to arise from the domain of filial piety.

The extent of the economic impact of ancestor worship on a family depended on the wealth of that family. Reserved exclusively for the maintenance of such worship and for the performance of its ceremonies were revenues from property (rice fields, houses, etc.) that constituted the *huong-hoa* (Chin., *xianghuo*), the portion of the incense and the fire transmitted by inheritance from the father to his eldest son. It should be noted that Confucianism did not succeed in lowering the Vietnamese woman to the inferior rank occupied by her Chinese counterpart. Even in wealthy families the wife had the same status as her husband in family ceremonies, including those pertaining to ancestor worship in its strict sense. As the ideology of the mandarin type of government, Confucianism, by its very nature, became a target of Marxist-Leninist regimes. In Vietnam the offensive has been less virulent and of shorter duration than in the People's Republic of China; it is true that Vietnam has not experienced any extremist phenomenon comparable to that of the Cultural Revolution in China.

Responsive as the literati were to the abstract universal order proposed by Confucianism, the idealized transposition of the bureaucratic hierarchy, they were equally responsive to the concrete universal order conceived by Daoist doctrine, with its correspondences (the human body, the microcosmic replica of the macrocosm) and its complementary contradictions (*âm* and *duong*, the Vietnamese equivalents of *yin* and *yang*). The peasant, on the other hand, retained of Daoism principally the imagery presented in the temples (*đên*) in various forms. Dominating the whole ensemble was the August Jade Emperor, Ngọc-Hoang (Chin., Yuhuang), assisted by his two chief ministers, Nam-Tao (Chin., Nancao, the Southern Constellation) and Bac-Đâu (Chin., Beidou, the Northern Constellation), who were charged respectively with keeping account of the birth and death of human beings and of governing a multitude of deities ranked according to an organization duplicating the imperial bureaucracy. Among these deities a special place must be assigned to Tao-quân (Chin., Zaojun), the hearth deity, who at the end of each year reports on the acts and deeds of humans; the days surrounding this event are a period of transition that provides an occasion for the Vietnamese to celebrate their most spectacular collective feast, the Têt Nguyên Đan (Chin., Yuandan), the celebration of the New Year. In popular Vietnamese consciousness Tao-quân is actually a composite of three personages, a woman and her two husbands, whose unhappy marriages were the subject of legends. The other important category in Vietnamese practice is represented by the immortals, whose Chinese nucleus of eight personalities has been enlarged by the addition of native deities.

The recourse to mediums and ritual decorative features representing the pantheon dominated by the Jade Emperor made possible the assimilation of Daoist elements into a certain number of Vietnamese popular cults. The one that came closest in form to a Daoist cult was that attributed to Trân Hung Đạo, a spirit served by a male medium (*ông đông*). Trân Hung Đạo is a Vietnamese national hero from the thirteenth century, conqueror of the Han armies of the Mongol dynasty. The medium would perform a violent ritual in the course of which he inflicted on himself bloody ordeals and healed the sick by exorcising them of the traitor or vanquished general who possessed them.

The cult of the *chu vi*, dignitaries served by female mediums (*ba đông*), borrowed from Daoism some elements of the decor, and at least in the north, the possession of the mediums by some immortals (whereas in the south it was spirits rather than immortals who descended). Here the medium (a *ba đông* in this case) is mounted not by one god but successively, in the course of the same séance, by different spirits of both sexes and of different ages.

At the collective level, the cult of the tutelary deity (*thanh-hoang*; Chin., *shenghuang*), the protector of the commune, held an eminent place in Vietnamese popular religion. Indeed, the most important public building in a village was the *đinh*, both a communal house and a place of worship; it sheltered the altar of the tutelary deity and served as a meeting place of the notables for the settlement of questions of administration and internal justice. The *đinh* was the center of collective life on the social as well as the religious level. It constituted the core of the system of peasant relations with the world beyond (through the intervention of the *thanh-hoang*) as well as with the state (the tutelary deity was confirmed by an imperial warrant obtained at the request of the notables).

The *thanh-hoang* could be a celestial deity, a deified legendary or historical personage, or even a disreputable person, such as a thief or a scavenger, whose violent death at a sacred hour endowed him with occult powers. It even would happen, although quite rarely, that an influential mandarin who had rendered an important service to the village became a guardian spirit during his lifetime. A deity who failed to protect the village at a critical moment or whose perfidy was denounced by a mystical revelation would be chased away and replaced by another deity.

A maintenance service for the fire and the incense was celebrated throughout the year, and ceremonies were held at the *đinh* on the first and fifteenth day of each month and on certain calendar feasts. The most important feast of the year was the Vao Đam, or Vao Hội (to be in festivities), which took place in spring or autumn, or on the anniversary of the birth or death of the tutelary deity. This feast lasted for two weeks, during which time it was forbidden to hold any funeral ceremonies. It was celebrated in great pomp with a series of processions, offerings, and prayers. Many villages undertook the organization of various entertainments: theater, cockfights, bullfights, and chess games with the people themselves acting as the chess pieces. Particular to this feast was a rite called Hem, often held secretly, recalling the salient features of the deity's life. It was celebrated at night when commemorating a dishonorable act: a scene of robbery for a thief deity, an enactment of excrement collection (with the excrement replaced by peeled bananas) for a scavenger deity, and so forth.

Certain trees, rocks, and natural boundaries were objects of cults that could lead to the construction of small altars. This veneration, very often fearful, could have varied origins. The tree, for example, could influence by the simple force of its being. It could also shelter a malevolent spirit, such as a *ma*, the soul of an unburied dead person, or of a *con tinh*, the soul of a young girl or woman who died before having experienced the joys of marriage. The man she succeeded in seducing would lose his reason and die unless exorcised in time. Sometimes, however, the tree or stone was not simply the habitat of a spirit but was in itself a deity: a deity-tree or deity-stone, such as one finds among the Proto-Indo-Chinese of the hinterlands.

The dominant features of Vietnamese religion were its openness to all forms of spirituality and its profusive character that resulted from this openness. These features were manifested on the level of the literati, whose most erudite members sought to abide by the texts of the Triple Religion or at least of one of the religions, as well as on the popular level, where the cult of the tutelary deity was observed and that was above all responsive to the different spirits peopling the environment as well as to the counsels of specialists. A village might possess a temple of one or another of the Three Ways, peopled with saints of the other two. There might at the same time be a temple by the seaside dedicated to the whale deity washed up and stranded on the shore. It should be noted that the intransigence of Christianity would eliminate from the territory of a converted village all monuments consecrated to another cult. This did not, however, prevent the majority of Christian peasants from having at least a minimum of respect for the spirits haunting the premises.

This general tendency toward syncretism made possible a strong implantation of Catholicism (but not of Islam) and encouraged Vietnamese, when emigrating in large numbers to foreign countries, to worship local deities until these were assimilated. This tendency has resulted, likewise, in the rise of new forms of syncretisms such as the Hoa-hao or Cao Dai, the first grafted on a Buddhist core, the other on a Daoist one.

SEE ALSO Ancestors, article on Ancestor Worship; Buddhism, article on Buddhism in Southeast Asia; Chinese Religion, overview article and article on Popular Religion; Chinese Religious Year; Confucianism, overview article; Daoism, overview article; Southeast Asian Religions, article on Mainland Cultures; Yinyang Wuxing; Yuhuang.

BIBLIOGRAPHY

Cadière, Leopold Michel. *Croyances et pratiques religieuses des Viêtnamiens.* 3 vols. Saigon, 1955–1958.

Dumotier, Gustave. "Essai sur les Tonkinois: Superstitions." *Revue indochinoise* 9 (1908): 22–76, 118–142, 193–214.

Durand, Maurice. *Technique et panthéon des médiums viêtnamiens.* Paris, 1959.

Nguyên Dông Chi. *Luoc khao ve thân thoại Viêt Nam.* Hanoi, 1956.

Nguyên Du. *Vaste recueil de légendes merveilleuses.* Translated by Nguyên Tran Huan. Paris, 1962.

Nguyên Tung. "Les Viêtnamiens et le monde surnatural." In *Mythes et croyances du monde entier.* Paris, 1986.

Nguyên Van Huyên. *La civilisation annamite.* Hanoi, 1944.

Nguyên Van Huyên. *Le culte des immortels en Annam.* Hanoi, 1944.

Nguyên Van Khoan. "Essai sur le *Đình* et le culte du génie tutélaire des villages au Tonkin." *Bulletin de l'École Française d'Extrême-Orient* 30 (1930): 107–139.

Nguyên Van Khoan. "Le repêchage de l'âme, avec une note sur les hôn et les phách d'après les croyances tonkinoises actuelles." *Bulletin de l'École Française d'Extrême-Orient* 33 (1933): 11–34.

Phan Ke Binh. *Việt-Nam phong-tục.* Saigon, 1970.

Simon, Pierre J., and Ida Simon-Barouh. "Les Génies des Quatre Palais: Contribution à l'étude du culte viêtnamien des *bà-dông.*" *L'homme* 10 (October–December 1970): 81–101.

Tran Van Giap. "Le bouddhisme en Annam, des origines au treizième siècle." *Bulletin de l'École Française d'Extrême-Orient* 32 (1932): 191–268.

New Sources

Condominas, Georges. *We Have Eaten the Forest: The Story of a Montagnard Village in the Central Highlands of Vietnam.* Translated by Adrienne Foulke. New York, 1994.

Do, Thien. *Vietnamese Supernaturalism: Views from the Southern Region.* London, 2003.

Ho, Tai H.T. "Religion in Vietnam: A World of Gods and Spirits." *Vietnam Forum* 10 (1987):113–145.

Matthews, Bruce. "The Power of Religion in Vietnam." In *Contacts between Cultures. Eastern Asia: Literature and Humanities,* vol. 3, edited by Bernard Hung-Kay Luk, pp. 102–107. Lewiston, N.Y., 1992.

Maurice, Albert-Marie. *Croyances et pratiques religieuses des Montagnards du centre-Vietnam.* Paris, 2002.

Ngyuen, Tai Thu. *History of Buddhism in Vietnam.* Washington, D.C., 1997.

Nguyen, The Anh. "Thien-Y-A-Na, ou la récupération de la déesse cam Po Nagar par la monarchie confuceenne vietnamienne." In *Cultes populaires et sociétés asiatiques: appareils culturels et appareils de pouvoir,* edited by Alain Forest, Yoshiaki Ishizawa and Leon Vandermeersch, pp. 73–86. Paris, 1991.

Pelzer, Kristin. "On Defining 'Vietnamese Religion': Reflections on Bruce Matthews' Article 'The Place of Religion in Vietnam Today.'" *Buddhist-Christian Studies* 12 (1992):75–79.

GEORGES CONDOMINAS (1987)
Translated from French by Maria Pilar Luna-Magannon
Revised Bibliography

VIJÑĀNABHIKṢU (c. sixteenth century CE) was an Indian philosopher and exponent of a syncretic Sāṃkhya-Yoga and Vedānta system. Nothing is known of the birthplace of Vijñānabhikṣu, but some scholars have suggested that he was a native of Bengal. His direct disciple was Bhāvāgaṇeśa, who may be the same as Gaṇeśa Dīkṣita, the author of a commentary on the *Tarkabhāṣā.*

Vijñānabhikṣu holds a significant position in the history of Indian philosophy. A Sāṃkhya-Yoga thinker, he is nonetheless recognized as having developed a distinct philosophical position all his own. He was the author of as many as sixteen or eighteen works, four or five of which are available as printed texts. The most notable are *Yogavārttika, Sāṃkhya-pravacana-sūtrabhāṣya,* and *Sāṃkhyasārah.* He also wrote commentaries on the *Brahma Sūtra* and on many Upaniṣads, including the *Kaṭha, Kaivalya,* and *Taittirīya.*

Although Vijñānabhikṣu was undoubtedly an original thinker, his originality was strongly tempered by his syncretic tendencies, as seen in his combining of Sāṃkhya-Yoga with Vedānta thought. One of his unique views was that the individual's ultimate goal is not the cessation of sorrow (*duḥkha*), but the cessation of the *experience* of sorrow. He maintained that the state of *mokṣa* ("liberation") is not blissful and that when the scriptures talk about the blissful state of the self (*ānandamaya*), what they really mean is the absence of sorrow.

Vijñānabhikṣu was primarily a yogin, both in theory and practice. In his *Yogavārttika,* he claimed that Yoga (as taught by Patañjali) is the best path to liberation. He believed that it was necessary to reconcile Vedānta philosophy with Yoga philosophy in order to combine knowledge and praxis. He was critical of Advaita Vedānta and charged that the Advaitins were crypto-Buddhists.

For Vijñānabhikṣu, sentient beings (*jīvas*) are not identical with *brahman* (Īśvara or Parameśvara) but are just parts of *brahman.* The relationship is one of the-part-and-the-whole, not total identity; the *jīvas* are the sparks of the fire that is *brahman. Brahman* creates the world, often referred to as *māyā* ("illusion"). However, according to Vijñānabhikṣu, the world is not illusory, because *prakṛti* ("matter, nature"), being part of *brahman,* is eternal and real. The creation is a real, not an illusory, transformation *(pariṇāma),* as in the Sāṃkhya view.

Bhikṣu's interpretation of the *Yoga Sūtra* differed from that of either Vācaspati Miśra or Bhoja. His interpretation of *vikalpa* ("mental discrimination") indicates a Buddhist influence. The Yoga school regards *suṣupti* ("dreamless sleep") as a *vṛtti* ("transformation") of consciousness, while the Vedānta school argues that it is not a *vṛtti* at all. Bhikṣu reconciles these viewpoints by saying that there are two states of dreamless sleep: *ardha* ("half") and *samagra* ("full"). The Yoga school talks about the first, while the Upaniṣads talk about the second.

God, the creator, is not simply an agent (as the Nyāya-Vaiśeṣikas hold) who creates the universe as a potter produces a pot. The causality of God is said to be very different from the three types of causality mentioned by Nyāya-Vaiśeṣika: *samavāyin* ("inherent"), *asamavāyin* ("non-inherent"), and *nimitta* ("efficient cause"). Rather, Vijñānabhikṣu refers to *adhiṣṭhāna kāraṇa* ("ground cause, container"). For Śaṃkara too, *brahman* is the ground for all changes and causation. But while Śaṃkara believes that all changing phenomena are unreal and the ground cause is real, Bhikṣu asserts that all changes are real and that the unchangeable ground cause, *brahman,* sustains this principle of change within its individual unity. By rejecting nondualism, Bhikṣu also fostered the *bhakti* movement. He interpreted *bhakti* as true devotion in the service of God, and referred to the Bhāgavata description of *bhakti* as "the emotion that melts the heart and brings tears to the eyes."

SEE ALSO Patañjali the Grammarian.

BIBLIOGRAPHY

Dasgupta, Surendranath. *A History of Indian Philosophy,* vol. 3. London, 1940. See chapter 22.

Rukmani, T. S., trans. *Yogavārttika of Vijñānabhikṣu.* Delhi, 1981. Text and translation.

BIMAL KRISHNA MATILAL (1987)

VILNA GAON SEE ELIYYAHU BEN SHELOMOH ZALMAN

VINAYA SEE BUDDHIST BOOKS AND TEXTS, *ARTICLE ON* CANON AND CANONIZATION—VINAYA

VINOBA BHAVE SEE BHAVE, VINOBA

VIOLENCE. Humans, as individuals and as groups, have the potential to be violent. Physical violence is disruptive and damaging to other individuals and groups because it conflicts with some of their basic rights. Individuals try to protect themselves from injury, and societies try to channel and curb violence both through symbolic action and through concrete counterviolence. Individuals and groups, on the other hand, may feel the necessity to resort to physical violence, while ritualization and symbolism may make violent acts easier to perform.

Religion is the most powerful symbolic system humans have developed. Throughout history, religion and violence have been in close contact. The detailed history of this contact still has to be written, although there is no lack of research on individual epochs and episodes, often stimulated by contemporary events. Recent examples include the surge in religiously motivated violence during the 1990s, reflected in the destruction of Yugoslavia or the conflict between Israelis and Palestinians. Both the actors on the ground and commentators from the outside understood these conflicts as religious confrontations, at least in part. During the same period, the rapid spread of religious fundamentalism, Christian as well as Islamic, led to further reflection on the relationship between religion and violence. The trauma of the attacks on the World Trade Center in New York and the Pentagon in Washington, D.C., which were quickly interpreted as religious as well as political phenomena, provoked yet another body of studies. On the other hand, general studies of the relationship between religion and violence are rare, and they often appear to be somewhat one-sided. Religion is usually perceived either from the perspective of those institutionalized monotheist religions that dominate the contemporary world, or from a secular position. Since even general research has grown out of actual necessities in most cases, relatively little attention has been given to the place of violence within polytheistic religious systems.

INTRODUCTION. Earlier philosophical reflection treated violence within the wider context of ethics or anthropology. Ethological research, in which Konrad Lorenz's investigation of aggression as a basic biological drive was the perhaps most influential theory in the mid-twentieth century (Lorenz, 1959), was a later field for the study of violence. In the early twenty-first century, however, research on societal and political violence has been carried out primarily in the area of conflict and peace studies. These disciplines evolved as a response to World War II—the Stockholm International Peace Research Institute (SIPRI) being founded in 1959 and the *Journal for Peace Research* in 1961—and gained momentum during the Vietnam War. The origin of these fields of study in actual political events accounts for their perspective. Researchers in these areas are interested in the political and social conditions under which collective violence originates as well as finding ways to counteract collective violence. They challenge Lorenz's assumption that violence is a biological given of the human condition. Most of these researchers, however, regard religion as relevant only as a social or political variable, and often overlook the consequences of the possibility that it might be an anthropological constant (Burkert, 1996).

As a heuristic approach—that is, one intended to stimulate exploration—the topic of religion and violence can be subdivided into three different questions: (1) religion can be used to legitimate and condone or even to stimulate and incite to violence—this is the most common view, and examples range from the role of priests in warfare to religious riots and wars; (2) violence, both direct and symbolic, through rituals, narrations and images, can be seen as inherent to religion; (3) religion can be a healing force after violence has been committed, as part of its function to create or restore social cohesion.

DEFINITIONS. In current research, violence is understood in several different ways. In common speech, violence usually refers to physical force directed against another human being in order to inflict bodily harm or, in extreme cases, death. This narrow use of the term is easily extended to include physical violence against other living beings and material objects. Violence may be a spontaneous emotional reaction to a provocation; premeditated; or institutionalized and ritualized, as in the violence associated with warfare, torture, or punishment. In conflict research, the term tends to be used in an even wider sense. Johan Galtung, the founder of peace studies, introduced the concept of *structural violence* as a supplement to *direct* (physical) *violence.* Structural violence refers to the coercion inherent in societal structures that is used without the agreement of the victims and against their interests, such as the exploitation of workers in capitalistic economies or the exclusion of foreigners from a state. Its effectiveness relies on the threat and plausibility of direct violence (Galtung, 1969).

A third type of violence is *cultural violence,* which is structural violence of such long duration that it is embedded in and protected by cultural institutions. Religious violence, or the violence inherent in the three institutionalized monotheistic religions of the West, is the most obvious example of cultural violence (Galtung, 1990). The contrast between direct and structural violence is useful because it demonstrates that direct violence is not necessarily an aberration but a direct consequence of structural violence, and thus of social developments and institutions. This connection has consequences for those who wish to combat violence. Cultural violence, on the other hand, might appear as a simple extension of structural violence to a specific content; it might be seen as inherent in such cultural institutions as those associated with religions. The consequences for the question of religion and violence, however, have to be explored in considerably greater depth than has been done hitherto (Galtung, 1997–1998). As to the social conditions under which direct collective violence is likely to develop, studies converge to show that such violence is likely to occur when "political power is centralized, non-democratic, and highly dependent on one's group membership, be it race, ethnicity, religion, or some cultural division" (Rummel, 1997, p. 170). This summary suggests that religion, not only in its monotheistic variants, is one among several possible triggers for violence, but fails to explore the question as to whether there is a privileged connection between the two.

RELIGION IN THE SERVICE OF VIOLENCE. Every society is committed to the use of direct violence, if only to defend itself against outside and inside enemies. In developed societies, however, the state usually claims a monopoly on the use of violence. Violence inside the state is regulated by its laws and structured by its justice system, violence against other states by concepts of warfare, among which the Roman notion of the *bellum iustum,* or just war, had the most important transhistorical consequences. In polytheistic systems, both law and warfare are protected by such specific deities as the Greek Zeus, the guardian of justice inside society, and Athena, the goddess of properly conducted defensive wars of the city-state of Athens. Monotheist systems place both areas under the tutelage and protection of their respective gods. This divine protection finds expression in the rituals surrounding both the performance of justice and warfare. War often was constructed as a time outside of society's normal order and taking place outside civic space; rituals opened and ended this period, such as the Spartan sacrifices to Artemis Agrotera, "Wild Artemis," before a battle, or the many rituals of integration performed for returning warriors (Parker, 2000). Religion thus marks the borders of war's confined territory. This role of religion was rarely contested in the name of a nonviolent and pacifist theology, as in the Buddhist concept of *ahiṃsā.* As long as early Christianity remained at the margins of the state, it was mostly a pacifist faith, following the nonviolent teachings of the New Testament (Swift, 1979). This attitude changed, however, when the Roman Empire adopted Christianity as its official faith. Christian leaders were then confronted with the necessity of violence related to warfare. The prosecution of war was left to the laity but was legitimated from Scripture, albeit under very clearly stated conditions (e.g., Augustine of Hippo [354–430], *Letter* 189). Unlike Christianity, Judaism and Islam never had a tradition of nonviolence; war thus presented many fewer theological problems. Nevertheless, in these religions too war needed sanction and regulation. Islam in particular developed the concept of *jihād* (literally, "the exercise of faith"), the just defense of the faith (Colpe, 1994; Lewis, 2003).

Despite these restrictions on open violence, Christian and to a lesser extent Muslim history is full of religious wars, most conspicuously the crusades that also turned against Orthodox Christian Byzantium and the European wars of religion that followed the Reformation, such as the Thirty Years' War of 1618–1648. The development of explicitly religious wars changes the relationship between religion and violence: religion now is the very source of violence, at least in the reading of the actors themselves. It has always been easy to find political and economical motives for these religious wars, in contrast to the indigenous understanding of them. The key problem then has been to assess the extent and sincerity of the combatants' religious motivations. To some extent, the answer has always been determined by axiomatic choices.

In the past, historiography tended to emphasize "rational" political and economical motives. More recently, however, indigenous insistence on religious motives has been taken more seriously: religion has come to be seen as more than just a thin veil hiding more important motivations (Holt, 1993). This reevaluation of motives is true also for the riots that accompanied religious practice before the rise of monotheist systems. When two neighboring villages in Roman Egypt fought each other over the killing of a sacred animal (Plutarch, *On Isis* 72; Dio Cassius 42.34; Juvenal, *Satire* 15), or when the killing of a sacred cat by a Roman soldier triggered riots (Diodorus Siculus 1.83.8), later scholars often pointed to rival political and economic ambitions, tensions created by the presence of foreign armies in Egypt, or popular impressions that local traditions were threatened. But in all cases, the native discourse as well as the discourse of the Roman administrators and commentators was religious. The same was true of the riots against the early Christians that triggered such major persecutions as the one in Lyons in 177 CE. The objections against the Christians were usually couched in the language of sacrifice and perverted sexuality; economic problems entered only marginally, as when Paul threatened the prosperous business of the Ephesian silversmiths (*Acts* 19).

But it was not until Natalie Zemon Davis published a seminal paper in 1973 on religious riots in early modern France that historians were compelled to take religion seriously as a motive for violence. With the establishment of the secularized state, matters became more complicated. Research on religious violence in nineteenth-century France has shown that as a consequence of the French Revolution, "the boundary between religious, social and political violence was extremely porous" (Ford, 1998, p. 105). Anticlerical riots in the name of a secularized state against the Catholic Church confused the distinction between political and religious violence more than the riots against Roman occupiers that were triggered by the killing of a sacred animal. In the latter case, violence was used against foreigners who were seen to violate the norms of the indigenous religion. In the former case, violence resulted from the political desire to curb the influence of a religious institution.

VIOLENCE AS INTRINSIC TO RELIGION. The key question in this debate is whether religion as such contains violence or whether it is only associated with it. The answers given by various scholars range from agreement to fierce denial, but the question may be too simplistic. Many religions contain rituals, stories, and representations that are directly violent. The pantheon of a polytheistic religion usually contains one or several *violent divinities;* these are often connected with the irrational violence of warfare, such as Ares in Greece or Erra in Mesopotamia. But these gods represent a violence kept at a distance and with which humans are uncomfortable. Civic cults of Ares are extremely rare, and gods as well as humans are said to hate him (*Iliad* 5.889). The myth of Erra describes his rule as only short-lived and characterized by senseless destruction that necessitates the reconstruction of Babylon (Maschinist and Sasson, 1985). These divinities define a world in which war is a bitter necessity that should be as infrequent as possible.

Other stories, however, place violence at the foundation of the present-day cosmic order. Marduk, the god of Babylon, creates the world from the body of his opponent Tiamat and human beings from the blood of her closest ally, while in Greek mythology Zeus fights the Titans and the monster Typhon before he can establish his rule (Trumpf, 1959). In one possible reading of the New Testament, the Christian God must let his son die as a victim of human violence in order to found the new messianic world order. Order can be created only through the destruction of its antecedents and its enemies. This order is also precarious because these hostile forces are still active and must be kept at bay. Thus protective violence is always necessary; for example, the Indian goddess Durgā is a powerful demon killer who protects the world "every time when demons create danger" (*Devīmāhātmya* 11.55).

Animal and human sacrifice. The notion of protective violence leads to the practice of *animal sacrifice,* a rite that is widespread in agricultural cultures. The victims are usually domesticated animals. The performers often regard the killing of animals as unproblematic because it prepares them for a common meal with the gods. Moreover, meat is a staple food in these cultures. Ritualization and mythologization explain and legitimate the public slaughter of animals, as does the ritualization of hunting and warfare. The very fact of ritualization, however, might point to the existence of a latent problem, in that the ritual and the discourse about it must give some kind of meaning to the killing. Sometimes, the indigenous discourse about animal sacrifice and its practice point to the awareness of the problem. In some Polynesian cultures, the victim—a pig—is never killed and sometimes never eaten by its owner because it is considered "a brother of humans." The complex ritual behavior allows the owner of a pig, however, to also eat pork (Lanternari, 1976, pp. 298–303).

In Indo-European sacrificial ideology, the stories talk about the killing of a human being (Lincoln, 1991, pp. 167–175). Thus the problem of killing interferes with the necessity of eating to the point that animal sacrifice is altogether abolished. This abolition leads to vegetarianism, as with the Pythagoreans in Greece or the Buddhists and Jains in India. In these instances, animals are regarded as too closely related to humans to be killed. But with the exception of Buddhism, the rejection of animal sacrifice remained an option only for individuals, and could be given up again (e.g., Findley, 1987).

Human sacrifice as the ultimate form of sacrificial violence exists at least in the discourse about sacrifice, even in societies in which actual human sacrifice is unattested. Greek and Roman myths, for example, establish some violent rituals on a past history of human sacrifice that the present and less cruel rite replaced. Stories that legitimate direct violence against others (Christians, Jews, Gnostics, religious reformers, political rebels) typically accuse them of practicing child sacrifice and even cannibalism. Accusations of Satanism in the 1980s and 1990s adopted the same strategy to trigger (and, presumably, legitimate) judicial violence in private relationships (Frankfurter, 2005). In other societies (Celts, Aztecs), human sacrifice is attested with varying explanations of the practice. In some cases, the foundational violence is taken more seriously and avoided by exchanging an animal for a human victim (Lincoln, 1991, pp. 176–207).

Not all modern theories of animal sacrifice pay attention to its inherent violence. The two best-known theories that address the problem, Burkert's and Girard's, were both published in 1972; their connection with the wider cultural interest in violence seems obvious. Although their theories assume different origins for animal sacrifice (hunting rituals in Burkert's case, scapegoat rituals in Girard's), they both arrive at similar conclusions regarding the function of sacrificial violence—namely that the ritualized killing of a living being channels the group's innate violence and renders it harmless. Violence is inherent in the religious act because violence as a threat is innate in humans, and religion offers a symbolized way to domesticate and defuse it. In the meantime, other scholars have challenged some of the premises of these constructions (Hamerton-Kelly, 1987), and the debate continues. The main thrust of this group of theories is that religion does not contain or breed violence, but is rather a powerful instrument to counteract it.

The problems surrounding questions of violence in the major monotheistic religions, Judaism, Christianity, and Islam, are more intricate and more controversial. Contemporary critics underscore the fact that the two main characteristics of monotheistic faiths, revelation and universalism, make them by their very nature potentially violent. Revelation can lead to conflicts with those who contest this revealed truth, and universalism can lead to missionary expansion (Galtung, 1997; Assmann, 2002). These consequences, however, are not inevitable; the certainty of revealed truth generates conflicts only when the claim of another truth becomes threatening to one or both parties. Early Christianity collided with the Roman religious system when its refusal of sacrifice to the emperor was seen as a threat to the divine protection of the empire (Fox, 1986, pp. 452–455). The Roman Catholic Church came into conflict with such other Christian groups as the Montanists, or with pagan diviners (Fögen, 1993) whose rituals or beliefs challenged its monopoly of truth.

In all cases, the situation is more complex than a simple conflict between religious systems. Modern analysts perceive political and economical reasons for outbreaks of violence as well as a conflict of personalities; the Montanist claim of charismatic prophecy, for example, challenged the established hierarchy of the church (Trevett, 1996). But again, when indigenous actors give religious motivations for violent behavior, they should be taken at their word. The religious motivations of the Islamic terrorists who attacked the United States on September 11, 2001, were intended to be taken seriously, as were the claims of Mormon fundamentalists who killed "recalcitrant" wives (Krakauer, 2003). Although Islam has a tradition of avoiding religious conflicts with non-Muslims, Islamic fundamentalism as it developed in early twentieth-century Egypt expressed its resistance to Western values in a religious key (Ali, 2002), as did Western fundamentalism with respect to the modernization of society.

Religious imagery and violence. A key role is often attributed to the *religious imaginary* of narrations and images. All societies possess traditional (or even sacred) stories about the violent acts of their gods, demons, heroes, or ancestors. Many of these tales value these acts positively and regard them as a necessity, as in foundation myths or stories about defense against spiritual or human enemies. Even when violence is perpetrated by others against members of one's own group, the result can be turned into a positive statement, as in the narratives of Christ's crucifixion or the deaths of Christian, Jewish, or Muslim martyrs. Another type of positive narrative of violence is found in apocalyptic visions from the Jewish-Christian *Book of Enoch,* which was composed in the second century BCE, to the contemporary series of "Left Behind" novels that are popular among American Christian fundamentalists in the early twenty-first century. In apocalyptic visions, violence serves as a deterrent from sin or as a tool of mission and conversion. In martyrologies, the stories (whose recitation was part of the liturgy of the early Church) encouraged their audiences to withstand the violence of persecution in order to preserve the faith. Stories, however, can always be reenacted; violent stories can, under certain circumstances, generate real violence (Lüdemann, 1997; Ellens, 2004, vol. 1). The texts do not always function as directly as they did during the French wars of religion, however, when executions and mutilations reproduced the details related in apocalyptic narratives (Crouzet, 1990).

The early Christians sometimes provoked the Roman authorities in order to suffer martyrdom in a sort of passive violence. In a theologically highly contested move, contemporary Palestinian suicide bombers turned active violence against their enemies and themselves in order to become martyrs. The investigators of persons suspected of witchcraft in early modern Europe projected their own concepts of demonic behavior on their victims in order to legitimate their own punitive violence (Frankfurter, 2005). The reasons for this "dark side" of religion are complex, but a major factor appears to be the tradition of reading sacred books in order to find models for religiously (and thus ethically) correct action. This pattern of reading is central to Christian, Muslim and Jewish religious education. To deny that some of the stories taken as models encourage violence, or even to point out that the sacred books contain at least as many stories that inculcate nonviolence, compassion, and love, serves only an apologetic function. The researcher seeks to analyze why certain epochs, circumstances and charismatic personalities preferred one type of story or the other, and why certain epochs and circumstances actualized the dormant potential of the religious imaginary. It is instructive to see how one of the most violent symbolic systems, Tantrism, is serving in its Himalayan version as the most powerful spiritual guide to total ascetic calm (Huntington and Bangdel, 2003), while Bengali Tantrism served as an ideological source for political violence during the struggle for Indian independence, its goddess Kālī coming to represent Mother India as a violent rebel (Urban, 2003, pp. 73–133).

RELIGION AND THE END OF VIOLENCE. Religion plays a vital but relatively unexplored role in the aftermath of violence. On one level, rituals mark the end of such periods of violence as warfare. Cathartic rituals and rituals of thanksgiving reintegrate the returning warriors into the fabric of peaceful society; the ringing of church bells and modern peace celebration liturgies also preserve this religious symbolism.

On another level, religion is used to heal the wounds caused by a violent conflict. In early nineteenth-century France, Catholic missionaries kept the memory of the horrors of the reign of terror alive by staging processions that retraced the way to the guillotine of prominent victims. The declared aim of these ritual processions was to remember the violent acts and, through confession, to expiate them. According to Catholic teaching, forgiveness and expiation are possible only after penitence, and penitence presupposes memory of the sinful deed, even if this remembrance contradicted the official policy of *oubli,* forgetting, as practiced by the Restoration monarchy (Kroen, 1998). After the violent civil wars in Zimbabwe in the 1980s, both the official Catholic Church and the country's indigenous religions were concerned with healing; because, in an indigenous reading, the violence had unleashed the demons of the murdered, Catholic exorcists and traditional diviners and spirit mediums stepped in (Ranger, 1992, pp. 705–706). The extraordinary situations that prevailed in both nineteenth-century France and twentieth-century Zimbabwe after a period of unusually high levels of violence generated new rituals within the matrix of traditional ritualism. The same dynamics are visible elsewhere; for example, Andean peasant communities readapted "new discourses and practices . . . according to community memory about ancient practices" after the violence of the *Sendero Luminoso* (Shining Path) insurrection (Gamarra, 2000, p. 286). It appears that most communities can deal with "ordinary" levels and forms of violence with the help of their traditional symbolic systems. On the other hand, extraordinary violence, especially the violence generated by prolonged periods of intensive or brutal civil war, demands adaptations of the symbolic language that gives meaning to violence.

SEE ALSO Apocalypse, overview article; Martyrdom; New Religious Movements, article on New Religious Movements and Violence; Nonviolence; Sacrifice; War and Warriors, overview article.

BIBLIOGRAPHY

Ali, Tariq. *The Clash of Fundamentalisms: Crusades, Jihads, and Modernity.* London and New York, 2002.

Assmann, Jan. *Die Mosaische Unterscheidung oder der Preis des Monotheismus.* Munich, 2003.

Bowersock, Glen Warren. *Martyrdom and Rome.* Cambridge, U.K., 1995.

Burkert, Walter. *Homo Necans. Interpretationen altgriechischer Opferriten und Mythen.* Berlin, 1972.

Crouzet, Denis. *Les guerriers de Dieu: La violence au temps des troubles de religion.* Seyssel, France, 1990.

Davis, Natalie Zemon. "The Rites of Violence: Religious Riot in Sixteenth-Century France." *Past & Present* 59 (1973): 51–91.

Ellens, J. Harold, ed., *The Destructive Power of Religion: Violence in Judaism, Christianity, and Islam.* 4 vols. Westport, Conn., 2004.

Findly, Ellison B. "Jahāng r's Vow of Non-Violence." *Journal of the American Oriental Society* 107 (1987): 245–256.

Fögen, Marie Therese. *Die Enteignung der Wahrsager: Studien zum kaiserlichen Wissensmonopol in der Spätantike.* Frankfurt, Germany, 1993.

Ford, Caroline. "Violence and the Sacred in Nineteenth-Century France." *French Historical Studies* 21 (1998): 101–112.

Frankfurter, David. *Structure of Evil.* Princeton, N.J., 2005.

Galtung, Johan. "Violence, Peace and Peace Research." *Journal of Peace Research* 6 (1969): 167–191.

Galtung, Johan. "Cultural Violence." *Journal of Peace Research* 27 (1990): 291–305.

Galtung, Johan. "Religions, Hard and Soft." *Cross Currents* 47 (1997–1998).

Gamarra, Jeffrey. "Conflict, Post-Conflict and Religion: Andean Responses to New Religious Movements." *Journal of Southern African Studies* 26 (2000): 271–287.

Girard, René. *La Violence et le Sacré.* Paris, 1972.

Goodman, Martin D., and A. J. Holladay. "Religious Scruples in Ancient Warfare." *Classical Quarterly* 36 (1986): 151–171.

Hamerton-Kelly, Robert G., ed. *Violent Origins: Walter Burkert, René Girard and Jonathan Z. Smith on Ritual Killing and Cultural Formation.* Stanford, Calif., 1987.

Holt, Mack P. "Putting Religion Back into the Wars of Religion." *French Historical Studies* 18 (1993): 524–551.

Huntington, John C., and Dina Bandel. *The Circle of Bliss: Buddhist Meditational Art.* Columbus, Ohio, and Chicago, 2003.

Krakauer, Jon. *Under the Banner of Heaven: A Story of Violent Faith.* New York, 2003.

Kroen, Sheryl T. "Revolutionizing Religious Politics during the Restoration." *French Historical Studies* 21 (1998): 27–53.

Langlois, Claude. "De la violence religieuse." *French Historical Quarterly* 21 (1998): 113–123.

Lanternari, Vittorio. *La grande festa. Vita rituale e sistemi di produzione nelle società tradizionali* (1959). Bari, Italy, 1976.

Lewis, Bernard. *The Crisis of Islam: Holy War and Unholy Terror.* New York, 2003.

Lincoln, Bruce. *Death, War, and Sacrifice: Studies in Ideology and Practice.* Chicago, 1991.

Lorenz, Konrad. *Das sogenannte Böse: Zur Naturgeschichte der Aggression.* Vienna, 1963.

Lüdemann, Gerd. *The Unholy in Holy Scriptures: The Dark Side of the Bible.* Louisville, Ky., 1997

Maschinist, Peter, and J. M. Sasson. "Rest and Violence in the Poem of Erra." *Journal of the American Oriental Society* 103 (1985): 221–226.

Parker, Robert. "Sacrifice and Battle." In *War and Violence in Ancient Greece,* edited by Hans van Wees, pp. 299–314. London, 2000.

Pérez Jiménez, Aurelio, and Gonzalo Cruz Andreotti, eds. *La religión como factor de integración y conflicto en el Mediterráneo.* Madrid, 1996.

Ranger, Terence. "War, Violence and Healing in Zimbabwe." *Journal of Southern African Studies* 18 (1992): 698–707.

Rummel, Rudolph J. "Is Collective Violence Correlated with Social Pluralism?" *Journal of Peace Studies* 34 (May, 1997): 163–175.

Swift, Louis J. "War and the Christian Conscience. I: The Early Years." In *Aufstieg und Niedergang der Römischen Welt* 2:23:1, edited by Wolfgang Haase, pp. 835–868. Berlin, 1979.

Trevett, Christine. *Montanism: Gender, Authority, and the New Prophecy.* Cambridge, U.K., 1996.

Trumpf, Jürgen. "Stadtgründung und Drachenkampf." *Hermes* 86 (1958): 129–157.

Urban, Hugh B. *Tantra: Sex, Secrecy, Politics and Power in the Study of Religion.* Berkeley, Calif., 2003.

FRITZ GRAF (2005)

VIRACOCHA is the name or title in the Quechua language of the Inca creator god at the time of the Spanish conquest of Peru in the sixteenth century. According to Inca beliefs, Viracocha (also called Ticciviracocha) made earth and sky, then fashioned from stone a race of giants. Displeased with them, he turned some giants back into stone and destroyed the rest in a flood. He then caused the sun and the moon to rise from Lake Titicaca, and created, at nearby Tiahuanaco, human beings and animals from clay. He painted clothing on the people, then dispersed them so that they would later emerge from caves, hills, trees, and bodies of water. He gave the people social customs, food, and other aspects of civilization. Appearing as a bearded old man with staff and long garment, Viracocha journeyed from the mountainous east toward the northwest, traversing the Inca state, teaching as he went. At Manta, on the coast of Ecuador, he spread his cloak and set out over the waters of the Pacific Ocean.

Viracocha is described by early Spanish chroniclers as the most important Inca god, invisible, living nowhere, yet ever-present. Texts of hymns to Viracocha exist, and prayers to him usually began with the invocation "O Creator." A temple in Cuzco, the Inca capital, was dedicated to him. He also appeared as a gold figure inside Cuzco's Temple of the Sun. Near this temple, a *huaca* (sacred stone) was consecrated to Viracocha; sacrifices were made there, particularly of brown llamas. At the festival of Camay, in January, offerings were cast into a river to be carried by the waters to Viracocha.

Viracocha may have been identified with the Milky Way, which was believed to be a heavenly river. His throne was said to be in the sky. The sun, the moon, and the star deities were subservient to him. Inti, the sun, was the imperial god, the one whose cult was served by the Inca priesthood; prayers to the sun were presumably transmitted by Inti to Viracocha, his creator.

Because there are no written records of Inca culture before the Spanish conquest, the antecedents of Viracocha are unknown, but the idea of a creator god was surely ancient and widespread in the Andes. Viracocha—who was related to Illapa ("thunder," or "weather")—may have been derived from Thunupa, the creater god (also the god of thunder and weather) of the Inca's Aymara-speaking neighbors in the highlands of Bolivia, or from the creator god of earlier inhabitants of the Cuzco Valley. The god's antiquity is suggested by his various connotations, by his imprecise fit into the structured Inca cult of the solar god, and by pre-Inca depictions of a deity very similar to Inca images of Viracocha. Viracocha is sometimes confused with Pachacámac, the creator god of adjacent coastal regions; they probably had a common ancestor.

The eighth king in a quasi-historical list of Inca rulers was named for Viracocha. The god appeared in a dream or vision to his son, a young prince, who (with the help of the god, according to legend) raised an army to defend Cuzco successfully when it was beleaguered by the rival Chanca people. This prince became the ninth Inca ruler, Pachacuti Inca Yupanqui (r. 1438?–1470?), the great man of Inca history, who glorified architecturally the Temple of Viracocha and the Temple of the Sun and began the great expansion of the Inca empire. According to some authors, he was called Yupanqui as a prince and later took the name *Pachacuti* ("transformer"). He is usually referred to simply as Pachacuti (Pachacutic or Pachacutec), although some records refer to him more fully as Pachacuti Inca Yupanqui. It was he who provided the list of Inca rulers.

See Also Inti.

Bibliography

The relative importance of Viracocha and Inti, the sun god, is discussed in Burr C. Brundage's *Empire of the Inca* (Norman, Okla., 1963); Arthur A. Demarest's *Viracocha* (Cambridge, Mass., 1981); Alfred Métraux's *The History of the Incas* (New York, 1969); and R. Tom Zuidema's *The Ceque System of Cuzco* (Leiden, 1964). Gary Urton's *At the Crossroads of the Earth and Sky: An Andean Cosmology* (Austin, 1981) interprets Viracocha in the light of present-day Quechua-speaking sources.

Elizabeth P. Benson (1987)

VIRGIN GODDESS is a nonhomogeneous, highly problematic concept for scholarly use, for it was partly made up by the religious politics of Greek city-states in order to further their patriarchal aims, and for the other part has been popularized by a certain kind of feminist interest promoted by followers of the contemporary goddess religion. Goddess worshipers in Western postmodern societies promote a biologistic understanding of femaleness that is focused on the procreative capacity of the female body, and therefore venerate one or several goddesses as givers and takers of life. In relating all possible functions of goddesses from all times and religions to sexuality and fertility, the goddess movement(s) reveal an outlook on the essence of femaleness that resembles that of ancient Greek gender ideology, even though it arrives at a different evaluation of it.

History and Critical Reevaluation of the Notion of the Virgin Goddess. The use of the term *virgin goddess* is grounded in the assumption that prehistoric societies in Europe and elsewhere worshiped a goddess who could appear in three forms: as maiden (often used synonymously with *virgin*), mother, and aged wise woman. A dyad of the goddess as mother and maiden had already been introduced by Jane Harrison (1903), and then taken up by the Jungian scholar Mary Esther Harding (1935), but the idea of a female divine trinity was for the first time formulated by the poet and essayist Robert von Ranke-Graves in his work *The Greek Myths* (1955). The origin of this construction is unclear, but it was very probably influenced by the trinitarian structure of God according to Christian dogma. Ranke Graves connected the threefold manifestation of the divine matriarch to the phases of the moon (waxing moon, full moon, waning moon) and to the three cosmic spheres: the "upper air" for the maiden, earth and sea for the mother, and the underworld for the old woman. Admittedly owing this construction mainly to his intuition, Graves also may have been inspired by the popular ideas of Johann Jakob Bachofen (1861) about the religion of a matriarchal age in early human history. Bachofen claimed that the relations of the sexes always found a cosmic expression in the relations between sun and moon, and according to his hypothesis the *gynaikokratia*, the Greek term for matriarchy, a social order that is dominated by assumignly female values, was characterized by the reign of the moon (and the night) over the sun (and the day). More recently, these kinds of ideas have been taken up by Heide Göttner-Abendroth (1993) and Marija Gimbutas (1989; 1991). Gimbutas, who used a great deal of nineteenth-century theory (Hegel, Bachofen, and James George Frazer) in her interpretations of Stone Age artifacts, promoted the idea of a parthenogenetic primal goddess that might have emerged in the Paleolithic era. According to her hypothesis, the primal goddess, who was avirgin in the sense that she did not have sexual intercourse with a male, was equated with nature as a whole and therefore did not have a particular shape. The earliest goddess images, the so-called Paleolithic Venuses (dated before 10,000 BCE), are images of the awesome creative power associated with woman and nature. The goddess could be represented by triangular stones or by stone or bone carvings emphasizing her vulva, buttocks, and breasts. In the Neolithic or early agricultural era (which began c. 9000 BCE in the Near East), goddess images symbolized the cosmic energy of birth, growth, death, and regeneration, on which farming, and indeed all life, depends. She was often depicted in zoomorphic shape or with animals as her companions (these figures are known as Ladies of the Animals). The anthropomorphic goddess images, according to Gimbutas, gradually became differentiated into two functions, one as "the giver and taker of all," and the other as rebirth and regeneration. Eventually these two images were characterized as the Mother and the Maiden. The Mother was the sustaining power, represented especially by the enduring earth, the bedrock that underpins all life. The Maiden, related to the forces of renewal and regeneration, was represented especially by new life, plant and animal, that emerges in spring. The Mother, the eternal, and the Maiden, the ephemeral power of nature, were understood to be two aspects of the same whole. Gimbutas's theories are very popular among people interested in female spirituality, but they have provoked criticism from professional historians and archaeologists, who argue that hardly anything can be said with any certainty about Neolithic female figurines because of the lack of written information about them.

But some adherents of contemporary goddess religions have taken up Gimbutas's conception and believe that farming societies of the Neolithic venerated a threefold goddess as maiden, mother, and old woman. Moreover, they argue that this pattern is still recognizable in religions of the ancient world. Within the context of a constructed female monotheism, all astral, war, and hunting goddesses venerated in ancient cultures are viewed as expressions of the Maiden, and as a particular focus of interest, this maiden goddess is interpreted as an antecedent of the virginal goddesses of Olympic religion in Classical Greece. Thus, the concept of the Virgin Goddess emerged, although so-called virgin goddesses share no other feature than their youthful virginity, and even this is interpreted in peculiar and inconsistent ways. In various contexts, virginity can mean maidenhood in the sense of prematurity, it can mean temporary or constant willful abstinence from sexual activity, and it can denote a struggle for independence from male domination. By their divine functions, so-called virgin goddesses do not form a coherent group at all, and they have no automatic connection to the category of mother goddesses. The assumption that mother and daughter (maiden)are two aspects of the same deity was taken from certain images in Minoan religion, where a woman figure appears with one or two maidens. The interpretation of these groups is uncertain, and their occurence is by no means universal, but culturally restricted to the Minoan and early Cycladic sphere. Generally, ancient polytheistic religions possessed a great number of highly differentiated female and male deities, and the accessible evidence does not allow for interpretations along the lines of monotheism.

In sum, ideas about the Virgin Goddess are based on several shortcomings and conflations. The monotheistic character of a Neolithic goddess cannot be proven. It remains an hypothesis that may be of some relevance in the interpretation of prehistoric religions, but the evidence from those early civilizations that can inform their modern interpreters through written testimonies reveals a different picture. There is every reason to assume that the idea of the Goddess as one whose mythology focuses on the theme of fertility and procreation is a rather late concept which appeared no earlier than in Hellenistic times (from about 300 BCE). Divine oneness as the source for the multiplicity of goddesses and gods is an outcome of philosophical speculations undertaken to systematize and rationalize mythological traditions. Early panthea and also the figurines and statuettes of the Stone Age show a great variety. In Mesopotamia and Egypt there was a vast number of female and male deities with most diverse powers and responsibilities. It seems unlikely that the prehistoric figurines and statuettes that may represent female godheads—even that is uncertain—should indicate a uniform concept of the female divine. Nothing suggests that the numerous sky goddesses, patronesses of war, and Ladies of the Animals and Hunting, as well as several female astral deities, were to be subsumed under anything like the concept of the Maiden or Virgin Goddess.

Moreover, chastity and virginity only became a feature of Olympic goddesses in Greek and then particularly in Hellenistic cults; in other ancient religions, particular sexual or antisexual attitudes of goddesses were not addressed. Instead, it seems that sexuality was considered an integral part of godheads as well as of humans. Thus, linking later virginal goddesses to earlier figures who were supposedly parthenogenetic (i.e., able to create life exclusively out of themselves) is problematic. The assumption of a Virgin Goddess with a history beginning earlier than in Classical Greece lumps together phenomenologically and historically different qualities. It must be concluded that a pre-Greek concept of virgin goddesses did not exist, and that even from the Classical Greek period onwards, virgin goddesses were never categorized as a group. If anything, it could be stated that goddesses of the ancient Mediterranean with virginal features are peculiar developments of archaic mistresses of the animals and the goddesses of the early city-states in Mesopotamia (Inanna-Ishtar) and Asia Minor (Cybele), whose power over natural forces was also called upon for the protection of the urban sphere, but great caution is required to avoid generalizations inapplicable to highly differentiated divine figures.

GREEK VIRGINITY AND ITS IMPACT ON GODDESSES. Nevertheless, it is interesting to see on which types of goddesses the Greeks imposed virginity and in which ways they thereby influenced their appearances and their spheres of action. But first, the implications of virginity, and specifically of Greek virginity, need to be clarified. Ideas about the interrelatedness of female sexuality and threat become apparent as ancient iconographic motifs, which are known from northern Mesopotamian representations on seals and also in evidence during the orientalizing period in Greece (eighth century BCE), but in the Classical era they became a generally recognizable cultural feature.

Two issues are important when considering the meanings of Greek virginity. The first regards the status and reputation of women in the urban milieus of Classical Greece, both of which were formed and dominated by patrilineal and patriarchal order. Greek societies were structured by the *oikoi* (households), and each *oikos* was ruled by a male head of the family. Girls were born and raised in one household, but later, through marriage, they passed into another domain of living, bringing a dowry as their share of the patrimonial inheritance into another man's household. Thus, a daughter was a threat to men's possessions and to their wishes for a stable existence. In order to guarantee the procreation of the society of the *poleis,* it was naturally necessary to have women crossing the borders between the *oikoi.* As a consequence, the female sex was associated with all things hated and abhorred: with changeability, unboundedness, pollutedness, formlessness, uncontrolledness, and natural chaos—all oppositions to cultural order represented by men. According to patriarchal ideology, femininity stood for the ability or rather the fate to cross boundaries. The means to control this necessary but dangerous inclination of women was first and foremost a control of their sexuality through the institution of legitimate marriage. In this context the polarity between virgin and wife developed. This polarity is expressed in Greek in the opposition between *gunē,* which means both "woman" and "wife" and is used to refer to married women, and *parthenos,* which means "maiden, girl, or virgin" and "virgin" and is used to refer to unmarried girls. Only by a rigid control control of women's sexuality could a man be certain that his children were his. Therefore, it was decreed that a woman must be a virgin at marriage and refrain from sexual intercourse with any man but her husband. Since marriage meant subjection of the female and her control by the male-defined cultural order, virginity made her an outsider and a potential threat. In other words, for the Greeks, virginity became a means to express what was to their standards a paradox—a female who is independent from and even capable of exercising power over men.

For those Greek goddesses who were perceived according to the virgin pattern, this meant that they never became fully subordinated. Consequently, virgin goddesses do not always necessarily abstain from sexuality; they may be virgins in the sense of being unmarried, or even in the sense of not being confined through marriage to a male god. The complex nature of the virgin goddesses is further explicated by the fact that the unmarried girl or woman poses a threat to patriarchal social order because her sexuality is not under the control of man. They carry the connotation of being wild or untamed. This wildness can manifest itself in at least three forms: as a connection to wild places and wild animals not tamed or under control of the city; as passion for the ritual shedding of blood, which draws hunters and warriors away from the city and the family; and as untamed sexuality, by which men are seduced and can be endangered.

A second issue that is important for the rise of Greek virgin goddesses has to do with intellectual currents towards more transcendental conceptualizations of the divine. This move took place in a number of ancient civilizations which are known as the cultures of the Axial Age, according to a theory by the German existentialist philosopher Karl Jaspers (1883–1969). The gender-specific implications of this theory have not yet been analyzed, but it can be said that in the majority of the civilizations of Jaspers's Axial Age the transcendental is ascribed to male godheads, whilst female deities were linked to nature and the material world. The emergence of the idea of transcendence and the transcendental in the intellectual history of humankind thus supported the polarization of the genders, that is, the belief in fundamental differences in female versus male nature. One way of mediating between the two became the construction of virginity as a "male femaleness," and thus with a kind of physical femaleness that was not acted out and lived as such.

Greek goddesses in general, and the Greek virgin goddesses in particular, combine protective and transgressive qualities in their relation to the cultural standards of the *poleis.* This results from the ability to overcome boundaries, which in Classical Greek culture was ascribed to women and goddesses alike. Virginity could underline as well as constrain this trait. It allowed for a kind of freedom, independence, and power that was usually refused to females, but it also ensured that married women, who represented by definition the kind of femininity that was demanded by their society, remained securely cut off from these privileges. Goddesses, however, unlike ordinary women, could make exceptions here.

INDIVIDUAL VIRGIN GODDESSES AND HEROINES. It is helpful to consider in more detail the expression of virginity by, or the impact of the virginity concept on, some mythological figures.

Kore. Strangely, the Greek goddess Kore, whose very name translates as "maiden," has so far attracted comparatively little attention by propagators of the threefold goddess. Kore was closely related to death, which corresponds with general Greek ideas about human *parthenoi.* Their state of being was regarded as very similar to being condemned to death. In rites that should prepare them for marriage, girls from aristocratic families underwent rites connected with the cults of either Artemis or Athena, initiating them to the theme of sexuality by exposing them to a death-like experience. In Kore's myth this is symbolized by her abduction by Hades, the god of the underworld. The sixth century BCE saw a very rich production of Kore statues, mainly, apparently, for a grave cult. On the Athenian Parthenon there were six Korai, who probably functioned as grave-servants for Erechteus, the legendary first king of Athens.

Hestia, Artemis and Iphigeneia, and Athena. Greek goddesses virgin in the sense of sexual abstinence by an adult woman were Hestia, Artemis, and Athena.

Hestia, the personification of the hearth and the sacrificial fire, transcends the boundary between humankind and the goddesses and gods. She had a major role in female rites of passage such as marriage and childbirth. Because the mythology as well as the iconography of the goddess Hestia are poorly developed, further implications of her virginity are not traceable.

Artemis was the goddess of wild places, flocks, and the hunt; she was named Potnia Theron ("lady of the wild animals") in the *Iliad,* and "slayer of wild beasts" in the Homeric hymns. She had particularly close ties to deer, as indicated by the legend that pregnant does swam to her island in order to give birth, and to bears. Bears play a significant role in the rites and roles of a cult dedicated to Artemis Brauronia, which were performed by young girls. The stages of the ritual are not clear, but it included libations and spinning and weaving, and it was finalized with a goat sacrifice. In Artemis's mythology, even human—and particularly maiden—sacrifices are significant. According to a study by Ken Dowden (1989), such plots can be interpreted as literary encodings of girls' initiation rites performed in the service of this goddess. Near the temple of Artemis Brauroneia there was a shrine for Iphigeneia, the daughter of Agamemnon and Klytaimnestra, who on her way to her wedding with Achilleus was almost sacrificed to Artemis. A deer was then slaughtered instead of the girl, and Iphigeneia was whisked away by the goddess herself in order to serve her on the Tauris Peninsular. Artemis was there venerated under the name *Parthenos,* or as Iphigeneia, which confirms the closeness of the two figures. Artemis was a virgin herself and shunned men except for her brother Apollo, and she insisted ruthlessly on the chastity of her mythical attendents, the nymphs. Yet, the goddess as well as the nymphs were intimately familiar with sexuality, the female cycle, and childbirth. The sexual appeal of nymphs is apparent in, for example, the story of Odysseus and Kalypso, in which Artemis was explicitely invoked as Elei-theia and Locheia, goddess of childbirth. She was one of the most powerful patronesses of life and death and all passages between them.

The Greek Artemis is clearly the heiress of the Mistress of the Animals, but her wildness was acceptable in a patriarchal culture only if it was understood that she was not like other women. Thus she was superficially bereft of her female sexuality, and although she always remained the goddess of women and female affairs, she was often portrayed as a masculinized huntress, clad in a short tunic, slaying wild animals with arrows from her quiver. However, the image of the Ephesian Artemis, which stressed her nurturing qualities by depicting her as a mature female with many breasts, proves that the Homeric shape of the goddess was not authoritative.

Worshiped in her temple, the Parthenon, Athena Parthenos was a very different expression of a virgin goddess than Artemis, for she was very much identified with the city and its distinct, male-defined culture. Athena was said to have been born from the head of her father Zeus, and in the *Eumenides* of Aeschylus she was said to have declared that she sided with her father against her mother in all things except marriage, which she shunned. She was born fully armed as a warrior and was usually depicted wearing a helmet and holding a spear and shield. Her title *polias* indicated that the city was her home; her titles *promachos* and *nike* named her victorious against its enemies. She avoided the company of women but nurtured such heroes as Odysseus, Theseus, Herakles, Perseus, and Erichthonius. Her virginity meant that she could consort with men as an equal and engage in the masculine pursuit of war. However, she also figured in important initiation rites for girls, the *Arrhephoria,* the theme of which seems to have been an encounter with overpowering and frightening aspects of male sexuality. Moreover, she was patroness not only of the masculine art of warfare but also of the arts and crafts associated with women, including pottery, weaving, and healing. One of the rituals performed in her honor involved the weaving and presentation of a new robe *(peplos)* for her ancient wooden statue; girls and women played important roles in these rites.

Hera and Aphrodite. If the designation *virgin goddess* is interpreted in the sense of a refusal to be submissive to a male partner, two other Olympians deserve mention here, although both are sexual and, according to Olympian mythology, sexually active.

Hera, known as wife of Zeus and as mother of Hebe, Eleitheia, Ares, and Hephaistos, was also known as an independent goddess. Before Zeus entered Greece, Hera was the indigenous goddess of the island of Samos, which was once called Parthenia, and of Argos; even at Olympus, her temple is older than that of Zeus. Her union with Zeus as presented in the *Iliad* was a sacred marriage that brought fertility to the earth. However, another legend reports that every year she renewed her virginity at a sacred spring called Canathus in Nauplia.

Aphrodite, too, although fully and joyously sexual, can be viewed as virginal in the sense of self-determined. Her sexuality is unbridled, untamed, and her own. She is married to Hephaistos, according to Olympian mythology, but she is neither submissive nor faithful to him. Although she is a mother, her child Eros ("love, desire") is but a reflection of her sexuality. Aphrodite is related to the Lady of the Animals, as indicated in the Homeric *Hymn to Aphrodite,* where she is portrayed as followed by wolves, lions, bears, and leopards, in whom she awakens the spark of desire, and she is also connected to the Near Eastern goddesses of sexuality and of warfare such as Anat, Ishtar, and Astarte. Like Inanna-Ishtar and Astarte, she is identified with the morning and evening stars, which mark the transition between night and day. Aphrodite is an island goddess who entered Greece through Phoenician ports in Cythera and Cyprus; her temples were often found in the marshy ground where sea transforms into land, or on the cliffs where the sea rises as mist to the land. Thus, the nature of her sacred places underlines her transcending capacities as they are also expressed through her irresistable sexual appeal.

Sophia. Although in the classical culture of Greece the meaning of virginity was not necessarily confined to sexual abstemiousness, certain currents in Hellenism and particularly in Hellenistic Judaism became obsessed with the religious benefits of chastity. This development applied to men and women alike, but in the context of virgin goddesses only the implications for female virginity are relevant.

Due to the "ascetic tension" (Fraade, 1989) in Judaism in the Hellenistic age, the feminine aspect of the Old Testament God acquired an independent identity, with a huge impact also on Gnosticism and emerging Christianity. In several Jewish texts of that period (e.g., *Proverbs*, Ben Sira, c. 200 BCE, *Wisdom of Solomon*, c. 150 BCE), Sophia as a personification of divine wisdom figures prominently, and chastity is described as one of her important traits. Another female figure in a number of writings (e.g., *Proverbs* 9; fragment from cave four in Qumran) is clearly recognizable as Sophia's counterpart: the "strange woman," one of whose most obvious marks is her lasciviousness, as opposed to the wise woman's purity. Thus, a discourse developed in which virginity was regarded as a means to, and even as a code for, salvation. According to Gnostic mythology, the origination of the lower worlds of psychic and material quality (as opposed to the upper world of spiritual substance) results from the fall of a female soul—later replaced by the Jewish Sophia—and her involvement in passion and sexual activity. In the end, the soul is restored by union with a male salvational figure in a "virginal" bridal chamber. In Sethian Gnostic texts, the original, purely spiritual creation of the *pleroma*, or fullness, is ascribed to the goddess Barbelo, who is characterized as a "male virgin." The *Apocryphon of John*, the *Gospel of the Egyptians*, and *The Three Tablets of Seth* know of her as the "thrice male" and the "masculine female virgin."

The Virgin Mary. Many features of ancient virginal goddesses survive to the present day in the Virgin Mary. Throughout the Near East, Europe, and Latin America, churches to the Virgin Mary were built at the holy places of the goddesses. Even though she is not prominent in the New Testament, Mary eventually became the repository for all the lingering images of the goddesses. To the Greeks she is *panaghia,* which means simply "the all-holy." In the *Gospel of Matthew,* a prophecy from Isaiah that reads "Behold, a virgin shall conceive and bear a son" (*Mt.* 1:23) is applied to the birth of Jesus. Although the Hebrew word *almanah* in the original prophecy might be translated "young woman" without the necessary imputation of *virgin,* both the Greek translation of the Hebrew Bible, the Septuagint, and the *Gospel of Matthew* use *parthenos.* Lest there be any ambiguity as to its interpretation, the author of *Matthew* clarifies, Joseph "knew her not until she had borne a son" (1:25). The theme of Mary's continual virginity despite of Jesus' birth emerged already in second-century theological discourse, there. The church agreed at the Council of Ephesus in 431 that Mary would be called *theotokos* ("God bearer"), and confirmed this title at the Council of Chalcedon in 451.

The dogmatic establishment of Mary's virginity is a continuation of the Greek strategies to mark particular and powerful women as virgins, but it also needs to be understood as a confirmation and even superelevation of the most important function of Greek goddesses: the mediation between different spheres of existence, which in Mary's case is the mediation between humans and the divine.

Kumari. A different kind of virgin goddess, which is completely detached from the specific cultural conditions of the eastern Mediterranean, can be found in Nepal. Here, the goddess Taleju, an aspect of Durga, inhabits a human virgin who is correspondingly worshiped as the goddess herself. The custom of having an immature girl residing in Taleju's temple in Kathmandu is said to go back to a legend from the late sixteenth century about the king Jaya Prakash Malla, who used to play dice with the goddess when she regularly visited him in his palace. On one occasion he developed "unholy thoughts" about his companion; she recognized this and then disappeared. When the remorseful king begged forgiveness, Taleju said she would return only in the form of a virginal little girl who would have to live next to the royal palace. Since then, the living Kumari is chosen from the Sakya community in the Kathmandu valley. Although Taleju is a Hindu goddess, the living Kumari comes from a Buddhist family (the Sakyas are descendents from the Buddha's clan) and is selected by high-level Vajracharya priests. Apart from her virginity, further criteria are an unblemished body and a fearless mind. When the girl approaches puberty, she ceases to be Kumari and in theory can live a normal life. However, she does not receive school education or any other training that would prapare her for such a life, and moreover she is unlikely to get married because she is still believed to be possessed by supernatural powers.

Possible meanings of virginity in Indian and Himalayan religions are less well researched than for Greek and Hellenistic antiquity, and particularly the political aspect of it—as it is suggested by the close bond with the Nepalese royals—has so far been neglected. Interpretations given agree on the assumption that the phenomenon should be explained in the context of shaktism. According to this branch of tantrism, the goddess is understood as creative energy. This energy remains untouched and therefore complete, as long as the goddess is virgin.

SEE ALSO Goddess Worship, overview article; Lady of the Animals; Mary, overview article; Virginity.

BIBLIOGRAPHY

The concept of Virgin Goddess was developed by the works cited above, including Johann Jakob Bachofen, *Das Mutterrecht: Eine Untersuchung über die Gynaikokratie der alten Welt nach ihrer religiösen und rechtlichen Natur* (Stuttgart, Germany, 1861); Jane Harrison, *Prolegomena to the Study of Greek Religion* (Cambridge, U.K., 1903); Mary Esther Harding, *Women's Mysteries, Ancient and Modern* (New York, 1935); Karl Jaspers, *Vom Ursprung und Ziel der Geschichte (About the Origin and Aim of History,* Zurich, 1949); Robert von Ranke-Graves, *The Greek Myths* (New York, 1955); Ken Dowden, *Death and the Maiden: Girls' Initiation Rites in*

Greek Mythology (New York, 1989); and Heide Göttner-Abendroth, *Die Göttin und ihr Heros,* 10th edition (Munich, 1993). Most influential were the popular books by Marija Gimbutas, *The Language of the Goddess* (San Francisco, Calif., 1989) and *The Civilization of the Goddess* (San Francisco, Calif., 1991). Positive assessments of Gimbutas's views can be found in several articles in issue 12 (1996) of the *Journal of Feminist Studies in Religion,* pp. 33–119.

A critical reconsideration of the threefold Goddess in general and the Virgin Goddess as one of her forms has not yet been written. Thorough reexaminations about the Goddess in prehistoric religions can be found in the collection *Ancient Goddess,* edited by Lucy Goodison and Christine Morris (London, 1998). Very insightful on the broader context of interpreting goddesses is the volume *Engendering Archaeology. Women and Prehistory,* edited by Joan M. Gero and Margaret W. Coney (Oxford, 1991). For the Near Eastern context see Tikva Frymer-Kensky, *In the Wake of the Goddesses* (New York, 1992).

The standard work on understandings of Greek virginity is Giulia Sissa, *Greek Virginity,* translated from the French by Arthur Goldhammer (Cambridge, Mass., 1990). For several thorough analyses of Greek interpretations of the female body—including its state as a virginal body—and female roles in Greek culture and religion consult Helen King, *Hippokrates' Women: Reading the Female Body in Ancient Greece* (London, 1998).

Julia Iwersen, *Die Frau im alten Griechenland. Religion, Kultur, Gesellschaft* (Düsseldorf, Germany, 2002) deals with virgin goddesses, virginity, and maidenhood in various contexts of Greek religion. Several important articles on the meaning of virginity and maidenhood in Greek religion can be found in the volume *The Sacred and the Feminine in Ancient Greece,* edited by Sue Blundell and Margaret Williamson (London and New York, 1998); see particularly the contribution of Susan Guettel Cole, "Domesticating Artemis," pp. 27–43. Nannó Marinatos, *The Goddess and the Warrior. The Naked Goddess and Mistress of Animals in Early Greek Religion* (London and New York, 2000) is interesting about functions of Artemis in male-dominated Greek society and also about how the image of this goddess was changed and adapted to Greek gender ideology. As for the maiden Kore, see Katerina Karakasi, *Archaische Koren* (Munich, 2001) and Andreas Scholl, *Die Korenhalle des Erechtheion auf der Akropolis. Frauen für den Staat* (Frankfurt am Main, Germany, 1998). For a classical interpretation of the virginity of a Greek goddess see Karl Kerenyi, *Sie Jungfrau and Mutter der greichischen Religion* (Zurich, 1952), translated as *Athene: Virgin and Mother in Greek Religion* (Zurich, 1978).

Wolfgang Beinert and Heinrich Petri, eds., *Handbuch der Marienkunde* (Regensburg, Germany, 1984), and Marina Warner, *Alone of All Her Sex* (New York, 1976) compile a vast amount of material on the Virgin Mary. For a comprehensive phenomenology of the type in the ancient Mediterranean milieu (from Isis and Cybele to Mary the Virgin and Mother of God) see Stephen Benko, *The Virgin Goddess: Studies in the Pagan and Christian Roots of Mariology* (Leiden, Netherlands, 1993).

The Nepalese Kumari is examined and interpreted in terms of cultural anthropology by Michael Allen, *The Cult of Kumari. Virgin Worship in Nepal* (Kathmandu, 1975, with several reprints), and for a more descriptive approach, see Siddhi B. Ranjitkar, *Kumari. The Virgin Goddess* (New Delhi, 2002).

Discussion of ascetic tension in Judaism in the Hellenistic age can be found in Steven D. Fraade, "Ascetical Aspects of Ancient Judaism" in *Jewish Spirituality from the Bible through the Middle Ages,* vol. 1, edited by Arthur Green, pp. 253–288 (New York, 1989).

JULIA IWERSEN (2005)

VIRGINITY is the condition of young male and female persons who have not had sexual intercourse and have preserved their sexual innocence. This state is partly biologically determined, in that children do not yet have sexual potency; but that condition can be voluntarily or obligatorily extended until marriage, so that virginal status becomes a social fact. The significance of virginity, therefore, has to be understood in a wider social context, in which it bears specific symbolic meanings. A basic fact in every society is the organization of the relationship of men and women into various kinship systems to guarantee the reproduction of the human species. Being a complete man or woman presupposes sexual potency and activity. A virgin boy or girl has not yet reached the condition of full maturity, and therefore retains a purity that makes him or her more suited for certain religious functions or specific activities.

In Classical Greece and Rome, virgin children of living parents often assisted with religious ceremonies. In Greece, they had the task of cutting the olive branches with which the victors at Delphi and at the Olympic games were crowned. They also had a ceremonial role at weddings comparable to that of bridesmaids and pages, who are supposed to be unmarried and consequently virgins. In Christianity, virgin children or eunuchs (i. e., artificial virgins) often functioned as singers in the choir, because their pure status made them more appropriate for contact with the divine world.

Virginity is also believed to bring a man or woman into closer contact with nature, because he or she is still unspoiled by sexuality. In the Babylonian *Epic of Gilgamesh* Enkidu, who was created by the gods as Gilgamesh's opponent, lived among the animals until he was seduced by a prostitute. After that the animals left Enkidu, who was forced to join human society. For the same reason the Kaluli, a tribe of Papua New Guinea, believe that virgin youths are the most effective hunters, and the belief is endorsed by a Kaluli myth featuring Dosali, the mythical model of perfect manhood, and Newelesu, his clownish, violent, and uncivilized antithesis. Both stay a night with the Mother of the Animals. Dosali behaves like a decent guest and gets a lot of game. Newelesu forces the old woman to have intercourse with him, and all the animals flee the house. A virginal man still has close rapport with the animal world, because he is less entangled in the social world of marriage, exchange of property, alliance, and all other issues linked with the world of settled married people.

The virginity of an unmarried girl is likewise temporary, a transitory biological condition with a strong social value. The virginity of young women often acts as a symbol of the social purity of the whole group to which the women belong. In some societies, therefore, the chastity of the young women is a matter of concern for the whole group. In India, the purity of the social group, the caste, is dependent on the purity of the women, who transmit caste membership. Therefore the whole group scrupulously guards the chastity of the young girls until their marriage, and often kills them if they break the interdiction of sexual intercourse. In other societies, for example, in Samoa, a group of islands in the Pacific Ocean close to the equator, the virginity of the daughter of the chief was a symbol of the integrity of the whole society, whereas other girls were permitted to have sexual relationships as they pleased.

In all societies where men exchange women, as is the case in almost all Mediterranean and Arab countries, and where virginity is expected at marriage, the virginity of the woman is an essential part of the marriage contract between the families and the chastity of the young woman is of direct family concern. A bride who is not a virgin breaks the contract and is often severely punished, even with death.

Virginity, however, has yet another aspect, in addition to sexual purity as a link to nature or as a symbol of social purity. Because of their lack or renunciation of sexual experience, virgins are not completely male or female, and consequently defy in a sense gender specificity. In a state of ambiguity, they have aspects of both genders, as sometimes becomes clear in mythology. Persephone, the corn maiden of Greek mythology, lives half the year with her mother Demeter and the other half with Hades, god of the underworld. As a virgin she belongs to both the female and the male world; she is a typically intermediary figure, a go-between. This mediating function of virgins makes them particularly appropriate for contact with the supernatural and implies their sacredness.

In imitation of this quality, chastity or temporary sexual renunciation is often a prerequisite for a visit to a temple or for the performance of religious rites. The participants in the Eleusinian mysteries were obliged to observe a period of chastity, just as in the Middle Ages lay people who wanted to take the Holy Communion had to remain chaste for some days before and after. The priests in Israel had to live apart from their wives during the period of their service in the Jerusalem Temple, and the priests of the Dea Syria, the Syrian mother goddess of fertility, were the so-called Galli, men who had emasculated themselves in the service of the goddess and had in this way made themselves into artificial virgins.

Priestesses of various cults in Greco-Roman antiquity had to be virgins. The Vestal Virgins are a good example of how an intermediary position implies sacredness and contact with the divine world. The Vestals were virgins, but they also had the main characteristics of married women: Their dress was similar and they had some legal rights. They were also treated as brides. For example, they wore permanently the hairstyle typical of a bride on her wedding day. They even showed some male characteristics: Like male magistrates they had the right to be escorted by a lictor. They were in every respect ambiguous, and so especially fit to mediate between human society and the powers that watched over it.

As brides the Vestal Virgins were permanently on the brink between the unmarried and married status. Their anomalous sacred position also entailed living outside a normal household: They lived together in a special house separated from common society. The same ambiguity is symbolized by the sacred fire that the Vestals guarded. Fire is life-giving and life-destroying; it is pure and sterile and a symbol of fertility, and thus a sacred symbol linking two spheres. The Vestals were not an isolated case. The priestess at the Delphic oracle, the Pythia, was required to be an elderly woman of over fifty who might have been married but had to dress as a young virgin. In this way she acted as an intermediary between divine decisions and human affairs.

All these examples of virginity refer to a temporary status—even the Vestals were allowed to leave their service after thirty years and to marry if they wished. The symbolic aspect of virginity was often a motive for a permanent virginity, or what is often called celibacy. A permanent status of virginity, for instance, occurs in Buddhism as a requisite for monks and in the Roman Catholic Church. Virginity was a widespread phenomenon in the early Christian church and was based upon specific concepts of human status and salvation. In view of the impending end of the world the apostle Paul considered the status of unmarried virgin as the most desirable (*1 Cor.* 7), in accordance with certain ascetical trends in the New Testament. Baptism in Christ represents the reunification of male and female, "being one in Christ Jesus" according to *Galatians* 3:28, and implies the abolition of sexual differentiation.

In particular during the second and third centuries CE, the ideal of following Christ as a virgin became a dominant element in the nascent Christian church. This development required broadening the idea of virginity to include those who had been sexually active but now chose to abstain. Just as Christ was unmarried and single, so his followers too should be virgins. But *imitatio Christi* means more than just an ascetic life of sexual renunciation. It is actually a reversion of the fateful division of humankind into sexually active males and females after the Fall, which started with the creation of Eve from Adam as described in *Genesis* 2:21f. According to an apocryphal logion of Christ quoted in *2 Clement,* a treatise dating back to the middle of the second century CE, the kingdom of God will come "when the two will be one, and the outer like the inner, and the male will be united with the female, so that there will be neither male nor female, but the two will be one."

The same language occurs in logion 22 of the *Gospel of Thomas,* an apocryphal gospel that originated in the Syriac-speaking East and dates from about 200 CE. The reunification of male and female is explained as the transformation of women into men. When Simon Peter said to Jesus and the disciples, "Let Mary go out from among us, because women are not worthy of the Life," Jesus said, "See, I shall lead her, so that I will make her male, that she too may become a living spirit, resembling you males. For every woman who makes herself male will enter the kingdom of Heaven" (logion 114).

This transcendence of sexuality is also described as becoming like children who do not yet know sexual shame. In the same *Gospel of Thomas* the disciples ask Jesus, "When wilt Thou be revealed to us and when will we see Thee?" And Jesus said, "When you take off your clothing without being ashamed, and take your clothes and put them under your feet as the little children and tread on them, then shall you behold the Son of the Living One and you shall not fear" (logion 37). When the apostle Thomas converted a royal bridal couple from "filthy intercourse" to a pure virginal life, as is related in the apocryphal *Acts of Thomas,* written in the Syrian East around 225 CE, the bride took off her veil, because "the veil of corruption is taken away from her, and the deed of shame has been removed." According to her own words, she is "betrothed to the true Husband," a situation recalling *Genesis* 2:24f.: ". . . and they shall be one flesh. And they were both naked, the man and his wife, and were not ashamed."

The union between the virgin and Christ the true bridegroom was often celebrated in the ritual of the Bridal Chamber that is attested in nascent Syrian Christianity as well as in sectarian gnostic groups. It represented the union with Christ the Second Adam that restored the asexual androgynous condition of humankind in paradise before the Fall. Where there is no longer male or female, a new world has come that is paradise regained. The life of the virgins is, therefore, often characterized as angelical life (*bios aggelikos*), referring to *Luke* 20:27–40.

The Christian virgins who had overcome gender differentiation demonstrated their paradisiacal state in different ways. They sometimes lived chastely together in one house or community, to show how they could live without passions. Often they lived singly outside common human society in isolation, for example, in the desert, because neutralization of sexuality implies a renunciation of all ties that link a person with society, since marriage and procreation are linked with its survival. Sexually and socially the virgins were ambiguous: They were neither male nor female, and they lived an angelical eternal paradisiacal life among or on the outskirts of human mortal society. They even demonstrated the new life in their dress: The virgin Thecla in the apocryphal *Acts of Paul and Thecla* dressed like a man and had her hair cut short. She is reminiscent of Joan of Arc, the virgin of Orléans, who also dressed like a man and played an intermediate role.

The virginal life meant perpetual struggle with bodily passions, the manifestations of Satan. Like Christ, Christian virgins could win that struggle and undo the inheritance of Adam's fate of sexuality and death. Their life is, therefore, often depicted as a permanent war or struggle, a motif that had its roots in the antique world and exercised a deep influence on Christian tradition. The virgins became saints who mediated between this world and God because they kept an intermediate, ambiguous position. Their symbolic behavior pointed to their mediating function, as did that of the stylites, early Christian ascetics who lived on the tops of pillars representing the link between heaven and earth.

But the most anomalous phenomenon connected with virginity is virgin birth. A virgin mother is a powerful symbol of the relationship between the natural (human) and supernatural (divine) world. Through the Virgin Mary, Christ became the mediator *par excellence,* being God and human at the same time. Thus virginity is also a sign of the power to cross the boundary of biological existence, to mediate between body and socioreligious ideals, between what is and what ought to be. In this way people can order their biological existence and social world through the most powerful symbols they have, the sexual bodies that are their only way of survival and their eternal fate.

See Also Celibacy; Chastity; Eremitism; Virgin Goddess.

Bibliography

A comprehensive study of virginity does not exist. For understanding the religious significance of the ambiguous status of virgins, modern cultural anthropology is useful, particularly the works of Mary Douglas: *Purity and Danger: An Analysis of Concepts of Pollution and Taboo* (New York, 1966), *Natural Symbols: Explorations in Cosmology* (New York, 1970), and *Implicit Meanings: Essays in Anthropology* (Boston, 1975). Kirsten Hastrup's article "The Semantics of Biology: Virginity," in *Defining Females: The Nature of Women in Society,* edited by Shirley Ardener (London, 1978), uses Douglas's theoretical insights with great profit, as does Mary Beard's "The Sexual Status of Vestal Virgins," *Journal of Roman Studies* 70 (1980): 12–27. A bit out of date but a useful collection of material and sources is Eugen Fehrle's *Die kultische Keuschheit im Altertum,* "Religionsgeschichtliche Versuche und Vorarbeiten," vol. 6 (Giessen, 1910). Aline Rousselle's *Porneia: De la maîtrise du corps à la privation sensorielle deuxième-quatrième siècles de l'ère chrétienne* (Paris, 1983) is excellent for the social and medical background of virginity and asceticism in general in the antique and early Christian world. For a good survey of the topic, see Peter Nagel's *Die Motivierung der Askese in der alten Kirche und der Ursprung des Mönchtums,* "Texte und Untersuchungen," vol. 95 (Berlin, 1966), and Bernhard Lohse's *Askese und Mönchtum in der Antike und in der alten Kirche* (Munich, 1969). Peter Brown's *The Making of Late Antiquity* (Cambridge, Mass., 1978) is quite interesting.

New Sources

Brown, Peter. *The Body and Society: Men, Women, and Sexual Renunciation in Early Christianity,* New York, 1988. Indispensable.

Clark, Elisabeth. *Reading Renunciation. Asceticism and Scripture in Early Christianity.* Princeton, N.J., 1999. A brilliant exploration of the consequences of late ancient sexual renunciation for the interpretation of Bible.

Elm, Susanna. *Virgins of God: The Making of Asceticism in Late Antiquity.* Oxford, 1994. Female ascetic life in Asia Minor and Egypt. A very comprehensive bibliography is included.

Sfameni Gasparro, Giulia. *Enkrateia e antropologia.* Rome, 1984. A systematic study of asceticism and virginity in early Christianity and Gnosticism. Select bibliography.

Sissa, Giulia. *Le corps virginal.* Paris, 1987. Virginity in Greece.

HAN J. W. DRIJVERS (1987)
Revised Bibliography

VIRGIN MARY SEE MARY

VISION QUEST. The personal vision is a fundamental feature of American Indian cultures across the continent and across all linguistic boundaries. While there are always people who have visions of a quality that sets them apart from others, people in all American Indian communities treasure their own visions and respect those of others. Whether wake-state or sleep-state, the vision in American Indian cultural contexts is always a communication between a human person and one or more nonhuman spirit persons.

While these vision experiences sometimes occur spontaneously, they occur most frequently in the context of intentional seeking done in a carefully arranged ceremonial manner in what is called in English the *vision quest* or *rite of vigil.* The details are always dependent on the particular purpose for the quest and the particularities of community custom. The general structures, however, tend to be similar across the continent. Adolescents might undertake the rite of vigil for one or two days and nights; adults might extend the ritual, which includes fasting, from four to seven days, and occasionally even longer. These occasions typically were, and are yet today, life-altering experiences for Native women and men. Fletcher and La Flesche report that a young man's vision became his personal connection with the "vast universe" of the immaterial spirit world, "by which he could strengthen his spirit and his physical powers" (p. 131).

The vision quest is a common American Indian ceremonial tradition that is or was practiced in nearly every tribal community. Indeed, Ruth Benedict, an early ethnographer, could claim that the vision was the single unifying factor in all North American Indian religious experience. While the ceremony varied from community to community and according to the particularity of the occasion, Benedict is essentially correct in claiming that it was, and is, structurally and functionally similar across all these communities, even as she distinguishes characteristics unique to the Plains. In every case, these were intense occasions of personal retreat from human community, of intentional self-deprivation, and of prayer.

A number of consistent factors tie these phenomena together. In almost every case the faster is separated from the human community and isolated in places remote from the civic center of the village. Lakota peoples sometimes refer to it as "going on the hill." A total abstinence from food and water is fundamental to the ceremonial exercise. The ceremony is one of constant prayer. The duration of the ceremony—usually dependent on the prior commitment of the faster—varies from one day and night (for an adolescent) up to four to seven days and sometimes longer (for an adult).

Finally, the American Indian vision phenomenon is always predicated on an understanding of the world as peopled by both material and immaterial beings, with the visionary moment as that which allows a human person to communicate with, and especially to receive communication from, immaterial spirit beings. Thus, the occasion always includes the possibility of receiving some sort of personal power as a gift from a spirit.

Much of the literature concerning the vision quest is somewhat unsatisfactory, either because of its great superficiality or because it attempts to impose colonial structures of meaning on indigenous phenomena. For instance, the majority of professional literature on the vision quest presumes the accuracy of nineteenth-century ethnographic collections of vision recitations as if the whole of the recitation is accurately represented in the brief paragraph typically recorded by the ethnographer; and as if the typically language-deficient ethnographer has also accurately translated the native language in which the vision would have been recited.

These anthropological renditions are typically rather short and cannot have been the whole of the vision experienced by the informant. In fact, it is a universal Native American characteristic that the vision, as an intensely personal experience, is never shared fully but is kept throughout life as a private revelation. Thus, the ethnographer was almost always not privy to the whole of the vision encounter. Moreover, few ethnographers, most of whom were Native Americans themselves, were fluent in the languages of those they presumed to study, meaning that almost all translations relied on others whose English may have been only nominally better than the ethnographer's understanding of the native language. The most egregious example of this is John Neihard's poetic and romanticized interpretation of Lakota elder Nicholas Black Elk's words in *Black Elk Speaks.* The work is based on Neihard's daughter's stenographic notes of Ben Black Elk's relatively naive boarding-school English translation of his father Nicholas's sophisticated and abstract Lakota spoken narrative, a sophistication that is inexorably stripped away on its path toward the English printed version.

Perhaps the most significant shortcoming of the professional literature is its proclivity, from the late nineteenth century to the present, to treat all Native American cultural phenomena, including the vision quest, as historical artifacts that have no place in contemporary American Indian societies. The more recent academic treatments almost universally base their interpretations on these older nineteenth- and early-twentieth-century ethnographic texts, treating them as if they actually represented a "textus receptus," an absolutely authoritative text, with regard to Native religious traditions.

While many early ethnographers included interpretive commentaries about visions and the vision quest, there is only one important recent interpretation, in Lee Irwin's *The Dream Seekers: Native American Visionary Traditions of the Great Plains.* Unfortunately Irwin's book, for all of its innovative insight, falls into the pattern just described. It is not an analysis of new data but merely rehashes the old ethnographies, presupposing their authority and veracity, but this time using modern psychiatric and neurological investigations of human dreaming as an interpretive device for understanding the vision as a sleep-state experience. This leads Irwin to place the Plains visionary experience under the more general category of dreaming. It should be clearly emphasized here that the vision as experienced in American Indian communities is not invariably, nor even usually, a sleep-state phenomenon, but is often experienced while one is awake.

It is a common theme in the professional literature to see the vision quest as definitive evidence of the radical individualism of Plains Native people. Nothing could be further from reality; in fact just the opposite is true. There is always a symbiotic relationship between the person engaging in the fast and the community to which she or he belongs, even though the ceremony involves the deeply personal sacrifice of rigorous fasting and prayer over several days. The vision itself certainly is a deeply personal experience, and the learning that comes from the experience affects the life of that one person directly. The effort expended in such serious fasting (total abstinence from food and liquid) is obviously a personal commitment and a personal trial. Moreover, the adult faster may have decided on the undertaking either by personal direction from the spirit world or because of some personal crisis. Or the person may have made an entirely voluntary choice to engage in the ceremony as a distinct personal moment to engage in prayer and to seek some spiritual communication that might provide that person's life with meaning, direction, and even personal spiritual power. Yet in each case the person undertaking the ceremony understands the benefits that also accrue to the communal whole. Whatever personal power the faster may gain is ultimately intended to serve the interests of the community.

One quintessential sign of the communal nature of the vision quest is the common practice in Lakota and other communities for the people to greet the faster with a handshake and a thank-you for the faster's accomplishment as she or he completes the ceremony. In a typical vision quest, moreover, the community or some part of the community participates in preparing the person to engage in the ceremony. There may be teachings that need to be shared and even preliminary ceremonies that have to be performed. Then through the duration of the fast the community will constantly be conscious of and in prayer for the one who is actually performing the ceremony in isolation.

A short word must be added with respect to the great appeal of this particular ceremony to non-Native adherents of New Age movements and practices. The vision quest is traditionally a ceremonial act performed by a single person in isolation, but always as a part of a particular community and acting for the good of the whole. Given that personal power and assistance is sought from the Mysteries for the ultimate benefit of the whole community, when a non-Native New York City resident flies off to South Dakota, for instance, to perform the rite of vigil on a Lakota reservation under the guidance of a Lakota spiritual leader, one must wonder what close community of political and spiritual existence has made such rigorous claims on this person's spiritual strength and why he or she has chosen to make the rite so far away from his or her community of residence. From a Native American perspective, this particular performance of the rite has little or no meaning, and thus it must be invested with an entirely new and non-Native meaning. Thus, while non-Native rites that are modeled after American Indian vision quests may provide a response to various spiritual urges and needs, and may correlate well with a Euro-American sense of individualism, ritual practices of that sort bear faint resemblance to the vision quests undertaken in Native communities.

On the other hand, the vision quest, with its resultant access to vision experiences, was and is an egalitarian and democratic phenomenon in American Indian communities. That is, against Albers and Parker (1971), it is a rite that is available to every member of a Native tribal community and was never reserved only for an elite few, such as medicine people or other spiritual leaders, even though certain kinds of medicine power do seem to run in families for a variety of reasons. Indeed, in many tribal communities it was common practice to require every adolescent male to make this rite of vigil as a rite of passage from childhood to adulthood. Georges Sioui, among others, correctly notes that the vision quest might be required of males but was always equally available to females, for whom the exercise would not be mandatory simply because of the privileged status of women in most Native tribal communities.

Historically then, all males in many Native American communities would have made a vision quest as a rite of passage before entering into adult responsibilities and possibly community leadership of any kind. Recognized spiritual leaders, on the other hand, would all have engaged in at least one vigil of some length during which they would have received a vision that communicated their specific medicine power, a situation that continues in the present. Moreover, they would usually engage in repeated exercises of the vigil (today this is sometimes done annually), even if for much shorter durations. While this may also be true of other community members who do not receive such medicine visions, the substantial difference in the visioning of these recognized healers is their more open line of communication with those spirit beings who have selected them as interpreters. Thus, the annual vigil might be an occasion for some new spirit being to introduce itself to the healer and offer a different sort of spiritual power not previously accessible to that healer. This increases the healer's personal repertoire of power to help the community.

At the same time, there is no sense of class stratification embedded in the vision experience, as some contemporary interpreters with a Marxist orientation would suggest. Healers would have been supported historically by the rest of a community because of their inherent practical usefulness to the community, and community gifts served to free them from the pressures of subsistence hunting and the like. Becoming a political leader was not predicated on access to vision power. On the other hand, leadership in Native American communities was spread in such diffuse ways through the community that different sorts of leadership were exercised by a variety of people at any given time. And it needs to be said clearly that questing for a vision was a very egalitarian phenomenon, something that was available to every person.

This ceremony continues today in many American Indian communities and continues in forms that are consistent with the historical practice of the rite in these communities.

BIBLIOGRAPHY

Albers, Patricia, and Seymour S. Parker. "The Plains Vision Experience: A Study of Power and Privilege." *Southwestern Journal of Anthropology* 27, no. 3 (1971): 203–233.

Benedict, Ruth. "The Vision in Plains Culture." *American Anthropologist* 24, no. 1 (1922): 1–23.

Benedict, Ruth. *The Concept of the Guardian Spirit in North America.* Menasha, Wis., 1923.

Fletcher, Alice, and Francis La Flesche. *The Omaha Tribe* (1911). Lincoln, Neb., 1992.

Harrod, Howard. *Renewing the World: Plains Indian Religion and Morality.* Tucson, Ariz., 1987.

Horse Capture, George, editor. *The Seven Visions of Bull Lodge, as Told by His Daughter, Garter Snake.* Gathered by Fred P. Gone. Lincoln, Neb., 1980.

Irwin, Lee. *Dream Seekers: Native American Visionary Traditions of the Great Plains.* Norman, Okla., 1994.

Johnston, Basil H. *Ojibway Ceremonies.* Toronto, 1987. Written by a member of the Ojibwe tribe.

Sioui, Georges E. *For an Amerindian Autohistory: An Essay on the Foundations of a Social Ethic.* Translated by Sheila Fischman. Montreal, 1992. Written by a member of the Wendot tribe.

TINK TINKER (2005)

VISIONS.

VISIONS. Usage of the term *vision* goes back to the thirteenth-century Italian theologian Thomas Aquinas, who first used the word to refer to a "supernatural" manifestation. It describes a religious experience that involves seeing and, frequently, the other senses as well. The quality of the experience suggests that the content of the perception is real, a direct, unmediated contact with a nonordinary aspect of reality that is external and independent of the perceiver. "[Vision] is very real," says Lame Deer, a medicine man of the Sioux nation. "It hits you sharp and clear like an electric shock. You are wide awake and, suddenly, there is a person standing next to you who you know can't be there at all" (*Lame Deer, Seeker of Visions,* New York, 1972, p. 65).

The explanation that visions are due to imaginings, pseudoperception, or errors of perception is an expression of the cultural difference between the visionary and the present-day Western psychologist in their views concerning the nature of reality, a topic that would stray too far afield here. But a stand should be taken against those psychiatrists who clinically equate vision with hallucination. In hallucination the content of what is reported is something to which nothing real corresponds; it is a delusion. For the health professional the presence of delusions is a sign of insanity, and in an application of the so-called pathology model of religious experience, visionaries are classified as mentally ill—a diagnosis often imputed to shamans. Yet in clinically healthy subjects visions dissolve spontaneously (as will be seen below), and, what is even more important for the institutionalization of the visionary experience, they can be induced and terminated ritually. This cannot be said of the hallucinations that are associated with insanity. Furthermore, one should be wary when encountering references to dreams in religious contexts. Semantically, the English word *dream* includes the notion that its content does not represent anything real. Non-Westerners, however, often set in opposition a dream category that is taken to be "real" or "valid" with one that is considered "ordinary." The latter category includes fleeting, or "invalid," dreams. The dreams referred to in such remarks as "Old Spotted Wolf had a painted lodge, which he was advised to make by the buffalo, in a dream" (George B. Grinnell, *The Cheyenne Indians,* vol. 1, 1972, p. 234), the dreams known from shamanistic traditions of flying, initiation, and dismemberment, and even the many revelatory dreams of the Hebrew scriptures (Old Testament) should all properly be considered visions.

VISIONARY EXPERIENCE. Contrary to commonly held Western views, having a vision is not a singular or rare event. The father of this Western misconception is once more Thomas Aquinas, who held that the human world and the sacred realm are separated by a wide chasm. A report of a vision was therefore indicative of a rare event, something that could take place only under extraordinary circumstances. In reality, visions are known to all societies, and their use in ritual is widespread.

When a type of behavior thus crosses boundaries, irrespective of ethnic or religious divisions, one may have to look to physical rather than cultural reasons. After all, human beings constitute one species only. Humans all have the same kind of body, the same nervous system. And, indeed, countless reports and modern field observations by anthropologists indicate that, when a person has a vision, certain physical changes occur. In what is popularly called a trance, the pupils may widen, muscles become rigid, and breathing seem shallow. Some visionaries will fall into what appears to be a deep sleep or even a dead faint. In such a trance, as Barbara W. Lex, a medical anthropologist, maintains, two opposing arousals of the nervous system are experienced. Their alternating action produces relaxation, and this accounts for the trance's beneficial effect. Simultaneously, the brain synthesizes β-endorphins (the body's own painkillers), as this writer learned in a study in which the trance experience was induced in a religiously neutral environment. (See Ingrid Müller's M. D. dissertation, University of Freiburg im Breisgau.) These endorphins are thought to be responsible on the biological level for the joy, euphoria, and "sweetness" that are often reported in the visions of Christian mystics. As this writer learned from fieldwork, these physiological changes must be produced before the visions can occur. In some mysterious way, then, the body becomes a perceiving organ for the sacred dimension of reality.

This manner of viewing the visionary event runs counter to another cherished notion inherited from the Middle Ages, namely that humans are dualistic in nature, consisting of a body and a separate soul. Rather, it seems to modern science that human beings are biopsychological systems. This view echoes ideas put forth by Galen, a Greek physician of the second century CE, who contended that mind and matter are different aspects of the same stuff. In other words, not the soul but the entire human being is having the vision.

The ritual trance, or ecstasy, as an altered state of consciousness, is responsible for even basic perceptions of a nonordinary quality. "Hearing" voices is not plain hearing. Those who experience voices can readily distinguish them from ordinary speech. "I do not hear it in so many words," explained a German university student who reported being possessed by demons and hearing Jesus and Mary speaking to her; "I am given to know." (See Felicitas D. Goodman, *The Exorcism of Anneliese Michel,* New York, 1981.) "Seeing" also takes place on a different level. As a blind !Kung San explained, the great god kept his eyeballs for him in a little pouch, giving them to him only during the medicine dance; and when the dance was over, he had to return them to the god. That is, he could see only while in trance. A changed quality is also reported during experience with an incubus—that is, when a spirit has sexual intercourse with a human being. In classical Greek tradition such sexual contact might make a diviner out of a woman, as happened when Apollo "raped" Cassandra. The Inquisition endlessly quizzed women accused of witchcraft concerning intercourse with Satan. When given the chance, these women testified that this was not like making love in ordinary reality.

Under certain circumstances, about which very little is known, clinically healthy human beings may inadvertently create the necessary biopsychological preconditions for a visionary experience—that is, they may "stray" into it. When this happens, as this writer found during fieldwork observations of a millenarian movement in the Yucatán, in Mexico, a regular pattern will assert itself, which, if experienced in its entirety, will take about thirty-five or forty days. The trance episode is apparently most intense at the beginning, and what is seen by participants during this time typically is white. The man who started the Yucatán millenarian movement initially saw white demons. A woman from another apostolic congregation in the same area saw "white angels on white horses galloping by, carrying white flags, very, very white." From the New Testament it is known that when the women went to Jesus' tomb, whatever they saw there—an angel, two angels, two men, or one young man—the vision was bathed in dazzling light, white as snow. The initial vision of Kotama, the founder of Sūkyō Mahikari, one of the "new religions" of Japan, was of a white-haired old man standing in a white cloud. The next phase of the trance is characterized by a gold or orange glow: The Yucatecan apostolic saw burning candles; Kotama's old man was washing clothes in a golden tub. Finally, there is a "double" vision, with ordinary and nonordinary perception overlapping. The Yucatecan went to the cathedral in Mérida and saw a procession of priests whose heads were those of demons. The woman from the other apostolic congregation saw a big Bible fastened above the entrance to the hospital where she was taken. The prophet Muḥammad watched the angel Gabriel astride the horizon, and no matter which way he turned, the angel was always there on the horizon. The widely reported voices are probably also part of this last phase in many instances, as another superimposition of a visionary (i.e., auditory) perception on the ordinary environment. Kotama's episode, for instance, concluded with a voice telling him his new name and giving him instructions. Eventually the vision dissolves, leaving only ordinary reality as the perceptual field.

Not everyone goes through the entire visionary sequence. It is possible to stray into it anywhere along the way. But whether complete or not, its extraordinary and impressive character can result in a conversion experience for the visionary and if the social configuration is right, religious innovation follows. According to legend, the Buddha's enlightenment came at daybreak after a sequence of visions in which he saw first all his own rebirths, then other beings dying and passing into the five destinies of existence, and finally the chain that bound all beings to continued, recurrent death and rebirth. Muḥammad's prophethood was heralded by a complete visionary sequence. First he experienced "true visions" resembling the brightness of daybreak. Several days later the angel Gabriel came to him with a coverlet of brocade (gold?) with some writing on it and commanded him to read it. Still later, Muḥammad beheld Gabriel on the horizon. A hundred years ago Wovoka, the Ghost Dance messiah, told of his vision that, "when the sun died, I went up to heaven and saw God and all the people that had died a long time ago. God told me to come back and tell my people they must be good and love one another, and not fight, or steal, or lie. He gave me this dance to give to my people." And in this century, the cargo cults of Melanesia have been characterized by spontaneously occurring visions. Leaders of various cults have told of hearing voices, seeing lights, and meeting native gods and fairylike beings of the forests and waters. They have spoken, too, of journeys to heaven (an idea borrowed from Westerners) and of visits to the Hiyoyoa, their own otherworld.

While these spontaneous episodes of visionary experience dissolve without the aid of ritual, there is another class of vision in which this is not the case. This is the so-called shamanistic illness, reported predominantly in Asia but also in Africa, North America, and, sporadically, other areas as well. Medical anthropologists suspect that in some instances the triggering mechanism may be biochemical, for example, resulting from a socially prescribed change in nutrition, but such causes cannot often be pinpointed. Its onset is variously signaled by high fever, swelling of either the limbs or the entire body, prolonged unconsciousness, and inability to eat; at times, there is also an indomitable urge to flee into the wilderness. These changes are preceded, accompanied, or followed by visions. The condition, which may linger for years, is classed not only as an illness but also as a sign that the sufferer is destined, singled out by an agency of the sacred ranges of reality, for a future as a religious specialist. Cure is effected by a ritual that is usually initiatory in nature.

One example among many comes from the German ethnographer Peter Snoy. In his book *Bagrot* (Graz, 1975), Snoy tells of a Yeshkun shaman from the Karakoram Mountains (part of the Himalayan system). When this man was about twenty he was walking home one day when suddenly he saw five fairies dancing in the fields. They did not talk to him, but the next day he had the unconquerable urge to run away into the mountains to join them. He started raging, and five men finally managed to tie him up. He was kept tied up in his house for a whole year, and the fairies visited him several times each day, descending through the smoke hole and singing and dancing for him. Eventually, the man's village arranged an initiation feast for him. A goat was sacrificed, and he drank its blood, which the fairies told him was milk. And for the first time he danced, performing what is in his society an important part of shamanistic séances. Subsequently, the man worked as a healer and diviner.

Reporting from Africa, the British social anthropologist Adrian Boshier, in "African Apprenticeship" (in *Parapsychology and Anthropology,* New York, 1974), tells the story of Dorca, a Zulu *sangoma,* that is, a diviner and healer. For three years, Dorca was sick in bed. During this time her spirit left her body every night, and she saw many things and visited places where she had never been. One night in a vision her dead grandfather came to see her. He told her that he liked her very much and that his spirit would enter her body so that she would be able to help her people. She refused, but spirit *sangomas* came to her every night, showed her beads and herbs and a feather headdress she was to make, and sang her a song that she was to learn. Finally her grandfather's spirit threatened to kill her if she continued to resist. Her mother thereupon took her to the house of an aunt who was also a *sangoma.* There Dorca sang the spirit song and danced for many hours. This was the beginning of her training as a *sangoma.*

In most non-Western societies, visions are an integral part of religious ritual. As Lame Deer says, "By themselves these things [rituals] mean nothing. Without the vision and the power this learning will do no good" (1972, p. 13). It is understandable, therefore, that such societies cannot rely on the fortuitous occurrence of visionary experiences but need ways for inducing them.

Many strategies for inducing visions utilize rhythmic stimulation. Inuit (Eskimo) ritual specialists use drums, as do various Siberian shamans, for whom the drum represents the magic horse on which they ride to the beyond. Such stimulation is so effective that by merely shaking a gourd rattle and using traditional postures, a visionary experience can be induced in volunteers in a religiously neutral environment. (See this writer's article "Body Posture and the Religious Altered State of Consciousness: An Experimental Investigation," *Journal of Humanistic Psychology,* 1984.) Other methods involve sensory deprivation, as used by the Shakers and by the Spiritual Baptists of Saint Vincent Island in their mourning ritual; isolation and fasting, as practiced by the Oglala Indians and other societies; and fasting and self-mortification, as in the initiation ritual of the Plains Indians, during which adolescents seeking a vision would fast, bathe in icy streams, and crawl naked over jagged rocks in order to acquire a guardian spirit. Christian mystics employed similar strategies. The German monk Suso (Heinrich Süse, c. 1295–1366), for instance, was able to achieve several visions daily for a period of about sixteen years by fasting extensively and by sleeping in a tight undergarment through which nails protruded into his skin.

Even intense concentration in combination with nothing more than certain breathing techniques may bring about visions, as has been learned from the Chinese Daoist philosopher and mystic Zhuangzi (369–286? BCE). Zhuangzi told of a master called Ciqi, who "sat leaning on his armrest, staring up at the sky and breathing—vacant and far away." The changes wrought in him were striking to his companion, who asked, "What is this? Can you really make the body like a withered tree and the mind like ashes? The man leaning on the armrest now is not the one who leaned on it before" (quoted in *Poetry and Speculation of the Rg Veda* by Willard Johnson, Berkeley, 1980, p. xxvii). Ciqi explained that by virtue of this change he was able to hear the piping of the earth and the piping of the heavens.

Other societies employ a number of different psychedelics to achieve visions. The use of such drugs goes back to antiquity and is widely distributed geographically. Mushrooms such as the fly agaric *(Amanita muscaria)* were probably known to Mesolithic Paleosiberians (about 8000 BCE). Mesoamerica and South America are particularly rich in plants that contain the requisite alkaloids, and many societies there utilize them ritually. But there are also reports of their religious application from every other continent. At first glance, the use of psychedelics seems to represent an easy way of achieving visions, and for this reason many North American Indians reject them. As Lame Deer said contemptuously, "Even the butcher boy at his meat counter will have a vision after eating peyote" (1972, p. 64). Actually, though, matters are not quite that simple. Many of the substances bring about an undifferentiated condition of intoxication, and seeing the right vision requires training. Thus Gerardo Reichel-Dolmatoff, in his book *Amazonian Cosmos* (Chicago, 1971), discusses the use of *Banisteriopsis caapi* by the Desana Indians of South America. He tells that during intoxication, the Desana religious specialist needs to learn to see the Milky Way as a road, the hills and pools as communal houses of the spirits, and the animals as people. Those who are unable to go so far in their visions see only clouds and stones, "and the birds laugh at them." In another instance reported by Reichel-Dolmatoff, during a communal rite of the same society, the men take the drug, and the priest, who has abstained, talks them through their visions.

FORMS OF VISIONS AND TYPES OF SOCIETY. It appears that, cross-culturally, the neurophysiology of visionary experience remains the same. Neither does the form in which it is expressed vary much, if one contemplates only the religions of a particular type of society, of agriculturalists, for instance. However, salient differences appear when comparing the religious expression of one societal type with that of another, that of agriculturalists, for example, with that of hunters. There are, of course, syncretic patterns, for societies change, and so do their religions. But it is still possible to recognize certain fundamental forms.

(In the following passages, the "ethnographic present" is used in giving examples from non-Western societies, although in many instances the rituals mentioned have fallen victim to Western conquest and aggressive missionizing.)

Visions of hunter-gatherers. The way of life of the hunter-gatherer is the most ancient and venerable of all human adaptations. Humans' antecedents were hunters and gatherers for a million years or more before any cultivation of the soil was introduced. In such societies that are still extant, visionary experiences are varied, involving a highly sophisticated use of religious trance. Hunter-gatherers understand the ordinary and the nonordinary aspects of reality to be closely intertwined, indeed to coexist in time and space, as one Pygmy elder from the Ituri rain forest expressed it. All adult men can easily switch from seeing ordinary reality to seeing its nonordinary aspect, having learned to do so early on, usually during initiation rites. In the sacred range a man can see the "spirits," that is, the nonordinary aspects of stones, mountains, waters, and winds, of plants, insects, and animals. He sees the spirits of the unborn, one of which he has to take to his wife before she bears his child. The spirits of the dead gather around when a feast is being prepared or during a medicine dance, and they need to be invited to take part. An individual spirit of a dead loved one may appear to teach a man or a woman a new song, game, or ritual. A murderer's essence may loiter at the tomb of his victim, and beings of curious shape may warn the living of danger. If they penetrate someone's body, they make him ill by leaving behind a bone, visible to the healer, who will remove it in a curing ritual by sucking it out. People also tell of seeing strange neighbors, such as the "no-knees" of the San, beings who catch the sun as it sets and kill it. After the sun has been cooked, the no-knees eat it and throw its shoulder blade to the east, where it rises once more.

The most spectacular institutionalized visionary experience of hunter-gatherers, however, is the spirit journey, a perfect expression of the hunter's life way, in which individual initiative is of paramount importance. The Pygmies embark on this journey by "crossing a river." On the "other side," they may visit the realm of the spirits of the dead, where everything is reversed but still as orderly as is earthly existence. For the !Kung San of the Kalahari Desert the great god used to let down a cord from the sky by which he allowed the medicine man to climb up to visit him. Nowadays, however, during the medicine dance, medicine men send their spirits out to fly into the veld while their bodies lie lifeless, for there is nothing to hold them up. They might see the spirits of the dead there, or the great god, or perhaps they go because they need to order a lion to stop disturbing people by roaring at night. An Australian medicine man takes a postulant up to the sky by assuming the form of a skeleton and fastening a pouch to himself into which he places the postulant, who is reduced to the size of a very small child. Sitting astride a rainbow, the medicine man pulls himself up with an arm-over-arm action. When near the top, he throws the young man out onto the sky as part of his initiation. An Inuit shaman will swim muscle-naked through rock to the underworld in order to seek out Tornassuq, the earth spirit, and inquire of him the reasons for recent misfortunes of his band. Other spirit journeys, as told of by North American Indians, are undertaken to recover a lost soul, whose absence makes its owner sick.

Visionary experiences serve many important functions within hunter-gatherer society. On the individual level, a vision bestows well-being and strength as well as power to speak impressively, to cure and to divine, and to protect the group against danger from the outside. For the community, visions are a part of many rituals. A spirit journey, for example, is an important communal event. When an Inuit shaman starts out on his trip, the entire village is present, and all are there when he comes back to tell of his adventures. Among the Salish, a tribe of North American Indians, the dramatization of the journey in a spirit canoe in quest of a lost soul is a most impressive performance. What was perceived in a vision is represented on cave walls, or on rocks, painted on bark, or carved in bone for all to see. For a while, such innovative iconography will be confined to the originating group, but unencumbered by written tradition, it eventually diffuses to neighboring bands and even to the wider cultural area, continually reinvigorating religious life.

Visions of horticulturalists. About ten to twelve thousand years ago human beings began growing some of their own food instead of merely collecting it. The areas cultivated were no more than gardens, hence the name *horticulturalist.* Horticulturalists also continued hunting, some extensively, others less so, depending on the ecology of their respective region. While European tradition retains no memory of the hunter-gatherer past, the horticulturalist way of life is reflected in recorded history. What is known of the Celtic, Germanic, and Greek societies clearly indicates their horticulturalist character. Societies of this type survive in Southeast Asia and, especially, in Mesoamerica and South America. Their members' visions have much in common with those of hunter-gatherers, but not all horticulturalists learn the behavior. Instead, there is a more or less pronounced tendency for religious specialists to assume the spiritual role that is performed by all male hunter-gatherers.

The spirit journey of the hunter-gatherer has undergone significant permutations in various horticulturalist societies. Their legends tell of full-fledged spirit journeys like those of the hunter-gatherers: of the Teutonic god Óðinn (Odin) who travels the earth, of a famous medicine man of the South American Guaraní who calls on First Woman in her maize garden in the mythical East. But horticulturalists cannot explore such distant ranges with impunity. Just as Orpheus cannot retrieve Eurydice from the underworld, no Amazonian Akwe-Shavante can ever visit the village of the spirits of the dead, although some have had offers from the spirits of friendly departed relatives to take them there. Instead, horticulturalists undertake a lesser experience, an actual journey that culminates in the desired vision. Initiates of the Eleusinian mysteries of ancient Greece descended into caves; the Huichol Indians of Mexico travel over land in search of peyote; adherents of Shinto climb Mount Fuji. Even the North American Indians' vision quest and their search for the guardian spirit is of this nature. The spirit journey may also be entirely vicarious, as when the Brazilian Yanomamö Indians send their friends, the miniature *hekura* spirits who live under stones and in mountains, to enemy villages to eat the souls of the children there. (See Napoleon A. Changnon, *Yanomamö: The Fierce People,* New York, 1977.) Visions are given shape in paintings on rock and in carvings, embroidery, and clay. They invest the practitioner not only with personal stature but also with power that leads to success in curing, hunting, and war, all in the service of the community.

Visions of nomadic pastoralists. Nomadic-pastoralist societies appear in a number of different adaptations. Some such societies arose from hunters who had attached themselves to wild herds of animals, such as reindeer, or from hunters who had acquired pet animals, such as horses, which had expanded into domesticated herds. Other nomadic-pastoralist societies arose as extensions of agriculturalist societies, and still others developed in which only the men are pastoralists, while the women cultivate the soil. The visionary experiences of nomadic pastoralists correlate with the differences in their origins.

Among reindeer herders, for instance, such as the Evenki of northern Siberia, the hunter's richly appointed sacred dimension is still preserved, although it is accessible only to the shaman. In his visions, the shaman constructs the fence that surrounds his clan's territory and protects it against enemy shamans. He communicates with the ruling spirits, the "masters" of waters, mountains, forests, and species of beasts. In his spirit journeys he guides departing souls to the lower world, at which time he must ask the mistress of that world for permission for the soul to enter. He also travels to the upper world, where he calls on Grandfather Spirit and the supreme spirit ruler of all animal and plant life as well as on the spirits of the sun, moon, stars, thunder, clouds, sunset, and daybreak. He even knows the way to the storehouse of the unborn, which is guarded by Bear. In addition, he masters the art of the vicarious spirit journey by swallowing his helping spirits and then sending them out to hunt down a disease spirit or fight an enemy shaman. He is healer and diviner, and the marvelous ritual dramas of his visions were, until their destruction by Soviet authorities, at the heart of his society's social life.

Traditions die hard, however. The Hungarian horse nomads have been cut off from their own cultural area in Inner Asia for over a millennium. By the year 1000 they had been converted to Roman Catholicism, and their economy changed radically. Yet to this day they retain a clandestine shamanistic tradition, with one *táltos* (shaman) fighting the other in visionary battles, and with "women of knowledge" who are able to see the spirits of the dead.

In passing to a discussion of nomadic-pastoralist societies with important ties to agriculture, this article leaves the visionary world of the hunters entirely behind. The Nilotic Dodoth, for instance, whose women garden while the men tend the cattle—a pattern found only in Africa—have but one god. This god is so remote and vague that little is known about him. He communicates with humans by such messengers as shooting stars, and no shaman ever visits him, although his worshipers send him sacrificial oxen. The most important ritual specialist among the Dodoth is the diviner, whose oracles have a literal quality: "[Lomotin] would see it raining in a dream, then see a red ox being sacrificed and he would know, when he awoke, that the sacrifice of such an ox would bring rain. He was uncannily right" (Elizabeth Marshall Thomas, *Warrior Herdsmen,* New York, 1965, p. 173).

For the Tuareg, nomads of the Sahara and nominally Islamic, God (Allāh) is equally a distant overseer, who sends the spirits of Islamic saints as messengers, or angels, who are often identified with lightning. In a faint outline of pre-Islamic religion, Tuareg men have dealings with spirits called *kel asouf,* which attach themselves to their hair, help them divine, and are seen doing battle with each other.

The messenger complex is reminiscent of Judeo-Christian tradition, and, indeed, both Judaism and Islam have their roots in nomadic pastoralism. Angels as messengers abound in both the Hebrew scriptures and the New Testament, from the one that spoke to Hagar, the mother of Ishmael, to the heavenly host who announced the birth of Jesus and the white-haired angel wearing a golden girdle who appeared to John according to the *Book of Revelation.* Muḥammad's numerous contacts with the angel Gabriel have been mentioned before.

Spirit journeys are reported both of Moses and of Muḥammad, with the former, for instance, going up Mount Sinai and there encountering God, and the latter rising through the night, ascending to heaven, and conversing with God. Traces of these journeys are even contained in the New Testament, as in *Matthew* 4:1–3: "Then Jesus was led into the desert by the Spirit to be tempted by the devil. And he fasted forty days and forty nights and afterwards he was hungry. And the tempter came to him."

The spirit journey was later taken up by the Islamic Ṣūfī mystics. The first one of these to give a personal account of such experiences was Najm al-Dīn (c. 1145–1223), the famous mystic and teacher of the city of Khorezm, an important center of learning at the time. Among the many mystic experiences he reported are visions of Muḥammad as well as numerous spirit journeys. (See *Die fawā'ih al-ǧamāl wa fawātiḥ al-ǧalal des Naǧmuddīn al-Kubrā,* translated by Fritz Meier, Wiesbaden, 1957.) Kubrā's spirit journeys were not metaphorical but were entirely real to him. He experienced the sensations of being lifted off the ground into the air, of being borne aloft by angels, and of flying. It was not his body that flew but "he himself, his heart or holy spirit, which leaves the body through a hole on the right side, opened by the formula of contemplating God." Once in heaven, he encountered God's properties at various locations, and while passing them he incorporated them into his being. Kubrā, who traveled widely and who carried Classical Greek and medieval Christian ideas back with him to Inner Asia, no doubt also knew about the Jewish mystics of his time, such as Mosheh ben Naḥman (Nahmanides) and perhaps also of the Italian friar Francis of Assisi.

By the early thirteenth century, however, mysticism was no longer part of European popular culture but was, rather, an enterprise of the intelligentsia, who induced mystical experiences for personal enlightenment. In fact, Moses ben Naḥman was criticized for having made mysticism accessible to the masses, because it gave rise to visionaries, who supposedly were followed blindly by the credulous. Thomas Aquinas's premise that visions are a rarely occurring bridge between the human and the divine must be seen in this context. Barely two generations later, Suso warned some nuns not to attempt any mystic experiences, although he himself had extensive visions. Once, while in a faint, "it seemed to him in a vision that he was being conducted to a choir, where the mass was being sung. A large number of the heavenly host was present in that choir, sent by God, where they were to sing a sweet melody of heavenly sound. This they did, and they sang a new and joyous melody that he had never heard before, and it was so very sweet that it seemed to him that his soul would dissolve for great joy" (*Briefbüchlein,* translation by this writer). The mystics soon found themselves in opposition to orthodoxy in all three monotheistic traditions, and within the century both Franciscans and Ṣūfīs were being executed for blasphemy. The pagan traditions of popular culture, with its legends of a wild huntsman and witches' sabbaths, deteriorated without institutionalization or support from the larger society, eventually to be wiped out by the Inquisition.

Visions of agriculturalists. As humans turn to tilling ever larger open fields and to the consuming task of exerting control over their habitat, the institutionalization of the visionary experience disappears entirely, and even spontaneous occurrence is suppressed because of its perceived threat to the written tradition. It is difficult, for instance, to gain recognition for a new shrine from the Vatican authorities, because claims of "genuine" visions are rarely credited. The predominant experience in the religions of large agricultural societies, such as Chinese popular religion, Christianity, and Hinduism, is instead spirit possession.

The urban adaptation. The situation in modern urban centers is similar to that in agriculturalist religions. Large urban movements such as pentecostalism or Umbanda, an Afro-Brazilian healing cult, as well as some Japanese "new religions," rely on possession. If visions occur at all, they usually come about outside the religious context, as was the case with the near-death experiences investigated by the physician Raymond A. Moody, Jr.

In general, it seems that as human beings develop various adaptations to their habitat beyond that of hunting and gathering, the frequency and rich variety of visionary experience in their world begins to diminish. Indeed, this reduction appears to be in inverse proportion to their control over the habitat, for as control over ordinary reality increases, the grasp on the sacred dimension as it is expressed in visions starts to slip away. In the spirit journey the initiative belongs to humans; in spirit possession humans are manipulated. Institutionalization of the visionary experience causes it to dissolve even faster—in the West, ending with the mystics. Since the biological capacity described earlier remains intact, however, a resurgence of all modes of ecstasy may be seen as more leisure time becomes available in the postindustrial era. Tendencies toward such a development are evident in the countercultures of both the United States and Europe.

See Also Angels; Cargo Cults; Drums; Hierophany; Images; Psychedelic Drugs; Revelation; Shamanism; Spirit Possession.

BIBLIOGRAPHY

A well-written biography of Francis of Assisi incorporating much recent research is Adolf Holl's *The Last Christian,* translated by Peter Heinegg (Garden City, N. Y., 1980). The *Complete Works of Saint Teresa of Jesus,* 3 vols., translated and edited by E. Allison Peers (New York, 1946), contains illuminating accounts of the mystic experiences of Teresa of Ávila. In the section entitled "Interior Castle" she describes her pioneering attempt to protect her nuns from the Inquisition by pointing to illness as a possible cause for visions. Hans Peter Duerr's *Dreamtime* (Oxford, 1984), reviews the prehistory and later struggles of pagan religion in Europe that involved contact with the sacred dimension, with special regard to the role of women. The footnotes in particular contain a wealth of interesting material. An excellent study of Sufism is Annemarie Schimmel's *Mystical Dimensions of Islam* (Chapel Hill, N. C., 1975).

Carlos Castaneda's work, especially *The Teachings of Don Juan: A Yaqui Way of Knowledge* (Berkeley, Calif., 1968) and *A Separate Reality: Further Conversations with Don Juan* (New York, 1971), whether entirely reliable ethnographically or not, still represents a graphic description of the feel of altered states of consciousness. For an unimpeachably authentic view of American Indian visionary experience, *Black Elk Speaks* (1961; reprint, Lincoln, Nebr., 1979), as told by the holy man of the Oglala Lakota through John G. Neihardt, the poet laureate of Nebraska, remains unsurpassed. The anthropologist Michael Harner, in *The Way of the Shaman: A Guide to Power and Healing* (New York, 1980), provides instructions for self-experimentation on the basis of what he learned in his fieldwork with Indian societies of South America. The interest of the counterculture in such experiments is reviewed in Tom Pinkson's study *A Quest for Vision* (San Francisco, 1976). A readable collection of case histories of near-death experiences was put together by Raymond A. Moody, Jr., in *Life after Life* (New York, 1975).

New Sources

Amat, Jacqueline. *Songes et visions. L'au-delà dans la littérature latine tardive.* Paris, 1985.

Benz, Ernst. *Vision und Offenbarung. Gesammelte Swedenborg-Aufsätze.* Zürich, 1979. Vision as revelation in the experience of Swedenborg.

Casadio, Giovanni. "Patterns of Vision in Some Gnostic Tractates from Nag Hammadi." In *Actes du IVe Congrès copte, II. De la linguistique au gnosticisme,* pp. 395–401. Louvain-la-Neuve, Belgium, 1992. Including a selected bibliography on visions in Gnosticism.

Couliano, Ioan Petru, *Expériences de l'extase.* Paris, 1984. A typology of visionary experiences from Greek antiquity until Middle Ages.

Goodman, Felicitas. *Ecstasy, Ritual, and Alternate Reality.* Bloomington and Indianapolis, Ind., 1988. An theory of religion based on the study of religious trances and controlled dreams in a cross-disciplinary perspective.

Holm, Nils G. *Religious Ecstasy.* Stockholm, 1982. A collection of essays by Scandinavian scholars tackling visionary experiences in psycho-physiological research and historical case-studies from primal cultures to Book religions.

Zinser, Hartmut. "Ekstase." In *Handbuch religionswissenschaftlicher Grundbegriffe,* vol. 2, pp. 253–258. Stuttgart, 1990. Stuttgart, 1990.

Sogni, visioni e profezie nell'antico cristianesimo edited by the Institutum Patristicum augustinianum. Rome, 1989. Dreams, visions and prophecies in early Christianity and Gnosticism.

FELICITAS D. GOODMAN (1987)
Revised Bibliography

VIṢṆU. In the age of the *Ṛgveda,* India's oldest religious document (c. 1200–1000 BCE), Viṣṇu must already have been a more important divine figure than it would appear from his comparatively infrequent appearances in the texts. He is celebrated in a few hymns, of which stanzas 1.22.16–21 came to be a sort of confession of faith, especially among the Vaikhānasa Vaiṣṇavas, who adapted them for consecratory purposes and for invoking the god's presence and protection. These stanzas eulogize the essential feature of the character of the Vedic Viṣṇu: namely, his taking, from the very place where the gods promote human interests, three steps, by which he establishes the broad dimensional actuality of the earthly space in which all beings abide (see also *Ṛgveda* 1.154.1 and 3, etc.). His highest step is in the realm of heaven, beyond mortal ken. Thus, his penetration of the provinces of the universe, in accordance with the traditional Indian interpretation of the character of the original god as the representative of pervasiveness, must be considered a central feature in the vast complex of ideas for which the name of the early Viṣṇu stood.

Virāj, the idea of extending far and wide the female principle of creation and the hypostasis of the universe conceived as a whole, came to be one of Viṣṇu's epithets. Being essential to the establishment and maintenance of the cosmos and beneficial to the interests of humans and gods, his pervasiveness obtained ample room for the former and divine power for the latter. To the sacrificer, who ritually imitates Viṣṇu's three strides and so identifies with him, the god imparts the power to conquer the universe and attain "the goal, the safe foundation, the highest light" (*Śatapatha Brāhmaṇa* 1.9.3.10). Viṣṇu's pervasiveness also manifests itself in the central cosmic axis, the pillar of the universe, whose lower end is visibly represented by the post erected on the sacrificial ground. This axis reaches the earth in the center or navel of the universe, putting the cosmic levels into communication with each other; it thus provides a means of traveling to heaven as well as a canal through which heavenly blessings reach humanity. In this navel is located the sacrifice with which Viṣṇu is constantly identified.

In the *Ṛgveda* Viṣṇu is Indra's ally and intimate friend. In the later Vedic Brāhmaṇa literature, two Ṛgvedic myths connected with Viṣṇu, or with Viṣṇu and Indra, are further developed so as to become, like two other myths, the seeds of some of the god's *avatāras.* After Indra slew a boar that kept the goods of the *asuras* (antigods), Viṣṇu, (i. e., the sacrifice) carried the animal off, with the result that the gods obtained the goods of their enemies. This boar, then identified with the creator god Prajāpati, is also said to have raised up the earth (*Śatapatha Brāh.* 14.1.2.11); in course of time Viṣṇu fuses with Prajāpati, and in the *Mahābhārata* (3.142.56, Bombay ed.) it is he who saves the overcrowded earth by raising it up. The great fish (*Śatapatha Brāh.* 1.8.1) that delivers Manu, the first human, from the deluge appears later as a form of Brahma (*Mahābhārata* 3.185) and becomes in the postepic Purāṇas an *avatāra* of Viṣṇu.

A conglomeration of religious currents contributed to the development of post-Vedic Viṣṇuism. In the centuries before the beginning of the common era, Viṣṇu fused with several divine, mythical, and heroic or legendary figures. Among them are (1) the primeval cosmic man (Puruṣa), embodying the idea that creation is the self-limitation of the transcendent person (*Ṛgveda* 10.90), which became the keystone of Vaiṣṇava philosophy; (2) the creator god Prajāpati; (3) Nārāyaṇa, a divine figure featured in the narrative of three ascetics who do not succeed in beholding him because this is a privilege of those who follow the path of *bhakti* (*Mahābhārata* 12.321ff.); and (4) Kṛṣṇa, who in the *Bhagavadgītā* (*Mahābhārata* 6.23–40) teaches, in human shape, how to combine a socially normal life with a prospect of final liberation. Although the names of these figures, when borne by Viṣṇu, came to represent particular aspects of his character and activities, they often also continued to indicate the principal persons of sometimes almost independent mythical themes. This plurality of names also helped to overcome incongruities caused by the fact that Viṣṇu is both the supreme being and a deity responsible for particular duties and activities: "the only [triune] God, Janārdana [Kṛṣṇa], is called Brahmā, Viṣṇu, and Śiva, accordingly, as he creates, preserves, or brings to an end" (*Viṣṇu Purāṇa* 1.2.62).

In the epic period (c. 500 BCE–200 CE) Viṣṇu definitely assumed that aspect of the godhead that he holds up to the present day, that of preserver and protector of the world, lord and ruler of all. Yet many of his names and epithets continue to refer to character traits proper to a great god in the mythological sphere. Moreover, the deeds and characters of parochial gods, especially those of Indra, are transferred to him. Whereas in the *Ṛgveda* he is not credited with warlike activities of his own but rather assists Indra in his encounters with demons, he is already at an early date described as fighting and killing antagonists who, like Jambha, the disturber of sacrifice, were in older versions slain by Indra.

In the extensive postepic Vaiṣṇava literature many mythical episodes are inserted to show that God, when devoutly worshiped, is willing to appear in one of his forms in order to help or protect his devotees. For instance, in the story of the two demons Madhu and Kaiṭabha—who in the older version (*Mahābhārata* 3.194) intimidated Brahmā and in the later version (*Jayākhya Saṃhitā* 2.45ff.) stole the Veda so that the world fell to a bad state—the gods and demons praise Viṣṇu, who by his supernormal knowledge restores the Veda and who, after a battle of many thousands of years, kills the demons with a body consisting of *mantras* that represent his *śakti* (superempirical creative power). From this story originates his epithet *Madhusūdana,* or "destroyer of Madhu."

Viṣṇu is usually depicted as a four-armed, dark blue young man bearing in his hands a conch (an auspicious object that represents fertility and is supposed to strengthen the divine powers), a discus (his invincible flaming weapon), a mace, and a lotus (which, rising from the depths of the waters, evidences their life-supporting power). He wears the miraculous jewel Kaustubha (which emerged from the churning of the ocean). The characteristic curl of hair on his chest is called the *śrīvatsa* ("favorite of the goddess Śrī"), and characterizes him as the universal sovereign. These mythological attributes are often used as aids to devotion. The mere presence of Viṣṇu riding the eagle Garuḍa, the theriomorphic manifestation of his nature and energy, suffices, in myth, literature, and plastic arts, to subdue the demoniac serpents.

In the post-Vedic period Viṣṇu's consort is known by two names, *Śrī* and *Lakṣmī;* originally these were two different goddesses, the former representing fortune and prosperity, the latter being closely connected with the ripe corn. Like Viṣṇu, Śrī-Lakṣmī is eternal and omnipresent. Associated in every possible way with the lotus symbol, she is said to have risen from the ocean to preside over earthly welfare. It is with the Goddess in such form that Viṣṇu is united in all of his incarnations: He, "the husband of Śrī," is the creator; she, creation; she is the earth, he, its support; he is one with all male beings, she, with all female beings; and so on. In mythical imagery, Lakṣmī never leaves Viṣṇu's side. In later Hinduism, she is, as Viṣṇu's *śakti,* the instrumental and material cause of the universe, God himself being the efficient cause. Indissolubly associated with each other, they constitute the personal *brahman,* also called Lakṣmī-Nārāyaṇa. Nevertheless, they are distinct: She alone acts, but everything she does is the expression of his wishes. Lakṣmī also makes an appearance in various mythical stories under different names (Mahālakṣmī, Bhadrakali, etc.). Many of these denote special aspects of Prosperity (Śrī-Lakṣmī); some appear, as companions of Viṣṇu, as the goddesses Victory (Jayā), Renown (Kīrti), and so on. While his alliance with his second consort, Bhūdevī, the Earth, stamps him as a bigamist, Viṣṇu's relations with many incarnations of his spouse are often characterized by youthful passion, reckless adventure, and human—often too human—emotions. He ravishes Rukmiṇī—even though she has been intended for Śiśupāla, whom he beheads—and marries her (*Mahābhārata* 2.37ff.); soon she is said to be an incarnation of Śrī, destined to marry Viṣṇu-Kṛṣṇa (*Harivaṃṣa* 104ff).

In his supreme and at the same time triune character, Viṣṇu, the Lord and highest Person, the unmanifest primordial principle, absorbs the universe at the end of a *yuga* (age of the world) by successively becoming the glowing sun, the scorching wind, and a torrential rain (*Matsya Purāṇa* 1.67).

When the world has again become the undifferentiated water from which it once arose, Viṣṇu—according to some, together with Lakṣmī—sleeps on a thousand-headed serpent called Śeṣa, "the remainder" (because it represents the residue that remained after the universe and all its beings had been shaped out of the cosmic waters of the abyss), or Ananta, "the endless one" (who, symbolizing eternity, is identical with the ocean out of which the world will evolve as temporal existence and ultimately also with Viṣṇu himself). With the serpent and the ocean upon which this animal floats, Viṣṇu then constitutes the triune manifestation of the single divine cosmic substance and energy underlying all forms of phenomenal existence. During his sleep the world is "thought," nonexistent. When he awakes, he engages in meditation for its recreation. A lotus grows from his navel, and on this flower is born the demiurge Brahmā, who creates the world. Then, while residing in the highest heaven (Vaikuṇṭha), Viṣṇu in the form of Puruṣa preserves the world until it is once again ripe for dissolution.

The development of many myths and mythical narratives attests to Viṣṇu's adaptability and versatility. For instance, the older sources (*Mahābhārata* 1.16ff.) state only that Viṣṇu-Nārāyaṇa advised the gods and the *asuras* to churn the ocean in order to acquire from it *amṛta;* then, in the form of an anonymous woman, he recovered this drink of continued life from the *asuras*. Later versions relate his appearance as a fascinating young woman, Mohinī ("the deluding one"), tricking the *asuras* and distributing the *amṛta* among the gods.

In innumerable tales attesting to the popular belief in Viṣṇu's intervention in the vicissitudes of individual lives, the mythical element is no less mixed up with legend than in the many hagiographic compilations, which, like devotional literature in general, reactivate the power inherent in the mythical stories. Invocation of the god's protection is therefore often accompanied by a reference to one of his great exploits or important mythical aspects. Thus Kṛṣṇa-Viṣṇu, who made the gods happy by slaying Kaṃsa (*Mahābhārata* 2.13.29ff.), will no doubt prove a competent and reliable helper. Hearing the holy story of the *Rāmāyaṇa*—the heroic deeds of Viṣṇu descending to the earth to save humankind—is said to be a dependable way to long life, moral purity, and good fortune (*Rāmāyaṇa* 7, final chap.).

Synthesizing its theology, philosophy, mythology, and religious practice, Vaiṣṇavism distinguishes five forms of God:

(1) God in his transcendent form with the six attributes: omniscience, activity based on independent lordship, ability, force, virtue combined with energy, and brilliant self-sufficiency.

(2) The *avatāras*, in which God sends forth his Self to save the *dharma* (order, stability) and humankind and to protect the good and destroy the wicked, evidencing his providential concern with humanity as a whole. However full of the wonderful and miraculous, the *avatāra* myths represent Viṣṇu as an essentially human character whose actions are within the limits of human understanding.

(3) The emanations (*vyūha*) of his power, namely, Vāsudeva (Kṛṣṇa), Saṃkarṣaṇa, Pradyumna, and Aniruddha (Kṛṣṇa's brother, son, and grandson), which, like the *avatāras*, represent an attempt at maintaining a fundamental monotheistic principle while incorporating manifestations of his being. This is also an attempt to harmonize theology with mythology and philosophy, for by assigning to these figures functions in a systematic explanation of the universe, theologians can account for Viṣṇu's part in its creation, preservation, and absorption.

(4) The immanent God, the inner ruler.

(5) The *Mūrti* (image or statue), God's most concrete form.

SEE ALSO Avatāra; Bhagavadgītā; Goddess Worship, article on The Hindu Goddess; Indian Religions, article on Mythic Themes; Kṛṣṇa; Mahābhārata; Mūrti; Prajāpati; Vaikhānasas; Vaiṣṇavism.

BIBLIOGRAPHY

Bhattacharji, Sukumari. *Indian Theogony: A Comparative Study of Indian Mythology from the Vedas to the Purāṇas.* New York, 1970.

Gonda, Jan. *Aspects of Early Viṣṇuism.* Utrecht, 1954.

Gonda, Jan. *Die Religionen Indiens.* 2 vols. Stuttgart, 1960–1963. Volume 1 has been issued in a second revised edition (Stuttgart, 1978).

Gonda, Jan. *Viṣṇuism and Sivaism: A Comparison.* London, 1970.

Gonda, Jan. *Medieval Religious Literature in Sanskrit.* In *A History of Indian Literature,* vol. 1, fasc. 1. Wiesbaden, 1977.

Singer, Milton, ed. *Krishna: Myths, Rites, and Attitudes.* Honolulu, 1966.

Zimmer, Heinrich. *Myths and Symbols in Indian Art and Civilization* (1946). Edited by Joseph Campbell. Reprint, Princeton, N. J., 1972.

New Sources

Gupta, Shakti M. *Vishnu and His Incarnations.* Bombay, 1993.

Patel, Sushil Kumar. *Hinduism in India: A Study of Visnu Worship.* Delhi, 1992.

Pattanaik, Devdutt. *Vishnu: An Introduction.* Mumbai, 1999.

JAN GONDA (1987)
Revised Bibliography

VISUAL CULTURE AND RELIGION

This entry consists of the following articles:

VISUAL CULTURE AND RELIGION: AN OVERVIEW

If the word *culture,* as Raymond Williams once pointed out (Williams, 1976, p. 76), is among the most complicated words in the English language, what can anyone hope to achieve by clapping the word *visual* in front of it? Not surprisingly, the use of the term *visual culture* among scholars of art, film, and media is quite varied. For many it simply refers to forms of imagery beyond the pale of traditional fine art, such as film, mass-produced prints, and advertisements. For others the term signifies something procedural: the method of study or the set of questions and themes that occupy a particular body of scholarship. For yet others the term marks a significant turn in the practice of art history, which involves pedagogical as well as political commitments that depart from traditional art historical practice. No discipline takes images with the single-minded seriousness of art history, and because art historians have been prominent in debating the use of the term, a review of developments in that discipline is a helpful way of approaching the definition of visual culture. From there it will be possible to consider the implications of visual culture for the study of religion.

VISUAL CULTURE AND ART HISTORY. The rise of interest in popular culture, film, women's studies, ethnicity and race, and sexuality challenged the dominance of traditional scholarship in the humanities, which was historically invested in the canon of fine art and literature. For a long time art historical interpretation had also avoided political interpretation of images and had largely ignored contemporary imagery, especially mass-produced imagery, because it lacked the craftsmanship of fine art. Nor did it accommodate the categories of genius, professional artist, and masterpiece or the criteria of museum value that dominated the discipline and its canon of fine art. But during the 1960s and 1970s art historians and art critics who were engaged by contemporary art's disavowal of traditional tastes or the celebration of political critiques of established authority in cultural and social affairs became interested in issues of reproduction, the conceptualization of viewing as a social and psychological act, and the ways of seeing that shaped the meaning of images. The social history of art sought to situate works of art within the ideological constructions of class and gender that were inseparable from any act of representation.

By the 1980s a rising tide of scholarship in art history had begun to explore canon formation, gender, sexuality, and the art of marginalized cultures, races, and ethnicities. A "crisis in the discipline" was discussed in professional forums, and the first instances appeared of what came to be known as the "new art history" (Rees and Borzello, 1988). Of special importance was the application of deconstruction, semiotics, and psychoanalytic theory (of greatest influence were the writings of Jacques Derrida, Roland Barthes, and Jacques Lacan). Practitioners of the new art history were intrigued by the visual construction of power relations, which they conceptualized as the "gaze," the visual field that evaluates space and object as intelligible forms.

Work in the 1980s and 1990s also explored the nature of representation, often in connection with the discussion of postmodernism and inspired by the oracular writing of Jean Baudrillard. A number of important studies during this time complemented the social history of art with greater attention to audience and reception, finding an important connection to the interest in the gaze and the visual construction of reality. At issue was the status of art history, the authority of its claims, its autonomy from the prevailing interests of the elite that controlled cultural institutions, as well as a host of questions about the nature of representation.

The reflection on ideology, the nature of vision, the gendered gaze, and the constructedness of representation led some art historians to greater awareness of the audience and its role in the interpretation of art. Prominent theoretical studies in the sociology of art assisted art historians along this line of thinking. Anthropological studies have produced ethnographies of image users. David Freedberg's *The Power of Images* (1989) problematized for art historians the capacity of images to incite fear and desire among viewers, for whom the appeal of images was not a matter of taste or connoisseurship but their ability to act upon people, other images, or the viewer's own desires and anxieties. Freedberg's book and several other studies in the next years helped art historians redefine the scope of art history. The study of response (Freedberg, 1989; Elkins, 2001) and reception (Heinich, 1996; Doss, 1999) decentered the traditional focus of the discipline as the discourse on images to a discourse on the use and conceptualization of images.

The 1990s and early 2000s witnessed a surfeit of publications under the new rubric of "visual culture" (Evans and Hall, 1999; Sturcken and Cartwright, 2001; Bryson, Holly, and Moxey, 1994; Mirzoeff, 2002). Generally speaking, scholars have made use of the term to designate the subject of their interpretation as well as the method or interpretive framework on which they have relied. But the definition of visual culture (not to mention its value) remains contested ("Visual Culture Questionnaire," 1996). Perhaps the most common meaning of the term is the most simple and least helpful: visual culture is whatever traditional art history does not do—film, advertisements, cartoons, tattoos. Another approach improves modestly on that one: visual culture is any treatment of imagery or of viewing imagery that is especially mindful of such concepts as the gaze, gendered practice of viewing, postmodern accounts of representation, and so forth. A third, common definition identifies visual culture as distinctly modern, as the product of modernity or postmodernity, as the hypervisual world of simulacra and mass-produced images whose principal purpose is propaganda for state and commerce, which, in radical political economy, are regarded as the same thing. Such a view ignores the ancient power of images in human culture and assumes a presentist perspective and one that tends strongly to reduce images to a means of persuasion. Those who criticize visual culture as an approach to studying imagery argue that the term is incapable of clear definition and is inclined to level artistic quality in a reading of images that regards distinction as unacceptable because it is elitist ("Visual Culture Questionnaire," 1996).

Defining Visual Culture. None of the definitions listed above is strongly compelling. And none of them offers much of substance to the study of religion. Indeed religion plays no role whatsoever in the great majority of visual culture studies cited above. Art historians who identify their work as the study of visual culture have largely concentrated on revisionist analyses of major works of art, the visual construction of gender, the cultural politics of imagery, and the dynamics of the gaze. All of these are quite applicable to the study of religious visual culture, but because many art historians assume that post-Enlightenment modernity is characterized by secularization, religion is considered vestigial and reactionary and therefore uninteresting. By contrast, the following definition of visual culture seeks to offer a way of interpreting images that will contribute to the understanding of religion. Given the dominance of art history as a discipline in the discussion over the last two decades of the twentieth century, the definition of visual culture outlined here is grounded in the development of art history. Defining the term turns on differentiating studies according to the object of their scrutiny.

As it was practiced for much of the twentieth century, art history focused on considerations of style, subject matter, patronage, and the meanings to be derived from these coordinates. Such an approach privileges the visual object—the painting or sculpture—as the principal concern, as the object of explanation. Iconography and stylistic analysis are the primary tools of this approach and serve well to scrutinize the work of art as a highly intentional object, one bearing the intent of the artist, the impress of the artist's visual tradition, and the aims and preferences of the patron, whether prince, collector, church, or state. This manner of analysis preserves the artist as a genius, a skilled maker who endows the work with a supreme intention, a meaning to be excavated by the art historian and matched to the material evidence of the image as the definitive meaning of the work.

Skill at formal analysis, detailed knowledge of the history of style and iconography, facility with the vast tools at the art historian's disposal for such research—iconographical indexes and lexicons, archival collections, museum holdings—form the skills base for competence in this line of inquiry. Art historians proceed by comparing one image under question with the preceding history of visual types in order to determine the relatively unique treatment of the image, positing that every change in its presentation of its subject corresponds to a particular intention of the image maker. The artist's monograph, one of the standard productions of art history in the twentieth century, develops a narrative of artistic production along the biographical lines of the artist's life. Juvenilia, professional formation, early work, mature work, and late productions, analyzed largely in terms of style and subject matter, are the familiar categories of this genre of art historical inquiry. The aim is a definitive edition of the artist's "oeuvre." In any genre of art historical inquiry that focuses on the image, stylistic features of the image are customarily considered to be freighted with intent: style is a kind of signature, the imprimatur of the image maker as well as the visual preference of the image's patron and its primary audience, those who bring to it a visual literacy that maker and patron can presume. With these assumptions and techniques, art historians are able to produce highly detailed analyses of objects, sorting out their histories, makers, and the genres of meaning that proceed from object-centered analysis and interpretation.

Another approach privileges ideas over the object. This approach might be called the intellectual history of art, or the history of ideas about art, or the history of art theory and aesthetics. Whatever one prefers to call it, this avenue of inquiry makes important contributions to the understanding of taste, evaluation, and the interpretation of art. In sum it seeks to delineate the theory of images that informs a particular philosophy, theology, culture, historical moment, or taste. The theory-centered approach may not tell in as detailed a fashion as stylistic or iconographic study why an image looks the way it does, but the intellectual history of art has much to offer regarding why art was valued or not at a particular time, how it was justified or criticized, and how it was interpreted. When conducted by skilled interpreters, this approach enhances studies of art objects by scrutinizing the intellectual schemes that deployed various iconographies, preferred certain styles, interpreted them in a certain manner, and offered rationales for the importance and use of art in the contemporary culture. The intellectual history of art can have everything to do with the history of patronage and the formation of subcultures for whom artistic taste and literacy were definitive. Moreover the history of great interpreters of art—from philosophers like G. W. F. Hegel or Arthur Schopenhauer to important theorists such as Charles Baudelaire or Walter Benjamin—is a special topic of study among intellectual historians of art.

A third approach to the study of the visual arts may be called institution-centered because it scrutinizes the social formations of patronage, art instruction, art criticism, and the many organizations that sponsor and regulate the production and presentation of art, including guilds, museums, galleries, exhibitions, collectors, dealers, and artists' societies. Art historians and sociologists of art study the ways in which these institutions exert an influence over the training and career of artists as well as the public display of art and the evolution of taste.

Finally, the approach defined here as visual culture takes yet another form. Although it makes important use of and relies on object-centered and theory-centered studies of imagery, the visual culture approach focuses primarily on visual practices, that is, the things people do with images. A practice-centered approach scrutinizes the social siting of images, the rituals that engage them, behaviors and attitudes toward images, all manner of use, such as devotion and healing, and the power of images as protective devices. Questions of central interest include the migration of images, how they are displayed or hidden from view, the trade or traffic in images, and their hoarding, destruction, and exchange. These queries explore the range of visual practices that help build, maintain, and transform the lifeworlds of those who use them.

Scholars of visual culture are also interested in the ways of seeing that inform images and their reception. Vision is not a passive operation but a creative and constructive one. Seeing orders the world and imposes structures and expectations upon human experience. This is evident in the widely varying systems of composing the visual field in images. Linear perspective, the system privileged in the West since the Italian Renaissance but continually modified and subverted by artists ever since, remains one important perceptual scheme, but one whose artifice and historicity become clear when compared to other models from different parts of the world and different historical epochs.

Methodologically the study of religious visual culture will make use of those procedures that examine the object (iconography, stylistic analysis, archeological analysis) as well as those methods that scrutinize the image's cultural or social function and its reception, including ethnography and sociological methods, such as sample surveys. Scholars of visual culture require the skills of visual analysis practiced by art historians as well as facility with the intellectual history of art and visual theory. Each of those approaches provides necessary interpretive practices to the visual cultural approach because a visual practice presumes a particular theory of the power or efficacy of images and puts an image to work in part because of its appearance and material presence. Examples include Allen F. Roberts and Mary Nooter Roberts (2003); Erika Doss (1999); David Morgan (1998); Donald J. Cosentino (1995); and Sally M. Promey (1993).

The Interpretation of Religious Visual Culture. What does the application of this definition of visual culture do for the study of religion? Religion is often defined as a system of beliefs or organized propositions to which believers assent. But this manner of describing religion reduces it to an intellectual dimension of human experience, ignoring the embodied, lived aspects that are much more characteristic of the experience of religion reported by or observed among practitioners. Scholars of religion engaged by the material culture of belief have made this case (McDannell, 1995; Kieschnick, 2003) and have sought to show that objects of everyday use and commercial nature play an important role in the practice of religion. Inexpensive, common objects, such as devotional pictures, commemorative statuary, prayer beads, wall hangings, and photographs of saints or loved ones, participate fundamentally in rituals of memory, devotion, and the formation and instruction of the young.

An important way of understanding religious objects and images is grasping their social or communal function (Morgan and Promey, 2001, pp. 1–17; Huyler, 1999; Tanabe, 1998; Eck, 1981, pp. 33–43). Another way is narrating their stories, as objects, in the ongoing history of a community or place (Davis, 1997). Still other scholars focus on the community's circulation or traffic of images (Roberts and Nooter Roberts, 2003; Cosentino, 1995) or the importance of cult or devotional images in the public performance of identity (Dean, 1999; Phillips, 1995) or in an extended community or loosely identified cohort, such as admirers of Elvis Presley (Doss, 1999). In every such case the image is not an end in itself but part of a larger fabric of social life. The scholar examines the image as a totem or joint property or shared emblem or ritual artifact or commodity—that is, as part of a social practice. The object of interpretation is not so much an image as the act of using an image, what may be called a visual practice. The image itself is incomplete without its ritual context or practice. Not only is this the case with the need to consecrate images such as statues or icons of Buddha (Kieschnick, 2003, p. 60; Freedberg, 1989, p. 82), but as far as explanation is concerned, the image's meaning is not to be limited to the image itself, such as its style or subject matter.

Because an image gains significance in its circulation, exchange, veneration, and narration, those must each be studied in order to understand the image in situ. And an image's meaning is never fixed or complete but forever undergoing mutation and stratification, as the meandering narratives that Richard Davis relates in his 1997 study of the "lives" of Hindu statuary. Sculptures of Hindu deities were consecrated after having been fashioned, then installed in temples, where they might become well known for their power to act on behalf of petitioners. When Muslims invaded the subcontinent, priests tried to anticipate the destruction of the cult statuary by removing it from the temple, deconsecrating it, and burying it. Sometimes the statues were forgotten where they lay until their rediscovery, when a new chapter in their lives would begin with reconsecration and reinstallation in a temple or, during the British Empire period, their appropriation by the colonial force and exhibition in museums or palaces as ethnographic objects or as trophies. Images created to illustrate an early book on Hindu myth and culture by a British missionary (Ward, 1817–1820) circulated in Europe and the United States, serving as one of the earliest visualizations of Hindu deities. Such images illustrated the Protestant imagination of "pagan idolatry," which was rudimentary to the Protestant understanding of mission. It is important to understand images in a robust way, as sustaining many, often staunchly rival, cultural perspectives. Images, in other words, are the lens through which cultures perceive one another.

Images are actually deposits, pastiches, thickly sedimented repositories of previous lives consisting of fragments of memory that are made to adhere to one another. This allows them to be forms of resistance as well as subordination. The story of Our Lady of Guadalupe illustrates this dynamic of imagery. One account written over one hundred years after the apparition was said to have taken place (1531) was produced, according to one scholarly authority, by a Mexican Creole, Miguel Sánchez, whose purpose was to advocate the propriety of *criollismo,* those born in Mexico of Spanish-born parents. An alternative account, the *Nican mopohua,* written at the same time, portrayed the Virgin's revelation as directed to the indigenous population (Poole, 1995, p. 126). Modern advocates of liberation theology and Chicano and neo-Aztec identities have seen Guadalupe as yet another kind of symbol and have relied on the *Nican mopohua* (Brading, 2001, pp. 342–360).

Not only are images historical pastiches, they also frequently integrate other forms of representation. Word and image, for examples, can be made to cooperate in powerful ways in order to avoid proscriptions against imagery that are sometimes enforced by religious traditions that consider the written or spoken word to be the privileged medium of divine revelation and authority. Such traditions include Sikhism, Islam, Judaism, and certain versions of Protestant Christianity, such as Puritanism and other Calvinist sects. As anxious as each of these traditions may profess to be regarding the inappropriateness of visual imagery, each contains abundant examples of devotional and instructional uses of imagery. Recalling the contribution of Islam to their spirituality, Sikhs, for instance, stress the importance of avoiding imagery in worship. Yet images of the gurus and Sikh history abound in temples and in private homes. Among the most interesting figures in the tradition, the man who is portrayed more than any other Sikh, is Gurū Nānak, the founder of the faith and an immensely charismatic leader and teacher, who is shown emanating an aura, his eyelids half closed, his large eyes focused on the blissful state of his soul (Brown, 1999). The image models the visual presence or demeanor of peace that Sikhs recognize in those who have achieved spiritual wisdom. One image of Nānak consists of the text of one of his writings contained in the *Gurū Granth Sāhib,* the collection of hymns and verse that form the central document and authority of the faith. Nānak is his word, his wisdom is manifest in his visual appearance. The intermingling of word and image stresses this unity and both enforces and obviates the injunction against imagery in worship: one sees Nānak and his wisdom, but one sees his word, which one is not allowed to confuse with an image and thereby lose sight of the true goal of the spiritual life (Singh, 1990, p. 12).

The capacity of images to embody teachers, prophets, saints, or deities goes to the heart of the power of images in religious life. Relics and icons are among the most universal features in world religions. In many Buddhist traditions, for example, relics of the Buddha and paintings and sculptures of him form the core practices of devotion among both elite and popular Buddhists. Images are able to incite and direct devotion precisely because they take the place of the holy one, inviting the believer's physical acts of veneration or adoration, which are relayed through the image to the person. Mahāyāna Buddhism has a long tradition of regarding the Buddha's sūtras as his embodiment (Tanabe, 1988). Orthodox and Catholic Christians revere different versions of the image of Christ imprinted miraculously on a veil or burial cloth. Relics are considered especially powerful sacred points where petitions can secure blessing. In such instances images participate in a metaphysical economy of dispensing merit accrued by saints or deities whose good works and holiness are a kind of spiritual capital that can be accessed through the veneration of imagery. In the case of Buddhist visual piety, a common practice among Southeast Asian Theravāda Buddhists is the ritual application of gold leaf to statues of the Buddha. This act is accompanied with prayers for blessing and karmic merit. Children accompany their parents and grandparents on these occasions and are taught the practice.

In addition to encouraging the cultivation of devotional relationships with the saint or deity, images are able to prompt and guide memory as well as creative thought or association. Used on such ritual occasions as marriage, baptism, and rites of passage, images mark the occasion and then commemorate it by virtue of domestic or public display thereafter. Images are also commonly exchanged or given as gifts on these occasions, signifying important relationships and status within family, clan, or community. If they serve to shape and secure memory and therefore operate as conservative devices, images can act as generative engines of creative or figurative thinking. Tarot cards are a good example of this, as are maṇḍalas in meditative visualization. On these occasions, images invite associative processes of thinking that are virtually unlimited. Images such as those on tarot cards provoke association and suggest narratives. Because they literally assert nothing, images invite interpretation. Their ambivalence urges a proliferation of conjecture and association. The result in the case of visual imagery, as well as in literary imagery in such apocalyptic literature as the *Book of Revelation* or the figurative language in such sacred poetry as the *Psalms* or allegory as in the *Song of Songs,* is an open-ended generation of interpretive possibilities. The text or image can be made to mean virtually anything, allowing a fit to be tailored to any occasion or situation. Images and texts like this offer powerful creative resources to religious traditions. It is evident in traditions as diverse as various astrologies or the Yi Jing's system of divination or the Hasidic practice of numerology in which the numeric value of scriptural words discloses deeper levels of meaning. Many religious traditions, or popular subcultures within them, practice sortilege, the apparently random selection of a passage in a book such as the Bible or the Qur'ān, which is then read as an oracle speaking to the person who selected it. In every case chance is incorporated into a material practice that reduces open-ended possibility into a suggestive prompt. Chance is transformed into a revelatory process.

CHALLENGES TO THE STUDY OF RELIGIOUS VISUAL CULTURE. The place of images in religious study is fascinating in part because of the flurry of misconceptions associated with images, many of which hinge on the idea that images mark an inferior religion or an inferior subculture within a religion. The study of religion is often hampered by prevailing notions like this, which garner an appearance of authority but are often ideological mirages, conjured to serve particular interests. For instance, it is a commonplace that Islam, Judaism, and Protestantism do not engage in religious uses of images. Another such commonplace is that religions that do employ images do so only at the level of popular piety. The "higher" forms of Buddhism, Hinduism, and Christianity are sometimes said to eschew any role for imagery. Misleading claims like these need to be traced to their sources in order to recognize the cultural work they are intended to perform. All of these assertions originate in polemic: Protestant polemic against Catholicism; an academic elite's polemic against popular, devotional religion; a Buddhist elite's polemic against popular practice; the polemic of the Brahmanic revival against Hindu "polytheism," and so forth. Any study of the visual culture of religion must anticipate this especially tenacious feature of scholarly and theological discourse. Moreover one does well to avoid the art historian's tendency to focus exclusively on objects and the religion scholar's traditional emphasis on doctrine, philosophy, or theology. The aim inspiring the study of the visual culture of religion is deeper understanding of the lifeworlds that religious peoples construct and sustain in their visual practices and in the aesthetic imagination that envisions their worlds or those they seek to create.

SEE ALSO Art and Religion; Iconography; Icons; Idolatry; Images; Media and Religion; Popular Culture.

BIBLIOGRAPHY

Brading, D. A. *Mexican Phoenix: Our Lady of Guadalupe, Image and Tradition across Five Centuries.* Cambridge, U.K., 2001.

Brown, Kerry, ed. *Sikh Art and Literature.* London, 1999.

Bryson, Norman, Michael Ann Holly, and Keith Moxey, eds. *Visual Culture: Images and Interpretations.* Hanover, N.H., 1994.

Cosentino, Donald J., ed. *Sacred Arts of Haitian Voudou.* Los Angeles, 1995.

Davis, Richard H. *Lives of Indian Images.* Princeton, N.J., 1997.

Dean, Carolyn. *Inka Bodies and the Body of Christ: Corpus Christi in Colonial Cusco, Peru.* Durham, N.C., 1999.

Doss, Erika. *Elvis Culture: Fans, Faith, and Image.* Lawrence, Kans., 1999.

Eck, Diana L. *Darśan: Seeing the Divine Image in India.* Chambersburg, Pa., 1981.

Elkins, James. *Pictures and Tears: A History of People Who Have Cried in Front of Paintings.* New York, 2001.

Evans, Jessica, and Stuart Hall, eds. *Visual Culture: The Reader.* London, 1999.

Freedberg, David. *The Power of Images: Studies in the History and Theory of Response.* Chicago, 1989.

Heinich, Nathalie. *The Glory of Van Gogh: An Anthropology of Admiration.* Translated by Paul Leduc Browne. Princeton, N.J., 1996.

Huyler, Stephen P. *Meeting God: Elements of Hindu Devotion.* New Haven, Conn., 1999.

Kieschnick, John. *The Impact of Buddhism on Chinese Material Culture.* Princeton, N.J., 2003.

McDannell, Colleen. *Material Christianity: Religion and Popular Culture in America.* New Haven, Conn., 1995.

Mirzoeff, Nicholas, ed. *The Visual Culture Reader.* 2d ed. London, 2002.

Mitchell, W. J. T. *Iconology: Image, Text, Ideology.* Chicago, 1986.

Morgan, David. *Visual Piety: A History and Theory of Popular Religious Images.* Berkeley, Calif., 1998.

Morgan, David, and Sally M. Promey, eds. *The Visual Culture of American Religions.* Berkeley, Calif., 2001.

Phillips, Ruth B. *Representing Women: Sande Masquerades of the Mende of Sierra Leone.* Los Angeles, 1995.

Poole, Stafford. *Our Lady of Guadalupe: The Origins and Sources of a Mexican National Symbol, 1531–1797.* Tucson, Ariz., 1995.

Promey, Sally M. *Spiritual Spectacles: Vision and Image in Mid-Nineteenth-Century Shakerism.* Bloomington, Ind., 1993.

Rees, A. L., and Frances Borzello, eds. *The New Art History.* Atlantic Highlands, N.J., 1988.

Roberts, Allen F., and Mary Nooter Roberts. *A Saint in the City: Sufi Arts of Urban Senegal.* Los Angeles, 2003.

Singh, Santokh, trans. *Nitnaym Baanees, Daily Sikh Prayers.* Princeton, Ontario, Canada, 1990.

Sturcken, Marita, and Lisa Cartwright. *Practices of Looking: An Introduction to Visual Culture.* Oxford, U.K., 2001.

Tanabe, Willa J. *Paintings of the Lotus Sutra.* New York, 1988.

"Visual Culture Questionnaire." *October* 77 (Summer 1996): 25–70.

Ward, William. *A View of the History, Literature, and Religion of the Hindoos: Including a Minute Description of Their Manners and Customs, and Translations from Their Principal Works.* 4 vols. London, 1817–1820.

Williams, Raymond. *Keywords: A Vocabulary of Culture and Society.* New York, 1976.

DAVID MORGAN (2005)

VISUAL CULTURE AND RELIGION: OUTSIDER ART

One of the defining characteristics of the emergent academic field of visual culture studies is its insistence on a methodological principle of complete inclusion. Everything within the realm of visual objects and practices is worthy of consideration—especially imagery traditionally neglected or felt to be outside the purview of "classical," "fine," "canonical," or "high art." Those who are concerned about all that has been ignored and devalued in the domain of image making have a special affinity for the maverick and controversial movement called contemporary folk, grassroots, self-taught, vernacular, or outsider art. Outsider art has no easily definable stylistic tradition or distinct movement in the conventional art history sense but instead refers to a loose grouping of persons, practices, and attitudes distinguished primarily by their peripheral relationship to elite culture and the mainstream art world. This marginality is largely determined by various psychological (e.g., psychosis, mental-physical disability, or visionary experience) and sociological (ethnic-racial, demographic, economic, class, age, or educational) factors. This unruly field is rambunctious, resisting any consistent definition or nomenclature, a situation that has given rise to an almost incessant and, at times, tedious, "term warfare."

The current vogue for the terminology of "outsider art" in the English-speaking world originates from the title of the British scholar Roger Cardinal's 1972 book, which roughly translated the expression *Art Brut.* Art Brut was first used by the French avant-garde artist and cultural critic Jean Dubuffet (1901–1985) (Danchin, 2001). For Dubuffet, Art Brut was art that expressed raw creativity and imagery supposedly uncontaminated by bourgeois culture—an art perhaps best found within mental wards. Cardinal and others expanded on Dubuffet by using the "outsider" terminology in neoromantic ways that eventually embraced a motley assortment of artists and practices. In addition to psychotic, mediumistic, spiritualist, and children's art, outsider art—especially in North America—came to include naive, folk, tramp, African American, prison, Hispanic American, vodou, tattoo, yard, and circus artwork done by persons often self-taught in the use of artistic methods and materials. The unfettered creativity, obsessive drive, and apparent primitivity of this kind of art are striking. Equally important, however, are the connections with religious experience and practice as seen by the prominence of nonordinary states of consciousness and different kinds of visionary experience, the use of conventional and unconventional religious imagery, and the drive to construct alternative and often strange paradisial worlds (Beardsley, 1995).

Outsider art may at times draw upon bits and pieces of the history of mainstream art, but rarely is it self-consciously ironic or concerned with the kind of referential "originality" associated with academic art making (Russell, 2001; DeCarlo, 2002). It is an art that has its own ambiguous inner intentions and private passions. In this sense, outsider artists often strive to communicate something deeply personal, hidden, unseen, or repressed about this and other worlds. There is almost always something more than just "art as art" going on. Moreover, this obsessively intense "something more" often takes various stylistic forms and quirky contents that may be most meaningfully called "visionary," "spiritual," "ecstatic," "revelatory," or "religious." The increasing popularity of outsider art in Europe and the United States during the last twenty years or so of the twentieth century appears in fact to be rooted in an almost quasi-religious "quest for authenticity" or "nostalgia for paradise" among a secularized middle-class audience of enthusiasts, collectors, and dealers. Artist and audience in the outsider field often seem similarly driven by unconscious, and sometimes conscious, motivations that are broadly religious and redemptive (Fine, 2004).

History of the Self-Taught and Outsider Field of Art. The diverse history of the self-taught and outsider field is yet to be written (Rhodes, 2000; Hartigan, 1991; Peiry, 2001; Russell, 2001). Aside from some very general associations with shamanistic phenomena, human eccentricity, psychosis, and compulsive image making, the origins of this movement in Western tradition go back to the discovery of primitive culture, art, and religion (in both a tribal and orientalist sense) by the newly conceived human sciences toward the end of the nineteenth century (e.g., psychology and psychiatry, comparative religions, anthropology, folklore studies, and critical-historical disciplines such as art history). The impact and influence of primitivism as both a disturbing and a liberating break with classical traditions established in the Renaissance and the eighteenth century were profound in many different cultural domains at the beginning of the twentieth century. Primitivism was therefore a formative factor in the development of modern art, as seen in the concerns and methods of individual artists, such as Paul Gauguin, Henri Rousseau, Pablo Picasso, and Paul Klee. At the same time, there were clear connections between primitivism and the Dada and surrealist movements (Rhodes, 1994). These associations, as well as the affinity with what would be called outsider art, is seen in surrealism's passionate interest in a primal creativity rooted in the unconscious mind, in occult or "automatic" forms of religious experience and behavior, and in various disruptive and unconventional artistic practices.

The other major influence on the genre of outsider art was the identification of so-called "psychotic art" after the cataclysm of World War I (MacGregor, 1989). Several groundbreaking psychological studies appeared at this time, the most important of which was *The Artistry of the Mentally Ill (Bildnerei der Geisteskranken),* written in 1922 by the German psychiatrist Hans Prinzhorn (1886–1933). Prinzhorn focused his attention on the artistic productions of schizophrenics and spent considerable time developing an elaborate expressionist theory of image making that tried to identify a set of basic artistic impulses. Another highly influential German psychotherapeutic study was Walter Morgenthaler's (1882–1965) *A Mentally Ill Person as Artist (Ein Geisteskranker als Künstler),* published in 1921. This work concentrated on the brilliantly obsessive drawings by the Swiss mental patient Adolf Wölfli (1882–1965), now recognized as one of the grand European masters of the outsider tradition of art.

Dubuffet said that he happened to see a copy of Prinzhorn's book and was haunted by the images. This epiphany eventually led to Dubuffet's dramatic declaration of Art Brut in the 1940s—a theretofore unrecognized tradition of artistic production in which creativity and image making were theoretically free from the asphyxiating influences of elite culture (Peiry, 2001). Dubuffet's definition of Art Brut was initially associated with the art of the mentally ill as witnessed by Prinzhorn and Morgenthaler, but over the years his understanding of the field wavered between dogmatic rigidity and inclusive flexibility—as, for example, seen in the supplemental category of *Neuve Invention* (Fresh Invention), intended to include artists less radically cut off from mainstream cultural tradition. The Art Brut tradition—and its institutional embodiment in the Collection De L'Art Brut in Lausanne, Switzerland—continues as an increasingly conspicuous aspect of the European art scene.

Self-taught or outsider art in the United States gradually came into prominence from the 1970s through the 1990s in association with various artistic movements and eclectic interests. Perhaps the most important of these movements was the changing nature of what was originally called "folk art," rural traditions that were becoming more individualistic, eccentric, and aesthetic in their methods and subject matter. These transformations within the realm of contemporary folk art were already evident in early exhibitions of naive and primitive folk art in the 1940s and 1950s (Janis, 1999) and then even more significantly in the later work of rural craftspeople, such as the Kentucky wood-carver Edgar Tolson (1904–1984) (Ardery, 1998). Another important trend emerged from the maverick interests and curatorial philosophy of Herbert Hemphill (1900–1900) at the new Museum of American Folk Art in New York City (Hemphill and Weissman, 1974; Hartigan, 1991). Hemphill boldly stretched the parameters of folk art to include, within the jumbled cultural situation of the last quarter of the twentieth century, all manner of strange and forlorn artistic production.

In the 1980s several innovative art dealers on the margins of the mainstream New York art world, most notably Phyllis Kind, who was originally based in Chicago, daringly started to exhibit European Art Brut along with various homegrown talent. These exhibits included such artists as the Chicago Imagists; newly discovered psychotic masters, such as Martin Ramirez (1895–1963) and Henry Darger (1892–1973); and a number of so-called "contemporary folk artists" from the American South, such as the amazingly prolific, self-taught visionary preacher-painter Howard Finster (1916–2001). During this same period, there was also an increasing awareness of numerous environmental works by compulsive creators around the world (e.g., Ferdinand Cheval [1879–1912] in France, Simon Rodia [c. 1879–1965] in North America, and Nek Chan in India) and, ever since the groundbreaking show in 1982, Black Folk Art at the Corcoran Gallery in Washington, D.C., an increasing recognition of the rich tradition of self-taught African American artists (e.g., Bill Traylor [1854–1947], Sam Doyle [1905–1986], Jimmy Lee Sudduth, Thornton Dial, Mose Tolliver, Purvis Young, Charlie Lucas, Gregory Warmack or Mr. Imagination, and Lonnie Holley).

By the early 1990s these movements had awkwardly coalesced into the field called self-taught/vernacular/outsider art. During the late 1990s and after the beginning of the twenty-first century, there has been an increased outpouring of exhibitions, catalogs, articles, and books. These developments were mirrored by a growing number of organizations, journals, and cultural institutions—including the emergence of a lively but sporadic secondary market of auctions and trade fairs (Maizels, 2002). Unfortunately most of the published discourse about self-taught and outsider art has been largely within the popular genre of pretty picture books replete with potted anecdotal biographies of the artists. There is still very little serious commentary on self-taught and outsider art, especially from multidisciplinary and cross-cultural perspectives that comparatively and critically analyze the artists and artworks with an eye to artistic quality, cultural embeddedness, and historical significance. The field of self-taught and outsider art also raises many interesting but largely unexplored questions about the nature of intense visionary experience, psychosis, and artistic creativity as related to religious traditions, such as shamanism, mysticism, and other forms of ecstatic cult practice.

Self-Taught and Outsider Art and Religion. Self-taught and outsider art frequently expresses specific religious belief systems by using traditional, eclectic, hybrid, or even wildly strange imagery. Examples from the spectrum of religious iconography and intention are seen in the mostly conventional Protestant evangelical apocalypticism of Myrtice West's paintings, which are based on the *Book of Revelation,* the idiosyncratic religious allusions in Saint OEM's art (Eddie Owen Martin, 1908–1986), the pop cultural appropriations in Howard Finster's scrappy "messages" from God and Elvis, and the dark distortions of Roman Catholic themes in Henry Darger's illustrations of cosmic conflict involving "little girls with penises." Outsider art's early association with madness, ecstatic experience, spiritualism, mediumship, conspiratorial occultism, and syncretistic religion also indicates that there are many connections with, to borrow from William James, the "varieties of religious experience"—that is, states of extraordinary and visionary consciousness, obsessive practice, and unusual imagery on the margins of mainstream or organized religious traditions. Witness, among many possible examples, the detailed divine cosmology constructed by Wölfli, the "Bible code" imagery seen in Norbert Kox's work, or the architectural spiritualism pervading Achilles Rizzoli's (1896–1981) meticulous drawings. Another very evocative but controversial, example of these associations is the apparent allusion to various "Africanisms" or fragmented or creolized aspects of traditional African religious forms seen in African American art (Thompson, 1984). Finally, self-taught and outsider art involves specific stylistic features (such as a penchant for compositional *horror vacui* [the avoidance of empty space], a juxtaposition of image and word, an emphasis on sign as subject, and thematic repetition), the use of cast off or recycled materials, and a tendency to construct monumental assemblages and environmental works that often have religious and visionary significance.

Even more provocative than these associations with conventional and unconventional forms of religion are the suggestions in outsider art of deeper links between religious and aesthetic experience. Most broadly, art and religion deal with imaginative creations that are felt or sensed to surpass (emotionally, spiritually, essentially, or aesthetically) the merely material or rational. The underlying conviction for both is that there is some experienced dimension of meaning, sacredness, power, sublimity, or beauty in or beyond the surface of things. Art and religion—and in a heightened way, outsider art and visionary experience—are therefore overlapping interpretive categories that partially name or define certain important aspects of human experience, expression, and practice in both a quotidian and extraordinary sense. To some extent it seems that all religious behavior originally draws on visionary experience and involves aesthetically expressive practices of making invisible spirit or meaning visual and therefore memorable and real in persons, things, and actions. Indeed effective religion is (perhaps) always artistic in its expressive ways and ritual means, whereas the most powerful art (perhaps) always manifests some real ecstatic motivation and performative intensity. One should look then to what is artistic in religious practice and to what is experientially and practically religious in art. Both art and religion involve the basic everyday human drive for order. Both refer to the possibility of feeling "in place" and seeing "something more" within and behind the changing surface of things (something unexpected, something strange, something special, something sacred). And it is this kind of creative "meaning making" that is related to the imaginative "world building" or "making special" aspects of religion and art (Dissanayake, 1992; Morgan, 1998).

Significantly the special synergy of artistic and religious experience and expression seems particularly vivid within the field of self-taught and outsider art. Whereas most people are relatively content to live within the fractured and often depressing worlds given to them, outsider artists, who in their art compulsively–ecstatically construct new self-identities and elaborate artistic environments, are those few brave, tormented, and virtuosic souls who are driven to transgress the confining boundaries of all conventional worlds. Their special romantic, nostalgic, or primitive appeal is that they are primordial creators, inventors, or world makers in a rough and unexpected sense. These marginalized and often psychologically wounded artist-healers can be metaphorically placed in a lineage embracing the Paleolithic shaman, tribal blacksmith, trickster-fool, medieval mystic, Renaissance magus, and romantic artist. All have that conjoined religious and artistic ability to make their visions real and therapeutic for others.

BIBLIOGRAPHY

Ardery, Julia S. *The Temptation: Edgar Tolson and the Genesis of Twentieth-Century Folk Art.* Chapel Hill, N.C., 1998. Provocative sociocultural analysis of the transformation of folk art.

Beardsley, John. *Gardens of Revelation: Environments by Visionary Artists.* New York, 1995. Insightful and gracefully written study of outsider environments.

Cardinal, Roger. *Outsider Art.* New York, 1972. Foundational work.

Danchin, Laurent. *Jean Dubuffet.* Paris, 2001. Helpful overview of Dubuffet's life and work.

DeCarlo, Tessa. "Outsider Biographies vs. Outsider Art." *Raw Vision* 41 (Winter 2002): 22–27. Interesting attempt to distinguish outsider art from mainstream tradition.

Dissanayake, Ellen. *Homo Aestheticus: Where Art Comes from and Why.* New York, 1992. Pioneering study of the origins of art as related to ritual tradition.

Fine, Gary. *Everyday Genius: Self-Taught Art and the Politics of Representation.* Chicago, 2004. Important sociological analysis of the outsider art world.

Hemphill, Herbert W., and Julia Weissman. *Twentieth-Century American Folk Art and Artists.* New York, 1974. Foundational book in the emergence of the outsider field.

Hartigan, Lynda Roscoe. *Made with Passion.* Washington, D.C., 1991. Good source of information on Herbert Hemphill and his influence.

Janis, Sidney. *They Taught Themselves: American Primitive Painters of the 20th Century* (1942). New York, 1999. Influential work on American naive artists.

MacGregor, John. *The Discovery of the Art of the Insane.* Princeton, N.J., 1989. Scholarly history and analysis of the tradition associated with the art of the mentally ill.

Maizels, John, ed. *Raw Vision Outsider Art Sourcebook.* Radlett, U.K., 2002. Overview of the state of the field by the leading outsider journal.

Morgan, David. *Visual Piety, a History and Theory of Popular Religious Images.* Berkeley, Calif., 1998. See page xv. Groundbreaking study of religion and art as related to American Protestant tradition.

Peiry, Lucienne. *Art Brut: The Origins of Outsider Art.* Paris, 2001. Accessible and knowledgeable discussion of the European tradition.

Rhodes, Colin. *Primitivism and Modern Art.* New York, 1994. Broad survey study of the influence of primitivism.

Rhodes, Colin. *Outsider Art: Spontaneous Alternatives.* New York, 2000. Excellent introduction to the field with special emphasis on the European tradition.

Russell, Charles, ed. *Self-Taught Art: The Culture and Aesthetics of American Vernacular Art.* Jackson, Miss., 2001. Collection of important articles on aesthetic theory as related to outsider tradition.

Thompson, Robert Farris. *Flash of the Spirit.* New York, 1984. Influential study of the African religious roots of African American vernacular art and tradition.

NORMAN J. GIRARDOT (2005)

VISUALIZATION SEE BUDDHISM, SHOOLS OF; DAOISM; MEDITATION

VITAL, ḤAYYIM (1543–1620), noted Jewish mystic. Ḥayyim Vital was born in Safad, the Galilean town north of Tiberias that was the site of an important renaissance of Jewish mystical activity in the sixteenth century. His teacher in rabbinic subjects was Mosheh Alshekh, who ordained him as a rabbi in 1590. In 1564 he became a student of Mosheh Cordovero, the most important teacher of Qabbalah (Jewish mysticism) in Safad before the arrival of Isaac Luria. When Luria came to Safad in 1570, Vital became his chief disciple, the role for which he is best known.

Following Luria's death two years later, Vital was one of several disciples who assembled a written version of the master's teachings, since Luria himself had recorded almost nothing on his own. Vital's corpus, the *Shemonah she'arim* (Eight gates), is the most detailed version and the main one in which Lurianic teachings were circulated widely from about the year 1660. During his lifetime Vital sought to guard Luria's teachings jealously and to assume authority as the sole legitimate interpreter of his master's ideas. Thus in 1575 he secured the pledge of twelve of Luria's former disciples to study Lurianic teachings only with him, as well as a promise not to reveal more of Luria's doctrines than Vital wished. Such tactics were rooted partly in Vital's conviction that he alone was capable of explaining Luria's work, as well as in personal rivalries among Luria's disciples. In any case, this study fellowship lasted only a short time, for in 1577 Vital moved to Jerusalem where he served as a teacher and head of a school. In later years he lived again in Safad and in Damascus, where he died in 1620.

Besides his work as a teacher of Lurianic ideas and practices, Ḥayyim Vital composed a number of qabbalistic treatises on his own. He wrote a commentary to the *Zohar,* the classical text of thirteenth-century Qabbalah, based upon the teachings of Mosheh Cordovero, to which he subsequently added notes in accordance with Luria's ideas. An interesting and important treatise intended to appeal to a wide audience is Vital's *Sha'arei qedushah* (The gates of holiness). This book presents Vital's cosmological and anthropological views, culminating in an account of the process by which an individual might achieve a state of prophetic illumination. An adept, according to Vital's four-part program, must repent for all sins, meticulously observe all religious obligations, practice acts of purification such as ritual baths and the wearing of clean clothes, and enter into a state of perfect silence and solitude. Following these preparatory exercises the soul begins an ascent to its personal source in the divine realm as the adept meditates upon the ten *sefirot,* the divine qualities of personality that characterize the qabbalistic system. Successful contemplation results in various experiences of mystical inspiration, including having a revelation of the prophet Elijah.

Vital also composed a diary, *Sefer ha-ḥezyonot* (Book of visions), which reveals his interest in all manner of magic and esoterica. Here Vital discloses his youthful enthusiasm for alchemy, which he later lamented, as well as his habit of visiting fortune-tellers and magicians in order to learn about the past history of his soul and promises for the future. *Sefer ha-ḥezyonot* also records his rich dream life, in which Vital communicates with various teachers and sages.

BIBLIOGRAPHY

The biographical details of Ḥayyim Vital's activities are found in Gershom Scholem's *Kabbalah* (Jerusalem, 1974), pp. 443–448, and Scholem's *Major Trends in Jewish Mysticism* (1941; reprint, New York, 1961), pp. 254ff. Vital's theory of prophetic illumination, as presented in his book *The Gates of Holiness,* is detailed in R. J. Zwi Werblowsky's *Joseph Karo* (London, 1962), pp. 65ff. An interesting technique of contemplation that Vital taught is examined in my article "Recitation of *Mishnah* as a Vehicle for Mystical Inspiration: A Contemplative Technique Taught by Ḥayyim Vital," *Revue des études juives* 141 (January–June 1982): 183–199. For a study of the religious climate in which Vital worked, see my book *Safed Spirituality: Rules of Mystical Piety; The Beginning of Wisdom* (New York, 1984).

New Sources

Bos, Gerrit. "Hayyim Vital's 'Practical Kabbalah and Alchemy': A 17th Century Book of Secrets." *JJTP* 4 (1994): 55–112.

Faierstein, Morris Moshe. "Rêves et dissonance dans le 'Livre des visions' de Hayyim Vital." *Cahiers du Judaïsme* 13 (2003): 32–40.

Wexelman, David M. *The Jewish Concept of Reincarnation and Creation: Based on the Writings of Rabbi Chaim Vital.* Northvale, N.J., 1999.

LAWRENCE FINE (1987)
Revised Bibliography

VIVEKANANDA was the religious name of Narendranath Datta, or Dutt (1863–1902), a leading spokesman for modern Hinduism and neo-Vedānta in the late nineteenth century, and the founder of the Ramakrishna Mission in India and the Vedanta Society in the West.

LIFE. Narendranath came from a Bengali family, *kāyastha* by caste, that since the early nineteenth century had improved its social status through the process of westernization. Narendranath's great-grandfather had clerked for an English attorney in Calcutta, while his grandfather took the vow of *saṃnyāsa* (renunciation) and abandoned his family shortly after the birth of his son, Vishwanath, who would be Narendranath's father. Vishwanath became a prosperous lawyer in the Calcutta High Court. The Datta home was a cosmopolitan one, in which the worlds of Bengali Hinduism and Indo-Muslim culture merged with European learning. Vishwanath knew Sanskrit and Arabic, enjoyed the poems of Ḥāfiẓ, and read the Bible and Qur'ān for pleasure. Narendranath received schooling in both Bengali and English, eventually earning his bachelor's degree in 1884. Narendranath had a prodigious intellect; he loved to read, ranging over Sanskrit texts, English literature, philosophy, and history. His reading in the cultures of ancient Egypt, Rome, the Muslim world, and modern Europe all provided insights into the trajectory of Indian history and contributed to his understanding of the relationship between East and West. Later in life he would elaborate these conclusions in a well-known Bengali work, *Prācya o pāścātya* (East and West).

During his college years, Narendranath belonged to the Brāhmo Samāj, a reformist movement begun in 1828 by Rammohan Roy (1772–1833) that promoted a vision of Hindu monotheism and rejected such practices as image worship and renunciation. Narendranath approved of the Brāhmos' rationalism and concern for social service, but he could not accept their repudiation of *saṃnyāsa,* a path for which he—like his grandfather—felt some affinity. In the 1870s the Brāhmos found themselves torn between the relative importance of social reform, emphasized by Sivnath Sastri (1847–1919), and devotional worship, promoted by Keshab Chandra Sen (1838–1884). While Narendranath shared Sivnath's goals, he also found himself drawn to Keshab's eclectic spiritual vision. After 1875 Keshab began visiting a little-known holy man named Ramakrishna (1834/6–1886), a celibate devotee of the goddess Kālī, a man unlearned in a formal sense but wise in religious experience. Narendranath first met Ramakrishna in 1881. Although impressed by the depth of Ramakrishna's renunciation and spiritual attainments, he was disturbed by Ramakrishna's image-oriented worship of Kālī and his apparent lack of social concern. While Narendranath believed in the formlessness of God, Ramakrishna urged him to meet God in person by worshiping Kālī.

Official accounts say that at their first meeting Ramakrishna took Narendranath aside and said to him, "Lord, I know you are that ancient sage, Nara, the Incarnation of Narayana, born on earth to remove the miseries of mankind." Narendranath was reportedly "altogether taken aback" by this and concluded that Ramakrishna was a madman (*Life,* 1989, vol. 1, p. 76). At the same time, Narendranath was captivated by Ramakrishna; here was a man who claimed to have seen God and who spoke of religion as something real to be experienced directly. Nevertheless, such mystic talk was far removed from the safety of Narendranath's rationalism.

Unable fully to come to terms with Ramakrishna's views, Narendranath withdrew periodically during his college years to immerse himself in Western philosophy and science, as well as in Indian music, for he excelled as a singer. Narendranath's singing affected Ramakrishna deeply, and he pursued Narendranath as someone who had the potential for spiritual greatness.

In 1884, Keshab died; two months later, Narendranath's father died. Keshab's death meant his followers were deprived of the spiritual charisma that united them, while the death of Vishwanath plunged Narendranath's family into financial ruin. Narendranath, at twenty-one, had to abandon his plans to go to England to study law. There were lawsuits within the family over property. In such a context, the loss of two father-figures plunged Vivekananda into the depths of spiritual uncertainty. In 1885 he accepted Ramakrishna as his *guru* and began a period of intensive religious training that lasted until Ramakrishna's death in August 1886. During the intervening months, Ramakrishna brought Narendranath to a personal experience of Kālī that he considered his pupil's final test.

The origins of the Ramakrishna Mission lie in the final months of Ramakrishna's life, when he nurtured Narendranath's spiritual development and prepared for his own death. Ramakrishna asked Narendranath to look after the welfare of the disciples, but left no explicit instructions beyond saying, "Keep my boys together" and "Teach them" (Williams, 1989, p. 325). Official accounts report that just before his death Ramakrishna transferred his spiritual powers to Narendranath, saying, "by the force of the power transmitted by me, great things will be done by you" (*Life,* 1989, vol. 1, p. 182). With his passing, Narendranath was left to make sense of the powerful mystical experiences induced by his master and to ensure that the other disciples lived up to the master's ideal of renunciation. The precise date for the emergence of the monastic movement differs "according to the perspective of the chroniclers" (Pangborn, 1976, p. 98). Some choose the day in January 1886 when Ramakrishna distributed ochre robes to the disciples; some choose Christmas eve of that year, when Narendranath led the disciples in a vigil of renunciation around a bonfire; others emphasize the day in January 1887 when the disciples held a fire ceremony at which they adopted monastic names, prefixed by the title *swami* (Skt., *svāmī,* "master"). Narendranath would initially be known as Swami Vividishananda, though this would change.

Narendranath taught the disciples as best he could for several years, yet he remained uncertain of his own religious views. In 1890 he set off from Calcutta with nothing but a staff and begging bowl on an extended pilgrimage throughout India, during which he attempted to reconcile the philosophical and devotional insights of Ramakrishna with the social concerns of the Brāhmo movement. Internally, he sought realization of the absolute; externally, he sought knowledge of India and the world. This search would eventually take him far beyond India, though India remained the focus of his patriotic spiritual vision. When he heard that a World's Parliament of Religions was to be held in Chicago in the autumn of 1893, Narendranath conceived a plan to seek Western material support for the revitalization of Hinduism and in return to share Hindu spiritual insights with the world. He obtained travel funds from the *māharājā* of Khetri, who suggested he adopt the religious name *Vivekananda* (Skt., "he whose bliss lies in discerning knowledge"). With his patron's support and a new monastic name, he left for the United States.

Although Vivekananda was not the only Hindu representative at the World's Parliament of Religions in Chicago, he was the most dynamic. In contrast to the learned dissertations by other Hindu speakers, Vivekananda gave a powerful argument for the universal truth of Hinduism, which he claimed was grounded in experience, not dogma. "The Hindu religion does not consist in. . .attempts to believe a certain doctrine. . .but in realizing," he claimed (*Complete Works*, 1964, vol. 1, p. 7). His lectures brought him widespread attention in the press and numerous speaking engagements. Having attracted a dedicated group of Western followers, he shifted his plans from raising money for India to creating a worldwide religious movement based on the eternal truths of Hinduism. With that purpose, and with his new Western disciples as the core, he founded the Vedanta Society in New York in 1895. He soon had chapters in London and Boston, for which he summoned two swamis from India to help direct their work. The mission to the West was well under way by the end of 1896 when Vivekananda left for India to begin the second phase of his program.

Vivekananda's arrival in India early in 1897 with a group of Western disciples was treated by the Indian press as a triumphal return, but not all Hindus were happy with his aggressive proselytizing of Westerners or with his unorthodox ideas. Ramakrishna's former disciples, whom Narendranath had left seven years earlier, were themselves uncertain how to respond to Narendranath-turned-Vivekananda and his Western disciples. They were even more uncertain when Vivekananda revealed his plan to turn them into a band of modern *saṃnyāsins* dedicated to social service (*sevā*), a plan he claimed Ramakrishna had intended.

Vivekananda's dynamism and persuasive powers carried the day; the disciples were won over to his program of *sevā*. To implement this program, Vivekananda instituted the Ramakrishna Mission on May 1, 1897, organizing the monks in a new Ramakrishna Math (Skt., *maṭha*, "monastery"). In 1898, with money from Western disciples, he purchased a site on the Ganges near Calcutta for a center to house what would become the Ramakrishna Math and Mission. The worldwide organization was established by 1899, at which point Vivekananda turned over the active work of the movement to his Indian and Western disciples. After visiting friends in the United States and Europe from 1899 to 1900, Vivekananda returned to India in semiretirement. He died on July 4, 1902.

TEACHINGS. In less than forty years of life, and in less than ten years of intensive effort, Vivekananda redefined India's relationship to the West, prescribing Hindu spirituality as the antidote to Western materialism. Vivekananda's teaching was not the Hinduism of the orthodox, nor was it the reformed monotheism of the Brāhmos. In its eclectic universalism it shares much with Keshab Chandra Sen's spirituality, yet its spiritual fountainhead lay in the mystic insights of Ramakrishna.

Vivekananda taught the virtues of what he called "Practical Vedānta," a universal Hinduism that combined practical work for the world with the quest for ultimate union with the One. Put simply, Practical Vedānta teaches that while humans may proclaim *śivo'ham*, "I am God," this very insight also obliges them to acknowledge the truth of *daridra nārāyaṇa*, "God dwells within the poor." Thus, nondual insight provides an ethical imperative for social service. With fiery rhetoric, Vivekananda exhorted listeners to "Arise, awake, and stop not till the desired end is reached" (*Complete Works*, 1964, vol. 3, p. 318). He called upon his followers to promulgate a manly religion that would have the energy and courage to overcome India's discriminatory caste practices and interreligious strife. Such would be true service to Ramakrishna's Divine Mother as embodied in India herself.

By adopting Vedānta as the essence of Hindu spirituality, Vivekananda built upon a revalorization of Vedānta that had begun with Rammohan Roy and the Brāhmo movement. However, Vivekananda's neo-Vedānta combines Brāhmo worldliness with the mysticism of Ramakrishna, which Vivekananda understood in terms of the classical system of nondual philosophy known as Advaita Vedānta. Scholars debate whether Ramakrishna viewed himself as a Vedāntin; the case can be made that his nondualism was more Tantric than Vedāntic. What is clear is that Vivekananda's Practical Vedānta represents a creative transformation of Ramakrishna's teaching. Some argue that the officially sanctioned neo-Vedānta of the Ramakrishna movement reflects the impact upon Vivekananda of Western reconstructions of Advaita Vedānta as found in influential writers like Arthur Schopenhauer and Paul Deussen. Others view Vivekananda's concern with social service as a result of his exposure to Christianity and modern Western thought as a young man. The influence of Brāhmo thought must also be acknowledged. Clearly the genesis of Vivekananda's teaching lies in a context of cultural change in which competing Hindu philosophies like Vedānta and Tantra were actively converging with Western norms of egalitarianism, positivism, and rationality, as well as with Orientalist constructions of Hinduism and Indian culture more broadly.

LEGACY. Vivekananda's teaching of the universal truths of Hinduism and his example of a selfless love for the Indian people had an immense impact on modern Hindu discourse and apologetics in the early twentieth century, gaining appreciation and reinforcement from figures like Mohandas Gandhi (1869–1948) and Sarvepalli Radhakrishnan (1888–1975). One of his greatest legacies may be seen in the place accorded to religious experience (*anubhava*) within modern Hindu thought. As we have seen, to Vivekananda, experience was the source of truth, not books or dogmas; "until your religion makes you realize God, it is useless" (*Complete Works*, 1964, vol. 1, p. 326). For Vivekananda, it was Hinduism's genius to have discovered the deepest truths of yogic experience through the teachings of Vedānta. In Radhakrishnan and other early twentieth-century Hindu apologists, this neo-Vedānta appeal to experience would be elevated to the very core of religion itself, providing colonized Hindus with a powerful strategy for responding to Western, Christian denunciations of Hinduism. Indeed, the neo-Vedānta evocation of India's spiritual wisdom became something of a spiritual rallying cry for nationalist mobilization.

Recognizing the degree to which the Indian nationalist movement came to be couched in Hindu idioms, scholars have raised questions regarding Vivekananda's responsibility for the subsequent development of more aggressive forms of Hindu chauvinism and for the increased polarization of Hindus and Muslims. The question is both legitimate and complex. On the one hand, Vivekananda's Vedāntic universalism does carry an implicit claim for the superiority of Hinduism; on the other, he regularly praised the spiritual ideals of Islam, the possibilities for Hindu-Muslim cooperation, and the need for religious tolerance more broadly. If Vivekananda's name and message are occasionally used to promote the idea that India is a Hindu nation, this is perhaps a case of unintended consequences, a reminder us of the complex dynamics of religion and politics in the colonial and postcolonial context.

In a similar fashion, feminist scholarship has encouraged the exploration of issues of gender, power, and identity as these are manifested in the life and teachings of Vivekananda and the Ramakrishna movement. Himself a spiritual seeker drawn to a celibate *guru* with a visceral fear of women and heterosexual contact, Narendranath toured the West as the dynamic and alluring Vivekananda, whose colorful silk robes and turbans captivated women in audiences from Boston to Pasadena. Indeed, he attracted a number of devoted women disciples in the West, such as Christine Greenstidel, Marie Louise, and Margaret Noble. Noble, who adopted the name Sister Nivedita, was very close to Vivekananda, traveling extensively with him in India and participating in his broader attempt to Indianize the notion of womanhood in the service of mother India. Such relationships, when set over against Vivekananda's rhetoric of masculinity, provide fruitful ground for exploring the gendering of nationalist projects, as well as the limitations imposed on women agents by this very process. As with Vedānta and Hinduism, the legacy of Vivekananda with respect to issues of gender and Indian identity is a complex and fascinating one.

See Also Brāhmo Samāj; Ramakrishna; Saṃnyāsa.

Bibliography

Details of Vivekananda's life and career were compiled in two volumes by his followers as *The Life of Swami Vivekananda, by His Eastern and Western Disciples,* 6th ed. (Calcutta, 1989). Older biographical studies by disciples and enthusiasts include Swami Nikhilananda, *Vivekananda: A Biography* (New York, 1953) and Romain Rolland, *The Life of Vivekananda and the Universal Gospel,* 6th ed. (Calcutta, 1965). Amiya P. Sen provides a brief, unannotated biography in *Swami Vivekananda* (New Delhi, 2000), while Rajagopal Chattopadhyaya scrutinizes received accounts in *Swami Vivekananda in India: A Corrective Biography* (Delhi, 1999). For a critical interpretation, see Narasingha P. Sil, *Swami Vivekananda: A Reassessment* (Selinsgrove, Pa., 1997). These may be compared with Tapan Raychaudhuri's sketch of Vivekananda in *Europe Reconsidered: Perceptions of the West in Nineteenth-Century Bengal* (New Delhi, 1988). Early scholarly studies of Vivekananda's career and philosophy include George M. Williams, *The Quest for Meaning of Svami Vivekananda* (Chico, Calif., 1974) and, "Svami Vivekananda: Archetypal Hero or Doubting Saint?" in *Religion in Modern India,* edited by Robert D. Baird, 2d rev. ed. (New Delhi, 1989), pp. 313–342. The essays in *Swami Vivekananda and the Modernization of Hinduism,* edited by William Radice (New Delhi, 1998), explore Vivekananda against the backdrop of education and socioreligious reform, while Gwilym Beckerlegge, *The Ramakrishna Mission: The Making of a Modern Hindu Movement* (New York, 2000) provides perspectives on several critical issues. Vivekananda's relationship to the broader Ramakrishna Mission received early attention in Cyrus Pangborn, "The Ramakrishna Math and Mission: A Case Study of a Revitalization Movement," in *Hinduism: New Essays in the History of Religions,* edited by Bardwell L. Smith (Leiden, 1976), pp. 98–119. In the wake of postcolonial studies, the question of Vivekananda's relationship to Indian nationalism, communal politics, and Hindu universalism has been revisited by Shamita Basu in *Religious Revivalism as Nationalist Discourse: Swami Vivekananda and New Hinduism in Nineteenth-Century Bengal* (New Delhi, 2002) and Brian A. Hatcher in *Eclecticism and Modern Hindu Discourse* (New York, 1999). For Sister Nivedita's view of Vivekananda, see her *The Master as I Saw Him* (Calcutta, 1910), while issues of gender are explored in Indira Chowdhury, *The Frail Hero and Virile History: Gender and the Politics of Culture in Colonial Bengal* (New Delhi, 1998); Parama Roy, *Indian Traffic: Identities in Question in Colonial and Postcolonial India* (Berkeley, 1998); and Kumari Jayawardena, *The White Woman's Other Burden* (New York, 1995). For Vivekananda's writings, the standard source is *The Complete Works of Swami Vivekananda,* 8 vols., 14th ed. (Calcutta, 1964). Vivekananda's scriptural hermeneutics are investigated in Anantanand Rambachan, *The Limits of Scripture: Vivekananda's Reinterpretation of the Vedas* (Honolulu, 1994).

Thomas J. Hopkins (1987)
Brian A. Hatcher (2005)

VLADIMIR I (d. 1015), founder and saint of the Russian Orthodox church. Vladimir (Volodimir, Valdimar?; meaning "he who rules the world") was the Varangian, or Scandinavian, prince of Kiev who established Christianity in the lands of Rus' and is thereby recognized as the founder of the Russian (and Ukrainian) Orthodox church. According to the legends recorded in the Russian *Primary Chronicle* (c. 1111), Vladimir, in his search for a religion for his pagan people, was courted by Latin Christians from the West as well as Jewish Khazars and Muslim Bulgars. He chose Greek Christianity when, the chronicle declares, his ambassadors reported to him after visiting the Cathedral of the Holy Wisdom (Hagia Sophia) in Constantinople: "We knew not whether we were in heaven or on earth. For on earth there is no such splendor or such beauty. . . . We cannot forget that beauty" (quoted in Dvornik, 1956, p. 205).

Vladimir married the Byzantine princess Anna and was baptized, with the Byzantine emperor as his godfather, by the bishop of the Greek city of Kherson, whose clergy came, at Vladimir's command, to christen the Kievan peoples in the Dnieper River in the year 988. Vladimir was partly motivated in his choice of religions by the political, military, and economic advantages of an alignment with the Byzantines, and he is also considered to have been influenced by the baptism of his grandmother Olga, who had become Kiev's ruler in 945 upon the death of her husband, Igor. Olga was a committed Greek Christian baptized in 957, perhaps in Constantinople with the empress Helen as her godmother.

Russian legends magnify the radical change in Vladimir after his conversion and the establishment of Christianity in Kiev, both in the prince's personal life and in his public policies. He is said to have abolished torture and the practice of capital punishment, an unheard-of action for his time and one allegedly opposed by the Greek bishops. He also gave up his five wives and hundreds of concubines (the *Primary Chronicle* speaks of eight hundred) in favor of monogamous fidelity to his Christian bride. He publicly desecrated statues to Perun and the other local gods and constructed a new cathedral for his Christian bishop. He also introduced the use of the Slavonic language into church worship, using the literary language developed a century earlier by the Greek missionary brother-saints, Cyril and Methodius, for their Slavic converts in Moravia and Bulgaria. The introduction of this language is considered to be the single most important factor in guaranteeing the Christian unity and development of the various peoples under his rule.

Vladimir was succeeded by his son Iaroslav the Wise (1036–1054) after a bloody war between Vladimir's sons from 1015 to 1036, during which his son Sviatopolk, who was ultimately defeated by Iaroslav, killed two other younger sons, Boris and Gleb. Boris and Gleb, who, in order to save the lives of their followers, refused to enter into battle against Sviatopolk, became the first canonized saints of the Russian church, known in tradition as the "passion-bearers." Vladimir, with his grandmother Olga, is a canonized saint of the Russian Orthodox church with the liturgical title of "equal to the apostles" because of his role in Christian conversion.

Bibliography

The Russian *Primary Chronicle* contains the story of the reign of Vladimir and the beginnings of Christianity in "the land of Rus'." The Laurentian text has been translated by Samul Hazzard Cross and Olgerd P. Sherbowitz-Wetzor as the Medieval Academy of America's Publication no. 60 (Cambridge, Mass., 1953). A critical study of Vladimir's time focusing on the conversion of the Kievan peoples is provided in Nicolas de Baumgarten's *Saint Vladimir et la conversion de la Russie* (Rome, 1932). This work contains 310 bibliographical items. A general study of the period is given in Francis Dvornik's *The Slavs: Their Early History and Civilization* (Boston, 1956). This work contains an extensive bibliography.

Thomas Hopko (1987)

VOCATION

VOCATION is a divine call or election, of a revelatory character, addressed to religiously gifted or charismatic personalities. It forms the first phase of their initiation into an often unwillingly accepted intermediary function between human society and the sacred world. Unlike functionaries with a special, well-defined religious task in a given group or culture (such as priests or even heads of families and elderly men, who bring offerings and give religious instruction), vocation is often felt by persons outside or on the fringe of the established institutions, whose charismatic and often abnormal psychic character makes them appear as prophets, founders or reformers of religion, saints, or shamans. Those called, therefore, often make their appearance in periods of social turmoil or crisis. Sometimes they start a new religious movement that implies a break with the past, or else they exorcise illness, famine, or drought, which destabilize personal or social health.

Vocation is experienced as divine revelation through various media (voices, visions, and dreams, exceptional accidents, severe illness, absentmindedness or insanity, and attacks of epilepsy), and it is sometimes accompanied by special cosmic phenomena such as a solar eclipse, an earthquake, or lightning. It usually provides the persons "called," often after initial resistance and unwillingness, with special knowledge and missionary zeal for the rest of their lives.

A true prophet was the Iranian Zarathushtra (Zoroaster), who probably lived at the beginning of the first millennium BCE and was called by his god, Ahura Mazda, to preach the coming of his reign. Zarathushtra's prophecy is characterized by an intimate personal relationship with his god and a highly moral and intellectual tone. It was Zarathushtra "who first thought the good, spoke the good and did the good, . . . the first revealer" (*Yashts* 13.88). Although of a wealthy aristocratic family, his vocation brought him into poverty, permanent conflict with the established priesthood, and even exile.

Further important material is provided by the reports on the vocation of the prophets of Israel and other chosen persons, as told by themselves or contained in the historical books of the Hebrew Bible. The prophet Isaiah tells about his vocation which took place in a vision in which he heard the voice of the Lord:

> In the year that King Uzziah died I saw also the Lord sitting upon a throne, high and lifted up, and his train filled the temple. Above it stood the seraphim, . . . and one cried to another and said, Holy, holy, holy is the Lord of hosts. . . . Then said I, Woe is me! for I am undone; because I am a man of unclean lips. . . . Also I heard the voice of the Lord, saying, Whom shall we send, and who will go for us? Then said I, Here am I, send me. (*Is.* 6:1–8)

Seeing visions, hearing voices, and being filled with a divine spirit are the most frequent media through which the prophets of Israel received their vocation to preach the word and will of their God, whose appearance often has ecstatic character. Their activities are sometimes accompanied by miracles, as in the story of Elijah and the priests of Baal (*1 Kgs.* 18), where Elijah brings down the fire of the Lord from heaven and performs the role of rainmaker, bringing a period of serious drought to its end. Like most of the other prophets of Israel, Elijah was in strong opposition to the religious establishment and practices of his time.

In the New Testament, Jesus' baptism in the river Jordan, during which he saw the heavens open, the Spirit descending like a dove upon him, and a voice from heaven saying: "Thou art my beloved Son, in whom I am well pleased" (*Mk.* 1:9–11 and parallels), is a traditional vocation with the fixed elements of a vision, the Spirit, and a voice immediately followed by the temptation in the wilderness, which forms Jesus' initiation into his public role, again in opposition to the Jewish establishment of his days. The persecutor Saul became the apostle Paul through a vocation consisting of a vision of heavenly light, a voice calling to him, and a temporary blindness. After three days he was cured and filled with the Holy Spirit (*Acts* 9). The vocation initiates a process of rebirth, making Saul into the second founder of Christianity.

Mani (b. 216 CE), the founder of Manichaeism, received his first vocation at the age of twelve when an angel appeared to him like "a flash of lightning," ordering him to leave the community in which he was reared. The angel was sent by the King of Light and in Manichaean sources is called the Twin or the Paraclete. It was a kind of heavenly double that guarded him during his youth, showed him many "visions and sights" and appeared again to him "in great glory" when he was twenty-four years old. The Twin revealed to him all the mysteries of the world: "what my body is, in what way I have come, . . . who my Father on high is, . . . the boundless heights and the unfathomable depths." The spirit sends Mani, who is very hesitant about his vocation, out into the world to proclaim his saving message, promising him: "You, then, expound all that I have given to you. I shall be your ally and protector at all times." Here again the first vocation is followed by a period of mental preparation in close relationship with the spirit, who functions as a guarding spirit and eventually brings about the revelation of perfect divine knowledge.

Muḥammad, the prophet of Islam, obtained his vocation (in 609 or 610 CE when he was about forty years old) after a long period of mental crisis and growing unhappiness with religious practice in his birthplace, Mecca; as a result, there ensued serious conflicts with the local tribal establishment and his eventual departure (Hijrah) for Medina in 622 CE. The Qurʾān contains some scanty allusions to the Prophet's vocation, which took place in a nocturnal vision, perhaps at Jerusalem, in which he saw Allāh or the angel Gabriel, who gave him the essence of the Qurʾanic message (*sūrahs* 17:1, 53:1–18, 81:19–26). Muḥammad was so confused that he believed himself mad. Later Islamic tradition developed this theme into the legend of Muḥammad's nightly ascension to heaven and descent with the heavenly Qurʾān.

The history of Christianity and its various offspring shows a wide variety of vocations of saints, reformers, and prophets. Joan of Arc (1412–1431) received a vocation as a little girl in a garden. She heard a loud voice and saw a brilliant light and the archangel Michael escorted by a legion of angels. Michael the Archangel announced the arrival of Saint Catherine and Saint Margaret, who urged her to help the French king and save France, a task she accepted after long hesitation.

Most nativistic cults and messianic movements that are the result of an acculturation conflict are initiated by the vocation of a prophetic leader, involving a remarkable amalgam of elements from the old and the new religion. Such is the case in the Shaker religion in the northwestern United States and in the Ghost Dance movement among the North American Indians. The second wave of the Ghost Dance was initiated by the Indian laborer Wovoka in 1890. During a solar eclipse he had an attack of fever and heard his fellow tribesmen make a loud noise to drive away the monster that devoured the sun. Then he had the following vision:

> When the sun died, I went up to heaven and saw God and all the people who had died a long time ago. God told me to come back and tell my people they must be good and love one another and not fight, or steal or lie. He gave me this dance to give to my people.

Other less peaceful messianic movements also began with the vocation of a prophet. W. W. Harris of Cape Palmas in Liberia was jailed in 1912 because his preaching was suspected of inciting rebellion against the Liberian government. In a nocturnal vision the angel Gabriel appeared to Harris and called him to become the prophet of Africa; thus began his very successful missionary travels along the west coast of Africa, which lasted for two years.

Also well-known is the vocation of the shaman, which forms the first phase of a long and difficult initiation into this ecstatic religious function that mediates between the world of the spirits and the world of men. Shamanism occurs all over the world, but principally in northern and Inner Asia and in North America. The vocation of the future shaman manifests itself in a significant change of behavior, in mental illness, hallucinations, epileptic attacks, strange accidents or ordeals, in all of which the activities of the guardian spirit are experienced. A shaman of the Yakuts in Siberia told how he became ill at the age of twenty, saw visions and heard strange voices, and struggled with the spirit for nine years. In the end he almost died; finally he began to be a shaman, and his illness was cured. The vocation of the shaman is in almost all cases associated with an initiatory sickness that brings him to the threshold of death, often resulting in a complete disintegration of his personality, which is then reintegrated in the initiation. It is a process of death and rebirth. The future shaman sometimes sees in dreams or visions his head chopped off, his body reduced to a dismembered skeleton or boiled in a kettle, symbols belonging to archaic cultural patterns in which the myth of life out of death is predominant. The powerful symbolism of the shamanic vocation as the initiatory phase of a process of rebirth is the most profound expression of the meaning of every vocation: being called and reborn into a new condition of life in order to minister to and save fragile human lives with the help of the divine world to which the vocation gives entrance.

BIBLIOGRAPHY

A comprehensive study of the various forms of vocation is still lacking. William James's *The Varieties of Religious Experience* (New York, 1902) remains basic for the correct understanding of the psychology of the divine call. For the phenomenon of the Hebrew prophets and related persons, see Erich Fascher's *Prophetes: Eine sprach- und religionsgeschichtliche Untersuchung* (Giessen, 1927) and Johannes Lindblom's *Prophecy in Ancient Israel* (Philadelphia, 1962). Arthur Darby Nock offers an excellent introduction to the early Christian and Hellenistic world in *Conversion: The Old and the New in Religion from Alexander the Great to Augustine of Hippo* (Oxford, 1933). For vocation in messianic movements, see Peter Worsley's *The Trumpet Shall Sound: A Study of "Cargo" Cults in Melanesia* (London, 1957); Bengt M. Sundkler's *Bantu Prophets in South Africa,* 2d rev. ed. (London, 1961); Wilson D. Wallis's *Messiahs: Their Role in Civilization* (Washington, D.C., 1943), a general work; and I. M. Lewis's *Ecstatic Religion* (Harmondsworth, 1971). For the various forms of shamanistic vocation, Mircea Eliade's *Shamanism: Archaic Techniques of Ecstasy,* rev. & enl. ed. (New York, 1964), is fundamental. Eliade's *Birth and Rebirth: The Religious Meaning of Initiation in Human Culture* (London, 1958) is a good introduction in the complex field of vocation and initiation.

New Sources

Harper-Bill, Christopher. *Christian Religious Beliefs and Ecclesiastical Careers in Late Medieval England.* Studies in the History of Modern Religion. Rochester, N.Y., 1991.

Harran, Marilyn. "The Contemporary Applicability of Lutheran Pedagogy; Education and Vocation." *Concordia Jounral* 16 (1990): 319–332.

Mahon, Brain J. *Forgetting Ourselves on Purpose: Vocation and the Ethics of Ambition.* New York, 2002.

Schwehn, Mark. *Exiles from Eden: Religion and the Academic Vocation in America.* New York, 1993.

HAN J. W. DRIJVERS (1987)
Revised Bibliography

VODOU is a sometimes misleading, but nevertheless common, name for the religious practices of the majority of Haitians. Outsiders have given the name Vodou to the complex web of traditional religious practices followed in Haiti. Only recently, and still to a limited extent, have Haitians come to use the term as others do. Haitians prefer a verb to identify their religion: they speak of "serving the spirits."

A mountainous, poverty-stricken, largely agricultural country of approximately eight million people, Haiti has a land area of 10,700 square miles and occupies the western third of the island of Hispaniola, which it shares with the Dominican Republic.

This is where Caribbean Vodou began, but Haiti is not the only place Vodou in practiced. Vodou is also a central part of everyday life in Haitian diaspora communities in New Orleans and Santiago, Cuba, both products of the upheaval caused by the Haitian Revolution (1791–1804). More recent political and economic struggles in Haiti have also led to Vodou communities in New York City, Miami, Montreal, and Paris.

In Haiti, *vodou* originally referred to one ritual style among many in their syncretic religious system, the style most closely connected to Dahomey and the Fon language. The word *vodou* is derived from the Fon *vodun,* which means "god" or "spirit." *Hoodoo* is a related term from the same Fon word, yet, in the United States, it is almost always used as a derogatory term that focuses on black magic spells and charms.

Sensationalized novels and films, as well as spurious travelers' accounts, have painted a negative picture of Haitian religion. Vodou has been depicted as primitive and ignorant. Vodou rituals have been described as arenas for uncontrolled orgiastic behavior, and even cannibalism. The same writers stir up fear of Vodou and suggest that if whites get too close to a Vodou ceremony terrible things could happen. These distortions are attributable to the fear that the Haitian slave revolution sparked in whites. Haiti achieved independence in 1804, and thus became the first black republic in the Western Hemisphere at a time when the colonial economy was still heavily dependent on slave labor.

In Vodou there are three (not always clearly distinguished) categories of spiritual beings: *lemò, lemistè,* and *lemarasa* (respectively, "the dead," "the mysteries," and "the sacred twins"). While certain Vodou prayers, songs, and invocations preserve fragments of West African languages, Haitian Creole is the primary language of Vodou. Creole is the first and only language of more than one half the population of Haiti. It has a grammatical structure familiar to speakers of West African languages and an eighteenth-century French vocabulary mixed with a smattering of English words and expressions.

Although individuals and families regularly serve the Vodou spirits without recourse to religious professionals, throughout most of Haiti there is a loosely organized priesthood open to both men and women. The male priest is known as an *oungan* and the female priest is a *manbo.* There is a wide spectrum of Vodou ritualizing. There are individual acts of piety, such as lighting candles to petition particular spirits, and elaborate feasts, sometimes lasting days and including the sacrifice of several animals as part of the meals offered to the spirits. Energetic singing, dancing, and polyrhythmic drumming accompany the larger rituals. In the countryside, rituals often take place outdoors, on family land set aside for the spirits, and there is often a small cult house on that land where the family's altars are kept. Urban Vodou rituals tend to take place in an *ounfò* ("temple"). Urban altars, dense with sacrificial food and drink, sacred stones, and chromolithographs of the Catholic saints and other images, are maintained in *jèvo* ("altar rooms") off the central dancing and ritualizing space of the temple, the *peristyl.* In the cities, those who serve the spirits also tend to keep more modest altars in their own homes.

The goal of Vodou drumming, singing, and dancing is to *chofè,* to "heat up," the situation sufficiently to bring on possession by the spirits. As a particular spirit is summoned, a devotee enters a trance and becomes that spirit's *chwal* ("horse"), thus providing the means for direct communication between human beings and the spirits. The spirit is said to ride the *chwal.* Using the person's body and voice, the spirit sings, dances, and eats with the people and also deals out advice and chastisement. The people in turn offer the spirit a wide variety of gifts and acts of obeisance, the goal being to placate the spirit and ensure his or her continuing protection.

There are marked differences in Vodou as it is practiced throughout Haiti, but the single most important distinction is that between urban and rural Vodou. Haitian society is primarily agricultural, and the manner in which peasants serve the spirits is determined by questions of land tenure and ancestral inheritance. Urban Vodou is not tied to specific plots of land, but the family connection persists in another form. Urban temple communities become substitutes for the extended families of the countryside. The priests are called "papa" and "mama"; the initiates, who are called "children of the house" or "little leaves" refer to one another as "brother" and "sister." In general, urban Vodou is more institutionalized and often more elaborate in its rituals than its rural counterpart.

AFRICAN INFLUENCE. Haiti's slave population was built up in the eighteenth century, a period in which Haiti supplied a large percentage of the sugar consumed in Western Europe. Vodou was born on sugar, sisal, cotton and coffee plantations out of the interaction among slaves who brought with them a variety of African religious traditions, but due to inadequate records, little is known about this formative period in Vodou's history. It has been argued by Haitian scholars such as Michel-Rolph Trouillot that the religion did not coalesce until after the revolution, but others suggest it had an effective presence, particularly in northern Haiti, during the latter part of the eighteenth century. James G. Leyburn in *The Haitian People* (1941) and Carolyn Fick in *The Making of Haiti* (1990) argue that Vodou played a key role in the organization of the slave revolt.

Among the African ethnic groups brought to Haiti as slave laborers, the most influential in shaping Haitian culture, including Vodou, were the Fon, Mahi, and Nago from old Dahomey (the present Republic of Benin), those who came to be known as the Yoruba (Nigeria), and Kongo peoples (Angola, and the Democratic Republic of the Congo). Many of the names of Vodou spirits are easily traceable to their African counterparts; however, the spirits have undergone change in the context of Haiti's social and economic history. For example, Ogun among the Yoruba is a spirit of ironsmithing and other activities associated with metal, such as hunting, warfare, and modern technology. Neither hunting nor modern technology plays much of a role in the lives of Haitians. Haiti, however, does have a long and complex military history. Thus, the Haitian spirit Ogou is first and foremost a soldier whose rituals, iconography, and possession-performance explore both the constructive and destructive uses of military power, as well as its analogues with human relations—anger, self-assertion, and willfulness.

Africa itself is a powerful concept in Vodou. Haitians speak of Ginen ("Guinea") both as their ancestral home, the Guinea coast of West Africa, and as the watery subterranean home of the Vodou spirits. Calling a spirit *franginen,* ("fully and completely African") is a way of indicating that the spirit is good, ancient, and proper. The manner in which an individual or a group serves the spirits may also be called *franginen,* with similar connotations of approval and propriety.

ROMAN CATHOLIC INFLUENCE. For the most part, the slaveholders were Catholics and baptism for slaves was mandatory by French law. Many have argued that slaves used a veneer of Catholicism to hide their traditional religious practices from the authorities. While Catholicism may well have functioned in this utilitarian way for slaves on plantations, it is also true that the religions of West Africa from which Vodou was derived, already had a tradition of borrowing the deities of neighbors and enemies alike. Whatever Catholicism represented in the slave world, it was most likely also used as a means to expand Vodou's ritual vocabulary and iconography, thus helping captive laborers function in a nominally Catholic world. In 1804, immediately after Haiti declared its liberation, the Catholic Church withdrew all of its clergy from the new republic. Yet Catholicism survived in Haiti for fifty years without contact with Rome and it did so through the imitative ritualizing of a Vodou figure known as *prêt-savan* ("bush priest") as well as the competitive market for healing charms and talismans that was kept going by defrocked Catholic priests and the self-appointed "clergy" who ended up in Haiti in the early nineteenth century.

Catholicism has had the greatest influence on the traditional religion of Haiti at the level of rite and image rather than theology. This influence works in two ways. First, those who serve the spirits call themselves Catholic, attend Mass, and undergo baptism and first communion. Because these Catholic rituals at times function as integral parts of larger Vodou rites, they can be even directed to participate by their Vodou spirits. Second, Catholic prayers, rites, images, and saints' names are integrated into the common ritualizing of Vodou temples. The prêtsavan is an active figure in Vodou. He achieves his title by knowing the proper, that is the Latin or French, form of Catholic prayers.

Over the years, a system of parallels has been developed between the Vodou spirits and the Catholic saints. For example, Dambala, the ancient and venerable snake deity of the Fon people, is venerated in Haiti both as Dambala and as St. Patrick, who is pictured in the popular chromolithograph with snakes clustered around his feet. In addition, the Catholic liturgical calendar dominates in much Vodou ritualizing. Thus the Vodou spirit Ogou is honored in Haiti and in the Haitian diaspora on July 25, the feast day of his Catholic counterpart.

Bondye, "the good God" is identified with the Christian God, and is said to be the highest, indeed the only, god. The spirits are said to have been angels in Lucifer's army whom God sent out of heaven and down to Ginen. Although the Vodou spirits may exhibit capricious behavior, they are not evil. Rather, they are seen as intermediaries between the people and the high god, a role identical to the one played by the so-called lesser deities in the religions of the Yoruba and Fon. Bondye is remote and unknowable. Although evoked daily in ordinary speech (almost all plans are made with the disclaimer *si dye vle* ("if God wills"), Bondye's intervention is not sought for help with life's problems. That is the work of the spirits.

Both the Catholic Church in Haiti and the government of Haiti have participated energetically in the persecution of those who serve the Vodou spirits. The last "antisuperstition campaign" was in the 1940s, but clerical and upperclass disdain for the religion has persisted much longer. In the twentieth century, Catholic clergy routinely preached against serving the spirits, and those who served them remarked, "That is the way priests talk." Many Catholic holy days have a Vodou dimension that church officials routinely manage to ignore.

For years Catholicism was the only religion in Haiti with official approval. Thus, the degree to which Vodou has been attacked, oppressed, tolerated, or even encouraged through the years has been largely a function of local politics. Presidents Dumarsais Estime (1946–1950) and Francois Duvalier (1957–1971) stand out from other Haitian heads of state because of their sympathy with Vodou. Jean-Bertrand Aristide, who was first elected president in 1990, was also a supporter of Vodou; in fact he changed the balance of religious power. On April 5, 2003, President Aristide fully recognized and fully empowered Vodou as a Haitian religion that could legally exercise its influence throughout Haiti according to the constitution and the laws of the republic.

VODOU SPIRITS. The Vodou spirits are known by various names*:* *lwa,* a common name with an uncertain origin; *sen,*"saints"; *mistè,* "mysteries"; *envizib,* "invisibles"; and more rarely, *zanj,* "angels." At some point in the development of Vodou the spirits were sorted into *nanchon,* "nations." The nanchon at an early point in their development appear to have functioned primarily as ethnic slave categories. The majority of the nation names are easily traceable to places in Africa: Rada, Ibo, Nago, Kongo. Later, however, these so-called nations became religious categories, diverse ritual styles of drumming, dancing, and honoring the Vodou spirits.

The Rada spirits (named after the Dahomean principality Allada, once a busy slave depot) comprise a collection of ancient, sweet-tempered, wise, and usually patient *lwa.* Then there are the fiery and powerful Petwo spirits. The origin of the name "Petwo" is contested, but the strong Kongo influence is not. The home of the Ogou, also hot spirits, is the Nago *nanchon,* a Dahomean name for Ketu Yoruba. Most big feasts end with the playful Gede, inveterate rule breakers, who insist they are a *fami* ("family"), not a *nanchon.* In rural Vodou, a person may inherit responsibilities to one or more of these *nanchon* through maternal or paternal kin. Familial connections to the land, where the *lwa* are said to reside in trees, springs, and wells, may determine which particular spirits are served. In urban Vodou, there are a few important spirit *nanchon* that make their appearance, according to seniority and importance, in most major rituals. In Port-au-Prince, two *nanchon,* the Rada and the Petwo, have emerged as dominant largely by absorbing other *nanchon.* Rada and Petwo spirits contrast sharply. The Rada are *dous,* "sweet," and the Petwo, *cho,*"hot." When an individual, family, or temple is described as ritualizing in a mode that is *Rada net* ("straight Rada"), a great deal is being said about how that person or group functions socially as well as ritualistically. Each spirit has drum rhythms, dances, and food preferences that relate to its identifying characteristics. For example, Danbala, the gentle Rada snake spirit, is said to love *orja,* thick sugary almond syrup. His devotees perform a graceful spine-rippling dance called *yanvalu.* By contrast, the Petwo rhythm played for rum-drinking spirits is energetic and pounding, and the accompanying dance is characterized by fast, strong body movements.

THE VODOU VIEW OF PERSON. In Vodou teachings the human being is composed of various parts: the body, that is, the gross physical dimension of the person who perishes after death, in addition to two to four souls, of which the most widely acknowledged are the *gwo bonanj,* and *ti bonanj. The gwo bonanj* ("big guardian angel") is roughly equivalent to consciousness or personality. When a person dies the *gwo bonanj* lingers, and immediately after death it must be protected because it is most vulnerable to capture and misuse by sorcerers. During possession, it is the *gwo bonanj* who is displaced by the spirit and sent to wander away from the body, as it does routinely during sleep. The *ti bonanj* ("little guardian angel") may be thought of as the spiritual energy reserve of a living person and, at times, as the ghost of a dead person.

Each person has one special *lwa* who is their *mèt-tet,* "master of the head." (The top of the head and the back of the neck are places where spirits may enter and leave.) The *mèt-tet* is the most important *lwa* served by a particular person and it reflects that person's personality to some degree. A Haitian whose family serves the spirits may inherit spiritual responsibilities to a deceased family member's *mèt-tet.* That is a big responsibility, but there are also things that can be gained. If the *mèt-tet* is conscientiously fed and honored, good luck and protection from both ancestor and *lwa* will be gained. In addition to the so-called masters of the head, most people who serve the spirits have a small number of other *lwa* with whom similar reciprocity has been established.

Unlike Catholic saints who are usually known through formulaic hagiography, Vodou *lwa* have richly developed histories, personalities, needs, desires, character strengths, and flaws, and even taste in food and drink. Because the *lwa* are fully developed characters and interact so intimately with *vivan-yo,* "the living," the practice of Vodou also functions as a system for categorizing and analyzing human behavior, in the individual and in the group. One of the characteristics of virtually all Caribbean African-based religions is the great amount of care given to analyzing social behavior and dealing with the results of that behavior.

VODOU AND THE DEAD. Cemeteries are major ritual centers in both urban and rural Haiti. The first male buried in any cemetery is known as Bawon Samidi. Bawon's wife (or sister) is Gran Brijit, the first woman buried in the cemetery. Most cemeteries have a cross for Bawon either in the center of the cemetery or near its gate. Lakwa Bawon ("Bawon's Cross") marks the site's ritual center. Lighted candles and food offerings are left at the base of this cross. People stand with their hands on the cross praying aloud. Rituals for healing, love, or luck performed in rural cult houses or urban temples are not considered complete until physical remnants of the "work" are deposited at crossroads or at Bawon's Cross, which is itself a kind of crossroads marking the intersection of the land of the living and the land of the dead.

Haitians who serve the *lwa* usually make a clear distinction between the dead and the spirits. Yet a few of the ancestors, particularly if they were exceptional people when alive, actually evolve into spirits or *lwa.* Jean-Jacques Dessalines, Toussaint L'Ouverture, and John Kennedy have all been reported making cameo appearances through possession in Vodou ceremonies. The group of spirits, known as the Gede, have Bawon as their leader and are spirits of the dead as might be expected, but they are not ancestral spirits. Instead, they stand in for the entire community of human beings now deceased and in this context, Gede's crude comic performances make some sense. They are designed to bring the haughty to their knees and convince them that in the end, human beings all face the same fate. The Gede are inclusive, with no limits, and therefore almost any image will work on a Gede altar. Statues of the Buddha, LaoTzu, King Kong, St. Gerard, and Elvis Presley have all been sighted on Vodou altars. In and around Port-au-Prince, the capital of Haiti and its largest city, the Gede are the object of elaborate ritualizing in the cemeteries and Vodou temples during the season of the Feast of All Souls, Halloween.

The Gede are not only spirits of death but also boosters of human sexuality, protectors of children, and irrepressible social satirists. Dances for Gede tend to be boisterous affairs, and new Gede spirits appear every year. The satirical, and often explicitly sexual, humor of the Gede levels social pretense. The Gede use humor to deal with new social roles and to challenge alienating social structures. Through possession-performance, they not only appear as auto mechanics and doctors, they also critique government bureaucrats, military figures, and Protestant missionaries.

VODOU CEREMONIES. In some parts of rural Haiti, the ideal Vodou ceremony is one that serves the spirits as simply as possible because simplicity is said to reflect discrete but strong spiritual power, the African way of doing things (Larose, 1977). In practice, rural ritualizing tends to follow the fortunes of extended families. Bad times are often attributed to the displeasure of family spirits. When it is no longer possible to satisfy the spirits with small conciliatory offerings, the family will hold a large drumming and dancing feast that includes animal sacrifice. Urban Vodou, by contrast, has a more routine ritualizing calendar, and events tend to be larger and more elaborate. Ceremonies in honor of major spirits take place annually on or around the feast days of their Catholic counterparts and usually include sacrifice of an appropriate animal—most frequently a chicken, a goat, or a cow.

In both rural and urban settings, a rich variety of ceremonies meet specific individual and community needs: For example, healing rites, dedications of new temples and new ritual regalia, and spirit marriages in which a devotee is wed to a spirit usually of the opposite sex and must pledge sexual restraint one night each week, when he or she receives that spirit in dreams. There is also a cycle of initiation rituals that has both public segments and segments reserved for initiates. The latter include the *kanzo* rituals, which mark the first stage of initiation into Vodou, and those in which the adept takes the *ason,* the beaded gourd rattle symbolizing Vodou priesthood. Certain rituals performed during the initiation cycle, such as the *bule zen* ("burning the pots") and the *chirè ayzan* ("shredding the palm leaf") may also be used in other ritual contexts. Death rituals include the *desounen,* in which the soul is removed from the corpse and sent under the waters of Ginen, which is followed by the *wète mò nan dlo* ("bringing the dead from the waters"), a ritual that can occur only after a person has been dead for one year and one day. Herbal good-luck baths are routinely administered during the Christmas and New Year season. Elizabeth McAlister's 2002 book on Rara has convinced scholars, in the habit of dismissing Rara as an entertaining aspect of Carnival, of the deeply religious character of these irreverent parades that pour from the Vodou temples into the cemeteries and streets during the Catholic Lent.

Annual pilgrimages draw thousands of urban and rural followers of Vodou. The focal point of these Catholic-Vodou events is often a church situated near some striking feature of the natural landscape that is sacred to the *lwa.* The two largest pilgrimages are one held for Ezili Danto (Our Lady of Mount Carmel) in mid-July in the small town of Saut d'Eau, named for its spectacular waterfall, and one held for Ogou (St. James the Elder) in the latter part of July in the northern town of Plain du Nord, where a shallow, muddy pool adjacent to the Catholic church is dedicated to Ogou.

VODOU AND MAGIC. Serge Larose (1977) has demonstrated that magic is not only a stereotypic label that outsiders have applied to Vodou, but also a differential term internal to the religion. Thus an in-group among the followers of Vodou identifies its own ritualizing as "African" while labeling the work of the out-group as *maji* ("magic"). Generally speaking, this perspective provides a helpful way to grasp the concept of magic within Vodou. There are, however, those individuals who, in search of power and wealth, self-consciously identify themselves with traditions of what Haitians would call "the work of the left hand." This includes people who deal in *pwen achte* ("purchased power points"), which means spirits or powers that have been bought rather than inherited, and people who deal in *zonbi.* A *zonbi* may be either the disembodied soul of a dead person whose powers are captured and used for magical purposes, or a soulless body that has been raised from the grave to do drone labor in the fields. Also included in the category of the left hand are secret societies known by such names as Champwel, Zobop, Bizango, and Zanglando. In Urban settings in the late twentieth century secret societies began to operate as if they were a branch of the Mafia, but their deep history is quite different: They once represented religiously enforced rural law and order. The secret societies were groups of elders who used their power not for personal gains but to enforce social sanctions. For example, Wade Davis (1985) says that *zonbi* laborers were created by secret society tribunals who voted to use *zonbi* powder against a sociopath in their community.

The "work of the left hand" should not be confused with more ordinary Vodou ritualizing that can have a magical flavor, such as divination, herbal healing, and the manufacture of *wanga,* charms for love, luck, or health, or for the protection of the home, land, or person. Much of the work of Vodou priests is at the level of individual client-practitioner interactions Theirs is a healing system that treats problems of love, health, family, and work. Unless a problem is understood as coming from God, in which case the Vodou priest can do nothing, the priest will treat it as one caused by a spirit or by a disruption in human relationships, including relations with the dead. Generally speaking, Vodou cures come about through ritual adjustment of relational systems.

VODOU IN THE HAITIAN DIASPORA. Drought and soil erosion, poverty, high urban unemployment, and political oppression have led to massive emigrations from Haiti in the last half-century. Vodou has gone along with the Haitians who, in search of a better life, have come to major urban centers of North America. In New York, Miami, and Montreal, the cities with the greatest concentrations of Haitian immigrants, Vodou ceremonies are carried on in storefronts, rented rooms, high-rise apartments, and basement storage areas. North American rituals are often somewhat truncated versions of their Haitian counterparts. There may be no drums, and the only animals sacrificed may be chickens. However it is possible to consult a manbo or oungan in immigrant communities with ease, and the full repertoire of rituals can be followed there, in one form or another. Even the pilgrimages are duplicated. On 16 July, rather than going to the mountain town of Saut d'Eau to honor Ezili Danto, New York Vodou practitioners take the subway to the Italian-American Church of Our Lady of Mount Carmel in East Harlem.

SEE ALSO Santería; Yoruba Religion.

BIBLIOGRAPHY

Alfred Metraux's *Voodoo in Haiti* (New York, 1959) is a complete and accurate, if not sympathetic, treatment of Haitian Vodou. Melville J. Herskovits's *Life in a Haitian Valley* (New York, 1937) is an early and popular ethnography of the Mirebalais Valley located fifty-five kilometers inland from Port-au-Prince. Herskovits worked there during a period when Vodou influence had been significantly repressed by Christian missionaries and consequently he saw it as a dying religion. Maya Deren, dancer and filmmaker, wrote a rich and insightful work on her encounter with Vodou, *Divine Horsemen: The Living Gods of Haiti* (1953; reprint, New Paltz, N.Y. 1983). In addition, Harold Courlander's *The Drum and the Hoe: Life and Lore of the Haitian People* (Berkeley, Calif.,1960) provides much helpful information about Vodou and its larger cultural contexts. It is especially good on music. To greater and lesser extents all of the above works are outdated. Donald Cosentino's, *The Sacred Arts of Haitian Vodou* (Los Angeles, 1995), a selection of essays by leading Haitian scholars and also the catalog from Cosentino's highly successful exhibition of the same name, is the richest and most diverse academic work on Vodou. A classic article by Serge Larose, "The Meaning of Africa in Haitian Vodu," can be found in *Symbols and Sentiments: Cross-Cultural Studies in Symbolism,* edited by Ioan Lewis, 85–116, (New York, 1977).

The most complete, although not necessarily the best, history of Haiti and Haitian Vodou is still James G. Leyburn's *The Haitian People* (1941, rev. ed. with a new introduction by Sidney Mintz, New Haven, 1966). Joan Dayan's *Haiti, History, and the Gods* (Berkeley, Calif., 1998) brings postmodern analytic skills and fresh archival work to her gendered account of Haiti's revolutionary history. Carolyn Fick's *The Making of Haiti: The San Domingue Revolution From Below* (Knoxville, Tenn., 1990) makes a carefully researched and convincing argument that Vodou played a significant role in Haiti's revolution and did so from the beginning. Michel-Rolph Trouillot, who argues that Vodou came together only in the first half of the nineteenth century, does a brilliant job in *Silencing the Past: Power and the Production of History* (Boston, 1997) of problematizing other versions of Haiti's taken-for-granted history.

Anne Greene's *The Catholic Church in Haiti: Political and Social Change* (East Lansing, Mich., 1993) provides important information about the role of Catholicism in Haiti, as does Terry Rey's *Our Lady of Class Struggle: The Cult of the Virgin Mary In Haiti* (Trenton, N. J., 1999). Leslie G. Desmangles's *The Faces of the Gods: Voudou and Roman Catholicism in Haiti* (Chapel Hill, N.C., 1993) explores the syncretism dimension of the relationship between Vodou and Catholicism. Robert Ferris Thompson's *Flash of the Spirit: African and Afro-American Art and Philosophy* (New York, 1981) contains the best analysis yet done on the specific African retentions within Haitian Vodou.

A handful of scholarly works cover new areas in Vodou scholarship. E. Wade Davis opened the world of the secret societies in *The Serpent and the Rainbow* (New York, 1985) and *Passage of Darkness* (Chapel Hill, N.C., 1988). Elizabeth McAlister's *Rara: Vodou Power and Performance in Haiti and the Diaspora* (Berkeley, Calif., 2002) changes the relationship between Vodou temples and Carnival, and thus, to some extent, between the sacred and the secular. My own work, *Mama Lola: A Vodou Priestess in Brooklyn* (Berkeley, Calif., updated edition, 2001), provides an extensive case study of Vodou in diaspora.

KAREN MCCARTHY BROWN (1987 AND 2005)

VOGUL RELIGION SEE FINNO-UGRIC RELIGIONS; KHANTY AND MANSI RELIGION; SOUTHERN SIBERIAN RELIGIONS

VOLOS SEE VELES-VOLOS

VON GLASENAPP, HELMUTH SEE GLASENAPP, HELMUTH VON

VON GÖRRES, JOSEPH SEE GÖRRES, JOSEPH VON

VON HARNACK, ADOLF SEE HARNACK, ADOLF VON

VON HÜGEL, FRIEDRICH SEE HÜGEL, FRIEDRICH VON

VOODOO SEE VODOU

VOTIVE OFFERING SEE VOWS AND OATHS

VOWS AND OATHS.

With the vow to accomplish something, a person dedicates himself to the task wholly. Whoever takes an oath to accomplish something is required to answer for it, for he has named himself or some one of his belongings as a pledge of his commitment and is thus bound by his very life, his honor, and his property.

Vows and oaths therefore affect a person's whole being; they put one's very existence in pawn. There is a distinct difference, however, between an oath and a vow: a vow is merely a personal promise, whereas an oath is a promise made before some institutional authority. In taking an oath, a person not only assumes an obligation but also becomes liable to prosecution; the state and society have an interest in his act. Oaths serve as objective guarantees of what is promised. Swearing to tell the truth, one guarantees that what one says is true. Oaths are self-endorsing.

The practice of oath taking by which a person places his very life at risk is an extremely ancient one. It is an institution of coercion, "the most powerful coercion known to primitive man" (Thurnwald, 1925, vol. 2, p. 39). Oaths are encountered among all peoples and in all cultures. They are a primal symbol of religion.

Because they are absolutely binding by nature, and because they are subject to both misuse and overuse, oaths are nevertheless looked upon with some suspicion in the fields of ethics, politics, and jurisprudence. They have to be judged in themselves, in relation to the particular substance of the promise they contain and the nature of the guarantee, as both tend to vary considerably depending on the level of the given culture and the conventions of the applicable code of law.

GIVING AND RECEIVING—AN INSTITUTION OF LIFE. In the archaic scheme of things, objects of barter, things that must be paid for, are not simply goods but rather gifts. They establish a substantial bond between giver and receiver, for the latter is obligated to provide something in exchange for the gift. Such exchange affects the social position of the participants: it turns the giver into a receiver and makes of the receiver a giver.

In this economy of mutual giving, the objects exchanged have both an objective and a subjective significance; they not only create the partnership, they also serve to insure it. They are subject to recall. They give rise to rights and obligations. They are pledges.

Vows and oaths have the same archaic structure. They create and solidify partnerships based on reciprocal giving. One swears by specific things, and in the exchange these pledges become extremely important. They guarantee the peace, subjectively and objectively. The bond of order they establish is affirmed in the oath itself, so that the oath, like the things by which it is sworn, is part blessing and part curse: it obligates one to a bond, and binds one to an obligation.

In many languages the word for "oath" is somehow associated with fate. The Assyrian *mamuti* translates as "oath," but it also means "obsession" and "curse." The related term *tamitu* is also used for "oath," but in addition it can refer either to a divine oracle or the question put to the god (Pedersen, 1914, p. 2). Clearly one is oneself possessed by what one possesses. Property can have a fatal power.

The Arabic word *baiʿ* translates as both "purchase" and "sale," but it also means "convenant." The exchange of wares, accompanied by ceremonial gestures of bonding such as reciprocal touching and shaking of hands, confers certain rights and obligations to both parties. One sells a certain object, but one also sells oneself. The bond linking buyer and seller is an oath. Implicit in the word *baiʿ* are both the sealing of a compact and an exchange of oaths (ibid., pp. 52–58). The former secures the connection, while the latter constitutes "religion" (from *religare,* "to tie fast") in the truest sense, bondage to the gift of life. The Anglo-Saxon verb *swerian* ("to swear") suggests something of the magic in such a bond, for at one time it meant to recite mystic charms and spells in a strange, singsong kind of chant. Old Frisian *swera* meant simply "to sing"—in the service of religion.

Oaths in early Germanic times were not only a religious rite, they were themselves the religion. An oath was an *actus religiosissimus* in the truest sense (Lex, 1967, p. 24). The Middle High German word for "oath" contains the Indo-European root **it* or **lig,* meaning bond. An oath is an added confirmation, an absolute guarantee, of the word and intent of the person swearing, and it is also the fetter that binds him to the truth. The Latin term for "oath" is *ius iurandum* ("sworn law"). Oaths were firmly established legal instruments with statutory force: "An oath is an assurance backed by religious sanctity; and a solemn promise given, as before God as one's witness, is to be sacredly kept" (Cicero, *De officiis* 3.104). The oath of allegiance was known as the *sacramentum.*

The things one swears by are pledges, and the promises to which one binds oneself in swearing by things are oaths. With the specific things to which he appeals, a person guarantees that to which he has committed himself. They can be demanded of him; they become objects for litigation. Greek mythology (according to Hesiod) speaks therefore of the oath as the offspring of contention. It issues from conflict over things to which one is obligated, namely heaven and earth, life and death, gods and men. The obligation to them is binding, and the bond with them brings with it obligation. The very earth avenges itself on the perjurer, for with his oath he has placed it in pawn. The Greeks speak of having to pass through the portals of the oath, for *horkos,* their word for "oath," designates a separate space before which one has a sense of dread (*aidōs*), a border region. The strongest oaths of all were those sworn on the bank of the Styx, the underworld stream whose waters expose the guilty and cleanse the innocent of false accusations.

Oaths are a divine judgment. The good and evil that they decide between amount to fortune and misfortune. Hence one speaks of eating and drinking one's oath. It either confirms or threatens one's very existence.

Oath taking may entail trial by fire, duels, symbolic destruction of specific objects, or hypothetical self-condemnation. The Maasai of East Africa bite off a few blades of grass, then exclaim: "May this grass prove poisonous to me if I have lied before God!" (Lasch, 1908, p. 80).

The reciprocal giving and taking in the economy of barter is something that serves to solidify society, for the one who gives also has a right to receive. Gifts are therefore challenges: they bind the receiver to the giver; they are what establishes a compact with him. They are an opening ceremony. While they serve to guarantee the fulfillment of oaths, they also anticipate the fulfillment of a vow, which is not a pledge to the past, but to the future. A vow presumes a compact that is yet to be. Votive gifts are only down payments on future covenants. They serve as symbols in the here and now of future fulfillment, and they have personal meaning. They give objective reality to a subjective religion.

Like votive gifts, magical rites and animal and human sacrifice are typical examples of such objectivization. So are the conjuring of rain in Arizona, New Mexico, and southern Europe, and so were temple prostitution in the Near East, cult chastity among the Romans, continence in preparation for specific tasks (as in war vows), or the habit in Latin countries of placing votive offerings in the form of garments and models of healed limbs on altars and temple walls. Popular faith abounds with customs of this kind. In them, promises take the form of gifts, and gifts serve as promises, concrete expressions of personal religion.

VOWS AND PERSONAL RELIGION. Gifts initiate the reciprocity of giving and receiving, and they have been used for that purpose since archaic times. They have personal importance, for the promises they imply must be kept only if the gifts are found acceptable.

Vows are promises of the same kind. Whether they are fulfilled is not a matter for the law but rather hinges on the person governing the giving and receiving. Nothing is given that is found unacceptable, and nothing is accepted that cannot be given. All involuntary vows are invalid. All voluntary ones are valid provided they satisfy the controlling authority, the religion, under which they are made. The same authority has the option of annulling them.

The Bible, Judaism, Christianity, Islam, and Buddhism all limit the use of vows. They have rules applying to the pledges of individuals as well as those of whole groups, such as communal orders and sects.

The terms for *vow* in the Bible are the Hebrew *nazir* and the Greek *euchē* ("prayer"). There a vow is an unconditional pledge of special submission to Yahveh. The Nazirite, or the man who has made such a vow, must refrain from drinking wine (*Nm.* 6:3), cutting his hair (*Nm.* 6:5), and coming into contact with a corpse (*Nm.* 6:6). The charismatic warrior Samson is an example of such a man (*Jgs.* 13ff). What distinguishes a person under such a vow is not his asceticism but rather his symbolic strength, his total commitment to the advancement of Yahveh's cause. This same vow is met with in the New Testament as well: Paul had placed himself under one (*Acts* 18:18) even before the Jerusalem congregation required it of him (*Acts* 21:23–24). Such a vow can be either for life or for only a specified period.

The Talmud and Mishnah treat all kinds of vows, that is, vows of abstinence as well as vows of consecretion, under the single rubric of *nedarim,* "vows" (*Ned.* 3.4). They advise that any such pledges be restricted as much as possible to basic religious practices. While admitting their usefulness as insurance of unconditional compliance with sacred obligations, the Jewish texts warn that vows must not be undertaken lightly and add that they have only limited validity when made by minors.

Christian vows consist of promises to obey the so-called gospel counsels: poverty, chastity, and obedience. They are taken in the various monastic orders and are implicit in their rules. Affirmation of the counsels is a sign of the Christian's calling within the church to give himself to God, to preach the gospel, and to personify the Lord's dominion. It constitutes an anticipation of heavenly existence. By referring to the calling and thereby underscoring the voluntary and charismatic aspects of monastic life, this article deliberately skirts the notion of ascetic self-indulgence and personal gain rejected by Luther in his Reformation tract *De votis monasticis.* There is such a thing as an unconditional pledge that is of necessity only temporal and is therefore not binding for all eternity.

The Qur'ān and the six canonical works of the *sunnah* warn against excessive use of vows (*nudhūr;* sg., *nadhr*) and make quite clear just what the nature of such pledges ought to be. According to the earliest thinking, they are best related to the basic religious duties and devotions, the intensity of which they tend to heighten. Thus one might vow to pray at specified places and times, to fast on unusual occasions, to undertake pilgrimage to shrines other than Mecca, or—most important of all—to provide additional, voluntary alms. Moreover, it is acceptable to vow to free slaves or to be especially attentive to fellow Muslims, to visit the sick, to attend services for the dead, and to accept invitations to weddings. Restrictive vows, entailing abstinence from certain foods, celibacy, extreme penance, and professions of contrition, are not considered binding. They are rejected for the simple reason that a person who presumes to declare forbidden what is generally allowed is no different from the one who allows what is in fact forbidden. Therefore the Qur'ān explains that monasticism is an innovation "that was not instituted by God, one that was only invented by the generations before you" (*sūrah* 57:27).

In the broadest sense, vows are unconditional promises to do something specific—good or evil. In the narrower sense, they are unqualified pledges to do good, not evil, and as such they are directed solely to God. Often they are cast in hypothetical terms: one "promises to do this or that under the condition that this or that is forthcoming" (Gottschalk, 1919, p. 30). Muḥammad is supposed to have said that a vow does not hasten anything and cannot forestall anything. However the miser's vow makes him better, for essentially he tells God: "Give, that I may give—*da ut dem!*" (ibid., p. 4).

Vows encourage the fulfillment of obligations and the accomplishment of certain tasks. War vows and vows of revenge are clear examples of this; they enlist self-sacrifice and deprivation in the cause of securing just retribution. The *bodhisattva* vow of Mahayana Buddhism consists of the promise not to wish to enter *nirvāṇa* until all creatures have been released from the cycle of rebirth and have attained perfection. It first appears in the legend of the Buddha Amitabha in the second century BCE, and it continues to characterize the aspirations of major sects in China and Japan. It is the key to the salvation doctrine of Amida Buddhism. For if one gives what one receives, so does one receive what one gives. In promising to wait for salvation, one finds salvation in the waiting. Such a vow has cosmic significance. It constitutes sacrifice and self-denial.

Oaths and Their Institutional Forms. Oaths have both a constitutive and an instrumental force. They convey the truth of an assertion, but they also serve as a means whereby it can be determined whether or not that assertion is true. They confirm a promise, and at the same time provide by their very form proof positive of the accuracy of its content.

The instrumental nature of oaths becomes particularly apparent when a judicial system becomes detached from the life of the community, when state and culture are no longer one and the same. In such cases, oaths no longer reveal their constitutive force. In a state trial they function as legally binding proofs. They are one method of arriving at the truth in legal proceedings, and as such they take on regulative importance.

The ritual of oath taking takes numerous forms. In every case there are strict rules governing the behavior of all participants, the rights and obligations of the person swearing, and the specific form in which he pronounces and confirms his pledge. There is a mystique associated with the taking of oaths, one that was especially pronounced in the Indo-European cultural sphere. An obsession with form is typical of such rites, each role being carefully prescribed. An oath could miscarry if for some reason it was impossible to observe strict conventions in the swearing of it.

These conventions applied not only to the person taking the oath but also to his oath-helpers. The use of witnesses is characteristic of the Germanic peoples and is in fact unique to them. They might be members of the oath taker's family or men with whom he has sworn brotherhood. They were not obliged to confirm the substance of his assertion but only to attest to this credibility. Once his oath had been taken, they were called upon to swear—by twos, threes, sixes, or twelves—that it was "pure and not forsworn."

Such oaths of purification could still count for naught in the event of so-called *eidschelte* (ON, "oath challenge"). If the accused chose to force down the raised hand of the person swearing, a duel had to be fought to decide the issue.

The spot where an oath could be sworn, its wording, and all of the attendant gestures were strictly prescribed. The setting was called the *malstat* ("justice site"), *dingstat* ("trial site"), or *richtstat* ("judgment site"). This was where the community regularly gathered for its *Þing*, or legislative assembly, and it was here that sacrifices were offered to the gods and trials were held. An oath circle would be inscribed on the ground and the person swearing required to stand inside it. Under no conditions could he leave the circle or even place a foot outside its perimeter until the ritual was ended.

The wording of oaths differed considerably depending on the authority before which they were sworn and the persons or objects serving as pledges. A man might swear by his sword, his threshold, the plank of his ship, his wife and children, his own life, or one of the gods. The oath taker was required to stand and recite the *argumentum iuramenti*, called the *eidstab* ("oath stave"), in a clear voice and without assistance. On occasion the phrases might first be spoken by either the judge or the accuser, then repeated word for word by the accused. This type of oath was known as a *gestabter eid* ("directed oath").

While swearing, the oath taker had to be touching his pledge with his free hand. It was this physical contact "that established the supernatural bond of the oath, the *mysterium iuramenti*, and gave it its magical force" (Brunner, 1906–1928, vol. 1, p. 257). If the oath was sworn by a god, such contact was accomplished through substitution. An animal was sacrificed to the god and the so-called *eidring* ("oath ring") dipped in its blood. The oath taker then took hold of the ring with one hand while raising the other. Local custom dictated how many of the fingers of his raised hand were to be extended, whether two, three, or all of them.

Everyone participating in the rite had to perform his role in accordance with fixed rules. No distinction was made between the miscarriage of an oath and outright perjury. Form and content were considered one and the same. If one of the oath-helpers swearing overstepped the margin of the oath circle by a fraction of an inch, forgot a portion of the formula, used a wrong word, lowered his hand too quickly, or failed to touch the pledges as required, the oath was useless and the guilt of the accused was established. It was clear that he had perjured himself, and he was required to leave the settlement in dishonor, stripped of all communal ties. Later it became customary to punish a perjurer by chopping off either the fingers he had used in swearing or his entire hand.

In Germanic law a man's whole life might hinge on his oath. Depending on its force in a trial, he could be either saved or doomed. Oaths of fealty and vassalage have the same constitutive importance, as does the citizen's oath of the Middle Ages. The Swiss *Eidgenossenschaft* ("sworn confederacy") takes its strength from the constitutive force of the citizen's oath, and the country's civil code is based on it.

There are, however, a number of traditions in which oaths are accorded only instrumental importance. This is the case in Greek rhetoric, Roman and Islamic law, and in the various modern judicial systems. For them an oath is not proof in itself but only a means of proof. It can be of assistance in determining the truth, yet it is not considered the truth itself.

In Roman civil cases the oath "occupies a less important position than in Germanic ones, for while in the latter it is a statutory right of the accused that regularly takes precedence over other proofs, in the former it only appears at the request of the adversary or the judge when there are no other means for bringing the truth to light" (Bethmann-Hollweg, 1864–1874, vol. 2, p. 573). It serves as a kind of confirmation, strengthened by the fact that God is called to witness it. Here the form and content of oaths, their religious and legal significance, and their ethical and political aspects are distinctly separate.

The ancient writers produced numerous logical, rhetorical, philological, philosophical, and theological treatises on the problem of intent in oaths (*restrictio mentalis*), on the meanings of their terms and their differing connotations, on the degree to which an oath is binding depending on the rank of the deity by which it is sworn, and on the question of how frequently oaths may be required. They speak of sophistic oaths, in which the sense and the wording differ, of involuntary oaths (unlike Plato and Aristotle, Democritus considered all oaths to be valid, even involuntary ones), and finally of the proper form for the naming of pledges. One reads of Rhadamanthys's struggle against the misuse of oaths and of Herakles' effort to do away with them altogether. The Hippocratic oath sworn by physicians has a venerable tradition, surviving as it does into the current time. Always there have been disputes over just what one ought to swear upon (as in the oath of allegiance or loyalty oath) and the degree to which one commits oneself (oaths of office, oaths of vassalage, the oath to the Führer).

In the Bible, oaths are treated in both their constitutive and instrumental senses. The Lord swears an oath by himself (*Dt.* 29:9ff.). That oath is the basis of the covenant with Israel, and he is bound and obligated by it. But for it, he would not have stood behind his chosen people and liberated them from bondage. That divine oath has constitutive force even for God himself. Men are permitted to swear oaths only as long as they call upon God in doing so, but they have not always observed this restriction. Hence Jesus' admonition not to swear at all (*Mt.* 5:34–37). Oaths are to be sworn before the Lord as God; they are not suited for the reinforcement of an intention that does not relate to him (*Mt.* 23:16–22). Jesus rejects the instrumental use of oaths. He nevertheless admits them when they serve to reaffirm the promise implicit in the Lord's name (*Mt.* 5:33). He also admits affirmation in the form of "Yea, yea," "Nay, nay." (*Mt.* 5:37).

This rule is applied by the early Christian church both positively (*Heb.* 6:13–19) and negatively (*Jas.* 5:12). Swearing is permitted, yet oaths are still rejected. Meanwhile the oath had come to serve in an instrumental sense as a confirmation of faith. In 251 CE the antipope Novatian required an oath of allegiance from his followers; he was the first pontiff to do so. Later it became customary for bishops and teachers to take oaths of office, Christian significance was given to the fingers extended when swearing, and oaths were sworn on the Gospels and on relics.

One persistent problem has been whether priests ought to be required to swear oaths to secular authority, as in the oath to the emperor in antiquity, to the Republic during the French Revolution, or to the Führer under National Socialism. The Reformation rejected papal oaths. Various Christian sects—Anabaptists, Jehovah's Witnesses, Mennonites—refuse to take oaths of any kind.

See Also Binding; Covenant.

Bibliography

Bethmann-Hollweg, Moritz August von. *Der Civilprozess des gemeinen Rechts in geschichtlicher Entwicklung.* 6 vols. Bonn, 1864–1874.

Brunner, Heinrich. *Deutsche Rechtsgeschichte.* 2 vols. 2d ed. Leipzig, 1906–1928.

Gold, I. *Das Gelübde nach Bibel und Talmud.* Berlin, 1926.

Gottschalk, Walter. *Das Gelübde nach älterer arabischer Auffassung.* Göttingen, 1919.

Hirzel, Rudolf. *Der Eid: Ein Beitrag zu seiner Geschichte.* Leipzig, 1902.

Lasch, Richard. *Der Eid: Seine Entstehung und Beziehung zu Glaube und Brauch der Naturvölker: Eine ethnologische Studie.* Stuttgart, 1908.

Lex, Peter. *Die Versicherung an Eides statt und ihr Verhältnis zum Geloben und zum feierlichen Eid: Eine rechtshistorische Untersuchung.* Zurich, 1967.

Lichtenthaeler, Charles. *Der Eid des Hippokrates: Ursprung und Bedeutung.* Hippokratische Studien, no. 12. Cologne, 1984.

Mauss, Marcel. *Essai sur le don: Forme et raison d'échange dans les sociétés archaïques.* Paris, 1925. Translated as *The Gift: Forms and Functions of Exchange in Archaic Societies* (New York, 1954).

Pederson, Johannes. *Der Eid bei den Semiten in seinem Verhältnis zu verwandten Erscheinungen sowie die Stellung des Eides im Islam.* Strasbourg, 1914.

Plescia, Joseph. *The Oath and Perjury in Ancient Greece.* Tallahassee, 1970.

Schimmel, Annemarie. "Das Gelübde im türkischen Volksglauben." *Die Welt des Islam,* n. s. 6 (1959–1961): 71–90.

Shirley, Francis A. *Swearing and Perjury in Shakespeare's Plays.* London, 1979.

Thudichum, Friedrich. *Geschichte des Eides* (1911). Reprint, Aalen, 1968.

Thurnwald, Richard. "Eid: Allgemein." In *Reallexikon der Vorgeschichte,* edited by Max Ebert, vol. 2. Berlin, 1925.

Wendel, Adolf. *Das israelitisch-jüdische Gelübde.* Berlin, 1931.

New Sources

Aithen, Robert. "Formal Practice; Buddhist or Christian." *Buddhist-Christian Studies* 22 (2002): 63–77.

Benoritz, Moshe. *Kol Nidre: Studies in the Development of Rabbinic Votive Traditions.* Atlanta, 1998.

Berlinerblau, Jacques. *The Vow and the Popular Religious Groups of Ancient Israel: A Philological and Sociological Inquiry.* Sheffield, U.K., 1996.

Cartledge, Tony. *Vows in the Hebrew Bible and the Ancient Near East.* Sheffield, U.K., 1992.

Cott, Nancy. *Public Vows: A History of Marriage and the Nation.* Cambridge, Mass., 2000.

Fagan, Patrick. *Divided Loyalties: The Question of the Oath for Catholics in the Eighteenth Century.* Dublin, 1997.

Merkl, Judity. *A Different Touch: A Study of Vows in Religious Life.* Collegeville, Minn., 1998.

Stuart, Gershon. *Kol Nidre: Its Origin, Development and Significance.* London, 1994.

Elmar Klinger (1987)
Translated from German by Russell M. Stockman
Revised Bibliography

VRIES, JAN DE (1890–1964), was a Dutch folklorist and historian of religions. Jan Pieter Marie Laurens de Vries was born in Amsterdam on February 11, 1890, and died in Utrecht on July 23, 1964. In 1926, de Vries was appointed to the chair for ancient Germanic linguistics and philology (comprising also Indo-European comparative grammar) at the University of Leiden. Among the numerous positions he held was the editorship of the fifth edition of Winkler Prins's *Algemene Encyclopedie* (General Encyclopedia; 16 vols, 1932–1938); this function occupied him for the entire period of publication. He established also a famous series of classical Dutch literary works, "Bibliotheek der Nederlandsche letteren" (1938–), sponsored by the Society for Dutch Literature and the Royal Flemish Academy of Language and Literature. Internationally famous as a Germanist, he became known in even wider circles as a folklorist. During the 1930s he pleaded fervently and often that the study of folklore (*volkskunde*) be considered a separate discipline, after having already championed the subject in congresses of philologists. The interest in the creativity of the *volk* (from which during this part of his life he excluded the intelligentsia and the urban proletariat, a view evinced in *Volk van Nederland,* published in 1937, which was a work by various authors that de Vries organized and edited, and of which he wrote a major part) was no doubt in tune with some scholarly and general interest fostered all over Europe at the time.

Unlike most scholars, de Vries had a career and lived in a time of history in which one's true colors could not always be kept concealed. After World War II, he was dismissed from his position at the University of Leiden because of his stance and his acts during the war. Under German occupation (1940–1945) he had served as vice-chairman of the Kultuurkamer (the body whose approval was required for any artistic or literary production). In the summer of 1940, shortly after the German invasion, he wrote a pamphlet, *Naar een betere toekomst* (Toward a Better Future), that promulgated his antidemocratic views and hailed the newly opened way toward a world in which the individual would be subordinate to a more encompassing, national structure. He published with National Socialist publishers, worked for a National Socialist journal, and by the end of the war even became a "sympathizing member" of the Schutzstaffel (SS). Many of de Vries's readers, and especially his students, have observed a mystifying inner contradiction in him.

No doubt, there is a conflict that is at the same time an essential ingredient in his work. De Vries was not only an industrious scholar but a very critical mind, a man who despised the crowd, yet longed for a truly harmonious community, which he thought was reflected among ancient Germanic and Norse tribes. Solitary, romantic in his tastes, and of superb intelligence, he seemed blind to the vulgarity of Nazism, to which he committed himself with a fatalistic faithfulness, even seeing its impending defeat, and all the while incapable of realizing the harmony with people for which he longed. It is quite remarkable that de Vries's scholarly work does not show any feature of Nazi ideology or any of the kitsch it spawned. He pursued his scholarly goals unabated during, and also after, the war.

After his retirement in 1955 from a position as secondary schoolteacher in Dutch literature that he held for seven years, he wrote an impressive number of important books. Among them are his *Kelten und Germanen* (1960); *Forschungsgeschichte der Mythologie* (1961), in which his admiration for romantic impulses in history stands out clearly; and *Nederlands etymologisch woordenboek* (1963–1971). The best-known handbook of Germanic religion is the second edition of his *Altgermanische Religionsgeschichte* (2 vols., 1956–1957). De Vries is among the foremost scholars who recognized the importance of Georges Dumézil's work. Throughout his career, however, de Vries maintained his own originality and erudite, critical competence in details. For instance, he points out the lack of clear evidence in Germanic sources for the existence of secret men's societies, yet, with implicit as well as explicit criticism on theoretical models employed by others, he demonstrates various other specific expressions of socioreligious cohesiveness.

SEE ALSO Indo-European Religions.

BIBLIOGRAPHY

Important works by de Vries that have been translated into English include *Heldenlied en Heldensage* (Utrecht, 1959), translated by B. J. Timmer as *Heroic Song and Heroic Legend* (London, 1963), and *Godsdientsgeschiedenis in vogelvlucht,* translated by me as *The Study of Religion: A Historical Approach* (New York, 1967) and later reissued as *Perspectives in the History of Religions* (Berkeley, Calif., 1977).

Other important untranslated works by de Vries include *Altnordische Literaturgeschichte,* 2 vols. (1941–1942; rev. ed., Berlin, 1964–1967), *Het sprookje: Opstellen* (Zutphen, Netherlands, 1929), *Keltische Religion* (Stuttgart, 1961), and *Kleine Schriften* (Berlin, 1965).

Further biographical information about de Vries can be found in my article "Jan de Vries (1890–1964)," *History of Religions* 5 (1965): 173–177, and in P. J. Meerten's article "Jan de Vries," *Volkskunde* 65 (1964): 97–113.

KEES W. BOLLE (1987)

VṚNDĀVANA

VṚNDĀVANA is both a mythical site, mentioned in the Purāṇas, and a town in modern India that is one of the most important Hindu pilgrimage centers of North India and the focus of much religious activity. As a sacred locality known in scripture, Vṛndāvana is ancient, but as a town it is comparatively new.

MYTHICAL SITE. Vṛndāvana (literally, "sacred basil grove") is described in the Purāṇas, most notably in the *Bhāgavata Purāṇa,* as a beautifully forested land associated with the cowherd god Kṛṣṇa. According to the *Bhāgavata Purāṇa,* Kṛṣṇa was born in the royal city of Mathura, but to avoid slaughter by his wicked uncle Kaṃsa his father secretly took him across the Yamuna River to the cowherd settlement of Gokula, where he passed the early years of his infancy. Kaṃsa soon learned of Kṛṣṇa's whereabouts, however, and began to send various demons to destroy him. When the danger grew too great, the cowherds who had taken in Kṛṣṇa moved to a new site—the beautifully forested land of Vṛndāvana—and there set up an idyllic village. In the land of Vṛndāvana, Kṛṣṇa charmed the elders of the village with mischievous pranks and frolicked in the forest herding cattle with his young companions. Most important, though, it was in the forests of Vṛndāvana that Kṛṣṇa would meet with the adolescent *gopīs* (cowherdesses) of the village under the autumn moon for love trysts. Kṛṣṇa's passionate affairs with the *gopīs* have been elaborated on extensively since medieval times, and one *gopī* in particular—Rādhā—rose to the position of Kṛṣṇa's favorite. The intimate relationships exemplified between Kṛṣṇa and his lovers in Vṛndāvana came to symbolize the human's true relationship with the divine. For the practicing Vaiṣṇava, Vṛndāvana is an eternal world, a heavenly paradise that the liberated soul achieves after ultimate success.

MODERN-DAY TOWN. The modern-day town of Vṛndāvana (also known as Brindavan) is located on the west bank of the Yamuna River, about eighty miles south of Delhi and forty miles north of Agra, and is situated in the modern Indian state of Uttar Pradesh. Vṛndāvana can best be understood, however, by viewing it as part of Vraja (Braj), a distinct cultural region, complete with a distinct language (Vrajabhāṣa, or Brajbhāṣa) and history, defined by its association with the Kṛṣṇa myth. Through complex historical developments of the sixteenth century, this region came to be identified as the very land where Kṛṣṇa actually lived long ago. The town of Vṛndāvana, in particular, was built on a site identified as the forest where Kṛṣṇa met with Rādhā and the other *gopīs* for their nightly trysts.

The historical development of Vṛndāvana was due primarily to the disciples of the Bengali saint Caitanya (b. 1486 CE), who came to be known as the Gauḍīya Vaiṣṇavas. The "reclaiming" of the sites of Kṛṣṇa's exploits on earth was a cherished dream of Caitanya. Although the saint himself visited the area surrounding Vṛndāvana only once, he had sent before him a close disciple named Lokanātha Ācārya and then later, a group of theologians known as the Six Gosvāmins of Vṛndāvana. The establishment of Vṛndāvana as an important religious center is chiefly the work of this group of theologians, especially two brothers among them, Rūpa and Sanātana Gosvāmin. These brothers were to have the first of the magnificent temples of Vṛndāvana built in the sixteenth century with the help of wealthy rajas of Rajasthan. They were also responsible for establishing the location of many of the sites associated with the Kṛṣṇa myth and for creating a center of Vaiṣṇava learning in Vṛndāvana.

Three other Vaiṣṇava sects were involved in the development of Vraja culture that took place in and around Vṛndāvana, namely, the Rādhāvallabhas, the Vallabhācāryas, and the Nimbārkas. Vṛndāvana continued to grow and develop as an important center for all Vaiṣṇavas, and with the construction of a large Śrī Vaiṣṇava temple in Vṛndāvana in the mid-nineteenth century, all major sects of Vaiṣṇavism came to be represented in Vṛndāvana.

Today hundreds of pilgrims flock into Vṛndāvana daily, their numbers increasing substantially during the four monsoon months when, as legend has it, all other pilgrimage sites come to reside in Vṛndāvana. These pilgrims come to walk the very land trodden by Lord Kṛṣṇa and to see the natural objects transformed by his contact. They come also to see Kṛṣṇa in another important form—as an image (*mūrti*) residing for the benefit of his worshipers in the many famous temples of Vṛndāvana. But most important, they come during the rainy season to see the numerous plays staged all over Vṛndāvana that depict stories of Kṛṣṇa and his intimate companions. Vṛndāvana continues to thrive—many new temples are being constructed today—making it a living center of traditional Hindu culture.

SEE ALSO Caitanya; Hindi Religious Traditions; Kṛṣṇa; Rādhā; Vaiṣṇavism, article on Bhāgavatas.

BIBLIOGRAPHY

William G. Archer's *The Loves of Krishna in Indian Painting and Poetry* (New York, 1957) remains one of the best introductions to the Kṛṣṇa myth. See especially chapter 3 for a good (if brief) description of Kṛṣṇa's exploits in Vṛndāvana. The best sourcebook for the modern-day town of Vṛndāvana is still Fredrick S. Growse's *Mathurā: A District Memoir,* 3d rev. ed. (Allahabad, 1883). Although this work is now quite dated, it provides detailed descriptions of the history and temples of Vṛndāvana. Charlotte Vaudeville's article "Braj: Lost and Found," *Indo-Iranian Journal* 18 (1976): 195–213, is useful for understanding the cultural condition of the area surrounding Vṛndāvana before its development by the Vaisnava Gosvāmins. For a good description of the Kṛṣṇa dramas of Vṛndāvana, see Norvin Hein's *The Miracle Plays of Mathurā* (New Haven, Conn., 1972) and John Stratton Hawley's *At Play with Krishna: Pilgrimage Dramas from Brindavan* (Princeton, N. J., 1981).

New Sources

Case, Margaret H. *Seeing Krishna: The Religious World of a Brahmin Family in Vrindaban.* New York, 1999.

Das, R. K. *Temples of Vrindaban.* Delhi, 1990.

Entwistle, A. W. *Braj: Centre of Krishna Pilgrimage.* Groningen Oriental studies, v. 3. Groningen, 1987.

Mahanidhi, Swami. *The Gaudiya Vaisnava Samadhis in Vrindavana.* Vrindavan, 1993.

DAVID L. HABERMAN (1987)
Revised Bibliography

VṚTRA, whose name is probably derived from the Sanskrit verbal root *vṛ,* meaning "hold back, restrain, envelop," is a serpent slain by Indra in the *Ṛgveda.* This act, which is Indra's most famous, most important, and most frequently mentioned achievement, is the subject of several complete Ṛgvedic hymns (notably *Ṛgveda* 1.32 and 10.124). Vṛtra had coiled around a mountain, preventing the waters from flowing down; Indra pierced him with his thunderbolt and released the waters. This act has many symbolic resonances: slaying the dragon, releasing the waters or rains, bringing the ambrosial *soma* down from heaven or the mountains (an act that Indra is elsewhere said to accomplish by stealing it, on the back of an eagle), conquering the enemies of the invading Indo-Aryans (for Vṛtra is called a *dāsa,* or "slave," the name given to the indigenous non-Aryans), creating the world out of the body of the slain dragon, or rescuing it from the dragon who had swallowed it. The thunderbolt of Indra is a cloud, which, as a phallic symbol, is a source of seed as well as rain; Vṛtra is a cloud pierced in his loins or his bellies; and the cows to which the waters are compared are also rain clouds. Vṛtra, who is depicted as a serpent or as a dragon whose arms and legs Indra has cut off, is a symbol of danger, constriction, drought, and loss. The battle is waged with magic as well as with physical weapons; Indra uses magic to make himself as thin as a horse's hair, and Vṛtra uses magic to create lightning and fog. Indra wins, of course, and the hymns end on a note of affirmation for Indra's victory.

The killing of Vṛtra was closely associated with the killing of other demonic enemies, particularly Triśiras Viśvarūpa (the "three-headed, many-formed" son of Tvaṣṭṛ, the artisan of the gods), Namuci ("don't-let-go"), and Ahi (the Serpent, perhaps just another name for Vṛtra). Vṛtra is the younger brother of Triśiras, created by their father to take revenge upon Indra for the killing of Triśiras. This mythology is elaborated in the Brāhmaṇas (c. 900 BCE), where it is said that when Indra killed Visvarupa he cut off his three heads, which became three birds; Tvaṣṭṛ performed a sacrifice to create Vṛtra. Namuci is a demon whom Indra is said to have killed with foam (*Ṛgveda* 8.14.13); later, Indra kills both Vṛtra and Namuci with foam at the juncture of day and night (*Taittirīya Brāhmaṇa* 1.7.1–7), when he had promised Namuci that he would kill him neither by day nor by night, neither with anything dry nor with anything wet (*Śatapatha Brāhmaṇa* 12.7.3.1–2). In the *Mahābhārata* (5.9–13), Indra kills Vṛtra alone by tricking him in this way. The cosmogonic implications of the killing of Vṛtra are spelled out in the Brāhmaṇas: Vṛtra lay covering all the space between heaven and earth until Indra killed him (*Śatapatha Brāhmaṇa* 1.1.3.4–5); when Indra killed Vṛtra, Vṛtra said to him, "You are now what I was; now cut me in two" (ibid., 1.6.3.1–17).

The killing of Vṛtra, particularly when combined with the accessory acts of killing Trisiras and Namuci, fits a pattern that has strong resonances in other Indo-European mythologies. In the Avesta, Thraetaona kills a three-headed demon and sets free the cows that have been imprisoned. In Greece, Herakles kills the three-headed Geryon, and the Roman Hercules kills Cacus, the son of Vulcan (who is, like Tvaṣṭṛ, the blacksmith of the gods). Þórr (Thor), Indra's parallel in Eddic literature, kills the World Serpent. And in a more general way, Vṛtra can be assimilated to all the dragons killed by all the great heroes—to Python slain by Apollo, to the dragon killed by Saint George, and so forth.

As Indra's powers diminished during the period of transition from the *Ṛgveda* to the Brāhmaṇas, the killing of Vṛtra was no longer regarded as an act that he could accomplish in single combat. Other gods help him (*Aitareya Brāhmaṇa* 2.3.5), or he uses the power of sacrifice rather than brute force (*Śatapatha Brāhmaṇa* 2.5.4.1–9); finally, as with Namuci, he hedges with words to break his treaty (ibid., 1.6.3.10). In the *Mahābhārata,* Indra is so overpowered by Vṛtra's superior magic and prowess that the demon can be slain only with the aid of Śiva (who creates a fever in Vṛtra) and Viṣṇu (who places his own power in Indra's thunderbolt). Moreover, even after killing Vṛtra, Indra is so weakened and defiled (polluted by the sin of brahmanicide for having killed Vṛtra, a priest) that he runs away and hides in a lotus stalk; still the fury (*kṛtyā*) of brahmanicide incarnate seizes Indra until Brahmā distributes the sin among fire, water, the trees, and the celestial nymphs, and purifies Indra with a horse sacrifice (*Mahābhārata* 12.272–273).

Thus the ancient myth of the dragon whose body is dismembered to form the world (as Tiamat's body does in the Mesopotamian myth) is transformed into an epic myth in which the sin of the warrior who kills the dragon is dismembered, as it were, to provide the substances that guarantee the fertility of the world. In either case, it is, ultimately, the dragon that is the source of that fertility; the darker side of creation and the sin that inevitably arises in dealing with it, rather than the hero and his virtue, is the source of life.

SEE ALSO Indian Religions, article on Mythic Themes; Indra; Snakes.

BIBLIOGRAPHY

Vṛtra et Verethraghna by Émile Benveniste and Louis Renou (Paris, 1934) remains the classic study of this myth; it has been imaginatively augmented and extended by Georges Dumézil's writings, particularly *The Destiny of the Warrior,* translated by Alf Hiltebeital (Chicago, 1970). The major myths of Indra and Vṛtra, together with a lengthy bibliography of the secondary literature, are assembled on pages 74–90 and 320–321 of my *Hindu Myths* (Baltimore, 1975) and discussed on pages 102–111 of my *The Origins of Evil in Hindu Mythology* (Berkeley, Calif., 1976). Sukumari Bhattacharji's *The Indian Theogony* (Cambridge, 1970) summarizes the details of the encounter on pages 251–259.

WENDY DONIGER (1987)

VULVA SEE YONI

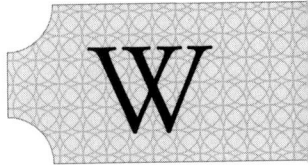

W

WACH, JOACHIM [FIRST EDITION] (1898–1955), German-American historian of religions. Wach was born in Chemnitz, Saxony, and died while vacationing in Orselina, Switzerland. He was a descendant of Moses Mendelssohn, a lineage that affected his life and career both positively and negatively. His paternal grandfather, the noted jurisconsult Adolph Wach, married Lily, the daughter of Felix Mendelssohn, the composer. His father, Felix, married Kathe, granddaughter of the composer's brother, Paul. Young Wach was early exposed to music, literature, poetry, and both classical and modern languages. After two years of military service (1916–1918), Wach enrolled at the University of Leipzig, but in 1919 and early 1920 he studied with Friedrich Heiler at Munich and with Ernst Troeltsch at Berlin. He then returned to Leipzig to study Oriental languages and the history and philosophy of religion. For a time he came under the spell of the enigmatic poet Stefan George, whose writings spoke of a heightened sense of "experience," through which one perceives the multiple threads of the tapestry of life as a transparent whole. Wach received his Ph.D. degree in 1922 from Leipzig with a thesis entitled "The Foundations of a Phenomenology of the Concept of Salvation," published as *Der Erlösungsgedanke und seine Deutung* (1922).

When Wach started teaching at Leipzig in 1924, the discipline of the history of religions *(Religionswissenschaft),* still in its infancy, faced serious dangers. On the one side, its right to exist was questioned by those who insisted that whoever knows one religion (i.e., Christianity) knows all religions; on the other, its religio-scientific methodology was challenged by reductionist psychological and social-scientific approaches. Thus in his habilitation thesis, *Religionswissenschaft: Prolegomena zu ihrer wissenschaftstheoretischen Grundlegung* (1924), Wach insisted on the integrity and autonomy of the history of religions, liberated from theology and the philosophy of religion. He emphasized that both historical and systematic dimensions are necessary to its task, and he argued that the discipline's goal was "understanding" *(Verstehen):* "The task of *Religionswissenschaft* is to study and to describe the empirical religions. It seeks descriptive understanding; it is not a normative discipline. When it has understood the historical and systematic aspects of the con-

---

CLOCKWISE FROM TOP LEFT CORNER. Engraving of a commune of witches, undated. *[©Bettmann/Corbis]*; Tenth-century ivory diptych showing the crucifixion, the Madonna and Child, and Christian saints. Biblioteca Apostolica Vaticana, Vatican Museums. *[©Scala/Art Resource, N.Y.]*; *The Four Horsemen of the Apocalypse,* woodcut, c. 1496, by Albrecht Dürer. *[©Burstein Collection/Corbis]*; Dogon altar object from Mali. *[©Werner Forman/Art Resource, N.Y.]*; King Gudea with a vase overflowing with water and fish, c. 2140 BCE. Louvre, Paris. *[©Erich Lessing/Art Resource, N.Y.]* .

crete religious configurations, it has fulfilled its task" (p. 68). His *Religionswissenschaft* is still regarded as a small classic in the field.

Wach's agenda centering on understanding led him to produce a three-volume work on the development of hermeneutics in the nineteenth century (*Das Verstehen,* 1926–1933). The first volume traced the hermeneutical theories of such major figures as Friedrich Schleiermacher, G. A. F. Ast, F. A. Wolf, August Boeckh, and Wilhelm von Humboldt. The second volume dealt with theological hermeneutics from Schleiermacher to Johannes von Hofmann, while the third volume examined theories of historical hermeneutics from Leopold von Ranke to historical positivism. Understandably, Wach felt it absolutely necessary to establish solid hermeneutical foundations for the history of religions.

Wach was convinced that the history of religions *(Religionswissenschaft)* should not lose its empirical character. He felt that C. P. Tiele and P. D. Chantepie de la Saussaye had failed to make an adequate distinction between the history of religions and the philosophy of religion. He was critical both of those who started with philosophy and developed science and of those who started with science and moved toward philosophy. In his view, the history of religions lay, rather, precisely between the two. In this respect he followed Max Scheler, who posited a "concrete phenomenology of religious objects and acts" between a historical study of religions (a positive *Religionswissenschaft*) and the essential phenomenology of religion *(die Wesensphänomenologie der Religion).* According to Scheler, this intermediate discipline aims at the fullest understanding of the intellectual contents of one or more religious forms and the consummate acts in which these intellectual contents have been given. It was Wach's conviction that an inquiry such as Scheler envisaged could be carried out only by employing the religio-scientific method of *Religionswissenschaft.*

Wach's reputation for erudition attracted many students to Leipzig. However, his productive career there came to an abrupt end in April 1935. The government of Saxony, under pressure from the Nazis, terminated Wach's university appointment on the ground of his Jewish lineage, even though his family had been Christian for four generations. Fortunately, through the intervention of American friends, Wach was invited to teach at Brown University in Providence, Rhode Island, where he stayed until 1945. His adjustment to the new environment was by no means easy; he was especially anxious about his mother, sister, and brother, who were suffering under the Nazi tyranny. From 1945 until his death ten years later, Wach taught the history of religions at the Divinity School of the University of Chicago.

Wach always asserted that the method of the history of religions must be commensurate with its subject matter, that is, the nature and expressions of the religious experience of humankind as that experience has been unfolded in history. Following his mentor, Rudolf Otto, Wach defined religious experience as the experience of the holy. Throughout his life, he never altered his views on the basic structure of the discipline: its twin tasks (historical and theoretical); the centrality of religious experience and its threefold expressions (theoretical, practical, and sociological); and the crucial importance of hermeneutics. But Wach emphasized three different methodological accents in three successive phases of his career.

During his first phase, Wach was preoccupied with the hermeneutical basis for the descriptive-historical task of the discipline. He was greatly influenced by the philological hermeneutics of August Boeckh, who defined the hermeneutical task as "recognizing" that which had previously been "cognized," that is, as articulating what has been recognized in its pristine character, even to the extent of "reconstructing" in its totality that which does not appear as a whole. Accordingly, Wach insisted that the historian of religions must first try to assimilate that which had been recognized as a religious phenomenon and "reproduce" it as one's own. Then he must observe and appraise that which has become one's own as an objective something apart from oneself.

During his second phase, Wach attempted to develop the systematic dimension of the history of religions by following the model of sociology. In Wach's view, the sociological (systematic) task of *Religionswissenschaft* had two main foci: (1) the interrelation of religion and society, which requires an examination, first, of the sociological roots and functions of myths, doctrines, cults, and associations, and, second, of the sociologically significant function and effect of religion in society; and (2) the study of religious groups. In dealing with religious groups, and especially with the variety of self-interpretations advanced by these groups, Wach employed the typological method. As he stated in his *Sociology of Religion* (1944), he was convinced of the need to develop a closer rapport between *Religionswissenschaft* and other disciplines, especially with the social and human sciences. In this sense, his *Sociology of Religion* was an attempt to bridge "the gulf which still exists between the study of religion and the social sciences" (p. v). Yet the ultimate aim of his sociological (systematic) study of religion was "to gain new insights into the relations between the various forms of expression of religious experience and eventually to understand better the various aspects of religious experience itself" (p. 5).

During the third phase, Wach's concern for an integral understanding of the various aspects of religious experience and its expressions led him to reassess not only the relationship of *Religionswissenschaft* with the social sciences but also its relationship with normative disciplines such as philosophy of religion and the various theologies. After Wach's sojourn in India, where he delivered the Barrows Lectures at various universities in 1952, this concern became more pronounced. It was, in fact, one of the key motifs of his lectures on the history of religions sponsored by the American Council of Learned Societies in 1954. Increasingly the vocabulary of "explaining" *(Deuten, Erklären)* came to be used side by side with that of "understanding" *(Verstehen)* in his lectures. Wach shared his dream of pursuing a new grand synthesis for the study of the human religious experience, a sequel to earlier works such as *Religionswissenschaft* and *Das Verstehen,* with friends during the Seventh Congress of the International Association for the History of Religion, held in Rome in the spring of 1955. But death came that summer and robbed him of this venture.

BIBLIOGRAPHY

Among Wach's important contributions to the study of religion are *Der Erlösungsgedanke und seine Deutung* (Leipzig, 1922) and *Das Verstehen: Grundzüge einer Geschichte der hermeneutischen Theorie im 19. Jahrhundert,* 3 vols. (1926–1933; reprint, Hildesheim, 1966). Neither of these works has been translated into English. The following books by Wach are available in English: *Sociology of Religion* (Chicago, 1944), *Types of Religious Experience: Christian and Non-Christian* (Chicago, 1951), and the posthumously published *The Comparative Study of Religions* (New York, 1958) and *Understanding and Believing: Essays* (New York, 1968).

Treatments of Wach's thought include the following: my "Joachim Wach et la sociologie de la religion," *Archives de sociologie des religions* 1 (1956): 25–41; Kurt Rudolph's "Joachim Wach," in *Bedeutende Gelehrte in Leipzig,* vol. 1 (Leipzig, 1965); my "Verstehen and Erlösung: Some Remarks on Joachim Wach's Work," *History of Religions* 11 (1971): 31–54; and Rainer Flasche's *Die Religionswissenschaft von Joachim Wach* (New York, 1978).

JOSEPH M. KITAGAWA (1987)

WACH, JOACHIM [FURTHER CONSIDERATIONS]. True to his highly cultured family background, Joachim Wach remained a passionate devotee of music, literature, and the arts throughout his life. This devotion dovetailed with his scholarly interest in religions. During his years as a student at Leipzig, where he majored in the history of religions and minored in philosophy of religion and "Oriental" studies, his friends included poets, musicians, and dancers, in addition to scientists and physicians. After taking his doctorate, he spent two years studying at the University of Heidelberg, where he attended lectures by the eminent historian and literary scholar Friedrich Gundolf (1880–1931), who had a lastingly influence on Wach. It was during those Heidelberg years that Wach became associated with the poet Stefan George (1868–1933), who, with his famous circle, or *Kreis,* of disciples (including Gundolf, one of Wach's closest links to the group), aspired to create a new world and culture of pure, sublime art. The most significant aesthetic commitment of his life, Wach's allegiance to the George-*Kreis* is thought to have been largely the source of his lasting concern with the problem and mission of understanding (*Verstehen*), and to have stamped his whole personality for life (see Flasche, 1978, p. 14).

There is abundant lore about Wach's lifelong active interest in literature and the arts. During his years as professor at the University of Chicago (1945–1955), he was known for listening as he worked to recordings of music by his ancestor Felix Mendelssohn, and for being able to quote from memory lengthy passages from the verse of Goethe, Schiller, and other classic German poets. Nonetheless, the bearing of his aesthetic reflections upon his formation as a historian of religions is generally underappreciated. In this respect he was not alone among some of the most influential mid-twentieth-century comparatists of religions. To him, as to Gerardus van der Leeuw, would apply what Joseph Kitagawa once said of Mircea Eliade, namely, that he had a passion for culture (*paideia*) in the Greek sense of the word. As with van der Leeuw, the accomplished poet and musician, and Eliade, the celebrated novelist and short-story writer, Wach's passion for *paideia* meant that his vocation of studying and interpreting a universal range of religious phenomena was complemented by, and inextricably related to, a rich variety of aesthetic concerns.

Presumably, the influence of the George-*Kreis,* especially through Gundolf, was among the chief factors that led Wach from the outset of his career to liken the investigation of religions to the contemplation of literature and the arts. As the *Kreis* is thought to have instilled in Wach a preoccupation with hermeneutics, so is it clear that Gundolf's ideas about the relation between the artist and the artist's work stimulated Wach's thinking about the relation between religious experience and the various forms of religious expression (practical, theoretical, and sociological). Wach opined that the great experiences from which all religious traditions originate "exist for others only in the degree to which they are expressed and where there is genuine religion, it will necessarily be expressed" (Wach, 1958, p. 59). He ascribed this idea to C. P. Tiele. However, it also calls to mind the claim in Gundolf's classic biography *Goethe* (1922) that, while the artist's experience (*Erlebnis*) may be superficially distinguishable from the artist's work, the artist exists only insofar as he "expresses himself" (*sich ausdrückt*) through the work (p. 2).

Wach associated the study of religions with the study of the arts as early as in his Habilitation thesis *Religionswissenschaft* (1924), known in translation as *The History of Religions.* Dismissing the common notion of understanding as empathy (*Nachfühlen*) or imitative experience (*Nacherleben*), and characterizing understanding instead as "an entirely spontaneous, productive act," he contends in this work that to interpret a religion or a work of art requires no consideration of its originator's "psychological condition" (Wach, 1988b, p. 111). While he followed Wilhelm Dilthey in likening the interpretation of a religion to that of an art work, Wach discounted the common analogization of having a religious sense to possessing an ear for music. Inasmuch as he dismissed the assumption that persons who profess no religious faith or confession are "religiously unmusical" (p. 115), he differed from Max Weber. The latter considered some people, including himself, to be "religiously unmusical," and cast them as antithetical to the religious "virtuoso" (a term adapted from musicology). Wach instead remained in harmony with the theory of Rudolf Otto, contending that "humanity, by nature, is attuned to religion," and therefore: "The study of music knows that there is no such thing as an unmusical person; such a person often lacks only the training and development of an ear for music. It would be good, too, if historians of religions would realize that a poorly developed religious sense never means that such a sense is lacking altogether" (p. 115).

Of all the arts, Wach invoked poetry the most extensively to illustrate his notion of understanding. To counter a common misinterpretation of Dilthey's view of the relation between experience (*Erlebnis*) and understanding, he contended that the possibilities of human experience are not limited to the totality of a person's external experience of life (*äussere Lebenserfahrung*): one need not have been in love, waged battle, or grown old to understand a lover, a general, or the aged. Poets afford practical illustrations of, and in some instances reflect theoretically upon, the fact that external experiences (*Erfahrungen*) can be presaged by internal experience (*inneres Erleben*). This is not to deny the formative bearing of external experience upon poetry. In probing the theoretical ramifications of this problem of imagination (*Phantasie*), experience (*Erlebnis*), and poetry, Wach was well aware of Dilthey's observation that poetic creation invariably originates from "life-experience" (*Lebenserfahrung*). Like Dilthey, who qualified that "only those moments of [the poet's] existence [*Dasein*] that disclose to him one of life's characteristics possess a deeper relationship to his poetry" (quoted in Wach, 1988b, p. 218n.), Wach emphasized that what ultimately matters for poetry is what the poet makes of external experiences through inner, imaginative power: "It is by imagination that experiences first bear fruit. To an amazing degree, imagination may supplement experiences and even substitute for them" (Wach, 1988b, p. 113).

Such reflections were germane to Wach's conception of his *religionswissenschaftlich* enterprise. His distinction between life-experiences and what the poet imaginatively makes of them harks back to Aristotle's distinction between history as that which conveys particular truths (telling what happened), and poetry as that which conveys universal truths (telling what might happen). Much as Aristotle viewed poetry as something graver and more scientific than history (see *Poetics* 1451a–b), so Wach deemed *Religionswissenschaft* to be hermeneutically more sophisticated than the positivist, historicist approach to religion. While the historicist was preoccupied with thoroughness of arbitrarily selected data, Wach urged the scholar of religions "to determine by comparison and phenomenological analysis if anything like a structure can be discovered in all these forms of expression, to what kind of experience this variegated expression can be traced, and, finally, what kind of reality or realities may correspond to the experiences in question" (Wach, 1951, p. 30).

Wach indicated how his pondering of poetry informed his conception of his scholarly vocation. In his view, the novelist Thomas Mann's idea of the poet's yearning (*Sehnsucht*) "signified the soul's inner ability and readiness to transcend itself," a task the soul accomplishes through the imagination: "For imagination allows ideas to be grasped, feelings to be felt, and realms of the soul to be traversed that actual experience [*Erfahrung*] could never teach the poet" (Wach, 1988b, p. 113). In this respect the poet resembles the scholar, whose "interest is stimulated by the appearance of a great personality, of significant processes, or of a tragic event" (p. 113). Given the same "inner affinity" as that between the poet and the poet's object, "the person who wishes to understand enters into a mysterious communication with the object of study that allows him to penetrate to its core" (p. 113). With an imagination thus aroused, the person feels drawn to seek a broader, deeper, more precise understanding of the object of interest, and "yearns to develop further those dispositions of the soul that have not yet been realized. Thus, the limits of the empirical personality are expanded" (p. 113). This analogy between poetic yearning and the aroused scholarly imagination anticipates Eliade's well-known construal of literary creation and aesthetic imagination as cognitive, epistemological instruments useful to the scholarly enterprise.

Although Wach often appealed abstractly to the categories of "poet" and "poetry," sometimes particular works by specific literary artists proved revelatory to him as a historian of religions. For example, he found Friedrich Hölderlin's poetic depiction of the bond between Empedocles and Pausanias to exemplify the typal master-disciple relation (Wach, 1988a, pp. 15–16, 19, 22), and his essay on "religious existence" in Fyodor Dostoevsky's novels praises the German Catholic theologian Romano Guardini for revealing in those texts the "groundlines of a Christian anthropology" (Wach, 1934, p. 196). Wach's *Sociology of Religion* (1944) is replete with allusions to prevalent symptoms of the interplay between religions and the arts, such as the "aesthetic finish" of Trobriand magic; the priestly fostering of sacred song, music, dance, and literary and visual arts; Australian Aboriginal totemic practices; and certain rituals associated with prophets. However, Wach elsewhere qualified that the practical, "activistic" orientation of religious experience, involving "an imperative, a commitment which impels man to act," distinguishes it from "aesthetic experience, of which it shares the intensity, and joins it with moral experience" (Wach, 1951, p. 33).

Bibliography

Among the studies by Wach that reflect his interest in the arts are his essay "Religiöse Existenz: Zu dem Dostojewskij-Buch Romano Guardinis," *Zeitschrift für Missionskunde und Religionswissenschaft*, 40th issue, 7th installment (1934): 193–201; *Sociology of Religion* (Chicago, 1944); *Types of Religious Experience: Christian and Non-Christian* (Chicago, 1951); *The Comparative Study of Religions* (New York, 1958); *Essays in the History of Religions*, edited by Joseph M. Kitagawa and Gregory D. Alles (New York, 1988a); and *Introduction to the History of Religions*, edited by Joseph M. Kitagawa and Gregory D. Alles (New York, 1988b), the first part of which constitutes a translation of Wach's Habilitation thesis *Religionswissenschaft: Prolegomena zu ihrer wissenschaftstheoretischen Grundlegung* (Leipzig, 1924). Wach's undated paper, "Stefan George (1863–1933): Poet and Priest of Modern Paganism," was published posthumously in his *Understanding and Believing: Essays* (New York, 1968), pp. 11–29.

Aside from Rainer Flasche's *Die Religionswissenschaft von Joachim Wach* (New York, 1978) and the other secondary sources cited in the bibliography to Kitagawa's entry on Wach above, two pertinent studies include Flasche, "Joachim Wach (1898–1955)," in *Klassiker der Religionswissenschaft von Friedrich Schleiermacher bis Mircea Eliade*, edited by Axel Michaels (Darmstadt, 1997), pp. 290–302; and Eric Ziolkowski, "Wach, Religion, and 'The Emancipation of Art,'" *Numen* 46 (1999): 345–369.

ERIC ZIOLKOWSKI (2005)

WAHHĀBĪYAH. An Islamic renewal group established by Muḥammad ibn ʿAbd al-Wahhāb (d. AH 1206/1792 CE), the Wahhābīyah continues to the present in the Arabian Peninsula. The term *Wahhābī* was originally used by opponents of the movement, who charged that it was a new form of Islam, but the name eventually gained wide acceptance. According to the teachings of Ibn ʿAbd al-Wahhāb, however, the movement is not a new Islamic school but, rather, a call or mission *(daʿwah al tawḥīd)* for the true implementation of Islam. The Wahhābīyah often refer to "the mission of the oneness of God" *(daʿwat al-tawḥīd)* and call themselves "those who affirm the oneness of God," or *muwaḥḥidun.*

HISTORICAL BACKGROUND AND CONTEXT. Renewal movements have deep roots in Islamic experience. The Qurʾān and the *sunnah,* or normative practice of the prophet Muḥammad, provide standards by which the belief and actions of Muslims in any age can be judged. A strict interpretation of these fundamentals has often provided the basis for an active call for reform. The Wahhābī call is one of the most famous of these so-called fundamentalist movements. Specifically, it can be seen as a continuation of the strict Sunnī tradition associated with the Ḥanbalī school of law based on the teaching of Aḥmad ibn Ḥanbal (d. 855 CE).

Aḥmad ibn Taymīyah (d. 1328) was a Ḥanbalī scholar whose works have had a major influence on the thinking of fundamentalist advocates of renewal. He became well known for his opposition to devotional innovations and popular religious customs not specified in the Qurʾān or *sunnah.* His preaching against even established scholars made his work controversial, while his polemical skills made him popular.

The core of his teaching was the "science of the oneness of God" *(ʿilm al-tawḥīd),* which stresses the comprehensive nature and unity of the Islamic message. Rationality, mystic intuition, and the legal prescriptions are seen as parts of a single whole. Ibn Taymīyah rejected claims by Islamic mystics that "the law" and "the [mystical] path" were somehow separate. He also stressed that independent interpretation *(ijtihād)* by scholars was possible, although subject to clear rules. He actively opposed what he considered innovations in devotional practices, such as the visitation of the tombs of famous figures. In these and other themes Ibn Taymīyah provided a basis for later Sunnī fundamentalism, including the Wahhābīyah.

The Ḥanbalī school did not gain a mass following in the Islamic world, but groups of Ḥanbalī scholars had local influence in some regions. One such region was the Najd in central Arabia, where the Ḥanbalī tradition continued in towns with established families of Ḥanbalī teachers. Nevertheless, the local lifestyle in the Najd did not reflect a fundamentalist spirit. People commonly believed that trees and rocks possessed spiritual powers and that the graves of holy men were places of special holiness. Such a society contained many elements that Islamic fundamentalists view as manifestations of polytheism (*shirk*) and the ignorance of the pre-Islamic era (Jāhīliyah).

Najd was not unique in the eighteenth-century Islamic world. While Islam had flourished in the strong empires of the fifteenth and sixeenth centuries, by the eighteenth century, compromises with local religious customs and ineffective political organizations led Muslims from West Africa to Southeast Asia to call for Islamic renewal. The Wahhābī movement emerged at the very center of this world.

HISTORY OF THE MOVEMENT. Wahhābī history can be divided into three periods, in each of which the movement is associated with the establishment of a state as well as a community of believers. While the call has been Wahhābī, the state in each case was based on leadership by the Saʿūd family.

The era of Muḥammad ibn ʿAbd al-Wahhāb. Muḥammad ibn ʿAbd al-Wahhāb, born in the central Arabian town of al-ʿUyaynah in 1703, traveled and studied widely. In the process, he developed a belief in the need for purification of Muslim beliefs and practices, and this belief became his life's mission.

At first the mission took the form of preaching opposition to popular religious practices and Shīʿī Islam, in Basra and eastern Arabia. Returning to his homeland to continue this call, he initially won some support from the ruler of al-ʿUyaynah, but the vigor of his purification efforts soon aroused opposition, and he was forced to leave.

Ibn ʿAbd al-Wahhāb then went to al-Darʿī yah, where the ruler was Muḥammad ibn Saʿūd. In 1744 the two men formed an alliance that became the basis for both the subsequent Saudi states and the Wahhābī movement. The ruler and the teacher worked together in the creation of the first Saudi-Wahhābī state.

The deaths of Ibn Saʿūd in 1765 and of Ibn ʿAbd al-Wahhāb in 1792 did not stop the expansion of the mission or the state. Political leadership remained in the hands of the Saʿūd family, while the family of Ibn ʿAbd al-Wahhāb, subsequently called "the family of the shaykh," or Āl al-

Shaykh, maintained a position of intellectual leadership in the later history of the state and movement.

By the beginning of the nineteenth century, the Saudi-Wahhābī community controlled most of the Arabian Peninsula and the holy cities of Mecca and Medina. This central position and attacks on Ottoman territories in Iraq and Syria brought a reaction, however: The Ottoman sultan ordered the governor of Egypt, Muḥammad ʿAli, to use his newly reformed army to defeat the Wahhābīyah. In 1812, the Egyptian army took Medina and in 1818 captured the Saudi capital of al-Darʿī yah. With this defeat, the first phase of Wahhābī history came to an end.

The second Saudi-Wahhābī state. The Egyptian army did not remain long in central Arabia, and Saudi leaders soon reestablished their state with a new capital at Riyadh. Key figures in this restoration were a grandson of Muḥammad ibn Saʿūd, Turkī (d. 1834), and his son Fayṣal (d. 1865). Although smaller than the first, the new state restored the political and religious mission of the original one. An important part of the Wahhābī heritage is the work of administering and consolidating a functioning fundamentalist state in the nineteenth century.

In the last quarter of the nineteenth century the Saudi ruling family divided, and in the conflicts that followed the death of Fayṣal, other Arabian chieftains began to take control of Saudi lands. By the 1890s, the leaders of the Saʿ ūd family were forced into exile and the second state came to an end.

The twentieth-century revival. The third period of Wahhābī history began in 1902, when a young Saudi prince recaptured Riyadh. This man was ʿAbd al-ʿAzīz ibn ʿAbd al-Raḥman, often called Ibn Saʿūd (1879–1953). ʿAbd al-ʿAzīz reconquered many of the lands of the first Saudi state in a series of bold diplomatic and military moves. The final steps came in the 1920s when, among other areas, Mecca and Medina again came under Saudi-Wahhābī control. Although geographic expansion stopped during that decade, the new Wahhābī state continued to develop.

The twenty-first century state is based on the pillars of Saudi leadership and the Wahhābī mission. ʿAbd al-ʿAzīz consciously adhered to Wahhābī teachings, and the official constitution of the state is the Qurʾān. The "family of the shaykh" and the learned teachers play important roles as advisers and legitimizers of the state. At first they were important in administration but later were active primarily in traditional education and legal interpretation. A key to early Saudi military success was the creation of the Ikhwān, tribal soldiers organized in special settlements as warriors for the faith. A critical transition in the development of the state came in 1929, when the Ihwān unsuccessfully revolted against the pragmatism of ʿAbd al-ʿAzīz's policies. Because the Wahhābī program is identified with the Saudi state, state policies represent an important definition of its mission. Thus the pragmatic style became characteristic of the Wahhābī movement during the twentieth century. In the spectrum of Islamic reform movements, however, the Saudi state continued to reflect a fundamentalist orientation.

Since the consolidation of the Saudi monarchy, the predominant tone of the Wahhābīyah has evolved significantly. Generally, fundamentalism works to change the existing social order. It is not a conservative style. However, the success of ʿAbd al-ʿAzīz and his successors in creating a relatively prosperous state has favored a more pragmatic and conservative policy. While still within the tradition of Ibn ʿAbd al-Wahhāb, the twenty-first century version of the Wahhābī mission works within the framework of a modernizing state.

A major factor in this development is the impact of Saudi oil revenues. Exploitation of oil resources began during the lifetime of ʿAbd al-ʿAzīz, and Saudi Arabia became a major oil-exporting state under his sons and successors, Saʿūd (r. 1953–1964) and Fayṣal (r. 1964–1975). Saudi policy in the early twenty-first century is designed to implement the fundamentalist call in a wealthy and modernizing state. An example is Fayṣal's ten-point program presented in 1962, which, like subsequent policies of Fayṣal's successors, Khālid (r. 1975–1982) and Fahd (r. 1982-), affirms that a modernizing state can be based on the Qurʾān and the *sunnah.*

BASIC IDEAS AND CONCEPTS. Despite the development of a more pragmatic ideology, the basic concepts of the Wahhābī program have remained quite constant. The oneness of God, or *tawḥīd,* is the fundamental concept in Wahhābī writings. It is an affirmation of the comprehensive nature of the statement "There is no god but [the one] God." *Tawḥīd* means that the political and economic realms are as much subject to God as are the realm of creeds. Any action or belief that seems to recognize ultimate authority or spiritual power in something other than God becomes polytheism.

In the eighteenth century the concept of *tawḥīd* provided the basis for opposition to saint worship and other popular religious customs. In the consolidation efforts of the nineteenth century, *tawḥīd* formed the logical basis for the legal decisions and religious positions of the scholars in the state ruled by Turkī and Fayṣal. In the twenty-first century pragmatic fundamentalism of the Saudi state *tawḥīd* provides an Islamic basis for comprehensive planning and a Muslim orientation to all aspects of policy.

A second basic concept is *ijtihād,* or independent informed reasoning, which directs a person with the proper training to base opinions on direct analysis of the Qurʾān and the *sunnah.* The analyst using *ijtihād* is not required to accept the conclusions of the great medieval scholars. In fact, blind adherence to the teachings of such scholars could be regarded as polytheism.

The Wahhābīyah have not carried the emphasis on *ijtihād* to the extreme of rejecting all medieval Islamic scholarship. Instead, they have stayed within the Ḥanbalī tradition but have felt free to go beyond its limits at times. In the thinking of Ibn ʿAbd al-Wahhāb, this flexibility opened the way for a more vigorous rejection of Sufism (mysticism) than is found generally among the Ḥanābilah. It also allowed the shaykh more freedom in developing the Islamic policy of the first Saudi-Wahhābī state and in later years has given the Wahhābīyah some freedom in adjusting to the changes of the modern era.

A different set of concepts involves aspects of life that the Wahhābīyah reject, including innovation (*bidʿah*), idolatry or polytheism (*shirk*), and sinful ignorance (*jāhilīyah*). These concepts are in counterpoint to the positive positions involved in *tawḥīd* and *ijtihād.* The opposition to innovation is not simply a rejection of all change. After all, the Wahhābī movement began with the call for major changes in society. The Wahhābīyah oppose innovations for which a justification cannot be found in the Qurʾān or the *sunnah.* In this way many medieval devotional practices were rejected as "innovations." At the same time, the exercise of *ijtihād* can provide justification for changes that fall within Islamic limits.

Idolatry and sinful ignorance represent a violation of *tawḥīd;* they are the identifying features of the real nonbeliever. In the early days of the Wahhābī mission, opposition to idolatry and ignorance focused on concrete issues such as saint worship, veneration of trees and stones, and ignoring explicit Qurʾanic commands. In the twentieth century these concepts have been expanded to include ideologies that are viewed as atheistic (such as communism). Originally in Islamic history the so-called Age of Ignorance or Jāhilīyah was the period before the time of Muḥammad. However, in modern fundamentalist thought, the concept of Jāhilīyah has been broadened to include willfully ignoring the guidance for human life given in the Qurʾān and the *sunnah.* Such defiance makes people nonbelievers to be opposed by Muslims of the Wahhābī tradition.

General Impact and Significance. The establishment of the Saudi-Wahhābī state in the Arabian Peninsula represents the most concrete heritage and impact of the Wahhābī movement. Since the eighteenth century the Wahhābīyah have represented the spirit of fundamentalism in the central lands of Islam, establishing the tradition of a community based on the Qurʾān and the *sunnah.* However, the significance of the movement goes beyond the state. In the rigor of their attachment to the renewal mission, the Wahhābīyah have provided an example of what was and is possible. The implementation of the call for renewal contributed to the general spirit of fundamentalism in the eighteenth century. Some Muslims were directly inspired by Wahhābī teachings while others were affected more by their general effort. The fame of the Wahhābīyah spread to such an extent that by the nineteenth century almost any movement of rigorous fundamentalist reform came to be called a "Wahhābī movement."

The Wahhābīyah are the best-known example of a Muslim movement calling for strict recognition of the oneness of God, with all of the social and moral implications of that belief, and advocating the reconstruction of society on the basis of a strict and independent interpretation of the fundamentals of Islam. This message helped to inspire movements ranging from holy wars to modernist rethinking of medieval formulations. Following the Shīʿī fundamentalist revolution in Iran in 1979, the Wahhābī movement as represented by the policies of the Saudi state became a more conservative influence in a context of more radical Islamic revivalism. However, the Wahhābī mode of activist renewal also became identified with many of the militant Islamic movements of the early twenty-first century. As happened in the nineteenth century, "Wahhābī" came to be the term used to describe terrorist and militant groups as well as puritanical advocates of Islamic renewal. Both as the followers of the specific movement that developed in the Arabian Peninsula and as the adherents of movements of the "Wahhābī-type," the Wahhābīyah have had and continue to have a significant role in the modern history of the Islamic world.

See Also Ibn ʿAbd al-Wahhāb, Muḥammad.

Bibliography

There are a number of important primary sources for the teachings and history of the Wahhābīya. Of particular interest are the numerous works of Muḥammad ibn ʿAbd al-Wahhāb, but few of these have been translated. His works are listed in an important biographical study, ʿAbd Allah al-Ṣaliḥal-ʿUthaymin's *Al-Shaykh Muḥammad ibn ʿAbd al-Wahhāb, ḥayātuhu wafikruhu* (Riyadh, n. d.). A large collection of legal decisions and letters by a number of important nineteenth-century Wahhabi leaders is contained in *Majmūʿāt al-rasāʾil wa-al-masaʾil al-najdīyah* (Cairo, 1927). Two important histories are ʿUthmān ibn Bishr's *Kitab ʿunwan al-majd fī taʾrīkh Najd* (Mecca, 1930) and Ḥasan ibn Ghannām's *Rawḍat al-afkār* (Bombay, 1919).

Major secondary sources include the works of H. St. John Philby, a close associate of ʿAbd al-ʿAzīz Ibn Saʿūd; see, for example, *Arabia* (New York, 1930). For the Ḥanbalī background, the standard work on Ibn Taymīyah and his impact is Henri Laoust's *Essai sur les doctrines sociales et politiques de Taki-d-Din Ahmed ibn Taymiyya* (Cairo, 1939). The life of Muḥammad ibn ʿAbd al-Wahhāb is covered in the biographical study by al-ʿUthaymin. The life and thought of Ibn Abd al-Wahhāb and the subsequent movement's impact is discussed in Natana J. Delong-Bas, *Wahhabi Islam: From Revival and Reform to Global Threat* (New York, 2004). The second Saʿūdi-Wahhābī state is described in R. Bayly Winder's, *Saudi Arabia in the Nineteenth Century* (New York, 1965). For the twentieth century, there are many studies dealing with specific aspects of the movement, such as John S. Habib's *Ibn Saʿūd's Warriors of Islam* (Leiden, 1978) and Christine Moss Helms's *The Cohesion of Saudi Arabia* (Baltimore, 1981), which contains an excellent summary of Wahhābī teachings. A useful general survey of the history of the movement and of the three Saudi states is Alexei Vassiliev, *The History of Saudi Arabia* (New York, 2000).

John O. Voll (1987 and 2005)

WAKANDA SEE POWER

WALĀYAH,

WALĀYAH, or *wilāyah,* an Arabic verbal noun derived from the root *wly,* carries the basic meanings of "friendship, assistance" and "authority, power." A fundamental notion of Islamic social and spiritual life, the term is used with a complex variety of meanings related to the function, position, authority, or domain of authority of a *walī* (pl., *awliyā'*; "next of kin, ally, friend, helper, guardian, patron, saint"); a *mawlā* (pl., *mawālī;* "cousin, close relation, ally, client, patron, master"); or a *wālī* (pl., *wulāh;* "administrator, governor, ruler"). It appears in Persian as *valāyat, vilāyat,* and in Turkish as *vilayet.*

A distinction is often made between *walāyah* and *wilāyah,* with the latter form generally preferred to convey the meaning of "power," "authority," or "domain of authority" (e.g., a political subdivision of a country). However, the vocalization is not normally indicated in the texts, and the classical Arab lexicographers are not unanimous on this point.

QUR'ANIC USAGE. Although the verbal noun *al-walāyah,* thus vocalized according to the standard text, occurs only twice in the Qur'an (surahs 8:72 and 8:44), other derivatives of the root *wly* are found in more than two hundred instances. Most frequently, the verbal forms *wallā* and *tawallā* are used, in the sense of "turning" either one's back or face—properly or metaphorically speaking—toward somebody or something (e.g., a hostile army, a sacred place, a prophetic message; God himself "turns to" or "takes care of" the pious, as in 7:196 and 45:19).

The nominal forms *walī* and *mawlā* are used, without apparent distinction, for the two partners of a close social relationship, such as kinship and alliance, but also for those of the God-human relationship. A *walī* or *mawlā* can claim certain rights of inheritance and has certain duties or responsibilities to assist an ally against enemies, in such cases as the retaliation for unjust killing of kinsmen (*wilāyat al-dam;* see 17:33). Inheritance and assistance expected of a *walī* may also be of a spiritual kind, as in the Qur'anic version of the birth of John the Baptist, which seems to echo a messianic idea implicit in the Judeo-Christian background of that theme: Zacharias, having no (natural) son and fearing therefore the claims of his *mawālī* (secondary heirs, perhaps priest colleagues), asks God to give him a "noble offspring" (3:38), a "*walī* from thee, who will be my heir and will inherit [prophethood?] from the family of Jacob" (19:5–6).

Similarly in 4:75, but without the notion of kinship and inheritance, the oppressed (Meccan Muslims), left alone after the prophet Muḥammad's emigration, ask God to bring them out of "the city of the unjust" and to provide for them "a *walī* from thee and a helper [*naṣīr*] from thee" (see also 17:80). According to 41:28–31, the enemies of God will dwell forever in the fire, whereas the angels will descend upon the righteous as their "friends [*awliyā'*] in this life and the next," so that they shall have no fear; indeed, according to 10:62, the "friends of God [*awliyā' Allāh,* i. e., the pious] shall have no fear"—a verse frequently quoted in Ṣūfī manuals.

God's unique position as the most powerful friend and helper *(walī naṣīr)* is one of the major themes of Qur'anic preaching, and several verses make it clear that those who "turn away" (e.g., 9:74) and/or "are lead astray by him" (e.g., 18:17) have no *walī* (42:8) or *mawlā* (47:11), that is, no one to turn to for help or guidance. The same message is also conveyed by the parable of the rich but impious owner of the two gardens and his poor but godfearing companion (18:32ff.), which closes with one of the two Qur'anic verses in which *al-walāyah* actually occurs: it is the rich man who ends up the loser in spite of the prosperity of his gardens and the power of his clan, for, "Ultimately, the *walāyah* belongs to God, the Truth!" (18:44).

While this verse gives an idea of the prophet Muḥammad's attitude during the early stages of his career as a religious "warner" at Mecca, the other verse in which *al-walāyah* occurs (8:72) reflects the situation immediately after his emigration (Hijrah) in 622 CE from Mecca to Medina, where he began to organize his new community. The verse defines the relationship between three groups of believers (Muslims) in terms of *walāyah*: (1) those who emigrated and "fought on the path of God," (2) those who gave them asylum (in Medina) and helped them, and (3) those who did not emigrate. The first two groups, who came to be known later as the emigrants *(muhājirūn)* and the helpers *(anṣār)*—the nucleus of the future Muslim community *(ummah)*—are, according to this verse, allies or friends of each other *(awliyā')*; but "as for those who believed but did not emigrate, you have no *walāyah* with them [or: you should disregard their *walāyah*] until they emigrate!"

Traditional interpretation of this verse refers to a ceremonial "brothering" *(mu'ākhāh)* supposed to have taken place between the emigrants and their Medinese helpers. This event was to cancel the old ties of *walāyah* linking the emigrants to their blood relations back in Mecca; this radical measure was, however, later abrogated or modified through verses 8:75 and 33:6, which state that blood relations are "closer [*awlā*] in the Book of God." Regarding this "brothering," W. Montgomery Watt suggests that "Muḥammad was prepared to use the kinship principle to increase the cohesion of his religious community in Medina" ("The Charismatic Community in Islam," *Numen* 7, 1960, p. 84). However, since it is not clear who "those who believed but did not emigrate" were in the first place, the ties of *walāyah,* to be ignored "until they emigrate," may have been those of friendship or alliance rather than kinship, as is also suggested by the parallel passage 4:89.

At any rate, emigrants and helpers were the "true believers" (8:74), and "those fighting" *(mujāhidūn)* were definitely placed in a higher rank than "those sitting" (at home), according to 4:95–4:96. Clearly, the new charismatic community of true believers was an alliance of those following the Prophet and was directed against his opponents. Further, it should be noted that these opponents were also seen as forming such an alliance of "*awliyā'* of each other," whether they were "the disbelievers" (8:73), "the hypocrites" (9:67–72), "the unjust" (45:19; 6:129), or "the Jews and Christians" (5:51). As is well known, the new Muslim community was patterned after the model of the nation of Abraham, but with Abraham as neither Jew nor Christian (see 3:64–68). The Jews in particular are frequently challenged in the Medinese surahs, notably to prove their claim to be "the exclusive friends of God" (*awliyā' Allah min dūn al-nās,* 62:6–8; 2:94–95).

Walāyah as a socioreligious concept seems indeed exclusive: one turns either to the right or to the wrong side, and the two sides are always engaged in battle: "Those who believe fight on the path of God, while those who disbelieve fight on the path of al-Ṭāghūt; thus, fight against the *awliyā'* of Satan!" (4:76). (*Al-Ṭāghūt,* perhaps derived from Ethiopic *ṭā'ōt,* "idols," is used for Satanic powers and often applied to tyrants or unlawful rulers, especially in Shīʿī interpretations.)

God and his antagonist(s) lead their respective allies or friends their way: God as the "*walī* of the believers" leads them from darkness to light, whereas the disbelievers, who have al-Ṭāghūt as *awliyā'*, are led by them from light to darkness (2:257). The world seems to be divided into two antagonistic groups: the party of God (*ḥizb Allāh,* 5:56) and the party of Satan (58:19), but the party of God, that is, "whoever turns to [or follows, *yatawallā*] God and his messenger [the prophet Muḥammad] and those who believe," is winning (5:56), while "whoever takes Satan rather than God as *walī* is surely going to lose!" (4:119). As though the divine *walāyah* were spread among the charismatic community, verse 5:55 states that "Your *walī* is only God, his Messenger, and those who [truly] believe, who perform the prayer and give alms, bending the body." Thus, unlike the purely God-oriented *walāyah* of the "poor companion" of Mecca, the Medinese *walāyah* seems to be the charisma of the party of God, in which the person of the Prophet himself plays the central role. Though never elevated to divine status, this role of the Prophet is stressed in the later parts of the Qur'an generally; it culminates in the solemn pledge of allegiance *(mubāyaʿah)* made to him in lieu of God in 628 at al-Ḥudaybīyah (surah 48:9–10). The ceremonial contract of allegiance *(bayʿah)* made with his successors—caliphs, imams, and later also Ṣūfī shaykhs—all of whom would claim *wilāyah* of a certain kind, was to reiterate this charismatic basis of Islam symbolically.

LEGAL USAGE. A trace of the pre-Islamic kinship principle may be seen in the fact that the Qur'anic commandments preserve the blood feud in restricted form, namely, as a right of the victim's *walī* to kill the murderer personally (17:33). In Islamic law, this particular right of the *walī*, which is known as *wilāyat al-dam* or "*wilāyah* of blood," is one among other forms in which the requital *(qiṣāṣ)* may be exercised.

Sunnī laws of inheritance, which were elaborated in the second Islamic century by the jurist al-Shāfiʿī (757–820), generally follow Arab tradition. The primary heir is the *walī* as the nearest male agnate in descending or ascending order *(ʿaṣabah);* but shares *(farā'iḍ)* are also provided for secondary heirs in accordance with the Qur'anic dispositions in surah 4:7ff. Under certain conditions, the inheritance of a manumitted slave goes to his former owner, who has become his patron *(mawlā)* and is counted as such among the agnates according to Shāfiʿī law. A similar kind of legal kinship was presumed in the early Umayyad period between non-Arab converts to Islam and their Arab patrons, who "adopted" them as clients *(mawālī).*

Al-Jurjānī (1339–1413) defines *walāyah* as legal kinship *(qarābah ḥukmīyah)* resulting from either manumission or "adoption." *Wilāyah,* on the other hand, he defines as the legal power "to carry through a decision affecting another person, whether the latter wishes or not." The notion of *wilāyah* as legal power is not, as such, Qur'anic but was probably developed from the early second century AH onward in two different, though not unrelated, social spheres: family law and political thought.

Family law. The Qur'anic laws of inheritance are laid down in 4:1ff., together with general rules and indications concerning marriage and the gift of the bridal dower to the brides (or wives), as well as the protection of the goods of orphans and fair treatment of the mentally weak *(safīh),* who should be represented by their *walī* in legal matters (2:282). A number of specific legal responsibilities of a *walī* regarding brides, orphans, minors, and otherwise legally incompetent persons *(safīh)* were eventually defined as a kind of guardianship or trusteeship. Among these, the most important socially is undoubtedly the "guardianship of marriage" *(wilāyat al-nikāḥ),* the office of the bride's nearest relative, her *walī*, who must give her in marriage by contractual agreement with the bridegroom. The *walī* may refuse consent or, as *walī mujbir,* force his ward into marriage under certain circumstances. According to Joseph Schacht, the *wilāyat al-nikāḥ* was not, as a legal institution, "originally as self-evident as it became later," and "marriage without a legal *walī* continued the easygoing practice of the pre-Islamic Arabs" during the early Islamic period (Schacht, p. 182f.).

Political thought. *Wilāyah* in the sense of political authority and sovereign power refers first of all to the authority of the "successor of the Messenger of God" *(khalīfat rasūl Allāh),* that is, the caliph, who is to be obeyed *(muṭāʿ)* as leader or guide *(imām)* of the Muslim community and as "commander of the faithful" *(amīr al-mu'minīn).* Although there is fundamental disagreement between Sunnī and Shīʿī Muslims concerning the nature and scope of this authority, and the persons invested with it, both refer to the same *locus classicus* to justify their claims: "Obey God and the Messenger and 'those in command' [*ūlī al-amr]* among you!" (surah

4:59); it is therefore called *wilāyat al-amr.* This usage of *wilāyah* should be seen in relation to the development of the charismatic alliance of those who "follow [*yatawallā*] God, the Messenger, and the [true] believers," or the party of God (5:55–56).

The question of who "those in command" were and how the alliance was to be preserved after the death of the Prophet was, perhaps not surprisingly, the primary concern of the early opposition parties. Among these, there were notably those who sided with Muḥammad's paternal cousin *(mawlā)* and son-in-law through Fāṭimah, ʿAlī ibn Abī Ṭalib (d. 661), known as the party of ʿAlī *(shīʿat ʿAlī),* later simply known as the Shīʿah, and those known as the dissidents (*khawārij,* Khārijīs). The early Shīʿah seem to have assumed that ʿAlī was entitled to inheritance from the Prophet not only as his kin but also as his "emigrant brother"; his preeminent position is thus unique.

But the kinship principle alone was evidently not sufficient to guarantee ʿAlī's exclusive right to what came to be known as *wilāyat al-amr:* it had to be completed by the principle of designation. This was made possible thanks to an inherent ambiguity of the term *mawlā.* According to a famous *ḥadīth* (prophetic tradition), the Prophet had made the following declaration at a solemn meeting after his last pilgrimage to Mecca and shortly before his death: "Am I not closer [*awlā*] to the believers than they are to themselves? . . . He whose *mawlā* I am, ʿAlī is his *mawlā!* God, befriend the one who befriends him [*wālī man wālāhu*], and treat as an enemy the one who treats him as an enemy!" (see also surah 33:6). The earliest sure evidence for an interpretation of this *ḥadīth* as asserting ʿAlī's *wilāyah* or right to be obeyed is found in the *Hāshimīyāt* of the pro-ʿAlid poet of Kufa, al-Kumayt ibn Zayd al-Asadī (680–743). ʿAlī, however, was elected caliph only after the assassination of ʿUthmān, the third of the four Rāshidūn ("rightly guided") caliphs in Sunnī Islam. ʿAlī's caliphate was overshadowed by civil war, and he was himself assassinated by a Khārijī.

In the heresiographical literature the Khārijī movement is associated with the doctrine that anyone, "even an Abyssinian slave," could serve as imam as long as that person was found to be a true believer. As may be seen from the earliest available Khārijī (Ibāḍī) texts (of uncertain date, between AH 70 and 150), a distinction between the "imams of truth" and the "imams of error" was essential to their doctrine, with the understanding that the first were to be obeyed as "*awliyā*ʾ of the believers" and the second to be fought as unbelievers. The Khārijīs also developed the principle of *walāyah* in the sense of "associating with" or "following" *(muwālāh, tawallī)* prophets and "true believers," and its correlative, "dissociating" or "freeing oneself" from the opposite powers *(barāʾah, tabarruʾ).* Exactly the same double principle (later known in Persian as *tawallā* and *tabarrā*) was adopted by the Shīʿah, but with the essential difference that the true believers to be followed were necessarily ʿAlī and subsequent imams issuing from his "holy family" *(ahl al-bayt, āl Muḥammad).*

The assassination of ʿAlī, far from helping the Khārijī cause of Muslim "integralism," led to its very opposite. The successful Umayyads established the dynastic principle in the Sunnī caliphate and introduced the practice of the designation of the heir apparent *(walī al-ʿahd)* by the reigning caliph. Although the authority of an Umayyad caliph was hardly religious in nature, he was considered not only "successor of the Messenger of God," but also "representative of God" on earth *(khalīfat Allāh),* a Qurʾanic phrase that refers specifically to David as God's "viceroy among men" (38:26) and that continued to be applied to the caliph well into the Abbasid period.

The dissatisfaction of the religious community with Umayyad worldliness, as well as the hopes of the Shīʿah, helped, among other factors, to bring about the so-called Abbasid Revolution in the Eastern caliphate. The descendants of Muḥammad's paternal uncle al-ʿAbbās were presented as members of the "providential family"; they showed, once in power, a marked zeal for religious affairs. The *ʿulamāʾ* (religious scholars) were now elaborating a Sunnī doctrine of *wilāyat al-amr* in close collaboration with the caliph. Harūn al-Rashīd is addressed by the jurist Abū Yūsuf (d. 798), a disciple of Abū Ḥanīfah, as "*khalīfah* of God on his earth," to whom God has "delegated the command" *(tawliyāt al-amr)* and "given a light" to guide the subjects through clarification of the law and its enforcement. At the same time, Abū Yūsuf also strikes a Ṣūfī note. He exhorts the caliph to fulfill the duties of his high office and expresses the hope that God will not "abandon him to himself" (i. e., to his human weakness); that he will, rather, take care *(yatawallā)* of him as he takes care of his friends *(awliyāʾ),* "given that he is the [ultimate] *walī* in the matter."

During the later Abbasid period, when the real power was no longer exercised personally by the caliph, he was still considered the representative or guardian of the law *(walī al-sharʿ).* According to al-Māwardī (975–1080), it is the religious law itself that requires entrustment of all matters or delegation of general authority *(wilāyah ʿāmmah)* to the elected or designated imam from the Quraysh, that is, the Abbasid caliph. The caliph in his turn delegates authority *(tawliyah)* to viziers, military commanders, governors, and judges, so that all public functions *(wilāyāt)* emanate in theory from the authority entrusted to him and are legally validated by it. But al-Ghazālī (1058–1111), recognizing that the caliph has no longer the military power *(shawkah)* to defend religion, justifies the transfer of this legal authority to the Seljuk sultan or king *(pādishāh).* Al-Ghazālī argues, with traditional Persian wisdom, that "religion [*dīn*] and kingship [*mulk*] are twin brothers in need of each other"; in effect, non-Arab sultans and kings were now to play the role of the "shadow of God on earth."

SHĪʿĪ CONCEPTS. Contrary to the Sunnī acceptance of *wilāyah* as a state-building idea, the mark of Shiism is *walāyah* as devotion to ʿAlī and "the imams from the house of the Prophet," that is, descendants of ʿAlī who are considered imams. Despite several unsuccessful ʿAlid attempts to seize power, or perhaps because of them—the martyrdom of ʿAlī's second son Ḥusayn (d. 680) is an important aspect of Shīʿī Islam—imams of various lines of descent became the focus of a veneration that went far beyond the charismatic alliance of surah 5:55–56, from which "orthodox" Shīʿī doctrine nevertheless takes its pedigree: in effect, it became the apotheosis of the imam. In this process, through which Shiism became the major receptacle of messianic hopes and gnostic ideas in Islam, converts *(mawālī)*, especially those of Iraq, seem to have played an essential role.

The transfer of *wilāyah* from Muḥammad to ʿAlī was understood as part of a more general *Heilsgeschichte*, a universal process of revelation to be completed by the imams as inheritors of the hidden *(bāṭin)* substance and knowledge of previous prophets, Arab and non-Arab, or as a process of transmigration *(tanāsukh)* that leads up to the final revelation of truth and justice with the coming, or return, of "the one who stands up" (*al-qāʾim*, probably the gnostic *hestōs*). Despite the repudiation of the more extremist ideas of their enthusiastic followers *(ghulāt)* by the imams themselves, and although the imams are not placed above Muḥammad's law according to standard Shīʿī doctrine, its major dogma insists that only the transfer of *wilāyah* from Muḥammad to ʿAlī and subsequent imams makes Islam the "perfect religion" (surah 5:3). In fact, *walāyah*, as adherence to the imams and as recognition of their mission as the true "holders of the [divine] Command" *(ūlī al-amr)* and the exclusive possessors of the true meaning of the Qurʾan and the "knowledge of the hidden" *(ʿilm al-ghayb)*, remains the key to salvation, without which no pious act of obedience to God *(ṭāʿah)* is truly valid. It is for these reasons that *walāyah*, and not the profession of monotheism *(tawḥīd)* as in Sunnī Islam, appears as the principal "pillar of Islam" in the classical collections of Shīʿī traditions, both those of the Ithnā ʿAsharīyah, or Twelvers (e.g., al-Kulaynī, d. 940), and those of the Fatimid Ismāʿīlīyah (e.g., Qāḍī al-Nuʿmān, d. 974), who follow a common line of imams up to Jaʿfar al-Ṣādiq (d. 765).

The concrete meanings and functions of *walāyah*, however, were quite different in the two cases. Contrary to the generally quietist or neutral attitude of the Twelvers, the Ismaʿīlīyah were politically active and succeeded in establishing, by the end of the third century AH, a Shīʿī counter-caliphate in North Africa and later in Egypt that constituted a serious challenge to the Abbasid order. For the function of *walāyah* in this process, it seems significant that the Fatimid campaign in North Africa is seen in Ismāʿīlī sources (Qāḍī al-Nuʿmān) as a parallel to the prophet Muḥammad's emigration (Hijrah) from Mecca to Medina: just as the Qurʾanic emigrant fighters are placed above those sitting at home, the front fighters of the Fatimid agent Abū ʿAbd Allāh al-Shīʿī (d. 911) are distinguished as *awliyāʾ* from the ordinary (Ismāʿīlī) believers *(muʾminūn)*. The Fatimid caliph, referred to as *walī Allāh* and imam "of the time," was evidently seen in the role of the Prophet himself. He was not only the political head of a counter-caliphate, but also the spiritual center of an esoteric hierarchy, the *daʿwah* (lit., the "call" or "mission"), initiation into which was expected to provide gradual access to gnosis *(ʿilm)*—a cause that al-Ghazālī feared would undermine Islam from inside.

From the point of view of an Ismāʿīlī missionary *(dāʿī)* such as Qāḍī al-Nuʿmān, *wilāyah* was indeed much more than the legal foundation of the imamate: standing esoterically *(bāṭin)* for the true knowledge *(ḥaqīqat al-ʿilm)* bestowed primordially on Adam and inherited by prophets and imams, it is the very foundation of the sacred history of prophecy itself and its necessary fulfillment in the imamate. According to the grand *dāʿī* al-Muʾayyad fī al-Dīn al-Shīrāzī (d. 1077), prophets and imams, each in their time, are the examples of "absolute human being" (*al-insān al-muṭlaq*, the gnostic Anthrōpos). As the prophet Muḥammad is the Seal of the Prophets (surah 33:40), so the final (?) imam of resurrection *(qiyāmah)* is the Seal of the Imams *(khātam al-aʾimmah)*.

The idea of the imam in Twelver Shiism, by contrast, is marked by the "occultation" *(ghaybah)* or absence of the twelfth imam, believed to have "disappeared" in AH 260 (873/874 CE); at his return *(rajʿah)* at the end of time he will "fill the earth with justice as it is now filled with injustice." In the absence of the imam, the *ʿulamāʾ* assumed authority in theological and juridical matters much like their Sunnī counterparts before; they insisted, however, on the presence of the infallible *(maʿṣūm)* Hidden Imam as a "grace necessary upon God" *(luṭf wājib)* that would validate their consensus *(ijmāʿ)*. Gnostic Shiism, alien to the rationalism of the *ʿulamāʾ*, reappears within Twelver Shiism by the fourteenth century in a Ṣūfī form. Sayyid Ḥaydar Āmulī (d. after 1385) interprets Ibn ʿArabī's doctrine of the "two seals of *walāyah*" in terms of Twelver Shīʿī imamology, with ʿAlī as the "seal of absolute *walāyah*" and the twelfth imam as the "seal of particular Muḥammadan *walāyah*"; *walāyah* itself is both the "inner dimension of prophethood" *(bāṭin al-nubūwah)* and the transcendental vocation of humankind, or the trust offered (*al-amānah, sūrah* 33:72).

At the same time, Ṣūfī orders such as the Ṣafawīyah and the Kubrawīyah gradually turned Shīʿī, possibly as an indirect result of the Mongol invasions. The Ṣafawīyah, supported by Türkmen "tribal Shiism" and claiming descent from the imams, became even "extreme Shīʿī"; once its leaders assumed rule of Iran (with Shah Ismaʿīl I in 1501), they introduced Twelver Shiism, in a form hardly compatible with "orthodox" Shīʿī doctrine, as state religion; their prayer carpet *(sajjādah)*, symbol of the dignity of the Ṣūfī *shaykh*, or Ṣūfī *wilāyah*, became the symbol of the quasi-divine throne of Persia *(qālīčah-i salṭanat)*. Their success also brought about, perhaps paradoxically, the establishment of a real Shīʿī "clergy" and its eventual politicization. For the first time in Twelver Shīʿī history, the rationalist (Uṣūlī) school of the clergy formally acknowledged in 1817/1818 a division of labor between the *ʿulamāʾ* and the rulers—a long-established Sunnī practice—claiming general viceregency *(wilāyah ʿāmmah)* of the Hidden Imam for themselves, against the more traditionalist ideas of the Akhbārī school, and against the Ṣūfīs.

The very complex religious, social, and political situation in nineteenth-century Iran is also highlighted by the tensions between the majority of the clergy and the Shaykhī school, who developed a mystical concept of the "perfect Shīʿah" on the basis of Akhbārī traditionalism and the philosophy of Mullā Ṣadrā (d. 1640). In the Shaykhī scheme, the imam presides over the realization of an individual's vocation in the realm between matter and spirit, or the *mundus imaginalis (ʿālam al-mithāl),* not over the realization of a political project.

It should be noted that the leader of the Islamic Revolution of 1978–1979, Ayatollah Khomeini, made a fundamental, albeit theoretical, distinction between two kinds of *wilāyah:* that of the learned jurist *(wilāyat al-faqīh),* called relative *wilāyah (wilāyah iʿtibārīyah)* and that of the traditional imams of the prophetic house, called real or creative *wilāyah (wilāyah takwīnīyah).*

ṢŪFĪ CONCEPT. *Walāyah/wilāyah* is also a key concept for Sufism; indeed, it is the very principle of Sufism itself according to al-Hujwīrī's eleventh-century systematic exposition of its doctrine, the *Kashf al-maḥjūb* (Unveiling of the Veiled). Yet once again, two notions appear to be involved. To use the typological distinction made above between "Meccan" and "Medinese" *walāyah,* one might suggest that the spiritual attitude of early Sufism, with its ideal of poverty *(faqr, darvīshī)* and reliance upon God *(tawakkul),* is more in line with the former. The Khorasani saint Ibrāhīm ibn Adham (d. 776), quoted by the reputed teacher of most of the Baghdad Ṣūfīs, the theologian al-Muḥāsibī (d. 857), puts it succinctly this way: "If you wish to be God's friend [*walī*] and care that he loves you, then leave this world and the next and do not heed either; free yourself from both and turn your face to God, so that he turns his face to you!"

A number of prophetic traditions, often in the form of *ḥadīth qudsī* (non-Qurʾanic "words of God" transmitted by a prophet), suggest that there are indeed such friends of God. As with the Qurʾanic notion of *awliyāʾ,* there is a certain ambiguity as to whether these friends of God are human or angelic beings. "Approaching [God] and approached by him," they have reached such a stage that God says: "I am his ear by which he hears, his eye by which he sees, his tongue by which he speaks, his heart by which he understands"; even the prophets will envy them at the Day of Resurrection. No tradition refers to them by name; indeed, according to a famous tradition, they are hidden "under God's tents, unknown to anyone but him." On the other hand, they are reminders of God for people and stand under his special protection: whoever turns against them, turns against God. "Marvelous is their story, and they know marvelous stories. The [heavenly] Book stands through them, and they stand through it; the Book speaks through them, and they speak through the Book."

Many of the traditions regarding these "friends of God," the first comprehensive collection of which is found in Abū Nuʿaym al-Iṣbahānī's *Ḥilyat al-awliyāʾ,* are attributed to pre-Islamic prophets, especially Yaḥyā ibn Zakarīyāʾ (John the Baptist) and Jesus. This may suggest a gnostic origin; some are clearly of a mythological nature. According to the tradition known throughout the Ṣūfī literature as the *ḥadīth* of ʿAbd Allāh ibn Masʿūd, there are 355 or 356 such figures, upon whom life and death of all nations depends: 300 "whose heart is after the heart" of Adam; 40 who are in the same relationship to Moses (or Noah); 7 to Abraham; 5 (or 4) to the angel Gabriel; 3 to Michael; and one to Seraphiel (Isrāfīl, the angel of resurrection). If one of them dies, God substitutes for him one of the next lower class. The substitutes of the lowest class (the 300) are taken from the common people *(al-ʿāmmah).* The single one is commonly called the "pole" *(quṭb)* or the "rescue" *(ghawth),* while terms such as *abdāl* (usually for the 40 or the 7) and *ṣiddīqūn* (see surah 4:69) refer either to a class, or to saints generally, like *awliyāʾ.*

Wilāyah, then, is the special charismatic quality of a Ṣūfī, that which enables him to be the subject of miracles or, more precisely, charismata *(karāmāt).* The classical Ṣūfīs, especially the Khorasani school, were divided over the question of whether *awliyāʾ* should themselves be aware of their sainthood and whether the charismata should become public knowledge. For Bāyazīd al-Basṭāmī (or Bisṭāmī, d. 875 or earlier), the *awliyāʾ* should be hidden like the "brides of God"; he was extremely critical of public shows. By contrast, Tirmidhī al-Ḥakīm (ninth century), the reputed founder of the Ṣūfī doctrine of *wilāyah,* dismissed such restraint as a subtle form of self-consciousness. According to the definition of Timidhī's contemporary and disciple Abū ʿAlī al-Juzjānī (which became more or less authoritative), a *walī* is "in oblivion [*fanāʾ*] of himself but subsisting [*baqāʾ*] in contemplation." Other well-known definitions distinguish an "active" from a "passive" aspect (al-Qushayrī), or a *walāyah* of "lordship" (*sūrah* 18:44) from a *wilāyah* (?) of "love" (al-Hujwīrī).

Typical connotations of Ṣūfī *wilāyah* are "insight into the hidden" (*al-ʿilm bi-al-ghayb,* Tirmidhī) and control of souls *(taṣarruf),* psychognostic and pedagogic abilities, and the power to drive Satan away. Medieval Ṣūfī "saints" are famous for having the power to help the Muslim armies, and to intercede *(shafāʿah)* on behalf of the sinners. In postclassical Ṣūfī texts, *walāyah* or *wilāyah* generally refers either to the highest mystical stage that may be attained or to the authority exercised by a Ṣūfī master, or to both at the same time. Najm al-Dīn Kubrā (d. 1221) identifies its highest stage with the experience of divine creative power *(takwīn).* By contrast, his followers in the late thirteenth and early fourteenth centuries, receptive to Shīʿī ideas but not yet themselves Shīʿah, notably ʿAlāʾ al-Dawlah al-Simnānī (d. 1336), emphasize the double experience of the prophet Muḥammad—his *walāyah* or mystical experience and his

WORD AND IMAGE

In both oral and literate societies, the tendency to intermingle word and image is irresistible. Spoken words, whether song, chant, or prose, contain the life-force or spirit of the speaker and are commonly joined to images by incantation and by rituals designed to charge images with power. Written words are themselves signifiers that can be pictorialized in many different ways in order to compound the potency of images. Word and image are imbricated or patterned one on top of the other for the purpose of enhancing memory, expanding the capacity of visual narrative, or avoiding the injunctions against visual representation that some religions enforce. By visualizing spoken or written language in the form of symbolic devices, image makers are able to create a hybrid form of discourse—pictographs, hieroglyphs, ideograms, or characters. Finally, naming is a universal practice in human culture. Visualizing names in graphic symbols or pictorial tableaux is often a way of remembering or evoking the deceased or tapping the power of the spirit by accessing its essence contained within the name.

Many religions find ways of integrating the written word and the image to create composite forms of representation. In the case of Sikhism, Judaism, and Islam, such composites are motivated by the desire to avoid committing idolatry, reducing the divine to a human invention. Influenced by Islam, Sikhism, for instance, eschews cult imagery, but engages in intense forms of devotion to its *gurūs*, the ten historical teachers who led Sikhs through times of tribulation and martyrdom. The hymns of several *gurūs* compose the eleventh and final *gurū*, the collection of holy writings, known as the *Gurū Granth Sāhib* (Great Reverend Teacher). Copies of this book are kept in every *gurdwara* or Sikh temple, where they are ritually displayed on throne-like altars **(a)** during Sikh worship and even

(a) *Gurū Granth Sāhib* on display during worship in a Sikh *gurdwara* in Merrillville, Indiana, in 2003. *[Photograph by David Morgan]*

attended by a fly whisk as if the book were the body of one of the *gurūs*. This reverence for the book displaces the role of images in worship. But Sikhism finds a place for images, as shown by a gilded plaque at the Golden Temple in Punjab **(b)**, portraying the revered Gurū Nānak with attendents. Another (unpictured) example is a deft intermingling of sacred text with an image of Nānak. The resulting "imagetext" strikes a higher unity that avoids confusing image with deity. The image consists of the opening scripture of the Sikh holy book, composed by Nānak himself. To see his image congealing in his words makes the *gurū's* wisdom appear palpable.

Micrographs are a common Jewish counterpart to the Sikh image described above and may have inspired it. One example shows the prophet Jeremiah lamenting the ruins

(b) **Top.** An early-seventeenth-century gilded plaque depicting Gurū Nānak (center) with two attendants. Golden Temple, Amritsar, Punjab, India. *[©Michael Freeman/ Corbis]* **(c)** **Left.** *Jeremiah Mourning the Destruction of the Temple in Jerusalem*, a mid-nineteenth-century lithograph by Beryl Reiss. ***[Courtesy of The Library of the Jewish Theological Seminary]***

of the Jewish temple **(c)**. Ironically, every aspect of the image consists of Hebrew text from the book of Jeremiah. If the second commandment (*Dt.* 5:8–9) proscribes the worship of images, or even the creation of images, the micrograph eludes the proscription by only writing sacred text. A similar evasion of the injunction against imagery informs the paper amulet reproduced here **(d)**, a Jewish print of symbols and objects portrayed by textual inscriptions, used for protection during childbirth. Muslims could produce comparable imagetexts, though attitudes varied greatly among Muslims in Persia, Turkey, India, and Africa, on the one hand, and Arabic Muslims, on the other. Among the most familiar examples of the Muslim imagetext is the sumptuous calligraphy and decoration of the Qurʾanic page **(e)**. A *qiblah*-compass from Istanbul

(d) **Top.** A late-nineteenth-century paper amulet from Jerusalem, used by Jewish women for protection during childbirth. *[©Erich Lessing/Art Resource, N.Y.]* **(e)** **Right.** *In the Name of the Almighty*, seventh-century CE calligraphy in the form of a hoopoe, ink on paper, Iran. *[©Bildarchiv Preussischer Kulturbesitz/Art Resource, N.Y.]*

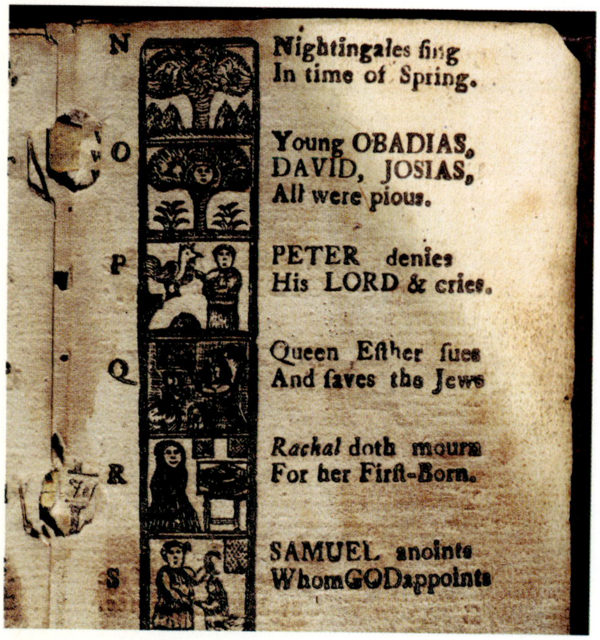

(f) Top. Cardboard *qiblah*-compass in a brass case, 1808–1809, from Istanbul, Turkey. *[©The Nour Foundation: Nasser D. Khalili Collection of Islamic Art. Accession number: sc1275]* **(g) Above.** Alphabet page from the 1782 editon of the *New England Primer*, first published in Boston in about 1690. *[Courtesy American Antiquarian Society]*

(f) shows how word and image could be combined in order to provide an important form of information for Muslim piety. This compass was able to find the direction of Mecca anywhere in the world when adjusted to the coordinates indicated on its face.

In another form of image dedicated to generating a kind of useful information, American Protestants relied on the alphabet page of the *New England Primer* **(g)** to teach their children to read. The page aligns the alphabet on the left with a central column of imagery, which corresponds, in turn, to rhymed phrases on the right. By embedding imagery in the semantic field of text, American Puritans and their theological descendents did not mistake image for divine referent, but applied the image as a form of graphic information to promote literacy, and to instill in children greater knowledge of the Bible and morality while doing so. The lesson also affirmed the important ideology of print: that words correspond clearly to images, and that both combine to create a uniform, reliable system of representing the physical and moral world. Cultural literacy was neatly enfolded in textual literacy.

The continuity of word and image in Protestant the-

ology began with Martin Luther, who is shown preaching in Wittenberg in a print by Lucas Cranach the Younger **(h)**. Luther preaches a dramatic sermon of propagandistic rage against the papal party, which is glimpsed in the smoking maw of a hellish monster, while the Lutheran party appears below the pulpit and to the left, receiving the elements of the Eucharist (wine and bread). The image was intended to register the fine points of doctrinal controversy between Catholics and Lutherans. The crucified Jesus flutters above the altar in order to underscore the Lutheran doctrine of consubstantiation (that the elements of the sacrament were joined with the substance of Christ's body and blood). The laity receives both wine and bread in contrast to the Catholic practice of distributing only the bread. The balance of word and image is tipped in favor of the word in the work of the twentieth-century Baptist preacher and artist Howard Finster, who, though he includes a standing figure of Jesus behind the cross, foregrounds a cross composed of text and recast as a graphic lesson on moral choice **(i)**. Recalling many popular prints before it, the subject of Finster's work is not the cross or figure of Christ, but, as the title signals, *The Way of Jesus* and the viewer's need to choose to follow

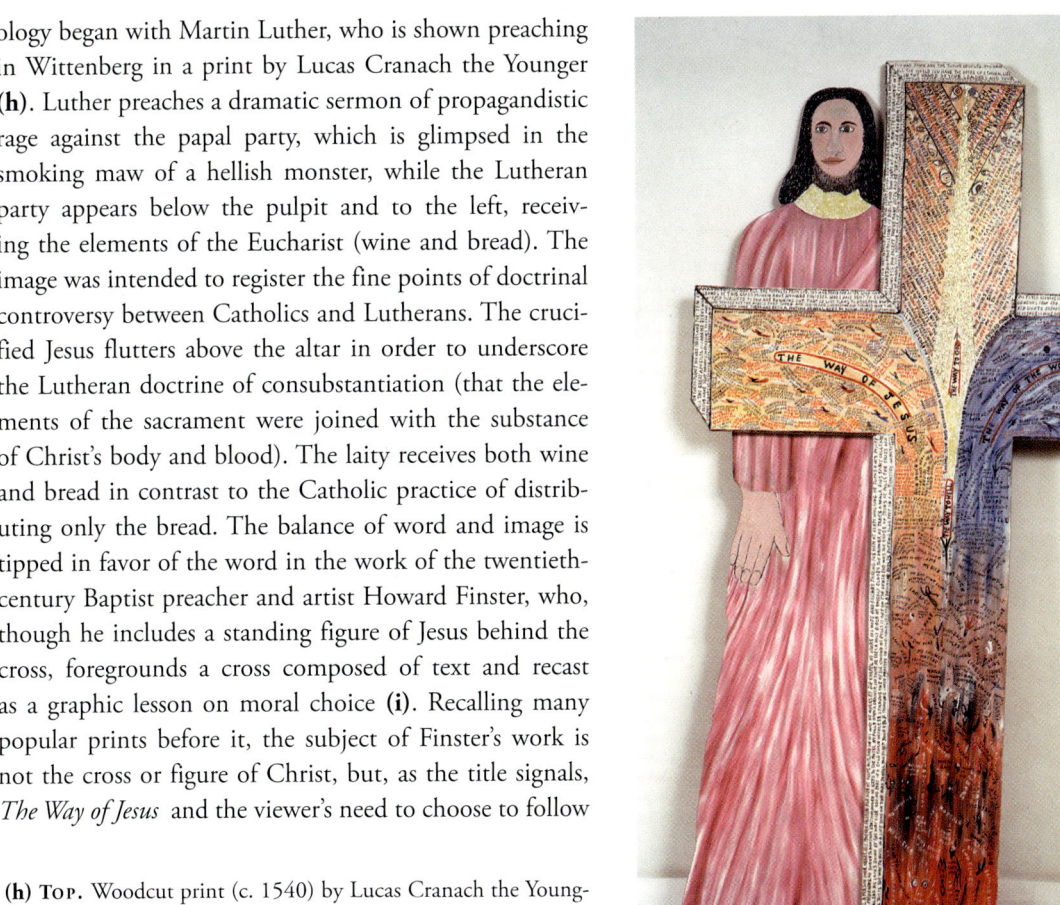

(h) **Top.** Woodcut print (c. 1540) by Lucas Cranach the Younger depicting Martin Luther preaching to the true church and the false church. *[©Bettmann/Corbis]* **(i)** **Right.** Howard Finster, *The Way of Jesus*, enamel and glitter on plywood, 1982. *[Lehigh University Art Galleries Museum Operation]*

(j) Visitors in 2002 at the Vietnam Veterans Memorial, designed by Maya Ying Lin and built on the National Mall in Washington, D.C., in 1982. *[©2004 Landov LLC. All rights reserved]*

it. The top of the cross, the direction toward God, as one arrow indicates, consists of densely inscribed text, while the bottom of the cross fades into a dark field of imagery. Encased in this single work is the radical Protestant antagonism toward the image. Though Jesus is present, he is relegated to the rear of the cross, which Finster has visualized as an obdurate block of words.

The capacity of written text to stand for objects was exploited by Japanese painters of the *Lotus Sūtra*, an important Buddhist scripture that encouraged the identification of the Buddha's body with the stupa and its relics and the very text of his teachings laid down in the written sūtras. In many scroll paintings of the sūtra, artists composed images of stupas from the Japanese characters of the Buddhist text, creating a visual unity of word, image, and the object that housed a relic of the Buddha's body. To see the sūtra was to see the stupa that contained the remains of the teacher. Pilgrims to the Vietnam Veterans Memorial **(j)** in Washington, D.C., gaze upon the names of the dead and see behind the inscribed names the reflections of themselves looking at the names in this moving, mausoleum-like memorial. The reflections encourage the idea that there is a space behind the wall, that the wall of names is a screen through which survivors may sense the proximity of their lost loved ones. Image and text intermingle to suggest a presence that makes remembering a poignantly embodied rite.

Symbolic imagery can possess a suggestive power by virtue of its appearance as a code. Tarot cards, for example, are clusters of emblematic devices and allegorical figures whose meanings are general and indeterminate until the cards are progressively configured in a serial reading that gradually tailors the cards to the personal reflections of the tarot reader's client **(k)**. The secrecy and mystery of the cards is revealed as a divination of the client's past, present, and future. Another kind of secrecy applies to the script of the golden plates found at Hill Cumorah by Joseph Smith, which he transcribed in 1828 in order for the text to be inspected by a Columbia University professor of ancient languages. Written in what the text itself called "Reformed Egyptian," the script could be translated only when Smith made use of mysterious

(k) The High Priestess card from the Rider-Waite Tarot Deck®. *[©1971 U.S. Games Systems, Inc.]*

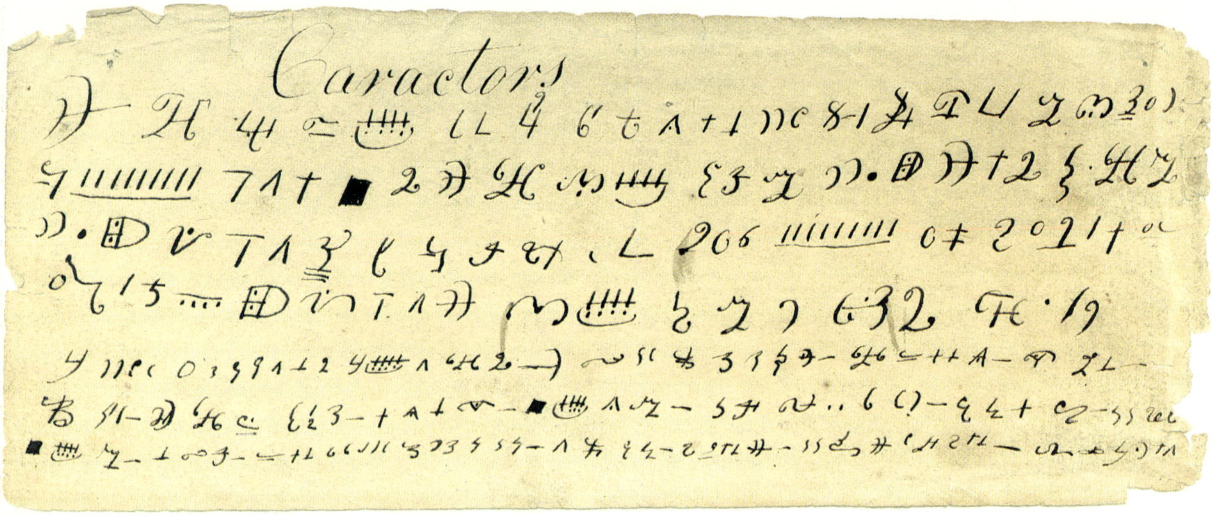

(I) The Anthon transcript, which some Mormons believe was copied in 1828 by Joseph Smith from the *Book of Mormon* plates. *[Courtesy Community of Christ, Independence, Mo.]*

interpretive devices that he called "Urim and Thummim." The putative golden plates, their allegedly ancient script, and the translation of the now-lost text shroud the *Book of Mormon* in a mystery that only enhances its authority as divine revelation for believers. The tantalizing trace of the transcript shown here **(I)** imbues the actual absence of proof with an antiquarian aura. The ancient ciphers evoke a past in which myth and history are virtually indistinguishable. Religion without suggestion is very little religion.

BIBLIOGRAPHY

Avrin, Leila. *Micrography as Art*. Jerusalem, 1981.

Brown, Peter. "Images as a Substitute for Writing." In *East and West: Modes of Communication, Proceedings of the First Plenary Conference at Merida*, edited by Evangelos Chrysos and Ian Wood, pp. 15–34. Leiden, 1999.

Givens, Terryl L. *By the Hand of Mormon: The American Scripture that Launched a New World Religion*. New York, 2002.

Murck, Alfreda, and Wen C. Fong, eds. *Words and Images: Chinese Poetry, Calligraphy, and Painting*. New York and Princeton, 1991.

Rogers, J. M. *Empire of the Sultans: Ottoman Art from the Collection of Nasser D. Khalili*. Alexandria, Va., and London, 2000.

Tanabe, Willa J. *Paintings of the Lotus Sutra*. New York, 1988.

Turner, J. F. *Howard Finster: Man of Visions*. New York, 1989.

DAVID MORGAN (2005)

nubūwah or prophetic authority—as a necessary model for their own double experience of mystical attainment and Ṣūfī authority.

One of the major theoretical problems discussed in Ṣūfī circles from the beginning was the exact nature of the relationship between the *awliyā'* and the prophet Muḥammad, that is, between the Ṣūfī and the prophet Muḥammad. The imam Jaʿfar al-Ṣādiq is quoted by Abū Nuʿaym as follows: "Whoever lives in the 'outward' [*ẓāhir*] of the Messenger [Muḥammad] is a Sunnī, and whoever lives in the 'inward' [*bāṭin*] of the Messenger is a Ṣūfī." In the Qur'anic commentary of the Ṣūfī Sahl al-Tustarī (d. 896 in Basra), the heart or spiritual reality of Muḥammad is seen as the divine element enshrined in him and the source for the illumination of human hearts; his pre-Adamic Light-nature *(nūr Muḥammad)* is the source of the prophetic ancestors of humankind, and of "those desired [by God]," that is, *awliyā'*.

Divine *walāyah,* on the other hand, is conferred directly on the elect, who are also those who have the right understanding of God and of the Qur'ān, according to al-Tustarī. The fact that the Prophet is "the *walī* of the believers" (surah 5:55) means only that he was notified (in this world) by God to befriend those whom God had befriended (or elected) in the first place. There does not seem to be an essential distinction in al-Tustarī's view between prophets generally and *awliyā',* although *ṣiddīqūn* occupy a lower rank; the charismata of the *awliyā'* are signs *(āyāt)* of God's power, and al-Tustarī himself claims to be the "proof of God" *(ḥujjat Allāh).* The Baghdad Ṣūfī Abū Sa'īd al-Kharrāz, (d. 890/891), on the other hand, polemizes against "certain Ṣūfīs" who "place the *awliyā'* above the prophets." For al-Kharrāz, prophecy is a grace additional to *wilāyah,* since prophets are *awliyā'* before they become prophets. The *awliyā'* are always placed under a prophet known by name, on whose behalf they call people to God, and their charismata are clearly of a secondary nature in comparison with the signs that are given exclusively to prophets.

Tirmidhī goes a step further in elevating the status of Muḥammad the lawgiving prophet, while at the same time elevating his own status: on the one hand, *awliyā'* and ordinary prophets rank lower than lawgiving prophets, among whom Muḥammad is unquestionably the greatest. All parts of prophecy are united in him; he is perfect in this sense, and impeccable *(maʿṣūm).* But his being "the Seal of the Prophets" means just this, not that he was the last in time, Tirmidhī insists. There is also a mysterious "Seal of the *Awliyā',*" to be sent by God at the end of time. Tirmidhī often uses Shīʿī (although not necessarily Ismāʿīlī) language, but clearly not with a Shīʿī intention: he explicitly denies that the "family of the Prophet" is the "kinship family." But the danger of a confusion with the Ismāʿīlīyah was evidently felt by al-Hujwīrī, who, writing in the mood of the "Sunnī Revival," omits the doctrine of the Seal from his summary of Tirmidhī's teaching. Yet it was brought to light again, and enriched with elements of a breathtaking complexity, by Ibn ʿArabī (1164–1240), the real master *(shaykh akbar)* of subsequent Ṣūfī thought. Ibn ʿArabī summarizes his concept of the relationship between the two Seals with the following proposition: "The Seal of the Prophets, considered from the point of view of his own *walāyah,* is toward the One who seals the *walāyah* in the same position as all other prophets and lawgiving messengers are toward him, for he is *walī,* lawgiving messenger, and prophet." But *walāyah* itself is divided into two, and, accordingly, there are two Seals of *Walāyah* in the shaykh's doctrine: Jesus, Seal of "General *Walāyah,* and Ibn ʿArabī himself, or his spiritual reality, Seal of "the Particular Muḥammadan *Walāyah.*" This doctrine, provocative as it sounds, is, however, balanced by the self-evident necessity for both Seals of *Walāyah* to follow the law of the Seal of Prophecy; and everything is placed under the primordial "reality of Muḥammad," also called "reality of realities," or the *logos.*

SEE ALSO Caliphate; Ghaybah; Imamate; Iṣmah; Nubūwah; Ummah.

BIBLIOGRAPHY

There is no single text in which all the aspects of *walāyah* are discussed in detail. For Qur'anic usage of the term, the passages cited in the text should serve as a guide. Willi Heffening's "Wilāyah" in the first edition of the *Encyclopaedia of Islam* (Leiden, 1913–1934) focuses on the legal usage; Joseph Schacht's *The Origins of Muhammadan Jurisprudence* (1950; reprint, Oxford, 1979), an invaluable work, contains much important information on the legal aspects of *walāyah.*

Walāyah in the sense of political authority is discussed in Dominique Sourdel's "L'autorité califienne dans le monde sunnite," in *La notion d'autorité au Moyen Âge: Islam, Byzance, Occident,* edited by George Makdisi et al. (Paris, 1982), pp. 101–116. An assessment of al-Ghazālī's ideas on political authority can be found in Henri Laoust's *La politique de Gazālī* (Paris, 1970) and W. Montgomery Watt's "Authority in the Thought of al-Ghazālī," in *La notion d'autorité au Moyen Âge,* already cited, pp. 57–68.

The Shīʿī concept of *walāyah* as a "pillar" of Islam is discussed by Henry Corbin in his *En Islam iranien, aspects spirituels et philosophiques,* 4 vols. (Paris, 1971–1972), a comprehensive work in which much valuable information on Ṣūfī concepts can also be found. See also Uri Rubin's "Prophets and Progenitors in the Early Shīʿa Tradition," *Jerusalem Studies in Arabic and Islam* 1 (1979): 41–66; Wilferd Madelung's "Authority in Twelver Shiism in the Absence of the Imam," also in *La notion d'autorité au Moyen Âge,* pp. 163–173; Said Amir Arjomand's *The Shadow of God and the Hidden Imam* (Chicago, 1984); Mangol Bayat's *Mysticism and Dissent* (Syracuse, N. Y., 1982); and, for recent developments, Murtaza Muṭahharī's *Wilāyah,* translated by Yaḥyā Cooper as *The Station of the Master* (Tehran, 1982).

Walāyah in Sufism is discussed in detail in al-Hujwīrī's eleventh-century *Kashf al-maḥjūb,* translated by Reynold A. Nicholson as *Kashf al-Mahjūb: The Oldest Persian Treatise on Sufism,* 2d ed. (1936; reprint, Lahore, 1976). See also Tor Andrae's *Die person Muhammeds in lehre und glauben seiner gemeinde* (Stockholm, 1918); Ignácz Goldziher's "Saint

Worship in Islam," in his *Muslim Studies,* vol. 2, translated by C. G. Barber and S. M. Stern (Chicago, 1973); Gerhard Böwering's *The Mystical Vision of Existence in Classical Islam: The Qur'ānic Hermeneutics of the Ṣūfī Sahl at-Tustarī* (Berlin and New York, 1980), pp. 149ff.; Bernd Radtke's *Al-Ḥakīm at-Tirmidī: Ein islamischer Theosoph des 3./9. Jahrhunderts* (Freiburg, 1980), pp. 85–86; and my *Nûruddîn Isfarâyinî: Le révelateur des mystères* (Paris, 1986).

HERMANN LANDOLT (1987)

WALDENSIANS. The Waldensians, also called the Poor Men of Lyons, originated with Pierre Valdès, or Peter Waldo, a wealthy merchant of Lyons, France. The dates of his birth and death are not known, nor is his exact name. The name Peter was given to him later by his followers, probably to stress his affinity with Peter, first of Christ's disciples. About 1170 Valdès was converted from his worldly life after hearing the story of Saint Alexis, who on his wedding day abandoned his bride and all his worldly possessions to become a pilgrim. The account led Valdès to seek the advice of a priest on how he, too, could obey God and become perfect. The reply he received was the same text from *Matthew* (19:21) that Francis of Assisi was to come upon forty years later: "If you wish to be perfect, go, sell your possessions, and give to the poor, and then you will have treasure in heaven; and, come, follow me." Valdès acted on the injunction, and took to a life of wandering poverty and preaching, living on alms, in emulation of Christ's life on earth.

He was soon joined by others, among them priests who translated into French passages from the Bible for the group's use in preaching. Vernacular translations from the Bible were one of the Waldensians' hallmarks. Before long their unauthorized preaching alarmed the local clergy, and the archbiship of Lyons ordered them to cease. Valdès refused, with the reply that was to be the central Waldensian tenet, that God was to be obeyed before humans (a reference to *Acts* 5:19).

The Waldensians decided to take their case to the pope, Alexander III, and a party of them traveled to Rome for that purpose. They arrived during the Third Lateran Council in 1179, were heard, and their beliefs were examined. Alexander confirmed their vow of poverty, but he also, in effect, confirmed the archbishop of Lyons's ban on their preaching by declaring that they could preach only if they first gained the permission of the local clergy. That, however, was not enough for Valdès; he continued to preach, and although he made a profession of faith before a synod at Lyons in 1180, he and his followers were excommunicated in 1182 or 1183. At the Council of Verona in 1184, where the first concerted attack on heresy was begun, the Waldensians were included among the heretical sects condemned, a condemnation to be repeated many times during the next three centuries.

The Waldensians are the classic case of popular piety become heresy. What had begun as one more attempt, not uncommon in the twelfth century, by a few individuals to return to evangelical principles, ended outside the church. The Waldensians differed in that they, alone among these groups and individuals, were neither absorbed into a religious order nor eventually disappeared as a sect, but survived the Middle Ages to become one of the new reformed churches—albeit a small one—of the sixteenth century. They did so, in part at least, because, of all the heretical sects, they remained closest to the teachings of the gospel which they sought simply to preach and practice without theological or metaphysical overtones. Theirs was above all a moral and spiritual Christianity. In that there were strong similarities between Valdès and Francis of Assisi. But where Francis and his band were accepted both by the local church hierarchy and by the pope, Innocent III, Valdès was not, and he rebelled. Even so, there is no evidence that he ever departed from the church's teachings, and every indication that during his lifetime he devoted himself to combating heresy, especially that of the Cathari. The closeness of the Waldensians to orthodox belief is suggested by the reconversion of two groups under Durand of Huesca and Bernard Prim in 1207 and 1210, and their formation into separate religious orders by Innocent III to oppose the Cathari.

That was probably the period when Valdès died. By then the Waldensians had spread from Lyons into Languedoc and northern Italy as well as into Germany, in due course extending into central Europe. They became the nearest thing to a popular counterchurch, with their own congregations and priests and their own religious forms. But they did not operate as a single church. That was due partly to circumstances and partly to their popular, almost exclusively lay, character. In 1205 there was a schism between the Lombard Waldensians and those from north of the Alps, the followers of Valdès. The Lombards had instituted their own sacraments and ceased to lead the life of wandering preachers but lived in towns and by manual labor. The followers of Valdès maintained their original pattern of mendicant preaching and poverty. The Lombards elected their own head, whereas for Valdès only Christ could be the head. Despite a further attempt to heal the split in 1218 and some degree of contact, the two different wings went their own ways.

The Waldensians were the one genuinely popular heresy (before the Hussites) who drew their support from artisans and peasants. Although they had their base in the cities, especially in Lombardy, they were also of the countryside, especially north of the Alps and in the Alpine valleys of Piedmont, where geography protected them. Cohesion was maintained by the Waldensian priests, often called the "perfect," an analogy with the Catharist perfect but having a very different character. The Waldensian perfect, especially north of the Alps—and by the fourteenth century the Waldensians had in effect become a northern phenomenon, with their main strength in Germany and central Europe—were preachers acting as Christ's apostles as Valdès had done. But now they acted clandestinely. They visited individual Waldensian believers and administered their simplified version of the sacraments. In return they were supported by the believers materially, sometimes by a voluntary tax or payment. Otherwise, the ordinary Waldensian led an ordinary life, earning his living and observing outward obedience to the Roman church. That may well have involved less of a conflict than among the ordinary Cathar believer. The difference between being a Waldensian and an orthodox Christian was less one of belief than of adherence to the Waldensian perfects, regarded by the Waldensian believers as Christ's true representatives. The opposition between them and the Roman church was the main source of Waldensian belief as it developed after the death of Valdès.

The Waldensians claimed that they were the one true church to whom the apostolic succession had passed after the so-called Donation of Constantine, which gave to the pope headship of the western Roman Empire. Although a forgery, the Donation was believed to be true until the fifteenth century, and the Waldensians were not alone in treating it as the cause of the Roman church's decline. From it they argued that the Roman priests were not true priests and, following Valdès, further held that any man, and, indeed, woman, pure in spirit and in the quality of his or her life, was a priest and ordained by God. Like the Cathari, the Waldensians accepted women as perfect, although there seems to have been a decline in the number of female perfect in the fourteenth century. Once adopted, those Waldensian beliefs became irreconcilable with those of the Roman church. The Waldensians also came to reject the Roman church's sacramental forms and most of its prayers and ceremony, including prayers for the dead, a belief in purgatory, or the very need for churches. In their place they had their own modified spiritual forms of baptism (and only for adults, not children), confession, and marriage. At the same time, true to the literal interpretation of Christ's own gospel teaching, they rejected all nonspiritual activities, including the swearing of oaths, the exercise of legal authority, the waging of war, or the taking of life.

In all those ways they sought to obey God rather than human authority by turning away from the laws of the Roman church to direct communion with Christ through God's word in the Bible. Their influence is to be seen upon the Hussites.

SEE ALSO Cathari; Hus, Jan.

BIBLIOGRAPHY

Lambert, Malcolm. *Medieval Heresy: Popular Movements from Bogomil to Hus.* New York, 1977. The fullest and most up-to-date account of medieval popular heresies.

Moore, R. I., ed. *The Birth of Popular Heresy.* London, 1975. A representative selection of translated sources, mainly from the twelfth century, with a useful introduction.

Russell, Jeffrey B. *Dissent and Reform in the Early Middle Ages.* Berkeley, 1965. A useful, wide-ranging survey of early medieval heresies to the end of the twelfth century.

Thouzellier, Christine. *Catharisme et Valdéisme en Languedoc.* Paris, 1966. A very full analysis of the sources.

Wakefield, Walter L., and Austin P. Evans. *Heresies of the High Middle Ages.* New York, 1969. The largest collection of translated sources, particularly valuable for their fullness.

New Sources

Cameron, Euan. *Waldenses: Rejections of Holy Church in Medieval Europe.* Oxford and Malden, Mass., 2000.

Shahar, Shulamith. *Women in a Medieval Heretical Sect: Agnes and Huguette the Waldensians.* Woodbridge, U.K., and Rochester, N.Y., 2001.

Stephens, Prescott. *The Waldensian Story: A Study in Faith, Intolerance and Survival.* Lewes, U.K., 1998.

Tourn, Giorgio. *The Waldensians: The First 800 Years.* Translated by Cpillo B. Merlino. Edited by Charles W. Arbuthnot. New York, 1980.

GORDON LEFF (1987 AND 2005)
Revised Bibliography

WALDMAN, MARILYN ROBINSON (1943–1996)

WALDMAN, MARILYN ROBINSON (1943–1996), was an American-born historian of religion with unusually strong commitments, knowledge, and convictions regarding Islam and Muslims. Born in Dallas, Texas, Marilyn Robinson Waldman was of Eastern European Jewish descent. Following undergraduate studies in African history at Radcliffe, she studied Islamic and African history at the University of London (1964–1965) and earned a PhD in Islamic history at the University of Chicago, where Marshall G. S. Hodgson was her most influential teacher. In her work, she combined clarity and toughness of mind with humanity and humor. She loved to find laughter where she could.

Though her life was cut short by cancer at age fifty-three, Waldman established a remarkably prolific record as a speaker, traveler, teacher, consultant, organizer, and university administrator. She was famously active in the American Academy of Religion, the American Society for the Study of Religion, the American Institute of Iranian Studies, and the World History Association. Additionally she served on the editorial boards of numerous journals and consulted on curriculum and program reform for a number of schools. At The Ohio State University (OSU), where she spent her entire professional career, she served on literally dozens of committees and held appointments in the Department of History, the Middle East Studies Program, and the Center (later Division) of Comparative Studies in the Humanities, an experimental interdisciplinary unit that she directed for several years and, in large measure, reinvented.

Professor Waldman's radical reconfiguration of the Center of Comparative Studies is telling of her broader intellectual concerns. Though staunchly committed to a strong presence for religious studies in the public university, she took the bold step of rejecting familiar arguments about the autonomy and "irreducibility" of religion, and thus argued against the need for an autonomous department of religion. She worked to establish an alternative institutional structure that would fully integrate the comparative study of religion with the comparative studies of literature and science, and indeed all versions of human inquiry. Committed to this truly interdisciplinary vision, she invested the same passion, vigor, and skill and the same quality of attention, care, and time in nurturing the Center as she did in raising her family or growing her garden. Overcoming much resistance, she shaped Comparative Studies according to her vision of a "meandering mainstream," a phrase that served as the title of her inaugural address to OSU's College of Humanities in 1988. She urged that comparison be embraced, not avoided; in fact, she regarded comparison as not just an academic exercise, but a ubiquitous human activity, a strategically deployed, socially consequential undertaking in which people are constantly involved. Though her vision has proven difficult to sustain, she regarded such a non-conventional academic unit as Comparative Studies to be not just an option but a necessity, and fought for its integrity and continuation when it was threatened by the wave of restructuring at Ohio State in the early 1990s.

Deeply concerned to find ways of framing the study of religion that avoided the problems of essentialism and reification, Professor Waldman was impressed by the claim that the category of *religion* is created for the scholar's analytic purposes through imaginative acts of comparison and generalization. In a plenary address at the Midwest American Academy of Religion (1990) she reminded her audience that "religion" is a word that the people whom scholars study do not use, or at least do not use in the way scholars do; in short, religious studies does not have a fixed or fixable object of its attention. Accordingly, she advocated what she termed "stipulative definitions" of religion, which would allow for adjustment or change over time. In her view, religion is neither a thing, nor even a phenomenon, but rather a construct that, imagined by scholars, provides, among others things, "an angle of vision" or a "take" on human beings' ways of living in the world.

Of special concern for Marilyn Waldman were the connections between religion, power, and authority, most notably in relation to prophethood and religious leadership. In fact, informed especially by years of studying Islam, she explained in the same plenary address (1990) that,

> Given my own research, I would say that the imagination and study of religion focuses us on strategies for dealing with power and authority that rely on the ability to perceive and/or generate paradoxes, disjunctions, contradictions, conflicts, competition, and discontinuities, and to make sense of them, and in making sense of them, to make connections not otherwise possible. . . . Perhaps the most fundamental paradox of all is the insistence on establishing human priorities on the basis of an extra-human source and standard . . . , that is, an insistence on distinguishing special from ordinary, and degrees of specialness and ordinariness, up and down the line, not just a focus on ultimate concern which has been the basis of many efforts to define religion. All sorts of other paradoxes flow from this one.

Given this set of interests, among Dr. Waldman's primary and enduring concerns was to bring Islam out of its marginal position in the academic study of religions. In a 1989 address to the North American Society for the Study of Religion (NASSR) entitled "Islam and the Comparative Study of Religion" she noted that Islam has seldom played a prominent role in the theorizing of the broader history of religions. In her view this was a missed opportunity for both Islamicists and comparativists, especially those like herself with special interests in religious leadership and prophethood; but once again she argued that the situation might be rectified by "reconsidering how we do comparison." Providing an early formulation of what she would term comparison via "catchments" in her final book project, *Power and Prophecy,* she argued for the creation of heuristic contexts of comparison wherein scholars, including scholars of Islam, could carry on a kind of hypothetical conversation or, as she wrote, operate with "an extra-language that will allow speakers of other languages to converse with each other in new ways." Ever mindful of the ways in which uncareful comparative strategies could reify and distort the specifics of Islamic history, she insisted that "Above all, I want my system to be fluid and tentative, to be able to account for the historical changes and momentary variation of internal systems of thought."

With the Iranian revolution, Marilyn Waldman's enduring historical and theoretical concerns about Islam were intensified and widened into more practical concerns. Her efforts to put her knowledge of Islam into more general circulation led her to cultivate a second career as a public speaker on issues of broad general concern; in all, she gave more than five hundred community presentations. The titles of some of her public lectures give a sense of how she projected her academic interests into the wider community: "Human Rights and Islamic Law" (1980), "Women Leaders: Why Are There More outside the U.S.?" (1989), "Behind and beyond the Gulf War" (1992), and "Islam in International Affairs" (1993).

This sense of obligation and her relentless efforts "to carry our knowledge into the wider world" earned her the 1992 Richard Bjornson Distinguished Service Award from the Ohio Humanities Council. As she stated in her acceptance speech, she believed in "disseminating the public significance of academic scholarship as widely as possible." Her public scholarship, she said, improved her academic scholarship, "not just the other way around." In 1987 she addressed Ohio State's summer commencement and in 1989 she served as guest lecturer on OSU's Alumni Association tour of Egypt. The Islamic Council of Ohio recognized her in 1989 for her efforts to advance public understanding of Islamic history.

If scholarship is judged by the questions it stimulates rather than the answers it provides, then Marilyn Waldman was a true scholar, for in her effort to fight stereotypes, she thrived on raising questions and complicating them through comparison. Underneath all of her pursuits was her desire to get to the heart of what it means to be human. "For me," she said, "it's not just a question of *whether* we survive, but *how* we survive, and what human possibilities we open up for ourselves in the process" ("The Meandering Mainstream: Reimagining World History," OSU Inaugural Address, 1988). She believed, as she wrote in the preface to her final book, "the commitment to cross-cultural interpretation is a moral act, a practical necessity, and an intellectual challenge; the circumstances of our time make it possible for us to address all three, and unwise to neglect any of them" (2005). A quote from Spinoza, which she had pinned to the bulletin board outside her office, sums up her investments, both personal and professional: "I have made a ceaseless effort not to ridicule, not to bewail, nor to scorn human actions, but to understand them."

BIBLIOGRAPHY

The Exemplary Faculty Award that Marilyn Waldman received from OSU's College of Humanities (1996) attests to the delicate balance she negotiated in the ways that she imparted her knowledge and understanding. Her enduring influence probably owes more to the people she affected in conferences, meetings, and classes than to her published writings. Nonetheless, the following titles are worth consulting, as they reflect the scope and depth of her thinking.

The Islamic World, which she coedited with William H. McNeill (Oxford, 1973; reprint, Chicago and London, 1983), contains translations of representative works by Muslim writers from all periods of Islamic history. *Toward a Theory of Historical Narrative: A Case Study in Perso-Islamicate Historiography* (Columbus, Ohio, 1980) challenges prevailing practice in Islamic historiography by undertaking a multifaceted analysis of a single text, *Tārīkh-i Bayhaqī,* written by a tenth-century premodern Muslim historian. It urges historians to abandon traditional attempts to deduce supposed historical realities from historical narratives, and argues that such narratives should be seen rather as part of a history of images and representations of the past.

Together with her colleague Richard Bjornson, Marilyn Waldman conceived and edited the series *Papers in Comparative Studies,* which explored issues of fundamental human concern from a variety of disciplinary and cultural perspectives. For example, *Religion in the Modern World,* edited by Waldman and Hao Chang (Columbus, Ohio, 1984), explores the relationship of religion to modernity; *Rethinking Patterns of Knowledge,* edited by Waldman and Bjornson (Columbus, Ohio, 1989), straddles fields such as medical research, mathematics, environmental engineering, zoology, psychology, history, literature, religious studies, and the performing arts; *The University of the Future: Problems and Prospects,* edited by Waldman and Bjornson (Columbus, Ohio, 1990), comments on the relationship of higher education with government and corporate America; *Judaism and Islam: Fostering Understanding,* edited by Waldman and Helena Schlam (*Jewish Education News,* 13[1], Columbus, Ohio, 1992) and *Muslims and Christians, Muslims and Jews: A Common Past, a Hopeful Future,* edited by Waldman alone (Columbus, Ohio, 1992), offer a clear, nontechnical, and accessible public scholarship; and *Understanding Women: The Challenge of Cross Cultural Perspectives,* edited by Waldman, Artemis Leontis, and Müge Galin (Columbus, Ohio, 1992), investigates the study of women, advocacy for women, and women themselves around the globe, touching on issues of colonialism, Orientalism, racism, modernization, and feminism.

At the time of her death, Dr. Waldman was working on yet another re-visioning of her thoughts on religion, authority, and comparison, under the working title of *Inviting Prophets and Entertaining Comparisons.* In this study of religious leadership, prophecy, and prophethood, comparison figures large as both subject and method. She uses the theme of "privileging communicator" to help her meditate on the benefits and perils of cross-cultural comparison, category formation, and the role of perspective in constructing knowledge in *Power and Prophecy: A Comparative Study of Islamic Evidence* (Cambridge, Mass., 2005).

MÜGÉ GALIN (2005)

WALĪ ALLĀH, SHĀH. Shāh Walī Allāh (AH 1114–1176/1703–1762 CE), Quṭb al-Dīn Aḥmad, was born in a village called Phulit in the district of Muzaffarnagar and was raised in Delhi under the close supervision of his father, Shaykh ʿAbd al-Raḥīm, an erudite scholar-educator, Ṣūfī, and accomplished jurist, and one of the compilers of *Fatāwā-i ʿĀlamgīrī,* a major work on Ḥanafī *fiqh,* commissioned by the Mughal emperor Awrangzeb (r. 1658–1707).

Walī Allāh memorized the entire text of the Qurʾān by the age of seven; studied the texts of the Qurʾān and *ḥadīth* (prophet's sayings); and was initiated into three Ṣūfī orders, the Chishtīyah, Qādirīyah, and Naqshbandīyah, by his father. In 1719, after his father's death, Walī Allāh assumed the responsibilities of full-time teaching and the running of Madrasah-i Raḥīmīyah, founded by his father. He traveled to Mecca and Medina for pilgrimage in 1730, stayed there for fourteen months, studied *ḥadīth* and Islamic law with prominent Muslim scholars belonging to the Mālikī and Shāfiʿī schools of law, and was initiated to the Shaṭṭārīyah and Shādhilīyah Ṣūfī orders. These experiences proved to be a catalyst in expanding Walī Allāh's intellectual horizons. The most productive period of his intellectual output started after his return to India, resulting in forty-one major and minor works on wide-ranging topics, including biography, ethics, law, metaphysics, mysticism, and sociopolitical issues that confronted the Muslims of his period.

Walī Allāh was an heir to the intellectual and theological heritage of such Indian Muslim thinkers as Maulana ʿAbd al-Ḥakīm Sialkotī (d. 1657), Shaykh ʿAbd al-Ḥaqq Muḥaddith Dihlawī (d. 1648), Naqshbandī master Khawājah Baqī-billāh (d. 1603), and his teachers in the Ḥijāz. His scholarship reflects the influence of many of the ideas of his predecessors; however, he differed from them in his integrative and analytical approach to various branches of the Islamic sciences, and he devised methods to reconcile conflicting opinions. In his writings he demonstrated that *ḥadīth*, *fiqh*, Qurʾān, *sunnah*, *taṣawwuf*, and Islamic history were all indispensable for the proper understanding and practice of Islam. He asserted that legislative interpretations ought to be compatible with the needs of a given period, and that jurists ought to express their independent opinion freely.

Walī Allāh lived during a period of rapid decline of Muslim political power. He was convinced of his divinely ordained role in Indo-Islamic society and embarked upon a comprehensive plan for religious renewal of the Muslim community. A serious thinker of the eighteenth century, Walī Allāh took upon himself the role of *mujaddid* (renewer and purifier of faith) of the twelfth century AH, a master of time (*qāʾim al-zamān*), and the pivot and head of the mystical hierarchy (*quṭb*). As a *mujaddid* he was concerned about practical ways of directing and enriching the tradition of scholarship and developing leadership for the community. He was especially interested in training the *ʿulamāʾ* (singular *ʿālim*, a traditionally educated Islamic scholar) by devising proper curricula and by spelling out a method of writing Qurʾanic exegesis in *al-Fawz al-Kabīr fī Uṣūl al-Tafsīr* (written in Persian), rather than writing glosses over the exegeses. With the rise of Shīʿī political power in Northern India, Walī Allāh stressed the importance of proper understanding of classical Islamic history in *Izālat al-Khafāʾ ʿan Khilāfat al-Khulafāʾ* (written in Persian) and *Qurrat al-ʿAynayn fī Tafḍīl al-Shaykhayn* (written in Persian). These two books were written not to reject Shiism, but to curb the spread of "innovation [*bidʿah*] of Shiism," which had created doubts on the legitimacy of the caliphate of the first four caliphs (632–661) in the minds of the Sunnīs. Based on reasoned discussion, Walī Allāh dealt with controversial issues in *Izālat al-Khafāʾ* (vol. 1, pp. 8–9). He argued that these caliphs played a crucial role in: (1) the compiling of Qurʾanic text and practicing the Qurʾanic ordinances; (2) establishing *ḥadīth* as a systematic source of Islamic law; and (3) developing the judicial process and juridical ordinances. To deny the key role of the caliphs in the history of Islam, in his view, amounted to destroying the very foundation of Islamic religious sciences.

Above all, in his monumental work *Ḥujjat Allāh al-Bālighah* (written in Arabic), Walī Allāh integrated the spiritual and material domains of human life; the dynamic and evolutionary relationship of human beings, life, and the universe; and the relationship of metaphysics, politics, and economics. His emphasis on the need to exercise independent reasoning on religious issues (*ijtihād*), his stress on the benefits of making the Qurʾanic text available to the community through translation (a controversial move at that time), and his belief in the power of the prophet Muḥammad's sayings and his practical model (*sunnah*) to reform communal behavior and morals made Walī Allāh the forerunner of the modernists and reformers of the nineteenth and twentieth centuries.

Madrasah-i Raḥīmīyah served as an institution of learning and research for the *shāh* and his descendants for over a century and half. Walī Allāh's career as a full-time educator lasted twelve years, until 1730, when he left for Mecca for *ḥājj*. During his absence and after his return, he assigned teaching responsibilities to a few of his pupils who were trained as teachers, while he himself concentrated on writing works of lasting value. After Walī Allāh's death, his son ʿAbd al-ʿAzīz and his younger three brothers not only managed the *madrasah* but also brought about changes in the methods and content of instruction. They maintained high standards of scholarship, took interest in social and political issues much like their father, and saw the number of students increase from thirty-five during Walī Allāh's period to many thousands drawn from across India. This institution reached new heights in prominence under the leadership of Muḥammad Isḥāq (d. 1845), who succeeded his maternal grandfather, ʿAbd al-ʿAzīz, after his death in 1824.

Shāh Walī Allāh's Legacy. Although today Walī Allāh is ranked as the most influential thinker of the modern period, he was not well-known in his lifetime, even in his home country of India. His works did not become the core of the curriculum even in his own *madrasah*, and they were not discussed, critiqued, or annotated by his progeny, as was the practice in traditional schools. His ideas, however, became attractive to modernists, reformers, and traditionalists of diverse schools of thought about three generations later. The prominent reformers and thinkers of the nineteenth and twentieth century, such as Aḥmad Khān (d. 1898), Iqbāl (d. 1938), and Mawdūdī (d. 1979), among many others, acknowledged their indebtedness to Walī Allāh. At the beginning of the twenty-first century, with Islam becoming a world religion, reference to Walī Allāh's works is a symbol of legitimacy for thinkers and organizations in Indo-Pakistan and abroad.

Bibliography

Alvi, Sajida. "The *Mujaddid* and *Tajdīd* Traditions in the Indian Subcontinent: An Historical Overview." *Journal of Turkish Studies (Schimmel Festschrift)* 18 (1994): 1–15. For a discussion on Walī Allāh's claims of *mujaddid* and *Qāʾim al-Zamān*, see pages 7–8.

Baljon, J. M. S. *Religion and Thought of Shāh Walī Allāh Dihlawī, 1703–1762.* Leiden, 1986. For details of Walī Allāh's teachers in the Ḥijāz, see page 6; for an annotated chronological listing of Walī Allāh's works, see pages 7–14.

Barakātī, Ḥakīm Maḥmūd Aḥmad. *Shāh Walī Allāh aur unkā Khāndān.* Lahore, Pakistan, 1973. For the history of Madrasah-i Raḥīmīyah, its leadership, and changes in its curriculum and fortunes until it was closed down in 1894, see pages 80–95.

Barakātī, Ḥakīm Sayyid Maḥmūd Aḥmad. *Ḥayat-i Shāh Muḥammad Isḥāq Muḥaddis Dihlawī.* Delhi, 1992. This short work is a valuable source for information on the descendants of Walī Allāh, especially Muḥammad Isḥāq, and Madrasah-i Raḥīmīyah and its evolution. Noteworthy are the following points: (1) Shāh Isḥāq received instruction in

Torah, Injīl (New Testament), and Zabūr (Psalms of David); familiarity with these scriptures was a prerequisite for the study of Qur'anic exegesis at the *madrasah* (p. 22); (2) Sayyid Aḥmad Khān, the towering modernist of the nineteenth century, attended lectures of Muḥammad Isḥāq, along with a large number of men and women in Delhi (p. 30); instruction of girls at his house in the morning was part of Shāh Isḥāq's daily routine (p. 78).

Geaves, Ron. "A Comparison of Maulana Mawdudi (1903–1980) and Shah Wali-Allah (1703–1762): A Pure Islam or Cultural Heritage." *Islamic Quarterly* 41, no. 3 (1997): 167–186.

Hermansen, Marcia K., trans. *The Conclusive Argument from God: Shāh Walī Allāh of Delhi's Ḥujjat Allāh al-Bālighah.* Leiden, 1996. For a concise overview of Walī Allāh's life, see Hermansen's introduction; for Walī Allāh's legacy and the claim of various movements and educational institutions in subsequent centuries for connection with him, see pages xxxiii–xxxvi; for a list of Walī Allāh's works and references to those available in English translation and pertinent secondary sources, see pages 479–481.

Iqbāl, Muḥammad ʿAllama. *The Reconstruction of Religious Thought in Islam.* Edited by M. Saeed Sheikh. Lahore, Pakistan, 1986; 2d ed., 1989. Iqbāl, the great philosopher-poet of twentieth century was deeply influenced by Walī Allāh's thought. He frequently referred to Walī Allāh in this work, as well as in 1,200 of his letters, more than to any other major Muslim thinker. See pages 196–197, note 47.

Rizvi, Saiyid Athar Abbas. *Shāh Walī-Allāh and His Times: A Study of Eighteenth Century Islām, Politics, and Society in India.* Canberra, 1980. A comprehensive study of Walī Allāh's life and times with the author's slight subjective slant; for an annotated chronological listing of Walī Allāh's works, see pages 220–228; for a discussion of teaching methods and curricula in the eighteenth century, see pages 358–378.

SAJIDA S. ALVI (2005)

WALKER, JAMES R. (1849–1926) was a physician with the Indian Service of the United States government who became an important scholar of Native American religion. He was born near Richfield, Illinois, on March 4, 1849. He joined the Union Army in 1864 at the age of fourteen and was eventually assigned to the U.S. Sanitary Commission to care for the sick and wounded during the Civil War. Walker resumed his schooling after he returned to Illinois at the end of the war and earned the degree of Doctor of Medicine from Northwestern University Medical School in 1873. He joined the government's Indian Service in 1877 and first served as a physician at Leech Lake Indian Reservation in Minnesota. In 1893 he was transferred to the Colville Reservation in Oregon, in 1896 to the Indian Industrial School at Carlisle, Pennsylvania, and later in 1896 to the Pine Ridge Reservation in South Dakota. It was at Pine Ridge that Walker developed a lifelong interest in the Lakota (Oglala Sioux) Indians and ultimately became one of the foremost scholars of Lakota religion, preserving a multifaceted documentary record as important to the Lakota people themselves as to academic researchers.

When Walker arrived at Pine Ridge, he found that health conditions were abysmally low. Tuberculosis afflicted almost half the Lakota population, particularly children. The Oglalas had no confidence in white doctors, preferring to rely on their medicine men (traditional religious healers). While Walker at first felt antagonistic toward the medicine men, he soon realized that if he could win them over he would have powerful allies in combating the disease. He learned that they attributed the symptoms of tuberculosis to a worm eating away the patient's lungs. By mounting sputum samples from infected individuals on slides and inviting the medicine men to examine them under a microscope, Walker was able to demonstrate to the medicine men that their theory was correct, although the "worms" were many times smaller than they had believed.

On this common ground Walker was able to gain the cooperation of the medicine men in imposing sanitary precautions to control the spread of tuberculosis. His interest in the Lakotas' medical and religious systems grew. He decided that to be effective as a physician on the reservation, he himself must become a medicine man. In the fall of 1896, some of the leading medicine men at Pine Ridge told him, "We have decided to tell you of the ceremonies of the Oglalas. . . . We will do this so you may know how to be the medicine man for the people" (Walker 1980, p. 68).

Walker's scholarly investigations intensified after 1902, when he met Clark Wissler, an anthropologist from the American Museum of Natural History in New York. Wissler was collecting objects for the museum and recording ethnographic notes. He recognized in Walker a kindred spirit and invited him to collaborate by recording vital statistics for physical anthropology studies and undertaking studies of traditional children's games, mythology, and religious ceremonies. These activities occupied Walker for the remainder of his life.

Walker's method of data collection was to transcribe interviews, commission drawings and written texts in Lakota, and make sound recordings of songs on a graphaphone, which was a device invented in 1886 that could record sound waves directly on a wax-coated cylinder. He relied on a few close consultants—Short Bull, who had been a leader of the Ghost Dance; George Sword, who wrote down many texts in Lakota and served as Walker's mentor; Thomas Tyon, who wrote texts and functioned as an interpreter—but also recorded material from more than thirty other individuals.

The study of the Sun Dance, the central Lakota religious ceremony held each summer as a ritual for renewal, was a particular challenge for Walker since the dance had been banned by the Office of Indian Affairs and was no longer performed. Of necessity Walker had to reconstruct the ritual and its meanings on the basis of interviews with the medicine men and others who had participated in the ceremony. This aspect of Walker's work complemented a series of studies of the Sun Dance among Plains tribes sponsored by the American Museum. The unparalleled richness and comprehensiveness of Walker's account of the Oglala Sun Dance, in comparison to other monographs in the series (Wissler 1915–1921), reveals his unique degree of insight into American Indian religion.

Published in 1917, Walker's "Sun Dance and Other Ceremonies of the Oglala Division of the Teton Dakota" situated the ritual in its fullest social, philosophical, and religious contexts. He laid out the common people's understanding of the ritual and of the religious system it represented, then outlined the esoteric knowledge of the medicine men. The meaning of each ritual detail was explicated with references to sacred myths. To structure the description, Walker synthesized all of his data to produce a systematized account that might be considered an instructional manual for performing the Sun Dance. In the process of compiling his systematic account, he eliminated the inconsistencies that were so apparent in his interview notes. He appended accounts of the Hunka (adoption) and Buffalo (girl's puberty) ceremonies, together with some brief philosophical and religious texts, an important interview with a medicine man named Finger, and a series of longer myths and tales.

Walker retired from the Indian Service in 1914 at the age of sixty-five and moved to a ranch in Colorado. By then, most of the medicine men with whom he had worked had died. In 1916 he completed writing his Sun Dance monograph; two years later ill health forced him to retire to Wheatridge, a suburb of Denver. Much of his time in Wheatridge was devoted to writing an Oglala mythology about the creation of the world and the origin of human beings. Walker used the same method as before, systematizing conflicting versions. The many overlapping drafts that survive attest to his struggle to synthesize all he had learned about Lakota religion. He died on December 11, 1926, leaving the mythology unfinished.

Walker's work is valued in the early twenty-first century not only for his own writings, but even more for the mass of interview material and other manuscripts that he left behind. Three volumes of documents have been published (Walker 1980, 1982, 1983) that have become primary sources for the study of Lakota religion. The often conflicting and very personal voices recorded in these documents add nuance and richness to Walker's syntheses. They are part of his legacy, a historical record of an American Indian religion remarkable for its detail and depth of insight. The record of his studies fulfils the commitment he made to the medicine men that their knowledge would be preserved in writing, "that future generations of the Oglalas should be informed as to all that their ancestors believed and practiced" (Walker 1980, p. 47).

See Also Lakota Religious Traditions; North American Indian Religions, article on History of Study.

Bibliography

Dooling, D. M., ed. *The Sons of the Wind: The Sacred Stories of the Lakota.* Norman, Okla., 2000. A popular edition of Walker's Oglala mythology for nonspecialist readers.

Walker, James R. "The Sun Dance and Other Ceremonies of the Oglala Division of the Teton Dakota." In *Anthropological Papers of the American Museum of Natural History,* vol. 16, no. 2 pp. 51–221. New York, 1917. Walker's synthesis of Lakota religion, together with important religious and mythological texts.

Walker, James R. *Lakota Belief and Ritual.* Edited by Raymond J. DeMallie. Lincoln, Nebr., 1980. Includes most of Walker's interview material on religion, together with a variety of lectures and short writings. The introduction includes a biographical sketch of Walker and an assessment of his significance.

Walker, James R. *Lakota Society.* Edited by Raymond J. DeMallie and Elaine A. Jahner. Lincoln, Nebr., 1982. Includes a common man's account of participation in the Sun Dance, a variety of ritual practices, and material on sacred time that includes pictorial calendars (winter counts).

Walker, James R. *Lakota Myth.* Edited by Elaine A. Jahner. Lincoln, Nebr., 1983. Presents the fullest surviving drafts of Walker's Oglala mythology, together with mythological texts from a number of religious leaders.

Wissler, Clark, ed. "Sun Dance of the Plains Indians." *Anthropological Papers of the American Museum of Natural History,* vol. 16 (1915–1921). Description of the Sun Dance among the Plains tribes with historical and comparative discussion.

Raymond J. DeMallie (2005)

WANDJINA.

Australian Aborigines traditionally believed that a person's spirit existed before entering the human life-cycle and that it survived after bodily death. Life-spirits were identified as originating in a number of mythological beings, of which those called *wandjina* were important in central and northern Kimberley, with the mythical snake Ungud and other animal spirits playing less significant parts.

Identification of a person's life-spirit, or conception totem, was revealed to his or her father or to another senior male of the group during a dream. Dream communication with the mythological beings played a significant role in Aboriginal religion, for although the events of the creation period, or *lalai,* were generally known, the present state of the beings was of ongoing significance, and that could be revealed only through the dreaming process. The father-to-be was entitled to identify the origin of a life-spirit, but in other circumstances, a specialist, or *banman* ("dreamer"), could communicate with the mythological beings. Life-spirits of *wandjina* origin came from the clouds, (that is, the sky) to live in water. They entered the mother-to-be either directly or through food gotten from water: for example, fish. In his dream, the father would see the spirit and identify its place of origin, from which he could deduce the mythological being who then became the conception totem. One Aboriginal man summarized the sequence of events as follows: "Our fathers found us in the form of fish or turtles, but the Wandjina is our real father. He put us in the water from the sky. . . . We came from heaven through the water by dreams." The life-spirit is regarded as a reincarnated *wandjina,* and a person whose spirit is so derived will speak in a way that indicates continuity of the (mythological) past and the present.

The *wandjina* are depicted in paintings on the walls of caves. On approaching these shrines, Aborigines call out to the *wandjina* to announce the arrival of visitors. If this is not done by a person with the correct status, the spirits become upset and take revenge on the Aborigines. Sometimes Aborigines perform a ritual in which smoke from green branches is held beneath the paintings. Similar gestures are made as placatory gestures at the end of mourning ceremonies.

Many of the paintings are spectacular. The *wandjina* are anthropomorphic in form and are usually larger than life size. Individual figures may be as large as six meters long. Against a whitened background, the figures are painted in red ochre and black charcoal. The faces and heads are emphasized, with large eyes (usually black, sometimes also engraved) and haloes around the heads. On these haloes, and projecting from them, may be radiating lines. A curious feature of each face is the absence of a mouth, although the nose is invariably present. The *wandjina* may be represented by a face only, but often the whole body is shown. The shoulders are always white, and there is a small shieldlike motif high on the chest. The body is filled-in with a dot or short-dash pattern, and body ornamentation is indicated by waist and arm bands.

In Aboriginal mythology, the *wandjina* are said to have lived during the creation period. They came from the sky or the sea, traveled a short distance (usually), and then transformed themselves into the paintings. For the most part, the *wandjina* set examples of disruptive behavior, seducing others' wives and quarreling among themselves. All myths about the *wandjina* share one central action, in which the *wandjina* round up the Aborigines and slaughter them with lightning and flood because two Aborigine boys have offended them by torturing an owl, their sacred bird. Other episodes are purely local in significance. The paintings, are the transformation of the living spirits into a new form. Their general human appearance is unmistakable, and Aborigines identify many of the features in the paintings as human characteristics. In these intepretations, the haloes are hair, the lines radiating from the heads are feathers, the dots on the bodies are body paint, and the bands around the waists and limbs are body ornaments. However, the human model is not the only one the Aborigines use in interpreting the paintings. *Wandjina* may take the form of clouds, and so the paintings may be interpreted as depicting the spirits in cloud form. In this case, the eyes are seen as dark patches of cloud, the haloes as the edges of clouds, the radiating lines as lightning, and the dot patterns as falling rain. Yet another model for interpretation is the owl, the bird sacred to the *wandjina.* Attention is then drawn to the round white faces, the large eyes, and the presence of beaks but the absence of separate mouths. In this interpretation, the body decoration represents the dappled markings of an owl's breast feathers.

The *wandjina* are often referred to as "the rainmakers." Toward the end of the dry season, when the heat has intensified, Aboriginal men who have *wandjina* as their conception totems may sing songs and perform rituals which are intended to entice the *wandjina* to send rain and alleviate their condition. Kimberley receives monsoonal rains starting in late December. Their arrival is a dramatic event. In the weeks preceding the arrival of the "wet," there are local showers and spectacular displays of lightning. With the rain come the banks of cumulonimbus clouds, which change shape rapidly and appear to have a life of their own. In them, the Aborigines see the *wandjina.* The call to the spirits, made in the songs and rituals, has been answered.

The rain that the *wandjina* bring is recognized by the Aborigines as a major factor in the fertility of the land. By the end of the dry season, when the Aborigines have burned off all the grass, the earth is parched and hot. Nothing grows, and animals hide from the heat. When the rains come, the earth, which is itself alive, drinks. Plants flourish. Animals emerge from their hiding places. To shelter from the rain the Aborigines build huts of bark or thatch or move into caves. Where the caves are painted, the figures on the walls appear brighter: In many cases, the painters have used huntite, a hydroscopic mineral, as the pigment for the white background, and so there is a noticeable change in the hue of the paintings when the humidity intensifies. As the wet season progresses, there may be flooding. The *banman* then must try to reduce the rain through further songs and rituals. These songs narrate episodes in the mythology of the *wandjina.*

Physical evidence implies that the *wandjina* have been repainted many times. Aborigines say that the original figures came into existence when the spirits transformed themselves into the paintings, and that the role of the Aborigines in the past has been restricted to maintenance. Some of the pigments are quite unstable in the presence of the high humidity that prevails during the wet season, and for this reason regular maintenance would always have been necessary. The custodian of a painting might invite a noted artist to carry out the restoration, in which case a payment of goods to the artist would have been required.

The *wandjina* are seen by the Aborigines as fertility gods. By sending rain, they ensure the survival of life on earth. More directly, by sending the life-spirits for humans, they ensure the continuity of human life. The enormous powers of the *wandjina* can be seen in the displays of thunder and lightning that precede the monsoon and in the rains themselves. If provoked, the *wandjina* could use their powers to destroy life as they did in the mythological past. Through the rituals performed at the caves, through the songs, and, especially, through the mechanism of dream-communication, Aborigines have traditionally sought to influence the *wandjina* and thus to gain for themselves some measure of control over the natural world.

BIBLIOGRAPHY

Crawford, I. M. *The Art of the Wandjina: Aboriginal Cave Paintings in Kimberley, Western Australia.* Melbourne, 1968. An overall coverage of *wandjina* and other cave art of the Kimberleys, together with a discussion of their mythology and meaning. Illustrated.

Elkin, A. P. "Grey's Northern Kimberley Cave Paintings Refound." *Oceania* 19 (1948): 1–15. Discusses the rediscovery of the *wandjina* paintings, first reported to the outside world by the European explorer George Grey in his *Journals of Two Expeditions of Discovery in Northwest and Western Australia* (London, 1841).

Lommel, Andreas. *Die Kunst des Fünften Erdteils.* Munich, 1959. Contains, among other material, both illustrations and discussion of *wandjina* paintings.

Petri, Helmut. *Sterbende Welt in Nordwest-Australien.* Braunschweig, 1954. A detailed study of northwestern Australian Aboriginal society and culture, in which *wandjina* paintings and their significance are placed in context.

Schulz, Agnes S. "North-west Australian Rock Paintings." In *Memoir of the National Museum of Victoria,* pp. 7–57. Melbourne, 1957. Further discussion on the mythological relevance of the *wandjina* and their expression through art.

I. M. CRAWFORD (1987)

WANG BI (226–249 CE) was the scion of an important Shandong clan with great intellectual ambitions and "over eighty members" who reached the highest echelon of power in the preceding Han dynasty (206 BCE–220 CE). The collapse of this dynasty resulted in the division of the country into three competing states, as well as the collapse of the state-sponsored and privately sponsored educational system, together with the authority of official teaching. It was chance that put arguably the richest and most intellectually diverse manuscript library to survive the conflagration and civil war of the collapsing Han dynasty into Wang's possession. His talents thus flourished during a rare and short moment in history, a time when philosophical originality and iconoclasm were much appreciated and youthful genius was revered. Wang Bi was spurred on by a rich and open competition, and a government reform project that was guided from 240 to 249 CE by He Yan (d. 249), a man considered by his contemporaries to be the ultimate *arbiter elegantiarum,* as well as a brilliant philosophical debater. The closure of the project came with a coup and the execution of its leaders in 249, the same year in which Wang Bi, just twenty-three years of age, died in an epidemic.

In a reaction to the bookwormishness of the Han scholars, Wang Bi rediscovered the warnings of such philosophical writings as the *Laozi* (*Dao de jing*), the *Analects* (*Lunyu*), and the *Book of Changes* (*Zhouyi*) about the inability of definitory language to deal with the necessarily unspecific root of all specificity. This root was thus linguistically "dark" (*xuan*), and the entire philosophical enterprise around Wang Bi was therefore later called *Xuanxue,* the "scholarly exploration of that which is dark," rather than being associated with any of the traditional philosophical "schools." In this philosophical, rather than school-dominated, enterprise, the appropriation of different texts by the different schools was rejected, and so was their habit of ranking their own founder highest. In Xuanxue, Confucius ranked philosophically higher than Laozi because—by not writing a book but only editing what became the "classics" and allowing his *verba et gesta* to be recorded by his students (*Analects*)—he proved himself superior in understanding the philosophical problem of language.

Xuanxue scholars reread the classics as writings that made conscious and sophisticated use of a flawed instrument—written language—because it was the only way to preserve the sage teachings of old. These works thus had to be viewed as pointing beyond themselves, and they received their unity not from the textual surface, but from their elusive common object. Wang Bi outshone his contemporaries in the philological brilliance and consistency of this type of "commentary of meaning," and his commentaries on the *Laozi* and the *Book of Changes,* together with an essay each on their structure, have time and again found copyists and sponsors, so that they alone of the plethora of commentaries written by his peers survive to this day, together with fragments of his commentary on the *Analects.*

Wang Bi extracted from these classical texts a political philosophy that was rooted in ontological analysis. The teachings of the "schools" about political strategies aimed at bringing about and maintaining social order lack a dialectical understanding of the dynamics of the relationship of the ruler to the people. Wang Bi argued that rulers following these teachings end up bringing about the very chaos they are trying to overcome. Only by going back to the fundamental dynamics prevailing between the "one" and the "many" can the laws be found that govern the dynamics between the one ruler and the multitude of the people. Wang Bi thus explores the ontological question of the necessary features of that by which the entities ("the ten thousand kinds of things") are, and by which they are in a regulated and orderly fashion. This exploration of the "one" provides the basis to determine the features and acts necessary for a ruler to secure social and political order. The "one" of the ten thousand kinds of entities can only be the "one" by being their—and their regulated order's—condition of possibility, and by not specifically interfering with the regulated order of the remaining entities. Otherwise, the "one" would only be another entity among the multitude. The emulation of this non-interference (*wuwei*) by the ruler in his relations with society thus becomes a philosophical imperative. Given the ruler's theoretically absolute powers and the commonsense assumption that their active use will be instrumental in establishing order, Wang Bi's proposal is philosophical by being counterintuitive, while its necessity is shown by the evident presence of chaos.

The thirty-year civil war ending Han rule (at great loss) was a timely reminder. In any given historical situation, however, the vicious circle between a ruler's efforts to establish order and the counterproductive dynamics these efforts set in motion is already in operation. The ruler's generous encouragement of some virtuous persons provokes the resentment of those not so favored; his use of surveillance machinery to ward off evildoers calls forth a rise in the arts of dissimulation. Accordingly, an actual historical ruler must not just "maintain" order, he must "bring back" society ("the hundred families" from the historically real chaos to find rest and order in his *wuwei*. *Wuwei* thus is a proactive policy of projecting the non-use of the absolute powers of the ruler through a public performance of this non-use; projections of "simplicity," "uncouthness," "dumbness," "femaleness," and the pointed abolition of state surveillance (an eyesore for many intellectuals in a state of Wie during Wang Bi's time) are some of the particular proactive forms of "non-interference" that Wang Bi extracts from the texts he analyzed. In this manner, the ruler will erase his own function as the point of orientation of all social competition, with the consequence that the hundred families will fall back to their "natural" station. Then the self-regulating mechanisms come into play in the same manner as they do in nature, where, as Wang Bi writes, "heaven and earth do not make grass for cattle, but cattle still eat the grass." The implied addressee of Wang Bi's philosophy is the ruler, and the quest is for the philosophical bases of social order. Philosophical questions are only pursued to the point where relevancy for the political application ceases.

Wang Bi's *Commentary to the Zhouyi* entered the canon in the seventh century, and it influenced all later commentaries on this text. His *Commentary to the Laozi* had a similar impact. His commentarial method is characterized by an insistence on internal coherence, a refusal to randomly impose terms or methods to solve problems of consistency, and full attention given to clues within the texts that help determine the appropriate manner of reading these texts.

See Also Guo Xiang; Laozi.

Bibliography

Lynn, Richard J., trans. *The Classic of Changes: A New Translation of the I Ching as Interpreted by Wang Bi.* New York, 1994.

Wagner, Rudolf. *The Craft of a Chinese Commentator: Wang Bi on the Laozi.* Albany, N.Y., 2000.

Wagner, Rudolf. *A Chinese Reading of the* Daode jing: *Wang Bi's Commentary on the* Laozi, *with Critical Text and Translation.* Albany, N.Y., 2003.

Wagner, Rudolf. *Language, Ontology, and Political Philosophy: Wang Bi's Scholarly Exploration of the Dark (Xuanxue).* Albany, N.Y., 2003.

Wang Baoxuan. *Zhengshi xuanxue.* Jinan, China, 1987.

Rudolf G. Wagner (1987 and 2005)

WANG CHE See WANG ZHE

WANG CHONG

WANG CHONG (27–100? CE), critic and skeptic who proposed naturalist explanations for the relation between Heaven and man. Born into a poor family in Guiji (in modern Zhejiang), Wang studied in the Imperial Academy but then held office for a brief period only. Most of his life he lived in seclusion, devoting himself to writing. He wrote three works, *Zhengwu* (The conduct of government), *Lunheng* (Critical Essays), and *Yangsheng* (On the cultivation of life). Of these only *Lunheng* has been preserved.

According to Wang himself, the spirit of his *Lunheng* may be summed up in one sentence: he detests what is fictitious and false. The fiction that Wang detested most was the theory of "mutual response between Heaven and man," which had dominated the mind of Han China since Dong Zhongshu had first propounded it 150 years earlier. According to this theory, aberrant natural phenomena (such as floods or the appearance of strange creatures) were omens, Heaven's comments on man's behavior. Wang wholly rejected this teleological cosmology, arguing instead that the Way of Heaven is one of spontaneity (*ziran*) and nonactivity (*wuwei*). "Heaven," he wrote, "does not desire to produce things, but things are produced of their own accord; Heaven does not desire to create things, but things are created of themselves." Because he defines Heaven in terms of spontaneity and nonactivity, Wang's philosophy usually has been characterized in modern times as naturalistic, even though he was traditionally classified as an eclectic (*zajia*).

Wang's definition of Heaven led him to a thorough denunciation of all theories that claimed conscious interactions between Heaven and man. He compared man's place in the universe to a louse in the folds of a garment: if a louse cannot, by its actions, affect the movements of the man who wears the garment, then how can a man who lives on the earth's surface affect, much less cause, by his actions, the movements and changes of Heaven? For this reason, it is simply false to suppose that a causal relationship exists between auspicious or calamitous natural events on the one hand and good or bad government on the other. All the seeming coincidences between natural phenomena and human actions must be understood as pure chance.

Another area of Wang's philosophy that has been influential is his conception of life and death. Several of his essays are devoted to a vigorous refutation of the popular belief of his time that the soul can survive the body. He maintained that a man's soul exists within his body and that at death, when the body decomposes into dust and earth, his soul also disintegrates. He used a famous metaphor to illustrate this body-soul relationship: human death is like the extinction of a fire; when a fire is extinguished, its light ceases to shine, and when a man dies, his consciousness also ceases to exist. To assert that the soul survives the body is like saying that the light survives the fire. Wang also argues against the existence of ghosts, another form in which the human spirit was believed to survive the body. According to Wang, since all accounts of ghosts report that like living persons they wear clothes, and since clothes certainly have no souls that can survive decomposition, how then can ghosts be seen with clothes on? In taking this atheistic position, however, Wang follows the Confucian rather than the Daoist tradition. In the Daoist thought of Han times, the soul leaves the body at death and returns to its "true home," where it continues a mystical existence.

Writing against the predominant beliefs of the day, Wang was indeed a bold thinker in his attempts to demolish a great variety of unfounded superstitious beliefs. But in other respects he was very much a product of his time. He accepted without question some of the fundamental assumptions of the yin-yang dualism and the theory of the Five Elements. He shared the contemporary view that life, whether cosmic or individual, arises out of the interaction and combination of the basic vital forces *(qi)* of yang and yin, and all things are made up of the five elements of wood, fire, soil, metal, and water. What essentially distinguishes Wang's cosmology is the absence of a cosmic purpose.

In Wang's naturalism is also grounded his theory of predetermined fate. Success or failure in the life of an individual or even of the whole state is, according to Wang, determined by what he called "fate" *(ming).* Fate, to Wang, controlled even precise areas of life. He held, for example, that a man's longevity, intelligence, social position, and wealth is fixed at birth by the kind of *qi* with which he is endowed. Order or disorder in the state is also predetermined. Thus Wang did assume a connection between celestial phenomena and human fate. However, he interpreted auspicious or calamitous natural events merely as signs of a predetermined fate, not purposive expressions of Heaven's pleasure or displeasure.

Wang was relatively obscure during his life, but his *Lunheng* was rediscovered in the early third century and paved the way for the growth of neo-Daoist naturalism during the Wei-Jin period (220–420).

SEE ALSO Afterlife, article on Chinese Concepts; Soul, article on Chinese Concepts; Yinyang Wuxing.

BIBLIOGRAPHY

Fung Yu-lan. *A History of Chinese Philosophy*, vol. 2. 2d ed. Translated by Derk Bodde. Princeton, 1953. See pages 150–167 for a concise treatment of Wang's thought and its historical context.

Needham, Joseph. *Science and Civilisation in China*, vol. 2, *History of Scientific Thought.* Cambridge, 1956. See pages 368–386.

Wang Ch'ung. *Lun-heng.* 2 vols. 2d ed. Translated by Alfred Forke. New York, 1962. A complete English translation with a useful introduction.

YÜ YING-SHIH (1987)

WANG CH'UNG SEE WANG CHONG

WANG FU-CHIH SEE WANG FUZHI

WANG FUZHI

WANG FUZHI (*zi*, Erhnung; *hao*, Chuanshan; 1619–1692), a Neo-Confucian philosopher. Now recognized along with Huang Zongxi and Gu Yanwu as one of the major thinkers to emerge in seventeenth-century China, Wang was almost unknown in his own lifetime outside of a small circle of followers in his native Hunan. He devoted his life to the task of revitalizing and restoring the cultural heritage and political autonomy of a Confucian China whose decline and fall, culminating in the overthrow of the Ming dynasty and the Manchu conquest, left him a virtual refugee in his own country. He was only thirty-one when in 1650 his patriotic foray into the political arena of the court of the Ming pretender Yungli ended in temporary imprisonment as a result of factional strife. Thereafter he had to content himself with propounding his ideas in a prodigious number of works, none of which was published during his lifetime owing largely to the fiercely anti-Manchu sentiments and politically subversive theories expressed in them. Nevertheless, as he himself declared, "With my country ruined and my home destroyed, I set forth my opinions for posterity . . . In the future there will arise those who will carry on the task." In the late nineteenth and early twentieth century, however, such historical and political writings as his *Du Tongjian lun* (On reading the *Comprehensive Mirror*), *Song lun* (On the history of the Song dynasty), *Huangshu* (Yellow book), and *E-meng* (Strange dream)—all published for the first time in 1865—fired the imagination of patriotic reformers and revolutionaries who regarded Wang as a prophet of modern Chinese nationalism. Tan Sitong, Zhang Binglin, and Mao Zedong all acknowledged him as a source of inspiration.

The same patriotic fervor that has attracted modern Chinese originally impelled Wang to undertake a radical reappraisal of the whole history of Chinese civilization. What had gone wrong? What were the remedies?—these were the two questions that inspired and informed all Wang's studies, which spanned the whole range of traditional Chinese scholarship. In typical Confucian fashion, however, his central concern was ideological: what had gone wrong with the transmission of the Confucian tradition, and what constituted the true development of orthodox Confucianism? This concern was shared by many scholars at the close of the Ming dynasty, particularly by those associated with the Donglin Academy who, reacting against Buddhist influences and contemporary tendencies in the school of Wang Yangming, tried to give Confucianism a new direction. Wang Fuzhi admired their efforts to encourage scholar-officials to abandon the selfish pursuit of personal fulfillment and absolute truth and commit themselves to a social and political program in which moral philosophy was applied to contemporary realities. Indeed, as a young man he was certainly influenced by them. But whereas these scholars tended to arrive at various compromises between the Cheng-Zhu tradition and the more moderate forms of the Wang Yangming tradition, Wang Fuzhi went further. He came to the conclusion that the moral decline of China could be traced to Sung times, when the Cheng-Zhu school had first turned away from the "true doctrines" of Zhang Zai (1020–1077).

Although there had been some revival of interest in Chang's thought among Wang's contemporaries, Wang went so far as to declare himself a latter-day disciple of the Song philosopher, according him precedence over Zhuxi (1130–1200), whose systematization of the Confucian tradition in a grand synthesis (incorporating certain of Chang's ideas in the process) had created the Cheng-Zhu school of Neo-Confucianism, the dominant orthodoxy until the twentieth century. Wang, however, proceeded to elaborate his own extremely coherent philosophical system on the basis of his Sung mentor's cosmology. He adopted Chang's concept (itself a refinement of such early Daoist naturalist views as found in the first-century-CE *Lunheng* of Wang Chong) of a universe that consisted of one vast mass of ether (*qi*) in a perpetual state of flux, agglomerating to form objects and dispersing to return to the "void" of apparent nonbeing as its *yin* and *yang* aspects interacted. Wang explicitly rejected the Cheng-Zhu school's doctrine on principle (*li*) and ether, which entailed a dualistic approach both in its basic metaphysics and in its treatment of human nature. For Wang there was no duality: principle lay within the ether, and all ether was principle. His monistic conception of the universe led him to attack both Zhuxi's attribution of evil to the physical nature and his consequent rejection of human desires.

Wang held that nothing was inherently evil: evil arose simply as excessive or incongruous activity in natural encounters within the movement of the organic whole. Man's vital role as an integral part of this dynamic universe was to ensure its harmonious functioning through cultivating himself and ordering human society. To fulfill this role required an understanding of the universal processes; these could be observed at work in the course of history and in codified form in the ancient divinatory classic the *Yi jing* (Book of Changes). Zhang Zai too had set great store by this text, but his treatment of the archetypal patterns and symbols of the *Changes* had been mystical, the expression of his ideas poetical—as in his influential *Ximing* (Western Inscription)—and he had paid little attention to history. Wang's approach was altogether more analytical, rational, and pragmatic—even utilitarian. Wang's emphasis on variable factors of time and place and prevailing conditions in determining what was appropriate, and hence, in a morally ordered universe, right, led him to make a critical evaluation of political institutions throughout Chinese history and to formulate his own proposals for reform based on radical changes in the system of land-tenure and taxation. In contemporary China Wang has been admired, patriotism apart, as a major contributor to the native tradition of philosophical materialism and as a historian critical of the old society.

BIBLIOGRAPHY

The most comprehensive edition of Wang's works is the *Chuanshan i-shu*, published by the Tai pingyang bookstore (Shanghai, 1933); a facsimile edition was published in Taipei in 1965. A full bibliography of secondary sources in Chinese, Japanese, and Western languages can be found in my "Wang Fuzhi and his Political Thought" (Ph.D. diss., Oxford, 1968). Liu Zhijisheng's appendix to *Wang Chuanshan yanjiu can kao liao* (Changsha, 1982) includes a comprehensive list of recent studies on Wang both in and outside China. For additional studies, see Tang Junyi's *Zhongguo zhexue yuanlun: yuan jian pain* (Hong Kong, 1975) and my essay "Wang Fuzhi and the Neo-Confucian Tradition," in *The Unfolding of Neo-Confucianism*, edited by Wm. Theodore de Bary (New York, 1975).

IAN MCMORRAN (1987)

WANG YANGMING (1472–1529), literary name, Wang Shouren; the most influenctial Confucian thinker in Ming-dynasty China and one of the most important scholar-officials in Chinese history. Wang's intellectual impact on East Asian culture and his transformation of the spiritual orientation of the Confucian tradition in China made him one of the greatest philosophers of the relation between knowledge and action in any age or culture.

Born to a prominent gentry family in the Yangtze River delta, Wang was subject as a youth to great social pressure to excel in Confucian learning. Hagiographical accounts relate that in his early teens Wang startled his teacher when, in response to the teacher's admonition that the most important thing in life was to study hard in order to pass the examinations with distinction, Wang said: "To learn to become a sage is of the utmost importance." Wang's competitiveness with his father, who had himself won highest honors in the triennial metropolitan (jinshi) examinations, and his rebelliousness against the conventions of the time led him to the pursuit of a spiritual path characterized by Daoist and Chan practices. His failure to pass the metropolitan examinations three times before he succeeded and his dissatisfaction with the vulgarity of other officials after he eventually obtained an official post further enhanced his determination to search for an alternative form of life.

Wang is noted for his lifelong quest to understand the mind and nature. His biography records that on his wedding day he became so absorbed in conversing with a Daoist priest about prolonging life through nourishing the vital force in one's body that he did not return home until the next day. At an early age he began a traditional education grounded in the Confucian classics, but he also studied military affairs, literary style, Buddhist philosophy, and Daoist technique of longevity. In 1492, intent on putting Zhu Xi's (1130–1200) doctrine of the investigation of things (*gewu*) into practice, he devoted himself to the study of the principle (*li*) inherent in things by meditating in front of a bamboo grove for seven days. His abortive attempt to understand Zhu Xi's assertion that personal knowledge can be acquired through an understanding of external phenomena compelled him to probe the internal resources of his own mind-and-heart (*xin*).

Wang started his official career at the age of twenty-eight. His primary goal in life, however, was to become an exemplary teacher so that he could share his intellectual insight and spiritual quest with friends and students. In fact, it took him some time to come to terms with his role as a scholar-official. While cultivating the Daoist arts of overlasting life in a cave near his home, he contemplated forsaking the world altogether. It was only after he had fully convinced himself that his longings for his father and the grandmother who had raised him were irreducible human feelings, necessary for the survival and well-being of the human community, that he decided to return to society permanently in order to transform it from within.

One of the most important events in this initial stage of his official career was his friendship with Zhan Ruoshui, the disciple of the eminent Confucian master Chen Bosha (Chen Xianzhang, 1428–1500). Wang sealed a covenant with Zhan to promote true Confucian learning, the kind of learning that stresses an experiential understanding of the body and mind. Such learning they clearly differentiated from the study of the classics for the sake of passing the examinations.

Wang advocated his first doctrine, "the unity of knowing and acting," shortly after his decision to return to society. According to his famous dicta, "knowledge is the beginning of action; action is the completion of knowledge" and "knowledge in its genuine reality and earnest practicality is action; action in its brilliant self-awareness and refined discrimination is knowledge," have become defining characteristics of Wang's philosophy of mind, what Wing-tsit Chan refers to as his dynamic idealism.

However, far from being a speculative thinker who made no attempt to put his ideas into practice, Wang described his doctrine as the result of a hundred deaths and a thousand hardships. Indeed, he once almost lost his life when he protested against a powerful eunuch. For this, the emperor had him flogged forty times at court and banished to a small postal station in a remote mountainous area in present-day Guizhou. However, it was there that he experienced enlightenment and developed a unique approach to Confucian learning that emphasized the learning of the body and mind.

A salient feature of Wang's thought is his inquiry into the internal landscape of the mind as the center of moral creativity. This emphasis is predicated on a vision that encompasses both the ontological reality of Heaven and the social reality of human relationships. In his philosophy, which is religious as well as ethical, self-cultivation is a holistic process of learning to be fully human. Wang argued that self-cultivation begins with a critical understanding of one's selfhood, but he remained fully within the Confucian tradition in placing the self at the center of relationships. Thus, for Wang the quest for self-knowledge necessarily involves active participation in the human community.

The Confucian idea of the human is not anthropocentric. Rather, humanity in its full realization here signifies an anthropocosmic reality often symbolized by the notion of the unity of people and Heaven. This realization requires that we as humans respond to the ultimate source of creativity, namely, the way of Heaven (*tiandao*). Thus, Wang's second important doctrine is "the preservation of the heavenly principle and the elimination of human desires." Human desires are egoistic demands and private, selfish ideas. The true self, which is not only the deepest source of moral creativity but also the heavenly principle (*tianli*) inherent in our nature, is an open system. It extends horizontally to the human community as a whole and, simultaneously, it reaches upward to Heaven. Therefore, the unity of people and Heaven is not merely an idea but an experienced ethico-religious reality.

Wang's attempt to integrate heavenly principle (ontological reality) and human relationships (social reality) in the moral creativity of the self (subjectivity) is well articulated in his third and most mature doctrine, often translated as "the extension of the innate knowledge of the good" (*zhi liangzhi*; Chan, 1969, p. 656). Actually, the doctrine can well be stated as the full realization of our primordial awareness, an awareness that we are capable of self-perfection. This doctrine may be regarded as a creative interpretation of the classical Mencian thesis of the goodness of human nature. Following Mengzi's notion that the moral feelings of the mind-and-heart are humanity at its best, Wang insisted that the uniqueness of being human lies in our ability to perfect ourselves through self-effort. The reason that some of us have become sages (the most genuinely realized humans) is because inherent in our heavenly endowed nature is our great body (*dati*), which never ceases to guide us toward the highest excellence of humanity. Wang underscores this dimension of Mengzi's teaching by adding the verb *zhi* (to extend, to fully realize) to the original Mencian term liangzhi (innate goodness or primordial awareness), thus transforming it into an active, dynamic, and creative principle of self-cultivation.

Wang formulated his interpretation of the Confucian way by wrestling with Zhu Xi's balanced approach to Confucian learning. Briefly stated, Zhu Xi held that moral development could only be attained through the simultaneous activities of dwelling in the spirit of reverence (*jing*) and investigating the principle inherent in all things. Wang, however, maintained that establishing the will to be good must be the focus of moral self-cultivation: neither the pursuit of empirical knowledge in and of itself nor the psychology of being serious and respectful will automatically bring about a good moral life.

In maintaining that the primary purpose of moral education is to establish in ourselves that which makes all humans great Wang aligned himself with Zhu Xi's intellectual rival, Lu Xiangshan (Lu Jiuyuan, 1139–1193). This concept that the quest for moral creativity begins with self-awareness was criticized by fellow Confucians as being Buddhistic, but Wang himself never doubted the authenticity of his Confucian message. He conscientiously defended the content and method of his teaching by reference to the very books chosen by Zhu Xi to represent the core of the Confucian tradition. Since the thirteenth century, the Four Books—the *Lunyu* (Analects), the *Mengzi* (Mencius), the *Zhongyong* (Doctrine of the Mean), and the *Daxue* (Great Learning)—had served as virtual scripture for the educated elite in East Asia. Wang's challenge to Zhu Xi's interpretive authority was only partially successful, but the mark that he left on the overall design of Confucian education in indelible. His celebrated *Daxue wen* (*Inquiry on the Great Learning*), which recapitulates the major themes in his philosophy, has become one of the most frequently cited treatises on Confucian humanism.

Inquiry on the Great Learning was written in 1527, roughly a year before Wang's death. It addresses the Confucian's ultimate concern, forming one body with Heaven and earth and the myriad things, with great sensitivity:

> That the great man can regard Heaven, Earth, and the myriad things as one body is not because he deliberately wants to be so, but because it is natural to the humane nature of his mind that he do so. Forming one body with Heaven, Earth, and the myriad things is not only true of the great man. Even the mind of the small man is no different. Only he himself makes it small. (Chan, 1969, p. 659)

Wang uses a descending scale of human sensitivity to depict the ordinary human responses to a variety of situations that easily evoke sympathetic feelings in us: encountering a child about to fall into a well, hearing pitiful cries and encountering frightened birds and animals, seeing plants broken and destroyed, seeing tiles and stones shattered and crushed. The feelings of alarm, commiseration, pity, and regret aroused in us vary in their emotional intensity, but indicate that fellow human beings, animals, plants, and stones all form one body in our primordial awareness.

This seemingly romantic assertion of the unity of all things is actually predicated on an ontological vision rooted in classical Confucian humanism. What Wang advocated was a representation of the Mencian thesis that if we fully realize the sprouts (*duan*) of humanity in our minds and hearts, we can experientially understand our human nature; if we understand our nature, then we know Heaven. Knowing Heaven, in the perspective of Wang's *Inquiry on the Great Learning*, is to regard Heaven, earth, and the myriad things as one body, the world as one family, and the country as one person.

Yet this explicit emphasis on commonality and communality was not abstract universalism. On the contrary, a major contribution of Wang's philosophy is its subtle appreciation of concrete personal experience in moral self-cultivation. Wang's insistence that only through polishing and disciplining in actual affairs of life can one learn the art of being human suggests a strong existential quality in his teaching. Wang himself, as a witness to his own teaching, acquired much practical knowledge: he concerned himself with local administration, legal cases, and military tactics. In fact, he was the only civilian official to be awarded a military lordship because of his unusual meritorious achievements in suppressing a rebellion that could have fundamentally changed the history of the Ming dynasty.

The Yangming school, known as the Yomeigaku in Japan, has profoundly influenced modern East Asia. The spirit of the samurai, which emphasises firm purpose, self-mastery, and loyalty, and the dynamic leadership of the Meiji Restoration in 1868 were partly Wang Yangming's gifts to Japan. In China, reformers such as Liang Qichao (1873–1929) and Tan Sitong (1865–1898), revolutionaries such as Sun Yat-sen (1866–1925), and philosophers such as Xiong Shili (1885–1968) and Liang Souming (b. 1893) have all been inspired by Wang's legacy, the *Chuanxi lu* (Instructions for Practical Living), which consists of his dialogues with students, scholarly letters to friends, and several short essays.

SEE ALSO Confucianism; Li; Lu Xiangshan; Mengzi; Zhu Xi.

BIBLIOGRAPHY

Wang Yangming's collected works can be found in his *Yangming quanshu*, Sibu Beiyao edition. Useful interpretive studies include the following:

Araki Kengo, et al., comps. *Yomeigaku taikei.* 12 vols. Tokyo, 1971–1973.

Chan, Wing-tsit, trans. *Instructions for Practicial Living and Other Neo-Confucian Writings by Wang Yang-ming.* New York, 1963.

Chan, Wing-tsit. *A Source Book in Chinese Philosophy.* Princeton, 1969. See pages 654–691.

Ching, Julia. *To Acquire Wisdom: The Way of Wang Yang-ming.* New York, 1976.

Okada Takehiko. *Oyomei to minmatsu no jugaku.* Tokyo, 1970.

Shimada Kenji. *Shushigaku to Yomeigaku.* Tokyo, 1967.

Tu Wei-ming, *Neo-Confucian Thought in Action: Wang Yangming's Youth.* Berkeley, 1976.

New Sources

Cua, A.S. "Between Commitment and Realization: Wang Yangming's Vision of the Universe as a Moral Community." *Philosophy East and West* 43:4 (1993): 611–647.

Geaney, Jane. "Chinese Cosmology and Recent Studies in Confucian Ethics: A Review Essay." *Journal of Religious Ethics* 28:3 (2000): 451–470.

Hauf, Kandice. "'Goodness Unbound': Wang Yangming and the Redrawing of the Boundary of Confucianism." In *Imagining Boundaries: Changing Confucian Doctrines, Texts, and Hermeneutics,* edited by Kai-wing Chow, On-cho Ng, and John B. Henderson, pp. 121–146. Albany, 1999.

Ivanhoe, Philip J. *Ethics in the Confucian Tradition: The Thought of Mencius and Wang Yangming.* Atlanta, 1990.

Kim, Youngmin. "Redefining the Self's Relation to the World: A Study of mid-Ming neo-Confucian Discourse (China)." Ph.D. diss., Harvard University, 2002.

Liu, Shu-Hsien. "On the Final Views of Wang Yangming." *Journal of Chinese Philosophy* 25:3 (1998): 345–360.

TU WEI-MING (1987)
Revised Bibliography

WANG ZHE (1112–1170), also known by his clerical name, Zhongyangzi; Daoist master of the Jin period (1115–1234) and founder of the Quanzhen sect. The third son of a great landowner in Xianyang, Shaanxi province, Wang received a Confucian education and entered the district school in Xianyang at the age of twenty. Following a disagreement with his teacher, however, Wang was denied permission to sit for the civil service examination and had to settle for success in the less prestigious military examination. Although at first enthusiastic about a career in the military, Wang grew discouraged by his failure to advance in rank and resolved to abandon the military for a life of seclusion on Mount Zhongnan. He practiced Buddhism for a time, but in the sixth month of 1159 he received secret oral teachings from Lü Chunyang and Zhong Liquan. Thereafter, he converted to Daoism and was ordained a priest *(daoshi).*

Accounts of Wang's career as a Daoist emphasize the ascetic character of his practice. On one occasion he is said to have slept on ice; at another time he dug a hole two meters deep in which to meditate, naming this austere cell "the grave of a living corpse." In 1163 he filled in this hole and built a small hermitage in the village of Liujiang, where he began to proselytize his newly attained religious faith. These efforts won him few converts at first, however, for he was regarded as little more than a madman. In 1167 he burned the hermitage and journeyed alone to Shandong province, where Ma Danyang of Ninghai became his disciple. Thereafter, in contrast to his experience in the Shaanxi region, many potential disciples came forward. Of these, Wang chose six to receive his transmission. With Ma Danyang they were called the Seven Perfected Ones of Quanzhen Daoism. Wang was successful in organizing five Daoist societies in the northern coastal area of Shandong. These include the Sanjiao Jinlian Hui (Golden Lotus Society of the Three Teachings) and the Sanzhai Pingdeng Hui (Equality Society of the Three Teachings). Following his success in Shandong, he decided to return to his home in Shaanxi. He set out with Ma Danying and four other disciples but died en route at Kaifeng in Henan province.

The Quanzhen school drew upon Confucianism, Daoism, and Buddhism, the so-called Three Teachings, for its doctrine and practice. With a strong affinity for Chan practices, it emphasized meditation, clerical itinerancy, and nonreliance on the scriptures. The teachings of this school are summarized in Wang's *Lijiao shiwu lun.* Wang Zhe was also an accomplished poet. Even today his anthologized poetry, especially the *Zhongyang quanzhen ji* and the *Zhongyang jiaohua ji,* are highly regarded.

SEE ALSO Daoism, article on the Daoist Religious Community.

BIBLIOGRAPHY

Chen Yuan. *Nan Song chu Hebei xin daojiao kao.* Beijing, 1958.

Kubo Noritada. *Chugoku no shukyo kaikaku.* Tokyo, 1967.

Kubo Noritada. *Dokyoshi.* Tokyo, 1977.

New Sources

Sharma, A., and H. G. Cox. *Our Religions.* San Francisco, Calif., 1993.

KUBO NORITADA (1987)
Translated from Japanese by James C. Dobbins
Revised Bibliography

WAQF. The Arabic term *waqf* (pl. *awqāf*) denotes in Islamic law the act of founding an endowment, the endowment itself, and also the endowment institution. A synonym, mainly used by Mālikī jurists, and hence in North Africa, is *ḥabs, ḥubs, ḥubūs, ḥabīs* (pl. *aḥbās*). The literal meaning of both roots is "stop," "block," or "suspend." In the context of the endowment institution, these terms refer to the legal situation of the property (*al-ʿayn*), which by the act of endowing is blocked from taking part in any commercial transaction, while its yields (*al-manfaʿah*) are devoted to charitable purposes.

The *waqf* is conceived of as a continuous, voluntary charity for the sake of Allāh and his religion. The founding of endowments is highly recommended to believers, and they are promised rewards for their meritorious acts in the hereafter.

For a long time, studies of the Islamic endowment institution centered on its legal aspects. In the last few decades of the twentieth century, a large number of scholars turned their attention to economic, social, political, and cultural aspects of the *waqf.* Discrete studies revealed the true dimensions of the institution, its actual working, ways in which the letter of *waqf* laws was made to coexist with the requirements of real life, the broad spectrum of purposes financed by endowments, and their impact on the public sphere and on the discourse between rulers and society. A great deal of traditional wisdom concerning the *waqf* was questioned, and differentiation was introduced into general statements traditionally accepted and repeated over and over again. Moreover, new insights were gained on a variety of other subjects, such as gender relations, urban studies, and many economic, social, and cultural aspects of the regions studied. A true picture thus emerged of the central importance of the endowment institution as a means for financing Islam as a society and as an integrative institution of the community of believers (the *ummah*) in the premodern era.

The origins of the endowment institution are traced traditionally to early *ḥadīth*s (traditions deriving from the

Prophet and his companions). The rules governing endowments were elaborated in the course of the eighth and ninth centuries. Modern research points to either the Byzantine *piae causae*, ancient Arabic customs, or pre-Islamic Iranian law as the main inspirations or influences on the legal form of the *waqf*.

Waqf law is an integral part of the *sharīʿah* (the sacred law). Application of the law, and difficulties and conflicts arising from it, have thus been handled by the *ʿulamāʾ* (the *sharīʿah* specialists), who alone were qualified to interpret the laws. The law covers every aspect of the *waqf* and differs in detail according to the schools of law and even within one school. Major elements of the law concern the beneficiaries of endowments, their administration, and the type of property that may be constituted as *waqf* and its legal status.

An endowment enters into effect immediately upon its foundation (unless it is a testamentary *waqf*). It is considered irrevocable by most jurists and must be perpetual. A valid purpose for the benefit of which the proceeds of an asset can be endowed is defined as *qurbah;* that is, anything likely to bring the founder nearer to God. This very broad definition includes contributions toward the general welfare of the community of believers, as well as care for the family or other individuals. The founder of an endowment is thus allowed almost complete freedom to determine its beneficiaries. The founder can designate a general charity of his or her choice as immediate beneficiary of the endowment. The *waqf* would then be referred to as *waqf khayrī* (charitable endowment). Alternatively, the founder can designate a succession of beneficiaries, the primary and intermediary of whom are either specific members of the founder's family or other individuals, male or female. The endowment would then be described as *waqf ahlī* or *dhurrī* (family *waqf*). However, families are not conceived of as permanent. Since no endowment is valid unless it is perpetual by nature, the founder has to name, as ultimate beneficiary, at the end of the chain of family members, the poor or a general charity *(khayrī)* of an equally permanent character. A third kind of endowments—*waqf mushtarak*—consists of a combination of *ahlī* and *khayrī* elements.

Endowments soon became by far the most popular form of voluntary charity in Islam. They were made by all strata of the population—rulers, high officials, men and women, rich people as well as people of modest means. Endowed assets covered considerable proportions of all kinds of properties in every Muslim town, as well as vast agricultural areas. They included large as well as modest properties. Endowments benefited individuals and groups, such as family members, freed slaves, and other individual Muslims, members of professional guilds, inhabitants of specific neighborhoods, groups of common origin, the poor in general, or the poor belonging to a specific social groups, even groups of animals. They were also the principal vehicle for financing public services, political and economic interests, including the religious cult, education and learning, welfare and health services, municipal services, colonization, urbanization, and economic infrastructure. The scope of voluntary charity in Islam, the purposes it served, and its importance in the public sphere thus reached proportions beyond what was common in other civilizations.

Non-Muslims living under Muslim rule (*ahl al-dhimmah*) could and actually did found *waqfs*. Their beneficiaries had, however, to qualify as *qurbah* according to both Islam and the founder's religion. An endowment by a non-Muslim in favor of his offspring, of the poor of his religious community, the poor of his church, synagogue, or neighborhood, or the poor in general, was valid under these rules. Endowments by a non-Muslim to benefit a mosque or in favor of a synagogue, a church, priests, or monks were invalid. Ways were found, however, to circumvent these limitations so that non-Muslim religious establishments could benefit from endowments.

Charity, piety, and the hope for recompense in the world beyond were the ideological motivations for founding endowments. Several, more practical reasons are mentioned in the literature to explain the proliferation of endowments in the Muslim world. Political reasons, such as enhancing their prestige and securing local support, followers, or clients, were found to have been at the root of endowments by rulers, governors, high officials, and local notables. Circumvention of the inheritance laws was a major motive for establishing *waqfs*, particularly, though not exclusively, among the common people. Islamic inheritance law divides the estate among a very large number of heirs. Disposition by testament is limited to one-third of the estate and may not be made in favor of a legal heir. Testamentary endowments had to follow these rules. Regular *waqfs*, that is, endowments that enter into effect immediately on their pronouncement, put no restrictions on the founder as far as the beneficiaries or their shares are concerned. The natural inclination to determine who will inherit one's property could, thus, be satisfied. Moreover, according to Abū Yūsuf—one of the founders of the Ḥanafī school of law, whose rulings have been widely followed—founders can name themselves as first beneficiaries of their endowments, and thus enjoy the income from the property as long as they live. This regulation prompted people belonging to the Malīkī school of law, particularly in Algeria and Tunisia under Ottoman rule, to establish their endowments with a Ḥanafī *qāḍī* and according to Abū Yūsuf's ruling. Moreover, contrary to inheritance, the endowment kept the property intact, dividing among the beneficiaries the income thereof only. It could thus secure a regular income to the founder's descendants in generations to come. Modern research put differentiation into some of the traditional, sweeping arguments, which listed the protection of property from confiscation or exemption of endowments from taxes as motivations for founding *waqfs*. Endowments were shown not to have been immune from confiscations. They were, in fact, subject to taxation, unless special exemption was granted by the authorities.

Founders of endowments are free to appoint a succession of administrators (*nāẓir, mutawallī, qayyim*) to his *waqf.* The first administrators are frequently the founders themselves (according to the Malīkīs this invalidates the endowment). When no administrator is provided by the founder, the *qāḍī* appoints one. The necessary qualifications of administrators, the limits of their freedom of action, and the circumstances in which they can be dismissed are all laid down in the law. Administrators are entitled to about 10 percent of the income from the endowment under their control. They are responsible for the maintenance of the property, renting it out, and distributing the proceeds among the beneficiaries according to the provisions laid down by the founder in the endowment deed (*waqfīyyah*). Major institutions financed by endowments, such as those benefiting large mosques, soup kitchens, or the poor of the holy places of Islam, were, however, handled differently. All endowments whose beneficiary was one of these institutions were lumped together to form the patrimony of that particular institution. The political authorities usually had either direct or indirect say in the appointment of their administrators and hence also in some matters concerning their management and the distribution of their income. Administrators of family and public *waqfs* acted under the *qāḍī*'s supervision, who alone was entitled to approve extraordinary transactions. *Qāḍīs* in the Ottoman Empire were assigned specific duties concerning public foundations: they audited the administrators' financial statements, assisted in preparatory works preceding major repair and maintenance works on *waqf* properties, and kept a watchful eye on the administrators appointed by the Ottoman center.

Basically, only immovable property of a permanent, eternal nature that yields a usufruct (*manfa'ah*) can be endowed. There are, however, some exceptions, such as horses and weapons for holy war; movables that follow endowed property (trees, slaves, animals, agricultural tools), books, various utensils, and *mīrī* land in the Ottoman Empire, whose ownership (*raqabah*) belonged to the state (these endowments were called *waqf ghayr ṣaḥīḥ*). The most notable exception are cash *waqfs* (*waqf al-nuqūd*), which were widespread, particularly in the core lands of the Ottoman Empire.

Among classical jurists, opinions differ as to the ownership of the endowed property. Many jurists hold that upon endowing the asset, ownership is transferred to God. Others claim that it is transferred to the beneficiaries or remains with the founder; neither, however, has actual rights of disposal. All jurists agree that once the property is endowed it becomes inalienable and is thus withdrawn from any commercial transaction. It cannot be sold, mortgaged, or the like. Moreover, no long-term or permanent leases are allowed in principle, for fear that they would eventually lead to the loss of the asset to the *waqf.* Administrators of endowed property were thus left with one option only for engendering profit from assets under their control—letting them for a short period, usually limited to one year for urban properties and three years for rural ones. In time, two main ways were, however, devised by jurists in order to overcome economic problems arising from the rule of inalienability: long-term or perpetual leases (differing in some details and known by different names in various parts of the Islamic world; for example, *ḥikr, 'anā', ijāratayn, khulū* or *murṣād, inzāl, jalsah*) and exchanges (*istibdāl, mu'āwaḍah*) of endowed assets. (The Shāfi'ī and the Shī'ī schools do not allow *istibdāl;* in the other schools, conditions governing exchanges vary slightly.) These transactions were allowed only in very exceptional circumstances, when the property was dilapidated and there was no other way for the *waqf* to secure income from the asset. Each such case had to come before the *qāḍī,* who, before approving the proposed transaction, examined all elements of the contract and made sure it was in the best interest of the *waqf.*

For a long time, criticism of the endowment institution, by both Muslim and Western writers, focused on the administration of public *waqfs,* its inefficiency, neglect of the endowed properties, and particularly on abusive practices on the part of administrators, rulers, and governors, who frequently enlisted in their manipulations the assistance of corrupt *qāḍīs.* Allowing for the proliferation of long-term or perpetual leases and exchanges of good and undamaged properties came under particularly heavy fire. Indeed, modern studies have documented the dismemberment of *waqfs* as a result of such corruptive practices. However, other discrete studies have shown that inefficiency, neglect, and embezzlement were neither inherent to the system, nor necessarily the rule. Instances were documented attesting to careful and dynamic management of public endowments, rational use of their funds, and the introduction of policies that, by means of a flexible interpretation of *waqf* laws, catered to the economic and social needs of the population and at the same time secured the interests of the *waqf.*

In the course of the nineteenth century, institutional reforms were introduced in both the Ottoman Empire and Egypt with a view to concentrating endowments under governmental supervision. An important by-product of these reforms was the publication of semi official codifications of *waqf* laws. Attempts were made under protectorate and mandatory rule to further improve the management of *waqf* properties. Much more radical steps were taken by colonial regimes, for instance the French in colonial Algeria. With the establishment of modern states in the Middle East, and particularly after the overthrow of monarchical regimes in some of these states, public criticism of the *waqf* increased. It now centered around the most basic characteristics of the institution and their incompatibility with economic development, budgetary policy of a modern state, and the social and political objectives of the new regimes. Consequently, reforms in *waqf* law were undertaken, particularly in the course of the second half of the twentieth century. Administration of endowed property was concentrated under special governmental ministries. In some countries (e.g., Turkey, Egypt, Syria, and Iraq) reforms amounted to the nationalization of public *waqf* properties, the total or partial abolition of family endowments, and, in some cases, prohibition of their establishment in the future. Former *waqf* lands were distributed as part of agrarian reforms. Various, less radical reforms in the law pertaining to endowments were introduced in other countries (e.g., Kuwait, the United Arab Emirates, and Yemen).

SEE ALSO Islamic Law, article on Personal Law.

BIBLIOGRAPHY

Semi official codifications of the Ḥanafī *waqf* law are: Muḥammad Qadrī Pāshā, *Kitāb Qānūn al-ʿAdl wa-al-Inṣāf lil-Qaḍāʾ ʿalā Mushkilāt al-Awqāf*, 3d ed. (Bulaq, Egypt, 1902); and Ömer Hilmi, *A Gift to Posterity on the Laws of Evqaf*, translated by C. R. Tyser and D. G. Demetriades, 2d ed. (Nicosia, Cyprus, 1922). A good introduction to broader knowledge on the subject, including an extensive bibliography, can be found in R. Peters et al., "Waḳf," in *The Encyclopaedia of Islam*, new edition, vol. 11, pp. 59–99 (Leiden, 2000). A detailed bibliography on the subject can also be found in Miriam Hoexter, "*Waqf* Studies in the Twentieth Century: The State of the Art," *Journal of the Economic and Social History of the Orient* 41, no. 4 (1998): 474–495. Special issues of the following journals are dedicated to the *waqf* and include a number of important studies on the subject: *Journal of the Economic and Social History of the Orient* 38, no. 3 (1995); and *Islamic Law and Society* 4, no. 3 (1997). Edited volumes comprising essays on the *waqf* are: *Le waqf dans l'espace islamique: Outil de pouvoir socio-politique*, edited by Randi Deguilhem (Damascus, 1995); and, with emphasis on the modern period, *Le waqf dans le monde musulman contemporain (XIXe–XXe siècles): Fonctions sociales, économiques, et politiques*, edited by Faruk Bilici (Istanbul, 1994). For the role of *waqf* in the public sphere, see *The Public Sphere in Muslim Societies*, edited by Miriam Hoexter, Shmuel N. Eisenstadt, and Nehemia Levtzion (Albany, N.Y., 2000), particularly the following articles: Haim Gerber, "The Public Sphere and Civil Society in the Ottoman Empire," pp. 65–82, and Miriam Hoexter, "The Waqf and the Public Sphere," pp. 119–138. On the contribution of the *waqf* toward alleviating poverty, see several articles in *Poverty and Charity in Middle Eastern Contexts*, edited by Michael Bonner, Mine Ener, and Amy Singer (Albany, N.Y., 2003).

MIRIAM HOEXTER (2005)

WAR AND WARRIORS

This entry consists of the following articles:

AN OVERVIEW
INDO-EUROPEAN BELIEFS AND PRACTICES

WAR AND WARRIORS: AN OVERVIEW

For the purposes of this article, war may be defined as organized and coherent violence conducted between established and internally cohesive rival groups. In contrast to numerous other modes of violence, it is neither individual, spontaneous, random, nor irrational, however much—like all varieties of violence—it involves destructive action, even on a massive scale. Being a complex phenomenon, war has multiple dimensions that are deeply interrelated, chief among them being economic, ideological, and social factors.

Of these, perhaps the most obvious and important (at least according to the majority of modern analysts) are the economic factors that precipitate war, war being the most extreme form of competition for chronically scarce resources, such as women, territory, movable wealth (including livestock), and/or the labor power of subjugated populations. One must note, however, that scarce and valued resources are not exclusively of a material nature, prestige being a crucially important example of a nonmaterial resource that is highly desired and that figures prominently in warfare. It is possible, in fact, to speak of a prestige economy that exists not only side by side but intimately interwoven with the material economy of any given people, and warfare provides a convenient means of reaping rewards in both. Thus, for instance, success in raiding was requisite for a Crow warrior to advance his position, for this provided him first with goods—above all, horses—that not only enriched him but also could be used to place others in his debt through a process of redistribution. Further, raiding furnished the successful warrior with a set of heroic deeds of which he could boast on regular, formalized occasions, thereby further elevating his standing in the group. Success in battle also opened up religious prerogatives for him, insofar as many important and prestigious ritual roles were reserved for those who had accomplished specific, highly regarded feats of war, such as touching coup, winning horses, killing an enemy, or leading a successful raiding expedition.

Indeed, accomplishments in battle provide a common means, in many cultures and periods in history, whereby individuals can seek to elevate not only their own individual prestige above that of their peers but also that of their group above others (conquered rivals, as well as those who remain outside the fray). Thus, for instance, among the Jalé-speaking peoples of highland New Guinea, the performance of stereotyped, formulaic songs is a prominent part of every public celebration. These songs, which preserve the memory of past warfare, are a crucial element in the local prestige economy as well as a stimulus to further conflicts, for they celebrate the glory of the group that sings them, while also heaping derision upon their foes:

> The man Wempa will never eat again,
> nor will Alavóm ever eat again.
> But we live to see the sweet potatoes roast,
> The sweet potatoes from Wongele and Tukui (Koch, 1974, p. 85)

One may observe similar processes in the well-wrought poetry of praise for successful warriors and blame for those who are less than successful (e.g., Hector's rebukes of Paris), which figures prominently in the Homeric epic. Moreover, the heroes depicted there are presented as acutely self-conscious with regard to issues of prestige, as is evident, for example, in Sarpedon's speech just prior to the Trojan assault on the Greek camp, an assault that leads to his death. Here is related a description of a warrior, himself the son of Zeus, weighing the relative value of the material and nonmaterial rewards of combat and setting greatest stock on the winning of a prominent and enduring reputation. In the last analysis, the pursuit of such a reputation—elsewhere called "undying fame" (*kleos aphthitos*)—becomes nothing less than a quest for immortality, although, ironically, it is a quest that regularly costs the quester his life. Among the most interesting aspects of this passage, however, is the absence of any tension or contradiction between the warrior's pursuit of material gain (booty, also land and privileged banquet portions) and his pursuit of glory. On the contrary, one sees an effective coalescence of the material and the prestige economy, encompassed within an ideology and a poetics that decidedly emphasize the latter:

> Glaukos, why is it you and I are honoured before others
> with pride of place, the choice meats and the filled wine cups
> in Lykia, and all men look on us as if we were immortals,
> and we are appointed a great piece of land by the banks of Xanthos,
> good land, orchard and vineyard, and ploughland for the planting of wheat?
> Therefore it is our duty in the forefront of the Lykians to take our stand, and bear our part of the blazing of battle,
> so that a man of the close-armoured Lykians may say of us:
> Indeed, these are no ignoble men who are lords of Lykia, these kings of ours, who feed upon the fat sheep appointed
> and drink the exquisite sweet wine, since indeed there is strength of
> valour in them, since they fight in the forefront of the Lykians.
> Man, supposing you and I, escaping this battle
> would be able to live on forever, ageless, immortal,
> so neither would I myself go on fighting in the foremost
> nor would I urge you into the fighting where men win glory.
> But now, seeing that the spirits of death stand close about us
> in their thousands, no man can turn aside nor escape them,
> let us go on and win glory for ourselves, or yield it to others. (Homer, *Iliad,* trans. Lattimore)

The assignation of prestige to deeds of valor (the etymological connections between *valor, valiance,* and *value* are significant, as are those between *virtue* and *virility*) is but one means whereby ideological factors influence warfare, albeit a tremendously important one. No less important is the way in which other ideological constructs supply the means necessary to persuade individuals to join in combat, providing them with motivation sufficiently great that they are willing to risk their lives, even in situations (as is true for the vast majority of warriors over the course of history) wherein they stand to reap quite little in the way of personal gain—material or immaterial—from even the greatest of military successes.

It is in this fashion that religion has played a most important role in war throughout history, and the examples of religious justifications that have been used to legitimate even the most tawdry of struggles are legion. Among these must be noted calls to convert the heathen (as in the Christian Crusades and more recent European wars of colonial expansion); promises of a favorable afterlife for warriors who die in battle (as within Islam, Shintō, or among the ancient Aztec, Germans, and others); and ethical dualisms whereby warfare is cast as an unremitting struggle between good and evil (as in ancient Iran or the modern United States).

Among the most contemporary students of war, ideological factors are generally viewed as subordinate or epiphenomenal to material ones, religious and other forms of legitimation being understood as the convenient or even necessary means that serve to mask or mystify the acquisitive competition that is the primary motivation for armed conflict. Others, however, have challenged this view, particularly with regard to warfare in the ancient and preindustrial world, where (in their view) religious motivations played a much more powerful and directly causal role. A favorite example cited by adherents of this position is the case of Aztec warfare, which they claim was pursued above all else to obtain the victims necessary for the performance of human sacrifice, the central ritual act of the Aztec empire. Such a line of analysis, however, has been rendered untenable by the most recent studies of Aztec sacrifice, which reveal it to have been not an act of transcendent religiosity performed for its own sake and at any cost but, as John Ingham has cogently argued, an expression and an instrument of the same drives for wealth, power, and prestige that prompted Aztec warfare and imperial expansion in general. In Ingham's words:

> Whatever else it may have been, human sacrifice was a symbolic expression of political domination and economic appropriation and, at the same time, a means to their social production. . . . The sacrificing of slaves and war captives and the offering of their hearts and blood to the sun thus encoded the essential character of social hierarchy and imperial order and provided a suitable instrument for intimidating and punishing insubordination. (Ingham, 1984, p. 379)

In this case, then, and others like it, one must conclude that, far from having been the ultimate cause of war, religion was intimately bound up with other causal factors more familiar to the world of *Realpolitik.*

Beyond the material and ideological factors, there are also powerful social factors that must be taken into account. Briefly, two social conditions are necessary for the occurrence of war, given the definition proposed above ("organized and coherent violence conducted between established and internally cohesive rival groups"). First, a given group of individuals must understand themselves as a group; that is, they must be bound together in some abiding fashion by sentiments, traditions, kinship ties, institutions, residence patterns, language, and the like. Second, they must understand members of some other group ("the enemy") as radically alien to them, outsiders to whom they are not connected and with reference to whom they need not refrain from violence. As the Jalé put it in a striking proverb: "People whose face is known should not be eaten." Moreover, prior to the outbreak of hostilities or at the very least shortly thereafter, this same set of conditions—internal solidarity coupled with external alienation and hostility—will prevail on the other side as well.

In short, warriors must be persuaded not only to risk their own lives but also to take the lives of others, and not merely random others but those whose otherness is most radically marked. Involving organized and relatively large-scale lethal violence as it does, warfare always poses serious ethical problems within the already thorny set of issues surrounding homicide. As a starting point, it must be noted that humans kill one another for many reasons and under many sets of circumstances, and all groups possess certain norms regulating how such killings are to be regarded and judged. Sometimes they are defined as murder (i. e., illicit homicide); in other instances they are not, for there are conditions under which the taking of a life is legally, morally, culturally, and/or religiously sanctioned or even (this is particularly relevant to the case of war) celebrated.

A fundamental concern in such adjudications, and one infinitely more complex and malleable than is ordinarily acknowledged, is the question of whether the victim(s) or would-be victim(s) of a given homicide are truly human. In any number of instances (e.g., infants, slaves, prisoners, outlaws, heretics and other social deviants, the aged and infirm, etc.), an individual may conveniently be defined by the killer (and the community that passes judgment upon the killing) as something less than human: a "monster," a "beast," a "vegetable," and so forth. Patterns of verbal abuse, in fact, whereby such persons are referred to as animals, rotting matter ("garbage," "trash"), and the like, regularly accompany and assist the lethal redefinitions whereby it is established that effecting the death of such an individual is a permissable or even a worthy act.

Nor is it only individuals who may be defined as somehow less than human and thus freely killable. On the contrary, social borders are regularly constructed and maintained such that entire groups of others ("aliens" in the fullest sense of the word) are regarded thus by their neighbors and enemies. Such a state of affairs is evidenced, for example, in the frequent occurrence of self-referential ethnonyms by which a given people denote themselves as "humans," implicitly (and in many instances, explicitly) relegating all others to the category of nonhumans—nonhumans who may, moreover, be freely killed as the occasion arises.

An instructive case is that of the Yanoama of the Amazon Basin, who not only call themselves "humanity" (the meaning of their name) and all others "lesser subhuman beings" (*nabä*) but carry the process still further: Members of one Yanoama village habitually accentuate the minor differences of dialect (or the like) that separate them from residents of other villages, then they deride the others for being less than fully *Yanoama,* which is to say, somewhat subhuman. Relations between Yanoama villages are always tense, partly as a result of this pattern of marking social borders and partly as a result of pronounced competition over women, for it is the goal of all Yanoama males to retain the women of their village while obtaining those of other villages through marriage or war. The central value of Yanoama life is *waiteri* ("fierceness"). To survive in this fiercely competitive atmosphere, a village must ally itself with others to resist the aggression of still others. As a means of overcoming the suspicions that normally prevail between villages, allies seek to bind themselves to one another through trade, marital exchanges, and reciprocal feasting, but the process is never a simple one. To form an alliance is to signal weakness, and allies, sensing this weakness, press ever-increasing demands for women as a condition for the alliance's continuation. Alliances thus often end in enmity, in warfare, or in an act that the Yanoama view as the ultimate form of fierceness and violence, being a parody and an inversion of the fragile festivals of intervillage solidarity: that is, a treacherous feast in which the male guests are all slaughtered and their women taken.

Again, with regard to the radical nature of social boundaries in situations of conflict and war, one may note the case of the Anggor in western New Guinea. As Peter Birkett Huber reports, each Anggor village "can be considered a cosmos in itself, an autonomous and essentially harmonious moral system confronted by a uniformly hostile, dangerous, and chaotic outside world. Violence between these villages is consequently not a form of policy or a distinct kind of political situation, but an inescapable feature of man's existential condition" (in Nettleship, Givens, and Nettleship, 1975, p. 620). Most violence perpetrated by residents of one Anggor village on those of another takes the form of sorcery, but revenge expeditions are ultimately organized and battles ensue in which Anggor warriors venture out from their homes to confront chaos itself and, by means of this confrontation, reassert the solidarity of their group and the order of their cosmos by inflicting retaliatory deaths on their enemies outside.

Although these are somewhat extreme cases, they are by no means unique, and all warfare involves sociopolitical suspensions of the ethical, whereby the otherness of the enemy is radically accentuated, a situation that permits and legitimates their victimization. War is, in truth, that situation in which the killing of other people on a grand (or even total) scale is rendered not only licit but requisite, even glorious, by virtue of the fact that they belong to a rival group to whom ethical norms do not extend, the enemy having been effectively defined as subhuman or even nonhuman.

Yet another example of these principles is found in the shields that form a crucial part of a warrior's equipment among the several Dayak peoples of Borneo. In general, shields function not only as an important implement of defense in warfare prior to the introduction of gunpowder but also as a movable social border that separates one's self, one's group, and that territory in which one feels some measure of security from the enemy. In an advance, shields mark the incorporation of conquered territory, booty, and prisoners into one's own group; in retreat, they mark the group's contraction, as land, stragglers, and the fallen are left outside. In the classic warfare of the Zulu, for instance, and in other powerful kingdoms of southern Africa, rival armies assumed formation in lines opposite to one another, each warrior holding a five-foot rawhide shield in front of him with his left arm. Standing behind this row of shields, the opponents exchanged insults with one another, verbal combat (in the forms I have discussed) preceding physical. Thereafter, the regiments closed, and each one tried to break through the enemy's walls of shields. Finally, when an army felt itself defeated, its members dropped their shields in token of surrender, whereupon the battle would cease. What was signified in this action was that the vanquished group renounced the social borders that they had previously maintained, thereby relinquishing their independence and accepting incorporation as a subjugated part of the victors' polity.

Dayak shields are used in similar fashion and bear similar significance but are remarkable for the iconographic content of the designs painted and carved upon them. Most noteworthy is the bifurcation of design, for on the inside of most Dayak shields—that is, the side facing toward the bearer—is the image of two protective ancestral figures; on the outside is a snarling monster. The import of the ancestors is not hard to judge; being the founders of the bearer's social group, they define that group and represent it. Insofar as there are others who descend from these same ancestors, the warrior has comrades who will take up arms together with him to defend their group against outsiders (i. e., those descended from other ancestral lines). The group's sense of identity and solidarity are thus nothing more than the sentiments called forth by the image of these ancestors, and it is such sentiments—much more than the wooden shields—that provide protection and security in battle and beyond.

The monsters on the outer face of Dayak shields are more difficult to interpret, however, for they are susceptible to multiple readings. On the one hand, these ferocious figures, marked most prominently by bulging eyes and exaggerated fangs, would seem to represent the enemy, particularly when considered in juxtaposition to the ancestral figures. Accordingly, one may posit a series of correlated binary oppositions, the effect of which is to dehumanize the enemy (in fashions similar to those discussed above) and thereby render his killing licit:

Inside: Outside::
Ancestors: Monsters::
Own Group: Enemy::
Protection: Menace::
Solidarity: Hostility::
Deaths Suffered Deaths Inflicted
:
must be avenged constitute revenge
Killings illicit: Killings licit or even requisite

In light of such observations as this, this writer is inclined to propose certain revisions to a classic text of Simone Weil, her justly celebrated meditations on "The Iliad, or The Poem of Force," written in 1940, shortly after the fall of France to Nazi arms and also after her own combat experience during the Spanish Civil War. In this essay, reflecting on death in battle, particularly as described in this epic, Weil came to define force as "that *x* that turns anybody who is subjected to it into a *thing*," going on to observe, "excercised to the limit, it turns man into a thing in the most literal sense: it makes a corpse out of him. Somebody was here, and the next minute there is nobody at all; this is a spectacle the *Iliad* never wearies of showing us" (Weil, 1983). To be sure, there is a power and a grandeur in so stark a formulation, yet, given what has been outlined above, particularly regarding the nature of social borders in warfare and those patterns of dehumanization whereby an enemy is defined as subhuman, nonhuman, and/or monstrous, one must reject the idea that it is force itself, acting as some sort of quasi-personified agent, that "turns a man into a thing." Rather, the process is quite the reverse, and one can say with more justice and precision, *pace* Weil, that it is only when human actors come to regard others as "things" that they become capable of employing force, particularly lethal force, against them. Force here only completes that process of "turning into a thing" that begins in the sentiments and social patterns of human subjects.

To return to the Dayak shields, however, there is more that can be said. Thus far, this article has suggested that the image of the monster may be taken to represent the enemy, as seen through the dehumanizing gaze of the warrior. Such an interpretation, moreover, is consistent with a view of the shields as a marker of social borders, for in this instance one may clearly perceive the tenuous nature of such borders, something that becomes particularly obvious within the situation of the battle, for it is then quite literally only the thickness of the shield itself that separates the ancestral (representation of) community from the monstrous (figure of the) outside, safety from danger, self from other. In addition, there is significant material evidence to support such a view, for in the construction of many Dayak shields the monster images are rendered more grotesque still by the use of human hair as ornament: hair taken from the trophy skulls of slain enemies. Such enemies, having been viewed as monsters, were treated as monsters, and their corpses were used to depict the monsters that they were.

This datum, however, suggests another line of interpretation that may be advanced regarding the complex and polyphonous image of the monster. For it is obvious that the outer side of any shield is directed toward the enemy, especially toward one's immediate adversary in hand-to-hand battle. Further, it is equally obvious that the intended (and also, one assumes, quite real) effect of such an image is to intimidate or even terrify opponents, for in its very material substance (the actual hair of fallen victims), this shield announces the force, the valor, and also the cruelty of its bearer. It supplies graphic and tangible witness to the fact that he has taken enemy lives in the past and stands ready and able to do so once more. The shield thus displays the bearer's face as seen through the eyes of his opponent or (to put it differently) the face that he wishes to present to all enemies: for he becomes a monster against those whom he regards as monstrous, even as they do conversely to him.

Here is reached the final paradox of war and the warrior: a corollary to the pattern that has been observed whereby one must dehumanize one's enemies in order to employ force against them. In practice, it appears that a warrior must also dehumanize himself before he can become an instrument of slaughter, effectively eradicating such human tendencies as guilt, fear, and compassion. A well-articulated example of this is found in the samurai ideal of "no-mind," this being that psychomental state—cultivated by years of meditation and training in martial arts—in which the samurai's body and arms act as if automatically, with no hesitation born of thought, weakness, or doubt. Elsewhere, warriors frequently speak of themselves as animals: "lions" or "leopards" (East Africa); "two-footed wolves" (India and Iran); berserkers, of "those who wear the bear's shirt" (Scandinavia); or "crazy-dogs-wishing-to-die" (Crow), to cite but a few examples. To these data one might add the fact that Yanoama warriors march off to battle imitating the noises of a host of carnivorous beasts, from insects on up. The war song of the Yanoama is also noteworthy as a supreme statement of the warrior's auto-dehumanization, being entitled "I am a meat-hungry buzzard."

SEE ALSO Human Sacrifice; Martial Arts; Violence.

BIBLIOGRAPHY

Not surprisingly, some of the best attempts at academic analysis of the nature and ideology of warfare were made at the time of the Vietnam War. Among the valuable collections that appeared during this period, one should note *Law and Warfare,* edited by Paul Bohannan (Garden City, N. Y., 1967); *War: The Anthropology of Armed Conflict and Aggression,* edited by Morton Fried, Marvin Harris, and Robert Murphy (Garden City, N. Y., 1968); *Problèmes de la guerre en Grèce ancienne,* edited by Jean-Pierre Vernant (The Hague, 1968); and *War: Its Causes and Correlates,* edited by Martin A. Nettleship, R. Dale Givens, and Anderson Nettleship (The Hague, 1975). A slightly later work, and in a different vein, is *The Warrior Tradition in Modern Africa,* edited by Ali A. Mazrui (Leiden, 1977). Special attention should also be given to Pier Giorgio Solinas's "Guerra e matrimonio," in *Potere senza stato,* edited by Carla Pasquinelli (Rome, 1986), pp. 21–47.

Among the most important case studies are those drawn from Melanesia, which, given the relatively late date of "pacification" there by colonial authorities, provided an extremely informative field for gathering data. Here, one ought to note Klaus Koch's *War and Peace in Jalémo: The Management of Conflict in Highland New Guinea* (Cambridge, Mass., 1974); Andrew P. Vayda's *War in Ecological Perspective* (New York, 1976); and M. J. Meggitt's *Blood Is Their Argument: Warfare among the Mae Enga Tribesmen of the New Guinea Highlands* (Palo Alto, Calif., 1977). Other valuable case studies include Peter Birkett Huber's discussion of the Anggor in *War: Its Causes and Correlates* (cited above), pp. 619–661; Napoleon A. Chagnon's essay on the Yanoama in *War: The Anthropology of Armed Conflict and Aggression* (cited above), pp. 109–159; and Fred W. Voget's "Warfare and the Integration of Crow Indian Culture," in *Explorations in Cultural Anthropology,* edited by Ward H. Goodenough (New York, 1964), pp. 483–509.

John Ingham's study of Aztec sacrifice is found in his "Human Sacrifice at Tenochtitlan," *Comparative Studies in Society and History* 26 (1984): 379–400. A brief discussion of the Dayak shields is W. Münsterberger's "Die Ornamente an Dayak–Tanzschilden und ihre Beziehung zu Religion und Mythologie," *Cultureel Indië* (Leiden) 1 (1939): 337–343. Simone Weil's essay "The Iliad, or The Poem of Force," translated by Mary McCarthy, can be found in *Revisions: Changing Perspectives in Moral Philosophy,* edited by Stanley Hauerwas and Alasdair MacIntyre (Notre Dame, Ind., 1983).

New Sources

Lincoln, Bruce. *Death, War, and Sacrifice: Studies in Ideology and Practice.* Chicago, 1991.

Partner, Peter. *God of Battles: Holy Wars of Christianity and Islam.* Princeton, N.J., 1998.

BRUCE LINCOLN (1987)
Revised Bibliography

WAR AND WARRIORS: INDO-EUROPEAN BELIEFS AND PRACTICES

As Georges Dumézil, the leading contemporary expert on comparative Indo-European mythology, long ago demonstrated, war gods and the ideology that is associated with them played an extremely important role in the pantheons of most, if not all of the early Indo-European-speaking societies. To cite several well-attested examples: the ancient Indic war god Indra, by far the most prominent of the Vedic divinities, the ubiquitous Roman god Mars, the Greek war god Ares, and the Norse god

Þórr (Thor), thunderbolt-wielder *par excellence* and the most popular of the ancient Scandinavian divinities. Moreover, heroes and demigods, like Arjuna, Herakles, Siegfried, Cú Chulainn, Arthur, and Achilles, all occupied important positions in their respective traditions. Indeed, like most pastoral nomads, modern as well as ancient, the ancestors of the Greeks, Hittites, Aryans, Celts, Germans, and so forth, seem to have regarded warfare as a fundamental fact of life and to have held both the war band and its collective representations in high esteem.

THE INDO-EUROPEAN MÄNNERBUND. As Stig Wikander pointed out (1938), the *Männerbund,* or war band, was clearly among the most important of ancient Indo-European social institutions. Examples of this phenomenon are legion, from the *kṣatriya* caste (or class, at least in the earliest period) of traditional India to the ancient Germanic *comitatus.* Moreover, the presence of such a social stratum—that is, a class of military specialists whose prime purpose was to exercise physical prowess, either in defense of the society or in order to conquer new territory—was a uniquely Indo-European phenomenon. Armed with the shaft-hole battle-ax, among other weapons, and propelled by the light, horse-drawn battle chariot, this warlike elite greatly facilitated the spread, beginning around 3500 BCE, of the several Indo-European communities from the Proto-Indo-European homeland in what is now southern Russia to the territory associated with this widespread language family in historic times.

AMBIVALENT ATTITUDES TOWARD THE WARRIOR. Nevertheless, despite his importance in the scheme of things, there seems to have been a deep-seated ambivalence in the Indo-European attitude toward the warrior, if not toward warfare, and this, too, is reflected in the belief system. On the one hand, the war leader, or **reĝ,* from which Latin *rex,* Sanskrit *rāj,* Old Irish *rig,* and so forth, derive, together with his war band, was generally regarded as the immediate secular authority, and his commands were typically obeyed without question. On the other hand, the *rex, rāj,* and so forth, was everywhere subordinate to—or at least no more prestigious than—the priests or holy men (e.g., the Indic brahmans, the Celtic druids, the Roman *flamines maiores*). And it is clear that ultimate sovereignty was vested in this most sacred of the ancient Indo-European social strata. Moreover, one finds everywhere a tension between the two classes in question, a sense that although the warrior was vital to the survival of the community, he was nevertheless a thoroughly ambivalent figure and prone to commit random acts of violence or treachery against nonwarrior members of his own society when not engaged in fighting external enemies. Indeed, throughout the ancient Indo-European-speaking domain one repeatedly encounters such concepts as *furor* (Latin) and *ferg* (Old Irish), as well as the Norse image of the *berserkir,* all of which are expressions of what was believed to be the warrior's inherent (and, on occasion, uncontrollable) ferocity.

Thus, the role of the warrior, and especially the warrior-leader, was steeped in paradoxes. He was at once at the apex of the social order and a potential threat to that order. Indeed, the contradiction here, which is reflected throughout Indo-European religious beliefs, is inherent in the profession of arms: it involves a social institution dedicated to the destruction of society. What follows is, in the main, a survey of these warrior-related beliefs, as interpreted by Dumézil.

THE IDEOLOGY OF THE SECOND FUNCTION. According to Dumézil, the ancient Indo-Europeans conceived of the world and their relationship to it in terms of three fundamental, hierarchically ranked ideological principles, or "functions." In descending order, the so-called first function includes the social and supernatural manifestations of ultimate sovereignty and is typically manifested in a pair of divinities, such as the Vedic divinities Mithra and Varuṇa, the Norse gods Tyr and Óðinn (Odin), and so forth, as well as in the priestly social strata mentioned above. The final function, or third function, reflects the sum total of activities and beliefs relating to the mass of society, the maintenance and promotion of fertility, physical well-being, and so on. However, it is the intermediate function, or second function, which includes the social, religious, and mythological manifestations of the exercise of physical prowess, that is of concern here, for it contains the ideology underlying the Indo-European conception of warfare and warriors.

As has been noted, that ideology is inherently ambivalent, for the canonical representations of the warrior figure are two in number. One is the apotheosis of the chivalrous warrior, the warrior who for the most part confines his violent behavior to the battlefield and does not habitually attack "civilians." This figure is perhaps best reflected by the aforementioned divinities Indra, Mars, and Þórr, as well as in the Indian epic hero Arjuna, and, at least to an extent, in the Greek figures Herakles and Achilles. The other representation of the warrior is diabolical in nature; the emphasis here is on unpredictability and sheer nastiness. Examples are to be found in the Vedic figure Vāyu, who is equated with the wind, especially the ill wind that blows up suddenly out of nowhere and does indiscriminate damage; the Norse antihero Starkaðr; and the aforementioned Greek divinity Ares, whose companions were Deimos ("fear") and Phobos ("fright"). Thus, the warrior has both a "light" and a "dark" side to his nature.

In several recent works, chief among them the second volume of the *Mythe et épopée* series (1971), Dumézil has suggested that this "dark/light" dichotomy can be detected throughout Indo-European ideology. That is, certain divinities are more remote from man, more unpredictable, and therefore "dark" in character (e.g., Varuṇa as well as Vāyu in the Indic tradition), while others, like Mitra and Þórr, are closer to humans and therefore "light" in character. Thus, the distinction between the two types of warrior figures, which almost certainly is rooted in a perception of social reality, may be but one example of a much more deep-seated Indo-European ideological theme.

THE THREE SINS OF THE WARRIOR. However, even the most chivalrous of Indo-European warrior figures, divine as well as heroic, sometimes manifest "dark" traits. Typically, this involves the commission of three "sins," one against each of the three ideological functions. The best example, perhaps, can be seen in the ancient Indic traditions about the recalcitrant behavior of the otherwise "light" divinity Indra. In *Mahābhārata* 5.9.1–40, Indra slays Viśvarupa, the monstrous, three-headed son of Tvaṣṭṛ, who has been threatening the divine community. However, as Tvaṣṭṛ is chaplain to the gods, his son is by definition a divine brahman, and Indra has therefore committed an act of brahmanicide, an unpardonable sin (and act of rebellion) against the first function and its representatives. Later, Indra is confronted by the warrior demon Namucī with whom he had earlier sworn a pact of eternal friendship. As that pact contained the promise not to kill Namucī with anything either wet or dry, Indra forges a weapon made of foam—which, in the eyes of the ancient Indians at least, was neither wet nor dry—and, when the unsuspecting demon's attention is diverted, he decapitates him. This, of course, is a sin against his own function, as the slaying was done by trickery, rather than in a fair fight. Finally, the god assumes the form of a man called Gautama and, so disguised, has intercourse with the man's wife. This is an abuse of the ideology of the third function, that is, Indra performs an illicit act of procreation.

As a result of these transgressions, Indra progressively lost his first function, majesty, or *tejas;* his second function, physical prowess, or *bālam;* and his third function, beauty, or *rūpam;* all of which, as Wikander and Dumézil have demonstrated, were eventually reincarnated in the offspring of the epic hero Paṇḍu (Yudhisṭhira, Arjuna, Bhīma, Nakula, and Sahadeva). The important thing here is that, from the standpoint of the Indo-European ideological system, Indra had by these acts clearly demonstrated his inherent recalcitrance and therefore his ultimate inferiority to Mitra, Varuṇa, and other representatives of the first function in the divine scheme of things. The lesson, of course, is that warriors, even the best of them, are capable of disrupting the social and natural order and therefore not to be fully trusted.

Another canonical example of the "three sins" can be found in the Greek traditions about Herakles, who (1) refuses to obey his sovereign, Eurystheus, (2) slays a fellow warrior, Iphitos, in violation of what amounts to a truce, and (3) although legally married to Deianira, abducts and then violates Astydamia after killing her father and sacking his city. The third prime example involves the Norse warrior Starkaðr, who sacrilegiously sacrifices his sovereign to the god Óðinn, abandons his cohorts in battle, and, for money, slays the Danish king Olo while he is relaxing in a bath. Still other examples have been noted in the careers of Ares, Agamemnon, Siegfried, Sir Gawain, and Achilles.

As Dumézil puts it, what is the case here is a "drama in three acts," as it were, and in a very real sense it is a tragedy, as with each "sin" the warrior in question—god as well as hero—loses his powers or his life force. Thus, after violating Astydamia, Herakles is rendered powerless by his outraged wife and eventually causes himself to be burned on a funeral pyre, while Starkaðr commits suicide after killing Olo. The net effect is what amounts to a "cautionary tale": warriors, even the best of them, are ultimately unreliable, and if their *furor,* and so forth, is allowed to go unchecked, the social order as a whole may very well collapse.

THE KILLING OF THE THREE-HEADED MONSTER. Among the more important themes involving Indo-European warrior figures is the killing of a three-headed monster. As has already been seen, Indra's first "sin" stemmed from such a slaying. But the theme in question is distinct from that of the "three sins" and needs to be considered separately. Indeed, Indra is by no means the only Indic figure who slays a tricephalus. In *Ṛgveda* 10.8.8 Viśvarupa's slayer is called Trita-Āptya, or the "third" of three Āptya brothers, and although the figure is sometimes held to be a hypostasis of Indra, there is no clear implication that Trita-Āptya's action is considered a "sin." The same can be said for the behavior of the onomastically related Iranian figure Thraetaona, who kills a three-headed monster called Aži Dahaka ("foreign snake").

Other reflexes of this theme can be found in the Greek story of Herakles versus the three-headed figure Geryon, the Norse myth of how Thor bested the giant Hrungnir, who is described as having a "three-horned" heart, the Irish account of the hero Cú Chulainn versus the three sons of Nechta Scéne, and the well-known Roman pseudo-historical account of the conflict between Horatius and the three Curiatii. The last two accounts are, or course, euhemerized, in that the three-headed monster has been transformed into a threefold set of human adversaries (in the Roman version they are a set of Alban triplets). Nevertheless, in the other accounts, the slayer performs the same service to his community: he eliminates a threat to the three fundamental elements of the tradition (i.e., the three functions)—hence presumably the three heads or triple character of the adversary.

But the recalcitrance and, indeed, antisocial proclivities of the Indo-European warrior are also very much in evidence here. In the Roman version, for example, when the victorious Horatius (also the last survivor of a set of triplets) learned that his sister mourned the death of one of the Curiatii—she had been betrothed to him—he slew her in a fit of rage. As a result the Roman hero was forced to walk under a beam to divest himself of his *furor* before returning to polite society. Similar rituals of purification seem to have been characteristic of other early Indo-European societies; indeed the later Roman custom wherein a victorious army had to pass under a "triumphal" arch before it disbanded seems, in light of this evidence, to have been rooted as much in a need to divest the army of its collective *furor* as in a desire to humiliate the war captives that marched in chains behind the general's chariot.

THE WAR OF FOUNDATION. Another widespread Indo-European theme in which warrior figures necessarily play an important part is what Dumézil variously calls "the war of foundation" and the "war between the functions," that is, a conflict between representatives of the first two functions and those of the third. The best examples come from the Germanic and Roman traditions. In the former, the Æsir, including Óðinn, Tyr, and, of course, Þórr, fight a war with the so-called Vanir divinities, the most prominent of whom are Njǫrðr, his son Freyr, and his daughter Freyja. As described in the *Ynglingasaga,* the Æsir fight their Vanir opponents to a standstill, and then, in reconciliation, incorporate them into the pantheon, rendering it complete.

Although scholars such as the late Karl Helm have interpreted this myth as a reflection of the conflict that must have occurred between the earliest Germans and the indigenous inhabitants of northern Europe, Dumézil has found a parallel in the Roman pseudo-historical account of the Sabine War, as preserved by Livy and others, and is therefore convinced that the theme is in fact Indo-European. In the latter case, shortly after founding the city of Rome, Romulus and his companions trick their wealthy neighbors, the Sabines, steal their wives and daughters, and then, as part of the truce following an inconclusive war, incorporate the whole Sabine community into the Roman body politic. In both examples, the defeated groups clearly represent the third function—neither the Vanir nor the Sabines were famed for their military prowess, and each was closely associated with fertility and the mass of society—while the victors represent the first two. Indeed, the Sabines eventually came to form one of the three founding tribes of Rome, the Titienses (named for the Sabine king Titus Tatius), completing a triad that also included the Ramnes (founded by Romulus and charged with priestly duties), and the warlike Luceres (reputedly named for the Etruscan hero Lucomon).

Thus, while the Roman version of the theme masquerades as history, it is as mythological in its roots as the Norse account of the conflict between the Æsir and the Vanir and ultimately stems from the same Indo-European mythologem. This conclusion is buttressed by several other examples of what appear to be "wars of foundation"—or at least traditions about an internecine struggle that broadly conforms to the pattern just discussed. One is the Vedic reference to a conflict between "two forces," or *ubhe vīrye,* that are expressed in the principles later incarnated, respectively, in the *vaisya* (third function) and in the *brahmaṇa* and *kṣatriya* (first and second functions). Another can be found in the Homeric accounts of the Trojan War (e.g., the *Iliad* and the *Odyssey*), as well as in accounts of its aftermath (e.g., Euripides' *The Trojan Women*). The Greeks, led by Agamemnon and, after he returns to the fray, championed by the famed warrior Achilles, represent the first two functions, while the Trojans, consistently described as possessing vast wealth, are, like the Vanir and the Sabines, almost certainly representatives of the third function. Moreover, the fate of the Trojan women closely parallels that of their Sabine sisters: they are abducted by the victorious Greek kings and heroes.

Yet another possible example of a "war of foundation" can be seen in the Irish accounts of the conflict between the Tuatha Dé Danann and the Fomhoire, which culminated in the Second Battle of Magh Tuiredh. After this battle, the defeated Fomhoiran figure Bres, who together with his kind seems generally to reflect the third function, is incorporated into the body politic created by the victorious Tuatha (first and second functions), rendering it complete.

Sword Cults. An important feature that appears in several ancient Indo-European traditions is what can best be described as the cult of the named, magical sword. Found among the Celts, Germans, and particularly the North Iranian-speaking steppe peoples (Scythians, Alans, Sarmatians, etc.), the cult seems to have spread westward in the early centuries CE. Perhaps the best-known example here is contained in the medieval tradition surrounding King Arthur's magical sword, Excalibur. Another example is Roland's famous sword, Durandel. But as early as the fifth century BCE Herodotus described the Scythian practice of worshiping swords as manifestations of "Ares," and in the fourth century CE Ammianus Marcellinus described the Alanic custom of thrusting swords into the earth and worshiping them as "Mars." The modern Ossets, a Caucasian people who have the distinction of being the last descendants of the ancient Alans, still preserve an epic tradition in which magical swords play an important role (see, for example, Dumézil, *Légendes sur les Nartes,* Paris, 1930, pp. 61–63).

Although this theme cannot be documented throughout the ancient Indo-European domain and may well be rooted in the steppe traditions, its subsequent distribution from Britain to the Caucasus renders it a potentially important element in the Indo-European warfare mystique.

The Warrior-Divinity as a Fertility Figure. To conclude this brief survey of Indo-European warrior figures and the beliefs and practices associated with them, it is necessary to point out that several of the best known of these figures also had strong associations with plant, animal, and human fertility. Mars, for example, in certain of his aspects (e.g., the so-called Agrarian Mars) was regularly worshiped as a fertility figure. The Norse god Þórr was also invoked as an agricultural deity, and his sexual prowess is in some respects as remarkable as his fighting ability. The same can be said for several other Indo-European figures who are otherwise clear-cut representatives of the "second function," including, as has been seen, the demigod Herakles.

The warrior also has important connections with the principle of sovereignty, that is, the first function. As Dumézil points out, the Indo-European king is everywhere drawn from the warrior elite and must undergo a ritual wherein he acquires symbols of the other two functions as well as those relevant to his own. He thus necessarily becomes a transfunctional (or better, perhaps, a parafunctional) figure. Indeed, all Indo-European royal consecration ceremonies, from ancient India to modern Britain, emphasize this element.

Thus, Dumézil's conception of this most important component of the Indo-European ideology is much more complex than it might seem at first glance. There was, for example, a *Mars qui praeest paci* and there were *arma Quirini* (that is, armed representatives of the "third function"). Moreover, most of the female warrior figures—such as the Greek goddess Athena, who leaped into existence fully armed from the forehead of Zeus and who was typically portrayed in the costume of a warrior maiden—were also trifunctional figures in that they incarnated divine wisdom and the domestic arts as well as military prowess (cf. the three Irish Macha figures and the triple-figured Hindu goddess Durga). For the most part, however, these fertility attributes seem to have been secondary, and the prime function of figures such as Mars and Þórr, if not Athena, was to ensure military success.

In sum, despite their periodic bouts of antisocial behavior and occasional double-duty as agricultural divinities, to say nothing of their periodic elevation to the transfunctional role of king, the great Indo-European war gods, as well as their heroic counterparts (Arjuna, Achilles, Siegfried, Cú Chulainn, et al.), everywhere occupied a fundamental niche in the belief systems in question. And this niche was paralleled by that occupied by the warrior stratum in the real world of the ancient Indo-Europeans. Although never at the apex of the social or divine pyramid (unless elevated to the kingship), the warrior, mortal as well as divine or legendary, was a figure to be reckoned with, and the ideology associated with his was (and still is) perhaps the most distinctive feature of the Indo-European worldview.

SEE ALSO Berserkers; Blades; Frenzy; Indo-European Religions, article on History of Study; Secret Societies.

BIBLIOGRAPHY

Dumézil, Georges. *Aspects de la fonction guerrière chez les Indo-Européens.* Paris, 1956. Dumézil's basic statement on the Indo-European warrior; a fundamental contribution to "the new comparative mythology." Revised and expanded as *Heur et malheur du guerrier* (Paris, 1969) and translated by Alf Hiltebeitel as *The Destiny of the Warrior* (Chicago, 1970).

Dumézil, Georges. "L'enjeu du jeu des dieux—un héros." In his *Mythe et popeé,* vol. 2, pt. 1. Paris, 1971. Dumézil's discussion of the "light" and "dark" aspects of the warrior figure. Translated by David Weeks as *The Stakes of the Warrior* (Berkeley, 1983). Includes an excellent introduction by Jaan Puhvel.

Evans, David. "Agamemnon and the Indo-European Threefold Death Pattern." *History of Religions* 19 (November 1979): 153–166. An analysis of an Indo-European warrior-related theme in Greek epic.

Helm, Karl. "Mythologie auf alten und neuen Wegen." *Beiträge zur Geschichte der deutschen Sprache und Literatur* 77 (1955): 333–365. A critique of Dumézil's conception of the Indo-European warrior figure. Claims that the war between the Æsir and the Vanir reflects the Germanic conquest of Scandinavia rather than an Indo-European theme.

Littleton, C. Scott. "Some Possible Indo-European Themes in the *Iliad.*" In *Myth and Law among the Indo-Europeans,* edited by Jaan Puhvel, pp. 229–246. Berkeley, 1970. Discusses the extent to which the Trojan War reflects the Indo-European "War of Foundation/War between the Functions" theme. Also analyzes Achilles as a trifunctional "sinner."

Littleton, C. Scott. *The New Comparative Mythology: An Anthropological Assessment of the Theories of Georges Dumézil.* 3d ed. Berkeley, 1982. A comprehensive assessment of Dumézil's theories. Includes a detailed discussion of the ideology of the "second function" (see, for example, pp. 120–129).

Littleton, C. Scott. "From Swords in the Earth to the Sword in the Stone: A Possible Reflection of an Alano-Sarmatian Rite of Passage in the Arthurian Tradition." In *Homage to Georges Dumézil,* edited by Edgar C. Polmé, pp. 53–68. Washington, D.C., 1982. Discusses North Iranian sword cults and the extent to which the pulling of a sword from the earth may have been part of an Alano-Sarmatian (or possibly Indo-European) warrior initiation ritual.

Miller, Dean A. *The Epic Hero.* Baltimore, 2000. A recent overview of the Indo-Eurtopean warrior *ethos,* with emphasis on epic heroes.

Strutynski, Udo. "Ares: A Reflex on the Indo-European War God?" *Arethusa* 13, (Fall 1980): 217–231. A discussion of the Greek divinity Ares and the extent to which he commits the three canonical "sins." Methodologically important.

Strutynski, Udo. "Honi Soit Qui Mal y Pense: The Warrior Sins of Sir Gawain." In *Homage to Georges Dumézil,* edited by Edgar C. Polomé, pp. 35–52. Washington, D.C., 1982. Discusses the extent to which Gawain commits the three characteristic sins of the Indo-European warrior. An important work, as it demonstrates the persistence of this theme into medieval times.

Wikander, Stig. *Der arische Männerbund.* Lund, 1938. Established the presence of the Indo-European warrior band throughout the ancient Indo-European-speaking domain. Had a tremendous influence on Dumézil's subsequent theories about the Indo-European conception of the warrior class and its mythological reflections.

C. SCOTT LITTLETON (1987 AND 2005)

WARAO RELIGION.

The Orinoco Delta, a landscape of swamps, islands, and waterways, is the territory of the Warao. Located between the modern republics of Venezuela, Guyana, and Surinam, the Warao today number approximately sixteen thousand. Heirs to a seven-thousand-year tradition of fishing adaptation, some twenty dialectal subgroups of Warao have been identified (Kirchoff, 1948, p. 869). Warao formerly was considered a linguistic isolate; recent research however indicates certain vocabulary correspondences with the Chibchan languages of northwestern South America (Wilbert, 1970, p. 22). Cultural and dialectical differences exist among the various Warao groups, but they are linked by a system of common beliefs.

Information on Warao religion is derived from three major areas: traditional narrative, cosmology, and shamanism.

TRADITIONAL NARRATIVE. Traditional narrative is clearly cosmogenic in nature in that it recounts the origin of the plants, animals, and spirits that occupy the Warao universe. It also relates the feats of culture heroes, outlines the taboos people must observe, defines the soul, death, and reincarnation, and depicts other realms of being.

Myth explains that in precultural times the Warao lived in the sky, where a hunter's shot went wide one day. While searching for his arrow, the man found a hole. Descending by a rope to the earth, he discovered an abundance of food.

On his return he informed the Warao of his extraordinary find. The other Warao immediately began lowering themselves to earth, until at one point a pregnant woman became stuck in the hole. Only her anus protruded, which became the morning star; or, in another version, her legs extruded, forming the stars in the Big Dipper. Thus some of the Indians were forced to remain behind. On earth, the Warao learned from the spirit of palm leaf fiber that they must suffer and work. And so the first baby was born, the first sickness was inflicted by evil spirits, and the first death occurred (Wilbert, 1970, p. 309).

According to another tale, the sun was originally the property of one man. The world was dark, and men could procure food only with difficulty. One man, hearing the complaints of his wife, decided to send his two daughters in search of the sun. The first failed because she took the wrong turn and was raped by a monster. The second successfully reached the house of the sun's owner, had sexual intercourse with him, and received, as a gift, the sun in a container. Before she left, the man advised the girl not to break the sun. But on the girl's return home, amid the family's rejoicing, a piece of the sun broke off and escaped into the sky.

Aloft in the sky, the sun moved so swiftly through the day that men were unable to procure food. To remedy this situation, the Indians caught a turtle that they presented to the sun as a pet. Now obliged to wait for his slow-moving pet, the sun moved across the sky much more slowly, giving the Warao many hours of daylight in which to fish and to gather food (Wilbert, 1970, p. 311).

In another tale, the origin of the moon is sketched. Every night a young man was having incestuous relations with his two sisters as they slept. Anxious to learn the identity of their violator, the women smeared black genipa juice on their bodies. Waking the next day, they discovered the incriminating dye on their brother. Overcome with shame, their brother flew into space, where he became transformed into the moon. On occasions when the moon turns pink, the Warao believe that it bleeds. They therefore consider all women to be daughters of the moon, because they bleed periodically in menstruation (Wilbert, 1970, p. 63).

With profound sentiment, the Warao narrative also describes the origin of death. At the beginning of the world, the Warao chief warned his people not to sleep that night for they all would be visited first by death and then by a good spirit. To gain immortality, he urged them not to answer the first call but to respond to the second. That night silence reigned through the settlement. Toward midnight a voice was heard. One youth who had fallen asleep woke with a start and answered the first call, the call of death. In fulfillment of the chief's prediction, from that time on all Indians have had to die (Wilbert, 1970, p. 192).

COSMOLOGY. According to Warao cosmology, the earth is a disk floating on water; its crust is fractured by the many waterways of the Orinoco Delta. The sea extends to the horizon, where, contained within a vast gorge, it is bordered by mountains. At the cardinal and solstice points, these mountains soar upwards in the form of petrified trees.

The Warao universe is divided into various realms. The celestial realm is a smaller disk that parallels the terrestrial one. The maximum height of the solsticial suns determines the bell-shaped cosmic vault, which rests on the world's axis. Located to the northeast of the zenith is an ovoid house that is two-storied; the lower level is inhabited by a plumed serpent and the upper level by the Creator Bird, the ancestral shaman and his wife, and four pairs of insects. In the central space of the upper floor the male residents assemble to play a game that perpetuates humanity on earth. At the end of each game the plumed serpent emerges from below to produce a luminous ball. Ropes of tobacco smoke connect the house with the zenith and with the world's axis.

Coiled around the earth disk is a huge marine serpent that controls the tides and is the source of all forms of life. Below the terrestrial-aquatic is the subterranean realm, at the center of which resides the four-headed serpent-goddess of the nadir; her heads, crowned with deer horns, mark the four cardinal directions. The northern seas of the summer solstice are inhabited by the Butterfly God, and the southern seas of the winter solstice by the Toad God. The eastern and western seas are the domains, respectively, of the Avian God of Origin and the Scarlet Macaw. The ancient forefathers, called *kanobotuma,* reside at the four mountains at the cardinal points and once a year visit the Warao. At festival time, the forefathers enter the house of worship in a barrel of roasted palm pith, and, as carved images nailed to a central platform, they participate in the sacred dances of propitiatory ritual in which the Warao implore their gods of origin for protection (Wilbert, 1981, pp. 37–40).

SHAMANISM. Among the Warao common maladies are treated with simple herbal remedies. A serious illness or death, however, is always attributed to the malevolent action or intention of a supernatural agent. Three major types of sickness, and three specialists to treat them, are distinguished. *Bahana,* which results from the introduction of material objects into the body, is cured by the healer *bahanarotu. Hoa,* inflicted by plant and animal theophanies, must be attended by a shaman called *hoarotu.* And *hebu,* the possession by an ancestor spirit, is treated by the *wisiratu,* who is the shaman or priest who presides over the house of worship and who acts as the mediator between the *kanobotuma* and the Warao (Wilbert, 1970, p. 24). When someone is sick, all three practitioners assemble to diagnose the illness and to determine which specialist must perform the appropriate ceremony.

At the beginning of the Warao cultural epoch, the primordial shaman ascended to the zenith, called the "bosom of the world," from which radiates a network of paths across the celestial canopy. Deities travel along these pathways, as do Warao shamans in their journeys to other worlds. Amid this traffic, men provide offerings for the gods, and the gods bestow life and health on humankind (Wilbert, 1981, p. 39).

Bibliography

As is evident from the above text, Johannes Wilbertt is unquestionably the most important contemporary source on Warao religion. The bibliography of his own works supplied at the end of his article "Warao Cosmology and Yekuana Roundhouse Symbolism," *Journal of Latin American Lore* 7 (Spring 1981): 37–72, is comprehensive. Especially useful among these works is *Folk Literature of the Warao Indians* (Los Angeles, 1970). See also less recent publications by Basilio Maria de Barral, *Guarao guarata: Lo que cuentan los indios Guaraos* (Caracas, 1960), and Henry Osborn, "Textos folklóricos en Guarao," *Boletín indigenista venezolano* (Caracas) 3, no. 5 (1958): 163–170, no. 6 (1960): 157–173, and no. 7 (1961): 169–189; and Osborn's "Textos folklóricos Guarao," *Antropológica* (Caracas) 9 (1960): 21–38 and 10 (1960): 71–80. Paul Kirchoff's article "The Warrau," in volume 3 of the *Handbook of South American Indians*, edited by Julian H. Steward (Washington, D.C., 1948), pp. 869–881, provides a general historical account and description of settlement and subsistence patterns. Earlier ethnographic works are Walter E. Roth's "An Inquiry into the Animism and Folklore of the Guiana Indians," in *Thirtieth Annual Report of the Bureau of American Ethnology, 1908–09* (Washington, D.C., 1915), pp. 103–386, and Louis Plassard's "Les Guaraunos et le delta de l'Orénoque," *Bulletin de la Société de Géographie* (Paris) 15 (1868): 568–592. Finally, it should be mentioned that in recent years many articles on various aspects of Warao culture have appeared in the aforementioned Venezuelan journal *Antropológica*, which is published by the Fundación La Salle, Instituto Venezolano de Investigaciones Científicas (Caracas). The Fundación La Salle has also published *Actas I Congreso Warao* (Caracas, n. d.), the record of the First Warao Congress, which was held in Tucupita, Venezuela, 10–12 October 1980.

New Sources

Vaquero Rojo, Antonio E. *Manifestaciones religiosas de los Waraos, y Mitología Fundante.* Caracas, 2000.

Wilbert, Johannes. *Mystic Endowment: Religious Ethnography of the Warao Indians.* Cambridge, Mass., 1993.

Wilbert, Johannes. *Mindful of Famine: Religious Climatology of the Warao Indians.* Cambridge, Mass., 1996.

Andrés Alejandro Pérez Diez (1987)
Translated from Spanish by Gabriela Mahnand Pita Kelekna
Revised Bibliography

WARBURG, ABY. Aby Moritz Warburg (1866–1929) was a German art historian and *Kulturwissenschaftler* (scholar of cultural studies) who developed new concepts in the understanding of the cultural expression of human consciousness and behavior. Although he was not well known during his lifetime and long after that remained a mere name to all but a small circle of art historians, Warburg has gradually become recognized as a major figure in the study of religion. His importance for contemporary research lies not only in issues connected with iconology; his profound curiosity for both psychology and anthropology allowed him to develop new and successful strategies for deciphering complex and impenetrable imagery, and his interest in the nature of communication and the transformation of the symbolic meaning of signs established him as an exponent of the modern study of symbolism.

Warburg was born in Hamburg on June 13, 1866, the firstborn son of the banker Moritz Warburg and Charlotte Oppenheim Warburg. According to the Warburg legend, Aby Warburg rejected his birthright as his father's successor in the firm at the age of thirteen. He instead demanded not only an allowance according to his financial needs but also the financing of an expensive life devoted to research, which achieved its climax in the public activities of the Kulturwissenschaftliche Bibliothek Warburg (KBW, later known as the Warburg Institute) and the outstanding scholars associated with it.

Warburg's Work. In 1886 Warburg began his studies in art history, history, and archaeology in Bonn at one of the most famous German universities of the late nineteenth century. From 1888 to 1889 he attended a seminar of August Schmarsow in Florence. From the writings of Giorgio Vasari interpreting the rise of painting as an increase in the ability of artists to copy nature, Warburg learned that the artists of the Florentine Quattrocento were not the faithful and dedicated imitators of natural appearance that they were reputed to be. In particular the drapery style of Filippino Lippi and Sandro Botticelli deviated from realism in the addition of swirling garments and flying hair. In his Ph.D. thesis, concerning Botticelli's *Geburt der Venus* und *Der Frühling*, Warburg made a convincing argument for this unexpected observation by uncovering the historical circumstances of its making. He was able to prove that antiquity was visualized with the aid of dynamizing formal additions because the poets and philosophers in the immediate circle of Botticelli's patrons derived a certain mental image from ancient writers who delighted in descriptions of enchanting movement. Only in the High Renaissance was the illustration of imaginary themes as visualized through fantasy developed into a language of idealization that became the typical stylistic idiom of the period.

Warburg's new inclination to explain stylistic elements and their change in psychological terms was partly influenced by his teachers in Bonn and later Strasbourg, where he completed his dissertation. Hermann Usener, whose lectures on Greek mythology Warburg had attended, focused on the problem of mental mechanisms as reflected in the origins of mythology. Influenced by the Italian evolutionist Tito Vignoli and Charles Darwin's *The Expression of the Emotions in Man and Animals* (1872), Warburg was able to trace human expression back to animal reactions deriving ultimately from fear. By interposing an interval of reflection between impulse and action, human beings are capable of turning the uncontrolled reactions of emotion into symbols of gesture and art. Warburg's monistic psychology of art, however, is not only based on this early theory of stimulus and response, a predecessor of ethology, but also on theories derived from John Locke's associationism, as specified by the German philosopher Johann Friedrich Herbart. According to the historian Karl Lamprecht, one of Warburg's teachers in Bonn, the collective mentality of a society was determined by the character of inherent mental images (*Vorstellungen*) as symbolized in art. Warburg used these new and scientific approaches to get at the mental images that become apparent behind art, literature, and religious ceremonies.

In conveying his program Warburg concentrated mainly on the elucidation of the rather narrowly confined cultural circle of the Renaissance. After his marriage to the artist Mary Hertz in 1897, he moved to Florence (1897–1904) to bring the famous patrons of Florentine art and their concerns to life. The complexity of the Florentine society of the fifteenth century was reflected in the famous works of art commissioned by Lorenzo de' Medici and his circle. At the artists' studios in Florence a new style emerged out of a renewed study of antiquity that contradicted the usually accepted costume realism *alla franzese* (French style of representation) that dominated art up to that time. It was not the dismissal of a too earthbound and materialistic fashion in order to reveal the body and its language of passion that puzzled Warburg but the discovery that the artistic loyalties of Lorenzo's circle were by no means undivided. On the contrary, the classical ideal had to overcome a heavy medieval style of calm realism originating in Flanders, and this struggle against strong opposing forces was the reason for the assertiveness and strength of the finally triumphant style *alla antica* (antique style of representation). Antiquity, with its language of passion, therefore could only be welcomed when it helped to squash the tendency toward nonreflective, shallow realism. Without a counterpoise, or in Warburg's terms, without a sense of distance, the same images would lead to empty rhetoric and eventually to the degradation of art.

The classical elements and their change of meaning in particular led Warburg to a line of research that nearly dominated his career after about 1908. The Quattrocento frescoes in the Palazzo Schifanoia depict the Greek planet deities in their typical manner of representation according to medieval traditions of mythology but also the illustrations of fictitious constellations, the Decans, astrological imagery that reached the Renaissance through Arabic sources. Only the High Renaissance succeeded in surmounting the demons of astrology and allocating them to the aesthetic and distanced sphere of pure beauty. The different renderings of the planet gods from medieval disguise to their former Olympian form is a perfect illustration of how primitive anxieties influence people's mental images. From a psychological point of view, the constellations that humans project onto the bewildering quantity of stars and their identification with mythical beings has to be understood as a first step toward orientation in a hostile world. This distance, as acquainted by the power of reflection, gets lost again if the same images evolve into a mere screen for contemporary fears and wishes.

During that time Warburg's interest in questions of mastering fear with the help of cultural media was not only theoretical. Personal experience with a life-threatening illness and the ubiquitous menace of Jewish existence had frequently led to attacks of anxiety that colored his philosophy of culture. With the collapse of Germany after World War I, Warburg's mind was unable to withstand the threatening impressions, and his referral into psychiatric clinics in Hamburg and Jena became inevitable. Only the skilled Swiss psychologist Ludwig Binswanger finally succeeded in reintegrating Warburg's personality. During his stay at the sanatorium in Kreuzlingen, Warburg struggled to regain clarity by giving his lecture "A Serpent Ritual" to his fellow patients. This lecture was based on a journey he took in 1895 and 1896 to the United States, where he had studied the culture of American Indians at the Smithsonian Institution and in the Indians' genuine Lebensraum on the arid plateaus of New Mexico. The recourse to his visit to the Hopi Indians in 1895–1896, which supplied him with material for later reflection, was significant when considered under different aspects. The study of traditional religion and art, with its primitive and violent emotions, led him back to the supposed origins of culture, where ritual and symbolic processes develop a particular sense of distance, acquired through reflection, that allows the sublimating transformations of frightening impressions into a fragile *sophrosyne* (the antique virtue of self-possession and composure).

During Warburg's illness his assistants Fritz Saxl (1890–1948) and Gertrud Bing (1892–1964) did much more than continue the work of the KBW, which had such an eminent and probably even sacral meaning for their mentor. The library was more than a systematic collection of books shaped for Warburg's special research program; it was the reflection of his thought and mental process. Warburg, who never tired of shifting and reshifting his books in accordance with his actual system of thought, looked upon his library as a fortress against the forces of darkness and hell. In this sense the library, with its ties both to science and to an obscure and demonic world, became a "consecrated space" where the fight against demonic forces in his struggle for clarity derived its greatest strength.

In the years of Warburg's recovery Saxl completed a paper by Warburg on astrological prophesies in the period of the German Reformation. In addition Saxl and Bing began preparations for an extensive project that was planned as a comprehensive study of the results of Warburg's former work. As soon as Warburg's health improved, he and his assistants began to pave the way for the *Mnemosyne-Atlas*, a reflection of the ancient images and symbols as preserved in the collective memory of the European race. According to Warburg's theory, any experience leaves an engram in the nervous system, which acts as a sort of energy storage space. This accumulated energy becomes tangible in paintings and symbols. In this context the act of painting, as well as the act of symbolizing in ritual, is a process of progress in the sense that it is an attempt to control a threatening energy that is fed by the collective memory of the societies under question. Warburg was not able to finish his life's work. He died in Hamburg in October 1929 at the age of sixty-three.

CONTINUING HIS WORK. Warburg's death, although a great loss for his family, friends, collaborators, and disciples, was by no means the end of the research program he had summoned into existence. During Warburg's illness Saxl had opened the KBW to the public and had transformed the formerly private institution into one of high-level research. It is mainly due to Saxl that an interdisciplinary circle of scholars, including Ernst Cassirer (1874–1945) and Erwin Panofsky (1892–1968), became attached to the Warburg Institute. During their long cooperation Saxl not only looked after Warburg's publications and popularized his research but, together with Bing and Edgar Wind (1900–1971), carried on Warburg's mission and saved the library for generations to come.

Even after Warburg's death and the successful emigration of his library to London, Warburg's former disciples and assistants kept close links to the work and thinking of their mentor. Many of the publications of Bing, Wind, Saxl, and Carl Georg Heise (1890–1979) grew from the distribution and reception of Warburg's ideas. Mainly by elaborating upon and systematizing Warburg's theoretical and conceptual assumptions were they able to acquire new and authentic positions in art history that made them into the leading experts in their subjects. Saxl, first interested in astrological and mythological Scripture, later included ancient religions as one of his main subjects of research. His work *Saturn and Melancholy* (1964), which he wrote together with the skilled historians of art and culture Erwin Panofsky (1892–1968) and Raymond Klibansky (1905–), became influential in future research. Wind, who joined the Warburg Institute in 1928, focused on the Italian Renaissance but was also influential in developing iconography as a method in art history and the history of religions. Ernst Gombrich (1909–2001), a young art historian with close ties to the Viennese school, gained a leading position in the world of art historians by writing the *Intellectual Biography* of Warburg, which has continued to be influential in the reception of Warburg's works. Gombrich's psychological view of art as a mutuality of creativity allowed for a new concept of the history of art that includes prehistorical and non-European art and its iconography. Panofsky, probably the most renowned art historian of his century, became associated with the Warburg circle during his scholarship at the University of Hamburg. His main concern was to safeguard methodological approaches in art history. It was Panofsky who finally established iconology as a method of research and who elaborated upon its theoretical foundation. Chiefly through his synopsis of the manifold disciplines of research, Panofsky was able to carry on the inheritance of Warburg.

SEE ALSO Iconography.

BIBLIOGRAPHY

Böhme, Hartmut. "Aby M. Warburg (1866–1929)." In *Klassiker der Religionswissenschaft: Von Friedrich Schleiermacher bis Mircea Eliade*, edited by Axel Michaels, pp. 133–156. Munich, 1997.

Ferretti, Silvia. *Cassirer, Panofsky, Warburg: Symbol, Art, and History.* Translated by Richard Pierce. London and New Haven, Conn., 1989.

Forster, Kurt W. "Introduction." In *The Renewal of Pagan Antiquity: Contributions to the Cultural History of the European Renaissance* (1932), by Aby Warburg, translated by David Britt, pp. 1–75. Los Angeles, 1999.

Ginzburg, Carlo. "From Aby Warburg to E. H. Gombrich: A Problem of Method." In *Clues, Myths, and the Historical Method*, translated by John Tedeschi and Anne C. Tedeschi, pp. 17–59. Baltimore, Md., 1989.

Gombrich, Ernst H. *Aby Warburg: An Intellectual Biography, with a Memoir of the History of the Library by F. Saxl.* London, 1970; 2d ed., Chicago, 1986.

Kultermann, Udo. *Geschichte der Kunstgeschichte: Der Weg einer Wissenschaft.* Düsseldorf, Germany, 1966; 2d ed., 1970. Translated into English as *The History of Art History* (New York, 1993).

Saxl, Fritz, Raymond Klibansky, and Erwin Panofsky. *Saturn and Melancholoy: Studies in the History of Natural Philosophy, Religion, and Art.* New York, 1964.

Warburg, Aby. *Die Erneuerung der heidnischen Antike: Kulturwissenschaftliche Beiträge zur Geschichte der europäischen Renaissance.* 2 vols. Edited by Gertrud Bing. Berlin, 1932. Translated into English by David Britt as *The Renewal of Pagan Antiquity: Contributions to the Cultural History of the European Renaissance* (Los Angeles, 1999).

Warburg, Aby. "A Lecture on Serpent Ritual." *Journal of the Warburg Institute* 3 (1938–1939): 222–292.

Warburg, Aby M. *Ausgewählte Schriften und Würdigungen.* Edited by Dieter Wuttke and Carl Georg Heise. Baden-Baden, Germany, 1980.

Wessels, Antje. *Ursprungzauber: Zur Rezeption von Hermann Useners Lehre von der Regigiösen Begriffsbildung.* Berlin and New York, 2003.

Wuttke, Dieter. *Aby M. Warburg-Bibliographie 1866 bis 1995: Werk und Wirkung, mit Annotationen.* Baden-Baden, Germany, 1998.

INA WUNN (2005)

WARD, MARY. Mary Ward (1585–1645) was the founder of the Institute of the Blessed Virgin Mary, earlier known as the "English Ladies." She is recognized for pioneering the active, unenclosed life for nuns within the Roman Catholic Church, and her institute was the first systematic attempt to adopt for women the Jesuit missionary purpose and governance, with its emphasis on mobility and centralized structure under a superior general answerable directly to the pope. Traditionally, and in canon law, the members of women's religious orders were enclosed and monastic, a definition that was reinforced by the Council of Trent (1545–1563) as part of its reform of Catholicism. Mary Ward's was not the only contemporary initiative to challenge the status quo, but it was the most far-reaching and controversial—and remained so long after her death. She was convinced that "women in time to come will do much," but it was not until the aftermath of the French Revolution, in response to a powerful female movement to revitalize Catholicism, that the centralized active model was approved for women, and her vision was fully realized.

Born into a family of minor landed gentry in the northeast of England, Mary Ward was educated at home, where she learned Latin and showed a gift for modern European languages. The Wards belonged to the persecuted English Roman Catholic minority, and Mary was taught her faith by the Jesuit chaplains secretly employed in their households, and by female relatives, several of whom served prison sentences for persistent nonconformity to the established Church of England. A culture of heroism for their faith was evident within the Ward kinship network, most notably when three of her uncles died resisting arrest for their part in the Gunpowder Plot of 1605 to blow up the Houses of Parliament in an attempt at the political restoration of Catholicism.

In the same year Mary rejected a proposal of marriage favored by her father and her confessor in order to pursue a religious calling. She traveled to Stt Omer in Flanders, first joining the Poor Clares and then in 1607 to 1608 successfully founding a new Poor Clare convent in Gravelines for Englishwomen. She seemed settled, but in 1609 she experienced the first of a series of mystical illuminations, which she described as "seeing intellectually," that determined her subsequent decisions: "there happened to me a thing of such a nature that I know not, and never did know, how to explain. It appeared wholly Divine, and came with such force that it annihilated and reduced me to nothing" (Wright, 1997, p. 3). Understanding that she was to leave the convent to undertake some work willed for her by God, she returned to London. After a second illumination she gathered a group of young women of similar social background who trusted her leadership. In 1610, with the support of the Jesuits and the local bishop, they opened a quasi-religious house in St. Omer giving instruction and teaching girls evangelical activism and prowress. A third illumination in 1611, reinforced by a fourth in 1615, led Mary to understand that her community should adopt, with some adaptations, the constitutions of the Society of Jesus, their *Formula Instituti.* The vision made clear to her that the Society would not approve, as indeed it could not, since its founder had forbidden it to direct the work of nuns.

After 1615 Mary developed her institute, writing constitutions and forming its members as teachers and domestic missioners for work in England. Between 1616 and 1628 it expanded, attracting support from leading churchmen and nobility. New houses and schools were opened across the continent: in Liège (1616), Cologne and Triers (1620–1621), Rome (1622), Naples (1623), Perugia (1624), Munich (1627), and Vienna (1627). At the same time it attracted a good deal of hostility, and petitions were received in Rome from Jesuits, English clergy suspicious of the Jesuits, and individuals scandalized by their boldness and public life. New names—"Jesuitesses" and "galloping" or "gadding girls"—were added to that of "English Ladies," and they were accused of usurping priestly roles.

From the outset Mary sought papal approval for the institute. In 1621 she made a journey of 1,000 miles on foot from Brussels to Rome to present her constitutions to Pope Gregory XV, who, impressed with her character, referred the documents for consultation. But by 1628 the controversy had damaged the institute beyond recovery, so that Mary's re-presentation of her case to Pope Urban VIII in 1629 could not avert condemnation. Individual houses of the institute were firstly warned and from 1628 onwards suppressed by the Spanish Inquisition, culminating in the promulgation of the papal bull *Pastoralis Romani Pontificis* in January 1631 emphatically suppressing the whole institute and leading to Mary's imprisonment on heresy charges.

Although Mary was cleared of heresy by Urban and continued to live in Rome with companions, the remainder of her life was dominated by ill health. In 1637 she returned to England, where she died close to her Yorkshire home on January 20, 1645. Loyal companions slowly restored the institute from a base of strength in Munich under the protection of Maximilian of Bavaria. In 1749 Pope Benedict XIV issued a landmark judgement, *Quamvis Justo,* approving the restored institute's members as active unenclosed religious, provided they worked under local bishops and ceased to claim that their institute had been founded by Mary Ward. It was a further 160 years before another pope, Pius X, rehabilitated her as founder of the Institute of the Blessed Virgin Mary. Interest in Mary Ward grew during the twentieth century and, in the context of changing attitudes, her reputation grew to the point where in 1982 John Paul II extolled this "remarkable Yorkshire woman . . . a pioneer of the active unenclosed congregations for women."

SEE ALSO Nuns, article on Christian Nuns.

BIBLIOGRAPHY

Chambers, Mary C. E. *The Life of Mary Ward (1585–1645),* edited by Henry Coleridge. 2 vols. London, 1882–1885. The biographical work, written by a member of the institute and based on original archival research, that played a crucial role in rehabilitating Mary Ward.

Orchard, Mary Emmanuel, ed. *Till God Will: Mary Ward Through Her Writings,* introduced by James Walsh. London, 1985.

Peters, Henriette. *Mary Ward. A World in Contemplation,* translated by Helen Butterworth. Leominster, U.K., 1994. A comprehensive and detailed biographical study that synthesizes all previous scholarship and draws on new sources.

Wright, Mary. *Mary Ward's Institute: The Struggle for Identity.* Darlinghurst, Australia, 1997. An accessible history of the canon law dimension of Mary Ward's initiative containing all the significant papal documents and covering the later history of her institute and its branches.

SUSAN O'BRIEN (2005)

WARLPIRI RELIGION. While the boundaries of Warlpiri territory have moved through time, the central-western part of the Northern Territory has generally been regarded as the heart of Warlpiri country. Until they were forced to sedentarize by the Australian government in the early 1940s, the Warlpiri people led an independent hunting and gathering life in an area spreading over approximately 53,200 square miles (137,800 square kilometers). While mandatory sedentarization deprived Warlpiri men and women of their socioeconomic roles as gatherers and hunters, they sustained what continues to give them their raison d'être: their connections to the land, their cosmology, and their ancestors. The Warlpiri reside mainly in the settlements of Yuendumu, Lajamanu, Ali-Curang, Willowra, and Nyirrpi (and their outstations) and represent the most populous Aboriginal group in central Australia. The fact that most Warlpiri continue to reside on lands they traditionally inhabited accounts in part for the vigor of Warlpiri ritual life.

THE *JUKURRPA*. When discussing their religion, Warlpiri men and women invoke a key concept: the *Jukurrpa*. The *Jukurrpa* provides the Warlpiri with links to their ancestral past and land, as well as to their ancestors and to each other, reifying contemporary social relations and articulating omnipresent connections at the core of Warlpiri sense of identity (Dussart, 2000). A thorough grounding in the notion of *Jukurrpa* in all its iterations and contexts is necessary to understand the richness of Warlpiri ritual life.

Jukurrpa has often been translated in English as "Dreaming," "Dreamtime," or "Ancestral Times" (Mulvaney, Morphy, and Petch, 1997), but these translations obscure rather than explain the richness of Warlpiri cosmology. *Jukurrpa*, as explained by contemporary Warlpiri, has five related distinct and interrelated usages. Contrary to the simplified definitions appropriated by Western "spiritualists" in the 1990s, *Jukurrpa* refers first to an ancestral period during which the world was fashioned by Ancestral Beings who instituted social and religious orders for humans. Although *Jukurrpa* refers to a fictitious past, the Warlpiri maintain that it continues to exist in the present. According to an immutable law, when the *Jukurrpa*, which has always existed, manifested itself, the ground was flat and shapeless. Mythical heroes and heroines emerged from the earth, traveled around the countryside, performed marvelous acts, and continue to live in the *Jukurrpa* (Stanner, 1966, p. 266). Their travels transformed the shapeless ground into features (hills, watercourses, trees, and so on) and left behind them "ancestral powers." Features in the landscape readily apparent are proof that the *Jukurrpa* is true (*yijardu*) and that its essence is ever present.

The second usage is to designate the whole category of Ancestral Beings. The actions of these legendary beings, who emerged from the earth, shaped the landscape, and performed marvelous acts, are still reenacted by the Warlpiri in their ritual performances. Every spot visited became a sacred site and every sacred site became part of a specific *Jukurrpa* itinerary. Some Ancestral Beings remained near their place of emergence, while others traveled through territories that belong to neighboring Aboriginal groups. In their travels, Ancestral Beings left behind "life forces" (Peterson, 1969, p. 27). The Warlpiri identify three main kinds of life forces: *kuruwarri*, *pirlirrpa*, and *kurruwalpa*.

The *kuruwarri* are the marks, signs, and designs mythical beings left behind, while the unseen aspect of the *Jukurrpa* is invoked by the use of the word *pirlirrpa*. *Kuruwarri* and *pirlirrpa* are complementary categories, with the former referring to the visible (and the latter to the invisible) traces of the *Jukurrpa*. *Pirlirrpa*, however, has a more specific application: to the "spirit" or "essence" of the individual, a spirit that enters via the semen of the father and the egg of the mother and that localizes itself in the two kidneys. Male and female elements are thus found in every individual. The *pirlirrpa* is believed to imbue people, Dreaming stories, and the ceremonies that invoke the *Jukurrpa*. It is the potency of *pirlirrpa* that guarantees the effectiveness of a ritual in the maintenance of the *Jukurrpa*.

The essence of the *Jukurrpa*, called *kurruwalpa*, is associated exclusively with the act of conception. Whereas the *pirlirrpa* is linked physically to the individual wherever that individual may be, the essence or spirits associated with conception are all site-specific. While a mother is walking along, a *kurruwalpa* will penetrate her—through the womb, foot, or navel—in a fashion that animates the fetus. When the *kurruwalpa* emerges, that particular site becomes known as the conception site of the soon-to-be-born child. Later on, the child will have special rights and ritual obligations over the site and the Ancestral Beings associated with it.

Even though it is often argued in anthropological literature that ancestors (i.e., deceased humans) and Ancestral Beings are fused indistinguishably, the actual relationships between ancestors (*nyurnupatu*) and Ancestral Beings (*Jukurrpa*) are far more complex. It is true that, while telling a *Jukurrpa* story, a Warlpiri person may refer to his or her deceased father as, say, "an Ancestral Emu" (*Yankirri*), implying the *Jukurrpa* Ancestral Being of that name. Such reference is particularly common when the cosmologically constituted connection to that Being can strengthen the narrator's ceremonial and territorial rights associated with the myth of a particular Ancestral Emu. This does not mean, however, that the deceased is instantly folded into, or immediately becomes one with, some larger cosmological force situated in the *Jukurrpa.* In point of fact, further interrogation reveals that at least two generational levels must exist between the deceased and a speaker for the former to merge fully with the *Jukurrpa,* a process of genealogical amnesia that transforms humans into Ancestral Beings.

The third sense of the *Jukurrpa* employs the term to denote specific narratives or Dreaming stories—as, for example, in the myth of an Ancestral Rain Being—such that not only the Being, but also the *ngurrara* (homes) it created in its travels are referred to as *Ngapa Jukurrpa* (Ancestral Rain Dreaming, or Rain Dreaming). Before returning to their site of emergence, Ancestral Beings may travel far, traversing many other homes (each portion of which represents a particular portion of the itinerary and a particular story) and many other countries owned and overseen by different kin groups, including many who are not Warlpiri. Other Ancestral Beings do not stray far from their site of emergence.

The fourth usage refers to a specific segment of an ancestral itinerary at a given site and its vicinity. One or several songs, designs, and dance sequences are associated with a segment of a Dreaming, which are enacted during ritual ceremonies. The same basic elements of designs, songs, and dances performed by men and women are stylistically arranged according to age and gender that characterize a specific ritual activity.

Finally, *Jukurrpa* is used to refer to nocturnal dreams. When asleep, dreamers may have a dream in which they "see and hear" Ancestral Beings. If the dreamers can remember song(s) sung by the Ancestral Beings as they wake, their dreams, after thorough examination by *Jukurrpa* experts, are usually integrated within an existing *Jukurrpa* itinerary. It is through such dreams that the Warlpiri have learned about (and continue to learn about) the *Jukurrpa.* The Warlpiri maintain that nothing is new, but simply forgotten. The *Jukurrpa* is believed to be immutable, whereas the reality of life is that cosmology and religious order are dynamic.

RITUAL MANAGEMENT. While the *Jukurrpa* has and will always be, humans in specific kin formations have the responsibility to reproduce and maintain it by enacting Dreaming stories in ritual performances as prescribed by the Ancestral Beings. Through the performance of ceremonies, the Warlpiri reaffirm their ties to the land, the *Jukurrpa,* and to one another. This is achieved following specific patterns of kinship—patterns that have been modified since sedentarization. Before being forced to settle, the Warlpiri lived a seminomadic life traveling in small groups of up to thirty relatives and in-laws (like most central Australian Aborigines). They camped for short or long periods of time with either spouse's families, and they would gather in great numbers with other central desert Aborigines for ceremonial purposes. Ritual activities such as initiations and betrothals usually took place at specific sites along the itinerary evoked in performances orchestrated by groups of kin responsible for the area and the associated *Jukurrpa.* Since sedentarization, ceremonial performances tend to be performed near settlements.

Dreaming stories, sites, and associated rituals are owned and managed along complex lines of subsection and kinship association. The Warlpiri have an Arandic system of kin classification (first identified by Mervin J. Meggitt [1962]). The Warlpiri divide the world into two groups of people: those they are related to and those who are not their relatives. Relationships with kin may be actual (when both parents are shared), close (when they share one relative, even distant), or "classificatory" (when kinship ties are established through land and daily life). The basic egocentric distinctions of the Arandic system are grouped into a set of sociocentric terms known as subsections, which in turn are further grouped into patrilineal, matrilineal, and generational moieties. Each descent group is associated with one or other of the four patrisubsection couples used to identify patterns of landownership.

The basic structure of landownership, and by implication ritual transmission and social organization, is constituted along lines of patrilineal descent. A person's patrimoiety is referred to as *kirda,* while the opposite patrimoiety is referred to as *kurdungurlu.* The real significance of *kirda* and *kurdungurlu* in the organization of religious life and land tenure derives from the more specific uses and the rights associated with them. Generally, a man or a woman inherit rights as *kirda* to more than one country and associated *Jukurrpa.* A *kurdungurlu* is a person who has inherited responsibilities through a matrilaterally traced interest. So each Warlpiri person has rights and responsibilities over countries and Dreamings as *kirda* and as *kurdungurlu.* However, acquisition of knowledge and responsibilities to act as *kirda* or *kurdungurlu* for sites and *Jukurrpa* acquired through classificatory kin associations is common and the result of residential alliances developed since forced sedentarization.

A *kirda* is often referred to in Aboriginal English as the "owner" of a *Jukurrpa* and its associated sites. Owners are responsible for the maintenance of the well-being of the land and its people by performing ritual ceremonies. The *kurdungurlu* is like a "manager" of a *kirda*'s Dreamings and associated sites and ritual performances. Reenactment of a *Jukurrpa* by *kirda* requires the surveillance and advice of *kurdungurlu.* The *kirda-kurdungurlu* relationship is, in theory, reciprocal, but in practice (and since sedentarization) this relationship is more often based on alliance rather than on descent.

In all their discussions of landownership, *Jukurrpa,* and ceremonial responsibilities and rights, Warlpiri men and women explain how transmission lines to obtain and pass on religious knowledge in no way restrict the role of either gender in the inheritance or performance of that knowledge. While men and women are identified as *kirda* or as *kurdungurlu* for specific Dreamings and related sites, certain segments along the *Jukurrpa* geospecific itinerary may be shared by both genders, while others are exclusively enacted in men- or women-only performances.

Ceremonies. The *Jukurrpa* is primarily maintained through the singing, dancing, and painting performed during land-based ceremonies. By enacting their Dreaming stories, Warlpiri men and women resolve conflicts, maintain and restore the health of the land and all that live on it, and uphold their ties to the land, to their ancestors, and to one another. In theory, *kirda* and *kurdungurlu* should never be negligent. If they do not enact their *Jukurrpa* correctly (*junga*) not only the land may become ill, but the people, animals, flora, and resources attached to it are put at risk as well. As one important Yuendumu ritual leader, who passed away and thus cannot be named, explained "if you do not care for country, that country will simply die. We cannot forget our *Jukurrpa* [and our obligations to it]."

Colonial and postcolonial forces have irrevocably changed Warlpiri ritual activities. A number of ceremonies have disappeared, and others have been altered. Regardless, initiation ceremonies with plural motives—such as male circumcision and betrothal, men- and women-only ceremonies, ceremonial cycles performed by both men and women, and rituals surrounding conception, death, love songs, and curing—now form the core of Warlpiri religious activity.

Some of these performances may last weeks, while others are performed in less than half a day. Ritual cycles tend to occur during a specific time of the year, such as during the wet season, which also coincides with Western-style holidays; adults and children are able to participate in these long initiation ceremonies. Other ceremonies, such as women-only performances called *yawulyu*, may occur throughout the year.

Three main distinctions are generally made when identifying who can participate, orchestrate, and witness ritual activities. These distinctions are defined by three ceremonial events: *tarruku*, *wiri*, and *warraja*.

Tarruku events are considered dangerous, potent, and powerful. Only the most senior persons knowledgeable in the specific segments of a *Jukurrpa* can orchestrate *tarruku* performances. *Tarruku* events associated with male initiation cannot be witnessed by women, though senior women are aware of their content and purposes. Others, such as *wiri*, can take place during ceremonies orchestrated by initiated men and enacted by both men and women. *Wiri* performances are considered potent but not as dangerous as *tarruku* events.

Senior Warlpiri men and women use the term *warraja* to refer to ritual events open to all: initiated, noninitiated, non-Warlpiri, and non-Aboriginal people. *Warraja* events are public but remain imbued with the potency of the *Jukurrpa*. These events may be performed by men or women or both.

As in all typologies, the ones for *tarruku*, *wiri*, and *warraja* are at best truncated. Explanations of ritual activities and terms employed to categorize them are done by specific persons for a specific audience. For example, a person who has not been given the rights to sing and dance in ritual activities because of his or her age could use *tarruku* to designate all ceremonies performed by the senior Aborigines. In brief, many religious Warlpiri terms, such as *tarruku*, *wiri*, and *warraja*, are imbued with supplemental meanings according to the ritual status, age, and gender of who uses them and in front of whom they are used.

Even though Warlpiri men and women unfailingly maintain that the *Jukurrpa* has not changed, they readily admit that their ritual repertoire has undergone transformation since forced sedentarization. Biomedical Western practices have reduced the frequency of birth and health-curing rituals. The performances of love and sorcery rituals, which increased in the early years of sedentarization, are now in decline. While certain ritual activities have faded away, some have been modified and others added to the religious repertoire. Inter-Aboriginal ceremonial cycles described as *tarruku* and *wiri* (which cannot be described here) and *warraja* have been organized since settled life. Creolized ceremonies blending elements of Christianity and Warlpiri religion have emerged and have had a measured impact on Warlpiri ritual life as a whole). Regardless, even though ritual repertoires may be smaller and the duration of performative events are shorter, the vitality of and the importance of the *Jukurrpa* has retained its intensity.

Initiation and conflict-resolution rituals continue to be regularly performed, as they play crucial roles in the production of Warlpiri identity in neocolonial Australia. These ceremonies are usually enacted during school breaks and near settlements to maximize participation and valorize the importance of such events.

Ritual Performances. There are two main groups of ceremonial performances. The first set is associated with rites of passage (initiation, betrothal, and death), and the second includes performances outside elemental ones connected to the cosmological construction of Warlpiri identity.

The main ritual cycle linked to initiation is called *kurdiji*. This is a ritual in which men and women perform gender-specific and joint ceremonies and that marks the first stage of a boy's initiation into manhood through the act of circumcision. Warlpiri boys have to undergo this procedure, which is restricted to men when they are between twelve and fifteen years old. It is during *kurdiji* that preferred marital associations are sealed between the initiand's family and the future spouse's family, whether the future wife is born or not. After the circumcision of their first son, mothers, if they wish, will be able to begin their ritual career. Mothers give away their sons; sisters dance so their brothers enter manhood; fathers, mothers' brothers, and future in-laws seal their newly articulated kin and spiritual responsibilities. After *kurdiji* ceremonies, both male and female participants have acquired sets of kinship obligations as well as spiritual responsibilities.

The young circumcised men, aided by their relatives, will have to go through other initiation ceremonies to be able to participate fully in their thirties in the ritual life of their settlement. The second stage of initiation is called *kajirri* and *kankarlu*, or "high school" in Aboriginal English (Meggitt, 1966; Peterson, 1970). *Kajirri* is associated with a set of Dreaming itineraries and *kankarlu* with others. Young men will be initiated in one or both of these cycles. Their participation will be predicated on their associations with the *Jukurrpa* itineraries evoked, the timing of the events, and their availability. *Kajirri* and *kankarlu* require planning on a grand scale because they demand the participation of Aboriginal people outside Warlpiri territory. They are usually performed only once every few years, and young men in their late teens are strongly encouraged to participate to further their understanding of their *Jukurrpa* and their responsibilities to the land and their ancestors, and to undergo other genital transformation. Young men who have undergone the initiation ceremonies of *kurdiji* and *kajirri* (or its variant, *kankarlu*) can be subincised, a highly restricted surgical intervention. Senior men and women active in ritual life participate in initiation ceremonies and perform gender-specific ceremonies in which they reenact restricted versions of Dreaming stories. Kinship ties among Warlpiri and other Aboriginal families are cemented and reaffirmed during *kajirri* and *kankarlu* events, prompting participants to perform other rituals together.

There are no marriage ceremonies among the Warlpiri, unless future spouses get married in a church as Christians. Betrothal takes place during initiation ceremonies. The ceremonies marking a person's death are called *malamala*, or "sorry business" in Aboriginal English. *Malamala* ceremonies are performed by a dead person's relatives. Widows, mothers, and mothers-in-law go to a "sorry camp," where they are placed under a speech taboo that can last from several weeks to several months (Kendon, 1988). Men conduct "sorry business" but are not put under a speech taboo. Male relatives self-inflict wounds to their bodies to show their sorrow at the loss of their relative. The name of the deceased as well as all words sounding the same are placed under a speech taboo. All individuals sharing the name of the deceased or something that sounds similar are subsequently identified as *kumanjayi*, or "no name" (Nash and Simpson, 1981). All performances of the *Jukurrpa* associated with the deceased are suspended until proper "finishing-time" rituals are conducted to lift the various bans imposed after death. With death, the *pirlirrpa*, or "essence of the individual," enters a liminal state identified as *yama* or *marnparrpa*. Since Warlpiri do not regard death as "natural," male relatives conduct a ritual in which they accuse various individuals of neglectful and malign actions that led to the death of their relative.

Every place and object owned by the deceased is put under taboo, and the ground where he or she walked has to be swept to ensure that the spirit of the deceased does not remain among the living. Plagued with social problems and deadly diseases, the Warlpiri are involved in *malamala* almost on a monthly basis. At the "finish-time" ceremonies, women are relieved from their speech taboo and other restrictions on remarriages are lifted, as is the ban on enacting the itineraries of the *Jukurrpa* associated with the deceased. Other individuals bearing the name of the deceased can resume the use of the name. The "finish-time" event can take place a few months or many years after the death of the individual whose country is "opened up" again. This process of reintegration has wide-ranging implications, offering insight into the relationship between the living, the dead, and the Ancestral Beings.

The second set of rituals mentioned earlier are the following ceremonial cycles: *jardiwanpa*, *kura-kurra*, *ngajikula*, and *puluwanti*. These are undertaken jointly by senior men and women. These four ceremonial cycles are distinguished by the Ancestral Beings they invoke. Most of the ceremonies are restricted, except for the last night of the cycles when the initiated, both young and old, are engaged in the final steps of conflict resolution. These ceremonial cycles contain a great deal of intra- and intersettlement importance, and their highly valued content is regularly exchanged with neighboring Aboriginal groups.

Since sedentarization, there has been a steady decrease of public performances called *purlapa*. *Purlapa* events are performed only by men and, like most public performances, they proclaim the richness of the *Jukurrpa* beyond the settlement, circulate ritual knowledge, and in the process sustain if not revivify social networks. In this sense, public performance simultaneously functions as a mirror and a projector of Warlpiri culture. Today, women's public rituals called *yawulyu* play such roles. The transfer of performative responsibility reflects more than the mutability of Warlpiri ceremonial life under postcolonial pressures, as it underscores the gender-specific methods by which sedentarized Warlpiri kin groups sustain their religion and their prestige within and beyond the confines of their settlements.

Yawulyu rituals are only performed by women. These ceremonies can be either restricted or public, and they have plural functions. In their *yawulyu* ceremonies, women enact the myths for which they are *kirda* assisted by their *kurdungurlu*, and most of them are performed in the settlements where the participants live. *Yawulyu* are performed to enhance women's knowledge of the *Jukurrpa*, sexuality, fertility, well-being, and physical and spiritual growth, as well as to educate non-Aboriginal peoples about the importance of the land and the *Jukurrpa*. Through the performance of public *yawulyu* ceremonies, Warlpiri women have come to play crucial roles as gatekeepers of Warlpiri identity beyond the confines of the settlement.

Church *purlapa* is the Aboriginal English term used for creolized performances merging some components of Christian and Warlpiri religions. Only formally constituted in the late 1970s, church *purlapa* are performed by both men and women. Missionaries representing various branches of the Christian church have long struggled to convert the Warlpiri and have had a small but noticeable impact within certain settlements. Since the mid-1990s, the younger generations have been far more actively engaged in orchestrating Christian ritual activities, such as church bands.

CONCLUSION. Despite colonial and postcolonial pressure, the *Jukurrpa* as a cultural form continues to provide a fundamental structure to the lives of the Warlpiri people. The *Jukurrpa* cannot change and gives to Warlpiri men and women feelings of continuity in a world of uncertainty. In their enactment of *Jukurrpa* itineraries, the Warlpiri reaffirm their ties to their lands, their ancestors, themselves, and other Aboriginal people. Even though the frequency of ceremonial performances has diminished and the length and site of performances modified, the power of the *Jukurrpa* remains strong. Through their ritual activities, Warlpiri participants demonstrate the importance of the *Jukurrpa* and their land to the world at large.

SEE ALSO Australian Indigenous Religions, overview article; Cosmology, article on Australian Indigenous Cosmology; Dreaming, The.

BIBLIOGRAPHY

Anderson, Christopher, and Françoise Dussart. "Dreamings in Acrylic: Contemporary Western Desert Art." In *Dreamings: The Art of Aboriginal Australia*, edited by Peter Sutton, pp. 89–142. New York, 1988.

Bell, Diane. *Daughters of the Dreaming.* Sydney, 1983.

Charlesworth, Max, Françoise Dussart, and Howard Morphy, eds. *Aboriginal Religions in Australia: Recent Writings.* Burlington, Vt., 2004.

Dussart, Françoise. *The Politics of Ritual in an Aboriginal Settlement: Kinship, Gender, and the Currency of Knowledge.* Washington, D.C., 2000.

Glowczewski, Barbara. *Du rêve à la loi chez les Aborigènes: Mythes, rites et organisation sociale en Australie.* Paris, 1991.

Kendon, Adam. *Sign Languages of Aboriginal Australia.* Cambridge, U.K., 1988.

Laughren, Mary. "Warlpiri Kinship Structure." In *Languages of Kinship in Aboriginal Australia*, edited by Jeffery Heath, Francesca Merlan, and Alan Rumsey. Oceania *Linguistic Monographs* 24 (1982): 72–85.

Meggitt, Mervin J. *Desert People: A Study of the Walbiri Aborigines of Central Australia.* Sydney, 1962.

Meggitt, Mervin J. *Gadjari among the Walbiri Aborigines of Central Australia.* Sydney, 1966.

Mulvaney, John, Howard Morphy, and Alan Petch. *"My Dear Spencer": The Letters of F. J. Gillen to Baldwin Spencer.* Melbourne, 1997.

Munn, Nancy. *Walbiri Iconography: Graphic Representation and Cultural Symbolism in a Central Australian Society.* Ithaca, N.Y., 1973.

Nash, David, and Jane Simpson. "No-Name in Central Australia." In *The Parasession on Language and Behavior*, edited by Carrie S. Masek, Roberta A. Hendrick, and Mary Frances Miller, pp. 165–177. Chicago, 1981.

Peterson, Nicolas. "Secular and Ritual Links: Two Basic and Opposed Principles of Australian Social Organization as Illustrated by Walbiri Ethnography." *Mankind* 7 (1969): 27–35.

Peterson, Nicolas. "Buluwandi: A Central Australian Ceremony for the Resolution of Conflict." In *Australian Aboriginal Anthropology: Modern Studies in the Social Anthropology of the Australian Aborigines*, edited by Ronald M. Berndt, pp. 200–215. Perth, 1970.

Peterson, Nicolas. "Demand Sharing: Reciprocity and the Pressure for Generosity among Foragers." *American Anthropologist* 95 (1993): 860–874.

Peterson, Nicolas, et al. *A Claim to Areas of Traditional Land by the Warlpiri, Kartangarurru-Kurintji.* Alice Springs, Australia, 1978.

Poirier, Sylvie. *A World of Relationships: Itineraries, Dreams, and Events in the Australian Western Desert.* Toronto, 2004.

Spencer, Walter Baldwin, and Francis J. Gillen. *The Native Tribes of Central Australia.* London, 1899.

Stanner, W. E. H. "On Aboriginal Religion." *Oceania Monographs* 11 (1966).

Swain, Tony. *A Place for Strangers: Towards a History of Australian Aboriginal Being.* Cambridge, U.K., 1993.

Tindale, Norman B. *Aboriginal Tribes of Australia: Their Terrain, Environmental Controls, Distribution, Limits, and Proper Names.* Canberra, 1974.

Wild, Stephen. "Walbiri Music and Dance in their Social and Cultural Nexus." Ph.D. diss., Indiana University, 1975.

FRANÇOISE DUSSART (2005)

WATER.

In the mythical narratives in which it is frequently employed, the image of water takes on many different aspects. This article shall try to classify its appearances and seek to understand how the diverse functions that it fulfills are ordered.

AT THE TIME OF ORIGINS. Many peoples tell how the world, already created in ancient times, was transformed and became what it is now. According to certain Australian traditions, the earth was originally surrounded by water, and in it were many spirits. Through the action of one of these spirits, the earth grew warm, and the first humans emerged from it. According to the Zuni Indians, a complex network of waterways circulates underground; the first Zuni were born there, at the lowest level. A pair of twins created by the Sun then made them climb to the surface. A pond marks the spot where they finally saw the light of day. A northern Australian myth tells the story of a *dema* (ancestral) deity. After one of his sons struck him with a lance, he threw himself into the sea; there, another of his children drew the lance out of his flesh where it had remained embedded. During the voyage the god then undertook, a spring appeared everywhere he rested. Finally, he plunged into the river Victoria, whose waters he proceeded to stir up until they formed deep branches in the forest; he then disappeared under a rock. From time to time he rises to the surface and causes storms; according to some accounts, he also occupies the region of the rainbow, where rain is formed.

Myths of this type show us water as present in the world from the most ancient times on, but they ascribe to it many different situations. Whether peripheral to the land or underground, water is first a significant element of the universal order. Sometimes it figures simply as a geographical feature—the sea or a river defining the shape of a country. However, there is something more to take note of. Water can be passive, with a spirit independent of it taking the sole initiative in the act of transformation. And yet water is tied mysteriously to the birth of the first humans or to the destiny of a god, who, after disappearing into its depths, remains bound up with storms and rain. The scope of these differences becomes clear when considering lengthier accounts.

In seeking the origin of all things, many peoples relate how water appeared in the course of cosmogonic events. Their explanations fall into three principal mythic systems. According to the first system, the world is created by a god who remains largely transcendent to it. In this case water, like the entire world, is a product of divine action. According to the Desána of South America, "Sun created the universe. . . . [He] created the earth, its forests and its rivers. . . . He also created the spirits and water demons" (Gerardo Reichel-Dolmatoff, *Desana: Simbolismo de los Indios Tukano del Vaùpès,* Bogotá, 1968, pp. 48–49). An African lament evokes "the one eternal God, the creator of the ocean and of dry land, of the fish in the sea and the beasts in the forest" (Louis Vincent Thomas, *Les religions d'Afrique noire,* Paris, 1969, p. 218).

In the second mythic context, the cosmogony takes on the aspect of a genealogy. The first ancestor is an entity whose simultaneously cosmic and divine attributes appear in the proliferation of his offspring. The waters that are then born throughout the generations are themselves generative. In a Greek system, the ancestral Earth gives birth to Heaven and to Pontos, the realm of the sea, composed of salt water. Earth then couples with each of these male principles. The first of the children she conceives from Heaven is Okeanos, a freshwater river, with deep eddies; he becomes the father of all the springs and rivers. Thus the deity who goes beyond the world remains immanent within it: In a way, he is present in the waters.

Finally, spirit may be presented as one of the primary agents of the formation of the world. Take for instance this Bambara myth: Out of the original void and motion a force, and then spirit, come forth. While the principles of things are being ordered, a mass falls and gives birth to the earth. However, a part of spirit arises; this is Faro, who builds the heaven. Faro then falls to earth in the form of water, thus bringing life to it. Dispenser of life, water is a manifestation of the divine spirit itself.

It is, however, in another type of cosmogony that the breadth and diversity of the functions of water become most intelligible. Here, water symbolizes what existed before the unleashing of the cosmogonic process, or the state of the world in the first phases of its history. There are numerous variations on this theme.

1. In its fluidity and elusiveness water may suggest the absence of form, the unsubstantiality and confusion from which the world will emerge. Inert, water has no power; a god or other beings independent of water will be the sole agents of creation. For instance, the following tale was told in the Admiralty Islands. In the beginning, there was nothing but an immense sea; in it swam a great serpent. Wanting a place where he could rest, he said, "Let a reef arise!" A reef then arose from the water and turned into dry land.

Biblical cosmogony illustrates the meaning of water in myths of this sort. The Bible brings together various symbols, including the desert, the void and darkness, the abyss, and the mass of water that the abyss contains and above which hovers the breath of God. This divine breath alone signifies reality. The other images have a negative value, evoking the idea of nonexistence; theologians will see in them a symbol of nothingness. Vedic language can go even further:

> Neither Non-Being nor Being existed then.
> Neither air nor the firmament above existed.
> What was moving with such force? Where? Under whose care?
> Was it the deep and fathomless water? (*Ṛgveda* 10.121.1)

In this question, the image of water alludes to the state of things prior to the distinction between being and nonbeing.

2. Water has no form of its own, but rivers have a bed and the sea has a bottom. This simple fact inspires several myths. Here is a Siberian example:

> In the beginning, water was everywhere. Doh, the first shaman, flew over the primordial ocean in the company of some birds. Finding nowhere to rest, he asked the red-breasted loon to dive into the ocean and bring back some earth from the bottom. This the loon did, and on his third attempt, he managed to bring back a little mud in his beak. Doh made of this an island on the original ocean which became the earth.

The original ocean can thus cover some solid element. Moreover, despite its fluidity, water itself has substance; it is itself matter, and may contain suspended matter. In some myths the gods capture this matter or condense it. Thus the *Atharvaveda* (12.1) reads: "[The Earth] was originally a wave in the heart of the Ocean; the Sages went looking for it with their magic." A Guinean myth tells how Ha made an immense sea of mud and, then, by solidifying the mud, created the earth. According to the *Kojiki,* Izanagi and Izanami drove a lance into the sea that extended below them. When they withdrew it, the salty drops that fell from it solidified and formed the first land: the island of Onogoro. A Greek commentator on the myth of Proteus expresses himself in more abstract terms:

> There was a time when all that existed was formless and muddy . . . there was nothing but matter that had been spilled out. A formless inertia reigned until the artisan of all things, having attracted order in order to protect life, imposed its imprint on the world. He disjoined the heavens from the earth, separated the conti-

nent from the sea, and each of the four elements . . . assumed its own form. (Heraclitus, *Homeric Allegories* 64ff.)

In this type of myth, water no longer signifies nothingness; it possesses a true existence. The gods use it, but it remains inert; they alone are active.

3. Very similar accounts, or even variants of the same myth, however, endow water with a certain spontaneity. This is the case in a story told by the Muskogee of North America. Before creation, they say, a vast expanse of water was the only thing visible, and two pigeons flew over the waves. At one end, they noticed a blade of grass growing on the surface of the waves. From this grass the earth gradually took shape, and at last the islands and continents took on their present form. One may also refer to an Orphic Greek cosmogony, according to which the primordial water appears to have been muddy. The matter it contained was condensed to become earth, and then from water and earth was finally born the mysterious god who would engender the cosmic egg. Despite their very different styles, both of these myths share one feature: Something happens in the original waters, without the intervention of any power external to the waters themselves. They therefore possess a certain intrinsic power. Other myths go on to explain the nature of this power.

4. In Hindu cosmogonies, waters are often represented as a receptacle of the divine egg or seed, which grows in the waters, carrying the god full of activity. But they do not give birth to what they carry. "In the beginning, he created only the waters, and then, in the waters, he laid his seed. And this became a golden egg. . . . In this egg Brahmā was born of himself, the ancestor of all living things" (*Mānava Dharmaśāstra* l.8–9). Auspicious for the development of the divine embryo, such waters fulfill an almost amniotic function. Egyptian mythology has a similar body of water, known as Nun. The primordial water is considered divine. It bears its own name and assumes human attributes. It can speak, and it can form a couple with its feminine double, the goddess Naunet. In Heliopolitan tradition, it is in Nun that the autogenous solar god is born and later rests. There he begins his creative or generative activity, and there, perhaps, the first gods begin their existence.

5. The image of a vivifying water that favors the birth of a god or the growth of an embryo is in fact very close to that of a fecund and procreative water. Some Egyptian texts give the impression that Nun himself engendered the solar god, whom he calls "my son." Nun has thus been called the "father of the gods." For a more clear-cut example of an image of procreative water, however, one may turn to the Babylonians. The Babylonians recognized two beings, Apsu and Tiamat, who existed prior to the formation of heaven and earth. They are at one and the same time waters, whose currents, in the beginning of time, mingled in a single mass, and two personified divinities, one masculine and one feminine. Their union produces another divine couple, who in turn will have their own offspring, so that Apsu and Tiamat become the ancestors of all creatures and, in this sense, the first authors of the cosmogonic process. Greece had a similar system, which Homer has preserved. Simultaneously currents of water and anthropomorphic deities, Okeanos and Tethys couple and give birth; their descendants will include all beings who will constitute, rule, or people the universe.

Essential to the life of plants, animals, and humans alike, water can be identified with the life-bearing forces and with fecundity itself. The regenerative nature can appear in a less biological fashion. One reads in the *Śatapatha Brāhmaṇa* (11.1.6.1): "In the beginning, the waters and the ocean alone existed. The waters had a wish: 'How shall we procreate?' They made an effort. They practiced ascetic heating [*tapas*], and so it happened that a golden egg appeared." This egg contained Prajāpati. Thus not only is water filled with the desire for procreation (*kāma*), it is also capable of truly creative effort and ascetic heat (*tapas*).

When looking at the role water plays in the later phases of the creation of the world, one sees these observations confirmed. Within one and the same cosmogonic system, waters can successively assume attributes that enable one to distinguish different systems within the most ancient phases. For example, it was seen that the embryo of Prajāpati developed in the primordial waters. But then Prajāpati himself undertakes the creation of the waters. In the *Śatapatha Brāhmaṇa* (11.1.6.16–19), Paramestin, son and hypostasis of Prajāpati, wished to become all things on earth. So he became water. Similarly, Prajāpati will become breath, and Indra, the word. These notions are not contradictory; they represent different stages in creation. Whatever their amniotic qualities, the primordial waters are formless and not especially substantive, since Prajāpati still remains an embryo within them. After his birth, however, the god creates more defined and concrete waters outside of himself. In this way the text shows that the deity penetrates the waters just as he penetrates the entire universe.

Other narratives make simpler distinctions among the successive states of water. If primordial waters are an inert mass, it would be logical for them, during the course of creation, to be influenced by the actions of the gods who rule them. In the Bible, God creates a space in the midst of the original waters, dividing it into two masses, the upper and the lower waters. After creating a solid mass, he then separates that from the lower waters, thereby forming the sea and dry land.

Waters also submit to the demiurgical action in more ambiguous accounts. Here is a Fali (African) myth: One of the first animals, the tortoise, gave the world its first structure by laying out a ditch on the waters. After the first crisis, when rain threatened to submerge all things, the toad—another of the first animals—completed the structure. He separated standing water from running water and opened up a second path for the waters, cutting through the earlier ditch. Thus he divided the world into four parts.

Passive waters can also be mere instruments in the hands of those who confront each other in the course of great cosmogonic battles. In Hindu mythology, the demon Vṛtra holds back the waters and prevents them from irrigating the earth. Indra, who is waging a difficult war against him, is finally victorious and gives life to the world by releasing the waters. Mesopotamian myths are more complex. When the god Enlil decides to destroy humanity, he first holds back the rains and prevents underground waters from reaching the surface. Then, in a second attempt, he unleashes the waters, causing a flood.

Although waters thus appear to be temporarily mastered by the gods who use them, they are not completely inert. Not only do they seem to help Indra in his combat, but they are used by the gods primarily because they have a power of their own. The gods retain them because they are fertilizing; they unleash them because they are destructive.

The life-bearing and generative qualities that have been recognized in some of the primordial waters become manifest in the later phases of the cosmogony. Thus in a later stage of the Sumerian cosmogony, Enki, the Sumerian water god, impregnates Nintur, a goddess close to the earth, by scattering his seed on a riverbank; he then becomes the father of the goddess Nimu. With Nimu he begets Ninkurra, and with Ninkurra, Ottu. Similarly in Greece, whether they be the primordial pair (as in Homer) or be born of Heaven and Earth (as in Hesiod), the river Okeanos and his spouse Tethys have many offspring in the form of springs and rivers; the latter also procreate. In this manner waters contribute to the growth and enrichment of the universe. They also do so in another way: Enki fills ditches, canals, and fallow land with water, thus participating in the organization of the world.

Amma, the Dogon creator god, also has close affinities with heaven and water. His children, the snake-shaped Nommo, who are associated both with water and with the primal word, are the most active and successful agents of the cosmogonic impulse. They contribute to the birth of sexuality and permit the birth of the first ancestors. The latter, who in turn acquire the dignity of Nommo, keep close ties with water. After eating the first dead person, one of them furnishes society with the principles of its structure by vomiting up water—a prefiguration of torrents and ponds, the source of the five rivers, and of the waters of parturition.

Finally, water is sometimes tied more specifically to the birth of humanity. A trout out of water couples with a man from the underground lakes to beget the first clans of the Desána. According to some New Guinea traditions, the *dema* deities once lived under the earth, except for one of them who dug a hole in the ground. The others came out through the hole; then it filled up with water, and fish began to swim in it. After a complex sequence of events the fish became men. Finally, in Greek mythology, men often appear by coming out of a river.

One may now consider instances in which waters are portrayed as destructive. Several examples can be found in the ancient Near East. The Ugaritic Baal, god of the storm and of rain, symbolizes the forces of life. He periodically struggles against Mot, the incarnation of drought and death. He must also combat and conquer Prince Yamm, that is, the sea prince. Because of the gaps in knowledge it is difficult to locate this conflict within the mythical history of the world. So much, however, is certain: Yamm is threatening, and Baal's victory is necessary to the survival of the universe.

Things are clearer in the *Enuma elish.* Troubled by the proliferation and activity of their offspring, Apsu and Tiamat, whose mingled waters had given birth to the most ancient beings of the Babylonian myth, one day tried to destroy their descendants. Apsu, who was the first to try, was quickly conquered by Ea's magic. Ea then built his temple on the waters of Apsu, which were henceforth underground. Tiamat, who tried next, was more formidable, but was killed in the end by Marduk. By blowing into and swelling up the monstrous body of Tiamat, the young god separated the celestial waters from the earth; he opened the way to mountain rivers as he imposed his order on the entire universe. The primordial beings thus appear to want to abolish the agitation that accompanies the rise of the world in order to recover the peace they knew in the undifferentiated state of the first ages. Their inertia proves destructive. Tiamat appears as a monster in the army of monsters she has raised. The original divine waters must be conquered before the organizing gods can accomplish their work by pushing them back to the ends of the world.

WATER IN THE PRESENT WORLD. One again encounters the different qualities, functions, and powers of water when looking at the position it holds in the completed world. Waters are one of the great domains of the ordered universe. Evoking the totality of the world, an Egyptian tale lists the sky, the earth, the domain of night, the mountains, and the waters. The *Ṛgveda* refers more simply to the sky, the waters, the earth. But despite such seemingly straightforward classifications, water is not thereby reduced to its palpable appearance; it continues to occupy places that are inaccessible to us; it possesses unsuspected qualities and powers.

The cosmic waters. For many peoples waters constitute the limits of the universe. They make up a vast expanse, in the middle of which lies the earth, like an island. They may be divided into two oceans on either side of the world, or they may flow in a river that surrounds the world, like the Greek Okeanos. They also frequently occupy the lower regions of the world in a more or less complex network of waterways underground. Or again, sometimes the entire earth is believed to rest on water. Finally, water is also found in the upper regions, above the heavens. Thus water can surround the world in any of the three dimensions of space. For the Desána Indians, a region bathed in water extends under the earth; water also circulates in the filaments of the Milky Way. In Mesopotamian texts the earth is built on the waters of Apsu, while the waters of Tiamat occupy the space above the heavens.

Waters can also help to define the center of the world. According to the Fali myth already cited, this center is located at the intersection of two open trenches in the waters. A character from an Iroquois myth runs around a lake to make the earth grow; the earth then develops on all sides under his steps. The great Ugaritic god El dwells at the source of the rivers in the midst of the course of the two oceans. The Guaraní Indians call the original abode of their ancestress the "Gushing Spring." It is the true center of the earth, the true center of the land of their first last father.

Because they occupy highly significant parts of the universe, waters help to define cosmic order. The *Śatapatha Brāhmaṇa* says categorically: "The waters are the order of the world" (11.1.6.24). In particular, bodies of water often establish important boundaries. In one widespread image, a lake or river separates the land of the living from the world of the dead. Examples of such a body of water include the river one crosses to reach the Babylonian Land of No Return and the Acheron of the Greeks. Furthermore, just as one must cross the waters to enter the realm of death, one must also cross the waters to enter the land of the living; according to the Ewe people, a child crosses a river when it is born.

Not all peoples make an explicit relationship between cosmic waters and the waters nearer at hand. Several do, however. Thus rains are sometimes believed to come from the celestial waters, and rivers from waters underground, if not from the waters surrounding the earth. Some texts provide more complex images. In a Babylonian poem, springs and rivers arise from the head of Tiamat's corpse; they therefore seem to come from the waters that occupy the upper regions of the world, even if these are near the earth, at the ends of the horizon. In ancient India, the Ganges was thought to descend from the heavens.

Waters and the divine. Wherever they are found, waters are often bound up with divine powers. The Hindu world generally holds them to be goddesses. More explicitly, in other cases, it is the sea, certain rivers, and certain springs that are considered to be gods. People in Vedic India, for instance, sacrificed to rivers. The Tigris and the Euphrates appear in a list of Hittite deities. Rivers are invoked in one Homeric oath.

There is something remarkable about these water deities. They are something more than representations of a purely natural element. Thus while the Egyptian Nun is a waterway on which the boat of the Sun sails at night, he is also a personage who can speak. Similarly, the name of the Ugaritic god Yamm means the sea itself; another of his names evokes the image of a river, but he also appears with the features of a prince or judge who sends ambassadors to the divine assembly. The Greek Pontos is the salty expanse of the sea; he is also a masculine being who couples with Earth and sires offspring. In Egypt, the Nile (and its floodwaters) is honored as Hapi, an anthropomorphic god. Water is thus the manifestation of a divine power that does not exactly coincide with the tangible appearance of the liquid element. Nevertheless, its immanence within this element is such that water can be perceived as the divinity itself.

In other cases, however, waters simply serve as the abode of spirits or sacred powers. Such spirits may inhabit a lake, a river, or the waves of the sea, or like others may live in a grove, a rock, or a mountain. Several gods that exercise a more extended authority should be mentioned separately. First of all, there are lords of rain, who are in some sense believed to cause it. However, rain also depends on beings whose powers are not restricted to the control of rain. In order to obtain rain, therefore, one must invoke several gods together, or certain ancestors who have become powerful spirits. Rain is sometimes conceived of as a gift from the supreme being, or the god of rain may be made into the supreme being itself.

Several ancient Mediterranean and Near Eastern peoples had a storm god. He rides or gathers the clouds, causes thunder and lightning to strike, and makes the rain fall. This storm god occupies a preeminent position among the gods; he can reign over them, protect the cities or their kings, and extend his power over the entire universe. Less prominent in the Hindu pantheon, the storm god Parjanya is a destroyer of demons; in some texts, he seems to be in command of the whole world.

The power of the gods that reign over the waters in a more general fashion is similarly extensive. The Sumerian god Enki, who comes by sea from a faraway land, established his residence or temple on the underground waters of Apsu, whom he has subdued. Enki is the lord of the waters. After being the major organizer of the world and one of the creators of humanity, he remains the master of fate. Along with An and Enlil, he belongs to the supreme triad. The same can be said of Ea, his Akkadian counterpart. King of the abyss, god of the vast sea, lord of the terrestrial waters, Ea has his place in the celestial world, and his counsel is heeded by the gods. Thus the power of the god of water usually transcends the domain of water.

The inverse phenomenon is also found. The authority of a more universal god is exercised in privileged fashion on the aquatic world. In the Veda, for example, Varuna is a major god who rules over nature, gods, and humans; he is the guardian of *ṛta*, the religious order of things. He is often closely linked to water. With Mitra, he can cause rain; with Indra, he can declare: "It is I who have swelled the rushing waters" (*Ṛgveda* 4.42). He rests on the waters, and his golden house is built on them. The two oceans are his entrails; he is hidden in each drop of water.

The situation is more highly defined in Greece. Poseidon, the god of the sea, is not essentially an aquatic deity. His name and several myths prove that he has close affinities with the earth. Son of the ancient king Kronos, he was given sovereignty over the seas when the paternal heritage was divided up; one of his brothers got the netherworld and the other, the heavens. Thus he commands the waters and raises tempests, but he is not immanent in them. Other gods—Pontos, Nereus, and Proteus—are more intimately tied to water. But in the case of Poseidon, sovereignty originates in a region beyond the domain where it is exercised. Whatever their wealth and power, waters are not the source of a political type of power. Political power is closer to the heavens; this is why it cannot be held by a god of the storm.

The qualities and powers of water. In their varied manifestations, the water gods and the waters themselves possess in the present world qualities or traits comparable to those that have been seen in the primordial cosmogonies. The waters that extend beyond the world and delimit it may in some cases be a symbol of the void, as they once were of nothingness; but this is not certain. These faraway waters sometimes feed terrestrial waters: They must have the same density. Water's fluidity and elusiveness are, however, manifested in the faculty of metamorphosis found in certain aquatic spirits or divinities. In a Vietnamese tale, a water spirit takes the shape of a seductive boy. Hindu nymphs turn into birds, and Greek sea gods, Proteus, Nereus, and his daughter Thetis, assume several forms in succession to escape those who attempt to detain them. This ability can be transferred. In Burmese narratives, the water of a certain pond transforms the person or animal who drinks it, the former into an ape, and the latter into a human.

Water is essential for human life; it ensures human nourishment by fertilizing the land. It is more than nourishment, because it is the source of nourishment. It may, therefore, be compared not only to milk, but more particularly to the cow. Because of its utility, it is perceived as a privileged support of vital forces. The Vendas, for instance, equate water with the blood, while the Desána view the rivers as umbilical cords joining people to the amniotic waters underground. In both Hindu and African texts, it is common to speak of the waters giving life and engendering humankind.

This is why water is found associated with sexuality. The Diola sing: "Women's sexual organs are full of water . . . , if Ata Sembe sleeps with a woman, he will always get her pregnant" (Louis Vincent Thomas, *Les religions d'Afrique noire*, Paris, 1969, p. 202). In this respect, waters often assume a feminine character. The Apsarasas of India and the Greek Naiads and Nereids are young women, caught up in erotic adventures. But the waters can also be masculine. "They rest on sperm, as Varuṇa rests on the waters," says the *Bṛhadāraṇyaka Upaniṣad* 3.9.22. To the Greek poets, the heavens send rain, like seed, to the earth, in an amorous outburst. The Egyptian god of the floodwaters of the Nile—Hati, the dispenser of life—is androgynous, and the Nile is imagined as half man and half woman. Its waters are male, and its arable land is female. Together, they are father and mother. In Greece the rivers are strongly masculine, and like the gods of the storm and of rain, have the attributes of a bull.

As vital principle, water allows people to ward off illness and to keep death away. Because water makes the plants of the pharmacopoeia grow, or because of the effects of its intrinsic qualities, the Veda associates it with the origin of medicine. In particular, water is believed to be highly effective against the venom of snakes. In a more positive sense, water is said to give vigor, make old men young, and prolong life.

Water is even capable of conferring immortality. Gilgamesh finds the herb of life, which enables people to escape death, at the bottom of the waters. Several peoples speak of a "water of life" that bestows immortality. Similarly, to give her son Achilles eternal life, Thetis wants to plunge him into the waters of the Styx. The Greeks in general establish a relationship between Okeanos and ambrosia, as the Indians do between water and *soma*.

There is a more enigmatic aspect of water: It possesses wisdom and knowledge. Water seeks the truth, one reads in the Vedas. The Mesopotamian water god Ea, full of wisdom, dispenses counsel to the gods. As a sage, he protects the mythical old wise men who were born in the abyss in the form of fish. The most ancient Greek water gods engender daughters whose names denote qualities of intelligence. Among the Oceanids, these are Metis ("prudence") and Idyia ("the knowing one"); among the Nereids, Panopeia ("the all-seeing one") and Nemertes ("the veracious one"). The latter, says Hesiod, has the same quality of spirit as her father. Nereus is in fact frank, loyal, and gentle, always concerned with justice. He resembles Proteus, who knows the present, the past, and the future.

Where does this wisdom of water come from? A Guaraní narrative establishes a relationship between the freshness of water and the freshness of the soul accompanied by moderation. In a Vedic text the waves, which stave off all evils, also keep away lies. A Greek text associates the extent of knowledge with the immensity of the depths of the sea. But perhaps the wisdom of the water gods is a function of their age. In the Hellenic world, the wisest among them are called "the old men of the sea."

Waters, which at one and the same time are sages and generative forces—to the point of symbolizing at times the creative power itself—are close to the word. To the Dogon, water and the word are joined in the person of the Nommo, whose civilizing activity simultaneously links the arts of civilization with the word and with wetness; one finds similar associations among the Bambara. In *Ṛgveda* 10.125, the ritual word itself, whose efficacy is cosmic, says of itself: "My origin is in the waters, in the ocean." Water is not always beneficent, however. In the present world, water can be hostile to humans, just as it could be destructive in the remote time of myth. There are catastrophic rains and floods; people drown in rivers and seas. These are not simply accidents but the manifestation of evil powers allied with the liquid element. One example alone illustrates this: Indigenous peoples of the north of Australia have a serpent-shaped spirit that lives in the clouds during the dry season and in marshes during the rainy season. It is he who drowns humans in floods, he who swallows them up when they venture out into swamps.

The negativity of water can take other forms. For the Desána, water is a symbol of illness. In one Mesopotamian text, bad coughs are caused by Apsu. An account from Gabon goes even further: The water spirit embodies rain, cold, and death. Mesopotamia also has waters of death, just as it has waters of life.

This hostile power is sometimes incarnated in monstrous creatures. The Desána believe that a formidable centipede lives in the sea; they also talk of maleficent serpentine creatures, some of whom eat children. The descendants of Pontos, the Greek god of the sea, include several hybrid beings with destructive powers, such as the Gorgons, who dwell near the waters of Okeanos, and the Hydra, in the marsh of Lerna. One recalls that Tiamat took on the form of a monster. Such monsters survive in the beliefs of ancient Israel; they are the leviathan, Rahab, and the dragon Tannin.

In the Hebrew scriptures, the ocean itself is often represented as an adversary of Yahveh. Of course, in imposing his order on the world, Yahveh conquered the waters and subdued the monsters they harbor; he is henceforth their master. However, their menace continues; the sea monster might reawaken, and if he does, God, who watches him, will kill him.

At times beneficent and at others maleficent, close to the principles of life and to creative power but nonetheless capable of destruction, a relative of gods and monsters, water bears within it all the ambiguities of the sacred. It is an agent of purification not only because it bathes, dissolves, and carries off material filth; its cathartic power is even more mysterious. According to a Babylonian text, water banishes all evils, even those that have not yet had an impact but that have been foretold by bad omens. In a Vedic hymn, water frees humanity from the consequences of false oaths and from all the sins people have committed.

The purity conferred by water is a positive trait. Water conveys to humankind certain of its virtues. It causes vision, according to a Vedic text. In a Greek legend, Pherecydes predicts an earthquake after drinking some water from a well. When Okeanos and Tethys purify Glaucus, they render him capable of undergoing the deification process to which he is subject. Thus, waters are fully purifying to the extent that they are also, to a certain extent, sacralizing.

Several of the qualities of water just discussed are manifest in the world of the dead. For certain Zuni societies, the ancestors inhabit a village at the bottom of a lake. The members of the society believe that when they die they will go to sleep and wake up as young children in this village, at the bottom of the "whispering waters." These waters seem to be the symbol of a blissful condition where ancestral life and childhood commingle. The beliefs of the Desána go even further. A region bathed in water, Axpicon-dia, extends beneath the earth; from there came the first organizer of the world. It is a uterine domain, the source of all life, to which the people yet to be born are tied by a sort of umbilical cord. The best of the Desána will go there after death. Happy death is thus conceived as a return to the amniotic waters. Among the Polynesians, the dead inhabit a sad region, located beyond the seas; the chiefs, however, go to a different land, where the god Tane gives them a water of life that brings them back to life.

Nun, the primordial water, crosses through the Egyptian land of the dead. At night, the boat of the sun sails over its waves to the east. In some texts, the dead board this boat and make its journey with it. In other texts, they bathe in Nun, into which the sun god also dives. Assimilated to him, they come out again, regenerated. But the infernal waters are not always beneficent and life-giving. They contain reefs that the ferryman's boat must steer clear of; they contain dangers and are disquieting. The Nun was supposed to be the site of mysterious drownings.

Among the Greeks, Hades contains rivers and lakes. The names of two of these rivers reveal their nature: *Pyriphlegethon* (*Puriphlegethōn*) means "burning and flaming like fire"; *Cocytus* (*Kōkutos*) means "groan, lamentation." The rivers terminate in the abyss of Tartaros where, according to Plato, evil souls suffer a temporary punishment. Other souls, however, purify themselves on the banks of the lake Acherousias, where they pass before reincarnation. Proclus states more clearly that the souls purified in Acheron attain a better fate.

One frequently recurring idea is that the dead are thirsty. Drink refreshes them; thanks to it, they regain some form of life, as suggested by Egyptian texts. Not all waters, however, are equally beneficent to the dead. In certain Greek traditions, there are two springs in the netherworld; the initiate knows he must drink from the one that comes from the Lake of Memory. Plato mentions a Plain of Forgetfulness where the Lake of Negligence is found. One of the infernal waters thus suppresses memory while the other maintains and reaffirms it, acting like the water of wisdom and knowledge already discussed. The importance of this opposition is apparent in the privilege granted to Pythagoras and Empedocles, who were said to have been allowed to retain the memories of their previous existences. It would appear from a reading of Empedocles that this privilege belongs to the souls who will shortly escape reincarnation.

Conclusion. In conclusion, the wide range of meaning given to the image of water is not without limits, and even opposing meanings given in different myths are not incoherent. These diverse meanings are in large part suggested by the diversity of human experience of water as a natural phenomenon.

Water can be ambiguous. As a fluid, it can symbolize a pure absence or an as yet still amorphous material that will be used by the gods. It may fulfill a positive function. It bathes, dissolves, and purifies. Essential to human life and necessary for the growth of plants, it symbolizes a generative or life-giving quality, very similar to creative power. It is thus divine and sacralizing. Yet it is also capable of playing a negative role. The gods can utilize the destructive power of its waves. Active in itself, whether divine or monstrous, water erodes everything that takes form and tends to annihilate all distinctions in its own inconsistency. Finally, just as rivers and seas contribute to defining the contours of a country, so the dividing of the waters helps to define cosmic order.

The image of water therefore is not univocal. It can never be interpreted without considering the totality of the myth in which it figures. But it is not indifferent, defined only by the position it holds in the mythic system of a given society. Capable of calling forth the memory of various concrete experiences and numerous emotions, it carries specific meanings within it in a potential state. Each narrative actualizes some of these meanings.

No rule of logic requires that the meaning that water assumes in the evocation of the time of origins must remain unchanged during the course of the cosmogonic process or in the present world. On the other hand, in the small number of mythic systems that this author has studied in some depth, it has been striking that the uses of the image of water, often quite diverse, nevertheless remain coherent, owing to the theological intention that inspires the whole of a given system.

SEE ALSO Ablutions; Baptism; Flood, The; Lakes; Rain; Rivers; Spittle and Spitting; Tears.

BIBLIOGRAPHY

Bachelard, Gaston. *L'eau et les rêves.* 4th ed. Paris, 1978.

Eliade, Mircea. "Baptism, the Deluge, and Aquatic Symbolism." In his *Images and Symbols: Studies in Religious Symbolism,* pp. 151–169. New York, 1961.

Kaiser, Otto. *Die mythische Bedeutung des Meeres in Ägypten, Ugarit und Israel.* 2d ed. Berlin, 1962.

Lüders, Heinrich. *Varuṇa,* vol. 1, *Varuna und die Wasser.* Göttingen, 1951.

Ninck, Martin. *Die Bedeutung des Wassers im Kult und Leben der Alten.* Leipzig, 1921.

Nola, Alfonso di. "Acqua." In *Enciclopedia delle religioni,* vol. 1. Florence, 1970.

Raymond, Philippe. *L'eau, sa vie, et sa signification dans l'Ancien Testament.* Leiden, 1958.

Rudhardt, Jean. *Le thème de l'eau primordiale dans la mythologie grecque.* Bern, 1971.

New Sources

Capdeville, Gérard, ed. *L'eau et le feu dans les religions antiques. Actes du premier colloque international d'histoire des religions organisé par l'Ecole Doctorale Les Mondes de l'Antiquité, Paris 1995.* Paris, 2004. 22 contributions in French and one in Spanish concerning the role played by water and fire mostly in the Greek and Roman worlds but also in China, India, Iran, Israel, and ancient Gaul.

Ginouvès, René, ed. *L'eau, la santé et la maladie dans le monde grec. Actes du colloque de Paris 1992.* Athens, 1994.

Loicq, Jean. "Eaux (Culte chez les Celtes et les Gallo-Romains)." In *Dictionnaire des religions,* edited by Paul Poupard, pp. 561–566. 3rd edition, Paris, 1993.

Lurker, Manfred. "Wasser." In *Wörterbuch der Symbolik.* Stuttgart, Germany, 1983, pp. 753–754.

Masson, Denise. *L'eau, le feu, la lumière d'après la Bible, le Coran et les traditions monotheistes.* Paris, 1985.

Ries, Julien. "Eau." In *Dictionnaire des religions,* edited by Paul Poupard, pp. 559–561. 3rd edition, Paris, 1993.

Varenne, Jean. "Eaux (Dans l'hindouisme)." In *Dictionnaire des religions,* edited by Paul Poupard, pp. 566–567. 3rd edition, Paris, 1993.

Wild, R. A. *Water in the Cultic Worship of Isis and Sarapis.* Leiden, 1981.

JEAN RUDHARDT (1987)
Translated from French by Erica Meltzer
Revised Bibliography

WAWALAG

WAWALAG. The most important myth and ritual constellation in Australia's north-central Arnhem Land belongs to the Dua moiety. (Everyone and everything in this entire region belongs through patrilineal descent to one or the other of the two moieties, Dua and Yiridja.) The myth focuses on two sisters in human form who were swallowed by the Great Python, Yulunggul. The sisters are known in northeastern Arnhem Land as the Wawalag and in north-central Arnhem Land as the Wagilag. The dramatic story line, told in narrative or song form or in a combination of both, is now a popular subject of bark paintings created for sale to non-Aborigines.

SUMMARY OF THE WAWALAG STORY. The two sisters leave their home near the Roper River in Wawalag country for their long journey toward the north coast. In some versions the elder, Waimariwi, is pregnant and in some versions already has a small child (or two). The younger, Boaliri, has just reached puberty. (In one version, she is pregnant.) Along with digging sticks and long food-collecting baskets (signifying a feminine domestic role) and one or two dogs, they bring heavy baskets of stone spear blades (also of the Dua moiety) from the stone-chipping quarries in Ridarngu-language territory, home of the Yiridja moiety, a source of eligible spouses for Dua moiety Wawalag people. The sisters give names to the places along their way, as well as to all the vegetable foods and small creatures they collect. They are tired when at last, late one afternoon, they come to a quiet water hole shaded by paperbark trees and cabbage palms. They do not know it is the home of the Great Python. They collect stringybark to make a small hut, paperbark for comfortable sleeping mats, and firewood to cook their meal.

At this juncture the emotional tone of the myth changes sharply. Either shortly before the sisters arrive at the complex of named sites centering on the water hole (Mirara-minar, or Muruwul), or soon after that, the elder sister (or the younger, according to which version is followed) gives birth to a child; in some versions, one of the sisters is menstruating. Now, blood (or the smell of blood) comes close to the water hole or falls into it.

The sisters begin to worry about the possible proximity of a Snake, but since it is too late to move on, they settle down to eat their supper. However, every item of food, as they reach out their hands for it, jumps from the hot coals and makes for the water hole. Dark clouds gather, and rain begins to fall, lightly at first, then heavily, with wind, thunder, and lightning engulfing the hut in a fierce storm sent by the Great Python. During the night the sisters, in turn, dance, sing, and call out ritually in an attempt to calm the storm. In one version the younger sister performs in men's singing style, using two clapping sticks. The elder sister's efforts are more successful. They sing songs with increasingly greater sacred power: songs about the Great Python, about circumcision ritual, about blood, Kunapipi (Gunabibi) songs, secret-sacred songs. Then, thinking all is quiet, they fall asleep while the Great Python, who has emerged from his water hole, sings. Finally, he coils around the hut, puts his head inside, bites their noses, drawing blood, and swallows them—along with the stone spear blades, the baskets, the child(ren), and the dog(s). Later, when an ant bites him, he jumps and vomits them but then he swallows the sisters again.

He raises himself, with his head toward the sky, and talks with other great snakes to the east and southeast about what each of them had been eating. He mentions other food, but finally admits he has eaten the Wawalag and their stone spear blades. Lowering himself to the ground again, he sinks into his water hole with the sisters still inside him. An additional section in versions recorded by William Lloyd Warner (1937, pp. 257–259) tells how the women and children are revived. Then Yulunggul kills them again, swallows them, and takes them back along an underground watercourse to Wawalag country, where he leaves the women, who turn to stone, but keeps the boys inside him because they are of the Yiridja moiety and he is Dua. Then come the linking episodes between the myth as such and its ritual counterparts, including dreams in which the Wawalag sisters teach men the secret-sacred songs and rites that become the responsibility of men of appropriate ritual and territorial status.

Comments and Interpretations. The Wawalag myth is usually long and quite detailed, covering small as well as large events, conversations, songs (referred to by name or included within the text), names of places and foods, brief descriptions of the environmental setting, and symbolic and ritual allusions. This simplified outline constitutes merely a set of clues to the content of the myth. As far as Aboriginal people in north-central and northeastern Arnhem Land are concerned, the range of acceptable versions—and therefore of acknowledged and potential meanings—hinges on factors of sex, age, ritual status, and regional perspectives. This last includes recognition of priority of rights and priority of ownership of the myth, accorded to a cluster of clans in north-central Arnhem Land.

The most extensive published account of the myth and associated rites derives from Warner's field research in the region, conducted in the late 1920s (Warner, 1937, e.g., pp. 248–259, pp. 376–411). He notes a number of differing versions but adds that "all the fundamental features and most of the secondary ones were always present, no matter how poor the narrator." Ronald M. Berndt (1951) studied the myth from the northeastern Arnhem Land side, with special reference to the Kunapipi complex. In both accounts, the principal meaning to local people lies in the dynamic interrelationship between the myth and three major ritual complexes: the initiatory Djunggawon, the Kunapipi, and the Ngurlmag; Warner adds (p. 249) a fourth, which he calls the Marndiella (Mandiwala). But these ritual meanings themselves include social implications and ramifications that are noted or hinted at in the myth. For example, in some versions the Wawalag sisters would have circumcised their son(s) if the Great Python had not intervened.

In men's versions (Berndt, 1951; Warner, 1937), the sisters commit incest before they begin their journey northward, and it is this "wrongdoing," as well as the "polluting" of the water hole with blood, that is responsible for their being swallowed by the Snake. Women's versions, however (Berndt, 1970), do not mention incest. They imply that, if there had been incest, it would have taken place at the Snake's water hole. Warner actually mentions that "incest" had occurred, in the sense that the women and children swallowed by the Snake are called "sisters" and "sisters' children" by him (pp. 193, 253). In the subsequent conversation between the Snakes (p. 257), when the Wessel Island Snake hears the truth, he is "disgusted. 'You've eaten your own [sisters and sisters' children],' he said. This was a terrible thing." Men's versions do not dwell on this point; instead they blame the women for their earlier "sin."

In regard to the blood in the water hole, the situation is less straightforward than it seems. Men's versions, reported by men, tend to emphasize pollution, uncleanliness, or the "profaning" effect of menstrual or afterbirth blood. In many versions, and in associated discussions, the expressions used include "attraction" as well as "anger" and "repulsion," an approach that is certainly compatible with "eating" rather than with more direct killing; moreover, the terms for "eating" in these dialects can apply to sexual intercourse as well as to the ingestion of food. Attitudes toward blood are a central feature in definitions of sacredness in this region. Distinctions between men's blood and women's blood in relation to ritual and natural circumstances of bloodletting or blood emission have been associated with an arbitrary division between sacred and profane that needs much more rigorous scrutiny.

Nancy D. Munn (1969) is concerned with the general issue of the nexus of the Wawalag myth and its ritual interconnections; taking "collective symbolic forms as instruments for transforming subjective experience," says Munn, "the myth conveys body destruction images saturated with negative feeling which the rituals convert into feelings of well-being" (p. 178). She also comments specifically on the importance of blood in the combination of myth and ritual. Basing her analysis on Warner's material, Munn notes that ritual swallowing by the Snake in contemporary settings is a men-only affair. Women's biological association with menstruation, for instance, aligns them closely with the Wawalag sisters, so that mythically they have already been swallowed: To be swallowed again in a ritual context would lead to their physical death, as it did for the Wawalag. Men's ritual bloodletting is symbolically equivalent to the emission of blood by the Wawalag, but in real life the two are incompatible. In terms of seasonal renewal, Munn says, it is men's blood, drawn and applied in the course of specific rites, that revitalizes the creatures who left the Wawalag sisters' fire and that "swings the wet season back into the dry, while women's blood regenerates the cycle of food loss and death and so turns the dry season into the rainy one." (p. 198). In its nonsymbolic state women's blood is too close to natural physical reality; it must be transformed and brought under men's control in its ritual equivalent. On the other hand, Munn has already referred to "the significance of blood as a symbolic inheritance binding the two sexes as parties to an exchange: the two women gave men their blood and naming powers (or lost these powers through their death) and men, in return, memorialize the two women" (p. 184).

The theme of blood as an important but contentious issue in myth-based rites and relations between men and women, with special reference to the Wawalag myth, is also treated by Chris Knight, who suggests that "the symbolic potency of the menstrual flow was central to the establishment of culture itself." He argues (1983, pp. 42, 43) that women, because of their basic natural periodicity, have a life potency that is far stronger than that of men. And he asserts (1984, p. 154) that such myths have to do with women's ability to synchronize their menstrual cycles in a natural process used by men as a basis on which to construct their own ritual models.

Natural blood from women and ritual blood from men can be powerful in different ways—and mutually dangerous. They represent different kinds of sacredness, a possibility that Émile Durkheim began to explore in his distinction between "positive" and "negative" sacredness but did not carry through to a more comprehensive conceptualization. The Wawalag story has as its central focus a powerful mixture: blood, water, and the Snake. It is this mixture that produces the wet season, crucial for human beings and all other living things in the natural environment. The fertility of the land and all its inhabitants could not be achieved either by the Wawalag alone or by the Snake alone. It came about as a result of the conjunction between them. And it can be ensured, in local belief, only through regular ritual reenactment of the event and its mythic and symbolic interconnections.

SEE ALSO Australian Indigenous Religions, overview article; Gadjeri; Yulunggul Snake.

BIBLIOGRAPHY

Berndt, Catherine H. "Monsoon and Honey Wind." In *Échanges et Communications: Mélanges offerts à Claude Lévi-Strauss,* edited by Jean Pouillon and Pierre Maranda, vol. 2, pp. 1306–1326. The Hague, 1970. Summarizes information from several northeastern Arnhem Land women, including their versions of the Wawalag myth, and suggests differing interpretations from those of Warner, as restated by Lévi-Strauss, as well as the need to take into account closely related myth constellations in any analysis and interpretation.

Berndt, Ronald M. *Kunapipi: A Study of an Australian Aboriginal Religious Cult.* Melbourne, 1951. Mainly concerned with content, performance, and spread of this religious complex, together with participants' statements, songs, and the relevance of the Wawalag myth.

Berndt, Ronald M., and Catherine H. Berndt. *The World of the First Australians* (1964). Rev. ed., Adelaide, 1985. Includes one version of the Wawalag myth and discusses its links with other local myths and associated rituals.

Knight, Chris. "Lévi-Strauss and the Dragon: *Mythologiques* Reconsidered in the Light of an Australian Aboriginal Myth." *Man* 18 (March 1983): 21–50. An enthusiastic but in parts empirically careless discussion, which includes (p. 41) a parallel between Lévi-Strauss's contrast between the "raw" and the "cooked" and the creatures who jumped from the Wawalag's fire; Knight sees this as illustrating the sisters' ability through "the power of blood to negate or invert the cooking-process, defining meat as sacred/taboo on account of its being raw."

Layton, Robert. "Myth as Language in Aboriginal Arnhem Land." *Man* 5 (1970): 483–497. On the Wawalag, using Warner's account.

Layton, Robert, and Chris Knight. "Correspondence." *Man* 19 (March 1984): 150–157. Layton's criticism of Knight's views and Knight's response. Specifically in regard to the Wawalag, part of the argument hinged on the equivalence of snakes and women in creation myths, rather than rigid contrasts between them; on "underlying logic" as opposed to "superficial separateness"; and on alternating motifs and images in "cyclical alternation," including "menstrual cyclicity."

Lévi-Strauss, Claude. *La pensée sauvage.* Paris, 1962. Translated into English with the unfortunate title *The Savage Mind* (London, 1966). The Wawalag reference is on pages 91–94, and 96. Lévi-Strauss accepts not only Warner's account of the Wawalag myth but also his interpretation.

Munn, Nancy D. "The Effectiveness of Symbols in Murngin Rite and Myth." In *Forms of Symbolic Action,* edited by Robert F. Spencer, pp. 178–207. Seattle and London, 1969. An ingenious interpretation of the Wawalag myth in relation to its sociocultural setting: for example, sorcery narratives, mortuary rites, "symbolic space" as "time," and male initiation rites as ritual transformation in the context of social hierarchy. Munn uses diagrams to illustrate her main contentions. Her chief source of data is Warner's volume.

Warner, William Lloyd. *A Black Civilization: A Study of an Australian Tribe* (1937). New York, 1958. Includes a very detailed discussion of versions of the Wawalag myth (Wawilak, in his spelling) told to him by men and of the rituals connected with it, as well as men's interpretations of all of these. A remarkably full and sympathetic study, considering Warner's admitted difficulty in coming to terms with the local dialects (for example, he apparently did not hear initial "ng" sounds), but his treatment of the Wawalag constellation exemplifies his negative view of women's religious roles in that region.

CATHERINE H. BERNDT (1987)

WAYANG KULIT

SEE DRAMA, *ARTICLE ON* JAVANESE WAYANG

WEALTH.

The relationship between religion and wealth can be analyzed in various ways. Economists of all persuasions have stressed the negative impact of religion on wealth. Adam Smith believed that clergymen, like lawyers and buffoons, are members of an unproductive, frivolous profession. Today, many argue that religion is one of the principal causes of economic underdevelopment. For example, in places like rural Burma, more than 30 percent of the regional income is spent on monks, monasteries, and religious festivals. In India, belief in *karman* (the sum of one's actions in successive states of existence), *dharma* (duties defined by the religious caste system), and *saṃśara* (a cyclical sense of time and rebirth) has been widely criticized as a major cause of poverty. In Muslim countries, some believe that the Islamic law (*sharīʿah*), insofar as it sanctifies the religious secular customs of the past, has made modernization difficult and slow.

While the German sociologist Max Weber emphasized the negative role of the religions of the East, he also called attention to the positive impact that religions based on this-worldly asceticism have had on economic development. Weber contended that Calvinism provided the "spirit" necessary for the initial rise of capitalism in the West. His argument, which has been criticized by many as being misinformed and ethnocentric, has nevertheless inspired many attempts to find analogies of the Protestant ethnic in successful non-Western countries. Some scholars who have accepted Weber's general thesis have modified its logic. For example, R. H. Tawney, who was reluctant to talk about the causal impact of Calvinism, recognized its importance as a "tonic" in the building of capitalism. Other scholars have found fault with Weber's idea that the rise of capitalism is necessarily accompanied by a decline in religion and magic. While Weber credited sectarianism with a positive role in the rise of capitalism, Liston Pope and others have pointed out the political conservatism and economic passivity of such groups in the southern United States.

If, on the other hand, scholarship on the impact of wealth upon religion is examined, one finds this impact characterized both positively and negatively. Karl Marx and Friedrich Engels believed that Protestantism was the "most fitting form of religion" for the capitalist and that in the religions of the masses one could hear the "sigh of the oppressed creature." Along similar lines, twentieth-century scholars have drawn attention to the influence of economic deprivation on the spread of messianic and millenarian movements. Both Marxists and Weberians believe that an increase in wealth discourages a truly religious spirit. Some scholars, however, argue that a comfortable income seems to encourage piety and have drawn attention to the "de-churching" of the working classes.

Finally, there are scholars who have addressed the differences between religion and economics rather than their interrelationship. Emile Durkheim, for example, contrasted the centrifugal impact of economic life with the centripital or integrating force of religion. Historians and sociologists of a materialistic bent have tended simply to ignore the problem of religion.

CHARACTERISTIC RELATIONS BETWEEN RELIGION AND WEALTH. There is no simple way to characterize the relationship between religion and wealth in light of the determinate role played by the specific historical and social context. Religion's effect on the wealth or poverty of a country is usually achieved through, or in conjunction with, a complex of other social factors including secular institutions, modal personality systems, and values in general. Among the possible relations between religion and wealth, one that is generally overlooked is the ability, or inability, of religion to step out of the way of economic development. In such a relationship, religion plays the quiescent part of *laissez faire, laissez passer* that classical economics assigned to the state. Examples of this kind of passive collaboration with economic development can be seen in civilizations like Europe or Japan in which religious law does not absolutize or sanctify secular conditions of the past, it can also be seen when religious leaders do not interfere in the work of development; when religion abandons traditional, communitarian values; when it ignores the ethical problem of the unequal burdens imposed by development; or when its rituals and taboos passively give way before the requirements of industry. It could be argued against Weber that the most significant contributions made by Protestantism to the development of capitalism were its general indifference to the social problem of poverty, its hostility to the labor movement, and its assumption that individualism is as "natural" in economics as it is in religion.

Since the relation between religion and wealth changes from one type of society to another, one must also attend to the historical stage and specific socioreligious traditions involved. In primitive, archaic, or prehistoric societies, religion tends to be diffuse and undifferentiated from the "material" side of life. Ownership and wealth are woven into a rich tapestry of myth, ritual, and values. Taboos and religious sanctions ensuring the common good and survival of the group put limits on possessions, competition, and market functions. Primitive myths and rituals often express the importance of a proper "ecological" relationship between nature and possessions. In hunter-gatherer societies, the lord of the animals not only guarantees a good hunting season, but also protects the animals from extinction. As the technological base of society changes—from, for example, hunting to agriculture—new religious symbols begin to appear. While hunters revere the symbols of animals (often their blood and bones), seeds and plants become the foci of the magic and religion of the cultivator. Since religion and wealth were so closely related in prehistoric societies, it has been strongly debated whether the "laws" of modern economics and the alleged natural instincts of "economic man" can be directly applied to people in less developed societies.

With the advent of cities, settled agriculture, writing, and the historic religions (e.g., Hinduism, Buddhism, Confucianism, Christianity, and Islam), the relation between religion and wealth changes. To coordinate societies and economies that were increasingly complex, sacred kings appeared who had in their control not only political power, but also magical power over the well-being of crops, society, and the cosmos itself. Literate priestly classes created sacred texts and laws on the proper use and distribution of wealth. From Africa to the Far East, ancestral spirits were worshiped in order to bring wealth and prosperity to the family. Other deities appeared who had specific functions as gods of wealth and good fortune; by offering tokens of their wealth to these gods (or to priests), people hoped to receive still more wealth and good luck. This ritual exchange is expressed in the sacred Latin formula *do ut des* ("I give to you so that you will give to me") and in the Sanskrit phrase *dadami se, dehi me,* which has almost the identical meaning. In general, the traditional religions sanctioned the family ownership of wealth, not individually owned private property. In Israel and Greece, religious authority guaranteed the integrity of family property with inviolable sacred landmarks and herms (phallic representations of Hermes). In the ancient Near East, and later in the Far East and Catholic Europe, religious institutions themselves became powerful landlords, controlling trade and the use of large tracts of land.

Reflecting the structure of society, ethical relationships (whether in ancient India, China, or the first-century Roman empire) were both hierarchical and reciprocal. Louis Dumont has called this an ethic of "hierarchical complimentarity." Masters and slaves, husbands and wives, older and younger brothers, teachers and students, rulers and the ruled all had responsibilities for each other. This responsibility included the distribution of scarce resources. In Islam, for example, an alms tax (*zakāt*) was used to support the poor (as well as to spread and defend the faith).

Hinduism. Throughout the ancient world, scattered proverbs and "wisdom literature" served as the only ethical guides to economics. Because traditional society was based on a zero-sum economy, greed was roundly condemned in scripture, myth, and folklore. As time passed, more specific guidance was offered. In India, Kauṭilya's *Arthaśāstra* (c. 300 BCE to 300 CE) described an economy based on agriculture, guilds, family ownership, and a bureaucratically centralized state. Most interesting is the way that this text elevates the pursuit of wealth and power (*artha*) above traditional duty (*dharma*). Like the much earlier Code of Hammurabi in the Near East, the *Arthaśāstra* recognizes the taking of interest on loans. In contrast, the *Laws of Manu,* which took final shape during the period from about 200 BCE to 200 CE, reverses the relationship between *artha* and *dharma* and idealizes a more or less static economy based on caste duties (*varṇa dharma*). Generally insensitive to economic opportunity, the *Laws of Manu* limits moneylending to the *vaiśya* caste, allowing brahmans and the *kṣatriya* to lend money only for sacred purposes and then only "to a very sinful man at a small interest."

Buddhism. While Buddhism has often been regarded as an "otherworldly" religion, it was first propagated by merchants and depended for its existence upon the financial support of lay householders. Sacred texts specified for the laity "right livelihoods," which excluded the caravan trade, trafficking in slaves, weapons, poisons, or alcohol, and tanning, butchering, and other occupations, and directed how to make, reinvest, and share their wealth with others. Donations to the monastic community (*saṃgha*) became the layperson's primary way of building up merit. In Mahayana Buddhism, the aspirant to Buddhahood, the *bodhisattva,* was sometimes described as a rich man who provided material and spiritual sustenance for others. As was the case in the Hindu tradition, it was not wealth, but the "attachment" to wealth that was believed to be an impediment to enlightenment.

Confucianism and Daoism. In China, Confucianism and Daoism tended to favor a primitive system of "private" property that has been described as "free enterprise." This description, however, must be qualified. The Confucians were generally opposed not only to state monopolies but also to competition for profit. The development of a free labor market was delayed by the strength of the family and by the belief that each person should follow the rites, morality, and etiquette *(li)* of his family. As in medieval Catholicism, the merchant was assigned a lowly role. However, Chinese society did have some of the rudiments of a *laissez-faire* system. The Confucian historian Sima Qian (145 BCE to c. 90 BCE) claimed that government intervention in the economy would be unnecessary if farmers, merchants, and other workers fulfilled their duties. The Daoists, emphasizing frugality and voluntary simplicity, were also opposed to the direct intervention by the state. The succinct expression, "the more laws are promulgated, the more thieves and bandits there will be," is found in the *Dao de jing.*

Judaism and Islam. In Judaism and Islam, wealth was regarded as part of creation and therefore as good. Since God was the "owner" of the world, absolute property rights were impossible. Wealth was a sign of divine approval and poverty was thought to be the result of sin. The identification of wealth and righteousness, sin and poverty was disputed by only a few religious leaders, such as the prophet Amos, who spoke of the poor as "the righteous." Because property was deemed inalienable, it could not be taken from a family even by the king. The biblical custom of the Year of Jubilee (*Leviticus* 25) indicates that religious tradition established limitations on the possession of land and slave. In both Judaism and Islam, religious laws concerning usury restricted markets in money.

Christianity. The New Testament radically inverted the traditional attitude toward wealth and power. In the Magnificat (*Luke* 1:52), it is stated that with the coming of the Son of man, God has "put down the mighty from their thrones and exalted those of low degree." Some pericopes, such as *James* 5:1-4 and *Revelation* 18, express an openly hostile attitude toward the rich. Soon, however, leaders like Clement of Alexandria (c. 150–c. 213) began to soften the hard sayings of Jesus about riches to accommodate well-to-do converts. The problem with wealth now became one of "attitude," a position that was not unlike the Hindu and Buddhist problem of "attachment."

Although the early church fathers rarely addressed the issue of economic justice, they shared the antichrematistic outlook of the New Testament and often taught a Stoic indifference (*apatheia*) to the things of this world. Another Stoic idea in their writings would have important consequences for radical sectarians much later on: the notion that the earth is a "common treasury" given by God to all people. Laboring under fervent eschatological expectations, the early Christians were more concerned about the injustice experienced by the oppressed than about the philosophical definition of the justice that was their due. Poverty, as the result of pride and greed, could be alleviated only by the voluntary charity of the church. Soon bishops became administrators of elaborate welfare systems. Only a few Christians, such as Ambrose (339–397), Victricius (c. 400), and Gregory I (c. 540–604) imply that poverty is a matter of justice. When the Parousia failed to occur as expected and as the Roman empire began to collapse, the church was forced to deal more positively with a world that had not come to its expected end. As part of a strategic compromise, the church borrowed deeply from such pagan doctrines as Stoic natural law, which provided a quasi-secular theory of juridical equity. Later, in the scholastic period, the distribution of wealth was treated from a point of view that combined scripture and the writings of the church fathers with the works of Aristotle and Islamic thinkers. One result of the synthesis was a hardening of the church's position against usury.

While the Protestant reformers were generally stricter in matters of economic morality than the casuists of the late scholastic period, they were followed by others who opened the door of compromise. Usury became legal in Protestant countries, which were fast becoming the most economically advanced in Europe. Protestants repudiated indiscriminate almsgiving and took repressive measures against the indigent. It is debatable whether concern for their own election or simple indifference to poverty contributed more to the economic success of the Protestant nations. Methodists, Baptists, Pietists, and other sectarians developed an economic rigorism that was similar to the medieval Catholic doctrine of "good works." Although by the nineteenth century English Methodists and Dissenters had risen to the level of the prosperous middle class, some supported political reforms that would primarily benefit the victims of economic development. Most Dissenters and Nonconformists assumed a conservative, antilabor stand or a position of indifference. This was especially true when they themselves became the majority or the "Establishment," as in the American South.

CONTEMPORARY RELIGIOUS ATTITUDES TOWARD WEALTH. In modern times, traditional religious attitudes toward wealth and power have come under heavy criticism. This is largely due to structural changes in society's industrial base, especially the growth of competition and rapid social mobility, and to the spread of possessive individualism and hedonism in consumer-oriented economies. In communist societies, religious values have been attacked as feudalistic or bourgeois. But in capitalist countries too, modern social roles make the ethics of brotherhood and the spirit of "hierarchical complementarity" seem unrealistic. Traditional charity seems to put the poor at the mercy of the rich. Other traditional attitudes, such as the eschatological indifference of the New Testament and the otherworldly asceticism of the Middle Ages, seem incredible if not irresponsible. Considerations such as these have led to a secularization of economic values in both capitalist and socialist countries. R. H. Tawney claimed that the religious ethic has declined because the church has ceased to think, but it could be asked whether even a "thinking" religion has anything significant to say about contemporary economic problems. The Social Gospel movement of the early twentieth century had some impact on the clergy and on intellectuals but failed to make contact with the working class itself. The "liberation theology" coming out of Latin America and other developing areas has been sympathetically received by only a few in the industrialized West. Many have criticized it as Marxism disguised as Christian social concern. In Asian countries, several forms of "Buddhist socialism" have appeared. Muslims have developed various forms of "Islamic socialism" (which generally recognizes private property rights) and other kinds of "Islamic economics," often based on the welfare state and religionationalistic idealism. Such relatively recent movements in Islam have vehemently rejected Western hedonism and exploitation.

In North America, popular religious groups generally emphasize spiritual inwardness or salvation techniques, ignoring questions about economic and social justice in this world. The secularization of social and economic thought in the academic world is all but absolute. Theories that have the greatest impact in contemporary professional circles usually have the least explicit religious content. This lack of religious influence is especially poignant since religious ethics, both in the East and in the West, have sometimes been the last repositories of the common good.

SEE ALSO Almsgiving; Charity; Economics and Religion; Mendicancy; Morality and Religion; Tithes; Zakāt.

BIBLIOGRAPHY

Max Weber sets forth the major issues on wealth in *The Protestant Ethic and the Spirit of Capitalism* (1930; New York, 1958), *Ancient Judaism* (1952; New York, 1967), *The Religion of India* (1958; New York, 1967), and *The Religion of China* (1951; New York, 1968), all originally published in German between 1904 and 1920. Important modifications of Weber's ideas are found in Ernst Troeltsch's *The Social Teachings of the Christian Churches,* 2 vols. (1931; Chicago, 1981) and R. H. Tawney's *Religion and the Rise of Capitalism* (1926; Harmondsworth, 1980). Robert N. Bellah's *Tokugawa Religion* (New York, 1957) is an application of the insights of Max Weber and Talcott Parsons to Japan. *Global Economics and Religion,* edited by James Finn (New Brunswick, N.J., 1983), contains insightful essays on religion and the economies of developing nations. Jacob Viner's *The Role of Providence in the Social Order* (Princeton, 1972) contains important information about Western religious thought on economics, as does his *Religious Thought and Economic Society,* edited by Jacques Melitz and Donald Winch (Durham, N.C., 1978). Joseph J. Spengler's *Origins of Economic Thought and Justice* (Carbondale, Ill., 1980) deals with the ancient economies of Mesopotamia, India, China, and Greece.

New Sources

González, Justo. *Faith and Wealth: A History of Early Christian Ideas on the Origin, Significance, and Use of Money.* San Francisco, 1990.

Graeber, David. *Toward an Anthropology of Value: The False Coin of Our Own Dreams.* New York, 2001.

Murphy, Catherine. *Wealth in the Dead Sea Scrolls and in the Qumram Community.* Boston, 2002.

Needleman, Joseph. *Money and the Meaning of Life.* New York, 1991.

O'Toole, Patricia. *Money and Morals in America: A History.* New York, 1998.

Sizemore, Russell, and Donald Swearer. *Ethics, Wealth, and Salvation: A Study in Buddhist and Social Ethics.* Columbia, S.C., 1990.

Starobinski, Jean. *Largesse.* Translated by Jane Marie Todd. Chicago, 1997.

WINSTON DAVIS (1987)
Revised Bibliography

WEBER, MAX (1864–1920), German sociologist, was the most influential (and in many respects the most profound) of twentieth-century social scientists. Educated as a legal historian, Max Weber made original contributions to the study of modern social structure, to the analysis of the economy and the law, to the comparative analysis of civilizations, and to the methodology of the social sciences. Engaged in the politics of his place and time, he brought to his inquiries into authority and power an acute sense of reality. What gave significance and unity to his entire work, however, were his dark reflections on the problem of meaning in human culture. He was acutely aware of the conflict between what he called the metaphysical needs of the human spirit and the constraints of social existence, with the limits of human historical automony. It was in this context that his studies of religion acquired a depth and a pathos unmatched to this day.

Weber was the son of a prominent Berlin lawyer typical of the educated bourgeoisie of the German empire under Wilhelm I, immobilized between his abstract attachment to liberal values and his actual predilection for national power. His mother was a devout Lutheran given to charitable works. The view that the dualism that permeated his life and work, between a sublime sensitivity to ethics and a no less pronounced regard for the iron demands of power, came from the conflict of values in his family is no doubt too simple. The dualism, however, was there, and another aspect of it was expressed in his own marriage to the strikingly independent feminist, Marianne Weber. The politicians and scholars of late nineteenth-century Berlin were familiar figures in the household of the Weber's father. Max himself eventually became a leading, if not the leading, figure of the cultural and political elite of early twentieth-century Germany. Ernst Troeltsch was his colleague and friend at Heidelberg, and the great figure of modern German social Protestantism, Friedrich Naumann, was a close associate. The young Georg Lukàcs, the revolutionary Ernst Toller, and the poet Stefan George frequented his home. Holding chairs successively at Freiburg, Heidelberg, and Munich, Weber quickly rose to fame as both scholar and publicist. He was an editor of the most distinguished social scientific journal of the time, the *Archiv für Sozialwissenschaft und Sozialpolitik.* He did some of his own most important writing for the encyclopedic project that he planned with Joseph Schumpeter, Werner Sombart, and others, the *Grundriss der Sozialökonomik,* 14 vols. (1914–1928). His political activity included work with Naumann's Evangelischer Sozialkongress and with the "Socialists of the Chair" (a group of university professors advocating social reforms, using the Verein für Sozialpolitik as their main instrument of collective reseach). He frequently contributed articles and editorials to the press. A member of the German delegation to the Versailles peace conference (he abjured the treaty), Weber died before he could participate in the tormented politics of the Weimar republic—or the Third Reich. This bare sketch of his career suggests the complexities with which he struggled: His work is best understood as a desperate effort to effect a precarious synthesis between the contradictory ideas and warring impulses that threaten to sunder modern culture.

Weber's methodological work is often portrayed as an attempt to obtain detachment and distance from the flux and passions of history. This is perhaps true, but his methodology is inseparable from his metahistorical vision of the world. In opposition to those whom he dismissed as enthusiasts or sectarians, he espoused a politics of realism. For Weber, social science is a disciplined way to know reality, but its scientific status does not entail the promulgation of articulated general laws of the kind developed in physics. Rather, social science for him is concerned with particular historical complexes and sequences. Their unique status does not preclude, and indeed makes more necessary, empirical analysis of their origins and structure. The manifold nature of social phenomena means that the starting point of empirical analysis is a question or a problem generated by the interests and values of the social scientist and his public. Once a particular set of interests and values generates a problem, however, its elements and terms can be stated with relative objectivity. A probable sequence of causation can be reconstructed, often with the aid of an instrumental abstraction that Weber terms an "ideal type." Against this model, the complexity and nuance of reality are illuminated.

Weber, then, insists on the distinctiveness of the human and social sciences but rejects a capitulation to total subjectivism or relativizing historicism. Social science relies on understanding of human motive in social contexts; he conceives of motive as the beliefs or values underlying action rather than a system of biological drives. Weber is therefore an exponent of an empirical and systematic hermeneutics that provides the essential elements for his reconstruction of institutions in their historicity. His methodological strictures, however, cannot be understood apart from his own empirical inquiries.

These inquiries are a singular amalgam of cultural and social analyses. In them the social organization, politics, and culture of the modern Western world are depicted as results of an irreversible process of rationalization. Behavior is controlled by explicit and formal norms, the person is legally separated from the function or office, and the relationship of ends to means is subject to continuous examination and revision. Rationalization makes possible an enormous expansion of market relationships and, therewith, the explosive productivity of the capitalist economy. The separation of market from community, household, and state is the work of modern law and lawyers. Bureaucracy, with its rules, is the opposite of a hindrance to economic development; it is its precondition.

In these arguments Weber is describing, of course, many of the processes others have termed secularization. Indeed, much modern analysis of secularization leads back to his work. His unmatched portrayal of the autonomy of modern social structures and his relentless critique of oversimplified notions of social conflict contributed to that systematic reinterpretation of Marxism that is one of the more enduring achievements of twentieth-century thought. Weber insists on the relatively restricted historical focus of Marxism and argues that the modern bureaucratic state (and ideologies like nationalism) has attenuated class conflict where it has not subordinated it to other social processes. The struggle of bureaucrats against citizens, he argues, is often as important as class conflict proper. Withal, his notion of the nature of social causation is far from linear. His structural approach to the history of institutions is infused with a large component of Social Darwinism. Society is a system of meanings imparted to routine and of legitimations attached to power. It is also the locus of perpetual conflict in which groups and nations struggle for their very existence.

It was in this intellectual framework that, despite his description of himself as "religiously unmusical," he undertook those studies of religion and society that still read as if they were new. He began with the studies of Protestantism exemplified but hardly terminated in *The Protestant Ethic and the Spirit of Capitalism* (1905). It is not his intention, he writes, to oppose a one-sided idealistic interpretation of the rise of capitalism to an equally one-sided materialistic one. In fact, his work on Protestantism employs many of the sociological concepts later expanded in his studies of ancient Judaism, and of Chinese and Indian religions.

The analysis of the social identity of the bearers of Protestantism, the distinctive tasks imposed by its beliefs, and above all, the practical consequences drawn by Protestants from doctrine for the conduct of their lives, anticipates the recurrent elements of his sociology of religion. The idea of inner, worldly asceticism in *The Protestant Ethic* and of the pursuit of sanctification by ceaseless devotion to the world's work ultimately leads to the exquisitely passionate typology of paths to salvation that crowned his comparative studies.

Weber's early work on Protestantism places much emphasis on the differences between Calvinism and Lutheranism, the archetypical Protestant sects, and has much to say on Roman Catholicism as well. When Troeltsch, in his *The Social Teaching of the Christian Churches* (1912), achieved what was for the time being a definitive sociology of Christianity, Weber sought more distant horizons. He began to study the "universal historical relationship of religion and society." He dealt with prophets and priests in ancient Judaism, with the alternation and fusion of world rejection and world affirmation in Buddhism and Hinduism, with Mandarin rationality and Daoist pantheism in China, and with much else as well. He contrasted the religions of virtuosi with those of popular strata and explored the world religions' very different consequences for communal life, economic system, and political structure. He examined their origins in the psychological response to social conflict, considered their compromises with social constraints, and showed how religions generated entire systems of belief and value, indeed, how they gave institutional structure and cultural content to civilizations.

Weber's studies of the world religions, like his work on Protestantism, reflect his spiritual critique of modern culture. The world religions were theodicies, and in general attempted to answer the implacable questions of human existence. They sometimes affirmed their worlds, sometimes rejected them, and invariably formed them. Some believers thought of themselves as active instruments of the supernatural and others as passive vessels of divinity. All struggled against accident and appearance and sought the essence of things. Religions invariably conflicted with the concrete structures of existence, with family and the state, with economic forces, and with the immediate demands of sexuality. The "disenchantment of the world" effected by Calvinism also banished from the world the metaphysical pathos of religion. Contemporary bureaucratic and capitalist society is calculable and efficient. It is also without poetry and speaks only banal prose. Religious revivals, because inauthentic, are bound to fail. The substitute religions of aesthetics and sexuality in the modern world cannot perform the moral functions of the historical religions. In any event, they are baubles for the intelligentsia, not doctrines that can move nations. The West's course of cultural and social development is indeed unique, but it is impossible not to be skeptical about its ultimate value. Contemplation of the world religions can teach one stoicism about his or her own fate and admiration for the deep spirituality of other civilizations. The refusal of artificial spirituality and of nostalgia is the necessary corollary of the political attitude that Weber so favors. His ethic of responsibility is a piece of residual Protestantism, a determination to do the work of the world even when that world is brutal, corrupt, or merely profane.

Weber's influence on modern thought is ecumenical and large; it is also contradictory. Thinkers as different as Raymond Aron, Georg Lukàcs, Karl Mannheim, and Carl Schmitt have fashioned or refashioned his ideas to suit their purposes. His comparative and historical work influenced the *Annales* school in France well before World War II. The initial introduction of Weber's thought into the United States was the work of the reflective political economist G. A. Frank Knight. The European émigrés of the 1930s not only brought Weber with them, but they also brought the world of thought (and politics) that rendered his work significant. Talcott Parson's reading of Weber was, by contrast, narrow and even tendentious. Among the American social scientists who have both grasped and extended Weber's legacy are Robert N. Bellah, Reinhard Bendix, Clifford Geertz, Alvin Gouldner, and C. Wright Mills. Not surprisingly, American Protestant theologians such as H. Richard Niebuhr and Reinhold Niebuhr and historians such as Perry Miller have recognized the implications of Weber's oeuvre for their evaluation of the fate of the churches in the New World. They (with, to be sure, many of their Continental counterparts) have developed Weber's ideas for purposes true to one of Weber's main intentions: the self-critique of Protestantism.

BIBLIOGRAPHY

A new edition of Max Weber's complete works began publication in Tübingen in 1984 under the general title *Gesamtausgabe.* Of the following lists, the first consists of English translations of those works by Weber most relevant to the study of religion; the second provides an extremely abbreviated selection of secondary works on Weber in English.

Works by Weber

The Religion of China. Edited and translated by Hans H. Gerth. Glencoe, Ill., 1951.

Ancient Judaism. Edited and translated by Hans H. Gerth and Don Martindale. Glencoe, Ill., 1952.

The Religion of India. Edited and translated by Hans H. Gerth and Don Martindale. Glencoe, Ill., 1958.

The Protestant Ethic and the Spirit of Capitalism. Translated by Talcott Parsons. New York, 1958.

The Sociology of Religion. Translated by Ephraim Fischoff. Boston, 1963.

Economy and Society. Edited by Guenther Roth and Claus Wittich; translated by Ephraim Fischoff et al. Berkeley, 1978.

Critical Studies

Antoni, Carlo. *From History to Sociology.* Detroit, 1959.

Aron, Raymond. *Main Currents in Sociological Thought,* vol. 2. Garden City, N. Y., 1970.

Baumgarten, Eduard, ed. *Max Weber: Werk und Person.* Tübingen, 1964.

Bendix, Reinhard. *Max Weber: An Intellectual Portrait.* Garden City, N. Y., 1960.

Bendix, Reinhard, and Guenther Roth. *Scholarship and Partisanship.* Berkeley, Calif., 1971.

Fleischmann, Eugène. "De Weber à Nietzsche," *Archives européennes de sociologie* 5 (1964): 190–238.

Freund, Julien. *The Sociology of Max Weber.* New York, 1968.

Jaspers, Karl. *Max Weber.* 2d ed. Bremen, 1946.

Käsler, Dirk. *Einführung in das Studium Max Webers.* Munich, 1979.

Löwith, Karl. "Max Weber und Karl Marx." *Archiv für Sozialwissenschaft* 67 (1932): 53–99.

Mitzman, Arthur. *The Iron Cage: An Historical Interpretation of Max Weber.* New York, 1969.

Parsons, Talcott. *The Structure of Social Action.* 2d ed. New York, 1966.

Stammer, Otto, ed. *Max Weber and Sociology Today.* New York, 1971.

Schluchter, Wolfgang. *The Rise of Western Rationalism.* Berkeley, Calif., 1981.

Weber, Marianne. *Max Weber: A Biography.* New York, 1975.

Wrong, Dennis, ed. *Max Weber.* Englewood Cliffs, N. J., 1970.

New Sources

Berlinerblau, Jacques. "Max Weber's Useful Ambiguities and the Problem of Defining 'Popular Religion.'" *Journal of the American Academy of Religion* 69/3 (2001): 605–626.

Brubaker, Rogers. *The Limits of Rationality and an Essay on the Social Moral Thought of Max Weber.* St. Leonards, Australia, 1984.

Buss, Andrea. "The Concept of Adequate Causation and Max Weber's Comparative Sociology of Religion." *British Journal of Sociology* 50/2 (1999): 317–329.

Kasler, Dirk. *Max Weber: An Introduction to His Life and Work.* Translated by Phillipa Hurd. Chicago, 1988.

Weber, Max. *The Protestant Ethic and Spirit of Capitalism.* Los Angeles, 1995.

NORMAN BIRNBAUM (1987)
Revised Bibliography

WEBS AND NETS. In general symbology, the act of weaving is usually understood to represent processes of creation and growth. Cognate symbols such as net, web, rope, fabric, and the like are frequently employed to suggest the unfolding of individual human lives and of the universe as a whole. These symbols bear also negative connotations as instruments of binding or tools of entrapment. Included in the symbolism of the net, for instance, are those negative forces that interact with positive ones to make of life the ambiguous reality that it is, a condition composed of pleasure and pain, health and disease, life and death, and so on.

In ancient Greece, the net of life and death is said to have been fashioned by the Moirai, personifications of the abstract concept *moira* ("fate, destiny"). These three stern, grim-faced women spin the web of destiny for each person at the time of his or her birth. In Homer, it is the gods who do the spinning (*Iliad* 24.525f.). Sometimes this is done by Zeus (*Odyssey* 4.207f.), but *moira* itself may also be the agent (*Iliad* 24.209f.). Odysseus declares to his blind psychopomp, Tiresias, "My life runs on as the gods have spun it" (*Odyssey* 11.104). In Plato (*Symposium* 196b), the art of weaving as practiced by the goddess Athena is attributed to Eros, the god of love.

Images of the crafts of weaving, plaiting, and interlacing strands to form nets, webs, sieves, and fabrics appear frequently in the literature of ancient Hinduism. In one creation hymn of the *Ṛgveda,* the cosmogonic agent is described as "stretching the warp and drawing the woof. . . . spreading [the fabric of heaven] upon the dome of the sky" (*Ṛgveda* 10.90.15). Elsewhere in this source (1.164.5), the "concealed footprints of the gods" seem to be thought of as an analogue for the sacrificial laws that are "woven" whenever the gods, in their function as divine priests, perform the sacrifice by the weaving of words.

In the *Mahābhārata, kāla* ("time, destiny") is represented as a cosmic weaver who composes the fabric of life for each individual and for the entire universe by intertwining the white threads of light, life, and well-being with the black threads of darkness, death, and sorrow.

Echoing earlier images such as *indrajāla* ("Indra's net") and *brahmājāla* ("Brahmā's net"), Vedānta texts sometimes compare the ultimate basis of the universe to a cosmic spider that in the beginning spins forth the multitudinous lineaments that form the fabric of the world and at the end withdraws those same threads back into its body.

Indian Buddhism makes similar use of these symbols, as an epithet of the *bodhisattva* Mañjuśrī—Māyājāla ("net of illusion")—and the title of a canonical text, the *Sandhinirmocana* (Untying the knots), attest. Echoing the term *bhavajala* ("net of existence") contained in the *Mañjuśrīnāmasaṃgīti,* Śāntideva, a Mahāyāna poet-philosopher of the seventh century CE, employs the image of a fisher's net to describe the desperate plight of living beings: "chased by fishers, the emotional defilements, into the net of birth . . ." ("klesavagurikaghra-tah pravisto janmavaguram"; *Bodhicaryāvatāra* 7.4).

In defining the essential elements of the process of enlightenment, the *Mahāyānasūtrālaṅkāra* (9.35) likens the realization of voidness (*śūnyatā*) and the cultivation of skillful means (*upāya-kauśalya*) to the warp and woof, respectively, of a fabric: "Just as the particulars of its knotting [*paṃśu*] determine whether a cloth [*vastra*] is colorful or not, so the liberating gnosis is determined as colorful [i. e., endowed with positive qualities] or colorless by the power of motivation."

SEE ALSO Binding; Fate; Knots.

BIBLIOGRAPHY

Eliade, Mircea. "The 'God Who Binds' and the Symbolism of Knots." In his *Images and Symbols.* New York, 1961.

Greene, William C. *Moira, Fate, Good and Evil in Greek Thought.* Cambridge, Mass., 1944.

Reynolds, Frank E., and Earle H. Waugh, eds. *Religious Encounters with Death.* University Park, Pa., 1977.

J. BRUCE LONG (1987)

WEIL, SIMONE (1909–1943), essayist and religious mystic. Born in Paris of secularized Jewish parents, Simone Weil was part of a family whose outstanding trait was intellectual precocity. As a student at France's École Normale, a school noted for its lofty intellectualism and academic rigor, she scored highest on a nationwide entrance examination and in 1931 graduated with the highest rank. The most remarkable quality of this woman, beyond her surpassing intellectual brilliance, was her disposition to extend herself physically in following her sympathies. She also suffered from excruciating headaches, which added to the frailty and exhaustion that came from nervous disability and undernourishment.

From 1931 to 1934, Weil taught school in several French towns and engaged in political activity in behalf of unemployed and striking workers. This political activity, together with her eccentricities of dress and manner, did not make for a successful teaching career. Weil's growing concern with Marxism led her to take a job in a Paris factory, which she stayed with only four months. In 1936 she went to Spain to join Loyalist frontline troops as a battalion cook, but colossal ineptitude for this work, plus a growing conviction that neither side wore the mantle of righteousness, led to her withdrawal from this venture as well.

Beginning in 1937, after several mystical experiences, she became a Christian, relating that in one of these experiences "Christ himself came down and he took me." After this experience her writing was largely concerned with religion. Weil did not write any books. What we know about her thought comes from her letters, journal, and essays, which may account for the lack of a coherent and developed statement of her religious views. The closest she came to a formal religious affirmation was to the Roman Catholic church but, curiously, she refused its baptism, partly on the grounds that Christianity claimed the Old Testament as the foundation of its truth. She rejected this because she felt that the Old Testament contained too much of war and was too tribal to sustain the Catholic claim to universality.

As a thinker in religion Weil is especially significant for her insights into the effect of mass material culture on the human spirit, especially in terms of the vitiating of freedom and the fragmenting of the idea of community. She died in England during World War II from what is now presumed to have been anorexia nervosa.

BIBLIOGRAPHY

The best statement of sources on Weil is "Simone Weil's Bibliography: Some Reflections on Publishing and Criticism" by George Abbott White in his *Simone Weil: Interpretations of a Life* (Amherst, Mass., 1981). See also John Hellman's *Simone Weil* (Atlantic Highlands, N.J., 1982).

WILLIAM D. MILLER (1987)

WELLHAUSEN, JULIUS (1844–1918), was a German Orientalist of signal importance for the study of the history of ancient Israel and early Islam. Wellhausen began his career as professor of Old Testament at the University of Greifswald (1872–1882) and continued as Semitist at the universities of Halle (an der Saale, 1882–1885), Marburg (1885–1892), and Göttingen (1892–1913). He received his early training from Heinrich Ewald (1803–1875) in Göttingen. Wellhausen represents a high point in the literary-critical method in Protestant historical theology: For Wellhausen the critical analysis of literary tradition according to motives and sources, whether in the Old and New Testaments or early Islam, constituted the basis for any historical research. He was critical of the Religionsgeschichtliche Schule (e.g., the work of Hermann Gunkel) that was in the early stages of development at this time.

Wellhausen's work began with his Old Testament studies. With his works "Die Composition des Hexateuchs" (in *Jahrbücher für deutsche Theologie,* 1876–1877; published as a book in 1885) and *Geschichte Israels* (vol. 1, 1878; 2d ed. published as *Prolegomena zur Geschichte Israels,* 1883), he provided the final breakthrough in the Pentateuch criticism that had been initiated by Edvard Reuss, Karl Heinrich Graf, Abraham Kuenen, and Wilhelm Vatke. With this advance in research Wellhausen also created the basis for a modern view of the history of ancient Israel, which he himself then presented in his work *Israelitische und jüdische Geschichte* (1894). Wellhausen was the first to make use of the insight that the "law" (*torah*) as it dominates the Pentateuch as it is known, does not represent the earliest constituent of this collection but rather the final (postexilic) stage of its composition. He recognized, too, that the remaining historical sources (Yahvist, Elohist, and Deuteronomic sources) are older than this, the so-called Priestly source. For Wellhausen, Judaism is a new stage in the history of Israel and is to be distinguished from ancient Israel. For this reason Wellhausen also carried through the notion of historical development to its logical end.

In order to better understand ancient, pre-exilic Israel he applied himself increasingly to the study of Old Arabian and early Islamic history. Employing here a method that was characterized by a critical analysis of the sources, he gave impetus to the study both of pre-Islamic religious history (*Reste arabischen Heidentums,* 1887) and of the life of Muḥammad (*Muhammad in Medina,* 1882; *Medina vor dem Islam,* 1889), and early Islamic history (*Prolegomena zur ältesten Geschichte des Islams,* 1889; *Die religiös-politischen Oppositionsparteien im alten Islam,* 1901). The consequences of these works are still felt today. His most significant achievement, *Das arabische Reich und sein Sturz* (1902), provides the crowning finish to his work.

Following this, Wellhausen devoted himself primarily to study of the New Testament. His explanations and translations of the Gospels and the histories of the apostles brought him less acclaim than his earlier works, but these, too, still belong in the inventory of indispensable historical-critical research. Wellhausen's works are outstanding not only for their masterful command of the source materials but also for an excellent and impressive style that is particularly conspicuous in his translations.

SEE ALSO Religionsgeschichtliche Schule.

BIBLIOGRAPHY

A bibliography of Wellhausen's publications can be found in *Beihefte zur Zeitschrift für die Alttestamentliche Wissenschaft* 27 (1914): 351–368. This bibliography leaves out Wellhausen's article, "Über den bisherigen Gang und gegenwärtigen Stand der Keilentzifferung," *Rheinisches Museum für Philologie* 31 (1876): 153–175. A collection of important essays by Wellhausen was published in *Skizzen und Vorarbeiten,* 6 vols. (Berlin, 1884–1899).

Publications on Wellhausen and his thought include Friedemann Boschwitz's *Julius Wellhausen: Motive und Mass-Stäbe seiner Geschichtsschreibung* (1938; reprint, Darmstadt, 1968); Horst Hoffmann's *Julius Wellhausen: Die Frage des absoluten Massstabes seiner Geschichtsschreibung* (Marburg, 1967); William A. Irwin's article, "The Significance of Julius Wellhausen," *Journal of Bible and Religion* 12 (1944): 160–173; a special issue of *Semeia* entitled "Julius Wellhausen and his Prolegomena to the History of Israel," edited by Douglas A. Knight, *Semeia* 25 (1983); and my *Wellhausen als Arabist* (Berlin, 1983).

New Sources

Lothar Perlitt's *Vatke und Wellhausen. Geschichtsphilosophische Voraussetzungenn und historiographische Motive für die Darstellung der Religion und Geschichte Israels durch Wilhelm Vatke und Julius Wellhausen* (Berlin, 1965); Helmut Weidmann's *Die Patriarchen und ihre Religion im Licht der Forschung seit Julius Wellhausen* (Göttingen, 1968); and Kurt Rudolph's *Wellhausen als Arabist* (Berlin, Germany, 1983). Ernest Nicholson, *The Pentateuch in the Twentieth Century: The Legacy of Julius Wellhausen* (Oxford, 1998), argues that Wellhausen's work remains the securest basis for understanding the Pentateuch. See also Hans Georg Kippenberg, *Die Entdeckung der Religionsgeschichte* (Munich, 1997), pp. 100–103 (stressing the revolutionary consequences of Wellhausen's Bible criticism).

Betz, Hans Dieter. "Wellhausen's dictum Jesus was not a Christian, but a Jew in light of present scholarship." *STh* 45 (1991): 83–110.

Smend, Rudolf. "Der Alttestamentler Julius Wellhausen und Wilamowitz." In *Wilamowitz in Greifswald. Akten der Tagung zum 150. Geburtstag Ulrich von Wilamowitz-Moellendorffs in Greifswald, 19.–22. Dezember 1998,* edited by William M. Calder et al., pp. 197–215. Hildesheim, 2000.

KURT RUDOLPH (1987)
Translated from German by Matthew J. O'Connell
Revised Bibliography

WENSINCK, A. J. (1882–1939), was a Dutch Semiticist, historian of Syriac mystical theology, and Islamicist. Arent Jan Wensinck, born in Aarlanderveen, the Netherlands, began his scholarly career with a year's study of theology in Utrecht. He then changed to Semitic studies, including Arabic, working first in Utrecht under M. T. Houtsma (1850–1943) and then in Leiden under M. J. de Goeje (1835–1909) and Christiaan Snouck Hurgronje (1857–1936). He obtained his doctorate at the University of Leiden in 1908 and subsequently became privatdocent for Syriac and Aramaic at the University of Utrecht. In 1908 he became secretary of *The Encyclopaedia of Islam.* From 1912 until 1927 Wensinck was professor of Hebrew, Aramaic, and Syriac at the University of Leiden, and in 1927 he succeeded Snouck Hurgronje as professor of Arabic and Islam at the same university, at which post he remained until his death.

Wensinck is best known as an Islamicist. He studied Muḥammad's life; he was familiar with the immense *ḥadīth* literature; and he wrote a masterly study on the development of Islamic creeds (*ʿaqīdah*s) and their theological background. Against the same background he described the rise of a distinct Islamic culture during the first centuries of Islam, paying much attention to the development of liturgy and ritual. Wensinck also contributed significantly to the accumulated the knowledge of Syrian mystical theology, after this field was opened by the works of Paul Bedjan and others.

Wensinck's major importance, however, seems to lie in his combination of various specializations within the historical study of religions. He was able not only to establish historical affiliations but also to reveal patterns within the Semitic religious world, patterns common to Israelite, Christian, and Islamic religious data. He explored areas as varied as cosmology, ritual behavior, ethics, mysticism, and folk religion, writing on such varied topics as New Year celebrations, the veneration of martyrs, and the notion of intention in law. Focusing on data relating to devotional and mystical life and thought, Wensinck showed the historical relationship between Muslim and Syriac Christian mysticism: Just as Isaac of Nineveh influenced Muslim mystics, Abū Ḥāmid al-Ghazālī influenced Bar Hebraeus in a later period. Wensinck contributed much to the understanding of al-Ghazālī as a mystic.

At the end of his life Wensinck provided an incentive to study the Aramaic background of the New Testament, which has proved to be a fruitful field of research. Thanks to his sharp, refined mind Wensinck was particularly suited for research in the field of religion, where he let the texts speak for themselves.

BIBLIOGRAPHY

After his dissertation, *Mohammed en de Joden te Medina* (Leiden, 1908), Wensinck published two major studies on Syriac Christian mysticism: *Bar Hebraeus's Book of the Dove* (Leiden, 1919) and *Mystic Treatises by Isaac of Niniveh* (Amsterdam, 1923). There followed three important books in the field of Islamic studies. *A Handbook of Early Muhammadan Tradition, Alphabetically Arranged* (1927; reprint, Leiden, 1971) gives a broad classification in English of Islamic traditions *(ḥadīths)* according to themes. In 1932 he published the excellent study *The Muslim Creed: Its Genesis and Historical Development* (reprint, New York, 1965). His *La pensée de Ghazzali* was published posthumously (Paris, 1940).

Wensinck was an editor of both *The Encyclopaedia of Islam,* 4 vols. with supplement (Leiden, 1913–1934), and the *Handwörterbuch des Islam* (Leiden, 1941); he contributed numerous articles to each. In 1916 Wensinck had initiated another international project, the *Concordance et indices de la tradition musulmane,* 6 vols. (Leiden, 1936–1971), and he remained the supervisor of it until the end of his life. *Semietische studiën uit de nalatenschap van Prof. Dr. A. J. Wensinck, 7 Augustus 1882–19 September 1939* (Leiden, 1941) contains a number of Wensinck's papers in English and French, as well as a bibliography of Wensinck's published work. For a study, in Dutch, of Wensinck's work, see W. C. van Unnik's essay "Professor A. J. Wensinck en de studie van de Oosterse Mystiek," in his *Woorden gaan leven, 1910–1978* (Kampen, 1979), pp. 238–263.

JACQUES WAARDENBURG (1987)

WESLEY BROTHERS. John Wesley, English clergyman (1703–1791), attempted to revive the spiritual life of the Church of England but instead founded Methodism, a worldwide family of independent churches. His father, Samuel (1662–1735), and his mother, Susanna Annesley (1669–

1742), changed their allegiance to the Church of England quite independently of each other before their marriage in 1688. John was probably their fifteenth child, and his brother Charles (1708–1788) the eighteenth. John was educated at the Charterhouse School, London, going on to Christ Church, Oxford; Charles attended Westminster School, and also went on to Christ Church, as had their elder brother Samuel (1691–1739), an ordained clergyman, a schoolmaster at Westminster and Tiverton, and a competent minor poet.

John Wesley's preparations for ordination in 1725 led to a deepened spiritual awareness. He was elected fellow of Lincoln College, Oxford, in 1726, served two years as his father's curate at Epworth and Wroot in Lincolnshire, and returned to Oxford in 1729 to resume his tutorial duties. He also took over the leadership of a religious study group organized by Charles. Similar groups soon arose. They were collectively known as "The Holy Club" and "Methodists," because of the methodical way in which they immersed themselves in the devotional classics and attempted to recreate the life of the apostolic church. In 1735 his sense of a mission to Oxford caused Wesley to refuse nomination at Epworth as his dying father's successor, but later that year he agreed to assume the spiritual leadership of the new colony of Georgia, recruiting as colleagues several Oxford Methodists, including his brother Charles, who was speedily ordained for the task.

John Wesley returned from Georgia after two frustrating years, realizing that his ministry lacked the spark of the personal assurance of salvation which he had witnessed among the Moravians there. Spurred on by another Moravian, Peter Böhler (1712–1775), who was in England on his way to America, he prayed for and received this spiritual certainty on May 24, 1738: "I felt my heart strangely warmed. I felt I did trust in Christ, Christ alone, for salvation; and an assurance was given me that he had taken away *my* sins, even *mine,* and saved *me* from the law of sin and death."

After a three-month pilgrimage to the Moravian headquarters in Germany, Wesley persuaded many of the old religious societies in London to adopt his modification of the Moravian "choirs" to form cells known as "bands" for intensive spiritual sharing among five or six persons of the same sex and marital status. This fostered his own eager attempts to bring others to a personal experience of Christ as Savior and Lord—which offended more formal church people as "enthusiasm." He also formed new societies from those who asked for his spiritual direction. He enriched his followers' faith and worship with song, and with his brother Charles published a new volume of hymns and sacred poems every year from 1737 to 1742.

Pulpits were repeatedly closed to Wesley because he preached on salvation by faith. Encouraged by his former pupil, George Whitefield (1714–1770), on April 2, 1739, in Bristol, he "proclaimed in the highways the glad tidings of salvation . . . to about three thousand people." Nor did he respect parish boundaries, writing, "I look upon all the world as my parish." His "field-preaching" was supported by a wide-ranging preaching itinerancy, spreading from London to Oxford and Bristol, and thence in 1739 to Wales, in 1742 to Newcastle, in 1743 to Cornwall, in 1747 to Ireland, and in 1751 to Scotland.

To aid him in his task Wesley strove to enlist other clergy in a similar preaching itinerancy, or at least to convince them to maintain deeply spiritual ministries in their own parishes. it soon became clear that his ordained colleagues were too few for the proliferating societies, and Wesley turned to laymen as preaching helpers, thereby scandalizing many otherwise sympathetic clergy. In 1744 he invited the handful of cooperating clergy to meet with him in London to confer about the whole work and its lay helpers, the first of the annual conferences which in 1784 he incorporated as the governing body for Methodism after his death. The early conferences defined Methodist teaching on sin and salvation, teaching which he embodied especially in his *Sermons.* The *Sermons* formed a major part of his huge publishing enterprise, begun at Oxford, which undergirded Methodist private devotions, public worship, evangelistic mission, and the organization of the network of society and preachers.

From the outset Wesley's purpose had been to revive his beloved church from within. However, he was not content to go through normal channels—so frustratingly slow—but maintained an unshaken determination to follow what he believed to be providential guidance in experimentation. Thus he began field-preaching, the employment of lay preachers, the development of his own "connexion" of societies not answerable to church authorities, the building of his own "preaching-houses," the constitution of his own administrative annual assembly, legally incorporated in 1784, the ordination of his own preachers in that same year, as well as his publication of a revised *Book of Common Prayer.* All these things, together with his eventual readiness to open his own buildings during normal times of worship in the established church, proved that although he protested to his dying day that he was a loyal member and minister of the Church of England, his loyalty was certainly not to the church's outward form as it was familiar to him, but to what he considered its essence. Yet there seems little doubt that his remarkable ministry of sixty-five years brought about not only the formation of a new denomination but also the desired reformation of his native church.

SEE ALSO Methodist Churches.

BIBLIOGRAPHY

Works by John Wesley

Under my editorial supervision, a new edition of *The Works of John Wesley* (Oxford, 1975–1983; Nashville, 1984–) is in progress. Thirty-five volumes are projected, of which volumes 1, 2, 7, 11, 25, and 26 have so far appeared. The most useful selection of Wesley's theological writings currently available is to be found in *John Wesley,* edited by Albert C. Outler (New York, 1964).

Works about John Wesley

No one has yet succeeded in presenting a full and fair portrayal of John Wesley in one volume, even a large one, although biographies by both Colwyn E. Vulliamy and Vivian H. H. Green can be recommended. Vulliamy's *John Wesley* (London, 1931) will please the general reader; Green's *John Wesley* (London, 1964), a more penetrating though brief study, will suit the scholar. Both will perhaps benefit from my own book, *John Wesley and the Church of England* (Nashville, 1970), in which I trace Wesley's life against the background of his gradual and largely unacknowledged estrangement from the established church.

FRANK BAKER (1987)

WEST AFRICAN RELIGIONS. West Africa lies between 5° to 23° north latitude, 23° east longitude, and 20° west longitude. It covers about one-fifth of the territory of sub-Saharan Africa and has a population of slightly more than 120 million people, about half of the total intertropical population of Africa. West Africa contains about six hundred ethnic groups, a loose designation with no scientific specificity. Throughout West Africa one finds large cultural variety with various local features.

Traditional religions in West Africa are original systems of relations between human beings and the not ordinarily seen—but not wholly invisible—realm of the divine. There is no concept of original sin for either the individual or the group, but there is a central notion of redemption. The idea of humanity is equated with the lineage, especially with the clan, which is perceived as a social entity bearing the spiritual principle that defines the clan's originality and distinguishes it from other clans. In this context redemption is based in the individual; through the individual as intermediary, redemption extends to the level of the entire family or clan. Individuals can be seen, then, as their own redeemers; eschatology is thus a short-term operation, part secular and part religious. The role of this eschatology is to assure individuals of their reincarnation as ancestors or, still better, of their return to the earth to be among their people at some future time. Because of the diversity of West African peoples and religions, it is impossible to treat them all in a general review such as this one. Hence, in the interest of providing a panoramic view of West African religious experience, it has been necessary to emphasize some traditions and overlook others.

THE CREATOR AND CREATION. Knowledge of the supreme being does not center on a particular set of religious teachings. Rather, one might say, religious adherents achieve their knowledge of God's nature indirectly through iconic images, symbols, metaphors, and metonyms. The principal element of this knowledge is the belief in the distance of God. Compared with a human, earth creature par excellence, the supreme being is so far away in space and in emotional perception that it sometimes cannot even be given a name, much less invoked or honored in worship. The Bwa of Mali, for example, have a name for God, but no cult is directed to God. The strategy of the African thought process concerning the nature of God is evident. The distance of God generates a religious need in humans; the absence of the divine gives birth to a quest for what is absent, a quest often satisfied through intermediaries more accessible than God.

The supreme being is not uniformly remote throughout West Africa. In a number of traditions, the supreme being is directly involved in everyday life, acting instead of, or in conjunction with, the lesser spirits. In these traditions, people feel a proximity to God that is analogous to the feelings they might have for their kin, and they appeal to and consult God through cults and rituals. Such is the case with Amma, supreme being of the Dogon, whose cults exist throughout all the villages of the Bandiagara cliffs in Mali. Similiar, though less striking, examples are the cult of Rog among the Serer, that of Ata Emit among the Diola, and that of Chukwu among the Igbo. In other traditions, as among the Ashanti, for example, contact with the supreme being is even more intimate: nearly every morning elders pour libations and offer prayers to Nyame (and often Asase Yaa), thanking him for his beneficence and asking for continued prosperity. Supreme beings who are not remote are accorded a variety of characteristics; it is often believed that they control rain and fertility, are a source of appeal in times of affliction, a force for justice in the world, and the guardians of the moral order.

Intermediary spirits are often punctual divinities or gods of specific circumstances, for example, patrons of such important events as war and hunting (Ogun of the Yoruba and Edo; Ta Tao of the Ashanti; Aflim, Dade, Kumi, and Otu of the Fanti; Gua of the Ga, and others). They may also be associated with atmospheric phenomena such as rain and wind, thunder and lightning, and rainbows (So of the Ewe, Xevioso of the Fon, Ṣango of the Yoruba, and others). Finally, they may be deities of natural phenomena central to human life, such as the earth (Asase Yaa of the Ashanti, Tenga of the Mossi, Oduduwa of the Yoruba, Odua of the Gu, Ayi or Li of the Ewe, and others), the river (Faro of the Bambara, Yemọja and Ọya of the Yoruba), the sea (Xu of the Fon), and the sun (Wende of the Mossi, Olorun of the Igbo, and others).

Reference should also be made here to the masters of smallpox, which is a feared and sacralized disease in West Africa. Smallpox is incarnated in the Sakpata divinity of the Fon and Ewe, in Ojuku of the Igbo, and in Ṣọpọna of the Yoruba. The religious importance of this illness lies in its royal character. In the myths of origin of the Kouroumba royalty (Yatenga kingdom in northern Burkina Faso), the first king descended from the sky carrying smallpox and was cured by agriculturalists. Smallpox is believed to be a sickness from the heavens that brings the mark of the starry firmament to the skin. Because its cure was provided by earth dwellers, the divinity who incarnated the disease is both God of the sky and of the earth.

Unlike all the secondary divinities, the supreme being is the creator. The creator alone enjoys this prerogative, although he does not constantly become involved in the details of creation. For example, the creator assigns the task of organizing the creation to a lesser spirit, or monitor, who thus becomes the first means of contact between the supreme being and humans. This occurs among the Bambara (Faro is the monitor for Bemba), the Yoruba (Oduduwa is the monitor for Ọlọrun), the Dogon (the Nommo are the monitors for Amma), and the Bwa (Do is the monitor for Debwenu).

Questions about the relations between the supreme being and the lesser spirits have been phrased in a number of ways. Are the lesser spirits extensions of the supreme being, or emissaries? Are they children of the supreme being? Do they have independent wills, and is there antagonism between them and the supreme being? In a sense, there is no one answer; questions such as these cannot be answered according to set theological principles but vary according to the believer's level of knowledge. Noninitiates and those who have little training tend to believe that the lesser spirits are separate from the supreme being (whether they are in a collaborative or conflicting situation with the supreme being) rather than being refractions of his power. Only initiates possessing great knowledge abandon this anthropomorphic view of divine realities. For them, the separation is an artificial concern brought about by the language of theology, invented by people who are unable to speak of God without humanizing God.

Africanists have often tried to establish complete inventories of the divinities encountered in one group or another. Some, for example, have found three hundred divinities among the Ewe, while others have identified from five to six hundred. This passion for inventories and numerical estimation is praiseworthy enough, but it is of no scientific interest. What seems clear in the present state of research is that the different cultures in West Africa all possess the idea of a creator divinity in a more or less developed fashion. This creator is not worshiped with altars, prayers, and sacrifices in all parts of West Africa, which can give the mistaken impression that relations between the human and the divine are not fully articulated.

We must take great caution when we use the word God in speaking of the supreme being of Africans, to whom this word does not have the same meaning as it does, for example, to Christians. Among the two best-studied populations of West Africa, the Bambara and the Dogon, it appears that God is a being who engendered himself; the creation he produced was contained in himself in the form of symbols before it was externalized. Analogous reservations must be made concerning the terms *to create* and *creation.* We often tend to associate these with the verbs to do or to make, but while this association is often accurate in African cosmological myths, it is not always so. Among the Bambara and the Dogon, for example, creation occurs by the thought and the word of God rather than by a manual act.

THE LIVING AND THEIR ANCESTORS. Not all deceased persons are elevated to the rank of ancestor, and death is not always a requirement for becoming an ancestor. In each society it is the living who select members for the rank of ancestor. Thus the notion of ancestralization relates, above all other considerations, to a social and religious model rooted in the idea of exemplarity, that is, in a model to be imitated in order to avoid perdition. Conduct in the human realm determines whether one is ancestralized and reincarnated (a good fate) or exiled into the bush to wander alone, eaten by animals and plagued by mosquitoes (as among the Diola), or condemned to the peppery place of potsherds (as among the Yoruba)—all bad fates. It is significant to note here that a bad fate is never eternal; the concept of eternal damnation is foreign to African religious thought.

To become an ancestor, one must possess certain qualities. The first requirement is longevity; this cannot be achieved through human measures to conserve health but must be bestowed by God. Thus only the elderly can become ancestors. Also important is the individual's physical integrity and morality. Those who die from an ignominious disease (such as leprosy), the insane, those who suffer an accidental death (after a fall or by being struck by lightning), thieves, and those who have committed reprehensible acts cannot become ancestors. Finally, the person's social standing in the community is important. An outsider (a slave, for example), although accepted by, and integrated within, the society, is excluded from the ranks of the ancestors. But above all, the preeminent attribute that allows one to become an ancestor is the self-knowledge that gives a person self-control; this poise is the moral quality par excellence. All ancestors were, during their lifetime on earth, models of wisdom, self-control, dignity, and purity.

Since death does not mark the end of human existence but only its changed status, death usually constitutes the necessary condition of being an ancestor. However, this is not true in all West African societies. In a sense, to become an ancestor, an individual must achieve a certain distance from his descendants. This distance is not created solely by death: age itself can provide sufficient reason for becoming an ancestor. Thus, among the Mossi of Burkina Faso a great-great-grandfather can become an ancestor during his lifetime but only in a marginal sense. Such an ancestor can, should the occasion arise, be reborn during his lifetime in one of his descendants. This assertion is based on research among the Mossi, among it research conducted by Doris Bonnet. When an old person returns during his own lifetime in the body of a newborn, the infant is not likely to live long. These beliefs deserve more extensive study, particularly because the Mossi are not the only group in sub-Saharan Africa to hold them. Recent research reveals a similar situation among the Mongo people. The ancestor cannot, however, benefit from the worship of his family group until after his physical death, which is marked by a second funeral or by rituals performed at the burial sites (such as libations and sacrifices, both widely prevalent in sub-Saharan Africa) and modifications to the burial site itself (for example, construction of altars on top of the ancestor's tomb).

Another important characteristic of the world of the ancestors is its representation as a perfect community. Unlike the society of the living, the community of ancestors is cleansed of antagonism and tension. Ancestors can, of course, become angry or even suffer, but such feelings arise only as the result of neglect or of negative actions on the part of their living descendants.

The universe of the ancestors, sometimes seen as slow moving, is quite active. Although recollection of the ancestors fades because of the weakness of the collective memory of those on earth, the world of the ancestors is constantly renewed and kept vivid in the minds of the living through fresh deaths and reincarnations. Indeed, both worlds are enhanced by this process. For example, each death brings an ancestor into play in the world of the living; by dying or crossing the boundary caused by age, ancestors gain greater access to spiritual power and can thus assist their descendants as intermediaries. But at the same time, by gaining additional ancestors in their ranks, the ancestors acquire new cultural experiences and their world becomes enriched just as the world of the living is enriched by new births. Lastly, ties between the world of the living and that of the ancestors are further reinforced by reincarnation, or the return of the ancestor. Each ancestor can take corporeal form and return to the world when a suitable occasion arises or when he simply longs to return to earth. In a general way each society possesses rules that regulate the ancestor's method of return. These are usually very precise; among the Sara of Chad, for example, a grandfather always inhabits the body of the first grandson born after his death. Among the Yoruba, the process of return involves consultation with the supreme being. Before an ancestor is reborn, the ancestral guardian soul appears before Ọlọrun to receive a new body, a new breath, and its destiny for its new life on earth. The guardian soul kneels before the supreme being and asks for whatever destiny it wishes, but Ọlọrun will refuse to grant its desires if they are made arrogantly or selfishly. In most cases, the ancestor makes the decision concerning his or her own incarnation, while the living, with the help of various mediums or diviners, attempt to determine the ancestor's will.

The living interact with ancestors by offering them libations and sacrifices. Libations generally precede sacrifices and constitute an overture to dealings with the ancestors. The sacrifice, which is the high point of the ceremony, actively unites the living, in their quest and anticipation, with the dead, in their obligation to respond favorably. Dealings between the ancestors and the living should not be seen as one-sided attempts by weak humans to seek aid from the heavenly powers (as is the case in revelatory religions). These interactions are, in fact, bilateral obligations: humans need the ancestors because of powerlessness and his indigence; ancestors need to be remembered by humans so they can return to earth by being reborn within the bodies of children within their lineage. The relations between the living and the dead can thus be seen as a kind of individual redemption brought about by humankind's quest for immortality.

Fresh water, millet flour mixed with water, and millet beer or palm wine are usually used in the libations. Fresh water, which usually precedes and sometimes introduces the other two offerings, is an emollient; when poured on the altar it serves as a tender and affectionate gesture to the ancestor. Water and millet flour rise when they are combined, evoking the act of swallowing and its immediate involuntary result, digestion. This offering pushes the ancestor into action. Millet beer and palm wine are stimulants that excite and exalt the ancestors. In a way these drinks make the ancestors lose control and behave as the living wish them to. This last libation represents the final resort to the will of the ancestors before the noblest offering, animal sacrifice, is made.

Animal sacrifice is the most profound means of communicating with the invisible world. The most frequent sacrificial victims are white chickens (male and female) and goats. Sometimes a royal family may sacrifice horses or, as was once the case among the Mossi, human beings. Sometimes cattle are sacrificed, but this occurs only on rare occasions. As sacrificial animals, cattle are reserved for extraordinary events and people (for example, the absolution of an incestuous act, the funeral ceremonies of a chief). The rarity and great significance of these sacrifices can be explained by the fact that West Africa is largely a region of agriculturalists, not pastoralists.

Altars for the ancestors vary but most often consist of one or several stones placed on the ground. They can also be chairs (Ashanti, Ewe, Attie), pottery, clay stools, or doorposts. The officiating priests are either the eldest of the lineage (clan) or a person specifically designated by the group. There are cases, however, as among the Dogon, in which the role is filled in part by a person designated by the ancestor himself.

Places of Worship. Generally West Africans have given more attention to the altar as the locus of the divine than to the sanctuary built to shelter it. There are exceptions: in Nigeria, Benin, Ghana, and Mali, there exist religious buildings in which one part is meant for the public and the rest for protection of cultic materials. (Public here refers to the faithful who have been or will be initiated.) Usually admission to the public parts of the sanctuary is available to the faithful who have been introduced to knowledge of the mystery evoked by the place of worship. The reserved part is only accessible to the high dignitaries of the community of the specific cult. In practice this separation suggests that religion does not merely pose problems of faith and adherence to a system of beliefs; more importantly, it raises questions about knowledge and power. Religion is parceled out in as many sectors, either exclusive of one another or complementary over time, as there are different domains of knowledge.

The linkage between religion and knowledge, particularly prominent in West Africa, is not surprising. Indeed, one can say that it constitutes the characteristic trait of sub-Saharan cultures. The higher one's position becomes in the religious hierarchy, the more knowledge one possesses. The greater one's knowledge, the more likely one will be invested with religious power. All this reveals, on the one hand, the connection between sacred knowledge and power (including political power)—every sage exercises real power over the community he is part of—and, on the other hand, the ways that knowledge is distributed. For example, during initiation rites, knowledge is distributed to the adept drop by drop, as if such instillation were the only possible method of instruction. If any other pedagogic method were used, the adept would reject the knowledge, much like his body would reject the intrusion of a foreign element such as a different blood type. However, there is another reason why knowledge is parceled out bit by bit. The adept is tested at each level to see how he or she reacts to it to ensure that the power that comes with such knowledge is not misused. In many West African societies, for instance, the sacred power to cure affliction through the manipulation of spiritual powers and material substances is not far removed from the practice of sorcery. Both sorcery and the practice of healing often involve the use of similiar techniques and medicines; what distinguishes them is the practitioner's intention to do good or evil. Hence, before giving an adept religious knowledge, measures must be taken to ensure that he or she will use this power for the good of the community. An individual with sacred knowledge who is deluded by his or her own power, greed, envy, or malice can have disastrous effects upon the community.

Worship sites are numerous and varied and can be classified according to the four elements: water, earth, air, and fire. Throughout West Africa, water inspires feelings of uncertainty, fear, reassurance, and security; most importantly, it is seen as the source of life. Each body of water has its own spirit. Metonymically speaking, the body of water is both a sort of water god worshiped by riverine peoples and a temple of water in which the faithful, bearing offerings, immerse themselves. For example, the part of the Niger River that crosses Bambara country is said to be the body of Faro, the water spirit, who is responsible for the fecundity, multiplication, and proliferation of all living things. Among the Yoruba of Nigeria it is thought that Yemọja, daughter of Ọbatala and Oduduwa, gave birth to all the waters of the country and that she is the patroness of the River Ogun, her favorite sanctuary. For the Edo of Nigeria, the waters of the regions belong to Oba. In Ghana and the Ivory Coast, the rivers, streams, and still waters are the property of Tano and Bia. Fresh water, by its very nature favorable to life, is humane. Seawater is inhumane and savage; it needs to be tamed. This negative view of seawater may have been formed during the era of colonization and slavery (both the early Europeans and slave traders arrived by sea); more likely, however, it may simply stem from the profound attachment to land that is often found throughout Africa.

Sanctuaries related to the land have as much, if not more, variety as those related to water. One must remember that at least 90 percent of the West African population is composed of sedentary agriculturalists and that for them land is the true reservoir of life. Land sanctuaries share one special feature. They are not temples in the true sense of the word because the land has no edifice; the land itself is a religious and sacred monument and thus it would be unseemly to try to limit it, to pretend to enclose it within walls. The sanctuaries of the earth are everywhere that human beings carry out gestures of deference to the nourishing soil. Mountains, grottoes, rocks, and stones that strike the religious imagination, pits and crevasses open to the unknown—all lend themselves admirably to being transformed into places of worship. Cultivated fields are particularly designated for sacralization.

The temples of the air, namely sacred trees and groves, are the most numerous sites of worship and the closest to the religious affections of West Africans. They are considered to have an airy nature because they are in harmony with atmospheric changes and with the seasons. There is not a single human community in West Africa that does not have high regard for this vegetation. The tree stands as an intermediary between the human being and spiritual powers. This mediation is often so central that humans are considered to be an emanation of the vegetation. The Bambara believe in a kind of metempsychosis, or transmigration of souls, in which one guidepost in the journey is a tree. One also encounters this belief among the Fon, for whom certain myths speak of how men and women descended from the branches of a tree in former times. Similarly, West African women desirous of becoming pregnant often implore a tree to give them a child. Trees acquire even more intense religious value when nature integrates them into sacred groves, which are the scenes of religious assemblies and initiation rites.

In West Africa, where there are no volcanoes, temples connected with fire are the most humble, the closest to daily life, and also the most ubiquitous. They are associated with the part of the home in which women prepare food. The fire, which transforms food, brings light and warmth to its users and mediates between the living and the dead. If the faithful lack the resources to provide a sacrificial victim, they can use ashes from the hearth fire as a replacement. The omnipresence of this temple of fire is matched by the reality of the forge in almost all West African groups, even though the profession of blacksmithing is generally considered to be limited to members of a guild. The forge is more than a workshop; it is also a place of worship, a shelter in which human justice gives way to the gentleness of heaven. The most typical characteristic of the forge lies in the fact that it constitutes a place of creation comparable to that held by the creator when the foundations of the world were established. This explains why fire becomes a sanctuary wherein the prayer of an empty womb beseeching fecundity will, according to the beliefs of the faithful, surely be answered.

Generally speaking, religion in West Africa is men's business. Nevertheless, women, especially after menopause, often become ritual specialists (for example, among the Guere, Ubi, and Wobe of the Ivory Coast; the Dogon of Mali; the Mende of Sierra Leone; and especially, the Yoruba and Igbo of Nigeria). Religious duties, which are numerous and complex, are ordinarily the responsibility of the eldest member of the group. All cultic practices include an oral liturgical element that is of central importance because the word, invested with the characteristics of both water and heat, has fertilizing power.

INITIATION AND SPIRITUAL LIFE. Initiation rites engender an internal disposition that guarantees a way of life different from ordinary existence. This disposition is acquired through the development of spiritual techniques that train the body and promote a sense of the abolition of finitude.

Initiation rites in West Africa fall into two types. In Nigeria, Benin, Togo, and Ghana (that is, among the Yoruba, Hausa, Ewe, Fon, Ashanti, and related groups), initiation is of a type one may term *epispanic*. Here the initiates attract (Gr., *epispaō*) the divinity to themselves, and the impact of the meeting between the human and divine translates into what is commonly called possession or trance. The introduction to and training for the spiritual life are accomplished either by individual training (as, for example, among the Ashanti and the eastern Yoruba) or by collective training in convents, as is the rule among the Ewe, Fon, western Yoruba, and Itsha. This form of initiation is available to both men and women. The physical tests that neophytes undergo during their initiation have a specific goal, even though the initiates may not be aware of it. It involves a spiritualization of the senses, particularly vision, hearing, and taste.

The second type of initiation, termed *allotactic* (Gr., *allos*, other; *taktikē*, from *tassein*, to marshal), is common from Ghana to Guinea. Here the neophytes go to seek God. Clearly the physical tests here are equally rigorous as those in epispanic initiation, but what matters above all in allotactic initiation is the accession of the neophytes to a transforming knowledge that permits them to get closer to particular spiritual beings and even to become a bit like them, in other words, to become immortal, for only through immortality do human beings guarantee their chances for reincarnation. Such transforming knowledge cannot be gained in several months or even in several years. Among the Senufo of Mali and northern Ivory Coast, initiation into the Poro society lasts more than twenty years. For the Bidjogo of Guinea-Bissau initiation takes almost the same time. Men and women are segregated in this form of initiation. Allotactic initiation clearly demonstrates the leitmotiv of African spirituality, the human struggle against total disappearance from the earth.

African spirituality demonstrates that human beings are not born spiritual; rather, they must become spiritual. Hence, adherents to West African religions find recourse to initiatory techniques that view the body as the starting point of religious and mystical feelings. The body becomes the authentic symbol of the elevation of the human being to the peak of spirituality. Mystical life in African religion does not detach humanity from the earth; instead, it permits human beings to live and relive indefinitely on earth.

SEE ALSO Akan Religion; Bambara Religion; Diola Religion; Dogon Religion; Edo Religion; Fon and Ewe Religion; Fulbe Religion; Igbo Religion; Mawu-Lisa; Tiv Religion; Yoruba Religion.

BIBLIOGRAPHY

Awolalu, J. Ọmọṣade. *Yoruba Beliefs and Sacrificial Rites.* London, 1979.

Bellman, Beryl L. *Village of Curers and Assassins: On the Production of Fala Kpelle Cosmological Categories.* The Hague, 1975.

Bonnet, Doris. "Le Retour de l'Ancêtre." *Journal de la Société des Africanistes* 51 (1981): 133–147.

Field, Margaret Joyce. *Search for Security: An Ethno-Psychiatric Study of Rural Ghana.* London, 1960. A study of religion and psychology among the Akan peoples, particularly centered on Ashanti shrines and the *obosom.*

Fortes, Meyer. *Oedipus and Job in West African Religion.* Cambridge, U.K., 1983. A reprint of Fortes's classic 1959 work on Tallensi religion.

Griaule, Marcel. *Conversations with Ogotemmêli.* Translated by Robert Redfield. London, 1965. Dogon religion as interpreted by a Dogon sage.

Henderson, Richard N. *The King in Every Man: Evolutionary Trends in Onitsha Ibo Society and Culture.* New Haven, Conn., 1972.

Horton, Robin. "Destiny and the Unconscious in West Africa." *Africa* 31 (April 1961): 110–116.

Horton, Robin. "The Kalabari World-View: An Outline and Interpretation." *Africa* 32 (July 1962): 197–220.

Nadel, Siegfried Frederick. *Nupe Religion: Traditional Beliefs and the Influence of Islam in a West African Chiefdom.* London, 1954.

Parrinder, Geoffrey. *West African Religion.* 2d ed., rev. London, 1961. A classic on West African religion, focusing primarily on three groups: the Akan, the Yoruba, and the Ewe.

Pelton, Robert D. *The Trickster in West Africa: A Study of Mythic Irony and Sacred Delight.* Berkeley, Calif., 1980.

Thomas, Louis-Vincent, and René Luneau. *La terre africaine et ses religions.* Paris, 1974.

Thompson, Robert Farris. *African Art in Motion.* Los Angeles, 1974. Superb analysis of African dance and art drawn exclusively from West Africa.

Thompson, Robert Farris. *Flash of the Spirit: African and Afro-American Art and Philosophy.* New York, 1981. An excellent work dealing primarily with the movement of African thought and art into the New World, using examples from Yoruba, Ejagham, and Mande cultures.

Zahan, Dominique. *The Religion, Spirituality, and Thought of Traditional Africa.* Translated by Kate Ezra Martin and Lawrence M. Martin. Chicago, 1979.

New Sources

Brenner, Louis. "Controlling Knowledge: Religion, Power and Schooling in a West African Muslim Society." Bloomington, Ind., 2001.

Fisher, Robert B. "West African Religious Traditions: Focus on the Akan of Ghana." Maryknoll, N.Y., 1998.

Murphy, Joseph M. "Osun across the Waters: A Yoruba Goddess in Africa and the Americas." Bloomington, Ind., 2001.

Stoller, Paul. "Embodying Colonial Memories: Spirit Possession, Power, and the Hauka in West Africa." New York, 1995.

ter Haar, Gerrie, ed. "Strangers and Sojourners: Religious Communities in the Diaspora." Louvain, 1998.

DOMINIQUE ZAHAN (1987)
Translated from French by F. A. Leary-Lewis
Revised Bibliography

WEST SYRIAN CHURCH SEE SYRIAC ORTHODOX CHURCH OF ANTIOCH

WHEATLEY, PAUL (1921–1999) was a professor at the University of Chicago who specialized in comparative urbanism and historical urban geography. If ever there was a contemporary scholar outside the field of religious studies itself who made a persuasive and elegant case for relating the study of religion to comparative worldviews and complex social processes, it was Paul Wheatley. His magisterial book *The Pivot of the Four Quarters: A Preliminary Enquiry into the Origins and Character of the Ancient Chinese City* still stands as a model for comparative studies of the social and religious dimensions of traditional urban settlements. The excellence of this book can be attributed in part to Wheatley's extraordinary linguistic abilities, his insightful handling of primary texts, and his elegant application and testing of his theories on the nature of the city, social stratification, and the religious imagination. Wheatley came to this achievement through his intensive study of historical geography. He was the first British geographer to explore sources in Chinese and Arabic, which he combined with Latin and Greek texts in his early book *The Golden Khersonese: An Historical Geography of the Malay Peninsula Before AD 1500.*

EARLY CAREER. Paul Wheatley was born in 1921 in Gloucestershire, England. He spent part of his youth in the village of Enham (later also named Alamein), a community set aside for families of seriously injured veterans of World War I. During Wheatley's youthful excursions around Coatswell and Salisbury, he developed interests in two landscapes: the geography of that part of England and the celestial landscapes that he observed during nighttime travels. In his early schooling he excelled in Latin and Greek; by 1939 to 1940 he had completed his first college degree in classics (Latin and Greek, philosophy and religion) in a two-year accelerated program offered by Kings College, London. Wheatley also studied two subjects that became foundational for his later study of urbanism, namely geology and geomorphology (the study of the origin and development of the earth's surface features). In 1940 Wheatley volunteered for service in the Royal Air Force (RAF). He served as a navigator, a parachute instructor in North Africa and Italy, and a trainer for British paratroopers preparing for the invasion of France in June 1944. He saw intense combat as a member of Squadron 150 of the RAF's Bomber Command and Pathfinder Group 205, surviving a crash landing in Iraq as well as forced parachute jumps behind the German lines in Italy and later in Yugoslavia.

POSTWAR WORK. After Wheatley returned from his war service, he met Henry Clifford Darby (1909–1992), a distinguished professor of geography, and became involved in Darby's historical geography project, which made use of the 1068 Domesday Book of William I, King of England from 1066 to 1087. Wheatley's interest in local geography and place names coupled with his knowledge of Latin allowed him to assist in the reading of the medieval manuscripts that Darby was analyzing. Wheatley eventually contributed the Staffordshire chapter and coauthored the Somerset chapter in Darby's book *The Domesday Geography of England,* which was published in 1954. In 1949 Wheatley received the Alexander von Humboldt Prize and was awarded his bachelor's degree with first class honors in geography from the University of Liverpool. He then joined the faculty of University College, London, where Darby had relocated. In 1952 Wheatley left England for the University of Malaya in Singapore (now the National University of Singapore), where he first served as the "neophyte colonial lecturer" and later as lecturer in geography.

During the next seven years Wheatley traveled extensively in the Malay Peninsula, did field archaeology, expanded his linguistic abilities, taught courses at the university, and founded the *Malayan Journal of Tropical Geography.* He also made use of classical Greek, classical Malay, Arabic, and Chinese sources to prepare two works that served both as source books and as innovative interpretations of the historical geography of the region. These were *The Golden Khersonese* and *Impressions of the Malay Peninsula in Ancient Times* (Singapore, 1964). In 1957 Wheatley married Margaret E. Ashworth, a member of the geography faculty at the University of Malaya. They moved to the United States in 1958, where Wheatley served on the faculty of the University of California at Berkeley until 1966. While helping to raise his two sons, Julian and Jonathan, Wheatley became deeply interested in the problem of urban origins. He discovered an intricate set of relationships between the rise of permanent social stratification and the organizing capabilities of religious thought as manifested in monumental ceremonial centers. He began an intensive analysis of the origins of cities as indicated in Chinese sources and expanded his focus to deciphering the process of primary urban generation in Mesoamerica, Mesopotamia, the Indus Valley, Nigeria, Peru, and Egypt.

MATURE WORK. Wheatley's most influential monograph was *The Pivot of the Four Quarters: A Preliminary Enquiry* *into the Origins and Character of the Ancient Chinese City* (Chicago, 1971). In this study Wheatley sought to understand the complex forces that led to the genesis of the first cities, especially the factors associated with permanent social differentiation. In each instance of urban origins, he found that "the earliest foci of power and authority took the form of ceremonial centers, with religious symbolism imprinted deeply on their physiognomy and their operation in the hands of organized priesthoods." Priestly elites in all seven areas of primary generation (northern China, Mesopotamia, Egypt, the Indus Valley, southwestern Nigeria, central Mexico, and Peru) had developed "greatly amplified ethical systems" which were part of a "new instrument for the organization of sacred, economic, social and political space" (p. 305). Wheatley stated concisely that these ceremonial centers "functioned as instruments for the dissemination through all levels of society of beliefs which, in turn, enabled the wielders of political power to justify their goals in terms of the basic values of that society, and to present the realization of class-directed aims as the implementation of collectively desirable policies" (p. 305).

Wheatley found the key to the efficacy of these ceremonial centers in a religious mode of thought that he called "cosmo-magical symbolism." This mode of thought "presupposes an intimate parallelism between the mathematically expressible regimes of the heavens, and the biologically determined rhythms of life on earth (as manifested conjointly in the succession of the seasons and the annual cycles of plant regeneration)" (p. 414). In Wheatley's understanding, there were at least three patterns of urban order that emerged from cosmo-magical thought: the pattern of building monumental capitals around supremely important ritual structures; the use of cardinal axiality (designing the city with fixed reference lines to the four principal points of the compass) to organize large urban populations, transportation systems and even general systems of market exchange; and the imprinting of episodes from the culture's mythology in the layout and ornamentation of major buildings. Wheatley illustrated these complex interrelations with the use of maps and narratives, showing the ways in which the morphology of specific ceremonial cities influenced the formation of economic and social order as well as reflecting cosmo-magical thought.

Wheatley's position was and remains a major challenge to materialist interpretations of the causes and nature of urban organization and authority. While several of his major books resulted from intensive analysis of the geographic and economic, especially exchange patterns of and within urban centers, Wheatley insisted that the evidence showed repeatedly that rulers just as often subordinated their technology and economic practices to religious symbolism as the other way around.

From 1966 to 1971 Wheatley served on the faculty at University College, London, where he produced several definitive essays in urban studies, including "City as Symbol" (1969) and "The Concept of Urbanism" (1972). He also contributed a prefatory essay to *An Historical Atlas of China* (1966). From 1971 until his retirement in 1991, he served as professor of geography and social thought at the University of Chicago. During Wheatley's years on the Chicago faculty, he was a member of the Committee on Social Thought and its chairman from 1977 to 1991. The novelist Saul Bellow was one of the distinguished members of this committee and included a flattering literary portrait of Paul Wheatley in his novel *Ravelstein* (2000). Wheatley was remarkably productive during his Chicago years, publishing on various questions of urban origins and history in *From Court to Capital: A Tentative Interpretation of the Origins of the Japanese Urban Tradition* (1978), *Nagara and Commandery: Origins of the Southeast Asian Urban Traditions* (1983), and the monumental two-volume *Melaka: The Transformation of a Malay Capital, c. 1400–1980* (1983), which he edited with Kernial Singh Sandhu. His editorial collaboration with Sandhu continued in *Management of Success: The Moulding of Modern Singapore* (1989). Wheatley's final book, published posthumously, was *The Places Where Men Pray Together: Cities in Islamic Lands, Seventh to Tenth Centuries* (2001). During these years he also served on numerous external committees, including the Jerusalem Committee, a group that advised Mayor Teddy Kollek (b. 1911) on the future organization of the city; the Ford Foundation, on academic fellowships for Vietnamese refugees; and the regional advisory board of the *Southeast Asian Journal of Ethnicity*. In addition, Wheatley served on the editorial boards of *Urbanism and Social Change*, the *Journal of Urban History*, the *Journal of Oriental Studies*, and other scholarly periodicals.

Wheatley was highly skilled in the use of human language, and wrote elegantly and movingly in his essays and books about the topics that engaged him. After his death in 1999, a eulogy about him stated, "Wheatley was a man of ideas, of exacting standards and often of forceful expression. . . . Only the grand thesis was good enough for him. A belief in the value of a comparative world view and an inter-disciplinary approach inspired his lifelong exploration of urbanism and his conviction that the emergence of the city was a turning point in the history of human society."

See Also Chinese Religion, overview article; Cities; Geography.

Bibliography

Wheatley, Paul. *The Golden Khersonese: An Historical Geography of the Malay Peninsula Before AD 1500.* Kuala Lumpur, Malaysia, 1961.

Wheatley, Paul. "City as Symbol." Inaugural lecture delivered at University College, London, November 20, 1967. London, 1969.

Wheatley, Paul. *The Pivot of the Four Quarters: A Preliminary Enquiry into the Origins and Character of the Ancient Chinese City.* Chicago, 1971.

Wheatley, Paul. *From Court to Capital: A Tentative Interpretation of the Origins of the Japanese Urban Tradition.* Chicago, 1978.

Wheatley, Paul. *Nagara and Commandery: Origins of the Southeast Asian Urban Traditions.* Chicago, 1983.

Wheatley, Paul. *The Places Where Men Pray Together: Cities in Islamic Lands, Seventh through the Tenth Centuries.* Chicago, 2001.

Wheatley, Paul, and Kernial Singh Sandhu, eds. *Melaka: The Transformation of a Malay Capital, c. 1400–1980.* 2 vols. New York, 1983.

Wheatley, Paul, and Kernial Singh Sandhu, eds. *Management of Success: The Moulding of Modern Singapore.* Pasir Panjang, Singapore, 1989.

DAVÍD CARRASCO (2005)

WHEEL SEE CAKRAS; CIRCLE

WHITE, ELLEN GOULD (1826–1915), prophetess and cofounder of the Seventh-day Adventist church. Ellen Gould Harmon was born November 26, 1827, on a farm near Gorham, Maine. As a child she moved with her family to Portland. When she was nine or ten, an angry schoolmate hit her in the face with a rock, knocking her unconscious for several weeks. The accident left her a semi-invalid, unable to continue her schooling (except for a brief period at the Westbrook Seminary and Female College) and unlikely to fulfill her ambition of becoming a scholar.

Raised a Methodist, Ellen in 1840 joined the Millerites, who believed that Christ would return to earth in 1843 or 1844. When he failed to appear on October 22, 1844, the date finally agreed upon, disappointment and confusion swept through the Millerite camp. In December, while praying with friends for guidance, seventeen-year-old Ellen went into a trance, the first of many visions during which she claimed to receive divine illumination. In this state God assured her that the Millerites' only mistake lay in confusing the second coming of Christ with the beginning of the heavenly judgment, which had indeed begun on October 22. In 1846 Ellen was shown the importance of observing the seventh-day sabbath. In both instances her visions supported doctrines that others were already teaching, a pattern that came to characterize her role as a religious leader.

In 1846 Ellen married James White, who became her editor, publisher, and manager. For several years they traveled throughout the Northeast preaching their sabbatarian message. When children began arriving, Ellen reluctantly left them with friends. In 1852 the weary, impoverished couple settled in Rochester, New York, where they collected their children about them and James acquired a printing press. After three discouraging years, the Whites moved to Battle Creek, Michigan, where in the early 1860s they formally created the Seventh-day Adventist church, then numbering about 3,500 members.

Health concerns dominated Ellen White's life during the 1860s. Since her childhood accident she had suffered almost constantly from an array of illnesses: heart, lung, and stomach ailments, frequent "fainting fits" (sometimes once or twice a day), paralytic attacks, pressure on the brain, breathing difficulties, and bouts of anxiety and depression. At times she feared that Satan and his evil angels were trying to kill her. In 1863, only months after using water treatments to nurse her children through a diphtheria epidemic, she received a special vision on health. Adventists, she learned, were to give up eating meat and other stimulating foods, shun alcohol and tobacco, and avoid drug-dispensing doctors. When sick, they were to rely solely on nature's remedies: fresh air, sunshine, rest, exercise, proper diet, and, above all, water. A second vision on health led her in 1866 to establish the Western Health Reform Institute in Battle Creek, the first of a worldwide chain of Adventist sanitariums.

During the 1870s the Whites spent considerable time proselytizing on the West Coast. In 1881, James died. Following a yearlong depression, Ellen White resumed her ministry through missions to Europe (1885–1887) and to Australia and New Zealand (1891–1900). Upon returning to the United States in 1900, she purchased a farmhouse near Saint Helena, California, from whence she continued to guide her growing church. Although she never assumed formal leadership of the Adventist organization, White wielded enormous influence, especially late in her career, in matters relating to both doctrine and policy. While in semiretirement, she directed a major campaign to build an Adventist sanitarium "near every large city" and to open a medical school, the College of Medical Evangelists (now Loma Linda University), in southern California. She died on July 16, 1915, at age eighty-seven; over 136,000 Seventh-day Adventists mourned her passing.

Although better at speaking than writing—her modest reputation among non-Adventists derived largely from her lectures on temperance—Ellen White enjoyed her greatest success as an author. Between the late 1840s, when her first broadsides appeared, and 1915, she published over a hundred books and pamphlets and contributed thousands of articles to church periodicals. Since her death the Ellen G. White Estate has brought out dozens of additional books, compiled from her letters, sermons, and articles. Few subjects escaped her attention. Among her most notable works were three sets of books on biblical history and eschatology: *Spiritual Gifts* (1858–1864), *Spirit of Prophecy* (1870–1884), and the "Conflict of the Ages Series" (1888–1917), which included *The Great Controversy between Christ and Satan,* her major eschatological work. Her health writings began with a tract on the perils of masturbation, *An Appeal to Mothers* (1864), and culminated with the widely circulated *Ministry of Healing* (1905). In *Education* (1903), she emphasizes "the harmonious development of the physical, the mental, and the spiritual powers." Between 1855 and 1909 she published thirty-seven volumes of *Testimonies for the Church,* in which she relayed counsel that she had received in visions. The most popular of her books was *Steps to Christ* (1892), a brief devotional work that sold in the millions.

Since early in Ellen White's career critics have alleged that she sometimes contradicted herself, failed to acknowledge—and on occasion denied—her indebtedness to other authors, and allowed her testimonies to be manipulated by interested parties close to her. In response, she insisted on the consistency, originality, and independence of her inspired writings. "I do not write one article in the paper expressing merely my own ideas. They are what God has opened before me in vision—the precious rays of light shining from the throne" (*Testimonies for the Church,* vol. 5, p. 67). In recent years scholars have uncovered evidence that she borrowed extensively from other authors and that her literary assistants provided more than routine editorial and secretarial services.

Although Ellen White preferred to style herself as "the Lord's messenger" rather than as a prophetess, she classed herself with the biblical writers. "In ancient times God spoke to men by the mouth of prophets and apostles," she wrote in 1876. "In these days he speaks to them by the Testimonies of his Spirit" an unambiguous reference to her own work (*Testimonies,* vol. 4, p. 148). Many early Adventists, including her own husband, resisted efforts to equate her writings with the Bible and to make acceptance of her inspiration a "test of fellowship." Nevertheless, by the early twentieth century Adventist churches were "disfellowshipping" members who questioned her gift, and were relying on her views to determine the correct reading of scripture. Among the faithful the very phrase "Spirit of Prophecy" became synonymous with Ellen White and her writings, which they regarded as authoritative not only in theology but in science, medicine, and history as well.

SEE ALSO Seventh-day Adventism.

BIBLIOGRAPHY

To date, no full-scale biography of Ellen White has appeared. Of the several autobiographical accounts, the most complete is *Life Sketches of Ellen G. White* (Mountain View, Calif., 1915), the last part of which was compiled by assistants. In 1981 Arthur L. White, a grandson of the prophetess, brought out the first installment (volume 5, covering the years 1900–1905) of a projected six-volume official biography, *Ellen G. White* (Washington, D. C., 1981–), which, though unabashedly apologetic, presents considerable new detail. My own work *Prophetess of Health: A Study of Ellen G. White* (New York, 1976) offers a nonapologetic interpretation of White's health-related activities. For guidance in using White's own writings, there is a splendid three-volume *Comprehensive Index to the Writings of Ellen G. White* (Mountain View, Calif., 1962–1963).

RONALD L. NUMBERS (1987)

WHITE BUFFALO CALF WOMAN is a central figure in Lakota Indian history and contemporary life. Known in the Lakota language as *Pte-san win-yan,* she brought the Sacred Buffalo Calf Pipe and the Seven Sacred Rites to the Lakota people. The Lakota consider her extremely holy. Some regard her as the reappearance of *Wohpe* (Falling Star or Beautiful Woman) who, like *Pte-san win-yan,* embodies the ideals of Lakota womanhood. White Buffalo Calf Woman is one of many female sacred powers in Native American myth and ritual, including Corn Woman (Cherokee), Changing Woman (Navajo), White Painted Woman (Apache), Our Grandmother (Shawnee), and Thought Woman (Keres).

Some tribal histories indicate that *Pte-san win-yan* arrived among the Lakota in the late 1700s during their difficult transition from the Great Lakes to the Great Plains. Buffalo were integral to Lakota life on the plains, providing everything the people needed for survival. According to written accounts of Lakota oral tradition, White Buffalo Calf Woman appeared to the Lakota long ago when the people were very hungry. Two men who were scouting for food one day noticed a beautiful woman approaching them from a distance. She wore a dress of fine white buckskin and carried a bundle on her back. As she drew closer, one of the hunters felt desire for her, but the other scout cautioned him, recognizing that she was sacred or *wakan.* As the desirous scout reached for her, he and the woman were enveloped in a swirling cloud which lifted to reveal a pile of bones beside the sacred woman. She then directed the remaining scout to return to the camp and instruct the people to prepare a large tipi for her arrival. The sacred woman appeared the following day, singing as she entered the camp and then the tipi:

> With visible breath I am walking.
> A voice I am sending as I walk.
> In a sacred manner I am walking.
> With visible tracks I am walking.
> In a sacred manner I am walking.
>
> (DeMallie, p. 284)

Sent from the buffalo, she gave the Lakota the White Buffalo Calf Pipe Bundle and taught them how to pray with the Sacred Pipe, *Ptehincala hu cannunpa.* Through the Sacred Pipe, humans became related to and at one with the entire cosmos. She instructed the people on how to live in good relation with one another, and she taught them the Seven Sacred Rites that accompany the Pipe. Finally, she pledged to return to the Lakota in the future. As she left the camp, she stopped, lay down, and rolled over, becoming a black buffalo. Stopping a second time, she changed into a red buffalo. The third time she was transformed into a yellow buckskin buffalo; and finally, the fourth time, before walking out of sight, she became a white buffalo. The Sacred Pipe is now in the possession of Arvol Looking Horse, Nineteenth-Generation Keeper of the White Buffalo Calf Pipe Bundle.

As Lakota mythology suggests, White Buffalo Calf Woman plays an important role in Lakota ritual. The Seven Sacred Rites, which she either brought to the people or modified through the addition of the Sacred Pipe, include ceremonies for purifying the body and spirit (*inika(tm)e*), commonly known as the sweat lodge; dancing looking at the sun, or the Sun Dance (*wiwanyag wachipi*); crying for a vision, or the vision quest (*hanbleceyapi*); making of relatives (*hunkapi*); throwing of the ball (*tapa wanka yap*); preparing a girl for womanhood (*i(nati awichalowan*); and keeping of the spirit (*wana(tm)i gluhapi*). The Sacred Pipe is integral to each of these rites and to the annual ceremonial cycle as a whole, which begins in early spring when the sun enters the Lakota constellation that implies the Pipe, thereby igniting the celestial Sacred Pipe and renewing life on earth. White Buffalo Calf Woman is particularly crucial to the Sun Dance and girls' puberty ceremonies, wherein a woman is the embodiment of *Pte-san win-yan,* bringing the Sacred Pipe to the Sun Dance arena in one rite and instructing the girl on Lakota women's codes of conduct in the other.

Many events seemingly threatened the interrelatedness of the Lakota and the buffalo: the outlawing of Lakota ceremonies in the nineteenth century, the imposition of Christianity, the prohibition against traditional buffalo hunting, the decimation of the buffalo herds by non-Indians, and acts of genocide against the Lakota people. However, White Buffalo Calf Woman and the buffalo in general remain the center of Lakota cultural survival. In fact, the birth of several rare white buffalos in the 1990s signaled to some Lakotas the return of *Pte-san win-yan.* Lakotas are working to protect and restore buffalo herds and their natural habitats and to revitalize and strengthen Lakota ceremonies. The White Buffalo Calf Woman Society has been established to support women victimized by domestic violence. In addition, Arvol Looking Horse has emerged as a highly visible religious leader among the Lakota. He and others have led many Big Foot Memorial Rides to help heal the wounds of the 1890 Wounded Knee Massacre and to foster leadership among Lakota youth.

See Also Gender and Religion, article on Gender and Native American Religious Tradition; Lakota Religious Traditions; North American Indians, article on Indians of the Plains.

Bibliography

Brown, Joseph Epes, recorder and editor. *The Sacred Pipe: Black Elk's Account of the Seven Rites of the Oglala Sioux* (1953). Baltimore, Md., 1971.

DeMallie, Raymond J., ed. *The Sixth Grandfather: Black Elk's Teachings Given to John G. Neihardt.* Lincoln, Nebr., 1984.

DeMallie, Raymond J., and Douglas R. Parks, eds. *Sioux Indian Religion: Tradition and Innovation.* Norman, Okla., 1987.

Goodman, Ronald. *Lakota Star Knowledge: Studies in Lakota Stellar Theology.* 2d ed. Rosebud, S.Dak., 1992.

Lame Deer, John (Fire), and Richard Erdoes. *Lame Deer, Seeker of Visions.* New York, 1972.

St. Pierre, Mark, and Tilda Long Soldier. *Walking in the Sacred Manner: Healers, Dreamers, and Pipe Carriers: Medicine Women of the Plains Indians.* New York, 1995.

Walker, James R. *Lakota Belief and Ritual.* Edited by Raymond J. DeMallie and Elaine A. Jahner. Lincoln, Nebr., 1980.

Mary C. Churchill (2005)

WHITEFIELD, GEORGE

WHITEFIELD, GEORGE (1714–1770), English evangelist and itinerant revivalist in America. Born in humble circumstances in Gloucester, England, Whitefield received his bachelor of arts degree from Oxford in 1736, the same year in which Bishop Martin Benson ordained him as deacon in the Church of England. Associated with John and Charles Wesley in an effort to revive a sedate and passionless Anglicanism, Whitefield followed with keen interest the missionary labors of the Wesley brothers in the newly founded colony of Georgia in North America. After nearly three years of preaching in the New World, the Wesleys returned to England discouraged and dismayed by the enormity of the religious challenge abroad. Neither they nor Whitefield's own admirers, however, could discourage the twenty-three-year-old Whitefield from setting out for Georgia on the first of seven voyages to America.

After an absence of less than one year, Whitefield returned to England late in 1738 to receive his ordination as priest, to strengthen his ties with the trustees of the Georgia colony, and to learn that England's hierarchy looked askance at his cavalier attitude toward canon law and the liturgical form of the national church. No less an authority than London's bishop, Edmund Gibson, published in 1739 a pastoral letter condemning "enthusiasm," a dangerous zeal associated with young Methodism in general, and with young Whitefield in particular. For evidence that Whitefield claimed a special and direct guidance from the Holy Spirit, Bishop Gibson turned to the young zealot's first journal, written from December 1737 to May 1738, in which "enthusiasm" seemed so conveniently and convincingly represented. Whitefield responded to this and to many other charges contained in the letter: that he preached extemporaneously in the open fields, that he criticized the national clergy, and that he claimed to "propagate a new Gospel, as unknown to the generality of ministers and people"—all this, said the bishop, in what is surely a Christian country already. Even as Whitefield sought to defend himself against the bishop's attack, he found pulpits in England closed to him and the clergy there growing increasingly wary of him. Overtures from the Georgia trustees enticed him once more, as he was now offered a pastoral charge in Savannah, together with a promise of five hundred acres of land for a proposed orphanage. Two weeks after the Gibson letter was published, Whitefield was on his way back to America.

This second visit, lasting from November 1739 to January 1741, was Whitefield's most successful evangelical tour of the American colonies. Wherever he went up and down the Atlantic coast, his reputation as a dramatic, divine messenger preceded him. Enormous crowds gathered in eager anticipation, in churches or outdoors, in town squares or country meadows. Calvinist in his own theological stance, Whitefield found his greatest reception from similarly oriented denominations: Congregationalists, Presbyterians, Dutch Reformed, and (later) Baptists. While the first Great Awakening could certainly have occurred without him, it is difficult to imagine that burst of intercolonial and interdenominational pietism arising so swiftly and to such heights apart from the labors of this thundering, persuasive, and tireless traveler.

Even as Bishop Gibson found in Whitefield's own writings his best evidence for the evangelist's excesses, so critics of revivalism in America rifled through his published journals for the ammunition so amply supplied there. Whitefield, for his part, repeatedly and needlessly alienated those who stopped short of uncritical adulation and applause. And although he eventually moderated his censorious tone (and even more important, stopped publishing his journals), damage was done to the evangelical cause on both sides of the Atlantic Ocean. Whitefield also damaged his relationship with the Wesleys by publishing an attack in 1741 upon the Arminianism evident in John Wesley's sermon "Free Grace."

Still, by the thousands the people came to hear and to believe, in Ireland, Scotland, Wales, and England as well as throughout the American colonies. For an entire generation Whitefield not only created an evangelical Atlantic community, he embodied it. Any pious project that required broad support found George Whitefield either assisting or directing the effort. He raised funds for Princeton University, helped Dartmouth emerge as a school open to Native Americans, promoted union in England among Calvinist Methodists, pleaded for more support of the Bethesda (Georgia) orphanage, took up collections for victims of natural disasters in Europe or elsewhere, and sustained the hopes of hundreds of thousands that a great and sweeping revival of piety would enliven and awaken all of Christendom.

In 1770 Whitefield made his seventh and final trip to America. After preaching on Saturday, September 29, to an impromptu crowd gathered in the fields of Exeter, New Hampshire, he urged his horse on to Newburyport, Massachusetts. The next morning at six o'clock, he died. He lies buried beneath the pulpit in the town's Presbyterian church.

BIBLIOGRAPHY

Two recent scholarly biographies elevate Whitefield studies to a higher plauteau: Harry S. Stout, *The Divine Dramatist: George Whitefield and the Rise of Modern Evangelicalism* (Grand Rapids, Mich., 1991); and Frank Lambert, *Pedlar in Divinity: George Whitefield and the Transatlantic Revivals, 1737–1770* (Princeton, N. J., 1994).

EDWIN S. GAUSTAD (1987 AND 2005)

WHITEHEAD, ALFRED NORTH (1861–1947),

English mathematician and philosopher, much of whose influence has been on theology. Whitehead grew up in a vicarage in the south of England and studied at Trinity College, Cambridge, where he subsequently became a fellow and taught mathematics. In 1890 he married Evelyn Wade. The couple had three children, Eric, North, and Jessie. After 1914 Whitehead taught mathematics at the Imperial College of Science and Technology in Kensington. In 1924, at the age of sixty-three, Whitehead moved to Harvard University, where he taught philosophy until 1936. The death of his son Eric in World War I is reported to have deepened Whitehead's religious interests.

Whitehead did not make any major contribution to mathematics as such. His early writings were chiefly on the philosophy of mathematics (*Treatise of Universal Algebra,* 1898) and logic (with Bertrand Russell, *Principia Mathematica,* 1910–1913). Later he involved himself increasingly in the rethinking of the natural world required by developments in physics, publishing *An Enquiry Concerning the Principles of Natural Knowledge* (1919), *The Concept of Nature* (1920), and *The Principle of Relativity* (1922). His writings also expressed still broader interests, as, for example, in *The Organization of Thought* (1922), which was largely included with other writings in *The Aims of Education* (1929). After moving to Harvard he developed a full-fledged cosmology in such works as *Science and the Modern World* (1925), *Religion in the Making* (1926), *Symbolism, Its Meaning and Effect* (1927), *The Function of Reason* (1929), *Process and Reality* (1929), *Adventures of Ideas* (1933), and *Modes of Thought* (1938).

Whitehead's cosmology may be understood best by contrasting it with the doctrine of mechanism. The world appears to contain both living, self-activating entities, such as birds and dogs, and inanimate, passive objects, such as stones and drops of water. Mechanism took the latter as fundamental and analyzed everything into inanimate and passive units. In classical atomism the ultimate entities are indestructible bits of matter. Contact imparts motion, but otherwise the atoms do not affect one another. Whitehead described his position as a philosophy of organism, arguing that not only living cells but also molecules and subatomic entities are internally interconnected with their environments.

All philosophies must explain both enduring things and events. Most Western philosophies have taken enduring things as basic and have explained events as the interaction of these. Mechanists see events as changing spatial configurations of unchanging material substances. Whitehead proposed that events are fundamental and that the relatively unchanging entities are "societies" of events exhibiting constancy of pattern.

A particular problem for mechanism is conscious experience. Some mechanists hold that this lacks full-fledged reality. Others accept a dualism of mind and matter. Whitehead rejected both positions, holding that an instance of human experience is an organic event and that it provides the model for discerning the basic structure of all individualized events.

Whitehead believed that cosmology and religion are bound closely together, whether or not the cosmology is theistic. Some who respond religiously to Whitehead's vision of the world want to separate it from talk of God, either because they are offended by such talk or because they are committed to other doctrines of God. Whitehead, on the other hand, believed that his cosmology was incomplete without God, although the God of organic events is quite different from that of the world machine. Instead of imposing laws of motion, God is the source of novelty, purpose, and freedom. God radically transcends each creature, but it is the divine presence that directs and enables each to reach toward richness in its own immediacy and in those future events to which it contributes. This cosmic urge to life is called by Whitehead the "primordial nature" of God.

Whitehead holds that God is not an exception to the principle of interrelatedness of actual things. Just as God is effective in the world of temporal events, so temporal events in turn enter into the divine life. What perishes in the world is everlasting in God. This aspect of God Whitehead calls God's "consequent nature." Apart from the consequent nature of God the utter transitoriness of events would undercut the human sense of meaning and importance.

Whitehead described God as lure for adventure and ideal companion in polemical contrast to a supernatural will untouched by the suffering of creatures. His doctrine also differed systematically from the understanding of God as being itself developed especially by Thomas Aquinas. Since the ideas of sovereign will and being itself have shaped much of Christian theology, some have denied that Whitehead's doctrine can be accepted by Christians. Others have been attracted to Whitehead's idea of a conscious, all-loving, all-knowing, everlasting actuality from whom creatures derive all that is good. His image of God as "the fellow sufferer who understands" has gained increasing acceptance.

Whitehead's thought played an important role in the Divinity School of the University of Chicago from the late 1920s. Charles Hartshorne systematically developed Whitehead's dipolar theism. Elsewhere, however, Whitehead's influence was sharply circumscribed by dominant intellectual trends. Analytic philosophy and positivistic science rejected the cosmological enterprise. Neo-Thomist Catholics reemphasized the idea of God as being itself. Neoorthodox Protestants stressed God's sovereign will. However, beginning in the mid-1960s, analytic philosophy and positivistic science lost their hegemony; Vatican II, the writings of Teilhard de Chardin, and the rise of liberation theology generated a dynamic openness among Roman Catholics; and a somewhat chaotic pluralism replaced the neoorthodox consensus among Protestants. In this new context Whitehead's influence has grown among philosophers, scientists, and humanists, as well as among theologians. His Christian followers employed his conceptuality in reformulating many Christian doctrines. They led in discussions of problems of religion and science, especially with regard to ecology. They found allies among feminists and points of contact with Teilhardians and liberation theologians. They have helped shape interreligious dialogue.

Although most of Whitehead's influence has been among North American Protestants, he has a following among Catholics and Jews as well. There is also increasing interest in Europe, Asia, and Latin America. His influence is institutionalized in the Society for the Study of Process Philosophies, the European Society for Process Thought, the Japan Society for Whiteheadian and Process Thought, the Center for a Post-Modern World in Santa Barbara, and the Center for Process Studies in Claremont, California, and its journal, *Process Studies.*

BIBLIOGRAPHY

Cobb, John B., Jr., and David R. Griffin. *Process Theology: An Introductory Exposition.* Philadelphia, 1976.

Leclerc, Ivor. *Whitehead's Metaphysics: An Introductory Exposition.* New York, 1958.

Lowe, Victor. *Understanding Whitehead.* Baltimore, 1962.

JOHN B. COBB, JR. (1987)

WICCA. Wicca originated in 1940s England as an attempt to recreate what was believed to be an ancient religious system indigenous to Britain and Europe, characterized by the veneration of nature, polytheism, and the use of magic and ritual. It was heavily influenced by the occult revival of the late nineteenth century, including secret, magical societies such as the Hermetic Order of the Golden Dawn (established in 1888), the notorious magician Aleister Crowley (1875–1947), Freemasonry, and Spiritualism. The rediscovery of classical ideas of nature and deity in Romantic literature and archaeology provided additional sources, as did British folklorist and Egyptologist Margaret Murray's (1862–1963) "anthropological" study of witchcraft in Europe, *The Witch-Cult in Western Europe* (1921).

These threads were woven into early Wicca by Gerald Brosseau Gardner (1884–1964), a British civil servant who had spent much of his working life in the Far East and had a lifelong passion for folklore and archaeology, visiting many sites of archaeological significance on travels to the Near East. Gardner returned to England when he retired in 1936, living in London and the New Forest before moving to the Isle of Man in 1954. Once back in England, Gardner, already a Freemason, joined the Folklore Society, the Co-Masons, the Druid Order, and the Rosicrucian Fellowship of Crotona. This latter group, he claimed, contained a hidden, inner group of hereditary witches who initiated him in 1939. They also allegedly allowed Gardner to publish their rituals in fictional form in his novel *High Magic's Aid* (1949), which he wrote under the pseudonym Scire. Gardner was not able to publish more open accounts of witchcraft under his real name until the 1736 Witchcraft Act was repealed in 1951 and replaced with the Fraudulent Mediums Act, which gave freedom for individuals to practice witchcraft as long as no harm was done to person or property. Released from a law that subjected any person alleged to have magical powers to prosecution, Gardner wrote *Witchcraft Today* (1954), which contains an introduction by Margaret Murray, followed by *The Meaning of Witchcraft* (1959), taking both himself and witchcraft into the public spotlight.

In *Witchcraft Today* Gardner set out his belief that witchcraft was not only the original indigenous religion of Britain, dating from the Stone Age, but that it had survived the persecutions of the Great Witch Hunt in early modern Europe, continuing in secret but now threatened with extinction. These claims followed closely Murray's thesis that an old religion involving worship of a horned god representing the fertility of nature had survived persecution and existed throughout western Europe. Murray argued that the witch-cult was organized in covens that met according to the phases of the moon and the changing seasons, conducting rituals that involved dancing, feasting, sacrifices, and ritualized sex in honor of the horned god. Later, in *The God of the Witches* (1933), Murray traced the development of this vegetation god and introduced the idea of a fertility goddess into the cult.

Gardner's absolute belief in and perpetuation of Murray's argument led many early Wiccans to believe that they were continuing this ancient tradition of witchcraft, although scholars had refuted the validity of her use of trial records since *The Witch Cult* was first published and dismissed most of her evidence over time. Most, though not all, Wiccans today acknowledge that there is little evidence for a continuous, pre-Christian witchcraft tradition indigenous to western Europe, but Gardner's aim of reviving what he believed to be a dying religion appears to have been fulfilled. His numerous media appearances brought Wicca to public attention throughout the 1950s, during which time he encouraged people to set up covens operating according to the outlines in his books and initiated many people into Wicca. One of these was Doreen Valiente (1922–1999), one of the key figures in modern Wicca. She worked with Gerald Gardner as his high priestess and revised the Book of Shadows, a book of rituals, information, and lore for which he claimed ancient provenance, which she felt to be too influenced by the writings of Aleister Crowley. Valiente eventually left his coven in 1957, after falling out with him over ever-increasing publicity seeking, and periodically withdrew from the public face of Wicca throughout her life. She was nevertheless consistent in her support for what she termed the old pagan religions: in 1964 she was president of the Witchcraft Research Association, she was a founding member of the Pagan Front in 1971, and in November 1998 she spoke at the annual Pagan Federation conference in London. Her life within Wicca, witchcraft, and paganism is documented in many of her books, including *The Rebirth of Witchcraft* (1989), *Witchcraft for Tomorrow* (1978), and *Witchcraft: A Tradition Renewed* (1990, with Evan Jones).

Another key figure is Patricia Crowther (b. 1932), who was initiated by Gerald Gardner in 1960 and established covens in Yorkshire and Lancashire. She was an actress and dancer whose husband, Arnold Crowther, was an old friend of Gerald Gardner. Patricia Crowther is the author of a number of books on witchcraft, including *Lid Off the Cauldron* (1981) and her autobiography, *One Witch's World* (1998), published as *High Priestess: The Life and Times of Patricia Crowther* (2000) in the United States. In the early twenty-first century, she continued to run a coven in Sheffield, and it was an ex-member of her coven, Pat Kopanski, who was instrumental in the initiation into Wicca of Alex Sanders (1926–1988), who developed a second branch of Wicca in the 1960s.

Sanders was a resident of Manchester who claimed a witch ancestress from Snowdonia, in North Wales. His branch of Wicca was based on Gardnerian lines, but Alexandrian Wicca, as it came to be known, was more heavily influenced by ceremonial, ritual magic—Sanders worked for the John Rylands library in Manchester, where he read classical texts on ritual magic, and he had been trained as a medium through visits to a Spiritualist church with his mother during childhood. In 1961 Sanders allegedly wrote to local Wiccans whom he had seen on television, but they took a dislike to him, and it was apparently not until 1963 that he was initiated into Wicca by a priestess in Derbyshire. Sanders went on to act as high priest to a coven in Nottinghamshire, but the group dissolved in 1964, and he then met the seventeen-year-old Arline Maxine Morris (b. 1946). They began running a coven together in 1965, were discovered by a local newspaper, and went on to manipulate the media to such an extent that they became the most famous witches in the world by 1966. Such media attention attracted many people and led to a whole network of covens springing up around them, although longer-established Gardnerian Wiccans denounced Alex as a charlatan. Like Gardner, Sanders sought publicity for Wicca, often of a sensational nature, and by the 1970s he had become known as the King of the Witches.

In 1967 Alex and Maxine Sanders moved to London, and in 1969 Alex Sanders was sensationally publicized in a newspaper article. This article led to many media appearances, a romanticized biography, *King of the Witches,* by June Johns (1969), and a film, *Legend of the Witches* (1969), as a result of which Alexandrian Wicca grew exponentially. In 1973 the relationship between Alex and Maxine broke down, and they divorced in 1982 but remained friends. While Maxine continued to run the coven, Alex retired from the limelight to Sussex, where he continued to teach Wicca until his death from lung cancer on Beltane Eve 1988. He was also a prolific initiator, and many covens in Germany, the Netherlands, and elsewhere in northern Europe sprang from visits to him during this period.

A number of the Sanderses' initiates—particularly Stewart Farrar (1916–2000), Janet Farrar, and Vivianne Crowley—have been responsible for writing extremely influential books on Wicca. Stewart met Alex and Maxine Sanders while working as a journalist in 1969 and was initiated by Maxine in 1970. He and Janet ran their own coven in London, married in 1974, and subsequently moved to Ireland in 1976. Here, they continued to train and initiate people in Wicca and became prolific Wiccan authors whose many books include *What Witches Do: A Modern Coven Revealed* (1971), *Eight Sabbats for Witches* (1981), *The Witches' Way* (1984), *The Witches' Goddess* (1987), *The Witches' God* (1989), *Spells and How They Work* (1990), and, with Gavin Bone, *The Pagan Path* (1995) and *The Healing Craft* (1999). *The Witches' Way* contains the bulk of the contemporary Gardnerian rituals and was published with the active help of Doreen Valiente, who wrote most of them and had herself made a large amount of material available in her 1978 book, *Witchcraft for Tomorrow.* It thus made the core ritual format and texts of Gardnerian Wicca available to all. After Stewart's death, Janet married Gavin Bone, and they continue to initiate, write, and speak at pagan conferences.

Wiccan priestess, psychologist, and university lecturer Vivianne Crowley was initiated into both Alexandrian and Gardnerian Wicca, and in 1979 she founded a Wiccan coven that combined the two traditions. In 1988 she founded the Wicca Study Group along with her husband, Chris, and it is now Europe's largest Wiccan teaching organization. She is a member of the Pagan Federation council, serving as honorary secretary (1988–1994), prison chaplaincy coordinator (1991–1995), and interfaith coordinator (1994–1996). Crowley has a doctorate in psychology and has trained in transpersonal counseling with the Centre for Transpersonal Psychology in London. Her books include the best-selling *Wicca: the Old Religion in the New Millennium* (1989; 1996), *Phoenix from the Flame: Pagan Spirituality in the Western World* (1994), *Principles of Paganism* (1996), *Principles of Wicca* (1997), and *A Woman's Guide to the Earth Traditions* (2001).

Wicca is not, however, confined to northwestern Europe. It has become a global phenomenon and can be found in most countries populated by people of European descent, including the United States, Canada, Australia, New Zealand, and South Africa. It has spread through such people as Ray Buckland, an initiate of Gerald Gardner, who subsequently emigrated to the United States in 1967, taking Gardnerian Wicca with him. Buckland later became disillusioned with the perceived hierarchy in Gardnerian Wicca and went on to form a more egalitarian tradition of Wicca, which he called Seax, or Saxon Wica [sic]. He is the author of several do-it-yourself guides to Wicca, including *The Tree: Complete Book of Saxon Witchcraft* (1974). The explosion in how-to books on Wicca since the 1980s and, more recently, internet sites has become the main means by which Wicca has spread and grown, evolving and at times mutating quite dramatically.

During the late 1970s and 1980s, for example, a further important development in Wicca took place as the feminist consciousness movement influenced the emergence of feminist Wicca and witchcraft in North America. The Hungarian-born American feminist activist Zsuzsanna Budapest was one of the prime movers behind the development of feminist witchcraft, forming the women-only Susan B. Anthony Coven, running a shop called The Feminist Wicca in California, and self-publishing *The Feminist Book of Light and Shadows* (1978). The book was a reworking of available Gardnerian Wicca, which excluded all mention of men and male deities and included her own rituals, spells, and lore. It was later expanded and published as *The Holy Book of Women's Mysteries* in 1986.

Starhawk (Miriam Simos) (b. 1951) is one of the most prominent feminist pagan activists in the United States. Her feminist activism in the 1970s led her to the Goddess movement, and she studied feminist witchcraft with Budapest and Faery Witchcraft with Victor Anderson. After practicing as a solitary, Starhawk formed Compost, her first coven, from participants in an evening class on witchcraft and then a second, Honeysuckle, for women only. She was elected president of the Covenant of the Goddess in 1976–1977, published her first book, *The Spiral Dance,* in 1979, and was one of the founders of the Reclaiming Collective in San Francisco in 1980. *The Spiral Dance* has proved to be an ever-popular volume since it was first published in 1979, selling over 100,000 copies in its first ten years of publication. The book is based on Anderson's Faery tradition but incorporates strictly feminist principles into modern witchcraft, principles that are expanded in her later books *Truth or Dare* (1987) and *Dreaming the Dark* (1988). Starhawk combines nature worship, politics, activism, psychology, and goddess worship in an attempt to heal spiritual and political divisions in society and individuals. Such themes come out even more strongly in her two novels, *The Fifth Sacred Thing* (1993) and *Walking to Mercury* (1997). European Wiccan attitudes towards Starhawk's redirection of witchcraft toward political activism tend to be cautious. Recently, Starhawk has actively reclaimed her Jewish roots as well as being a witch, an exploration that has led to her sometimes referring to herself as a "Jewitch."

The religion described by Gardner and developed since the 1950s positions nature as central, through deities representative of nature and rituals associated with seasonal change, and through the growing concern for the environment since the 1970s. Although some versions of feminist Wicca focus exclusively on the divine female, perceptions of deity in Wicca are directly linked to nature and are generally regarded as empowering for both men and women, since they include both goddesses and gods. For example, *The Great Charge,* rewritten by Doreen Valiente from earlier versions, focuses specifically on the goddess as the embodiment of nature, and is one of Wicca's most well-known liturgical texts. It describes the goddess as "the beauty of the green earth, the white moon among the stars, the mystery of the waters" and as "the soul of nature who gives life to the universe." Her counterpart is Lord of the Greenwood, Sun King, Corn King, Leader of the Wild Hunt, and Lord of Death, a god intimately connected with nature represented through the seasonal cycle of festivals.

Each year most Wiccans celebrate eight festivals, known as sabbats; these make up a ritual cycle known as the Wheel of the Year. Four main rituals are celebrated at the four seasonal festivals described by Murray as the witches' sabbats and based on the agricultural year. These are Candlemas on February 1, May Day on May 1, Lammas on August 1, and Hallowe'en on October 31. During the 1980s these festivals became Celticized as a result of the Farrar's relocation to Ireland and North American interest in Celtic ancestry; they thus tend now to be known as Imbolc, Beltane, Lughnasadh, and Samhain respectively. The four other festivals that make up the Wheel are astronomically fixed: the Winter and Summer Solstices around December 21 and June 21, and the Spring and Autumn Equinoxes around March 21 and September 21. The Winter Solstice is often called Yule and, particularly in North America, the Summer Solstice tends to be called Litha, with the equinoxes known as Ostara (Spring) and Mabon (Autumn).

At each of the festivals, deities are addressed in aspects appropriate to the season. For example, at Hallowe'en or Samhain, gods and goddesses associated with death and the underworld such as Hekate, Hades, Rhiannon, or Anubis might be addressed, as Wiccans celebrate death as part of the cycle of life and seek to prepare themselves for the dark winter months ahead. The Wiccan sabbats are intended to deepen the participants' understanding of the cycle of life, death, and rebirth as revealed in the changes evident in nature, for deities, humans, and the natural world are all seen as interconnected. For this reason many Wiccans living in the Southern Hemisphere have reversed the festivals. For example, Summer Solstice rituals take place on December 21 to celebrate the fullness of life reflected in nature at that time of the year in such countries as in Australia, New Zealand, and South Africa.

Most Wiccans live in urban areas, and rituals that celebrate nature and venerate nature deities help them to feel more in touch with the natural world. This, along with a rise in active concern for the environment since the 1970s, has been a major reason for the growth in popularity of Wicca and Neopaganism in general throughout the latter half of the twentieth century and into the twenty-first. However, Wiccans demonstrate a range of attitudes toward protecting the natural world, from radical environmentalism and direct protest to more abstract views derived from the idealized nature of Romanticism or from Western esotericism. In the latter, nature is a reflection of a greater divine reality, being at once both an intermediary between humanity and divinity and being imbued with divinity itself. Thus, environmental activism does not necessarily follow from a ritual or spiritual engagement with nature, although this is often the case in North American Wicca as practiced and taught by Starhawk, for example. Nature, and Wiccans' understandings of it, are extremely complex; one cannot assume that Wicca and environmentalism go hand in hand.

Such complexity is evident in the diversity of Wiccan traditions that have emerged around the world. Practices borrowed from Native Americans have been adopted and adapted by Wiccans in North America, for example, while many European Wiccans turn to Saxon, Celtic, or Germanic traditions, seeking inspiration from the supposed indigenous traditions of northern Europe. The classical pagan cultures of Greece, Egypt, and Rome are also mined for inspiration. Feminist witchcraft has had a great impact on Wicca in North America, which has then spread to New Zealand and Australia, but has been less influential in Britain, where the Gardnerian and Alexandrian traditions remain strong. Nevertheless, the multitude of North American Wiccan derivations—including Starhawk's Reclaiming, Faery Wicca, Dianic Wicca, and Seax Wica—have crossed back to Europe, and Starhawk's version in particular has grown in popularity because of its stress on political and environmental action.

Wicca has no centralized, institutional structure, and Wiccans have only a few beliefs to which they all adhere. These include the Wiccan Rede or Law—"Do what thou wilt an it harm none"—and the Law of Threefold Return, which states that whatever a person does, for good or ill, will return to them threefold. The lack of any central organizational structure allows for an enormous level of variety, and Wicca at the beginning of the twenty-first century looks likely to retain its complexity and differentiate further as it continues to spread and grow.

See Also Crowley, Aleister; Freemasons; Neopaganism; Rosicrucians; Spiritualism.

Bibliography

Adler, Margot. *Drawing Down the Moon: Witches, Druids, Goddess-Worshippers, and Other Pagans in America Today.* 2d ed. Boston, 1986. A comprehensive study of neopaganism in North America in the early 1980s.

Crowley, Vivianne. *Wicca: The Old Religion in the New Millennium.* London, 1996. Provides an account of the combined Alexandrian/Gardnerian tradition, with a strong Jungian flavor.

Gardner, Gerald B. *Witchcraft Today.* London, 1954.

Gardner, Gerald B. *The Meaning of Witchcraft.* London, 1959. The second of two fact-based accounts of Wicca by its founder.

Greenwood, Susan. *Witchcraft, Magic and the Otherworld: An Anthropology.* Oxford, 2000. An anthropological study of modern magic as practiced by British pagans.

Hanegraaff, Wouter J. *New Age Religion and Western Culture: Esotericism in the Mirror of Secular Thought.* New York, 1998. A comprehensive critical examination of the links between New Age and the Western Esoteric Traditions.

Harvey, Graham. *Listening People, Speaking Earth: Contemporary Paganism.* London, 1997. A broad introduction to the range of modern pagan traditions and their expression.

Hutton, Ronald. *The Triumph of the Moon: A History of Modern Pagan Witchcraft.* Oxford, 1999. The first scholarly history of Wicca and its development since the mid-nineteenth century.

Luhrmann, Tanya M. *Persuasions of the Witches' Craft: Ritual Magic in Contemporary England.* Basingstoke, 1994. An ethnographic account of ritual magic groups in London in the early 1980s, which explores the nature of belief.

Murray, Margaret A. *The Witch Cult in Western Europe: A Study in Anthropology.* Oxford, 1921. A key text in the development of Wicca, which directly influenced Gerald Gardner.

Pearson, Joanne E., Richard H. Roberts, and Geoffrey Samuel, eds. *Nature Religion Today: Paganism in the Modern World.* Edinburgh, 1998. An examination of paganism as "nature religion," with contributions from scholars in a wide range of disciplines.

Pearson, Joanne E. *A Popular Dictionary of Paganism.* London, 2002. A short-entry dictionary encompassing terms and ideas commonly found within paganism and providing information on key figures and historical developments.

Pearson, Joanne E., ed. *Belief Beyond Boundaries: Wicca, Celtic Spirituality and the New Age.* Aldershot, 2002. A textbook exploring forms of spirituality including paganism, Celtic spirituality, the appropriation of Native Indian peoples' practices, and New Age.

Starhawk. *The Spiral Dance: A Rebirth of the Ancient Religion of the Great Goddess.* New York, 1979. A classic text on feminist Faery Wicca.

JOANNE E. PEARSON (2005)

WIDENGREN, GEO. One of the most famous historians of religions of the twentieth century, Geo Widengren (1907–1996) was born on April 24, 1907, in Stockholm, Sweden. From his early youth, he devoted his entire life to conducting research and teaching in the universities of Sweden. He studied Iranian and Semitic languages and religions under the supervision of Henrik Samuel Nyberg (1889–1974), the patron of the Uppsala Oriental school for many decades. Immediately after graduating in 1936, Widengren published his Ph.D. thesis under the title *The Accadian and Hebrew Psalms of Lamentation as Religious Documents.* His most important book from his early career, however, is *Hochgottglaube im alten Iran,* one of the most influential monographs of the Swedish school of Iranian studies. Widengren was appointed professor of the history of religions at the University of Uppsala in 1940, a post he held until 1973. During his tenure at the University, Widengren supervised many dissertations, including *Feuerpriester im Kleinasien und Iran* (1943, published 1946), written by his younger colleague, Stig Wikander (1908–1983).

In his early writings, Widengren was influenced not only by the works of scholars such as Nyberg and Tor Andrae, but also by Richard Reitzenstein and Raffaele Pettazzoni. Consequently, his books include themes, motifs, and methodological assumptions that often appear in the influential paradigms of the history of religions in the interwar period. His strongest influence came from Nyberg; like him, his mentor specialized in several philological fields and wrote critical appraisals of textual sources pertaining to both the Semitic and Iranian religions. Widengren's work, however, was usually much more accurate, insightful, and innovative than that of most of his predecessors. After publishing his first monographs, Widengren became inspired to synthesize the philological, historical, archaeological, and ethnological studies pertinent to the Near and Middle East using the phenomenological method—involving description, arrangement, interpretation and typology of historical data—that he applied in his imposing treatise *Religionens värld* (World of religion; Swedish edition 1945, German revised translation 1969). If, for instance, the formula *Hochgottglaube* (Faith in a high God) as a recurrent pattern in Near Eastern religions depends at least partially on the impact of the Germanic ethnologic school (as postulated by Wilhelm Schmidt and his followers of the Vienna school), Widengren illustrates the hypothesis by a more comprehensive and insightful usage of the sources.

As Jacques Duchesne-Guillemin wrote in his 1996 obituary, Widengren had a comprehensive knowledge of all the religions and literatures of the ancient Near and Middle East. His academic expertise encompassed the whole territory conquered by Alexander the Great, from Greece on the west to the eastern border of Iran and Central Asia, for over a thousand years. Widengren's oeuvre must therefore be viewed as sustaining the Swedish school of history of religions, located mainly in Uppsala (see Widengren, 1953; and Carl-Martin Edsman, 2001), although he could sometimes be polemic, as were his fellow renowned representatives of the Uppsala school, Stig Wikander and Carl-Martin Edsman.

Widengren's series of monographs titled *King and Saviour* (Parts I-V, 1945–55) represents probably the best example of his fine mastery of sources and method. Writing about a major theme in such an extensive cultural geography as that of the "Heavenly Book," for instance, he reviewed religious concepts and symbols from Accadian, Arabic, Aramaic (Mandaic, Samaritan, Syriac), Armenian, Greek, Hebrew, Iranian, Sumerian, and Ugaritic vocabularies, but never lost sight of the local oral traditions that are so influential to the formation of a religious corpus.

Widengren also wrote extensively on Gnosticism (authoring various books and many inspiring articles despite his avowed distance from the new approaches adopted by scholars after the publication of the Coptic editorial tractates), Manicheism (including a short but valuable encompassing survey), and Mandeism. His main contribution to the latter field, published in 1982, discussed all the favorite motifs of the German and Nordic *Religionsgeschichtliche Schule* related to astronomical symbolism, apocalypticism, the destiny of the soul after death, the influence of Mesopotamian and Iranian motifs in Mediterranean religions of antiquity and Middle Ages, and special topics such as the origin and diffusion of *The Hymn of the Pearl* or the vividly disputed shamanic patterns in Zoroastrianism. Widengren's long-lasting familiarity with several ancient and early medieval Iranian civilizations allowed him to study the cultural ties between the Islamic and Iranian beliefs as represented in motifs such as the "tree of life" or the "heavenly ascension" of Muḥammad, (Widengren, 1950 and 1951). For a time, he explored the relevance of Jungian psychology to the study of religions (Widengren, 1967), but he never participated in the Ascona Eranos meetings, nor contributed to the *Eranos Jahrbücher.* Instead of assuming a nonhistorical description of religion after studying ancient documents, Widengren expressed his immense erudition by outlining an evolution of ideas and by linking his conclusions to historical events. His book *Iranisch-semitische Kulturbegegnung in parthischer Zeit* (1960) remains a seminal study, and his many articles on sacral kingship were planned to comprise a great autonomous book, never published.

Religious scholars in the 1960s critiqued these themes, but Widengren continued to defend the importance of Iranian influence throughout his career (see Widengren et al., 1995). In Europe, as in North America, his view supported a pan-Iranist model of historical diffusion. In the twenty-first century, however, religious scholars have largely refuted his vision of ancient Iran as the source of many ancient and modern religious motifs.

Monographs like Widengren's *Mani and Manicheism* proved his ability to elegantly master in a rather small space the complex problem of the Manichean relationship to Zoroastrianism, Judaism, and Christianity, including developing a political and historical synopsis of Iran under Shapur.

Together with his Italian and Dutch colleagues Raffaele Pettazzoni, Gerardus van der Leeuw, and C. J. Bleeker, Widengren founded the International Association of the History of Religions (IAHR), and he participated in the first IAHR congress, held in 1950 in Amsterdam. He also helped establish the international journal of the IAHR, *Numen.* First published in 1954, the journal quickly developed into one of the major periodicals in the field of religious studies. In this journal, Widengren published a long article (which scholars continue to consult) pertaining to the state and future tasks of Iranian religious history (*Stand und Aufgaben der iranischen Religionsgeschichte,* 1954 and 1955).

Contributing to the initiative of Erik Gren and of other colleagues in close connection with the Nordic School of Oriental and Religious Studies, including Alfred Haldar, Ivan Engnell, Nils Simonsson, and Stig Wikander, Widengren assumed the role of co-editor of *Orientalia Suecana,* which soon became a major scholarly organ and promoter of research. His erudite skills and intellectual stamina were represented in the journal by his rare and illuminating studies such as his micro-monograph on clowns, harlequins and dervishes and their habits in the ancient and medieval near and middle east.

Widengren served as the president of the IAHR from 1960 to 1970. He presided over the Twelfth Congress of the International Association for the History of Religions in Stockholm in August 1970, at which time he resigned his post. Widengren also worked as one of the editors of those proceedings, thus helping to ensure international recognition of the Swedish school of religious studies.

During the last twenty years of his life, Widengren refined some previously developed themes, including the role of Zoroastrianism under the Sassanids and Syriac religious literature. His successor in the chair of Uppsala, the Egyptologist Jan Bergman, edited a double-volume Festschrift, *Ex Orbi Religionum. Studia Geo Widengen oblata,* and dedicated it to Widengren in 1972 to commemorate his sixty-fifth birthday. Having received worldwide acclaim from his fellow historians, Widengren died on January 28, 1996. Unfortunately, however, no comprehensive record of his publications exists.

BIBLIOGRAPHY

Books and Selected Articles of Geo Widengren

The Accadian and Hebrew Psalms of Lamentation as Religious Documents: A Comparative Study. Diss. Uppsala, Sweden, 1936.

Hochgottglaube im alten Iran. Eine religions-phänomenologische Untersuchung. Uppsala-Leipzig, 1938.

The Great Vohu Manah and the Apostle of God. Uppsala-Leipzig, 1945.

Religionens värld. Religionsfenomenologiska studier och översikter. Stockholm, 1945 (German translation, 1969).

Religionens Ursprung. En kort framställning av de evolutionistiska religionsteorierna och kritiken mot dessa. Stockholm, 1946 (2d ed. Stockholm, 1973).

Mesopotamian Elements in Manicheism (King and Saviour II). Uppsala-Leipzig, 1946.

The Ascension of the Apostle and the Heavenly Book (King and Saviour III). Uppsala-Leipzig, 1950.

The King and the Tree of Life in Ancient New Eastern Religion (King and Saviour IV). Uppsala-Wiesbaden, 1951.

"Iranischer Hintergrund der Gnosis." *Zeitschrift für Religions- und Geistesgeschichte* 20 (1952): 97–114.

"Die Religionswissenschaftliche Forschungen in Skandinavien in der letzten zwanzig Jahren." *Zeitschrift für Religion und Geistesgeschichte* 5 (1953): 1–30.

Muhammad, the Apostle of God, and his Ascension (King and Saviour V). Uppsala-Wiesbaden, 1955.

Sakrales Königtum im Alten Testament und im Judentum. Stuttgart, 1955.

Stand und Aufgaben der iranischen Religionsgeschichte. Leiden, 1955. (Previously published in *Numen* 1 (1954): 16–83 and 2 (1955): 47–134.)

"Recherches sur le féodalisme iranien." *Orientalia Suecana* 5 (1956): 70–172.

"Quelques rapports entre Juifs et Iraniens à l'époque des Parthes." *Vetus Testamentum,* Suppl. IV (1957): 197–241.

Iranisch-semitische Kulturbegegnung in parthischer Zeit. Cologne, 1960.

"The Fate of the Soul after Death." *OS* 9 (1960): 102–106.

Iranische Geisteswelt. Baden-Baden, 1961.

Mani und der Manichäismus. Stuttgart, 1961 (English translation by Charles Kessler; London, 1965).

"The Principle of Evil in Eastern Religions." In *Das Böse,* foreword by Carl Gustav Jung. Zürich, 1961. (Translated into English by Ralph Manheim and Hildegard Nagel as "Studies in Jungian Thought," edited by James Hillman. Evanston, Ill., 1967).

Die Religionen Irans, Die Religionen der Menschheit Band 14. Stuttgart, 1965.

Religionsphänomenologie. Berlin, 1969.

Der Feudalismus im alten Iran. Cologne, 1969.

"The Death of Gayōmart." *Myths and Symbols: Studies in Honor of Mircea Eliade,* pp. 179–193. Chicago, 1969.

"The Establishement of the Sassanian Dynasty in the Light of the New Evidence." In *Atti del Convegno internazionale sul tema 'La Persia nel Medioevo'* (31 March–5 April, 1970): 711–82.

Editor, with C. Jouco Bleeker. *History of Religions.* 2 vols. Leiden, 1972.

"La méthode comparative: entre philologie et phénoménologie." In *Problems and Methods in History of Religions,* edited by Ugo Bianchi, C. Jouco Bleeker, and Alessandro Bausani, pp. 5–14. Leiden, 1972.

The Gnostic Attitude. Translated by Birger A. Pearson. Santa Barbara, Calif., 1973.

Editor, with C. Jouco Bleeker and Eric J. Sharpe. *Proceedings of the XIIth International Congress of the International Association for the History of Religions.* Leiden, 1975.

"Iran, der große Gegner Rom: Königsgewalt, Feudalismus, Militärwesen." In *Aufstieg und Niedergang der römischen Welt (ANRW)* II.9.1 (1976), pp. 219–306.

Editor. *Der Manichäismus.* Wege der Forschung Band 168. Darmstadt, 2d ed. 1977.

Editor. *Proceedings of the International Colloquium on Gnosticism, Stockholm, August 20–25, 1973.* Stockholm, 1977.

Editor. "Der Manichäismus. Kurzgefasste Geschichte der Problemforschung." In *Gnosis. Festschrift für Hans Jonas,* edited by Barbara Aland et al., pp. 278–315. Göttingen, 1978.

"Révélation et prédication dans les Gīthās." In *Iranica,* edited by Gherardo Gnoli and Adriano V. Rossi, pp. 339–364. Naples, 1979.

Der Mandäismus. 2d ed. Wege der Forschung Band 167. Darmstadt, 1982.

"Leitende Ideen und Quellen der iranischen Apokalyptik." In *Apocalypticism in the Mediterranean World and the Near East.* Proceedings of the International Colloquium on Apocalypticism, Uppsala (August 12–17, 1979), edited by David Hellholm, pp. 77–162. Tübingen, Germany, 1983.

"Bardesanes von Edessa und der syrisch-mesopotamische Gnostizismus." In *The Many and the One. Essays on Religion in the Graeco-Roman World, presented to H. Ludin Jansen,* edited by P. Borgen, pp. 153–181. Trondheim, 1985.

"Aramaica et Syriaca II." *Orientalia Suecana* 33–35 (1984–1986): 479–86. A sharp critique, but not so convincingly argued, of Carl-Martin Edsman's 1940 Ph.D. thesis, *Le baptême de feu* (Uppsala-Leipzig).

"On Some Astrological Correspondence in the Writings of Pure Brethren." In *Orientalia Iosephi Tucci memoriae dicata,* vol. 3, edited by Gherardo Gnoli and Lionello Lanciotti, pp. 1551–1559. Rome, 1988.

Apocalyptique iranienne et dualisme qoumrânien. Paris, 1995. (Widengren contributed a general introduction and the article "Les quatre âges du monde.")

Contributions on Geo Widengren, the Swedish School of History of Religions, and Current Exegesis

Ardvisson, Stefan. *Ariska Idoler. Den indoeuropeiska mytologin som vetenskap och ideologi.* Stockholm, 2001.

Bergman, Jan, et al., eds. *Ex Orbe Religionum. Studia Geo Widengren oblata.* 2 vols. Leiden, 1972. Includes a complete bibliography of Widengren through 1972.

Duchesne-Guillemin, Jacques. "Geo Widengren (1907–1996)." *Studia Iranica* 25 (1996): 263–72. Includes a selected bibliography focusing on Widengren's Iranian studies.

Edsman, Carl-Martin. "Ein halbes Jahrhundert Uppsala-Schule." In *Festschrift für Anders Hultgård,* pp. 194–209. Berlin, 2001.

Eliade, Mircea, and Raffaele Pettazzoni. *L'histoire des religions a-t-elle un sens? Correspondence 1926–1959.* Paris, 1994.

Filoramo, Giovanni. "Geo Widengren e la fenomenologia storica della religione." In *Fenomenologia della religione,* edited by Geo Widengren, pp. 13–62. Bologna, 1984.

Gnoli, Gherardo. "Geo Widengren." *East and West* (1996): 495–497.

Hultgård, Anders. "In Memoriam, Geo Widengren." *Orientalia Suecana* 43–44 (1994–1995): 7–9.

Kahle, Sigrid. *H.S. Nyberg: en vetenskapsman biografi.* Stockholm, Sweden, 1991.

Pearson, Birger A., ed. *Religious Syncretism in Antiquity: Essays in Conversation with Geo Widengren.* Institute of Religious Studies, University of California, 1972. Missoula, Mont., 1975.

Timus, Mihaela, and Eugen Ciurtin, eds. "The Unpublished Correspondence between Mircea Eliade and Stig Wikander." *Archaeus. Études d'Histoire des Religions* (Bucharest), 4 (2000), fasc. 3, p. 157–185, fasc. 4, p. 179–211; 5 (2001), fasc. 1–2, p. 75–119; 6 (2002), p. 325–394.

EUGEN CIURTIN (2005)

WIKANDER, STIG. Oscar Stig Wikander (1908–1983) was born in Nörrtalje, a small town close to Stockholm, Sweden, on August 27, 1908. He entered the University of Uppsala in 1925, majoring in classical and oriental languages. Wikander's mentor in Asian studies was the great Iranologist and Semitist Henrik Samuel Nyberg, whose principal ideas, expressed in the synthesis *Irans forntida religionen* (1937), exemplify the Uppsalian school's specific contribution to religious studies. In 1931, Wikander became a member of the prestigious Société Asiatique in Paris. He also studied at the University of Copenhagen under the guidance of Arthur Christensen, where he delivered on February 24, 1936, a paper entitled "*Karnamak-i-Artaxer* och den iranska historietradition" (*Karnamak-i-Artaxer* and the Iranian historical tradition). In 1938 Wikander defended his Ph.D. thesis on the Aryan *Männerbund,* under the supervision of Nyberg, but was awarded only a medium qualification: *med beröm godkänd* (*cum laudatur approbatur*).

In Lund in 1943 Wikander submitted another paper, *Feuerpriester in Kleinasien and Iran* (The Fire Priests in Asia Minor and Iran), under the guidance of his colleague, Geo Widengren, which he hoped would establish his academic career. This paper was published with the same title in 1946. While writing *Der arische Männerbund* (The Aryan warrior bands) and before the beginning of World War II, Wikander built strong ties with the German academic community, in particular with Otto Höfler and Walther Wüst from Munich. Wikander's private correspondence as well as his articles published in Swedish journals before the war provide concrete testimony on his ambiguous position on the Nazi political, as well as academic, situation. In February 1944 he left for the Eastern Front (Greece and Turkey), enrolling in the Swedish Red Cross organization. After teaching Iranian languages at the University of Lund from 1941 to 1953, he was appointed professor of Sanskrit and Indo-European languages at the University of Uppsala. Wikander held this position until late 1974. He died on December 20, 1983, in Uppsala, after suffering during the last years of his life from the painful loss of his mental clarity.

During his life Wikander published numerous articles, but only three books: *Der arische Männerbund* (1938); *Vāyu: Texte und Untersuchungen* (1941), and *Feuerpriester in Kleinasien und Iran* (1946). They made him known as an eminent Iranist, although he was a controversial representative of the Uppsalian school. Even though he published no further books after World War II, these three works represent a common methodology: a historical and even social reconstruction on the basis of predominantly philological data. In these works, Wikander embraced Nyberg's distinction between *Mithragemeinde* and *Gathasgemeinde,* the general theory of a pre-Zoroastrian religion, and he used it as a basis for a philological analysis aimed at reconstructing the social institution and religious cults of the pre-Zoroastrian (Indo-Iranian or Arian) warrior communities, whose principles were very different from the moral Zoroastrian rules. Wikander aimed to prove that such warrior organizations had an important social, political, and religious role within Arian society. He argued that analysis of these structures should be the main focus of research into Indo-Iranian religions. At the same time Wikander supported Widengren's theory about the high gods of ancient Iran presented in *Hochgottglaube im alten Iran* (1938).

Wikander's 1938 thesis had been preceded by various ethnological and anthropological investigations undertaken during the nineteenth and early twentieth centuries (i.e., the work of such scholars as Leo Bittremieux, Leo Frobenius, Heinrich Schurtz, and Hutton Webster), most of them concerned with African secret societies. Though benefiting from many of these works Wikander was inspired mainly by Otto Höfler's *Kultische Geheimbünde der Germanen* (1934). Both Wikander and Widengren took into consideration the relevance of primitive African materials; while Widengren found identical structures between African and ancient Iranian ideas concerning the high gods, Wikander considered the political role of Arian warrior bands to be deeper than that of primitive African secret communities, emphasizing in this way the superiority of Arian structures.

Apart from his book on Vāyu, whom he treated as a high god of the war, Wikander continued to examine the paradigm of warrior bands and masculine society, but with a different theoretical approach. The conclusion of his controversial "Études sur les mystères de Mithras" (1950), meant to criticize Franz Cumont's theory of the Iranian origin of the Western Mithraic cults, suggests that this Western phenomenon could have had its origin among warrior bands from the Balkans that worshipped the god Sabazios. The existence of an Iranian influence could be certified in the Balkans by the common symbol of the Thracian or Danubian cavalier. Wikander's article on Indo-Iranian twin-gods, published as a tribute to Georges Dumézil, points out how the main attributes of Nakula and Sahadeva received, from *Ṛgveda* to *Mahābhārata,* new warlike connotations. Finally, at the Congress of Mithraic Studies (Teheran, 1975), Wikander presented the Avestan text *Mihr Yasht* as indicating a purely masculine society, comparable to the Roman society of mysteries and following the general pattern of the archaic *Männerbund,* but from a phenomenological, not historical or sociological, point of view.

Wikander conceived his other two books, *Vāyu* and *Feuerpriester in Kleinasien und Iran,* as complementary and circumscribed to the same purpose: to broaden the reconstruction of the morphology of the socio-religious observances of ancient Indo-Iranians, centered on the cults devoted to the high gods Mithra and Vāyu-Anahita. Though this general theory is considered outdated, Wikander's work on fire-priests can still be used as an introduction to the cults related to Anahita, being valuable for the multiplicity of sources (Greek, Latin, Byzantine, and Arabic) upon which Wikander built his arguments.

Almost all of these theories have been criticized or rejected, including the relevance of the high gods for the ancient Iranian area, the discontinuity between Indo-Iranian preexistent religious forms and Zoroastrian reform, the consistency of a particular cult specific to masculine societies devoted to the Vāyu-Anahita gods, and so on. In addition, Wikander's philological interpretation of key terms, such as the Vedic *maryá,* the Old Iranian *mairya-,* and the Middle Iranian *mērak* (or *mērag*), which he thought proved the existence of warrior bands, seems doubtful. After World War II, Wikander abandoned the philological perspective of socio-religious reconstruction. On this point, he faced the same theoretical difficulties as Dumézil (at least before his *Naissance d'archanges,* 1945) in presuming to be able to reconstruct, on the basis of mere textual evidence, the three functions as social estates, real institutions of the ancient Indo-Europeans—that is, the *sacerdotium,* the caste of warriors, and the caste of growers and breeders (*brāhmaṇa, kṣatriya,* and *vaiśya*). However, by revising his methodology toward a more structural approach, Wikander could begin a fruitful dialogue with Dumézil.

In an article first published in the Swedish journal *Religion och Bibel* under the title "Pāṇḍava-sagan och Mahābhāratas mytiska förutsättningar" ("The legend of the Pāṇḍava and the mythical substructure of Mahābhārata," 1947) and later only partially translated by Dumézil in his *Jupiter, Mars, Quirinus* (1941), Wikander proposed the principle of homogeneity and coherence from old Vedic theology to the epic construction of *Mahābhārata.* By assuming Dumézil's theory of trifunctional partition, Wikander attempted to demonstrate that the five principal actors in *Mahābhārata* (Pāṇḍavas Yudhiṣṭira, Arjuna and Bhīma, and Nakula and Sahadeva) are the exact epic transposition of the trifunctional Vedic gods, namely Mitra and Varuṇa, Indra, and the twin-gods Nasatyas. A second important article, published in *Nouvelle Clio,* "Sur le fonds commun indo-iranien des épopées de la Perse et de l'Inde" (1949), shows the extent to which Wikander preserved the relevance of the hypothesis of the common Indo-Iranian mythology, but from a new, Indo-European, comparative perspective. In this field, Wikander made a major contribution with his article "Germanische und indo-iranische Eschatologie" (1960), in which he emphasized the structural, mythological correlation between the Indo-Iranian and German-Scandinavian epic from an eschatological point of view. He expanded this view of Indo-Iranian eschatology in one of his six 1967 Haskell Lectures, "Indo-European Eschatology."

Few aspects of Wikander's work were sympathetic to the *Religionsgeschichtliche Schule,* as was certainly the case with his compatriot, Widengren. One could invoke Wikander's criticism of Cumont's theory about the Iranian origin of the Western Mithraic cult or his general suspicion of the fervent pan-Iranian theories of Michael Rostovtzeff or Lars-Ivan Ringbom. More eloquent is a short passage from "The Indo-European Eschatology": "I am not qualified to take up those problems about Iranian influence on the religions of the Bible and the religions of the Greco-Roman syncretism. But, I cannot refrain from regretting that the discussion follows an all too old and antiquated pattern."

During the last period of his life Wikander turned his attention mainly to the phenomenon of Gnosticism. He published four articles on Gnostic symbols in the work of Erik Johan Stagnelius, the famous Romantic poet of Sweden. Wikander's "Ingmar Bergman's Mythic Ironies" on the Gnostic symbolism in some of Bergman's films, belongs to the same area of interest. It was based on a conference entitled "Bergman, a Gnostic?" held in Chicago in 1967. Wikander was also interested in Mircea Eliade's scholarly works on religious symbolism (in particular for their examination of the transition from archaic to modern societies). In addition, Wikander worked on projects concerning the epic literature of the Kurds, which he analyzed while traveling in Syria and Lebanon. He transcribed and translated several epic texts in an attempt to reveal the correspondence between the religious observances of contemporary Kurdish communities and Old Iranian ones. Many of Wikander's studies on Kurdish folklore remain unpublished.

There are many unpublished manuscripts in Wikander's archive at Uppsala University Library. The most relevant for the history of religions are the Haskell Lectures ("The Ideology of the National Epic," "Heroic Age or Mythic Age?" "Problems of Indian Epics," "Problems of Iranian Epics," "From Myth to History," and "The Indo-European Eschatology"), held in Chicago at the invitation of Eliade. These lectures show the influence of Eliade's work (in particular his *Le mythe de l'éternel retour* [1949] and parts of *Aspects du mythe* [1963]) on Wikander's thought (especially regarding the relation between myth and history). Another important manuscript entitled "Den ariska romantiken" (The Arian Romanticism) is a sort of history of nineteenth-century European oriental studies, with special attention given to Swedish authors. Wikander mainly analyzed the European adoption of the term *Arian* and the ideological development of its meaning according to English, French, German, and Italian Romantic and post-Romantic writers.

In 1947, Wikander and the Swedish linguist Bertil Malmberg founded the journal *Studia Linguistica* in Lund. Wikander also planned to publish with Kasten Rönnow a series called *Quæstiones indo-iranicæ,* but only one work was eventually published—Wikander's book on Vāyu. For several years he served on the advisory board for the Uppsalian journal for Asian studies, *Orientalia Suecana.* In 1974 the president of the Society for Mithraic Studies, Harold W. Bailey, invited him to join the advisory board of the *Journal for Mithraic Studies.* He also served with Franz Altheim, Dumézil, and Eliade on the scientific committee of *Mankind Quarterly* during the first years of its publication.

Wikander took part in a number of congresses, including the International Congress for Oriental Studies (Paris, 1948; Munich, 1957), the IAHR congresses (Amsterdam, 1950; Marburg, 1960), the first International Congress for Sanskrit Studies (New Delhi, 1972), and the second International Congress of Mithraic Studies (Teheran, 1975). He also served as visiting professor at Columbia University in New York (1959–1960), at Colegio de México (spring-summer, 1967), and at the University of Chicago (fall-winter 1967).

In conclusion, Wikander's academic works reveal a surprisingly complex personality, whose place in the framework of the history of religions should be fully reconsidered. Until then, the correspondence between Wikander and Eliade proves it to be extensive.

See Also Indo-European Religions; Mithraism.

Bibliography

As of 2004 no monograph had been published on the life and work of Stig Wikander, in part because Wikander left few autobiographical traces. The Eliade-Wikander correspondence, discovered in 2001, brings forth, to the best of our knowledge, the most comprehensive biographical documentation published so far on Wikander.

Arvidsson, Stefan. *Ariska Idoler: Den indoeuropeiska mytologin som vetenskap och ideologi.* Stockholm, 2001.

De Jong, Albert. *Traditions of the Magi: Zoroastrianism in Greek and Latin Literature.* Leiden, 1997.

Dumézil, Georges. *Mythe et épopée.* 3 vols. Paris, 1986.

Hiltebeitel, Alf. *The Ritual of Battle: Krishna in the Mahābhārata.* Albany, N.Y., 1990.

Kahle, Sigrid. *H. S. Nyberg: En vetenskapsmans biografi.* Stockholm, 1991.

Lincoln, Bruce. "Warriors and Non-Herdsmen: A Response to Mary Boyce." In *Death, War, Sacrifice: Studies in Ideology and Practice,* pp. 147–166. Chicago, 1991.

Littleton, C. Scott. *The New Comparative Mythology: An Anthropological Assessment of the Theories of Georges Dumézil.* 3d ed. Berkeley, 1982.

Nyberg, H. S. *Irans forntida religioner.* Stockholm, 1937. Translated as *Die Religionen des alten Iran.* Leipzig, 1938; 2d ed., Osnabrück, 1966.

Timus, Mihaela. "La bibliographie annotée de Stig Wikander." *Stvdia Asiatica: Revue internationale d'études asiatiques* 1 (2000): 209–234.

Timus, Mihaela. "Addendum II: Other unpublished letters sent or received by Stig Wikander." *Archævs: Études d'histoire des religions* 6 (2002): 383–394.

Timus, Mihaela, ed. *The Unpublished Correspondence Eliade-Wikander.* Iassy, Romania, 2004.

Timus, Mihaela, and Eugin Ciurtin. "The Unpublished Correspondence between Mircea Eliade and Stig Wikander (1948–1977)." *Archævs: Études d'histoire des religions* 3/4 (2000): 157–185, 179–211; 5 (2001): 75–119; 6 (2002): 325–362.

Waldmann, Helmut. *Heilgeschichtlich verfasste Theologie und Männerbünde: Die Grundlagen des gnostischen Weltbildes.* Tübingen, Germany, 1994.

Widengren, Geo. *Hochgottglaube im alten Iran.* Uppsala, Sweden, 1938.

Wikander, Stig. *Der arische Männerbund: Studien zur indoiranischen Sprach- und Religionsgeschichte.* Lund, Sweden, 1938.

Wikander, Stig. *Vāyu: Texte und Untersuchungen zur indoiranischen Religionsgeschichte.* Lund, Sweden, 1941.

Wikander, Stig. *Feuerpriester in Kleinasien und Iran.* Lund, Sweden, 1946.

Wikander, Stig. "Pāṇḍavasagan och Mahābhāratas mystika förutsättningar." *Religion och Bibel* 6 (1947): 27–39.

Wikander, Stig. "Sur le fonds commun indo-iranien des épopées de la Perse et de l'Inde." *La Nouvelle Clio* 1–2 (1949): 310–329.

Wikander, Stig. "Études sur les mystères de Mithras." *Vetenskaps Societetens i Lund Årsbok* (1951): 37–56.

Wikander, Stig. "Histoire des Ouranides." *Cahiers du sud* 36 (1952): 9–17.

Wikander, Stig. "Mithra en vieux-perse." *Orientalia suecana* 1 (1952): 66–68.

Wikander, Stig. "Nakula et Sahadeva." *Orientalia suecana* 6 (1957): 66–96.

Wikander, Stig. "Germanische und indo-iranische Eschatologie." *Kairos* 2 (1960): 81–88.

Wikander, Stig. "Kurdish Tales on Animals." Edited by Marita Wikander and Jan Stolpe. *Orientalia suecana* 51–52 (2002–2003): 429–435.

MIHAELA TIMUS (2005)

WILĀYAH SEE WALĀYAH

WILLIAM OF OCKHAM (1280?–1349?), English philosopher and theologian.

William of Ockham was born between 1280 and 1285 at Ockham in Surrey, England. He entered the Franciscan order and studied at the Franciscan house in Oxford but without taking his doctorate; hence his title of "Venerable Inceptor," which indicated that he had not received a degree.

Ockham's career is divided into two phases. During the first phase he wrote his major theological, philosophical, and logical works; the most important were his *Commentary on the Sentences* and his *Sum of Logic.* The second phase began when in 1328 he fled from the papal court at Avignon with the general of the Franciscan order, Michael of Cesena, to the German emperor Ludwig of Bavaria, at Munich. Ludwig had become the adversary of John XXII, and Ockham joined the other Franciscan dissidents there who had quarreled with the pope over his denial of the Franciscan claim to be following Christ's life of absolute poverty. Ockham, who had originally been summoned to Avignon to answer accusations of error in some of his theological and philosophical doctrines, spent the remainder of his life polemicizing against papal claims to absolute jurisdiction in temporal and spiritual matters. He died at Munich, probably in 1349.

Ockham was the most influential thinker of the later Middle Ages. Philosophically, he was the first to found his outlook upon the discrepancy between the individual nature of all created being and the universal nature of the concepts and terms constituting our proper knowledge. Since, he said, only individuals were real, all universal and general notions only had real, as opposed to conceptual or grammatical, meaning if they referred to real individual things. In contrast to the overwhelming weight of medieval tradition, Ockham held that there were no such things as universal natures or essences. Instead, therefore, of seeking to explain the individual as the particularization of the universal, as in the statement that the individual man Socrates is the expression of the essence humanity, or that a white object is the manifestation of the quality whiteness, Ockham inverted the order and sought to explain how the mind arrives at the universal concept of humanity or whiteness from exclusive experience of individual men or white objects. He did so psychologically,

logically, and grammatically by seeking to show how the mind forms concepts and what their relation is to the terms and propositions in which knowledge of them is expressed. He thereby gave a new direction to philosophical inquiry, which effectively denied an independent place to metaphysics.

Theologically, the effect was to undermine the bases for a natural theology, since whatever lay outside intuitive experience of individual things lacked evidential status. Not only did that exclude proofs, as opposed to persuasions, for God's existence, but it confined theological discourse to the elucidation of the meaning of the articles of faith rather than providing rational support for their truth. Their truth was a matter of belief. And central to belief was thc Christian's recognition of God's omnipotence. By Ockham's time, the affirmation of God's omnipotence had assumed a new importance, partly at least in response to the determinism of Greek and Arabic philosophy. It had come to be expressed in the distinction between God's ordained power *(potentia ordinata),* the power by which he governed the workings of the universe he had created, and his absolute power (*potentia absoluta*), which denoted his omnipotence taken solely in itself without relation to any order, and so is limited by nothing other than logical self-contradiction, which would have impaired it.

It was Ockham who more than anyone gave this distinction the currency which it acquired in the middle of the fourteenth century. He applied it to restate the accepted Christian truth that God could do directly (or indeed differently or not at all) what, ordinarily, by his ordained power, he did by secondary causes. Ockham was thereby reaffirming God's role as the direct ruler as well as creator of the universe. What was novel was the range and frequency of Ockham's application of God's omnipotence to virtually every aspect of creation: nature, knowledge, and matters of belief. Thus God himself could directly cause or conserve an effect that normally had a natural cause: the Eucharist, for example, where the appearance of the elements of the bread and wine could remain after consecration without any longer existing as physical substances. Similarly, absolutely, God could cause direct intuitive knowledge of an object that was not immediately present to the knower. He could do so, not by creating an illusion that what appeared to exist did not really exist, but by himself directly conserving knowledge of an object that was real but not present, such as someone seen in Oxford who was at Rome. Theologically, the implications were perhaps most far-reaching of all—and here Ockham was following Duns Scotus—by substituting God's immediate agency for the agency of the church, above all in directly accepting individuals for eternal life without the requisites of sacramental grace. God was thereby rewarding an individual action or will and not the preceding grace that ordinarily an individual had first to receive as the condition of the reward. Although neither Duns Scotus nor Ockham went beyond stating such a conclusion as the consequence of God's freedom from created forms, many of their successors gave the notion much wider application, which virtually denuded sacramental grace of its intrinsic efficacy. The effect was to reinforce the tendency in the religious outlook of the later Middle Ages to make God's will the sole arbiter in individual justification and predestination. It had as its accompaniment a corresponding stress upon individual religious experience based upon faith as the foundation of all theological discourse and alone bringing certainty in a contingent universe.

The extent of Ockham's influence during the fourteenth and fifteenth centuries can be seen in the dominance of the so-called nominalist school that developed first at Paris University and then spread to the new universities founded throughout the German-speaking lands. Its hallmarks were precisely an emphasis upon God's absolute power and therefore on the immediacy of God's will in deciding whom to justify and accept for eternal life. With Ockham's attack upon the concept of the pope's plenitude of power, and his insistence upon the sole authority of faith residing in every believer to decide questions of doctrine, he did perhaps more than any other single thinker to transform the philosophical and theological outlook of the later Middle Ages.

SEE ALSO Nominalism.

BIBLIOGRAPHY

Authoritative accounts of Ockham's philosophy can be found in Marilyn McCord Adams's *William Ockham,* 2 vols. (Notre Dame, Ind., 1987), Léon Baudry's *Guillaume d'Occam* (Paris, 1949), Philotheus Boehner's *Collected Articles on Ockham,* edited by Eligius Buytaert (New York, 1958), Jürgen Miethke's *Ockhams Weg zur Sozialphilosophie* (Berlin, 1969), Paul Vignaux's article "Occam" in *Dictionaire de théologie catholique* (Paris, 1931), and my own *William of Ockham: The Metamorphosis of Scholastic Discourse* (Manchester, 1975).

GORDON LEFF (1987 AND 2005)

WILLIAMS, ROGER (1603–1683), English and American Puritan minister and prophet of religious liberty, founder of Rhode Island. Born in London, Roger Williams was the son of Alice and James Williams, a merchant tailor. Of his early education little is known, but his ability at shorthand probably attracted the attention of Sir Edward Coke, then lord chief justice, who enabled him to attend Charterhouse School, from whence he won a scholarship to Cambridge (B.A., 1627). After several years' further study in divinity at that Puritan stronghold, Williams became chaplain in the household of Sir William Masham, and he married Mary Barnard, who was to bear him six children. As a convinced Puritan at the time when Bishop William Laud was vigorously opposing the movement, he found it advisable to join the great migration to New England in December 1630.

Called to serve the church at Boston, Williams refused to accept the post because the Massachusetts Bay Puritans had not fully broken with the Church of England or rejected legal religious establishment, and Williams was by then a thorough Separatist. Instead, he ministered for several years at Plymouth Colony, where the Separatist element was stronger, and undertook missionary work among the Algonquin Indians, learning their language. Williams returned to Massachusetts Bay Colony in 1633, however, accepting a call to the church at Salem. But he angered colonial leaders by insisting that the churches profess separation, by claiming that the royal charter did not provide a valid title to the land, by denying that the unregenerate could take an oath of loyalty (which for him was an act of worship), and by arguing that magistrates could not punish breaches of the first commandments (which deal with religious obligations), but only of those that deal with moral or civil matters. Brought to trial in October 1635, he was banished. Williams fled southward, purchased land from the Indians, and founded Providence, Rhode Island, in 1636. In a departure new in Christian civilization, no church was established in the new colony—religious liberty was for all, even those with whom Williams was in sharp theological disagreement.

Williams earned his living by farming and (until 1651) trading with Indians at a lonely outpost on Narragansett Bay. His knowledge of Indian ways and his friendship with them permitted him to mediate among them, as well as between them and the English, on many occasions. His skill prevented what could have been a powerful Indian alliance against the colonies in 1637. His political abilities were also exercised in helping to keep order among the growing towns of Rhode Island. To secure a charter so that Rhode Island would not be swallowed up by Massachusetts Bay Colony, he journeyed to England in 1643–1644. He became known to the rising Puritan leadership through such writings as *A Key into the Language of America* (1643) and *The Bloudy Tenent of Persecution, for Cause of Conscience* (1644), a hastily written but forceful scriptural argument for religious freedom. Successful in obtaining the charter, Williams returned home, but political changes soon jeopardized that achievement. he sold his trading post to finance a return to England (1651–1654), where he associated with such powerful figures as John Milton and Oliver Cromwell. Again he published extensively, notably *The Bloody Tenent Yet More Bloody, Experiments of Spiritual Life and Health,* and *The Hireling Ministry None of Christs,* all in 1652. Called home by political turmoil and family need, he left John Clarke of Newport to complete the diplomatic mission; Clarke remained until 1663, finally securing a permanent charter for Rhode Island from the Restoration government. Meanwhile Williams served three years as president of the colony he had founded.

Williams's deepest concern throughout his life was with matters of religion, the central theme of his extensive writings. He remained faithful to common Puritan presuppositions but doggedly pursued their implications to radical conclusions few could accept. A Calvinist in theology, he emphasized the authority of the Bible as the means by which the spirit of God speaks, interpreting many of its passages in typological and millenarian ways. His greatest divergence with other Puritans was over the doctrine of the church. He sharply differentiated the pure church from the secular world, but he had difficulty identifying it amid the warring sects of his time. Briefly in 1639 he believed that the Baptists came the closest to his ideal of the church. Williams was baptized by affusion (pouring), baptized others, and participated in the founding of the first Baptist church in America at Providence. He soon left the congregation, however, and became known as a "seeker," but was not a member of any Seeker group, although he was acquainted with the Calvinist Seekers in England in the early 1650s.

Williams became convinced that the apostasy of the churches since Constantine had engulfed Christendom and that until God raised up new apostles the true church could not be discerned. Meanwhile, God called "prophets in sackcloth" to preach and witness to the truth, but not to gather churches. As a "prophet in sackcloth" Williams ministered among both English and Indians, but he remained highly critical of Christendom in all its forms, as well as of clergy who earned their livings by ministering. he believed that the truly faithful must be prepared for misunderstanding and persecution, having as their sole defense the sword of the spirit—the word of God. Magistrates have no competence in matters of religion, he insisted, for their rule extends only to civil matters.

Although Williams believed ardently in religious freedom, he was not a tolerant man; he could attack vigorously with tongue and pen (though never by force) those with whom he disagreed in matters of theology and biblical interpretation. He was deeply opposed to George Fox and the Quakers; as a Calvinist he objected to their separation of Word and Spirit, as well as to what was for him their inadequate Christology. He hoped to debate Fox when the latter was in Rhode Island in 1672, but had to settle for sharp exchanges with other Quaker leaders, about which he wrote in his most polemical work, *George Fox Digg'd out of His Burrowes* (Boston, 1676).

Williams's role as a pioneer of religious liberty and the separation of church and state has been rightly celebrated as his major contribution; the twentieth-century renaissance in Puritan studies has made clear how deeply his work was rooted in his religious commitments.

Bibliography

Almost all of Williams's extant writings are in *The Complete Writings of Roger Williams,* 7 vols. (New York, 1963); the first six volumes are reprints of nineteenth-century editions, but the seventh adds tracts not included in previous collections and was edited by Perry Miller with an interpretive introduction. Miller had previously written *Roger Williams: His Contribution to the American Tradition* (1953; reprint, New York, 1966), which includes brief, modernized passages from Williams's major works. A well-delineated interpretation of Williams's thought, based on his writings, is Edmund S. Morgan's *Roger Williams: The Church and the State* (New York, 1967). A thoughtful treatment that includes informed attention to the English as well as to the American locales of Williams's life is John Garrett's *Roger Williams: Witness beyond Christendom, 1603–1683* (New York, 1970). A study of his religious and biblical views is W. Clark Gilpin's *The Millenarian Piety of Roger Williams* (Chicago, 1979).

ROBERT T. HANDY (1987)

WILLIBRORD (658–739), pioneer of the English missionaries who crossed the seas to proclaim the gospel to the non-Christian peoples of the continent of Europe. Born in Northumbria, Willibrord as a boy came under the influence of the great Wilfrid, archbishop of York. From 678 to 690 he was in Ireland, and while there he became filled with the desire, which never left him, to preach the gospel to non-Christians.

In 690 Willibrord went to Friesland in the Netherlands, which became his home for forty-nine years. This part of Europe was in a state of great disorder from which it was emerging through the rise of Carolingian power, destined to reach its climax in the empire of Charlemagne. Pepin I gave Willibrord the land near Utrecht on which later Willibrord was to build his cathedral. In 695 he was consecrated archbishop by the pope, who intended to establish Utrecht as a regular province of the church with archbishop and diocesan bishops. This goal was never attained, and after the death of Willibrord, Utrecht gradually lost its importance.

None of the correspondence of Willibrord has survived, and we have hardly anything from his hand. This makes it difficult to get a clear idea of his personality and his work. He seems to have been characterized not so much by brilliance as by steadfast continuance in the work that he had set himself to do. It is clear that his aims were greater than his achievements. He penetrated Denmark and brought back thirty boys who presumably were to be trained as missionaries to their own people, but nothing came of this. It is not clear whether he ever consecrated other bishops. He did, however, in 698 found the Monastery of Echternach in Luxembourg, which later became a great center of missionary work.

Willibrord opened a door to the evangelists of the rising English church, worked out a model of what a missionary should be, and set an example followed by many successors. The churches in the Netherlands are right in regarding him as the apostle of Frisia and the founder of the church in their land.

BIBLIOGRAPHY

The two lives of Willibrord by Alcuin (735–804), *Vita sancti Willibrordi*, "Monumenta Alcuiniana," vol. 6, are hagiographical, full of stories of miracles, and inadequate from the point of view of historical detail and reliability. Of modern works, William Levison's *England and the Continent in the Eighth Century* (Oxford, 1946), pp. 1–69, is authoritative. Reference may be made also to Alexander J. Grieve's *Willibrord, Missionary in the Netherlands* (Westminster, 1923) and to *The Anglo-Saxon Missionaries in Germany*, edited and translated by Charles H. Talbot (New York, 1954).

STEPHEN C. NEILL (1987)

WINE SEE BEVERAGES; EUCHARIST

WINTER SOLSTICE SONGS. In Europe the celebration of the winter solstice, the longest night of the year, is a heritage that goes back to prehistoric times. The classical Greek and Latin authors, as well as the fathers of the church, attest to the fact that the festivities centered around the winter solstice in antiquity perpetuated traditions still more ancient that were deeply rooted in folk practice. Despite regional differences in the evolution of these feasts and in their cultural significance, they all included elements of sun worship, revels, masquerades, and divination since the winter solstice was considered to be a time of great importance. The fertility of the fields, the reproduction of the cattle, the health of the people, and the conclusion of marriages in the coming year were all deemed to depend on the observance of the solstice rituals.

The celebration of the winter solstice also included the singing of special songs. Unfortunately, very little is known about the songs performed during the cycle of the Roman imperial feasts, the Saturnalia, the Dies Natalis Solis Invicti (the birthday of the Iranian god Mithra), and the Calendae Ianuari, which occasioned the exchange of congratulations and the start of the new administrative year. All that has come down to the present day are the texts of certain congratulation formulas. From Augustine one learns that in the fifth century CE, on the day of such feasts, songs that from the Christian point of view were "most vain and filthy" were still performed. In comparison with the celebration of the winter solstice in northern Europe, however, the Roman feasts, through their insertion into the official calendar and through their fusion with elements imported from different provinces of the empire, may be considered a relatively late cultural synthesis.

The winter solstice feasts celebrated in northern Europe display different features and have a much more archaic character. Nearly all records of the winter solstice feasts in this area relate only to the Germanic peoples. Nevertheless, this article shall try to demonstrate, most of these customs and beliefs can also be found in the folk traditions of eastern Europe.

According to Latin historians and church chronicles, as well as evidence derived from the laws and capitularies prohibiting pagan practices and early Anglo-Saxon and northern

European literature such as the Icelandic sagas, the Germanic midwinter Yule feast celebrated the reappearance of the sun and had a marked funeral character. It was commonly believed that the spirits of the dead were most haunting during the period of the winter solstice. They would return to their former dwelling places in order to participate in the feasting, and unless they were treated with due honor, they would do harm to the living. On the other hand, the welcoming of the spirits, who were impersonated with masks, was believed to insure peace, health, prosperity, and fertility in the coming year.

Despite the relative richness of data about the mythology and customs of the Germanic peoples, precise information about the specific myths, tales, or songs that were performed during the Yule feast is lacking. Sources that mention the performance of Icelandic sagas on Yuletide are not really an exception. The Icelandic sagas, however, cannot be considered specialized songs of the winter solstice since they were also performed on other occasions, such as weddings and night gatherings. It must also be borne in mind that the Icelandic sagas, although partly based on older oral literature, were composed during the twelfth and thirteenth centuries and thus cannot properly be included among the pagan folk traditions of the winter solstice.

Through missionary propaganda and the skillful strategy of the church, these traditions were partly obliterated and partly assimilated into the patterns of Christian ideology. The winter holy days of the church were originally based on the calendar of the later Roman empire. While ostensibly expelling pagan winter customs, the winter holy days actually adopted some of them under Christian cover, first those of the Mediterranean area, then some of the ancient winter solstice traditions of the Germanic peoples. Thus in the sounds of modern hibernal holy days one can still hear the echoes of the pagan celebrations of the winter solstice.

But the link that still connects the ancient winter solstice celebration to the present day must be sought in the traditions of the peasantry. If in the urban world the church succeeded in gradually assimilating pagan customs, wiping out their memory and finally supplanting them, its success among the peasants came later and was less definitive. Judging by the repeated admonitions that medieval priests addressed to the country folk, it seems clear that the peasants continued to cling to the pagan customs of the winter solstice, especially in northern Europe, where conversion to Christianity came late. Some of these customs still linger in the folk traditions of the Germanic peoples: To this day, the peasants of those countries attribute magical powers to the ashes of the old "Yule log" burned on Christmas and to the bread especially baked for this holy day.

It is not by chance that only in eastern Europe is found a living folk tradition that in part continues the ancient pagan winter solstice traditions. In this outlying region of the continent, at the turn of the twentieth century, and in some areas even until the onset of World War I, the numerically superior peasant class continued to live in relative isolation, under conditions that were in many ways archaic. Owing partly to this gap in socio-historical evolution, elements of the sun worship referred to among the Germanic peoples in the sixth and seventh centuries can still be found in eastern European folklore. The survival here of winter solstice traditions is also to be explained by the fact that in this area the fight against pagan customs was far less methodical than in the west. Lacking adequate theological training, the village priests of eastern Europe were not intransigent adversaries of paganism; they themselves sometimes contributed unintentionally to the survival of pagan customs or to their symbiosis with Christianity.

The eastern European solstice songs, performed by organized groups of adults during the winter holy days, resemble Christmas carols in the time of their performance and in some minor parallels in subject matter. Unlike Christmas carols, however, which circulated mainly in manuscript and in printed editions, the eastern European songs belonged to oral tradition. At their core, they preserved pagan rituals and myths that are integrated into a rich complex of folk customs of eastern Europe.

Circulating in impoverished form among the Poles, Bylorussians, Moravians, and Serbians, and still in use in certain districts of Greece, the repertoire of winter solstice songs of eastern Europe is rich and well preserved among the Ukrainians, Bulgarians, and especially among the Romanians. The composer and ethnomusicologist Béla Bartók, who collected Romanian folklore from before World War I, noted that "among all the eastern European peoples, the Romanians have preserved best till this day these partly ancient songs of the winter solstice" (Bartok, 1968, p. xxviii).

It can be demonstrated on linguistic grounds that the terms designating the winter repertoire in eastern Europe (i.e., the Ukrainian *koliada* or *koliadka,* the Belorussian *kaliada,* the Bulgarian *koleda,* and the Romanian *colinda* or *corinda*) are all derived from the Latin *calendae.* When one adds to this the fact that early Christian documents, as well as archaeological evidence, prove that the Roman winter feasts enjoyed great popularity in the Eastern Roman Empire, one can conclude that the folk terminology designating the eastern European repertoire of winter solstice songs almost certainly referred originally to the Calendae Ianuari. However, whether or not the eastern European songs themselves derived from the Roman winter feasts may be decided only by an analysis of the genre at the level of ritual acts and at the level of verbal expression.

The performance of the eastern European repertoire of solstice songs, which this article shall conventionally call "winter carols," is governed by unwritten regulations and occasionally shows traces of rituals, representations, and beliefs of mythological origin. Because of the present-day decline in the performance of the winter carol, in what follows this article shall take into consideration not only contemporary evidence but also certain data concerning regulations and beliefs that were obtained from the older generation of carolers or that were recorded in archives.

Owing not only to local circumstances but also to the multiform, diffuse character of the myth itself, the performance of winter carols differs not only from people to people but very frequently from district to district inside the borders of the same country. Thus while this article shall insist on the commonality of the custom among the Ukrainians, Romanians, and Bulgarians, the writer shall also point out certain local peculiarities that eventually could contribute to clarifying the significance of the winter carol.

As mentioned above, the winter carols are performed during the period of the Christian holy days. According to certain witnesses, this period was once dedicated exclusively to winter carols, the performance of other songs being forbidden. In the past, various benefits were attributed to the performance of winter carols during the traditional period: an increase of the wheat and hemp harvest, welfare and health, the fecundity of the cattle. On the other hand, the performance of the carols at other times could harm the harvest and impair the health of children. Such opposing effects—beneficial and harmful—occasioned by the observance or neglect of the time period prescribed by tradition bears witness to the sacred character of the carols.

According to tradition, winter carols are performed by groups of varying composition and organization. Widely distributed and well structured among the Bulgarians, Romanians, and Ukranians are groups composed of young men, and this may be considered the predominant traditional type. Some of the traditional rules connected with this type of group emphasize the ritual character of the caroling. Thus among the Bulgarians, illegitimate children and those having a physical defect were not permitted to join the group of young men. Archival records and frequent references in the carols to "lads" and "youngsters" show that in the past, at least in certain districts of Romania, caroling was the exclusive prerogative of young unmarried men. In certain districts of Romania, during the winter holy days, the young men of the group were obliged to live together in one dwelling and avoid sexual relations with women. During the same period, young carolers were permitted to behave rather wildly, even to cause minor damage, without being punished.

Today the group of young carolers includes married as well as unmarried men. The organization of such groups starts at the beginning of the Christmas fast (November 15) or at the latest a couple of days before Christmas. On this occasion different duties are assigned to the members of the group. Among the Bulgarians, Romanians, and Ukrainians, it is standard to elect a chief invested with absolute authority over the group and to name a young caroler whose task will be to carry the presents that are given as rewards to the carolers. Among the Ukrainians, the local priest traditionally arbitrated the election of the chief, and the carolers carried the cross with them.

Caroling often entails more than simply singing songs. In certain districts of eastern Europe the caroling is accompanied by the noise of bells, drums, or trumpets, probably aimed at neutralizing the influence of the spirits of the dead, who are widely believed to be especially dangerous during the winter solstice. The Hutzuls, a Ukrainian ethnic group living in the northeastern Carpathian Mountains, associate caroling closely with dance and perform hieratic dances while singing the carols. In certain districts of Romania young carolers would dance with girls after singing the carols in order to bestow upon them joy and good health. In some areas caroling has also been associated with masks. In various districts of Romania, for instance, the dance of the Turka or the Stag (both zoomorphic masks) is performed while, or after, a certain carol is sung.

In Bulgaria, Romania, and the Ukraine, the actual performance of the winter carols takes place on the night of Christmas Eve, on Christmas Day, and sometimes on New Year's Day as well. In certain regions of Romania, groups of carolers sing a special carol at dawn while facing in the direction of the rising sun. The carols may be performed while standing by a window outside a house, in the house itself, or on the road as the carolers go from house to house. By custom the carolers must perform their carols at all the houses of the village, and in turn the people must welcome and reward them. The most common gift is a pastry especially baked for Christmas. It is believed that by eating morsels of this cake or, alternatively, by burying it in the ground or feeding it to cattle, one can ensure the good health of one's children and animals, as well as increase the fertility of the fields. Possibly related to Mediterranean and Near Eastern vegetation rituals is a custom recorded at the beginning of the twentieth century in certain districts of Romania: At the time the young men's group is disbanded, a simulation of the death and resurrection of one of the carolers is enacted. Finally, at the end of the holiday period, the carolers hold a banquet to which they invite the girls of the village.

Winter carols are classified in different ways. Some are named in accordance with the time or place of their performance, for example, "Carol at Night," "Carol at Dawn," "Carol at the Window." Most of the titles refer to the person addressed, such as "Carol for a Girl," "Carol for a Young Man," "Carol for a Widow." Very often the titles refer to the profession of the addressee: "Carol for a Shepherd," "Carol for a Plowman," "Carol for a Midwife," "Carol for a Priest," and so forth. Here and there, in houses where a member of the family has died, the carolers sing a special piece called "Carol for the Dead." Such titles, which have become rare in modern times, derive from an earlier period when the carols were connected with funeral rituals. While some of the winter solstice rituals were intended to repel the spirits of the dead, others were aimed at winning their good will by inviting them to join the feasts and honoring them with songs, offerings, and banquets. The belief that during the period between December 24 and January 6 the souls of the dead come out of their graves and haunt the living is widespread in eastern Europe. In order to appease them, both Slavic peoples and the Romanians used to leave a table laden with food and drink on the night of December 23.

Despite the Latin etymology of the terms designating the eastern European winter carol, the analysis of beliefs and rituals that underlie the performance of the genre does not support the hypothesis of a Roman origin of the custom. It may be assumed that the substratum of the winter carol precedes the romanization of the Thracian populations of eastern Europe. The regulations regarding the organization of young men's groups, as well as other related features, suggest the preservation of vestiges of puberty rituals. Most of the rituals and beliefs associated with the gift of the cake to the carolers, as well as certain remnants of sun worship (e.g., "Carol at Dawn"), seem to belong to a much more archaic stratum than do the Roman winter feasts, and they bear striking resemblances to the northern European celebration of winter solstice. One may deduce that the introduction of Roman winter festivals would not have entailed the abolition of the local festivals. The coincidence of data and certain analogies between the two traditions (revels and masquerades) could not but favor the perpetuation of the local folk tradition under the emblem of the conquerors. The Romans, for their part, were adept at assimilating foreign customs, rituals, and gods through their well-known system of *interpretatio Romana.* It seems very probable that, due to the political and cultural prestige of the imperial winter festivals, local customs relating to the winter solstice, as well as rituals performed at other periods of the year (such as the agrarian rituals performed on the vernal equinox, the old New Year), came to be focused around the new Roman New Year.

The foregoing considerations can be extended through an analysis of the actual repertoire of the winter carols themselves, their fundamental types and motifs. Here one encounters the same problems that are involved in the description of the practice of caroling but now at the linguistic level of the carol itself.

Students of the winter carols generally divide them into two groups: secular and religious. In doing so they mean to distinguish between winter carols that were not influenced by the church and those in which Christian characters or references do appear. A good number of both secular and religious carols contain properly mythological materials, such as the types of carols that present a non-Christian myth of creation in Christian dress. One type of carol, for example, tells how, at the beginning of the world, Judas plunged the universe into darkness by stealing the sun and the moon. Saint John or Saint Elijah then brought the celestial bodies back and thus dispersed the darkness. Another type relates how God created the world by placing the sky on four silver pillars. Despite the references to saints or to God, the versions of creation disclosed by the winter carol have nothing in common with the biblical account in *Genesis* and obviously convey pagan myths about the foundation of the world.

Another category of winter carols, very possibly produced by peasant women, may be connected to feminine rites. In Romania until World War I a female folk society, called Ceata Fetelor, preserved traces of initiation rites for girls, practiced matchmaking charms, and was deeply involved in caroling. Apparently similar societies once existed among other east European peoples as well. Of course, only some of the carols dedicated to unmarried women may be associated with feminine rites. Most of the Romanian, Ukrainian, and Bulgarian carols in this category bear the mark of the traditions and history peculiar to each of these peoples. Common to all three is the well-known allegory of the wedding, which presents the bridegroom in the form of a hunter who pursues a deer.

The Romanian and Bulgarian repertoires contain a large number of carols that deal with hunting. Usually dedicated to young men, these carols were no doubt originally connected with puberty rites. The ritual significance of the hunt as a task preliminary to marriage can still be discerned in the carols that culminate with the killing of the game. As a rule, the victim is an edible wild animal, very often a stag, and the young man plays the part of an accomplished hunter. In a further extension of meaning, the hunter is frequently called the bridegroom, and the hunt is sometimes viewed as a preliminary condition for marriages. Particularly relevant for the relation between the hunt and marriage is the ending of this type of carol: In its death agony, the wounded animal announces the impending marriage of the hunter. It follows that the young man hunts as a candidate for marriage and that the shooting of the game makes him eligible as a bridegroom.

In a distinct group of carols, the hunter-quarry relation is associated with the miracle of metamorphosis. The hunter is confronted by an ambiguous character whose human or social identity is hidden behind the outer form of a wild animal, usually a stag. The creature's ambiguity is manifest from the very beginning: The stag has white or golden horns (colors with a well-known ritual significance); it laughs, sings, and openly defies the hunter. At the revelation of the animal's hidden identity, which entails the recognition of its prestige and authority, the hunter silently gives up the hunt, sometimes breaking his bow into pieces. Here the hunt becomes the scene of a young man's encounter with the sacred. There is undoubtedly a relation between such metamorphoses described in the hunting carols, the dances with zoomorphic masks that sometimes accompany caroling, and the confrontations with disguised characters that often take place in puberty rites.

In addition to carols focused on hunters, shepherds have produced a repertoire of carols of their own. Many of these are clearly related to rites intended to encourage the growth of the shepherd's flock. Others have a cryptic character. For instance, in "Mioritza, the Clairvoyant Lamb," a carol known only to the Romanians, a shepherd is ritually condemned to death for reasons that remain obscure.

While the exact ritual significance of some of the carols sung within the restricted circle of the shepherds remains unclear, the significance of caroling within the context of the more ample agrarian rituals is more explicit. This is especially true of the Bulgarian, Romanian, and Ukrainian carols. These carols tell how God, the saints, or the carolers themselves sprinkle the courtyards and fields with water in order to increase the harvest. Quite often, the carol text preserves not only the ritual formula but a descriptive trace of the ritual actions as well:

Water in his mouth he has taken.
The cornfield he has sprinkled.
And thus he spake:
"Wheat, grow you up to my belt
And you, hemp, up to my armpits."

In the Romanian and Bulgarian repertoires one frequently encounters references to the sun, the sister of the sun, and sometimes to the daughter of the sun. Such personifications are typical of the sun worship that is proper to cultivators and seem to have been connected with the winter solstice celebration. In certain Romanian winter carols, the sun is presented as descending from the sky with a sickle under its arm or as the owner of a ship that harbors the soul of the deceased. Some of the refrains of the Romanian winter carols refer to the sun, its rays, or the dawn, and in certain contexts the sun is referred to as "sacred." It would be impossible to distinguish a category of carols exclusively on the basis of references to the sun or to agricultural rituals. Rather, one finds such references scattered throughout carols of all sorts—hunting carols as well as those influenced by Christianity. It is clear that the point of view and the mentality of an agrarian society are predominant in the winter carol and that it is still rooted in prehistory. Nevertheless, an analysis of hunting carols reveals that many motifs that were passed down from prehistory were reinterpreted to reflect interests of herdsmen and plowmen.

Even the archaic Romanian carol about the hunters who were turned into stags, a carol that served Béla Bartók in 1930 as the libretto of his *Cantata Profana,* did not escape the influence of herdsmen and plowmen. All the versions tell of an old man who, in teaching his sons to hunt, neglected other professions:

And he taught them not
Any kind of trade:
Neither husbandry
Nor herding of cattle
Only [taught them] hunting.

From the perspective of herdsmen and plowmen, hunting as an exclusive profession becomes a culpable activity.

Another important change can be seen in another set of carols in which the hunter is confronted with strange animals: Not only miraculous stags but also fish that jump out of the sea in order to graze on flowers or pick apples, or (among the Romanians) a lion endowed with horns or equated with a human being or a dragon. Unlike the animals in the carols that feature the metamorphosis of the hunter's prey, however, these creatures do not pretend to have a hidden identity, and consequently they are neither spared nor feared. They are characterized by the harmful role they play. They are considered malefactors not so much because they steal to eat but because of the damage they do. The fish is blamed less for stealing apples than for spoiling them, and the lion is deemed guilty not only for plundering the vineyard but also of ravaging it.

Although it is possible to draw a parallel between the wild behavior ascribed to these creatures and the disorders permitted to neophytes in a puberty ritual, it is nevertheless evident that the relations between the harmful animals and the hunter described in this category of carols overstep the bounds of the ritual. While the hero continues to play the part of the hunter, he is at the same time represented as the owner of a house or a vineyard or as the protector of an apple tree. Crossing the borderline that separates what is wild from what is cultivated, the harmful animals endanger the interests of the farmers. The ritual matrix of the hunting carol is reduced to an empty shell in order to make way for the message of an agrarian society. The young hero has not dropped the emblem of the hunter; he has nonetheless become a manifest representative of the farmers' interests.

It was not only the agrarian mentality that brought about change in the winter carol but other factors as well; first among these was the influence of Christianity, which took several forms. It is probable that the earliest direct influence of the new faith was the introduction of Christian refrains into the carols. One of the oldest of these is the "hallelujah," which one finds preserved in a corrupted form. In a more indirect way, Christianity served as a vehicle for conveying legends and beliefs from the Mediterranean and Near East to eastern Europe. For instance, the story found in an apocryphal gospel, which tells of the Mother of God asking a palm tree to lend her its shade, reappears in a winter carol, where the palm tree has become the poplar and fir common to eastern Europe. Such apocryphal legends form the basis of many of the carols.

Only a part of the corpus of religious carols was inspired by Christian apocrypha spread through the Slavonic-Byzantine church. Many others combine Christian themes with the local folk culture of eastern Europe. Here the distinction between religious carols and secular carols breaks down. Symbolic of this lack of a clear boundary is a magnificent robe, described in the carols as adorned with the heavenly bodies, which may be worn in turn by God himself, by Jesus, by a shepherd, or by the boy who, in the carol, is chosen as chief of the army. Similarly, the fusion of Christian motifs with older beliefs could result in surprising, hybrid characters. Judas, for instance, may be equated with a subterranean demon, with a serpent, or with an aquatic monster.

One occasionally encounters carols that betray a degree of tension between Christianity and the folk mythology.

Thus in some of the hunting carols a stag pretends at first to be Saint John, and then denies it and reveals itself to be a sacred beast that measures the earth and the sky. In a large number of the carols, however, there is no such tension. Jesus is depicted dancing with the sister of the sun, Saint Nicholas saves the ships of the sun from sinking, and the birth of Jesus is announced by a fairy. In the mild climate of folk Christianity, which survived until quite late in eastern Europe, the association of the saints with mythological characters was neither resented nor felt to be inappropriate or desecrating.

One of the most straightforward forms of interaction between Christianity and folk motifs was the simple substitution of Christian saints for earlier mythological figures. At a deeper level, however, the Christian ideas of sin and punishment could occasionally give a new meaning to both the motivation and the denouement of the original myth.

Judging by a textual analysis of the carols and related documents, it appears that the process of the christianization of the carols has intensified in the last three or four centuries as a consequence of the increased influence of the church. Yet one can detect in the carol repertoire an old Christian nucleus. The fact that some of the "religious" types conform well to the patterns of the genre and bear folk titles apparently proves their penetration into the winter carol's repertoire at an early date. Among these old Christian carols we may mention the type that represents Jesus surrounded by sheep, a type eventually inspired by the early Christian symbol of the good shepherd, and those that tell of a monastery by the sea or describe the Mother of God with the baby Jesus in her arms.

What one might call the "poetics" of the genre of the winter carol is in fact an ensemble of canons closely connected with the ritual function that the winter carol is intended to serve. Each carol consists of two parts: a first part that is sung, and that includes one or more descriptive or narrative sequences, and a second part that is spoken, and that includes a congratulation formula.

Although relatively concise and placed at the end of the carol, the congratulation formula was of the utmost importance. In a context where ritual formulas were believed to have concrete effects, the wish expressed through the congratulation formula was not intended as the mere expression of a desire but as a means of influencing reality.

The first part of the carol is in a sense the incarnation of the wish expressed in the congratulation formula. Thus, the carol's descriptions and narratives present a series of models, which may be ritual, social, heroic, professional, moral, or physical. Like the fairy tale, the winter carol conveys the singer or listener into a world where dreams come true. But contrary to the fairy tale, which projects the wish into the realm of fiction and places the events in a remote age, the winter carol presents one with a concrete and immediate model of an ideal of life or behavior, an ideal that is supposed to be realized through the compulsory influence attributed to the congratulation formula.

In practice, the carol is always addressed to a specific person, and the name of this person is usually assigned to the hero in the carol. Thus the hero who shoots the stag or captures the lion in the carol is symbolically identified with the person at whose house the carol is performed. A happy ending is dictated by the logic of the ritual: In order to confirm and support the wish expressed in the congratulation formula, the hero, identified with the addressee, must attain victory and receive its rewards. It is to be noted that today this ritual symbolism is perceived as a mere stylistic device, however, or as an homage paid to the host.

There are, of course, exceptions to the aforementioned canons. Some of these are the result of the carols' different ritual functions. As noted, the winter carol can also have a funerary function. In the carols for the dead the rule of the happy ending must naturally be canceled. Other exceptions are to be explained on the basis of the process of a carol's composition. Compiled in stages and from different sources, a carol sometimes includes characters or sequences incongruous with the canons of the genre. The saints, for instance, cannot be identified with the addressee of the carol and consequently cannot take on their names. Various devices are employed to circumvent such difficulties. Thus in various Christian carols, in order to comply with the canons of the genre and at the same time avoid desecrating the sacred character of the saints, a human character is introduced—usually "the Good Man"—who receives the name of the addressee.

The vision presented by the winter carol is one in which harmony and peace reign over the world. The heroes appear in a halo of happiness, beauty, and glory, and conflicts are attenuated or resolved. Even tragic endings are accompanied by serene images: In "Mioritza, the Clairvoyant Lamb" the moon keeps watch over the corpse of the slain shepherd, and according to a winter carol on the theme of the foundation sacrifice, the baby of the immured victim is not abandoned but is nursed by full-uddered deer that descend from the mountains.

The sparkling festive atmosphere peculiar to the winter carol is enhanced by a profusion of gold and white (both originally magical colors) that pour over the most humble objects and turn them into sources of light and wonder. The broom, for instance, is made of gold, as is the spindle and the cradle, while the sea and the heath are all white.

Typical of the winter carol is its refrain. Although part of the refrains that survive are preserved in distorted versions, one occasionally detects certain analogies with the invocations. The refrains, as well as the versification in general, are closely intertwined with the melody, which, by itself, deserves the highest interest of the specialist.

From a stylistic point of view one may distinguish two types of carols: the Ukrainian type, which has a pronounced descriptive character and long final formulas, and the Romanian-Bulgarian type, which includes epic segments and closes with concise formulas. The stylistic and typological analogies between the Romanian and Bulgarian repertoires suggest that the basic form of the eastern European winter carol was the creation of the Thracians, on either side of the Danube. The fact that a number of mythological carols are common to the Ukrainians, Romanians, and Bulgarians suggests that the Slavs took the custom of the carol from the Thracians at an early date, enriched it with their own traditions, and dispersed it over a wide area. The rich and original character of the Romanian repertoire recommends it as the best source for study of the genre.

This general survey of the complex elements involved in the performance and texts of the eastern European winter carol requires that certain distinctions be made. Thus one may conclude that if the Christian influence is rather insignificant at the level of the customary practices associated with the carol, it cannot be neglected at the level of the text. Without shattering the mythological basis of the genre, the church succeeded in giving a Christian hue to a portion of the winter carol repertoire and, here and there, exerting an even stronger influence. The part played by the congratulation formulas in the structure of the carols may be seen as an echo of the Roman custom of exchanging congratulations on the occasion of the Calendae Ianuari. But in the empire's eastern provinces, the Roman New Year provided only a new label and framework for the well-rooted autochthonous celebration of the winter solstice.

Judging by certain aspects of the custom, and by references within the texts, the eastern European winter songs seem to have served as incantations directed against the evil influences of the dead and to have included elements of sun worship. Viewed from this perspective, the eastern European carol still displays its link with the ancient rituals of the winter solstice, but it has a diffuse ritual character. It incorporated not only the winter solstice rituals but also rituals of puberty, agrarian rituals of the vernal equinox, and the rituals and myths of the New Year.

In the folk traditions of eastern Europe the winter carol represents one of the oldest cultural strata. In it are found the vestiges of prehistoric rituals and cosmogonic myths, and this fact alone makes it important to the history of religions, ethnology, ethnomusicology, and linguistics. But the winter carol is more than a fossilized genre that provides data for the reconstruction of an earlier age. It has conveyed elements of myth and ritual that express fundamental experiences of humankind and thus still appeal to the contemporary reader. Moreover, the eastern European winter carol contains more than ancient myths and rituals; over the centuries, it has integrated a vast range of motifs into a complex synthesis. It may be fairly judged to be one of the purest voices that, emerging from the depths of magical belief, ever reached the heights of poetry. Had it not been embedded in provincial languages, the eastern European winter solstice song would have long ago joined the choir of those perennial songs inspired by faith that delight and strengthen the spirit of humankind.

BIBLIOGRAPHY

Bartók, Béla. "Melodien der rumänischen Colinda (Weihnachtslieder)." In *Ethnomusikologische Schriften Faksimile Nachdrücke,* vol. 4. Budapest, 1968.

Bartók, Béla. *Rumanian Folk Music,* vol. 4, *Carols and Christmas Songs (Colinde).* Edited by Benjamin Suchoff. The Hague, 1975.

Bîrlea, Ovidiu. "Colindatul în Transilvania." In *Anuarul Muzeului etnografic al Transilvaniei pe anii 1965–1967.* Cluj, Romania, 1969. One of the most valuable contributions to the literature.

Brailoiu, Constantin. "Sur une ballade roumaine (La Mioritza)." In *Problèmes d'ethnomusicologie.* Geneva, 1973.

Bratulescu, Monica. *Colinda Românească.* Bucharest, 1981. The most complete work on the subject. Offers a typological and bibliographic index with important sections translated into English.

Caraman, Petru. *Colindatul la Români: Slavi si alte popoare.* Bucharest, 1983.

Dragoi, Sabin V. *303 colinde cu text si melodie.* Craiova, Romania, 1925.

Eliade, Mircea. *Zalmoxis, the Vanishing God: Comparative Studies in the Religions and Folklore of Dacia and Eastern Europe.* Chicago, 1972.

Usener, Hermann. *Das Weihnachtsfest.* Bonn, 1889.

MONICA BRĂTULESCU (1987)

WINTI SEE AFRO-SURINAMESE RELIGIONS

WISDOM. The term *wisdom* has been used with a great variety of meanings in the course of history. A survey quickly shows that every culture has or has had its ideal of wisdom and recorded it in oral or written sapiential literature. In particular, the relation, both historical and systematic, between wisdom on the one hand and religion and philosophy on the other, varies a great deal. This article can give only a limited selection from the broad range of sapiential traditions and ideas.

GENERAL TERMINOLOGY. As far as we can judge from the terms used and their history, wisdom was originally a practical matter, namely "insight" into certain connections existing in human life and in the world and modes of behavior derived from this insight and put into the service of instruction and education. The Indo-European root of the word *wisdom,* **ueid-*, connotes "perceiving, seeing" (compare Greek *idein,* "idea," and Latin *videre,* "to see"). The German language has preserved the ancient connection between *Weisheit* ("wisdom"), *Wissen* ("knowledge"), and *Wissenschaft* ("science"). A person's wisdom depends on what he or she has seen and thereby come to know. It is therefore a practical knowledge, the primordial shaper of human behavior toward the environing world (to the extent that this knowledge resists the pressures for immediate action). The same practical element is manifest in other cultures as well. Thus the Hebrew *ḥokhmah* has to do with "skill, ability" (*ḥkm*); the Akkadian *némequ* with "dexterity and skill"; Greek *sophia* with "cleverness" or "skill" in any of the arts or professions of life (carpentry, medicine, poetry, music, etc.). The Akkadian word for a teacher of wisdom or learned person, *ummanu*, was borrowed from Sumerian and originally meant "master craftsman." The cultivation and transmission of cumulative experience in coping intellectually with the world was done mainly in schools that were the seedbeds of literary culture and the forerunners of the later "schools of wisdom" or universities. Oral tradition was likewise controlled by specific groups that were responsible for the maintenance of tradition.

WISDOM, RELIGION, AND PHILOSOPHY. If religion can be broadly conceived as a way of coping, theoretically and practically, with the problems of the world, nature, and society, then wisdom is one part of this effort. In fact, wisdom and the various contents of the religions have historically been closely connected. Wisdom was regarded as an area of religious tradition and derived its authority from its relation to particular gods (especially the sun, as in Mesopotamia and Egypt) or religious principles (e.g., concepts of world order, such as the ancient Egyptian *maat*). In this form, wisdom contributed to the development of theological thought and is part of its history ("priestly wisdom"). Particular divinities were venerated in cult and magic (the two are difficult to distinguish) as protectors or representatives of religious knowledge (Ea and Marduk in Babylonia, Ptah in Egypt). The legitimation of wisdom by more or less religious figures, such as kings, teachers, and priests, belongs in the same context. We know instances of wisdom being personified as a divine hypostasis (e.g., in Buddhism, Judaism, gnosticism, Zoroastrianism). In many religions wisdom is an attribute of the divinities; in monotheistic religions it is an attribute of the supreme God. The wisdom of God transcends that of human beings and makes it pale into insignificance; in Christianity the wisdom of God even turns human wisdom into folly (see below). This Christian revaluation of the value set upon wisdom in antiquity did not, however, lead to an abandonment of wisdom but to its relativization and to a radical transformation of the whole concept.

This more or less positive relation between wisdom and religion is only one side of the coin. Just as often, wisdom went its own way alongside official religion; it was even, as in the ancient Middle East, in tension or conflict with it. To the extent that this was true, it was a profane, secular way of coping with the world that avoided or excluded any appeal to traditional religious entities (gods, cult, priests). It thus paved the way for philosophical and ultimately also for scientific thinking (see the etymological connection mentioned earlier between the German words for wisdom and science). This development is most easily seen among the Greeks, where the concept of philosophy, or "love of wisdom," took shape. According to tradition (Diogenes Laertius, 1.12; Cicero, *Tusculanae Disputationes* 5.3.8) the term went back to Pythagoras and was then taken over by Plato and Aristotle, who gave it its normative meaning. It is clear that the projection of the Platonic conception of philosophy and science back onto Pythagoras meant a reinterpretation of the latter's simple, prescientific notion of wisdom. Pythagoras was undoubtedly a teacher of wisdom, not a scientist or mathematician in the later sense of these words; his explanation of the cosmos had at its center a number symbolism that could not yet be called scientific, since in it number, ritual, and doctrine of the soul still formed a unity (Burkert, 1972). In any case, *philosophy* retained its practical meaning of "way of life" down through the centuries and has not lost it even today. Ancient Greek wisdom, documented in gnomic poetry (Hesiod, Mimnermos, Solon, Phocylides, Theognis), with its simple key idea of "moderation" (*mēden agan*) or "fitness of act to time and situation" (*kairon gnōthi*), found its extreme application in the so-called Sophists, who converted wisdom (*sophia*) into practical rationality and thereby brought its dangers to light for the first time. In contrast to the Sophists, Socrates avoided the concept of wisdom and reserved this quality for God alone (Plato, *Apology* 20–22). For Plato wisdom was the supreme virtue (*Republic* 441c–d). Aristotle distinguished between the practical wisdom of everyday life (*phronēsis*) and speculative wisdom (*sophia*), which concerns itself with "first things" (*Nicomachean Ethics* 4.5.2, 15.1.5). The distinction marked the transition to systematic wisdom, or philosophy. Nonetheless, in the history of philosophy its ancient root—"wisdom for living"—has repeatedly surfaced; in particular it has found ever new expression in ethical systems and endeavors (e.g., those of Spinoza, Kant, Fichte, and Schopenhauer). In his *Wörterbuch der Philosophie* ([1910–1911] 1980, vol. 1, p. 446), Fritz Mauthner formulates the difference between wisdom and practical "prudence," and between wisdom and philosophy or science with their goal of theoretical knowledge, as follows:

> In my opinion, *wisdom* seems to mean not only that those who have this quality, possession, or way of thinking are able on every occasion to act or think with rare prudence in pursuing their theoretical or practical goals; it means that in addition they are able to judge the value of the theoretical and practical goals in question. It also means perhaps that such persons act according to their judgments. Schopenhauer was certainly a philosopher but hardly a wise man. Montaigne was a wise man but not really a philosopher. We think of Socrates as being both wise man and philosopher.

PROBLEMS OF A TYPOLOGY. Since it is not possible at present (or ever, in my opinion) to write a history of the various ideas of wisdom, scholars have quickly settled for providing at least a typology of the concepts of wisdom. Wisdom has taken these broad forms: an anthropological ability to cope with life (the oldest and most widespread form); a rational system (interpretation of the cosmos, philosophy, beginnings of science); and a personification, hypostasis, goddess, or attribute of God.

Any attempt at greater detail becomes mired in the problems of the given historical context. It is possible, for example, with Edward Conze to compare the Buddhist (Mahāyāna) Prajñāpāramitā ("perfect wisdom") with the figure of Sophia in early Judaism and to find surprising similarities (Conze, 1968, pp. 207–209). There are even chronological correspondences: the hypostatization of both ideas of wisdom began about 200 BCE and yielded similar conceptions. Yet differences of content are unmistakable: Prajñāpāramitā is a personification of Buddhist insight into the "emptiness" of the world and has no connection with an idea of God; the Jewish Sophia became a divine hypostasis that can also be mediator of creation and identifiable with the Law (Torah). The situation is the same with parallels between Egyptian, Mesopotamian, and Iranian ideas of wisdom, each of which retains its own special character and cannot be wholly assimilated to the others and made to coincide with them. By and large, the only common element is the shift in the thematization of wisdom from an anthropological skill to a central religious figure or person who mediates wisdom. In this shift wisdom changes from subject to object; an anthropological capacity for insight becomes a form of revelation about the cosmos or God. The content of wisdom as insight into the coherence of the world and life takes on a religious and, to some extent, esoteric character (as in the *Wisdom of Solomon*, gnosticism, and Mahāyāna Buddhism). This development did not occur wherever ideas of wisdom existed (thus except for Israel and Iran it did not occur in the Near East or in Greece). It looks as if a necessary condition of this development is the existence of a canonical literature that accepts the idea of wisdom. "Revelation" is identified with wisdom inasmuch as wisdom becomes the content of revelation and as a result either heightens the importance of canonicity or permits an extension of canonicity (as, for example, in the Prajñāpāramitā literature or the gnostic writings).

This literary documentation for the idea of wisdom makes possible some typological classifications that should not be overlooked. Thus the "typical" wisdom genre is the *gnōme* (Lat., *sententia*), that is, the tersely formulated "sentence" or maxim, or, more generally, the proverb. The oldest collections of wisdom traditions are collections of proverbs that can be developed into literary works on the theme of wisdom or can at least supply material for such ("teachings," "disputations," dialogues). Omens, riddles, fables, parables, and metaphors are also frequently storehouses of wisdom. Wisdom is thus not limited to a particular literary form, although it is closely linked with the proverb and maxim. Its origin in the oral tradition of the preliterary period of history can be demonstrated only through inference from the presence of such traditions among contemporary nonliterate peoples. There is hardly a people that does not possess some stock of wisdom traditions; this stock is the source of wisdom in the original sense of the term. Its beginnings are lost in the darkness of prehistory. The question whether the often asserted "international" character of wisdom literature is to be explained by evolution (from an original common possession) or by diffusion (through spread and borrowing) cannot be further answered. There are many arguments for the second hypothesis, but the first theory can also be helpful in examining many cultures. In any case, both forms of development can be seen at work in the course of history (the ancient Near East is a classic example of the borrowing of wisdom traditions). The important thing, however, is what particular cultures, literatures, and religions did with the common treasury of wisdom; these results are attractively multifaceted and pluralistic.

THE MANY FORMS OF WISDOM. Space allows only a limited survey of some of the principal forms taken by ideas of wisdom. The emphasis will be on the ancient Near East, which decisively molded the image of wisdom (transmitted through the biblical heritage). Only a brief glance can be taken at India and East Asia, which developed an independent form of wisdom that has influenced the culture and life of these peoples down to our own day.

Mesopotamia (Sumer and Babylonia). The Near East possessed expressions of wisdom at a very early date, although these did not lead later on to a unitary concept of wisdom. The dominant element in this wisdom was skilled proficiency in insightful understanding of the world, human beings, and society. No one doubted the divine origin of wisdom, even if an increasing awareness of the difference between divine and human wisdom manifested itself in later literature and led to a crisis in the wisdom tradition. The basic idea of the wisdom tradition was what scholars have named the "act-consequence connection," that is, the early insight that specific actions have or can have specific consequences in the lives of human beings. People attempted to find rules of behavior by observing their human environment, but they did not advance as far as systematic reflection or even develop an ethic of behavior (this step was left for the Greeks and the Chinese). Their observations, handed down in the form of aphorisms, provided valuable counsel for kings, officials, and scribes. The storehouse for this wisdom was the school, and its teachers were the scribes, who were therefore regarded as wise beyond others. Wisdom derived its authority from its being traced back to divinities (especially Utu, Shamash, Ninurta, Enki, Inanna) or prehistoric wise men (Shuruppak, Gilgamesh). Because of its origin and approach this wisdom had a eudaimonistic and at times even a mantic character, but in the late period it turned pessimistic and skeptical. The dogma of the act-consequence connection to a great extent prevented the raising of new questions; when these were finally asked they led to a helpless skepticism (the problem of Job, the suffering just man; the problem of a just world order). Modesty, uprightness, consideration for others (love of neighbor), and deliberation were the principal virtues; their cultivation brought life, happiness, children (sons), and God's providential care.

The decisive force in the development of ancient Mesopotamian wisdom was that of the Sumerians. The Akkadians for their part mainly translated, transmitted, and interpreted, while adding a few new forms of their own (*Wisdom of Ahikar*, omen literature). The beginnings of wisdom are to be found in the early "lists" or "inventories" in which language was used as a means of "inventorying" the world and thus to some extent ordering or systematizing it. This kind of wisdom has therefore been called "list wisdom" and understood as a first approach to scientific effort (Soden, 1936). More developed approaches led from a simple listing of objects to an appraisal of them; this has come down to us in the form of disputations (literature of disputes over relative values). This kind of wisdom has been described as "value wisdom" (Hans Heinrich Schmid, *Wesen und Geschichte der Weisheit*, Berlin, 1966). The rise of proverbs relating to occurrences in nature and society brought for the first time the formulation of simple factual situations (called therefore the "wisdom of events"). This stage paved the way for wisdom sayings in the narrower sense. The latter emerged from observation of human behavior (initially without thematizing the act-consequence connection), first in proverbs and then clearly in various "counsels," which unfortunately have come down to us only in fragmentary form (*Counsels of Shuruppak, Counsels of Wisdom*). Wisdom gradually made its way into various other genres; meanwhile links were also established between wisdom and ideas of a socio-ethical and legal kind from royal and legal texts (e.g., conceptions of protecting the weak, widows, and orphans; doing good and hating evil; practicing righteousness). Wisdom thus sought to formulate and thereby give insight into the basic rules governing the cosmos. The gods had established a just world order; it was for human beings to learn this order and act accordingly. The challenge to this outlook by, for example, historical events led to a crisis of wisdom, since the act-consequence connection came into question and the theme of the "suffering just man" became topical. This was the subject of the "Job poems," which followed the "complaint and response paradigm" (*ersha-hunga*). To this genre belong the following: *Sumerian Job, the Poem of the Righteous Sufferer* (also called *I Will Praise the Lord of Wisdom* [*Ludlul bel nemeqi*], from its opening words), the *Babylonian Theodicy*, and the satirical *Dialogue of a Master and Slave* (or *Dialogue of Pessimism*), which probably does not belong to the wisdom literature but is nonetheless very informative in regard to it. The conclusion reached in these works is that God's action is inscrutable and his wisdom different from that of human beings. The act-consequence connection is pushed into the background but not abandoned, since insight into the order governing the world is denied to human beings. In all this we can see wisdom in the process of leaving our earth and becoming a supratemporal system and part of the divine world (to which in fact it had always belonged).

Egypt. Unlike Mesopotamia, Egypt did not have a "list wisdom" as a preliminary stage of wisdom; instead the sapiential saying (maxim) served as the starting point of a wisdom literature (the various "counsels"). The sapiential saying either contained a simple statement about the world and social relationships or it already connected consequences with specific actions that were either recommended or disapproved. Unlike the Mesopotamians, the ancient Egyptians developed the concept of a cosmic order (*maat*) that became basic to the idea of wisdom. The goddess Maat was a daughter of Re, the sun god, and symbolized truth, justice, and order in cosmos and society. The pharaoh was her representative on earth. The wise had to act like Maat; agreement with her bestowed success, disagreement brought punishment (unhappiness). Subordination to Maat was therefore the mark of the wise. Wisdom supplied the needed rules, which were based on tradition and experience (which included successive reinterpretations). Examples of wisdom or, as Egyptologists prefer to say, of "counsels" or "instructions," go back to about 2800 BCE. Only the names of the earliest have come down to us (*Instructions of Imhotep, Instructions of Djedefhor*). The *Instruction of Ptahhotep* is the oldest surviving document of this genre (fifth dynasty). It is filled with optimism about the order (*maat*) that exists and is known and with an unbroken confidence in the act-consequence connection. Modesty, uprightness, self-control, subordination, silence, are virtues of the wise. The idea of the silent sage influenced Egyptian biographical literature. Citations from the wisdom literature can be demonstrated in numerous inscriptions.

Most of the remaining "instructions" are from the Middle Kingdom (c. 2135–1660 BCE) and are "tendentious writings" that discuss problems of wisdom and are therefore also called "disputation literature." Among them are the *Instruction for Merikare* (tenth dynasty), in which the first mention is made of the judgment of the dead; the *Instruction of King Amenemhet to His Son Sesostris* (twelfth dynasty), which was probably a model for *Proverbs* 22:17–24:22, although the former is more pessimistic and materialistic; and the *Instruction of Cheti, Son of Duauf*, a piece of publicity for the civil service. The threat to the old order shows through in the *Admonitions of an Egyptian Sage* and the *Protest of the Eloquent Peasant.*

To the period of the New Kingdom (c. 1570–1085 BCE) belong the *Instruction of Ani* (eighteenth dynasty), which defends traditional authority against criticism, and the *Instruction of Amenemope* (twenty-second dynasty), which is strongly pietistic and calls for humility toward the hidden rule of the sun god. From the late period (first millennium CE) we have only the very homespun *Instruction of the Papyros Insinger* and the instruction of a certain Ankhsheshonk. Characteristic of later wisdom (from the eighteenth dynasty on) is the realization, in Egypt no less than in Babylonia, of the limitations of human knowledge and the freedom of the divinity; this meant that the act-consequence connection, though weakened, was not completely abandoned, but was considered to reside in the impenetrable recesses of the godhead. Authority, tradition, humility, circumspection, and silence continued to be themes of wisdom. In fact, in the late period wisdom and piety came to be more closely identified.

Maat yielded to the godhead (Re). Devout individuals had as their partner no longer Maat but God; God became the guarantor of the act-consequence connection, which was hidden from the devout but which they nonetheless humbly accepted as existing. Wisdom now consisted in this knowledge of God and his free will, a knowledge that was familiar to the Bible and probably exerted an influence on it. For that matter, a monotheistic or henoheistic current runs through the entire wisdom literature.

Ancient Israel, Judaism. Israelite wisdom literature (*Proverbs, Job, Ecclesiastes*) underwent developments comparable to those in Babylonia and Egypt. In its earliest, preexilic form, wisdom is here, as in the ancient Near East generally, not specifically religious but focused on the act-consequence connection in the cosmos and in individual lives (see *Prv.* 22:13–23:11). It is not opposed to faith in Yahveh but on the other hand has only peripheral contacts with it (see *Prv.* 16:1–22, 16:28–29). Yahveh, like the ancient Near Eastern and Egyptian sun god, is guarantor of the cosmic order that governs the lives of human beings. Wisdom is primarily concerned with this-worldly questions affecting the order and security of human life; observation and insight into what goes on in the world and society play their part here. From a literary standpoint the proverb or maxim is the basic form of transmission (*Proverbs, Ecclesiastes*; later on, the *Book of Ben Sira* and the *Wisdom of Solomon*). Ascription to Solomon (c. 970 BCE) has a historical basis to the extent that international communication (especially with Egypt) flourished during that period (see the *First Book of Kings* 5:9–14). From that time on in Israel, as elsewhere, the "wise man" (*ish ḥakham*) had his place alongside the priest and the prophet, and the area of tradition with which he dealt soon became one of the most important in Israelite literature (see *Ben Sira* 24:3–7).

In its historical development this literature reflects shifting approaches to wisdom until the latter's crisis and disintegration (*Job, Ecclesiastes*). To begin with, ancient wisdom is increasingly theologized, that is, connected with the Yahvistic faith, but also systematized or dogmatized and reduced to a series of anthropological contrasts (see *Prv.* 10–15). The wise and the foolish are turned into contrasting types, as are the devout and the ungodly, the sensible and the ignorant, and so on. The act-consequence connection changes (in the post-exilic period) to a connection between behavior and its results (*Prv.* 10:30, 11:3–4). Corresponding dualistic traits make their appearance as human beings are divided into the just and the wicked, and the cosmos into good and evil, just and unjust. Wisdom itself withdraws into heaven and is personified (see below). The ancient program of wisdom, which urged insight into human beings and the world through observation and its application, comes under the control of strict monotheism and the doctrine of creation, both of which leave little room for independent human thought. As a result, the crisis of dogmatized wisdom becomes radical and leads in the *Book of Job* to its rejection. As in the Babylonian world, an appeal is made at this point to the inscrutability of God (see *Jb.* 40), a solution that is accepted in later Judaism. At the same time, however, a return to the ancient, authentic concept of wisdom is urged (*Jb.* 38–39): understanding of the world consists in the acknowledgement of its given order, even though insight into it is limited. The most radical break with the wisdom tradition comes in the Hellenistic period in the person of Qohelet (the purported author of *Ecclesiastes*), who abandons the act-consequence connection as a means of insight, is skeptical about an order in the world, and demonstrates the meaninglessness of human existence. Wisdom is no longer available in this world (see also *Jb.* 28). Reverence is still shown toward creation and its distant creator, but the "historicality of human existence" and its transitory character are thematized for the first time. Qohelet offers no solution for the crisis; the world and human beings remain unintelligible.

This situation, which we meet only in the Bible, had consequences that probably led to the disintegration of the biblical worldview in gnosticism. But Jewish apocalypticism too had some of its roots in wisdom: the removal of wisdom from the world led to an eschatological hope; the introduction of dualism into the cosmos (see above) led to the apocalyptic doctrine of the two kingdoms; historical events had deprived the scribes, who were the transmitters of wisdom, of their ancient theater of operations, the royal court, and they dreamed of its future restoration. Gnosis and apocalyptic were connected.

Hellenistic influence probably played a part also in the complete transformation of the figure of wisdom (Ḥokhmah). It becomes a suprahuman, otherworldly personage, a divine hypostasis (*Prv.* 8:22–31; *Ben Sira* 4:11–19, 24:3–22; *Wis.* 6–9), a mediator of revelation and creation (*Prv.* 3:19, *Ben Sira* 24:3); it is even identified with the Torah, or Law, as the content of the word of God (*Ben Sira* 24:8, 24:23; *1 Bar.* 3:9–4:4). It takes on the traits of a goddess (perhaps Isis Panthea) and, as Lady Wisdom, becomes the antagonist of Lady Folly, another personification, modeled on Aphrodite or Astarte (*Prv.* 7:9–13, 9:1–18). "Kinship" with her, such as the just or the wise have, bestows immortality (*Wis.* 6:17) and even makes one like God (*Wis.* 6:18). This shift from a horizontal role, as an anthropological skill in understanding of the world, to a vertical role leads in the *Wisdom of Solomon* (first century BCE) and then especially in the work of Philo Judaeus (first century CE) to the idea of wisdom (Gr., *sophia*) as an otherworldly figure accessible only through esoteric "knowledge." Communication with this distant heavenly wisdom is accomplished in the philosophy of Philo through the Logos (the divine intelligible word), which represents "wisdom close to us." Sophia is thus accessible only through revelation and knowledge of the Logos. It is no longer available in this world, but has vanished from it (Ethiopic *Apocalypse of Enoch* 42:1–8, 4 Ezr. 5:9–10, Syriac *Apocalypse of Baruch* 48:36). At this point the way is already being paved for the gnostic conception of wisdom.

Christianity and gnosis. Early Christianity accepted the early Jewish conception of wisdom at various levels. On the one hand, the early Jesus tradition (the purported source of the sayings of Jesus, known as the Q source) took over the ancient Israelite proverbial wisdom (explicit reference is made to Solomon in *Mt.* 12:42, *Lk.* 11:31); on the other hand, Jesus himself is understood as the embodiment of wisdom (*Lk.* 7:35 and parallels; cf. *Mt.* 23:34–36 with *Lk.* 11:49). He is "filled with wisdom" from his childhood (*Lk.* 2:40, 2:52) and surpasses even Solomon in this respect (*Mt.* 12:42, *Lk.* 11:31). His deeds and teachings demonstrate his wisdom (*Mk.* 6:2, *Mt.* 13:54). Scholars therefore speak of a "wisdom-Christology" as one of the earliest forms of christological statement. In the letters of Paul wisdom plays an important role in his dispute with the community in Corinth (*1* and *2 Corinthians*), where a wisdom that was probably already interpreted in a Gnostic manner was being preached and was finding expression in ecstatic utterances (revelations). In response, Paul conceives the momentous idea that Christian wisdom, represented by the Redeemer, is foolishness (*mōria*) to the world, this wisdom being the cross that as sign of the "weakness of God" (*1 Cor.* 1:25) is the very sign of his "strength." God has destroyed "the wisdom of the wise" and turned it into "foolishness" (*1 Cor.* 1:18–22, 2:6–8). In the presence of the true wisdom of God, which has been revealed in Christ, the traditional wisdom of this world has been reduced to naught, but at the same time it has also been fulfilled. Those who believe in Christ possess "the power of God and the wisdom of God" (*1 Cor.* 1:24, 1:30, 2:10–12, 3:18). Old Testamental and Jewish wisdom literature of two centuries before the common era is here given a completely new interpretation and thereby rescued from the crisis into which it had fallen; on the other hand, limits are also set for any future Christian conception of wisdom. The critical acceptance of ancient wisdom traditions and the ambivalent response of Christian theology to philosophy both have their roots here (see Thomas Aquinas on the one side and Martin Luther on the other). Meanwhile, as the *Letter of James* in particular shows, the principle is still accepted that wisdom shows its truth in ethico-moral practice: Christian life is wisdom made manifest (*Jas.* 3:13–17; cf. *Jas.* 1:5). The ancient idea of wisdom is thus revived here; it becomes a Christian virtue for coping with life.

In my opinion, Gnosticism has its roots in those parts of early Jewish sapiential teaching that, like *Ecclesiastes*, challenged the traditional picture of the world. Independently of this heritage from tradition and the history of ideas, Gnostic literature too continues to present wisdom in the guise of transmitted sayings, for the most part in Christian form (from the Nag Hammadi corpus, the *Gospel of Thomas* and the *Gospel of Philip;* see also *Silvanus* and the *Sentences of Sextus*), but also in new forms of its own (*The Thunder, Perfect Mind*). Most notable, however, is the figure of Sophia, or Pistis Sophia ("faith wisdom"), an ambivalent embodiment of the Gnostic Pleroma, especially in the Barbelo and Valentinian forms of gnosis. According to some heresiological accounts and original (Nag Hammadi) texts, Sophia is a companion of the most high God; more precisely, she is the feminine aspect of his first manifestation or emanation, whose masculine aspect or consort may be identified with the Primal Man, the Son of man, or Christ (Seth). A second, lesser Sophia must also be included in the series of "syzygies" (paired aeons) that derive from the first pair. Other passages— and these are in the majority—describe Sophia variously as one of the final aeons: the one that, as mother of the demiurge (Ialdabaoth), is indirectly involved in the fate of the created world. But she is simultaneously active in the work of redemption, repairing the harm done by the loss of the spark of light, inasmuch as Sophia herself, split into two parts—an upper and a lower, a greater and a lesser, a part of life and a part of death, of truth and of lie, or simply as Sophia and Achamoth (the Aramaic word for "wisdom")—suffers in an exemplary fashion the fate of the fall and redemption. This version is characteristic of the so-called Barbelo Gnostics and of the Valentinians; it is also attributed to the Cainites and the Ophites, as well as to the Sethians. Several texts from Nag Hammadi also belong here (e.g., *Apocryphon of John, Hypostasis of the Archons, Gospel of the Egyptians, Trimorphic Protennoia*). Gnostic wisdom (*sophia*) serves to express many sides of gnostic thought. It serves as an image of the self-estrangement of God in emanation and reflection; thus it represents the feminine aspect in God, while leaving his perfect unity undiminished. But Wisdom is also (as aeon) the consort of the Savior and is intimately connected with both demiurgic (cosmological) and soteriological processes. This has nothing to do with feminist ideas; behind it, rather, stands the heritage of the Jewish wisdom tradition in its later form.

Iran and Zoroastrianism. It is often forgotten that Iran too has produced an extensive wisdom literature that goes by the Middle Persian name of *handarz* (early New Persian, *andarz*), meaning "advice, instruction." This too has been handed down in various forms of *gnomai.* It is preserved only in Middle Persian, but it doubtless had Avestan (Old Iranian) precursores (such as the now lost *Barish nask*). At the center of this literature is "wisdom" (MPers., *khrad*, or *xrat*), whose representatives or transmitters were kings of the prehistoric period (e.g., Jam, Ōshnar) and the Sasanid period (e.g., Chosrau I), viziers (e.g., Wazurgmihr ī Bokhtagān), and priests (e.g., Ādurbad ī Mahraspandān). Here again collection and transmission were the work of priestly schools or the (fire) temples. Since thought, along with speech and action, played a dominant role in Zoroastrianism, great attention was paid to the teaching of religious knowledge. This knowledge was identified with wisdom. But in fact the "knowledge" in question was not only religious, theological, and cultic. Iran had either taken over (via Hellenism) or had itself produced a great deal of secular knowledge.

Nonetheless, the religious framework within which the wisdom tradition was placed played a very important role. According to one of the principal works, *Mēnōg ī Khrad*

(Spirit of Wisdom), all wisdom flows from a single wisdom that goes back to God. Two works in particular are important in this context. One is the sixth book of the encyclopedia *Dēnkard* (Acts of Religion); the other is *Dādistān ī Mēnōg i Khrad* (Book of Judgments of the Spirit of Wisdom). Both originated in the Sasanid period but preserve older material as well. Book 6 of the *Dēnkard* goes back in part to the Avestan Barish nask; other material comes from oral tradition. Its content is largely religious and has to do with Zoroastrian teaching on cleanliness; it is therefore highly ritualistic in character. In this context wisdom is correct knowledge and correspondingly correct behavior in things religious. "This world was created by Ōhrmazd the Lord [Av., Ahura Mazdā] with knowledge (*dānāgih*). He maintains it with sagacity (*frazānagīh*) and manliness (*mardābagīh*); ultimately He will become joyful through it" (Shaked, 1979, sec. 311). This is interpreted as follows by the sages (*dānāgān*): "The thing of Wisdom (*khrad*) is this: sagacity (*frazānagīh*), manliness (*mardābagīh*) and the hope of the Renovation" (ibid., sec. 312). The same passage goes on to say: "The substance of wisdom (*khrad*) is similar to that of fire. For nothing in this world may become so perfect as that which is done by wisdom (*khrad*)" (ibid., sec. 313). In the *Dēnkard*, "character" (*khēm* or *xēm*) is superior even to wisdom, since "wisdom is in character; and religion is in both wisdom and character" (ibid., sec. 6; see also sec. 2). Ōhrmazd creates creatures through "character," "holds them with wisdom, and takes them back to himself by religion" (ibid., sec. 11).

In other, more secular *handarz* texts wisdom is at the head of the virtues and leads human beings to a knowledge of their duties. Ōhrmazd created the following spiritual realities that help human beings to that goal: "innate wisdom, acquired wisdom, character, hope, contentment, religion [*dēn*], and the consultation of the wise" (*Āyadgar ī Wazurgmihr* 43, cited in Shaked, 1979, p. xxvi). Acquired wisdom is gained through education; innate wisdom preserves human beings from fear and sin. Clearly, in Zoroastrianism wisdom is firmly embedded in a religious context (although secular wisdom is not completely absent). Wisdom is primarily a matter of Zoroastrian knowledge; the latter defines its essence. It is therefore the duty of the faithful to follow the "wise" (teachers, priests) and ask them questions; association with them brings God close to one. Parts of Iranian wisdom literature, however, are also marked by a fatalistic pessimism reminiscent of *Ecclesiastes* (Shaked, 1979, sec. D). "Destiny" (*bakht, brēh, zamān*) determines human beings; their action is geared to its accomplishment. We see here the influence of Iranian teaching on fate (i. e., Zurvanism), an influence also to be seen in modern Persian literature wherever this is in continuity with ancient Iranian wisdom traditions (proverbial literature, didactic poetry).

Wisdom clearly emerges as a heavenly person or hypostasis, the Spirit of Wisdom (Mēnōg ī Khrad), in the work of the same name. Wisdom is here viewed as one of the "holy immortals" (Amahraspandān; Av., Amesha Spentas); in fact, the author devotes more prayers to her than to the others (1.53). She is "original wisdom (*āsn khrad*) from the heavens and the worlds"; she dwells with Ōhrmazd and combines all wisdom in herself (57.3–32); she was created by Ōhrmazd (8.3, 8.8), and through her he created the world (1.11, 1.49, 57.5); through her Ōhrmazd keeps the world in existence (1.12). Her most important function is instruction or, as the case may be, revelation. Each of the sixty-two chapters following upon the introduction to the work begins with questions by an (anonymous) "wise man" (*dānāg*), which Wisdom then answers at length. The book is thus a compendium or catechism of Zoroastrianism and derives its authority from the heavenly wisdom of God. The "wise man" who passes its contents on is evidently a representative of the Zoroastrian community or priesthood. He had wandered through the world, from land to land and city to city, looking for wisdom, until he realized that true wisdom was to be found in his religion; then this wisdom appeared to him in bodily form as Ōhrmazd's Spirit of Wisdom (Mēnōg ī Khrad) and instructed him (1.14–61). The most likely equivalent of this Wisdom in the Avesta is Vohu Manah (Vahuman, Vahman), the Good Mind; "primordial or inherent wisdom" *(āsn khrad)* is found in Yasna 22.25 and 25.18 (*āsnō khratush*) in connection with the Zoroastrian concept of faith ("the innate understanding Mazda-made").

India. Some of the earliest Indian wisdom literature is found in the collections of proverbial wisdom that were made for rulers or kings, as, for example, the well-known *Pañcatantra* or the *Hitopadeśa* (Instruction in What Is Beneficial). The *Mahābhārata*, the Indian national epic, contains in its didactic sections a good deal of ancient wisdom tradition; this includes the *Bhagavadgītā* in particular. The important part played by knowledge or insight (*jñāna*) in ancient Indian thought (especially in the Upaniṣads) has given wisdom a central position in India. It is difficult to distinguish this wisdom from philosophy, and philosophy in turn from religion; each shares in the character of the others. The *Bhagavadgītā* praises "the way of knowledge or wisdom" in preference to the way of action (*karman*): "A man of faith, intent on wisdom (*jñāna*), his senses (all) restrained, wins wisdom; and, wisdom won, he will come right soon to perfect peace" (4.39; trans. Robert C. Zaehner, The *Bhagavad-Gita*, London, 1973). Brahmanic philosophy or religion did not, however, reach the point of personifying wisdom or knowledge. This step was taken only in Buddhism, in which the Indian ideal of knowledge, the way to deliverance from the cycle of births (*saṃsāra*) without reliance on the priestly tradition or extreme asceticism took new forms. But the objectification (hypostatization) of redemptive knowledge or transcendental wisdom (*prajñā*; Pali, *pañña*) came only in Mahāyāna Buddhism, beginning in about 100 BCE in southern or northern India. A whole literature arose (originally in Sanskrit) consecrated to what it termed the "perfection of wisdom" (*prajñapāramitā*; lit., "the wisdom that has gone beyond"). The earliest Prajñapāramitā works were composed between 100 BCE and 150 CE; from the fourth to the seventh centuries CE compendia and short versions were redacted under the influence of the Mādhyamika school; from the sixth century on, Tantrism also gained control of these texts and gave them ritualistic interpretations (to the extent even of introducing antinomian practices). As mentioned above, there are a number of parallels between the Buddhist and the early Jewish conceptions of wisdom. The Buddhist "wisdom books" (Conze, 1975) introduce a specifically new type of knowledge about redemption: an insight into the "emptiness" (*śūnyatā*) of existence that promises deliverance. These teachings are presented in the form of dialogues between the Buddha and some of his disciples. The manner of presentation lends authority to the new teaching and gives it canonical status. Here the virtue (*pāramitā*) of "insight" (*prajñā, paññā*), perhaps under the influence of the South Indian mother goddess, is sometimes personified as a goddess of wisdom, Prajñapāramitā. In this form she is regarded as "mother" of all the Buddhas (*buddhāmati, jināna mātā*) and *bodhisattvas.*

> If a mother with many sons had fallen ill, They all, sad in mind, would busy themselves about her: Just so also the Buddhas in the world-systems in the ten directions Bring to mind this *perfection of wisdom* as their mother. The Saviours of the world who were in the past, and also those that are (just now) in the ten directions, Have issued from her, and so will the future ones be. She is the one who shows the world (for what it is), she is the genetrix, the mother of the Jinas, And she reveals the thought and action of other beings. (Conze, 1973, p. 31)

Prajñapāramitā is depicted iconographically with two, four, six, ten, or twelve arms. Her color is gold or white; her symbols are the lotus and a book (colored blue or red). She often resembles depictions of Mañjuśrī (the male personification of wisdom) or Sarasvatī (the Hindu goddess of learning, eloquence, and intelligence) or Avalokiteśvara, Tārā, and Cunda. To ordinary Buddhists she is a goddess who can be invoked and who bestows merit, well-being, and blessing. Buddhist theologians, however, see in her simply a "spiritual" manifestation of redemptive or enlightening ("*bodhi*-giving") wisdom, which contains and sustains all things and is called "mother of enlightenment." Here the very essence of Buddhist doctrine is manifested and personified. The various interpretations of this doctrine in the Mahāyāna schools (Mādhyamika, Yogācāra, Tantra) are also reflected in the figure of Prajñapāramitā and the literature about her. One of the best-known hymns to her was composed by Rāhulabhadra (c. 150 CE):

> Homage to Thee, Perfect Wisdom, Boundless, and transcending thought! All Thy limbs are without blemish, Faultless those who Thee discern. . . . Teachers of the world, the Buddhas, Are Thine own compassionate sons; Then art Thou, O Blessed Lady, Grandam thus of beings all. . . . When as fearful Thou appearest Thou engender'st fear in fools; When benignly Thou appearest Comes assurance to the wise. . . . By all Buddhas, Single Buddhas, By Disciples courted, too, Thou the one path to salvation, There's no other verily. . . . By my praise of Perfect Wisdom All the merit I may rear, Let that make the world devoted To this wisdom without peer. (Conze, 1959, pp. 168–171)

The Tantric school produced magical incantations or formulas (*mantras*) for Prajñapāramitā, which were given by the goddess herself. The recitation of these sayings has liberating power; it is also meritorious on behalf of others. In this form of Buddhism the figure of Wisdom unites in itself all aspects of religion, both in theory and in practice. In fact, Prajñapāramitā is probably its most notable expression.

China. Finally, I shall add a brief word on China, where, in contrast to India, wisdom has minimal connections with religion. In Confucianism it has an unambiguously ethico-moral character. We are reminded of the Greeks when we find wisdom consisting in the avoidance of extremes and the following of the mean. *Chih* ("wisdom") is one of the five cardinal virtues that characterize the Confucian "wise man" (*chün-tzu*). It includes knowledge of human nature and society, a command of language, and a practical behavior that obeys the Confucian rules *(li)*. "The sense of right and wrong is the beginning of wisdom (*chih*)" (Fung Yu-lan, 1952, vol. 1, p. 121). Every human being has the native ability to become wise and needs only instruction and practice, since in the prevailing Chinese view human nature is good (another point reminiscent of Greek thought). Confucianism nonetheless also offers the ideal of the "noble man" or "holy man" (*sheng-jen*) who surpasses even the wise man, since he complies perfectly with all the principles *(li)*, lives in harmony with nature and society, and thus is the peerless teacher of an age. The ancient meaning of wisdom as the practical management of life through knowledge of the world and human beings has probably found its most impressive development in China and has for thousands of years profoundly shaped the character of the people. Wisdom is embodied in behavior and can be acquired by practice; it then becomes a habitual attitude.

SEE ALSO Avalokiteśvara; Buddhism, Schools of, article on Mahāyāna Philosophical Schools of Buddhism; Goddess Worship, article on The Hindu Goddess; Ḥokhmah; Jñāna; Knowledge and Ignorance; Li; Mañjuśrī; Mengzi; Prajña; Sarasvatī; Sophia; Tārā; Tathatā; Upāya; Wisdom Literature.

BIBLIOGRAPHY

There is no monograph that completely covers the concepts of wisdom that are found among various peoples and cultures. Only A. R. Gordon's "Wisdom," in the *Encyclopaedia of Religion and Ethics,* edited by James Hastings, vol. 12 (Edinburgh, 1921), attempts a survey; the areas most fully studied and described are the ancient Near East (including Israel), Greek thought, and early Christianity. The following bibliography lists other articles and books that I have found helpful and that can serve as an introduction to the subject.

Burkert, Walter. *Lore and Science in Ancient Pythagoreanism.* Translated by Edwin L. Minar, Jr. Cambridge, Mass., 1972.

Conze, Edward. *Buddhist Scriptures.* Harmondsworth, 1959.

Conze, Edward. *The Prajñapāramitā Literature.* The Hague, 1960.

Conze, Edward. *Thirty Years of Buddhist Studies: Selected Essays.* Columbia, S. C., 1968.

Conze, Edward, trans. *The Perfection of Wisdom in Eight Thousand Lines and Its Verse Summary.* Bolinas, Calif., 1973.

Conze, Edward, trans. and ed. *Buddhist Wisdom Books, Containing the Diamond Sutra and the Heart Sutra.* London, 1975.

Conze, Edward, trans. *The Large Sutra on Perfect Wisdom.* Berkeley, 1975.

Dijk, Jan van. *La sagesse suméro-accadienne.* Leiden, 1953.

Fohrer, Georg, and Ulrich Wilcken. "Sophia." In *Theological Dictionary of the New Testament,* vol. 7. Nashville, 1967.

Fung Yu-lan. *A History of Chinese Philosophy.* 2 vols. 2d ed. Translated by Derk Bodde. Princeton, 1952–1953.

Gese, Hartmut. "Weisheit." In *Die Religion in Geschichte und Gegenwart,* 3d ed., vol. 6. Tübingen, 1962.

Gladigow, Burkhard. *Sophia und Kosmos.* Hildesheim, 1965.

Küchler, Max. *Frühjüdische Weisheitstraditionen.* Freiburg, 1979.

Lambert, W. G. *Babylonian Wisdom Literature.* Oxford, 1960.

Langdon, Stephen H. "Babylonian Wisdom." *Babyloniaca* (1923): 129–194.

Mack, Burton L. *Logos und Sophia: Untersuchungen zur Weisheitstheologie in hellenistischen Judentum.* Göttingen, 1973.

Noth, Martin, and D. Winton Thomas, eds. *Wisdom in Israel and in the Ancient Near East.* Leiden, 1955.

Rad, Gerhard von. *Wisdom in Israel.* Nashville, 1972.

Ringgren, Helmer. *Word and Wisdom.* Lund, 1947.

Rudolph, Kurt. "Sophia und Gnosis." In *Altes Testament-Frühjudentum-Gnosis: Neue Studien zu "Gnosis und Bibel,"* edited by K.-W. Tröger, pp. 221–237. Berlin, 1980.

Sasson, Jack M., ed. *Oriental Wisdom.* Special issue of the Journal of the American Oriental Society 101, no. 1 (1981).

Shaked, Shaul, trans. *The Wisdom of the Sasanian Sages: Dēnkard Book Six.* Boulder, 1979.

Soden, Wolfram von. "Leistung und Grenze sumerischer und babylonischer Wissenschaft." *Welt als Geschichte* 2 (1936): 411–464, 509–557.

West, Edward W., trans. and ed. *The Book of the Mainyô-i-khard* (1871). Amsterdam, 1979.

Wilcken, Ulrich. *Weisheit und Torheit.* Tübingen, 1959.

New Sources

Collins, John Joseph, *Seers, Sybils and Sages in Hellenic-Roman Judaism.* New York, 1997.

Curnow, Trevor. *Wisdom, Intuition, and Ethics.* Brookfield, Vt., 1999.

Day, John, Robert P. Gordon, and H. G. M. Williamson, eds. *Wisdom in Ancient Israel: Essays in Honor of J. A. Emerton.* New York, 1995.

Harrington, Daniel J. *Wisdom Texts from the Qumran.* New York, 1996.

Kekes, John. *Wisdom and Good Lives.* Ithaca, N.Y., 1995.

Kinnard, Jacob N. *Imaging Wisdom: Seeing and Knowing in the Art of Indian Buddhism.* Curzon Critical Studies in Buddhism. Richmond, U.K., 1999.

Langan, Thomas. *Tradition and Authenticity in the Search for Ecumenic Wisdom.* Columbia, 1992.

Murphy, Roland Edmund. *The Tree of Life: An Exploration of Biblical Wisdom Literature.* New York, 1990.

Raphals, Lisa Ann. *Knowing Words: Wisdom and Cunning in the Classical Traditions of China and Greece.* Ithaca, N.Y., 1992.

Reichert, John. *Milton's Wisdom: Nature and Scripture in* Paradise Lost. Ann Arbor, 1992.

Kurt Rudolph (1987)
Translated from German by Matthew J. O'Connell
Revised Bibliography

WISDOM LITERATURE

This entry consists of the following articles:

BIBLICAL BOOKS [FIRST EDITION]
BIBLICAL BOOKS [FURTHER CONSIDERATIONS]
THEORETICAL PERSPECTIVES

WISDOM LITERATURE: BIBLICAL BOOKS [FIRST EDITION]

Certain books within the Hebrew scriptures stand out as significantly different from the narrative and legal material comprising the Pentateuch as well as from prophetic and apocalyptic literature. This "alien corpus" is altogether silent with regard to the dominant themes found in the rest of the Bible, for example the promise to the patriarchs, the deliverance from Egypt, the Mosaic covenant, the centrality of Jerusalem and the Davidic dynasty, the prophetic word, and so forth. In the place of such emphases one finds ideas and literary forms that are closer to certain Egyptian and Mesopotamian works. That literary corpus contains a rational principle of the cosmic order that is worthy of study (*ḥokhmah* in ancient Israel, *maat* in Egypt, *me* in Mesopotamia) and expresses a belief that conduct in accord with this principle brings well-being. Or the literature gives voice to various levels of doubt about the validity of this understanding of reality, a skepticism spawned by life's inequities. Since study of the underlying principle of the universe rather than proclamation of the divine word comes to prominence here, modern scholars designate these texts as wisdom literature.

Characteristics of Wisdom Literature. Decisive differences do exist between Israel's sapiential literature, on the one hand, and certain texts written in Egypt and Mesopotamia on the other. Egyptian wisdom functioned almost exclusively at the royal court. Its aim was to provide proper education for future bureaucrats in the pharaoh's court. Accordingly, this literature largely assumed the form of instruction (e.g., the *Instruction of Ptahhotep,* the *Instruction of King Amenemhet to His Son Sesostris,* and the *Instruction for Merikare*) and its setting was usually the scribal school (praise of which occurs in Papyrus Sallier, Papyrus Anastasi, and the *Instruction of a Man for His Son.*) In Mesopotamia the study of school texts also played an important role, but the fundamental feature of wisdom was cultic, indeed, magical, and the goal of wisdom was to manipulate the paraphernalia of the cult in order to ensure one's existence.

Israelite wisdom finds primary expression in the books of *Proverbs, Job,* and *Ecclesiastes* within the Palestinian (Masoretic) canon and in *Ben Sira* (*Ecclesiasticus*) and the *Wisdom of Solomon* in the Alexandrian canon (the Septuagint). Its influence extends beyond these texts to *Psalms* (*Ps.* 1, 19, 33, 39, 49, 127) and various other books. The precise extent of this influence is the subject of considerable discussion; scholars have claimed much of the Hebrew scriptures for the sages (*Genesis* 1–11, the Joseph story, *Deuteronomy, Amos, Isaiah, Micah, Jonah, Habakkuk, Esther,* the succession narrative in *2 Samuel* 9–20, *1 Kings* 1–2, and more). While such claims appear to be exaggerated, they do serve as a reminder that the sages did not dwell in isolation from the prophets, priests, and raconteurs in ancient Israel.

With the exception of *Job,* these Israelite wisdom books are pseudonymous. There is no historical basis for the attribution of the older collections within *Proverbs* to Solomon or for Solomonic authorship of *Ecclesiastes* and *Wisdom of Solomon;* in Egyptian wisdom literature pseudonymity and literary fiction of royal authorship also play a significant role. The unique example of pride of authorship is Yehoshu'a ben Sira, the author of *Ben Sira,* who claims to have run a school about 190 BCE during the high priesthood of Shim'on II. Confirmation of this date comes from information provided by Ben Sira's grandson, who translated the Hebrew text into Greek around 132 BCE, and from the hymn in praise of Shim'on. *Proverbs* contains several different collections from various times, some of which may be preexilic. *Ecclesiastes* probably comes from the end of the third century BCE, while *Wisdom of Solomon* is known to be considerably later, because it was written in Greek and because its thought patterns and rhetoric are thoroughly hellenized. In dating *Ecclesiastes,* grammar and syntax seem conclusive. *Job* is particularly hard to date, but a combination of things, including both language and thought, suggest the sixth century BCE or slightly later.

THEMES, LITERARY TYPE, AND FUNCTION. In general, wisdom literature comprises two quite distinct types: brief observations about the nature of reality and instructions deriving from experience or extensive reflection on the deeper meaning of life. The former are formulated in parallel half lines for the most part; one statement is thus balanced by another, either synonymously or antithetically. Three variants are "Better is this than that" (e.g., *Prv.* 15:16); a graded numerical proverb, such as "Three things . . . yea, four" (e.g., *Prv.* 30:18–19); and "There is . . ." (e.g., *Prv.* 20:15). Most of these brief aphorisms are complete in themselves, although larger paragraphs appear in the latest collection in *Proverbs* 1–9, *Ecclesiastes,* and, especially, *Ben Sira,* constituting paragraphs that resemble brief essays on a specific topic. Speculative wisdom literature (*Job* and *Ecclesiastes*) prefers dialogue and monologue as its peculiar mode of expression.

Another way of categorizing various types of wisdom literature derives from the four uses to which the texts were put: juridical, experiential, theological, and natural. Since the king was the final court of appeal, and since society relied on royal power to implement justice, the judicial ability to ferret out the truth amid competing claims was greatly prized, as the widely disseminated story about Solomon's royal verdict in the case of two harlots' dispute over a surviving infant suggests (*1 Kgs.* 3:16–28). Experiential wisdom encompasses the overwhelming majority of biblical proverbs. These represent conclusions based on experience, and they endeavor to assist others in the difficult task of coping. Some are content with stating the way things are; others engage the pedagogic enterprise with zeal, offering warnings and motivations for following a particular path of conduct. Theological wisdom is concerned with the first principle of knowledge in religious devotion, the fear of the Lord. It speculates on the presence or absence on earth of the divine rational principle (personified wisdom), and sometimes equates revelation of Torah and human reasoning. Natural wisdom refers to encyclopedic data about heavenly bodies, atmospheric conditions, wild animals, and so forth. Although prominent in Egypt and Mesopotamia, such noun lists (onomastics) did not survive in biblical wisdom, although the divine speeches in the *Book of Job* resemble them in some ways.

The function of Israelite wisdom literature is by no means clear, partly because of the difficulty in tracing the history of this sort of thinking. At least three distinct stages seem likely. Wisdom's earliest phase seems to have coincided with early clan existence, when parents instructed their children in the ways of the world. The vast majority of proverbs attributed to Solomon may well have arisen in this early period because they rarely reflect the situation of the royal court. In the second phase, with Solomon perhaps, and certainly with Hezekiah, wisdom makes itself at home in the court. This phase placed a distinct mark on only a few proverbs, although it did evoke a tradition about "men of Hezekiah" who transmitted the collection in *Proverbs* 25–29. With *Ben Sira* the third phase comes to light, school wisdom. Precisely when this phenomenon first surfaced remains hidden. Certainly, the first epilogue to *Ecclesiastes* (12:9–12) identifies the unknown author of that book as a "wise man" who taught "the people," and the strange pen name *Qohelet* has often been interpreted as one who summoned people to a place of worship and study. (It is more likely that the word alludes to his assembling of proverbs about life's absurdity.)

SCHOOL TEXTS. For various reasons, several scholars have proposed that biblical wisdom literature originated in Israel in monarchic or premonarchic times as texts for study in schools. This theory is based on analogy with schools in the pharaoh's court and in the Mesopotamian temple precincts. Israel's familiarity with international wisdom cannot be denied; witness Solomon's relations with Egypt, the incorporation of a portion of the *Instruction of Amenemope* in *Proverbs* 22:17–23:33, and the *Sayings of Agur and of Lemuel's Mother* in *Proverbs* 30:1–4 and 31:1–9. Corroborative evidence has come from the nature of canonical wisdom—its exceptional literary quality, its conscious rhetoric and pedagogic thrust. To these have recently been added data from Palestinian inscriptions (alphabetic series, drawings, inaccurate spellings, transposed letters, large and poorly formed consonants, and so forth). None of this evidence is altogether compelling, although its cumulative force merits consideration. The preservation of wisdom literature implies such a group of individuals, whether they attended a formal institution or not. At least one scholar has simply called this phenomenon "Israel's intellectual tradition."

Internal evidence suggests that the *Book of Proverbs* was written for the instruction of young men. That conclusion seems inevitable for at least two reasons: the direct address to "my son" and the extensive warning against the foreign woman, Dame Folly, together with the erotic language about Dame Wisdom, which is appropriate only if the audience is male. This erotic language becomes fully evident in the *Wisdom of Solomon* where readers are invited to strive for marriage with Sophia ("wisdom"), here a divine attribute. Male dominance also explains the misogyny within canonical wisdom, particularly in *Ben Sira* but also in *Ecclesiastes* (although this explanation has been disputed). If the author of the epilogue to *Ecclesiastes* is trustworthy, a democratization may have taken place under this collector of sayings who taught "the people."

WISDOM AS A WAY OF THINKING. Just what did the teachers wish to communicate to their students? The sages endeavored to discover ways to secure one's existence and to enrich it, as in *Ecclesiastes'* question "What is good for humans?" Their ultimate goal was to achieve life's good things: a good name, longevity, wealth, wise children. Believing that the creator had implanted within the universe the secrets to success, these sages looked for analogies that unlocked the doors to such insight. Observation of nature and human nature, the study of animals and insects—these were the ways in which they obtained information that was then applied to their own concrete situation. They also moved beyond the visible universe to speculate about God's nature and activity, and even their quest for pleasure was grounded in religious conviction. Since order in society, like cosmic order, is divinely ordained, the wise individual is not disruptive of society. Entirely missing, therefore, is the prophetic sense of social revolution. In its place prudence reigns, and a calculated use of bribes, silence, and the concealment of real thoughts and feelings. Self-control and the right word were their aim. The seekers of wisdom sought to know the appropriate word or proper deed for a given occasion, the one that would confirm their membership in the company of the wise and therefore the righteous.

A CRISIS OF THE INTELLECT. Experience was sometimes ambiguous, forcing the wise to question their own hardened dogmas. That was especially the case with regard to the conviction that virtue flourished and vice resulted in calamity. Belief in reward and retribution evoked powerful protests from the authors of *Job* and *Ecclesiastes.* In Mesopotamia a similar crisis of faith produced such works as the Sumerian *A Man and His God, I Will Praise the Lord of Wisdom,* the Babylonian *Theodicy,* and the *Dialogue of a Master and Slave.* Furthermore, to the biblical sages life was infinitely more complex than their proverbial formulations might suggest. They therefore ventured to speculate about things that could not be verified in experience. Religion thus emerged into prominence, both as the essential ingredient of all knowledge and as a faith claim. Whereas Yahvism tended to ground its claims in history, the wise took creation as their starting point. They even posited a feminine principle (*ḥokhmah*) as active in the process of creation (*Prv.* 8:22–31), eventually identifying it with the Torah of Moses (*Sir.* 24:23). In general, creation faith functions to undergird belief in divine justice; only the creator has sufficient power and knowledge to assure justice on earth. As long as sages believed in the power of the human intellect to secure their existence, grace remained in the background. In time, loss of faith in the power of wisdom creates a vacuum into which competing forces come. These opposing responses are pessimism and divine mercy, and their spokesmen are *Ecclesiastes* and *Ben Sira,* respectively.

Skepticism's roots go back a long way prior to the time of *Ecclesiastes* (e.g., *Jgs.* 6:13, *Prv.* 14:1, 14:13, 16:9, 16:33). Integral to the earliest sapiential expression is the concession that human ingenuity has its definite limits. Those who devise plans for battle must ultimately acquiesce before an incalculable divine will. Life has its mystery, which cannot be penetrated. Even instances of injustice cropped up now and then. In time, those cracks in the fundamental conviction of the sages became more frequent, and the idea of wisdom's hiddenness suddenly emerged as a viable epistemological option. The poem, probably by another author, that has been inserted into the *Book of Job* (28) marvels at the remarkable achievements humans have to their credit but expresses the opinion that wisdom is accessible to God alone. The author of *Ecclesiastes* admits that wisdom is very deep, so much so that it cannot be fathomed. Ben Sira cannot endorse such skepticism, although he does advise against trying to understand that which is too difficult. In a sense, the nature of human knowledge has been greatly qualified as a consequence of man's limited powers.

Sometimes an inability to comprehend life's mysteries ends in awe rather than skepticism. That is the insight put forth with poetic brilliance in the *Book of Job.* The decisive issue here is whether faith can transcend self-interest. To be sure, the book offers counsel on how to respond when trouble strikes innocent victims, but even more central is the issue of whether anyone will serve God for nothing. Job's final submission before a self-manifesting deity points to a wholly different response from that of skepticism or banality: a bowed knee and silenced protest, a seeing with the eye of faith. A similar response occurs in Psalm 73, which is often included in discussions of wisdom literature, where the believer comes close to abandoning the faith because of the prosperity of the wicked but in the end recognizes God's presence as the highest good.

Wisdom as a Tradition. Such shifts in perspective indicate that the wise were very much aware of history even if they did not ground their teachings in it. Indeed, a decisive transition takes place in the early second century with Ben Sira. In part a result of the Hellenistic environment within which he wrote, this borrowing of various features from Yahvism, for example, references to the primeval history, patriarchs, and prophets, was Ben Sira's way of salvaging the ancient teaching in a changing society. By means of mythological speculation he was able to identify earlier revelation with divine wisdom (*Sir.* 24:23) and locate its residence in Jerusalem (*Sir.* 24:1–12). Again and again Ben Sira alludes to biblical stories, until finally he compiles a hymn in praise of ancient heroes of the faith (*Sir.* 44:50).

The unknown author of *Wisdom of Solomon* continued Ben Sira's reliance on canonical tradition as a framework, particularly the account of Egyptian bondage and divine deliverance. This Exodus material generated unusual interest for the Jews who resided in Alexandria a millennium later. In this instance the author reflects on the events of the Exodus in Midrashic style; the running comments on scripture are designed to evoke psychological factors such as dread even though the central focus is a frontal attack on idolatry. Nevertheless, the Hebraic tradition shares equal billing with the Hellenic, and this is entirely new for the wisdom literature. The Greek influence is considerable: the style is replete with Greek rhetoric, and the content is equally Greek in origin, including the four cardinal virtues, the notion of immortality, the twenty-two attributes of deity, the description of the curriculum in a local school, the rhetorical device called *sorites*, and much more.

Personified Wisdom. The change within wisdom thinking from the sixth to the first century BCE is nowhere clearer than in the notion of personified wisdom. In the latest collection of *Proverbs* (1–9) Wisdom appears in the guise of a teacher; here she invites and threatens young men, seeking to deliver them from Dame Folly. In *Proverbs* 8 Dame Wisdom is a celestial figure who assists God in creation; she is the manifestation of divine thought, depicted in veiled erotic language. Interpreters have often compared this theologoumenon to the Isis myth and to the teachings about the Egyptian goddess Maat. Elsewhere in *Proverbs* (3:16), Wisdom holds life in her right hand, riches and honor in her left hand, just as Maat is depicted as holding in each hand emblems that symbolize these qualities. In the *Book of Job* there is mention of an impenetrable wisdom who is known to the underworld by rumor but to whom only God has direct access (*Jb.* 28:20–28).

In contrast, Ben Sira writes that wisdom existed in heaven but searched the whole earth for a place of residence and finally chose Jerusalem as a permanent abode. This celestial figure then loses her enigmatic character, however, and becomes identical with the Mosaic law. Divine wisdom is thereby domesticated on earth, and Greek philosophy and the Hebraic tradition become equal in this aspect. In *Wisdom of Solomon* this heavenly figure is a divine attribute that guides the chosen people to their destiny. Those who desire to succeed in life must win her favor, and she is therefore to be courted like a bride.

To sum up, poetic imagery in *Proverbs* has by the time of *Wisdom of Solomon* become an actual figure who functions to bring well-being to God's people. By way of *Ben Sira* this imagery was particularized to refer to an actual body of literature, the Mosaic law. From first to last, however, wisdom's role in the initial act of creation was an active one. The intention was to give a name to the order that governs reality itself and thus to suggest a universe in which right thinking and acting would prosper. The author of *Ecclesiastes*, who did not endorse such faith, maintained silence with regard to personified wisdom. Instead, he echoes one feature of the poem in *Job* 28: the profundity of wisdom and, therefore, its hiddenness (*Eccl.* 7:23–29).

A Corpus of Literature. The thesis of a shift in wisdom thinking that took place with *Ben Sira* and *Wisdom of Solomon* does not imply monolithic thought prior to the second century, but it does assume that certain essentials held the literature together despite individual characteristics. A closer look at the actual contents of this literature may illustrate this point.

Proverbs. The *Book of Proverbs* comprises at least nine separate collections, four major ones—(I) 1–9, (II) 10:1–22:16, (III) 22:17–24:22, (IV) 25–29—and five minor ones—(V) 24:23–34, (VI) 30:1–9, (VII) 30:10–33, (VIII) 31:1–9, (IX) 31:10–31. Two (VI and VIII) are attributed to foreign authors (Agur and King Lemuel's mother, respectively), and another (III) makes extensive use of an Egyptian source (Amenemope). Three (I, II, and IV) are credited to King Solomon, and one (V; cf. III) is simply called "More Sayings of the Wise." Only two brief collections (VII and IX) have no superscriptions. The probable order of dating is IV, II, III, and V, from oldest to most recent; the relative ordering of the others is uncertain. The initial collection is probably the latest one, with the possible exception of IX. Affinities with Canaanite literature suggest an early date for VI and VIII, but their religious content renders the issue unclear. In any event, much of the material probably arose in preexilic times.

In the older collections the dominant form is a single verse parallel with another. The parallel verse may be synonymous, antithetical, or ascending (climactic). Each brief aphorism registers an observation that compels assent; therefore, the sentence argues from what is presumed to be a general consensus. The other major proverb type is the instruction, which urges a particular course of action and reinforces it with threats of punishment or promises of reward. Instruction pervades the latest collection, but the decision about the date of composition is not based on form. In Egypt "instructions" (a form that has its own genre identification, and covers a wide spectrum of texts) date from very early times, while the late *Teaching of ʿOnkhsheshonqy* resembles the brief aphorisms in the earliest collections of *Proverbs.* Thus we see that dating from form is tricky. In the later biblical material single proverbs give way to brief essays, some of which make their point by citing a proverb and developing it. *Ben Sira* develops this trend so that paragraph units result. In *Proverbs* one finds extended treatments of such themes as the relative value of various professions (38:24–39:11), the place of physicians in society since God punishes the wicked by sending illness (38:1–15), duty to parents, drunkenness (19:1–3), headstrong daughters (42:9–11), dreams, discipline (30:7–13), passions (40:1–11), and shame (41:16–42:8). The different form in *Proverbs* 1–9 is accompanied by a more self-conscious theology. Whereas wisdom literature throughout the ancient Near East prefers the general name for God, these chapters use the name *Yahveh* quite freely. Furthermore, they insist that the fear of the Lord is the *sine qua non* of true intelligence. It is possible that one passage (6:20–35) draws on language from *Deuteronomy* in juxtaposing the fire of lust and the lamp of parental instruction. In these chapters, too, personified wisdom functions to mediate divine presence. Accordingly, she addresses the people in the manner of a prophet or a prophetic depiction of God, and she offers life itself.

There are some brief sayings elsewhere in the *Book of Proverbs* that are wholly secular in tone. That does not necessarily indicate an early date. It is more likely that religious and secular proverbs existed simultaneously but that they served different constituencies. Some of these secular sayings call attention to social inequities without any indication that such situations should be rectified. Other proverbs identify areas in which humans confront their limits. Those who wage war can make careful plans, but the battle's outcome rests in divine hands. This awareness of finitude crops up in Egyptian wisdom as well, where royal wisdom abounds. The attribution of wisdom to Solomon is therefore an interesting parallel, although it cannot be known whether this tradition of Solomonic authorship has any basis in history. One thing appears certain: the supposed Solomonic enlightenment never existed, and the type of wisdom credited to that king in *1 Kings* 4:29–34 (English version) does not correspond with sayings in the collections bearing his name. Nevertheless, Solomon may have sponsored a group of sages in his court, as Hezekiah did in the late eighth century. These sages may have shown their appreciation by attaching the king's name to their compositions. Unfortunately, these collections do not require an assumption of courtly provenance, although they do contain an occasional reference to royalty. The same is true of *Proverbs* 25:2, which states that God's glory consists in concealing things, whereas a king's glory lies in searching them out.

In general, the thrust of the sayings in the *Book of Proverbs* has a universal quality. Similar aphorisms exist in Egyptian wisdom and, to a lesser extent, in Mesopotamian. The biblical proverbs contrast the wise and the foolish (called the silent and the heated in Egyptian wisdom literature), offer advice on table manners, warn against laziness and sexual debauchery, endorse eloquence, observe human foibles for what they are, talk about responsibilities in given vocations, compare human conduct to that of animals or insects, encourage strict discipline of children, inculcate respect for parents and persons in authority, and treat social relations in all their complexity. Extended treatises occur outside the initial collection on significant issues, for instance, the dangers of strong drink and the virtues of a good wife.

The Book of Job. The fundamental presupposition underlying virtually all these proverbs is a belief in reward and retribution. The universal creator oversees the governance of the universe and makes certain that those who merit life's good things receive them. The author of the *Book of Job* questions this principle, although at first the argument set forth by his hero rests on the very premise it refuses to acknowledge. Were it not for this principle, Job would have no basis on which to complain, since there would be no anticipated correlation between conduct and life situation. The author of *Ecclesiastes* is much more thorough in rejecting this dogma, for in his view time and chance strike everyone without respect to behavior. In both cases, later tampering with the author's final product has radically altered its meaning.

The *Book of Job* resembles disputes in Mesopotamian wisdom (such as *I Will Praise the Lord of Wisdom*), but it also has elements of a lament (one critic has called the book a paradigm of an answered lament). An old folk tale in epic prose sets the stage for the poetic dispute: a patient Job loses everything and praises God nonetheless until God rewards him by doubling his original possessions. Apart from this narrative framework, *Job* consists of a dispute between Job and his three friends and a second dispute between God and Job. Speeches by the youthful Elihu interrupt these two disputes; like the poem in *Job* 28, these speeches (*Jb.* 32–37) are probably secondary. The hero of the poetic speeches is far from patient. Instead, he complains bitterly because God has become a stranger to him for no discernible reason. Although his three friends encourage him to pray for forgiveness, Job insists that he has done nothing to deserve such harsh treatment. His bitterness arises from a sense of an oppressive divine presence and an awareness that the deity he once knew can no longer be found. Now and again Job entertains the notion that a vindicator will set things right and establish his innocence. At last, despairing of assistance from his friends, Job utters an oath of innocence highly reminiscent of Egyptian cultic practice and challenges God to slay him or confirm his oath of purity (*Jb.* 31). God responds to the challenge but hardly in the way Job expected (*Jb.* 38–41). In a style similar to school questions in Egyptian texts, the deity addresses Job with a host of questions that force him to look beyond his own situation and survey the vast scope of creation. The shift in focus corrects Job's anthropocentricity while acknowledging divine solicitude for wild creatures beyond the parameters of human habitation. The divine speeches evoke a feeling of unworthiness in Job, who confesses that this new insight about God overshadows his former knowledge as immediate information does secondhand information. The resolution comes through repentance, if that is the true meaning of Job's final response to God. The Mesopotamian parallels to *Job* find their answer in the cultic realm, and proper ritual plays a significant role.

Ecclesiastes. Israel's contribution to skeptical literature, the *Book of Ecclesiastes*, presents reflections on life's vanity and concludes that everything is empty, like breath itself. Purporting to be written by the wisest and wealthiest king in Israel, it claims that all pursuits achieve no lasting results. For this book's author, wisdom no longer possesses the power to guarantee success; all human endeavors amount to a senseless "chasing after wind." He feels that even though some sages claim to know the truth about reality, they do not really penetrate to the heart of things (8:17). The great shadow hanging over life is death, which makes no distinctions between good and bad people or between animals and humans. The universe is out of kilter, and God is indifferent to what takes place on earth (9:11–12). As a consequence humans are advised to follow a path of moderation, to be neither overly righteous (like Job) nor excessively wicked (7:15–18). Such dark thoughts eventuate in hatred for life (2:17), and stillborns are considered more fortunate than the living (6:1–6). To be sure, wisdom does bestow a relative advantage over folly, as light is usually superior to darkness. But oppression runs rampant, and there is no comforter. The positive advice given is to enjoy life during one's youth, before death wields its awesome power. The book closes with a poem about old age and death (comparable texts have been found in ancient Sumer and Egypt). Unhappy with the negative note on which the book ends, someone added an epilogue that characterizes the teacher and his work (12:9–12), to which yet another epilogue has been attached (12:13–14). This final word neutralizes the entire book by summing up its contents as fearing God (piety) and keeping the commandments (praxis).

Ben Sira. The author of *Ben Sira* strives mightily to combine traditional religious belief and the wisdom tradition. Although capable of soaring to lofty heights in poetic verse, his heart is especially stirred when priestly interests and prerogatives come to mind. This fact has led some critics to the view that religion (the "fear of the Lord"), not wisdom, was central to Ben Sira. The same emphasis occurs in the long poem celebrating heroes of the past, a poem that concludes with a lavish description of the high priest in attendance at the altar (44–50). Competing traditions are held in check in *Ben Sira*. This accounts for the acceptance of old belief in the functioning of reward and retribution, along with special attention to divine mercy.

In some respects *Ben Sira* resembles *Proverbs*, even with regard to the subject matter. Nevertheless, whereas *Proverbs* for the most part couches its teaching in succinct observations, *Ben Sira* systematically elaborates upon one topic after another. In so doing *Ben Sira* occasions a decisive stylistic change: refrains occur with regularity. The same phenomenon is typical of Egyptian instructions; in fact, Egyptian influence in *Ben Sira* is likely (cf. *The Satire on the Trades* and Papyrus Insinger).

One important concern in *Ben Sira* is theodicy, the defense of divine justice. *Ben Sira* employs an ancient form of debate to achieve the defense and adds two distinct answers, one metaphysical and the other psychological, to the problem of theodicy: that the universe itself fights on the side of virtue and punishes wickedness, and that reward or punishment may be inner states of tranquillity or anxiety. Furthermore, God will set things right in a moment, so that one cannot be adjudged righteous or sinful until death; a similar expectation of future divine action furnishes comfort to the author of Psalm 73. Such faith finds appropriate expression in prayer and in hymnic praise; both modes of worship characterize Ben Sira the teacher. Wisdom has now become an integral facet of Yahvistic faith.

Wisdom of Solomon. The combination of piety and practical ethics continues in *Wisdom of Solomon*, which presents Hebraic ideas in Hellenistic dress. In this Hellenistic setting religious syncretism poses a problem of grave proportions; to combat the attractiveness of idols as an expression of devotion to the gods, the author ridicules this type of worship mercilessly. A similar attitude pervades the author's references to Egyptian rulers; like the earlier sages, this unknown author deals with only two categories of people, wise and foolish, who are, respectively, good and evil. The new element is an identification of good and evil along ethnic lines, a precedent for which occurs in *Ben Sira*. The earlier universalism that was an identifying mark of wisdom has faded under the mighty impact of national religious tradition.

Perhaps the single most radical departure from older sapiential teachings is the elevation of the erotic dimension as the dominant metaphor for the educational enterprise. Knowledge is a highly desirable bride of the one who is favored by the deity. The paradigm that functions effectively in this respect is grounded in the legend about King Solomon, wisest of men. But such intellectual superiority came as a divine gift in response to humble prayer. The power of wisdom transcends the personal inasmuch as it governs the affairs of a nation. In fact, wisdom functions in the same way that the holy spirit is described as functioning in the rest of the Hebrew Bible: as a personification guiding the prophets and leaders of Israel. Once again, an earlier characteristic of wisdom literature, its individualism, gives way to the nation of Israel.

With increased stress on divine activity come two further transformations of ancient wisdom: humanism bows before revelation, and eudaemonism bows before duty. Belief in immortality relieves the human finitude of its tragedy, because pleasures may be delayed until the next life.

LATER DEVELOPMENTS. The Jewish Alexandrian philosopher Philo Judaeus, who was born about 20 BCE, avails himself of Logos speculation from Greek and Jewish thinkers to present wisdom as the ordering principle of the universe and an expression of the divine will. Comparison with the Stoic Logos principle was almost inevitable, because this similarity in the two intellectual systems served as a bridge to bring them closer together. Like the author of *Wisdom of Solomon,* Philo was steeped in Hellenistic thought and expression. Nevertheless, the content of his thought is often thoroughly Judaic. Scholars cannot decide whether the language of mystery religions belongs to the heart of his message or is mere window dressing.

Philo does not borrow exclusively from Israelite wisdom literature but makes free use of the patriarchal stories. His elaborate allegorical exegesis of biblical texts is largely Greek, although certain writings from Qumran also employ a complex kind of hermeneutics (cf. the *Habakkuk Commentary*). This ancient sect in the region of the Dead Sea largely ignored the wisdom literature, with one possible exception—the erotic dimension of knowledge.

Late Jewish narratives—*Tobit,* for example—make occasional use of motifs and data from canonical and noncanonical wisdom. Certain affinities between older wisdom and *Pirqei avot* (Sayings of the Fathers) have often been cited, but these seldom extend beyond surface resemblances. Within the Apocrypha, *2 Esdras* (*4 Ezra*) wrestles with the difficult problem of theodicy, and the pseudepigraphic *Testaments of the Twelve Patriarchs* contains ethical teachings that resemble wisdom texts.

The New Testament. The wisdom tradition seems to have influenced the unknown author of the earliest source for the Gospels, known as Q. Jesus is credited with a number of gnomic sayings, most of which function to orient by disorientation: they challenge listeners by forcing them to rethink their own presuppositions about a given situation. One noteworthy feature of these sayings attributed to Jesus is their unusual attitude toward women. Whereas aphorisms concerning women in the first-century Greco-Roman world and in Jewish literature contain a strong misogynistic element, the brief sayings placed in Jesus' mouth are remarkably free of this sentiment.

The prologue to the *Gospel of John* utilizes Logos speculation to express the belief that Jesus was an earthly incarnation of the deity, and the *Gospel of Matthew* dares to identify Jesus with divine wisdom, the embodiment of Torah (*Mt.* 11:25–30). Outside the Gospels, Paul's letters rely on Judaic speculation about wisdom to express Jesus' role in creation itself. Furthermore, just as the sages had developed a theory in opposition to theodicy as an extreme response to evil (that is, the very wish to defend God's honor is blasphemous, since the deity is by definition just), Paul ridicules human wisdom and proclaims that God's love and power are demonstrated by Jesus' death on the cross. It is conceivable that Paul's opponents were witnessing the birth of Christian Gnosticism, perhaps even performing midwife service. One other New Testament text is strongly influenced by Hebrew wisdom, the short *Letter of James,* which draws freely upon brief aphorisms to inculcate certain teachings in the minds of listeners.

Gnosticism. The influence of the wisdom tradition in Gnosticism is somewhat anomalous. In Jewish tradition wisdom played a vital role during the creation of the world. For the Gnostics the present material universe is the product of demiurges, inferior divine beings. Nevertheless, wisdom speculation was too appealing for Gnostics to ignore, although they soon found ways to overlook wisdom's role in creating the universe. Three documents deserve consideration here: the *Gospel of Thomas,* the *Sentences of Sextus,* and a nongnostic text from Nag Hammadi, the *Teachings of Silvanus.* The influence of the wisdom tradition on Thomas may explain why instead of a passion story one finds a collection of sayings. The *Sentences of Sextus* (second century) contains over four hundred maxims of non-Jewish origin whose purpose is to describe the ideal Christian. The *Teachings of Silvanus* is a text that manifests typical Jewish stylistic forms: the address to "my son," which is reminiscent of the *Book of Proverbs;* poetic parallelism; and certain subjects and expressions that correspond to canonical ones. All this indicates that early Christians may have been drawn to some features of Hebrew wisdom and that they agree with their predecessors who believed that the intellect was a sufficient means of coping with reality and achieving the good life.

SEE ALSO Biblical Literature; Ecclesiastes; Job; Psalms.

BIBLIOGRAPHY

The most comprehensive discussions are James L. Crenshaw's *Old Testament Wisdom* (Atlanta, 1981) and Gerhard von Rad's *Wisdom in Israel,* translated by James D. Martin (Nashville, 1972). Three older treatments contain much valuable material: Johannes Fichtner's *Die altorientalische Weisheit in ihrer israelitisch-jüdischen Ausprägung,* "Beihefte zur Zeitschrift für die Alttestamentliche Wissenschaft" (BZAW), vol. 62 (Giessen, 1933); Oliver S. Rankin's *Israel's Wisdom Literature* (Edinburgh, 1936); and Hilaire Duesberg and Irénée Fransen's *Les scribes inspirés,* 2d ed. (Maredsous, Belgium, 1966). Three colloquiums have illuminated many disputed points; these are *Les sagesses du Proche Orient ancien,* edited by François Wendel (Paris, 1963); *La sagesse de l'Ancien Testament,* edited by Maurice Gilbert (Gembloux, 1979); and *Sagesse et religion,* edited by Edmond Jacob (Paris, 1979). Three additional collected works are highly informative: *Studies in Ancient Israelite Wisdom,* edited by James L. Crenshaw (New York, 1976); *Israelite Wisdom: Theological and Literary Essays in Honor of Samuel Terrien,* edited by John G. Gammie et al. (Missoula, Mont., 1978); and *Aspects of Wisdom in Judaism and Early Christianity,* edited by Robert L. Wilkin (Notre Dame, Ind., 1975).

The finest survey of current research on Egyptian wisdom is R. J. Williams's "The Sages of Ancient Egypt in the Light of Recent Scholarship," *Journal of the American Oriental Society* 101 (1981): 1–19, while Glendon E. Bryce's *A Legacy of Wisdom* (Lewisberg, Pa., 1979) is an update of Paul Humbert's pioneer study of Egyptian influence on Israelite wisdom, *Recherches sur les sources égyptiennes de la littérature sapientiale d'Israël,* "Mémoires de l'Université de Neuchâtel," vol. 7 (Neuchâtel, 1929). For Mesopotamian wisdom three references are noteworthy: W. G. Lambert's *Babylonian Wisdom Literature* (Oxford, 1960); Giorgio Buccellati's "Wisdom and Not: The Case of Mesopotamia," *Journal of the American Oriental Society* 101 (1981): 35–47; and Bendt Alster's *Studies in Sumerian Proverbs,* "Mesopotamia," vol. 3 (Copenhagen, 1975). Leo G. Perdue's *Wisdom and Cult* (Missoula, Mont., 1977) remains the fullest discussion of that issue, and the related matter of royal wisdom has been studied by Leonidas Kalugila in *The Wise King,* "Co-niectanea Biblica, Old Testament Series," vol. 15 (Lund, 1980).

Several examinations of school wisdom have appeared; Roger N. Whybray's *The Intellectual Tradition in the Old Testament,* BZAW, vol. 135 (New York, 1974), opposes such a view, while Hans-Jürgen Hermisson's *Studien zur israelitischen Spruchweisheit,* "Wissenschaftliche Monographien zum Alten und Neuen Testament," vol. 28 (Neukirchen-Vluyn, 1968), Bernhard Lang's *Frau Weisheit* (Düsseldorf, 1975), and André Lemaire's *Les écoles et la formation de la Bible dans l'ancien Israël,* "Orbis Biblicus et Orientalis," vol. 39 (Göttingen, 1981), defend the existence of a school in Israel.

Heinrich Schmid's *Wesen und Geschichte der Weisheit,* BZAW, vol. 101 (Berlin, 1966), has documented the crisis throughout the ancient Near East that resulted from a collapse in the dogma of reward and punishment. The pervasive presence of sapiential themes and theology has been examined in Donn F. Morgan's *Wisdom in the Old Testament Traditions* (Atlanta, 1981); Gerald T. Sheppard's *Wisdom as a Hermeneutical Construct: A Study in the Sapientializing of the Old Testament,* BZAW, vol. 151 (New York, 1980); and Max Küchler's *Frühjüdische Weisheitstraditionen,* "Orbis Biblicus et Orientalis," vol. 26 (Göttingen, 1979). The problem of theodicy is discussed in an anthology edited by James L. Crenshaw, *Theodicy in the Old Testament* (Philadelphia, 1983). Burton L. Mack's *Wisdom and the Hebrew Epic* (Chicago, 1985) discusses Ben Sira's hymn in praise of the fathers.

JAMES L. CRENSHAW (1987)

WISDOM LITERATURE: BIBLICAL BOOKS [FURTHER CONSIDERATIONS]

The subject of wisdom literature in the Bible has flourished in the last decades of the twentieth century and the beginning of the twenty-first century. New material and approaches have helped bring some aspects into clearer focus, while others remain just as obscure as ever.

It was previously thought that the authors of the Dead Sea Scrolls were uninterested in wisdom; with the fuller publication of more Qumran texts, however, they discovered that the opposite was true. In addition to copies of the biblical wisdom books and some Targums (Aramaic translations) of *Job,* wisdom texts from the Qumran Dead Sea scrolls also include: some sapiential psalms from Cave 11 (11Q5); parts of six copies of a large instruction known as "Sapiential Work A" (1Q26, 4Q415–418, 423); descriptions of a wicked woman the wise are to avoid and a woman the wise are to follow (4Q184 and 4Q185), perhaps to be identified with the Dame Folly and Dame Wisdom of *Proverbs*; a series of beatitudes (4Q525); other collections of maxims or instructions (4Q424 and 4Q420–421); a hymn about acquiring knowledge (4Q413); and several others. Many of these works were probably not composed by the Qumran community; rather, they likely existed beforehand and were merely copied by them. Unique among Jewish instructions, a fragment of Sapiental Work A (4Q415 2 ii 1–9) seems to be directly addressed to a woman; a wife is given conventional advice: to cling to her husband, to honor her father-in-law, and so on.

Scholars continue to investigate biblical wisdom's relation to the wisdom traditions in the neighboring Near Eastern literatures, as well as its place in world religions. In the case of Ancient Egypt, further explorations of the subgenre of instructions have yielded more specific similarities in language and form with those in the Bible. Moreover, the tale of Aḥiqar,

the earliest text of which is written in Aramaic and dates to the fifth century BCE in Egypt, but which was subsequently transmitted in over a dozen languages, contains a series of proverbs that demonstrate the popularity and continuity of the proverb tradition in the Near East across the centuries. With regard to Mesopotamia, the Sumerian "proverb" or "rhetoric collections" have been more fully published and studied, and other wisdom pieces have been considered in connection with the Bible. For instance, the so-called Sumerian poem about early rulers, preserved in three Old Babylonian copies and in seven Sumero-Akkadian bilingual fragments from thirteenth-century Syria, constitutes a particularly interesting case. In this composition, the universal literary motif of the fleeting nature of glory and fame, epitomized by the medieval theme *ubi sunt qui ante nos fuerunt?* (where are they who were before us?), seems to lead to a more optimistic corollary, the *carpe diem* (seize the day) theme, which can be compared to several passages in *Ecclesiastes.* Outside the ancient world, scholars have found many parallels to the biblical *Proverbs* in Arabic and African sapiential traditions, and they have shown that proverbial sayings and their many settings are cross-culturally quite similar, as are the multiple settings from which they arise. These correspondences do not necessarily imply genetic or historical relationships between the traditions, however; instead, they may actually indicate cross-cultural commonplaces.

New approaches to the Bible's wisdom tradition also include feminist interpretations, among other. For example, the existence of female sages has been explored, as has women's verbal use of proverbs. While some scholars have looked to ancient Near Eastern goddesses as precursors of Dame Wisdom and Dame Folly (the Egyptian Isis, the Canaanite Astarte, and the Mesopotamian Inanna, among others), others have suggested that Dame Wisdom is a hypostasis of Yahweh or a literary device, or a "literary compensation for the eradication of the worship of these goddesses" (Hadley in Day et al., *Wisdom in Ancient Israel,* p. 236).

Still, despite numerous recent monographs and articles on biblical wisdom literature, little consensus has been reached on some of the important issues; namely, the setting of wisdom in ancient Israel, the existence of a school or court tradition as in Mesopotamia or Egypt, the existence of sages as a professional class, the precise definition of "wisdom literature" (including its specific rhetoric, vocabulary, and themes), and the appropriateness of the generic label "wisdom" or the unity of all ancient Near Eastern texts deemed such, and so forth. One of the most basic questions yet to be answered definitively is whether there were schools in ancient Israel.The best supporting epigraphic evidence may perhaps be found in several inscriptions with sequences of numbers and measurements especially from the regions of Kadesh Barnea and Kuntillet ʾAjrud, as well as abcedaries (rudimentary alphabets) from various locations. These scarce indications, however, cannot compare to the abundance of evidence that exists for the scribal traditions in ancient Egypt and Mesopotamia.

Concerning vital questions about the nature of biblical wisdom literature, therefore, one can anticipate continued lively debate among scholars, and hopefully subsequent advancement of our understanding.

Bibliography

Some of the most important recent discussions on wisdom or the sage in the Bible are: J.G. Gammie and L.G. Perdue, editors of eds. *The Sage in Israel and the Ancient Near East* (Winona Lake, 1990); Stuart Weeks, *Early Israelite Wisdom* (Oxford, 1994); Roland E. Murphy, *The Tree of Life: An Exploration of Biblical Wisdom Literature,* 2d ed. (Grand Rapids, 1996); Leo G. Perdue, *Wisdom and Creation: The Theology of Wisdom Literature* (Nashville, 1994); John Day, Robert P. Gordon and H.G.M. Williamson, editors of *Wisdom in Ancient Israel: Essays in Honour of J. A. Emerton* (Cambridge, U.K., 1995); Joseph Blenkinsopp, *Wisdom and Law in the Old Testament: The Ordering of Life in Israel and Early Judaism* (Oxford, 1995); John J. Collins, *Jewish Wisdom in the Hellenistic Age* (Louisville, Ky., 1997); James L. Crenshaw, *Education in Ancient Israel: Across the Deadening Silence* (New York, 1998); Carol Fontaine, *Traditional Sayings in the Old Testament* (Sheffield, U.K., 1982).

For wisdom at Qumran see: Charlotte Hempel, Armin Lange, and Hermann Licthenberger, editors of *The Wisdom Texts from Qumran and the Development of Sapiential Thought* (Louvain, 2002); and Daniel J. Harrington, *Wisdom Texts from Qumran* (London, 1996).

As for the ancient Near Eastern parallels, see: Riad Aziz Kassis, *The Book of Proverbs and Arabic Proverbial Works* (Leiden, 1999); Nili Shupak, *Where Can Wisdom Be Found? The Sage's Language in the Bible and in Ancient Egyptian Literature* (Fribourg/Göttingen, Germany, 1993); Hellmut Brunner, *Die Weisheitsbücher der Ägypter: Lehren für das Leben,* 2d ed. (Zürich, 1991); and Miriam Lichtheim, *Late Egyptian Wisdom Literature in the International Context: A Study of Demotic Instructions* (Freiburg/Göttingen, Germany, 1983). For the Sumerian proverbs, see Bendt Alster, *Proverbs of Ancient Sumer,* 2 vols. (Bethesda, Md., 1997).

Tawny L. Holm (2005)

WISDOM LITERATURE: THEORETICAL PERSPECTIVES

There is great ambiguity in defining wisdom literature within Jewish and Christian studies. This literary corpus has been defined alternately as (1) a precise canonical division of biblical books attributed to Solomon (traditional view); (2) the literary product of a particular social class (i.e., the sages of Israel); (3) an empirical literature developed to address the problems of government and administration; (4) an instructional literature developed to teach social conduct in the family unit; (5) a literary observation on creation in reaction to the failure of prophecy; (6) an international literature often characterized as universal, eudaemonistic (i.e., happiness as life's goal), secular, or humanistic; (7) a literature whose goal is to facilitate the reading and interpretation of sacred tradition and scripture itself; (8) a literature expressive of an intellectual tradition distinguishable from other types of thought in Hebrew culture; and, (9) most broadly, any literature that expresses a particular view toward reality (especially in clan, court, or scribal settings) in answer to the question "What is good for men and women?"

This representative—but by no means exhaustive—list of definitions reflects the lack of consensus about what wisdom is and how the wisdom tradition can be said to have shaped a literary genre called wisdom literature. The problem of definition may be elucidated by examining the relevant wisdom terms and patterns of usage in canonical deuterocanonical and extra-canonical texts through the Second Temple period (536 BCE–70 CE).

Professional Class or Canonical Division? Despite the pervasive use of the words *hokhmah* (wisdom) and *hakham* (wise) and the Greek equivalents *sophia* (wisdom) and *sophos* (wise) in the Bible and Septuagint (third-century BCE Greek translation of the Hebrew scriptures), they do not technically describe either a professional class or a canonical division of scripture. Although the word *hak-ham* appears in *Jeremiah* 18:18 in a context that to some scholars suggests three professional classes (priests, prophets, and sages), such a reading is by no means conclusive and has been forcefully challenged by Roger Whybray (1968), among others. Other texts suggestive of a professional class of *ha-khamim* (sages) are similarly inconclusive (see *Is.* 5:21, 29:14, 31:2; *Jer.* 8:8, 9:22). Aside from these biblical references, certain external evidence of international school and scribal structures has been used to posit similar biblical institutions. However, lack of direct biblical evidence makes these theories somewhat speculative.

Whether wisdom constitutes an intra-canonical category is likewise debatable. Not until the apocryphal *Book of Ben Sira* (second century BCE) is there even an allusion to the tripartite canonical division: law, wisdom, and prophets (expressed in this unusual order at 39:1)

Wisdom-Torah Identification. A related and more sharply defined issue in *Ben Sira* is the clear and striking identification of Torah and wisdom in chapter 24. Here

Wisdom, personified as a preexistent entity with God at creation, is said to have found a resting place in Israel (*Book of Ben Sira* 24:9). Furthermore, wisdom is peculiarly merged with Torah so that there is no Torah study without the study of wisdom. Beyond the early association of wisdom and Torah in *Deuteronomy* 4:6, the logic of this identification may be sought in the second-century BCE encounter between Judaism and Hellenism, whose rich philosophical traditions challenged Israel to provide a philosophical foundation for its own sacred history. In such a setting wisdom takes on a decidedly apologetic task. For the author of Ben Sira, Torah is mediated or interpreted by wisdom—the same wisdom perhaps that provides the international standard for the conduct of human affairs. The concerns of *Ben Sira* are echoed in *Baruch* (*Bar.* 3:9–4:4) and perhaps even in the final stages of earlier biblical books in which wisdom interprets sacred tradition.

This wisdom-Torah association persists in the later rabbinic literature. More typical of rabbinic interpretation, the Mishnah tractate *Avot* entertains the same wisdom-Torah juxtaposition but comes to the opposite conclusion: Rather than wisdom leading inevitably to Torah, knowledge of Torah now must precede and temper wisdom. In the words of the rabbinic sage Simon the Just:

> He whose wisdom takes precedence over his fear of sin, his wisdom will not endure. . . . That is why a person should first . . . carry out the commandments, even if he does not understand the reasons why. . . . He whose wisdom exceeds his works is one who does not carry out what he learns; therefore his knowledge of the Torah will not keep. (*Avot* 3.12)

In the Dead Sea Scrolls at Qumran, in which the wisdom tradition is variously supplemented or even supplanted by apocalypticism, there is surprisingly little *hokhmah/hakham* vocabulary. Nevertheless, selected scrolls (1 QS, 1 QH, 1 QM) are strongly reminiscent of the late wisdom writings (e.g., Book of *Ben Sira, Baruch, Wisdom of Solomon*). Here an esoteric wisdom aids in the interpretation of Torah; what can be known about the origin and end of the world is not clearly discernible either in creation itself or in Torah plainly interpreted. Torah mysteries are revealed to the sectaries who become by membership in the community initiates into divine mysteries (1 QS 9:17–18; 1 QH 1:21). And yet, this esoteric wisdom is still linked to ethics and piety as in the older wisdom–Torah dialectic. The created order is still cause for praise despite its secrets (1 QH 1:11–12), and the secrets will finally be revealed to the remnant of those who obey to the commandments:

> But with the remnant of those who held fast to the commandments of God He made his Covenant with Israel forever, Revealing to them the hidden things In which all Israel had gone astray. (1 CD 3:13–14; as cited in Vermes, 1962, p. 85)

A similar wisdom-Torah dialectic, now with different aims, may be at work in the New Testament *Gospel of Matthew* in which Jesus is depicted as both a new Moses (e.g., *Mt.* 5:17–20; 23:34–40) and as Wisdom's representative (*Mt.* 11:19, 25–30; 23; cf. *Book of Ben Sira* 51) and in the *Letter of James* in which the "wisdom from above" (*Mt.* 3:17) seems to replace explicit Torah language.

The coexistence of such varied perspectives on the role of wisdom testifies to the highly pluralistic milieu of Hellenistic Judaism. Ultimately, for Judaism, Torah remained the standard by which all other scripture was to be interpreted, for despite the eventual recognition of the prophets and the writings as canonical divisions, at no time were these placed on equal footing with Torah. To the contrary, the challenge at Yavneh in the first century to the canonicity of Song of Songs and Ecclesiastes testifies to their tentative status, although the view that these books "defile the hands" (i.e., are to be revered as sacred writings) prevailed.

WISDOM ATTRIBUTED TO SOLOMON. The ascription of three books to the hand of Solomon, Judaism's preeminent wise man (*1 Kgs.* 3–5), is evidence of another link between wisdom and sacred history. *Proverbs, Song of Songs,* and (obliquely) *Ecclesiastes* all claim or allude to Solomonic authorship. The curious circumstance that *Ecclesiastes* is ascribed not to Solomon but to Qohelet, who is nevertheless described in language appropriate only to Solomon ("Son of David, king in Jerusalem"), is regarded by Brevard S. Childs (1979) as evidence of canonical shaping. By means of this device, the reader who knows the tradition of wisdom surrounding Solomon is instructed to read *Ecclesiastes* as an authoritative part of that tradition. If this assessment is correct, the assignment of texts to Solomon provides the earliest glimpse of a biblical category functioning as (what is now referred to as) wisdom literature.

Although modern scholars such as Whybray, Gerhard von Rad, Walter Bruggemann, and Joseph Blenkinsopp have tended to attribute a secular humanistic orientation to the literature of the Solomonic enlightenment, Jewish historian Josephus Flavius (37/38–c. 101), the rabbis, and the early church fathers offer evidence for the inadequacy of this assessment. Both Flavius and Origen (c. 185–c. 254) refer to the Solomonic works as theologically didactic, that is, teaching divine wisdom. In his famous discussion of the twenty-two books of scripture "justly accredited" and "containing the record of all time," Josephus observes that "four contain hymns to God and precepts for the conduct of human life [*hypothekas*]" (*Against Apion* 1.39). These four are thought to be *Psalms, Proverbs, Ecclesiastes,* and *Song of Songs.*

In the prologue to his *Commentary on Song of Songs,* Origen places "three books written by Solomon's pen [in] didactic order" from *Proverbs* to *Ecclesiastes* to *Song of Songs.* In this order, he writes, the books present three general disciplines by which one attains knowledge of the universe. The Greeks call them ethics, physics, and enoptics (Origen, *Commentary on Song of Songs*).

Origen's thought was further systematized in the fourth century by Gregory of Nyssa (c. 335–c. 395), who writes that

God used Solomon as an instrument to show "in systematic and orderly fashion, the way which leads upward to perfection." These three books, analogous to stages of growth in the physical body, reveal a particular order of development that brings human beings to virtuous life. From *Proverbs*'s neophyte wisdom, suitable for the child, to *Ecclesiastes*'s teaching that "beauty is that beyond anything grasped by the senses," to *Song of Songs*'s "initiation of the mind into the innermost divine sanctuary," the human soul is directed gradually toward its final "mingling with the divine" (Gregory of Nyssa, *Homily on the Song of Songs*).

WISDOM SINCE THE ENLIGHTENMENT. With the Enlightenment and the rise of modern biblical scholarship came a departure from the traditional definition of wisdom literature as material attributed to Solomon. Attention turned now to the issues of form and redaction criticism and particularly to newly discovered ancient Near Eastern wisdom parallels (especially Egyptian texts). In this period the term *wisdom literature* came to be a standard designation for a vaguely defined type of Old Testament literature.

Interest in the implications of scientific findings for the standing of wisdom in biblical theology also arose in the modern period, doubtless in reaction to the Enlightenment preoccupation with historical critical method. Von Rad's (1972) three-part chronological division of Old Testament wisdom history into old (secular) wisdom, theological wisdom, and apocalyptic wisdom is perhaps the most comprehensive result of such study, although it has received sharp criticism by such scholars as James Crenshaw and Gerald Sheppard.

In the 1950s a new and extensive exploration of wisdom influence on biblical texts generally not defined as wisdom literature was initiated by von Rad's (1966) study of the Joseph narrative in *Genesis*. Von Rad's claim that the *Genesis* narrative, through its use of wisdom themes and vocabulary, presents Joseph as one trained in the wisdom of the Egyptian court drew much criticism but also gave rise to a generation of similar studies. Studies of other narrative texts, like Whybray's (1968) *Succession Narrative* and Talmon's (1963) study of the *Book of Esther*, followed von Rad's lead. Legal and prophetic texts were similarly explored by Moshe Weinfeld, Joseph Jensen, William Whedbee, and others.

CROSS-CULTURAL STUDIES OF WISDOM IN THE ANCIENT NEAR EAST. The international context of biblical wisdom is already suggested by the claim in *1 Kings* 4:30 that Solomon's wisdom surpassed that of all the peoples of the East and Egypt. The comparison of Egyptian instructional literature to *Proverbs* by Adolf Erman (1924) and Paul Humbert (1929) opened a new phase of inquiry into wisdom literature as a genre. From the Egyptian *sebayit* (teaching) with its central idea of *maat* (the divine order of truth established by God) to the Sumerian and Assyro-Babylonian instructional texts of Mesopotamia, parallels to nearly every presumed wisdom category in the Hebrew scriptures have been found. Egyptian texts relating advice to the student were found to bear strong resemblance to the biblical *Proverbs,* whereas texts listing the works of nature, such as the *Onomasticon of Amenemope,* were compared to texts such as *Job* 38–39. Likewise, the biblical theme of the suffering of the righteous and the skeptical tradition of Qohelet found rough parallels in certain Egyptian texts (such as the papyrus *Dispute over Suicide*) and even stronger resonance in Mesopotamian texts like the poem *Ludlul bel nemeqi* (the Babylonian Job), the *Dialogue of Human Misery,* and the *Dialogue of Pessimism.*

Despite these strong family resemblances, however, many scholars have objected that ancient Near Eastern parallels have been exaggerated in the secondary literature. W. G. Lambert's (1960) pivotal study of Babylonian literature stresses the inapplicability of biblical definitions of wisdom to the Akkadian word *nemequ,* usually translated "wisdom." Unlike biblical wisdom, *nemequ* most often refers to skill in cult and magic lore in which the wise man is the initiate. Although Babylonian literature exhibits thought patterns similar to those often characterized as biblical wisdom (e.g., proverbs, advice on living), "there is no precise canon by which to recognize them" as wisdom texts (Lambert, 1960). In any case Lambert cautions that the term *nemequ* does not adequately define these writings.

Equally problematic is the attempt to equate proverbial or folk sayings with wisdom. Once again the cross-cultural resemblance is undeniable and yet one cannot limit wisdom to proverbs without depriving the term *wisdom* of its rich nuance. Proverbs, after all, occur in the widest variety of cultures, often without any religious content or implication. The discovery of Egyptian parallels to biblical proverbs is far from establishing an international standard for wisdom.

WISDOM AS A CATEGORY IN THE HISTORY OF RELIGIONS. If it is somewhat problematic to speak of a cross-cultural wisdom literature in the ancient Near Eastern context, it is even more difficult to do so in the context of contemporary comparative religions. It would be tempting, for example, to draw a correspondence between Buddhism's *prajñā,* sometimes personified as a goddess who brings enlightenment to all buddhas, and the personified Wisdom of *Proverbs* 8. Both figures are praised in hymns that endow them with feminine traits, and yet the practices directed toward achieving the two states—*prajñā* and biblical wisdom—are near opposites. Buddhism, particularly Mahāyāna Buddhism, undertakes to awaken *prajñā* "found slumbering under ignorance and karma which come from our unconditioned surrender to the intellect" (Suzuki, 1958 p. 5), whereas biblical wisdom is often characterized as an intellectual tradition. In other words, wisdom in the biblical tradition is often associated with knowledge, and *prajñā*—more like antiknowledge—is characterized by detachment from the intellect and the cultivation of a transcendental insight into things "just as they are" (*yatha bhutam*), without conceptual distortion.

Closer to what scholars associate with biblical wisdom is the wisdom of Zoroastrianism, which is manifest in perfect control over the will, shown in "good deeds, righteousness and good repute," according to *Denkard,* a ninth-century encyclopedia of Zoroastrianism. The source of this wisdom is the Creator "who is essential wisdom"; the created "receive it through their own faculties" (*Denkard* 380.19–382.3). As in much of the Bible, wisdom and righteousness go hand in hand.

Islamic mysticism offers another example of wisdom as anti-intellectualism. For the Ṣūfīs, all wisdom (*aqul;* universal reason) is included in the letter *alif,* the first letter of the Arabic alphabet and symbol for God. It requires no study of books or philosophical quest because knowledge is immediately derived from God. Furthermore, it is typical of Persian mystical literature to elevate love over intellect or to substitute "rapture for reasoning" (Schimmel, 1975, p. 431).

Each of these traditions undoubtedly exhibits internal diversity and nuance in its definition of wisdom equal to or exceeding the variations in biblical and other ancient Near Eastern texts. The problems encountered in the comparison of the latter, texts from similar temporal and geographical settings, are only exacerbated in the broader cultural context of contemporary history of religions. If there is no consistent use of the term in the ancient Near East, there is far less consistency of definition about a wisdom genre outside of that milieu. The question remains, then, whether wisdom can be spoken about as a category of literature either within the Bible or in the broader and more problematic cross-cultural context of world religions.

See Also Ḥokhmah; Prajñā; Sophia.

Bibliography

Blenkinsopp, Joseph. *Sage, Priest, and Prophet: Religion and Intellectual Leadership in Ancient Israel.* Louisville, Ky., 1995.

Blenkinsopp, Joseph. *Wisdom and Law in the Old Testament: The Ordering of Life in Israel and Early Judaism.* 2d ed. New York, 1995.

Brenner, Athalya, ed. *A Feminist Companion to Wisdom Literature.* Sheffield, U.K., 1995.

Bruggemann, Walter. *In Man We Trust: The Neglected Side of Biblical Faith.* Richmond, Va., 1972.

Camp, Claudia. *Wisdom and the Feminine in the Book of Proverbs.* Sheffield, U.K., 1987.

Childs, Brevard S. *Introduction to the Old Testament as Scripture.* Philadelphia, 1979.

Collins, John J. *Jewish Wisdom in the Hellenistic Age.* Louisville, Ky., 1997.

Crenshaw, James L. "Method in Determining Wisdom Influence upon 'Historical' Literature." *Journal of Biblical Literature* 88 (1969): 129–142.

Crenshaw, James L. "Prolegomenon." In *Studies in Ancient Israelite Wisdom,* edited by James L. Crenshaw, pp. 1–60. New York, 1976.

Crenshaw, James L. *Old Testament Wisdom: An Introduction.* Atlanta, Ga., 1981.

Deutsch, Celia M. *Lady Wisdom, Jesus and the Sages: Metaphor and Social Context in Matthew's Gospel.* Valley Forge, Pa., 1996.

Erman, Adolf. "Das Weisheitsbuch des Amen-em-ope." *Orientalische Literaturzeitung* 27 (May 1924): 241–252.

Gammie, John G., and Leo G. Perdue, eds. *The Sage in Israel and the Ancient Near East.* Winona Lake, Ind., 1990.

Gerstenberger, Erhard. "Covenant and Commandment." *Journal of Biblical Literature* 84 (1965): 38–51.

Greer, Rowan A., ed. and trans. *Origen: An Exhortation to Martyrdom.* New York, 1979.

Harrington, Daniel J. *Wisdom Texts from Qumran.* London, 1996.

Hempel, Charlotte, Armin Lange, and Hermann Lichtenberger, eds. *The Wisdom Texts from Qumran and the Development of Sapiential Thought: Studies in Wisdom at Qumran and its Relationship to Sapiential Thought in the Ancient Near East, the Hebrew Bible, Ancient Judaism and the New Testament.* Louvain, 2001.

Humbert, Paul. *Recherches sur les sources égyptiennes de la littérature sapiéntiale d'Israël.* Neuchâtel, Switzerland, 1929.

Jensen, Joseph. *Isaiah 1–39.* Wilmington, Del., 1984.

Lambert, Wilfred G. *Babylonian Wisdom Literature.* Oxford, 1960.

McKane, William. *Prophets and Wise Men.* Naperville, Ill., 1965.

Murphy, Roland E. *The Tree of Life: An Exploration of Biblical Wisdom Literature.* New York, 1990.

Norris, Richard A., ed. *The Song of Songs Interpreted by the Early Church and Medieval Commentators.* Grand Rapids, Mich., 2003.

O'Connor, Kathleen. *Wisdom Literature.* Wilmington, Del., 1988.

Pritchard, James B., ed. *Ancient Near Eastern Texts Relating to the Old Testament.* 3d ed. Princeton, N.J., 1969.

Robert, A. "Les attaches littéraires bibliques de *Proverbs* I–IX." *Revue Biblique* 43 (1934): 42–68, 374–384; 44 (1935): 344–365, 502–525.

Schimmel, Annemarie. *Mystical Dimensions of Islam.* Chapel Hill, N.C., 1975.

Schroer, Silvia. *Wisdom has Built Her House.* Collegeville, Pa., 2000.

Sheppard, Gerald T. *Wisdom as a Hermeneutical Construct: A Study in the Sapientializing of the Old Testament.* Berlin, 1980.

Suzuki, Daisetz Teitaro. *Zen and Japanese Culture.* 2d ed., rev. and enl. Princeton, N.J., 1958.

Talmon, Shemaryahu. "'Wisdom' in the *Book of Esther.*" *Vetus Testamentum* 13 (1963): 419–455.

Vermes, Geza. *The Dead Sea Scrolls in English.* London, 1962.

Von Rad, Gerhard. "The Joseph Narrative and Ancient Wisdom." In *The Problem of the Hexateuch and Other Essays,* translated by E. W. Trueman Dicken. Edinburgh, 1966.

Von Rad, Gerhard. *Wisdom in Israel.* Translated by James D. Martin. Nashville, 1972.

Weinfeld, Moshe. *Deuteronomy and the Deuteronomic School.* Oxford, 1972.

Whedbee, J. William. *Isaiah and Wisdom.* Nashville, 1971.

Whybray, Roger N. *The Succession Narrative: A Study of II Samuel 9–20; I Kings 1 and 2.* Naperville, Ill., 1968.

Whybray, Roger N. *The Intellectual Tradition in Israel.* Berlin, 1974.

Zaehner, Robert C. *The Dawn and Twilight of Zoroastrianism.* London, 1961.

ALEXANDRA R. BROWN (1987 AND 2005)

WISE, ISAAC M. (1819–1900), pioneer and leading organizer of American Reform Judaism. Born near Eger, Bohemia (now Cheb, Czech Republic), Isaac Mayer Wise led an impoverished childhood. He received a traditional Talmudic education, which, though irregular, gave him an extensive acquaintance with rabbinic literature and an appetite for wider knowledge. In 1846, after holding a minor rabbinical position in Radnitz, he left for America.

Essentially Wise was an autodidact. He appears to have imbibed Mendelssohnian ideas in Europe, but on his arrival in New York there was nothing to distinguish him from conventional Orthodoxy. The mainspring of his Reform inclinations, which surfaced in America, appears to have been a sense of the needs of Judaism in the New World. He became the rabbi at a synagogue in Albany, New York, and not only instituted reforms there but began to write and lead efforts designed to bring direction to the scattered elements of American Jewry—to formulate a particularly American Judaism. A quarrel within his synagogue over certain of these reforms led to his being forcibly ejected from his position in 1850; he thereupon started his own congregation. In 1854 he moved to Cincinnati, where he remained until his death. During the course of his lifetime Wise was twice married; he had ten children with his first wife and four with his second.

In Cincinnati, Wise started a weekly, *The Israelite* (later renamed *The American Israelite*), which was quickly followed by a German periodical for Jewish women, *Die Deborah.* He wrote voluminously: history, theology, poetry, catechisms, and liturgical writings issued from his pen. Wise's overriding concerns were to provide the American Jewish community with a synod that would set qualifications for American rabbis and to establish a college that would train them and legitimize changes in ritual. This program incurred the suspicion not only of Orthodox Jews but also of the more doctrinaire Reform Jews, and it led to violent polemics with his colleagues.

Nevertheless, as a result of Wise's propaganda the Union of American Hebrew Congregations was established in 1873 in Cincinnati, and in 1875 the union opened Hebrew Union College, with Wise as its president. His energy, resilience, and single-minded devotion to his tasks nursed the college through a difficult beginning, and when in 1889 the Central Conference of American Rabbis was established Wise became its president. His place in the history of American Judaism rests on his intuition of the needs of an as yet inchoate community and his persistence in bringing his ideas to fulfillment.

BIBLIOGRAPHY

Heller, James G. *Isaac M. Wise.* New York, 1965.

Knox, Israel. *Rabbi in America: The Story of Isaac M. Wise.* Boston, 1957.

Philipson, David. *Reform Movement in Judaism.* 2d rev. ed. (1931). Reprint, New York, 1967.

Temkin, S. D. "Isaac Mayer Wise and the Civil War." *American Jewish Archives* 15 (November 1963): 120–142.

Wise, Isaac M. *Reminiscences.* Translated by David Philipson. Cincinnati, 1901. Covers the period between 1846 and 1857.

New Sources

Wolf, Alfred. "A Newly-Discovered Letter by Isaac M. Wise." *Journal of Reform Judaism* 37 (1990): 1–8.

S. D. TEMKIN (1987)
Revised Bibliography

WISE, JOHN (1652–1725), Congregational clergyman and proponent of ecclesiastical liberty in the Massachusetts Bay Colony. A graduate of Harvard College in 1673, Wise by the end of the 1670s had settled in the town of Ipswich as its parish minister, remaining in that capacity and locale until his death. Wise is remembered chiefly for his defense of a pure "congregational" polity, each local church being left free to conduct its own affairs without hindrance or help from "higher" or more numerous clerical authorities. In *The Churches Quarrel Espoused* (1710) and again in *A Vindication of the Government of New-England Churches* (1717), Wise ridiculed the notion that pastors were unable to lead their own flocks, perform their proper duties, or steadily "steer in all weather that Blows." It was quite unnecessary, he argued, and indeed potentially dangerous, to resort to councils or synods—to consociations or committees—to "advise" or "assist" the independent congregation. If people cannot direct their own worship, he continued, perhaps they are incapable even of choosing their own spouses. Some may even think that a committee is needed to "direct all Wooers in their Choice for the Marriage Bed; for that there is many a fond Lover who has betrayed the glory of Wedlock by making an unwise and unfortunate Choice; and why not particular Beds be overruled, as well as particular Churches?"

With such wit joined with even more convincing arguments from antiquity, from nature, and from Christian scripture, Wise argued narrowly for the congregational way, but he also argued broadly for local rule and individual liberty. That Wise's plea for ecclesiastical liberty had inescapable implications for civil liberty found explicit recognition in the republication in 1772 of both works noted above. After the Sugar Act (1764), the Stamp Act (1765), the Townshend acts (1767), and the Boston Massacre (1770), New Englanders welcomed the assurance that a natural person is "a Free-Born Subject under the Crown of Heaven, and owing Homage to none but God Himself."

BIBLIOGRAPHY

The only modern biography of John Wise is George A. Cook's *John Wise: Early American Democrat* (New York, 1952, 1966). For a fuller assessment of Wise's significance, see Perry Miller's *The New England Mind: From Colony to Province* (Cambridge, Mass., 1953).

EDWIN S. GAUSTAD (1987 AND 2005)

WISE, STEPHEN S.

WISE, STEPHEN S. (1874–1949), American rabbi, Zionist leader, and social activist. Scion of a family of European rabbis, Stephen Samuel Wise was brought to America as an infant from Budapest to join his father, Aaron Wise. Educated at Columbia University, he received private rabbinic training and was ordained by Adolf Jellinek of Vienna. From service as assistant rabbi at the Conservative synagogue B'nai Jeshurun in New York, he moved to the pulpit of Reform Temple Beth Israel in Portland, Oregon, and returned to New York in 1907 to found and head the Free Synagogue. Its pulpit would be free, said Wise; its pews would welcome all; its purpose would be to make its congregants more "vitally, intensely, unequivocally Jewish."

A religious liberal and social activist, Wise used the pulpit and lecture platform to promote both liberalism and social justice. As an American clergyman he involved himself in civic affairs and social and economic issues, helping to found both the National Association for the Advancement of Colored People (1909) and the American Civil Liberties Union (1920); as a rabbi he made the plight of brethren abroad, Jewish rights at home, and the democratization of Jewish communal life his central concerns. Above all was his lifelong devotion to the cause of Zionism. He was a founder of the Federation of American Zionists in 1898, and he twice served as president of the Zionist Organization of America (1913–1920; 1936–1938).

To help democratize the structure of the American Jewish community, Wise took leadership in the organization of the American Jewish Congress. He was its president from 1921 to 1925 and honorary president until his death. In the wake of the rise of Nazism, he organized the World Jewish Congress in 1936 and served as its president. To bring greater unity to American Jewry, he founded a nondenominational rabbinical seminary, the Jewish Institute of Religion, in 1922. Wise was acclaimed as one of the most stirring of pulpit orators and platform lecturers of his generation.

BIBLIOGRAPHY

Polier, Justine Wise, and James Waterman Wise, eds. *The Personal Letters of Stephen Wise.* Boston, 1956.

Urofsky, Melvin I. *A Voice That Spoke for Justice.* Albany, N.Y., 1982.

Voss, Carl H. *Rabbi and Minister.* Cleveland, 1964.

Voss, Carl H., ed. *Stephen S. Wise, Servant of the People: Selected Letters.* Philadelphia, 1969.

New Sources

Moffic, Evan. "The Progressive Zionism of Louis Brandeis and Stephen Wise." *CCAR Journal* 47 (2001): 15–24.

ABRAHAM J. KARP (1987)
Revised Bibliography

WISSOWA, GEORG

WISSOWA, GEORG (1859–1931), was a German philologist and historian of Roman religion. Georg Otto August Wissowa was born near Breslau, the son of a civil servant. His grandfather was a noted Tacitus scholar and the director of Breslau's Catholic Gymnasium, where Wissowa himself was educated, graduating with superior marks in 1876. That same year he entered the University of Breslau, where he studied under the classical philologist August Reiffersheid, who introduced him to the study of Roman religion. In 1880 Wissowa successfully defended his doctoral dissertation, "De Macrobii Saturnalium fontibus." He subsequently continued his studies in Munich under Heinrich von Brunn, then one of Germany's foremost students of Roman antiquities. From Brunn he gained an appreciation of the importance of art and monuments for the understanding of Roman religious life, and in 1882 he produced a habilitation thesis on the images of Venus in Roman art ("De Veneris simulacris romanis"). Through Brunn, Wissowa also met that towering genius of Roman historical studies, Theodor Mommsen, whose methods he later applied to the study of Roman religion.

Upon the acceptance of his thesis, Wissowa joined the faculty at Breslau as a privatdocent, but he spent his first year in that position doing research in Italy (his only trip to the homeland of Roman civilization). In 1886 he accepted a post as associate professor at Marburg, where he was promoted to professor ordinarius in 1890. In 1895 he left Marburg for the University of Halle (Saale), where he spent the remainder of his career.

During the early part of his career Wissowa wrote nearly a dozen articles dealing with Roman religious antiquities. There were, in fact, preliminary studies for what was to be his chief contribution to the science of religion, *Religion und Kultus der Römer* (1902; 2d ed., 1912). In this work he traced the development of Rome's religion and described in detail its gods and practices. The book's importance lies in Wissowa's successful identification of the several strata of Roman religion, his clarity and precision in delineating the nature of its various facets, and his masterful treatment of its evolution by adoption of foreign forms. He demonstrated once and for all the essential dissimilarity of Greek and Roman religion, emphasizing that the latter was highly legalistic and almost totally lacking in mythology. In an era dominated by the comparative approach to religion popularized by James G. Frazer's *The Golden Bough,* Wissowa anticipated more recent anthropology by insisting on the need to understand Roman religion on its own terms and as an organic unit (cf. his remarks on Frazer in *Religion und Kultus,* 2d ed., p. 248,

n. 3). *Religion und Kultus der Römer* soon became the foundation for all subsequent work in its field. Though other general treatments of the subject have appeared since its publication, it remains a standard and indispensable authority.

Hardly less important for the study of religion was Wissowa's decision to take on the task of reediting August Pauly's *Realencyclopädie der klassischen Altertums-wissenschaft.* The resulting compendium, not completed until 1972, became a standard reference for all students of the ancient world. It naturally included numerous articles on ancient gods and cults, many of them written by Wissowa himself. He was, in addition, a contributor to W. H. Roscher's *Ausführliches Lexikon der griechischen und römischen Mythologie* and to James Hastings's *Encyclopaedia of Religion and Ethics.*

Wissowa continued to be an active author and teacher until 1923, when his health failed. He spent the last eight years of his life as an invalid. It is to be regretted that his physical condition prevented him from participating in the discussion of new archaeological evidence unearthed during the 1920s that was to prove of major significance for the history of Roman religion.

BIBLIOGRAPHY

In addition to the works cited above, Wissowa wrote a collection of articles, *Gesammelte Abhandlungen zur römischen Religions- und Stadtgeschichte* (1904; reprint, New York, 1975), which supplement *Religion und Kultus.* Of his many other valuable articles, I would single out as particularly interesting "Zum Ritual der Arvalbrüder," *Hermes* 52 (1917): 321–347.

A bibliography of Wissowa's works (nearly complete, but add the articles listed in the index to the *Encyclopaedia of Religion and Ethics,* edited by James Hastings, Edinburgh, 1908–1927) may be found at the end of Otto Kern's obituary for Wissowa in the *Biographisches Jahrbuch für Altertumskunde* 60 (1934): 120–145. This article and Kern's *Georg Wissowa: Gedächtnisrede* (Halle, 1931) are the fullest treatments of Wissowa's life.

New Sources

See now the various contributions (by Johns Scheid, Fritz Graf, Mary Beard, among others) intended to form a sort of monographic section in *Archiv f. Religionsgeschichte* 5 (2003): 1–211; as well as Gert Audring, *Gelehrtenalltag. Der Briefwechsel zwischen Eduard Meyer und Georg Wissowa (1890–1927)* (Hildesheim, 2000).

HENRY JAY WATKIN (1987)
Revised Bibliography

WITCHCRAFT

This entry consists of the following articles:

WITCHCRAFT: CONCEPTS OF WITCHCRAFT

The term *witchcraft* embraces a wide variety of phenomena. Its meaning varies according to historical and cultural context. The word *witch* derives from the Old English noun *wicca* (sorcerer) and the verb *wiccian* (to cast a spell). The original concept of witchcraft corresponds to what anthropologists call *sorcery*: the attempt to influence the course of events by ritual means. Sorcery is widespread and found in almost every culture and historical period. Two other, quite different, phenomena have also been called *witchcraft.* The first is the alleged diabolical witchcraft of early modern Europe and its colonies; the second is Neopagan witchcraft, a twentieth-century revival. This article will distinguish sharply among these three phenomena, because the connections between them are few and tenuous.

ANTHROPOLOGICAL CONCEPTS OF SORCERY AND WITCHCRAFT. Anthropologists distinguish between sorcery and witchcraft. Sorcery is a system of beliefs and practices whose goal is to manipulate nature in order to bring about specific changes that benefit the sorcerer or her or his clients. Witchcraft is the belief that certain members of society are inherently able to harm others. Sorcery involves a set of skills that can be learned; witchcraft is usually thought to be inborn and inherited. In practice, however, sorcery and witchcraft beliefs often exist side by side, and it is sometimes difficult to separate the two.

The simplest forms of sorcery involve the performance of one action in order to bring about another, such as performing sexual intercourse in a sown field to assure a good harvest, or putting pins in an image to cause injury. However, sorcery often goes beyond the performance of magical acts and invokes the help of spirits. In order to cure illness, a Guatemalan sorcerer may perform rituals invoking the aid of San Simon, a Catholic saint who has absorbed the characteristics of an indigenous Mayan deity. If a member of the Lugbara tribe of Zaire and Uganda were injured, he might appeal to the shrines of his dead ancestors for help. This type of magic has much in common with prayer: both magic and prayer attempt to assure a spirit's assistance. However, while prayer usually implores a deity's cooperation, magic sometimes attempts to compel the gods to collaborate.

Sorcery implies an underlying belief system in a coherent universe in which all parts are interrelated, and influencing one part can affect another. In such a universe, relationships exist linking human beings with stars, plants, minerals, animals, and other natural phenomena, as well as supernaturals, such as gods, nature spirits, and angels. This belief system is known as the "magical worldview." Its thought processes are intuitive rather than analytical, but they have their own internal logic, and are thus not inherently irrational. They can arise out of an emotionally charged experience: for example, if in a rage you curse someone who has offended you, and shortly afterwards this person dies, you may feel both guilty and powerful, and henceforth assume that certain powers are available to you. Empirical science ignores such events because they cannot be verified through experimentation, but societies whose worldviews are not exclusively empirical regard them as direct and convincing evidence of a coherent, magical universe.

Almost all societies have some form of sorcery; in many, it plays an important function. In cultures without access to medical technology, sorcerers may function as healers. Even when medical cures are available, people may still resort to sorcerers to heal certain kinds of illnesses that do not respond readily to pharmaceutics or surgery. Healers, medicine men, and so-called witch doctors are sorcerers who by definition have a positive function in society, for their work is to cure victims of the effects of witchcraft or malevolent magic. Individuals may consult healers to obtain relief from disease or other misfortunes attributed to witchcraft or sorcery; tribal and village authorities may summon them to combat drought or other public calamities. Dances and other rituals serve to detect and repel witches and evil spirits. Such protective sorcery assumes special social importance in times of famine, war, or severe stress in the community.

In some cultures, sorcery and religion come together: a priest or priestess may perform ritual acts to make rain, ripen the crops, procure peace, or ensure victory in war. When such acts are performed publicly, for the public good, they are generally viewed as benevolent and have a positive social function. But when they are performed privately and for the benefit of a few individuals, they are often regarded with suspicion. The distinction between public and private magic often becomes the distinction between "good" and "bad" magic. Both Vodou and Santeria, Afro-Caribbean religions in which elements of magic exist within a religious framework, make formal distinctions between public religious ceremony and private sorcery done against certain individuals; the latter is condemned. Private sorcery provides the poor, the weak, and the powerless with a tool of resistance and revenge. During periods of great social tension, such as plague or warfare, recourse to sorcery tends to increase and intensify, as more individuals feel powerless at the mercy of larger forces.

Periods of social strain are also characterized by a rise in witchcraft accusations. Unlike sorcerers, witches do not actually have to perform any actions to harm their victims. The Azande of southern Sudan believed that witchcraft was a psychic act; it required no magic spells or actions, and could even be done involuntarily. Witchcraft was inherited from the parent of the same sex. Witches were believed to possess *mangu*, a substance thought to be lodged in the intestines and to confer the spiritual power to harm. Witches were also believed to be able to send their spirits out at night to eat the souls of their victims, causing them to sicken and die. The Azande often blamed any kind of misfortune, from cracked pots to serious illness and death, on witchcraft. Their suspicions fell first upon neighbors with whom they had a disagreement. In order to identify whether witchcraft was responsible for their problems, they would consult oracles. If the oracle's response indicated that witchcraft was to blame, the Azande would confront the alleged witch and ask him to blow water over an offering in order to "cool" his emotions towards the victim. This act alone was usually enough to undo the witchcraft and mend social relations. Only in severe cases would disagreements result in the trial and execution of the witch.

The Navajo Indians of the American Southwest believed in witches called *skinwalkers* who would transform into wolves or coyotes at night in order to stalk their victims. Skinwalkers were said to assemble secretly in order to concoct a poison made from corpses that they used to kill their enemies. They were thought to fly through the air at night to blow the corpse poison into the smoke holes of their victims' hogans (a hogan is a Navajo dwelling). Both the Azande and the Navajo had healers who specialized in curing cases of witchcraft; however, among the Navajo, these specialized healers sometimes became suspected of witchcraft themselves. This occurs in many societies where sorcerers are enlisted to undo witchcraft, because it is assumed that those who have the power to heal can also use that power to harm.

Cultures with a belief in witchcraft often imagine witches as the very opposite of everything considered right in society. A witch is someone who disregards social rules, flouting even the most basic rules regarded as standards of decency in a particular society. Witches are often said to commit murder and incest, to engage in cannibalism and indiscriminate orgies, to have the ability to transform into animals, and to eat or otherwise abuse corpses. In other words, witches are people who violate the most basic rules in human society. Because the basic rules that maintain social order are similar cross-culturally, witches tend to be imagined in similar ways. It follows that individuals who flout other kinds of social rules, or who appear anomalous in other ways, stand a chance of being accused of witchcraft. For example, among the Azande, those who did not behave as good neighbors, who had many quarrels within the village, or who had a history of violent behavior were more frequently accused of witchcraft. Among the Navajo, those who appeared greedy, selfish and refused to share with their families, or who were marginal to the community and lived in peripheral areas were vulnerable to witchcraft accusations. Belief in witchcraft thus serves as a form of social control, reinforcing sanctioned behaviors and creating a threat against those who violate social norms.

Witchcraft beliefs also function as an attempt to explain the reasons behind otherwise unexplained negative events: illness, calamities, natural disasters, and death. Some anthropologists have argued that witch beliefs disappear once more scientific explanations for illness and natural phenomena are available. But even when humans understand the physical causes of a misfortune, the question remains: why does it strike some people, but not others? When a granary collapsed, killing a man inside it, the Azande were perfectly capable of understanding that it had given way because it was in a state of disrepair and weakened by termites. Still, the question for them remained: why had it collapsed at that very moment, and why when that particular man was inside? It is this question, the question why things happen as they do, that witchcraft beliefs attempt to tease out.

Witchcraft beliefs may also serve to explain the unexplainable. In all human cultures there are some experiences that are difficult to explain. These include experiences as diverse as sleep paralysis, near-death experiences, and dissociative states that produce very strong physical sensations that can lead believers to interpret them as signs of a spiritual reality that is contiguous to our material reality. Such experiences figure prominently in folklore about witches and witchcraft. In Newfoundland, for example, people often attribute the experience of sleep paralysis to being "hagged" or "hag ridden," believing that a malevolent witch sends her spirit out at night to torment them in their sleep. Because sleep paralysis often produces a physical sensation of a weight on the chest or a presence pressing down on the sleeper, the belief that witches cause this phenomenon may have arisen as an attempt to explain it.

Unlike sorcery, witchcraft beliefs are not true universals; that is, they do not occur in all cultures. They are most often found in small-scale agricultural societies with a stable settlement pattern, where neighbors have intimate knowledge of one another and social relationships are intense and multilayered. They also tend to be more frequent in cultures with little access to Western scientific knowledge and technology. Witchcraft beliefs are rare in large-scale societies with a great deal of social mobility. But similar phenomena, or so-called witch-hunts, do occur in developed societies with excellent access to information and scientific knowledge, for some of the same reasons they occur in small-scale societies: the desire to effect social control and to blame others for factors causing social tensions.

WITCHCRAFT AS A HISTORICAL PHENOMENON. Patterns of sorcery have existed in virtually all societies in the past, including Western society. The classical Greco-Roman and Hebrew societies from which Western civilization sprang entertained a great variety of beliefs and practices about sorcery, from public rituals that melded with religion to legends about hideous *striae* and *lamiae* reported by the poet Horace. He portrayed these witches as clothed in rotting shrouds, with disheveled hair, clawing the soil with taloned fingers as they invoked the gods of the underworld. The Greeks distinguished between three varieties of magic. The highest was *theourgia*, a kind of public liturgy "working things pertaining to the gods" (*theoi*), in which magic and religion blended. *Mageia* was the next variety; its practitioners worked technical magic privately to help themselves or their clients. *Goeteia* was the lowest form; "howlers" of incantations and mixers of potions, its practitioners were widely feared.

The sorcery of most cultures involved incantations supposed to summon spirits to aid the sorcerer. In many societies the connection between sorcery and the spirits was not explicitly formulated. But in both Greco-Roman and Hebrew thought the connection was defined or elaborated. The Greeks believed that all sorcerers drew upon the aid of spirits called *daimones* or *daimonia*. A Greek *daimon* could be either malevolent or benevolent. It could be almost a god (*theos*), or it could be a petty spirit. In the thought of Plotinus (205–270 CE) and other Neoplatonists, the demons occupied an ontological rank between the gods and humanity. The Hebrews gradually developed the idea of the *mal'akh*, originally a manifestation of God's power, later an independent spirit sent down as a messenger by God. In Greek translations of Hebrew, *mal'akh* became *angelos*, "messenger." Christians eventually identified "angels" with the Greek *daimones* and defined them as beings ontologically between God and humanity.

But a different element gained influence through the apocalyptic writings of the Hellenistic period (200 BCE–150 CE): the belief in evil spirits led by Satan, lord of all evil. The idea had limited precedents in earlier Jewish thought but gained prominence in the Hellenistic period under the influence of Iranian Mazdaism, or Zoroastrianism. Under such influence, the Christians came to divide the Greek *daimones* into two groups, the good angels and the evil demons. The demons were supposed to be angels who, under Satan's leadership, had turned against God and thereby become evil spirits. Sorcerers sought to compel spirits to carry out their will, but angels under God's command could not be compelled; thus it was supposed that sorcerers might well be drawing upon the aid of evil demons. This was the central idea of the second main variety of witchcraft, the alleged diabolism of the late medieval and Renaissance periods in Europe.

EUROPEAN WITCHCRAFT. Although simple sorcery had always existed, a new concept of witchcraft evolved in medieval and early modern Europe. The Christian concept of the devil transformed the idea of the sorcerer into that of the witch, consorter with demons and subject of Satan. Since 1880 this kind of diabolical witchcraft has been subject to four major schools of interpretation. The first, rooted in classical nineteenth-century liberalism, perceived witchcraft as an invention of superstitious and greedy ecclesiastics eager to prosecute witches in order to augment their own power and wealth. The second school, that of Margaret Murray, argued that witchcraft represented the survival of the old pagan religion of pre-Christian Europe. This religion (which never existed in the coherent form she believed) she supposed to be the religion of the majority of the people down into the seventeenth century, although subject to constant persecution by the Christian authorities. Murray's theory had great influence from the 1920s through the 1950s; unsupported by any credible evidence, it is now rejected by scholars. The third school emphasizes the social history of witchcraft, seeking to analyze the patterns of witch accusations in Europe much as anthropologists have done for other societies. The fourth school emphasizes the evolution of the idea of witchcraft from elements gradually assembled over the centuries. Most scholars currently belong to one or the other of the last two schools.

Historical development. The first element in diabolical witchcraft was sorcery, which existed in Europe as it did elsewhere. It persisted through the period of the witch craze and indeed has persisted to the present. Without this fundamental element, belief in diabolical witchcraft could not have existed. The second, related aspect was the survival of elements from pagan religions in the folklore of Christian Europe. In some parts of Europe, women believed that they participated in nighttime spiritual journeys led by the goddess Diana or by other supernatural female figures. These nighttime spiritual assemblies would dance, feast, and occasionally enter the homes of neighbors, rewarding the hospitable and punishing the slovenly. The wild ride with Diana was a form of folk belief in the "wild hunt," a troop of spirits led by a female or male deity that rode out at night, striking terror in those who encountered it.

During the Middle Ages, the Christian view of these beliefs changed. Early in the period they were seen as merely superstitious and mistaken, but towards the tenth and eleventh centuries they began to be considered heretical. The *Canon Episcopi,* a legal document of the Frankish kingdom issued about 900 CE, condemns "wicked women. . .who believe that they ride out at night on beasts with Diana, the pagan goddess. . . .Such fantasies are thrust into the minds of faithless people not by God but by the Devil." Gradually, the folk concept of the wild hunt, with its feasting, music, and dancing, was transformed into the diabolical sabbat, a nocturnal assembly of witches under the direction of the devil where horrible acts took place.

Another element in the development of diabolical witchcraft in Europe was Christian heresy. The classical formulation of diabolical witchcraft had been established by the fifteenth century. Its chief elements were: (1) a pact with the devil; (2) formal repudiation of Christ; (3) the secret nocturnal meeting; (4) the ride by night; (5) the desecration of the Eucharist and the crucifix; (6) orgy; (7) sacrificial infanticide; and (8) cannibalism. Each of these elements derived from one or another charge made against medieval heretics. Heresy became the medium through which sorcery was linked with the devil.

At the first formal trial of heretics in the Middle Ages, at Orléans in 1022, the accused were said to hold orgies underground at night, to call up evil spirits, to kill and cremate children conceived at previous orgies and use their ashes in blasphemous parody of the Eucharist, to renounce Christ and desecrate the crucifix, and to pay homage to the devil. The history of such charges goes at least as far back as the court of Antiochus IV Epiphanes of Syria (176–165 BCE), who made similar accusations against the Jews; the pagan Romans used them against the Christians, and the early Christians used them against the Gnostics. An early eleventh-century pedant must have resurrected the charges from patristic accounts of Gnostic heresy and applied them to the Orléans group, applying the archetypal thinking common in the Middle Ages: a heretic is a heretic, and whatever one heretic does another must also do. Thus the *idea* of heresy, more than any actual heresy itself, became the basis for the connection of heresy with witchcraft. Some later heretical groups, such as the sect of the Free Spirit, also were accused of similar diabolical crimes. Not all heretics were so charged, however. On the whole, the accusations were limited to those who had some connection with dualism, the doctrine that not one but two eternal principles existed. The two principles, one evil and one good, struggled for control of the cosmos. Dualist influence on most medieval heresies was indirect, but upon Catharism it was both direct and pronounced.

Catharism was a dualist heresy imported into western Europe from the Balkans in the 1140s. Strong in southern France and northern Italy for well over a century, it dominated the culture of Languedoc and the Midi in the years around 1200; it was suppressed by the Albigensian Crusade and eradicated by the Inquisition. The Cathari believed that matter, and the human body in particular, were creations of the evil god, whose intent was to hold the spirit imprisoned in the "filthy tomb of the flesh." The evil god is Satan, lord of this world, ruler of all material things and manipulator of human desires for them. Money, sex, and worldly success were the domain of the devil. These doctrines brought the devil closer to the center of attention than he had been since the time of the "Desert Fathers" a thousand years earlier. If only to refute Catharist theories, Scholastic theologians had to give the devil his due. The Catharist designation of Satan as the lord of the things of this world may also have led some who desired those things in the direction of Satan worship.

Scholastic theology was the next major element in the formation of the witch concept. Tradition going back to the early church fathers had suggested that the Christian community, which formed the mystical body of Christ, was opposed by an opposite group forming the mystical body of Satan and consisting of pagans, heretics, Jews, and other unbelievers. It was not only the right but the duty of the Christian to struggle against this evil host. Saints' lives and legends of the intense struggles of the Desert Fathers against demonic forces kept this tradition alive, and it was reinforced by Catharist dualism. In the twelfth through fourteenth centuries the Scholastics developed the tradition of the body of Satan, refined its details, and supplied it with a rational substructure. They extended the devil's kingdom explicitly to include sorcerers, whom they considered a variety of heretic. Simple sorcerers became, in the dominant Scholastic thought of the later Middle Ages, servants of Satan.

The link between sorcerers, heretics, and Satan was the idea of pact. The notion of pact had been popularized in the eighth century by translations of the sixth-century legend of Theophilus. In this story, Theophilus was a clergyman who sold his soul to the devil in exchange for ecclesiastical preferment. He met the devil through a Jewish magician and signed a formal pact with "the evil one" in order to fulfill his desires. The Scholastics derived a number of sinister ideas from the legend of Theophilus. Their theory transformed the person making the pact from a relatively equal contracting party to an abject slave of Satan who abjured Christ, did feudal homage to "the dark lord," and kissed his master's genitals or backside in token of his submission. The Scholastics also broadened the idea of pact to include implicit as well as explicit consent. One did not actually have to sign a contract to be a member of Satan's army; anyone—heretic, sorcerer, Jew, Muslim—who knowingly opposed the Christian community—that is, the body of Christ—was deemed to have made an implicit pact with the devil and to number among his servants.

The shift from Platonic to Aristotelian philosophy in the thirteenth and fourteenth centuries encouraged the process of demonizing witches. Platonic thought allowed for the existence of a natural, morally neutral magic between divine miracle and demonic delusion; but Aristotelianism dismissed natural magic and denied the existence of occult natural forces. If no natural magic existed, it followed that wonders were worked either through divine miracle or demonic imposture. Magicians compel or exploit supernatural powers, and since God and the angels cannot be compelled or exploited, the powers with which sorcerers deal must be demonic, whether they know this explicitly or not. Thus, Scholastic logic dismissed simple sorcery as demonic witchcraft.

Theology, then, made a logical connection between witchcraft and heresy. Heresy is any persistently held belief counter to orthodox doctrine. One who used demons serves the devil rather than God, and if one serves the devil, one acknowledges that correct theology involves serving the devil rather than God: this was the worst imaginable heresy.

The final element in the transformation of sorcery into diabolical witchcraft was the Inquisition. The connection of sorcery with heresy meant that sorcery could be prosecuted with much greater severity than before. Late Roman laws against sorcery were extremely severe, but during the early Middle Ages simple sorcery, or natural magic, was treated with relative leniency. Often it was ignored; when detected, it might bring no more than a fairly stiff penance. Elements of simple sorcery were incorporated into Christian practice, as seen in the combination of Christian prayer and pagan spells commonly said by parish priests in England during the tenth and eleventh centuries. Penalties for heresy, on the other hand, were severe. Suppression of heresy in the earlier Middle Ages was inconsistent, but in 1198 Innocent III ordered the execution of those who persisted in heresy after having been convicted and excommunicated. Between 1227 and 1235 a series of decrees established the papal Inquisition. In 1233 Gregory IX accused the Waldensian heretics, who were in fact evangelical moralists, of Satan worship. In 1252 Innocent IV authorized the use of torture by the Inquisition, and Alexander IV (1254–1261) gave it jurisdiction over all cases of sorcery involving heresy. Gradually almost all sorcery came to be included under the rubric of heresy.

The Inquisition was never well organized or particularly effective; in fact, most cases of witchcraft were tried before the secular courts. Nonetheless, the Inquisition provided one essential ingredient of the witch craze: the inquisitors' manuals. These manuals told inquisitors what signs of Satanism to look for, what questions to ask, and what answers to expect. Having obtained the answers they expected by using torture or the threat of torture, the inquisitors duly entered the answers in formal reports, which then added to the body of "evidence" that witches flew through the air, worshiped the devil, or sacrificed babies. It is unlikely that no one in the period ever practiced Satanism, but it is even more unlikely that any widespread Satanism existed. The great majority of the accused were innocent, at least of diabolism.

The witch craze. The number of executions for witchcraft was measured in the hundreds until the end of the mid-fifteenth century, but from 1450 to 1700—the period of the Renaissance and the origins of modern science—as many as a hundred thousand may have perished in what has been called the great witch craze. The witch craze can be explained by the dissemination, during a period of intense social unrest, of the intellectual elements summarized above by the Inquisition, the secular courts, and above all the medium of the sermon. The popularity of the sermon during the later Middle Ages and the Reformation explains how beliefs about witches spread in a period when the leading intellectual movements, such as nominalism and humanism, downplayed or even ignored witchcraft. The invention of the printing press also did its part in spreading the evil. In 1484 Pope Innocent VIII issued a bull confirming papal support for inquisitorial proceedings against witches, and this bull was included as a preface to the *Malleus maleficarum* (The Hammer of Witches), a book by two Dominican inquisitors. Published in 1486, the *Malleus* went into many editions in many languages, selling more copies in Protestant and Catholic regions combined than any other book except the Bible. The *Malleus* colorfully detailed the diabolical, orgiastic activities of witches and helped persuade public opinion that a cosmic plot directed by Satan threatened all Christian society.

Fears of cosmic plots increase in periods of high social tension. The fifteenth and sixteenth centuries witnessed a growth of existential anxiety, a widespread belief that the antichrist, the return of the savior, and the transformation of the world were at hand. As the religious split between Catholicism and Protestantism widened during the sixteenth century and flared up into religious warfare, eschatological fears deepened. Catholics saw the Protestants as soldiers of Satan sent to destroy the Christian community; Protestants viewed the pope as the antichrist. Terror of witchcraft and prosecution of witches grew in both Catholic and Protestant regions, reaching heights between 1560 and 1660, when religious wars were at their worst. No significant differences distinguished Catholic from Protestant views of witchcraft. The Protestants, who rejected so many of the accretions of doctrine in the Middle Ages, accepted beliefs about witches almost without modification. Martin Luther (1483–1546) declared that all witches should be burned as heretics in league with Satan; persecutions in the regions ruled by the Calvinists were comparable to those in Catholic and Lutheran areas.

Tens of thousands were persecuted and hundreds of thousands terrified and intimidated during one of the longest and strangest delusions in history.

The discourse of diabolical witchcraft was often invoked by ordinary people to prosecute neighbors for petty jealousies and resentments characteristic of small-scale societies. The craze was restricted almost exclusively to western Europe and its colonies. Since diabolism is virtually meaningless outside a Christian conceptual framework, it could not spread to non-Christian areas. Although the Eastern Christian church shared the same beliefs in the powers of Satan as the Western church, it experienced no witch craze. The absence of the witch craze in the Eastern church illustrates the hypothesis that for a craze to break out, three elements are required: (1) the appropriate intellectual structure; (2) the mediation of that structure from the elite to the people at large; and (3) marked social tension and fear.

Skeptics such as Johann Weyer (fl. 1563) and Reginald Scot (fl. 1584), who wrote against belief in witchcraft, were rare and were often rewarded for their efforts by persecution; Weyer, for example, was accused of witchcraft himself. More typical of the period were the works of the learned King James I of England and VI of Scotland (d. 1625). Personally terrified of witches, James encouraged their prosecution, wrote a book against them, encouraged the statute of 1604 against pact and devil worship, and commissioned a translation of scripture (the Authorized Version or King James Bible) that deliberately rendered certain Hebrew words (such as *kashshaf*) as "witch" in order to produce texts such as "Thou shalt not suffer a witch to live" (*Ex.* 22:18), which supported the king's design of suppressing witchcraft legally. In 1681 Joseph Glanvill was still able to publish a popular second edition of a work supporting belief in diabolical witchcraft. But by that time the craze was beginning to fade. Cartesian and scientific thought had no room for witchcraft; ecclesiastical and civil authorities agreed that witch prosecutions had got out of hand; and European society was settling down to two centuries (1700–1900) of relative peace and prosperity. The greatest outburst in those centuries was the French Revolution; it occurred in an intellectual context (the Enlightenment) in which revival of witch beliefs was impossible. European society found other rationales by which to demonize aristocrats, Jews, communists, capitalists, imperialists, or whomever was selected as an object of hatred. The date of the last execution for witchcraft in England was 1684, in America 1692, in Scotland 1727, in France 1745, and in Germany 1775.

Witchcraft and Society. The most important social function of the belief in diabolical witchcraft was scapegoating. Sometimes this process was conscious and cynical, as when Henry VIII added witchcraft to the list of charges trumped up against Anne Boleyn. Much more often it was unconscious. If one is impotent, or one's crops fail, or one becomes ill, it helps to blame a witch, not only because it relieves one of guilt but also because the belief that a witch has caused one's problems gives one the illusion of being able to solve them. If God or fate has caused your illness, you may have no remedy; if a witch caused it, then you may recover once the witch has been found and punished. Some scholars have hypothesized that witchcraft accusations function as a form of psychological projection: according to this unconscious mechanism, reviled characteristics are projected onto another individual or social group. "I hate you" becomes "You hate me," leading to suspicions and accusations of witchcraft against the target. During the period of the witch craze, projection had the important function of promoting the cohesion of Christian communities by the postulation of a powerful external foe. Witches thus served a purpose similar to that of external enemies in modern warfare, for they united the people against a common threat.

Historians have noted correlations between witch accusations and social position. Persons between the ages of forty and sixty were most commonly accused; the accused had fewer children than normal; children were seldom accused of witchcraft but were often believed to be its victims; people accused of witchcraft had been previously accused of other crimes more frequently than normal, especially offensive language, lying, theft, and sex offenses. Chronic grumbling, abrasive personality, quarreling, and cursing also increased one's chances of being accused. The social status of accused witches was usually low or lower middle, though sometimes magistrates, merchants, and other wealthy persons were involved. Anyone connected with medicine, especially midwives, was prone to suspicion, because illness and death could so easily be blamed upon witchcraft.

The most striking social correlation is between witchcraft and women. Although in certain areas and for brief periods of time more men were accused than women, over the entire history of the witch craze 75 percent of the accused were women. In the sixteenth century many more women were living alone than men. Given the patriarchal structure of European society at the time, a woman living alone without the support of father or husband had little influence and little legal or social redress for wrongs. Such women were often reduced to begging and depending on the charity of their neighbors. They also naturally tended to grumble or curse more than persons having effective influence in society. A physically weak, socially isolated, financially destitute, and legally powerless old woman who provoked resentment in her neighbors became an easy target for projection.

But the explanation lies only partly in specific social conditions. The misogyny underlying the association of women with witchcraft sprang from deep and ancient psychological roots. C. G. Jung, Mircea Eliade, Wolfgang Lederer, and others have commented on the powerful ambivalence of the feminine in religions, mythologies, and literatures dominated by males. The male view of the archetypal feminine is tripartite: she is the sweet, pure virgin; she is the kindly mother; she is the vicious, carnal hag. From the twelfth century, Christian society developed a compelling symbol incarnating the first two types in the Blessed Virgin Mother of God. As the power of the symbol of the Virgin Mother grew, the shadow side, the hag symbol, had to find outlet for its corresponding power. In ancient polytheistic religions the dark side of the female archetype had been integrated with the light side in the images of morally ambivalent goddesses such as Artemis. Split off from the positive side of the archetype, the Christian image of the hag became totally evil. In the period of the witch craze, this one-sided image was projected upon human beings, and the witch, no longer simply a sorceress, became the incarnation of the hag. Other androcentric assumptions in male-dominated religions encouraged the connection. The biblical narrative of creation blamed Eve for having succumbed to the temptation of the serpent, resulting in the expulsion of humans from the Garden of Eden. God, the chief power of good, was imagined in masculine terms, and so the devil, the chief power of evil, was supposed to be masculine also. Since it was believed that the devil's followers submitted to him sexually, it was naturally supposed that they should be women, some of whom described their intercourse with the devil in lurid detail.

The outbreak of witch trials in Salem, Massachusetts, during 1692 has been the subject of careful social analysis. Although the first hanging of a witch in New England occurred in 1647, it was at Salem in 1692, when the craze was already fading in Europe, that the colonies produced their most spectacular series of witch trials, in which nineteen persons were executed. After a group of young girls suffered an unusual combination of symptoms and visions, their elders suggested that they might be the victims of witchcraft, and the witch-hunt began. At the time, Salem village was in the throes of a long dispute concerning the church. An unpopular minister, John Burroughs, was succeeded by a controversial one, Samuel Parris, in 1689, just at the time when England was undergoing a revolution and the lines of authority were blurred. The villagers split into factions supporting and opposing Parris, and, since no structured means of expressing dissent existed, its release took the form of vituperation and slander. Continuing incursions of hostile Indians further exacerbated the situation, leading some settlers to conclude that a diabolical conspiracy was to blame.

The outbreak was the violent expression of deeply felt moral divisions; the moral divisions were generated by the quarrel over the governance of the church, and the quarrel over governance was exacerbated by the Indian wars and deep-seated conflicts between prominent families. Salem was a small, premodern village in which everyone knew everyone else, a situation that encouraged people to correlate unfortunate events with unpopular individuals and to blame them for their misfortunes. Intensely religious to a degree seldom paralleled in Europe at the time, the New England Puritans could not view the strife in their village in purely personal or political terms. They interpreted it in religious terms, as a manifestation of the cosmic struggle between Christ and Satan, good and evil. The tradition of belief in the existence of witchcraft was a vehicle perfectly adapted to the expression of such assumptions. Many towns and villages had political controversies without becoming centers of the witch craze; clearly such controversies do not automatically produce witch accusations and cannot be considered their cause. Most sophisticated scholars give full weight to the history of religious concepts and avoid simplistic correlations between external phenomena and witch beliefs. Disasters and controversies can produce witch accusations only in the presence of certain value systems. But such social tensions, once those value systems are there, can provoke the outbreak of a witch persecution.

MODERN WITCHCRAFT. The eighteenth and nineteenth centuries in Europe, with their secularism, scientism, and progressivism, were not conducive to witch beliefs of any kind. Yet Romanticism, an intellectual movement that arose in Europe at the end of the eighteenth and the beginning of the nineteenth century, laid the groundwork for a new permutation, which became the third main variety of witchcraft: Neopaganism.

Romanticism located authenticity in the folklore of European peasants, which was presumed to contain elements of ancient pagan religions. This led to a renewed interest in both folklore and paganism, reflected in the art and literature of the time, and to a revisionist interpretation of the witch. Franz-Josef Mone, Jules Michelet, and other writers of the mid-nineteenth century suggested that European witchcraft was really a widespread fertility cult surviving from pre-Christian paganism. Such arguments influenced anthropologists and folklorists at the turn of the century, such as James Frazer, Jessie Weston, and Margaret Murray. In 1899, amateur folklorist Charles Leland published *Aradia: The Gospel of the Witches*, a text claiming to present evidence that witchcraft was the survival of a pagan cult of Diana. *Aradia* influenced Murray and other twentieth-century anthropologists. Meanwhile, interest in the occult gained fashion among intellectuals and poets such as Algernon Blackwood and Charles Baudelaire. By the early part of the twentieth century, occultism enjoyed a certain popularity, especially among bohemians; magicians such as Aleister Crowley, who styled himself "the Great Beast," attracted a following. Their doctrines were a mixture of ritual magic, sorcery, dubious historical and philosophical arguments, and a longing for enchantment in an increasingly mechanized world.

Out of the crucible of early twentieth-century British occultism emerged modern Neopagan revival Witchcraft, or Wicca. Around the time that the poet Robert Graves was writing his imaginative *White Goddess* (1948) about an alleged worldwide cult of the moon goddess, the Englishman Gerald Gardner was recording the first documents that led to the formation of this new religious movement. According to his followers, Gardner, who was born in 1884, was initiated into the ancient religion in 1939 by a witch of the New Forest named Dorothy Clutterbuck. In fact, Gardner probably cobbled together elements of revival Witchcraft from his experiences with various occult and theatrical groups, including the Co-Masons, the Rosicrucian Theatre, and the Crotona Fellowship. Gardner's claim to be the mediator of an ancient religion was spurious, but he launched a growing religious movement that has gained many adherents throughout the world. Whatever its origins, it has become a legitimate religious movement in its own right.

The overall world numbers of revival Witches are difficult to calculate, but scholars estimate that in North America alone there are about 500,000. There are numerous denominations of Neopagan Witchcraft, including Gardnerian Craft, which traces its lineage to Gardner's 1950s coven; Reclaiming Witchcraft, an American variant with an ecofeminist perspective; and Dianic Witchcraft, an all-female tradition. The tenets of Witchcraft as it has evolved include a reverence for nature expressed in the worship of a goddess and (sometimes) a god; the practice of group magic aimed at healing or other positive ends; colorful rituals whose goal is to produce ecstatic experience; and an acceptance of the sensual, bodily aspects of human existence. It rejects diabolism and even belief in the devil on the grounds that the existence of the devil is a Christian, not a pagan, doctrine. It offers a sense of the feminine principle in the divine, a principle almost entirely forgotten in the masculine symbolism of the great monotheistic religions. And its eclectic paganism promotes a sense of the variety and diversity of the sacred.

Modern Neopaganism has no connections with diabolism. Diabolism, in fact, has almost ceased to exist in the late twentieth century. Though a few groups claiming to practice Satanism, such as the American Church of Satan and the Temple of Set, do exist, their practices are more like ironic rejection of bourgeois conventions than true devil worship. Sorcery, on the other hand, continues to flourish worldwide. *Curanderos* in Mexico and the American Southwest still practice healing with herbs and charms. Fear of sorcerers persists as widely as sorcery itself. In many parts of Africa, sorcery and counter-sorcery continue to be a part of everyday life, especially away from urban centers.

During the 1980s and 1990s, fears of Satanic activities briefly reemerged in North America. In these so-called Satanic panics, rumors spread about far-reaching diabolical conspiracies whose activities allegedly included the sexual abuse and murder of children, the practice of cannibalism, and the induction of new victims into the cult through role-playing games and rock music. The panics were most intense in small towns whose industrial base had been eroded by economic transformation, resulting in financial collapse. They were exacerbated by social changes, such as the rising divorce rate, the increasing number of women in the work force and of children in day care, and new definitions of gender roles, which led to social tensions. Some fundamentalist Protestant ministers fomented the panics by acting as conduits for the rumors. The panics culminated in a series of lengthy trials against the operators of several preschools and day-care centers, who were charged with sexually abusing children in the context of Satanic rituals. Though the charges were later proved to be completely false, a number of people were sentenced to prison. As in most cases of witchcraft accusations, Satanic panics projected fears and anxieties that arose out of social transformation onto completely innocent people. No evidence of diabolical conspiracies or Satanic ritual abuse rings has ever been found.

CONCLUSIONS. One of the most surprising aspects of the study of witchcraft is that African, Asian, European, and Native American cultures all postulate similar behaviors on the part of witches. Witches are often elderly and socially isolated; they meet at night in small groups to plot evil deeds; they are able to leave their bodies or change their shapes; they can suck the blood, drain the energy, or devour the internal organs of their victims; and they murder family members, commit cannibalism, fly through the air, hold indiscriminate orgies, and seduce sleeping people. These similarities go beyond the possibility of coincidence. While some anthropologists believe they are the result of diffusion from a single early Paleolithic human culture, others argue that they are the product of projection, a psychological defense mechanism that helps human beings maintain an image of themselves as good by projecting negative, undesirable impulses away from the self and onto an other. All societies designate certain behavior as bad, undesirable, or negative; however, the impulses behind the behavior are part of human nature, and cannot be completely banished from human consciousness. In projection, the forbidden thoughts or impulses are attributed to an "other," whether a group or an individual. Projection may work on both an individual level and a societal one. For example, a person may have long-standing disagreements with a neighbor. One day, the neighbor curses at some chickens that have wandered into the yard; the next day, some of the chickens sicken and die. The individual may assume the neighbor caused the loss. On a societal level, a village may blame a bad harvest or a plague on the presence of witches in the community. In both cases, the witch is imagined as an antisocial force embodying the essence of evil. When the witch is construed as the opposite of right society, projection is at work.

All cultures grapple with the problem of evil. We observe people performing monstrous acts of destruction and cruelty against their own self-interest as well as that of the community. We watch illness and natural disaster strike randomly without any sense of justice or fairness; around us, good people suffer and die while the wicked prosper. Many feel that evil exists in the world to a degree far beyond what one might expect in nature. This pervasive power, whose purpose seems to be to corrupt and destroy the cosmos, can be perceived as coming from an external being. The witch as an embodiment of this evil is a powerful metaphor whose power may be diminished from time to time, but is unlikely to disappear.

SEE ALSO Cathari; Healing and Medicine; Magic; Neopaganism; Theurgy; Vodou; Wicca.

BIBLIOGRAPHY

Anthropological Perspectives on Witchcraft and Sorcery

Douglas, Mary, ed. *Witchcraft: Confessions and Accusations.* London, 1970.

Evans-Pritchard, E. E. *Witchcraft, Oracles, and Magic among the Azande.* Oxford, 1937.

Kilpatrick, Alan. *The Night Has a Naked Soul: Witchcraft and Sorcery among the Western Cherokee.* Syracuse, N.Y., 1997.

Kluckholn, Clyde. *Navaho Witchcraft.* Cambridge, Mass., 1944.

Mair, Lucy Philip. *Witchcraft.* New York and Toronto, 1969.

Middleton, John, ed. *Magic, Witchcraft, and Curing.* Austin, Tex., 1967.

Rush, John A. *Witchcraft and Sorcery: An Anthropological Perspective of the Occult.* Springfield, Ill., 1974.

European and North American Witchcraft

Boyer, Paul, and Stephen Nissenbaum. *Salem Possessed: The Social Origins of Witchcraft.* Cambridge, Mass., 1974.

Briggs, Robin. *Witches and Neighbors: The Social and Cultural Context of European Witchcraft.* London, 1996.

Caro Baroja, Julio. *The World of the Witches.* Translated by O. N. V. Glendinning. Chicago, 1964.

Cohn, Norman. *Europe's Inner Demons: An Enquiry Inspired by the Great Witch-Hunt.* London and New York, 1975.

Davies, Owen. *Witchcraft, Magic and Culture, 1736–1951.* Manchester, U.K., 1999.

Ginzburg, Carlo. *The Night Battles: Witchcraft and Agrarian Cults in the Sixteenth and Seventeenth Centuries* (1966). Translated by John and Ann Tedeschi. Baltimore, 1983.

Ginzburg, Carlo. *Ecstasies: Deciphering the Witches' Sabbath* (1989). Translated by Raymond Rosenthal. New York, 1991.

Hennigsen, Gustav, and Bengt Ankarloo, eds. *Early Modern European Witchcraft: Centres and Peripheries.* Oxford, 1990.

Macfarlane, Alan. *Witchcraft in Tudor and Stuart England: A Regional and Comparative Study.* London, 1970.

Norton, Mary Beth. *In the Devil's Snare: The Salem Witchcraft Crisis of 1692.* New York, 2002.

Russell, Jeffrey B. *A History of Witchcraft: Sorcerers, Heretics, and Pagans.* London, 1980.

Thomas, Keith. *Religion and the Decline of Magic: Studies in Popular Beliefs in Sixteenth and Seventeenth Century England.* New York, 1971.

Trevor-Roper, Hugh R. *The European Witch Craze of the Sixteenth and Seventeenth Centuries, and Other Essays.* London and New York, 1969.

Modern Witch-Hunts

Ellis, Bill. *Raising the Devil: Satanism, New Religions, and the Media.* Louisville, Ky., 2000.

Victor, Jeffrey. *Satanic Panic: The Creation of a Contemporary Legend.* Chicago, 1993.

Neopagan Witchcraft

Adler, Margot. *Drawing Down the Moon: Witches, Druids, Goddess-Worshippers, and Other Pagans in America Today.* Rev. ed. Boston, 1986.

Hutton, Ronald. *Triumph of the Moon: A History of Modern Pagan Witchcraft.* Oxford, 1999.

Luhrmann, T. M. *Persuasions of the Witches' Craft: Ritual Magic in Contemporary England.* Cambridge, Mass., 1989.

Magliocco, Sabina. *Witching Culture: Folklore and Neo-Paganism in America.* Philadelphia, 2004.

Orion, Loretta. *Never Again the Burning Times: Paganism Revived.* Prospect Heights, Ill., 1995.

Salomonsen, Jone. *Enchanted Feminism: The Reclaiming Witches of San Francisco.* London and New York, 2001.

JEFFREY BURTON RUSSELL (1987)
SABINA MAGLIOCCO (2005)

WITCHCRAFT: AFRICAN WITCHCRAFT

As a set of beliefs that varies region by region and has a good many consequences in everyday life, African witchcraft is in many respects similar to corresponding sets of beliefs found among peoples of other continents. African systems, however, are of great interest because they have some unique features and because they have provided material for the formulation of definitions and the development of theories of worldwide application.

GENERAL CHARACTERISTICS. Most African societies—though not all—hold the cardinal belief that certain members of the community are in the habit of using supernatural means for illicitly destroying the interests, or even the lives, of their fellows. This basic tenet has led Africans to attribute to persons designated by terms we might translate as "witches" or "sorcerers" characteristics that resemble those of their counterparts elsewhere. Beliefs about witches are, of course, not directly observable, but they may have overt consequences in everyday life.

Subjective aspects. Thus African witches (in the generic sense, including sorcerers) are believed to harm others either because they possess powers (of which they may not be aware and which their fellows find incomprehensible) that emanate from their aberrant personalities or because they perform antisocial magic, technically referred to as "sorcery" (see below). Furthermore, they resemble witches in other continents in that they are believed to employ certain species of animals and, in some instances, spirits or humanoid creatures as their servants, messengers, or familiars. Familiars are sometimes reputed to drive their owners to their evil practices.

Like their counterparts elsewhere, African witches are believed to belong to associations that meet periodically (usually around a fire) to discuss the promotion of their interests, the regulation of relations among them, and to celebrate recent antisocial accomplishments by, for example, having a ghoulish feast of the revived body of someone they have killed supernaturally. These associations form distorted reflections of the societies in which they are believed to exist. On the one hand, they may mirror the authority structure of the polity of which they are a part, as when, among the Chewa, their meetings are presided over by a village headman who is himself a witch. On the other hand, among some peoples the organization of witch societies may contrast with that of everyday society; among relatively egalitarian peoples witch societies are more hierarchical and vice versa. In any case, witch societies invariably invert normal ethical standards by delighting in the practice of promiscuous sexual activity (including incest), by going naked, by frequenting forbidden places such as graveyards, and by murdering and eating their fellow human beings, often their close relatives (African witches are believed to attack their neighbors and kinsmen rather than distant and unrelated persons).

As in other parts of the world, African witches are often reported to be preponderantly women (although there are notable exceptions, such as among the Azande, Bemba, and Tonga). However, it is important to note that the actual summation of cited cases of witchcraft may yield a gender ratio that is at variance with the traditional one expressed in general statements made by informants. Thus, although Chewa tradition holds that most witches are women, it is men, the more socially and politically active sex, who form a clear majority of those cited in instances of witchcraft.

Finally, in Africa as elsewhere, the belief in witchcraft—together with other components of the religious system—provides an explanatory framework, a means by which the misfortunes that befall people may be understood and, in terms of their beliefs, avoided in the future. African societies vary in the degree that witchcraft (as opposed to the other elements of religious belief) plays in the explanation of everyday events and, more importantly, crises. Thus, among the Lugbara, misfortunes appear to be attributed more often to the intervention of ghosts rather than witches, whereas among the Chewa the reverse is true. But in all societies where witchcraft is a component of the belief system—and this applies to the majority of African societies—witchcraft beliefs are of paramount importance insofar as they explain the persistence of evil and the inability of humans to eradicate it. As J. D. Krige (1947) puts it:

> Witches and sorcerers are considered [by the Lovedu] to be the embodiment of malignant forces ever on the alert to enter into unholy matrimony with the criminal impulses of the human heart. Witchcraft particularly [as opposed to sorcery—see below] is the essence of evil, vicious and inscrutable, that whirls through the universe and seeks asylum in sinful souls in which the germs of wickedness lie ready to be quickened into life.

Overt consequences of belief. Some of the consequences of witch belief are visible to the ethnographer. This is because, given that people believe in and are concerned about witches, they take steps to protect themselves from them and (as individuals or assisted by professionals such as diviners, or perhaps backed by the political authorities) to detect, prosecute, and sometimes destroy by vengeance-magic those they assume to be bringing them harm. Many of the processes involved in self-protection, divination, and revenge are spiritual, usually involving magical substances (often translated as "medicines") of botanical origin, though activated by ingredients of animal or human origin which are of symbolic significance, such as a piece of human caul (protective in function) added to the powdered root of a particular species of tree to make a protective amulet.

Protective steps include not only wearing amulets but also taking "medicines" orally, washing the body in infusions of them, or rubbing them into incisions made in the skin. Huts and field crops can also be treated to make them invisible to, or impenetrable by, witches. Divination includes the use of oracles such as those of the Azande of the southern Sudan (adjective and singular noun, Zande), the best known of which consists of feeding benge, a poisonous substance, to chickens, mentioning the name of a suspect each time, and determining the guilt of a particular suspect by noting whether the chicken poisoned in accompaniment to his name dies.

Elsewhere in central Africa an ordeal is held in which a poison (*mwafi*, *mwabvi*, etc.) is administered to the human suspects themselves (and sometimes to the accuser as well to check that he is acting in good faith), and a person is deemed guilty if he retains the poison (an action that will cause him eventually to purge, faint, or actually die) and innocent if he vomits it. In southern Africa witches may be "smelled out" in a public ceremony by a diviner, who is guided by his audience's verbal responses to his tentative naming of the suspects. All over Africa diviners use a variety of techniques—dreaming, manipulating various kinds of apparatus, throwing dice ("bones"), opening the Bible or the Qur'an at random—to help clients identify their attackers.

From several parts of Africa it has been reported that persons found to be guilty of witchcraft were traditionally burned. This penalty is also suffered by convicted witches in some other parts of the world.

Distinctive Features. A comparison by E. E. Evans-Pritchard (1929) of Zande and Trobriand magic (and thus of the variant of witchcraft sometimes separately designated as sorcery—destructive magic illegitimately applied) suggests that whereas Melanesians regard the verbal element, or spell, in an act of magic (in general and sorcery in particular) as all-important and insist on its being word perfect, Africans place greater emphasis on the material element, or "medicines." Hence in Africa the verbal element is less important, more properly being regarded as a relatively informal address made to the "medicines" to activate them and make them attack the proper victim.

Another feature setting off African witch beliefs from those found elsewhere is the range of animal species that witches are assumed to use as familiars. Whereas in Europe, cats, dogs, and weasels are commonly believed to be witches' familiars (dogs and foxes in Japan), in Africa hyenas, owls, and baboons are commonly listed. While not unparalleled elsewhere, witches in some African societies are believed to be served by familiars of human origin or appearance, such as a "zombie" (*khidudwane*) among the Lovedu of the northern Transvaal or a "hairy dwarf" (*tokoloshe, tikoloshe*) among the Zulu and Xhosa-speaking peoples of Natal and the eastern Cape Province of South Africa. Within Africa, regional variations apply to the main list of familiars, with hyenas cited more often in central Africa and baboons in southern Africa.

There are similar regional differences in other aspects of witch beliefs and their everyday concomitants. For instance, while in most parts of the continent people accused of witchcraft are likely to refute the accusation and with it the long list of crimes (e.g., murder, incest, necrophagy) that it implies, there is a tendency, reported mainly from West Africa, for people to confess their witchcraft, sometimes voluntarily.

DEBATE OVER A BASIC DISTINCTION. An outstanding instance of how African ethnography has stimulated worldwide debates over terminology is provided by Evans-Pritchard's seminal book on the Azande (1937). In witchcraft theory, the Azande make a distinction between two entities, *mangu* and *ngwa. Mangu,* a hereditary substance which can be discovered by autopsy in the stomach of a witch, exerts a baleful mystical influence over the lives of others in the community when it is activated by hatred. On the other hand, *ngwa* ("magic") is not identified with a particular substance; less of an object, it is subdivided into "good" magic (*wene ngwa*) and "bad" or "criminal" magic (*gbigbita ngwa*). Evans-Pritchard translates *mangu* as "witchcraft" and *gbigbita ngwa* as "sorcery." He sums up:

> To Azande themselves the difference between a sorcerer and a witch is that the former uses the techniques of magic and derives his power from medicines, while the latter acts without rites and spells and uses hereditary psycho-physical powers to attain his ends. Both alike are enemies of men, and Azande class them together. (Evans-Pritchard, 1937, p. 387)

Although Evans-Pritchard emphasized that he expressed no opinion on the applicability of this distinction to peoples other than the Azande, several anthropologists working in Africa have found parallels to it, and this would, at first sight, justify its more general use. Thus the distinction between "night witch" and "day witch" made by the Sotho-speaking peoples of the plateau of South Africa, as well as the Lovedu, parallels that made by the Azande between witch and sorcerer. Similarly, among the Chewa of east-central Africa the distinction between *nfiti yeniyeni* ("real witch") and *mphelanjilu* ("killer for malice") is similar, though not as clear since both are commonly referred to as *nfiti.* However, among the Nguni-speaking peoples of South Africa (including the Zulu, Pondo, Bhaca, Xhosa, etc.) the distinction is tenuous, applying simply to the mode of attack, that is, "with animals (familiars)" or "with medicines."

Some anthropologists question the value of employing the witch-sorcerer distinction more widely than in the context to which Evans-Pritchard limited it. This position is taken by both Victor Turner (1964) and Mary Douglas (1967) in their respective review articles on the books by John Middleton and E. H. Winter (1963) and Maxwell Gay Marwick (1965). Turner's conclusion is that "almost every society recognizes such a wide variety of mystically harmful techniques that it may be positively misleading to impose upon them a dichotomous classification" (Turner, 1964, p. 323); Douglas suggests that it would be better to use traditional English terms freely and to classify beliefs according to whatever criterion is significant (Douglas, 1967, p. 73).

A related debate has stemmed from the reports by Godfrey Wilson (1936) and Monica Wilson (1951a, 1951b) that the Nyakyusa of southern Tanzania believe that "the defenders" of the village, by exercising a supernatural power known as "the breath of men," protect their fellows and punish those who transgress; it is claimed that this power "comes from the same source as the power of the witches" (Wilson, 1951a, p. 97). In its antisocial form, that is, if it is illicitly used (and victim-transgressors are often likely to assert this), this power is indistinguishable from the witchcraft of other societies. Thus the Nyakyusa, who like peoples all over the world divide magic into good and bad forms, also dichotomize mystical influence in the same way, with "the breath of men" as its approved form and witchcraft as its disapproved form. Wilson reminds us that Henri A. Junod, in his classic study of the Tsonga of southeast Africa, first published in 1912–1913, came to the tentative conclusion that these people believe that the power of the magician, who protects the interests of society, and that of the witch, who destroys them, is derived from the same source (Junod, 1927, pp. 504–505, 516).

Alan Harwood (1970) has found a belief parallel to that of the Nyakyusa among the neighboring Safwa. Like the Azande, the Safwa distinguish between the power derived from medicine (*onzizi*) and a power that they refer to as *itonga* and that they believe to be inherited and hidden in its operation. But unlike the Azande (according to Evans-Pritchard's account) and like the Nyakyusa, the Safwa subdivide not only medicine but also "hidden power" into approved and disapproved forms. As to hidden power, "good *itonga*," according to Harwood, is believed to be used in divination to protect members of the community from external attack and to punish some of them for uncooperative behavior; "bad *itonga*" is used to introduce foreign substances into another person's body or into his gardens to diminish their effectiveness and is said to enable its possessors to "consume" members of their own lineage (Harwood, 1970, pp. 59–60). *Itonga* is thus conceived of as a neutral spiritual power and, since it is innate and can harm people, its bad (antisocial) form can reasonably be equated with the witchcraft of other societies. Harwood believes that, "appearances to the contrary, the Safwa are not alone with their neighbours the Nyakyusa in believing that the mystical power of 'witches' is morally neutral, and that perhaps the ethnocentric preconceptions of ethnographers are responsible for the dim light in which African 'witches' have traditionally been painted" (Harwood, 1970, p. 69). In particular, after carefully reexamining Evans-Pritchard's account of Zande witchcraft, Harwood concludes that Evans-Pritchard's finding that the Zande word *mangu* denotes an exclusively antisocial power—and should therefore be translated as "witchcraft"—is mistaken and comes from his having taken the perspective of the witch doctor (diviner) rather than that of the ordinary villager.

THEORETICAL APPROACHES TO AFRICAN WITCHCRAFT. With its rich variety of social structures and belief systems, Africa has provided useful material for the development of theories that account for the continued existence of witch beliefs and contribute to our understanding of the dynamics of society in general.

Evans-Pritchard's approach (1937) explains Zande witch beliefs mainly by showing their concordance with the basic assumptions and modes of reasoning, or philosophy of life, prevailing in the society and, somewhat incidentally, by relating them to social conditions, including stratification. The theoretical approaches to witchcraft taken by J. D. Krige (1947) in reference to the Lovedu, Monica Wilson (1951) in her comparison of the Mpondo of South Africa with the Nyakyusa, and Siegfried Frederick Nadel (1952) in his comparison of four West African peoples are of a more psychological orientation, showing varying degrees of similarity to Clyde Kluckhohn's analysis of Navajo witchcraft (1944). These writers explain witch beliefs as giving expression to the stresses, strains, and predilections that arise in the particular circumstances of the society concerned. The basic defect in these psychological approaches is that, based as they are on speculative propositions, for example, those of depth psychology, they do not generate hypotheses that are testable. More recently this approach has developed into, or been displaced by, a Lévi-Straussian structuralist model in which a society's cognitive system is taken to be a logical system in its own right rather than just a secondary reflection of social relations. This approach is found in Edwin Ardener's analysis of the witch beliefs of the Bakweri of west Cameroon (1970) and in subsequent studies by W. David Hammond-Tooke on the Cape Nguni of South Africa (1974) and by Michael D. Jackson on the Kuranko of northeast Sierra Leone (1975).

A more sociological orientation is found in the approaches of James Clyde Mitchell (1956), Middleton (1960), and Marwick (1952, 1965). By comparing the incidence of accusations and believed attacks of witchcraft in different categories of relationship, these writers relate witch beliefs to periodic social processes, such as the division of lineages into segments as their size increases in successive generations. Associated with this approach is a reemphasis of the principle, implicit in the writings of most students of witchcraft, that a society's conception of the characteristics of the witch reinforces its norms by providing a negative example.

All three types of approach try to make sense of what in modern society are regarded as bizarre and fallacious beliefs, and because they provide functionalist justifications of the continuance of witch beliefs, they have been criticized. For instance, James R. Crawford (1967) has argued that placing too much emphasis on the idea that an allegation of witchcraft is merely a symptom of social malaise leads to a failure to recognize that the allegation usually embitters social relations and increases social tension by adding a new dynamic dimension to them, for example, making a previously private quarrel public. Similarly Douglas (1963) has pointed out that, though an accusation of witchcraft may facilitate developmental processes, such as lineage segmentation, "it is also an aggravator of all hostilities and fears, an obstacle to peaceful co-operation . . ." and "orderly social relations."

Turner warns against the use of any single explanation of the complex circumstances leading to an accusation of witchcraft, arguing that "each instance or set of accusations has to be examined within a total context of social action, which includes the operation of biotic, ecological, and intergroup processes, as well as intra-group developments" (Turner, 1964, pp. 315–316).

In the light of the criticisms that have been made of prevailing theories, we would do well to adopt a more comprehensive model for the analysis of African witchcraft. Ecological circumstances, including the prevalence of disease vectors and the level of medical understanding and associated hygiene, contribute to morbidity and mortality rates and thus provide the raw material of misfortunes requiring explanation; social structure and associated tradition lay down the general direction that the explanations (including accusations of witchcraft) will take. But far from resolving the tensions that cause them, accusations may often exacerbate them.

WITCHCRAFT UNDER MODERN CONDITIONS. The colonial authorities in Africa banned many divinatory practices such as the poison ordeal and smelling-out ceremonies, and they usually declared the imputation of witchcraft legally punishable. This led Africans to adopt alternative, and usually secret, ways of identifying those whom they believed to be witches. Antiwitchcraft cults developed and often recurred in many African societies, and some writers attribute their rise to the suppression of the traditional means of detection. Some of the African churches independent of the missions include witch finding among their activities.

The impression of most ethnographers has been that Africans' preoccupation with witch beliefs has increased in modern times and that this is to be explained by the conflict between the values of the economically egalitarian indigenous societies and the more individualistic ones of the intruders. Certainly people who have advanced educationally and financially are often concerned about protecting themselves from the witchcraft of those retaining a more traditional way of life.

This majority view was contested by Godfrey and Monica Wilson (1945, p. 120), who believed that the relative importance of witchcraft was declining and that of science increasing. Some statistical evidence has come forward recently (Mitchell and Mitchell, 1980; Hammond-Tooke, 1970), and this supports the Wilsons' view in that it demonstrates that modern social changes tend to be accompanied by a progressive, if slow, secularization of the beliefs that traditionally explained misfortunes.

SEE ALSO Nyakyusa Religion; Southern African Religions, overview article; Tswana Religion.

BIBLIOGRAPHY

Note: Asterisked items are particularly recommended for further consultation.

Ardener, Edwin. "Witchcraft, Economics and the Continuity of Belief." In *Witchcraft Confessions and Accusations*, edited by Mary Douglas, pp. 141–160. New York, 1970.

*Crawford, James R. *Witchcraft and Sorcery in Rhodesia.* London, 1967. Based on more than a hundred records of court cases, supplemented by sound knowledge of the cultures of the persons involved. The author is well acquainted with the literature and has a refreshingly independent stance in theoretical debates. Excerpted in Marwick (1982).

Douglas, Mary. "Techniques of Sorcery Control in Central Africa." In *Witchcraft and Sorcery in East Africa*, edited by John Middleton and E. H. Winter, pp. 123–142. London, 1963.

Douglas, Mary. "Witch Beliefs in Central Africa." *Africa* 37 (1967): 72–80.

*Douglas, Mary, ed. *Witchcraft Confessions and Accusations.* New York, 1970. A diverse, somewhat uncoordinated collection of papers, half of which are concerned with African societies.

Evans-Pritchard, E. E. "The Morphology and Function of Magic: A Comparative Study of Trobriand and Zande Ritual and Spells." *American Anthropologist* 31 (1929): 619–641. Reprinted in Middleton (1967).

*Evans-Pritchard, E. E. *Witchcraft, Oracles and Magic among the Azande.* Oxford, 1937. A skilled analysis of the thinking behind Zande witchcraft-related behavior. The starting point for any serious study of witch beliefs and, apart from Margaret Murray's romantically misleading works, quite the most influential study of witchcraft yet written. For an appreciation of Evans-Pritchard's work, see Max Gluckman's review, "The Logic of African Science and Witchcraft," *Human Problems in British Central Africa* 1 (1944): 61–71; reprinted in Marwick (1982).

*Gelfand, Michael. *The African Witch: With Particular Reference to Witchcraft Beliefs among the Shona of Rhodesia.* Edinburgh, 1967. Shona witch beliefs and practices related to them, especially divination. Based on long medical experience among the Shona.

Hammond-Tooke, W. David. "Urbanization and the Interpretation of Misfortune: A Quantitative Analysis." *Africa* 40 (1970): 25–39. Reprinted in Marwick (1982).

Hammond-Tooke, W. David. "The Cape Nguni Witch Familiar as a Mediatory Construct." *Man*, n. s. 9 (March 1974): 128–136. Reprinted in Marwick (1982).

*Harwood, Alan. *Witchcraft, Sorcery and Social Categories among the Safwa.* London, 1970. A thorough study of beliefs in their social context, involving a searching inquiry into the theoretical issues they raise. Excerpted in Marwick (1982).

Jackson, Michael D. "Structure and Event: Witchcraft Confession among the Kuranko." *Man*, n. s. 10 (March 1975): 387–403.

Junod, Henri A. *The Life of a South African Tribe.* 2d ed., rev. & enl. 2 vols. London, 1927. First published as Les Ba-Ronga (1898; reprint, New Hyde Park, N. Y., 1962).

Krige, J. D. "The Social Function of Witchcraft." *Theoria* (Pietermaritzburg, South Africa) 13 (1947): 8–21. Reprinted in Marwick (1982).

Kluckhohn, Clyde. *Navaho Witchcraft.* Boston, 1944. Excerpted in Marwick (1982).

Marwick, Maxwell Gay. "The Social Context of Ceŵa Witch-Beliefs." *Africa* 22 (1952): 120–135, 215–233.

*Marwick, Maxwell Gay. *Sorcery in Its Social Setting: A Study of the Northern Rhodesian Ceŵa.* Manchester, 1965. Sorcery related to traditional matrilineage segmentation, wider social tensions, political organization, and modern changes. Based on nearly two hundred explanations of misfortunes, which, critics say, came from too few informants. Comparisons of informants' general statements with the summation of specific cases in statistical tables. Reviewed in Douglas (1967).

*Marwick, Maxwell Gay, ed. *Witchcraft and Sorcery: Selected Readings.* 2d ed. Harmondsworth, 1982. A collection of forty-two papers and excerpts from the writings of anthropologists, historians, and others, eighteen of which have reference to African societies.

Middleton, John. *Lugbara Religion: Ritual and Authority among an East African People.* London, 1960.

*Middleton, John, ed. *Magic, Witchcraft and Curing.* Garden City, N. Y., 1967. Six of the sixteen papers included are concerned with the social setting of African witchcraft, sorcery, or divination.

*Middleton, John, and E. H. Winter, eds. *Witchcraft and Sorcery in East Africa.* London, 1963. Makes a brave if not foolhardy attempt to link witchcraft with unilineal societies and sorcery with others, but, as these two categories are in dispute and as contributors show no uniform deference to the editors' thesis, the reader may remain unconvinced. For an excellent critical review, see Turner (1964).

Mitchell, Hilary Flegg, and J. Clyde Mitchell. "Social Factors in the Perception of the Causes of Disease." In *Numerical Techniques in Social Anthropology*, edited by J. Clyde Mitchell, pp. 49–70. Philadelphia, 1980. Reprinted in Marwick (1982).

Mitchell, J. Clyde. *The Yao Village: A Study in the Social Structure of a Nyasaland Tribe.* Manchester, 1956.

Nadel, S. F. "Witchcraft in Four African Societies: An Essay in Comparison." *American Anthropologist* 54 (1952): 18–29. Reprinted in Marwick (1982).

*Parin, Paul, Fritz Morgenthaler, and Goldy Parin-Matthèy. *Fear Thy Neighbor as Thyself: Psychoanalysis and Society among the Anyi of West Africa.* Translated from German by Patricia Klamerth. Chicago, 1980. Gives an interesting comparative glimpse of a former French territory in regard to both traditional witch beliefs and modern conflicts of values.

*Reynolds, Barrie. *Magic, Divination and Witchcraft among the Barotse of Northern Rhodesia.* London, 1963. A thorough account of witch beliefs and practices related to them, such as divining. Includes an analysis of court records arising from a sudden spate of witchcraft cases in Rotseland in the mid-1950s. Illustrated with useful drawings of related material culture.

Turner, Victor. "Witchcraft and Sorcery: Taxonomy versus Dynamics." *Africa* 34 (1964): 314–325.

Wilson, Godfrey. "An African Morality." *Africa* 9 (1936): 75–99.

Wilson, Godfrey, and Monica Wilson. *The Analysis of Social Change.* Cambridge, 1945.

Wilson, Monica. *Good Company: A Study of Nyakyusa Age-Villages.* London, 1951. Cited in the text as Wilson (1951a).

Wilson, Monica. "Witch-Beliefs and Social Structure." *American Journal of Sociology* 56 (January 1951): 307–313. Cited in the text as Wilson (1951b). Reprinted in Marwick (1982).

New Sources

Bastian, Misty L. "The Daughter She Will Eat Agousie in the World of the Spirits: Witchcraft: Confessions in Missionised Onitsha, Nigeria." *Africa,* 72 (2002), 83–111.

Cristoph, Henning, and Hans Oberländer. *Voodoo: Secret Power in Africa.* Kohl, 1996.

Delius, Peter. "Witches and Missionaries in Nineteenth Century Transvaal." *Journal of Southern African Studies,* 27 (September 2001): 429–444.

Geschiere, Peter. Peter Geschiere and Janet Roitman, trans. *The Modernity of Witchcraft: Politics and the Occult in Postcolonial Africa.* Charlottesville, 1997.

Lemert, Edwin. *The Trouble with Evil: Social Control at the Edge of Morality.* Albany, 1997.

Monter, William. "Reconceptualizing British Witchcraft." *Journal of Interdisciplinary Studies,* 35 (Summer 2004): 105–112.

Niehaus, Isak A. "Witch-Hunting and Political Legitimacy: Continuity and Change in Green Valley, Lebowa, 1930–1991." *Africa,* 63 (1993): 498–531.

Sweet, James. *Recreating Africa: Culture, Kinship, and Religion in the African-Portuguese World, 1441–1770.* Chapel Hill, 2003.

MAXWELL GAY MARWICK (1987)
Revised Bibliography

WITTGENSTEIN, LUDWIG

WITTGENSTEIN, LUDWIG (1889–1951), one of the most influential philosophers of the twentieth century. Born of a wealthy family in Vienna, Wittgenstein did most of his philosophical work at Cambridge, England. He became a British subject in 1938 and succeeded G. E. Moore as professor of philosophy at Cambridge in 1939. His two principal works were largely responsible for the "linguistic revolutions" in twentieth-century Anglo-American philosophy. The *Tractatus Logico-Philosophicus* (German edition 1921, English translation 1922, second English translation 1961), completed in the Austrian army during World War I, was the only one of Wittgenstein's books published during his lifetime. It inaugurated a logical-structuralist approach to philosophical analysis. The *Philosophical Investigations* (Oxford, 1953) initiated what came to be called ordinary language philosophy. Some dozen other books of lectures, notes, letters, and various manuscripts and manuscript fragments have been published posthumously; the most important is probably *On Certainty* (Oxford, 1969). This material, on which Wittgenstein was working at the time of his death, seems to point the way toward still a third period of his philosophy.

Wittgenstein concerned himself primarily with the nature of language, a concern that for him entailed the understanding and clarification of meaning. Thus he believed language to be the proper subject of philosophy, for it is according to the terms of language that the world and human life become comprehensible. The function of philosophy is to see language clearly and thereby dissolve (particularly at certain critical nodes) metaphysical problems and anxieties created by deep misunderstandings about the grammatical possibilities of language. Wittgenstein excelled in the subtle examination of how ordinary words with ordinary uses come to seem fraught with metaphysical complexities.

The spirit in which these profound philosophical (and not merely linguistic) studies were carried out was the very reverse of a positivistic or scientistic one, though some of Wittgenstein's early interpreters, such as Bertrand Russell, misunderstood him on this point. In his notebooks, excerpts from which have been published under the title *Culture and Value* (1977; Eng. ed., 1980), he declared himself out of sympathy with the scientific and progressivistic spirit of the age. Even in his early letters to Paul Engelmann and Ludwig Flicker, he made it clear that the purpose of the *Tractatus* was an ethical and not a scientific or positivistic one.

Wittgenstein once told a friend that he could not help seeing everything from a religious point of view. He belonged to no religious group or institution, though his mother was Catholic and he had been baptized a Catholic. (Three of his grandparents are said to have been of Jewish extraction.) During World War I he came under the influence of Tolstoi's writings on the Gospels and adopted a Tolstoyan mode of life, giving away his considerable inheritance and living ascetically as a village schoolteacher in southern Austria. To his friends he expressed admiration for Kierkegaard and Augustine and for some of the writings of George Fox and the prayers of Samuel Johnson. Engelmann reported that Wittgenstein believed in the Last Judgment but could make little out of the biblical doctrine of creation.

Wittgenstein wrote very little specifically on religion; the most important documents in this regard are *Lectures on Religious Belief* (Oxford, 1966) and *Remarks on Frazer's "Golden Bough"* (London, 1979). Yet his philosophy is permeated with a religious spirit. It was one of his strongest convictions that religion should be shown and demonstrated in everything rather than talked about as a separate matter. He advised his students that philosophical problems must arise out of a genuine need rather than as an expression of wit and cleverness. The important question about a philosopher, he said, is how much his ideas cost him. Wittgenstein believed that a philosophy is no better than the life out of which it arises and that in order to see things clearly it is necessary, above all, to destroy vanity. Unexamined biases and commitments are a mortgage against clarity.

Wittgenstein's reserve on the subject of religion arose not only from his feeling that it is more important to talk to God than to talk about God, but also from his awareness that in the present age religious expressions are almost certain to be misunderstood. Thus he considered dedicating one of his books, later published after his death as *Philosophical Remarks,* "To the glory of God," but decided against it.

What is evident from the study of Wittgenstein's life and work is that he was a clear-cut "supernaturalist," in the sense that he sharply separated God from the world. He told a student, Friedrich Waismann, that it is more profound to believe that something is good because God commands it than to believe that God commands it because it is good.

Religion for Wittgenstein was a matter of belief, and such beliefs outranked any explanations, reasons, or logic. Wittgenstein had no patience with either sociological or psychological "explanations" of religion, and even less with scientific attempts to bolster religion or to create religious emotions as responses to scientific wonders. Religion had to do with a different and more important dimension than that of fact: the dimension of how we are to live.

His most important contribution to the philosophy of religion was in his analysis of belief in *Lectures on Religious Belief,* included in *Lectures and Conversations,* compiled by Yorick Smythies, Rush Rhees, and James Taylor (Oxford, 1966). Here Wittgenstein examines the role played by religious beliefs in the guidance of life and attempts to disentangle them from all factual matters, including claims about existence. He makes the important point that denying a religious belief or disagreeing with it is not contradicting anything, since the essence of religious belief has nothing to do with whether something is or is not the case, or was or will be the case. Rather, it has to do with how we live and die. When people are willing to suffer and die for their religious beliefs, it is not for some factual proposition that they are willing to suffer and die, though it may appear so. Thus a belief in the Last Judgment should not be taken as an assertion that a certain event is or is not going to take place, but as something like an icon guiding our thoughts and actions, particularly in times of crisis. The attempt to make religious beliefs appear reasonable Wittgenstein regarded as often "ludicrous."

BIBLIOGRAPHY

Hacker, P. M. S. *Insight and Illusion: Wittgenstein on Philosophy and the Metaphysics of Experience.* Oxford, 1972.

Kenny, Anthony. *Wittgenstein.* London, 1973.

Malcolm, Norman. *Ludwig Wittgenstein: A Memoir.* London, 1958. Includes a biographical sketch by G. H. von Wright.

Rhees, Rush, ed. *Ludwig Wittgenstein: Personal Recollections.* Totowa, N. J., 1981.

HENRY LE ROY FINCH (1987)

WOLFF, CHRISTIAN (1679–1754), rationalist philosopher of the German Enlightenment. Born in Breslau, Wolff was educated there and at the University of Jena. Though he had studied theology and philosophy, Wolff's main interest while at the university was in mathematics. Wolff earned his master's degree from the University of Leipzig in 1703; in 1707, with the help of a recommendation from Gottfried Wilhelm Leibniz, he was appointed professor of mathematics and natural sciences at the relatively new University of Halle, where he taught until 1723. In that year he moved to the University of Marburg, subsequently returning in 1740 to Halle, where he remained until his death.

Wolff's education familiarized him with Lutheran, Calvinist, and Roman Catholic viewpoints in theology, with Aristotelian and Cartesian school traditions in philosophy, and with emerging empirical methods in Newtonian science. The most important single influence on Wolff's thought was Leibniz, but it is too simple to say that Wolff merely systematized the views of his great predecessor.

Wolff began lecturing on philosophy in 1709. In 1713 he published his first major work in the field, a German logic. Later German works dealt with metaphysics (1720), ethics (1720), politics (1721), physics (1723), teleology (1724), and physiology (1725).

In 1728 Wolff turned his attention beyond the borders of Germany to the larger intellectual world. This new international audience was addressed in Latin in a series of works that are larger, more extensive in scope, and some would say more "objective" or "scholastic" in character than their German predecessors. They include treatises on logic (1728), ontology (1729), cosmology (1731), empirical and rational psychology (1732 and 1734), natural theology (2 vols., 1736–1737), universal practical philosophy (2 vols., 1738–1739), natural law (8 vols., 1740–1748), *jus gentium* (1749), and ethics (5 vols., 1750–1753).

Two aspects of Wolff's life and thought are perhaps most significant for the history and development of religious thought. The first of these is his clash with Pietist theologians at Halle. Wolff's commitment to rational method, the content of his metaphysics, his success with students, and an abrasive personal style soon generated criticism. Among the issues at stake were Wolff's acceptance of the Leibnizian doctrine of preestablished harmony and his emphasis on God's intellect as the controlling framework for divine freedom and power. Wolff was accused of idealism, fatalism, determinism, Spinozism, and atheism—all fairly standard charges at the time, though in this case not without some basis in fact. When their efforts to alter his views or to limit his influence within the academic world did not succeed, some of Wolff's opponents made an external appeal to political authority. The result, in 1723, was an order from King Frederick William I—issued without a hearing—that removed Wolff from his professorship and banned him from Prussia within forty-eight hours on pain of death. This was perhaps a more serious escalation than even Wolff's enemies might have desired, with ominous implications for academic freedom. In fact, another post was immediately available at Marburg in Hesse-Cassel, and exile only heightened Wolff's popularity. Moreover, upon the accession of Frederick the Great to the Prussian throne in 1740, Wolff was recalled in triumph to Halle. In the meantime, he had switched from German to Latin in his writing and had published an eloquent essay on the freedom to philosophize in his "Preliminary Discourse on Philosophy in General" (1728).

The second issue worth noting is Wolff's commitment to natural theology. Wolff saw his philosophy as a support rather than a hindrance to religion. His account of God's existence and attributes was meant to lay the basis for a secure theology and ethics. This is in keeping with his goal to achieve through philosophy both a science and a wisdom. In retrospect, what Wolff has given posterity is the epitome of a rationalist tradition in philosophical theology. His demonstrations of the existence of God, for example, include both *a priori* and *a posteriori* proofs, forms of the ontological, cosmological, and teleological arguments. Their exposition presented Kant with a ready-made target for his well-known critique.

In both his teaching and early writings, Wolff made a major contribution toward establishing the German language as an accepted instrument for scientific work. The common opening phrase in the titles of his central German works ("Rational thoughts on . . .") and the equally common subtitle of his Latin volumes ("Treated according to the scientific method") mark Wolff's abiding concerns for method, order, and system. Wolff divided human knowledge into three parts: history (knowledge of the fact), philosophy (knowledge of the reason for the fact), and mathematics (knowledge of the quantity of things). He subdivided philosophy into metaphysics, physics, and practical philosophy; further divided metaphysics into ontology, cosmology, psychology, and natural theology; and popularized the distinction between empirical and rational modes of knowing. These divisions are implemented in both his German and Latin writings, which themselves enjoyed a huge success, often appearing in multiple editions right up to the time of his death. Wolff's views soon dominated the academic scene in Germany; his students filled key posts in institutions of higher education, and his prestige was immense. Kant called Wolff "the greatest of all the dogmatic philosophers." Despite contemporary adversities and relative obscurity today, Wolff was undoubtedly the most influential philosopher in Germany between the death of Leibniz in 1716 and the publication of Kant's *Critique of Pure Reason* in 1781.

BIBLIOGRAPHY

A new edition of Wolff's *Gesammelte Werke* is well under way (Hildesheim, 1962–) in three series: (1) German works, (2) Latin works, and (3) related materials and documents. The *Preliminary Discourse on Philosophy in General* is available in an English translation by Richard A. Blackwell (Indianapolis, 1963). The only comprehensive study of Wolff's thought is Mariano Campo's *Cristiano Wolff e il razionalismo precritico,* 2 vols. (Milan, 1939); reprinted in *Gesammelte Werke,* series 3, vol. 9. For historical context, see Lewis White Beck's *Early German Philosophy: Kant and His Predecessors* (Cambridge, Mass., 1969) and my article "Christian Wolff and Leibniz," *Journal of the History of Ideas* 36 (1975): 241–262. For his metaphysics, see *Le métaphysique de Christian Wolff* (1990; *Gesammelte Werke,* series 3, vol. 12.1 & 12.2) by Jean École, the editor of Wolff's Latin metaphysics volumes. École has also edited a collection of essays by experts on Wolff's philosophy, *Christian Wolff: Autour de la philosophie Wolfienne* (2001; *Gesammelte Werke,* series 3, vol. 65). For Wolff's philosophical theology, see James D. Collins's *God in Modern Philosophy* (1959; reprint, Westport, Conn., 1978), pp. 133–143; Anton Bissinger's *Die Struktur der Gotteserkenntnis: Studien zur Philosophie Christian Wolffs* (Bonn, 1970); my article "The Existence of God, Natural Theology, and Christian Wolff," *International Journal for Philosophy of Religion* 4 (1973): 105–118; and two articles by Jean École, "De la démonstration *a posteriori* de l'existence et des attributs de Dieu, ou la *Theologia naturalis, Pars I* de Christian Wolff," *Giornale di metafisica* 28 (1973): 363–388, 537–560, and "De la démonstration *a priori* de l'existence et des attributs de Dieu, et des erreurs sur Dieu, ou la *Theologia naturalis, Pars II* de Christian Wolff," *Giornale di metafisica* 32 (1977): 85–109, 237–272.

CHARLES A. CORR (1987 AND 2005)

WOLVES. Wolf symbolism embraces the dual aspects of good and evil human nature. Although the dark, menacing image of the fearless predator and ravening killer preponderates, wolves also personify a protective spirit and the nurturing mother. In classical times the wolf, perceived in both aspects, symbolized transition. The "hour of the wolf," for example, is the time of emergence from darkness into light or, contrarily, of reversion to the world of darkness and ignorance. The biblical verse "The wolf also shall dwell with the lamb" (*Is.* 11:16) is a metaphor for the assimilation of the lower to the higher and participates in the symbolism of the center. The Roman *signa* represents the wolf mounted on a cube (earth) and on a sphere (heaven). As an alchemical symbol, the wolf, together with the dog, stands for the dyadic nature of Mercurius, the philosophical mercury, the *nous* ("intelligence").

Many of the ancient war gods bore the name Wolf. Apollo, more widely known as a sun god, was associated with the wolf, and the epithets "wolf-born" and "wolfish Apollo" occur in Greek and Roman literature. In the *Aeneid,* the god assumed the form of a wolf in order to destroy the sorcerers of Rhodes, and a bronze statue of a wolf still stands at his shrine at Delphi. The Romans associated the wolf with the god Mars, and their legions marched into battle under the protection of the sacred wolf displayed on their banners. The Lupercalia, a festival of ancient Rome, has been interpreted as a wolf festival with wolf priests. Wolf deities were worshiped in Iran and Scythia, and in Japan the wolf was long regarded as a great god. The Teutonic war god Woðan (whose name derives from *wut,* "fury") and his Scandinavian counterpart, Óðinn (Odin), were accompanied by wolves when waging war. The Finns called wolves "dogs of the death spirit." American Indian tribes whose gods bore wolf names preceded their war sorties with wolf dances to ensure victory.

The most sinister wolf image is that of Fenrir, or Fenrisúlfr (Fenriswolf), in Norse mythology. The son of the trickster Loki, this monster embodied the destructive potential of chaos in the universe. Immured by the gods in the bowels of the earth, he broke out of his prison and devoured the sun and so brought about the twilight of the gods. In the thirteenth-century Icelandic Eddas, the cyclic cosmic battle between the gods and antigods is called "the war with the wolf."

Exaltation of wolves rather than fear of them prevailed in archaic times, for, as hunters, humans identified themselves with the wolf, the exemplary predator. Animals were considered divine in those early societies and were the nucleus around which religious belief crystallized. The discovery of Neolithic figurines of men wearing wolf masks and wolf skins suggests ceremonies of a religious and initiatory character. When wolf totems were created and the name of the animal taken by the tribe, it was often in the belief that the tribe was descended from a wolf ancestor, an idea that reflects a religious concept of great antiquity. The Chinggisids attributed their origin to a wolf who had come down from heaven to mate with a doe. Analogous myths existed among various tribal peoples of Inner Asia. The wolf also figured in the mythology of the American Indian hunting societies, such as the Cheyenne, and for some tribes of the Plains and the Eastern Woodlands, it was a clan or gens animal. Awed by the skill of the wolf as predator, these tribes incorporated its image into their rituals and ceremonial dances with the aim of acquiring the animal's stamina and courage. Conversely, the wolf was anathema for agricultural societies, although, according to Herodotus, the priests of Ceres had wolf guides.

In ancient Egypt, Greece, and Rome, the wolf, symbolizing the warrior-hero, was a guardian figure on monuments. An emblem of valor, it was a dominant image in the *Volsungasaga* and in the Teutonic military societies, the Berserkers and Männerbünde. Fostering the cult of the fanatical warrior, these martial brotherhoods held initiation ceremonies for the purpose of transforming the neophyte into a wolf. By donning the skin of the invulnerable animal, the initiate was thought to acquire its ferocity and power. Such traditions of initiatory transformation are documented in cultures as remote as those of Iceland and Africa.

The widespread and enduring association of wolves with ferocity and greed, darkness and death, prevailed among the Hindus and Celts. For the Chinese, the animal signified avarice and voracity, for the Zoroastrians and Armenians, evil more malign than that of the serpent charms used to destroy it. The Abyssinians regarded wolves as demons in animal form. In Judaism, wolves connoted bloodthirstiness and the spirit of persecution, and the biblical epithet "stiff-necked" derived from the belief that the animal was unable to turn its head. In both testaments of the Bible, wolves are characterized as "ravening." The image of the wolf as Satan or his henchman, a devourer of human souls, pervaded Christianity. The wolf represented the heretic, despoiler of the sheepfold of the faithful, of which Christ was the shepherd-protector. In "The Parson's Tale" Chaucer speaks of "the devil's wolves that strangle the sheep of Jesus Christ." Dante, in the first canto of his *Inferno,* names the she-wolf "laden with all craving" as one of the three dangerous beasts in the dark wood of fear; and in the eighth circle of Hell, thieves, liars, and hypocrites are condemned for "the sins of the wolf."

In many societies, the wolf was the symbol of outlaws, fugitives, and exiles, all of whom were believed to be under the protection of wolf gods. In the laws of the Hittites as well as those of Edward the Confessor, such men were required to wear a wolf-headed mask. Around 350 CE, the first bishop of the Goths applied the term *wolf* to any man who had committed a capital crime.

Early associated with sorcery and superstition, wolves were said to be the mounts of warlocks and witches. In Norse mythology, they consorted with the Norns, and Circe's palace was surrounded by tame wolves that she had subdued by enchantment. "Tooth of wolf" is an ingredient of the witches' brew in Shakespeare's *Macbeth,* and various parts of the animal's body were included in the armaments of magic of American Indian medicine men.

Perhaps the most colorful of the beliefs relating to wolves is that of lycanthropy, the ancient belief in the transformation of human into werewolf. This fearsome, night-roaming beast, avid for human blood, has been an almost universal specter. Legends of werewolves are known in almost every part of the world, and where no wolves have existed, the belief in were-animals has been associated with the fiercest native animal: the tiger in India, the jaguar in South America, the hyena in Africa, and the fox in Japan and China, where stories of the werefox have been preserved in the lore of popular Taoism. Werewolves played a role in the shamanism of Asia, and Inuit (Eskimo) and Chukchi shamans transformed themselves into wolves when in trance. Herodotus wrote of the Neuri turning into wolves annually, which suggests periodic religious ceremonies in which wolf masks and wolf skins were worn. Socrates refers to werewolves in Plato's *Republic;* Pliny gives an account of werewolfry in his *Natural History;* and Vergil wrote that the creatures were produced by means of magic herbs. Such beliefs may have had their origin in the mythico-religious complex of wolf gods or in rituals of the return of the dead. But it was in medieval Christian Europe that the werewolf most obsessed the human mind, and the Catholic Inquisition exploited the panic it aroused to further the suppression of heresy.

Wolves have been represented in Christian art as susceptible to spiritual persuasion and reform. The wolf of Gubbio, which had terrorized that Italian village, was converted by Francis of Assisi and is often depicted as his companion. Odo of Cluny, the tenth-century French saint, is said to have been rescued by a wolf when assailed by foxes, and the manuscript of the life of Edmund the Martyr (ninth century) contains an illustration of a wolf guarding the saint's severed head.

Wolves as nurturing figures occur in myth and legend, often mothering human infants who become founders of dynasties or nations. The best known of these, the Capitoline wolf that nursed Romulus and Remus, the legendary founders of Rome, is by no means the only surviving monument to this widespread legend. Coins antedating the founding of Rome bear the images of wolves with twin children. Apollo's children by human mothers were also said to have been suckled by wolves.

Siberian and American Indian shamans regarded wolves as guardians or helpful spirits and a source of great power. The doctoring societies of the Quileute and Makah Indians of the Northwest Coast performed wolf dances to heal the sick, and the image of a wolf head was believed to be a safeguard against evil. For many Indian tribes the wolf represented the corn god. The Keresan Pueblo tribe of the Southwest ordered the world according to the four cardinal points plus the zenith and nadir, and each of the six points was said to be dominated by a god, with the wolf in the west.

Wolves are often represented in fairy tales and fables as helpful animals; they manifest a sagacity and acumen superior to human knowledge.

BIBLIOGRAPHY

Eisler, Robert. *Man into Wolf* (1951). Reprint, New York, 1969. An exhaustive account of the belief in lycanthropy in various parts of the world and of ethnic names derived from the various names for the wolf.

Eliade, Mircea. *Zalmoxis, the Vanishing God: Comparative Studies in the Religions and Folklore of Dacia and Eastern Europe.* Chicago, 1972. An analysis of wolf rituals in archaic mythico-religious traditions predating Near Eastern and Mediterranean civilizations: their relation to the rites of martial initiations and to beliefs in the periodic return of the dead.

Gubernatis, Angelo de. *Zoological Mythology or Legends of Animals,* vol. 2, *The Animals of the Earth (cont.), The Animals of the Air, The Animals of the Water.* London, 1872. Treats the benevolent aspect of wolves as guides or guardians of saints and priests and the relation of wolves to curative beliefs.

Ovid. *The Fasti,* vol. 2. Edited by Sir James Frazer. London, 1929. An extensive review of legends of the nurturing wolf, predating and including the Capitoline wolf as well as histories of "wolf children" from ancient to modern times.

Summers, Montague. *The Werewolf* (1933). Reprint, New Hyde Park, N. Y., 1966. An excellent exposition of the prevalent view of the wolf in the Middle Ages as a projection of human fears and anxiety. A survey of shamanic wolf rituals.

New Sources

Busch, Robert. "The Wolf in Human Culture." In *The Wolf Almanac,* pp. 85–112. Guilford, Conn., 1998.

Daniels, Edwin. *Wolf Walking.* New York, 1997.

Hall, Jamie. *Half Human, Half Animal: Tales of Werewolves and Related Creatures.* Bloomington, Ind., 2003.

Savage, Candace. *Wolves.* 1988; reprint, San Francisco, 1996.

Steiger, Brad. *The Werewolf Book: The Encyclopedia of Shape-Shifting Beings.* 1999; reprint, Detroit, 2003.

ANN DUNNIGAN (1987)
Revised Bibliography

WOMAN SEE FEMININE SACRALITY

WOMEN'S STUDIES IN RELIGION.

Women's studies in religion comprise the many and varied scholarly approaches to the study of religion that arise from commitment to the equal dignity of the sexes, that employ the category of gender as a necessary and key variable in the inquiry, and that focus explicitly on the dynamic and reciprocal interplay between religion and women's lives. Taken together these diverse approaches constitute a major body of research that has irreversibly altered the landscape of religious studies.

Women's studies emerged as a new field of inquiry across a number of academic disciplines in the late 1960s and early 1970s, when the entry of greater numbers of women into higher education coincided with the second wave of feminism. The largely Western phenomenon of the women's liberation movement politicized women (and men) as they became aware of the historical legacy and cultural pervasiveness of sex discrimination and gender stereotyping. Recognizing these damaging features within their own disciplines, female students and teachers began to explore these and the many other ways that gender matters shape their subjects and the manner in which they are taught and on this basis to develop critiques of and alternative approaches to the subject matter and the methods of its study. As a result women are the focus of study as never before, and in most fields of academic research gender is considered an indispensable analytical category.

The initial impetus for women's studies in religion was (and to some extent remains) the need to counter what Rosemary Radford Ruether described as "the buried continent of unconscious androcentrism" that has shaped religion and its study (Ruether, 1985, p. 706). Feminist conscientization rendered this latent male bias visible, and women's scholarship began to expose its full extent. It became clear, for example, that there was a dearth of research into women's religious experience and participation, leading to gaps in knowledge and understanding. In part this was due to the paucity of available source material relating to women's religious lives, but it was also the result of scholarly neglect. Where such material had been the subject of scholarly attention, there was a tendency to impose false assumptions about innate sex differences and gender roles onto the interpretation of data, based on Western constructions of femininity and masculinity.

A disproportionate amount of research was devoted to men's religion and to the elite males who had shaped religions. Those aspects of religion that were singled out as characteristic, significant, and worthy of study were often male-dominated, with females less prominent and portrayed as occupying inferior or supporting roles. As Rita Gross, one of the founders of the field of women's studies in religion and a graduate student of Mircea Eliade during the late 1960s, stated, "One did not receive a coherent, connected account of women's religious lives and activities, but only glimpses, as they entered or left the stage of men's lives" (Gross, 2002a, p. 45). This (often inadvertent) male focus created a skewed picture of the religions of the world. Human religiosity was described (unwittingly) in terms of male religious experience. For instance, the state of knowledge about religious initiation was based largely on research into male initiation. To a significant degree, it was the religious experience of males and not humankind that was being recorded for posterity, thereby distorting the historical record. Furthermore religious texts and traditions, themselves largely the products of male authorship and systematization, are often framed in predominantly androcentric terms and are often carriers of patriarchal, sexist, and even misogynistic material. Women scholars of religion were faced with the dual problem that androcentrism was a feature of both the shapers of religion and the shapers of its study. One of the continuing tasks therefore of women's studies in religion is to seek out and correct androcentric bias in primary and scholarly sources.

The academic community of scholars of religion was made aware of its own partiality and blindness to gender injustice thanks to the pioneering research of scholars such as Carol P. Christ, Rita Gross, Judith Plaskow, Rosemary Radford Ruether, and Valerie Saiving, who pointed to the suspect nature of previous generalizations, theories, and models that were based on incomplete or erroneous pictures of religion. In light of this critique, women's studies began to reconfigure approaches to studying religion by introducing new data, methodologies, and alternative organizing principles to those that had traditionally constituted the theoretical framework of religious studies.

In 1972 the first Working Group on Women and Religion was held at the Annual Meeting of the American Academy of Religion (AAR)—the largest professional body for scholars of religion; the first signs of the anticipated integration of women's studies into the mainstream of the discipline. A year later, in 1973, the Women's Studies in Religion Program was founded at Harvard Divinity School, the foremost research center for the study of gender and religion in the early twenty-first century.

THE CONTEMPORARY PURVIEW OF WOMEN'S STUDIES IN RELIGION. From these beginnings, women's studies in religion have proliferated and diversified. The heterogeneity of the field extends far beyond the differences that exist as a result of religious diversity. Neither can women's studies scholars be characterized as a homogeneous group. While the majority of scholars in the field are women, there are growing numbers of men whose research concentrates on the study of women's religion, such as David Kinsley and Arvind Sharma. As with all subject disciplines, there are ideological divisions that give rise to internal debate and disagreement on theoretical, methodological, and programmatic issues. In order to discuss the contemporary diversified nature of women's studies in religion and examine the questions that enliven scholarly debate, it will be necessary to classify the field into four chief areas of study, though it is well to note that many women's studies scholars are engaged in research that spans these categories.

Recording and analyzing the diversity of women's religious lives. First and foremost, what unites all scholarly approaches to women's studies in religion is that such studies seek to contribute to human knowledge and understanding of the rich global diversity and complexity of women's religious lives cross-culturally and historically and, where necessary, to correct any absence from or distortion in the historical record. The extraordinary diversity of women's religious lives, in the present and in the past, is one of the chief findings of women's studies in religion (see Durre Ahmed, 2002; King, 1987; Plaskow and Christ, 1989). There is burgeoning scholarship on contemporary women's participation in the religions of the world (e.g., Holm, 1994; Sharma, 1987, 1994a, 1994b), in women's involvement in new religious movements (e.g., Palmer, 1994; Puttick, 1997), and in the recovery of women's religious history from all periods—including prehistory (e.g., Bynum, 1992; Kraemer, 1992; Newman, 1995). After centuries of neglect, women's religious lives—be they those of extraordinary mold breakers or those of the conventional majority—are being indelibly written into human history, allowing for the first time comparative study of materials and practices that have yielded, across cultures and historical periods, patterns of commonality in female religious experience and expression (e.g., Falk and Gross, 2001). Prompted by the feminist critique of androcentrism in religion, much of the initial focus in women's studies was on the negative influence of religion on women's lives. Subsequent primary research has disclosed more fully the positive motivations for women belonging to religions, including the role played by religions in conferring value to women's lives, in legitimating everyday female activities, in nurturing identity, in providing sanctuary from life's frustrations, and in empowering resistance to oppression in all its forms.

Although most religions are male-dominated in terms of power structures, female adherents are the majority participants in many religions, and a small number of religious movements and sects—such as Afro-Brazilian healing cults, Japanese *Ryūkyū* religion, Christian Science, and Black Carib religion—can be described as women's religions to the extent that the leaders and most of the adherents are female (see Sered, 1994). Women's sacral power is honored cross-culturally through specialist roles as ascetics, diviners, healers, mystics, prophets, shamans, and witches. Frequently women are leading organizers and participants in purification, fertility, birth, and funerary rites and carry the burden of preserving oral traditions. Within many religions women prepare ritual food and observe low-profile and often private rites within the household (e.g., praying, fasting, chanting) as a means of protecting their families and their livelihoods from harm.

Although leadership positions are more associated with male religious roles, women share with men authority and leadership positions in many religions, whether as bishops, priests, and preachers in certain Christian denominations, as priestesses in traditional African religion and Haitian vodou, as Conservative, Reform, and Reconstructionist Jewish rabbis, as Buddhist teachers, and in the rare but not unheard of cases of Hindu gurūs and Daoist priests. Some religions offer females certain roles and communities that allow them to be independent from the conventional domestic arrangements of marriage and childbearing, as in women's religious orders in Buddhism and Christianity. Stories of powerful female heroes, teachers, and saints are preserved in many traditions. Women have been active as founders of new religious movements, including Mother Ann Lee, the eighteenth-century founder of the Shakers in North America, and Nakayama Miki, the nineteenth-century founder of Japanese Tenrikyō. In the late twentieth century women-dominated goddess-based feminist spiritualities became popular. Amid this colorful diversity it is clear that the reasons women become involved with and remain in religions are many and complex and are subject to the influence of various social, political, and economic factors that inform women's needs and desires (see Woodhead, 2001, 2002).

If women's studies, particularly ethnographic and sociological research, have uncovered the diverse nature of women's participation in religion, they have also demonstrated the shadow side of the role that gender ideology plays in patterning and stratifying religious participation. Religions can be sites of discrimination against women, who frequently find themselves subject to male domination, excluded from certain (prestigious) roles and sacred spaces, and recipients of fewer legal privileges and their putative nature, bodies, and sexuality devalued and subject to ritual proscriptions. Even in religions such as Bahā'ī, Islam, Jainism, Sikhism, and Zoroastrianism that introduced improvements in women's rights over the prevailing culture, male dominance persists. As a result women may be positioned in ambiguous and complicated relationships with their religions that require them to adopt creative strategies in negotiating fitting places for themselves within their traditions.

The application of gender analysis to religious traditions. A second major strand of women's studies in religion is the application of gender analysis to religious traditions. This entails analysis of the ways in which religions in the past and in the present have developed and deployed gendered systems of thought, symbolism, and religious practices and how these (and other forces) have shaped women's religious lives for good or ill. This in turn leads to evaluation of humanity's pluriform religious heritage and the envisaging of its future forms in light of this gender-based inquiry.

Much (though not all) of this analysis arises from women's dissatisfaction with the gendered organization of their religions and initially was carried out predominantly by feminist scholars in North America and Europe examining the negative impact of religion on women's lives. Faced with the realization that androcentric and patriarchal values were as deeply embedded within religions as within the rest of human culture, these feminists sought to delineate and critique their malign omnipresence in religious scriptures, texts, teachings, rituals, forms of worship, institutional hierarchies, the construction of religious language and symbolism, and so on. An influential early feminist critique of religion was Mary Daly's *The Church and the Second Sex* (1968), which built on Simone de Beauvoir's *The Second Sex* (1949) to argue for an end to what Daly described as "Catholic antifeminism." Five years later Daly's position was firmly post-Christian. Her landmark *Beyond God the Father* (1973) advocated a radical feminist spirituality disconnected from patriarchal religion. Daly's contribution catalyzed feminist reactions to religion; numerous scholars set to work unpicking the fabric of religions and pointing to their distorted patterns of thought. No historical religion has since escaped feminist scrutiny.

Alongside the feminist critique and deconstruction of religious traditions, men and women sensitive to questions of gender (not all of whom identify as feminist) are engaged in the study of the positive elements in their tradition that offer resources for a renewed, nonoppressive contemporary religious expression. For example, there is considerable interest in the study of divine females such as Buddhist bodhisattvas, Hindu goddesses, and Daoist celestials. Mostly this research involves the recovery and restoration of previously overlooked or neglected elements of religion and includes, for instance, the retrieval of women's histories (including the documentary recording of the legacy of the women's movement itself), the rehabilitation of suppressed or marginal female characters (e.g., mythical female figures such as Lilith), the reappropriation and, where necessary, reinterpretation of scriptures and teachings, and the preservation of endangered but valuable religious traditions and practices that are meaningful for and often performed by women but threatened by forces such as urbanization and industrialization.

As a result of this work of critique and recovery, women are actively engaged in reconstructing and transforming religions so that they are in line with gender justice and better nurture female identities. This is occurring in an enormous variety of ways: through the rethinking and reformulation of the philosophical and theological aspects of religion—increasingly achieved by bringing other academic disciplines into creative conversation with the theoretical elements of religion (e.g., reinterpreting the meaning of and employing new images for the divine); through the creation of new religious practices (e.g., the use of new forms of prayer, ritual, and worship); and through the establishment of new social organizations (e.g., women's support, networking, and campaign groups). Correspondingly the aim is to replace all institutional practices and thought patterns that deny or undermine women's full participation and flourishing. As such this constructive and corrective task is praxis-based and politico-ethical in character, involving advocacy for women's rights (e.g., campaigning for the greater presence of females in leadership positions) as women worldwide seek to make their religions more conducive to women's authentic agency and development.

This threefold project of critique, recovery, and reconstruction has been carried out most extensively within Christianity and Judaism, where it has often (though not unproblematically) gone by the name of feminist theology. However, the same process is occurring to some degree in all religions and constitutes the greater bulk of writing in women's studies in religion (e.g., Gross, 1993; Mernissi, 1991; Plaskow, 1991; Robinson, 1999; Ruether, 1983; el Saʿdāwī, 1980).

Some women, like Daly, have found the feminist critique of religion to be decisive. They argue that the historical religions cannot be reformed in line with gender justice and identify as postreligious and secular (e.g., Taslima Nasrin) or prefer to express their religious experience and spirituality through means other than traditional religion (e.g., Carol P. Christ; Daphne Hampson).

The development and study of new religious movements that express women's spiritualities. This brings us to a third area of activity in women's studies in religion: the development and study of new religious movements that draw on the articulation of women's spiritualities. Within the Western world, the demise of organized religion has been accompanied by a growth in unofficial spiritualities, many of which largely attract female adherents. For example, one of the fastest growing is the mind-body-spirit movement that offers holistic means to self-improve one's bodily and spiritual well-being using techniques such as yoga, meditation, Tai Chi, and reflexology.

The most studied strand of new women's spiritualities is often termed *feminist spirituality.* Feminist spirituality, while of importance in its own right as a religious phenomenon, offers women's studies an important example of a form of religious expression that has been created explicitly by (mainly Western) women for women who have chosen to jettison the negative patriarchal inheritance of historical religions and create anew an inclusive worshipping community based on feminist principles. Some of the chief exponents of spiritual feminism are Zsuzsanna Budapest, Carol P. Christ, Naomi Goldenberg, Asphodel Long, Melissa Raphael, and Starhawk. The way spiritual feminists choose to express their religious sense varies. Thus while the label spiritual feminism unites adherents under a common identity, it is more accurate to speak of feminist spirituality movements in the plural since there are differences in approach and focus. Feminist spirituality movements reject institutional structures, organizational hierarchies, creeds, and fixed forms of worship. The form of spirituality these movements espouse is gynocentric and ecological. The focus is on the celebration of female sacral power, which is accompanied by a positive evaluation of the female body, sexuality (including the erotic), and fecundity. Nature is revered for its powers of birth and regeneration, and humanity is understood to be intimately connected to and responsible for the natural world.

As a response to and reaction against patriarchal religion and, more specifically, as a result of the rejection of the use of male imagery and language for the divine, spiritual feminists often draw instead on the symbolic power of the Goddess. For instance, female gods such as Ishtar, Diana, or the Great Mother may be invoked in feminist rituals, and appeal may be made to various ancient Goddess traditions (e.g., Gimbutas, 1974; Spretnak, 1981). The way the Goddess is conceptualized in these movements varies. She may be worshipped as supreme being, personification of the earth, or alternatively, function as a nonrealist symbol of female perfection. In any case the Goddess is visualized through immanent or other means than traditional, transcendent categories. The term *thealogy* (in contradistinction to theology), coined by Naomi Goldenberg (1979, p. 96), is now widely employed to signal the importance of Goddess worship and symbolism to the movements and to refer to the growing body of literature that offers scholarly reflection on spiritual feminism (e.g., Christ 1979, 1997; Eller, 1993; Goldenberg, 1979; Long, 1994; Raphael, 1999). However, some spiritual feminists prefer not to be defined in relation to the enterprise of theology to the degree that it is viewed as an inherently patriarchal discipline that entails a retreat from praxis into systematic theorizing about doctrine. Other elements that have proved attractive to spiritual feminists include pagan and Wiccan traditions. Participatory rituals, occasionally with magical overtones, are often held to coincide with pagan feasts such as the spring equinox and summer solstice. Some of the key figures in feminist spirituality identify as witches (e.g., Zsuzsanna Budapest; Starhawk). This both reclaims the witch as a positive female role and at the same time honors those women who were historically persecuted for witchcraft because of their refusal to succumb to (often religious) authority.

Feminist spirituality movements are deliberately eclectic and syncretistic, and this, combined with the rejection of institutional organization, accounts for their variety. To a certain extent these feminist strategies of connection and appropriation are similar to those employed by women who seek to rebuild the traditional religions. Both entail the recovery of suppressed or forgotten symbolism and traditions and the construction of new religious expressions on this basis. However, the borrowing of religious symbols—such as the incorporation of goddess traditions into feminist spirituality—risks offending those from the indigenous cultures of Africa, America, Australia, China, and India whose symbols have been reappropriated for use by Western women if it is done without due sensitivity to their proper context. There is also debate about whether spiritual feminists are engaged in the recovery or imaginative re-creation of religious history. Controversially the archaeologist Marija Gimbutas postulated the existence of peaceful goddess-worshipping matrifocal cultures in Neolithic Europe that were superseded by warfaring patriarchal tribes that worshipped male gods. That a prepatriarchal golden age of female-affirming religious culture ever existed has been disputed—even by feminists sympathetic to Goddess spirituality (e.g., Eller, 2000; Hewitt, 1993). Irrespective of whether conjecture plays a part in such hypotheses, innovation in ritual celebration is of more importance to feminist spirituality movements than appeal to historically verifiable traditions.

The critique and transformation of the academic study of religion. A fundamental task of women's studies scholarship has been to interrogate and overhaul the presuppositions, explanations, key principles, and accepted canons and methods that shape the academic study of religion. As has been indicated, women's studies in religion arose from the realization that the academic study of religion was an androcentric enterprise. A central goal of women's studies has therefore been to dismantle the epistemological and methodological architecture of the discipline constructed from within the parameters of androcentrism and to rebuild religious studies so as to incorporate into its framework critical awareness of the role gender plays both in shaping religion and in shaping its study in order to offer a fuller and truer account of the religious experiences of humankind.

As women's studies entered the scholarly arena, the academic study of religion was dominated by the *Religionswissenschaft* school, led by scholars such as Mircea Eliade, Joseph Kitagawa, and Charles Long. The laudable ambition of this influential movement was to study any and all human religious phenomena dispassionately, impartially, and nonjudgmentally, free from religious and all other bias that might interfere with the goal of the objective and scientific study of religion. Religion was understood to be a universal human phenomenon that, despite its cross-cultural and historical variety, has distinctive transcultural features in common (such as initiation rites) that are shared by the timeless, supposedly genderless, and otherwise decontextualized *homo religiosus,* "religious man." This ahistorical, undifferentiated generic subject was soon subjected to critical scrutiny by women's studies scholars and *homo religiosus* exposed as the false universal it was.

The androcentrism of the *Religionswissenschaft* school was diagnosed by Gross: "*Homo religiosus* as constructed by the history of religions does not include women as religious subjects, as constructors of religious symbol systems and as participants in a religious universe of discourse" (Gross, 1977, p. 10). While it was claimed that women were included under the generic *man*, examination of scholarship by historians of religion demonstrated that this was not the case. For instance, Saiving found that Eliade's *Rites and Symbols of Initiation* (1958) devotes just 9 of its 175 pages to female initiations (Saiving, 1976, p. 184). While this is attributable to the lack of reliable ethnographic data on women's rites, Saiving takes issue with Eliade's extrapolation from the more extensive data on male initiation rites to his conclusions about initiation as a human phenomenon: "What he says about the *human* meaning of initiation corresponds almost exactly to what he says about *male* initiation" (Saiving, 1976, p.189). Similarly, though Eliade's magisterial three-volume work *A History of Religious Ideas* (1978–1985) seeks to relate "the spiritual history of humanity" (Eliade, 1978, p. xvi), Christ finds: "The history of religion which Eliade tells is distorted by dualism, Idealism, and false universalization of male experience" (Christ, 1991, p. 94). If women's religious data is omitted from the construction of models and theories about religion, it comes as no surprise when women are treated as curious exceptions to the (male) norm. Thus Gross notes: "Most of the time, Eliade writes about women as symbols to *homo religiosus*, rather than as real people. When he does, infrequently, write about women as real people, it is because their behavior represents a special case that does not fit his general descriptions or theories" (Gross, 2002a, p. 46).

While the *Religionswissenschaft* school had been sensitive to the dangers of allowing Christian models of religion to function as a key to the interpretation of other religious traditions, the movement had been blind to the way gender affects scholarship. The quest for a universal account of religion as such was conducted using inadequate data, erroneous inferences and dubious hypotheses. Women's studies scholarship demolished the assertion that the discipline of religious studies was scientific and impartial and demonstrated the illusory nature of the claim to objectivity. As Kinsley indicates: "The effect [of women's studies] has been to show, often in shocking and dramatic ways, the extent to which history of religions has not been true to its own mandate. It has been neither all-inclusive nor objective in its study of human religiousness" (Kinsley, 2002, p. 2).

This powerful feminist critique of the scientific study of religion crystallized a thoroughgoing reconceptualization of the subject, initiating a change in the discipline that has been characterized by several scholars as no less than a conceptual paradigm shift (see Christ, 1987, 1991; Gross, 1983; King, 1995; Warne, 1989). Within religious studies as a whole there is an increased sensitivity to the influence of gender in shaping religious and research perspectives and greater caution in the formulation of generalizations about religious beliefs, symbolism, and practices. The methods of studying religion have been expanded as women's studies scholarship has penetrated the specialist academic disciplines in the study of religion. While the study of religious texts remains an important element in religious studies, it has been recognized that, to the extent that it exists, sacred literature is of limited use for ascertaining the reality of ordinary women's (and men's) religious lives on the ground. Women are often absent from holy writings, and when women are mentioned in texts and teachings, there is the danger of distorted or idealized portrayals of their lives.

Women's studies have helped to dislodge the discipline's overemphasis on and priority given to text-based research by shifting the focus to other sources and methods of obtaining information about women and their religions. Within the specialisms of anthropology and sociology of religion, more extensive use of fieldwork has improved data gathering through the increased use of interview techniques and the collection of oral testimonies. With greater numbers of female researchers engaged in fieldwork, there is wider access to women's spaces, allowing more detailed study of female-dominated religious subcultures. Scholarly interest in popular and folk religion, where women are often more prominent, has also aided the documentation of women's religious participation.

One important methodological question that arises with respect to the conduct of fieldwork concerns the relationship between the researcher and the subject of research—the observer and the observed. Women's studies scholarship exposed the false claims to objectivity made by scholars within the so-called scientific study of religion, and this has given rise to a wider hermeneutical suspicion of the ethos of objectivity, including a questioning of whether the methodological values of impassive detachment and scholarly neutrality are genuinely attainable (and desirable) in the field and whether fieldwork observations can supply an accurate account of religion uninfluenced by the observer's presuppositions, values, and evaluative and interpretive faculties (see Franzmann, 2000; Knott, 1995). The issues at stake can be ethically perplexing, involving, for example, matters of whether fieldwork necessarily objectifies women who are studied; whether the establishment of trust and friendship have a place in ethnographic research; whether scholarly noninvolvement implies tacit approval of unjust power relations between those who are studied; and how far a researcher should stand back from cultural practices that she or he judges to be harmful, degrading, or otherwise questionable (see Jacobs, 1991).

Feminist and other researchers committed to social justice for women may find the research values of noninterference and neutrality conflict with a perceived duty to engage in the consciousness-raising of research subjects and to speak out against the discrimination and oppression of women. Some female scholars suggest the values of engagement and empathy—as important feminist commitments—should replace the ethos of objectivity as the appropriate feminist and morally responsible means of conducting research in religion (e.g., Christ, 1987, 1997). In order to take proper cognizance of the inherent presence of scholarly subjectivity and the perspectival nature of human knowing, it has become common for women's studies scholars (and other scholars of religion) as creators of knowledge, in an act of self-reflexivity, to disclose to their readership as prolegomenon to their research, their authorial standpoint, social position, interests, background, and any other relevant features in order to make explicit those factors that may shape and color the research questions, objectives, methods of study, and conclusions. The theoretical aspects of feminist epistemology and standpoint theory find an important place in feminist philosophy of religion (see Anderson, 1998; Jantzen, 1998).

Experience, Identity, and Difference. The process of articulating one's standpoint as a situated subject has become a critically important exercise in women's studies, not least as a means of shedding light on three dominant but problematic analytical themes: experience, identity, and difference. To be a person in the world necessarily entails location in a particular place and time, and humans are further shaped (though not determined) by social identities and roles that contribute to self-understanding and form identities, that make one subject to different life experiences, that give one particular outlooks or perspectives on the world, and that enable differences to be discerned between oneself and other differently situated subjects. A greater appreciation of the role of social location in creating and shaping human diversity has allowed women's studies in religion to offer more sophisticated analyses of the factors that affect women's religious lives and to dispel some of the generalizations about "women's experience" that characterized certain less-critical early feminist critiques of religion (see Davaney, 1987). If previously more sweeping assertions were made about women's lives on the basis of a monolithic understanding of womanhood, there is now recognition of the analytical inadequacy of "woman" as a unified category. Women have diverse needs, desires, ideals, and so on and are embodied subject to differentials such as sexuality, religion, nationality, ethnicity, "race," class, caste, and age. As such women's religious lives are shaped by a complex interaction of forces, and they cannot be understood adequately using the category of gender alone. For example, the plight of *dalit* women in India is as much concerned with issues of economics and caste as it is with gender (see Jogdand, 1995).

It is clear that women who belong to religions in the advanced industrialized countries of the Northern Hemisphere are affected differently by political, economic, and environmental forces than those within the more rural economies of eastern Europe and the Southern Hemisphere. Traditional forms of religion and ritual practices and the family units that preserved them are subject to transformation through the impetus for economic development and the demise of rural communities. While many women are affected by these changes transculturally, the effects are often most acute in developing countries since it is women in traditional societies who tend to safeguard and preserve religious customs and values from the modernizing and Westernizing tendencies that globalization brings. In this context, in countries such as India and Pakistan, women have found themselves pedestalized by religious nationalisms eager to promote them as antisecular symbols of national pride, identity, and purity. When it comes to ecological activism, religious women have campaigned more vigorously for sustainable development and global resource management in countries that are directly affected by the destruction of habitat through deforestation, the industrial pollution of rivers, and the stripping of natural resources compared to those in more affluent nations, where a sense of connection to and responsibility for the environment has to a large extent been compromised by mass consumption and consumerism (see Ruether, 1996).

Crucially the way geopolitical economic forces affect contemporary religions cannot be understood without recognition of the influence of the shameful history of Western imperialism, colonial expansion and exploitation, racism, slavery, and the imposition of Christianity onto indigenous peoples. These wrongdoings were perpetrated under the guise of promoting civilization and religious salvation, and their enduring legacy has been Third World debt, apartheid, racial discrimination, religious unrest, the emergence of fundamentalisms, tribal warfare, genocide, displaced peoples, and an obscene discrepancy between the economies of the rich North and poor South. The historical legacy of Western imperialism and its contemporary afterlives cast a long shadow over international relations and religious identities.

This historical background has had a profound influence on women's studies and continues to act as an obstacle to the global solidarity of women. While women are united in fighting sexism, they are divided by injustice with regard to "race," religion, class, nationality, economics, sexual orientation, and so on. In these respects women can be the perpetrators as well as the victims of discrimination and injustice—as were white Western women during the colonial era. For those women still experiencing the aftermath of colonial empire building, the Western message of women's liberation is an ambivalent one. Feminism is a suspect category for a significant number of nonwhite and non-Western women who associate the term with the bourgeois liberal individualistic claims of white, educationally privileged, and economically elite middle-class women whose gender analyses do nothing to address the racism, classism, and economic injustice suffered by most of the world's women. For some, feminism also stands for sexual licence and family breakdown. For these reasons, many nonwhite and non-Western women—including some who campaign for women's liberation—eschew the feminist label (see Isasi-Díaz, 1993, p. 4).

In the early days of the women's movement many Western women were unaware of these sensitivities. Western feminists would often write as though gender were the only lens through which women's lives could be understood, whereas for some women the discriminating factors were as much associated with economic injustice, racial prejudice, and imperialistic domination. The idealism of the women's movement tended to neglect these conflictual elements, and those involved in women's studies failed to see the monopoly of power that Western women possessed as shapers of the new discourse (see Williams, 1985). Feminist theory, it was thought, included all women and could address their universal concerns.

In the same way that the *Religionswissenschaft* school had initiated a flawed attempt to distill the essential nature of pure religion, uncontaminated by social, political, or any other context that gives religion its variety and complexity, so too Western feminists constructed anemic accounts of women's nature and experience that had the blood of real lives drained out of them. Women's studies scholars were falling into the same homogenizing traps and reproducing the same errors as their male predecessors. The social, political, and other contextual elements that form women's lives and create distinct identities were submerged under the rhetoric of a nebulous undifferentiated "women's experience." In a repeat performance of the mistakes of androcentric scholarship, the formulations of feminism that were articulated represented the interests and perspectives of the white Western women who had created them, and the dominant feminist critiques of religion were based on the predominant religion of the West, Christianity. These analyses lacked the standpoints of other women from different contexts whose life experiences could provide additional perspectives that previously had been omitted.

Contextuality as a Characteristic of Women's Studies in Religion. The scope of women's studies broadened as new writings emerged from women keen to assert their distinct identities and name their particular experiences (see Kwok, 2002). These built on the feminist critique of religion but also reacted against it. For example, African American women (avoiding feminist nomenclature) adopted Alice Walker's term *womanist* to describe their theological and ethical projects, located in the experiences of not only sexism by males but also racial and economic oppression by the white majority in the United States (e.g., Cannon, 1988; Grant, 1989; Williams, 1993). Initially united by their Christian heritage, womanists have since shed their exclusively Christian focus. Similarly Ada María Isasi-Díaz and colleagues coined the term *mujerista* theology to express the religious reflection and liberative praxis that arises from the ethnically diverse Latina women living in the United States who are united by their common experience of sexism, poverty, and racism (Isasi-Díaz et al., 1992). Numerous other local and contextualized women's theologies also emerged differentiated on geographical, ethnic, and other grounds that reflect the pluralism of Christianity (humanity's most populous and geographically dispersed religion) and that express the shared perspectives of women united by marginalization, communal struggle, and religious empowerment (e.g., Brock et al., 1987; Katoppo, 1979; King, 1994; Oduyoye, 2001; Kwok, 2000).

As a result of this proliferation of contextualized approaches, women's studies in religion are more diverse, complex, and internally divided but also more inclusive as the many social allegiances and religious loyalties of women are given expression. Further diversification seems inevitable as increasing numbers of women from traditions other than Christianity organize themselves into distinct local constituencies.

The ideological diversity that exists leads to dissonant responses to religious issues that concern women. For example, there is no consensus on the use of the *ḥijāb* (veil) in Islam, which has become a particularly contested and polysemic religious symbol. The requirement that Islamic women dress modestly in public is interpreted differently in different social and historical locations. The practice of veiling is frequently characterized by non-Muslims as nothing other than an illustration of the religion's oppression of women. While some Muslim feminists may agree with this assessment and applaud the influential action of Egyptian feminists who first cast off the veil in the 1920s, other Muslim women, where veiling is not compulsory, have reclaimed the practice both as a symbolic act asserting Islamic identity over against Western liberalism and in order to enter public life free of the male gaze (see Leila Ahmed, 1992; Hoodfar, 2001).

The veiling issue illustrates the complexity and multiple layers of meaning that religious symbols can have for women and also demonstrates the need for women's studies scholars to actively foster intercultural and interreligious sensitivity and dialogue as a means of overcoming prejudicial intolerance and supremacist tendencies and of learning from encounters with those who are other. This has been theorized by writers such as Rita Gross, Ursula King, and Maura O'Neill and put into practice by initiatives such as the Asian Women's Consultations on Interfaith Dialogue (AWRC) (AWRC, 1990, 1995; Gross, 2002b; King, 1999; O'Neill, 1990). Nevertheless further critical reflection and practical measures by women are required in this area—especially given the continuing augmentation and exploitation of religious suspicions and hostilities for political, terror, and militaristic purposes.

To the extent that religions have sought to control and circumscribe female sexuality, women who have chosen to live outside the framework of heterosexuality and straight conventions have found themselves doubly oppressed by religious teachings, ideals, and practices that concern sex and gender. Yet lesbians and other queer women have found homes in religions and have drawn on their marginal experience to theorize about religion and sexuality and to campaign for societal acceptance and civil rights. Women who have identified as lesbians, such as Rebecca Alpert, Mary Daly, Beverley Harrison, Carter Heyward, Mary Hunt, Audre Lorde, and Elizabeth Stuart, have made important contributions to what has become a subject discipline in its own right: in 1986 the American Academy of Religion Lesbian-Feminist Issues and Religion Group was established (see Alpert, 1997; Daly, 1978; Harrison, 1985; Heyward, 1984; Hunt, 1983; Lorde, 1984; Stuart, 2003). In addition to exploring the intersection of religious and sexual identity, these writers have expanded the understanding of terms such as *eros, embodiment, desire,* and *friendship.*

INTERDISCIPLINARITY AS A CHARACTERISTIC OF WOMEN'S STUDIES IN RELIGION. As women's studies in religion have embraced these new identities and contingencies, the purview of the field has grown and diversified by the welcome introduction of new intellectual resources and interdisciplinary approaches that have preserved women's studies from becoming stagnant and irrelevant. For example, the insights of postcolonial theory are commonly employed by female scholars from non-Western contexts (e.g., Donaldson and Kwok, 2002). The Argentinean liberation theologian Marcella Althaus-Reid has combined the class analysis of liberation theology with feminism, postcolonial theory, and queer theory to offer new insights into the oppression of the economically and sexually disenfranchised (Althaus-Reid, 2000, 2004). Sharon Welch and Mary McClintock Fulkerson have both incorporated poststructuralist theory into their influential feminist liberation theologies, and Fulkerson has also drawn on the empirical social sciences (Fulkerson, 1994; Welch, 1985). Terms such as *woman, experience, identity, subjectivity,* and *difference* are critically examined using the tools of postmodern feminist theory (see Chopp and Davaney, 1997). Religious feminists are examining issues of sexual difference, the symbolic order, and the divine through the psychoanalysis and philosophy of French feminists such as Luce Irigaray and Julia Kristeva (e.g., Joy et al., 2002, 2003; Kim, et al., 1993). Perhaps most significantly for women's studies, the intellectual vibrancy of gender studies—which continues to anchor theoretical work in women's studies—is leading to increased interdisciplinary collaboration between male and female scholars of religion (e.g., Peskowitz and Levitt, 1997).

FROM WOMEN'S STUDIES TO GENDER STUDIES IN RELIGION. The evolution of gender studies as an academic discipline in its own right has had a considerable impact on women's studies in religion. If women's studies scholars have learned that factors other than gender must also be taken into account when seeking to understand women's religious lives, gender studies have shown that gender itself is not a straightforward category: sexed identities are more diverse, fluid, and performative attributes than previous scholarship and religious or cultural prescriptions had appreciated (e.g., Butler, 1990). These insights, which gave birth to queer theory, have resourced lesbians and other women who point to the inadequacies of religious attitudes to sexual orientation. Feminist theory has benefited from the more nuanced accounts of gender that now exist, which have challenged the feminist fundamentalisms that stress either secure and normative sex differences or that appeal to aspirations of androgynous sameness. The advent of gender studies has also created a much-needed intellectual space for men's studies in religion to flourish (e.g., Boyd et al., 1996). This, along with the synergistic collaboration of male and female scholars of religion who employ gender theory in their work, has raised important foundational questions about the future of women's studies in religion.

One question involves whether gender theory as a discourse might subsume feminist theory and how such a scenario would affect women's studies. It has already been noted that some female scholars of religion do not identify themselves or their work as feminist. It is for this reason that the phrase *feminist studies in religion* was considered an inadequate title for this encyclopedia entry. The question of appropriate nomenclature for the discipline is more than an exercise in terminology. The term *gender studies in religion* better reflects the fact that both females and males are affected (albeit diversely) by the many ways gender matters shape religions. It also addresses the concerns of the significant numbers of female and male students who (rightly or wrongly) find feminism threatening and women's studies courses exclusionary. Increasingly academic work in women's studies is based in gender studies departments. In these respects gender studies in religion is a more inclusive subject discipline and offers a more adequate terminological label than either feminist or women's studies in religion. However, while the trend toward gender studies may attract more students into the field, it may also call into question the continued need for separate women's studies courses on educational curricula, leading to closures or mergers of academic programs. The danger is that absorption into gender studies may further dilute the status and visibility of scholarship that concentrates on women's religion or lead to a loss of provision altogether.

The Academy and Women's Studies in Religion. As a cross-disciplinary subject, work in women's studies in religion is often carried out as a subsidiary aspect of established cognate disciplines within religious studies, theology, or (less frequently) women's and gender studies departments. As a result the subject has struggled for acceptance in the academy, and it remains marginalized and underfunded. Nevertheless women's scholarship is supported and shared through numerous international and faith-based organizations, networks, and conferences. The World Wide Web has proved particularly effective in making widely available religious and other online resources to large numbers of interested women inside and outside of academia.

Of the enormous body of literature devoted to women and religion, Serinity Young's *Encyclopedia of Women and World Religion* (1999) deserves mention as the first comprehensive reference work in the subject. And if women's studies in religion have often been forgotten within the wider women's studies discourse, this oversight has been corrected in the *Routledge International Encyclopedia of Women*, in which "Religion and Spirituality" comprises one of its thirteen major sections (Kramarae and Spender, 2000). Established periodicals that publish on women and religion include Arvind Sharma and Katherine Young's *Annual Review of Women in World Religions*, the American *Journal of Feminist Studies in Religion*, and in the British Isles *Feminist Theology*, which has a broader compass than its name suggests. From Australia come the biannual *Women-Church: An Australian Journal of Feminist Studies in Religion* and the annual online journal *Seachanges: The Journal of Women Scholars of Religion and Theology*. Christian journals include the *Yearbook of the European Society of Women in Theological Research; In God's Image*, the Asian women's theological journal; *Revista Con-spirando: Latin American Review of Ecofeminism, Spirituality, and Theology*. *Hawwa: Journal of Women of the Middle East and the Islamic World* and *Al-Raida*, published by the Institute for Women's Studies in the Arab World, are English-language journals. Within Judaism there exists *Bridges: A Journal for Jewish Feminists and Our Friends; Nashim: A Journal of Jewish Women's Studies and Gender Issues;* and *Women in Judaism*, a multidisciplinary electronic journal. While such journals facilitate scholarly exchange, it is still mainly Western women who have access to these and other resources.

While few doubt that the entry of women's studies in religion into the academic arena constituted a major event in the history of the study of religion, the extent to which women's studies have transformed the discipline of religious studies is a moot point (see Plaskow, 1999; Warne, 1998). The pattern across specialisms is uneven. Whereas anthropological, psychological, and historical studies of religion have integrated feminist insights into mainstream scholarship, feminist writings remain on the fringes of sociology and philosophy of religion (see Sharma, 2002). There is more work to be done before the marginalization of women's scholarship finally comes to an end. However, much has been achieved. One need only compare the revised edition of this encyclopedia with its first edition (1987) to see the abundant growth and reconceptualization of the subject on the grounds of gender. Ursula King's trenchant criticisms of the neglect of women's scholarship in the first edition did not go unheeded (King, 1990). This second edition of *The Encyclopedia of Religion* gives eloquent testimony to the manifest influence of women's scholarship in engendering religious studies.

See Also Androcentrism; Ecology and Religion, overview article; Eliade, Mircea; Feminine Sacrality; Feminism, article on Feminism, Gender Studies, and Religion; Feminist Theology, overview article; Gender and Religion, overview article, article on History of Study; Gender Roles; Goddess Worship, overview article; Gynocentrism; Lesbianism; Men's Studies in Religion; New Religious Movements, article on New Religious Movements and Women; Patriarchy and Matriarchy; Spirituality; Thealogy; Wicca.

Bibliography

The literature on women's studies in religion is vast and varied.

The most comprehensive treatment of the subject is in the

Encyclopedia of Women and World Religion. For an indication of how the field has changed since its inception, compare this entry with its forerunner "Women's Studies" by Constance H. Buchanan in the first edition of the *Encyclopedia of Religion.* Gross's *Feminism and Religion* offers a detailed overview of the impact women's (and especially feminist) studies have had on religion; and their direct influence on the subject specialisms and methods of religious studies are discussed by Sharma (2002). The edited collections listed here typically offer a combination of essays on theoretical questions in gender and religion and on the contemporary and historical impact of religions on women's lives. All the works below are referred to in the *Women's Studies in Religion* entry.

Ahmed, Durre S., ed. *Gendering the Spirit: Women, Religion, and the Post-Colonial Response.* London, 2002.

Ahmed, Leila. *Women and Gender in Islam: Roots of a Modern Debate.* New Haven, Conn., 1992.

Alpert, Rebecca. *Like Bread on the Seder Plate: Jewish Lesbians and the Transformation of Tradition.* New York, 1997.

Althaus-Reid, Marcella. *Indecent Theology: Theological Perversions in Sex, Gender, and Politics.* New York, 2000.

Althaus-Reid, Marcella. *From Feminist Theology to Indecent Theology.* London, 2004.

Anderson, Pamela Sue. *A Feminist Philosophy of Religion: The Rationality and Myths of Religious Belief.* Oxford, 1998.

Asian Women's Resource Centre for Culture and Theology (AWRC), ed. *Faith Renewed I: A Report on the First Asian Women's Consultation on Interfaith Dialogue, November 1–8, 1989, Kuala Lumpur, Malaysia.* Kuala Lumpur, Malaysia, 1990.

Asian Women's Resource Centre for Culture and Theology (AWRC), ed. *Faith Renewed II: A Report on the Second Asian Women's Consultation on Interfaith Dialogue, November 1–7, 1991, Colombo, Sri Lanka.* Kuala Lumpur, Malaysia, 1995.

Beauvoir, Simone de. *The Second Sex.* Translated by H. M. Parshley. New York, 1953. First published as *Le deuxieme sexe.* Paris, 1949.

Boyd, Stephen B., W. Merle Longwood, and Mark W. Muesse, eds. *Redeeming Men: Religion and Masculinities.* Louisville, Ky., 1996.

Brock, Rita Nakashima, Yasuko Morihara Grosjean, Patria Agustin, Kwok Pui-lan, Soon-Hwa Sun, and Naomi Southard. "Special Section: Asian Women Theologians Respond to American Feminism." *Journal of Feminist Studies in Religion* 3, no. 2 (Fall 1987): 103–150.

Budapest, Zsuzsanna E. *The Feminist Book of Lights and Shadows.* Venice, Calif., 1976. Republished as *The Holy Book of Women's Mysteries: Feminist Witchcraft, Goddess Rituals, Spellcasting, and Other Womanly Arts.* Berkeley, Calif., 1989.

Butler, Judith. *Gender Trouble: Feminism and the Subversion of Identity.* New York, 1990.

Bynum, Caroline Walker. *Fragmentation and Redemption: Essays on Gender and the Human Body in Medieval Religion.* New York, 1992.

Cannon, Katie G. *Black Womanist Ethics.* Atlanta, 1988.

Chopp, Rebecca S., and Sheila Greeve Davaney, eds. *Horizons in Feminist Theology: Identity, Tradition, and Norms.* Minneapolis, 1997.

Christ, Carol P. "Why Women Need the Goddess: Phenomenological, Psychological, and Political Reflections." In *Womanspirit Rising: A Feminist Reader in Religion,* edited by Carol P. Christ and Judith Plaskow, pp. 273–287. San Francisco, 1979.

Christ, Carol P. "Toward a Paradigm Shift in the Academy and in Religious Studies." In *The Impact of Feminist Research in the Academy,* edited by Christie Farnham, pp. 53–76. Bloomington, Ind., 1987.

Christ, Carol P. "Mircea Eliade and the Feminist Paradigm Shift." *Journal of Feminist Studies in Religion* 7, no. 2 (1991): 75–94.

Christ, Carol P. *Rebirth of the Goddess: Finding Meaning in Feminist Spirituality.* New York, 1997.

Daly, Mary. *The Church and the Second Sex.* New York, 1968.

Daly, Mary. *Beyond God the Father: Toward a Philosophy of Women's Liberation.* Boston, 1973.

Daly, Mary. *Gyn/Ecology: The Metaethics of Radical Feminism.* Boston, 1978.

Davaney, Sheila Greeve. "The Limits of the Appeal to Women's Experience." In *Shaping New Vision: Gender and Values in American Culture,* edited by Clarissa W. Atkinson, Constance H. Buchanan, and Margaret R. Miles, pp. 31–49. Ann Arbor, Mich., 1987.

Donaldson, Laura E., and Kwok Pui-lan, eds. *Postcolonialism, Feminism, and Religious Discourse.* New York, 2002.

Eliade, Mircea. *Rites and Symbols of Initiation: The Mysteries of Birth and Rebirth.* Translated by W. R. Trask. New York, 1958.

Eliade, Mircea. *A History of Religious Ideas.* vol. 1: *From the Stone Age to the Eleusinian Mysteries.* Translated by W. R. Trask. Chicago, 1978.

Eller, Cynthia. *Living in the Lap of the Goddess: The Feminist Spirituality Movement in America.* New York, 1993.

Eller, Cynthia. *The Myth of Matriarchal Prehistory: Why an Invented Past Won't Give Women a Future.* Boston, 2000.

El Sa'dāwī, Nawāl. *The Hidden Face of Eve: Women in the Arab World.* Translated by Sherif Hetata. London, 1980.

Falk, Nancy Auer, and Rita M. Gross, eds. *Unspoken Worlds: Women's Religious Lives* (1980). 3d ed. Belmont, Calif., 2001.

Franzmann, Majella. *Women and Religion.* New York, 2000.

Fulkerson, Mary McClintock. *Changing the Subject: Women's Discourses and Feminist Theology.* Minneapolis, 1994.

Gimbutas, Marija. *The Gods and Goddesses of Old Europe, 7000–3500 BCE,* Berkeley, Calif., 1974.

Goldenberg, Naomi R. *The Changing of the Gods: Feminism and the End of Traditional Religions.* Boston, 1979.

Goldenberg, Naomi R. "Witches and Words," "Embodying Feminist Liberation Theologies: A Special Edition of Feminist Theology," edited by Beverley Clack. *Feminist Theology* 12, no. 2 (January 2004): 203–211.

Grant, Jacquelyn. *White Women's Christ and Black Women's Jesus: Feminist Christology and Womanist Response.* Atlanta, 1989.

Gross, Rita M. "Androcentrism and Androgyny in the Methodology of History of Religions." In *Beyond Androcentrism: New Essays on Women and Religion,* edited by Rita M. Gross, pp. 7–19. Missoula, Mont., 1977.

Gross, Rita M. "Women's Studies in Religion: The State of the Art, 1980." In *Traditions in Contact and Change: Selected Proceedings of the XIVth Congress of the International Association for the History of Religions,* edited by Peter Slater and Donald Wiebe with Maurice Boutin and Harold Coward, pp. 579–591. Waterloo, Ontario, 1983.

Gross, Rita M. *Buddhism after Patriarchy: A Feminist History, Analysis, and Reconstruction of Buddhism.* Albany, N.Y., 1993.

Gross, Rita M. "Feminist Issues and Methods in the Anthropology of Religion." In *Methodology in Religious Studies: The Interface with Women's Studies,* edited by Arvind Sharma, pp. 41–66. New York, 2002a.

Gross, Rita M. "Feminist Theology as Theology of Religions." In *The Cambridge Companion to Feminist Theology,* edited by Susan Frank Parsons, pp. 60–78. Cambridge, U.K., 2002b.

Hampson, Daphne. *Theology and Feminism.* Oxford, 1990.

Hampson, Daphne. *After Christianity.* 2d ed. London, 2002.

Harrison, Beverley Wildung. *Making the Connections: Essays in Feminist Social Ethics.* Edited by Carol S. Robb. Boston, 1985.

Hewitt, Marsha A. "Cyborgs, Drag Queens, and Goddesses: Emancipatory-Regressive Paths in Feminist Theory." *Method and Theory in the Study of Religion* 5, no. 2 (1993): 135–154.

Heyward, Carter. *Our Passion for Justice: Images of Power, Sexuality, and Liberation.* New York, 1984.

Holm, Jean, with John Bowker, eds. *Women in Religion.* London, 1994.

Hoodfar, Homa. "The Veil in Their Minds and on Our Heads: Veiling Practices and Muslim Women." In *Women, Gender, Religion: A Reader,* edited by Elizabeth A. Castelli with Rosamond C. Rodman, pp. 420–446. New York, 2001.

Hunt, Mary. "Lovingly Lesbian: Toward a Feminist Theology of Friendship." In *A Challenge to Love: Gay and Lesbian Catholics in the Church,* edited by Robert Nugent, pp. 135–155. New York, 1983.

Isasi-Díaz, Ada María, Elena Olazagasti-Segovia, Sandra Mangual-Rodriguez, Maria Antoinetta Berriozábal, Daisy L. Machado, Lourdes Arguelles, and Raven-Anne Rivero. "*Mujeristas*: Who We Are and What We Are About." *Journal of Feminist Studies in Religion* 8, no. 1 (Spring 1992): 105–125.

Isasi-Díaz, Ada María. *En La Lucha/In the Struggle: A Hispanic Women's Liberation Theology.* Minneapolis, Minn., 1993.

Jacobs, Janet L. "Gender and Power in New Religious Movements: A Feminist Discourse on the Scientific Study of Religion." *Religion* 21 (1991): 345–356.

Jantzen, Grace. *Becoming Divine: Towards a Feminist Philosophy of Religion.* Manchester, U.K., 1998.

Jogdand, P. G., ed. *Dalit Women in India: Issues and Perspectives.* New Delhi, 1995.

Joy, Morny, Kathleen O'Grady, and Judith L. Poxon, eds. *French Feminists on Religion: A Reader.* London, 2002.

Joy, Morny, Kathleen O'Grady, and Judith L. Poxon, eds. *Religion in French Feminist Thought: Critical Perspectives.* London, 2003.

Katoppo, Marianne. *Compassionate and Free: An Asian Woman's Theology.* Geneva, Switzerland, 1979.

Kim, C. W. Maggie, Susan M. St. Ville, and Susan M. Simonaitis, eds. *Transfigurations: Theology and the French Feminists.* Minneapolis, Minn., 1993.

King, Ursula. "Women Scholars and the Encyclopedia of Religion." *Method and Theory in the Study of Religion* 2, no. 1 (1990): 91–97.

King, Ursula. "Introduction: Gender and the Study of Religion." In *Religion and Gender,* edited by Ursula King, pp. 1–38. Oxford, 1995.

King, Ursula. "Interreligious Dialogue." In *Encyclopedia of Women and World Religion,* 2 vols., edited by Serinity Young, pp. 477–479. New York, 1999

King, Ursula, ed. *Women in the World's Religions, Past and Present.* New York, 1987.

King, Ursula, ed. *Feminist Theology from the Third World: A Reader.* Maryknoll, N.Y., 1994.

Kinsley, David. *Hindu Goddesses: Visions of the Divine Feminine in the Hindu Religious Tradition.* Berkeley, Calif., 1986.

Kinsley, David. "Women's Studies in the History of Religions." In *Methodology in Religious Studies: The Interface with Women's Studies,* edited by Arvind Sharma, pp. 1–15. New York, 2002.

Knott, Kim. "Women Researching, Women Researched: Gender as an Issue in the Empirical Study of Religion." In *Religion and Gender,* edited by Ursula King, pp. 199–218. Oxford, 1995.

Kraemer, Ross Shepard. *Her Share of the Blessings: Women's Religions among Pagans, Jews, and Christians in the Greco-Roman World.* New York, 1992.

Kramarae, Cheris, and Dale Spender, eds. *Routledge International Encyclopedia of Women: Global Women's Issues and Knowledge.* New York and London, 2000.

Kwok Pui-lan. *Introducing Asian Feminist Theology.* Cleveland, Ohio, 2000.

Kwok Pui-lan. "Feminist Theology as Intercultural Discourse." In *The Cambridge Companion to Feminist Theology,* edited by Susan Frank Parsons, pp. 23–39. Cambridge, U.K., 2002.

Long, Asphodel P. "The Goddess Movement in Britain Today." *Feminist Theology* 5 (1994): 11–39.

Lorde, Audre. *Sister Outsider: Essays and Speeches.* Trumansburg, N.Y., 1984.

Mernissi, Fatima. *Women and Islam: An Historical and Theological Enquiry.* Translated by Mary Jo Lakeland. Oxford, 1991.

Nasrin, Taslima. "Ending Silence." *Time Magazine,* August 23–30, 1999.

Newman, Barbara. *From Virile Woman to WomanChrist: Studies in Medieval Religion and Literature.* Philadelphia, 1995.

Oduyoye, Mercy Amba. *Introducing African Women's Theology.* Sheffield, U.K., 2001.

O'Neill, Maura. *Women Speaking, Women Listening: Women in Interreligious Dialogue.* Maryknoll, N.Y., 1990.

Palmer, Susan Jean. *Moon Sisters, Krishna Mothers, Rajneesh Lovers: Women's Roles in New Religions.* Syracuse, N.Y., 1994.

Peskowitz, Miriam, and Laura Levitt, eds. *Judaism since Gender.* New York, 1997.

Plaskow, Judith. *Standing again at Sinai: Judaism from a Feminist Perspective.* San Francisco, 1991.

Plaskow, Judith. "The Academy as Real Life: New Participants and Paradigms in the Study of Religion." *Journal of the American Academy of Religion* 67, no. 3 (September 1999): 521–538.

Plaskow, Judith, and Carol P. Christ, eds. *Weaving the Visions: New Patterns in Feminist Spirituality.* San Francisco, 1989.

Puttick, Elizabeth. *Women in New Religions: In Search of Community, Sexuality, and Spiritual Power.* Basingstoke, U.K., 1997.

Raphael, Melissa. *Introducing Thealogy: Discourse on the Goddess.* Cleveland, Ohio, 2000.

Robinson, Catherine A. *Tradition and Liberation: The Hindu Tradition in the Indian Women's Movement.* Richmond, U.K., 1999.

Ruether, Rosemary Radford. *Sexism and God-Talk: Toward a Feminist Theology.* London, 1983.

Ruether, Rosemary Radford. "The Future of Feminist Theology in the Academy." *Journal of the American Academy of Religion* 53, no. 3 (1985): 703–713.

Ruether, Rosemary Radford, ed. *Women Healing Earth: Third World Women on Ecology, Feminism, and Religion.* Maryknoll, N.Y., 1996.

Saiving, Valerie. "Androcentrism in Religious Studies." *Journal of Religion* 56, no. 2 (1976): 177–197.

Sered, Susan Starr. *Priestess, Mother, Sacred Sister: Religions Dominated by Women.* New York, 1994.

Sharma, Arvind, ed. *Women in World Religions.* Albany, N.Y., 1987.

Sharma, Arvind, ed. *Religion and Women.* Albany, N.Y., 1994a.

Sharma, Arvind, ed. *Today's Woman in World Religions.* Albany, N.Y., 1994b.

Sharma, Arvind, ed. *Methodology in Religious Studies: The Interface with Women's Studies.* New York, 2002.

Spretnak, Charlene. *Lost Goddesses of Early Greece: A Collection of Pre-Hellenic Myths.* Boston, 1981.

Starhawk. *The Spiral Dance: A Rebirth of the Ancient Religion of the Great Goddess.* San Francisco, 1979.

Stuart, Elizabeth. *Gay and Lesbian Theologies: Repetitions with Critical Difference.* Aldershot, U.K., 2003.

Walker, Alice. *In Search of Our Mothers' Gardens: Womanist Prose.* San Diego, Calif., 1983.

Warne, Randi R. "Toward a Brave New Paradigm: The Impact of Women's Studies on Religious Studies." *Religious Studies and Theology* 9, nos. 2–3 (1989): 35–46.

Warne, Randi R. "(En)gendering Religious Studies." *Studies in Religion/Sciences Religieuses* 27 (1998): 427–436.

Welch, Sharon D. *Communities of Resistance and Solidarity: A Feminist Theology of Liberation.* Maryknoll, N.Y., 1985.

Williams, Delores S. "The Color of Feminism." *Christianity and Crisis* 45, no. 7 (April 29, 1985): 164–165.

Williams, Delores S. *Sisters in the Wilderness: The Challenge of Womanist God-Talk.* Maryknoll, N.Y., 1993.

Woodhead, Linda. "Feminism and the Sociology of Religion: From Gender-Blindness to Gendered Difference." In *The Blackwell Companion to Sociology of Religion,* edited by Richard K. Fenn, pp. 67–84. Oxford, 2001.

Woodhead, Linda. "Women and Religion." In L. Woodhead et al., eds., *Religions in the Modern World: Traditions and Transformations,* edited by Linda Woodhead et al., pp. 332–356. London, 2002.

Young, Serinity, ed. *Encyclopedia of Women and World Religion.* 2 vols. New York, 1999.

JULIE CLAGUE (2005)

WŎNHYO (617–686), Buddhist philosopher and putative founder of the Pŏpsŏng (Dharma-Nature, also called Haedong) school of Korean Buddhist thought. Wŏnhyo is indisputably the greatest Buddhist exegete produced by the Silla kingdom's Buddhist tradition, if not Korea's premier philosopher of all time.

Wŏnhyo was born into the Sŏl clan, a tribal league of the Chinhae region of the southern Korean peninsula, which had been assimilated into the Silla aristocratic system *(yuktu p'um)* in the early years of the common era. After his ordination into the Buddhist order, Wŏnhyo and his close friend, Ŭisang (625–702), founder of the Korean Hwaŏm (Chin., Huayan) school, twice decided, we are told, to undertake a pilgrimage to China in order to study with the renowned Chinese translator Xuanzang (d. 664). On their first trip in 650 the two Silla pilgrims were arrested as spies by Koguryŏ border guards and spent several weeks in prison before being repatriated. During their second attempt in 661 it is said that the friends traveled to a port in the Paekche region, where they hoped to board a ship bound for the mainland. Forced by a heavy downpour to spend the night in what they thought was an earthen sanctuary, they learned the next morning that it was actually an ancient tomb littered with human skulls. Marveling at his mind's ability to transform a thoroughly gruesome site into a comfortable haven, Wŏnhyo realized his world was created by the mind alone. His enlightenment rendered his planned pilgrimage to China unnecessary, and he returned to his home country to undertake a life of writing, preaching, and proselytizing. Sometime during his career, a liaison with a widowed princess led to the birth of a son, Sŏl Ch'ong (c. late sixth to early seventh century), who developed the Idu system of transcribing Korean, the first indigenous writing system used on the peninsula. Along with lecturing on Buddhism to the Silla aristocracy, which had only recently (and grudgingly) converted to the religion, Wŏnhyo also traveled among the peasant populace, instructing them with popular songs and verses. Hence, Wŏnhyo's prodigious efforts at proselytism helped to cement Buddhism's place as the national religion of Korea during the early years of the Unified Silla period (668–935).

Wŏnhyo was a prolific writer and commentator, authoring some one hundred works, of which over twenty are still extant. His interests ran the gamut of Buddhist materials then available in East Asia, from Mādhyamika, to Yogācāra, to Pure Land. Wŏnhyo played a major role in introducing to the Korean intelligentsia to Buddhist scriptures and commentaries, which, prior to his time had been virtually nonexistent in Silla. Wŏnhyo was the first Korean Buddhist to attempt to reconcile the disparate teachings of Chinese and Indian Buddhist philosophy, in particular the Mādhyamika and Yogācāra traditions. In his commentaries he eschewed the explication of scriptures according to the hermeneutics of any particular school; rather, he attempted to reveal the unifying principle, the "one mind," that vivified each of those texts. In one of his principal works devoted to his synthetic philosophy, *Simmun hwajaengnon* (Ten approaches to the reconciliation of doctrinal controversy), Wŏnhyo states that his fundamental intent is to harmonize the differences that characterize the various schools of Buddhist philosophy and merge their views into two all-inclusive perspectives. These were, first, the dependent origination approach *(saenggi-mun),* in which the myriads of qualities were shown to be the products of a perdurable causal process, and, second, the return to the source approach *(kwiwŏn-mun),* in which all such phenomenal characteristics were abandoned so that one could return to their ultimate source, the one mind. This dichotomy is seen, with slight variations, in many of Wŏnhyo's writings.

Perhaps Wŏnhyo's most influential works were his commentaries to the *Tasheng qixin lun* (Awakening of faith in Mahāyāna) and the *Huayan jing* (Skt., *Avataṃsaka Sūtra, Flower Garland Sūtra*). In the former commentary, Wŏnhyo outlines a four-stage soteriology—from nonenlightenment, to apparent enlightenment, advanced enlightenment, and finally ultimate enlightenment—that demonstrates how ordinary persons can hope to achieve spiritual liberation. Both of these texts had such a profound effect on the philosophical development of Fazang (643–712), the systematizer of the Chinese Huayan school of Buddhist thought, that Wŏnhyo is now considered to be an important vaunt-courier of that school. Wŏnhyo's many outlines *(chongyo)* to Buddhist sūtras also sought to treat those texts in terms that would result in fraternal harmony rather than sectarian controversy. The synthetic tendencies in Wŏnhyo's thought were to inspire all future Korean Buddhist writers and establish doctrinal synthesis as the hallmark of the Korean Buddhist tradition. It is for this reason that Wŏnhyo is traditionally regarded as the founder of the synthetic Pŏpsŏng school, one of the five Buddhist scholastic schools of the mature Silla tradition.

SEE ALSO Buddhism, article on Buddhism in Korea; Fazang; Huayan; Ŭisang.

BIBLIOGRAPHY

Buswell, Robert E., Jr. *The Formation of Ch'an Ideology in China and Korea: The Vajrasamādhi-Sūtra, a Buddhist Apocryphon.* Princeton, 1989. Chapters two and three discuss Wŏnhyo's life and thought.

Buswell, Robert E., Jr. "Hagiographies of the Korean Monk Wŏnhyo." In *Buddhism in Practice,* edited by Donald S. Lopez, Jr., pp. 553–562. Princeton, 1995.

Hong, Jung-shik. "The Thought and Life of Wŏnhyo." In *Buddhist Culture in Korea,* pp. 15–30. Seoul, 1982.

Koh, Ik-jin. "Wŏnhyo's Hua-yen Thought." *Korea Journal* 23, no. 8 (August 1983): 30–33.

Nam, Dong-shin. "Wŏnhyo's Ilsim Philosophy and Mass Proselytization Movement." *Seoul Journal of Korean Studies* 8 (1995): 143–162.

Rhi, Ki-yong. "Wŏnhyo and His Thought." *Korea Journal* 11, no. 1 (January 1971): 4–9.

ROBERT EVANS BUSWELL, JR. (1987 AND 2005)

WORD SEE LANGUAGE; LOGOS

WORK.

Once, at the dawn of creation, in the Golden Age, when earth and sky were conjoined (or when there was only sky), when only children, or the first human pair, inhabited the world, there was no "work." Only God, or the gods, worked their divine eternal play, the uncompelled sport of inexhaustible creativity. Only the primordial smith, the primal maker, seeded or molded the earth as archetypal sower or first craftsman. The fruits of the earth were available to all.

The world range of the myth indicates the universality of the theme. In ancient narratives from the Vedic, Greek, and Judeo-Christian traditions, from Africa, from North and South America, the subsequent fall from this paradisiacal state is widely associated on the one hand with some false move or a human choice based on some petty, selfish desire and on the other with the plunge into the *condition humaine*—nakedness, the loss of immortality, the withdrawal of the sky, the opening of Pandora's box of woes, the cycle of birth and death, and the sentence to hard labor for life.

The tale is compelling on several counts. Most people experience lack of ease in their endeavors—as Marsilio Ficino notes in a letter on the work of the mind (*Epistolae* 2.1), they seem to be rolling the stone of Sisyphus up the steep slopes of the mountain—and wish to find rest. Equally it can be argued that on some level everyone, even the unemployed, the idle rich, and the thief, is working at something and longs to find fulfillment in that work. Indeed, the history of labor, from Adam and Eve to the arts (or, by extension, to the most advanced technology), is literally the history of humankind.

At the same time, myth provides the notion of a deeper level of universality: The sentence to work symbolizes humanity's physicality in the world in the sense its separation from the divine, the cosmic, the natural. From this breach follows all suffering and toil. Significantly, in some versions of the story the point is made that in fact some form of work was originally designated for human beings. The *Book of Genesis,* for instance, indicates that Adam was first placed in the garden to work (or till) and keep it (2:15; cf. 2:5); only after the Fall is there talk of toil or suffering *('itstsavon)* and the sweat of the brow. Similarly, according to a common African theme God originally meant the world to be a tilled garden, with no bloodshed, work, or sorrow. Depicting a reversed sequence of the human encounter with toil and ease, ancient Chinese myth relates that the primal figure Gun labored in vain to tame the great flood; only his son Yu, by going with the flow of things, was able to complete the task and make the earth suitable for cultivation. A distinct line is drawn between the first human participation in divine work—the easy yoke of conformance to the cosmic order—and the labor under which humans burden. In the words of the Hebrew scriptures, this is the heathen world of the "work of men's hands" (*Dt.* 4:28, *2 Kgs.* 19:18, *Is.* 2:8), the cosmos bereft of hierophany. It is a treadmill on which humans are bound to do it all themselves, including the manufacture of their own clay gods.

PHYSICAL WORK. Removed from sacred context, human activity is in itself simply neutral bodily movement. Whether the task is slopping the pigs or pushing papers around in a corporate office, work may be experienced as exhausting or, if the natural and efficient operation of the body is discovered, it may be felt as easy, enjoyable, even rewarding, at least up to the point when muscle fatigue or mental torpor takes over. But work unrelated to any higher meaning threatens to inspire the "work ethic" that so fascinated Max Weber: Labor itself becomes the end of life, at best valorized as the worship of accomplishment, success, or physical prowess, at worst crystallized into a nightmare of the most menial physical chores, undertaken in a tortured attempt to keep one's own body (and perhaps the body of one's immediate family) alive "between a sterile earth and an uncontrollable sky" (Agee, 1960, p. 325).

By contrast, esoteric traditions in both primal myth and organized mystical discipline assign human activity to a hierarchy of levels among which physical human bodies constitute only the most readily discernible plane. Transcending that plane is the world of the mind, which has its own work and rest; beyond that, the realm of the inner self, or spiritual being. Within this context, religious work is the actualization of principle through action, to be realized on all three levels.

Physical work may be taken as a starting point of experience, since one has to begin where one is: in the physical world. But bodily work serves as a metaphor for work on some other level, as in the New Testament parables about laborers, or in this passage by the Palestinian tanna Ṭarfon: "The day is short, and the work is great, and the laborers are sluggish, and the reward is much, and the Master is urgent" (*Avot* 2.20, cited in *Sayings of the Fathers*, New York, 1945, p. 43). The performance of physical work may even be experienced as metaphor, as when sweeping the floor is taken as a spiritual task and becomes a means of revelation (cleansing myself, or the face of God).

Religiously viewed, physical work serves outwardly to maintain the world, in the sense of renewing its structure (maintaining the order of the cosmos) or in the simple sense of paying creation back for the life than one has received as a gift. Both work itself, as a reflection of the primal structuring of the world, and the cycles of rest that punctuate it are ways of acknowledging the creative source as supreme. The injunction to serve the earth directly, to earn one's daily bread literally, is an expression of this inexorable law of just returns. It is honored by the apostle Paul ("If any would not work, neither should he eat"; *2 Thes.* 3:10), the Chan master Hyakujo ("No work, no food"; in Paul Reps, *Zen Flesh, Zen Bones*, New York, 1957, p. 70), and Gandhi in his invocation of the *Bhagavadgītā* 3.12 ("He who eats without offering the sacrifice eats stolen food"). Since the world itself is based on sacrifice (the supreme deity's creation of everything from nothing, or from his own substance), "this body, therefore, has been given us, only in order that we may serve all Creation with it" (Gandhi, 1960, p. 12). This fullhearted acceptance of the human condition as a call to labor in the sweat of one's face may be the supreme act of obeisance (the Ṣūfī servant of God prostrate in the dust of the desert), or it may be an act of total obedience in penance for the original sin of disobedience, as Simone Weil proposed (Weil, 1952).

In another view, physical work expresses the primary function of the human being among all creatures: Humans are enjoined to subdue the earth and thus to reassert the hierarchical order of creation. At the same time, work subdues the earth of the human body, as anyone who has engaged in extended physical exertion will testify. Not only Western monastics but the Eastern Fathers as well called for severe labor (along with weeping) as ascetic practice. The early Shakers (for whom the terms *work* and *worship* were as synonymous as they were for the Benedictines) called their frenzied exercises *laboring* and communally shook off their physicality to the tune of such songs as *The Zealous Laborer* ("Oh, how I long to be released / from every feeling of the beast"). Yet consciously applied physical work is more than simple mortification of the flesh. It can be a strengthening, cleansing, a temporary bypass of the usual, interfering complex of mental associations, comparable to any other form of meditation.

MENTAL WORK. In an essay that serves to define work at the mental level, Simone Weil reflected that the purpose of academic study is ultimately to "help form . . . the habit of that attention which is the substance of prayer" (Weil, 1973, p. 108). From the view of esoteric tradition, the function of mental work is to direct activity to the level of spirit (or the harmonious universe, or the gods). This is accomplished, first, by practicing a condition of attention at rest in which physical or intellectual activity can proceed naturally, and second, by deliberately dedicating the activity to the sacred realm. The outward work may be offered for the welfare of all (the bodhisattva's vow) or to the god or goddess in charge of the specific field of endeavor; or its fruits may be sacrificed to the supreme self. By this direction of attention or intention, outward work of whatever kind is acknowledged to be sacred or construed as living prayer in the sense of the Christian monastics' *laborare est orare* or what the Tibetan monk

Chögyam Trungpa has called "meditation in action." Such mental work serves the heart of orthodox spiritual praxis, which decrees all activity to be valorized at every moment by dint of its relationship to the divine and all work to have for its goal the realization of one's natural being. This is the alchemical *opus* of transformation to a higher state.

SPIRITUAL WORK. Preparation for the spiritual event of self-realization is traditionally the only real work there is. It demands the most stringent of efforts, calling as it does for the elimination of such obstacles as egocentrism and attachment to results and the abandonment of compulsive human activity (the attempt to make things go as one would like them to). In the Ṣūfī classic *Manṭiq al-ṭayr* (The conference of the birds) Farīd al-Dīn ʿAṭṭār warns that on the path to God "a hundred difficulties will assail you. . . . You will have to make great efforts. . . . The Spiritual Way reveals itself only in the degree to which the traveller has overcome his faults and weaknesses, his sleep and his inertia, and each will approach nearer to his aim according to his effort" (trans. Nott, New York, 1954, pp. 98, 107).

Yet it is in keeping with the mystical paradox that whenever this spiritual effort is encountered consciously, the outward effort is negated. When the simple working of the laws of nature are perceived through attention, experienced as my own nature, and allowed to act unimpeded by personal interference, work on any level becomes "not doing," "nonaction," "inaction." In the words of Zhuangzu, "The mind of a perfect man is like a mirror. It grasps nothing. It expects nothing. It reflects but does not hold. Therefore, the perfect man can act without effort" (trans. Watson). Similarly, the *Dao de jing* refers repeatedly to the sage who works without doing; the *Bhagavadgita* states that "the knower of truth, seated in the Self, thinks 'I do nothing at all, though seeing, hearing, touching, smelling, eating, going, sleeping, breathing, speaking, letting go, grasping, opening and closing the eyes' "(5.8f).

Nondoing is an entirely pragmatic matter, as witnessed even by the dry psychological records of Mihaly Csikszentmihalyi's "flow experience" reports, descriptions of moments in which subjects engaged fullheartedly in activity have experienced a release from habitual limitations and the work is seen to "flow by itself." "The secret of power," wrote Emerson, "is delight in one's work. . . . Place yourself in the stream of power and wisdom which animates all whom it floats, and you are without effort compelled to truth, to right and a perfect contentment." The arts have been classically sacralized in this sense, of course. The spirit of the Shaker craftsmen no less than that of medieval scribes fostered an atmosphere of meditative stillness in which the direction of the work would present itself effortlessly in the moment of the creative act. Similarly, Simone Weil's statement that "attention consists of suspending our thought, leaving it detached, empty, and ready to be penetrated by the object" has the ring of an instruction in Zen art. In a frequently translated passage from Zhuangzu, Prince Wenhui learns the art of life from his cook, who explains his observation of the Dao in carving up an ox: There are natural spaces through which the blade simply passes, and the carcass falls apart of itself.

Surely this is the message of Jesus' invitation "Come unto me, ye that labor and are heavy laden, and I will give you rest" (*Mt.* 11:28). If the Dao can arise in the interstices between a cleaver blade and the joint of the bullock, why not in the space between an iron and a shirtsleeve, or between an editor's blue pencil and the manuscript page? In that space, work itself literally constitutes rest, earth and sky are conjoined, and the sentence of human work resolves back into its source, becomes what it has always been in reality: God's work, the play of his creation.

SEE ALSO Art and Religion; Attention; Fall, The; Golden Age; Shabbat.

BIBLIOGRAPHY

The richness of the subject is hardly matched by the number of works that directly address it at any length. Dennis Clark's *Work and the Human Spirit* (New York, 1967) offers a very general sociocultural discussion from the Christian view. Etymological considerations are well served by Klaus R. Grinda's study *Arbeit und Mühe: Untersuchungen zur Bedeutungsge-schichte altenglischer Wörter* (Munich, 1975), which demonstrates that words in English meaning "work" and those meaning "effort, labor, suffering" stem from entirely separate semantic fields. Readers who wish to address the theme of sacred and profane meanings of work may be moved by James Agee's intense, poetic vision of physical toil at a level utterly bereft of sacrality; see the section "Work" in Agee and Walker Evans's *Let Us Now Praise Famous Men* (1941; Boston, 1960), pp. 319–325.

Max Weber's *The Protestant Ethic and the Spirit of Capitalism* (1958; New York, 1976) presents his classic interpretation of the development of the "work ethic" of modern capitalism through the influence of ascetic Protestant doctrine. Gandhi's plea for widespread commitment to "bread labor" as a service to creation is offered in a small collection of his published statements and newspaper essays, *Bread Labour: The Gospel of Work* (Ahmedabad, 1960). For a document of the Catholic view of work, see the encyclical *Laborem exercens* from the pen of John Paul II, published as *On Human Work* (Washington, D.C., 1981). Much of the discussion is devoted to social-humane issues, but see pages 9–15 and the section "Elements for a Spirituality of Work" on pages 53–60.

Simone Weil's *The Need for Roots* (1952; New York, 1971) presents her vision of physical labor as simultaneously the most torturous "subjection to matter" and the most transcendent human activity. Her wonderful essay "Reflections on the Right Use of School Studies with a View to the Love of God," in *Waiting for God* (1951; New York, 1973), pp. 105–116, offers profound insights regarding attention in work at any level. The same volume includes a brief discussion of physical work on page 170.

Finally, two books explore in depth the theme of craft as a way of self-knowledge: Carla Needleman's *The Work of Craft* (New York, 1979) and D. M. Dooling's *A Way of Working: The Spiritual Dimension of Craft* (New York, 1979), a collection of essays by various hands.

New Sources

Fox, Matthew. *The Reinvention of Work: A New Vision of Livelihood for Our Time.* San Francisco, 1994.

His Holiness the Dalai Lama and Howard Cutler. *The Art of Happiness at Work.* New York, 2003.

Schnall, David. *By the Threat of Your Brow: Reflections on Work and the Workplace in Jewish Thought.* New York, 1991.

Volf, Miroslav. *Work in the Spirit: Toward a Theology of Work.* New York, 1991.

KAREN READY (1987)
Revised Bibliography

WORLD RELIGIONS. There are three overlapping yet divergent senses in which the term *world religions* is commonly used today. In its broadest sense, it is shorthand for the "religions of the world," that is, any religion that currently exists or formerly existed somewhere in the world. The emphasis, however, tends to be on extant religions rather than those that flourished in the past, and in this connotation another often favored synonym is "living religions" or "living faiths." In the second, somewhat more restrictive and evaluative sense, only a certain number of religions is meant: usually, "the major religions of the world," meaning the type of religions that can claim to have played a distinct and significant role in the historical process of a nation or a region, or the type of religions that purportedly have had universal aspirations and an appeal that transcends the limits of a particular locality or ethnic group. Thirdly, especially when the term appears in the context of an academic curriculum, course title, book title, and so on, *world religions* is often adopted expressly to signal that the subject matter covered therein is not limited to Christianity, the Biblical tradition, or the so-called Judeo-Christian perspective, but is inclusive of all or many other religions. Whichever sense of the term is meant, it is far more frequently used in the plural form than in the singular. In fact, the cardinal presupposition underlying the concept of world religions is the multiplicity of religion; it is predicated on the idea that *religion* is a genus comprising many species, and that Christianity, for example, is but one of them. This idea, though a truism nowadays, is distinctly modern, if not to say altogether unprecedented in the history of the West.

Although regularly mentioned in scholarly tracts as well as in nonscholarly media, *world religions* is not a technical term. There has been little critical discussion of the concept or its history; nor is there an established definition agreed upon by religion specialists. The term itself originated in certain academic contexts of the nineteenth century, and it was indeed a matter of considerable scholarly debate among European scientists and theologians then, but those arguments are now largely forgotten and further obscured by contemporary usage, which appears to take little account of past concerns. It is therefore best to understand that the meaning of this term at present is largely determined by conventional practice rather than by any scholarly consensus or rigorous analytic considerations. At the same time, the notion of world religions can be shown to have a complex historical relation to some earlier conceptual schemes for delineating the variety of religious traditions, schemes that it presumably has replaced.

Until the early decades of the nineteenth century, a well-established convention going back to the Middle Ages had been to divide the world population into four groups: Christians, Jews, Muḥammadans (as Muslims were commonly called then), and, finally, those others who were attached to countless varieties of idolatry (also called pagans, heathens, or polytheists). This four-part classification implied, however, not a recognition of four distinct religions as we think of them now, but a division of the world's nations into, first, the correctly faithful believers in the true and only God (i.e., Christians of various sorts), then two major groups with errant or heretical opinions and attitudes toward God (Jews and Muḥammadans), and then the rest, who were altogether ignorant of God and therefore paid inappropriate reverence to various substitute objects, or idols. In effect, in this frame of mind, there was only one religion—the true one—and others were various ways of straying from it. The plurality of religions presupposed by the concept of world religions, therefore, came as a sea change in the way in which Europeans thought about themselves—understood first and foremost as Christendom—and about their relation to the rest of the world.

ORIGIN AND EARLY USES OF THE TERM. The coinage of the term *world religion*—in German, *Weltreligion*—was probably not unrelated to the advent of similar terms, such as *world history* (*Weltgeschichte*, a concept especially associated with G. W. F. Hegel) and *world literature* (*Weltliteratur*, associated with Goethe), which began to circulate in the early nineteenth century. Whatever this relation may have been, there is little doubt that the term originated in German. In summarizing the nineteenth-century controversy over the notion of world religions, the Dutch historian of religion P. D. Chantepie de la Saussaye, in his *Manual of the Science of Religion* (1891, p. 54), credibly notes that the word was first introduced by Johann Sebastian von Drey in 1827. A prominent German Catholic theologian and cofounding editor of the *Tübingen Theological Quarterly*, Drey in that year published in this journal a two-part article entitled "Von der Landesreligion und der Weltreligion" (loosely translated, "on the religion of a country and the religion of the world"), wherein he argued that the Christian Church, in its true catholicity, was an institution pertaining to what was universally human, and as such it differed fundamentally from the cult of any particular nation. In effect, *world religion* was the term he applied uniquely and exclusively to Christianity (*Christentum*), in contradistinction from all the indigenous religions of Europe and elsewhere, roundly called paganism or heathenism (*Heidentum*). What is significant here, therefore, is not only the appearance of the term—albeit in the singular—but also the pairing of *world religion* with its presumed other, *Landesreligion,* or, literally, "religion of the land," meaning "religion of a country," or more commonly, "national religion."

Half a century later, this pairing of terms was to acquire further significance in the context of a debate among certain Dutch and German scholars. The debate had to do with the distinction between two supposedly different *types* of religion: purportedly "universalistic" religions on the one hand and religions that were said to be ethnically, nationally, or racially particular on the other. Meanwhile, the most pertinent development in the intervening decades was the European "discovery" of Buddhism. As Philip Almond has shown in *The British Discovery of Buddhism* (1988), it was only in the course of the nineteenth century that Europeans came to believe that: (1) that certain traditions of ritual practice and cultic observance, philosophic systems, legends, and clerical institutions found in various parts of Asia actually constituted a single religion; (2) the essential identity of these greatly divergent and diffuse phenomena could be traced back to a particular historical moment and location in northern India, indeed, to a specific historical personage who lived several centuries before Jesus of Nazareth; and (3) the successful dissemination of this religion in Asia was such that it either rivaled or possibly surpassed Christianity in the size of its adherents. Among the ramifications of this understanding of Buddhism as a distinct religion was a sudden awareness that there was another religion in some way comparable to Christianity. Like Christianity, which grew out of an older religion unique to the ancient Israelites, it was thought that Buddhism grew out of Hinduism (more commonly called Brahmanism then), the quintessential religion of India. Buddhism, too, supposedly began as a reform movement initiated by an extraordinary but historical figure, Gautama, bearing a moral message and spiritual appeal to all humanity. Like Christianity, it was also observed, Buddhism disappeared eventually from the land of its origin but spread swiftly beyond national, ethnic, and regional boundaries, not to mention among people of different social strata. In effect, European scholars came to recognize in Buddhism a second world religion, though this did not necessarily lead them to relinquish the claim for the unique and absolute superiority of Christianity.

The discovery of Buddhism was among the most important achievements of the European scholarship on India, which had gained momentum since Sir William Jones's celebrated pronouncements in 1786 suggesting the affinity—and hence the likely commonality of origin—between the classical languages of India and of Europe. This was to be the basis of the idea of the Indo-European (or Aryan) language family, a group of related languages purportedly characterized and distinguished from other groups by the purity of their grammatical form (i.e., inflection). This idea helped redefine Europeanness, aligning Europe with ancient India and Persia, while separating it from the Semitic (those who spoke languages allegedly marred by "imperfect inflection," exemplified by Arabic and Hebrew), as well as from all the rest—that is, the speakers of the noninflectional (or agglutinative) languages of Asia and Africa. In the course of the nineteenth century these groupings of languages became increasingly understood not only in the linguistic sense, but also in an ethnic and, finally, a racial sense. In view of the newly emergent idea of Aryan Europe and, concomitantly, the possible ancestral relation to the "noble race" ("Arya") of ancient India, the recognition of Buddhism as a world religion had implications far beyond the technical question of how to classify religions of the world.

The question of religious versus racial identity was brought into even sharper focus by a related notion—also based on the new understanding of language groups—that Christianity, insofar as it began as one of the numerous Jewish sects, is Semitic in its historical origin, no less so than Islam and Judaism. This notion was at once intriguing and disturbing to many nineteenth-century Europeans who considered themselves Aryan yet claimed Christianity as their own, so much so that various theories were advanced implying that Christianity was only incidentally and tangentially related to the religion of the ancient Israelites. Some argued that Christianity grew not so much out of ancient Judaism as out of Panhellenism—that is, the widespread Greek culture of the Mediterranean world in late antiquity (for example, Emile Burnouf, *La Science des religions: Sa méthode et ses limites,* 2nd edition, 1872). Others propounded a theory of the Indian origin of Christianity (Louis Jacolliot, *La Bible dans l'Inde: Vie de Iezeus Christna,* 1869) or even went so far as to suggest that Christianity began in a community of Buddhist missionaries residing in Egypt (Arthur Lillie, *Buddhism in Christendom, or, Jesus, the Essene,* 1887).

Although these enormously popular nineteenth-century speculations have been largely discredited by mainstream scholarship, it is important to remember that such efforts to Hellenize and Aryanize Christianity and to separate it from its presumed Semitic parentage was not unrelated to the new recognition of Buddhism as a world religion, and, moreover, to the understanding that Buddhism was an Aryan religion in its essential beginning, though now extant only among the non-Aryan nations of eastern Asia in its various corrupted forms. At the same time, Islam—the powerful domain of an alien religion well known to European Christians for centuries—came to be increasingly represented as the religion of the Arabs, therefore, as a quintessentially Semitic religion. This opinion—which formed the basis of the argument that it was not a world religion—was held by some prominent scholars, despite the widely acknowledged fact that the great majority of Muslims, then as now, were not Arabs.

These newly emergent trends of thought were largely implicit, and yet essential to the scholarly debate about world religions that took place in the 1870s and 1880s. The scholars who engaged in this debate appear to have been uniformly of the opinion that Buddhism, in addition to Christianity, was a world religion, thus differing in their conception of the term from that of Drey half a century earlier. The controversy was above all over the status of Islam. Some scholars counted, as a matter of course, Christianity, Buddhism, and Islam as world religions (presumably on the grounds that all three were major religions, each with a transnational spread, thus de facto demonstrating their "universalistic" aspirations and capabilities); other scholars, however, strenuously maintained that Islam was not a world religion but instead quintessentially a national religion specific to the Arabs, that it was adopted by non-Arabs only for extraneous political reasons or because it was imposed upon them by force (see Kuenen, 1882; Pfleiderer, 1907). These contentious arguments led some others to question the cogency of distinguishing world religions from national religions in the first place, and to mitigate the earlier claims for the scientific usefulness of these categories (see Rauwenhoff, 1885; Tiele, 1885; Jastrow, 1901).

There was no clear resolution to the debate in the end; rather, it appears that the matter was decided by default. For, by the early decades of the twentieth century, when the use of the term *world religions* in the plural became well established, it was simply taken for granted that Christianity, Buddhism, and Islam were world religions. Ernst Troeltsch, for example, in his essay entitled "The Place of Christianity among the World Religions" (1923), named all three as world religions without any explanation. More fundamentally, the demarcation between *world religions* and *national religions* was effectively undermined, as the latter category dropped out of use entirely.

Perhaps no one was more instrumental in making this turn definitive and authoritative than Max Weber. In the last decade of his life, he undertook an ambitious multivolume project under the general title *The Economic Ethic of the World Religions* (*Wirtschaftsethik der Weltreligionen*), which remained unfinished at the time of his death in 1920. As can be discerned from his introductory essay of the same name, originally published independently in 1915, he treated *world religions* strictly as a conventional nomenclature referring to the major religions of the world, and he included Hinduism and Confucianism in the list; in addition, he found it necessary to consider in the same context "Ancient Judaism," though he stopped short of naming it a bona fide world religion. Weber was of the opinion that any numerically substantial or otherwise significant religion was of interest precisely because of its uniquely characteristic ethos, each specific to the history and culture of a particular people. Put differently, all of those Weber called "world religions" were, in his view, what nineteenth-century scholars called "national religions."

ADAPTATION OF THE TERM IN ENGLISH. The use of the term *world religions* in English most probably began with its appearance in C. P. Tiele's article "Religions," published in the ninth edition of the *Encyclopaedia Britannica* (1885). This was a rather literal translation of the term *wereldgodsdiensten* from his native Dutch; for, until then and sometime thereafter, the usual translation of *wereldgodsdiensten* and *Weltreligionen* was either "universal religions" or, as Tiele himself sometimes preferred, "universalistic religions." Although the nineteenth-century Dutch and German scholarly debate over the notion of world religions did not extend to the English-speaking world, it was known among the scholars (Jastrow, 1901, pp. 122–123), and perhaps more importantly, a parallel distinction between what continental European scholars called "national religions" and "world religions" had been drawn under different names. To cite two of the most prominent examples, the renowned Christian socialist and progressive Anglican Frederick Denison Maurice published his Boyle Lectures under the title *The Religions of the World and Their Relations to Christianity* (1847). He argued that, although all religions purported to unite and encompass all humankind in their aspiration to rise above the merely human, only Christianity actually achieved this goal, and that all other "religions of the world" were but melancholy testimonies to the impossibility of fulfilling their ideals on their own terms. In short, in his view, Christianity alone accounted for the whole, and was therefore universal, while all other religions were limited and particularistic. A second example is from across the Atlantic: the distinguished Unitarian minister James Freeman Clarke of Boston published a series of articles in 1868—issued in 1871 in a single volume as *Ten Great Religions: An Essay in Comparative Theology* and reprinted many times—where he drew the same distinction between the truly universal religion, which he termed "catholic religion," namely Christianity, and all the rest, which he called "ethnic religions."

It was in this sense of "universal religion" that the term *world religion*, in the singular, first came to be used by certain Anglophone theologians toward the end of the nineteenth century. John Henry Barrows—an American Presbyterian minister who served as the president of the World Parliament of Religions in 1893—lectured in India under the title "Christianity, the World-Religion" (1897), signaling his conviction that Christianity alone was the truly universal religion. Similarly, William Fairfield Warren—the occupant of arguably the first chair of comparative religion at an American university and later president of Boston University—gave the same appellation to Christianity when he wrote *The Religions of the World and the World-Religion* (1892). Far from being a synonym for "religions of the world," then, for these authors, *world-religion* (in both cases hyphenated) signified one unique religion, their own, which, in their opinion, happened to be universally viable. In effect, they viewed the contrast between Christianity and all other religions as Maurice and Clarke had, and at the same time, their usage of the term *world-religion* was consistent with Drey's original sense of *Weltreligion*.

It is difficult to determine with certainty how this exclusivist or Christian supremacist connotation of *world-religion* came to be displaced or overridden by the other pluralistic use of the term assumed by Tiele and others, or, for that matter, how the novel theory originating in the scientific discourse of continental Europe—suggesting, specifically, that Buddhism at least should be regarded as a world religion in addition to Christianity—was first received in the English-speaking world generally. As it happened in the German-speaking world, the claim for the "uniquely universal" status of Christianity eventually became less pronounced in the notion of world religion(s), while the other, seemingly indifferent sense of the term, comprising any numerically significant religions, eventually prevailed.

It was during the decades between the two world wars that the use of the term *world religions*, as well as the standard list of about a dozen religions so designated, became conventional. What is remarkable about this turn of events is, first, the relatively precipitous establishment of the convention, and secondly, its unchallenged stability to this day. It is also striking that the rhetorical emphasis shifted, suddenly turning to what was regarded as current, alive, and immediately present, whereas during the nineteenth century all of the non-Christian religions—with the conspicuous and ever troublesome exception of Islam—were represented as bygone religions, as fossil-like remnants of "ancient," "archaic," "defunct," or "past" religions that had been superceded by the coming of Christ.

Since the beginning of the early twentieth century, then, there has been a list of world religions that could be called standard or customary, albeit with some individual variations—some addition, subtraction, further division, or merging. The typical list almost invariably includes Christianity, Buddhism, Islam, Hinduism, and Judaism; it also frequently identifies Confucianism, Daoism, and Shintō (at times grouped together as "Chinese and Japanese religions" or "East Asian religions"), as well as Parsiism (or Zoroastrianism), Jainism, and Sikhism.

In addition to these purportedly major religions, a typical world religions textbook or curriculum often includes discussion of traditions that are supposedly minor in scale, numbers, or world-historical significance. In earlier times, these minor traditions were often referred to as "savage" or "primitive" religions, though nowadays these appellations are generally avoided and variously replaced by "primal," "preliterate," "tribal," or even "basic" religions. The content of the category, under whatever name, has remained more or less constant; it refers to those cultic practices, mythic lore, and cosmologies that fall outside of the above-named major religions. Such small-scale religions are recognized generically as a type, and examples of this type are said to be found in profusion, particularly in Africa, the Americas, the Pacific islands, Oceania, Central and Southeast Asia, and other pockets of indigenous tribal life. Within this group, individual cases and examples are specified by their geographical location or by certain subcategories coined by European scholars in the eighteenth and nineteenth century, such as shamanism and animism. Whether these minor traditions en masse are treated as part of world religions or as constituting a category in addition to world religions depends on whether a given author defines the term *world religions* as "all religions of the world" or as "major religions." In any case, the supplementary status of "the rest" seems inevitably to have remained anomalous and problematic, thereby threatening the symmetry and stability of each classification system, whether it be the fourth category (idolaters) in the traditional system, that of national religions in the nineteenth-century scientific system, or the generic category of tribal religions among world religions in the system in use at the beginning of the twenty-first century.

See Also Comparative Religion; Study of Religion.

Bibliography

There has been little scholarly discussion or critical examination of the idea of *world religions*. Regarding the ideological implications of applying this concept to a specific geographical location, Timothy Fitzgerald considers the case of India in "Hinduism and the World Religion Fallacy," *Religion* 20 (1990): 101–118. Russell T. McCutcheon critiques an aspect of the current pedagogic practice of religious studies, as predicated on the notion of world religions, in *Manufacturing Religion: The Discourse on Sui Generis Religion and the Politics of Nostalgia* (New York, 1997). For an overall history of the idea of world religions, see Tomoko Masuzawa, *The Invention of World Religions* (Chicago, 2005).

It is important to consider this history in relation to the formation of the concept of religion(s) more generally, and for this purpose particularly informative are two articles by Jonathan Z. Smith, "Religion, Religions, Religious," in *Critical Terms for Religious Studies*, edited by Mark C. Taylor, pp. 269–284 (Chicago, 1998), and "Classification," in *Guide to the Study of Religion*, edited by Willi Braun and Russell T. McCutcheon, pp. 35–44 (London, 2000).

Historically, F. Max Müller has been regarded by many scholars as the progenitor of the science of religion and of the modern scholarly classification of religions, as delineated in his *Introduction to the Science of Religion* (London, 1873); it is all the more notable, then, that Müller expressly avoided engaging in the debate concerning the notion of world religions and that he never made use of the term. For critical discussions by his contemporaries of the category of world religions and systems of classification, the following texts may be consulted: C. P. Tiele, *Geschiedenis van den Godsdienst tot aan de heerschappij der Wereldgodsdiensten* (Leiden, 1876), translated by J. Estlin Carpenter as *Outlines of the History of Religion to the Spread of the Universal Religions* (London, 1877), as well as Tiele's entry, "Religions," in the ninth edition of the *Encyclopaedia Britannica* (Edinburgh, 1885); Abraham Kuenen, *Volksgodsdienst en Wereldgodsdienst* (1882), translated by P. H. Wicksteed as *National Religions and Universal Religions* (London, 1882); L. W. E. Rauwenhoff, "Wereldgodsdiensten" (in Dutch), *Theologisch Tijdschrift* 19 (1885): 1–33; P. D. Chantepie de la Saussaye, *Lehrbuch der Religionsgeschichte*, vol. 1 (Freiburg, Germany, 1887), translated by Beatrice S. Colyer-Furgusson as *Manual of the Science of Religion* (London, 1891); Maurice Vernes, *L'Histoire des religions; son espirit, sa méthode, et ses divisions, son enseignement en France et à l'etranger* (Paris, 1887); Morris Jastrow

Jr., *The Study of Religion* (New York, 1901); and Otto Pfleiderer, *Religion und Religionen* (Munich, 1906), translated by Daniel A. Huebsch as *Religion and Historic Faiths* (New York, 1907).

Regarding the earliest examples of texts employing the modern notion of world religions (though not necessarily adopting the term) and exhibiting more or less the same list of religions as is encountered today, the following were among the most renowned and authoritative: George Foot Moore, *History of Religions*, 2 vols. (New York, 1913–1919); Robert Ernest Hume, *The World's Living Religions: An Historical Sketch* (New York, 1924); and John Clark Archer, *Faiths Men Live By* (New York, 1934). Whereas nineteenth-century books, pamphlets, and lectures on the subject of world religions were often intended for future Christian missionaries and for others likewise seeking a confirmation of Christian superiority in comparison to other religions, the texts just mentioned are meant expressly for liberal arts college students and for the general public. In this connection, also noteworthy is what appears to be the first correspondence course in world religions and an early instance of a university extension enterprise based in Chicago. The textbook for the course—twelve monthly issues containing essays by prominent scholars, including Müller (Oxford), Jastrow (Pennsylvania), and Chantepie de la Saussaye (Amsterdam), among others, and edited by Edmund Buckley—is entitled *Universal Religion: A Course of Lessons, Historical and Scientific, on the Various Faiths of the World* (Chicago, 1897).

The earliest books that mention *world religions* in the title—in English and in the contemporary sense of the term—are Charles Samuel Braden's *Modern Tendencies in World Religions* (New York, 1933) and *Modern Trends in World-Religions*, edited by A. Eustace Haydon (Chicago, 1934).

Meanwhile, the extant portion of Max Weber's unfinished project, *Die Wirtschafisethik der Weltreligionen* (literally, *The Economic Ethic of the World Religions*), was published posthumously as *Gesammelte Aufsätze zur Religionssoziologie*, 3 vols. (Tübingen, Germany, 1921). The introductory essay by the same name as the overall project had been previously published independently in *Archiv für Sozialwissenschaft und Sozialpolitik* (1915); it has been translated as "The Social Psychology of the World Religions" and included in *From Max Weber: Essays in Sociology*, edited and translated by H. H. Gerth and C. Wright Mills (New York, 1946), pp. 267–301. Weber's most famous work, *The Protestant Ethic and the Spirit of Capitalism*, translated by Talcott Parsons (New York, 1930), constitutes but a segment of this massive project, as do three other monograph-length works by him that were separately published in English: *The Religion of China*, translated by Hans H. Gerth (New York, 1951); *Ancient Judaism*, translated by Hans H. Gerth and Don Martindale (New York, 1952); and *The Religion of India*, translated by Hans H. Gerth and Don Martindale (New York, 1958).

The subject of world religions in general gained much popularity in the English-speaking world in the second half of the twentieth century. In the decades following World War II, curricula for the secular study of religions proliferated, particularly in American colleges and universities. Concurrently, there appeared a number of texts that came to have enduring influence and that have undergone many reprints and revised editions. Those include *The Religions of Man* by Huston Smith (1st ed., New York, 1958); *The Concise Encyclopedia of Living Faiths*, edited by R. C. Zaehner (New York, 1959); *The Religious Experience of Mankind* by Ninian Smart (1st ed., New York, 1969); and *Religions of the World* by E. Geoffrey Parrinder (New York, 1971).

TOMOKO MASUZAWA (2005)

WORLD'S PARLIAMENT OF RELIGIONS.

Held in Chicago from September 11 to 18, 1893, in conjunction with the Columbian Exposition, the World's Parliament of Religions was a milestone in the history of interreligious dialogue, the study of world religions, and the impact of Eastern religious traditions on American culture. The parliament's several delegates from Asia were among the first authoritative representatives of their traditions to travel to the West. The earliest Vedāntist and Buddhist organizations in the United States to cater primarily to Westerners can be traced directly or indirectly to the conference and its delegates.

Though awakened by the "Yankee Hindoo" motif of New England transcendentalism during the early part of the nineteenth century and furthered by the educational efforts of the Theosophical Society (founded in New York in 1875), American interest in Eastern spirituality was enhanced by the publicity created by the conference. The number of courses in "comparative religion" at American colleges rose appreciably as a result of the event. At the same time the parliament provided an occasion for dialogue, enabling Christian apologists to present forceful counterarguments to those of their Eastern colleagues, linking faith in Christ with "progress" and moral superiority and justifying missionary endeavor. Indeed, while the parliament was undeniably liberal Protestant in tone, it was also a pioneering ecumenical event, international in scope. Roman Catholic and Jewish spokespeople took their places alongside representatives of those "mainstream" Protestant denominations that were, at that time, usually perceived as the dominant form of American religious life.

The idea of sponsoring a parliament of religions was proposed to the Columbian Exposition by Charles C. Bonney (1831–1903), a civic leader and devout layman of the Swedenborgian Church; his role could be said to epitomize the rising influence of the laity in American religion at the time. Paul Carus (1852–1919), the Open Court Press editor and publisher, influential through his early introduction of Eastern classics to Western readers, was also an active promoter of the event. The leadership of the parliament itself, however, was clerical—preeminently in the person of John Henry Barrows (1847–1902), a prominent Chicago Presbyterian minister.

Nonetheless, the most lasting impression at the conference was made by three colorful, articulate representatives of

Hinduism and Buddhism: Swami Vivekananda (1863–1902), Anagārika Dharmapāla (1864–1933), and Shaku Sōen (1859–1919). Vivekananda, a disciple of the saintly Ramakrishna Paramahaṃsa (1836–1886), was the founder of the Ramakrishna Mission, which has planted outposts of intellectual Hinduism (frequently known as Vedanta Societies) throughout the West. Dharmapāla, a Singhalese reformer, was the founder of the Maha Bodhi Society, which aimed at revitalizing and promoting Buddhism in dialogue with modern thought; the society came to have a great deal of interaction with Western Buddhists. Shaku, a Japanese Zen priest, was particularly influential through his students, who included the first Zen monks to settle in America (a decade or so later) and the layman D. T. Suzuki (1870–1966), whose books have done much to introduce Zen to the West.

The parliament was not without difficulty or dissent. Islam was inadequately represented; the participation of Roman Catholics sparked much controversy within their church; and many conservative Protestants were horrified by the entire project. The gathering's coincidental connection with the American "triumphalism" of the Columbian Exposition, in the heyday of Western expansion, sent a strangely ambiguous message. But the parliament's American fruits, in the form of both increased academic study of world religion and non-Western religious presences in America, foreshadowed the religious pluralism of the twentieth century and remain visible in the twenty-first.

At the same time, non-Western delegates like Vivekananda (though often seen by conservative coreligionists as too prone to universalism and modernism) became key promoters of reform within their own faiths. Moreover, the parliament was viewed by nationalists as legitimating their homeland's spiritual culture against colonialism, and so played a role in the cultural and, ultimately, political renaissance of nations like India and Sri Lanka.

In 1993, on the centenary of the first parliament, a second Parliament of the World's Religions (apart from one or two smaller interreligious events called congresses or parliaments) brought some six thousand attendees to Chicago. The effects of a hundred years were evident. Among the most conspicuous delegates were Tibetan Buddhists, Western Neopagans, and Native Americans, all unrepresented in 1893. The distinguished student of American religious pluralism Diana Eck noted in a major address that when Swami Vivekananda came to Chicago there were no known Hindus in that city, while in 1993 some twenty Hindu temples served the Chicago area. The same was true also with Buddhism, Islam, and other religions once mysterious to most Americans.

The twentieth-century event was far more participatory than the earlier one, despite the dramatic opening procession in 1893. The halls of the hotel in which the 1993 event was held echoed with the sounds of chants, gongs, drums, and prayers as well as speeches. This parliament focused not only on getting acquainted but also on the application of the world's religious energies to the world's problems. A parliamentary document, "Toward a Global Ethic," called on the planet's spiritual leaders to work assiduously toward universal justice, peace, nonviolence, and ecological awareness. The major address at the closing ceremony was given by the Dalai Lama, who urged the implementation of these values.

For all that, it cannot be said that the 1993 parliament had the impact of the first. It was but one voice and one interreligious experience among many in the late-twentieth-century world, whereas the first parliament in a real sense created, or epitomized, a new era in world spiritual interaction.

A third Parliament of the World's Religions, inspired by the second, was held in Cape Town, South Africa, in December 1999. While inspiring for the some six thousand attendees, it too was of less historical significance than the first.

See Also Ramakrishna; Suzuki, D. T.; Vivekananda.

Bibliography

Barrows, John Henry, ed. *The World's Parliament of Religions.* 2 vols. Chicago, 1893. Original publication of parliament talks and papers.

Seager, Richard Hughes. *The World's Parliament of Religions.* Bloomington, Ind., 1995. An excellent scholarly study of the parliament in historical context.

Seager, Richard Hughes, ed. *The Dawn of Religious Pluralism.* La Salle, Ill., 1993. A new collection of key parliament addresses.

Teasdale, Wayne, and George F. Cairns, eds. *The Community of Religions: Voices and Images of the Parliament of the World's Religions.* New York, 1996. Documents of the 1993 parliament.

Ziolkowski, Eric J., ed. *A Museum of Faiths: Histories and Legacies of the 1893 World's Parliament of Religions.* Atlanta, 1993. Collection of essays on the 1893 parliament, emphasizing its subsequent influence.

Robert S. Ellwood (1987 and 2005)

WORSHIP AND DEVOTIONAL LIFE

This entry consists of the following articles:

JEWISH WORSHIP
CHRISTIAN WORSHIP
MUSLIM WORSHIP
HINDU DEVOTIONAL LIFE
BUDDHIST DEVOTIONAL LIFE IN SOUTHEAST ASIA
BUDDHIST DEVOTIONAL LIFE IN EAST ASIA
BUDDHIST DEVOTIONAL LIFE IN TIBET
DAOIST DEVOTIONAL LIFE

WORSHIP AND DEVOTIONAL LIFE: JEWISH WORSHIP

Although never discouraging private, incidental prayer, Judaism gives absolute priority to the formal worship of the community. Jewish law (*halakhah*) establishes that even individuals praying privately must first recite the fixed texts, meeting their own needs through added intentionality (*kavvanah*) before adding freely composed prayers only in restricted locations. This worship functions as a constant reminder to Jews of their existential situation: they are members of the people Israel, living a life enabled by God in a divinely created and maintained world, corporately heirs to the irrevocable covenants between God and Israel. The formal prayers grow from this relationship, expressing praise, petition, and thanksgiving to God, as well as reminding Jews of the expectations it places on them for a life lived constantly in the divine presence. In reciting these prayers, Jews locate themselves within a sacred history that extends from creation, through the exodus and Sinai revelation, to the future messianic fulfillment of God's promises.

Jewish worship includes prayers by which to respond to the inherent holiness found in every moment of life, from the seemingly mundane (like the proper functioning of bodily orifices), to the seemingly miraculous (like seeing rainbows and flowering trees). It touches on every moment of normal waking life, from rising, dressing, eating, and studying to interpersonal relations. The Babylonian Talmud (Menaḥot 43b) cites the second-century CE Rabbi Meir that everyone must recite one hundred blessings daily. By this practice, one acknowledges the sanctity of all these moments, praising God as sovereign of the universe for all aspects of the divine relationship with creation.

The first preserved Jewish prayer books, from the ninth century CE, begin as lists of these hundred blessings. Jewish worship calls for the regular recitation of many of these blessings during statutory formal worship of God, thrice daily with additional services on holidays. Concatenations of blessings structure the central statutory prayers. These prayers ideally are recited with a *minyan*, a quorum of ten worshipers, usually but not necessarily in a synagogue, in the presence of a Torah scroll. Individuals, however, may recite most of these prayers for themselves. Any member of the *minyan* (adult Jews, traditionally only men) may lead public prayers, taking on the role of the *sheliaḥ tsibbur*, the emissary of the congregation. No clergy are necessary, although a congregation may appoint a *hazzan*, or cantor, as a professional *sheliaḥ tsibbur*, and in modern liberal contexts rabbis often lead services.

ORIGINS. This system of worship apparently developed in response to the destruction of the Jerusalem Temple by the Romans in 70 CE. While the Temple functioned, Jewish corporate worship of God was sacrificial, consisting of daily and festival sacrifices offered by the priestly families on behalf of the nation and in response to God's biblical covenantal commands. These sacrifices, like those of the Jews' neighbors, required scrupulous attention to detail, both in the choice of unblemished sacrificial victims and in the performance of the cultic acts. Priests offered lambs morning and afternoon, as well as incense and grain offerings and additional sacrifices to mark Sabbaths and holidays. Individual Jews who could attend brought various other offerings, either from personal obligation or in celebration. Many holy days called for special Temple rituals: the sacrifice of paschal lambs at Passover, the complex expiatory offerings of the high priest on Yom Kippur, the blowing of the *shofar* (ram's horn) on Ro'sh ha-Shanah, circumambulation with *lulav* (palm branches) at Sukkot, or the singing of *hallel* (*Psalms* 113 to 118) on most festivals.

We know of few settings where Jews gathered for worship outside of the Temple while it functioned. Synagogues existed in Israel and in the Diaspora, but probably as places for reading and studying scripture or for meetings, not for regular communal prayer. Communities whose local priests were serving in Jerusalem (the *ma'amad*) apparently gathered for a scripture-centered worship during those weeks. At least one dissident group, objecting to the administration of the Temple, retreated to the Dead Sea and conducted regular, nonsacrificial worship. Textual evidence from the Dead Sea Scrolls, as well as from liturgical passages in contemporary Jewish literature, suggests that a recognized register of prayer language was emerging, in Hebrew and in continuity with biblical prayer texts. Jewish prayer in Greek likely also existed in some circles, but evidence is sparse.

RABBINIC PRAYER. With the destruction of the Temple, the covenantal, biblically-mandated worship of God ceased, creating a spiritual crisis. Many competing substitute methods of worship were likely proposed, most of which failed to gain authority. Some Jews may also have chosen simply to wait for a restoration of the cult, as had happened after the destruction of the Solomonic Temple by the Babylonians. The worship system that became universal Jewish prayer seems to have begun as a substitution for sacrifices among the rabbinic class under the leadership of Rabban Gamli'el at Yavneh in the last decades of the first century CE. In a revolutionary move, Rabban Gamli'el decreed that instead of priestly, sacrificial worship in Jerusalem, now every Jew everywhere was responsible for daily verbal prayer (Mishnah *Berakhot* 4:3). Sages of his academy organized a prayer of eighteen blessings, known then as "the prayer" (*ha-t'fillah*) to be recited at every weekday service, with shorter versions for holy days. Later Jewish communities call this prayer the *'amidah*, for the standing posture in which it is recited, or *sh'moneh 'esreh*, the eighteen. The recitations of this prayer assumed the names of the daily sacrifices and were recited at corresponding hours while facing Jerusalem's Temple Mount. The content of this prayer is complex, but its focal point on weekdays is a petition for messianic redemption, including the rebuilding of the Temple. On Sabbaths and holidays, a single blessing reflecting on the holiness of the day replaces its thirteen petitionary blessings.

Scholars today debate whether Rabban Gamli'el's court decreed simply the thematic structure of this prayer, enabling individuals to develop their own precise language, or whether they promulgated a verbatim tightly composed set of prayers. Classical rabbinic texts preserve only snippets of these prayers. The sheer variety of language that developed in subsequent centuries around the common Yavnean structure suggests some freedom. In either case, we know little about how quickly Jews throughout Israel, let alone throughout the Diaspora, responded to this revolutionary decree. Materials embedded in the late-fourth-century Christian Apostolic Constitutions (VII:33–38) suggest that Greek versions were also extant.

It is possible that rabbinic prayers became Jewish prayers more broadly and became the worship of the preexistent synagogue only as rabbinic influence grew in the third and fourth centuries. Archaeological evidence points to a flowering of synagogue construction in Byzantine Palestine, and these synagogues show some evidence of rabbinic presence. Rabbinic tradition records that only in the third century did rabbis rule that only blessings formulated as "Blessed are You, Lord our God, King of the universe" were appropriate (Babylonian Talmud *Berakhot* 40b). This is also the period where rabbis finalized the protocols for joining the *t'fillah* with the recitation of *sh'ma'*.

The *sh'ma'*, the recitation of *Deuteronomy* 6:4–9, 11:13–31, and *Numbers* 15:37–41, forms the second major component of rabbinic prayer. Its origin is obscure, but its recitation morning and night as a liturgical unit surrounded by blessings is presumed in the earliest rabbinic texts. In reciting these biblical passages, one declares loyalty to God and God's commandments. The passages command Jews to surround themselves physically with reminders, placing the text on the entrances to their house (*mezuzah*), wearing it on their forehead and arm (*t'fillin*), and knotting fringes on the corners of their clothes (*tsitsit*). The complex blessings surrounding the biblical passages focus on Judaism's central theological tenets: God is creator, the revealer of Torah, and the one who saves.

Whether or not all synagogue communities conducted rabbinic prayer, the rabbis presumed early that their worship would take place in the presence of the Torah scroll and that the *sheliaḥ tsibbur* for the *t'fillah* would stand before the ark housing it—presumably located in the communal synagogue. The third major component of rabbinic prayer is native to the synagogue: the public reading and exposition of scripture. This apparently had its roots in the Second Temple period. The rabbis maintained the pattern of reading Torah on the Sabbath and the Monday and Thursday market days. Cyclical reading of the entire Torah apparently developed gradually during the rabbinic period, with two cycles emerging: an annual cycle with the entire Pentateuch being read in one year, and a so-called triennial cycle with the entire text being read twice in seven years. Originally, each community followed its own cycle. By the Geonic period (late sixth to eleventh centuries), the Babylonian annual cycle gradually displaced all alternatives. Since then, on Simḥat Torah (Rejoicing of the Torah) at the conclusion of the fall festivals, Jews complete *Deuteronomy* and immediately begin *Genesis.* Evidence for ritual reading from the Prophets (*haftarah*) appears first in *Luke* 4:17. These readings, only performed on Sabbaths and festivals, are not cyclical. They correspond either to the content of the Torah reading or to the day and are not uniform universally. They include only a small fraction of the prophetic corpus.

A specified number of congregants participates in the lection each time, either by personally reading a section of the text or, more frequently, by reciting blessings over the text read by a designated reader. The pentateuchal text must be chanted from a properly prepared parchment scroll that contains a perfect copy of the entire Torah; the scroll itself, like ancient Hebrew texts, contains neither vowels nor musical notation. In this way, the reading ritually recapitulates the revelation of Torah at Mount Sinai. Today, the rest of the congregation follows in printed Bibles that often include vernacular translation or commentaries. Until medieval Jews adopted other vernaculars, Aramaic translation (*targum*) accompanied all readings of scripture. The scrolls of *Song of Songs, Ruth, Lamentations, Ecclesiastes,* and *Esther* are read on Passover, Shavu'ot, the Ninth of Av, Sukkot, and Purim, respectively.

Psalms also play an important role in Jewish worship, but not in a lectionary context. The synagogue perpetuates the Temple's festival recitation of *hallel* (*Psalms* 113 to 118), as well as the daily psalms originally recited by the Levites there (*Psalms* 24, 48, 82, 94–95:3, 81, 93, 92). Other psalms eventually became standard as introductory morning prayers (*p'suqei d'zimra,* verses of song). Although the full list varies from rite to rite and is expanded on Sabbaths, all today include daily the core of *Psalms* 145 to 150 as well as *Exodus* 15.

Other nonsacrificial Temple rituals specific to various holidays were also integrated into the synagogue service, often in the additional service *(musaf).* The Ro'sh ha-Shanah *musaf* includes an elaborate ritual for the blowing of the *shofar*; the Yom Kippur *musaf* includes an extended recollection of the high priest's rituals in the Temple; Sukkot rituals include waving the four species (*lulav*) during *hallel* and parading with them with special songs before or after *musaf.* Jews of priestly descent also pronounce the priestly benediction (*Nm.* 6:24–26) over the assembled congregation. Outside of Israel this occurs only during the *musaf* of festivals; in Israel, Sabbaths are added. In Jerusalem, in proximity to the location of the Temple, priests pronounce it daily.

The Hebrew of the core prayers described above also alludes deeply to biblical language but rarely cites verses verbatim. Probably in the mid-first millennium it became common to construct new prayers as florilegia of biblical verses. Prayers of this style appear around the earlier core, both in the introductory psalms and in the supplicatory prayers (*taḥanun*) that came to follow the *'amidah.* However, allusions to the Bible and to midrashic comment on it continued to inform the rich body of liturgical poetry (*piyyut*) that embellished the core prayers on Sabbaths and holidays in that period and later. Prayers constructed of verses characterize the liturgy of Karaite Jews, a group rejecting rabbinic teachings that emerged in the closing centuries of the first millennium.

Medieval Additions. Various elements of private liturgy also became part of public prayer in the medieval period, out of concern for their popular neglect. These include the series of blessings intended to accompany one's actions while rising in the morning (*birkhot hashaḥar*) and a symbolic study of both written and oral Torah. This Torah study provides another opportunity to recall and vicariously participate in the Temple sacrifices by reciting the biblical and rabbinic texts describing them.

This complex of prayers constituted public worship for all Jews until modernity. All the regional rites preserved this basic structure, differing only in specific wording and, especially, in their poetic additions. Medieval Jews increasingly considered their received rites to be authoritative and unalterable, appropriately meeting God's desire for worship. Medieval and early modern Jews adapted their fixed prayers to new situations through interpretative strategies, investing their received prayers with new, frequently mystical, meanings. These meanings could find expression through meditations on the fixed texts or though additions in the interstices of the prayer book of *qavvanot,* texts expressing the mystical intentions of the prayers. Frequently, one generations' innovative response became the fixed liturgy of their descendents. Most widely accepted were memorial prayers added in the wake of the Crusades and liturgies influenced by the customs of sixteenth-century Lurianic Qabbalah, like the *Psalms* and songs welcoming the Sabbath (*qabbalat shabbat*).

Especially with the expulsion of Jews from Spain in 1492, the regional nature of the rites changed. Rather than adapting to the rites of their new homes, the refugees who were dispersed throughout the Mediterranean and Europe preserved their Sephardi (Iberian) rites. This led to the demise of almost all Mediterranean and Eastern rites and meant that communities now sometimes supported multiple synagogues with different customs. Heredity more than location determined liturgical details. Influenced by Lurianic mysticism, Hasidism, beginning in the eighteenth century, deliberately adopted elements of Sephardi-rite liturgy into their eastern European Ashkenazi context.

Little is known about women's participation in this system. Women seem to have attended services more in late antiquity and in Christendom than under Islam. From the twelfth century, there is evidence in the Rhineland both for women's sections of synagogues and for women who led other women in prayer there. In some places women prayed the statutory prayers but in their vernacular; others learned Hebrew; others were probably regularly "prayerful" but did not know the official prayers. Prayer books produced for women presume their participation in the normative liturgy, but such early modern Yiddish prayers (*teḥines*) often parallel rather than participate in the "men's" liturgy.

Modernity. With Napoleon (1769–1821), western European Jews became citizens and sought to become full members of greater society. This meant, for some, transforming Jewish worship into something less strange in Christian eyes. Elements of this transformation included increased decorum, more formal music, more preaching, and shortened prayers (by removing much *piyyut* and mystical accretions). Reform Judaism adopted vernacular prayer and theologically driven changes to its contents. This allowed for radical abbreviation of the traditional liturgy, but the structure described above usually remained discernable. Rabbis and cantors were increasingly liturgical experts performing for a largely passive audience. After 1948, the presence of the State of Israel encouraged a cultural expression of Judaism, generating a return to Hebrew prayer and concepts of Jewish peoplehood. In this period, women too became full participants in the non-Orthodox synagogue, counting for the *minyan* and serving as its professionals. Feminism has generated another set of changes to prayer language with demands for egalitarian language. While Orthodox Judaism (as it became known in this period) can allow only aesthetic changes to the worship service, a full spectrum now exists between it and the most radical Reform settings, where immediate response to cultural change is normative.

See Also Biblical Temple; Domestic Observances, article on Jewish Practices; Folk Religion, article on Folk Judaism; Priesthood, article on Jewish Priesthood; Rites of Passage, article on Jewish Rites; Siddur and Maḥzor; Synagogue.

Bibliography

Since the publication of a series of Hebrew articles by Ezra Fleischer beginning in 1990, there has been significant scholarly disagreement over the origins of rabbinic liturgy. For a review of these articles, see Ruth Langer, "Revisiting Early Rabbinic Liturgy: The Recent Contributions of Ezra Fleischer," *Prooftexts* 19, no. 2 (1999): 179–194; and Ezra Fleischer and Ruth Langer, "Controversy," *Prooftexts* 20, no. 3 (2000): 380–387. Among those disagreeing with Fleischer are Stefan C. Reif, *Judaism and Hebrew Prayer: New Perspectives on Jewish Liturgical History* (Cambridge, U.K., 1993), which provides the most comprehensive recent scholarly survey of Jewish prayer, including important discussions of medieval and early modern dynamics. See also Reuven Kimelman, "The Literary Structure of the Amidah and the Rhetoric of Redemption," in *The Echoes of Many Texts: Reflection on Jewish and Christian Traditions, Essays in Honor of Lou H. Silberman,* edited by William G. Dever and J. Edward Wright (Atlanta, 1997), pp. 171–218. Also of importance are Kimelman's "The *Shema'* Liturgy: From Covenant Ceremony to Coronation," *Kenishta: Studies of the Synagogue World* 1 (2001): 9–105. Fleischer challenges the still influential theory, informed by form-critical methods, of Joseph Heinemann, *Prayer in the Talmud,* translated by Richard S. Sarason (Berlin, 1977). Earlier methods are generally no longer accepted. However, Raymond Scheindlin's translation of Ismar Elbogen, *Jewish Liturgy: A Comprehensive History* (Philadelphia, Jerusalem, and New York, 1993; German ed., 1913), incorporates the editorial updates of the 1972 Hebrew edition. Even though Elbogen's historical reconstructions are now deemed unreliable, his descriptions of the liturgy remain valid. Important discussions also appear in Lee I. Levine, *The Ancient Synagogue: The First Thousand Years* (New Haven and London, 2000). Another dimension of attention to the nonverbal dynamics of early liturgy appears in Uri Ehrlich, *The Non-Verbal Language of Jewish Prayer* (in Hebrew; Jerusalem, 1999).

The subsequent history of Jewish prayer is less well studied. Reif's *Judaism and Hebrew Prayer* provides the only comprehensive overview. Hebrew liturgical poetry is the focus of many recent important publications in Hebrew. On the dynamics of this genre, see Joseph Yahalom, *Poetry and Society in Jewish Galilee of Late Antiquity* (in Hebrew; Tel Aviv, 1999). On early medieval liturgy, see Lawrence A. Hoffman, *The Canonization of the Synagogue Service* (Notre Dame, Ind., and London, 1979); Naphtali Wieder's collected articles, *The Formation of Jewish Liturgy in the East and the West* (in Hebrew; Jerusalem, 1998); and Ezra Fleischer's *Eretz-Israel Prayer and Prayer Rituals as Portrayed in the Geniza Documents* (in Hebrew; Jerusalem, 1988). On dynamics of liturgical development see Ruth Langer, *To Worship God Properly: Tensions between Liturgical Custom and Halakhah in Judaism* (Cincinnati, 1998). Collections of important studies include E. D. Goldschmidt, *On Jewish Liturgy: Essays on Prayer and Religious Poetry* (in Hebrew; Jerusalem, 1980) and Israel Ta-Shma's *The Early Ashkenazic Prayer: Literary and Historical Aspects* (in Hebrew; Jerusalem, 2003). On the impact of mysticism on the liturgy, see especially Meir Bar-Ilan, *The Mysteries of Jewish Prayer and Hekhalot* (in Hebrew; Ramat Gan, Israel 1987); Moshe Hallamish, *Kabbalah: In Liturgy, Halakhah, and Customs* (in Hebrew; Ramat Gan, Israel, 2000); and Louis Jacobs, *Hasidic Prayer* (London and Washington, 1972; reprint, 1993). On women and prayer, see *Daughters of the King: Women and the Synagogue*, edited by Susan Grossman and Rivka Haut (Philadelphia, New York, and Jerusalem, 1992); and Chava Weissler, *Voices of the Matriarchs: Listening to the Prayers of Early Modern Jewish Women* (Boston, 1998).

On the liturgies of the modern liberal movements, see Jakob J. Petuchowski, *Prayerbook Reform in Europe: The Liturgy of European Liberal and Reform Judaism* (New York, 1968); Eric L. Friedland, "*Were Our Mouths Filled with Song: Studies in Liberal Jewish Liturgy*" (Cincinnati, 1997); and Eric Caplan, *From Ideology to Liturgy: Reconstructionist Worship and American Liberal Judaism* (Cincinnati, 2002).

RUTH LANGER (2005)

WORSHIP AND DEVOTIONAL LIFE: CHRISTIAN WORSHIP

The death of Jesus of Nazareth by crucifixion and his resurrection on the first day of the week constitute the root paradigm of Christianity and, as such, are central to Christian worship in all its dimensions. Because that death and resurrection occurred at Jerusalem at the time of the Jewish Passover (Heb., Pesaḥ; *pascha* in the Greek transliteration of the Aramaic), this paradigm is frequently referred to as "the paschal mystery." Paul's *First Letter to the Corinthians* (5:7) identifies the death of Jesus with the sacrifice of the Passover lambs, and that same identification is made in the *Gospel of John* (19:32–36 refers to the prohibition against cracking the bones of the lamb eaten at Passover). References in early Christian literature to the Cross or to the death of Jesus should most frequently be understood as including Jesus' resurrection and glorification, the total paschal mystery as that paradigm of salvation in which the Christian participates.

CHRISTIAN INITIATION. The public ministry of Jesus began with his baptism by John in the river Jordan. The accounts of that baptism report that when Jesus came up from the water the Holy Spirit descended upon him and the voice of God proclaimed him to be the Son of God. This outpouring of the Holy Spirit is referred to (*Acts* 10:38) as an anointing by virtue of which Jesus is the expected "anointed one" (the Messiah, or Christ). Such ritual washings as the baptism of John were common in Judaism in the first century of the common era, and many scholars suppose that the early Christian baptismal rituals were influenced by the initiatory ritual employed for converts from paganism to Judaism, where circumcision was followed by a ritual washing.

Early Christian baptism. The earliest accounts of Christian baptism focus on the confession of Jesus as Lord, usually in response to preaching, and on the ritual washing. The earliest church order, *Didache* (before CE 100), describes that washing, following extended catechesis, as preferably accomplished by immersion in running water, but it allows for water to be poured over the initiate three times. In either case, the baptism is to be performed "in the name of the Father, and of the Son, and of the Holy Spirit." It is uncertain whether such references to the anointing and sealing of Christians as that in *2 Corinthians* 1:21 refer to an actual anointing with oil in first-century initiatory ritual, but such anointings do appear in the course of the second century. In Syria an anointing prior to the water bath was called *rushma* ("mark") and has been interpreted as a Christian surrogate for the circumcision that preceded the water bath in Jewish proselyte baptism. Elsewhere such baptismal anointing was associated with the outpouring of the Holy Spirit upon Jesus and so was performed after the water bath. Such postbaptismal anointing (referred to as the "seal") was frequently accompanied by imposition of the baptizer's hands upon the initiate. Such is the pattern reported for North Africa by Tertullian (*On Baptism* 7–8).

The most extensive of the early church orders, the *Apostolic Tradition* (third century), usually assigned to Hippolytus at Rome, reveals a more extensive initiatory process. After three years as catechumens (learners), candidates for baptism are selected after careful scrutiny and enter a final period of intensive preparation under direct supervision of the bishop. At the end of that period, concluded with a two-day fast, the initiates keep vigil through the night from Saturday to Sunday until cockcrow. Then, stripped of their clothing and having renounced Satan and his service, they are anointed with an exorcised oil. Next, entering the water, they profess belief in each of the persons of the Trinity in response to a threefold creedal examination and are immersed after each profession. Coming up from the water, they are anointed with another oil, the "oil of thanksgiving" (later known as *chrisma* or *muron*), and reassume their clothing. They are then led to the bishop before the gathered congregation and anointed again by him with the imposition of his hands upon their heads. The bishop then kisses each initiate, and they take their places in the congregation to participate in the prayer of the community and in the eucharistic meal for the first time. This complex initiatory ritual set the pattern discernible, with significant variations, in later centuries. The Eastern churches maintain only one postbaptismal anointing, while the anointing by the bishop was eventually separated from baptism in the Western church, coming to be known as "confirmation."

It is widely supposed that the initiation described in the *Apostolic Tradition* took place on Easter at the conclusion of the paschal vigil. In the course of the third century such paschal baptism became the norm in most churches, and many scholars have suggested that the custom was much more ancient. Such a time for baptism is rendered particularly appropriate by the baptismal theology of Paul (*Rom.* 6), which associated baptism with participation in Christ's burial and resurrection, and by Jesus' references to his coming passion and death as his "baptism" (*Lk.* 12:50).

Normalization of infant baptism. While primitive baptismal practice with its extensive catechesis took adult baptism to be normative, in the third century the baptism of young children, although opposed by some, was practiced frequently. By the fifth century it was perhaps more common than the baptism of adults, and by the sixth century the catechumenate was reduced to a formality. Vestiges of that formative process perdured, nonetheless, and were still evident in the rites used by Western Christians at the time of the Reformation. The reforms of the sixteenth century removed from the baptismal rite many of the ceremonies that had belonged formerly to the catechumenate, and the postbaptismal anointings were also dropped from Protestant baptismal practice. Infant baptism continued to be the norm, however, and increasingly a postbaptismal formative process of instruction and discipline led to a rite of confirmation after age seven for both Catholics and Protestants, although for Catholics that rite usually followed well after admission to the Eucharist.

Opposition to the baptism of those too young to make a personal profession of faith occurred from time to time in the Middle Ages and became a significant wing of the Reformation with the Anabaptists. Since the seventeenth century, such refusal to practice pedobaptism and the insistence on believers' baptism has been characteristic of several Protestant churches, the Baptists being the most numerous. While Roman Catholics, Anglicans, and churches of the Evangelical and Reformed traditions continue to baptize infants, as do the Eastern churches, liturgical studies in the twentieth century have focused attention on the rich initiatory rituals of the patristic age, and restoration of that classic passage through catechesis to baptism, anointing, and eucharist has held an important place in the agenda of recent liturgical reform, the Rite of Christian Initiation of Adults in the Roman Catholic church being a significant instance.

THE HOLY EUCHARIST. As early as the *Didache,* participation in the communion meal, or Eucharist, was limited to the baptized, and such participation in the Eucharist is regularly found as the conclusion of the initiatory process. The Eucharist is, indeed, the locus of that *koinōnia,* or communion, which is the mode of the Christian's unity with other Christians in the unity of the church, and of the church's unity with Christ: a unity expressed and realized in the believer's feeding on Christ's body and blood through the eucharistic signs of bread and wine. The *Didache* speaks of the Eucharist as a sacrifice, and this may reflect a sense of continuity with the *zevaḥ todah,* the "thank offering" of the Second Temple period in which those who offered a sacrifice consumed part of it, thus keeping communion with God, to whom the victim was offered.

In later centuries both this offering of the eucharistic gifts of bread and wine to God as a memorial of and thanksgiving for Christ's death and resurrection, and the consecration of these gifts to identify them with Christ's body and blood, would achieve explicit expression in the eucharistic prayer, the central prayer of the Eucharistic liturgy. The *Apostolic Tradition* presents the text of a eucharistic prayer that opens with a dialogue between the officiating celebrant and the congregation which has remained virtually unchanged in the West, and proceeds to a thanksgiving for the redemptive work of Christ, which comes to its climax in a recitation of the charter narrative describing the institution of the Eucharist by Jesus on the night before his crucifixion. The earliest such institution narrative is that in Paul's *First Letter to the Corinthians* (chap. 11), written around 55 CE, which many exegetes consider to have been a text transmitted through liturgical tradition.

In the *Apostolic Tradition* that narrative's concluding command, "When you do this, make my memorial," is followed at once by the clause that accompanies the narrative in virtually all early liturgies, although the wording varies considerably. Such a clause, known technically as *anamnēsis* ("memorial"), is generally believed to have been attached to the institution narrative from the first inclusion of that narrative within the body of the eucharistic prayer. In the prayer of the *Apostolic Tradition* the *anamnēsis* reads, "Remembering therefore his death and resurrection, we offer to thee this bread and cup, giving thanks to thee that thou hast made us worthy to stand before thee and to minister to thee." This is the earliest extant example of such an inclusion of the narrative and the *anamnēsis* in the body of the eucharistic prayer, but it is typical of the prayers of the fourth century and later. In the *Apostolic Tradition* the *anamnēsis* is followed by an invocation of the Holy Spirit upon the oblation of the church, praying that all who receive the holy gifts, being united, may be filled with the Holy Spirit for the strengthening of faith.

Such an invocation of the Holy Spirit is referred to as an *epiklēsis.*

That pattern for the eucharistic prayer was expanded in most of the Eastern empire in the fourth century. In the first place, after the opening dialogue, a praise of God as creator, hymned by the heavenly hosts, was added before the christological thanksgiving. Such an opening praise of the creator, ending in the singing of the Sanctus (a liturgical hymn already in the Temple liturgy reflected in *Isaiah* 6:3 and continued in the synagogue liturgy after the destruction of the Temple), is characteristic of eucharistic prayers of Cappadocia, Syria, Palestine, and eventually Alexandria. A second development in these fourth-century prayers is the focusing of the *epiklēsis* on the oblations of bread and wine, invoking the Holy Spirit for their consecration as the body and blood of Christ. Also, the older content of that supplication, the gathering of the church into union with God, was expanded into a series of intercessions.

Influenced perhaps by a transitional phase in liturgical evolution at Alexandria, a different pattern for the eucharistic prayer emerged in the West. First visible in northern Italy in the late fourth century (in *De sacramentis,* a series of postbaptismal instructions commonly ascribed to Ambrose of Milan), this Western eucharistic prayer appears in virtually its final form in the *Gelasian Sacramentary,* an eighth-century document reflecting usages of sixth-century Rome. In this Western pattern the opening dialogue leads into a variable prayer of praise and thanksgiving, sometimes general in its content but more frequently phrased to reflect the varying emphases of particular feasts or seasons of the liturgical year. This variable praise leads into the Sanctus, and thereafter the prayer is relatively invariable and comes to be known as the Canon Actionis or Canon Missae, titles that reflect its regularity. This canon is supplicatory throughout, with intercessions and commendations of the eucharistic gifts preceding and following a prayer for their consecration, the institution narrative, and *anamnēsis.*

This Canon Missae became the standard eucharistic prayer for all the Western church from the ninth century. Unlike the Eastern prayers discussed above, this Western prayer contained no explicit invocation *(epiklēsis)* of the Holy Spirit for the consecration of the eucharistic gifts as Christ's body and blood. Theological reflection associated that conversion of bread and wine increasingly with the words of Jesus in the narrative of the institution: "This is my body" and "This is the chalice of my blood of the new and eternal covenant." While occasional theologians expressed the view that such identification of the gifts with the body and blood of Christ was to be understood symbolically or typologically, a more realistic interpretation prevailed, especially from the eleventh century, and this encouraged a perception of the Eucharist as a sacramental representation of Christ's redemptive sacrifice, complete and efficacious even if none but the celebrating priest received Communion. That the people were disinclined to frequent Communion is indicated by the requirement of the Fourth Lateran Council (1215) that all must communicate at least once annually.

In spite of the moderating expressions of sensitive theologians, such emphasis on the sacrificial character of the Mass (as the Eucharist was known in the West) and diminution of its character as communion meal grew stronger in the later medieval period and established the eucharistic agenda of the Reformation. While the reformers' understandings of Christ's presence in the Eucharist varied widely, there was broad agreement on two matters: the suppression of all reference to the Eucharist itself as a sacrifice and insistence on general reception of Holy Communion as constituting the divinely instituted memorial of Christ's death on Calvary, itself the sole and sufficient sacrifice for the sins of the world. For the reformed liturgies the narrative of the institution of the Eucharist, already central in medieval tradition as the formula of consecration, achieved even greater prominence, its scriptural origin excepting it from the general reaction against liturgical elements that could be ascribed to human composition.

Protestant eucharistic liturgies in general sought to give expression to the cardinal principle that it is only faith in the sufficiency of Christ's redeeming work which justifies sinners. Protestants opposed all liturgical practice that could be interpreted as a human "good work." Even so, such major reformers as Martin Luther and John Calvin assumed that the Eucharist would continue to form the core of the Christian observance of Sunday as it had from the first century, but the popular disinclination to frequent Communion proved too strong in the end, and in Protestant worship the Eucharist became an occasional observance, being celebrated only monthly or even less frequently. This brought the reading and preaching of the word of God much more strongly to the fore and established the contrast between Roman Catholic and Protestant forms of worship still visible today, although the extent of that contrast has been reduced vastly in the twentieth century, especially as a result of the Second Vatican Council (1962–1965).

The Liturgy of the Word. As early as the second century the eucharistic meal was preceded by readings from the scriptures, preaching, and extended prayers of intercession. Justin Martyr, in chapter 67 of his first *Apology,* addressed to the emperor Antoninus Pius around 155 CE, describes the assembly of Christian worshipers on Sunday and tells us that on such occasions there were readings from the "memoirs of the apostles" or the prophets for as long as time permitted. Then the "president of the brethren" preached about what had been read, exhorting the congregation to perform good deeds. After that, the congregation prayed in common for themselves and for all the church. At that point, the gifts of bread and wine for the Eucharist were placed on the table, and the eucharistic prayer was begun.

The basic outline of the Liturgy of the Word has remained largely the same to the present, although introductory entrance rites (chants and prayers) appropriate to rich new architectural settings of the liturgy were added from the fifth century on. By that time, too, other musical elements, such as the singing of psalms or verses with "Alleluia" between scripture readings, as well as within the Eucharist proper, had begun to appear in many areas. In spite of these enrichments and eventual variation in the number of scripture readings, the basic picture given by Justin is still clearly discernible.

PREACHING. While in most traditions today the sermon retains the place it had in the second century, at the conclusion of the scripture readings, preaching has never been limited to that liturgical context. Throughout Christian history the gift of prophetic proclamation has been exercised within, parallel to, and apart from the regular ritual patterns of Christian worship. While preaching has regularly been considered a responsibility of officiating clergy, it has not been limited to them. At times, patterns in the official cultus have come to leave little place for preaching, and in such circumstances preaching has flourished alongside that cultus and on occasion as a vehicle of opposition to it. Even where preaching continued within the traditional Latin liturgy in the later Middle Ages, it frequently formed the centerpiece of a larger bloc of catechetical and devotional material in the vernacular, known by the collective term *prone.* Its variable content established by the preacher, a prone might include such didactic materials as the Ten Commandments or the Apostles' Creed, practical pastoral elements such as the announcement of proximate fasts or festivals or the publication of the banns of marriage, and devotional elements such as intercessions (replacing the Latin prayers of the faithful, which had fallen into desuetude in the early medieval period). Such a prone, including the sermon, might be found before the eucharistic liturgy, at its midpoint following the scripture readings, or apart from the liturgy. This provided the format for the Preaching Service, which achieved great popularity in some quarters of the Protestant Reformation where proclamation of the word of God in preaching took on the character of an alternative to the liturgical tradition. Such a preaching tradition continues to form the mainstream of much Protestant worship today, set in a context of instructional and devotional elements of the free composition that characterized the medieval prone. Other strongly homiletical traditions have set the sermon in the context of the Liturgy of the Word, even when no eucharist followed, or in the context of the traditional Liturgy of the Hours.

LITURGY OF THE HOURS. Scholars disagree in their reconstructions of the regimen of daily prayer among Christians of the first two centuries, but there is broad agreement that this regimen, however described, grew out of the Christian continuation of patterns of daily prayer in first-century Judaism and the daily service of the synagogue, which furnished the public framework of that prayer.

The *Didache* (chap. 8) orders the Lord's Prayer three times a day, but it is not clear what hours are intended. The third-century *Apostolic Tradition* speaks of seven times for prayer during the day, the frequently mentioned third, sixth, and ninth hours, plus evening, midnight, cockcrow, and morning. These hours, interpreted as commemorative of moments in Christ's passion or focused on expectation of his triumphant return, are set forth as occasions for private prayer, although it seems that the morning hour (and occasionally the evening) were also times of public assembly. In the fourth and following centuries, public offices of prayer in the morning and evening form the daily pattern of the church's liturgical prayer, although monastic influence led to a much more complex regimen. The fully developed monastic liturgy consisted of a major vigil at cockcrow, and other assemblies for prayer at around 6:00 AM and at every third hour thereafter until the hour of retiring. The establishment of urban monasteries in connection with major basilicas brought a conflation of this monastic regimen with the simpler cathedral hours of prayer, and in the medieval period all clergy were obligated to recite a liturgy of the hours deeply shaped by the presuppositions of the monastic tradition.

Sixteenth-century reforms of the hours of prayer, such as that by Thomas Cranmer in the English *Book of Common Prayer,* returned to the simpler regimen of two hours in the day, morning and evening, but Cranmer's work still betrayed such monastic characteristics as the systematic reading in course of all the psalms (albeit within the space of a month, rather than a week as had been the custom). Twentieth-century reform of the Liturgy of the Hours in the Western churches has continued this emphasis on the morning and evening offices as times of public liturgical prayer, while providing for certain of the intervening hours for private use.

LITURGICAL ARTICULATION OF TIME. The Liturgy of the Hours reveals the Christian perception of times as themselves symbolic of the paschal mystery and as the framework within which the church watches for the coming of Christ. However, derived as this daily regimen was from the traditions of Judaism, the hours of the day were not the only time cycle to receive Christian expression. This was equally true of two other important cycles in the Old Testament, the week and the year.

Liturgical week. None of the numerous scholarly efforts to get behind the Jewish seven-day week and to discover its origin apart from the history of Israel has achieved definitive success. That seven-day cycle seems to have been present with the earliest settlement of Israel in Canaan, and the question of the ultimate origin of the week must remain unsettled. What can be said more surely is that the cycle was defined by the treatment of every seventh day as a day of rest for servants and draft animals and, by extension, for the whole people. This Sabbath (meaning "to stop" or "that which stops") recurs every seventh day without regard to other time cycles, such as the month or the year, making the week an independent cycle. Not originally a day distinguished by obligations of worship, the Sabbath came to afford peculiar opportunity for public worship because of the rest from ordinary employment which it demanded.

While early Christians participated in the worship of the synagogue as opportunity afforded, it is likely that the Sabbath, with its extended synagogue liturgy, was an especially important occasion for Christian witness. Some have suggested that the Christian observance of the first day of the week, Sunday, found its beginnings in the gatherings of Christians for their characteristic table fellowship following the conclusion of the liturgy at the closing of the Sabbath at sundown. Others have insisted that it was in the evening from the first day to the second (Sunday to Monday) that Christians began to assemble, on the model of the appearances of the risen Christ reported in *John* 20. What seems sure in either case is that the first Christians continued to observe the week as defined by the Sabbath and that, once growth of the movement required gatherings at a longer interval than daily, assemblies of a specifically Christian character were on the first day of the week, the day of Christ's resurrection.

Several writers have suggested that, because that weekly assembly was the time of the Eucharist, the Lord's Supper *(kuriakon deipnon; 1 Cor.* 11:20), the first day of the week came to be known as "the Lord's Day" *(kuriakē hēmera).* Whether that is the reference of that phrase in *Revelation* 1:10 or not, it is clear that the term was used for the first day of the week as early as the *Didache* (chap. 14). Sources from the second century speak of that first day of the week, the first day of creation, as the Eighth Day, the day beyond the creation itself and the day of the new creation accomplished by Christ's paschal sacrifice (*1 Cor.* 5:7). Such thought reflects the strong sense of Christ's spiritual presence in the community constituted by the outpouring of the Holy Spirit (*Acts* 2), a "realized eschatology" that throughout Christian history expresses the sense of the presence in worship of both Christ's redeeming action in the past and a prolepsis of his future appearing in judgment at the end of history. The meeting of that memory of the past and that hope for the future in the Eucharist on each Lord's Day has been a constant dimension of classical Christian liturgical experience.

Beyond that festal Sunday, the weekly celebration of the paschal mystery, Christians very early began to observe every Wednesday and Friday as fast days (*Didache* 8). Friday was the day of Jesus' crucifixion, and most early interpreters of this custom treat Wednesday as the day of his betrayal by Judas Iscariot. However, one third-century source, *Didascalia apostolorum,* places Jesus' arrest in the early hours of Wednesday, a chronology that would put his last supper with his disciples on Tuesday night rather than on Thursday, as is the more common tradition. This alternative chronology, Annie Jaubert has suggested, may reflect the impact on early Christianity of the Essene community at Qumran. The unique calendar of that group always situated the Passover in the night from Tuesday to Wednesday and was so arranged that all important liturgical days occurring on fixed dates of the month would fall on Wednesday, Friday, or Sunday. (It remains unclear how such a calendar of exactly 52 weeks, only 364 days, would adjust for its significant error.) Tertullian speaks of these Wednesday and Friday fasts as "stations," a term encountered earlier in the *Shepherd of Hermas,* and it is clear that in the third century they were days of liturgical assembly, even for the Eucharist, in addition to the assembly on Sunday. While always secondary to Sunday, the primitive prominence of Wednesday and Friday continued in the later history of the Christian week and is still manifest in various ways in the several traditions.

According to Tertullian (*On Fasting* 14.3) it appears that some Western Christians (probably Romans) were deviating from the common practice of the church by ordering certain Sabbaths (i.e., Saturdays) in the year to be observed with fasting, a custom that Innocent I (*Epistle* 25, CE 416) reports for every week at Rome. Tertullian had complained that fasting on the Sabbath was forbidden except for the Sabbath before Easter. In this he seems to reflect correctly a tradition still followed in all the Eastern church, a tradition probably rooted in the Jewish prohibition against fasting on the Sabbath. This suggests a much stronger continuation of Sabbath observance among Christians than some writers (e.g., Willy Rordorf) have supposed. Such continuation of observance, if there was any, would concern the Sabbath rest rather than a day for liturgical worship. The association of rest from secular employment with Sunday rather than the Sabbath stems from the time of Constantine, but the direct identification of Sunday as the Christian Sabbath and its rigorous observance according to Old Testament norms appears first in English and Scottish Protestantism, especially in the seventeenth century. Apart from that, the term *Sabbath* has continued to be understood to refer to the seventh day of the week and was employed to designate that day in all medieval liturgical books.

Liturgical year. While it seems likely from such texts as *Acts* 20:7 that the beginnings, at least, of the Christian week go back to the apostolic period, other passages such as *Colossians* 2:16 suggest that liturgical time patterns of Judaism were considered, at least in the gentile mission, to be matters of little importance, given the expectation of the proximate Parousia. Still other texts, however, make it clear that even Paul, the apostle to the gentiles, was far from insensitive to the festivals of Israel and did not hesitate to relate them to the paschal mystery.

The Christian Pascha. Many scholars have, with modifications, held to the notion that the celebration of the annual paschal festival of Easter was established on the Sunday after Passover at Rome in the apostolic period. This assertion can be documented only from the fifth century, and many other scholars consider it to be contravened by documents of the second century that seem to assert that there was no annual observance of Pascha (Easter) at Rome prior to Soter, bishop there from 165. According to Karl Holl, the Passover, continued by Christians at Jerusalem in the night from 14 to 15 Nisan, was accommodated to the structure of the week, by moving the feast to Sunday, only after the establishment of a gentile hierarchy in Jerusalem following the Bar Kokhba Revolt (c. 132–135). Prior to that, the Christian Pascha would have been observed annually on the same date as the Jewish Passover, being in fact a continuation of the Jewish festival, reinterpreted in light of the tradition that identifies the crucifixion of Jesus as coinciding with the slaughter of the lambs for the festival of Passover at the Temple. By the time of such an adjustment of the Christian Pascha to the structure of the week, Christians of Jewish background had been driven out of Aelia Capitolina, the new Roman city built on the ruins of Jerusalem, to settle elsewhere, some in Mesopotamia, others in Asia Minor. It is in that latter area, especially, that we discover our earliest documents of a Christian celebration of Pascha, kept on the Jewish date in the night following 14 Nisan, the anniversary of the Crucifixion. Late in the second century, controversy developed over whether the Christian Pascha should be observed on that date or whether its preliminary fast should be terminated only on Sunday, the weekday of the Resurrection. This controversy was finally concluded by a decision in favor of a Sunday Pascha by the first ecumenical council at Nicaea in 325. By that time, however, the Pascha was almost universally observed on Sunday, and the original one day of fasting (now the Sabbath) had been extended to six days, the Holy Week that is still the most solemn time of the year for Christians.

Even when transferred to Sunday, the paschal solemnity continued to be spoken of as a memorial of the passion of Jesus. Much more than that was included in the content of the festival, however, and it can best be described as a total festival of Christ celebrating the incarnation, passion, death, resurrection, and glorification of the Savior. That unitive content was refracted, especially during the fourth century, and distinct events came to be associated with particular days: the death of Jesus with Friday of Holy Week, his resurrection with Easter Sunday, his ascension into heaven with the fortieth day after Easter, and the outpouring of the Holy Spirit upon the church with the fiftieth day, corresponding to the Jewish Feast of Weeks (Shavu'ot), or Pentecost. From the end of the second century, at least, that entire fifty-day period from Pascha to Pentecost had been kept as the extended paschal rejoicing, and recent reforms of the liturgical year have sought to restore the integrity of that festal period.

Christmas and Epiphany. Since the eighteenth century it has been commonly observed that the celebration of the nativity of Christ on December 25, first discernible at Rome around 336, represents a Christian adaptation of the winter solstice festival established by the emperor Aurelian in 274 CE. Some more recent studies have revived interest in the hypothesis of Louis Duchesne, who suggested that the date was arrived at by counting forward nine months from March 25, a date taken in the West in the third century to be that of Jesus' death. Duchesne held that the impatience of symbolic number systems for fractions made this to be as well the date of Christ's conception. However arrived at, that date would have coincided with the solar festival at Rome, and later data make it clear that the themes of the two festivals merged in the celebration of Christmas.

Coincidence with pagan festivals has also been argued for the early Eastern date for the nativity of Jesus, January 6, the Epiphany (Gk., *epiphaneia,* "manifestation"), although the argument is much less firm in this case. Here again, Duchesne's computation from a fixed date for Christ's death (April 6 in Asia Minor, according to the fifth-century church historian Sozomen), taken to be as well the date of the Incarnation, would yield the nativity nine months later, on January 6. That date seems to have been treated as the beginning of the year and, with that, the beginning of the reading of the gospel. Preference for a particular gospel in a particular church would lead to the association of different themes with the festival of Epiphany: at Jerusalem the reading of *Matthew* led to an emphasis on the nativity; at Alexandria a preference for *Mark* emphasized the baptism of Jesus; at Ephesus the predominance of *John* stressed the Cana wedding feast. While such an explanation is only hypothetical, those three themes are associated with Epiphany in the later fourth century. By that time the December 25 festival of the nativity had been accepted in the East (with the exception of Jerusalem and Armenia), and the January 6 festival of Epiphany had been adopted in the West. At Milan, Epiphany celebrated the baptism of Jesus, but at Rome it formed a duplication of the nativity observance, limited to the commemoration of the visit of the Magi. That visit of the Magi, the baptism of Jesus, and the miracle at Cana formed the *tria miracula* that were celebrated at Epiphany in Gaul. There a preparatory period, eventually six weeks, preceded the nativity festival, and this was adopted in the seventh century at Rome, though shortened first to five weeks and later to the present four. As Epiphany and Christmas had been considered the beginning of the liturgical year, so this season of preparation came to be considered the beginning of the year, and it is with the first Sunday of Advent that Western liturgical books begin.

Lent. The emergence of Pascha as the preferred time for the rites of initiation, in accordance with the death/resurrection theology of baptism taught by Paul, led to the development of a period for final catechesis and ascetical formation prior to paschal baptisms. While such a period is indicated as early as the third-century *Apostolic Tradition,* its length is indefinite prior to Nicaea. Thereafter it is spoken of as the fast of forty days and spans a period of six weeks either prior to Easter (as in Rome and fourth-century Alexandria) or prior to Holy Week (as in Syria, Constantinople, and eventually all the Eastern churches). The forty-day duration of the fast has traditionally been associated with Jesus' fast immediately following his baptism by John, and recent studies have supported Coptic sources that place the original fast of forty days immediately following Epiphany (celebrating Jesus' baptism) at Alexandria. After Nicaea the prepaschal situation of the fast is universal, although its separation from the six-day paschal fast in the Eastern rites may still reflect the wider separation of them in early Alexandria. There, Coptic tradition maintains, the fast of forty days concluded with the administration of baptism in the sixth week and the Feast of Palms on the following Sunday, an arrangement similar to the later Byzantine conferral of baptism on the Saturday of Lazarus, the day before Palm Sunday. After Nicaea that Palm Sunday is the day before the paschal fast and, in the late fourth century, is considered to be the first day of Holy Week at Jerusalem.

Although preparation for baptism constituted the original agenda of the Lenten period, by the end of the fourth century in the West it was also a period for the ritual humiliation of penitents, those who for grave sin had been severed from the communion of the church. Such penitents were publicly reconciled in Holy Week so as to be able to celebrate Easter as restored Christians, and their penitential exercises during Lent gave that color to Lenten piety. In Byzantine tradition, which has known no such formal reconciliation of penitents in Holy Week, the Western penitential concern was long absent from Lent, although similar penitential piety did enter that tradition through monasticism from the eighth century on.

Christian liturgical traditions that observe the Lenten fast experience Lent as a time of ascetical development, of "dying to self," so as to participate fully in the renewal of life in the celebration of Christ's resurrection. This participation in Christ's dying and rising, focused in the annual observance of Lent, Holy Week, and the fifty days of Easter rejoicing, is that same paschal mystery experienced by each Christian in baptism, in every celebration of the Eucharist, and indeed in every dimension of the complex of worship and sacramental life for which the paschal mystery of Christ's redemptive death and resurrection is the root paradigm.

SEE ALSO Anamnesis; Baptism; Christian Liturgical Year; Christmas; Church, article on Church Membership; Cult of Saints; Easter; Epiphany; Eucharist; Initiation; Jesus; John the Baptist; Liturgy; Lord's Prayer; Monasticism, article on Christian Monasticism; Pilgrimage, articles on Eastern Christian Pilgrimage, Roman Catholic Pilgrimage in Europe, Roman Catholic Pilgrimage in the New World; Sacrament, article on Christian Sacraments.

BIBLIOGRAPHY

The principal liturgical texts relevant to Christian initiation are presented in English in Edward C. Whitaker's *Documents of the Baptismal Liturgy,* 2d ed. (London, 1960), and John D. C. Fisher's *Christian Initiation: The Reformation Period* (London, 1970). Texts relevant to the Eucharist can be read in English in *Prayers of the Eucharist, Early and Reformed,* 2d ed., edited by Ronald C. D. Jasper and Geoffrey J. Cuming (New York, 1980), and *Liturgies of the Western Church,* edited by Bard Thompson (New York, 1961). The best survey of the whole range of the history of Christian worship is *The Study of Liturgy,* edited by Cheslyn Jones, Geoffrey Wainwright, and Edward Yarnold (London, 1978). The limitations of the magnificent overview by Gregory Dix, *The Shape of the Liturgy* (Glasgow, 1945), have been addressed in a new edition (New York, 1982) with appended notes by Paul Marshall taking account of some more recent developments. Josef A. Jungmann's *The Early Liturgy: To the Time of Gregory the Great* (1959; reprint, London, 1966) is an excellent survey, less detailed than his magisterial two-volume *Missarum Sollemnia: Eine genetische Erklärung der römischen Messe,* rev. ed. (1949; reprint, Freiburg, 1958), translated as *The Mass of the Roman Rite,* 2 vols., rev. ed. (New York, 1959).

For more particular studies of rites of initiation, G. R. Beasley-Murray's *Baptism in the New Testament* (New York, 1962) is the standard treatment of that period. For the patristic period, see Hugh M. Riley's *Christian Initiation* (Washington, D.C., 1974), and for the medieval, John D. C. Fisher's *Christian Initiation: Baptism in the Medieval West* (London, 1965). Aidan Kavanagh's *The Shape of Baptism: The Rite of Christian Initiation* (New York, 1978) examines reforms since the Second Vatican Council against the background of the earlier tradition. Much recent concern with the Eucharist has focused on the eucharistic prayer, and several contributions to this discussion, which have appeared in the liturgical journal *Worship,* have been collected in *Living Bread, Saving Cup: Readings on the Eucharist,* edited by R. Kevin Seasoltz (Collegeville, Minn., 1982). For a systematic treatment of the evolution of that central prayer of the Eucharist, see Allan Bouley's *From Freedom to Formula* (Washington, D.C., 1981).

New Sources

Bond, Gilbert I. *Community, Communitas, and Cosmos: Toward a Phenomenological Interpretation and Theology of Traditional Afro-Christian Worship.* Lanham, Md., 2002.

Bradshaw, Paul K. *The New SCM Dictionary of Liturgy and Worship.* London, 2002.

Davies, Horton. *Worship and Theology in England.* 3 vols. Grand Rapids, Mich., 1996.

Hurtado, Larry W. *At the Origins of Christian Worship.* Grand Rapids, Mich., 2000.

Lang, Bernard. *Sacred Games: A History of Christian Worship.* New Haven, Conn., 1997.

Old, Hughes Oliphant. *The Reading and Preaching of Scriptures in the Worship of the Christian Church.* Grand Rapids, Mich., 1997.

Swanson, R. N., ed. *On Continuity and Change in Christian Worship: Papers Read at the 1997 Summer Meeting and the 1998 Winter Meeting of the Ecclesiastical History Society.* Woodbridge, U.K., 1998.

Thompson, Bard, ed. *A Bibliography of Christian Worship.* Metuchen, N.J., 1989.

Webber, Robert, ed. *The Complete Library of Christian Worship.* 7 vols. Peabody, Mass., 1993.

THOMAS J. TALLEY (1987)
Revised Bibliography

WORSHIP AND DEVOTIONAL LIFE: MUSLIM WORSHIP

The nature of Muslim devotional life in Islam is rooted in its basic theological presuppositions. The three primary fundamentals of religion (*uṣūl al-dīn*) are *tawḥīd* (belief in the unity of God), *nubūwah* (belief in prophets), and *qiyāmah* (belief in the Day of Judgment). The acceptance of these three beliefs is required of all Muslims. Collectively, they constitute the essence of the Islamic worldview.

Tawḥīd is the core concept of Islam. The sovereignty of a monotheistic God, who is omnipotent, omniscient, and simultaneously transcendent and immanent, is Islam's definitive tenet. For Muslims there is one and only one true God, who is identical with the God of Abraham, Moses, and Jesus. The necessity of obedience to God's will is thus the foundation for all devotion in Islam. Every human being should aspire to live as a servant *(ʿabd)* of God. For this reason, the required ritual acts of worship are referred to collectively as *ʿibādah,* which can be translated as either "worship" or "service." According to the concept of *nubūwah,* God communicates through prophets (*nabīs*) and messengers (*rasūls*). Thus, human agency is essential to the process of revelation. The centrality of this concept can be seen in the fact that the first human being, Adam, is also the first prophet, as humanity should never be without divine guidance. It is through the prophets in their roles as messengers and models of behavior, especially the final prophet, Muḥammad, that humanity learns how to live in obedience to God's will. Devotional life in Islam rests simultaneously upon the worship of and obedience to God, and allegiance to and veneration of the Prophet Muḥammad, who serves both as a teacher and an exemplar.

The doctrine of *qiyāmah* asserts that there will come a time when all human beings will be judged according to their beliefs and actions. Thus, whether interpreted literally or figuratively, *qiyāmah* asserts that human beings are fully responsible before God for their actions. Despite the apparent logical contradiction between an omniscient and omnipotent God and human free will, Islam clearly asserts that, however this contradiction is resolved, individuals must act as if they had free will and fulfill their ritual and ethical obligations with clear intention.

Within this theological context, acts of devotion and worship serve two interrelated purposes. The first is as the fulfillment of God's commandments. As such, they are evidence of obedience to God in preparation for the Day of Judgment. But devotional actions also serve to transform the worshipper, bringing him or her into greater conformity with the divine will. Devotion in Islam is not simply an end in itself; it is also a means for facilitating proper ethical behavior. God calls on humanity not only to follow commands related to the proper performance of ritual, but also to live lives devoted to justice *(ʿadl)* and ethical behavior (*akhlāq*). One who lives his life in the constant remembrance of God will develop the virtue of *ihsān* (beneficence) and become a more perfect human being. Devotional actions within Islam are thus simultaneously evidence of obedience to God and mechanisms for the spiritual education of believers.

ʿIBĀDAH. The most obvious form of worship and devotion within Islam are those actions commonly referred to as "the Five Pillars of Islam." These are: the confession of faith (*shahādah*), ritual prayer (*ṣalāt,* or *namāz*), the fast (*ṣawm*) during the month of Ramaḍān, the *ḥajj,* or pilgrimage to Mecca, and the paying of alms to the needy (*zakāt*). These are the minimal required devotional practices of exoteric Islam. Collectively, they are referred to as *ʿibādah* because they indicate and affirm the worshipper's status as a servant *(ʿabd)* before God. All of these actions require the worshipper to first make an intention to perform them (*nīyah*), thus affirming the doctrine of human responsibility inherent in the doctrine of *qiyāmah.* All of the actions of the *ʿibādah* result in *thawāb,* or spiritual benefit, for the worshipper.

It is through the recitation of the Shahādah—also called the *kalimah,* or word of belief—that one becomes a Muslim. The Shahādah contains two declarations, which must be recited publicly in Arabic. The first, "*ashhadu an lā ilāha illā Allāh*" (I bear witness that there is no god but God), is an affirmation of *tawḥīd.* The second, "*ashhadu an Muḥammadan rasūl Allāh*" (I bear witness that Muḥammad is the Messenger of God), is an affirmation of *nubūwah.* This public recognition of the unity of God and the spiritual authority of Muḥammad, made with proper intention, is sufficient to make one a member of the Muslim community.

ṢALĀT is the daily ritual prayer. Many Muslims consider prayer to be the most important of all Islamic devotional actions. Each prayer consists of a sequence of prescribed actions coupled with the recitation of devotional phrases in Arabic and short *sūrahs* from the Qurʾān. Each of these sequences is referred to as a *rakʿah.* Sunnī Muslims are required to pray five times a day—after dawn, at noon, in the afternoon, at sunset, and in the evening. Each of these prayers consists of between two and four *rakʿahs.* Twelver Shīʿī Muslims pray the same number of *rakʿahs* each day but combine their prayers into three sessions. The fact that prayer punctuates the day at regular intervals affirms the importance of the Qurʾanic concept of *dhikr,* or the remembrance of God. Generally, within Islam the root of human disobedience and sin is seen as forgetfulness. Prayer at regular intervals encourages Muslims constantly to remember the presence of God.

The time of each prayer is announced by the *adhān* or "call to prayer." Each *adhān* is recited in Arabic and includes declaration of the Shahādah and the *takbīr*—the affirmation that "God is Greater" (*Allāhu akbar).* Recited by the *muʾadhdhin* publicly from a minaret, the sound of the *adhān* has become one of the defining characteristics of living in a Muslim environment.

As with all acts of *ʿibādah,* the act of prayer begins with the making of proper intention or *nīyah.* This is followed by *wuḍūʾ,* or ablutions, as one must approach God in a state of physical purity. One prays facing in the direction of the Kaʿbah in the holy city of Mecca. This directional focus is called the *qiblah.* Within a mosque, the *qiblah* is marked by a niche called the *miḥrāb.* Thus, Muslims in communal prayer throughout the world stand in straight lines, except in the sacred precinct surrounding the Kaʿbah itself, where it becomes apparent that Muslims in prayer are actually arranged in concentric circles facing the Kaʿbah and each other.

The act of *ṣalāt* in Islam is a physical performance. Worshippers use their bodies and their voices to physically express obedience to God. The performance of prayer calls for the worshipper to engage in a series of postures culminating in complete prostration as physical evidence of submission and obedience to God. The language used in *ṣalāt* is not the vernacular of the individual worshipper but rather the Qurʾanic Arabic of the time of the Prophet. In performing *ṣalāt* individual believers repeat actions initially performed by the Prophet Muḥammad. Whenever Muslims engage in prayer they form a chain of piety back to the very origins of Islam and affirm a single ritual community with all other Muslims both spatially and temporally. It is an affirmation of *tawḥīd* and *nubūwah,* which links together all Muslims into a common devotional community.

Prayer can be either individual or communal. On Fridays the congregational prayer may take place in a special building called a *masjid,* literally a "place of prostration." Prayers are said behind an *īmām khaṭīb,* who stands at the *miḥrāb* and leads the community through the actions of the *ṣalāt.* At these Friday prayers the *īmām khaṭīb* delivers a sermon called a *khuṭbah,* which generally takes the form of a commentary on a Qurʾān verse, exhorting believers to lead more devout and ethical lives. It should be noted that the *khuṭbah* can also be used for political purposes. For this reason, Muslim rulers have generally attempted to maintain a degree of control over the content of the *khuṭbah.*

Along with the five daily prayers and the Friday congregational prayer, there are special prayers associated with religious holidays and funerals. There are also prescribed supererogatory prayers, which, while not required, are recommended and can be performed at other times of the day. Finally it should be noted that *ṣalāt,* the ritual prayer in Arabic, is not the only form of prayer in Islam. While the term *duʿāhamza* has a variety of meanings, it most commonly refers to personal prayer recited in one's own language. The saying of *duʿāhamza* is an essential aspect of piety of Islam, which affirms the personal relationship of individual believers with God.

While literalist traditions within Islam have seen the act of *ṣalāt* as the simple fulfillment of a divine command, Muslim mystics and esoteric interpreters have noted that there are both exoteric (*ẓāhirī*) and an esoteric (*bāṭinī*) dimensions to *ṣalāt.* For them, prayer is a mystery that imprints upon the bodies and the souls of worshippers and assists in their spiritual transformation.

RAMAḌĀN AND *ZAKĀT*. Muslims fast during the lunar month of Ramaḍān, abstaining from food, drink, and sexual intimacy from sunrise until sunset. They should also attempt to avoid negative and hostile emotions. The fast is incumbent upon all adult Muslims, although the sick, the aged, pregnant and nursing women, and travelers are exempt from its demands. The Ramaḍān fast acts to remind believers of their dependence upon God and affirms their servitude before the divine will. According to some Muslim commentators, it also helps to build an attitude of self-discipline and patience (*ṣabr*) and nurtures a sense of empathy and compassion for the sufferings of the poor.

The fast has both individual and social dimensions, as individual believers experience the fast in the context of community. Families tend to wake collectively to prepare breakfast before sunrise. The breaking of the fast at sunset, called *ifṭār,* is the occasion for shared meals with family and friends. It is not unusual for people to gather in the evening to listen to recitations of the Qurʾān. The Qurʾān is, in fact, traditionally divided into thirty equal portions, each called a *juzʾ,* so that the entire text may be recited over the month-long period of the fast. The end of the Ramaḍān fast is marked by the festival of ʿĪd al-Fiṭr. This is a day for giving charity, exchanging gifts and cards, and visiting one's friends and relatives. The sense of a shared ritual duty helps to create the sense of a single community bound by common practice and belief.

Zakāt refers to the payment of a percentage of one's wealth as alms to the poor. The giving of *zakāt* may appear to be an ethical rather than a devotional act. It is, however, almost always mentioned in the Qurʾān in tandem with *ṣalāt.* The giving of *zakāt* cleanses one's wealth and renders it legitimate. The giving of *zakāt,* like *ṣalāt* and *ṣawm,* affirms the notion that humans are not autonomous beings but rather servants of God. One's wealth is in fact only an *amānat* (trust) from God, who is the real owner. Therefore, while almsgiving is an ethical action designed to support the community, it is also an affirmation of *tawḥīd.*

THE *ḤAJJ*. At least once in a lifetime Muslims should, if possible, make the pilgrimage to Mecca during the month of Dhū al Ḥijjah to perform the rites of the *ḥajj.* There is a lesser pilgrimage called the *ʿumrah,* which can take place any time, from which a believer also gains *thawāb*; but it is the collective and communal action of the *ḥajj* that is required (*wājib*) by Islamic law.

In no other ritual context are the doctrines of *tawḥīd, nubūwah,* and *qiyāmah* so clearly apparent. The *ḥajj* takes place in the city of Mecca and its environs, where the religion of Islam was born. Having faced all of their lives in the direction of the Kaʿbah for prayer, worshippers now travel to the site of the *qiblah.* Here they encounter the structure containing the room that once housed the polytheistic deities of the Arabs, until cleansed of them by the Prophet Muḥammad and left empty to symbolize the unity of God—the essential symbol of *tawḥīd.* The most common image associated with the *ḥajj* is the circumambulation of the Kaʿbah, called the *ṭawāf.* As they circle the Kaʿbah seven times, each pilgrim recites the *talbiyah*, proclaiming in Arabic, "Here I am. O my Lord, Here I am."

However, the central act of the *ḥajj* takes place on the ninth day of Dhū al-Ḥijjah at the Mount of Mercy, on the plain of ʿArafāt, where the Prophet delivered his farewell sermon. This event is called the *wuqūf* (standing). Having previously entered into a state of ritual sanctity known as *iḥrām*, the pilgrims stand draped only in two seamless pieces of white cloth. Dressed identically, all traces of worldly hierarchy are eradicated and each stands equally before God, awaiting divine mercy. This action is not only an affirmation of *tawḥīd*; it is also an evocation of the *qiyāmah*, when all believers will stand at their graves dressed in their funeral shrouds to await the judgment of God.

The events of the *ḥajj* are also evocative of *nubūwah*. Because Mecca is the birthplace of Muḥammad, wherever one looks one is confronted with the remembrance of the Prophet. Although it is not technically part of the *ḥajj*, most pilgrims travel to the city of Medina to visit his tomb. Elements of the *ḥajj* also evoke the memory of other prophets as well, especially Ibrāhīm. Near to the Kaʿbah is the *maqām* of Ibrāhīm, where he stood to lay its cornerstone. The well of Zamzam marks the place where Hagar and Ismāʿīl were rescued from thirst by the angel Jibrīl, who struck the earth with his wing to bring forth water.

On the tenth day of Dhū al-Ḥijjah, pilgrims sacrifice an animal in memory of Ibrāhīm's sacrifice. This is the feast of ʿĪd al-Aḍḥā, the second major festival in Islam after ʿĪd al-Fiṭr. On this day Muslims throughout the world make their own sacrifices, sharing the meat with their own families and giving a portion to the poor.

The Qurʾān as an Object of Devotion within Islam. Devotional piety within Islam is not restricted to the *ʿibādah*. For example, the veneration of the Qurʾān is a ubiquitous form of piety. As the concrete presence of the word of God the Qurʾān is not only a source of knowledge, it is also a focus of devotion and veneration. As God's word it must be treated with respect. One should not handle it while in a state of ritual impurity. It is a violation of religious etiquette to place anything else, even another book, upon the Qurʾān. Devout Muslims wrap the Qurʾān in silk and store it as the highest object in the room. The recitation of the Qurʾān is an act of piety; professional reciters of the Qurʾān are considered great artists, whose recordings are popular throughout the Muslim world.

Phrases from the Qurʾān are used in numerous formulaic ways throughout the day. For example, the opening *sūrah*, *al-Fātiḥah*, is recited on numerous occasions, such as when visiting the tombs of Ṣūfī saints. Pious Muslims will often evoke the phrase *bismillāh* (in the name of God) before initiating any activity—especially at the beginning of a journey. One should not speak of future actions without saying *inshāʾallāh* (God willing), affirming thereby that only God is the true author and knower of future events. The evocation of God's word is, in a very real sense, the evocation of God, and as such it facilitates *dhikr*. Such actions are thus invocations of *tawḥīd*.

Vernacular Traditions within Islam. Because Arabic is the language of the Qurʾān, and because *ṣalāt* is performed in Arabic, Islam's rich vernacular devotional traditions are often overlooked. In the South Asian musical tradition of *qawwālī*, the Prophet Muḥammad and Ṣūfī saints are praised in Urdu and Panjabi. The Shīʿī tradition has produced moving poetry of mourning for Imām Ḥusayn in Urdu and Persian called *marsiyeh*. The Ismāʿīlī tradition includes the recitation of devotional poetry called *ginān*s. There is a rich tradition of devotional poetry in Swahili connected with the birthday of the Prophet. Among the Alevis of Anatolia there is a profound musical tradition called *nefes* in which songs about the Twelve Imāms and the great *pir* Haci Bektash Veli are sung in Turkish to the accompaniment of the *saz*. While *ʿibādah* provides evidence of the unity underlying the world of Islam, these vernacular practices are examples of its rich diversity. Much of this vernacular literature is connected with that aspect of Islamic piety that involves devotional allegiance to persons.

The piety of devotional allegiance. Many of the most popular forms of Muslim devotion are those associated with devotional allegiance to holy persons, especially the Prophet Muḥammad. The person of the Prophet is as important as the Qurʾān in Islamic piety. As one Shīʿī scholar has pointed out, when the earliest Muslims accepted Islam there were only a few verses of the Qurʾān. At that time the fundamental action of accepting Islam was to give allegiance to the Prophet. This is the root of the piety of devotional allegiance.

Certain radical reform movements within Islam, most notably Wahabism, have been critical of devotion to the Prophet, seeing it as a form of *shirk* (associating partners with God). But for most Muslims, devotion to Muḥammad follows instinctively from their love for God. If all Muslims should love God, what better expression of that love can there be than to love the one whom God loves best? And that person is Muḥammad, who bears the title *Ḥabībullah*, the beloved of God.

There are a variety of expressions of devotion to Muḥammad. In many places the birthday of the Prophet is celebrated as a holiday (ʿĪd Mīlād al-Nabī), with special vernacular poetry recited for the occasion. *Naʿt*, the a cappella recitation of devotional verse about the Prophet Muḥammad in Arabic and vernacular languages, is especially popular in South Asia. Another important form of devotion to the Prophet is the recitation of *durūd*, the formulaic blessing of the Prophet recited in Arabic. Muslims often recite *durūd* in conjunction with pilgrimage (*ziyārat*) to the tomb of the Prophet or Ṣūfī saints. It is commonly believed that if one recites *durūd* at the tomb of the Prophet in Mecca he will actually hear it. The recitation of *durūd* is also thought to produce spiritual effects, such as the appearance of the Prophet to the devotee in a dream.

One of the central beliefs associated with this concept of devotional allegiance is the belief in the continuing spiritual existence of the Prophet Muḥammad. Although the Prophet died a physical death like any other human being, most Muslims believe that he is still available to his devotees as a spiritual presence. He is said to be "present and watching" (*hāḍr-o nāẓir*). Despite the fact that radical groups like the Wahabis firmly reject this notion, its supporters point to *ḥadīths* that state that the Prophet is a manifestation of a preexistent light—the prophetic *nūr*. Thus the Prophet is not merely a model of behavior, he is also an object of veneration.

Devotional allegiance in Shīʿī Islam. For many Muslims the piety of devotional allegiance extends beyond the person of the Prophet Muḥammad to include those who are identified as his legitimate representatives and successors. Once again, if one is to love the Prophet, should one not express that love by loving those whom he loved? Within Shīʿīsm this love focuses on the *ahl al-bayt* (the family of the Prophet; literally, "the people of the house") especially the Shīʿī *imāms*. The first *imām*, ʿAlī ibn Abī Ṭālib, Muḥammad's cousin and son-in-law, is especially venerated. He is identified as *Mushkil Kusha*, the remover of obstacles. It is not uncommon in Asia for Muslims—Sunnīs as well as Shīʿah—to say *"Ya ʿAlī Madad"* ("Oh ʿAlī, help me") when attempting a difficult task. Not only is the tomb of ʿAlī in Najaf in Iraq a center of pilgrimage, but his purported tomb in Mazār-I Sharīf in southern Afghanistan is also a major pilgrimage site for Muslims.

The Prophet's grandson, Imām Ḥusayn, also has a major role in Shīʿī devotional life. As the martyr of Karbalāʾ, killed by the Caliph Yazīd on the tenth of the lunar month of Muḥarram, he has a special place in the hearts of Shīʿī Muslims. While the Shīʿah believe that all the *imāms* share in the same spiritual light, Imām Ḥusayn was the last of the immediate *ahl al-bayt* who lived with the Prophet in Medina. This immediate family—consisting of Muḥammad, his daughter Fāṭimah, her husband ʿAlī, and their two children, Ḥasan and Ḥusayn—are often represented iconographically by the image of a five-fingered hand. In South Asia these five persons are venerated as "the five pure ones" (*panjatan pāk*). As the final surviving grandson of the Prophet, Ḥusayn's murder is an axial event and has deep spiritual significance.

During the first ten days of Muḥarram, Shīʿī Muslims enter into a state of ritual mourning. People dress in black and recite mournful poetry. They also gather in mourning assemblies to hear the retelling of the story of Karbalāʾ. It is commonly believed that Fāṭimah attends these assemblies and gathers the tears of the mourners to present them before God on the Day of Judgment. The day of ʿĀshūrāʾ on the tenth of Muḥarram is a particularly fervent day of devotional activity, when the community gathers to mourn and share food.

The precise nature of mourning for Imām Ḥusayn varies from region to region. In Iran there are stylized *taʿziyah* plays, which depict the events of Karbalāʾ. In South Asia there are processions culminating in ritual funerals for the *imām*. But for Shīʿī Muslims everywhere, participation in these events is a crucial marker of religious identity. There is a famous aphorism: "Every day is ʿĀshūrāʾ, every place is Karbalāʾ." The events of Karbala are not seen as mere historical events. Beneath the appearances of ordinary reality the eternal struggle between "Good and Evil" that took place paradigmatically at Karbalāʾ is always reoccurring. Humanity is always being asked to choose between the path of Imām Ḥusayn and the path of Yazīd, the path of light and the path of darkness. The ritual recreation of the events of Karbalāʾ during the month of Muḥarram is a way of preparing for participation in the eternal spiritual struggle between "Good and Evil."

It should be noted that devotion to ʿAlī and his descendants extends into the Sunnī community as well. For example, the day of ʿĀshūrāʾ is commemorated by many Sunnīs. More importantly, the great majority of Sunnīs who accept the validity of the Ṣūfī tradition accept ʿAli as the master of the esoteric sciences. He is venerated as *Shāh-i Awliyāʾ* (King of the Saints). Within the Ṣūfī traditions, devotional allegiance extends to include the various *awliyāʾ* (sing. *walī*; saints) of the Islamic mystical traditions. Like the Prophet, they are simultaneously models of behavior and objects of devotion; and, as with the Prophet, people seek their intercession. Within the worldview of Sufism it is believed that the *awliyāʾ*, who trace their spiritual lineage back to the Prophet through a chain of spiritual transmission, have achieved a state of annihilation in God. For those who practice it, devotion to the *awliyāʾ* is intimately connected to notions of *tawḥīd* and *nubūwah*.

Devotion to Ṣūfī saints takes a variety of forms. Some people visit living saints to formally become their disciples (*murīds*) on the Ṣūfī path (*ṭarīqah*). Those on this path practice specific devotional exercises. Chief among these is *dhikr*, which involves the individual or collective repetition of the names of God in order to produce an altered state of consciousness called *ḥāl* or *wajd*. But many people visit the *awliyāʾ* simply to seek their blessing or to request some material benefit, such as the birth of sons, better jobs, or successful marriages.

More common than visitation to living spiritual masters is pilgrimage (*ziyārat*) to the tombs of deceased *awliyāʾ*. The gravesites of important Ṣūfīs have, over time, become the locations of major tomb complexes. Such *ziyārats* are found in nearly every corner of the Islamic world. The tombs of such major figures as Aḥmad Yasavī in Central Asia, Aḥmad al-Badawī in North Africa, Muʿīn al-Dīn Chishtī in India, and Jalāl al-Dīn Rūmī in Anatolia are not only local but regional and even international centers of pilgrimage. It is commonly believed that, like the Prophet, the *awliyāʾ* continue to exist as spiritual presences at their tombs. As with visits to living *awliyāʾ*, pilgrims come to seek both spiritual and material blessings. Pilgrims may make vows in connection with their requests, which they later fulfill by performing pious action. Ṣūfī shrines have thus become centers for the feeding of the poor, as pilgrims often fulfill their vows by feeding the less fortunate.

There is a general air of piety and devotion within the precincts of a Ṣūfī tomb. The *awliyāʾ* are the true rulers of this world, and one approaches them as one does a monarch, with humility and respect. There is thus a proper etiquette (*adab*) for interacting with the *awliyāʾ*, whether as living masters or at their tombs.

In many parts of the world the death or birth anniversary of the *awliyāʾ* is celebrated with religious festivals that at first glance may seem to conflict with the piety inherent in *ziyārat.* In South Asia, for example, these celebrations, called *ʿurs,* include fairs (*melas*) and carnival attractions, as well as pious devotions. Not surprisingly, aspects of these manifestations of the piety of devotional allegiance are frequently attacked by Muslim reformers, who see in them, at the very least, a form of popular innovation, and at the worst a kind of *shirk* that violates *tawḥīd.* Defenders of these traditions, however, have argued that those who take part in these popular expressions of piety are ultimately expressing their devotion to God and his Prophet. As such, their actions are within the proper purview of Islamic piety.

SEE ALSO Attributes of God, article on Islamic Concepts; Dhikr; God, article on God in Islam; Islamic Religious Year; Kaʿbah; Pilgrimage, article on Muslim Pilgrimage; Ṣawm; Shahādah.

BIBLIOGRAPHY

Calverley, Edwin Eliot, trans. and ed. *Worship in Islam* (1925). 2d ed. London, 1957. Reprint, Westport, Conn., 1981. Translation of the *Book of Worship* from the great Sunnī scholar and proponent of Sufism al-Ghazzālī's *Iḥyaʾ ʿulūm al-dīn,* an important book dealing with the esoteric dimension of *ʿibādah.* Al-Ghazzālī's book has been widely translated and remains popular in the Muslim world.

Cragg, Kenneth, and R. Marston Speight, eds. *Islam from Within: Anthology of a Religion.* Belmont, Calif., 1980. A useful anthology of Islamic sources containing a variety of important texts on devotion and worship.

Currie, P. M. *The Shrine and Cult of Muʿīn al-Dīn Chishtī of Ajmer.* Delhi, 1989. This book provides fascinating insight into the role of the *awliyāʾ* and pilgrimage to their tombs in Islamic piety.

Denny, Frederick Mathewsen. *An Introduction to Islam.* 2d ed. New York, 1994. Although this is a textbook it provides detailed and accurate descriptions of *ʿibādah.*

Hodgson, Marshall G. S. *The Venture of Islam: Conscience and History in a World Civilization,* vol. 1, *The Classical Age of Islam.* Chicago, 1974. The chapters "The Sharʿi Islamic Vision" and "Muslim Personal Piety" are still among the best commentaries on Muslim piety.

Kassam, Tazim R. *Songs of Wisdom and Circles of Dance: An Anthology of Hymns by the Satpanth Ismāʿīlī Muslim Saint, Pir Shams.* Albany, N.Y., 1995.

Peters, F. E. *The Hajj.* Reprint, Princeton, N.J., 1995.

Schimmel, Annemarie. *Mystical Dimensions of Islam.* Chapel Hill, N.C., 1975. Excellent overview of the Ṣūfī tradition.

Schimmel, Annemarie. *And Muhammad Is His Messenger: The Veneration of the Prophet in Islamic Piety.* Chapel Hill, N.C., 1985. Rich source on the role the Prophet in Muslim devotional life.

Schubel, Vernon James. *Religious Performance in Contemporary Islam: Shiʿi Devotional Rituals in South Asia.* Columbia, S.C., 1993. Provides a detailed account of Muḥarram rituals in South Asia in the larger context of Shīʿī piety. Includes a lengthy explanation of the concept of the piety of devotional allegiance.

VERNON JAMES SCHUBEL (2005)

WORSHIP AND DEVOTIONAL LIFE: HINDU DEVOTIONAL LIFE

Although there is great variety in the forms of devotional life in Hinduism, some common themes may be identified that characterize the general religious impulse behind their variety. One important theme is that of ritual enhancement: Devotional practice aims at sustaining or improving the circumstances of the worshiper. These aims may be immediate and practical, such as the healing of disease, avoidance of the destructive influences of malevolent forces, fertility of crops, animals, and persons, and maintenance of family solidarity; or they may be more soteriological in character, such as the pursuit of liberation (*mokṣa*) from the bondage of rebirth. In this way, devotional life may be seen as a series of elaborate strategies for the enhancement of an individual's or group's situation as defined in terms of both worldly and transcendent goals.

A second theme centers on the ordering function of devotional life. Ceremonies frequently require the creation and/or maintenance of conditions of ritual purity. This purity may be temporary, brought about through bathing, cleaning, and providing substances deemed pure and religiously efficacious for the various rites, or it may be of a more permanent sort, such as the employment of members of castes, especially in their roles as priests, who are deemed sufficiently pure within the caste hierarchy to make their participation in devotional performances ritually effective.

A third theme is that of negotiation or exchange, in which devotional performances become occasions for giving human resources of food, gifts, and devotion to supernatural entities and powers in exchange for human well-being, which is understood to flow from those persons and powers as a consequence of the rite. While this negotiation process may have as its goal the pursuit of order and the existential enhancement of the worshiper, it may also involve episodes that are chaotic and/or playful.

The major forms of devotional practice in the Hindu tradition include sacrifice (*yajña*); ceremonies for the ancestors (*śrāddha*); life cycle rituals (*saṃskāra*); meditational or ascetic practices (*tapas*); worship of deities (*pūjā*); pilgrimage (*yātra*); personal vows (vrata); festivals and fairs (*utsava, melā*); sacred calendars (*pañcāṅga*); and religious healing or exorcism (*cikitsā*). Some of these devotional practices have ancient textual warrants for their authority that date back to the period of the Vedas and that are perpetuated by members of the traditional priestly castes, especially brahmans. Others are preserved in oral tradition among castes and communities further removed from the ritual texts and practices of the traditional religious elite groups. In both cases, these devotional traditions rest on the assumptions of their participants that they possess long-standing authority and efficacy.

SACRIFICE. As both the Vedas and the Brahmanas, books of ritual instruction and commentary, attest, sacrifice (*yajña*) is among the earliest forms of devotional life. The sacrifices are distinguished in the later literature between those performed in temporarily constructed enclosures or in the open air for larger communities (the *śrauta,* lit. "solemn," rites) and those that are restricted to individual households and are performed indoors. At the center of Vedic sacrifice is the use of fire and the ritual transformation of the patron or sacrificer (*yajamāṇa*), who is given rebirth through the sacrifice into the world of the gods. Fire is personified as the god Agni, who mediates between the worlds of gods and humans and who is associated with the warmth of the world and its creatures. Priests who maintain sufficient purity act on behalf of the patron who sponsors the sacrifice and for whom the benefits of the rite accrue. The Vedic *śrauta* sacrifices frequently employed sixteen or seventeen brahmans in various specialized roles. The priests offered oblations of milk, butter, honey, grains, fruits, animals, water, and soma, the elixir of immortality (*amṛta*), along with recitations of mantras. The *śrauta* sacrifices included the Agnihotra, a relatively simple morning and evening series of offerings; the Aśvamedha, in which a horse roamed for a year to measure the boundaries of the kingdom and then was captured and sacrificed to the gods for the protection and well-being of the kingdom; the Rājasūya, which consecrated the king by putting him through a ritual rebirth that included the rebirth of the cosmos; and the Agnicayana, which reinvigorated the cosmos by constructing an altar of fire, feeding the gods offerings of divine drink, and providing a voice for divine speech through the sustained recitation of sacred formulas.

Usually a king or tribal leader served as the sponsor of such sacrifices on behalf of his clan and the world as a whole. In this way, the sacrifice had as a specific goal the enhancement of a particular individual and as a general goal, universal enhancement. The fire served as the symbol connecting personal, political, cosmological, and metaphysical understandings of the world through its capacity to serve as element, deity, animating power in all beings, and receptacle of offerings. These offerings usually involved the blood sacrifice of animals and the brewing of soma, a beverage having hallucinogenic properties and believed to contain immortalizing power much desired by the gods. The aim of the *śrauta* rites was to reestablish or maintain the welfare of the universe. They provided food, long life, sons, cattle, and power; they did not seek to confer release from the world (*mokṣa*) but to sustain it in its optimal form. The sacrifice, with its fire at the center, served as the axis around which the cosmos, containing all that moves and does not move, journeyed through time and space. Since the Vedic period these rites have undergone gradual eclipse, and in the present day they are performed only occasionally by groups of brahmans who raise the funds for their performance through contributions.

Following similar patterns resting on the same religious beliefs and assumptions, the domestic (*gṛhya*) rituals articulated the religious concerns of people rooted in the world of family and kingdom. The head of the household served as the patron or sacrificer before the household fire by offering butter and grain cakes variously directed at the gods, ancestors, all beings, sages, and humans, all of whom often appear in the guise of guests and beggars. These rites, along with the life-cycle rituals (*saṃskāras*), continue to be performed by traditionalist brahmans. In addition, the Vedic tradition of sacrifice has had a profound influence over other forms of devotional life beyond the boundaries of Brahmanical practice, from temple worship to popular fairs and festivals.

ANCESTOR RITUALS. The Śrāddha rites, or ceremonies performed for the dead, begin at the conclusion of the corpse's cremation. According to the textual traditions of the Gṛhyasūtras, which were contemporary with the Brahmanas, the rites should last for a year, although twelve days as a symbolic year is the more common pattern. These Śrāddha rites continue to be performed among brahmans and other castes traditionally understood to be "twice-born" and therefore eligible for the benefits of Vedic rites and knowledge. After the eldest son, serving as the sacrificer, has ignited the cremation fire and the body is consumed, a temporary ritual body (*piṇḍa*) fashioned from cooked rice is assembled over a period of ten days. This body contains the ghost (*preta*) and serves as a receptable for subsequent offerings, thus enabling the deceased to be nourished on the long journey to join the ancestors in the divine world. On the final day the assembled body is cut into three pieces and merged with *piṇḍas* representing the deceased's father, grandfather, and great-grandfather dwelling in the earth, atmosphere, and heavens, respectively. These rites establish the deceased harmoniously within their appropriate worlds and prevent them from becoming hungry and haunting their living descendants. In this way the ceremony honors and serves the needs of the ancestors, seeks their influence within the world of the dead for the benefit of the living, and protects the living community from potential peril wrought by ancestors insufficiently sustained in their respective worlds.

Other ceremonies, performed on the new-moon day of each month, provide ritual veneration of the ancestors as part of the regular rhythms of the religious calendar. In these rites a brahman—and in some parts of India, a crow—represents the ancestor and receives offerings of pindas, water, and sesame seeds from his descendants. Annually the descendants journey to sacred sites and rivers to have pinda ceremonies performed.

LIFE-CYCLE RITES. The literal meaning of *saṃskāra* is "refined" or "well-accomplished," and thus the *saṃskāras*, or life-cycle rites, are directed at the ritual perfection or consecration of an individual at various moments in life. The traditional number of these rites varies with different texts and performance traditions, most of them having from twelve to sixteen rituals that might be performed throughout a person's life. These include rites for auspicious conception, the birth of a son, safe delivery, birth (Jātakarman), naming the child, first solid food, first haircut, initiation into learning the Vedas (Upanayana), and first hearing of the sacred Gayatrī mantra—thus marking the transition into the first of the four life stages (*asrāmas*), namely, studentship (*brahmacarya*). The marriage rite (Vivāha) marks the onset of the second stage, that of the householder (*gṛhastha*). *Saṃskāra* performance calls for fire, offerings, and brahmans to receive the offerings that remain after the gods and ancestors have been honored.

Although today only a relatively few groups of brahmans maintain the *yajña* traditions, the larger patterns of Vedic sacrifice have continued to shape later devotional life. The sacrifice's concern for achieving ultimate conceptual order and performative effectiveness found new voice in the speculative and ascetic traditions making use of a number of meditative techniques, the best-known of which is yoga. The concern for the constituency of the ancestors continued to be articulated in the Śrāddha rites, in which descendants construct new and purified bodies for the dead. The worship of the gods, which is not emphasized in yoga and Śrāddha practices, becomes highly developed in the tradition of *pūjā*, which makes use of permanent or disposable images of gods and goddesses.

ASCETIC AND MEDITATIONAL PRACTICES. The practice of sacrifice in ancient India yielded a tradition of speculation on the sources and meanings of the sacrifice itself. The ritual commentaries (Brāhmaṇas) invited meditations on the homologies between elements of the sacrifice and those of the cosmos and the individual in order to identify that which lay at the source of all reality. Knowledge paralleled ritual exactitude as a source of power to participate in and even transcend profane time and space. The practice of asceticism (*tapas*) provided the moral, physical, psychological, and intellectual environment in which the one who knows the inner meanings of the sacrifice might achieve proximate or ultimate religious transformation.

Ascetic and meditational practice is probably the most ancient Hindu religious practice. Evidence from images and cylinder seals from the Indus Valley of the third millennium BCE suggests that ascetic practices were part of this pre-Vedic culture. As speculation about the homologies between the sacrifice and the *yajamāṇa* (patron or sacrificer) grew during the late Vedic and Brahmanic periods, the fire of the sacrifice became identified with the bodily warmth produced during prolonged periods of meditation. As an acquired skill resulting from intense practice, *tapas* was principally a technique for achieving power and therefore had no inherently moral quality; it became a means by which one might appropriate the creative heat that animates the Vedic fire and thereby direct its power toward one's own ends. In the epic and Puranic traditions, gods and demons alike make use of ascetic practice in order to overpower or resist their opponents. As the internalization of the creative heat of the cosmos, *tapas* came to be recognized by virtually every religious and philosophical tradition in South Asia as a valuable or necessary component in the pursuit of both proximate and ultimate religious goals. The *Bhagavadgītā* classifies *tapas* according to its uses or goals; it recognizes the purpose of release from rebirth, which it considers to be a "pure" goal; the purpose of obtaining supernatural powers; and the purpose of increasing one's enjoyment of worldly pleasures. These three goals are classified as *sattva* ("luminosity"), *rajas* ("energy"), and *tamas* ("inertia"), respectively.

The traditions of *tapas* that have been most systematically formulated are those of *rajāyoga*, that is, the classical system of Yoga as taught by Patañjali; the controlling of bodily and mental states, or *haṭhayoga;* and the use of complex visual and aural symbolization drawing upon sexual and ritual imagery in order to achieve powerful and highly desirable religious experiences, or Tantra. As a form of *tapas,* Yoga draws upon ancient traditions of South and Central Asian shamanism in which trances were induced through strict regulation of diet, breathing, bodily movement, and autosuggestion in order to ascend into ecstatic states. During the Upaniṣadic period (c. 800 BCE–200 CE) there emerged further systematic formulations that classified bodily and mental states in a finely distinguished hierarchy leading to *mokṣa* (release from rebirth) as its ultimate goal. One of the most important of these various meditational traditions found precise articulation by Patañjali in his *Yoga Sūtra,* written probably during the Gupta period (320–540 CE), with important later commentaries such as the sixteenth-century *Yogavārttika* of *Vijñānabhikṣu.* The social contexts of yogic devotional practice were small communities of ascetics assembled around a *guru* ("teacher") who was highly regarded for his skills in the practice and for personal religious charisma. This classical formulation of Yoga remained largely compatible with Brahmanical orthodoxy and orthopraxis.

The practice of asceticism found particular favor among sectarian devotees of Śiva, the mythological embodiment of ascetic power. This tradition combined the classical with the more esoteric and eroticized practices and postures of the non-Vedic traditions of Tantra.

Unlike the ascetic traditions of Brahmanic culture, which held sensory experience suspect and emphasized celibacy and the restraint of erotic impulses, Tantric practice pursued the senses by integrating erotic desire into ascetic transcendence. Building on the techniques of *haṭhayoga,* the *vāmamarga,* or "left-path"—indicating deviation from the "right-path," or Brahmanic orthopraxis—provides for practitioners to become initiated into "circles" (*cakras*) in which males identify with Śiva and females with Śakti, his consort. While Vedic and Tantric mantras are chanted the adept heightens his or her sense experience by consuming *Cannabis sativa* followed by fish, meat, aphrodisiacs, and liquor, and by engaging in sexual union with the consort. The female practitioners, called *śaktis*, imitate the active role of the Goddess in the cosmos by initiating sexual union with the males who take the role of Śiva. By a highly stylized process the male adept simultaneously retrains his mind, his breath, and the flow of his semen. The intensity of these forms of control is understood to pull up the animating power of the universe (*kuṇḍalinī*) through the physical body into the subtle body and finally to merge with the Śiva-Śakti principles at the center of the cosmos. This experience is believed to result in a quick, though potentially quite dangerous, path to *mokṣa.*

Tantric practice and imagery inspired much of India's erotic art, much of which is founded on the iconography of Śiva's ithyphallic emblem (*liṅga*) located in the center of Śakti's "seat" or "vulva" (*pīṭhā*). By reversing the logic of orthoprax asceticism, which stressed renunciation of sensuality as the means of overcoming attachment to the world and its consequences for karman and suffering, Tantra exploited sensual experience and placed the practitioner in the midst of heightened sensuality, using its power for mystical ends. This radical reinterpretation of the traditions of *tapas* never won favor in the Brahmanical tradition, but remained a marginal movement. It did, however, influence temple devotional life, especially in South India.

WORSHIP OF DEITIES. Derived from the Sanskrit root meaning "honor" or "worship," *pūjā* involves the ritual offerings of foods, service, and gestures of respect usually bestowed upon deities in their iconic forms. As a devotional tradition, *pūjā* appears to have emerged during the late Brahmanic period from the practice of honoring brahmans during their visits to the home. The practice then became amalgamated into later *bhakti,* or devotional Hinduism, through its classical textual formulation from the sixth century onward in ritual sections of the Puranas. Today, *pūjā* is one of the most pervasive forms of Hindu worship, and is observed with varying degrees of complexity by most Hindus. The enduring popularity of *pūjā* as a devotional undertaking may be in part its ability to combine elements of Vedic practice with popular religious sentiment.

Pūjās vary widely in ritual complexity, from simple offerings of sips of water, flowers, food, the recitation of mantras, the singing of devotional songs (*āratīs, kīrtanas*), and the waving of lighted camphor before the image, to extended ritual episodes that draw on Vedic texts involving offering hospitality, invocations, bathing and dressing the image, and offering many kinds of foods, flowers, and leaves. The image of the deity is frequently made of perishable materials such as clay or wood, and may be brought ceremoniously into the home. It is placed in a part of the household set aside for the deity's residence and then ritually enlivened by establishing in it vital breath (*prāṇapratiṣṭhā*). There it dwells as a living member of the household for a period of time and is then taken to a nearby river, temple tank, or ocean to be immersed, thereby dissolving back into its primal elements.

Similar patterns of hospitality and praise may be seen in *pūjās* performed in temples. The temple traditions rely heavily on the images and mythologies of divine kingship: The deity is the king or queen of the universe and the shrine is his or her palace. The temple images are periodically enthroned and taken in procession around the ritual boundaries of the kingdom, where they are seen and adored by multitudes of worshipers. The priests perform the duties associated with *pūjā* in both large public settings and small private ones for client worshipers.

Central to the religious appeal of *pūjā* for many Hindus is the experience of *darśana* ("auspicious seeing"). When an image of a deity is prepared and placed on view in the home or temple, appropriately honored and attired in festive costume, the deity makes himself or herself available to be seen by worshipers. The deity "sees" them and extends his or her grace to them, tangibly in the form of *prasāda,* the sacred food that, having been offered to the god or goddess and thus become sanctified by its proximity to the deity, is now returned to the worshiper. At the same time, the deity is "seen" by the worshiper, thereby establishing a visual and personal moment of mutual religious contact.

PILGRIMAGE. As with many other religious traditions, Hinduism has long valued visits to sacred places. These places are frequently associated with geographical features such as rivers (Gangotri, Allahabad, Banaras), places marking land's end (Kanya Kumārī, Rameśvaram, Dvarkā), and mountains (Bādrināth). Other shrines derive their sanctity from the deities who reside there, for example, Viṣṇu at Puri and Tirupati, Kṛṣṇa at Vrndāvana, Śiva at Ujjain and Nāsik, the Goddess at Kāmakhya, Madurai, and Kālighaṭ. Some pilgrimage centers have appeal throughout the subcontinent, drawing pilgrims from upper classes and providing religious merit for those who journey the distance to receive the *darśana* of the deity enshrined there. Other centers are more regional, or local; they serve pilgrims from the more immediate areas and may have large constituencies from particular castes and groups of castes. The pan-Indian shrines are generally the centers for the "high gods and goddesses" of the Hindu pantheon who are celebrated in the Sanskrit lore of the epics and Purāṇas, whereas the regional and local shrines house deities whose lore is carried more commonly through oral and non-Sanskritic literary sources; these regional deities are, however, frequently associated with one of the "high gods." Pilgrimages (*yātra*) may be made at any time, but those undertaken in conjunction with sacred times in the religious year are understood to be particularly efficacious.

Pilgrims make the often arduous journey to shrines for many reasons: in order to honor the deity who lives there, to bring offerings, to celebrate the magnificent and heroic deeds performed there as told in the sacred lore of the shrine, to receive the deity's grace through the experience of *darśana,* or "beholding," to gain personal religious merit, to derive specific benefits such as healing or the expiation of past misdeeds, or to enhance their personal status in their home communities when they return. Pilgrims often visit shrines as part of the performance of a vow (*vrata*) in which the pilgrimage becomes a gesture of gratitude given in exchange for benefits bestowed by the deity. Pilgrimages also serve as occasions in which Hindus temporarily move out of the hierarchical structures of home and village and enter into a more amorphous realm in which the pilgrims encounter one another as parts of a single generic religious community with the shrine as its symbolic center. Finally, pilgrimages to shrines serve as occasions for religious educations and microcosms of the religious life; they are journeys, at once personal and collective, through auspicious temporal and spatial contexts that enhance the devotees' religious appropriation of their lives.

VOWS. A *vrata,* or vow, is a ritual practice undertaken for a specific length of time in order to achieve a particular goal. It is usually undertaken by an individual and may include various forms of renunciation, such as fasting, celibacy, and an increased intensity of religious awareness that usually takes the form of reciting stories (*kathā*). A *vrata kathā* ("vow story") can be either ancient or contemporary, and its purpose is to disclose the origin of the vow and its efficacy. As a form of devotional practice, *vrata* is more commonly observed by women, and is often directed toward goddesses. The aims to be achieved through their observance of *vratas* are often quite immediate and pragmatic: the birth of children, particularly sons; success in business and on examinations; abundant harvests; healing of illness; return of an errant spouse; and so forth. The *vrata* involves a basic exchange in which the devotee demonstrates her (or his) heightened religious devotion and faith which the deity receives as a gift and in which she or he delights. In return, if the deity is satisfied that the vow was pure in its intent and execution, she or he rewards the devotee according to the request made in the vow. In this way the tradition of *vrata* makes use of the Hindu renunciatory impulse in order to contribute to the maintanence and enhancement of the everyday world.

FAIRS AND FESTIVALS. Just as nature passes through seasons of cold weather, heat, and the rains, Hindu religious life passes through seasons marked by various collective religious observances. Each deity has his or her own month or season. Which festivals are observed is shaped in some measure by caste and sectarian affiliation. In North India, for example, the religious year begins in the month of Caitra (March–April), with the first festival being Navarātri, or "Nine Nights," in honor of the Goddess. As the hot season approaches the festival life takes on a more austere and ascetic character. It is the season for honoring the goddess Śītalā, the bringer of fever diseases. Her images are cooled with water in an effort to prevent her (and the cosmos she embodies) from becoming overheated and thus conveying fever to worshipers. The monsoon, occurring during the months of Āśādha (June–July) and Śrāvaṇa (July–August), disrupts travel from place to place. It is the time when the various mendicants cease their pilgrimages and settle in shrines and hermitages for the rainy season to observe Cāturmāsya, or the "four-month" retreat. This period has its mythical parallel in Viṣṇu's cosmic sleep. The full-moon night of the month of Āśādha (June-July) is called Guru Pūrṇimā and is the time when Hindus pay homage to their religious teachers.

With the conclusion of the rainy season, festival life increases in intensity through the relatively cool and dry months that follow. The months of Śrāvaṇa (July–August) and Bhādrapada (August–September) are filled with religious fairs (*melās*) held at shrines and temples, where the images of the deities are displayed for worshipers to receive their *darśana* (auspicious viewing). *Melās* are also recreational and commercial occasions for merchants and traders to set up temporary booths and sell their wares. An important festival during the waxing fortnight of the month of Śrāvaṇa is Nāga Pañcamī ("serpent's fifth"), because it falls on the fifth night of the fortnight. Snakes are particularly dangerous during the rainy season because the flooding forces them out of the subterranean holes in which they had taken refuge during the preceding hot, dry months. Although especially associated with Śiva, the veneration and propitiation of the serpent is acknowledged by Hindus from many different ranks. The full moon of the month of Śrāvaṇa is the occasion for the honoring of brothers and sisters in the celebration of Rakṣā Bandhana ("tying the amulet"), in which sisters tie elaborately decorated wrist-ornaments on their brothers.

The goddess Gaurī and the gods Gaṇeśa and Kṛṣṇa are celebrated during the month of Bhādrapada (August–September), followed in the fall season by the month of Āśvina (September–October) with the rituals of remembrance of the ancestors (Pitṛ Pakṣa) in which the annual Vedic *śrāddha* ceremonies are performed. This is followed by the second Navarātri, or nine-night worship of the Goddess, called Durgā Pūjā. Rāma is worshiped with sacred dramas and processions celebrating his victory over the demon Rāvaṇa. During the following month of Kārtika (October-November), the popular festival of Dīvālī, a Vaiṣṇava celebration particularly popular among merchant castes, marks another year's return of Lakṣmī, the goddess of wealth and good fortune. It is a time of housecleaning and refurbishing, the purchase of new clothing and cooking pots, and general renewal of life. It is a highly auspicious time in the Hindu year, and Hindus, especially in the north, celebrate it with great enthusiasm.

The cold season lasts through the months of Mārgasīrṣa, Pauśa, and Māgha, and brings about a decrease in the rhythm of fair and festival activity. The sun is worshiped especially during this season, and it is a good time for Hindus to undertake pilgrimages to near or distant shrines. As the weather begins to warm again during the months of Phālguna (February–March) and Caitra (March–April) the major celebration is Māhaśivarātrī ("great night of Śiva"), the principal festival in honor of the god Śiva. Kṛṣṇa, the erotic cowherd, is celebrated with the dionysian festival of Holī in which devotees dance, play pranks, and douse one another with colored water. Although the new year does not actually begin for another fortnight, Holī serves as the event of chaotic renewal that marks the end of the old year and begins the new year with appropriate exuberance.

As classified and prescribed by the sacred calendar, the Hindu year provides a temporal structure for an array of religious moods and activities to take place. As one moves through the days and weeks of the year, various occasions—both solemn and raucous—affirm the many gods, goddesses, ancestors, and auspicious as well as inauspicious powers. As a totality of time, the religious calendar provides an eternal architecture through which time as the experience of irreversible duration may pass. Every year is new and different from the last, yet through the observances of sacred festivals and fairs each year is a repetition of the enduring and paradigmatic forms of religious experience and community life.

Sacred Calendars. The Hindu sacred calendar is called the Pañcāṅga ("five limbs"). It contains the temporal structure of opportunities for religious enhancement by identifying those segments of time that are appropriate for various undertakings, whether they be moments of auspicious power or moments of danger. The Hindu year is based on the twelve lunar months, which are slightly shorter than the solar months of the Western calendar. Each month is made up of two fifteen-day fortnights (*pakṣas*, "wings"). The first is the waning or dark (*kṛṣṇa*) fortnight moving toward the new moon night (*amāvāsyā*); the second is the waxing or bright (*śukla*) fortnight, which culminates in the full moon night (*pūrṇimā*). Each day of the month is thus described by its place in fortnight (e.g., "the fourth day in the bright fortnight"). Days occurring during the bright half of the month are generally regarded as inherently auspicious, because time, like the moon, is moving toward fulfillment; days occurring during the dark or waning half of the month tend to be associated with danger and inauspiciousness and often call for more cautious behavior and an increase in asceticism. Because the lunar months are shorter than the solar, the calendar adds an extra month every two to three years to make it coincide with the solar calendar.

The lunar days and weeks move through cycles overseen by deities. For example, Sunday is ruled by the Sun (Ravi) and is therefore called Ravivāra; Monday is governed by the Moon (Soma) and is called Somavāra; Tuesday is overseen by Mars (Maṅgala) and is known as Mangalavāra; Wednesday, ruled by Mercury (Budha), is called Budhavāra; Thursday, ruled by Jupiter (Bṛhaspati), is called Bṛhaspativāra; Friday, ruled by Venus (Śukra), is called Śukravāra; and Saturday, ruled by Saturn (Śani), is called Śanivāra. The Pañcāṅga details the auspicious and inauspicious powers inherent in each lunar day (*tithi*). This information is useful to Hindus in planning new undertakings such as setting out on journeys, opening businesses, and, especially, performing weddings. Because time is not merely neutral duration but already carries with it certain identifiable—and to some extent predictable—powers, the moment of one's birth serves to define or characterize one's character and destiny. Astrological information regarding the precise time of one's birth carries considerable weight in arranging marriages, and it is commonplace for the horoscopes of prospective brides and grooms to be scrutinized to determine if the potential marriage carries sufficient auspicious powers to ensure its success and its capacity to enhance the lives of others in the extended family. In cases where the astrological signs may be inauspicious, avoidance or compensatory ritual undertakings may be recommended by astrological specialists.

Religious Healing and Exorcism. The Hindu cosmos is a complex structure of interacting, and at times competing, powers with which (or whom) Hindus must align themselves to their maximum advantage through devotional actions that generate personal and collective enhancement. This enhancement is frequently represented through imagery and ritual strategies having to do with purity, renunciation, and propitiation. The pursuit of these forms of enhancement shape particular ritual actions, diets, and social associations. Nevertheless, even when these efforts are undertaken, but especially if they are neglected or held in contempt, individuals can fall prey to malevolent forces. These malevolent forces take the forms of "hungry ghosts"—those spirits who are trapped in the interstitial realm between the living and the dead—witches, demons, and sometimes deities (such as Śītala, the goddess of smallpox) who themselves have been victims of misfortune. They tend to inhabit territories of maximal pollution such as graveyards and cremation grounds, places where violent and untimely deaths have taken place, or in marginal areas, such as forests, at the edge of the inhabited worlds. They appear under cover of darkness, frequently attacking their victims in dreams. Diseases, particularly diseases of a psychosomatic or psychological character for which precise empirical diagnosis is lacking, are often understood to be the result of the malevolent intervention of one of these spirits, either out of the spirit's own bad temper or as the consequence of a curse of a worldly opponent.

Individuals are diagnosed as possessed by malevolent entities if, in addition to physical symptoms such as fever, they exhibit erratic behavior such as falling into trance and verbally abusing members of their family. Certain exorcist-healers are called upon to induce the evil spirit to come out. These healers, frequently from low-caste or tribal communities, are recruited on the basis of their personal charisma and their knowledge of and fearlessness within the territory of the demonic. They bring a specialized knowledge of mantras and medicines to the treatment of their clients or patients. Often the exorcist goes into shamanic trance and takes onto himself the voice and persona of the demon or argues with it in a way suggestive both of juridical proceedings and drama. The patient is frequently accompanied by members of his or her family, so that the diagnosis and treatment of the illness serve to integrate into rather than isolate the patient from his or her family. In some cases, shamanic healers maintain regular practices in or around religious shrines and pilgrimage centers and serve clientele who come to the shrine for general religious merit and treatment for specific disorders.

CONCLUSION. While each of these general types of devotional practice has nearly infinite variations in textual tradition and local custom, they all serve as structures for symbols, actions, and understanding that help to locate Hindus in complex and at times conflicting worlds of meaning. The devotional practices of Hinduism hold in common the goal of moving individuals, groups, and the whole cosmos toward conditions of greater well-being. This movement is always undertaken in the face of counter movements, symbolized by particular forces such as demons or the more abstract formulations of cosmological entropy expressed in theories of the yugas or in the belief in the deterioration of wisdom, virtue, and well-being through the mere passing of time. Devotional practices give Hindus something to do in the face of the desire for enhancement and the anxiety over its erosion or nonattainment, something to do that brings them together as siblings, families, castes, communities, and as the whole culture itself.

SEE ALSO Bengali Religions; Bhakti; Cakras; Dīvālī; Domestic Observances, article on Hindu Practices; Haṭhayoga; Hindi Religious Traditions; Hindu Religious Year; Holī; Iconography, article on Hindu Iconography; Indian Religions, article on Rural Traditions; Kuṇḍalinī; Marathi Religions; Music, article on Music and Religion in India; Navarātri; Patañjali the Grammarian; Pilgrimage, article on Hindu Pilgrimage; Poetry, article on Indian Religious Poetry; Pūjā, article on Hindu Pūjā; Rites of Passage, article on Hindu Rites; Saṃnyāsa; Tamil Religions; Tantrism, article on Hindu Tantrism; Tapas; Temple, article on Hindu Temples; Vedism and Brahmanism; Yoga.

BIBLIOGRAPHY

Descriptions of Hindu devotional practices are scattered throughout the literature on Hinduism, but some sources distinguish themselves as places to begin in pursuit of further study. On Vedic sacrifice (*yajña*), see P. V. Kane's *History of Dharmasastra,* vol. 2 (Poona, 1941), pt. 1, chaps. 17–18, and pt. 2, chaps. 19–35, which provides detailed discussions of ritual procedures, although it may appeal less to nonspecialist readers. *Agni: The Vedic Ritual of the Fire Altar,* 2 vols., edited by Fritz Staal (Berkeley, Calif., 1983), provides the fullest textual and ethnographic documentation on traditions of Vedic ceremonialism in India today. On ancestor worship, see David M. Knipe's " *Śapiṇḍikaraṇa:* The Hindu Rite of Entry into Heaven," in *Religious Encounters with Death,* edited by Frank E. Reynolds and Earl H. Waugh (University Park, Pa., 1977). A good treatment of Hindu life-cycle rites can be found in Raj Bali Pandey's *Hindu Saṃskāras,* 2d rev. ed. (Delhi, 1969). For a discussion of asceticism in its orthoprax and Tantric forms, see Mircea Eliade's *Yoga: Immortality and Freedom,* 2d ed. (Princeton, N. J., 1969); Agehananda Bharati's *The Tantric Tradition* (London, 1965); and Philip Rawson's *The Art of Tantra* (London, 1973). For a discussion of *pūjā,* see P. V. Kane's *History of Dharaśāstra,* vol. 2 (Poona, 1941), and Jan Gonda's *Viṣṇuism and Śivaism* (London, 1970). Little systematic research has been done on vrata, but a useful introduction may be found in Diana L. Eck's *Banaras: City of Light* (New York, 1982).

Discussions on Hindu pilgrimage may be found in Agehananda Bharati's "Pilgrimage in the Indian Tradition," *History of Religions* 3 (Summer 1963): 135–167, and Surinder M. Bhardwaj's *Hindu Places of Pilgrimage in India* (Berkeley, Calif., 1973). Festivals and fairs are best discussed in sources with specific ethnographic focus. Two good books are Lawrence A. Babb's *The Divine Hierarchy: Popular Hinduism in Central India* (New York, 1975) and Ákos Östör's *The Play of the Gods* (Chicago, 1980). Sacred calendars are discussed by both Eck and Babb, in works cited above, and in Muriel Marion Underhill's *The Hindu Religious Year* (Calcutta, 1921). Discussions of healing and exorcism may be found in Sudhir Kakar's *Shamans, Mystics, and Doctors: A Psychological Inquiry into India and Its Healing Traditions* (Boston, 1982).

New Sources

Bühnemann, Gudrun. *Puja: A Study in Smrta Ritual.* Vienna, 1988.

Gold, Ann Grodzins. *Fruitful Journeys: The Ways of Rajasthani Pilgrims.* Berkeley, 1988.

Rodrigues, Hillary. *Ritual Worship of the Great Goddess: The Liturgy of the Durga Puja with Interpretations.* Albany, N.Y., 2003.

Tachikawa, Musashi. *Puja and Samskara.* Delhi, 2001.

van der Meij, Dick, ed. *India and Beyond: Aspects of Literature, Meaning, Ritual and Thought: Essays in Honour of Frits Staal.* London; New York, 1997.

PAUL B. COURTRIGHT (1987)
Revised Bibliography

WORSHIP AND DEVOTIONAL LIFE: BUDDHIST DEVOTIONAL LIFE IN SOUTHEAST ASIA

Mainland Southeast Asia comprises the modern countries of Thailand, Laos, Cambodia, Burma (Myanmar), and Vietnam, as well as parts of Malaysia and Yunnan province in China. However, it is more useful to examine the Buddhism of the region in terms of language group or culture than of these relatively recent nation-states. This Buddhism is in no sense monolithic, and one may reasonably speak of "Buddhisms" of the Thai, Lanna Thai, Shan, Lao, Khmer, Mon, Arakanese, and Burmese. These Buddhisms are "Theravādin" in the sense that they are transmitted by monastic orders that descend from Sri Lankan ordination lineages, and in the sense that these orders are custodians of a foundational literature, the Pali canon. The use of Pali, the classical Indic language of Theravāda Buddhism, links the Buddhisms of the region and gives them common access to the rich narrative and philosophical heritage of Sinhalese Buddhism, to which they ultimately refer. But each Buddhism also has its own Pali and vernacular compositions, preserved in manuscript, inscription, and recitation, and in its own practices and rites.

Until the late colonial period, "Theravāda" was not the marker of identity for either members of the order or lay followers. For them what we call *Buddhism* was the *sāsana*, the teaching of the Buddha, and the system of ethics and mental culture that he instituted. Even the monastic ordination lineages did not describe themselves as Theravādin; instead they identified themselves with ethnic or geographic terms, such as "Sinhala monks," "Mon lineage," or "Lanka lineage." By the late nineteenth century, Theravāda developed as a self-conscious religion in the European sense of the term, and the term is now a potent marker of identity in South and Southeast Asia and, increasingly, the West.

Devotion is essential to the Buddhisms of Southeast Asia (as it is to all Buddhisms). In a certain sense the whole edifice of Buddhism rests upon devotion, insofar as devotion is one of the primary driving forces of the ideology of merit, which has produced much of the region's material and spiritual culture. As part of a complex of beliefs and practices, however, it resists reification and isolation, and must be viewed in its ritual and social contexts.

ACTS OF DEVOTION. Devotion may be public or private. Public devotion is a social act that announces an individual's active participation in a Buddhist community. Private devotion confirms and strengthens an individual's consciousness as a Buddhist. In both cases it is ritualized and formulaic, but at the same time it is flexible and renewable.

Devotion is expressed through rituals that engage the "three doors" of body, speech, and mind. It is enacted physically through prostration, raising the hands with palms pressed together, and sitting with legs tucked behind. With speech one murmurs or recites formulas. The mental workings of devotion—the worshipper's wishes and aspirations—are ultimately private, but, as seen below, they have often been recorded in inscriptions.

The simplest act of devotion is homage in front of an image, usually of the Buddha, accompanied by offerings of flowers, incense, and candles. Its focus is the "three jewels": the Buddha, the *dhamma*, and the *saṃgha* (always in the same order), and for that reason three incense sticks are usually offered. Reflections on the virtues of these three are the "three recollections" that structure daily chanting programs. First, praises will be offered to the Buddha, and his blessing and protection will be invoked; the same will then be done for the *dhamma* and the *saṃgha*.

The Buddha is seen as the acme of wisdom, power, and compassion. His many names express his many virtues: the Awakened One, the Blessed One, the Teacher, the Protector, the Omniscient One, the Ten-Powered One, and so on. His power comes from his practice of the perfections (*paramī*) during countless previous births. This aspect of the Buddha is seen in the *Ṃhākāruṇiko Ṇātho* (Stanzas on the greatly compassionate protector):

> For the welfare, benefit, and happiness
> Of all breathing things
> The Greatly Compassionate Protector
> Fulfilled all of the perfections
> And realized ultimate awakening:
> By virtue of these words of truth
> May all afflictions never be.

The Buddha's virtues are so many that he is ultimately beyond praise. This idea is expressed in a Pali stanza included in old Thai liturgical manuscripts (Skilling, 1998):

> If a person had a thousand heads—
> Each head with a hundred mouths,
> Each mouth with a hundred tongues— If he could live
> as long as an aeon
> And possessed great supernormal power:
> He would still be unable to enumerate The virtues of
> the
> Teacher in full.

DEVOTION AND LITURGY. Devotion has produced a vast liturgical corpus in Pali and in vernaculars. The shared use of Pali does not mean that the regional Buddhisms chose the same texts for recitation or gave the Pali the same pronunciation and cadence. Texts and recitation styles differ widely in the Mon, Khmer, Burmese, Thai, and Lao traditions. Even within a single tradition they vary according to ordination lineage and individual temple custom.

Liturgy lies at the heart of Buddhist practice. An integral part of living Buddhism, it is a teaching vehicle for both monastics and lay followers. In public rituals there is often a leader—a layperson, nun, or monk—who recites the formulas through a microphone, to be followed by the assembly. The recitation of formulas is a powerful vehicle of inspiration. Choral chanting by well-trained monks or nuns has a musical aesthetic that, combined with the fragrance of incense, the serenity of images, and the rich tapestry of mural paintings, is one of Buddhism's most sensuous expressions.

Throughout the region liturgy opens with a simple statement of reverence towards the Buddha, repeated three times: *Namo tassa bhagavato arahato sammā-sambuddhassa* (Homage to the Blessed One, the Worthy One, the Truly and Fully Awakened One). In public rituals this is followed by the taking of the five, eight, or ten precepts. After this a specific ritual will take place: offering food, offering robes, recitation of texts appropriate to the occasion, and so on, enacted with appropriate formulas. Some rituals end with the spreading of loving kindness towards all beings, or a brief session of silent meditation. At the end of an offering ceremony the monks chant verses that rejoice in the merit performed (*anumodanā*). The liturgy closes with invocations of blessing through the power of the three jewels:

> May all blessings come to be, may all deities protect:
> By the power of all buddhas (*dhammas*, and *saṃghas*)
> May you always be well.

The generic name for apotropaic texts is *paritta* (protection). The core texts of the *paritta* come from the *tipiṭaka*, and have been used in all traditions of the region for centuries. These are supplemented by noncanonical protections, among which the *Jinapañjara*, *Sambuddhe*, and *Bāhuṃ* are three of the most popular. The *Jinapañjara* (Cage of the conquerors) stations buddhas, arhats, and the *parittas* themselves around the body at specific points, thereby making a protective cage. The *Sambuddhe* stanzas (Skilling, 1996) invoke the power of multitudes of buddhas, and the *Bāhuṃ* invokes the eight victories of the Buddha, such as his defeat of Māra or his taming of the maddened elephant Nālāgiri. The interdependence of liturgy and art is seen in the fact that the eight victories are depicted in temple murals in Cambodia and Thailand.

The formula requesting the chanting of *paritta,* recited by lay followers to the monks three times at the beginning of the ceremony, succinctly expresses the function of *paritta*:

> To ward off disaster, to accomplish all blessings,
> To eradicate all suffering, fear, and illness:
> Please recite the auspicious *paritta.*

A bewildering variety of chanting books, in all shapes and sizes, is readily available in the region's bookstalls. In Thailand the sixteenth printing of the *Royal Chanting Book* (ten thousand copies) is 427 pages long; first published in 1880, it is available in Pali only and in Pali with Thai translation. Other popular sellers are the *Seven* or the *Twelve Protections* and the *Manual for Laymen and Laywomen.* Cambodian *paritta* collections include the *Anthology of Pali Paritta* and *Pali Recitations*; for laypeople there is the *Householders' Practice.* A comprehensive collection used in Burma is the *Great Paritta.* Popular throughout the region are books devoted to magic diagrams, talismans, and spells.

Many of these collections are bilingual. Translations may follow the Pali, or face it on the opposite page. In one translation style the Pali is embedded in the translation: Pali and vernacular follow each other phrase by phrase. An early Thai collection in this style, the *Translated Chants,* dates to the beginning of the nineteenth century. Other devotional poems or chants are composed directly in the vernacular. There is, however, no body of devotional literature, either authored or anonymous, comparable to the vernacular Indian *bhakti* literature.

Books serve as aids to memory. Monastery regulations and ritual needs require monks and novices to commit liturgical repertoires to memory. Long-term monks memorize the *pātimokkha,* the monk's code, which takes up to an hour to recite. Nuns are adept at chanting, and in Thailand today it is primarily nuns who preserve the vernacular *Phra Malay* recitation, often chanted at funerals. The presence of nuns at ceremonies was noted by early Western travelers to Siam, such as Jeremias van Vliet, an agent for the Dutch East India Company at Ayutthaya from 1629 to 1634:

> Besides these male priests, there are connected with the principal temples many old women, who also have to shave their heads. They are dressed in white linen, and they are present at all sermons, songs, ceremonies and other occasions connected with the religion. They are not, however, subject to any extraordinary rules, and they do everything out of religious fervour and free will. Also they have to live on the alms which they receive from the people. There are no young maidens or pregnant women among them. (van Vliet, 1910, p. 77)

Lay knowledge of chanting varies. Most people are familiar with the basic chants—the three refuges, the precepts, and the formulas of offering—and can at least repeat them after a leader. Many memorize short texts like the *Jinapañjara, Sambuddhe,* or *Bāhuṃ* stanzas, and recite them in their private devotions. The same text can be recited more than once. In Thailand the number of repetitions may be determined by one's day of birth; for example, a person born on a Monday should recite the Pali stanzas beginning "*yaṃ dunimittaṃ*" ("Whatever ill omens. . .") fifteen times daily. Some learn to recite chants backwards, in the belief that this increases the efficacy of the syllables.

Demonstration of devotion is not limited to temple ritual. Verses of homage to the three jewels open classical and popular texts. The *Cintāmaṇi,* a manual of Thai language and prosody dating to seventeenth-century Ayutthaya, contains many examples of homage to the Buddha, some quite elaborate, in a range of meters. Thai religion has always been inclusive and eclectic, and homage does not neglect the classical deities of India or local spirits of all stripes. Reverence is also due to teachers and parents, and when they are invoked five joss-sticks or five candles may be offered.

The opening of *Samutthakhot Kham Chan,* a metrical adaptation of the nonclassical *Samuddaghosa Jātaka,* offers extravagant praise to the Buddha followed by homage to Brahmā, Śiva, and Viṣṇu. A Southern Thai verse version of a well-known *jātaka,* "The Story of the Six-Tusked Elephant King" (*Phraya Chaddanta*), invokes the protection of a catalogue of deities:

> I pay homage to my teachers
> Who have trained and instructed me
> That I might compose this tale.
> I pay homage to the Buddha,
> To the *dhamma,* and the *saṃgha,*
> To my Mother who protected me—
> May I be free from danger.
> I pay homage to my Father
> Who cared for me until I grew up. I pay homage to
> Goddess of Grain
> Who guards us all and always.
> I pay homage to all spirits
> Who dwell on earth up to the sky:
> To Vessuvanna, to Thousand Eyes,
> To Indra and Brahmā who always
> Protect against danger, obstacles,
> Disaster, and misfortune. May that called danger
> Never approach or trouble me!

Modern studies tend to compartmentalize divinities, goddesses, and spirits as "Hindu," "non-Buddhist," or "animistic," assigning them static textbook identities that miss the point. In the tolerant pluralism of Southeast Asian culture they are part of a seamless hierarchy of power and merit, with the Buddha, at least ideally, at the top.

THE CULT OF IMAGES. The production and worship of images of the Buddha has fired the religious imagination to the point that images are everywhere—not only in temples, but in the open air, homes, and schoolyards. Altars bear not just one image, but dozens. In Thailand nearly every roadside shop boasts a shelf lined with deities, raised up on a wall facing the entrance. Many of these shrines are extraordinarily eclectic, with a profusion of figures from the revered King Rāma V (r. 1868–1910) to bearded Chinese deities. A seventeenth-century Persian visitor to Ayutthaya observed that:

> The Siamese persevere in worshipping idols. . .They are not even like the other idolaters who worship one special idol which has a determined shape and form. In Siam anyone who pleases makes an image out of plaster, wood, or mud, sets it up in a particular spot and worships it. . .The scholars of Siam exclaim, "Since we cannot experience direct contact with God in all His glory and perfection, we are obliged to seek him through substitutes, which we can behold with our own eyes. Therefore we make the idols our masters and gods." (Ibn Muhammad Ibrahim 1972, p. 114)

Although Ibn Muhammad Ibrahim's understanding of the Buddha as "God" may not be strictly accurate, he does grasp one important point: images can be made by anyone. The production of images is deemed a source of great merit; according to a uniquely Theravādin belief, it helps to preserve the *sāsana* for its allotted five-thousand-year life span. The result of this potent authorization is that those who are able to do so sponsor images, often as a family or group project. In most cases an altar is not the product of a conscious and finite iconographic program. Living altars continue to grow, to accumulate new images in accordance with the imperatives of merit. Since to restore an image is also a source of merit, the images themselves undergo periodic repair and are never finished. This is also true of temple buildings, mural paintings, and manuscripts: they must constantly be renovated, restored, and rewritten, in the insatiable quest for merit and perfection.

In the middle of the twentieth century a Thai scholar remarked that:

> Perhaps more than any other country in the world, Thailand is the land of Buddha images. They range in size from tiny miniatures to huge giants. They are made of many different kinds of materials—stone, plaster or terracotta, wood, crystal or jade, silver, or gold. . .For more than 1300 years the artists of our country have concentrated on making Buddha images, to such an extent that at the present time the images far outnumber the human population. (Luang Boribal Buribhand, 1956, p. 3)

If one counts the small amulets highly prized by the Thai, the statement may well be true. But the other cultures of the region share the same ideology of merit, and also produce images in large numbers. A popular custom was to turn spacious limestone caves into cathedrals filled with images, such as the Pak U grottoes on the Mekong River near Luang Prabang in Laos, or, in Burma, the Pindiya Caves in the Shan States and the Kaw-gun caves on the Salween River near Moulmein. The latter was eloquently described by a "bygone traveler":

> Everywhere, on the floor, overhead, on the jutting points, and on the stalactite festoons of the roof, are crowded together images of Gautama—the offerings of successive ages. Some are perfectly gilded; others encrusted with calcareous matter; some fallen, yet sound; others mouldered; others just erected. Some are of stupendous size; some not larger than one's finger; and some of all the intermediate sizes—marble, stone, wood, brick, and clay. Here and there are models of temples, some not larger than half a bushel, and some ten or fifteen feet square, absolutely filled with small idols, heaped promiscuously one on the other. A ship of five hundred tons could not carry away the half of them. (O'Conner 1904 [1993], p. 289, condensed)

When an image is installed there is an inauguration ceremony and a celebration, which may last a week or more. At certain times of the year, often the solar New Year, images may be carried in procession on land or water with grand festivity and merrymaking. Such a procession was witnessed by Ibn Muhammad Ibrahim:

> There are also special occasions when the idols are mounted on traveling palanquins and brought in from the outlying temples to the city temples where the king and monks worship. In such a case the Siamese say that one idol has come to visit another. . . .Then the city population gathers together and they play drums and flutes. The devout bring flowers and leaves from the trees and fasten them on the temple walls to make festoons. They also fashion artificial flowers from paper. (Ibn Muhammad Ibrahim, 1972, pp. 118–119)

Other foci of devotion are *cetiyas,* bodhi trees, and replicas of the Buddha's feet or footprints. In Southeast Asia *cetiya* and *stupa* are generally synonymous, and refer to solid freestanding structures built to house relics. *Cetiyas* come in all shapes and sizes; as reliquaries they are often called *Phra That* (from Pali and Sanskrit *dhātu,* "relic") or *Phra Mahathat* (from *mahādhātu,* "great relic") in Thai, Lao, and Lanna Thai. *Cetiyas* can enshrine images, scriptures, and other objects of reverence, as well as rich offerings of gold, gems, and pearls. Relics are frequently installed in Buddha images, sometimes (if the chronicles are to be believed) miraculously. A well-known verse venerates most of the sacred objects together: "I pay homage to all *cetiyas,* all and always, wherever they are established— / Physical relics, Great Awakening Trees, and images of the Buddha."

Relics and images are installed with pomp and celebration. In 1718 in the central Thai principality of Chainat, for example, high-ranking monks were invited from the capital (at that time Ayutthaya) to lead the festivities for the Great Relic. These included one day each of recitation of the "(Summarized Account of) the Buddhist Councils" (*Saṅgāyanā*), of the *tipiṭaka,* and of the "Great Birth" or *Vessantara Jātaka.* The site was decorated with offerings, parasols, banners, flowers, torches, and candles, and there were performances of masked dance, shadow-puppet plays, and drama. The event was carefully recorded in a large stone inscription that stands at the temple today (*Prachum Silacharuk* 4, no. 97, 1970, pp. 73–74).

Cetiyas fill temple compounds and dot the countryside of the region. Bodhi trees are planted in temple precincts. A liturgical genre, both Pali and vernacular, offers homage to the trees of past and future buddhas. Theravādin tradition lists ten future buddhas, starting with Metteyya (this does not mean that there are no others—there are, but they are not named). A class of texts known as *Anāgatavaṃsa* (Chronicle of the future) is devoted to them. A Thai-language version of one such text explains at the end that, "Any human beings, female or male, who offer homage and bow in respect to the ten Lord Buddhas along with the ten Glorious Great Awakening Trees . . . will gain fruit and benefit. They will not be born in hell for as long a period as one hundred thousand aeons. This is a result of the wholesome intentions of the person who recollects the ten Lord Buddhas."

Shrines housing replicas of the soles of a Buddha's feet (positive models) or of his footprints (negative impressions) as the primary icon are common. The replicas are made on stone slabs, wooden panels, or cloth painting. In addition to replicas, there are also "natural" footprints, believed to have been left by a buddha—not only Śākyamuni, but also his three predecessors in this "Auspicious Aeon." According to old traditions, Śākyamuni left the impression of his foot or feet at five sites in India and Sri Lanka. These are listed in chants that venerate the five prints "from afar": that is, it is possible to render homage and request protection without going on pilgrimage, although several of the sites have been localized in Burma and Thailand and are relatively accessible.

Other verse compositions, in Pali, Khmer, Burmese, and Thai, list the one hundred and eight auspicious signs that adorn the soles of the Ten-Powered One's feet and invoke their protection. A Southern Thai text on the signs opens as follows:

> May I offer obeisance to the supreme feet of the Buddha,
> The glorious and resplendent pair.
> My ten fingers raised in a row are bright like golden candles;
> My two eyes are alight like a pair of lamps: these I offer.
> My hair-knot is like a flower-garland, like beautiful golden nenuphars.
> My melodious voice is like an offering of incense and candles.
> My heart I dedicate like fragrant scents.

The text ends with the promise that whoever recites the names of the signs will gain vast merit and meet the future Buddha Metteyya. Such texts can be recited at home, or in the presence of one of the replicas of the Buddha's footprints enshrined in temples and pavilions throughout the region.

DEVOTION AND CUSTOM. Devotion has its own protocols—it invests parts of the body, direction, and space with its own values. Shoes must be removed before entering a temple or shrine, or—mainly in Burma—at the very first gate, before entering the precincts of monasteries and pagodas. Feet should not be pointed at images or objects of respect, which should be placed higher than the worshipper. One should keep to the right of revered objects, and use the right hand when making offerings. Damaged or discarded objects of reverence are not thrown away or sold: they are left in temples or at the foot of bodhi trees. To steal or damage an image of the Buddha, a bodhi tree, a *cetiya*, or a religious text is a heinous crime that will send the culprit straight to hells of unremitting torment. Such values were incorporated into legal codes, for example the *Three Seals Code* of medieval Siam, which stipulated severe if not gruesome punishments for those guilty of such crimes.

In some cultures access to sanctuaries is determined by gender. In Burma, only males are allowed onto the upper platforms of pagodas—for example, at the Shwedagon Pagoda in Rangoon, where they can sit in meditation or apply gold leaf directly to the revered shrine. In Northern Thailand, women are barred from the raised platform upon which the images are installed; in Northeastern Thailand, females cannot enter the ordination hall; and in Central Thailand they cannot sit on the raised platform within the ordination hall.

Devotion has its own vocabulary. Special terms, often derived from Sanskrit, are used to describe images: one does not buy an image, one *rents* or *reveres* it. One does not take it home: one *invites* it into one's house. The features of the image are spoken of in a special language used also for members of the royal family. Venerated images are addressed directly, in the second person, with kinship terms identical to those used for revered monks, such as "Great Father."

DEVOTION AND MATERIAL CULTURE. Worship has had an immense impact on material culture and technology, and thereby on the economy. Special utensils, crafted from bronze, silver, or gold, fulfill ritual functions. Offerings to monks or idols require fine trays and bowls made from lacquer or metal. At the end of a merit-making ceremony, water is poured from a bronze vessel into a small bowl, both purpose-made. In Thailand the monks hold ornate fans in front of themselves when performing certain ceremonies; the fans are a unique art form.

Skilled bronze casters, stonecutters, and woodcarvers produce images in a range of styles, sizes, and materials. Gold beaters produce delicate squares of gold leaf to apply to images. Garland makers station themselves at pagoda gates, threading fragrant flowers such as jasmine and roses into beautiful shapes. Annual rituals have led to the development of unique products, such as the giant candles offered to monasteries at the beginning of the three-month rains-retreat, or the fine threaded sweets prepared at Nakhon Si Thammarat in Southern Thailand to offer to *pretas* (so-called hungry ghosts, tormented by hunger because their mouths are the size of needles).

The premodern landscape was transfigured by devotion. Land, groves, fields, and villages were offered to temples and exempted from taxation. The architecture of the region is in part a response to the needs of devotion. Monastic complexes include buildings for public worship, from simple open-sided pavilions to grand and ornately decorated halls. Large stupas have broad circumambulatories. In Thailand, distinctive shrines—often miniature versions of grander structures—stand raised on pillars in gardens: these are the spirit houses, which accommodate the spirit of the land. Opulent shrines to Brahmā, Indra, or other deities stand in front of banks and office buildings.

Special shops cater to the needs of the faithful, offering a wide range of paraphernalia, including incense, candles, images, monastic requisites, and shrine tables. Crafts and trades were integrated into city plans: the gold beaters' quarters in Mandalay and Bangkok, the religious supplies stores in central Bangkok, and the image makers district in Thonburi, across the river from Bangkok. The economy of worship played a role in the exploitation of natural products and translocal trade. Lime, laterite, and stone were quarried for use as construction materials (lime for the manufacture of stucco to decorate religious structures). Gold, bronze, and tin were mined, exported, or imported, and from antiquity the tropical forests of Southeast Asia supplied the international market with aromatics and exotic timber.

Daily Routines and Ritual Calendars. The daily monastic routine includes morning and evening chanting structured around homage to the three jewels. The time of the chanting (from four in the morning on) and the selection of texts vary from temple to temple. Lay people may start their day with chanting and meditation before a private altar. In Thailand the day ends with an act of homage, as recommended by the nineteenth-century poet Sunthorn Phu in his *Svasti Raksa*, a book of stanzas on etiquette for the maintenance of one's well-being:

> When you go to bed,
> Don't forget to salute the pillow,
> While saying your praise and gratitude
> To your parents and your teachers. (Umavijani, 1990, p. 86)

The lunar calendar is used for religious purposes. Special offerings are made on the "holy days" of the four quarters of the moon, especially the lunar fortnight, when the monks recite the *pātimokkha.* The Thai cycle of court festivals is described in several late-nineteenth-century texts, including an elegant verse composition by Prince Maha Mala and two detailed historical studies by King Chulalongkorn (Rāma V). In Thailand today the highlights of the year are the great full-moon celebrations or *pūjā* of the months of Māgha, Visākha, and Āsāḷha. On these nights, lay people throng to circumambulate *uposatha* halls and *cetiyas*, carrying candles, incense, and flowers. The monks recite Pali texts and give sermons explaining the significance of the ceremonies, which mark events in the life of the Blessed One. Visākhā Pūjā, which usually falls in April, commemorates the birth, awakening, and passing away of the Master, while Āsāḷha Pūjā marks his first sermon in the Deer Park at Sārnāth near Vārāṇasī—the "Turning of the Wheel of the *Dharma.*" The rich ritual calendar includes the day-long "Sermon on the Great Birth"—the *Vessantara Jātaka*—formerly one of the greatest entertainments of the year, and in the countryside still indispensable as a rainmaking festival. At the New Year people fashion *cetiyas* from sand, and decorate them with papers parasols, flags, and banners.

For the monks the most important event is the three-month Vassa, or "rains-retreat," during which they remain in their home-temple and do not travel. In Thailand males often ordain as monks especially for this three-month period in order to deepen their understanding of the Awakened One's teaching. Male government officials may obtain fully paid leave for this purpose. Although the Vassa is originally and primarily a monastic retreat, during this period devout lay followers may stay overnight in the temple each lunar quarter to chant and meditate. A few take extra vows of abstention or devote themselves to meditation throughout the three-month period. In Northern Thailand, collections of texts to be chanted during this period are called *Nangsu non wat* (Books for staying overnight in the temple), and special quarters are erected for females within the temple precincts. Other monastic rites that take place after the rains are Pavāraṇā, when monastics invite their fellows to point out any wrongs they may have committed during the rains-retreat, and Parivāsa, penitence for having concealed breaches of certain monastic rules. In Thailand and Cambodia the latter has become ritualized; large numbers of monks from many temples gather at a designated site for the period. Another important festival is the offering of Kaṭhina robes to the monks.

People make special offerings on their birthdays, or in memory of their parents or loved and respected ones on the anniversary of their deaths. They may offer food to the monks on the early morning alms-round, or to the *saṃgha* in general at a temple. Monks are invited to bless newlyweds at wedding ceremonies. At funerals the monks recite texts for the benefit of the deceased. In Thailand they recite extracts from the *abhidhamma*, often every night for forty-nine days in front of the coffin in special funerary pavilions in the temple precincts. For the final passage, the cremation, monks recite a simple stanza on impermanence. On this occasion sons may "ordain in front of the fire," that is, become a monk for a few hours or a few days in order to offer the merit to a deceased parent.

In Thailand a major source of temple income is the annual festival (*ngan wat*), a full-fledged fair with Ferris wheels, rock music concerts, and entertainments of every description. For several days the temple becomes a noisy hive of activity. Another grand affair is the consecration of the monastic boundary, or *sima.* In Central Thailand this has become a weeklong fund-raising event usually held to coincide with the Chinese New Year in order to attract the wealth of the powerful business and merchant communities of Chinese origin. Less frequent are image-consecrations, for which revered monks are invited to chant special Pali stanzas.

PILGRIMAGE. From chronicles and inscriptions we know that pilgrims from Southeast Asia regularly visited the holy sites of India and Sri Lanka. Royal missions were sent to repair the temple at Bodh Gayā, the "Diamond Seat" where Śākyamuni achieved awakening. In the Pala and Sena periods, Southeast Asian monks traveled to study at the famed universities of Northern India and the monasteries of Sri Lanka, carrying images, scriptures, practices, and ideas back and forth. Pilgrims and monks also traveled throughout Southeast Asia, which had its own study centers and pilgrimage sites.

The most important pilgrimage sites are reliquary shrines (*cetiya*, stupa) and footprints of the Buddha. *Cetiyas* housing hair and bone relics of Śākyamuni are found throughout the region; many boast a chronicle that validates their claims to the pilgrims' devotions and offerings. In lower Burma two of the greatest attractions are the old Mon stupa of Shwedagon, which enshrines the relics of four buddhas, and the extraordinary pagoda of Kyaiktiyo, which perches precariously on a massive boulder at the top of a hill. In upper Burma pilgrims are drawn to the Mahamuni image in Mandalay and to Mandalay hill. But there are many others: "Most of the commanding heights in Burma have long since been crowned with pagodas, and a visit to any of these gratifies the innate piety and gaiety of the people" (O'Connor, 1904, p. 347).

For the Lao, one of the holiest stupas is Phra That Phanom on the western bank of the Mekong River. Northern Thailand has a tradition of pilgrimage to twelve sites determined by one's year of birth according to the twelve-year cycle. These include the Shwedagon Pagoda in Burma, the old Mon stupa at Hariphunchai in northern Thailand, and the stupa at Wat Suthep overlooking the Chiang Mai Valley. In Southern Thailand the tall, tapering reliquary at Nakhon Si Thammarat draws busloads of pilgrims from the Thai and Chinese Buddhist communities in Malaysia and Singapore. On the way they stop at other sites, such as Wat Pa Kho in the narrow Sathing Phra peninsula, where a footprint was left on top of a hill by a revered seventeenth-century monk named Luang Pu Thuat. To attract wealthy Chinese pilgrims, temples along the route have built statues of Kuanyin, the "Goddess of Mercy," some of them immense.

Pilgrimage centers in central Thailand include Thung Yang in Uttaradit province, where there is a large stone slab where the four buddhas have sat, and the fifth, Metteyya, will sit. Thung Yang was formerly the goal of royal pilgrimage (e.g., during the reign of King Borommakot of Ayutthaya, who restored the complex of sites). Its foundational legend is narrated in both Pali and Thai texts. To the west of the old capital of Ayutthaya and the present capital of Bangkok is Phra Taen Dong Rang, a localized site of the Buddha's passing away, which was visited in 1836 by the poet Nai Mi, who wrote:

> We brought incense, candles, and choice flowers
> And gathered to pay homage to the stone couch
> Between a pair of Rang trees.
> Their branches, twigs, and sprouts bowed low in homage.
> Oh, the Rang trees still adore the Teacher—
> How sad that we were born too late to meet him!
> All we can see is the stone couch,
> Our minds overwhelmed with sorrow and dismay.
> Tears stream down as we call to mind
> The Holy Omniscient One.

Rang tree is the Thai name for the Indian sala tree. At the same site the poet saw a stone held to be the blood that the Buddha vomited during his final illness, and the site of his cremation on a nearby hill.

From the seventeenth century on, the leading Thai pilgrimage site has been Phra Phutthabat, in Saraburi province to the east of Ayutthaya, identified with one of the five places where the Omniscient One left his print. The annual pilgrimage was a grand affair. Commoners streamed in by boat, horse, and oxcart, and on foot. Stalls were set up at the approach to the shrine, and for a week there were festivities of all kinds—acrobatics, shadow and puppet theatre, dance-drama, and fireworks. King and court made the pilgrimage regularly, first by boat and then by elephant with opulent pageantry. The king would make grand offerings, and perform a unique sword-dance on elephant-back in homage to the footprint. Surviving records—poems, official documents, and a seventeenth-century Dutch account—leave no doubt about the significance of the pilgrimage.

IDEOLOGIES OF BENEFIT AND EXCHANGE. The human predicament is a life of insecurity, suffering, and impermanence, inevitably ending in death. The Buddha taught people to recognize the predicament, identify its roots, and then to practice in order to free themselves from it. Therefore it is said that the Buddha arose in the world "for the benefit of the many, for the happiness of the many, from compassion for the world, for the welfare, benefit, and happiness of gods and humans." Buddhism is a quest for security and benefit, and it is the Buddha who explains the "ultimate blessings" (*maṅgala*).

Tradition lists "three bases for the performance of merit" (*puññakiriyavatthu*): giving or charity, precepts or ethical conduct, and mental culture or meditation. The performance of these leads to three types of felicity (*sampatti*): felicity as a human, felicity in heaven, and the felicity of *nirvāṇa*. Worship and devotional life are directed towards these three goals, which are often referred to in sermons and narrative literature. They are inspired and guided by the ideology of benefit or advantage. The Pali term for this is *ānisaṃsa* (Skt., *ānuśaṃsa*, Tib., *phan yon*). It is a key concept not only in Theravāda Buddhism but in all Buddhisms; it is prominent in the earliest texts—the sūtras of the Pali

Nikāyas and Sanskrit Āgamas—for example in the *Metta-ānisaṃsa-sutta* of the former, which promises eleven benefits for those who practice loving kindness: they will sleep well, they will wake happily, they will not have bad dreams, and so on. Thai Buddhists developed a genre of sermon, both in Pali and in Thai, that lauds the specific benefits of specific meritorious acts, such as producing an image of the Buddha, offering candles at the beginning of the rains-retreat, or erecting sand *cetiyas. Anisamsa* texts are known in other traditions, such as the Sanskrit *Triratnabhājana-ānuśaṃsa* (Advantages of revering the three gems) from Nepal, or the *Advantages of the Diamond Sūtra* from Tibet.

Another key term in the pragmatics of offering is *paṇidhāna* (Skt., *praṇidhāna*): wish, aspiration, or prayer. When making offerings, one makes a silent wish for specific benefits. This is the private and personal aspect of devotion mentioned above. There are also generalized and public aspirations, such as prayers for the health and welfare of teachers, preceptors, parents, rulers, and all sentient beings. Many of the earliest Buddhist inscriptions (starting from the second century BCE) in India record aspirations. The practice was followed in Southeast Asia; some of the Thai and Cambodian aspirations recorded on stone are long and elaborate verse compositions.

The ideology of *ānisaṃsa* and *paṇidhāna* is one of exchange. One takes refuge in the three jewels, and in return they grant protection or fulfill wishes. When supplicants pray before an image they promise something in return—special food, servants, or entertainment, for example—if their wish is fulfilled. In earlier periods servitors, livestock, groves, fields, and land were granted to images. Such grants were recorded in inscriptions and legal documents, which today are primary sources for the study of economic history. Today live music and dance are offered in some temples; in others one sees small model dancers.

Together, the complex of worship—the chants of refuge and homage, the prayers and aspirations—invokes and constructs an intricate universe of relations and obligations. Offerings are made to the Buddha, and merits are shared with relatives, deities, and spirits, who in turn are asked to offer protection or grant wishes. Offerings to the monks transmit merit to deceased relatives; Buddha images convey benefits. The question of whether it is the image or the Buddha that is addressed and responds can never be resolved, since in the imagination they are both the same and different.

MODERNITY AND BEYOND. *Modernity* and its cognates are troubled and troublesome terms. In this entry they are used as unavoidable conventions for a modernity that begins in the early nineteenth century and continues through the twentieth century to the present. In the last half of the twentieth century the impact of new ideologies and technologies effected enormous change throughout the region.

The Western calendar and the "working week" have broken the rhythm of the lunar calendar, especially in the cities, where urban life has its own priorities. Urban migration has disrupted the agricultural calendar and the transmission of knowledge within village communities, as has compulsory secular education. This—along with the rapid spread of modern communications, culminating in the internet—has contributed to the erosion of community memories. People have less time for festivals and religious practice; ceremonies and chants have been simplified and abridged, and also standardized as a result of centralized monastic education and print technology. This has led to an impoverishment of liturgical and ritual repertoires, since many of the older chants and rites have fallen into disuse. Old temple districts and craft quarters have been savaged by ruthless construction of roads and commercial buildings, and temple precincts have become parking lots. Festivals are packaged for tourist consumption.

The commercialization of worship in the cash economy has led to questions about the nature of devotion. Is Buddhism being packaged and sold like any other product? Have devotees turned into consumers? Have values gone awry? Do people equate the degree of merit with the financial value of their offering? Some temples, such as Wat Chonlaprathan in Nonthaburi, Thailand, explicitly discourage lay followers from offering commercialized products. The temple donates excess offerings to orphanages, prisons, or victims of natural disasters; on festival days this amounts to several truckloads.

But the human predicament remains. Buddhist teachings address human needs, and they have always shown resilience and adaptation. The vitality of Buddhist worship and practice is undaunted by modernity. On offering-days devotees bring traffic jams into temple compounds. Radio, television, and the internet are used to propagate Buddhist values. New generations explore the relationship between the teachings of Buddhism and contemporary understandings of society and the universe, proposing compatibilities with science, ecology, feminism, and human rights. Throughout Thailand there has been a rapid development of the cult of Kuan-yin, whose image graces separate shrines or altars beside the presiding Buddha. Migration has led to the construction of Khmer, Lao, Burmese, and Thai temples abroad, especially in the United States, where new forms of worship are developing.

SEE ALSO Buddhist Religious Year; Pilgrimage, article on Buddhist Pilgrimage in South and Southeast Asia; Pūjā, article on Buddhist Pūjā; Saṃgha, overview article.

BIBLIOGRAPHY

The primary sources for the study of devotional life in Southeast Asia are inscriptions, chronicles, royal orders, poetry, and the accounts of foreign travelers. Very little research on the subject has been published. The best comprehensive English-language source remains a work first published in 1939: Kenneth Wells, *Thai Buddhism: Its Rites and Ceremonies* (Bangkok, 1975). Wells describes the main ceremonies and translates many formulas and chants. One of the few works dealing with *anisamsa*—specifically that connected with erecting sand *cetiyas*—is Louis Gabaude, *Les cetiya de sable au Laos et en Thaïlande: Les textes* (Paris, 1979). The present entry is based on Pali and Thai sources and field observations. Translations are the author's unless otherwise noted; in some cases the translations are condensed.

The chanting books mentioned in the essay are as follows:

Bhanavara Pali (Pali recitations)

Chet tamnan, Sattaparitta, Cularajaparitta (Seven protections)

Gihipatipatti (Householders' practice)

Khu mu ubasok ubasika (Manual for laymen and laywomen)

Mahaparitta (Great *paritta*)

Parittasamodhana Pali (Anthology of Pali *paritta*)

Sipsong Tamnan, Dvadasaparitta, Maharajaparitta (Twelve protections)

Suat mon chabap luang (Royal chanting book)

Suat mon plae (Translated chants)

References

Luang Boribal Buribhand. *Thai Images of the Buddha.* Bangkok, 1956.

Ibn Muhammad Ibrahim. *The Ship of Sulaiman.* Translated by John O'Kane. New York, 1972. Translation of a seventeenth-century account of a journey to Siam.

O'Conner, V. C. Scott. *The Silken East: A Record of Life and Travel in Burma* (1904). Gartmore, Stirling, U.K., 1993.

Phraya Chaddanta (The six-tusked elephant king). Nakhon Si Thammarat, 1992.

Prachum Silacharuk (Corpus of inscriptions). Vol. 4. Bangkok, 1970.

Skilling, Peter. "The Sambuddhe Verses and Later Theravādin Buddhology." *Journal of the Pali Text Society* 22 (1996): 151–183.

Skilling, Peter. "Praises of the Buddha Beyond Praise." *Journal of the Pali Text Society* 24 (1998): 195–200.

Umavijani, Montri. *Sunthorn Phu: An Anthology.* Bangkok, 1990.

van Vliet, Jeremias. "Description of the Kingdom of Siam." 1636. Translated by L. F. van Ravenswaay in *Journal of the Siam Society* 7, no.1 (1910) 1–105.

PETER SKILLING (2005)

WORSHIP AND DEVOTIONAL LIFE: BUDDHIST DEVOTIONAL LIFE IN EAST ASIA

Buddhist practice in East Asia extends across almost two millennia and several different religious cultures and languages. This means that there is a rich and complex set of practices to consider—far too many to attempt a comprehensive presentation within the scope of this article. The character of East Asian Buddhist practice differs both from that of the Western traditions, which have informed the way in which ritual and practice are understood in religious studies, and from many of the popular representations of Buddhism. These differences constitute a series of theoretical issues, which include the relation between the categories of ritual and meditation, the relation between local and translocal traditions of practice, the complex relation between practice and ideology, the social dimensions of East Asian Buddhist practice, the multivalence of practices, and the emic categories for types and structures of ritual practice. The following will discuss specific instances of East Asian Buddhist practice in relation to these issues.

RITUAL AND MEDITATION. Contemporary Western religious discourse frequently differentiates between ritual and meditation as mutually exclusive categories, often implicitly valuing meditation and dismissing ritual. However, the cultic practices of East Asian Buddhism cannot be so clearly distinguished, as they have both ritual and meditative aspects. For example, the most familiar Buddhist practice is doubtless sitting meditation as found in the Zen (Chin., Chan; Kor., Sŏn) tradition. Often considered the epitome of meditation, upon examination one finds such meditation to be a highly ritualized practice. All aspects of behavior during Zen meditation are prescribed, from bodily posture while sitting to the manner of walking while circumambulating the temple between sitting sessions and the manner in which one enters the meditation hall and takes one's seat. Even outside of the meditation period, the manner of one's behavior in all activities—particularly during meals, and excepting only break periods—is carefully prescribed.

Conversely, the rituals of the Japanese Tantric tradition of Shingon are filled with meditative elements. For example, the Full Moon Visualization practice (Jpn., *gachirin kan*), which is one of the introductory practices in the training of a Shingon priest (Skt., *ācārya*; Jpn., *ajari*), includes gazing at a white circle until one is able to see the image mentally, without the support of the visual object. One then imagines this white circle expanding to fill the entirety of the universe and shrinking to a tiny spot at the very center of one's visual field. The Full Moon Visualization practice also exemplifies the continuity between Indian and East Asian Buddhist practices. The practice matches the *kasiṇa* practice recorded for example in Buddhaghosa's *Path of Purification* (Pali, *Viśudhimagga*). The *kasiṇas* are a set of ten visualizations of a circular device made of a variety of substances and colors (Skt., *rūpa*), one of which is a white circle. Thus, it forms part of a tradition of practice that, while originating in a specific historical and cultural location, was relocated across China to Japan, becoming thereby translocal.

LOCAL AND TRANSLOCAL. All religion is local. Some practices, however, are portable, and being carried across linguistic and cultural boundaries become translocal. Frequently, this process of movement between religious cultures leads to confrontation, interaction, and appropriation of practices, symbols, and ideas. In East Asia many practices are shared by Buddhist, Daoist, neo-Confucian, Shintō, and Shugendō traditions. Despite this long history of religious interaction, Buddhist practices do demonstrate a high level of continuity between their Indian origins and their East Asian instantiations. This continuity, however, should neither be interpreted as providing a basis for claims of authority or authenticity, nor taken as grounds for claims that some practices are pure while others are syncretic. It is simply the case that Buddhist practitioners both maintained practices originating in India and integrated East Asian religious elements into Buddhism.

One example of the interaction between local and translocal traditions of practice is the Ghost Festival (Skt., Avalambana or Ullambana; Chin., Yu lan pen; Jpn., Urabon or Obon). While drawing on Indian antecedents, the Ghost Festival originated in medieval China and continues in present-day Japan and in Japanese Buddhist temples in the United States. The founding story for the Ghost Festival is that of the monk Maudgalyāyana (Chin., Mulien), who saves his mother from her current birth as a hungry ghost (Skt., *preta*; Jpn., *gaki*) by making offerings to monks coming out of their summer retreat (Skt., *varṣā*; Chin., *anju*)—a three month period of reclusion and intensified practice. The rainy-season retreat dates from the time of the historical Buddha, Śākyamuni, and was in fact common to other groups of wandering ascetics in fourth century BCE India.

While based on Indian monastic antecedents, the Ghost Festival complex was adapted to local values and local practices. Developed in response to the Chinese emphasis on filial devotion (*xiao*), the Ghost Festival was promoted to high levels of popularity. Additionally, the involvement of laity and the emphasis on the agricultural cycle with its symbolism of renewal are aspects of the Chinese Ghost Festival that distinguish it from the Indian precedents. In China the schedule of the Ghost Festival correlates strongly with the agricultural cycle. There, the monastic summer retreat began in the middle of the fourth lunar month and ended in the middle of the seventh lunar month, while in India and Central Asia there was much more variation in the monastic schedule.

One of the specific rites that frequently forms part of the Ghost Festival in some contemporary Japanese Buddhist traditions is the feeding of the hungry ghosts. The dead are conceived under two categories: those who have a relation with a living family and those who do not (Jpn., *muenbotoke*). The former can proceed through a cycle of rituals over a period of thirty-three years and become a member of the anonymous collectivity of the ancestors. In the contemporary Japanese Shingon tradition of Tantric Buddhism, these memorial rites proceed through an increasingly extended cycle and are associated with a group known as the Thirteen Buddhas (though technically not all are buddhas): first seventh day, Acala (Fudō); second seventh day, Śākyamuni (Shaka); third seventh day, Mañjuśrī (Monju); fourth seventh day, Samantabhadra (Fugen); fifth seventh day, Kṣitigarbha (Jizō); sixth seventh day, Maitreya (Miroku); seventh seven day, Bhaiṣajyaguru (Yakushi); hundredth day, Avalokiteśvara (Kannon); first anniversary, Mahāsthāmaprāpta (Seishi); third anniversary, Amitābha (Amida); seventh anniversary, Akṣobhya (Ashuku); thirteenth anniversary, Mahāvairocana (Dainichi); and thirty-third anniversary, Ākāśagarbha (Kokūzō).

However, those who do not have family relations who can insure that this process is completed are in danger of becoming hungry ghosts—dangerous and dissatisfied—wandering the human realm at the time of the Ghost Festival. During the Ghost Festival in contemporary Japan one can see offerings to hungry ghosts placed outside the homes of those who also have offerings to their own ancestors on their family altar.

Hungry ghosts are described as having huge bellies, indicative of their hunger, at the same time they have exceedingly slender necks, blocking them from taking in as much as their hunger drives them to desire. In another description, whenever they do take food their mouths burst into flames, giving them their alternate name of "flaming mouths." By the power of the ritual, the throats of the hungry ghosts are opened and they are able to consume the offerings made to them. Indeed, after consuming the offerings, their evil *karma* is extinguished and they are reborn in a Pure Land.

Another practice that combines local and translocal religious forms, and also continues into the present, is pilgrimage. Classic Chinese pilgrimage sites for Buddhists were Mount Tiantai and Mount Wutai. The former was important as the location in which Zhiyi (538–597) established the Tiantai tradition (Jpn., Tendai). Consequently, monastic pilgrims, even from Japan, were drawn to Mount Tiantai. For example, Ennin (794–864) of the Japanese Tendai tradition centered on Mount Hiei outside Kyoto spent nine years in China and recorded his travels in a historically important journal. Of more popular appeal was Mount Wutai, widely considered to be the residence of Mañjuśrī, the *bodhisattva* of wisdom. So popular was Mount Wutai that it drew pilgrims not only from within China itself, but also from Mongolia, Inner Asia, and Tibet.

In Japan, Mount Kōya is an important pilgrimage site, particularly the tomb of Kūkai (774–835; posthumous title, Kōbō Daishi, founder of the Japanese Tantric Shingon tradition), where he is said to remain in perpetual meditation. Although the most important center of Shingon Buddhism, because of Kūkai's wide appeal, Mount Kōya serves as a pan-Buddhist pilgrimage site. Also associated with Kūkai is the pilgrimage route encircling the island of Shikoku. Beginning and ending on Mount Kōya, the route comprises eighty-eight temples. Despite the association with Shingon, specific temples along the route are affiliated with a variety of Japanese Buddhist sects, and have an equally wide variety of chief deities (Jpn., *honzon*). Specific sites along the route mark events in Kūkai's life, and thus the entire route is often asserted to have been established by him. However, the route only became a pilgrimage circuit much later, becoming most popular in the first half of the nineteenth century. The circuit character of the Shikoku pilgrimage is shared with many South and East Asian pilgrimages, and distinguish these from Western pilgrimages, which tend to be linear.

Throughout its history in East Asia, Buddhist practice interacted with other religious traditions, with borrowing being done in both directions. In Japan the rise of distinct, self-identified Shintō traditions in the fifteenth century saw the adaptation of Buddhist practices into Shintō forms. For example, Yuiitsu and other Shintō lineages developed their own rituals of fire offerings (Skt., *homa*; Jpn., *goma*), clearly modeled on Tantric Buddhist practices. Practice of the *homa* seems to have been entirely exterminated from the Shintō tradition by the suppression of Buddhism (Jpn., *shinbutsu bunri*) in the second half of the nineteenth century, which involved the enforced "purification" of Shintō. Shugendō, the way of mountain ascetics, also developed a *homa*, this one being performed out of doors (Jpn., *saitō goma*). Shugendō *saitō gomas* continue to be performed in contemporary Japan, sometimes on the grounds of Buddhist temples or Shintō shrines, and they have also become part of the Japanese new religions (Jpn., *shin shūkyō*). Conversely, in interaction with Chinese religious culture, within which the Northern (Big) Dipper was a key element—Buddhist practitioners created a *homa* with that constellation as the chief deity.

Understanding the relation between local and translocal practices requires an examination not only of the textual record but also of the artistic record. While sometimes appearing to be normative, textual sources may in fact only represent one local version of a practice. Like other visualization practices, visualization of the Land of Bliss (Skt., Sukhāvatī; Jpn., Gokuraku) originated in India, was practiced in Central Asia, and was subsequently transmitted to East Asia. The artistic record found in Central Asian cave temples at Turfan show great variety in the visualization sequence and in the elements to be visualized. As Pure Land visualization was transmitted further east—to Dunhuang, China, and Japan—the practice became much more standardized, closely matching the version found in the *Contemplation Sūtra* (Skt., *Amitāyur dhyāna sūtra*; Chin., *Kuan wu liang shou ching*; Jpn., *Kammuryōju kyō*).

PRACTICE AND IDEOLOGY. The relation between practice and ideology, or doctrine, is complex. Both practice and ideology influence one another. For example, practices are molded by conceptions of the path to awakening, while cosmological conceptions reflect states of mind created through meditative practice. Likewise, practices appropriated from another religious tradition or relocated into a new religious milieu may be reinterpreted in order to fit into their new setting. An emphasis on the integrity of practice and ideology is found within Buddhist conceptions of the path to awakening. One of the traditional Buddhist ways of talking about the path is to organize it under the three categories of precepts, meditation, and wisdom (Skt., *śīla*, *samādhi*, and *prajñā*). These are known as the three learnings (Skt., *trīṇiśikṣāṣi*; Jpn., *sangaku*). Contrary to the idea propagated by some that meditation alone is adequate, the three learnings are understood to form an integrated whole and to all be equally necessary.

The *Contemplation Sūtra* provides a doctrinal justification for both recitation of the name of Buddha Amitāyus (Amitābha) and visualization of his image. Both kinds of practices are forms of "keeping the Buddha in mind" (Skt., *buddhānusmṛti*; Chin., *nianfo*; Jpn., *nembutsu*), and as such are considered to imbue the practitioner's mind with the qualities of the Buddha. This is very similar to the idea of "becoming a buddha in this body" (Jpn., *soku shin jo butsu*), which informs Tantric Buddhist practice in East Asia. This idea is reflected in the identification of the practitioner's body, speech, and mind with the body, speech, and mind of the Buddha, which is key to many East Asian Tantric Buddhist rituals.

SOCIAL DIMENSIONS. An additional consideration is the common conception of Buddhist practice as primarily being a matter of a solitary practitioner seeking awakening. The vast majority of Buddhist practices in East Asia are social activities, either involving the monastic community or the larger community. Even the practice of seated meditation as found in the Zen lineages, often considered paradigmatic of Buddhist practice, is rarely performed as an individual practice in East Asia the way it is in the contemporary West. Rather, it is performed as part of a larger, monastic context, meaning that it is performed both communally and as part of a larger set of monastic practices. What has formed the popular image of the solitary practitioner is the noteworthy exception that becomes legendary for that very reason.

Buddhist practitioners and institutions have also long been deeply involved with the state, being institutionally dependent on the court for approval of monks and for economic support. As a consequence, there are many rituals directed toward the protection of the state, from the alleviation of droughts to protecting the state from invaders. Sometimes called "national protection" (Chin., *hu guo*) Buddhism, this meant providing ritual services for the benefit of the court. Perhaps the most important ritual for national protection is the Humane Kings ritual, such as that created by Amoghavajra (Chin., Bukong) when he reworked the *Scripture for Humane Kings* in eighth-century China. The scripture is classed as one of the perfection of wisdom (Skt., *prajñāpāramitā*) sūtras, though it is apparently unique in promoting not wisdom (Skt., *prajñā*) as key to movement along the path to awakening, but rather forbearance (Skt., *kṣānti*; Chin., *ren*) as most important. This plays on the homophone with the Confucian virtue of humaneness (also *ren*). The equation of these two virtues allowed for the promotion of Buddhism in fifth-century China, when the first version of the *Scripture for Humane Kings* (traditionally considered a translation by Kumārajīva) appeared—a time when Buddhism was struggling for legitimacy in a Confucian world.

For most of East Asian Buddhism, the Pure Land practice of reciting the name of the Buddha Amitābha serves to advance the search for rebirth in the Land of Bliss. Both in China and Japan, mixed groups of monastic and lay adherents were formed to support their members in this practice, in some instances meeting monthly for extended periods of recitation. Some groups combined lectures on the *Lotus*

Sūtra with recitation practice. Of particular importance was supporting dying members so they could pass away either reciting the name Amitābha or at least hearing the name recited. The earliest of these groups is thought to have been established in 402 CE by the monk Huiyuan on Mount Lu. Comprising 123 adherents, both lay and monastic, it is known by its later appellation, White Lotus Society. Half a millennium later in Japan a similar group was formed on Mount Hiei. Known as the Samādhi Society of Twenty-Five (Jpn., Nijūgozanmai-e), this group was founded in 986 and reorganized in 988 by the monk Genshin.

MULTIVALENCE OF PRACTICES. Some of the most common categories for the discussion of religious practices are based on distinctions between elite and popular (social status) or between monastic and lay (institutional affiliation) forms of practice. These categories, however, are often misleading in the case of East Asian Buddhism, where—as we have seen with the Pure Land recitation societies described above—the same practices were commonly engaged in by both monks and laity. Geoffrey Samuel has proposed a more nuanced three-part division based on goal or motivation. Of course, all category systems are provisional. The limiting factor in this case is that motivations may differ between different people, and the same practice may be engaged in with different goals in mind. Thus, rather than utilizing Samuel's threefold division as a means of categorizing ritual practices per se, it provides us with a means of acknowledging the multivalence of ritual practices. The strength of this categorization is that it is based on Buddhist categories themselves, rather than being imposed from outside.

Samuel's three categories are: pragmatic, *karma*-oriented, and *bodhi*-oriented. Pragmatic practices are directed toward providing immediate benefits in this life. *Karma*-oriented practices deal with the issues of death and rebirth, such as past and future lives. *Bodhi*-oriented practices are those in which the goal is awakening. Understanding East Asian Buddhist practices as having these three dimensions is important because it demonstrates the breadth of religious practices and concerns in Buddhism, a breadth often obscured by the typical representation of Buddhism in contemporary Western religious culture, which focuses solely on an individualized quest for awakening. Some of the practical concerns include healing, exorcism of demonic possessions, and apotropaic protection from demonic attack and possession.

Healing has been a primary human concern in Buddhism, as in other religious traditions. In medieval Chinese Buddhism, for example, there are many stories of recitation of *mantras* and sūtras healing the practitioner, either lay or monastic, from illness or demonic possession. Common among these recitative practices are recitation of the name of the Buddha Amitābha (Chin., Amitou; Jpn., Amida) and the *Diamond Sūtra* (*Prajñāpāramitā hṛdaya sūtra*). Like constructing roads and bridges, and providing economic support for monks and monasteries, such recitative practices were understood to generate merit that could benefit the practitioner either in this life or the next.

Recitative practices also served karmic functions, and their efficacy was not considered to be limited to Buddhist settings, but rather extended across the Chinese cosmology. An anecdote tells of a man of good standing who, upon entering a Daoist temple while drunk, playfully pulled the writing brush from the hand of the statue of the judge of evil. Later he is met by a messenger who has been ordered by the judge to bring him before the otherworldly court. Reciting the *Diamond Sūtra* in secret, he is reprimanded severely by the judge of evil, but eventually forgiven when he promises to recite the *Diamond Sūtra* seven times a day for the rest of his life. Many other texts, including the *Lotus Sūtra* and its "Guanshiyin" chapter, which itself circulated as an independent text, were the object of recitation practice.

This recitation of sūtras is one part of what has been called the "cult of the book," in which texts were given religious significance in ways other than being read for their didactic content. Both hagiographic collections, such as the *Lives of Eminent Monks* (*Gaoseng zhuan*) by Huijiao (496–554), and miracle tales written by laypersons record a variety of devotional practices directed toward sūtra texts. Sūtra texts were collected, preserved, and displayed, which seems to continue the equation made between the Buddha and his teachings—sūtra texts themselves were treated as comparable to relics; that is, as vehicles for the presence of buddhas and *bodhisattvas.* The physical presence of a sūtra text also provided protection when worn on the body like an amulet, and miraculous punishments were said to follow on acts of desecration against sūtra texts.

Similar to healing, exorcistic, and apotropaic rites are practices related to personal hygiene, which are found throughout East Asian monastic Buddhism. One particular set of these practices is focused on avoiding the polluting and demonic forces of the toilet. A sixteenth-century Korean Sŏn manual reflects beliefs and practices inherited from China, which are still found in some Japanese temples as well. Before entering the latrine, a monk is to snap his fingers three times to warn the demons dwelling there. This is followed by a series of five *mantras*—for entering the latrine, for purification, for cleansing the hand, for getting rid of filth, and for a pure body.

Illness and demonic possession do not seem to have been clearly distinguished, as illness was often understood as a sign of demonic possession—seen, for example, in the Japanese *Tale of Genji* (*Genji monogatari*), written by Murasaki Shikibu at the very beginning of the eleventh century. Exorcistic rituals date back much further in China, however. Compiled in the middle of the fifth century CE, the Buddhist *Book of Consecration* employs a practice of impressing a seal empowered with the names of powerful spirits. Despite the text's use of the Sanskrit term *mudrā*, which literally means "seal," the Buddhist form of this ritual draws on earlier Chinese practices. Seals were used as the symbol of authority and power, and by carving seals with the names of powerful spiritual entities, such as the Yellow God, Monarch of Heaven, and impressing these either directly on buildings or on pieces of paper hung on a house, one could be protected from demonic forces. Such apotropaic uses clearly match exorcistic uses in which the seal is applied to the body of the afflicted person.

TYPES AND STRUCTURES. Buddhist practitioners have categorized ritual practices according to their purposes. These native taxonomies demonstrate the continuity of Buddhist thought, which originated in Indian Buddhism and is found in Tibet as well as East Asia. These categories are applied, for example, to the *homa,* which has its origins in pre-Buddhist Vedic votive rituals employing fire as a means by which the offering is transferred from the officiant to the deities evoked. In the esoteric Buddhist traditions, there are five purposes for which the *homa* may be performed: for pacification (Skt., *śāntika;* Jpn., *soku sai*); for increase (Skt., *pauṣṭika;* Jpn., *zō yaku*); for subjugation (Skt., *ābhicāruka;* Jpn., *gō buku* or *jō buku*); for subordination (Skt., *vaśikaraṇa;* Jpn., *kei ai*); and for acquisition (Skt., *aṅkuśa;* Jpn., *kō shō*). The use of the same ritual for differing purposes is evidenced by this practice. Each of these five kinds of *homa* are interpreted as having both a practical purpose and as conducive to awakening. For example, the *homa* of pacification functions practically to protect the practitioner—or the ritual sponsor—from accidents, disasters, and misfortunes. The esoteric interpretation is that the ritual extinguishes obscurations (Skt., *kleśa;* Jpn., *bonnō*). Indeed, the ideology of esoteric Buddhism presents a view in which there is no real difference between these two effects, based on the equation of *saṃsāra* and *nirvāṇa* found in the Madhyamaka tradition. An instance of the practical application of the *homa* of pacification is found at the Shin Daibutsu temple in Mie prefecture, where the ritual is performed for the protection of truck drivers who work in the logging industry.

The contents and organization of many of the rituals of East Asian Buddhism were based on a common set of elements and structures. In China, one of the most widely practiced monastic rites was repentance. Repentance rituals were built up out of a set of common elements. The earliest set of these elements appears in the *triskandha* ritual found in the *Ugra-paripṛcchā Sūtra,* translated into Chinese in the last decades of the second century CE. Typically, the *triskandha* is a three-part ritual involving repentance, rejoicing in the merits of others, and requesting the buddhas to teach. This was not a fixed form, however. In some versions, rejoicing in the merits of others is replaced with committing oneself to changing one's future behavior. Requesting the buddhas to have pity on the practitioner replaces requesting the buddhas to teach. The formulaic character of repentance rites indicates that these are not confessions of particular sins that one has committed, but rather a ritualized repenting of all of the karmic offenses that one may have performed—not only in this lifetime, but indeed in all previous lifetimes throughout beginningless time.

The ritual format of repentance rites expanded over time, coming to include from four to eleven ritual actions, known as "limbs." While there are eleven elements in both the Indian and Chinese forms, differences between the two traditions lead to a total of fourteen. These are making offerings (Skt., *pūja, pūjanā;* Chin., *gongyang*), going for refuge (Skt., *śāraṇa-gamana;* Chin., *sangui*), receiving the five precepts (Chin. only, *shou wujie*), relying on the Buddha's path (Skt. only, *mārgāśrayaṇa*), offering praise (Skt., *vandanā;* Chin., *zan fo*), performing veneration through prostrations (considered part of the offerings in Sanskrit; distinguished in Chinese, *li fo*), confessing or repenting (Skt., *pāpa-deśanā;* Chin., *chanhui*), rejoicing in the merits of others (Skt., *puṇyānumodanā;* Chin., *suixi*), requesting the buddhas to teach (Skt., *adhyeṣanā;* Chin., *quanzhu, qing*), requesting the buddhas to remain in the world (Skt., yācanā, not distinguished from requesting the buddhas to teach in Chinese), sacrificing the self (Skt., *atmatyāga, ātmabhāvananiryātana;* Chin., *sheshen*), giving rise to the thought of awakening (Skt., *bodhicittotpāda;* Chin., *fa putixin*), transfering merit (Skt., *pariṇāmanā;* Chin., *huixiang*), and making vows (Skt., *praṇidhāna;* Chin., *fayuan*).

The structure of the *homa* ritual demonstrates another organizing structure. The fundamental ritual metaphor is that of feasting an honored guest, which originates in Vedic ritualism and was adopted into all Tantric traditions. The ritual proceeds through a regular sequence beginning with preparing the site and offerings, inviting the deities into the ritual space, making offerings and ritually identifying with the chief deity, separating from the chief deity and returning the deities to their place in the *maṇḍala,* and finally ending the ritual and opening the ritual space.

CONCLUSION. The range and variety of East Asian Buddhist practice can be exemplified by examination of a specific cult, such as that of Kṣitigarbha, the Earth Treasury *Bodhisattva.* There are three primary axes of this cult: devotional practices, repentance rituals, and funerary rituals. The devotional practices include recitation of the name of the *bodhisattva,* creation of different kinds of representations of the *bodhisattva* and their veneration, and recitation and copying of the *Sūtra of the Bodhisattva Kṣitigarbha.* Recitation of the name and veneration of the image of Kṣitigarbha seem to have been influenced by the Pure Land tradition's practices. The link between Pure Land and the cult of Kṣitigarbha is indicated by the changes to the standard Amitābha triad of Amitābha Buddha and his two attendant *bodhisattvas,* Avalokiteśvara and Mahāsthāmaprāpta. In some cases Mahāsthāmaprāpta is replaced by Kṣitigarbha. A variety of repentance rituals focusing on Kṣitigarbha were also written.

The diversity of East Asian Buddhist practices constitute a rich field of study, especially given the difference between these practices and both the intellectual heritage of Western religious studies and the popular representation of Buddhism in the West. The issues raised by the study of East Asian Buddhist practice include the integrity of ritual and meditation, the dynamics of local and translocal practices, the complex relation between practice and ideology, the social dimensions of practice, the multivalence of practice, and the emic categories for types and structures of practice.

SEE ALSO Amitābha; Buddhist Meditation, article on East Asian Buddhist Meditation; Buddhist Religious Year; Nianfo; Priesthood, article on Buddhist Priesthood; Sūtra Literature; Temple, articles on Buddhist Temple Compounds.

BIBLIOGRAPHY

Boucher, Daniel. "The Praītyasamutpādagātha and its Role in the Medieval Cult of Relics." *Journal of the International Association of Buddhist Studies* 14, no. 1 (1991): 1–27.

Buswell, Robert E., Jr. *The Zen Monastic Experience: Buddhist Practice in Contemporary Korea.* Princeton, 1992.

Campany, Robert F. "Notes on the Devotional Uses and Symbolic Functions of Sūtra Texts as Depicted in Early Chinese Buddhist Miracle Tales and Hagiographies." *Journal of the International Association of Buddhist Studies* 14, no. 1 (1991): 28–72.

Dōgen. *Dōgen's Pure Standards for the Zen Community: A Translation of the Eihei Shingi.* Translated by Taigen Daniel Leighton and Shohaku Okumura. Albany, N.Y., 1996.

Faure, Bernard, ed. *Chan Buddhism in Ritual Context.* London and New York, 2003.

Gimello, Robert M. "Chang Shang-ying on Wu-t'ai Shan." In *Pilgrims and Sacred Sites in China,* edited by Susan Naquin and Chün-Fang Yü, pp. 89–149. Berkeley, 1992.

Jones, Charles B. "Buddha One: A One-Day Buddha-Recitation Retreat in Contemporary Taiwan." In *Approaching the Land of Bliss: Religious Praxis in the Cult of Amitābha,* edited by Richard K. Payne and Kenneth K. Tanaka, pp. 264–280. Honolulu, 2004.

Orzech, Charles. *Politics and Transcendent Wisdom: The Scripture of Humane Kings in the Creation of Chinese Buddhism.* University Park, Pa., 1998.

Reader, Ian, and Paul L. Swanson, eds. *Japanese Journal of Religious Studies.* Special issue on Pilgrimage 24, nos. 3–4 (1997).

Samuel, Geoffrey. *Civilized Shamans: Buddhism in Tibetan Societies.* Washington and London, 1993.

Stone, Jacqueline I. "By the Power of One's Last Nenbutsu: Deathbed Practices in Early Medieval Japan." In *Approaching the Land of Bliss: Religious Praxis in the Cult of Amitābha,* edited by Richard K. Payne and Kenneth K. Tanaka, pp. 77–119. Honolulu, 2004.

Strickmann, Michel. *Mantras et mandarins: Le bouddhisme tantrique en Chine.* Paris, 1996.

Strickmann, Michel. *Chinese Magical Medicine.* Edited by Bernard Faure. Stanford, Calif., 2002.

Teiser, Stephen F. *The Ghost Festival in Medieval China.* Princeton, 1988.

Ter Haar, B. J. *The White Lotus Teachings in Chinese Religious History.* Leiden, 1992.

Unno, Mark. *Shingon Refractions: Myōe and the Mantra of Light.* Somerville, Mass., 2004.

Wang-Toutain, Françoise. *Le bodhisattva Kṣitigarbha en Chine du Ve au XIIIe siècle.* Paris, 1998.

Weber, Claudia. *Buddhistische Beichten in Indien und bei den Uiguren: Unter besonderer Berücksichtigung der uigurischen Laienbeichte und ihrer Beziehung zum Manichäismus.* Wiesbaden, Germany, 1999.

Welch, Holmes. *The Practice of Chinese Buddhism, 1900–1950.* Cambridge, Mass., 1967.

Williams, Bruce Charles. "Mea Maxima Vikalpa: Repentance, Meditation, and the Dynamics of Liberation in Medieval Chinese Buddhism, 500–650 CE." Ph.D. diss., University of California, Berkeley, 2002.

Yamabe, Nobuyoshi. "Practice of Visualization and the Visualization Sūtra: An Examination of Mural Paintings at Toyok, Turfan." *Pacific World: Journal of the Institute of Buddhist Studies,* 3rd ser., no. 4 (2002): 123–152.

RICHARD K. PAYNE (2005)

WORSHIP AND DEVOTIONAL LIFE: BUDDHIST DEVOTIONAL LIFE IN TIBET

Tibetan Buddhism is a continuation of the form of Buddhism that gradually developed over fifteen hundred years in India. The Indian masters who came to Tibet as missionaries encountered folk traditions and beliefs and either suppressed them or incorporated them, in modified form, into the Buddhist universe. Tibetan Buddhism is therefore a complex and layered set of philosophical concepts, rituals, and local beliefs symbolically represented by a pantheon of deities who are either considered Buddhist or have been integrated into Buddhism. The faith of the people is rooted in the historical presence of the Buddha Śākyamuni, his teachings, and the monastic community (i.e., "the three refuges"). Their faith focuses on the celestial Tantric emanations of Śākyamuni, especially on the "wrathful tutelary deities" and the *bodhisattvas,* in particular Avalokiteśvara, Mañjuśrī, Vajrapāṇi, and Tārā in all her forms; these *bodhisattvas* symbolize compassion, knowledge, and power to overcome obstacles. Tibetans also believe in numerous spirits of the land, sky, and underworld. While they consider these spirits to be inferior to the elevated Buddhist pantheon, Tibetans believe that they can have more immediate influence on their daily mundane life than the *bodhisattvas,* and therefore they worship them.

There is a complementarity between the monastics who live in communities and the lay people. According to the Tibetan Buddhist idea of spiritual evolution, merit and wisdom must be gathered for a person to advance towards better rebirths and eventual buddhahood. A lay person mainly concentrates on merit, while also gathering wisdom by supporting the members of the monastic community, who pursue study, reflection, and contemplation in order to gain wisdom. The duty of monastics is to attend to the spiritual aspect of humankind, while lay people provide material support to the religious communities.

Karma, the consequence of the actions of past lives, along with the consequences of this life's actions in a subsequent life, form the theological basis of the people's beliefs. The maintenance of the right attitude and the right mind so as to accumulate merit is the key to a better future life; few people hope to reach the enlightened state, by which they will escape the wheel of reincarnation. Each being has to practice religion in the best way possible at the level reached in this present life. The worship and devotional life of Tibetans reflect these specificities of Tibetan Buddhism.

For most people, including monastics, worship as an individual or a community revolves around thanksgiving and pleasing the deities in order to be safeguarded; worship also involves beliefs concerning protection against evil influences, which can take the form of spirits, and the accumulation of meritorious actions. Most of the devotional life of Tibetans is made up of rituals or actions directed toward these aims.

In monastic communities, besides individual practices, worship takes the form of common daily rituals to the Buddha, *bodhisattvas*, and deities who are specific to each religious tradition within Tibetan Buddhism. The recitation and chanting of prayers accompanied by music is one of the best-known features of Tibetan Buddhism. Certain sequences of prayers and gestures form a liturgy, also called ritual, which can be performed for different purposes and be more or less elaborated. Sacrificial cakes (*gtor ma*) made of cereals and butter are erected and offered to deities by the monastics. Each deity has a specific sacrificial cake. Sand *maṇḍalas*, which take days to make according to a prescribed text, are sometimes offered and then destroyed at the end of the ritual, demonstrating the impermanence of all things. Monastics have other important ceremonies as well: rituals of ordination (for novices and fully ordained monks), monthly rituals of purification, summertime rituals of retreat, and rituals of accession to higher ranks and offices within the monastic hierarchy.

Lay people visit temples on auspicious days to offer butter lamps and incense sticks, and to prostrate in front of the deities, asking for their blessings. They can also offer tea or make any other kind of offering to the whole monastic community, actions that will bring them merit. Out of devotion, lay people often use all their extra earnings to make religious contributions towards new statues or paintings in a temple, or toward building a Buddhist memorial *mchod rten* (chorten, in Sanskrit, stupa), or to go on pilgrimage. These actions are believed to not only add merit to a person's *karma*, but also to increase positive influences for the whole community and beyond to all sentient beings. Collective or individual practices are based on the same belief. Devotional actions are not only meant for oneself but for humankind, and they take different forms.

Nyung gnas (*nyungne*, prayer and fasting), which can last for several days, is practiced mainly by groups of village women and nuns for the benefit of all. *Dbyar gnas* (*yarne*) is the summer retreat made by monastic communities after the model of Buddha's life. The *Phyag 'bum* (*cha bum*, 100,000 prostrations) are also performed by individuals as a spiritual and devotional exercise that should be done once in a lifetime; it is very strenuous and usually takes three months to complete. A person performing a large number of prostrations can wear a leather apron and gloves, especially during pilgrimages.

Recitation of formulas called *mantras*, which are dedicated to a single deity, is performed with a 108-bead rosary or a prayer wheel and is the most common and ubiquitous form of worship. The two main formulas are *oṃ maṇi padme hūṃ*, the six-syllable *mantra* of Avalokiteśvara, the *bodhisattva* of compassion, who can release sentient beings from the six realms of rebirth, and *oṃ vajra gurū siddhi hūṃ*, the *mantra* of Padmasambhava, whom Tibetans call Gurū Rinpoche. Women have a special devotion for Tārā, the savior and female aspect of Avalokiteśvara, and they recite her *mantra* as protection. These *mantras* can be recited whenever people have free time and while traveling. Elderly people devote most of their time to recitations for their own accumulation of merit, as well as for the merit of all sentient beings. Collective 100,000 recitations are also organized by monastic communities.

Circumambulations around holy places are the third most popular form of devotion, following prostration and recitation; all three are often combined. The holy place could be a monastery, a temple, a *mchod rten* (Buddhist memorial), even a whole city like Lhasa or a mountain like Kailash in Western Tibet. Buddhists perform their circumambulation with the holy place on the right-hand side (Bonpos keep it on the left-hand side). The manner of performing circumambulation is left to each person's initiative; the practice may be performed daily or on auspicious days, and may include fast walking and half or complete prostrations individually or in a group.

The cult of relics is another manifestation of worship in Tibetan Buddhism. Miraculous imprints of parts of the body of a saint are found in rocks, and people touch them with their forehead in order to attain blessings. Bones found after the cremation of high lamas and even mummies are enshrined in *mchod rten* and are objects of great veneration and a source of blessings. One impressive example is the temple containing the reliquary *mchod rten* of the Dalai Lamas in the Potala in Lhasa. Tibetans, in an uninterrupted flow, pass in front of them, touch them with their forehead, burn incense sticks, and pour butter and oil into the butter lamps. This manifestation of faith is all the more poignant now that the Potala is officially a museum and people have to move very quickly through the temple. In addition, designated holes and passages in rocks at "power places" are associated with a means to purify oneself from sins. They are matrices symbolizing rebirth to a new life.

All these devotional manifestations find their apex in pilgrimages. During pilgrimages, monastics and lay people alike combine all of them. This is probably one reason why pilgrimages are so highly regarded in Tibetan Buddhism. They often represent a lifelong dream, the realization of which demands financial investment and hardship for most people. But these material conditions make the pilgrimage even more meritorious, and the devotion shown by pilgrims amply demonstrates the total spiritual fulfillment of this act.

Holy cities like Lhasa, monasteries like Bsam yas (Samye), and sacred mountains like Gang Tise (Kailash), A myes ma chen (Amnye Machen) in northeastern Tibet, and Tsa ri (Tsari) in southeastern Tibet are the most rewarding in terms of blessings and merit. But people also make pilgrimages to sites that are not far from their region, and some pilgrimage destinations are purely local. Travel to a distant pilgrimage site, which can take weeks to reach, is usually organized by a group of villagers headed by a monk. With the assistance of a religious guidebook, the monk points out the important places en route and explains their symbolic meaning. The skor ra (kora), or circumambulation of a mountain (mountains are considered the abode of a manifestation of the Buddha), can take several days.

Only the most determined do the full prostration all the way; helped by a friend, they may live off alms on a physically exhausting but spiritually fulfilling journey. Today in Lhasa one can still meet such leather-clad pilgrims who have prostrated all the way from their home regions to the holy city, continuing their devotion through the fumes and the noise of the traffic. The pilgrim is oblivious to the ugly aspects of the modern city and sees only the holy places. India and its historical Buddhist sites, such as Bodh Gayā, are the ultimate pilgrimage destinations for Tibetan Buddhists.

One of the strongest aspects of Tibetan devotional life is the veneration in which high incarnate lamas (addressed as *rinpoche*, "precious jewel") are held. Such a lama is a *sprul sku (tulku),* which, in Tibetan, means a body of incarnation, implying that he is a human embodiment, a quintessential representative, of the Buddha or a *bodhisattva,* or the present form of a saint. The Dalai Lama is the best known of such high lamas: he is the incarnation of the *bodhisattva* Avalokiteśvara, the all compassionate, and the Buddhist protector of Tibet. However, there are hundreds of incarnate lamas. Some are the embodiment of a long lineage of past lamas, some are more reputed for their spiritual achievement and teachings than others, but all command a veneration that is difficult to describe in rational terms. Being in their presence, listening to their teaching, and getting blessed by them are among the greatest benedictions a devotee can hope for. This explains the gathering of thousands of people who come from all over the world when one of these high incarnates gives a public initiation. It also explains the blessing on the head given by the touch of a lama's photograph.

According to Tibetan Buddhism, rites fall into four main categories: (1) pacification rites (to pacify, bless, and heal); (2) augmentative rites (to increase lifespan and good luck, and to generate bounty and wealth); (3) empowering rites (to enhance control of divine and human individual and social forces, and to tame and discipline); and (4) wrathful rites (to protect against evil and remove obstacles; exceptionally, these rites may involve the taking of sentient life). This four-fold philosophical categorization of rites is understood by most educated monks, but common people often do not perceive the rites in this way. They see rites as a means to remedy a particular situation.

An important aspect of devotional life is made up of rituals performed at home. Each house has an altar room or, in the case of very poor people, a corner devoted to religious activities. Monastics, or simply religious practitioners in some areas, are called into a family's house and stay there for one or several days, depending on the length of the ritual they have been asked to perform. The reading of a specific text, often a version of the *Prajñāpāramitā* in 100,000 verses (*'bum*) or 8,000 verses (*brgyad stong pa*) is done, if possible, once a year in each household to insure blessings to the family. On a grander scale, a noble family can ask for the reading of the 120 volumes of the Bka' 'gyur (*Kanjur),* considered to be in the Tibetan Buddhist canon the words of the Buddha. There are religious communities that specialize in reading the scriptures.

Other rituals have different purposes, and they usually involve lengthy preparations in the making of sacrificial cakes, effigies, or thread crosses, and the gathering of special ingredients and vessels. A ritual has more value if it is presided over by a reincarnate lama. The purpose of these rituals is to cleanse the house after a birth or a death; to ensure the prosperity of the family, the harvest, and the cattle; to ward off evil spirits who have caused sickness or misfortune; to call back prosperity and fortune or *g-yang* (*yang*); to protect members of the family while they travel; or to redeem sins. It may be in the rituals that the assimilation of pre-Buddhist or non-Buddhist beliefs into Buddhism is most obvious. The best example might be the state oracle ceremony, still performed today. During every New Year festival, the oracle monk of Gnas chung (Nechung) monastery, next to 'Bras spung (Drepung) near Lhasa and now rebuilt at Dharamsala in India, dressed in ceremonial garments and crowned by heavy headgear, is brought before the Dalai Lama in public. While in a trance, possessed by the deity Rdo rje drag ldan (Dorje Dragden), he blesses the state and the people and shoots a symbolic arrow at the heart of the scapegoat effigy in which all the evil of the previous year is magically entrapped. The effigy is then burned in a bonfire. In coded language, the oracle monk provides information to the state, responds to questions, and gives warnings of impending dangers.

Many rituals that Tibetans perform as part of their devotional life find their origins in the pre-Buddhist religion, commonly called Bon. Once a year, community rituals dedicated to the local guardian deity of the territory are performed; these involve the burning of incense and juniper, as well as the erecting of prayer flags near the abode of the deity, usually on a mountain. The burning of juniper, called *bsangs (sang)*, is also done daily by each family in order to please the local deity. This does not prevent Buddhist prayers being said every morning in the family altar room, where butter lamps and water bowls are placed as offerings to the Buddha and *bodhisattvas*.

The great capacity of Tibetans to assimilate or maintain, side by side, different beliefs in a religion called Tibetan Buddhism has led to a rich devotional life that is supported by an unwavering faith in meritorious acts and compassionate beings.

SEE ALSO Buddhism, article on Buddhism in Tibet; Buddhism, Schools of, articles on Early Doctrinal Schools of Buddhism, Tibetan and Mongolian Buddhism; Maṇḍalas, article on Buddhist Maṇḍalas; Tibetan Religions, overview article.

BIBLIOGRAPHY

Avedon, John F. *In Exile from the Land of Snows.* New York, 1984; reprint, 1997.

Bazin, Nathalie, ed. *Rituels tibétains: Visions secrètes du Ve Dalai Lama* (Catalogue de l'exposition du Musée Guimet, 6 novembre 2002– 26 février 2003). Paris, 2002.

Beer, Robert. *The Encyclopedia of Tibetan Symbols and Motifs.* London, 1999.

Beyer, Stephen. *The Cult of Tārā: Magic and Ritual in Tibet.* Berkeley, 1973.

Blondeau, Anne-Marie, ed. *Tibetan Mountain Deities: Their Cults and Representations.* Vienna, 1998.

Blondeau, Anne-Marie, and Ernst Steinkellner, eds. *Reflections of the Mountain: Essays on the History and Social Meaning of the Mountain Cult in Tibet and the Himalayas.* Vienna, 1996.

Brauen, Martin. *The Mandala: Sacred Circle in Tibetan Buddhism.* Translated by Martin Wilson. London, 1997.

Buffetrille, Katia. *Pèlerins, lamas, et visionnaires: Sources orales et écrites sur les pèlerinages tibétains.* Vienna, 2000.

Dowman, Keith. *The Sacred Life of Tibet.* London, 1997.

Gyatso, Tenzin. *My Land and My People.* New York, 1962; reprint, 1983. The autobiography of the fourteenth Dalai Lama.

Huber, Toni, ed. *Sacred Spaces and Powerful Places in Tibetan Culture: A Collection of Essays.* Dharamsala, India, 1999.

Huber, Toni. *The Cult of Pure Crystal Mountain: Popular Pilgrimage and Visionary Landscape in Southeast Tibet.* Oxford, 1999.

Karmay, Samten G. *Secret Visions of the Fifth Dalai Lama.* London, 1988; reprint, 1998.

Karmay, Samten G. *The Arrow and the Spindle: Studies in History, Myths, Rituals, and Beliefs in Tibet.* 2 vols. Kathmandu, 2004.

Lopez, Donald S., ed. *Religions of Tibet in Practice.* Princeton, 1997.

McKay, Alex, ed. *Pilgrimage in Tibet.* Richmond, U.K., 1998.

Nebesky-Wojkowitz, René de. *Oracles and Demons of Tibet: The Cult and Iconography of the Tibetan Protective Deities.* Graz, Austria, 1956; reprint, Kathmandu, 1993.

Ricard, Matthieu, Olivier Föllmi, and Daniele Föllmi. *Buddhist Himalayas.* London and New York, 2002

Ricard, Matthieu. *Monk Dancers of Tibet.* Translated by Charles Hastings. Boston, 2003.

Richardson, Hugh. *Ceremonies of the Lhasa Year.* London, 1993.

Samuel, Geoffrey. *Civilized Shamans: Buddhism in Tibetan Societies.* Washington, D.C., 1993.

Samuel, Geoffrey, Hamish Gregor, and Elisabeth Stutchbury, eds. *Tantra and Popular Religion in Tibet.* New Delhi, 1994.

Stein, Rolf A. *Tibetan Civilization.* Translated by J. E. Stapleton Driver. Stanford, Calif., 1972.

Tucci, Giuseppe. *The Religions of Tibet.* Translated by Geoffrey Samuel. Berkeley, 1980.

FRANÇOISE POMMARET (2005)

WORSHIP AND DEVOTIONAL LIFE: DAOIST DEVOTIONAL LIFE

The Chinese have traditionally rendered a cult to a vast array of spiritual beings that includes, in addition to their own ancestors, great heroes of the past, spirits of place, and the souls of the unfortunate dead. Every geographical unit had its own god of the soil; every social grouping has its patron deity and temple. There were gods who judged the souls of the dead and gods who kept watch on the conduct of the living; there were gods of healing and gods who spread epidemics. Even the latrine, as a distinct place, had its guardian spirit.

Chinese popular religion is essentially concerned with the cultivation of the good graces of these spirits, most of whom are at once potentially harmful and potentially beneficial. Their cults represent alliances or covenants between the worshipers and the worshiped: in exchange for the protection and assistance of the spiritual potentate, the faithful render it a cult. It is a reciprocal relationship, with obligations on both sides. These features of the religion of the people also characterize state-sponsored religion from very early times, as may be seen in the third-century BCE descriptions of the gods of the realms' mountains and rivers in the *Shanhai jing* (Classic of mountains and seas): sovereignty over a given territory required knowing the nature of the local gods and making the prescribed sacrifices to them.

Daoism, by contrast, is the cult of the Dao ("way"); it denies neither the existence of the gods nor the legitimacy of the cults rendered them. It simply accords them an insignificant place in the world of the Dao. "In a world governed according to the Way," says Laozi (fourth century BCE), "spirits are impotent, or rather, it is not that they are impotent, but that they have no power to harm people."

Unlike the gods of the popular pantheon, the Dao "gives life yet lays no claim, is generous but exacts no gratitude" (*Laozi* 2); it "clothes and feeds the myriad creatures but does not lord it over them" (*Laozi* 34). The natural model for this "highest good" is water. "Because water excels in benefiting the myriad creatures without contending with them and collects in a place ordinary people despise, it comes close to the Way" (*Laozi* 8). "Greatly virtuous behavior," therefore, "consists in following the Way" (*Laozi* 21), and the Daoist is simply one who, because he "acts in accord with the Dao, is like the Dao" (*Laozi* 23).

A book of philosophical maxims, the *Laozi* says nothing of the practices that most probably lie behind Laozi's principles. Recent studies of hitherto neglected texts, such as the *Neiye* ("inward training"), said to date to about the same time as the *Laozi*, have helped to fill this gap by showing that meditation practices were already highly developed at that time. The discovery in tombs dating to the early imperial period (early second century BCE) of medical texts and texts of macrobiotic hygiene has also opened up new perspectives on what some now call "proto-Daoism." These new sources show that the human body was already then understood as a kind of microcosm, subject to the same rules of order and disorder as the macrocosm. In both worlds, the normal circulation of *qi* (breath, vapor, energy) was seen as essential to health, and techniques were therefore proposed for ensuring and improving this circulation. Prominent among these techniques were breath and sexual cultivation.

The *Liexian zhuan* (Biographies of the immortals), a second-century collection of seventy hagiographic sketches, gives a good idea both of the range of these practices and of their social function. All the practices focus on the human body, which is conceived of as a kind of "energy bank" whose original capital can either be spent—the result is death—or "nourished" and so augmented until one obtains immortality. Adepts "nourished their energy" (*yang qi*) with a great variety of natural products thought to be particularly potent. The most remarkable of these products is without doubt the "essence of the mysterious female," obtained by means of the "arts of the bedroom." But most of the products were of either a plant or mineral variety: roots, thistles, chrysanthemums, pine seeds, mica, and cinnabar are among those mentioned. Inasmuch as most of these products could be found only by patient searching in uninhabited regions, the future immortals (*xian*) appear as solitary individuals who, having learned the techniques of searching and use from a master, disappear into the mountainous wilds or the "Far West" and are never seen again. But some return on occasion to cure people or save them from a natural disaster.

One Cui Wen Zi, for example, after having lived for a long time in obscurity at the foot of Mount Tai—also called the Eastern Peak and considered to be the dwelling place of the souls of the dead—returns one day to human society to sell his "yellow potions and red pills." When later a great epidemic breaks out and the deaths number in the tens of thousands, the civil authorities come to Cui begging him to save the people. Carrying a red banner in one hand and his yellow potion in the other, Cui goes from house to house, and all who drink his potion are saved.

Cui later goes off to Sichuan in western China to sell his pills. Although no cult is established in his honor, many of the immortals do become cult objects. Huang Yuanqui, a Daoist (*daoshi*) who descends occasionally from his mountain to sell drugs, comes to be worshiped because he saves the local people from an earthquake by giving them advance warning of its imminence. A female Daoist (*daoren*) by the name of Changrong likewise becomes the object of a cult when, over a period of two hundred years, she wins fame by giving away to widows and orphans all the money she makes selling a special plant from her mountain as a dye. Another mountain-dwelling Daoist first appears to give one Shantu a recipe or an herbal drug that not only heals his wounds but also completely satisfies his hunger. When Shantu returns to become his disciple, the Daoist reveals himself to be an "angel of the Five Peaks," that is, one of the divine messengers of the five sacred mountains of China.

HEAVENLY MASTER DAOISM. If most of the immortals of the *Biographies* were hermits of the distant past, the second century CE also witnessed the appearance of the first mass movements in Daoism. The most important proved to be that of the Way of the Heavenly Masters (*Tianshi dao*), which has survived to the present. Sometime in the middle of the second century—the traditional date is 142 CE—Zhang Daoling, on the basis of a revelation received from the Most High Lord Lao (the religious title of the philosopher Laozi), founded a "church" composed of twenty-four "governances" (*zhi*). The twenty-four governances on earth corresponded to twenty-four energies in heaven, and the term therefore implied that the world of the Heavenly Masters was "governed" according to the same principles as heaven.

Behind this program for an orderly world lay a detailed cosmology. The Dao was conceived of as a giant body containing three pure energies in a chaotic state. Over time, these energies separated out to form a three-layered universe composed of the heavens above, the earth beneath, and the waters under the earth. Each of these three layers spread out to the "eight confines," that is, the four directions plus the four corners. The twenty-four governances are the replica of these twenty-four regions of the universe; both are expressions of the twenty-four celestial energies, each of which is dominant in turn for fifteen days each year: 24 x 15 = 360.

The new religion was called the *zhengyi mengwei dao* ("way of the alliance of the orthodox one with the gods"). The Orthodox One was the "unique energy" of Lord Lao—his revelation—communicated to Zhang Daoling. The gods were taken over from the popular pantheon, but they included only the gods who assisted in governing the universe, that is, the gods of the hearth and of the soil, who reported at regular intervals to heaven on the conduct of the family or the community of which they had charge. In addition, there were the Four Generals, who "hold the year-star in place," that is, regulate time, and the Three Officers, who control the Three Realms of heaven, earth, and the waters. Explicitly excluded from this pantheon were the souls of the dead, which played so large a part in popular religion. They were considered "stale energies" that needed to be recycled, and whose worship, as it retarded their recycling and so contravened the natural order, could only cause harm to the living.

The Three Officers were particularly important because they were cosmic inspector gods. It was to them that ill adepts had therefore to address documents of confession, for all illness was considered to be the result of sin. Each of the Three Officers governed a portion of time, as well as a portion of space. Every year, at the beginning of their respective reigns, assemblies of the gods were held to bring the registers of merit and demerit of all beings up to date. On those days, called the days of the Three Assemblies, the Daoist faithful gathered for communal rituals and meals called *zhai* or *chu.* The word *chu* means "kitchen" and therefore refers primarily to the communal meal. The word *zhai* came to mean "vegetarian meal," in part because Daoist meals did not involve animal sacrifices like the meals associated with popular cults; however, its basic meaning is "to equalize," in the sense of "to compose oneself" in preparation for an important encounter, especially with the gods. The term "merit meals" was also used because, as with the meals in the popular cults, the food eaten was first offered to the gods. It was thus consecrated food that brought merit and blessing to its partaker.

The days of the Three Assemblies were also the occasions for bringing the registers of the faithful up to date. This was the job of the *jijiu* (libationers), as the heads, male or female, of the twenty-four governances were called. Everyone in his or her governance, layperson or priest, had a register that corresponded to his or her level of initiation. The texts concerning these registers are unfortunately late (sixth to eighth century) and contradictory, but we can deduce from them that the faithful were organized in a military hierarchy, conceived, no doubt, on the model of the heavenly host that was holding its assembly at the same time.

According to some texts, the body of the Dao—the universe—contains a grand total of 36,000 energies. The bodies of earth dwellers, however, contain only half that number, and adepts must, therefore, learn how to recognize the energies within their bodies so as to "hold them in place" and attract their 18,000 celestial counterparts to come and "attach themselves" to them. This latter term indicates how Daoism borrowed the practices of popular cults and rationalized them by making them controlled techniques in the context of a complete cosmological system, because it is the same term used to describe the phenomenon of possession—the god "attaches himself" to the medium—on which many popular cults are based.

The expedition of petitions was also a characteristic feature of Heavenly Master Daoism. One surviving collection lists the names of some three hundred such texts, together with the offerings that were to accompany them. The petitions are confessions of sin, statements of merit obtained by the performance of a given ritual, and prayers for children, for long life, and for deliverance from every imaginable kind of difficulty (drought, locusts, rats, tigers, sorcery, epidemics, etc.). The offerings invariably include rice, silk, money, incense, oil, and the paper, brushes, and ink needed to write the petition. The generic term for such offerings came to be *jiao,* a word that originally referred to the ceremonial offerings made in connection with a marriage or with male puberty rites. What distinguished such an offering from other offerings was that it was not performed "in response" to someone or "in exchange" for something. It was, in that sense, a gratuitous act, as opposed to an act of gratitude.

Jiao offerings of this kind remain to the present day the one truly distinguishing feature of Daoism in general. Nowadays, in addition to rice, they include tea, fruits, wine, precious objects, candles, even the texts used during the rituals. They are called "pure offerings" in order to distinguish them from the offerings of popular religion, which still include meat, either cooked or raw. These two different types of offering show better than anything else the real differences between the alliances of ordinary people with their gods and the Alliance of the Orthodox One with the Powers: ordinary alliances are "deals" between nonequals, and the offerings are often described quite frankly as "payoffs," such as one would make to a local hoodlum or mandarin. At the same time, such an alliance has nothing permanent about it: it can be broken by either of the contracting parties for "breach of contract."

The Alliance of the Orthodox One with the Powers, being based on the structure of the universe itself, cannot be broken; it can only be recognized. Ritual action that is in accord with this structure automatically brings a response of "merit," for like is attracted to like. Adherents of the Alliance, therefore, must transcend the expectations of reciprocity and mutual obligation that normally determine social and spiritual relations and take responsibility for their own destiny. They must learn to become, like a king, "solitary, single" (*Laozi* 42). All of this is expressed in the "pure offering," an offering that is pure because it includes no blood sacrifices, but also because it expresses the pure intentions of the participants in the offering. It is these pure intentions that will ineluctably attract to the participants the pure energies that bring fortune, health, and salvation. The *jiao* offering continues to celebrate, thus, both a marriage and a coming of age.

In addition to the vast range of rituals performed, either on the occasion of set feast days or at moments of crisis, Heavenly Master Daoism involved private practices. Recitation of sacred texts (of the *Laozi* in the first place, but also of rhymed verses describing the spirits inside the body) was one of them. By recitation, the adept assimilated the text and thereby gained mastery over the spirits described in it. Cycles of recitation imitated the gestational cycles in the body of the Dao, and mastery over the energies within attracted their counterparts without.

Great emphasis was also placed on moral behavior, and each step up in the hierarchy of registers brought with it an increase in the number of commandments to be observed

(180 for libationers). The basic idea of these many commandments was to preserve and nourish the pure energies within rather than squandering them on the outside in the pursuit of pleasure. Because infractions of the commandments were thought to lead to illness, rituals of confession were from the very beginning a central part of the movement. In the "vegetarian vigils" *(zhai)* that became characteristic of Daoism from the mid-fifth century on, partly under Buddhist influence, litanies of confession came to play a major role in all Daoist liturgies.

INDIVIDUAL PRACTICES. The rise of communal Daoism did not put an end to the kinds of individual practice alluded to in the *Biographies of the Immortals.* Beginning in the fifth century, individual eremetism gradually gave way to monastic communities called *guan.* The word means "to observe" or "to visualize"; it refers especially to the "inner vision." Such inner vision being the fruit of individual practice, the constitution of "hermitages" clearly did not put an end to the individual practice of the arts of immortality. These arts included techniques of visualization, breath control and circulation, gymnastics, special diets, intercourse, and alchemy. Early forms of external alchemy involved a fairly broad range of minerals and metals, with cinnabar and lead being central to the process. Later forms used lead and mercury. Internal alchemical methods ranged from the relatively empirical, scarcely distinguishable from the more ordinary techniques of breath circulation, to the extremely abstract and symbolic, virtually indistinguishable from traditional cosmological speculation. What these various techniques and recipes shared was a common symbolic and cosmological framework and the fact that they were transmitted from master to disciple in separate lineages.

Breathing techniques included purely internal methods such as embryonic breathing and circulating the energy while ceasing to breathe. Other methods involved the absorption of outside energies followed by the wedding of these energies to their internal counterparts. Such techniques were usually practiced at times determined by the system of symbolic correspondences. Absorption of the energies of the five directions, for example, was linked to the cycle of the sun, whereas that of the energies of the sun and the moon was linked to the phases of the moon. The adept was to inhale the energies of the four directions on the first and central days of the corresponding season (the "eight segmental days" [*ba jie ri*] because they divided the year into eight equal segments) and those of the center on a day in the sixth month when the central element, earth, was dominant.

The adept who practiced the "method [*dao*] of the absorption of the essences of the sun and the moon" did so on set days on each month: on days 1, 3, 5, 7, 9, and 15. At daybreak, according to the fourth-century *Tai-shang lingbao wufu xu* (Preface to the five symbols, potent treasure of the most high), the adept would face the sun, close his eyes, and visualize a small boy, dressed in red, inside his heart. He would massage himself with both hands from his face to his chest twelve times; then,

> the yellow energies of the true red of the solar essence come before his eyes. They enter his mouth, and he swallows them eighteen times, sending them downward with a massaging movement. He prays, "Original Yang of the Solar Lord, join your power to mine so that together we may nourish the young boy in my Scarlet Palace." After a moment, he visualizes [the energies] going down to the crucible [*dan tian,* in the depths of the belly], where they stop. This leads to eternal life. (*Tai-shang lingbao wufu xu* 1.19a)

From very early times, imaginative visualization played a central role in the Daoist's search for transcendence. In the *Laozi zhongjing* (second century CE), for example, the adept learns to visualize a whole series of gods, from the Supreme Great One above his head to the spirit of his feet. Inside his body, at each of several levels and with constantly shifting names, he visualizes a kind of holy family composed of a Mother of the Dao and Father of the Dao, together with their infant Real Person. The resultant familiarity with the divine forces of his body becomes vital to survival during a three-day retreat at the time of the autumn equinox, when celestial gods come to inspect the human world: by "holding these forces in his mind's eye" (*cun*), he prevents them from leaving his body. Having thus preserved all his own energies, the adept ultimately succeeds in attracting their celestial counterparts and thereby achieves immortality.

The visualizations in the eleventh-century *Lingbao bifa* are very different, focused not on individual gods but on metaphorical representations of the energies of the viscera that combine in an extraordinary variety of ways. After a first cycle of visualizations concentrated within the trunk of the body, a second cycle expands to include the head. In the third and final cycle the adept achieves complete unity of concentration and energy. This enables him to make, cautiously at first, journeys of the mind outside the body and, finally, complete liberation.

A similar process of interiorization occurs in the rituals of communal Daoism, partly as a result of Tantric influence. The esoteric aspects of rituals for presenting memorials, for example—the hand gestures, the dance steps, the visualizations—become ever more important and complex. In extreme cases the external, written memorial disappears altogether. Perhaps most remarkable of all is the appearance, in the thirteenth and fourteenth centuries, of rituals of "universal salvation" (*pudu*) performed by individual laypeople in the quiet of their own meditation rooms. Down to the present day the ritual of universal salvation is normally the most public, not to say noisy, of all rituals.

It is probably also during the Song dynasty that communal Daoism of the kind described above died out. (It seems to have survived only among the Yao tribes of southern China, Thailand, and Laos into the twentieth century.) Lay initiation disappeared, and the priest became a ritual specialist serving a community that had by and large ceased to understand the nature of the rituals for which it still felt a need. The result was not only an increase of ritual secrecy and esoterism, but also a proliferation of rituals. (Urbanization and mercantilization of the economy were also factors in this.) One of the most interesting cases of a new ritual is that of the posthumous ordination of laymen. People became thereby in the next life what they had ceased to be in this life, members of a Daoist community. The religious affiliation of common people in this life tended now only to be with the temples and gods of the very popular religion Daoism had originally set out to combat and replace. Daoism was on its way to becoming what it is in modern times, the servant of the religion of the people, called on primarily to perform offerings that legitimize the gods of the people by showing them how the order of the Dao works, and integrating them thereby into that order.

See Also Alchemy, article on Chinese Alchemy; Daoism, overview article; Jiao; Priesthood, article on Daoist Priesthood; Xian; Zhenren.

Bibliography

The best general introduction to religious—especially Heavenly Master—Daoism is Kristofer Schipper's *Le corps taoïste* (Paris, 1982), translated as *The Taoist Body* by Karen Duval (Berkeley, 1993). On pre-imperial meditation techniques, see Harold D. Roth, *Original Tao: Inward Training (Nei-yeh) and the Foundations of Taoist Mysticism* (New York, 1999). On early macrobiotic techniques of longevity, see Donald Harper, *Early Chinese Medical Literature: The Mawangdui Medical Manuscripts* (London and New York, 1998). On Daoist practice in the formative Six Dynasties period, see Stephen R. Bokenkamp with Peter Nickerson, *Early Daoist Scriptures* (Berkeley, 1997). On Daoist alchemy, see Joseph Needham's *Science and Civilisation in China,* vol. 5, pts. 3 and 4: *Alchemy and Chemistry* (Cambridge, U.K., 1976–1980), and Fabrizio Pregadio, "Elixirs and Alchemy," in Livia Kohn, ed., *Daoism Handbook* (Leiden, 2000), chap. 7, pp. 165–195. On Maoshan practice, see Isabelle Robinet's *Méditation taoïste* (Paris, 1979), translated by Julian F. Pas and Norman J. Girardot as *Taoist Meditation: The Mao-shan Tradition of Great Purity* (Albany, N.Y., 1993). On symbolic alchemy, see Farzeen Baldrian Hussein, trans., *Procédes secrets du joyau magique: Traité d'alchimie taoïste du XIe siècle* (Paris, 1984). On the *Laozi zhongjing,* see John Lagerwey's "Deux écrits taoïstes anciens," in *Cahiers d'Extrême-Asie* 14 (2003).

John Lagerwey (1987 and 2005)

WOVOKA (c. 1856/8–1932), Paiute religious prophet and messiah of the Ghost Dance of 1890; also called Jack Wilson by white settlers. Although he often referred to himself as Kwohitsauq ("big rumbling belly"), after his paternal grandfather, he was given the name Wovoka (or Wuvoka, "cutter") by his father, Tävibo ("white man"), who was reported to have trained his son in Paiute shamanistic practices. Tävibo had been an active participant in the 1870 Ghost Dance led by the Paiute shaman-prophet Wodziwob. Central tenets of this earlier Ghost Dance were related to the later teachings of Wovoka, which in turn led to the Ghost Dance movement of 1890. Among these earlier revelations was the prediction of the return of the ancestral dead. This imminent return was to be assisted through the practice of a round dance, which would also effect an earthly cataclysm and so result in the removal of white men.

In addition to Paiute shamanic practices and the Ghost Dance of 1870, Wovoka was influenced by his contact with Skokomish Shakers, Mormons, and other Christians. The Puget Sound Shaker religion of the Skokomish leader Squsacht-un (called John Slocum by whites) was primarily concerned with healing. It combined native shamanistic and Christian religious practices. These Shakers produced twitching-ecstasies and trances that sometimes lasted for days. Wovoka's later teachings were also similar to Mormon doctrines regarding the rejuvenation of the American Indians, the radical transformations in the earth's terrain, and the return of the Messiah. Moreover, Paul Bailey indicates in his biography of Wovoka (1957) that the famous Plains Ghost Dance shirt bears a resemblance to Mormon holy garments. Finally, after his father died, Wovoka was hired by a white family named Wilson. This position brought him into close contact with Presbyterian Christianity, which involved Bible reading, moral exhortations, and pietistic stories about Jesus.

Around 1888 Wovoka is reported to have undergone his first deathlike trance-journey to heaven. From this point his teachings were derived from conversations with the ghosts of the dead. Wovoka's oral revelations were associated with the ritual performance of the round dance, which promoted moral and spiritual renewal. His teachings were transmitted by means of a syncretic mythology and dramatized through the skillful use of his personal power symbols.

Wovoka's foremost revelations came in a deathlike coma experienced while he was suffering from scarlet fever during the solar eclipse of 1889. During this trance-coma Wovoka related that he saw God on a transformed earth where Indians and game animals abounded. Wovoka's messages increasingly focused on the presence of the Messiah, a role he himself gradually assumed. His mythology centered on the imminent revival of deceased Indians, who would be reunited with their living kin in an earthly paradise. His description of the fate of whites varied. He predicted that they would be either swept away by the cataclysm or amalgamated into the restored humanity. Many of these doctrines, such as the transformed earth, were more fully explicated by Wovoka's disciples, who disseminated the Ghost Dance in the years following 1889.

The later Ghost Dance, similar to that of the Ghost Dance of 1870, was a kind of round dance that lasted for five nights. Men and women, their fingers intertwined, shuffled sideways around a fire, dancing to the songs that Wovoka received from the dead. While the Paiute participants themselves did not go into a trance, Wovoka did occasionally journey in a trance state to the ghosts, who assured him that Jesus was already on the earth with the dead, moving about as in a cloud. Moreover, along with their remonstrations against lying, drinking, and fighting, the dead said that Indians should work for the whites and have no more trouble with them.

Wovoka's personal power-symbols were typical of native shamanic practices. Along with his sombrero he used eagle, magpie, and crow feathers and red ocher paint from the traditional Paiute holy mountain (now called Mount Grant). As with so many visionary symbol systems, their meaning is not fully known, but Wovoka often incorporated these symbols into his teaching so as to foster belief in his messianic role among his followers.

Wovoka went somewhat into hiding when news of the Wounded Knee massacre of 1890 reached him. He vigorously condemned the misunderstanding of his teachings, especially as reflected in the Lakota armed resistance. He also denied any influence in the development of the Ghost Dance shirts. He later reemerged as the continuing leader of the much diminished Ghost Dance. He readjusted his predictions of imminent earthly transformation, explaining that Indian ritual and ethical behavior had not conformed properly to his visions. Wovoka died on September 20, 1932, in Schurz, Nevada; his death was preceded a month earlier by that of his wife, Mary, his companion for over fifty years.

More is known of Wovoka than of other similar religious figures, but he can be seen as part of a larger revivalistic movement of the period. Various tribal groups, caught in the death throes of their traditional cultures and the inescapable morass of governmental reservation policy, responded to Wovoka's revelations from a variety of motivations that mediated between their present distress and their future hopes. Wovoka's injunctions against warfare, immoral behavior, and some traditional medicine practices enabled many who participated in the Ghost Dance to begin the psychic transitions needed to respond to the changing circumstances of life. Most important in this connection was Wovoka's orientation away from exclusive tribal recognition toward a pan-Indian identity.

SEE ALSO Ghost Dance; North American Indian Religions, article on New Religious Movements.

BIBLIOGRAPHY

The most authoritative treatment of Wovoka is still James Mooney's *The Ghost Dance Religion and the Sioux Outbreak of 1890* (1896; reprint, Chicago, 1965). A biography of limited value because of its popularizing tone is Paul Bailey's *Wovoka: The Indian Messiah* (Los Angeles, 1957). A good overview of Wovoka can be found in Bryan R. Wilson's *Magic and the Millenium* (New York, 1973). For an informative account of Wovoka's continuing involvement, by mail, in Ghost Dance activities after 1890, see Grace M. Danberg's edition of *Letters to Jack Wilson, the Paiute Prophet, Written between 1908–1911* (Washington, D.C., 1957).

JOHN A. GRIM (1987)

WRITING, SACRED

SEE CALLIGRAPHY; SCRIPTURE

WUNDT, WILHELM

WUNDT, WILHELM (1832–1920), German physiologist, philosopher, and psychologist, was best known as the founder of experimental psychology. Born the son of a Lutheran pastor, near Mannheim, Wundt studied at Tübingen, Heidelberg, and Berlin, took his Ph.D. and M.D. degrees at Heidelberg, and taught at the universities of Heidelberg, Zurich, and Leipzig. Early in his teaching career at Heidelberg he wrote *Beiträge zur Theorie der Sinneswahrnehmung* (1858–1862), considered to be the first treatment of psychology as an experimental science, and *Vorlesungen über die Menschen- und Tierseele* (1863). Perhaps his most important work for psychology was *Grundzüge der physiologischen Psychologie* (1874), in which he advocated investigating the immediate experiences of consciousness using a method of introspection. In 1874 he was made professor of inductive philosophy at Zurich. In the following year, he accepted a professorship at Leipzig, where in 1879 he founded what is generally regarded as the world's first psychological laboratory. In 1881 he founded a journal of psychology, *Philosophische Studien,* which primarily published the results of research conducted at his Leipzig institute and which helped to establish experimental psychology as a separate discipline.

During his long career at Leipzig, Wundt's most important works were *Grundriss der Psychologie* (1896) and his *Völkerpsychologie* (10 vols., 1900–1920). These two works represent diverse streams that Wundt held together: his interest in physiological psychology and his more philosophical approach to the analysis of ethnic groups. For him, they were not so disparate; he considered psychology the science that could study the phenomena of human consciousness in both its individual and its group manifestations. In his *Völkerpsychologie* Wundt considered an immense amount of anthropological data. He viewed religion, myth, morality, art, and language as phenomena of long duration and therefore as constituting a psychic reality distinct from individual consciousness. Wundt discerned a "folk soul," which for him was not a substance but rather a psychic actuality that could be studied. The idea of a collective unconscious was quite foreign to Wundt, who rejected any idea of the unconscious, advising his students that its study by psychology was a mistake. Wundt focused instead on the objective forms of language, morality, and religion. Nevertheless, his earlier association studies anticipated and inspired the work of his student, Emil Kraepelin, in psychopathology, and stimulated the development of the association test used by C. G. Jung and his associates in Zurich.

Although social psychologists (except possibly for those in Germany during the Nazi period) have rejected any notion of a folk soul and have operated from premises different from those established by Wundt, social psychology has continued the study of the objective forms of religion in society.

Wundt's interests in the universality of mythological motifs and the nature of the language of religion have been taken up by students in the fields of history of religions (although the evolutionary approach implicit in Wundt's more philosophical works has been rejected) and psychology of religion, especially from Freudian and Jungian perspectives.

BIBLIOGRAPHY

The best recent studies of Wundt's work are two publications stemming from the celebration of the founding of his psychological laboratory in 1879: *Wundt Studies: A Centennial Collection,* edited by Wolfgang G. Bringmann and Ryan D. Tweney, with a foreword by Ernest R. Hilgard (Toronto, 1980), and *Wilhelm Wundt and the Making of a Scientific Psychology,* edited by R. W. Rieber in collaboration with Arthur L. Blumenthal, Kurt Danziger, and Solomon Diamond (New York, 1980). Both are critical of Edwin G. Boring's evaluation of Wundt in *A History of Experimental Psychology,* 2d ed. (New York, 1950), which, however, provides considerable biographical data. A good summary of Wundt's legacy is found in Daniel N. Robinson's *Toward a Science of Human Nature: Essays on the Psychologies of Mill, Hegel, Wundt, and James* (New York, 1982).

New Sources

The most comprehensive recent monograph is Robert W. Rieber and David K. Robinson, *Wilhelm Wundt in History. The Making of Scientific Psychology,* New York, 2001. In German see Alfred Arnold, *WilhelmWundt. Sein philosophysches System,* Berlin, 1980, and the authoritative biography by Georg Lamberti, *Wilhelm Maximilian Wundt (1832–1920),* Bonn, 1995.

WALLACE B. CLIFT (1987)
Revised Bibliography

WYCLIF, JOHN (1330?–1384), English scholastic theologian, trenchant critic of abuses in the church, and promoter of a vernacular translation of the Bible. Wyclif was the most learned man of his generation in England. The rigor of his scholastic logic and, in his last years, his appeal to scripture as the sole authority for the church's life, led him into heresies. During his time and to this day, he has had both sympathetic admirers and caustic critics. Nonetheless, the real, human Wyclif remains an enigma. We know little about him except that he led an austere life marked by tireless study, lecturing, and writing.

Nothing certain is known about Wyclif's family or its resources. John Wyclif (or Wycliffe) was born near Richmond in North Riding, Yorkshire. At an early age he entered Balliol College, Oxford, and then served as its regent master from 1360 to 1361. The date of his ordination is unrecorded. Later he resided at Queen's College, where he studied for and received his bachelor of divinity degree (1369) and his doctor of divinity degree (1372). Early connections with Merton College and Canterbury Hall are disputed.

University scholars without means of their own were dependent upon "provisions to livings" of parishes or prebends and canonries in collegiate churches or cathedrals. From this income they were expected to pay vicars for service during their absence. Wyclif was no exception. In 1361 Balliol gave him its choicest living at Fillingham, Lincolnshire. The following year he received from Pope Urban V a prebend at Aust in the collegiate church of Westbury-on-Trym near Bristol, but he neither resided there nor ever provided a vicar. In 1368 Wyclif exchanged Fillingham for Ludgershall, a less lucrative living in Buckinghamshire, because it was nearer to Oxford. He left this in 1374 for a royal provision at Lutterworth, Leicestershire. There he spent the last three years of his life. He died on December 31, 1384, after a massive paralytic stroke.

In philosophy Wyclif was a realist and in theology an advocate of Augustine's doctrines of predestination and grace. Only in the mid-1370s did he come into prominence outside Oxford for his views on *dominium* (lordship and ownership). Between 1376 and 1379 he published successively *On Divine Lordship, On Civil Lordship, On the Duty of the King,* and *On the Church.* In these treatises Wyclif argues that only God is the true Lord and owner of his whole creation. Whatever authority and property human beings possess they have from God, to whom they owe faithful service. Only the predestined have any right to them, but, like Augustine, Wyclif believed that no one could know who was and who was not among the elect. Hence one should suffer patiently under unjust and greedy masters until they repent or are removed and dispossessed.

Both estates of the realm, civil and ecclesiastical, should be under the authority of the king in all temporal matters. The ecclesiastical estate (including theologians) is of greater dignity because it is called to serve in spiritual teaching and guidance. It should be stripped of all temporal possessions, except what was necessary for food, clothing, and lodging, and no clergy should hold any civil office. The king should remove all unworthy clergy. All ecclesiastics, from the pope on down, should live in poverty as Peter and the other apostles did.

Although Wyclif's views were largely theoretical and not altogether unprecedented, they were noticed by Edward, Prince of Wales (the "Black Prince," 1330–1376), and his younger brother John of Gaunt (1340–1399), who became duke of Lancaster in 1362. The two virtually ruled England during the declining years of Edward III (1312–1377) and probably saw in Wyclif a front for their aim to plunder the church's wealth. In February 1377, Wyclif was summoned before the bishops at Saint Paul's, London, to answer for his views. He arrived accompanied by four friar doctors of theology and by John of Gaunt with some of his supporters. At once a bitter altercation broke out between Gaunt and Bishop William Courtenay of London, and the duke's party with Wyclif left before Wyclif could be heard or condemned.

In May, Gregory XI sent bulls to England denouncing nineteen propositions from Wyclif's writings and asking for a thorough investigation and Wyclif's arrest. Before the bulls arrived, however, ten-year-old Richard II had become king, and nothing became of the pope's directives. The archbishop of Canterbury, Simon of Sudbury, asked the faculty at Oxford to give an opinion on the propositions. They were unanimous in stating that some of them "sounded ill" but that they "were all the same true." In March, Wyclif appeared before Sudbury and Courtenay at Lambeth, just as a message arrived from the king's mother forbidding them to pass judgment on Wyclif. A mob broke into the meeting, and the bishops concluded the meeting by merely enjoining Wyclif from publicly disputing and preaching about his controverted views.

If Wyclif's mouth was shut for a time, his pen was not stilled. In 1378 he wrote *On the Truth of Holy Scripture,* in which he affirms that the Bible taken literally is the sole law of the church and that a translation without interpretation is needed so that the humblest person can learn from it. The treatise *On the Eucharist* (1379) cost him much support. In it he denies the dogma of transubstantiation: it is unscriptural, unknown in the church before the twelfth century, idolatrous, and contrary to his realist position that no substance can be changed into another substance. Yet he affirms the real presence of Christ's body and blood sacramentally in bread and wine. His last major work, the *Trialogus* (1382), gives a summary of his views.

Wyclif's enemies blamed him for the Peasants' Revolt in 1381, but there is no evidence to support the connection. After Archbishop Sudbury's murder during the rebellion, Courtenay succeeded to the primacy (1382–1396), determined to root out Wyclif's teachings at Oxford. In May 1382 he presented twenty-four propositions from Wyclif's writings to a council of bishops and theologians in London. Ten were voted heretical, the others erroneous. Leading Oxford supporters of Wyclif were summoned to appear and persuaded to recant. In November, Courtenay held the Convocation of Canterbury at Oxford, where all doctors, masters, and bachelors made their submission.

Yet Courtenay never moved against Wyclif personally. Wyclif had retired to Lutterworth in 1381 and suffered his first stroke in 1382. In his last years Wyclif may have supervised the translation of the Latin Vulgate Bible and the training of "poor preachers," cleric and lay (the Lollards), to spread the gospel, but his personal involvement has been disputed. The translation has come down in two principal versions, a literal version and a later, more idiomatic English version.

The marriage of Richard II to Anne of Bohemia (1382) brought several leaders of the Czech reform movement to England who took many of Wyclif's writings back home. Jan Hus, the principal champion of that movement, admired Wyclif and quoted extensively from his writings, but he used them with care, especially those on the Eucharist. The Council of Constance in 1415 burned Hus as a "Wycliffite" heretic and ordered that Wyclif's remains be exhumed and burned. Bishop Richard Fleming of Lincoln did this in 1428 and cast the ashes into the Swift River.

The extent of Wyclif's influence on the sixteenth-century Reformation is open to debate. Luther knew of him through Hus's writings. In England, Thomas Cranmer, archbishop of Canterbury (1533–1556), owned a copy of the *Trialogus* printed at Basel in 1525. Yet references to Wyclif, always with approval, are scanty in his writings. Cranmer's views on the Eucharist were similar to Wyclif's, and he too worked for an English translation of the Bible. He would have supported the reform of the church by the king, but not its disendowment and reduction to apostolic poverty.

After Elizabeth I's settlement of the church in 1559, Wyclif became a hero and a martyr to those who dissented from it. Yet even they, contrary to Wyclif, would have had the church the dominant power in the kingdom. Wyclif's importance lies partly in his influence on Jan Hus, but even more in his propagation of reformed principles.

See Also Cranmer, Thomas; Hus, Jan.

Bibliography

The numerous Latin writings of Wyclif have not been completely edited in modern editions. Most of them have been published by the Wyclif Society of London since 1884. A complete listing of Wyclif's Latin works, based on notes of S. Harrison Thomson, has been completed by his son, Williell R. Thomson, in *The Latin Writings of John Wyclyf: An Annotated Catalog* (Toronto, 1983). It notes all manuscripts and editions, with commentary on them. The authenticity of many, if not all, of Wyclif's English works is disputed. The best selection is Herbert E. Winn's *Wyclif: Select English Writings* (Oxford, 1929). A comprehensive bibliography is that of C. C. Scott in *Cambridge Medieval History,* vol. 7 (Cambridge and New York, 1932), which goes with Bernard L. Manning's chapter "Wyclif" in the same volume, pp. 486–507. Translations of Wyclif's Latin writings are few, but see the excerpts from *On the Pastoral Office* and *On the Eucharist* in *Advocates of Reform from Wyclif to Erasmus,* edited by Matthew Spinka, "The Library of Christian Classics," vol. 14 (Philadelphia, 1953), pp. 32–88.

The standard biography is Herbert B. Workman's *John Wyclif: A Study of the English Medieval Church,* 2 vols. (Oxford, 1926). Less sympathetic to Wyclif is K. B. McFarlane's *John Wycliffe and the Beginnings of English Nonconformity* (London, 1952), reprinted under the title *The Origins of Religious Dissent in England* (New York, 1966). McFarlane gives good background material about Oxford and church-state relations in Wyclif's time and, based on original research, carries the story through the Lollard movement until 1417, when it is driven underground. John Stacey's *John Wyclif and Reform* (Philadelphia, 1964) is informative and well balanced.

The influence of Wyclif on the Bohemian reformers is carefully researched by Matthew Spinka in *John Hus and the Czech Reform* (1941; Hamden, Conn., 1966). On the English version of the Bible associated with Wyclif, see Henry Hargreaves's "The Wycliffite Versions," in *The Cambridge History of the Bible,* vol. 2, *The West from the Fathers to the Reformation*

(Cambridge, 1970), edited by G. W. H. Lampe, pp. 387–415, with bibliography, pp. 527–528.

MASSEY H. SHEPHERD, JR. (1987)

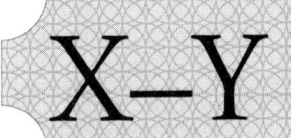

X–Y

XAVIER, FRANCIS (1506–1552), cofounder of the Roman Catholic Society of Jesus (the Jesuits), missionary, and saint. Francisco de Jassu y Xavier was born in the family castle in the kingdom of Navarre (now northern Spain), the fifth and youngest child of noble, wealthy, and pious Catholic parents. His early education took place at home and under the tutelage of local priests. In 1525 the keen, ambitious student left home permanently, bound for Paris. A handsome, slender, athletic youth, about five feet four inches tall, he was noted then, as throughout his life, for his cheerful and vivacious personality. At the University of Paris, Xavier gained a master of arts degree in philosophy in 1530, taught this subject for several years (1530–1534), and then studied theology until 1536.

During his years at the university, Ignatius Loyola, a fellow student since 1528, became an increasingly important influence on Xavier, and by 1533 Xavier had become one of his disciples. In 1534 Xavier made the Spiritual Exercises under the direction of Ignatius and on August 15 he joined Ignatius and five other students in a chapel in Montmartre, a district of Paris, where all of them vowed to lead lives of apostolic poverty, to labor for the salvation of their neighbors, to make a pilgrimage to Jerusalem, and to place their services at the disposition of the pope. Together with three other students who joined the group when it renewed its vows a year later, these men were the ten founders of the Society of Jesus.

Beginning the pilgrimage to Jerusalem, Xavier left Paris in November 1536 with eight of his companions and, traveling by foot, reached Venice nearly two months later. Ignatius met them there. In Venice, Xavier, along with Ignatius and four other companions, was ordained a priest in June 1537. War with the Turks ruled out a voyage across the Mediterranean to Palestine, so in 1538 Xavier went to Rome and there shared in the discussions that led to the founding of the Society of Jesus. Until his departure from Rome in 1540, he served as secretary of the new religious order.

When the pious King John III of Portugal put out a call for missionaries, especially for the care of recently converted Paravas (Bhavatas) in southern India, Xavier left Rome

Clockwise from top left corner. Scupture of a *yakṣa* at the Great Stupa at Sāñcī, India. *[©Charles & Josette Lenars/Corbis]*; Detail of a nineteenth-century Chinese ceramic plate with the yin-yang symbol. *[©Werner Forman/Art Resource, N.Y.]*; Postclassic Mixtec sculpture in gold of Xiuhtecuhtli, the fire god. Museo Nacional de Antropologia, Mexico City. *[©Werner Forman/Art Resource, N.Y.]*; Eighteenth-century Tibetan bronze of Yama, the Lord of Death. *[©Werner Forman/Art Resource, N.Y.]*; Nineteenth-century Yoruba wood carvings commemorating the death of twins. Nigeria. *[©Werner Forman/Art Resource, N.Y.]* .

for Portugal, traveling overland to Lisbon in the entourage of the Portuguese ambassador. While awaiting the annual departure of the India fleet, Xavier performed various priestly tasks in the city and at the royal court. His ship set sail in April 1541, rounded the Cape of Good Hope, and wintered in Mozambique, where Xavier's two Jesuit colleagues remained. After further stops at Melinde (Malindi, in modern-day Kenya) and the island of Socotra (off the coast of modern-day Somalia, where Xavier had to be dissuaded from remaining), the voyage ended in May 1542 in Goa, a district on the west coast of India and the main Portuguese center in that country.

Until the end of the rainy season in September, Xavier ministered to the Portuguese and native Christians in Goa. Accompanied by three native helpers, he then sailed to the southern tip of the continent. For the next three years his apostolate was centered in Malabar and Travancore, the coastal regions northwest of Cape Comorin; in the regions northeast of the cape as far as São Thomé (modern-day Madras); and on the neighboring island of Ceylon. Much of his ministry consisted of instructing the thousands of Parava pearl divers and fishermen who had been converted to Roman Catholicism around 1535 but whose religious knowledge remained minimal. Spectacular numbers of conversions were made: Xavier reported baptizing over ten thousand villagers in Travancore in one month.

In September 1545 Xavier sailed from São Thomé to Malacca, a Portuguese settlement on the Malay Peninsula; then to the Moluccas, or Spice Islands, in the East Indies, where his main concern was the native Christians, left without clergy in the Portuguese centers of Amboina and Ternate; and then as far north as the Moro Islands. He returned to Malacca in June 1547 and to Goa in March 1548. After further work along the Fishery Coast he returned to Goa once again. In April 1549 he set sail with three Japanese converts and two fellow Jesuits to inaugurate the Christian mission in Japan. When he departed from Japan for Goa twenty-seven months later, he left behind some two thousand converts. Hoping to initiate a Christian mission to China, he took ship from Goa in April 1552, but he was not allowed to disembark on the Chinese mainland. After three months of fruitless waiting on the desolate island of Sancian (near Canton), he died on December 3 following a brief illness. His incorrupt body was taken in 1554 to Goa, where it is still enshrined and greatly venerated.

Xavier is ranked among the greatest missionaries in Christian history. His numerous far-ranging journeys were not those of a spiritual adventurer, restlessly seeking new fields to conquer. He served not only as missionary but also as apostolic nuncio and Jesuit superior, with the duty of investigating mission possibilities in areas then little known to Europeans. He was both a pioneer and organizer of the Jesuit missions in the Far East, intent on obtaining suitably trained European co-workers. He was eager to supply mission stations with churches, schools, and personnel and to be kept informed about them. Both his actions and his writings show practicality, prudence, and sound spirituality. His success was promoted also by his exemplary apostolic zeal, his personal holiness, and his ability to mix easily with persons of all classes, races, and beliefs. In addition, he was a man much devoted to prayer, a mystic. Unlimited confidence in God, his most basic spiritual trait, freed him from discouragement in the face of obstacles and reverses. These characteristics, together with his reputation as a wonder-worker, led Christians, Muslims, and pagans alike to refer to him as "the holy father," and "the great father." Since his death, he has been venerated as the ideal missionary and, as such, has inspired thousands to devote their lives to spreading the gospel far afield. In 1622 he was canonized, and in 1927 he was designated by Pius XI as patron of all missions. His annual liturgical feast is celebrated on December 3.

See Also Jesuits.

Bibliography

The critical edition of the letters and other writings of Xavier that supplants earlier, defective editions is *Epistolae S. Francisci Xaverii aliaque eius scripta,* 2 vols., edited by Georg Schurhammer and Joseph Wicki (Rome, 1944–1945), published as volumes 67 and 68 of *Monumenta historica Societatis Iesu.* Applicable bibliographies include *Archivum historicum Societatis Iesu* (Rome, 1932–) and *Bibliographie sur l'histoire de la Compagnie de Jésus, 1901–1980,* 7 vols., by László Polgár (Rome, 1982–). A readable, brilliantly written biography, the one most widely read in English, which has also been translated into several languages, is James Brodrick's *Saint Francis Xavier, 1506–1552* (New York, 1952); it should be studied with some caution, however, because of questionable accuracy in its characterizations of Xavier. *The Life and Letters of Saint Francis Xavier,* 2d ed., 2 vols. (1881; reprint, London, 1927), by Henry J. Coleridge is useful still because of its translation into English of all the letters of Xavier, although the collections of letters used by Coleridge have now been superseded by that edited by Schurhammer and Wicki. *Francis Xavier: His Life, His Times,* 4 vols., by Georg Schurhammer (Rome, 1973–1982) is the definitive biography by the leading authority on Xavier, the result of decades of study. Schurhammer's *Saint Francis Xavier: The Apostle of India and Japan* (Saint Louis, Mo., 1928) and Margaret Yeo's *Saint Francis Xavier: Apostle of the East* (New York, 1932) are both good, popular biographies.

John F. Broderick (1987)

XENOPHANES

XENOPHANES (c. 580–470 BCE), Ionian poet, satirist, philosopher, and theologian, was born in Colophon, a wealthy city of Ionia under the influence of the Lydian kingdom. Because of Persians' invasion of the city, he had to flee to South Italy. He spent much of his life wandering through Sicily and Greece until he joined a Phokaian colony sent to Elea in Lucania, and he taught there, founding the Eleatic school. His pupil Parmenides was the founder of Western metaphysics. A friend of Empedocles, Xenophanes attacked

Pythagoras and was attacked by Heraclitus. He has been considered both an amateur thinker and "a paradigm of the [pre-Socratic] genius" (Barnes, 1982, p. 82). In fact, he was a significant thinker and an innovator in many fields of research, such as natural sciences, morality, and gnosiology. His approach to the problems of human knowledge is so particular (and somewhat contradictory) that he can be defined as a sceptic, an empiricist, a rationalist, a fallibilist, a critical philosopher—or, more accurately, a natural epistemologist. A precise definition of his epistemological attitude clearly influences any evaluation of his theology (see fragment 34: "No man has seen, or ever will see, the exact truth about the gods").

As a religious thinker, Xenophanes has been identified as the founder of the Greek enlightenment, prior to Heraclitus and Hecataeus. From the complex of his polymath oeuvre (of which only 43 fragments and 52 controversial *testimonia* have been preserved) he emerges as a critical thinker, sceptical about any claims to knowledge in religious matters. As a consequence of the elusiveness and versatility of his thought in these matters, an ample variety of opinions has risen about his religious positions. If one emphasizes single facets of his teaching, it is possible to consider him a traditional polytheist, a revolutionary monotheist, a pantheist, or even an atheist or precursor of negative theology. What is clear is that with him there emerged in Greece the first form of scientific inquiry into indigenous and alien religious realities.

Xenophanes' first concern was God and the divine. He wrote: "One god is greatest among gods and men" (fragment 23). This does not mean that he was a monotheist. The fragments warrant attributing to Xenophanes the novel idea of a single god of unusual power (*henotheism*), but not the stronger view that beyond this one god there could be nothing else worthy of the name. God is a body (testimonium 28), spherical in form, being alike and perceptive in all his parts (testimonia 1, 28, 33, and 34) and in a way coextensive with the whole universe (testimonium 31), and identical with the One (testimonia 30, 34 and 35). God is ungenerated and eternal (testimonia 28 and 31), motionless (fragment 26), and at the same time "shaking all things by the thought of his mind" (fragment 25). Apparently, this view anticipates Anaxagoras's Nous (intellect, mind—the intellectual principle that is separate from the mass that it governs), which is the ultimate source of movement, and the Aristotelian doctrine of the prime unmoved mover. Xenophanes was the first to regard the soul *(psuchē)* as "breath" (*pneuma*), that is, moving air, full of vital energy (testimonium 1). His concept of time is cyclic: there is an unlimited number of worlds existing successively without overlapping one another, and a new generation begins again after each cosmic catastrophe (testimonia 1, 33, and 37)—the first manifestation of the doctrine of the Eternal Recurrence, later adopted by the Pythagoreans, the Stoics, and Friedrich Nietzsche (1844–1900). Earth (Gaia) is the root and the ultimate destination of all things (fragments 27, 28, 29, 33)—perhaps a survival of ancient pre-Olympian religiosity.

From the theological reflection combined with the scientific speculation, Xenophanes moved to scathing criticisms of the most objectionable aspects of Greek religion. He attacked poets (including Homer and Hesiod) for saying false and immoral things about the gods in their tales of divine warfare with Titans, giants, and centaurs (fragment 1); as well as in their attributions to the gods of things that are matters of reproach even among men—theft, adultery, and mutual deceit (fragments 11 and 12). Further, he repudiated the whole enterprise of divination through natural signs (testimonium 52) and the connected popular belief in the godship of celestial bodies (fragment 32 and testimonia 32 and 38–46). Subjects of stern rebuke are also the contemporary outbreaks of ecstatic religion such as the naturalism of the Bacchic cult (fragment 17) and the Pythagorean belief in the reincarnation of the human soul in any animal form (fragment 7). Had Xenophanes limited himself to these assertions, he would have emerged only as an innovative theologian, albeit one less insightful and less audacious than his near contemporary and fellow Ionian, Heraclitus of Ephesus. Nor would he have found a place among the pioneers of the comparative study of religion. As can be inferred from Aristotle's and Plutarch's testimonies (testimonium 13), the Ionian thinker perceived a marked affinity between the cult of the Greek Leucothea, worshipped with funeral dirges (*threnoi*) although considered a deity (ergo, immortal for the Greeks), and the cult of the Egyptian Osiris, who was ritually mourned by his worshippers (as befitted a dead god) but was at the same time honored as a very high-ranking god. Thus, Xenophanes seems to have virtually highlighted—two and a half millennia before James Frazer (1854–1941)—the typological category of the dying/rising gods present on both sides of the Mediterranean. This ability for critical perception, which earned Xenophanes the mantle of "precursor of comparative ethnology" (Pettazzoni, 1954, p. 134), is certainly connected with his experience as an Ionian citizen who since birth had been familiar with the beliefs and customs of the other peoples of Anatolia: the Lydians, the Carians, and the Median-Persian invaders. Xenophanes could autoptically realize that the routes through which humans (and, by paradoxical analogy, the other animals) reach the representation of the divine are numberless. Starting with his criticism of the anthropomorphism typical of the Greek conception of divinity (fragment 14), Xenophanes came to make two famous assessments: "The Ethiopians say that their gods are snub-nosed and black, the Thracians that theirs are blue-eyed and red-haired"(fragment 16); and "But if horses or oxen or lions had hands or could draw with their hands and do the works that men can do, horses would draw the forms of the gods like horses, and oxen like oxen, and they would make their bodies such as they each had themselves"(fragment 15). This can be viewed as the first application of a comparative perspective to the study of religion.

SEE ALSO Atheism; Images; Knowledge and Ignorance; Monotheism; Parmenides; Plato; Pythagoras; Sociology; Stoicism; Transmigration.

BIBLIOGRAPHY

All the fragments (21 B: 1–45) and the *testimonia* on Xenophanes' life and teaching (21 A: 1–52) are collected in *Die Fragmente der Vorsokratiker*, vol. 1, edited by Hermann Diels and Walther Kranz (6th ed., Berlin, 1951), which has an indispensable critical apparatus and German translation of the text. Diels's and Kranz's numeration is still the standard system of reference. A personal selection, in English translation and with substantial interpretation, is provided by Geoffrey S. Kirk in *The Presocratic Philosophers: A Critical History with a Selection of Texts*, 2d edition, edited by Geoffrey S. Kirk, John E. Raven, and M. Schofield (Cambridge, U.K., 1983), pp. 163–181. A complete edition with Greek text and Italian translation is given by Mario Untersteiner, *Senofane's Testimonianze e frammenti* (Firenze, Italy, 1956). The commentary and the introduction (especially "Senofane di fronte alla religiosità preellenica. Il politeismo" and "Il dio di Senofane," pp. 134–212) are important from the religiohistorical point of view. James H. Lesher, in *Xenophanes of Colophon: Fragments: A Text and Translation* (Toronto, 1992), provides a very informative and perceptive commentary on most of the fragments (Greek text of all the fragments, with critical annotations) and the *testimonia* (English translation only). The interest of this work is philosophical but the main theological questions are examined with subtlety. Extensive bibliographies are provided by Untersteiner and Lesher.

Among the numerous general interpretations, Hermann Fränkel, *Early Greek Poetry and Philosophy* (Oxford, 1975), pp. 325–337, and Jonathan Barnes, *The Presocratic Philosophers* (London, 1982), pp. 82–99, are representative of two divergent approaches: for the German scholar, even as a theologian, Xenophanes was "a staunch empiricist"; for the British philosopher, he was "the initiator of natural theology." Relevant themes of Xenophanes' religious thought are examined in various recent contributions. Michael Eisenstadt, in "Xenophanes' Proposed Reform of Greek Religion," *Hermes* 102 (1974): 142–150, argues for Xenophanes' approval of the worship of the Olympian gods in spite of the philosophical inadequacy of traditional religion. In "The Xenophanean Religious Thought: A Field of Various Interpretations," *Kernos* 2 (1989): 89–96, Aikaterini Lefka outlines the main approaches to the philosopher's teaching about god. Mark J. Edwards, in "Xenophanes' Christianus?," *Greek, Roman, and Byzantine Studies* 32 (1991): 219–228, seeks to demonstrate (somewhat unconvincingly) that the three crucial fragments cited by of Alexandria in the *Stromateis* (fragments 14, 15, 23) are attributable to a Christian or Jewish forger. Massimo Di Marco, in *Sapienza italica. Studi su Senofane, Empedocle, Ippone* (Rome, 1998), pp. 9–31, contributes a useful discussion on the controversial issue of Xenophanes' relationship with the Eleatic school. In a series of insightful articles—"Elea, Senofane e Leucothea," *Annali Istituto Universitario Orientale Napoli* 16 (1994): 137–155; "Senofane ed Elea," *Quaderni urbinati di cultura classica* 95 (2000): 31–49; and "Il frammento Lebedev di Senofane," *Quaderni urbinati di cultura classica* 98 (2001): 25–34—Giovanni Cerri reconstructs the polytheistic background (Leucothea, Persefone) against which Xenophanes built his characteristic theology.

Xenophanes is acknowledged as the founder of religious criticism by Raffaele Pettazzoni, in *La religione nella Grecia antica fino ad Alessandro*, Bologna, 1922, 2d ed. Turin, 1954, pp. 133-134, and in two standard histories of the comparative study of religion: Jan de Vries, *Perspectives in the History of Religions* (New York, 1967; 2d ed., Berkeley, Calif., 1977), pp. 3–5; and Eric J. Sharpe, *Comparative Religion. A History* (London, 1975; 2d ed., 1986), pp. 3–4.

GIOVANNI CASADIO (2005)

XIAN. Usually written using the characters for "man" and for "mountain," the character for *xian* is said originally to have been composed of those for "man" and for "ascend." An early dictionary explains that it refers to those who, "when they grow old, do not die." *Xian* means "to move into the mountains"; that is why it is written with the character for "man" next to that for "mountain." Together, these etymologies circumscribe a field of meaning that links the search for survival beyond death to mountains and to the heavens—a range that quite accurately reflects both the practice and the status of *xian* throughout Chinese history. It also explains why the term is translated in English either as "immortal" or "transcendent."

The *xian* is in the first place a human being. But unlike ordinary human beings who die and become ancestors (or roving ghosts), the *xian* survives beyond death and becomes, as a result, the focus of tales and even of worship. The earliest images of these extraordinary beings date to the Han dynasty (206 BCE–220 CE) and sometimes portray them with wings, a feature expressed in later texts that refer to them as *yuren*, or "feathered humans" (this term is also a synonym for Daoists). One of the earliest tales describes them as living on distant, perhaps imaginary isles in the sea off the eastern coast of China. The First Emperor (r. 221–206 BCE), having heard of them and being desirous of surviving beyond death like them, dispatched three thousand lads and lasses to find them, but the ships never returned, and rumor had it, in later times, that they had found and populated what is now known as Japan.

Other early tales recount the earthly lives of future *xian*. Not surprisingly, many of them were indeed mountain-dwellers: people who had left their homes and families to become hermits and devote themselves to the search for survival. They went to the mountains not only to find the necessary solitude, but also because they could find there the herbs and minerals they needed to secure, at the very least, longevity. *Xian* who had lived several centuries became a standard trope in hagiographies, as were the capacity to foresee the future, ubiquity, and "ascension to the heavens in broad daylight."

Of the seventy immortals whose legends are recounted in the earliest collection, the *Liexian zhuan* (Biographies of the immortals; second century CE), over twenty may be classified as gods. Some, such as Chisongzi (Red Pine), the Master of Rain, are known to have been the focus of official worship, but most are worshiped as local saints. A woman by the name of Changrong, for example, is said to have been a "person of the Dao" living on Mount Chang. For over two hundred years she was seen coming and going, "and her complexion was that of a twenty-year-old." For generations, she sold plants used for dyeing and gave the money thus earned to widows and orphans. "Thousands worshiped her." Hanzi, a lover of dogs, was led by one into a cave where he discovered a magic world of palaces, forests, and immortals guarding the gates. He also encountered his dead wife, who urged him to join her. A year later he did so, and from then on only left the mountain on occasion "to succor his lineage. The people of Shu built a temple for him at the mouth of the cave. Over several thousand *li* in the southwest, people worship him."

The immortals of the *Liexian zhuan* are prescient, and this enables them to save local populations from floods by giving advance warning. Others provide drugs that save people from epidemics. Of some it is said simply that they disappear without a trace, of others that their corpse disappears and only a sacred writ or some clothing are found in the grave, of still others that people catch a glimpse of them now and again over decades or centuries.

Immortals are usually thought of as a quintessentially Daoist category, a classification that is probably legitimate in modern times, when the Eight Immortals with their drunken whimsicality and endearingly unorthodox behavior come to be almost synonymous with Daoism, at least in the popular mind. A Daoist work of the Yuan, the *Lishi zhenxian tidao tongjian* (Comprehensive mirror of the real persons and immortals who have embodied the Dao through the ages) by Zhou Daoyi (fl. 1294–1307), would seem to confirm this Daoist identity by linking *xian* and *zhen*, immortals and real persons, to the idea of "embodying the Dao." In fact, the term *zhen* has an even longer pre-Daoist history than *xian*. At the time of the compilation of the *Liexian zhuan*, Daoism did not yet exist as a self-conscious religious movement or institution, and only two or three of its *xian* were explicitly said to have been "people of the Dao" while alive. A good number of the immortals in the *Liexian zhuan* turn up again in two works of the fourth century: the *Sou Shen Ji* (In search of the gods) of Gan Bao (b. 280) and the *Shenxian zhuan* (Biographies of the gods and immortals) of Ge Hong (283–343). While Ge Hong's work is generally classified as Daoist, that of Gan Bao is not: it is said to belong to the category mirabilia. Classifications aside, what the titles of their texts confirm is that *xian* and *zhen*, immortals and gods, were not hermetically sealed categories. *Xian*, insofar as they do constitute a distinct type of divine entity, should probably be distinguished from *zuxian*, or ancestors: both once lived on earth, and both continue to interact with humans after their death (both are also referred to as *shen*, "gods"). But in the case of ancestors, this interaction occurs primarily, though not exclusively, within the lineage, while in the case of immortals, virtually all links with lineage are severed: they belong to and embody the Dao; that is, they "live as long as Heaven and Earth."

SEE ALSO Daoism, overview article and article on The Daoist Religious Community.

BIBLIOGRAPHY

Campany, Robert Ford, trans. and ed. *To Live as Long as Heaven and Earth: A Translation and Study of Ge Hong's Traditions of Divine Transcendents.* Berkeley, 2002. A complete translation with an excellent introduction and textual notes.

Kaltenmark, Max, trans. *Le Lie-sien tchouan: Biographies légendaires des immortels taoïstes de l'antiquité.* Beijing, 1953; reprint, Paris, 1987. Contains superb notes on each of the seventy biographies of the immortals.

Mathieu, Rémi, trans. and ed. *A la recherche des esprits: Récits tirés du Sou shen ji par Gan Bao.* Paris, 1992.

JOHN LAGERWEY (2005)

XIAO. For the three thousand years of China's recorded history, *xiao* (filial piety) has been the cornerstone of Chinese religious, social, and ethical life. According to China's oldest dictionary, *xiao* simply means "to serve one's parents well." This concept's unchanging spirit has been that one surrenders pleasures and even necessities to ensure the happiness of one's parents. Within the family, this moral value has subordinated the young to the old and the individual to the collective. Since Confucianism maintained that the ruler-subject relationship was merely an extension of that between parent and child, within the larger community, *xiao* has produced loyal and obedient citizens. Due to its overwhelming importance, each of China's great religious traditions—Buddhism, Confucianism, and Daoism—appropriated and popularized its understanding of it. Moreover, *xiao*'s appeal extended well beyond China to all of East Asia.

Although long a salient feature of Chinese society, *xiao*'s meanings and requirements have undergone much change. Around the year 1000 BCE, *xiao* probably originated as a form of sacrifice given to the powerful dead, which included one's ancestors, in-laws, and allies. Soon its focus narrowed to service to one's senior patrilineal kin, both living and dead. By the fifth century BCE, Confucians began to remold filial practices into specific ceremonial forms, which their ritual codes spelled out in great detail. Through daily morning and evening audiences, sons and daughters (in-law) were supposed to nourish their parents, obey their instructions, anticipate their wishes, and ensure their comfort. This service did not end with death; rather, it intensified. For three years, a son or daughter was supposed to serve the parents' spirits through ascetic mourning rituals: he or she should dress in rough hemp clothes, live in a hut near the parent's tomb, and forego meat, alcohol, music, and sex. After the conclusion of these rites, he or she continued to serve the dead by preserving the patrimony and producing heirs—acts that ensured that the ancestral sacrifices would be ceaseless. During the third century BCE, most notably in the *Xiao jing* (Classic of filial piety), a short work that almost every imperial dynasty promoted, Confucians assimilated *xiao* to the lord-retainer tie. They argued that, since in a larger sense a ruler parents his people through the care he lavishes on them, a retainer should serve his ruler as he would his father. Hence, by definition, a filial child should also be a loyal subject.

After China's unification in 221 BCE, imperial governments found *xiao*'s hierarchy-affirming message to be irresistible; consequently, dynasty after dynasty lavished awards on outstanding filial children. The Han dynasty (206 BCE–220 CE) even selected its officials on the basis of their reputation for filiality. By the fourth century, each officially sanctioned dynastic history devoted a chapter to the previous era's filial paragons. By the Tang (618–907), unfilial behavior, such as failing to sufficiently nourish one's parents or marrying while mourning them, became punishable by law. Buddhists, too, discovered that to appeal to Chinese sensibilities they had to emphasize filial piety; thus, they stressed that their religion best served one's parents because it saved them from the torments of purgatory and delivered them to Buddhist heavens. Daoists likewise insisted that mastery of the immortality arts would not only secure salvation for oneself, but also for seven generations of one's ancestors.

By the late imperial period (960–1911), the overwhelming emphasis placed on filial piety led to increasingly extreme manifestations of it. Inspired by Buddhist tales of self-sacrifice, filial children would slice off part of their flesh and feed it to their parents to cure them of incurable diseases. Moreover, although classical texts stressed the need for filial children to remonstrate with their errant parents, late imperial filial piety emphasized the inviolable obedience owed to parents and discounted the possibility that they could ever be wrong. At the same time, filial directives increasingly fell upon women in their role as daughter-in-law. Hence, women were credited with increasingly extreme and self-destructive forms of filiality. In the twentieth century it is precisely this fanaticism that lead intellectuals such as Lu Xun (1881–1936) to condemn filial piety (and Confucianism, which it exemplified) as an impediment to modernization and westernization.

SEE ALSO Chinese Religion, overview article.

BIBLIOGRAPHY

For a simple overview see Kenneth L. Traylor, *Chinese Filial Piety* (Bloomington, Ind., 1988). For a more detailed study of *xiao*'s propagation and functions in early imperial China, see Keith Knapp's *Selfless Offspring* (Honolulu, 2005). Stephen F. Teiser's *The Ghost Festival in Medieval China* (Princeton, 1988) and Alan Cole's *Mothers and Sons in Chinese Buddhism* (Stanford, Calif., 1998) extensively discuss Buddhist adaptations of *xiao*. T'ien Ju-k'ang's *Male Anxiety and Female Chastity: A Comparative Study of Chinese Ethical Values in Ming-Ch'ing Times* (Leiden, 1988) looks specifically at the extremism that was associated with late imperial expressions of filiality. Norman Kutcher's *Mourning in Late Imperial China: Filial Piety and the State* (Cambridge, U.K., 1999) examines how governments tried to regulate *xiao*'s demands.

KEITH KNAPP (2005)

XIAO BAOZHEN (d. 1166 CE), Daoist master of the Jin period and founder of the Taiyi sect of Daoism. A native of Ji prefecture (present-day Henan province), he was also called Yuan Sheng. Neither his occupation before becoming a Daoist master nor the training he undertook to that end is known. During the Tianjuan period (1138–1140) of Emperor Xizong's reign, Xiao established the Taiyi sect in Ji prefecture. Of the three new Daoist sects established in the northern reaches of the Jin kingdom (Quanzhen, Zhenda, and Taiyi), Taiyi was the most similar in character to existing Daoist teachings. Its practices centered on the talisman called Taiyi Sanyuan that had allegedly been transmitted to Xiao from an immortal. Although the contents of the talisman are not known, it is clear that the sect placed great importance on talismans and incantations. Because of Xiao's ability to relieve people's suffering, disperse evil spirits, and cure illnesses, he gradually attracted many disciples and succeeded in establishing the Taiyi sect. As Xiao's teachings became a source of salvation for people wracked by the social unrest of the time, his sect's power grew apace. Hearing of his growing reputation, Emperor Xizong invited him to the court during the eighth year of his reign (1148). While at court, Xiao demonstrated his spiritual prowess by curing a sick person. Deeply impressed, the emperor presented Xiao with a name plaque inscribed "Taiyi wanshou gong," the name he bestowed on Xiao's Daoist temple in Ji prefecture, thereby indicating official recognition and patronage of Xiao's sect. Xizong is also said to have been converted to Taiyi Daoism by Xiao.

Although part of Xiao's teachings centered on the use of talismans, he did not adopt elixirs of immortality or other elements of the immortality cult. Instead, he upheld the "middle way," forbidding the drinking of intoxicants and the consumption of the five pungent substances. He also forbade priests to marry. It is clear that the rules of conduct that he taught were strict and aimed at transforming Daoist speculative theories into a disciplined monastic practice. He also required that successive head priests of his school take his own name. Unfortunately, many elements of his life remain unclear.

SEE ALSO Daoism, overview article and article on the Daoist Religious Community.

BIBLIOGRAPHY

Chen Yuan. *Nan Song chu Hebei xin daojiao kao.* Beijing, 1958.

Kubo Noritada. *Chugoku no shukyo kaikaku.* Tokyo, 1967.

Kubo Noritada. *Dokyoshi.* Tokyo, 1977.

New Sources

Pas, Julian F. *Historical Dictionary of Taoism.* Lanham, Md., 1998.

KUBO NORITADA (1987)
Translated from Japanese by James C. Dobbins
Revised Bibliography

XINXING (540–594), Chinese Buddhist monk and founder of the Sanjie Jiao, or Three Stages sect. A native of Henan Province, Xinxing entered the religious life at an early age and eventually took full monastic orders *(upasampadā)* at the Fazang Si near the city of Ye, the capital of the Northern Qi dynasty and a thriving center of Buddhist learning. With the eclipse of the Northern Qi by the Northern Zhou dynasty and the initiation, in the year 574, of a vigorous proscription of Buddhism by the new government, Xinxing renounced his vows and lived as a common laborer. It was during this period that he formulated the religious doctrines that would form the basis for the Sanjie Jiao.

The foundation of Xinxing's thought was the conviction, common to many segments of the Buddhist community during the latter half of the sixth century, that the Buddha's teachings had recently entered a period of degeneration and decline foretold in several Buddhist scriptures. This period, known as *mofa,* or the Latter Days of the Law, was believed to be one in which the spiritual capacities of sentient beings would be so far diminished as to render them incapable of observing the Vinaya or of distinguishing good from evil and truth from falsehood. Because it was an age far removed from that of Śākyamuni (fifteen hundred years from the date of his *parinirvāṇa* by the reckoning of many of Xinxing's contemporaries), sentient beings were deemed no longer subject to his guidance and unable even to practice Buddhism as it had traditionally been taught, let alone to attain enlightenment. Adherents of this doctrine believed that *mofa* would last for ten thousand years, at the end of which time the teachings of Śākyamuni would disappear from this world.

Against this starkly eschatological background, Xinxing argued for a reappraisal of contemporary Buddhist practice, one that would bring it into conformity with the greatly altered historical conditions prevailing during the *mofa.* He believed that it was only when religious practices matched the capacities of sentient beings and the historical conditions under which they lived that genuine enlightenment was possible. Unlike thinkers of the Pure Land tradition, who saw in the onset of *mofa* the need to replace the traditional range of Buddhist practices with a single, "easy," discipline, the worship of the Buddha Amitābha, Xinxing claimed that the practice most appropriate to the *mofa* age was a radical recognition of the Buddhahood inherent in *all* sentient beings. Calling his teaching that of the Universal Dharma *(pufa),* Xinxing advocated rigorous moral training to combat the degeneracy of the age and a catholic embracement of "all Buddhas and all *dharmas,*" predicated upon the underlying Buddha nature in all things. Members of his school were thus conspicuous for the public obeisance they made to others as a recognition of their potential Buddhahood, and for their strong emphasis on charitable activities. The sect came to receive lavish donations and eventually instituted *wujin zangyuan* ("inexhaustible treasuries") as a means of dispensing its charities to the needy and to the *saṃgha.*

With the reunification of the empire under the Sui (589), Xinxing was summoned to Chang'an by the emperor Wen (581–604). At the suggestion of one of his ministers, five temples were built in the capital for followers of the sect, thus providing an institutional base around which the sect flourished for the next decade. During this brief period of official favor and patronage Xinxing produced many of his most important works, including the *Sanjie fofa* and the *Duigen qixin fa.* In all, his works are believed to comprise at least forty fascicles, some of which were only recovered in this century among the documents unearthed at Dunhuang.

In the year 600, the Three Stages sect suffered the first in a series of proscriptions. The enormous wealth of the sect, its essentially negative assessment of the moral condition of society, and its contention that human institutions, particularly governments, were incapable of conferring any lasting spiritual benefits, made it a conspicuous target for the civil authorities. Throughout the Tang dynasty the sect suffered numerous attempts to seize its wealth and outlaw its writings, until it finally succumbed under the general suppression of Buddhism in the year 845.

SEE ALSO Mappō.

BIBLIOGRAPHY

For the traditional account of Xinxing's life, see his biography in Daoxuan's *Xu gaoseng zhuan* (T.D. 50. 559c–560b). Among modern studies of Xinxing and his sect, none surpasses Yabuki Keiki's *Sangaikyō no kenkyū* (1927; reprint, Tokyo, 1973). This monumental study includes some four hundred pages of original texts found at Dunhuang.

New Sources

Lewis, Mark Edward. "The Suppression of the Three Stages Sect: Apocrypha as a Political Issue." *Chinese Buddhist Apocrypha* (1990): 207–238.

MIYAKAWA HISAYUKI (1987)
Revised Bibliography

XI WANG MU, whose name is usually rendered as "queen mother of the west," appeared in the earliest stages of Chinese mythology and was a focus of intense religious devotion during the first few centuries of the present era. It is possible that she is mentioned in the oracle bone inscriptions of about 1500 BCE, but she appears with more certainty in the *Zhuangzi* (fourth century BCE) and later writings. Xi Wang Mu is described as one who had "attained the Dao," but nothing is known of her beginning or her end; she was said to dwell in the never-never land of the far west. In some sources she is described as a being of hybrid form. Usually her realm is pictured at the summit of a mountain called Kunlun, but there are also references to a cave residence. She is said to possess certain magical powers and to live in material splendor, surrounded by rare jewels. She may be accompanied by spirits, also of hybrid form, and Kunlun is sometimes described as a being protected by encircling waters, or as beyond human reach.

The queen was also credited with various cosmic powers. She may have controlled certain constellations, and she may have been able to maintain or to disrupt the rhythms that kept the universe in operation. She is also believed to have held the secret of the elixir of immortality, which she made available to suppliants in the form of a potion.

These characteristics feature in several versions of a Chinese myth relating a meeting between partners. According to one version, in order to keep the cosmic rhythms in motion it was necessary for two stars (who were otherwise separated by the Milky Way) to meet annually at a crucial point during the summer. The same theme is seen in accounts of meetings held during the summer between the Queen Mother of the West and various earthly monarchs. Sometimes the queen is described as receiving a king in her own abode; sometimes she travels to earth in all her glory to meet a king or emperor in his realm. The purpose of these ceremonial meetings was to enable the human partner to obtain the drug of immortality. In another version the queen is partnered by a mythical consort known as the King Father of the East.

According to several accounts, a soteriological movement that centered on the invocation of the queen swept through wide areas of northern China in 3 BCE. Descriptions of this movement refer to such practices as the exchange of tokens or talismans, the performance of religious services, and singing or dancing, as well as a certain amount of permissive or unrestrained behavior. The purpose of these gatherings was to prepare for the arrival of the queen and to convey or to acquire the promise of deathlessness. But it was not until the middle of the first century CE that the queen began increasingly to be associated with immortality.

Early Chinese notions of an afterlife had envisaged a "paradise of the east" situated in islands such as Penglai. In addition to the attempts made by talismanic means to guide the souls of the deceased to paradise by way of those islands, considerable effort was stimulated by a completely different notion, one that sprang from intellectual rather than religious motives. It was hoped that the provision of symbolic objects of a different sort, notably a particular type of bronze mirror, would set a deceased person within the most favorable cosmic circumstances. By this means a correspondence would be forged between the individual's personal circumstances of life and death and the eternal cyclical movements of heaven and earth. But from perhaps the middle of the second century BCE emphasis was being directed to the acquisition of immortality through the agency of the Queen Mother of the West, in one of two ways. Either she might be induced to provide the elixir that would ensure continuity of life on earth, or the soul might journey to the land where the queen presided, a realm populated by mythical beings who took part in a superhuman existence.

The custom of burying talismans to ensure the happiness of the deceased was established in China long before the first century CE, but from this time on the Queen Mother of the West appears repeatedly in funerary iconography. Her attributes, as shown on stone reliefs, frescoes (rarely), and bronze mirrors, include a characteristic headdress or crown and sometimes a throne, composed of part dragon and part tiger, on which she is seated in majesty. She is accompanied by one or more hares who are engaged in compounding the elixir, a three-legged bird (sometimes three separate birds), and a nine-tailed fox, all of whom have special duties and properties. She may be attended by an armed guardian. Sometimes suppliants are shown beside the queen, praying for the drug or drinking a dose in a cup. In a few instances she is portrayed at the top of a pillar that is virtually inaccessible to man; rarely, her partner is shown beside her, similarly enthroned.

In time the symbolic power of this type of iconography weakened, so that the details that originally possessed talismanic significance were reduced to decorative motifs and reproduced inaccurately. At the same time it is likely that the queen's religious significance and her popularity began to decline as Buddhist influence began to grow in China, beginning perhaps in the third century CE. Traces of Buddhist characteristics can be seen in versions of the myth of the queen that appeared from the third century CE. This shift in emphasis culminates in the well-known account of a banquet given by the queen during which Monkey steals the peaches of immortality from her table. Monkey's subsequent punishment and adventures are all placed within a Buddhist context.

SEE ALSO Afterlife, article on Chinese Concepts; Chinese Religion, article on Mythic Themes.

BIBLIOGRAPHY

For further discussion, see chapter 4, "The Queen Mother of the West," of my book *Ways to Paradise: The Chinese Quest for Immortality* (London, 1979).

MICHAEL LOEWE (1987)

XUANZANG (596?–664), religious name of the Chinese pilgrim-monk who became a leading cleric of the early Tang dynasty after returning from an eighteen-year journey to the homeland of Buddhism in India. Famous in his own day as a Buddhist scholar and adviser to the emperor, Xuanzang eventually came to be best known as the historical prototype for the legendary Tripiṭaka, Master of the Three Collections of the Buddhist Dharma, whose mythical adventures with his companion, the supernatural monkey king Sun Wukong, are elaborated in the great sixteenth-century Chinese folk epic, the *Xiyou ji* (Journey to the West).

Born into a family of relatively important government officials and court scholars under the Sui dynasty (581–618), Xuanzang grew up during a period of great turmoil and transition, a time that saw the reunification of the Chinese empire after almost three centuries of division. With the encouragement perhaps of his father, he decided early to follow the example of an elder brother in pursuing a monastic career. The young monk is depicted as a precocious, even impetuous student, one who diligently sought out the best scholars of the realm, only to decide while still in his twenties that he had already exhausted the resources available to him in China. To truly master the Buddhist teaching, he felt, he would have to travel to the source of the tradition, to the Ganges River valley, thousands of miles away across some of the most inhospitable terrain in Asia.

In 627 Xuanzang set out on his pilgrimage, surreptitiously crossing the western frontier of China after failing to secure the official bureaucratic approval he had sought. After an arduous journey across mountain and desert with several long sojourns at the oases of Central Asia, he finally reached India two years later, there slowly to make his way to the various sites associated with the career of the Buddha and also to spend a number of years studying with Buddhist teachers, including the aged Yogācāra master Śīlabhadra at the great university-monastery of Nālandā. We are told that the gifted Chinese monk mastered the intricacies of Buddhist philosophy, both Hīnayāna and Mahāyāna, while also pursuing studies in the standard curriculum of the day: Vedic literature, logic, grammar, medicine, and mathematics. Excelling at philosophical debate, an important spectator sport in the prosperous urban centers, Xuanzang's fame increased steadily. He was chosen to represent Nālandā in important contests, and in 642, fourteen years after leaving China, he was summoned to the court of King Harṭa, a patron of the arts and ruler of most of northern India. With the generous patronage of Harṭa, which ensured his victory at a royal debate held in Kanauj later that year, Xuanzang reached the apogee of his career in India and began to make plans for a return to China.

After traveling for more than a year, Xuanzang arrived back in China in 645 bringing an extensive collection of Buddhist texts and artifacts. The new Tang dynasty was a powerful and recently consolidated regime ready to initiate an expansionist policy in the west, a campaign that would eventually extend China's frontier across much of the very terrain that Xuanzang had come to know so well. The emperor Taizong was quick to recognize the strategic military value of his extensive knowledge of the geography, customs, and politics of the many kingdoms to the west, but Xuanzang politely declined to return to lay life in order to serve as a court official. The monk did agree, however, to record his knowledge in a long and detailed travelogue, the *Da Tang xiyu ji* (Record of western realms), a document that remains one of the best historical sources for Central and South Asia during this period. In recognition of his unique knowledge, Xuanzang was received as a national hero and eventually installed as the director of a lavishly funded translation project that greatly expanded the Chinese Buddhist canon.

Taizong's imperial patronage gave Xuanzang a position of great prestige and power within the Chinese Buddhist establishment of Chang'an. As a Buddhist philosopher and scholar, he is probably best characterized as a radical conservative. The radical aspect of his character was evident already in the restlessness of his youth, in the dissatisfaction with the state of Chinese Buddhism that inspired his long pilgrimage to India. His primary concern was to preserve faithfully the roots of the tradition, and he had little interest in the new, more indigenous Chinese Buddhist thought that was being formulated in the late sixth century. It was surely no accident that once in India he allied himself with the most conservative faction of Mahāyāna thought then current, the scholastic Yogācāra doctrine represented by Śīlabhadra, a school that was vigorously resisting the innovations of *tathāgata-garbha* thought and Tantric practice. The Yogācāra thought he followed sought to revitalize the old Abhidharma program of systematic soteriology, undertaken anew in light of the Mahayana concept of emptiness (*śūnyatā*). His respect for older Buddhist traditions is demonstrated further by his devotion to the Maitreya cult and by the conspicuous absence of any reference to the increasingly popular Amitābha cult in his travelogue and his biographies.

In spite of his prestige, Xuanzang's best efforts to restore a more Indian style of scholastic Buddhism in China were swept away by the new schools of Chinese Buddhism, schools that better addressed the Chinese philosophical problematic. Court patronage proved fickle, the influence of his disciples waned quickly, and in the end his teaching survived as a distinct lineage only in Japan, where it was known as the Hossō school. Modern scholars have gained an invaluable picture of early India through Xuanzang's prodigious efforts. Yet it is not as scholar or philosopher that he is most venerated within the tradition. For East Asian Buddhists, Xuanzang came to epitomize the sincerely devout and pious pilgrim, the itinerant seeker ever in arduous pursuit of ultimate enlightenment.

SEE ALSO Kuiji; Yogācāra.

BIBLIOGRAPHY

The grandeur of the Tang dynasty and the drama of Xuanzang's journey are well captured by René Grousset in his popular history, *Sur les traces du Bouddha* (1929; reprint, Paris, 1977), translated by Mariette Leon as *In the Footsteps of the Buddha* (London, 1932) and translated again under the same title by J. A. Underwood (New York, 1971). The best scholarly survey currently available is *Genjō* by Kuwayama Shōshin and Hakamaya Noriaki (Tokyo, 1981). On Xuanzang's relationship to the Tang court, see Stanley Weinstein's *Buddhism under the T'ang* (Cambridge, U.K., 1987).

In addition to his many translations, Xuanzang wrote a record of his journey and several philosophical treatises, including most notably an essay reconciling Mādhyamika and Yogācāra. Only the travelogue has survived, however, and of it there are several translations, all now rather dated and in need of revision. The best is Samuel Beal's *Si-yu-ki: Buddhist Records of the Western World*, 2 vols. (1884; reprint, Oxford, 1906). There is no complete translation of the main biographical document, that written by Xuanzang's contemporaries Huili and Yanzong. Beal published a partial translation of this work also, *The Life of Hiuen-Tsiang* (London, 1911). Preferable, though difficult to obtain, is the more complete and more accurate version published by the Chinese Buddhist Association of the People's Republic of China in commemoration of Xuanzang's anniversary: *The Life of Hsüan-tsang*, translated by Li Yung-hsi (Beijing, 1959).

Xuanzang's understanding of the Vijñaptimātratā school of Yogācāra thought is best seen in the *Cheng weishi lun*, a synoptic edition of ten Indian commentaries on the *Thirty Verses* of Vasubandhu prepared by Xuanzang and his main disciple, Kuiji. This work was translated by Louis de La Vallée-Poussin as *Vijñaptimātratāsiddhi: La Siddhi de Hiuan-tsang*, 2 vols. with separate index (Paris, 1928–1929), and less adequately by Wei Tat as *Ch'eng Wei-Shih Lun: The Doctrine of Mere Consciousness* (Hong Kong, 1973).

On the complex problems with Xuanzang's chronology, see especially Luo Xianglin's "Xuanzang Fashi niandai kao," published with an English summary in the *Journal of Oriental Studies* 3 (1956): 34–47. For further research on the geographical and historical data in Xuanzang's travelogue, see Thomas Watter's monograph *On Yuan Chwang's Travels in India* (London, 1904) along with the extensive review by Paul Pelliot in *Bulletin de l'École Française d'Extrême-Orient* 5 (1905): 423–457. On Xuanzang's rather tenuous relation to the mythical Tripiṭaka in the folk epic *Xiyou ji*, see the introduction to Anthony C. Yu's four-volume translation, *The Journey to the West* (Chicago, 1977–1983).

New Sources

Barat, Kahar, ed. and trans. *The Uygur-Turkic Biography of the Seventh-Century Chinese Buddhist Pilgrim Xuanzang, Ninth and Tenth Chapters.* Bloomington, Ind., 2000.

Kuwayama, Shoshin. "How Xuanzang Learned about Nalanda." In *Tang China and Beyond: Studies on East Asia from the Seventh to the Tenth Century*, edited by Antonino Forte, pp. 1–33. Kyoto, 1988.

Lusthaus, Dan. *Buddhist Phenomenology: A Philosophical Investigation of Yogācāra Buddhism and the Ch'eng Wei-shih lun. New York*, 2002.

Rongxi, Li, trans. *A Biography of the Tripiṭaka Master of the Great Ci'en Monastery of the Great Tang Dynasty.* Berkeley, 1995.

Wriggins, Sally. *Xuanzang: A Buddhist Pilgrim on the Silk Road.* Boulder, Colo., 1996.

ALAN SPONBERG (1987)
Revised Bibliography

XUNZI ("Master Xun") was, after Confucius and Mencius (Mengzi), the third great Ru or "Confucian" of the classical period of Chinese thought. Despite conflicting and fragmentary evidence regarding his exact dates, Xunzi appears to have lived from approximately 310 to 220 BCE, through the climax of the Warring States period of Chinese history. This was a time of social turmoil and terrible interstate warfare, culminating in 221 BCE with the annexation of all the original "central states" of China by the western state of Qin. Xunzi rose to a position of intellectual and cultural eminence during his own lifetime, three times serving as head libationer among the assembled scholars in the state of Qi, traveling widely to different states, and even briefly holding a significant administrative post in the state of Chu.

Xunzi saw himself as defending the true Confucian heritage from threats both internal and external to the tradition. He appears familiar with all the known currents of thought of the period, and often aggressively attacks some central point of a previous thinker while quietly borrowing other elements of their thought that seem valuable to him when properly assimilated into his Confucianism. He wrote focused, well-constructed essays in a pugnacious and frequently colorful style, which taken as a group present a remarkably coherent and powerful religious philosophy. His intellectual goal was to rearticulate Confucianism on a more sophisticated and realistic anthropological, political, and cosmological basis, while preserving the hopeful humaneness of the Confucian Way.

In contrast to Mencius, who retains the Zhou dynasty idea of a purposive *tian* or "Heaven" that lifts up worthy leaders at regular intervals to put the Confucian Way into practice, Xunzi argues that Heaven is not humanlike and is unconcerned with human affairs. It follows its own path, does not reward goodness or punish evil, and does not send meaningful omens or respond favorably to appropriate sacrifices. To view the arts of sacrifice and divination as techniques to manipulate spiritual or material realities, Xunzi thinks, is a profound error; such ceremonies, as well as other rituals, are done to bring order to human life and thereby give it beauty and proper form. For Xunzi, Heaven does occupy the supreme position in the cosmos, and along with Earth deserves ritualized respect as one of the "three roots" of human existence; this is so because Heaven and Earth through their interactions mysteriously generate all life, including human life. But humans have a crucial role to play, governing themselves and indeed ordering the whole world, on the basis of steady cycles of change within the cosmos. Heaven, like a ruler, occupies the central position of the cosmos; but human beings, like ministers of state, actively order the natural and social worlds according to the Way. This Confucian Way is for Xunzi the human Way, in explicit contrast with the Heavenly Way, and it is crucial for us "not to compete with Heaven over responsibilities."

For Xunzi the Way is the ultimate human tradition, created over time by the ancient sages in response to human nature and the environment, and yet still universally binding on all human beings. This Way is both necessary and suitable for us, Xunzi argues (notoriously in the view of later Chinese commentators), because humanity's innate impulses are *e,* "bad," in the sense of "ugly" or "foul." This is a direct attack on Mencius, who taught that people all possess four "sprouts" or "beginnings" of virtue within their hearts, which we must attend to and follow if we are to become good (in Mencian terms, we will "cultivate" our "sprouts" until they are fully grown). Xunzi adamantly rejects these agricultural metaphors for self-cultivation, and the whole anthropological edifice they are meant to symbolize. Following our uncultivated intuitions and impulses will lead only to strife, Xunzi thinks, as people struggle with each other for social dominance and limited material resources. We have no reliable inborn moral intuitions; we must learn the Way from others, and only over time will its fittingness and power become apparent to us.

Xunzi speaks of the formation of virtuous people as a long, initially difficult and unpleasant process akin to crafting beautiful and useful implements out of less than ideal raw materials. Mere indoctrination or coercion will be insufficient, however; people must be exposed to the gracious humaneness of the Confucian Way, and judge for themselves that it is more desirable than their current anxious, dangerous, and painful lives, even from an ignorant starting point.

A beginning Confucian student needs above all to find and follow a wise teacher, and congregate with fellow students of the Way. Xunzi describes in some detail the practices of self-cultivation he recommends, the most prominent of which are textual study of the Confucian classics, the practice of ritual, and musical performance and appreciation.

Xunzi's treatment of ritual is particularly noteworthy. His use of the term is very broad, encompassing not only sacrifices and discrete ceremonies, but also deportment, etiquette, speech, and even dress; such matters of interpersonal "style" are crucial elements of Xunzian ethics. According to Xunzi, ritual works at personal, social, and even cosmic levels, properly ordering all things into harmonious wholes. Over time, by means of diligent ritual practice, the Xunzian student will "cut and stretch" his dispositions to feel, judge, and act so that they come to perfectly accord with the rites; by doing this he will come to follow and "enact" the Way. For Xunzi, Confucian learning is a sham unless it is grounded in a bodily appropriation of the Way, so that a person's every movement and word is appropriate; this sort of self-mastery can only be attained by practicing ritual and music. Fully cultivated leaders will both exemplify and implement the Way in society at large, ushering in a humane society where the poor, weak, and infirm never lack for basic necessities, the strong are restrained from predation and redirected to more public service, and the surplus bounty of a harmonious state will be used to elevate and enrich the lives of all, according to their virtue and social standing (which ought, in a Xunzian world, to coincide). Even the natural world will share in greater fecundity and order when brought under Confucian stewardship, as people's needs are met in harmony with natural processes. This ideal state of affairs, which Xunzi calls "forming a triad with Heaven and Earth," is the fullest flowering of the human Way.

Xunzi's ideas had a significant impact on the formation of later Confucian imperial bureaucracy and methods of education. Moreover, his students preserved texts (such as the *Odes*) that proved indispensable to later Chinese tradition. Nevertheless, his two most famous students were viewed by later Confucians as apostates from the Way who brought disgrace upon their teacher by aiding Qin's ruthless drive to unify China. And later, during the Confucian revival of the Song dynasty (960–1279 CE), Mencius's views on human nature became canonical, with Xunzi's thereafter considered heterodox. He was thus occasionally disparaged but largely ignored until modern times. He is the subject of considerable current scholarly interest in the West because of his philosophically complex and sophisticated version of Confucianism.

BIBLIOGRAPHY

John Knoblock's three-volume *Xunzi: A Translation and Study of the Complete Works* (Stanford, Calif., 1988–1994) is invaluable, particularly in its voluminous notes to the commentarial tradition, even if particular translations are sometimes debatable or excessive; Knoblock includes ample introductory material on Xunzi's context, and the fullest collected bibliography of Xunzi studies available. Burton Watson's partial translation is also very good (*Hsün-Tzu: Basic Writings,* New York, 1963), as are the precisely rendered but brief selections translated by Eric Hutton in *Readings in Classical Chinese Philosophy,* edited by Philip J. Ivanhoe and Bryan W. Van Norden (New York, 2001). The best collections of secondary works are *Virtue, Nature, and Moral Agency in the Xunzi,* edited by T. C. Kline III and Philip J. Ivanhoe (Indianapolis, Ind., 2000), and *Ritual and Religion in the Xunzi,* edited by T. C. Kline III (New York, 2004). Other helpful works concerning Xunzi's understanding of ritual include A. R. Radcliffe-Brown's classic and insightful "Religion and Society," in Radcliffe-Brown, *Structure and Function in Primitive Society: Essays and Addresses* (1952), pp. 153–177 (New York, 1968), and Robert F. Campany, "Xunzi and Durkheim as Theorists of Ritual Practice," in *Discourse and Practice,* edited by Frank Reynolds and David Tracy, pp. 197–231 (Albany, N.Y., 1992). Edward Machle's *Nature and Heaven in the Xunzi: A Study of the Tian Lun* (Albany, N.Y., 1993) is a searching treatment of Xunzi's views of *tian* or "Heaven" that argues Xunzi should be seen as a religious thinker, and that his *tian* is better understood as a Chinese sort of high god than as an amoral, law-governed "Nature."

AARON STALNAKER (2005)

YAʿAQOV BEN ASHER (c. 1270–1343), Hispano-Jewish codifier. Yaʿaqov was a son of the great German halakhist Asher ben Yeḥiʾel, who settled with his family in Toledo in 1303. Yaʿaqov ben Asher never accepted rabbinical office and at times suffered economic adversity, but he continued his father's lifework—the revival of Talmudic studies in Castile and the fusion of Franco-German and Spanish *halakhah.*

Ya'aqov's *magnum opus* was his code, the *Arba'ah ṭurim* (lit., "four rows"; see *Ex.* 28:17). It consists of four books: *Oraḥ ḥayyim,* on liturgy and holidays; *Yoreh de'ah,* on "the prohibited and permitted" and other topics, including mourning, charity, education, and filial piety; *Even ha-'ezer,* on family law; and *Ḥoshen mishpaṭ,* on civil law. Ya'aqov sought to attain coherence and order in Jewish law, but in a manner less radically reductive and homogenizing than that of Maimonides in his *Mishneh Torah* a century and a half earlier. Instead of excising all disagreement and discussion, as Maimonides had done, Ya'aqov skillfully integrated into his code brief discussions of legal cruxes and of the divergent views of major authorities who represented different schools, generally concluding with his father's view.

The language of the *Ṭurim* is clear and simple. Unlike *Mishneh Torah,* its arrangement aims at functionality rather than conceptual categorization. This practical orientation is evident also in its omission of all laws not applicable since the destruction of the Temple. Nor does the *Ṭurim* attempt the grand synthesis of law and theology to which *Mishneh Torah* aspires. It does, however, contain many homiletical and hortatory passages (especially in the section prologues) based on classical *aggadah* and the author's own pure and simple piety. Only rarely are there reflections of the Ashkenazic Hasidism of Ya'aqov's German forebears and of his opposition to philosophical rationalism. The spirituality underlying Ya'aqov's piety occasionally breaks through the surface, as in his recommendation, inserted matter-of-factly in "the laws of prayer," that one emulate the "men of piety and good deeds [who] would so meditate and concentrate in prayer, that they achieved a stripping away of corporeality and an intensification of the rational soul, which brought them close to the level of prophecy."

The *Ṭurim* became an immensely popular work among both Sephardic and Ashkenazic Jews and occasioned many commentaries. It was the second Hebrew book published (Piove di Sacco, 1475) and in the sixteenth century served as the basis for Yosef Karo's classic code, the *Shulḥan 'arukh.*

Ya'aqov also composed a commentary on the Torah (1806) that clearly summarizes the brilliant but difficult thirteenth-century Pentateuch commentary of Moses Nahmanides, without the latter's qabbalistic exegesis. To each section, Ya'aqov prefaced homiletical interpretations based on the numerical value of letters *(gemaṭriyyah)* and the orthographic peculiarities of the Masoretic text. Ironically, these interpretations, mentioned as a relatively inconsequential afterthought in Ya'a-qov's introduction, became extremely popular, eclipsing the main body of the commentary.

Bibliography

Abrahams, Israel, ed. and trans. *Hebrew Ethical Wills* (1926). Reprint, with a foreword by Judah Goldin, Philadelphia, 1976. Includes the testament of Ya'aqov to his children (pp. 202–205) as well as testaments of Ya'aqov's brother and father.

Elon, Menachem. *Ha-mishpaṭ ha'Ivri,* vol. 3. 2d ed. Jerusalem, 1973. A good description of the *Ṭurim* as a code, pp. 1058–1082.

Freimann, Alfred. "Die Ascheriden, 1267–1391." *Jahrbuch der jüdisch-literarischen Gesellschaft* 13 (1920): 142–254. Still the basic study of Ya'aqov and his family.

Twersky, Isadore. "The *Shulḥan 'Aruk:* Enduring Code of Jewish Law." *Judaism* 16 (1967): 141–158. Reprinted in *The Jewish Expression,* edited by Judah Goldin (New York, 1970), pp. 322–343. Contains valuable comments on the *Ṭurim* and its use by Yosef Karo.

Urbach, E. E. "Darkhei pesiqah: Sefer ha-Ṭurim." In *American Academy for Jewish Research Jubilee Volume,* edited by Salo W. Baron and Isaac E. Barzilay, vol. 2, pp. 1–14 (Hebrew section). Jerusalem, 1980. Explores, among other things, the question of structural parallels between the *Ṭurim* and Roman and Spanish law codes.

New Sources

Amrán, Rica. "Un estudiante ruso en la Yesiba de Toledo en tiempos de Asher ben Yehiel, ha-Rosh." *Anuario de Estudios Medievales* 20 (1990): 9–13.

Ta-Shma, Israel Moses. "Between East and West: Rabbi Asher b. Yehi'el and His Son Rabbi Ya'akov." In *Studies in Medieval Jewish History and Literature,* vol. 3, edited by Isadore Twersky and Jay M. Harris, pp. 179–196. Cambridge, Mass., 2000.

Bernard Septimus (1987)
Revised Bibliography

YAKṢAS See NĀGAS AND YAKṢAS

YAKUT RELIGION.

The Yakuts, who numbered 328,000 during the 1979 census, are the northernmost of Turkic peoples. Beginning in the twelfth and thirteenth centuries, under pressure caused by Buriat encroachment, they gradually emigrated northward from the Lake Baikal region of southern Siberia. They moved upstream along the course of the Lena River and finally settled in northeastern Siberia, the coldest region in the world. The horses and cattle bred by these semisedentary people have successfully adapted to the rigorous climate; however, hunting and fishing provide the Yakuts with a significant additional source of income. The Yakuts are organized in patrilineal and exogamic clans regrouped into tribes.

Under pressure from the Russians, who subjugated them during the first half of the seventeenth century, the majority of Yakuts were baptized by the end of the eighteenth century. They adopted Christianity primarily for material reasons (e.g., gifts of crosses, shirts, and various privileges). At the same time, they secretly preserved their own religious system, shamanism, which was modified superficially as the result of contact with Russian Orthodoxy. The practitioners of shamanism accepted the new idea of a reward after death and attributed the traits of God, the Virgin Mary, and the guardian angels to some of their spirits.

COSMOLOGY. The Yakut universe is composed of three superimposed worlds. The "upper world" comprises nine skies of different colors. Spirits reside in each sky: In the east are the *aĭyys*, bright, creative spirits, and in the west are the *abaasys*, dark, harmful spirits. (The Yakuts are situated in the east.)

The "middle world," flat and octagonal, is populated by humans and by a host of spirits. The forest of this world is a formidable territory because the greatest number of spirits are found there: Although they grant game, they also capture the souls of hunters who have pleased them.

The "lower world" is a crepuscular region solely inhabited by the harmful spirits who roam among a metallic, iron vegetation. Here, the "sea of death," composed of children's cadavers, churns its waves. The term employed for "lower world," *allaraa,* signifies "below, downstream, in the north." (The rivers of Siberia flow northward, hence the use of the same term for both "downstream" and "north.") It is possible that the lower world is not conceived of as a sinister and subterranean replica of the middle world but rather as a watery abyss in the northern regions. In any case, the contrasts of above and below and of upper and lower do not figure predominately in the Yakut religion. More important is the division of the sky into east (good) and west (evil): This division allows for the classification of the spirits.

THE PANTHEON. The bright, creative spirits, *aĭyys* (from the Turkic root "ai," "to create"), assure the Yakuts their survival by granting them the souls of children and also of horses, cattle, and dogs, the Yakuts' only domesticated animals. However, the Yakuts must pay homage to the aiyys with milk offerings and prayers and must consecrate animals to them from their herd. The consecrated animal (yzykh) is not slain; it is sent back to the herd and is treated with respect, for it no longer belongs to humans but to the spirit to which it was consecrated. This spirit will reward the people for their care by granting fertility to the herd. The *aĭyy* cult, called "white shamanism," disappeared in the eighteenth century and never was studied properly.

The White Lord Creator, Iurung Aiyy Toion, is the master of all the *aĭyys* who are imagined to be like rich Yakuts and are organized in clans, as are the Yakuts themselves. Associated with the sun and the heat of summer, the White Lord Creator resides in the ninth sky, where "the grass is as white as the wing of a white swan." He rules the world, sends the soul (kut) to children, and assures fertility in cattle and the growth of plants, but he does not interfere in human affairs on his own initiative. During the great spring feasts called "libations" (*ysyakh*), he is first offered libations of fermented mare's milk; later, horses are consecrated to him. Occasionally a goddess, the wife of this god, is mentioned; she would become an avatar of the goddess of the earth. Such an identification of the goddess may be a vague indication of a marriage between the sky and the earth.

The *aĭyysyts*, a group of spirits, female for the most part, attend to human reproduction and the reproduction of certain species of animals (especially the domestic species). The *aĭyysyt* who attends to human reproduction brings the soul of the child created by Aĭyy Toĭon. She also comes to help women during childbirth. She is often associated with Ieĭiëkhsit, and is occasionally confused with her. When they are associated, Aĭyysyt is the one who grants the soul and Ieĭiëkhsit is the one who delivers it. (The latter has been likened to a guardian angel.) Aĭyysyt and Ieĭiëkhsit are both proper nouns and epithets that can be applied even to male personages: When one is begging for offspring one uses the epithet Aĭyysyt, and when one desires an intermediary the epithet Ieĭiëkhsit is used. The three *aĭyysyts* of man, of horned livestock, and of dogs are all feminine spirits, but the spirit that grants horses, "the formidable Dzhësëgëĭ," is masculine. When mares and cows reproduce, and each time a child is born, relatives and cousins come together to offer a ritual of renewal to the spirit that granted the soul. However, the ritual for the spirit-master of horses is conducted by the (male) ruler of the house, while the other two rituals are celebrated by the women.

The goddess of the earth, who lives among beautiful white birches far from the evil spirits, takes care of the traveler, blesses the harvests, and occasionally decides the fate of the newborn. The spirit-master of the domestic fire assures the survival of the household: In his embers tremble the souls of children and calves yet to be born. He removes harmful spirits and purifies the accessories of the hunt that are soiled by the presence of a menstruating woman. This spirit-master also serves as an intermediary for other spirits by delivering offerings to them that are thrown into his flames in their honor. In exchange, one must not forget to feed him by throwing him a mouthful of food before each meal; otherwise, he may take revenge by, for example, burning down the house.

On the opposite side, in the western sky, loom the black spirits, *abaasys* (the Turkic root is probably *ap,* "enchantment"), "gigantic as the shadows of larches under the full moon." In fact, they appear to be more terrible than they really are, because once they have sent diseases (most often, various types of insanity), they will take them away if the shaman sacrifices horses with suitable coats. The supreme ruler of the nine clans of *abaasy* is Ulu Toion ("powerful lord"), who gave the Yakuts fire and perhaps one of the three souls that the Yakuts believe each person possesses (according to some, the soul he gave was the *siur,* vital energy). He is the protector of the black shamans, *abaasy oĭun* (lit., "shamans in contact with the *abaasys*").

Other harmful abaasys populate the earth and the lower world. The two most celebrated are the ruler of the lower world, Arsan Duolan (a pale replica of Ulu Toĭon), who sends infant mortality and obstinacy, and Kudai Bagsi, the ruler of the smiths, who cures the apprentice smith of his initiatory illness if the shaman offers him a black bull.

Among the harmful spirits are the unsatisfied deceased (*iuërs*) those who died without completing a full life cycle, such as young girls who died without having been married. The souls of suicides and of shamans become the most formidable *iuërs*.

In the domestic environment and in natural phenomena that directly influence humanity's well-being, there exists a supernatural force that the Yakuts call *ichchi* ("master, possessor"). This force is personified in the spirit-masters who reside in the object, house, or territory they possess. To ensure that a tool be effective or that a house not collapse, to avoid being crushed by a tree or hurled into the waters when crossing the forest or the river, one must make an offering to one's spirit-master.

Since the Yakuts believed the spirits were organized in clans as they themselves were, they recognized their right to have tribal property. This property was the game and fish existing in the territory of these spirits. They accorded part of this to humans in exchange for food (milk products, alcohol, flesh of domestic animals) in an alliance that is similar to that formed between bartering human tribes. However, the spirits never give enough souls of game, cattle, and children. This is where the shaman intervenes.

THE SHAMAN. To obtain the souls of wild game, the shaman provides the master of the particular kind of animal in question with food in return: He smears the blood of a sacrificed animal on a wooden statuette where he has caused the spirit-master of the forest, the rich Baianaĭ or Baryllakh, to descend. He then gives a symbol of these souls (e.g., feathers, etc.) to the members of the clan. To obtain the souls of children and additional cattle, the shaman himself goes to the beyond to confront the *aĭyysyts*. At first the spirits refuse, remembering the wrongs that humans have committed. Then, after considering the supplications of the shaman, they give him the souls. The position of the shaman has changed: He no longer barters, he implores, because the *aĭyy* spirits, dispensers of cattle and human offspring, are venerated, unlike the spirits of the hunt or of illnesses, whom the shaman treats as equals.

To cure illness, which the Yakuts conceive as the installation of an evil spirit in the body of the ailing person and also as the theft of the soul by a spirit "soul-eater," the shaman trades the soul of the sick person for that of a sacrificed animal, which he sends into the otherworld. These negotiations with the spirits take place during the shamanic séance, which is generally held nocturnally at the afflicted person's home, with relatives and neighbors in attendance. The séance includes a purification ceremony; a convocation of the spirits through the shaman's chanting, accompanied on the tambourine; a voyage of the shaman himself into the otherworlds to find the spirits (a voyage mimicked by the shaman's dance); and an act of divination.

The shaman is aided by his principal spirit (*ämägät*), generally the shaman's ancestor, who chose the shaman from among his descendants in order to pass on the shamanic gift, a gift that always remains in the same family. Women also can become shamans (*udaghans*), but female shamans are less numerous because the clans are patrilineal. Once chosen by the ancestor, the soul of the future shaman takes on the form of a young bird and is educated atop either the mythic larch of the upper world or the pine tree of the lower world. It is during his initiation that the shaman seals his alliance with the spirits. In the course of his sleep, his body is cut up in the lower world and consumed like a sacrificial animal by several spirits. The spirits then reconstitute his body. Recreated in this manner, the shaman acquires rights over the spirits who have consumed his flesh and who will subsequently help him remove illnesses.

The shaman is also aided by zoomorphic spirits who transport him in the air or under the ground and who fight at his side. Moreover, the shaman possesses an animal double (usually a male moose or bull); it is in this form that he fights against shamans of enemy clans. If the shaman's animal double has been killed, he himself dies. The shaman also fights against the souls of dead avengers, the spirits of illnesses and epidemics. He also assures the survival of his clan by divination—predicting the future, the areas where game will be most plentiful, and so forth. In this dark universe, where mad spirits who populate three-fourths of the sky in the west predominate, where the bright spirits (*aĭyys*) often refuse to grant offspring and prosperity, and where "soul-eating" spirits lurk about the earth and in the lower world, the shaman is the Yakuts' only support.

SEE ALSO Shamanism, article on Siberian and Inner Asian Shamanism; Southern Siberian Religions.

BIBLIOGRAPHY

Alekseev, N. A. *Traditsionnye religioznye verovaniia iakutov v deviatnadtsatom-nachale dvadtsatogo v.* Novosibirsk, 1975. A work giving a detailed description, from an evolutionist perspective, of Yakut beliefs.

Ksenofontov, G. V. *Legendy i rasskazy o shamanakh u iakutov, buriat i tungusov.* 2d rev. ed. Moscow, 1938. Very valuable work for the study of Yakut, Buriat, and Tunguz shamanism, consisting of a series of accounts by indigenous informants, collected between 1921 and 1926 and accompanied by notes from the author, a Yakut himself.

Pekarskii, E. K. *Slovar' iakutskago iazyka.* 3 vols. Saint Petersburg (Leningrad), 1907–1930. Dictionary that contains many facts on the ethnography and religion of the Yakuts.

Popov, A. A. "Materialy po religii iakutov Viliuiskogo okruga." *Sbornik Muzeia Antropologii i Etnografii* 11 (1949): 255–323. Important article including information on the Yakut world, spirits, souls, and certain rituals, collected by the author during the time of a survey conducted from 1922 to 1925 on the Yakuts living in the region of the Viliui, a western tributary of the Lena River.

LAURENCE DELABY (1987)
Translated from French by Sherri L. Granka

YAMA. In the earliest Ṛgvedic hymns, Yama is a benign god who looks after the well-being of the dead, whom he entertains with food and shelter. His abode and its environment are pleasant and comfortable; survivors supplicate him for the care of their departed relatives.

Yama is the son of Vivasvat and Saraṇyū; he has a twin sister, Yamī. In the *Ṛgveda,* Amṛta ("ambrosia") is Yama's son, but in the *Atharvaveda,* Yama has a son, Duḥsvapna ("bad dream"), by Varuṇānī. In the epic-Puranic literature, the Aśvins are his brothers, and Śani and Manu are his half brothers. The Aṅgirasas are his associates.

The name *Yama* is derived from a stem meaning "twins"; Latin *gemini* and the Avestan names *Yima* and *Yimeh* are cognates. In a Ṛgvedic hymn, Yamī implores Yama to unite with her, but he rejects her advances. The hymn has an abrupt, inconclusive end. In Buddhist literature, Yama is identified with Kāma ("desire") and Māra ("death"). In the Vedic literature, Yama has close relations with Rudra, Soma, Agni, Kāla, and Nirṛti. Yama also bears a remote relationship to Varuṇa.

Yama in the Vedas was the first mortal to die. He then went to heaven, where he ruled over the dead. But toward the close of the Vedic period sinister traits began to appear in him, and they grew stronger with time. Yama then became the god of death and the lord of Hell. In the *Kaṭha Upaniṣad,* as death personified, he holds a long discourse with the boy Naciketas, whom he initiates into the mysteries of life, death, and immortality. Prayers are offered to Yama for longevity and deliverance from recurring deaths. Yama also grants release from *aśanāyā* (hunger). In many rituals of ancestor worship, oblations are offered to Yama with prayers for averting recurring deaths. In the Gṛhyasūtras, oblations are offered to Yama's men, presumably his associates, in the realm of the dead.

Of the two paths in later Vedic eschatology, Devayāna and Pitṛyāṇa, the latter is that of the fathers and of spirits doomed to rebirth. These spirits proceed through Soma, the moon, and are judged by Yama. In the epics and Purāṇas, Yama has a palace, Śubhāvatī, in the netherworld. Yama's realm begins, in Buddhist literature, to shift from the heaven of the gods until, in the Hindu epics and Purāṇas, it assumes distinctly sinister characteristics. As god of death and lord of Hell, Yama is dark and malevolent, yet still a giver of boons.

The south is the region of Yama (as it is that of the Avestan Yima) and the region of death. Yama has two dogs, Śyāma and Śabala, who are associated with the final judgment of souls, as are Hades' dog, Kerberos, the Egyptian Anubis, and Yima's four dogs. Yama is also associated with oil and with the dove, eagle, and raven (all of which are endowed with sinister traits). The epic and Puranic Yama has a buffalo for a mount. Dread monsters (*rākṣasas*), semidivine *yakṣas*, demons, cruel messengers, the Aṅgirasas, and the souls of the departed throng his realm. His ritual oblations in ancestor worship are gruesome and evil. The symbols associated with his various aspects as Kāla, Mṛtyu, and Antaka are images of repulsiveness, cruelty, and deformity. In descriptions of Yama red and black colors predominate.

In the final stage of his evolution, Yama shares two significant characteristics with Śiva: He is Kāla ("time") and Dharmarāja ("lord of righteousness"). As Kāla, he is also Antaka, the "ender" (i. e., Death). As Dharmarāja, he takes over Varuṇa's role as the moral judge and punisher whose assistants torture the wicked in hell. At this stage his name is clearly derived differently, from the root *yam* ("to control"), from which are derived *yantraṇa* ("constriction") and *yantraṇā* ("torture"). As Dharmarāja, Yama can also be lenient to supplicants and revoke his own order (as he did for Sāvitrī) or modify it (as he did for Pramadvarā in the *Mahābhārata*).

Numerous episodes in the epics and Purāṇas contribute to Yama's almighty and sinister image. This image contrasts with his early Vedic appearance as a minor god who is simply a "gatherer of men." A cluster of hymns in the tenth and last book of the *Ṛgveda* presents him as a benign god like any other in the pantheon. But from the *Yajurveda* (especially in the Puruṣamedha sacrifice), where different oblations are prescribed for each of the various aspects of Yama, his personality undergoes a radical change: From the benevolent god of the dead he becomes the dread god of death. The theophany of Yama as Kāla, Antaka, and Dharmarāja brings him closer to Śiva.

BIBLIOGRAPHY

Barua, P. R. "The Conception of Yama in Early Buddhism." *Journal of the Asiatic Society* (Pakistan) 9 (December 1964): 1–14.

Bhattacharji, Sukumari. *The Indian Theogony: A Comparative Study of Indian Mythology from the Vedas to the Purāṇas.* Cambridge, 1970. The chapter on Yama (pp. 48–64) seeks to trace Yama's evolution from the Vedic to the epic-Puranic period and his transformation from a benign god of the dead to an agent of Śiva.

Chapekar, N. G. "Pitārāḥ and Yama." In *Belvalkar Commemoration Volume, Benares,* 1957, pp. 36–42. Deals with Yama's relationship with ancestral spirits.

Dandekar, R. N. "Yama in the Veda." In *B. C. Law Commemorative Volume,* edited by D. R. Bhandarkar. Calcutta, 1945. A critical and comprehensive account.

Dumézil, Georges. "La sabhā de Yama." *Journal asiatique* 253 (1965): 161–165.

Ehni, Jacques. *Die ursprüngliche Gottheit des vedischen Yama.* Leipzig, 1896. One of the earliest studies.

Heras, Henry. "The Personality of Yama in the Ṛgveda." In *Jadunath Sarkar Commemoration Volume,* edited by Gupta Hari Ram, vol. 2. Hoshiarpur, 1958. Discusses the Vedic antecedents of Yama.

Karmarkar, A. P. "Yama—The God of Death of the Dravidians." *Indica* 4 (March 1967): 7–10.

Varma, M. *Yama.* Allahabad, 1939. A fairly full study of some important aspects of Yama's personality.

Wayman, Alex. "Studies in Yama and Māra." *Indo-Iranian Journal* 3 (1959): 44–73, 112–131. A critical and comparative treatment of the Vedic Yama and his transformation into Māra in Buddhist literature.

New Sources

Merh, Kusum P. "Yama, the Glorious Lord of the Other World." *Reconstructing Indian History & Culture* no. 12. New Delhi, 1996.

SUKUMARI BHATTACHARJI (1987)
Revised Bibliography

YAMAGA SOKŌ (1622–1685), Japanese Confucian of the school of Ancient Learning (Kogaku). Sokō was born in Aizu, the son of a masterless warrior named Yamaga Sadamochi (1585–1664) and Sadamochi's mistress, Myōchi (d. 1677). He began studying the Confucian classics at the age of five or six, and at eight he was en rolled at the Hayashi school in Edo (present-day Tokyo). As a youth, he also studied Japanese literature, Shintō, and military science—the latter with Obata Kagenori (1572–1663) and Hōjō Ujinaga (1609–1670).

Sokō first achieved fame in 1642 when he published *Heihō yūbishū* (Collected Writings on Military Methods and Preparedness), a fifty-volume work on military science that treated a whole range of subjects from castle defense to warrior organization. Over the next two decades his lectures on military affairs and the Chinese classics attracted growing numbers of local warriors and lords. In 1652 Sokō entered the service of Asano Naganao (1610–1672), lord of the Akō domain, and served him until 1660, when he resigned to devote himself to teaching. Despite his service in the Asano house and his success as a teacher, Sokō longed to become a direct retainer of the shogun. Although he nearly realized this ambition on several occasions, his hopes were dashed in 1666 when the senior councillor Hoshina Masayuki (1611–1672) had him exiled to the Akō domain. The ostensible reason for this was the publication of *Seikyō yōroku* (Essentials of the Sages' Teachings), in which Sokō criticized the officially sanctioned Neo-Confucianism. During his exile Sokō was well cared for by the Asano family, had an endless stream of visitors from Edo, and wrote more than seventeen books, the most important of which were *Takkyō dōmon* (A Child's Queries During Exile), *Chūchō jijitsu* (The Truth about Japan), and *Haishō zanpitsu* (Last Testament in Exile). When he was pardoned in 1675 he returned to Edo, where he resumed his teaching career, once again lecturing on military science and Confucianism. He died of jaundice in 1685.

Sokō is best known as a military thinker, Confucian scholar, and nationalist. Early in his life he concentrated on formalizing and systematizing the essentially medieval mores, customs, and institutions of the warrior class. In the early 1650s, he developed the notion of what he called *bushidō* ("way of the warrior"), which, borrowing heavily from Neo-Confucianism, provided a philosophical basis for military science and described the ideal behavior of a class whose chief function was no longer to fight but to govern.

Sokō is also known as an advocate of Ancient Learning. While he had once subscribed to Neo-Confucianism, he came to oppose it, calling for a return to the teachings of the ancient Chinese sages and Confucius. In *Seikyō yōroku*, he attacked Neo-Confucianism's introspective concerns and in their stead, advanced a new utilitarianism, stressed the importance of social relationships, and recommended the revival of ancient Chinese regulations and rituals. Sokō began the work that Itō Jinsai (1627–1705) and Ogyū Sorai (1666–1728), his successors in the school of Ancient Learning, would complete. While in exile, Sokō became an ardent nationalist. In *Chūchō jijitsu* and *Takkyō dōmon* he argued that Japan's idigenous religion, Shintō ("way of the gods"), was superior to Confucianism and that Japan itself was superior to China and all other countries in the world.

Sokō's writings reveal, first, an impressive eclecticism that reflects his having studied, at different times, Neo-Confucianism, Shintō, military science, Buddhism, and even Taoism. They also reflect his concern, associated with his utilitarianism, with the actual affairs of daily life and the larger problem of how best to govern the country. Finally, Sokō's writings give evidence of his fierce loyalty to the shogun and the government he headed. Although Sokō never became a direct retainer of the shogun, he taught hundreds, perhaps thousands, of Tokugawa retainers and formulated political principles aimed at strengthening shogunal rule.

SEE ALSO Bushidō; Confucianism in Japan; Itō Jinsai; Ogyū Sorai.

BIBLIOGRAPHY

de Bary, Wm. Theodore. "Sagehood as a Secular and Spiritual Ideal in Tokugawa Neo-Confucianism." In *Principle and Practicality: Essays in Neo-Confucianism and Practical Learning*, edited by Wm. Theodore de Bary and Irene Bloom, pp. 127–188. New York, 1979. An important revision of Maru-yama Masao's interpretation of Tokugawa intellectual history, in which Yamaga Sokō is treated.

Maruyama Masao. *Studies in the Intellectual History of Tokugawa Japan.* Translated by Mikiso Hane. Princeton, 1974. A classic study of Tokugawa intellectual history.

Uenaka Shuzo. "Last Testament in Exile: Yamaga Sokō's *Haishō Zampitsu.*" *Monumenta Nipponica* 32 (Summer 1977): 125–152. An annotated translation of Sokō's *Haishō zanpitsu*, with full biographical introduction.

SAMUEL HIDEO YAMASHITA (1987)

YAMATO TAKERU. Yamato Takeru, whose name means "brave man from the Yamato region," is a legendary character described in the records of the Yamato kingship, including the *Nihonshoki* (720 CE) and *Kojiki* (712 CE). According to the *Nihonshoki* and *Kojiki*, Yamato Takeru was the son of Keiko Tenno, the twelfth emperor. He laid the foundations for the Yamato kingship to rule almost all of the Japanese islands by conquering previously unsubjugated peoples, such as the Kumaso in the southwest and the Emishi in the northeast. Yamato Takeru's conquests finally ended when he died after his defeat by a mountain god just before returning to the Yamato region. Today, Yamato Takeru is not considered to have been an actual living person, but his character may reflect memories of Yuryaku Tenno, who lived during the fifth century.

The descriptions of Yamato Takeru's character are similar in the *Kojiki* and *Nihonshoki*, but his relationship with his father, Keiko Tenno, is described very differently in the two books. In the *Nihonshoki*, Yamato Takeru is the one and only crown prince who is relied on by his father as a man of perfected character in terms of the ideal Chinese Confucian. But in the *Kojiki*, Yamato Takeru is just one of many princes, and he is hated by his father because of his extraordinary powers as a trickster-like character. Yamato Takeru's expedition is also described differently in the two books. In the *Nihonshoki*, he leads his father's army, whereas in the *Kojiki* he is forced to enter enemy territory almost alone, as if he had been expelled from the Yamato region, even though he had shown obedience to his father. The relationship described in the *Kojiki* could be thought of as an Oedipus complex in reverse, with the father showing hatred for the son regardless of the son's affection towards him.

Legends of Yamato Takeru are also found in the *Fudoki*, a compilation from the early eighth century CE explaining the origins of the names of places across the Japanese islands. There are some suggestions in the *Fudoki* that Yamato Takeru was classified as an emperor. From the evidence of the *Nihonshoki*, *Kojiki*, and *Fudoki*, there are at least three different types of legends concerning Yamato Takeru. Although they are not unified, all of these books concern the Yamato kingship.

In the medieval era, there were repeated attempts to unify the numerous records of Yamato Takeru. Most of the stories of the period, in the *Heike monogatari* and other works, were based on the *Nihonshoki* account. They emphasize the Yamato Takeru legend as a story about the miraculous powers of the Kusanagi sword, one of three items making up Japan's imperial regalia. This emphasis reflected the fact that at this point in history the warrior class controlled the political power of Japan, and the imperial family feared losing cultural power as well. Thus, the imperial family and their supporters sought to exemplify the family's strength and lineage through their possession of the legendary sword.

Beginning in the middle of the early modern period, Yamato Takeru came to be characterized as a figure with rich human emotions, especially the feeling of sorrow. Scholars of Japanese classical studies, such as Motoori Norinaga, drew more upon the *Kojiki* account. In the modern era and moving into World War II, the Japanese government used the figure of Yamato Takeru to represent and glorify the loyal subject, implying that it was honorable to die in war for the country and the emperor. After Japan's defeat, Marxists historians, such as Ishimoda Shō, re-presented the story of Yamato Takeru as crystallizing memories of pre-imperial Japan. Ishimoda believed that the national epics of Japan were equal to the Greek and Roman mythologies. They could be traced back to the stage before the construction of an artificial national identity through the *Kojiki* and *Nihonshoki*, when there was, according to Ishimoda, a pure national sensibility. The image of Yamato Takeru has been transformed through interpretive acts in every period of Japanese history and used to legitimate the standpoint of each interpreter. For many, the legend of Yamato Takeru was thought to preserve historical traces of national memories of how ancient Japanese society was established. The image of Yamato Takeru will no doubt continue to change over time in order to meet new needs.

BIBLIOGRAPHY

Aston, W. G., trans. *Nihongi: Chronicles of Japan from the Earliest Times to A.D. 697.* 1896; reprint, Rutland, Vt., and Tokyo, 1972.

Ishimoda Shō. *Kodai kizoku no eiyuu jidai: Kojiki no ichi kousatsu.* 1948; reprint, Tokyo, 1989.

Isomae Jun'ichi. "Myth in Metamorphosis: Ancient and Medieval Versions of the Yamato Takeru Legend." *Monumenta Nipponica* 54, no. 3 (1999): 361–385.

Isomae Jun'ichi. "Re-appropriating the Japanese Myths: Motoori Norinaga and the Creation Myths of the *Kojiki* and *Nihon shoki.*" *Japanese Journal of Religious Studies* 27, nos. 1–2 (2000): 15–39.

Motoori Norinaga. *Kojiki-den. Motoori Norinaga zenshū,* vol. 11. Tokyo, 1969.

Philippi, D. L., trans. *Kojiki.* Princeton, 1969.

Tsuda Sōkichi. *Nihon koten no kenkyū* (1948). Tokyo, 1993.

Ueda Masaaki. *Yamato Takeru no Mikoto.* Tokyo, 1960.

Uegaki Setsuya, ed. *Fudoki. Shinpen Nihon koten bungaku zenshū,* vol. 5. Tokyo, 1997.

ISOMAE JUN'ICHI (2005)

YAMAZAKI ANSAI (1618–1682), Japanese Confucian and Shintō scholar of the early Tokugawa period. The son of a samurai who lost his position in the turbulence of the early Tokugawa period, Ansai was set at a young age on a career as a Zen priest. However, in his twenties he became acquainted with the anti-Buddhist writings of the Song Chinese Neo-Confucian scholar Zhu Xi. Inspired by them, he rejected Buddhism in favor of Confucianism, left the monastery, and devoted himself to the study and explication of the ideas of Zhu Xi. He attracted many disciples, drawn primarily from the samurai class, and developed close relations with a number of important political figures. He thus played a significant part in the spread of Confucian learning among the Tokugawa samurai class. Ansai was also deeply interested in the fusion of Confucianism and Shintō that had been developed by contemporary Shintō scholars such as Yoshikawa Koretaru. From Yoshikawa, Ansai received the Shintō religious name of Suika Reisha, and Ansai's own version of Confucian-flavored Shintō is known as Suika Shintō.

Insisting that, like Confucius, he sought only to transmit, not to create, Ansai wrote little of a systematic, interpretive nature. His preferred method was to compile selections of excerpts from the writings of Zhu Xi and to express his own views on Zhu Xi's teachings through lectures on these excerpts and a few chosen texts. Ansai's ideas were thus conveyed primarily in the form of lecture notes taken down by his disciples. As reflected in these notes, Ansai's lectures, delivered in a forceful, colloquial style, sought both to come to terms with the complexities of Zhu Xi's metaphysics and to deliver them to a relatively uneducated audience in a simple, direct fashion. This approach was undoubtedly an important factor behind the popularity and influence of his school.

Similarly, Ansai stressed mastery of a few basic texts rather than wide reading. Whereas other Tokugawa Confucian scholars, such as Hayashi Razan, emphasized the importance of erudition and thereby presented Confucian learning as the special province of the professional scholar, Ansai decried the pursuit of erudition as encouraging dilettantism and as counterproductive to the development of a firm sense of moral priorities. Confucian scholars of other schools criticized his position as narrow and rigid, but it did serve to offer a large audience entry into the forbidding body of Chinese Confucian literature.

Ansai insisted that his selection of the core teachings of Zhu Xi constituted the orthodox tradition. In fact, however, he modified Zhu Xi's ideas in several important ways. For instance, he gave added emphasis to the moral importance of the relation between lord and vassal, depicting the obligation of the vassal to the lord in absolute terms comparable to that between parent and child. The Ansai school position on this subject contributed to the growth of the idea, found widely in the late Tokugawa period, of the absolute, eternal nature of the obligation of loyalty to the imperial line.

Another area in which Ansai deviated significantly from Zhu Xi was in emphasizing the importance of "reverence" over "investigation of the principle of things" in the process of the individual's cultivation of his innate moral nature. The resulting stress on cleaving to the norms of Confucianism and on rigorous introspection to ensure that one's behavior conformed to those norms contributed to the characteristically stern and dogmatic tone of the Ansai school.

Ansai's linking of Confucianism and Shintō was another distinctive feature of his teachings. Unlike other Confucian scholars such as Hayashi Razan, who sought to equate Shintō and the Confucian way, Ansai presented them as two distinct manifestations of a universal truth, each particular to the country in which it originated. Ansai's joining of Shintō and Confucianism added a note of mystery and religious authority to Confucianism that furthered its acceptance in Tokugawa society, while his insistence on the particularly "Japanese" character of Shintō endowed his school with a nationalistic flavor that tended to increase with the passage of time. However, many of the connections Ansai made between Shintō and Confucianism were forced and far-fetched, and his leading disciples, although declaring themselves faithful to the essence of Ansai's teachings, broke with him over the question of the relationship between Confucianism and Shintō. This break led in later years to the division of the Ansai school into two major branches, one Confucian and one Shintō.

BIBLIOGRAPHY

An introduction in English to Yamazaki Ansai's major ideas can be found in Okada Takehiko's "Yamazaki Ansai," in *Principle and Practicality: Essays in Neo-Confucianism and Practical Learning,* edited by Wm. Theodore de Bary and Irene Bloom (New York, 1979). For an account of the ideological orientation of his school, see Herman Ooms, *Tokugawa Ideology: Early Constructions, 1570–1680* (Princeton, N. J., 1985). Bitō Masahide's *Nihon hōken shisōshi kenkyū* (Tokyo, 1961) presents an incisive treatment of Ansai's place in the development of Tokugawa thought and of the points where Ansai diverges from Zhu Xi.

KATE WILDMAN NAKAI (1987 AND 2005)

YĀMUNA (fl. c. 1022–1038), known in Tamil as Āḻavandār; Hindu philosopher, theologian, and devotional poet. Yāmuna lived in the Tamil-speaking area of South India and represented a learned family of brahmans who played a leading role in the formulation of the Śrī Vaiṣṇava tradition and of the Viśiṣṭādvaita school of Vedānta, which is most widely associated with the name of Rāmānuja. The Śrī Vaiṣṇavas made a major contribution to the development of Hindu religion by being the first Brahmanic movement to integrate fully into the classical Vedic tradition a popular, predominantly non-Brahmanic religious movement, the ecstatic devotion (*bhakti*) of the Tamil hymnists called the Āḻvārs. This synthesis of popular or vernacular elements with Vedic or Sanskritic ones provided a highly influential model for a number of later Hindu theistic sectarian movements.

Yāmuna is recognized as the fourth in the preceptorial line of *ācāryas*, or teachers, who provided the intellectual leadership of the Śrī Vaiṣṇava sect, and is the first for whom there are extant works. His incompletely preserved literary corpus thus provides the major beginning point for a study of the formulation of this important movement and its school of philosophical theology, Viśiṣṭādvaita Vedānta. Yāmuna's name is closely linked with that of his grandfather, Nāthamuni (c. tenth century), who is acknowledged as the first teacher in the Śrī Vaiṣṇava line. Nāthamuni, in addition to propounding a system of logic and epistemology (*nyāya*), was the head of a family of prestigious Bhāgavata brahmans devoted to Hare Krishna and is the one to whom tradition ascribes the canonization of the Tamil hymns of the Āḻvārs in the collection entitled the *Divyaprabandha.* While the evidence for this traditional ascription is inconclusive, Yāmuna's two devotional hymns to Visnu and Śrī, the *Stotraratna* and the *Catuśślokī,* reflect the influence of the Āḻvārs' ecstatic devotional style.

According to the tradition, Yāmuna's greatest contribution lay in attracting to the Śrī Vaiṣṇava sect Rāmānuja (eleventh to twelfth centuries), their sixth teacher and the classical exponent of Viśiṣṭadvāita. Although the two never met, it is clear from the literary evidence that Yāmuna was the seminal thinker who provided the primary inspiration for Rāmānuja's major Vedantic writings. The basic structure for Rāmānuja's commentary on the *Bhagavadgīta* was provided by Yāmuna's versified summary, the *Gitarthasamgrahā;* and in his other works Rāmānuja regularly refers to and quotes from Yāmuna's major Vedantic philosophical writings, the *Siddhitraya,* a triad of critical works *(Ātmasiddhi, Saṃvitsiddhi,* and *Īśvarasiddhi)* that are now only fragmentarily preserved, having been eclipsed by Rāmānuja's own definitive works.

Another of Yāmuna's major contributions as represented by his largest completely preserved work, the *Āgamaprāmāṇya,* was his defense of the Pañcarātra revelation or scriptures (Āgamas) as being equal to the Vedas in authority. These Pañcarātra Āgamas, also called Tantras or Saṃhitās, provide the scriptural basis for the earliest post-Vedic, Tantric tradition to arise during the first millennium CE. Yāmuna's defense of these temple-oriented ritual texts as compatible with the Vedas and Vedānta facilitated a radical enlargement and enrichment of the Hindu scriptural base, as did the incorporation of the Tamil hymns of the Āḻvārs.

SEE ALSO Āḻvārs; Rāmānuja; Śrī Vaiṣṇavas; Tamil Religions; Vaiṣṇavism, articles on Bhāgavatas, Pāñcarātras.

BIBLIOGRAPHY

Works by Yāmuna

Gitarthasamgraha. Edited with an English translation by J. A. B. van Buitenen in his *Ramanuja on the Bhagavadgita,* pp. 177–182. Delhi, 1968.

Siddhitraya. Edited, translated, and annotated by R. Ramanujachari and K. Srinivasacharya. Annamalainagar, 1943. Reissued with a new introduction by Ramanujachari as *Sri Yamunacharya's Siddhi Traya* (Madras, 1972). Contains Yāmuna's three major but fragmentarily preserved Vedantic works: *Atmasiddhi* (pp. 1–151), *Isvarasiddhi* (pp. 153–174), and *Samvitsiddhi* (pp. 175–213), "The Definitive Determinations of the Self, of the Lord, and of Consciousness."

Yāmuna's Agama Pramanyam, or, Treatise on the Validity of Pañcaratra. Sanskrit text with English translation by J. A. B. van Buitenen. Madras, 1971.

Works about Yāmuna

The most complete survey of Yāmuna's extant literary corpus, written from a traditional perspective, is M. Narasimhachary's *Contribution of Yamuna to Visistadvaita* (1971; 2d ed., Hyerabad, 1998). The most comprehensive critical work is Walter G. Neevel, Jr.'s *Yāmuna's Vedānta and Pāñcarātra: Integrating the Classical and the Popular* (Missoula, Mont., 1977). A critical study of Yāmuna's theory of consciousness is Roque Mesquita's *Yāmunācāryas Philosophie der Erkenntnis: eine Studie zu seiner Saṃvitsiddhi* (Vienna, 1990).

WALTER G. NEEVEL, JR. (1987 AND 2005)

YANTRA.

YANTRA. Geometrical diagrams known as *yantras* form a very special class of religious symbols in Hinduism. Their forms and functions within the tradition vary according to their uses. The most important ones are those that serve as supports for daily ritual worship and as meditational aids to stimulate inner visualizations; others are employed in astrology and temple rites; some are meant for proficiency in occult arts, and many of these are used as talismans.

Meditational *yantras* are an indispensable constituent of Tantric worship and are a substitute for the deity's iconographic image. Basically, a *yantra* used in this context is an abstract icon of some personification or aspect of the deity. Most Indian divinities have been assigned aniconic symbols in their specific *yantras*. Whereas an anthropomorphic image is a static presentation, the *yantra* is a dynamic symbol of the totality of the cosmos. Hence it is represented as an expanding form emanating from the central nucleus, a dimensionless point, the *bindu*. A linear configuration, the *yantra* usually has around its center several concentric primal shapes, such as triangles, hexagons, circles, octagons, and rings of lotus petals. The figure's periphery is a square enclosure with four sacred doors opening toward the four cardinal directions. The centrifugal *yantras* are conceived of as a sacred dwelling in which the presiding deity and its retinue take up residence. The seat of the principal deity is in the center, while those of its emanations, or *parivāra devatās,* are arranged concentrically in successive circuits known as *āvaraṇas* ("veils"), so called because they conceal the luminous splendor of the deity in the center.

At the subtlest level, *yantras* translate into visual terms the theory of cosmogenesis. They are to be read as dynamic graphs of the creative process of cosmic evolution and involution that takes place from the center and moves outward. The creative process is represented by the unity of the male and female principles, which, descending into the world of multiplicity, are symbolized by the concentric geometric circuits. The best example of this type of *yantra* is the Śrīcakra of the cult of the goddess Tripurasundarī. It is composed by the interlacing of two sets of triangles: Four apexes point upward, representing Śiva, the male principle, and five apexes point downward, representing sakti, the female principle. The Śrīcakra is devised to give a vision of the totality of existence, so that the adept may internalize its symbols for the ultimate awareness of his own unity with the cosmos. Every meditational *yantra* is in essence a psychic improvisation in which the closed concentric circuits of various geometric shapes, from the periphery to the center, correspond to the planes of the adept's consciousness.

Architectural *yantras* contribute substantially to the conceptual basis of the Hindu temple. An early example is the Vāstupurusa Maṇḍala, of which Hindu manuals of architecture provide thirty-two variations. The *maṇḍala* represents the diagram of the ordered cosmos. In Tantric temple rites, *yantras* were laid into the foundation of the womb chamber and were also embedded in cult figures installed in the shrine. *Yantras* were also used as compositional diagrams in the execution of sculptural images adorning the walls of the temple. The architectural *yantra* functions as an ideogram, while the temple is a materialization of the concepts it embodies.

Occult *yantras* are distinguished from all other *yantras* by their practical applications. They serve as powerful diagrams of magical potency, used mainly in preventive medicine, as good luck charms, for exorcism, to ward off calamities, and so forth. The occult figures are not stereotyped; their designs vary according to the object of worship. One of the most popular is the Dhāraṇa Yantra; worn as an amulet for protection, this *yantra* is given to a person after the priest has consecrated it in a life-giving ceremony. Another kind that serves the same purpose is the magical square. The proven efficacy of such *yantras* is explained in psychological terms. To the individual who wears a *yantra* as a talisman or an amulet, the diagram manifests itself as a repository of power through which the presence of the divinity can be invoked at will. Ultimately, the efficacy of the *yantra* is brought about by the adept's own willpower, working through faith.

Yantras are most commonly drawn on paper or engraved on metals or rock crystals, although any flat surface, such as a floor or wall, can be used. The *yantras* are always used in conjunction with mantras, or mystical sound-units, that correspond to the deity's subtle form. Mantras are employed to energize the latent force inherent in the deity's *yantra.* Indeed, it is said that a *yantra* without its seed mantra is as lifeless as a corpse.

See Also Maṇḍalas, article on Hindu Maṇḍalas; Mantra; Temple, article on Hindu Temples.

Bibliography

Sanskrit and Hindi Sources

Especially recommended for an overview of the theory and cultic significance of *yantras* are Rāmacandra Kaulācāra's *Śilpa Prakāśa,* translated by Alice Boner and S. R. Śarmā (Leiden, 1966); the *Yantra Saṁskārapaddhiti* (Moradabad, 1899); the *Yantracintāmaṇi,* with Hindi translation by B. P. Misra (Bombay, 1967); and the "Yantrasāra Tantram," in *Tantrasāra,* edited by R. Chattopadhyaya (Calcutta, 1922). See also Arthur Avalon's translation of Puṇyānanda's *Kāmakalāvilāsa,* 2d ed. (Madras, 1953), which includes a translation of Naṭanānanda's commentary, the *Cidvallī.*

Secondary Sources in English

Boner, Alice, and S. R. Sarma with R. P. Das, trans. and eds. *New Light on the Sun Temple of Koṇārka.* Varanasi, 1972.

Cammann, Schuyler. "Islamic and Indian Magic Squares." *History of Religion* 8 (February 1969): 275–286, (May 1969): 271–299.

Khanna, Madhu. *Yantra, the Tantric Symbol of Cosmic Unity.* London, 1979.

Kramrisch, Stella. *The Hindu Temple* (1946). 2 vols. Columbia, Mo., 1980.

New Sources

Bühnemann, Gudrun. *Mandalas and Yantras in the Hindu Traditions.* Leiden; Boston, 2003.

Bunce, Fredrick W. *The Yantras of Deities and Their Numerological Foundations: An Iconographic Consideration.* New Delhi, 2001.

Ramachandra Rao, Saligrama Krishna. *The Yantras: Text with 32 Plates.* Delhi, India, 1988.

Madhu Khanna (1987)
Revised Bibliography

YAO AND SHUN were legendary sage-rulers of antiquity in China. According to traditional Chinese historiography, Tang Yao (Yao of the Tang clan or state; personal name, Fang Xun) or Tang Dao ruled from 2356 to 2256 BCE. A ruler of great virtue, he considered his son Dan Zhu (or, in some versions, his ten sons) unworthy to rule the empire, and thus selected Shun to be his successor, having first given to him his two daughters in marriage. Yu Shun (personal name, Zhong Hua) served Yao first as a minister, then in Yao's old age as regent, finally succeeding him and ruling for fifty years. Shun in turn considered his son Shang Xun (or, in some versions, his nine sons) unworthy to rule and so he selected Yu as his successor. Yu became the founder of the Xia, traditionally considered to be the first hereditary dynasty in China.

In Zhou dynasty (eleventh to third century BCE) texts, history conventionally begins with the time of Yao. All the great cosmological events took place during his rule. The ten suns appeared, nine of which were shot down by the archer Yi; Buzhou Mountain, the pillar of the northwest, was brought down by Gonggong; and the great flood occurred, which was eventually controlled by Yu. During the Warring States period (403–221 BCE), however, other rulers, some of whom were originally the mythical ancestors of other houses, began to be placed before Yao, and in the *Shi ji,* the universal history compiled by Sima Qian during the second century BCE, Yao and Shun are but the most recent of five emperors.

Yao abdicated to Shun because of Shun's virtue. An exemplar of filial piety since the Zhou period, Shun often appears on temple frescoes, usually following a plow drawn by an elephant. His filial piety is exemplary because his wicked father, Gu Sou ("blind man"), and his younger brother Xiang ("elephant") both tried to murder him. They first tried to kill him by removing the ladder and setting fire to a granary while he was repairing its roof; then they filled in a well that he had been sent to dredge. The earliest version of this story is in the *Mengzi.* In the more elaborate Han dynasty version found in *Lienu zhuan* (Biographies of exemplary women), Yao's daughters advised Shun how to escape his father's evil schemes. Shun continued to serve his father as a son should and without resentment; according to the *Mengzi,* his father was in the end pleased.

Although Shun is a symbol of filial piety, in accepting the succession to Yao and in marrying Yao's two daughters, he both went against his father's will and displaced Yao's son from the succession. His role therefore is paradoxical, and his story exemplifies the conflict between the principles of rule by virtue and rule by hereditary right that is a common theme in the succession legends recorded in Zhou dynasty texts. Motifs in the story of Shun's succession, such as the ruler's perception of his successor's virtue in spite of his lowly position and his willingness to rely on a man of low birth, also occur in the legends that surround the foundation of the hereditary dynasties.

Elements in the stories of Yao and Shun in early texts suggest still earlier legends concerning clan origins. The earliest record of the story of Yao and Shun is found in the "Yao dian" chapter of the *Shang shu,* a Zhou dynasty text. In this text, Yao is called *di* (lord), a title that suggests Shangdi, the high lord of the Shang dynasty (c. sixteenth to eleventh century BCE) who is later equated with Tian (Heaven). The succession story of Yao to Shun may contain the remnants of an earlier cosmogonic myth in which the Lord on High first gave the rule to Shun, the progenitor of the Shang people. Shun has been identified with Di ku (who gave birth to the first Shang ancestor, Xie, by means of the egg of a black bird) and with Zhun, the husband of Xihe (who gave birth to the ten suns) and possibly the highest ancestor claimed by the Shang kings in their oracle-bone inscriptions. Shun is also closely associated with the Eastern Yi tribe. His two wives are sometimes identified with the goddesses of the Xiang River in the "Nine Songs" of the *Zhuzi.*

The philosophers of the Warring States period recounted the story of Shun's succession to Yao with differing emphasis and attitudes concerning the role of the sage and the right to hereditary succession. Recently discovered philosophical texts written on bamboo slips and buried in tombs around the end of the fourth century BCE include several accounts of Shun's accession to Yao with many details not found in the traditional texts. These suggest that the idea that a virtuous ruler should appoint a sage rather than an heir as his successor was an important philosophical position in this period.

SEE ALSO Chinese Religion, article on Mythic Themes; Kingship, article on Kingship in East Asia.

BIBLIOGRAPHY

Allan, Sarah. *The Heir and the Sage: Dynastic Legend in Early China.* San Francisco, 1981. A discussion of the Warring States legend and its meaning in philosophical texts.

Allan, Sarah. *The Shape of the Turtle: Myth, Art, and Cosmos in Early China.* Albany, N.Y., 1991. Includes the hypothesis that the legend of Yao and Shun was based upon an earlier cosmogonic myth.

SARAH ALLAN (1987 AND 2005)

YATES, FRANCES AMELIA was born on November 29, 1899, in Southsea, Hampshire, and died in Surbiton, Surrey, on September 29, 1981. By the time a brief illness ended a long life of intense and single-minded scholarly endeavor, her reputation had reached almost cult status.

Yates was the fourth and youngest child of James Alfred Yates and Hannah Eliza Malpas. Her father, having entered Portsmouth Naval Dockyard as an apprentice, had risen to chief constructor of the British navy. One of her elder sisters was a schoolteacher and novelist, the other an art-student-turned-missionary. On the death in action of her only brother in 1915, the ambitions of a close-knit family came to center on her. Hopes of following her brother to Oxford having been disappointed, partly because of interruptions to early formal schooling, she took a London first-class degree in French by correspondence, following it with a graduate thesis on French religious drama of the sixteenth century. She never married.

Yates would often later pay tribute to the material and intellectual support of her family and its tradition of what she called "effort." Observantly Anglican, liberal in their opinions, interested in ideas, devoted to Shakespeare, and sympathetic to matters French, they left their mark on her strongly individual mind and personality. They enabled her to begin the life of a modestly circumstanced private scholar; from a newly purchased family house in Claygate, in the countryside outside London, where she lived uninterruptedly from 1925 until almost the day of her death, she would go to read in the British Museum Library and the Public Record Office. The hallmark of her work was always firsthand acquaintance with her sources.

On those sources was based her first book: the prize-winning and still standard *John Florio: The Life of an Italian in Shakespeare's England* (1934). Here, as throughout her work, the religious dimension—the Florios were Protestant refugees—is a major concern. *A Study of Love's Labour's Lost* (1936), her second book, explored Shakespeare's ideas about language. Less successful, it led her in 1937 to the Warburg Institute, then newly escaped to England from Nazi Germany, which became her intellectual second home. She began to use its excellent library and to learn from Fritz Saxl, Gertrud Bing, Edgar Wind, and Rudolf Wittkower how to apply an encyclopedic historical approach to the study of Giordano Bruno, which had led her there in the first place. When, in 1941, she was given a part-time place on the staff, it was virtually her first paid employment; she remained part of the institute until she died, bequeathing to it her residual estate to found research fellowships.

The new approach she learned there, combined with her innate intellectual courage, is already clear in her independent line on Giordano Bruno's religious and philosophical position in essays she wrote in 1937–38; it was consolidated in "Queen Elizabeth as Astraea" (1945), a ground-breaking inquiry into the messianic ideas behind the cult of the English ruler. The French Academies of the Sixteenth Century, which followed in 1947, was a remarkable, original, and wide-ranging investigation of how academic study had once been directed at promoting religious and civil harmony; it was also a demonstration of the historical significance of ideas and ideals judged worthless and ineffectual by progressist opinion. The power of heterodox thought, already a theme in her early work on Bruno, is again apparent in her pioneering essays of 1954 and 1959, for which she learned Catalan, on the universalist mystic Ramon Lull, whom she judged important for later philosophers, especially Bruno. *Giordano Bruno and the Hermetic Tradition,* published in 1964 when she was in her mid-sixties, is—along with *The Art of Memory* of 1966—the book for which she is best known. In each she argued at length for the importance of Hermeticism as the secret heart of Renaissance Neoplatonism, especially invoking Giulio Camillo Delminio in relation to the Renaissance transformation of artificial memory systems. Her opening for Anglophone scholars of Renaissance occult belief, studied historically and not from the believer"s point of view, as a legitimate subject for investigators of Renaissance thought in general has had a profound effect, not least in arousing the opposition of historians of science.

In the background of everything that Frances Yates wrote was a vision: peace and harmony denied by faction and fanaticism. *The Valois Tapestries* (1959) was a study of the politico-religious context and purpose of these great works of art; she republished it in 1975, at the same time as a collection of related essays, *Astraea: The Imperial Theme in the Sixteenth Century. Shakespeare's Last Plays: A New Approach* of the same year was the closest she came to the definitive work on the mind of Shakespeare she had always hoped to write. In her *Theatre of the World* (1969), the grand theme is hardly apparent; this book was rather aimed at showing influence from the Vitruvian tradition on the structure of Elizabethan public theaters. The magus figure of John Dee is, however, seen as important for the transmission of these ideas. In the politico-religious context of the age of James I and the Winter Queen of Bohemia, which is the subject of *The Rosicrucian Enlightenment* (1972), Dee plays an expanded role, which is further enlarged in Yates's final book, *The Occult Philosophy in the Elizabethan Age* (1979).

Frances Yates, it has been said, created her own discipline. She was widely honored for it by invitations, honorary degrees, and international prizes from universities, academies, and other bodies in Britain, Europe, and the United States, and by her appointments as OBE (Officer of the Order of the British Empire) in 1972 and DBE (Dame Commander of the Order of the British Empire) in 1977; her writings have been translated into many languages. Despite a certain personal diffidence, she was undeterred by opposition, retaining a conviction that her approach was both right and fruitful.

BIBLIOGRAPHY

Frances Yates's writings are listed in her posthumously published *Ideas and Ideals in the North European Renaissance,* volume 3 of her *Collected Essays* (London, 1984, pp. 325–336); her books and articles have been many times reprinted in English and in translation. The most important are:

John Florio: The Life of an Italian in Shakespeare's England. Cambridge, England, 1934.

"Queen Elizabeth as Astraea." *Journal of the Warburg & Courtauld Institutes* 10 (1947): 27–82; reprinted with other essays in *Astraea: The Imperial Theme in the Sixteenth Century.* London, 1975.

"The French Academies of the Sixteenth Century." In *Studies of the Warburg Institute* 15. London, 1947; reprinted London and New York, 1988.

"The Art of Ramon Lull." *Journal of the Warburg & Courtauld Institutes* 17 (1954): 115–173; reprinted with other essays in Collected Essays, vol. 1. London, 1982.

"The Valois Tapestries." In *Studies of the Warburg Institute* 22. London, 1959; reprinted London, 1975.

Giordano Bruno and the Hermetic Tradition. London and Chicago, 1964.

The Art of Memory. London and Boston, 1966.

Theatre of the World. London and Chicago, 1969.

The Rosicrucian Enlightenment. London and Boston, 1972.

Shakespeare's Last Plays: A New Approach. London and Boulder, Colo., 1975 (published in Boulder as *Majesty and Magic in Shakespeare's Last Plays*).

The Occult Philosophy in Elizabethan England. London, 1979.

Collected Essays, 3 vols. *Lull and Bruno.* London, 1982. *Renaissance and Reform: The Italian Contribution.* London, 1983. *Ideas and Ideals in the North European Renaissance.* London, 1984.

"Biography and Assessment: 'Autobiographical Fragments,'" in *Collected Essays,* vol. 3 (1984), pp. 272–301; J. B. Trapp, "Frances Amelia Yates 1899–1981," Proceedings of the British Academy, 120, in *Biographical Memoirs of Fellows,* vol. 2 (2003), pp. 527–554; Robert S. Westman and J. E. McGuire, *Hermeticisn and the Scientific Revolution: Papers Read at a Clark Library Seminar March 9, 1974* (Los Angeles, 1977); Hilary Gatti, "Frances Yates's Hermetic Renaissance in the Documents Held in the Warburg Institute Archive," *Aries,* n.s., 2 (2002), pp. 193–210; Hilary Gatti, "The Notes on Camillo and Hermes Trismegistus in the Yates Archive at the Warburg Institute in London," *Annali della Scuola Normale Superiore di Pisa: Classe di lettere e filosofia,* Serie IV, 6, no. 1, 2001 (2004), pp. 171–194.

J. B. TRAPP (2005)

YAZATAS. The term *yazata* occurs in the Avesta, the collection of sacred books of Zoroastrianism, as an attribute or designation of divine beings. From this term is derived the Middle Persian *yazd* ("god"; pl., *yazdān*). The word appears frequently in the Avesta, although not in the five *Gāthās* ("songs") attributed to Zarathushtra (Zoroaster); in Gathic it appears only in the *Yasna Haptanhāiti* (Yasna of the Seven Chapters), ascribed to Ahura Mazdā. Its meaning in this text is "worthy of worship, worthy of sacrifice" (from the verb *yaz,* "to venerate, sacrifice"), identical to that of its Vedic counterpart, *yajata.* This is the general meaning of the term, which is used to refer to divine beings, usually secondary gods, personifications, or cult gods of the pre-Zoroastrian Indo-European pantheon that had been absorbed into the religion. Thus, as Zoroastrianism reached a compromise with ancient polytheism, *yazata* came to designate a deity who was readmitted to the cult. At the beginning of the hymn dedicated to Vayu (*Yashts* 15), for example, the god is called *yazata* in a sentence that is evidently meant to justify the integration of the hymn within the canonical list of the *Yashts*, a section of the Avesta.

In the Zoroastrianism that evolved following the prophet's reforms, some of the ancient *daivas*—the word is used here in its most general and archaic sense, to mean "gods"—became or were reinstated as *yazatas*. That is, they were transformed from beings whose worship was forbidden (*daivas* in the later sense of "demons") back into beings whose worship was permitted or even recommended. The *Yashts* is very instructive in this regard: many passages in various hymns provide justification for the readmission to the cult of one or another *daiva*, and often it is Ahura Mazdā himself who is said to approve such a reintegration.

The meaning of *yazdān* in Pahlavi texts (from the ninth and tenth centuries CE) is derived from this general meaning of *yazata*. It is used for various categories of divine beings: for the gods in general, for the ancient *yazatas* in particular, and for the Amesha Spentas (MPers., Amahraspandan). The *yazdans* rule over the months, the days, and five liturgical periods of the day.

But in the Avesta *yazata* has a precise meaning: any entity to whom a hymn is dedicated. Besides Ahura Mazdā and Vayu, *yazata* refers, as has been noted (Kellens, 1976), to the following beings: Mithra, Sraosha ("discipline"), Arshtāt ("justice"), Nairyōsanha ("of manly utterance"), Verethraghna ("victory"), Ātar ("fire"), Apąm Napāt ("son of the waters"), Zam ("earth"), and Gairi Ushidarena ("mountain dawn-abode"). But in the so-called Younger Avesta it is, above all, the deities who form the escort of Mithra who are defined as *yazatas*. From this it follows that not all the beings to whom a hymn in the Avesta is dedicated are in a strict sense *yazatas* and that *yazata* is not the Avestan equivalent of the Old Persian *baga*; the latter has no specific meaning but only carries the general sense of "god," as does the parallel Avestan *bagha*.

SEE ALSO Amesha Spentas; Daivas.

BIBLIOGRAPHY

Boyce, Mary. *A History of Zoroastrianism*. 2 vols. Leiden, 1975–1982.

Kellens, Jean. "Trois réflexions sur la religion des Achémé-nides." *Studien zur Indologie und Iranistik* 2 (1976): 113–132.

Kellens, Jean. *Le panthéon de l'Avesta ancien*. Wiesbaden, 1994.

Lommel, Herman. *Die Religion Zarathustras nach dem Awesta dargestellt*. Tübingen, 1930.

Narten, Johanna. *Die Aməṣ̌a Spəṇtas im Awesta*. Wiesbaden, 1982.

Nyberg, H. S. *Irans forntida religioner*. Stockholm, 1937. Translated as *Die Religionen des alten Iran* (1938; 2d ed., Osnabrück, 1966).

Widengren, Geo. *Die Religionen Irans*. Stuttgart, 1965. Translated as *Les religions de l'Iran* (Paris, 1968).

GHERARDO GNOLI (1987)
Translated from Italian by Roger DeGaris

YEHOSHUʿA BEN ḤANANYAH (first and second centuries CE), Palestinian tanna who taught in Jerusalem and later at Yavneh and Peqiʿin. Legend has it that when he was a child his mother carried him to the study hall so that he would become accustomed to hearing words of the Torah (J.T., *Yev.* 3a). Because he was a Levite, it is assumed that he sang in the Temple before it was destroyed. He is said to have made his living as a needlemaker or blacksmith.

Yehoshuʿa achieved prominence as a leading rabbinic authority of his day. He was one of the five prominent disciples of Yoḥanan ben Zakkʾai (*Avot* 2.8). With Eliʿezer ben Hyrcanus, Yehoshuʿa is alleged to have carried Yoḥanan ben Zakkʾai out of Jerusalem in a coffin in 68 CE during the siege of the city by the Romans (B.T., *Git.* 56a). During Yehoshuʿa's later career he was the center of contention within rabbinical circles. Several sources recount how he was humiliated by the *nasi*ʾ Gamliʾel (B.T., *R. ha-Sh.* 25a). Yehoshuʿa's dispute with Gamliʾel over whether the evening prayer was compulsory or voluntary brought about the events that led to the deposition of Gamliʾel and the ascension of Elʿazar ben ʿAzaryah to the office of *nasi*ʾ (B.T., *Ber.* 28a).

Yehoshuʿa was involved in many legal disputes with Eliʿezer ben Hyrcanus; one celebrated argument concerned the ritual cleanness of the ovens of ʿAkhnʾai (a kind of tiled oven). Yehoshuʿa ruled that the ovens were ritually unclean; Eliʿezer said that the ovens could not become ritually unclean (B.T., *B.M.* 59a–b). Eliʿezer announced that a heavenly voice had declared his own position correct. Yehoshuʿa responded with the famous declaration: "It [the Torah] is not in heaven" (a quotation from *Dt.* 30:12)—that is, the rabbis alone have the authority to decide matters of law, not a supernatural voice or even a direct revelation.

An important teaching attributed to Yehoshuʿa shows a positive attitude toward outsiders: He declared that pious Gentiles will be able to enter heaven (Tosefta, *San.* 13.2). According to tradition, he engaged in many discourses with political figures and various groups, including the Roman emperor Hadrian, the elders of Athens, and the Jews of Alexandria.

Recent scholarship has questioned the legitimacy of attempts at reconstructing the lives of Yehoshuʿa and his fellow rabbis from the scattered traditions in rabbinic literature. No systematic analysis has been made of Yehoshuʿa's philosophical or religious beliefs.

SEE ALSO Tannaim.

BIBLIOGRAPHY

Joshua Podro's *The Last Pharisee: The Life and Times of Rabbi Joshua Ben Hananyah* (London, 1959) is an early attempt at Yehoshu'a's biography. William S. Green's *The Traditions of Joshua ben Hananiah* (Leiden, 1981) represents a hypercritical approach to rabbinic sources concerning this master, following some of the methods used in Jacob Neusner's *Eliezer ben Hyrcanus: The Tradition and the Man* (Leiden, 1973).

New Sources

Flensberg, Hayim Yirmeyahu ben Avraham. *Sefer Nezer hanitsahon: al vikuah Rabi Yehoshu'a ben Hananyah im save de-ve Atuna.* Lakewood, NJ, 2001.

TZVEE ZAHAVY (1987)
Revised Bibliography

YEHOSHU'A BEN LEVI,

YEHOSHU'A BEN LEVI, Palestinian amora of the early third century. A native of Lydda (modern-day Lod), Yehoshu'a reflects the interests and traditions of Judaea at a time when rabbinic activity was becoming increasingly concentrated farther north in Galilee.

Yehoshu'a's son married into the patriarchal house (B.T., *Qid.* 33b), a fact that may explain the notorious incident in which Yehoshu'a arranged for a wanted Jewish nationalist to be handed over to the Romans (J.T., *Ter.* 8.10, 46b). In general, he was an active representative of Jewish interests before the Roman authorities, both in the regional capital at Caesarea (J.T., *Ber.* 5.1, 9a) and, apparently, even in Rome (*Gn. Rab.* 33.1, 78.5). On the other hand, by ordaining his own disciples (J.T., *Ned.* 10.8, 42b), Yehoshu'a contributed to one of the important developments in Palestine in the third and fourth centuries—the weakened prestige of the patriarchate among the rabbis of the Land of Israel.

Yehoshu'a's main distinction was as a master of *aggadah* (nonlegal rabbinic thought), a rubric of learning that he associated with the "honor" promised in *Proverbs* 21:21 (B.T., *B.B.* 9b). He was a fervent advocate of Torah study (B.T., *Mak.* 10a, *Meg.* 27a, *'Eruv.* 54a). His descriptions of the fates of the righteous and the wicked after death (B.T., *'Eruv.* 19a) and his reported conversations with the Angel of Death and with the prophet Elijah (B.T., *Ber.* 51a, *Ket.* 77b; J.T., *Ter.* 8.10, 46b) made him a favorite subject of later legend. It was to him that Elijah allegedly made his famous remark that the Messiah might come any day—any day, that is, that Israel was ready to listen to God's commands (B.T., *San.* 98a).

Although Yehoshu'a was technically not a tanna, he lived close enough to the tannaitic period, and his teachings were honored enough, that one of his sayings was added to the closing paragraph of the Mishnah (*Uqts.* 3.12) and another was included in the supplementary chapter added to the Mishnaic tractate *Avot* (known as *Ethics of the Fathers,* 6.2).

SEE ALSO Amoraim.

BIBLIOGRAPHY

Fraenkel, Yonah. "Demuto shel R. Yehoshu'a ben Levi besippurei ha-Talmud ha-Bavli." In *Proceedings of the Sixth World Congress of Jewish Studies,* vol. 3, pp. 403–417. Jerusalem, 1977.

Hyman, Aaron. *Toledot tanna'im ve-amora'im.* 1910. Reprint, Jerusalem, 1964.

Safrai, Samuel. "Ha-qehillah ha-qedoshah be-Yerushalayim." *Zion* 22 (1957): 183–191.

New Sources

Rozenfeld, Ben Tsiyon. *Lod and Its Sages in the Period of the Mishnah and the Talmud* (in Hebrew). Jerusalem, 1997.

ROBERT GOLDENBERG (1987)
Revised Bibliography

YEHUDAH BAR IL'AI (second century CE), Palestinian tanna. Born in Usha, in the lower Galilee, he was a student of 'Aqiva' and Ṭarfon and was ordained as rabbi by Yehudah ben Bava' during the Hadrianic persecutions in the aftermath of the Bar Kokhba Revolt.

Numerous traditions attributed to Yehudah are preserved in rabbinic literature where he is usually referred to without patronymic. Along with Me'ir, Shim'on, and Yose, he is one of the most frequently quoted authorities of his generation. His importance is reflected in the tradition that tells us that his contemporaries were called "members of Yehudah bar Il'ai's generation" (B.T., *San.* 20a). Yehudah is also one of the most important transmitters of rabbinic teachings from the Sanhedrin at Yavneh before the Bar Kokhba Revolt to the Sanhedrin at Usha afterward. He cites numerous legal rulings in the names of 'Aqiva', Ṭarfon, and other masters of the period of rabbinic activity at Yavneh.

To date, no systematic analysis has been made of Yehudah's traditions, probably because of the sheer size of the corpus of sayings attributed to him. There are, for example, some 180 disputes recorded between Yehudah and Neḥemyah, yet these represent only a fraction of the entire collection ascribed to Yehudah. Jacob Epstein (1957) believes that the corpus of his traditions was one of the primary documents used in the redaction of the Mishnah by his student Yehuda ha-Nasi'. Several of his rulings deal with the standardization of rabbinic liturgy (*Ber.* 4.1), the regulation of prayer (*Ber.* 4.7; Tosefta, *Ber.* 1.9; Tosefta, *Ber.* 3.5), and the regulation of daily liturgical blessings (Tosefta, *Ber.* 6.18). Other rules ascribed to Yehudah emphasize the importance of concentration and intention during the performance of rituals (Tosefta, *Ber.* 2.2) and the importance of maintaining the proper frame of mind during recitation of prayers (*Ber.* 2.2). Yehudah is also associated with legislation concerning the recitation of blessings over foods (*Ber.* 6.4; Tosefta, *Ber.* 4.4–5) and with blessings over natural wonders, both those for which one is permitted to recite blessings (*Ber.* 9.2) and those for which one is forbidden to recite blessings because it would appear to be a form of idolatry (Tosefta,

Ber. 6.6). Yehudah's legal, exegetical, and theological sayings range across the whole spectrum of rabbinic thought and life.

SEE ALSO Tannaim.

BIBLIOGRAPHY

Jacob N. Epstein's *Mavo' la-sifrut ha-tanna'im* (Jerusalem, 1957) discusses the role of Yehudah's materials in the development of the Mishnah. In *Rabbi Yehudah bar Ilai: Collected Sayings* (in Hebrew) (Jerusalem, 1965), Israel Konovitz collects all the references to Yehudah in rabbinic literature. My own *Studies in Jewish Prayer* (1990) analyzes some of the major contributions of Yehudah to the development of early Jewish prayer.

New Sources

Silverberg, David. "Rabbi Akiva's Students: What Went Wrong?" *Alei Etzion* 9 (2000): 67–85.

TZVEE ZAHAVY (1987)
Revised Bibliography

YEHUDAH BAR YEḤEZQE'L

YEHUDAH BAR YEḤEZQE'L (c. 220–c. 299), a leading second-generation Babylonian amora, based in Pumbedita. He studied chiefly with Rav and then Shemu'el. Although remaining subservient to the exilarch (B.T., *Qid.* 70a–70b), the leader of the Jewish community appointed by the Persian authorities, Yehudah was empowered by him to apply rabbinic law in the marketplace and in civil and other matters that fell under his jurisdiction, especially through the enforcement of documents (B.T., *Mo'ed Q.* 4b, *Yev.* 39b).

As a teacher of rabbinic tradition, Yehudah cited the Mishnah to draw out its subtle legal points and to emend or explain it to make it fit the physical and social conditions of Babylonian Jewry or extra-Mishnaic tannaitic traditions (Epstein, 1964). In interpreting and rewording the comments of Rav and Shemu'el, Yehudah played a crucial role in preserving and employing their teachings (Bokser, 1980, esp. pp. 399–406, 414–415).

Yehudah was accorded high status due to his communal role, expertise in tracing people's genealogy, and devotion to Torah study (see, e.g., B.T., *Mo'ed Q.* 16b–17a, *Ḥag.* 15b). People believed that he was able to communicate with the dead, intercede for rain, and give insightful advice on health and other practical matters (B.T., *Ber.* 20a and parallels, *'A. Z.* 28b–29a). He lectured in the *pirqa'*, a popular instructional gathering for both aggadic and halakhic subjects aimed at the general public but to which disciples were also expected to attend (B.T., *Shab.* 148a).

Notably, Yehudah speculated on the creation (B.T., *Shab.* 77b), handed down teachings on sacred objects such as the *mezuzah* and fringes *(tsitsit)* (B.T. *Men.* 35b, 39b, 41a), and proposed additional blessing formulas for the wedding ceremony (B.T., *Ket.* 7b–8a) and other situations. He reportedly concentrated on *neziqin* (Torts)—the area in which he had received actual authority from the exilarch. Stating that the laws of *neziqin* had to be carried out to obtain saintliness (B.T., *B.Q.* 30a), Yehudah asserted that equity in one's daily life was a criterion of one's faith. This rootedness in the practical realm and concern that people relate to the society in which they live may be further reflected in his teachings that discouraged his disciples from emigrating from Babylonia to Palestine (B.T., *Ber. 24b; B.T., Ket.* 110b–111a); he believed they should not hold their personal religious goals over the needs of the community in the here and now, in the Diaspora.

SEE ALSO Amoraim.

BIBLIOGRAPHY

A comprehensive treatment and bibliography of Yehudah bar Yehezqe'l and his teachings can be found in Jacob Neusner's *A History of the Jews in Babylonia,* 5 vols. (Leiden, 1966–1970), esp. vol. 3. Note in particular Jacob N. Epstein's *Mavo' le-nusaḥ ha-Mishnah,* 2 vols. (1948; reprint, Jerusalem, 1964), pp. 318–343. See also David M. Goodblatt's *Rabbinic Instruction in Sasanian Babylonia* (Leiden, 1975) and my *Post Mishnaic Judaism in Transition* (Chico, Calif., 1980).

New Sources

Goodblatt, David. "Local Traditions in the Babylonian Talmud." *HUCA* 48 (1977): 187–217.

BARUCH M. BOKSER (1987)
Revised Bibliography

YEHUDAH HA-LEVI

YEHUDAH HA-LEVI (c. 1075–1141), Jewish poet, theologian, and physician. Born in either Tudela or Toledo, Spain, to a wealthy and cultured family, Yehudah ben Shemu'el ha-Levi was well educated. He studied the Bible, rabbinic literature, Arabic poetry, philosophy, and medicine. During his early travels in southern Spain he won acclaim for his poetic talent and was warmly received by many prominent Jewish families. However, in the wake of the Almoravid invasions of the area to halt the Christian *reconquista,* his enjoyment of courtly life was cut short. Eventually he settled in Christian-held Toledo, supporting himself as a physician and continuing to write. But he viewed with growing alarm the disruption of Jewish life throughout Andalusia. Sometime after 1125, in response to the queries of a Karaite thinker, ha-Levi began to draft a defense of Judaism, which developed into his most famous work, the *Kuzari.* In the summer of 1140, various personal, political, and religious considerations prompted him to depart for Palestine. Legend claims that he was killed within sight of Jerusalem, although recent studies suggest that he died *en route,* in Egypt.

Ha-Levi's poetry is generally regarded as the finest Hebrew verse written in the Middle Ages. Besides addressing all the traditional secular and religious themes of his day, he also developed, in his poems of Zion, an entirely new genre expressing both his own and his people's longing for renewal in their ancestral home. This longing was intensified by the upheavals and persecution suffered by Jews on both sides of the Mediterranean following the Almoravid invasion of Andalusia and the First Crusade. As ha-Levi observes,

> Between the hosts of Seʿir [Christians] and Qedar [Muslims], My host is utterly lost. . . . When they wage their wars, we fall with their fall.

Dismayed by the upheavals within Spanish Jewish life and sensing its eventual dissolution, ha-Levi began to question the value of some of its main cultural pursuits, especially philosophic speculation about religion:

> Let not the wisdom of the Greeks beguile you Which has no fruit, but only flowers. . . . Why should I seek out crooked ways And forsake the mother of paths?

While philosophy could produce a tantalizing array of opinions, it could not satisfy the spiritual hunger of men seeking concrete guidance for their actions. This required a return to the wellsprings of traditional Jewish piety, since one could approach God only by following "the mother of paths," the Torah.

> I have sought Your nearness. With all my heart have I called You; And going out to meet You I found You coming toward me.

Still, for ha-Levi, the path of return and religious renewal inevitably led to the Land of Israel as the chief site of past revelations and as the focus of God's promised redemption:

> Have we either in the East or the West A place of hope wherein we may trust, Except the land that is full of gates Toward which the gates of Heaven are open?

Ha-Levi's only theological work, the *Kuzari* (Book of the Khazars, or Book of refutation and in defense of the despised faith), develops these and other themes in a five-part dialogue, mainly between a pagan Khazar king who is converted to Judaism and the Jewish sage who instructs him. The king's conversion was factual, but ha-Levi created this dialogue with him to answer contemporary criticism of Judaism by representatives of philosophy, Christianity, Islam, and Karaism. The philosopher is clearly the most formidable spokesman of those who leave it to human reason to determine how best to serve God. The fact that a pagan king must evaluate their competing claims aids ha-Levi in giving all the participants, and notably Judaism, a fair hearing. It also underscores, inasmuch as a king is preeminently a man of action, the importance of practice over theory.

The story opens as the king repeatedly dreams that an angel is telling him that his intention is pleasing to God but his mode of worship is not. Convinced that this vision is genuine, he invites first an Aristotelian philosopher and then scholars of Christianity and Islam to instruct him.

The philosopher, expressing views reflecting the influence of Ibn Sīnā and Ibn Bājjah, denies the presuppositions of the king's dream. God as a perfect and changeless First Cause has neither likes nor dislikes, he says, or even knowledge of the king's mutable behavior, for all these would imply deficiency and imperfection in God. Still, a human may perfect him or herself and even achieve prophecy by studying the eternal system of necessary causes that emanate from God, thus attaining union with the Active Intellect, the source of all human knowledge. Since the principal requirement for achieving that union is the purification of one's soul, it does not matter from a purely rational standpoint which religious regimen one follows.

The king finds the philosopher's argument plausible, but says it does not provide what he seeks. Nor does he find that philosophers are able to prophesy. Consequently, he turns to the Christian and Muslim scholars. Their expositions directly address his concern, but they do not provide adequate evidence for their respective claims. Still, because both scholars agree that their beliefs are based on God's well-attested revelation to Israel, the king finally consults a Jewish scholar.

The rabbi declares his faith in the God of Abraham, Isaac, and Jacob, who led the Israelites out of Egypt, miraculously sustained them, and gave them his law in the Torah of Moses. Subsequent discussion of these claims eventually convinces the king of their truth because they are supported by what he regards as compelling grounds: public, empirical, direct, and miraculous evidence. Over 600,000 initially skeptical Israelites saw and heard God personally reveal his commandments at Mount Sinai and transmitted a unanimous, reliable report of that occasion to subsequent generations.

The king regards the rabbi's account as superior not only to that of the other scholars but also to that of the philosopher. The philosopher infers the existence and nature of God from some aspect of the world's order, but such speculation is tenuous and uncertain, and it evokes no reverence for its object. By contrast, there is nothing tenuous or uncertain about the veracity of a collective experience of God, transmitted by a reliable, uninterrupted tradition.

The rabbi goes on to depict those few who are able to prophesy as quite literally belonging to the divine realm. Relying heavily on conceptions current in Shiism, he argues that in relation to the traditional hierarchy of inorganic matter, plants, animals, and human beings, this elect group *(ṣafwah)* constitutes an essentially separate order, manifesting extraordinary faculties and behavior. Because they are by nature conjoined with "the divine thing" *(al-amr al-ilāhī)*—ha-Levi's multivalent term for diverse aspects of divine immanence—they alone can communicate God's will to ordinary persons, whereas human speculation and cosmic powers, like the Active Intellect, cannot. Tradition identifies Adam as the first to possess this prophetic faculty or inner eye. From him it passed to the biblical heroes until it reached the children of Israel. Prophecy flourished among them because, like choice fruit, it was cultivated in the ideal climate of the Land of Israel, through use of the Hebrew language and adherence to the regimen of God's own laws. With exile and the neglect of many commandments, prophecy ceased, yet it will reappear once the original conditions are restored.

After converting, the king learns more about these matters and also that Israel remains a living focus of divine providence in the world, despite its exile and degradation. While other nations and religions imitate its religious institutions, they are "dead" by comparison; they rise and fall according to chance and natural causes, being subject neither to miraculous deliverances nor to catastrophic defeats. Israel, however, like a seed cast upon the ground, is governed by a secret, providential wisdom, whereby it transforms its surroundings and will eventually produce a unified humanity obedient to God's will.

The pious human personifies this obedience with a faith that is natural and wholehearted, neither the product of speculation nor vulnerable to it. Ruling one's self and one's inclinations, the individual is uniquely suited to rule the city, for like Plato's philosopher-king he or she gives everything its due by exercising rational choice. The behavior of the pious human thus conforms to the rational, political laws (such as decrees of justice) that are preambles to the divine traditional laws (such as ritual rules), preceding them in nature and in time. The former constitute the indispensable prerequisite for the existence of any group, even a den of robbers. But the divine laws are more important than the rational laws, because they specify the application of the latter and also bring people to communion with God and to happiness in ways that reason cannot explain.

In their knowledge of God, both the pious and the prophets apprehend all that the philosophers do and more. They, too, recognize God generically as Elohim, the governing cause of the universe from whom the natural forms of all things emanate in regular ways, indifferent to the needs and merits of human beings. But they also experience God individually as YHVH (Adonai), who reveals himself to those suitably prepared and who overrides natural causes on their behalf at predetermined times. Only as YHVH does God evoke love and service, for in communion with him humans find their greatest happiness, and in separation from him, their greatest misery.

The rabbi's final exposition and critique of philosophy attempts to show the king that he need not be persuaded by many of its key claims, since they are untenable. Earlier he had suggested that the philosopher seeks wisdom only because he lacks a reliable tradition embracing wisdom, while Israel has received divine wisdom in a Torah that contradicts nothing truly demonstrated by philosophy. Apparently influenced by al-Ghazālī's *Incoherence of the Philosophers,* he now suggests that what has been so demonstrated is confined largely to mathematics and logic. In physics, he argues, the philosophers' account of the four elements is empirically unsubstantiated. In psychology, their theory of the Active Intellect entails numerous absurdities, and in metaphysics, their views on divine causation are riddled with inconsistency. The most we can know regarding metaphysics is that only God governs material things by determining their natural forms. Since philosophy offers little wisdom about matters of such importance, a turn toward the divine wisdom embodied in Israel's ancestral tradition is called for. But, as the rabbi recognizes, a wholehearted turn toward the ancestral tradition can be completed only by a return to the ancestral land. Accordingly, as the dialogue closes, he follows the logic of his position and departs for the Holy Land.

Ha-Levi was the first medieval Jewish thinker to appreciate fully the challenge posed to Judaism by Aristotelian rationalism and to address it in a philosophically literate way. Speaking as a religious empiricist and working from the sources of Judaism, he produced what has become a classic theological defense of Judaism as a suprarational religion of revealed practice.

BIBLIOGRAPHY

The definitive edition of the original Judeo-Arabic text of ha-Levi's *Kuzari* is the *Kitāb al-radd wa-al-dalīl fī al-dīn al-dhalīl,* edited by David H. Baneth and prepared for publication by Haggai Ben-Shammai (Jerusalem, 1977). Hartwig Hirschfeld's *The Kuzari (Khitab al-Khazari): An Argument for the Faith of Israel* (1905; reprint, New York, 1964) is a complete but largely outdated English translation of his own earlier edition of this work. An abridged but far more adequate translation of Hirschfeld's edition, accompanied by a brief but useful commentary, has been provided by Isaak Heinemann in *Three Jewish Philosophers,* edited by Hans Lewy et al. (New York, 1960). Heinemann's translations of ha-Levi's poetry have served as the basis for some of the translations offered by me in this article.

The groundbreaking studies of ha-Levi's religious philosophy by Harry A. Wolfson, collected in volume 2 of *Studies in the History of Philosophy and Religion,* edited by Isadore Twersky and George H. Williams (Cambridge, Mass., 1977), remain valuable, as does Leo Strauss's classic analysis of ha-Levi as an esoteric writer in "The Law of Reason in the *Kuzari,*" in Strauss's *Persecution and the Art of Writing* (1952; reprint, Westport, Conn., 1973), pp. 95–141. The best recent study of the literary structure of the *Kuzari* is Eliezer Schweid's Hebrew article "Ummanut ha-di'alog bi-sefer 'ha-*Kuzari*' u-mashma 'utah ha-'iyyunit," in *Ṭa'am ve-haqashah* (Jerusalem, 1970). Aryeh L. Motzkin's "On Halevi's Kuzari as a Platonic Dialogue," *Interpretation* 9 (August 1980): 111–124, is a valuable study of ha-Levi's philosophical aims in employing the dialogue form. Two works focusing on ha-Levi's use of Arabic sources in connection with various issues in the *Kuzari* are Herbert A. Davidson's "The Active Intellect in the Cuzari and Hallevi's Theory of Causality," *Revue des études juives* 131 (June–December 1972): 351–396, and Shlomo Pines's "Shiite Terms and Conceptions in Judah Halevi's Kuzari," *Jerusalem Studies in Arabic and Islam* 2 (1980). A valuable resource for the study of ha-Levi's religious poetry is Matitiahu Tsevat's "An Index to the Religious Poetry of Judah Halevi," *Studies in Bibliography and Booklore* 13 (1980).

New Sources

Brann, Ross. "Judah Halevi, the Compunctious Poet." *Prooftexts* 7 (1987): 123–143.

Galli, Barbara Ellen. *Franz Rosenzweig and Jehuda Halevi: Translating, Translations, and Translators.* With a foreword by Paul Mendes-Flohr. Montreal, 1995.

Newmyer, Stephen T. "Climate and Zion in the 'Kuzari.'" *Koroth* 10 (1993–1994): 9–18.

Scheindlin, Raymond P. "Contrasting Religious Experience in the Liturgical Poems of Ibn Gabirol and Judah Halevi." *Prooftexts* 13 (1993): 141–162.

Silman, Yochanan. *Philosopher and Prophet: Judah Halevi, the Kuzari, and the Evolution of His Thought.* Translated by Lenn J. Schramm. Albany, N.Y., 1995.

BARRY S. KOGAN (1987)
Revised Bibliography

YEHUDAH HA-NASI' (135?–220?), called "Rabbi" or "Our Holy Rabbi," was a Palestinian tanna. Yehudah was the son of Shim'on ben Gamli'el of Yavneh. With Yehudah the office of *nasi'* (patriarch, head of the court) reached its zenith. Reestablished by the Romans after the disastrous defeat of the Bar Kokhba Revolt in 135 CE, the position of *nasi'* by the end of the century afforded Yehudah an authority recognized by Jews and Romans alike. Even the Jewish community in Babylonia looked to him as the head of the Jewish people.

As *nasi'* Yehudah first established his court in Beit Shearim. However, for reasons of health he spent the last seventeen years of his life in Sepphoris (J.T., *Ket.* 12.3, 35a). Yehudah's major task as *nasi'* was to secure the economic recovery of Israel after the destruction caused by the Bar Kokhba Revolt. He and his court exempted several places from tithes (J.T., *Dem.* 2.1, 22c–d), enacted laws that allowed Jews to regain ownership of land confiscated by the Romans during the Bar Kokhba Revolt (B.T., *Git.* 58b), eased the laws of the sabbatical years to increase the food supply in Israel (J.T., *Ta'an.* 3.1, 66c), took over the important task of proclaiming the new month and intercalating the year (J.T., *San.* 1.2, 18c), and introduced regulations that eased taking testimony and dispatching messengers to declare the court's decision concerning the new months (J.T., *R. ha-Sh.* 2.1, 58a). His support of the rabbinic class found expression in his exempting the sages from some taxes (B.T., *B. B.* 8a).

The significance of Yehudah's tenure as *nasi'* is seen in the many stories that depict his close relationship with the Roman emperor (B.T., *'A. Z.* 10a–b, *San.* 9 1a–b; J.T., *Meg.* 1.11, 72b; J.T., *San.* 10.5, 29c; *Gn. Rab.* 11.4, 67.6, 75.7, 84.3). For example, the following is in *Berakhot* 57b of the Babylonian Talmud: "And YHVH said to her, 'Two nations are in your womb' [*Gn.* 25:23]. Do not read nations *[goyim]*, but 'lords' *[ge'im]*, and Rav Yehudah [third-century amora] said in the name of Rav: 'These are [Marcus Aurelius] Antoninus and Rabbi, whose table never lacked either radish, lettuce or cucumbers either in summer or winter.'" These many stories are meant to equate Yehudah (Rabbi) with the leader of the most powerful political force of his time. Whether or not the conversations reported in these texts actually occurred is open to question. However, the point they make is clear: Our patriarch is as powerful and important as their emperor.

At the same time that the sages picture Yehudah as an outstanding political leader, they also describe him as an exceptionally learned rabbi. One proverb stated that "from the days of Moses until the days of Rabbi we did not find both Torah and Greatness in one place" (B.T., *Git.* 59a). It is recorded that Yehudah wandered from academy to academy so he might learn from all five of 'Aqiva' ben Yosef's major students as well as from the other leading sages of his time (B. T., *'Eruv.* 53a, *Yoma'* 79b, *Yev.* 84a, *Shab.* 147b, *Meg.* 20a).

In addition Yehudah ha-Nasi' exhibited the qualities of the "ideal sage." Shi'mon ben Menasya' said, "All of the seven characteristics which the sages attributed to the righteous—comeliness, strength, riches, wisdom, old age, honor, and children—all of them were established in Rabbi and his sons" (*Avot* 6.9). Although Yehudah was so wealthy that his house steward was said to be richer than the Persian ruler Shāpūr I (r. 241–272 CE; B.T., *B. M.* 85a), his generosity was also well known. He invited the sages to his table, and during years of need he opened his private storehouses to the hungry (B.T., *'Eruv.* 73a, *B. B.* 8a). When a person strayed from the correct path, Yehudah was there to guide him or her gently back to God (B.T., *B. M.* 85a). He showed kindness and compassion to all of God's creatures, even to the insects (*Gn. Rab.* 33.3). He was willing to learn from all, and he never treated his contemporaries with disrespect or contempt; he often accepted their teachings when those differed from his own (B.T., *Ket.* 93a). One proverb stated that "when Rabbi died humility and fear of sin ceased" (B.T., *Sot.* 49b). He was noted for his support of the Hebrew language (in place of the vernacular Aramaic). It was claimed that he spoke only Hebrew in his house and that the sages came to him seeking explanations of Hebrew words and phrases (B.T., *B.Q.* 82b, *R. ha-Sh.* 26b; J.T., *Shevi'it* 9.1 38c).

No other political leader so captured the minds and imaginations of the ancient rabbis. Upon Yehudah's death the sages decreed a fast and offered prayers of supplication, and a voice from heaven proclaimed that "whoever has been present at Rabbi's death is destined to enjoy life in the world to come" (B.T., *Ket.* 103b–104a). His burial place in Beit Shearim was visited by generations of Jewish pilgrims.

Among the tannaim and the amoraim, only Yehudah is pictured as combining the learning of a rabbinic sage who mastered the oral Torah with the skill of a seasoned politician who was an equal to the emperor of Rome. Other sages interacted with Roman and Sassanian leaders, while other rabbis were noted for their areas of knowledge. But Yehudah alone among the rabbis is praised equally for his knowledge and piety and for his political skills. His uniqueness is attested by his often being cited merely as Rabbi, the only sage who is cited merely by title without a reference to his name. Similarly he is the only patriarch known as Ha-Nasi, the Patriarch, par excellence. The tradition presents a unique rabbi whose knowledge of the rabbinic tradition and whose political skills permitted him to bring together the rabbinic and nonrabbinic classes of society and to rebuild the Palestinian Jewish community after the devastating defeat of Bar Kokhba. Even though he could be intimidating and arrogant (B.T. *Ket.* 103b, *Yeb.* 9a, J.T. *Naz.* IX:57d), these traits are played down by the tradition.

During Yehudah's tenure as *nasi'*, the foundation document of postbiblical rabbinic Judaism, the Mishnah, was created. This collection of primarily legal statements formed the basis of both the Babylonian and the Jerusalem (Palestinian) Talmuds, repositories of Jewish law and lore from the first six centuries of the common era organized as commentaries on the Mishnah. The appearance of the Mishnah also marked a crucial stage in the process of the development of Judaism from a temple-oriented cult to a Torah-oriented culture of study and exposition.

Generations of scholars have maintained that Yehudah was the sole editor of the Mishnah. Many have attempted to explain the processes by which he created this document from sources composed by Hillel the Elder, ʿAqivaʾ ben Yosef, and Meʾir. Basing their theory largely on the letter of Sheriraʾ Gaon (tenth century CE), these scholars have argued that Yehudah merely did what others before him had done—he faithfully preserved and transmitted what he had received from his teachers. Although nothing was written down before Yehudah, the earlier oral traditions were part of a memorized corpus that was carefully preserved and that included the names of those who had written opinions or of the majority. Yehudah organized this material into a unified text according to comprehensive principles.

Jacob Neusner, in *Judaism: The Evidence of the Mishnah* (1981), concluded, on the basis of detailed literary analyses, that the Mishnah is not the work of one person. However, there is no doubt that the Mishnah's reputation was enhanced by its completion at Yehudah's court and that its importance in the history and development of Judaism stems from the central place Yehudah and his colleagues occupied in the minds and imaginations of subsequent generations of Jews.

SEE ALSO Judaism, overview article; Mishnah and Tosefta; Rabbinic Judaism in Late Antiquity; Tannaim.

BIBLIOGRAPHY

For traditional views of Yehudah, see Aaron Hyman, *Toldoht Tanaʿim ve-Amoraʿim,* vol. 2 (London, 1910; reprint, Jerusalem, 1964), pp. 575–606; Hyman, "Judah Ha-Nasi," in *Encyclopaedia Judaica,* vol. 10 (Jerusalem, 1971), cols. 366–371; and Mordechai Margalioth, ed., *Encyclopedia of Talmudic and Geonic Literature,* vol. 1 (Jerusalem, 1945; Tel Aviv, 1995), pp. 436–446. On Yehudah as patriarch, see Michael Avi-Yonah's *The Jews of Palestine* (New York, 1976) and E. Mary Smallwood's *The Jews under Roman Rule* (Leiden, Netherlands, 1976). On the Mishnah, see Jacob Neusner's *Judaism: The Evidence of the Mishnah* (Chicago, 1981). On the problem of rabbinic biography, see William Scott Green's "What's in a Name? The Problematic of Rabbinic 'Biography,'" in his *Approaches to Ancient Judaism,* vol. 1 (Missoula, Mont., 1978), pp. 77–96.

GARY G. PORTON (1987 AND 2005)

YE SHES MTSHO RGYAL (YESHE TSOGYAL)

YE SHES MTSHO RGYAL (YESHE TSOGYAL) (777–873) is a leading female figure and role model for Tibetan Buddhists. She is especially important for the Rnyingma (Nyingma) school of Tibetan Buddhism as a key figure in myth, dreams, iconography, and meditative practice. But she is also significant for Tibetans more generally, especially for her role in the stories of the establishment of Tibetan Buddhism in the eighth century CE.

Yeshe Tsogyal is said to have been one of the queens of the pivotal Tri Songde Tsan (eighth century), the king who brought Indian masters of Buddhism to Tibet and who built the first monastic community at Bsam yas (Samye). There are no contemporary inscriptions that mention her, and so there is some question about whether she is really a historical figure. But she appears at a relatively early point—by at least the twelfth century—in the mythologized accounts of the conversion of Tibet to a Buddhist country, and references to her clan title Mkhar chen Bza' (Karchen Za) also make her historicity credible. It is certainly possible that there was such a queen who became involved in Buddhist meditative practices, even if her story was elaborated greatly as the narrative of Tibet's conversion developed.

The earliest known reference to her life appears in a one-page notice in a history by the Treasure-discoverer Nyangrel Nyima Özer (1136–1204). A full-length presentation of her life from the fourteenth century has recently been identified, but she is best known for the version by Tagsham Nuden Dorje (b. 1655), a visionary of the seventeenth century. This work has been translated into English twice. In this story her early rejection of suitors and her desire to practice Buddhism are recounted, placing her story squarely within the norms of standard Buddhist hagiography, albeit with a number of twists specific to women's situations. Yeshe Tsogyal's plight is noticed by King Tri Songde Tsan, who takes her as one of his queens, but he soon offers her in turn to the Indian Tantric master Padmasambhava, whom the king had invited to Tibet to teach Tantric Buddhism. Padmasambhava and Yeshe Tsogyal become a Tantric couple and Padmasambhava transmits to her the full range of Tantric teachings. Early lineage stories of one of those teachings, on the Indic deity Vajrakā, lists Yeshe Tsogyal as a primary lineage holder.

Yeshe Tsogyal then proceeds alone to a mountain hermitage to practice what she has learned. She practices austerities and endures extreme hardship, reaching key stages of realization. At a certain point she is advised through visionary means to take a Tantric consort of her own. In a rare twist from the usual androcentric rendition of this stage on the path, Yeshe Tsogyal sets out to procure a partner, who turns out to be an attractive but indigent man in Nepal, and she brings him back to the caves of Tibet to teach him the requisite techniques of sexual yoga.

Yeshe Tsogyal's hagiography deals with several specifically female situations, one of which is found in its provocative account of her rape by seven bandits. During this ordeal she turns the situation into a teaching for the bandits and ultimately helps them on their own path to buddhahood. She also continues to serve as a premier disciple of the master Padmasambhava. An important element of her story is that she assists the master in recording and then concealing Treasure (*gter ma*) teachings for future generations of Buddhists in Tibet. After Padmasambhava's departure to the Pure Land, Yeshe Tsogyal remains as a teacher of many, and finally dies surrounded by a large number of disciples.

One more element of her life story in the Tagsham version is that she defeats in debate certain rival teachers from the Bon religion. This episode seems to be missing in earlier renditions of her life, but it connects her to larger conceptions about Tibet's past and its identity vis-à-vis Buddhism. Nonetheless, Yeshe Tsogyal was also adopted as a heroine for Tibetan followers of Bon, and another full-length version of her life was recently identified in the Bonpo canon of scriptures.

The appeal of Yeshe Tsogyal is undoubtedly tied primarily to her image as a female master of meditation and yoga. That she serves as a role model for Tibetan women involved in the lay yogic path can be seen from the fact that outstanding female religious leaders in Tibet have been regularly identified as her "emanation," up to the twenty-first century. But she is also a popular source of visionary revelation for both male and female meditators. Yeshe Tsogyal often appears in the dreams and visions of yogis of the Nyingma school, during which she gives indications of how to uncover a Treasure revelation of their own, along with other key teachings. In addition, practitioners of visualization meditation in the Nyingma tradition will often use her image as the object of their imagination in the Tantric rites known as *sādhana* meditation. One of the most popular cycles of meditation that contains instructions for visualization of Yeshe Tsogyal is the Heart Sphere Teachings (Klong chen Snying thig), revealed by Jigme Lingpa (1729–1798) in the eighteenth century. Tantric empowerment rites that focus on her image continue to be given to students in Tibet today, as well as in the exile communities of Tibetan Buddhists in South Asia.

SEE ALSO Padmasambhava; Treasure Tradition.

BIBLIOGRAPHY

Dowman, Keith. *Sky Dancer: The Secret Life and Songs of the Lady Yeshe Tsogyel.* London, 1984.

Gross, Rita M. "Yeshe Tsogyel: Enlightened Consort, Great Teacher, Female Role Model." *The Tibet Journal* 12, no. 4 (Winter 1987): 1–18.

Gyatso, Janet. *Apparitions of the Self: The Secret Autobiographies of a Tibetan Visionary.* Princeton, N.J., 1998.

Gyatso, Janet. "A Partial Genealogy of the Lifestory of Yeshe Tsogyal." *Journal of the International Association of Tibetan Studies* 2 (2004).

Nam-mkha'i snying-po. *Mother of Knowledge: The Enlightenment of Ye-shes mTsho-rgyal.* Translated by Tarthang Tulku. Berkeley, Calif., 1983.

Tsogyal, Yeshe. *Dakini Teachings: Padmasambhava's Oral Instructions to Lady Tsogyal.* Translated by Erik Pema Kunsang. Boston, 1990.

JANET GYATSO (2005)

YESHIVAH.

YESHIVAH. In contemporary usage, the Hebrew term *yeshivah* refers to an academy for the advanced study of Jewish religious texts, primarily the Talmud. Since the destruction of the Second Temple in 70 CE, the *yeshivah* has been one of the most important institutions of Jewish communal life. Although many *yeshivah* students go on to become rabbis and although the texts taught in *yeshivot* are among those a rabbi is expected to master, it should be emphasized that a *yeshivah,* an all-male institution, is not a rabbinical seminary. Its function is not to train professional religious leaders but rather to provide a framework for study. In the Jewish religious tradition, study of the Torah is seen as a central and meritorious religious act in and of itself, regardless of its relevance to the student's career plans. While *yeshivot* have been a common feature of Jewish communities, they have not been equally prevalent in every location and time. In various communities and at various times, aspiring scholars would study individually under the guidance of more advanced scholars and rabbis without taking part in a formal educational framework. The *batei midrash,* or communal study halls, that were common in many communities facilitated this practice. However, for much of Jewish history, advanced study rarely occurred outside the framework of the *yeshivot.*

The term *yeshivah* appears in tannaitic sources, where it refers to a rabbinical court *(beit din),* not to an institution of learning. The Jews of Palestine in the first and second centuries CE made no distinction between higher education and judicial activity, and they had no tradition of academic career training. Study of Jewish law *(halakhah)* was not seen as something that could or should be isolated from its practical applications.

Little is known of the precursors of the *yeshivot. Yeshivot* became central institutions in Palestine after the destruction of the Second Temple and in the absence of other central institutions. The academy founded by Yoḥanan ben Zakk'ai at Yavneh in 68 CE and its successors, first in Judaea and later in the Galilee, functioned, according to rabbinic tradition, as the continuation of the Sanhedrin (the legislative body that convened in the Temple) and as the training ground for future scholars and leaders.

***YESHIVOT* IN BABYLONIA.** After the death of Yehuda ha-Nasi', the patriarch of Judaea (c. 220 CE), the *yeshivot* of Babylonia began to grow in importance and soon became the most highly esteemed authorities in the Jewish world. For a period of eight hundred years, Babylonian *yeshivot* functioned not only as the central religious-legal institutions of Babylonian Jewry, alongside the lay authority of the exilarchate, but also as the final arbiters of halakhic questions for most of the Jewish communities of the world.

Amoraic period. At any given time during the Talmudic period, there were usually two leading *yeshivot* that often competed for honor and prestige. The first of these was the *yeshivah* of Nehardea, which flourished in the first half of the third century under the leadership of the Babylonian sage Shemu'el (d. 263?). Although the date of its foundation is unknown, it was already regarded in Shemu'el's time as a venerable institution and as an important center for the transmission of Babylonian Jewish traditions. In 219 Abba' bar Ayyvu (c. 155–247), known as Rav, a Babylonian who had spent many years in Palestine and was familiar with Palestinian traditions, settled in Nehardea. Shortly after, he moved to the town of Sura and opened a *yeshivah* there. Both Rav and Shemu'el had able successors, and even though the institutions they led sometimes changed location or were temporarily closed, they endured until perhaps the thirteenth century. The *yeshivah* of Nehardea moved to Pumbedita in the wake of the destruction of Nehardea in 259, and in the late ninth century it moved to Baghdad, followed soon after by the *yeshivah* of Sura.

The degree to which these Babylonian *yeshivot* (or *metivtot,* as they were known in Aramaic) can be classified as educational institutions is still a subject of debate. They certainly continued to function as courts, and the scholars who were clustered around them formed an equivalent to the Sanhedrin. It would appear, though, that from early on young students came to study with the eminent *ro'shei yeshivah* (masters of the *yeshivah*) and that the pedagogic function of the *yeshivah* was seen as important.

According to later sources (which may not be completely reliable), the *ro'shei yeshivot* in Babylonia were often appointed by the exilarch (*ro'sh ha-golah,* lit., "head of the exile"). The veteran scholars of the *yeshivah* sat at assigned seats in the study hall in a seating order based on age and scholarly reputation, wherein the more advanced sat in the front rows (this seating plan was also characteristic of non-Jewish academies in Babylonia). The contact between the *ro'sh yeshivah* and the students was often indirect. It was apparently a common practice for the *ro'sh yeshivah* to deliver his lecture in a soft voice and to have his words declaimed by an *amora'* (speaker) in a loud voice. Since many of the authoritative teachings of the Jewish tradition were transmitted orally, recourse was made to *tanna'im* (repeaters) who had committed them to memory.

Twice a year, in the spring and the fall, this pattern of study changed radically, with Jewish laymen flocking to the *yeshivot,* apparently by the thousands, for a month of popular and intensive study. These months were known as *yarḥei kallah* ("months of assembly").

Geonic period. From roughly 550 to 1050 CE, Babylonian *yeshivot* continued to flourish as centers of both education and legal decision making. Students came not only from Babylonia but from Egypt, North Africa, Spain, Italy, and elsewhere to study and to prepare themselves for leadership roles in their home communities. Legal questions (accompanied by donations) were sent from many Jewish communities in the Mediterranean basin, and the *responsa* were copied down for the guidance of later generations. The Geonim, as the heads of the *yeshivot* were called in the post-Talmudic period, wrote legal treatises and other works that were widely distributed. The widespread respect and authority that the Geonim enjoyed no doubt contributed to the acceptance of the Babylonian Talmud as the authoritative source of Jewish legal and aggadic thought. Their institutions were funded not only by donations but by tax revenues from certain Babylonian Jewish communities. Much less is known about the *yeshivot* in the Land of Israel in this period.

The general decline of the Abbasid empire, long centered in Baghdad, anti-Jewish persecutions in the tenth and eleventh centuries in Iraq, and the rise of new Jewish centers elsewhere led to the decline of the Babylonian *yeshivot* and a corresponding rise in the importance of *yeshivot* in other locations. However, none of these newer *yeshivot* achieved the centrality and influence that the *yeshivot* of Babylonia had enjoyed. According to Avraham ibn Daud's account in *Sefer ha-qabbalah* (The book of tradition; c. 1161), around the year 990 a ship bringing four scholars to a *kallah* month was captured by pirates. Three of the scholars were sold as slaves in various ports—one in Egypt, one in North Africa, and one in Spain (the fourth met an unknown fate)—where each became the leader of an important *yeshivah.* While the legend is not a reliable historical source, it does illustrate the continuity between later *yeshivot* and their Babylonian predecessors as well as the weakening of the ties between other Jewish communities and Babylonia.

***YESHIVOT* IN THE MEDIEVAL DIASPORA.** From the tenth century onward, *yeshivot* were to be found in most Jewish communities. In Spain, one of the first important *yeshivot* to develop was that of Cordova; others were located in Lucena, Toledo, Barcelona, and elsewhere. These *yeshivot* were often located in or near community structures such as synagogues. The curriculum of these *yeshivot* centered on the Babylonian Talmud and its legal application and at times included qabbalistic literature. The well-known interest of some Spanish Jews in secular subjects found no expression in the *yeshivot;* their study of languages and sciences was usually carried out with the help of tutors or, occasionally, through enrollment in a non-Jewish school. The size and importance of a *yeshivah* was directly related to the fame and prestige of its head, the *ro'sh yeshivah.* Most of the central rabbinical figures of Spanish Jewish history, including Nahmanides (Mosheh ben Naḥman, c. 1190–1270), Shalomoh ben Avraham Adret (c. 1235–1310), and Nissim Gerondi (d. 1380?), headed *yeshivot.* The notes taken by students were passed from hand to hand and formed the basis for many of the Spanish glosses on the Talmud.

In North Africa, *yeshivot* were often located close to Muslim academies, though the question of intellectual relations between Jewish and Muslim schools has yet to be explored. The first important *yeshivah* in North Africa was that of Kairouan, which had close ties with Babylonian *yeshivot.* The *yeshivah* of Kairouan rose to importance in the tenth century and upon its decline in the following century, the *yeshivot* of Fez and Tlemcen in Morocco became prominent. Fusṭāṭ, near present-day Cairo, was also the site of an important *yeshivah.*

In the Ashkenazic communities of northern Europe, the great intellectual flowering that produced Gershom ben Yehudah (c. 965–1028), Rashi (Shelomoh ben Yitsḥaq, 1040–1105), and the Tosafists was achieved to a large extent within the *yeshivot.* These *yeshivot* differed from their predecessors in that they were chiefly educational institutions and no longer functioned as courts or as facilities for scholarly assembly. They tended to be small institutions with just a few tens of students who often lived with the *ro'sh yeshivah* and studied in a separate room in his house. Many of these students were Talmudic scholars in their own right, and they were not so much disciples of the *ro'sh yeshivah* as his partners in study. Beginners would prepare for admission to the *yeshivah* by studying with special teachers. The course of study in the *yeshivot* centered on Talmud and led to the conferment of formal degrees. The lowest, corresponding roughly to the bachelor of arts degree granted by universities of the time, was that of *ḥaver* ("fellow"), while more advanced students looked forward to receiving the title *morenu* ("our teacher"), which entitled them to open their own *yeshivot.* As in the medieval universities, the curriculum emphasized discussion and disputation rather than literary creativity; this phenomenon is reflected in the Jewish scholarly literature of the period, which was mainly in the form of commentaries and glosses and not extended expository works. Like their counterparts in the universities, *yeshivah* students were highly mobile and often studied in many schools in the course of their academic careers.

Both in Mediterranean countries and in northern Europe, *yeshivot* stressed creative study for their advanced students rather than rote learning. Often students were required to resolve logical problems and contradictions in a text, or between authoritative texts, in a manner that led to a deeper understanding of the issues. In a very real sense, this kind of intellectual development was an organic continuation of earlier patterns. The members of the medieval *yeshivah* related to the Talmud in very much the same way as the tannaim (the rabbis whose teachings are collected in the Mishnah) related to the Hebrew Bible and as the amoraim (the rabbis whose teachings are collected in the *gemara'*) related to the Mishnah.

There was a significant flow of ideas between the *yeshivot* of various areas. Rashi, who lived in northern France, was accepted in Spain and North Africa as the authoritative commentator on the Talmud, and the work of his successors in northern Europe, the Tosafists, was eventually carried on in Spain. This tradition concentrated on reconciling texts and statements scattered through the rabbinic literature so that it would form a harmonious whole.

One of the distinctive characteristics of the curriculum of the late medieval Ashkenazic *yeshivah* (thirteenth to seventeenth century) was the development of *pilpul,* a type of argumentation that uses highly contorted, often hair-splitting reasoning to resolve hypothetical cases or to reconcile opposing views. Most *pilpul* took place in oral debates, and few texts from the period survive. Many scholars found *pilpul* a fascinating intellectual stimulus, but others criticized it for its artificiality. *Pilpul* was eventually abandoned in favor of the more logical approach of the Spanish scholars, whose works were widely disseminated in northern Europe after the development of the printing press. Another activity popular in *yeshivah* circles of the time was the collection and study of *minhagim,* or local customs.

YESHIVOT IN THE MODERN WORLD. The continuity of the Ashkenazic *yeshivah* was broken in the seventeenth and eighteenth centuries in two different ways. In German-speaking lands, there was a gradual decline of interest in Talmudic and rabbinic literature, exacerbated by the Haskalah (Jewish Enlightenment movement) and the increasing assimilation of Jews into the general community. In Polish lands there was a sharper break that was associated with (but not totally explained by) the Cossack rebellion of 1648, which destroyed many communities and their *yeshivot.* The failure of the Polish Jewish community to reestablish the network of *yeshivot* immediately after the rebellion was due, in part, to the economic decline of the Jewish community and perhaps also to the spread of Hasidism, which encouraged the study of Talmud but placed less emphasis on formal education.

The nineteenth century saw important growth in the number and role of European *yeshivot.* In central Europe a key part was played by Mosheh Sofer (1762–1839), the rabbi of Pressburg, Hungary (now Bratislava, Slovakia). He was appointed to the position in 1806, and as his fame grew he became a major force in developing an active Orthodoxy in reaction to the Reform movement, which was gaining adherents in his native Germany and Hungary. One of the elements of his program was the development and expansion of the Pressburg *yeshivah,* whose student body soon numbered several hundred. Sofer's students went on to occupy many of the important rabbinical posts in the Habsburg Empire. The *yeshivot* they founded were a great influence on the lives of students who studied there during their formative adolescent years and were a major factor in the stability and cohesiveness of Hungarian Orthodoxy. In Germany, however, no major *yeshivot* developed. The rapid pace of acculturation, the need for a general education for economic advancement, and the lack of prestige for Talmudic knowledge among wide sectors of the Jewish community were largely responsible for this.

The revival of *yeshivot* of eastern Europe began in the early nineteenth century with the foundation in 1803 of a *yeshivah* in Volozhin, White Russia, by Ḥayyim ben Yitsḥaq (1749–1821). It differed from earlier Ashkenazic *yeshivot* in that it was neither a private institution nor a communal one, but rather a regional institution supported by donations collected by fundraisers from Jews throughout Lithuania and later even farther afield. As such, the *yeshivah* of Volozhin was free from local pressures. This organizational model was not immediately imitated, and most Talmud students continued to study in *batei midrash* (local study halls). In the latter part of the nineteenth century there was a sharp rise in the number of *yeshivot* that were founded to counteract the appeal of secular education and Haskalah. Important *yeshivot* were founded in Telz, Slobodka, Ponevezh, Slutsk, Novorodok, and elsewhere. Many were founded to advance the aims of the Musar movement, founded by Yisraʾel Salanter (1810–1883), which called for the study and practice of ethical behavior. These *yeshivot* appointed special preceptors *(mashgiḥim)* to teach and supervise ethical behavior; they functioned alongside the standard Talmud teachers, not always without friction. Other *yeshivot* emphasized new methods of study that stressed analysis of texts rather than legal casuistry. At the same time, and because of the same stimulus of competition from secular education and nontraditional influences, the Hasidic communities also began to establish *yeshivot*.

In the period between the world wars, all *yeshivot* in areas controlled by the Soviet Union were closed. However, in Poland, Lithuania, Hungary, and Czechoslovakia, *yeshivot* continued to flourish. These *yeshivot* were funded largely by subventions from Jews in the United States. The Holocaust led to the destruction of all of these institutions.

Today the two main centers of *yeshivot* are Israel and the United States. Until after World War II, *yeshivot* in the United States were relatively unsuccessful in attracting students and had little influence on Jewish life. Most of the Jews who came to America from eastern Europe in the late nineteenth and early twentieth century were not well educated, and the conditions of immigrant life in America were not conducive to the perpetuation of traditional customs. Those *yeshivot* that did exist followed the established patterns of the Old World. One important exception was the Rabbi Isaac Elhanan Theological Seminary, which grew into Yeshiva University. This institution, founded in the late nineteenth century in New York City, successfully introduced a new curriculum that included traditional Talmudic studies in the morning and secular studies, leading to the bachelor of arts degree, in the afternoon. After World War II there was a major increase in the number of American *yeshivot* and in the size of their student populations, as well as an improvement in the quality of instruction. These changes were due in part to the arrival of refugees from eastern Europe, who brought with them a strong commitment to tradition and expertise in Talumdic learning, and in part to the emergence of a native-born and self-confident American Jewish Orthodox community.

A similar pattern is found in the Land of Israel. In the early modern period, Sefardic Jews and Jewish communities in North Africa and Asia continued their traditional practice of financially supporting *yeshivot*, many of which were in the Land of Israel. They tended to be academies of established scholars rather than educational institutions in the Ashkenazic mold. These *yeshivot*, with their mature student bodies, often emphasized the study of Qabbalah or of Jewish law, not Talmudic study exclusively. The scholars who constituted the membership of the *yeshivot* were given stipends. When the Ashkenazic immigration to the Land of Israel began in the late eighteenth century, Ashkenazic *yeshivot* began to appear. They were intended for younger students, and the program of study was devoted almost completely to Talmud.

As the Jewish community in Palestine grew, there was a corresponding growth in the number of *yeshivot*. In the interwar period there was even a case of a *yeshivah* that was transferred *in toto*—student body and staff—from Slobodka in Lithuania to Hebron in Palestine. After the establishment of the State of Israel in 1948 this growth continued, now with the financial support of the Israeli government. As in America, the *yeshivah* high schools drew many of the sons of observant families. The special security problems of Israel led to the establishment of *yeshivot* for soldiers, who were permitted to interrupt their military service for periods of Talmud study.

Today almost all *yeshivah* students are unmarried. Another institution, the *kolel* (pl., *kolelim*), provides married students with stipends to enable them to study full-time. Unlike *yeshivah* students, they usually study independently, without formal guidance or supervision. The *yeshivot*, with the *kolelim*, are now among the most important institutions of contemporary Orthodoxy. They play a major role in securing the loyalty of the younger generation to traditional patterns and values. It has become standard practice for groups within the Orthodox community to establish separate *yeshivot* for their youth. Now, for example, every Hasidic sect has its own *yeshivah*. *Roʾshei yeshivah* are among the most important leaders of Orthodox Jewry, and they often supplant the authority of communal rabbis.

There are probably more young men studying Torah (and especially the Talmud) full-time today than ever before. Only a small minority go on to serve as rabbis. While in traditional *yeshivot* the student body continues to be all male, similar institutions of study for women have been developed. Recently, the term *yeshivah* has often been applied to Jewish day schools, on both the elementary and high school level, that have a program that includes general studies as well as

Jewish studies. But the Orthodox *yeshivot* have managed to adapt to new conditions without compromising their basic commitment to the perpetuation of tradition.

SEE ALSO Amoraim; Hasidism, overview article; Holocaust, The, article on History; Judaism, overview article, articles on Judaism in the Middle East and North Africa to 1492, Judaism in Northern and Eastern Europe to 1500; Musar Movement; Rabbinate; Rabbinic Judaism in Late Antiquity; Schenirer, Sarah; Shemu'el the Amora; Tosafot.

BIBLIOGRAPHY

Relatively few works have been written that deal specifically with *yeshivot.* However, almost anything written on the history of Jewish education touches on *yeshivot,* and so do many studies of Jewish history or religion. The best starting point for bibliographies on particular *yeshivot* or on higher education in a given community or area is Shlomo Shunami's *Bibliography of Jewish Bibliographies,* 2d ed. (Jerusalem, 1965; suppl., Jerusalem, 1976), which directs the reader to bibliographies on almost any topic of Judaica. The most useful guides to current literature are *Kiryat Sefer,* a quarterly listing of recent books of Judaica and Hebraica, and the annual *Index of Articles on Jewish Studies.* Both are arranged topically and are published by the Jewish National and University Library in Jerusalem.

There are a number of valuable monographs on *yeshivot.* The most recent book on the Babylonian *yeshivot* is David M. Goodblatt's *Rabbinic Instruction in Sasanian Babylonia* (Leiden, 1975). For the other end of the time spectrum, William B. Helmreich's *The World of the Yeshiva* (New York, 1982) provides a useful description of modern American *yeshivot.* A number of unpublished Ph.D. dissertations are relevant: Armin Harry Friedman's "Major Aspects of Yeshiva Education in Hungary, 1848–1948" (Yeshiva University, 1971), M. Breuer's "The Ashkenazi Yeshiva toward the Close of the Middle Ages" (Hebrew University, 1967), I. Gafni's "The Babylonian Yeshiva" (Hebrew University, 1978), and my own "Three Lithuanian Yeshivot" (Hebrew University, 1982); the latter three are in Hebrew with detailed English summaries. The most valuable collection of primary sources on the history of Jewish education, which includes a great deal of material on *yeshivot,* is Simha Assaf's *Megorot le-toledot ha-ḥinukh be-Yisra'el,* 4 vols. in 2 (Tel Aviv, 1936–1954).

New Sources

Avital, Moshe. *Yeshiva and Traditional Education in the Literature of the Hebrew Enlightenment Period* (in Hebrew). Tel-Aviv, 1996.

Gil, Moshe. "The Babylonian Yeshivot and the Maghrib in the Early Middle Ages." *PAAJR* 57 (1991): 69–120.

Kanarfogel, Ephraim. *Jewish Education and Society in the High Middle Ages.* Detroit, 1992.

Paretzky, Zev T. *Reservoirs of Faith: The Yeshiva through the Ages.* Jerusalem and New York, 1996.

Rodik, Yohai. *Hayim shel yetsirah: Yeshivat "Merkaz ha-Rav" le-doroteha: hagut, hinukh u-ma'as.* Jerusalem, 1998.

Schiffer, Varda. *The Haredi Educational [system] in Israel: Allocation, Regulation and Control.* Translated by David Hornick. Jerusalem, 1999.

SHAUL STAMPFER (1987)
Revised Bibliography

YETSIRAH, SEFER SEE SEFER YETSIRAH

YHVH SEE ATTRIBUTES OF GOD, *ARTICLE ON* JEWISH CONCEPTS; GOD, *ARTICLE ON* GOD IN POSTBIBLICAL JUDAISM; GOD, *ARTICLE ON* GOD IN THE HEBREW SCRIPTURES

YI SEE REN AND YI

YIJING (635–713), Chinese Buddhist translator and traveler to India. Born Zhang Wenming, a native of Qizhou (modern Shandong province), Yijing left his family at the age of seven and lived in a Buddhist monastery, where he studied under the guidance of two monks, Shanyu (d. 646) and Huizhi. The former was a learned scholar with a broad range of religious and secular knowledge; the latter was an expert on monastic discipline (Vinaya). Yijing was ordained at the age of fourteen and was urged by Huizhi to follow the Vinaya strictly. He studied the monastic rules for another five years and became well versed in its regulations as well as in the interpretations given by Fali (d. 635) and Daoxuan (d. 667), the two leading and influential masters of monastic discipline. He was then allowed to lecture on the subject at the monastery. With the encouragement of his teacher, Yijing left the monastery for Chang'an, the capital of Tang-dynasty China. It was a time when Xuanzang's (d. 664) famed journey to India and his translation of Buddhist texts into Chinese were still held in highest esteem, especially in the capital. Xuanzang's legacy inspired Yijing to make his own mission to India. He first returned to his monastery at Qizhou, then proceeded to Guangfu (Canton) with the blessings of his teacher. Although other monks had planned to join Yijing, all but one dropped out at the last moment.

In 671 the two monks boarded a Persian merchant ship and arrived at the kingdom of Śrīvijaya (South Sumatra), where Yijing's companion died. Yijing stayed on for six months and then embarked alone for Tāmraliptī in eastern India via the kingdoms of Malayu, Kacha, and one of the Nicobar islands. At Tāmraliptī he studied Sanskrit for a year. He then traveled to Nālandā with another Chinese monk, Dachengdeng (d. 675). They went on pilgrimages to Gṛdhrakūṭa at Rājagṛha and to Mahābodhi at Bodh Gayā. Thereafter, they traveled to Vaiśālī, Amaraba, and Kāśī (Banaras), visited Jetavana Monastery at Śrāvastī and the "heavenly stairs" (said to have been built by the god Śakra for the Buddha to use in descending from Heaven) at Sāmkāśya, and journeyed to Sārnāth and Kukkuṭapāda.

At the end of his journey, Yijing settled at Nālandā, where for a period of nine years he studied the five prevailing Buddhist curricula. These were Buddhist logic, the *Abhidharmakośa*, monastic discipline (Vinaya), and the Mādhyamika and Yogācāra philosophies. Yijing pointed out that each of these disciplines is for a specific purpose, but that none is absolute by itself.

With the manuscripts he had collected at Nālandā, Yijing left central India for Tāmraliptī in 685. He embarked on a ship from the same port in 686, and after short stops at Kacha and Malayu, arrived at Śrīvijaya in 687. When he had been there a little over two years, however, Yijing found himself short of supplies for copying Sanskrit manuscripts. He went to the port to send word to China for supplies, but the ship that was to carry his message unexpectedly set sail while he was still on board. This accident brought Yijing back to Guangfu on August 10, 689, leaving behind his collection of Sanskrit manuscripts, amounting to half a million words. He recruited four assistants and returned to Śrīvijaya on December 18, 689. Yijing remained in the country, copied scripture, and studied under the distinguished teacher Śākyakīrti. He also wrote an account of Buddhist practices and a report regarding a group of Chinese monks who had traveled to India in search of Buddhism. Yijing sent these reports, together with his translations of Buddhist texts, to China through one of his assistants in 692.

Accompanied by two assistants, Yijing himself returned to Guangfu in 694. Five months later he traveled to Luoyang, the eastern capital, where in 695 he was personally received with great honor by the empress Wu Zetian (r. 684–704). He was accommodated at Foshouji Monastery and worked as an assistant translator in the bureau of translations headed by Siksananda. From 700 until his death, Yijing headed his own bureau of translation of Buddhist canons at Luoyang and Chang'an. Altogether he translated fifty-six works in 230 fascicles, among them scriptures, commentaries, and Vinaya texts. The empress and her successors patronized his work and even provided forewords to Yijing's translations. Various honors and rewards were bestowed upon the monk, and he was awarded the title "Master of the Tripiṭaka."

The works translated by Yijing include a broad range of Buddhist texts, including the Āgamas, the Avadānas, and Mahāyāna sūtras and *sastras*. Also translated were eleven Buddhist *tantras* and eighteen works on monastic discipline, as well as exegetic works that are important not only for Chinese Buddhism but also for the religion as a whole. His version of the *Suvarnapra-bhasa-uttamaraja Sūtra* (Golden light sūtra) is widely acknowledged by scholars as the best Chinese translation of that scripture and one that has influenced all East Asia. His translation of the Sarvāstivāda Vinaya texts has systematically preserved one of the most influential monastic traditions in India. His translations of the Yogācāra texts and of Buddhist logic are quite significant. Yijing's own writings are also valuable. His two records, of Buddhist practices in South Asia and of Chinese monks who traveled to India in the seventh century, are extremely important sources for historians of religion. His glossary, the *Fanyu qianziwen* (A thousand Sanskrit words), is the earliest extant Sanskrit-Chinese dictionary. Although Yijing's translations have been overshadowed by those of his predecessor, Xuanzang, a sample examination of both renderings of the *Viṃśatikā* (Liebenthal, 1934) concluded that Yijing was a better translator than Xuanzang.

Yijing died on February 16, 713. He was buried with grand honors, and was posthumously honored with the title Director of Foreign Office (*honglu qing*). A memorial inscription was composed by Lu Can at imperial request. A temple called Jin'guangming ("gold light") was raised at his burial site in 758.

SEE ALSO Pilgrimage, article on Buddhist Pilgrimage in South and Southeast Asia.

BIBLIOGRAPHY

The best account of the life of Yijing in a European language and a translation of his record of his journey is Junjirō Takakusu's *A Record of the Buddhist Religion as Practised in India and Malay Archipelago, A.D. 671–695* (1896; reprint, Delhi, 1966). Other studies and translations are *Mémoire composé à l'époque de la grande dynastie T'ang, sur les Religieux éminents qui allèrent chercher la loi dans les pays d'occident par I-Tsing*, translated by Édouard Chavannes (Paris, 1894), and *Suvarṇaprabhāsottamasūtra: Das Goldglanz-Sūtra, ein Sanskrittext des I-tsing's Chinesische version*, 2 vols., translated by Johannes Nobel (Leiden, 1958). For discussion of the merit of Yijing's translated works, see Johannes Nobel and Walter Liebenthal's "The Versions of the Viṃśatikā by I-ching and Its Relation to That of Hsüan-tsang," *Yenching Journal of Chinese Studies* 17 (1934): 188ff. For a list of the works translated by Yijing, see Prabodh Chandra Bagchi's *Le canon bouddhique en Chine*, vol. 2 (Paris, 1938), pp. 525–540. Additional Chinese materials related to the monk are contained in the Zhenyuan catalog of Buddhist canons by Yuanzhao (T. D. 55.867b–872a); no translation yet exists.

JAN YÜN-HA (1987)

YIN-YANG WU-HSING

SEE YINYANG WUXING

YINYANG WUXING.

Yinyang (umbral and bright) and *wuxing* (Five Phases: water, fire, wood, metal, and earth) are the core concepts of traditional Chinese cosmology. This cosmology perceives the universe as an organic whole, in which the spiritual, natural, and human worlds are ordered into a single, infinitely interconnected system. Modern scholars retrospectively call it *correlative cosmology*, since it is based on "correlative thinking."

Correlative thinking is by no means uniquely Chinese; it has appeared in all civilizations and still underlies the operations of language and serves as one of the building blocks of thought. Chinese cosmology is a distinctive and extraordinary elaboration of such a mode of thinking. It groups phenomena into heuristic or analogistic categories, within and among which relationships are held to be relatively regular and predictable. Eventually, all things in the universe are categorized and correlated, and everything affects everything else. Entities, processes, and classes of phenomena found in the human world (the human body, behavior, morality, the sociopolitical order, and historical change) are set in correspondence to various entities, processes, and classes of phenomena in nature (time, space, the movements of heavenly bodies, seasonal change, plants and animals, etc.).

This elaborate classification and correlation structure is based on various numerical systems, such as interlaced pairs (correlated to *yinyang*), sets of fours (correlated to the four directions and four seasons, and further divided into twelve months, twelve Earthly Branches, and *jieqi* seasonal nodes), sets of fives (correlated to *wuxing* or Five Phases), and sets of eights (correlated to the Eight Trigrams). While these numeral systems had different origins and represented divergent ways of classification and correlation building, the systems of *yinyang* and *wuxing* were combined and used to synthesize all other systems into an elaborate and coherent cosmology. Therefore the Chinese have used *yinyang* and *wuxing* as a general term to refer to this cosmology as a whole and the correlative thinking beneath it.

ORIGIN AND DEVELOPMENT. The words *yin* and *yang* first appeared in texts of the Warring States period (403–221 BCE), with their root meanings of "a hillside in shade" and "a hillside in sunlight," or, by extension, "cool" and "warm." A reference to a physician named Ho, in his speech dated 541 BCE, shows the first link of *yin* and *yang* to the six *qi*, the energetic fluids in the atmosphere and inside of the body. With this linkage to the *qi*, *yin* and *yang* acquired cosmological meaning. By the third century BCE, a wide variety of dualistic phenomena were being characterized in terms of *yin* and *yang*, as demonstrated in a comprehensive list (see Table 1) from an excavated text from Mawangdui.

The chain shown in Table 1 could go on infinitely, until everything is paired and divided accordingly. More often the *yang* chain is superior to the *yin* chain, but the two are mutually dependent. The use of the terms *yin* and *yang*, with their connotations of the changing ratio of shadow and sunshine on a hillside during the course of a day, aptly suited the Chinese concept of dualism, which was never absolute or antagonistic. Chinese culture tends to treat opposites as relativistic and complementary, while the West treats them as conflicting. Coolness exists only relatively to its complement, warmth—a minister is *yin* in relation to his ruler, but *yang* in relation to his wife. The *yin* of winter moves inevitably to the *yang* of summer, and back again: each contains the germ of the other.

Wuxing, the categories of five, also appeared during the Warring States period. Like *yingyang*, these categories had ancient roots. They may derive from astronomical considerations of the five visible planets, or from the numerology of the magic squares (a 3 x 3 grid arrangement of the integers 1 through 9, with 5 at the center; each row, column, and diagonal yields a sum of 15), or more likely, from the ancient spatial concepts of the four quarters of the world and four cardinal directions, with a fifth, the center, added to the four.

Towards the end of the Warring States period and during the first empires immediately following (221 BCE–220 CE), *yinyang* and *wuxing* were integrated and elevated to become the core system for synthesizing the divergent classification systems. From their initial appearance as loosely defined and unsystematically used terms, and through the long process of synthesis and standardization, these concepts went through many changes. Their meanings varied in different historical periods, as well as in different applications during the same period. For example, the Chinese term *wuxing* literarily means five "goings," "doings," or "conducts." The Confucians used the term to refer to the Five Virtues (benevolence, righteousness, propriety, wisdom, and sagehood), rather than water, fire, wood, metal, and earth. At the same time, the set of water, fire, wood, metal, and earth were called by different terms, including *wuxing*, *wucai* (Five Materials), *wude* (Five Powers), and *wuwei* (Five Positions).

This is why the translation of these concepts is extremely controversial. While *yin* and *yang* are left untranslated, *wuxing* has many translations: formerly as Five Elements, and then as Five Materials, Five Forces, Five Agents, Five Entities, Five Powers, Five Processes, or Five Phases ("Five Phases" has gained increasing acceptance). But the term is only appropriate from the Han (206 BCE–220 CE) onward, referring to cosmic cycles; using "Five Phases" to translate *wuxing* in pre-Han sources poses the danger of anachronism. Scholars more often prefer to leave *wuxing* untranslated, so that its exact meaning can be determined by the specific historical period and context.

Like *yinyang*, the term *wuxing* was used to classify phenomena that shared a common attribute (see Table 2). Although lacking the apparent inevitability found in the binary oppositions of *yinyang*, the classification of phenomena into categories of five spread widely throughout Chinese civilization. Medical practitioners described Five Viscera, musical experts worked with a scale of Five Tones, political theorists spoke of Five Powers of dynastic transmission, religious specialists named Five Gods.

More than just categories for classification, *yinyang* and *wuxing* explain the changes in all the phenomena and interactions among them. Things within the same category affect one another through resonance, because they share the same kind of *qi*. For example, if a ruler acts benevolently during the months of spring, the *qi* of the wood phase that is thus engendered will encourage the growth of plans. If, on the contrary, during the spring months he inappropriately engages in war and punishment, thus generating the metallic *qi* of autumn, then the springtime growth of plants will be hindered.

Yinyang and *wuxing* are seen as existing in interactive cycles of succession, through which things in different categories interact and transform one another. These cycles are regular and predictable, various permutations of the pair and the set of five formed cyclical orders to be applied in specific circumstances. *Yin* and *yang* were used to describe cyclical dualistic phenomena, such as the shifting proportions of sunlight and darkness throughout the solar year and the waxing and waning of the seasons. The Five Phases exist in various kinds of cycles, and the two most common and widely used were the mutual conquest and mutual generation cycles. In the former, water conquers fire (extinguishing), fire conquers metal (melting), metal conquers wood (chopping), wood conquers earth (plowing), and earth conquers water (damming). In the latter, wood generates fire (burning), fire generates earth (ash), earth generates metal (ore), metal generates water (melting), and water generates wood (irrigation). The conquest cycle was applied to, for example, the sequential planting and harvesting of crops throughout the growing year, and the generation cycle was applied to the succession of the seasons.

The inventor of the *yinyang* and *wuxing* system remains unknown. Traditionally, the invention was attributed to Zou Yan (fourth century BCE), the believed founder of a school of "naturalist" philosophy called *yinyang* and *wuxing jia*, a philosophical system that combines science and magic. But archaeological discoveries in the last decades of the twentieth century provided a body of new sources challenging this attribution. Some scholars identified affiliations of *yinyang* and *wuxing* with other philosophical schools, such as Confucianism. But many others found ample evidence in the new sources that the cosmology originated from the world outside of philosophical schools, the world of technical tradition occupied by court historians, astronomers, diviners, physicians, and music masters. Scholars have been debating whether the cosmology originated from technical professions and later was adopted and synthesized by philosophers, or whether it entered the technical world from philosophy. But whether the technical tradition and philosophy had such a clear distinction in the Warring States period is itself a debatable question. Even if they were differentiated, they both were overwhelmingly concerned with politics, history, and morality, rather than pure technical or philosophical speculations.

SIGNIFICANCE IN CHINESE CIVILIZATION. *Yinyang* and *wuxing* have played a significant role in Chinese civilization; as a twentieth-century Chinese scholar put it, they are "the law of Chinese thinking." During the formation of the first empires, *yinyang* and *wuxing* formed the cosmological foundation for the imperial ideology. Zou Yan and his followers used the conquest cycle of Five Phases to articulate their theory of dynastic transmission. According to this theory, a dynasty that was ruled by the power of the wood phase would be conquered by a new ruling house associated with metal, which in turn would be conquered by a dynasty of fire. For the rise of each new dynasty, heaven would show favorable signs to verify its legitimacy. The sign would be yellow for a dynasty ruled by the power of earth, and green for a dynasty of wood. Accordingly, Zou Yan arranged ancient history in such a cycle of conquest and predicted that a new dynasty of water, in black color, was due to rise. The first empire of Qin (221–206 BCE) adopted this theory and claimed the phase water and the ritual color black.

Attributes of *Yin* and *Yang*

A *Yang*	B *Yin*
Heaven	Earth
Spring	Autumn
Summer	Winter
Day	Night
Big states	Small states
Action	Inaction
Ruler	Minister
Above	Below
Man	Woman
Father	Child
Older	Younger
Noble	Base
Controlling others	Being controlled

TABLE 1. *Derived from Graham, 1989, p. 331. Table provided courtesy of the author.*

This imperial ideology was by no means a homogenous one. *Yinyang* and *wuxing* provided the shared discourse for political debates and struggles throughout the Han dynasty. The dispute over the two cycles of the Five Phases, conquest and generation, articulated the competition between two concepts of sovereignty and two ways of government. The conquest cycle represented a sovereignty based on force and punishment, and the generation cycle represented one based on ethical principles, rituals, and hierarchies. Confucian philosopher Dong Zhongshu (179–104 BCE) rejected the implication of Zou Yan's theory that there are different ways of government, each legitimate. He stated that a change of government would serve only to illuminate the Dao of heaven, rectifying the deviations from it by the preceding dynasty. Dong's followers further used the generation cycle of Five Phases to explain dynastic transmission, thus shifting the ground for imperial sovereignty from conquering force to nurturing morality. This system of dynastic transmission and imperial symbolism was adopted by Wang Mang in establishing the New Dynasty (Xin, 9–23 CE), and was continued by the later Han (25–220 CE) and all dynasties of the remaining imperial history.

Outside of political ideology, *yinyang* and *wuxing* were fully integrated into every domain of Chinese culture and the

Attributes of *Wuxing*

Phase	Planet	Color	Season	Direction	Taste
Wood	Jupiter	Green	Spring	East	Sour
Fire	Mars	Red	Summer	South	Bitter
Earth	Saturn	Yellow	Midsummer	Center	Sweet
Metal	Venus	White	Autumn	West	Acrid
Water	Mercury	Black	Winter	North	Salty

TABLE 2. *Table provided courtesy of the author.*

everyday practice of the people, becoming a common property of Chinese philosophy, religion, medicine, and science as a whole. *Yinyang* and *wuxing* were used by court historians, astronomers, diviners, ritual experts, physicians, and music masters in predicting, planning, and checking government functions. By ordering time, space, body, and all phenomena into a single predictable order, the state used this cosmology as the means of creating a tightly integrated order and of controlling the actual daily practice of administration. *Yinyang* and *wuxing* also penetrated a wide terrain of technical, mantic, and religious practice; they were integrated into the calendar, medicine, and divination, and were used to order the daily affairs of the populace in marriage, funerals, rituals, travel, diet, healing, trade, house building, farming, hunting, and the making of food, wine, and clothing. Even after the introduction of modern science and the decline of *yinyang* and *wuxing* as a political ideology towards the end of the imperial era, *yinyang* and *wuxing* remained the conceptual foundation of popular religion, martial arts, geomancy, and traditional Chinese medicine, all of which are still operating today.

SEE ALSO Daoism, overview article; Dong Zhongshu; Onmyōdō.

BIBLIOGRAPHY

Bodde, Derk. "Types Chinese Categorical Thinking." In *Essays on Chinese Civilisation,* edited by Charles Le Blanc and Dorothy Borei, pp. 141–160. Princeton, 1981.

Bodde, Derk. *Chinese Thought, Society, and Science: The Intellectual and Social Background of Science and Technology in Pre-modern China.* Honolulu, 1991.

Fung Yu-lan. *A History of Chinese Philosophy,* 2d ed., 2 vols. Translated by Derk Bodde. Princeton, 1952–1953.

Graham, A. C. *Yin-Yang and the Nature of Correlative Thinking.* Singapore, 1986.

Graham, A. C. *Disputers of Tao: Philosophical Argument in Ancient China.* La Salle, Ill., 1989.

Harper, Donald. "Warring States, Natural Philosophy, and Occult Thought." In *The Cambridge History of Ancient China: From the Origins of Civilization to the 221 B.C.,* edited by Michael Loewe and Edward Shaughnessy, pp. 813–883. Cambridge, U.K., 1999.

Henderson. John B. *The Development and Decline of Chinese Cosmology.* New York, 1984.

Kalinowski, Marc, trans. and ed. *Cosmologie et divination dans la Chine ancienne: Le compendium des cinq agents.* Paris, 1991.

Major, John S. "Myth, Cosmology, and the Origins of Chinese Science." *Journal of Chinese Philosophy* 5 (1978): 1–20.

Major, John S. *Heaven and Earth in Early Han Thought: Chapters Three, Four, and Five of the Huainanzi.* Albany, N.Y., 1993.

Needham, Joseph. *Science and Civilisation in China,* vol. 2, *History of Scientific Thought.* Cambridge, U.K., 1956.

Puett, Michael. *The Ambivalence of Creation: Debates Concerning Innovation and Artifice in Early China.* Stanford, Calif., 2001.

Schwartz, Benjamin I. *The World of Thought in Ancient China.* Cambridge, Mass., 1985.

Sivin, Nathan. "State, Cosmos, and Body in the Last Three Centuries B.C." *Harvard Journal of Asiatic Studies* 55, no. 1 (1995): 5–37.

Sivin, Nathan. "The Myth of the Naturalists." In *Medicine, Philosophy, and Religion in Ancient China: Researches and Reflections,* pp. 2–7. Aldershot, U.K., 1995.

Reconsidering the Correlative Cosmology of Early China. Special issue of *Bulletin of the Museum of Far Eastern Antiquity* 72 (Stockholm, 2000).

Wang, Aihe. *Cosmology and Political Culture in Early China.* Cambridge, U.K., 2000.

Yates, Robin D. S. "Body, Space, Time and Bureaucracy: Boundary Creation and Control Mechanisms in Early China." In *Boundaries in China,* edited by John Hay, pp. 56–80. London, 1994.

AIHE WANG (2005)

YISHMAʿEʾL BEN ELISHAʿ (c. 50–c. 135 CE), Palestinian tanna. Yishmaʿeʾl was ʿAqivaʾ ben Yosef's most famous contemporary; rabbinic tradition has constantly placed the sayings of these masters in opposition to each other.

Although some have argued that Yishmaʿeʾl was a member of the priestly class, nothing in the traditions attributed to him supports this claim except for a number of dubious passages (B.T., *Ber.* 7a, *Ḥul.* 49a–b; Tosefta *Ḥal.* 1.10; *Avot de-Rabbi Natan* 38 [cf. *Mekhiltaʾ de-Rabbi Yishmaʿeʾl, Nez.* 18]). One story recalls that as a child he was captured by the

Romans and placed in prison, where he was discovered by Yehoshuʿa, who predicted great things for the child (B.T., *Giṭ.* 58a); however, not all manuscripts containing this story mention Yishmaʿeʾl, and his appearance here is suspect. He is said to have studied with Yehoshuʿa, Eliʿezer, and, especially, Naḥunyaʾ ben ha-Qanah, who is said to have taught him the importance of exegesis of the Torah by means of logical arguments (B.T., *Shav.* 26a). The Talmud states that he rejected the study of Greek wisdom; he argued that one should study Torah day and night (B.T., *Men.* 99b), and his sayings demonstrate a tendency to reject Gentiles and their wisdom (*ʿA.Z.* 1.2, 2.3, 4.1).

Yishmaʿeʾl's importance has been based on his role as a biblical exegete. The opening of *Sifraʾ*, a collection of exegetical comments on *Leviticus,* states that Yishmaʿeʾl's exegesis of the Bible relied on thirteen principles. Based on this passage, most scholars of rabbinic Judaism have contrasted Yishmaʿeʾl's "logical" method of interpreting scripture with the more "imaginative" techniques employed by ʿAqiva.ʾ Yishmaʿeʾl is said to have ignored such things as the repetition of words or phrases in biblical verses and the appearance of certain adjectives, adverbs, and conjunctions, while these supposedly were crucial to the exegetical enterprises of ʿAqiva.ʾ Yishmaʿeʾl's statement that such features of biblical Hebrew should be ignored because "Scripture speaks in the language of common men" (*Sifrei Nm.* 112) is taken as the underlying assumption of his exegetical techniques. However, recent scholarship has challenged this traditional picture.

It has been demonstrated that Yishmaʿeʾl and ʿAqivaʾ often used the same "logical" exegetical techniques normally attributed to Yishmaʿeʾl and that they both employed the more "imaginative" exegetical methods usually assigned to ʿAqiva.ʾ In addition, it has been shown that we have no evidence that Yishmaʿeʾl employed the majority of the thirteen exegetical techniques attributed to him in the opening of *Sifraʾ*. In fact, he most often employed methods not found in that list, such as the analogy, but that were commonplace among the Hellenistic rhetoricians of his age.

Given the fact that the traditions attributed to Yishmaʿeʾl and ʿAqivaʾ do not support the common scholarly picture, we must consider what has happened. It is likely that toward the end of the rabbinic period, two major schools of biblical exegesis had developed, one "logical" and one "imaginative." In an attempt to claim that these opposing views were very old, the later sages attributed their creation to Yishmaʿeʾl and ʿAqiva,ʾ for the importance of ʿAqivaʾ in all areas of rabbinic thought, including biblical exegesis, had by then been well established. Thus Yishmaʿeʾl's importance probably stems from the frequent juxtaposition of his sayings with those of ʿAqiva,ʾ one of the most important sages of Jewish history, and not from anything he actually said or did, or at least not from anything attributed to him in the sources we have at hand.

SEE ALSO Tannaim.

BIBLIOGRAPHY

For traditional views of Yishmaʿeʾl, see the *Encyclopedia of Talmudic and Geonic Literature,* edited by Mordechai Margalioth (Tel Aviv, 1945), vol. 2, pp. 599–605; Aaron Hyman's *Toledot tannaʿim ve-amoraʾim* (1910; reprint, Jerusalem, 1964), vol. 2, pp. 817–824; and Samuel Safrai's "Ishmael ben Elisha," in *Encyclopaedia Judaica* (Jerusalem, 1971), vol. 9, cols. 83–86. Marcus Petuchowski began the serious study of Yishmaʿeʾl with *Der Tanna Rabbi Ismael* (Frankfurt, 1894). For a critical modern approach to the corpus of his work, see my four-volume study *The Traditions of Rabbi Ishmael* (Leiden, 1976–1982) and the bibliography given therein. On the problem of rabbinic biography, see William S. Green's "What's in a Name? The Problematic of Rabbinic 'Biography,'" in his *Approaches to Ancient Judaism* (Missoula, Mont., 1978), vol. 1, pp. 77–96.

New Sources

Abusch, Raʿanan. "Rabbi Ishmael's Miraculous Conception: Jewish Redemption History in Anti-Christian Polemic." In *The Ways That Never Parted; Jews and Christians in Late Antiquity and the Early Middle Ages,* edited by Adam H. Becker and Annette Yoshiko Reed, pp. 307–343. Tübingen, 2003.

Finkelstein, Louis. "Rabbi Akiba, Rabbi Ishmael, and the Bar Kochba Rebellion." In *Approaches to Ancient Judaism, New Series,* vol. 1, edited by Jacob Neusner, pp. 3–10. Atlanta, 1990.

Ilan, Tal. "'Daughters of Israel, Weep for Rabbi Ishmael:' The Schools of Rabbi Akiva and Rabbi Ishmael on Women." *Nashim* 4 (2001): 15–34.

GARY G. PORTON (1987)
Revised Bibliography

YISRAʾEL BEN ELIʿEZER SEE BAʿAL SHEM TOV

YI T'OEGYE,

pen name of Yi Hwang (1501–1570), founder of the Yŏngnam school of Korean Neo-Confucianism. T'oegye is credited with having established in Korea the orthodox Neo-Confucian tradition as propounded by the Cheng-Zhu school, so-called after its putative founders Cheng I (1033–1107) and Zhu Xi (1130–1200), and is widely regarded as the greatest of all Korean Neo-Confucian thinkers.

Yi T'oegye was born in Yean in Kyongsang Province, in the southeastern part of Korea. He began his studies with his uncle, Yi U, and continued them at the Royal College in Seoul, which he entered in 1523. He passed the preliminary civil service examination in 1528 and the final examination in 1534, after which he joined the small governing elite by embarking upon a long official career. His career, which followed the pattern typical of the elite of the period, included posts in such metropolitan bureaus as the Office of Diplomatic Correspondence, the Censorate, the Office of the Crown Prince Tutorial, and the Royal College. He also served as a magistrate in local government. Despite the rather volatile political atmosphere of the time, his career was a smooth one. The highest positions he held included appointments as Minister of Rites, Fifth State Councillor, Director of the Office of Royal Decrees, and Director of Special Councillors. In 1569 he retired from public life and returned to his place of origin. The kings he served, Chungjong (r. 1506–1544), Myŏngjong (r. 1545–1567), and Sŏnjo (r. 1567–1608), all treated him with great respect. Legend has it that King Myŏngjong, to whom T'oegye submitted his celebrated *Ten Diagrams of Sage Learning (Sŏnghak sipto),* was supposed to have been a devotee.

Despite his long and illustrious public career, T'oegye is remembered as having maintained, or perhaps even initiated, the tradition of scholarly independence from the state. While he did not shy away from public life, T'oegye seems to have been constantly attracted to independent scholarship and educational activity. He frequently professed his desire for the life of a private scholar devoted to learning and teaching. Whenever possible, either between official posts or during his service, he attempted to pursue this ideal. During his tenure as the magistrate of P'unggi County, T'oegye successfully campaigned for government support of a private academy in the area, setting a frequently observed precedent. Eventually, he founded the Tosan Academy in his place of birth, which attracted numerous students through the generations. It was to this academy that he retired periodically in pursuit of scholarship. His alleged preference for the scholarly life influenced the attitudes of later scholars; indeed, the majority of the scholars of the Yŏngnam school (School of Principle) remained private scholars. This of course reflected political realities such as violent factionalism and fierce competition for office. But these scholars also preserved a certain pride in their independence from the state and in their exclusive devotion to scholarship. They believed they were true heirs of T'oegye not only in their scholarship but also in their mode of life.

T'oegye based his philosophy largely on that of Zhu Xi. He endorsed Zhu Xi's dual theory of *li* (Kor., *i;* "principle") and *qi* (Kor., *ki*; "material force"), but labored over the question of whether Zhu Xi's priority of principle over material force referred to a valuative or existential priority. He concluded that the priority of principle obtained in the realm of values. His belief in the superiority of principle, which he identified with original nature and the moral mind, defined his position on the *sadan* (Chin., *ssu-tuan*; "four beginnings") and the *ch'ilchong* (Chin., *qi-qing*; "seven emotions") in the famous debate with Ki Taesung (1527–1572). Here, T'oegye argued for their separate origins, proposing that the Four Beginnings were initiated by principle and the Seven Emotions by material force. In order to maintain this position, however, T'oegye saw principle as having a generative power of its own. This position became a focus of the scholarship of the Yŏngnam school.

A perhaps more meaningful aspect of his scholarship is his position on moral cultivation. Dismissing Wang Yang-ming's (1472–1529) theory of the unity of knowledge and action as irresponsible in its disregard for the rationality of man, T'oegye was firmly committed to the need for a daily regimen of moral cultivation, a slow and painstaking process. He regarded sincerity and reverence as fundamental necessities in the acquisition of knowledge, which could be sought only through laborious step-by-step inquiry and meditation. The rather quiescent and meditative quality of his scholarship was inherited by his followers and remained a distinctive feature of the Yŏngnam School.

See Also Confucianism in Korea.

Bibliography

Works by Yi T'oegye are collected in *T'oegye chonso,* 2 vols. (reprint, Seoul, 1958). An authoritative study on him is Yi Sang-un's *T'oegye ui saengae wa hangmun* (Seoul, 1973). Articles discussing his philosophy in English are Tomoeda Ryutaro's "Yi T'oegye and Zhu Xi: Differences in Their Theories of Principle and Material Force," Tu Wei-ming's "Yi T'oegye's Perception of Human Nature: A Preliminary Inquiry into the Four-Seven Debate in Korean Neo-Confucianism," and Sa-Soon Youn's "T'oegye's Identification of 'To Be' and 'Ought': T'oegye's Theory of Values," all in *The Rise of Neo-Confucianism in Korea,* edited by Wm. Theodore de Bary and me (New York, 1985), pp. 243–260, 261–282, and 223–242, respectively.

New Sources

Chung, Edward Y. J. *The Korean Neo-Confucianism of Yi T'oegye and Yi Yulgok: A Reappraisal of the "Four-Seven Thesis" and Its Practical Implications for Self-Cultivation.* Albany, 1995.

Kalton, Michael C., trans. *The Ten Diagrams on Sage Learning by Yi T'oegye.* New York, 1988.

Lee, Kwang-Sae. "Yi T'oegye [1501–1570]." In *Great Thinkers of the Eastern World: The Major Thinkers and the Philosophical and Religious Classics of China, India, Japan, Korea, and the World of Islam,* edited by Ian P. McGreal, pp. 413–417. New York.

JaHyun Kim Haboush (1987)
Revised Bibliography

YI YULGOK pen name of Yi I (1536–1584), Korean Neo-Confucian thinker whose stature in the tradition is equalled only by that of Yi T'oegye. Yulgok is credited with having established the Kiho ("material force") school in Korea. Born in Kangnŭng in Kangwon Province in western central Korea, not far from the capital, Yulgok began his studies with his mother, Sin Saimdang, a well-known poet and painter. Her death when he was sixteen seems to have brought about a profound personal crisis. After three years of mourning, Yulgok retreated into a Buddhist mountain temple intending to become a monk. Although he changed his mind after a year of studying the Buddhist scriptures, his resulting familiarity with Buddhism supposedly influenced his scholarship. In 1564 he placed first in both the preliminary and final civil service examinations and thus acquired the nickname Lord First Candidate of the Nine Examinations. His ensuing reputation as a brilliant scholar and a quick study led to his meteoric rise in the bureaucracy. He served in numerous offices in both metropolitan and provincial government. In 1568 Yulgok traveled to China on an ambassadorial mission. His official posts included appointments as minister of military affairs, minister of public works, and minister of personnel, in which post he died at the age of forty-nine. He enjoyed a close relationship with King Sŏnjo (r. 1567–1608), whom he served as a royal tutor.

As was typical of Yi dynasty officials, Yulgok's illustrious public career was interrupted by short periods of retirement either for personal reasons or because of an unfavorable political climate at court. Nevertheless, he is regarded as representing the activist tradition of Confucian scholar-statesmanship. In this respect, Yulgok is viewed as the opposite of T'oegye, his scholarly rival, who is known for his preference for private life. This reputation seems to be based on Yulgok's wide range of interests and concerns. Unlike T'oegye, whose scholarship was confined mainly to philosophical issues, Yulgok was keenly interested in the practical aspect of government. He wrote copiously on such matters as fiscal reform, the problems of resettlement of landless peasants, military organization and finance, questions of disseminating Confucian mores to the populace, the relationship of the monarch and the bureaucracy and their respective roles, potential frictions within the bureaucracy, and the regulation and curricula of private academies. His proposal for a strong army of one hundred thousand, although unheeded, is often cited as prophetic in view of the disastrous Japanese invasions of the 1590s. He is said even to have written a memorial on his deathbed emphasizing the need for more effective government policies. His successors, the scholars of the Kiho school, inherited this activist tradition, and perhaps it is not purely coincidental that they maintained power throughout the Yi dynasty.

While Yulgok remained within Cheng-Zhu orthodoxy (named for the Chinese thinkers Cheng I and Zhu Xi) he rejected the dual theory of *i* (Chin., *li;* "principle") and *ki* (Chin., *qi;* "material force") held by Zhu Xi and T'oegye. While he accepted a conceptual distinction between the two, he maintained that they were inseparable in both function and manifestation. Rather than seeing principle as one, unchanging and immanent in all things, he saw the principle in each thing as distinct, conditioned by its material force and thus always changing. His belief in the primacy of material force as the determinant of an entity led to a corresponding theory of the *sadan* (Chin., *situan;* "four beginnings") and the *ch'ilchŏng* (Chin., *qi-qing;* "seven emotions"). Taking issue with T'oegye's position that the Four Beginnings and the Seven Emotions had separate origins, Yulgok insisted that they are both manifestations of material force that contain principle. Moreover, he held that the Four are "good" manifestations of material force. The difference between the Four and the Seven lies in how they are manifested, that is, the Four Beginnings are the Seven Emotions themselves manifested as good. This was a clear departure from the idea that principle and material force were the sources, respectively, of good and evil. The scholars of the Kiho school continued to develop the primacy of material force, posing a scholarly as well as political alternative to the Yongnam school of Yi T'oegye.

SEE ALSO Confucianism in Korea; Yi T'oegye.

BIBLIOGRAPHY

Works by Yi Yulgok are collected in *Yulgok chonso,* 2 vols. (Seoul, 1961). A comprehensive study is Kim Kyongt'ak's *Yulgok ui yon'gu* (Seoul, 1960). Articles discussing his philosophy and activities are Julia Ching's "Yi Yulgok on the 'Four Beginnings and Seven Emotions' " and Sakai Tadao's "Yi Yulgok and the Community Compact," both in *The Rise of Neo-Confucianism in Korea,* edited by Wm. Theodore de Bary and me (New York, 1985), pp. 303–322 and 323–348, respectively.

New Sources

Chung, Edward Y. J. *The Korean Neo-Confucianism of Yi T'oegye and Yi Yulgok: A Reappraisal of the "Four-Seven Thesis" and Its Practical Implications for Self-Cultivation.* Albany, 1995.

JAHYUN KIM HABOUSH (1987)
Revised Bibliography

YOGA. Etymologically, the Sanskrit word *yoga* derives from the root *yuj,* meaning "to bind together," "hold fast," or "yoke," which also governs the Latin *iungere* and *iugum,* the French *joug,* and so on. In Indian religion the term *yoga* serves, in general, to designate any ascetic technique and any method of meditation. The "classical" form of yoga is a *darśana* ("view, doctrine"; usually, although improperly, translated as "system of philosophy") expounded by Patañjali in his *Yoga Sūtra,* and it is from this "system" that this article must set out if the reader is to understand the position of yoga in the history of Indian thought. But side by side with classical Yoga there are countless forms of sectarian, popular (magical), and non-Brahmanic yogas such as Buddhist and Jain forms.

Patañjali is not the creator of the Yoga *darśana.* As he himself admits, he has merely edited and integrated the doctrinal and technical traditions of yoga (*Yoga Sūtra* 1.1). Indeed, yogic practices were known in the esoteric circles of Indian ascetics and mystics long before Patañjali. Among these practices Patañjali retained those that the experiences of centuries had sufficiently tested. As to the theoretical framework and the metaphysical foundation that Patañjali provides for such techniques, his personal contribution is of the smallest. He merely rehandles the Sāṃkhya philosophy in its broad outlines, adapting it to a rather superficial theism and exalting the practical value of meditation. The Yoga and Sāṃkhya *darśanas* are so much alike that most of the assertions made by the one are valid for the other. The essential differences between them are two: (1) Whereas Sāṃkhya is atheistic, Yoga is theistic, since it postulates the existence of a "Lord" (Īśvara); (2) Whereas according to Sāṃkhya the only path to final deliverance is that of metaphysical knowledge, Yoga accords marked importance to techniques of purification and meditation.

Thanks to Patañjali, Yoga, which had been an archaic ascetic and mystical tradition, became an organized "system of philosophy." Nothing is known of the author of the *Yoga Sūtra,* not even whether he lived in the second or third century BCE or in the fifth century CE, although claims to both datings have been vigorously defended. The earliest commentary known is the *Yogabhāṣya* of Vyāsa (seventh to eighth century CE), annotated by Vācaspatimiśra (ninth century) in his *Tattvavaiśāradī.* These two works, indispensable for understanding the *Yoga Sūtra,* are complemented by two works of later centuries. At the beginning of the eleventh century King Bhoja wrote the commentary *Rājamārtaṇḍa,* which is very useful for its insights into certain yogic practices, and in the sixteenth century Vijñānabhikṣu annotated Vyāsa's text in his remarkable treatise the *Yogavārttika.*

Ignorance and Suffering. "All is suffering for the sage," writes Patañjali (*Yoga Sūtra* 2.15), repeating a leitmotif of all post-Upanṣadic Indian speculation. The discovery of pain as the law of existence has a positive, stimulating value. It perpetually reminds the sage and the ascetic that the only way to attain freedom and bliss is withdrawal from the world, radical isolation. To liberate the self from suffering is the goal of all Indian philosophies and magico-mystical techniques. In India, metaphysical knowledge always has a soteriological purpose, for it is by knowledge of ultimate reality that humanity, casting off the illusions of the world of phenomena, awakens and discovers the true nature of spirit (*ātman, puruṣa*). For Sāṃkhya and Yoga, suffering has its origin in ignorance of spirit, that is, in confusing spirit with psychomental states, which are the most refined products of nature (*prakṛti*). Consequently, liberation, absolute freedom, can be obtained only if this confusion is abolished. As the structure and unfolding of nature and the paradoxical mode of being of the self (*puruṣa*) are discussed elsewhere, here only the yogic practices themselves will be examined.

The point of departure of yogic meditation is concentration on a single object: a physical object (the space between the eyebrows, the tip of the nose, something luminous, etc.), a thought (a metaphysical truth), or God (Īśvara). This determined and continuous concentration, called *ekāgratā* ("on a single point"), is obtained by integrating the psychomental flux, *sarvārthatā* ("variously directed, discontinued, diffused attention"; *Yoga Sūtra* 3.11). This is the precise definition of yogic technique, and is called *cittavṛtti-nirodha,* "the suppression of psychomental states" (*Yoga Sūtra* 1.2). The practice of *ekāgratā* tends to control the two generators of psychomental life: sense activity (*indriya*) and the activity of the unconscious (*saṃskāra*). A yogin is able to concentrate his or her attention on a single point and become insensible to any other sensory or mnemonic stimulus. It goes without saying that *ekāgratā* can be obtained only through the practice of numerous exercises and techniques. One cannot obtain *ekāgratā* if, for example, the body is in a tiring or even uncomfortable posture, or if the respiration is disorganized, unrhythmical. This is why yogic technique implies several categories of physiological practices and spiritual exercises, called *aṅgas,* "members," or elements. The eight "members" of classical Yoga can be regarded both as forming a group of techniques and as being stages of the ascetic and spiritual itinerary whose end is final liberation. They are (1) restraints (*yama*), (2) disciplines (*niyama*), (3) bodily attitudes and postures (*āsana*), (4) rhythm of respiration (*prāṇāyāma*), (5) emancipation of sensory activity from the domination of exterior objects (*pratyāhāra*), (6) concentration (*dhāraṇā*), (7) yogic meditation (*dhyāna*), and (8) enstasis (*samādhi;Yoga Sūtra* 2.29).

In addition to this classical Yoga comprising eight *aṅgas,* there exist a number of *ṣaḍaṅgayogas,* that is, yogic regimens having only six members. Their main characteristic is the absence of the three first *aṅgas (yama, niyama, āsana)* and the introduction of a new "member," *tarka* ("reason, logic"). Attested already in the *Maitrāyani Upaniṣad* (second century BCE-second century CE), the *ṣaḍaṅgayoga* appears especially in certain sects of Hinduism and in the Buddhist Tantras (Grönbold, 1969, 1983).

Restraints and Disciplines. The first two groups of practices, *yama* and *niyama,* constitute the inevitable preliminaries for any asceticism. There are five "restraints," namely, *ahiṃsā* (restraint from violence), *satya* (restraint from falsehood), *asteya* (restraint from stealing), *brahmacarya* (restraint from sexual activity), and *aparigraha* (restraint from avarice). These restraints do not bring about a specifically yogic state but induce in the adept a purified state superior to that of the uninitiated. In conjunction with the *yamas,* the yogin must practice the *niyama,* that is, a series of bodily and psychic disciplines. "Cleanliness, serenity, asceticism [*tapas*], study of Yoga metaphysics, and an effort to make Īśvara [God] the motive of all his actions constitute the disciplines," writes Patañjali (*Yoga Sūtra* 2.32). Obviously, difficulties and obstacles arise during these exercises, most of them produced by the subconscious. The perplexity arising from doubt is the most dangerous. To overcome it, Patañjali recommends implanting the contrary thought (*Yoga Sūtra* 2.33). To vanquish a temptation is to realize a genuine, positive gain. Not only does the yogin succeed in dominating the objects that he or she had renounced, but also obtains a magic force infinitely more precious than all these objects. For example, he who successfully practices *asteya* "sees all jewels coming near to him" (*Yoga Sūtra* 2.37).

Āsana and Prāṇāyāma. The specifically yogic techniques begin with *āsana,* the well-known bodily posture of the Indian ascetics. *Āsana* gives a rigid stability to the body while at the same time reducing physical effort to a minimum and finally eliminating it altogether. *Āsana* is the first concrete step taken with a view to abolishing the modalities peculiar to the human condition. On the bodily plane, *āsana* is an *ekāgratā;* the body is "concentrated" in a single position. Thus, one arrives at a certain neutralization of the senses; consciousness is no longer troubled by the presence of the body. Furthermore, a tendency toward "unification" and "totalization" is typical of all yogic practices. Their goal is the transcendence (or the abolition) of the human condition, resulting from the refusal to obey one's natural inclinations.

The most important—and certainly the most specifically yogic—of these various "refusals" is the disciplining of respiration (*prāṇāyāma*), the refusal to breathe like the majority of humankind, that is, unrhythmically. Patañjali defines this refusal as follows: "*Prāṇāyāma* is the arrest [*viccheda*] of the movements of inhalation and exhalation and it is obtained after *āsana* has been realized" (*Yoga Sūtra* 2.49). He speaks of the "arrest," the suspension, of respiration; however, *prāṇāyāma* begins with making the respiratory rhythm as slow as possible; and this is its first objective.

A remark in Bhoja's commentary (on *Yoga Sūtra* 1.34) reveals the deeper meaning of *prāṇāyāma:* "All the functions of the organs being preceded by that of respiration—there being always a connection between respiration and conciousness in their respective functions—respiration, when all the functions of the organs are suspended, realizes concentration of consciousness on a single object." The special relation of the rhythm of respiration to particular states of consciousness, which has undoubtedly been observed and experienced by yogins from the earliest times, has served them as an instrument for "unifying" consciousness. By making respiration rhythmical and progressively slower the yogin can penetrate—that is experience in perfect lucidity—certain states of consciousness that are inaccessible in a waking condition, particularly the states of consciousness that are peculiar to sleep.

Indian psychology recognizes four modalities of consciousness (besides enstasis): diurnal consciousness, consciousness in sleep with dreams, consciousness in sleep without dreams, and "cataleptic consciousness." Through *prāṇāyāma,* that is, by increasingly prolonging inhalation and exhalation (since the purpose of this practice is to allow as long an interval as possible to elapse between the two phases of respiration) the yogin can experience all the modalities of consciousness. For the uninitiated, there is a discontinuity between these several modalities; one passes from the state of waking to the state of sleeping unconsciously. The yogin must preserve continuity of consciousness; that is, he must penetrate each of these states with determination and awareness.

But the immediate goal of *prāṇāyāma* is more modest; it induces the respiratory rhythm by harmonizing the three "moments" of breathing: inhalation (*pūraka*), retention (*kumbhaka*), and exhalation (*recaka*) of the inhaled air. These three moments must each fill an equal space of time. Practice enables the yogin to prolong them considerably. The yogin begins by holding his or her breath for sixteen and a half seconds, then for thirty-three seconds, then for fifty seconds, three minutes, five minutes, and so on. (Similar respiratory technique were familiar to the Daoists, to Christian hesychasts, and to the Muslim contemplatives; see Eliade, 1969, pp. 59–65).

YOGIC CONCENTRATION AND MEDITATION. Making respiration rhythmical and, as far as possible, suspending it greatly promotes concentration (*dhāraṇā; Yoga Sūtra* 2.52–53). The yogin can test the quality of his concentration by *pratyāhāra,* a term usually translated as "withdrawal of the senses" or "abstraction" but more acurately rendered as the "ability to free sense activity from the domination of external objects." According to the *Yoga Sūtra* (2.54) and its commentators, the senses, instead of directing themselves toward an object, "abide within themselves" (Bhoja, on *Yoga Sūtra* 2.54). When the intellect (*citta*) wishes to know an exterior object, it does not make use of sensory activity; it is able to know the object by its own powers. Being obtained directly, by contemplation, this knowledge is, from the yogic point of view, more effective than normal knowledge. "Then the wisdom [*prajñā*] of the yogin knows all things as they are" (Vyāsa, on *Yoga Sūtra* 2.45). Thenceforth, the yogin will no longer be distracted or troubled by the activity of the senses, by the subconscious, and by the "thirst of life"; all activity is suspended. But this autonomy of the intellect does not result in the suppression of phenomena. Instead of knowing through forms (*rūpa*) and mental states (*cittavṛtti*) as formerly, the yogin now contemplates the essence (*tattva*) of all objects directly.

Such autonomy allows the yogin to practice a threefold technique that the texts call *saṃyama.* The term designates the last three "members" of yoga (*yogāṅga*), namely concentration (*dhāraṇā*), yogic meditation (*dhyana*), and stasis (*samādhi*). They do not imply new physiological practices. *Dhāraṇā,* from the root *dhṛ,* meaning "to hold fast," is in fact an *ekāgratā,* undertaken for the purpose of comprehension. Patañjali's definition of *dhāraṇā* is "fixation of the thought on a single point" (*Yoga Sūtra* 3.1). According to some authors (cf. Eliade, 1969, pp. 66–68), a *dhāraṇā* takes the time of twelve *prāṇāyāmas* (i. e., twelve controlled, equal, and delayed respirations). By prolonging this concentration on an object twelve times, one obtains yogic meditation, *dhyana.* Patañjali defines *dhyana* as "a current of unified thought" (*Yoga Sūtra* 3.2) and Vyāsa adds the following gloss to the definition: "continuum of mental effort to assimilate the object of meditation, free from any other effort to assimilate other objects." It is unnecessary to add that this yogic meditation is absolutely different from any secular meditation.

SAMĀDHI AND THE LORD OF THE YOGINS. Yogic enstasis, *samādhi,* is the final result and crown of all the ascetic's spiritual efforts and exercises. The term is first employed in a gnoseological sense: *Samādhi* is the state in which thought grasps the object directly. Thus, there is a real coincidence between knowledge of the object and the object of knowledge. This kind of knowledge constitutes an enstatic modality of being that is peculiar to yoga. Patañjali and his commentators distinguish several sorts, or stages, of *samādhi.* When it is obtained with the help of an object or idea (that is, by fixing one's thought on a point in space or on an idea), it is called *samprajñāta samādhi,* "enstasis with support." When, on the other hand, *samādhi* is obtained apart from any relation to externals, when it is simply a full comprehension of being, it is *asamprajñāta samādhi,* "undifferentiated stasis."

Because it is perfectible and does not realize an absolute and irreducible state, the "differentiated enstasis" (*samprajñāta samādhi*) comprises four stages, called *bīja samādhi* ("*samādhi* with seed") or *sālambana samādhi* ("*samādhi* with support"). By accomplishing these four stages, one after the other, one obtains the "faculty of absolute knowledge" (*ṛtambharāprajñā*). This is in itself an opening toward *samādhi* "without seed," pure *samādhi,* for absolute knowledge discovers the state of ontological plenitude in which being and knowing are no longer separated. According to Vijñānabhikṣu, *asamprajñāta samādhi* destroys the "impressions [*saṃskāra*] of all antecedent mental functions" and even succeeds in arresting the karmic forces already set in motion by the yogin's past activities (Eliade, 1969, p. 84).

Fixed in *samādhi,* consciousness (*citta*) can now have direct revelation of the self (*puruṣa*). For the devotional yogins, it is at this stage that the revelation of the Supreme Self, Īśvara, the Lord, takes place. Unlike Sāṃkhya, Yoga affirms the existence of a God, Īśvara. He is not a creator god, for the cosmos, life, and humanity proceed from the primordial substance, *prakṛti.* But in the case of certain persons (i. e., the yogins), Īśvara can hasten the process of deliverance. Īśvara is a self (*puruṣa*) that has been eternally free. Patañjali says that the Īśvara has been the guru of the sages of immemorial times (*Yoga Sūtra* 1.26) and that he can bring about *samādhi* on condition that the yogin practice *īśvarapraṇidhāna,* that is, devotion to Īśvara (*Yoga Sūtra* 2.45). But it has been seen that *samādhi* can be obtained without such mystical exercises. In the classical Yoga of Patañjali, Īśvara plays a rather minor role. It is only with the later commentators, such as Vijñānabhikṣu and Nilakaṇṭha, that Īśvara gains the importance of a true God.

The Yogic Powers; Deliverance. By practicing *saṃyama*—that is, by means of concentration, meditation, and the realization of *samādhi*—the yogin acquires the "miraculous powers" (*siddhis*) to which book 3 of the *Yoga Sūtra,* beginning with *sūtra* 16, is devoted. The majority of these powers are related to different kinds of supranormal or mystical knowledge. Thus, by practicing *saṃyama* in regard to his or her own subconscious residues (*saṃskāra*), the yogins come to know their previous existences (*Yoga Sūtra* 3.105). Through *saṃyama* exercised in respect to "notions" (*pratyaya*), the yogin knows the mental states of other people (3.19). *Saṃyama* practiced on the umbilical plexus (*nābhicakra*) produces knowledge of the system of the body (3.28), on the heart, knowledge of the mind (3.33), and so forth. "Whatever the yogin desires to know, he should perform *saṃyama* in respect to that object," writes Vācaspatimiśra (on *Yoga Sūtra* 3.30). According to Patañjali and the whole tradition of classical Yoga, the yogin uses the innumerable *siddhis* in order to attain the supreme freedom, *asamprajñāta samādhi,* not in order to obtain a mastery over the elements (*Yoga Sūtra* 3.37). A similar doctrine is found in Buddhism (Eliade, 1969, pp. 177–180; Pensa, 1969, pp. 23–24).

Through the illumination (*prajñā*) spontaneously obtained when reaching the last stage of his or her itinerary, the yogin realizes "absolute isolation" (*kaivalya*), that is, liberation of the self (*puruṣa*) from the dominance of nature (*prakṛti*). But this mode of being of the spirit is not an "absolute emptiness"; it constitutes a paradoxical, because unconditioned, state. Indeed, the intellect (*buddhi*), having accomplished its mission, withdraws, detaching itself from the *puruṣa* and returning into *prakṛti.* The self remains free, autonomous; that is, the yogin attains deliverance. Like a dead person, the yogin has no more real relation with life, but is a *jīvanmukta,* one "liberated in life." The yogin no longer lives in time and under the domination of time, but in an eternal present.

To recapitulate, the method recommended by the classical form of Yoga comprises a number of different techniques (physiological, mental, mystical) that gradually detach the yogin from the processes of life and the rules of social behavior. The worldly person lives in society, marries, establishes a family; Yoga prescribes solitude and chastity. In opposition to continual movement, the yogin practiced *āsana;* in opposition to agitated, unrhythmical, uncontrolled respiration, the yogin practices *prāṇāyāma;* to the chaotic flux of psychomental life, the yogin replies by "fixing thought on a single point"; and so on. The goal of all these practices always remains the same—to react against normal, secular, and even human inclinations. The final result is a grandiose, although paradoxical, mode of being. *Asamprajñāta samādhi* realizes the "knowledge-possession" of the autonomous Self (*puruṣa*); that is, it offers deliverance, freedom, and, more specifically, the consciousness of absolute freedom.

See Also Cakras; Īśvara; Jīvanmukti; Patañjali the Grammarian; Puruṣa; Sāṃkhya.

Bibliography

Patañjali's *Yoga Sūtra,* with the commentary *(Yogabhāṣya* or *Yogasūtra-bhaṣya)* of Vyāsa and the gloss *(Tattvavaiśāradī)* of Vācaspatimiśra have been translated into English by James H. Woods as *The Yoga System of Patañjali,* 3d ed. (Dehli, 1966), and by Rāma Prasāda as *Patanjali's Yoga Sutras* (Allahabad, 1910). A listing of editions and translations of other, later commentaries can be found on page 372 of my *Yoga: Immortality and Freedom,* 2d aug. ed. (Princeton,

N. J., 1969), which also includes bibliographies on pages 372, 437–480, and 533–555.

On the Yoga Upaniṣads, see *Yoga Upaniṣads with the Commentary of Srī Upaniṣad-Brahma-Yogin,* translated and edited by Allādi Mahādeva Sāstrī (Madras, 1920). Among the different works on Yoga, written from different perspectives, one may cite Richard Garbe's *Sāṃkhya und Yoga* (Strasbourg, 1896); Surendranath Dasgupta's *Yoga as Philosophy and Religion* (1924; reprint, Calcutta, 1973) and *Yoga Philosophy in Relation to Other Systems of Thought* (1930; reprint, Delhi, 1974); Hermann Jacobi's "Über das ursprüngliche Yogasystem," *Sitzungsberichte der preussischen Akademie der Wissenschaften* 26 (1929): 581–627; Sigurd Lindquist's *Die Methoden des Yoga* (Lund, 1932) and *Siddhi und Abhiññā: Eine Studie über die klassischen Wunder des Yoga* (Uppsala, 1935); Heinrich Zimmer's *Kunstform und Yoga im indischen Kultbild* (Berlin, 1926); J. W. Hauer's *Der Yoga, als Heilweg: Nach den indischen Quellen dargestellt,* 2d. ed. (Stuttgart, 1958); Jean Varenne's *Yoga and the Hindu Tradition,* translated by Derek Coltman (Chicago 1976); and Georg Feuerstein's *The Philosophy of Classical Yoga* (Manchester, 1980).

On Īśvara, see my *Yoga,* 2d aug. ed. (Princeton, N. J., 1969), pp. 68ff., and especially Jan Gonda's "The Īśvara Idea," in *Change and Continuity in Indian Religion* (The Hague, 1965), pp. 131–163.

On different types of yogic meditation, the best work is *Strukturen yogische Meditation* by Gerhard Oberhammer (Vienna, 1977). See also A. Janácek's "The 'Voluntaristic' Type of Yoga in Patañjali's *Yoga-Sūtras,*" *Archiv Orientálni* 22 (1954): 69–87, and Corrado Pensa's "On the Purification Concept in Indian Tradition, with Special Regard to Yoga," *East and West,* n. s. 19 (1969): 1–35. On the recent scientific observations in regard to the physiological and psychological aspects of yogic technique, see Thérèse Brosse's *Études instrumentales des techniques du Yoga: Expérimentation psychosomatique* (Paris, 1963).

On *ṣaḍaṅgayoga,* see Anton Zigmund-Cerbu's "The Ṣaḍaṅgayoga," *History of Religions* 3 (Summer 1963): 128–134; *Ṣadaṅga-yoga,* edited by Günter Grönbold (Munich, 1969), an edition and German translation of *Guṇabharaṇi-nāma-Ṣaḍaṅgayogatippanī* of Raviśrījñāna and Grönbold's "Materialen zur Geschichte des Ṣaḍaṅga-yoga, I–III," *Indo-Iranian Journal* 25 (April 1983): 181–190 (also published in *Zentralasiatische Studien* 16, 1982, pp. 337–347), and "Der sechsgliedrige Yoga des *Kālacakra-Tantra,*" *Asiatische Studien / Études asiatiques* 37 (1938): 25–45.

My *Yoga,* cited above, includes discussion of the different forms of yogic practices in Brahmanism, Hinduism, Buddhism, and Tantrism (pp. 101–274, 384–414) and of the yoga of the Jains (pp. 209–210, 404–405). On the yoga of the Jains, see also Robert H. B. William's *Jaina Yoga: A Survey of the Medieval Śrāvākācaras* (London, 1963).

New Sources

Bajpai, R. S. *The Splendours and Dimensions of Yoga.* New Delhi, 2002.

Burley, Mikel. *Hatha-Yoga: Its Context, Theory, and Practice.* Delhi, 2000.

Coward, Harold G. *Yoga and Psychology: Language, Memory, and Mysticism.* Albany, 2002.

Yoga: Discipline of Freedom: The Yoga Sutra attributed to Patanjali. Translated by Barbara Stoler Miller. Berkeley, 1996.

Yoga: The Indian Tradition. Edited by Ian Whicher and David Carpenter. London; New York, 2003.

The Yogasastra of Hemacandra: A Twelfth Century Handbook of Svetambara Jainism. Translated by Olle Quarnström. Cambridge, Mass., 2002.

Mircea Eliade (1987)
Revised Bibliography

YOGĀCĀRA. The Yogācāra school is, with the Mādhyamika, one of the two main traditions of Indian Buddhism. As the name indicates (*yogācāra* means "one whose practice is yoga"), this school attaches importance to the religious practice of yoga as a means for attaining final emancipation from the bondage of the phenomenal world. The stages of yoga are systematically set forth in the treatises associated with this tradition. The particular doctrinal stance of the school is suggested by its alternate name, Vijñānavāda, or the "doctrine" (*vāda*) that all phenomenal existence is fabricated by "consciousness" (*vijñāna*).

In concert with those who uphold the doctrine of "voidness" (*śūnyatā*), the Vijñānavādins maintain that phenomenal existences are devoid of intrinsic nature, but unlike the Mādhyamika, they admit the reality of the consciousness by which phenomenal existences, subjective as well as objective, are fabricated. This consciousness, however, is not deemed to exist in the ultimate sense. It subsists for but a moment and is replaced by the consciousness in the next moment. It has no substantiality and its origination is dependent on the consciousness of the preceding instant. To use the Yogācāra terminology, consciousness is of dependent nature (*paratantra-svabhāva*) and, as such, is not ultimately real. The Prajñāpāramitā Sūtras teach the voidness, or the nonexistence, of all entities. However, it is a fact of experience that phenomenal existences appear as if they were real. By admitting the reality of the consciousness, the Yogācāra clarified the foundation of our daily experience.

According to the *Saṃdhinirmocana Sūtra,* a Yogācāra text, the Buddha set the "wheel of the doctrine" (*dharmacakra*) in motion three times. On the first turning, the Buddha taught the doctrine of the four noble truths (*catvāry āryasatyāni*), the Hīnayāna path culminating in arhatship; on the second, he taught the doctrine of universal voidness designed to advance practitioners along the path to Buddhahood. But because the complete meaning of the Buddha's teaching was not fully elucidated during these "turnings," the Buddha set the wheel in motion a third time, with the intention of making explicit (*nītārtha*) what was only implicit (*neyārtha*) in the *sūtras* composed in earlier times.

Formative Period. The Yogācāra philosophy was systematized by Asaṅga and Vasubandhu, thinkers who lived in the fourth or fifth century. However, some important Yogācāra works, namely, the *Saṃdhinirmocana Sūtra,* the *Yogā-*

cārabhūmi, and the treatises ascribed to Maitreya(nātha), predate them.

The *Saṃdhinirmocana Sūtra*'s major contribution to the Yogācāra school is its formulation of the doctrine of the three "characteristics" (*lakṣaṇa*) of entities: the imaginary character (*parikalpita-lakṣaṇa*), the dependent character (*paratantra-lakṣaṇa*), and the perfected character (*pariniṣpanna-lakṣaṇa*). (All are explained in chapter 6.) The imaginary character is the assignation of conventional names to things with respect to their intrinsic nature (*svabhāva*) and specific qualities (*viśeṣa*). The dependent character is the conditioned origination (*Pratītya-samutpāda*) of things. The perfected character is the "thusness" (*tathatā*) of things or the emptiness of intrinsic nature in things. These three characteristics are closely related to the "triple unreality" discussed in chapter 7. Since the characteristic features of things are established merely by the act of assigning them conventional names, these features are ultimately unreal. Thus, the imaginary character of things is related to the unreality of their characteristic features (*lakṣaṇa-niḥsvabhāvatā*). Since the origination of things is dependent on causes and conditions, it is also not real. Thus the dependent character is related to the unreality of origination (*utpatti-niḥsvabhāvatā*). The ultimate reality is manifested through the thusness of things or the emptiness of intrinsic nature in things. Thus, the perfected character is related to the unreality of intrinsic nature, which is the ultimate reality (*paramārtha-niḥsvabhāvatā*).

The doctrine of three characteristics and triple unreality expresses what the Buddha had in mind when, in the Prajñāpāramitā Sūtras, he taught that all entities are devoid of intrinsic nature. It is understood that the Prajñāpāramitā Sūtras put forth a teaching, the meaning of which is inexplicit and must be drawn out (*neyārtha*). The *Saṃdhinirmocana Sūtra* unfolds (*nirmocana*) the "intention" (*saṃdhi*) of the Buddha that was hidden in the doctrine of voidness. This purpose is brought to full expression through the doctrine of triple unreality. Thus, this *sūtra* is of explicit meaning (*nītārtha*).

Chapter 5 of the *Saṃdhinirmocana Sūtra* presents the concept of *ālaya-vijñāna* ("storehouse consciousness"), which is characteristic of the Yogācāra teachings. It describes this consciousness as possessing "all the seeds" (*sarvabījaka*) from which future phenomenal existences will grow. The storehouse consciousness is attached to the sense faculties and to the impressions of "differentiations" (*prapañca*) left by the conventional usages regarding phenomenal existences and is called "attachment consciousness" (*ādāna-vijñāna*). Chapter 9 gives a detailed explanation of the practices of tranquilization (*śamatha*) and contemplation (*vipaśyanā*) through which a practitioner acquires the ability to concentrate his mind on certain ideas and to visualize and efface them at will. This practice forms the basis of the Yogācāra view that there is no external object.

The *Yogācārabhūmi* (Stages of the follower of yoga practice) is a voluminous, comprehensive work comprising five parts. The main part, which is called "Basic Text of the Stages," treats the seventeen stages (*bhūmi*) to be successively passed through by a follower of yoga practice. It begins with the stage of sense perceptions, proceeds through many stages of meditation and other practices, reaches the stage of "disciples" (*śrāvaka*), then of "isolated Buddhas" (*pratyekabuddha*), then of *bodhisattvas*, and ends with the stage of complete *nirvāṇa* (*nirupadhiśeṣa-nirvāṇa*, or "*nirvāṇa* with no residue"), the ultimate goal.

The Buddhist tradition in China attributes this work to Maitreya, but in Tibet it is known as a work of Asaṅga. Regarding the composition of a treatise dealing with seventeen stages, Paramārtha's *Life of Vasubandhu* (T.D. no. 2049) and Xuanzang's *Da Tang xiyu ji* (T.D. no. 2087) provide the following account. Asaṅga often went up to the Tuṣita Heaven, where he was taught the Mahāyāna doctrines by the *bodhisattva* Maitreya. Complying with the request of Asaṅga, who wanted Mahāyāna Buddhism to spread among the people, Maitreya came down to the continent of Jambudvīpa and gave a series of lectures on the seventeen stages. He lectured every night for four months; the next day Asaṅga, for the sake of the other attendants, gave a full explanation of what the *bodhisattva* had taught. (Asaṅga was the only attendant who had access to the *bodhisattva;* the others could merely hear him from afar.) This account may explain why the Chinese and the Tibetan traditions differ on the authorship of the *Yogācārabhūmi.* Some scholars assume that Maitreya, from whom Asaṅga is said to have received instruction on the Yogācāra doctrine, was a historical person; others, however, debate Maitreya's historicity. Recent studies of the *Yogācārabhūmi* have proved that it was not the work of a single person; it is now supposed that the text was gradually enlarged by successive generations of Yogācāra scholars.

The *Yogācārabhūmi* enumerates, classifies, and explains all elements that relate to the practice of each of the seventeen stages in the same manner as that of Abhidharma treatises. The doctrine of *ālaya-vijñāna* is found in the first two chapters of the "Basic Text" and in some sections of the "Compendium of Ascertainment" (an auxiliary division), while the doctrine of the three characteristics of entities is mentioned only in the latter division. The chapter dealing with the "stage of *bodhisattvas*" *(bodhisattvabhūmi)* is devoted to the detailed analysis of the religious practices of *bodhisattvas*, systematically explaining the matters with which their practices are concerned, the ways that their practices are to be conducted, and the results to be attained by the practices. It is known that this chapter once existed as an independent text.

In the Tibetan Buddhist tradition the following five works are ascribed to Maitreya(nātha): *Mahāyānasūtrālaṃkāra, Madhyāntavibhāga, Dharmadharmatāvibhaṅga, Ratnagotravibhāga,* and *Abhisamayālaṃkāra.* The last two are not considered Yogācāra works.

The *Mahāyānasūtrālaṃkāra* (Ornament of Mahāyāna Sūtras), which presents a systematic exposition of the practices of *bodhisattvas*, consists of about 800 verses and is divided into 21 chapters. According to the Tibetan tradition, the verse text was written by Maitreyanātha and the prose commentary by Vasubandhu; the Chinese tradition assigns both to Asaṅga. This treatise has the same structure as the chapter in the *Yogācārabhūmi* dealing with the stage of *bodhisattvas (bodhisattvabhūmi)*. The subject matter of chief concern to *bodhisattvas*—ultimate reality—is expounded in chapter 6, and the state of having attained the ultimate reality—enlightenment *(bodhi)*—is elucidated in chapter 9. The theoretical basis of the practices of *bodhisattvas* is given in chapter 11. The *Madhyāntavibhāga* (Discrimination of the middle and the extremes), which gives the Yogācāra interpretation of the doctrine of voidness (*śūnyatā*), consists of about 110 verses and is divided into 5 chapters. Both the Chinese and the Tibetan traditions ascribe the verse text to Maitreya and the prose commentary to Vasubandhu. This treatise places voidness in the middle (*madhya*) of the two extremes (*anta*), that is, existence and nonexistence. The *Dharmadharmatāvibhaṅga* (Discrimination of phenomenal existence and ultimate reality), a short treatise written in concise *sūtra* style, is commented upon by Vasubandhu. It was not transmitted to China. It shows that phenomenal existences, which are characterized by the duality of subject and object or of denoter and denoted, are in reality modifications of a conscious principle called "unreal imagination" (*abhūta-parikalpa*). Through the cognition of the true nature of phenomenal existences, the ultimate reality—the "thusness" (*tathatā*) that is free from the duality—is realized.

These works, attributed to Maitreya, describe the ultimate reality with such positive terms as "sphere of religion" (*dharmadhātu*), instead of characterizing it merely as "void" or "empty" (*śūnya*). Like space, ultimate reality is all-pervasive, and there is no phenomenal existence independent of it. It is also called the "essence of phenomenal existences" (*dharmatā*). The idea that the mind (*citta*) is essentially pure (*prakṛti-viśuddha*) and brilliant (*prabhāsvara*), a stance neglected in the dogmatics of the Abhidharma treatises, is fully supported, and the ultimate reality is identified with this pure and brilliant mind.

Whereas the concept of *ālaya-vijñāna* is not found in these works, the concept of "unreal imagination" (*abhūta-parikalpa*) plays an important role. The opening verse of the *Madhyāntavibhāga* clearly states that in emptiness (*śūnyatā*) there exists the unreal imagination. However, the unreal imagination is not admitted to exist in the ultimate sense. It is essentially "unreal," but it is supposed to exist as the basis of the wrong assumption of the reality of phenomenal existences, which are characterized by the duality of subject and object, denoter and denoted, and so on. Much importance is attached to the doctrine of the three characteristics (*lakṣaṇa*) or natures (*svabhāva*) of entities. In chapter 3 of the *Madhyāntavibhāga* this doctrine is considered the fundamental truth (*mūlatattva*), and some important doctrines, such as that of the four noble truths, the two truths (ultimate and conventional), and so on, are elucidated in terms of the three natures. The stages of yogic practice (*yogabhūmi*) through which a practitioner is led to the "transformation of the basis of his existence" (*āśraya-parāvṛtti*) and attains the ultimate reality, are explained systematically in chapter 11 of the *Mahāyānasūtrālaṃkāra*.

Period of Systematization. Asaṅga and Vasubandhu are the most prominent figures in the history of the Yogācāra school. Asaṅga first belonged to the Mahīśāsaka school of Hīnayāna Buddhism, but later, under the influence of the *bodhisattva* Maitreya, he became an advocate of the Mahāyāna. His treatises combine Abhidharmic analysis of the elements constituting phenomenal existences with Mahāyāna ideas. He composed, among others, the *Mahāyānasaṃgraha* (Compendium of the Mahāyāna), a comprehensive work on Yogācāra doctrines and practices. In the first two chapters of this work he gives a full treatment of the doctrines of *ālaya-vijñāna* and of the three natures (*trisvabhāva*) of entities, thus laying the firm foundation of the philosophical system of the Yogācāra school.

According to Paramārtha's *Life of Vasubandhu*, Vasubandhu was a younger brother of Asaṅga. He wrote two Yogācāra treatises: the *Viṃśatikā* (Treatise of twenty verses) and the *Triṃśikā* (Treatise of thirty verses). The *Viṃśatikā* repudiates the realist view that the image of an object in the consciousness has a corresponding reality in the external world and demonstrates that the image of an object appears in the consciousness as the result of a particular change (*pariṇāma-viśeṣa*) that occurs in the stream of the successive moments (*saṃtati*) of consciousness. The *Triṃśikā* presents a lucid, concise exposition of Yogācāra dogmatics. The first half of this treatise analyzes the structure and the function of consciousness; the second elucidates the three-nature doctrine and the stages of practice. Regarded as the standard textbook of the Yogācāra school, the *Triṃśikā* has been the subject of many commentaries by post-Vasubandhu scholars. Vasubandhu also composed a short treatise in verse dealing with the three-nature doctrine, the *Trisvabhāvanirdeśa*.

A number of other Yogācāra works have been handed down under the name of Vasubandhu, such as commentaries on the treatises attributed to Maitreya, on the *Mahāyānasaṃgraha* of Asaṅga, and on some Mahāyāna *sūtras*. The philosophical ideas expressed in these commentaries are not identical with those presented in the *Viṃśatikā* and the *Triṃśikā*. In the last two works, the influence of the Sautrāntika school of Hīnayāna Buddhism is noticeable, but this is not the case with the commentaries. Accordingly, some modern scholars believe that there were two Vasubandhus: one, Asaṅga's brother, composed the commentaries on *sūtras* and treatises; the other, the author of the *Viṃśatikā* and the *Triṃśikā*, also wrote the *Abhidharmakośa*, a summary of Sarvāstivāda dogmatics, and an autocommentary written from the Sautrāntika viewpoint. However, further investigations must be made before a more definite conclusion can be drawn. The fundamental doctrines of the Yogācāra school as formulated by Asaṅga and Vasubandhu are surveyed below.

Representation only (vijñaptimātra). The Yogācāras maintain that phenomenal existences, which are generally supposed to have objective reality in the external world, are no other than the "representations" (*vijñapti*), or images, of objects appearing in our consciousness (*vijñāna*). According to the Yogācāras, the image of an object is produced by the consciousness itself; there is no external object independent of the consciousness.

The *Mahāyānasaṃgraha* indicates that the image of an object in the consciousness does not presuppose the existence of the object in the external world. Some of the reasons mentioned are as follows;

1. The one and the same thing is represented differently by beings in different states of existence; for instance, that which is perceived by a man as a stream of clean water is represented as a flaming river by an inhabitant of hell and as a stream of pus and filth by a *preta.* This shows that an object represented in the consciousness is a product of mental construction.

2. It is a fact of experience that a cognition arises even when there is no object, as in the case of a recollection or dream. It is also known that a person who has advanced in yoga practice perceives a future object.

3. Through the practice of meditation (*dhyāna*) or tranquilization of the mind (*śamatha*), man comes to acquire the ability to visualize an object at will.

4. A practitioner who has stepped into the "path of insight" (*darśana-mārga*) attains "supermundane cognition" (*lokottara-jñāna*), in which there is no image of an object. This cognition, which has no corresponding reality in the external world, is thus experienced in daily life as well as in the process of religious practice.

Consequently, it is known that the form of an object that appears in the consciousness does not belong to a thing in the external world but is attributed to the consciousness itself.

Modification of consciousness *(vijñāna-pariṇāma).* The Yogācāra maintains that human beings and objective things, to which various terms—such as "self" (*ātman*), "living being" (*jīva*), "pot," and "cloth"—are applied, are in reality the "modifications of consciousness." The consciousness that undergoes modification consists of three strata: (1) the six kinds of consciousness produced through the visual, auditory, olfactory, gustatory, and tactile senses and the mind; (2) the "I-consciousness," called *manas,* which accompanies the six kinds of consciousness; and (3) the subliminal consciousness, called *ālaya-vijñāna* ("store consciousness"), in which the "impressions" (*vasana*) of past experiences are accumulated as the "seeds" (*bija*) of future experiences. While the *ālaya-vijñāna* is latent, the six kinds of consciousness and the I-consciousness are in manifest activity and are thus called the "consciousness-in-activity" (*pravṛtti-vijñāna*). The *ālaya-vijñāna* and the consciousness-in-activity are dependent on each other: the latter is produced from the seed preserved in the former and leaves, in turn, its impression on the former. Thus the *modification* (*pariṇāma*), or "change," of consciousness takes place in two ways: (1) a seed planted by the consciousness-in-activity becomes ripe in the *ālaya-vijñāna;* and (2) the consciousness-in-activity arises from the seed. The term "modification" was first used by Vasubandhu, but the idea of the mutual dependence of the *ālaya-vijñāna* and the consciousness-in-activity was formulated by Asaṅga in the *Mahāyānasaṃgraha.*

The *ālaya-vijñāna* subsists only for a moment, then is replaced by another consciousness in the next moment. The successive moments of the *ālaya-vijñāna* form a stream that continues to flow until the seeds planted in it are completely destroyed. In each moment there arises the consciousness-in-activity, and thus a consciousness complex is formed. A human being is a stream of the consciousness complex, and the things that are thought to exist in the external world are but the images that appear in this stream of consciousness.

Three natures *(trisvabhāva).* The three natures of entities, that is, the imagined nature (*parikalpita-svabhāva*), the dependent nature (*paratantra-svabhāva*), and the perfected nature (*pariniṣpanna-svabhāva*), were expounded in the *Saṃdhinirmocana Sūtra,* but this text does not discuss the interrelation of the three natures and consequently the doctrine's religious significance is not quite clear. In the *Mahāyānasaṃgraha,* in which the three-nature doctrine is a major topic, Asaṅga sets forth the view that the imagined and the perfected natures are two aspects of the dependent nature; the dependent nature, he explains, appears as the imagined nature by dint of a false imagination and as the perfected nature when the false imagination is removed. It is thus shown that the three-nature doctrine is closely related to Yogācāra soteriology. The doctrine, as formulated by Asaṅga and Vasubandhu, may be briefly summarized as follows. The consciousness that arises in each moment with the image of an object is of dependent nature because its origination is dependent on the impressions of past experiences preserved in the *ālaya-vijñāna.* Because of his false imagination, man ordinarily takes this image for a real object and applies a name to it. The object thus superimposed upon the image in the consciousness is of imagined nature. When the false imagination is completely removed through the practice of yoga, man realizes the absence of the superimposed object, that is, the perfected nature.

TRANSFORMATION OF THE BASIS *(ĀŚRAYA-PARĀVṚTTI).* The stages of yogic practice leading to the "transformation of the basis of existence" are systematized in some early Yogācāra works, and no substantial changes were made by Asaṅga and Vasubandhu. After passing the stage of accumulating merits and learning the Buddha's teaching, a yogācāra proceeds to the stage of "preparatory exercise" (*prayoga*). Through this stage he comes to understand clearly that a name or a concept has no corresponding reality in the external world and that the intrinsic nature and specific qualities of things are products of subjective construction. Thus, he realizes that there is no real object to be "seized" (*grāhya*) and, consequently, that the consciousness as the "seizer" (*grāhaka*) is also devoid of reality. At this moment he steps forward into the "path of insight" (*darśana-mārga*) and attains the immediate awareness of the ultimate reality. There arises in him the force to destroy the seeds of defilement that have accumulated from beginningless time in the *ālaya-vijñāna*. This force gradually becomes more powerful as he proceeds to the "path of intensive practice" (*bhāvanā-mārga*). Finally, the seeds are completely destroyed and the stream of the *ālaya-vijñāna* no longer constitutes the basis (*āśraya*) of his existence. In its place the ultimate reality reveals itself as the real, undifferentiated basis of all living beings. Through this transformation of the basis (*āśraya-parāvṛtti*) the *yogācāra* reaches the final stage of his yogic practice and attains Buddhahood.

Later Period: Transmission into China and Japan. After Vasubandhu, scholars in the Yogācāra school formed two subschools. One maintained that the consciousness (*vijñāna*) is necessarily endowed with the "form" (*ākāra*) of an object and that of a subject; the other held that the forms of object and subject are of imagined nature and false and that the consciousness itself, which is a pure luminosity, is real. Proponents of the former were called, from the eighth century onward, the Sākāra-vijñānavādins (that is, the upholders of the doctrine that the consciousness is endowed with forms) and proponents of the latter were termed the Nirākāra-vijñānavādins (that is, the upholders of the doctrine that the consciousness possesses no form). Dignāga (c. 480–540) and Dharmapāla (c. 530–561), prominent scholars in Nālandā, are recognized as the early representatives of the former and Sthiramati (c. 510–570) in Valabhī as an advocate of the latter. The Sākāra-vijñānavāda is doctrinally related to the Sautrāntika school, and a branch of the Nirākāra-vijñānavāda, represented by Śāntirakṣita (c. 725–788) and Kamalaśīla (c. 740–795), is united with the Mādhyamika. Scholarly activities continued in both subschools until the twelfth century, when Buddhism declined in India. In the last period, Ratnakīrti and Jñānaśrīmitra (eleventh century) maintained the former, and Ratnākārasanti (c. eleventh century) was a powerful advocate of the latter. Dharmakīrti (c. 600–660) and Prajñākāragupta (c. eighth century) are recognized by both subschools as exponents of their respective doctrines.

As early as the fifth century some Yogācāra works were translated into Chinese, but a real interest in Yogācāra was not aroused until Bodhiruci (?–527) arrived in China in 508 and translated Vasubandhu's commentary on the *Daśabhūmika Sūtra*, the *Shi di jing lun* (T.D. no. 1522), in which the doctrine of the *ālaya-vijñāna* is presented. This work was accepted as an authority among Buddhist circles in North China, and gave rise to the Dilun sect. In the meantime, Paramārtha (c. 499–569), who came to South China in 546, introduced several Yogācāra treatises to the Buddhist circles. He attached importance to the *Mahāyānasaṃgraha*, and his translation of this treatise, namely, the *She dasheng lun* (T.D. no. 1593), was treated as the basic text of the Shelun sect. In the seventh century, Xuanzang (602–664) traveled to India and studied Yogācāra doctrines at Nālandā under Śīlabhadra, a disciple of Dharmapāla. After returning to China in 645, Xuanzang translated a number of important Yogācāra works. In his translation of Dharmapāla's commentary on the *Triṃśikā Vijñaptimātratāsiddhiḥ* of Vasubandhu, he incorporated the views of ten other commentators and composed the *Cheng weishi lun*. This work was recognized as authoritative for Yogācāra dogmatics by the Faxiang sect, which was founded by Kuiji (632–682), a disciple of Xuanzang. Both the Dilun sect and the Shelun sect were absorbed into and replaced by the Faxiang sect, which itself soon declined under the new trend of Buddhism represented by the Huayan and Chan sects.

The dogmatics of the Faxiang (Jpn., Hossō) sect were introduced into Japan during the Nara period (710–784) by some monks who had studied in China. The *Cheng weishi lun* was earnestly studied there by Buddhist scholars of different sects until recent years.

See Also Ālaya-vijñāna; Asaṅga; Buddhism, article on Buddhism in India; Buddhism, Schools of, article on Chinese Buddhism; Buddhist Philosophy; Dharmakīrti; Dharmapāla; Dignāga; Indian Philosophies; Kamalaśīla; Kuiji; Mādhyamika; Maitreya; Paramārtha; Pratītya-samutpāda; Śāntirakṣita; Sautrāntika; Śīlabhadra; Sthiramati; Śūnyam and Śūnyatā; Tathatā; Vasubandhu; Xuanzang.

Bibliography

Frauwallner, Erich. *Die Philosophie des Buddhismus.* 3d rev. ed. Berlin, 1969. The philosophical ideas presented in the Yogācāra works of the early period and maintained by the principal figures of the Yogācāra school are clearly explained. Some passages extracted from important treatises are translated into German on pages 264–407.

Fukaura Seibun. *Yuishikigaku kenkyū.* Kyoto, 1976. The dogmatics of the Faxiang sect are explained in detail.

Hamamya Noriaki. *Yuishiki-shisō Ronkō* (Studies in philospohical ideas of the Vijñānavā). Tokyo, 2001. Collection of articles discussing some textual problems and philosphical ideas found in the Vijñānavā treatises.

Hirakawa Akira. *Indo bukkyōshi*, vol. 2. Tokyo, 1979. A brief description of the Yogācāra teachers and their works and an exposition of the fundamental doctrines are given on pages 92–169, 228–250.

Jacobi, Hermann, trans. *Triṃśikāvijñapti des Vasubandhu, mit bhāṣya des acarya Sthiramati.* Stuttgart, 1932.

Lamotte, Étienne. *Saṃdhinirmocana Sūtra: L'explication des mystères.* Louvain, 1935.

Lamotte, Étienne. *La somme du Grand Véhicule d'Asaṅga* (*Mahāyānasaṃgraha*). 2 vols. Louvain, 1938–1939.

La Vallée Poussin, Louis de. *Vijñaptimātratāsiddhi, la siddhi de Hiuan-tsang.* 2 vols. Paris, 1928–1929.

Lévi, Sylvain. *Un système de philosophie bouddhique: Materiaux pour l'étude du système Vijñaptimātra.* Paris, 1932.

Lévi, Sylvain, ed. and trans. *Asaṅga: Mahāyāna-sūtralaṃkāra,* vol. 2, *Exposé de la doctrine du Grand Véhicule selon le système Yogācāra.* Paris, 1911.

May, Jacques. "La philosophie bouddhique idéaliste." *Asiatische Studien* 25 (1971): 265–323. A sketch of the historical development of the Yogācāra school in India; elucidates the fundamental doctrines.

Nagao Gadjin. *Chūkan to yuishiki.* Tokyo, 1978. Contains articles discussing some philosophical ideas of the Vijñānavāda.

Nagao Gadjin. *Mādhyamika and Yogācāra: A Study of Mahāyana Philosophies.* Edited, collated, and translated by L. S. Kawamura in collaboration with G. M. Nagao. Albany, 1991. English versions of some articles published in *Chūkan to yuishiki* are included.

Nagao Gadjin. *Shōdai jōron. Wayaku to chūkai.* (Mahāyānasaṃgraha. A Japanese translation with annotations.) 2 vols. Tokyo, 1982–87. A translation based on the comparison of all available texts in Chinese and Tibetan—Tibetan text and reconstructed Sanskrit text (Introd., chaps. I. II) are added as an appendix.

Nagao Gadjin, Kajiyama Yūichi, and Aramaki Noritoshi. *Seshin ronshū.* Tokyo, 1976. Vasubandhu's *Viṃśatikā, Triṃśikā* (with Sthiramati's commentary), and *Trisvabhāvanirdeśa,* and Maitreya's *Madhyāntavibhāga* (with Vasubandhu's commentary) are translated into lucid modern Japanese.

Powers, John, trans. *Two Commentaries on the Saṃdhinirmocana-sūtra by Asaṅga and Jñānagarbha.* Lewiston, 1992.

Sakuma Hidenori. *Die Āśrayaparivṛtti-Theorie in der Yogācārabhūmi.* 2 Stuttgart, 1990.

Schmithausen, Lambert. *Der Nirvāṇa-Abschnitt in der Viniścayasaṃgrahani der Yogācārabhūmiḥ.* Vienna, 1969.

Schmithausen, Lambert. "Zur Literaturgeschichte der álteren Yogācāra-Schule." *Zeitschrift der Deutschen Morgenländischen Gesellschaft; Supplement* 1 (1969): 811–823. A careful examination of the composition of the *Yogācārabhūmi.*

Schmithausen, Lambert. *Ālayavijñāna. On the Origin and Early Development of a Central Concept of Yogācāra Philosophy.* 2 Pts. Tokyo, 1987.

Stcherbatsky, Theodore, trans. *Madhyanta-vibhaṅga: Discourse on Discrimination between Middle and Extremes, Ascribed to Maitreyanātha and Commented by Vasubandhu and Sthiramati.* Moscow, 1936.

Suguro Shinjō. *Shoki Yuishiki-shisō no kenkyū.* Tokyo, 1989.

Yamaguchi Susumu. *Bukkyō ni okeru mu to u to no tairon.* Kyoto, 1941. A detailed study of a chapter of Bhāvaviveka's *Madhyamakahṛdaya,* intended for the refutation of the Yogācāra doctrine.

Yamaguchi Susumu, and Nozawa Jōshō. *Seshin yuishiki no genten kaimei.* Kyoto, 1953. Contains a Japanese translation of the *Viṃśatikā* with Vinītadeva's *ṭīkā* and the *Triṃśikā* with Sthiramati's *bhāṣya* and Vinitadeva's *ṭīkā.*

HATTORI MASAAKI (1987 AND 2005)

YOGANANDA (1893–1952) was one of the earliest and most influential of the Hindu gurus to come to the West. Growing up in Calcutta in Bengal, India, he was a product of the Bengali Neo-Vedāntic Renaissance and was influenced by the saint Sri Ramakrishna (1836–1886).

The Neo-Vedāntic Renaissance originated in Bengal, one of the areas of India with the most exposure to Western culture as a result of British colonialism. The movement sought to reassert the vigor and worth of Hindu spirituality and philosophy while being open to influences from other religions and Western science and values. Yogananda was affiliated with a lineage of gurus that sought to integrate Hindu spirituality with a modern, Western-influenced lifestyle. Yogananda felt that he had a special destiny: to introduce Hindu concepts and spiritual techniques to westerners. He did this by disseminating a practice called *kriyā yoga* through his organization, the Self-Realization Fellowship, and by the publication of his books. His most famous published work is his *Autobiography of a Yogi,* first published in 1946, which has been translated into eighteen languages.

YOUTH IN INDIA. Yogananda was born Mukunda Lal Ghosh, the son of a railway executive in Bengal. His parents were disciples of Lahiri Mahasaya (1828–1895), a householder guru (he continued his married family life while being a guru) who taught a spiritual technique called *kriyā yoga.*

As a boy, Mukunda's first mentor in spirituality was "M." or Mahendra Nath Gupta, a disciple of Sri Ramakrishna and author of *Śrīśrīrāmākṛṣṇakathamṛta,* which was shaped by Swami Nikhilananda into *The Gospel of Sri Ramakrishna.* M. took Mukunda to worship at the Kālī temple at Dakshineswar, which had been Ramakrishna's residence, and stimulated Mukunda's first mystical experience. One day after M. and his young protégé were exiting a bioscope (an early motion picture), M. tapped Mukunda on his chest. Suddenly all noise on the busy street stopped for Mukunda. He saw the pedestrians and vehicles, but all was silent, and he observed a luminous glow emanating from all phenomena. This experience was the basis of Yogananda's later teaching that the physical world has the reality of a motion picture or a dream.

In 1910 Mukunda became the disciple of Swami Sri Yukteswar (1955–1936), who was a direct disciple of Lahiri Mahasaya. Mukunda completed his A.B. degree at Serampore College. He then took vows of *sannyasa* (renunciation) and became Swami Yogananda. In 1917 Yogananda demonstrated his considerable administrative ability by founding a boys' school, which he ran under the auspices of an organization he named the Yogoda Satsanga Society.

MISSION IN THE UNITED STATES. After Swami Yogananda came to the United States from India in 1920, he attracted numerous disciples by means of his public lectures and writings. Yogananda built up an organization called the Self-Realization Fellowship (SRF) to disseminate his presentation of the wisdom and spiritual techniques of Hinduism. Yogananda first came to the United States to deliver an invited lecture to the International Congress of Religious Liberals, sponsored by the American Unitarian Association. He subsequently spoke to large audiences across the United States from 1924 to 1927. In 1925 an estate was acquired at Mount Washington in Los Angeles, California, to be the headquarters of his organization, which was incorporated in 1935 as the Self-Realization Fellowship. In that same year his guru gave him the title Paramahansa ("supreme swan") indicating that he had achieved the highest enlightenment and, while in India on a visit, he initiated Mohandas Gandhi into *kriyā yoga.* In 1946 Yogananda published his most famous book, *Autobiography of a Yogi,* in which he describes his meetings with Eastern and Western saints and discusses visions and miracles that demonstrate the availability of supernormal powers and enlightenment to adepts of all religious traditions. In the ensuing years the SRF established a hermitage at Encinitas, California, a temple in San Diego, the Church of All Religions in Hollywood, and the Lake Shrine at Pacific Palisades, California, where a portion of Gandhi's ashes are kept. By 2004 the SRF additionally had forty-four centers and meditation groups in the United States as well as centers and groups in seventeen other countries.

Yogananda is regarded by his disciples as a *premavatār,* an incarnation of divine love. Yogananda stressed the deep emotional love for God that is associated with Hindu *bhakti yoga.* Members of the SRF rever Krishna and Christ as the two great gurus from whose works the teachings of Yogananda's lineage of gurus are derived. The SRF offers instruction in *kriyā yoga* and related philosophy and practices conveyed in a correspondence course called the SRF Lessons. Students pledge to keep the *kriyā yoga* technique secret from non-initiates. The SRF also has a monastic order for women and men headquartered at Mount Washington.

Yogananda passed away on March 7, 1952, after speaking at a banquet of the India Association of America at the Biltmore Hotel in Los Angeles. His devotees believe that the lack of corruption displayed by his body for twenty days after his death was the physical manifestation of his yogic mastery. Rajarsi Janakananda (formerly James J. Lynn) took over the leadership of the SRF until his death in 1955. An American woman, Sri Daya Mata, has served as SRF president since 1955. The Self-Realization Fellowship continues to disseminate Yogananda's books and to offer instruction in *kriyā yoga* and other spiritual techniques. Although Yogananda has passed from the material world, he is regarded as a still-living master who continues to guide his disciples.

SEE ALSO Gandhi, Mohandas.

BIBLIOGRAPHY

Self-Realization Fellowship. *Pictorial History of Self-Realization Fellowship (Yogoda Satsanga Society of America).* Los Angeles, 1975. Helpful history of Yogananda and the SRF.

Wendell, Thomas. *Hinduism Invades America.* New York, 1930. Yogananda approved the chapter appearing on pages 177 to 245, which discusses his work.

Wessinger, Catherine. "Hinduism Arrives in America: The Vedanta Movement and the Self-Realization Fellowship." In *America's Alternative Religions,* edited by Timothy Miller. Albany, N.Y., 1995, pp. 173–190. Essay on Yogananda and Swami Vivekananda and the other swamis who first brought Hinduism to the United States.

Yogananda, Paramahansa. *The Divine Romance.* Los Angeles, 1986. Describes Yogananda's basic approach to loving God.

Yogananda, Paramahansa. *Autobiography of a Yogi,* 12th ed. Los Angeles, 1990. Yogananda's most famous and widely influential book.

Yogananda, Paramahansa. *The Science of Religion.* Los Angeles, 1990. Text of Yogananda's first lecture in America.

CATHERINE WESSINGER (2005)

YOḤANAN BAR NAPPAḤA'

YOḤANAN BAR NAPPAḤA' (d. 279?), leading Palestinian amora. Yoḥanan's father and mother had both died by the time he was born (B.T., *Qid.* 31b), and his apparent patronymic refers either to his trade as a smith *(nappaḥa')* or to his legendary, "inflaming" good looks. Yoḥanan is always referred to either by his given name or by the epithet *bar Nappaḥa',* never both.

Yoḥanan's studies began during the lifetime of Yehuda ha-Nasi', known as "Rabbi," the redactor of the Mishnah. Later, Yoḥanan remembered having attended Rabbi's lectures and not understanding them (B.T., *Ḥul.* 137b). A native of Sepphoris, Yoḥanan began his studies there, but ultimately he became head of a prestigious rabbinic academy in Tiberias, where he spent the major part of his career. The only Babylonian for whom he spontaneously expressed respect was Rav, with whom he had studied under Yehuda ha-Nasi'; he later came to acknowledge the mastery of Shemu'el (B.T., *Ḥul.* 95b), but the two never met. In general, Yoḥanan's career was limited to the rabbinate of the Land of Israel, though his reputation traveled far beyond that country and even in Babylonia equaled that of the great Babylonian masters (B.T., *'A.Z.* 40a).

Yoḥanan inherited a considerable amount of wealth but was said to have allowed it to dissipate in his pursuit of advanced learning. He became the teacher, senior colleague, and brother-in-law of Shim'on ben Laqish. The latter, according to Talmudic tradition, was originally attracted to Yoḥanan because he was so handsome. Shim'on became Yoḥanan's colleague and eventually the two were inseparable. It is recorded that Shim'on died because of a slight from his companion. Later legend explained Yoḥanan's own death as the result of his grief over this incident. Yoḥanan was also embittered by the death within his lifetime of ten of his children (B.T., *B.M.* 84a, *Ber.* 5b).

In his halakhic teaching, Yoḥanan devised a number of rules for determining which of several conflicting opinions in the Mishnah was to be followed—for example, when Me'ir and Yehuda disagree, the *halakhah* ("law") follows Yehuda; when Yehuda and Yose disagree, the *halakhah* follows Yose (B.T., *'Eruv.* 46b); whenever Shim'on ben Gamli'el gives a ruling in the Mishnah, the *halakhah* follows him except in three cases (B.T., *Giṭ.* 75a); when Yehuda ha-Nasi' disagrees with his colleagues, the *halakhah* follows him (J.T., *Ter.* 3.1, 42a). He also formulated the much-quoted norm that the law always follows anonymous Mishnaic rulings (see, for instance, B.T., *Shabbat* 46a, and J.T., *Shabbat* 3.7, 6c). Yoḥanan's influence on the development of rabbinic scholarship in the Land of Israel was so great that Moses Maimonides considered him the redactor of the Jerusalem Talmud, although this is surely an exaggerated report.

According to one tradition, the custom of placing decorative art on walls (probably the walls of synagogues) arose in Yoḥanan's time "and he did not object" (J.T., *'A.Z.* 3.3, 42d). Yoḥanan also became an authority on calendrical astronomy (J.T., *R. ha-Sh.* 2.6, 58a-b; B.T., *Hul.* 95b). With respect to nonlegal lore, Yoḥanan was known as a student of *merkavah* mysticism, which he unsuccessfully offered to teach to his own student El'azar ben Pedat. The long *aggadah* (nonlegal rabbinic thought) on the destruction of Jerusalem that starts in the Babylonian Talmud tractate *Giṭṭin* 55b is attributed to him, as are other narratives that purport to recount important events in the history of the rabbinate (B.T., *Hor.* 13b) or the circumstances that gave rise to particular rabbinical enactments (B.T., *B.Q.* 94b, *Bekh.* 30b). Yoḥanan also gave considerable attention to the etiquette of prayer and to methods for increasing its effectiveness. According to legend, his final instructions were that he was to be buried in neither a black nor a white shroud so that he would not be ashamed to find himself in the company of either the righteous or the wicked.

SEE ALSO Amoraim.

BIBLIOGRAPHY

Aaron Hyman's *Toledot tanna'im ve-amora'im* (1910; reprint, Jerusalem, 1964) is an altogether uncritical compendium of traditional lore concerning Yoḥanan. It is almost useless as a tool for modern, critical biography, but it remains valuable as an encyclopedic gathering of information. The "Johanan ben Nappaḥa" articles in the *Jewish Encyclopedia* (New York, 1906) and in *Encyclopaedia Judaica* (Jerusalem, 1971) are also useful.

New Sources

Baumgarten, Albert I. "Yohanan and Resh Lakish on Anonymous 'mishnayot.'" *Jewish Law Association Studies* 2 (1986): 75–88.

Friedman, Shamma. "The Further Adventures of Rav Kahana: Between Babylonia and Palestine." In *The Talmud Yerushalmi and Graeco-Roman Culture,* vol. 3, edited by Peter Schäfer, pp. 247–271. Tübingen, 2002.

Kimelman, Reuven R. "Problems in Late Rabbinic 'Biography': The Case of the Amora Rabbi Yohanan." *SBLSP* 2 (1979): 35–42.

ROBERT GOLDENBERG (1987)
Revised Bibliography

YOḤANAN BEN ZAKK'AI

YOḤANAN BEN ZAKK'AI (c. 1–80 CE), sage and leader of Judaism in the Land of Israel after the destruction of the Jerusalem Temple in 70 CE. Known to us only from sources brought to closure two and more centuries after his death, beginning with the Mishnah (c. 200), two facts about his life are certain: he lived before the destruction, and survived it.

Yoḥanan was the principal figure in the formation, in the aftermath of the calamity, of a circle of disciples with whom he laid the foundations of the Judaism presented by the Mishnah. This work of legal-theological formation defined Judaism as it would be known from the second century onward. Yoḥanan himself is represented in the Mishnah principally through attributions to him of certain temporary ordinances, meant mostly to take account of the destruction of the Temple as an event in the sacred calendar of Judaism. These reforms, involving very trivial matters, signified a policy of surviving and carrying on. They meant that even without the Temple it would be possible to worship God and observe the festivals formerly focused upon the Temple. To Yoḥanan are attributed, also, certain interpretations of biblical stories, one of which stressed that Job had served God out of awe and reverence, not (merely) love. Finally, he is represented as having attempted to exercise authority even over the priesthood, which had formerly run the country. His rulings in matters of genealogy, on which priestly authority rested, indicate that he held that sages' mastery of Torah was paramount, priests' genealogical standing derivative. In these aspects Yoḥanan carried forward the position of the Pharisees of the period before the destruction. They had maintained that lay people might observe at home certain rules that were kept by the priests in the Temple, so indicating that the priests enjoyed no monopoly over access to the sacred.

In compilations of stories produced much later than the Mishnah, Yoḥanan's career is fleshed out. His surviving the destruction is represented as an encounter between Israel, the Jewish nation, and Rome, with a sage, Yoḥanan himself, negotiating on behalf of the Jews with a Roman general. In the principal version Yoḥanan is portrayed as having escaped from Jerusalem before it was fully invested and as having come before the Roman general Vespasian. He asked for the right to go to Yavneh, a coastal town where loyalists were held. There he would teach his disciples, establish a house of prayer, and carry out the commandments, the religious deeds of Judaism. He further informed Vespasian that the general would become emperor. (In other versions Yoḥanan is supposed to have asked for "the chain of Rabban Gamli'el and physicians to heal Rabbi Tsadoq.")

Yoḥanan's message to Israel, portrayed in other late sources, involved three elements. First, not to take too seriously the claims of messiahs: "If you have a sapling in your hand and people say to you, 'Behold, there is the Messiah,' go on with your planting, and afterward go out and receive him." Second, to obey God's will as the response to defeat: "Happy are you, O Israel! When you obey the will of God, then no nation or race can rule over you! But when you do not obey the will of God, you are handed over into the hands of every low-born people." Third, what God wants is acts of loving kindness. Yoḥanan held that even though sin could no longer be atoned through sacrifice in the Temple, "We have another atonement as effective as this. And what is it? It is acts of loving-kindness, as it is said, 'For I desire mercy, not sacrifice'" (*Hos.* 6:6).

Whether or not these tales go back to the person, or even the time, of Yoḥanan ben Zakk'ai, we do not know. But they are the foundation legends of the kind of Judaism that has been paramount from the second century to the present, and Yoḥanan, above all, is credited with the definition of that Judaism.

BIBLIOGRAPHY

The most original and important scholarship on Yoḥanan ben Zakk'ai is in Gedalyahu Alon, *Jews, Judaism and the Classical World,* translated from the Hebrew by Israel Abrahams (Jerusalem, 1977), pp. 252–343. The principal tales appear in *The Fathers according to Rabbi Nathan,* translated from the Hebrew by Judah Goldin (New Haven, 1955). This work is a compilation of rabbinical fables, loosely organized around the Mishnah tractate *Avot.* Two works of my own concern Yoḥanan: all of the sources on the man are collected and analyzed, in the rough sequence of their formation, in *Development of a Legend: Studies on the Traditions concerning Yoḥanan ben Zakkai* (Leiden, 1970) and are collected into a biography in *A Life of Yoḥanan ben Zakkai, ca. 1–80 C.E.* (Leiden, 1970).

New Sources

Cervelli, Innocenzo. "Dalla storiografia alla memoria: a proposito di Flavio Giuseppe e Yohanan ben Zakkai." *Studi Storici* 31 (1990): 919–982.

Finkel, Asher. "The Departures of the Essenes, Christians and R. Yohanan ben Zakkai from Jerusalem." In "Wie gut sind deine Zelte, Jaakow. . ." *Festschrift zum 60 Geburtstag von Reinhold Mayer,* edited by Ernst Ludwig Ehrlich [et al.], pp. 29–40. Gerlingen, 1986.

Herscher, Uri D. "Yohanan ben Zakkai at Yavneh: Merkavah and Messiah." In *Bits of Honey: Essays for Samson H. Levey,* edited by Stanley F. Chyet and David H. Ellenson, pp. 25–42. Atlanta, 1993.

JACOB NEUSNER (1987)
Revised Bibliography

YOM KIPPUR SEE RO'SH HA-SHANAH AND YOM KIPPUR

YONI is a Sanskrit word with various meanings such as "womb, vulva, vagina; place of birth, source, origin, spring; abode, home, lair, nest; family, race, stock, caste," and so on. It is etymologically derived from the verbal root *yu* ("join, unite, fasten, or harness"), from which is derived the English *yoke; ni* is added to the root to form a noun with active meaning. Thus *yoni* is "what joins or unites." The word *yoga,* derived from the same root, means "union, connection." The two words *yoni* and *yoga* are thus similar to the word *religion,* from the Latin *religio* ("binding, fastening, reuniting, or relinking").

Icons representing the *yoni* alone or in conjunction with the male generative organ, the *liṅga,* are widespread in both popular Hinduism and in the Tantric traditions of India; such images, known in English as yonis and lingams, stand for the generic goddess, Devī, in her many aspects, and the god Śiva. These traditions are the heirs of a female-dominated symbol system characteristic of the pre-Vedic worldview. Before the Indus and Ganges valleys were populated from the north by Aryan pastoral nomads, bearers of a more androcentric religion, there flourished an agricultural civilization known as the Indus Valley civilization (c. 4000–1000 BCE). Archaeological remains from the sites at Harappa and Mohenjo Daro abound in mother-goddess figurines, large stone yonis (and lingams), and a variety of seals. One of the most intriguing of these seals bears the figure of a man in a cross-legged posture typical of yogic discipline. The religious complex of ideas and practices called *yoga* has been identified as being pre-Vedic in origin; the yogic posture of the figure on this Indus Valley seal is one of the strongest pieces of evidence for the pre-Vedic origins of yoga. Scholars have until recently identified this horned yogic person as a proto-image of Śiva. More recent research has identified the scene depicted on the seal as being linked with an archaic form of the still-practiced buffalo sacrifice to the Goddess. On the seal the Goddess is represented next to her mount, the lion, which is shown in a dynamic posture facing the seated figure on its right, corresponding to the northern direction with the Goddess. The yogic posture of the buffalo-horned god has been interpreted as expressive of the destructive and creative power entailed by the sacrifice. The sacrifice itself aims at a symbolic unification with the Goddess. In many popular South Indian myths concerning this sacrifice, the buffalo is depicted as desiring or actually uniting with the Goddess in the guise of a lower-caste husband or suitor. As David Shulman has shown in his discussion of South Indian mythology (1980), Śiva becomes the buffalo. Through sacrificial death, Śiva as the buffalo consort of the goddess is reborn from her. In these myths and representations one seems to be able to apprehend the common etymology of the terms *yoni* and *yoga.* Union with the Goddess is the ultimate aim of the sacrifice; it is at one and the same time an abstract concept and a concrete act of union with the Goddess's icon, namely her yoni.

The symbolism on this famous Harappan seal, thus interpreted in the light of contemporary ritual practices and myths, brings up the extremely widespread symbolic themes of the mysterious and potent link between the yoni and death, and sacrificial death in particular. Perhaps the earliest evidence of the theme is to be found in the European Paleo-

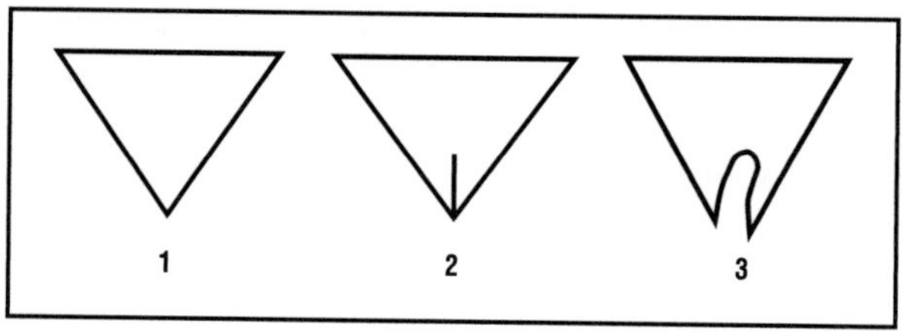

FIGURE 1. Yoni symbols.

lithic caves dating from about 20,000 to 11,000 BCE. Yoni symbols have been found in profusion in these caves, many of them identical to some of the Indian representations of the *yoni.* The most often found Paleolithic *yoni* symbol is the same as the Tantric symbol, namely a downward-pointing triangle (see figure 1.1), with variations (figure 1.2, 1.3). What is even more remarkable is the association between the yonic triangle and representations of the bison found at several Paleolithic caves, since the bison is the Western cousin of the Eastern buffalo.

The most striking such representation is the one found at the Abri du Roc aux Sorciers at Angles-sur-Anglin, France, dating from about 13,000 to 11,000 BEC. A colossal group of three female torsos with exaggerated *yonis*, all represented as cleft downward-pointing triangles (figure 1.2), are etched in the living rock wall. The three female figures are standing on a bison. The relief of two recumbent female figures dates from the same period; they flank both sides of the entrance to a shallow cave at La Madeleine in France. The figure to the right has at its center the same downward-pointing cleft triangle to represent the *yoni* (the left image is too damaged to discern the sexual parts); below the figure on the left is a bison.

The famous "Woman with the Horn," dating some five to seven thousand years earlier, depicts a nude female holding a bison horn in her right uplifted hand; it is incised on the rock wall of a shelter at Laussel in France. The bison horn is marked with thirteen lines, most likely representing the thirteen lunar months in the year. The crescent shape of the horn bears an unmistakable likeness to the lunar crescent. The analogy between the cycles of the moon and the menstrual cycle of women is found in most cultures of the world. The parallelism is most directly stated by the !Kung hunters and gatherers of the Kalahari Desert of southern Africa, among whom the menses are simply called "the moon."

Only a few miles from the Laussel rock shelter is situated the most grandiose of all Paleolithic painted caves, that of Lascaux. That caves were symbolic of the earth's womb is strongly suggested by the cave at La Madeleine, with its entrance flanked by two nude women. On the rim of the entrance to the Lascaux cave is incised a cluster of what André Leroi-Gourhan has termed "female vulvas in the shape of claviforms." Thus to enter a cave was to enter the deep, labyrinthine, dark womb of Mother Earth.

In India in the early twenty-first century there are several popular pilgrimage sites where the icon of the Goddess is situated deep in a cave whose access is through an extremely narrow, dark, and winding passageway. The most famous such natural icon of the Goddess's *yoni* is found in Assam in eastern India, at the shrine of Kāmakhya Devī. It is a natural cleft in the rock that is said to menstruate once per year, the period coinciding with the main festival of the Goddess in June at the time of the arival of the monsoon. The shrine of Kāmakhya Devī is linked with the myth of Satī, the consort of Śiva, who immolated herself after her father scorned her husband by not inviting him to a great sacrifice. The disconsolate Śiva carried Satī's corpse with him in his wanderings, and parts of her body fell to earth. Her *yoni* fell where the shrine of Kāmakhya Devī is located. At the shrine of Vaishno Devī in Jammu, pilgrims crawl on their bellies along a dark and wet narrow corridor to reach the cave of the Goddess. A spring originates there, completing the birth-rebirth imagery. Clearly the yonic symbolism of caves is extraordinarily ancient.

The cave at Lascaux is immense, with several corridors and large chambers covered with spectacular rock paintings of animals. These caves were not habitats but ritual centers for the Paleolithic hunters and gatherers. The painted herds found in their depths, visible only by the flickering light of torches, may represent the animals in the earth's womb out of which animals come in the daylight and into which they return at night, only to reemerge in the morning. A painted scene in the innermost recess of this complex of caves, called "the Crypt" because it is sixteen feet below the general level of the cavern floor, has been interpreted by Joseph Campbell as representing a similar theme, that of the regenerative power of death. The scene shows a bison with a spear entering through its anus and emerging from its genitals, where its entrails hang out in the form of four concentric ovals. Next to the bison lies a bird-headed or bird-masked ithyphallic man and next to him a spear-thrower and a bird-topped staff. The figure in all likelihood represents a shaman, since birds are in contemporary shamanistic contexts the typical vehicles for the shaman's trance flight to the underworld or the heavens.

The symbolic equivalence between spear and phallus is ethnographically widespread, as is the analogy between concentric ovals or other labyrinthine or spiral patterns and the female generative organs. The association between the *yoni* and a wound is widespread as well. It is an analogy still expressed today in South India and Sri Lanka. An ancient Tamil poem brings together the phallus-spear and *yoni*-wound analogies by depicting a man who views his newborn son for the first time wearing full warrior attire, a bloody spear in his hand and a freshly self-inflicted wound on his neck. Leroi-Gourhan, who has made an intensive study of the Paleolithic cave paintings, identifies the bison's hanging entrails as a *yoni* symbol. The speared bison, most probably a sacrificial victim, represents in death a sexual union. The scene is hauntingly reminiscent of the sacrifice of the buffalo-man to the Indian Goddess, also equivalent to sexual union. The womb-cave of the earth is a generative power, which brings forth life through death.

The view of the womb as the originator of both life and death is succinctly captured in the following Hindu saying: "Again birth, again death, again sleep in the mother's womb." In many so-called primitive cultures, the departed ancestors live in a place from which they come back to enter the *yonis* of women to be reborn. In the Trobriand Islands of Melanesia unborn and the dead are the very same beings. After death and the observation of the proper funerary rituals, the departed ancestor or ancestress goes to the island of Tuma. It is from that island that the departed return in the form of the soul of unborn children to enter the *yonis* of Trobriand women. In aboriginal Australia, the sacred engraved ancestral stones called *tjurungas* are hidden in hollows and caves; by visiting these sites the women become impregnated. It is in the light of such cyclical views of generation and regeneration that one can understand rituals in which death and the act of generation are made to coincide as they apparently do in the Lascaux crypt; the end is also the beginning.

Entering the womb/caves of the Paleolithic hunters and gatherers must have been a numinous experience for the participants, who had to creep through dangerously narrow, dark passageways to a world beyond night and day, beyond time itself. It is indubitable that the nearly universal analogy between the earth and woman implicit in the womb/cave identification is at least as old as those remotest of cultures.

The theme of the earth as a womb into which the dead are placed is found throughout the Neolithic period. In her work summarizing the archaeological finds in southeastern Europe and the eastern Mediterranean areas (6500 to 3500 BCE), Marija Gimbutas (1982) gives ample evidence of the prominence of triangular *yoni* designs as well as of goddess images in the act of giving birth, legs wide apart. The dual nature of the goddess as both giver and taker of life is most vividly represented in the many shrines found at the site of Çatal Hüyük in Anatolia. Breasts rising out of the shrine wall have open nipples out of which vultures' beaks protrude; the skull of the vulture is inside the breast. The wall paintings in these shrines show vultures pecking at the flesh of headless corpses. The evidence from burial sites in the shrines led the excavator of Çatal Hüyük, James Mellaart, to the conclusion that before burial in the earth, the corpses were exposed on elevated platforms for the purpose of excarnation. This is a practice still followed by Zoroastrians. In some of the shrines, images of the naked goddess are represented giving birth to a bison or a ram's head. In other sites of this area, designated by Gimbutas as Old Europe, the dead are placed in egg-shaped pithoi in a fetal position. Like the grave pit, the pithos was considered to be a womb from which the child or adult could be born again. Often the body was sprinkled with red ocher, a symbol of blood, to assure the restoration of life.

Cave mouths and clefts in rock walls are not the only yonic associations one encounters cross-culturally. Mountains themselves have been associated with the *yoni,* as the Latin term *mons veneris,* meaning the yonic triangle, attests, since it literally means "mountain of Venus." Springs, rivers, ponds, lakes, and seas have female meanings in many cultures of all levels of complexity. From the *yoni* gush forth the maternal waters at the time of birth. The earth's stones and metals have been analogized to the Goddess's bones. In the realm of vegetation some of the best-known yonic icons are fruits whose shape are in some ways analogous to that of the *yoni.* Some of the best-known are the pomegranate (Europe and West Asia), the mango (South Asia), the kidney bean (Rome), the fig and the almond (the Mediterranean world), and the peach and the apricot (Europe).

The active character of the etymology of the word *yoni* reveals itself in the mythological realm as the *śakti,* or power of the Goddess. These are contemporary Hindu concepts that seem to be the heirs of one of the oldest religious traditions of humankind. In the Tantric tradition—and much popular Hinduism as well—the Goddess is the active principle in the cosmos without whom her male consort Śiva would be just a corpse. The life-giving, animating power of the cosmos is Śakti, a personification that in its most concrete manifestation resides in the *yoni.* In the esoteric Tantric traditions in both Hinduism and Buddhism, the *yoni* is worshiped in an elaborate secret ritual in the form of several symbolic representations. It is worshiped literally as well: a woman sits nude and cross-legged, exposing her *yoni,* to which the worshipper makes a series of offerings. For Tantrics, all women are living incarnations of the Goddess. In popular Hinduism, the *yonis* of sculpted female figures on entrance gates are ritually fingered by worshipers as they enter a place of worship.

Popular belief in Hindu India holds that vaginal fluids enter the man's penis during intercourse. This belief corresponds to the standard Indian poetic image for sexual union, that of the male bumblebee gathering honey in female flower buds. In intercourse, through the woman's vaginal fluids a man receives the *śakti* that is his wife's. Such ideas underlie the custom of the establishment of concubines for kings, chiefs, and other important males, a practice found not only in India but in certain West African and Pacific cultures as well. These ideas are by no means encountered solely among complex cultures based on agriculture, such as traditional Hindu India, but are also found among hunters and gatherers. A !Kung woman from the Kalahari Desert, named Nisa by her anthropologist biographer (Marjorie Shostak), says the following about women's genitals: "Women possess something very important, something that enables men to live: their genitals. A woman can bring a man life, even if he is almost dead. She can give him sex and make him live again. If she were to refuse, he would die!"

The life-giving power of vaginal fluids is most concretely exemplified among the Kiwai people of New Guinea. Vaginal secretions are used extensively in garden rituals. For example, when the first shoots of yams, the culture's staple diet, have sprouted above ground, the mother of the owner of the garden smears her hands with her vaginal fluids and tugs at one of the shoots. At the time of planting taro, the mother lies down nude in the garden; and her husband inserts the digging stick in her vulva and then digs the hole in the ground between her legs. The fertile powers of the vulva and its secretions could not possibly be more concretely stated.

In most agricultural societies the furrow or the seed hole stand for the vulva. The seed stands for semen, and the plough or digging stick for the phallus. Sītā, the heroine of the Indian epic the *Rāmāyaṇa,* was born in a furrow; indeed, her name means "furrow." When she was abducted by the demon king Rāvaṇa, the vegetation wilted and the animals ceased to reproduce. Rāma, her royal husband, unable to unite with her, had to endure a barren realm until he was able to bring her back.

Underlying the symbolic associations between the earth, its caves, furrows, and waters and the vulva is the notion of the transformative powers of female sexuality. In the furrow the seed transforms itself into fruit or grain; in the cave/womb of the earth death transforms itself into life; in the womb of woman, male and female sexual fluids transform themselves into a human being. The transformative powers of the vulva account for much of the symbolism of initiation rites cross-culturally. The transformation of a child into a sexually potent adult or of an uninitiated person into an initiated one is very often effected by a symbolic return into the womb, the original transformative matrix. It is interesting to note that in Hindu India both the Vedic initiation for a *brahman* male and the Tantric initiation rite use basically the same womb symbolism. The following passage from the *Aitareya Brāhmaṇa* (1.3), most graphically describes this process:

> Him whom they consecrate the priests make into an embryo again. He should be bathed in water. . . , anointed with *navanita* or clarified butter [a symbol of embryo, according to the text] and purified with *darbha* or *kusa* grass. Then collyrium is to be put in his eyes, just as it is in the eyes of the new born. After this, the candidate will have to enter and stay in a hut shaped like a female organ.

The absence of any other openings except for the eastern entrance can only be explained in terms of a womb symbolism. The native North American Navajo myth of Changing Woman makes it clear that impregnation by the Sun took place through the hogan's eastern entrance. Thus the initiand is transformed into a bringer of fertility to herself, the people, and the earth in a fashion identical to that of Changing Woman. The transformation was accomplished through a stay in a symbolic vulva that, through song, became the primordial hogan at the womb-gate of the earth.

Aside from the transformative religious mysteries of sacrifice and initiation, the obvious life-giving and growth-promoting powers of the vulva and its secretions have given rise to a widespread use of representations of the female genitalia as apotropaic devices. The custom of plowing a furrow for magical protection around a town was practiced all over Europe by peasants. It was still observed in the twentieth century in Russia, where villages were thus annually "purified." The practice was exclusively carried out by women, who, while plowing, called on the moon goddess. A similar apotropaic function seems to have prompted the placing of squatting female figures prominently exposing their open vulvas on the key of arches at church entrances in Ireland, Great Britain, and German Switzerland. In Ireland these figures are called Sheelagh-na-gigs. Some of these figures represent emaciated old women. These images are illustrations of myths concerning the territorial Celtic goddess who was the granter of royalty. When the goddess wished to test the king-elect, she came to him in the form of an old hag, soliciting sexual intercourse. If the king-elect accepted, she transformed herself into a radiantly beautiful young woman and conferred on him royalty and blessed his reign. Most such figures were removed from churches in the nineteenth century.

This Celtic tradition bears a remarkable resemblance to certain Hindu myths and rites. The goddess Lakṣmī is also a granter of sovereignty. In union with her, a man becomes a king. If she leaves such a man, he loses his sovereignty and/or the power to ensure the fertility and well-being of his realm. Lakṣmī's iconography is intimately associated with the lotus, one of the most ubiquitous South Asian *yoni* symbols. The lotus itself can stand for Lakṣmī. Her consort, Viṣṇu, who is an embodiment of sovereignty, has as one of his four attributes the lotus, which he holds in one of his hands. This denotes his union with the Goddess, the source of his sovereignty. Such beliefs underlie the apotropaic character of the couples engaged in sexual intercourse often found sculpted on the outer walls and entrances of Hindu temples. The magical protective function of the female genitalia is dimly preserved in the European folk custom of hanging a horseshoe over the threshold. The horseshoe, made from a substance from deep inside the womb of the earth—iron—is shaped like the loop in the yonic triangles.

A remarkable parallel to the Celtic Sheelagh-na-gig is found in the Palauan archipelago. The wooden figure of a nude woman, prominently exposing her vulva by sitting with legs wide apart and extended to either side of the body, is placed on the eastern gable of each village's chiefly meeting house. Such figures are called *dilugai.* Interestingly, the *yoni* is in the shape of a cleft downward-pointing triangle. These female figures protect the villagers' health and ward off all evil spirits as well. They are constructed by ritual specialists according to strict rules, which if broken would result in the specialist's as well as the chief's death. It is not coincidental that each example of signs representing the female genitalia used as apotropaic devices are found on gates. The vulva is the primordial gate, the mysterious divide between nonlife and life.

A final major cluster of meanings associated with the vulva relates to its association with wealth. Such an association expresses itself in a broad variety of cultures and in different ways. Shells in general have been and still are symbols of the vulva; the earliest known example is a Magdalenian (Upper Paleolithic) fragment of bone from Arudy in southwestern France depicting a horse's head in the act of licking a yonic shell. However, the link between the vulva and wealth has been represented perhaps most prevalently by the cowrie shell, which has served as a medium of economic exchange in several cultures, particularly in West Africa and India. This smooth univalve bears in its shape and coloring an unmistakable resemblance to the vulva, which undoubtedly accounts for the association in as widely separated regions as West and North Africa, South Asia, Japan, and the Pacific Islands.

The complex of ideas relating wealth and fertility to the vulva is further illustrated by an example from the West African Tiv culture. One of their most sacred objects, symbolizing the fertility of their tribal land and the well-being of its inhabitants, is a human tibia, decorated and ornamented in the shape of a woman, with cowrie shells for the eyes and sometimes on the front of the body as well. It has a hole at the place of the navel; the decorations around it are the same as the scarifications produced on women's bodies at puberty. When disaster threatens or has taken place, and also in annual renewal ceremonies, this object, called the *imborivungu* ("owl pipe") is used ritually. In a secret ritual the elders pour blood from a miscarried fetus into its navel hole. The *imborivungu* is then shaken over fields and in wells to ensure the fertility of the land and of the women. In this example, the yonic cowries, along with the abdominal designs, identify the sacred object as a fertile woman. The ritual is intended to bring about both material abundance—since good crops are the primary source of wealth in agricultural societies—and the fertility of women. Here again one finds the nearly universal equation between the fertility of the earth, the source of wealth, and the fertility of women.

SEE ALSO Caves; Feminine Sacrality; Paleolithic Religion; Prehistoric Religions, article on Old Europe.

BIBLIOGRAPHY

There is no single work available that deals primarily with this topic. Information is widely scattered in many different works of ethnography, history of religion, and art history, to mention the most relevant disciplines. On the Tantric religion of India a thorough and reliable work is N. N. Bhattacharyya's *History of the Tantric Religion* (New Delhi, 1982). A useful study of female initiation rites in five cultures—India, Navajo, Tiv, Amazon Basin, and ancient Greece—is Bruce Lincoln's *Emerging from the Chrysalis: Studies in Rituals of Women's Initiation* (Cambridge, Mass., 1981). For an inspiring and superbly illustrated treatment of the Paleolithic cave paintings, Joseph Campbell's *The Way of the Animal Powers*, vol. 1 of his *Historical Atlas of World Mythology* (New York, 1983), provides an excellent summary of scholarly research to date. Marija Gimbutas's book *The Goddesses and Gods of Old Europe, 7000–3500* B.C.: *Myths, Legends, Images* (Berkeley, Calif., 1982) is a must for a richly illustrated and clearly presented treatment of goddess imagery during the Neolithic period in Europe. *Primitive Erotic Art*, edited by Philip S. Rawson (New York, 1973), has seven essays covering prehistory, Celtic and northern regions, North America, Mesoamerica, the Central Andean region, Africa south of the Sahara, and the equatorial islands of the Pacific. Rawson's own essay on Paleolithic and primitive symbolism is an excellent introduction and can be used for further research. For a convenient compendium of information on female-centered religious myths and rituals, Barbara G. Walker's *The Woman's Encyclopedia of Myths and Secrets* (San Francisco, 1983) is quite useful; each entry is footnoted, and the bibliography is extensive. Elinor Gadon's *The Once and Future Goddess* (San Francisco, 1989) has an excellent survey of Goddess' icons, including the *yoni* throughout prehistory and history. An important article on a reevaluation of the so-called proto-Śiva Harappan seal is Alf Hiltebeitel's "The Indus Valley 'Proto-Śiva,' Reexamined through Reflections on the Goddess, the Buffalo, and the Symbolism of *Vahanas*," *Anthropos* 73 (1978): 767–797. For a comprehensive treatment of the links between the West Asian, the Harappan and the Hindu Goddess see the following three articles by the vedic scholar Asko Parpola: "The Metamorphoses of Mahisa Asura and Prajapati" in Hoek, A. W. van den, D. H. A. Kolff and M. S. *Oort* (1992): 275–308; "Vac as a Goddess of Victory in the Veda and Her Relation to Durga" *Annals of the Institute for Research in Humanities, Kyoto University* 1999: 34(2): 101–143; "Pre-Proto Iranians of Afghanistan as initiators of Sakta Tantrism: On the Scythian/Saka affiliation of the Dasas, Nuristanis and Magadhans" *Iranica Antiqua* 37 (2002): 233–324. On the royal symbolism of goddess Lakṣmī, see Frédérique Apffel, *Marglin Wives of the God-King: The Rituals of the Devadasis of Puri* (Oxford, 1985). For an in-depth treatment of yonic rituals in Tantric Buddhism, see Miranda Shaw, *Passionate Enlightenment* (Princeton, N.J.,1995). For an exhaustive treatment of the theme of sacrificial death, sexual union, and rebirth, David Dean Shulman's *Tamil Temple Myths: Sacrifice and Divine Marriage in the South Indian Saiva Tradition* (Princeton, N.J., 1980) is indispensable.

FRÉDÉRIQUE APFFEL-MARGLIN (1987 AND 2005)

YORUBA RELIGION.

The twelve to fifteen million Yoruba people of southwestern Nigeria, the Republic of Benin (formerly Dahomey), and Togo (topographically the area is defined as that between 6°0–9°5' 2°41'–6° east longitude) are the heirs of one of the oldest cultural traditions in West Africa. Archaeological and linguistic evidence indicate that the Yoruba have lived in their present habitat since at least the fifth century BCE. The development of the regional dialects that distinguish the Yoruba subgroups and the process of urbanization, which developed into a social system unique among sub-Saharan African peoples, took place during the first millennium BCE. By the ninth century the ancient city of Ile-Ifẹ was thriving, and in the next five centuries

Ifẹ artists would create terracotta and bronze sculptures that are now among Africa's artistic treasures.

Both Yoruba myth and oral history refer to Oduduwa (also known as Odua) as the first king and founder of the Yoruba people. Some myths portray him as the creator god and assert that the place of creation was Ile-Ifẹ, which subsequently became the site of Oduduwa's throne. Oral history, however, suggests that the story of Oduduwa's assumption of the throne at Ifẹ refers to a conquest of the indigenes of the Ifẹ area prior to the ninth century by persons from "the east." While it is increasingly apparent that the sociopolitical model of a town presided over by a paramount chief or king (*ọba*), was well established in Ifẹ and present among other Yoruba subgroups, the followers of Oduduwa developed the urban tradition and enhanced the role of the king. In later years, groups of people who sought to establish their political legitimacy (even if they were immigrants) were required to trace their descent from Oduduwa. Such people were known as "the sons of Oduduwa," and they wore beaded crowns (*adenla*) given to them by Oduduwa as the symbol of their sacred authority (*aṣẹ*).

Origin myths, festival rituals, and oral traditions associate the indigenous peoples with Ọbatala, the deity (*oriṣa*) who fashions the human body. And because he too was an *ọba,* his priests wear white, conical, beaded crowns similar to those reserved for "the sons of Oduduwa." The myths and rituals also refer to a great struggle between Ọbatala and Oduduwa at the time of creation, following Oduduwa's theft of the privilege granted by Ọlọrun (Olodumare), the high god, to Ọbatala to create the earth and its inhabitants. In the town of Itapa, the sequence of rituals that composes the annual festival of Ọbatala reenacts a battle between Oduduwa and Ọbatala, Oduduwa's victory over and the banishment of Ọbatala, and the rejoicing that took place among the gods and humankind with the return of Ọbatala at the invitation of Oduduwa. And there is the tradition among the Ọyọ Yoruba of the unwarranted imprisonment of Ọbatala by Ṣango and the thunder god's release of the wandering, ancient king after famine and barrenness threatened field and home.

In these myths and rituals there is a historical remembrance of a usurpation of power and the acknowledgment that a violent conflict and a tenuous reconciliation gave birth to modern Yoruba culture. The remembrance, however, has not only to do with a past time, with historical and cultural origins; it is also a statement about the nature and limits of the authority of kings in defining the moral basis of Yoruba society. It is also about the importance of Ile-Ifẹ as the symbol of Yoruba cultural homogeneity, while acknowledging the distinctiveness and the independence of other Yoruba subgroups.

There are approximately twenty subgroups, each identifiable by its distinctive variation in linguistic, social, political, and religious patterns born of the history of the region. Among the principal groups are the Ẹgba and Ẹgbado in the southwest, the Ijẹbu in the southern and southeast, the Ọyọ in the central and northwest, the Ifẹ and the Ijẹṣa in the central, the Owo in the eastern, and the Igbomina and Ekiti in the northeast regions. Throughout Yorubaland, the social system is patrilineal and patrilocal, although among the Ẹgba and Ẹgbado there are elements of a dual descent system. The extended family (*idile*), which dwells in the father's compound so long as space and circumstance permit, is the essential social unit and the primary context in which self-awareness and social awareness are forged. Thus, Ọdun Egungun, the annual festival for the patrilineal ancestors, is the most widespread and important festival in the Yoruba liturgical calendar. Elaborate masquerades (*egungun*), are created of layers of cloths of dark colors with white serrated edges. The costume covers the dancer, who moves about the compound or town with stately pace, occasionally performing whirling movements, causing the cloths to splay out in constantly changing patterns. In movement and appearance the masquerade depicts the presence and power (*aṣẹ*) of the ancestors. The ancestors are those persons who established the "house" (*ile*) and the family and who continue to stand surety for its integrity and survival against threats of witchcraft and disease, so long as their heirs acknowledge the ancestral presence.

While masquerades for the patrilineal ancestors are found among all the Yoruba, there are other masked festivals that are distinctive to particular areas, reflecting the regional history that has shaped the Yoruba experience. The Yoruba peoples of the southwest (the Anago, Awori, Ẹgbado, Kẹtu, and Ẹgba) celebrate the Gẹlẹdẹ festival at the time of the spring rains. The festival honors *awon iya wa* ("the mothers"), a collective term for the female power (*aṣẹ*) possessed by all women but especially manifest in certain elderly women and in female ancestors and deities. It is the awesome power of woman in its procreative and destructive capacities that is celebrated and acknowledged. Among the Ijẹbu peoples of the south the annual festival for Agẹmọ, an *oriṣa* whose power is represented by the chameleon, brings sixteen priest-chiefs famed for their magical or manipulative powers from towns surrounding the capital city of Ijẹbu-Ode into ritual contests of curse and masked dance with one another and then into the city, where they petition and are received by the Awujale, the *oba* of Ijẹbu-Ode. The secret power of the priest-chiefs meets the sacred power of the crown. Each is required to acknowledge the role of the other in the complex balance of power that constitutes Ijẹbu political life. The Ẹlẹfon and Ẹpa festivals are masquerades performed in the towns of such Yoruba subgroups as the Igbomina and Ekiti in honor of persons and families whose lives embodied the social values by which Yoruba culture has been defined in the northeastern area. The helmet masks with their large sculptures are balanced on the dancers' heads and are the focus of ritual sacrifice (*ẹbọ*) and songs of praise (*oriki*) throughout the festival. They are images of the sacred power of those who founded the town or contributed to its life in important ways. Thus, while individual masks are associated with particular families, they also refer to the roles of hunter, warrior, king, herbalist-priest, and leader of women, roles that transcend lineage ties and express in their collectivity cultural achievement. Their powers are akin to those of the *orișa,* the gods of the Yoruba pantheon.

According to the Yoruba, there are 401 *orișa* who line the road to heaven. All of them are thought to have been humans who, because they led notable lives, became *orișa* at the time of their death. For example, Șango, the god of thunder, was a legendary king of Ọyọ before he became an *orișa.* The extraordinary number of *orișa* reflects the regional variation in their worship. Șango is the patron deity of the kings of Ọyọ, and his shrines are important in those towns that were once part of the old Ọyọ empire (c. 1600–1790). But in Ile-Ifẹ, or in communities to the south and east, the role of Șango and the degree to which he is worshiped diminishes markedly. As one moves from one part of Yorubaland to another, it will be Ọșun, goddess of medicinal waters, or Oko, god of the farm, or Erinle, god of forest and stream, or Ọbatala or Agẹmọ whose shrines and festivals shape the religious life of a people. Furthermore, the *orișa* have multiple names. Some call Șango Ọba Koso ("king of Koso"); others greet him as Balogunnile Ado ("leader of warriors at Ado"). Șango is also addressed as Abinufarokotu ("one who violently uproots an *iroko* tree"), Ọkọ Iyemọnja ("husband of Iyemonja"), or Lagigaoogun ("he who is mighty in the use of magical powers"), names that reveal the varied and distinctive experiences of his devotees and their relationship to the *orișa.* The multiplicity (or fragmentation) of the *orișa* is also a consequence of the historical dislocation of peoples that occurred during the intertribal wars of the nineteenth century. When persons and groups were forced to move from one area to another, their *orișa* went with them, shaping and being shaped by the new world of their devotees' experience.

Of all the *orișa* it is Ogun, god of iron and of war, whose worship is most widespread. It is said that there are seven Ogun, including Ogun of the blacksmiths, Ogun of the hunters, Ogun of the warriors, and Ogun Onire. Ire is a town in northeast Yorubaland where Ogun was once the leader of warriors and where he "sank into the ground" after killing persons in a great rage, having misunderstood their vow of ritual silence as a personal affront. As with other *orișa,* Ogun expresses and shapes a people's experience with respect to a particular aspect of their lives. In the case of Ogun, it is the experience of violence and culture: His myths and rituals articulate for the Yoruba the irony that cultural existence entails destruction and death. One must kill in order to live. And such a situation carries with it the danger that the destruction will go beyond culturally legitimate need, destroying that which it should serve. Thus, to employ Ogun's power, one must be aware of Ogun's character (*iwa*) and be cognizant that the beneficent god can become the outraged *orișa* who bites himself.

As with Ogun, each of the *orișa,* in the diversity and individuality of their persons and attributes, may be understood as providing an explanatory system and a means of coping with human suffering. Rarely does only one *orișa* lay claim to a person. Ogun or Șango or Ọșun may dominate one's life and shape one's perception of self and world, but other *orișa* will have their artifacts on the shrine, as well as their claims and influence upon one's life. Just as the Yoruba dancer must respond to the multiple rhythms of the drums, so must the soul attentive to the powers of the *orișa* respond to their diverse claims. The complexity of the response may overwhelm one. But as in the ability of the dancer to be conscious of and respond to every instrument of the orchestra, so in sacrificing to all the *orișa* who call, the worshiper (*olusin,* "he who serves") can know the richness of life and its complexity and can achieve the superior poise, the equanimity of one who possesses *ase* amid the contradictions of life. Thus, when one considers the configuration of *orișa* symbols on a devotee's shrine or the cluster of shrines and festivals for the *orișa* in a particular town or the pantheon as a whole, as a total system, one discerns that the total assemblage of *orișa* expresses in it totality a worldview. And it is in the reality of this worldview that Yoruba experience, at the personal and social levels, is given coherence and meaning.

In addition to the *orișa* of the pantheon, there is one's personal *orișa,* known as *ori inun* ("inner head"), which refers to the destiny that one's ancestral guardian soul has chosen while kneeling before Ọlọrun prior to entering the world. It is a personal destiny that can never be altered. Birth results in the loss of the memory of one's destiny. But one's "*ori*-in-heaven," which is also referred to as *ekejimi* ("my spiritual other"), stands surety for the possibilities and the limits of the destiny that one has received. Hence, one must make one's way in life, acknowledging one's *ori* as an *orișa* who can assist one in realizing the possibilities that are one's destiny. One can have an *ori buruku* ("a bad head"). In such a case a person must patiently seek to make the best of a foolish choice and seek the help of the other *orișa.*

In *orișa* worship it is the wisdom of Ọrunmila, the *orișa* of Ifa divination, and the work of Eșu, the bearer of sacrifices, that stand for the meaningfulness of experience and the possibility of effective action. The vast corpus of Ifa poetry, organized into 256 collections called *odu* (also known as *orișa*) is a repository of Yoruba cultural values. It is the priest of Ifa, the *babalawo* ("father of ancient wisdom"), who knows Ifa and performs the rites of divination. Using the sixteen sacred palm nuts or the *opele* chain, the priest divines the *odu* whose verses he will chant in addressing the problem of the suppliant and determining the sacrifices that must be made. For the Yoruba, every ritual entails a sacrifice, whether it is the gift of prayer, the offering of a kola nut, or the slaughter of an animal. In the Ifa literature, sacrifice (*ẹbọ*) has to do with death and the avoidance of such related experiences as loss, disease, famine, sterility, isolation, and poverty. It is an acknowledgment that human existence is ensnared in the interrelated contradictions of life and death. But sacrifice is also viewed as the reversal of the situation of death into life. Sacrifice is the food of the *orișa* and other spirits, and one sacrifices that which appropriately expresses the character (*iwa*) of the particular *orişa* or spirit of one's concern. Hence, Ogun receives a dog, the carnivorous animal that can be domesticated to assist the hunter and warrior. Sacrifice is the acknowledgement of the presence of powerful agents in the world, and the sacrificial act brings the creative power of the *orişa*, the ancestors, or the mothers to the worshiper; sacrifice can also temporarily stay the hand of Death and ward off other malevolent spirits (*ajogun*). Such is the power of Eşu, the bearer of sacrifices, the mediator and guardian of the ritual way, the "keeper of *ase*."

Those who have observed the ritual way and achieved the status of elders in the community may also become members of the secret Oşugbo (Ogboni) society. Although Oşugbo is found throughout Yorubaland, its role and rituals vary from one region to another. Oşugbo members, who come from various lineage groups, worship Onile ("the owner of the house"). The "house" (*ile*) is the image of the universe in its totality, of which the Oşugbo cult house is a microcosm. The *ẹdan* of the Oşugbo society, which are small, brass, linked staffs that depict male and female figures, are the sign of membership and the symbol of the Oşugbo understanding of reality. The secret of the Oşugbo appears to be that its members know, and are in touch with, a primordial unity that transcends the oppositions characterizing human experience. Expressing the unity of male and female, the *ẹdan* and their owners possess the power of adjudicating conflicts among persons or groups; when blood has been shed illicitly (as in a murder) it is the Oşugbo members who must atone for this "violation of the house."

The worldview of the Yoruba is a monistic one. The universe of their experience is pervaded by *aşẹ*, a divine energy in the process of generation and regeneration. *Aşẹ* is without any particular signification and yet invests all things and all persons and, as the warrant for all creative activity, opposes chaos and the loss of meaning in human experience. Thus, for the Yoruba the universe is one, and it is amenable to articulation in terms of an elaborate cosmology, to critical reflection, and to innovative speculation.

BIBLIOGRAPHY

The best general introductions to Yoruba religion are E. Bọlaji Idowu's *Olódùmarè: God in Yoruba Belief* (London, 1962) and Robert Farris Thompson's *Black Gods and Kings: Yoruba Art at UCLA,* 2d ed. (Bloomington, Ind., 1976). Idowu's study contains a wealth of primary data and is an important contribution by a Yoruba scholar, although the presentation is compromised by an uncritical use of Christian theological concepts and categories. Thompson's highly readable, insightful, and brief essays analyze the Yoruba worldview in terms of Yoruba art. This approach has been further developed by William B. Fagg and John Pemberton III in *Yoruba Sculpture of West Africa,* edited by Bruce Holcombe (New York, 1982). In addition to an anthology of Fagg's essays on Yoruba art, this volume includes texts by Pemberton, which discuss seventy works of art in the context of Yoruba history, rituals, and cosmology, and an extensive bibliography.

The most important specialized studies on Yoruba religious thought and practice include those on Ifa poetry and divination rites by 'Wande Abimbọla, *Ifá: An Exposition of Ifá Literary Corpus* (Ibadan, 1976), and William R. Bascom, *Ifa Divination: Communication between Gods and Men in West Africa* (Bloomington, Ind., 1969). Abimbola has edited an extensive collection of essays, *Yoruba Oral Tradition* (Ifẹ, 1975), that provides an excellent introduction to Yoruba scholarship in the areas of archaeology, history, art, and religion. Of special note for their substantive and methodological contribution are the essays by Babatundi Agiri on the early history of Ọyọ and by Rowland Abiodun on Ifa art objects. Specialized studies of *orişa* worship by John Pemberton III and Karin Barber offer contrasting approaches and alternative interpretations to that of Idowu; Pemberton's "A Cluster of Sacred Symbols: *Orişa* Worship among the Igbomina Yoruba of Ila-Ọrangun," *History of Religions* 17 (August 1977): 1–26, pursues a structuralist analysis, and Barber's "How Man Makes God in West Africa: Yoruba Attitudes towards the *Orişa,*" *Africa* 51 (1981): 724–745, combines a sociological with an oral history approach. The best study of masked festivals is Henry John Drewel and Margaret T. Drewal's *Gèlèdé: A Study of Art and Feminine Power among the Yoruba* (Bloomington, Ind., 1983). See also the special issue of *African Arts* 11, no. 3 (April 1983), edited by Henry John Drewal, on the arts and festivals for Egungun.

New Sources

Adeoye, C. Laogun. *Igbagbo and Esin Yoruba.* Ibadan, Nigeria, 1985.

Ajuwon, Bade. *Funeral Dirges of Yoruba Hunters.* New York, 1982.

Apter, Andrew. *Black Critics and Kings: The Hermeneutics of Power in Yoruba Society.* Chicago, 1992.

Barnes, Sandra T., ed. *Africa's Ogun: Old World and New.* 2d ed. Bloomington, Ind., 1997.

Gleason, Judith Illsley. *OYA: In Praise of an African Goddess.* San Francisco, 1992.

Komolafe, Kolawole. *African Traditional Religion: Understanding Ogboni Fraternity.* Lagos, Nigeria, 1995.

Matory, James Lorand. *Sex and the Empire That Is No More: Gender and the Politics of Metaphor in Oyo Yoruba Religion.* Minneapolis, 1994.

Murphy, Joseph M. *Osun Across the Waters: A Yoruba Goddess in Africa and the Americas.* Bloomington, Ind., 2001.

Olupona, Jacob K. *Kingship, Religion and Rituals in a Nigerian Community: A Phenomenological Study of Ondo Yoruba Festivals.* Stockholm, 1991.

Peel, J.D.Y. *Religious Encounter and the Making of the Yoruba.* Bloomington, Ind., 2000.

Pemberton III, John, and Funso Afolayan. *Yoruba Sacred Kingship: A Power Like That of the Gods.* Washington, D.C., 1996.

JOHN PEMBERTON III (1987)
Revised Bibliography

YOSE BEN ḤALAFTA' (second century CE), Palestinian tanna. Born in Sepphoris, Yose was a student of Yoḥanan ben Nuri, ʿAqivaʾ ben Yosef, and Ṭarfon. Like many of his contemporaries, he worked at a humble occupation—he was a tanner (B.T., *Shab.* 49a–b)—but he was also a leader of the rabbinic court at Sepphoris (B.T., *San.* 32b). He is associated with early mystical traditions, and it is said that he studied with Elijah the prophet (B.T., *Ber.* 3a, *Yev.* 63a).

Numerous traditions attributed to Yose are preserved in rabbinic literature. He is one of the most frequently quoted authorities of his generation, along with Meʾir, Shimʿon, and Yehudah. Jacob Epstein believes that the corpus of his traditions was one of the primary documents used in the redaction of the Mishnah.

Yose was a product of rabbinic learning and culture in a time of adjustment after two devastating wars with Rome. His rulings and teachings, like those of other rabbis of the time, reflect the struggle to overcome the uncertainty of Jewish life in the Land of Israel and the attempt to establish a sense of order in religious and social life. Yose's legal, exegetical, and theological sayings contributed greatly toward this goal.

Yose's traditions evince a special interest in the events of biblical history, as well as in the entire range of theological topics, including the nature of God, the centrality of the Torah, and the special nature of Israel. His legal rulings reflect the concerns and activities of the rabbis of his generation, from agricultural taboos, table manners, and rules for holidays and family life to regulations for the rabbinic system of purities. Yose is associated, for example, with legislation concerning the recitation of blessings over foods in which he rules that one who alters the formula for blessings established by the sages does not fulfill his obligation (Tosefta, *Ber.* 4.4).

To date, no systematic analysis has been made of Yose's traditions, probably because of the sheer size of the corpus of sayings attributed to him.

SEE ALSO Tannaim.

BIBLIOGRAPHY

Jacob N. Epstein's *Mavoʾ le-sifrut ha-tannaʾim* (Jerusalem, 1957) discusses the role of Yose's materials in the formation of the Mishnah. In *Rabbi Yose ben Halaftaʾ* (in Hebrew; Jerusalem, 1966), Israel Konovitz collects all the references to Yose in rabbinic literature. My own *Studies in Jewish Prayer* (1990) analyzes the role of Yose's rulings in the development of early rabbinic liturgy.

New Sources

Levine, Hillel. "Rabi Yose's Laundry: The History of a Flagrant Voice and the History of an Idea." In *Celebrating Elie Wiesel: Stories, Essays, Reflections*, edited by Alan Rosen, pp. 113–122. Notre Dame, Ind., 1998.

TZVEE ZAHAVY (1987)
Revised Bibliography

YOUNG, BRIGHAM (1801–1877), second president of the Church of Jesus Christ of Latter-day Saints (hereafter LDS); chief architect of the form of Mormonism that flourished in the intermountain region of the western United States in the nineteenth century and expanded throughout the United States and into many other countries.

Although he insisted on baptism by immersion, which he thought scripture required, Brigham Young joined the Methodists several years before he heard about Joseph Smith's "golden bible." A skilled carpenter, painter, and cabinetmaker, Young came from a family of devout Methodists whose extreme poverty impelled them to leave New England for western New York, a family history that paralleled that of the Smith family. While Mormonism attracted many of his family members, Young held back. He read the *Book of Mormon* soon after its publication in 1830 but waited two full years before becoming a Latter-day Saint. Thus he was not converted in the very beginning when Mormonism's primary appeal was its claim that it had restored the priesthood of ancient Israel and that it was the only true church of Jesus Christ. He became a follower of the Mormon prophet, Joseph Smith, in 1832, when the character of the new movement was becoming as Hebraic as it was Christian, given the emphasis being placed on its "gathering" doctrine, its temple-building plans, its patriarchal office, and its assertion that Mormons are God's only chosen people. Convinced that these elements separating Mormonism from traditional Christianity were scripturally correct, Young accepted them wholeheartedly. Moreover, when temple ordinances were introduced that added plural marriage and baptism for the dead to Mormonism, and when the movement organized itself into a political kingdom, he accepted these innovations as well, albeit somewhat less enthusiastically.

After his rebaptism, Young devoted his entire energies to Mormonism. Following a preaching mission in the eastern United States, he moved to Ohio, assisting with the construction of the Kirtland temple and much else. He went with Zion's Camp, a paramilitary expedition that failed to rescue beleaguered Missouri Saints from their enemies, but nevertheless tested the mettle of future LDS leaders. Called to the highest council in Mormondom, the Quorum of the Twelve, in 1835, and made its president in 1841, Young rendered signal service, particularly in organizing the exodus when the Saints were driven from Missouri in 1839 and in establishing a successful Mormon mission in England in the early 1840s. In Nauvoo, Illinois, during the final years of Smith's life, Young served in the prophet's inner circle as the LDS political kingdom was organized and the secret practice of plural marriage instituted.

The struggle for succession to LDS leadership after Smith's murder in 1844 intensified a division within the movement. On one side were Saints who, regarding Mormonism as an idiosyncratic version of primitive Christianity, opposed plural marriage and the political organization of a kingdom in an Old Testament mode; on the other were Saints who supported these innovations as a part of the restoration of the "ancient order of things." Although most historical accounts present Young as the clear winner in this succession struggle, recent demographic studies reveal that he was the acknowledged leader of the latter group, but that he by no means led the whole of the LDS community after Smith's death.

For the thousands who followed him, however, Young managed to effect the transfer of Mormon culture from Illinois to the Great Salt Lake Valley while preserving the vision of Mormonism that Joseph Smith held at the end of his life. He did this by assuming ecclesiastical, political, and spiritual leadership of his followers. In Nauvoo, he took practical charge of the chaotic situation and arranged the departure of the Saints. In 1847, he was sustained as president of the church by those who went west with him. In 1851, the federal government recognized his leadership by appointing him as governor of Utah Territory. From these dual positions of power, he established a new "Israel in the tops of the mountains" in which, in the manner of Solomon of old, he reigned supreme as prophet, church president, and political leader. Unlike Joseph Smith, however, Young was not a prophet who delivered new revelations and added lasting theological elements to the movement he headed. His great contribution was realizing Smith's vision through the creation of a literal LDS kingdom. Even changed, as it was at the end of the nineteenth century, this kingdom continues to animate and inspire Mormonism in much the same way that Solomon's kingdom has animated and inspired Judaism and Christianity across the ages.

See Also Mormonism.

Bibliography

Until very recently, historical accounts of Young's life and career were either faith-promoting paeans of praise, based on nineteenth-century official LDS publications, or ill-concealed attacks, based on published sources unfriendly to the Mormons. Neither genre has disappeared, but as much of the primary source material on which studies of Young must rely is now available to scholars, new studies presenting a more balanced assessment of this important Mormon leader are appearing. The most significant of these new studies are Leonard J. Arrington's *Brigham Young: American Moses* (New York, 1985); Newell G. Bringhurst's *Brigham Young and the Expanding American Frontier* (Boston, 1985); and Ronald K. Esplin's "The Emergence of Brigham Young and the Twelve to Mormon Leadership, 1830–1841" (Ph. D. diss., Brigham Young University, 1981). Two valuable editions of primary source materials are *Letters of Brigham Young to His Sons,* edited by Dean C. Jesse (Salt Lake City, 1974); and *Diary of Brigham Young, 1857,* edited by Everett L. Cooley (Salt Lake City, 1980). Stanley P. Hirshson's *The Lion of the Lord: A Biography of Brigham Young* (New York, 1969) is not recommended; despite its reputable publisher and respected author, it is based on published sources, most of which are unfriendly to the Mormons.

The results of recent demographic studies are reported in Dean L. May's "A Demographic Portrait of the Mormons, 1830–1980," in *After 150 Years: The Latter-day Saints in Sesquicentennial Perspective,* edited by Thomas G. Alexander and Jessie L. Embry (Provo, Utah, 1983).

Jan Shipps (1987)

YOUTH, FOUNTAIN OF See REJUVENATION

YU, also known as Yu the Great; demiurge who rid China of a great flood, legendary founder of the Xia dynasty, and oldest pan-Chinese culture hero. (Huangdi, Yao, and Shun are in fact of later origin.) According to traditional accounts, Yu combated the flood by following the examples found in nature. Draining fields, dredging rivers, and cutting passes through the mountains, he thus succeeded where his father, Kun, who used dikes to restrain the floods and block their course, had failed (*Shu jing, Yu gong*; *Shi ji*). Credited with the shaping of China's waterways and irrigation systems, he became the patron saint of all hydraulic engineering (*Shi zi, Huainanzi*). Yu also was a miner and a master of metals. He invented bronze weapons and cast the Nine Caldrons of Xia, symbols of his sovereignty, on which the various regions of his empire were pictured (*Zuo zhuan*). The famous *Shanhai jing* (Book of Mountains and Seas) is said to be the text corresponding to these images. Founder of metal-working confraternities, Yu is the patron saint of esoteric and magical arts that are at the roots both of alchemy and of Daoist longevity techniques.

Yu is one of the legendary model sovereigns upon whom the Yellow River and the Luo River deities bestowed the mystical diagrams Hetu ("river chart") and Luoshu ("Lo writing"). In Daoist traditions, these sacred emblems were reinterpreted into the *lingbao wufu* ("five talismans of *lingbao*"), which Yu received from a god as a source of magical aid in his Herculean labors. He is said to have hidden them in a sacred mountain, whence they were rediscovered to become the nucleus of a Daoist corpus of sacred scriptures (*Wu Yue chunqiu*; *Lingbao wufu xu*).

One of the oldest rituals of Chinese culture, still practiced today by Daoist priests, is the Yubu, or "pace of Yu." Exhausted by his labors, Yu is said to have been stricken by hemiplegia, which gave him a limping gait (*Shi zi*). Others say that spirits gave him control over men and nature by teaching him a hopping dance with one foot trailing behind the other. The ancient sovereigns danced in order to subdue rebels (*Huainanzi*), and sorcerers performed this dance to enter into trance. The Daoists adopted the Pace of Yu both to gain access to supernatural powers such as those granted by plants that confer immortality and to overcome demonic forces (*Baopuzi*). For them, it was not merely the gait that was important but also the labyrinthine pattern traced by the officiant's feet, the pattern of a hexagram, or, more often, the meander of the Big Dipper. The Pace of Yu or the "shaman's pace" (*wubu*) is considered to contain the magic rhythm for creating cosmic order and for summoning and subduing gods and demons. It became the favorite gait for the *daoshi*'s liturgical procession through the heavens (*Daozang* 987, *Taishang zongzhen biyao* 8, 1116 CE). The Pace of Yu is still performed today as part of Daoist rituals in Taiwan.

SEE ALSO Chinese Religion, article on Mythic Themes.

BIBLIOGRAPHY

The myths of Yu the Great have been studied by Marcel Granet in his *Danses et légendes de la Chine ancienne* (1929; reprint, Paris, 1959), pp. 466–590. His role in Daoism is mentioned in Max Kaltenmark's "*Ling-pao*: Note sur un terme du taoïsme religieux," *Mélanges publiés par l'Institut des Hautes Études Chinoises*, vol. 2 (Paris, 1960), pp. 561–565. Granet has used the Pace of Yu as an example demonstrating the roots of the Daoist religion in the rituals of high antiquity. See his "Remarques sur le taoïsme ancien," *Asia Major* 2 (1925): 146–151, reprinted in *Études sociologiques sur la Chine* (Paris, 1953). Much information on Yu is to be found also in volumes 2, 3, and 4 of Joseph Needham's *Science and Civilisation in China* (Cambridge, 1956–1971).

ANNA SEIDEL (1987)

YUHUANG, the Jade Emperor, has been the supreme deity of the Chinese popular pantheon since at least the tenth century CE.

An essential and deeply rooted feature of Chinese culture is the concept of a single, centralized empire under the sovereignty of an emperor who is a sacerdotal as well as a secular ruler. This concept influenced religion in many ways. Both the Daoist and the popular pantheon are modeled on the civil bureaucracy of the Chinese state. Communication between the gods and encounters between deities and mortals often involve ritual similar to that between the vassal and his sovereign or the administrator and his superior.

The highest deity of the religion of antiquity, the Emperor on High (Shangdi) already was the ruler of a heavenly court. About the supreme deity of folk religion we know nothing until the ninth century CE. Belief and cult of the Jade Emperor took shape during the time of the most perfect realization of the bureaucratic universal empire, the Tang dynasty (618–906). Poems and paintings of the tenth century attest to a fully developed myth, in which the Great Jade Emperor (Yuhuang Dadi) is attended by his heavenly court composed of all the deities who rule above and below the earth, the gods of stars, wind, rain and thunder, mountains and lakes, and others. The Song emperor Zhenzong (r. 998–1022) reinforced his own authority by claiming descent from mythical culture heroes, a lineage that had been revealed to him by an emissary of the Jade Emperor. In 1017, a state cult was instituted for the Jade Emperor, and he was canonized under the title Great Heavenly Emperor, Majesty of [the Heaven of] Jade Purity (Yuqinghuang Da tiandi).

Jade Emperor is not a name but the title of a ruler with a particular function. Patterned after the terrestrial emperor, the Jade Emperor is the supernatural ruler of the universe, including the divine pantheon. His foremost role is to confer all advancement in the supernatural bureaucracy and in the religious hierarchies of this world, and to oversee the investiture of emperors and of gods, as in the popular novel *Fengshen yanyi* (The Investiture of the Gods). Supreme arbiter, judge, and sovereign of the universe, he is nevertheless merely the executor of orders emanating from the highest heavenly triad, the Daoist Three Pure Ones (San Qing) who are deities too remote and formidable for the popular cults.

His feast day is the ninth day of the first lunar month. His popular name is Master Heaven (Tiangong). He is represented in the dragon-embroidered robe and pearly headgear of the Chinese emperor, seated on a throne and surrounded by his courtiers. His canonical scripture, the *Yuhuang benxing jing* (twelfth to thirteenth century; *Daozang* nos. 10, 11, 12), plays an important role in Daoist ritual.

SEE ALSO Chinese Religion, article on Mythic Themes; Kingship, article on Kingship in East Asia.

BIBLIOGRAPHY

There is yet no monograph on this important deity. The best description is still that by Henri Maspero in "The Mythology of Modern China," in *Taoism and Chinese Religion*, translated by Frank A. Kierman (Amherst, Mass., 1981). Some additional material has been presented by H. Y. Feng in "The Origin of Yü Huang," *Harvard Journal of Asiatic Studies* 1 (1936): 242–250.

ANNA SEIDEL (1987)

YULUNGGUL SNAKE. Yulunggul is the Great Python of north-central Arnhem Land, who swallowed the Wawalag sisters and their child(ren). Yulunggul is most often identified as male, with or without female counterparts. One northeastern Arnhem Land version specifies Yulunggul as female but with symbolic male (phallic) implications.

William Lloyd Warner's account (1937, e.g. p. 257) notes a variety of snakes, goannas, and snails as sons of Yulunggul. In a couple of women's versions, Yulunggul's python children, who live in the water hole with him, ask him to regurgitate what he has eaten so that they can eat it too. Warner refers to Yulunggul as "great father" (Yindi Bapa or Bapa Yindi), but it is possible that he misheard the more usual expression, "great snake" (Yindi Baapi).

Unlike so many of the great mythic characters, who came from elsewhere to sites that were to be spiritually associated with them, Yulunggul had always been at his special water hole, known as Mirara-minar and Muruwul; there is a cluster of names and waters in that area. The Wawalag sisters, in contrast, were travelers from a distant country and were strangers: the kinship terms identifying them as sisters of Yulunggul's were not consanguineously based. Nevertheless, all of the mythic Snakes in north and northeastern Arnhem Land, including Yulunggul, were good site guardians and knew who the travelers were.

The Wawalag sisters brought with them inland-type songs. These are in the compressed, key-word style typical of the Kunapipi (Gunabibi)—unlike the long, drawn-out songs of north-central and northeastern Arnhem Land, such as Yulunggul sang. The longer songs include names for physical and other attributes of the Snake that are used as personal names by present-day Aborigines of appropriate social and territorial status, and they include singing words for the monsoon, the coasts and offshore islands, and the rough seas. This introduction to inland people and inland songs and religious rites was not achieved without trauma, in the context of the myth, but it marked the acceptance of "new" items on a longterm basis.

In one of his roles Yulunggul is, explicitly, a culture-area indicator, or a boundary marker. During his conversation with the other great Snakes after he has swallowed the Wawalag, he faces east. This conversation is like a statement about a broad cultural zone that shares a range of common understandings and rules, though there are local variations. Its principal binding force is its religious system, actively expressed through ritual collaboration. The Snakes (in Warner's version, p. 253) underline this accord, agreeing that although they speak "different languages" (dialects), they share the same religious commitments. Significantly, then, Yulunggul looks to and talks to his counterparts in the east, turning his back on western Arnhem Land. That region is clearly outside the eastern Arnhem Land bloc, notwithstanding its mythic swallowing and vomiting Rainbow Snakes and some cultural exchange and transmission; traditionally the westerners did not circumcise, and their marriage rules and language patterns were very different.

There are divergent views on whether Yulunggul is a Rainbow Snake manifestation. In the Milingimbi versions, when the two men from Wawalag country came to Mirara-minar, the water "shone like a rainbow. When they saw this they knew there was a snake there." (Warner, p. 258, also 385). Where his Rainbow Snake identification is not accepted, mainly on the eastern side of Arnhem Land, it is sometimes explained with, "Yulunggul is separate: he is *himself*."

As a weather symbol, Yulunggul has his own personal niche in the pantheon of deities (Warner, p. 378). He has both freshwater and saltwater affiliations. Although he is anchored spiritually to a special site, he is also spiritually mobile. He is the spirit of the monsoon, the west and northwest wind that brings the fertilizing rains of the wet season. Just as the copulations of the Snakes and clouds during the wet season ensure fertility in the dry season, so Yulunggul's "union" with the Wawalag transformed him into a symbol of seasonal fertility. He continued to inhabit his water hole but gained prominence in two additional dimensions. One was his role in the ritual constellations "given" to posterity by the Wawalag sisters. The other was spiritual mobility. In some Milingimbi versions (Warner, p. 254), he flies across the country with the Wawalag and their child(ren) inside him, naming various places and allocating local dialects. More generally, in all available versions he is identified in spirit with the *baara,* the fast-moving, rain-bearing monsoon storms and clouds from the west and northwest.

The full force of the monsoon can have a formidable impact on the people, creatures, landscape, and waters in its path. A skillful storyteller can convey the force dramatically in narrative versions of the Yulunggul myth. Warner (pp. 379–381) tried to communicate the power of the monsoon through a quotation from a geographer about the Darwin area, but the cycle of the seasons is much less "uniform" than his source suggests. It is the variability and unpredictability of the monsoon that has convinced Aborigines of the need to work ritually to regularize it.

In his Milingimbi study, Warner (pp. 381–382) mentions a number of named seasons, but his whole emphasis is on a twofold division between "wet" and "dry." Men are identified with the Snake, as a "purifying element" (p. 387), "with the positive higher social values," ritual cleanliness, the sphere of "the sacred" (p. 394), women with the dry season, "uncleanliness," and "the profane." Lévi-Strauss recognized the contradiction between these statements and the claim that Aborigines regarded the wet season as bad (too much rain, no food) and the dry season as good (plenty of food, greater mobility). But the seasonal picture and other suggested dichotomies are oversimplified and unreal.

Yulunggul's territorial, seasonal, and religious-ritual roles make him a powerful and majestic figure. Much of his ritual symbolism is secret-sacred, not to be discussed publicly, but his public persona is awesome enough. All of this gives rise to some intriguing questions. For example, in a Milingimbi version that is found only in Warner, after Yulunggul had regurgitated the sisters and they lay "dead," a great Yulunggul *didjeridu* (drone pipe) came out of Yulunggul's water hole of its own volition and revived them with the help of green ants. Yulunggul was angry. He "killed" the sisters and swallowed them again. The *didjeridu* that features so prominently in Kunapipi and associated rituals, however, *is* Yulunggul, and its sound is his voice. How to reconcile the contradiction? Contradiction is, up to a point, the essence of myth, and perhaps it merely reflects the approach of Yulunggul to the Wawalag sisters in the events of the myth as usually told and interpreted, in a relationship about which there is still much more to be said.

See Also Rainbow Snake.

Bibliography

Berndt, Catherine H. "Monsoon and Honey Wind." In *Échanges et Communications: Mélanges offerts à Claude Lévi-Strauss,* edited by Jean Pouillon and Pierre Maranda, vol. 2, pp. 1306–1326. The Hague, 1970. Comments on Yulunggul as an intermediary between the interlinked dialect units and clans of eastern Arnhem Land and on the sociocultural scene in western Arnhem Land and its proliferation of Rainbow Snake myths. Notes briefly some points in Wawalag and Yulunggul songs from women's perspectives, as well as the issue of "incest" at the water hole rather than in Wawalag country.

Berndt, Ronald M. *Kunapipi: A Study of an Australian Aboriginal Cult.* Melbourne, 1951. Includes discussion of Yulunggul in the context of *Kunapipi* ritual and in relation to the Wawalag myth.

Berndt, Ronald M., and Catherine H. Berndt. *The World of the First Australians* (1964). Rev. ed., Adelaide, 1985. Includes discussion of Yulunggul and of the Wawalag myth in their sociocultural context and in their ritual manifestations and interconnections.

Hiatt, L. R. "Swallowing and Regurgitation in Australian Myth and Rite." In *Australian Aboriginal Mythology,* edited by L. R. Hiatt, pp. 143–162. Canberra, 1975. Summarizes a number of Aboriginal myths, including two versions of the Wawalag myth, and discusses various interpretations of the swallowing and regurgitation behavior attributed to certain mythic characters, among them Snakes and old woman (mother) figures who are "also cosmic creators."

Lévi-Strauss, Claude. *La pensée sauvage.* Paris, 1962. Translated anonymously into English with the unfortunate title *The Savage Mind* (London, 1966). The references to Yulunggul and the Wawalag myth are on pages 91–94 and 96. Lévi-Strauss follows Warner's interpretation, reframing it to some extent but accepting his statements and his male-dominated perspective.

Munn, Nancy D. "The Effectiveness of Symbols in Murngin Rite and Myth." In *Forms of Symbolic Action,* edited by Robert F. Spencer, pp. 178–207. Seattle and London, 1969. This perceptive analysis of the Wawalag myth and other features of northeastern Arnhem Land culture, ritual and social relationships includes an examination of the role of the Snake and its bearing on power relations between men and women, and between older and younger men.

Warner, William Lloyd. *A Black Civilization: A Study of an Australian Tribe* (1937). New York, 1958. Devotes a great deal of attention to Yulunggul (Yurlunggur, in his spelling) in the context of the Wawalag myth and associated rituals and their social and environmental implications.

CATHERINE H. BERNDT (1987)

YUNUS EMRE (d. 1321), Turkish mystic, initiator of popular mystic poetry in Turkish literature, and one of the greatest poets in that language. Apart from a few notes in sixteenth-century biographical works, the life of Yunus Emre remains shrouded in legend. More reliable biographical data can be gathered from his own corpus, which recent research (particularly by Abdülbâki Gölpınarlı) has sifted out from the mass of poems produced by contemporary or later anonymous authors who attributed their own work to him.

According to available evidence, he was born in the village of Sarıköy (modern Emre) in central Anatolia, educated in the classical Islamic sciences, and later trained in the mystic path by a certain Tapduk Emre, whom he often mentions in his poems with great veneration. He seems to have lived mostly in the region of his birth and to have died and been buried in the same village. There is also evidence that he traveled to Syria and Azerbaijan, as well as to Konya, where he may have met the great mystic poet Jalāl al-Dīn Rūmī, whose thought and mystic fervor exercised considerable influence on him.

Yunus Emre's writings include a short didactic *mathnavī* and his *dīvān,* or collected poems. The *mathnavī, Risalet ün-nushiyye* (Book of Counsels), written in 1307, is an allegorical poem of 575 couplets in classical Persian meter, with a prose introduction. Elaborating on certain human virtues and vices along orthodox Muslim lines, it is rather sober and uninspired in style and not typical of his work. Rather, his fame rests primarily on his *dīvān,* which is the first one in Turkish literature. It consists of about 350 poems, most of which dwell on variations of pantheistic thought, the tribulations of the initiate, the various stages of the mystic path, guidance to the "straight path," the nature of real knowledge (*ʿirfān*) as different from worldly science (*ʿilm*), the confession of one's errors and shortcomings and the enjoyment of self-accusation (*melāmet*), and nostalgic and evocative themes of the years away from home. Smaller numbers elaborate on orthodox religious themes, with frequent reference to the Qurʾān and the traditions of the Prophet, and to popular stories of prophets and saints, or address the obsessive idea of death, otherworldliness, and eternity.

These poems are addressed to the masses of ordinary people. They are mainly written in the spoken Turkish of the early fourteenth century, with a moderate number of Arabic/Persian loanwords, and the predominant meter follows the traditional Turkish syllabic form. Their great popular appeal over the centuries can be ascribed to Yunus's simple and direct style, his enthusiastic lyricism, and the skill with which he made mystic and pantheistic philosophy accessible. Both the style and the language of his poems continued to exert a tremendous influence on most of the popular mystic poets down to the eighteenth century.

BIBLIOGRAPHY

Gölpınarlı, Abdülbâki. *Yunus Emre: Hayati.* Istanbul, 1936.

Gölpınarlı, Abdülbâki, ed. *Yunus Emre divani.* Istanbul, 1943. With a facsimile of a fifteenth-century manuscript.

Gölpınarlı, Abdülbâki. *Yunus Emre ve tasavvuf.* Istanbul, 1961.

Régnier, Yves, ed. and trans. *Le divan de Yunus Emré.* Paris, 1963.

Schimmel, Annemarie. "Yunus Emre." *Numen* 8 (1961): 12–33.

Schimmel, Annemarie. *Mystical Dimensions of Islam.* Chapel Hill, N. C., 1975.

Sefercioğlu, Nejat, and İsmet Binark. *Yunus Emre hakkinda bir bibliyoğrafya denemesi.* Ankara, 1970.

FAHIR IZ (1987)

YURUPARY is the lingua franca name for an Amazonian culture hero who established order in nature and society and taught men rules of ritual conduct. The term refers also to sacred flutes and bark trumpets, taboo to women and children, played in a secret men's cult into which boys are periodically initiated, and to the celebrations held by the cult. These instruments, kept hidden under water, represent Yurupary in spirit form, and their sound is his voice. By extension the term is used throughout Amazonia to refer to cannibal forest spirits. Christian missionaries have also erroneously identified Yurupary with the devil and attempted to eradicate his cult.

The Yurupary cult is found among nearly all the Indians of northwest Amazonia living in the area of the Japurá, Negro, and middle Orinoco rivers. In particular, it is characteristic of the Arawakan groups (Baníwa, Baré, etc.) of the upper Río Negro and of their Tucanoan-speaking neighbors (Cubeo, Tucano, Desána, Barasana, etc.) of the Uaupés, whose culture shows strong Arawakan influence. The Arawakans call Yurupary Kowai, and a number of other names are used by the Tucanoans. These Indians share many cultural features, including division into patrilineal, exogamous phratries made up of a series of ranked clans, patrilocal marriage, and residence in communal longhouses.

Similar secret men's cults with flutes, trumpets, bullroarers, and masks are a typical feature of many Indian groups of lowland South America, most notably the Mundurucú of the lower Tapajós, the Yagua and Tikúna of the upper Amazon, the tribes of the upper Xingu, and the nearly extinct Selk'nam of Tierra del Fuego.

Yurupary Myth. Numerous versions of the Yurupary myth have been published. What follows is a synthesis of these myths, designed to bring out the major episodes and themes. Yurupary was the child of Ceucy (the Pleiades), who was made pregnant by the juice of a *caimo* (*Pouteria caimito*) or *cucura* (*Pourouma cecropiaefolia*) fruit. She was a virgin, and a disguised incestuous union with a father, brother, or son identified with the sun, moon, thunder, or the constellation Scorpius is implied. Yurupary is himself often identified with the Sun. Lacking a vagina, Ceucy had a painful labor and had to be pierced by a fish. Her baby, taken from her at birth, was brought up by his shaman father or brother. Yurupary had no mouth so he had to be fed on tobacco smoke. He was asked if he was man, animal, or fish, but by shaking his head he indicated that he was none of these. Only when asked if he was Yurupary did he nod his head in agreement, an agreement that, by a process of elimination, also suggested that he was connected with the vegetable world. When given a mouth, he emitted a terrible sound, and sounds emerged from holes in his body, which was that of a monkey but with human face, feet, and hands.

He grew very rapidly and became a shaman leader who taught his people rituals and a regime of taboos and fasts and decreed that no woman should see him or hear his secrets on pain of death. He ordered the men to collect fruit from trees, and he conducted the first initiation rite, at which young boys saw him dressed in full costume.

While the boys were still under initiation taboos, he took them to collect *uacú* fruit (*Monopteryx angustifolia*), which, despite prohibitions, they roasted and ate. Angered by their disobedience, Yurupary sent a thunderstorm, and the boys took shelter in his mouth (or, in some versions, his anus), which they mistook for a cave. Having ingested all but one of them, Yurupary disappeared to his house in the sky, and the lone survivor returned home with the dreadful news.

The parents, angered by their loss and fearful of this cannibal monster, resolved to kill him. They tempted him back with offers of ever more exotic kinds of beer until, offered one he had never tried, Yurupary agreed to return. He knew they wished to kill him and made it known that he could be killed only with fire.

Arriving at dusk, Yurupary vomited up the boys (or their bones), into either an initiates' seclusion enclosure or flat baskets, along with the fruit the boys had collected. He danced and sang all night, getting increasingly drunk on beer and *yagé*, a hallucinogenic drink, and at dawn his hosts threw him on a fire. There followed a huge conflagration, which was the prototype of all future slash-and-burn fires. The burning of a cultivation site is now identified with this first fire. As he died, Yurupary announced that henceforth, though he would be immortal, all men would die.

From the ashes a *paxiuba* palm (*Iriartea exorrhiza*) grew, together with vines for ritual whips and for poison and stinging ants, snakes, and other noxious creatures that shed their skins. The palm was his bone, and the poisonous plants and animals were his soft parts. The palm ascended rapidly to the sky, taking with it Yurupary's soul, which became a star in the constellation Orion. Squirrels cut the palm into sections, which were distributed among men and animals as their different voices. This distribution marked the differentiation of men from animals and, among men, the distinction between the different clans and phratries, which have corresponding linguistic differences. The sections of paxiuba palm, which correspond to paired parts of Yurupary's anatomy—arm and leg bones and fingers—make up the *yurupary* instruments, which are also in pairs, and their sound is his voice. From other parts of his body—skull, brain, tongue, and so on—were made gourds, tobacco snuff, coca, and beeswax, which play an important role in the rites.

Later on, the Sun told his son to rise early and play the *yurupary* instruments at the river. His daughter overheard and got up while her lazy brother slept on. She found the instruments and ran away with them, accompanied by the other women. With the women in possession of the instruments, the social order was reversed: While the women dedicated their lives to ritual, the men menstruated and did all the heavy agricultural work.

The men then set about regaining the stolen flutes. With the aid of ritual whips and small piston whistles, they frightened the women into submission. In punishment for the rebellion, the men caused the women to menstruate and declared that if women should ever see the Yurupary rites and instruments they would be killed.

Yurupary Cult. A number of themes emerge from this myth that relate to the symbolic significance of the cult. Most notable are the astronomical character of the major protagonists; the importance of the vegetable world and its links with human fertility and growth; the links between periodicities in the human and natural worlds; the contrasts between men and women, humans and animals, life and death, and hard and soft parts of the body; and the ambiguity of Yurupary as both benevolent lawgiver and cannibal monster. The myth also serves as a charter for rituals which form the most important expression of the religious life of the people concerned and accounts for the origin of the sacred objects used by them.

There are two kinds of Yurupary ritual, one less sacred than the other. In the former, quantities of forest fruit, gathered by the men, are brought to the longhouse to the sound of the flutes and trumpets. During the day women and children are excluded from the house, but at dusk the instruments are removed and the women join the men to dance and drink manioc beer. The men chant origin myths and drink *yagé* to put them in contact with the spirit world. They also whip one another and the women and children to make them grow strong. The rites are held to increase the abundance of fruit and mark the ripening of each species. They also represent an exchange, in that the fruits are a gift from the spirits and in that fruit is often exchanged between longhouse communities.

These rites also form the first stage of initiation into the cult. Young boys are brought into the house along with the fruit, shown the flutes, given coca, snuff, and yagé, and whipped to make them grow. After participation in one or more such rites they then graduate to the more sacred rites, which are held once per year at the start of the rainy season as the Pleiades set at dusk. For these latter rites greater numbers of more sacred instruments are used, together with gourds of snuff, coca, and beeswax. These and other items, when assembled together, make up the body of the first ancestor, Yurupary or his equivalent. At the climax of the rites the ancestor appears in the form of two men dressed in full ceremonial regalia and adopts the initiates as his sons. The boys are shown the flutes and whipped, then taken to the river to bathe while water poured from the flutes is "vomited" over their heads.

The initiates are then secluded for two months in an enclosure that is out of sight of the women. They must fast; rigid taboos govern various aspects of their behavior; and they are taught to make baskets, an exclusively male task. The adult men are also under strict taboos and all are in a state described as being like that of menstruating women. The women fend for themselves and a state analogous to the matriarchy of the myth pertains. This period is brought to an end when the initiates are given chili peppers to eat and hot liquids to drink, ending a taboo on contact with sources of heat. There follows a festive dance at which the initiates give women the basketry they have made, and thereafter the food taboos are progressively lifted and life returns to normal.

Themes and Interpretations. A number of different interpretations have been proposed for this cult and, given the simultaneous operation of a number of different symbolic levels, they are not necessarily incompatible. At a sociological level, the cult involves the ritualized opposition between men and women, an opposition that permeates the Indians' secular and ritual life. The *yurupary* instruments are the means whereby men dominate women. Not only are women excluded from important rituals but they are also excluded from the knowledge of mythology and shamanism that this entails. Such knowledge is also a source of prestige and power. In the same vein the cult emphasizes the equivalent status of women and uninitiated children and allows the subjection of young men by their elders, who have greater ritual knowledge and experience.

Among the Tucanoan Indians Yurupary is also an ancestral cult related to their patrilineal ideology. The death of the ancestor and the distribution of his flute-bones provides a model for the division of human society into discrete phratries and, at a lower lever, for the segmentation of each phratry into a number of clans descended from a common ancestor. The ritual adoption by the ancestor of his sons, the initiates, each one the potential founder of a new patriline, reenacts and repeats this initial process of segmentation. The instruments, each set of which is owned by a clan, are the sons of the ancestor and founders of the clans, and they bear the names of these ancestors.

The exclusion of women further emphasizes clan solidarity and patrilineal ideology by implying that the clan can reproduce itself without the intervention of women from outside. Latent in the Yurupary and related myths is a tension between the extremes of incest—as in the start of the myth—and its opposite, reproduction without the intervention of women—as when Yurupary is burned and becomes his sons, the flutes. Note too that Yurupary's bones become masculine flutes while his soft parts become things with feminine (and poisonous) connotations. This tension relates to that between a patrilineal ideology and the requirement that women must be brought in from outside for sexual reproduction. The symbolism of the cult plays upon this by dividing men and women into opposed groups while stressing the complementarity between male and female principles.

The Yurupary rituals can be seen as reenactments of elements of the central myth, and the symbolism of swallowing and regurgitation, a familiar theme of many initiation rites, is clearly present. The ritual, the myth, and statements by indigenous informants all suggest that the initiates are killed and swallowed and reborn by being vomited up again, a theme that can be linked to the etymology of Yurupary—from *yuru* ("mouth") and *pary* (initiates' enclosure, or a trap made of woven palm splints). The vegetable nature of Yurupary, shown in his fast growth and his associations with fruit, is clearly related to the association of the initiates with fruit and the stress on their growth. The cult involves magic designed to increase the fertility of nature and to ensure the growth and fertility of human beings. Whipping to promote growth is common throughout Amazonia, as is the use of stinging ants for the same purpose.

The myth accounts for the origin of human mortality and links it with human and natural periodicity. While death is final, society endures through sexual and social reproduction. Ritually this process is accomplished by a symbolic death and rebirth whereby young boys come to replace their ageing elders. The myth implies that death is not final: Yurupary's soul becomes an immortal star and his bones become flutes, and are his representatives on earth. The myth draws a parallel between his death and slash-and-burn agriculture, whereby new plants grow from the ashes of dead trees. The instruments thus mediate between life and death and turn their opposition into an alternating cycle.

The theme of periodicity also relates to that of menstruation, which figures in both the myth and the rites. The myth implies that menstruation and possession of the flutes are equivalent but inversely distributed between the sexes. Women are held to approximate Yurupary's immortal state both because they reproduce themselves through their children and because menstruation is seen as analogous to the sloughing of their skins by the immortal snakes and other creatures who came from Yurupary's ashes. Though men lost the power to menstruate they gained the *yurupary,* which, although clearly masculine symbols, have an important feminine aspect appropriated and controlled by the men. The cult implies that whereas women give birth to children, only men can "give birth" to fully social adults.

That Yurupary and his mother and father are all identified with heavenly bodies further relates to this theme of periodicity. The myths and rites relate to the apparent movement of the stars in relation to that of the sun. The azimuth of the Pleiades corresponds with the winter solstice, Orion moves along the celestial equator, the azimuth of Scorpius corresponds with the summer solstice, and the heliacal rise of the Pleiades corresponds with the setting of Scorpius. Throughout northwest Amazonia the Pleiades are a seasonal marker, their heliacal rise coinciding with the start of the dry season and their setting with the rains, and the "opposition" between the Pleiades and Scorpius is a common symbolic theme in South American Indian cultures. Yurupary himself has both solar and masculine characteristics and a lunar, more feminine side.

Many of the themes mentioned above reappear in secret men's cults elsewhere in lowland South America. Among the Mundurucú the opposition between the sexes is more pronounced and antagonistic and corresponds with an apparent fear and jealousy of female sexuality and reproduction on the part of the men. With them, as with the Yagua, the link between sacred instruments and fruit is replaced by a link between the instruments and game animals. The flutes guarantee an abundance of game and luck in the hunt, in return for which they must be constantly fed. In the Xingu area the cults are again linked with the fertility of fruit. Among the Tikúna, sacred instruments are associated with female initiation involving the pulling out of the girls' hair. Female hair figures also in the Yurupary cult, for sacred masks representing Yurupary were made from hair shorn from girls at first menstruation. Finally, myths of matriarchy are common to all these groups.

Bibliography

Of the many versions of the Yurupary myth published to date, the most complete is contained in *La leggenda del Jurupary e outras lendas amazonicas* (São Paulo, 1964) by Ermanno Stradelli (1852–1926). Wilhelm Saake's article "Die Juruparilegende bei den Baniwa des Rio Issana," in *Proceedings of the Thirty-second International Congress of Americanists, Copenhagen 8–14 August 1956* (Copenhagen, 1958), pp. 271–279, is also an important source. This version is translated into English in Robin Michael Wright's work "History and Religion of the Baniwa Peoples of the Upper Río Negro Valley," 2 vols. (Ph.D. diss., Stanford University, 1981), which also contains another very full version of the myth, an ethnography of Baníwa religion, and some important material on the links between the Yurupary cult and messianic movements. Jonathan David Hill's study "Wakuenai Society: A Processual-Structural Analysis of Indigenous Cultural Life in the Upper Rio Negro Region of Venezuela" (Ph. D. diss., Indiana University, 1983) gives an ethnography of the Wakuenai (Curipaco) with good material on Yurupary and a valuable ethnomusicological analysis.

No really full and general account of the Yurupary cult, dealing equally with mythology, ritual, and its social structural context, exists. Silvia Maria da Carvalho's *Jurupari: Estudos de mitologia brasileira* (São Paulo, 1979) is a comparative analysis of the Yurupary and related myths. The analysis, while not based on primary field research, provides a comprehensive survey and makes a number of significant points of interpretation but is marred by thinly supported discussions concerning population movements, evolution, and diffusion. Hector Orjuela's *Yurupary: Mito, leyenda y epopeya* (Bogotá, 1983) relies also on published works and again provides a valuable compilation of the relevant myths. The interpretation is, however, patchy, and includes unsubstantiated assertions concerning the supposed Colombian origins of the myth. Jacqueline Bolens's "Mythe de Jurupari: Introduction à une analyse," *Homme* 7 (1967): 50–66, is a structuralist analysis of several classic versions of the Yurupary myth that, though short, contains some important insights concerning the symbolism involved.

My book *The Palm and the Pleiades: Initiation and Cosmology in Northwest Amazonia* (Cambridge, 1979), based on field research, provides a full account of Yurupary myths and rituals among the Tucanoan Barasana and their neighbors and is perhaps the most accessible and rounded interpretation of the cult. It also gives a comprehensive bibliography.

There is no general account of secret men's cults in South America, but Yolanda Murphy and Robert F. Murphy's *Women of the Forest* (New York, 1974) and Anne Chapman's *Drama and Power in a Hunting Society: The Selk'nam of Tierra del Fuego* (Cambridge, 1982) provide accounts and interpretations, both based on primary research of such cults among the Mundurucú and Selk'nam.

Finally, *Rituals of Manhood*, edited by Gilbert H. Herdt (Berkeley, Calif., 1982), describes secret men's cults, this time in the New Guinea highlands, which show striking parallels with their South American counterparts.

New Sources

Caicedo de Cajigas, Cecilia. *Origen de la Literatura Colombiana: El Yurupary*. Pereira, Colombia, 1990.

Clastras, Hélène. *The Land-without-Evil: Tupí-Guaraní Prophetism.* Translated by Jacqueline Grenez Brovender. Urbana, Ill., 1995.

Vesga Nuñez, Omar. *Yurupary, el Hijo de las Pléyades que Fundo una Nación en el Vaupés: Breve Estudio Comparado.* Bogotá, 2003.

STEPHEN HUGH-JONES (1987)
Revised Bibliography

Z

ZAEHNER, R. C. (1913–1974), was an English Orientalist and historian of religions. Robert Charles Zaehner, born April 8, 1913, began studies in Persian while on a scholarship in classics at Oxford and received a master's degree in Oriental languages. After leaving his position as research lecturer at Christ Church, Oxford, in 1939, he entered government service and was attached to the British embassy in Tehran during World War II. He accepted appointment as lecturer in Persian at Oxford in 1950; and, after serving briefly as acting counselor in the British embassy in Tehran, he was designated to succeed Sarvepalli Radhakrishnan as Spalding Professor of Eastern Religions and Ethics at Oxford in 1952, a professorship he held until his death on November 24, 1974.

At the least, Zaehner was a controversial figure during his remarkably productive two-decade career as Spalding Professor, and an altogether equitable assessment of his substantial publications on mysticism, the religions of India, Islam, and the comparative study of religions is difficult. If a historian of religion should be thoroughly grounded as a specialist in at least one major religious tradition, then Zaehner's credentials, in this respect, can scarcely be criticized: His primary research on Zoroastrianism, especially evident in his invaluable *Zurvan* (1955), unquestionably demonstrated his specialist's knowledge. If, too, a historian of religions may be expected to learn the original language or languages of primary sources in traditions that have special significance for his research, then Zaehner's study of Sanskrit in order to read classical Hindu sources again adds to his credentials. And, if an unwavering concern to allow source materials to speak in their own voices is essential to the prospering of serious primary and comparative investigations of religions, then Zaehner served his field of study well.

But if it is supposed that proper comparative history of religions must be so conducted as almost to render invisible the interpreter's presence, then Zaehner poses a problem. He is neither bland nor unobtrusive. In an age of increasingly "objective" and almost anonymous scholarship, Zaehner seldom left his readers uncertain of his position. He lauded, lamented, scolded, praised, and condemned. Unquestionably, he took seriously the materials he studied. Above all, he seems to have wanted the sources to present them-

---

CLOCKWISE FROM TOP LEFT CORNER. Relief of the third-century Zoroastrian high priest Kerdēr. Naqsh-e-Radjab, Iran. *[The Art Archive/Dagli Orti]*; Bronze Zeus or Poseidon from the Artemisius at Cape Sounion, 460 BCE. National Archaeological Museum, Athens. *[©Erich Lessing/Art Resource, N.Y.]*; Relief depicting the Zoroastrian god Ahura Mazdā at the ruins of Persepolis. Takht-i Jamshid, Iran. *[©Charles & Josette Lenars/Corbis]*; Zen garden at Ryoanji in Kyoto, Japan. *[©Archivo Iconografico, S.A./Corbis]*; Ziggurat of Nanna at Ur, c. 2100 BCE. Iraq. *[©Charles & Josette Lenars/Corbis]*.

selves fully and authentically and not partially or tendentiously. What Zaehner himself took to be authentic, of course, was disputed on more than one occasion. Thus, for example, Zaehner's struggle with the specter of Sarvepalli Radhakrishnan's happy Neo-Hindu universalism provoked counter-assertions from Zaehner about the theistic dimension of Hindu thought that have been found extreme by many specialists.

For Zaehner, his source documents and what they represented were alive and not safely dead or distant. Misunderstood, his attitude could appear to be no more than a throwback to apologetic comparative studies of an earlier day. And it often was misunderstood. But in fact it seems that—his conversion to Roman Catholicism in the mid-1940s notwithstanding—Zaehner conceived his own "mission" to be the pursuit of comparative religious studies in ways that would not violate the uniqueness and integrity of the individual religions he studied. Unshakably convinced of the authenticity of his own youthful mystical experiences and the truth of his conversion (as he was certain that chemically induced altered states of consciousness were worse than bogus mysticism), Zaehner was altogether ready to take religious documents completely seriously. And, believing himself to be a religious man, he had no difficulty accepting the existence and (occasionally wrongheaded) sincerity of other religious men.

BIBLIOGRAPHY

Zaehner's command of Zoroastrian material is indisputably documented in *Zurvan: A Zoroastrian Dilemma* (Oxford, 1955) and his more accessible and wide-ranging *The Dawn and Twilight of Zoroastrianism* (London, 1961). Among the latter's several strengths not the least is its thorough and unusually entertaining bibliography. Zaehner's *Hinduism* (London, 1962) is among the most helpful overviews; and his *The Bhagavad-Gita,* a translation and commentary (Oxford, 1969), is one of the most significant scholarly encounters with this text. Vigorous and insightful also are Zaehner's Jordan Lectures, *Hindu and Muslim Mysticism* (London, 1960) and his *Mysticism: Sacred and Profane* (Oxford, 1957). The complex range of Zaehner's thought and style is nowhere better illustrated than in his stimulating and controversial Gifford Lectures, *Concordant Discord* (Oxford, 1970). Possibly the most engaging introduction to Zaehner's work, however, may be the eight late essays published posthumously as *The City within the Heart* (London, 1980), which is introduced by philosopher Michael Dummett's warm tribute.

G. R. WELBON (1987)

ZAKĀT is a Qurʾanic term that signifies the specific obligation of giving a portion of an individual's wealth and possessions for primarily charitable purposes. The word is derived from a root meaning "to be pure" and also carries additional connotations of "increase" and "virtue," as well as "giving." It is also used in the Qurʾān together with other terms such as *ṣadaqāt* that also carry the connotation of giving and of charity.

The Qurʾān links *zakāt* to other primary acts of belief: "Piety does not consist of merely turning your face to the east or to the west. Rather, the pious person is someone who believes in God, the last day, the angels, the book, and the prophets and who out of his love gives his property to his relatives, orphans, the needy, travelers, supplicants, and slaves; and who performs the required prayers and pays the *zakāt*" (Qurʾān 2:177).

The verb *zakā* suggests the idea of growth to emphasize that the giving of one's resources is simultaneously an act that entails the cleansing of oneself and one's property and, through sharing, an enhancement of the capacity of others. More specifically, this kind of giving is considered in the Qurʾān to be analogous to a fertile garden whose yield is increased by abundant rain (Qurʾān 2:265). It is this multiple connotation of *zakāt* that is reflected in subsequent interpretations in the institutionalization of the principle in Muslim thought and practice. The centrality of *zakāt* is underscored by the many times it is coupled with the command for prayer and also identified as a continuation of the practice of past prophets.

It is clear that the Qurʾān envisaged a broad framework both for those who might benefit from the more formalized practice that was evolving in the early Muslim community and for the fiscal support of the community's needy. *Zakāt* and other forms of giving served to benefit the early Muslims who had migrated from Mecca with the Prophet. It was also used to encourage others to join the Muslim community and to support the Muslims in the conflict against Mecca. The Qurʾān specifies the types of recipients who ought to benefit from it: those afflicted by poverty; those in need and incapable of assisting themselves; those who act, sometimes in a voluntary capacity, as stewards and custodians to ensure the collection and appropriate expenditure of funds; those who should be attracted to the faith; captives who need to be ransomed; debtors; travelers; and finally those engaged in serving God. All of these categories came to be strictly defined in later legal and exegetical literature. But other verses also suggest broader uses that might include those who during periods of hardship or transitions were not visibly in need and who nonetheless either required assistance to enhance their livelihood or needed to be directed towards new occupations and economic opportunities. While one aspect of *zakāt* was clearly projected towards charitable acts for the poor and the needy, the practice also encompassed the wider goal of applying the donations to improve the general condition and economic well-being of other recipients and constituencies and those working to foster the growth of the new community.

The fact that the Prophet eventually organized the collection and distribution of *zakāt* suggests that the process was being cast into specific institutional forms even in his day. It was, according to early Muslim sources, applied to crops, animals, merchandise, gold and silver, and so on. Such wealth and possessions qualified only when they were above a certain minimum number or amount. The collector was urged to be fair and to persuade rather than impose. According to the Qurʾān, some of the Bedouin groups that had converted to Islam remonstrated about the paying of *zakāt.* Al-Bukhārī (d. 870), the compiler of the most respected collection of Sunnī prophetic *ḥadīth,* cites a report in which the Prophet sent a representative to Yemen to invite the local tribes to convert to Islam and pay *zakāt.* When Abū Bakr became caliph after the Prophet's death, a number of tribes refused to pay the *zakāt* because they felt that the death of the Prophet absolved them from the obligations contracted with him. In order to ensure adherence to the practice and to put down the rebellion Abū Bakr was compelled to send forces against the rebels, restoring order and proper remission of *zakāt.* It appears therefore that based on the example of the Prophet and the early Muslim community, while the practice of *zakāt* had become well-established, its particulars and regularization were still in the process of development.

The juristic literature produced by succeeding generations of scholars further formalized the collection and disbursement of *zakāt* as part of the larger systematization of legal obligations. While in some instances rulers and states collected *zakāt,* inefficiencies and corruption resulted throughout Muslim history in a variety of collection practices, so that individuals were still free to disburse *zakāt* as individuals or in community contexts through appropriate intermediaries.

The work of the Hanafī jurist Abū Yūsuf (d. 808), *Kitāb al-Kharāj,* which was written during the reign of the Abbasid caliph Hārūn al-Rashīd (r. 786–809), is an instructive example of the collaboration between jurists and rulers to appropriate and extend such practices as *zakāt* as part of the fiscal working of the state. A jurist such as al-Shāfiʿī (d. 820) was able to systematize and rationalize prevailing practice in his work. Generally, such works built upon the references to *zakāt* and *ṣadaqāt* in the Qurʾān, detailing the payments based on the ownership of property, possessions, precious stones and money, animals, and income generated from farming and trading. They prescribed when an amount was to be paid and to whom, as well as what minimum amounts were due in each category. It is interesting to note that the *zakāt* was also extended to include underground resources, such as minerals and treasure troves. These juristic works enumerate in great deal the character and terms of *zakāt,* developing into an elaborate formalized obligation, presented as a religious duty. Many of the sources however continue to emphasize the moral agency of the act, linking its obligatory character to religious merit and reward. Moreover, they often identified *ṣadaqāt* and *zakāt* as a means of seeking God's pleasure and the reward of the afterlife.

Developments in legal theory also reflect the way different groups in Islam interpreted *zakāt.* Shīʿī sources, citing ʿAlī ibn Abī Tālib and the other early *imāms,* emphasize the need to pay the *zakāt* to the rightful authorities. Among the Shīʿah, this was to be entrusted to the *imām* or those designated by him and disbursed in accordance with the spirit of Qurʾanic values. Among the Ithna Ashari Shīʿah, who believe that the *imām* is in a state of physical absence from the world (*ghayba*), *zakāt* was to be entrusted to those considered his trusted worldly representatives. Their role was to ensure that *zakāt* reached the appropriate recipients. Among the Ismāʿīlī Shīʿah, *zakāt*'s formal aspect is complemented by a spiritual significance, and it was the role of the *imām* to interpret and sustain the values of *zakāt* in changing contexts. The Zaydi tradition insisted that it must be paid to official collectors representing the Zaydi state under a legitimate *imām.*

The Sūfīs emphasize the mystical value of *zakāt.* In certain circles, individuals were known to distribute their entire possessions as *zakāt.* Some groups sanctioned the acceptance of *zakāt* as a gift emanating directly from God. Over the period of Muslim history, the practices relating to *zakāt* evolved into various forms, but it remained an important practice, mirroring beyond all the formal details the principle and moral commitment to share one's wealth.

As Muslims seek to address questions of identity and development in the modern world, *zakāt* has afforded them the opportunity to rethink the relevance of past practices within their changed contexts, which include living in nation-states or as minorities in many parts of the world. A majority of Muslims live in areas of the world that are considered to be less developed than the more industrialized regions. Hence, issues of social justice and the equitable distribution of resources figure prominently in discussions of the present-day significance for building civil society according to the values of past tradition. Some Muslim theorists have advocated the reintroduction of the obligatory *zakāt* tax as one element of a general tax policy to add the moral aspect of social benevolence to a modern economic policy.

Additionally, some countries have developed nonstate financial agencies to allow for individuals to voluntarily contribute *zakāt.* In Pakistan, Saudi Arabia, Sudan, and Yemen, legislation was created to encompass *zakāt* as part of the state fiscal practice. The majority of Muslims, however, continue the practice of *zakāt* as a voluntary act of giving and as an expression of personal faith, intending it to serve the needs of those less privileged in their communities and elsewhere in the world.

BIBLIOGRAPHY

For primary sources in translation see, Abū Yūsuf Yaʾqūb ibn Ibrahīm, *Kitāb al-Kharāj,* translated by E. Fagnan (Paris, 1921); Bukhārī, *Sahīh,* translated by A. Houdas and W. Marçais as *Les traditions islamiques,* 4 vols. (Paris, 1903–1914); al-Ghazālī, Abū Hāmid Muhammad, *Ihyāʾ ʿulūm al-dīn,* translated by Nabih A. Faris as *The Mysteries of Almsgiving* (Beirut, 1966); al-Nuʾmān, Abū Hanīfa (Qadī), *Daʾāʾim al-Islām,* translated by Asaf A. A. Fyzee and I. K. Poonawala (Delhi, 2002); al-Shāfi-ī, *al-Risāla,* edited by A. M. Shākir (Cairo, 1940), translated by Majid Khadduri as *al-Shāfiʿī's* Risāla: *Treatise on the Foundations of Islamic Jurisprudence* (Baltimore, 1961; 2d ed., Cambridge, U.K., 1987; reprint, 1997); Tabarī, *Taʾrīkh,* translated by W. M.

Watt and M. V. McDonald as *The History of al-Tabarī*, vols. 6 and 7 (Albany, N.Y., 1988–1990).

Secondary sources include Mahmoud Ayoub, *The Qur'ān and its Interpreters*, 2 vols. (Albany, N.Y., 1984–1992); Norman Calder, "Zakāt in Imāmī Shīʿī Jurisprudence from the Tenth to the Sixteenth Centuries A.D.," *BSOAS* 44 (1981): 468–480; Hartley Dean and Zafar Khan, "Muslim Perspectives on Welfare," *Journal of Social Policy* 26 (1997): 193–209; Clifford Geertz, *Local Knowledge: Further Essays in Interpretive Anthropology* (New York, 1983; 3d ed., 2000); Marshall Hodgson, *The Venture of Islam*, 3 vols. (Chicago, 1974); Azim Nanji, "Ethics and Taxation: The Perspective of the Islamic Tradition," *Journal of Religious Ethics* 13 (1985): 161–178; Javed A. Khan, *Islamic Economics and Finance: A Bibliography* (London, 1995); Abdul Aziz bin Muhammad, *Zakāt and Rural Development in Malaysia* (Kuala Lumpur, 1993); Abdulaziz Sachedina, *The Just Ruler in Shīʿite Islam* (New York, 1988); Nasim Shah Shirazi, *Systems of Zakāt in Pakistan: An Appraisal* (Islamabad, 1996); and Norman A. Stillman, "Charity and Social Service in Medieval Islam," *Societas* 2 (1975): 105–115.

AZIM NANJI (2005)

ZALMAN, ELIYYAHU BEN SHELOMOH

SEE ELIYYAHU BEN SHELOMOH ZALMAN

ZALMOXIS

ZALMOXIS was the founder, possibly legendary, of a priestly line of succession closely linked with kingship of the Getae and the Dacians, the northernmost Thracian peoples of the ancient world. Whether he is a figure of legend or of history is moot, as are questions of his religious functions. Associated both with priesthood and with kingship, he was divinized and became the object of a widespread cult among both northern and southern Thracian peoples.

NAME. The name *Zalmoxis* is attested by ancient authors from Herodotus and Plato (fifth-fourth centuries BCE) to Diodoros of Tyre (second century CE) and Jordanes (sixth century CE). Herodotus spells the name *Salmoxis;* Strabo gives it as *Zamolxis.* The genuine form, however, is *Zalmoxis,* support for which is found in such Thracian names as *Zalmodegikos* and *Zelmutas* and in numerous composites formed with *-zelmis, -zelmos,* and *-selmios. Zamolxis* is only a metathesis, frequent since Strabo (first century BCE), with no parallels in Thracian onomastics.

Porphyry (third century CE) explains the etymology of *Zalmoxis* through the Thracian word *zalmos* ("skin"; Gr., *dora*), and in supporting this thesis he offers an etiologic legend that tells of the covering of Zalmoxis at birth with a bearskin (*Life of Pythagoras* 14–15). Dimiter Detschew (1957, p. 175) has proved that Indo-European correspondents of *zalmos* also mean "shield, protection," which is perfectly fitting to both a god and the highest priest. But Porphyry also gives another explanation of the meaning of the name: "foreigner" (Gr., *xenos aner*). On this basis Paul Kretschmer compared the metathetical form *Zamolxis* with the Phrygian *zemelen* ("barbarian slave"; Gr., *barbaron andrapodon*), with *Zemelo,* the name of a Thraco-Phrygian earth goddess (compare the Greek *Semele*), and with the Slavic *zemlja* ("earth") and thus explained *Zamolxis* as meaning "lord of men" (for *-xis,* compare the Avestan *xshaya-,* "lord, king"). Hence was developed (mainly by I. I. Russu) the theory of the chthonic character of this god, which led to the ongoing dispute over his real functions.

According to Herodotos (*Histories* 4.94), some Getae also gave Zalmoxis the name *Gebeleizis* or *Beleizis,* which Kretschmer has related to the same Indo-European root, **g'hem-el-* ("earth"), that he traced in *Zamolxis.* Given that Herodotus spoke about a thundering god, Wilhelm Tomaschek corrected the name to *Zibeleizis,* meaning "thunder sender" (compare the Lithuanian *žaibas,* "thunderbolt," which has no clear etymology). More recently, Cicerone Poghirc (1983) has proposed, for reasons of textual criticism, the reading *Nebeleizis,* meaning "god of the [stormy] sky" (compare the Slavic *nebo,* "sky," and the Greek *nephele,* "cloud").

TESTIMONIES. Herodotos (4.95) refers to a story told by the Greeks in the Pontic colonies (on the western shore of the Black Sea) according to which Zalmoxis was a Getic slave of the Greek Pythagoras, who lived in Samos. After Zalmoxis was freed, he became wealthy and went back to his native country, where he taught the northern Thracians the Greek way of life based on Pythagorean ideas about immortality, vegetarianism, and so forth (see Strabo, *Geography* 7.3–5). In his homeland Zalmoxis had an *andreion* built (a room for the exclusive use of men), where he received the chiefs of the Getae and taught them that neither they nor their posterity would die. This concept of immortality refers in all probability to a paradise where warriors would enjoy eternal life and everlasting pleasure after death. While he imparted this teaching of the afterlife, Zalmoxis had an underground chamber constructed. When it was finished, he retired to it for three years, during which the Thracians mourned his death, but in the fourth year he reappeared, showing that death is not irreversible.

With slight variations, this legend is repeated by several Greek and Latin writers. Herodotos, however, opines that Zalmoxis was not a slave of Pythagoras but did in fact live long before him. Strabo adds that Zalmoxis learned from Pythagoras and from the Egyptians, whom he visited. He says that Zalmoxis was a prophet who became a priest of the principal god of the Getae and an associate of the king; later he was divinized. He dwelled in a cave, on the holy mountain Kogaionon, where scarcely anyone but the king and his messengers could join him (7.3–5). The kingship of Zalmoxis and his teaching on immortality are confirmed by Plato (*Charmides* 156d–e), who adds further that Zalmoxis had taught a highly praised method of psychosomatic medicine based on charms (*epoidai,* 157a).

Another piece of basic information provided by Herodotus (4.94) concerns the principal rite of the Getae, which consisted of killing a messenger every four years (or five years, according to Greek computation). A man chosen by lot from among the warriors was given a message to be delivered to the god. Then he was cast on top of three spears. If he died instantly, this was interpreted as a good omen. If he failed to die, the sacrifice had to be repeated, and the first messenger was cursed. This cursing suggests that purity of some kind was required.

According to the Roman geographer Pomponius Mela (first century CE), Getic warriors were not afraid of death. Pomponius gives three different explanations for their contempt of life, each one believed by some among them: belief in metensomatosis (reincarnation); belief that the soul survives after death in a happy place; and belief that life is worse than death, although the soul is mortal. Of these interpretations, only the second refers to the genuine teaching of Zalmoxis according to Herodotus (4.95).

Herodotus's reference to Zalmoxis/Gebeleizis introduces the latter as a heavenly god. This description is supported by the claim that during thunderstorms the Getae shot arrows into the sky, thus threatening their god (4.94).

Decaeneus (also known as Dekaineous, Deceneus, and Dicineus), a high priest of Zalmoxis during the reign of the Getic king Burebista (c. 80–44 BCE), is mentioned in an account by Strabo (7.3–5), his near contemporary. According to a Greek commonplace, Egypt was a land where wisdom could be acquired, and Strabo also says that Decaeneus wandered there and learned soothsaying (7.3–11). The story that he ordered grape vines cut down in the kingdom of Burebista and an allusion to the vegetarianism of the Getae may be based on actual facts. It is also not impossible that Decaeneus was acquainted with the idea of metensomatosis, which fits well in the Pythagorean pattern of the religion of the Getae. An authentic feature of Getic high priesthood was Decaeneus's dwelling in a cave on Mount Kogaionon (Strabo, 7.3–5).

INTERPRETATIONS. The history of the interpretations of Zalmoxis is somewhat disappointing. Distinguished scholars have disagreed about whether Zalmoxis's cult was a form of monotheism or of polytheism (it was not more monotheistic than, say, the Cretan cult of Zeus Idaeus); about whether Zalmoxis was a god or a man, perhaps a religious reformer; and about whether he was connected with the earth or with the sky (in fact he was associated with both). Spiritualistic evolutionists have tried to show that the cult of Zalmoxis represented for the Daco-Roman population a sort of primordial revelation and a *praeparatio evangelica.* Rationalists and Marxist evolutionists have tried to demonstrate that it was, on the contrary, much more "primitive" than some testimonies indicate. Hadrian Daicoviciu, for instance, shared this last hypothesis even though it contradicted his own pertinent interpretation of the calendar temple of Sarmizegetusa Regia (modern-day Gradistea Muncelului, Romania), according to which the Dacian priests were steeped in sophisticated astronomical speculations (*Dacii,* 2d ed., Bucharest, 1972).

The excellent study *Zalmoxis, the Vanishing God* (Chicago, 1972) by Mircea Eliade put an end to these discussions by showing that the testimonies concerning the cult of Zalmoxis have to be trusted and interpreted on the basis of a close comparison with other religious materials. According to Eliade, Zalmoxis was a mystery god in whose cult the divinity's "occultation" and "epiphany" were celebrated. In his attempt to decipher the Greek interpretation of Zalmoxis in its genuine dimensions, Eliade established important links between Zalmoxis and Archaic Greek traditions concerning soothsayers and medicine men like Pythagoras himself.

ZALMOXIS AND THE GREEK SEERS. In the most ancient testimonies, Zalmoxis is constantly related to Pythagoras. Pythagorean features of his cult are further specified until the times of Strabo and Pomponius. A corpus of these features can be established as follows: Zalmoxis has an underground chamber built, disappears for three years, and then reappears (katabasis, occultation, and epiphany); he makes prophecies; he and his priests and successors live in a mountain cave, practice psychosomatic medicine, and make astronomical computations; there is among the Getae a group of ascetics who live in poverty and continence, abstaining from animal food. The core of the Zalmoxean teaching is the doctrine of immortality of the soul, which should actually be interpreted as a promise to the brave warriors that they would survive in paradise. Later, some among the Getae may have been acquainted with the idea of metensomatosis. All this sounds so Pythagorean that the Greeks were even disposed to understand the less attractive practice of human sacrifice without much ethical comment.

One of the false problems connected with Zalmoxis that has received much attention from scholars is whether the god—if he was a god at all—ought to be interpreted as a chthonic or as a heavenly divinity. In fact, from the perspective of the history of religions, this is not a logical contradiction, since divinities of the sky can be strongly connected with the earth, and vice versa. Furthermore, even in Greek religion, which is usually the model according to which Zalmoxis is interpreted, such heavenly divinities as Zeus and Apollo were worshiped in caves, whereas such a typically chthonic divinity as Persephone was associated very early with heavenly immortality. Pythagoras himself, who was apparently connected with Apollo of Hyperborea, is also the character who descends to the underworld and who exhibits important features that establish his relationship with a chthonic goddess, or "great mother." Zalmoxis's "Pythagorean" structure connects him with both the earth and the sky.

Among the Greek characters belonging to the same class of seers, soothsayers, medicine men, and semidivinities as Pythagoras, the one who most closely resembles Zalmoxis is Epimenides of Crete, worshiped as a god in a local cult. Epimenides is said to have dwelled in the grotto of the infant

Zeus on Mount Ida, where he slept for several decades. He avoided food and used only a plant called *alimos,* or hungerbane, to keep hunger in abeyance. He could foretell the future, he practiced purifications, and he was able to remember his previous existences as a human being. In one of these incarnations he was Aeacus, brother of Minos, who was a son of Zeus. Minos visited his godly father in the Idaean cave every eight years, and thus it is not surprising that Epimenides used this place for incubation. During his catalepsy, his soul was reported to be together with the gods, listening to their speeches.

According to another legend, once when Epimenides was about to dedicate a sanctuary to the nymphs a heavenly voice instructed him to dedicate it to Zeus instead. This could be interpreted as an indication that the Idaean cave did not belong to the sphere of influence of those divinities who normally preside over such places, that is, the nymphs, but to the heavenly god *par excellence,* Zeus. In fact, Epimenides was considered a "new infant" (*neos kouros*), the Idaean Zeus reborn. It is, then, no surprise to learn that he was the guide of Pythagoras when the latter descended into the Idaean cave. Nor is it surprising that Epimenides, the author of oracles and theogonies, worshiped by the Cretans as a god, was nevertheless transformed by the Neoplatonic Iamblichus (c. 250–330 CE) into a pupil of Pythagoras in precisely the same way as this happened with Zalmoxis; among Greek seers of pre-Socratic times Pythagoras was simply more famous than Epimenides.

The chthonic side of Epimenides is revealed by his dwelling in a cave and by his relationship with the nymphs. In the legends of Pythagoras and Zalmoxis this chthonic side is revealed by a detail that has only recently received a consistent interpretation. Walter Burkert (1972) has shown that Pythagoras was probably viewed as a representative of the chthonic goddess Demeter, a hypothesis confirmed by the tradition that Pythagoras once exhibited a "golden thigh." This probably means that the legend attributed to Pythagoras a tattoo on his thigh, which was the mark, or seal, of the Anatolian great goddess. At the same time it was an indication that Pythagoras could travel to Hades (Burkert, 1972, pp. 160–161).

In his *Life of Pythagoras* (15), the Neoplatonist Porphyry reports a strange legend according to which Zalmoxis was a disciple of Pythagoras; at the time of the revolt of the citizens of Croton against Pythagoras, Zalmoxis was captured by bandits who tattooed him on his face, which he kept covered ever after. This brief account seems to be extremely important, since tattooing among southern Thracian nobles is attested as early as Herodotus (5.6) and confirmed by several testimonies, and yet Artemidorus of Ephesus (fl. 100 BCE) reports that, whereas the southern Thracian nobles had their children tattooed, the Getae tattooed only the children of their slaves. From a fragment attributed to Clearchus of Soloi (sixth century BCE) one could infer that Getic women were tattooed over the whole body. The rhetorician Dio Chrysostom (first century CE) specifies that only the wives of Thracian nobles were tattooed, with red-hot irons.

Tattooing among the Thracians was probably a religious mark; among the northern Thracians, the Getae and the Dacians, it could have been associated with the pain once inflicted upon Zalmoxis by his captors. Since tattooing among the Getae is twice mentioned in relationship to slavery, one could infer that the ancient legend making Zalmoxis a slave was based on this character's genuine myth, which might have originally included suffering and imprisonment. Plutarch of Chaeronea (first century CE) reports that the Thracians tattooed their women in order to avenge the sufferings inflicted by Thracian women upon Orpheus. Plutarch, who was far better acquainted with Orpheus than with Zalmoxis, could have misinterpreted here an actual tradition connected with Zalmoxis. It is possible to a certain extent to state that the Getae tattooed their slaves and perhaps their wives as a religious record and possibly as revenge for the mark impressed upon Zalmoxis while he was a captive.

Much less convincing is the interpretation of Rhys Carpenter in his *Folk-Tale, Fiction, and Saga in the Homeric Epics* (Berkeley, Calif., 1946), which is based on the testimony of Porphyry (*Life of Pythagoras* 14), according to which a bearskin was put on Zalmoxis at his birth. According to Carpenter, Zalmoxis actually was a bear, whose hibernation (i.e., occultation) was taken by the Getae as a religious model.

CONCLUSION. God or man, possibly also a religious reformer of the Getae, Zalmoxis fits almost perfectly into the Pythagorean pattern of a Greek seer and medicine man such as Epimenides, who was also worshiped as a god. His myth is scarcely known, but it could have contained an episode of captivity and, possibly, suffering. Ritual tattooing among the Getae was related to this episode, and might have been inflicted upon slaves and women as an expiation of a mythical sin. Zalmoxis probably taught immortality for valiant warriors. He was worshiped in a grotto, which might have played an important part in the initiation of priests and warriors. A chief priest, his representative in the grotto, was considered a prophet, and he gained such influence in political matters that the state of Burebista could be properly called a theocracy. A sanctuary, possibly the old sanctuary with an underground chamber at Sarmizegetusa Regia, described by Ion Horaţiu Crişan in *Burebista and His Time* (Bucharest, 1977), was provided with a subterranean room, a substitute for the grotto. This indicates that the legend of the occultation of Zalmoxis referred to by Herodotus was connected with the existence of such an ancient sanctuary.

SEE ALSO Geto-Dacian Religion; Thracian Religion.

BIBLIOGRAPHY

The bibliography relating to the etymology of the name *Zalmoxis* is discussed by Dimiter Detschew in *Die thrakischen Sprachreste* (Vienna, 1957) and by Cicerone Poghirc in "Considérations philologiques et linguistiques sur Gebeleizis," which appears in Poghirc's *Philologica et Linguistica* (Bochum,

1983), pp. 169–172. All Greek and Latin testimonies concerning Zalmoxis are reported and translated in *Fontes Historiae Dacoromanae,* 2 vols., edited by Virgil C. Popescu et al. (Bucharest, 1964–1970).

The widest historico-religious interpretation of this divinity of the Geto-Dacians, together with an impressive bibliography, is to be found in Mircea Eliade's *Zalmoxis, the Vanishing God* (Chicago, 1972). For alternative interpretations, see Walter Burkert's *Lore and Science in Ancient Pythagoreanism* (Cambridge, Mass., 1972) and Ioan Petru Culianu's "Iatroi kai manteis," *Studi storico-religiosi* (Rome) 4 (1980): 287–303. In a more recent book, *Psychanodia,* vol. 1 (Leiden, 1983), pp. 24–39, Culianu has examined the historico-religious context in which the testimonies connected with Zalmoxis are to be placed. See also, by the same author, *Expériences de l'extase* (Paris, 1984), pp. 25–43.

New Sources

Alexandrescu, Petru. "La nature de Zalmoxis selon Hérodote." *Dialogues d'histoire ancienne* 6 (1980): 113–122.

Dana, Dan. "Zalmoxis in Antonius Diogenes' *Wonders Beyond Thule.*" *Studii clasice* 34–36 (1998–2000): 79–119. Basing on the study of various literary traditions he criticizes Eliade's and Culianu's strictly religious interpretations.

Pippidi, D. M. "Réflexions d'hier et d'aujourd'hui sur le culte de Zalmoxis." *StudClas* 14 (1972): 205–210.

IOAN PETRU CULIANU (1987)
CICERONE POGHIRC (1987)
Revised Bibliography

ZAMAKHSHARĪ, AL-

ZAMAKHSHARĪ, AL- (AH 467–538/1075–1144 CE), fully Abū al-Qāsim Maḥmūd ibn ʿUmar al-Zamakhsharī; Muslim philologist and Qurʾān commentator. Born in Khorezm in northern Persia, al-Zamakhsharī traveled little outside his native province except for several years spent studying and writing in the holy city of Mecca. He was a native Persian speaker, but he believed strongly in the superiority of the Arabic language and excelled in Arabic philology. According to various historical records, he wrote some fifty works; thirty of these are known to exist today, a majority of which have been published in the original Arabic. Most of these works deal with the Qurʾān or the Arabic language in general.

Al-Zamakhsharī's major work, and the one for which he is most famous, is his book of Qurʾān interpretation (*tafsīr*), *Al-kashshāf ʿan ḥaqāʾiq ghawāmiḍ al-tanzīl* (The unveiler of the realities of the secrets of the revelation), a work completed during a two-year stay in Mecca around 1134. The work is a phrase-by-phrase philosophical and philological commentary on the entire text of the Qurʾān, written in a concise, careful, and somewhat difficult style. Notable is its lack of tradition-oriented material; virtually no reports are attributed to the early authorities on interpretation; rather, all comments are directly stated with no concern for their authority in the past. Generally, al-Zamakhsharī presents first what he considers to be the obvious meaning of a verse and then notes other possible interpretations on the basis of grammar and textual variant readings, while always paying full attention to the notion of the rhetorical beauty *(iʿjāz)* of the Qurʾān.

The distinctiveness of al-Zamakhsharī's Qurʾān commentary lies in his Muʿtazilī theological leanings. Beginning in the tenth century, the Muʿtazilah were apparently a powerful theological force in al-Zamakhsharīs birthplace. He states explicitly that *Al-kashshāf* was written in order to provide the needed comprehensive Muʿtazilī commentary to the Qurʾān. The most obvious result of this theological position in the commentary is the way in which he resolves apparent conflict between various verses of the Qurʾān. The Muʿtazilī doctrines of the unity and justice of God and the consequent ideas of the human free will and the need to deanthropomorphize the Qurʾān become the prime themes of the distinctive passages of interpretation. A typical example is found in his treatment of surah 6:125:

> *Whomever God desires to guide:* those upon whom God bestows his benevolence, which only happens with those who are worthy. *He expands his breast to Islam:* bestowing his benevolence on them so that they long for Islam, and their souls feel at home there, and they desire to be Muslims. *Whomever he desires to lead astray:* those whom God leaves alone and wishes to abandon to their own deeds. What is meant is one who is not worthy of his benevolence. *He makes his breast narrow, tight:* He keeps his benevolence from them, so that their hearts harden, and they refuse and resist truth, and thus faith finds no path into them.

Here the emphasis is always upon the prior moral condition of the individual, to which God responds by enhancing the condition that the individual has already chosen.

Likewise the doctrine of the created Qurʾān (as opposed to the orthodox dogma of the preexistent, uncreated Qurʾān) is present throughout al-Zamakhsharī's work; apparently *Al-kashshāf* originally began, "Praise be to God who created the Qurʾān," but this was changed to "God who gave" or "God who sent down" in order to temper the tone somewhat.

Despite its theological argumentation, al-Zamakhsharī's Qurʾān commentary has been widely read and copied, especially in the eastern parts of the Islamic world. The work has consistently been subject to both explication and attack by later authors, who have provided many supercommentaries and derivative commentaries. The work by al-Bayḍāwī (d. sometime between 1286 and 1316), *Anwār al-tanzīl wa-asrār al-taʾwīl* (The lights of the revelation and the secrets of the interpretation), is the most famous attempt to distill the essence of al-Zamakhsharī's work while attempting to omit those views which were reprehensible to orthodoxy. For the Muʿtazilah, on the other hand, *Al-kashshāf* represents the peak of intellectual achievement in Qurʾān commentary.

BIBLIOGRAPHY

Al-kashshāf an ḥaqāʾiq ghawāmiḍ al-tanzīl has been edited and published a number of times, but no particular edition has emerged as the standard one. No extensive portions have ever been translated, and the usefulness of such translations would be quite limited because of the precise and technical nature of much of the original. Short passages of the work are available in English throughout Helmut Gätje's *The Qur'ān and Its Exegesis: Selected Texts with Classical and Modern Muslim Interpretations,* translated and edited by Alford T. Welch (Berkeley, 1976), and in Kenneth Cragg's *The Mind of the Qur'ān: Chapters in Reflection* (London, 1973), pp. 64–69, where the commentary on Qur'ān surah 90 is translated. The most significant and extended treatment of al-Zamakhsharī's work on the Qur'ān is to be found in Ignácz Goldziher's *Die richtungen der islamischen Koranauslegung* (Leiden, 1920), pp. 117–177. Jane I. Smith's *An Historical and Semantic Study of the Term "Islām" as Seen in a Sequence of Qur'ān Commentaries* (Missoula, Mont., 1975), pp. 89–101, gives a useful summary of al-Zamakhsharī's work, provides examples of his method of interpretation, and locates it within the general historical framework of *tafsīr.* A number of articles by Lutpi Ibrahim have appeared on al-Zamakhsharī and his theological relationship to al-Bayḍāwī: "Al-Bayḍāwī's Life and Works," *Islamic Studies* (Karachi) 18 (1979): 311–321; "The Concept of Divine Justice according to al-Zamakhsharī and al-Bayḍāwī," *Hamdard Islamicus* 3 (1980): 3–17; "The Relation of Reason and Revelation in the Theology of al-Zamakhsharī and al-Baiḍāwī," *Islamic Culture* 54 (1980): 63–74; "The Concept of *Iḥbāṭ* and *Takfīr* according to al-Zamakhsharī and al-Bayḍāwī," *Die Welt des Orient* 11 (1980): 117–121; and "The Questions of the Superiority of Angels and Prophets between al-Zamakhsharī and al-Bayḍāwī," *Arabica* 28 (1981): 65–75.

ANDREW RIPPIN (1987)

ZAPATISMO AND INDIGENOUS RESISTANCE.

ZAPATISMO AND INDIGENOUS RESISTANCE. The EZLN's (Zapatista Army of National Liberation) seizure of five municipalities on January 1, 1994, in Chiapas follows a tradition of insurrections and armed rebellions dating back to the arrival of Europeans to the region. Examples of these insurrections include the Zoque community rebellion, 1532–1534; Mayan descendants executed a Spanish mayor in 1693; the Cancuquero people, in alliance with other communities, rose up in 1712; and in 1869–1870 the Chamulas and Tzotziles rebelled. San Cristóbal de las Casas, the main city in which the first EZLN uprising played out, is named for Bartolomé de las Casas (sixteenth-century Spanish archbishop and defender of the thesis that the indigenous peoples, contrary to the Catholic Church's position, indeed possessed souls). The experience of the indigenous struggle against the Spanish crown and then the Mexican nation-state took on more clear articulations with the leadership of Emiliano Zapata, who drew upon Zapotec cultural traditions, and the modern anticapitalist conceptualizations of Marxism, Leninism, and anarchism during the Mexican Revolution. Zapata brought the indigenous traditions that informed the politics of the *ejidos* and the autonomy of the land together with modern revolutionary articulations of the seizure of power. This mode seeks either to maintain the state structure according to Leninist inspiration or to eliminate it according to Bakuninian thought and indigenous beliefs and convictions surrounding land autonomy. Zapata agreed with the anarchist Flores-Magón brothers and favored the dissolution of the state. The most important document of this period (which divides the urban and the *villista* camps from the land-based Zapatista camp during the Mexican civil war) was the "Plan de Ayala," written by the Zapatista Army of the South on December 11, 1911. The plan sustains that the people must remain armed until the land is concretely transferred back into the hands of the indigenous peoples.

In the 1960s, during the worldwide intellectual movements, the student movements, the inspiration of the Cuban revolution, and the Soviet and Chinese forms of Marxism, the ELN (Army of National Liberation) and other groups developed in Mexico. This party became one of the few that remained active in the 1970s after the student massacre at Tlatelolco under the Diaz Ordaz presidency in 1968. When the urban revolutionaries, among them the future subcomandante Marcos, arrived in Chiapas in the early 1980s with the intent to develop an armed Zapatista uprising, they found the region in a state of political agitation. The diocese of San Cristóbal formed part of the political action inspired by Liberation Theology, and the Mayan communities were clear about the urgent need for liberation in order to continue to exist as autonomous cultures with their own worldviews and pertinent social structures. The Zapatista revolutionaries installed themselves in Las Cañadas and learned from the local peoples. The EZLN began to take shape in accordance with the beliefs and worldviews of the people—the value of the word and the ethical responsibility of language making up a central axis of the movement.

President Carlos Salinas de Gotari eliminated Article 27 from the Mexican constitution (which prohibits the privatization of the *ejido* lands) in 1992, making possible the liquidation of these common lands and thus facilitating the pauperization and eventual cultural and physical disappearance of the inhabitants. On January 1, 1994, NAFTA (North American Free Trade Agreement) took effect for the United States, Canada, and Mexico and with it the Anglo–North American exploitation of Chiapas, a state rich in uranium, petroleum, jungle, and hydroelectric resources. The EZLN opened its campaign at dawn with eighteen thousand Mayan men and women—masked and armed with automatic guns, single-shot rifles, and wooden replicas painted black—making known the First Declaration from the Lacandon Jungle against neoliberalism and globalization.

THE WORD. In *Balún Canan* (1957) the Chiapas author Rosario Castellanos wrote of the ongoing plight of the indigenous people of the region:

> *Y entonces, coléricos nos desposeyeron, nos arrebataron lo que habíamos atesorado: la palabra, que es el arca de la memoria. Desde aquellos días arden y se consumen con el leño en la hoguera. Sube el humo en el viento y se deshace.*

> *Queda la ceniza sin rostro. Para que puedas venir tú y les baste un soplo, solamente un soplo.*
>
> And then, furiously they dispossessed us, they carried off what we had treasured: the word, which is the ark of memory. Ever since those days they smolder and are consumed with the logs of the bonfire. The smoke rises in the wind and dissolves. Faceless ash remains. So that you can come, and with only a puff, just a puff. (Castellanos, 1984/1957, p. 9)

Globalization, like other words of its kind—*modernization, pacification,* or *industrialization*—connote neutral if not humanitarian processes in the world of mass media and consumer culture; people take them for granted without seeing their morphology and ideological weight. Such words appeal to first world consciousness, and people accept them, act upon them, and live with them as though they were trees that express the passage of time. If one attends the words carefully, looks at the meaning attached to each root, prefix, and suffix, and reinserts them into the memory and the narrative of time, one can reestablish the connection between word and deed, and one can recover meaning.

Within modernization are assumptions of backwardness. Within industrialization lies the classification of inefficiency and "primitive," small-scale production. Within the idea of normalization is assumed erraticness, abnormality, diversity, and the need to establish patterns in what is unpredictable through Western paradigms. Calling for stabilization attributes chaos to the object of that stabilization and the need to make it secure. Pacification deems the people and place in question warlike. Secularization identifies the necessity to eliminate religious thought and the sacrality of the everyday: sunrise, harvest, slaying animals, and eating. Secularization also proposes science as truth and unideologically suspect.

The postmodern era of the world economy has its socially accepted words, as did the era of modernity and colonial economy. The moral high ground of the civilization depended on the belief in the savagery and cannibalism of the Other. Christianization assumed paganism, idolatry, and witchcraft. Supporting colonization assumed the inferiority of cultures and the inaptitude of targeted "races" for self-government and for the management of the resources of the land they inhabit. Inside the mission of population lies the assumption that the people of the targeted lands are not people.

These words are euphemisms, coded signifiers that say nicely, according to their contemporary social mores, what may otherwise offend the morality and self-image of the people whose cultures promote and support these market-driven processes. This long-standing language strategy belongs to the strategies of discourse and rhetoric, particularly writing discourse in its character of self-reflective materiality and class-constructed hegemony.

When these words are naturalized, they become necessary, indisputable, and unavoidable. Embedded in language, they form part of the macronarrative into which every culture's history is made to conform, describing how all the world's peoples fit into the history of the Western tradition. The words originate in the language of the dominant narrative (Spanish from the sixteenth century to the early nineteenth century and English in the era of the American economic system). These are the words of the macronarrative that deems the social organization of non-Western peoples as "underdeveloped" or "developing." The unavoidability of the terminology becomes another layer in the mission of modernity, science, and progress—the belief in the superiority of secular society and republican governance. This conviction, bolstered by self-professed objectivity, overlooks the fact that modernity is a historical phenomenon not unlike the previous era's belief in the Catholic Church.

To see globalization or any other such terms as natural, neutral, or necessary, one accepts the implicit negation that such cultural processes of transformation are dual, involving a subject and an object: the one who globalizes, modernizes, democratizes, and so on and the one that is globalized, modernized, or democratized. They are not horizontal dialogues between subjects as the colorful image of "global culture" suggests. One entity carries out the project, and another entity purportedly receives the benefits. The straightforward characterization of subject and object, however, overlooks the histories that demonstrate quite the opposite, that the modernizer, for example, benefits more economically from the modernization project than does the object of that modernization.

Globalization is a capitalist project requiring expansion in order to grow (key word of the economic vocabulary). Growth, acquired by the institution of profit, is the core of globalization. When internal markets and tariffs become a barrier for the health of accumulation and the movement of the capitalist economical machinery, expansion is imperative. This expansion goes hand in hand with the justification of political and military invasion—a traditional way of creating markets and resource pools with positive industrial and commercial results.

This phenomenon is paradoxical because what is discussed is the globalization of capital, and capital is an object, not a subject. Given that paradox, globalization is not the expansion of the will of a subject over an object but the contrary, the globalization of an object (capital) over subjects (the people and cultures of the world). Globalization is the action of an agent of capital over nature, resources, people, language, ideas, and imagination in order to expand the sphere of influence of that capital to increase the amount of capital in return. It is an operation where humans are agents of an object that oppresses them, that robs them of subjectivity and agency, and that functions through them. The will of the object loosely follows "the economical laws," it is the invisible hand. In practice, in a highly racialized, socially divided and gendered society, the rationale for participating—ideologically speaking—is given by the most prestigious and influential part of society. Women, people of color, and other social classes unenfranchised with the international corporate economic forces only participate, consciously or unconsciously, as collaborators or assimilated people. The project is not in their interest but in the interest of inertia. Even though some reap more material benefit as agents of capital, they are all oppressed by it, all doubly objectified.

ZAPATISTA WORLDVIEW. Subcomandante Insurgente Marcos wrote in "Como nace la palabra en la montaña" from *Relatos de El Viejo Antonio*:

> *Decía el Viejo Antonio que los viejos más viejos de los dioses enseñaron a los hombres a leer el cielo y el suelo. en esas dos grandes hojas del cuaderno del mundo (dijo el Viejo Antonio que dijeron los más grandes dioses, los que nacieron el mundo), los hombres y mujeres verdaderos pueden leer la orientación para que su corazón camine. Cuando el cielo calla, cuando el sol y la luna reinan con silencio, y cuando el suelo se esconde tras su dureza su quehacer interno, los hombres y las mujeres de maíz guardan la palabra y la trabajan pensando. Cuando el techo de la tierra se agrieta con nubes, lluvias y viento, cuando la luna y el sol sólo asoman cada tanto, y cuando la tierra se abre con verde y vida, los hombres y mujeres verdaderos nacen de nuevo la palabra en la montaña que es su casa y camino.*
>
> Old Man Antonio used to say that the old ones older than the gods taught men to read heaven and the ground. In those two big pages of the notebook of the world [Old Man Antonio said that the biggest gods said this, the ones who gave birth to the world] the true men and women can read the directions so that their heart can walk. When heaven becomes quiet, when the sun and the moon rule with silence, and when the ground hides its inner workings behind its hardness, the men and women of the corn hold the word and work thinking. When the roof of the earth cracks open with clouds, rain and wind, when the moon and the sun only appear once in a while, and when the earth opens up with green and life, the true men and women bare the word again in the mountains which are their home and their path. (p.131)

The recovery of the word is central to the project of democracy, liberty, and justice for the Zapatistas of Chiapas. Changing the world and countering the force of the global economy that have been destructive to indigenous cultures and their integrated worldviews means changing the word. Achieving democracy, one of the central goals of the movement, necessitates mending the relationship between language (oral and written) and meaning. This recuperation establishes a move from a liberal (formal) democracy to a participative or authentic democracy as signified by the word itself: *demos*, coming from the Greek root meaning "people," and *–cracy*, meaning "from government." The search for the true word is the search for collective participation and consensus. The Zapatista practice *mandar-obedeciendo* (to command-obeying) better explains this idea: the leader has to be part of the bases and represent them according to their will. Thus Subcomandante Marcos has a secondary rank (deputy commander) in the Zapatista army, because the *comandante* are the Mayan people of Chiapas. The recovery of the word then means that this subordinated rank of Marcos is not a rhetorical construction to justify his power but instead a word, which represents a real subordination of an individual to the collective.

The recovery of the word is deeply rooted in the historical silence and invisibility in which the original people autochthonous to the Mayan homelands and the Americas were compelled to remain for five hundred years. The silence was enacted by European conquerors, their descendants, and their religious-cultural-governmental structures that are the foundation for the New World governments and institutions that have developed into a dialogical relationship of imitation, counteridentification, and reform with the worldview and corresponding structures of the conquerors. They have established a religion, which separates the natural and the social from the divine. This religion allows for the brutal exploitation of the planet, creating an economic system that separates producers from consumers and making room for profit and poverty, and institutionalizing a political system that has divided the representatives from the represented, allotting space for the burial of local holistic worldviews and the fragmentation of communities.

The weight assigned to the truth in the act of recuperation of the word is a frontal challenge to the hegemonic ideology that sustains itself in the double standard of domination and justification. It is not enough that the word represent reality or that its utterer have honest intentions to do so; only with the practice of horizontal (not hierarchical) dialogue can democracy be held accountable.

The recovery of the word not only implies the return of the original inhabitants to the scene of the continent but also the return of the autochthonous worldviews, which present new ways of dealing with human liberation in the postmodern world. This implies a new praxis beyond the structure of the liberation movements that are born of modernity and based on a historical trajectory anchored in the European, such as Marxism and industrialization.

The Zapatista collective (wearing masks in order to emphasize the collectivity of the group and to reflect the government's rhetoric of hiding meaning, holding weapons, and taking over five municipalities) forced the dialogic exercise of democracy with the formal democratic government of the Republic of Mexico, which is complicit in global economics. In this way the movement recovered the meaning of the word, putting indigenous beliefs about the necessary connection between language and meaning at the forefront and holding the formal democratic institution accountable to the word with which it describes itself. The Zapatistas are willing to remove their masks if the government does the same: the Zapatista mask functions as a metaphor for the hiding of the true face: "Detrás de nuestras máscaras estamos ustedes (Behind our masks are you)," writes Marcos. The mask is a means for maintaining the memory of the lies behind the official truths that are based in different forms of privilege. The purpose of the word is to communicate, to exchange ideas, to understand, and to create consensus. With the social distortion of oppression in any of its forms (class, race, and gender), the word also has been distorted to fulfill the will of the privileged groups, creating the need of ideology or false consciousness to make people collaborate willingly with their own oppressors. Dialogue, on the other hand, set within a horizontal arrangement, is a tool for democracy where participation is exercised with respect and human dignity.

The recovery of the word becomes an ethical imperative in the modern and postmodern world, a world that has privileged economic goals and systematically forgotten the promise of meaning. Proponents of globalization have arranged the world in a way that enables them to live relatively unaffected by the consequences of the enactments of falsely named operations, operations like democratization or stabilization. They have established a monologue and constructed a dehumanized common sense through euphemism and other distortions. Ironically the proponents of globalization have become the emblematic figures for human perfection, spreading the institutionalization of the misuse of words like *democracy* and *peace* in the targeted path of economic expansion. The expansion in turn has fractured the integrated worldviews of the indigenous peoples of the locations of economic homogenization. They have created an equation that imposes a Western particularism as the universal standard: socioeconomic improvement means capitalism, security means militarism, humanity means ideologically in agreement with the globalizing forces.

For the original people, the reintegration of meaning and the word is essential for liberation on all fronts, including the cultural, spiritual, economic, and intellectual. Their naked exploitation at the hands of the agents of capitalism makes the confrontation with meaning inescapable. Their experiences reveal the incongruous relationship between the Western word and its manifestations. The word has to represent reality: killers must be killers, abusers must be abusers, and democracy must be democracy. Original people do not need to sever meaning from word to live. They, because of their place in the structures of globalization, live with the violent consequences of the separation of word and meaning. NAFTA came into being on January 1, 1994. At the dawn the same day the EZLN invaded San Cristóbal de las Casas in Chiapas, Mexico, and the four other municipalities. The NAFTA agreement, they explained, was a sentence to death to more than a million Mayan people and their worldviews. For the NAFTA project, Chiapas was one of the most important states to be incorporated into this new brand of hegemony called globalization due to the unusually rich and diverse natural resources of the land. These natural resources and the Mayan people to work in a new setting of *maquiladoras* were all part of the strategic plan to make southeast Mexico a participant in the global economy. The EZLN understood well the move and confronted the army, starting a rebel movement that has attracted sympathizers from all over the world in its years of resistance, motivating indigenous movements the world over to struggle against globalization.

BIBLIOGRAPHY

Bonfil Batalla, Guillermo. *Méxcio profundo: Una civilización negada.* Mexico City, 1987.

Castellanos, Rosario, ed. *Balún Canán* (1957). Mexico City, 1984.

De Vos, Jan. *Vivir en la frontera: La experiencia de los indios de Chiapas.* Mexico City, 1997.

EZLN. "First Declaration from the Lacandon Jungle: EZLN's Declaration of War." Chiapas, Mexico, 1993.

EZLN. http://www.ezln.org.

Marcos, Subcomandante Insugente. *Relatos de El Viejo Antonio.* San Cristóbal de las Casas, Mexico, 1998.

Marcos, Subcomandante Insugente. "El mundo: Siete pensamientos en mayo de 2003." *Revista Rebeldía* 7 (May 2003).

Marcos, Subcomandante Insugente. "Otra geografía." *Revista Rebeldía* 5 (May, 2003).

Rodríguez Lasacano, Sergio. "¿Puede ser verde la teoría? Sí, siempre y cuando la vida no sea gris." *Revista Rebeldía* 8 (June 2003).

Wienberg, Bill. *Homage to Chiapas: The New Indigenous Struggles in México.* New York, 2000.

AMADO J. LÁSCAR (2005)
AMANDA NOLACEA HARRIS (2005)

ZARATHUSHTRA. Zarathushtra (known in the West under his Graeco-Latin name of Zoroaster) is seen by all Zoroastrians and by most modern scholars as the founder or the prophet of Zoroastrianism, the dominant religion in the Iranian world up to the ninth century CE. Since modern scholarship dates the earliest texts of Zoroastrianism (attributed to Zarathushtra himself) to the beginning of the first millennium BCE and there is broad agreement over the fact that these texts were not written down before the fifth century CE, it is not surprising that the historicity of Zarathushtra has been doubted by several modern scholars. Two different approaches are available for an introduction to this pivotal person in the development of one of the oldest and most influential of all religions. The first is based on the Zoroastrian traditions concerning his life and mission and the second on the findings of modern scholarship. These two approaches, which often interlock in both religious and academic writings, need to be discussed separately here not only to avoid anachronisms but also because modern assumptions about Zarathushtra's activities tend to distort the image of the prophet in premodern Zoroastrianism itself. Modern scholars agree on the fact that Zarathushtra can only count as the author of a tiny portion of the corpus of the Avesta. However, in premodern Zoroastrianism the text of the entire Avesta and its commentaries were seen as the revelation brought to the world by Zarathushtra according to the wish of the supreme god Ahura Mazdā. Therefore the "sources" available for reconstructing his life and activities cannot be immediately settled.

ZARATHUSHTRA IN ZOROASTRIANISM. The focus here is on the image of Zarathushtra in "classical" Zoroastrianism, that is, the Zoroastrianism of the Pahlavi books (dated to the ninth century CE), with additional materials from earlier texts and evidence from non-Zoroastrian sources. If Zarathushtra counts as the "founder" of Zoroastrianism at all in these sources, it is usually in his capacity of the chosen person who brings Ahura Mazdā's revelation to the world. This revelation is usually referred to as *dēn*, a word that has a wide range of meanings but most often simply means "religion." This is not a banal detail: most Zoroastrian texts use the words "it is revealed in the religion" as an introductory formula to the claim that what is being transmitted is part of the "original" revelation of Ahura Mazdā to Zarathushtra. This revelation, the religion, was prepared by Ahura Mazdā even before the work of creation. Small parts of it were revealed by Ahura Mazdā to earlier persons from the mythical history of the Iranians as is told explicitly in the Pahlavi books and follows naturally from the fact that Ahura Mazdā regularly speaks to such important early humans as the first man (Gayōmard), the first human couple (Mašya and Mašyāna), and the first king (Yima). It is also part of the evolved theology of Zoroastrianism: if Ahura Mazdā is good and the religion is necessary for the benefit of humankind, Ahura Mazdā should be protected from the reproach that he had left humankind unaware of his intentions up to the time of Zarathushtra.

Other traditions, however, mention that all "prophets" before Zarathushtra refused to bring his revelation into the world and that it was only Zarathushtra who took this work upon himself. The revelation he brought consisted of the whole Avesta (in its own special language) with its commentaries (in the vernacular). This is evident especially from later texts (in Pahlavi), which had to account for the fact that the religion was formulated and that priestly decisions were based on the *Zand*, the (exegetical) translation of the Avesta, rather than on the Avestan texts themselves (several of which had been lost). The *Gāthās* were occasionally attributed to Zarathushtra in a more direct sense than the other parts of the revelation. In the Avesta, Zarathushtra is presented "while singing the Gāthās" (Y. 9.1), and the recitation of the *Gāthās* in the *Yasna* liturgy is preceded by important introductory formulae. But the suggestion by a nameless heretic that one should accept as Zarathushtra's revelation only the *Gāthās* is firmly rejected in the *Dēnkard*, one of the most important Pahlavi texts (*Dēnkard* 3.7).

As bringer of the revelation, Zarathushtra occupies a pivotal place in the history of the world. From the early texts onward, this aspect of his life is stressed regularly. In order to emphasize his importance, the world before Zarathushtra is portrayed as a world where demons roam freely. With the first utterance of the sacred Ahuna Vairya-prayer, Zarathushtra smashed the shape of the demons and repelled them from the face of the earth.

The Zoroastrian tradition has preserved a lengthy legendary biography of the prophet, the value of which is enormous for a proper understanding of Zoroastrianism and its sense of history. Every aspect of his life is characterized by miracles and portents. His coming to the world came to be seen as preordained: his guardian spirit (*fravashi*) was created millennia before his actual birth. His birth in itself was miraculous in many ways: the various constituent elements of his human life (body, soul, guardian spirit, "glory") were all transmitted by Ahura Mazdā and several of his divine helpers in a very complicated process, which involved his father and mother and various elements from the natural world.

During the pregnancy of his mother, the demons and evil priests were struck by terror and feelings of impending disaster for their ways of life. At birth, Zarathushtra laughed, and as a boy, he showed every sign of great accomplishments. The most crucial episodes from his life took place when he was thirty years old. Having moved to the "land of the Aryans," he entered a river to draw water for the morning rituals. Purifying himself, he encountered a shining figure on the banks of the river who introduced himself as Wahman (Vohu Manah, "good thought") and brought him to heaven, before Ahura Mazdā. There were a total of seven meetings between Zarathushtra and Ahura Mazdā. During these, Ahura Mazdā gave Zarathushtra the revelation and ordered him to spread it in the world.

This was not an easy task. Zarathushtra had to overcome the opposition of the wicked priests and their secular overlords of the religion(s) he meant to replace and was, initially, not very successful in doing this. Success only came after a lengthy stay at the court of King Wištāsp. After a series of philosophical debates, an episode of treachery leading to his arrest and incarceration, and Zarathushtra's success in curing the king's favorite horse, he finally found an audience willing to listen to his words. He recited the revelation for the king and his family, and they were the first to convert outside his own family. From the conversion of Wištāsp onward, the history of Zoroastrianism was to be a history of growth and success, but hostilities continued nonetheless. According to late traditions, Zarathushtra lived to be an old man but was eventually murdered and received into heaven.

A part of Zarathushtra remained, however: his semen is kept in a lake, where it will rest until the period of the separation of good and evil begins. When this time arrives, a virgin will bathe in the lake and become pregnant, giving birth to Zarathushtra's son(s), the Savior(s), who will lead humankind in bringing about the Renovation of the world. Thus Zarathushtra is represented, in Zoroastrian traditions, in all periods of world history, from the beginning of creation up to the desired end.

Many elements from these Zarathushtra legends can be found already in the Avesta. His meetings with Ahura Mazdā are alluded to in what is undoubtedly an old text, the confession of faith (*Fravarānē*, Y. 12). Parts of the Avesta are cast in the literary genre of questions and answers between Zarathushtra (asking the questions) and Ahura Mazdā (giving the answers) and thus stress the fact that he was responsible for the whole revelation. Although the *Gāthās* contain little if any information relevant for his personal life according to modern opinions, many elements from the Zarathushtra legends can be traced back to (often obscure) passages from the *Gāthās*. Although Zarathushtra played a role in the Zoroastrian version of the history of the world that is almost incommensurate with human capacities, there is no evidence that he was ever seen as something other than human.

In contemporary Zoroastrianism, pictures of Zarathushtra are omnipresent in houses as well as fire-temples and sanctuaries. It is not certain how old this custom is, but the iconography used in the Iranian and Parsi communities cannot be traced to a period before the late eighteenth century. Small devotional rituals can be performed in the presence of these pictures: lighting a candle or an oil lamp or decorating the picture with a garland of flowers. On the sixth day of the first month of the Zoroastrian calendar, Zoroastrians commemorate Zarathushtra's birth and the beginning of his meetings with Ahura Mazdā.

In ancient and medieval non-Zoroastrian sources, Zarathushtra is often mentioned. Usually he is presented as the founder of the Persian priesthood (the magi) and the founder of the religion of the Persians. From an early period, Zoroaster was also annexed in Western traditions. Among Greeks and Romans, he came to be known as an early sage, who invented magic and astrology. The Western traditions on Zoroaster owe little to Zoroastrian ideas. This is true for antiquity but also for the remarkable popularity of Zoroaster in western European traditions from the Renaissance up to the late eighteenth century.

ZARATHUSHTRA IN MODERN SCHOLARSHIP. The traditional biography of Zarathushtra is of course a myth. This myth is of great importance for a proper understanding of Zoroastrianism, but it yields little information on the historical Zarathushtra. Modern scholars (and indeed most modern Zoroastrians) do not accept the entire Avesta as the work of Zarathushtra, not to mention the vast body of exegetical literature in the *Zand*. When the Avesta and other Zoroastrian texts reached Europe in the late eighteenth century, the study of these texts remained under the influence of traditional Zoroastrian understanding only for a short while. The academic study of Zarathushtra and his message had to disengage itself more and more from the tradition that grew out of it. In the middle of the nineteenth century the German Orientalist Martin Haug demonstrated that a small part of the *Yasna* (sacrifice), the text of the daily high ritual, was written in a different language than the rest of the Avesta; that this language was more archaic; and that the texts in this more archaic language were the only texts that could be accepted as Zarathushtra's own words. These are the *Gāthās* (songs), five in number, to which modern scholarship has now added a few prayers and a short ritual prose text, all written in the same archaic dialect. These texts have now been recognized as the only possible source of information for the earliest period of Zoroastrianism. They are attributed to Zarathushtra himself by many scholars, but others have voiced doubts about the historicity of Zarathushtra or about the possibility of gaining accurate knowledge about him from these texts.

The corpus of relevant texts is thus small and unfortunately difficult. It is not only full of words of disputed or unknown meaning, but especially the difficulty of the poetic *Gāthās* is seen as intentional. Although earlier scholars thought of these texts as "verse sermons" or solemn declarations of new religious insights, it is now generally assumed that the poems are to be interpreted as visionary poetry composed in a ritual setting. The Old Avestan prose text, by contrast, is much less opaque. Since the texts do not refer to historical or geographical settings known from other sources, the possibility of contextualizing these texts is slim. Even though there is no shortage of speculation on this matter, it seems impossible to date the texts with precision or to situate them in a geographical environment. The texts mention the names of several persons, all known from the later Zoroastrian tradition, but it is a moot point whether that tradition has preserved knowledge of these persons or has invented a narrative in which these persons could fit.

In order to confront these difficulties, most scholars use two different sets of comparative materials. The first of these are the later Zoroastrian traditions, which reflect the religion that grew out of these early texts. The second set of comparative texts is offered by the hymns of the *Ṛgveda*, which were composed in a language that resembles Old Avestan closely and are full of set expressions and poetic usages that both traditions share.

There are certain dangers in using either approach to the exclusion of the other. Both sets of *comparanda* are, in a sense, quite far removed from the Old Avestan texts. Using both sets of data in combination seems to be the best option to guard against anachronisms (by reading later developments into the early texts) and against reading into these texts Vedic ideas that may never have been present in them. The truth is that the *Gāthās* are different from the Vedic hymns. There are certain similarities in poetic expressions and in the grammar of the texts, but the poems as compositions are completely different, as are the main components of the contents of the *Gāthās*.

Since contexts are unavailable, only rough indications of dating and localization, based on the content of the texts and the archaisms of their language, can be given. There seems to be a broad agreement that the texts (and therefore Zarathushtra himself) should be dated around the beginning of the first millennium BCE in an eastern part of the Iranian world, perhaps the area known as Bactria-Margiana (present-day Afghanistan and Turkmenistan).

Two names stand out in importance in the *Gāthās.* The first of these is the name of the god who is celebrated in these hymns: Ahura Mazdā, "the Wise Lord." The second is the name of the most important man in these hymns: Zarathushtra, who occurs regularly as singer of the hymns and as performer of the rituals that the hymns accompanied. Following an established poetic pattern, the singer of the hymns declares that he is going to proclaim certain truths about the gods, the world and reality. In these proclamations, Ahura Mazdā is extolled as the creator of the world, dispenser of justice, lord of all that is good, and rightful recipient of prayer and sacrifice. But he is not alone: there are his children and his (spiritual) creations, personifying mental attitudes and human virtues, who aid him in the struggle against evil, which is taking place in front of one's own eyes. For there are evil beings in this world and in the spiritual world; although they are worshipped by those of little intellect, they should not be worshipped, for they cause nothing but harm to humankind and to the world at large. These evil beings are called *daēvas* and they too appear to be ruled by a separate being, who is chiefly alluded to as the "evil one," "the deceitful one," or "the one of evil doctrine" and who is said to have destroyed existence once (but will not do so again: [Y. 45.1]; the interpretation of this verse is debated). In several passages, two spirits are referred to who are each other's total opposites and between which humans must choose. If one makes the wrong choice, this has consequences for his or her afterlife. Indeed many passages have a marked focus on the implications of human choices for their fate in the other world.

The marked polarity between good and evil in these texts, focusing chiefly on the options for "righteousness" or "deceit," also splits human society. Even though some scholars have doubted the interpretation of the *Gāthās* as containing elements from Zarathushtra's biography, there are many passages that hint at an acute crisis, instigated by enemies and borne by the majority of the people surrounding Zarathushtra. In these passages, various individuals and groups of enemies are mentioned, together with examples of their hostilities. This may reflect an actual struggle between competing groups of religious specialists, divided over matters of ritual and ideas about the gods and reality.

Many passages of the *Gāthās* show that rituals and religious views mattered not only for this world but also for the afterlife. Those who oppose truth will certainly be held accountable for their wrong choice through an ordeal and a judgment of their souls. A blessed existence is promised the righteous ones and a life of woe the wicked.

In a number of passages, all rather cryptic, there are allusions to the most influential of all Zoroastrian ideas: that the world as humans know it will come to an end in a decisive, collective transformation according to the wish of its creator. The most important passage is Y. 30.7–11, which contains the famous words "thus may we be those who will make existence brilliant" (Y. 30.9). Although other suggestions have been made, it is most likely that these verses indeed refer to the notion that the battle between good and evil, and therefore the world and "history," will eventually come to an end. This is certainly how it has always been understood in the tradition.

In spite of the many lexical parallels with hymns from the *Ṛgveda,* these are all aspects from the *Gāthās* for which one would look in vain in the Vedic corpus. The god Ahura Mazdā is as absent from India as the important Indian gods are from the *Gāthās.* Although ideas on the importance of ritual for the life and well-being of the people are characteristic for both traditions, the pervasive focus on the distinction between good and evil, their existence as (the only) two "primal" spirits, and their impact on the lives of humans in this world—in the afterlife and in the transformation of the world—is wholly specific for the *Gāthās.* Something resembling the Gathic insistence on the primary nature of Ahura Mazdā and his sole responsibility for the origins of everything—and especially the idea that history would come to an end—is likewise difficult to find in early Indian literature. There are no indications whatsoever that these were ideas that had grown slowly among the Iranians. For these reasons, the idea that a single person, Zarathushtra, was responsible for the *Gāthās* and in a real sense the founder of the religion that grew out of them raises fewer historical difficulties than the idea that such a person did not exist. One can question the suitability of the concept of "originality" in the writing of history but not doubt the possibility of real innovations. All the evidence suggests that the oldest Zoroastrian texts, which were preserved in a different language among a much larger body of ritual literature, offered a new vision of reality, using traditional words and concepts for the (successful) propagation of an innovative message.

SEE ALSO Amesha Spentas; Avesta; Saoshyant; Zoroastrianism.

BIBLIOGRAPHY

The literature on the subject is enormous and shows a wide variety of approaches and interpretations. The selection given here assembles some fundamental works and examples of the various methods scholars have used to make sense of the data.

There are many translations of the Old Avestan texts, ranging from intensely personal interpretations with an almost mystical message to elaborate philological studies. The most recent of these certainly show great improvements over earlier attempts.

Humbach, Helmut, Josef Elfenbein, and Prods Oktor Skjaervø. *The Gāthās of Zarathushtra and the Other Old Avestan Texts.* 2 vols. Heidelberg, Germany, 1991.

Insler, Stanley. *The Gāthās of Zarathustra.* Leiden, 1975.

Kellens, Jean, and Eric Pirart. *Les textes vieil-avestiques.* 3 vols. Wiesbaden, Germany, 1988–1991.

Studies of Zarathushtra

These include discussions of his historicity and, where accepted, his most likely dates and place.

Boyce, Mary. *A History of Zoroastrianism,* vol. 1: *The Early Period.* Leiden, 1975.

Boyce, Mary. *Zoroastrianism: Its Antiquity and Constant Vigour.* Costa Mesa, Calif., 1992.

Gnoli, Gherardo. *Zoroaster's Time and Homeland: A Study on the Origins of Mazdaism and Related Problems.* Naples, 1980.

Gnoli, Gherardo. *Zoroaster in History.* New York, 2000.

Kellens, Jean. *Essays on Zarathustra and on Zoroastrianism.* Costa Mesa, Calif., 2000.

Lommel, Herman. *Die Religion Zarathustras: Nach dem Awesta dargestellt.* Tübingen, Germany, 1930.

Molé, Marijan. *Culte, mythe, et cosmologie dans l'Iran ancien: Le problème zoroastrien et la tradition mazdéenne.* Paris, 1963.

Schlerath, Bernfried, ed. *Zarathustra.* Darmstadt, 1970.

Skjaervø, Prods Oktor. "The State of Old Avestan Scholarship." *JAOS* 117 (1997): 103–114.

Studies of the Image of Zarathustra in Zoroastrian and Non-Zoroastrian Traditions

De Jong, Albert. *Traditions of the Magi: Zoroastrianism in Greek and Latin Literature.* Leiden, 1997.

Molé, Marijan. *La légende de Zoroastre selon les textes pehlevis.* Paris, 1967.

Rose, Jenny. *The Image of Zoroaster: The Persian Mage through European Eyes.* New York, 2000.

Stausberg, Michael, ed. *Faszination Zarathushtra: Zoroaster und die europäische Religionsgeschichte der Frühen Neuzeit.* Berlin, 1998.

Zoroastrian Works on Zarathustra

There are many modern Zoroastrian studies of Zarathustra and his importance for the Zoroastrian tradition. Most of these appear in Persian or Gujarati. Some representative examples are:

Dhalla, Maneckji Nusservanji. *Zoroastrian Theology.* New York, 1914.

Kapadia, Shapurji Aspandiarji. *The Teachings of Zoroaster and the Philosophy of the Parsi Religion.* London, 1905.

Mehr, Farhang. *The Zoroastrian Tradition: An Introduction to the Ancient Wisdom of Zarathustra.* Costa Mesa, Calif., 2003.

Mistree, Khojeste. *Zoroastrianism: An Ethnic Perspective.* Bombay, 1982.

Nanavutty, Piloo. *The Gathas of Zarathustra: Hymns in Praise of Wisdom.* Ahmadabad, 1999.

Taraporewala, Irach Jehangir Sorabji. *The Divine Songs of Zarathustra.* Bombay, 1951.

Albert de Jong (2005)

ZĀWIYAH See KHĀNAGĀH

ZAYNAB BINT ʿALĪ (c. AH 5–62; 626/7–682 CE),

daughter of ʿAlī ibn Abī Ṭālib and Fāṭimah al-Zahrāʾ, was the first granddaughter of the prophet Muḥammad. She is best known for her courageous and eloquent role supporting her brother, the second Shīʿah Imām Ḥusayn, at the time of his martyrdom in the Battle of Karbala, and for protecting his family in the following months of Umayyad imprisonment.

Life. Zaynab was born in Medina a few years after Muḥammad's immigration thereto in the early days of Shaʿbān of the year AH 5 (626 or 627 CE). She was the third child born to ʿAlī and Fāṭimah—after Ḥasan (the first Shīʿah *imām*) and Ḥusayn—with about a year's interval between each child. Her birth was followed by that of a sister, Umm Kulthūm. Tradition states that Zaynab was named by Muḥammad, who attributed her name to divine inspiration.

Little is known of her early life. Muḥammad died when she was about five, followed by Fāṭimah a few months later. She married her paternal cousin ʿAbd Allāh (whose father was ʿAlī's brother Jaʿfar al-Ṭayyār ibn Abī Ṭālib, and whose mother was then ʿAlī's wife and hence Zaynab's own stepmother, Asmāʾ ibn ʿUmays). Zaynab is reported to have had five children with ʿAbd Allāh: ʿAlī (known as ʿAlī al-Zaynabī, whose numerous descendants took pride in tracing their lineage to Zaynab), ʿAwn al-Akbar (killed at Karbala), Abbās (no information about him), Muḥammad (possibly killed at Karbala), and one daughter named Umm Kulthūm (married to her paternal cousin Qāsim ibn Muḥammad ibn Jaʿfar ibn Abī Ṭālib, after rejecting the suit of the Umayyad Yazīd ibn Muʿāwiya).

When Zaynab's father ʿAlī became caliph in 656 and moved his capital from Medina to Kūfah, Zaynab and ʿAbd Allāh accompanied him there. She lived in Kūfah through four years of military confrontations with the insurgent governor of Syria, Muʿāwiya ibn Abī Sufyān, and with the Iraqi Kharijite rebels, until ʿAlī was killed in 661 by one of the latter. She was then thirty-five years old.

Zaynab is mentioned a few times in the accounts of ʿAlī's caliphate as a devoted and beloved daughter. Moreover, it is reported that ʿAlī taught her a devotional poem that she often recited, and that she herself taught Qurʾān interpretation to women in her house in Kūfah. It is thus likely that she was trained by her father (who is considered the most learned of sages), and that she herself played a teaching role among the women of the early Muslim community.

After ʿAlī's death, his son Ḥasan stepped down from the caliphate and Muʿāwiya became the first Umayyad caliph. Ḥasan returned to Medina with the family, and was subsequently poisoned by Muʿāwiya in 669. There are reports of Zaynab's caring attendance on Ḥasan during his last few days.

Ḥasan was followed as head of the Prophet's family by his brother Ḥusayn. In 680, Muʿāwiya died, having appointed his son Yazīd to the caliphate. At that time—according to some sources, after consulting with Zaynab—Ḥusayn refused to pledge allegiance to Yazīd, and set off with his family and supporters for Mecca and then Kūfah to meet up with his Kūfan supporters and overthrow Yazīd. Some of Ḥusayn's well-wishers tried to dissuade him from going, and these included Zaynab's husband ʿAbd Allāh (who had by then lost his sight, according to some sources), but when Ḥusayn remained adamant, ʿAbd Allāh sent Zaynab and his two sons ʿAwn and Muḥammad with him (there is conflicting evidence regarding whether this Muḥammad was ʿAbd Allāh's son from Zaynab or another wife).

En route to Kūfah, Ḥusayn's entourage was stopped at Karbala and surrounded by a military unit sent by the Umayyad governor of Kūfah, ʿUbayd Allāh ibn Ziyād. On 10 Muḥarram 61 (680), after three days without food or water in the scorching desert, Ḥusayn, his supporters, all but one of the men from his family, and many of the male children were slaughtered. They were reported to be seventy-two in number, including the family members, who numbered eighteen. ʿAwn and Muḥammad were among those killed, according to some reports, encouraged by their mother to fight in defense of their uncle. Zaynab was then fifty-four years old. Her grief-filled speeches are recorded by many historians.

After the massacre, the Umayyad army looted Ḥusayn's camp and set off with his women and children for the court of Ibn Ziyād. Upon reaching Kūfah, Zaynab, with the other women, was paraded unveiled and shackled through the very town where her father had ruled, with the heads of Ḥusayn and his companions raised on spears beside them. Ibn Ziyād then ordered the execution of Ḥusayn's only remaining son, the 23-year-old ʿAlī Zayn al-ʿĀbidīn (the third Shīʿah *imām*); Zaynab protected his life saying Ibn Ziyād would have to kill her before he killed ʿAlī, which shamed him into withdrawing the execution order. A moving oration delivered by Zaynab in Kūfah is recorded in some sources. The prisoners were next sent to the court of the Umayyad caliph Yazīd in Damascus, where one of his Syrian followers asked for Ḥusayn's daughter Fāṭimah al-Kubrā, and once again it was Zaynab who came to the rescue and protected her honor. The family remained in Yazīd's prison for a time; the sources do not specify the number of days or months. The first assembly (*majlis*) of mourning for Ḥusayn is said to have been held by Zaynab in prison. In Damascus, too, she is reported to have delivered a poignant oration.

Zaynab and her family were eventually released and escorted back to Medina. After her return to Medina, little is known of her in the year and a half before her death, except through much later, conflicting reports. According to one report, she stayed and died there. Another report states that due to persecution from the governor of Medina, she traveled to Fustat (later Cairo) in Egypt with several other women from the family of the Prophet; she lived in Fustat for over a year, narrating the Karbala tragedy and preaching the love of the family of the Prophet, and died there. A third report states that she went with her husband to his Syrian estates in a year of drought and died there. Sources also differ as to the year of her death. According to most of them, she died on 15 Rajab AH 62 (682 CE), when she was fifty-six years old.

ROLE IN MUSLIM PIETY. Zaynab is best remembered for her role in Karbala. Through the centuries, she has continued to hold a prominent place in Muḥarram orations, as well as in lamentation poetry composed in Arabic, Persian, Urdu, and other languages commemorating the Karbala tragedy. She is portrayed in these variously as an object of pity, a compassionate saint, and a powerful intercessor. On a somewhat more militant note, she was used in pre-revolution Iran as a model for inspiring political opposition among women—in the Iranian revolution of 1979, female commandos came to be known as "the commandos of her holiness Zaynab" (*Komāndo-hāye Hazrat-e Zaynab*).

Every day, hundreds of Muslim men and women, but especially women, visit the mausoleums dedicated to Zaynab in Damascus and Cairo. In fact, some scholars call Zaynab the patron saint of Muslim women. At the shrine, visitors ask for her help *(madad)*, and they beseech her intercession (*shafaʿa*) with God on their behalf for a myriad of petitions, such as curing illness, passing school examinations, or finding a good husband or wife for themselves or their children. Many miracles are attributed to her, such as the curing of chronic illness. Mostly Shīʿah visit the Damascus shrine, and Egyptian Sunnīs of a Ṣūfī bent visit the Cairo shrine, where tens of thousands celebrate Zaynab's birthday *(mawlid)* for seven days annually.

Zaynab is known by several titles. She is called Zaynab al-Kubrā (the senior Zaynab) to distinguish her from Zaynab al-Ṣughrā (the junior Zaynab, the name of her full sister, Umm Kulthūm, and also perhaps of another half-sister). Zaynab is called al-ʿAqīla (literally, "secluded one," or "pearl," perhaps connected to a suggested etymology of her name: *zayn* + *ab*, "adornment of father"), as well as Thānī-ye Zahrāʾ (the second Fāṭimah Zahrāʾ). In Egypt she is known as al-Ṭāhirah (the pure one) and by a number of "mother" epithets (Umm Hāshim, mother of the Prophet's family; Umm al-ʿawājiz, mother of the weak; Umm al-masākīn, mother of the poor; Umm al-yatāmā, mother of the orphans; and Umm Miṣr, mother of Egypt). She is also known simply as al-Sayyida (the Lady), a fitting title for a woman who came to be considered a role model for Muslim women, typifying courage, fortitude, leadership, eloquence, devotion, and faith.

BIBLIOGRAPHY

The primary source of information on the Karbala tragedy, and of Zaynab's role in it, is the account of the Umayyad author Abū Mikhnaf Lūṭ ibn Yaḥyā preserved in the early medieval historical works; Abū Mikhnaf's original work *Maqtal al-Ḥusayn* (The killing of al-Ḥusayn) is probably lost, and the various manuscripts and editions thereof are most likely reworked and corrupted versions (see Ursula Sezgin, *Abū Miḥnaf: Ein Beitrag zur Historiographie der umaiyadischen Zeit*, Leiden, 1971, pp. 116–123). Much of the original Abū Mikhnaf account rendered by al-Ṭabarī is found in English translation in *The History of al-Ṭabarī: An Annotated Translation*, vol. 19, *The Caliphate of Yazīd b. Muʿāwiyah*, translated by I. K. A. Howard (Albany, N.Y., 1990). Al-Balādhurī also narrates the Karbala tragedy on Abū Mikhnaf's authority in *Ansāb al-Ashrāf*, vol. 2, edited by M. B. al-Maḥmūdī (Beirut, 1977). The text of Zaynab's Damascus oration is recorded by the early scholar Aḥmad ibn Abī Ṭāhir Tayfūr in his *Kitāb Balāghāt al-nisā'*, edited by ʿAbd al-Ḥamīd Hindāwī (Cairo, 1998, pp. 70–73). A book devoted to the Karbala tragedy that includes the texts of Zaynab's Kūfah and Damascus orations (pp. 56–57, 69–71) is *al-Luhūf fī qatlā al-ṭufūf* (Beirut, 1992) by the later medieval historian Ibn Ṭāwūs al-Ḥusaynī, who also bases his narrative on Abū Mikhnaf's authority.

In European languages, there are no monographs about Zaynab's life. There is one anthropological study of her birthday celebrations in Cairo and the rituals associated with visiting her shrine: Nadia Abu Zahra, *The Pure and Powerful: Studies in Contemporary Muslim Society* (Berkshire, U.K., and Ithaca, N.Y., 1997). There are also several articles about various aspects of Zaynab's role in Muslim piety, including David Pinault, "Zaynab bint Alī and the Place of the Women of the Households of the First Imāms in Shiʿite Devotional Literature," in *Women in the Medieval Islamic World: Power, Patronage, and Piety*, edited by Gavin Hambly (New York, 1998), pp. 69–98; Diane D'Souza, "The Figure of Zaynab in Shīʿī Devotional Life," *Bulletin of the Henry Martyn Institute of Islamic Studies* 17, no. 1 (1998): pp. 31–53; Andreas D'Souza, "'Zaynab I Am Coming!': The Transformative Power of Nawḥah," *Bulletin of the Henry Martyn Institute of Islamic Studies* 16, nos. 3 and 4 (1997): 83–94; Anna Madoeuf, "Quand le temps revele l'espace: Les fetes de Ḥusayn et de Zaynab au Caire," *Geographie et Cultures* 21 (1997): 71–92; Irene Calzoni, "Shiʿite Mausoleums in Syria with Particular Reference to Sayyida Zaynab's Mausoleum," *Convegno sul tema la Shʿia nell 'Imapero Ottomano* (Rome, 1993): 191–201; and Valerie J. Hoffman-Ladd, "Devotion to the Prophet and His Family in Egyptian Sufism," *International Journal of Middle Eastern Studies* 24 (1992): 615–637.

In Arabic, there are several monographs about the life of Zaynab, and these also address the issue of her burial place with differing conclusions. These include: Ḥasan Mūsā Ṣaffār, *al-Mar'a al-ʿAẓīma: Qirā'a fī Ḥayāt al-Sayyida Zaynab bint ʿAlī* (London and Beirut, 2000); Aḥmad Shukr al-Ḥusaynī, *al-Shams al-Ṭāl iʿa wa al-Anwār al-Sāṭ ʿa: ʿAqīlat al-Imāma wa al-Wilāya al-Sayyida Zaynab al-Kubrā* (Beirut, 1999); Muḥammad Ḥasanayn al-Sābiqī, *Marqad al-ʿAqīla Zaynab* (Beirut, 1979); and ʿAlī Aḥmad Shalabī, *Ibnat al-Zahra' Baṭalat Karbalā' Zaynab raḍiya Allāh ʿanhā* (Cairo, 1972). An encyclopedia entry on Zaynab is provided by Ḥasan al-Amīn in his *Aʿyān al-Shīʿa*, vol. 7 (Beirut, 1983), pp. 137–142.

B. Tahera Qutbuddin (2005)

ZEALOTS. The Zealots were Jewish revolutionaries in first-century Israel whose religious zeal led them to fight to the death against Roman domination and to attack or kill other Jews who collaborated with the Romans. Scholars disagree as to whether the name *Zealots* designated all revolutionary groups of the first century or only one of the factions active during the Roman-Jewish War of 66–70 CE. Josephus Flavius (37–c. 100 CE.), the Jewish general who surrendered to the Romans and whose official Roman history of the war furnishes the major source, is ambiguous in his use of terminology. References in the New Testament, the Pseudepigrapha, and the rabbinic literature add to the confusion.

In 6 CE, Judah (Yehudah) the Galilean showed zeal for God's law and land when he led a revolt against the Roman census in Judaea. He and his followers fought to cleanse the land by taking vengeance against Jews who cooperated with the Romans. Judah considered such cooperation to be idolatrous recognition of a lord (Caesar) other than God. By such vengeance, he and his followers sought to appease God, who would thereby honor their cause against the Romans. The revolt failed, but Judah had originated the so-called Fourth Philosophy ("No Lord but God") based on the first commandment. Judah's descendents emerged again after all of Judaea became a Roman province in 44 CE. Their subsequent revolutionary actions against the corrupt and incompetent Roman authorities contributed to the outbreak of war in 66 CE. Josephus usually refers to Judah's group as Sicarii, after the *sikkah* ("dagger") used in assassinations.

Although Josephus refers to Judah's faction as a Jewish sect, it is not clear that his group is to be identified with a revolutionary faction called the Zealots or indeed that there was such an organized group early in the first century. Many Jews venerated "zealous action" as a model of piety, using the biblical figure Phineas as a prototype (*Num* 25:1–15). Such persons endured persecution for the Law or sought to destroy those who violated the Law as a means to cleanse the land of defilement and thereby turn back God's wrath. Individuals, such as Simon the "zealot" (a disciple of Jesus: *Luke* 6:15; *Acts* 1:13), were zealous for God over a variety of legal issues. Sometimes, as was the case with the Maccabean revolt in 167–142 BCE, zeal was a dominant motivation for revolution. However, not all zealots were revolutionaries, and not all revolutionaries were motivated by zeal. It is not until his account of the war period that Josephus refers to one of the wartime revolutionary groups formally as "the Zealots."

Amid the growing unrest in the decades leading up to the war, there was broad resistance to Roman occupation, including protests against provocative actions by the procurator Pilate (ruled 26–36 CE), a threatened strike against raising crops for the Romans when the emperor Gaius Caligula sought to put a statue of Zeus in the Temple (41 CE), riots at feast time in Jerusalem in reaction to offenses by Roman soldiers, official delegations to Rome protesting inept procurators, prophetic actions and oracular pronouncements by apocalyptic figures, banditry, kidnappings, and assassinations. Resistance to Roman rule was widespread and cut across all sectors of society. The war broke out in 66 CE when the procurator Florus tried to seize money from the Temple treasury, after which the populace drove Florus out of Jerusalem and successfully held off Cestius Gallus, the Legate of Syria, when he arrived to restore Roman order. The Jewish declaration of war came when the lower priests ceased the sacrifices to God on behalf of the emperor. Subsequently, the traditional high priests assumed control of the wartime government and prepared for the Romans to return.

For the war period, Josephus identifies (in addition to the wartime government) five revolutionary groups, each with its own social and geographic origins, motivations, methods, and goals (*Jewish War* 7:262–267). Not all the groups embraced a "zealous" mentality, and they were often in conflict with each other except when confronted with the common Roman enemy. Josephus mentions the Zealots last in order.

1. The Sicarii fought for "No Lord but God" under the messianic leadership of Judah the Galilean's descendants. When other revolutionary groups forced them out of Jerusalem in 66 CE, they remained during the rest of the war on the fortress Masada, where in 74 CE they chose suicide rather than capture by the Romans.
2. John of Giscala (Yoḥanan ben Levi), leader of a Galilean contingent, gained the confidence of the wartime government, which he then betrayed to the Zealots.
3. Simeon bar Giora, from Gerasa in the Decapolis, raised an army of freed slaves and peasants, then overran Idumea. In 69 CE, he was joined by some nobles and seized most of Jerusalem. A messianic strongman, Simeon led the coalition of revolutionary groups in the defense of Jerusalem in 70 CE.
4. The Idumeans, a local militia, helped the Zealots to overthrow the provisional government.
5. The Zealots, primarily priests from Jerusalem and the Judaean peasantry, declared war by stopping the official sacrifices for Caesar. Later, under democratic leadership, they occupied the Temple, chose a high priest by lot, and, in 68 CE, overthrew the wartime government.

The war lasted four years. From 66 to 68 CE, the Roman general Vespasian overran the countryside of Galilee and Judaea, thereby isolating Jerusalem. When he became emperor in 69 CE, his son Titus assumed the siege of Jerusalem, eventually destroying the city in 70 CE, burning the Temple, executing Jewish warriors, and consigning many families to slavery after a triumphal procession in Rome. Flavius Sylva led Roman troops to overcome Jewish holdouts in a few fortresses, including Masada, by 74 CE.

The causes of the war were many and complex: incompetent and corrupt Roman governors, deteriorating Roman policies toward Jews, a determined Jewish opposition to foreign domination, economic exploitation of peasants (the war was also a peasant revolt against the Jewish elites), widespread banditry, apocalyptic expectations, the conviction that God would honor the Jewish cause, and a zealous commitment to cleanse the land of idolatry.

Major scholarly controversies, arising primarily from the biased and often unreliable accounts of Josephus (in *The Jewish War,* as well as his *Jewish Antiquities* and *The Life*), have centered on the ancient usage of the term "Zealot," the extent of religious zeal among the revolutionaries and the populace, the nature and makeup of each revolutionary group, whether the wartime government was moderate or revolutionary, and the relative importance of social, economic, political, and religious factors as causes of the war.

BIBLIOGRAPHY

Borg, Marcus. "The Currency of the Term 'Zealot.'" *Journal of Theological Studies,* n. s. 22 (October 1973): 504–512. Concludes that the term did not come into use as a title until the time of the war.

Goodman, Martin. *The Ruling Class of Judea: The Origins of the Jewish Revolt against Rome, A. D. 66–70.* Cambridge, 1987. Assesses the role the Jewish elite class, their successes and failures, and their involvement in the war effort.

Hengel, Martin. *The Zealots: Investigations into the Jewish Freedom Movement in the Period from Herod I until 70 A. D.* Translated by D. Smith. Leiden, 1976. The most thorough depiction, gleaned from many sources, of the mentality of "zeal." Argues that the Zealots were a unified and organized prewar sectarian minority that splintered at the time of the war.

Horsley, Richard, and John Hanson. *Bandits, Prophets, and Messiahs: Popular Movements in the Time of Jesus.* Minneapolis, Minn., 1985. Details the nature of the diverse expressions of resistance against Roman rule in first century Israel.

Rhoads, David M. *Israel in Revolution, 6–74 C. E.: A Political History Based on the Writings of Josephus.* Philadelphia, 1976. Thorough treatment of the positions that the revolutionary movement was disparate and that support for the war was widespread.

Rhoads, David M. "Zealots." In *The Anchor Bible Dictionary,* Vol. VI, pp. 1043–1054. New York, 1992. Identifies the variety of scholarly positions on diverse issues. Extensive bibliography appended.

Smith, Morton. "Zealots and Sicarii: Their Origins and Relation." *Harvard Theological Review* 64 (January 1971): 1–19. Seminal article arguing for a disparate and unorganized revolutionary movement.

Stern, Menachem. "Zealots." In *Encyclopaedia Judaica Yearbook.* Jerusalem, 1973. A balanced treatment claiming that the Sicarii had prewar connections with those who came to be called Zealots and that it is appropriate to speak about a Zealot movement and yet appreciate the uniqueness of each revolutionary group.

DAVID M. RHOADS (1987 AND 2005)

ZEKHUT AVOT (Ancestral merit). *Zekhut avot* is a Hebrew phrase that refers to the merits of the ancestors of Israel. Biblical teaching frequently presupposes that reward and punishment have a collective dimension. Many passages are directed to the people of Israel as a whole—for example, *Deuteronomy* 11:13–17. Some passages suggest that later generations benefit or suffer as a result of the actions of their ancestors, as in *Exodus* 20:5–6 and 34:7; *Deuteronomy* 7:8–10; and *Lamentations* 5:7. Other statements that deny or downplay transgenerational recompense, such as *Ezekiel* 14 and 18, balance these judgments. Later rabbinic and medieval interpretation tended to restrict the penal aspect, limiting it to grievous sins like idolatry and to cases in which the sons perpetuated the sins of their fathers. Examples include B.T. *Makkot* 24 and the commentaries of Abraham Ibn Ezra (1093–1167) and Naḫmanides on *Exodus* 20. Some biblical verses single out the particular benefit derived from the merit of the patriarchs Abraham, Isaac, and Jacob, as in Leviticus 26: 42. Several rabbinic debates argued for and against the possibility that the attainments of later generations justified divine solicitude for their forebears.

The rabbinic concept of *zekhut avot* (merits of the fathers, with occasional mention of their wives) in the narrow sense of the term derives from the special standing of the original progenitors. Nonetheless, the term is occasionally applied to other Jewish figures such as the sons of Jacob, to Noah's merit in preserving humanity, or to any kind of inherited merit. Examples of the latter can be found in M *Eduyot* 2:9 and Maimonides' commentary. Some sources speak of the merit of descendants justifying the fathers; others disagree. To the extent that *zekhut avot* is construed narrowly, it is distinguished from universal philosophical concepts of divine justice; it belongs rather to concepts related to the idea of election. When *zekhut avot* is assimilated to natural mechanisms of collective or transgenerational deserving, it is more easily regarded as an application of general principles. In this framework one must also consider the negative impact of unworthy parents on their children's destiny.

Solomon Schechter's century-old dictum that ". . . the notion of imputed righteousness and imputed sin. . . have. . . never attained such significance in Jewish theology or in Jewish conscience as is generally assumed" remains true. (Schechter, 1909, p. 170) Consequently the rabbinic material has not generated a systematic theological consensus. In classic medieval Jewish philosophy, *zekhut avot* is not central to the major discussions of providence and theodicy. The explorations of exegetes, nonphilosophical theological thinkers, and modern academic scholars have shed light on aspects of the theme by adopting both synchronic and diachronic approaches.

TERMINATION OF *ZEKHUT AVOT*. Several amoraim (third- and fourth-century interpreters of the Mishnah) claimed that *zekhut avot* no longer applies, although they differed as to the date in the First Temple period when it ceased to operate (B.T. *Shab.* 55a and *Leviticus Rabba* 36). These views limited appeal to the merits of the fathers; they are better suited to conceptions of *zekhut avot* rooted in the principle of election than to universal models of reward and punishment. Medieval commentators noted that the cessation of *zekhut avot* flies in the face of Jewish liturgy, which frequently cites *Leviticus* 26:42, especially in the *selihot* (penitential) service. Rabbi Jacob Tam, who was a twelfth-century French commentator, posited that while the merits of the fathers were depleted, the covenant with them (*berit avot*) is irrevocable (*Tosafot Shab.* 55). He thus shifted a crucial employment of the concept from consideration of merit by itself to the abiding remembrance of divine promise.

DIACHRONIC FACTORS. Some scholars have detected an evolution in rabbinic thought regarding the specific merits of the patriarchs behind the concept of *zekhut avot*. Thus Urbach maintains that statements made after Bar Kokhba's revolt (132–135 CE), were more likely to anchor the *zekhut* in willingness to offer up one's life in obedience to God, in accordance with the increasing emphasis on martyrdom in the second century. At this stage the binding of Isaac described in *Genesis* 22 became the paradigm of *zekhut avot*. The liturgy described in the Talmud refers to the merit of the ashes of Isaac's virtual immolation; one passage, commenting on *Isaiah* 63:16, imagines Abraham and Jacob declining to intervene on behalf of Israel while Isaac alone offers his merit (B.T. *Shab.* 89b). Kasher likewise discerns a movement away from defining Abraham's merit as faith towards an emphasis on heroic action, a development interpreted as a reaction against the early Christian understanding of *Genesis* 15:6.

It has also been argued that different sources offer different accounts of the benefits of *zekhut avot* for the people of Israel. Goshen-Gottstein observes that biblical sources stress the value of patriarchal merit in the inheritance of the land of Israel. This theme, however, is downplayed in the rabbinic literature.

***ZEKHUT AVOT* AND COLLECTIVE RESPONSIBILITY.** Rabbi Avraham Yitsḥaq Kook (1865–1935) developed an influential theory regarding the place of *zekhut avot* in Jewish theology. For Kook, *zekhut avot* finds its place within a metaphysical doctrine of social organisms. Inherited spiritual traits affect the Jewish people, as well as non-Jewish social entities and humanity as a whole. Negative traits also leave their imprint on later generations. Faithful to the rabbinic principle that "the measure of beneficence is greater than that of retribution," Kook maintained that the favorable impact far exceeds the negative (*Yoma,* 76a). With the Babylonian exile it was judged preferable to loosen the ties between the generations; this interpretative development is reflected in *Ezekiel* 18 and B.T. *Makkot* 24a.

An earlier Hasidic master, Rabbi Judah Alter of Gur (1847–1905), likewise reflected a metaphysical orientation presented from a social perspective. He insisted that even if one accepts the view that *zekhut avot* ended, the merit of the seventy grandchildren of Jacob who arrived in Egypt remains operative. That is because the passage of time weakens the Jewish people's connection to the forefathers, but not their connection to the more "accessible" merit of the intermediate generations.

SEE ALSO Election; Kook, Avraham Yitsḥaq; Merit, overview article.

BIBLIOGRAPHY

Solomon Schechter, *Some Aspects of Rabbinic Theology* (New York, 1909), Chapter 12 ("The Zachuth of the Fathers: Imputed Righteousness and Imputed Sin"), pp. 170–198, remains the best survey of rabbinic material on the topic of *zekhut avot*. See also A. Marmorstein, *The Doctrine of Merits in Old Rab-*

binic Literature (London, 1920). Among recent scholars, see E. E. Urbach, *The Sages* (Jerusalem, 1975) 15:7, pp. 483–511; R. Kasher, "Miracles, Faith and Merit of the Fathers," (Hebrew) *Jerusalem Studies in Jewish Thought* 5 (1986):15–23; A. Goshen, "The Covenant with the Fathers and the Inheritance of the Land—Between Biblical Theology and Rabbinic Thought," (Hebrew) *Daat* 35 (1995): 5–28; S. Carmy, "Merits of the Mothers" (Hebrew) *Or haMizrah* 5665 (Spring 2005). Rabbi Avraham Yitsḥaq Kook's major treatment of the topic can be found in his *Iggerot Ha-Re'ayah,* §379 (Jerusalem, 1943). It is available in English translation in T. Feldman, *Rav A. Y. Kook: Selected Letters,* pp. 141–161 (Ma'ahleh Adumim, Israel, 1986). For the Rabbi of Gur, see *Sefat Emet,* the sermon on *Shemot* 5645 (=1885) (Jerusalem, 1971).

SHALOM CARMY (2005)

ZEME. In Baltic religion, earth (Latv., *zeme;* Lith., *žeme*) is sacralized. On this basis, the Latvian goddess Zeme and the Lithuanian goddess Žemýna (diminutive, Žemynele) evolved. Called in Latvian Zemes Māte ("earth mother"), she takes a central place in the religious system of the Baltic peoples. Attested by Tacitus, who reports that the ancient Balts venerated a *deum matrem,* her role is determined by her femininity: Like a mother she is connected with the promotion of fertility. Everything in nature that is born, grows, and dies belongs to her. Thus humanity, too, is drawn into this all-embracing cult, beginning at birth and ending with death.

Description of Zeme as *māte* is dependent on which of a variety of mother roles she plays, a variety that can be seen particularly clearly in Latvian traditions. Here appear such descriptions as *Lauku māte* ("field mother"), *Meža māte* ("forest mother"), *Krūmu māte* ("bush mother"), *Ogu māte* ("berry mother"), and *Sēņu māte* ("mushroom mother"), among a number of others. In the main, these are poetic personifications of aspects of nature without any religious connotations. The juxtaposition of religious and poetic personifications is a well-known occurrence, but this does not deny that in differentiating the variety of functions of Zeme as *māte,* new beings are created. These then become independent and assume the particular specialized function that is appropriate in a given tradition.

The central place of Zeme is revealed especially in cultic practices; together with those of Laima, these are the most fully developed in Baltic religion. There was, for example, a notion that children are created from springs, lakes, trees, and hills, all places that are connected with the earth. It is therefore understandable that at the birth of a child offerings were made to Zeme. These offerings were placed either by trees and stones close to the home or were thrown into the hearth fire. The offerings were accompanied by prayers: "My dear earth, my mother, sustain me, feed me." More widespread still were rituals concerned with encouraging fertility in both crops and animals. Thus, at the commencement of work in the fields in spring, the farmer plowed a piece of bread into the first furrow. On this day, too, a special meal was eaten at which the first measure of ale was thrown on the earth together with a small piece of meat. In the spring, when the animals were sent out to pasture for the first time, offerings were made, normally eggs, a special gruel, and ale. The entire household, led by the paterfamilias, joined in the sacral meals, for which a piglet or cockerel was occasionally slaughtered.

More frequent still were rituals connected with the gathering of the harvest in autumn. After the last sheaf had been taken in, bread and salt were buried in the soil in its place, to the accompaniment of a prayer: "Dear earth, as you have given, so also do I give to you." A kind of cultic drama, in two parts, was then enacted. The first part, in which the female head of the household also generally participated, took place in the field. A festive meal was eaten, including special cakes, and, as at all country feasts, ale was drunk. This meal of thanksgiving was made festive by singing and dancing. The songs were commonly characterized by bravado directed at neighboring farmers who had not yet succeeded in harvesting their crops. After the feast, the participants returned home crowned with garlands made from ears of grain and bearing their tools, scythes and rakes, similarly decorated. The second part of the drama took place at the homestead. At the gate, the workers were met by the head of the household, who offered them a drink, usually ale, but often vodka in a later tradition. Afterward, the festivities continued inside the house, with more singing and dancing.

This résumé of the fertility cult of the Baltic earth mother shows that it embraced the countryman's whole life from the time of his birth, including all aspects of his activities at work. The practice of customary rites attests to the fact that by following them the individual believed that he secured the patronage of Zeme, the mother goddess. So intensive was this cult that even until the eighteenth century country people first said prayers to the earth and then kissed it both in the morning, at the beginning of their work, and in the evening, when their work was done. In these religious instances, the holy earth is the mother of all life. As the extensive collection of nineteenth- and twentieth-century folklore materials demonstrates, this understanding was never completely lost, in spite of centuries of Christian missionizing.

Complementing this positive aspect of the cult of the sacred earth, the giving of life, is its negative counterpart, the taking of life, for the rhythm of nature shows that everything that comes from the earth must at some point return to it. Zeme, the mother of life, is ruler of everything created on earth and of everything that takes place there. That is her positive aspect. Yet experience of life forces the conclusion that the earth is also responsible for the individual's negative experiences, that is, death and one's fate thereafter. Thus the earth goddess adopts simultaneously her other morphological role, that of a chthonic goddess. In this role she rules what takes place below the earth, and she is given titles appropriate to this function. In Latvian she is called Smilšu Māte ("sand mother"), a name arising from the custom of burying the dead in sandy knolls, or she is described directly as Kapu Māte ("mother of the grave") or Nāves Māte ("death mother"). Thus the mother of life, promoter of bounty and fertility, becomes her opposite, the mother of death. Although paradoxical, this morphological transformation is nonetheless understandable, for in the eyes of the Baltic farmer the processes of birth and death were manifest both in nature and in his immediate and extended families. The dead were buried in a nearby grave mound, and were thus ever-present as a reminder to the living.

In Baltic religion there is no metaphysical ontology contrasting the notions of life and death. Instead, these notions are simply two aspects of a single goddess. In the sources this is stated metaphorically: Not only may one address petitions and give thanks to Zeme as Zemes Māte, but one may have an amicable discussion with her as Nāves Māte, offering her substitutes for a dying person—an oak log to decompose or an ax or a plow to rust away. This final, unique trait of the Baltic earth goddess is explicable by reference to the farmer's close ties to the land.

BIBLIOGRAPHY

Biezais, Haralds. *Die Hauptgöttinnen der alten Letten.* Uppsala, 1955. The basic concept of the goddess is discussed on pages 325–342.

Gimbutas, Marija. *Die Bestattung in Litauen in der vorgeschichtlichen Zeit.* Tübingen, 1946. The role and functions of the goddess in Lithuanian burial customs.

Šmits, Pēteris. *Latviešu tautas ticējumi IV.* Rīga, 1941. Croyances populaires Lettonnes IV. Latvian Folk Beliefs.

Straubergs, Karlis. *Lettisk folktro om de döda.* Nordiska Museets Hanlingar, vol. 32. Stockholm, 1949. An extensive comparative study, but lacking a critical interpretation of the sources.

New Sources

Ankrava, Sigma. *Vai Lāčplēsis bija karalis Artūrs?* (*Was Bearslayer the King Arthur?: A Study in Comparative Mythology*) Riga, 2000. Pp.176–196.

Kusīte, Janīna. *Mītiskais folklorā, literatūrā, mākslā.* (*The Mythical in Folklore, Literature, Art*) Riga, 1999. Pp. 30–93.

Rudzīte, Anta, ed. *Latviešu tautas dzīveszina. Vol. 2.* (*Latvian World Perception. Vol. 2.*) Riga, 1990.

HARALDS BIEZAIS (1987)
Revised Bibliography

ZEN.

[*This article treats the development of the Zen sect in Japan. The historical antecedents of this school, the practices and institutions of Chinese Chan Buddhism, are discussed in* Chan.]

The Zen Buddhist sect in Japan consists of three main schools and several additional smaller movements. The largest denomination is the Sōtō school, founded by Dōgen Kigen (1200–1253), which has two head temples, Eiheiji in Fukui prefecture and Sōjiji in Kanagawa prefecture, and claims nearly fifteen thousand temples, over thirty monasteries and (six) nunneries, and more than eight million adherents, making it one of the largest of the traditional Japanese Buddhist schools. The second largest Zen denomination is the Rinzai school, founded by Myōan Eisai (1141–1215), which is divided into fifteen streams associated with different head temples and claims about six thousand temples, forty monasteries and (one) nunnery, and two million adherents. The largest of the streams is Myōshinji temple in Kyoto, which claims about half of the total Rinzai temples and monasteries and over one-third of the adherents. The third Zen school is the Ōbaku school, founded by Yinyuan Longqi (Jpn., Ingen Ryūki, 1592–1673), which has a head temple of Manpukuji in the town of Uji outside Kyoto and claims nearly five hundred temples, two monasteries, and under half a million adherents. In addition, there are several modern movements or "brotherhoods" (*kyōdan*) based on Zen meditation or other training techniques that all together claim about one hundred temples and 200,000 adherents.

The Zen sect was first established in the early medieval period as a controversial form of "New Kamakura Buddhism," along with the fledgling Pure Land and Nichiren cults. Zen was proscribed in the 1190s for a few years, and for several decades thereafter it was vigorously opposed by the dominant Tendai sect at Enryakuji temple located on Mount Hiei to the northeast of Kyoto. During the 1240s and 1250s, major Rinzai and Sōtō Zen temples were built in Kyoto, Kamakura, and Echizen province, and by the beginning of the fourteenth century, Zen had become the leading religious institution in Japan with an ever-expanding network of temples and a wide-ranging, nearly all-pervasive influence on many different levels of society and culture.

During the late medieval and early modern eras, Zen underwent various periods of apparent decline and renewal, especially when it stood in competition with diverse forms of Japanese religiosity in other Buddhist, as well as Shintō and Confucian, movements during the Tokugawa era (1600–1868). In the modern period, Zen has spread to become a worldwide phenomenon greatly admired for its unique features of spiritual practice, including strict monastic discipline and contemplation of pedagogical riddles, or *kōans,* that have a resonance with contemporary spiritual and intellectual trends in psychotherapy, phenomenology, and environmentalism. At the same time, the Zen sect has received criticism both from within and outside of Japan for contributing to social ills ranging from nationalism and nativism to discrimination against women and outcastes.

FORMATIVE PERIOD (LATE TWELFTH AND THIRTEENTH CENTURIES). The origins of Zen in Japan stem from the Nara and early Heian eras, when sitting meditation and some representative early Chan texts were introduced by monks who had traveled to China, including Saichō (767–822), and were practiced or studied for several centuries under the auspices of the Tendai sect as one of several styles of training available to novices. Zen began to be established as a separate, autonomous sect by the end of the twelfth century (corresponding to the beginning of the Kamakura era) when several prominent Tendai monks made pilgrimages to the mainland in search of authentic Buddhism after a hiatus in exchange with China that lasted nearly two hundred years. These monks, including Eisai and Dōgen, returned with the newly fashioned Song dynasty (960–1279) approach to Chan. The style of Song Chan that was brought to Japan included an emphasis on monastic institutional structure and rules of conduct, as well as voluminous texts containing biographies of eminent monks and records of their sayings and dialogues, in addition to extensive poetic and prose commentaries on *kōan* cases.

The earliest Zen schools were created either by Japanese monks who went to China and returned to establish important temples and lineages or by Chinese monks who came to Japan and played a crucial role in the rapid development of Zen. Monks in the first category, in addition to Eisai and Dōgen, include: Enni Ben'en (1202–1280), who studied at Mount Jing, the leading temple of the Chinese Chan Five Mountains (Chin., *Wushan*; Jpn., *Gozan*) system and became abbot of Tōfukuji temple in Kyoto; Shinchi Kakushin (1207–1298), who introduced to Japan the most prominent *kōan* collection, the *Wumen guan* (Jpn., *Mumonkan*); and Nampo Jōmin (also known as Daiō Kokushi, 1235–1308), who received transmission from the Chinese master Xutang (1185–1269) and created the lineage that founded Daitokuji temple in Kyoto.

Notable among Chinese monks who came to Japan are: Lanxi Daolong (Jpn., Rankei Dōryū, 1213–1278), who was the founding abbot of Kenchōji temple in Kamakura in 1253 with the support of regent Hōjō Tokiyori (1226–1263); Wuan Puning (Jpn., Gottan Run'ei, 1197–1276), who came at the request of Tokiyori but spent only four years in Japan trying to introduce authentic Chinese-style Zen, serving for a time as abbot of Kenninji temple, which Eisai had founded in Kyoto in 1202 as the first major Zen monastery in Japan; Daxiu Chengnian (Jpn., Daikyū Shōnen, 1214–1289), who founded Jōchiji temple in Kamakura; and Wuxu Zuyuan (Jpn., Mugaku Sogen, 1226–1286), who was the founding abbot of Engakuji temple in Kamakura with the support of regent Hōjō Tokimune (1251–1284).

Even before Eisai spent four years studying Chan during his second trip to China, which lasted from 1187 to 1191, a monk named Kakua (b. 1142) reached the Chinese mainland in 1171 and, on his return, had an audience with Emperor Takakura (1161–1181). In response to a question about the meaning of Zen, Kakua responded by simply playing his flute, while the emperor and his retainers looked on in puzzlement. This anecdote is contained in the valuable historical record of Buddhism in Japan, the *Genkō shakusho*, produced by the Zen monk, Kokan Shiren (1278–1345).

Around the time of Kakua's and Eisai's travels, an anomalous monk not mentioned in Kokan's record, Dainichi Nōnin (d. 1196?), started the first organized Zen movement, known as the Daruma school. Nōnin was not considered legitimate because he never traveled to China, but instead sent two of his disciples to receive transmission from Zhuan Deguang (1121–1203) of the Dahui Zonggao lineage. His movement was prohibited by imperial decree in 1194, and its temples were destroyed, although some followers persisted at Hajakuji, a Tendai temple in remote Echizen province (currently Fukui prefecture) until 1241 when they all joined Dōgen's upstart Sōtō school. Nōnin sought to create a pure Zen school free of Tendai esoteric ritualism, but by abandoning requirements to follow the precepts or practice meditation, his approach was accused of antinomian tendencies by both Eisai and Dōgen, as well as by Tendai leaders.

Early Rinzai school. Eisai, who is probably best known for introducing tea to Japan, received transmission in the Huanglong (Jpn., Ōryū) lineage of the Linji (Jpn., Rinzai) school of Chan and, like Nōnin, tried to create a pure Zen approach in Japan. However, to distinguish his role from Nōnin's and gain acceptance from the mainstream Buddhist institution, in the *Kōzen gokokuron* that was composed in 1198 Eisai repudiated the Daruma school's antinomianism and argued for the consistency of Zen meditation with established Tendai practices. Eisai also emphasized the importance of following the Chinese Chan way of administering the mixed precepts (that is, the 250 Hīnayāna and forty-eight Mahāyāna precepts), after several centuries in Japan during which only the bodhisattva vows were followed. In the two main temples Eisai established with the support of Hōjō Masako (1157–1225)—Kenninji and Jufukuji in Kamakura—there was an eclectic training known as *Enmitsu-zenkai* that combined Tendai perfect practice *(engyō)* and esotericism *(mitsu* or *mikkyō)* with Zen-style sitting meditation (*zazen*) and disciplinary rules *(jukai)*.

The next major development in the spread of Rinzai Zen involved Enni Ben'en, who like Eisai and Dōgen started out studying Tendai Buddhism in Japan and traveled to China from 1235 to 1241 to gain transmission from the Five Mountains temple system. On his return, Enni was awarded the abbacy of Tōfukuji temple, constructed along the lines of a grand Song Chan compound. For the first time in the three-quarters of a century since Kakua, a major temple was built exclusively for Zen training with the support of Buddhist and imperial authorities. However, in the end, Tōfukuji also provided facilities for the observance of Shingon and Tendai rituals, in accord with the wishes of its patron, Fujiwara Michiie (1192–1252). Since it was located near Kenninji, Enni often made daily visits and tried to restore the authentic Zen practice that had declined somewhat following the death of Eisai. Tōfukuji was also situated near Dōgen's first temple, Kōshōji, in southeast Kyoto. In the following years, Shinchi, who traveled to China from 1249 to 1254, was frequently summoned to lecture on *kōans* and related Zen topics before the imperial court, which further legitimated the Rinzai school.

Based on the intense interest of Hōjō Tokiyori in promulgating Zen by building Song-style temples and lending other forms of patronage and support, Zen became firmly ensconced in Kamakura, which was the temporary capital for several decades in the thirteenth century. For Tokiyori, Zen was the ideal ideology for the emerging samurai class because of its focus on self-control and creative self-expression in a highly disciplined communal environment. Lanxi and the other monks who arrived from China tended to emphasize the importance of monastic discipline governing every aspect of the daily behavior of monks. Because of their Chinese provenance, the Kamakura temples became the most prominent ones in the Japanese version of the Five Mountains system, outranking Kyoto temples, with the exception of Nanzenji.

Early Sōtō school. Whereas numerous prominent Japanese and Chinese monks were involved in the establishment of the Rinzai school, the development of the Sōtō school was primarily based on the efforts of Dōgen, who traveled to China from 1223 to 1227 with one of Eisai's disciples, Myōzen (1184–1225). After an itinerant phase during which he traveled around several of the Five Mountains Chan temples in search of an authentic teacher, in the summer retreat of 1225 Dōgen gained enlightenment under the tutelage of Caodong (Jpn., Sōtō) school master Ju-ching through the experience of "casting off body-mind" (*shinjin datsuraku*). On returning to Japan, Dōgen stayed for a few years at Kenninji before opening Kōshōji, which was the first Zen temple in Japan to have a Chan style monks' hall for *zazen* training, where Dōgen began delivering sermons and indoctrinating disciples in Chinese discipline. He preached a message of the universality of enlightenment for all those who practice "just sitting" (*shikan taza)*, including women and laypersons.

At the peak of his career in the summer of 1243, Dōgen departed from his temple in Kyoto with a small, dedicated band of disciples and moved to Echizen province, where he established Eiheiji temple. The reasons for the move are obscure, but it seems to be connected with several factors that occurred in the couple of years previous. These include the rapid ascendancy to the Tōfukuji abbacy of Enni after his return from China, which may have intimidated Dōgen since the massive Rinzai temple dwarfed Kōshōji, and the conversion of former Daruma school monks at Hajakuji to Dōgen's movement, which may have given him an incentive to take up residence in Echizen. Dōgen's patron Hatano Yoshishige also owned land in the Echizen region, which was the vicinity of the sacred mountain Mount Hakusan, long a center of *yamabushi* activity affiliated with a branch of the Tendai sect centered at Onjōji (also known as Miidera) temple, east of Kyoto and near Lake Biwa.

During a transitional year, until he settled in the summer of 1244 in his new temple, Dōgen was extremely creative in producing over a third of the fascicles included in his major text, the *Shōbōgenzō*, which consists of informal sermons delivered in the vernacular (*kana*) in the abbot's quarters. At Eiheiji, Dōgen turned to another style of literature that was included in the *Eihei kōroku*, which consists of formal sermons delivered in the dharma hall in Sino-Japanese (*kanbun*), as prescribed by Chinese Chan monastic rules texts. During the Echizen/Eiheiji period, Dōgen stressed that enlightenment is available only for male monastics, but he also developed methods for evangelizing and administering precepts to the lay community. According to some reports, Dōgen visited Hōjō Tokiyori in Kamakura for half a year in 1247 to 1248, but he turned down an invitation to head a temple there due to misgivings about the mixing of Zen and the new samurai lifestyle. This would have occurred just a few years before Kenchōji was constructed and became a leading Rinzai center under Lanxi.

Zen Practice and Training. Much of the difference in the styles of theory and practice that has evolved between the Rinzai and Sōtō schools, such as the Rinzai emphasis on *kōan* training and the Sōtō emphasis on just-sitting meditation without a focus on *kōan* cases, reflects historical developments subsequent to the formative period of Zen in Japan. The differences tend to stem especially from the Tokugawa and early Meiji eras, periods when all forms of Buddhism had to define themselves in distinctive ways in a competitive religious environment strictly supervised by civil authorities. Discrepancies in style should not be imposed retrospectively, which might obscure the fact that the two schools are linked by fundamental similarities in approach.

On the level of doctrine, both schools stress the importance of post-enlightenment cultivation, as found in Dōgen's teaching of *shushū ittō* (oneness of practice and realization) and the doctrine proclaimed by Daitō Kokushi (Shūhō Myōchō, 1282–1337) of *shōtaichōyō* (sustained nurturing of the seed of truth). Genuine practice must not end at the time of realization, but should continue after the initial experience of enlightenment and be integrated with each aspect of daily life. This practice can take the form of meditation, performing daily chores on the monastic compound, collecting alms from the lay community (*takuhatsu*), participating in the way (*dō* or *michi*) of the arts, communing with nature during a mountain retreat (*yamazato*), or residing in a secluded hermitage on or off the temple grounds.

Monastic regulations. For both schools, all aspects of monastery life are governed by the codes of discipline and ethics, as covered in detail in an extensive body of texts dealing with monastic regulations (*shingi*). These codes were originally imported from China, most notably the 1103 text, *Chanyuan qinggui* (Jpn., *Zen'en shingi*), which was derivative of early Buddhist Vinaya rules and supposedly based on a much shorter source text attributed to the Tang dynasty master Baizhang (749–814), known for his injunction, "a day without work is a day without food." The *Chanyuan qinggui* was adapted in Japanese texts and required for all monks by numerous thirteenth-century Rinzai and Sōtō leaders, including Eisai in 1195, Dōgen with several texts beginning in 1237, Lanxi in 1278, and Enni in 1280. The seminal source of Chan rules was also referenced in *shingi* texts by Sōtō master Keizan Jōkin (1264–1325) in 1325, Rinzai master Musō Sōseki (1275–1351) in 1339, and the *Ōbaku shingi* in 1672.

Whether or not it was literally followed, the spirit of "no work, no food" pervades the *shingi* collections, which include rules on the observance of precepts and ethical conduct, as well as on daily activities and annual ceremonies. These works depict a communal life of meditation, frugality, manual labor, and active debate between master and disciple, with regularly scheduled public assemblies and impromptu lectures and instruction. They also describe the functions of abbot, officers, stewards, rank-and-file monks, and novices, in addition to the management of kitchens, the dharma hall, and the larger monastery estate. The *shingi* rules provide requirements for the dharma transmission and awarding of seals (*inka*), as well as commissioning portraits of masters (*chinsō*) and selecting successors to the abbot. Topics such as quarreling and discipline, wandering, and the role of women are given careful consideration. Furthermore, the relation between a school's head temple (*honji*) and branch temples (*matsuji*) is delineated in both the *shingi* records and the laws of the civil society.

Zen monasteries in Japan follow the style of the "seven-hall compound" (*shichi-dō garan*) originally developed in China. The schema below bears anthropomorphic symbolism in that each of the seven buildings is associated with a part of the Buddha's body, so that entering the temple grounds is considered the equivalent of communing directly with the Buddha. The halls include on the main axis: the mountain gate or entrance associated with the groin, the Buddha hall for displaying icons and hosting banquets associated with the heart, and the dharma hall for sermons before the assembly associated with the head. The right leg is associated with the bathhouse and the right arm with the kitchen, whereas the left leg is associated with the latrine and the left arm with the monks' hall.

Four additional mainstays of the structure of Zen temples are: the abbot's quarters, known as the "ten-foot square hut" (*hōjō*), following a passage in the *Vimalakīrti Sūtra* in which an informed layman holds forth in a humble abode with the ability to outsmart bodhisattvas; the hall to commemorate the local earth deity (*dōjishin*) associated with protection of the temple grounds; a bell tower that houses a large Buddhist bronze bell rung at the New Year and other festivals, as well as purification ceremonies; and a reading room for the study of sūtras and related Buddhist and literary works. The abbot's quarters is usually located above the dharma hall, with the earth deity hall and bell tower to the right, and reading room to the left.

***Zazen* and *kōan* practice.** Life in Zen monasteries is centered on *zazen* meditation, which is conducted at least four times daily, as well as for longer, more intensive weeklong sessions known as *sesshin*, especially on special occasions such as Rohatsu (December 8 celebration of the anniversary of the Buddha's enlightenment). During these special occasions, meditation may be prolonged for up to twenty hours a day, leaving time only for minimal sleeping and eating. In addition to the traditional seated posture, there is a form of meditation known as *kinhin*, which is a walking exercise developed in Japanese Zen.

Another main ingredient of Zen practice is the use of *kōans* as both a literary device and a tool for contemplative training. Diverse styles of commentary were developed during the medieval period (discussed below), involving the use of prose, poetic, and sometimes diagrammatic remarks on the inner meaning of case narratives found in a handful of collections preserved from China, such as the *Wumen guan*, *Biyan lu* (Jpn., *Hekiganroku*), and *Zongrong lu* (Jpn., *Shōyōroku*). A new *kōan* exercise developed in Japan is the brief face-to-face interview of the disciple by the master. This is known in the Rinzai school as *dokusan* (literally "individual study"), which is similar to the Sōtō school practice of *nyūshitsu* (literally "entering the room [of the abbot]"). Both terms refer to private instruction in which the teacher evaluates and motivates the aspiring student to attain a higher level of understanding.

Furthermore, nearly all Japanese Zen monasteries and temples have performed a myriad of functions related to the spirits of the dead, including funerary rites that bestow a posthumous ordination name (*kaimyō*) to ensure that the deceased attains *nirvāṇa* (*nehan*) in the afterlife. Zen temples are also involved in memorial services, as well as the annual Obon or Ghost Festival, held either on July 15 or August 15 (the ceremony was originally held at the time of the full moon of the seventh month of the Chinese calendar). It is believed that during this period the spirits of deceased ancestors visit the living, and Buddhist rituals play an important purification function. Despite an apparent emphasis on uniformity and ritualism, several of the most prominent masters of the medieval period were known for a rugged individuality and eccentricity in their commitment to a life of poverty and reclusion, as well as the creative expression of self-awareness.

MEDIEVAL PERIOD (TO 1600). Beginning with the rise of the new political leadership of the Ashikaga government in 1338, which consolidated its power through alliances with Zen clergy and consciously emulated the Song way of propagating the religion, Zen became a dominant force affecting both the aristocratic elite in the urban centers and the rural population. Zen contributed to the fine, literary, applied, performing, and martial arts, ranging from calligraphy, poetry, gardening, tea ceremony, theater, and sword fighting, among numerous other forms, and also assimilated and domesticated many aspects of popular religion and folklore, including autochthonic gods, demons, and exorcistic rites. Furthermore, Zen began its involvement in constructing the *bushidō* code of honor and loyalty to the warlord by integrating and adapting traditional art of war strategies to monastic training. Nō theater, which is often based on plays dealing with ghosts of defeated samurai wrestling with demons in the afterlife, and which is written and performed with an uncannily studied contemplative simplicity, represents a realm of the arts where many of these cultural elements have converged.

The developments that took place in establishing Zen in the thirteenth century ensured that the Rinzai school would grow mainly in the Kyoto and Kamakura areas with the support of the shogunate, whereas the Sōtō school would spread in the northwestern region, as well as other outlying territories, based on proselytizing to an agrarian population. The two schools were separated by other factors in addition to geography and patterns of patronage and participation, yet there were underlying points of connection both institutionally and in terms of styles of religious practice disseminated through a network of temples known as the *Rinka* monasteries.

Five Mountains system. The Rinzai school formed the main hierarchical institutional structure known as the Five Mountains system, which was patterned after the Chinese Chan monastery system At its peak it claimed a network of over three hundred temples centered at Nanzenji in Kyoto under the protection of the military regime (*bakufu*). The third Ashikaga shogun, Yoshimitsu (1358–1408), established in 1386 a definitive ranking of five temples each in Kyoto (Tenryūji, Shōkokuji, Kenninji, Tōfukuji, Majuji) and Kamakura (Kenchōji, Engakuji, Jufukuji, Jōchiji, Jōmyōji). A head administrative monk (*sōroku*) was appointed superintendent or the supreme official ruling over the system.

The hallmark of the Five Mountains system was the creation of multiple artistic forms referred to collectively as *Gozan bunka*, with special emphasis on literature, especially *kanbun* poetry, known as the tradition of *Gozan bungaku*. *Gozan* poetry, which usually consists of four-line verses containing seven characters (*kanji*) in each line, deals with Buddhist doctrines and practice, as well as themes that are more general and are used to articulate indirectly an understanding of Zen awareness. One of the main topoi is the contemplation of nature as perceived in secluded landscapes or mountain retreats, as in the following verse by one of the luminaries of the movement, Musō Sōseki (1275–1351):

> Autumn's colors dropping from branches in masses of falling leaves, Cold clouds bringing rain into the crannies of the mountains: Everyone was born with the same sort of eyes—Why do *mine* keep seeing things as Zen *kōans*? (Pollack, 1985, p. 37).

Musō, founder of Tenryūji temple in Kyoto, was immensely successful and popular with all factions as an abbot who gained the attention of Emperor Hanazono and political leaders, monks in training, and the general populace. His book *Muchū mondō* (Dialogues in a dream) explains Zen in everyday language in response to questions raised by the warrior Ashikaga Tadayoshi. He was said to have left ten thousand followers at the time of his death. However, Musō was also criticized by rivals such as Daitokuji master Daitō for not rising above a doctrinal understanding of Zen—that is, for failing to embody a genuinely creative Zen approach that was evident in some of the leading Rinka temple masters.

Rinka monasteries. In addition to the Five Mountains temples of the Rinzai school, which were considered the leading rank in the Zen network, another series of temples that included representatives from both the Rinzai and Sōtō schools was known as *Rinka* or *Sanrin* temples; both designations refer to "forests" (*rin*) of Zen monks. The term, which implies the legions of monasteries in the countryside or hinterlands that were outside, and probably resentful of, the domain of the shogun, is perhaps applied most accurately to Eiheiji and other Sōtō temples. But the term is at least in part a misnomer because this group also included prominent Rinzai temples in Kyoto that enjoyed imperial patronage, especially Daitokuji of the Daiō-Daitō line and Myōshinji temple. Myōshinji was impressively developed by Daitō's disciple, Kanzan Egen (1277–1360), and eventually it broke off to become an independent head temple that surpassed Daitokuji in the size and scope of its network.

Whereas the Five Mountains temples were known for their poetry, one of the main features of the Rinka temples was the formation of a curriculum of *kōan* studies that took on many different dimensions. Daitō is particularly notable for writing two commentaries on the *Biyan lu* collection of 100 *kōan* cases by using the style of capping phrases (*jakugo*), originally developed by Chinese Chan commentators as ironic remarks that illuminate each line of the case narrative. In Sōtō Zen, there were various styles of commentary known as *shōmono*, which included formal/public and informal/private styles. One of the main examples of *shōmono* literature was the subgenre of *kirigami* (literally "strips of paper") commentaries, in which a master would write down quickly an esoteric comment, usually accompanied by a drawing or illustration, that was handed to a disciple as a training tool or an emblem of attaining transmission. Given the transitory quality and secretive nature of this style, the *kirigami* were left uncollected and were lost until recent scholarship rediscovered and interpreted numerous examples.

A prominent example of medieval Zen art is the famed rock garden at Ryōanji temple in Kyoto, which was perhaps designed by the painter Sōami (1472–1525). A classic of the *kare-sansui* (dry mountains-rivers) style that contains only rocks and sand constructed in patterns but no living form except moss, the Ryōanji garden is surrounded by earthen walls in three directions and faced with the corridor of the *hōjō* (abbot's quarters) building. In the rectangular space measuring thirty meters from east to west and ten meters from north to south, fifteen rocks of various sizes are arranged on white sand in five groups, each comprising five, two, three, two, and three rocks. The most popular explanation of this garden is that the rocks represent a mother tiger and her cubs, swimming in the river of the white sand toward a fearful dragon. The asymmetric composition achieves a certain balance and harmony that creates energy and rhythm in the midst of subtlety and simplicity.

Another important development of the Rinka period was the way creative Rinzai masters sought to recapture the iconoclasm and eccentricity of early Chinese Chan figures, as epitomized by Ikkyū (1394–1481), who was said to have destroyed his transmission seal for being an empty symbol devoid of significance and to have refused to award such a symbol to any of his disciples. Ikkyū became an acolyte at the age of five and excelled at Chinese poetry and calligraphy as well as painting. Throughout his life he railed against the corruption of priests and the meaningless formalities of Zen monastic life, yet he succeeded to the abbacy of Daitokuji and also won widespread acceptance by the common folk for his inventiveness and independence.

One of Ikkyū's noted calligraphies contains the saying, "Entering the realm of Buddha is easy, entering the realm of the demon [*ma*] is difficult." On one level, this expression, along with Ikkyū's lifestyle, which included the celebration of visits to brothels and the "red thread" of passion, could be interpreted as endorsing the kind of antinomianism that was consistently rejected by Zen monastic leaders. However, another implication of the saying is that, for Ikkyū, asserting the priority of purity while occupying a state of transcendence is a relatively simple task that is not necessarily as demanding as maintaining a genuinely authentic state of mind while being tempted and tested in the midst of impurity. An underlying theme is that Buddha and demon are not distinct, but symbolize interior forces of wisdom and delusion that are inextricably and dialectically linked as complementary opposites embraced by a deeper level of nondual awareness.

Sōtō school assimilationism. Within the Sōtō school, the fourth generation patriarch Keizan maintained Dōgen's twin emphasis on continuing a commitment to rigorous meditation and adhering to monastic regulations, but he also assimilated many elements of Tendai esotericism, as well as folklore religiosity in his approach to Zen. Before joining Sōtō, Keizan had been a follower of the remnants of the Daruma school. Through Keizan's efforts, Sōtō Zen spread primarily northward from Echizen to the Noto peninsula, where Sōjiji temple was established. Long a rival with Eiheiji for the designation of the school's head temple—Eiheiji enjoyed the prestige of the founder's legacy, but Keizan's temple could claim more than nine times as many branch sites—Sōjiji was moved at the end of the nineteenth century. It was relocated in a neighborhood outside Yokohama in the Kanto region, which had become over the centuries a major center of Sōtō school activity.

A key to the success of this lineage was Keizan's evangelical disciple Gasan Jōseki (1275–1365), who was abbot of Sōjiji for forty years. Along with his followers, such as Tsūgen Jakurei (1322–1391), Gasan helped the rapid spread of Sōtō Zen in the countryside areas by taking over many abandoned Tendai and Shingon temples and assimilating folklore divinities, which were called upon to protect the welfare of the sacred sites. While greatly concerned with construction projects for bridges, dams, and irrigation canals to help win popular support, Gasan was also a scholastic monk who promulgated the dialectical doctrine of the "five ranks" *(go-i)* rooted in Chinese texts.

One of the legacies of the popularization campaign is that some of the most prominent Sōtō temples are associated with shamanistic and esoteric practices. They are best known to their congregations of lay followers for espousing a syncretic approach to attaining worldly benefits (*genze riyaku*), such as prosperity, fertility, or safety during travels, rather than for traditional Zen practices of meditation and monastic discipline. A prime example is Saijōji temple near the town of Odawara, which was founded by Ryōan Emyō (1337–1411), who was said to have transformed into a winged *tengu* (the mountain goblin of Japanese lore) to enhance his powers for protection of the temple grounds.

Another such example is Myōgonji temple in the town of Toyokawa in Aichi prefecture, anomalously affiliated with Eiheiji rather than Sōjiji, which is also called Toyakawa Inari because the main icons on the compound are not images of Buddha but rather the fox deity (Inari), originally a Shintō fertility symbol that became a force spiritually protecting the Buddhist teachings. Followers who flood these prayer temples (*kitō jiin*) for New Year's Day or other annual festivals may not even be aware that rituals and chants are being performed by monks trained at head temples or monasteries, where the primary training is in meditation with the aim of overcoming worldly attachments.

One of the features of medieval Sōtō Zen was the role played by female monastics at several nunneries who sought to keep alive the integrity of the tradition of clerical discipline espoused by Dōgen, and who also developed unique rituals for healing and purification. It is unclear, however, whether and to what extent Dōgen himself endorsed the equality of women, as there are several seemingly contradictory passages in his writings on this topic.

EARLY MODERN PERIOD (1600–1868). Zen Buddhism during the Tokugawa era was affected by several trends that influenced all Buddhist schools, including the rise of Confucianism and the return to prominence of Shintō under the banner of National Learning (*kokugaku*) thought. Both ideologies were taught at academies that helped support the rule of the shogunate. The *danka* (loosely "parish") system in which all families were assigned to a Buddhist temple strengthened the numbers of Buddhist affiliates but tended to weaken the spirituality and integrity of Zen monastic life. It has long been said that Zen apparently entered a prolonged period of decline (*daraku*), but the early modern period was actually characterized by many important luminary figures and elements of revitalization.

Ōbaku school. One of the new developments was the formation of a third movement, the Ōbaku school, which was based on the teachings of Chan masters of the Ming dynasty (1368–1644). The reintroduction of Chinese religion and culture was an anomalous event, since the Tokugawa regime restricted all foreign travel, but Yinyuan and his followers were able to enter Japan after receiving an invitation from Sōfukuji in Kyushu and exert great influence. This school emphasizes the preservation of the sūtras, as well as the combination of *zazen* meditation with Pure Land, other-power (*tariki*) practices for the veneration of Amida (Skt., Amitābha) Buddha, and the recitation of the *nembutsu* chant, which is generally thought to stand in contrast with the Zen self-power (*jiriki*) approach.

Rinzai monks. The Rinzai school of this period featured several prominent monks, including Takuan Sōhō (1573–1645), whose writings synthesize Zen principles of mental cultivation and swordsmanship. This is a form of training in which a warrior must be able to respond to a rival or threat spontaneously and with an unclouded and imperturbable mind that can be attained through meditation. According to Takuan, controlling the battleground and the sense of winning and losing is a matter of mastering the impulses of the mind and casting off fetters and delusions. While Takuan found the Zen mind in the highly specialized world of the warrior, another key monk of the day, Bankei Yōtaku (1622–1693), stressed the role of the mind manifested in ordinary activity, such as walking, standing, sitting, and lying down, which are all exemplary of the imperishable "unborn" Zen state of awareness.

The most important monk of the Tokugawa era was Hakuin Ekaku (1686–1768), who single-handedly reformed Rinzai school practice in a way that has persisted for over three centuries. Hakuin was known for both his appropriation of the strict training style of the Chinese masters of the Tang and Song periods and his appeal to the common folk, who found him a charismatic spiritual leader. Hakuin perfected a new system of *kōan* study by cataloging and rating the challenging quality of several hundred cases available in the primary collections, as well as creating one of the most famous riddles, "We know the sound of two hands clapping, what is the sound of one hand?" Hakuin gave form to a training method that integrates the techniques of practice sessions (*sesshin*) and master-disciple pedagogy (*dokusan*), along with public sermons (*teishō*) and capping phrase (*jakugo*) commentary provided by the master.

Hakuin also emphasized the role of intense mystical experience in developing Zen awareness. The experience begins with the Great Doubt, in which all perceptions are called into question and stripped away of conventional attitudes. The Great Doubt may seem to lead to a nihilistic state of perpetual anxiety, and this condition is identified by Hakuin as the Zen Sickness, which can affect enlightened and unenlightened alike. However, the goal of the spiritual path is to move beyond debilitating anxiety and attain a more advanced level of insight through experiences that are sudden and dramatic. Hakuin had several instances of subitaneous awakening; for example, it is recorded in his biography, "One night, he sat up in complete absorption until dawn. Suddenly, he heard the bell from a far off temple. As soon as this distant sound entered his ears, it penetrated to the core and made all perceptions of the external world fall away. It was like the ringing of a magnificent bell resounding in his ears."

Sōtō scholasticism. The Sōtō school underwent a significant revival of scholastic studies, producing many new editions and interpretations of the seminal works by and about Dōgen's life and thought. Manzan Dōhaku (1636–1714) was the originator of this movement and was responsible for acquiring a new rule of transmission and succession for the post of temple superior from the shogun government. Tenkei Denson (1648–1735) developed a novel, if idiosyncratic, view of Dōgen's *Shōbōgenzō* by favoring the controversial 60-fascicle edition, and Menzan Zuihō (1683–1769) was the premier cataloger and revisionist of the writings and biographies of Dōgen. The Sōtō school also published a comprehensive 95-fascicle edition of the *Shōbōgenzō* in 1690, which was reissued in the early nineteenth century, although the authenticity of this version has been questioned by modern scholars.

The Tokugawa era also saw several highly creative Zen spirits, including the lay practitioner and humanist thinker Suzuki Shōsan (1579–1655), who practiced an unorthodox style of meditation that owed to both samurai culture and Buddhist chanting rituals; the great *haiku* poet Bashō (1644–1694), who followed a Zen lifestyle as a lay disciple that influenced the inspiration and manner of his verse; and Ryōkan (1758–1831), a Sōtō monk affectionately called the Great Fool (Daigu) for the childlike innocence expressed in deceptively simple poems that celebrated the Zen values of poverty and nonattachment. Like other early modern Zen leaders who paid obeisance to Chan and early medieval Zen heroes and icons, Ryōkan expressed his gratitude for Dōgen in some of his poetry.

MODERN PERIOD (1868–PRESENT). Zen Buddhism in the Meiji era (1868–1912) was greatly affected by the response of Japanese society to modernization and westernization that resulted in the emerging of a nationalistic, pro-Shintō stance and the suppression or modification of traditional Buddhist institutions in several campaigns. These included the persecution of *haibustu kishaku*, which led to the destruction of Buddhist iconography, the new regulations of *shinbutsu bunri*, or the separation of Buddhist temples from Shintō shrines that had long been amalgamated; and the legislation of *nikujiki saitai*, forcing marriages and meat-eating upon Buddhist clergy and nearly ending centuries of celibacy and pacifism.

Reactions to modernity. One reaction to the disturbing trends was embodied by Ōtori Sessō (1814–1904), a Sōtō monk who worked for the Ministry of Doctrine to modernize Buddhism and eliminate the dissonance between traditional monasticism and secularized, industrialized society. Ōtori was also active in creating linkages between monks and laypersons, and in 1891, the Sōtō sect produced an abbreviated version of Dōgen's *Shōbōgenzō* as a source of guidance for lay practitioners. This very short text, the *Shushōgi*, does not even mention the need for *zazen* but instead emphasizes a life of gratitude and penitence. Several lay or *kyōdan* organizations became established as autonomous movements.

By the end of the nineteenth century, Zen had begun to emerge out of the cocoon of the Asia/Pacific cultural context to become a religious phenomenon that was spreading worldwide. Several factors influenced this development. One factor was that immigrant communities in Hawai'i, the American West Coast, and Brazil were serviced by missionaries and international outreach components of Zen temple institutions, especially for funerals and memorials.

Another factor was that non-Japanese were introduced to and became fascinated with the philosophy and practice of Zen. A key turning point was the 1893 World Parliament of Religions in Chicago, an interreligious congress that was attended by the widely traveled Shaku Sōen (1859–1919), a disciple of the eminent Rinzai monk, Imakita Kōsen (1816–1892), who was abbot of Engakuji temple in Kamakura. The parliament was also attended by the young D. T. Suzuki (1870–1966), who served as Sōen's interpreter. Suzuki went on to stay for long periods in the United States and have a lengthy career as the main exponent of Zen Buddhism in the West. He published dozens of books in English on various dimensions of Zen in relation to Japanese culture as seen from comparative theoretical perspectives. He also greatly influenced the famous 1956 essay by Alan Watts (1915–1973) on different styles of the appropriation of Zen practice in the West, "Beat Zen, Square Zen, and Zen." Famous American Beat poets were indebted to Suzuki, whose role was inherited by Masao Abe (b. 1915), who specialized in interfaith dialogue involving various Western religious traditions.

In the post–World War II period, historical accounts of Chan and Zen were significantly improved through the scholarship of Yanagida Seizan (b. 1922), a professor of Kyoto University, who was associated with scholars at Komazawa University in Tokyo, which specialized in Sōtō studies. Yanagida established an institute for international studies of Zen, as well as mentoring a number of influential Western scholars.

In addition to the efforts of Suzuki, Yanagida, and Abe, among others the spread of international interest in Zen was enhanced by the comparative philosophy of the Kyoto school led by Nishida Kitarō (1870–1945) and his main follower, Nishitani Keiji (1900–1990). Their works explicating the notion of "absolute nothingness" (*zettai mu*) as the key to understanding the Zen experience of enlightenment have been analyzed in relation to leading Western philosophers from ancient to modern times. The significance of Zen thought is now frequently examined in conjunction with the main trends of Western thought.

SOCIAL CRITICISMS OF ZEN. At the same time, since the 1970s a social criticism of Zen's role in relation to political and cultural affairs has been taken up by commentators in Japan and the West. Ichikawa Hakugen (1902–1986) was a Rinzai monk writing during the Vietnam War era. Ichikawa reflected on the role of Japan as an aggressor against China in World War II and argued that leaders of Zen, including Kyoto school thinkers who treated the theme of national polity in their works during the 1930s, when they were under considerable political pressure, needed to accept responsibility for contributing to prewar nationalism and imperialism. A movement that began within the Sōtō school in 1985 known as Critical Buddhism (*Hihan Bukkyō*) has demanded that Zen temples reform the practice of distributing posthumous ordination names because it discriminates against the outcaste (*burakumin*) community. In a related development, Sōtō nuns have criticized the misogynist aspect of Zen rules and customs as part of a broader gender criticism of Japanese Buddhism.

A wave of books published in the West beginning in the 1990s, including Brian Victoria's *Zen at War* (1997), James W. Heisig and John C. Maraldo's *Rude Awakenings* (1995), Jamie Hubbard and Paul L. Swanson's *Pruning the Bodhi Tree* (1997), Christopher Ives's *Zen Awakening and Society* (1992), and Bernard Faure's *Chan Insights and Oversights* (1993), has called attention to apparent limitations in the Zen view of transcendence. In striving to rise above the pettiness of worldly strife and conflict, Zen may overlook—and therefore implicitly sanction—problematic issues in everyday society. Some elements of this critique were anticipated in the famous novel *Temple of the Golden Pavilion* (*Kinkakuji*, 1956) by Yukio Mishima (1925–1970), which is based on the true story of an acolyte who burned down the most elegant temple in Kyoto. In that sense, the charge of antinomianism leveled at the fledgling Zen movements at the end of the twelfth century has resurfaced in a contemporary context.

SEE ALSO Buddhism, articles on Buddhism in Japan, Buddhism in the West; Bushidō; Dōgen; Eisai; Gozan Zen; Ikkyū Sōjun; Musō Sōseki; Suzuki, D. T.

BIBLIOGRAPHY

To cite some representative examples of the voluminous literature on Zen in Japanese, important reference works include *Zengaku daijiten* (Tokyo, 1978); *Ōbaku bunka jinmei jiten*, edited by Ōtsuki Mikio, Katō Shōshun, and Hayashi Yukimitsu (Kyoto, 1988); and *Zengo jiten*, compiled by Koga Hidehiko (Kyoto, 1991). Also, *Kōza Zen*, edited by Nishitani Keiji (Tokyo, 1974) is an important collection of essays, and two historical studies by Tekenuki Genshō are *Nihon shushūshi* (Tokyo, 1989) and *Nihon Zenshūshi no kenkyū* (Tokyo, 1993). Collections of original sources include *Nihon no Zen goroku*, 20 vols. (Tokyo, 1977), and two collections edited by Yanagida Seizan, *Zengaku sōsho*, 13 vols. (Kyoto, 1973–1980), and *Zen no goroku*, 17 vols. (Tokyo, 1969–1981).

Information on Zen demographics is included in T. Griffith Foulk, "The Zen Institution in Modern Japan," and in Kenneth Kraft, ed., *Zen Tradition and Transition: A Sourcebook by Contemporary Zen Masters and Scholars* (New York, 1988), pp. 157–177. Standard historical studies in English include Heinrich Dumoulin, *Zen Buddhism: A History,* Vol. 2: *Japan,* translated by James W. Heisig and Paul Knitter (New York, 1989), and Daigan Matsunaga and Alicia Matsunaga, *Foundation of Japanese Buddhism,* Vol. 2: *The Mass Movement* (Los Angeles, 1978). Cultural criticism of Zen is explored in Bernard Faure, *The Rhetoric of Immediacy: A Cultural Critique of Chan/Zen Buddhism* (Princeton, 1991).

Illustrated materials on the early history of the Rinzai school are contained in a partially bilingual catalogue prepared for an exhibit at the Tokyo National Museum of Art on *Kamakura Zen no genryū* (*The Art of Zen Buddhism*; Tokyo, 2003). An analysis of the interactions among early Zen movements is discussed in Bernard Faure, "The Daruma-shū, Dōgen, and Sōtō Zen," *Monumenta Nipponica* 42, no. 1 (1987): 25–55. Works on Dōgen include Hee-Jin Kim, *Dōgen Kigen—Mystical Realist* (Tucson, Ariz., 1975); Carl Bielefeldt, *Dōgen's Manuals of Zen Meditation* (Berkeley, 1988); and Steven Heine, *Dōgen and the Kōan Tradition: A Tale of Two Shōbōgenzō Texts* (Albany, N.Y., 1994). A selection of Dōgen's writings in translation is found in Kazuaki Tanahashi, ed., *Moon in a Dewdrop: Writings of Zen Master Dōgen,* translated by Robert Aitken et al. (San Francisco, 1985).

Institutional practices are discussed in Martin Collcutt, *Five Mountains: The Rinzai Zen Monastic Institution in Medieval Japan* (Cambridge, Mass., 1981). Intellectual practices of Zen are discussed in T. P. Kasulis, *Zen Action/Zen Person* (Honolulu, 1980); Miura Isshū and Ruth Fuller Sasaki, *Zen Dust: The History of Kōan Study in Rinzai (Lin-chi) Zen* (New York, 1966); Robert Aitken, trans. and ed., *The Gateless Barrier: The Wu-men kuan (Mumonkan)* (New York, 1991); and Ishikawa Rikizan, "Transmission of *Kirigami* (Secret Initiation Documents): A Sōtō Practice in Medieval Japan," in *The Kōan: Texts and Contexts in Zen Buddhism,* edited by Steven Heine and Dale S. Wright (New York, 2000), pp. 233–243. Syncretic practices are discussed in a book dedicated to the 500th anniversary of Saijōji, a Sōtō temple, *Daiyūzan: Saijōji kaisō roppyakunen hōzan* (Kanagawa-ken, Japan, 1994), and Karen Smyers, *The Fox and the Jewel: Shared and Private Meanings in Contemporary Japanese Inari Worship* (Honolulu, 1998).

The poem by Musō is cited from David Pollack, *Zen Poems of the Five Mountains* (New York, 1985). *Muchū mondō* is translated by Thomas Cleary in *Dream Conversations* (New York, 1994). Other works on this period of Rinzai Zen include Joseph Parker, *Zen Buddhist Landscape Arts of Early Muromachi Japan (1336–1573)* (Albany, N.Y., 1999); Kenneth Kraft, *Eloquent Zen: Daitō and Early Japanese Zen* (Honolulu, 1993); and Sonja Arntzen, *Ikkyū and the Crazy Cloud Anthology: A Zen Poet of Medieval Japan* (Tokyo, 1987). For an examination of the Sōtō school, see William M. Bodiford, *Sōtō Zen in Medieval Japan* (Honolulu, 1993).

An analysis of the development of the Ōbaku school is in Helen Baroni, *Ōbaku Zen: The Emergence of the Third Sect of Zen in Tokugawa Japan* (Honolulu, 1998). Zen's relation to samurai culture is discussed in Takuan Sōhō, *The Unfettered Mind: Writings of the Zen Master to the Sword Master,* translated by William Scott Wilson (New York, 1988), and Winston L. King, *Zen and The Way of the Sword: Arming the Samurai Psyche* (New York, 1993). Translations of Hakuin's writings are contained in Philip B. Yampolsky, *Zen Master Hakuin: Selected Writings* (New York, 1971), and Norman Waddell, *Essential Teachings of Zen Master Hakuin* (New York, 1994). William M. Bodiford's article treats changes in the transmission process in the Sōtō school, "Dharma Transmission in Sōtō Zen: Manzan Dōhaku's Reform Movement," *Monumenta Nipponica* 46, no. 4 (1991): 423–451. A translation of Ryōkan is found in *Great Fool: Zen Master Ryōkan: Poems, Letters, and Other Writings,* translated by Ryūichi Abe and Peter Haskel (Honolulu, 1999).

On changes in Meiji era Zen, see Richard Jaffe, *Neither Monk Nor Layman: Clerical Marriage in Modern Japanese Buddhism* (Princeton, 2001), and Steven Heine, "Abbreviation or Aberration? The Role of the *Shushōgi* in Modern Sōtō Zen Buddhism," in *Buddhism and the Modern World: Adaptations of an Ancient Tradition* (New York, 2003). The advent of Zen in the West is discussed in Rick Fields, *How the Swans Came to the Lake: A Narrative History of Buddhism in America,* rev. ed. (New York, 1986). The outlook of modern Zen in a comparative religious context is expressed in Masao Abe, *Buddhism and Interfaith Dialogue: Part One of a Two-Volume Sequel to Zen and Western Thought* (Honolulu, 1995). For Kyoto school philosophy, see James W. Heisig, *Philosophers of Nothingness: An Essay on the Kyoto School* (Honolulu, 2002), and Michiko Yusa, *Zen and Philosophy: An Intellectual Biography of Nishida Kitarō* (Honolulu, 2002).

On social criticism, see Ichikawa Hakugen, *Bukkyōsha no sensō-sekinin* (Tokyo, 1970), and a special (*tokushō*) issue of the journal *Bukkyō* 14, no. 5 (1994). Some of the recent works on a social criticism of Zen in English include Brian A. Victoria, *Zen at War* (New York, 1997); James W. Heisig and John C. Maraldo, eds., *Rude Awakenings: Zen, the Kyoto School, and the Question of Nationalism* (Honolulu, 1995); Jamie Hubbard and Paul L. Swanson, eds., *Pruning the Bodhi Tree: The Storm over Critical Buddhism* (Honolulu, 1997); Christopher Ives, *Zen Awakening and Society* (Honolulu, 1992); and Bernard Faure, *Chan Insights and Oversights: An Epistemological Critique of the Chan Tradition* (Princeton, 1993). Also, a translation of Mishima's novel *Kinkakuji* (Tokyo, 1956) is by Ivan Morris, *The Temple of the Golden Pavilion* (New York, 1959; reprint, 1994).

STEVEN HEINE (2005)

ZEUS, the son of Kronos and Rhea, is the main divinity of the Greek pantheon. Besides Hestia, he is the only god in the Greek pantheon with an undisputed Indo-European provenance, to judge from his name: it derives from the root **diéu-* (day; Latin *dies,* meaning "[clear] sky") and has close parallels in the Latin *Iu-piter* or the Ancient Indian (*Ṛgveda*) *Dyaus* (*pitar*). The Homeric and later epithet *pater* (father) closely corresponds to the Latin or early Indian way his name is expanded: his mythical and religious role as father must be already Indo-European. Despite the frequent Homeric formula "Zeus, father of men and gods," however, Zeus is father not in a theogonical sense, but, as the Homeric variant Zeus *ánax* (Lord Zeus) shows, in the sense of having the power of a father in a strict patriarchal system. This explains why all the Olympian gods are either his siblings (Poseidon, Hera, Demeter) or his children by different mothers (Athena, Apollo, Artemis, Hermes, Dionysos, Aphrodite, Ares, Hephaistos). This role—which implies unrestricted power over all members of the family, but also its check through father-like benignity—continues as the fundamental role of Zeus throughout antiquity and finds its expression in the standard iconography of Zeus as a bearded and powerful middle-aged man.

MAIN FUNCTIONS. In Greece, however, the Indo-European role of Zeus as the god of the bright sky is transformed into the role of Zeus as the weather god, whose paramount place of worship is a mountaintop; cult worship in such a peak sanctuary is specific to him. Among the many mountains connected with Zeus, many are reflected only in an epithet that does not necessarily imply the existence of a peak sanctuary, since few such sanctuaries are excavated. Those attested in literature are mainly connected with rain rituals (Zeus Hyetios or Ombrios), although the sanctuary on the Arcadian Mount Lykaion had a much wider function: it preserves traces of earlier initiatory rituals, and it turned into the federal sanctuary of all Arcadians, just as the sanctuary of Jupiter Latiaris on the top of the Mons Sacer, the "Sacred Mountain," was the federal sanctuary of the cities of archaic Latium. As Zeus "the Gatherer of Clouds" (*nephelêgeretas,* a common Homeric epithet), he was generally believed to cause rain, both in serious expressions ("Zeus rains") and in the comic parody of Aristophanes (*Clouds* 373). With the god of clouds comes the god of thunder (*hupsibremétês,* or "He Who Thunders High Up") and of lightning (*terpsikéraunos,* or "He Who Enjoys Lightning"). A spot struck by lightning and thus touched by the god is inaccessible for humans (*ábaton*) and often sacred to Zeus Kataibates ("He Who Comes Down"). As the Master of Lightning, Zeus has the Cyclopes at his command, the divine blacksmiths who fabricate for him the lightning as his main weapon. As the Master of Tempest, he also is supposed to give signs to mortals through thunder and lightning, and to strike evildoers, as he struck the giants and the monstrous Typhon at the beginning of his reign.

This entire complex finds expression in the myth that Zeus has his (palatial) home on Mount Olympus, together with all the gods of his household. Olympus had been transformed from a real mountain into a mythical place even before Homeric poetry. Homer described it as a place that "neither winds assail nor rains drench nor snow covers, but cloudless clarity and brilliant light surround it" (*Odyssey* 6.43). The myth, in turn, generated cult on one of the several peaks of the mountain (Hagios Antonios) that is archaeologically attested for the Classical period.

But for the early archaic Greeks, and conceivably for the Mycenaeans, Zeus was a much more fundamental divinity. According to the succession myth in the Hesiodeic *Theogony,* Zeus deposed his father Kronos—who in turn had deposed and castrated his father Uranus, and who had swallowed all his children to prevent them from deposing him. Baby Zeus escaped only because his mother Rhea fed Kronos a swaddled stone in place of the infant. After his accession to power, Zeus fought the giants and the monster Typhon who attacked his reign, and he disposed the actual order of things by attributing to each divinity his or her respective sphere: to his brothers Poseidon and Hades/Plouton, he allotted two-thirds of the cosmos—to Poseidon the sea, and to Hades the netherworld; to his sisters Hera (who was also his wife) and Demeter and to his many divine children he gave their respective domains in the world of the humans (mankind had been preexistent to Zeus's reign). The main outline of this myth is known also in the Homeric poems that either precede or follow Hesiod's *Theogony* closely; thus, early Greek narrative poetry, and through it, early Greek society, shared this fundamental myth. It makes Zeus the ruler ("king": *anax* or, after Homer, *basileus*) over both the other gods (whom he overrules by sheer force, if necessary) and the world of man: the order of things as they are now is the order of Zeus.

Closely related succession myths are attested from Hittite Anatolia and from Mesopotamia. In Hittite mythology, the succession passed through Anu (Sky), who was deposed and castrated by Kumarbi, finally to Teshub, the storm god, who corresponds to Zeus; other myths tell of the attacks of Kumarbi and his followers on Teshub's reign, which corresponds to the Greek myths of how young Zeus had to defend his rule against Typhon and the Titans. Myths from Mesopotamia present a similar, though more varied structure; the Babylonian *Enuma elish* moves from a primeval pair, Apsu and Tiamat, to the reign of Marduk, the city god of Babylon and in many respects a Zeus-like figure. A later version of the Typhoeus myth (preserved in Apollodorus's *Bibliotheke* 1.6.3) locates part of it on Syrian Mount Kasion (Phoen., Sapon), the seat of a peak cult of Baal Saphon, who the Greeks named Zeus Kasios; Baal shares traits also with Marduk. The Greek concept of Zeus the kingly ruler of the present world is as unthinkable without Oriental influence as is the figure of Zeus the Master of Storms.

In many instances, human affairs follow the plan of Zeus (for example, the Trojan War, or the return of Odysseus in Homeric poetry), despite apparent setbacks. He might help to bring things to perfection, if asked in a prayer to do so (Zeus Teleios, "He Who Perfects"), and he might signal his will, either asked for or not, in dreams, augural signs, or thunder and lightning, but also but by provoking ominous human utterances (*pheme*). In cult, this function is expressed in rare epithets such as Phanter (He Who Signals), Terastios (He of the Omina), and Phemios or Kledonios (He Who Gives Oracular Sayings).

CULTS. Zeus has few major polis festivals, and only a few month names attest an important early festival of Zeus: the

Bronze Age month Diwos (attested in Knossos on Crete) to which the Macedonian, Aetolian, and Thessalian month name Dios corresponds; the Attic month Maimakterion which derives from the minor festival of a rather shadowy Zeus Maimaktes (presumably a storm god); the Cretan month [V]elchanios which belongs to a typically Cretan (Zeus) Velchanos who perhaps originally was an independent storm god. Of some interest among city festivals are also the sacrifice of a bull of Zeus Polieus in Kos and the festival of Zeus Sosipolis in Magnesia on the Maeander, both attested by sacrificial prescriptions preserved by Hellenistic inscriptions; these texts show the pomp with which Hellenistic cities celebrated the god whose cult expressed their identity and their hopes for the future. In both cases, the texts emphasize the choice and importance of the sacrificial animal as the center of Zeus's cult.

The Diasia, "the greatest Athenian festival of Zeus" (Thucydides 1.126.6), had a much less auspicious character. The festival was celebrated in honor of Zeus Meilichios, who took the form of a huge bearded snake. The cult place was outside the town, and the cult contained either animal sacrifices or bloodless cakes; sacrificial animals were entirely burnt. This meant that the festival did not culminate in a common banquet that released the tension of the sacrifice. Instead, there is evidence of common meals in small family circles and of presents given to the children—in this phase of the ritual, the community has disintegrated and nuclear families have become highly visible. Such a mood fits the date of the festival, Anthesterion 23 (February/March); the main event of the month had been the Anthesteria, which had a similar, but even more marked character of uncanny disintegration: on its first day, every participant was drinking, and ghosts were roaming the city. Phenomenologically, both festivals belong to a New Year-like transition at the turn from winter to spring.

Thus, although Zeus's polis festivals were not very widespread, he was from early times prominent as a Panhellenic deity who transcends the single polis (as he is the only Olympic divinity who, in the Homeric poems, sides with neither side in the war). The *Iliad* mentions the oracular sanctuary of Dodona in northwestern Greece that was dedicated to Zeus Naios, and its strange, barefoot priests who slept on the ground (*Iliad* 16.233–5, *Odyssey* 19.296–301); later, priestesses derived the oracles from the sound of a holy oak, the flight of doves, and the sound of a bronze basin. Questions from and answers to the many private worshipers were written on lead tablets that are preserved in considerable number. But Zeus's main Greek sanctuary was in Olympia, in the southwestern Peloponnese, with its games that were held every four years. The games began with an impressive sacrifice to Zeus Olympios on an ash altar whose growing height made it an impressive sight; a Panhellenic contest followed whose main events were a foot race and a chariot race. Their foundation (in the year 776 BCE, according to tradition) marked the end of the isolation of the Dark Age communities; the common festival took place at a spot well-removed from a single polis and was under the protection of a superior god. The analysis of the sacrifices points to an origin in initiation rituals of young warriors. The sanctuary contained an archaic temple of Hera and a large temple of Zeus, built in the 460s BCE; its cult state, an enthroned Zeus, was a major work of the Athenian sculptor Phidias and evoked wonder and admiration throughout antiquity.

Inside the polis, Zeus has his own specific province and cares for the smaller units whose lawful unification forms the polis. His own domain is the agora: as Zeus Agoraios, he presides over the just political dealings of the community; in this function, he can be counted among the main divinities of a city, including Hestia Prytaneia and Athena Poliouchos, or Polias. On the level of smaller units, he is one of the patrons of phratries (Zeus Phratrios or Zeus Patr[o]ios), sometimes together with Athena Phratria or Patr[o]ia (see Plato, *Euthydemus* 302d); or of clans (Zeus Patr[o]ios). In this function, he also protects the single households. As Zeus Herkeios (He in the Yard), he receives sacrifices on an altar in the courtyard, which had to be in every Athenian family home (Aristotle, *Constitution of Athens* 55); as Zeus Ephestios (He on the Hearth), sacrifices were offered on the hearth of a house.

There are functions of Zeus on the level of the family that easily are extended both to individuals and to the polis. Since property is indispensable for the constitution of a household, Zeus is also Zeus Ktesios, the protector of property. As such, he receives cults from families, from cities, and from individuals. In many places, Zeus Ktesios has the appearance of a snake—property is bound to the ground, at least in the still-agrarian conception of ancient Greece, and its protectors belong to the earth (see Ploutos ["Riches"], whose mother is Demeter, and Plouton ["The Rich One"] one of the many names of the god of the netherworld). The same holds true for Zeus Meilichios (The Gentle One). On the level of the individual, Xenophon attests Zeus Meilichios's efficiency in providing funds (*Anabasis* 7.8.1), and in many communities, Zeus Melichios protects families or clans. In Athens he receives the polis festival of the Diasia; there and elsewhere, he also has the form of a snake. And finally, one might add Zeus Philios, protector of friendship between individuals (as among an entire polis).

The Zeus cults of Crete fit only partially into this picture. Myth places both his birth and his grave in Crete: according to Hesiod, in order to save him from Kronos, Rhea gave birth to Zeus, then entrusted the baby to Gaia, who hid it in a cave near Lyktos, on Mount Aigaion (Hesiod, *Theogony* 468ff.). Later authors replaced Gaia by the Kouretes—armed demons, whose noisy dance kept Kronos away—and name other mountains, usually Mount Ida or Mount Dikte. This complex of myths reflects cult in caves that partly go back to Minoan times, and armed dances by young Cretan warriors, like those attested in the famous hymn for Zeus from Palaikastro (sanctuary of Zeus Diktaios), which belong in the context of initiatory rituals of young warriors; in the actual oaths of Cretan ephebes, Zeus plays an important role. In this function, Zeus exceptionally can be young: the Palaikastro hymn calls him *koûros* (young man); the statue in the sanctuary of Zeus Diktaios was beardless, and coins from Knossos show a beardless (Zeus) Welchanos. There certainly are Minoan (and presumably Mycenaean) elements present in the complex, but it would be wrong to separate Cretan Zeus too radically from the rest of the Greek evidence; both the cults of Mount Lykaios and of Olympia contain initiatory features.

THEOLOGICAL REFLECTIONS. In Homer's epics (much more than in actual cult), Zeus had reached a nearly overpowering position. During the Classical and Hellenistic ages, religious thinkers developed this into a sort of "Zeus monotheism." By the time of Aeschylus (525–456 BCE), Zeus had begun to move away from simple human knowledge ("Zeus, whoever you are . . . ," *Agamemnon* 160) to a nearly universal function ("Zeus is ether, Zeus is earth, Zeus is sky, Zeus is everything and more than that," *Fragment* 105); and Sophocles (c. 496–406 BCE) sees Zeus's hand in all human affairs ("Nothing of this which would not be Zeus," *Women of Trachis* 1278). The main document of this monotheism is the hymn to Zeus by the Stoic philosopher Kleanthes (d. 232/231 BCE), where Zeus, mythical image of the Stoic logos, becomes the commander over the entire cosmos ("no deed is done on earth . . . without your office, nor in the divine ethereal vault of heaven, nor at sea") and its "universal law," while at the same time he is the guarantor of goodness and benign protector of man ("protect mankind from its pitiful incompetence"). This marks the high point of a development—other gods, though briefly mentioned, become insignificant beside universal Zeus.

SEE ALSO Greek Religion; Hades; Hera.

BIBLIOGRAPHY

Arafat, Karim. *Classical Zeus. A Study in Art and Literature.* Oxford, 1990.

Bianchi, Ugo. *Dios Aisa. Destino, Nomini e Divinità nell'epos, nelle Teogonie e nel Culto dei Greci.* Rome, 1953.

Cook, Albert B. *Zeus. A Study in Ancient Religion.* 3 vols. Cambridge, U.K., 1914; reprint, 1926, 1940.

Kérenyi, Karl. *Zeus and Hera. Archetypal Image of Father, Husband, and Wife.* London, 1975.

Lolyd-Jones, Hugh. *The Justice of Zeus.* Sather Classical Lectures 41. Berkeley, Calif., 1971; reprint, 1983.

Parke, H. W. *The Oracles of Zeus.* Oxford, 1967.

Schwabl, Hans, and Erika Simon. "Zeus." *Pauly-Wissowa* 10A (1972): 253–376; suppl. 15 (1978): 993–1481.

Tiverios, M. "Zeus." *Lexicon Inconographicum Mythologiae Classicae* (*LIMC*) 8 (1997): 310–470.

Verbruggen, Henri. *Le Zeus crétois.* Paris, 1981.

FRITZ GRAF (2005)

ZHANG DAOLING,

semilegendary figure of the second century CE, depicted in hagiographies as a master of long life (*changsheng*) who put his disciples to tests, vanquished demons, and prepared the elixir of immortality. He is said to have received in 142 CE a revelation from Taishang Laojun the deified Laozi, who bestowed on him the title of Celestial Master (*tianshi*). The god gave him the "Doctrine of the Orthodox One [Resting on] the Authority of the Alliance" (*zhengyi mengwei dao*), revealing that the demoniac Six Heavens had been abolished and their reign replaced by a golden age governed by the Three Heavens. The people were to honor no gods other than those of the Alliance, the masters were to eschew all payment, and blood sacrifices were to be banished.

Subsequently, Zhang Daoling gathered together many disciples in Sichuan and launched a campaign for the reform of the religious practices of a people described as having lapsed into degeneracy. He started a health cult and wrote several books; however, his works are now lost and consequently nearly nothing is known about his doctrines. He is said to have established the basis of a theocratic state divided into twenty-four parishes corresponding to the twenty-four breaths of the year (one every fifteen days). This was later altered to twenty-eight, to correspond to the divisions of the Chinese zodiac. The followers of the sect were obliged to pay a tax of five pecks of rice, whence came the description of the sect as the Way of Five Pecks of Rice (Wudoumi Dao).

Zhang Daoling is considered the founder of the Daoist sect of the Celestial Masters (Tianshi Dao). His eldest son, Zhang Heng, succeeded him, and Zhang Heng in turn was succeeded by his son, Zhang Lu. Under Zhang Lu's leadership the movement rose in rebellion against the Han. The Way of the Celestial Masters was the first organized Daoist movement and has continued down to the present day in Taiwan through a succession of Daoist masters who are allegedly lineal descendants of Zhang Daoling. Many texts in the *Daozang* (the Daoist canon) derive from this religious movement, whose tendency is liturgical, demonological, and more or less shamanistic.

SEE ALSO Daoism, overview article and article on The Daoist Religious Community; Laozi.

BIBLIOGRAPHY

Imbault-Huart, Camille. "La légende du premier pape des taoïstes et l'histoire de la famille pontificale des Tchang." *Journal asiatique* 2 (1844); 389-461.

Welch, Holmes. "The Chang tien-shih and Taoism in China." *Journal of Oriental Studies* 4 (1957-1958): 188-212.

ISABELLE ROBINET (1987)

ZHANG JUE

(d. 184 CE), founder of the Yellow Turban sect. Zhang Jue was heir to the doctrines of Yu Ji, a sorcerer and healer who preached and practiced in Shandong and who was probably the author of the *Taiping qingling shu* (Book of Great Peace, or Book of Great Equality), a text now lost. Having received a revelation that the "blue heaven" of the Han dynasty was to be replaced by a "yellow heaven" (yellow is the color of the Center) in the first (*jiazi*) year of the next new cycle of sixty years (i.e., 184 CE), around the year 175 Zhang Jue dispatched eight apostles to convert the people of the central and eastern provinces of China. They preached doctrines closely related to those of the Five Pecks of Rice sect in Sichuan. Like the leader of the latter sect, Zhang Lu, Zhang Jue healed the sick by group confession (sins were believed to be the cause of sickness), organized collective worship under a quasi-military church hierarchy, and used sexual techniques to achieve sanctity.

Zhang Jue's followers were called Yellow Turbans (Huangjin) from the yellow kerchiefs they wore on their heads in token of their expectation of the "yellow heaven." They worshiped Huang-Lao and were intent on inaugurating a golden age—the age of Great Peace—and a utopian state based on egalitarian ideas, as opposed to the Confucian ideas of social hierarchy. They regularly retired to oratories ("pure chambers," *jingshi*) where they healed the sick by confession of sins and recitation of sacred scriptures. The followers of the sect were governed by moral codes and divided into thirty-six *fang* (a word that means both "regions" and "magic recipes"), local communities headed by "generals." The "three Zhangs," Zhang Jue and his two brothers, Liang and Bao, were respectively generals of Heaven, Earth, and Man, symbolizing their embodiment of the all-embracing triad.

Over a ten-year period, Zhang Jue enjoyed great success. He had several hundred thousand followers in eight provinces by the time he initiated the Yellow Turban rebellion in 184. Although Zhang Jue and his brothers were caught and executed in the same year, they left behind a great number of communities of believers, and as late as 205 the Yellow Turbans still posed a military problem for the government. The Yellow Turban uprisings in eastern and northern China, taken together with Zhang Lu's uprisings in the west, weakened the Han dynasty and contributed to its fall.

SEE ALSO Daoism, overview article and article on The Daoist Religious Community; Millenarianism, article on Chinese Millenarian Movements; Taiping; Zhang Lu.

BIBLIOGRAPHY

Eichhorn, Werner. "Bemerkungen zum Aufstand des Chang Chio und zum Staate des Chang Lu." *Mitteilungen des Instituts für Orientforschung* 3 (1955): 291–327.

Fukui Kojun. *Dokyo no kisoteki kenkyu.* Tokyo, 1952. See pages 62–92.

Levy, Howard S. "Yellow Turban Religion and Rebellion at the End of the Han." *Journal of the American Oriental Society* 76 (October-December 1956): 214–227.

Michaud, Paul. "The Yellow Turbans." *Monumenta Serica* 17 (1958): 47–127.

ISABELLE ROBINET (1987)

ZHANG LU (fl. 184–220), grandson of Zhang Daoling, founder of the sect of the Celestial Masters, and the sect's third Celestial Master. In 184 CE Zhang Lu led the sect in rebellion against the Han dynasty and established an independent state in Hanzhong, in the west, which he governed for thirty years. In 215 he surrendered to the Han general Cao Cao and was rewarded with honors that included a fiefdom. After the founding of the Wei dynasty in 220 by Cao Cao's son, Zhang Lu lived some years at the Wei court. It may be said that both the existence of the sect as an organized church and its official recognition by the government were due to his efforts. The Celestial Masters sect became the first institutionalized Daoist movement, distinguished on this point from the other popular beliefs and messianic movements of the time, and especially from the Daoist seekers after long life, who were unorganized and scattered. The movement of the Celestial Masters spread to North China by the end of the third century and, by the end of the fourth century, to all of China. It counted among its adherents many powerful families.

The church was divided into twenty-four dioceses (later twenty-eight), corresponding to the twenty-four breaths of the year (one every fifteen days) and, later, to the twenty-eight divisions of the Chinese zodiac. The hierarchy of the church and its way of addressing the powers on high were modeled on imperial and bureaucratic usages. The church set up wayside inns all over the state where food and shelter were available to travelers at no charge. Each household of followers contributed a tax of five pecks of rice, whence the name of the sect, the Way of Five Pecks of Rice (Wudoumi Dao).

The focal center of each diocese was the oratory, presided over by "libationers" (*jijiu*), a married hereditary priesthood. These priests mediated between the faithful and the divine and knew as well how to ward off demons. The petitions of the faithful, transmitted by the rising smoke of incense and by the spirits exteriorized from the priest's body, were borne to the Three Heavens. Letters could be sent to the Three Officials of Heaven, Earth, and Water (*san guan*). One copy, placed on a mountain, rose to Heaven, another was buried in the ground for the Earth official, and a third was cast into the river for the Official of Water. Other rituals involve talismans drawn by priests; these were burned, their ashes were mixed with water, and the talismanic holy water was then drunk by believers. The sung liturgies were based on religious texts, in particular on the *Dao de jing.* The *Xiang'er,* a commentary on the *Dao de jing* attributed to Zhang Lu, was used as a kind of catechism in the instruction of the faithful. Morals and law were combined: diseases were believed to be caused by evil deeds, and hence the sick were healed by rites of expiation, ceremonials, confessions, and punishment. The misdeeds of the faithful, such as theft and drinking, also fell under the jurisdiction of the sect. Road repair or imprisonment was the usual punishment.

The year was marked by a religious calendar. At the equinoxes, offerings were made to the god of the earth and the god of the soil, and healing talismans were distributed to the sect's followers. At the solstices, sacrifices were made for the salvation of the souls of the dead. Communal feasts (*chu*) were offered during the first, seventh, and tenth months, and also on religious occasions such as an initiation or the consecration of an oratory. At each new moon a communal sexual ritual was celebrated, the Union of the Breaths (*heqi*), which Buddhist sources describe as a licentious orgy, but which some texts still extant show to be a ceremony of highly stylized erotic choreography of religious and cosmic significance.

The sect of the Celestial Masters is still in existence, and its leaders claim direct descent from Zhang Daoling and Zhang Lu. Many of the present rituals, sacrifices, and festivals derive from rituals of the Celestial Masters of the third century.

SEE ALSO Daoism, overview article and article on The Daoist Religious Community.

BIBLIOGRAPHY

Eichhorn, Werner. "Bemerkungen zum Aufstand des Chang Chio und zum Staate des Chang Lu." *Mitteilungen des Instituts für Orientforschung* 3 (1955): 291–327.

Fukui Kojun. *Dokyo no kisoteki kenkyu.* Tokyo, 1952. See pages 62–92.

Stein, Rolf A. "Remarques sur les mouvements du taoïsme politico-religieux au deuxième siècle ap. J. C." *T'oung pao* 50 (1963): 1–78.

Xiong Deji. "Taiping jing de zuozhi he sixiang ji qi yu Huangjin he Tianshidao de guanxi." *Lishi yanjiu* 4 (1962): 8–25.

ISABELLE ROBINET (1987)

ZHANG XUECHENG (1738–1801), Chinese historian and philosopher. A native of Shaoxing (Kuaiji district), Zhejiang Province, and son of a district magistrate, Zhang went to Beijing as a student in 1762, and in the next ten years became acquainted with many of the leading writers of the day. Among his associates and mentors were, notably, Zhu Yun (1729–81), whom he acknowledged as his master, and the philosopher and philologue Dai Zhen (1724–77), whom Zhang admired for his philosophical essays but criticized strongly for his opposition to the ideas of the Song dynasty Confucian moralist Zhu Xi (1130–1200). As a youth Zhang developed a keen interest in the art and theory of historical writing, admiring the Tang dynasty historiographer Liu Zhiji (661–721). As early as 1770 he had begun to formulate a theory of the development of civilization based on the Han court librarian Liu Xin's theories of the history of types of writing. In 1778 he passed the examinations for the highest civil service degree (*jinshi*), but he never took office, and supported himself usually through teaching appointments in local academies, commissions to compile local and family histories, and research and writing sponsored by patrons (notably Bi Yuan, 1730–97).

Zhang articulated his vision of the human past in his local history of Hezhou (1775; only fragments are extant), his *Jiaochou tongyi* (Philosophy of Bibliography, 1779), and especially in his monograph-length essay *Yuandao* (The Analysis of the Way, 1789). He saw all moral conventions, institutions, traditions of learning, and genres of writing as taking form in an early state of the human condition in which there was no distinction between public (official) and private aspects of life, when all kinds of writing were naturally beautiful or useful according to their function, anonymous and unmarred by personal vanity. This ideal state of affairs ended some centuries before Confucius. Thereafter, "officials were no longer teachers," and there was no longer a "unity of government (*zhi*) and doctrine (*jiao*)"—Zhang's idiom (following the Song polymath Ouyang Xiu, 1007–1072) for saying that the primal unity of the human spirit was sundered forever, in an alienation of intellect from action. Intellectual history since that time has been a dialectical process of always incomplete vision of the truth, ages of philosophy, of scholarship, and of literary art succeeding each other endlessly, each age blind to the values it fails to realize. Zhang crystalizes his vision in the famous one-line evaluation of the Confucian Classics, opening his collected essays, *Wenshi tongyi* (General Principles of Literary and Historical Criticism): "The Six Classics are all history." By this he means that they are not authored books that formulate the *dao* of human society, but are exemplifications of this *dao,* being documents, residues of the functioning of the ancient society and state, an age when "the *dao* and its embodiments were one" (*dao qi heyi*). This *dao* cannot be reduced to "empty words" (*kong yan*) and formulas; it must be grasped intuitively through the study of institutions and human acts, which the historian must present just as they were, without bias.

In this aspect of his thought Zhang is close to the Ming dynasty Confucian moralist Wang Shouren (Wang Yangming, 1472–1529); but unlike Wang he never himself had a religious drive toward self-cultivation. Zhang had several Buddhist friends, whom he teased good-naturedly, but he was open-mindedly willing to own that Buddhism might be saying something true and valuable in its own way. He could hardly be called a Daoist, but his vision of intellectual history owes not a little to Zhuangzi. He had strong conservative prejudices about the status of women, expressed in several vigorous essays attacking the poet Yuan Mei (1716–1798). Zhang was impatient with the philological scholarship fashionable in his time, his thinking being more akin to the so-called Tongcheng circle of literary men. He much admired the early Qing historian Huang Zongxi (1610–1695) and other Zhejiang authors, and is sometimes classed as a "member" of an "Eastern Zhejiang school" of historical learning.

SEE ALSO Wang Yangming.

BIBLIOGRAPHY

Demiéville, Paul. " Chang Hsüeh-ch'eng and His Historiography." In *Historians of China and Japan,* edited by W. G. Beasley and E. G. Pulleyblank, pp. 167–185. Oxford, 1961.

Nivison, David S. *The Life and Thought of Chang Hsüeh-ch'eng, 1738–1801.* Stanford, 1966. Includes an annotated bibliography of important Chinese and Japanese sources.

Yü Ying-shih. *Lun Dai Zhen yu Zhang Xuecheng.* Hong Kong, 1976. An English edition of this work is forthcoming.

New Sources

Mann, Susan. "Women in the Life of Zhang Xuecheng." In *Chinese Language, Thought, Culture: Nivison and His Critics,* edited by Philip J. Ivanhoe. LaSalle, Ill., 1996.

Nivison, David S. "The Philosophy of Zhang Xuecheng." In *The Ways of Confucianism: Investigations in Chinese Philosophy.* La Salle, Ill., 1996.

Wong, Young-tsu. "Discovery or Invention: Modern Interpretation of Zhgang Xuecheng (1738–1801)." *Historiography East and West,* 1 (September 2003), 178–203.

DAVID S. NIVISON (1987)
Revised Bibliography

ZHANG ZAI

ZHANG ZAI (1021–1077), also known as Zhang Hengqu, the second major Neo-Confucian thinker in the traditional lineage of Neo-Confucian teachers. Zhang Zai was a native of Chang'an in modern Shaanxi. His study of what became central Neo-Confucian texts began at the age of twenty-one when he corresponded with and then met Fan Zhongyan (989–1052), a prominent Confucian official. Fan suggested that Zhang Zai begin his study with the *Zhongyong* (Doctrine of the mean). This advice led Zhang Zai to study Confucianism, but like many Neo-Confucians he also studied Buddhism and Daoism, particularly their religious practices such as meditation. Eventually, however, he rejected their philosophies and returned to Confucian classics. Zhang Zai was appointed to office in 1057 and became widely recognized as one of the major interpreters of Confucian teachings. He eventually resigned from office over disagreement with the reform measures of Wang Anshi (1021–1086), a figure of major political influence during the Song dynasty. Zhang was appointed once again, only to retire and die on the trip home from the capital in 1077.

For Zhang Zai, the focus of his return to Confucian teachings was his interest in two of the classics, the *Yi Jing* (Book of changes) and the *Zhongyong,* works that served as the foundation of his philosophical and religious thought. Zhang Zai's prominent position in the lineage of Neo-Confucian teachers, a position in part the result of the lineage drawn up by the great synthesizer of Neo-Confucianism, Zhu Xi (1130–1200), derives from the interpretive stance he developed toward these works and from his position as teacher to both Zheng Hao (1032–1085) and Zheng Yi (1033–1077), two of the most prominent figures in the development of Neo-Confucian thought.

Like Zhou Dunyi (1017–1073), the first major Neo-Confucian teacher, Zhang Zai based much of his philosophy upon the *Yijing.* For Zhang Zai, the *taiji,* or Great Ultimate, refers to the source of all existence, which he takes to be *qi,* the material or vital force of existence itself. Thus *taiji* is identified with *qi* and yin and yang, the symbols of polar opposites in Chinese thought, as well as with the Five Elements *(wuxing),* the basis of an early cosmological theory of the nature of change. Although later modified by other thinkers, this *qi*-based monism continued to play an important role in Neo-Confucian metaphysics.

Zhang Zai's thought had far-reaching religious implications as well. While Neo-Confucianism has often been thought to be primarily a rationalistic system whose major influence was intellectual, a more recent reassessment of the tradition suggests that Neo-Confucianism also contains a profound religious dimension. The focus of this religious perspective is the central role assigned to the figure of the sage *(sheng)* and to the goal of sagehood. To become a sage became increasingly important as the goal of Neo-Confucian learning and self-cultivation.

When Neo-Confucianism is considered in this context, Zhang Zai's philosophical system is fully religious. In Zhang Zai's most celebrated work, the *Ximing* (Western inscription), the monistic metaphysical structure of *qi* is enlarged to include a poetic vision of the unity and interdependence of the universe and its multifaceted phenomena:

> Heaven is my father and Earth is my mother, and even such a small creature as I finds an intimate place in their midst.
>
> Therefore that which extends throughout the universe I regard as my body and that which directs the universe I consider as my nature.
>
> All people are my brothers and sisters, and all things are my companions. (de Bary and Bloom, 1999, p. 683)

Some have called this passage the foundation of Neo-Confucian ethics. Others have expanded its meaning to include not only ethics but a religious dimension that ultimately comprehends the religious goal of sagehood.

Later Neo-Confucians primarily valued Zhang Zai's doctrine of the sage "forming one body with the universe." This doctrine represents both the Neo-Confucian contiguity with its classical Confucian heritage and an enlargement of the Neo-Confucian system. At the center of Zhang Zai's teaching is the idea of *ren,* humaneness or human-heartedness, in many ways the salient teaching of the classical Confucian tradition. This basic quality, which was for Confucius and Mencius the bond between human society and the ways of Heaven *(tian)* and hence fundamental to the underlying moral structure of the universe, was expanded by Zhang Zai to encompass the universe itself, since for the sage to form "one body with the universe" suggests the complementarity and fundamental identify of microcosm and macrocosm. The doctrine illustrates as well Zhang Zai's belief in the fundamental goodness and purpose of the universe and in the potential of the individual to realize the ideal of the sage.

In the teaching of "forming one body with the universe," Zhang Zai also claimed to distinguish Confucianism clearly from Buddhism and Daoism. For him the universe and its processes have a real existence. In turn, human life is looked upon as intrinsically valuable and ultimately the very foundation for the realization of sagehood. For Zhang Zai, such a view is clearly distinguishable from Daoism and Buddhism, both of which require a radical departure from the universe as it is given in order to fulfill the soteriological quest. In Zhang Zai's terms, Daoism and Buddhism both emphasize escape from the world, while Confucianism finds fulfillment and ultimate identity precisely within the changes found in this world, a world of *qi* rather than of emptiness. The sage accepts the ultimate reality of *qi* and its inherent goodness, he acknowledges the infusion of *ren* throughout the very structure of the universe itself, and thus he can fulfill the ideal of the sage, "forming one body with the universe."

SEE ALSO Confucianism; Qi; Ren and Yi; Taiji.

BIBLIOGRAPHY

The thought of Zhang Zai is introduced with a translation of the *Western Inscription* as well as of his other major work, *Correcting Youthful Ignorance,* in *A Source Book in Chinese Philosophy,* translated by Wing-tsit Chan (Princeton, 1963), pp. 495–517, and *Sources of Chinese Tradition from Earliest times to 1600, 2d ed.,* compiled by Wm. Theodore de Bary and Irene Bloom (New York, 1999), vol. 1, pp. 682–689. Selections from Zhang Zai's writings are included in the major anthology of Song dynasty Neo-Confucianism compiled by Zhu Xi and Lü Zu-qian, translated into English by Wing-tsit Chan as *Reflections on Things at Hand* (New York, 1967). Discussions of Zhang Zai's thought may be found in Fung Yu-lan's *A History of Chinese Philosophy,* 2d ed., vol. 2, *The Period of Classical Learning,* translated by Derk Bodde (Princeton, 1953), pp. 477–498, and in Carsun Chang's *The Development of Neo-Confucian Thought,* vol. 1 (New York, 1957), pp. 159–183. More detailed discussions of specific problems in the thought of Zhang Zai may be found in Siu-chi Huang's "The Moral Point of View of Chang Tsai," *Philosophy East and West* 21 (April 1971): 141–156, and Chun-i T'ang's "Chang Tsai's Theory of Mind and Its Metaphysical Basis," *Philosophy East and West* 6 (1956): 113–136. For general discussions see Xinzhong Yao, *An Introduction to Confucianism* (Cambridge, 2000) pp. 98–104; John H. Berthrong, *Transformations of the Confucian Way* (Boulder, Colo., 1998), pp. 6–114. and Rodney L. Taylor, *The Illustrated Encyclopoedia of Confucianism,* 2 vols (New York, 2003), pp. 107–108.

RODNEY L. TAYLOR (1987 AND 2005)

ZHENREN. The term *zhenren* ("real person") is first encountered in parts of the *Zhuangzi* that are thought to date from the third century BCE. *Zhenren* may also be translated "perfect person" or "true person" (most Sinologists now translate it "Perfected"). Zhuangzi's "real person" is one who does not oppose the human and the natural, who knows how to accept both defeat and victory, joy and sorrow, life and death without being affected by them. Ordinary people, according to Zhuangzi, "wallow in their passions because they are out of touch with the workings of Heaven. The 'real person' of ancient times knew neither to love life nor to hate death. . .He took pleasure in what he received; he forgot what he gave back. This is what it means not to throw away the Dao with the heart, not to use what is human to help out what is heavenly. This is what is called a 'real person'" (chap. 6). The "real person" is thus one who possesses what is for Zhuangzi the highest form of knowledge, the knowledge that enables him to "make all things equal" and so renders him invulnerable to the vicissitudes of human life.

Zhuangzi uses a range of terms to refer to this ideal person, among them "divine person" (*shenren*), "accomplished person" (*zhijen*), and "saintly person" (*shengren*). The last term in particular, being the standard term in the *Laozi,* appears much more frequently than "real person." But the term *saintly person* had the disadvantage, at a time when the battle between the different schools of philosophy had reached its pitch, of referring also to the Confucian ideal person. In the *Laozi* itself, in fact, it refers indifferently to the ruler of men and the person who, even if he does not rule, is worthy of ruling. By Zhuangzi's time the feudal system of the Zhou dynasty (c. 1150 to 256 BCE) was in its final agony, and interstate relationships were characterized by ruse and violence. This political context forced philosophers to choose between "man" and "nature," between politics and integrity, and the term *saintly person* came increasingly to serve only as the designation of the Confucian (that is, political) ideal. In its place the Daoists put the "real person." This person does not yet, by definition, refuse all contact with human society and politics, but if he should happen to "get involved," he will not allow himself to "feel involved."

In chapter 21 of the *Zhuangzi* we thus read of Sun Shu Ao, who had "thrice been named prime minister without considering it glorious and thrice been dismissed without looking distressed." Someone asks Sun Shu Ao whether he has some special way of "using his heart." "Why should I be any better than anyone else?" he responds. "When [the nomination] came, I could not refuse it; when it left, I could not keep it. Neither getting it nor losing it had anything to do with me." Such a man, comments Zhuangzi through the mouth of none other than Confucius, is "a real person of old."

This phrase, "a real person of old," shows that the concept of the "real person" is associated from the very first with the notion of a golden age in times past, a paradise lost. On the individual level, it is linked with the preservation of one's original purity and integrity; "The way of whiteness and purity consists exclusively in keeping one's spirit. If you keep your spirit and do not lose it, you will become one with your spirit" (*Zhuangzi,* chap. 15).

Zhuangzi makes no explicit reference to the techniques that enable one to maintain one's purity and "keep" one's spirit, but they are implicit in the vocabulary used to describe the "real persons of old." The reference to these techniques is even clearer in another third-century BCE text, the *Lushi chunqiu* (Annals of Mr. Lu): "One who daily renews his seminal energy and gets rid entirely of perverse energies, and [so] lives out his heaven [-appointed] years, is called a 'real person.'" The reference is all the more interesting in that the next line reads: "The saint-kings of the past perfected their persons, and the empire then perfected itself. They regulated their bodies, and the empire was regulated." To solve the crisis of the body politic, says this author, we must find individuals who, like the saints of old, concentrate on the vital energies of their own bodies.

A long dissertation on the Daoist ideal in chapter 7 of the *Huainanzi* by Liu An (c. 180–122 BCE) adds little of substance to Zhuangzi's conception of the "real person." Liu An's language, however, is more explicitly physiological and cosmological: the essence of the "saintly person" or "real person"—the terms remain interchangeable—is "one with the root of Great Purity, and he wanders in the realm of no-form. . .He makes ghosts and gods to do his bidding." In chapter 14 we learn that the "real person" has such cosmic powers because he has "never become distinct from the Great One." By "closing up his four gates"—the eyes, ears, mouth, and heart—and keeping his vital forces from being wasted on the outside, he "regulates what is within and knows nothing of what is without" (chap. 7).

The *Huainanzi* is no more specific about how to become a "real person" than the *Zhuangzi.* But Liu An's "real person" is obviously far less concerned with the world of politics and society than the "real person" of Zhuangzi, and he is correspondingly more concerned with his interior world of spirits, souls, and oneness. Within the scope of that world, moreover, he has attained what can only be called superhuman powers. These powers are precisely those later ascribed to exorcists and Daoist priests.

A wide range of techniques leading not just to supernatural powers but to immortality are described in the *Liexian zhuan* (Biographies of the immortals, second century CE). The "way of the immortals" might involve a diet of pine seeds or sap, of mushrooms, or simply of clouds; it might mean the ingestion of a variety of elixirs or mineral drugs, the "circulation of energy and the transmutation of the body," the elimination of the five cereals from one's diet, or "nourishing one's energy." "Nourishing one's energy" usually refers to an art of intercourse in which the semen, rather than being allowed to flow out of the body, is "returned" by way of the spinal column to "repair the brain." In the *Liexian zhuan* this technique is specifically attributed to Laozi, who is one of only three immortals in this text to be called a "real person."

The second, Master Fuju, makes a living as a wandering mirror-polisher in the region of Wu (southeastern China). He also regularly heals sick clients with "purple pills and red drugs," and the local people first recognize in him a "real person" when he saves thousands from an epidemic with his medicine. Later, before leaving for one of the "isles of the immortals" in the Eastern Sea, he creates a stream with miraculous healing powers for the local people, who, after his departure, set up dozens of sanctuaries for his worship. The third "real person," Zhuhuang, is himself first cured of an ailment by a "Daoist" *(daoshi)* living on a mountain and is then given a book called *Laojun huangting jing* (The Yellow court classic of Lord Lao). When he finally returns home eighty years later, "his white hair had all turned black."

In his *Lunheng* (Critical disquisitions), Wang Chong (27–97 CE) refers to the belief that Laozi became a "real person" by "nourishing his spermatic essence and being chary of his energy" (chap. 7). A commentary from the second century CE on the *Laozi,* the *Heshang gong,* confirms that the "real person" is one who "cultivates the Dao within his body by being chary of his energy and by nourishing his spirits" (chap. 54). The first glimpse of what all this means comes from the oldest extant version of *The Yellow Court Classic,* which alludes to the "Real-Person Infant Elixir" inside the body.

The *Laojun zhong jing* (Classic on the center of the person, second century CE) identifies the "Real-Person Infant Elixir" as the "father and mother of the Dao, [those who] give birth to the infant" (1.6b). He (or she) is also called the "master of the real self, who is constantly instructing me in the techniques of eternal life, the way of gods and immortals" (1.7b). This internal "real person" also appears in the *Taishang lingbao wu-fu xu* (Preface to the five symbols of the numinous treasure of the Most High), a work of the fourth century. The main technique for obtaining immortality described in this text involves absorption of the energies of the heavens of the five directions. The energies of the center are used to nourish the "real person" whose name is Infant Elixir, and who dwells in the Yellow Court.

Every adept thus contains within his or her body a "real person" in embryo. It is the adept's "real self," and if it is properly fed and instructed, it will grow up to replace entirely the "old self." For this nourishment and instruction it relies on what Zhuangzi called "real persons of the past": in the text of *The Five Symbols,* for example, it is the Real Person of Bell Mountain who reveals to the legendary Emperor Yu the "oral instructions for the way to eternal life" (1.6a). When a hermit later explores a cave in which Yu had buried a set of the five symbols called "real writs," he discovers it to be a "residence full of real persons" (1.9a). The most important of the myriads of "real persons" who come thus to inhabit Daoist caves and heavens is Laozi himself, who is in fact already the real self the adept will become.

In general, the religious content of the term *real person,* implicit already in the *Zhuangzi,* becomes entirely explicit by the fourth and fifth centuries: he or she is the revealer of sacred texts. The revelations on Mount Mao (Maoshan), for example, which date to the years 364 to 370 and which form the scriptural basis for the Maoshan tradition, are almost all attributed to *zhenren,* many of whom are female. The Lingbao canon of the late fourth/early fifth century also contains texts ascribed to real persons. But an even more important development is their appearance on the ritual arena, where "flags of the real persons" are hung up to mark the Gate of All Real Persons. According to a text attributed to Lu Xiujing (406–477), this gate represents the divinized spirits of the sacred mountains and rivers of China. The gods of the Five Sacred Peaks, in particular, are referred to as real persons, a usage that was continued in the Tang dynasty (618–907 CE), when Sima Chengzhen convinced Emperor Xuanzong (r. 713–756) to replace the worship of the blood-eating gods of these mountains with the vegetarian real persons of Daoist worship. The same emperor in fact considered himself a *zhenren* and had his statue set up next to that of his divine ancestor, Laozi, to illustrate his semi-divine status. He also conferred the title real person on four Daoist philosophers, among them Zhuangzi.

By the Song dynasty (960–1279), living Daoists were also being called "real persons." The title of the massive Yuan collection of Daoist hagiographies, the *Lishi zhenxian tidao tongjian* (Comprehensive mirror of the real persons and immortals who have embodied the Dao through the ages), shows that *real person* and *immortal* had become synonymous terms that could be combined to refer to any Daoist of some renown. Among the most famous were the seven disciples of the founder of the Quanzhen movement, known collectively as the Seven Real Persons.

SEE ALSO Alchemy, article on Chinese Alchemy; Daoism, overview article; Laozi; Priesthood, article on Daoist Priesthood; Zhuangzi.

BIBLIOGRAPHY

Translations

Erkes, Eduard, trans. *Ho-shang kung's Commentary on Lao tse.* Ascona, Switzerland, 1950.

Forke, Alfred, trans. *Lun-hêng* (1907–1911). 2d ed. 2 vols. New York, 1962.

Lau, D. C., trans. *Tao-te ching* (1963). Reprint, New York, 1976.

Le Blanc, Charles, Rémi Mathieu, et al., trans. *Huainan zi.* Paris, 2003. Complete translation with excellent introductions to each chapter.

Ware, James Roland, trans. *Alchemy, Medicine, Religion in the China of A. D. 320: The Nei P'ien of Ko Hung* (1967). Reprint, New York, 1981.

Watson, Burton, trans. *The Complete Works of Chuang Tzu.* New York, 1968.

Wilhelm, Richard, trans. *Frühling und Herbst des Lü Bu We* (1928). Reprint, Düsseldorf, Germany, 1971. A translation of the *Lushi chunqiu*

Translations with Studies

Chan, Alan K. L. *Two Visions of the Way: A Study of the Wang Pi and the Ho-shang Kung Commentaries on the Lao-Tzu.* Albany, N.Y., 1991.

Kaltenmark, Max, trans. *Le Lie-sien tchouan, biographies légendaires des immortels taoïstes de l'antiquité.* Beijing, 1953; reprint, Paris, 1987. Contains superb notes on each of the seventy biographies of the immortals.

Schipper, Kristofer. *Le corps taoïste.* Paris, 1982. Translated by Karen Duval as *The Taoist Body.* Berkeley, 1993. Contains good introductions to and partial translations of the *Huang-t'ing ching* (chap. 6) and the *Laojün zhong jing* (chap. 8).

The Tang Changes

Benn, Charles David. "Taoism as Ideology in the Reign of Emperor Hsüan-tsung (712–755)," Ph.D. diss., University of Michigan, Ann Arbor, 1977.

Benn, Charles David. *The Cavern-Mystery Transmission: A Taoist Ordination Rite of A.D. 711.* Honolulu, 1991.

JOHN LAGERWEY (1987 AND 2005)

ZHENYAN Buddhism is a form of Vajrayāna Buddhism that flourished in China from the seventh to the twelfth century. The term *zhenyan* is a translation of the Sanskrit word *mantra* and literally means "real word." The school is also called Mijiao (esoteric teaching) to distinguish it both from all other forms of Buddhism, which are regarded as exoteric, and from Indo-Tibetan Vajrayāna. The Chinese translation of *mantra* by the word *zhenyan* underscores the importance of a realized ontology. *Zhen* designates the real, apprehended through words, meditation, and action: it is reality realized.

Although the term *zhenyan* is conventionally used to designate sectarian lineages during the Tang (618–907) and Song (960–1278) dynasties, it may also indicate Tantric precursors of the organized lineages and the continued presence of Zhenyan elements in other sects and in popular cults.

HISTORY. Buddhism spread across Asia on two levels: clerics with a theological bent missionized the literate elite while healers and wonder-workers ministered to the peasants. Early proto-Tantric materials in China appear at both levels, although their application is largely associated with wonder-workers. Zhu Lüyan translated the first text containing *dhāraṇīs,* the *Modengqie jing* (T.D. no. 1300), in 230 CE, yet there is little evidence that it aroused interest at the Wu court in the South. Fotudeng (d. 348) worked among the people and served the rough latter Zhao emperors Shi Luo (r. 330–333) and Shi Hu (r. 333–348) with a repertoire of mantras and *dhāraṇīs.* Like later Zhenyan masters, he used ritual to bring rain, to make military prognostications, to heal, and to influence politics.

During the Six Dynasties period (221–584), the magical use of mantra and *dhāraṇī* found greater acceptance in North China while other Buddhist traditions dominated the literary culture of the South. The unification of China under the Sui (584–618) and Tang dynasties wedded the interests, culture, and family lines of the barbarian North with those of the Han South. Meanwhile in India, Tantric ritual, spurned earlier as heterodox by the Buddhist establishment, was being codified and blended with Mahāyāna theology, resulting in the formation of the Vajrayāna. During the first century of Tang rule other Buddhist schools held sway, and Daoists were patronized by emperors who made much of the fact that they bore the surname (Li) of the sage Laozi.

Tantric teachings remained eclipsed until the arrival of Śubhākarasiṃha (Shanwuwei) in 716 and his translation of the *Mahāvairocana Sūtra* (T.D. no. 848). Vajrabodhi (Jin'gangzhi) and his disciple Amoghavajra (Bukong) arrived in 720 and produced two selective translations of the *Sarvatathāgatatattvasaṃgraha* (T.D. no. 866, 865). For the next fifty years the wonder-working abilities of these *ācāryas* (teachers) and the prestige of their newly imported teachings bolstered the school until, under Amoghavajra and Emperor Daizong (r. 762–779), Zhenyan replaced Daoism as the dominant religious force among the elite.

During the Tang there were two closely related Zhenyan lineages. Śubhākarasiṃha and his disciple Yixing concentrated on the *Mahāvairocana Sūtra* and its *Commentary* (T.D. no. 1796) and on the *Susiddhikāra Sūtra* (T.D. no. 893). Vajrabodhi, Amoghavajra, and Amoghavajra's disciples Hanguang, Huiguo, and others concentrated on the *Sarvatathāgatatattvasaṃgraha* and also incorporated teachings associated with the *Mahāvairocana Sūtra.* Thus, each lineage had a characteristic textual emphasis. Only the best disciples were initiated into both. Amoghavajra's synthesis was the most influential, although the lineage and teachings of Śubhākarasiṃha continued to be transmitted. Both lineages had links to non-Esoteric sects; that of Śubhākarasiṃha has great influence in Tiantai, while that of Vajrabodhi developed links to Huayan. A similar situation developed in Japan as the Shingon and Tendai Esoteric lineages (Tōmitsu and Taimitsu, respectively) interacted with each other and with other sects. Following Amoghavajra's death in 774 his disciples continued to perform rituals in the Imperial Chapel, at the Green Dragon and Da Xingshan temples in Chang'an, and at the Golden Pavilion on Mount Wutai. At the beginning of the ninth century Japanese clerics such as Saichō (767–822), the founder of Tendai, and Kūkai (774–835), founder of Shingon and disciple of Huiguo, studied the teachings in China. Zhenyan continued to be popular at the court and spread among the upper classes in the provinces. It suffered during the Huichang persecution of 845 but was not completely extinguished.

Zhenyan showed renewed vitality during the Song dynasty owing to a final wave of missionaries from India. Shihu, Fatian, and Faxian presided over an Esoteric revival, translating new scriptures and producing complete translations of earlier works, such as Shihu's 1002 CE version of the *Sarvatathāgatatattvasaṃgraha* (T.D. no. 882). Zhenyan ritual elements continued to penetrate other Buddhist sects and when its lineages died these elements continued in the other sects and in popular traditions. Esoteric Buddhism had two further revivals. The first was under the impact of Lamaism during the Yuan (1206–1368), the second during the nineteenth century with the reintroduction of the school from Japan.

TEXTS. Zhenyan teachings are drawn from two major texts, the *Mahāvairocana Sūtra* and the *Sarvatathāgatatattvasaṃgraha.* The *Mahāvairocana Sūtra* was probably written in North India during the seventh century. The text begins with a theological prolegomenon describing Mahāvairocana Buddha's palace at the summit of the cosmos (Akaniṣṭha Heaven). The palace and the cosmos are manifestations of Mahāvairocana's wondrous transformation power (*adhiṣṭhāna*), which is based on the realization of ultimate unconditioned reality (*śūnyatā*; emptiness). The unconditioned and the cosmos manifested through transformative power are presented as a *maṇḍala,* first as an exterior *maṇḍala,* then as the *maṇḍala* realized ritually in the heart of the practitioner. The massive *Commentary* (T.D. no. 1796), giving Śubhākarasiṃha's oral explanations as recorded by Yixing, is indispensable. Another arrangement of the *Commentary* by Zhiyan and Wengu was influential in Tiantai circles.

There are three versions of the *Sarvatathāgatatattvasaṃgraha,* those of Vajrabodhi (T.D. no. 866), of Amoghavajra (T.D. no. 865), and the complete version of Shihu (T.D. no. 882), which dates from the Song. Those of Vajrabodhi and Amoghavajra are highly abridged selections from the text. The *Saravatathāgatatattvasaṃgraha,* apparently written in South India, also begins in the Akaniṣṭha Heaven and presents a series of *maṇḍalas* based on a fivefold visionary structure through which the *bodhisattva* Sarvārthasiddha realizes his identity with Mahāvairocana as the unconditioned *dharmakāya.* Thus, he also realizes his identity with all of the Buddha's wondrous transformations, which form the conditioned world. Amoghavajra's *Shibahui zhigui* (T.D. no. 869) is important in understanding the *Tattvasaṃgraha.*

A third text important to the Zhenyan school is the *Susiddhikāra Sūtra* (T.D. no. 893), a ritual compendium translated by Śubhākarasiṃha and closely associated with the *Mahāvairocana Sūtra.* During the ninth century some lineages regarded the *Susiddhikāra Sūtra* as the synthetic conjunction of the *Mahāvairocana Sūtra* and the *Sarvatathāgatatattvasaṃgraha,* calling Zhenyan the "Triple Great Dharma." Some of Amoghavajra's disciples referred to the total Zhenyan teaching as "the Manuals of *Siddhi,* the Eighteen Assemblies [of the *Sarvatathāgatatattvasaṃgraha*], and the Mahākaruṇāgarbha Maṇḍala [of the *Mahāvairocana Sūtra*]" (T.D. 50.294b).

TEACHINGS. The basic teachings of Zhenyan are common to both textual traditions. Zhenyan teaches the ritual realization of the paradoxical identity of *nirvāṇa* and *saṃsāra,* of the unconditioned and the world, of Buddha and humans. This conjunction is a primary organizing motif in the major texts and in Chinese commentary and ritual adaptions.

The Three Mysteries. Zhenyan proclaims the goal of enlightenment in this world, in this body, not in some distant land aeons hence. According to the *Mahāvairocana Sūtra,* "the complete Zhenyan altar is first established in your own body. . . . [Mahāvairocana] is in this body" (T.D.

18.36c). This immanental realization and a closely guarded initiatory structure distinguish Zhenyan from exoteric Buddhism. Enlightment is actualized in ritual through the three mysteries (Chin., *sanmi*; Skt., *triguhya*) of body, speech, and mind. The practitioner realizes that his body, speech, and consciousness in meditation are identical with those of Mahāvairocana. The Three Mysteries therefore allow the practitioner to realize that *bodhi,* the thought of enlightenment, exists within us. Enlightenment is accomplished through a ritual realization of the enlightened state guided by iconographic, mantric, and meditational conventions.

A key to realizing the Three Mysteries is meditation on the Sanskrit seed syllable *A.* The *Mahāvairocana Sūtra* says, "What is the Zhenyan Dharma? It is [the teaching of] the letter *A*" (T.D. 18.10a). *A,* the first letter in the Sanskrit alphabet, is also a negative prefix. Thus, it represents the conjunction of the conditioned and the unconditioned, of *saṃsāra* and *nirvāṇa,* and is the symbol of Mahāvairocana and of *bodhi.* Through ritual and meditation this seed is nurtured in the heart, and the meditator becomes Mahāvairocana.

Bodhisattva path. In Mahāyāna Buddhism the path toward Buddhahood is the arduous one of the *bodhisattva.* It begins with the arousal of the thought of enlightenment (*bodhicitta*) and passes through ten stages over a period of three great *kalpa*s (aeons). Zhenyan collapses the path into a ritual process; the three *kalpa*s are interpreted not as units of time but as defilements to be eliminated. "If one transcends the three *kalpa*s in one's lifetime, then in one life one attains Buddhahood. Why should time be discussed?" (T.D. 39.600c). From the Esoteric perspective, the last stage of the path is contained in the first. Thus, there are two interpretations of the statement in the *Mahāvairocana Sūtra* that "*bodhi* is the cause, compassion (*karuṇā*) the root, skill in means (*upāya*) the outcome" (T.D. 18.1b–1c). The exoteric view indicates the development of the *bodhisattva* through time. From the Esoteric viewpoint, all three—*bodhi,* compassion, and skill in means, the beginning, middle, and end of the path—are accomplished ritually as a piece. They are a whole, as are roots, trunk, and branches of a tree. Zhenyan collapses the beginning and end of the path: the disciple and the Buddha are really identical.

The goal: siddhi. Success in Zhenyan ritual is called *siddhi* (accomplishment; Chin., *chengjiu*). There are two major typologies of *siddhi.* The first is found in the *Mahāvairocana Sūtra* and is associated with the lineage of Amoghavajra; the second is propounded in the *Susiddhikāra Sūtra* and in Śubhākarasiṃha's *Commentary.* According to the *Mahāvairocana Sūtra,* mundane, or outer *siddhi* (*laukikasiddhi*) is overtly aimed at the application of wondrous transformative powers (skill in means) to aid in the salvation of beings. Supermundane, or inner, *siddhi* (*lokottarasiddhi*) is aimed at the achievement of enlightenment. All Zhenyan ritual has both components. Burnt offerings (*homa*), for example, involve placing things in a fire and might be performed to expel invading armies. The same rite has an inner meaning: one's defilements are incinerated and enlightenment attained. Ritual activity in the world, which is performed for the salvation of beings, is paradoxically an exercise in one's own enlightenment. The second typology of *siddhi,* which may reflect Tiantai or even Daoist influence, posits three levels of *siddhi*: superior, middling, and inferior. Superior *siddhi* is said to lead to transcendence and emptiness. Middling *siddhi* leads to the various heavenly realms, while inferior *siddhi* leads to command of illusion. We are further told that inferior *siddhi* may yield superior attainment and vice versa (T.D. 18.614a–614c).

BUDDHOLOGY. Zhenyan teaching on the nature and function of the Buddha is similar to that of other Vajrayāna traditions. Zhenyan posits two theories concerning the Buddha's bodies. The first is the triple-body theory. The *dharmakāya,* or body of *dharma,* represents the unconditioned thought of enlightenment in itself; *saṃbhogakāya,* or body of bliss, represents the wondrous powers achieved through compassionate deeds; *nirmāṇakāya* is the form taken by a Buddha to apply those powers in aid of suffering beings. The three bodies thus parallel the triade *bodhi,* compassion, and skill in means. In Zhenyan ritual, the three bodies are realized simultaneously. Enlightenment and salvific activity form a conjunction in compassion. The consecration ritual (*abhiṣeka*) is therefore the paradigm of all ritual, for in it the disciple is consecrated as *saṃbhogakāya. Bodhi* (*dharmakāya*) and skill and means (*nirmāṇakāya*) are joined in compassion (*saṃbhogakāya*). The second theory distinguishes three wheel bodies (*san lunshen, tricakrakāya*). The first wheel, *svabhāvacakrakāya,* is Buddhahood in itself. It manifests itself in beneficent or horrific forms. Beneficent manifestations such as Avalokiteśvara (Guanyin) practice compassion and, according to Amoghavajra, are equivalent to the *saṃbhogakāya.* Horrific manifestations such as the *vidyārāja*s Trilokyavijaya and Acala, utilize skill in means to chastise and discipline beings. The Three Wheels are ultimately one. Much of Zhenyan ritual is devoted to the third wheel.

The two *maṇḍalas*. Unlike most Vajrayāna traditions, Zhenyan focuses on a pair of *maṇḍala*s, the Womb Maṇḍala, drawn primarily from the *Mahāvairocana Sūtra,* and the Diamond Maṇḍala, drawn from the *Sarvatathāgatatattvasaṃgraha.* The Womb Maṇḍala of Great Compassion (Mahākaruṇā-garbhodbhāva Maṇḍala) is a graphic representation of the cosmos as the wondrous transformations, born of compassion and based on *bodhi,* of Mahāvairocana. The term *garbha* has two meanings. It is *bodhi,* the embryo of enlightenment present in all beings, as well as the womb of compassion and skill in means in which the embryo grows. The *maṇḍala* has three courts. The first is an eight-petaled lotus on which Mahāvairocanais enthroned amid four buddhas and four *bodhisattvas.* This court represents the seed of *bodhi,* of enlightened wisdom present in the cosmos. An intermediate court is dominated by beneficent manifestations that embody compassion, such as Avalokiteśvara, Mañjuśrī, and Kṣitigarbha. The Court of the Outer *Vajra*s represents

Māhavairocana's skill in means as manifested through the *vidyārājas* and the Hindu gods in the traditional Buddhist six destinies (*gati*). Thus the *maṇḍala* embodies the triade *bodhi,* compassion, and skill in means.

The Diamond Maṇḍala is actually a selection of nine *maṇḍalas* from the many presented in the *Sarvatathāgatatattvasaṃgraha.* The central *maṇḍala,* the Vajradhātu Mahāmaṇḍala, is the most important since the others are derived from it. The Vajradhātu Mahāmaṇḍala represents the fivefold wisdom that is the basis of enlightenment. The *maṇḍala* has three courts. The first is the Akaniṣṭha Palace of Mahāvairocana, who is enthroned on a lunar disk and surrounded by four Buddhas representative of aspects of his wisdom. Surrounding the palace are the Buddhas of the past, present, and future (the *bhadrakalpa*), whose compassion causes the enlightenment of beings. The outer perimeter of the *maṇḍala* is populated by twenty Hindu divinities who act as protectors of the Dharma. Each of the other *maṇḍalas* described in the *Sarvatathāgatatattvasaṃgraha* focuses on a particular aspect of the whole.

Both the Womb Maṇḍala and the Diamond Maṇḍala are external projections of a reality that must be realized internally through the Three Mysteries. Each *maṇḍala* and each of the two texts has a separate initiatory tradition through which the disciple ritually realizes the reality of Mahāvairocana in the center of the cosmos.

ZHENYAN AS CHINESE VAJRAYĀNA. The Zhenyan *ācāryas* lived in a great cosmopolitan city, Chang'an, a milieu in which Confucian, Buddhist, and Daoist, and even Muslim and Nestorian ideas were freely exchanged. Many of Zhenyan's distinctive teachings were articulated for this audience. Zhenyan's preoccupation with two *maṇḍalas* is a distinctively Chinese adaption of Vajrayāna teachings. Since the two textual lineages came to be regarded as a pair, the *maṇḍalas* drawn from them also constitute a pair. Just as each *maṇḍala* expresses the conjunction of conditioned and unconditioned reality, so too, during the late eighth century, did the pair became a graphic shorthand for that conjunction. Through a reinterpretation of Chinese philosophical categories the Womb Maṇḍala was said to represent Mahāvairocana's numinous reality *(li), bodhi* as universally present in the Buddha's compassionate activities. The Diamond Maṇḍala represented the enlightened mind in itself, wisdom *(zhi).* There is evidence that this synthesis was taught by Amoghavajra's disciple Huiguo, and it may even have been initiated by Amoghavajra.

Another distinctive innovation is the selection of nine *maṇḍalas* from the *Sarvatathāgatatattvasaṃgraha* and their arrangement in a three by three square. The configuration is clearly based on the *Luoshu,* one of a pair of ancient Chinese cosmograms representing the earthly realm. This cosmogram was the basis of an imperially sponsored Daoist cult of Taiyi (surpassing unity), in which the sovereign of the universe circulated through a court of nine thrones. Moreover, Amoghavajra changed the *maṇḍala*'s traditional Indian attributions. Mahāvairocana, formerly associated with the color blue and the element ether, was now associated with yellow and earth, the traditional attributes of the Chinese sovereign and those chosen by the Tang rulers. It is even possible that the paired cosmograms, the *Hetu* and the *Luoshu,* influenced Zhenyan's pair of *maṇḍalas*.

Another Chinese development was Amoghavajra's promotion of Vajrayāna as the best method both for the attainment of enlightenment and for the protection of the state. Such a teaching appealed to the mid-Tang emperors, for it joined lofty theological pursuits with practical application, and after the An Lushan rebellion the emperor needed all the aid he could get. A series of rites was developed for the protection of the state, for the prolongation of the emperor's life, for the salvation of the imperial ancestors, and for the propagation of rain. The emperor was hailed as a *cakravartin,* the universal worldly ruler and counterpart of the Buddha. The state was portrayed as a Buddha land.

The promotion of the state cult focused on deities who were compassionately active in the world. The *vidyārājas*, or protectors, were important, as were Avalokiteśvara and Kṣitigarbha, both of whom figured prominently in rites for dead imperial ancestors. Mañjuśrī and Samantabhadra, representing wisdom and the fulfillment of vows, were frequently paired, as for instance, at the Golden Pavilion on Mount Wutai and in Taiyuan, the imperial clan seat.

THE LEGACY OF ZHENYAN. Although sectarian Zhenyan disappeared after the Song dynasty, it had widespread influence on Chinese Buddhism. The use of mantra and *dhāraṇī* permeated other Buddhist groups, including some Pure Land and Chan sects. Tales of wonder-working *ācāryas* added to popular lore. Zhenyan and Daoism influenced each other. During the Six Dynasties, Tantric rituals such as consecration (*abhiṣeka*) and pseudo-Sanskrit mantras were already in use in Daoist circles. Zhenyan ritual structures, used in rites for imperial ancestors, and even some of the divinities, such as Dizang (Kṣitigarbha), were emulated in Daoist Esoteric rites dating from the Song. These ancestor rites have remained an economic mainstay for both the Daoists and the Buddhists. The tremendous increase in the popularity of Guanyin during the Tang and Song is also attributable in part to Zhenyan. Guanyin, in one form or another, is invoked in many of Zhenyan's public rites. Thus, even after its demise as a recognizable sect, Zhenyan continued to shape Chinese tradition. Finally, it transformed Japanese Buddhism through the teachings of such clerics as Saichō and Kūkai, who formally introduced the sect to Japan.

SEE ALSO Amoghavajra; Avalokiteśvara; Bodhisattva Path; Buddhas and Bodhisattvas; Buddhism, Schools of; Karuṇā; Kṣitigarbha; Mahāsiddhas; Mahāvairocana; Maṇḍalas, article on Buddhist Maṇḍalas; Mañjuśrī; Nirvāṇa; Prajñā; Saichō; Shingonshū; Soteriology; Śubhākarasiṃha; Upāya; Vajrabodhi.

BIBLIOGRAPHY

Works in Western Languages

The only work available in a Western language that is devoted exclusively to Zhenyan is Chou I-liang's monograph-length article "Tantrism in China," *Harvard Journal of Asiatic Studies* 8 (March 1945): 241–332, an annotated translation of the standard biographies of Śubhākarasiṃha, Vajrabodhi, and Amoghavajra. Amoghavajra's role in the court with particular reference to the Golden Pavilion on Mount Wutai and the cult of Mañjuśrī is discussed in Raoul Birnbaum's *Studies on the Mysteries of Mañjuśrī* (Boulder, Colo., 1983). The Japanese monk Ennin gives us an eyewitness account of Zhenyan just before the persecution of 845 in his diary, translated by Edwin O. Reischauer as *Ennin's Diary: The Record of a Pilgrimage to China in Search of the Law* (New York, 1955). Fotudeng's exploits are recounted by Arthur F. Wright in "Fo-t'u-têng: A Biography," *Harvard Journal of Asiatic Studies* 11 (1948): 321–371. There are several studies of Shingon, the Japanese offspring of Zhenyan, that cover material in Zhenyan history and texts. These studies present valuable material but must be used with caution, as they advance Shingon interpretations of Zhenyan; these interpretations are not always faithful to those of the Zhenyan masters. In English, see Yoshito S. Hakeda's *Kūkai: Major Works* (New York, 1972) and Minoru Kiyota's *Shingon Buddhism* (Los Angeles, 1978).

On the *maṇḍalas*, Beatrice Lane Suzuki's article on the Womb Maṇḍala, "Shingon School of Mahāyāna Buddhism: II, The Mandara," *Eastern Buddhist* 7 (May 1936): 1–38, is helpful. Anesaki Masaharu's "Buddhist Cosmotheism and the Symbolism of Its Art," in his *Buddhist Art in Relation to Buddhist Ideals* (1915; reprint, New York, 1978), is brief but insightful. More difficult to find are two works in French by the Shingon priest Tajima Ryūjun: *Les deux grands maṇḍalas et la doctrine de l'ésotérisme Shingon* (Paris, 1959) and *Étude sur le Mahāvairocana-sūtra* (Paris, 1936). The best full-color illustrations appear in Pierre Rambach's *The Sacred Message of Tantric Buddhism,* translated by Barbara Bray (New York, 1979).

Works in Asian Languages

There is as little secondary material on the Zhenyan school in Chinese as there is an overabundance of it in Japanese. Chinese scholarship on Buddhism has suffered through a period of relative decline in interest during the nineteenth and early twentieth century and then through a period of outright supression during the second half of the twentieth century. Scholarship on Buddhism, Daoism, and other religious traditions is beginning to revive, but for the moment one must make do with a few works that present a decidedly Marxist reading of Zhenyan in particular and of Chinese Buddhism in general. The most extensive and informative work is Guo Ming's treatment of Esoteric Buddhism in his *Sui-Tang fojiao* (Ji'nan, 1980), pp. 573–610. More heavy-handed Marxist interpretations are Gao Guanru's entry on Esoteric Buddhism in *Zhongguo fojiao,* vol. 1 (Beijing, 1980), pp. 312–318, and Fan Wenlan's *Tangdai fojiao* (Beijing, 1979), pp. 36–46.

There is a wide range of secondary works in Japanese, but nearly all treat Zhenyan from the perspective of Shingon. The best of these, however, are distinguished by careful scholarship and sophisticated historical and doctrinal reasoning. Matsunaga Yūkei's *Mikkyō no rekishi* (Kyoto, 1969) is comprehensive, readable, and views Esoteric Buddhism in the context of the Tantric systems of India and Tibet. Although old, somewhat hard to find, conservative, and written in Classical Chinese, Omura Seigai's *Mikkyō hattatsushi,* 5 vols. (1918; reprint, Tokyo, 1972) is by far the best textual history of Zhenyan. Finally, I would still recommend two old works by Toganoo Shoun. His *Himitsu bukkyōshi* (Kyoto, 1933), which was reprinted as vol. 9 of *Gendai bukkyō meicho zenshū,* edited by Nakamura Hajime, Masutani Fumio, and Joseph M. Kitagawa (Tokyo, 1964), provides excellent historical coverage, and his *Mandara no kenkyū* (Kyoto, 1936), which chronicles the development and use of *maṇḍalas* in Esoteric Buddhism beginning in India, has yet to be surpassed. Most Japanese works still hold that Tantra emerged in Buddhism at the time of its first textual appearance, that is in the seventh century. Alex Wayman has recently put forward persuasive arguments for dating some Buddhist Tantric texts some three to four centuries earlier in "The Early History of the Buddhist Tantras, Especially the Guhyasamāja Tantra," in his *The Buddhist Tantras: Light on Indo-Tibetan Esoterism* (New York, 1973).

New Sources

Abe, R. *The Weaving of Mantra: Kukai and the Construction of Esoteric Buddhist Discourse.* New York, 1999.

Brown, R. L. *Ganesh: Studies of an Asian God.* Albany, N.Y., 1991.

Chen, Jinhua. "The Construction of Early Tendai Esoteri Buddhism: The Japanese Provenance of Saicho's Transmission Documents and Three Esoteric Buddhist Apocrypha Attributed to Subhakarasimha." *Journal of the International Association of Buddhist Studies* 21, no. 1 (1998): 21–76.

Lopez, Donald S., Jr., ed. *Buddhism in Practice.* Princeton, 1995.

Meisig, M. *Die "China-Lehre" des Saktismus: Mahacinacara-Tantra.* Wiesbaden, 1988.

Orzech, Charles D. "Seeing Zhenyan Buddhism: Traditional Scholarship and the Vajrayana in China." *History of Religions* 29 (1989): 87–114.

Watt, Paul B. "Tantric Buddhism in China." In *Buddhist Spirituality,* edited by Takeuchi Yoshinori, pp. 397–404. New York, 1993.

Yamamoto, C., and International Academy of Indian Culture. *Mahavairocana-sutra: Translated into English from Ta-p'i lu che na ch'eng-fo shen-pien chia-ch'ih ching, the Chinese Version of Subhakarasimha and I-hsing, A.D. 725.* New Delhi, 1990.

CHARLES D. ORZECH (1987)
Revised Bibliography

ZHIYAN (602–668), second patriarch of the Huayan school of Buddhism in China. Born in the town of Tianshui near Chang'an, the capital of the Tang dynasty, Zhiyan was the son of an official in Shenzhou province. When Zhiyan was twelve years old his family was visited by the first patriarch of the Huayan school, Dushun, who claimed that Zhiyan was his son and should be returned to him. This declaration was taken by Zhiyan's parents to mean that Zhiyan was to become a Buddhist monk, and they thus entrusted him to Dushun.

Ordained in 615, Zhiyan studied Buddhism, mainly the thought of the *She dasheng lun (Mahāyānasaṃgraha)* and, later, the thought of the *Huayan jing (Mahāvaipulya-buddhagaṇḍavyūha Sūtra),* under many famous Buddhists. During this period he also mastered Sanskrit. His reading of the *Huayan jing shu* (Commentary on the *Huayan jing*) by Huiguang, the founder of the Nandao branch of the Dilun school, greatly contributed to his religious development. Shortly after this he met a monk who taught him to consider the meaning [of] the Huayan teaching of *liuxiang* ("six aspects" of reality). At the age of twenty-seven, having followed this monk's teaching, he is said to have realized the truth of the "One Vehicle." Thereafter, he wrote his commentary on the *Huayan jing,* the *Souxuan ji.* By pursuing this religious path Zhiyan became the leader of the Huayan school at the Zhixiang Si on Mount Zhongnan. Although Zhiyan did not seek social influence, honor, and wealth, he did engage in social activity when, late in his life, he became a private teacher of Xian, the king of Pei. This occurred while he was staying at the Yunhua Si in Chang'an.

Zhiyan's greatest influence was in the development and systematization of Huayan doctrine. His work was to pave the way for Fazang's subsequent completion of Huayan thought. Zhiyan created the method of classifying the Buddhist teachings into five grades, arranged according to the subtlety of the doctrines, and founded the teaching of *fajie yuanqi* ("dependent origination of the True Realm"). These doctrines were given their final form by Fazang, one of his disciples. However, Zhiyan had his own character, one different from both those of his teachers and of his disciples. For example, he placed high emphasis on Tanqian's *Wangshifei lun,* a work that praised what it termed *wuxin* ("the mind beyond functions"), a mental state based upon the thought of Zhuangzi, and esteemed Xinxing's Sect of the Three Stages, which was generally treated as heretical. Zhiyan's extant works are as follows:

1. *Souxuan ji* (T.D. no. 1732)
2. *Yisheng shixuan men* (T.D. no. 1868)
3. *Wushiyao wenda* (T.D. no. 1869)
4. *Huayan jing kongmu zhang* (T.D. no. 1870)
5. *Jin'gang jing lüeshu* (T.D. no. 1704)

Zhiyan had two disciples of special importance for the tradition. The first, Fazang (643–712), went on to become the great systematizer and so-called third "patriarch" of Huayan Buddhism in China. Through his efforts, Huayan became one of the prestigious and lavishly patronized traditions of the Tang dynasty (618–907). The other, Uisang (625–702), returned to his native Korean state of Silla and was instrumental in establishing Huayan as one of the most important Buddhist traditions there.

See Also Fazang; Huayan; Ŭisang.

Bibliography

Kamata Shigeo. *Chugoku kengonshisoshi no kenkyu.* Tokyo, 1965. Pages 79–106 discuss Zhiyan's importance to the Huayan tradition.

Kimura Kiyotaka. *Shoki chugoku kegonshiso no kenkyu.* Tokyo, 1977. This work, a comprehensive study of early Huayan Buddhism, focuses on Zhiyan's thought.

Kimura Kiyotaka (1987)

ZHIYI

ZHIYI (538–597), third patriarch of the influential Tiantai school of Chinese Buddhism. This man is often regarded as having united Chinese Buddhism into a coherent whole by resolving doctrinal and practical strains that had plagued Buddhism virtually from the time of its introduction into China. His literary output was prodigious: about one thousand pages of the *Taishō* edition of the Chinese Buddhist canon are devoted to his extant works, a sum that would correspond to about nine thousand pages in unannotated English translation.

More important, however, than the sheer volume of his works is their synthesizing nature. Zhiyi was born at a time when Chinese Buddhism was beginning to move from unquestioning fidelity to Indian Mahāyāna doctrines and practices toward a more mature synthesis of Indic and Chinese religious values. Zhiyi was not the only man of his era to contribute to this synthesis: it is well known, for instance, that he borrowed heavily from the "three southern and seven northern" teachers in constructing his own system of doctrinal classification (*panjiao*). However, Zhiyi's scheme of doctrinal classification proved to be more comprehensive and influential than those of his predecessors and contemporaries, in part because of his success at incorporating religious practice as well as doctrine into his great synthesis. In short, he is credited with having united practice with doctrine and doctrine with practice, whereas his predecessors had attempted only to arrange the various doctrines in the sūtras into an understandable and consistent whole. His role in uniting these two tendencies in Chinese Buddhism has often been compared to the political achievement of his patron Sui Wendi, the first emperor of the Sui dynasty, who succeeded in uniting the north and south of China for the first time in some three and a half centuries. The analogy is apt in that Buddhist historiography commonly views the north of China before the Sui as having been oriented toward the practical side of Buddhism, just as its leaders were men of action, often non-Chinese in ancestry, while the South then tended toward the theoretical or doctrinal side, its leaders and upper classes being aristocrats and Chinese scholar-officials. Thus in uniting doctrine and practice, Zhiyi united southern and northern religious cultures in a way comparable to the feat of his imperial patron. In his own words, these two aspects of Buddhism must be considered analogous to the "two wings of a bird" or the "two wheels of a cart," each valueless without the other. Zhiyi, therefore, was a kind of nodal point in the development of Chinese Buddhism, embracing in his synthesis virtually all that went before, and influencing virtually all that came after.

In terms of formal lineage Zhiyi stands third in the line of Tiantai patriarchs, following the semilegendary Huiwen and the historically attested Huisi. However, Zhiyi is generally regarded as the de facto founder of the Tiantai school, named for the mountain where Zhiyi built his most important monastery. Because it was associated so closely with the rulers of the Sui, Tiantai suffered an eclipse with the rise of the Tang dynasty (618–907 CE), whose rulers were eager to dissociate themselves from the ideological underpinnings of Sui rule. The school was revived a century and a half later by the monk Zhanran (711–782), one of whose disciples transmitted the Tiantai teachings to the Japanese monk Saichō (767–822). Saichō in turn introduced the lineage to Japan, where it soon became the dominant tradition. Its center, Mount Hiei near Kyoto, became the training ground for most of the key figures in the development of Kamakura Buddhism. The Tiantai lineage continues to the present day, with active branches in Taiwan and especially Japan, although nothing is known about the situation in China proper.

Among Zhiyi's works the two most prominent are the *Fahua xuanyi* (Profound meaning of the *Lotus Sūtra*) and the *Mohe zhiguan* (The great calming and contemplation, or The practice of meditation according to the Mahāyāna). The former is his principal work on doctrine, the latter his principal work on practice, but Zhiyi was careful to relate each aspect to the other in both works. He applied a tripartite analysis to both doctrine and practice, which he classified as sudden, gradual, or variable. The "sudden" doctrine (or teaching) refers to the *Avataṃsaka Sūtra*, understood by Zhiyi and some of his predecessors as the text expounded by the Buddha to a mostly uncomprehending audience immediately after his enlightenment. It is referred to as "sudden" because it purports to reveal the Buddha's direct experience of enlightenment just as it is, without making any concessions to the need of its audience for a more "gradual" exposition of the nature of the experience. "Gradual" doctrines (or teachings) refer to the succeeding four stages of the Buddha's teaching, during which he was said to have gradually trained his listeners, in sūtra after sūtra of deepening truth, for the final revelation of the *Lotus* and *Nirvāṇa Sūtras*, commonly believed to be the last discourses of the Buddha. "Sudden meditation" is the kind of meditation expounded in the *Mohe zhiguan*, in which preliminary practices are dispensed with and "ultimate reality is taken as the object of meditation from the very beginning." Gradual meditation, like the gradual teaching, moves step by step toward the goal. Finally, by "variable" Zhiyi meant certain texts and practices that could function as either sudden or gradual, depending upon the level of religious attainment of the practitioner.

The strength of Zhiyi's system lies in its comprehensiveness. By showing how a variety of disparate texts and practices, each of which had its own adherents, could be the product of a historically continuous revelation, beginning with the Buddha's preaching of the *Avataṃsaka Sūtra* and culminating in the message of the *Lotus* and *Nirvāṇa Sūtras*, Zhiyi was able successfully to integrate them all into a single, coherent system. His great synthesis made it possible for the many branches of Chinese Buddhism to be regarded by their adherents as aspects of a loosely integrated, self-consistent whole.

A related and highly influential teaching of Zhiyi is the doctrine of the Three Truths: Empty, Provisional, and—Zhiyi's addition—Middle. This may be regarded as a Chinese emendation, or even improvement, on the pivotal Indian Mahāyāna concept of the Two Truths, first expounded by Nāgārjuna. While the Indians discerned two levels of meaning in the sūtras (i.e., in the Buddha's pronouncements) and regarded the Empty (*śūnya*) as superior to the Provisional, Zhiyi and the Chinese Buddhist tradition after him were uncomfortable with this Indian equation of ultimate truth and emptiness. To them, such a formulation seemed too nihilistic. Zhiyi was able to find passages in Nāgārjuna's works that justified the addition of a third Truth, namely the Middle, which he also styled the Perfect Teaching. This third level of truth became characteristic of the fundamental orientation of Chinese Buddhism, affirming as it does that ultimate reality (or truth) is not to be found apart from mundane reality (or truth), that the world as it is is already identical to the Absolute. The corollary of this doctrine is the assertion that all beings have the buddha nature, that is, that without exception all beings have the capacity for buddhahood. Scarcely any school or teacher in East Asian Buddhism has deviated from these two related teachings, and their influence upon Chan and Zen was particularly significant. While Zhiyi cannot be said to have originated them—he was always careful to provide scriptural citations for his doctrines, and other Chinese monks were exploring similar notions before him—he argued them with greater eloquence and made them an essential part of his incalculably influential summation of Buddhist doctrine and practice.

See Also Tiantai.

Bibliography

Ch'en, Kenneth. *Buddhism in China: A Historical Survey.* Princeton, 1964. The most readable and comprehensive survey available on Chinese Buddhism. One chapter is devoted to Tiantai and discusses Zhiyi.

Hurvitz, Leon N. *Zhiyi (538–597): An Introduction to the Life and Ideas of a Chinese Buddhist Monk.* Brussels, 1962. A wealth of biographical information. However, the sections on Zhiyi's teachings must be used with caution, as the "five periods and eight teachings" delineated here have recently been found to represent not Zhiyi's thought, but that of a much later Korean Tiantai monk.

New Sources

Donner, Neal, and Daniel B. Stevenson. *The Great Calming and Contemplation: A Study and Annotated Translation of the First Chapter of Zhiyi's "Mo-ho chih-kuan."* Honolulu, 1993.

Penkower, Linda. "In the Beginning. . . Guanding (561–632) and the Creation of Early Tiantai." *Journal of the International Association of Buddhist Studies* 23, no. 2 (2000): 245–296.

Swanson, Paul L. *Foundations of T'ien-T'ai Philosophy: The Flowering of the Two Truths Theory in Chinese Buddhism.* Berkeley, 1989.

Swanson, Paul L. "Understanding Zhiyi: Through a Glass, Darkly?" *Journal of the International Association of Buddhist Studies* 17, no. 2 (1994): 337–360.

Swanson, Paul L. "What's Going On Here? Zhiyi's Use (and Abuse) of Scripture." *Journal of the International Association of Buddhist Studies* 20, no. 1 (1997): 1–30.

NEAL DONNER (1987)
Revised Bibliography

ZHOU DUNYI (1017–1073), also known as Zhou Lianxi, was the first major neo-Confucian thinker generally credited with formulating a Confucian cosmology and metaphysics. Zhou Dunyi was a native of Daozhou in modern Hunan province in China. Zhou held a series of modest official positions throughout his career but because he refused to participate in the official civil service examinations, he was limited in the positions he could occupy and never achieved high level appointments with their accompanying status and recognition. He briefly served as tutor to both Cheng Hao (1032–1085) and Cheng Yi (1033–1107), the brothers who were to become major exponents of what later became known as the two principal schools of neo-Confucianism. Apart from his interactions with the Cheng brothers, he was generally not a well known figure until Zhu Xi (1130–1200) later raised his status to one of the founding figures of the neo-Confucian movement. It seems to have been primarily for his role in the development of a neo-Confucian cosmology and metaphysics that Zhou Dunyi was considered by Zhu Xi to be the first teacher in the traditional lineage of neo-Confucians. Zhou Dunyi's major exposition of this cosmology and metaphysics, an interest new to the Confucian school, is found in his two major works, the *Taijitu shuo* (An explanation of the diagram of the Great Ultimate) and the *Tongshu* (Penetrating the book of changes).

At the center of Zhou Dunyi's system of thought lies what is called the Diagram of the Great Ultimate, which may have been transmitted to him by a Daoist priest. For Zhou, the Great Ultimate (*taiji*) is seen as the source of all things in the universe, that which lies both within and behind all things. In its capacity for tranquillity it gives rise to *yin,* the symbol of the mysterious and the female in Chinese thought. In its capacity for activity it gives rise to *yang,* the symbol of the rational and the male. It is the source of the basic patterns or phases of change known as the Five Elements (*wuxing*) and forms the foundation of the two major symbols of the *Yi jing* (Book of changes): *qian,* the heavenly principle, and *kun,* the earthly principle, themselves again symbols of male and female. Humankind in Zhou Dunyi's system receives the highest, most rarefied form of the Five Elements, and thus is seen as capable of playing a critical role in the life of the universe. On this point the system finds its characteristically Confucian focus, for in humankind lies the foundation for understanding the universe as a whole. Particularly in the ideal form as a sage, the human being is the central figure in the universe. In this way, a metaphysical framework is established that incorporates the Confucian emphasis upon the unique relation of humankind and heaven (*tian*) that forms the basic moral structure of the universe.

One of the most frequently debated points of Zhou Dunyi's thought is the first sentence of his *Explanation of the Diagram of the Great Ultimate.* The sentence reads "The Ultimate of Non-being and also the Great Ultimate!" (Chan, 1963, p. 463). The *wuji,* or Ultimate of Non-being, is often cited as evidence of Daoist influence, for it first occurs in the *Dao de jing.* To simply identify its source does not, however, explain what particular meaning it has for Zhou Dunyi. From Zhou's point of view the entire universe, all being itself, is ultimately derived from the Great Ultimate. By suggesting that the Great Ultimate is also the Ultimate of Non-being, Zhou affirms the all-inclusive nature of the source of things. The measure of its all-inclusiveness is that even its own opposite is included: there is nothing that is excluded from the Great Ultimate. This interpretation of the Great Ultimate also has a very practical side to it, for by suggesting that the Great Ultimate includes the Ultimate of Non-being, Zhou Dunyi emphasizes the degree to which Confucianism already includes Buddhist and Daoist symbols. Thus, what the Buddhists refer to as emptiness (*kong*) or the Daoists as voidness (*xu*) is, according to Zhou, already subsumed in the Great Ultimate. This is not to be understood as some kind of syncretism, but instead as a reaffirmation of the Confucian claim for the ontological priority of the Great Ultimate and thus of the Confucian affirmation of life itself as the ultimate ground for the achievement of sagehood.

There are other areas of Daoist influence in Zhou's thought beyond that evinced in his interpretation of the Great Ultimate. At the center of his practices and teachings are the ideas of quietude or tranquillity (*jing*) and desirelessness (*wuyu*). The sage is defined by Zhou Dunyi as one who is able to achieve a state of profound quietude and who is without desires. Zhu Xi felt that such ideas if carried to excess could lead dangerously close to the ways of the Buddhists and the Daoists. It may be because of this reservation that Zhu Xi chose to emphasize the metaphysical structure of Zhou Dunyi's thought and qualified Zhou's views by insisting upon the need for serious study rather than the cultivation of states of quietude and desirelessness.

The religious significance of Zhou Dunyi's thought for the development of neo-Confucianism is found in part in the degree to which he isolates the Great Ultimate as a symbol of ultimate meaning. The significance of this symbol persists throughout the course of the neo-Confucian tradition and reaffirms the central Confucian idea of the ultimate importance of life. But Zhou Dunyi's own life serves as a neo-Confucian religious model as well. In Zhou Dunyi we have someone who told his disciples that the whole purpose of learning is to achieve the goal of sagehood, and someone who in his own life displayed a seriousness and a humility that speak directly to the authenticity of the neo-Confucian religious perspective. When asked at one point why he refrained from cutting the grass outside his window, Zhou said that the grass's feeling and his own were the same. This has suggested to most readers Zhou Dunyi's extraordinary respect for and love of all forms of life, not to the detriment of the unique role of humankind, but rather as the extension and enlargement of humankind's own focus. It also suggests Zhou Dunyi's own religious sense of the continuity of all life and its common root in the Great Ultimate.

See Also Zhu Xi.

Bibliography

Introductory essays on Zhou Dunyi with a partial translation of his major writings are found in the two major sourcebooks on Chinese thought: *A Source Book in Chinese Philosophy,* translated by Wing-tsit Chan (Princeton, 1963), pp. 460–480, and *Sources of Chinese Tradition, From Earliest Times to 1600,* 2d ed., edited by Wm. Theodore de Bary and Irene Bloom (New York, 1999), vol. 1, pp. 669–678. Both contain selections from *An Explanation of the Diagram of the Great Ultimate* and *Penetrating the Book of Changes.* Zhou Dunyi's writings are included in part in a thirteenth-century anthology of neo-Confucianism compiled by Zhu Hsi and Lü Zuqian, translated into English by Wing-tsit Chan as *Reflections on Things at Hand* (New York, 1967). Discussions of specific aspects of Zhou Dunyi's thought may be found in Fung Yu-lan's *A History of Chinese Philosophy,* 2d ed., translated by Derk Bodde (Princeton, 1953), vol. 2, pp. 434–451; and Carsun Chang's *The Development of Neo-Confucian Thought,* 2 vols. (New York, 1957–1962), vol. 1, pp. 137–158. General studies including material on Zhou Dunyi are Xinghong Yao, *An Introduction to Confucianism* (Cambridge, UK, 2000), pp 98–104; John H. Berthrong, *Transformations of the Confucian Way* (Boulder, Colo., 1998), pp. 86–114.

Rodney L. Taylor (1987 and 2005)

ZHUANGZI. Zhuangzi is both the name of the second foundational text of the Daoist philosophical and religious tradition and the name of the putative author of this text after whom the book was titled, who, according to early historical sources, flourished between about 369 and 286 BCE. While what we know of the philosophy of Zhuangzi comes primarily from this work, it is important to realize that the *Zhuangzi* text is not the work of a single author. At the very least there are five authorial voices: the historical Zhuangzi; his disciples; a "Primitivistic" Daoist author with ideas akin to those of the *Dao de jing,* who responded to the challenge of the followers' individualist thinker Yang Zhu; and the "Syncretic" Daoist authors who likely compiled the original recension of the text. The received version in thirty-three chapters was established by the commentator Guo Xiang (d. 312 CE), who revised a fifty-two chapter original recension first listed in imperial bibliographies circa 110 CE by removing material he thought was superstitious and generally not of philosophical interest. This received Guo version is traditionally divided into three sections: "Inner Chapters" (1–7), "Outer Chapters" (8–22), and "Miscellaneous Chapters" (23–33). This division is longstanding and is likely to have been part of the original recension.

The *Zhuangzi* has become renowned for a series of original insights into human nature and the nature of the cosmos, and many of these are found in the "Inner Chapters." These insights are communicated in a variety of literary styles: didactic narratives, poetry, and very short prose essays. Like its famous companion, the *Dao de jing,* the *Zhuangzi* is grounded in the complementary ideas of Dao and De. Dao, the "Way," is an ineffable monistic principle that infuses and guides the spontaneous processes of all phenomena; De, "Inner Power," is the manifestation of this Way within all phenomena. Despite sharing these foundational ideas, these two Daoist works discuss them very differently. The *Dao de jing* often presents the characteristics and features of the Way in a discursive style (e.g.; DDJ 1: "The Way that can be told of is not the Constant Way"). On the other hand, the *Zhuangzi* often approaches the Way indirectly through narratives and poetry. Witness the following rumination on epistemological relativity that ends with a vivid pointing to the Way:

> What is It is also Other, what is Other is also It. There they say, "this is true and that is false" from one point of view; here we say, "this is true and that is false" from another point of view. Are there really It and Other? Or really no It and Other? Where neither It nor Other finds its opposite is called the axis of the Way. When the axis is found at the center of the circle there is no limit to responding with either, on the one hand no limit to what is it, on the other no limit to what is not. . . . (chapter 2)

This questioning of the certainty of knowledge from any normal human viewpoint is another hallmark of the "Inner Chapters," as is the considerable degree of humor and irony with which the most profound insights into the cosmos are presented. This is true as well for Zhuangzi's presentation of Inner Power, which is done through narratives in which the paragons of its cultivation are skilled tradesmen and the outcasts of society. This flaunting of societal prejudices is another way in which Zhuangzi challenges entrenched beliefs and demonstrates the breathtaking freedom from fixed conventions that has delighted readers for two millennia.

The Zhuangzi of the "Inner Chapters" is also known for a thorough questioning of the canons, methods, and value of discursive logic as practiced by contemporary thinkers in the traditions of the Mohists, Confucians, and Terminologists (*ming jia*). He skewers the presumed objectivity of their categories, arguing that names are purely arbitrary and reveal no inherent truths about the things that are named. Furthermore, no matter how sophisticated the logic involved, no argument can establish objective truths because all knowing remains confined to the standpoint of the knower:

> how do I know that what I call knowing is not ignorance? How do I know that what I call ignorance is not knowing? . . . Gibbons are sought by baboons as mates, elaphures like the company of deer, loaches play with fish. Maoqiang and Lady Li were beautiful in the eyes of men but when the fish saw them they plunged into the deep, and when the birds saw them they flew away. Which of these four knows what is truly beautiful in the world? (chapter 2)

Inspired by such ideas, comparative philosophers have engaged in spirited debate about whether Zhuangzi is a skeptic, a relativist, or a perspectivist. Scholars of religion further maintain that Zhuangzi's philosophical relativism does not apply to the higher level of cognition he calls "great knowledge," which is attained through the "inner cultivation" practices that lead to mystical gnosis. These practices involve sitting quietly and systematically circulating the breath until mind and body become tranquil and the contents of consciousness gradually empty. Taken to its ultimate levels, this practice leads to a direct experience of the Way. In the "Inner Chapters" Zhuangzi epitomizes this meditative practice as "the fasting of the mind" and as "sitting and forgetting:" "I let organs and members drop away, dismiss hearing and eyesight, part from the body and expel knowledge, and merge with the Great Pervader. This is what I mean by 'just sit and forget'" (chapter 6).

Yet for Zhuangzi this experience of "merging with the Great Pervader" (the Way), although profound, is relatively easy compared to the challenges of bringing this gnosis into the everyday world: "to stop making footprints is easy but it is difficult to walk without touching the ground" (chapter 4). This type of ungrounded "walking" has a significant epistemological dimension: a distinctive mode of cognition that Zhuangzi refers to as "flowing" (*yin-shi:* literally "to affirm by following along") in contrast to the "fixed" mode of cognition (*wei-shi:* literally "to affirm by forcing") that is bound to one individual perspective (chapter 2).

Zhuangzi further makes clear that abandonment of fixed cognition is concomitant with abandonment of attachment to the self and with the embracing of a new perspective grounded in the Way. From this perspective, just as the Way is able to "pervade and unify" all things, to see them just as they are, without bias and without preference, so too are sages able to see "all things as equal." It is just this kind of mystical seeing that is the essential defining characteristic of the "great knowledge" or "illumination" of the flowing cognition that is developed through inner cultivation practice. Zhuangzi's questioning of logic and his skepticism and relativism are based upon this shift from fixed cognition to flowing cognition, from self-centered perspective to "Way-centered" perspective. His epistemological critique is thus applied to knowledge derived from fixed cognition. Flowing cognition is exempted from this critique because it is this continually changing "Way-centered" perspective from which the critique is made.

These complementary mystical experiences (merging with the Great Pervader and pervading and unifying all things through flowing cognition) are critical for understanding other important philosophical themes for which the *Zhuangzi* is renowned. Political involvements are useless entanglements that only inhibit the opportunity to realize these experiences. Naturalness and spontaneity arise directly from the flowing cognition that is free of attachment to any one limited perspective. When sages act from this cognitive mode they can spontaneously respond without self-consciousness to whatever situation in which they find themselves. This freedom from attachment to any individual perspective also leads to the freedom from fear of death and acceptance of it as part of the natural processes of life that is another of the hallmarks of this work.

The Disciples of Zhuangzi. With writings as profound and vibrant as these, the historical Zhuangzi must have had quite a devoted group of followers. It is to them that we owe both the transmission of his ideas beyond his lifetime and at least six chapters of new material, much of it consisting of narratives written in the style of the "Inner Chapters" but generally not demonstrating the same creativity and rhetorical skill. Zhuangzi is a figure in about one quarter of these narratives, which were probably based on stories told by his immediate disciples and written down after his death. The chapters in this section, 17–22, are almost completely devoid of the philosophical essays, jottings, or even the diatribes we find in the first third of the book, yet they contain some of its most famous narratives.

Unlike the "Inner Chapters," which contain no references to Laozi the man and to the text of the *Dao de jing,* many of these disciple chapters use ideas and quotations from the *Dao de jing.* Thus they were most likely written after this work began circulating widely in China circa 260 BCE. To the extent that they recast material from the "Inner Chapters" in new narrative frameworks and frequently see it in light of ideas from the *Dao de jing,* these chapters represent a unique blending of the two intellectually foundational sources of early Daoism. Chapters 23 through 27 and 32 are much more heterogeneous in their content and contain fragmentary writings of the followers of Zhuangzi mixed with passages from the other authorial voices in the text.

The Primitivist Chapters. Four chapters (8–10, 16) and half of a fifth (11) espouse a philosophical position similar to that found in the *Dao de jing,* differing principally in that it is not addressed to the ruler. Because of their advocacy of a return to a government and social organization similar to that found in primitive tribal utopias, they have been labeled "Primitivist." They shared a utopian vision and critique of the Confucians with the Yangists and, under their influence, developed the first Daoist theory of human nature that derived from "inner cultivation" and was cast in terms of the Way and Inner Power. Rather than totally eschewing political life, they advocated a government by non-action *(wuwei)* similar to that found in the *Dao de jing.*

The Primitivists argue that it is the inherent nature of all people to be "simple and unhewn." The "simple" (*so*) and the "unhewn" (*pu*) are important ideas in the *Dao de jing* wherein to be simple means to be unselfish (DDJ 19) and to be "unhewn" means to be without desires (DDJ 19, 38). These ideas suggest a state of mind totally devoid of self-consciousness, a state of mind in which people act spontaneously and without self-reflection. It is a state of mind that is reminiscent of the flowing cognition of the "Inner Chapters." For the Primitivists, it is human nature to attain this state of mind when people are left on their own, when the institutions of culture do not interfere with spontaneous human tendencies. To attain this state is to realize one's Inner Power.

Throughout their writings the Primitivists harken back to an earlier utopian age when people lived in selfless harmony with one another and with all things in the world and when the Way and Inner Power were fully realized. The Confucian sage-rulers, who established cultural norms and thereby forced people to think about how to attain them, destroyed this harmony and made it much more difficult for people to attain the simple and unhewn state of mind. However by doing away with the sages and their cultural norms we can return to a primitive utopia. Then society can be governed by a ruler who learns how to practice non-action.

Chapters 28–31 of the received recension of the *Zhuangzi* are similar in thought to five essays from the first two chapters of the compendium *Lüshi chunqiu* (240 BCE), which constitute the only surviving works of the lost Yangist tradition. While some regard these *Zhuangzi* chapters themselves as Yangist, close examination reveals that they are a heterogeneous collection of writings likely compiled and created by the Primivitists to respond to the intellectual challenges of the Yangists in the debates at the Qin court of Lü Buwei, where the *Lüshi chunqiu* was written.

THE SYNCRETIST CHAPTERS. The final stratum of the *Zhuangzi* contains a distinctive and largely consistent viewpoint that connects with the rest of the text and with a larger philosophical context. It is contained in three complete essays: (1) the first two-thirds of chapter 13, "The Way of Heaven"; (2) chapter 15 "Inveterate Ideas"; and (3) the final chapter, 33, "Below in the Empire," as well as in narratives that play key roles in chapters 12 and 14. This material shares a common cosmology of the Way and interest in inner cultivation that we have seen in most of the rest of the text but veers in a different direction in its political thought, advocating a hierarchical social and political structure that incorporates the best ideas of other earlier intellectual lineages within a Daoist cosmological framework. Nonetheless, it agrees with the Primitivist idea that government should be led by a sage enlightened through inner cultivation techniques. In its general intellectual viewpoint it exemplifies many of the characteristics of the Daoist tradition that were first enunciated by the Han dynasty historian, Sima Tan (d. 110 BCE), the man who coined the very term "Daoism" (*daojia*). According to him, Daoists assert that:

1. Humans can cultivate themselves to attain harmony of body and mind and to realize their essential connection to the Way and to the entire cosmos.
2. When rulers become adept at such "inner cultivation" they can govern dispassionately and humanely according to the greater patterns of heaven and earth, upon which they model their social and political institutions.
3. While remaining faithful to this general Daoist orientation rulers should make use of the best ideas of other early intellectual lineages.
4. With these institutions and practices established, rulers can govern by taking no action while leaving nothing undone.

All these ideas are found in the Syncretist *Zhuangzi.* Inner cultivation practice is advocated to attain a deep and tranquil state of mind to enable both sages and rulers to act efficaciously in the world. They then make use of this experience to act spontaneously and harmoniously while being guided by the greater patterns of the cosmos. This is the Syncretists' version of attaining the flowing mode of cognition advocated in the other parts of the text. The Syncretist author of chapter 13 argues that this flowing mode can be applied to a variety of life circumstances: ruler and minister, politician and hermit, sage and commoner can all utilize flowing cognition; but when it is applied to rulership, it attains its greatest flourishing. Government by enlightened sages who attain flowing cognition is the pinnacle of Daoist political thought for the Syncretist: it is symbolized by the phrase "in stillness a sage, in motion a king," which is elsewhere referred to as being inwardly a sage and outwardly a king. It is with this cultivated mind that the sage ruler establishes human society in parallel to the greater patterns of the cosmos. This coordination of human society with cosmic patterns is a characteristic tenet of the early Daoist syncretic lineage that historians first called the "Way of the Yellow Emperor and Laozi" (*Huang-Lao zhi dao*), and some scholars have argued that these Syncretist chapters are the products of this intellectual lineage.

The final chapter of the *Zhuangzi,* "Below in the Empire," exemplifies this kind of syncretism in its analysis of earlier intellectual traditions. After establishing its own position, the comprehensive "Way of Heaven and Earth," it analyzes how each of these earlier traditions understood one part of this comprehensive Way but ultimately failed to grasp the whole. Zhuangzi himself is included in this analysis. The Syncretist author praises Zhuangzi for his depth of mystical cultivation but chides him for failing to realize that there are practical affairs in the world that must be attended to. It is an interesting yet telling comment. The Syncretist criticizes the very impracticability for which Zhuangzi later became renowned.

Thus the text called the *Zhuangzi* is a multilayered work that transmits the ideas of an important early Daoist philosophical and religious lineage founded by the historical figure of Zhuangzi towards the end of the fourth century BCE. His writings were conveyed to later generations by his disciples who added to the work over the better part of a century, during which the developing text passed through the Qin court of Lü Buwei, circa 240 BCE, and was completed at the court of Liu An (c. 180–122 BCE), second king of Huai-nan, circa 150 BCE. While the lineage of Zhuangzi elaborated upon the master's original thought by developing Primitivist and Syncretist political dimensions, each in its own way remained true to his advocacy of cultivating the spontaneous flowing mode of cognition.

See Also Daoism, overview article.

Bibliography

There are three scholarly modern translations of the *Zhuangzi* currently in circulation that are worthy of consultation. All others are outdated, derivative, or not grounded in Sinological scholarship. There are the complete translations of Burton Watson, *The Complete Works of Chuang Tzu* (New York, 1968), and Victor Mair, *Wandering on the Way: Early Taoist Tales and Parables of Chuang Tzu* (Honolulu, 1998). Both are more literary than philosophical, and while each is appealing for its rendering of the humorous flair of the original, the Mair translation is preferable because of its well-founded semantic subdivisions within each chapter and Mair's tendency to translate the meaning of proper names, which skillfully helps to communicate the irony of these names in the original narratives.

The philosophically most interesting and the most linguistically precise translation is Angus Charles Graham, *Chuang Tzu: The Inner Chapters* (London, 1981; Reprint, Boston, 2000). Despite its title, it contains about eighty percent of the original text organized by each of the five philosophical positions Graham has identified in the work: (1) the historical Zhuangzi; (2) his disciples; (3) The Primitivist; (4) The Yangists; and (5) The Syncretists, with additional passages translated under narrative categories such as "stories about Zhuangzi," etc. This is at once a strength and a weakness of the Graham translation: it clearly distinguishes philosophical voices that most translations do not. However, organizing the translation along these lines makes it maddening to attempt to compare different translations or to check Graham's translation with the original Chinese text.

There are a number of excellent essay collections that deal with various aspects of the philosophy and the textual history of the *Zhuangzi:* Roger T. Ames, ed., *Wandering at Ease in the Zhuangzi* (Albany, N.Y., 1998); Scott Cook, ed., *Hiding the World in the World: Uneven Discourses on the Zhuangzi* (Albany, N.Y., 2003); Paul Kjellberg and Philip J. Ivanhoe, eds., *Essays on Skepticism, Relativism, and Ethics in the Zhuangzi* (Albany, 1996); and Victor Mair, ed., *Experimental Essays on the Chuang Tzu* (Honolulu, 1983). Each collects essays by at least a dozen specialists in either Chinese thought or in comparative philosophy, and each has its stronger and weaker contributions, with none standing out from the rest.

There is a thoughtful collection of essays on various aspects of the philosophy of *Zhuangzi* by Jean Francois Billeter titled *Études sur Tchouang-Tseu* (Paris, 2004). It assembles five of his essays published in academic journals and adds a number of new ones. Harold D. Roth's *A Companion to Angus C. Graham's Chuang Tzu: The Inner Chapters* (Honolulu, 2003) is a useful collection of Angus Graham's essays on *Zhuangzi* that also includes Graham's rare textual notes to his translation of *Zhuangzi* and an assessment of his text-analytical scholarship by Roth. In addition there are several other works on the textual history of the *Zhuangzi:* Angus C. Graham, "How Much of *Chuang Tzu* did Chuang Tzu write?" reprinted in Roth, *A Companion,* presents his ideas of the stratification of the text; Liu Xiaogan, *Classifying the Zhuangzi Chapters* (Ann Arbor, Mich., 1994) is a thorough book-length study of this same topic that reaches similar conclusions on the strata but sometimes different conclusions about the authorship of these strata; Harold D. Roth's "Chuang Tzu" in *Early Chinese Texts: A Bibliographical Guide,* compiled and edited by Michael Loewe (Berkeley, Calif., 1993), succinctly summarizes Western and East Asian scholarship on the textual history and textual analysis of the *Zhuangzi.* Finally, Harold D. Roth's "Who Compiled the *Chuang Tzu?*" in *Chinese Texts and Philosophical Contexts,* ed. Henry Rosemont, Jr. (LaSalle, Ill., 1991) argues that the Syncretist compilers of the *Zhuangzi* were members of the early Daoist Huang-Lao lineage who were part of the intellectual circle of Liu An, second king of Huai-nan in about 150 BCE.

Harold D. Roth (2005)

ZHUHONG (1535–1615), also known as Master Yunqi; an important Buddhist leader in the late Ming dynasty (1368–1644). A reformer of monastic Buddhism, a synthesizer of various Buddhist traditions, and a successful promoter of lay Buddhism, Zhuhong was also regarded posthumously as the eighth Pure Land patriarch. However, his influence has never been confined within any sectarian boundary. He has, in fact, been credited with the renewal of Buddhism in Ming China.

Zhuhong was a native of Hangzhou. He became a student in the local school at the age of sixteen and quickly achieved a reputation for his knowledge of Confucianism and Daoism. He sat for the higher civil examinations several times but was without success. His interest in Pure Land Buddhism dates from the time when he daily witnessed an old woman calling the name of the Buddha Amitābha (Chin., Emituofo). Thereafter, he kept a vegetarian diet, studied Buddhist scriptures, and practiced *nianfo* (recitation of Amitābha's name). When Zhuhong was twenty-seven his father died. Shortly afterward his wife and only son also passed away. He then remarried a pious Buddhist laywoman and resolved that if he failed to pass the provincial examinations by the age of thirty and the metropolitan examinations by the age of forty, he would become a monk. Three years later his mother died. When success in the examinations still eluded him he bade farewell to his wife (who later became a nun) and in 1566 entered the monastic order.

After he became a monk, Zhuhong followed the mendicant tradition, spending the next six years traveling throughout the country seeking instruction from prominent teachers. He achieved his first enlightenment on his way to Dongzhang in Shandong. He also took part in five sessions of Chan meditation held in different monasteries in the Zhejiang area. In 1571 he returned to Mount Yunqi in his native Hangzhou. It is said that through the performance of Tantric rituals and the invocation of the Buddha's name, Zhuhong cleared the region of tigers that had been harming men and beasts, and brought rain during a severe drought. In gratitude, villagers rebuilt an abandoned old temple, which he named Yunqi Monastery upon its completion in 1577. Zhuhong stayed there until his death in 1615, making it a model of monastic discipline and a center for the joint practice of Pure Land and Chan, a syncretic tradition that was initiated by the Chan master Yanshou (904–975) and that reached its culmination with Zhuhong.

The joint practice of Chan and Pure Land rested on the assertion that the two paths were essentially the same insofar as both led to the same goal: the stopping of wrong thoughts and the end of the cycle of *saṃsāra* (Chin., *shengsi*). Zhuhong wrote a four-volume commentary on the smaller *Sukhāvatīvyūha Sūtra* (Chin., *Emituofo jing*) in which he provided a creative interpretation of "one mind" (*yixin*). Using the Huayan categories of particularity (*shi*) and universality (*li*), Zhuhong divided the attainment of *nianfo* into the "one mind of particularity" and the "one mind of universality." The former is achieved through concentration, which suppresses ignorance, while the latter is achieved through insight, which destroys ignorance. By the "uninterrupted experience and embodiment" of the Buddha's name, he believed, one could attain insight into the true nature of things, the object of Chan meditation. The link between Chan meditation and *nianfo* practice was precisely this one mind. Zhuhong firmly believed that this one mind was nothing other than that to which Bodhidharma was "directly pointing."

Zhuhong was an energetic evangelist of vegetarianism and kindness to animals. Under his advocacy, the practice of "release of life" (*fangsheng*), that is, buying fish and other creatures from marketplaces and setting them free, became very popular among lay Buddhists. He wrote the *Zizhi lu* (Record of Self-knowledge), which was modeled on the ledgers of merit and demerit long favored by Daoists, to inculcate Buddhist values among the general populace.

Zhuhong was interested in harmonizing Buddhism with Confucianism. He was less impressed by Daoism and clearly hostile toward Catholicism, as can be seen from the four rebuttals supposedly addressed to Matteo Ricci and contained in Zhuhong's collected works, *Yunqi fahui.*

SEE ALSO Jingtu.

BIBLIOGRAPHY

Hurvitz, Leon. "Chu-hung's One Mind of Pure Land and Ch'an Buddhism." In *Self and Society in Ming Thought,* edited by Wm. Theodore de Bary, pp. 451–476. New York, 1970.

Yü, Chun-fang. *The Renewal of Buddhism in China: Chu-hung and the Late Ming Synthesis.* New York, 1981.

Zhuhong. *Yunqi fahui.* 34 vols. Nanjing, 1897. The collected works of Zhuhong.

CHUN-FANG YÜ (1987)

ZHU XI (1130–1200), philosopher, scholar, and formulator of what would for centuries be regarded as mainstream neo-Confucianism. The son of an official, Zhu Xi passed the highest civil service examination when he was only eighteen. In 1151 he was appointed a district registrar in Fujian province, where he served until 1158. He did not accept another official post until 1172, when he became prefect of Nankang in Jiangxi. Except for a month and a half in 1194, when Zhu Xi served at court, his government service was entirely at the local or regional level.

As a local official he built a strong record of conscientious service looking after the economic as well as moral welfare of the people. One notable acccomplishment was the establishment of communal granaries as a measure to combat famine. Less successful was his attempt to conduct a land survey. Most influential in the long run were his activities on behalf of education, especially the rehabilitation of private academies such as the White Deer Grotto Academy in Nankang. Such academies played a prime role in propagating neo-Confucianism.

In office or out, Zhu Xi was ever mindful of the plight of the Song dynasty, which had lost China's northern heartland to the non-Chinese Jin only three years before his own birth. In memorials and personal audiences he urged moral reform of the government beginning with the emperor himself. Both his ideas about moral government and his discussions on specific policy issues, however, had little influence on government. Zhu's brief period at court came to an end when a hostile faction came to power. Not content with purging their opponents from government, the men who ousted Zhu Xi went on to denounce him and fifty-eight other philosophers as guilty of "spurious" or "false" learning (*weixue*). Zhu Xi was still in political disgrace at the time of his death.

In his prolific writings and recorded conversations with disciples Zhu Xi ranged over many areas of inquiry encompassing a host of topics and issues. His greatest achievement lay in shaping the varied and diffuse ideas of his eleventh-century predecessors into a coherent, organic philosophy. In the process he not only defined neo-Confucianism but established the Confucian core curriculum. It was Zhu Xi who joined the *Daxue* (Great learning) and the *Zhongyong* (Doctrine of the mean), originally two chapters in the *Li ji* (Book of rites), with the *Lunyu* (Analects) of Confucius and the *Mengzi* to comprise the so-called Four Books, a collection that formed the basis for the education of the Chinese elite until 1905.

Zhu Xi's thought was deeply religious in several senses. On a personal level, his was a creed to guide people's conduct as well as thinking, a quest for wisdom as well as truth, focused on an ideal of self-perfection (sagehood) to be pursued with the most earnest dedication. Part and parcel of this attitude was his reverence for Confucius and other past sages as well as his passionate concern with proper behavior and ritual. Furthermore, his view of the world and man was grounded in a sense of a transcendent reality and a vision of the unity of the cosmos and humanity.

Like Cheng Yi before him, Zhu Xi considered both the physical world of nature and the moral world of human relations as structured by *li* ("principle"), but he went beyond Cheng Yi to identify principle with the "supreme polarity" (supreme ultimate; *taiji*) discussed by Zhou Dunyi (1017–1073) in his *Taijitu shuo* (Explanation of the diagram of the Supreme Polarity). Above and prior to form, the Supreme Polarity is itself without form. It contains all principles even as it is their source. It generates tranquillity and activity, the cosmic forces of yin and yang; indeed, its activity and tranquillity are yin and yang. It is transcendent but also immanent, for Zhu Xi stressed the unity of the one and the many. To illustrate this, he used the metaphor of the single moon that shines on and is reflected in rivers and lakes everywhere. Everything has the Supreme Polarity within it, yet the Supreme Polarity remains one whole.

Zhu's contemporary, Lu Jiuyuan (Lu Xiangshan, 1139–1193), objected to Zhou Dunyi's formulation, "the Non-Polarity [*wuji*, or Ultimate of Non-being] and yet the Supreme Polarity," as constituting the Daoist emphasis on non-being. But Zhu Xi insisted on retaining this formula because it makes clear that there is nothing beyond or prior to the *Taiji* and that *Taiji* cannot be limited or qualified in any way. As indicated in the diagram, the Non-Polarity and the Supreme Polarity are not two entities. According to Zhu Xi, in some contexts the *Taiji* need not itself be thought of as an entity at all.

Zhu Xi compared the relationship between *Taiji*, which he identified with principle or pattern *(li)*, and the flux of activity and tranquillity, which he identified with material force *(qi)*, to that of a man riding a horse, going wherever the horse goes in an inseparable union. In a crucial disagreement with Buddhists, Zhu Xi emphasized that principle is not something empty and detached, insisting instead that principle and concrete things never exist in isolation from one another. Without the material force *(qi)*, principle *(li)* would have nothing to attach itself to. Accordingly, *qi* plays an important role in Zhu Xi's thought, so much so that an extensive literature has debated whether his thought may be more properly characterized as monism or dualism. Perhaps one may say that he was capable of adopting both perspectives, but that in ultimate metaphysical terms he saw reality as one.

Human beings are, of course, very much part of this reality. Like all Neo-Confucians, Zhu Xi accepted Mengzi's teaching that human nature is fundamentally good and that it contains within it the "beginnings" of the virtues. He equates this nature with principle: it belongs to the individual but is also shared with the world. While nature is good in its original quiescent state, once aroused to activity, goodness consists in following it, while evil results from going against it. What makes evil possible is that in man, as in the cosmos, principle needs to attach itself to material force in order to become actualized. Just as water may be clear or turbid, the physical nature people receive at birth may be pure or gross in varying degree. The more turbid the physical nature, the more seriously will principle be obstructed, but human beings, unlike animals, are able to penetrate their turbidity to recover the underlying principles.

Essential to Zhu Xi's view of man and the process of self-perfection is the activity of the "mind-and-heart" (*xin*, hereafter "mind"). Drawing on Zhang Zai, Zhu Xi held that the mind unites and controls the nature and the feelings. Thus, unlike Lu Jiuyuan and the "school of Mind" (Xinxue), Zhu Xi does not identify the mind with principle. For him, principles are contained in the mind, which, however, is constituted of highly rarefied *qi*. While the nature, identified with substance *(ti)*, is good, the feelings, identified as function (*yong*), need to be maintained in proper balance. Some, such as the feeling of commiseration, are good, but there is always the danger posed by selfish desires. As a result, the human mind (*ren-xin*) is in a precarious state, ever subject to errors that prevent it from returning to the original "mind of the Way" (*dao-xin*, moral mind). The nature, as principle in general, is inert. Consequently, Zhu Xi places special emphasis on the mind as the active master whose role it is to engage in the strenuous effort to discriminate between moral error and the correct way and then to maintain constant correctness. Self-cultivation requires utmost exertion and commitment.

In his methodology of self-development Zhu Xi emphasized intellectual learning, but, in keeping with the general inclusive and synthetic cast of his mind, he by no means rejected meditation, or "quiet sitting" (*qingzuo*), as the neo-Confucians called it. He once even advised a student to spend half his day in quiet sitting and the other half in reading. As a young man Zhu Xi was greatly influenced by the concept of quietism, but changed his views under the influence of his friend Zhang Shi (1133–1180) and the ideas of the philosopher Hu Hong (1106–1162). It was not until 1169 that he worked out a doctrine of self-cultivation that involved watchfulness over one's emotions and feelings both before and after they have been aroused. Central to this doctrine was the cultivation and practice of "seriousness" (*jing,* also rendered as "reverence, mindfulness"). The *locus classicus* for the concept of seriousness, so prominent in the thought of Cheng Yi as well as Zhu Xi, is a passage in the *Yi jing* (Book of changes) that couples "seriousness to straighten the internal life" with "righteousness to square the external life."

Zhu Xi is especially noted for stressing "the investigation of things" (*gewu,* a term from *Daxue*), by which he meant the investigation of the principles of all things and events. It was on this issue that he had his famous debate with Lu Jiuyuan in 1175 at the Goose Lake Temple in Jiangxi. In contrast to Lu, whose philosophy of inwardness de-emphasized external learning or book knowledge, Zhu Xi maintained that principle was to be investigated in the external world as well as within one's self. According to Zhu, the extension of knowledge (*zhi-zhi,* another term from *Daxue*) is a gradual process of investigating the principles of one thing after another until a great breakthrough takes place and the perfection of knowledge is attained. Like other Confucians, he taught that such knowledge must necessarily be manifested in action, but unlike the Ming dynasty philosopher Wang Yangming (1472–1529), Zhu Xi taught that knowledge must precede action.

The prime virtue, the source of all other virtues and thus the object of all endeavor is "humaneness" (*ren,* also rendered as "humanity, benevolence"). In keeping with the centrality of this concept in Confucian thought, Zhu Xi gave much attention to working out his own theory of humaneness. Rejecting an interpretation given by one of Cheng Yi's disciples, who defined it as consciousness, as well as that of another disciple, who equated it to unity with all things, Zhu Xi characterized *ren* as the principle of love and the very character of the mind. Vital and creative, *ren* is the spirit of life found in the mind of Heaven and earth. Thus, through humaneness people partake of the creative process of the universe.

This creative process is natural and unending. Because the universe constantly rotates, the heaviest material force concentrates at the center to form the earth while the most rarefied *qi* is farthest out, forming the sky, sun, moon, and celestial bodies. When Zhu Xi discussed the "mind of heaven and earth," the word translated as "heaven" is *tian,* which, depending on the context, can also be rendered as "sky" or "nature." Asked about its meaning in the classics, Zhu Xi replied that in some cases it meant "the lord" and in some "principle." The question of whether Zhu Xi was a deist was much debated among Jesuit and other Western scholars of Chinese philosophy and forms an important chapter in the history of Western sinology rather than in that of neo-Confucianism in China or East Asia.

In both his official capacity and in his personal life Zhu Xi participated wholeheartedly in religious ceremonies, including, for instance, prayers for rain in times of drought, sacrifices to former sages, and ancestor worship. As a man of his time, he believed in the existence of ghosts but sought to explain natural phenomena in terms of *li.* He strongly rejected the Buddhist idea of reincarnation, Daoist beliefs in longevity, and shamanism. Living in disgrace in his old age, he wrote a memorial condemning the men in power, much to the alarm of his disciples, who were concerned for his safety. Finally, they persuaded him to let divination decide whether to risk sending the memorial. Zhu Xi accepted the negative verdict of the milfoil. It was a dramatic and poignant expression of his conviction of the unity of the universe and man.

A brief summary of as subtle and prolific a thinker as Zhu Xi inevitably runs into the danger of oversimplification. It also tends to disguise the extent to which the modern scholar is engaged in a task of interpretation and reconstruction, for Zhu Xi, like other Chinese thinkers, did not set forth his ideas in a systematic magnum opus. Although there are some essays on specific subjects, for the most part he developed his ideas in commentaries on the classics, letters to friends, prefaces and the like, as well as in conversations recorded by disciples. His works are a rich source for modern students of many aspects of twelfth-century China and continue to provide scholars within the tradition with numerous issues for cogitation and debate. Recent years have seen major advances in the study of Zhu Xi, but the work continues.

SEE ALSO Chinese Religion; Confucianism; Li; Lu Xiangshan; Mengzi; Qi; Ren and Yi; Taiji; Tian; Zhang Zai; Zhou Dunyi.

BIBLIOGRAPHY

Wing-tsit Chan's "The Study of Chu Hsi in the West," *Journal of Asian Studies* 35 (August 1976): 555–577, is a comprehensive survey and a most useful guide. Professor Chan has included translations from Zhu Xi in his *A Source Book in Chinese Philosophy* (Princeton, 1963) and translated Zhu Xi and Lü Ziqian's anthology of Northern Song neo-Confucianism, the *Jinsi lu,* under the title *Reflections on Things at Hand* (New York, 1967). Studies published since the appearance of Professor Chan's article include *Journal of Chinese Philosophy* 5.2 (June 1978), a special issue on Zhu Xi; Hoyt C. Tillman's *Utilitarian Confucianism: Chen Liang's Challenge to Zhu Xi* (Cambridge, Mass., 1982); Daniel K. Gardner's meticulous translations and insightful studies: *Zhu Xi and the Da-xue* (Cambridge, Mass., 1986); *Learning to Be a Sage: Selections from the Conversations of Master Chu* (Berkeley, 1990); and *Zhu Xi's Reading of the Analects: Canon, Commentary, and the Classical Tradition* (New York, 2003). Also see Kim Yuk-sik, *Natural Philosophy of Chu Hsi* (Philadelphia, 2000) and *Zhu Xi and Neo-Confucianism,* edited by Wing-tsit Chan (Honolulu, 1986).

Mu's *Zhuzi xin xuean* (Taipei, 1971) remains authorative. Wing-tsit Chan's *Zhu xue lunji* (Taipei, 1982) includes an essay on Zhu Xi's religious practice. An excellent study published in the Peoples' Republic is Zhang Liwen's *Zhu Xi sixiang yanjiu* (Beijing, 1981). Japanese scholars have made major contributions to the study of Zhu Xi. An extensive modern translation of Zhu Xi and others associated with him is the fifteen-volume *Shushigaku taikei* (Tokyo, 1974–1983).

Conrad Schirokauer (1987 and 2005)

ZIMMER, HEINRICH ROBERT (1890–1943), German Indologist and comparative mythologist. Son of the Sanskritist and Celticist Heinrich Friedrich Zimmer (1850–1910), Heinrich (Henry) Robert Zimmer was born in Greifswald, in present-day Germany, on December 6, 1890. Beginning his studies in Berlin in Hebrew literature, Germanics, and art history, he received his doctorate in 1913 with a thesis on India's traditional system of *gotras*. After service in World War I, he qualified as professor at Greifswald and then moved to Heidelberg in 1922. Zimmer's marriage to Christiane von Hofmannsthal, daughter of the Jewish poet Hugo von Hofmannsthal, and his consistent outspokenness as an anti-Nazi were causes for his eventual dismissal from the university in 1938. After lecturing at Oxford and Johns Hopkins universities, Zimmer was appointed visiting lecturer at Columbia University in 1941. He died of pneumonia two years later, on March 20, 1943.

Although the son of one of Germany's pioneering Indologists, whose *Altindische Leben: Die Kultur der vedischen Arier* is a landmark in Vedic studies, Heinrich Zimmer is most often linked rather to two other persons: Joseph Campbell and, particularly, C. G. Jung. Jung apparently first learned of Zimmer through the latter's *Kuntsform und Yoga im indischen Kultbild* (1926), a work that introduced Tantric studies to Jung and to much of educated Europe. Zimmer and Jung first met in 1932, and their deep friendship, based on shared strong interests, had important consequences for both; not least important was their joint founding of the Psychology Seminar of Zurich. As editor of Zimmer's posthumous English publications, upon which Zimmer's reputation principally rests, Joseph Campbell's role also has been extremely important.

Zimmer's passionate interest in Indian thought and spirituality as witnesses to the universal aspirations of the human spirit marked something of a departure from contemporary and immediately preceding continental approaches to the study of India's religions, and is reminiscent rather of the attitudes of such late eighteenth- and early nineteenth-century German Romantics as Wilhelm and Friedrich Schlegel. With Sir John Woodroffe (also known as Arthur Avalon), who seems strongly to have influenced his own thought, Zimmer was among the first in the twentieth century to urge that understanding the adventure of Indian religious and philosophical thought would help one better understand one's own situation in the world. This enthusiastic, personal element represents an early flowering of a new, "second-generation" attitude in the European study of non-European religious thought and culture. Rather than holding the "alien" cultural material at arm's length, Zimmer embraced it (though he was never able to fulfill his wish to visit India). While his enthusiasm led to certain excesses and disputable interpretations of India's religions, Zimmer's own example eloquently suggests the importance of such enthusiasm for true understanding. In Jung's words, Zimmer's was "a spirit that overcame the limitations of the specialist and, turning towards humanity, bestowed upon it the joyous gift of eternal fruit" (Jung, *Collected Works,* vol. 11, 1963, p. 577).

Bibliography

Had Zimmer written nothing else, his *The Art of Indian Asia,* 2 vols., completed and edited by Joseph Campbell (New York, 1950), would have assured his reputation and importance. Four others of his works are available in English. His important *Kuntsform und Yoga im indischen Kultbild* (Berlin, 1926) is now translated into English by Gerald Chapple and James B. Lawson as *Artistic Form and Yoga in the Sacred Images of India* (Princeton, N.J., 1984). Joseph Campbell also completed and edited three further works. Possibly the most engaging of these is Zimmer's *Myths and Symbols in Indian Art and Civilization* (New York, 1946), which remains among the more useful introductions to traditional Indian thought and culture. The essays constituting *The King and the Corpse* (New York, 1948) well illustrate Zimmer's broad interests in comparative mythology and folklore. No doubt the liveliest introduction to the sweep of classical Hindu, Buddhist, and Jain philosophy is his *Philosophies of India* (New York, 1951), though some of his interpretations must be treated with caution.

A charming autobiographical sketch written by Zimmer only three months before his death is included as an appendix in Chapple and Lawson's translation of *Kunstform und Yoga* along with a select bibliography (pp. 243–267). *Heinrich Zimmer: Coming into His Own,* edited by Margaret H. Case (Princeton, N.J., 1994) is a volume of illuminating essays stemming from a 1990 Columbia University conference celebrating Zimmer's birth centenary. Among these essays are two personal reminiscences (one by Zimmer's daughter), Zimmer's own estimate of Jung's significance for his work, and helpful assessments of Joseph Campbell's role in preserving and transmitting Zimmer's scholarship by Wendy Doniger and Gerald Chapple. Inter alia, Chapple notes the substantial amount of Zimmer's scholarly and popular writing in German that remains untranslated.

G. R. Welbon (1987 and 2005)

ZINZENDORF, NIKOLAUS (1700–1760), German nobleman, theologian, leader of the Moravian church; born Count Nikolaus Ludwig von Zinzendorf on May 26, 1700, in Dresden, Saxony. At his baptism his parents invited the electress of Saxony to be his godmother and the Pietist leader Philipp Jakob Spener to be his godfather. These choices represented the influences of noble lineage and pietistic devotion that were to be so decisive in Zinzendorf's later life.

Even as a child Zinzendorf displayed an extraordinary interest in religious matters. At the age of ten, following private tutoring, he was sent to the Halle boarding school run by the Pietist leader August Hermann Francke. In 1716 he transferred to the orthodox Lutheran University of Wittenberg to prepare for a career as a lawyer, but he continued to read theological literature in his free time. His perennially irenic approach to theological disputes showed up in his ultimately unsuccessful attempts to arrange colloquiums for the exchange of views between the Pietists of Halle and the orthodox of Wittenberg.

With his formal training completed, Zinzendorf studied briefly at various universities and developed friendships with leading personalities, including the Jansenist cardinal archbishop of Paris, Louis de Noailles. Although Zinzendorf would have probably preferred ordination as a Lutheran pastor or to work with Francke at Halle, his family did not consider such possibilities appropriate for a nobleman, and he became a legal counselor. In September 1721 he married Countess Erdmuth Dorothea Reuss, also a committed Pietist, with whom he fathered twelve children.

In 1722 Zinzendorf purchased the Berthelsdorf estate from his grandmother and soon found himself with an unexpected opportunity to exercise his religious leadership when a group of religious refugees from neighboring Bohemia settled on his estate. They were heirs of the traditions of the Unity of Brethren, a group that had thrived a century earlier during the Hussite reformation. Persecution had forced them to continue their religious practices underground and sometimes to leave their homeland as refugees. The leadership of these people consumed Zinzendorf's considerable energies for the rest of his life. The newly established town of Herrnhut, with its unique communal organization and economic self-sufficiency, became the center for the developing Moravian church, as it became known in the late 1740s.

In 1735, after examination by the theological faculties of the Universities of Stralsund and Tübingen, Zinzendorf's desire to receive Lutheran ordination was finally realized. With the revival of the Brethren's clerical orders, he was consecrated a Moravian bishop in 1737. These events signaled the emergence of a new denomination and created legal difficulties for Zinzendorf, resulting in banishment from Saxony from 1736 to 1747. During this period he visited Moravian settlements and missions in Europe, England, the West Indies, and America. From the mid-1740s to 1750, Zinzendorf and some of his followers displayed a marked tendency to carry certain of his ideas to emotional excess. This approach was finally rejected and years later came to be regarded as the "sifting time." The Moravians were granted religious freedom in Saxony in 1749, and six years later the count returned to spend his last days in Herrnhut. When the countess died in 1756, Zinzendorf entered into a morganatic marriage with Anna Nitschmann, a leader of the Single Sisters Choir, one of the church's residential groups.

Zinzendorf's extensive involvement in the practical life of the church and his belief that it was not possible to produce a system of theology kept him from producing a comprehensive presentation of his often-original ideas. Throughout his life he worked at new translations of the Bible, incorporating the use of popular language, rearrangements of the books in order of historical origin, harmonization of the Passion accounts, and an abridged Old Testament. He also produced attempts at Lutheran and Reformed catechisms, prepared numerous sermons, and wrote religious poetry and hymns.

In his theology Zinzendorf sought an alternative to the rationalism of the Enlightenment and the sterility of Lutheran orthodoxy. His answer was "heart religion." His christocentricity derived from his belief that God is a person, not a system, and can be known only through the Son, who reveals the Father. To experience Christ in the inner senses is the true essence of religion. From this central idea flows Zinzendorf's interest in experiential language, including reference to the Holy Spirit as "Mother." Likewise, "heart religion" knows no creedal or institutional boundaries; hence Zinzendorf's radical ecumenicity. The relationship with Christ produces joy in the believer; Zinzendorf's thought departed from traditional Pietism's emphasis upon struggle and conversion to focus on the results of this relationship. A startlingly creative thinker in his day, Zinzendorf's influences are apparent in the later theology of Friedrich Schleiermacher with his attention to religious feeling and in the Christocentric emphasis of Karl Barth.

SEE ALSO Moravians.

BIBLIOGRAPHY

Erich Beyreuther and Gerhard Meyer have edited Zinzendorf's *Hauptschriften,* 6 vols. (Hildesheim, 1962–1963), along with *Ergänzungsbände zu den Hauptschriften,* 12 vols. (Hildesheim, 1964–1972), photographically reproduced original editions. An excellent introduction to Zinzendorf's role within Pietism and a summary of his theology is provided by F. Ernest Stoeffler in his *German Pietism during the Eighteenth Century* (Leiden, 1973). See also Arthur J. Freeman *An Ecumenical Theology of the Heart: the Theology of Count Nicholas Ludwig von Zinzendorf* (Bethlehem, Pennsylvania, 1998) and Gary S. Kinkel *Our Dear Mother the Spirit: an Investigation of Count Zinzendorf's Theology and Praxis* (Lanham, Md., 1990). George W. Forell has translated Zinzendorf's sermons in *Nicholaus Ludwig Count von Zinzendorf: Nine Public Lectures on Important Subjects in Religion* (Iowa City, Iowa, 1973). *A Collection of Sermons from Zinzendorf's Pennsylvania Journey* has been published (Bethlehem, Pa., 2001) by Julie Tomberlin-Weber, translator, and Craig Atwood, editor. Stoeffler and Forell both provide helpful bibliographies. The best modern biography is *Count Zinzendorf* by John R. Weinlich (Nashville, Tenn., 1956).

DAVID A. SCHATTSCHNEIDER (1987 AND 2005)

ZIONISM.

The origin of the word *Zion* is unclear. It most likely derives from a word meaning "rock" or "stronghold" or perhaps "a dry place." The first occurrence of the name is in *2 Samuel* 5:7, where David captures the Jebusite city of Jerusalem. The "fortress of Zion" appears to have been the Jebusite name for the place that was henceforth to be called "the citadel of David." But although Jebusite in origin, the name Zion (Hebrew, *Tsiyyon*) was assimilated into the Israelite vocabulary and became associated with the Davidic monarchy and its capital in Jerusalem. In writings of such prophets as "First Isaiah" and Jeremiah and in *Psalms*, the name Zion is used as a synonym first for the Temple in Jerusalem, then for the kingdom of Judah, and finally, in postexilic literature, for the Land of Israel. In the Babylonian exile the psalmist wrote: "By the waters of Babylon / There we sat down, yea, we wept / When we remembered Zion" (*Ps.* 137:1). Thus what was first a specific place-name came to represent symbolically the whole Land of Israel, whose people had been exiled. The particular associations between Zion and the Davidic monarchy gave the word a special resonance in later messianic literature that expressed longing not only for the return of the people to their land but also for the reestablishment of the kingdom of David.

A particular tension has informed the Jewish relationship to Zion since biblical times. On the one hand, the Land of Israel is regarded as a land specially promised to the ancient Israelites and their descendants (the term *Holy Land*, however, only appears once in the Hebrew Bible). According to this position, the Israelite God can be worshiped only on this sanctified territory. Thus when David flees from Saul to the land of the Philistines, he laments that "[men] have driven me out this day that I should have no share in the heritage of the Lord, saying 'Go and serve other gods'" (*1 Sm.* 26:19). In Psalm 137, verse 4 the writer wonders, "How shall we sing the song of YHVH in a foreign land?" In both biblical and rabbinic law, much of the agricultural, ritual, and even civil law applied only to the Land of Israel.

On the other hand, a strong universalist tendency already developed in biblical times held that God rules over all the world and can be worshipped anywhere. This tendency became particularly prominent as a result of the Babylonian exile and found expression in such exilic writers as "Second Isaiah" (*Is.* 40ff.). In some of this literature there is even a hint of criticism against those who wished to limit worship of God to Zion: "Thus says YHVH: with heaven my throne and earth my footstool, what house could you build me, what place could you make for my rest?" (*Is.* 66:1).

The realities of Jewish life during and after the Second Temple period (538 BCE–70 CE) made a combination of these positions necessary. From the time of the Babylonian exile, a large Jewish community developed outside the Land of Israel and became particularly prominent during the Hellenistic and Roman Empires. Even before the destruction of the Second Temple in 70 CE and the Bar Kokhba Revolt (132–135 CE), the Jews of the Diaspora probably constituted a majority of the Jewish people. Nevertheless these Jews maintained a strong connection with the Land of Israel and its religious institutions. They made regular pilgrimages to the Temple and contributed money to it for sacrifices. After the Temple was destroyed, the Palestinian community remained important until the late third century, when it began to decline, and following the Muslim conquest in the seventh century, it ceased to play a significant role in Jewish life. Even after the Temple was destroyed, the Land of Israel continued to function as a religious center for Diaspora communities, owing in part to the continuing authority of the Palestinian rabbis. But at the same time the emerging rabbinic center in Babylonia challenged its Palestinian counterparts and insisted on the equal—or sometimes even the greater—importance of its own community. From a legal point of view, these rabbis did not legislate that one must live in the land in order to fulfill all those commandments that could only be realized there. But they did make the decision of a man to "go up" to the land binding on his wife.

The rabbis developed rituals that could be practiced anywhere and yet were designed to preserve the memory of the Temple *(zekher le-hurban)*. Such ceremonies included leaving a small area of wall unfinished in one's house. It was during this period that prayers were added to the daily service that pleaded with God:

> Sound the great shofar for our freedom; raise the standard for the gathering of our exiles, and assemble us from the four corners of the earth. . . . Restore our judges as of old. . . . And to Jersualem thy city return in mercy and dwell therein as thou has spoken, rebuild it soon in our days as an everlasting building, and speedily set up therein the throne of David. (The Daily Prayer Book)

MEDIEVAL PERIOD. The spiritual connection to Zion was kept alive during the Middle Ages primarily through literature. To be sure through the centuries there were individual Jews who made pilgrimages or actually settled in the Land of Israel, but no theology of pilgrimage developed, nor was it seen as religious obligation. The theme of Zion played an important role in the medieval liturgical poems *(piyyutim)* and especially in the lamentation poem *(qinot)* recited on the Ninth of Av (the day, according to tradition, on which the First and Second Temples were destroyed).

The best examples of secular poetry devoted to longing for Zion are found during the "classical age" of the Spanish Jews (900–1200 CE). Two themes intermingle in this poetry: descriptions of the beauty of Zion and lamentations for its ruin. Some of the Spanish Jewish writers achieved high positions in Spanish society, but their work reflects persistent attachment to the land of their forefathers. Shemuʾel ha-Nagid (933–1055/6 CE) was the vizier of Granada and the commander of its army. One of his poems, "My Heart Waxes Hot within Me," celebrates victory over his enemies, but the first part is a lament over the destruction of Zion. Thus Shemuʾel's pride over his military accomplishments was tempered by the feeling that they were incomplete as long as the Jews lived in exile.

Perhaps the most outstanding representative of this school of poets was Yehudah ha-Levi (c. 1075–1141), whose

Shirei Tsiyyon (Songs of Zion) inspired many imitations later in the Middle Ages. One of his poems, ("Zion, Will You Not Seek the Welfare of Your Prisoners?") was included in the liturgy of the Ninth of Av. In another, titled, "My Heart is in the East," he wrote:

> My heart is in the East and I am at the edge of the West
> How then can I taste what I eat, how can I enjoy it?
> How can I fulfill my vows and pledges, while Zion is
> in the domain of Edom [i.e., the Christian Crusaders]
> and I am in the bonds of Arabia [i.e., Muslim Spain]?
> It would be easy for me to leave behind the good things
> of Spain, just as It would be glorious to see the dust of
> the ruined Shrine. *(The Penguin Book of Hebrew Verse)*

Ha-Levi emigrated to the Land of Israel toward the end of his life, although whether he moved out of ideological or pragmatic reasons remains disputed.

Moses Nahmanides (1194–1270), the twelfth-century Spanish commentator, philosopher, and mystic, who died in the land in 1270, advanced the most radical position on settlement in the land. Not only did he view it as a religious obligation, but he held that it was perhaps the cardinal obligation. Where other thinkers had noted the fact that perhaps a third of the laws of biblical and rabbinic Judaism pertained to the land—and especially to its agriculture—Nahmanides suggested that all of the commandments required performance in the land if they were to achieve their full mystical effect on the divine.

This proto-Zionist sentiment cannot be dissociated from medieval Jewish messianism. All messianic thinkers in the Middle Ages considered the return to Zion to be among the primary tasks of the Messiah. Even as messianic expectations were embroidered with supernatural fantasies, such as the belief in the resurrection of the dead, the core of Jewish messianism remained political and nationalistic: the Messiah would return the Jews to Zion, reestablish the kingdom of David, and rebuild the Temple in Jerusalem. The movements mentioned here were all attempts to spark the messianic process by encouraging human beings to take the first steps of resettling the Land of Israel. In the seventeenth century the Shabbatean movement caused Jews throughout the world to prepare themselves for the imminent return to Zion, a hope largely dashed when the putative Messiah, Shabbetai Tsevi (1626–1676), converted to Islam in 1667.

On the other hand, another group of medieval thinkers deemphasized the importance of immigration to Zion. Some, such as Ḥayyim Kohen (twelfth century), saw no obligation to live in the Land of Israel since the commandments pertaining to the land could not be observed until the coming of the Messiah. Meir ben Baruch of Rothenburg (c. 1220–1293) argued that it is permissible to leave the Land of Israel to study the Torah. Similarly Moses Maimonides (Mosheh ben Maimon, 1135/8–1204), the most renowned of medieval Jewish philosophers and legal scholars, gave greater emphasis to the study of the Torah than to awaiting or hastening the coming of the Messiah. In his code of Jewish law *(Mishneh Torah, c. 1180),* Maimonides did not include settling in the land as one of the 613 commandments. For Maimonides the central event in Jewish history was at Mount Sinai, and the return to Zion in messianic times would be a means toward uninterrupted study of the law revealed at Sinai. Although Maimonides clearly believed in the coming of the Messiah (which he understood as a realistic and not solely supernatural process), he subordinated Zion to Sinai.

This trend of thought became even more pronounced in eighteenth-century Hasidism, which, as Gershom Scholem (1897–1981) has argued, frequently played down expectations of the imminent coming of the Messiah. Dov Ber, the *maggid* of Mezhirich (1704–1772), believed that the qabbalistic task of "raising the sparks" might be more effectively accomplished in the lands of the exile. Naḥman of Bratslav (1772–1810), who was perhaps the most messianic of the Hasidic masters, stretched the holiness of the Land of Israel to encompass all the lands in which the Jews lived, thus spiritualizing what had hitherto been a concrete concept.

The Nineteenth Century. In the nineteenth century the forces of modern nationalism, released by the French Revolution, awakened nationalist hopes among the Jews throughout Europe. Although emancipation and assimilation caused many Jews, particularly in western and central Europe, to identify with the national aspirations of the countries in which they lived, increases in anti-Semitism and the failure of emancipation to fulfill its promises refocused attention on Zion. The nineteenth century thus witnessed a fusing of traditional messianism with modern nationalism that culminated in the emergence of modern Zionism at the end of the century.

Two important intellectual developments in the nineteenth century, among both modernizing and traditional Jews, prepared the ground for Zionism. The first was the movement of Jewish Enlightenment (Haskalah), which began in Germany in the late eighteenth century and spread to eastern Europe in the nineteenth. The Haskalah developed in two directions with respect to Zion. On the one hand, there was a general tendency to promote the emancipation of the Jews in Europe by glorifying the European nations. The Reform movement in Germany, which was one product of enlightenment, deleted references to Zion in the prayer book and emphasized the patriotic attachment of Jews to their native countries. Some Haskalah writers used messianic language to describe European rulers, such as Joseph II of Austria (1741–1790) and Alexander II of Russia (1818–1881), who were perceived as particularly sympathetic to the Jews.

On the other hand, much of the new Hebrew literature written by Haskalah authors, especially in eastern Europe, harkened back to the land of the Bible. Avraham Mapu (1808–1867), the first Hebrew novelist, placed the plots of two of his novels, *Ahavat Tsiyyon* (Love of Zion, 1853) and *Ashmat Shomron* (Guilt of Shomron, 1865–1866), in romantic biblical settings. Hebrew newspapers such as *Ha-shahar* and *Ha-maggid*, published in Russia, also fostered interest in the Land of Israel and countered assimilationist tendencies by arguing for a Jewish national consciousness. In addition the activities of western European Jewish philanthropists, such as Edmund de Rothschild (1845–1934), Adolphe Crémieux (1796–1880), and Moses Montefiore (1784–1885), in settling Jews in Palestine fostered the beginnings of the modern settlement in the country. Thus both in literature and philanthropy modern "enlightened" Jews created the basis for a Zionist movement.

One secular Jewish thinker of particular importance was Moses Hess (1812–1875). Hess was one of the early leaders of European socialism. Following the 1848 revolutions, he withdrew from political activity and became interested in the history of national groups. He rediscovered his Jewish origins and became a fervent advocate of Jewish nationalism. In his *Rome and Jerusalem* (1862), he advanced a proposal for the renewal of the Jewish state, arguing that the continuation of the Jewish people could be justified only on national, rather than religious, grounds.

The second important nineteenth-century development was among traditional Jews. Tsevi Hirsch Kalischer (1795–1874) appealed to the Rothschild family to buy the Land of Israel from Muḥammad ʿAlī (1769–1849), the ruler of Egypt. Kalischer developed a plan to reinstitute the ancient sacrifices on the Temple mount as a way of hastening the coming of the Messiah. He based his messianic doctrine, which called for human initiative, on Moses Maimonides, who had argued that certain human actions might precede the actual coming of the Messiah. Later, following the Damascus blood libel affair of 1840 and the attempt by Western philanthropists to rescue the Damascus Jews, Kalischer advocated agricultural settlement in the Land of Israel. However, even in his later writings, which put forward this kind of practical suggestion, Kalischer never abandoned his messianic expectations, nor did he give up his hope that the sacrifices might be reinstituted by the new settlers.

A similar kind of religious "Zionism" can be found in the writings of Yehudah ben Shelomoh Alkalai (1798–1878), who until the Damascus Affair was an obscure preacher in the Balkans. Like Kalischer, Alkalai argued in numerous pamphlets for Jewish settlement in the Holy Land as a means toward bringing the Messiah.

The writings of Kalischer and Alkalai had little immediate effect, although there was an increase in immigration to Palestine by Orthodox Jews throughout the nineteenth century. New communities of religious Jews were established outside the walls of Jerusalem, in some cases with the help of philanthropists like Montefiore. In 1878 a group of Orthodox Jews established the first agricultural colony, Petach Tikva. Despite their traditionalist orientation, these religious Jews made important contributions in laying the groundwork for the later Zionist settlement.

MODERN SECULAR ZIONISM. The rise of anti-Semitism in France, Germany, and Russia in the last quarter of the nineteenth century raised serious questions about the prospects of Jewish integration into European society. Under the influence of modern nationalist ideas, a number of secular or partially secular Jews in several countries began to conceive of a Jewish homeland as the only answer to the Jewish situation. In addition to the political problem of anti-Semitism, many of these thinkers felt that the growing problem of Jewish assimilation could be addressed only by the creation of a Jewish society with its own national culture.

The new Zionist thinkers attempted to combine the ideas of secular nationalism with the messianic aspirations still cultivated by the large population of traditional Jews. Indeed it might be argued that Zionism emerged when it did as a result of the influence of modern nationalism, but that it emerged at all was a result of the persistence of the age-old religious longing for Zion. Yet the tensions between these seemingly similar national ideals were evident from the inception of modern Zionism, and they continue to characterize the conflict between the secular and the religious in modern Israel.

Following the pogroms in Russia in 1881, a group of eastern European intellectuals formed the Ḥibbat Tsiyyon (Love of Zion). The members of this movement came from both of the groups previously mentioned: followers of the Haskalah and religious figures. Ḥibbat Tsiyyon was primarily a practical movement that sought to foster settlement and agricultural development in Palestine. It borrowed its ideology of "productivization" of the Jews from the earlier Haskalah. The Ḥibbat Tsiyyon was a response to the mass emigration of Jews from Russia that began in the wake of the pogroms, and it tried to direct the immigration to Palestine instead of to western Europe and America. Although the Ḥibbat Tsiyyon sponsored a number of colonies in Palestine, it never became a mass movement, and its impact was largely on Russian Jewish intellectuals.

Modern Zionism really began with Theodor Herzl (1860–1904). The term Zionism was coined in 1890 by Nathan Birnbaum (1864–1937) in his journal *Selbstemanzipation* and was adopted by Herzl and his followers at the First Zionist Congress in 1897. Although some rabbis supported Herzl, most members of the movement, including Herzl himself, were secular and Westernized. Nevertheless Herzl was greeted by many eastern European Jews as a messianic figure. The first substantial Zionist emigration from eastern Europe to Palestine started after the pogroms of 1903 and 1905 to 1906 and was largely made up of young secular Russian Jews, many of whom were influenced by the Russian radicalism of the period.

The attitude toward religion among the early secular Zionist thinkers was frequently quite hostile. Traditional Judaism was viewed as the religion of the exile, and the Zionists saw themselves as a movement to "negate the exile" *(shelilat ha-golah).* This position received its sharpest expression in the writings of M. Y. Berdichevsky (1865–1921), J. H. Brenner (1881–1921), and Jacob Klatzkin (1882–1948). Berdichevsky, for example, saw the whole religious Jewish tradition, going back to Mount Sinai, as being opposed to a proud national life, and he wished to create a "new Hebrew man" based on a "Nietzschean" countertradition of strength and naturalism. Berdichevsky traced this countertradition back to the biblical period, when, he believed, the ancient Hebrews followed a revelation from Mount Gerizim, mentioned in *Deuteronomy* 27:11–26, that was opposed to the "ethical" Torah of Mount Sinai. The prophets, and later the rabbis, suppressed this Torah of nature, but it persisted in heretical movements and splinter sects, such as the first-century Zealots and the eighteenth-century Ḥasidim. This idea, that the Jews had been misled by the rabbis and had followed a tradition alien to their roots, had an important influence on the more radical secular Zionist attitudes toward the Jewish religion.

Nevertheless there were other secular Zionists who tried to base the new Zionist culture on elements from the religious tradition. Aḥad ha-ʿAm (the pen name of Asher Ginsberg, 1856–1927) tried to develop a secular Judaism based on certain principles from the Jewish heritage. He believed that the Jewish religion was one expression of a wider Jewish national culture. The elements that a secular Judaism might borrow from the tradition varied in Aḥad ha-ʿAm's writings (sometimes "absolute monotheism" was stressed, other times "liberal ethics"), but he held that the development of this culture was possible only in a Jewish national home. This national cultural center would in turn revitalize the Jewish Diaspora, which had been spiritually weakened by assimilation and the decline of the Jewish religion.

A number of the leaders of the secular Zionist labor movement also tried, with varying degrees of success, to incorporate a more positive attitude toward the Jewish religion into their secular ideologies. Aharon David Gordon (1856–1922), who was one of the pioneers of the early agricultural settlements, developed a religion of labor based on a mystical bond between the Jew and the Land of Israel. Physical labor on the national soil is a way of renewing the self and bringing it into harmony with the cosmos. Although Gordon was not a practicing Orthodox Jew, his philosophy relied heavily on Jewish mysticism and Hasidism as well as on Tolstoyan ideals.

Another labor leader, Berl Katzenelson (1887–1944), argued for the adaptation of traditional Jewish holidays and rituals to the new national home. Katzenelson, who was enormously influential as a cultural and ideological writer, laid the groundwork for a secular national culture that had its roots in Jewish tradition. Similarly the first prime minister of Israel, David Ben Gurion (1886–1973), sought to base the new national culture on a return to the Bible, a theme that had precedent among the Haskalah writers of the nineteenth century.

The ambivalence toward the Jewish tradition that one finds in many of these early secular Zionists had much to do with their biographies. In most cases they came from traditional homes and were educated in the *yeshivot* (rabbinic academies) of eastern Europe. Zionism was a radical revolution for them against the world of their childhood, but they never fully broke with their memories of this religious culture. Even if their way of life was secular, they wished to recreate an authentic Jewish culture on a new, national basis.

If the labor Zionists were ambivalent at best toward the Jewish religion, their counterparts in the Revisionist Zionist Party (organized in 1925) were militant. The Revisionists were led by Vladimir Jabotinsky (1880–1940), the Russian-Jewish journalist and poet, and they acquired the reputation of a right-wing, nationalist movement. Although Jabotinsky had a few religious followers, his movement was generally adamantly secular and opposed to religion. In the 1940s a splinter group under the poet Yonatan Ratosh (1908–1981) broke off from the Revisionists and formed the Young Hebrew, or "Canaanite," movement (the latter term was originally used by their opponents). The Canaanites saw the Jews as a religious group whose history was in the exile, whereas the new Hebrew community in Palestine was to break from the religious past and develop its own indigenous culture. The Canaanites were inspired by the myths of the ancient Canaanites that were uncovered in the Ras Shamra excavations of the 1930s. Although the Canaanites were an extreme nativist movement, their thought points to an important trend in Israeli culture away from traditional Jewish religion and toward a new national culture that might incorporate ancient Near Eastern myths.

RELIGIOUS ZIONISM. Although the majority of the Orthodox Jewish world was either indifferent or opposed to Herzl's Zionist movement, there was a significant group that responded favorably to the idea of a Jewish state. Among the first rabbis to join Herzl were Yitsḥaq Yaʿaqov Reines (1839–1915) and Shemuʾel Mohilever (1824–1898), who was perhaps the most prominent rabbi in the Ḥibbat Tsiyyon movement. In 1902 Reines formed Mizraḥi, a religious faction within the World Zionist Organization (the name is a composite of some of the Hebrew letters from the words *merkaz ruhani,* "spiritual center"). Mizraḥi consisted of two groups, one that opposed the introduction of any "cultural" issues into the Zionist movement, for fear that the secularists would set the tone in such endeavors, and another that saw that Zionism could not avoid confronting cultural questions and demanded that Mizraḥi try to influence the Zionist movement in a religious direction. Although the "political" faction was initially predominant, the Mizraḥi movement ultimately saw as its raison d'être the fostering of religious education and public religious practice in the Zionist settlement in Palestine and later the state of Israel.

Mizraḥi played a major role in mustering support for Zionism among Orthodox Jews in Europe and the United States. It created a network of schools in which Zionism was taught together with traditional religious subjects. At the same time Mizraḥi established schools in Palestine that formed the backbone of the religious educational system that is an important part of the general educational system in the contemporary state of Israel. The Mizraḥi youth movements, Young Mizraḥi and Benei Akiva, began establishing agricultural settlements in Palestine in the 1920s.

The Mizraḥi joined three other religious parties to create a religious faction in the first Israeli governing coalition. In 1956 they formed the National Religious Party (NRP) and Poʿel Mizraḥi (Mizraḥi workers). The NRP has sat in every Israeli government (with the exception of one year) to date and regularly receives approximately 10 percent of the vote. However, this percentage began to drop in the 1980s with the defection of more nationalist elements to other, nonreligious parties and the emergence of the ultraorthodox Shas Party, which appealed to Jews of Middle Eastern and North African origin. Despite its relatively small share of the national vote, the NRP has constituted an important "swing" element in Israeli governments since neither the Labor Alignment nor the Likud Party has been able to win a clear majority. Thus the NRP has exerted disproportionate influence on Israeli politics and on the role of religion in Israeli society.

Since its inception the Mizraḥi sought to avoid the problem of the relationship of Zionism to Jewish messianism. Much opposition to Zionism in the religious world stemmed from the belief that human beings should not "force the end" (i.e., initiate messianic times by secular means). Instead of answering this position with a new messianic theory, the adherents of Mizraḥi took a cautious stance, claiming that the Zionist movement constituted a "beginning of redemption." They saw their role as guaranteeing that the future redemption would not be ruined by the heretical actions of the secular Zionists.

There were, however, certain elements among the religious Zionists who took a bolder approach to the question of messianism. Primary among these was Avraham Yitsḥaq Kook (1865–1935), who became chief rabbi of Jaffa in 1904 and then chief Ashkenazic rabbi of Palestine from 1921 until his death in 1935. Kook held that redemption had begun with the Zionist movement, and in anticipation of imminent messianic times, he fostered study of the sacrificial laws in his *yeshivah.* Unlike other religious Zionists and religious anti-Zionists, Kook believed the secular pioneers were a necessary force to prepare the material foundation for messianic times. He argued dialectically that the profane was necessary for subsequent emergence of the sacred. Kook met frequently with leaders of the labor Zionist movement and developed close ties with them. As chief rabbi of Jaffa he played a central role in 1909 in the attempt to solve the problem of the *shemittah,* the agricultural sabbatical during which land owned by Jews in the Land of Israel is supposed to lie fallow. Kook arranged for sale of such land to a non-Jew, which allowed it to be worked by Jews and permitted the continuation of the agricultural settlements. Kook's unusually positive attitude toward the secular Zionist movement was based on his belief that, when Zionism succeeded, messianic times would come and the Zionist movement would itself return to its unconscious religious roots.

Kook's messianic philosophy had little direct impact on the religious Zionist parties, but it did influence a new generation of religious Israelis, particularly through the Merkaz ha-Rav Yeshivah in Jerusalem, established by Kook and headed by his son Tsevi Yehudah Kook (1891–1982) until the latter's death. This new generation did not accept the compromise position of the older leaders of Mizraḥi, who believed that the religious parties should primarily guard the religious status quo in the state of Israel. The young religious Zionists, who grew up after the creation of the state in 1948, believed strongly in Zionism as the fulfillment of traditional Jewish messianism. This belief took political expression after the Six-Day War of 1967. Young religious Israelis reestablished the settlements in the Etsion bloc south of Jerusalem and created a Jewish outpost in Hebron in 1968. (This illegal settlement was later recognized by the government and developed into the town of Qiryat Arba outside of Hebron.) In 1974, following the Yom Kippur War, these religious activists founded the Gush Emunim (bloc of the faithful) movement, which advocated the incorporation of Judea and Samaria (the West Bank of the Jordan River) into Israel. The Gush Emunim led a settlement drive in these areas, sometimes with the support of the Israeli government and sometimes illegally. They constituted a significant messianic force in Israeli politics and formed alliances with secular nationalist forces.

Religious Institutions in the State of Israel. Under both the Ottoman Empire and the British Mandate, Jewish religious courts enjoyed official jurisdiction over matrimonial and inheritance law. The office of the *hakham basi* in the Ottoman Empire was succeeded by the Ashkenazic and Sefardic chief rabbis under the British Mandate. These functions were carried over to the rabbinic courts and the chief rabbinate of the state of Israel, which were given jurisdiction over matters of personal law by a Knesset enactment of 1953. Rabbinical judges were given the same status as district court judges, and their decisions were enforced by the civil authorities. Thus in matters of marriage, divorce, and child custody, rabbinic courts—ruling according to Jewish law *(halakhah)*—have state sanction. Civil marriage and divorce do not exist, although civil marriages are recognized if contracted abroad. The Ministry of Religious Affairs deals with the needs of the various religious communities in Israel and funds the construction and maintenance of synagogues, *yeshivot,* and other religious facilities.

Although both the Conservative and Reform movements have small followings in Israel, their rabbis are not authorized by the rabbinate to perform marriages, and they do not benefit from the budgets available through the Ministry of Religious Affairs. Conversion to Judaism is supervised by the rabbinate, and thus Conservative and Reform conversions are not recognized as valid unless contracted abroad.

Although the majority of the Jewish citizens of Israel are secular or quasi-traditional, a religious status quo is maintained. The Sabbath is the national day of rest, and Jewish holidays are national holidays. Sabbath rules apply in public places at the discretion of local municipalities, but the various political parties have undertaken to maintain the practices that have existed since the creation of the state. In the 1977 and 1982 coalition agreements, the Agudat Yisra'el Party, which represents some of the most orthodox elements, demanded certain changes in the status quo, such as cancellation of Sabbath flights by the national airline, El Al.

The problem of religion in the state of Israel is connected more generally to the question of a Jewish state. According to the Orthodox interpretation, a Jewish state would have to be a "theocratic" state governed by Jewish law *(halakhah).* At the opposite extreme, the secular nationalist argument holds that Israel should be a secular state in which synagogue and state are strictly separated and whose Jewish character is determined purely by the sociological makeup of its population. For the Orthodox the identity of the Jews can only be determined by the *halakhah:* one is a Jew only if born of a Jewish mother or converted by a *halakhic* procedure. For the secular Zionists anyone who declares himself or herself a Jew should be considered as such. Moreover some secular nationalists argue that a new Israeli identity should take the place of Jewish identity, which they regard as a religious relic of the years of exile. In a case in the 1960s the Israeli Supreme Court ruled that Jewish identity is not determined by the *halakhah.* The case concerned a Carmelite monk, Brother Daniel, who was born a Jew and had fought against the Nazis as a partisan. He requested Israeli citizenship under the Law of Return, arguing that, according to the *halakhah,* he remained a Jew even though he professed another religion. The court ruled against him with the argument that the conventional understanding of who is a Jew contradicted the *halakhah* in such a case and, since Israel is not a *halakhic* state, that the common definition should prevail. Similarly in 1970 the court ruled that a child born of a Jewish father and a non-Jewish mother might be registered as of "Israeli" rather than "Jewish" national identity. This decision would have set aside the concept of a corporate Jewish state in favor of a new secular Israeli identity. As a result of pressure from the religious Zionist parties and of discomfort on the part of many secular Zionists, the Knesset passed a law providing that only persons recognized as Jews by the *halakhah* might be registered as Jews by nationality. In 1980 the Knesset passed a law stipulating that, in matters in which there is no specific law or precedent, judges should be guided by "Hebrew jurisprudence" *(mishpat 'ivri).* Judges were directed to follow traditional Jewish law, but by avoiding the term *halakhah,* the Knesset was able to satisfy the secular refusal to accept a theocratic state. Thus the judicial system has generally attempted a secular definition of Jewish identity, whereas the legislative system, responding to religious sentiments, has avoided such a break with tradition.

The immigration of nearly a million Russian Jews following the breakup of the Soviet Union posed new challenges to Israel's identity. Many of these Russian Jews were of mixed parentage, and a large percentage (perhaps as many as a third) was not Jewish at all. The courts faced problems of whether fallen soldiers of Israel's army could be buried in Jewish cemeteries. The state faced another problem in 1994 with the immigration of Ethiopian Jews, whose religious traditions did not include rabbinic law. The rabbinate ruled that they were to be considered Jews, even though the weight of historical evidence seemed to preclude such ethnic descent on religious grounds.

ANTI-ZIONISM. There are a number of expressions of anti-Zionism based on religious motivations. In both Europe and America nineteenth-century Reform Judaism was unalterably opposed to a national definition of Judaism. The Pittsburgh Platform of 1885 specifically rejected any expectation of a return of the Jews to Zion. By 1937, however, the Reform movement had moved to a more neutral position and adopted the Columbus Platform, in which the "group loyalty" of the Jews is recognized and the Jewish community of Palestine is supported "not only [as] a haven of refuge for the oppressed but also [as] a center of Jewish culture and spiritual life" (Plaut, 1963–1965). Nevertheless a wing of the Reform movement, which formed the American Council for Judaism, actively opposed the creation of Israel in the 1940s. Following the Six-Day War, the Reform movement became explicitly Zionist and joined the World Zionist Organization. Reform Jews established several *kibbutsim* and congregations in Israel.

Among the Orthodox, Zionism was initially greeted with skepticism or hostility. The initial plan to hold the First Zionist Congress in Munich was canceled as a result of opposition by the German rabbis. In 1912 Agudat Yisra'el was formed by rabbis from Germany, Hungary, and Poland as an organization to advance orthodoxy in Jewish life. The Agudah opposed secular Zionism but maintained an ambivalent attitude toward settlement in the Land of Israel. Following the establishment of the state, the Agudah became a political party advocating a state based on the *halakhah.* The ideology of the movement opposes participation in Zionist governments, although its representatives have nevertheless from time to time held cabinet seats and although they provided coalition support for the government after 1977. The Agudah has used its political influence to strengthen its educational and religious institutions and has sought religious concessions from the Knesset, such as exemptions for religious girls from national service and stricter adherence to Sabbath rules. As opposed to the National Religious Party, the Agudah considers itself non-Zionist and does not identify with the national goals of the state.

In the 1980s the Shas Party was formed under the spiritual leadership of Rabbi 'Ovadyah Yosef (b. 1920), an Iraqi-born sage who served as chief Sefardic rabbi of Israel. The Shas Party appealed primarily to Jews of Middle Eastern and North African origin and defined itself as non-Zionist, by which it meant that, like the Agudat Yisra'el, it favored a theocratic state in place of the secular state of Israel. But Shas was characterized more by pragmatism, seeking state subsidies for its extensive network of schools and social services for its constituents.

A more extreme anti-Zionist group is the Neturei Karta (guardians of the city), which broke off from Agudat Yisra'el in 1935. The Neturei Karta are largely followers of the Satmar Hasidic sect. Neturei Karta opposed the creation of the state of Israel and regarded Zionism as a heinous sin that prevents the coming of the Messiah. They believe the Nazi Holocaust was punishment for secular Zionism, and they declared their willingness to participate in an Arab government in Palestine. They clashed violently from time to time with the Israeli police in demonstrations against what they regard as violations of Jewish law in the state. The members of Neturei Karta live for the most part in Jerusalem, where they govern themselves, taking no services from the state and paying no taxes. They also have significant support from certain ultraorthodox Jews in the United States.

CONCLUSION. Modern Israel is the product of both secular and religious tendencies with origins in modern nationalism and in the traditional messianic connection to Zion. With the exception of the small anti-Zionist group, most Jews in the world, representing virtually the whole religious spectrum, support the basic aspirations of Zionism. Thus the character of the Jewish state—religious, secular, or some combination of both—remains an issue of political conflict among Zionists, but this conflict is also emblematic of the larger question of the relationship of religion to nationalism in the modern world.

SEE ALSO Agudat Yisra'el; Messianism, article on Jewish Messianism.

BIBLIOGRAPHY

Two books devoted to the subject of Zion throughout the history of Jewish thought are Abraham S. Halkin, ed., *Zion in Jewish Literature* (New York, 1961), which contains essays on the biblical and rabbinic periods, medieval secular and religious poetry, and nineteenth-century Hebrew poetry and prose; and the more synthetic Jean-Christophe Attias and Esther Benbassa, *Israel, the Impossible Land* (Stanford, Calif., 2003). An additional source of Zionist poetry is *The Penguin Book of Hebrew Verse*, edited by T. Carmi (New York, 1981), which includes poetry by Yehudah ha-Levi. For additional articles on the biblical period, see Shemaryahu Talmon's "The Biblical Concept of Jerusalem," *Journal of Ecumenical Studies* 8 (1971): 300–316; and Ben Zion Dinaburg's "Zion and Jerusalem: Their Role in the Historic Consciousness of Israel" (in Hebrew), *Zion* 16 (1951): 1–17. Other valuable discussions of medieval writings are Yitzhak F. Baer's "Erez Yisrael and the Diaspora in the View of the Middle Ages" (in Hebrew), *Zion Yearbook* 6 (1946): 149–171; and H. H. Ben-Sasson's "Exile and Redemption through the Eyes of the Spanish Exiles" (in Hebrew) in *Yitzhak F. Baer Jubilee Volume*, edited by S.W. Baron, B. Dinur, S. Ettinger, and I. Halperin (Jerusalem, 1960). A nationalist argument about the relationship between the Jews and Zion in Jewish history and especially the modern period is in Ben Zion Dinur's *Israel and the Diaspora* (Philadelphia, Pa., 1969). For the relationship of the Jewish Enlightenment to Zion, see Isaac F. Barzilay's "National and Anti-National Trends in the Berlin Haskalah," *Jewish Social Studies* 21 (1959): 165–192; and Jacob S. Raisin's *The Haskalah Movement in Russia* (Maple Shade, N.J., 2001), an old but still useful work. The attitude of nineteenth-century Reform is treated in W. Gunther Plaut's *The Rise of Reform Judaism* (New York, 1963–1965).

On the origins and history of the Zionist movement, see David Vital's *The Origins of Zionism* (Oxford, U.K., 1975) and *Zionism: The Formative Years* (Oxford, U.K., 1982). A good general history of Zionism is Walter Laqueur's *A History of Zionism* (New York, 1972). The history of Zionist thought has been treated by Shlomo Avineri in *The Making of Modern Zionism: The Intellectual Origins of the Jewish State* (New York, 1981) and by Ben Halpern in *The Idea of the Jewish State* (Cambridge, Mass., 1961). A good anthology of Zionist thought with a superb introductory essay is Arthur Hertzberg, ed., *The Zionist Idea* (Philadelphia, 1997). The specific issue of religion in the Zionist movement is treated by Ehud Luz, *Parallels Meet: Religion and Nationalism in the Early Zionist Movement (1882–1904)* (Philadelphia, 1988) and, in the state of Israel, by Ervin Birnbaum, *The Politics of Compromise: State and Religion in Israel* (Rutherford, N.J., 1970), Charles S. Liebman and Eliezer Don-Yehiya, *Religion and Politics in Israel* (Bloomington, Ind., 1984), and S. Zalmon Abramov, *Perpetual Dilemma: Jewish Religion in the Jewish State* (Rutherford, N.J., 1976). A good treatment of the relationship between Zionism and Jewish messianism is Aviezer Ravitzky, *Messianism, Zionism, and Jewish Religious Radicalism* (Chicago, 1996). An anthology of anti-Zionist thought is in Michael Selzer, ed., *Zionism Reconsidered* (New York, 1970). A semischolarly treatment of religion in Israel from the viewpoint of Neturei Karta is Emile Marmorstein's *Heaven at Bay: The Jewish Kulturkampf in the Holy Land* (London, 1969).

DAVID BIALE (1987 AND 2005)

ZODIAC SEE ASTROLOGY

ZOHAR.

Sefer ha-zohar (The book of splendor) is the central book in the literature of Jewish mysticism (Qabbalah). It is attributed to Shim'on bar Yoḥ'ai, a second century tanna, but modern scholarship has concluded that it is a compilation dating from thirteenth-century Spain. Quotations from the *Zohar* first appear in qabbalistic writings after 1280, and analysis of the book's terminology and prose style shows that its real author is Mosheh de León (1240–1305), a Castilian qabbalist.

Written mostly in Aramaic, the *Zohar* presents an elaborate and comprehensive, though not always coherent, mystical system that employs audacious anthropomorphic and sexual imagery to express a mythical and symbolic perception of divine reality without precedent in medieval Qabbalah. The *Zohar* was accepted by qabbalists as an authoritative ancient work, and its influence on the later evolution of Jewish mysticism was felt principally through the impact of its mythical conceptions on qabbalistic theosophy.

The *Zohar* encompasses a series of qabbalistic works that can be divided into three main layers:

(1) *Midrash ha-ne'elam* (The hidden Midrash) is considered to be the earliest stratum. Written partly in Hebrew, partly in Aramaic, it has overt affinities with Mosheh de León's early Hebrew works and an obvious tendency toward allegorical exegesis of biblical verses.

(2) The bulk of the *Zohar* consists mainly of a homiletical interpretation of the Pentateuch, written in Aramaic and using symbolic exegesis. To this layer belong several shorter compositions, of which the most important are *Sifra' de-tseni'uta'* (The occult book), *Idra' rabba'* and *Idra' zuṭṭa'*.

(3) The latest stratum is formed by two large compositions: *Tiqqunei zohar,* which is composed of seventy interpretations of the word *bere'shit* (the opening word of *Genesis*), and *Ra'ya' meheimna'* (The faithful shepherd), a qabbalistic interpretation of the rationale for the commandments.

Immediately after their appearance, the earlier strata of the *Zohar* were the subjects of commentaries by qabbalists. Yosef Angelino (early fourteenth century) compiled a commentary entitled *Livnat ha-sappir* on the portions of the *Zohar* that explain *Genesis* and *Leviticus.* In the late thirteenth century David ben Yehudah he-Ḥasid wrote *Sefer ha-gevul,* a commentary on *Idra' rabba'*. In the second half of the sixteenth century several important commentaries were composed including, Shim'on Lavi's *Ketem paz,* Mosheh Cordovero's *Or yaqar,* and works by Mosheh Isserles, Eliyyahu Loans of Worms, Avraham Axulai, Avraham Galante, and Ḥayyim Vital. All subsequent commentaries extant were written under the influence of the reinterpretation of qabbalistic ideas by Isaac Luria, a fact that diminishes their contribution to understanding the text. The most important of these are by Shalom Buzaglo (seventeenth century) Eliyyahu ben Shelomoh Zalman (known as the Gaon of Vilna [Vilnius]) in the eighteenth century, and Yitsḥaq Eiziḳ Safrin of Komarno in the nineteenth century.

There are several Hebrew translations of the *Zohar;* the earliest, dating from the late thirteenth or early fourteenth century, is that of David ben Yehudah he-Ḥasid, who incorporated parts of it in his own qabbalistic works. Parts of the *Zohar* have been translated into Latin by Guillaume Postel and Knorr von Rosenroth. Larger translations exist in English (by Harry Sperling and Maurice Simon, 1931–1934; by Daniel Chanan Matt, 1983); in French (by Jean de Pauly, 1906–1911; by Charles Mopsik and B. Maruani, 1981); in German (by Ernst Müller, 1932 and 1984); and in Italian (by L. Balducci, 1978).

BIBLIOGRAPHY

Jellinek, Adolf. *Moses ben Schem-Tob de Leon und sein Verhaltnis, zum Sohar.* Leipzig. 1851.

Liebes, Yehudah. "Peraqim be-milon *Sefer ha-Zohar.*" Ph. D. diss., Hebrew University of Jerusalem, 1976.

Liebes, Yehudah. "Ha-mashiaḥ shel ha-Zohar." In *Ha-re'ayon ha-meshihi ba-maḥshavah ha-Yehudit,* pp. 83–234. Jerusalem, 1982.

Liebes, Yehudah. "Christian Influences in the Zohar." *Immanuel* 17 (Winter 1983–1984): 43–67.

Matt, Daniel Chanan. *Zohar: The Book of Enlightenment.* Ramsey, N.J., 1983.

Scholem. Gershom. *Major Trends in Jewish Mysticism.* 3d ed. New York. 1961. See pages 156–243.

Scholem, Gershom, ed. *Zohar: The Book of Splendor.* Reprint. New York, 1963.

Secret, François. *Le Zôhar chez les Kabbalistes chrétiens de la Renaissance.* Paris, 1958.

Tishby, Isaiah. *Mishnat ha-Zohar.* 2 vols. 3d ed. Jerusalem, 1971.

MOSHE IDEL (1987)

ZOLLA, ELÉMIRE. Elémire Zolla (1926–2002), an Anglo-Italian polymath, writer, historian of ideas, metaphysical thinker, and spiritual seeker, has a unique place in twentieth-century religious, comparative, and cultural studies. His rigorous and passionate explorations of shamanism, Gnosticism, alchemy, and esoteric doctrines, and his original views on archetypes as the unifying patterns underlying historical processes, on the mystic state conceived as the crux and marrow of human experience, and on syncretism as the equalization of philosophies and religions on a trans-historical plan, make Zolla an unusual thinker, and a candidate for a nonparochial reconsideration of his spiritual anthropology. Zolla's work is imbued with the passion for truth that Abraham Joshua Heschel immediately recognized at the time of their first encounter in Rome in the late 1960s. In fact, Zolla was the dedicatee of the Italian edition of Heschel's *Passion for Truth* (1974).

A prominent and controversial figure on the Italian cultural scene from the late 1950s, Zolla became director of the Institute of Foreign Languages and Literatures at the University of Genoa, where he was also chair of Anglo-American literature and Germanic philology (1970–1974). In those same years, before transferring to the University of Rome to serve as professor of American literature, he directed the Ticinese Institute for Advanced Studies at Lugano, Switzerland, where he organized summer courses dealing with the metaphysical assumptions of Latin, Greek, Hindu, Chinese, Iranian, Hebrew, Islamic, and African civilizations. Zolla was also the founder and editor of an Italian-language journal in cultural and religious studies, *Conoscenza religiosa* (1969–1983), and he was a regular contributor to numerous other journals, many in English. He served on the board of editors of *Cahiers de l'hermetisme, Connaissance des religions, Incognita,* and *Quaderni di Italianistica,* and was a member of the advisory board of the African Institute for the Studies of Humanistic Values at the University of Cincinnati, as well as for the Centre for the Study of Eurasian Shamanism at the University of Rome Tor Vergata, and the scientific council of the Centre d'anthropologie et de civilization Européenne at the University of Strasbourg. Zolla became professor emeritus in American literature at the University of Rome after he retired in 1991.

ESSENTIAL BIOGRAPHICAL AND ACADEMIC DATA. Zolla was born in Turin on July 9, 1926. His father, Venanzio, was a well known Anglo-Italian painter; his mother, Blanche Smith, was a musician from Kent. Zolla was brought up speaking English, Italian, French, Spanish, and German. Later he would master several other languages, including Russian (he translated Pavel Florenskii's *Ikonostas* as *Le porte regali,* Milan, 1977). He graduated in law from the University of Turin, and also attended courses in psychiatry held at the town asylum. A severe lung disease contracted at the age of twenty-two gave him recurrent reminders throughout his life of the need to cherish every drop of vital energy. From a religious point of view, he was agnostic, but a fervent believer, as he used to say, in the boundless power of belief. In the prime of his life he wrote stories, including "An Angelic Visit on Via dei Martiri," and two novels, *Minuetto all'inferno* (Minuet in hell; 1956) and *Cecilia o la disattenzione* (Cecilia or inattention; 1961).

As a literary critic he freelanced for the main periodicals of the time, contributing essays on Franz Kafka, André Gide, Thomas Mann, Marcel Proust, and James Joyce. Zolla developed a keen interest in American matters from literary, historical, juridical, and ethnological angles. On the suggestion of Mario Praz, the leading Anglicist at the University of Rome, who had been highly impressed by Zolla's earlier investigations on Herman Melville's *Clarel,* on Emily Dickinson's poetry, and on Nathaniel Hawthorne's *Septimius Felton,* Zolla was offered the post of associate professor of American literature at the University of Rome in 1959. A full professorship followed in 1967.

Eloquence, bold knowledge, and a special gift for teaching made Zolla revered and popular among his assistants and students at the universities of Genoa and Rome. New branches of study, such as Native North-American studies and ethnopoetics, along with fecund intersections with comparative and Oriental studies, developed as a result of Zolla's work. He launched research projects involving teams of junior scholars on the superman theme in modern literature and on exoticism in American literature. He also edited and introduced *Novecento Americano* (American literature in the twentieth century; 1980–1983), a three-volume textbook providing monographs on fifty major American modern writers. The studies *in mortem* produced by some of Zolla's former disciples are noteworthy when considering the legacy of Zolla's work in this area.

KEY FIGURES IN ZOLLA'S THOUGHT. In a long interview with a journalist shortly before his death, Zolla teasingly predicted: "It won't be easy to retrace the lives I have lived and the directions of my thought" (Fasoli, 1995, p. 29). On another occasion, when asked who had been a key figure in his own quest, he replied by quoting two metaphors, both of them aquatic. The first is from Zolla's collection of essays *Che cos'è la tradizione?* (What is tradition?, 1971), a work that Bernard Wall described as a manifesto of a fearless program of reaction against the spiritual atrophy of modern civilization: "Humans are like carp," wrote Zolla, "who flourish and grow when there is a rock in the center of their pond that they can swim around in harmonious circles" (p. 9). The second metaphor, from Zolla's *Verità segrete esposte in evidenza* (Neglected truths exposed, 1990), is contained in a broader reflection, abbreviated here: "Every life," wrote Zolla, "comprises an invisible interiority that is substantial to it. The only way to grasp this is to sidestep tangible appearances, to take a leap against the current like the salmon, who is the living symbol of knowledge in the Old Norse Scriptures" (p. 154). The carp circling the rock and the salmon swimming upstream towards the source—no images could better express the two leading traits in Zolla's intellectual biography and at the same time the character of his peculiar philosophical vision.

Syncretism, which Zolla vigorously defended in his essay "Il sincretismo" (1986), and metaphysical experience, which in the first lines of "Archetypes" (1981) he described as "the gathering in of the aloof mind" when it "becomes absorbed in its self-existent identity and sameness," were as much leitmotifs in Zolla's pursuit of a unitive knowledge as was his incoercible drive toward the systematic exploration of otherness, a notion that he shaped into an extraordinarily vast array of implications, much beyond its strict ethnological meaning. In a memorable lecture given at the Interreligious Colloquium at the Rothko Chapel in Houston in 1974 (see Ibish and Marculescu, 1978), Zolla described otherness as an antipodal category of the human spirit, the paradigm of an inverted world where ordinary life might flow peacefully between action and contemplation, and the esoteric life as a joyous apprenticeship in metaphysical experience. This broader notion of otherness offers a key to an unbiased investigation of Zolla's accumulated research into alchemy, including Western, Indian, and Daoist notions of immortality; esotericism, with a special bent for ecstatic Qabbalah, Sufism, Zoroastrian, and Tantric traditions; mysticism, which he explored in a monumental anthology of pagan and Christian contemplatives (*I mistici dell'Occidente,* 1963); shamanism, particularly in the Native North American and Korean contexts; and tradition and metaphysics, fields par excellence of Zolla's lifelong spiritual quest. His encounters with survivals of the past among the North American Indians, in Africa (Nubia and Cairo), and especially in the East (Israel, Iran, India, Bali, Taiwan, Korea, and Japan), were analyzed in his quarterly journal *Conoscenza religiosa.* An international group of leading specialists contributed to its sixty-eight issues.

The most perceptive interpreter of the multifaceted identity of Zolla's spiritual anthropology was probably the Romanian historian of religions, Ioan P. Culianu (1950–1991). In his view Zolla was "perhaps the most original, versatile, and untimely of Italy's foremost intellectuals, displaying supreme indifference towards the fashion of the day and therefore—needless to say—controversial" (Culianu, 1990, pp. 222–224). In his reconstruction of the image of the Indian in American literature, which Zolla made in his celebrated book, *The Writer and the Shaman* (1968), he approached the categories from the point of view of the Native American. Moreover, Culianu emphasizes that this process of lucid identification with the indigenous point of view, or with the shaman who effects his ascent to heaven in trance, or with the mystic enraptured in a circle of contemplative bliss, was possible thanks to the new position that emerged as part of Zolla's method. It is the position of the "intelligence out of love" (a fairly faithful translation of Dante's "intelletto d'amore"). To kindle a certain quality of love in the process of comprehending the inner nature of otherness was the esoteric part of Zolla's intellectual achievement. He was well aware that such an achievement could not be pursued except by swimming upstream against the current of his time. No vision could be as antipodal to the spirit of the age which was dominant on the eve of the 1968 student revolts as the one Zolla depicted in *Le potenze dell'anima* (The powers of the soul, 1968), a crucial investigation of the spiritual morphology in the history of culture.

BIBLIOGRAPHY

Eighty percent of Zolla's writings are in Italian; approximately ten percent are in English, with the remaining works in Spanish, French, and German. Essays and papers provided to international conferences are scattered in several journals and volumes of proceedings. His articles in *Il corriere della sera, La nación,* and the Sunday supplement of *Il sole 24ore* (published between 2000 and 2002) have ranged from travel accounts to social, literary, and art criticism. An annotated bibliography in Italian, updated to 1991, is available in *La religione della terra: Vie sciamaniche, universi immaginali, iperspazi virtuali nell'esperienza sacrale della vita,* edited by Grazia Marchianò (Como, Italy, 1991), pp. 35–41. This title, translated as *Earth Religion: Shamanic Paths, Imaginal Worlds, Virtual Hyperspaces in the Sacred Experience of Life,* is a collection of interdisciplinary essays offered to Zolla on the occasion of his sixty-fifth birthday by Francisco Garcia Bazán, Ioan Petru Culianu, Terence DuQuesne, Moshé Idel, Toshihiko and Toyo Izutsu, Wolfgang J. Jilek, Louise Jilek-Aall, Luce López-Baralt, Adam McLean, Viviana Pâques, and Lawrence E. Sullivan.

For evidence of the mark Zolla left on a new generation of Italian specialists in Anglo-American studies, see Angelica Palumbo's "Elémire Zolla: An Initiation to Research"(in Italian). *Studi Europei: Annals of the Department of History of European Thought* 10 (Genoa, 2002): 129–144, and Fedora Giordano's "Zolla and the Native Americans"(in Italian), in *Gli Indiani d'America e l'Italia,* edited by F.Giordano and Alberto Guaraldi, Alessandria, 2002.

Bibliographies updated to the year of Zolla's death (2002) are available in *Viator* 6 (2002): 24–34; and *Idea viva: Gaceta de cultura* 14 (2002): 52–54, where, in addition, the relevance of Zolla's esoteric thought is examined by F. G. Bazán in "E. Zolla y el esoterismo," pp. 10, 12, and 48; and *Sheshat: Cross-Cultural Perspectives in Poetry and Philosophy* 6 (2003), a special issue in memory of Zolla, edited by Terence DuQuesne and Mark Angelo de Brito. See also *Religion, Fiction, and History: Essays in Memory of Ioan Petru Culianu,* 2 vols., edited by Sorin Antohi (Bucharest, 2001), a collection to which Zolla contributed his "Culianu" (pp. 176–205), which includes an essential bibliographical survey on page 589.

Ten new works by Zolla appeared between 1991 and 2002, the last being *Discesa all'ade e resurrezione* (Milan, 2002), a philosophical meditation on the hermetic motif of the journey of the human soul once the flesh has been discarded. Zolla's *Il dio dell'ebbrezza: Antologia dei moderni dionisiaci* (Turin, 1998) is an exegesis of the Dionysian traces in modern literature, and *Uscite dal mondo* (Milan, 1992) is a collection of essays focusing on the goal of life in light of the amazing new perspectives offered by virtual reality technology. Among Zolla's works in English, *The Eclipse of the Intellectual* (1959), translated by Raymond Rosenthal (New York, 1968), Zolla's first controversial book in social criticism, contains a fierce attack on modern mass civilization. Zolla's influence is acknowledged in Marshall McLuhan's *From Cliché to Archetype* (New York, 1970). Stefano Cochetti notices the strong influence of Theodor W. Adorno's and Max Horkheimer's negative dialectics on it. Zolla's *The Writer and the Shaman: A Morphology of the American Indian,* translated by Raymond Rosenthal (New York, 1973), is an impressive study of the images of the Indian in American literature from the beginning of colonization to 1969.

Zolla's *Language and Cosmogony* (Ipswich, U.K., 1976) is a philologically-based analysis of Indo-European roots leading to a reconstruction of the Vedic cosmogonical process. His *The Uses of Imagination and the Decline of the West* (Ipswich, U.K., 1978) is a concise discussion on the decay of creative imagination as distinct from and opposite to fancy in the modern West, with a learned, comparative approach to the theory of imagination in Iranian metaphysics and Indian Vedānta. Zolla's *Archetypes: The Persistence of Unifying Patterns* (New York, 1982) begins with a description of metaphysical experience in terms akin to *samādhi* in the Vedānta philosophy, then moves on to a consideration of the archetypal patterns and their modes of operation as mirrored in mathematics, poetry, history, and politics. Reviews include those by Paul D. Huss in *Library Journal* 5, no. 1 (1982): 897; Pamela van Schaik, *English Studies of the University of South Africa* 1 (1982); Philip Sherrard, *Temenos* 3 (1982): 186–190; and Victor H. Jones, *The Journal of Mind and Behavior* 3, no. 2 (1982): 175–177. *The Androgyne: Fusion of the Sexes* (London, 1981), published in the United States as *The Androgyne: Reconciliation of Male and Female* (New York, 1982), is a scholarly and beautifully illustrated pageant of the man-woman image throughout history and myth. Encyclopedic entries by Zolla include "Les religions des

Amériques: Tribus Indiennes du Canada et des Etats-Unis," in *Encyclopédie des religions*, edited by Frédéric Lenoir and Ysé T. Masquelier, vol. 1, pp. 1235–1250 (Paris, 1997); and "Chamanisme: Amérique du Nord: Cheyenne"; "Amérique du Nord: Inuit"; and "Amérique du Nord: Sioux"; in *Dictionnaire critique de l'esoterisme*, edited by Jean Servier, pp. 280–282 (Paris, 1998).

Zolla's essay, "Traditional Modes of Contemplation and Action" can be found in *Contemplation and Action in World Religions: Selected Papers from the Rothko Chapel Colloquium "Traditional Modes of Contemplation and Action,"* edited by Yusuf Ibish and Ileana Marculescu (Houston, Tex., and Seattle, Wash., 1978). See also Ioan P. Culianu, "Elémire Zolla: Neglected Truths Exposed," *Incognita* 1, no. 2 (1990): 222–224; and Doriano Fasoli, ed. *Un destino itinerante: Conversazioni tra occidente e oriente* (Venice, 1995).

Reviews on Zolla include Bernard Wall, "Against the Delirium of Negation," *Times Literary Supplement* (October 29, 1971). Excerpts from major reviews are quoted in the entry on Zolla in *Book Review Digest* (1974): 1351. See also Vine Deloria Jr., "Images of the Indian," *Boston Sunday Herald Advertiser* (March 2, 1974); Guy Davenport, *The Geography of Imagination* (1981): 353–358; Peter Nabokov, "Return to the Native," *New York Review of Books* 31 (September 27, 1984); and Ioan P. Culianu, "The Construction of the Other," *History of Religions* 30, no. 3 (1991): 308–311. In Cesare Médail's *Le piccole porte*, translated as *Small Doors* (Milan, 2004), Zolla's spiritual quest is closely examined in comparison with the ones of Mircea Eliade, Tenzin Gyatso, XIVth Dalai Lama, Thich Nhat Hanh, and Raimon Panikkar.

GRAZIA MARCHIANÒ (2005)

ZONGMI

ZONGMI (780–841), more fully, Guifeng Zongmi; Chinese Buddhist Chan and Huayan scholar, traditionally reckoned as the fifth "patriarch" both in the Heze line of Southern Chan and in the Huayan tradition. Zongmi was born in Xichong County, Guo prefecture, in Szechwan province. His family, the Ho, was one of local prominence, and as a youth he received a traditional education in the Confucian classics. He became interested in Buddhism as an adolescent, but he continued his Confucian studies at a local academy in preparation for the imperial examinations that would open the door to an official career. In 804, however, he met the Chan priest Daoyuan and was so impressed that he abandoned his worldly ambitions and became his disciple. Later, while still a novice monk, he experienced his first awakening after reading only two or three pages of the *Yuanjue jing* (The scripture of perfect enlightenment) at the home of a lay patron. Zongmi continued his Chan study under Daoyuan, receiving full ordination from him in 808. Two years later he was introduced to the commentary and subcommentary to the *Avataṃsaka Sūtra* written by the famous Huayan scholar Chengguan (738–839). This work so impressed him that in 812 he became a disciple of Chengguan and studied intensely with him for two years. In 816 he withdrew to Mount Zhongnan outside the eastern capital of Luoyang to read the Buddhist canon. He now began a productive career as a scholar, writing numerous commentaries on a wide range of Buddhist texts. His greatest exegetical energies, however, were devoted to the *Yuanjue jing*, which he regarded as better suited to the age than the *Avataṃsaka*. His scholarly activity came to an abrupt stop in 835, when he became implicated in an abortive attempt to oust the eunuchs from power at court. Afterward he withdrew from public life, and nothing further is known about him until his death in 841.

Zongmi's Chan training played a key role in the new thrust that he gave to Huayan metaphysics. His emphasis on the ultimate ground from which phenomena arise over their unimpeded interpenetration—an idea characteristic of the classical Huayan thought of Fazang (643–712)—reveals his interest in clarifying the ontological basis for religious practice. He also found in Huayan hermeneutics a framework in which to harmonize the conflicting tendencies evident in the Buddhist world of his day. His *Chanyuan zhuquanji duxu* (Preface to the collected writings on the source of Chan), for instance, in addition to affording valuable historical insight into the Chan of the late eighth and early ninth centuries, seeks to reconcile the split that had developed between Chan practitioners and textual scholars, as well as between the various Chan lineages. His efforts to articulate a comprehensive framework in which apparently opposing positions could be sublated also extended to non-Buddhist traditions, as can best be seen in his *Yuanren lun* (Inquiry into the origin of man). Zongmi's writings represent an important stage in the complex unfolding of the dialogue among the "Three Religions" (Buddhism, Daoism, and Confucianism) in Chinese history.

SEE ALSO Huayan.

BIBLIOGRAPHY

The most thorough study of Zongmi's life and thought is Kamata Shigeo's *Shūmitsu kyōgaku no shisōshiteki kenkyū* (Tokyo, 1975), which includes a summary in English. Although not entirely reliable in details, the best introduction to Zongmi in English is still Jan Yunhua's "Zongmi: His Analysis of Chan Buddhism," *T'oung pao* 58 (1972): 1–53. Two of Zongmi's most important works are also available in English translation. For a study and translation of his, see Jeffrey L. Broughton's "Guifeng Zongmi: The Convergence of Chan and the Teachings" (Ph.D. diss., Columbia University, 1975). For a study and translation of his *Yuanren lun*, see my own work, "Zongmi's *Inquiry into the Origin of Man:* A Study of Chinese Buddhist Hermeneutics" (Ph.D. diss., Harvard University, 1981).

New Sources

Gregory, Peter N. "Sudden Enlightenment Followed by Gradual Cultivation: Zongmi's Analysis of Mind." In *Sudden and Gradual: Approaches to Enlightenment in Chinese Thought*, edited by Peter Gregory, pp. 279–320. Honolulu, 1987.

Gregory, Peter N. *Zongmi and the Sinification of Buddhism*. Honolulu, 1991.

Gregory, Peter N. "Tsung Mi's Perfect Enlightenment Retreat: Ch'an Ritual during the T'ang Dynasty." *Cahiers d'Extreme-Asie* 7 (1993–1994): 115–148.

PETER N. GREGORY (1987)
Revised Bibliography

ZOROASTRIANISM. Zoroastrianism, known to its followers as the *Zarathushti din* (Zoroastrian religion), developed from the words, ideas, beliefs, and rituals attributed to a devotional poet named Zarathushtra (later Middle Persian or Pahlavi: Zardukhsht, Zardusht; New Persian or Farsi: Zardosht). Zarathushtra eventually came to be regarded as the founder and prophet of the devotionally monotheistic, doctrinally dualistic faith named after him. So, followers of the religion are termed Zoroastrians (New Persian: Zartoshtis, Zardoshtis; Gujarati: Jarthushtis). Zoroastrians also traditionally refer to their faith as *Mazdayasna daēnā* (Middle Persian: *dēn ī Māzdēsn*) (religion of Mazdā) and to themselves as *Mazdayasna* (Middle Persian: *Māzdēsn*) (worshipers of Mazdā), thus acknowledging worship of Ahura Mazdā (Wise Lord) as God and creator. The *Fravarānē* (Profession of faith) begins with the Avestan words: "I profess myself a worshiper of Mazdā, a follower of Zarathushtra, opposing the demons, accepting the doctrine of the Ahura."

Zoroastrianism developed into the major religion—theologically, demographically, and politically—of Iran and Central Asia between the sixth century BCE and the tenth century CE, enjoying royal patronage from various dynasties. During those centuries it influenced Hellenistic, Jewish, Christian, and Muslim beliefs through contact between members of those communities and Zoroastrians. Zoroastrians assimilated aspects of monotheism and hagiography from the Judeo-Christian and Islamic traditions. After the Arab conquest of Iran and Central Asia in the seventh century CE, Zoroastrianism gradually lost adherents through conversion to Islam. During the tenth century, some adherents migrated to India, forming the minority Parsi (Persian) community that flourishes there into the twenty-first century but became endogamic within Hindu society. By the thirteenth century, Irani Zoroastrians also had become a confessional minority. During the nineteenth and twentieth centuries, Zoroastrians relocated from Iran and India to other countries. Based on recent demographic assessments, the faith has a following of approximately 300,000 persons worldwide.

THE FOUNDER, HIS IDEAS, AND HIS REPRESENTATIONS. The issue of Zarathushtra's image is central to Zoroastrianism and Zoroastrians. Therefore, Zarathushtra requires discussion within any overview of the religion.

Zarathushtra's dates and place. Devotees do not doubt the basic reality of Zarathushtra's existence. Yet one line of modern scholarship has been to view Zarathushtra as a legendary character. This position has resulted in suggestions that a historical Zarathushtra was not the composer of the *Gāthās* (Songs) central to Zoroastrian belief. Rather, some scholars attributed the *Gāthās* to one or more anonymous poet-worshippers who allegedly presented an epic character named Zarathushtra as the prototypical poet-sacrificer. These conclusions are based on comparing aspects of the Gathic texts with certain Vedic poems and archaic Greek epics. However, analyses of compositional style and structure indicate that the *Gāthās* were the product of a single devotional poet named Zarathushtra (Possessor of Old Camels) who ensured that memory of him was perpetuated through self-references within his compositions.

When and where Zarathushtra lived is another problematic issue. The traditional place and date for Zarathushtra's life found in a variety of Iranian (including Zoroastrian), Mesopotamian, Greek, and later Arab sources is in Iran two hundred and fifty-eight years before Alexander the Great's conquest of Iran and the death of the last Achaemenian king, Dārayavaush or Darius III (in 330 BCE)—that is, 588 BCE. However, the traditional date for Zarathushtra's life seems to have been either of Greek or more probably of Babylonian origin. Moreover, it is unlikely that the Old or Gathic Avestan dialect was still spoken at that time, as evidenced by the rapid decline in use of its west Iranian cognate, Old Persian, during the Achaemenian period. So composition of the *Gāthās* must have predated the seventh century BCE.

Another set of dates for Zarathushtra's life arose among classical writers. Diogenes Laertius (fl. third century CE), based on Xanthus of Lydia (fl. fifth century BCE) and Hermodorus (fl. fourth century BCE), gave two dates for Zarathushtra's life—six thousand years before the Achaemenian king Xerxes' forces invaded Greece (in 480 BCE) and from five to six thousand years before the Trojan War (early second millennium BCE). Pliny the Elder (23–79 CE) cited Eudoxus (fl. fourth century BCE) in claiming that Zarathushtra had lived six thousand years before the death of Plato (in 348 or 347 BCE), or five thousand years before the Trojan War. All those dates fall within the seventh millennium BCE. Moreover, classical Greek and Roman authors regarded Zarathushtra as having been an Iranian magus. One major problem with accepting seventh millennium BCE dates for Zarathushtra's life is that his words and ideas should then be present not only in the *Gāthās* but also within early Vedic texts of Hinduism and be part of Indo-European devotional literature generally. Because the material data indicates that Proto-Indians separated from Proto-Iranians during the late third or early second millennium BCE, Zarathushtra's life cannot date to before that division.

The third possible place and date for Zarathushtra are the result of enhanced knowledge of both comparative Indo-Iranian linguistics and the archaeology of Central Asia. The linguistic data suggests that the *Gāthās* must have been composed after the Proto-Iranians were distinct from the Proto-Indians (that is, by the eighteenth century BCE) but before the *Gāthās* became part of the Zoroastrian religious canon (that is, between the tenth and sixth centuries BCE), following which Old Avestan fell into disuse. Descriptive reconstruction from the Avestan texts of the society in which Zarathushtra lived correlates with the archaeological remains of the Late Bronze Age in Central Asia. That Bronze Age culture extended from the Caspian Sea through Transoxiana to Afghanistan in 2000–1750 BCE, followed by a period of societal dispersion in 1750–1500 BCE. So, Zarathushtra probably lived and preached in Central Asia between the eighteenth and fifteenth centuries BCE.

Zarathushtra's teachings. Zarathushtra's *Gāthās* provided the Bronze Age people of Central Asia with a vivid and engaging system whereby religious belief and ritual activity were utilized to differentiate between *asha* (order) and *drug* (confusion) (*Gāthās* 33.4, 34.6). Zarathushtra established *mazdā* (wisdom) and Ahura Mazdā (later Old Persian: Auramazdā, Middle Persian: Ohrmazd, New Persian: Hormazd) as means of distinguishing right from wrong (*Gāthās* 33.13, 45.6). The primordial entity Ahura Mazdā was ascribed a creative hypostasis called Spenta Mainyu (originally Spanta Manyu, Middle Persian: Spenāg Mēnōg) (Holy Spirit). Opposing order and Ahura Mazdā, Zarathushtra suggested, were confusion and the primordial entity Angra Mainyu (later Middle Persian: Ahreman, New Persian: Ahriman) (the Angry Spirit). By medieval times Zoroastrian theologians would ascribe a destructive hypostasis called Ganāg Mēnōg (Harmful Spirit) to Angra Mainyu. According to Zarathushtra, the two primordial entities were "in thought, word, and deed, the better and the worse" respectively (*Gāthās* 30.3). Ahura Mazdā came to be venerated as the "father of order" and the "creator of all these [beneficial] things" (*Gāthās* 44.3, 7).

The *Gāthās* also suggested that the corporeal (Avestan: *gaēthya*) world be regarded as an extension of the spiritual (Avestan: *mainyava*) one, explaining the differential experiences of humans in terms of struggles between order and confusion. In so doing, Zarathushtra endowed human existence with meaning during life and hope for an afterlife. Zarathushtra even articulated the notion of pious souls journeying to a paradisiacal existence in the Abode of Song.

Zarathushtra's images. As the Zoroastrians of ancient and medieval Iran interacted with other religious communities such as Jews, Christians, and eventually Muslims, a pious biography or hagiography developed around Zarathushtra. Zoroastrian writers in antiquity and the Middle Ages drew upon glimpses of his life, the names of family members and followers like Jāmāspa, and the accounts of his opponents, such as the tribal leader Bēndva in the *Gāthās,* combining those with biblical notions of piety, devotional quest, revelation, opposition, ministry, and violent demise. This organized hagiography began to develop after the Achaemenian conquest of Babylonia (in 538 BCE) under influence of Israelite accounts of the Patriarchs, was augmented during the second through seventh centuries CE by the Christian image of Jesus' life as recounted in the Gospels, and was supplemented by images from the life of the prophet Muḥammad after Arab Muslims began ruling Iran in the seventh century.

According to that later hagiographic tradition, Zarathushtra's mother, Dughdōvā, was forced to flee her hometown for another village. There, she met a pious man named Pourushaspa, with whom she conceived Zarathushtra. A light supposedly shone from Dughdōvā's womb when she was pregnant, resulting in attempts by evildoers to harm mother and fetus. Upon birth, Zarathushtra's first breath apparently sounded like a laugh rather than a cry. Surviving several attacks upon his life, Zarathushtra eventually left home at the age of twenty. After a decade of wandering and contemplation, he received revelation via Vohu Manah (Middle Persian: Wahman, New Persian: Bahman) (Good Mind) and returned to preach the religion of Ahura Mazdā. Zarathushtra was opposed by the clergy of the older cults in his homeland and had to seek refuge at the court of a neighboring ruler named Vishtāspa, who accepted the religion. Here, Zarathushtra preached and gained many followers until he was assassinated by a priest of another sect at the age of seventy-seven, or so it was written. Through these stories, Zarathushtra's image was firmly established as that of a Near Eastern prophet and eventually recorded in the *Zardukhsht nāmag* or *Zardosht nāme* (Book of Zarathushtra) and other medieval texts like as the *Dēnkard* (Acts of the religion), written in the Middle Persian and New Persian languages. This hagiography has become increasingly popular among Zoroastrians. It is often reproduced in an assortment of pious literature from novels for adults to comics for children in which Zarathushtra is regarded as one of the earliest prophets.

There are no surviving descriptions or renditions of Zarathushtra's actual likeness. Images, however, were produced by devotees and others. Raphael Santi (1483–1520), the Italian Renaissance artist, depicted Zarathushtra—back turned to viewers, wearing a golden robe, holding a globe of the Earth, facing a depiction of Ptolemy, and standing next to an image of the artist himself—on the lower right corner of the *School of Artists* fresco at the Vatican in Rome, Italy. Modern Zoroastrians have generated their own images of Zarathushtra, the most popular of which is modeled on a rock relief of Mithra commissioned by the Sasanian king Ardeshir II (r. 379–383) at Taq-e Bostan in Iran. Various versions of that image adorn fire temples and homes of contemporary Zoroastrians showing Zarathushtra with rays of light emerging from a halo and, sometimes, pointing his right forefinger upward to heaven, much like the Greek philosopher Plato in Raphael's fresco.

PRIESTS, SECTS, AND LAY LEADERS. A Zoroastrian clergyman is termed a magus (Old Persian: *magush,* Middle Persian: *mowbed, mowmard,* New Persian and Gujarati: *mobed*) and is a member of a hereditary priestly subgroup among the Zoroastrians. Over time, subgroups developed among the magi based on theological divergences. Likewise, sects arose within the Zoroastrian community itself based on differences in beliefs and praxes. At various times, certain lay members of the Zoroastrian community have also gained followers for particular tenets and traditions.

The Magi in history Herodotos (c. 484–between 430 and 420 BCE), the Greek author, mentioned that no devotional rituals would be conducted by Iranians unless a magus was present. He also listed practices and beliefs specific to the magi such as consanguineous marriage, exposure of human corpses to wild creatures and the environment for desiccation, nondesecration of nature, and dislike of creatures regarded as noxious or harmful, such as wild animals, reptiles, and insects (*History* 1.101, 132, 140). Herodotos confirms that the magi (Greek: *magoi*) began as the priestly tribe among a tribal confederation known as the Medes. It appears that they appropriated the ideas of Zarathushtra after those concepts had begun to spread among the Proto-Iranians and that they were the sole clerics of the early Zoroastrians by the time the Medes had settled permanently in Iran (ninth century BCE). The magi claimed, erroneously, that Zarathushtra had been a member of their group and had lived among them in northwestern Iran as noted by Plato (c. 428–348 or 347 BCE) *Alcibiades* 1.121). The magi modified Zarathushtra's message to accommodate their own practices within the framework of dualism between order and confusion. They brought with them the notion of a hereditary priesthood that followed their established praxis of never including women in the ecclesiastic membership, claiming that menstruation and childbirth resulted in the discharge of blood that, once outside the body, could pollute priests, ritual actions, and holy places.

Greek and Roman authors learned of Zarathushtra through contact with the magi. Hellenistic scholars such as Pythagoras (c. 570–500 BCE) came to regard Zarathushtra as a mystical figure and as the original leader of magicians—a term deriving from the Old Persian word *magush* borrowed into Greek as *mágos* and Latin as *magus*. The name Zoroaster, by which the devotional poet is commonly identified in Western literature, derives from classical Greek Zōroástrēs, meaning "golden star" and symbolizing his association with spirituality. The magi were introduced into Christian belief as the wise men from the east who supposedly journeyed to Bethlehem; thus, the sages of Zoroastrianism were used to legitimize the founder of another Near Eastern faith.

Ranks within the early Zoroastrian magi seem to have included that of *āthravan* (fire priest) and *zaotar* (invoker, libation offerer). During the Achaemenian Empire, magi served as seers, counselors, and tutors to Iranian noble families. Magi staffed fire temples at urban centers such as Kangavar and Istakhr. The chief priest at each temple probably was titled *magupati* (head magus, master magus.) Seminaries developed for training magi, as did pious foundations for meeting the expenses of temples and seminaries. The color white was reserved for magian clothing to symbolize purity. Their dress, as evidenced from artistic representations, consisted of loose pants, a long-sleeve tunic bound by a belt, and a hooded cap with side flaps for covering the mouth to prevent breath and saliva from polluting ritual items. Because they lost royal favor and state support, the magi reacted adversely to Alexander's conquest of Iran. They denounced the Macedonian conqueror by claiming that his troops slaughtered many magi and burned copies of Zoroastrian scripture—a legend that became part of Iranian official history. Under the Achaemenians and, subsequently, with the Seleucids (fourth century–first century BCE), some magi moved to Ionia and Cappadocia (now in Turkey) where they staffed fire temples into the first century BCE (as noted by Strabo, (c. 63 BCE–24 CE), *Geography* 15.3.14–15).

By the Arsacid or Parthian period (238 BCE–224 CE), magi served in ranks bearing titles such as *hērpat* (later *hērbed*) (theologian), *magpat* (ritual priest), and *bagnapat* (shrine master.) They were present in large provincial temples such as those for the holiest fires in Iran—Ādur Farrōbay, Ādur Gushnasp, and Ādur Burzēnmihr—and in village *chahār tāq* (four-arch) fire precincts. They began working with clerics of other religious groups within Iran, such as the Jewish patriarchate, to regulate religious activity across confessional lines. They also served in the imperial judiciary. Leading magi were mentioned in Sassanid royal inscriptions and other official documents. Kirdīr, who functioned as royal *hērbed* under the second Sassanid ruler Shāpūr I (r. 240–272) and his immediate successors, commissioned Middle Persian inscriptions in which his religious duties, visions of the afterlife, and image were recorded. Kirdīr claimed to have zealously attacked religious sects regarded as heresies. By the fourth century, magi were led by an official titled the *mowbedān mowbed* (chief magus of the magi), or high priest—such as Ādurbād ī Māraspandān, who served during the reign of Shāpūr II (r. 309–379)—whose position was part of the royal court at Ctesiphon (near modern Baghdad). The title *dastwar* (high priest), denoting a cleric certified in both scripture and exegesis, was used as well.

When Zoroastrians lost political control of Iran and Zoroastrianism began to lose adherents to Islam, medieval magi compiled the faith's traditions and practices into the Pahlavi books. For example, Mardānfarrokh ī Ohrmazddādān (fl. ninth century) wrote the *Shkand Gumānīg Wizār* (Doubt dispelling exposition) to critique Judaism, Christianity, Manichaeism, and Islam while defending Zoroastrian tenets. Later, between the fifteenth and eighteenth centuries, magi in Iran sent the *Persian Revāyats* (Treatises) to their coreligionists—the Parsis—in India to advise the latter on religious observances. As the number of Zoroastrians in Iran declined through conversion to Islam, fire temples and seminaries (Middle Persian: *hērbedestān*) fell into disuse. After the Parsi Zoroastrians had settled in western India, their magi divided into five *panths* (ecclesiastic groups). Learned among the Indian magi was Neryōsangh Dhaval (fl. late eleventh century or early twelfth century), who translated portions of the Avesta into the Sanskrit language. According to Iranian tradition, the *dastur dasturān* (high priest of high priests) moved to the central Iranian village of Torkabad north of Yazd in the twelfth century and then to Yazd itself during the eighteenth century.

Contemporary magi. The present-day priesthood, whose members are still called *mobeds,* traces its lineage to the medieval magi of Iran. They form a class (New Persian and Gujarati: *āthornān*) (members of the priestly group) distinct from the laity (New Persian and Gujarati: *behdinān* (members of the good religion). Within the modern magi, ranks persist, including that of *ostā* (teacher, an uninitiated priest), *ērvad* (teacher priest, a priest who has undergone the first level of induction), and *dastur* (high priest, usually, but not always, associated with a temple for a holy fire of the *ātesh behrām* [fire of Verethraghna], or highest ritual level). Two categories of lay individuals traditionally have assisted magi in Iran: the *ātashband* (keeper of the flames) who tends ritual fires and the *dahmobed* (junior priest) who serves as temple warden. In the twentieth and twenty-first centuries, another category of priestly assistants has been created by the Mobed Councils in Iran and North America, namely the *mobedyār* (lay priest), to counter the growing shortage in the number of clerics by performing basic rituals for the laity.

Magi in both Iran and India continue to wear white robes and a white turban. They don a white mouth and nose mask (Middle Persian and New Persian: *padām,* Gujarati: *padān*) to avoid polluting implements (New Persian and Gujarati: *ʿālāt*) and offerings (Avestan: *myazda,* Middle Persian: *mēzd,* New Persian and Gujarati: *myazd*) during rituals. For high or inner rituals, they are required to be in a major state of ritual purity, which is obtained via the *Barashnūm ī nō shab* (Purification of the nine [days and] nights ceremony). During rites, an appropriately inducted and purified magus can serve in ranks including *zōt* (invoker, officiating priest), *rāspī* (assistant), and *bōywalla* (incense offerer). Passed from father to son, priesthood involves studying liturgies and rituals from childhood. Training usually occurs at a seminary (now known in New Persian and Gujarati as *madrasah*). Presently, there are only two functioning seminaries for the magi—the Athornan Boarding Madressa at Dadar in Bombay (Mumbai) and the M. F. Cama Athornan Institute at Andheri West in Bombay. Despite such training, because scripture is memorized, many magi comprehend only the gist of prayers. Clerical training may be followed by formal induction as a priest via the *Nāwar* and *Martab (Maratib)* ceremonies among the Parsis and the *Navezut* ceremony among Iranis. Most magi also obtain secular education and, after undergoing only the *Nāwar* or basic *Navezut* induction, serve as part-time priests or else leave the priesthood completely for secular employment that provides greater remuneration. The resulting shortage of magi has led to abbreviation of certain rites such as purificatory ones and to a focus on daily devotions. On a regular basis, magi serve lay Zoroastrians at fire temples in countries as diverse as Iran, India, Australia, Britain, and the United States, where they are employed by local congregations.

Leaders and groups. A large array of beliefs and practices seem to have been prevalent among the ancient and medieval magi. Only as the religion declined under Muslim rule in late medieval times were certain priests able to establish the more monolithic form of Zoroastrianism that is evidenced by the Middle Persian literature of the ninth through thirteenth centuries. As a result those texts, written for the most part by a handful of related clergymen, convey a false sense of uniformity in doctrine and ritual. One of the most widespread doctrinal variations was that called Zurvanism, which regarded Zurvan (Time) as a monist reconciliation of the dualism represented by Ahura Mazdā and Angra Mainyu and as a means of explaining the evil spirit's anger. Probably arising from theological speculation during the fifth century BCE, it was still subscribed to by magi such as Zādspram in the late ninth century CE. Another sect, that following Gayōmartiya and engaging in astrological and cosmological speculation, regarded Ahura Mazdā as eternal but Angra Mainyu as produced by divine doubt (in this respect perhaps drawing upon Zurvanite ideas) before waning in the ninth century.

Premodern and modern Parsis have experienced their own sectarian schisms. Disagreement relating to the calendar caused a division of the Parsi Zoroastrian community in 1746 into Kadmīs, who readopted the *qadīmī* (ancient) Iranian calendar, and Shenshaīs (also called Rasimīs) (traditionalists), who maintained the traditional Parsi calendar. Another group, called the Fasalīs or Faslīs, formed in 1906 to rely on a *fasl* (seasonal) calendar for rituals. Observance of rituals and festivals on different days because of these calendrical differences persists to the present, even among Parsis now residing in Western countries.

As priests' erudition on scripture and exegesis declined during the twentieth century, so did the Zoroastrian community's esteem for the magi, reliance on clerical learning, and acceptance of ecclesiastical authority. Contemporary *dasturs* still issue socioreligious injunctions on matters such as conversion to Zoroastrianism, marriage with members of other faiths, appropriate roles for women, and disposal of corpses, but by and large such rulings have only moral value for receptive laity and other magi. As a result, some magi have begun following sects established by lay Zoroastrians. One such sect arose when a Parsi named Behramshah Shroff (1858–1927) claimed to have been trained by spiritual sages on Mount Damavand in Iran and preached *Ilm-e Khshnum* (Knowledge of joy). *Ilm-e Khshnum* provides esoteric teachings that combine ideas of mysticism, astrology, reincarnation, and auras with the practice of vegetarianism and the compilation of new exegeses on the Avesta while granting religious authority to laypersons. One Khshnumist subgroup—whose members are identifiable by their red prayer caps and formulaic phrases of greeting such as *khshnaothra ahurahe mazda* (satisfaction unto Ahura Mazdā)—now follows the teachings of Minochehr Pundole and so are termed the Pundolites. Among twenty-first-century Irani Zoroastrians living in the United States, a Muslim convert to Zoroastrianism named Ali Jafarey is popular. He founded the Zarathushtrian Assembly based in Anaheim, California, in

1990. Its members advocate Zoroastrianism as a universalistic faith—a viewpoint rejected by mainstream Zoroastrians who do not favor unregulated proselytism.

Scripture, Exegeses, Commentaries, and Catechisms. Holy texts, interpretations of scripture, and discourses have developed and changed over the centuries. They have also been translated into a variety of languages to meet the confessional needs of linguistically diverse Zoroastrian communities.

The Avesta. Zoroastrian scripture, or Avesta (Middle Persian: *Abestāg,* probably from Old Iranian: **Upa-stāvaka,* "praise"), is a collection of texts regarded as holy and central to beliefs and practices. The canon may be divided into two groups based on linguistic differences: (1) the Old or Gathic Avestan materials, which were composed orally between the eighteenth and twentieth century BCE, transmitted and augmented for several centuries, then established as the main portion of the oral scriptural canon between the tenth and sixth centuries BCE, and (2) and the Young or Standard Avestan materials, which were composed orally, in some cases from existing verses, between the ninth and fifth centuries BCE, transmitted, augmented, then established in the oral scriptural canon by the third century BCE. The written text of the Avesta originated in the fourth century CE—probably from deliberations by magi under the royal patronage of Shāpūr II. All existing Avestan manuscripts derive from a base text dating to the ninth or tenth century.

Only about one-third of the Sassanid Avesta has survived. It consists of:

1. The *Yasna* (Middle Persian and New Persian: *Yasn,* Gujarati: *Ijeshne*) (Sacrifice, worship), comprising seventy-two chapters. *Yasna* 28–34, 43–50, 51, and 53 preserve the seventeen *Gāthās* of Zarathushtra. Chapters 35–41 comprise the *Yasna Haptanghāiti* (Yasna of seven chapters), composed in Old Avestan prose probably by devotional poets among the early Zoroastrian community. Four *mąthras* (holy words), also composed in Old Avestan perhaps by Zarathushtra himself, are preserved in the *Yasna*—namely, *Yathā Ahū Vairyō* (*Ahuna Vairya, Ahunawar*) (As is the Lord's will), *Ashem Vohū* (Order is good), *Yenghē Hātąm* (All the entities), and *Ā Airyēmā Ishyō* (May the invigorating Airyaman.) The other chapters of the *Yasna* were composed in the Young Avestan dialect. Because this scripture serves as the recitation for the central ritual of worship, *Yasna* chapter 1 invites Ahura Mazdā and other holy spiritual entities to the ritual that will be performed. *Yasna* chapters 70–72 bring the accompanying ritual to an end with worship of those spirits.
2. The *Vīsperad* (Avestan: *Vīspe Ratavō*) ([Prayers to] all the [spiritual] chiefs), comprising twenty-four short sections. It is a collection of supplementary materials, compiled in the Young Avestan dialect, to the *Yasna.* It is dedicated to Ahura Mazdā as the chief and master of all creation, and serves to extend the *Yasna.*
3. The *Khwurdag Abestāg* (New Persian and Gujarati: *Khorde Avesta*) (Concise or shorter Avesta), beginning with five prayers: *Ashem Vohū; Yathā Ahū Vairyō; Nirang-e Kusti Bastan* (Incantation for tying the cord), also known as *Ohrmazd Khwadāy* (Ahura Mazdā is the Lord); *Srōsh Bāj* (Recitation to Sraosha); and *Hōshbām* (Middle Persian: *Ōshbām*) (Dawn). Next come five *Niyāyishns* (New Persian and Gujarati: *Niyāyesh*) (Invocations of praise) to the sun, Mithra, the moon, water, and fire, in that order. Then follow prayers to the five *Gāhs* (periods, watches [of each day]). *Siroza* (Thirty days) 1 and 2 contain short invocations to thirty-three divine spirits individually. The words of four *Āfrīnagāns* (Blessings) are also given in the *Khorde Avesta.*

There are twenty-one surviving *Yashts* (Devotional poems) dedicated to various beneficent spirits in the *Khorde Avesta.* Those devotional poems are *Ohrmazd* (New Persian and Gujarati: *Hormazd*) *Yasht* to Ahura Mazdā; *Haft Amahraspand* (New Persian and Gujarati: *Haft Ameshaspand, Haftān*) *Yasht* to the seven Amesha Spentas (Holy Immortals); *Ardwahisht* (New Persian and Gujarati: *Ardibehesht, Ordibehesht*) *Yasht* to the male Amesha Spenta Asha Vahishta (Best Order, Prayer); *Hordād* (New Persian: *Khordād,* Gujarati: *Awerdād*) *Yasht* to the female Amesha Spenta Haurvatāt (Integrity, Wholeness, Perfection); *Ardwīsūr* (New Persian: *Ābān,* Gujarati: *Āwān, Āvā*) *Yasht* to the female water yazata (worship-worthy spirit) Aredvī Sūrā Anāhitā; *Khwarshēd* (New Persian and Gujarati: *Khorshed*) *Yasht* to Hvare Khshaēta, the yazata of the Sun; *Māh* (*Māh Bakhtār,* New Persian: *Māh Bokhtār,* Gujarati: *Mohor*) *Yasht* to Māh, the yazata of the Moon; *Tishtar* (New Persian and Gujarati: *Teshtar*) *Yasht* to Tishtrya the star Sirius, religiously often confused with the divine spirit Tīr (beneficent stars); *Druwāsp* (New Persian and Gujarati: *Drvāsp*) *Yasht* to the female yazata Drvāspā, associated with horses and cattle; *Mihr* (New Persian and Gujarati: *Meher*) *Yasht* to Mithra; *Srōsh* (New Persian and Gujarati: *Sarosh*) *Yasht Hādōkht* (that is, *Yasht* 11) or extract to Sraosha, together with *Srōsh Yasht Wadī* (*Yasna* 57) or the longer (greater) *yasht* to Sraosha, and *Srōsh Yasht ī Keh* (*Yasna* 56) or the shorter (lesser) *yasht* to Sraosha (this designation is found in *Yasna* manuscripts); *Rashn* (Gujarati: *Rashna*) *Yasht* to Rashnu, the male yazata of justice and spiritual judgment; *Frawardīn* (New Persian and Gujarati: *Farvardin*) *Yasht* to the fravashis (immortal human spirits); *Wahrām* (New Persian and Gujarati: *Behrām*) *Yasht* to Verethraghna, the male yazata of victory; *Rām Yasht* to Vayu (Middle Persian: Way, New Persian: Bād, Gujarati: Govād), the male yazata of the good celestial wind; *Dēn* (New Persian and Gujarati: *Din*) *Yasht* to the Cistā (Cisti), the female yazata of insight or religious knowledge; *Ard* (*Ahrishwang, Ahlishwang,* New Persian and Gujarati: *Ashishvang*) *Yasht* to Ashi, the female yazata of recompense; *Ashtād* (*Āshtād*) *Yasht* to Arshtāt, the female yazata of rectitude and order; *Zamyād* (*Zam*) *Yasht* to Khvarenah (glory); *Hōm Yasht* (*Yasna* 8.9–10.21) to Haoma (Parsis designate this as the *Mōtī* [larger, longer] *Hōm Yasht*) plus an extract from *Yasna* 9 (Parsis designate this as the *Nānī* or [smaller, shorter] *Hōm Yasht*); and the *Wanand Yasht* to Vega, the brightest star in the constellation Lyra.

4. The *Vidēvdād* (Middle Persian: *Wendīdād*, New Persian and Gujarati: *Vendidād*), consisting of twenty-two prose chapters in Young Avestan. The text is largely socioreligious in content, focusing on ritual purity with rules and rites for protecting the earth, cleansing after pollution by corpses and carrion, rites for exorcizing spiritual pollution, and fines for absolution from sin. Most of the ritual stipulations in the *Vidēvdād* can be attributed to practices specific to magi of the Proto-Iranian, Median, Achaemenian, and Parthian periods. Like the *Yasna*, the *Vidēvdād* is scripture that functions as the basis of a high ritual. Therefore, its manuscripts contain not only doctrine and exegesis but also performative directions for the magi to follow.
5. Additional texts for daily use that are included in premodern manuscripts and modern printed versions of the *Khorde Avesta. Nirangs* (Avestan: *nīrāngāni*, Middle Persian: *nērang*) (incantations, spells) are present, often as extracts from Avestan or Middle Persian passages. Pious believers regard them as highly efficacious in dispelling evil, producing good health, and fulfilling boons. The *Duā Nām Setāyeshne* (*Nām Stāyishn;* Invocation of praise to the names [of Ahura Mazdā]) and a list, *One hundred and One Names of Ahura Mazdā* (*Sād-ō Yek Nām-e Khodā*), were incorporated so that devotees could directly display respect for their creator. The text of the *Tandorosti* (Health of the body) is given so that it can be recited for both maintenance and return to well-being. The *Petīt* [or *Patēt*] *Pashēmānī* (Penance and repentance) also become part of many *Khorde Avestas* because it is believed that spiritual ailments which led to physical manifestations of illness could be expunged through regular confessionals. Eventually, *monājāts* (litanies) in New Persian and Gujarati (now even in English translations) were incorporated so that devotees can understand the gist of the prayers that are in languages which most individuals have not learned.
6. Several surviving Avestan texts and textual fragments, containing materials that probably were once part of scripture. A few should be mentioned. The Young Avestan *Hērbedestān* (Priestly code or book of religious education) and *Nērangestān* (Ritual code or book of ritual directions) were redacted between the sixth and ninth centuries CE. The *Pursishnīhā* (Questions [and answers]) on pious and sinful behaviors was redacted in the fifteenth century. The *Aogemadaēcā* (I profess) is a dirge that was redacted by the twelfth century. It has a Pāzand version as well. The *Hādōkht Nask* (Selection of scripture) provides an important synopsis of Zoroastrian notions of the afterlife.

Zand. Sassanid magi and learned laymen, writing in Middle Persian, produced a series of supplementary texts often drawing upon Avestan sources that no longer exist. Their endeavors were continued by other clergymen when Zoroastrians fell under Muslim overlordship in the seventh century. The major accomplishment of those priests was *Zand* (Avestan: *zantish*) (exegesis) on the Avesta. The purpose of each translation with commentary—often written interlinear with the Avestan text—into Middle Persian was to transmit the meaning of texts to members of the Zoroastrian community who no longer comprehended the Avestan language. Because of problems in determining equivalent lexical value, reconstituting the sentences, and explaining phrases, the translations often were not exact but served more as expository commentaries. Middle Persian *Zand* has survived to the present for the *Gāthās;* the *Yasna;* the *Khwurdag Abestāg*, including the *Ohrmazd, Ardwahisht, Srōsh, Wahrām, Hōm,* and *Wanand Yashts;* the *Videvdād;* the *Hērbedestān;* the *Nērangestān;* and a few other scriptures.

The Pahlavi books. Most of the Middle Persian or Pahlavi books were compiled and redacted by Zoroastrians in Iran between the ninth and thirteenth centuries. Such compilations aimed to preserve Zoroastrian doctrine, ritual, theology, mythology, history, and mores under circumstances in which the faith was becoming a minority. An encyclopedic collection, the *Dēnkard* preserves selections from the collective wisdom of the medieval magi as edited by two *hudēnān pēshōbāy* (leaders of the members of the good religion) in Fars—namely, Ādurfarrōbay ī Farrokhzādān (fl. early ninth century) and Ādurbād ī Ēmēdān (fl. early tenth century). Cosmogonical and eschatological texts include the *Bundahishn* ([Book of] primal creation; major redaction in 1078) and the *Wizīdagīhā* (Selections), by Zādspram (fl. late ninth century), which cover Zoroastrian mythical, legendary, and factual history from creation to the end of time. The *Ardā Wirāz Nāmag* (Book of righteous Wirāz, based on Sassanid-era materials but redacted in the ninth or tenth century) preserves the description of a spiritual voyage through heaven, limbo, and hell. The *Ardā Wirāz Nāmag* proved very popular as a didactic text, and so was translated into Pāzand and Old Gujarati and illustrated for the edification of premodern Parsis. A book on apocalypticism—also found in Pāzand—is the *Zand ī Wahman Yasn* (Exegesis on the devotional poem to Vohu Manah), an anonymous ninth-century compilation).

Among Middle Persian catechisms are the *Mēnōg ī Khrad* ([Book of the] spirit of wisdom, sixth century), which was composed in the form of an imaginary dialogue between the Spirit of Wisdom and a sage. A later Pāzand version of it is extant as well. The *Chīdag Handarz ī Pōryōtkēshān* (Select counsels of the ancient sages, ninth century), also known as the *Pand Nāmag* (Book of advice), provides a more basic synopsis of religious values, beliefs, and practices. Among the books providing religious guidance are *Nāmagīhā* (Epistles) of Manushchihr ī Juwānjamān (fl. ninth century); the *Rivāyat* (Treatise) of Ēmēd ī Ashawahishtān (fl. mid-tenth century); and the *Pahlavi Rivāyats of Ādurfarrōbay and Farrōbaysrōsh*, which contain replies by two Irani magi to questions posed by laypersons in the years 800 and 1008, respectively. Broader in theme is the *Dādestān ī Dēnīg* (Book of religious judgments), answers by Manushchīhr ī Juwānjamān to ninety-two questions from laypersons on matters of doctrine, ethics, legal issues, and social problems experienced by Zoroastrians in ninth-century Iran. Religious stipulations and ritual requirements are discussed in the *Shāyest nē Shāyest* (The proper and the improper) and its *Supplementary Texts;* both compilations, although written in the ninth century, contain Sassanid period (224–651 CE) rulings and mores.

Pāzand and Sanskrit versions. Magi living in Iran under Muslim rule produced *Pāzand* ([Text] with commentary) literature. Pāzand prayers include the *Paywand nāme,* or *Ashirwād,* which serves as the benediction for marriage ceremonies. This Pāzand tradition was continued by the Parsi priest Neryōsangh Dhaval. He transcribed select Pahlavi books into the Avestan script to make them accessible to twelfth-century magi who could not read Middle Persian. In addition to the Pāzand texts mentioned previously (in discussions of the Avesta and the Pahlavi books), there are among others the *Petīts,* the *Dibāches* (Prefatory recitations) to *Āfrīnagāns,* and *Nirangs.*

Neryōsangh Dhaval also translated portions of Avestan scripture into Sanskrit, including incomplete versions of the *Yasna,* the *Khorde Avesta,* the *Mēnōg ī Khrad,* and the *Shkand Gumānīg Wizār.* Fragments of Sanskrit translations of the *Vidēvdād,* perhaps also going back to Neryōsangh's efforts, have survived. His intension was to make Zoroastrian scripture and exegesis accessible to Parsis who knew the Indian language but not Avestan and Middle Persian. There are sixteen Sanskrit *ślokas* by Aka Adhyaru, verses dating to before the seventeenth century, dealing with miscellaneous socio-religious matters from prayer times to dress codes to purity. The *Ashirwād* was translated from Pāzand into Sanskrit by Dinidās Bahman (fl. early fifteenth century) prior to the year 1415.

New Persian and Gujarati texts. Many Zoroastrian religious documents were written in New Persian. Most famous is the Parsi community's founding legend, known as the *Qessa-e Sanjān* (Story of Sanjan) composed in 1600 CE by Bahman Kaikōbād Sanjāna, a Zoroastrian priest. Expository translations from Middle Persian texts include the late medieval *Saddar Bondahesh* ([Book of] primal creation [written] in one hundred chapters) and *Saddar Nasr* (One hundred chapters of assistance.) More original works of advice, yet drawing upon established traditions, form the *Persian Revāyats,* which date to between the late fifteen and late eighteenth centuries. Those treatises contain responses by learned Zoroastrians living in Yazd and Kermān to ecclesiastical questions posed by their Indian coreligionists. The *Farziyāt nāme* (Book of obligatory duties), by *dastur* Darab Pahlan (1668–1734), written in couplets at Navsari, India, lays out the religious duties of each individual—male and female, children and adults—through life and on every day of the month; it displayed Indian influence by advocating vegetarianism. It was translated and published in Gujarati for general readers about one century later. The Muslim scholar Ebrahim Pur-e Davoud (1885–1968) produced New Persian translations of the *Gāthās* and *Yashts* that became popular among Iranis and, upon reprint in Bombay, met with enthusiasm from educated Parsis.

In addition to translation into Gujarati of the *Khorde Avesta,* Zoroastrians in India wrote original tracts in the Gujarati language, which had replaced New Persian as their medium of communication. The *Rehbar-e Din-e Jarthushti* (Guide to the Zoroastrian religion) is a premodern catechism written by the high priest Erachji Meherjirana (1826–1900). That text was eventually translated into English with a commentary by the contemporary Parsi *dastur* Firoze Kotwal of Bombay.

English renditions. As English has become a major medium of communication among Zoroastrians—through British colonialism, Western-style secular education, globalization, and migration to the West—translations of scripture have been produced in that language. Among the most commonly utilized prayer books during the late twentieth and early twenty-first centuries—especially for teaching scripture to children before their initiation into the faith—with transcription of the Avestan and Middle Persian texts into the Roman (i.e., English) script and translation of those texts into English are *Daily Prayers of the Zoroastrians* by the Sri Lankan lay Parsi scholar Framroz Rustomjee (1896–1978) and *Khorde Avesta* by the Irani *mobed* Fariborz Shahzadi, who now lives in the United States. Major discourses on Zoroastrianism, written in English, have been published by *dastur* Khurshed Dabu (1889–1979) at Bombay. *Ervad* Godrej Sidhwa at Karachi and *mobed* Behram Shahzadi at Westminster, California, among many others, have also written Zoroastrian theological works in English during the twentieth century. Basically catechisms, those books serve to disseminate knowledge of Zoroastrianism—from a variety of perspectives—to clerical and secular Zoroastrians and to non-Zoroastrians who may not know any of their religion's traditional languages.

DOCTRINES AND MYTHOLOGY. Zoroastrian beliefs and myths were interconnected by ancient and medieval magi to provide believers with a unified explanation for the joys and sufferings of life while endowing existence with purpose. It is clear that Zarathushtra's own ideas were conjoined with the Indo-European and Indo-Iranian tenets that Zoroastrians inherited. Near Eastern millenary chronologies—beliefs in which a new millennium was regarded as a new age, following a violent end to the old one—then reshaped Zoroastrian beliefs as did historical events.

Dualism, pantheon, and demons. As the devotional tradition was amplified slowly after Zarathushtra's lifetime, it came to be believed that Ahura Mazdā, through Spenta Mainyu, had created six Amesha Spentas to generate and protect aspects of material creation: Vohu Manah, who oversees animals; Asha Vahishta, who symbolizes fire; Khshathra Vairya (Middle Persian: Shahrewar) (Desirable dominion, power), who manifests metals; Spenta Ārmaiti (Middle Persian: Spendarmad) (Holy disposition, later understood as Holy devotion), who represents the Earth as its mother; Haurvatāt, who characterizes water; and Ameretāt (Middle Persian: Amurdād, New Persian and Gujarati: Amardād) (Immortality, rejuvenation), who exemplifies plants. After incorporation of the *Yashts,* which originally served as devotional poems for Indo-Iranian divinities, into the liturgy of the descendants of Zarathushtra's early followers, it was assumed that Ahura Mazdā originally had created more beneficent spirits. These included the male and female yazatas like Mithra, Sraosha, Verethraghna, Daēnā, Ashi, and Aredvī Sūrā Anāhitā to assist in protecting the material creations. Zoroastrian doctrine records that, in response, Angra Mainyu supposedly produced numerous daēvas (Middle Persian: dēws, New Persian and Gujarati: divs). The daēvas (shinning ones) had been part of Indo-Iranian belief but were demonized by Zarathushtra (*Gāthās* 30.6). Such malevolent daēvas include female ones like Āzi (Middle Persian: Āz), who generates concupiscence and other desires; Jahikā (Middle Persian: Jēh) the "Whore," who supposedly misleads women to lust and prostitution; and Drukhsh Nasush (Middle Persian: Druz ī Nasush), who ferments carrion and pollution. There are also male ones, like Aēshma (Middle Persian: Khēshm), who instills wrath; Aka Manah (Middle Persian: Akōman), who instigates bad thoughts; and Būti (Middle Persian: But), who spreads idolatry. Essentially, spiritual entities venerated by the earliest Iranians were assimilated into the developing Zoroastrian faith and then assigned differential valence as either agents of order or confusion during antiquity and the Middle Ages.

During the modern period, the beliefs of Zoroastrians have gradually changed under the influences of Protestant Christianity—especially due to the activities of the Reverend Dr. John Wilson (who began preaching in Bombay in 1829, eventually converting some Parsis to Anglicanism) and other British missionaries—and colonial western ideas, moving from a dualism to an absolute monotheism in which Ahura Mazdā is regarded as the sole God. The Amesha Spentas and yazatas are now accorded a variety of positions, usually equivalent to archangels and angels, respectively. Angra Mainyu has come to be regarded as the Devil with his independent nature tempered by partial subservience to God. The daēvas have lost much of their demonic force, becoming minor bad spirits and ghouls. Yet most Zoroastrians living in the twenty-first century continue to believe that humans serve a vital function in the struggle between God and the Devil, representing order or good versus confusion or evil, respectively. Moreover, from the 1980s onward there has been a trend among orthodox Zoroastrians back to dualistic tenets while maintaining Ahura Mazdā's divine supremacy.

Cosmogony and sacred history. Human history is regarded as a divinely ordained, twelve-thousand-year period of finite time (Middle Persian: *zamān ī kanāragōmand*) bounded at its commencement and conclusion by eternity or infinite time (Middle Persian: *zamān ī akanārag*). Before finite time began, Ahura Mazdā and Angra Mainyu supposedly were separated from each other by the void or wind of Vayu and dwelt within heaven in "infinite light" (Middle Persian: *anagr rōshnīh*) and within hell in "infinite darkness" (Middle Persian: *anagr tārīgīh*), respectively.

When finite time began, creation (Middle Persian: *dahishn*) lasted six thousand years. The first three thousand years of creation were marked by the initial encounter between Ahura Mazdā and Angra Mainyu and an offer of peaceful coexistence in purity and righteousness that was rejected by the evil spirit. After Angra Mainyu had spurned Ahura Mazdā's overture of peace, the Angry Spirit was temporarily defeated by the Wise Lord, who chanted the *Ashem Vohū* prayer. On hearing these holy words, the Angry Spirit is said to have collapsed, stupefied, back into the darkness (*Wizīdagīhā* 1.1–4). The second three thousand years passed while Angra Mainyu lay in a stupor and Ahura Mazdā prepared spiritual creations—including the Amesha Spentas, yazatas, and the spiritual prototypes of all living creatures. Angra Mainyu revived and generated harmful spirits. When Angra Mainyu attacked again, Ahura Mazdā repelled the adversary for another three thousand years with the *Yathā Ahū Vairyō* prayer (*Bundahishn* 1.29–30). According to religious lore, Ahura Mazdā then transformed spiritual creations into the material universe by fashioning the Earth inside the sphere of the sky. That sphere, supposedly made of rock crystal, was thought to enclose the oceans, seven continents, and firmament with the Sun, Moon, planets, and stars. On the central continent called Khvaniratha (Middle Persian: Khwanirah), Ahura Mazdā apparently placed the first human—an androgyne named Gayō Maretan (Middle Persian: Gayōmard, New Persian: Gayumars, Keyumars) (Mortal life)—the primordial bovine, and the first plant (*Bundahishn* 1A.1–3.24). Angra Mainyu eventually was aroused from his second stupor by the demoness Jahikā.

Corporeal existence and humanity's purpose. The second six thousand years of finite time is said to be the current age of mixture (Middle Persian: *gumēzishn*) between good and evil. Angra Mainyu invaded the world, polluted it, and then slew Gayō Maretan, the primordial bovine, and the first plant with the demoness Āz's assistance, according to Zoroastrian cosmogonical accounts. Owing to Ahura Mazdā's intervention, humanity supposedly arose from the semen of the androgyne, animals and cereals from the body of the first bull, and other plants from the seed of the initial plant (*Wizīdagīhā* 2.1–22). The first human couple, Mashya (man) and Mashyāna (woman), who were born from Gayō Maretan's semen, are believed to have succumbed to lying and worshiping daēvas, resulting in their damnation (*Bundahishn* 14.11–30). Human history passed, in this scheme of religious chronology, with the rise and fall of legendary dynasties until Zarathushtra was born in the year 8,970.

Thirty years later, Zarathushtra received revelation from Ahura Mazdā and preached the Wise Lord's faith—thus beginning the final three-thousand-year sequence. According to sacral history, the era of Zarathushtra and the Kayanians was followed by the Achaemenian, Seleucid, Arsacid, and Sassanid dynasties. Thereafter, the Arabs conquered Iran establishing the Umayyad (661–750) and Abbasid (750–1258) caliphates, succeeded by semi-independent and independent Iranian Muslim states and then by Turkish invaders (tenth to fourteenth centuries). Those conquests, triggering the reduction of Zoroastrianism to a minor faith and Zoroastrians to the status of a religious minority through conversion to Islam between the eight and thirteenth centuries CE, were incorporated into the faith's mythohistory and explained in terms of a steady increase in evil (*Zand ī Wahman Yasn* 1.6–11, 3.20–29, 6.6–10). Thereafter, it is claimed, finite time will progress onward and Zoroastrianism will not be practiced widely—a situation that allegedly heralds the advent of the final days.

For devotees, the material world came to be viewed as not merely the arena in which humans combat evil. Zoroastrians regard it as the trap into which the evil spirit was lured. Once trapped in matter, Angra Mainyu ostensibly is vanquished gradually via good thoughts, good words, and good deeds by divine spirits and devotees acting in unison. This became the faith's and each practitioner's raison d'être. Zoroastrians, then, trust that humans were created by Ahura Mazdā as allies in God's cosmic struggle against Angra Mainyu and that humans consented to assume physical form to further this battle. The reward of heaven after death is offered to the souls of believers, albeit on gender-differential bases, who have upheld righteousness and combated evil during their lifetimes.

Afterlife. Zoroastrians have faith that when an individual dies, the life force leaves the corporeal body, which then becomes a corpse that demonic forces attack and cause to decay so that pollution occurs. His or her mortal soul (Avestan: *urvan,* Middle Persian: *ruwān,* New Persian: *ravān*) also leaves the body, remaining beside the head of the corpse for three days and nights (*Mēnōg ī Khrad* 2.111–114). The mortal soul of a righteous person is said to chant happily *Yasna* 43, "According to my wish," whereas the mortal soul of a sinful person wails *Yasna* 46, "To what land shall I flee? " (*Hādōkht Nask* 2.2–6, 3.2–6). On the dawn of the fourth day, the soul is led to the Bridge of the Compiler (Avestan: *Cinvat peretav,* Middle Persian: *Chinwad puhl).* Beneath this metaphysical transit point, which connects the earthly realm to the heavenly one, is said to lie hell. Individual tribunals are convened at the bridge's earthly base to determine each mortal soul's holiness. The yazatas Mithra (who presides to appraise whether the soul has kept its covenant to do good while in the corporeal world), Rashnu, and Sraosha—in some later traditions, Mithra and Sraosha are occasionally replaced by Arshtāt and Zamyād—comprise the spiritual court. Rashnu is described as weighing each soul's good and bad deeds in the pans of a scale (*Mēnōg ī Khrad* 2.118–122, 163).

If the soul's righteous acts outweigh its evil ones, the soul is greeted by its Daēnā or conscience in the form of a "a beautiful girl" (*Hādōkht Nask* 2.9) who personifies those pious actions. This good Daēnā, together with the yazatas, then escort the saved mortal soul across the bridge to heaven, where the soul will dwell until the end of time in union with its immortal spirit (Avestan: *fravashi,* Middle Persian: *frawahr,* New Persian: *farvarshi,* Gujarati: *farohar*) (*Mēnōg ī Khrad* 2.123). If a mortal soul's unrighteous acts outweigh its good ones, that soul is greeted by its Daēnā "in the form of an ugly naked whore" (*Hādōkht Nask* 3.9) who personifies the soul's evil actions. This bad Daēnā, together with other daēvas, toss the condemned mortal soul off the bridge into hell, where it will dwell and experience punishment as recompense until the end of time. In cases where a mortal soul's good and evil deeds are equal, it is consigned to limbo until the end of time.

Heaven or paradise, known as *Garō-nmāna* (also *Garō-demāna,* Middle Persian: *Garōdmān*) (Abode of song) and therefore termed *Wahisht* (the best [place]), is depicted as a physical location—a realm of joy, peace, happiness that is full of light, warmth, and all virtuous pleasures (*Hādōkht Nask* 2.15–18). Hell, known as *Drūjō-nmāna* (also *Drūjō-demāna,* Middle Persian: *Druzmān*) (Abode of Confusion) and therefore described as *Dushokh* (he Worst [place]), is also depicted as a physical location—a realm of grief, conflict, despair that is filled with darkness, cold, stench, plus harmful insects and animals like scorpions and serpents (*Hādōkht Nask* 3.15–36). Here demonic creatures, lead by Angra Mainyu, are said to gloat as they torment the impious soul together with his or her predeceased bad relatives and friends in a gloomy space. Limbo, known as *Nana* (different [place]), *Misvana Gātav* (Place of the Mixed), or *Hamēstagān* (Place of the Equally-Weighing Ones), is thought to be located between the Earth and heaven. It is described as a place where mortal souls are suspended, each in isolation, experiencing nothing at all.

Apocalypse and eschatology. Social strife, personal calamity, and pollution of body and soul are all viewed as originating from Angra Mainyu, whose presence in the material world is believed to increase as time passes. The present period will, in Zoroastrian belief, be followed by a time when three saviors—Ukhshyatereta (Middle Persian: Ushēdar) (He who makes order flourish); Ukhshyatnemah (Middle Persian: Ushēdarmah) (He who makes reverence flourish); and Astvatereta (He who embodies order), also called Saoshyant (Middle Persian: Sōshāns) (Savior)—will be born, one every thousand years, to gradually purify the world and its inhabitants (*Zand ī Wahman Yasn* 9.1–23). Eventually, during the religious year 11973, the eschaton supposedly will commence with Saoshyant resurrecting all the dead. The resurrection, performed by Saoshyant at Ahura Mazdā's command, results in each human's mortal soul and immortal spirit returning to earth from heaven, hell, or limbo and gaining a final body (Middle Persian: *tan ī pasēn*). Zoroastrians claim that Ahura Mazdā then will descend to Earth with the Amesha Spentas and yazatas. Saoshyant will separate righteous individuals from evil ones at a final, universal judgment of all humans. At that assembly, called the gathering of Isatvāstra (Middle Persian: Isadwāstar) after the prophet Zarathushtra's eldest son, each person will recognize his or her relatives and friends, and the pious shall rejoice in their goodness while the sinful lament their evil deeds. It is believed that the stars will fall from space onto the Earth, leveling the mountains into molten metal. Each sinner, having already suffered in hell after death, will be purified once more of his or her transgressions and impurities by means of an ordeal involving passage through the molten metal. A mythical bovine named Hadhayash (Middle Persian: Hadhayans) will be ritually sacrificed, and its fat mixed with a legendary white haoma to produce an elixir granting immortality of body and soul to all who consume it (*Bundahishn* 34.10–26).

Thereafter, Ahura Mazdā, the Amesha Spentas, and the yazatas will annihilate most of the daēvas and all the harmful corporeal creatures. The devil Angra Mainyu himself will be rendered innocuous and forced to scuttle out of creation back to hell. Finally, hell will supposedly be sealed shut with molten metal, safeguarding the spiritual and material worlds from evil, impurity, and pollution forever. According to Zoroastrian eschatology, once the separation (Middle Persian: *wizārishn*) of confusion or evil from order or good has been accomplished, Ahura Mazdā will renovate or "make excellent" (Avestan: *frasho-kereti,* Middle Persian: *frashagird*) the universe in the year 12000: "The renovation will take place in the world, [and the beings in] the material world will become immortal forever" (*Bundahishn* 34.32). Human history allegedly will then end, and eternity will recommence in absolute purity and perfection, with humanity dwelling in happiness upon a refurbished, flat earth.

Rituals. Worship (Middle Persian: *yazishn*) and purification (Middle Persian: *yōjdahrgarīh*) are central to all aspects of Zoroastrian piety. Worship may occur at home or even outdoors, but is most regularly performed inside fire temples (New Persian: *āteshkade*), where holy fires of the *ātesh behrām, ātesh ādarān* (fire of fires), and *ādurōg ī dādgāh* r (hearth fire) ranks burn upon altars in fire precincts (New Persian: *āteshgāhs*). Medieval injunctions urged devotees to "go each day to the fire temple and perform worship" (*Chīdag Handarz ī Pōryōtkēshān* 45). Yet in order for worship to be efficacious, the devotee must have ritual purity.

Purity and pollution. Elaborate rules were established by the magi to prevent pollution of the material world on the basis that Angra Mainyu had produced various types of defilement, particularly through Drukhsh Nasush, whose ill effects could spread from humans and animals to fire, water, and earth. A series of purificatory ceremonies were developed to ensure socioreligious purity for high ceremonies and rites of passage. Most of those rituals have fallen into disuse in the twentieth and twenty-first centuries, because beliefs regarding pollution have undergone modification as a consequence of modern science and have come to be regarded by many Zoroastrians as superstitious demonology.

The simplest ritual cleansing, known as the *Pādyāb* (Protection [preceding] water), takes only a few minutes to perform. It is undergone facing a source of light such as the Sun, Moon, stars, or lamp. After covering the head as a sign of deference, the performer dedicates his or her action to Ahura Mazdā. He or she washes the hands and forearms, the face, and the feet (if unshod), then wipes them dry. Original praxis in ancient and medieval times required that the ablution be performed first with *gōmēz* (urine from a bovine), or else with dust, before washing with water. Moreover, *gōmēz* (or else dust) and water had to be applied thrice. In modern practice, however, water is regarded as adequate for ensuring daily purity and so is applied only once due to simplification of the ritual. According to orthopractic codes, this cleansing is essential upon awakening each morning, prior to prayer and eating, after urination and excretion, and at the beginning of each period of each day. Most Zoroastrians now perform a perfunctory *pādyāb* only before entering a fire temple or after attending a funeral. After undergoing a *pādyāb,* the devotee must perform the ritual of untying and retying the *kustī* (see below).

More elaborate is the *Sade Nāhn* (Simple ritual bath). Conducted at home, fire temple, or funerary ground, it is administered during the daylight hours so that light can aid in dispelling evil. The ceremony lasts approximately half an hour. In orthodox practice, a priest who has attained the rank of purifier (Avestan: *yaozhdāthrya,* Middle Persian: *yōjdāhrgar,* New Persian: *yozhdāsragar*) must officiate. After performing a *Pādyāb* and untying the*kustī,* the candidate for purification recites the *Bāj* ([Consecratory] recitation) used for grace before meals, then chews a pomegranate leaf as a sign of wishing for immortality, drinks three sips of *nirangdin* or consecrated urine from a bovine for symbolic spiritual cleansing, and recites the *Pētit* for absolution from sin. He or she undresses, applies *gōmēz* over the body, washes with water, dries the body, dons a *sudre* or white undershirt, dresses in clean clothes, and reties the *kustī.* In modern performance, ablution with *gōmēz* is often omitted and all actions have been reduced from thrice to once. Moreover this *Nāhn* is undergone by most male and female Zoroastrians only prior to initiation and marriage. Until the mid-1900s, it was undergone by mothers forty days after childbirth (serving as a simplification of an even more detailed cleansing of thirty washings) and by pious devotees on holy days.

The most complex of Zoroastrian purification rituals is the *Barashnūm ī nō shab.* It generally was reserved for cleansing after direct contact with human carrion or to ensure that a priest was in the highest state of ritual purity. Purification was obtained via consuming *nirangdin,* followed by multiple cleansings with *gōmēz,* dust, and water while either standing within pits (in antiquity), crouching upon stones (during the

Middle Ages), or squatting on bricks (in modern times), followed by seclusion and additional ablutions for nine days and nights. The *Barashnūm ī nō shab* is still undergone, but with diminishing frequency, only by magi who conduct the most central Zoroastrian consecratory services.

Worship. Zoroastrian liturgical ceremonies can be divided into two categories: inner or high services that must be performed within a holy *gāh* (space, precinct), usually located within fire temples, and outer or regular services that can be performed at any clean location. Inner rituals include the *Yasna, Vīsperad, Vendidād, Nīrangdīn* (Consecration of liquids), and *Bāj.* Magi who conduct inner rituals have to be in high states of purity and grace. Outer rituals include the *Āfrīnagān, Staomi (Stūm;* Praise), *Farrokhsi* ([Recitation] for the Fravashis), and *Jashan* (Thanksgiving).

The *Yasna* ritual, the most fundamental of Zoroastrian devotional ceremonies, brings together fire, water, plants, animals, humans, and holy words. The *Yasna* liturgy has already been discussed. Originating among the Indo-Iranians, it was assimilated into Zoroastrianism and modified to remove immolation of sacrificial animals in the libation produced from the haoma (Vedic: soma) plant. In a variant form it is still present in Hinduism as the *yajña* ceremony. Conducted each dawn by two magi who are in the highest state of ritual purity, most of the ritual occurs within a precinct that had been made holy by demarcating and consecrating a small space from the rest of the area via furrows while reciting holy words. In ancient and medieval times, an animal regarded as beneficial, such as an ox, sheep, or goat, would be sacrificed as an offering. Since the early twentieth century, fruits, flat unleavened breads *(drōn),* and cooked foods have been substituted. Twigs from the *haoma* plant (now identified by Zoroastrians as ephedra) are purified and pounded to extract sap, which is strained and mixed with milk and water to form a libation called *parāhōm.* Aromas from the consecrated food and drink are believed to satisfy Ahura Mazdā, the Amesha Spentas, and yazatas to whom the worship is directed. Thereafter, the two priests and sponsoring laypersons consume the food offerings and infuse the liquid offering into a source of water, such as the temple's well.

The *Vīsperad* ritual's liturgy consists of the *Yasna* plus twenty-four additional passages from the Avesta. Dedicated to Ahura Mazdā, its performance comprises the *Yasna* ritual with the extended recitation. This inner ritual is performed whenever the *Vendidād* is conducted. It is performed at the *Gāhānbārs* (also pronounced *Gāhāmbārs*) (Communal feasts) too.

The *Vendidād* ritual is often conducted by an officiating priest and an assisting priest at midnight to dispel evil. Celebration of the ritual involves recitation of the *Vidēvdād* text from the Avesta with interpolation of chapters from the *Yasna* and *Vīsperad,* producing a total of forty-nine selections. The ritual is conducted in the presence of a *dādgāh* fire and lasts approximately seven hours.

Nīrangdīn rituals are conducted to obtain consecrated liquid used to purify symbolically the souls of devotees. Having purified themselves via the *Barashnūm ī nō shab* and obtained religious fortitude via a *Khūb* (Good [ritual power]), two priests obtain bull's urine. As part of the *Nīrangdīn* ceremony, the prefatory rite for the *Yasna* and other high rituals—known as the *Paragṇā* (Preceding the Yasna)—and the *Vendidād* are performed, consecrating the urine.

Bāj services involve consecration of *drōn, gōshudā* (animal products)—now usually butter—and fruits with dedication of those offerings to yazatas and fravashis. *Bājs* often are commissioned on death anniversaries by relatives of deceased Zoroastrians.

The *Āfrīnagān, Farrokhsi,* and *Staomi* outer rituals serve to honor the mortal souls and immortal spirits of both living and deceased Zoroastrians. For example, the *Staomi (Stūm)* ritual is a soliloquy of remembrance that links the present to the past and the future, uniting the living with the dead. That ritual may be conducted in any clean area where outer ceremonies are performed, such as at a Zoroastrian's house or inside a fire temple, upon a carpet or table or within a ritual precinct. At the turn of the twenty-first century, the *Staomi* consists of five stages: a *shnūman* (dedicatory formula), *Yasna* 26 or the rite proper, a *dībāca,* a series of propitiatory recitations, and a *Bāj* that serves as a closing recitation. Because of offerings and the fragrances of those offerings that are made holy during the ritual, it is believed that asymbolic gathering together of all fravashis occurs. At such gatherings, therefore, the immortal spirits can be propitiated by the living, and in turn those spirits presumably bless the living. Most frequently performed is the *Jashan* ritual, which also involves consecration of food by the officiating magus or magi who recite an *Āfrīnagān* and *Bāj.* Then the food is shared by the sponsors of the ritual, often at a communal gathering.

Festivals and popular rites. Prayer services like *Jashans* are performed in fire temples and homes on days such as *Nav Ruz,* the New Year's festival (at the vernal equinox); *Mihragān* (also called *Jash-e Mehr Ized*), the feast honoring Mithra (at the autumnal equinox), and the *Gāhānbārs.* The six *Gāhānbārs* are still celebrated by many Zoroastrians, especially those in Iran. On those occasions fruits, flowers, and cooked foods made from plants—and now less frequently from animals—are consecrated to the divinities and then consumed by the community. Originally, animals were sacrificed by Zoroastrians in both Iran and India on religious and communal festivals. But Hindu vegetarian influences on the Parsis led to the gradual phasing out of animal sacrifice, and Parsi abstention spread to Iranis in the twentieth century.

The spreading upon *Sofres* (clothes) of food offerings to beneficent spirits, often in conjunction with the *Gāhānbārs* and during pilgrimages to shrines, has become a frequent devotional practice among women, although not sanctioned by the magi. *Sofres* are widely performed by Zoroastrian women of all social classes in Iran. The rite serves as a locus of feminine spirituality, organized and attended mainly by women and their children.

Pilgrimages form part of the religious lives of devout Zoroastrians who are seeking favors from God or are fulfilling vows. Major shrines are located in the Iranian province of Yazd and each shrine has a founding legend associated with Zoroastrian attempts to withstand conversion to Islam. The six major *pirs* (shrines) are Pir-e Sabz, Pir-e Nawraki (Nāreke), Pir-e Narestan, Set-e (Se-tā) Pir, Pir-e Herisht (Hrisht), and Pir-e Bānu Pārs. Those shrines are administered by local *anjomans* (associations), often drawing upon funds from charitable foundations. Parsis consider the Irān Shāh *ātesh behrām* at the city of Udwada to be their most venerable holy fire, and so travel to worship Ahura Mazdā in its presence. In the late twentieth century, Parsis began making pilgrimages to Iran, where they visit the important functional fire temples and shrines at Yazd and Sharifabad, then view the ruins of ancient and early medieval archaeological monuments associated with the Zoroastrian dynasties of that country.

Rites of Passage. Zoroastrians past and present perform ceremonies to mark major points in their lives, much like members of other faiths. Birth, initiation into the religion, marriage, and death are important times during which religious beliefs are reaffirmed and membership in the confessional community is consolidated. Those rites of passage involve not only the Zoroastrian who is undergoing the life-altering event, but his or her family and friends as well.

Birth. Children are regarded as essential for "continuation of the corporeal lineage" to combat confusion in the material world (*Chīdag Handarz ī Pōryōtkēshān* 5). Therefore, abortion is discouraged (*Vidēvdād* 15.9–12). Birth rites still follow many guidelines found in medieval and premodern Zoroastrian writings, even though most births now occur in hospitals.

Once a woman conceives, an oil lamp or light is lit in her house to ward off evil. Also, the expectant mother should avoid contact with polluted items that may render her ritually unclean (*Saddar Nasr* 16.1, 17.2). Traditionalist Parsis mark the first days of the fifth and seventh months as auspicious, exchanging gifts between husband and wife and between each spouse's families. Upon the birth of a child, a lamp is kept lighted for between three to forty days, depending on the degree of orthopraxy in the family, so that mother and child will be protected from daēvas (*Farziyāt nāme* 2c–d). Because haoma is regarded as "death dispelling" (*Hōm Yasht* or *Yasna* 9.7), a few drops of its libation or *parāhōm* followed by a few grains of sugar would be placed upon the child's tongue by the parents, grandparents, or family priest while reciting the *Yathā Ahū Vairyō* prayer so that the child might experience a life free of sickness and full of joy. This practice was common into the eighteenth century (*Farziyāt nāme* 2a). Now, after prayers of thanks to God, breast milk or milk formulas are fed to the infant. Naming of the child occurs shortly thereafter (as noted even in the Achaemenian period by Herodotos, *History,* 1.139). Many families still consult astrologers who determine, based on the day and time of birth, the syllable with which the child's given name should commence.

Despite the positive aspects of childbirth among Zoroastrians, the accompanying discharge of tissue and blood came to be regarded as polluting. A period of isolation was prescribed for the mother—initially twelve days during antiquity (*Vidēvdād* 5.45–62, 7.60–72), extended to forty days by the Middle Ages (*Shāyest nē Shāyest* 3.15). This praxis continued into premodern times, to be followed by a ritual purification via the *Sade Nāhn* before the mother was reintroduced to the community (*Persian Revāyats* 223). Isolation and purification gradually ceased to be enforced during the early twentieth century. In the twenty-first century, most Zoroastrian women simply bathe to cleanse themselves after childbirth.

Initiation. Teaching of prayers to children by a magus or family elder usually begins at the age of seven years. Once the boy or girl has memorized at least the *Ashem Vohū, Yathā Ahū Vairyō, Kēm Nā Mazdā, Nirang-e Kustī Bastan* or *Ohrmazd Khwadāy, Jasa Mē Avanghe Mazdā* (Come to my aid, O [Ahura] Mazdā), and *Srōsh Bāj* prayers, he or she is initiated into the faith before puberty (*Farziyāt nāme* 2h–i). Failure to be initiated is thought to expose the child to demonic forces (*Vidēvdād* 18.31, 54). During the ceremony that symbolizes advent to adulthood, acceptance of religio-legal responsibilities, and spiritual rebirth, each child is vested with a cord (Avestan: *aiwyānghana,* Middle Persian: *kustīg,* New Persian: *koshti,* Gujarati: *kustī*) around the waist and a white undershirt (Middle Persian *shabīg,* New Persian: *sedra,* Gujarati: *sudre*). Origin of initiation into the sectarian community may date from the Central Asian Bronze Age, for a similar cord is tied around the shoulder of each Brahman boy during the *Upanayana* ceremony in Hinduism. Failing to wear these holy items was regarded as a sin and equated to "scrambling around naked" (*Shāyest nē Shāyest* 4.10). The *sudre* is sown from white cloth such as cotton and serves as religious armor against evil. Its neckline has a small pocket or *girehbān (girdo)* where the wearer's good deeds symbolically accumulate. The *kustī* is woven by priests' wives from wool and its seventy-two strands are said to represent the chapters of the *Yasna* (*Nērangestān* 3.1.11–21). An entire medieval text, the *Chīm ī Kustīg* (Meaning of the cord) discusses the *kustī's* theological significance.

In the twenty-first century, most Zoroastrian boys and girls undergo religious initiation between the ages of seven and fifteen. The ceremony is termed *Navjote* (new birth) or *Sedra-Pushi* (donning the white undershirt) and is conducted by one or more magi. Just before initiation, the boy or girl undergoes the *Sade Nāhn* to ensure that entrance into the devotional community occurs in a state of ritual purity. A *dādgāh* fire burns in a small altar during the ceremony; candles and oil lamps may also be lighted so that illumination drives away evil. Fruits and flowers are placed nearby as offerings to Ahura Mazdā, the yazatas, and the fravashis. Several Zoroastrians may be initiated together, irrespective of gender. Standing up, the priest(s) lead the initiate(s) in prayers while the undershirt is donned and the cord is looped around the waist thrice and tied at front and back with square knots. Family and friends gather to witness the initiation, share a festive meal, and bestow gifts upon the initiate. The initiation ceremony is still performed routinely by Zoroastrians all over the world early in the twenty-first century. Auspicious days, such as the days of each month dedicated to Ahura Mazdā and Verethraghna, often are chosen for the ceremony.

The *kustī,* which most Zoroastrians continue to wear, should be untied and retied after the *Pādyāb* purification and with the recitation of prayers at five canonical prayer times—sunrise, noon, afternoon, evening, and before sunrise—and prior to performing worship at fire temples (*Farziyāt nāme* 3). The majority of modern-day Zoroastrians wear the *sudre* and *kustī* under their clothes, but the rites of untying and retying the cord are usually performed facing the sun or another source of light by laity only upon awakening each morning, prior to sleeping at night, and for bathing. If a Zoroastrian apostate wishes to return to the community, he or she has to undergo another initiation ceremony. Admission to Zoroastrianism became patrilineal after its followers became a minority faith during the late Middle Ages. Orthodox contemporary Parsi magi initiate only children whose parents are both Zoroastrians. More liberal magi among the Parsis and Iranis initiate children whose fathers are of Zoroastrian descent. Rarely are persons whose parents were not non-Zoroastrians initiated—and such initiates still are denied entrance to Zoroastrian religious sites on the Indian subcontinent.

Marriage. The family unit has long been central to Zoroastrian communal structure, and so marriage is encouraged as a religious duty and divorce is discouraged, especially after children have been born (*Chīdag Handarz ī Pōryōtkēshān* 5). Royal records from ancient Iran, medieval religious manuals, and premodern marriage records indicate that Zoroastrian social praxis found polygyny fully acceptable. Wives were accorded differential status within the family based on their social class prior to marriage, whether they bore children, and the stipulations of their marriage contract. Only during the twentieth century was polygyny phased out under European influence, first among the Parsis and subsequently among Iranis.

Spring, reflecting fertility and growth, is regarded as an auspicious time for weddings. So are nights of the full and new moons. *Nav Ruz,* the "New Year's" festival day, is favored too. In India the monsoon seasons are avoided. Traditionally, weddings occur in the evening. Parsis conduct the service after nightfall owing to a legendary agreement with the first Hindu king whom their ancestors encountered in Gujarat. Iranis would conduct both the betrothal and wedding services at midnight, a practice now modified to early evening so that celebrations can be held with family and friends at a dinner reception. A white jacket (Gujarati: *duglī*) and trousers plus an ornate hat (Gujarati: *fethā, paghī*) are worn by Parsi grooms. White saris, with the trail draped over the head, are worn by Parsi brides. White jacket and trousers, with a simple green prayer cap, are worn by Irani grooms, although recently Western-style suits have become popular. White or green robes and shawl are worn by Irani brides, although in the twentieth and twenty first centuries Western-style wedding gowns have become popular. Symbolic items at an Irani wedding include a candelabra with candles to cast light upon the service, a tray with sweets (known as *lurk*) made of seven types of fruits and nuts representing Ahura Mazdā and the Amesha Spentas, a pomegranate and an egg symbolizing fertility, decorated sugar cones representing the sweetness of married life, a mirror for self reflection, a prayer book to provide guidance, and a needle with thread and scissors indicating domesticity. Symbolic items present at Parsi weddings include trays with coconuts and rice grains representing fertility and a censer or fire brazier. Parsi brides and grooms wear flower garlands and hold flower bouquets as well. The religious service for a wedding is conducted by one or more priests. Irani and Parsi wedding ceremonies display variations that reflect cultural differences between the two communities of Zoroastrians.

Among Iranis, the wedding service begins when Ahura Mazdā is invoked by the officiating magus. Recitations include *andarz* (advice) relating to the *gava giri* (marriage contract). Bride and groom are asked if they accept each other as partners. A wedding sermon by the priest on the benevolence of the Amesha Spentas follows. Selections from the *Srōsh Bāj* and *Yasna* 52 (which recounts a wedding homily by Zarathushtra) are chanted by the magus. Finally, the *Tandorosti* is recited. Then the couple is sprinkled with flower petals and rice symbolically to bring them good luck. Among Parsis, the *Āchu Michu* rite of Indian origin—in which eggs, leaves, nuts, sugar, coconut, rose petals and other flowers, water, and coins are utilized to symbolize aspects of creation and reproduction coupled with hopes of joy and wealth—is performed upon groom and bride by the bride's mother and the groom's mother. The officiating priest inquires from the bride and groom whether they consent to marrying each other. The bride and groom sit facing each other and the *Hathēvāro* (hand fastening) rite is performed: a white cotton sheet separates the seated bride and groom, while their right hands are bound together by the magus using white thread to indicate their holy union. The thread is then wrapped around them seven times in a clockwise manner while seven *Yathā Ahū Vairyō* prayers are recited. The sheet is then removed, the bride and groom toss rice at each other, the thread is removed as well, and the fire brazier brought close to the couple so that they may worship God in its presence. Next, with the couple seated side by side facing east, the Pāzand and Sanskrit versions of the *Ashirwād* are narrated by the officiating magus in the name of Ahura Mazdā, and the couple's oral consents are obtained for the marriage. Finally, *Tandarosti* is intoned to bless the newlyweds. A celebratory meal usually follows, hosted by the couple's parents, for their families and friends.

Death and funerary practices. If a Zoroastrian is known to be in the final hours of his or her life, the dying individual is supposed to recite the *Petīt Pashēmānīh* (also called *Patēt-e Vidardegān* [Penance for the deceased] by Iranis and *Patēt Ravān-ni* [Penance for the soul] by Parsis) in repentance for prior evil deeds, followed by several *Ashem Vohū* prayers. After the deceased's eyes are closed, the corpse is given a ritual cleaning (termed *sachkār* by the Parsis) either by professional corpse bearers (New Persian and Gujarati: *nasā sālārs*) and corpse cleaners (New Persian and Gujarati: *pākshus*) or by relatives or friends of the same sex, all of whom should be Zoroastrians. The chest is draped in a *sudre* and a *kustī* is tied around its waist. Thereafter, the deceased's body is dressed in white clothes, his or her hands are crossed over the chest, the legs are crossed by Iranian Zoroastrians but not by Parsi Zoroastrians, and the entire body is covered with a white shroud. The face remains exposed. If possible, handling of corpses is left to professional Zoroastrian corpse cleaners and bearers. Until the funeral service commences, a prayer vigil is maintained to safeguard the deceased's body and soul from demonic forces thought to be lurking in the vicinity. At the commencement of each period of the day, a rite known as *sagdīd* ([ritually] seen by the dog) is performed. The actual funeral service, termed *Gēh Sārnā* (Chanting of the Gāthās) by Parsis, occurs within twenty-four hours, during the three daylight periods, or morning, afternoon, and evening but not after sunset or after midnight. The body is placed upon a metal (which like stone is believe to withstand pollution) bier. The funeral service is followed by *sezdo* (*sijdā*) (last respects). Then the deceased's face is covered with the shroud. The bier may be carried to the funerary site with mourners following, after having recited the *Srōsh Bāj* and formed gender-specific pairs. Mourners must be led by a pair of priests or one priest plus a dog to ward off evil and pollution. Most often in the late twentieth and early twenty-first centuries the corpse is placed in a hearse, which is followed to the funerary site by relatives and friends in a motorcade.

In the early history of Zoroastrianism, human corpses were buried under the floors of disused buildings, following a practice prevalent among the Late Bronze Age people of Central Asia. Later, interment took place in village cemeteries. Achaemenian monarchs and their families were interred in rock sepulchers in the belief that the stone prevented the spread of pollution created by corpses' decay. Yet as praxis changed between the sixth and third centuries BCE, the original Avestan term *dakhma* for a grave or tomb came to designate a place for exposure of corpses. As initially remote locales came to be inhabited because of demographic growth, *dakhmas* developed into walled enclosures or funerary towers that came to be called "Towers of Silence" in popular parlance. The practice of exposure prior to gathering and disposal of the bones appears to have been introduced by the ancient magi in order to prevent pollution of the earth, fire, and water.

Further variations in Zoroastrian funerary practices occurred during the nineteenth and twentieth centuries. Exposure of corpses was gradually phased out in Sri Lanka (then Ceylon) during the late 1800s and in Iran during the 1970s. Iranis now bury their dead in graves walled with cement slabs to prevent the corpse from polluting earth and water. Parsis in India and Pakistan continue the tradition of exposing bodies to vultures in funerary towers, particularly at Bombay and Karachi, laying the bodies in specific areas or rows according to gender and age. However, in the United States, Canada, England, Australia, Sri Lanka, and even some locales in India and Pakistan, Zoroastrians—like their coreligionists in Iran—bury the dead irrespective of gender and age in rows of graves within graveyards known as *aramgāhs* (places of rest, cemeteries). In Western countries, deceased non-Zoroastrian spouses may also be buried in those graveyards.

HISTORICAL ASPECTS. Zoroastrianism was brought onto the Iranian plateau by tribes migrating southward from Central Asia around 1500 BCE. It became established as the dominant faith among the Medes, Persians, Scythians, and other Iranian groups who took up residence in various locations on that plateau. Through the Persians, Zoroastrianism spread to the indigenous Elamites of southwestern Iran as evidenced by renditions of the names of Ahura Mazdā and various yazatas preserved in Elamite ritual documents.

Ancient Iran. Median practice of Zoroastrianism is known from archaeological remains. At the citadel of Tepe Nush-e Jan (c. mid-eighth century to sixth century BCE), south of the northwest Iranian city of Hamadan, two rooms with ritual fire precincts have been excavated. Likewise, the capital city of Hagmatāna (Ecbatana, now Hamadan) had at least one small, open-sided building with four corner columns supporting a domed ceiling that seems to be a precursor of the *chahār tāq*–style of fire precinct. A relief carved above the entrance to a late Median or early Achaemenian rock tomb located at Qyzqapan in Iraqi Kurdistan depicts a priest on the left and a warrior on the right, both in Median garb appropriate to their occupations, flanking a fire altar with a stylized, semicircular flame.

Some modern scholars have questioned whether the Achaemenian rulers followed Zoroastrianism. Kūrush or Cyrus II (r. 550–530 BCE), who founded the dynasty, had magi at his royal court, according to classical writers. An open-air ritual precinct with stone fire plinths has been excavated at Parsarga (Pasargadae), the royal capital. The plinths' function is indicated by reliefs carved above the rock cliff tombs of seven subsequent Achaemenian rulers, including that of Darius I at Naqsh-e Rostam and that of Artakhshaçā or Artaxerxes III (r. 359–338 BCE) at Persepolis. The king or a magus climbed to the top of the southern plinth, faced the northern plinth, which bore a fire altar with flame, and performed devotions before Zoroastrianism's main icon. Implements such as mortars and pestles, whose dedicatory inscriptions confirm their ritual usage for pounding of *haoma* during the *Yasna* ritual, have been excavated at Persepolis. While Zarathushtra was not mentioned in imperial inscriptions, Ahura Mazdā was routinely praised in those writings. For instance, Darius I noted: "Ahura Mazdā is the great God who created this earth, who created that sky, who created humans, who created happiness for humanity, who made Darius king" (*Naqsh-e Rostam inscription A* 1–5). Following Egyptian depictions of Ra and Assyrian ones of Ashshur, Ahura Mazdā seems to have been depicted on Achaemenian royal reliefs standing within a disk which had a bird's wings, tail, and talons, although some scholars consider the symbol to represent Khvarenah (glory) and modern Parsis regard it as a farohar. Artaxerxes II (r. 404–359 BCE) and Artaxerxes III honored Mithra and Anāhitā in conjunction with Ahura Mazdā—a practice that parallels Zoroastrian liturgies—as evidenced by their official Old Persian inscriptions (*Susa inscriptions* A 4–5, D 3–4; *Hamadan inscriptions* A 5–6, B; and *Persepolis inscription* A 25). No form of Mazdā worship other than Zoroastrianism has ever been identified. It is safe, therefore, to regard the Achaemenian rulers and many of their Iranian subjects as Zoroastrians, even though a range of other religions—such as Judaism and Babylonian cults—were practiced within the empire and Cyrus II honored other divinities like Yahweh and Marduk when he was among their followers.

Religiosity during the Seleucid period was characterized by an amalgamation of Greek, Mesopotamian, and Iranian divinities. On the Iranian plateau and in Armenia, Anāhitā—whose name was Hellenized as Anaitis and whose attributes were augmented by those of other feminine divinities, such as Artemis and Inanna-Ishtar—became the focus of an extensive temple cult with statuary and votive offerings. Among the residents of Commagene in southeastern Anatolia, Ahura Mazdā was fused with Zeus as Zeus Oromasdes. Mithra was fused with Apollo Helios Hermes, and Verethraghna (called Artagnes by the people of Anatolia) was conjoined with Hercules Ares. Colossal images of all those composite divinities were placed on a platform in an open air Zoroastrian temple at the site of Nimrud Dagh in southeastern Anatolia during the reign of Antiochus I (c. 69–34 BCE), a king of the regional Orontid dynasty (c. 163 BCE–CE 72) who had descended from Achaemenian satraps. Antiochus also had images carved of him clasping the hands of divinities (Greek: *dekhiōsis*).

Such syncretism continued during the Parthian period. Women, for example, served as professional mourners at funerals. Augmentation of the ritual role of fire occurred between middle Achaemenian and early Parthian times with the construction of monumental temples. Holy fires of the highest ritual grade, called the fires of Verethraghna, (Parthian: *ādar warahrān,* Middle Persian: *ātakhsh wahrām,* New Persian and Parsi Gujarati: *ātesh behrām*) the yazata of victory, were placed in fire temples. The most famous *ādar warahrān* of antiquity were founded during that time: Ādur Farrōbay, considered the *ādar warahrān* of clergy and nobility, at the site of Kariyan; Ādur Gushnasp, linked to rulers as the *ādar warahrān* of warriors, at the site of Takht-e Sulayman southeast of Lake Urmiya (now in Iranian Azerbaijan); and Ādur Burzēnmihr, regarded as the holy fire of farmers and pastoralists, on Revand mountain northwest of Nishapur in Parthia (now Khorasan).

Advent of the Sassanid dynasty witnessed Zoroastrianism becoming the official religion of Iran. In addition to supporting the faith financially, Sassanid monarchs are credited by the magi as having commanded codification of the Avesta. Sacral kingship based on Zoroastrianism became normative. So Sassanid rulers like Ardeshīr I (r. 224–240), Shāpūr I (r. 240–272), and Khusrō II (r. 591–628) had themselves depicted on monumental rock reliefs at Naqsh-e Rostam, Naqsh-e Rajab, and Taq-e Bostan receiving diadems of kingship from anthropomorphized images of Ahura Mazdā and Anāhitā. Every Sassanid monarch referred to himself or herself as *māzdēsn bay* (Mazdā-worshipping Lord) on their coins. That coinage routinely depicted monarchs—for example, Hormizd II (r. 302–309)—performing worship in front of fire altars. Magian ranks were regularized. Fire temples and seminaries were funded by the state and by private foundations. Committing apostasy was forbidden. As a result, under the Sassanian dynasty, Zoroastrianism became the politically and demographically dominant faith on the Iranian plateau and in western Central Asia.

Conversion to Christianity and Islam. Yet as Christian missionaries began proselytizing among Zoroastrians, and individuals from the latter groups began to adopt Christianity, Zoroastrian fire temples were transformed into churches at locales like Ejmiacin and Dvin in Armenia after the year 300. In Sassanid Iran itself, converts to Nestorianism deliberately extinguished holy fires on occasion while refusing to return to Zoroastrianism—resulting in their martyrdom at the hands of magi as documented in the Syriac martyrologies.

Confessional realignment gained momentum with the Arab Muslim conquest of the Sassanid Empire during the seventh century. The Arab conquest came to be associated with prophetic and apocalyptic expectations. It gave rise to literature that presented claims of propitious birth, flourishing of a new religion and its followers, and disintegration of older dynasties and faiths. Islamic prophecy alluded to triumph, Zoroastrian apocalypticism to doom. The prophet Muḥammad and the Muslim caliphs were presented as successors to Zarathushtra and the Sassanid monarchs. These stories were construed to cast a veil of mystery over ordinary events involving the fall of one empire with its state religion and the rise of another empire with its new faith. Since people believed these statements, they acted on those beliefs. Many despondent Zoroastrians, concluding that a true deity would not have forsaken their religion or them, eventually chose to accept the new Islamic faith, which they felt had demonstrated its ascendance through political victory. Urban Irani Zoroastrians adopted Islam from the eighth through tenth centuries, and that faith spread among rural folk from the tenth through thirteenth centuries. Most Zoroastrian ecclesiastical institutions were either transformed into Islamic mosques and Sunni *madrasahs* or else destroyed or abandoned by the fourteenth century. The *chahār tāq* style of fire precinct with its domed roof was assimilated into Muslim religious architecture as domed mosques. Moreover, as residents' confessional alliance shifted to Islam, there was gradual diminishment in contributions to pious foundations that supported the magi.

Zoroastrian leaders turned to canon law in a futile attempt to circumscribe contact of their followers with Muslims, for they rightly perceived interaction as a conveyor of religious and social changes that threatened their traditional way of life. The magi outlawed marriage, sexual intercourse, and procreation with Muslims, encouraging all Zoroastrians to ostracize those who violated these bans. Muslim elites were, however, often in positions to stifle such endeavors and encourage conversion to Islam by the people whom they referred to generically as the *māgūs* (so named by Muslims after the priesthood).

Medieval migrations. The Arab Muslim occupation of Iran triggered migrations by Zoroastrians. Zoroastrianism had already reached China during the early sixth century, where the religion came to be known as Hsien. During and after the seventh century, there were many small, poorly documented migrations away from Iran over both land and sea. Some Zoroastrians, especially Sassanid nobles and military personnel, immigrated eastward through Central Asia to northern China. Other groups of Zoroastrians probably sailed from Iran to join expatriate communities already present in southern Chinese port cities like Canton. From China, small groups even relocated to Japan. From fifteen to eighteen fire temples functioned in China until Zoroastrianism, together with other foreign faiths, was proscribed there in 845. However, Zoroastrians survived in China as late as the mid-fourteenth century, after which they were completely assimilated into the local population. The situation proved different for other groups of immigrants, specifically those who went to India and formed the *Parsi* (Persian) community that flourishes into the twenty-first century. Those Zoroastrians who remained in Iran sought refuge from Muslim lifestyles by moving to out-of-the-way locales within Fars, Yazd, and Kermān provinces.

Medieval and premodern minorities in Iran. Between the fourteenth and seventeenth centuries, the lives of Zoroastrians as a *dhimmī* (minority) community were governed by religious tenets and a sectarian society dominated by Muslim men. All followers of Zoroastrianism had to pay the *jizya* (poll tax) to the Sunni Muslim authorities, and the Zoroastrians' standing under Islamic law was secondary to members of the new confessional majority. Invasion and rule of Iran by the Mongols (1219–1256), Ilkhanids (1256–1335), and Timurids (1370–1507) resulted in violence against Zoroastrians producing even further conversion to Islam.

Institutionalization of Shiism under the Safavids (1501–1722) did little to strengthen relations between the Muslim and Zoroastrian communities, for the latter increasingly feared the specter of forced conversion to Islam under the religious zealousness of specific Shīʿī clerics or *mollās.* Zoroastrians living in the Yazd and Kermān areas bore the brunt of religious persecution, resulting in adoption of Shiism by some villagers, the transformation of associated fire temples into mosques, and desecration or even demolishment of nearby funerary towers. A New Persian designation, *gabr* (hollow, empty), hence "one lacking faith, infidel," came to be used by Muslims to scorn Zoroastrians as nonbelievers in God despite the claim of the latter that the Avesta was a holy book just like the *Qurʾān.* Likewise, the term *ātashparast* (fire worshipper) became a slur directed against Zoroastrians by Shīʿī Iranians, despite the former's protestations that they worshipped God and not fire. Forcible relocation of Zoroastrians occurred during the reign of Shāh ʿAbbās I (r. 1587–1629) from Yazd and Kermān to the capital city, Isfahan, as laborers. In other cities of Safavid Iran, they also served as manual workers and textile weavers. Outside the cities, they toiled on farmland owned by Muslims.

European eyewitness accounts suggest that the Zoroastrian community of Iran was at its nadir during the Qajar period (1779–1921). Since Zoroastrians were considered *najes* (unclean) by the Shīʿah, they experienced hostility from the Muslim majority populace. Conversion to Islam was enforced periodically with transformation of fire temples to mosques. In the middle of the nineteenth century, Zoroastrians feared that their homes would be raided and religious texts burned. Religious rites were performed indoors, out of view of Muslims, so as not to attract the latter's attention. Only after intercession by Parsi Zoroastrians from British India was religious freedom enhanced and the *jizya* abolished by Qajar royal decree in 1882. Zoroastrian *anjomans* (associations) were established thereafter, as were women's societies and orphanages. More than three dozen schools for Zoroastrian boys and girls were founded with Parsi and Irani money. The curricula at such institutions combined Western secular knowledge and traditional religious instruction, stressing English as a language for societal advancement. Irani magi began traveling to and residing in India for clerical training—a trend that lasted until the latter part of the twentieth century, when the priesthood within Iran was able to strengthen its organizational and didactic bases. Zoroastrians, hoping for more equitable treatment under a secular national government, participated actively in the Constitutional Reform movement. Eventually, the community was allocated its own seat in the *majles* (national consultative assembly, parliament). Although the 1906 Constitution claimed "all citizens are equal before the law," the legal standing of Zoroastrians vis-à-vis Muslims remained unequal as evidenced by Article 8 of that Constitution, where Zoroastrians were assigned a legal status no different from that which they held previously as a *dhimmī* community. Therefore, during the nineteenth and early twentieth centuries, more Zoroastrians relocated from Iran to British India to live amidst the Parsis. Carving out a distinctive economic niche in India, they became restaurateurs and liquor merchants.

Modern Iran. A brief period of respite for Zoroastrians in Iran from socioeconomic hardship and pressure to adopt Islam was experienced under the Pahlavi dynasty (1925–1979). Attempts to secularize and westernize Iranian society resulted in citizens generally being regarded as equal under the law. The *ʿAyn nāme* (Uniform Legal Code) for Zoroastrians was put into practice during the mid-1930s, establishing a nationally approved framework for their rights in personal matters such as marriage, divorce, and inheritance. The Family Protection Law of 1967 and its revisions of 1975 were another central part of the restructuring of the community's legal relationship with the nation. Glorification of Iran's pre-Islamic past for sociopolitical reasons by the state, including introduction into the official calendar in 1925 of Zoroastrian names for the months, also raised the status of Zoroastrians in the eyes of many Muslim Iranians. The Pahlavi era was marked by rapid urbanization and reform for the Zoroastrian community as educational, employment, and business opportunities burgeoned. Westernization, urbanization, and secular education led to religious change, spread in part through elementary, middle, and high schools founded by Irani Zoroastrians for edification of their children during the Pahlavi period plus those schools that had been established earlier. Irani Zoroastrian communal leaders championed their religion as an early form of monotheism, brought about calendrical reform, and simplified or replaced rites deemed antiquated in favor of ones regarded as more suitable for a community with newfound societal and economic aspirations. Even conversion to Zoroastrianism by Muslims was tacitly permitted. Reform gradually spread from the community in Tehran to other urban settings such as the cities of Kermān and Yazd. Due to state pressure on behalf of its secularization program, access to most fire temples in Iran was opened in the 1960s to members of all faiths—although they were requested (but not required) to cover their heads and remove footwear as signs of respect for the holy fires. Together with open access, yet another change occurred wherein the *Pādyāb* purificatory ritual and *koshti* (cord rite) came to be ever-less-frequently performed prior to entering the presence of a holy fire. Thus, an attenuation in notions of purity and pollution took place. By the mid-1970s, the community was finally confident that its lot had genuinely changed for the better in a secularizing Iranian state. Hence, leading members of the community at Tehran, Yazd, and Kermān still recount that Iran's reversal in 1979 to a political system in which Islam predominated once more deeply shook the foundational psyche of the Zoroastrian community and brought back a collective, multigenerational memory of harsh times from centuries past.

The advent of the Islamic Republic of Iran witnessed a return to strict socioreligious minority status for Zoroastrians. Technically protected under Article 13 of the 1979 Constitution, the community is allocated one elected representative position among the two hundred and seventy members or national representatives of the legislative branch of government, the *majles.* Despite being officially recognized as a minority and represented in public settings, Zoroastrians in Iran often are offered only limited protection on a daily basis from their Muslim neighbors. As a result, they sporadically have been targets for persecution. Community records list cases of Zoroastrian women being compelled to marry Muslim men in the presence of Shīʿī clerics or *mollās* and to publicly adopt Islam. On a daily basis, more important are the legal distinctions between Muslims and Zoroastrians, which echo, in large part, ordinances that Zoroastrians have experienced under many Islamic regimes since the middle of the seventh century. Thus, for instance, a Zoroastrian who converts to Islam is regarded by Iranian law as the sole inheritor of his or her family's assets. Likewise, a Zoroastrian who even accidentally causes the demise of a Muslim faces the possibility of capital punishment, but not vice versa. The concept that Zoroastrians are *najes* has been revived, affecting their socioeconomic lives in daily interactions with Muslims, since items the former touch, especially food, may be regarded as unclean by the latter. The insults *gabr* and *ātashparast* have once again been used against them. Chronic unemployment has become prevalent among members of both genders. One major cause appears to be discrimination by the government in access to state jobs. While employment opportunities are withheld, Zoroastrians feel they have been targeted for especially hazardous assignments when performing the military service required of all young men in Iran. Therefore, yet again Zoroastrians have begun leaving Iran.

Globalization of the faith. The initial modern exodus from Iran was during the 1980s by elite families who had been associated with the Pahlavi state and therefore feared retribution. Relocations since then have been by young men and women who are growing increasingly pessimistic about the possibility of a viable socioeconomic future for their families and themselves in Iran. Some of the migrants, fleeing Iran overland to Turkey, Pakistan, and India, then spending many months or a few years in refugee camps or under the protective welfare of Parsi communities, eventually settle in North America and in Europe. Globalization of the Zoroastrian community has also occurred through emigration of Parsis from the Indian subcontinent. During the British Raj, Parsi trading families settled in Burma (now Myanmar); Singapore; Malaysia; Hong Kong (now united with the People's Republic of China) and mainland China; Taiwan; the Seychelles; and African countries such as Zaire, Tanzania (on the island of Zanzibar), and South Africa. Some Parsis relocated to England, Scotland, and Wales during the nineteenth and twentieth centuries, seeking better educational and economic opportunities. Beginning in the 1960s, yet other Parsis left to unite with relatives in Australia, New Zealand, Europe, and North America as a consequence of nationalism and religious fundamentalism in India, Pakistan, and Sri Lanka. Since the 1970s, Parsi immigrants have settled in the United States and Canada after gaining education and employment there.

Many among the first generation of recent Irani immigrants have settled in ethnic clusters—forming large communities in cities like Los Angeles, Toronto, and London—where they continue many of their native customs and speak New Persian. However, their children, the second generation, being born in Western countries, have tended to become better acculturated as native speakers of the English language. For them, Iran is a cultural legacy of their parents. While the first generation of Parsi immigrants remains bilingual in the Gujarati and English languages, maintaining customs from the Indian subcontinent, their children have limited facility in Gujarati and have integrated fully with local Western populations. Differences of language and custom still present challenges to the cultural and religious unity of the first generations of Parsi and Irani Zoroastrians in the West. Despite such divergences, they have worked together raising funds to establish community centers, fire temples, and cemeteries in most major cities in the United States, Canada, England, and Australia.

As Zoroastrians have spread globally, many issues have come to the fore. They include intermarriage between them and followers of other faiths and the religious identity of children from such unions; conversion to Zoroastrianism of persons who wish to adopt the religion; access to fire temples by non-Zoroastrians, including those who are the spouses and children of Zoroastrians; and ways in which the bodies of deceased Zoroastrians may be disposed, including inhumation and cremation. By and large the Parsis of India tend to be the most conservative and orthopractic. Theocratic positions taken by Zoroastrians in India are not uniformly accepted by lay and clerical Zoroastrians elsewhere, however. Occasionally, individuals who wish to join Zoroastrianism are initiated by magi outside the Indian subcontinent, but magi in the Indian subcontinent do not accept converts. Likewise, the frequency of marriage across confessional boundaries is on the rise; this is the case even among the Parsis of India. Outside the Indian subcontinent, Zoroastrians routinely permit non-Zoroastrian spouses to attend rituals at fire temples and cemeteries. Zoroastrian women, while still not part of the priesthood, now participate fully in community activities and governance.

In the late twentieth century, Zoroastrian organizations in countries around the globe began establishing and maintaining regular contact with one another. Recent demographic studies, national censuses, and community association membership rosters yield the following approximate population figures for Zoroastrians—Iranis, Parsis, and recent converts—worldwide in the early twenty-first century: 28,000 in Iran; 69,600 in India; 20,100 in the United States; 10,000 in Canada; 7,500 in England, Scotland, Wales, and Ireland; 4,500 in the other countries of the European Union; 2,800 in Pakistan; 2,100 in Australia; 1,200 in the United Arab Emirates; 250 in New Zealand; 190 in Hong Kong; 150 in Singapore; 130 in Bahrain; 110 in Zaire; 75 in South Africa; 70 in Sri Lanka; 50 in Myanmar; 30 in Japan; 30 in Malaysia; 30 in the Seychelles; 20 in Bermuda; 10 in Venezuela; 10 in the Peoples Republic of China; and even smaller numbers in Armenia, Azerbaijan, Belarus, Yemen, Tanzania (on the island of Zanzibar), Zambia, Mozambique, Mexico, and Brazil.

SEE ALSO Ahura Mazdā and Angra Mainyu; Ahuras; Airyana Vaējah; Amesha Spentas; Anāhitā; Ateshgah; Avesta; Chinvat Bridge; Daivas; Frashokereti; Fravashis; Gender and Religion, article on Gender and Zoroastrianism; Haoma; Khvarenah; Magi; Parsis; Saoshyant; Yazatas; Zarathushtra; Zurvanism.

BIBLIOGRAPHY

Amighi, Janet K. *The Zoroastrians of Iran: Conversion, Assimilation, or Persistence.* New York, 1990.

Bailey, Harold W. *Zoroastrian Problems in the Ninth-Century Books.* 2d ed. Oxford, 1971.

Bartholomae, Christian. *Altiranisches Wörterbuch.* Strasbourg, France, 1904; reprint, Berlin, 1979.

Benveniste, Emile. *The Persian Religion according to the Chief Greek Texts.* Paris, 1929.

Bidez, Joseph, and Franz Cumont. *Le Mages hellénisés: Zoroastre, Ostanès, et Hystaspe d'après la tradition grecque.* 2 vols. Paris, 1938; reprint Paris, 1973.

Boyce, Mary. *A Persian Stronghold of Zoroastrianism.* Oxford, U.K., 1977; reprint, Lanham, Md., 1989.

Boyce, Mary. *Zoroastrians: Their Beliefs and Practices.* London, U.K., 1979; reprint, Chicago, 1984.

Boyce, Mary. *Textual Sources for the Study of Zoroastrianism.* Manchester, U.K., 1984.

Boyce, Mary et al. *A History of Zoroastrianism.* 3 vols. Leiden, 1975–1991.

Boyd, James W., and Firoze M. Kotwal. "Worship in a Zoroastrian Fire Temple." *Indo-Iranian Journal* 26 (1983): 293–318.

Choksy, Jamsheed K. *Purity and Pollution in Zoroastrianism: Triumph over Evil.* Austin, Tex., 1989.

Choksy, Jamsheed K. "Doctrinal Variation within Zoroastrianism: The Notion of Dualism." In *K. R. Cama Oriental Institute: Second International Congress Proceedings,* pp. 96–110. Bombay, 1996.

Choksy, Jamsheed K. *Conflict and Cooperation: Zoroastrian Subalterns and Muslim Elites in Medieval Iranian Society.* New York, 1997.

Choksy, Jamsheed K. "Aging, Death, and the Afterlife in Zoroastrianism." In *How Different Religions View Death and Afterlife,* edited by Christopher J. Johnson and Marsha G. McGee, pp. 246–263. 2d ed. Philadelphia, 1998.

Choksy, Jamsheed K. "Sarnevesht-e Zartoshtiyān-e Irān moruri tārikhi (The Fate of the Zoroastrians of Iran over Time)." *Iran Nameh* 19 (2001): 61–78.

Choksy, Jamsheed K. *Evil, Good, and Gender: Facets of the Feminine in Zoroastrian Religious History.* New York, 2002.

Choksy, Jamsheed K. "Hagiography and Monotheism in History: Doctrinal Encounters between Zoroastrianism, Judaism, and Christianity." *Islam and Christian-Muslim Relations* 14 (2003): 407–415.

Choksy, Jamsheed K. "Incorporation of Medieval Science into Zoroastrian Scripture and Exegesis: Some Evidence from Dēnkard Book 4." In *The Spirit of Wisdom: Essays in Memory of Ahmad Tafazzoli,* edited by Touraj Daryaee and Mahmoud Omidsalar, pp. 58–63. Costa Mesa, Calif., 2004.

Christensen, Arthur. *Essai sur la démonologie iranienne.* Copenhagen, Denmark, 1941.

Clark, Peter. *Zoroastrianism: An Introduction to an Ancient Faith.* Sussex, U.K., 1998.

Darmesteter, James, trans. *The Zend-Avesta,* pts. 1–2. 2 vols. Oxford, 1884–1895; reprint, Delhi, 1981.

Darmesteter, James, trans. *Le Zend-Avesta.* 3 vols. Paris, 1892–1893; reprint Paris, 1960.

Daryaee, Touraj. "The Mazdean Sect of Gayōmartiya." In *Ātash-e Dorun—The Fire Within: Jamshid Soroush Soroushian Memorial Volumes,* vol. 2, edited by Carlo G. Cereti and Farrokh J. Vajifdar, pp. 131–137. Bloomington, Ind., 2003.

Dhabhar, Bamanji N., trans. *The Persian Rivayats of Hormazyar Framarz and Others: Their Version with Introduction and Notes.* Bombay, 1932.

Dhabhar, Bamanji N., trans. *Zand-i Khūrtak Avistāk.* Bombay, 1963.

Dhalla, Maneckji N., ed. and trans. *The Nyaishes or Zoroastrian Litanies: Avestan Text with the Pahlavi, Sanskrit, Persian, and Gujarati Versions.* New York, 1908; reprint New York, 1965.

Duchesne-Guillemin, Jacques. *The Western Response to Zoroaster.* Oxford, 1958.

Duchesne-Guillemin, Jacques. *Symbolik des Parsismus.* Stuttgart, 1961.

Duchesne-Guillemin, Jacques. *La religion de l'Iran ancien.* Paris, 1962.

Duchesne-Guillemin, Jacques. *Symbols and Values in Zoroastrianism: Their Survival and Renewal.* New York, 1966.

Dumézil, Georges. *Naissance d'archanges.* Paris, 1945.

Eduljee, Homi E. "The Date of Zoroaster." *Journal of the K. R. Cama Oriental Institute* 48 (1980): 103–160.

Fox, W. Sherwood, and R. E. K. Pemberton. "Passages in Greek and Latin Literature Relating to Zoroaster and Zoroastrianism Rendered into English." *Journal of the K. R. Cama Oriental Institute* 14 (1929): 1–145.

Geiger, Wilhelm. *Civilization of the Eastern Iranians in Ancient Times.* Translated by Peshotan Sanjana. 2 vols. London, 1882; reprint London, 1885–1886.

Gershevitch, Ilya. "Approaches to Zoroaster's Gathas." *Iran* 33 (1995): 1–29.

Gignoux, M. Philippe. "L'apocalyptique iranienne est-elle vraiment la source d'autres apocalypses?" *Acta Antiqua Academiae Scientiarum Hungaricae* 31 (1985–1988): 67–78.

Gignoux, M. Philippe. "Nouveaux regards sur l'apocalyptique iranienne." *Comptes rendus de l'Académie des inscriptions et belles-lettres* (1986): 334–346.

Gnoli, Gherardo. *Zoroaster in History.* New York, 2000.

Godrej, Pheroza P., and Firoza P. Mistree, eds. *A Zoroastrian Tapestry: Art, Religion, and Culture.* Bombay, 2002.

Gray, Louis H. *The Foundations of the Iranian Religions.* Bombay, 1929.

Haug, Martin. *Essays on the Sacred Language, Writings, and Religion of the Parsis,* 4th ed. London, 1907; reprint, Amsterdam, 1971.

Henning, Walter B. *Zoroaster: Politician or Witch-Doctor?* Oxford, 1951.

Herzfeld, Ernest. *Zoroaster and His World.* 2 vols. New York, 1947; reprint New York, 1973.

Hinnells, John. "Zoroastrian Influence on the Judeo-Christian Tradition." *Journal of the K. R. Cama Oriental Institute* 45 (1976): 1–23.

Hinnells, John. "Zoroastrian Influence on Judaism and Christianity: Some Further Reflections." *Journal of the American Academy of Religion* 53 (1985): 202–235.

Hinnells, John R. *Zoroastrians in Britain.* Oxford, 1996.

Hinnells, John. "The Zoroastrian Diasporas." In *South Asians in the Diaspora: Histories and Religious Traditions,* edited by Knut A. Jacobsen and P. Pratap Kumar, pp. 313–336. Leiden, Netherlands, 2004.

Hintze, Almut. "On the Literary Structure of the Old Avesta." *Bulletin of the School of Oriental and African Studies* 65 (2002): 31–51.

Hodivala, Shapurji K. *Indo-Iranian Religion.* Bombay, 1925.

Humbach, Helmut, and Pallan R. Ichaporia, eds. and trans. *The Heritage of Zarathushtra: A New Translation of His Gathas.* Heidelberg, 1994.

Insler, Stanley, ed. and trans. *The Gathas of Zarathustra.* Leiden, 1975.

Jackson, A. V. Williams. *Zoroaster: The Prophet of Ancient Iran.* New York, 1898.

Jamzadeh, Laal, and Margaret Mills."Iranian Sofreh: From Collective to Female Ritual." In *Gender and Religion: On the Complexity of Symbols,* edited by Caroline W. Bynum, Stevan Harrell, and Paula Richman, pp. 23–65. Boston, 1986.

Jong, Albert de. *Traditions of the Magi: Zoroastrianism in Greek and Latin Literature.* Leiden, 1997.

Kellens, Jean. *Le panthéon de l'Avesta ancien.* Wiesbaden, 1994.

Kellens, Jean. *Essays on Zarathustra and Zoroastrianism.* Translated by P. Oktor Skjærvø. Costa Mesa, Calif., 2000.

Kellens, Jean, and Eric Pirart, eds. and trans. *Les textes vieil-avestiques.* 3 vols. Wiesbaden, 1988–1991.

Kotwal, Firoze M., and James W. Boyd. *A Persian Offering, The Yasna: A Zoroastrian High Liturgy.* Paris, 1991.

Kreyenbroek, Philip G. "The Zoroastrian Priesthood after the Fall of the Sasanian Empire." In *Transition Periods in Iranian History,* pp. 151–166. Louvain, 1987.

Kriwaczek, Paul. *In Search of Zarathustra: The First Prophet and the Ideas that Changed the World.* London, 2002; reprint, New York, 2003.

Kuiper, Franciscus B. J. "The Bliss of Asha." *Indo-Iranian Journal* 8 (1964): 96–129.

Langer, Robert. "From Private Shrine to Pilgrimage Center: The Spectrum of Zoroastrian Shrines in Iran." In *Zoroastrian Rituals in Context,* edited by Michael Stausberg, pp. 563–592. Leiden, 2004.

Leslie, Donald D. "Persian Temples in T'ang China." *Monumenta Serica* 35 (1981–1983): 275–303.

Lommel, Herman, trans. *Die Yäsht's des Awesta.* Göttingen, Germany, 1927.

Malandra, William W. *An Introduction to Ancient Iranian Religion: Readings from the Avesta and Achaemenid Inscriptions.* Minneapolis, 1983.

Meherjirana, Erachji S. *A Guide to the Zoroastrian Religion: A Nineteenth-Century Catechism with Modern Commentary.* Translated by Firoze M. Kotwal and James W. Boyd. Chico, Calif., 1982.

Mehr, Farhang. "Zoroastrians in Twentieth-Century Iran." In *A Zoroastrian Tapestry: Art, Religion, and Culture,* edited by Pheroza P. Godrej and Firoza P. Mistree, pp. 278–299. Bombay, India, 2002.

Mehr, Farhang. *The Zoroastrian Tradition: An Introduction to the Ancient Wisdom of Zarathustra.* 2d ed. Costa Mesa, Calif., 2003.

Menasce, Jean de. "L'Église mazdéene dans l'empire sassanide." *Cahiers d'histoire mondaile* 2 (1955): 554–565.

Menasce, Jean de. "Problèmes des mazdéens dans l'Iran musulman." In *Festschrift für Wilhelm Eilers,* edited by Gernot Wiessner, pp. 220–230. Wiesbaden, 1967.

Menasce, Jean de. "Zoroastrian Literature after the Muslim Conquest." In *Cambridge History of Iran,*vol. 4, edited by Richard N. Frye, pp. 543–565. Cambridge, U.K., 1975.

Menasce, Jean de. "Zoroastrian Pahlavi Writings." In *Cambridge History of Iran,* vol. 3, pt. 2, edited by Ehsan Yarshater, pp. 1166–1195. Cambridge, U.K., 1975.

Mills, Lawrence H., trans. *The Zend-Avesta,* pt. 3. Oxford, 1887; reprint, Delhi, India, 1981.

Mistree, Khojeste P. *Zoroastrianism: An Ethnic Perspective.* Bombay, 1982.

Mistree, Khojeste P. "The Breakdown of the Zoroastrian Tradition as Viewed from a Contemporary Perspective." In *Irano-Judaica,* vol. 2, edited by Shaul Shaked and Amnon Netzer, pp. 227–254. Jerusalem, 1990.

Modi, Jivanji J. *The Social Life of the Ancient Iranians as Presented by the Avesta.* Poona, 1923.

Modi, Jivanji J. *The Religious Ceremonies and Customs of the Parsees.* 2d ed. Bombay, 1937.

Molé, Marijan. *Culte, mythe, et cosmologie dans l'Iran ancien: Le problème zoroastrien et la tradition mazdéene.* Paris, 1963.

Molé, Marijan., ed. and trans. *La légende de Zoroastre: Selon les textes pehlevis.* Paris, 1967.

Moreen, Vera B. "The Status of Religious Minorities in Safavid Iran." *Journal of Near Eastern Studies* 40 (1981): 119–134.

Munshi, Shehnaz N., and Sarah Stewart. "Observances of the Faithful." In *A Zoroastrian Tapestry: Art, Religion, and Culture,* edited by Pheroza J. Godrej and Firoza P. Mistree, pp. 384–397. Bombay, 2002.

Narten, Johanna. *Die Amesha Spentas im Avesta.* Wiesbaden, 1982.

Nigosian, Solomon A. *The Zoroastrian Faith: Tradition and Modern Research.* Montreal, 1993; reprint Montreal, 1999.

Nyberg, Henrik S. "Sassanid Mazdaism according to Moslem Sources." *Journal of the K. R. Cama Oriental Institute* 39 (1958): 1–63.

Nyberg, Henrik S. *Die Religionen des alten Iran.* 2d ed. Osnabrück, Germany, 1966.

Oshidari, Timsar. *Tārikh-e Zartoshtiyān* (History of Zoroastrianism). Tehran, 1976.

Pangborn, Cyrus R. *Zoroastrianism: A Beleaguered Faith.* New York, 1983.

Pavry, Cursetji. *The Zoroastrian Doctrine of a Future Life.* 2d ed. New York, 1929.

Rose, Jenny. *The Image of Zoroaster: The Persian Mage through European Eyes.* New York, 2000.

Russell, James R. *Zoroastrianism in Armenia.* Cambridge, Mass., 1987.

Russell, James R. "On Mysticism and Esotericism among the Zoroastrians." *Iranian Studies* 26 (1993): 73–94.

Rustomjee, Framroz. *Daily Prayers of the Zoroastrians.* 2 pts. Colombo, Sri Lanka, 1967.

Sanasarian, Eliz. *Religious Minorities in Iran.* Cambridge, U.K., 2000.

Sarianidi, Victor. *Margiana and Protozoroastrianism.* Translated by Inna Sarianidi. Athens, 1998.

Schmidt, Hanns-Peter. "Zaraθuštra and His Patrons." In *Ātash-e Dorun—The Fire Within: Jamshid Soroush Soroushian Memorial Volumes,* vol. 2, edited by Carlo G. Cereti and Farrokh J. Vajifdar, pp. 357–376. Bloomington, Ind., 2003.

Schwartz, Martin. "The Religion of Achaemenian Iran." In *Cambridge History of Iran,* vol. 2, edited by Ilya Gershevitch, pp. 664–697. Cambridge, U.K., 1985.

Shahbazi, A. Shapur. "Recent Speculations on the 'Traditional Date of Zoroaster.'" *Studia Iranica* 31 (2002): 7–45.

Shahzadi, Fariborz S., with Khojeste P. Mistree. *The Zarathushti Religion: A Basic Text.* Hinsdale, Ill., 1998.

Shaked, Shaul. "The Notions Mēnōg and Gētīg in the Pahlavi Texts and Their Relation to Eschatology." *Acta Orientalia* 33 (1971): 59–107.

Shaked, Shaul. *Dualism in Transformation: Varieties of Religion in Sasanian Iran.* London, 1994.

Skjærvø, P. Oktor. "The Literature of the Most Ancient Iranians." In *Proceedings of the Second North American Gatha Conference,* edited by Sarosh J. H. Manekshaw and Pallan R. Ichaporia, pp. 221–235. Womelsdorf, Pa., 1996.

Skjærvø, P. Oktor. "The State of Old Avestan Scholarship." *Journal of the American Oriental Society* 117 (1997): 103–114.

Skjærvø, P. Oktor. "Zarathustra: First Poet-Sacrificer." In *Paitimāna: Essays in Iranian, Indo-European, and Indian Studies in Honor of Hanns-Peter Schmidt,* edited by Siamak Adhami, pp. 157–194. Costa Mesa, Calif., 2003.

Soroushian, Jamshid S. *Farhang-e behdinān (Dictionary of the Members of the Good Religion).* Tehran, 1956.

Soroushian, Jamshid S. *Tārikh-e Zartoshtiyān-e Kermān dar in chand sad sāle* (History of the Zoroastrians of Kerman in Recent Centuries). Tehran, 1992.

Stausberg, Michael. *Faszination Zarathushtra: Zoroaster und die Europäische Religionsgeschichte der Frühen Neuzeit.* 2 vols. Berlin, 1998.

Stausberg, Michael, ed. *Zoroastrian Rituals in Context.* Leiden, 2004.

West, Edward W., trans. *Pahlavi Texts.* 5 vols. Oxford, 1882–1901; reprint, Delhi, 1994.

Williams, Ron G., and James W. Boyd. *Ritual Art and Knowledge: Aesthetic Theory and Zoroastrian Ritual.* Columbia, S.C., 1993.

Windfuhr, Gernot L. "The Logic of the Holy Immortals in Zoroastrianism." In *Proceedings of the Second North American Gatha Conference,* edited by Sarosh J. H. Manekshaw and Pallan R. Ichaporia, pp. 237–274. Womelsdorf, Pa., 1996.

Windfuhr, Gernot. "A Note on Aryaman's Social and Cosmic Setting." In *Aryan and Non-Aryan in South Asia: Evidence, Interpretation, and Ideology,* edited by Johannes Bronkhorst and Madhav M. Deshpande, pp. 295–336. Cambridge, Mass., 1999.

Writer, Rashna. *Contemporary Zoroastrians: An Unstructured Nation.* Lanham, Md., 1994.

Zaehner, Robert C. *The Teachings of the Magi: A Compendium of Zoroastrian Beliefs.* London, 1956; reprint, New York, 1976.

Zaehner, Robert C. *The Dawn and Twilight of Zoroastrianism.* London, 1961; reprint, New York, 2003.

JAMSHEED K. CHOKSY (2005)

ZULU RELIGION. After nearly 150 years of missionary activity the majority of the some 5.5 million Zulu-speaking South Africans are Christians. For many, however, the *amadlozi* (ancestors or shades of dead kin) who once dominated Zulu religion are still a force to be reckoned with and propitiated. The acceptance of the power of the *amadlozi* to intervene in the lives of their descendants and to help them is manifested in the beliefs and rituals of most of the African independent churches to which, indeed, over a quarter of all Zulu Christians belong. The basic concerns of traditional Zulu religion—the pursuit of health, fertility, and a balance between man and man and between man and nature—are as relevant today as ever. Since these are the very areas in which the ancestors are thought to be most powerful, offerings to the *amadlozi* occur in many contexts both traditional and Christian. These offerings take place both in the far-flung areas of rural KwaZulu (the geographical area situated on the east coast of South Africa between 28° and 31° south latitude from which most Zulu originated even if they have no ties there today) as well as in cosmopolitan urban centers where Zulu mingle with other South Africans as residents and work-seekers.

Attention is focused here upon the major enduring features of Zulu religion as first reported in the writings of early travelers and missionaries, and later in contemporary anthropological work in KwaZulu, notably that of Harriet Ngubane, whose study of the Nyuswa-Zulu provides a picture of how Zulu religion is practiced today and highlights the previously neglected role of women in belief and ritual.

In Zulu thought the ancestors are only one part of a more extensive system of beliefs. Within this system, the natural order is thought to impinge closely upon man for human beings are thought to be related both physically and psychically to their environment and to be vulnerable to harmful forces in nature. Such forces either operate automatically or are manipulated by sorcerers (*abathakathi*) who cause ill health, misfortune, and the general state of vulnerability known as *isifo.* The ancestors also harm the living but only as a warning when they are angry; in fact, the *amadlozi,* many of whom were once known to the living, are the major protectors against sorcery. Appropriate ancestral offerings are cattle or goats that are sacrificed, the meat being left overnight for the ancestors to "lick" (*khotha*) and to share with the living. Diviners called *izangoma* (sg., *isangoma*) are consulted whenever illness, misfortune, or unusual events occur, for it is they alone who can ascertain the cause. They also recommend paths of reparation in the case of ancestral anger and, in the event of sorcery, may point out the sorcerer or suggest countermeasures. Diviners are called to their profession by their own ancestors, who possess and guide them, and they undergo a lengthy training in their art. Herbalists (*izinyanga*) also treat disease and provide protective medicines but, because they are not possessed by the spirits, they lack powers of divination.

ZULU COSMOLOGY AND THE NATURAL ORDER. The Zulu say that in the beginning there was uMvelinqangi, literally the first "comer-out," who broke off from a reed bed followed by human beings, animals, and nature as a whole. He sent a chameleon to humanity with the message that they would live forever. Later, growing impatient with the chameleon's slowness, he sent a lizard with the message that all humans would die, and because it was the faster animal, the lizard arrived first. In some tales uMvelinqangi is portrayed as the source of the known social order, for he gave human beings their ancestors and decided how the ancestors should be approached and placated. There is, however, little evidence that uMvelinqangi was worshiped directly. Ideas about him probably served largely as explanatory constructs for the natural order (and some features of the social order), and in traditional times such ideas would have played a minor role in everyday religious practice. Another name for uMvelinqangi was uNkulunkulu ("the old, old one"), a term that missionaries used for "God," thus causing some confusion by conflating Zulu ideas of a pure creator with Christian notions of a creator and supreme being to whom regular worship must be directed. Distinct from uMvelinqangi is iNkosi yeZulu, the lord of the sky and personification of heaven. He is associated with thunder and lightning, which are greatly feared and against which specially trained herbalists offer protection.

Linked also with the sky or the "above" (*ezulwini*—a critical concept that contrasts with *phansi,* the "below," where the dead go before becoming ancestors) is iNkosazana yeZulu, or merely iNkosazana, the princess of heaven (uNomkhubulwana). The latter term is derived from *khubula* ("to sow again after rain or sun has destroyed crops"), and this female deity is closely associated with abundance and sufficient (but not too much) rain. She bestows fertility on crops, cattle, and human beings and is often actively placated in times of drought and searing heat. The patron of women and particularly of young girls, iNkosazana is said to appear in the fructifying mists of spring and to stand on the threshold of summer like a girl whose puberty ceremonies mark her entry to marriage and procreation. The same songs are sung both at girls' puberty ceremonies and at ceremonies held in honor of iNkosazana; in both cases the songs are thought to promote fertility and good rains. Before hoeing begins, women sometimes plant a small field for iNkosazana near a river, and a libation of beer is poured on the ground to the accompaniment of a prayer for a fruitful harvest. Other ceremonies connected with the goddess are aimed at warding off pests that affect crops, cattle diseases, and maladies common in spring and summer such as malaria and gastroenteritis. The word *ukushweleza* ("to make an apology"), which is used in connection with these rituals, suggests the placation of iNkosazana's anger and the setting of things in order so that the season will proceed without mishap. Because of its conceptual links with fertility and girls' puberty ceremonials, the cult of iNkosazana must be seen against the background of the widespread emphasis upon fertility in African cosmological systems. Her cult has a counterpart in the *uyali-vuhwera* fertility cult and the *gomana* drum cult of the northeastern Transvaal Lowveld, but the Zulu are unique among Bantu-speaking peoples in southern Africa in their conception of a female deity associated with fertility who is worshiped even today.

The natural order impinges on life in other ways which affect health and well-being. In contrast to illnesses caused by sorcery or ancestral anger, there is an extremely wide range of diseases stretching from the common cold to more serious epidemics like smallpox or measles, which are said to "just happen." These maladies may be due to natural causes such as the changing of the seasons or the inevitable processes of aging and maturation. Many are treated with medicines which are potent in themselves and do not necessarily require ritual or religious accompaniment, although protection against certain seasonal illnesses may be sought from iNkosazana. Another important class of natural illnesses are thought to result inevitably from imbalances in nature. All living things are believed to leave behind something of themselves and absorb something of the atmosphere through which they move. Such influences, called *imikhondo* ("tracks"), may be detrimental to the individual. Treatment, while bringing relief to one person, may release the dangerous element to affect others. To keep the immediate environment pure, people seek to discard *imikhondo* in public places such as highways and crossroads, where they are thought to mix with other noxious substances placed there by sorcerers; these areas are thus extremely dangerous to travelers. Moving into a new environment may in itself be dangerous, as one is not yet attuned to its influences. Several categories of people are particularly at risk from environmental influences including newcomers to an area, infants who have only recently entered the world, and all those who are temporarily in a weakened state, known as *umnyama.* This last category includes the bereaved, newly delivered mothers, homicides, and menstruating women. Although all people should be strengthened from time to time against alien environmental influences, these people must be given specific treatments, often both medicinal and ritual, aimed not only at strengthening them but also at achieving or restoring order or symmetry between them and their environment. The word commonly used to describe such treatment is *ukuzilungisa* (from *lunga,* "to be as should be," and *isa,* "to come to be"), which implies the restitution of balance not only between man and nature but sometimes between man and man or between man and his ancestors.

Certain natural processes are thought to weaken the individual. The most important and general is *umnyama,* to which reference was made above, and which may be literally translated as "darkness," "blackness," or "heaviness." This state results from contact with death or birth, which renders the individual open to sorcery, other malign influences, bad luck, and misfortune, and also makes him or her a danger to others. Women are extremely vulnerable to *umnyama* because of their biological association with procreation and because the chief mourners at funerals are always women. Indeed, Ngubane argues that because of this dual association with the beginning and end of life, women occupy a "marginal" position in Zulu cosmology and serve as a symbolic bridge between "this world" (the world of the living) and the "otherworld" (that of the spirits). Women, however, not only link this world and the otherworld, but in their roles as daughter in one kinship group and mother in another they form a bridge between two distinct patrilineages. Zulu society is strongly patrilineal, and marriage may occur only outside the clan. A bride is thus an outsider in her affinal home, yet it is only through her that her husband's group can reproduce itself. This social marginality is indicated by certain linguistic avoidances or restrictions (*hlonipha*) placed upon a bride and also by the fear that married women are potential sorcerers in their husband's homestead. Since the bearer of children is thus paradoxically also a threat to continuity of the patriline, Zulu social structure places married women in an ambiguous position which complements the marginality they derive from their biological and cultural association with birth and death. Diviners are also seen to be marginal in that they intercede between the living and the dead, between this world and the otherworld, and it is significant that most diviners are women and that men who are called to this position are transvestites.

ANCESTORS AND SOCIAL LIFE. As Eileen Jensen Krige has pointed out, "the real vital religion of the Zulus is their ancestor worship" (Krige, 1936). Indeed, when things are going well, the Zulu say that their ancestors are "with them," but when misfortune strikes, they say that the ancestors are "facing away." Revelations are made in dreams and visions as well as through misfortune, and what angers the ancestors most is neglect and failure to fulfill kinship obligations. Different aspects of the overall conception of the ancestors are indicated in the various Zulu words used for the dead. *Amadlozi* is derived from *dloza,* meaning "to care for, keep an eye on," but because the spirit world is thought to be situated "below" (*phansi*), the ancestors are often referred to simply as *abaphansi, "those of the below."* Another word frequently used is *amathongo,* from *ubuthongo,* "deep sleep," a reference to one of the ways in which the ancestors contact the living. Diviners address their ancestors as *makhosi,* from *inkhosi,* "chief," and *ubukhosi,* "authority, power, glory," thus emphasizing the major nuances of the unique relationship between them and the spirits which possess them. The word *isithunzi,* from *umthunzi,* "shadow," refers to the force or personality that leaves the body at death and wanders aimlessly until it is "brought home" (*buyisa*) by a special ceremony designed to integrate it (as an *idlozi,* or ancestor proper) into the body of powerful ancestors who have control over the living. Since the spirits are dependent upon their descendants to perform this and other ancestral rituals, the relationship between the living and the dead is one of mutuality which excludes non-kin and reflects the major emphases of Zulu kinship and particularly patrilineal organization.

A man's most important ancestors are his father, mother, father's father, and father's mother, as well as the father's brothers who act with and share sacrifices offered to deceased parents and grandparents. Among the Nyuswa-Zulu, about whom we have recent knowledge from the work of Ngubane, *amadlozi* more than three generations removed from a homestead head are not thought to be dangerous. They are said, however, to come to sacrifices along with closer ancestors, and may even possess a diviner as a supporting spirit. The living kin who gather for ancestral rituals largely include the patrilineal descendants of a grandfather, and the women who have married these men. At sacrifices, it is the genealogically senior male (*umnumzane*) who officiates. Among the Nyuswa-Zulu the married men of this cluster or segment (*umndeni*) of two or three generations often live close to each other and, under the headship of the *umnumzane,* act as a corporate group in the control and management of common resources (such as land) and in the settlement of internal disputes. The authority of the *umnumzane* is bolstered by his ritual position and the fact that younger agnates can approach the ancestors only through him. The rituals of the ancestor cult therefore both demonstrate and, in the Durkhemian sense, promote the corporate character and social continuity of the *umndeni.* On the political level, the ancestors of the king guard and protect the whole society and are sacrificed to at national festivals. Prior to the defeat of the Zulu nation and the disbanding of the army by the British, the king's ancestors were always called upon before warriors went into battle.

The ancestor cult reflects a number of other important aspects of Zulu social life. The role of the chief wife who bears the heir is emphasized, for it is on the *umsamo* of her hut (the rear part of the dwelling associated with the spirits) that sacrificial meat is placed for the ancestors to share. Individual social identities are often fixed unambiguously by calling on the ancestors. Thus a baby is placed formally under the control of the ancestors to whose line it belongs by the sacrifice of a goat known as *imbeleko,* the skin of which is used to secure the baby on its mother's back. This ceremony is usually performed by the child's father or father's father, but in the case of an unmarried woman, the responsibility lies with her father and his *umndeni* to which the child belongs.

In former times abandoned children were adopted by an *imbeleko* sacrifice, thus demonstrating that it is social rather than biological paternity which is important. By the same token, one of the objectives of wedding ceremonies is to introduce the bride, who comes from another descent group, to her husband's ancestors and to put her under their care. Neglect of this formality may result in failure on the part of her affinal ancestors to recognize and protect her and her children. Barrenness is sometimes, however, attributed to a married woman's own ancestors who may, for instance, be angry that the correct puberty ceremonies were not performed for her. They may also make her ill if they want her to become a diviner. In both cases it is her father's responsibility to set matters in order. The fact that a married woman can be affected by her own ancestors as well as those of her husband serves both to underline the separate identity of affinal groups linked by marriage and to indicate the married woman's role as a bridge between the two patrilineages. With time and the birth of children she is effectively transferred from the one descent group to the other. After menopause she may eat those parts of ancestral sacrifices reserved for members of her affinal kin group, and she may even call on the ancestors if no suitable male is present. At death she is fully incorporated into her affinal group when she is brought back by her son as one of his patrilineal ancestors. She has then completed the "long journey" (*udwendwe*) that she began as a bride, and in so doing she had mediated between the conflicting interests of patriliny and exogamy in Zulu society.

SPIRIT POSSESSION. Spirit possession is an important and dynamic aspect of Zulu life. The call to be a diviner takes the form of recognized mental and physical affliction, the cure for which are initiation and professional training. The traditional *isangoma* (and her counterpart in many Christian sects) is a pivotal force for order and rapprochement between man and the spirit world. There are, however, new forms of spirit possession that were first reported at the turn of the century, which have intensified since the 1930s. These are destructive and anarchic; Ngubane relates them to the disruptive effects of social and industrial change. *Indiki* and *ufufunyane* (or *iziwe*) are the most prevalent types, resulting from possession by the deceased spirits of foreigners, which have not been integrated into the body of the ancestors. *Indiki* are possessed by male spirits who enter the individual's chest by chance and manifest themselves in a deep bellowing voice which speaks in a foreign tongue. Treatment often involves replacing the alien spirit with an ancestral spirit, and the *indiki* may become a diviner. *Ufufunyane* is diagnosed as due to sorcery and is a particularly intractable form, for the alien spirit becomes violent when challenged. The possessed individuals become hysterical and may attempt suicide in a frenzy. Treatment involves dispelling the alien spirit—or often hordes of spirits of different race groups—and replacing them by spirits controlled by the doctor and referred to as a regiment (*amabutho*). The image is one of war against the sorcerer's evil medicine; no attempt is made to call an ancestral spirit, and no cult membership or professionalization results.

TRADITIONAL BELIEF AND ZULU CHRISTIANITY. Zulu cosmological ideas have been incorporated into Zulu Christian thought in a number of subtle ways. The word for "breath" (*umoya*) is translated as "Holy Spirit," and people said to be filled with the Holy Spirit become leaders in African independent churches that have split off from orthodox congregations. In these churches Christian beliefs coexist with aspects of traditional Zulu belief, and leadership reveals striking similarities to traditional divination in that the prophet, with the help of the Holy Spirit, explains misfortune and prescribes remedies. These may include ancestral offerings as well as orthodox Christian prayer. Protection against sorcery and misfortune is given by prayer and also medicine, and the blend of the two religious systems is basic to the vibrancy of African Christianity as it has developed, not only in the independent churches, but recently in orthodox congregations as well. Healing, purification, and the search for fertility are major issues in African Christianity, and many of the sects and churches that have proliferated in town and country serve not only the spiritual needs of their members but perform important social and welfare functions in the context of the chronic poverty and political subordination that has characterized the lives of many Zulu in the twentieth century.

BIBLIOGRAPHY

The most important of the early works on Zulu religion is the Reverend Henry Callaway's *The Religious System of the Amazulu* (1870; reprint, Cape Town, 1970), which presents original texts by Zulu informants together with translations and notes. A. T. Bryant's article "The Zulu Cult of the Dead," *Man* 17 (September 1917): 140–145, and his book *The Zulu People* (1948; New York, 1970), which gives details on Nomkhubulwane beliefs and ceremonies, provide a useful summary of what may be considered the main elements of the traditional belief system as described to early travelers and missionaries. An anthropological analysis, built up largely from these sources, but placing both belief and practice in their wider social context, is to be found in Eileen Jensen Krige's *The Social System of the Zulus* (Pietermaritzburg, 1936), pp. 280–296.

Two studies that deal with the present situation, both based on detailed anthropological research, are the Reverend Axel-Ivar Berglund's *Zulu Thought-Patterns and Symbolism* (London, 1976), and Harriet Ngubane's *Body and Mind in Zulu Medicine* (London, 1977). The first work offers an exhaustive compilation of detail, which provides some important insights, and also discusses a number of problematic conceptual issues. However, for scholars and laymen alike, Ngubane's book is the best starting point; an ethnographic study of one community, it is written lucidly and with the insight of a Zulu anthropologist. For doctors and those involved in the medical field, it is a *sine qua non* as it examines religious beliefs as part of Zulu ideas about the causation and treatment of disease.

Researchers seeking to become conversant with the details of Zulu thought patterns should consult Otto F. Raum's *The Social Functions of Avoidances and Taboos among the Zulu* (Berlin and New York, 1973), as it presents fascinating but very detailed data on a wide range of beliefs and their associated avoidances. The writings of Katesa Schlosser will also be of interest, especially *Zauberei im Zululand: Manuskripte des Blitz-Zauberers Laduma Madela* (Kiel, 1972), a study of Zulu mythology as told by a lightning doctor. Although the latter work shows how one Zulu philosopher has rethought and to some extent reinterpreted and expanded traditional Zulu cosmological notions, none of the above works concentrate specifically on change. Those interested in this aspect should consult Bengt Sundkler's *Bantu Prophets in South Africa*, 2d ed. (Oxford, 1961), and his more recent *Zulu Zion and Some Swazi Zionists* (Lund and Oxford, 1976). The sociological and welfare concomitants of many African independent churches are discussed in the work of James P. Kiernan; see in particular "Pure and Puritan: An Attempt to View Zionism as a Collective Response to Urban Poverty," *African Studies* 36 (1977): 31–41. The continuing influence of the conception of the ancestors in literature and worldview is demonstrated by a recent collection of poems by the Zulu poet Mazisi Kunene, *The Ancestors and the Sacred Mountain* (Exeter, N. H., 1982).

New Sources

Berglund, Axel-Iver. *Zulu Thought-Patterns and Symbolism.* Bloomington, 1989.

Canocini, Noverino N. *Zulu Oral Traditions.* Durban, 1996.

Hexham, Irving, ed. *Texts on Zulu Religion: Traditional Zulu Ideas About God.* Lewiston, N.Y., 1987.

Morris, Donald R. *The Washing of Spears: A History of the Rise of the Zulu Nation Under Shaka and Its Fall in the Zulu War of 1879.* New York, 1998.

Mountain, Alan. *The Rise and Fall of Zulu Empire.* Constantia, South Africa, 1999.

ELEANOR M. PRESTON-WHYTE (1987)
Revised Bibliography

ZURVANISM.

It is difficult to determine whether veneration of a deity of time and fate, literally a father "time" figure, named Zurvan (Avestan, Zrvan; Pahlavi, Zurwān—variant form, Zamān) developed chronologically or spatially into a distinct religious movement in ancient and medieval Iran that competed with Zoroastrianism or Mazdaism. Nevertheless, Zurvanism is attested in Iranian belief generally, and Zoroastrianism specifically, from at least mid-

Achaemenian times (late fifth century BCE). By the Sasanian period (224–651 CE), Zurvanite theology and mythology seems to have gained substantial followers among the magi or Zoroastrian priests along with Iranian nobles and scholars, possibly exerting influence on doctrines at times when fatalism seemed appropriate. As a monist sect, it possibly was one form of early medieval orthodoxy in southwestern Iran, among other locales. Yet there are no Iranian temples that can be associated specifically with worship of Zurvan. Neither are there images that can be identified clearly as representing Zurvan, not even the leontocephalic, or lion-headed, spirit (later known to be associated with western Mithraism). Nor can any particular rituals be attributed to the ration of Zurvan. The entire performative dimension of religiosity appears to be have been absent in the case of Zurvan.

SOURCES AND PRINCIPLES. The *Persepolis Fortification Tablets* (fifth century BCE) preserve the theophoric name Izrudukma (*Zru[va]taukhma, "of Zurvan's seed" [2084.4]) as an early reference to the importance of time in ancient Iranian society. Other ancient-to-medieval Iranian and Armenian names like Zrovandukht (daughter of Zurvan), Zarwandād (created or given by Zurvan), and Zrvandasht (preserved by Zurvan) also reflect devotees' association with this deity.

The Zoroastrian scripture, or *Abestāg* (Avesta; Praise), places only limited emphasis on Zurvan, mentioning him infrequently. One passage in the Young Avesta (composed between 900–400 BCE, with canonization lasting into the third century BCE) notes that after death the souls of the "confused ones and the orderly ones all journey along the road created by Zurvan to the bridge of the compiler created by [Ahura] Mazdā" (*Vidēvdād*, "Code to Ward Off Evil Spirits," 19.29). Another passage claims that Spenta Mainyu (holy spirit; the hypostasis of Ahura Mazdā), created Manthra Spenta (holy word)in Zurvan—that is, during time (*Vidēvdād* 19.9). Other Young Avestan references to Zurvan distinguish between Zrvan akarana (infinite or unlimited time) and Zrvan dareghō-khva-dhāta (time of the long dominion) (*Vidēvdād* 19.13, 19.16; *Yasna*, "Worship, Sacrifice" 72.10; *Sīrōza*, "[Invocations for] the Thirty Days of the Month," 1.21, 2.21; *Niyāyishn*, "Litany," 1.8). In these scriptural passages, Zurvan is associated with a range of divine spirits such as the Amesha Spentas (holy immortals), Daēna (religion, conscience), Rāman (peace), Vayu (wind or air), Thwasha (space), and Tishtrya (Sirius.) However, Zurvan is not presented as a preexisting deity, independent of Ahura Mazdā.

Clearer attestation of Zurvan's independent status comes from the reign of Artaxerxes or Artakhshaçā II (r. 404–359/8 BCE), through the writing of Theopompos (fl. fourth century BCE) as cited by Plutarch (c. 46–after 119 CE, where a millenary scheme of time—when Ohrmazd and Ahreman do battle—is the result of actions by a god who having "brought this to pass is quiet and at rest for a time" (*Isis and Osiris* 47). A few other classical sources, preserved in later redactions, also cite Zurvan. Antiochus I (c. 69–34 BCE) of Commagene referred to Kronos apeiros (unlimited time) on his Greek inscription at Nimrud Dagh in Anatolia—a document containing allusions to Iranian beliefs syncretized with Hellenistic ones. The broad dates for those documents have led to scholarly suggestions that chronological speculation may have culminated in a time-based cosmogony within the multinational, multireligious empire of the Achaemenians. Doctrinal augmentation could have occurred through confluence of Near Eastern, Greek, Iranian, and Indian notions of cosmic progenitors—such as Ra, Kronos, Zrvan, and Kāla, respectively—with the mythological Indo-European primal twins represented in the Old Avestan devotional poems as Spenta Mainyu and Angra Mainyu (*Gathas* 30.3, 45.2).

Zurvanism and medieval Zoroastrianism. Medieval Zoroastrian theology drew upon the Avesta to describe Zurvan in two forms: as Zurwān ī akanārag (infinite time) and as Zurwān ī dērang khwadāy (time of the long dominion)—an epithet shared with Vayu or Way—alternately termed Zurwān ī kanāragōmand or Zurwān ī brīnōmand (finite time). Such was the case in the *Greater Bundahishn* ([Book of] primal creation) (especially 3.14—on which see figure 1, Codex TD1 folio 14 verso, the oldest extant manuscript copy dating to 1531 CE, lines 2–3—and 3.6, 26.31), a text whose redactions spanned the Sassanian Empire and the Umayyad (661–750 CE) and Abbasid (750–1258 CE) caliphates.

In those forms, Zurvanite ideas are present in the *Mēnōg ī Khrad* (Spirit of wisdom), a Pahlavi or Middle Persian exegetical text from the sixth century CE, where Ahura Mazdā is said to have created the universe with the "blessing of infinite time," who is "infinite, ageless, undying, painless, unfeeling, incorruptible, and unassailable" (8.8, 8.9). Moreover, Zurvan was equated to Vayu as a weapon of Ahura Mazdā against falsehood (*Greater Bundahishn* 26.34).

In the ninth century CE, Zurvan was associated by Zoroastrians with the divine spirits Rām (peace), Spihr (sky), Māh (moon), and Gōsh (cow) in assisting the Amesha Spenta named Vohu Manah (Wahman; "good mind"; *Greater Bundahishn* 3.14). Likewise, the *Wizīdagīhā* (Selections) of Zādspram, a ninth-century CE *hērbed* (theologian) living at Sirkan, presented Ahura Mazdā's creative power as linked to Zurvan, who determines the course of the cosmic conflict between order and confusion (1.27–28, 2.19, 34.35). So, ultimately, these medieval sources do not clarify the degree of Zurvan's independence, in theology and ritual, from a Zoroastrian pantheon headed by Ahura Mazdā. However, even when not adopting an extreme monism of Zurvan with its ascription of the origin of all other entities to the actions of time, medieval Zoroastrianism in most sectarian forms employed a millenarian system of two, eternal, dualistic spirits in conflict during time (compare the standard account of cosmogony in the *Greater Bundahishn* 1.1–1a.14).

Christian and Muslim sources. Perhaps because of tensions within Zoroastrianism of reconciling Ahura Mazdā and Zurvan as progenitor spirits, the major extant textual

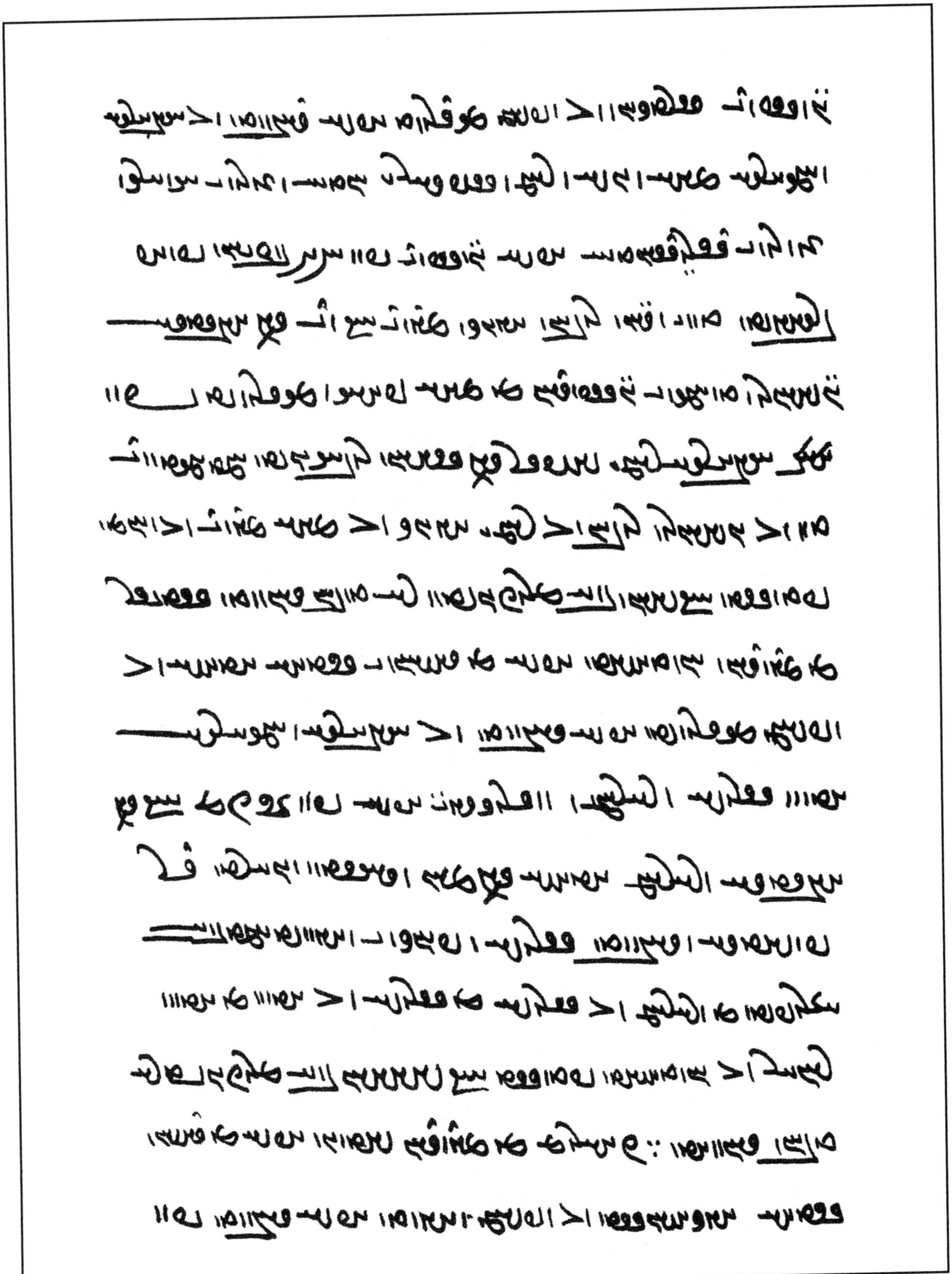

FIGURE 1. *Reproduced by permission of the archive of J. K. Choksy.*

sources for Zurvanism are those by Christian and Muslim writers. Armenian Christian authors who mentioned the Zurvanite creation myth include Eznik of Kołb (fl. fifth century CE) and Ełishē Vardapet (d. 480 CE). There are Syriac accounts, such as those by the Arab Christian bishop Theodore Abū Qurra (c. 740–820 CE), Theodore bar Kōnai (fl. ninth century CE), and the Nestorian monk Yohannān bar Penkayē (fl. c. seventh to ninth century CE). The Syriac documents mention divinities named Ashōqar, Frashōqar, and Zarōqar—whose names derive from Iranian words—as existing alongside Zurvan. All of the above-named writers may have utilized a common source, a work by the Cappadocian bishop Theodore of Mopsuestia (c. 350–428/9 CE), in addition to drawing upon each others' writings when possible. Syriac martyrologies of Nestorians, such as that of a woman named Anāhīd (d. c. 446 CE), mention portions of Zurvanite theology as well.

According to extant versions of the Zurvanite creation myth, as preserved by these authors, Ohrmazd (Ahura Mazdā, variously rendered as Ohrmizd, Ormizd, Hormizd, and Hormuz in the documents of Zurvanism) was conceived as the result of a rite that Zurvan had performed for a millennium to be granted a son who could create the universe. Ahreman (often written in those same sources as Ahriman, Ahrimen, Ahrman, Arhmn) was conceived unexpectedly, though not surprisingly within the ritual context, because Zurvan had doubted the efficacy of his devotive actions. Realizing that his wife would give birth to twins, Zurvan supposedly decided that the firstborn would rule the universe. Ahreman, upon learning of Zurvan's decision from a rather naïve Ohrmazd, ripped his way out of the womb and demanded his birthright. Zurvan, repulsed by this son's vileness, sought to restrict the evil twin's power by establishing a finite period of nine thousand years during which Ahreman would be in charge. Zurvan deemed that thereafter, his other son, Ohrmazd, would gain absolute power and appropriately determine the trajectory of events. Having set into motion the cosmic cycle and predetermined its outcome, Zurvan's relevance largely ended. No mention was made specifically of the origins of time or its female spouse, nor of the recipient of ritual, perhaps because it was assumed both that time in all its facets was eternal and that ritual could occur either for its own sake without a recipient or be directed at the performer.

Interestingly, a ninth-century CE Zoroastrian denunciation of this story is found in the *Dēnkard* (Acts of the religion; 9.30.4–5), where it is attributed to "the ranting of the demon Arashka" (Arashk or Areshk, "envy"). More important, Mardānfarrokh, the son of Ohrmazddād (fl. ninth century CE), author of the *Shkand Gumānīg Wizār* (Doubt dispelling exposition), condemned persons who subscribed to doctrines of time, referring to them as *Daharī* (6.2–3). This classification probably reflects a confluence of Islamic and Zoroastrian thought, because the *Dahriyya* (from the Arabic *dahr*, "time") were regarded as a heterodox sect by Sunni Muslims as well. The text of the critique itself preserves a variant of Zurvanite cosmogony. Even later, Iranian heresiographer Abū ʾl-Fatḥ Muḥammad al-Shahrastānī (d. 1153 CE) would categorize the *Zurwāniyya* as a specific sect.

Function of the Zurvanite myth. Mardānfarrokh's and Shahrastānī's comments reveal the central function of Zurvan for certain ancient and medieval Zoroastrians. It appears Zurvanism's teachings sought to reconcile the origins and functions of the dualism between Zoroastrianism's chief divinity Ahura Mazdā and chief demon Angra Mainyu through an entity whose actions created both. Zurvanism thus seems to have served as a theological and philosophical means of speculating about the origins, functions, and effects of the passage of time, the role of fate, the nature of duality, and the dilemmas of human existence within religiously constructed chronological frameworks. In other words, the Zurvanite myth provided those persons who accepted it with an explanation of how and why cosmogony occurred, stressing the roles of time as both medium and framework for creation. It proffered a theological explanation for the origins, purposes, interrelatedness, and interdependence of good and evil (Ohrmazd and Ahreman) and of their functions within human and cosmic frameworks of time. It also focused attention on the importance of performing rituals properly, for the case of Zurvan implied that if any aspect of a rite—thought, word, or deed—deviated, pandemonium could occur. Ultimately, the creation story would have been an attempt to overcome—through common origins, interrelated functions, and shared destinies that were linked and mediated by time—dilemmas posed by the creativeness and destructiveness ascribed in Zoroastrianism to spiritual forces and by the effects of those on human lives.

Manichaeism and Mandaeism. Other Iranian faiths also experienced the effect of time as a doctrinal force. Manichaeism drew upon Iranian beliefs in Zurvan, postulating a high god variously named Zurwān, Pidar Rōshn (Father of Light), and Pidar ī Wuzurgīh (Father of Greatness), who was "righteous" and dwelled "among the lights" (M 10R 11). Manichaeans believed that Zurvan was forced into conflict by an attacking Ahrimen and had created Ohrmizd to battle against the evil spirit but that the counteroffensive failed to stop evil at the beginning of time. As a result, life and death occur, Manichaeans had to strive toward purification of their spirits, and purity would set the stage for the final days of humanity. Manichaeism taught that eventually, and having enjoyed the assistance of devotees over the centuries, Zurvan would defeat Ahriman and purify all aspects of spirit or light from matter or darkness at the end of time (M 473, M 475, M 477, M 482, M 472, M 470). Likewise, Mandaean belief regarding the origins of both the good spirit and the evil spirit from a singular source, Pirā Rabbā, may bear an echo of Zurvanism. Both Manichaeism and Mandaeism may have assimilated aspects of Zurvanism through intercommunal contacts within southern and western Iran and in Iraq during the early Middle Ages.

DECLINE. Zurvanism's waning in Zoroastrianism is evidenced by very gradual omission of Zurvanite ideas in the writings of magi after the thirteenth century, perhaps because social turmoil created by the Mongol conquests facilitated the slow spread among the Zoroastrian minority of starker dualist ideas. The Muslim population of Iran, by then an absolute demographic majority, had little theological need for a figure such as Zurvan, because all aspects of life could be reconciled with the attributes of its monotheistic deity Allah. So entrenched was the notion of time as a creator spirit that doctrinal change appears to have been slow. Even texts contained in the *Revāyats* (Treatises)—compiled by Iranian magi for their counterparts in India from 1478 to 1773—while referring to time in the more generic sense of *zamān,* which had preceded corporeal creation and in which the material universe exists (*ʿUlamā-e Islām,* 2, pp. 72–80), also preserves the idea that "Zamān is the creator. . . . It created fire and water; once these combined, Ohrmazd came into existence" and goes on to echo the Zurvanite creation story (*ʿUlamā-e Islām,* 2, pp. 80–81). When the Gujarati *Rehbar-e Din-e Jarthushti* (Guide to the Zoroastrian religion) was composed by dastur Erachji Sohrabji Meherjirana in 1869 at Bombay (later Mumbai) in India, time had faded in importance. As veneration of time lapsed, Ahura Mazdā begun to emerge in Zoroastrian belief—especially under colonial, Christian, influences in the nineteenth and twentieth centuries—as a monotheistic god par excellence, the creator of all other spiritual entities, whether evil ones like Angra Mainyu or aloof ones like Zurvan.

SEE ALSO Zoroastrianism.

BIBLIOGRAPHY

Benveniste, Émile. *The Persian Religion according to the Chief Greek Texts.* Paris, 1929.

Bianchi, Ugo. *Zamān i Ōhrmazd: Lo zoroastrismo nelle sue origini e nella sua essenza.* Turin, Italy, 1958.

Boyce, Mary. "Some Reflections on Zurvanism." *Bulletin of the School of Oriental and African Studies* 19 (1957): 304–316.

Boyce, Mary. "Some Further Reflections on Zurvanism." In *Iranica Varia: Papers in Honor of Professor Ehsan Yarshater,* pp. 20–29. Leiden, 1990.

Boyce, Mary, et al. *A History of Zoroastrianism.* 3 vols. to date. Leiden, 1975–1991.

Choksy, Jamsheed K. "Doctrinal Variation within Zoroastrianism: The Notion of Dualism." In *K. R. Cama Oriental Institute: Second International Congress Proceedings,* pp. 96–110. Bombay, 1996.

Choksy, Jamsheed K. "Zurvan." In *Late Antiquity: A Guide to the Postclassical World,* edited by G. W. Bowersock, Peter Brown, and Oleg Grabar, p. 757. Cambridge, Mass., 1999.

Christensen, Arthur. *L'Iran sous les Sassanides.* 2d ed. Copenhagen, 1944.

Duchesne-Guillemin, Jacques. "Notes on Zervanism in the Light of Zaehner's Zurvan, with Additional References." *Journal of Near Eastern Studies* 15 (1956): 106–112.

Frye, Richard N. "Zurvanism Again." *Harvard Theological Review* 52 (1959): 63–73.

Gnoli, Gherardo. "L'évolution du dualisme iranien et le problème zurvanite." *Revue de l'Histoire des Religions* 201 (1984): 115–138.

Gray, Louis H. *The Foundations of the Iranian Religions.* Bombay, 1929.

Menasce, Jean de. "Reflexions sur Zurvān." In *A Locust's Leg: Studies in Honour of S. H. Taqizadeh,* edited by W. B. Henning and Ehsan Yarshater, pp. 182–188. London, 1962.

Molé, Marijan. "Le problème zurvanite." *Journal asiatique* 247 (1959): 431–469.

Nyberg, Henrik S. "Questions de cosmogonie et de cosmologie mazdéennes." *Journal asiatique* 214 (1929): 193–310 and 219 (1931): 1–34, 193–244.

Shaked, Shaul. *Dualism in Transformation: Varieties of Religion in Sasanian Iran.* London, 1994.

Widengren, Geo. *Die Religionen Irans.* Stuttgart, Germany, 1965.

Zaehner, Robert C. *Zurvan: A Zoroastrian Dilemma.* Oxford, 1955; reprint, New York, 1972.

JAMSHEED K. CHOKSY (2005)

ZWINGLI, HULDRYCH

ZWINGLI, HULDRYCH (1484–1531), Swiss Protestant theologian. Born in Wildhaus, Switzerland, Zwingli was educated in Vienna (1500–1502) and later in Basel (1502–1506), where he studied under Thomas Wyttenbach. He read Erasmus during his first pastorate in Glarus (1506–1516). During his second pastorate in Einsiedeln (1516–1518), he began to preach against indulgences. In 1518 Zwingli became preacher in the Zurich Cathedral, a post he retained until his death in 1531. He married Anna Reinhart in 1524.

From the beginning of his work in Zurich, Zwingli declared scripture to be the sole ultimate authority for the life and teaching of the church, thereby repudiating hierarchical authority. He preached against indulgences, stating that Christ's sacrifice is sufficient to remit all penalties for sin. He also preached against ascetic religious orders, fasting, the invocation of the saints, and the doctrine of purgatory. As a fervent Swiss patriot, Zwingli opposed Pope Leo X's recruitment of Swiss mercenaries.

In 1522 the civil authority of the canton of Zurich declared that a disputation should take place between those who advocated and those who opposed the Reformation principle that scripture alone should be the ultimate norm of church life and teaching. In preparation for this disputation, Zwingli, the leader of the Reformation group, wrote his lengthy *Sixty-Seven Conclusions,* in which he repudiated the authority of the pope, the transubstantiation of bread and wine, the veneration of the saints, the existence of purgatory, and the necessity of fasting. The disputation was held on 29 January 1523; the council of Zurich decided in favor of the Reformation, and Zurich became a canton of the Reformation.

Zwingli's attention then turned toward a radical Reformation group, the Anabaptists, which had begun to flourish in Zurich during the early 1520s. The Anabaptists opposed the baptism of infants and denied the validity of such baptisms. They opposed any jurisdiction of the civil authorities in church life. They placed ultimate church authority in the local congregation rather than in larger church or civil councils. They aspired to establish "sinless congregations." In 1526 the government of Zurich, with Zwingli's support, suppressed the Anabaptists. The government also suppressed Catholicism in the canton. In retaliation the papal forces made war on Zurich. In a battle at Kappel on 11 October 1531, Zwingli fell and was executed on the battlefield.

While Zwingli, Luther, and Calvin had in common such great Reformation themes as the justification of the sinner by faith rather than by works and the acknowledgment that the church in all of its teaching is subject to the greater authority of scripture, there were also disagreements among them, principally in their understandings of the church, the Lord's Supper, and the relationship between church and civil authority. Zwingli's influence on subsequent Protestant teaching is apparent chiefly in these areas.

Doctrine of the Church. Luther and Calvin identify the church with the preaching of the word and the administration of the sacraments. Zwingli agrees but offers a more developed understanding of the church as community. He does so by identifying three meanings of the word *church* and then interrelating those meanings. He defines the church as (1) the communion of saints, the heavenly church called and gathered by Christ, (2) the historical church, made up of those who throughout the world confess Christ as Lord, and (3) the local congregation. It is Christ who chooses the members of his church and gathers them into a fellowship with him. This is the heavenly church that must exist here and now as the historical church, the means by which Christ makes himself visible in the world.

There is no historical church, however, except as it comprises the many local congregations. The unity of the historical church exists not by the mere assertion that all these local congregations belong to it but rather by the fact, known through faith, that all local congregations have been chosen and gathered by the same Lord. Moreover, this unity is emphasized by the fact that every congregation has the same pattern of life to emulate. The earthly Jesus chose and gathered a local congregation, the apostles. Now the risen Lord, by the power of the Holy Spirit, continues to call and gather local congregations and commands them to emulate the pattern of the first congregation, as it is described in the New Testament. Zwingli, through his interrelation of these three meanings of *church,* represents Christ's choosing and gathering of his saints as the basic meaning of the church. He then explains preaching and the sacraments as means by which Christ calls and gathers his people into fellowship with him. These same means are to be used by his people to gather themselves around their invisible Lord, thereby making him visible. The invisible "being gathered" and the visible "gathering" constitute Zwingli's church.

Lord's Supper. For Zwingli, the Lord's Supper could not be understood in isolation but only as a moment in Christ's calling and gathering of his saints. The Lord's Supper is a pledge of loyalty by God's people made to their Lord, who commands this of them. It is one moment, but a central moment, of Christ's calling and gathering activity; it is not a moment in which Christ becomes suddenly present. Rather, Christ is understood to be present in the whole of that calling and gathering activity, which is the church. Zwingli does not deny that transubstantiation takes place in the Lord's Supper. He declares, however, that it is not the elements of bread and wine but rather the people who are changed; they are changed into saints by the calling and gathering activity of Christ. Luther and Calvin differed with Zwingli; both, in different ways, continued the tradition of the church that focuses attention upon the elements of bread and wine. Zwingli and Luther quarreled about this focus at the Marburg Colloquy of 1529.

Church and Civil Government. According to Zwingli, Christ not only gathers a church, he also ordains the existence of the civil community, a body of free citizens. The authority of the civil community, while ultimately Christ's, rests derivatively in the consent of the citizenry. The church and civil society each has responsibilities toward the other. The civil rulers are to keep the peace and rule according to a concept of justice derived from scripture. Preachers are, therefore, to proclaim not only the gospel but also the demands of human justice that are derived from the gospel announced in scripture. The members of the civil community are guided away from self-interest by such preaching. The civil rulers, then, have the power and responsibility to protect the church's preaching of justice and the responsibility to be guided by it. The church and its preachers have no direct power to rule in civil affairs, but they have the responsibility of preaching human justice to citizens and civil rulers.

Zwingli's emphasis on the preaching of God's justice as the basis of the human justice of the civil community and on the importance of the consent of the governed distinguishes his teaching from Luther's. Luther taught that the function of civil rulers is, primarily, to restrain disorder. Zwingli's emphasis on the preacher as the people's tribune before the civil rulers and his willingness to accept some civil jurisdiction over church life distinguish his teaching from Calvin's. Calvin advocated a stronger separation between the ecclesiastical and the civil authorities.

Bibliography

Works by Zwingli

Huldreich Zwinglis Sämtliche Werke. 14 vols. Corpus Reformatorum, vols. 88–101. Berlin, Leipzig, Zurich, 1905–1959.

Translations into English

Bromiley, Geoffrey W., ed. *Zwingli and Bullinger.* Library of Christian Classics, vol. 24. Philadelphia, 1953. Selected texts of Zwingli and Bullinger translated into English with a good, short introduction to the life, works, and theology of Zwingli.

Hadidian, Dikran, ed. *Huldrych Zwingli Writings.* 2 vols. Allison Park, Pa., 1984.

Works about Zwingli

Courvoisier, Jaques. *Zwingli, a Reformed Theologian.* Richmond, Va., 1963. A brief, competent introduction to Zwingli's theology.

Furcha, E. J., and H. Wayne Pipkin, eds. *Prophet, Pastor, Protestant: The World of Huldrych Zwingli after Five Hundred Years.* Pittsburgh, Pa., 1984. Essays by ten able Zwingli scholars.

Gäbler, Ulrich. *Huldrych Zwingli im 20. Jahrhundert: Forschungsbericht und annotierte Bibliographie, 1897–1972.* Zurich, 1975. Authoritative Zwingli bibliography.

Gäbler, Ulrich. *Huldrych Zwingli: His Life and Work.* Translated by Ruth C. L. Gritsch. Philadelphia, 1986. An intellectual biography by a leading Zwingli scholar.

Köhler, Walther. *Huldrych Zwingli.* Leipzig, 1943. Part of the foundation of twentieth-century Zwingli scholarship.

Locher, G. W. *Die Zwinglische Reformation im Rahmen der europäischen Kirchengeschichte.* Göttingen, 1979. A comprehensive and scholarly examination of Zwingli's theology.

Locher, G. W. *Zwingli's Thought: New Perspectives.* Leiden, 1981. An excellent, medium-length survey of Zwingli's thought.

Potter, G. R. *Zwingli.* New York, 1976. An accurate and thorough intellectual biography.

Stephens, W.P. *Zwingli: An Introduction to His Thought.* Oxford, 1984. A readable and reliable introduction to Zwingli's thought.

DAVID E. DEMSON (1987 AND 2005)

ISBN 0-02-865983-X
90000
9 780028 659831